PHILIP'S

CONCISE WORLD ATLAS

TWELFTH EDITION

IN ASSOCIATION WITH
THE ROYAL GEOGRAPHICAL SOCIETY
WITH THE INSTITUTE OF BRITISH GEOGRAPHERS

THE EARTH IN SPACE
Cartography by Philip's

Text
Keith Lye

Illustrations
Stefan Chabluk

Star Charts
John Cox
Richard Monkhouse

PICTURE ACKNOWLEDGEMENTS
Corbis Sygma /Thorne Anderson 47
Robert Harding Picture Library /PHOTRI 13, /Bill Ross 41, /Adam Woolfitt 43
Hutchison Library /John Hatt 46
Image Bank /Peter Hendrie 20, /Daniel Hummel 34, /Image Makers 8 top, /Pete Turner 39
Images Colour Library Limited 15
Japan National Tourist Organization 45
NASA/Galaxy Picture Library 8 bottom left
NPA Group, Edenbridge, UK 48
Panos Pictures /Howard Davies 35
Chris Rayner 19 top
Rex Features /SIPA Press /Scott Andrews 12
Science Photo Library /Martin Bond 14, /CNES, 1992 Distribution Spot Image 27 top, /Luke Dodd 3, 6, /Earth Satellite Corporation 25 bottom, /NASA 9 centre right, 9 top, 22, 23, 24, /David Parker 26, /Peter Ryan 27 below, /Jerry Schad 4, /Space Telescope Science Institute /NASA 9 centre left, 9 bottom right, /US Geological Survey 8 centre right
Space Telescope Science Institute /R. Williams /NASA 2
Starland Picture Library /NASA 8 centre left
Still Pictures /Francois Pierrel 28, /Heine Pedersen 31, 40
Tony Stone Images 33, /Glen Allison 38, /James Balog 16, /John Beatty 21, /Neil Beer 30, /Kristin Finnegan 11, /Jeremy Horner 42, /Gary Norman 36, /Frank Oberle 25 top, /Dennis Oda 17, /Nigel Press 37, /Donovan Reese 18, 19, /Hugh Sitton 32, /Richard Surman 44, /Michael Townsend 29, /World Perspectives 10
Telegraph Colour Library /Space Frontiers 9 bottom left

Published in Great Britain in 2002
by Philip's,
a division of Octopus Publishing Group Limited,
2–4 Heron Quays, London E14 4JP

Cartography by Philip's

ISBN 0-540-08233-3

A CIP catalogue record for this book is available from the British Library.

Printed in Hong Kong

Details of other Philip's titles and services can be found on our website at:
www.philips-maps.co.uk

Philip's World Atlases are published in association with The Royal Geographical Society (with The Institute of British Geographers).

The Society was founded in 1830 and given a Royal Charter in 1859 for 'the advancement of geographical science'. It holds historical collections of national and international importance, many of which relate to the Society's association with and support for scientific exploration and research from the 19th century onwards. It was pivotal in establishing geography as a teaching and research discipline in British universities close to the turn of the century, and has played a key role in geographical and environmental education ever since.

Today the Society is a leading world centre for geographical learning – supporting education, teaching, research and expeditions, and promoting public understanding of the subject.

The Society welcomes those interested in geography as members. For further information, please visit the website at: www.rgs.org

Philip's World Maps

The reference maps which form the main body of this atlas have been prepared in accordance with the highest standards of international cartography to provide an accurate and detailed representation of the Earth. The scales and projections used have been carefully chosen to give balanced coverage of the world, while emphasizing the most densely populated and economically significant regions. A hallmark of Philip's mapping is the use of hill shading and relief colouring to create a graphic impression of landforms: this makes the maps exceptionally easy to read. However, knowledge of the key features employed in the construction and presentation of the maps will enable the reader to derive the fullest benefit from the atlas.

MAP SEQUENCE

The atlas covers the Earth continent by continent: first Europe; then its land neighbour Asia (mapped north before south, in a clockwise sequence), then Africa, Australia and Oceania, North America and South America. This is the classic arrangement adopted by most cartographers since the 16th century. For each continent, there are maps at a variety of scales. First, physical relief and political maps

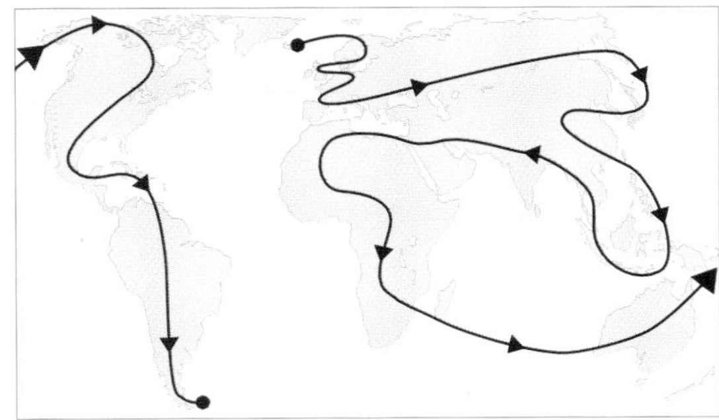

of the whole continent; then a series of larger-scale maps of the regions within the continent, each followed, where required, by still larger-scale maps of the most important or densely populated areas. The governing principle is that by turning the pages of the atlas, the reader moves steadily from north to south through each continent, with each map overlapping its neighbours.

MAP PRESENTATION

With very few exceptions (e.g. for the Arctic and Antarctic), the maps are drawn with north at the top, regardless of whether they are presented upright or sideways on the page. In the borders will be found the map title; a locator diagram showing the area covered and the page numbers for maps of adjacent areas; the scale; the projection used; the degrees of latitude and longitude; and the letters and figures used in the index for locating place names and geographical features. Physical relief maps also have a height reference panel identifying the colours used for each layer of contouring.

MAP SYMBOLS

Each map contains a vast amount of detail which can only be conveyed clearly and accurately by the use of symbols. Points and circles of varying sizes locate and identify the relative importance of towns and cities; different styles of type are employed for administrative, geographical and regional place names to aid identification. A variety of pictorial symbols denote landscape features such as glaciers, marshes and coral reefs, and man-made structures including roads, railways, airports, canals and dams. International borders are shown by red lines. Where neighbouring countries are in dispute, for example in parts of the Middle East, the maps show the *de facto* boundary between nations, regardless of the legal or historical situation. The symbols are explained on the first page of the *World Maps* section of the atlas.

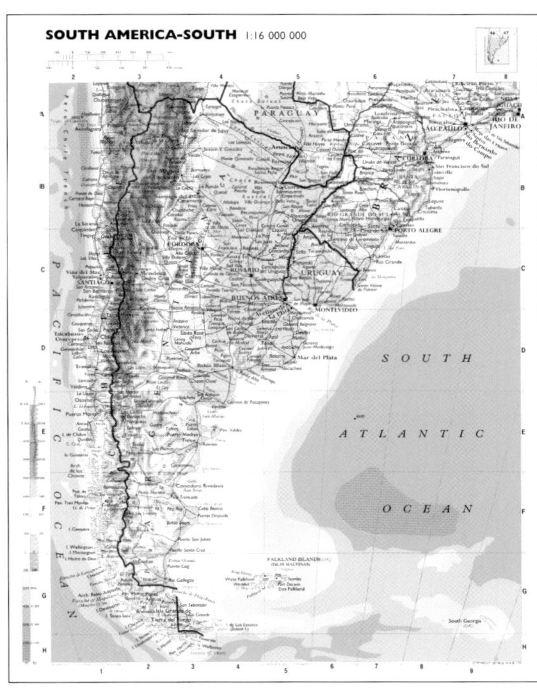

MAP SCALES

1:16 000 000
1 inch = 252 statute miles

The scale of each map is given in the numerical form known as the 'representative fraction'. The first figure is always one, signifying one unit of distance on the map; the second figure, usually in millions, is the number by which the map unit must be multiplied to give the equivalent distance on the Earth's surface. Calculations can easily be made in centimetres and kilometres, by dividing the Earth units figure by 100 000 (i.e. deleting the last five 0s). Thus 1:1 000 000 means 1 cm = 10 km. The calculation for inches and miles is more laborious, but 1 000 000 divided by 63 360 (the number of inches in a mile) shows that 1:1 000 000 means approximately 1 inch = 16 miles. The table below provides distance equivalents for scales down to 1:50 000 000.

LARGE SCALE

1:1 000 000	1 cm = 10 km	1 inch = 16 miles
1:2 500 000	1 cm = 25 km	1 inch = 39.5 miles
1:5 000 000	1 cm = 50 km	1 inch = 79 miles
1:6 000 000	1 cm = 60 km	1 inch = 95 miles
1:8 000 000	1 cm = 80 km	1 inch = 126 miles
1:10 000 000	1 cm = 100 km	1 inch = 158 miles
1:15 000 000	1 cm = 150 km	1 inch = 237 miles
1:20 000 000	1 cm = 200 km	1 inch = 316 miles
1:50 000 000	1 cm = 500 km	1 inch = 790 miles

SMALL SCALE

MEASURING DISTANCES

100 0 100 200 300 400 miles
100 0 100 200 300 400 500 600 km

Although each map is accompanied by a scale bar, distances cannot always be measured with confidence because of the distortions involved in portraying the curved surface of the Earth on a flat page. As a general rule, the larger the map scale (i.e. the lower the number of Earth units in the representative fraction), the more accurate and reliable will be the distance measured. On small-scale maps such as those of the world and of entire continents, measurement may only be accurate along the 'standard parallels', or central axes, and should not be attempted without considering the map projection.

MAP PROJECTIONS

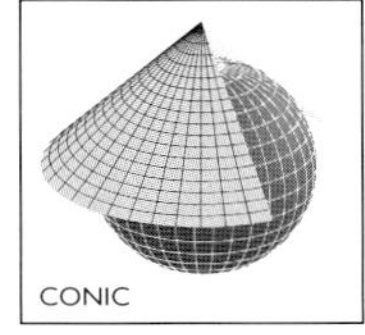

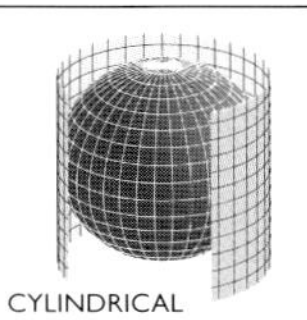

Unlike a globe, no flat map can give a true scale representation of the world in terms of area, shape and position of every region. Each of the numerous systems that have been devised for projecting the curved surface of the Earth on to a flat page involves the sacrifice of accuracy in one or more of these elements. The variations in shape and position of landmasses such as Alaska, Greenland and Australia, for example, can be quite dramatic when different projections are compared.

For this atlas, the guiding principle has been to select projections that involve the least distortion of size and distance. The projection used for each map is noted in the border. Most fall into one of three categories – conic, azimuthal or cylindrical – whose basic concepts are shown above. Each involves plotting the forms of the Earth's surface on a grid of latitude and longitude lines, which may be shown as parallels, curves or radiating spokes.

LATITUDE AND LONGITUDE

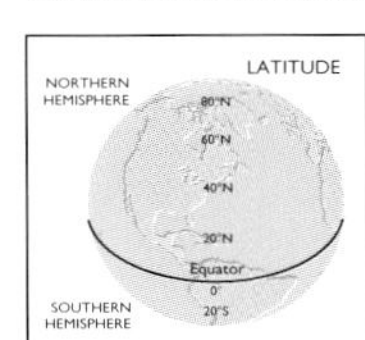

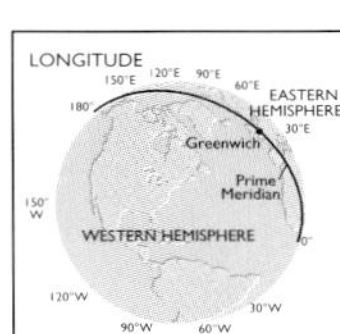

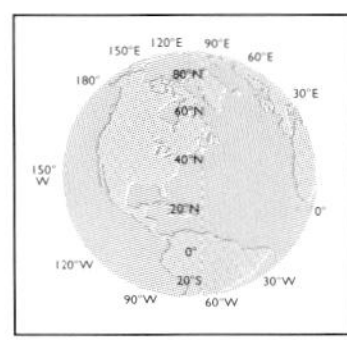

Accurate positioning of individual points on the Earth's surface is made possible by reference to the geometrical system of latitude and longitude. Latitude *parallels* are drawn west–east around the Earth and numbered by degrees north and south of the Equator, which is designated 0° of latitude. Longitude *meridians* are drawn north–south and numbered by degrees east and west of the *prime meridian*, 0° of longitude, which passes through Greenwich in England. By referring to these co-ordinates and their subdivisions of minutes (1/60th of a degree) and seconds (1/60th of a minute), any place on Earth can be located to within a few hundred metres. Latitude and longitude are indicated by blue lines on the maps; they are straight or curved according to the projection employed. Reference to these lines is the easiest way of determining the relative positions of places on different maps, and for plotting compass directions.

NAME FORMS

For ease of reference, both English and local name forms appear in the atlas. Oceans, seas and countries are shown in English throughout the atlas; country names may be abbreviated to their commonly accepted form (e.g. Germany, not The Federal Republic of Germany). Conventional English forms are also used for place names on the smaller-scale maps of the continents. However, local name forms are used on all large-scale and regional maps, with the English form given in brackets only for important cities – the large-scale map of Russia and Central Asia thus shows Moskva (Moscow). For countries which do not use a Roman script, place names have been transcribed according to the systems adopted by the British and US Geographic Names Authorities. For China, the Pin Yin system has been used, with some more widely known forms appearing in brackets, as with Beijing (Peking). Both English and local names appear in the index, the English form being cross-referenced to the local form.

Contents

World Statistics

Countries x
Cities xi
Climate xii–xiii
Physical Dimensions xiv–xv
Regions in the News xvi

The Earth In Space

The Universe 2–3
Star Charts and Constellations 4–7
The Solar System 8–9
The Earth: Time and Motion 10–11
The Earth from Space 12–13
The Dynamic Earth 14–15
Earthquakes and Volcanoes 16–17
Forces of Nature 18–19
Oceans and Ice 20–21
The Earth's Atmosphere 22–23
Climate and Weather 24–25
Water and Land Use 26–27
The Natural World 28–29
The Human World 30–31
Languages and Religions 32–33
International Organizations 34–35
Agriculture 36–37
Energy and Minerals 38–39
World Economies 40–41
Trade and Commerce 42–43
Travel and Communications 44–45
The World Today 46–47

World Maps

Map Symbols **1**

The World: Political
1:71 100 000 **2–3**

Arctic Ocean
1:31 100 000 **4**

Antarctica
1:31 100 000 **5**

Europe

Europe: Physical
1:17 800 000 — 6

Europe: Political
1:17 800 000 — 7

Scandinavia
1:4 400 000 — 8–9

Denmark and Southern Sweden
1:2 200 000 — 10–11

England and Wales
1:1 800 000 — 12–13

Scotland
1:1 800 000 — 14

Ireland
1:1 800 000

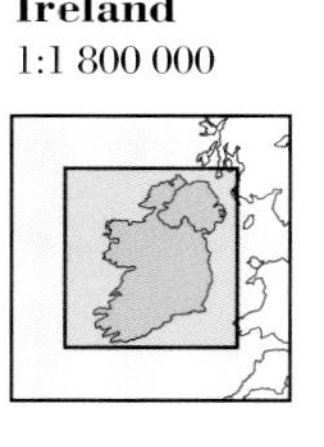

15

British Isles
1:4 400 000 — 16

Netherlands, Belgium and Luxembourg
1:2 200 000

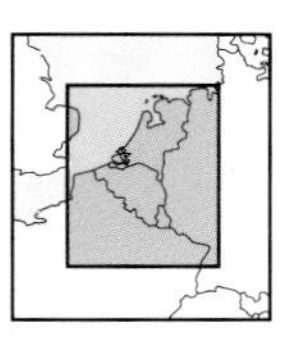

17

Northern France
1:2 200 000 — 18–19

Southern France
1:2 200 000 — 20–21

Middle Europe
1:4 400 000 — 22–23

Germany and Switzerland
1:2 200 000 — 24–25

Austria, Czech Republic and Slovak Republic
1:2 200 000 — 26–27

Northern Italy, Slovenia and Croatia
1:2 200 000 — 28–29

Southern Italy
1:2 200 000 — 30–31

Eastern Spain
1:2 200 000 — 32–33

Western Spain and Portugal
1:2 200 000 — 34–35

Malta, Crete, Corfu, Rhodes and Cyprus
1:900 000 / 1:1 200 000

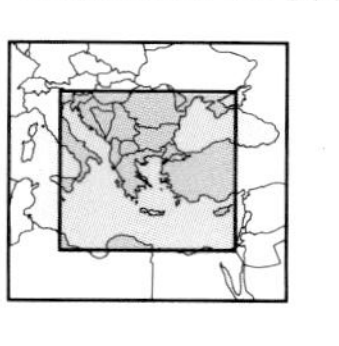

36

The Balearics, the Canaries and Madeira
1:900 000 / 1:1 800 000

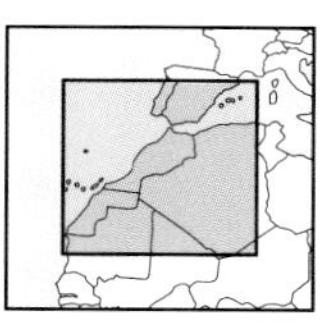

37

Southern Greece and Western Turkey
1:2 200 000

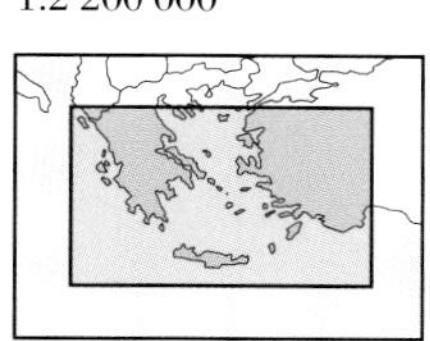

38–39

Northern Greece, Bulgaria and Yugoslavia
1:2 200 000

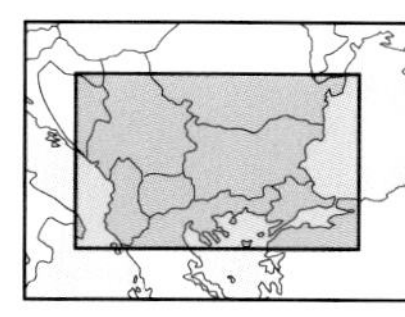

40–41

Hungary, Romania and the Lower Danube
1:2 200 000

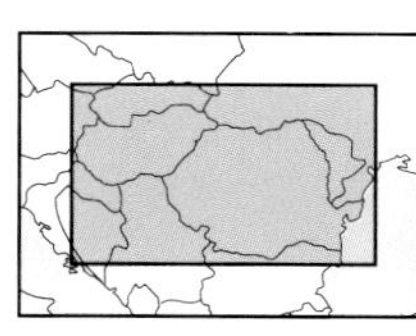

42–43

Poland and the Southern Baltic
1:2 200 000

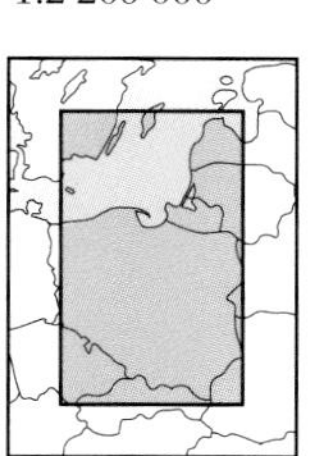

44–45

Baltic States, Belarus and Ukraine
1:4 400 000 — 46–47

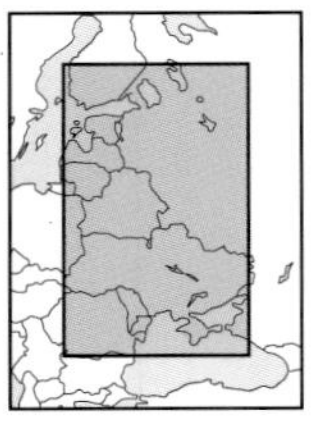

The Volga Basin and the Caucasus
1:4 400 000 — 48–49

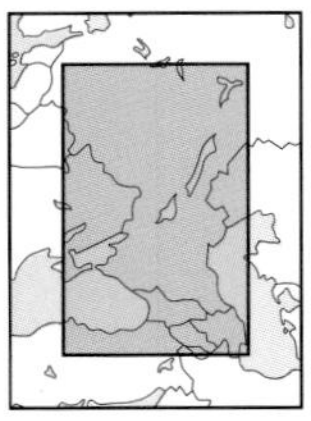

Asia

Russia and Central Asia
1:17 800 000 — 50–51

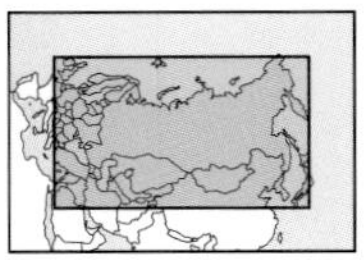

Asia: Physical
1:44 400 000 — 52

Asia: Political
1:44 400 000 — 53

Japan
1:4 400 000 — 54–55

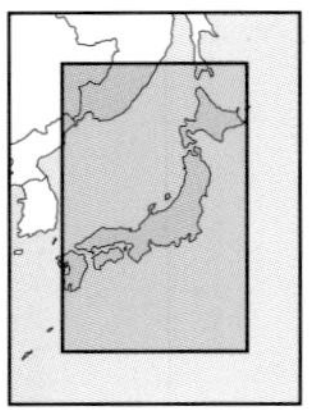

Northern China and Korea
1:5 300 000 — 56–57

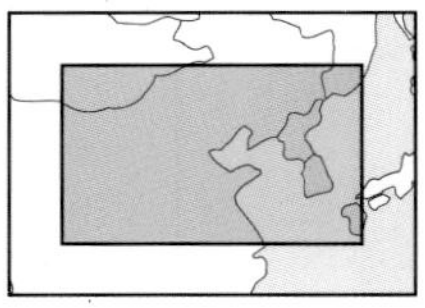

Southern China
1:5 300 000 — 58–59

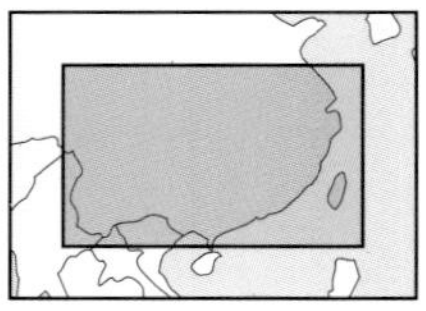

China
1:17 800 000 — 60

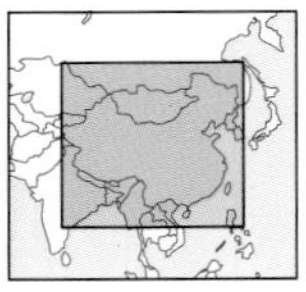

The Philippines
1:6 700 000 — 61

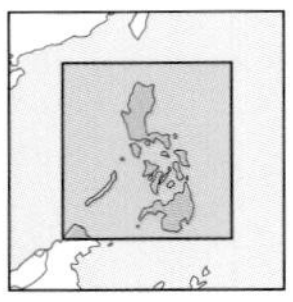

Indonesia and the Philippines
1:11 100 000 — 62–63

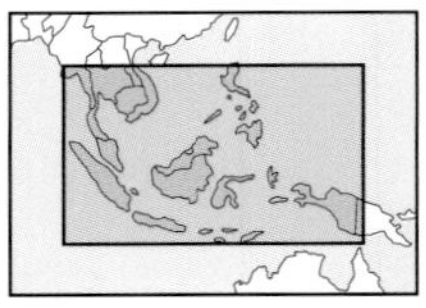

Mainland South-east Asia
1:5 300 000 — 64–65

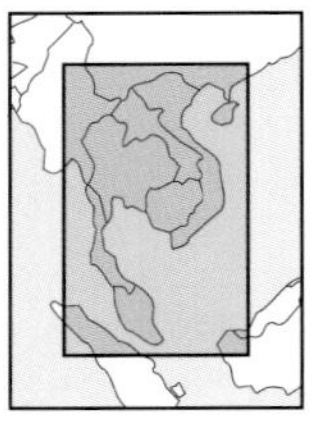

South Asia
1:8 900 000 — 66–67

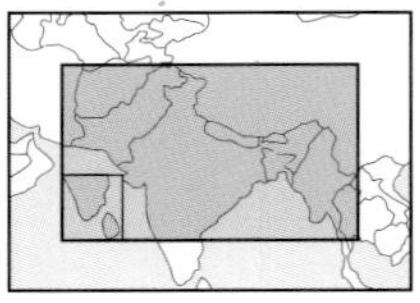

The Indo-Gangetic Plain
1:5 300 000 — 68–69

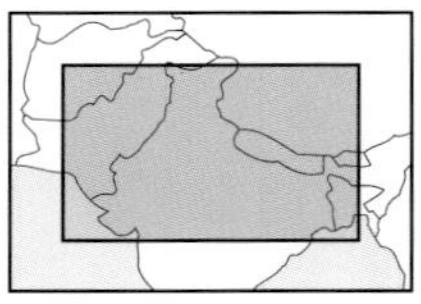

The Middle East
1:6 200 000 — 70–71

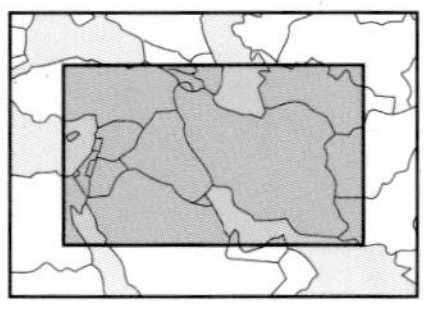

Turkey and Transcaucasia
1:4 400 000 — 72–73

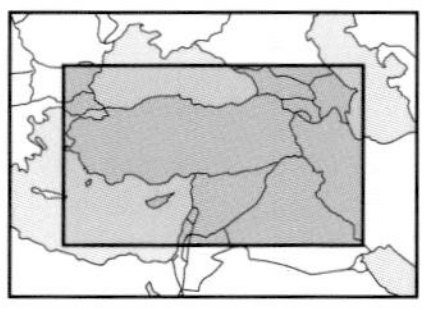

Arabia and the Horn of Africa
1:13 300 000 — 74

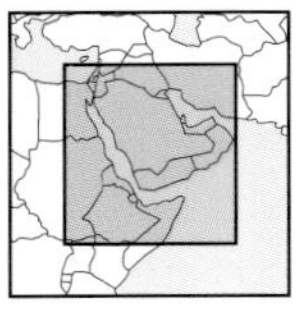

The Near East
1:2 200 000 — 75

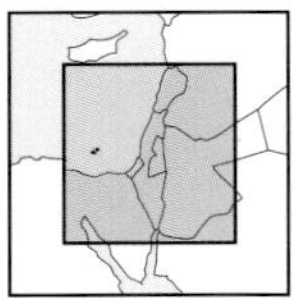

Africa

Africa: Physical
1:37 300 000 — 76

Africa: Political
1: 37 300 000 — 77

Northern Africa
1:13 300 000 — 78–79

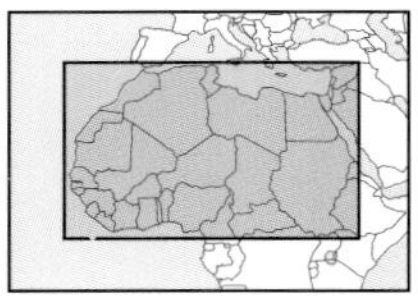

The Nile Valley and the Nile Delta
1:7 100 000 / 1:3 600 000 — 80–81

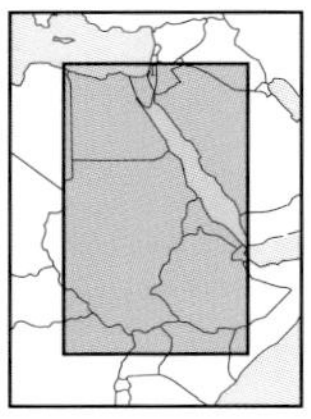

West Africa
1:7 100 000 — 82–83

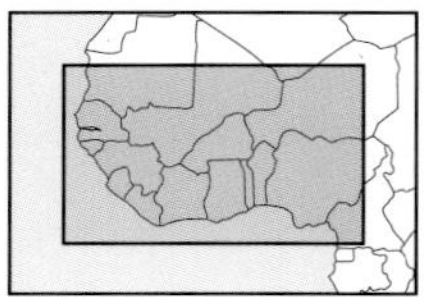

Central and Southern Africa
1:13 300 000 — 84–85

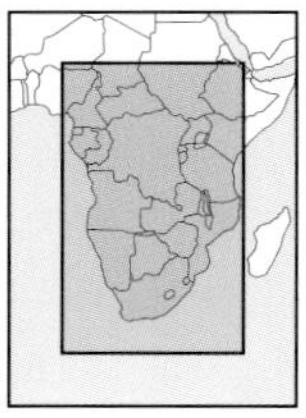

East Africa
1:7 100 000
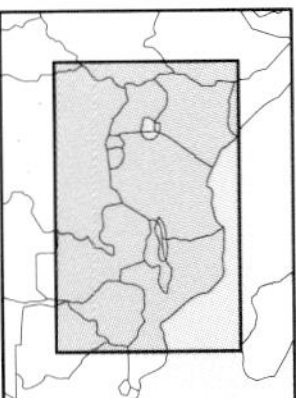
86–87

Southern Africa
1:7 100 000 / 1:7 100 000
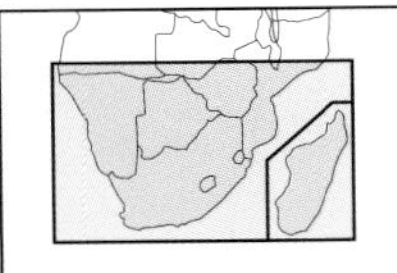
88–89

Australia and Oceania

Australia and Oceania: Physical and Political 90
1:44 400 000

New Zealand and Samoa, Fiji and Tonga
1:5 300 000 / 1:10 700 000
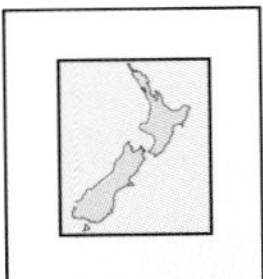
91

Western Australia
1:7 100 000
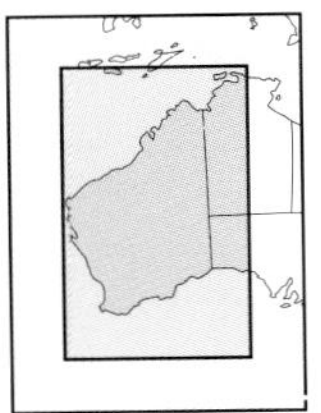
92–93

Eastern Australia
1:7 100 000
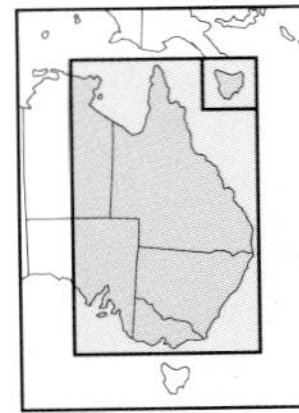
94–95

Pacific Ocean 96–97
1:48 000 000

North America

North America: Physical 98
1:31 100 000

North America: Political 99
1:31 100 000

Canada and Alaska
1:13 300 000 / 1:26 700 000
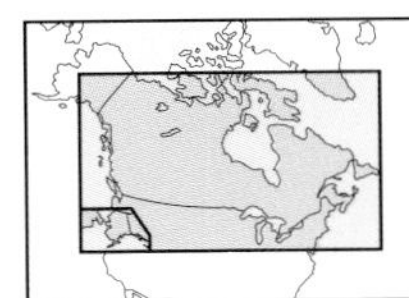
100–101

Eastern Canada
1:6 200 000
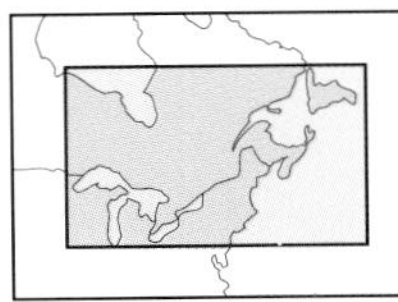
102–103

Western Canada
1:6 200 000
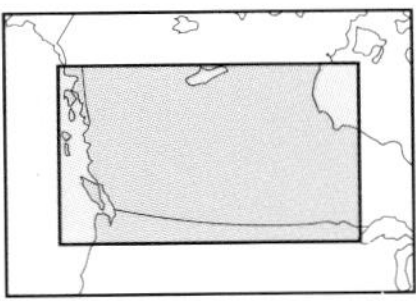
104–105

United States and Hawaii
1:10 700 000 / 1:8 900 000
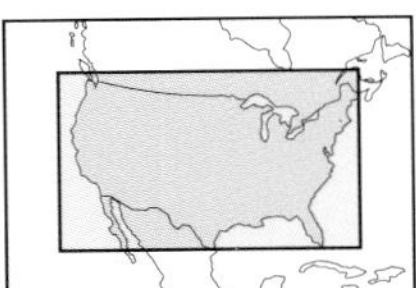
106–107

Eastern United States
1:5 300 000
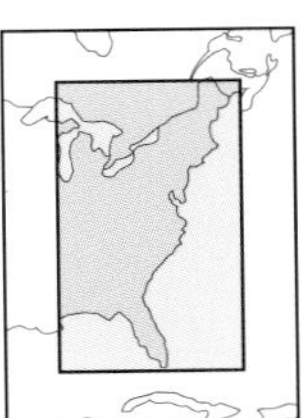
108–109

North-eastern United States
1:2 200 000
110–111

Middle United States
1:5 300 000
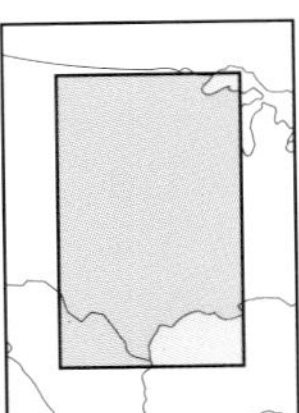
112–113

Western United States
1:5 300 000
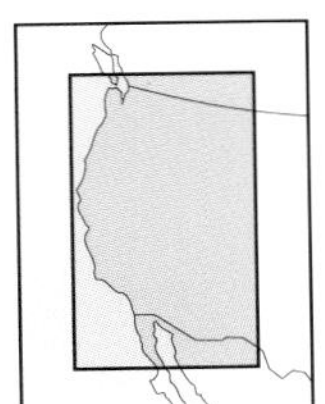
114–115

Central and Southern California and Western Washington
1:2 200 000
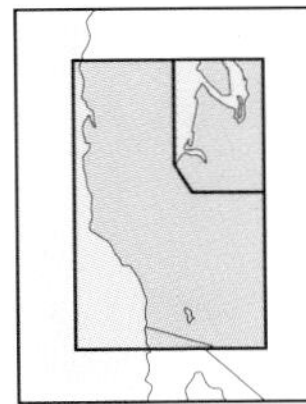
116–117

Mexico
1:7 100 000
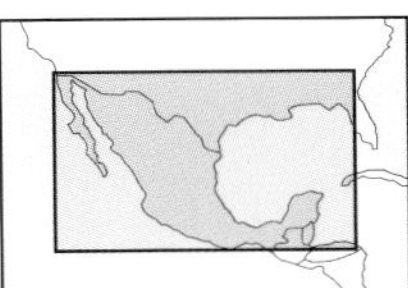
118–119

Central America and the West Indies
1:7 100 000
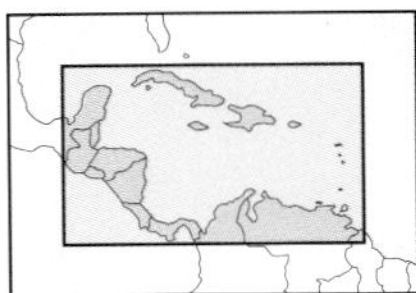
120–121

South America

South America: Physical 122
1:31 100 000

South America: Political 123
1:31 100 000

South America – North
1:14 200 000

124–125

Central South America
1:7 100 000
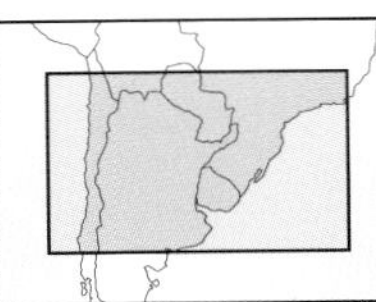
126–127

South America – South
1:14 200 000
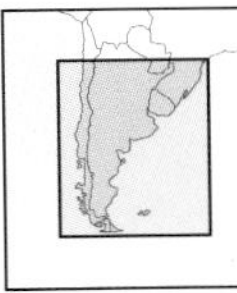
128

Index to World Maps

129–224

World Statistics: Countries

This alphabetical list includes all the countries and territories of the world. If a territory is not completely independent, the country it is associated with is named. The area figures give the total area of land, inland water and ice.

The population figures are 2001 estimates. The annual income is the Gross Domestic Product per capita† in US dollars. The figures are the latest available, usually 2000 estimates.

Country/Territory	Area km^2 Thousands	Area $miles^2$ Thousands	Population Thousands	Capital	Annual Income US $
Afghanistan	652	252	26,813	Kabul	800
Albania	28.8	11.1	3,510	Tirana	3,000
Algeria	2,382	920	31,736	Algiers	5,500
American Samoa (US)	0.2	0.08	67	Pago Pago	8,000
Andorra	0.45	0.17	68	Andorra La Vella	18,000
Angola	1,247	481	10,366	Luanda	1,000
Anguilla (UK)	0.1	0.04	12	The Valley	8,200
Antigua & Barbuda	0.44	0.17	67	St John's	8,200
Argentina	2,767	1,068	37,385	Buenos Aires	12,900
Armenia	29.8	11.5	3,336	Yerevan	3,000
Aruba (Netherlands)	0.19	0.07	70	Oranjestad	28,000
Australia	7,687	2,968	19,358	Canberra	23,200
Austria	83.9	32.4	8,151	Vienna	25,000
Azerbaijan	86.6	33.4	7,771	Baku	3,000
Azores (Portugal)	2.2	0.87	243	Ponta Delgada	11,040
Bahamas	13.9	5.4	298	Nassau	15,000
Bahrain	0.68	0.26	645	Manama	15,900
Bangladesh	144	56	131,270	Dhaka	1,570
Barbados	0.43	0.17	275	Bridgetown	14,500
Belarus	207.6	80.1	10,350	Minsk	7,500
Belgium	30.5	11.8	10,259	Brussels	25,300
Belize	23	8.9	256	Belmopan	3,200
Benin	113	43	6,591	Porto-Novo	1,030
Bermuda (UK)	0.05	0.02	64	Hamilton	33,000
Bhutan	47	18.1	2,049	Thimphu	1,100
Bolivia	1,099	424	8,300	La Paz/Sucre	2,600
Bosnia-Herzegovina	51	20	3,922	Sarajevo	1,700
Botswana	582	225	1,586	Gaborone	6,600
Brazil	8,512	3,286	174,469	Brasília	6,500
Brunei	5.8	2.2	344	Bandar Seri Begawan	17,600
Bulgaria	111	43	7,707	Sofia	6,200
Burkina Faso	274	106	12,272	Ouagadougou	1,000
Burma (= Myanmar)	677	261	41,995	Rangoon	1,500
Burundi	27.8	10.7	6,224	Bujumbura	720
Cambodia	181	70	12,492	Phnom Penh	1,300
Cameroon	475	184	15,803	Yaoundé	1,700
Canada	9,976	3,852	31,593	Ottawa	24,800
Canary Is. (Spain)	7.3	2.8	1,577	Las Palmas/Santa Cruz	17,100
Cape Verde Is.	4	1.6	405	Praia	1,700
Cayman Is. (UK)	0.26	0.1	36	George Town	24,500
Central African Republic	623	241	3,577	Bangui	1,700
Chad	1,284	496	8,707	Ndjaména	1,000
Chile	757	292	15,328	Santiago	10,100
China	9,597	3,705	1,273,111	Beijing	3,600
Colombia	1,139	440	40,349	Bogotá	6,200
Comoros	2.2	0.86	596	Moroni	720
Congo	342	132	2,894	Brazzaville	1,100
Congo (Dem. Rep. of the)	2,345	905	53,625	Kinshasa	600
Cook Is. (NZ)	0.24	0.09	21	Avarua	5,000
Costa Rica	51.1	19.7	3,773	San José	6,700
Croatia	56.5	21.8	4,334	Zagreb	5,800
Cuba	111	43	11,184	Havana	1,700
Cyprus	9.3	3.6	763	Nicosia	13,800
Czech Republic	78.9	30.4	10,264	Prague	12,900
Denmark	43.1	16.6	5,353	Copenhagen	25,500
Djibouti	23.2	9	461	Djibouti	1,300
Dominica	0.75	0.29	71	Roseau	4,000
Dominican Republic	48.7	18.8	8,581	Santo Domingo	5,700
East Timor	14.9	5.7	737	Dili	N/A
Ecuador	284	109	13,184	Quito	2,900
Egypt	1,001	387	69,537	Cairo	3,600
El Salvador	21	8.1	6,238	San Salvador	4,000
Equatorial Guinea	28.1	10.8	486	Malabo	2,000
Eritrea	94	36	4,298	Asmara	710
Estonia	44.7	17.3	1,423	Tallinn	10,000
Ethiopia	1,128	436	65,892	Addis Ababa	600
Faroe Is. (Denmark)	1.4	0.54	46	Tórshavn	20,000
Fiji	18.3	7.1	844	Suva	7,300
Finland	338	131	5,176	Helsinki	22,900
France	552	213	59,551	Paris	24,400
French Guiana (France)	90	34.7	178	Cayenne	6,000
French Polynesia (France)	4	1.5	254	Papeete	10,800
Gabon	268	103	1,221	Libreville	6,300
Gambia, The	11.3	4.4	1,411	Banjul	1,100
Gaza Strip (OPT)*	0.36	0.14	1,178	–	1,000
Georgia	69.7	26.9	4,989	Tbilisi	4,600
Germany	357	138	83,030	Berlin	23,400
Ghana	239	92	19,894	Accra	1,900
Gibraltar (UK)	0.007	0.003	28	Gibraltar Town	17,500
Greece	132	51	10,624	Athens	17,200
Greenland (Denmark)	2,176	840	56	Nuuk (Godthåb)	20,000
Grenada	0.34	0.13	89	St George's	4,400
Guadeloupe (France)	1.7	0.66	431	Basse-Terre	9,000
Guam (US)	0.55	0.21	158	Agana	21,000
Guatemala	109	42	12,974	Guatemala City	3,700
Guinea	246	95	7,614	Conakry	1,300
Guinea-Bissau	36.1	13.9	1,316	Bissau	850
Guyana	215	83	697	Georgetown	4,800
Haiti	27.8	10.7	6,965	Port-au-Prince	1,800
Honduras	112	43	6,406	Tegucigalpa	2,700
Hong Kong (China)	1.1	0.4	7,211	–	25,400
Hungary	93	35.9	10,106	Budapest	11,200
Iceland	103	40	278	Reykjavik	24,800
India	3,288	1,269	1,029,991	New Delhi	2,200
Indonesia	1,890	730	227,701	Jakarta	2,900
Iran	1,648	636	66,129	Tehran	6,300
Iraq	438	169	23,332	Baghdad	2,500
Ireland	70.3	27.1	3,841	Dublin	21,600
Israel	20.6	7.96	5,938	Jerusalem	18,900
Italy	301	116	57,680	Rome	22,100
Ivory Coast (= Côte d'Ivoire)	322	125	16,393	Yamoussoukro	1,600
Jamaica	11	4.2	2,666	Kingston	3,700
Japan	378	146	126,772	Tokyo	24,900
Jordan	89.2	34.4	5,153	Amman	3,500
Kazakstan	2,717	1,049	16,731	Astana	5,000
Kenya	580	224	30,766	Nairobi	1,500
Kiribati	0.72	0.28	94	Tarawa	850
Korea, North	121	47	21,968	Pyŏngyang	1,000
Korea, South	99	38.2	47,904	Seoul	16,100
Kuwait	17.8	6.9	2,042	Kuwait City	15,000
Kyrgyzstan	198.5	76.6	4,753	Bishkek	2,700
Laos	237	91	5,636	Vientiane	1,700
Latvia	65	25	2,385	Riga	7,200

*OPT = Occupied Palestinian Territory   N/A = Not Available

Country/Territory	Area km^2 Thousands	Area $miles^2$ Thousands	Population Thousands	Capital	Annual Income US $
Lebanon	10.4	4	3,628	Beirut	5,000
Lesotho	30.4	11.7	2,177	Maseru	2,400
Liberia	111	43	3,226	Monrovia	1,100
Libya	1,760	679	5,241	Tripoli	8,900
Liechtenstein	0.16	0.06	33	Vaduz	23,000
Lithuania	65.2	25.2	3,611	Vilnius	7,300
Luxembourg	2.6	1	443	Luxembourg	36,400
Macau (China)	0.02	0.006	454	–	17,500
Macedonia (FYROM)	25.7	9.9	2,046	Skopje	4,400
Madagascar	587	227	15,983	Antananarivo	800
Madeira (Portugal)	0.81	0.31	259	Funchal	12,120
Malawi	118	46	10,548	Lilongwe	900
Malaysia	330	127	22,229	Kuala Lumpur	10,300
Maldives	0.3	0.12	311	Malé	2,000
Mali	1,240	479	11,009	Bamako	850
Malta	0.32	0.12	395	Valletta	14,300
Marshall Is.	0.18	0.07	71	Dalap-Uliga-Darrit	1,670
Martinique (France)	1.1	0.42	418	Fort-de-France	11,000
Mauritania	1,030	398	2,747	Nouakchott	2,000
Mauritius	2	0.72	1,190	Port Louis	10,400
Mayotte (France)	0.37	0.14	163	Mamoundzou	600
Mexico	1,958	756	101,879	Mexico City	9,100
Micronesia, Fed. States of	0.7	0.27	135	Palikir	2,000
Moldova	33.7	13	4,432	Chişinău	2,500
Monaco	0.002	0.001	32	Monaco	27,000
Mongolia	1,567	605	2,655	Ulan Bator	1,780
Montserrat (UK)	0.1	0.04	8	Plymouth	5,000
Morocco	447	172	30,645	Rabat	3,500
Mozambique	802	309	19,371	Maputo	1,000
Namibia	825	318	1,798	Windhoek	4,300
Nauru	0.02	0.008	12	Yaren District	5,000
Nepal	141	54	25,284	Katmandu	1,360
Netherlands	41.5	16	15,981	Amsterdam/The Hague	24,400
Netherlands Antilles (Neths)	0.99	0.38	212	Willemstad	11,400
New Caledonia (France)	18.6	7.2	205	Nouméa	15,000
New Zealand	269	104	3,864	Wellington	17,700
Nicaragua	130	50	4,918	Managua	2,700
Niger	1,267	489	10,355	Niamey	1,000
Nigeria	924	357	126,636	Abuja	950
Northern Mariana Is. (US)	0.48	0.18	75	Saipan	12,500
Norway	324	125	4,503	Oslo	27,700
Oman	212	82	2,622	Muscat	7,700
Pakistan	796	307	144,617	Islamabad	2,000
Palau	0.46	0.18	19	Koror	7,100
Panama	77.1	29.8	2,846	Panamá	6,000
Papua New Guinea	463	179	5,049	Port Moresby	2,500
Paraguay	407	157	5,734	Asunción	4,750
Peru	1,285	496	27,484	Lima	4,550
Philippines	300	116	82,842	Manila	3,800
Poland	313	121	38,634	Warsaw	8,500
Portugal	92.4	35.7	9,444	Lisbon	15,800
Puerto Rico (US)	9	3.5	3,939	San Juan	10,000
Qatar	11	4.2	769	Doha	20,300
Réunion (France)	2.5	0.97	733	St-Denis	4,800
Romania	238	92	22,364	Bucharest	5,900
Russia	17,075	6,592	145,470	Moscow	7,700
Rwanda	26.3	10.2	7,313	Kigali	900
St Kitts & Nevis	0.36	0.14	39	Basseterre	7,000
St Lucia	0.62	0.24	158	Castries	4,500
St Vincent & Grenadines	0.39	0.15	116	Kingstown	2,800
Samoa	2.8	1.1	179	Apia	3,200
San Marino	0.06	0.02	27	San Marino	32,000
São Tomé & Príncipe	0.96	0.37	165	São Tomé	1,100
Saudi Arabia	2,150	830	22,757	Riyadh	10,500
Senegal	197	76	10,285	Dakar	1,600
Seychelles	0.46	0.18	80	Victoria	7,700
Sierra Leone	71.7	27.7	5,427	Freetown	510
Singapore	0.62	0.24	4,300	Singapore	26,500
Slovak Republic	49	18.9	5,415	Bratislava	10,200
Slovenia	20.3	7.8	1,930	Ljubljana	12,000
Solomon Is.	28.9	11.2	480	Honiara	2,000
Somalia	638	246	7,489	Mogadishu	600
South Africa	1,220	471	43,586	C. Town/Pretoria/Bloem.	8,500
Spain	505	195	38,432	Madrid	18,000
Sri Lanka	65.6	25.3	19,409	Colombo	3,250
Sudan	2,506	967	36,080	Khartoum	1,000
Surinam	163	63	434	Paramaribo	3,400
Swaziland	17.4	6.7	1,104	Mbabane	4,000
Sweden	450	174	8,875	Stockholm	22,200
Switzerland	41.3	15.9	7,283	Bern	28,600
Syria	185	71	16,729	Damascus	3,100
Taiwan	36	13.9	22,370	Taipei	17,400
Tajikistan	143.1	55.2	6,579	Dushanbe	1,140
Tanzania	945	365	36,232	Dodoma	710
Thailand	513	198	61,798	Bangkok	6,700
Togo	56.8	21.9	5,153	Lomé	1,500
Tonga	0.75	0.29	104	Nuku'alofa	2,200
Trinidad & Tobago	5.1	2	1,170	Port of Spain	9,500
Tunisia	164	63	9,705	Tunis	6,500
Turkey	779	301	66,494	Ankara	6,800
Turkmenistan	488.1	188.5	4,603	Ashkhabad	4,300
Turks & Caicos Is. (UK)	0.43	0.17	18	Cockburn Town	7,300
Tuvalu	0.03	0.01	11	Fongafale	1,100
Uganda	236	91	23,986	Kampala	1,100
Ukraine	603.7	233.1	48,760	Kiev	3,850
United Arab Emirates	83.6	32.3	2,407	Abu Dhabi	22,800
United Kingdom	243.3	94	59,648	London	22,800
United States of America	9,373	3,619	278,059	Washington, DC	36,200
Uruguay	177	68	3,360	Montevideo	9,300
Uzbekistan	447.4	172.7	25,155	Tashkent	2,400
Vanuatu	12.2	4.7	193	Port-Vila	1,300
Vatican City	0.0004	0.0002	0.89	Vatican City	N/A
Venezuela	912	352	23,917	Caracas	6,200
Vietnam	332	127	79,939	Hanoi	1,950
Virgin Is. (UK)	0.15	0.06	21	Road Town	16,000
Virgin Is. (US)	0.34	0.13	122	Charlotte Amalie	15,000
Wallis & Futuna Is. (France)	0.2	0.08	15	Mata-Utu	2,000
West Bank (OPT)*	5.86	2.26	2,091	–	1,500
Western Sahara	266	103	251	El Aaiún	N/A
Yemen	528	204	18,078	Sana	820
Yugoslavia (Serbia & Montenegro)	102.3	39.5	10,677	Belgrade	2,300
Zambia	753	291	9,770	Lusaka	880
Zimbabwe	391	151	11,365	Harare	2,500

† Gross Domestic Product per capita has been measured using the purchasing power parity method. This enables comparisons to be made between countries through their purchasing power (in US dollars), showing real price levels of goods and services rather than using currency exchange rates.

World Statistics: Cities

This list shows the principal cities with more than 500,000 inhabitants (only cities with more than 1 million inhabitants are included for Brazil, China, Indonesia, Japan and Russia). The figures are taken from the most recent census or estimate available, and as far as possible are the population of the metropolitan area, e.g. greater New York, Mexico or Paris. All the figures are in thousands. Local name forms have been used for the smaller cities (e.g. Kraków).

AFGHANISTAN	
Kabul	1,565
ALGERIA	
Algiers	1,722
Oran	664
ANGOLA	
Luanda	2,250
ARGENTINA	
Buenos Aires	10,990
Córdoba	1,198
Rosario	1,096
Mendoza	775
La Plata	640
San Miguel de Tucumán	622
Mar del Plata	520
ARMENIA	
Yerevan	1,256
AUSTRALIA	
Sydney	4,041
Melbourne	3,417
Brisbane	1,601
Perth	1,364
Adelaide	1,093
AUSTRIA	
Vienna	1,560
AZERBAIJAN	
Baku	1,713
BANGLADESH	
Dhaka	7,832
Chittagong	2,041
Khulna	877
Rajshahi	517
BELARUS	
Minsk	1,717
Homyel	502
BELGIUM	
Brussels	948
BENIN	
Cotonou	537
BOLIVIA	
La Paz	1,126
Santa Cruz	767
BOSNIA-HERZEGOVINA	
Sarajevo	526
BRAZIL	
São Paulo	10,434
Rio de Janeiro	5,858
Salvador	2,443
Belo Horizonte	2,239
Fortaleza	2,141
Brasília	2,051
Curitiba	1,587
Recife	1,423
Manaus	1,406
Pôrto Alegre	1,361
Belém	1,281
Goiânia	1,093
Guarulhos	1,073
BULGARIA	
Sofia	1,139
BURKINA FASO	
Ouagadougou	690
BURMA (MYANMAR)	
Rangoon	2,513
Mandalay	533
CAMBODIA	
Phnom Penh	570
CAMEROON	
Douala	1,200
Yaoundé	800
CANADA	
Toronto	4,881
Montréal	3,511
Vancouver	2,079
Ottawa–Hull	1,107
Calgary	972
Edmonton	957
Québec	693
Winnipeg	685
Hamilton	681
CENTRAL AFRICAN REPUBLIC	
Bangui	553
CHAD	
Ndjaména	530
CHILE	
Santiago	4,691
CHINA	
Shanghai	15,082
Beijing	12,362
Tianjin	10,687
Hong Kong (SAR)*	6,502
Chongqing	3,870
Shenyang	3,762
Wuhan	3,520
Guangzhou	3,114
Harbin	2,505
Nanjing	2,211
Xi'an	2,115
Chengdu	1,933
Dalian	1,855
Changchun	1,810
Jinan	1,660
Taiyuan	1,642
Qingdao	1,584
Zibo	1,346
Zhengzhou	1,324
Lanzhou	1,296
Anshan	1,252
Fushun	1,246
Kunming	1,242
Changsha	1,198
Hangzhou	1,185
Nanchang	1,169
Shijiazhuang	1,159
Guiyang	1,131
Ürümqi	1,130
Jilin	1,118
Tangshan	1,110
Qiqihar	1,104
Baotou	1,033
COLOMBIA	
Bogotá	6,005
Cali	1,986
Medellín	1,971
Barranquilla	1,158
Cartagena	813
Cúcuta	589
Bucaramanga	508
CONGO	
Brazzaville	938
Pointe-Noire	576
CONGO (DEM. REP.)	
Kinshasa	2,664
Lubumbashi	565
CROATIA	
Zagreb	868
CUBA	
Havana	2,204
CZECH REPUBLIC	
Prague	1,203
DENMARK	
Copenhagen	1,362
DOMINICAN REPUBLIC	
Santo Domingo	2,135
Stgo. de los Caballeros	691
ECUADOR	
Guayaquil	2,070
Quito	1,574
EGYPT	
Cairo	6,800
Alexandria	3,339
El Gîza	2,222
Shubra el Kheima	871
EL SALVADOR	
San Salvador	1,522
ETHIOPIA	
Addis Ababa	2,316
FINLAND	
Helsinki	532
FRANCE	
Paris	11,175
Lyons	1,648
Marseilles	1,516
Lille	1,143
Toulouse	965
Nice	933
Bordeaux	925
Nantes	711
Strasbourg	612
Toulon	565
Douai	553
Rennes	521
Rouen	518
Grenoble	515
GEORGIA	
Tbilisi	1,253
GERMANY	
Berlin	3,426
Hamburg	1,705
Munich	1,206
Cologne	964
Frankfurt	644
Essen	609
Dortmund	595
Stuttgart	585
Düsseldorf	571
Bremen	547
Duisburg	529
Hanover	521
GHANA	
Accra	1,781
GREECE	
Athens	3,097
GUATEMALA	
Guatemala	1,167
GUINEA	
Conakry	1,508
HAITI	
Port-au-Prince	885
HONDURAS	
Tegucigalpa	814
HUNGARY	
Budapest	1,885
INDIA	
Mumbai (Bombay)	16,368
Kolkata (Calcutta)	13,217
Delhi	12,791
Chennai (Madras)	6,425
Bangalore	5,687
Hyderabad	5,534
Ahmadabad	4,519
Pune	3,756
Surat	2,811
Kanpur	2,690
Jaipur	2,324
Lucknow	2,267
Nagpur	2,123
Patna	1,707
Indore	1,639
Vadodara	1,492
Bhopal	1,455
Coimbatore	1,446
Ludhiana	1,395
Cochin	1,355
Vishakhapatnam	1,329
Agra	1,321
Varanasi	1,212
Madurai	1,195
Meerut	1,167
Nasik	1,152
Jabalpur	1,117
Jamshedpur	1,102
Asansol	1,090
Faridabad	1,055
Allahabad	1,050
Amritsar	1,011
Vijayawada	1,011
Rajkot	1,002
INDONESIA	
Jakarta	11,500
Surabaya	2,701
Bandung	2,368
Medan	1,910
Semarang	1,366
Palembang	1,352
Tangerang	1,198
Ujung Pandang	1,092
IRAN	
Tehran	6,759
Mashhad	1,887
Esfahan	1,266
Tabriz	1,191
Shiraz	1,053
Karaj	941
Ahvaz	805
Qom	778
Bakhtaran	693
IRAQ	
Baghdad	3,841
As Sulaymaniyah	952
Arbil	770
Al Mawsil	664
Al Kazimiyah	521
IRELAND	
Dublin	1,024
ISRAEL	
Tel Aviv-Yafo	1,880
Jerusalem	591
ITALY	
Rome	2,654
Milan	1,306
Naples	1,050
Turin	923
Palermo	689
Genoa	659
IVORY COAST	
Abidjan	2,500
JAMAICA	
Kingston	644
JAPAN	
Tokyo	17,950
Yokohama	3,427
Osaka	2,599
Nagoya	2,171
Sapporo	1,822
Kobe	1,494
Kyoto	1,468
Fukuoka	1,341
Kawasaki	1,250
Hiroshima	1,126
Kitakyushu	1,011
Sendai	1,008
JORDAN	
Amman	1,752
KAZAKSTAN	
Almaty	1,151
Qaraghandy	574
KENYA	
Nairobi	2,000
Mombasa	600
KOREA, NORTH	
Pyŏngyang	2,741
Hamhung	710
Chŏngjin	583
KOREA, SOUTH	
Seoul	10,231
Pusan	3,814
Taegu	2,449
Inch'on	2,308
Taejŏn	1,272
Kwangju	1,258
Ulsan	967
Sŏngnam	869
Puch'on	779
Suwŏn	756
Anyang	590
Chŏnju	563
Chŏngju	531
Ansan	510
P'ohang	509
KYRGYZSTAN	
Bishkek	589
LAOS	
Vientiane	532
LATVIA	
Riga	811
LEBANON	
Beirut	1,500
Tripoli	500
LIBERIA	
Monrovia	962
LIBYA	
Tripoli	960
LITHUANIA	
Vilnius	580
MACEDONIA	
Skopje	541
MADAGASCAR	
Antananarivo	1,053
MALAYSIA	
Kuala Lumpur	1,145
MALI	
Bamako	810
MAURITANIA	
Nouakchott	735
MEXICO	
Mexico City	15,643
Guadalajara	2,847
Monterrey	2,522
Puebla	1,055
León	872
Ciudad Juárez	798
Tijuana	743
Culiacán	602
Mexicali	602
Acapulco	592
Mérida	557
Chihuahua	530
San Luis Potosí	526
Aguascalientés	506
MOLDOVA	
Chişinău	658
MONGOLIA	
Ulan Bator	673
MOROCCO	
Casablanca	2,943
Rabat-Salé	1,220
Marrakesh	602
Fès	564
MOZAMBIQUE	
Maputo	2,000
NEPAL	
Katmandu	535
NETHERLANDS	
Amsterdam	1,115
Rotterdam	1,086
The Hague	700
Utrecht	557
NEW ZEALAND	
Auckland	1,090
NICARAGUA	
Managua	864
NIGERIA	
Lagos	10,287
Ibadan	1,432
Ogbomosho	730
Kano	674
NORWAY	
Oslo	502
PAKISTAN	
Karachi	9,269
Lahore	5,064
Faisalabad	1,977
Rawalpindi	1,406
Multan	1,182
Hyderabad	1,151
Gujranwala	1,125
Peshawar	988
Quetta	560
Islamabad	525
PARAGUAY	
Asunción	945
PERU	
Lima	6,601
Arequipa	620
Trujillo	509
PHILIPPINES	
Manila	8,594
Quezon City	1,989
Caloocan	1,023
Davao	1,009
Cebu	662
Zamboanga	511
POLAND	
Warsaw	1,626
Lódz	815
Kraków	740
Wroclaw	641
Poznań	580
PORTUGAL	
Lisbon	2,561
Oporto	1,174
ROMANIA	
Bucharest	2,028
RUSSIA	
Moscow	8,405
St Petersburg	4,216
Nizhniy Novgorod	1,371
Novosibirsk	1,367
Yekaterinburg	1,275
Samara	1,170
Omsk	1,158
Kazan	1,085
Chelyabinsk	1,084
Ufa	1,082
Perm	1,025
Rostov	1,023
Volgograd	1,005
SAUDI ARABIA	
Riyadh	1,800
Jedda	1,500
Mecca	630
SENEGAL	
Dakar	1,905
SIERRA LEONE	
Freetown	505
SINGAPORE	
Singapore	3,866
SOMALIA	
Mogadishu	997
SOUTH AFRICA	
Cape Town	2,350
Johannesburg	1,196
Durban	1,137
Pretoria	1,080
Port Elizabeth	853
Vanderbijlpark-Vereeniging	774
Soweto	597
Sasolburg	540
SPAIN	
Madrid	3,030
Barcelona	1,615
Valencia	763
Sevilla	720
Zaragoza	608
Málaga	532
SRI LANKA	
Colombo	1,863
SUDAN	
Omdurman	1,271
Khartoum	925
Khartoum North	701
SWEDEN	
Stockholm	727
SWITZERLAND	
Zürich	733
SYRIA	
Aleppo	1,813
Damascus	1,394
Homs	659
TAIWAN	
T'aipei	2,596
Kaohsiung	1,435
T'aichung	858
T'ainan	708
Panch'iao	539
TAJIKISTAN	
Dushanbe	524
TANZANIA	
Dar-es-Salaam	1,361
THAILAND	
Bangkok	7,507
TOGO	
Lomé	590
TUNISIA	
Tunis	1,827
TURKEY	
Istanbul	8,506
Ankara	3,294
Izmir	2,554
Bursa	1,485
Adana	1,273
Konya	1,140
Mersin (Içel)	956
Gaziantep	867
Antalya	867
Kayseri	862
Diyarbakir	833
Urfa	785
Manisa	696
Kocaeli	629
Antalya	591
Samsun	590
Kahramanmaras	551
Balikesir	538
Eskisehir	519
Erzurum	512
Malatya	510
TURKMENISTAN	
Ashkhabad	536
UGANDA	
Kampala	954
UKRAINE	
Kiev	2,621
Kharkov	1,521
Dnepropetrovsk	1,122
Donetsk	1,065
Odessa	1,027
Zaporizhzhya	863
Lviv	794
Kryvyy Rih	720
Mykolayiv	518
Mariupol	500
UNITED ARAB EMIRATES	
Abu Dhabi	928
Dubai	674
UNITED KINGDOM	
London	8,089
Birmingham	2,373
Manchester	2,353
Liverpool	852
Glasgow	832
Sheffield	661
Nottingham	649
Newcastle	617
Bristol	552
Leeds	529
UNITED STATES	
New York	21,200
Los Angeles	16,374
Chicago–Gary	9,158
Washington–Baltimore	7,608
San Francisco–San Jose	7,039
Philadelphia–Atlantic City	6,188
Boston–Worcester	5,819
Detroit–Flint	5,456
Dallas–Fort Worth	5,222
Houston–Galveston	4,670
Atlanta	4,112
Miami–Fort Lauderdale	3,876
Seattle–Tacoma	3,554
Phoenix–Mesa	3,252
Minneapolis–St Paul	2,969
Cleveland–Akron	2,946
San Diego	2,814
St Louis	2,604
Denver–Boulder	2,582
San Juan	2,450
Tampa–Saint Petersburg	2,396
Pittsburgh	2,359
Portland–Salem	2,265
Cincinnati–Hamilton	1,979
Sacramento–Yolo	1,797
Kansas City	1,776
Milwaukee–Racine	1,690
Orlando	1,645
Indianapolis	1,607
San Antonio	1,592
Norfolk–Virginia Beach –Newport News	1,570
Las Vegas	1,563
Columbus, OH	1,540
Charlotte–Gastonia	1,499
New Orleans	1,338
Salt Lake City	1,334
Greensboro–Winston Salem–High Point	1,252
Austin–San Marcos	1,250
Nashville	1,231
Providence–Fall River	1,189
Raleigh–Durham	1,188
Hartford	1,183
Buffalo–Niagara Falls	1,170
Memphis	1,136
West Palm Beach	1,131
Jacksonville, FL	1,100
Rochester	1,098
Grand Rapids	1,089
Oklahoma City	1,083
Louisville	1,026
Richmond–Petersburg	997
Greenville	962
Dayton–Springfield	951
Fresno	923
Birmingham	921
Honolulu	876
Albany–Schenectady	876
Tucson	844
Tulsa	803
Syracuse	732
Omaha	717
Albuquerque	713
Knoxville	687
El Paso	680
Bakersfield	662
Allentown	638
Harrisburg	629
Scranton	625
Toledo	618
Baton Rouge	603
Youngstown–Warren	595
Springfield, MA	592
Sarasota	590
Little Rock	584
McAllen	569
Stockton–Lodi	564
Charleston	549
Wichita	545
Mobile	540
Columbia, SC	537
Colorado Springs	517
Fort Wayne	502
URUGUAY	
Montevideo	1,379
UZBEKISTAN	
Tashkent	2,118
VENEZUELA	
Caracas	1,975
Maracaibo	1,706
Valencia	1,263
Barquisimeto	811
Ciudad Guayana	642
Petare	176
Maracay	459
VIETNAM	
Ho Chi Minh City	4,322
Hanoi	3,056
Haiphong	783
YEMEN	
Sana'	972
Aden	562
YUGOSLAVIA	
Belgrade	1,598
ZAMBIA	
Lusaka	982
ZIMBABWE	
Harare	1,189
Bulawayo	622

* SAR = Special Administrative Region of China

World Statistics: Climate

Rainfall and temperature figures are provided for more than 70 cities around the world. As climate is affected by altitude, the height of each city is shown in metres beneath its name. For each location, the top row of figures shows the total rainfall or snow in millimetres, and the bottom row the average temperature in degrees Celsius; the average annual temperature and total annual rainfall are at the end of the rows. The map opposite shows the city locations.

CITY	JAN.	FEB.	MAR.	APR.	MAY	JUNE	JULY	AUG.	SEPT.	OCT.	NOV.	DEC.	YEAR
EUROPE													
Athens, Greece	62	37	37	23	23	14	6	7	15	51	56	71	402
107 m	10	10	12	16	20	25	28	28	24	20	15	11	18
Berlin, Germany	46	40	33	42	49	65	73	69	48	49	46	43	603
55 m	–1	0	4	9	14	17	19	18	15	9	5	1	9
Istanbul, Turkey	109	92	72	46	38	34	34	30	58	81	103	119	816
14 m	5	6	7	11	16	20	23	23	20	16	12	8	14
Lisbon, Portugal	111	76	109	54	44	16	3	4	33	62	93	103	708
77 m	11	12	14	16	17	20	22	23	21	18	14	12	17
London, UK	54	40	37	37	46	45	57	59	49	57	64	48	593
5 m	4	5	7	9	12	16	18	17	15	11	8	5	11
Málaga, Spain	61	51	62	46	26	5	1	3	29	64	64	62	474
33 m	12	13	16	17	19	29	25	26	23	20	16	13	18
Moscow, Russia	39	38	36	37	53	58	88	71	58	45	47	54	624
156 m	–13	–10	–4	6	13	16	18	17	12	6	–1	–7	4
Odesa, Ukraine	57	62	30	21	34	34	42	37	37	13	35	71	473
64 m	–3	–1	2	9	15	20	22	22	18	12	9	1	10
Paris, France	56	46	35	42	57	54	59	64	55	50	51	50	619
75 m	3	4	8	11	15	18	20	19	17	12	7	4	12
Rome, Italy	71	62	57	51	46	37	15	21	63	99	129	93	744
17 m	8	9	11	14	18	22	25	25	22	17	13	10	16
Shannon, Ireland	94	67	56	53	61	57	77	79	86	86	96	117	929
2 m	5	5	7	9	12	14	16	16	14	11	8	6	10
Stockholm, Sweden	43	30	25	31	34	45	61	76	60	48	53	48	554
44 m	–3	–3	–1	5	10	15	18	17	12	7	3	0	7
ASIA													
Bahrain	8	18	13	8	<3	0	0	0	0	0	18	18	81
5 m	17	18	21	25	29	32	33	34	31	28	24	19	26
Bangkok, Thailand	8	20	36	58	198	160	160	175	305	206	66	5	1,397
2 m	26	28	29	30	29	29	28	28	28	28	26	25	28
Beirut, Lebanon	191	158	94	53	18	3	<3	<3	5	51	132	185	892
34 m	14	14	16	18	22	24	27	28	26	24	19	16	21
Bombay (Mumbai), India	3	3	3	<3	18	485	617	340	264	64	13	3	1,809
11 m	24	24	26	28	30	29	27	27	27	28	27	26	27
Calcutta, India	10	31	36	43	140	297	325	328	252	114	20	5	1,600
6 m	20	22	27	30	30	30	29	29	29	28	23	19	26
Colombo, Sri Lanka	89	69	147	231	371	224	135	109	160	348	315	147	2,365
7 m	26	26	27	28	28	27	27	27	27	27	26	26	27
Harbin, China	6	5	10	23	43	94	112	104	46	33	8	5	488
160 m	–18	–15	–5	6	13	19	22	21	14	4	–6	–16	3

CITY	JAN.	FEB.	MAR.	APR.	MAY	JUNE	JULY	AUG.	SEPT.	OCT.	NOV.	DEC.	YEAR
ASIA (continued)													
Ho Chi Minh, Vietnam	15	3	13	43	221	330	315	269	335	269	114	56	1,984
9 m	26	27	29	30	29	28	28	28	27	27	27	26	28
Hong Kong, China	33	46	74	137	292	394	381	361	257	114	43	31	2,162
33 m	16	15	18	22	26	28	28	28	27	25	21	18	23
Jakarta, Indonesia	300	300	211	147	114	97	64	43	66	112	142	203	1,798
8 m	26	26	27	27	27	27	27	27	27	27	27	26	27
Kabul, Afghanistan	31	36	94	102	20	5	3	3	<3	15	20	10	338
1,815 m	–3	–1	6	13	18	22	25	24	20	14	7	3	12
Karachi, Pakistan	13	10	8	3	3	18	81	41	13	<3	3	5	196
4 m	19	20	24	28	30	31	30	29	28	28	24	20	26
Kazalinsk, Kazakstan	10	10	13	13	15	5	5	8	8	10	13	15	125
63 m	–12	–11	–3	6	18	23	25	23	16	8	–1	–7	7
New Delhi, India	23	18	13	8	13	74	180	172	117	10	3	10	640
218 m	14	17	23	28	33	34	31	30	29	26	20	15	25
Omsk, Russia	15	8	8	13	31	51	51	51	28	25	18	20	318
85 m	–22	–19	–12	–1	10	16	18	16	10	1	–11	–18	–1
Shanghai, China	48	58	84	94	94	180	147	142	130	71	51	36	1,135
7 m	4	5	9	14	20	24	28	28	23	19	12	7	16
Singapore	252	173	193	188	173	173	170	196	178	208	254	257	2,413
10 m	26	27	28	28	28	28	28	27	27	27	27	27	27
Tehran, Iran	46	38	46	36	13	3	3	3	3	8	20	31	246
1,220 m	2	5	9	16	21	26	30	29	25	18	12	6	17
Tokyo, Japan	48	74	107	135	147	165	142	152	234	208	97	56	1,565
6 m	3	4	7	13	17	21	25	26	23	17	11	6	14
Ulan Bator, Mongolia	<3	<3	3	5	10	28	76	51	23	5	5	3	208
1,325 m	–26	–21	–13	–1	6	14	16	14	8	–1	–13	–22	–3
Verkhoyansk, Russia	5	5	3	5	8	23	28	25	13	8	8	5	134
100 m	–50	–45	–32	–15	0	12	14	9	2	–15	–38	–48	–17
AFRICA													
Addis Ababa, Ethiopia	<3	3	25	135	213	201	206	239	102	28	<3	0	1,151
2,450 m	19	20	20	20	19	18	18	19	21	22	21	20	20
Antananarivo, Madag.	300	279	178	53	18	8	8	10	18	61	135	287	1,356
1,372 m	21	21	21	19	18	15	14	15	17	19	21	21	19
Cairo, Egypt	5	5	5	3	3	<3	0	0	<3	<3	3	5	28
116 m	13	15	18	21	25	28	28	28	26	24	20	15	22
Cape Town, S. Africa	15	8	18	48	79	84	89	66	43	31	18	10	508
17 m	21	21	20	17	14	13	12	13	14	16	18	19	17
Jo'burg, S. Africa	114	109	89	38	25	8	8	8	23	56	107	125	709
1,665 m	20	20	18	16	13	10	11	13	16	18	19	20	16

CITY	JAN.	FEB.	MAR.	APR.	MAY	JUNE	JULY	AUG.	SEPT.	OCT.	NOV.	DEC.	YEAR
AFRICA (continued)													
Khartoum, Sudan	<3	<3	<3	<3	3	8	53	71	18	5	<3	0	158
390 m	24	25	28	31	33	34	32	31	32	32	28	25	29
Kinshasa, Congo (D.R.)	135	145	196	196	158	8	3	3	31	119	221	142	1,354
325 m	26	26	27	27	26	24	23	24	25	26	26	26	25
Lagos, Nigeria	28	46	102	150	269	460	279	64	140	206	69	25	1,836
3 m	27	28	29	28	28	26	26	25	26	26	28	28	27
Lusaka, Zambia	231	191	142	18	3	<3	<3	0	<3	10	91	150	836
1,277 m	21	22	21	21	19	16	16	18	22	24	23	22	21
Monrovia, Liberia	31	56	97	216	516	973	996	373	744	772	236	130	5,138
23 m	26	26	27	27	26	25	24	25	25	25	26	26	26
Nairobi, Kenya	38	64	125	211	158	46	15	23	31	53	109	86	958
820 m	19	19	19	19	18	16	16	16	18	19	18	18	18
Timbuktu, Mali	<3	<3	3	<3	5	23	79	81	38	3	<3	<3	231
301 m	22	24	28	32	34	35	32	30	32	31	28	23	29
Tunis, Tunisia	64	51	41	36	18	8	3	8	33	51	48	61	419
66 m	10	11	13	16	19	23	26	27	25	20	16	11	18
Walvis Bay, Namibia	<3	5	8	3	3	<3	<3	3	<3	<3	<3	<3	23
7 m	19	19	19	18	17	16	15	14	14	15	17	18	18
AUSTRALIA, NEW ZEALAND AND ANTARCTICA													
Alice Springs, Aust.	43	33	28	10	15	13	8	8	8	18	31	38	252
579 m	29	28	25	20	15	12	12	14	18	23	26	28	21
Christchurch, N.Z.	56	43	48	48	66	66	69	48	46	43	48	56	638
10 m	16	16	14	12	9	6	6	7	9	12	14	16	11
Darwin, Australia	386	312	254	97	15	3	<3	3	13	51	119	239	1,491
30 m	29	29	29	29	28	26	25	26	28	29	30	29	28
Mawson, Antarctica	11	30	20	10	44	180	4	40	3	20	0	0	362
14 m	0	–5	–10	–14	–15	–16	–18	–18	–19	–13	–5	–1	–11
Perth, Australia	8	10	20	43	130	180	170	149	86	56	20	13	881
60 m	23	23	22	19	16	14	13	13	15	16	19	22	18
Sydney, Australia	89	102	127	135	127	117	117	76	73	71	73	73	1,181
42 m	22	22	21	18	15	13	12	13	15	18	19	21	17
NORTH AMERICA													
Anchorage, USA	20	18	15	10	13	18	41	66	66	56	25	23	371
40 m	–11	–8	–5	2	7	12	14	13	9	2	–5	–11	2
Chicago, USA	51	51	66	71	86	89	84	81	79	66	61	51	836
251 m	–4	–3	2	9	14	20	23	22	19	12	5	–1	10
Churchill, Canada	15	13	18	23	32	44	46	58	51	43	39	21	402
13 m	–28	–26	–20	–10	–2	6	12	11	5	–2	–12	–22	–7
Edmonton, Canada	25	19	19	22	43	77	89	78	39	17	16	25	466
676 m	–15	–10	–5	4	11	15	17	16	11	6	–4	–10	3
Honolulu, USA	104	66	79	48	25	18	23	28	36	48	64	104	643
12 m	23	18	19	20	22	24	25	26	26	24	22	19	22
Houston, USA	89	76	84	91	119	117	99	99	104	94	89	109	1,171
12 m	12	13	17	21	24	27	28	29	26	22	16	12	21

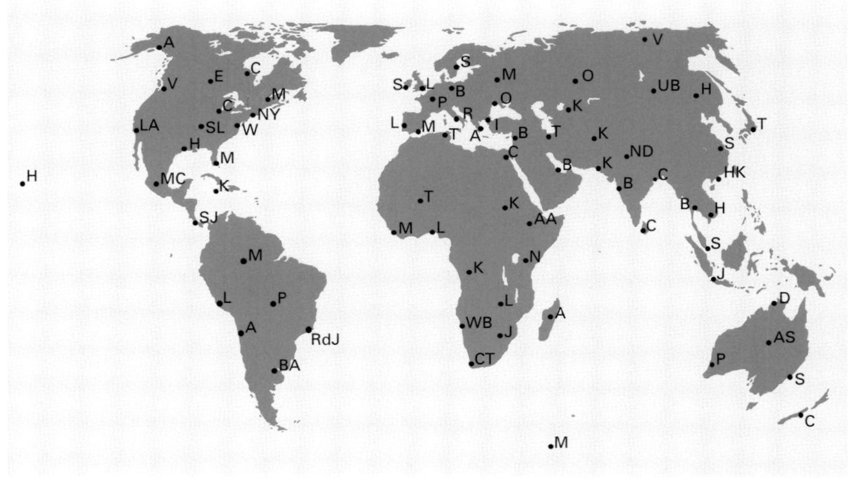

CITY	JAN.	FEB.	MAR.	APR.	MAY	JUNE	JULY	AUG.	SEPT.	OCT.	NOV.	DEC.	YEAR
NORTH AMERICA (continued)													
Kingston, Jamaica	23	15	23	31	102	89	38	91	99	180	74	36	800
34 m	25	25	25	26	26	28	28	28	27	27	26	26	26
Los Angeles, USA	79	76	71	25	10	3	<3	<3	5	15	31	66	381
95 m	13	14	14	16	17	19	21	22	21	18	16	14	17
Mexico City, Mexico	13	5	10	20	53	119	170	152	130	51	18	8	747
2,309 m	12	13	16	18	19	19	17	18	18	16	14	13	16
Miami, USA	71	53	64	81	173	178	155	160	203	234	71	51	1,516
8 m	20	20	22	23	25	27	28	28	27	25	22	21	24
Montréal, Canada	72	65	74	74	66	82	90	92	88	76	81	87	946
57 m	–10	–9	–3	–6	13	18	21	20	15	9	2	–7	6
New York City, USA	94	97	91	81	81	84	107	109	86	89	76	91	1,092
96 m	–1	–1	3	10	16	20	23	23	21	15	7	2	11
St Louis, USA	58	64	89	97	114	114	89	86	81	74	71	64	1,001
173 m	0	1	7	13	19	24	26	26	22	15	8	2	14
San José, Costa Rica	15	5	20	46	229	241	211	241	305	300	145	41	1,798
1,146 m	19	19	21	21	22	21	21	21	21	20	20	19	20
Vancouver, Canada	154	115	101	60	52	45	32	41	67	114	150	182	1,113
14 m	3	5	6	9	12	15	17	17	14	10	6	4	10
Washington, DC, USA	86	76	91	84	94	99	112	109	94	74	66	79	1,064
22 m	1	2	7	12	18	23	25	24	20	14	8	3	13
SOUTH AMERICA													
Antofagasta, Chile	0	0	0	<3	<3	3	5	3	<3	3	<3	0	13
94 m	21	21	20	18	16	15	14	14	15	16	18	19	17
Buenos Aires, Arg.	79	71	109	89	76	61	56	61	79	86	84	99	950
27 m	23	23	21	17	13	9	10	11	13	15	19	22	16
Lima, Peru	3	<3	<3	<3	5	5	8	8	8	3	3	<3	41
120 m	23	24	24	22	19	17	17	16	17	18	19	21	20
Manaus, Brazil	249	231	262	221	170	84	58	38	46	107	142	203	1,811
44 m	28	28	28	27	28	28	28	28	29	29	29	28	28
Paraná, Brazil	287	236	239	102	13	<3	3	5	28	127	231	310	1,582
260 m	23	23	23	23	23	21	21	22	24	24	24	23	23
Rio de Janeiro, Brazil	125	122	130	107	79	53	41	43	66	79	104	137	1,082
61 m	26	26	25	24	22	21	21	21	21	22	23	25	23

World Statistics: Physical Dimensions

Each topic list is divided into continents and within a continent the items are listed in order of size. The bottom part of many of the lists is selective in order to give examples from as many different countries as possible. The order of the continents is as in the atlas, Europe through to South America. The world top ten are shown in square brackets; in the case of mountains this has not been done because the world top 30 are all in Asia. The figures are rounded as appropriate.

WORLD, CONTINENTS, OCEANS

THE WORLD	km²	miles²	%
The World	509,450,000	196,672,000	–
Land	149,450,000	57,688,000	29.3
Water	360,000,000	138,984,000	70.7
Asia	44,500,000	17,177,000	29.8
Africa	30,302,000	11,697,000	20.3
North America	24,241,000	9,357,000	16.2
South America	17,793,000	6,868,000	11.9
Antarctica	14,100,000	5,443,000	9.4
Europe	9,957,000	3,843,000	6.7
Australia & Oceania	8,557,000	3,303,000	5.7
Pacific Ocean	179,679,000	69,356,000	49.9
Atlantic Ocean	92,373,000	35,657,000	25.7
Indian Ocean	73,917,000	28,532,000	20.5
Arctic Ocean	14,090,000	5,439,000	3.9

SEAS

PACIFIC	km²	miles²
South China Sea	2,974,600	1,148,500
Bering Sea	2,268,000	875,000
Sea of Okhotsk	1,528,000	590,000
East China & Yellow	1,249,000	482,000
Sea of Japan	1,008,000	389,000
Gulf of California	162,000	62,500
Bass Strait	75,000	29,000

ATLANTIC	km²	miles²
Caribbean Sea	2,766,000	1,068,000
Mediterranean Sea	2,516,000	971,000
Gulf of Mexico	1,543,000	596,000
Hudson Bay	1,232,000	476,000
North Sea	575,000	223,000
Black Sea	462,000	178,000
Baltic Sea	422,170	163,000
Gulf of St Lawrence	238,000	92,000

INDIAN	km²	miles²
Red Sea	438,000	169,000
The Gulf	239,000	92,000

MOUNTAINS

EUROPE		m	ft
Elbrus	Russia	5,642	18,510
Mont Blanc	France/Italy	4,807	15,771
Monte Rosa	Italy/Switzerland	4,634	15,203
Dom	Switzerland	4,545	14,911
Liskamm	Switzerland	4,527	14,852
Weisshorn	Switzerland	4,505	14,780
Taschorn	Switzerland	4,490	14,730
Matterhorn/Cervino	Italy/Switz.	4,478	14,691
Mont Maudit	France/Italy	4,465	14,649
Dent Blanche	Switzerland	4,356	14,291
Nadelhorn	Switzerland	4,327	14,196
Grandes Jorasses	France/Italy	4,208	13,806
Jungfrau	Switzerland	4,158	13,642
Barre des Ecrins	France	4,103	13,461
Gran Paradiso	Italy	4,061	13,323
Piz Bernina	Italy/Switzerland	4,049	13,284
Eiger	Switzerland	3,970	13,025
Monte Viso	Italy	3,841	12,602
Grossglockner	Austria	3,797	12,457
Wildspitze	Austria	3,772	12,382
Monte Disgrazia	Italy	3,678	12,066
Mulhacén	Spain	3,478	11,411
Pico de Aneto	Spain	3,404	11,168
Marmolada	Italy	3,342	10,964
Etna	Italy	3,340	10,958
Zugspitze	Germany	2,962	9,718
Musala	Bulgaria	2,925	9,596
Olympus	Greece	2,917	9,570
Triglav	Slovenia	2,863	9,393
Monte Cinto	France (Corsica)	2,710	8,891
Galdhöpiggen	Norway	2,468	8,100
Ben Nevis	UK	1,343	4,406

ASIA		m	ft
Everest	China/Nepal	8,850	29,035
K2 (Godwin Austen)	China/Kashmir	8,611	28,251
Kanchenjunga	India/Nepal	8,598	28,208
Lhotse	China/Nepal	8,516	27,939
Makalu	China/Nepal	8,481	27,824
Cho Oyu	China/Nepal	8,201	26,906
Dhaulagiri	Nepal	8,172	26,811
Manaslu	Nepal	8,156	26,758
Nanga Parbat	Kashmir	8,126	26,660
Annapurna	Nepal	8,078	26,502
Gasherbrum	China/Kashmir	8,068	26,469
Broad Peak	China/Kashmir	8,051	26,414
Xixabangma	China	8,012	26,286
Kangbachen	India/Nepal	7,902	25,925
Jannu	India/Nepal	7,902	25,925
Gayachung Kang	Nepal	7,897	25,909
Himalchuli	Nepal	7,893	25,896
Disteghil Sar	Kashmir	7,885	25,869
Nuptse	Nepal	7,879	25,849
Khunyang Chhish	Kashmir	7,852	25,761
Masherbrum	Kashmir	7,821	25,659
Nanda Devi	India	7,817	25,646
Rakaposhi	Kashmir	7,788	25,551
Batura	Kashmir	7,785	25,541
Namche Barwa	China	7,756	25,446
Kamet	India	7,756	25,446
Soltoro Kangri	Kashmir	7,742	25,400
Gurla Mandhata	China	7,728	25,354
Trivor	Pakistan	7,720	25,328
Kongur Shan	China	7,719	25,324
Tirich Mir	Pakistan	7,690	25,229
K'ula Shan	Bhutan/China	7,543	24,747
Pik Kommunizma	Tajikistan	7,495	24,590
Demavend	Iran	5,604	18,386
Ararat	Turkey	5,165	16,945
Gunong Kinabalu	Malaysia (Borneo)	4,101	13,455
Yu Shan	Taiwan	3,997	13,113
Fuji-San	Japan	3,776	12,388

AFRICA		m	ft
Kilimanjaro	Tanzania	5,895	19,340
Mt Kenya	Kenya	5,199	17,057
Ruwenzori (Margherita)	Uganda/Congo (D.R.)	5,109	16,762
Ras Dashan	Ethiopia	4,620	15,157
Meru	Tanzania	4,565	14,977
Karisimbi	Rwanda/Congo (D.R.)	4,507	14,787
Mt Elgon	Kenya/Uganda	4,321	14,176
Batu	Ethiopia	4,307	14,130
Guna	Ethiopia	4,231	13,882
Toubkal	Morocco	4,165	13,665
Irhil Mgoun	Morocco	4,071	13,356
Mt Cameroon	Cameroon	4,070	13,353
Amba Ferit	Ethiopia	3,875	13,042
Pico del Teide	Spain (Tenerife)	3,718	12,198
Thabana Ntlenyana	Lesotho	3,482	11,424
Emi Koussi	Chad	3,415	11,204
Mt aux Sources	Lesotho/S. Africa	3,282	10,768
Mt Piton	Réunion	3,069	10,069

OCEANIA		m	ft
Puncak Jaya	Indonesia	5,029	16,499
Puncak Trikora	Indonesia	4,750	15,584
Puncak Mandala	Indonesia	4,702	15,427
Mt Wilhelm	Papua NG	4,508	14,790
Mauna Kea	USA (Hawaii)	4,205	13,796
Mauna Loa	USA (Hawaii)	4,169	13,681
Mt Cook (Aoraki)	New Zealand	3,753	12,313
Mt Balbi	Solomon Is.	2,439	8,002
Orohena	Tahiti	2,241	7,352
Mt Kosciuszko	Australia	2,237	7,339

NORTH AMERICA		m	ft
Mt McKinley (Denali)	USA (Alaska)	6,194	20,321
Mt Logan	Canada	5,959	19,551
Citlaltepetl	Mexico	5,700	18,701
Mt St Elias	USA/Canada	5,489	18,008
Popocatepetl	Mexico	5,452	17,887
Mt Foraker	USA (Alaska)	5,304	17,401
Ixtaccihuatl	Mexico	5,286	17,342
Lucania	Canada	5,227	17,149
Mt Steele	Canada	5,073	16,644
Mt Bona	USA (Alaska)	5,005	16,420
Mt Blackburn	USA (Alaska)	4,996	16,391
Mt Sanford	USA (Alaska)	4,940	16,207
Mt Wood	Canada	4,848	15,905
Nevado de Toluca	Mexico	4,670	15,321
Mt Fairweather	USA (Alaska)	4,663	15,298
Mt Hunter	USA (Alaska)	4,442	14,573
Mt Whitney	USA	4,418	14,495
Mt Elbert	USA	4,399	14,432
Mt Harvard	USA	4,395	14,419
Mt Rainier	USA	4,392	14,409
Blanca Peak	USA	4,372	14,344
Longs Peak	USA	4,345	14,255
Tajumulco	Guatemala	4,220	13,845
Grand Teton	USA	4,197	13,770
Mt Waddington	Canada	3,994	13,104
Mt Robson	Canada	3,954	12,972
Chirripó Grande	Costa Rica	3,837	12,589
Pico Duarte	Dominican Rep.	3,175	10,417

NORTH AMERICA (continued)

SOUTH AMERICA		m	ft
Aconcagua	Argentina	6,960	22,834
Bonete	Argentina	6,872	22,546
Ojos del Salado	Argentina/Chile	6,863	22,516
Pissis	Argentina	6,779	22,241
Mercedario	Argentina/Chile	6,770	22,211
Huascaran	Peru	6,768	22,204
Llullaillaco	Argentina/Chile	6,723	22,057
Nudo de Cachi	Argentina	6,720	22,047
Yerupaja	Peru	6,632	21,758
N. de Tres Cruces	Argentina/Chile	6,620	21,719
Incahuasi	Argentina/Chile	6,601	21,654
Cerro Galan	Argentina	6,600	21,654
Tupungato	Argentina/Chile	6,570	21,555
Sajama	Bolivia	6,542	21,463
Illimani	Bolivia	6,485	21,276
Coropuna	Peru	6,425	21,079
Ausangate	Peru	6,384	20,945
Cerro del Toro	Argentina	6,380	20,932
Siula Grande	Peru	6,356	20,853
Chimborazo	Ecuador	6,267	20,561
Alpamayo	Peru	5,947	19,511
Cotapaxi	Ecuador	5,896	19,344
Pico Colon	Colombia	5,800	19,029
Pico Bolivar	Venezuela	5,007	16,427

ANTARCTICA	m	ft
Vinson Massif	4,897	16,066
Mt Kirkpatrick	4,528	14,855
Mt Markham	4,349	14,268

OCEAN DEPTHS

ATLANTIC OCEAN	m	ft	
Puerto Rico (Milwaukee) Deep	9,220	30,249	[7]
Cayman Trench	7,680	25,197	[10]
Gulf of Mexico	5,203	17,070	
Mediterranean Sea	5,121	16,801	
Black Sea	2,211	7,254	
North Sea	660	2,165	
Baltic Sea	463	1,519	
Hudson Bay	258	846	

INDIAN OCEAN	m	ft
Java Trench	7,450	24,442
Red Sea	2,635	8,454
Persian Gulf	73	239

PACIFIC OCEAN	m	ft	
Mariana Trench	11,022	36,161	[1]
Tonga Trench	10,882	35,702	[2]
Japan Trench	10,554	34,626	[3]
Kuril Trench	10,542	34,587	[4]
Mindanao Trench	10,497	34,439	[5]
Kermadec Trench	10,047	32,962	[6]

PACIFIC OCEAN (continued)	m	ft	
Peru–Chile Trench	8,050	26,410	[8]
Aleutian Trench	7,822	25,662	[9]

ARCTIC OCEAN	m	ft
Molloy Deep	5,608	18,399

LAND LOWS

		m	ft
Dead Sea	Asia	–411	–1,348
Lake Assal	Africa	–156	–512
Death Valley	N. America	–86	–282
Valdés Peninsula	S. America	–40	–131
Caspian Sea	Europe	–28	–92
Lake Eyre North	Oceania	–16	–52

RIVERS

EUROPE		km	miles	
Volga	Caspian Sea	3,700	2,300	
Danube	Black Sea	2,850	1,770	
Ural	Caspian Sea	2,535	1,575	
Dnepr (Dnipro)	Black Sea	2,285	1,420	
Kama	Volga	2,030	1,260	
Don	Black Sea	1,990	1,240	
Petchora	Arctic Ocean	1,790	1,110	
Oka	Volga	1,480	920	
Belaya	Kama	1,420	880	
Dnister (Dniester)	Black Sea	1,400	870	
Vyatka	Kama	1,370	850	
Rhine	North Sea	1,320	820	
N. Dvina	Arctic Ocean	1,290	800	
Desna	Dnepr (Dnipro)	1,190	740	
Elbe	North Sea	1,145	710	
Wisla	Baltic Sea	1,090	675	
Loire	Atlantic Ocean	1,020	635	

ASIA		km	miles	
Yangtze	Pacific Ocean	6,380	3,960	[3]
Yenisey–Angara	Arctic Ocean	5,550	3,445	[5]
Huang He	Pacific Ocean	5,464	3,395	[6]
Ob–Irtysh	Arctic Ocean	5,410	3,360	[7]
Mekong	Pacific Ocean	4,500	2,795	[9]
Amur	Pacific Ocean	4,400	2,730	[10]
Lena	Arctic Ocean	4,400	2,730	
Irtysh	Ob	4,250	2,640	
Yenisey	Arctic Ocean	4,090	2,540	
Ob	Arctic Ocean	3,680	2,285	
Indus	Indian Ocean	3,100	1,925	
Brahmaputra	Indian Ocean	2,900	1,800	
Syrdarya	Aral Sea	2,860	1,775	
Salween	Indian Ocean	2,800	1,740	
Euphrates	Indian Ocean	2,700	1,675	
Vilyuy	Lena	2,650	1,645	
Kolyma	Arctic Ocean	2,600	1,615	
Amudarya	Aral Sea	2,540	1,575	
Ural	Caspian Sea	2,535	1,575	
Ganges	Indian Ocean	2,510	1,560	
Si Kiang	Pacific Ocean	2,100	1,305	
Irrawaddy	Indian Ocean	2,010	1,250	
Tarim–Yarkand	Lop Nor	2,000	1,240	
Tigris	Indian Ocean	1,900	1,180	

AFRICA		km	miles	
Nile	Mediterranean	6,670	4,140	[1]
Congo	Atlantic Ocean	4,670	2,900	[8]
Niger	Atlantic Ocean	4,180	2,595	
Zambezi	Indian Ocean	3,540	2,200	
Oubangi/Uele	Congo (D.R.)	2,250	1,400	
Kasai	Congo (D.R.)	1,950	1,210	
Shaballe	Indian Ocean	1,930	1,200	
Orange	Atlantic Ocean	1,860	1,155	
Cubango	Okavango Swamps	1,800	1,120	
Limpopo	Indian Ocean	1,600	995	
Senegal	Atlantic Ocean	1,600	995	
Volta	Atlantic Ocean	1,500	930	

AUSTRALIA		km	miles
Murray–Darling	Indian Ocean	3,750	2,330
Darling	Murray	3,070	1,905
Murray	Indian Ocean	2,575	1,600
Murrumbidgee	Murray	1,690	1,050

NORTH AMERICA		km	miles	
Mississippi–Missouri	Gulf of Mexico	6,020	3,740	[4]
Mackenzie	Arctic Ocean	4,240	2,630	
Mississippi	Gulf of Mexico	3,780	2,350	
Missouri	Mississippi	3,780	2,350	
Yukon	Pacific Ocean	3,185	1,980	
Rio Grande	Gulf of Mexico	3,030	1,880	

NORTH AMERICA (continued)		km	miles
Arkansas	Mississippi	2,340	1,450
Colorado	Pacific Ocean	2,330	1,445
Red	Mississippi	2,040	1,270
Columbia	Pacific Ocean	1,950	1,210
Saskatchewan	Lake Winnipeg	1,940	1,205
Snake	Columbia	1,670	1,040
Churchill	Hudson Bay	1,600	990
Ohio	Mississippi	1,580	980
Brazos	Gulf of Mexico	1,400	870
St Lawrence	Atlantic Ocean	1,170	730

SOUTH AMERICA		km	miles	
Amazon	Atlantic Ocean	6,450	4,010	[2]
Paraná–Plate	Atlantic Ocean	4,500	2,800	
Purus	Amazon	3,350	2,080	
Madeira	Amazon	3,200	1,990	
São Francisco	Atlantic Ocean	2,900	1,800	
Paraná	Plate	2,800	1,740	
Tocantins	Atlantic Ocean	2,750	1,710	
Paraguay	Paraná	2,550	1,580	
Orinoco	Atlantic Ocean	2,500	1,550	
Pilcomayo	Paraná	2,500	1,550	
Araguaia	Tocantins	2,250	1,400	
Juruá	Amazon	2,000	1,240	
Xingu	Amazon	1,980	1,230	
Ucayali	Amazon	1,900	1,180	
Maranón	Amazon	1,600	990	
Uruguay	Plate	1,600	990	

LAKES

EUROPE		km²	miles²
Lake Ladoga	Russia	17,700	6,800
Lake Onega	Russia	9,700	3,700
Saimaa system	Finland	8,000	3,100
Vänern	Sweden	5,500	2,100
Rybinskoye Res.	Russia	4,700	1,800

ASIA		km²	miles²	
Caspian Sea	Asia	371,800	143,550	[1]
Lake Baykal	Russia	30,500	11,780	[8]
Aral Sea	Kazakstan/Uzbekistan	28,687	11,086	[10]
Tonlé Sap	Cambodia	20,000	7,700	
Lake Balqash	Kazakstan	18,500	7,100	
Lake Dongting	China	12,000	4,600	
Lake Ysyk	Kyrgyzstan	6,200	2,400	
Lake Orumiyeh	Iran	5,900	2,300	
Lake Koko	China	5,700	2,200	
Lake Poyang	China	5,000	1,900	
Lake Khanka	China/Russia	4,400	1,700	
Lake Van	Turkey	3,500	1,400	

AFRICA		km²	miles²	
Lake Victoria	E. Africa	68,000	26,000	[3]
Lake Tanganyika	C. Africa	33,000	13,000	[6]
Lake Malawi/Nyasa	E. Africa	29,600	11,430	[9]
Lake Chad	C. Africa	25,000	9,700	
Lake Turkana	Ethiopia/Kenya	8,500	3,300	
Lake Volta	Ghana	8,500	3,300	
Lake Bangweulu	Zambia	8,000	3,100	
Lake Rukwa	Tanzania	7,000	2,700	
Lake Mai-Ndombe	Congo (D.R.)	6,500	2,500	
Lake Kariba	Zambia/Zimbabwe	5,300	2,000	
Lake Albert	Uganda/Congo (D.R.)	5,300	2,000	
Lake Nasser	Egypt/Sudan	5,200	2,000	
Lake Mweru	Zambia/Congo (D.R.)	4,900	1,900	
Lake Cabora Bassa	Mozambique	4,500	1,700	
Lake Kyoga	Uganda	4,400	1,700	
Lake Tana	Ethiopia	3,630	1,400	

AUSTRALIA		km²	miles²
Lake Eyre	Australia	8,900	3,400
Lake Torrens	Australia	5,800	2,200
Lake Gairdner	Australia	4,800	1,900

NORTH AMERICA		km²	miles²	
Lake Superior	Canada/USA	82,350	31,800	[2]
Lake Huron	Canada/USA	59,600	23,010	[4]
Lake Michigan	USA	58,000	22,400	[5]
Great Bear Lake	Canada	31,800	12,280	[7]
Great Slave Lake	Canada	28,500	11,000	
Lake Erie	Canada/USA	25,700	9,900	
Lake Winnipeg	Canada	24,400	9,400	
Lake Ontario	Canada/USA	19,500	7,500	
Lake Nicaragua	Nicaragua	8,200	3,200	
Lake Athabasca	Canada	8,100	3,100	
Smallwood Reservoir	Canada	6,530	2,520	
Reindeer Lake	Canada	6,400	2,500	
Nettilling Lake	Canada	5,500	2,100	
Lake Winnipegosis	Canada	5,400	2,100	

SOUTH AMERICA		km²	miles²
Lake Titicaca	Bolivia/Peru	8,300	3,200
Lake Poopo	Bolivia	2,800	1,100

ISLANDS

EUROPE		km²	miles²	
Great Britain	UK	229,880	88,700	[8]
Iceland	Atlantic Ocean	103,000	39,800	
Ireland	Ireland/UK	84,400	32,600	
Novaya Zemlya (N.)	Russia	48,200	18,600	
W. Spitzbergen	Norway	39,000	15,100	
Novaya Zemlya (S.)	Russia	33,200	12,800	
Sicily	Italy	25,500	9,800	
Sardinia	Italy	24,000	9,300	
N.E. Spitzbergen	Norway	15,000	5,600	
Corsica	France	8,700	3,400	
Crete	Greece	8,350	3,200	
Zealand	Denmark	6,850	2,600	

ASIA		km²	miles²	
Borneo	S. E. Asia	744,360	287,400	[3]
Sumatra	Indonesia	473,600	182,860	[6]
Honshu	Japan	230,500	88,980	[7]
Sulawesi (Celebes)	Indonesia	189,000	73,000	
Java	Indonesia	126,700	48,900	
Luzon	Philippines	104,700	40,400	
Mindanao	Philippines	101,500	39,200	
Hokkaido	Japan	78,400	30,300	
Sakhalin	Russia	74,060	28,600	
Sri Lanka	Indian Ocean	65,600	25,300	
Taiwan	Pacific Ocean	36,000	13,900	
Kyushu	Japan	35,700	13,800	
Hainan	China	34,000	13,100	
Timor	Indonesia	33,600	13,000	
Shikoku	Japan	18,800	7,300	
Halmahera	Indonesia	18,000	6,900	
Ceram	Indonesia	17,150	6,600	
Sumbawa	Indonesia	15,450	6,000	
Flores	Indonesia	15,200	5,900	
Samar	Philippines	13,100	5,100	
Negros	Philippines	12,700	4,900	
Bangka	Indonesia	12,000	4,600	
Palawan	Philippines	12,000	4,600	
Panay	Philippines	11,500	4,400	
Sumba	Indonesia	11,100	4,300	
Mindoro	Philippines	9,750	3,800	

AFRICA		km²	miles²	
Madagascar	Indian Ocean	587,040	226,660	[4]
Socotra	Indian Ocean	3,600	1,400	
Réunion	Indian Ocean	2,500	965	
Tenerife	Atlantic Ocean	2,350	900	
Mauritius	Indian Ocean	1,865	720	

OCEANIA		km²	miles²	
New Guinea	Indon./Papua NG	821,030	317,000	[2]
New Zealand (S.)	Pacific Ocean	150,500	58,100	
New Zealand (N.)	Pacific Ocean	114,700	44,300	
Tasmania	Australia	67,800	26,200	
New Britain	Papua NG	37,800	14,600	
New Caledonia	Pacific Ocean	19,100	7,400	
Viti Levu	Fiji	10,500	4,100	
Hawaii	Pacific Ocean	10,450	4,000	
Bougainville	Papua NG	9,600	3,700	
Guadalcanal	Solomon Is.	6,500	2,500	
Vanua Levu	Fiji	5,550	2,100	
New Ireland	Papua NG	3,200	1,200	

NORTH AMERICA		km²	miles²	
Greenland	Atlantic Ocean	2,175,600	839,800	[1]
Baffin Is.	Canada	508,000	196,100	[5]
Victoria Is.	Canada	212,200	81,900	[9]
Ellesmere Is.	Canada	212,000	81,800	[10]
Cuba	Caribbean Sea	110,860	42,800	
Newfoundland	Canada	110,680	42,700	
Hispaniola	Dom. Rep./Haiti	76,200	29,400	
Banks Is.	Canada	67,000	25,900	
Devon Is.	Canada	54,500	21,000	
Melville Is.	Canada	42,400	16,400	
Vancouver Is.	Canada	32,150	12,400	
Somerset Is.	Canada	24,300	9,400	
Jamaica	Caribbean Sea	11,400	4,400	
Puerto Rico	Atlantic Ocean	8,900	3,400	
Cape Breton Is.	Canada	4,000	1,500	

SOUTH AMERICA		km²	miles²
Tierra del Fuego	Argentina/Chile	47,000	18,100
Falkland Is. (East)	Atlantic Ocean	6,800	2,600
South Georgia	Atlantic Ocean	4,200	1,600
Galapagos (Isabela)	Pacific Ocean	2,250	870

World: Regions in the News

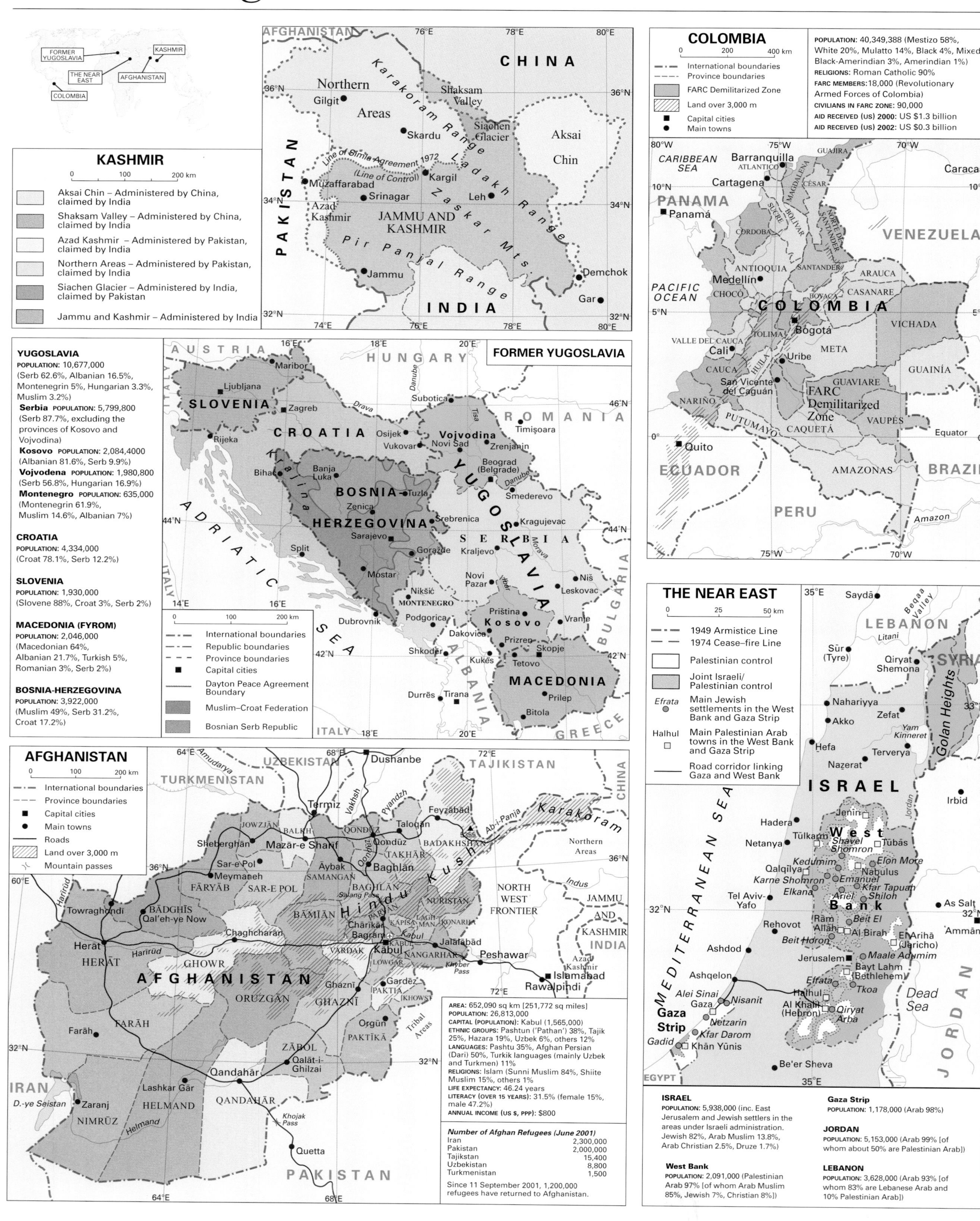

THE EARTH IN SPACE

The Universe 2

Star Charts and Constellations 4

The Solar System 8

The Earth: Time and Motion 10

The Earth from Space 12

The Dynamic Earth 14

Earthquakes and Volcanoes 16

Forces of Nature 18

Oceans and Ice 20

The Earth's Atmosphere 22

Climate and Weather 24

Water and Land Use 26

The Natural World 28

The Human World 30

Languages and Religions 32

International Organizations 34

Agriculture 36

Energy and Minerals 38

World Economies 40

Trade and Commerce 42

Travel and Communications 44

The World Today 46

The Universe

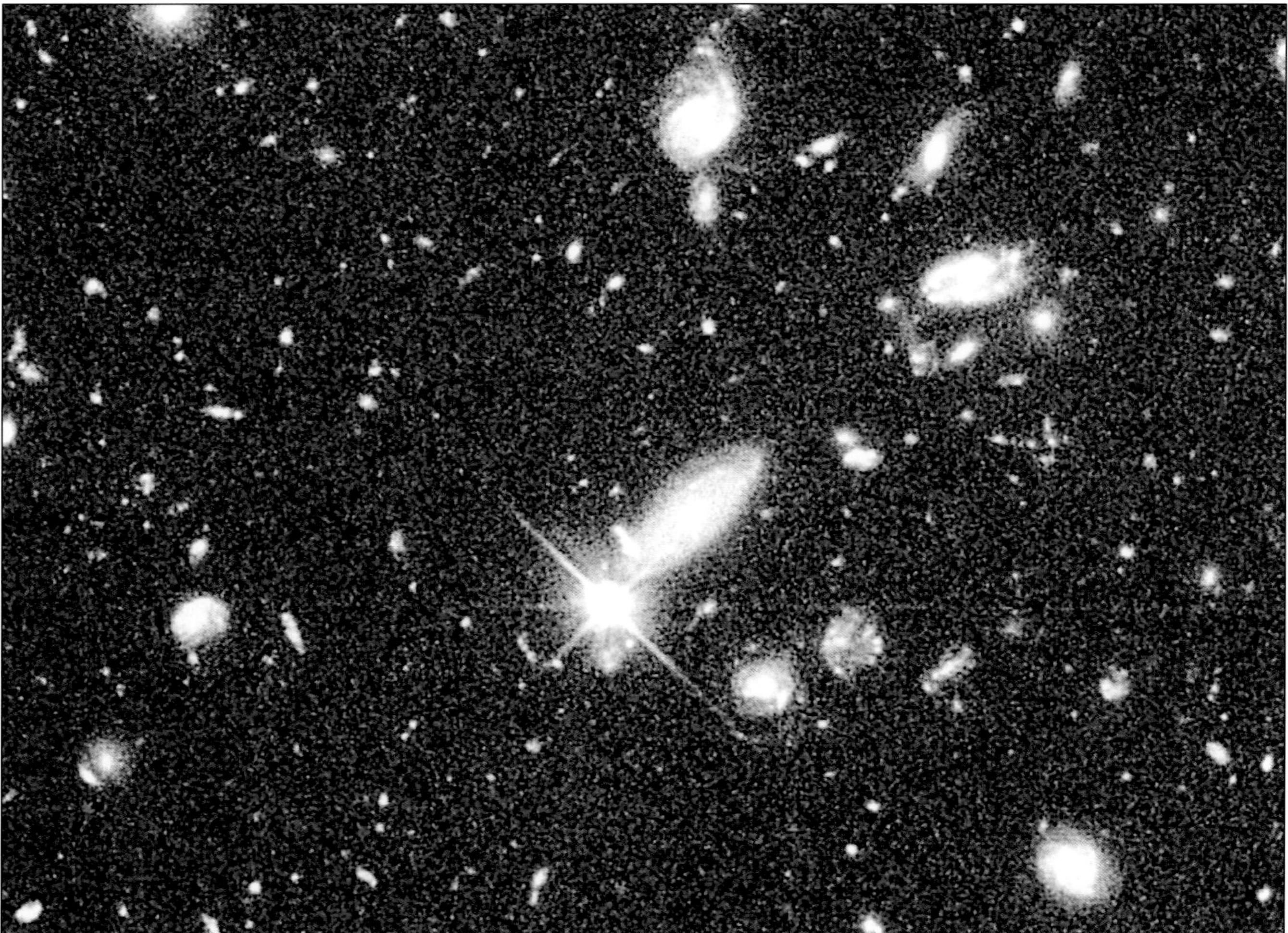

The depths of the Universe

This photograph shows some of the 1,500 or more galaxies that were recorded in the montage of photographs taken by the Hubble Space Telescope in 1995.

Just before Christmas 1995, the Hubble Space Telescope, which is in orbit about 580 km [360 miles] above the Earth, focused on a tiny area in distant space. Over a ten-day period, photographs taken by the telescope revealed unknown galaxies billions of times fainter than the human eye can see.

Because the light from these distant objects has taken so long to reach us, the photographs transmitted from the telescope and released to the media were the deepest look into space that astronomers have ever seen. The features they revealed were in existence when the Universe was less than a billion years old.

The Hubble Space Telescope is operated by the Space Telescope Science Institute in America and was launched in April 1990. The photographs it took of the Hubble Deep Field have been described by NASA as the biggest advance in astronomy since the work of the Italian scientist Galileo in the early 17th century. US scientists described these astonishing photographs as 'postcards from the edge of space and time'.

THE BIG BANG

According to research published in 2001, the Universe was created, and 'time' began, about 12,500 million (or 12.5 billion) years ago, though earlier estimates have ranged from 8 to 24 billion years. Following a colossal explosion, called the 'Big Bang', the Universe expanded in the first millionth of a second of its existence

THE NEAREST STARS

The 20 nearest stars, excluding the Sun, with their distance from the Earth in light-years*.

Proxima Centauri	4.2
Alpha Centauri A	4.3
Alpha Centauri B	4.3
Barnard's Star	6.0
Wolf 359	7.8
Lalande 21185	8.3
Sirius A	8.7
Sirius B	8.7
UV Ceti A	8.7
UV Ceti B	8.7
Ross 154	9.4
Ross 248	10.3
Epsilon Eridani	10.7
Ross 128	10.9
61 Cygni A	11.1
61 Cygni B	11.1
Epsilon Indi	11.2
Groombridge 34 A	11.2
Groombridge 34 B	11.2
L789-6	11.2

** A light-year equals approximately 9,500 billion km [5,900 billion miles].*

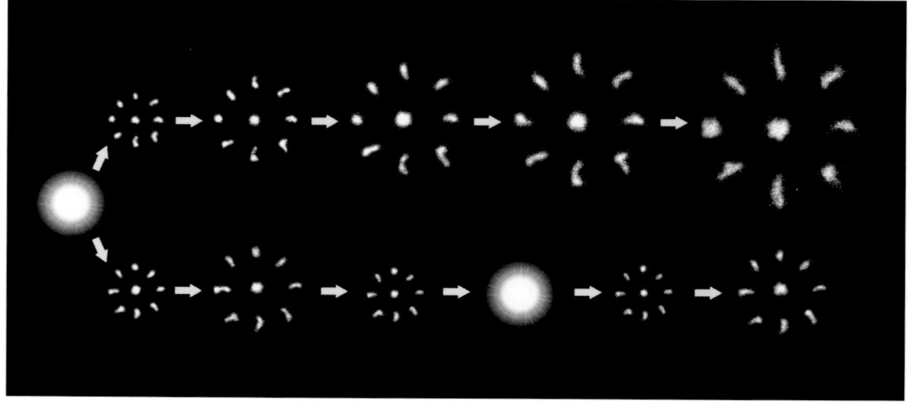

The End of the Universe

The diagram shows two theories concerning the fate of the Universe. One theory, top, suggests that the Universe will expand indefinitely, moving into an immense dark graveyard. Another theory, bottom, suggests that the galaxies will fall back until everything is again concentrated in one point in a so-called 'Big Crunch'. This might then be followed by a new 'Big Bang'.

from a dimensionless point of infinite mass and density into a fireball about 30 billion km [19 million miles] across. The Universe has been expanding ever since, as demonstrated in the 1920s by Edwin Hubble, the American astronomer after whom the Hubble Space Telescope was named.

The temperature at the end of the first second was perhaps 10 billion degrees – far too hot for composite atomic nuclei to exist. As a result, the fireball consisted mainly of radiation mixed with microscopic particles of matter. Almost a million years passed before the Universe was cool enough for atoms to form.

Solar System

The Home Galaxy
This schematic plan shows that our Solar System is located in one of the spiral arms of the Milky Way galaxy, a little less than 30,000 light-years from its centre. The centre of the Milky Way galaxy is not visible from Earth. Instead, it is masked by light-absorbing clouds of interstellar dust.

A few billion years later, atoms in regions where matter was relatively dense began, under the influence of gravity, to move together to form proto-galaxies – masses of gas separated by empty space. The proto-galaxies were dark, because the Universe had cooled. But a few billion years later, stars began to form within the proto-galaxies as particles were drawn together. The internal pressure produced as matter condensed created the high temperatures required to cause nuclear fusion. Stars were born and later destroyed. Each generation of stars fed on the debris of extinct ones. Each generation produced larger atoms, increasing the number of different chemical elements.

The Galaxies

At least a billion galaxies are scattered through the Universe, though the discoveries made by the Hubble Space Telescope suggest that there may be far more than once thought, and some estimates are as high as 100 billion. The largest galaxies contain trillions of stars, while small ones contain less than a billion.

Galaxies tend to occur in groups or clusters, while some clusters appear to be grouped in vast superclusters. Our Local Cluster includes the spiral Milky Way galaxy, whose diameter is about 100,000 light-years; one light-year, the distance that light travels in one year, measures about 9,500 billion km [5,900 billion miles]. The Milky Way is a huge galaxy, shaped like a disk with a bulge at the centre. It is larger, brighter and more massive than many other known galaxies. It contains about 100 billion stars which rotate around the centre of the galaxy in the same direction as the Sun does.

One medium-sized star in the Milky Way galaxy is the Sun. After its formation, about 5 billion years ago, there was enough leftover matter around it to create the planets, asteroids, moons and other bodies that together form our Solar System. The Solar System rotates around the centre of the Milky Way galaxy approximately every 225 million years.

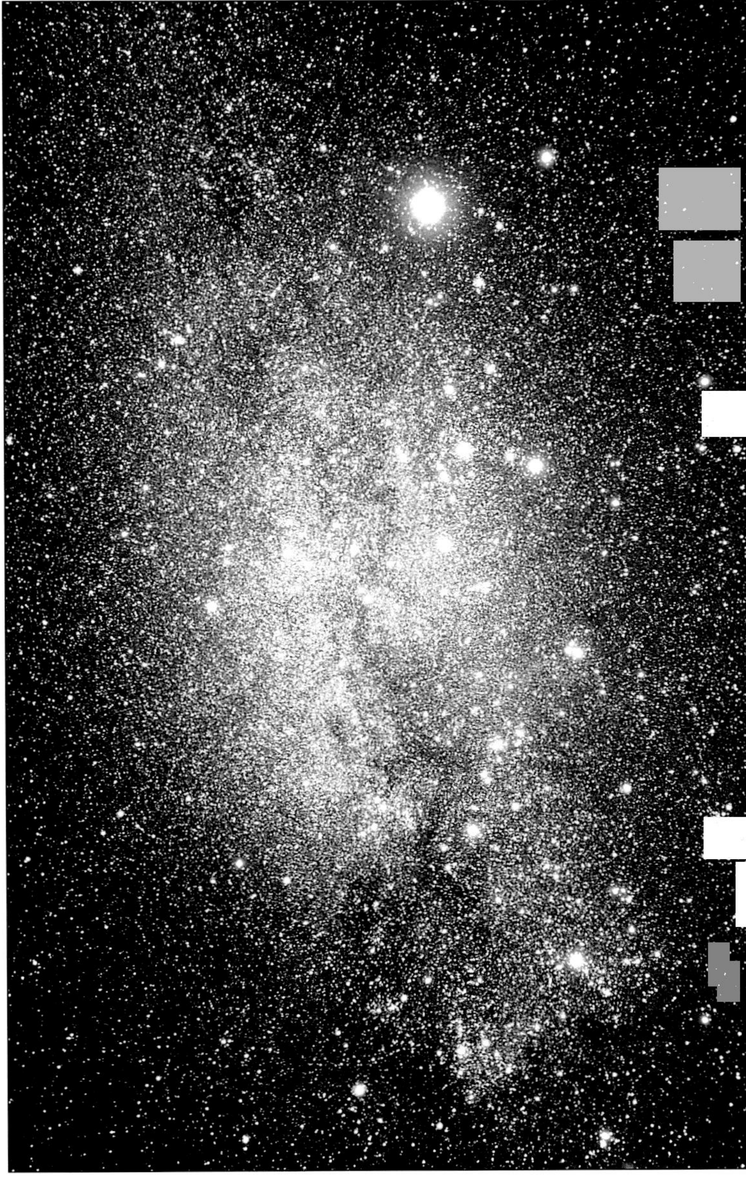

The Milky Way
This section of the Milky Way is dominated by Sirius, the Dog Star, top centre, in the constellation of Canis Major. Sirius is the brightest star in the sky.

Stars similar to our Sun are known to have planets orbiting around them. By the start of 2002, more than 70 extra-solar planets had been reported and evidence from the Hubble Space Telescope suggests that the raw materials from which planets are formed is common in dusty disks around many stars. This provokes one of the most intriguing questions that has ever faced humanity. If other planets exist in the Universe, then are they home to living organisms?

Before the time of Galileo, people thought that the Earth lay at the centre of the Universe. But we now know that our Solar System and even the Milky Way galaxy are tiny specks in the Universe as a whole. Perhaps our planet is also not unique in being the only one to support intelligent life.

Star Charts and Constellations

The Plough

The Plough, or Big Dipper, above glowing yellow clouds lit by city lights. It is part of a larger group called Ursa Major one of the best-known constellations of the northern hemisphere. The two bright stars to the lower right of the photograph (Merak and Dubhe) are known as the Pointers because they show the way to the Pole Star.

THE BRIGHTEST STARS	
The 15 brightest stars visible from northern Europe. Magnitudes are given to the nearest tenth.	
Sirius	–1.5
Arcturus	0.0
Vega	0.0
Capella	0.1
Rigel	0.1
Procyon	0.4
Betelgeuse	0.4
Altair	0.8
Aldebaran	0.8
Antares	1.0
Spica	1.0
Pollux	1.1
Fomalhaut	1.2
Deneb	1.2
Regulus	1.3

On a clear night, under the best conditions and far away from the glare of city lights, a person in northern Europe can look up and see about 2,500 stars. In a town, however, light pollution can reduce visibility to 200 stars or less. Over the whole celestial sphere it is possible to see about 8,500 stars with the naked eye and it is only when you look through a telescope that you begin to realize that the number of stars is countless.

Small and Large Stars

Stars come in several sizes. Some, called neutron stars, are compact, with the same mass as the Sun but with diameters of only about 20 km [12 miles]. Larger than neutron stars are the small white dwarfs. Our Sun is a medium-sized star, but many visible stars in the night sky are giants with diameters between 10 and 100 times that of the Sun, or supergiants with diameters over 100 times that of the Sun.

Two bright stars in the constellation Orion are Betelgeuse (also known as Alpha Orionis) and Rigel (or Beta Orionis). Betelgeuse is an orange-red supergiant, whose diameter is about 400 times that of the Sun. Rigel is also a supergiant. Its diameter is about 50 times that of the Sun, but its luminosity is estimated to be over 100,000 times that of the Sun.

The stars we see in the night sky all belong to our home galaxy, the Milky Way. This name is also used for the faint, silvery band that arches across the sky. This band, a slice through our

THE CONSTELLATIONS

The constellations and their English names. Constellations visible from both hemispheres are listed.

Constellation	English name	Constellation	English name	Constellation	English name
Andromeda	Andromeda	Delphinus	Dolphin	Perseus	Perseus
Antlia	Air Pump	Dorado	Swordfish	Phoenix	Phoenix
Apus	Bird of Paradise	Draco	Dragon	Pictor	Easel
Aquarius	Water Carrier	Equuleus	Little Horse	Pisces	Fishes
Aquila	Eagle	Eridanus	River Eridanus	Piscis Austrinus	Southern Fish
Ara	Altar	Fornax	Furnace	Puppis	Ship's Stern
Aries	Ram	Gemini	Twins	Pyxis	Mariner's Compass
Auriga	Charioteer	Grus	Crane	Reticulum	Net
Boötes	Herdsman	Hercules	Hercules	Sagitta	Arrow
Caelum	Chisel	Horologium	Clock	Sagittarius	Archer
Camelopardalis	Giraffe	Hydra	Water Snake	Scorpius	Scorpion
Cancer	Crab	Hydrus	Sea Serpent	Sculptor	Sculptor
Canes Venatici	Hunting Dogs	Indus	Indian	Scutum	Shield
Canis Major	Great Dog	Lacerta	Lizard	Serpens*	Serpent
Canis Minor	Little Dog	Leo	Lion	Sextans	Sextant
Capricornus	Sea Goat	Leo Minor	Little Lion	Taurus	Bull
Carina	Ship's Keel	Lepus	Hare	Telescopium	Telescope
Cassiopeia	Cassiopeia	Libra	Scales	Triangulum	Triangle
Centaurus	Centaur	Lupus	Wolf	Triangulum Australe	Southern Triangle
Cepheus	Cepheus	Lynx	Lynx		
Cetus	Whale	Lyra	Lyre	Tucana	Toucan
Chamaeleon	Chameleon	Mensa	Table	Ursa Major	Great Bear
Circinus	Compasses	Microscopium	Microscope	Ursa Minor	Little Bear
Columba	Dove	Monoceros	Unicorn	Vela	Ship's Sails
Coma Berenices	Berenice's Hair	Musca	Fly	Virgo	Virgin
Corona Australis	Southern Crown	Norma	Level	Volans	Flying Fish
Corona Borealis	Northern Crown	Octans	Octant	Vulpecula	Fox
Corvus	Crow	Ophiuchus	Serpent Bearer		
Crater	Cup	Orion	Hunter		
Crux	Southern Cross	Pavo	Peacock		
Cygnus	Swan	Pegasus	Winged Horse		

** In two halves: Serpens Caput, the head, and Serpens Cauda, the tail.*

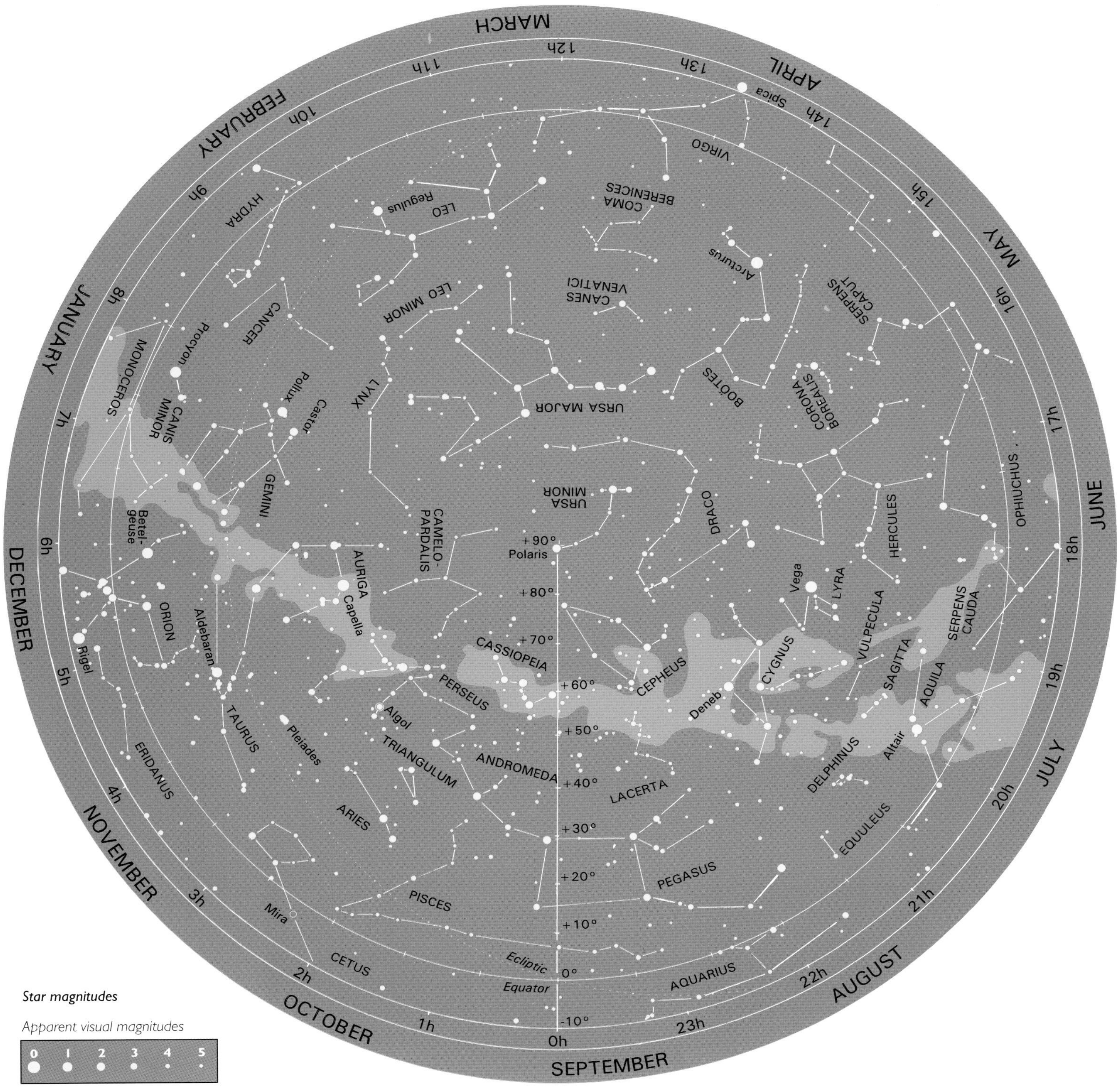

The Milky Way is shown in light blue on the above chart.

Star chart of the northern hemisphere

When you look into the sky, the stars seem to be on the inside of a huge dome. This gives astronomers a way of mapping them. This chart shows the sky as it would appear from the North Pole. To use the star chart above, an observer in the northern hemisphere should face south and turn the chart so that the current month appears at the bottom. The chart will then show the constellations on view at approximately 11pm Greenwich Mean Time. The map should be rotated clockwise 15° for each hour before 11pm and anticlockwise for each hour after 11pm.

galaxy, contains an enormous number of stars. The nucleus of the Milky Way galaxy cannot be seen from Earth. Lying in the direction of the constellation Sagittarius in the southern hemisphere, it is masked by clouds of dust.

The Brightness of Stars

Astronomers use a scale of magnitudes to measure the brightness of stars. The brightest visible to the naked eye were originally known as first-magnitude stars, ones not so bright were second-magnitude, down to the faintest visible, which were rated as sixth-magnitude. The brighter the star, the lower the magnitude. With the advent of telescopes and the development of accurate instruments for measuring brightnesses, the magnitude scale has been refined and extended. Very bright bodies such as Sirius, Venus and the Sun have negative magnitudes. The nearest star is Proxima Centauri, part of a multiple star system, which is 4.2 light-years away. Proxima Centauri is very faint and has a magnitude of 11.3. Alpha Centauri A, one of the two brighter members of the system, is the nearest visible star to Earth. It has a magnitude of 1.7.

These magnitudes are known as apparent magnitudes – measures of the brightnesses of the stars as they appear to us. These are the magnitudes shown on the charts on these pages. But the stars are at very different distances. The star Deneb, in the constellation Cygnus, for example, is over 1,200 light-years away. So astronomers also use absolute magnitudes – measures of how bright the stars really are. A star's absolute magnitude is the apparent magnitude it would have if it could be placed 32.6 light-years away. So Deneb, with an apparent magnitude of 1.2, has an absolute magnitude of –7.2.

The brightest star in the night sky is Sirius, the Dog Star, with a magnitude of –1.5. This medium-sized star is 8.64 light-years distant but it gives out about 20 times as much light as the Sun. After the Sun and the Moon, the brightest objects in the sky are the planets Venus, Mars and Jupiter. For example, Venus has a magnitude of up to –4. The planets have no light of their own however, and shine only because they reflect the Sun's rays. But whilst stars have fixed positions, the planets shift nightly in relation to the constellations, following a path called the Ecliptic (shown on the star charts). As they follow their orbits around the Sun, their distances from the Earth vary, and therefore so also do their magnitudes.

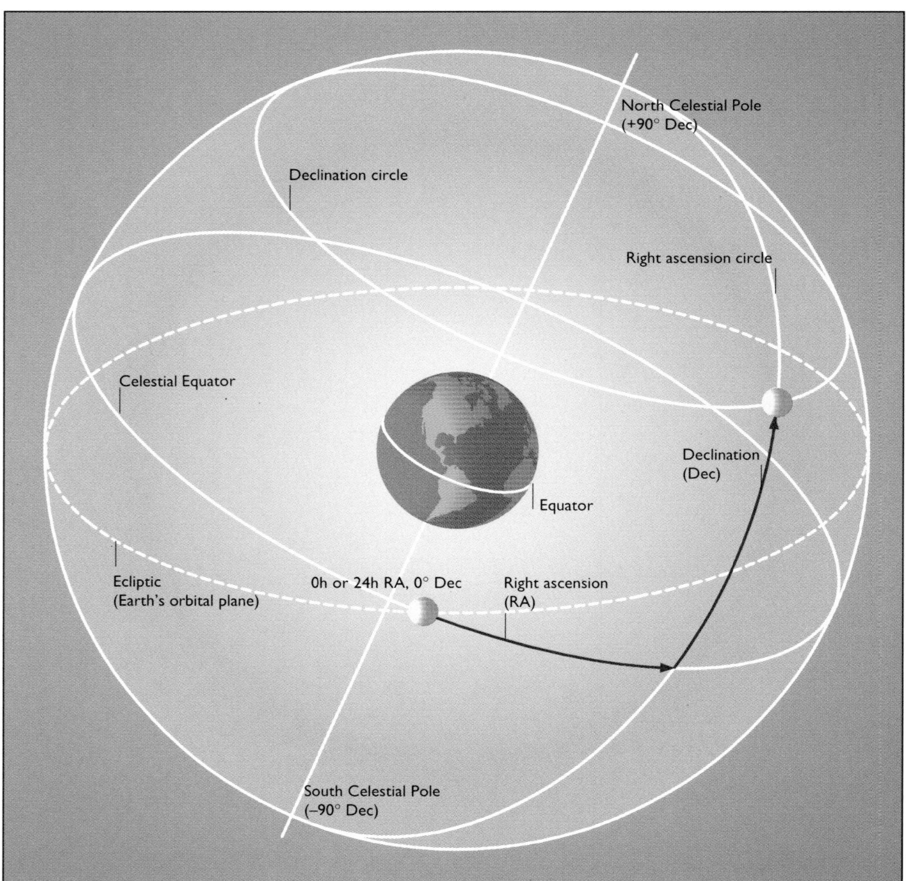

Celestial sphere
The diagram shows the imaginary surface on which astronomical positions are measured. The celestial sphere appears to rotate about the celestial poles, as though an extension of the Earth's own axis. The Earth's axis points towards the celestial poles.

While atlas maps record the details of the Earth's surface, star charts are a guide to the heavens. An observer at the Equator can see the entire sky at some time during the year, but an observer at the poles can see only the stars in a single hemisphere. As a result, star charts of both hemispheres are produced. The northern hemisphere chart is centred on the North Celestial Pole, while the southern hemisphere chart is centred on the South Celestial Pole.

In the northern hemisphere, the North Pole is marked by the star Polaris, or North Star. Polaris lies within a degree of the point where an extension of the Earth's axis meets the sky. Polaris appears to be stationary and navigators throughout history have used it as a guide. Unfortunately, the South Pole has no convenient reference point.

Star charts of the two hemispheres are bounded by the Celestial Equator, an imaginary line in the sky directly above the terrestrial Equator. Astronomical co-ordinates, which give the location of stars, are normally stated in terms of right ascension (the equivalent of longitude) and declination (the equivalent of latitude). Because the stars appear to rotate around the Earth every 24 hours, right ascension is measured eastwards in hours and minutes. Declination is measured in degrees north or south of the Celestial Equator.

The Southern Cross
The Southern Cross, or Crux, in the southern hemisphere, was classified as a constellation in the 17th century. It is as familiar to Australians and New Zealanders as the Plough (or Big Dipper) is to people in the northern hemisphere. The vertical axis of the Southern Cross points towards the South Celestial Pole.

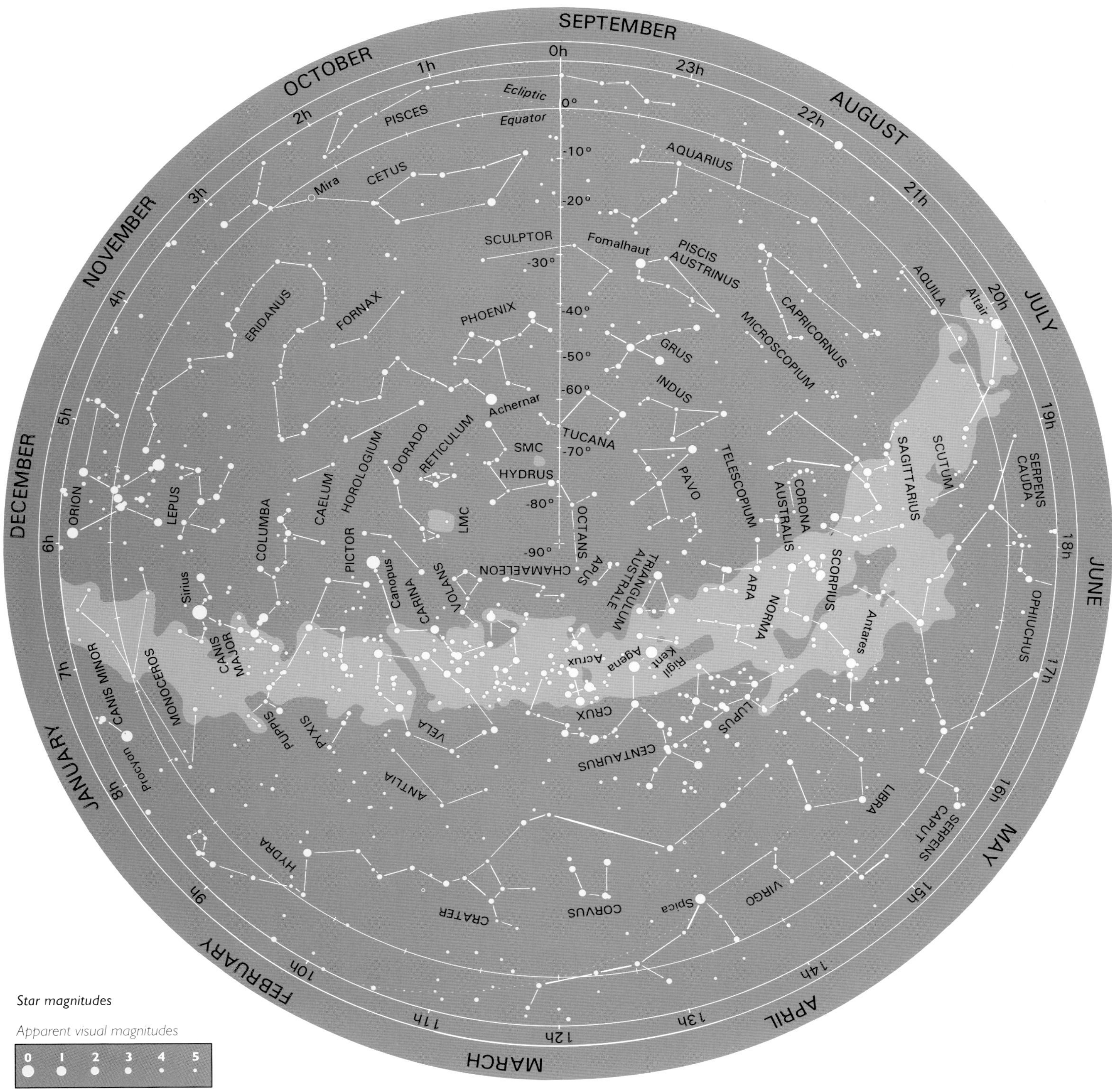

Star magnitudes

Apparent visual magnitudes

0 1 2 3 4 5

The Milky Way is shown in light blue on the above chart.

Star chart of the southern hemisphere

Many constellations in the southern hemisphere were named not by the ancients but by later astronomers. Some, including Antila (Air Pump) and Microscopium (Microscope), have modern names. The Large and Small Magellanic Clouds (LMC, SMC) are small 'satellite' galaxies of the Milky Way. To use the chart, an observer in the southern hemisphere should face north and turn the chart so that the current month appears at the bottom. The map will then show the constellations on view at approximately 11pm Greenwich Mean Time. The chart should be rotated clockwise 15° for each hour before 11pm and anticlockwise for each hour after 11pm.

Constellations

Every star is identifiable as a member of a constellation. The night sky contains 88 constellations, many of which were named by the ancient Greeks, Romans and other early peoples after animals and mythological characters, such as Orion and Perseus. More recently, astronomers invented names for constellations seen in the southern hemisphere, in areas not visible around the Mediterranean Sea.

Some groups of easily recognizable stars form parts of a constellation. For example, seven stars form the shape of the Plough or Big Dipper within the constellation Ursa Major. Such groups are called asterisms.

The stars in constellations lie in the same direction in space, but normally at vastly different distances. Hence, there is no real connection between them. The positions of stars seem fixed, but in fact the shapes of the constellations are changing slowly over very long periods of time. This is because the stars have their own 'proper motions', which because of the huge distances involved are imperceptible to the naked eye.

The Solar System

Although the origins of the Solar System are still a matter of debate, many scientists believe that it was formed from a cloud of gas and dust, the debris from some long-lost, exploded star. Around 5 billion years ago, material was drawn towards the hub of the rotating disk of gas and dust, where it was compressed to thermonuclear fusion temperatures. A new star, the Sun, was born, containing 99.8% of the mass of the Solar System. The remaining material was later drawn together to form the planets and the other bodies in the Solar System. Spacecraft, manned and unmanned, have greatly increased our knowledge of the Solar System since the start of the Space Age in 1957, when the Soviet Union launched the satellite Sputnik I.

The Planets

Mercury is the closest planet to the Sun and the fastest moving. Space probes have revealed that its surface is covered by craters, and looks much like our Moon. Mercury is a hostile place, with no significant atmosphere and temperatures ranging between 400°C [750°F] by day and –170°C [–275°F] by night. It seems unlikely that anyone will ever want to visit this planet.

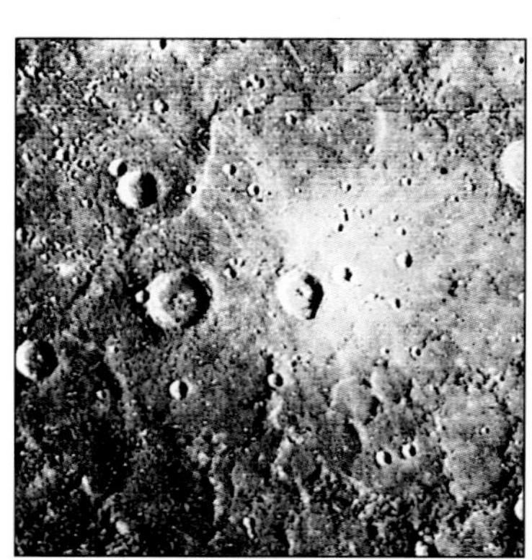

Venus is much the same size as Earth, but it is the hottest of the planets, with temperatures reaching 475°C [885°F], even at night. The reason for this scorching heat is the atmosphere, which consists mainly of carbon dioxide, a gas that traps heat thus creating a greenhouse effect. The density of the atmosphere is about 90 times that of Earth and dense clouds permanently mask the surface. Active volcanic regions discharging sulphur dioxide may account for the haze of sulphuric acid droplets in the upper atmosphere.

From planet Earth, Venus is brighter than any other star or planet and is easy to spot. It is often the first object to be seen in the evening sky and the last to be seen in the morning sky. It can even be seen in daylight.

Earth, seen from space, looks blue (because of the oceans which cover more than 70% of the planet) and white (a result of clouds in the atmosphere). The atmosphere and water make Earth the only planet known to support life. The Earth's hard outer layers, including the crust and the top of the mantle, are divided into rigid plates. Forces inside the Earth move the plates, modifying the landscape and causing earthquakes and volcanic activity. Weathering and erosion also change the surface.

Mars has many features in common with Earth, including an atmosphere with clouds and polar caps that partly melt in summer. Scientists once considered that it was the most likely planet on which other life might exist, but the two Viking space probes that went there in the 1970s found only a barren rocky surface with no trace of water. But Mars did have flowing water at one time and there are many dry channels – but these are not the fictitious 'canals'. There are also giant, dormant volcanoes.

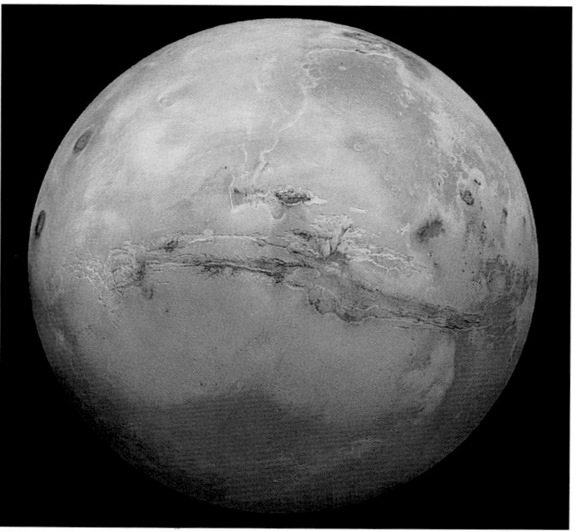

PLANETARY DATA

Planet	Mean distance from Sun (million km)	Mass (Earth=1)	Period of orbit (Earth yrs)	Period of rotation (Earth days)	Equatorial diameter (km)	Average density (water=1)	Surface gravity (Earth=1)	Number of known satellites
Sun	–	333,000	–	25.4	1,391,000	1.41	28	–
Mercury	57.9	0.055	0.2406	58.67	4,880	5.43	0.38	0
Venus	108.2	0.815	0.6152	243.0	12,104	5.20	0.90	0
Earth	149.6	1.0	1.00	1.00	12,756	5.52	1.00	1
Mars	227.9	0.107	1.88	1.028	6,792	3.91	0.38	2
Jupiter	778.3	317.8	11.86	0.411	142,800	1.33	2.69	27
Saturn	1,426.8	95.2	29.46	0.427	120,000	0.69	1.19	30
Uranus	2,869.4	14.53	84.01	0.748	51,118	1.29	0.79	21
Neptune	4,496.3	17.14	164.8	0.710	49,528	1.64	0.98	8
Pluto	5,900.1	0.002	2447.7	6.39	2,320	2.00	0.03	1

Asteroids are small, rocky bodies. Most of them orbit the Sun between Mars and Jupiter, but some small ones can approach the Earth. The largest is Ceres, 913 km [567 miles] in diameter. There may be around a million asteroids bigger than 1 km [0.6 miles].

Jupiter, the giant planet, lies beyond Mars and the asteroid belt. Its mass is almost three times as much as all the other planets combined and, because of its size, it shines more brightly than any other planet apart from Venus and, occasionally, Mars. The four largest moons of Jupiter were discovered by Galileo. Jupiter is made up mostly of hydrogen and helium, covered by a layer of clouds. Its Great Red Spot is a high-pressure storm. Jupiter made headline news when it was struck by fragments of Comet Shoemaker–Levy 9 in July 1994. This was the greatest collision ever seen by scientists between a planet and another heavenly body. The fragments of the comet that crashed into Jupiter created huge fireballs that caused scars on the planet that remained visible for months after the event.

Saturn is structurally similar to Jupiter but it is best known for its rings. The rings measure about 270,000 km [170,000 miles] across, yet they are no more than a few hundred metres thick. Seen from Earth, the rings seem divided into three main bands of varying brightness, but photographs sent back by the *Voyager* space probes in 1980 and 1981 showed that they are broken up into thousands of thin ringlets composed of ice particles ranging in size from a snowball to an iceberg. The origin of the rings is still a matter of debate.

Uranus was discovered in 1781 by William Herschel who first thought it was a comet. It is broadly similar to Jupiter and Saturn in composition, though its distance from the Sun makes its surface even colder. Uranus is circled by thin rings which were discovered in 1977. Unlike the rings of Saturn, the rings of Uranus are black, which explains why they cannot be seen from Earth.

Neptune, named after the mythological sea god, was discovered in 1846 as the result of mathematical predictions made by astronomers to explain irregularities in the orbit of Uranus, its near twin. Little was known about this distant body until *Voyager 2* came close to it in 1989. Neptune has thin rings, like those of Uranus. Among its blue-green clouds is a prominent dark spot, which rotates anticlockwise every 18 hours or so.

Pluto is the smallest planet in the Solar System, even smaller than our Moon. The American astronomer Clyde Tombaugh discovered Pluto in 1930. Its orbit is odd and it sometimes comes closer to the Sun than Neptune. The nature of Pluto, a gloomy planet appropriately named after the Greek and Roman god of the underworld, is uncertain. At Pluto's distance and beyond are many small, asteroid-like bodies the first of which was found in 1992.

Comets are small icy bodies that orbit the Sun in highly elliptical orbits. When a comet swings in towards the Sun some of its ice evaporates, and the comet brightens and may become visible from Earth. The best known is Halley's Comet, which takes 76 years to orbit the Sun.

The Earth: Time and Motion

The Earth is constantly moving through space like a huge, self-sufficient spaceship. First, with the rest of the Solar System, it moves around the centre of the Milky Way galaxy. Second, it rotates around the Sun at a speed of more than 100,000 km/h [more than 60,000 mph], covering a distance of nearly 1,000 million km [600 million miles] in a little over 365 days. The Earth also spins on its axis, an imaginary line joining the North and South Poles, via the centre of the Earth, completing one turn in a day. The Earth's movements around the Sun determine our calendar, though accurate observations of the stars made by astronomers help to keep our clocks in step with the rotation of the Earth around the Sun.

Spring/Vernal Equinox
Northern spring, southern autumn
Summer Solstice
N
21 March
Winter Solstice
21 June
SUN
22 December
23 September
Northern summer, southern winter
Northern winter, southern summer
Autumnal Equinox
Northern autumn, southern spring
S

The Seasons
The 23½° tilt of the Earth's axis remains constant as the Earth orbits around the Sun. As a result, first the northern and then the southern hemispheres lean towards the Sun. Annual variations in the amount of sunlight received in turn by each hemisphere are responsible for the four seasons experienced in the middle latitudes.

The Earth from the Moon
In 1969, Neil Armstrong and Edwin 'Buzz' Aldrin Junior were the first people to set foot on the Moon. This superb view of the Earth was taken by the crew of Apollo 11.

The Changing Year

The Earth takes 365 days, 6 hours, 9 minutes and 9.54 seconds to complete one orbit around the Sun. We have a calendar year of 365 days, so allowance has to be made for the extra time over and above the 365 days. This is allowed for by introducing leap years of 366 days. Leap years are generally those, such as 1992 and 1996, which are divisible by four. Century years, however, are not leap years unless they are divisible by 400. Hence, 1700, 1800 and 1900 were not leap years, but the year 2000 was one. Leap years help to make the calendar conform with the solar year.

Because the Earth's axis is tilted by 23½°, the middle latitudes enjoy four distinct seasons. On 21 March, the vernal or spring equinox in the northern hemisphere, the Sun is directly overhead at the Equator and everywhere on Earth has about 12 hours of daylight and 12 hours of darkness. But as the Earth continues on its journey around the Sun, the northern hemisphere tilts more and more towards the Sun. Finally, on 21 June, the Sun is overhead at the Tropic of Cancer (latitude 23½° North). This is

Tides
The daily rises and falls of the ocean's waters are caused by the gravitational pull of the Moon and the Sun. The effect is greatest on the hemisphere facing the Moon, causing a 'tidal bulge'. The diagram below shows that the Sun, Moon and Earth are in line when the spring tides occur. This causes the greatest tidal ranges. On the other hand, the neap tides occur when the pull of the Moon and the Sun are opposed. Neap tides, when tidal ranges are at their lowest, occur near the Moon's first and third quarters.

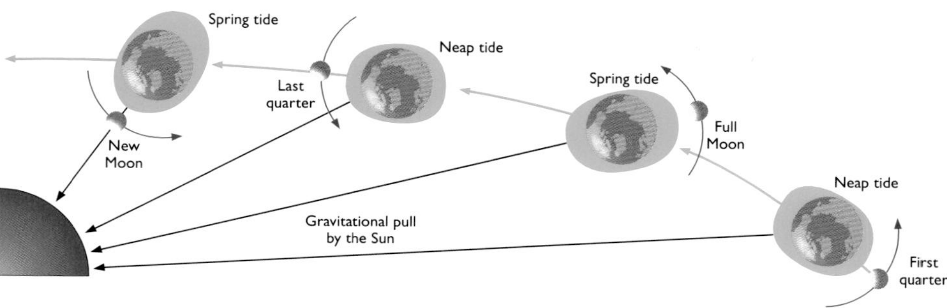

SUN DATA	
DIAMETER	1.391×10^6 km
VOLUME	1.412×10^{18} km^3
VOLUME (EARTH = 1)	1.303×10^6
MASS	1.989×10^{30} kg
MASS (EARTH = 1)	3.329×10^6
MEAN DENSITY (WATER = 1)	1.409
ROTATION PERIOD	
AT EQUATOR	25.4 days
AT POLES	about 35 days
SURFACE GRAVITY (EARTH = 1)	28
MAGNITUDE	
APPARENT	–26.9
ABSOLUTE	+4.71
TEMPERATURE	
AT SURFACE	5,400°C [5,700 K]
AT CORE	15×10^6 K

MOON DATA	
DIAMETER	3,476 km
MASS (EARTH = 1)	0.0123
DENSITY (WATER = 1)	3.34
MEAN DISTANCE FROM EARTH	384,402 km
MAXIMUM DISTANCE (APOGEE)	406,740 km
MINIMUM DISTANCE (PERIGEE)	356,410 km
SIDERIAL ROTATION AND REVOLUTION PERIOD	27.322 days
SYNODIC MONTH (NEW MOON TO NEW MOON)	29.531 days
SURFACE GRAVITY (EARTH = 1)	0.165
MAXIMUM SURFACE TEMPERATURE	+130°C [403 K]
MINIMUM SURFACE TEMPERATURE	–158°C [115 K]

the summer solstice in the northern hemisphere.

The overhead Sun then moves south again until on 23 September, the autumn equinox in the northern hemisphere, the Sun is again overhead at the Equator. The overhead Sun then moves south until, on around 22 December, it is overhead at the Tropic of Capricorn. This is the winter solstice in the northern hemisphere, and the summer solstice in the southern, where the seasons are reversed.

At the poles, there are two seasons. During half of the year, one of the poles leans towards the Sun and has continuous sunlight. For the other six months, the pole leans away from the Sun and is in continuous darkness.

Regions around the Equator do not have marked seasons. Because the Sun is high in the sky throughout the year, it is always hot or warm. When people talk of seasons in the tropics, they are usually referring to other factors, such as rainy and dry periods.

Day, Night and Tides

As the Earth rotates on its axis every 24 hours, first one side of the planet and then the other faces the Sun and enjoys daylight, while the opposite side is in darkness.

The length of daylight varies throughout the year. The longest day in the northern hemisphere falls on the summer solstice, 21 June, while the longest day in the southern hemisphere is on 22 December. At 40° latitude, the length of daylight on the longest day is 14 hours, 30 minutes. At 60° latitude, daylight on that day lasts 18 hours, 30 minutes. On the shortest day, 22 December in the northern hemisphere and 21 June in the southern, daylight hours at 40° latitude total 9 hours and 9 minutes. At latitude 60°, daylight lasts only 5 hours, 30 minutes in the 24-hour period.

Tides are caused by the gravitational pull of the Moon and, to a lesser extent, the Sun on the waters in the world's oceans. Tides occur twice every 24 hours, 50 minutes – one complete orbit of the Moon around the Earth.

The highest tides, the spring tides, occur when the Earth, Moon and Sun are in a straight line, so that the gravitational pulls of the Moon and Sun are combined. The lowest, or neap, tides occur when the Moon, Earth and Sun form a right angle. The gravitational pull of the Moon is then opposed by the gravitational pull of the Sun. The greatest tidal ranges occur in the Bay of Fundy in North America. The greatest mean spring range is 14.5 m [47.5 ft].

The speed at which the Earth is spinning on its axis is gradually slowing down, because of the movement of tides. As a result, experts have calculated that, in about 200 million years, the day will be 25 hours long.

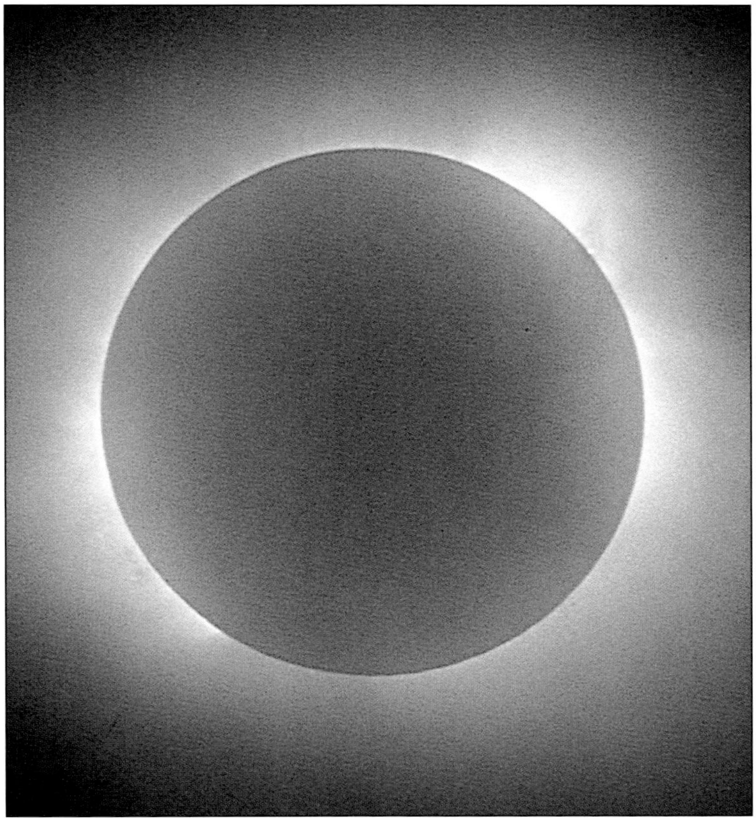

Total eclipse of the Sun

A total eclipse is caused when the Moon passes between the Sun and the Earth. With the Sun's bright disk completely obscured, the Sun's corona, or outer atmosphere, can be viewed.

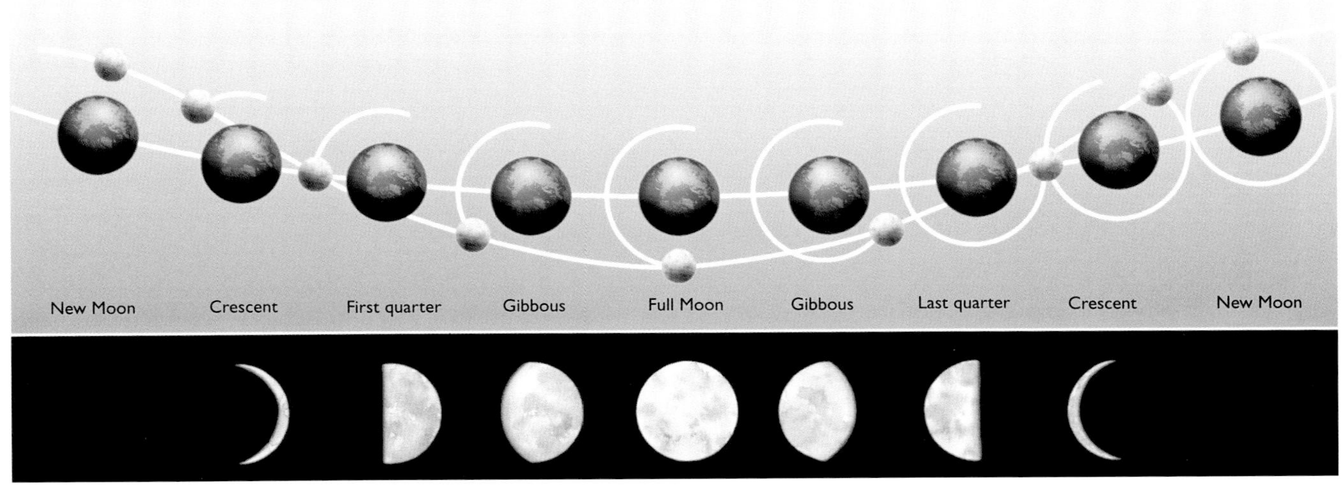

Phases of the Moon

The Moon rotates more slowly than the Earth, making one complete turn on its axis in just over 27 days. This corresponds to its period of revolution around the Earth and, hence, the same hemisphere always faces us. The interval between one full Moon and the next (and also between new Moons) is about 29½ days, or one lunar month. The apparent changes in the appearance of the Moon are caused by its changing position in relation to Earth. Like the planets, the Moon produces no light of its own. It shines by reflecting the Sun's rays, varying from a slim crescent to a full circle and back again.

The Earth from Space

Any last doubts about whether the Earth was round or flat were finally resolved by the appearance of the first photographs of our planet taken at the start of the Space Age. Satellite images also confirmed that map- and globe-makers had correctly worked out the shapes of the continents and the oceans.

More importantly, images of our beautiful, blue, white and brown planet from space impressed on many people that the Earth and its resources are finite. They made people realize that if we allow our planet to be damaged by such factors as overpopulation, pollution and irresponsible over-use of resources, then its future and the survival of all the living things upon it may be threatened.

Views from Above

The first aerial photographs were taken from balloons in the mid-19th century and their importance in military reconnaissance was recognized as early as the 1860s during the American Civil War.

Launch of the Space Shuttle Atlantis

Space Shuttles transport astronauts and equipment into orbit around the Earth. The American Space Shuttle Atlantis, *shown below, launched the Magellan probe, which undertook a radar mapping programme of the surface of Venus in the early 1990s.*

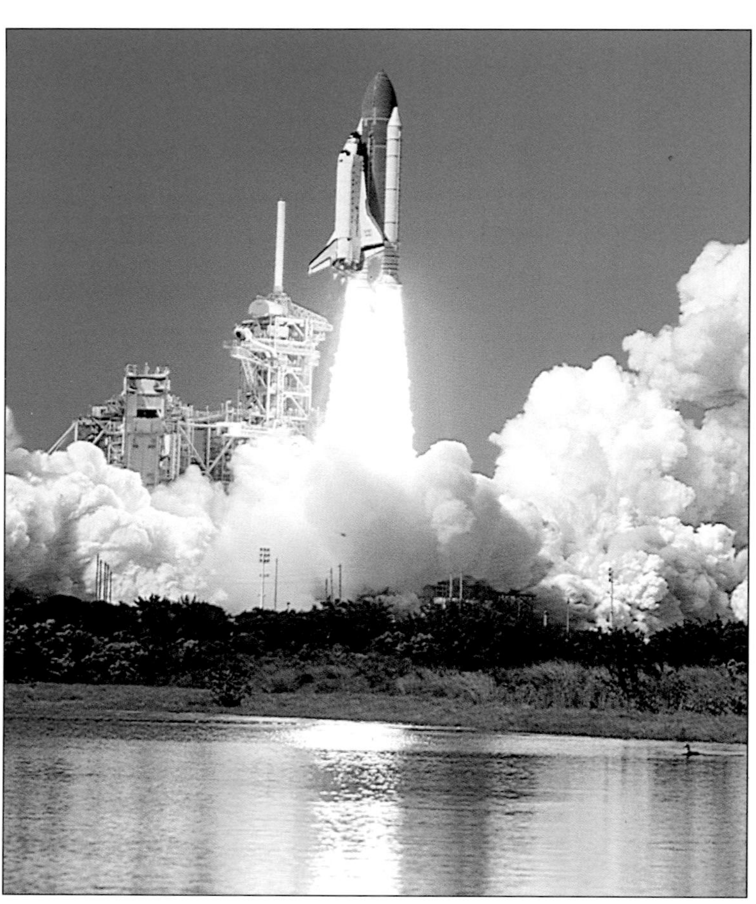

Since the end of World War II, photographs taken by aircraft have been widely used in map-making. The use of air photographs has greatly speeded up the laborious process of mapping land details and they have enabled cartographers to produce maps of the most remote parts of the world.

Aerial photographs have also proved useful because they reveal features that are not visible at ground level. For example, circles that appear on many air photographs do not correspond to visible features on the ground. Many of these mysterious shapes have turned out to be the sites of ancient settlements previously unknown to archaeologists.

Images from Space

Space probes equipped with cameras and a variety of remote sensing instruments have sent back images of distant planets and moons. From these images, detailed maps have been produced, rapidly expanding our knowledge of the Solar System.

Photographs from space are also proving invaluable in the study of the Earth. One of the best known uses of space imagery is the study of the atmosphere. Polar-orbiting weather satellites that circle the Earth, together with geostationary satellites, whose motion is synchronized with the Earth's rotation, now regularly transmit images showing the changing patterns of weather systems from above. Forecasters use these images to track the development and the paths taken by hurricanes, enabling them to issue storm warnings to endangered areas, saving lives and reducing damage to property.

Remote sensing devices are now monitoring changes in temperatures over the land and sea, while photographs indicate the melting of ice sheets. Such evidence is vital in the study of global warming. Other devices reveal polluted areas, patterns of vegetation growth, and areas suffering deforestation.

In recent years, remote sensing devices have been used to monitor the damage being done to the ozone layer in the stratosphere, which prevents most of the Sun's harmful ultraviolet radiation from reaching the surface. The discovery of 'ozone holes', where the protective layer of ozone is being thinned by chlorofluorocarbons (CFCs), chemicals used in the manufacture of such things as air conditioners and refrigerators, has enabled governments to take concerted action to save our planet from imminent danger.

Earth Data

MAXIMUM DISTANCE FROM SUN (APHELION)
152,007,016 km

MINIMUM DISTANCE FROM SUN (PERIHELION)
147,000,830 km

LENGTH OF YEAR – SOLAR TROPICAL (EQUINOX TO EQUINOX)
365.24 days

LENGTH OF YEAR – SIDEREAL (FIXED STAR TO FIXED STAR)
365.26 days

LENGTH OF DAY – MEAN SOLAR DAY
24 hours, 03 minutes, 56 seconds

LENGTH OF DAY – MEAN SIDEREAL DAY
23 hours, 56 minutes, 4 seconds

SUPERFICIAL AREA
510,000,000 km^2

LAND SURFACE
149,000,000 km^2 (29.3%)

WATER SURFACE
361,000,000 km^2 (70.7%)

EQUATORIAL CIRCUMFERENCE
40,077 km

POLAR CIRCUMFERENCE
40,009 km

EQUATORIAL DIAMETER
12,756.8 km

POLAR DIAMETER
12,713.8 km

EQUATORIAL RADIUS
6,378.4 km

POLAR RADIUS
6,356.9 km

VOLUME OF THE EARTH
1,083,230 $\times 10^6$ km^3

MASS OF THE EARTH
5.9 $\times 10^{21}$ tonnes

Satellite image of San Francisco Bay

Unmanned scientific satellites called ERTS (Earth Resources Technology Satellites), *or* Landsats, *were designed to collect information about the Earth's resources. The satellites transmitted images of the land using different wavelengths of light in order to identify, in false colours, such subtle features as areas that contain minerals or areas covered with growing crops, that are not identifiable on simple photographs using the visible range of the spectrum. They were also equipped to monitor conditions in the atmosphere and oceans, and also to detect pollution levels. This* Landsat *image of San Francisco Bay covers an area of great interest to geologists because it lies in an earthquake zone in the path of the San Andreas fault.*

The Dynamic Earth

The Earth was formed about 4.6 billion years [4,600 million years] ago from the ring of gas and dust left over after the formation of the Sun. As the Earth took shape, lighter elements, such as silicon, rose to the surface, while heavy elements, notably iron, sank towards the centre.

Gradually, the outer layers cooled to form a hard crust. The crust enclosed the dense mantle which, in turn, surrounded the even denser liquid outer and solid inner core. Around the Earth was an atmosphere, which contained abundant water vapour. When the surface cooled, rainwater began to fill hollows, forming the first lakes and seas. Since that time, our planet has been subject to constant change – the result of powerful internal and external forces that still operate today.

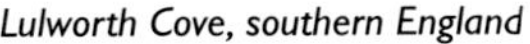

Lulworth Cove, southern England

When undisturbed by earth movements, sedimentary rock strata are generally horizontal. But lateral pressure has squeezed the Jurassic strata at Lulworth Cove into complex folds.

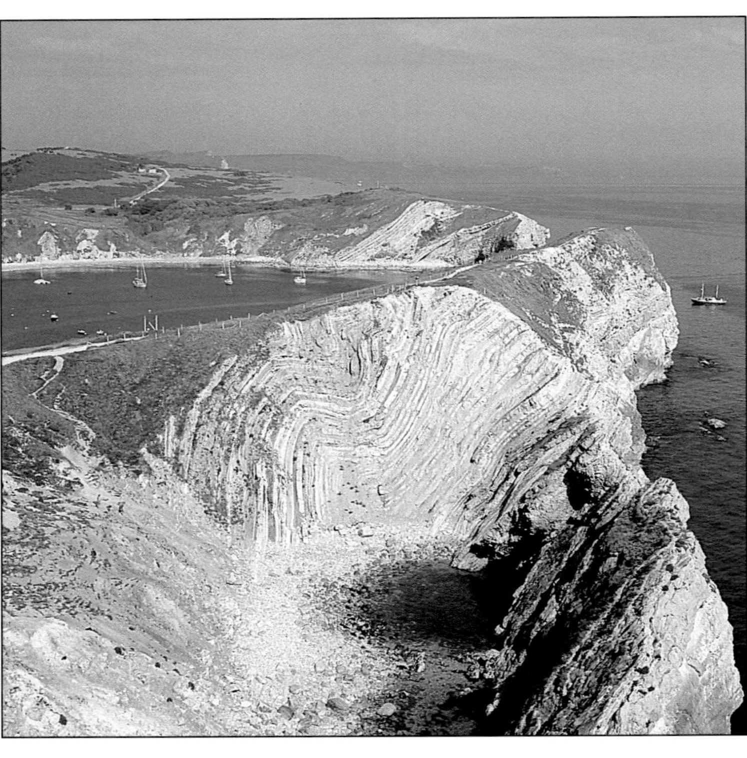

The History of the Earth

From their study of rocks, geologists have pieced together the history of our planet and the life forms that evolved upon it. They have dated the oldest known crystals, composed of the mineral zircon, at 4.2 billion years. But the oldest rocks are younger, less than 4 billion years old. This is because older rocks have been weathered away by natural processes.

The oldest rocks that contain fossils, which are evidence of once-living organisms, are around 3.5 billion years old. But fossils are rare in rocks formed in the first 4 billion years of Earth history. This vast expanse of time is called the Precambrian. This is because it precedes the Cambrian period, at the start of which, about 590 million years ago, life was abundant in the seas.

The Cambrian is the first period in the Paleozoic (or ancient life) era. The Paleozoic era is followed by the Mesozoic (middle life) era, which witnessed the spectacular rise and fall of the dinosaurs, and the Cenozoic (recent life) era, which was dominated by the evolution of mammals. Each of the eras is divided into periods, and the periods in the Cenozoic era, covering the last 65 million years, are further divided into epochs.

The Earth's Changing Face

While life was gradually evolving, the face of the Earth was constantly changing. By piecing together evidence of rock structures and fossils, geologists have demonstrated that around 250 million years ago, all the world's land areas were grouped together in one huge landmass called Pangaea. Around 180 million years ago, the supercontinent Pangaea, began to break up. New oceans opened up as the continents began to move towards their present positions.

Evidence of how continents drift came from studies of the ocean floor in the 1950s and 1960s. Scientists discovered that the oceans are young features. By contrast with the continents, no part of the ocean floor is more than 200 million years old. The floors of oceans older than 200 million years have completely vanished.

Studies of long undersea ranges, called ocean ridges, revealed that the youngest rocks occur along their centres, which are the edges of huge plates – rigid blocks of the Earth's lithosphere, which is made up of the crust and the solid upper layer of the mantle. The Earth's lithosphere is split into six large and several smaller

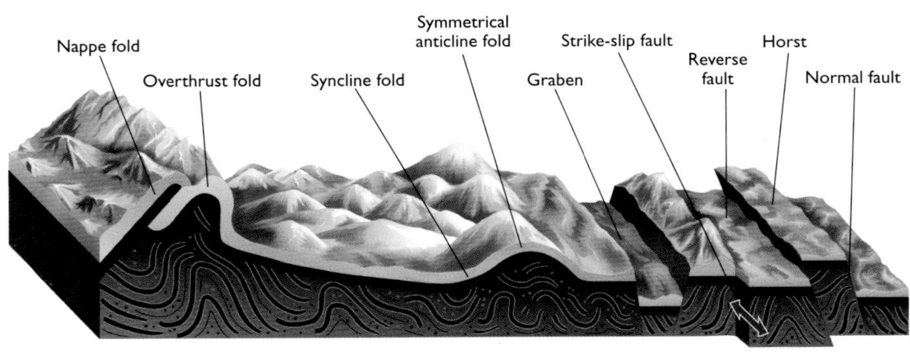

Mountain building

Lateral pressure, which occurs when plates collide, squeezes and compresses rocks into folds. Simple symmetrical upfolds are called anticlines, while downfolds are synclines. As the pressure builds up, strata become asymmetrical and they may be tilted over to form recumbent folds. The rocks often crack under the intense pressure and the folds are sheared away and pushed forward over other rocks. These features are called overthrust folds or nappes. Plate movements also create faults along which rocks move upwards, downwards and sideways. The diagram shows a downfaulted graben, or rift valley, and an uplifted horst, or block mountain.

The Himalayas seen from Nepal

The Himalayas are a young fold mountain range formed by a collision between two plates. The earthquakes felt in the region testify that the plate movements are still continuing.

plates. The ocean ridges are 'constructive' plate margins, because new crustal rock is being formed there from magma that wells up from the mantle as the plates gradually move apart. By contrast, the deep ocean trenches are 'destructive' plate edges. Here, two plates are pushing against each other and one plate is descending beneath the other into the mantle where it is melted and destroyed. Geologists call these areas subduction zones.

A third type of plate edge is called a transform fault. Here two plates are moving alongside each other. The best known of these plate edges is the San Andreas fault in California, which separates the Pacific plate from the North American plate.

Slow-moving currents in the partly molten asthenosphere, which underlies the solid lithosphere, are responsible for moving the plates, a process called plate tectonics.

Mountain Building

The study of plate tectonics has helped geologists to understand the mechanisms that are responsible for the creation of mountains. Many of the world's greatest ranges were created by the collision of two plates and the bending of the intervening strata into huge loops, or folds. For example, the Himalayas began to rise around 50 million years ago, when a plate supporting India collided with the huge Eurasian plate. Rocks on the floor of the intervening and long-vanished Tethys Sea were squeezed up to form the Himalayan Mountain Range.

Plate movements also create tension that cracks rocks, producing long faults along which rocks move upwards, downwards or sideways. Block mountains are formed when blocks of rock are pushed upwards along faults. Steep-sided rift valleys are formed when blocks of land sink down between faults. For example, the basin and range region of the south-western United States has both block mountains and down-faulted basins, such as Death Valley.

Geological time scale

The geological time scale was first constructed by a study of the stratigraphic, or relative, ages of layers of rock. But the absolute ages of rock strata could not be fixed until the discovery of radioactivity in the early 20th century. Some names of periods, such as Cambrian (Latin for Wales), come from places where the rocks were first studied. Others, such as Carboniferous, refer to the nature of the rocks formed during the period. For example, coal seams (containing carbon) were formed from decayed plant matter during the Carboniferous period.

Era	Pre-Cambrian	Paleozoic (Primary) – Lower				Paleozoic (Primary) – Upper		Mesozoic (Secondary)			Cenozoic (Tertiary, Quaternary)					
System	Pre-Cambrian	Cambrian	Ordovician	Silurian	Devonian	Carboniferous	Permian	Triassic	Jurassic	Cretaceous	Paleocene	Eocene	Oligocene	Miocene	Pliocene	Quaternary
Orogeny				CALEDONIAN FOLDING		HERCYNIAN FOLDING				LARAMIDE FOLDING			ALPINE FOLDING			

600 550 500 450 400 350 300 250 200 150 100 50

Millions of years before present

Earthquakes and Volcanoes

On 26 January, 2001, an earthquake rocked north-west India and south-east Pakistan. Bhuj, in Gujarat state, suffered the worst damage. The death toll was more than 14,000, and the 'quake was felt as far away as Karachi, Delhi and Mumbai. Earlier that month, an earthquake had struck El Salvador in Central America. Around 1,200 people died, 750 of them being buried by mudslides.

The Restless Earth

Earthquakes can occur anywhere, whenever rocks move along faults. But the most severe and most numerous earthquakes occur near the edges of the plates that make up the Earth's lithosphere. Japan, for example, lies in a particularly unstable region above subduction zones, where plates are descending into the Earth's mantle. It lies in a zone encircling the Pacific Ocean, called the 'Pacific ring of fire'.

Plates do not move smoothly. Their edges are jagged and for most of the time they are locked together. However, pressure gradually builds up until the rocks break and the plates lurch forward, setting off vibrations ranging from slight tremors to terrifying earthquakes. The greater the pressure released, the more destructive the earthquake.

Earthquakes are also common along the ocean trenches where plates are moving apart, but they mostly occur so far from land that they do little damage. Far more destructive are the earthquakes that occur where plates are moving alongside each other. For example, the earthquakes that periodically rock south-western California are caused by movements along the San Andreas Fault.

The spot where an earthquake originates is called the focus, while the point on the Earth's surface directly above the focus is called the epicentre. Two kinds of waves, P-waves or compressional waves and S-waves or shear waves, travel from the focus to the surface where they make the ground shake. P-waves travel faster than S-waves and the time difference between their arrival at recording stations enables scientists to calculate the distance from a station to the epicentre.

Earthquakes are measured on the Richter scale, which indicates the magnitude of the shock. The most destructive earthquakes are shallow-focus, that is, the focus is within 60 km [37 miles] of the surface. A magnitude of 7.0 is a major earthquake, but earthquakes with a somewhat lower magnitude can cause tremendous damage if their epicentres are on or close to densely populated areas.

San Andreas Fault, United States

Geologists call the San Andreas fault in south-western California a transform, or strike-slip, fault. Sudden movements along it cause earthquakes. In 1906, shifts of about 4.5 metres [15 ft] occurred near San Francisco, causing a massive earthquake.

NOTABLE EARTHQUAKES
(since 1900)

Year	Location	Mag.
1906	San Francisco, USA	8.3
1906	Valparaiso, Chile	8.6
1908	Messina, Italy	7.5
1915	Avezzano, Italy	7.5
1920	Gansu, China	8.6
1923	Yokohama, Japan	8.3
1927	Nan Shan, China	8.3
1932	Gansu, China	7.6
1934	Bihar, India/Nepal	8.4
1935	Quetta, India†	7.5
1939	Chillan, Chile	8.3
1939	Erzincan, Turkey	7.9
1964	Anchorage, Alaska	8.4
1968	N. E. Iran	7.4
1970	N. Peru	7.7
1976	Guatemala	7.5
1976	Tangshan, China	8.2
1978	Tabas, Iran	7.7
1980	El Asnam, Algeria	7.3
1980	S. Italy	7.2
1985	Mexico City, Mexico	8.1
1988	N. W. Armenia	6.8
1990	N. Iran	7.7
1993	Maharashtra, India	6.4
1994	Los Angeles, USA	6.6
1995	Kobe, Japan	7.2
1995	Sakhalin Is., Russia	7.5
1996	Yunnan, China	7.0
1997	N. E. Iran	7.1
1998	N. Afghanistan	6.1
1998	N. E. Afghanistan	7.0
1999	Izmit, Turkey	7.4
1999	Taipei, Taiwan	7.6
2001	El Salvador	7.7
2001	Gujarat, India	7.7
2002	Afyon, Turkey	6.0
2002	N. Afghanistan	5.2

† now Pakistan

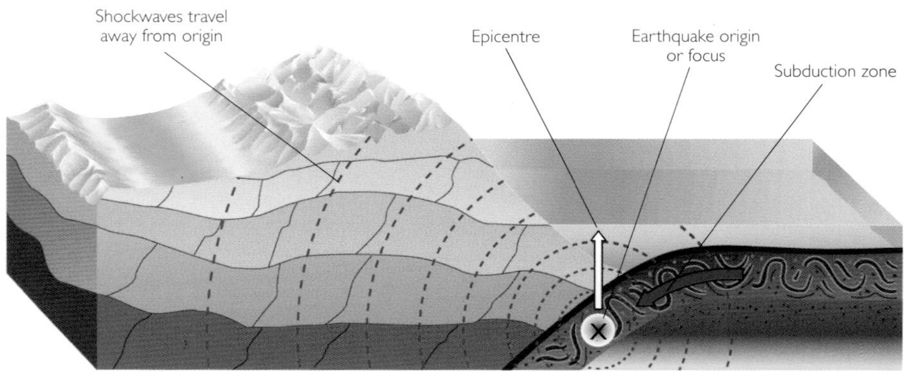

Earthquakes in subduction zones

Along subduction zones, one plate is descending beneath another. The plates are locked together until the rocks break and the descending plate lurches forwards. From the point where the plate moves – the origin – seismic waves spread through the lithosphere, making the ground shake. The earthquake in Mexico City in 1985 occurred in this way.

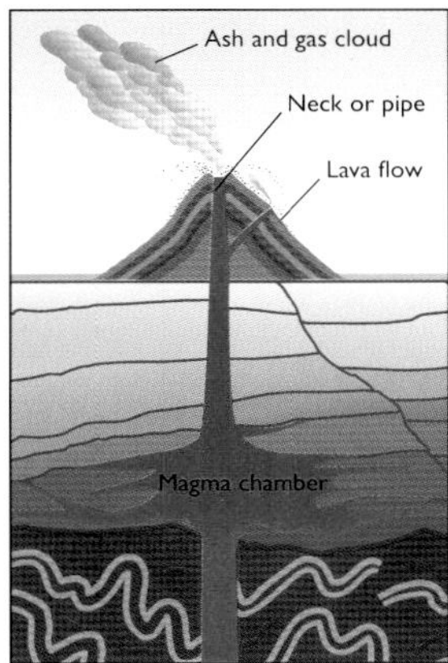

Cross-section of a volcano
Volcanoes are vents in the ground, through which magma reaches the surface. The term volcano is also used for the mountains formed from volcanic rocks. Beneath volcanoes are pockets of magma derived from the semi-molten asthenosphere in the mantle. The magma rises under pressure through the overlying rocks until it reaches the surface. There it emerges through vents as pyroclasts, ranging in size from large lumps of magma, called volcanic bombs, to fine volcanic ash and dust. In quiet eruptions, streams of liquid lava run down the side of the mountain. Side vents sometimes appear on the flanks of existing volcanoes.

Scientists have been working for years to find effective ways of forecasting earthquakes but with very limited success. Following the Kobe earthquake in 1995, many experts argued that they would be better employed developing techniques of reducing the damage caused by earthquakes, rather than pursuing an apparently vain attempt to predict them.

Volcanic Eruptions

Most active volcanoes also occur on or near plate edges. Many undersea volcanoes along the ocean ridges are formed from magma that wells up from the asthenosphere to fill the gaps created as the plates, on the opposite sides of the ridges, move apart. Some of these volcanoes reach the surface to form islands. Iceland is a country which straddles the Mid-Atlantic Ocean Ridge. It is gradually becoming wider as magma rises to the surface through faults and vents. Other volcanoes lie alongside subduction zones. The magma that fuels them comes from the melted edges of the descending plates.

A few volcanoes lie far from plate edges. For example, Mauna Loa and Kilauea on Hawaii are situated near the centre of the huge Pacific plate. The molten magma that reaches the surface is created by a source of heat, called a 'hot spot', in the Earth's mantle.

Magma is molten rock at temperatures of about 1,100°C to 1,200°C [2,012°F to 2,192°F]. It contains gases and superheated steam. The chemical composition of magma varies. Viscous magma is rich in silica and superheated steam, while runny magma contains less silica and steam. The chemical composition of the magma affects the nature of volcanic eruptions.

Explosive volcanoes contain thick, viscous magma. When they erupt, they usually hurl clouds of ash (shattered fragments of cooled magma) into the air. By contrast, quiet volcanoes emit long streams of runny magma, or lava. However, many volcanoes are intermediate in type, sometimes erupting explosively and sometimes emitting streams of fluid lava. Explosive and intermediate volcanoes usually have a conical shape, while quiet volcanoes are flattened, resembling upturned saucers. They are often called shield volcanoes.

One dangerous type of eruption is called a *nuée ardente*, or 'glowing cloud'. It occurs when a cloud of intensely hot volcanic gases and dust particles and superheated steam are exploded from a volcano. They move rapidly downhill, burning everything in their path and choking animals and people. The blast that creates the *nuée ardente* may release the pressure inside the volcano, resulting in a tremendous explosion that hurls tall columns of ash into the air.

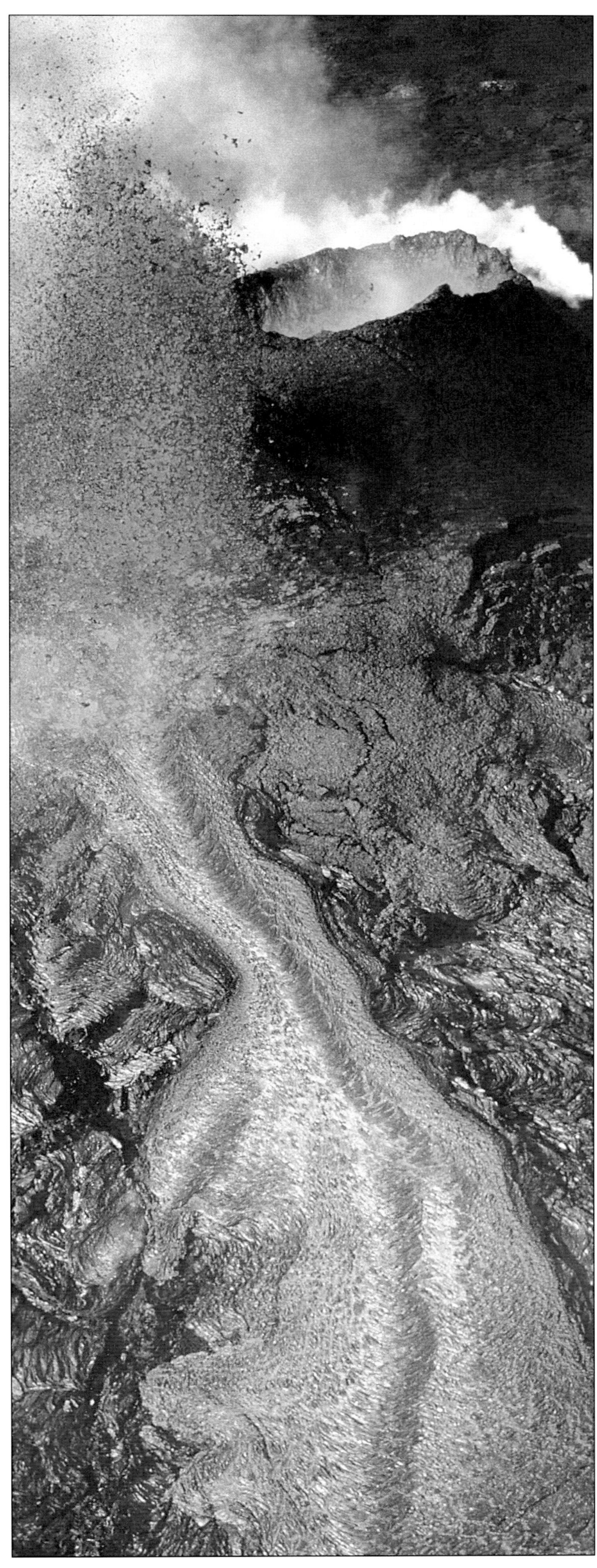

Kilauea Volcano, Hawaii
The volcanic Hawaiian islands in the North Pacific Ocean were formed as the Pacific plate moved over a 'hot spot' in the Earth's mantle. Kilauea on Hawaii emits blazing streams of liquid lava.

Forces of Nature

When the volcano Mount Pinatubo erupted in the Philippines in 1991, loose ash covered large areas around the mountain. During the 1990s and early 2000s, rainwater mixed with the ash on sloping land, creating *lahars*, or mudflows, which swept down river valleys burying many areas. Such incidents are not only reminders of the great forces that operate inside our planet but also of those natural forces operating on the surface, which can have dramatic effects on the land.

The chief forces acting on the surface of the Earth are weathering, running water, ice and winds. The forces of erosion seem to act slowly. One estimate suggests that an average of only 3.5 cm [1.4 in] of land is removed by natural processes every 1,000 years. This may not sound much, but over millions of years, it can reduce mountains to almost flat surfaces.

Weathering

Weathering occurs in all parts of the world, but the most effective type of weathering in any area depends on the climate and the nature of the rocks. For example, in cold mountain areas, when water freezes in cracks in rocks, the ice occupies 9% more space than the water. This exerts a force which, when repeated over and over again, can split boulders apart. By contrast, in hot deserts, intense heating by day and cooling by night causes the outer layers of rocks to expand and contract until they break up and peel away like layers of an onion. These are examples of what is called mechanical weathering.

Other kinds of weathering include chemical reactions usually involving water. Rainwater containing carbon dioxide dissolved from the air or the soil is a weak acid which reacts with limestone, wearing out pits, tunnels and networks of caves in layers of limestone rock. Water also combines with some minerals, such as the feldspars in granite, to create kaolin, a white

RATES OF EROSION

	SLOW ◄ WEATHERING RATE		► FAST
Mineral solubility	low (e.g. quartz)	moderate (e.g. feldspar)	high (e.g. calcite)
Rainfall	low	moderate	heavy
Temperature	cold	temperate	hot
Vegetation	sparse	moderate	lush
Soil cover	bare rock	thin to moderate soil	thick soil

Weathering is the breakdown and decay of rocks in situ. It may be mechanical (physical), chemical or biological

Rates of erosion
The chart shows that the rates at which weathering takes place depend on the chemistry and hardness of rocks, climatic factors, especially rainfall and temperature, the vegetation and the nature of the soil cover in any area. The effects of weathering are increased by human action, particularly the removal of vegetation and the exposure of soils to the rain and wind.

Grand Canyon, Arizona, at dusk
The Grand Canyon in the United States is one of the world's natural wonders. Eroded by the Colorado River and its tributaries, it is up to 1.6 km [1 mile] deep and 29 km [18 miles] wide.

clay. These are examples of chemical weathering which constantly wears away rock.

Running Water, Ice and Wind

In moist regions, rivers are effective in shaping the land. They transport material worn away by weathering and erode the land. They wear out V-shaped valleys in upland regions, while vigorous meanders widen their middle courses. The work of rivers is at its most spectacular when earth movements lift up flat areas and rejuvenate the rivers, giving them a new erosive power capable of wearing out such features as the Grand Canyon. Rivers also have a constructive role. Some of the world's most fertile regions are deltas and flood plains composed of sediments periodically dumped there by such rivers as the Ganges, Mississippi and Nile.

Glaciers

During Ice Ages, ice spreads over large areas but, during warm periods, the ice retreats. The chart shows that the volume of ice in many glaciers is decreasing, possibly as a result of global warming. Experts estimate that, between 1850 and the early 21st century, more than half of the ice in Alpine glaciers has melted.

ANNUAL FLUCTUATIONS FOR SELECTED GLACIERS

Glacier name and location	Changes in the annual mass balance† 1970–1	1990–1	Cumulative total 1970–90
Alfotbreen, Norway	+940	+790	+12,110
Wolverine, USA	+770	–410	+2,320
Storglaciaren, Sweden	–190	+170	–120
Djankuat, Russia	–230	–310	–1,890
Grasubreen, Norway	+470	–520	–2,530
Ürümqi, China	+102	–706	–3,828
Golubin, Kyrgyzstan	–90	–722	–7,105
Hintereisferner, Austria	–600	–1,325	–9,081
Gries, Switzerland	–970	–1,480	–10,600
Careser, Italy	–650	–1,730	–11,610
Abramov, Tajikistan	–890	–420	–13,700
Sarennes, France	–1,100	–1,360	–15,020
Place, Canada	–343	–990	–15,175

† The annual mass balance is defined as the difference between glacier accumulation and ablation (melting) averaged over the whole glacier. Balances are expressed as water equivalent in millimetres. A plus indicates an increase in the depth or length of the glacier; a minus indicates a reduction.

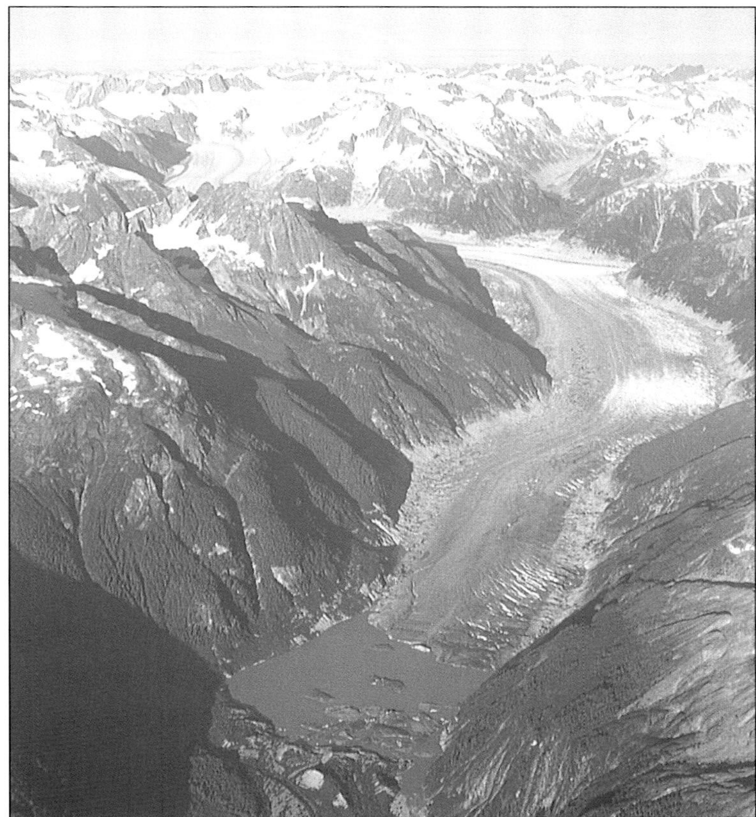

Juneau Glacier, Alaska

Like huge conveyor belts, glaciers transport weathered debris from mountain regions. Rocks frozen in the ice give the glaciers teeth, enabling them to wear out typical glaciated land features.

Running water in the form of sea waves and currents shapes coastlines, wearing out caves, natural arches, and stacks. The sea also transports and deposits worn material to form such features as spits and bars.

Glaciers in cold mountain regions flow downhill, gradually deepening valleys and shaping dramatic landscapes. They erode steep-sided U-shaped valleys, into which rivers often plunge in large waterfalls. Other features include cirques, armchair-shaped basins bounded by knife-edged ridges called *arêtes*. When several glacial cirques erode to form radial *arêtes*, pyramidal peaks like the Matterhorn are created. Deposits of moraine, rock material dumped by the glacier, are further evidence that ice once covered large areas. The work of glaciers, like other agents of erosion, varies with the climate. In recent years, global warming has been making glaciers retreat in many areas, while several of the ice shelves in Antarctica have been breaking up.

Many land features in deserts were formed by running water at a time when the climate was much rainier than it is today. Water erosion also occurs when flash floods are caused by rare thunderstorms. But the chief agent of erosion in dry areas is wind-blown sand, which can strip the paint from cars, and undercut boulders to create mushroom-shaped rocks.

Oceans and Ice

Since the 1970s, oceanographers have found numerous hot vents on the ocean ridges. Called black smokers, the vents emit dark, mineral-rich water reaching 350°C [662°F]. Around the vents are chimney-like structures formed from minerals deposited from the hot water. The discovery of black smokers did not surprise scientists who already knew that the ridges were plate edges, where new crustal rock was being formed as molten magma welled up to the surface. But what was astonishing was that the hot water contained vast numbers of bacteria, which provided the base of a food chain that included many strange creatures, such as giant worms, eyeless shrimps and white clams. Many species were unknown to science.

Little was known about the dark world beneath the waves until about 50 years ago. But through the use of modern technology such as echo-sounders, magnetometers, research ships equipped with huge drills, submersibles that can carry scientists down to the ocean floor, and satellites, the secrets of the oceans have been gradually revealed.

The study of the ocean floor led to the discovery that the oceans are geologically young features – no more than 200 million years old. It also revealed evidence as to how oceans form and continents drift because of the action of plate tectonics.

Vava'u Island, Tonga
This small coral atoll in northern Tonga consists of a central island covered by rainforest. Low coral reefs washed by the waves surround a shallow central lagoon.

The Blue Planet

Water covers almost 71% of the Earth, which makes it look blue when viewed from space. Although the oceans are interconnected, geographers divide them into four main areas: the Pacific, Atlantic, Indian and Arctic oceans. The average depth of the oceans is 3,370 m [12,238 ft], but they are divided into several zones.

Around most continents are gently sloping continental shelves, which are flooded parts of the continents. The shelves end at the continental slope, at a depth of about 200 m [656 ft]. This slope leads steeply down to the abyss. The deepest parts of the oceans are the trenches, which reach a maximum depth of 11,033 m [36,198 ft] in the Mariana Trench in the western Pacific.

Most marine life is found in the top 200 m [656 ft], where there is sufficient sunlight for plants, called phytoplankton, to grow. Below this zone, life becomes more and more scarce, though no part of the ocean, even at the bottom of the deepest trenches, is completely without living things.

Continental islands, such as the British Isles, are high parts of the continental shelves. For example, until about 7,500 years ago, when the ice sheets formed during the Ice Ages were melting, raising the sea level and filling the North Sea and the Strait of Dover, Britain was linked to mainland Europe.

By contrast, oceanic islands, such as the Hawaiian chain in the North Pacific Ocean, rise from the ocean floor. All oceanic islands are of volcanic origin, although many of them in warm parts of the oceans have sunk and are capped by layers of coral to form ring- or horseshoe-shaped atolls and coral reefs.

Ocean Water

The oceans contain about 97% of the world's water. Seawater contains more than 70 dissolved elements, but chloride and sodium make up 85% of the total. Sodium chloride is common salt and it makes seawater salty. The salinity of the oceans is mostly between 3.3–3.7%. Ocean water fed by icebergs or large rivers is less saline than shallow seas in the tropics, where the evaporation rate is high. Seawater is a source of salt but the water is useless for agriculture or drinking unless it is desalinated. However, land

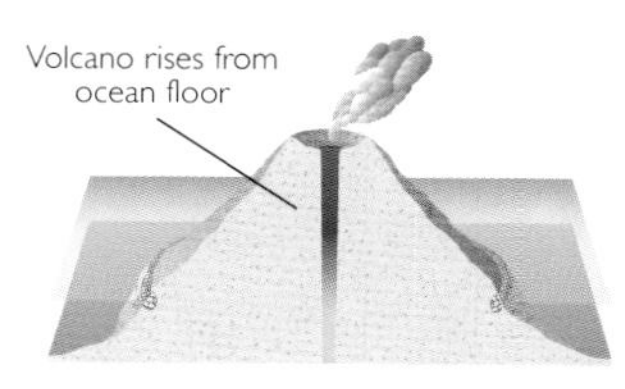

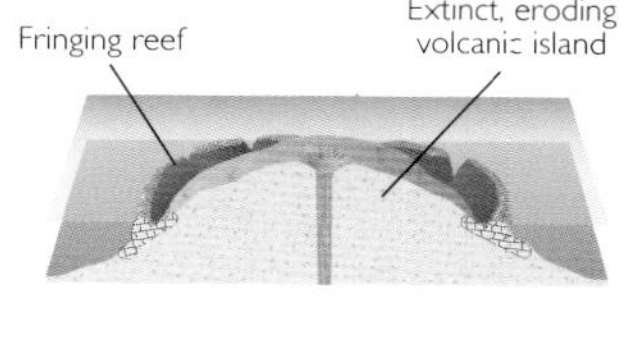

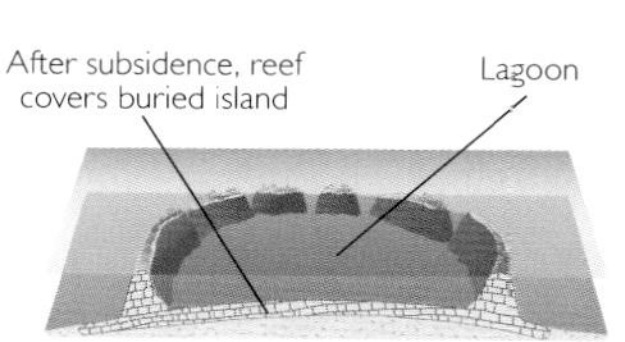

Development of an atoll
Some of the volcanoes that rise from the ocean floor reach the surface to form islands. Some of these islands subside and become submerged. As an island sinks, coral starts to grow around the rim of the volcano, building up layer upon layer of limestone deposits to form fringing reefs. Sometimes coral grows on the tip of a central cone to form an island in the middle of the atoll.

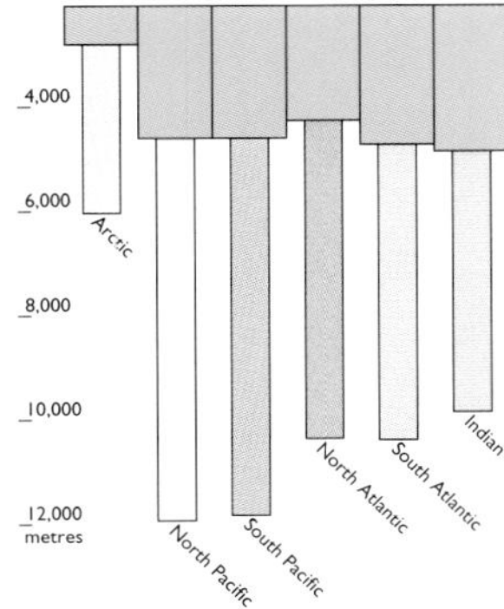

The ocean depths

The diagram shows the average depths (in dark blue) and the greatest depths in the four oceans. The North Pacific Ocean contains the world's deepest trenches, including the Mariana Trench, where the deepest manned descent was made by the bathyscaphe Trieste *in 1960. It reached a depth of 10,916 metres [35,813 ft].*

Relative sizes of the world's oceans:

PACIFIC	49%	ATLANTIC	26%
INDIAN	21%	ARCTIC	4%

Some geographers distinguish a fifth ocean, the Southern or Antarctic Ocean but most authorities regard these waters as the southern extension of the Pacific, Atlantic and Indian oceans.

areas get a regular supply of fresh water through the hydrological cycle (see page 26).

The density of seawater depends on its salinity and temperature. Temperatures vary from –2°C [28°F], the freezing point of seawater at the poles, to around 30°C [86°F] in parts of the tropics. Density differences help to maintain the circulation of the world's oceans, especially deep-sea currents. But the main cause of currents within 350 m [1,148 ft] of the surface is the wind. Because of the Earth's rotation, currents are deflected, creating huge circular motions of surface water – clockwise in the northern hemisphere and anticlockwise in the southern hemisphere.

Ocean currents transport heat from the tropics to the polar regions and thus form part of the heat engine that drives the Earth's climates. Ocean currents have an especially marked effect on coastal climates, such as north-western Europe. In the mid-1990s, scientists warned that global warming may be weakening currents, including the warm Gulf Stream which is responsible for the mild winters experienced in north-western Europe.

Ice Sheets, Ice Caps and Glaciers

Global warming is also a threat to the world's ice sheets, ice caps and glaciers that together account for about 2% of the world's water. There are two ice sheets in the world, the largest covers most of Antarctica. With the ice reaching maximum depths of 4,800 m [15,748 ft], the Antarctic ice sheet contains about 70% of the world's fresh water, with a total volume about nine times greater than the Greenland ice sheet. Smaller bodies of ice include ice caps in northern Canada, Iceland and Scandinavia. Also throughout the world in high ranges are many valley glaciers, which help to shape dramatic mountain scenery.

Only about 11,000 years ago, during the final phase of the Pleistocene Ice Age, ice covered much of the northern hemisphere. The Ice Age, which began about 1.8 million years ago, was not a continuous period of cold. Instead, it consisted of glacial periods when the ice advanced and warmer interglacial periods when temperatures rose and the ice retreated.

Some scientists believe that we are now living in an interglacial period, and that glacial conditions will recur in the future. Others fear that global warming, caused mainly by pollution, may melt the world's ice, raising sea levels by up to 55 m [180 ft]. Many fertile and densely populated coastal plains, islands and cities would vanish from the map.

Weddell Sea, Antarctica

Antarctica contains two huge bays, occupied by the Ross and Weddell seas. Ice shelves extend from the ice sheet across parts of these seas. Researchers fear that warmer weather is melting Antarctica's ice sheets at a dangerous rate, after large chunks of the Larsen ice shelf and the Ronne ice shelf broke away in 1997 and 1998 respectively. This was followed in March 2002 by the disintegration of the Larsen B ice shelf.

The Earth's Atmosphere

Since the discovery in 1985 of a thinning of the ozone layer, creating a so-called 'ozone hole', over Antarctica, many governments have worked to reduce the emissions of ozone-eating substances, notably the chlorofluorocarbons (CFCs) used in aerosols, refrigeration, air conditioning and dry cleaning.

Following forecasts that the ozone layer would rapidly repair itself as a result of controls on these emissions, scientists were surprised in early 1996 when a marked thinning of the ozone layer occurred over the Arctic, northern Europe, Russia and Canada. The damage, which was recorded as far south as southern Britain, was due to pollution combined with intense cold in the stratosphere. It was another sharp reminder of the dangers humanity faces when it interferes with and harms the environment.

The ozone layer in the stratosphere blocks out most of the dangerous ultraviolet B radiation in the Sun's rays. This radiation causes skin cancer and cataracts, as well as harming plants on the land and plankton in the oceans. The ozone layer is only one way in which the atmosphere protects life on Earth. The atmosphere also provides the air we breathe and the carbon dioxide required by plants. It is also a shield against meteors and it acts as a blanket to prevent heat radiated from the Earth escaping into space.

Layers of Air

The atmosphere is divided into four main layers. The troposphere at the bottom contains about 85% of the atmosphere's total mass, where most weather conditions occur. The troposphere is about 15 km [9 miles] thick over the Equator and 8 km [5 miles] thick at the poles. Temperatures decrease with height by approximately 1°C [2°F] for every 100 m [328 ft]. At the top of the troposphere is a level called the tropopause where temperatures are stable at around –55°C [–67°F]. Above the tropopause is the stratosphere, which contains the ozone layer. Here, at about 50 km [31 miles] above the Earth's surface, temperatures rise to about 0°C [32°F].

The ionosphere extends from the stratopause to about 600 km [373 miles] above the surface. Here temperatures fall up to about 80 km

N
S
FRONTAL RAIN
EASTERLY WINDS
SOUTH-WESTERLY WINDS
NORTH-EASTERLY TRADES
SOUTH-EASTERLY TRADES
NORTH-WESTERLY WINDS
EASTERLY WINDS
FRONTAL RAIN
CONVECTIONAL THUNDERSTORM

CIRCULATION OF AIR

HIGH PRESSURE
LOW PRESSURE
WARM AIR
COLD AIR
SURFACE WINDS
CLOUDS

The circulation of the atmosphere can be divided into three rotating but interconnected air systems, or cells. The Hadley cell (figure 1 on the above diagram) is in the tropics; the Ferrel cell (2) lies between the subtropics and the mid-latitudes, and the Polar cell (3) is in the high latitudes.

Moonrise seen from orbit

This photograph taken by an orbiting Shuttle shows the crescent of the Moon. Silhouetted at the horizon is a dense cloud layer. The reddish-brown band is the tropopause, which separates the blue-white stratosphere from the yellow troposphere.

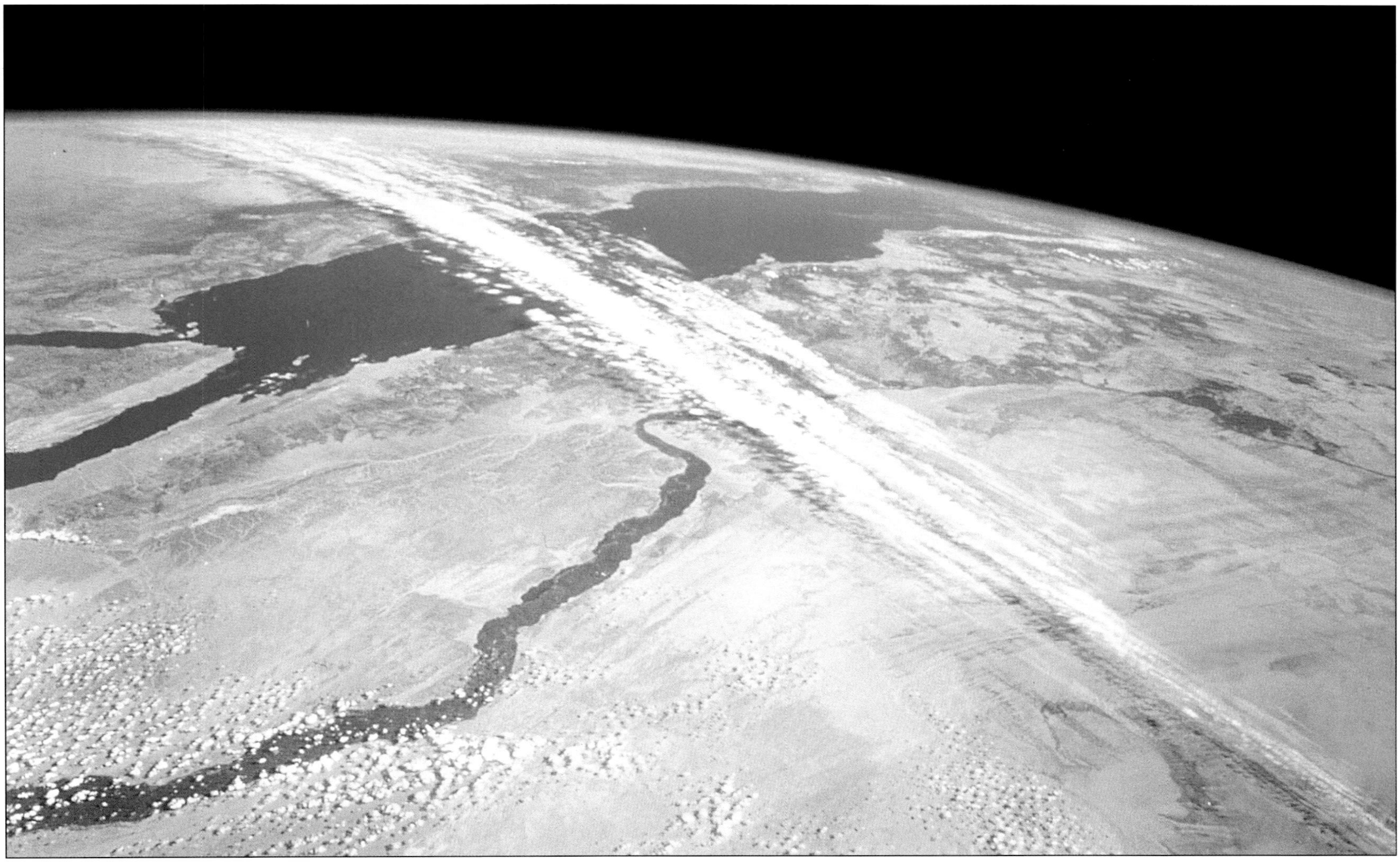

Jetstream from space
Jetstreams are strong winds that normally blow near the tropopause. Cirrus clouds mark the route of the jet stream in this photograph, which shows the Red Sea, North Africa and the Nile valley, which appears as a dark band crossing the desert.

[50 miles], but then rise. The aurorae, which occur in the ionosphere when charged particles from the Sun interact with the Earth's magnetic field, are strongest near the poles. In the exosphere, the outermost layer, the atmosphere merges into space.

Circulation of the Atmosphere

The heating of the Earth is most intense around the Equator where the Sun is high in the sky. Here warm, moist air rises in strong currents, creating a zone of low air pressure: the doldrums. The rising air eventually cools and spreads out north and south until it sinks back to the ground around latitudes 30° North and 30° South. This forms two zones of high air pressure called the horse latitudes.

From the horse latitudes, trade winds blow back across the surface towards the Equator, while westerly winds blow towards the poles. The warm westerlies finally meet the polar easterlies (cold dense air flowing from the poles). The line along which the warm and cold air streams meet is called the polar front. Depressions (or cyclones) are low air pressure frontal systems that form along the polar front.

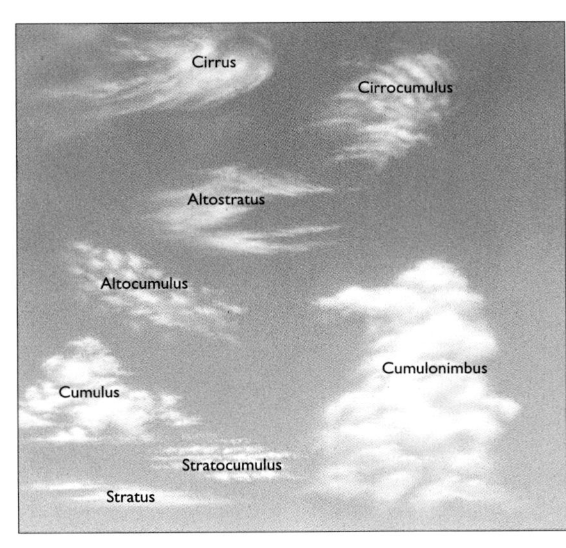

Classification of clouds
Clouds are classified broadly into cumuliform, or 'heap' clouds, and stratiform, or 'layer' clouds. Both types occur at all levels. The highest clouds, composed of ice crystals, are cirrus, cirrostratus and cirrocumulus. Medium-height clouds include altostratus, a grey cloud that often indicates the approach of a depression, and altocumulus, a thicker and fluffier version of cirrocumulus. Low clouds include stratus, which forms dull, overcast skies; nimbostratus, a dark grey layer cloud which brings almost continuous rain and snow; cumulus, a brilliant white heap cloud; and stratocumulus, a layer cloud arranged in globular masses or rolls. Cumulonimbus, a cloud associated with thunderstorms, lightning and heavy rain, often extends from low to medium altitudes. It has a flat base, a fluffy outline and often an anvil-shaped top.

Composition of the Atmosphere

The air in the troposphere is made up mainly of nitrogen (78%) and oxygen (21%). Argon makes up more than 0.9% and there are also minute amounts of carbon dioxide, helium, hydrogen, krypton, methane, ozone and xenon. The atmosphere also contains water vapour, the gaseous form of water, which, when it condenses around minute specks of dust and salt, forms tiny water droplets or ice crystals. Large masses of water droplets or ice crystals form clouds.

Climate and Weather

In 1992, Hurricane Andrew struck the Bahamas, Florida and Louisiana, causing record damage estimated at $30 billion. In September 1998, following heavy monsoon rains, floods submerged two-thirds of Bangladesh. The same month, in Central America, more than 7,000 people died in floods and mudslides caused by Hurricane Mitch. The economy of Honduras, already crippled by debt, was thought to have been put back by 15 to 20 years. In November 2001, violent storms in Algeria caused the deaths of more than 700 people in floods and landslides.

Every year, exceptional weather conditions cause disasters around the world. Modern forecasting techniques now give people warning of advancing storms, but the toll of human deaths continues as people are powerless in the face of the awesome forces of nature.

Weather is the day-to-day condition of the atmosphere. In some places, the weather is normally stable, but in other areas, especially the middle latitudes, it is highly variable, changing with the passing of a depression. By contrast, climate is the average weather of a place, based on data obtained over a long period.

Hurricane Elena, 1995

Hurricanes form over warm oceans north and south of the Equator. Their movements are tracked by satellites, enabling forecasters to issue storm warnings as they approach land. In North America, forecasters identify them with boys' and girls' names.

Climatic Factors

Climate depends basically on the unequal heating of the Sun between the Equator and the poles. But ocean currents and terrain also affect climate. For example, despite their northerly positions, Norway's ports remain ice-free in winter. This is because of the warming effect of the North Atlantic Drift, an extension of the Gulf Stream which flows across the Atlantic Ocean from the Gulf of Mexico.

By contrast, the cold Benguela current which flows up the coast of south-western Africa cools the coast and causes arid conditions. This is because the cold onshore winds are warmed as they pass over the land. The warm air can hold more water vapour than cold air, giving the winds a drying effect.

The terrain affects climate in several ways. Because temperatures fall with altitude, highlands are cooler than lowlands in the same

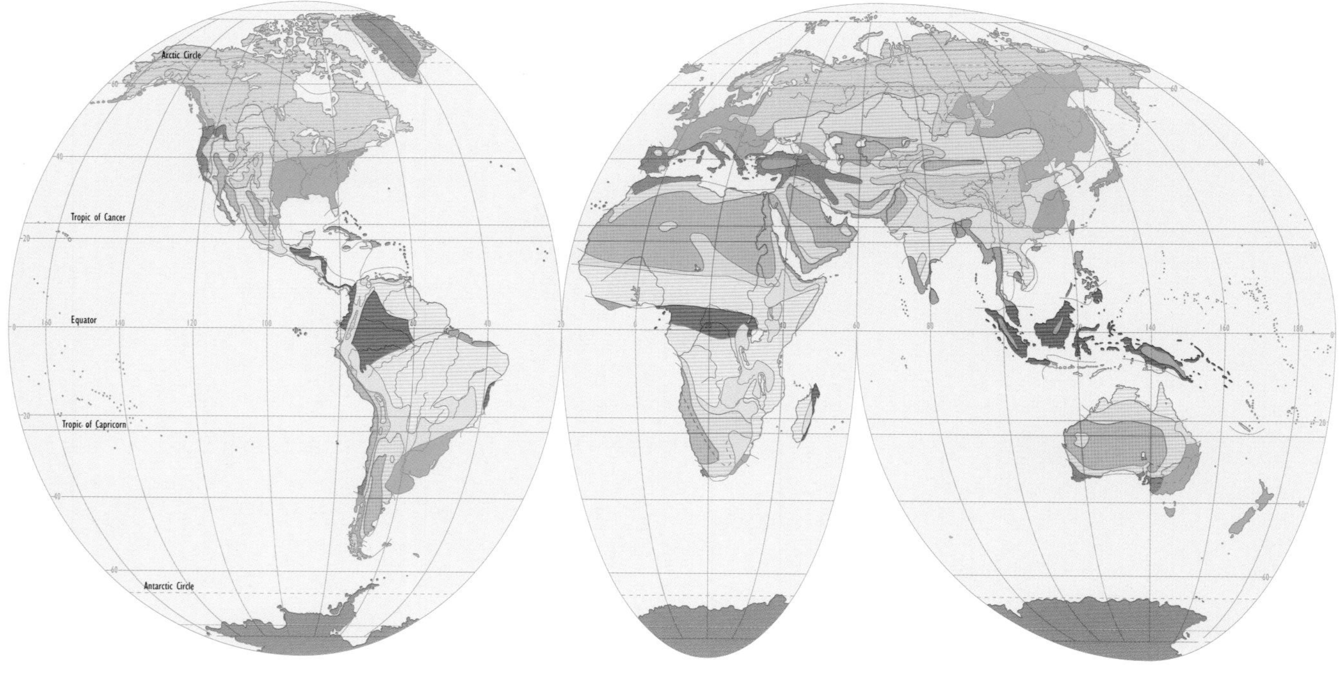

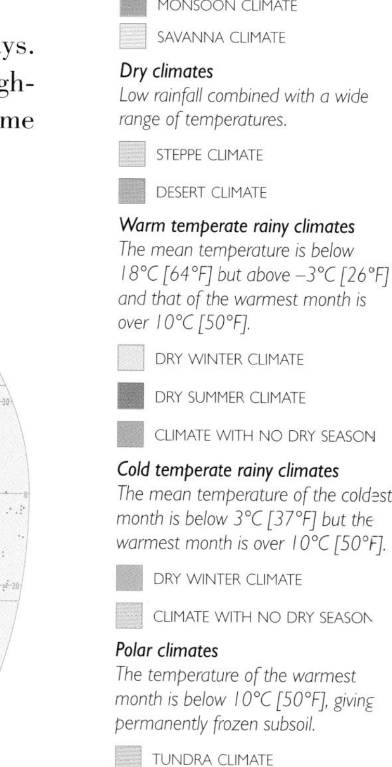

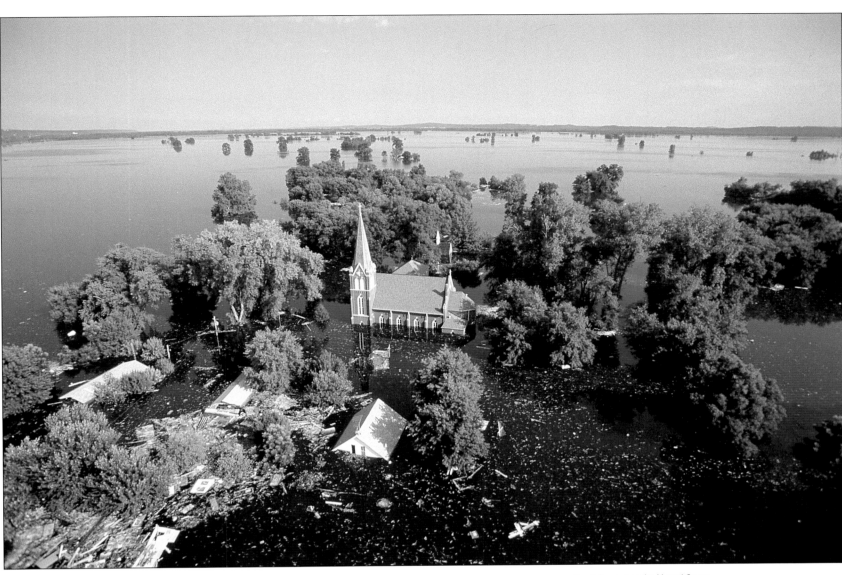

Flood damage in the United States

In June and July 1993, the Mississippi River basin suffered record floods. The photograph shows a sunken church in Illinois. The flooding along the Mississippi, Missouri and other rivers caused great damage, amounting to about $12 billion. At least 48 people died in the floods.

Floods in St Louis, United States

The satellite image, right, shows the extent of the floods at St Louis at the confluence of the Mississippi and the Missouri rivers in June and July 1993. The floods occurred when very heavy rainfall raised river levels by up to 14 m [46 ft]. The floods reached their greatest extent between Minneapolis in the north and a point approximately 150 km [93 miles] south of St Louis. In places, the width of the Mississippi increased to nearly 11 km [7 miles], while the Missouri reached widths of 32 km [20 miles]. In all, more than 28,000 sq km [10,800 sq miles] were inundated and hundreds of towns and cities were flooded. Damage to crops was estimated at $8 billion. The USA was hit again by flooding in early 1997, when heavy rainfall in North Dakota and Minnesota caused the Red River to flood. The flooding had a catastrophic effect on the city of Grand Forks, which was inundated for months.

latitude. Terrain also affects rainfall. When moist onshore winds pass over mountain ranges, they are chilled as they are forced to rise and the water vapour they contain condenses to form clouds which bring rain and snow. After the winds have crossed the mountains, the air descends and is warmed. These warm, dry winds create rain shadow (arid) regions on the lee side of the mountains.

Climatic Regions

The two major factors that affect climate are temperature and precipitation, including rain and snow. In addition, seasonal variations and other climatic features are also taken into account. Climatic classifications vary because of the weighting given to various features. Yet most classifications are based on five main climatic types: tropical rainy climates; dry climates; warm temperate rainy climates; cold temperate rainy climates; and very cold polar climates. Some classifications also allow for the effect of altitude. The main climatic regions are subdivided according to seasonal variations and also to the kind of vegetation associated with the climatic conditions. Thus, the rainforest climate, with rain throughout the year, differs from monsoon and savanna climates, which have marked dry seasons. Similarly, parched desert climates differ from steppe climates which have enough moisture for grasses to grow.

Water and Land Use

All life on land depends on fresh water. Yet about 80 countries now face acute water shortages. The world demand for fresh water is increasing by about 2.3% a year and this demand will double every 21 years. About a billion people, mainly in developing countries, do not have access to clean drinking water and around 10 million die every year from drinking dirty water. This problem is made worse in many countries by the pollution of rivers and lakes.

In 1995, a World Bank report suggested that wars will be fought over water in the 21st century. Relations between several countries are already soured by disputes over water resources. Egypt fears that Sudan and Ethiopia will appropriate the waters of the Nile, while Syria and Iraq are concerned that Turkish dams will hold back the waters of the Euphrates.

However, experts stress that while individual countries face water crises, there is no global crisis. The chief global problems are the uneven distribution of water and its inefficient and wasteful use.

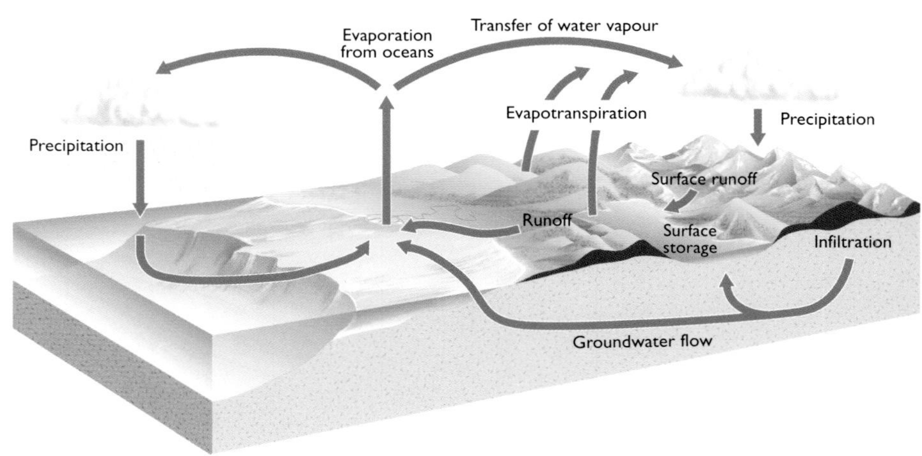

The hydrological cycle
The hydrological cycle is responsible for the continuous circulation of water around the planet. Water vapour contains and transports latent heat, or latent energy. When the water vapour condenses back into water (and falls as rain, hail or snow), the heat is released. When condensation takes place on cold nights, the cooling effect associated with nightfall is offset by the liberation of latent heat.

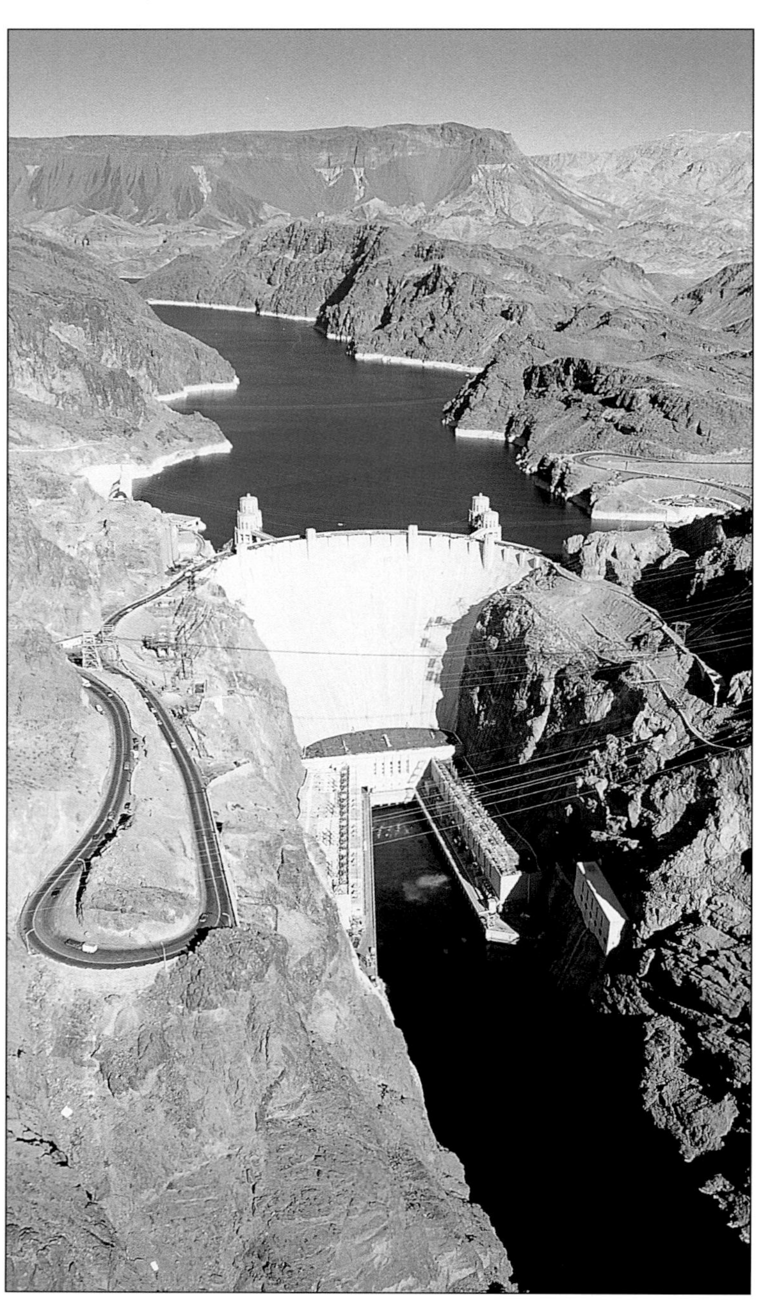

Hoover Dam, United States
The Hoover Dam in Arizona controls the Colorado River's flood waters. Its reservoir supplies domestic and irrigation water to the south-west, while a hydroelectric plant produces electricity.

The World's Water Supply

Of the world's total water supply, 99.4% is in the oceans or frozen in bodies of ice. Most of the rest circulates through the rocks beneath our feet as ground water. Water in rivers and lakes, in the soil and in the atmosphere together make up only 0.013% of the world's water.

The freshwater supply on land is dependent on the hydrological, or water cycle which is driven by the Sun's heat. Water is evaporated from the oceans and carried into the air as invisible water vapour. Although this vapour averages less than 2% of the total mass of the atmosphere, it is the chief component from the standpoint of weather.

When air rises, water vapour condenses into visible water droplets or ice crystals, which eventually fall to earth as rain, snow, sleet, hail or frost. Some of the precipitation that reaches the ground returns directly to the atmosphere through evaporation or transpiration via plants. Much of the rest of the water flows into the rocks to become ground water or across the surface into rivers and, eventually, back to the oceans, so completing the hydrological cycle.

WATER DISTRIBUTION
The distribution of planetary water, by percentage.

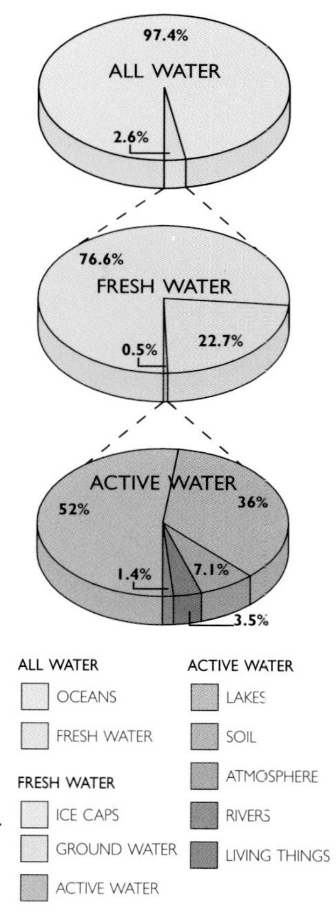

Water and Agriculture

Only about a third of the world's land area is used for growing crops, while another third

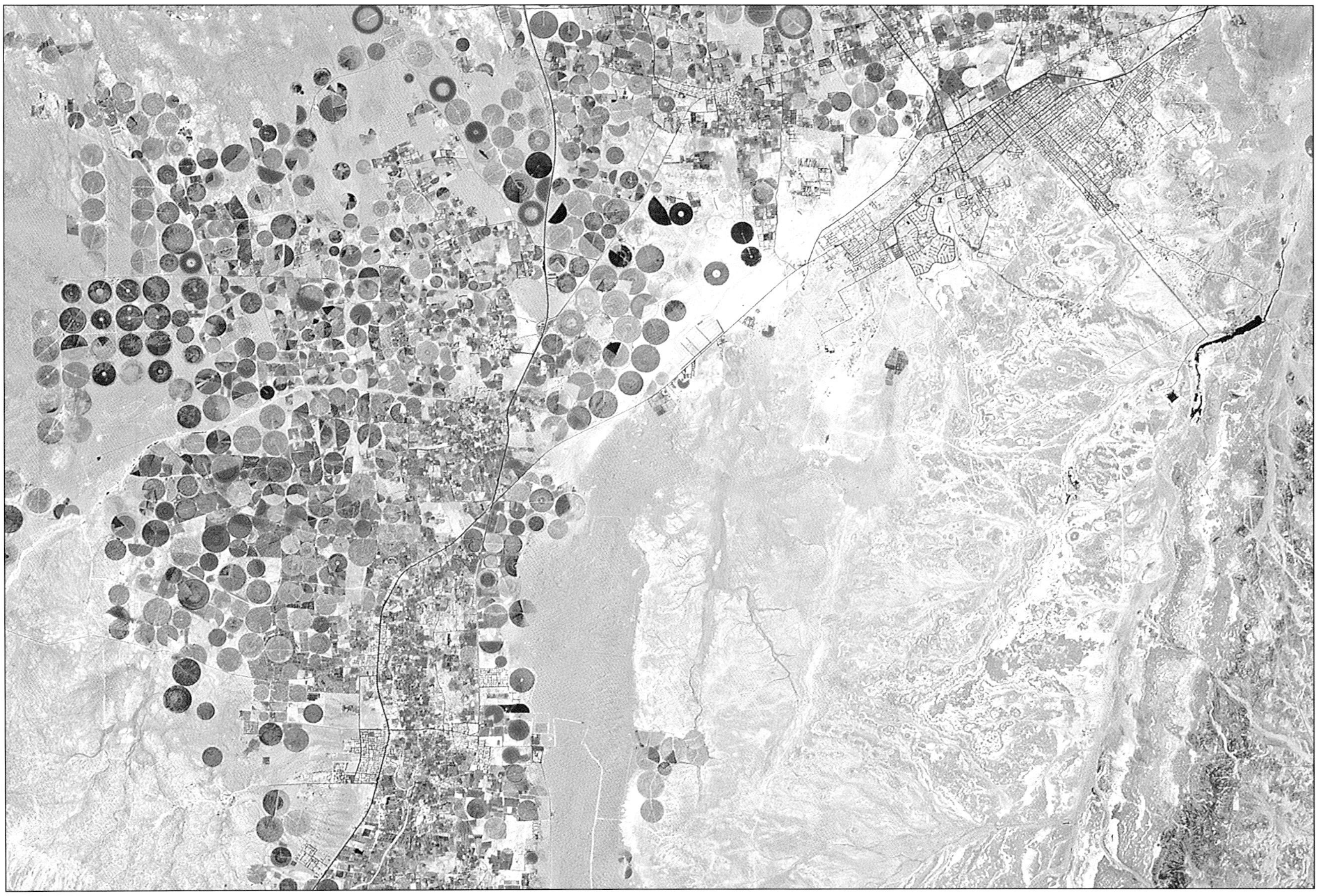

Irrigation in Saudi Arabia

Saudi Arabia is a desert country which gets its water from oases, which tap ground water supplies, and desalination plants. The sale of oil has enabled the arid countries of south-western Asia to develop their agriculture. In the above satellite image, vegetation appears brown and red.

Irrigation boom

The photograph shows a pivotal irrigation boom used to sprinkle water over a wheat field in Saudi Arabia. Irrigation in hot countries often takes place at night so that water loss through evaporation is reduced. Irrigation techniques vary from place to place. In monsoon areas with abundant water, the fields are often flooded, or the water is led to the crops along straight furrows. Sprinkler irrigation has become important since the 1940s. In other types of irrigation, the water is led through pipes which are on or under the ground. Underground pipes supply water directly to the plant roots and, as a result, water loss through evaporation is minimized.

consists of meadows and pasture. The rest of the world is unsuitable for farming, being too dry, too cold, too mountainous, or covered by dense forests. Although the demand for food increases every year, problems arise when attempts are made to increase the existing area of farmland. For example, the soils and climates of tropical forest and semi-arid regions of Africa and South America are not ideal for farming. Attempts to work such areas usually end in failure. To increase the world's food supply, scientists now concentrate on making existing farmland more productive rather than farming marginal land.

To grow crops, farmers need fertile, workable land, an equable climate, including a frost-free growing period, and an adequate supply of fresh water. In some areas, the water falls directly as rain. But many other regions depend on irrigation.

Irrigation involves water conservation through the building of dams which hold back storage reservoirs. In some areas, irrigation water comes from underground aquifers, layers of permeable and porous rocks through which ground water percolates. But in many cases, the water in the aquifers has been there for thousands of years, having accumulated at a time when the rainfall was much greater than it is today. As a result, these aquifers are not being renewed and will, one day, dry up.

Other sources of irrigation water are desalination plants, which remove salt from seawater and pump it to farms. This is a highly expensive process and is employed in areas where water supplies are extremely low, such as the island of Malta, or in the oil-rich desert countries around the Gulf, which can afford to build huge desalination plants.

LAND USE BY CONTINENT

	Forest	Permanent pasture	Permanent crops	Arable	Non-productive
North America	32.2%	17.3%	0.3%	12.6%	37.6%
South America	51.8%	26.7%	1.5%	6.6%	13.4%
Europe	33.4%	17.5%	3.0%	26.8%	19.3%
Africa	23.2%	26.6%	0.6%	5.6%	44.0%
Asia	20.2%	25.0%	1.2%	16.0%	37.8%
Oceania	23.5%	52.2%	0.1%	5.7%	18.5%

The Natural World

In 2002, a United Nations report identified more than 11,000 plant and animal species known to face a high risk of extinction, including 24% of all mammals and 12% of birds. Human activities, ranging from habitat destruction to the introduction of alien species from one area to another, are the main causes of this devastating reduction of our planet's biodiversity, which might lead to the disappearance of unique combinations of genes that could be vital in improving food yields on farms or in the production of drugs to combat disease.

Extinctions of species have occurred throughout Earth history, but today the extinction rate is estimated to be about 10,000 times the natural average. Some scientists have even compared it with the mass extinction that wiped out the dinosaurs 65 million years ago. However, the main cause of today's high extinction rate is not some natural disaster, such as the impact of an asteroid a few kilometres across, but it is the result of human actions, most notably the destruction of natural habitats for farming and other purposes. In some densely populated areas, such as Western Europe, the natural habitats were destroyed long ago. Today, the greatest damage is occurring in tropical rainforests, which contain more than half of the world's known species.

Modern technology has enabled people to live comfortably almost anywhere on Earth. But most plants and many animals are adapted to particular climatic conditions, and they live in association with and dependent on each other. Plant and animal communities that cover large areas are called biomes.

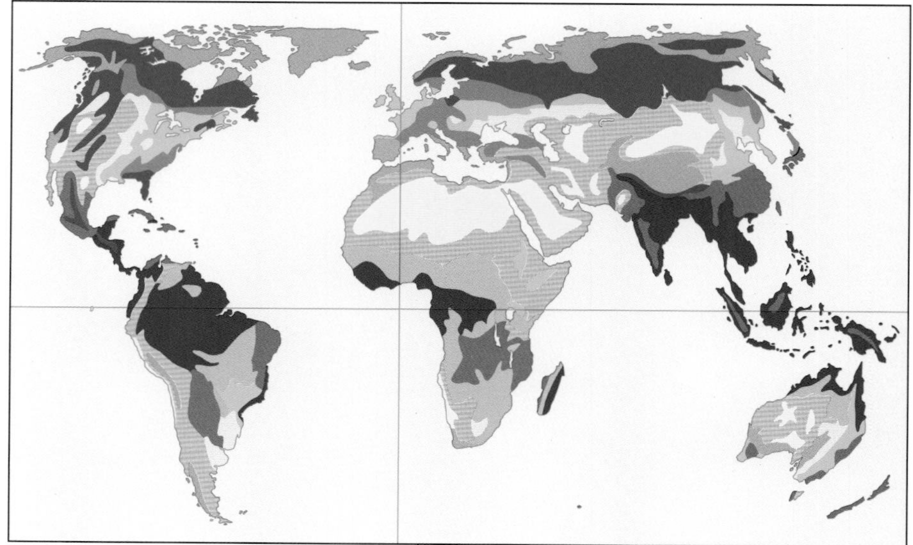

NATURAL VEGETATION

- TUNDRA & MOUNTAIN VEGETATION
- NEEDLELEAF EVERGREEN FOREST
- MIXED NEEDLELEAF EVERGREEN & BROADLEAF DECIDUOUS TREES
- BROADLEAF DECIDUOUS WOODLAND
- MID-LATITUDE GRASSLAND
- EVERGREEN BROADLEAF & DECIDUOUS TREES & SHRUBS
- SEMI-DESERT SCRUB
- DESERT
- TROPICAL GRASSLAND (SAVANNA)
- TROPICAL BROADLEAF RAINFOREST & MONSOON FOREST
- SUBTROPICAL BROADLEAF & NEEDLELEAF FOREST

The map shows the world's main biomes. The classification is based on the natural 'climax' vegetation of regions, a result of the climate and the terrain. But human activities have greatly modified this basic division. For example, the original deciduous forests of Western Europe and the eastern United States have largely disappeared. In recent times, human development of some semi-arid areas has turned former dry grasslands into barren desert.

The World's Biomes

The world's biomes are defined mainly by climate and vegetation. They range from the tundra, in polar regions and high mountain regions, to the lush equatorial rainforests.

The Arctic tundra covers large areas in the polar regions of the northern hemisphere. Snow covers the land for more than half of the year and the subsoil, called permafrost, is permanently frozen. Comparatively few species can survive in this harsh, treeless environment. The main plants are hardy mosses, lichens, grasses, sedges and low shrubs. However, in summer, the tundra plays an important part in world animal geography, when its growing plants and swarms of insects provide food for migrating animals and birds that arrive from the south.

The tundra of the northern hemisphere merges in the south into a vast region of needleleaf evergreen forest, called the boreal forest or taiga. Such trees as fir, larch, pine and spruce are adapted to survive the long, bitterly cold winters of this region, but the number of plant and animal species is again small. South of the boreal forests is a zone of mixed needleleaf evergreens and broadleaf deciduous trees, which

Rainforest in Rwanda

Rainforests are the most threatened of the world's biomes. Effective conservation policies must demonstrate to poor local people that they can benefit from the survival of the forests.

Tundra in subarctic Alaska

The Denali National Park, Alaska, contains magnificent mountain scenery and tundra vegetation which flourishes during the brief summer. The park is open between 1 June and 15 September.

shed their leaves in winter. In warmer areas, this mixed forest merges into broadleaf deciduous forest, where the number and diversity of plant species is much greater.

Deciduous forests are adapted to temperate, humid regions. Evergreen broadleaf and deciduous trees grow in Mediterranean regions, with their hot, dry summers. But much of the original deciduous forest has been cut down and has given way to scrub and heathland. Grasslands occupy large areas in the middle latitudes, where the rainfall is insufficient to support forest growth. The moister grasslands are often called prairies, while drier areas are called steppe.

The tropics also contain vast dry areas of semi-desert scrub which merges into desert, as well as large areas of savanna, which is grassland with scattered trees. Savanna regions, with their marked dry season, support a wide range of mammals.

Tropical and subtropical regions contain three types of forest biomes. The tropical rainforest, the world's richest biome measured by its plant and animal species, experiences rain and high temperatures throughout the year. Similar forests occur in monsoon regions, which have a season of very heavy rainfall. They, too, are rich in plant species, though less so than the tropical rainforest. A third type of forest is the subtropical broadleaf and needleleaf forest, found in such places as south-eastern China, south-central Africa and eastern Brazil.

NET PRIMARY PRODUCTION OF EIGHT MAJOR BIOMES

- TROPICAL RAINFORESTS
- DECIDUOUS FORESTS
- TROPICAL GRASSLANDS
- CONIFEROUS FORESTS
- MEDITERRANEAN
- TEMPERATE GRASSLANDS
- TUNDRA
- DESERTS

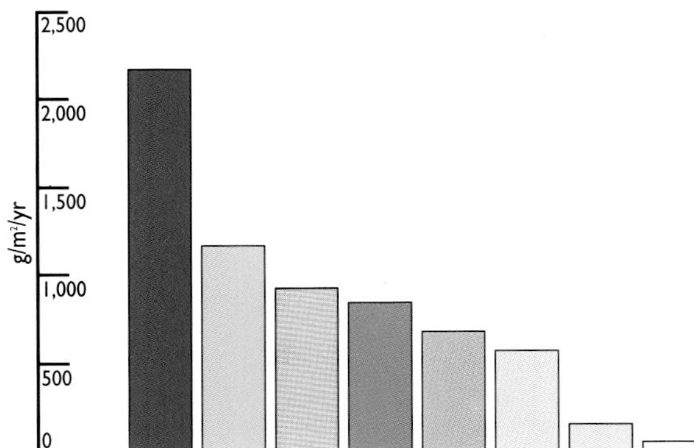

The net primary production of eight major biomes is expressed in grams of dry organic matter per square metre per year. The tropical rainforests produce the greatest amount of organic material. The tundra and deserts produce the least.

The Human World

Every minute, the world's population increases by between 160 and 170. While forecasts of future growth are difficult to make, most demographers are in agreement that the world's population, which passed the 6 billion mark in October 1999, would reach 8.9 billion by 2050. It was not expected to level out until 2200, when it would peak at around 11 billion. After 2200, it is expected to level out or even decline a little. The fastest rates of increase will take place in the developing countries of Africa, Asia and Latin America – the places least able to afford the enormous costs incurred by such a rapidly expanding population.

Elevated view of Ki Lung Street, Hong Kong
Urban areas of Hong Kong, a Special Administrative Region on the southern coast of China, contain busy streets overlooked by crowded apartments.

Average world population growth rates have declined from about 2% a year in the early 1960s to 1.4% in 1998. This was partly due to a decline in fertility rates – that is, the number of births to the number of women of child-bearing age – especially in developed countries where, as income has risen, the average size of families has fallen.

Declining fertility rates were also evident in many developing countries. Even Africa shows signs of such change, though its population is expected to triple before it begins to fall. Population growth is also dependent on death rates, which are affected by such factors as famine, disease and the quality of medical care.

The Population Explosion

The world's population has grown steadily throughout most of human history, though certain events triggered periods of population growth. The invention of agriculture around 10,000 years ago, led to great changes in human society. Before then, most people had obtained food by hunting animals and gathering plants. Average life expectancies were probably no more than 20 years and life was hard. However, when farmers began to produce food surpluses, people began to live settled lives. This major milestone in human history led to the development of the first cities and early civilizations.

From an estimated 8 million in 8000 BC, the world population rose to about 300 million by AD 1000. Between 1000 and 1750, the rate of world population increase was around 0.1% per year, but another period of major economic and social change – the Industrial Revolution – began in the late 18th century. The Industrial Revolution led to improvements in farm technology and increases in food production. The world population began to increase quickly as industrialization spread across Europe and into North America. By 1850, it had reached 1.2 billion. The 2 billion mark was passed in the 1920s, and then the population rapidly doubled to 4 billion by the 1970s.

Population Features

Population growth affects the structure of societies. In developing countries with high annual rates of population increase, the large majority of the people are young and soon to become parents themselves. For example, in Kenya, which had until recently an annual rate of population growth of around 4%, just over half

Largest Cities

Within 10 years, for the first time ever, the majority of the world's population will live in urban areas. Almost all the urban growth will be in developing countries. Below is a list of cities with their estimated populations in the year 2015, in millions.

1	Tokyo	28.7
2	Mumbai (Bombay)	27.4
3	Lagos	24.1
4	Shanghai	23.2
5	Jakarta	21.5
6	São Paulo	21.0
7	Karachi	20.6
8	Beijing	19.6
9	Dhaka	19.2
10	Mexico City	19.1
11	Kolkata (Calcutta)	17.6
12	Delhi	17.5
13	New York City	17.4
14	Tianjin	17.1
15	Metro Manila	14.9
16	Cairo	14.7
17	Los Angeles	14.5
18	Seoul	13.1
19	Buenos Aires	12.5
20	Istanbul	12.1

These city populations are based on figures for urban agglomerations rather than actual city limits.

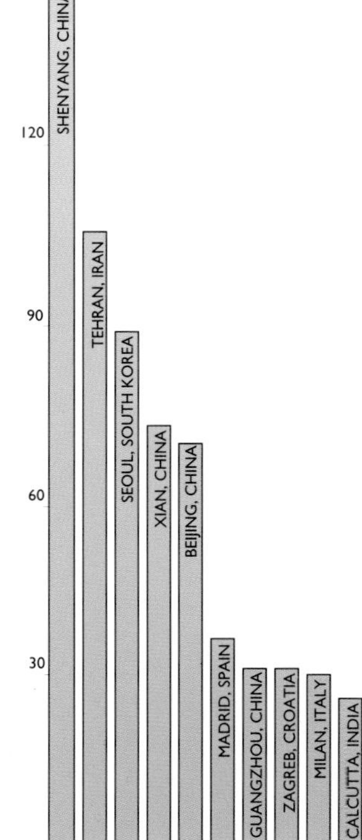

Urban air pollution
This diagram of the world's most polluted cities indicates the number of days per year when sulphur dioxide levels exceed the WHO threshhold of 150 micrograms per cubic metre.

Hong Kong's business district

By contrast with the picturesque old streets of Hong Kong, the business district of Hong Kong City, on the northern shore of Hong Kong Island, is a cluster of modern high-rise buildings. The glittering skyscrapers reflect the success of this tiny region, which has one of the strongest economies in Asia.

of the population is under 15 years of age. On the other hand, the populations of developed countries, with low population growth rates, have a fairly even spread across age groups.

Such differences are reflected in average life expectancies at birth. In rich countries, such as Australia and the United States, the average life expectancy is 77 years (74 years for men and 80 for women; women live longer, on average, than their male counterparts). As a result, an increasing proportion of the people are elderly and retired, contributing little to the economy. The reverse applies in many poor countries, where average life expectancies are below 60 years. In the early 21st century, life expectancies were falling in some southern African countries, such as Botswana, where they fell from nearly 70 to around 40 years because of the fast spread of HIV and AIDS.

Paralleling the population explosion has been a rapid growth in the number and size of cities and towns, which contained nearly half of the world's people by the 1990s. This proportion is expected to rise to nearly two-thirds by 2025.

Urbanization occurred first in areas undergoing the industrialization of their economies, but today it is also a feature of the developing world. In developing countries, people are leaving impoverished rural areas hoping to gain access to the education, health and other services available in cities. But many cities cannot provide the facilities necessitated by rapid population growth. Slums develop and pollution, crime and disease become features of everyday life.

The population explosion poses another probem for the entire world. No one knows how many people the world can support or how consumer demand will damage the fragile environments on our planet. The British economist Thomas Malthus argued in the late 18th century that overpopulation would lead to famine and war. But an increase in farm technology in the 19th and 20th centuries, combined with a green revolution, in which scientists developed high-yield crop varieties, has greatly increased food production since Malthus' time.

However, some modern scientists argue that overpopulation may become a problem in the 21st century. They argue that food shortages leading to disastrous famines will result unless population growth can be halted. Such people argue in favour of birth control programmes. China, one of the two countries with more than a billion people, has introduced a one-child family policy. Its action has slowed the growth of China's huge population.

POPULATION CHANGE 1990–2000

The population change for the years 1990–2000.

- OVER 40% POPULATION GAIN
- 30–40% POPULATION GAIN
- 20–30% POPULATION GAIN
- 10–20% POPULATION GAIN
- 0–10% POPULATION GAIN
- NO CHANGE OR LOSS

TOP 5 COUNTRIES	
Kuwait	+75.9%
Namibia	+62.5%
Afghanistan	+60.1%
Mali	+55.5%
Tanzania	+54.6%

BOTTOM 5 COUNTRIES	
Belgium	–0.1%
Hungary	–0.2%
Grenada	–2.4%
Germany	–3.2%
Tonga	–3.2%

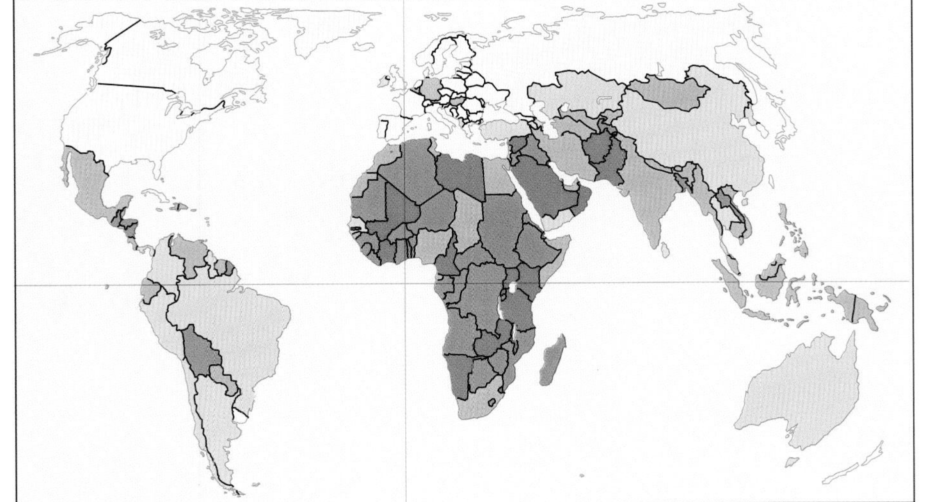

Languages and Religions

In 1995, 90-year-old Edna Guerro died in northern California. She was the last person able to speak Northern Pomo, one of about 50 Native American languages spoken in the state. Her death marked the extinction of one of the world's languages.

This event is not an isolated incident. Language experts regularly report the disappearance of languages and some of them predict that between 20 to 50% of the world's languages will no longer exist by the end of the 21st century. Improved transport and communications are partly to blame, because they bring people from various cultures into closer and closer contact. Many children no longer speak the language of their parents, preferring instead to learn the language used at their schools. The pressures on children to speak dominant rather than minority languages are often great. In the first part of the 20th century, Native American children were punished if they spoke their native language.

The disappearance of a language represents the extinction of a way of thinking, a unique expression of the experiences and knowledge of a group of people. Language and religion together give people an identity and a sense of belonging. However, there are others who argue that the disappearance of minority languages is a step towards international understanding and economic efficiency.

The World's Languages

Definitions of what is a language or a dialect vary and, hence, estimates of the number of languages spoken around the world range from about 3,000 to 6,000. But whatever the figure, it is clear that the number of languages far exceeds the number of countries.

RELIGIOUS ADHERENTS

Number of adherents to the world's major religions, in millions (1998).

Christian	**1,980**
Roman Catholic	1,300
Orthodox	240
African sects	110
Pentecostal	105
Others	225
Islam	**1,300**
Sunni	940
Shiite	120
Others	240
Hindu	**900**
Secular/Atheist/Agnostic/ Non-religious	**850**
Buddhist	**360**
Chinese Traditional	**225**
Indigenous/Animist	**190**
Sikh	**23**
Yoruba	**20**
Juche	**19**
Spiritism	**14**
Judaism	**14**
Baha'i	**6**
Jainism	**4**
Shinto	**4**

Buddhist monks in Katmandu, Nepal
Hinduism is Nepal's official religion, but the Nepalese observe the festivals of both Hinduism and Buddhism. They also regard Buddhist shrines and Hindu temples as equally sacred.

Countries with only one language tend to be small. For example, in Liechtenstein, everyone speaks German. By contrast, more than 860 languages have been identified in Papua New Guinea, whose population is only about 4.6 million people. Hence, many of its languages are spoken by only small groups of people. In fact, scientists have estimated that about a third of the world's languages are now spoken by less than 1,000 people. By contrast, more than half of the world's population speak just seven languages.

The world's languages are grouped into families. The Indo-European family consists of languages spoken between Europe and the Indian subcontinent. The growth of European empires over the last 300 years led several Indo-European languages, most notably English, French, Portuguese and Spanish, to spread throughout much of North and South America, Africa, Australia and New Zealand.

English has become the official language in many countries which together contain more than a quarter of the world's population. It is now a major international language, surpassing in importance Mandarin Chinese, a member of the Sino-Tibetan family, which is the world's leading first language. Without a knowledge of English, businessmen face many problems when conducting international trade, especially with the United States or other English-speaking countries. But proposals that English, French, Russian or some other language should become a world language seem unlikely to be acceptable to a majority of the world's peoples.

MOTHER TONGUES

First-language speakers of the major languages, in millions (1999).

- MANDARIN CHINESE 885M
- SPANISH 332M
- ENGLISH 322M
- BENGALI 189M
- HINDI 182M
- PORTUGUESE 170M
- RUSSIAN 170M
- JAPANESE 125M
- GERMAN 98M
- WU CHINESE 77M

OFFICIAL LANGUAGES: % OF WORLD POPULATION	
English	27.0%
Chinese	19.0%
Hindi	13.5%
Spanish	5.4%
Russian	5.2%
French	4.2%
Arabic	3.3%
Portuguese	3.0%
Malay	3.0%
Bengali	2.9%
Japanese	2.3%

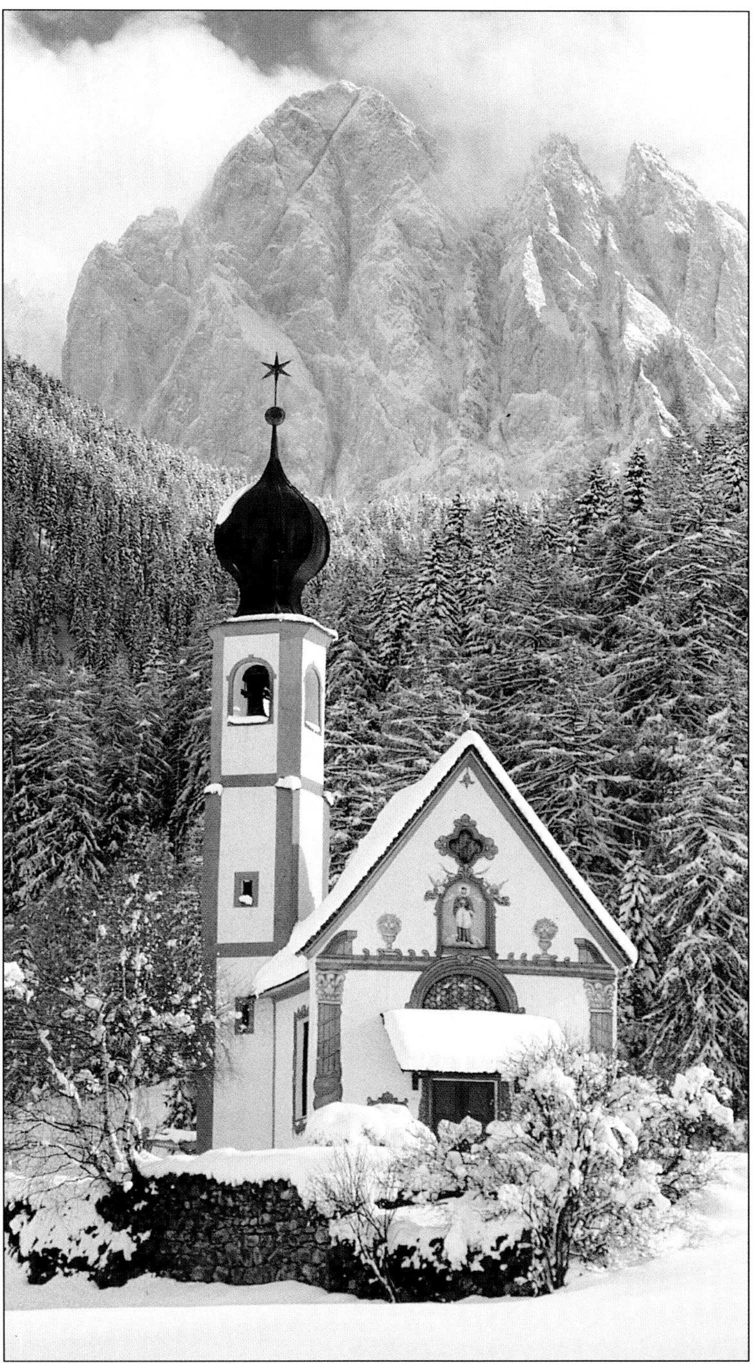

The Church of San Giovanni, Dolomites, Italy

Christianity has done much to shape Western civilization. Christian churches were built as places of worship, but many of them are among the finest achievements of world architecture.

World Religions

Religion is another fundamental aspect of human culture. It has inspired much of the world's finest architecture, literature, music and painting. It has also helped to shape human cultures since prehistoric times and is responsible for the codes of ethics by which most people live.

The world's major religions were all founded in Asia. Judaism, one of the first faiths to teach that there is only one god, is one of the world's oldest. Founded in south-western Asia, it influenced the more recent Christianity and Islam, two other monotheistic religions which now have the greatest number of followers. Hinduism, the third leading faith in terms of the numbers of followers, originated in the Indian subcontinent and most Hindus are now found in India. Another major religion, Buddhism, was founded in the subcontinent partly as a reaction to certain aspects of Hinduism. But unlike Hinduism, it has spread from India throughout much of eastern Asia.

Religion and language are powerful creative forces. They are also essential features of nationalism, which gives people a sense of belonging and pride. But nationalism is often also a cause of rivalry and tension. Cultural differences have led to racial hatred, the persecution of minorities, and to war between national groups.

Brazil (210)
Congo (Z.) (220)
Australia (230)
Mexico (240)
Cameroon (275)
India (410)
Nigeria (470)
Indonesia (701)
Papua New Guinea (862)

Polyglot nations

The graph, right, shows countries of the world with more than 200 languages. Although it has only about 4.6 million people, Papua New Guinea holds the record for the number of languages spoken.

International Organizations

Twelve days before the surrender of Germany and four months before the final end of World War II, representatives of 50 nations met in San Francisco to create a plan to set up a peacekeeping organization, the United Nations. Since its birth on 24 October 1945, its membership has grown from 51 to 189 in 2001.

Its first 50 years have been marked by failures as well as successes. While it has helped to prevent some disputes from flaring up into full-scale wars, the Blue Berets, as the UN troops are called, have been forced, because of their policy of neutrality, to stand by when atrocities are committed by rival warring groups.

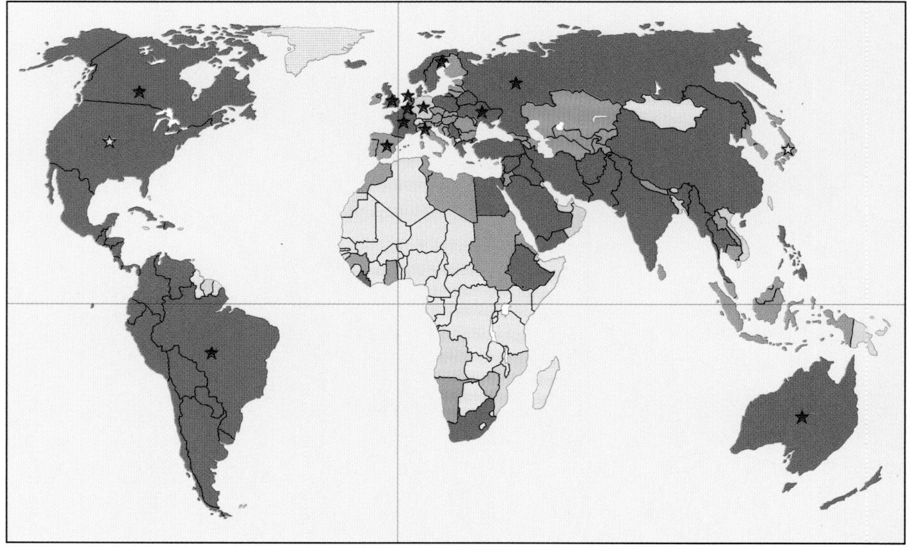

MEMBERS OF THE UN
Year of joining.

- 1940s
- 1950s
- 1960s
- 1970s
- 1980s
- 1990s
- NON–MEMBERS
- ★ 1% – 10% CONTRIBUTION TO FUNDING
- ★ OVER 10% CONTRIBUTION TC FUNDING

The Work of the UN

The United Nations has six main organs. They include the General Assembly, where member states meet to discuss issues concerned with peace, security and development. The Security Council, containing 15 members, is concerned with maintaining world peace. The Secretariat, under the Secretary-General, helps the other organs to do their jobs effectively, while the Economic and Social Council works with specialized agencies to implement policies concerned with such matters as development, education and health. The International Court of Justice, or World Court, helps to settle disputes between member nations. The sixth organ of the UN, the Trusteeship Council, was designed to bring 11 UN trust territories to independence. Its task has now been completed.

The specialized agencies do much important work. For example, UNICEF (United Nations International Children's Fund) has provided health care and aid for children in many parts of the world. The ILO (International Labour Organization) has improved working conditions in many areas, while the FAO (Food and Agricultural Organization) has worked to improve the production and distribution of food. Among the other agencies are organizations to help refugees, to further human rights and to control the environment. The latest agency, set up in 1995, is the WTO (World Trade Organization), which took over the work of GATT (General Agreement on Tariffs and Trade).

Other Organizations

In a world in which nations have become increasingly interdependent, many other organizations have been set up to deal with a variety of problems. Some, such as NATO (the North Atlantic Treaty Organization), are defence alliances. In the early 1990s, the end of the Cold War suggested that NATO's role might be finished, but the civil war in the former Yugoslavia showed that it still has a role in maintaining peace and security.

Other organizations encourage social and economic co-operation in various regions. Some are NGOs (non-governmental organizations), such as the Red Cross and its Muslim equivalent, the Red Crescent. Other NGOs raise funds to provide aid to countries facing major crises, such as famine.

Some major international organizations aim at economic co-operation and the removal of trade barriers. For example, the European Union has 15 members. Its economic success and the adoption of a single currency, the euro, by 12

Food aid

International organizations supply aid to people living in areas suffering from war or famine. In Bosnia-Herzegovina, the UN Protection Force supervised the movements of food aid, as did NATO on the borders of Kosovo a few years later.

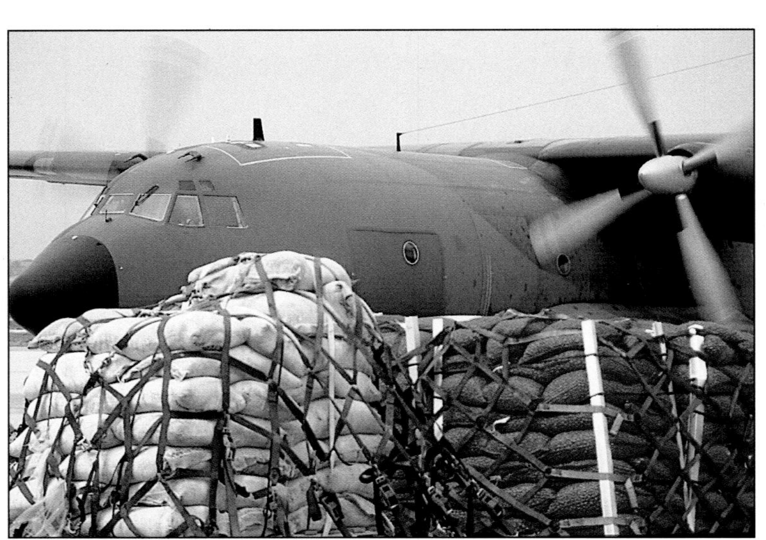

INTERNATIONAL AID AND GNP
Aid provided as a percentage of GNP, with total aid in brackets (1997).

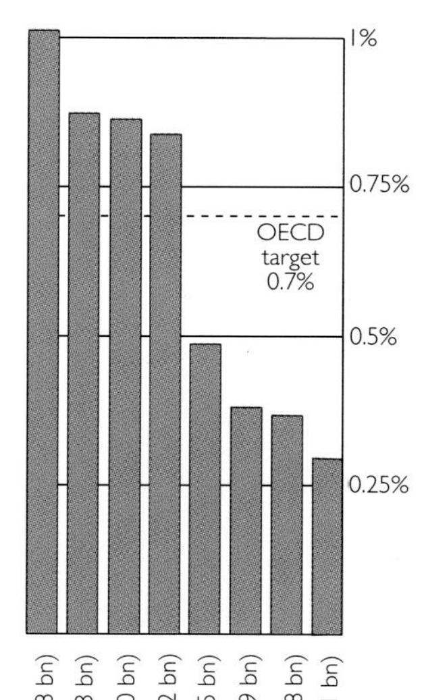

UNHCR-funded jetty, Sri Lanka

At the start of 2000, the number of people 'of concern' to the UN High Commission for Refugees totalled 22.3 million people. Sometimes, it has to provide transport facilities, such as this jetty, to get aid to the refugees.

of its members, has prompted some people to support the idea of a federal Europe. But others fear that political union might lead to a loss of national sovereignty by member states.

Other groupings include ASEAN (the Association of South-east Asian Nations) which aims to reduce trade barriers between its members (Brunei, Burma [Myanmar], Cambodia, Indonesia, Laos, Malaysia, the Philippines, Singapore, Thailand and Vietnam). APEC (the Asia-Pacific Co-operation Group), founded in 1989, aims to create a free trade zone between the countries of eastern Asia, North America, Australia and New Zealand by 2020. Meanwhile, Canada, Mexico and the United States have formed NAFTA (the North American Free Trade Agreement), while other economic groupings link most of the countries in Latin America. Another grouping with a more limited but important objective is OPEC (the Organization of Oil-Exporting Countries). OPEC works to unify policies concerning trade in oil on the world markets.

Some organizations exist to discuss matters of common interest between groups of nations. The Commonwealth of Nations, for example, grew out of links created by the British Empire. In North and South America, the OAS (Organization of American States) aims to increase understanding in the Western hemisphere. The OAU (Organization of African Unity) has a similar role in Africa, while the Arab League represents the Arab nations of North Africa and the Middle East.

COUNTRIES OF THE EUROPEAN UNION

	Total land area (sq km)	Total population (2001 est.)	GDP per capita, US$ (2000 est.)	Unemployment rate, % (2001)	Year of accession to the EU	Seats in EU parliament (1999–2004)
Austria	83,850	8,151,000	25,000	3.9%	1995	21
Belgium	30,510	10,259,000	25,300	6.9%	1958	25
Denmark	43,070	5,353,000	25,500	4.3%	1973	16
Finland	338,130	5,176,000	22,900	9.2%	1995	16
France	551,500	59,551,000	24,400	8.6%	1958	86
Germany	356,910	83,030,000	25,350	7.9%	1958	99
Greece	131,990	10,624,000	23,400	10.3%	1981	25
Ireland	70,280	3,841,000	21,600	3.8%	1973	15
Italy	301,270	57,680,000	22,100	9.4%	1958	87
Luxembourg	2,590	443,000	36,400	2.5%	1958	6
Netherlands	41,526	15,981,000	24,400	2.2%	1958	31
Portugal	92,390	9,444,000	15,800	4.4%	1986	25
Spain	504,780	38,432,000	18,000	13.0%	1986	64
Sweden	449,960	8,875,000	22,200	4.9%	1995	22
United Kingdom	243,368	59,648,000	22,800	5.1%	1973	87

Agriculture

Around the turn of the century, partly because of ongoing turmoil in the Russian economy, the increase in food production was less than the rise in world population, creating a small per capita fall in food production. Downward trends in world food production reopened an old debate – whether food production will be able to keep pace with the predicted rapid rises in the world population in the 21st century.

Some experts argue that the lower than expected production figures in the 1990s heralded a period of relative scarcity and high prices of food, which will be felt most in the poorer developing countries. Others are more optimistic. They point to the successes of the 'green revolution' which, through the use of new crop varieties produced by scientists, irrigation and the extensive use of fertilizers and pesticides, has revolutionized food production since the 1950s and 1960s.

The green revolution has led to a great expansion in the production of many crops, including such basic foods as rice, maize and wheat. In India, its effects have been spectacular. Between 1955 and 1995, grain production trebled, giving the country sufficient food reserves to prevent famine in years when droughts or floods reduce the harvest. While once India had to import food, it is now self-sufficient.

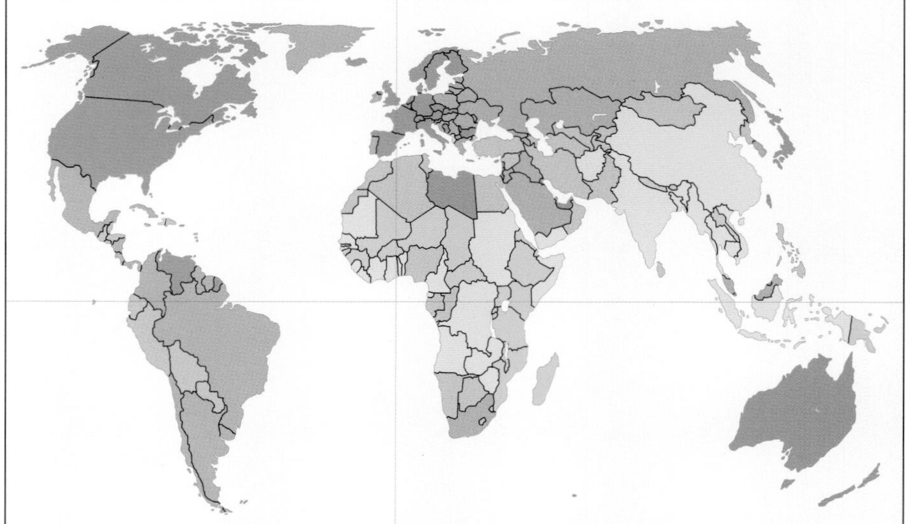

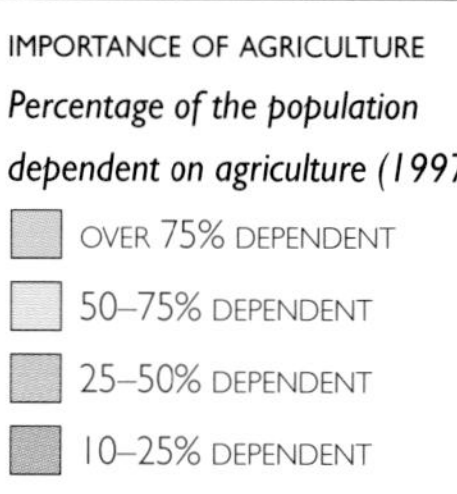

Rice harvest, Bali, Indonesia

More than half of the world's people eat rice as their basic food. Rice grows well in tropical and subtropical regions, such as in Indonesia, India and south-eastern China.

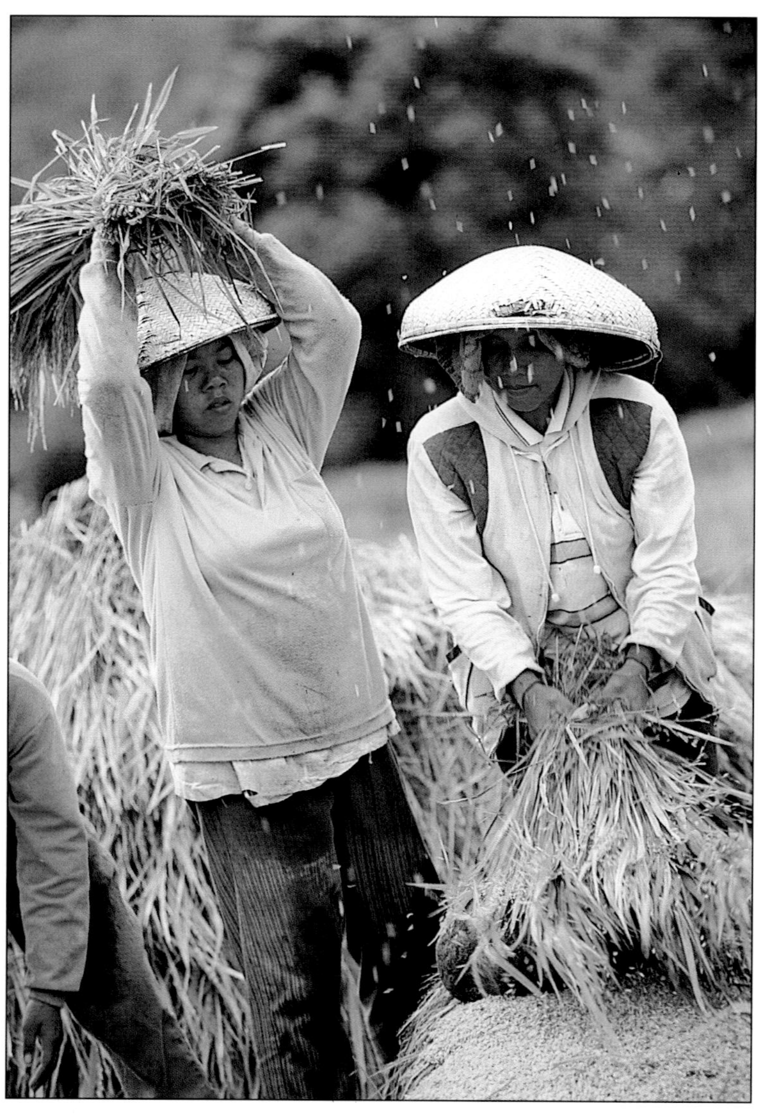

Food Production

Agriculture, which supplies most of our food, together with materials to make clothes and other products, is the world's most important economic activity. But its relative importance has declined in comparison with manufacturing and service industries. As a result, the end of the 20th century marked the first time for 10,000 years when the vast majority of the people no longer had to depend for their living on growing crops and herding animals.

However, agriculture remains the dominant economic activity in many developing countries in Africa and Asia. For example, by the start of the 21st century, 80% or more of the people of Bhutan, Burundi, Nepal and Rwanda depended on farming for their living.

Many people in developing countries eke out the barest of livings by nomadic herding or shifting cultivation, combined with hunting, fishing and gathering plant foods. A large proportion of farmers live at subsistence level, producing little more than they require to provide the basic needs of their families.

The world's largest food producer and exporter is the United States, although agriculture employs

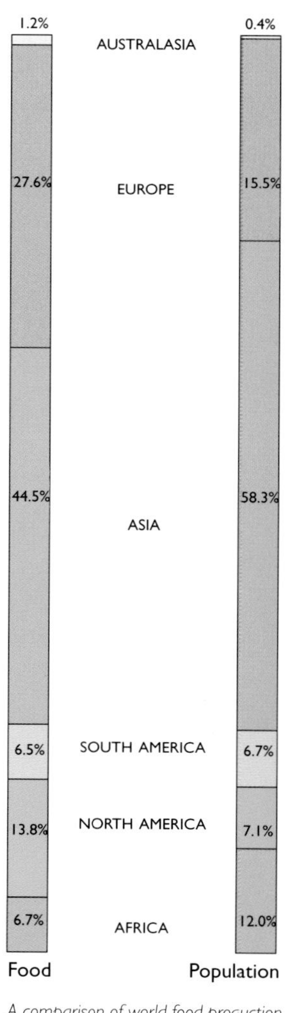

A comparison of world food production and population by continent.

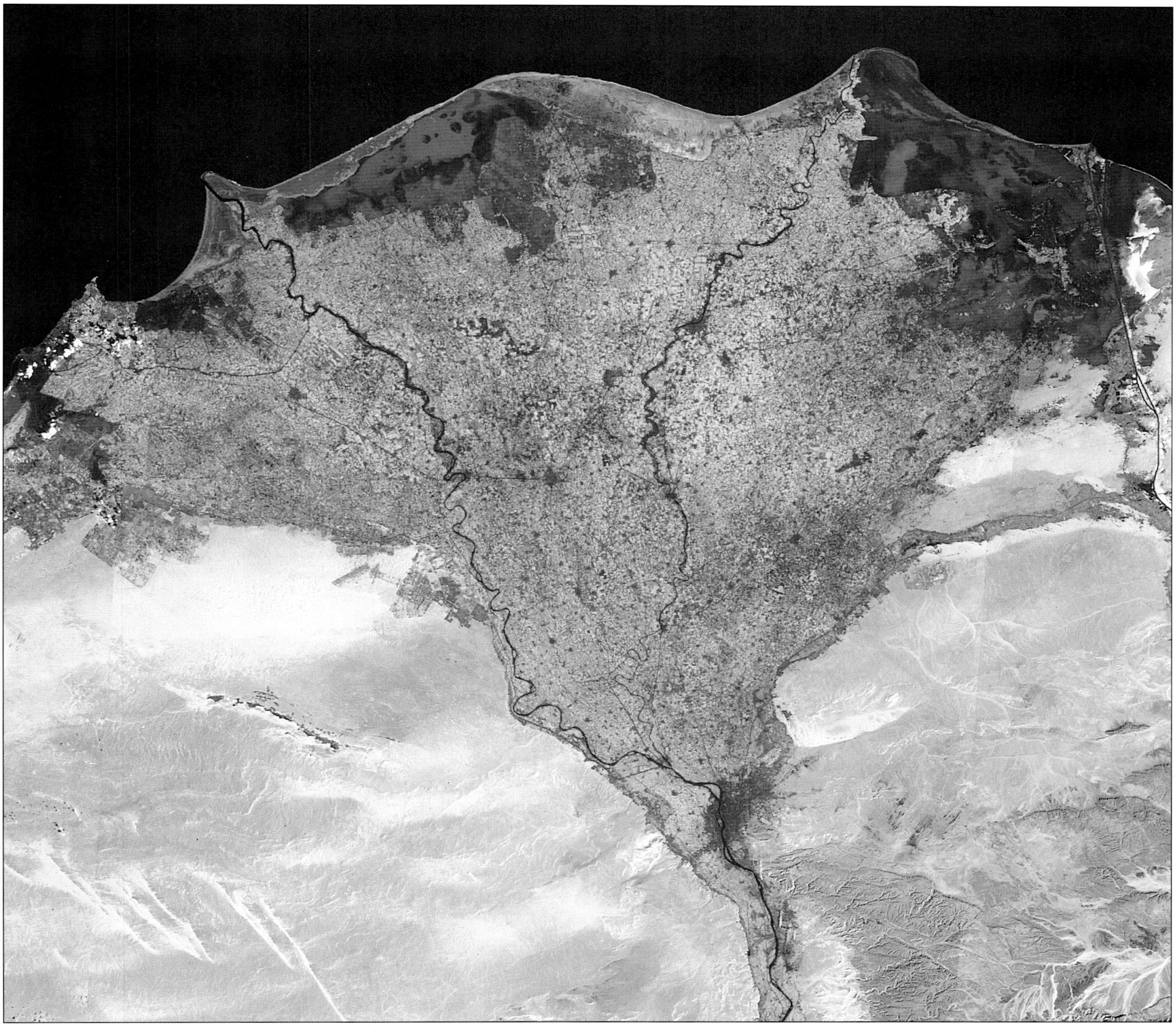

Landsat ***image of the Nile delta, Egypt***

Most Egyptians live in the Nile valley and on its delta. Because much of the silt carried by the Nile now ends up on the floor of Lake Nasser, upstream of the Aswan Dam, the delta is now retreating and seawater is seeping inland. This eventuality was not foreseen when the Aswan High Dam was built in the 1960s.

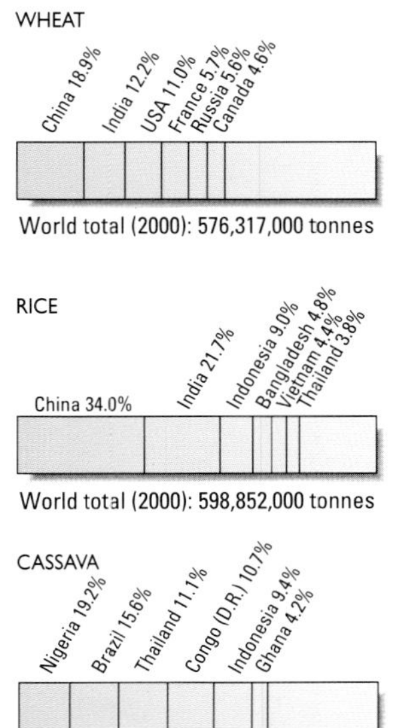

around 2% of its total workforce. The high production of the United States is explained by its use of scientific methods and mechanization, which are features of agriculture throughout the developed world.

Intensive or Organic Farming

In the early 21st century, some people were beginning to question the dependence of farmers on chemical fertilizers and pesticides. Many people became concerned that the widespread use of chemicals was seriously polluting and damaging the environment.

Others objected to the intensive farming of animals to raise production and lower prices. For example, the suggestion in Britain in 1996 that BSE, or 'mad cow disease', might be passed on to people causing CJD (Creuzfeldt-Jakob Disease) caused widespread alarm.

Such problems have led some farmers to return to organic farming, which is based on animal-welfare principles and the banning of chemical fertilizers and pesticides. The costs of organic foods are certainly higher than those produced by intensive farming, but an increasing number of consumers in the Western world are beginning to demand organic products from their retailers.

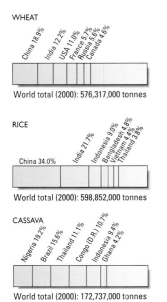

Energy and Minerals

In September 2000, Japan experienced its worst nuclear accident, when more than 400 people were exposed to harmful levels of radiation. This was the worst nuclear incident since the explosion at the Chernobyl nuclear power station, in Ukraine, in 1986. Nuclear power provides around 17% of the world's electricity and experts once thought that it would generate much of the world's energy supply. But concerns about safety and worries about the high costs make this seem unlikely. Some developed countries have already abandoned their nuclear programmes.

Fossil Fuels

Huge amounts of energy are needed for heating, generating electricity and for transport. In the early years of the Industrial Revolution, coal formed from organic matter buried beneath the Earth's surface, was the leading source of energy. It remains important as a raw material in the manufacture of drugs and other products and also as a fuel, despite the fact that burning coal causes air pollution and gives off carbon dioxide, an important greenhouse gas.

However, oil and natural gas, which came into wide use in the 20th century, are cheaper to produce and easier to handle than coal, while, kilogram for kilogram, they give out more heat. Oil is especially important in moving transport, supplying about 97% of the fuel required.

In 1995, proven reserves of oil were sufficient to supply the world, at current rates of production, for 43 years, while supplies of natural gas stood at about 66 years. Coal reserves are more abundant and known reserves would last 200 years at present rates of use. Although these figures must be regarded with caution, because they do not allow for future discoveries, it is clear that fossil fuel reserves will one day run out.

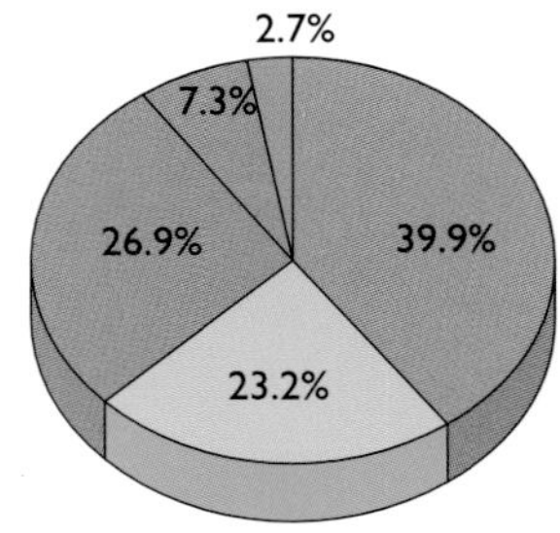

WORLD ENERGY CONSUMPTION

- OIL
- GAS
- COAL
- NUCLEAR
- HYDRO

The diagram shows the proportion of world energy consumption in 1997 by form. Total energy consumption was 8,509.2 million tonnes of oil equivalent. Such fuels as wood, peat and animal wastes, together with renewable forms of energy, such as wind and geothermal power, are not included, although they are important in some areas.

Wind farms in California, United States

Wind farms using giant turbines can produce electricity at a lower cost than conventional power stations. But in many areas, winds are too light or too strong for wind farms to be effective.

SELECTED MINERAL PRODUCTION STATISTICS (1997)			
Bauxite		**Diamonds**	
Australia	34.9%	Australia	33.9%
Guinea	15.1%	Congo (D.R.)	18.6%
Brazil	9.8%	Botswana	17.0%
Jamaica	9.4%	Russia	16.1%
China	7.1%	S. Africa	8.5%
Gold		**Iron ore**	
S. Africa	20.5%	China	22.1%
USA	14.9%	Brazil	17.4%
Australia	13.1%	Australia	14.0%
Canada	7.0%	Ukraine	10.3%
China	6.5%	Russia	6.7%
Manganese		**Zinc**	
Ukraine	27.0%	China	16.4%
China	25.6%	Canada	14.5%
S. Africa	11.4%	Australia	14.0%
Brazil	8.0%	Peru	11.7%
Australia	7.8%	USA	8.5%

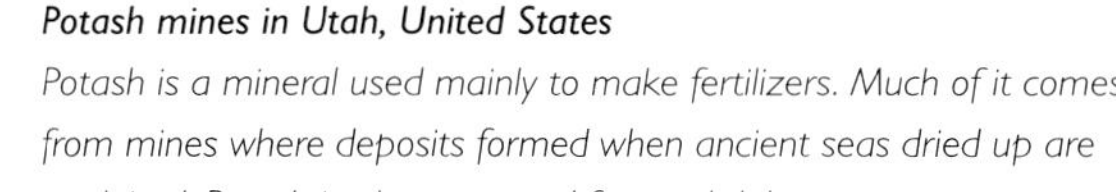

Potash mines in Utah, United States

Potash is a mineral used mainly to make fertilizers. Much of it comes from mines where deposits formed when ancient seas dried up are exploited. Potash is also extracted from salt lakes.

Alternative Energy

Other sources of energy are therefore required. Besides nuclear energy, the main alternative to fossil fuels is water power. The costs of building dams and hydroelectric power stations is high, though hydroelectric production is comparatively cheap and it does not cause pollution. But the creation of reservoirs uproots people and, in tropical rainforests, it destroys natural habitats. Hydroelectricity is also suitable only in areas with plenty of rivers and steep slopes, such as Norway, while it is unsuitable in flat areas, such as the Netherlands.

In Brazil, alcohol made from sugar has been used to fuel cars. Initially, this government-backed policy met with great success, but it has proved to be extremely expensive. Battery-run, electric cars have also been developed in the United States, but they appear to have limited use, because of the problems involved in regular and time-consuming recharging.

Other forms of energy, which are renewable and cleaner than fossil fuels, are winds, sea waves, the rise and fall of tides, and geothermal power. These forms of energy are already used to some extent. However, their contribution in global terms seems likely to remain small in the immediate future.

MINERAL DISTRIBUTION

The map shows the richest sources of the most important minerals. Major mineral locations are named. Undersea deposits, most of which are considered inaccessible, are not shown.

- GOLD
- SILVER
- DIAMONDS
- TUNGSTEN
- IRON ORE
- NICKEL
- CHROME
- MANGANESE
- COBALT
- MOLYBDENUM
- COPPER
- LEAD
- BAUXITE
- TIN
- ZINC
- MERCURY

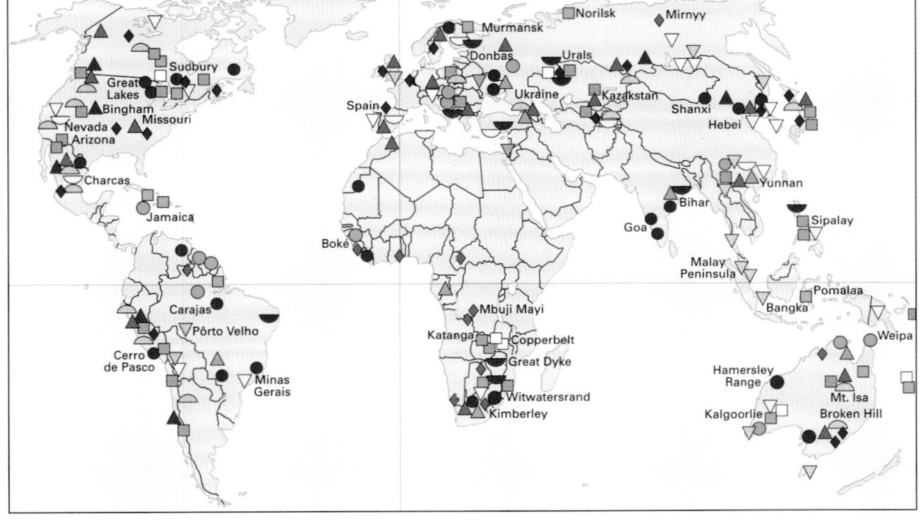

Minerals for Industry

In addition to energy, manufacturing industries need raw materials, including minerals, and these natural resources, like fossil fuels, are being used in such huge quantities that some experts have predicted shortages of some of them before long.

Manufacturers depend on supplies of about 80 minerals. Some, such as bauxite (aluminium ore) and iron, are abundant, but others are scarce or are found only in deposits that are uneconomical to mine. Many experts advocate a policy of recycling scrap metal, including aluminium, chromium, copper, lead, nickel and zinc. This practice would reduce pollution and conserve the energy required for extracting and refining mineral ores.

World Economies

In 1999, Tanzania had a per capita GNP (Gross National Product) of US$240, as compared with Switzerland, whose per capita GNP stood at $38,350. These figures indicate the vast gap between the economies and standards of living of the two countries.

The GNP includes the GDP (Gross Domestic Product), which consists of the total output of goods and services in a country in a given year, plus net exports – that is, the value of goods and services sold abroad less the value of foreign goods and services used in the country in the same year. The GNP divided by the population gives a country's GNP per capita. In low-income developing countries, agriculture makes a high contribution to the GNP. For example, in Tanzania, 40% of the GDP in 1999 came from agriculture. On the other hand, manufacturing was small-scale and contributed only 6.6% of the GDP. By comparison, in high-income economies, the percentage contribution of manufacturing far exceeds that of agriculture.

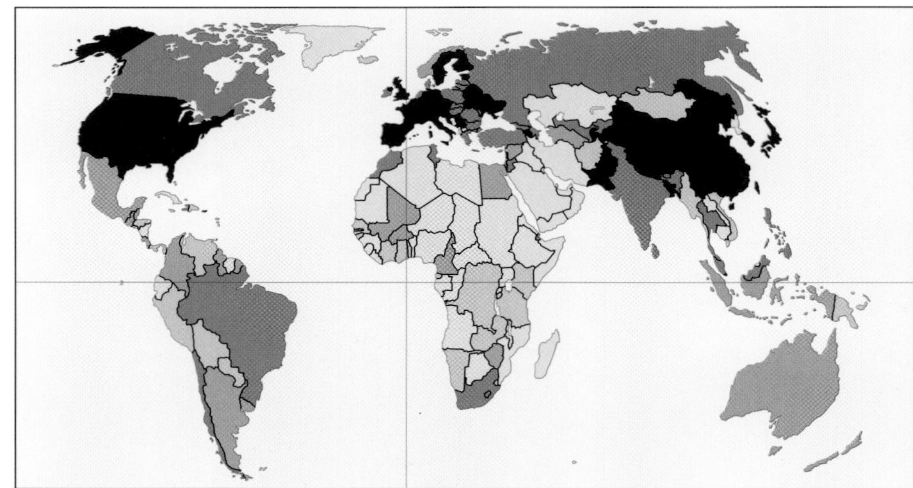

INDUSTRY AND TRADE

Manufactured goods (including machinery and transport) as a percentage of total exports.

- OVER 75%
- 50–75%
- 25–50%
- 10–25%
- UNDER 10%

Eastern Asia, including Japan (98.3%), Taiwan (92.7%) and Hong Kong (93.0%), contains countries whose exports are most dominated by manufactures. But some countries in Europe, such as Slovenia (92.5%), are also heavily dependent on manufacturing.

Microchip production, Taiwan

Despite its lack of resources, Taiwan is one of eastern Asia's 'tiger' economies. Its high-tech industries have helped it to achieve fast economic growth and to compete on the world market.

Industrialization

The Industrial Revolution began in Britain in the late 18th century. Before that time, most people worked on farms. But with the Industrial Revolution came factories, using machines that could manufacture goods much faster and more cheaply than those made by cottage industries which already existed.

The Industrial Revolution soon spread to several countries in mainland Europe and the United States and, by the late 19th century, it had reached Canada, Japan and Russia. At first, industrial development was based on such areas as coalfields or ironfields. But in the 20th century, the use of oil, which is easy to transport along pipelines, made it possible for industries to be set up anywhere.

Some nations, such as Switzerland, became industrialized even though they lacked natural resources. They depended instead on the specialized skills of their workers. This same pattern applies today. Some countries with rich natural resources, such as Mexico (with a per capita GNP in 1999 of $4,400), lag far behind Japan ($32,230) and Cyprus ($11,960), which lack resources and have to import many of the materials they need for their manufacturing industries.

Service Industries

Experts often refer to high-income countries as industrial economies. But manufacturing employs only one in six workers in the United

GROSS NATIONAL PRODUCT PER CAPITA US$ (1999 ESTIMATES)

		US$
1	Liechtenstein	50,000
2	Luxembourg	44,640
3	Switzerland	38,350
4	Bermuda	35,590
5	Norway	32,880
6	Japan	32,230
7	Denmark	32,030
8	USA	30,600
9	Singapore	29,610
10	Iceland	29,280
11	Austria	25,970
12	Germany	25,350
13	Sweden	25,040
14	Monaco	25,000
15	Belgium	24,510
16	Brunei	24,630
17	Netherlands	24,320
18	Finland	23,780
19	Hong Kong (China)	23,520
20	France	23,480

New cars awaiting transportation, Los Angeles, United States
Cars are the most important single manufactured item in world trade, followed by vehicle parts and engines. The world's leading car producers are Japan, the United States, Germany and France.

States, one in five in Britain, and one in three in Germany and Japan.

In most developed economies, the percentage of manufacturing jobs has fallen in recent years, while jobs in service industries have risen. For example, in Britain, the proportion of jobs in manufacturing fell from 37% in 1970 to 14% in 2001, while jobs in the service sector rose from just under 50% to 77%. While change in Britain was especially rapid, similar changes were taking place in most industrial economies. By the late 1990s, service industries accounted for well over half the jobs in the generally prosperous countries that made up the OECD (Organization for Economic Co-operation and Development). Instead of being called the 'industrial' economies, these countries might be better named the 'service' economies.

Service industries offer a wide range of jobs and many of them require high educational qualifications. These include finance, insurance and high-tech industries, such as computer programming, entertainment and telecommunications. Service industries also include marketing and advertising, which are essential if the cars and television sets made by manufacturers are to be sold. Another valuable service industry is tourism; in some countries, such as the Gambia, it is the major foreign exchange earner. Trade in services plays a crucial part in world economics. The share of services in world trade rose from 17% in 1980 to 22% in the 1990s.

THE WORKFORCE
Percentage of men and women between 15 and 64 years old in employment, selected countries (latest available year).

MEN
WOMEN

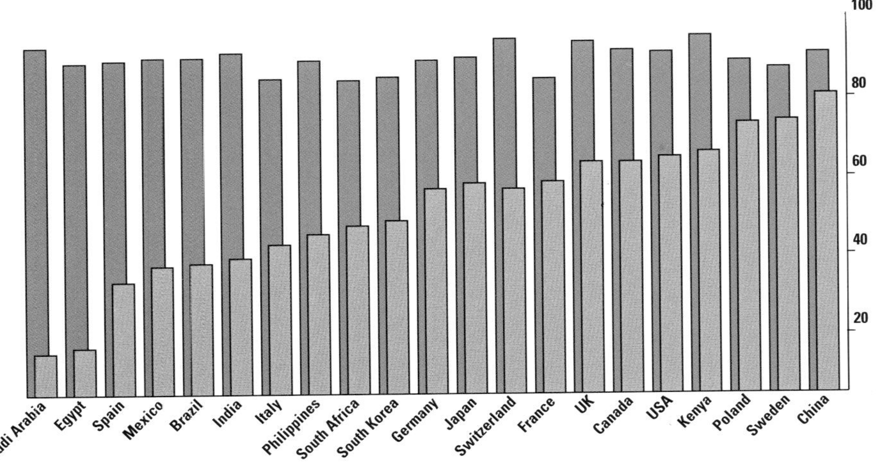

Trade and Commerce

The establishment of the WTO (World Trade Organization) on 1 January 1995 was the latest step in the long history of world trade. The WTO was set up by the eighth round of negotiations, popularly called the 'Uruguay round', conducted by the General Agreement on Tariffs and Trade (GATT). This treaty was signed by representatives of 125 governments in April, 1994. By the start of 2002, the WTO had 144 members.

GATT was first established in 1948. Its initial aim was to produce a charter to create a body called the International Trade Organization. This body never came into being. Instead, GATT, acting as an *ad hoc* agency, pioneered a series of agreements aimed at liberalizing world trade by reducing tariffs on imports and other obstacles to free trade.

GATT's objectives were based on the belief that international trade creates wealth. Trade occurs because the world's resources are not distributed evenly between countries, and, in theory, free trade means that every country should concentrate on what it can do best and purchase from others goods and services that they can supply more cheaply. In practice, however, free trade may cause unemployment when imported goods are cheaper than those produced within the country.

Trade is sometimes an important factor in world politics, especially when trade sanctions are applied against countries whose actions incur the disapproval of the international community. For example, in the 1990s, worldwide trade sanctions were imposed on Serbia because of its involvement in the civil war in Bosnia-Herzegovina.

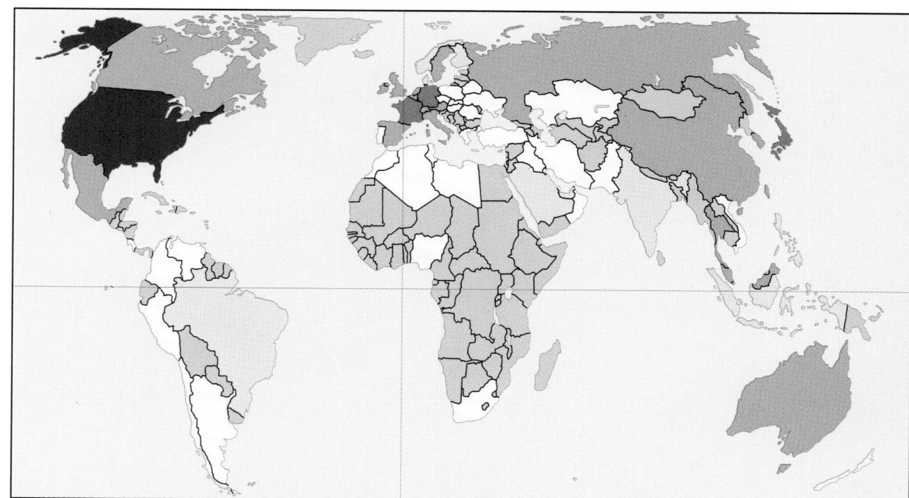

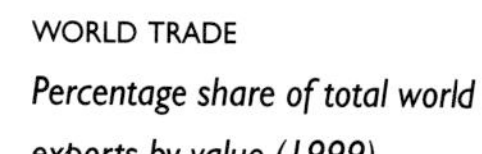

WORLD TRADE

Percentage share of total world exports by value (1999).

- OVER 10% OF WORLD TRADE
- 5–10% OF WORLD TRADE
- 1–5% OF WORLD TRADE
- 0.5–1% OF WORLD TRADE
- 0.1–0.5% OF WORLD TRADE
- UNDER 0.1% OF WORLD TRADE

The world's leading trading nations, according to the combined value of their exports and imports, are the United States, Germany, Japan, France and the United Kingdom.

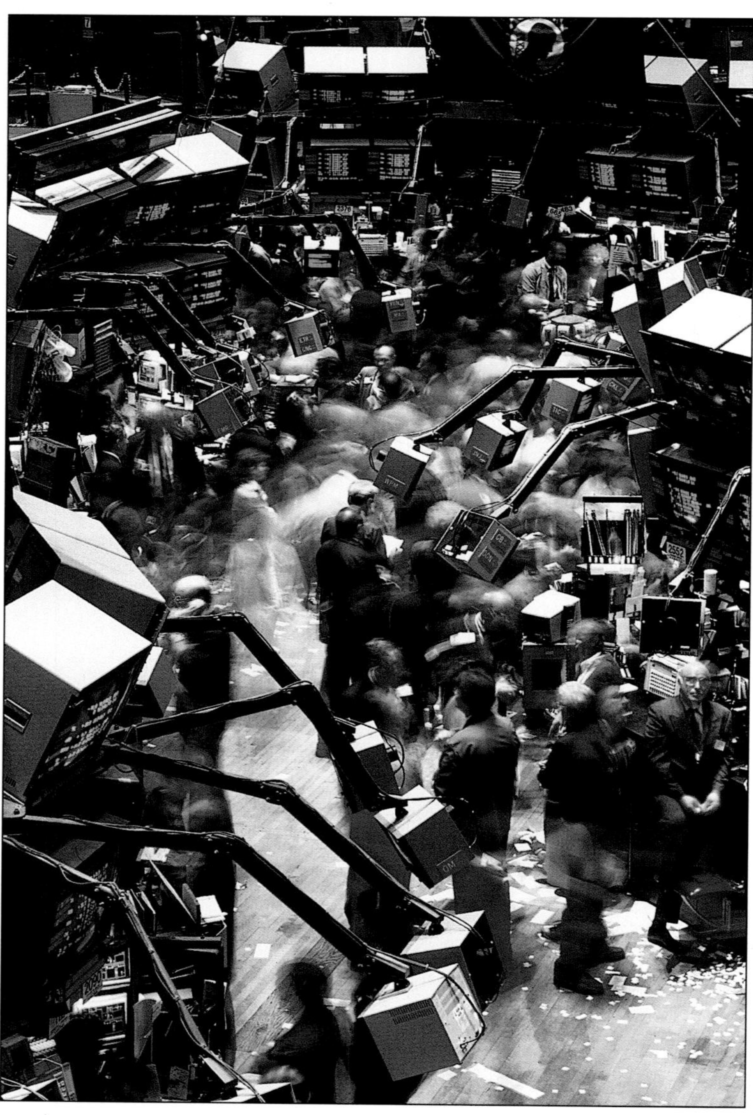

New York City Stock Exchange, United States

Stock exchanges, where stocks and shares are sold and bought, are important in channelling savings and investments to companies and governments. The world's largest stock exchange is in Tokyo, Japan.

Changing Trade Patterns

The early 16th century, when Europeans began to divide the world into huge empires, opened up a new era in international trade. By the 19th century, the colonial powers, who were among the first industrial powers, promoted trade with their colonies, from which they obtained unprocessed raw materials, such as food, natural fibres, minerals and timber. In return, they shipped clothes, shoes and other cheap items to the colonies.

From the late 19th century until the early 1950s, primary products dominated world trade, with oil becoming the leading item in the later part of this period. Many developing countries still depend heavily on the export of one or two primary products, such as coffee or iron ore, but overall the proportion of primary products in world trade has fallen since the 1950s. Today the most important elements in world trade are

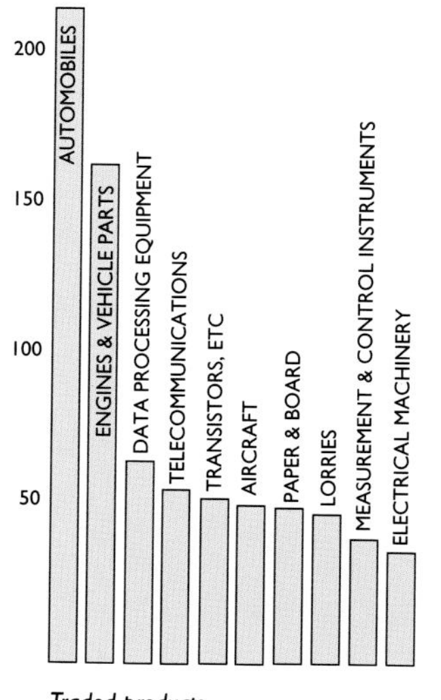

Traded products

Top ten manufactures traded by value in billions of US$ (latest available year).

Rotterdam, Netherlands

World trade depends on transport. Rotterdam, the world's largest port, serves not only the Netherlands, but also industrial areas in parts of Germany, France and Switzerland.

manufactures and semi-manufactures, exchanged mainly between the industrialized nations.

The World's Markets

Private companies conduct most of world trade, but government policies affect it. Governments which believe that certain industries are strategic, or essential for the country's future, may impose tariffs on imports, or import quotas to limit the volume of imports, if they are thought to be undercutting the domestic industries.

For example, the United States has argued that Japan has greater access to its markets than the United States has to Japan's. This might have led the United States to resort to protectionism, but instead the United States remains committed to free trade despite occasional disputes.

Other problems in international trade occur when governments give subsidies to its producers, who can then export products at low prices. Another difficulty, called 'dumping', occurs when products are sold at below the market price in order to gain a market share. One of the aims of the newly-created WTO is the phasing out of government subsidies for agricultural products, though the world's poorest countries will be exempt from many of the WTO's most severe regulations.

Governments are also concerned about the volume of imports and exports and most countries keep records of international transactions. When the total value of goods and services imported exceeds the value of goods and services exported, then the country has a deficit in its balance of payments. Large deficits can weaken a country's economy.

DEPENDENCE ON TRADE

Value of exports as a percentage of GDP (Gross Domestic Product) 1997.

- OVER 50% GDP FROM EXPORTS
- 40–50% GDP FROM EXPORTS
- 30–40% GDP FROM EXPORTS
- 20–30% GDP FROM EXPORTS
- 10–20% GDP FROM EXPORTS
- UNDER 10% GDP FROM EXPORTS
- ○ MOST DEPENDENT ON INDUSTRIAL EXPORTS (OVER 75% OF TOTAL)
- ● MOST DEPENDENT ON FUEL EXPORTS (OVER 75% OF TOTAL)
- ● MOST DEPENDENT ON METAL & MINERAL EXPORTS (OVER 75% OF TOTAL)

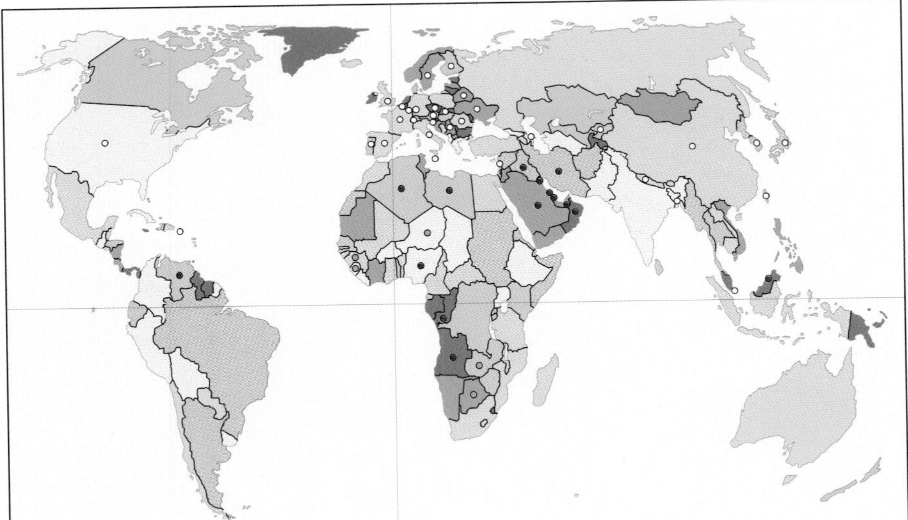

Travel and Communications

In the 1990s, millions of people became linked into an 'information superhighway' called the Internet. Equipped with a personal computer, an electricity supply, a telephone and a modem, people are able to communicate with others all over the world. People can now send messages by e-mail (electronic mail), they can engage in electronic discussions, contacting people with similar interests, and engage in 'chat lines', which are the latest equivalent of telephone conferences.

These new developments are likely to affect the working lives of people everywhere, enabling them to work at home whilst having many of the facilities that are available in an office. The Internet is part of an ongoing and astonishingly rapid evolution in the fields of communications and transport.

Transport

Around 200 years ago, most people never travelled far from their birthplace, but today we are much more mobile. Cars and buses now provide convenient forms of transport for many millions of people, huge ships transport massive cargoes around the world, and jet airliners, some travelling faster than the speed of sound, can transport high-value goods as well as holiday-makers to almost any part of the world.

Land transport of freight has developed greatly since the start of the Industrial Revolution. Canals, which became important in the 18th century, could not compete with rail transport in the 19th century. Rail transport remains important, but, during the 20th century, it suffered from competition with road transport, which is cheaper and has the advantage of carrying materials and goods from door to door.

Road transport causes pollution and the burning of fuels creates greenhouse gases that contribute to global warming. Yet privately owned cars are now the leading form of passenger traffic in developed nations, especially for journeys of less than around 400 km [250 miles]. Car owners do not have to suffer the inconvenience of waiting for public transport, such as buses, though they often have to endure traffic jams at peak travel times.

Ocean passenger traffic is now modest, but ships carry the bulk of international trade. Huge oil tankers and bulk grain carriers now ply the oceans with their cargoes, while container ships

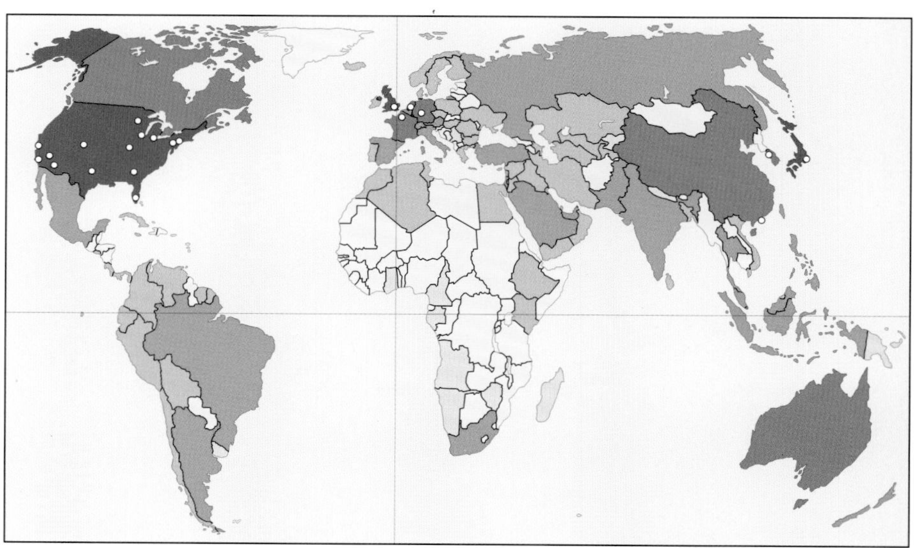

AIR TRAVEL – PASSENGER KILOMETRES* FLOWN (1997).

- OVER 100,000 MILLION
- 50,000–100,000 MILLION
- 10,000–50,000 MILLION
- 1,000–10,000 MILLION
- 500–1,000 MILLION
- UNDER 500 MILLION
- ∘ MAJOR AIRPORTS (HANDLING OVER 25 MILLION PASSENGERS IN 2000)

** Passenger kilometres are the number of passengers (both international and domestic) multiplied by the distance flown by each passenger from the airport of origin.*

Jodrell Bank Observatory, Cheshire, England

The world's first giant radio telescope began operations at Jodrell Bank in 1957. Radio telescopes can explore the Universe as far as 16 billion light-years away.

SELECTED NEWSPAPER CIRCULATION FIGURES (1995)

France		
Le Monde		357,362
Le Figaro		350,000
Germany		
Bild		4,500,000
Süddeutsche Zeitung		402,866
Italy		
Corriera Della Sella		676,904
La Republica		655,321
La Stampa		436,047
Japan		
Yomiuri Shimbun	(a.m. edition)	9,800,000
	(p.m. edition)	4,400,000
Manichi Shimbun	(a.m. edition)	3,200,000
	(p.m. edition)	1,900,000
Russia		
Pravda		1,373,795
Ivestia		700,000
Spain		
El Pais		407,629
United Kingdom		
The Sun		4,061,253
Daily Mirror		2,525,000
Daily Express		1,270,642
The Times		672,802
The Guardian		402,214
United States		
New York Times		1,724,705
Chicago Tribune		1,110,552
Houston Chronicle		605,343

Kansai International Airport, Japan
The new airport, opened in September 1994, is built on an artificial island in Osaka Bay. The island holds the world's biggest airport terminal at nearly 2 km [1.2 miles] long.

carry mixed cargoes. Containers are boxes built to international standards that contain cargo. Containers are easy to handle, and so they reduce shipping costs, speed up deliveries and cut losses caused by breakages. Most large ports now have the facilities to handle containers.

Air transport is suitable for carrying goods that are expensive, light and compact, or perishable. However, because of the high costs of air freight, it is most suitable for carrying passengers along long-distance routes around the world. Through air travel, international tourism, with people sometimes flying considerable distances, has become a major and rapidly expanding industry.

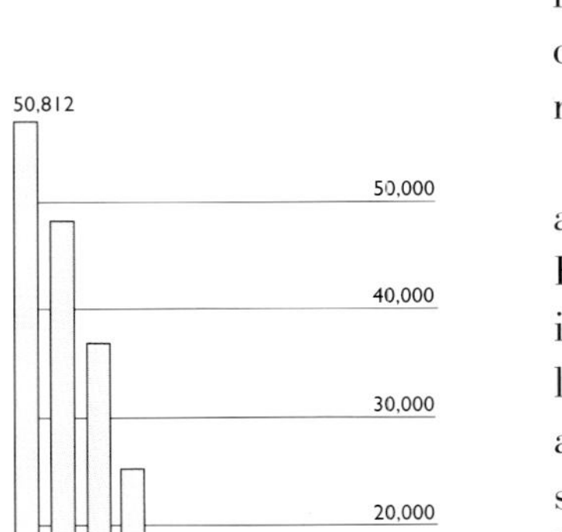

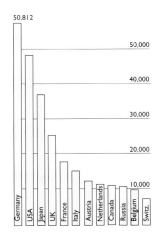

Spending on tourism
Countries spending the most on overseas tourism, US$ million (1996).

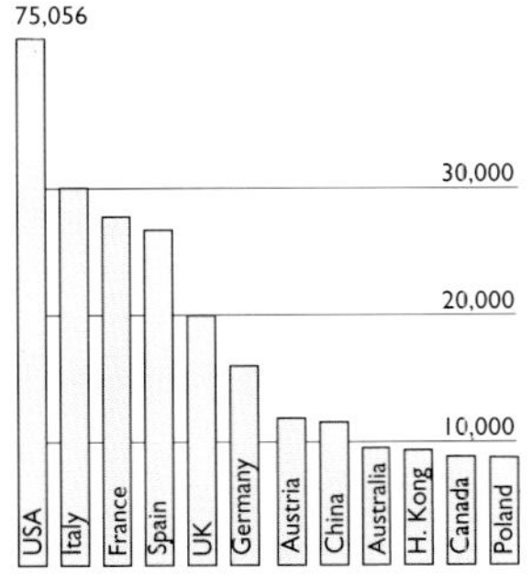

Receipts from tourism
Countries receiving the most from overseas tourism, US$ million (1996).

Communications

After humans first began to communicate by using the spoken word, the next great stage in the development of communications was the invention of writing around 5,500 years ago.

The invention of movable type in the mid 15th century led to the mass production of books and, in the early 17th century, the first newspapers. Newspapers now play an important part in the mass communication of information, although today radio and, even more important, television have led to a decline in the circulation of newspapers in many parts of the world.

The most recent developments have occurred in the field of electronics. Artificial communications satellites now circle the planet, relaying radio, television, telegraph and telephone signals. This enables people to watch events on the far side of the globe as they are happening. Electronic equipment is also used in many other ways, such as in navigation systems used in air, sea and space, and also in modern weaponry, as shown vividly in the television coverage of such military actions as that in Afghanistan in 2001.

The Age of Computers

One of the most remarkable applications of electronics is in the field of computers. Computers are now making a huge contribution to communications. They are able to process data at incredibly high speeds and can store vast quantities of information. For example, the work of weather forecasters has been greatly improved now that computers can process the enormous amount of data required for a single weather forecast. They also have many other applications in such fields as business, government, science and medicine.

Through the Internet, computers provide a free interchange of news and views around the world. But the dangers of misuse, such as the exchange of pornographic images, have led to calls for censorship. Censorship, however, is a blunt weapon, which can be used by authoritarian governments to suppress the free exchange of information that the new information superhighway makes possible.

The World Today

The early years of the 20th century witnessed the exploration of Antarctica, the last uncharted continent. Today, less than 100 years later, tourists are able to take cruises to the icy southern continent, while almost no part of the globe is inaccessible to the determined traveller. Improved transport and images from space have made our world seem smaller.

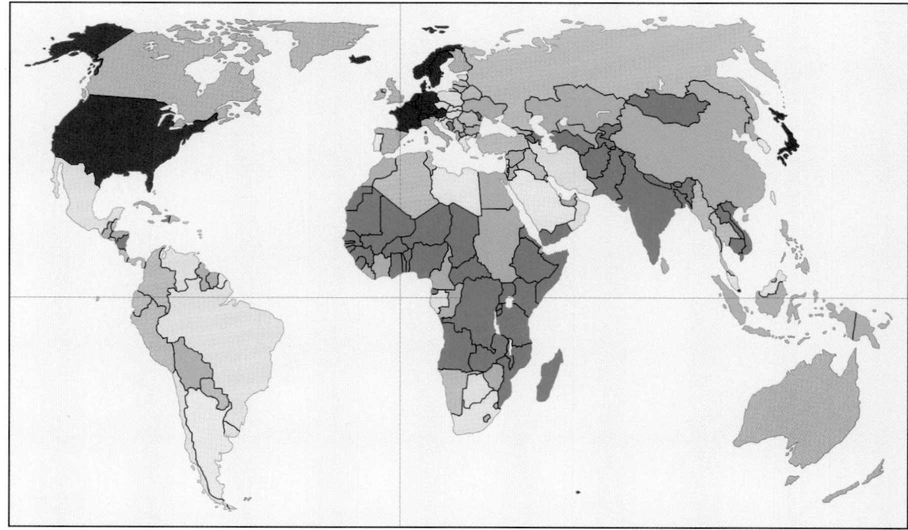

GROSS NATIONAL PRODUCT PER CAPITA

The value of total production divided by the population (1999).

- OVER 400% OF WORLD AVERAGE
- 200–400% OF WORLD AVERAGE
- 100–200% OF WORLD AVERAGE

[WORLD AVERAGE WEALTH PER PERSON US$6,316]

- 50–100% OF WORLD AVERAGE
- 25–50% OF WORLD AVERAGE
- 10–25% OF WORLD AVERAGE
- UNDER 10% OF WORLD AVERAGE

RICHEST COUNTRIES	
Liechtenstein	$44,640
Switzerland	$38,350
Bermuda	$35,590
Norway	$32,880
Japan	$32,230

POOREST COUNTRIES	
Ethiopia	$100
Burundi	$120
Sierra Leone	$130
Guinea-Bissau	$160
Niger	$190

A Divided World

Between the end of World War II in 1945 and the late 1980s, the world was divided, politically and economically, into three main groups: the developed countries or Western democracies, with their free enterprise or mixed economies; the centrally planned or Communist countries; and the developing countries or Third World.

This division became obsolete when the former Soviet Union and its old European allies, together with the 'special economic zones' in eastern China, began the transition from centrally planned to free enterprise economies. This left the world divided into two broad camps: the prosperous developed countries and the poorer developing countries. The simplest way of distinguishing between the groups is with reference to their per capita Gross National Products (per capita GNPs).

The World Bank divides the developing countries into three main groups. At the bottom are the low-income economies, which include China, India and most of sub-Saharan Africa. In 1999, this group contained about 40% of the world's population, but its average per capita GNP was only US$420. The other two groups are the lower-middle-income economies, with an average per capita GNP of $1,200, and the upper-middle-income economies with an average per capita GNP of $4,870. By contrast, the high-income economies, also called the developed countries, contain only 15% of the world's population but have the high (and rising) average GNP per capita of $26,440.

Economic and Social Contrasts

Economic differences are coupled with other factors, such as rates of population growth. For example, around the turn of the century, the low- and middle-income economies had a high population growth rate of 1.7%, while the growth rate in high-income economies was around 0.1%. Around 18 countries in Europe experienced a natural decrease in population in 1998.

Stark contrasts exist worldwide in the quality

Porters carrying luggage for tourists, Selous Park, Tanzania

Improved and cheaper transport has led to a boom in tourism in many developing countries. Tourism provides jobs and foreign exchange, though it can undermine local cultures.

Operation Enduring Freedom, Afghanistan

A joint patrol of US Marines and Army soldiers is seen here patrolling through the village of Cem, Afghanistan, some 10 km [6 miles] from the airport near Kandahar, in January 2002.

of life. Generally, the people in Western Europe and North America are better fed, healthier and have more cars and better homes than the people in low- and middle-income economies.

In 1999, the average life expectancy at birth in sub-Saharan Africa was 47 years. By contrast, the average life expectancy in the United States and the United Kingdom was 77 years. Illiteracy in low-income economies for people aged 15 and over was 39% in 1999. But for women, the percentage of those who could not read or write was 48%. Illiteracy is relatively rare for both sexes in high-income economies.

Future Development

In the last 50 years, despite all the aid supplied to developing countries, much of the world still suffers from poverty and economic backwardness. Some countries are even poorer now than they were a generation ago while others have become substantially richer.

However, several factors suggest that poor countries may find progress easier in the 21st century. For example, technology is now more readily transferable between countries, while improved transport and communications make it easier for countries to take part in the world economy. But industrial development could lead to an increase in global pollution. Hence, any strategy for global economic expansion must also take account of environmental factors.

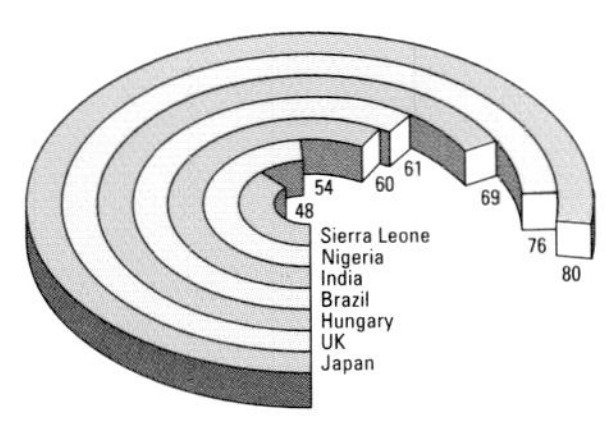

Years of life expectancy at birth, selected countries (1997).

The chart shows the contrasting range of average life expectancies at birth for a range of countries, including both low-income and high-income economies. Generally, improved health services are raising life expectancies. On average, women live longer than men, even in the poorer developing countries.

A World In Conflict

The end of the Cold War held out hopes of a new world order. But ethnic, religious and other rivalries have subsequently led to appalling violence in places as diverse as the Balkan peninsula, Israel and the Palestinian territories, and Rwanda–Burundi. Then, on 11 September 2001, the attack on those symbols of the economic and military might of the United States – the World Trade Center and the Pentagon Building – demonstrated that nowhere on Earth is safe from attack by extremists prepared to sacrifice their lives in pursuit of their aims.

The danger posed by terrorist groups, such as al Qaida, or by rogue states, possibly in possession of nuclear or biological weapons, has forced many countries into new alliances to combat the terrorists and the governments that give them shelter. Many people also recognize a pressing need to understand and correct the wrongs, real or perceived, that lead people to acts of martyrdom or murderous destruction.

WESTERN CAPE, SOUTH AFRICA

WORLD MAPS

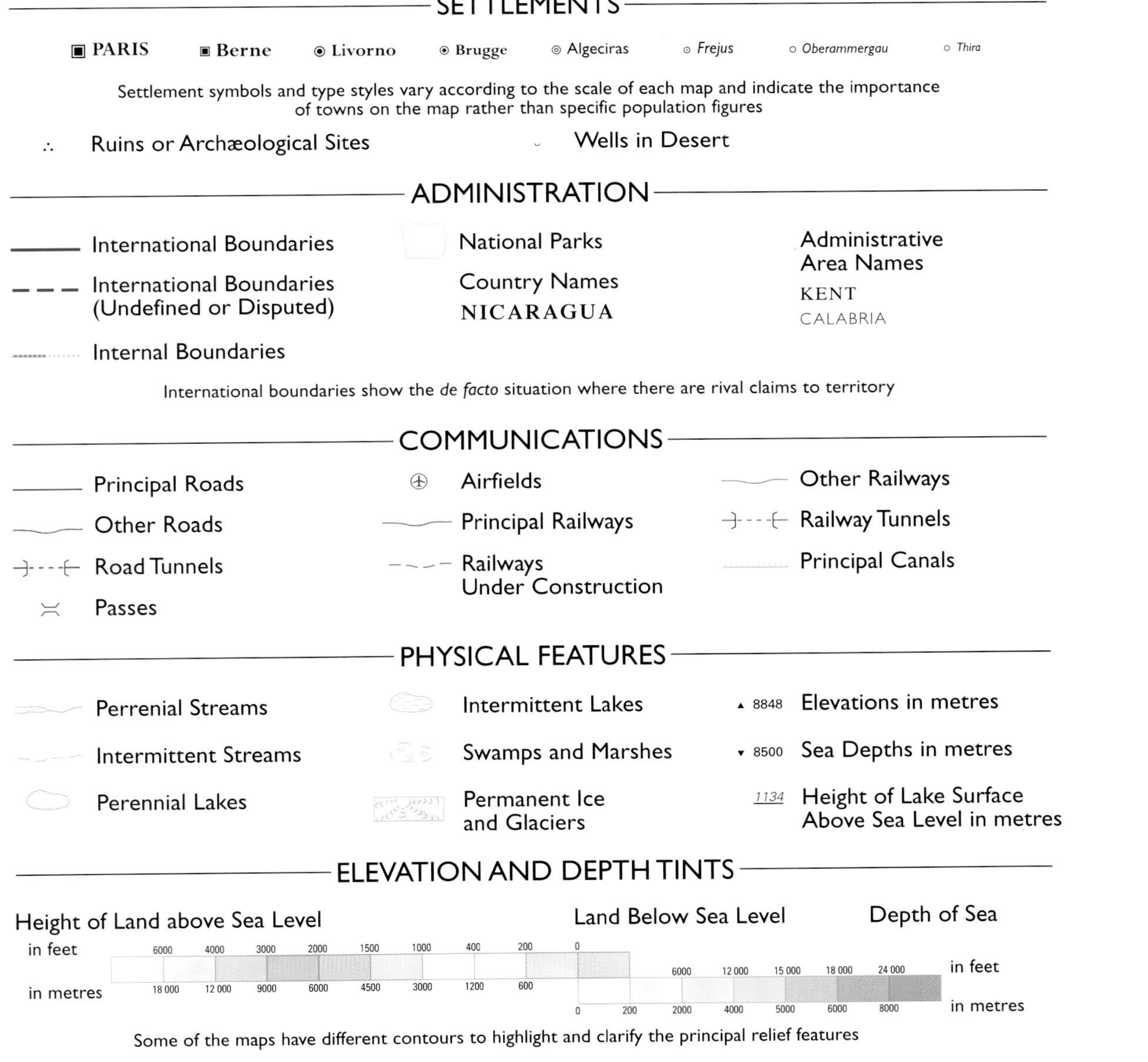
SETTLEMENTS
PARIS
Berne
Livorno
Brugge
Algeciras
Frejus
Oberammergau
Thira
Settlement symbols and type styles vary according to the scale of each map and indicate the importance of towns on the map rather than specific population figures
Ruins or Archæological Sites
Wells in Desert
ADMINISTRATION
International Boundaries
International Boundaries (Undefined or Disputed)
Internal Boundaries
National Parks
Country Names
NICARAGUA
Administrative Area Names
KENT
CALABRIA
International boundaries show the de facto situation where there are rival claims to territory
COMMUNICATIONS
Principal Roads
Other Roads
Road Tunnels
Passes
Airfields
Principal Railways
Railways Under Construction
Other Railways
Railway Tunnels
Principal Canals
PHYSICAL FEATURES
Perrenial Streams
Intermittent Streams
Perennial Lakes
Intermittent Lakes
Swamps and Marshes
Permanent Ice and Glaciers
8848 Elevations in metres
8500 Sea Depths in metres
1134 Height of Lake Surface Above Sea Level in metres
ELEVATION AND DEPTH TINTS
Height of Land above Sea Level
Land Below Sea Level
Depth of Sea
in feet
6000 4000 3000 2000 1500 1000 400 200 0
in metres
18 000 12 000 9000 6000 4500 3000 1200 600
6000 12 000 15 000 18 000 24 000
in feet
0 200 2000 4000 5000 6000 8000
in metres
Some of the maps have different contours to highlight and clarify the principal relief features

Projection: *Hammer Equal Area*

Hanoi ● Capital Cities

ARCTIC OCEAN 1:31 100 000

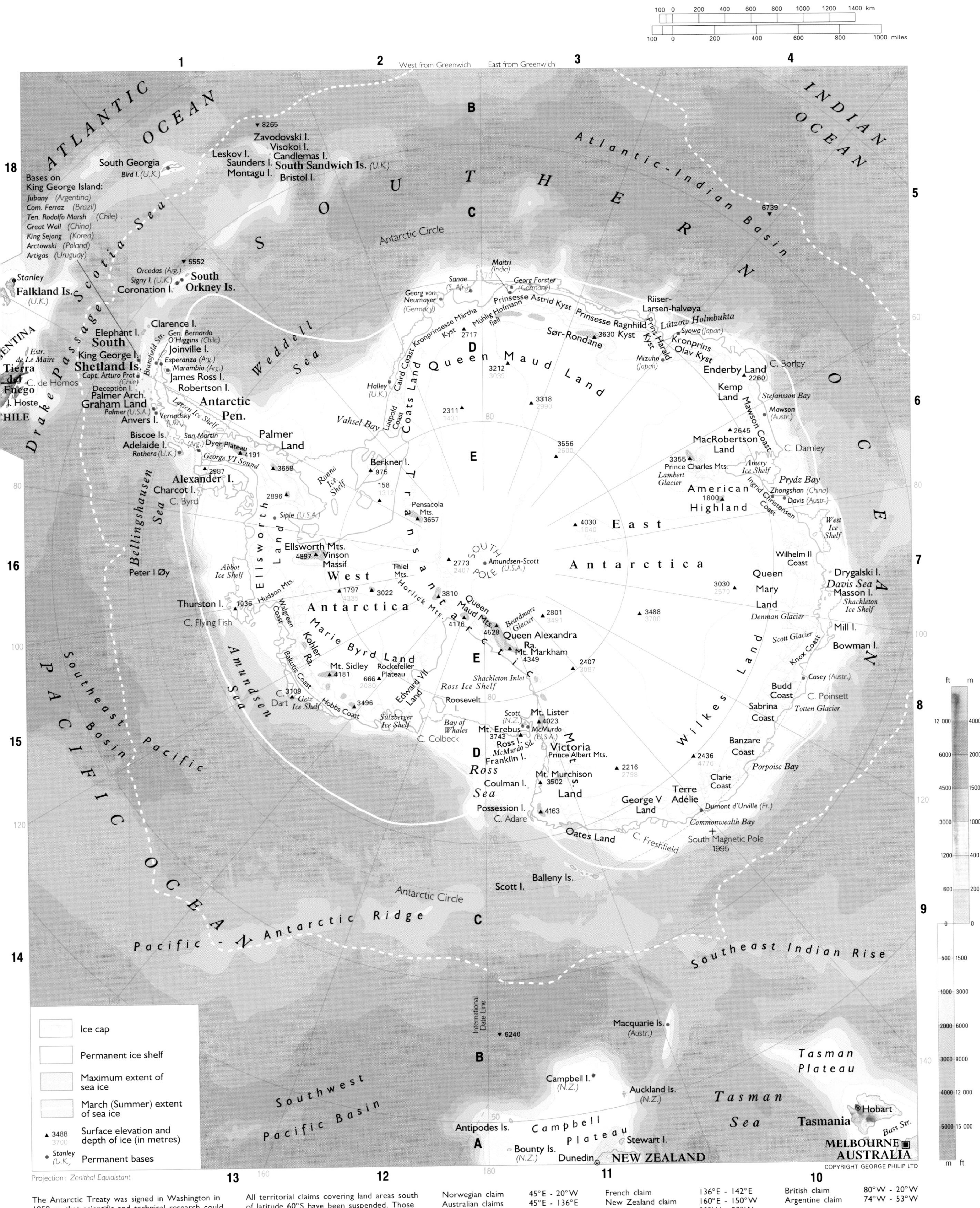

The Antarctic Treaty was signed in Washington in 1959 so that scientific and technical research could continue unhampered by international politics.

All territorial claims covering land areas south of latitude 60°S have been suspended. Those claims were:

Norwegian claim	45°E - 20°W	French claim	136°E - 142°E	British claim	80°W - 20°W
Australian claims	45°E - 136°E	New Zealand claim	160°E - 150°W	Argentine claim	74°W - 53°W
	142°E - 160°E	Chilean claim	90°W - 53°W		

EUROPE : Physical 1:17 800 000

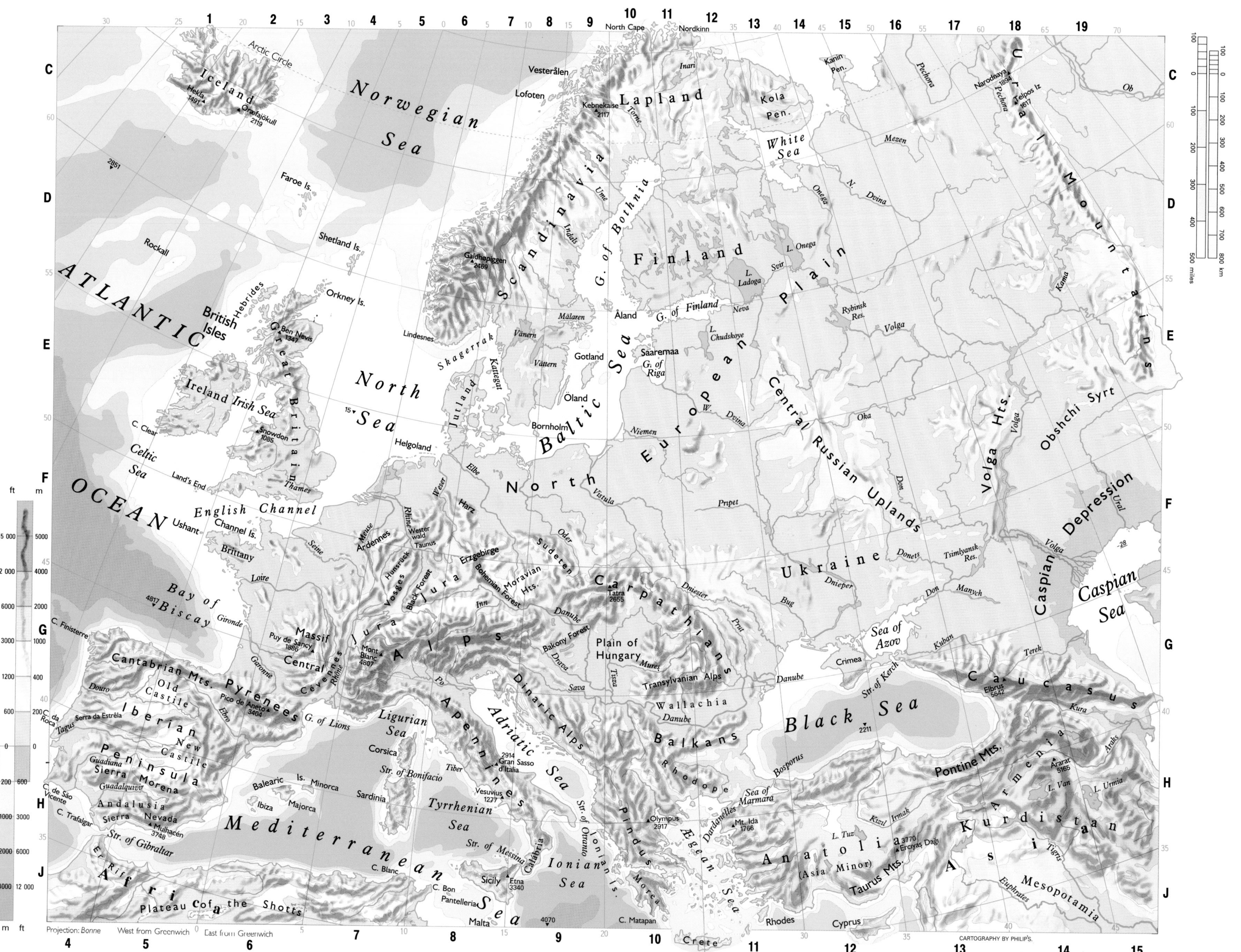

100 0 100 200 300 400 500 600 700 800 km
100 0 100 200 300 400 500 miles
ICELAND
Reykjavík
Arctic Circle
Norwegian Sea
Faroe Is. (Den.)
Shetland Is.
Orkney Is.
Hebrides
NORWAY
SWEDEN
FINLAND
G. of Bothnia
White Sea
ESTONIA
LATVIA
LITHUANIA
BELARUS
RUSSIA
MOSCOW
ST. PETERSBURG
UKRAINE
MOLDOVA
ROMANIA
BULGARIA
POLAND
GERMANY
CZECH REP.
SLOVAK REP.
HUNGARY
AUSTRIA
SWITZERLAND
LIECH.
LUX.
SLOVENIA
CROATIA
BOSNIA-HERZ.
YUGOSLAVIA
SERBIA
MONTE-NEGRO
MACEDONIA
ALBANIA
GREECE
ITALY
SAN MARINO
MONACO
ANDORRA
FRANCE
SPAIN
PORTUGAL
UNITED KINGDOM
SCOTLAND
ENGLAND
WALES
N. IRELAND
IRELAND
LONDON
PARIS
DENMARK
NETHERLANDS
BELGIUM
North Sea
Baltic Sea
English Channel
ATLANTIC OCEAN
Bay of Biscay
Adriatic Sea
Tyrrhenian Sea
Ionian Sea
Ægean Sea
Mediterranean Sea
Black Sea
Caspian Sea
TURKEY
ISTANBUL
KAZAKSTAN
GEORGIA
ARMENIA
AZERBAIJAN
IRAN
IRAQ
SYRIA
CYPRUS
MALTA
TUNISIA
ALGERIA
MOROCCO
Africa
Asia
■ LONDON Capital Cities
Projection: Bonne
West from Greenwich
East from Greenwich
CARTOGRAPHY BY PHILIPS.

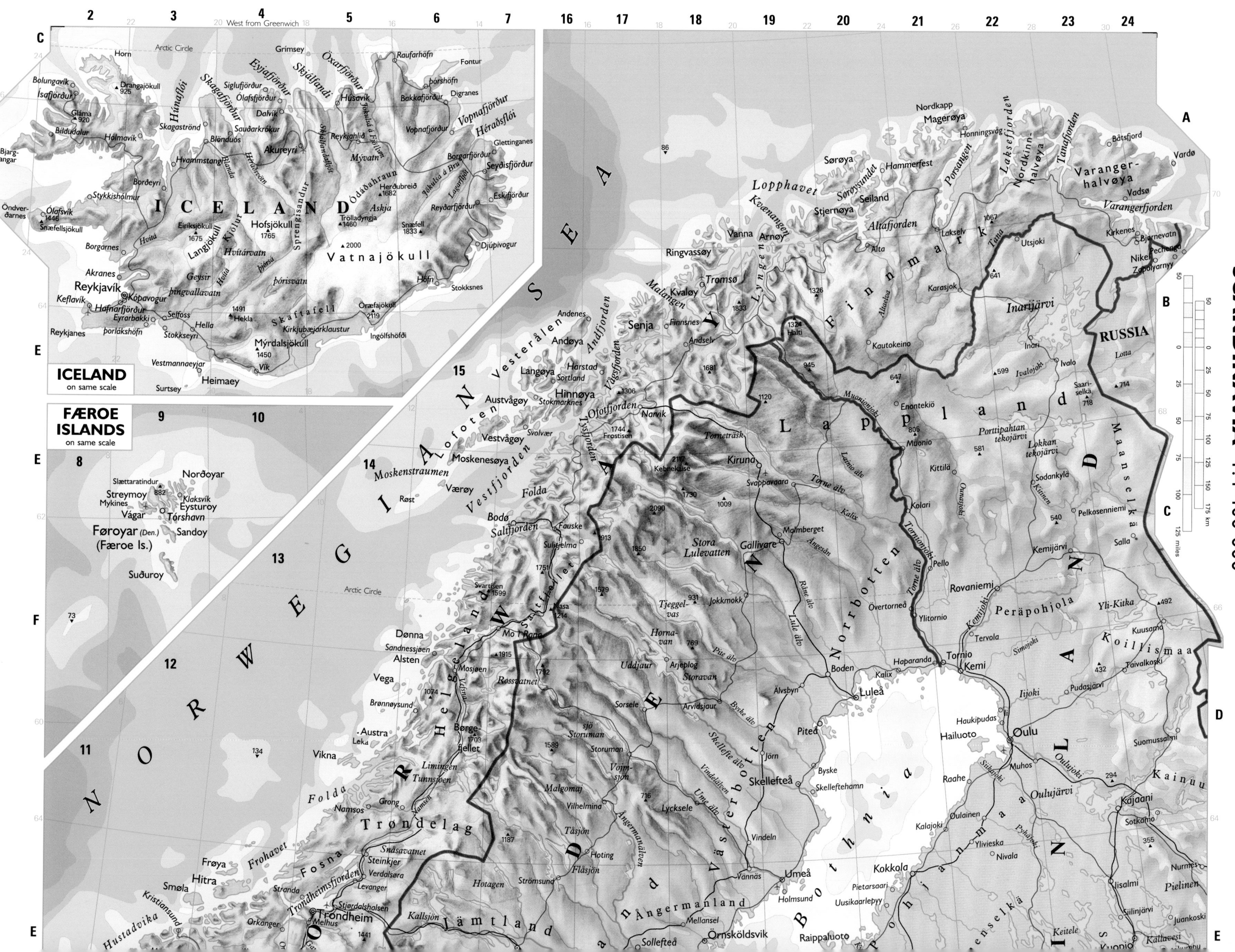

West from Greenwich
Arctic Circle
ICELAND
on same scale
FÆROE ISLANDS
on same scale
ICELAND
Vatnajökull
Reykjavík
Akureyri
Hofsjökull
Langjökull
Mýrdalsjökull
Hekla
Ísafjörður
Húsavík
Höfn
Heimaey
Vestmannaeyjar
Keflavík
Akranes
Borgarnes
Selfoss
Vík
Grímsey
Surtsey
Færoyar (Den.)
(Færoe Is.)
Tórshavn
Streymoy
Eysturoy
Vágar
Sandoy
Suðuroy
Norðoyar
NORWEGIAN SEA
RUSSIA
Nordkapp
Magerøya
Honningsvåg
Hammerfest
Sørøya
Seiland
Stjernøya
Loppahavet
Kvænangen
Altafjorden
Alta
Porsangen
Laksefjorden
Nordkinn-halvøya
Tanafjorden
Varanger-halvøya
Varangerfjorden
Vadsø
Vardø
Båtsfjord
Kirkenes
Nikel
Finnmark
Karasjok
Kautokeino
Tromsø
Ringvassøy
Kvaløy
Lyngen
Senja
Malangen
Andfjorden
Andøya
Andenes
Vesterålen
Harstad
Hinnøya
Langøya
Lofoten
Austvågøy
Vestvågøy
Moskenesøya
Moskenstraumen
Værøy
Røst
Vestfjorden
Narvik
Ofotfjorden
Tysfjorden
Bodø
Saltfjorden
Fauske
Folda
Mo i Rana
Mosjøen
Dønna
Alsten
Vega
Brønnøysund
Helgeland
Vikna
Namsos
Trøndelag
Steinkjer
Trondheim
Trondheimsfjorden
Fosna
Frøya
Hitra
Smøla
Kristiansund
Hustadvika
Lappland
Kiruna
Kebnekaise
Torneträsk
Gällivare
Stora Lulevatten
Jokkmokk
Norrbotten
Boden
Luleå
Piteå
Skellefteå
Västerbotten
Umeå
Örnsköldsvik
Sollefteå
Ångermanland
Ångermanälven
Lycksele
Vilhelmina
Storuman
Jämtland
Haparanda
Tornio
Kemi
Oulu
Hailuoto
Raahe
Kokkola
Kajaani
Oulujärvi
Kainuu
Rovaniemi
Kemijärvi
Peräpohjola
Koillismaa
Inarijärvi
Inari
Ivalo
Utsjoki
Muonio
Enontekiö
Kittilä
Sodankylä
Maanselkä
Gulf of Bothnia
Pohjanmaa

SWEDEN

NORWAY

FINLAND

ESTONIA

LATVIA

LITHUANIA

BELARUS

POLAND

GERMANY

DENMARK

BALTIC SEA

Gulf of Finland

Gulf of Bothnia

Gulf of Riga

Skagerrak

Kattegat

Ålands hav

Svealand

Götaland

Norrland

STOCKHOLM

Oslo

KØBENHAVN (Copenhagen)

Helsinki (Helsingfors)

Tallinn

Riga

Vilnius

ft	m
6000	2000
4500	1500
3000	1000
1500	500
600	200
0	0
150	50
300	100
600	200
1500	500
3000	1000
6000	2000
ft	m

Projection: Conical with two standard parallels

East from Greenwich

12 13 14 15 16 17 18 19 20 21

F G H J K

DENMARK AND SOUTHERN SWEDEN 1:2 200 000

10 0 10 20 30 40 50 60 70 80 90 km

10 0 10 20 30 40 50 60 miles

Gulf of Bothnia

STOCKHOLM

Uppsala

Gävle

Sundsvall

Östersund

Trondheim

Oslo

Drammen

Örebro

Karlstad

NORRLANDS

JÄMTLANDS LÄN

GÄVLEBORGS LÄN

KOPPARBERGS LÄN

VÄRMLANDS LÄN

ÖREBRO LÄN

VÄSTMANLANDS LÄN

UPPSALA LÄN

STOCKHOLMS LÄN

SÖDERMANLANDS LÄN

SØR-TRØNDELAG

MØRE OG ROMSDAL

OPPLAND

HEDMARK

AKERSHUS

BUSKERUD

TELEMARK

VESTFOLD

ØSTFOLD

Härjedalen

Hälsingland

Medelpad

Gästrikland

Dalarna

Uppland

Västmanland

Närke

Jotunheimen

Rondane

Dovrefjell

NORWAY

SWEDEN

m 2000 1500 1000 500 200 0

ft 6000 4500 3000 1500 600 0

50 150 100 300 200 600 500 1500

Skagerrak
Kattegat
BALTIC SEA
DENMARK
SWEDEN
GERMANY
POLAND
Jylland
Sjælland
Götaland
Småland
Skåne
Dalsland
Bohuslän
Vättern
Vänern
Öresund
Store Bælt
Lille Bælt
Fehmarn Belt
Hanöbukten
Bornholmsgattet
Kalmarsund
KØBENHAVN
Göteborg
Malmö
Helsingborg
Jönköping
Norrköping
Linköping
Kalmar
Karlskrona
Visby
Gotland (Sweden)
Öland (Sweden)
Bornholm (Denmark)
Læsø (Denmark)
Anholt (Denmark)
Ålborg
Århus
Odense
Esbjerg
Flensburg
Kiel
Lolland
Falster
Møn
Fyn
Samsø
Fehmarn
Sylt
Föhr
Rügen
Arendal
Grimstad
Lillesand
Tromøy
Kragerø
Risør
Nyköping
Västervik
Växjö
Halmstad
Varberg
Falkenberg
Borås
Trollhättan
Vänersborg
Uddevalla
Lidköping
Skövde
Mariestad
Motala
Kristianstad
Lund
Trelleborg
Ystad
Simrishamn
Slupsk
Ustka
Lebork
Projection : Lambert's Conformal Conic
East from Greenwich
COPYRIGHT GEORGE PHILIP LTD.
F
G
H
J
K
2
3
4
5
6
7
8
9
10
11

ENGLAND AND WALES 1:1 800 000

10 0 10 20 30 40 50 60 70 80 km
10 0 10 20 30 40 50 miles
NORTH SEA
IRISH SEA
North Channel
SCOTLAND
NORTHERN IRELAND
ISLE OF MAN
Key to English unitary authorities on map.
25. HARTLEPOOL
26. DARLINGTON
27. STOCKTON-ON-TEES
28. MIDDLESBROUGH
29. REDCAR AND CLEVELAND
30. BLACKPOOL
31. BLACKBURN WITH DARWEN
32. HALTON
33. WARRINGTON
34. KINGSTON UPON HULL
35. NORTH EAST LINCOLNSHIRE
36. STOKE-ON-TRENT
37. TELFORD AND WREKIN
38. DERBY CITY
39. CITY OF NOTTINGHAM
40. LEICESTER CITY
41. RUTLAND
42. PETERBOROUGH
43. MILTON KEYNES
44. LUTON
45. NORTH SOMERSET
46. CITY OF BRISTOL
47. BATH AND NORTH EAST SOMERSET
48. SWINDON
49. READING
50. WOKINGHAM
51. WINDSOR AND MAIDENHEAD
52. SLOUGH
53. BRACKNELL FOREST
54. THURROCK
55. SOUTHEND-ON-SEA
56. MEDWAY
57. PLYMOUTH
58. TORBAY
59. POOLE
60. BOURNEMOUTH
61. SOUTHAMPTON
62. PORTSMOUTH
63. BRIGHTON AND HOVE
Key to Welsh unitary authorities on map.
15. SWANSEA
16. NEATH PORT TALBOT
17. BRIDGEND
18. RHONDDA CYNON TAFF
19. MERTHYR TYDFIL
20. CAERPHILLY
21. BLAENAU GWENT
22. TORFAEN
23. CARDIFF
24. NEWPORT

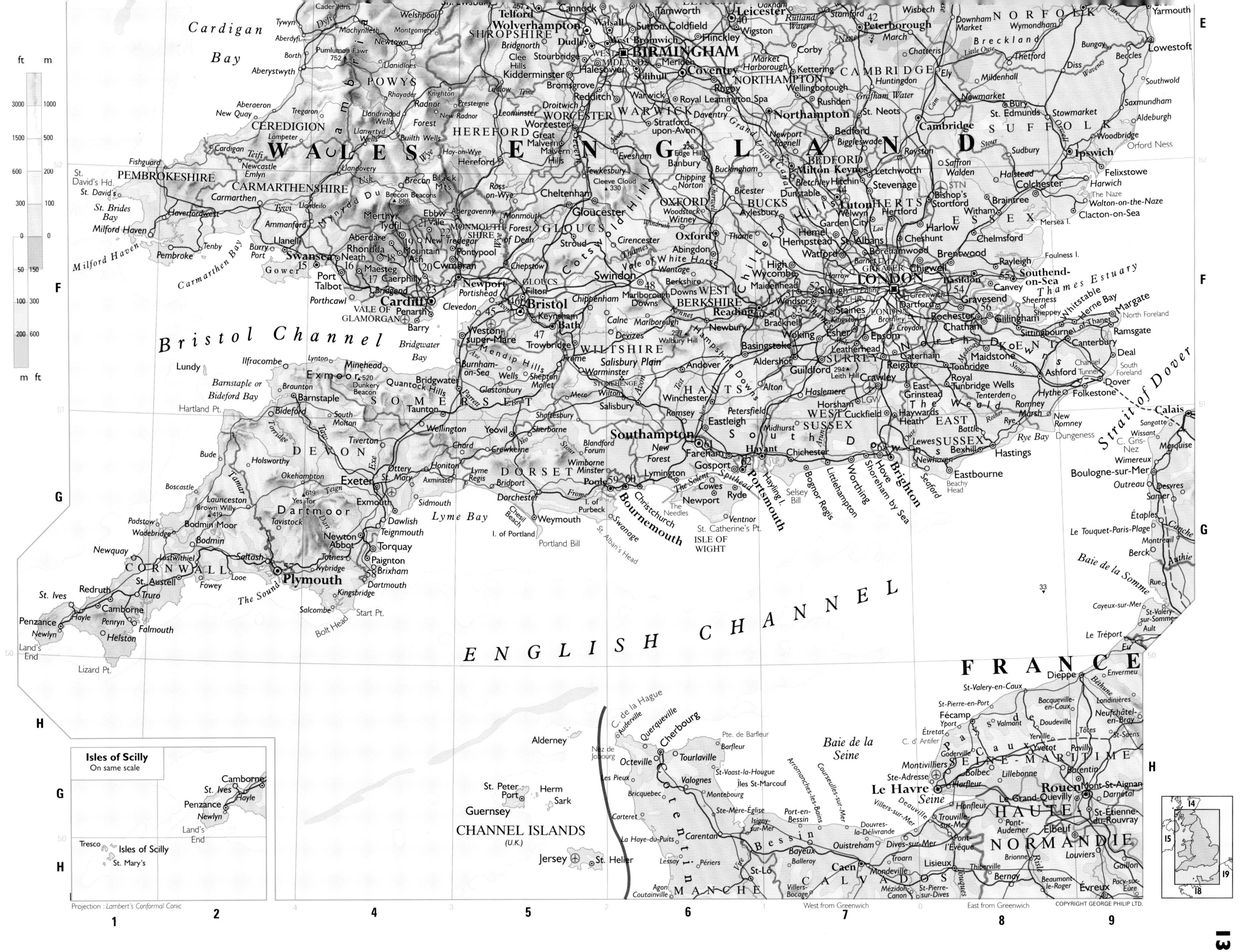
ENGLISH CHANNEL
FRANCE
ENGLAND
WALES
Bristol Channel
Cardigan Bay
Strait of Dover
Thames Estuary
Lyme Bay
Baie de la Seine
Baie de la Somme
CHANNEL ISLANDS
(U.K.)
Alderney
Guernsey
St. Peter Port
Herm
Sark
Jersey
St. Helier
LONDON
BIRMINGHAM
Bristol
Cardiff
Southampton
Portsmouth
Brighton
Bournemouth
Plymouth
Exeter
Oxford
Cambridge
Ipswich
Dover
Calais
Boulogne-sur-Mer
Dieppe
Le Havre
Rouen
Caen
Cherbourg
NORMANDIE
ISLE OF WIGHT
CORNWALL
DEVON
DORSET
WILTSHIRE
Isles of Scilly
On same scale
St. Mary's
Tresco
Projection : Lambert's Conformal Conic
West from Greenwich
East from Greenwich
COPYRIGHT GEORGE PHILIP LTD.
ft
m
3000
1500
600
300
1000
500
200
100
50
150
300
600

SCOTLAND 1:1 800 000

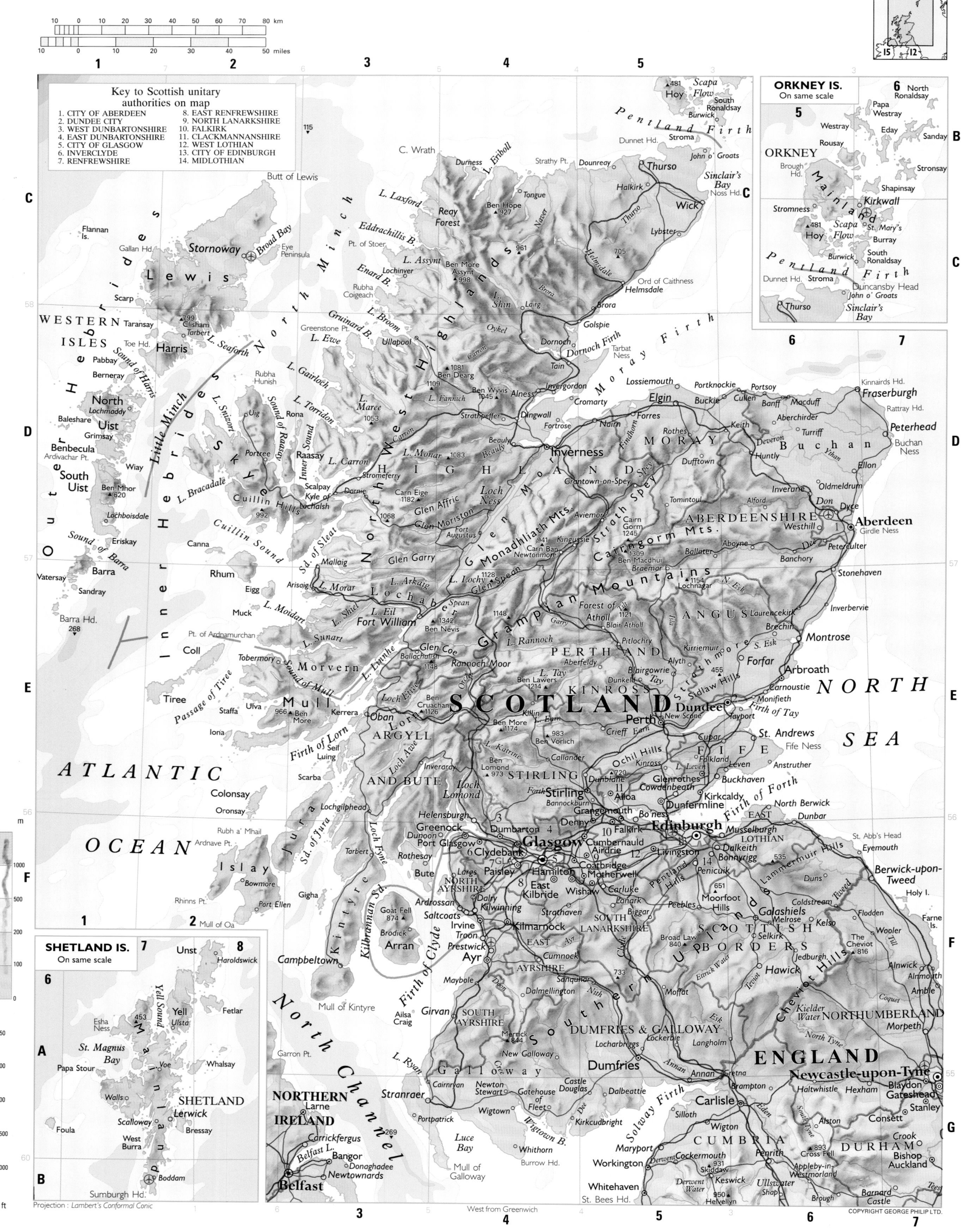

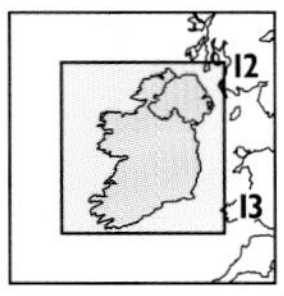

12
13

10 0 10 20 30 40 50 60 70 80 km

10 0 10 20 30 40 50 miles

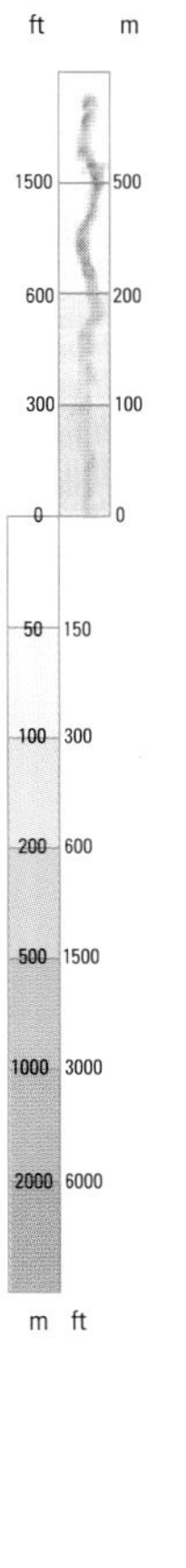

1 2 3 4 5 6

11 10 9 8 7 6 5

A B C D E

Mull of Oa
Kintyre
Campbeltown
Brodick
Arran
Firth of Clyde
Ailsa Craig
Mull of Kintyre
Rathlin I.
North Channel
Giants Causeway
Fair Hd.
Ballycastle
Portrush
Portstewart
Coleraine
Malin Hd.
Malin Pen.
Carndonagh
Inishowen Pen.
Moville
Buncrana
Lough Swilly
Fanad Hd.
Mulroy B.
Sheep Haven
Tory I.
Horn Hd.
Bloody Foreland
Inishfree B.
Gweedore
Errigal 752
The Rosses
Derryveagh Mts.
683
Rathmelton
Aran I.
Crohy Hd.
Gweebarra B.
Dawros Hd.
Loughros More B.
Rossan Pt.
Letterkenny
DONEGAL
Glenties
Lavagh More 676
Killybegs
Donegal
St. John's Pt.
Donegal Bay
Ballyshannon
Bundoran
Erne
Finn
Lifford
Strabane
Sion Mills
Newtownstewart
Mourne
Derg
Castlederg
L. Foyle
Limavady
LONDONDERRY
Londonderry
Roe
Bann
Mts of Antrim
Ballymoney
Trostan 554
Garron Pt.
ANTRIM
Main
Ballymena
Larne
Cairnryan
Stranraer
Portpatrick
Sawel Mt. 683
Sperrin Mts.
NORTHERN
Magherafelt
Randalstown
Ballyclare
Carrickfergus
269
Antrim
Belfast L.
Bangor
Donaghadee
Newtownards
Newtownabbey
Lough Neagh
Belfast
Comber
Lisburn
Saintfield
Strangford L.
Ards Pen.
Portaferry
Ballyquintin Pt.
Moneymore
Cookstown
Coalisland
TYRONE
Ulster
Omagh
Dromore
Irvinestown
Dungannon
IRELAND
Craigavon
Lurgan
Lagan
DOWN
Portadown
Banbridge
Ballynahinch
Tandragee
Downpatrick
Dundrum
Dundrum B.
St. John's Pt.
Aughnacloy
Armagh
ARMAGH
Blackwater
Middletown
Keady
Lower L. Erne
Enniskillen
FERMANAGH
Upper L. Erne
Monaghan
Clones
MONAGHAN
Newry
Mourne Mts.
852 Slieve Donard
Newcastle
577 Slieve Gullion
Warrenpoint
Kilkeel
Castleblaney
Cootehill
Dundalk
Greenore
Carlingford L.
Dundalk Bay
Downpatrick Hd.
Broad Haven
Erris Hd.
Killala B.
Belmullet
Mullet Pen.
Inishkea North
Inishkea South
Killala
Ballina
Blacksod Bay
L. Conn
806 Nephin
Achill Hd.
Achill I.
Corraun Pen.
MAYO
Newport
Castlebar
Clare I.
Clew Bay
Westport
Inishturk
Killary Harbour
Croagh Patrick 765
Mweelrea 819
Inishbofin
Inishshark
Sligo Bay
Sligo
Dromore West
544
Ox Mts.
Slieve Gamph
Collooney
SLIGO
Ballymote
L. Arrow
Moy
L. Allen
LEITRIM
Belturbet
Annalee
Cavan
Leitrim
Carrick-on-Shannon
Charlestown
Boyle
Swinford
Ballaghaderreen
Knock
ROSCOMMON
Ballyhaunis
Castlerea
Claremorris
Connacht
Ballinrobe
Glennamaddy
Roscommon
Lough Mask
Tuam
Lough Corrib
Lough Ree
Connemara
Clifden
Slyne Hd.
Oughterard
GALWAY
Suck
Athlone
Bertraghboy B.
Kilkieran B.
Galway
Athenry
Ballinasloe
Galway Bay
Black Hd.
Aran Is.
Inishmore
Inishmaan
Inisheer
Loughrea
368
Slieve Aughty
Portumna
Gort
Shannon
Clare
CAVAN
Carrickmacross
L. Gowna
Kingscourt
L. Sheelin
Louth
LOUTH
Ardee
Dunleer
Clogher Hd.
Drogheda
Granard
LONGFORD
Oldcastle
Ceanannus Mor (Kells)
Castlepollard
Longford
MEATH
An Uaimh (Navan)
Balbriggan
Boyne
IRELAND
Athboy
Inny
Mullingar
Trim
Rush
Lambay I.
Leinster
Malahide
Swords
DUB
Royal Canal
WESTMEATH
Moate
Maynooth
Howth Hd.
Dublin
Dun Laoghaire
Edenderry
Brosna
Liffey
Bog of Allen
Clondalkin
DUBLIN
KILDARE
Clara
Grand Canal
Daingean
Tullamore
Droichead Nua
Naas
Bray
Kippure 754
Greystones
OFFALY
Kildare
Portarlington
Monasterevin
WICKLOW
123
Birr
Mountmellick
Poulaphouca Res.
Slieve Bloom 528 Arderin
Port Laoise
Athy
Wicklow Mts.
Wicklow
Wicklow Hd.
Lugnaquilla 926
Rathdrum
Avoca
Roscrea
Mountrath
LAOIS
Mizen Hd.
Nenagh
Durrow
Carlow
Tullow
Arklow
Templemore
CARLOW
Shillelagh
Muine Bheag
Bunclody
Gorey
Hags Hd.
Liscannor Bay
Ennistimon
Lough Derg
Mal Bay
Milltown Malbay
Tulla
Mutton I.
Ennis
CLARE
Killaloe
Sixmilebridge
694 Keeper Hill
Shannon Airport
Kilkee
Kilrush
Limerick
TIPPERARY
Thurles
Kilkenny
KILKENNY
Loop Hd.
Foynes
LIMERICK
Rathkeale
Golden Vale
Callan
796 Mt. Leinster
Slaney
Cahore Pt.
Mouth of the Shannon
Kerry Hd.
Listowel
Feale
Munster
Newcastle West
Tipperary
Cashel
Slievenamon 722
Nore
Barrow
Enniscorthy
WEXFORD
Kilfinnane
Galtymore 920
Galty Mts.
Caher
Suir
Carrick-on-Suir
New Ross
Wexford
Wexford Harbour
Rosslare
Greenore Pt.
Smerwick Harbour
Brandon B.
Tralee B.
Tralee
953 Brandon Mt.
Slieve Mish 853
Dingle
Rath Luirc
Mitchelstown
Clonmel
Comeragh Mts. 792
Knockmealdown Mts. 795
Waterford
Tramore
Carnsore Pt.
Maine
Newmarket
Buttevant
KERRY
Laune
Kanturk
Fermoy
Blackwater
Lismore
WATERFORD
Hook Hd.
Saltee Is.
Great Blasket I.
Dunmore Hd.
Killorglin
Killarney
Mallow
Dungarvan
Tramore B.
Waterford Harbour
Inishvickillane
Dingle Bay
Carrauntoohill 1041
L. Leane
Boggeragh Mts.
646
Dungarvan Harbour
Valencia I.
Cahersiveen
Macgillycuddy's Reeks
CORK
Cork
Youghal
Youghal B.
Puffin I.
Kenmare
Macroom
Blarney
Midleton
Passage West
Cobh
Great Skellig
Ballinskelligs B.
Kenmare River
Caha Mts.
686
Glengarriff
Lee
Crosshaven
Cork Harbour
Dunmanway
Bandon
Bandon
Scariff I.
Bantry
Kinsale
Dursey I.
Castletown Bearhaven
Bear I.
Clonakilty
Old Head of Kinsale
Crow Hd.
Bantry Bay
Skibbereen
Clonakilty B.
Dunmanus B.
Skull
Galley Hd.
Mizen Hd.
Long I.
Baltimore
Sherkin I.
C. Clear
Clear I.
St. David's Hd.
St. David's
St. Brides Bay
115
ATLANTIC OCEAN
IRISH SEA
St. George's Channel
CELTIC SEA

55 54 53 52

ft m
1500 500
600 200
300 100
0 0
50 150
100 300
200 600
500 1500
1000 3000
2000 6000
m ft

Projection : *Lambert's Conformal Conic*

West from Greenwich

1 2 3 4 5 6

BRITISH ISLES 1:4 400 000

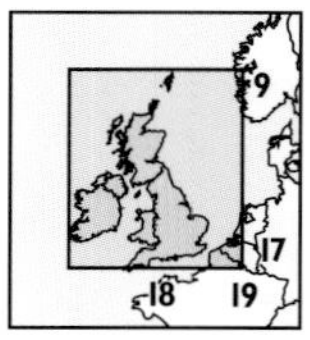

50 0 25 50 75 100 125 150 175 km
50 0 25 50 75 100 125 miles

ft m
3000 1000
1500 500
600 200
0 0
50 150
100 300
200 600
500 1500
1000 3000
2000 6000
m ft

ATLANTIC OCEAN
NORTH SEA
CELTIC SEA
IRISH SEA
English Channel
Bristol Channel
St. George's Channel
North Channel
North Minch
Pentland Firth
Moray Firth
Firth of Clyde
Str. of Dover
The Wash

Shetland Is.
Yell
Unst
Fetlar
Mainland
Lerwick
Foula
Fair Isle
1224
316
Orkney Is.
Westray
Sanday
Stronsay
Mainland
Kirkwall
Hoy
South Ronaldsay
C. Wrath
Thurso
Wick
Helmsdale
Outer Hebrides
Lewis
Stornoway
789
Harris
St. Kilda
North Uist
Benbecula
South Uist
Barra
Inner Hebrides
Skye
Portree
Rhum
Eigg
Mallaig
Coll
Tiree
Tobermory
Mull
Oban
Colonsay
Jura
Islay
Ullapool
Lairg
Golspie
Tain
Invergordon
Dingwall
North West Highlands
Inverness
Nairn
Elgin
Buckie
Banff
Fraserburgh
Peterhead
Huntly
Inverurie
Aberdeen
Stonehaven
L. Ness
1182
Aviemore
Spey
Don
Dee
1311
Ballater
SCOTLAND
Grampian Mts.
Ben Nevis
1342
Fort William
1214
Montrose
Arbroath
Forfar
Dundee
St. Andrews
Perth
Tay
Glenrothes
Kirkcaldy
L. Lomond
973
Stirling
Dunfermline
Edinburgh
Dunbar
Greenock
Clyde
Glasgow
Paisley
East Kilbride
Hamilton
Arran
Irvine
Kilmarnock
Ayr
Campbeltown
Girvan
Southern Uplands
Galashiels
Jedburgh
Hawick
840
816
Cheviot Hills
Berwick-upon-Tweed
Alnwick
Dumfries
Kirkcudbright
Stranraer
Annan
Carlisle
238

Malin Hd.
Buncrana
Coleraine
Aran I.
Letterkenny
Londonderry
Ballymena
Larne
Lifford
Donegal
NORTHERN IRELAND
Ulster
Lough Neagh
Antrim
Bangor
Omagh
Belfast
Lisburn
Bundoran
Lower L. Erne
Portadown
Lurgan
Enniskillen
Armagh
Newry
Sligo
Clones
Ballina
Achill I.
L. Conn
Castlebar
Leitrim
Cavan
Dundalk
Westport
Connacht
Roscommon
Longford
Ceanannus Mor
Drogheda
Lough Mask
Connemara
Lough Corrib
Athlone
Lough Ree
Mullingar
Boyne
Galway B.
Galway
Aran Is.
Ballinasloe
Tullamore
Liffey
Dublin
Dun Laoghaire
Bray
IRELAND
Birr
Leinster
Ennis
Lough Derg
Port Laoise
Athy
Wicklow Mts.
926
Kilrush
Limerick
Carlow
Kilkenny
Arklow
Shannon
Listowel
Thurles
Tipperary
Munster
Tralee
Carrick-on-Suir
Wexford
953
Dingle
Mallow
Clonmel
Waterford
Rosslare
Carrauntoohill
1041
Killarney
Blackwater
Macgillycuddy's Reeks
Dungarvan
Valencia I.
Cork
Youghal
Cobh
Bandon
Bantry
Kinsale
C. Clear
99

UNITED KINGDOM
Mull of Galloway
Workington
Whitehaven
Cumbrian Mts.
978
Douglas
I. of Man
Barrow-in-Furness
Lancaster
Pennines
893
Newcastle-upon-Tyne
South Shields
Sunderland
Hexham
Gateshead
Durham
Hartlepool
Redcar
Middlesbrough
Darlington
Stockton-on-Tees
16
Scarborough
Bridlington
Harrogate
York
Leeds
Beverley
Kingston upon Hull
Keighley
Blackpool
Preston
Burnley
Bradford
Blackburn
Halifax
Huddersfield
Scunthorpe
Humber
Bolton
Barnsley
Doncaster
Grimsby
Manchester
Oldham
Rotherham
Liverpool
Warrington
636
Stockport
Sheffield
Louth
Lincoln
Chesterfield
Skegness
Anglesey
Holyhead
Bangor
Colwyn Bay
Chester
Crewe
Mansfield
Snowdon
1085
Wrexham
Derby
Nottingham
Boston
Cromer
Pwllheli
Stoke on Trent
Stafford
Trent
Grantham
King's Lynn
Shrewsbury
Great Ouse
Norwich
Great Yarmouth
Cardigan Bay
Aberystwyth
Cambrian Mts.
Welshpool
Telford
ENGLAND
Leicester
Lowestoft
Wolverhampton
Nuneaton
Corby
Peterborough
Thetford
BIRMINGHAM
Coventry
Ely
Redditch
Rugby
Northampton
Bury St. Edmunds
Worcester
Royal Leamington Spa
Bedford
Cambridge
Ipswich
Hereford
Severn
Milton Keynes
Stevenage
Felixstowe
WALES
Cotswold Hills
Harwich
Fishguard
Cheltenham
Carmarthen
Brecon
886
Hemel Hempstead
Luton
Harlow
Colchester
Haverfordwest
Gloucester
Oxford
Chelmsford
Milford Haven
Merthyr Tydfil
Neath
Pembroke
Llanelli
Cwmbran
High Wycombe
Watford
Basildon
36
Swansea
Port Talbot
Rhondda
Newport
Slough
Southend-on-Sea
Cardiff
Bristol
Swindon
Thames
Margate
Barry
Bath
Newbury
Reading
LONDON
Chatham
Canterbury
Basingstoke
Reigate
Maidstone
Dover
Weston-super-Mare
Guildford
Ashford
Folkestone
Barnstaple
Exmoor
Salisbury
Winchester
Crawley
Taunton
Southampton
Fareham
Havant
Hastings
Bude
Yeovil
Bournemouth
Portsmouth
Worthing
Brighton
Eastbourne
Exeter
Poole
Newport
618
Dartmoor
Exmouth
Weymouth
Isle of Wight
Torbay
Newquay
Truro
Plymouth
St. Austell
Falmouth
Land's End
Penzance
Isles of Scilly

Channel Is. (U.K.)
Alderney
C. de la Hague
Guernsey
St. Peter Port
Sark
St. Helier
Jersey
Pte. de Barfleur
Cherbourg
Valognes
Cotentin
Bayeux
Trouville-sur-Mer
Caen
Le Havre
Bolbec
Lisieux
Elbeuf
Seine
Rouen
Fécamp
Pays de Caux
Dieppe
Le Tréport
Abbeville
Amiens
Somme
Picardie
FRANCE
St-Quentin
Cambrai
Valenciennes
Lens
Béthune
Bruay-la-Buissière
Lille
Villeneuve-d'Ascq
Roubaix
Tourcoing
Tournai
St-Omer
Calais
C. Gris-Nez
Boulogne-sur-Mer
Le Touquet-Paris-Plage
33
Dunkerque
Flandre
Oostende
Zeebrugge
Brugge
Gent
Antwerpen
Mechelen
BELGIUM
BRUSSEL (Bruxelles)
Vlissingen
Dordrecht
ROTTERDAM
Hoek van Holland
's-Gravenhage (Den Haag)
NETHERLANDS
Haarlem
Alkmaar
Den Helder
Texel

Askøy
Bergen
Osøyro
Stord
Bømlo
Leirvik
NORWAY
Haugesund
Kopervik
Åkrahamn
Bokna
Stavanger
Sandnes
Bryne
Nærbø

Projection: Conical with two standard parallels
East from Greenwich
West from Greenwich

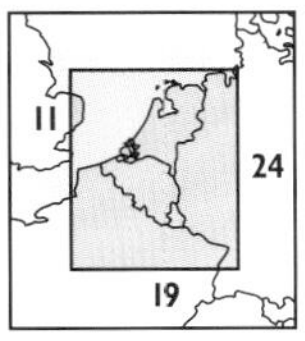

10 0 10 20 30 40 50 60 70 80 90 km

10 0 10 20 30 40 50 60 miles

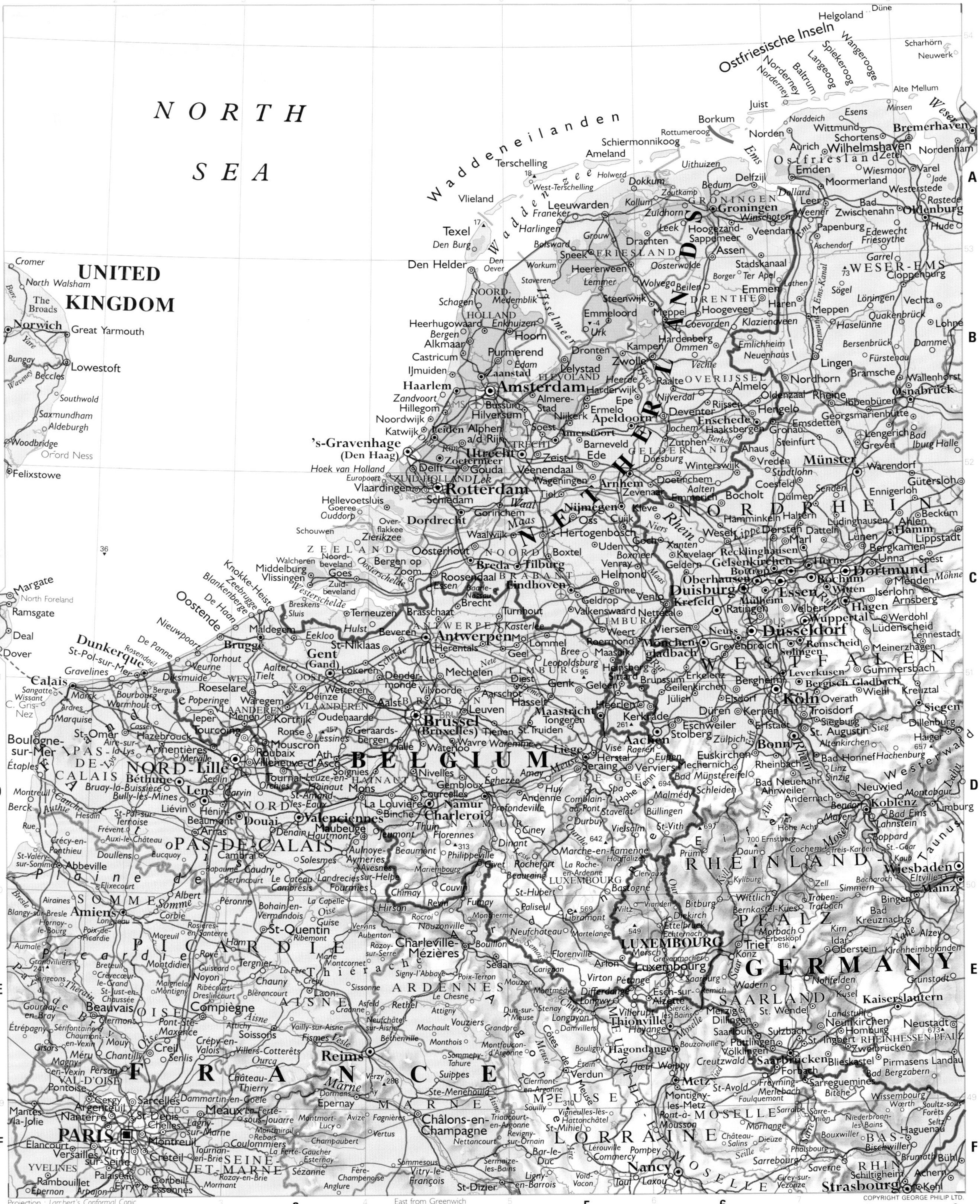

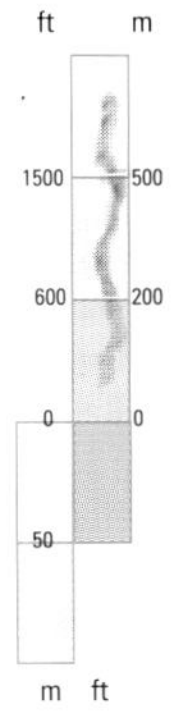

Projection : Lambert's Conformal Conic

East from Greenwich

Underlined towns give their name to the administrative area in which they stand.

DÉPARTEMENTS IN THE PARIS AREA

1. Ville de Paris
2. Seine-St-Denis
3. Val-de-Marne
4. Hauts-de-Seine

Underlined towns give their name to the administrative area in which they stand.

10 0 10 20 30 40 50 60 70 80 90 km
10 0 10 20 30 40 50 60 miles
1 2 3 4 5 6 7
B C D E F G
ATLANTIC OCEAN
Golfe de Gascogne
FRANCE
SPAIN
ANDORRA
POITOU-CHARENTES
LIMOUSIN
AQUITAINE
MIDI-PYRÉNÉES
AUVERGNE
LANGUEDOC-ROUSSILLON
CATALUÑA
NAVARRA
ARAGÓN
PYRÉNÉES
Bordeaux
Toulouse
Limoges
Poitiers
La Rochelle
Clermont-Ferrand
Bayonne
Pau
Perpignan
Zaragoza
Pamplona
Lleida
BARCELONA
Agen
Périgueux
Angoulême
Niort
Montauban
Tarbes
Carcassonne
Narbonne
Béziers
Sète
Huesca
Donostia-San Sebastián
Île de Ré
Île d'Oléron
Île d'Yeu
Costa Brava
Golfe du Lion
Projection : Lambert's Conformal Conic
West from Greenwich
East from Greenwich

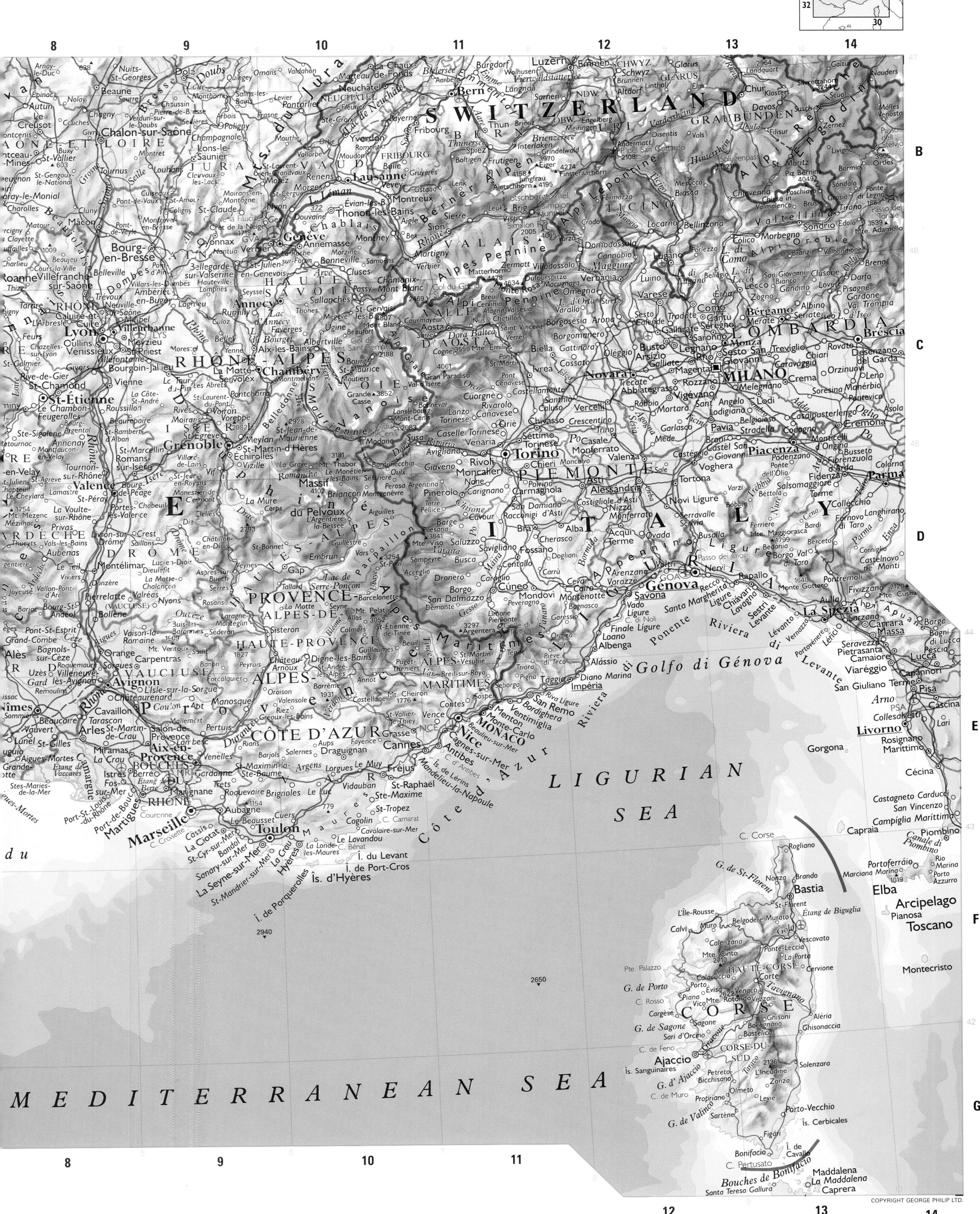

SWITZERLAND
ITALY
LIGURIAN SEA
MEDITERRANEAN SEA
Golfo di Génova
Riviera di Ponente
Riviera di Levante
Côte d'Azur
RHÔNE-ALPES
PROVENCE-ALPES-CÔTE D'AZUR
PIEMONTE
LOMBARDIA
LIGURIA
VALLE D'AOSTA
CORSE
HAUTE-CORSE
CORSE-DU-SUD
SAVOIE
HAUTE SAVOIE
ISÈRE
DRÔME
VAUCLUSE
HAUTES-ALPES
ALPES-DE-HAUTE-PROVENCE
ALPES-MARITIMES
BOUCHES-DU-RHÔNE
VAUD
VALAIS
BERN
FRIBOURG
TICINO
GRAUBÜNDEN
URI
SCHWYZ
GLARUS
NEUCHÂTEL
JURA
AIN
Alpes Pennine
Alpi Lepontine
Alpi Graie
Alpes Maritimes
Berner Alpen
Mts. du Jura
Massif du Pelvoux
L. Léman
L. Maggiore
L. di Como
Lac du Bourget
Lac d'Annecy
Milano
Torino
Génova
Marseille
Lyon
Grenoble
Genève
Lausanne
Bern
Luzern
Nice
Monaco
Cannes
Toulon
Avignon
Nîmes
St-Étienne
Chambéry
Annecy
Aosta
Novara
Alessandria
Asti
Cúneo
Savona
La Spezia
Livorno
Pisa
Lucca
Piacenza
Parma
Cremona
Bérgamo
Brescia
Monza
Pavia
Como
Lugano
Bellinzona
Sion
Valence
Aix-en-Provence
Arles
Ajaccio
Bastia
Corte
Bonifacio
Porto-Vecchio
Calvi
Elba
Capraia
Gorgona
Pianosa
Montecristo
Arcipelago Toscano
Îs. d'Hyères
Bouches de Bonifacio
Maddalena
Mte. Rosa
Matterhorn
Mont Blanc
Gran Paradiso
Mte. Viso
Mte. Cinto
Camargue
Rhône
Po
Arno
8
9
10
11
12
13
14
B
C
D
E
F
G

MIDDLE EUROPE 1:4 400 000

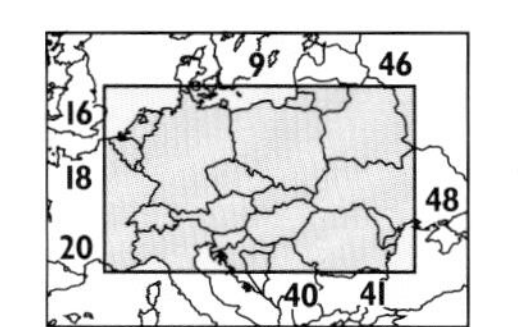

9 10 11 12 13 14 15 16

B C D E F G

LITHUANIA

BELARUS

POLAND

UKRAINE

SLOVAK REP.

HUNGARY

MOLDOVA

ROMANIA

YUGOSLAVIA

BOSNIA-HERZEGOVINA

BULGARIA

Carpathians

Transylvania

Carpaţii Meridionali

Vojvodina

Pripet Marshes

Podilska Vysochyna

Dobruja

Walachia

East from Greenwich

9 10 11 12 13 14 15

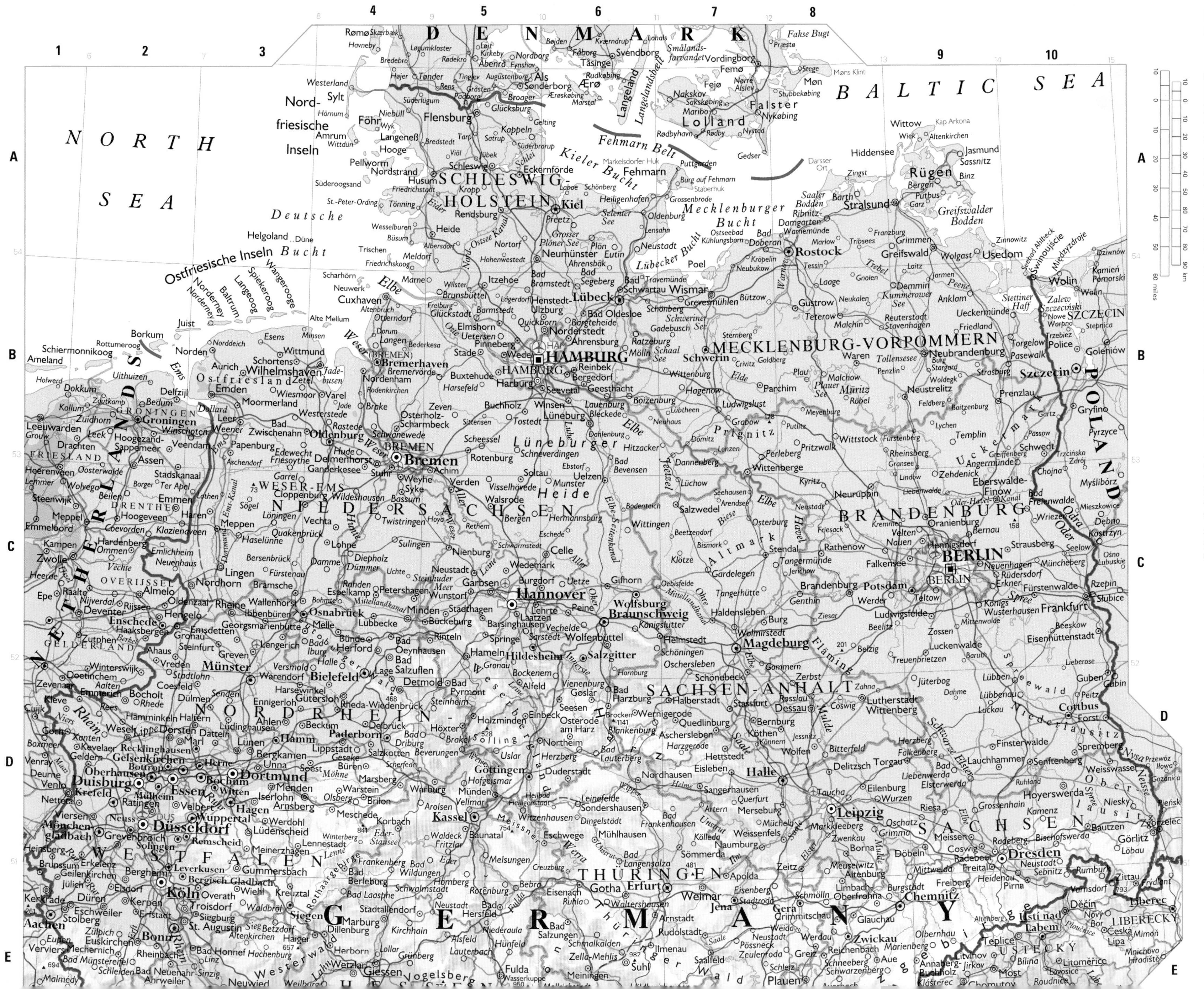
10 0 10 20 30 40 50 60 70 80 90 km
10 0 10 20 30 40 50 60 miles
NORTH SEA
BALTIC SEA
DENMARK
POLAND
NETHERLANDS
GERMANY
SCHLESWIG-HOLSTEIN
MECKLENBURG-VORPOMMERN
BRANDENBURG
NIEDERSACHSEN
SACHSEN-ANHALT
SACHSEN
THÜRINGEN
NORDRHEIN-WESTFALEN
BERLIN
HAMBURG
BREMEN
Hannover
Kiel
Lübeck
Rostock
Szczecin
Magdeburg
Leipzig
Dresden
Halle
Erfurt
Kassel
Dortmund
Düsseldorf
Köln
Bonn
Münster
Osnabrück
Bielefeld
Braunschweig
Chemnitz
Groningen
Deutsche Bucht
Mecklenburger Bucht
Kieler Bucht
Fehmarn Belt
Ostfriesische Inseln
Nordfriesische Inseln
Lüneburger Heide
Harz
Thüringer Wald
Elbe
Weser
Rhein
Oder

Underlined towns give their name to the administrative area in which they stand.

GERMANY
CZECH REP.
AUSTRIA
ITALY
SLOVENIA
SWITZERLAND
PRAHA
MÜNCHEN
Dresden
Nürnberg
Stuttgart
Salzburg
Innsbruck
Linz
Graz
Ljubljana
Venézia
Trieste
Zagreb
Projection : Lambert's Conformal Conic

Underlined towns give their name to the administrative area in which they stand.

NORTHERN ITALY, SLOVENIA AND CROATIA 1:2 200 000

Underlined towns give their name to the administrative area in which they stand.

dministrative divisions in Croatia:

Brodsko-Posavska
Koprivničko-Križevačka
Krapinsko-Zagorska
4. Međimurska
6. Požeško-Slavonska
7. Varaždinska
8. Virovitičko-Podravska
10. Zagrebačka

Inter-entity boundaries as agreed at the 1995 Dayton Peace Agreement.

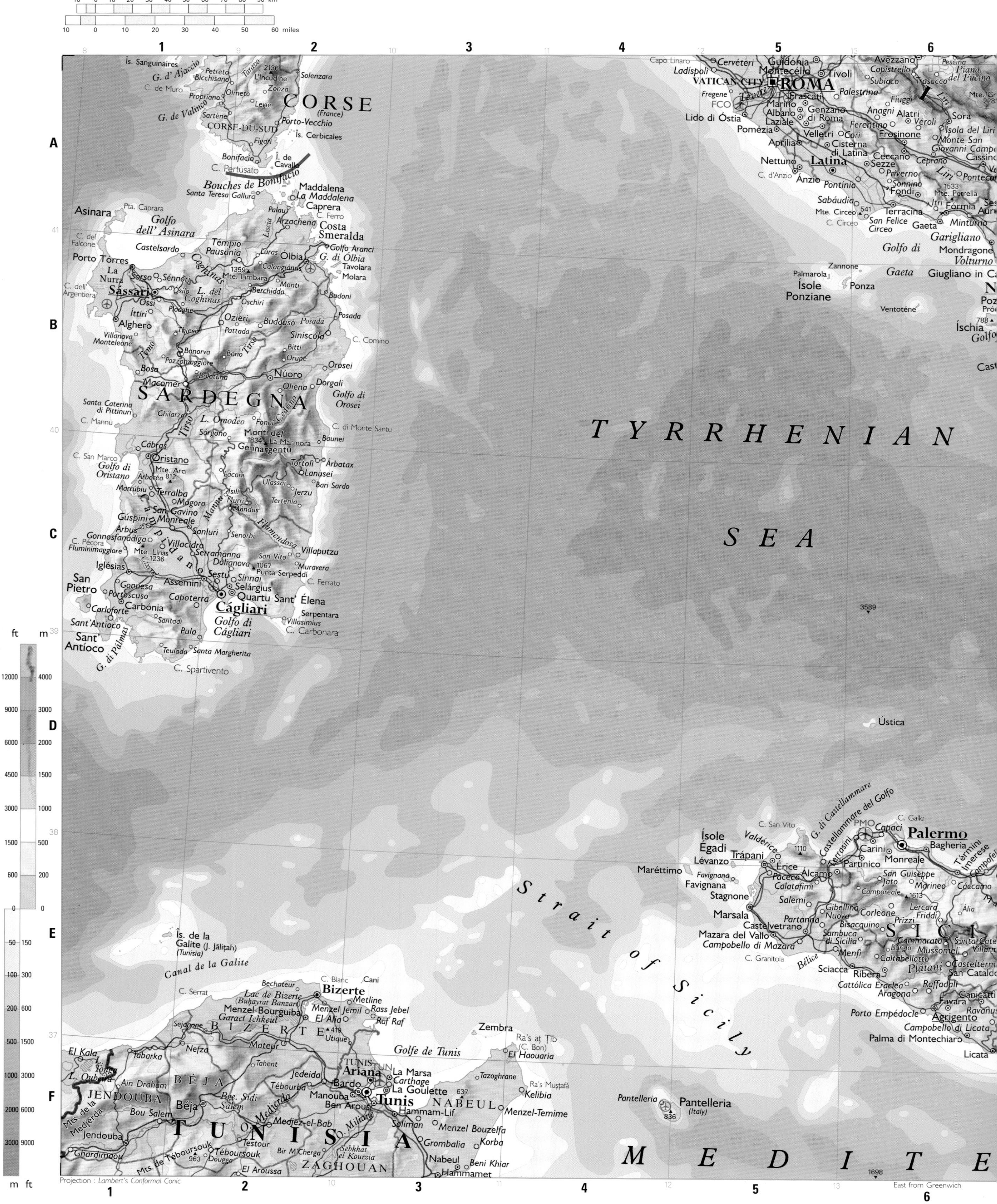

CORSE
SARDEGNA
TYRRHENIAN SEA
Strait of Sicily
TUNISIA
MEDITE
ROMA
Cágliari
Palermo
Tunis
Sassari
Bizerte
Pantelleria
Projection : Lambert's Conformal Conic
East from Greenwich

7 8 9 10 11 12

A B C D E F

COPYRIGHT GEORGE PHILIP LTD.

Underlined towns give their name to the administrative area in which they stand.

10 0 10 20 30 40 50 60 70 80 90 km
10 0 10 20 30 40 50 60 miles
FRANCE
SPAIN
ANDORRA
BARCELONA
Zaragoza
Toulouse
Perpignan
Tarragona
Pamplona
Bilbao
Donostia-San Sebastián
Vitoria-Gasteiz
Logroño
Burgos
Soria
Huesca
Lleida (Lérida)
Girona
Teruel
Castelló de la Plana
Guadalajara
MADRID
Cuenca
ARAGÓN
CATALUÑA
NAVARRA
LA RIOJA
PAÍS VASCO
CASTILLA Y LEÓN
Golfe de Gascogne
Costa Brava
Costa Dorada
Costa del Azahar
G. de Sant Jordi
MENORCA
MALLORCA
BALEARES

MEDITERRANEAN SEA
Golfo de Valencia
ISLA
Costa Blanca
Costa del Sol
CASTILLA LA MANCHA
CIUDAD REAL
ALBACETE
VALENCIA
ALICANTE
MURCIA
JAÉN
GRANADA
ALMERÍA
Sierra Nevada
Sierra de Segura
Sierra de Alcaraz
Valencia
Alicante
Elche
Murcia
Cartagena
Albacete
Granada
Almería
Benidorm
Lorca
Linares
Úbeda
Baeza
Guadix
Motril
Aguilas
Mar Menor
G. de Almería
G. de Mazarrón
C. de Gata
EIVISSA (IBIZA)
Eivissa (Ibiza)
Formentera
Cabrera
B. de Palma
ALGERIA
ALGER (Algiers)
Blida
Médéa
Oran (Ouahran)
Mostaganem
Relizane
Mascara
Sidi-bel-Abbès
Ech Cheliff
Aïn Defla
Tissemsilt
Tiaret
Aïn Témouchent
TIPASA
ECH CHELIFF
AÏN DEFLA
MÉDÉA
MOSTAGANEM
RELIZANE
ORAN
AÏN TÉMOUCHENT
MASCARA
TIARET
DJELFA
Golfe d'Arzew
Melilla (Sp.)
Nador
Alborán (Sp.)
Islas Chafarinas (Sp.)
Ghazaouet
2850
2726
Projection : Lambert's Conformal Conic
West from Greenwich
East from Greenwich
COPYRIGHT GEORGE PHILIP LTD.

10 0 10 20 30 40 50 60 70 80 90 km

10 0 10 20 30 40 50 60 miles

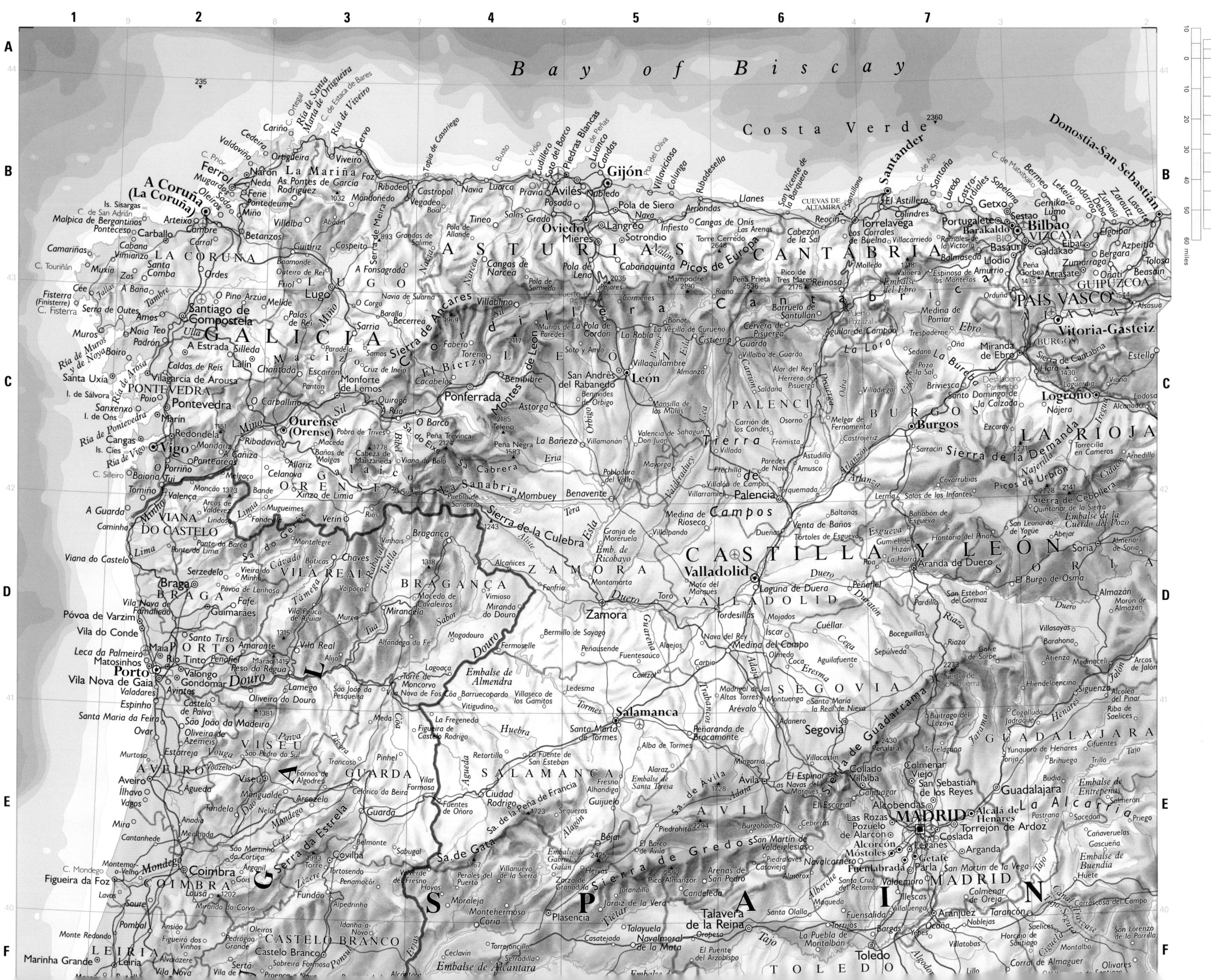

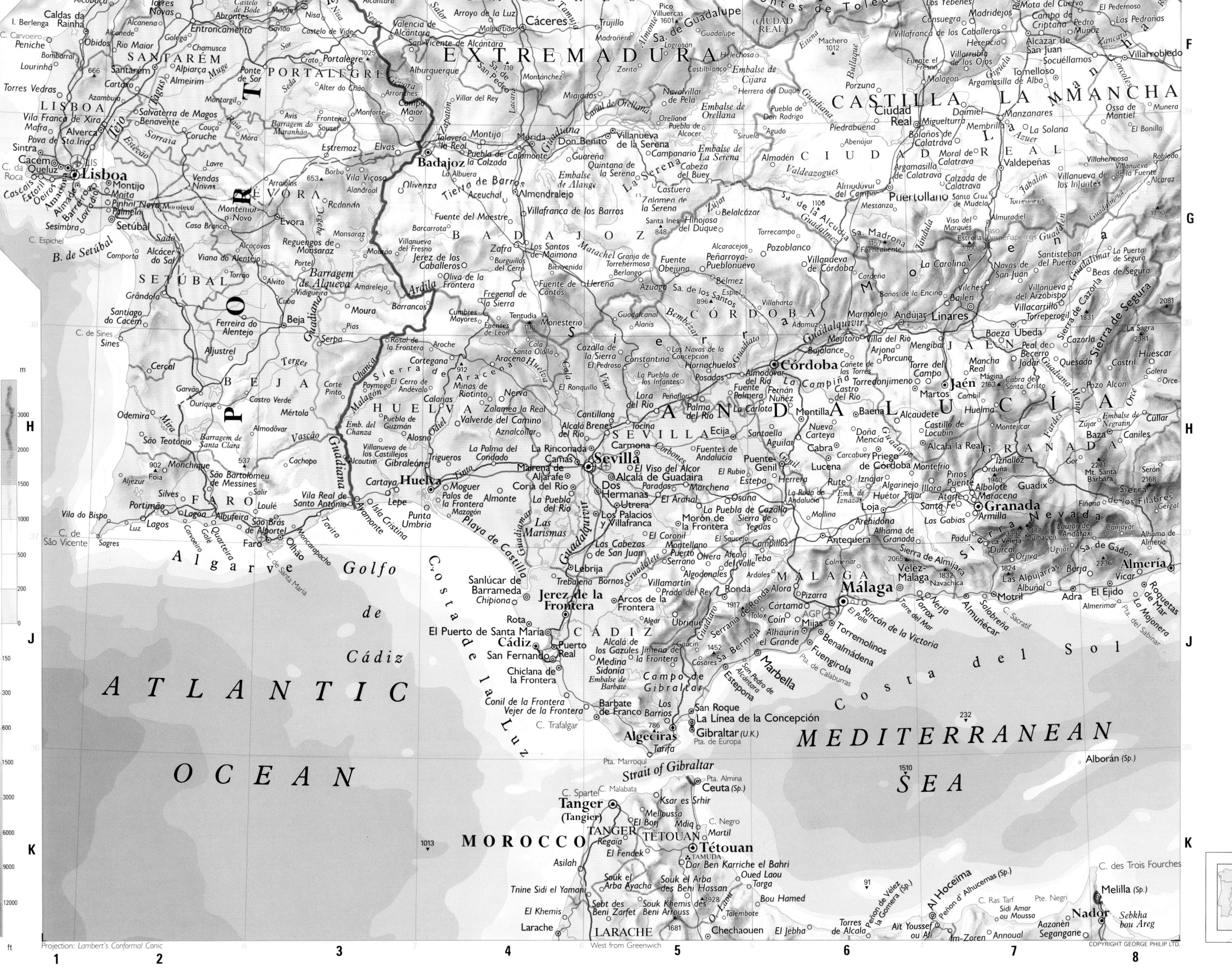
ATLANTIC OCEAN
MEDITERRANEAN SEA
Golfo de Cádiz
Costa de la Luz
Costa del Sol
Strait of Gibraltar
MOROCCO
EXTREMADURA
CASTILLA LA MANCHA
ANDALUCÍA
Sierra Nevada
Sierra Morena
Sierra de Segura
Montes de Toledo
Lisboa
Sevilla
Córdoba
Granada
Málaga
Cádiz
Huelva
Badajoz
Cáceres
Jaén
Almería
Gibraltar (U.K.)
Ceuta (Sp.)
Melilla (Sp.)
Tanger (Tangier)
Tétouan
Faro
Setúbal
Évora
Beja
Guadiana
Guadalquivir
Algarve
Projection: Lambert's Conformal Conic
West from Greenwich
COPYRIGHT GEORGE PHILIP LTD.

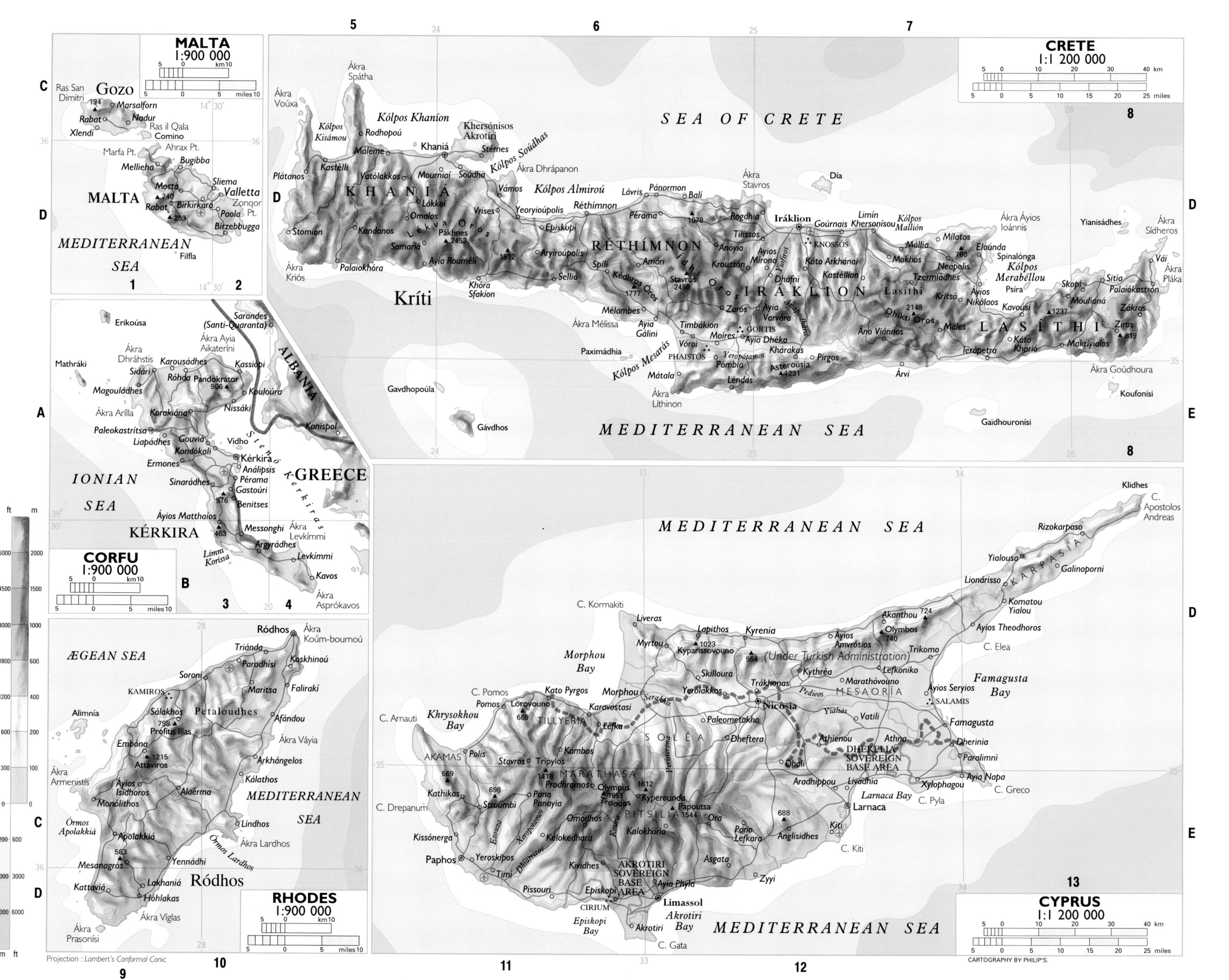
MALTA
1:900 000
Gozo
MALTA
MEDITERRANEAN SEA
CRETE
1:1 200 000
SEA OF CRETE
Kríti
MEDITERRANEAN SEA
CORFU
1:900 000
IONIAN SEA
KÉRKIRA
ALBANIA
GREECE
RHODES
1:900 000
ÆGEAN SEA
MEDITERRANEAN SEA
Ródhos
CYPRUS
1:1 200 000
MEDITERRANEAN SEA
Projection : Lambert's Conformal Conic
CARTOGRAPHY BY PHILIP'S

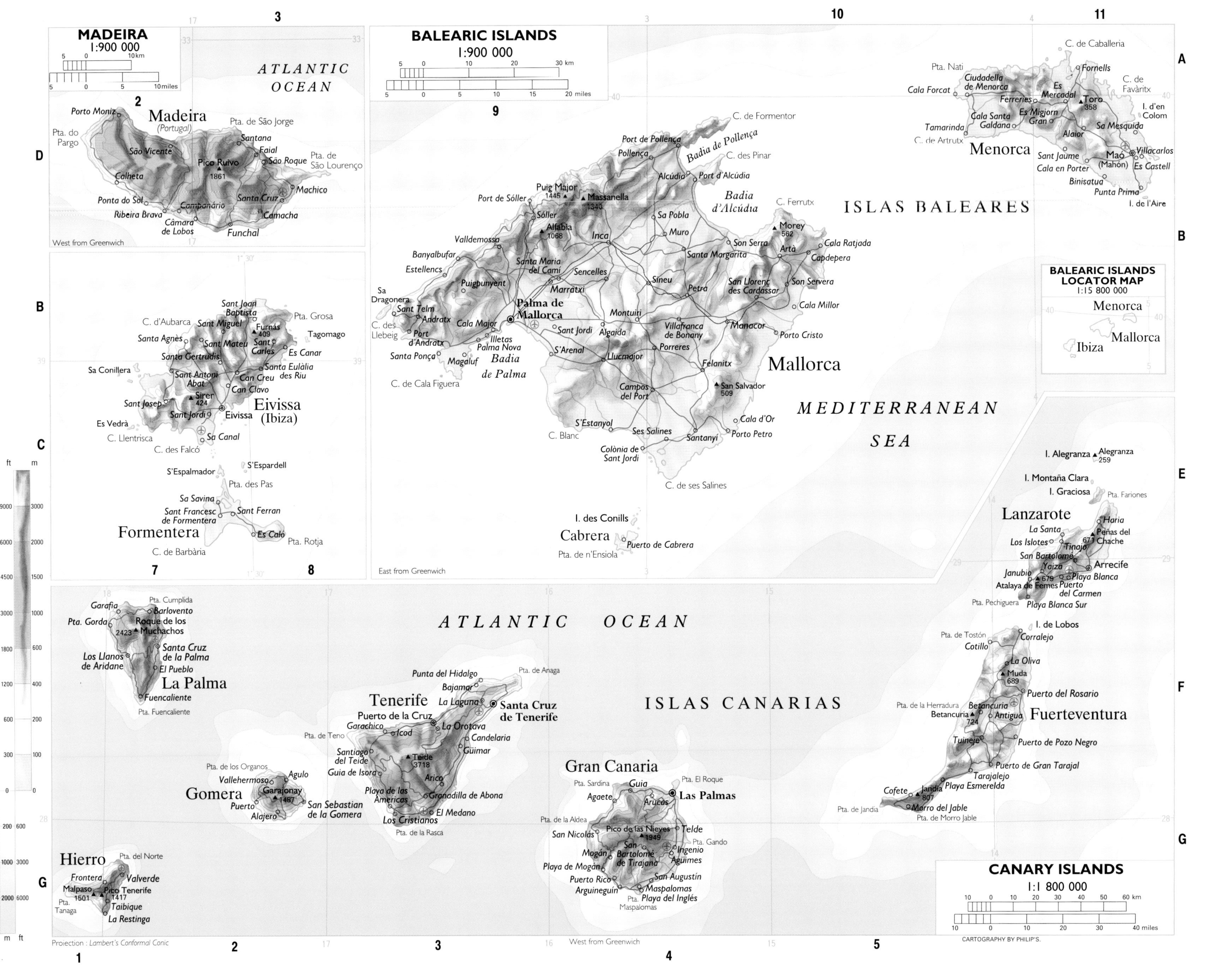

MADEIRA
1:900 000
ATLANTIC OCEAN
Madeira
(Portugal)
Porto Moniz
Pta. do Pargo
São Vicente
Pico Ruivo 1861
Pta. de São Jorge
Santana
Faial
São Roque
Pta. de São Lourenço
Machico
Calheta
Ponta do Sol
Ribeira Brava
Campanário
Câmara de Lobos
Funchal
Santa Cruz
Camacha
West from Greenwich
BALEARIC ISLANDS
1:900 000
C. de Formentor
Badia de Pollença
C. des Pinar
Port de Pollença
Pollença
Alcúdia
Port d'Alcúdia
Badia d'Alcúdia
Puig Major 1445
Massanella 1340
Port de Sóller
Sóller
Alfabia 1068
Valldemossa
Banyalbufar
Estellencs
Sa Dragonera
Sant Telm
Andratx
Port d'Andratx
C. des Llebeig
Santa Ponça
Magaluf
C. de Cala Figuera
Puigpunyent
Santa Maria del Camí
Palma de Mallorca
Cala Major
Illetas
Palma Nova
Badia de Palma
Inca
Sencelles
Marratxí
Sa Pobla
Muro
Sineu
Santa Margarita
Petra
Son Serra
C. Ferrutx
Morey 562
Artà
Cala Ratjada
Capdepera
Son Servera
Sant Llorenç des Cardassar
Cala Millor
Manacor
Porto Cristo
Montuïri
Algaida
Sant Jordi
S'Arenal
Villafranca de Bonany
Porreres
Llucmajor
Felanitx
Campos del Port
San Salvador 509
Cala d'Or
Porto Petro
Santanyí
Ses Salines
S'Estanyol
C. Blanc
Colònia de Sant Jordi
C. de ses Salines
Mallorca
ISLAS BALEARES
MEDITERRANEAN SEA
I. des Conills
Cabrera
Puerto de Cabrera
Pta. de n'Ensiola
East from Greenwich
C. de Caballeria
Pta. Nati
Ciudadella de Menorca
Cala Forcat
Fornells
Es Mercadal
Toro 358
C. de Favàritx
Ferreries
Es Migjorn Gran
Cala Santa Galdana
Tamarinda
C. de Artrutx
Alaior
Sa Mesquida
I. d'en Colom
Menorca
Sant Jaume
Cala en Porter
Binisatua
Mao (Mahón)
Villacarlos
Es Castell
Punta Prima
I. de l'Aire
BALEARIC ISLANDS LOCATOR MAP
1:15 800 000
Menorca
Mallorca
Ibiza
Sant Joan Baptista
C. d'Aubarca
Sant Miquel
Pta. Grosa
Furnàs 409
Tagomago
Santa Agnès
Sant Mateu
Sant Carles
Es Canar
Santa Gertrudis
Sa Conillera
Sant Antoni Abat
Santa Eulàlia des Riu
Can Creu
Can Clavo
Siret 424
Sant Josep
Sant Jordi
Eivissa
Eivissa (Ibiza)
Es Vedrà
C. Llentrisca
Sa Canal
C. des Falcó
S'Espalmador
S'Espardell
Pta. des Pas
Sa Savina
Sant Francesc de Formentera
Sant Ferran
Formentera
Es Caló
Pta. Rotja
C. de Barbària
ATLANTIC OCEAN
ISLAS CANARIAS
Pta. Cumplida
Garafia
Barlovento
Pta. Gorda
Roque de los Muchachos 2423
Santa Cruz de la Palma
Los Llanos de Aridane
El Pueblo
La Palma
Fuencaliente
Pta. Fuencaliente
Hierro
Pta. del Norte
Frontera
Valverde
Malpaso 1501
Pico Tenerife 1417
Pta. Tanaga
Taibique
La Restinga
Pta. de los Organos
Vallehermoso
Agulo
Gomera
Garajonay 1487
Puerto
Alajeró
San Sebastian de la Gomera
Punta del Hidalgo
Pta. de Anaga
Bajamar
La Laguna
Tenerife
Santa Cruz de Tenerife
Puerto de la Cruz
Garachico
Icod
La Orotava
Pta. de Teno
Candelaria
Güimar
Santiago del Teide
Teide 3718
Guia de Isora
Arico
Playa de las Americas
Granadilla de Abona
Los Cristianos
El Medano
Pta. de la Rasca
Gran Canaria
Pta. Sardina
Guia
Pta. El Roque
Agaete
Arucas
Las Palmas
Pta. de la Aldea
San Nicolás
Pico de las Nieves 1949
Telde
Pta. Gando
Mogán
San Bartolomé de Tirajana
Ingenio
Agüimes
Playa de Mogán
Puerto Rico
San Augustín
Arguineguín
Maspalomas
Pta. Maspalomas
Playa del Inglés
I. Alegranza
Alegranza 259
I. Montaña Clara
I. Graciosa
Pta. Fariones
Lanzarote
Haria
La Santa
Peñas del Chache 671
Los Islotes
Tinajo
San Bartolomé
Arrecife
Janubio
Yaiza
Atalaya de Femes 679
Playa Blanca
Puerto del Carmen
Pta. Pechiguera
Playa Blanca Sur
I. de Lobos
Pta. de Tostón
Corralejo
Cotillo
La Oliva
Muda 689
Puerto del Rosario
Pta. de la Herradura
Betancuria 724
Betancuria
Antigua
Fuerteventura
Tuineje
Puerto de Pozo Negro
Puerto de Gran Tarajal
Tarajalejo
Cofete
Jandia 807
Playa Esmerelda
Pta. de Jandia
Morro del Jable
Pta. de Morro Jable
CANARY ISLANDS
1:1 800 000
Projection : Lambert's Conformal Conic
West from Greenwich
CARTOGRAPHY BY PHILIP'S.

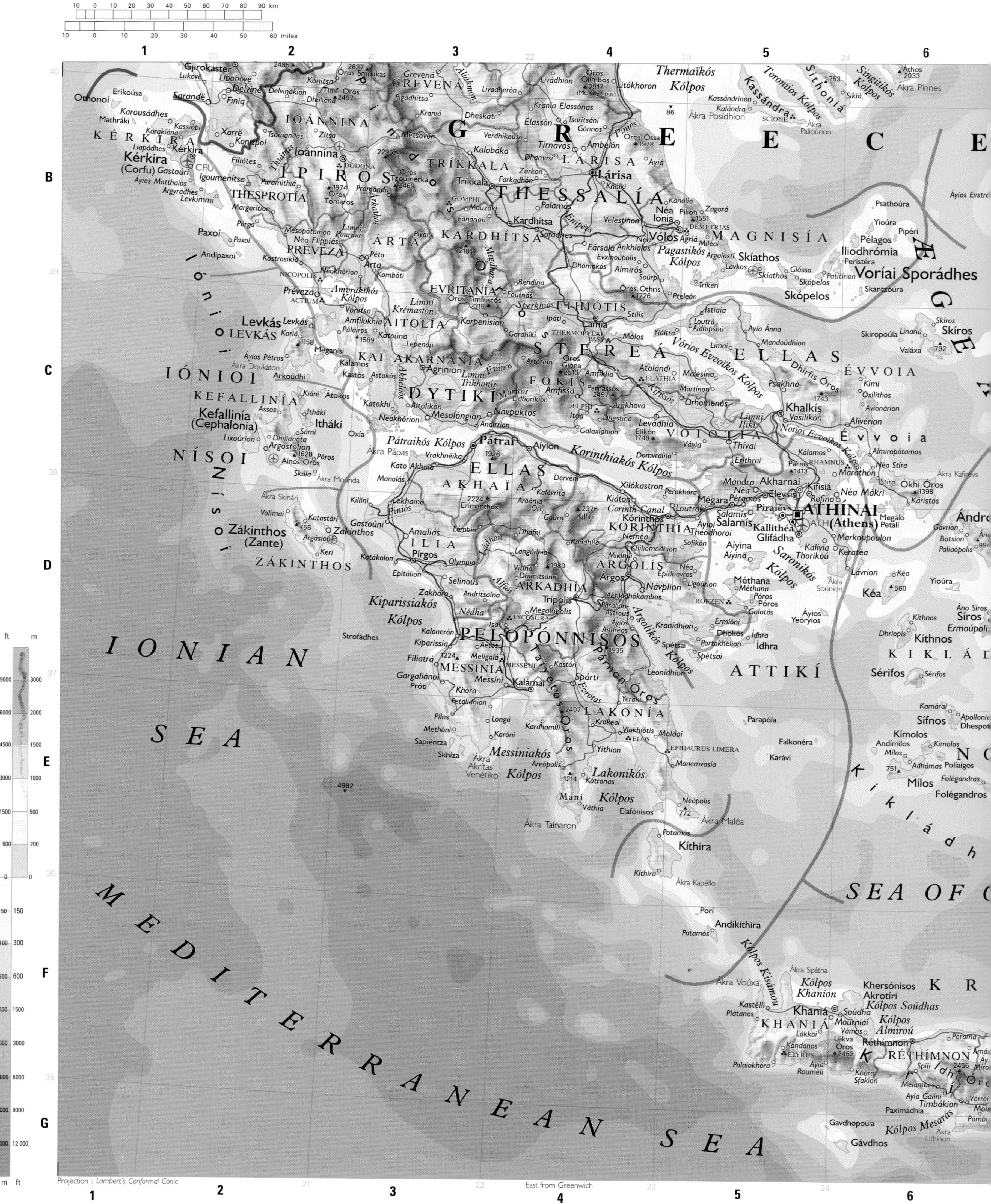
10 0 10 20 30 40 50 60 70 80 90 km
10 0 10 20 30 40 50 60 miles
IONIAN SEA
MEDITERRANEAN SEA
SEA OF
GREECE
Thermaïkós Kólpos
Kérkira (Corfu)
Ioánnina
ÍPIROS
THESPROTÍA
PRÉVEZA
ÁRTA
TRÍKKALA
THESSALÍA
KARDHÍTSA
LÁRISA
Lárisa
MAGNISÍA
Vólos
Pagastikós Kólpos
Skíathos
Skópelos
Vóriai Sporádhes
Skíros
EVRITANÍA
FTHIÓTIS
Lamía
AITOLÍA KAI AKARNANÍA
Agrinion
Levkás
LEVKÁS
IÓNIOI NÍSOI
KEFALLINÍA
Kefallinía (Cephalonia)
Itháki
Argostólion
Zákinthos (Zante)
ZÁKINTHOS
STERÉA ELLÁS
FOKÍS
DYTIKÍ ELLÁS
Mesolóngion
Návpaktos
Pátrai
Pátraïkós Kólpos
Korinthiakós Kólpos
AKHAÏA
VOIOTÍA
Thívai
Khalkís
ÉVVOIA
Évvoia
Kórinthos
KORINTHÍA
ATHÍNAI (Athens)
Piraiévs
Saronikós Kólpos
ATTIKÍ
ARGOLÍS
Návplion
Árgos
ARKADHÍA
Trípolis
ILÍA
Pírgos
PELOPÓNNISOS
MESSINÍA
Kalámai
Kiparissiakós Kólpos
Messiniakós Kólpos
LAKONÍA
Spárti
Lakonikós Kólpos
Kíthira
Andikíthira
Ídhra
Kéa
Kíthnos
Sérifos
Sífnos
Mílos
Folégandros
KIKLÁDHES
KHANIÁ
Khaniá
RÉTHIMNON
Gávdhos
Projection : Lambert's Conformal Conic
East from Greenwich

7 8 9 10 11 12
B C D E F G
TURKEY
Mysia
Lydia
Caria
Lycia
AIYAÍON
DHODHEKÁNISOS
MEDITERRANEAN SEA
Çanakkale
Gökçeada
Bozcaada
Límnos
Lésvos
Mitilini
Balıkesir
Edremit
Edremit Körfezi
Ayvalık
Bergama
Soma
Akhisar
Manisa
İZMIR (Smyrna)
Çeşme
Khíos
Psará
Kuşadası
Sámos
Ikaría
Aydın
Nazilli
Denizli
Uşak
Kütahya
Eskişehir
Afyon (Afyonkarahisar)
Isparta
Burdur
Muğla
Milas
Bodrum
Kos
Marmaris
Dalaman
Fethiye
Rhódos (Rhodes)
Sími
Tílos
Kárpathos
Kásos
Lindhos
Pátmos
Léros
Kálimnos
Astipálaia
Amorgós
Náxos
Míkonos
Thíra (Santoríni)
Iráklion
Áyios Nikólaos
Ierápetra
LASÍTHI
Stenón Kárpathos
Stenón Kásos
Gökova Körfezi
Güllük Körfezi
Büyük Menderes
Gediz
Boz Dağları
Aydın Dağları
Simav Dağları
Murat Dağı
Ak Dağ 3024
EPHESUS
MILETUS
HIERAPOLIS
APHRODISIAS
SARDIS
KAUNOS
XANTHOS
TROY
Megiste (Kastellórizon)
Kaş
Finike
Kumluca
Elmalı
Rhodes 4210

10 0 10 20 30 40 50 60 70 80 90 km
10 0 10 20 30 40 50 60 miles
CROATIA
VOJVODINA
BOSNIA-HERZEGOVINA
YUGOSLAVIA
SERBIA
MONTENEGRO
KOSOVO
MACEDONIA
ALBANIA
ITALY
ADRIATIC SEA
Strait of Otranto
BEOGRAD
Novi Sad
Sarajevo
Podgorica
Skopje
Tiranë
Durrës
Shkodër
Sofiya
Thessaloníki (Salonica)
Thermaïkós Kólpos
KENTRIKÍ MAKEDHONÍA
DYTIKÍ MAKEDHONÍA
Kérkira (Corfu)
Brindisi
Lecce
Craiova
Vidin
Niš
Priština
Ohridsko Jezero
Prespansko Jezero
Skadarsko Jezero
Projection : Lambert's Conformal Conic
East from Greenwich
Inter-entity boundaries as agreed at the 1995 Dayton Peace Agreement.

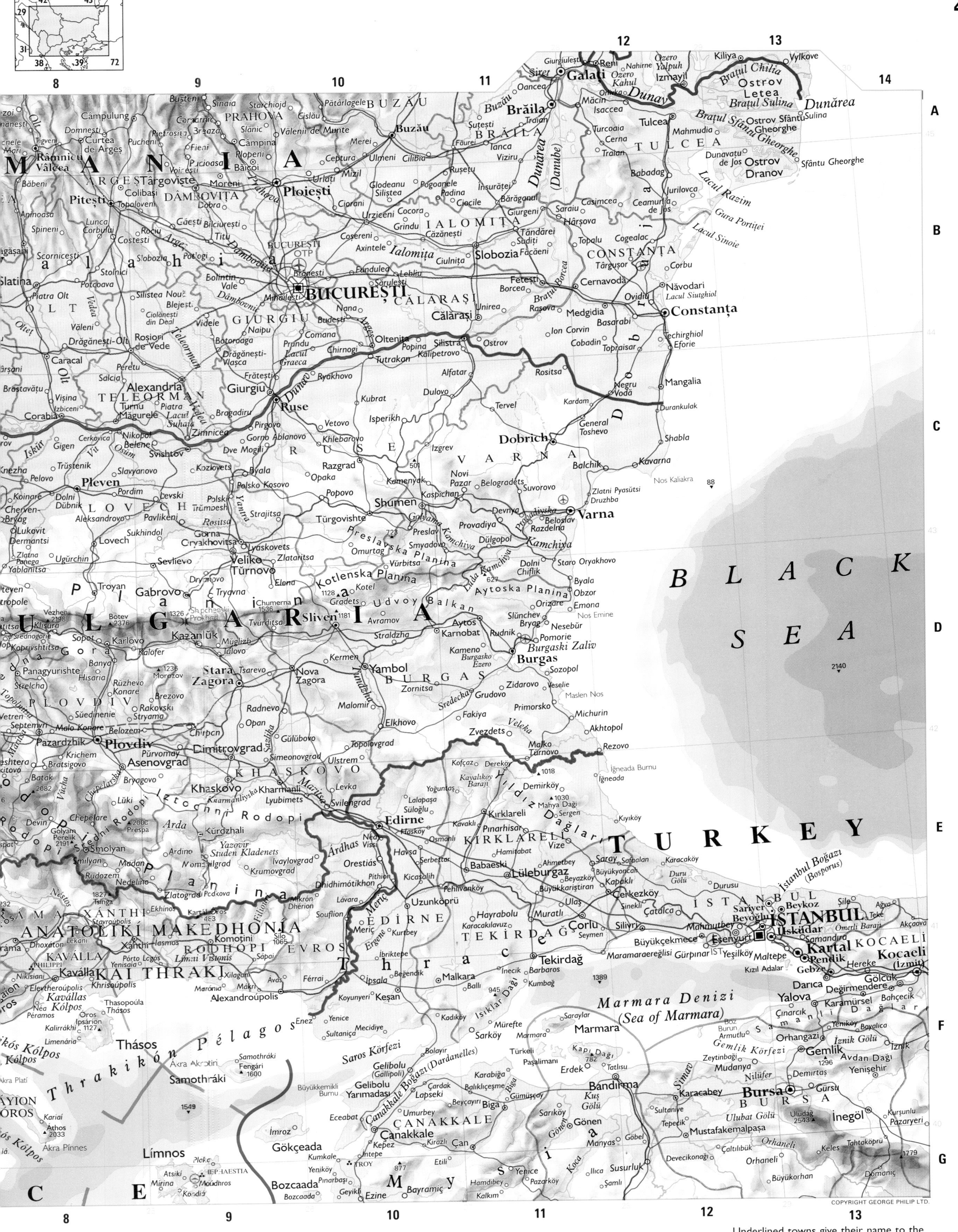

Underlined towns give their name to the administrative area in which they stand.

Administrative divisions in Croatia:
1. Brodsko-Posavska
2. Koprivničko-Križevačka
4. Međimurska
5. Osječko-Baranjska
6. Požeško-Slavonska
8. Virovitičko-Podravska
9. Vukovarsko-Srijemska

Inter-entity boundaries as agreed at the 1995 Dayton Peace Agreement.

Underlined towns give their name to the administrative area in which they stand.

POLAND AND THE SOUTHERN BALTIC 1:2 200 000

Underlined towns give their name to the administrative area in which they stand.

BALTIC STATES, BELARUS AND UKRAINE 1:4 400 000

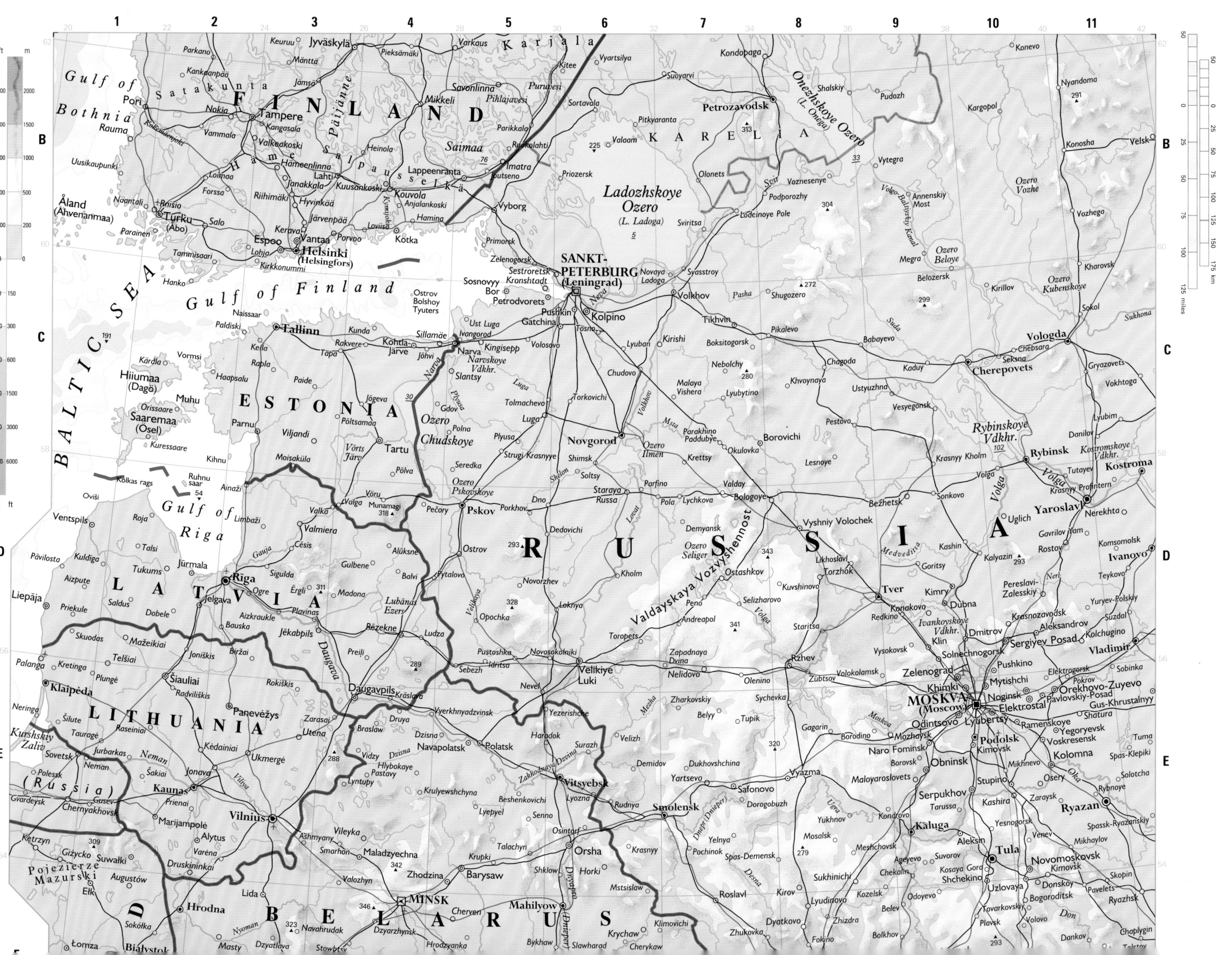

UKRAINE
MOLDOVA
ROMANIA
BULGARIA
POLAND
SLOVAK REP.
HUNGARY
BLACK SEA
Sea of Azov
CRIMEA
Krymskyy Pivostriv
Karkinitska Zatoka
Taganrogskiy Zaliv
Kerchenskiy Proliv
Arabatskaya Strelka
Pripet Marshes
Podilska Vysochyna
Transilvania
Carpații Meridionali
KYYIV (Kiev)
KHARKIV (Kharkov)
DNIPROPETROVSK
DONETSK
ODESA
ROSTOV
BUCUREȘTI (Bucharest)
Chișinău
Homyel
Voronezh
Kursk
Belgorod
Chernihiv
Zhytomyr
Lviv (Lvov)
Chernivtsi
Vinnytsya
Cherkasy
Poltava
Kremenchuk
Kirovohrad
Zaporizhzhya
Kryvyy Rih
Mykolayiv
Kherson
Mariupol
Luhansk
Simferopol
Sevastopol
Iași
Cluj-Napoca
Constanța
Dnipro
Dnister
Buh
Desna
Prut
Siret
Dunărea (Danube)
Don
Donets
Kremenchuksk Vdskh.
Kakhovske Vdskh.
Kyyivske Vdskh.
Dniprodzerzhynske Vdskh.
East from Greenwich
CARTOGRAPHY BY PHILIP'S
Projection: Conical with two standard parallels

THE VOLGA BASIN AND THE CAUCASUS 1:4 400 000

KAZAKSTAN
Ryn Peski
Caspian Depression
CASPIAN SEA
KALMYKIA
Chernyye Zemli
DAGESTAN
CHECHENIA
INGUSHETIA
NORTH OSSETIA
KABARDINO-BALKARIA
KARACHEY-CHERKESSIA
ADYGEA
ABKHAZIA
GEORGIA
ARMENIA
AZERBAIJAN
TURKEY
Caucasus Mountains
BLACK SEA
Sea of Azov
CRIMEA
Prikubanskaya Nizmennost
Kuzey Anadolu Dağları
VOLGOGRAD
Volzhskiy
Astrakhan
Volga
Elista
Stavropol
Krasnodar
ROSTOV
DONETSK
DNIPROPETROVSK
Zaporizhzhya
Mariupol
Luhansk
Taganrog
Novorossiysk
Sochi
Sokhumi
Batumi
Kutaisi
TBILISI
YEREVAN
BAKI
Sumqayıt
Gäncä
Makhachkala
Derbent
Grozny
Vladikavkaz
Nalchik
Pyatigorsk
Maykop
Kerch
Trabzon
Samsun
Rize
Elbrus 5642
Kazbek 5047
Tsimlyanskoye Vdkhr.
Taganrogskiy Zaliv
Kerchenskiy Proliv
Projection: Conical with two standard parallels
East from Greenwich
CARTOGRAPHY BY PHILIP'S.

100 0 100 200 300 400 500 600 700 800 km
100 0 100 200 300 400 500 miles
RUSSIA
1 Adygea
2 Karachey-Cherkessia
3 Kabardino-Balkaria
4 North Ossetia
5 Ingushetia
6 Chechenia
7 Dagestan
8 Mordvinia
9 Chuvashia
10 Mari El
11 Tatarstan
12 Udmurtia
13 Khakassia
AZERBAIJAN
14 Naxçıvan
GEORGIA
15 Ajaria
16 Abkhazia
UKRAINE
17 Crimea
ft m
12 000 4000
9000 3000
6000 2000
3000 1000
1200 400
600 200
0 0
200 600
2000 6000
4000 12 000
m ft
RUSSIA
KAZAKSTAN
UZBEKISTAN
TURKMENISTAN
KYRGYZSTAN
TAJIKISTAN
AFGHANISTAN
IRAN
TURKEY
FINLAND
SWEDEN
NORWAY
POLAND
BELARUS
UKRAINE
MOSKVA
SANKT-PETERBURG
Barents Sea
Kara Sea
Black Sea
Caspian Sea
Aral Sea
Gulf of Bothnia
Beloye More
Zemlya Frantsa Iosifa
Novaya Zemlya
Projection: Conical Orthomorphic with two standard parallels
East from Greenwich
D C B E F G 6 7 8 9

A
B
C
D
E
F
8
9
10
11
12
13
14
15
16
17
18
19
Mys Dezhneva (East C.)
Uelen
St. Lawrence I. (U.S.A.)
Chukchi Sea
Ostrov Vrangelya
East Siberian Sea
Ostrov Genrietty
Ostrov Zhannetty
Ostrova Delonga
Ostrov Zhokhova
Ostrov Bennetta
Novosibirskiye Ostrova
Ostrov Faddeyevskiy
Ostrov Novaya Sibir
Ostrov Malyy Lyakhovskiy
Ostrov Bolshoy Lyakhovskiy
Lyakhovskiye Ostrova
Proliv Dmitriya Lapteva
Ostrov Belkovskiy
Ostrov Kotelnyy
Ostrov Stolbovoy
Laptev Sea
OCEAN
Mys Arkticheskiy
Ostrov Shmidta
Ostrov Komsomolets
Ostrov Pioner
Ostrov Oktyabrskoy Revolyutsii
Ostrov Bolshevik
Severnaya Zemlya
Proliv Vilkitskogo
Mys Chelyuskin
Poluostrov Taymyr
Gory Byrranga
Oz. Taymyr
Ostrov Bolshoy Begichev
Mys Buorkhaya
3800
965
374
1146
Providenjya
Anadyrskiy Zaliv
Beringovskiy
Vankarem
Egvekinot
Chukotskoye Nagorye
Pevek
Ust Chaun
Anadyr
Koryakskoye Nagorye
Khatyrka
Bering Sea
Ostrova Medvezhi
Ostrov Ayon
Ambarchik
Cherskiy
Bilibino
Bolshoy Anyuy
Yeropol
Markovo
Penzhino
Kamenskoye
Tilichiki
Korf
Nizhne Kolymsk
Omolon
Kolymskoye Nagorye
Srednekolymsk
Chokurdakh
Indigirka
Kazachye
Ust Kuyga
Tiksi
Ust Olenek
Tit-Ary
Bulun
Kyusyur
Saskylakh
Novorybnoye
Khatanga
Nordvik
Volochanka
Kheta
Zhilinda
Norilsk
Gory Putorana
Olenek
Yessey
Zhigansk
Arctic Circle
Verkhoyanskiy Khrebet
Verkhoyansk
Batagai
Deputatskiy
Druzhina
Khonuu
Zyryanka
Pobeda 3147
Kolyma
Gora Chen 2682
Ust-Nera
Khrebet Cherskogo
Oymyakon
Susuman
Yagodnoye
Omsukchan
Orotukan
Evensk
Paren
Gizhiga
Penzhinskaya Guba
Gizhiginskaya Guba
Zaliv Shelikhova
Palana
Tigil
Sredinnyy Khrebet
Poluostrov Kamchatka
Klyuchevskaya
Ust-Kamchatsk
Komandorskiye Ostrova
Nikolskoye
Petropavlovsk-Kamchatskiy
Ust Khayryuzovo
Ust-Bolsheretsk
Severo-Kurilsk
Ostrov Paramushir
Ostrov Onekotan
Ostrov Simushir
Ostrov Urup
Ostrov Iturup
Kurilsk
Ostrov Kunashir
Kurilskiye Ostrova
Magadan
Palatka
Atka
Ust-Omchug
Kystatyam
Sangar
Lena
Batamay
Borogontsy
Khandyga
Okhotskiy Perevoz
Ytyk-Kyuyel
Yakutsk
Mayya
Amga
Aldan
Ust Maya
Okhotsk
Ulya
Arka
Sea of Okhotsk
Vilyuy
Vilyuysk
Verkhnevilyuysk
Namtsy
Nyurba
Pokrovsk
Suntar
Mirnyy
Sinsk
Chernyshevskiy
Noginsk
Nizhnyaya Tunguska
Tura
Yukta
Ust-Mil
Aim
Nelkan
Khrebet Dzhugdzhur
Ayan
Ostrov Bolshoy Shantar
Sakhalinskiy Zaliv
Okha
Sakhalin
Aleksandrovsk-Sakhalinskiy
Gora Lopatina
Poronaysk
Uglegorsk
Yuzhno-Sakhalinsk
Kholmsk
Korsakov
Vanino
Nikolayevsk-na-Amure
Chagda
Uchur
Olekminsk
Lensk
Tommot
Aldan
Yerbogachen
Kuyumba
Mutoray
Podkamennaya Tunguska
Vanavara
Severo-Yeniseyskiy
RUSSIA
Vitim
Yenyuka
Olekma
Neryungri
Stanovoy Khrebet
Chumikan
Tugur
Uda
Amgun
Khrebet Sikhote Alin
Kezhma
Korshunovo
Mama
Bodaybo
Chara
Nagornyy
Tynda
Zeya
Yeniseysk
Angara
Boguchany
Ust-Ilimsk
Kirensk
Strelka
Kondratyevo
Makarovo
Ust-Kut
Zheleznogorsk-Ilimskiy
Magistralnyy
Karalon
Ust-Nyukzha
Kalakan
Skovorodino
Dzhalinda
Ushumun
Norsk
Komsomolsk
Amursk
Kansk
Ilanskiy
Tayshet
Bratsk
Nizhneangarsk
Bagdarin
Yablonovyy Khrebet
Mogocha
Amur
Gulian
Shimanovsk
Svobodnyy
Belogorsk
Zavitinsk
Chegdomyn
Obluchye
Birobidzhan
Smidovich
Khabarovsk
Krasnoyarsk
Artemovsk
Nizhneudinsk
Tulun
Zima
Vostochnyy Sayan
Minusinsk
Abakan
Cheremkhovo
Usolye Sibirskoye
Angarsk
Irkutsk
Ulan Ude
Barguzin
Chita
Shilka
Nerchinsk
Sretensk
Bukachacha
Blagoveshchensk
Poyarkovo
Bikin
Vyazemskiy
Hegang
Jiamusi
Kyzyl
Turan
Toora-Khem
Munku-Sardyk 3491
Slyudyanka
Gusinoozersk
Kyakhta
Aginskoye
Olovyannaya
Petrovsk-Zabaykalskiy
Khilok
Borzya
Zabaykalsk
Manzhouli
Hailar
Hulun Nur
Nenjiang
QIQIHAR
Da Hinggan Ling
Hövsgöl Nuur
Hatgal
Uvs Nuur
Samagaltay
Zakamensk
Darhan
Khapcheranga
Hentiyn Nuruu
Onon
Choybalsan
Tamsagbulag
HARBIN
Dongbei
Mudanjiang
Dalnerechensk
Lesozavodsk
Spassk Dalniy
Ussuriysk
Vladivostok
Nakhodka
Artem
Olga
Terney
Amgu
Dalnegorsk
Hokkaidō
SAPPORO
Otaru
Rumoi
Obihiro
Abashiri
Kushiro
Wakkanai
Hakodate
Aomori
Hachinohe
Akita
Honshū
Niigata
Hangayn Nuruu
Hyargas Nuur
Uliastay
Tsetserleg
Ulaanbaatar
Lun
Öndörhaan
MONGOLIA
Altay
Saynshand
Xilinhot
Linxi
Chifeng
Tao'an
Nen Jiang
Ang'angxi
CHANGCHUN
Siping
JILIN
Yanji
Kraskino
Chongjin
FUSHUN
Tonghua
SHENYANG
ANSHAN
NORTH KOREA
Dandong
Wonsan
Kansong
Sea of Japan
Gobi
CHINA
Erenhot
Dalandzadgad
Hami
Gaxun Nur
Baotou
Hohhot
Zhangjiakou
Chengde
Yingkou
BEIJING
PYONGYANG
Nampo
DALIAN
SOUL
INCH'ON
SOUTH KOREA
TAEJON
TAEGU
PUSAN
JAPAN
Kanazawa
Fuji-San 3776
OSAKA
2999
2840
2800
3967
4266
1949
2744
2646
2078
3669
1054
2246
2389
2959
1853
1843
1852
1752
4750
3621
3456
1701
932
1104
1609
1780
2290
1620
1456

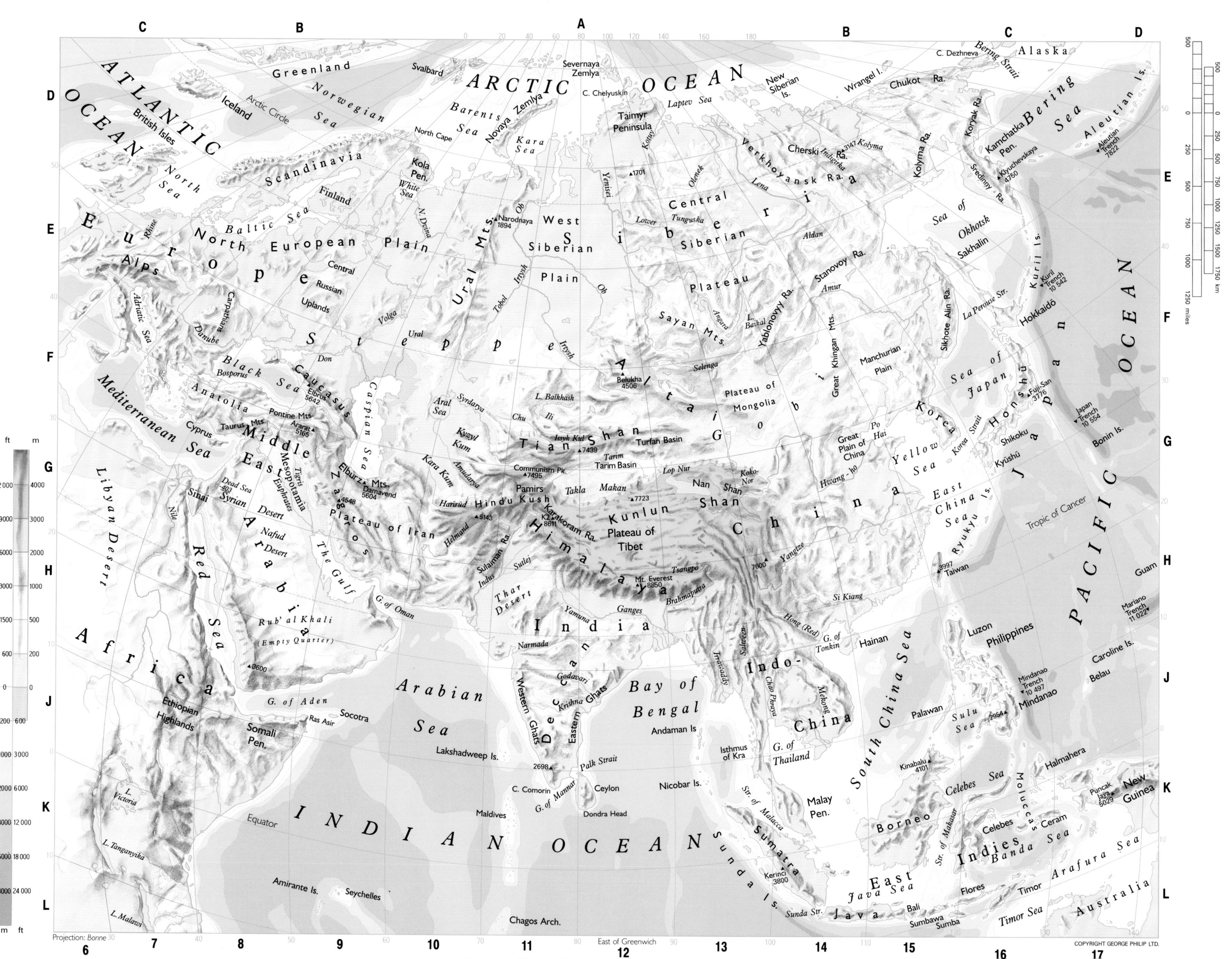

ARCTIC OCEAN
PACIFIC OCEAN
INDIAN OCEAN
ATLANTIC OCEAN
Greenland
Svalbard
Severnaya Zemlya
C. Chelyuskin
New Siberian Is.
Wrangel I.
Chukot Ra.
C. Dezhneva
Bering Strait
Alaska
Bering Sea
Aleutian Is.
Aleutian Trench 7822
Iceland
Arctic Circle
Norwegian Sea
Barents Sea
Novaya Zemlya
Kara Sea
North Cape
Laptev Sea
Taimyr Peninsula
British Isles
North Sea
Scandinavia
Kola Pen.
White Sea
Finland
Baltic Sea
Europe
North European Plain
Central Russian Uplands
Alps
Carpathians
Adriatic Sea
Danube
Black Sea
Bosporus
Caucasus
Elbrus 5642
Anatolia
Pontine Mts.
Taurus Mts.
Ararat 5165
Cyprus
Mediterranean Sea
Middle East
Mesopotamia
Tigris
Euphrates
Dead Sea 403
Sinai
Syrian Desert
Nafud Desert
Arabia
Rub' al Khali (Empty Quarter)
Libyan Desert
Nile
Red Sea
Africa
Ethiopian Highlands
Somali Pen.
G. of Aden
Ras Asir
Socotra
L. Victoria
L. Tanganyika
L. Malawi
Amirante Is.
Seychelles
Chagos Arch.
Maldives
Equator
Steppe
Don
Volga
Ural
Ural Mts.
Narodnaya 1894
N. Dvina
Caspian Sea
Elburz Mts.
Damavend 5604
Zagros
4548
Plateau of Iran
The Gulf
G. of Oman
Aral Sea
Syrdarya
Amudarya
Kyzyl Kum
Kara Kum
Harirud
Helmand
Hindu Kush
5143
Pamirs
Communism Pk. 7495
Tian Shan
Issyk Kul
7439
L. Balkhash
Chu
Ili
Karakoram Ra.
K2 8611
Sulaiman Ra.
Indus
Sutlej
Thar Desert
Himalaya
Mt. Everest 8850
Tsangpo
Brahmaputra
Yamuna
Ganges
India
Narmada
Godavari
Krishna
Deccan
Western Ghats
Eastern Ghats
2698
C. Comorin
G. of Mannar
Palk Strait
Ceylon
Dondra Head
Arabian Sea
Lakshadweep Is.
Bay of Bengal
Andaman Is.
Nicobar Is.
West Siberian Plain
Siberia
Ob
Irtysh
Tobol
Yenisei
Kotuy
1701
Lower Tunguska
Olenek
Central Siberian Plateau
Lena
Aldan
Verkhoyansk Ra.
Cherski Ra.
Indigirka
3147
Kolyma
Kolyma Ra.
Koryak Ra.
Kamchatka Pen.
Sredinny Ra.
Klyuchevskaya 4750
Sea of Okhotsk
Sakhalin
Kuril Is.
Kuril Trench 10 542
La Perouse Str.
Hokkaido
Sikhote Alin Ra.
Stanovoy Ra.
Amur
Yablonovyy Ra.
L. Baikal
Angara
Sayan Mts.
Selenga
Altai
Belukha 4506
Plateau of Mongolia
Gobi
Great Khingan Mts.
Manchurian Plain
Turfan Basin
Tarim
Tarim Basin
Lop Nur
Takla Makan
7723
Kunlun Shan
Plateau of Tibet
Nan Shan
Koko Nor
China
Great Plain of China
Po Hai
Hwang-ho
Yangtze
7600
Si Kiang
Korea
Yellow Sea
Korea Strait
Sea of Japan
Japan
Honshu
Fuji-San 3776
Shikoku
Kyushu
Japan Trench 10 554
Bonin Is.
East China Sea
Ryukyu Is.
Tropic of Cancer
Taiwan
3997
Guam
Mariano Trench 11 022
Hong (Red)
G. of Tonkin
Hainan
Irrawaddy
Salween
Chao Phraya
Mekong
Indo-China
G. of Thailand
Isthmus of Kra
Malay Pen.
Str. of Malacca
Sumatra
Kerinci 3800
Sunda Is.
Sunda Str.
Java
Java Sea
East Indies
Bali
Sumbawa
Sumba
Flores
Timor
Timor Sea
Arafura Sea
Australia
South China Sea
Luzon
Philippines
Palawan
Sulu Sea
2954
Mindanao
Mindanao Trench 10 497
Caroline Is.
Belau
Borneo
Kinabalu 4101
Celebes Sea
Str. of Makasar
Celebes
Moluccas
Ceram
Banda Sea
Halmahera
Puncak Jaya 5029
New Guinea
Projection: Bonne
East of Greenwich
COPYRIGHT GEORGE PHILIP LTD.

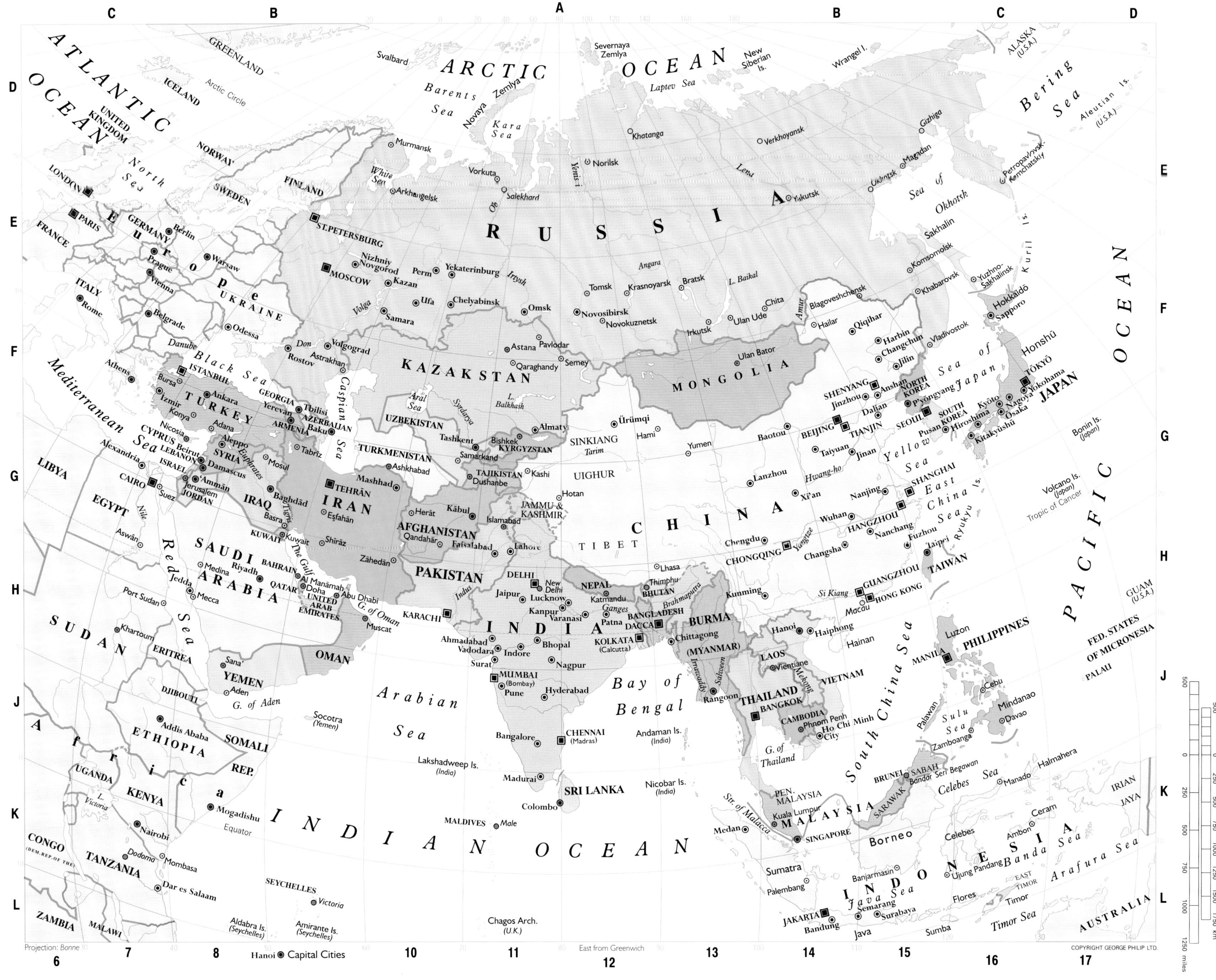

500 0 250 500 750 1000 1250 1500 1750 km
500 0 250 500 750 1000 1250 miles
ARCTIC OCEAN
PACIFIC OCEAN
INDIAN OCEAN
ATLANTIC OCEAN
Barents Sea
Kara Sea
Laptev Sea
Bering Sea
Sea of Okhotsk
Sea of Japan
East China Sea
Yellow Sea
South China Sea
Sulu Sea
Celebes Sea
Banda Sea
Arafura Sea
Timor Sea
Java Sea
Bay of Bengal
Arabian Sea
Red Sea
Mediterranean Sea
Black Sea
Caspian Sea
North Sea
RUSSIA
KAZAKSTAN
MONGOLIA
CHINA
JAPAN
NORTH KOREA
SOUTH KOREA
TAIWAN
PHILIPPINES
VIETNAM
LAOS
CAMBODIA
THAILAND
BURMA (MYANMAR)
MALAYSIA
SINGAPORE
BRUNEI
INDONESIA
INDIA
PAKISTAN
AFGHANISTAN
IRAN
IRAQ
SAUDI ARABIA
OMAN
YEMEN
TURKEY
SYRIA
JORDAN
ISRAEL
LEBANON
CYPRUS
GEORGIA
ARMENIA
AZERBAIJAN
TURKMENISTAN
UZBEKISTAN
TAJIKISTAN
KYRGYZSTAN
NEPAL
BHUTAN
BANGLADESH
SRI LANKA
MALDIVES
KUWAIT
BAHRAIN
QATAR
UNITED ARAB EMIRATES
EGYPT
SUDAN
ETHIOPIA
ERITREA
DJIBOUTI
SOMALI REP.
KENYA
TANZANIA
UGANDA
LIBYA
Europe
Africa
MOSCOW
ST. PETERSBURG
TOKYO
BEIJING
SEOUL
MANILA
BANGKOK
JAKARTA
DELHI
KOLKATA (Calcutta)
MUMBAI (Bombay)
CHENNAI (Madras)
KARACHI
TEHRĀN
CAIRO
ISTANBUL
SHANGHAI
HONG KONG
Tropic of Cancer
Equator
Arctic Circle
East from Greenwich
Projection: Bonne
COPYRIGHT GEORGE PHILIP LTD.
Hanoi ● Capital Cities

JAPAN 1:4 400 000

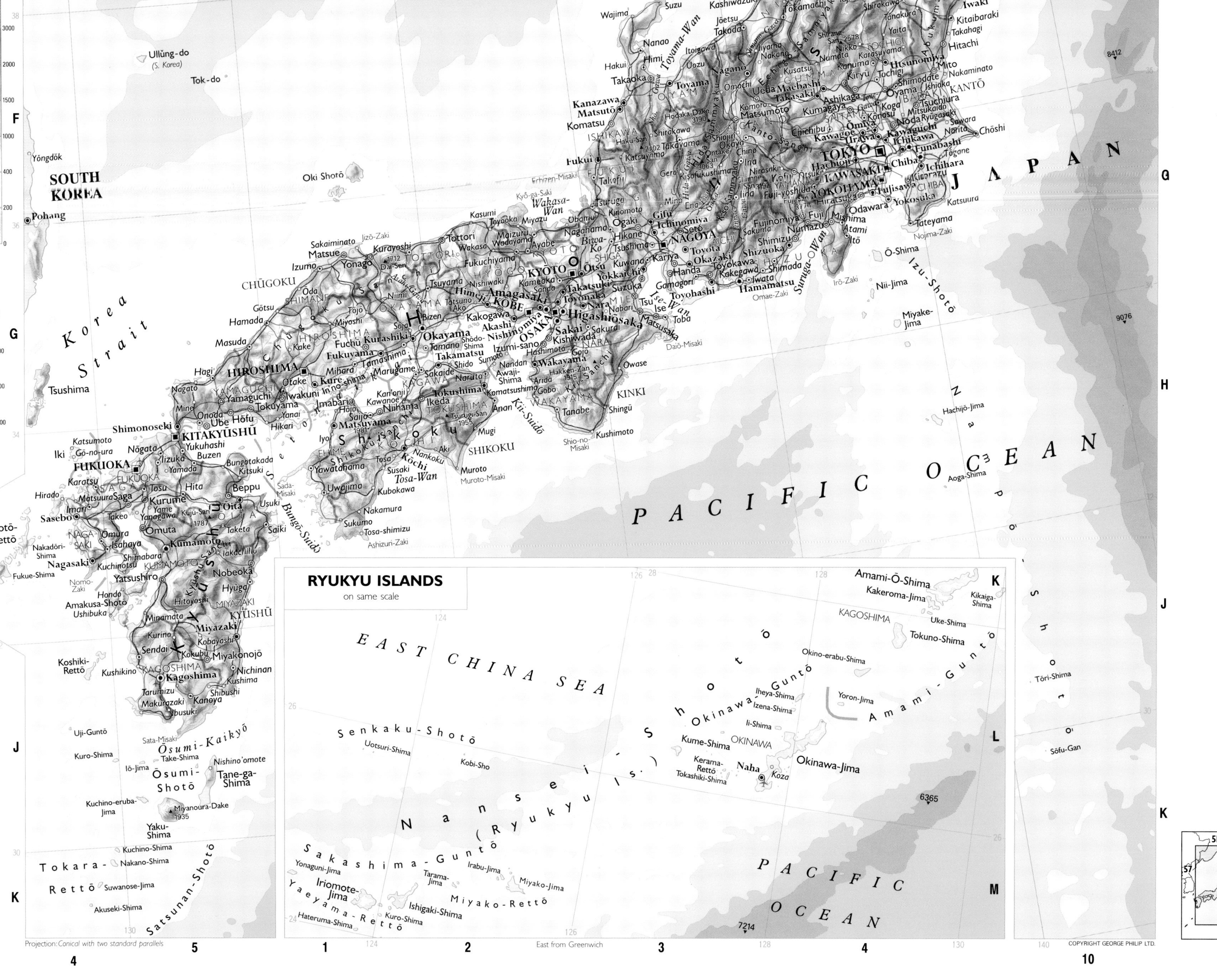

JAPAN
PACIFIC OCEAN
SOUTH KOREA
Korea Strait
Tsushima
Oki Shotō
TŌKYŌ
KYŌTO
ŌSAKA
NAGOYA
HIROSHIMA
FUKUOKA
KITAKYŪSHŪ
Shikoku
Kyūshū
Izu-Shotō
Nanpō-Shotō
RYUKYU ISLANDS
on same scale
EAST CHINA SEA
Senkaku-Shotō
Nansei-Shotō (Ryukyu Is.)
Okinawa-Guntō
Amami-Guntō
Sakashima-Guntō
Okinawa-Jima
Naha
PACIFIC OCEAN
Projection: Conical with two standard parallels
East from Greenwich
COPYRIGHT GEORGE PHILIP LTD.

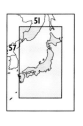

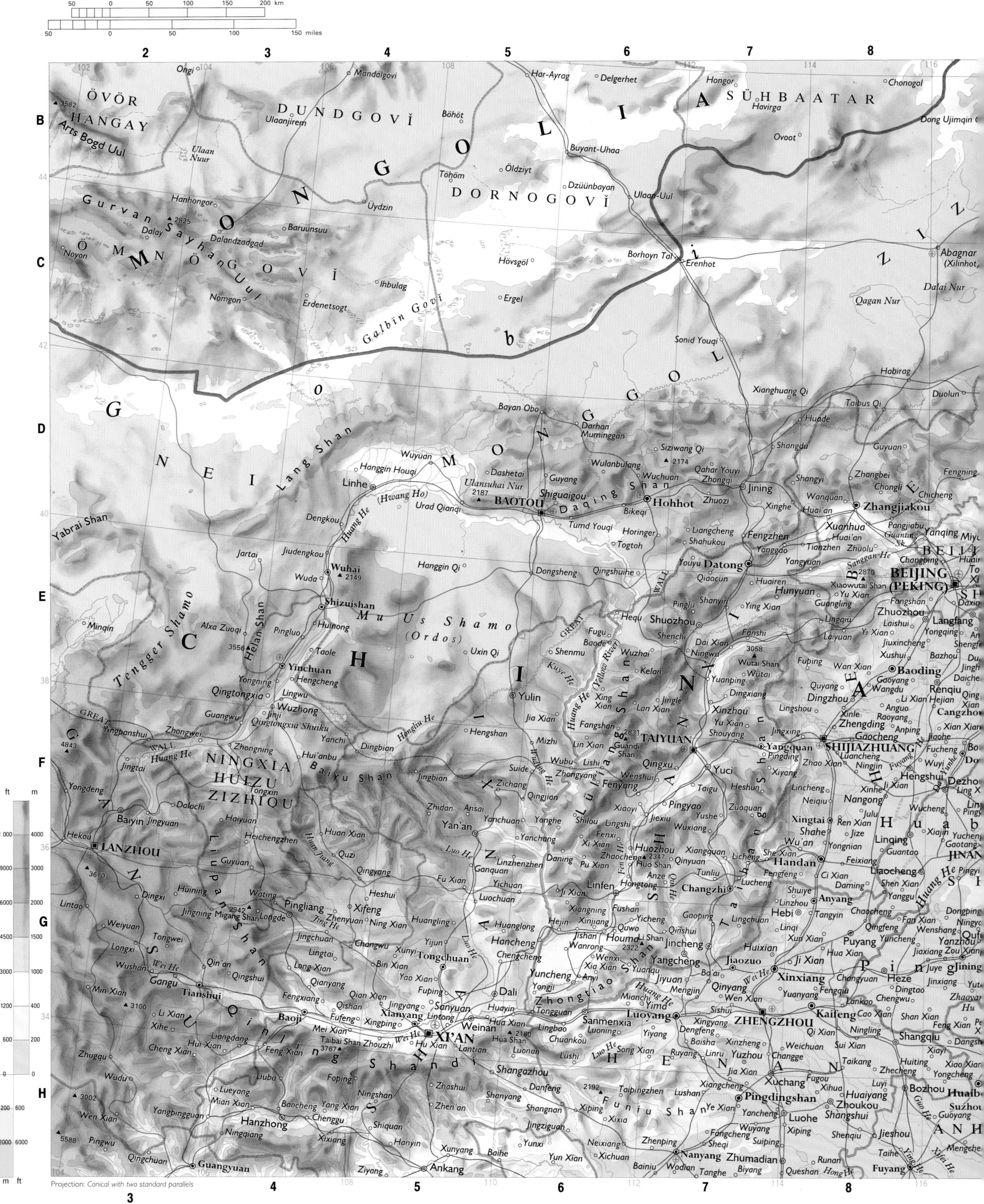

50 0 50 100 150 200 km
50 0 50 100 150 miles
ÖVÖR HANGAY
Arts Bogd Uul
DUNDGOVĬ
Mandalgovi
Ulaanjirem
Böhöt
Har-Ayrag
Delgerhet
Hongor
SÜHBAATAR
Havirga
Chonogol
Dong Ujimqin Qi
Ovoot
Ulaan Nuur
Buyant-Uhaa
Tõhöm
Öldziyt
Dzüünbayan
DORNOGOVĬ
Ulaan-Uul
Gurvan Sayhan Uul
Hanhongor
Dalay
Dalandzadgad
Baruunsuu
Üydzin
ÖMNÖGOVĬ
Noyon
Nomgon
Erdenetsogt
Ihbulag
Galbin Govi
Hövsgöl
Ergel
Borhoyn Tal
Erenhot
Abagnar Qi (Xilinhot)
Dalai Nur
Qagan Nur
Sonid Youqi
Habirag
Duolun
Xianghuang Qi
Taibus Qi
Huade
Bayan Obo
Darhan Muminggan
Siziwang Qi
Shangdu
Guyuan
NEI MONGGOL
Lang Shan
Wuyuan
Hanggin Houqi
Dashetai
Ulansuhai Nur
Linhe
Wulanbulang
Guyang
Wuchuan
Qahar Youyi Zhongqi
Jining
Shangyi
Zhangbei
Chongli
Fengning
Chicheng
Huang He (Hwang Ho)
Urad Qianqi
BAOTOU
Shiguaigou
Daqing Shan
Hohhot
Zhuozi
Xinghe
Wanquan
Zhangjiakou
Huai'an
Xuanhua
Dengkou
Tumd Youqi
Bikeqi
Horinger
Togtoh
Liangcheng
Shahukou
Fengzhen
Yanggao
Tianzhen
Yangyuan
Huailai
Yanqing
Yabrai Shan
Jartai
Jiudengkou
Wuhai
Hanggin Qi
Dongsheng
Qingshuihe
Youyu
Datong
Qiaocun
Huairen
Hunyuan
Xiaowutai Shan
Yu Xian
Guangling
BEIJING (PEKING)
Wuda
Shizuishan
Mu Us Shamo (Ordos)
Hequ
Pinglu
Shanyin
Ying Xian
Fangshan
Zhuozhou
Langfang
Minqin
Tengger Shamo
Alxa Zuoqi
Helan Shan
Huinong
Pingluo
Shuozhou
Shenchi
Fanshi
Lingqiu
Laiyuan
Yi Xian
Yongqing
Taole
Fugu
Baode
Shenmu
Wuzhai
Kelan
Dai Xian
Ningwu
Wutai Shan
Wutai
Fuping
Wan Xian
Baoding
Xushui
Uxin Qi
Yinchuan
Hengcheng
Yongning
Lingwu
Yulin
Yuanping
Dingxiang
Quyang
Dingzhou
Renqiu
Qingtongxia
Wuzhong
Guangwu
Jia Xian
Fangshan
Xinzhou
Lingshou
Jinji
Qingtongxia Shuiku
Yangpanshui
Zhongwei
Yanchi
Honqliu He
Hengshan
Mizhi
TAIYUAN
Shouyang
Jingxing
Yangquan
SHIJIAZHUANG
Zhengding
Gaocheng
Zhongning
Hui'anbu
Dingbian
Lin Xian
Pingding
Luancheng
Jingtai
NINGXIA HUIZU ZIZHIQU
Baiyu Shan
Jingbian
Suide
Wubu
Lishi
Qingxu
Yuci
Xiyang
Zhao Xian
Ningjin
Hengshui
Yongdeng
Tongxin
Zichang
Zhongyang
Fenyang
Wenshui
Taigu
Heshun
Xinhe
Ji Xian
Dalochi
Qingjian
Pingyao
Lincheng
Nangong
Zhidan
Ansai
Yan'an
Xiaoyi
Jiexiu
Yushe
Zuoquan
Neiqiu
Baiyin
Jingyuan
Haiyuan
Yanchuan
Yanghe
Shilou
Lingshi
Wuxiang
Xingtai
Ren Xian
Hekou
LANZHOU
Heichengzhen
Huan Xian
Yanchang
Fenxi
Xi Xian
Huozhou
Shahe
Jize
Linqing
Yongnian
Wu'an
Quzi
Luo He
Linzhenzhen
Daning
Zhaocheng
Huo Shan
Qinyuan
Xiangyuan
Licheng
She Xian
Handan
Feixiang
Guantao
Guyuan
Qingyang
Ganquan
Pu Xian
Anze
Tunliu
Fengfeng
Ci Xian
Liaocheng
JINAN
Liupan Shan
Fu Xian
Yichuan
Linfen
Hongtong
Changzhi
Lucheng
Daming
Shen Xian
Huining
Dingxi
Heshui
Luochuan
Ji Xian
Shuiye
Anyang
Yanggu
Lintao
Wating
Pingliang
Xifeng
Xiangning
Fushan
Linzhou
Jingning
Migang Shan
Longde
Zhenyuan
Ning Xian
Huangling
Hejin
Xinjiang
Quwo
Yicheng
Qinshui
Gaoping
Lingchuan
Hebi
Tangyin
Qingfeng
Weiyuan
Tongwei
Jingchuan
Changwu
Huanglong
Hancheng
Houma
Jincheng
Huixian
Puyang
Longxi
Lingtai
Yijun
Xunyi
Tongchuan
Chengcheng
Jishan
Wanrong
Yangcheng
Jiaozuo
Ji Xian
Hua Xian
Wushan
Wei He
Gangu
Qin'an
Qingshui
Bin Xian
Long Xian
Yao Xian
Wenxi
Xia Xian
Yuanqu
Jiyuan
Xinxiang
Changyuan
Heze
Min Xian
Tianshui
Fengxiang
Qianyang
Qian Xian
Fuping
Dali
Yuncheng
Yongji
Zhongtiao Shan
Mianchi
Mengjin
Qinyang
Bo'ai
Fengqiu
Dingtao
Li Xian
Qishan
Jingyang
Sanyuan
Huayin
Tongguan
Yima
Sishui
Wen Xian
Yuanyang
Lankao
Kaifeng
Chengwu
Xihe
Baoji
Fufeng
Xingping
Xianyang
Lintong
Weinan
Hua Xian
Lingbao
Sanmenxia
Luoyang
Xingyang
ZHENGZHOU
Cao Xian
Shan Xian
Liangdang
Mei Xian
Taibai Shan
Zhouzhi
Hu Xian
XI'AN
Hua Shan
Luoning
Yiyang
Dengfeng
Qi Xian
Ningling
Shangqiu
Cheng Xian
Hui Xian
Feng Xian
Qinling Shandi
Lantian
Luonan
Chuankou
Song Xian
Baisha
Xinzheng
Sui Xian
Zhugqu
Lushi
Ruyang
Linru
Yuzhou
Weichuan
Changge
Wudu
Liuba
Foping
Shangzhou
Jia Xian
Xuchang
Taikang
Zhecheng
Huiting
Lueyang
Zhashui
Danfeng
Taipingzhen
Lushan
Xiangcheng
Fugou
Xihua
Luyi
Bozhou
Mian Xian
Ningshan
Shanyang
Funiu Shan
Pingdingshan
Huaiyang
Wen Xian
Yangpingguan
Baocheng
Yang Xian
Zhen'an
Shangnan
Xiping
Ye Xian
Yancheng
Zhoukou
Hanzhong
Chenggu
Shiquan
Jingziguan
Xixia
Luohe
Shangshui
Ningqiang
Xixiang
Hanyin
Yunxi
Neixiang
Zhenping
Fangcheng
Wuyang
Xiping
Shenqiu
Jieshou
Pingwu
Qingchuan
Xunyang
Baihe
Yun Xian
Xichuan
Sheqi
Suiping
Guangyuan
Ziyang
Ankang
Bainiu
Wodian
Nanyang
Zhumadian
Runan
Tanghe
Biyang
Queshan
Fuyang
Projection: Conical with two standard parallels

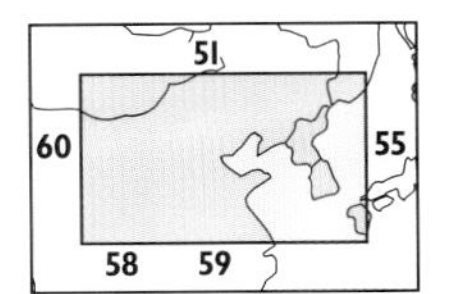

9 10 11 12 13 14 15 16

B C D E F G H

HEILONGJIANG
HARBIN
Horqin Youyi Qianqi (Ulanhot)
Zhenlai
Baicheng
Da'an
Maoxing
Zhaoyuan
Shuangcheng
Acheng
Bin Xian
Yanshou
Linkou
Jixi
Turiy Rog
Ozero Khanka
Shangzhi
Lalin
Yimianpo
Hulingol
Tuquan
Taonan
Anguang
Qagan Nur
Qian Gorlos
Changchunling
Fuyu
Sanchahe
Wuchang
Zhangguangcai Ling
Hengdaohezi
Mudanjiang
Muling
Maqiaohe
Xiachengzi
Pogranichnyy
Qian'an
Beitaolaizhao
Yushu
Shanhetun
Hailin
Ning'an
Suiyang
Suifenhe
Golenki
Tongyu
Shenjingzi
Kaoshan
Nong'an
Dehui
Shulan
Dongning
RUSSIA
Ussuriysk
Jarud Qi
Zhanyu
Beizhengzhen
Fulongquan
Jiutai
Gangyao
Wulajie
Jingpo Hu
Dongjingcheng
Luozigou
Razdolnoye
Artem
Changling
Horqin Zuoyi Zhongqi
Maolin
CHANGCHUN
Huaidezhen
JILIN
Jiaohe
Xinzhan
Emu
Huangsongdian
Chunyang
Tavrichanka
Vladivostok
Xinkai He
Bairin Zuoqi
Kailu
Tongliao
Fanjiatun
Shuangyang
Songhua Hu
Dunhua
Daxinggou
Wangqing
Shixian
Linxi
Bairin Youqi
Xiliao He
Shuangliao
Dongliao He
Gongzhuling
Yitong
Mingyuegue
Yanji
Tumen
Hunchun
Slavyanka
Lishu
Siping
Liaoyuan
Panshi
Huadian
Longjing
Helong
Namyang
Kraskino
Posyet
Xar Moron He
Jargalang
Bamiancheng
Xifeng
Dongfeng
Huifa He
Erdao Jiang
Antu
Hoeamdong
Sŏsura
Najin
Ongniud Qi
Laoha He
Wutonghaolai
Kangping
Zhangwu
Kaiyuan
Meihekou
Huinan
Baishan
Baihe
Hoeryong
Unggi
Musan
Pugodong
Hure Qi
Xiawa
Faku
Tiefa
Shanchengzhen
Liuhe
Jingyu
Fusong
Changbai Shan
Puryong
Chifeng
Fuxin
Liu He
Zhangwu
Liao He
Tieling
Qingyuan
Hunjiang
Linjiang
Paektu-san 2744
Pupyongdong
Nanam
Chŏngjin
Kyŏngsŏng
Chuuronjang
Heishui
Xinlitun
Xinmin
Chunggang-ŭp
Hachon
Irhyangdong
Ondaejin
Weichang
Ningcheng
Beipiao
Qinghemen
SHENYANG
FUSHUN
Xinbin
Tonghua
Dongbei
Changbai
Hyesan
Hapsu
Simpungdong
Kilchu
Musudan
Chaoyang
Daling He
Yi Xian
Beizhen
Heishan
Liaozhong
Goubangzi
Liaoyang
Benxi
Qinghecheng
Huanren
Inpundong
Huch'ang
Kasan-dong
Kapsan
Pujon-chŏsuji
P'ungsan
Kosongni
Kimch'aek (Songjin)
Lingyuan
LIAONING
Jinzhou
Panjin
ANSHAN
Anping
Tianshifu
Ji'an
Manp'o
Kanggye
Ch'ail-bong 2522
Chengde
Pingquan
Jinxi
Niuzhuang
Haicheng
Lianshanguan
Kuandian
Supung Shuiku
Yalu Jiang
Kuŭp-tong
Ch'osan
Pyŏktong
Changjin-chŏsuji
Kwangdaeri
Changhŭngni
Tanch'ŏn
Luanne
Luanping
Liugou
Shangbancheng
Kuancheng
Jianchang
Tianzhuangtai
Huludao
Yingkou
Dashiqiao
Fengcheng
Koin-dong
Sinhung
Pukch'ŏng
Sinp'o
Sinch'ang
Sŏhori
Xinglong
Xingcheng
Liaodong Wan
Gaizhou
Xiuyan
Cao He
Sakchu
Taegwan
NORTH KOREA
Hongwon
Shuangshanzi
Suizhong
Xiongyuecheng
Wanfu
Buyun Shan 1131
Dandong
Sinŭiju
Uiju
Pukchin
Hamhung
Hŭngnam
Tongchŏn-ni
SEA OF JAPAN
Jianchangying
Zunhua
Gushan
Donggou
Yongamp'o
Kusŏng
Kujang
Tŏkch'ŏn
Yŏnghŭng
Tongjosŏn Man
Yutian
Fengrun
Lulong
Funing
Qinhuangdao
Luan Xian
Changli
Wafangdian
Liaodong Bandao
Zhuanghe
Sŏnch'ŏn
Chŏngju
Pakch'ŏn
Anju
Sunch'on
Kowŏn
Munch'ŏn
Wŏnsan
TANGSHAN
TIANJIN SHI
Baodi
Leting
Pulandian
Pikou
Sukch'ŏn
Sinchang-ni
Songch'ŏn
Kangdong
Tongyang
Anbyŏn
Kojŏ
Wuqing
Hangu
TIANJIN
Jin Xian
P'YŎNGYANG
Sunan
Chunghwa
Koksan
Singosan
Hoeyang 1638
Kosŏng
Tanggu
Dagu
Lüshun
DALIAN
Korea Bay
Namp'o
Songnim
Suan
Sepo-ri
Chiha-ri
Pyŏnggang
Kansŏng
Sokch'o
Yangyang
Bo Hai
Cho-do
Sariwŏn
Chaeryŏng
Sinmak
Nam-ch'on
Ch'ŏrwon
Kumhwa
Hwach'ŏn-chŏsuji 1578
Chumunjin
Oikou
Changyŏn
Sinch'ŏn
Kŭmch'on
Haeju
Kaesŏng
Panmunjŏm
Ch'unch'ŏn
Kangnŭng
Huanghua
Miaodao Qundao
Ongjin
Yŏnan
Munsan
Uijŏngbu
Hongch'ŏn
Samch'ŏk
Ullŭng-do
Paengnyŏng-do
Kanghwa
Puch'on
SOUL
Songnam
Hoengsŏng
Chŏngsŏn
Yanshan
Penglai
Longkou
INCH'ŎN
Anyang
Wŏnju
Yŏngwol
Qingyun
Wudi
Zhanhua
Huang He
Daxindian
Yantai
Weihai
Ansan
Suwŏn
Ich'ŏn
Yoju
Osan
Chech'ŏn
Ulchin
Huimin
Laizhou Wan
Huang Xian
Muping
Chengshan Jiao
Ch'ungju
Yŏngju
Kenli
Dongying
Zhaoyuan
Fushan
Qixia
Wendeng
P'yŏngt'aek
Ch'ŏnan
SOUTH KOREA
Nakdong
Shanghe
Binzhou
Laizhou
923
Rongcheng
Sŏsan
Chŏngjiu
Yech'ŏn
Andong
Yŏngdŏk
Gaoyuan
Guangrao
Shandong Bandao
Rushan
Hongsŏng
Yesan
Sangju
Uisong
Chŏngha
Huantai
Shouguang
Changyi
Pingdu
Laiyang
Nanhuang
Shidao
Kongju
Anmyŏn-do
Nonsan
TAEJŎN
Sŏnsan
P'ohang
Linzi
Zhoucun
ZIBO
Yidu
Weifang
Laixi
Haiyang
Taechŏn-ni
Kanggyŏng
Yŏngdong
Kimch'ŏn
Kumi
Yŏngch'ŏn
Changgi-Ap
Fangzi
Lancun
Kyŏngju
Boshan
Linqu
Anqiu
Gaomi
Jimo
Kunsan
Iri
Chŏnju
Waegwan
TAEGU
Chŏngdo
Chengyang
Jiaozhou
Kimje
Puan
Kochang
Koryŏng
Miryang
Ulsan
Laiwu
1108
Zhucheng
QINGDAO
Chŏngŭp
Hamyang
Tai'an
Jiaozhou Wan
Chii-san 1915
Xintai
Mengyin
Yishui
Wulian
HUANG HAI (Yellow Sea)
Namwŏn
Chinju
Masan
Kimhae
Tongnae
Sishui
Sagŏ-ri
Tamyang
PUSAN
Ju Xian
Langcheng
Songjŏng-ni
KWANGJU
Ch'angwon
Samch'ŏnp'o
Pingyi
Yi He
Rizhao
Shijiusuo
Naju
Hodong
Ch'ungmu
Sasuna
Tangtou
Andongwei
Sunch'ŏn
Korea Strait
Fei Xian
Linyi
Mokp'o
Posong
Pŏlgyo-ri
Yŏsu
Saka
Tsushima
Tengzhou
Haizhou Wan
Changhŭng
Izuhara
Teng Xian
Ganyu
Haenam
Zaozhuang
Lianyungang
Hŭksan-chedo
Chindo
Tancheng
Weishan Hu
Hanzhuang
Jiawang
Pizhou
Haizhou
Ganyun
Chenjiagang
Iki
Xinyi
Xiangshui
Karatsu
Xuzhou
Yaowan
JIANGSU
Guannan
Binhai
JAPAN
Imari
Shuanggou
Suqian
Shuyang
Cheju
Cheju-do
Onpyŏng-ni
Sasebo
Suining
Lianshui
Funing
Hallim
Kashima
Da Yunhe
Sheyang
Taejŏng
Halla-san 1950
Ōmura
Lingbi
Huaiyin
Huai'an
Mosŭlpo
Sŏgwipo
Nakadōri-Shima
Isahaya
Hongze Hu
Yancheng
Nagasaki
Guzhen
Suzhou
Baoying
Kuchinotsu
Wuhe
Grand Canal
Liuzhuang
Fukue-Shima
Huaiyuan
Xinghua
Bengbu
Gaoyou Hu
Dongtai
Fengyang

118 120 122 124 126 128 130 132
44 42 40 38 36 34

East from Greenwich

9 10 11 12 13 14 15

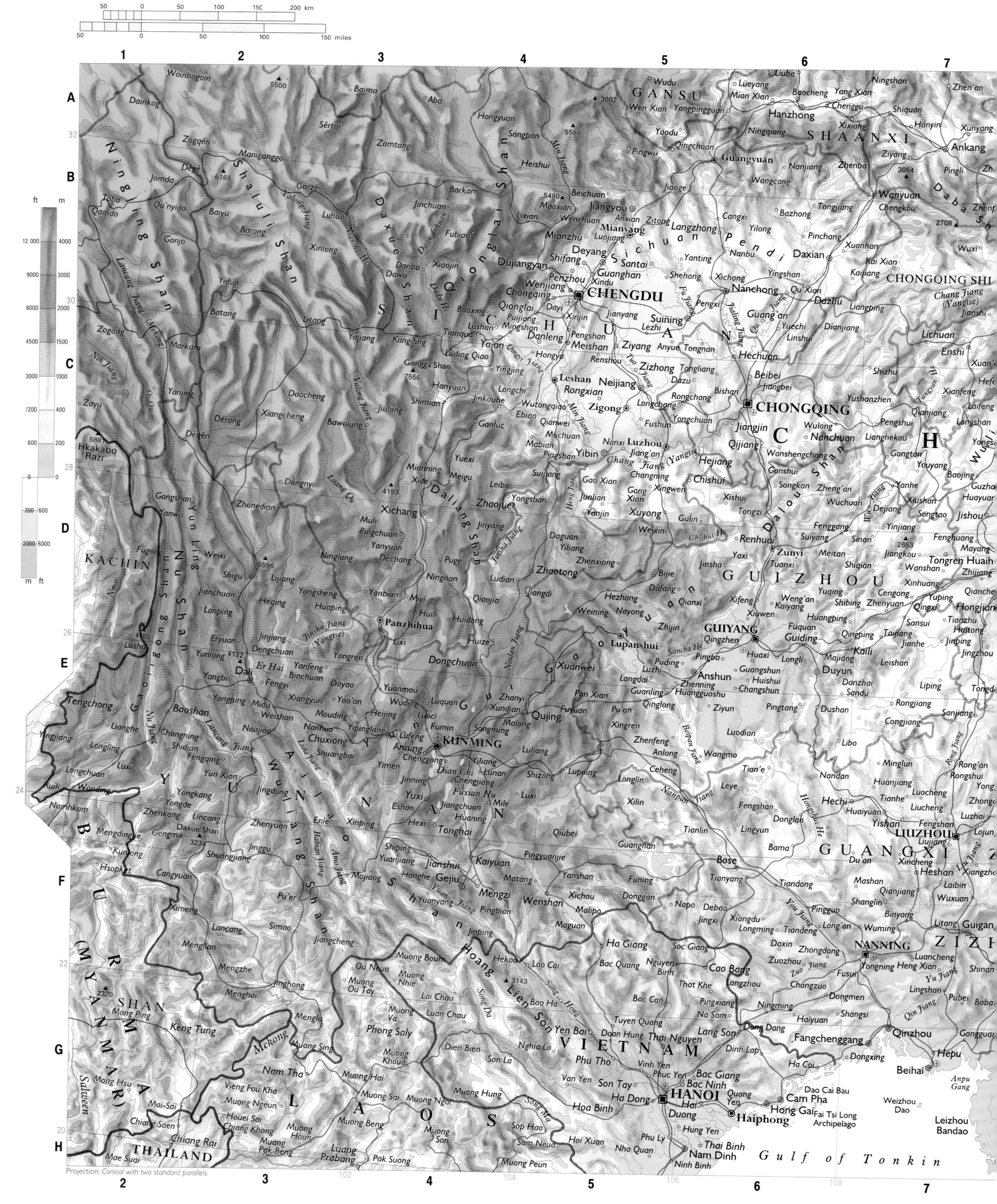
50 0 50 100 150 200 km
50 0 50 100 150 miles
ft m
12 000 4000
9000 3000
6000 2000
4500 1500
3000 1000
1200 400
600 200
0 0
200 600
2000 6000
m ft
1 2 3 4 5 6 7
A B C D E F G H
GANSU
SHAANXI
CHONGQING SHI
GUIZHOU
GUANGXI
YUNNAN
SICHUAN
Sichuan Pendi
KACHIN
SHAN
BURMA (MYANMAR)
LAOS
VIETNAM
THAILAND
Gulf of Tonkin
CHENGDU
CHONGQING
KUNMING
GUIYANG
NANNING
HANOI
Haiphong
Hanzhong
Ankang
Guangyuan
Mianyang
Deyang
Suining
Nanchong
Dazhou
Leshan
Zigong
Neijiang
Luzhou
Yibin
Zunyi
Anshun
Duyun
Kaili
Liuzhou
Panzhihua
Xichang
Zhaotong
Qujing
Dali
Lijiang
Baoshan
Tengchong
Jianshui
Gejiu
Kaiyuan
Mengzi
Wenshan
Bose
Hechi
Qinzhou
Beihai
Fangchenggang
Lao Cai
Cao Bang
Lang Son
Yen Bai
Thai Nguyen
Nam Dinh
Thai Binh
Ninh Binh
Hoa Binh
Dien Bien
Phong Saly
Luang Prabang
Chiang Rai
Chiang Saen
Mae Suai
Keng Tung
Mong Hsu
Nam Tha
Muong Sai
Ningjing Shan
Shaluli Shan
Daxue Shan
Qionglai Shan
Daliang Shan
Wuliang Shan
Ailao Shan
Hoang Lien Son
Dalou Shan
Daba Shan
Yun Ling
Nu Shan
Gaoligong Shan
Lancang Jiang (Mekong)
Nu Jiang
Jinsha Jiang (Yangtse)
Chang Jiang (Yangtse)
Min Jiang
Yalong Jiang
Dadu He
Jialing Jiang
Nanpan Jiang
Hongshui He
Yuan Jiang
Song Da
Song Hong
Mekong
Salween
Er Hai
Dian Chi
Fuxian Hu
Gongga Shan 7556
Hkakabo Razi 5881
Leizhou Bandao
Weizhou Dao
Fai Tsi Long Archipelago
Projection: Conical with two standard parallels

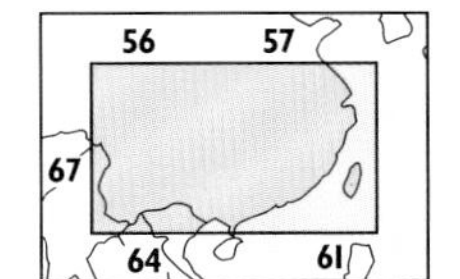
56
57
67
64
61

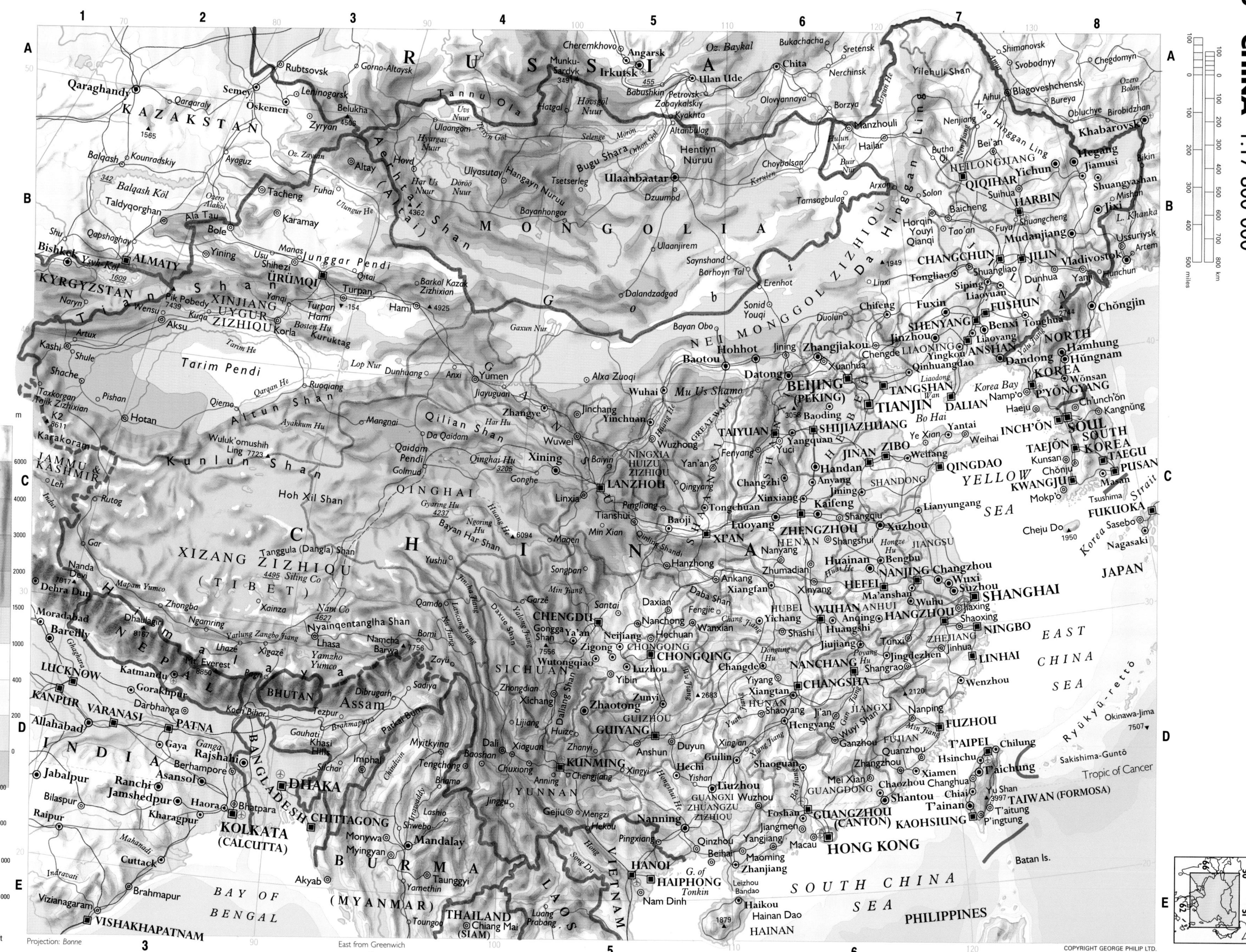

100 0 100 200 300 400 500 600 700 800 km
100 0 100 200 300 400 500 miles
RUSSIA
MONGOLIA
CHINA
KAZAKSTAN
KYRGYZSTAN
JAMMU & KASHMIR
NEPAL
BHUTAN
BANGLADESH
INDIA
BURMA (MYANMAR)
THAILAND (SIAM)
LAOS
VIETNAM
NORTH KOREA
SOUTH KOREA
JAPAN
PHILIPPINES
TAIWAN (FORMOSA)
BEIJING (PEKING)
SHANGHAI
HONG KONG
GUANGZHOU (CANTON)
KOLKATA (CALCUTTA)
YELLOW SEA
EAST CHINA SEA
SOUTH CHINA SEA
BAY OF BENGAL
Tropic of Cancer
Projection: Bonne
East from Greenwich

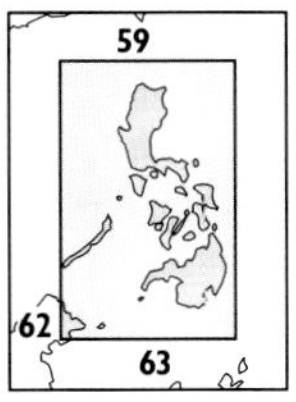

THE PHILIPPINES

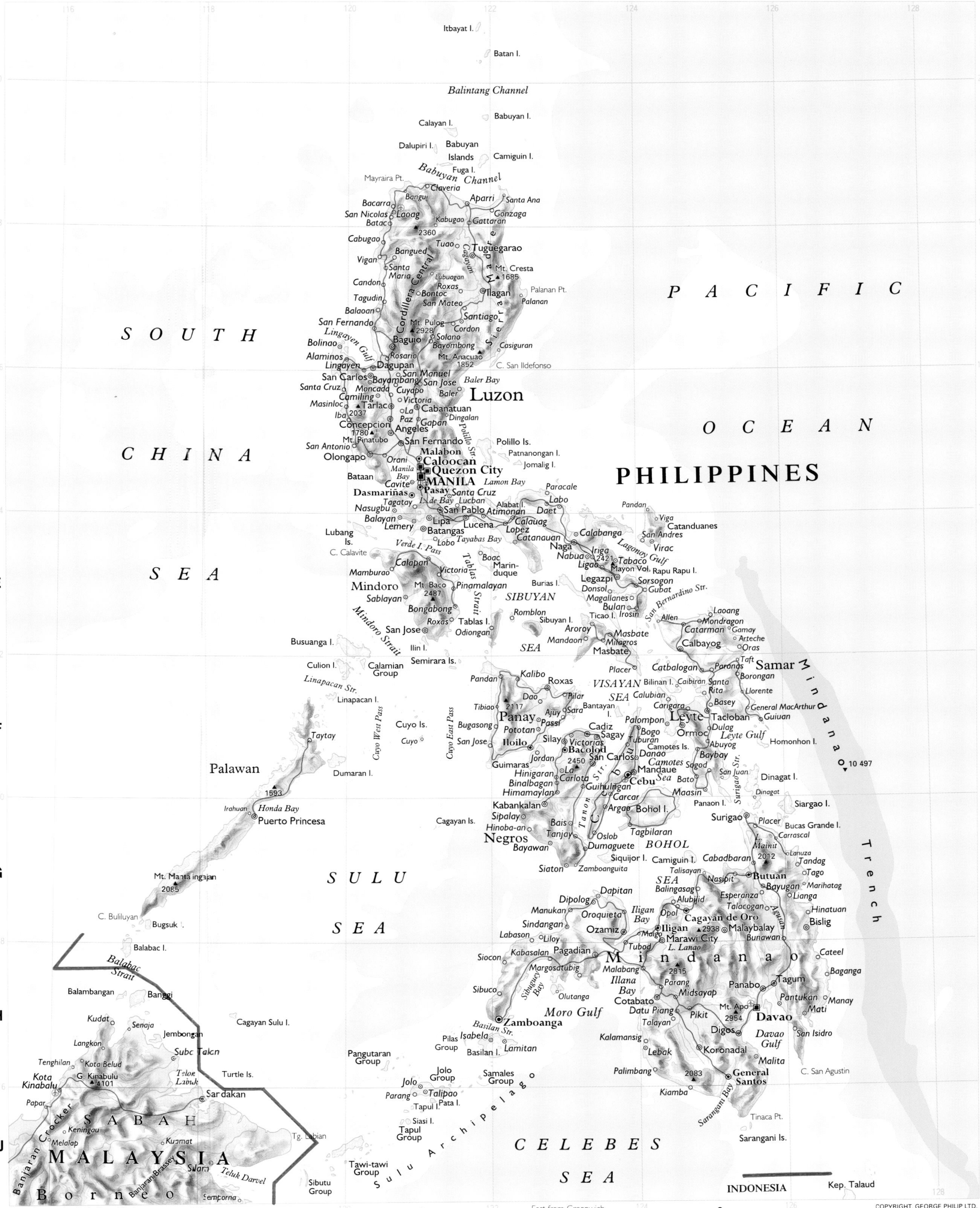

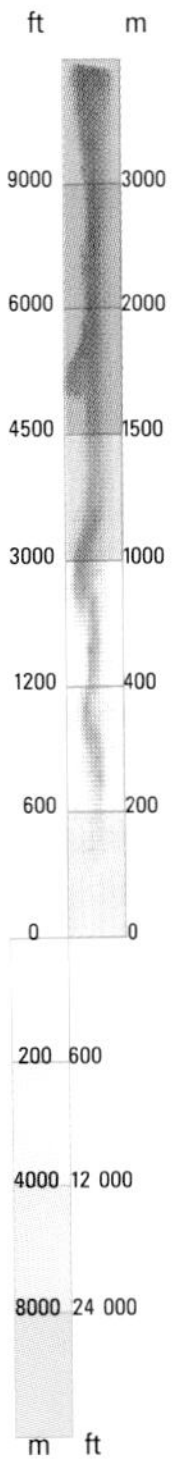

1:6 700 000

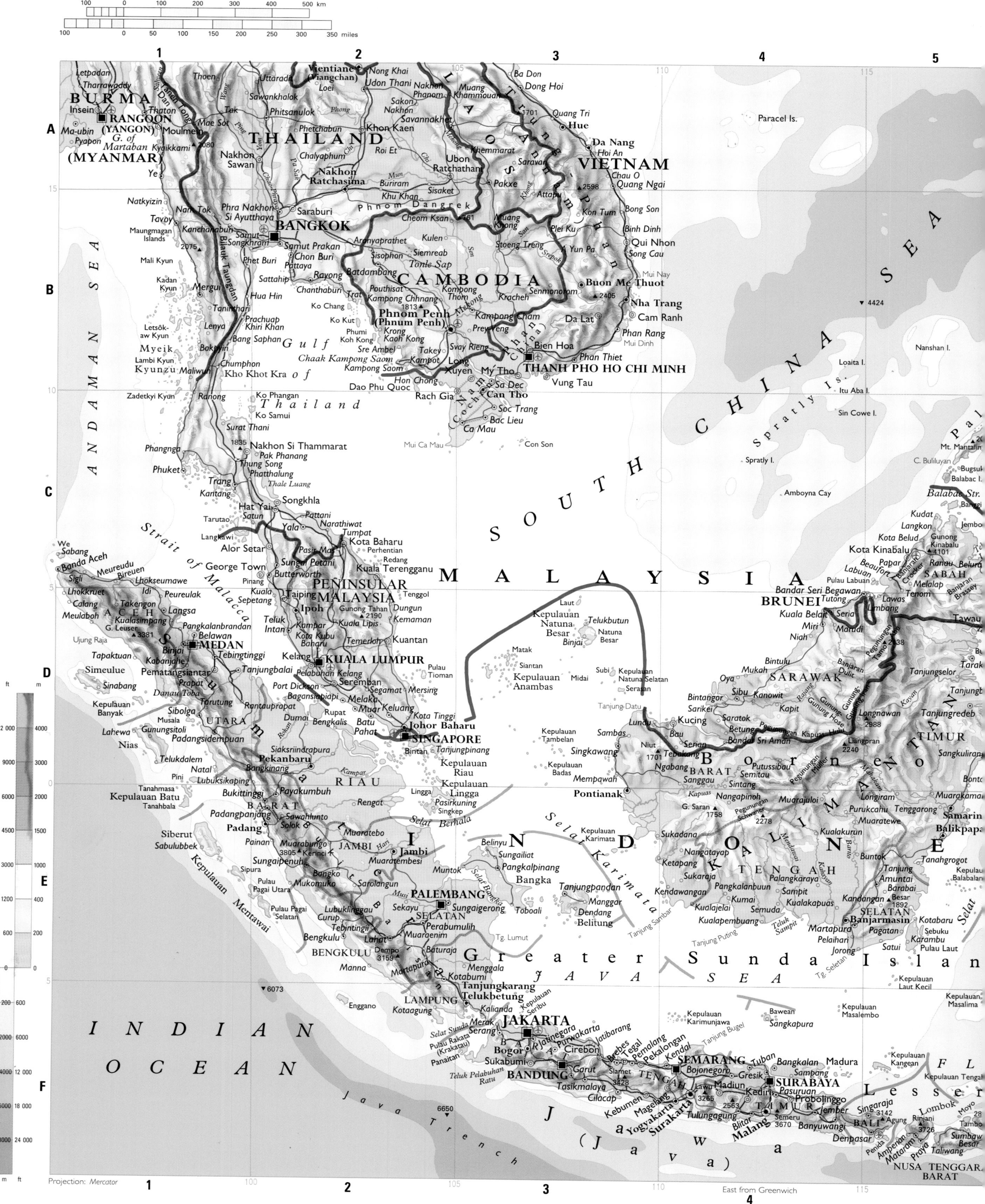

100 0 100 200 300 400 500 km
100 0 50 100 150 200 250 300 350 miles
1 2 3 4 5
A B C D E F
BURMA (MYANMAR)
RANGOON (YANGON)
G. of Martaban
Moulmein
THAILAND
Vientiane (Viangchan)
Nong Khai
Udon Thani
LAOS
Muang Khammouan
Savannakhet
Khon Kaen
Nakhon Ratchasima
Ubon Ratchathani
Pakxe
Attapu
Hue
Da Nang
Hoi An
VIETNAM
Quang Ngai
Dong Hoi
Ba Don
Quang Tri
Paracel Is.
Phnom Dangrek
Saraburi
Phra Nakhon Si Ayutthaya
BANGKOK
Samut Prakan
Chon Buri
Pattaya
Rayong
Chanthaburi
Trat
Aranyaprathet
Siemreab
Tonle Sap
Batdambang
Pouthisat
Kampong Chhnang
CAMBODIA
Kompong Thom
Kracheh
Senmonorom
Phnom Penh (Phnum Penh)
Kampong Cham
Prey Veng
Svay Rieng
Takeo
Kampot
Kampong Saom
Chaak Kampong Saom
Gulf of Thailand
Kon Tum
Plei Ku
Bong Son
Binh Dinh
Qui Nhon
Song Cau
Buon Me Thuot
Nha Trang
Cam Ranh
Da Lat
Phan Rang
Phan Thiet
Bien Hoa
THANH PHO HO CHI MINH
Vung Tau
My Tho
Sa Dec
Can Tho
Long Xuyen
Rach Gia
Hon Chong
Dao Phu Quoc
Soc Trang
Bac Lieu
Ca Mau
Mui Ca Mau
Con Son
ANDAMAN SEA
Tavoy
Mergui
Myeik
Kyunzu
Chumphon
Kho Khot Kra
Ranong
Ko Phangan
Ko Samui
Surat Thani
Nakhon Si Thammarat
Phangnga
Phuket
Trang
Hat Yai
Songkhla
Pattani
Narathiwat
Kota Baharu
Alor Setar
George Town
Strait of Malacca
Kuala Terengganu
PENINSULAR MALAYSIA
Ipoh
Kuantan
KUALA LUMPUR
Seremban
Melaka
Johor Baharu
SINGAPORE
SOUTH CHINA SEA
Spratly Is.
Spratly I.
Amboyna Cay
Itu Aba I.
Sin Cowe I.
Loaita I.
Nanshan I.
MALAYSIA
Kepulauan Natuna Besar
Kepulauan Anambas
Kota Kinabalu
Gunong Kinabalu
SABAH
Labuan
Bandar Seri Begawan
BRUNEI
Miri
Bintulu
Sibu
SARAWAK
Kuching
Pontianak
Borneo
KALIMANTAN
Samarinda
Balikpapan
Banjarmasin
Palangkaraya
Selat Karimata
Banda Aceh
ACEH
Lhokseumawe
Langsa
G. Leuser
MEDAN
Belawan
Tebingtinggi
Pematangsiantar
Danau Toba
Sibolga
Nias
Simeulue
Sumatera UTARA
Pekanbaru
RIAU
Kepulauan Riau
Kepulauan Lingga
Padang
Siberut
Kepulauan Mentawai
Jambi
JAMBI
Bangka
Pangkalpinang
PALEMBANG
Belitung
Bengkulu
BENGKULU
LAMPUNG
Tanjungkarang Telukbetung
Greater Sunda Islands
JAVA SEA
INDONESIA
INDIAN OCEAN
Java Trench
Enggano
JAKARTA
Bogor
Bandung
Cirebon
Semarang
Surakarta
Yogyakarta
Madiun
Malang
SURABAYA
Madura
Banyuwangi
Bali
Denpasar
Lombok
Jawa (Java)
NUSA TENGGARA BARAT
Lesser
Projection: Mercator
East from Greenwich

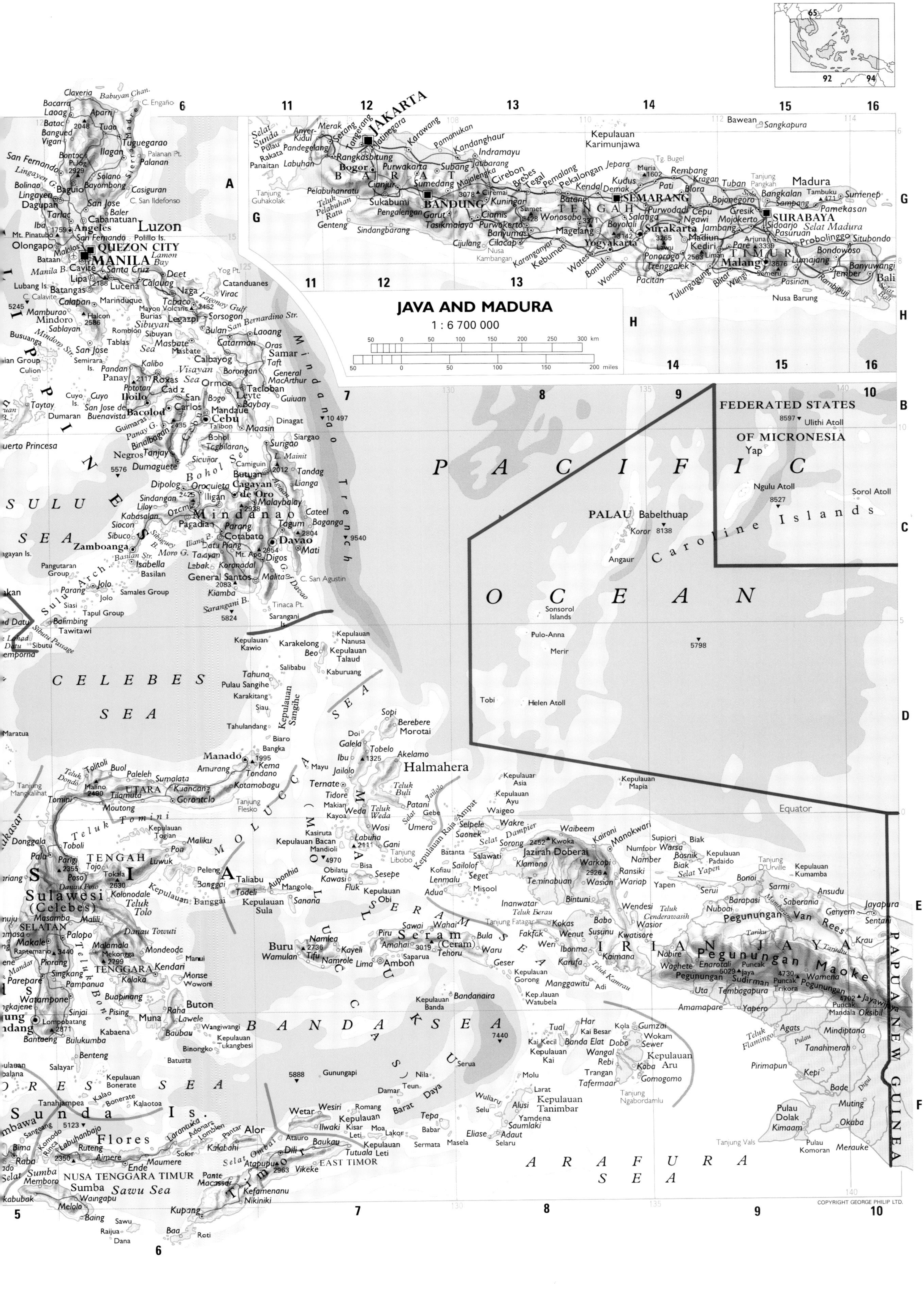

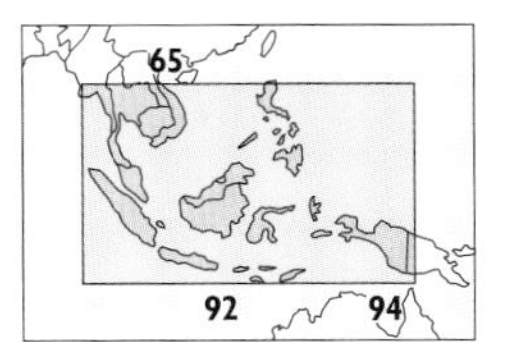

JAVA AND MADURA

1 : 6 700 000

50 0 50 100 150 200 km
50 0 50 100 150 miles
BURMA
(MYANMAR)
THAILAND
CAMBODIA
LAOS
VIETNAM
YUNNAN
GUANGXI ZHUANGZU ZIZHIQU
GUANGDONG
HAINAN
SHAN
KAYAH
MON
PEGU
G. of Tonkin
Mandalay
RANGOON (YANGON)
HANOI
Haiphong
Vientiane (Viangchan)
BANGKOK
Chiang Mai
Luang Prabang
Nakhon Ratchasima
Khon Kaen
Ubon Ratchathani
Da Nang
Hue
Haikou
Nanning
Zhanjiang
Moulmein
Tavoy
Mekong
Salween
Phnom Dangrek
Dawna Range
Bilauktaung
TENASSERIM
Khorat
Cao Nguyen
Tran Ninh

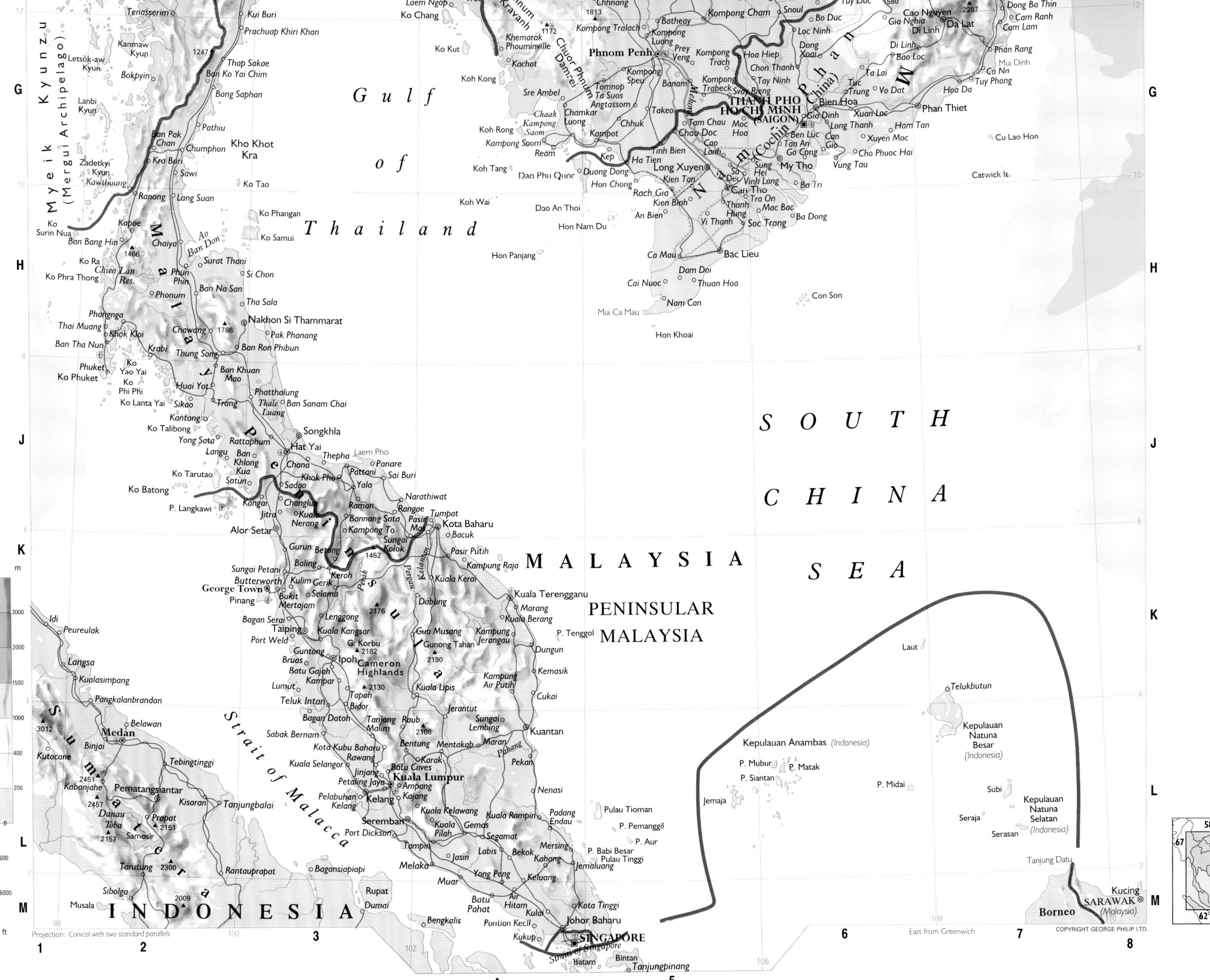
SOUTH CHINA SEA
Gulf of Thailand
MALAYSIA
PENINSULAR MALAYSIA
INDONESIA
Strait of Malacca
Borneo
SARAWAK (Malaysia)
Kuching
SINGAPORE
Johor Baharu
Kuala Lumpur
Phnom Penh
THANH PHO HO CHI MINH (SAIGON)
Kepulauan Anambas (Indonesia)
Kepulauan Natuna Besar (Indonesia)
Kepulauan Natuna Selatan (Indonesia)
Medan
George Town
Ipoh
Kuantan
Kota Baharu
Kuala Terengganu
Melaka
Seremban
Hat Yai
Songkhla
Nakhon Si Thammarat
Surat Thani
Ko Phuket
Myeik Kyunzu (Mergui Archipelago)
Can Tho
Bac Lieu
Ca Mau
Da Lat
Phan Thiet
Con Son
East from Greenwich
Projection: Conical with two standard parallels

50 0 100 200 300 400 km
50 0 50 100 150 200 250 miles
TURKMENISTAN
AFGHANISTAN
IRAN
PAKISTAN
INDIA
SRI LANKA
ARABIAN SEA
Tropic of Cancer
Hindu Kush
Karakoram
JAMMU & KASHMIR
Aksai Chin
NORTH WEST FRONTIER
Northern Areas
Kabul
Islamabad
RAWALPINDI
LAHORE
FAISALABAD
Multan
Quetta
KARACHI
Hyderabad
Herat
Qandahar
Srinagar
Amritsar
DELHI
New Delhi
Jaipur
Agra
Gwalior
Ahmadabad
Vadodara (Baroda)
Surat
MUMBAI (BOMBAY)
Pune (Poona)
Nagpur
HYDERABAD
Bangalore
Chennai (Madras)
Mysore
Madurai
Colombo
Kandy
Jaffna
Thar Desert
Great Indian Desert
Rann of Kachchh
Gulf of Kachchh
Gulf of Khambhat
Kathiawar
GUJARAT
RAJASTHAN
PUNJAB
HARYANA
HIMACHAL PRADESH
MADHYA PRADESH
MAHARASHTRA
KARNATAKA
TAMIL NADU
KERALA
ANDHRA PRADESH
DADRA AND NAGAR HAVELI
Western Ghats
Eastern Ghats
Malabar Coast
Coromandel Coast
Palk Strait
Gulf of Mannar
Adam's Bridge
Makran Coast Range
Central Makran Range
Siahan Range
Kirthar Range
Sulaiman Range
Toba Kakar
Satpura Range
Vindhya Range
Ajanta Range
Satmala Hills
Dasht-e Khāsh
Dasht-e Mārgow
Rīgestān
Mouths of the Indus
C. Comorin
Dondra Head
Continuation Southwards on same scale
Projection: Conical with two standard parallels
ft m
18 000 6000
12 000 4000
9000 3000
6000 2000
4500 1500
3000 1000
1200 400
600 200
0 0
200 600
m ft

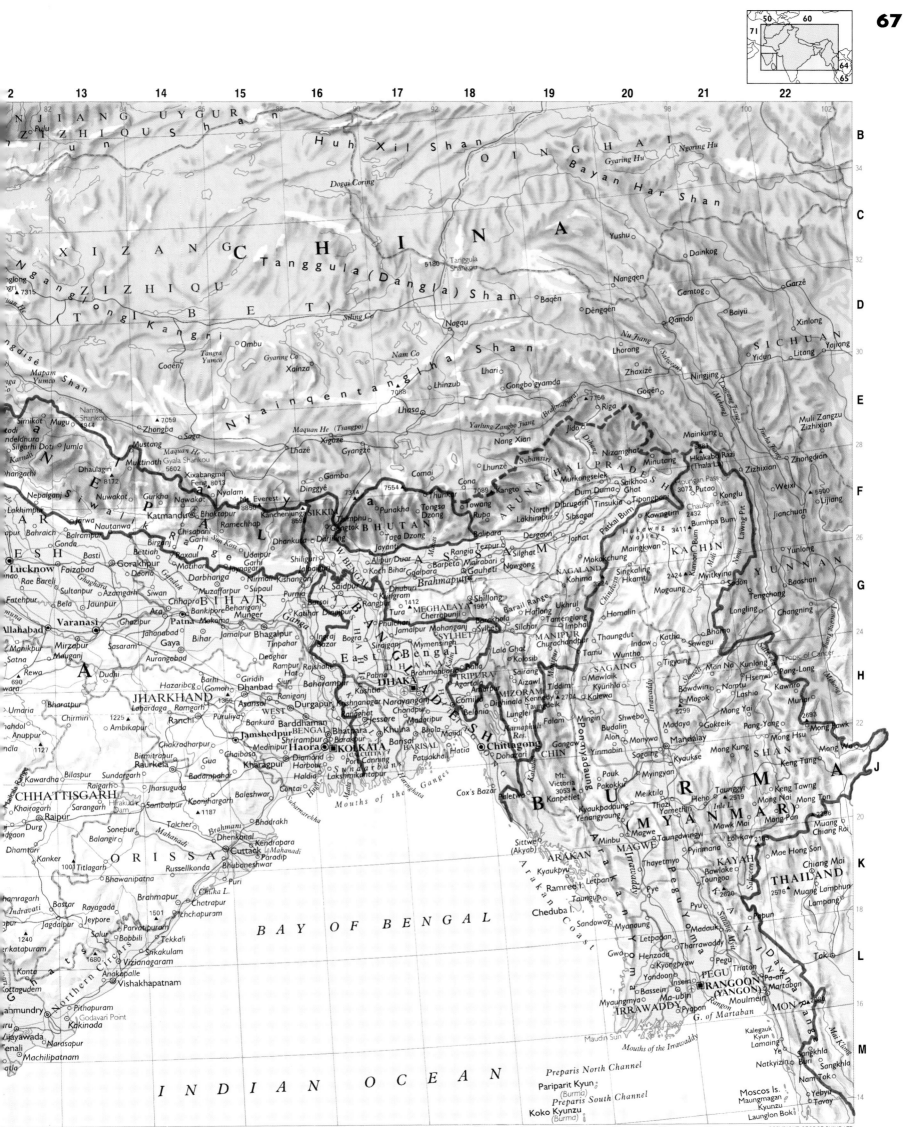

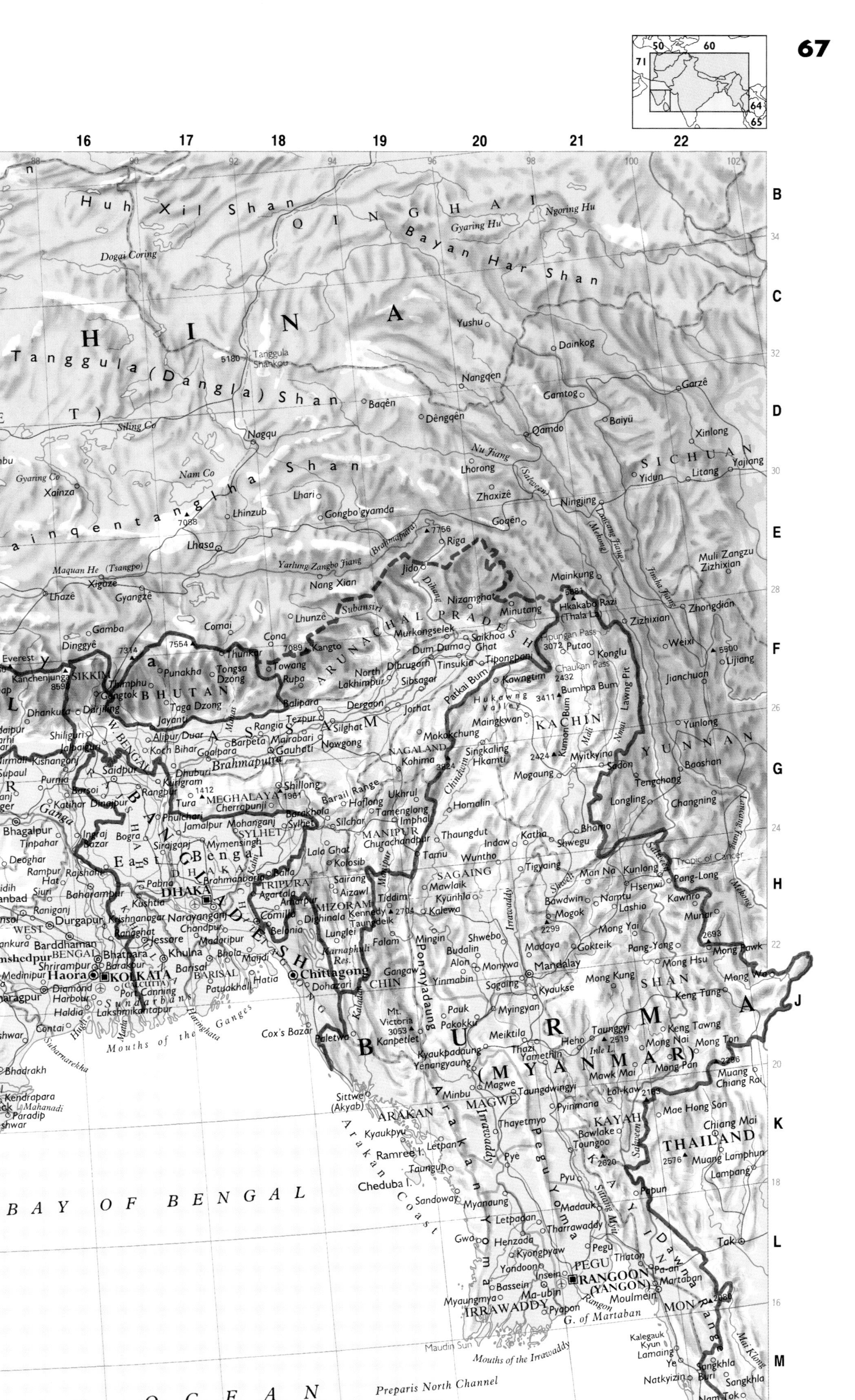
CHINA
XIZANG ZIZHIQU (TIBET)
QINGHAI
SICHUAN
YUNNAN
Tanggula (Dangla) Shan
Nyainqentanglha Shan
Bayan Har Shan
Hoh Xil Shan
Lhasa
NEPAL
Katmandu
BHUTAN
Thimphu
SIKKIM
ARUNACHAL PRADESH
ASSAM
MEGHALAYA
NAGALAND
MANIPUR
MIZORAM
TRIPURA
BANGLADESH
DHAKA
Chittagong
BIHAR
JHARKHAND
ORISSA
CHHATTISGARH
KOLKATA (CALCUTTA)
Varanasi
Patna
Lucknow
Allahabad
Cuttack
Vishakhapatnam
BAY OF BENGAL
INDIAN OCEAN
BURMA (MYANMAR)
RANGOON (YANGON)
Mandalay
KACHIN
SAGAING
SHAN
MAGWE
KAYAH
PEGU
IRRAWADDY
ARAKAN
CHIN
MON
THAILAND
Mouths of the Ganges
Mouths of the Irrawaddy
G. of Martaban
Preparis North Channel
Preparis South Channel
Brahmaputra
Ganga
Irrawaddy
Tropic of Cancer
East from Greenwich
COPYRIGHT GEORGE PHILIP LTD.

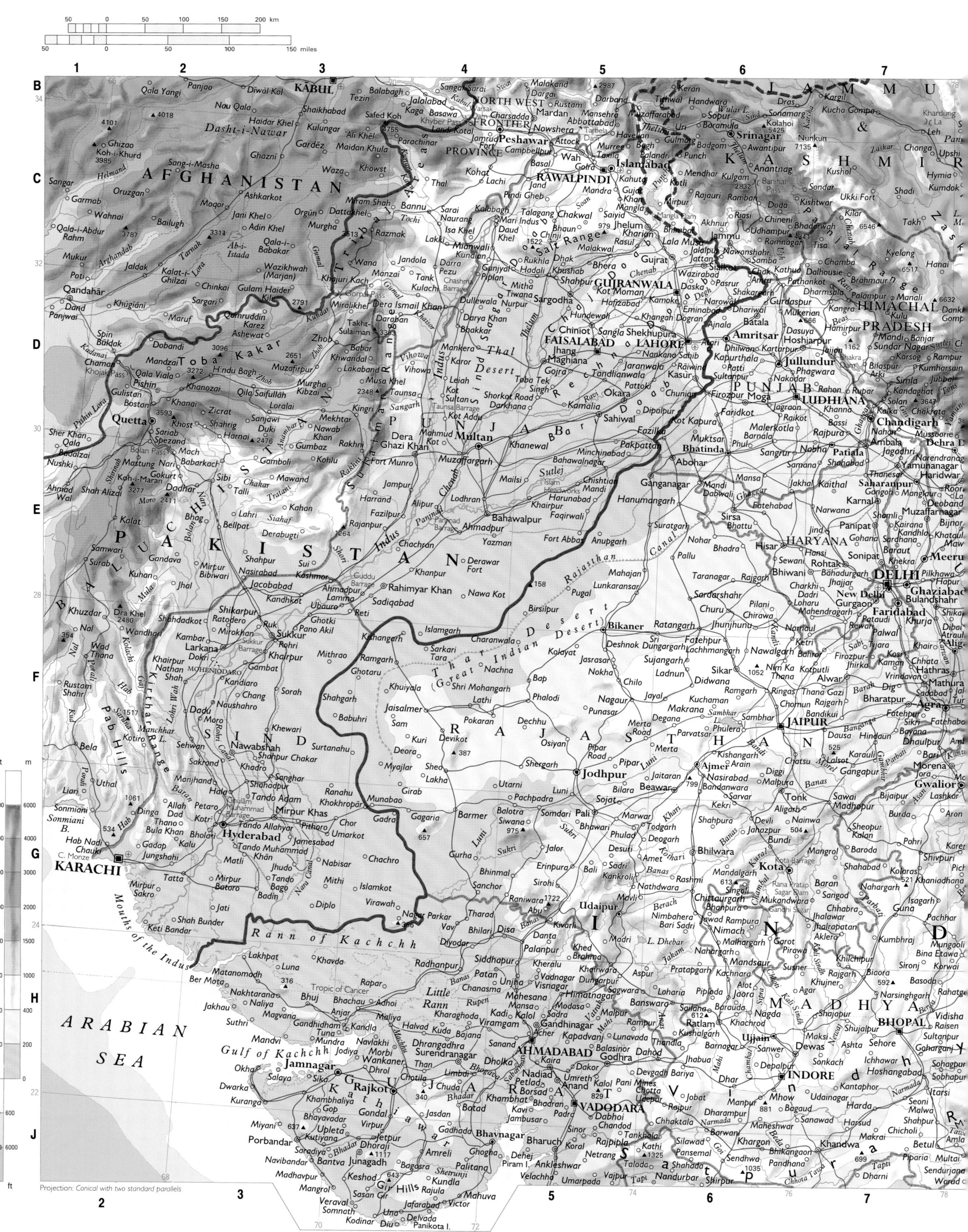

50 0 50 100 150 200 km
50 0 50 100 150 miles
AFGHANISTAN
PAKISTAN
BALUCHISTAN
PUNJAB
SIND
RAJASTHAN
INDIA
MADHYA PRADESH
HARYANA
HIMACHAL PRADESH
JAMMU & KASHMIR
NORTH WEST FRONTIER PROVINCE
ARABIAN SEA
Gulf of Kachchh
Rann of Kachchh
Little Rann
Thar Desert (Great Indian Desert)
Thal Desert
Kathiawar
Dasht-i-Nawar
Salt Range
Sulaiman Range
Toba Kakar
Kirthar Range
Pab Hills
Gir Hills
Mouths of the Indus
Tropic of Cancer
KABUL
Peshawar
RAWALPINDI
Islamabad
Srinagar
Quetta
Qandahār
Multan
FAISALABAD
LAHORE
GUJRANWALA
Amritsar
Jullundur
LUDHIANA
Chandigarh
DELHI
New Delhi
Agra
JAIPUR
Jodhpur
Bikaner
Ajmer
Hyderabad
KARACHI
Sukkur
Bahawalpur
AHMADABAD
VADODARA
Rajkot
Jamnagar
Bhavnagar
Udaipur
Kota
INDORE
Ujjain
BHOPAL
Gwalior
Projection: Conical with two standard parallels
ft m
18 000 6000
12 000 4000
9000 3000
6000 2000
4500 1500
3000 1000
1200 400
600 200
0 0
200 600
2000 6000
m ft

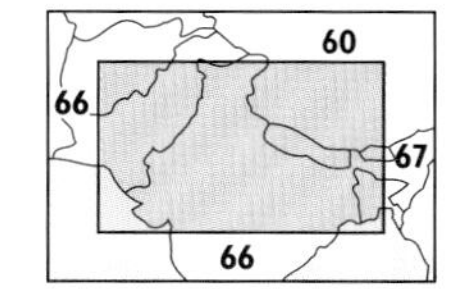

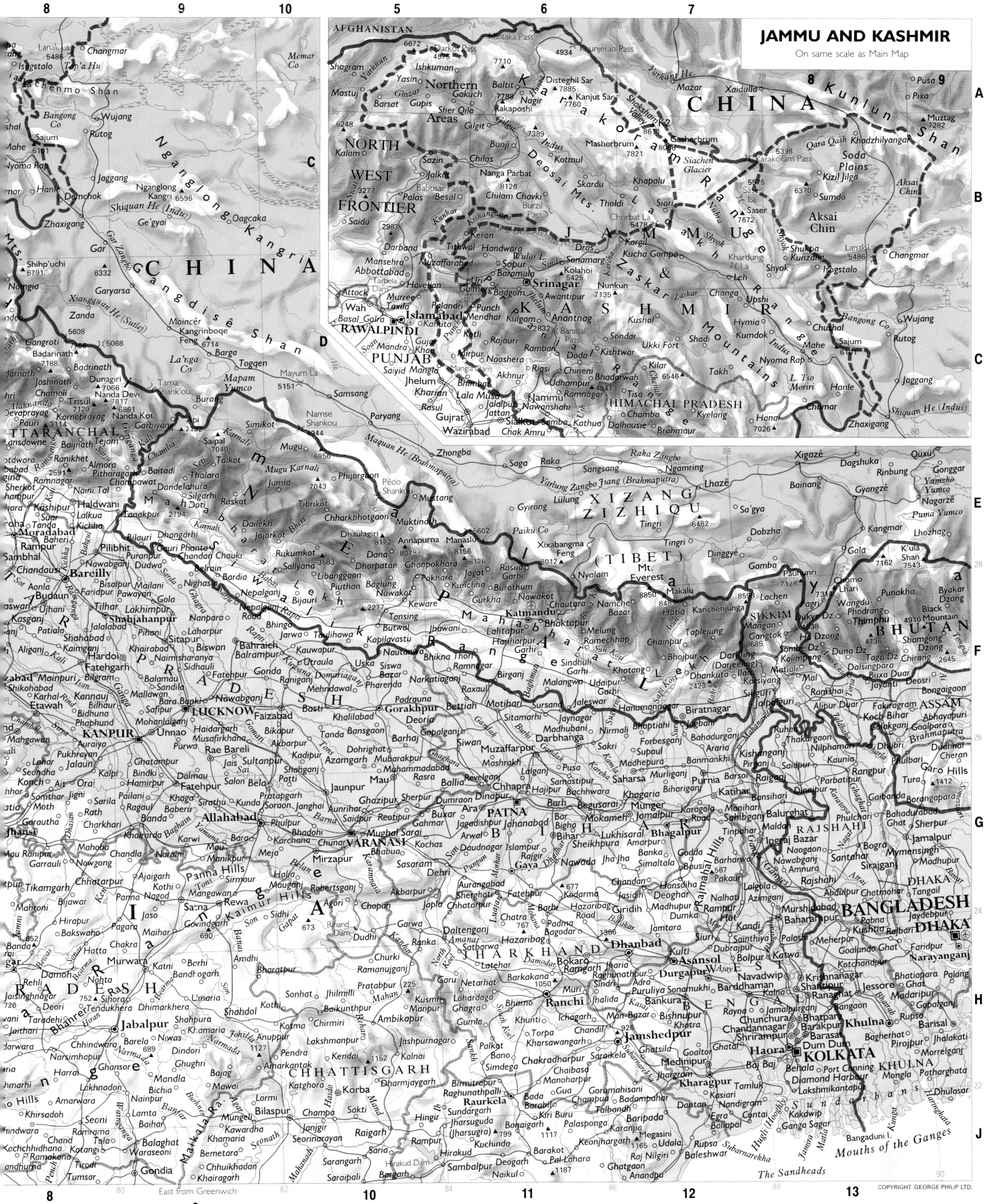

JAMMU AND KASHMIR

On same scale as Main Map

CHINA · NORTH WEST FRONTIER · Northern Areas · PUNJAB · JAMMU & KASHMIR · HIMACHAL PRADESH · XIZANG ZIZHIQU (TIBET) · NEPAL · SIKKIM · BHUTAN · BANGLADESH · UTTARANCHAL · UTTAR PRADESH · BIHAR · JHARKHAND · WEST BENGAL · CHHATTISGARH · MADHYA PRADESH · ASSAM

East from Greenwich

THE MIDDLE EAST 1:6 200 000

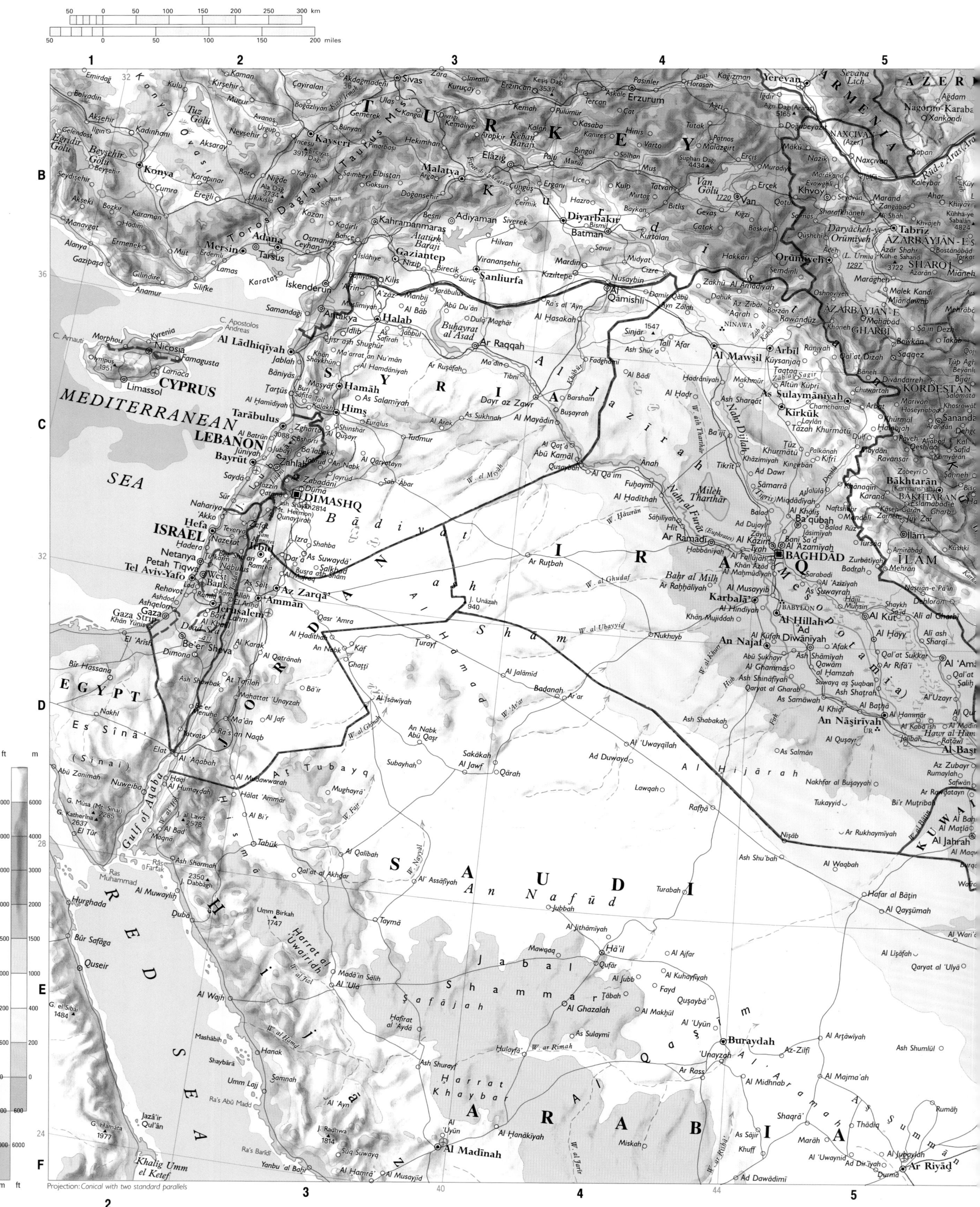

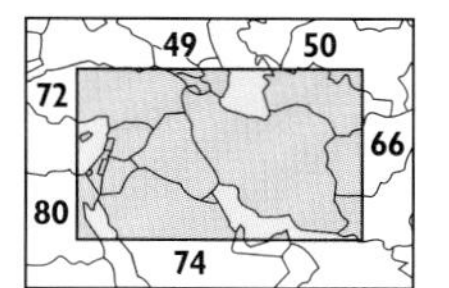

6 7 8 9 10

B C D E F

CASPIAN SEA

TURKMENISTAN

Kara Kum

Kopet Dagh

IRAN

Dasht-e Kavir

Dasht-e Lut

AFGHANISTAN

PAKISTAN

THE GULF

Gulf of Oman

QATAR

BAHRAIN

UNITED ARAB EMIRATES

OMAN

Reshteh-ye Kūhhā-ye Alborz

Kūhhā-ye Zāgros

Kūhhā-ye Bashākerd

Makran

TEHRĀN

MĀZANDARĀN

GĪLĀN

SEMNĀN

MARKAZĪ

KHORĀSĀN

EṢFAHĀN

YAZD

KERMĀN

FĀRS

HORMOZGĀN

SĪSTĀN VA BALŪCHESTĀN

KHŪZESTĀN

CHAHĀR MAHĀLL VA BAKHTĪĀRĪ

KOHKĪLŪYEH VA BŪYER AHMADĪ

BŪSHEHR

HERĀT

FARĀH

NĪMRŪZ

Bakı

Ardabīl

Rasht

Qazvīn

Karaj

Tehrān

Rey

Qom

Kāshān

Arāk

Eṣfahān

Najafābād

Yazd

Kermān

Shīrāz

Ahvāz

Ābādān

Khorramshahr

Dezfūl

Būshehr

Bandar-e 'Abbās

Zāhedān

Mashhad

Ashgabat

Mary

Chārjew

Herāt

Sārī

Gorgān

Babol

Semnān

Neyshābūr

Sabzevār

Bīrjand

Zābol

Chāh Bahār

Kuwayt

Ad Dammām

Al Manāmah

Ad Dawḥah

Dubayy

Abū Ẓaby

Ash Shāriqah

Al 'Ayn

Ra's Masandam (Oman)

Str. of Hormuz

Daryācheh-ye Namak

Daryācheh-ye Tashk

Daryācheh-ye Sīstān

Daryācheh-ye Namakzar

Namakzār-e Shahdād

Gowd-e Zirreh

Dasht-e Mārgow

Ḩāmūn-e Jaz Mūrīān

Al Ḩajar Al Gharbī

East from Greenwich

COPYRIGHT GEORGE PHILIP LTD.

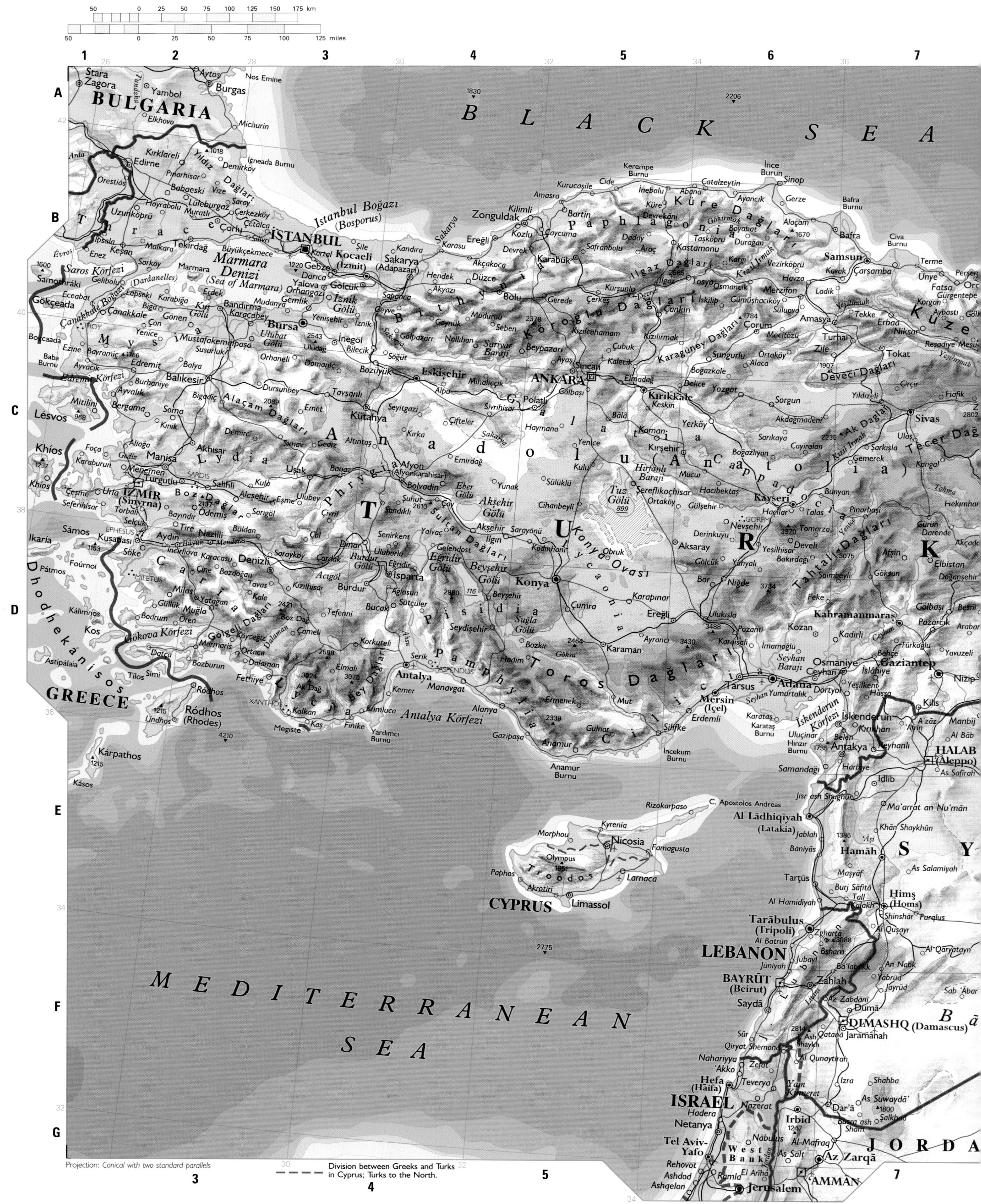

Projection: *Conical with two standard parallels*

— — — Division between Greeks and Turks in Cyprus; Turks to the North.

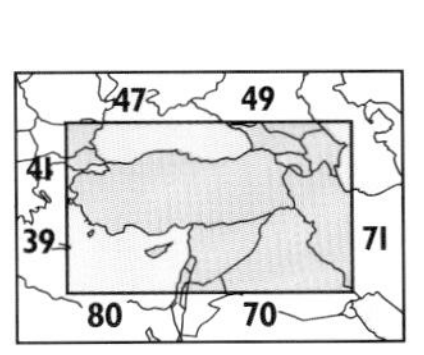

47 49 41 39 71 80 70

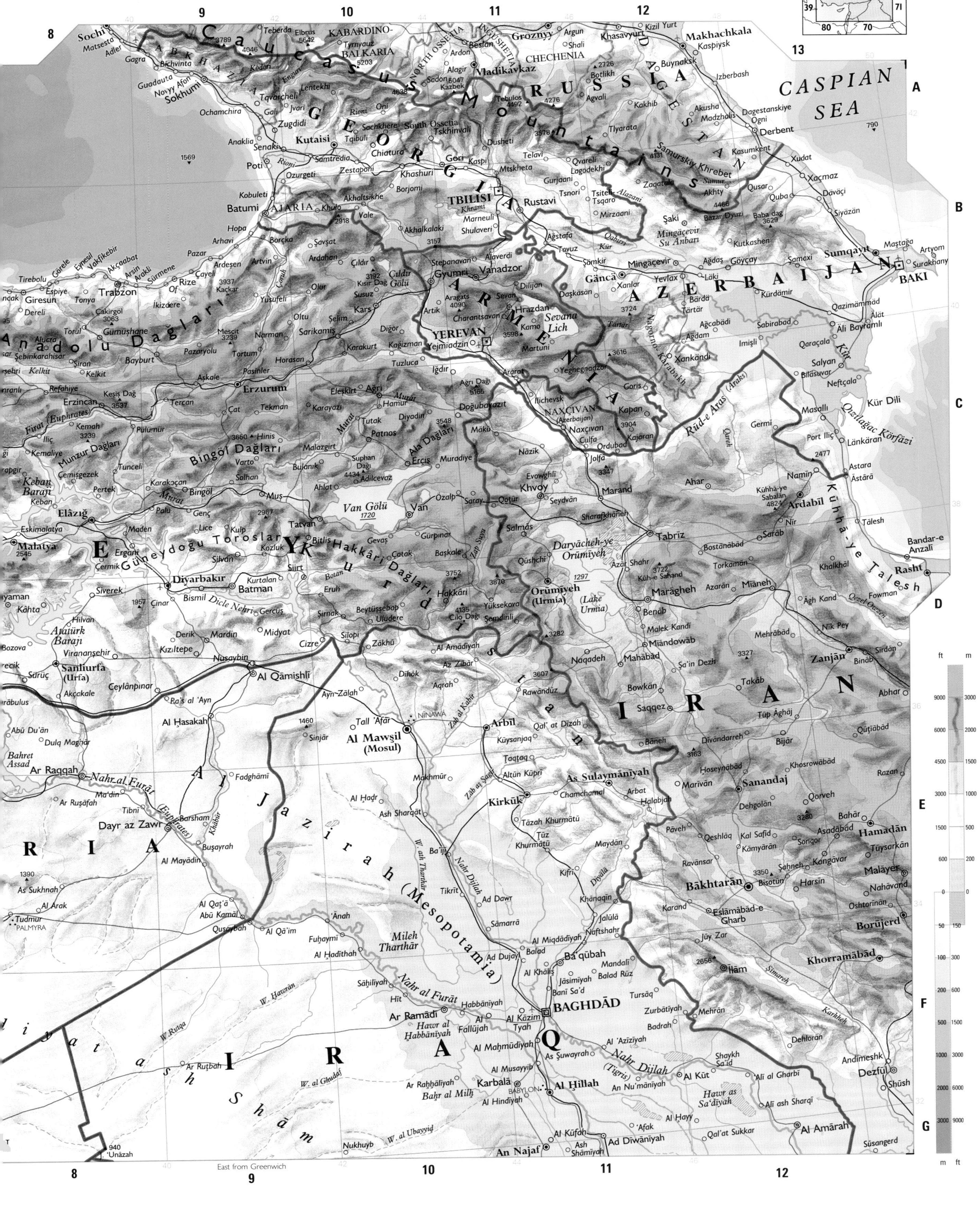

9 10 11 12 13 8

A B C D E F G

CASPIAN SEA
790

Caucasus Mountains
RUSSIA
GEORGIA
ARMENIA
AZERBAIJAN
IRAN
IRAQ
TURKEY
SYRIA
DAGESTAN
CHECHENIA
INGUSHETIA
NORTH OSSETIA
KABARDINO-BALKARIA
ABKHAZIA
AJARIA
South Ossetia
NAXÇIVAN (Azerbaijan)
Nagorno-Karabakh
Kurdistan
Al Jazīrah (Mesopotamia)
Bādiyat ash Shām

Sochi
Matsesta
Adler
Gagra
Bichvinta
Gudauta
Novyy Afon
Sokhumi
Ochamchira
Anaklia
Poti
Kobuleti
Batumi
Teberda
Elbrus 5642
Tyrnyauz
5203
3789
4046
Kodori
Enguri
Tqvarcheli
Gali
Jvari
Zugdidi
Senaki
Lentekhi
Rioni
Oni
Kutaisi
Samtredia
Ozurgeti
Zestaponi
Chiatura
Tqibuli
Sachkhere
Tskhinvali
Khashuri
Borjomi
Akhaltsikhe
Khulo
Vale
2918
Akhalkalaki
Gori
Kaspi
Mtskheta
Dusheti
TBILISI
Rustavi
Khrami
Marneuli
Shulaveri
Beslan
Alagir
Ardon
Sadon
Vladikavkaz
Kazbek 5047
4638
Tebulos 4492
4276
3578
Grozny
Argun
Shali
Khasavyurt
Kizil Yurt
Makhachkala
Kaspiysk
Buynaksk
Izberbash
2726
Botlikh
Agvali
Kakhib
Tlyarata
Akusha
Madzhalis
Dagestanskiye Ogni
Derbent
Kasumkent
4131
Samursky Khrebet
Samur
Akhty
4466
Bazar Dyuzi
Telavi
Qvareli
Lagodekhi
Gurjaani
Tsnori
Tsiteli-Tsqaro
Alazani
Mirzaani
Zaqatala
Qusar
Quba
Xudat
Xaçmaz
Däväçi
Siyäzän
Baba dag 3629
Şaki
Mingäçevir Su Anbarı
Qabırri
Kür
Kutkashen
Ağstafa
Tovuz
Şämkir
Gäncä
Xanlar
Daşkäsän
Mingäçevir
Yevlax
Ağdaş
Göyçay
Läki
Şamaxi
Sumqayıt
Maştağa
Artyom
Surakhany
BAKI
Bärdä
Tärtär
Kürdämir
Qazimämmäd
Älät
Äli Bayramlı
Sabirabad
Ağcabädi
Ağdam
Imişli
Xankändi
3724
3616
Tärtär
Qaraçala
Salyan
Biläsuvar
Neftçala
Kür Dili
Masallı
Qızılağac Körfäzi
Germi
Port Iliç
Länkäran
2477
Astara
Ästārā
Namīn
Kūhhā-ye Sabalan 4824
Ardabīl
Nīr
Tālesh
Bandar-e Anzalī
Rasht
Kūhhā-ye Tālesh
Fowman
Qezel Owzan
Āgh Kand
Khalkhāl
3157
Alaverdi
Stepanavan
Vanadzor
Gyumri
Dilijan
Aragats 4090
Artik
Charentsavan
Hrazdan
Sevan
Sevana Lich
Kamo
3598
Martuni
YEREVAN
Yejmiadzin
Ararat
Yeghegnadzor
Goris
Kapan
Ilichevsk
Naxçivan
Culfa
Ordubad
3904
Kajaran
Rūd-e Aras (Araks)
Qareh
Agri Dagi 5165
Iğdır
Doğubayazit
Tuzluca
Mākū
Nāzīk
Jolfā
3347
Ahar
Marand
Evowghlī
Khvoy
Seydvān
Qotūr
Saray
Sharafkhāneh
Salmās
Tabrīz
Bostānābād
Sarāb
Daryācheh-ye Orūmīyeh
Qūshchi
Azar Shahr
3722
Kūh-e Sahand
Torkamān
1297
Orūmīyeh (Urmia)
(Lake Urmia)
Marāgheh
Azarān
Mīāneh
Benāb
Malek Kandī
Mīāndowāb
3282
Naqadeh
Mahābād
Şā'īn Dezh
3327
Mehrābād
Nīk Pey
Zanjān
Sirdān
Bīnāb
Takāb
Bowkān
Saqqez
Abhar
Tūp Āghāj
Qūţībād
Bījār
Bāneh
Dīvāndarreh
3163
Hoseynābād
Khosrowābād
Razan
Marīvān
Sanandaj
Qorveh
Dehgolān
Bahār
Hamadān
3280
Asadābād
Tūysarkān
Pāveh
Qeshlāq
Kal Safīd
Kāmyārān
Songor
Kangāvar
Ravānsar
Şahneh
3350
Bīsotūn
Harsīn
Malāyer
Nahāvand
Bākhtarān
Karand
Eslāmābād-e Gharb
Oshtorīnān
Borūjerd
Jūy Zar
2656
Īlām
Khorramābād
Şīmareh
Karkheh
Mehrān
Dehlorān
Andīmeshk
Dezfūl
Shūsh
Sūsangerd
Trabzon
Rize
Of
Sürmene
Araklı
Arsin
Akçaabat
Vakfıkebir
Eynesil
Görele
Tirebolu
Espiye
Giresun
Tonya
Dereli
Çayeli
Ardeşen
Pazar
Hopa
Arhavi
Borçka
Artvin
Şavşat
Ardahan
Çıldır
3192
Kısır Dağ
Çıldır Gölü
Susuz
Kars
Olur
3937
Kaçkar
İkizdere
Yusufeli
Çoruh
Çakırgöl 3063
Gümüşhane
Torul
Alucra
Şebinkarahisar
Kelkit
Şiran
Bayburt
Mescit 3239
Pazaryolu
Tortum
Narman
Oltu
Sarıkamış
Şelim
Digor
Kağızman
Karakurt
Horasan
Pasinler
Aşkale
Erzurum
Tercan
Refahiye
Keşiş Dağ 3537
Erzincan
Fırat (Euphrates)
Kemah
Çat
Tekman
Karayazı
Eleşkirt
Ağrı
Murat
Hamur
Tutak
Diyadin
Patnos
3548
Ala Dağları
Malazgirt
Hinis
3660
Bingöl Dağları
Varto
Solhan
Bingöl
Karlıova
Munzur Dağları
3239
Pülümür
İliç
Kemaliye
Çemişgezek
Tunceli
Pertek
Keban Barajı
Keban
Elâzığ
Palu
Genç
Muş
2967
Murat
Bulanık
Suphan Dağı 4434
Adilcevaz
Ahlat
Erciş
Muradiye
Van Gölü
1720
Van
Özalp
Tatvan
Bitlis
Gevaş
Gürpınar
Çatak
Başkale
Zap Suyu
Hakkari Dağları
3752
Hakkâri
3870
Yüksekova
Şemdinli
4135
Cilo Dağı
Beytüşşebap
Uludere
Şırnak
Eruh
Siirt
Botan
Kozluk
Kurtalan
Batman
Bismil
Diyarbakır
Dicle Nehri
Gercüş
Silvan
Kulp
Lice
Maden
Ergani
Güneydoğu Toroslar
Eskimalatya
Malatya
2545
Çermik
Siverek
Kâhta
Hilvan
Atatürk Barajı
Çınar
1957
Derik
Mardin
Midyat
Kızıltepe
Nusaybin
Cizre
Silopi
Zākhū
Bozova
Viranşehir
Şanlıurfa (Urfa)
Suruç
Akçakale
Ceylânpınar
Al Qāmishlī
Ra's al 'Ayn
Al Ḥasakah
Abū Du'ān
Dulq Maghār
Bahret Assad
Ar Raqqah
Nahr al Furāt
Ma'din
Ar Ruşāfah
Tibnī
Fadghāmī
Barsham
Khābūr
Dayr az Zawr
Buşayrah
Al Mayādīn
1390
As Sukhnah
Al 'Arak
Tudmur
PALMYRA
Al Qaṭ'ā
Abū Kamāl
Qusaybah
Al Qā'im
'Ānah
Fuhaymī
Al Ḥadīthah
Mileh Tharthār
Al 'Amādīyah
Az Zībār
Dihōk
'Aqrah
3607
Rawāndūz
Ayn Zālah
1460
Sinjār
Tall 'Afār
NĪNAWĀ
Al Mawşil (Mosul)
Zāb al Kabīr
Arbīl
Qal' at Dizah
Kūysanjaq
Ţaqţaq
Altūn Kūprī
Zāb aş Şaghīr
As Sulaymānīyah
Chamchamal
Arbat
Ḥalabjah
Makhmūr
Al Ḥaḍr
Ash Sharqāţ
Kirkūk
Ţāzah Khurmātū
Ţūz Khurmātū
Maydān
Bā'ījī
W. ath Tharthār
Nahr Dijlah
Tikrīt
Ad Dawr
Kifrī
Diyala
Khānaqīn
Jalūlā
Sāmarrā
Naftshahr
Al Miqdādīyah
Balad
Ad Dujayl
Ba'qūbah
Mandalī
Al Khāliş
Jāsimīyah
Balad Rūz
Banī Sa'd
Tursāq
Zurbāţīyah
Badrah
Ṣāḥilīyah
Hīt
Nahr al Furāt
Habbānīyah
Ar Ramādī
Hawr al Ḥabbānīyah
Al Fallūjah
Al Kāẓim
Tyah
BAGHDĀD
Al Maḥmūdīyah
Al 'Azīzīyah
As Şuwayrah
Nahr Dijlah (Tigris)
Al Kūt
Shaykh Sa'd
'Alī al Gharbī
Al Musayyib
Karbalā
Ar Raḥḥālīyah
Baḥr al Milḥ
BABYLON
Al Ḥillah
An Nu'mānīyah
Al Hindīyah
Hawr as Sa'dīyah
'Alī ash Sharqī
Al Ḥayy
'Afak
Qal'at Sukkar
Al 'Amārah
Al Kūfah
Ash Shāmīyah
Ad Dīwānīyah
An Najaf
Nukhuyb
W. al Ubayyiḍ
W. al Ghudaf
Ar Ruṭbah
W. Ruṭqa
W. Ḥawrān
940
'Unāzah

East from Greenwich
40 42 44 46 48 50
42 40 38 36 34 32

ft m
9000 3000
6000 2000
4500 1500
3000 1000
1500 500
600 200
0 0
50 150
100 300
200 600
500 1500
1000 3000
2000 6000
3000 9000
m ft

ARABIA AND THE HORN OF AFRICA 1:13 300 000

100 0 100 200 300 400 500 600 km

100 0 100 200 300 400 miles

LEBANON
SYRIA
DIMASHQ (DAMASCUS)
BAYRŪT (BEIRUT)
ISRAEL
Tel Aviv-Yafo
Haifa
Ashdod
Jerusalem
West Bank
Gaza Strip
'AMMĀN
JORDAN
Jabal ad Durūz 1801
Bâdiyat ash Shām
Ar Ruṭbah
IRAQ
BAGHDĀD
Karbalā
An Najaf
Al Jazīrah
Mesopotamia
Nahr al Furāt
Nahr Dijlah
An Nāṣirīyah
Al 'Amarah
Al Baṣrah
Kūhhā-ye Zāgros
IRAN
EṢFAHĀN
4548
Ahvāz
Khorramshahr
Ābādān
Khvor
Bīrjand
Yazd
Dasht-e Lut
AFGHANISTAN
Farāh
Zābol
Daryācheh-ye Seīstan
Kermān
Zāhedān
Bam
PERSEPOLIS
Shīrāz
Kāzerūn
Būshehr
Neyrīz
Jahrom
Deyyer
Bandār 'Abbās
Bampūr
Qeshm
Khamir
Str. of Hormuz
Ra's Musandam (Oman)
Gābrīk
Ra's al-Khaymah
Ash Shāriqah
Dubayy (Dubai)
Abū Ẓaby (Abu Dhabi)
Ṣuḥār
Gulf of Oman
Maṭraḥ
Masqat
3019
Nazwá
Ṣūr
Ras al Hadd
UNITED ARAB EMIRATES
Būbiyān
Al Kuwayt
KUWAIT
J. Khārk
Hafar al Bāṭin
Rafḥā
Al Jawf
An Nafūd
Al Ḥasa
The Gulf
Al Qaṭīf
Ad Dammām
BAHRAIN
Al Manāmah
QATAR
Ad Dawḥah (Doha)
Al Mubarraz
Al Hufūf
Ḥaraḍ
AR RIYĀḌ (RIYADH)
Ḥā'il
Buraydah
'Unayzah
Najd
SAUDI ARABIA
Al Madīnah
Tropic of Cancer
Yanbu 'al Baḥr
Ḥijāz
Rābigh
JIDDAH (JEDDA)
Makkah (Mecca)
Aṭ Ṭā'if
2565
Turabah
Al Līth
Laylá
Al 'Ubaylah
As Sulayyil
Rub' al Khālī (Empty Quarter)
'Asīr
Abhā
Jīzān
Ẓufār
OMAN
Khalūf
Maṣīrah
Khalīj Maṣīrah
Ra's al Madrakah
J. Khurīyā Murīyā
Ṣalālah
Mirbāṭ
Ḥaḍramawt
Shibām
YEMEN
2469
Sayḥūt
Rās Fartak
Al Mukallā
Niṣāb
Shaqrā'
Aḥwar
Khamir
Ṣana'
Djebel Manar 3350
Ta'izz
Al Ḥudaydah
Kamaran
Farasān
Al Luḥayyah
Dahlak Kebir
Al Mukhā
Al' Adan (Aden)
Hanish
Gulf of Aden
Bab el Mandeb
Socotra (Yemen)
Hadiboh
Abd al Kūrī
Bereda
Ras Asir
Bosaso
Erigavo
2406
El Gal
Dante
Ras Hafun
Karin
Berbera
Hargeisa
Burao
Gardo
Bender Beila
Garoe
Eil
Galcaio
Las Anod
SOMALI REP.
Sinadogo
Obbia
El Dere
Belet Uen
Ferfer
Lugh Ganana
Baidoa
Bur Acaba
Bardera
MUQDISHO (MOGADISHU)
Merca
Wabi Scebeli
Giuba
Dif
INDIAN OCEAN
SINAI (Es Sînâ')
G. Mûsa 2637
2578
Elat
Al 'Aqabah
Ma'ān
Tabūk
Al Muwayliḥ
Al Wajh
Bûr Sa'îd (Port Said)
Qanâ es Suweis
Ismâ'iliya
El Suweis (Suez)
Khalig el Suweis
Hurghada
2187
Bûr Safâga
EGYPT
Qena
Quseir
El Uqsur
Idfû
Kôm Ombo
Sadd el Aali
Aswân
Ras Bânâs
Bîr Shalatein
Buheirat en Naser
RED SEA
Wadi Halfa
Halaib
Ras Hadarba
Es Sahrâ en Nûbîya
Kosha
Delgo
3rd Cataract
Muhammad Qol
2259
Abu Hamed
Dongola
4th Cataract
Kareima
Nahr en Nil
Bûr Sûdân
Suakin
Trinkitat
Sinkat
5th Cataract
Haiya
Ed Debba
Berber
Atbara
Adarama
Nahr 'Atbara
Karora
2780
Nakfa
Wad Hamid
6th Cataract
Shendi
Omdurmân
El Khartûm (Khartoum)
Kassalâ
Khashm el Girba
Akordat
Asmera
Massawa
Zula
ERITREA
El Gezira
Wad Medanî
Gedaref
Ed Dueim
Adigrat
Aksum
Adwa
Mekele
-116
Danakil Desert
Ras Dashen 4620
Gonder
Lalibela
4190
1830
L. Tana
Aseb
Debre Tabor
Bahir Dar
Tendaho
L. Abbé
-155
DJIBOUTI
Tadjoura
Djibouti
Dikhil
Zeila
Dese
Bure
Debre Markos
Singa
Kôstî
Umm Ruwaba
Nil el Azraq
Ed Damazin
Nil el Abyad
SUDAN
Malakâl
Sobat
Sûdd
Bahr el Jebel
Nekemte
ADDIS ABEBA
Debre Zevit
Dire Dawa
3381
Harer
Jijiga
Awash
3202
Dembidolo
Metu
Gore
ETHIOPIA
Nazret
L. Ziway
Asela
Shashemene
Ginir
Ogaden
Kebri Dehar
Imi
Scebeli
3686
Jima
Omo
Awasa
Yirga Alem
Mt. Batu 4307
Goba
Dila
L. Abaya
Arba Minch
L. Shamo
Kibre Mengist
Negele
Ganale
Chew Bahir
Dolo
Mega
Moyale
El Wak
Wajir
Pibor Post
Bôr
Tali Post
Mongalla
Kapoeta
Juba
Torit
3187
Kajo Kaji
Yei
Lokitaung
375
L. Turkana
Albert Nile
Gulu
Arua
Lira
Moroto
3084
Pakwach
Murchison Falls
2456
UGANDA
Soroti
619
L. Albert
Masindi
L. Kyoga
Mbale
4321
Lodwar
South Horr
Marsabit
3206
Kitale
KENYA

ft m
12 000 4000
9000 3000
6000 2000
4500 1500
3000 1000
1200 400
600 200
0 0
200 600
1000 3000
2000 6000
4000 12 000
m ft

Projection : Sanson-Flamsteed's Sinusoidal

East from Greenwich

CYPRUS
Paphos
Episkopi
Limassol
Akrotiri Bay
Episkopi Bay
C. Gata
MEDITERRANEAN
SEA
LEBANON
SYRIA
ISRAEL
JORDAN
EGYPT
SAUDI ARABIA
Hims
Tarābulus (Tripoli)
Al Minā'
Al Batrūn
Jubayl
Jūniyah
BAYRŪT (Beirut)
Ash Shuwayfāt
Ad Dāmūr
Saydā (Sidon)
Jazzīn
An Nabatīyah at Tahta
Sūr (Tyre)
Zahlah
Ba'labakk
Bsharri
Qurnat as Sawdā' 3088
Al Hirmil
Al Qusayr
Al Burayj
Al Labwah
Yabrūd
An Nabk
Al Qaryatayn
DIMASHQ (Damascus)
Dūmā
Dārayyā
Qatanā
Al Kiswah
Az Zabadānī
J. ash Shaykh (Mt. Hermon) 2814
Golan Heights
Al Qunaytirah
Marj 'Uyūn
Qiryat Shemona
As Sanamayn
Dar'ā
As Suwaydā'
Salkhad
Nahariyya
'Akko (Acre)
Hefa (Haifa)
Zefat
Teverya (Tiberias)
Yam Kinneret -210
Nazerat (Nazareth)
Irbid
Ar Ramthā
Afula
Bet She'an
Janīn
Hadera
Tulkarm
Netanya
Herzliyya
Nāblus
Tel Aviv-Yafo
Petah Tiqwa
Ramat Gan
Bat Yam
Rishon le Ziyyon
Lod
Ramla
Rehovot
Yavne
Ashdod
West Bank
Rām Allāh
El Arīhā (Jericho)
Jerusalem (Yerushalayim) (Al Quds)
Bayt Lahm (Bethlehem)
Al Khalīl (Hebron)
As Salt
Az Zarqā
'AMMĀN
Mā'dabā
Al Mafraq
Dead Sea -411
Ashqelon
Qiryat Gat
Gaza
Gaza Strip
Khān Yūnis
Rafah
Be'er Sheva (Beersheba)
Arad
Dimona
Sedom
Al Karak
HADAROM
At Tafīlah
Hanegev
Mizpe Ramon
Ma'ān
Ra's an Naqb
Al Mudawwarah
Elat
Al 'Aqabah
Gulf of Aqaba
Haql
Bûr Sa'îd (Port Said)
Bûr Fu'ad
El 'Arîsh
Sabkhet el Bardawil
Ismâ'ilîya
El Buheirat el Murrat el Kubra (Great Bitter L.)
El Suweis (Suez)
Es Sînâ' (Sinai)
Nakhl
Gebel el Tîh
Khalîg el Suweis
1974 Cease Fire Lines
Projection: Polyconic
East from Greenwich
COPYRIGHT PHILIP'S

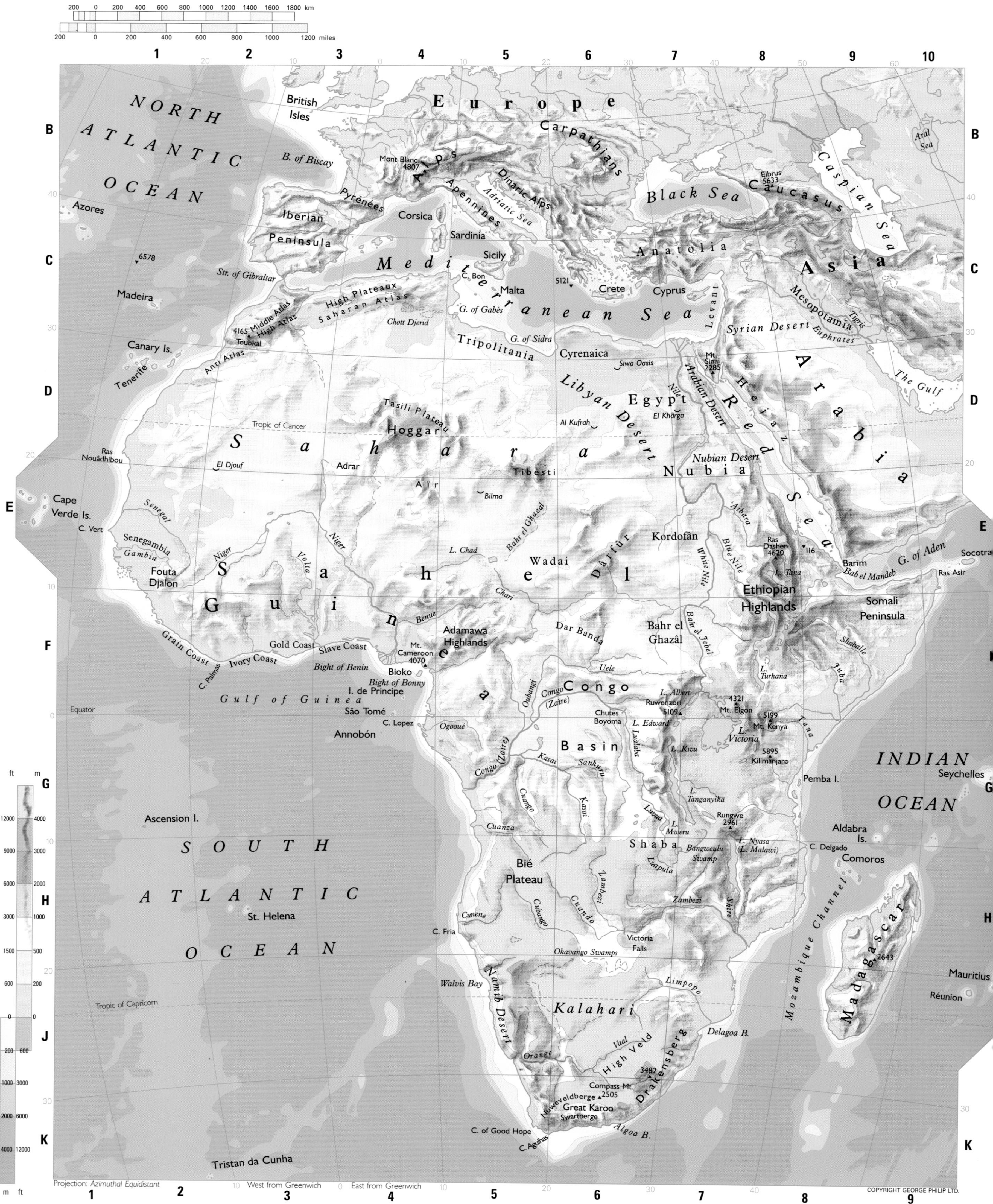
NORTH ATLANTIC OCEAN
British Isles
Europe
Carpathians
Aral Sea
Caspian Sea
B. of Biscay
Mont Blanc 4807
Alps
Apennines
Adriatic Sea
Dinaric Alps
Elbrus 5633
Black Sea
Caucasus
Azores
Iberian Peninsula
Pyrénées
Corsica
Sardinia
Sicily
Anatolia
Asia
6578
Str. of Gibraltar
Mediterranean Sea
C. Bon
Malta
5121
Crete
Cyprus
Madeira
Middle Atlas
High Plateaux
Saharan Atlas
G. of Gabès
Levant
Mesopotamia
Tigris
4165 Toubkal
High Atlas
Chott Djerid
Syrian Desert
Euphrates
Canary Is.
Tenerife
Anti Atlas
G. of Sidra
Tripolitania
Cyrenaica
Siwa Oasis
Mt. Sinai 2285
Arabian Desert
Hejaz
The Gulf
Arabia
Libyan Desert
Egypt
Nile
Tasili Plateau
Hoggar
Tropic of Cancer
Al Kufrah
El Khârga
Red Sea
Ras Nouâdhibou
Sahara
El Djouf
Adrar
Tibesti
Nubian Desert
Nubia
Aïr
Bilma
Cape Verde Is.
C. Vert
Senegal
Atbara
Senegambia
Gambia
Niger
Volta
L. Chad
Bahr el Ghazal
Kordofân
Blue Nile
White Nile
Ras Dashen 4620
116
Barīm
G. of Aden
Socotra
Bab el Mandeb
Ras Asir
Fouta Djalon
Sahel
Wadai
Dārfūr
L. Tana
Ethiopian Highlands
Somali Peninsula
Chari
Guinea
Benue
Adamawa Highlands
Dar Banda
Bahr el Ghazâl
Bahr el Jebel
Shaballe
Grain Coast
Gold Coast
Slave Coast
Ivory Coast
C. Palmas
Mt. Cameroon 4070
Bight of Benin
Bioko
Bight of Bonny
I. de Principe
Gulf of Guinea
São Tomé
Equator
C. Lopez
Annobón
Uele
Oubangi
Congo (Zaïre)
Congo Basin
L. Turkana
Juba
L. Albert
Ruwenzori 5109
4321 Mt. Elgon
5199 Mt. Kenya
Tana
Chutes Boyoma
L. Edward
L. Victoria
Ogooué
Lualaba
L. Kivu
5895 Kilimanjaro
Kasai
Sankuru
INDIAN OCEAN
Seychelles
Pemba I.
Cuango
L. Tanganyika
Rungwe 2961
Ascension I.
Cuanza
Lucuva
L. Mweru
Aldabra Is.
SOUTH ATLANTIC OCEAN
Shaba
Bangweulu Swamp
L. Nyasa (L. Malawi)
C. Delgado
Comoros
Bié Plateau
Luapula
Zambezi
Shire
Mozambique Channel
Madagascar
St. Helena
Cubango
Cuando
Cunene
C. Fria
Victoria Falls
Okavango Swamps
2643
Mauritius
Walvis Bay
Namib Desert
Limpopo
Réunion
Tropic of Capricorn
Kalahari
Delagoa B.
Vaal
Orange
High Veld
3482
Drakensberg
Compass Mt. 2505
Nuweveldberge
Great Karoo
Swartberge
C. of Good Hope
C. Agulhas
Algoa B.
Tristan da Cunha
Projection: Azimuthal Equidistant
West from Greenwich
East from Greenwich

NORTH ATLANTIC OCEAN
SOUTH ATLANTIC OCEAN
INDIAN OCEAN
Mediterranean Sea
Sahara
ALGERIA
LIBYA
EGYPT
MOROCCO
MAURITANIA
MALI
NIGER
CHAD
SUDAN
ETHIOPIA
SOMALI REP.
KENYA
TANZANIA
NIGERIA
CAMEROON
CENTRAL AFRICAN REP.
CONGO (DEM. REP. OF THE)
GABON
ANGOLA
ZAMBIA
ZIMBABWE
MOZAMBIQUE
NAMIBIA
BOTSWANA
SOUTH AFRICA
MADAGASCAR
SAUDI ARABIA
YEMEN
Projection: Azimuthal Equidistant
West from Greenwich
East from Greenwich
Dakar Capital Cities

ATLANTIC OCEAN
MOROCCO
ALGERIA
WESTERN SAHARA
MAURITANIA
MALI
SENEGAL
GAMBIA
GUINEA-BISSAU
GUINEA
SIERRA LEONE
LIBERIA
IVORY COAST
BURKINA FASO
GHANA
TOGO
BENIN
NIGERIA
NIGER
Tropic of Cancer
Projection : Sanson-Flamsteed's Sinusoidal
West from Greenwich
East from Greenwich

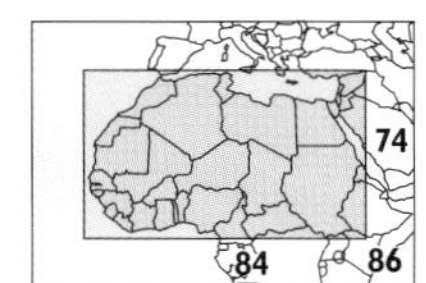

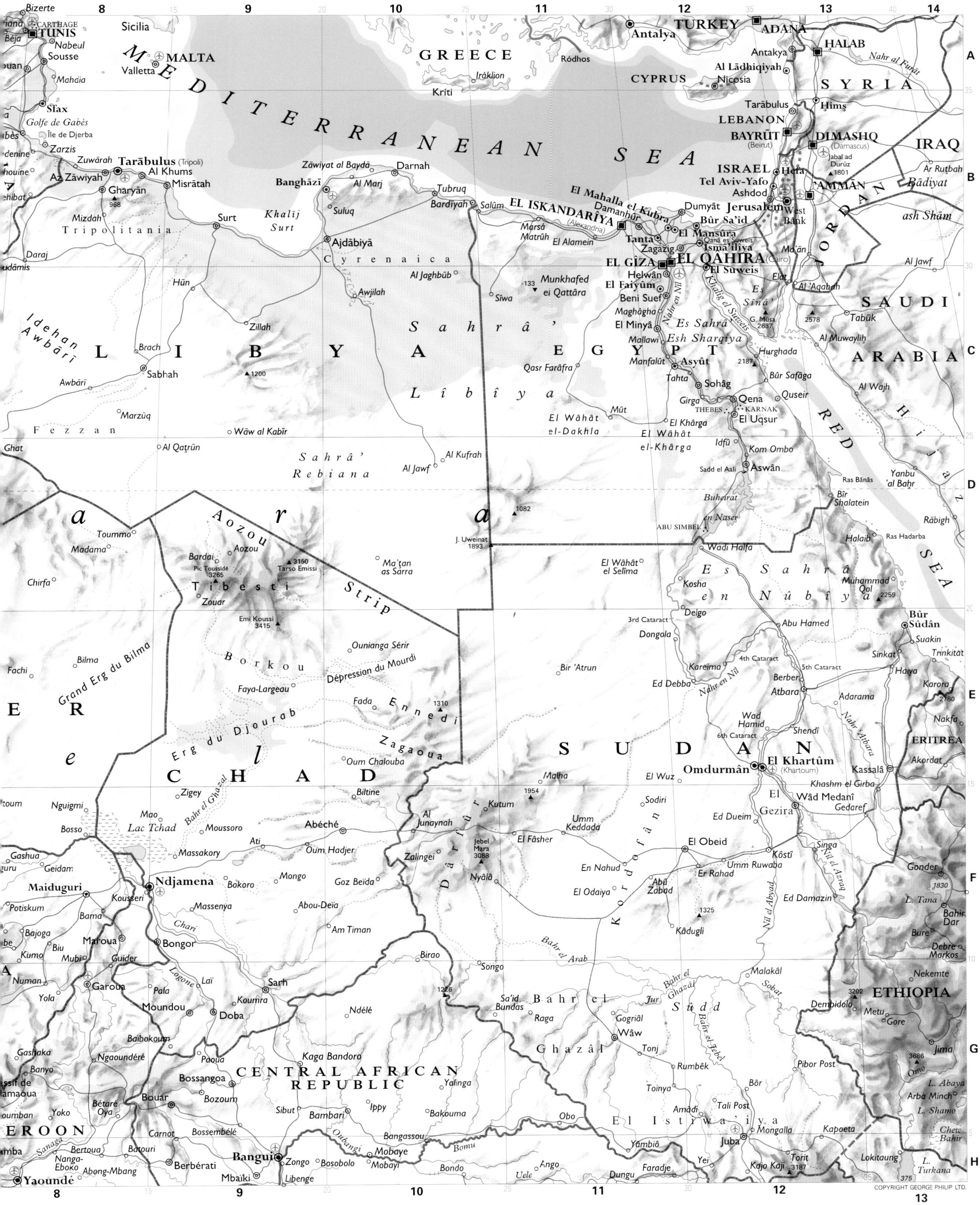

8 9 10 11 12 13 14

Bizerte
CARTHAGE
TUNIS
Béja
Nabeul
Sousse
Mahdia
Sfax
Golfe de Gabès
Île de Djerba
Zarzis
Sicilia
MALTA
Valletta
MEDITERRANEAN SEA
GREECE
Iráklion
Kríti
Ródhos
Antalya
TURKEY
ADANA
Antakya
HALAB
Nahr al Furat
Al Lādhiqīyah
CYPRUS
Nicosia
SYRIA
Tarābulus
Hims
LEBANON
BAYRŪT (Beirut)
DIMASHQ (Damascus)
IRAQ
Jabal ad Durūz 1801
Ar Rutbah
Bādiyat
ash Shām
ISRAEL
Haifa
Tel Aviv-Yafo
Ashdod
Jerusalem
West Bank
'AMMĀN
JORDAN
Zuwārah
Tarābulus (Tripoli)
Al Khums
Az Zāwiyah
Gharyān
Misrātah
968
Mizdah
Tripolitania
Surt
Khalīj Surt
Zāwiyat al Baydā
Darnah
Banghāzī
Al Marj
Tubruq
Bardīyah
Suluq
Ajdābiyā
Cyrenaica
Al Jaghbūb
Awjilah
Salûm
EL ISKANDARÎYA (Alexandria)
Marsá Matrûh
El Alamein
El Mahalla el Kubra
Damanhûr
Dumyât
Bûr Sa'îd
Tanta
El Mansûra
Zagazig
Isma'iliya
Qanâ es Suweis
EL GÎZA
EL QAHIRA (Cairo)
El Suweis
Helwân
El Faiyûm
Beni Suef
Maghâgha
El Minyâ
Mallawi
Manfalût
Asyût
Tahta
Sohâg
Girga
Qena
THEBES
KARNAK
El Uqsur
Idfû
Kom Ombo
Aswân
Sadd el Aali
-133
Munkhafed el Qattâra
Sîwa
Nahr en Nil
Khalîg el Suweis
Es Sînâ'
G. Mûsa 2637
Elat
Al 'Aqabah
Ma'ān
2578
Tabūk
SAUDI ARABIA
Al Muwaylih
Al Jawf
Es Sahrâ Esh Sharqîya
Hurghada
2187
Bûr Safâga
Quseir
Al Wajh
Hijaz
RED SEA
Yanbu 'al Bahr
Rābigh
Ras Bânâs
Bîr Shalatein
Halaib
Ras Hadarba
Muhammad Qol
2259
Bûr Sûdân
Suakin
Trinkitat
Sinkat
Haiya
Karora
2780
Daraj
Ghadāmis
Hūn
Zillah
Idehan Awbārī
Brach
Sabhah
Awbārī
LIBYA
1200
Marzūq
Fezzan
Wāw al Kabīr
Al Qatrūn
Ghat
Sahrâ' Lîbîya
EGYPT
Qasr Farâfra
Mût
El Wâhât el-Dakhla
El Khârga
El Wâhât el-Khârga
Sahrâ' Rebiana
Al Kufrah
Al Jawf
1082
Buheirat en Naser
ABU SIMBEL
J. Uweinat 1893
Wadi Halfa
El Wâhât el Selîma
Es Sahrâ en Nûbîya
Kosha
Delgo
Sahara
Toummo
Madama
Aozou Strip
Aozou
Bardai
Pic Toussidé 3265
3150
Tarso Emissi
Tibesti
Zouar
Emi Koussi 3415
Chirfa
Ma'tan as Sarra
3rd Cataract
Dongola
Abu Hamed
4th Cataract
5th Cataract
Kareima
Berber
Atbara
Nahr en Nil
Ed Debba
Bir 'Atrun
Ounianga Sérir
Dépression du Mourdi
Borkou
Bilma
Fachi
Grand Erg du Bilma
Faya-Largeau
Fada
Ennedi
1310
Erg du Djourab
Zagaoua
Oum Chalouba
NIGER
CHAD
SUDAN
Wad Hamid
6th Cataract
Shendi
Adarama
Nahr Atbara
Nakfa
ERITREA
Akordat
Kassalâ
Omdurmân
El Khartûm (Khartoum)
El Wuz
Khashm el Girba
El Gezira
Wâd Medanî
Gedaref
Malha
1954
Biltine
Zigey
Nguigmi
Mao
Lac Tchad
Bahr el Ghazal
Moussoro
Bosso
Abéché
Al Junaynah
Kutum
Dârfûr
Umm Keddada
Sodiri
Kordofân
Ed Dueim
Ati
Oum Hadjer
Massakory
Zalingei
Jebel Marra 3088
El Fâsher
El Obeid
Kôstî
Singa
Nîl el Azraq
Gashua
Geidam
Maiduguri
Ndjamena
Bokoro
Mongo
Goz Beïda
Nyâlâ
En Nahud
Umm Ruwaba
Er Rahad
Abû Zabad
El Odaiya
Ed Damazin
Gonder
1830
L. Tana
Bahir Dar
Kousseri
Potiskum
Bama
Massenya
Abou-Deïa
1325
Kâdugli
Nîl el Abyad
Chari
Am Timan
Bajoga
Maroua
Biu
Mubi
Kumo
Guider
Bongor
Bahr el Arab
Birao
Songo
Numan
Garoua
Logone
Laï
Sarh
Pala
Yola
Moundou
Koumra
Doba
Ndélé
1256
Sa'id Bundas
Bahr el Jur
Bahr el Ghazâl
Sudd
Raga
Malakâl
Sobat
Dembidolo
3202
ETHIOPIA
Metu
Gore
Bure
Debre Markos
Nekemte
Baïbokoum
Gogriâl
Wâw
Ghazâl
Tonj
Bahr el Jebel
Rumbêk
Pibor Post
Jima
3686
Omo
Gashaka
Ngaoundéré
Paoua
Kaga Bandoro
Banyo
Bossangoa
CENTRAL AFRICAN REPUBLIC
Yalinga
Bozoum
Toinya
Bôr
L. Abaya
Arba Minch
L. Shamo
Massif de l'Adamaoua
Bétaré Oya
Bouar
Sibut
Bambari
Ippy
Bakouma
Obo
Amâdi
Tali Post
Foumban
Yoko
CAMEROON
Carnot
Bossembélé
Ouaka
Bangassou
El Istiwa'iya
Mongalla
Kapoeta
Chew Bahir
Sanaga
Bertoua
Batouri
Oubangi
Mobaye
Bomu
Yambiô
Juba
Torit
3187
Lokitaung
Nanga-Eboko
Berbérati
Bangui
Zongo
Bosobolo
Mobayi
Bondo
Ango
Yei
Kajo Kaji
L. Turkana
375
Abong-Mbang
Yaoundé
Mbaïki
Libenge
Uele
Dungu
Faradje

A B C D E F G H

8 9 10 11 12 13

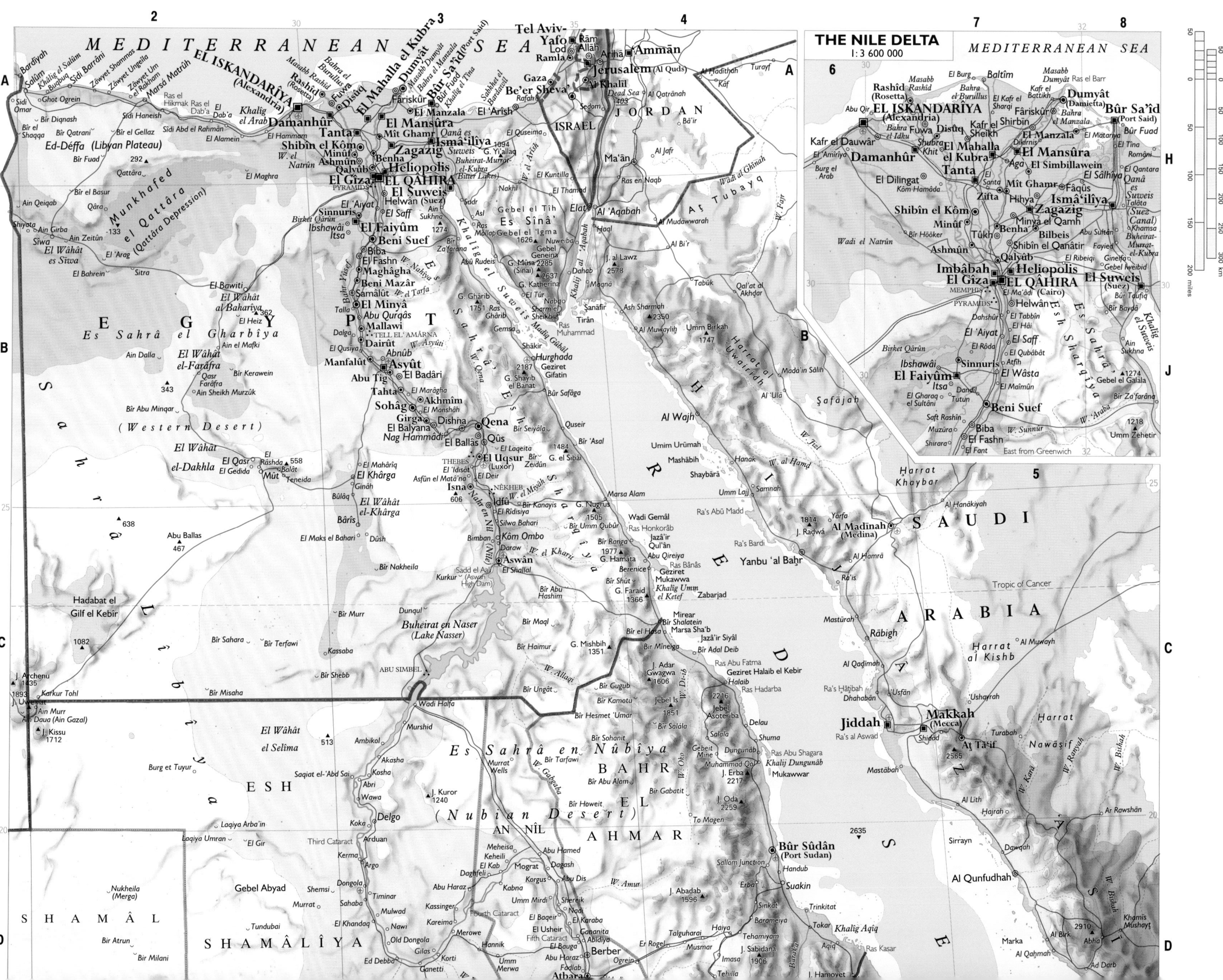
50 0 50 100 150 200 250 300 km
50 0 50 100 150 200 miles
THE NILE DELTA
1:3 600 000
MEDITERRANEAN SEA
EL ISKANDARÎYA (Alexandria)
Damanhûr
Tanta
El Mansûra
Bûr Sa'îd (Port Said)
Dumyât (Damietta)
Ismâ'ilîya
Zagazig
EL QÂHIRA (Cairo)
El Gîza
Heliopolis
El Suweis (Suez)
El Faiyûm
Beni Suef
Helwân
Imbâbah
Shibîn el Kôm
PYRAMIDS
MEMPHIS
East from Greenwich
M E D I T E R R A N E A N S E A
E G Y P T
L î b y a
S a h r â
Es Sahrâ el Gharbîya
(W e s t e r n D e s e r t)
Munkhafed el Qattâra (Qattâra Depression)
Ed-Déffa (Libyan Plateau)
El Wâhât es Sîwa
Sîwa
El Wâhât al Bahariya
El Wâhât el-Farâfra
el-Dakhla
El Wâhât el-Khârga
El Minyâ
Asyût
Sohâg
Qena
El Uqsur (Luxor)
Aswân
Isna
Kôm Ombo
Buheirat en Naser (Lake Nasser)
Nahr en Nîl (Nile)
Es Sahrâ en Nûbîya (Nubian Desert)
BAHR EL AHMAR
Khalîg el Suweis
Es Sînâ'
Hurghada
Bûr Sûdân (Port Sudan)
Wadi Halfa
Dongola
Atbara
Berber
Merowe
SHAMÂLÎYA
S H A M Â L
Gebel Abyad
Hadabat el Gilf el Kebîr
Tel Aviv-Yafo
Jerusalem (Al Quds)
Ammân
ISRAEL
JORDAN
Gaza
Be'er Sheva'
Al 'Aqabah
Elat
Ma'ân
SAUDI ARABIA
Al Madînah (Medina)
Yanbu 'al Bahr
Makkah (Mecca)
Jiddah
At Tâ'if
Al Qunfudhah
Râbigh
Al Wajh
Tabûk
Tropic of Cancer
A B C D
2 3 4 5 6 7 8
H J

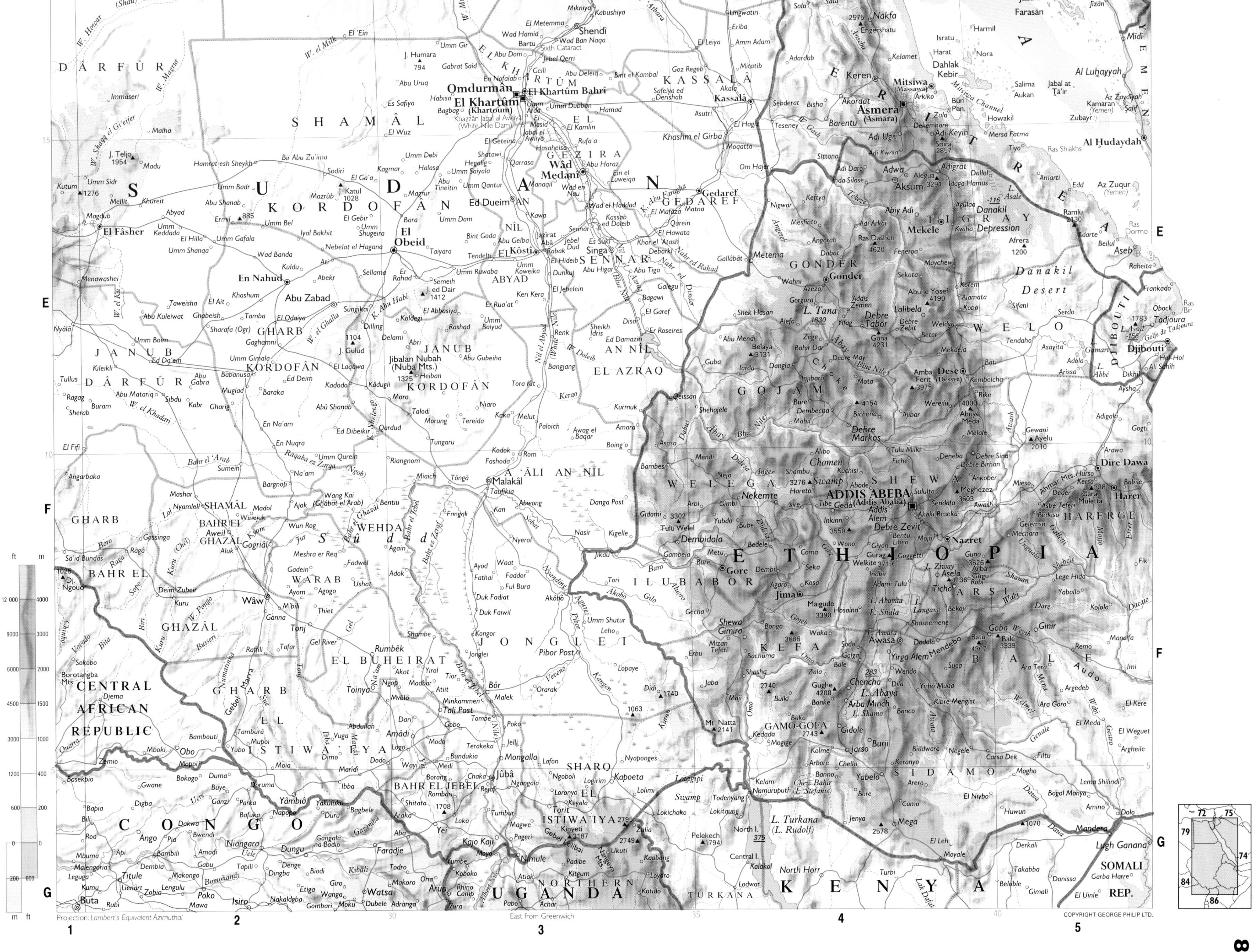

S U D A N
E T H I O P I A
E R I T R E A
DJIBOUTI
YEMEN
SOMALI REP.
K E N Y A
U G A N D A
C O N G O
CENTRAL AFRICAN REPUBLIC
D Â R F Û R
SHAMÂL KORDOFÂN
JANUB KORDOFÂN
GHARB KORDOFÂN
JANUB DÂRFÛR
GHARB DÂRFÛR
KASSALÂ
GEZIRA
GEDAREF
SENNAR
ABYAD
AN NÎL
EL KHARTÛM
AN NÎL EL AZRAQ
A'ÂLI AN NÎL
JONGLEI
EL BUHEIRAT
WARAB
BAHR EL GHAZÂL
SHAMÂL BAHR EL GHAZÂL
GHARB BAHR EL GHAZÂL
BAHR EL JEBEL
SHARQ EL ISTIWA'IYA
GHARB EL ISTIWA'IYA
NORTHERN
TURKANA
TIGRAY
GONDER
GOJAM
WELO
SHEWA
WELEGA
ILUBABOR
KEFA
GAMO-GOFA
SIDAMO
ARSI
BALE
HARERGE
Danakil Desert
Danakil Depression
Sudd
Omdurmân
El Khartûm (Khartoum)
El Khartûm Bahrî
Wad Medani
Kassalâ
Gedaref
El Obeid
En Nahud
Abu Zabad
El Fâsher
Malakâl
Wâw
Jûba
Rumbêk
Bôr
Tonj
Kôsti
Ed Dueim
Singa
Shendi
ADDIS ABEBA (Addis Ababa)
Asmera (Asmara)
Mitsiwa (Massawa)
Djibouti
Dire Dawa
Harer
Gonder
Dese (Dessye)
Mekele
Aksum
Adwa
Nazret
Jima
Gore
Nekemte
Debre Markos
Debre Zeyit
Awasa
Mega
Lalibela
Keren
Akordat
Barentu
Assab
Tadjoura
Obock
Al Hudaydah
Al Luhayyah
Lugh Ganana
Mandera
Isiro
Buta
L. Tana
L. Turkana (L. Rudolf)
L. Abaya
L. Shala
L. Ziway
L. Abbé
L. Assal
Blue Nile
White Nile
Bahr el Jebel
Bahr el Ghazâl
Sobat
Abay
Awash
Omo
Atbara
Dahlak Kebir
Mitsiwa Channel
Golfe de Tadjoura
Ras Dashen 4620
Nubian Mts.
Jibalan Nubah (Nuba Mts.)
Imatong Mts.
East from Greenwich
Projection: Lambert's Equivalent Azimuthal
COPYRIGHT GEORGE PHILIP LTD.
ft
m
12 000
9000
6000
4500
3000
1200
600
0
200
4000
3000
2000
1500
1000
400
200
0
600
1
2
3
4
5
E
F
G
72
75
79
74
84
86
18

50 0 50 100 150 200 250 300 km
50 0 50 100 150 200 miles
M A U R I T A N I A
T r a r z a
T a g a n t
A o u k â r
El Mreyyé
Nouakchott
Akjoujt
Oujeft
Et Tîdra
Râs Timirist
Nouâmghâr
Bennichchâb
Bou Rjeïmât
Sebkhet Te-n-Dghâmcha
Rachid
Tidjikja
Gâneb
Tîchît
Akreïjit
Aratâne
Moudjeria
Boutilimit
Magta Lahjar
Boûmdeïd
Tâmchekket
Tagouräret
Oualâta
Mederdra
Aleg
Mâl
Rosso
Dagana
Podor
Bogué
Kiffa
'Ayoûn el 'Atroûs
Néma
Timbedgha
Kaédi
Mbout
Kankossa
Kobenni
Sélibabi
Bassikounou
Araouane
Bou Djébéha
Tombouctou (Timbuktu)
Goundam
Diré
Niafounké
L. Faguibine
S E N E G A L
Sénégal
St. Louis
Louga
Linguère
Vallée du Ferlo
Dahra
Tivaouane
Thiès
C. Vert
DAKAR
Rufisque
Diourbel
Mbour
Fatick
Kaolack
Kaffrine
Guinguinéo
Foundiougne
Nioro du Rip
Koungheul
Koumpentoum
Tambacounda
Matam
Bakel
Kidira
Kayes
Ambidédi
Kédougou
GAMBIA
Banjul
Brikama
Georgetown
Basse Santa-Su
Kerewan
Casamance
Ziguinchor
Bignona
Sédhiou
Kolda
Velingara
GUINEA-BISSAU
Arquipélago dos Bijagós
Bissau
Bolama
Bafatá
Gabú
Cacheu
São Domingos
Bula
Mansoa
Farim
Nova Lamego
Buba
Catió
G U I N E A
F o u t a D j a l o n
Labé
Pita
Télimélé
Dalaba
Mamou
Kindia
Conakry
Îles de Los
Forécariah
Boké
Gaoual
Koumbia
Tougué
Dinguiraye
Dabola
Kouroussa
Kankan
Faranah
Siguiri
Kissidougou
Guékédou
Macenta
Beyla
Nzérékoré
Yomou
SIERRA LEONE
Freetown
Lungi Airport
Port Loko
Makeni
Kabala
Kambia
Magburaka
Kenema
Bo
Bonthe
Sherbro I.
Turtle Is.
Yonibana
Moyamba
NORTHERN
EASTERN
SOUTHERN
WESTERN
Koidu
Kailahun
L I B E R I A
Monrovia
Robertsport
Paynesville
Buchanan
Gbarnga
Sanniquellie
Zwedru
Greenville
Harper
Cape Palmas
River Cess
Tchien
St. Paul
St. John
Cestos
Cavally
Lofa
M A L I
Nioro du Sahel
Diéma
Bafoulabé
Kita
Kolokani
Banamba
Koulikoro
Bamako
Kati
Ségou
Sansanding Dam
Niger
Mopti
Djenné
San
Tominian
Bla
Koutiala
Sikasso
Bougouni
Kadiolo
Niono
Macina
Ténenkou
Bandiagara
Kolondiéba
Yanfolila
Yorosso
IVORY COAST
Odienné
Boundiali
Korhogo
Ferkéssédougou
Touba
Séguéla
Man
Danané
Duékoué
Daloa
Bouaflé
Yamoussoukro
Bouaké
Katiola
Dabakala
Bondoukou
Issia
Gagnoa
Soubré
Sassandra
San Pédro
Tabou
Divo
Lakota
Agboville
Dabou
ABIDJAN
Grand Bassam
Bingerville
Adzopé
Abengourou
Dimbokro
Tiassalé
Jacqueville
Grand Lahou
L. de Kossou
L. de Buyo
Bandama Blanc
Bandama Rouge
Sassandra
Bobo-Dioulasso
Banfora
Orodara
Houndé
Gaoua
Diébougou
Batié
Ouahigouya
Tougan
Koudougou
Black Volta
Sunyani
Kumasi
Wa
Berekum
Wenchi
Bole
Lawra
Tumu
ATLANTIC
OCEAN
Grain Coast
Ivory Coast
GULF
6363
C. Three Points
Half Assini
Axim
Projection : Lambert's Equivalent Azimuthal
West from Greenwich

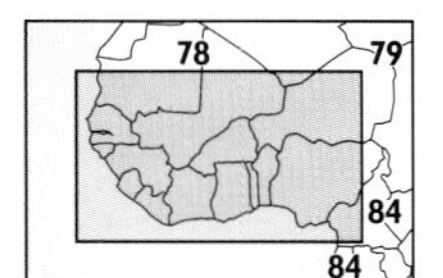

4 5 6 7

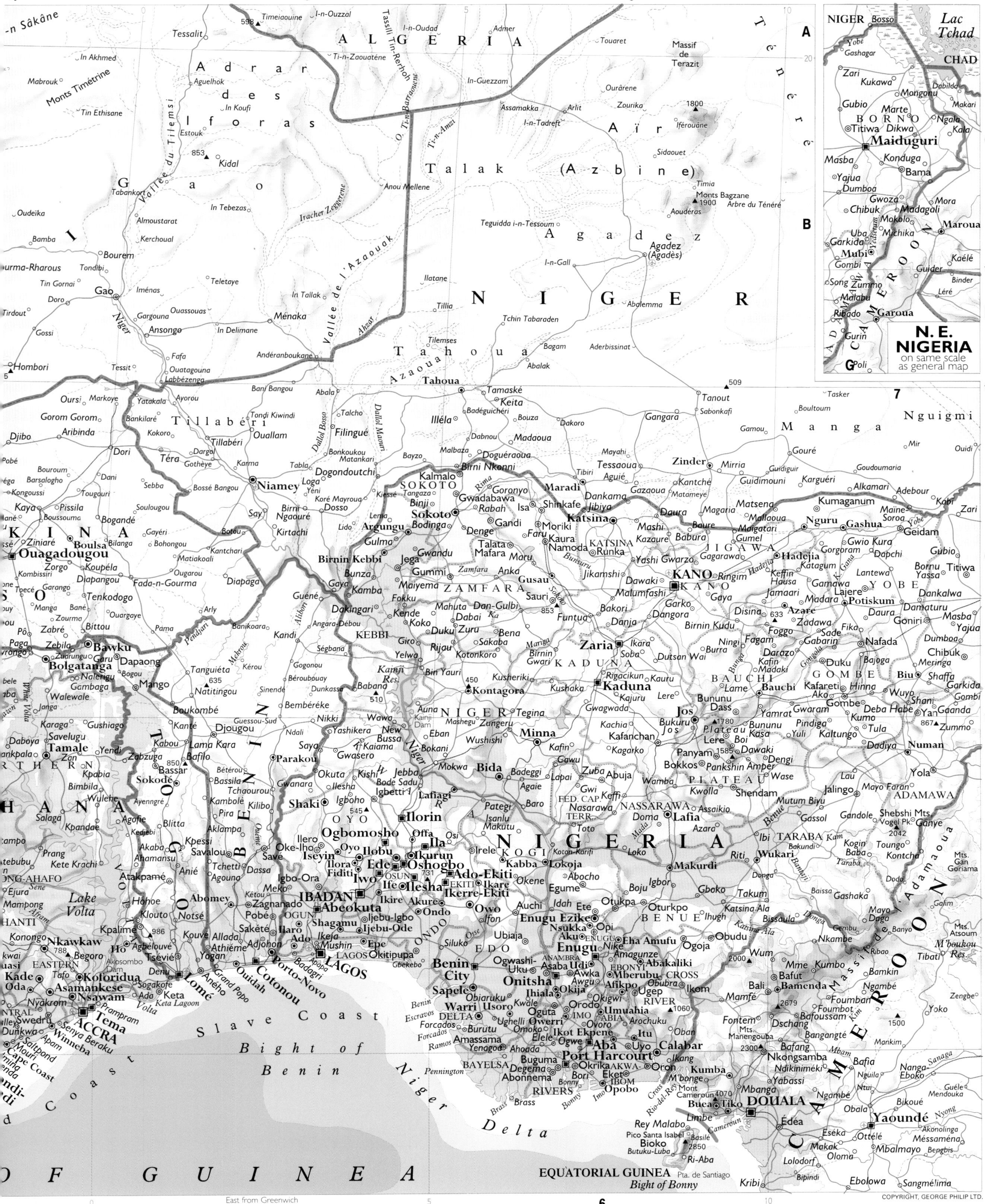

A B C D E

N.E. NIGERIA
on same scale
as general map

East from Greenwich

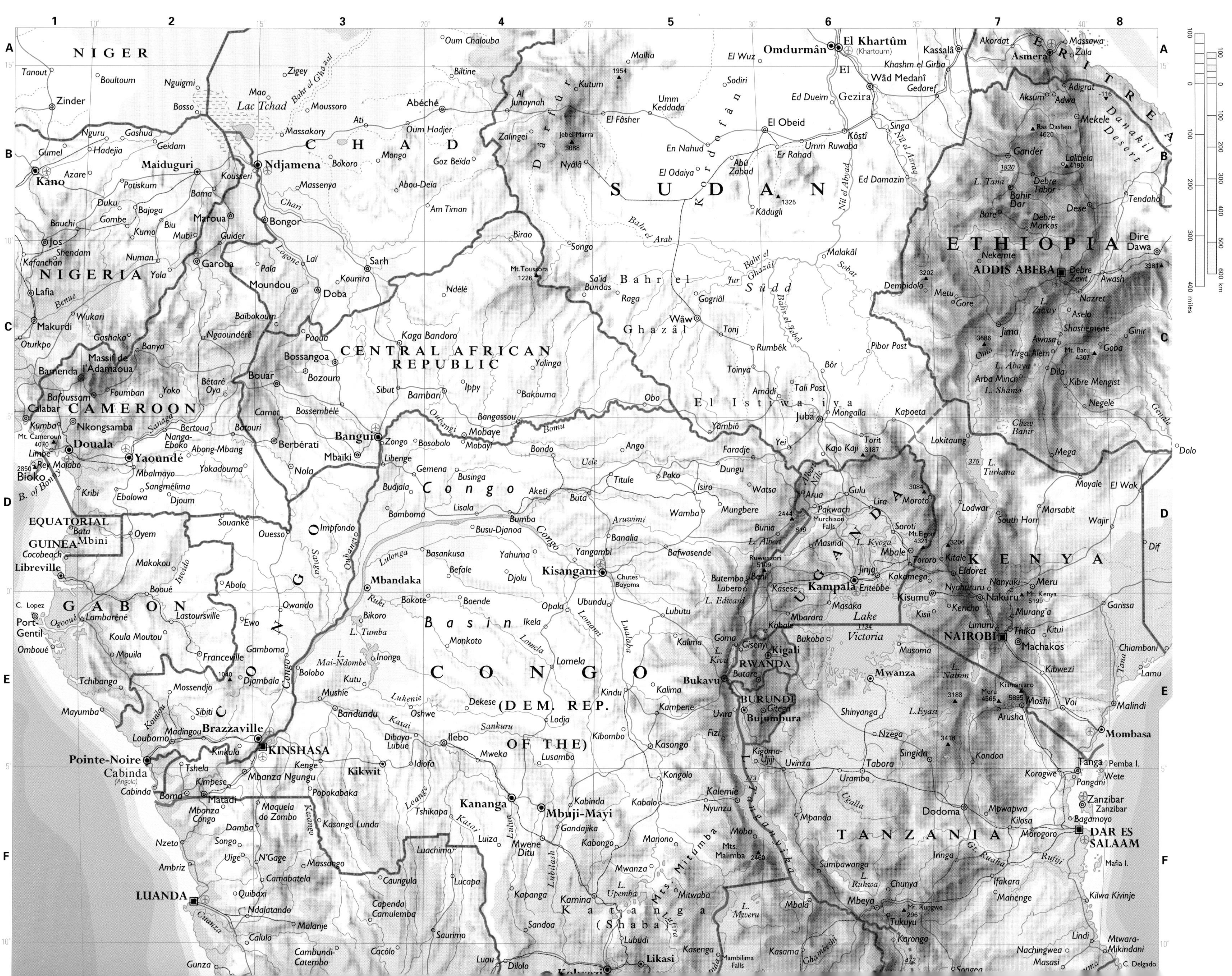

100 0 100 200 300 400 500 600 km
100 0 100 200 300 400 miles
NIGER
NIGERIA
CHAD
SUDAN
ETHIOPIA
ERITREA
CENTRAL AFRICAN REPUBLIC
CAMEROON
EQUATORIAL GUINEA
GABON
CONGO
CONGO (DEM. REP. OF THE)
UGANDA
KENYA
RWANDA
BURUNDI
TANZANIA
El Khartûm
Omdurmân
Ndjamena
Bangui
Yaoundé
Libreville
Brazzaville
KINSHASA
LUANDA
Kampala
NAIROBI
ADDIS ABEBA
Asmera
Kigali
Bujumbura
DAR ES SALAAM
Mombasa
Kisangani
Douala
Pointe-Noire
Kano
Lake Victoria
Lac Tchad
Congo Basin
Danakil Desert

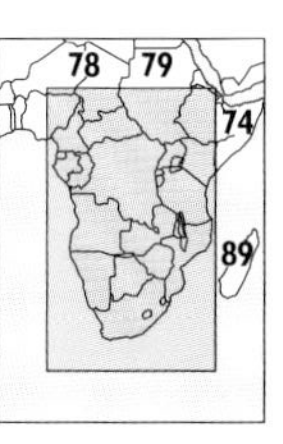

ATLANTIC OCEAN

INDIAN OCEAN

SOUTH AFRICA

NAMIBIA

BOTSWANA

ZIMBABWE

ZAMBIA

MOZAMBIQUE

MALAWI

LESOTHO

SWAZILAND

Kalahari

Namib Desert

Skeleton Coast

Namaland

Damaraland

Ovamboland

Caprivi Strip

Barotseland

Matabeleland

Mashonaland

Transvaal

Free State

Natal

Cape Province

Great Karoo

Stormberge

Drakensberg

Tropic of Capricorn

PRETORIA

JOHANNESBURG

Soweto

Vereeniging

CAPE TOWN

Table Mt. 1087

Cape of Good Hope

DURBAN

Pietermaritzburg

Port Elizabeth

East London

Bloemfontein

Kimberley

Maseru

Windhoek

Walvis Bay

Swakopmund

Lüderitz

Gaborone

HARARE

Bulawayo

Livingstone

Lusaka

Ndola

Kitwe

Lilongwe

Blantyre

MAPUTO

Beira

Nampula

Quelimane

Lubango

Huambo

Benguela

Lobito

Namibe

MADAGASCAR

On same scale as General Map

Antananarivo

Toamasina

Mahajanga

Antsiranana

Fianarantsoa

Toliara

Taolanaro

INDIAN OCEAN

Projection : Sanson-Flamsteed's Sinusoidal

East from Greenwich

ft	m
12 000	4000
9000	3000
6000	2000
4500	1500
3000	1000
1200	400
600	200
0	0
600	200
3000	1000
6000	2000
12 000	4000

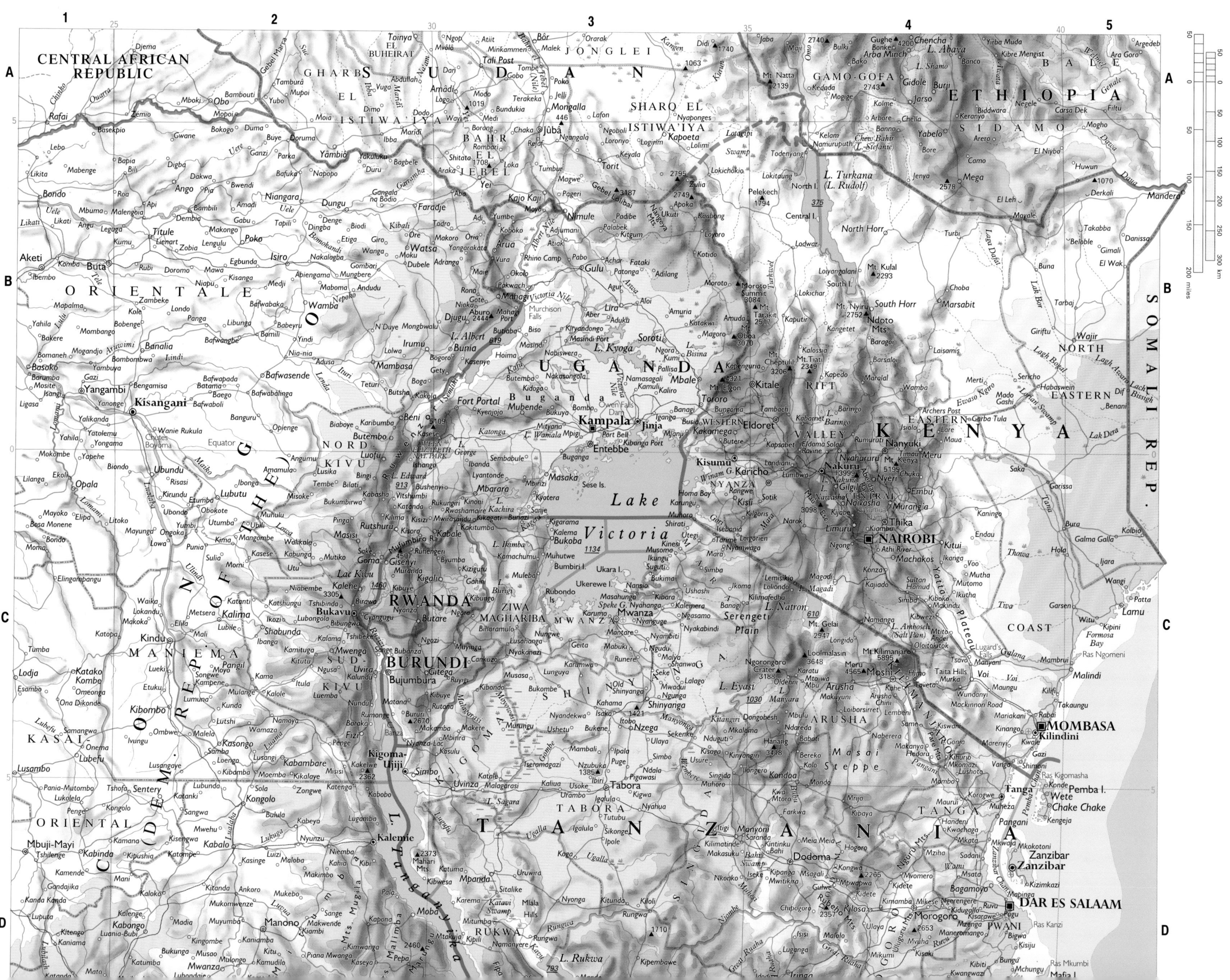
50 0 50 100 150 200 250 300 km
50 0 50 100 150 200 miles
SOMALI REP.
ETHIOPIA
KENYA
UGANDA
RWANDA
BURUNDI
TANZANIA
CENTRAL AFRICAN REPUBLIC
Lake Victoria
NAIROBI
MOMBASA
DAR ES SALAAM
Zanzibar
Kampala
Entebbe
Kisangani
Jubā
Kigali
Bujumbura
Kigoma-Ujiji
Mwanza
Tabora
Dodoma
Arusha
Moshi
Nakuru
Eldoret
Kisumu
Lamu
Malindi
Tanga
L. Turkana (L. Rudolf)
L. Tanganyika

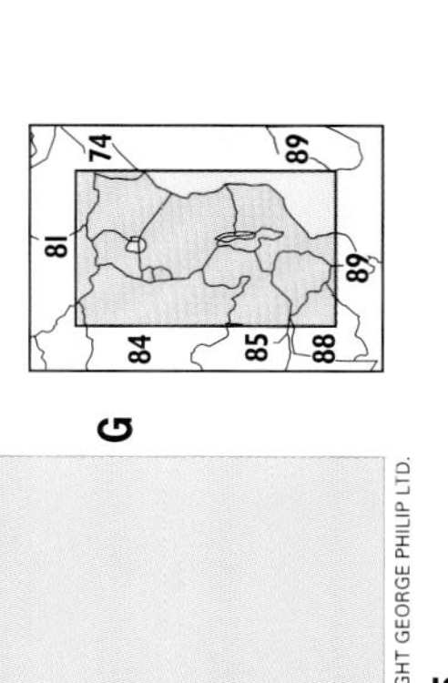

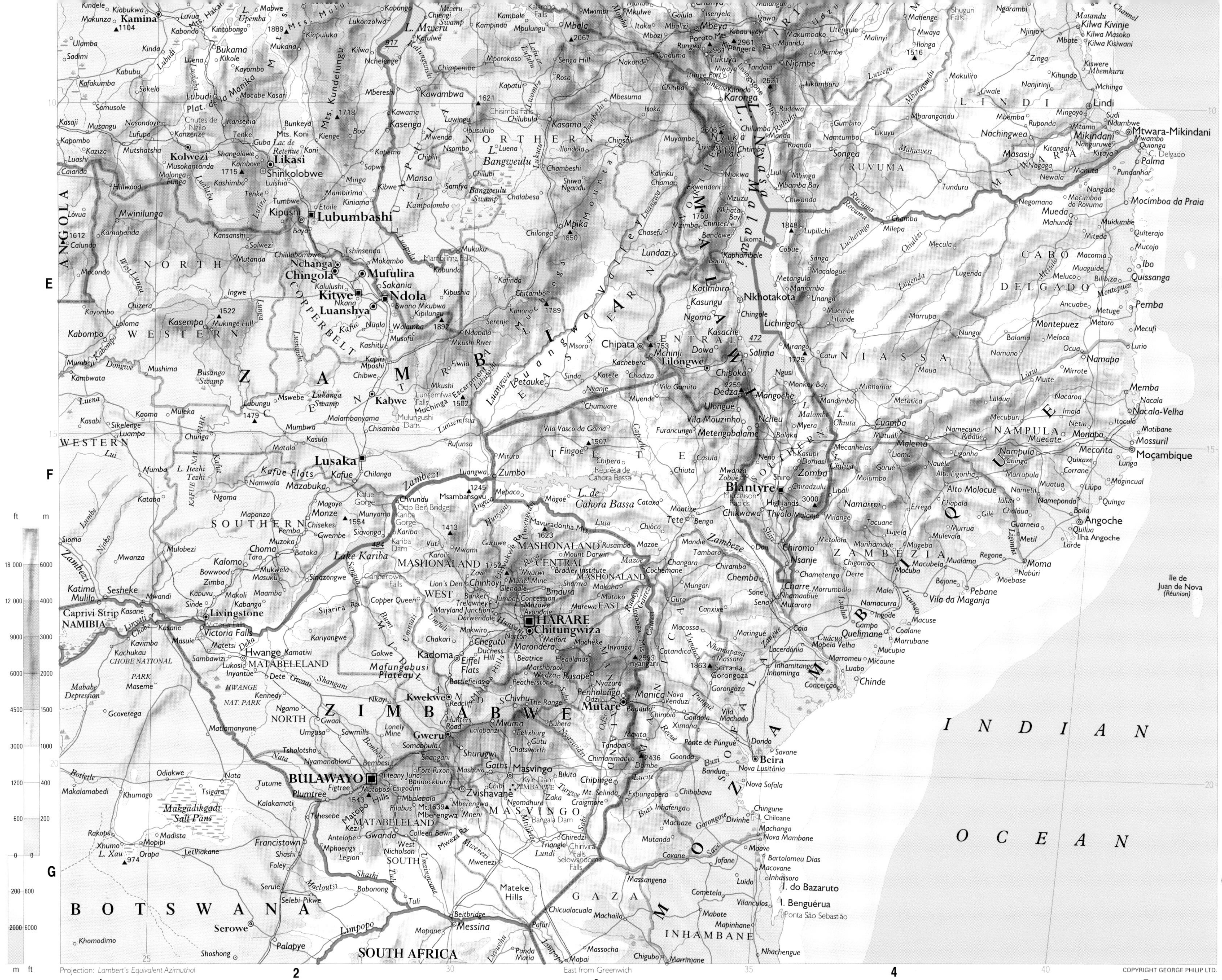
INDIAN OCEAN
L. Nyasa
HARARE
Lusaka
Lilongwe
Blantyre
Beira
BULAWAYO
Lubumbashi
Ndola
Kitwe
Kabwe
Kolwezi
Likasi
Chingola
Mufulira
Chipata
Mbeya
Livingstone
Victoria Falls
Lake Kariba
Zambezi
Tete
Quelimane
Moçambique
Mtwara-Mikindani
Lindi
Mutare
Masvingo
Gweru
Caprivi Strip
NAMIBIA
ANGOLA
BOTSWANA
SOUTH AFRICA
Projection: Lambert's Equivalent Azimuthal
East from Greenwich
COPYRIGHT GEORGE PHILIP LTD.

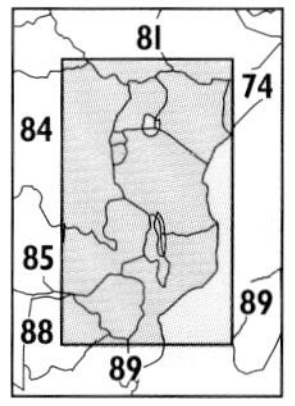

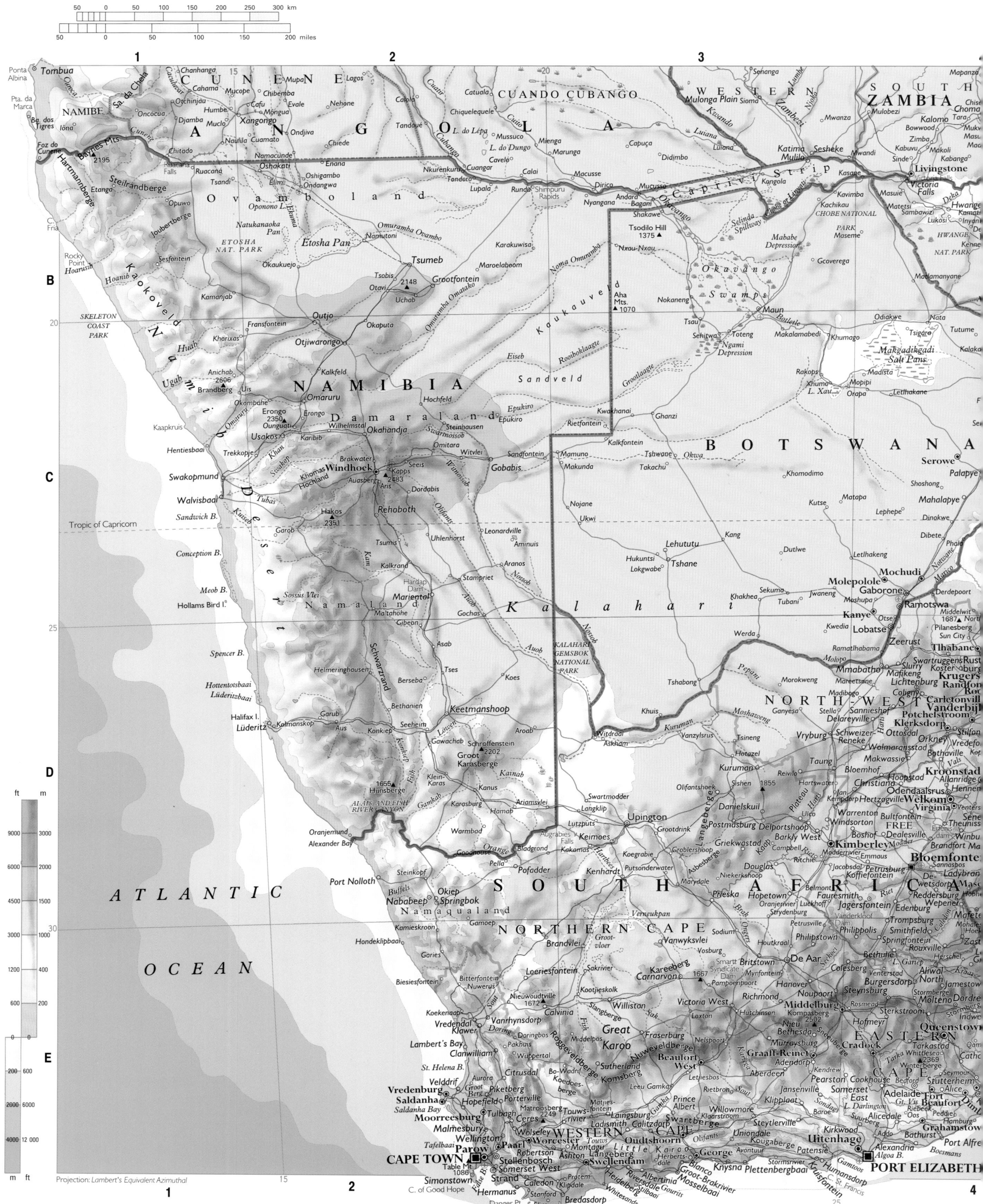

50 0 50 100 150 200 250 300 km
50 0 50 100 150 200 miles
1
2
3
4
B
C
D
E
ANGOLA
CUNENE
CUANDO CUBANGO
ZAMBIA
NAMIBIA
BOTSWANA
SOUTH AFRICA
ATLANTIC OCEAN
Tropic of Capricorn
Tombua
NAMIBE
Xangongo
Ondjiva
Oshakati
Ovamboland
Etosha Pan
ETOSHA NAT. PARK
Tsumeb
Grootfontein
Outjo
Otjiwarongo
Omaruru
Damaraland
Okahandja
Swakopmund
Walvisbaai
Windhoek
Rehoboth
Gobabis
Mariental
Namaland
Keetmanshoop
Lüderitz
Oranjemund
Alexander Bay
SKELETON COAST PARK
Kaokoveld
Namib Desert
Kalahari
Sandveld
Kaukauveld
Caprivi Strip
Okavango Swamps
Maun
Makgadikgadi Salt Pans
Ghanzi
Serowe
Mahalapye
Molepolole
Mochudi
Gaborone
Kanye
Lobatse
Ramotswa
Tshane
Livingstone
Victoria Falls
Katima Mulilo
KALAHARI GEMSBOK NATIONAL PARK
NORTH-WEST
NORTHERN CAPE
Namaqualand
Upington
Kimberley
Bloemfontein
Kuruman
Vryburg
Mmabatho
Klerksdorp
Welkom
Kroonstad
De Aar
Colesberg
Great Karoo
Beaufort West
Calvinia
Springbok
Port Nolloth
Vredendal
Clanwilliam
Vredenburg
Saldanha
Malmesbury
Paarl
Worcester
Stellenbosch
Somerset West
CAPE TOWN
Simonstown
C. of Good Hope
Hermanus
Bredasdorp
C. Agulhas
Swellendam
Oudtshoorn
George
Knysna
Mosselbaai
Plettenbergbaai
Uitenhage
PORT ELIZABETH
Grahamstown
Graaff-Reinet
Cradock
Queenstown
EASTERN CAPE
WESTERN CAPE
Middelburg
Hopetown
Prieska
Kenhardt
Carnarvon
Victoria West
Projection: Lambert's Equivalent Azimuthal

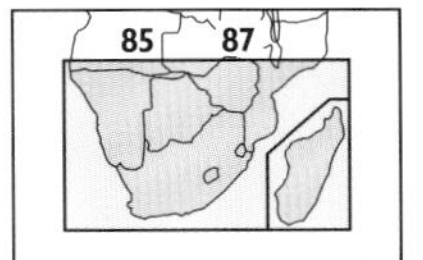

MOZAMBIQUE CHANNEL

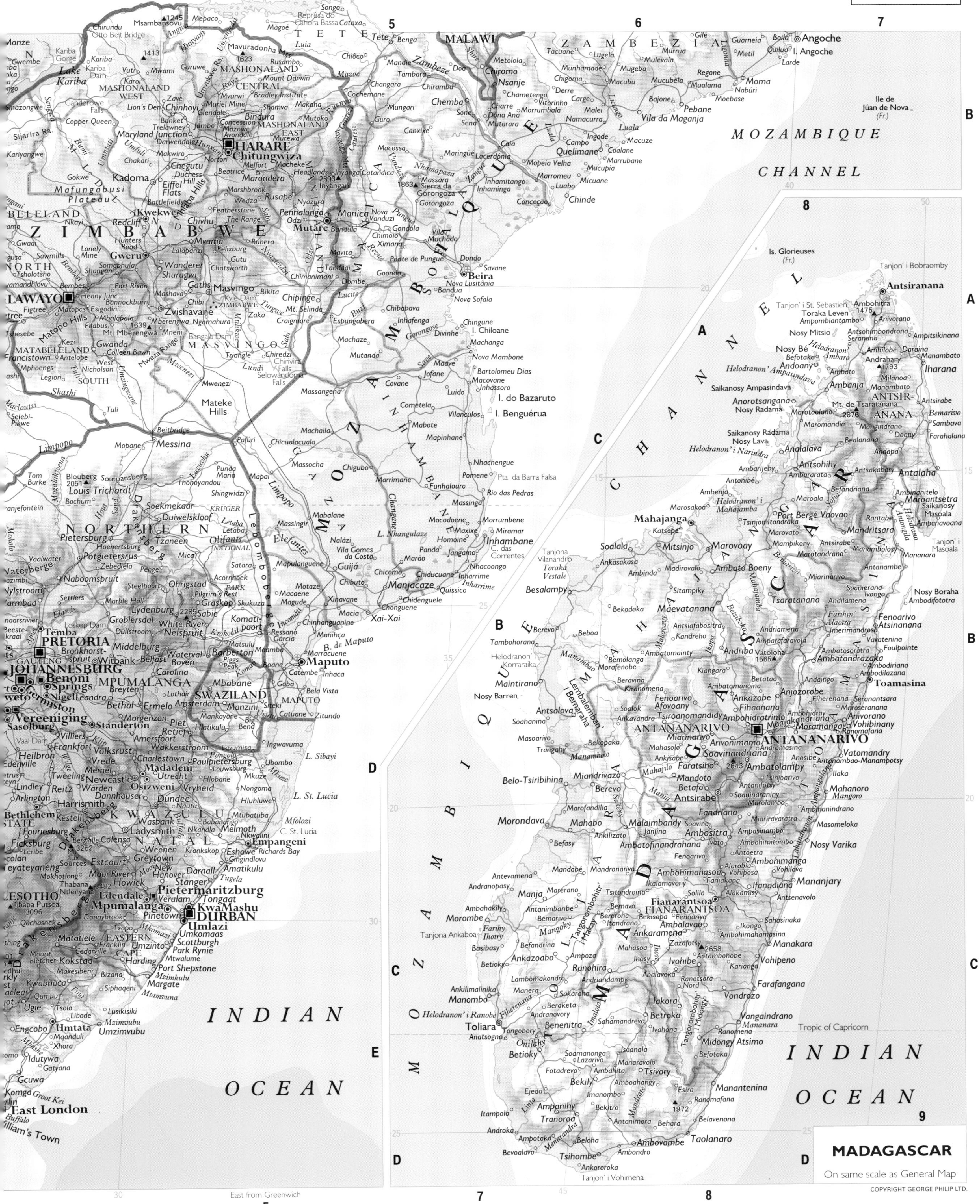

INDIAN OCEAN

MADAGASCAR

On same scale as General Map

East from Greenwich

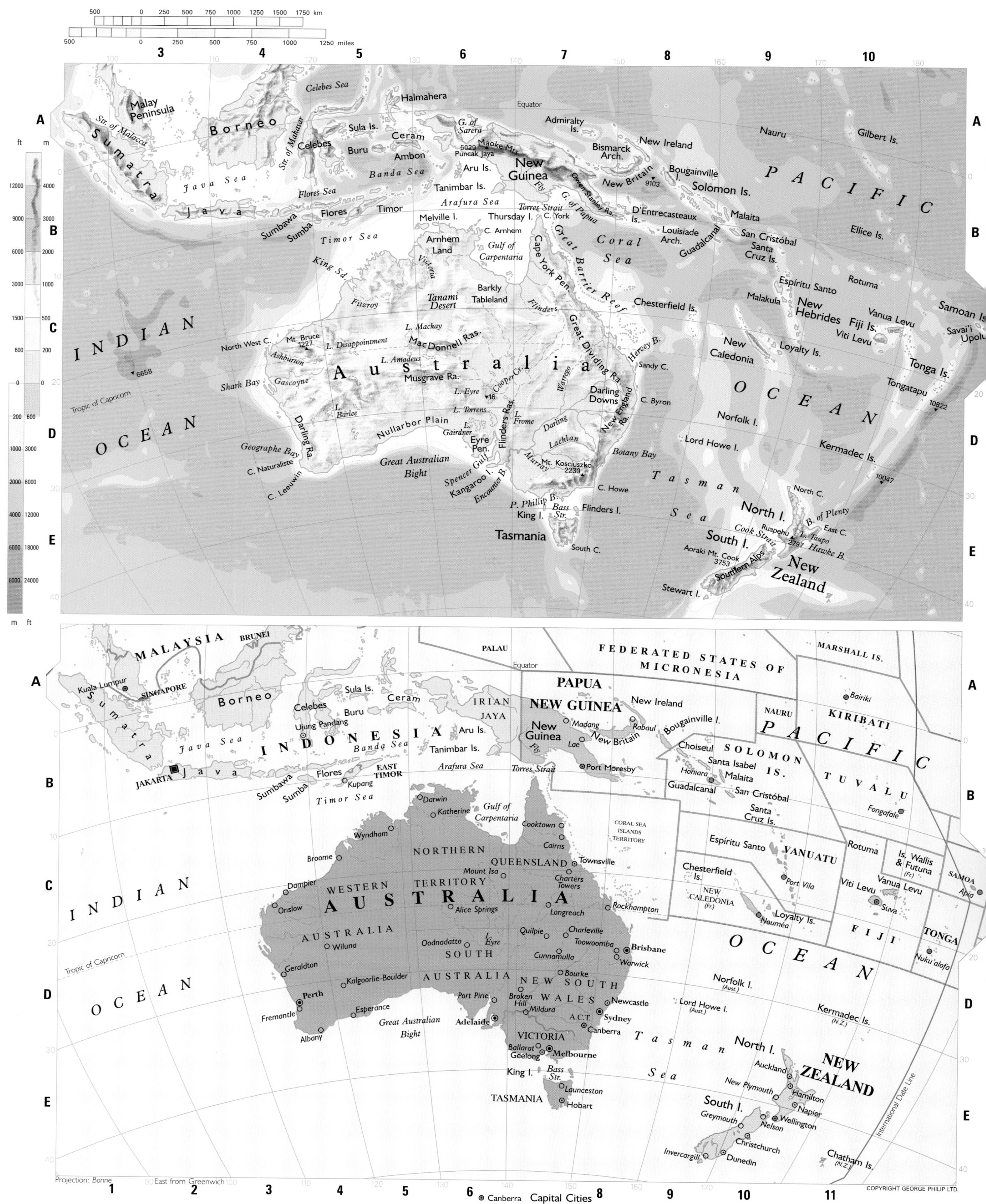
INDIAN OCEAN
PACIFIC OCEAN
Australia
New Guinea
New Zealand
Tasmania
Borneo
Sumatra
Java
Celebes
Coral Sea
Tasman Sea
Timor Sea
Arafura Sea
Great Australian Bight
Great Barrier Reef
Great Dividing Ra.
Mt. Kosciuszko 2230
AUSTRALIA
INDONESIA
PAPUA NEW GUINEA
NEW ZEALAND
FEDERATED STATES OF MICRONESIA
SOLOMON IS.
VANUATU
FIJI
TONGA
SAMOA
KIRIBATI
TUVALU
NAURU
PALAU
MARSHALL IS.
MALAYSIA
BRUNEI
SINGAPORE
EAST TIMOR
WESTERN AUSTRALIA
NORTHERN TERRITORY
QUEENSLAND
SOUTH AUSTRALIA
NEW SOUTH WALES
VICTORIA
TASMANIA
A.C.T.
Canberra
Sydney
Melbourne
Brisbane
Perth
Adelaide
Hobart
Darwin
Wellington
Auckland
Port Moresby
JAKARTA
Tropic of Capricorn
Equator
International Date Line
Projection: Bonne
East from Greenwich
Canberra Capital Cities
COPYRIGHT GEORGE PHILIP LTD.

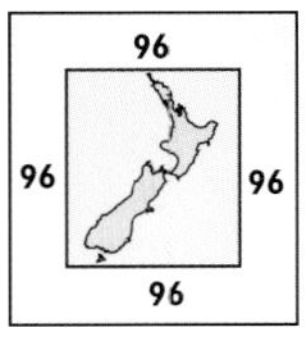
96
96
96
96

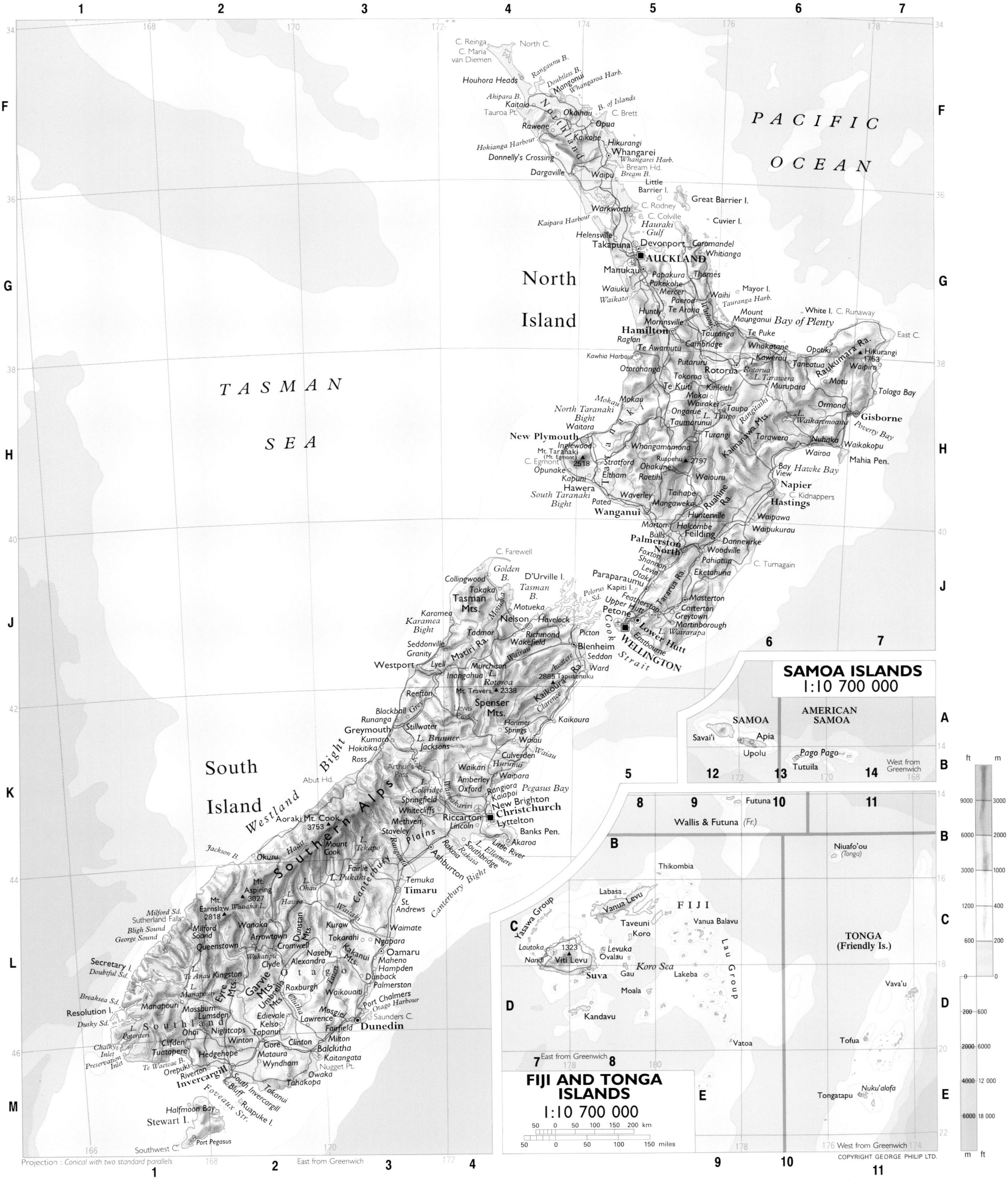
50 0 50 100 150 200 km
50 0 50 100 150 miles
PACIFIC OCEAN
TASMAN SEA
North Island
South Island
C. Reinga
C. Maria van Diemen
North C.
Rangaunu B.
Houhora Heads
Doubtless B.
Mangonui
Whangaroa Harb.
Ahipara B.
Kaitaia
Tauroa Pt.
B. of Islands
C. Brett
Okaihau
Rawene
Opua
Kaikohe
Northland
Hokianga Harbour
Hikurangi
Whangarei
Donnelly's Crossing
Whangarei Harb.
Bream Hd.
Bream B.
Dargaville
Waipu
Little Barrier I.
Great Barrier I.
Warkworth
C. Rodney
C. Colville
Kaipara Harbour
Hauraki Gulf
Cuvier I.
Helensville
Devonport
Coromandel
Takapuna
AUCKLAND
Whitianga
Manukau
Papakura
Thames
Pukekohe
Mercer
Waiuku
Waikato
Waihi
Mayor I.
Tauranga Harb.
Paeroa
Huntly
Te Aroha
Mount Maunganui
Bay of Plenty
White I.
C. Runaway
Morrinsville
Hamilton
Tauranga
Te Puke
East C.
Raglan
Cambridge
Whakatane
Opotiki
Raukumara Ra.
Hikurangi 1753
Kawhia Harbour
Te Awamutu
Kawerau
Te Teko
Waipiro
Putaruru
Rotorua
L. Rotorua
L. Tarawera
Otorohanga
Tokoroa
Murupara
Motu
Tolaga Bay
Te Kuiti
Kinleith
Mokau
Mokai
Wairakei
Ormond
North Taranaki Bight
Ongarue
Taupo
L. Taupo
Gisborne
Waitara
Taumarunui
Kaimanawa Mts.
Rangitaiki
L. Waikaremoana
Poverty Bay
New Plymouth
Turangi
Tarawera
Nuhaka
Waikokopu
Inglewood
Whangamomona
Wairoa
Mahia Pen.
Mt. Taranaki (Mt. Egmont) 2518
Ruapehu 2797
C. Egmont
Stratford
Ohakune
Bay View
Hawke Bay
Opunake
Eltham
Raetihi
Waiouru
Napier
Kaponga
Hawera
C. Kidnappers
Taihape
Hastings
South Taranaki Bight
Patea
Waverley
Mangaweka
Ruahine Ra.
Wanganui
Hunterville
Waipawa
Marton
Halcombe
Waipukurau
Bulls
Feilding
Palmerston North
Dannevirke
Foxton
Woodville
Shannon
Pahiatua
C. Turnagain
C. Farewell
Golden B.
D'Urville I.
Levin
Otaki
Eketahuna
Collingwood
Takaka
Tasman B.
Paraparaumu
Kapiti I.
Tasman Mts.
Motueka
Pelorus Sd.
Tararua Ra.
Masterton
Karamea
Karamea Bight
Nelson
Havelock
Upper Hutt
Featherston
Carterton
Greytown
Petone
Martinborough
Tadmor
Richmond
Wakefield
Picton
Lower Hutt
L. Wairarapa
Seddonville
Granity
Blenheim
Eastbourne
Seddon
WELLINGTON
Cook Strait
Westport
Lyell
Murchison
Ward
Inangahua
L. Rotoroa
2885 Tapuaenuku
Kaikoura Ra.
Reefton
Mt. Travers 2338
Clarence
Spenser Mts.
Blackball
Runanga
Greymouth
Stillwater
Lewis Pass
Kaikoura
Hanmer Springs
Kumara
L. Brunner
Hokitika
Jacksons
Waiau
Ross
Culverden
Arthur's Pass
Waikari
Hurunui
Abut Hd.
Amberley
Waipara
Westland Bight
Oxford
Rangiora
Kaiapoi
Pegasus Bay
Springfield
New Brighton
Whitecliffs
Christchurch
Aoraki Mt. Cook 3753
Methven
Riccarton
Lyttelton
Lincoln
Banks Pen.
Staveley
Canterbury Plains
Akaroa
Mount Cook
L. Ellesmere
Little River
Jackson B.
Okuru
Haast
Southern Alps
Fairlie
Southbridge
Rakaia
Ashburton
L. Tekapo
L. Pukaki
Temuka
Timaru
Canterbury Bight
Mt. Aspiring 3027
L. Ohau
St. Andrews
Mt. Earnslaw 2818
Wanaka L.
L. Hawea
Waitaki
Milford Sd.
Sutherland Falls
Bligh Sound
Milford Sound
Wanaka
Dunstan Mts.
Kurow
Waimate
George Sound
Arrowtown
Tokarahi
Ngapara
Queenstown
Cromwell
Naseby
Kakanui Mts.
Oamaru
Maheno
Hampden
Secretary I.
Doubtful Sd.
Wakatipu
Clyde
Alexandra
Otago
Dunback
Palmerston
Te Anau
Kingston
Eyre Mts.
Garvie Mts.
Umbrella Mts.
Roxburgh
Taieri
Manapouri
Breaksea Sd.
Mossburn
Waikouaiti
Port Chalmers
Otago Harbour
Resolution I.
Lumsden
Edievale
Lawrence
Mosgiel
Saunders C.
Dusky Sd.
Kelso
Dunedin
Southland
Ohai
Nightcaps
Tapanui
Fairfield
Winton
Clinton
Milton
Chalky Inlet
Tuatapere
Hedgehope
Gore
Balclutha
Preservation Inlet
Mataura
Kaitangata
Te Waewae B.
Orepuki
Riverton
Wyndham
Nugget Pt.
Owaka
Invercargill
Tahakopa
Bluff
South Invercargill
Tokanui
Foveaux Str.
Ruapuke I.
Halfmoon Bay
Stewart I.
Port Pegasus
Southwest C.
Projection : Conical with two standard parallels
East from Greenwich
SAMOA ISLANDS
1:10 700 000
SAMOA
AMERICAN SAMOA
Savai'i
Apia
Upolu
Pago Pago
Tutuila
West from Greenwich
Futuna
Wallis & Futuna (Fr.)
Niuafo'ou (Tonga)
Thikombia
Labasa
Vanua Levu
FIJI
Vanua Balavu
Yasawa Group
Taveuni
Koro
Lau Group
TONGA (Friendly Is.)
Lautoka
1323
Levuka
Nandi
Viti Levu
Ovalau
Koro Sea
Suva
Gau
Lakeba
Vava'u
Moala
Kandavu
Tofua
Vatoa
East from Greenwich
FIJI AND TONGA ISLANDS
1:10 700 000
50 0 50 100 150 200 km
50 0 50 100 150 miles
Tongatapu
Nuku'alofa
West from Greenwich
ft m
9000 3000
6000 2000
3000 1000
1200 400
600 200
0 0
200 600
2000 6000
4000 12 000
6000 18 000
m ft

50 0 50 100 150 200 250 300 km
50 0 50 100 150 200 miles
I N D O N E S I A
T I M O R S E A
I N D I A N O C E A N
NORTHERN TERRITORY
Tanami Desert
Great Sandy Desert
Gibson Desert
Kimberley
King Leopold Ranges
Hamersley Range
Pilbara
Bonaparte Archipelago
Joseph Bonaparte Gulf
Eighty Mile Beach
Tropic of Capricorn
Timor
Kupang
Roti
Sawu
Sumba
Waingapu
Waikabubak
Sumbawa
Lombok
Bali
Melville I.
Bathurst I.
Cobourg Pen.
Darwin
Katherine
Kununurra
Wyndham
Kalumburu
Halls Creek
Fitzroy Crossing
Derby
Broome
Port Hedland
Karratha
Dampier
Roebourne
Wickham
Newman
Onslow
Barrow I.
Exmouth Gulf
Exmouth
Mt. Hann 776
Mt. Ord 937
Mt. Wells 970
L. Argyle
Lake Mackay
Lake Disappointment
MacDonnell Ranges
Rowley Shoals
Ashmore Reef
Cartier I.

WESTERN AUSTRALIA
SOUTH AUSTRALIA
Great Victoria Desert
Nullarbor Plain
Great Australian Bight
INDIAN OCEAN
SOUTHERN OCEAN
PERTH
Fremantle
Kwinana
Rockingham
Mandurah
Bunbury
Busselton
Albany
Esperance
Geraldton
Carnarvon
Kalgoorlie-Boulder
Norseman
Merredin
Northam
Katanning
Narrogin
Collie
Manjimup
Hopetoun
Ravensthorpe
Southern Cross
Coolgardie
Kambalda
Menzies
Leonora
Laverton
Wiluna
Meekatharra
Cue
Mount Magnet
Sandstone
Yalgoo
Mullewa
Northampton
Kalbarri
Dongara
Jurien
Moora
Cervantes
Lancelin
Eucla
Cocklebiddy
Madura
Balladonia
Nullarbor
Penong
Ooldea
Maralinga
Forrest
Rawlinna
Ayers Rock 868
Mt. Olga 1069
Musgrave Ranges
Petermann Ranges
Everard Ranges
Hampton Tableland
Archipelago of the Recherche
Houtman Abrolhos
Dirk Hartog I.
Shark Bay
Hamelin Pool
L. Carnegie
L. Wells
L. Carey
L. Barlee
L. Moore
L. Austin
L. Cowan
L. Dundas
L. Lefroy
C. Leeuwin
Projection: Bonne
East from Greenwich
COPYRIGHT GEORGE PHILIP LTD.

50 0 50 100 150 200 250 300 km
50 0 50 100 150 200 miles
Arnhem Land
Gulf of Carpentaria
Groote Eylandt
Sir Edward Pellew Group
Wellesley Is.
Mornington I.
Cape York Peninsula
Great Dividing Range
Great Barrier Reef
CORAL SEA
Bass Strait
King Island
Flinders Island
Furneaux Group
TASMANIA
Launceston
Devonport
Hobart
Barkly Tableland
NORTHERN TERRITORY
QUEENSLAND
Great Artesian Basin
Simpson Desert
Cairns
Townsville
Mackay
Rockhampton
Gladstone
Mount Isa
Cloncurry
Charters Towers
Longreach
Emerald
Alice Springs
MacDonnell Ranges
Tennant Creek
Cumberland Islands
Northumberland Islands
Whitsunday I.
Hinchinbrook I.
Tropic of Capricorn

SOUTH AUSTRALIA
NEW SOUTH WALES
VICTORIA
AUSTRALIAN CAPITAL TERRITORY
TASMAN SEA
SOUTHERN OCEAN
Bass Strait
Great Dividing Range
Darling Downs
Grey Range
Flinders Ranges
Great Artesian Basin
Gippsland
BRISBANE
SYDNEY
MELBOURNE
ADELAIDE
Canberra
Gold Coast
Tweed Heads
Newcastle
Wollongong
Gosford
Geelong
Ballarat
Bendigo
Broken Hill
Mildura
Wagga Wagga
Albury
Dubbo
Tamworth
Armidale
Toowoomba
Coffs Harbour
Port Macquarie
Lismore
Maryborough
Hervey Bay
Gympie
Port Augusta
Port Pirie
Whyalla
Port Lincoln
Mount Gambier
Warrnambool
Kangaroo I.
King Island
Flinders Island
Furneaux Group
Lake Eyre (North)
Lake Eyre (South)
Lake Torrens
Lake Frome
Lake Gairdner
Darling
Murray
Spencer Gulf
Gulf St. Vincent
COPYRIGHT, GEORGE PHILIP LTD.
Projection: Bonne
East from Greenwich

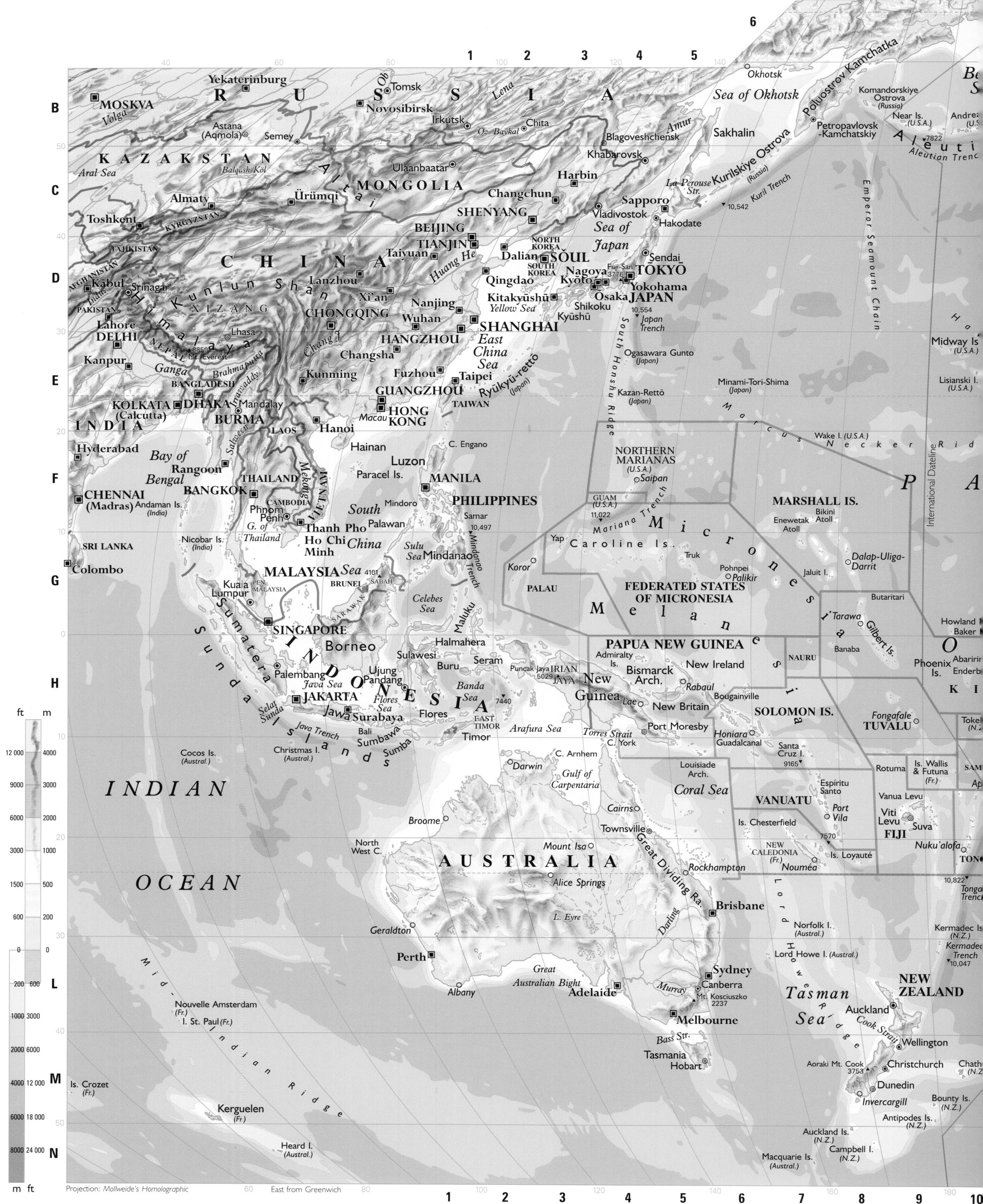
RUSSIA
KAZAKSTAN
MONGOLIA
CHINA
INDIA
JAPAN
PHILIPPINES
MALAYSIA
INDONESIA
AUSTRALIA
PAPUA NEW GUINEA
NEW ZEALAND
INDIAN OCEAN
Sea of Okhotsk
Sea of Japan
East China Sea
South China Sea
Coral Sea
Tasman Sea
Arafura Sea
Bay of Bengal
Micronesia
Melanesia
FEDERATED STATES OF MICRONESIA
MARSHALL IS.
SOLOMON IS.
VANUATU
FIJI
TUVALU
Projection: Mollweide's Homolographic
East from Greenwich

ALASKA (U.S.A.)
Anchorage
Gulf of Alaska
Juneau
Prince of Wales I. (U.S.A.)
Prince Rupert
Queen Charlotte Is. (Canada)
C A N A D A
Edmonton
Calgary
Regina
Winnipeg
L. Winnipeg
Vancouver
Victoria
Vancouver I.
Seattle
Portland
Boise
Salt Lake City
Minneapolis
Denver
Kansas City
CHICAGO
Detroit
Toronto
Ottawa
Montréal
Québec
Buffalo
Boston
Pittsburgh
NEW YORK CITY
PHILADELPHIA
Baltimore
Washington D.C.
St. Louis
Cincinnati
C. Mendocino
Sacramento
SAN FRANCISCO
UNITED STATES
Oklahoma City
Memphis
Atlanta
C. Hatteras
LOS ANGELES
San Diego
Phoenix
Dallas
Ciudad Juárez
Houston
San Antonio
New Orleans
Jacksonville
Newfoundland
St. John's
NORTH ATLANTIC OCEAN
Bermuda (U.K.)
Sargasso Sea
Gulf of Mexico
Miami
BAHAMAS
Monterrey
La Habana
CUBA
West Indies
Guadalajara
MEXICO
Mérida
Puebla
Acapulco
BELIZE
JAMAICA
Kingston
HAITI
DOMINICAN REP.
PUERTO RICO (U.S.A.)
Leeward Is.
HONDURAS
Caribbean Sea
GUATEMALA
Guatemala
San Salvador
EL SALVADOR
NICARAGUA
Managua
COSTA RICA
San José
PANAMA
Colón
Panamá
Barranquilla
Maracaibo
Caracas
Windward Is.
BARBADOS
VENEZUELA
Orinoco
Medellín
Bogotá
Cali
COLOMBIA
Quito
ECUADOR
Guayaquil
Iquitos
Amazonas
BRAZIL
Trujillo
PERU
LIMA
Cuzco
L. Titicaca
Arequipa
La Paz
BOLIVIA
Arica
Iquique
Antofagasta
PARAGUAY
Asunción
San Miguel de Tucumán
Porto Alegre
Córdoba
Rosario
Valparaíso
SANTIAGO
BUENOS AIRES
URUGUAY
Montevideo
Río de la Plata
Concepción
ARGENTINA
Patagonia
SOUTH ATLANTIC OCEAN
Falkland Is. (U.K.)
Punta Arenas
Est. de Magallanes
Tierra del Fuego
C. de Hornos
South Georgia (U.K.)
Tropic of Cancer
Tropic of Capricorn
Equator
Arctic Circle
Honolulu
Oahu
HAWAIIAN IS. (U.S.A.)
Hawaii
Guadalupe (Mex.)
C. San Lucas
Baja California
Golfo de California
Is. Revilla Gigedo (Mex.)
I. Clipperton (Fr.)
I. del Coco (Costa Rica)
I. de Malpelo (Colombia)
Galápagos (Ecuador)
C. Paliñas
Palmyra Is. (U.S.A.)
Teraina
Tabuaeran
Kiritimati
Jarvis I. (U.S.A.)
Malden I.
Starbuck I.
Tongareva
Pukapuka
Manihiki
Caroline I.
Vostok I.
Flint I.
Is. Marquises
Suwarrow Is.
Is. de la Société
Papeete
Tahiti
Is. Tuamotu
Cook Is (N.Z.)
FRENCH POLYNESIA
Rarotonga
Is. Tubuai
Mururoa
Rapa
Ducie I.
Pitcairn I. (U.K.)
Sala-y-Gómez (Chile)
I. de Pascua (Chile)
San Felix (Chile)
San Ambrosio (Chile)
Arch. de Juan Fernández (Chile)
East Pacific Ridge
Chile Rise
Pacific-Antarctic Ridge
Tuamotu Ridge
Austral Seamount Chain
Christmas Ridge
Peru-Chile Trench
Nevada Ancohuma 6550
Aconcagua 6960
PACIFIC OCEAN
ROCKY MTS
ANDES
Snake
Missouri
Colorado
Mississippi
Appalachian Mts.
St. Lawrence
L. Superior
L. Michigan
L. Huron
L. Ontario
L. Erie
Florida Str.
Canal de Yucatán
West from Greenwich

ARCTIC OCEAN
Beaufort Sea
Greenland
Baffin Bay
Hudson Bay
Labrador Sea
PACIFIC OCEAN
NORTH ATLANTIC OCEAN
Gulf of Mexico
Caribbean Sea
Rocky Mountains
Great Plains
Great Basin
Mackenzie Mts.
Alaska Range
Brooks Ra.
Queen Elizabeth Is.
Baffin Island
Hudson Strait
Davis Strait
Bering Sea
Bering Strait
Gulf of Alaska
Alaska Peninsula
Mt. McKinley 6194
Mt. Logan 5959
Mt. St. Elias 5489
Mt. Robson 3954
Mt. Waddington 3994
Mt. Rainier 4392
Mt. Shasta 4317
Mt. Whitney 4418
Mt. Elbert 4399
Blanca Peak 4378
Popocatepetl 5452
Citlaltépetl 5700
Mt. Washington 1917
Great Lakes
Appalachian Mts.
Laurentian Plateau
Sierra Nevada
Cascade Range
Coast Ranges
Colorado Plateau
Grand Canyon
Mexican Plateau
Western Sierra Madre
Eastern Sierra Madre
Lower California
Gulf of California
Yucatán Peninsula
Isthmus of Tehuantepec
Central America
Greater Antilles
Cuba
Jamaica
Hispaniola
Florida
Newfoundland
Nova Scotia
Iceland
Asia
Tropic of Cancer
Arctic Circle
Clarion Fracture Zone
Guatemala Trench
Projection: Bonne
West from Greenwich
COPYRIGHT GEORGE PHILIP LTD.

100 0 200 400 600 800 1000 1200 1400 km
100 0 200 400 600 800 1000 miles
RUSSIA
Asia
International Date Line
ARCTIC OCEAN
Beaufort Sea
Bering Sea
Bering Strait
St. Lawrence I.
ALASKA (U.S.A.)
Yukon
Porcupine
Fairbanks
Anchorage
Kodiak I.
Gulf of Alaska
Queen Elizabeth Is.
Ellesmere I.
Victoria I.
Baffin Island
Baffin Bay
GREENLAND (Denmark)
Nuuk
Davis Strait
Denmark Strait
Cape Farewell
ICELAND
Reykjavik
NUNAVUT
NORTHWEST TERRITORIES
Arctic Circle
YUKON TERRITORY
Mackenzie
Great Bear L.
Back
Whitehorse
Liard
Yellowknife
Great Slave L.
Dubawnt
Juneau
Hudson Strait
Hudson Bay
CANADA
BRITISH COLUMBIA
Skeena
Peace
L. Athabasca
Athabasca
Churchill
Nelson
ALBERTA
MANITOBA
Fraser
Edmonton
SASKATCHEWAN
Saskatchewan
Calgary
L. Winnipeg
Eastmain
QUÉBEC
Labrador
NEWFOUNDLAND
St. John's
St. Lawrence
PRINCE EDWARD I.
Charlottetown
St.-Pierre Et Miquelon (Fr.)
NEW BRUNSWICK
NOVA SCOTIA
Halifax
Fredericton
C. Sable
Victoria
Vancouver
Regina
Winnipeg
ONTARIO
Québec
Montréal
Ottawa
L. Superior
L. Huron
L. Ontario
L. Michigan
Toronto
WASHINGTON
Olympia
Seattle
Portland
Salem
Columbia
OREGON
MONTANA
Missouri
Helena
IDAHO
Boise
Snake
NORTH DAKOTA
Bismarck
MINNESOTA
Minneapolis
SOUTH DAKOTA
WISCONSIN
Madison
Milwaukee
MICHIGAN
Lansing
Detroit
Toledo
Cleveland
Erie
Buffalo
NEW YORK
PA.
Pittsburgh
MAINE
Augusta
VER.
N.H.
Concord
MASS.
Boston
Providence
CT.
R.I.
Hartford
NEW YORK CITY
PHILADELPHIA
N.J.
Baltimore
DE.
MD.
Washington D.C.
Richmond
WYOMING
Cheyenne
IOWA
CHICAGO
OHIO
Sacramento
Carson City
SAN FRANCISCO
San Jose
Salt Lake City
UNITED STATES
NEBRASKA
Lincoln
ILLINOIS
INDIANA
Columbus
NEVADA
UTAH
Denver
Kansas City
Springfield
Indianapolis
Cincinnati
W.V.
VIRGINIA
CALIFORNIA
COLORADO
Topeka
St. Louis
KENTUCKY
Raleigh
NORTH CAROLINA
Las Vegas
KANSAS
MISSOURI
Nashville
Charlotte
TENNESSEE
LOS ANGELES
Santa Fe
OKLAHOMA
ARKANSAS
Memphis
Columbia
SOUTH CAROLINA
Albuquerque
Oklahoma City
Little Rock
Atlanta
San Diego
Colorado
ARIZONA
NEW MEXICO
Birmingham
GEORGIA
Charleston
Phoenix
MISSISSIPPI
Mississippi
Montgomery
Tucson
El Paso
Dallas
Jackson
ALABAMA
Jacksonville
TEXAS
Baton Rouge
Tallahassee
Austin
LOUISIANA
New Orleans
FLORIDA
Houston
Tampa
Miami
Bermuda (U.K.)
NORTH ATLANTIC OCEAN
PACIFIC OCEAN
Guadalupe (Mex.)
Hermosillo
Rio Grande
MEXICO
Monterrey
Culiacan
Tropic of Cancer
Gulf of Mexico
Florida Str.
Nassau
BAHAMAS
Turks & Caicos Is. (U.K.)
Havana
CUBA
DOMINICAN REP.
San Juan
PUERTO RICO (U.S.A.)
HAITI
Port-au-Prince
Santo Domingo
Cayman Is. (U.K.)
JAMAICA
Kingston
Mérida
Guadalajara
MÉXICO
Puebla
Revilla Gigedo Is. (Mex.)
Belmopan
BELIZE
Acapulco
Caribbean Sea
GUATEMALA
HONDURAS
Guatemala
Tegucigalpa
San Salvador
EL SALVADOR
NICARAGUA
L. Nicaragua
Managua
Maracaibo
Barranquilla
VENEZUELA
COSTA RICA
San José
Panamá
PANAMA
South America
COLOMBIA
Medellín
Projection: Bonne
West from Greenwich
MÉXICO Capital Cities

PACIFIC OCEAN
ALASKA
YUKON TERRITORY
NORTHWEST TERRITORIES
BRITISH COLUMBIA
ALBERTA
SASKATCHEWAN
MANITOBA
WASHINGTON
MONTANA
NORTH DAKOTA
SOUTH DAKOTA
MINNESOTA
NEBRASKA
IOWA
UNITED STATES
Victoria Island
Banks Island
Prince of Wales I.
Great Bear L.
Great Slave L.
Lake Athabasca
Rocky Mountains
Mackenzie Mountains
Coast Mountains
Cassiar Mountains
Selwyn Mts.
Edmonton
Calgary
Vancouver
Victoria
Seattle
Winnipeg
Regina
Saskatoon
Whitehorse
Yellowknife
Anchorage
Minneapolis
Projection : Bonne
ALASKA
1:26 700 000
CHUKCHI SEA
BERING SEA
GULF OF ALASKA
West from Greenwich

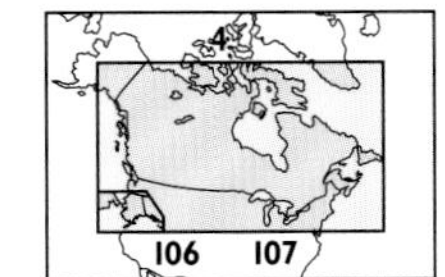

11 12 13 14 15 16

B

Devon I.
Lancaster Sound
Bylot I.
1890
Arctic Bay
Nanisivik
Borden Pen.
Eclipse Sd.
Pond Inlet
Brodeur Peninsula
2136
Baffin Bay
Nunavik
Uummannaq
Qeqertarsuaq
Qeqertarsuaq
Qeqertarsuup Tunua
Ilulissat
Qasigiannguit
Tasiilaq
GREENLAND
(KALAALLIT NUNAAT)
(Denmark)
Kangerlussuaq
2850
Kong Frederik VI's Kyst
C. Adair
Clyde River
C. Raper
Baffin Island
Davis Strait
Sisimiut
Maniitsoq
Home B.
Qikiqtarjuaq
C. Dyer
Fury and Hecla Str.
Igloolik
Sanirajak
Simpson Pen.
Pelly Bay
Committee B.
Melville Peninsula
Air Force I.
Prince Charles I.
Foxe
2591
Cumberland Peninsula
Pangnirtung
Hoare B.
Nuuk
Qeqertarsuatsiaat
Paamiut
Arsuk
Qaqortoq
Nanortalik
Alluitsup Paa
Uummannarsuaq
ATLANTIC
Basin
Nettilling L.
Mercy C.
Cumberland Sd.
Rae Isthmus
Repulse Bay
NUNAVUT
C. Dorchester
Amadjuak L.
Foxe Pen.
Iqaluit
Hall Peninsula
Wager B.
Roes Welcome Sd.
Foxe Channel
Cape Dorset
Meta Incognita Peninsula
Kimmirut
Frobisher Bay
Southampton I.
Salliq
Bell Pen.
Salisbury I.
Nottingham I.
Hudson Strait
Resolution I.
Labrador
3809
C. Chidley
Akpatok I.
Quaqtaq
Coats I.
Mansel I.
Ivujivik
Salluit
Kangiqsujuaq
Labrador Sea

C

Péninsule d'Ungava
Kangirsuk
Ungava Bay
1652
Kangiqsualujjuaq
Hebron
Puvirnituq
Arnaud
L. Payne
Hudson
Ottawa Is.
257
Feuilles
Koksoak
Kuujjuaq
Baleine
George
Nain
NEWFOUNDLAND
Inukjuak
Mélèzes
Caniapiscau
Hopedale
C. Harrison
Rigolet
Cartwright
Bay
L. Minto
Sleeper Is.
King George Is.
Baker's Dozen Is.
Sanikiluaq
Belcher Is.
Tatnam
Smallwood Res.
Labrador
North West River
Happy Valley-Goose Bay
Port Hope Simpson
Belle Isle
C. Bauld
St. Anthony
L. à l'Eau Claire
L. Bienville
Schefferville
Petitsikapau
Esker
Churchill Falls
Churchill
Grande Baleine
Kuujjuarapik
C. Henrietta Maria
Pte. Louis XIV
Rés. de Caniapiscau
Kanaaupscow
La Grande
Labrador City
Fermont
L. Ashuanipi
QUÉBEC
Natashquan
St-Augustin
Str. of Belle Isle
Notre Dame B.
Baie Verte
Lewisporte
Gander
Bonavista
Trinity B.
Carbonear
St. John's
Severn
Peawanuck
Winisk
Chisasibi
James Bay
1135
Gagnon
Moisie
Romaine
Havre-St-Pierre
Deer Lake
Grand Falls
Corner Brook
Newfoundland
Placentia
C. Race
Big Trout L.
Akimiski I.
Wemindji
Eastmain
Rés. Manicouagan
Î. d'Anticosti
814
Stephenville
Marystown
Placentia B.
Attawapiskat
Attawapiskat
Fort Albany
Charlton I.
Eastmain
Waskaganish
Rupert
L. Mistassini
L. Albanel
Péribonca
Manicouagan
Sept-Îles
Port-Cartier
Gulf of St. Lawrence
Channel-Port aux Basques
C. Ray
Cabot Str.
OCEAN

D

ONTARIO
Albany
Moosonee
Nottaway
Harricana
Missinaibi
Chibougamau
Baie Comeau
St. Lawrence
Gaspé
Matane
Pén. de Gaspé
Îs. de la Madeleine
North C.
ST.-PIERRE et MIQUELON (Fr.)
L. St. Joseph
Nakina
Kenogami
Matagami
L. Matagami
Dolbeau
L. St-Jean
Chicoutimi
Rimouski
Campbellton
Bathurst
Cape Breton I.
Glace Bay
Sydney
L. Nipigon
Geraldton
Hearst
Cochrane
Abitibi L.
Rés. Gouin
Roberval
Jonquière
Rivière-du-Loup
Edmundston
Miramichi
PR. EDWARD I.
Summerside
Charlottetown
Port Hawkesbury
Nipigon
Marathon
Kapuskasing
Oba
Timmins
Amos
1190
Québec
Grand Falls
NEW BRUNSWICK
Moncton
Northumberland Str.
Antigonish
New Glasgow
NOVA SCOTIA
Kirkland Lake
Rouyn-Noranda
Val-d'Or
La Tuque
Lévis
Thetford Mines
Woodstock
Fredericton
Amherst
Truro
Sable I. (Nova Scotia)
Thunder Bay
Chapleau
New Liskeard
Rés. Cabonga
Mont-Laurier
Shawinigan
Trois-Rivières
Joliette
St. Hyacinthe
MAINE
Saint John
B. of Fundy
Digby
Kentville
Dartmouth
Halifax
Bridgewater
Liverpool
Lake Superior
Wawa
Houghton
183
Sault Ste. Marie
Elliot Lake
Sudbury
Outaouais
MONTRÉAL
Sherbrooke
Bangor
Yarmouth
C. Sable
Ironwood
Marquette
L. Nipissing
North Bay
Hull
Granby
L. Champlain
Augusta
Lewiston
6309
MICHIGAN
Sault Ste. Marie
Manitoulin I.
Parry Sound
Georgian Bay
Pembroke
Ottawa
Cornwall
Montpelier
Portland
Manistique
Lake Huron
Huntsville
Burlington
VERMONT
NEW HAMPSHIRE
Rhinelander
Escanaba
Menominee
Petoskey
Traverse City
177
Barrie
Peterborough
Kingston
Concord
Manchester
WISCONSIN
Wausau
Green Bay
Cadillac
Owen Sound
Oshawa
L. Ontario
Belleville
Syracuse
MASS.
BOSTON
C. Cod
Appleton
L. Michigan
TORONTO
Kitchener
Hamilton
75
Albany
Springfield
Providence
Sheboygan
Grand Rapids
Saginaw
Flint
London
Niagara Falls
Rochester
NEW YORK
HARTFORD
R.I.
MILWAUKEE
Racine
Kenosha
Lansing
Sarnia
BUFFALO
Elmira
Binghamton
CONN.
New Haven
Madison
Rockford
CHICAGO
DETROIT
Windsor
174
L. Erie
Erie
Jamestown
Scranton
Bridgeport
NEW YORK
Gary
South Bend
Toledo
CLEVELAND
PENNSYLVANIA
Newark
N.J.
Allentown
Trenton
ILLINOIS
INDIANA
OHIO

E

West from Greenwich

11 12 13 14

HUDSON BAY
JAMES BAY
MANITOBA
ONTARIO
MINNESOTA
WISCONSIN
MICHIGAN
ILLINOIS
INDIANA
OHIO
NEW YORK
LAKE SUPERIOR
LAKE MICHIGAN
LAKE HURON
LAKE ERIE
LAKE ONTARIO
Georgian Bay
Belcher Islands
Akimiski I.
Fort Severn
Partridge I.
C. Henrietta Maria
Moosonee
Moose Factory
Fort Albany
L. Nipigon
Thunder Bay
Duluth
Superior
Isle Royale
Sault Ste. Marie
Marquette
Timmins
Kapuskasing
Hearst
Cochrane
Sudbury
North Bay
Rouyn-Noranda
Val d'Or
Chibougamau
Lac Mistassini
Réservoir Cabonga
La Tuque
Trois-Rivières
MONTRÉAL
Ottawa
Kingston
Peterborough
TORONTO
Hamilton
St. Catharines
Niagara Falls
BUFFALO
Rochester
Syracuse
Utica
Albany
Schenectady
London
Kitchener
Windsor
DETROIT
Flint
Saginaw
Lansing
Grand Rapids
Toledo
CLEVELAND
Erie
MILWAUKEE
CHICAGO
Green Bay
Manitoulin
Adirondack Mountains
Projection: Lambert's Equivalent Azimuthal

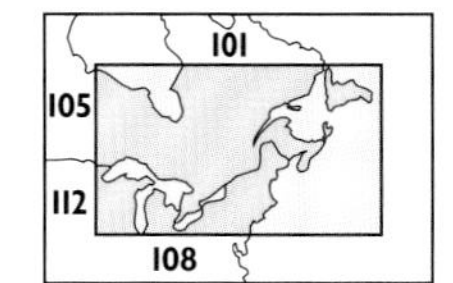

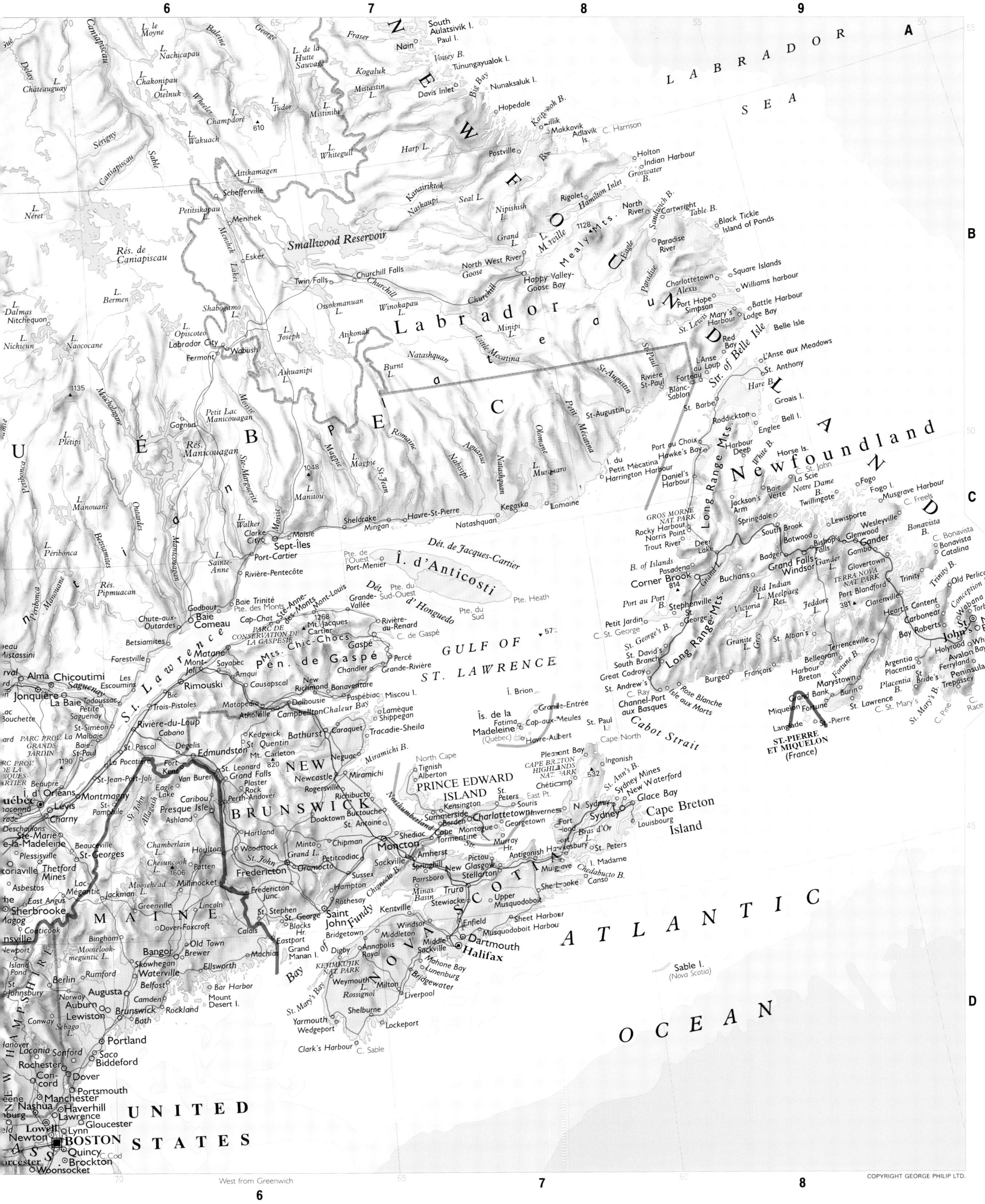

6 7 8 9

A B C D

LABRADOR SEA

NEWFOUNDLAND

Labrador

QUÉBEC

Smallwood Reservoir

Newfoundland

Î. d'Anticosti

GULF OF ST. LAWRENCE

Pén. de Gaspé

NEW BRUNSWICK

PRINCE EDWARD ISLAND

NOVA SCOTIA

Cape Breton Island

Cabot Strait

Str. of Belle Isle

ST-PIERRE ET MIQUELON (France)

Sable I. (Nova Scotia)

Bay of Fundy

MAINE

NEW HAMPSHIRE

UNITED STATES

ATLANTIC OCEAN

Sept-Îles

Halifax

BOSTON

Chicoutimi

Corner Brook

Gander

St. John's

Sydney

Charlottetown

Moncton

Saint John

Fredericton

Bangor

Portland

West from Greenwich

6 7 8

YUKON TERRITORY
NORTHWEST TERRITORIES
BRITISH COLUMBIA
ALBERTA
ALASKA (U.S.A.)
WASHINGTON
IDAHO
UNITED STATES
PACIFIC OCEAN
GREAT SLAVE LAKE
Queen Charlotte Islands
Queen Charlotte Sound
Vancouver Island
Alexander Arch.
Rocky Mountains
Coast Mountains
Skeena Mountains
Cassiar Mountains
Columbia Mts.
Monashee Mts.
Purcell Mts.
Caribou Mts.
Birch Mountains
Swan Hills
Clear Hills
Whitehorse
Yellowknife
Juneau
Prince Rupert
Prince George
Kamloops
Kelowna
Vancouver
Victoria
Seattle
Edmonton
Calgary
Red Deer
Lethbridge
Grande Prairie
Dawson Creek
Fort St. John
Fort Nelson
Projection: Lambert's Equivalent Azimuthal
West from Greenwich

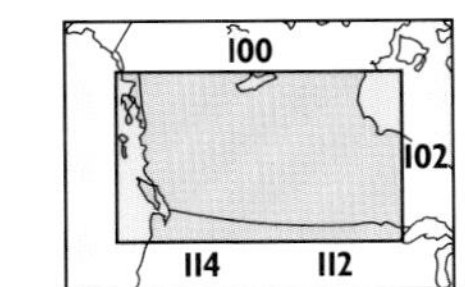

7 8 9 10 11

A

Walmsley L. Artillery L. Campbell L. Tyrrell L. Garde L. Thelon Mosquito L. Nicholson L. Dubawnt L. 213 Tulemalu L. Yathkyed L. Whale Cove Pistol B.
McLeod Bay Reliance Whitefish L. Snowdrift Kamilukuak L. Angikuni L. Kazan Kaminak L. Bibby I. Dawson Inlet
Lutselke Lynx L. Carey L. N U N A V U T North Henik L. South Henik L. Maguse L. Austin I. Maguse Pt.
Gagnon L. Nonacho L. Taltson Damant L. Barlow L. Kazan Arviat
Hjalmar L. Porter L. Rennie L. Firedrake L. Hicks L. Ennadai Tatinnai L. Thaolintoa L. Tha-anne Thlewiaza
Talston Manchester L. Dubawnt Snowbird L. Ennadai L. H U D S O N
Doran L. Smalltree L. Anaunethad L. Thekulthili L. Thoa Wholdaia L. Kasba L. 266 Nuetlin L. Nehon L. B A Y
Hill Island L. Abitau Selwyn L. Baralzon L.

B

Tazin L. Tazin Uranium City Scott L. Dodge L. Putahow L. Kasmere L. Thlewiaza Nejanilini L. Caribou Caribou L. Hubbart Pt.
Camsell Portage Bushell Fond-du-Lac Stony Rapids Black L. Porcupine Phelps L. Munroe L. Stony L. Seal Button B. Churchill C. Churchill
Lake Athabasca 213 Black Lake Fond-du-Lac Riou L. Hatchet L. Cochrane Misty L. North Seal Shethanei L. North Knife Bylot
Fort Chipewyan Davy L. Pine Lac Brochet Tadoule L. South Knife Churchill Deer
William McFarlane Pasfield L. Whiskey Jack L. South Seal Etawney L. Owl Herchmer C. Tatnam
Cree Waterbury L. 524 396 Wollaston L. Wollaston Lake Brochet Big Sand L. Northern Indian L. Little Churchill
Richardson Engemann L. Clearwater Reindeer Lake 350 Southern Indian L. 254 Churchill Weir River Weir Nelson Machichi Kaskattama Kettle Black Duck Niskibi
Firebag Lloyd L. Cree L. 478 Geikie Highrock L. Nokomis L. Kinoosao Goldsand L. Barrington L. South Indian Lake Gauer L. Waskaiowaka L. Limestone Stephens L. Bird Sundance Long Spruce Hayes Gods Beaver

C

Clearwater River Prov. Park Careen L. Black Birch L. Upper Foster L. Wathaman L. Oliver L. Lynn Lake Leaf Rapids Churchill Rat Split Lake Nelson Gillam Shamattawa Beaverstone
Clearwater Wasekamio L. Deception L. Laurie L. Granville L. Rat L. Baldock L. Split L. Ilford Fox
La Loche Turnor L. Frobisher L. Porter L. Daly L. Macoun L. Southend Kamuchawie L. Herriot Odei Thompson Arnot M A N I T O B A Stupart Echoing
Garson L. Peter Pond L. Dillon Churchill L. Patuanak Knee L. Pinehouse L. Sandfly L. McIntosh L. Brabant L. Reindeer Loon Russell L. Highrock L. Pukatawagan Nelson House Burntwood Paint L. Pikwitonei Thicket Portage Atik L. Knee L. Gods River Edmund L. Stull L. Sachigo Severn
Conklin Buffalo Narrows Ile-à-la-Crosse Besnard L. Nemeiben L. Stanley Otter L. Sandy Bay Sisipuk L. Kipahigan L. Burntwood L. Setting L. Sipiwesk L. Bear L. Oxford L. Gods L. Sharpe L. Severn L. Big Trout Lake
Winefred L. McCusker Canoe L. Beauval Lac la Ronge Prov. Park 365 La Ronge Pelican Narrows Mirond L. Sherridon Snow Lake Wabowden Cross L. Walker L. Beaver Hill L. Red Sucker L. Bearskin Lake Big Trout L.
Primrose L. Arsenault L. Lac la Plonge La Ronge Egg L. Wapawekka L. Jan L. Flin Flon Creighton Cranberry Portage Reed L. Wekusko L. Cross Lake Molson L. Ponask L. Sachigo L.
Keeley L. Doré L. Smoothstone L. Grass River Prov. Park Minago Stevenson L. Opasquia Prov. Park North Caribou L.
Cold L. S A S K A T C H E W A N Deschambault L. Amisk L. Namew L. Wanless Cormorant L. N. Moose L. Playgreen L. Norway House Bigstone L. Island L. Sandy Lake
Grand Centre Meadow Lake Prov. Park 680 Delaronde L. Crean L. Montreal L. Narrow Hills Prov. Park Cumberland L. Clearwater Prov. Park The Pas Gunisao Gunisao L. Finger L. Sandy L. Severn
Bonnyville Pierceland Meadow Lake Green Lake Waskesiu Lake Montreal Lake Candle L. Saskatchewan Moose Lake S. Moose L. Mukutawa Deer Lake Pipestone
Elk Point Loon Lake Cowan L. Prince Albert Nat. Park Big River Tobin L. Carrot Westray Cedar Lake Selkirk I. Grand Rapids Poplar O N T A R I O
St. Walburg Turtle L. Leoville Paddockwood Nipawin Carrot River Easterville LAKE WINNIPEG Deer L. McInnes L. MacDowell L.
Paradise Hill Glaslyn Spiritwood Debden Shellbrook Prince Albert Smeaton Arborfield Red Deer L. Dawson B. Berens River Fishing L.
Vermilion Lloydminster Turtleford Edom Meath Park Kinistino Hudson Bay Lake Winnipegosis Reindeer I. Berens I. 217 Berens Little Grand Rapids Stout L. Pikangikum Cat Lake Cat L.

D

Lashburn Maidstone North Battleford Leask Blaine Lake Duck Lake Birch Hills Melfort Star City Tisdale Red Deer Mafeking Swan L. Birch River 252 Birch I. Sturgeon B. Family L. Cairns L. Berens Birch L.
Wainwright Battle Battleford Wakaw Rosthern Lenore L. Naicam Greenwater Prov. Park Bowsman Pelican L. Waterhen Bloodvein Trout L. Bamaji L.
Chauvin Provost Denholm Wilkie Radisson Aberdeen Prud'homme Lake Lenore Rose Valley Swan River Camperville Grahamdale L. St. Martin Fisher B. Woodland Caribou Prov. Park Red L. Balmertown St. Joseph
Macklin Unity Saskatoon Humboldt Watson Wadena Kelvington Preeceville Sturgis Duck Mtn. Prov. Park Pine River Winnipegosis Fairford Black I. Manigotagan Gammon Red Lake Ear Falls Lac Seul
Luseland Salvador Biggar Asquith Colonsay Quill Lakes Buchanan Norquay Kamsack Ethelbert Sifton Steep Rock Hodgson Riverton Hecla I. Victoria Beach Sydney L. Sioux Lookout
Kerrobert Delisle Allan Lanigan Wynyard Foam Lake Canora Theodore L. of the Prairies Roblin 831 Dauphin L. Ste. Rose du Lac Dog L. Ashern Arborg Eriksdale Gimli Nopiming Prov. Park English
Dodsland Rosetown Conquest Young Watrous Nokomis Outlook Raymore Lestock Ituna Yorkton Grand View Dauphin Riding Mountain National Park Manitoba 248 Winnipeg Beach Pine Falls Winnipeg Red Lake Road Minnitaki L.
Kindersley Alsask Milden Imperial Davidson Last Mountain L. Strasbourg Cupar Melville Langenburg Russell Rossburn Wasagaming McCreary Amaranth St. Laurent Teulon Pinawa Whiteshell Prov. Park Minaki Vermilion Bay Dryden Wabigoon L. Dinorwic
Oyen Eatonia Eston Elrose Elbow Craik Regina Beach Qu'Appelle Balcarres Esterhazy Binscarth Shoal Lake Neepawa Gladstone Portage la Prairie Selkirk Beausejour Keewatin Kenora Eagle L. Ignace White Otter L.
Empress Leader S. Saskatchewan 876 Kyle Riverhurst Beechy Central Butte Lumsden Fort Qu'Appelle Grenfell Whitewood Birtle Minnedosa Stonewall Elma Falcon Lake Sioux Narrows Lower Manitou L.
Burstall Cabri Diefenbaker Herbert Chaplin Mortlach Regina Pense Indian Head Montmartre Moosomin Rivers Winnipeg Ste. Anne Steinbach Shoal L. 323 Lake of the Woods Rainy L. Atikokan
Schuler Pennant Fox Valley Swift Current Moose Jaw Rouleau Sedley Pipestone Elkhorn Carberry Assiniboine St. Claude Niverville Carman Morris Woodridge Rainy River Fort Frances Quetico Prov. Park
Redcliff Gull Lake Hodgeville Neville Old Wives L. Avonlea Milestone Kipling Moose Mt. Prov. Park Maryfield Virden Brandon Treherne Vassar Warroad Emo
Medicine Hat Irvine Piapot Vanguard Mossbank Weyburn Redvers Souris Wawanesa Pilot Mound Manitou Morden Winkler Emerson Roseau International Falls Lac la Croix
Cypress Hills Prov. Park 1468 Cypress Hills Maple Creek Pontelx Gravelbourg Assiniboia Stoughton Carlyle Reston Hartney Boissevain Killarney Pembina Pembina Greenbush Upper Red L. Big Falls Little Fork
Eastend Shaunavon Lafleche Bengough Radville Midale Lampman Oxbow Carnduff Melita Deloraine 762 Rolla Karlstad Thief River Falls
Frenchman Val Marie Grasslands Nat. Park Mankota Willow Bunch Minton Estevan North Portal Bowbells Mohall Langdon Grafton Lower Red L. Northome Virginia
Orion Pakowki L. Consul Climax Rockglen Coronach Outlook Westby Souris Cando Warren East Grand Forks Red Lake Falls M I N N E S O T A
Milk Turner Opheim Scobey Plentywood Kenmore N O R T H Rugby Grand Forks Lakota Bemidji Winnibigoshish L. Hibbing
Fresno Res. Chinook Harlem Malta Ray Granville Towner Devils Lake Larimore Northwood Crookston Erskine Bagley Cass Lake Deer River Grand Rapids
Hingham Chester Havre Milk Saco Glasgow Nashua Poplar Culbertson Williston Stanley Minot Velva D A K O T A Drake Harvey New Rockford Mayville Hillsboro Ada Mahnomen Leech L. Walker Hill City Floodwood Duluth Cloquet
M O N T A N A Fort Peck Lake Fort Peck Wolf Point Missouri Fairview Alexander Watford City L. Sakakawea Garrison Turtle Lake Carrington Cooperstown Red Park Rapids Pine River Mississippi Superior
Big Sandy

7 8 9 10

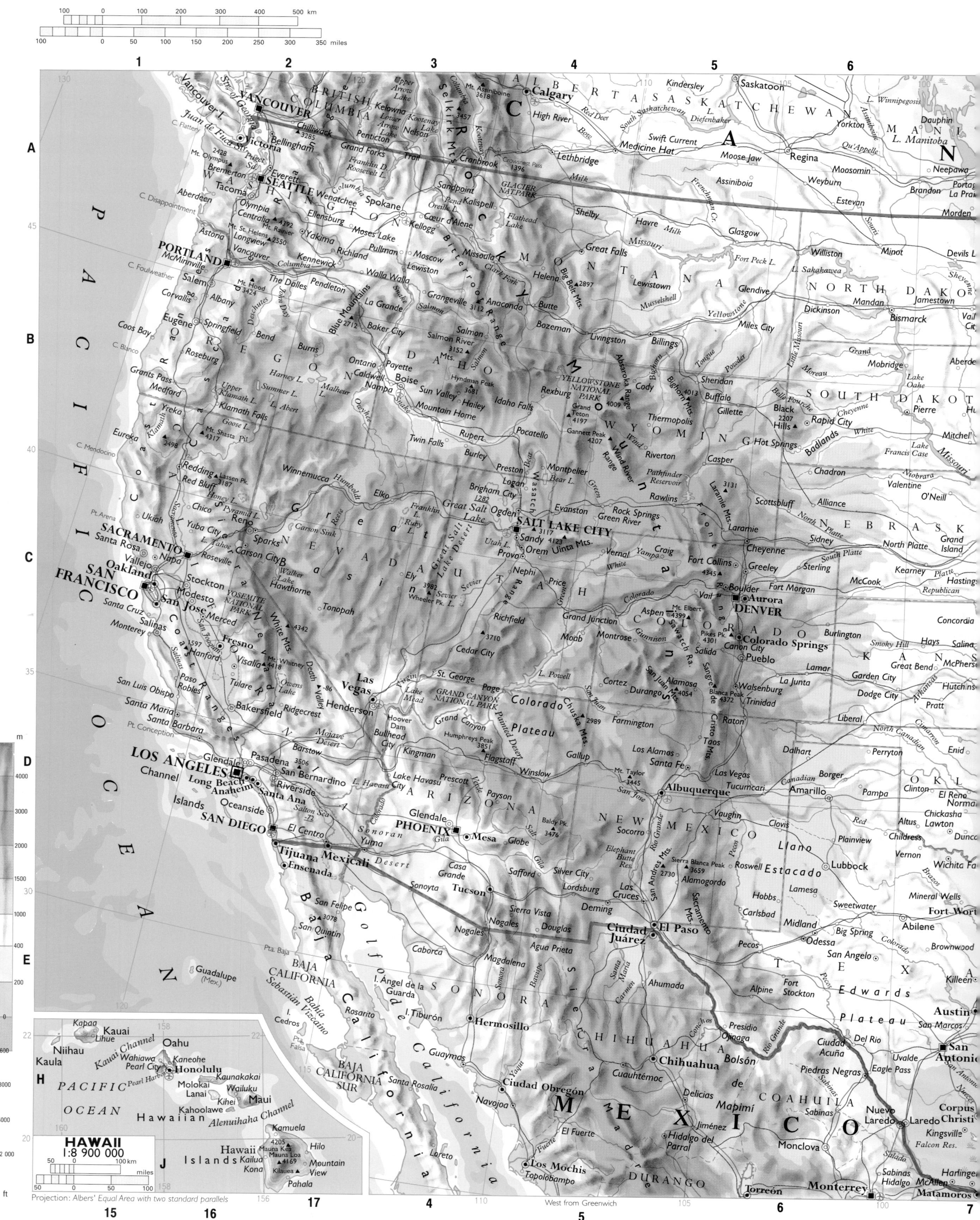
100 0 100 200 300 400 500 km
100 0 50 100 150 200 250 300 350 miles
1 2 3 4 5 6
A
B
C
D
E
H
J
15 16 17 4 5 6 7
P A C I F I C O C E A N
BRITISH COLUMBIA
ALBERTA
SASKATCHEWAN
MANITOBA
CANADA
WASHINGTON
OREGON
IDAHO
MONTANA
WYOMING
NORTH DAKOTA
SOUTH DAKOTA
NEBRASKA
NEVADA
UTAH
COLORADO
KANSAS
CALIFORNIA
ARIZONA
NEW MEXICO
TEXAS
OKLAHOMA
MEXICO
BAJA CALIFORNIA
BAJA CALIFORNIA SUR
SONORA
CHIHUAHUA
COAHUILA
DURANGO
Great Basin
Colorado Plateau
Llano Estacado
Edwards Plateau
Golfo de California
Rocky Mts.
Sierra Nevada
Coast Ranges
Cascade Range
Bitterroot Range
Wasatch Range
Uinta Mts.
Front Range
Sangre de Cristo Mts.
Sierra Madre
Mojave Desert
Sonoran Desert
Great Salt Lake
Great Salt Lake Desert
YELLOWSTONE NATIONAL PARK
GRAND CANYON NATIONAL PARK
YOSEMITE NATIONAL PARK
GLACIER NAT. PARK
VANCOUVER
Victoria
Calgary
SEATTLE
Tacoma
Spokane
PORTLAND
Salem
Eugene
Boise
Helena
Great Falls
Billings
Bismarck
Regina
Saskatoon
Pierre
Rapid City
Casper
Cheyenne
Laramie
SALT LAKE CITY
Ogden
Provo
Reno
Carson City
SACRAMENTO
SAN FRANCISCO
Oakland
San Jose
Fresno
Bakersfield
Las Vegas
LOS ANGELES
Long Beach
Anaheim
Santa Ana
San Bernardino
SAN DIEGO
Tijuana
Mexicali
Ensenada
PHOENIX
Mesa
Tucson
Flagstaff
Albuquerque
Santa Fe
El Paso
Ciudad Juárez
DENVER
Aurora
Boulder
Colorado Springs
Pueblo
Amarillo
Lubbock
Midland
Odessa
San Angelo
Abilene
Austin
San Antonio
Laredo
Nuevo Laredo
Corpus Christi
Monterrey
Torreón
Chihuahua
Hermosillo
Ciudad Obregón
Los Mochis
Matamoros
HAWAII
1:8 900 000
Kauai
Niihau
Oahu
Honolulu
Molokai
Lanai
Maui
Kahoolawe
Hawaii
Hawaiian Islands
Mauna Kea 4205
Mauna Loa 4169
Hilo
Projection: Albers' Equal Area with two standard parallels
West from Greenwich

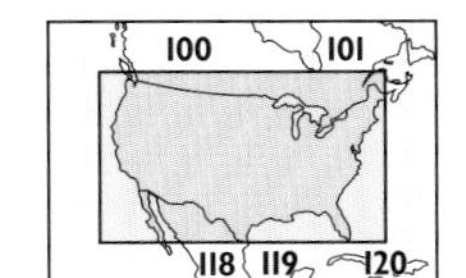

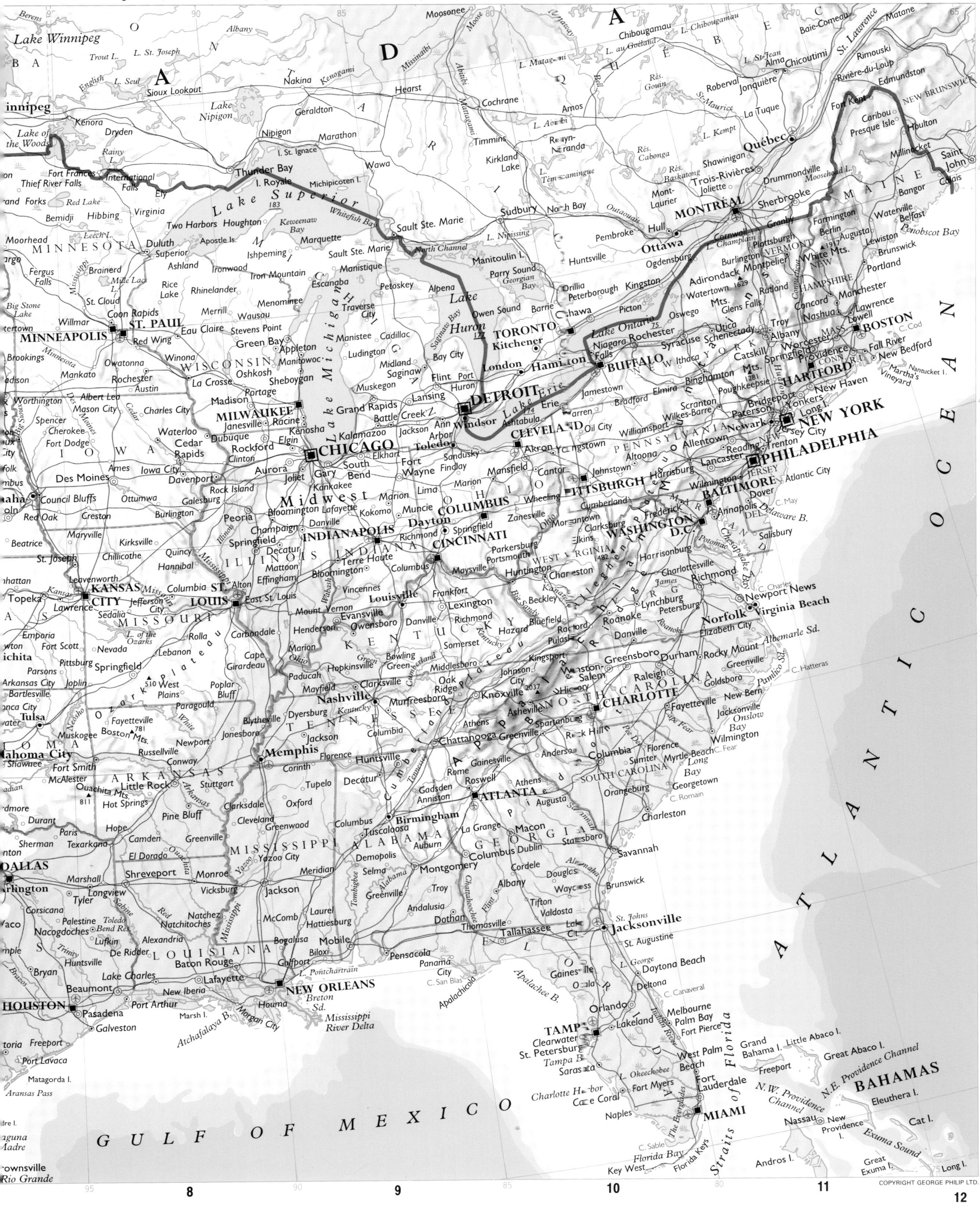

8 9 10 11 12 13

A B C D E F

CANADA
Lake Winnipeg
Berens
Trout L.
L. St. Joseph
Albany
English
L. Seul
Sioux Lookout
Lake Nipigon
Nakina
Kenogami
Geraldton
Hearst
Moosonee
Missinaibi
Abitibi
Mattagami
Cochrane
Timmins
Kirkland Lake
L. Matagami
Amos
L. Abitibi
Rouyn-Noranda
Chibougamau
L. Chibougamau
L. au Goéland
Rés. Gouin
QUEBEC
Baie-Comeau
St. Lawrence
Matane
Rimouski
Rivière-du-Loup
Edmundston
NEW BRUNSWICK
L. St-Jean
Alma
Chicoutimi
Jonquière
Roberval
St-Maurice
La Tuque
L. Kempt
Rés. Cabonga
Rés. Baskatong
Shawinigan
Québec
Trois-Rivières
Joliette
Drummondville
Mont-Laurier
MONTREAL
Sherbrooke
Fort Kent
Caribou
Presque Isle
Houlton
Millinocket
Saint John
Calais
Moosehead L.
MAINE
Bangor
Waterville
Belfast
Penobscot Bay
Farmington
Berlin
Augusta
Lewiston
Brunswick
Portland
Granby
Innipeg
Kenora
Lake of the Woods
Dryden
Rainy L.
Fort Frances
International Falls
Thief River Falls
Red Lake
Grand Forks
Bemidji
Hibbing
Virginia
Ely
Nipigon
Marathon
I. St. Ignace
Thunder Bay
I. Royale
Michipicoten I.
Wawa
Lake Superior
183
Whitefish Bay
Two Harbors
Houghton
Keweenaw Bay
Sault Ste. Marie
Sudbury
North Bay
L. Nipissing
Témiscamingue
Outaouais
Pembroke
Ottawa
Hull
L. Champlain
Cornwall
Plattsburgh
VERMONT
Moorhead
MINNESOTA
Leech L.
Duluth
Superior
Apostle Is.
Marquette
Ishpeming
North Channel
Manitoulin I.
Parry Sound
Georgian Bay
Huntsville
Ogdensburg
Burlington
Montpelier
White Mts.
1917
NEW HAMPSHIRE
Fergus Falls
Brainerd
Mille Lacs L.
Ashland
Ironwood
Iron Mountain
Manistique
Escanaba
Petoskey
Alpena
Orillia
Peterborough
Kingston
Adirondack Mts.
1629
Watertown
Rutland
Concord
Manchester
Big Stone Lake
Willmar
St. Cloud
Coon Rapids
Rice Lake
Rhinelander
Merrill
Wausau
Menominee
MICHIGAN
Lake Michigan
Traverse City
Lake Huron
Owen Sound
Barrie
Oshawa
Picton
Oswego
Glens Falls
Nashua
Lowell
Lawrence
MINNEAPOLIS
ST. PAUL
Red Wing
Eau Claire
Stevens Point
Green Bay
Appleton
Manistee
Cadillac
Saginaw Bay
171
TORONTO
Kitchener
Lake Ontario
Rochester
Utica
Schenectady
Troy
Albany
MASS.
Worcester
BOSTON
C. Cod
Brookings
Minnesota
Owatonna
Winona
WISCONSIN
Manitowoc
Ludington
Bay City
Midland
Saginaw
London
Hamilton
Niagara Falls
BUFFALO
Syracuse
Ithaca
NEW YORK
Catskill Mts.
1281
Springfield
Hartford
Providence
CONN.
Fall River
New Bedford
Martha's Vineyard
Nantucket I.
Mankato
Rochester
Austin
Oshkosh
La Crosse
Sheboygan
Muskegon
Flint
Port Huron
Binghamton
Poughkeepsie
Worthington
Albert Lea
Mason City
Charles City
Portage
Madison
MILWAUKEE
Grand Rapids
Lansing
DETROIT
Windsor
Lake Erie
Erie
Jamestown
Bradford
Elmira
Scranton
Wilkes-Barre
Bridgeport
New Haven
Yonkers
Long I.
NEW YORK
Paterson
Spencer
Cherokee
Fort Dodge
Des Moines
Cedar
Waterloo
Cedar Rapids
Janesville
Racine
Kenosha
Battle Creek
Kalamazoo
Jackson
Ann Arbor
Toledo
Ashtabula
174
CLEVELAND
Warren
Oil City
Williamsport
PENNSYLVANIA
Newark
Jersey City
Trenton
IOWA
Dubuque
Rockford
Elgin
Clinton
CHICAGO
Elkhart
Sandusky
Akron
Youngstown
Allentown
Reading
NEW JERSEY
PHILADELPHIA
Ames
Iowa City
Davenport
Aurora
Joliet
Gary
Kankakee
South Bend
Fort Wayne
Findlay
Mansfield
Canton
Altoona
Johnstown
Lancaster
Harrisburg
Atlantic City
Des Moines
Council Bluffs
Ottumwa
Galesburg
Rock Island
Midwest
Marion
Lima
OHIO
Wheeling
PITTSBURGH
Wilmington
BALTIMORE
Dover
C. May
Red Oak
Creston
Burlington
Peoria
Bloomington
Lafayette
Kokomo
Muncie
COLUMBUS
Zanesville
Cumberland
Frederick
Annapolis
DEL.
Delaware B.
Maryville
Kirksville
Champaign
Danville
INDIANAPOLIS
Dayton
Richmond
Springfield
Morgantown
Clarksburg
WASHINGTON D.C.
MARYLAND
Beatrice
St. Joseph
Chillicothe
Quincy
Hannibal
Springfield
Decatur
ILLINOIS
INDIANA
CINCINNATI
Parkersburg
Portsmouth
Elkins
WEST VIRGINIA
1482
Potomac
Salisbury
Chesapeake Bay
Mattoon
Effingham
Terre Haute
Bloomington
Columbus
Maysville
Huntington
Charleston
Harrisonburg
Charlottesville
Topeka
Kansas
Leavenworth
KANSAS CITY
Lawrence
Missouri
Columbia
Jefferson City
ST. LOUIS
Alton
East St. Louis
Mississippi
Vincennes
Wabash
Frankfort
Lexington
Louisville
Kanawha
James
Richmond
C. Charles
Newport News
Virginia Beach
Sedalia
MISSOURI
Mount Vernon
Evansville
Owensboro
Henderson
Danville
Richmond
KENTUCKY
Big Sandy
Beckley
Bluefield
Lynchburg
Petersburg
Norfolk
Emporia
Fort Scott
Nevada
L. of the Ozarks
Rolla
Carbondale
Marion
Somerset
Hazard
Radford
Roanoke
Pulaski
Danville
Elizabeth City
Albemarle Sd.
Wichita
Pittsburg
Springfield
Lebanon
Cape Girardeau
Ohio
Hopkinsville
Bowling Green
Cumberland
Middlesboro
Kingsport
Johnson City
Winston-Salem
Greensboro
Durham
Rocky Mount
Greenville
Pamlico Sd.
C. Hatteras
Parsons
Arkansas City
Joplin
Ozark Plateau
510
West Plains
Poplar Bluff
Paducah
Mayfield
Clarksville
Oak Ridge
Knoxville
2037
Raleigh
Goldsboro
New Bern
Bartlesville
Tulsa
Fayetteville
Paragould
Blytheville
Dyersburg
Nashville
Murfreesboro
TENNESSEE
Asheville
Hickory
NORTH CAROLINA
CHARLOTTE
Fayetteville
Jacksonville
Onslow Bay
Muskogee
Boston Mts.
781
Jonesboro
White
Jackson
Columbia
Athens
Spartanburg
Rock Hill
Cape Fear
Wilmington
C. Fear
Oklahoma City
Shawnee
Russellville
Newport
Memphis
Corinth
Florence
Huntsville
Chattanooga
Greenville
Anderson
Columbia
Pee Dee
Florence
Myrtle Beach
Long Bay
Fort Smith
McAlester
ARKANSAS
Conway
Little Rock
Stuttgart
Tupelo
Decatur
Gainesville
Rome
Roswell
Athens
Sumter
SOUTH CAROLINA
Georgetown
Ouachita Mts.
811
Hot Springs
Pine Bluff
Clarksdale
Oxford
Gadsden
Anniston
ATLANTA
Augusta
Orangeburg
C. Romain
Charleston
Ardmore
Durant
Hope
Cleveland
Greenwood
Columbus
Birmingham
La Grange
Macon
GEORGIA
Statesboro
Paris
Sherman
Texarkana
Camden
Greenville
MISSISSIPPI
Tuscaloosa
ALABAMA
Auburn
Columbus
Dublin
Savannah
DALLAS
El Dorado
Ouachita
Yazoo City
Demopolis
Arlington
Marshall
Longview
Shreveport
Monroe
Vicksburg
Jackson
Meridian
Selma
Montgomery
Cordele
Douglas
Waycross
Brunswick
Tyler
Troy
Albany
Corsicana
Palestine
Nacogdoches
Toledo Bend Res.
Natchez
Natchitoches
McComb
Laurel
Hattiesburg
Andalusia
Dothan
Tifton
Valdosta
Waco
Lufkin
Alexandria
LOUISIANA
Bogalusa
Mobile
Thomasville
Tallahassee
Lake City
St. Johns
Jacksonville
St. Augustine
Huntsville
De Ridder
Baton Rouge
Gulfport
Biloxi
Pensacola
Panama City
C. San Blas
Apalachicola
Apalachee B.
Gainesville
Ocala
L. George
Daytona Beach
Deltona
C. Canaveral
Bryan
Lake Charles
Lafayette
L. Pontchartrain
NEW ORLEANS
Breton Sd.
Beaumont
Port Arthur
New Iberia
Houma
Morgan City
Atchafalaya B.
Mississippi River Delta
Orlando
Melbourne
Palm Bay
HOUSTON
Pasadena
Galveston
Marsh I.
TAMPA
Lakeland
Clearwater
St. Petersburg
Tampa B.
Sarasota
FLORIDA
Fort Pierce
West Palm Beach
Grand Bahama I.
Little Abaco I.
Great Abaco I.
Freeport
Port Lavaca
Matagorda I.
Aransas Pass
L. Okeechobee
Charlotte Harbor
Cape Coral
Fort Myers
Naples
Fort Lauderdale
MIAMI
The Everglades
Straits of Florida
N.E. Providence Channel
N.W. Providence Channel
BAHAMAS
Eleuthera I.
Nassau
New Providence I.
Cat I.
Exuma Sound
GULF OF MEXICO
ATLANTIC OCEAN
C. Sable
Florida Bay
Florida Keys
Key West
Andros I.
Great Exuma I.
Long I.
Laguna Madre
Brownsville
Rio Grande

8 9 10 11 12

50 0 50 100 150 200 km
50 0 50 100 150 miles
LAKE SUPERIOR
ONTARIO
QUÉBEC
MICHIGAN
WISCONSIN
LAKE MICHIGAN
LAKE HURON
Georgian Bay
LAKE ONTARIO
LAKE ERIE
NEW YORK
PENNSYLVANIA
OHIO
INDIANA
KENTUCKY
WEST VIRGINIA
VIRGINIA
MARYLAND
DELAWARE
NEW JERSEY
VERMONT
NEW HAMPSHIRE
MASS.
CONN.
R.I.
Chesapeake Bay
Delaware Bay
NEW YORK CITY
PHILADELPHIA
BOSTON
BALTIMORE
WASHINGTON D.C.
PITTSBURGH
CLEVELAND
DETROIT
CHICAGO
MILWAUKEE
INDIANAPOLIS
CINCINNATI
COLUMBUS
BUFFALO
TORONTO
MONTRÉAL
Ottawa
Québec
HARTFORD

TENNESSEE
NORTH CAROLINA
SOUTH CAROLINA
GEORGIA
ALABAMA
MISSISSIPPI
FLORIDA
MAINE
NEW HAMPSHIRE
CANADA
ATLANTIC OCEAN
GULF OF MEXICO
BAHAMAS
Nashville
Knoxville
Chattanooga
Asheville
CHARLOTTE
Raleigh
Greensboro
Winston-Salem
Durham
Wilmington
Columbia
Charleston
Savannah
ATLANTA
Macon
Columbus
Augusta
Birmingham
Montgomery
Mobile
Huntsville
Pensacola
Tallahassee
Jacksonville
Gainesville
Orlando
TAMPA
St. Petersburg
MIAMI
Fort Lauderdale
West Palm Beach
Great Abaco I.
Grand Bahama
Portland
Augusta
Bangor
Continuation Eastwards On same scale.
Projection: Albers' Equal Area with two standard parallels
West from Greenwich
COPYRIGHT GEORGE PHILIP LTD.

10 0 10 20 30 40 50 60 70 80 90 km
10 0 10 20 30 40 50 60 miles
LAKE HURON
Georgian Bay
Bruce Peninsula
CANADA
ONTARIO
MICHIGAN
LAKE ONTARIO
LAKE ERIE
OHIO
PENNSYLVANIA
NEW YORK
TORONTO
Mississauga
Hamilton
BUFFALO
DETROIT
Windsor
London
Kitchener
CLEVELAND
PITTSBURGH
Rochester
Erie
Akron
Youngstown
Allegheny Plateau
Allegheny Mountains
Tuscarora Mts.
Projection: Bonne

102
108
108

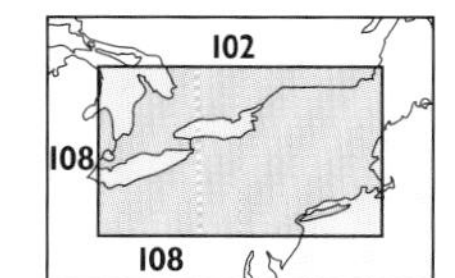

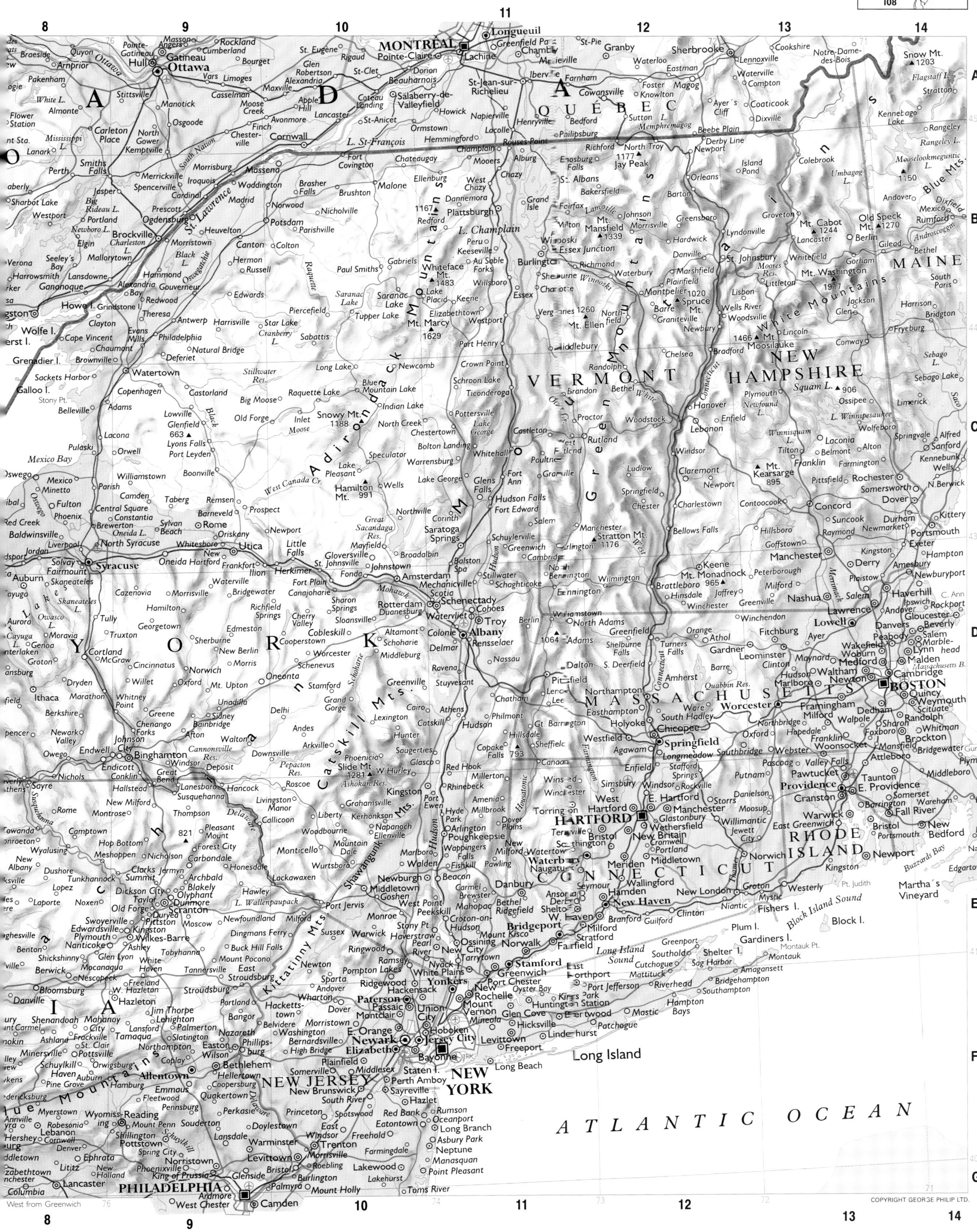

8
9
10
11
12
13
14
A
B
C
D
E
F
G
MONTREAL
Longueuil
Lachine
Pointe-Claire
Ottawa
Gatineau
Hull
Sherbrooke
Q U É B E C
Granby
Cornwall
Brockville
Ogdensburg
Massena
Plattsburgh
L. Champlain
Burlington
Montpelier
Mt. Mansfield
1339
Jay Peak
1177
Mt. Marcy
1629
Whiteface Mt.
1483
Saranac Lake
Lake Placid
Tupper Lake
Watertown
Syracuse
Utica
Rome
Oneida
Auburn
Ithaca
Cortland
Binghamton
Elmira
Schenectady
Troy
Albany
Amsterdam
Saratoga Springs
Glens Falls
Lake George
Ticonderoga
Rutland
Brattleboro
Bennington
Adirondack Mts.
Catskill Mts.
Kingston
Poughkeepsie
Newburgh
Middletown
Yonkers
New Rochelle
White Plains
Paterson
Newark
Jersey City
Elizabeth
Bayonne
NEW YORK
Long Island
Long Beach
Staten I.
NEW JERSEY
New Brunswick
Trenton
Princeton
PHILADELPHIA
Camden
Allentown
Bethlehem
Easton
Reading
Lancaster
Norristown
Scranton
Wilkes-Barre
Hazleton
Pottsville
Stroudsburg
Kittatinny Mts.
Shawangunk Mts.
HARTFORD
Springfield
Holyoke
Pittsfield
Worcester
BOSTON
Cambridge
Quincy
Lowell
Lawrence
Haverhill
Salem
Lynn
Framingham
Brockton
Taunton
Fall River
New Bedford
Providence
Pawtucket
Cranston
Warwick
Newport
RHODE ISLAND
Block I.
Block Island Sound
Martha's Vineyard
New Haven
Bridgeport
Stamford
Norwalk
Danbury
Waterbury
Meriden
New Britain
New London
Norwich
CONNECTICUT
MASSACHUSETTS
VERMONT
NEW HAMPSHIRE
MAINE
Manchester
Nashua
Concord
Portsmouth
Dover
Keene
Laconia
Mt. Washington
1917
White Mountains
Green Mountains
Mt. Monadnock
965
Stratton Mt.
1176
Mt. Ellen
1260
Lake Winnipesaukee
L. Memphremagog
St. Johnsbury
Newport
Fishers I.
Gardiners I.
Shelter I.
Montauk Pt.
Long Island Sound
Hudson
Connecticut
Delaware
Mohawk
St. Lawrence
Ottawa
Y O R K
A T L A N T I C   O C E A N
West from Greenwich
76
75
74
73
72
71
45
44
43
42
41
40

CANADA
NORTH DAKOTA
SOUTH DAKOTA
MINNESOTA
WISCONSIN
MICHIGAN
IOWA
NEBRASKA
ILLINOIS
KANSAS
MISSOURI
COLORADO
WYOMING
MONTANA
LAKE SUPERIOR
LAKE MICHIGAN
MINNEAPOLIS
ST. PAUL
MILWAUKEE
CHICAGO
KANSAS CITY
ST. LOUIS
DENVER
50 0 50 100 150 200 km
50 0 50 100 150 miles

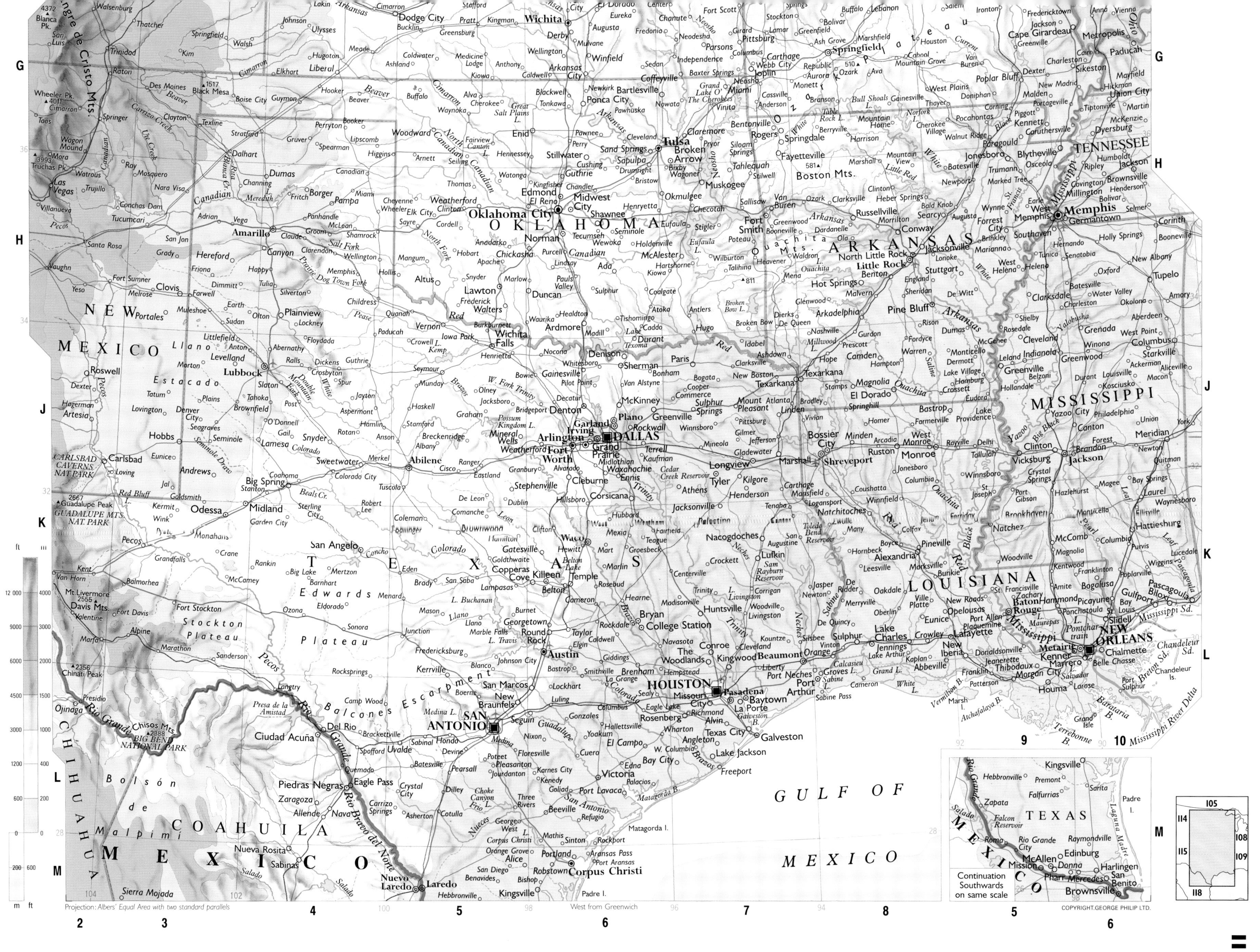

NEW MEXICO
TEXAS
OKLAHOMA
ARKANSAS
LOUISIANA
MISSISSIPPI
TENNESSEE
MEXICO
COAHUILA
CHIHUAHUA
GULF OF MEXICO
Llano Estacado
Edwards Plateau
Stockton Plateau
Balcones Escarpment
Bolsón de Mapimí
Sangre de Cristo Mts.
Ozark Plateau
Boston Mts.
Ouachita Mts.
Chisos Mts.
BIG BEND NATIONAL PARK
CARLSBAD CAVERNS NAT. PARK
GUADALUPE MTS. NAT. PARK
Guadalupe Peak 2667
HOUSTON
DALLAS
SAN ANTONIO
NEW ORLEANS
Oklahoma City
Tulsa
Fort Worth
Austin
Memphis
Little Rock
Shreveport
Jackson
Baton Rouge
Corpus Christi
Wichita
Amarillo
Lubbock
Odessa
Midland
Abilene
San Angelo
Waco
Beaumont
Galveston
Laredo
Nuevo Laredo
Brownsville
Rio Grande
Red
Canadian
Brazos
Colorado
Pecos
Arkansas
Mississippi
Continuation Southwards on same scale
Projection: Albers' Equal Area with two standard parallels
West from Greenwich
COPYRIGHT GEORGE PHILIP LTD.
m ft

WESTERN UNITED STATES 1:5 300 000

COLORADO
NEW MEXICO
ARIZONA
TEXAS
MEXICO
SONORA
CHIHUAHUA
BAJA CALIFORNIA
PACIFIC OCEAN
Golfo de California
Colorado Plateau
Sangre de Cristo Mts.
San Juan Mts.
Sawatch Range
Uncompahgre Plateau
Painted Desert
Grand Canyon
Mogollon Rim
Sacramento Mts.
San Andres Mts.
Manzano Mts.
Chuska Mts.
Black Range
Sonoran Desert
Mojave Desert
Death Valley
Coast Ranges
Santa Lucia Range
White Mts.
Inyo Mts.
New York Mts.
Chocolate Mts.
Sierra de Juárez
Sierra de San Pedro Mártir
Desierto de Altar
Channel Is.
Salton Sea
Rio Grande
Rio Bravo del Norte
Colorado
Gila
LOS ANGELES
SAN DIEGO
SAN FRANCISCO
PHOENIX
Tucson
Albuquerque
Santa Fe
El Paso
Ciudad Juárez
Chihuahua
Hermosillo
Tijuana
Mexicali
Las Vegas
San Jose
Fresno
Bakersfield
Flagstaff
Prescott
Yuma
Nogales
Ensenada
Las Cruces
Isla Guadalupe (Mexico)
I. Tiburón
I. Ángel de la Guarda
Projection: Albers' Equal Area with two standard parallels
West from Greenwich
COPYRIGHT GEORGE PHILIP LTD.

CENTRAL AND SOUTHERN CALIFORNIA AND WESTERN WASHINGTON 1:2 200 000

N E V A D A
C A L I F O R N I A
A R I Z O N A
M E X I C O
BAJA CALIFORNIA
P A C I F I C
O C E A N
Las Vegas
Henderson
North Las Vegas
Lake Mead
Lake Mohave
Bullhead City
Kingman
Needles
Lake Havasu City
Parker
Blythe
Yuma
Mexicali
El Centro
Calexico
Brawley
Salton Sea
Indio
Coachella
Palm Springs
Palm Desert
Death Valley
Amargosa Range
Mojave Desert
Sonoran Desert
Chocolate Mts.
Imperial Valley
Barstow
Victorville
Hesperia
Apple Valley
Lancaster
Palmdale
Bakersfield
Ridgecrest
San Bernardino
Riverside
Moreno Valley
Corona
Ontario
Pomona
Rancho Cucamonga
LOS ANGELES
Santa Monica
Long Beach
Anaheim
Santa Ana
Irvine
Huntington Beach
Newport Beach
Oceanside
Carlsbad
Escondido
SAN DIEGO
Chula Vista
Tijuana
Tecate
Santa Barbara
Ventura
Oxnard
Santa Maria
San Luis Obispo
Lompoc
Santa Clarita
San Fernando
Glendale
Pasadena
Tehachapi Mts.
San Gabriel Mts.
San Bernardino Mts.
San Jacinto
Santa Barbara Channel
San Pedro Channel
Channel Islands
Santa Catalina I.
San Clemente I.
San Nicolas I.
Santa Cruz I.
Santa Rosa I.
San Miguel I.
Gulf of Santa Catalina
Coachella Canal
Colorado
Projection: Bonne
West from Greenwich
COPYRIGHT GEORGE PHILIP LTD.
km
miles
m
ft

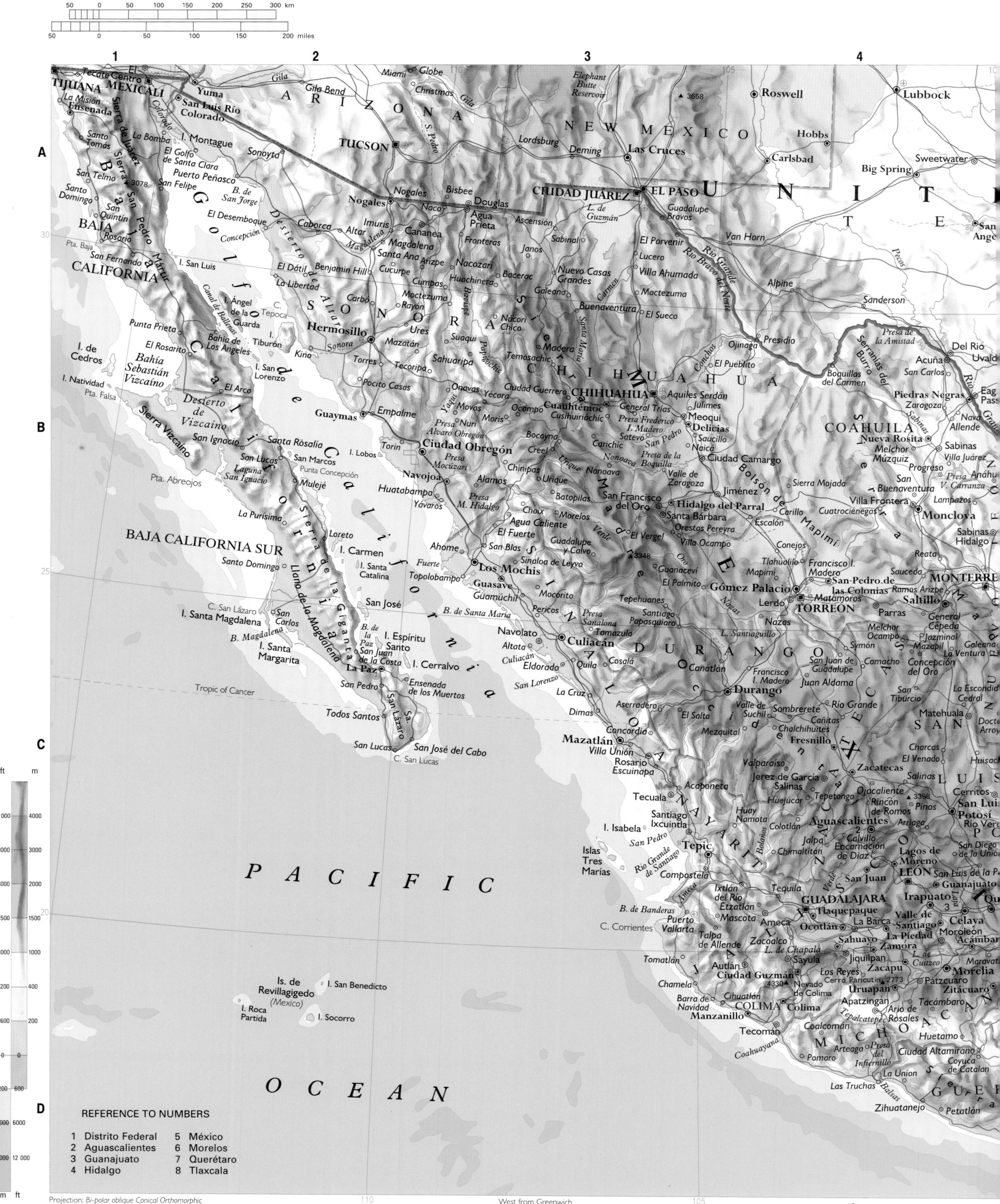
50 0 50 100 150 200 250 300 km
50 0 50 100 150 200 miles
1 2 3 4
A B C D
ARIZONA
NEW MEXICO
UNITED STATES
SONORA
CHIHUAHUA
COAHUILA
BAJA CALIFORNIA
BAJA CALIFORNIA SUR
SINALOA
DURANGO
NAYARIT
ZACATECAS
JALISCO
COLIMA
MICHOACÁN
SAN LUIS POTOSÍ
Golfo de California
Sierra Madre Occidental
Desierto de Vizcaíno
Bolsón de Mapimí
Tropic of Cancer
PACIFIC OCEAN
Is. de Revillagigedo (Mexico)
I. San Benedicto
I. Roca Partida
I. Socorro
Islas Tres Marías
TIJUANA
MEXICALI
TUCSON
CIUDAD JUÁREZ
EL PASO
Hermosillo
CHIHUAHUA
Ciudad Obregón
Los Mochis
Culiacán
Mazatlán
Durango
Gómez Palacio
TORREÓN
Hidalgo del Parral
Monclova
Saltillo
Zacatecas
Aguascalientes
GUADALAJARA
LEÓN
Morelia
Tepic
Manzanillo
La Paz
Guaymas
ft m
12 000 4000
9000 3000
6000 2000
4500 1500
3000 1000
1200 400
600 200
0 0
200 600
2000 6000
4000 12 000
m ft
REFERENCE TO NUMBERS
1 Distrito Federal
2 Aguascalientes
3 Guanajuato
4 Hidalgo
5 México
6 Morelos
7 Querétaro
8 Tlaxcala
Projection: Bi-polar oblique Conical Orthomorphic
110
West from Greenwich
105
2 3 4

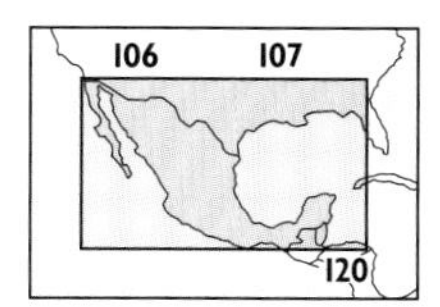

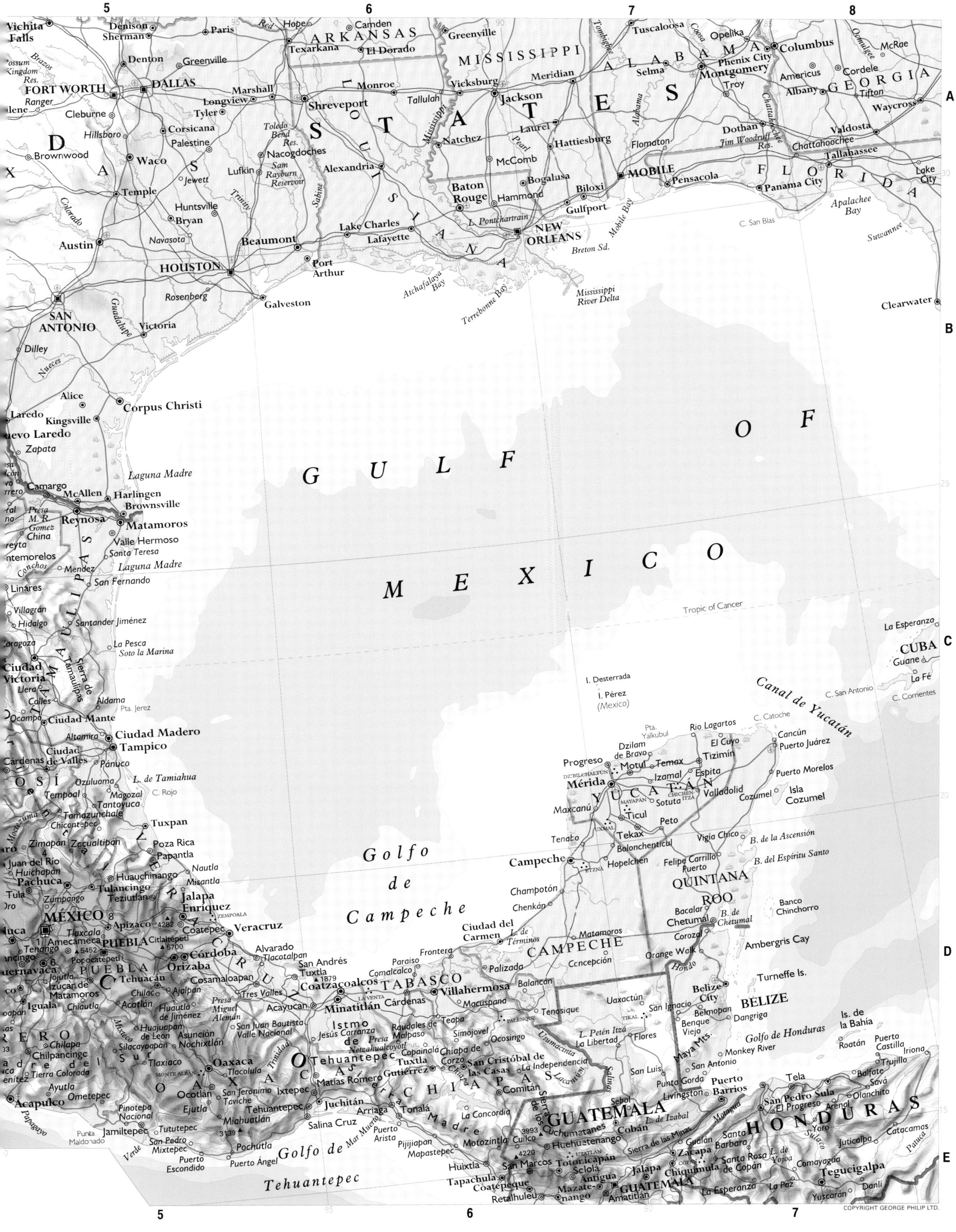

106
107
120

5
6
7
8
A
B
C
D
E
GULF OF MEXICO
Golfo de Campeche
Golfo de Tehuantepec
Golfo de Honduras
Tropic of Cancer
Canal de Yucatán
ARKANSAS
MISSISSIPPI
ALABAMA
GEORGIA
FLORIDA
LOUISIANA
STATES
TEXAS
CUBA
TAMAULIPAS
VERACRUZ
PUEBLA
OAXACA
TABASCO
CHIAPAS
CAMPECHE
YUCATÁN
QUINTANA ROO
GUATEMALA
BELIZE
HONDURAS
Wichita Falls
Denison
Sherman
Paris
Hope
Camden
Texarkana
El Dorado
Greenville
Tuscaloosa
Opelika
Columbus
McRae
Denton
Greenville
Phenix City
Montgomery
Selma
Americus
Cordele
FORT WORTH
DALLAS
Marshall
Monroe
Vicksburg
Meridian
Troy
Albany
Tifton
Longview
Shreveport
Tallulah
Jackson
Waycross
Tyler
Cleburne
Corsicana
Laurel
Dothan
Valdosta
Hillsboro
Palestine
Toledo Bend Res.
Nacogdoches
Natchez
Hattiesburg
Flomaton
Jim Woodruff Res.
Chattahoochee
Tallahassee
Brownwood
Waco
Sam Rayburn Reservoir
Alexandria
McComb
Lake City
Jewett
Lufkin
Bogalusa
MOBILE
Pensacola
Panama City
Temple
Huntsville
Baton Rouge
Hammond
Biloxi
Bryan
Gulfport
Apalachee Bay
Lake Charles
L. Pontchartrain
Austin
Navasota
Beaumont
Lafayette
NEW ORLEANS
C. San Blas
Breton Sd.
HOUSTON
Port Arthur
Atchafalaya Bay
Terrebonne Bay
Mississippi River Delta
Rosenberg
Galveston
SAN ANTONIO
Victoria
Clearwater
Dilley
Alice
Corpus Christi
Laredo
Kingsville
Nuevo Laredo
Zapata
Laguna Madre
Camargo
McAllen
Harlingen
Brownsville
Reynosa
Matamoros
Presa M. R. Gomez
China
Valle Hermoso
Santa Teresa
Montemorelos
Mendez
Laguna Madre
San Fernando
Linares
Villagrán
Hidalgo
Santander Jiménez
La Pesca
Soto la Marina
Ciudad Victoria
Sierra de Tamaulipas
Llera
Aldama
Pta. Jerez
Ocampo
Ciudad Mante
Altamira
Ciudad Madero
Tampico
Ciudad de Valles
Pánuco
L. de Tamiahua
Ozuluama
C. Rojo
Tempoal
Tantoyuca
Tamazunchale
Chicontepec
Tuxpan
Zimapán
Zacualtipán
Poza Rica
Papantla
San Juan del Río
Huichapán
Nautla
Pachuca
Huauchinango
Misantla
Tula
Tulancingo
Jalapa Enríquez
Zumpango
Teziutlán
MÉXICO
Apizaco
ZEMPOALA
Tlaxcala
4282
Coatepec
Veracruz
Amecameca
PUEBLA
Citlaltépetl
5700
Tenango
5452
Popocatépetl
Córdoba
Alvarado
Tlacotalpan
Cuernavaca
Orizaba
San Andrés Tuxtla
1879
Jojutla
Tehuacán
Cosamaloapan
Izúcar de Matamoros
Ajalpan
Coatzacoalcos
Tres Valles
Chilac
Iguala
Chiautla
Acatlán
Huautla de Jiménez
Presa Miguel Alemán
Acayucan
Minatitlán
Cárdenas
Villahermosa
Huajuapan de León
Asunción Nochixtlán
San Juan Bautista Valle Nacional
Istmo de Tehuantepec
Jesús Carranza
Presa Netzahualcóyotl
Chilapa
Silacayoapan
Chilpancingo
Tlaxiaco
Oaxaca
Tierra Colorada
MONTE ALBÁN
Tlacolula
Ayutla
Ometepec
Ocotlán
San Jerónimo Taviche
Ixtepec
Ejutla
Matías Romero
Juchitán
Acapulco
Tehuantepec
Pinotepa Nacional
Salina Cruz
Punta Maldonado
Jamiltepec
Tututepec
Miahuatlán
3139
San Pedro Mixtepec
Pochutla
Puerto Escondido
Puerto Ángel
Papagayo
Verde
Trinidad
Sierra Madre del Sur
Mar Muerto
Puerto Arista
Pijijiapan
Mapastepec
Arriaga
Tonalá
Sierra Madre
La Concordia
Motozintla
Huixtla
Tapachula
Coatepeque
Retalhuleu
Mazatenango
Amatitlán
GUATEMALA
Antigua
Sololá
Totonicapán
San Marcos
4220
Cuilco
3993
Cuchumatanes
Huehuetenango
Cobán
UTATLÁN
Jalapa
Chiquimula
COPÁN
Zacapa
Gualán
Santa Bárbara
Santa Rosa de Copán
La Esperanza
La Paz
Comayagua
Tegucigalpa
Yuscarán
Danlí
L. de Yojoa
Yoro
Juticalpa
Catacamas
Patuca
Sulaco
San Pedro Sula
El Progreso
Tela
Arenal
Olanchito
Balfate
Savá
Trujillo
Iriona
Puerto Castilla
Roatán
Is. de la Bahía
Sebol
L. de Izabal
Sierra de las Minas
Motagua
Livingston
Puerto Barrios
Punta Gorda
San Antonio
Monkey River
Maya Mts.
Dangriga
Belmopan
Belize City
BELIZE
Benque Viejo
San Ignacio
Turneffe Is.
Ambergris Cay
Corozal
Orange Walk
Hondo
San Luis
Flores
L. Petén Itzá
TIKAL
La Libertad
Uaxactún
Tenosique
Balancán
Usumacinta
Lacantún
Salinas
La Independencia
Comitán
San Cristóbal de las Casas
Ocosingo
Chiapa de Corzo
Tuxtla Gutiérrez
Copainalá
Simojovel
PALENQUE
Teapa
Macuspana
Raudales de Malpaso
Comalcalco
LA VENTA
Paraíso
Frontera
Palizada
Ciudad del Carmen
L. de Términos
Concepción
Matamoros
Chenkán
Champotón
Campeche
ETZNÁ
Hopelchén
Bolonchenticul
Tenabo
Tekax
UXMAL
Ticul
MAYAPÁN
Maxcanú
Sotuta
Peto
Mérida
DZIBILCHALTÚN
Progreso
Motul
Dzilam de Bravo
Pta. Yalkubul
Temax
Izamal
CHICHÉN ITZÁ
Espita
Valladolid
Tizimín
El Cuyo
Río Lagartos
C. Catoche
Cancún
Puerto Juárez
Puerto Morelos
Isla Cozumel
Cozumel
Vigía Chico
B. de la Ascensión
B. del Espíritu Santo
Felipe Carrillo Puerto
Bacalar
Chetumal
B. de Chetumal
Banco Chinchorro
I. Desterrada
I. Pérez (Mexico)
La Esperanza
Guane
La Fé
C. San Antonio
C. Corrientes
Red
Brazos
Colorado
Trinity
Sabine
Mississippi
Pearl
Tombigbee
Coosa
Alabama
Chattahoochee
Ocmulgee
Suwannee
Mobile Bay
Guadalupe
Nueces
Conchos
Possum Kingdom Res.
Ranger
Abilene
Moctezuma
Mixteco
95
90
85
30
25
20
15

1:7 100 000

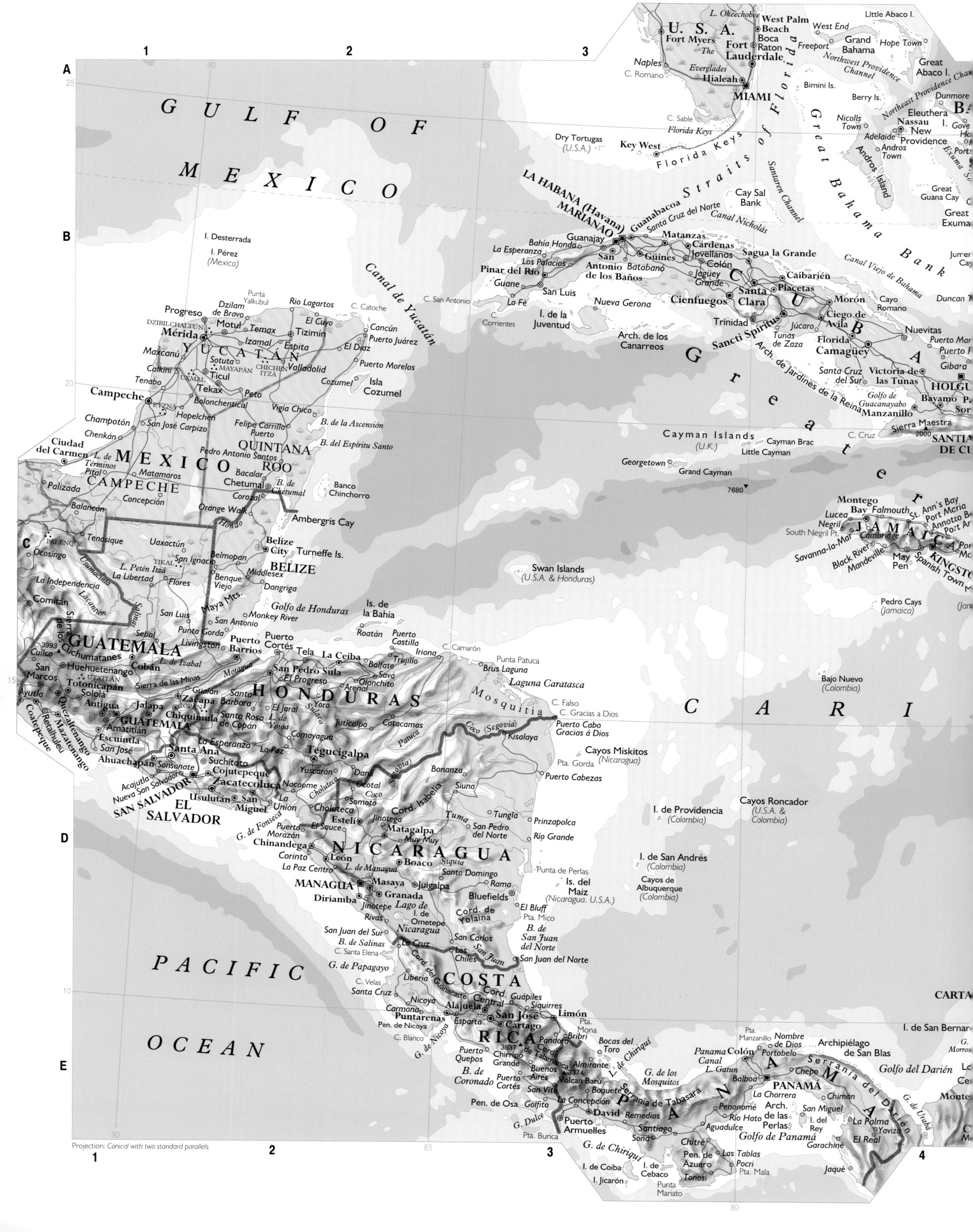

GULF OF MEXICO
Canal de Yucatán
Straits of Florida
Florida Keys
Great Bahama Bank
Greater Antilles
CARIBBEAN
PACIFIC OCEAN
U.S.A.
MIAMI
Fort Myers
Fort Lauderdale
West Palm Beach
Boca Raton
Hialeah
Naples
Key West
Grand Bahama
Freeport
Great Abaco I.
Nassau
New Providence
Eleuthera
Andros Island
Bimini Is.
Dry Tortugas (U.S.A.)
LA HABANA (Havana)
MARIANAO
CUBA
Matanzas
Cárdenas
Pinar del Río
Santa Clara
Cienfuegos
Sancti Spíritus
Camagüey
Holguín
Bayamo
Manzanillo
Sierra Maestra
I. de la Juventud
Nueva Gerona
Cayman Islands (U.K.)
Georgetown
Grand Cayman
Cayman Brac
Little Cayman
JAMAICA
Montego Bay
Kingston
Spanish Town
Mandeville
May Pen
Swan Islands (U.S.A. & Honduras)
Pedro Cays (Jamaica)
YUCATÁN
Mérida
Progreso
Campeche
Ciudad del Carmen
MEXICO
CAMPECHE
QUINTANA ROO
Chetumal
Cancún
Isla Cozumel
Cozumel
Valladolid
BELIZE
Belize City
Belmopan
Orange Walk
Ambergris Cay
Turneffe Is.
Dangriga
GUATEMALA
Flores
L. Petén Itzá
Puerto Barrios
Cobán
Huehuetenango
Quezaltenango
Escuintla
Antigua
HONDURAS
TEGUCIGALPA
San Pedro Sula
La Ceiba
Puerto Cortés
Tela
Is. de la Bahía
Roatán
Golfo de Honduras
Choluteca
Mosquitia
Laguna Caratasca
C. Gracias a Dios
Puerto Cabezas
Cayos Miskitos (Nicaragua)
EL SALVADOR
SAN SALVADOR
Santa Ana
San Miguel
Usulután
NICARAGUA
MANAGUA
León
Granada
Masaya
Chinandega
Matagalpa
Bluefields
Lago de Nicaragua
San Juan del Norte
Is. del Maiz (Nicaragua, U.S.A.)
I. de Providencia (Colombia)
I. de San Andrés (Colombia)
Cayos Roncador (U.S.A. & Colombia)
Cayos de Albuquerque (Colombia)
Bajo Nuevo (Colombia)
COSTA RICA
San José
Cartago
Alajuela
Puntarenas
Limón
Liberia
G. de Nicoya
PANAMA
PANAMÁ
Colón
Panama Canal
David
Santiago
Golfo de Panamá
G. de Chiriquí
Arch. de las Perlas
Archipiélago de San Blas
Golfo del Darién
I. de Coiba
Pen. de Azuero
Projection: Conical with two standard parallels

50 0 50 100 150 200 250 300 km
50 0 50 100 150 200 miles
5
6
7
8
A
B
C
D
E
ATLANTIC OCEAN
Tropic of Cancer
Puerto Rico Trench
Milwaukee Deep 9200
CARIBBEAN SEA
Greater Antilles
Hispaniola
Lesser Antilles
Leeward Islands
Windward Islands
MAS
Arthur's Town
The Bight
Cat I.
San Salvador I.
Conception I.
Rum Cay
Long I.
Clarence Town
Crooked I. Passage
Samana Cay
Crooked I.
Plana Cays
Albert Town
Snug Corner
Mayaguana I.
Acklins I.
Cay Verde
Mira por vos Cay
Caicos Passage
Turks & Caicos (U.K.)
Caicos Is.
Turks Island Passage
Turks Is.
Hogsty Reef
Little Inagua I.
Lake Rosa
Great Inagua I.
Matthew Town
Moa
Baracoa
Pta. de Maisí
Maisí
Guantánamo
Paso de los Vientos (Windward Passage)
Î. de la Tortue
Cap-Haïtien
Port-de-Paix
Jean Rabel
Monte Cristi
LA ISABELA
Puerto Plata
Santiago de los Caballeros
San Francisco de Macorís
Nagua
Samana
Sánchez
Sabana de la Mar
Hato Mayor
Fort Liberté
Gonaïves
Hinche
St-Marc
Cord. Central
3175
La Vega
HAITI
DOMINICAN REP.
PORT-AU-PRINCE
San Juan
L. Enriquillo
Jérémie
Î. de la Gonâve
Dame Marie
Massif de la Hotte
Les Cayes
Aquin
Petit Goâve
Jacmel
2280
Barahona
Pedernales
Î. à Vache
Pointe-à-Gravois
Azua de Compostela
Baní
San Cristóbal
San Pedro de Macorís
SANTO DOMINGO
La Romana
Higüey
C. Engaño
B. de Yuma
I. Saona
I. Beata
C. Beata
Navassa I. (U.S.A.)
Canal de la Mona
Isla Mona (U.S.A.)
Aguadilla
Arecibo
Bayamón
SAN JUAN
Carolina
Mayagüez
1338
Ponce
Caguas
Guayama
Fajardo
PUERTO RICO (U.S.A.)
St. Thomas
Virgin Gorda
Tortola
Anegada
Virgin Is. (U.K.)
Anegada Passage
Road Town
Charlotte Amalie
Virgin Is. (U.S.A.)
Christiansted
Frederiksted
St. Croix
Sombrero (U.K.)
Anguilla (U.K.)
St.-Martin (Fr.)
St. Maarten (Neth.)
St.-Barthélemy (Fr.)
Saba (Neth.)
St. Eustatius (Neth.)
Barbuda
ANTIGUA & BARBUDA
ST. KITTS & NEVIS
Basseterre
Nevis
St. John's
Antigua
Redonda
Montserrat (U.K.)
Guadeloupe Passage
Ste.-Rose
Le Moule
La Désirade
GUADELOUPE (Fr.)
Pointe-à-Pitre
Basse-Terre
Marie-Galante (Fr.)
Grand-Bourg
I. des Saintes (Fr.)
Dominica Passage
Portsmouth
DOMINICA
Roseau
I. de Aves (Venezuela)
Martinique Passage
Mt. Pelée 1397
Ste.-Marie
Le François
Fort-de-France
Rivière-Pilote
MARTINIQUE (Fr.)
St. Lucia Channel
Castries
ST. LUCIA
Soufrière
St. Vincent Passage
La Soufrière 1234
ST. VINCENT
Speightstown
Bridgetown
BARBADOS
Kingstown
& THE
Grenadines
GRENADINES
Hillsborough
St. George's
GRENADA
Aruba (Neth.)
Curaçao
Bonaire
Willemstad
NETH. ANTILLES
Pta. Gallinas
C. San Román
Pen. de Paraguaná
Pen. de la Guajira
Pta. Espada
Punto Fijo
Puerto Cumarebo
Punta Cardón
Coro
La Vela de Coro
Is. Las Aves (Ven.)
Is. Los Roques (Ven)
I. Orchila (Ven.)
I. Blanquilla (Ven.)
Is. Los Hermanos (Ven.)
Is. Los Testigos (Ven.)
Tobago
Scarborough
I. de Margarita
La Asunción
Porlamar
I. La Tortuga (Ven.)
NUEVA ESPARTA
DISTRITO FEDERAL
Dragon's Mouth
Port of Spain
Galera Point
Trinidad
Arima
Rio Claro
Pen. de Paria
Güiria
G. de Paria
San Fernando
TRINIDAD & TOBAGO
Serpent's Mouth
Ríohacha
Uribia
GUAJIRA
Golfo de Venezuela
SANTA MARTA
BARRANQUILLA
Ciénaga
Sierra Nevada de Santa Marta
5800
San Rafael
MARACAIBO
Altagracia
FALCÓN
Mene de Mauroa
Tocuyo
Tucacas
Puerto Cabello
Maracay
Maiquetía
La Guaira
CARACAS
Guatire
C. Codera
Higuerote
Puerto La Cruz
Cumaná
Carúpano
Caribe
Carioca
SUCRE
Baranoa
Soledad
Sabanalarga
ATLÁNTICO
Fundación
Valledupar
La Concepción
Santa Rita
Cabimas
Baragua
Carora
San Felipe
CARABOBO
Valencia
YARACUY
ARAGUA
MIRANDA
Los Teques
Río Chico
Ocumare del Tuy
Barcelona
Caripito
Caicara
Maturín
Calamar
MAGDALENA
Agustín Codazzi
Villa del Rosario
Ciudad Ojeda
LARA
BARQUISIMETO
Yaritagua
de los Morros
Villa de Cura
San Juan de los Morros
Altagracia de Orituco
Aragua de Barcelona
Anaco
MONAGAS
DELTA
Arjona
Plato
Zambrano
CÉSAR
Machiques
Lago de Maracaibo
Mene Grande
TRUJILLO
El Tocuyo
San Carlos
COJEDES
El Sombrero
Cantaura
Tucupita
Carmen
Sincelejo
Corozal
Mompós
Sincé
Sahagún
Magangué
El Banco
ZULIA
Betijoque
Valera
Trujillo
Acarigua
PORTUGUESA
Guanare
Portuguesa
El Baúl
Calabozo
GUÁRICO
Valle de la Pascua
Unare
El Tigre
Tigre
Pariaguán
ANZOÁTEGUI
AMACURO
Los Barrancos
Ciudad Guayana
Sierra Imataca
San Marcos
Planeta Rica
Ayapel
Majagual
BOLÍVAR
Simití
Caucasia
Sierra de Perijá
Encontrados
San Carlos del Zulia
MÉRIDA
Mérida
Cord. de Mérida
Barinas
Santa María de Ipire
Manapire
Guaritico
Soledad
El Pao
Upata
Caroní
NORTE DE SANTANDER
Ocaña
TÁCHIRA
Cúcuta
Santa Bárbara
Ciudad Bolivia
BARINAS
Libertad
Puerto de Nutrias
Bruzual
Achaguas
San Fernando de Apure
Apure
Orinoco
Mapire
Ciudad Bolívar
Caicara
Embalse de Guri
Guasipati
El Callao
Tumeremo
VENEZUELA
West from Greenwich
COPYRIGHT GEORGE PHILIP LTD
ft m
12 000 4000
9000 3000
6000 2000
4500 1500
3000 1000
1200 400
600 200
0 0
200 600
2000 6000
4000 12 000
6000 18 000
8000 24 000
m ft
109
119
124
125

NORTH ATLANTIC OCEAN
PACIFIC OCEAN
SOUTH ATLANTIC OCEAN
Caribbean Sea
Greater Antilles
Lesser Antilles
Cuba
Hispaniola
Jamaica
Puerto Rico
Turks & Caicos Is.
Guadeloupe
Dominica
Martinique
St. Lucia
St. Vincent
Barbados
Grenada
Tobago
Trinidad
I. Margarita
Yucatan Channel
Yucatán Peninsula
Gulf of Campeche
Isthmus of Tehuantepec
G. de Honduras
C. Gracias a Dios
Guatemala Trench
L. Nicaragua
Panama Canal
G. of Darién
Gulf of Panamá
C. de la Aguja
Sierra Nevada de Santa Marta
5800
L. Maracaibo
Cord. de Mérida
Cordillera Occidental
Cordillera Central
Cordillera Oriental
Magdalena
Llanos
Orinoco
Meta
Guaviare
Guiana Highlands
Mt. Roraima
2810
Sierra Pacaraima
Serra Tumucumaque
C. Orange
Essequibo
Courantyne
Branco
Negro
Caquetá
Putumayo
Japurá
Napo
Amazon
Marajó I.
Equator
C. de San Francisco
Cotopaxi 5897
Chimborazo 6267
Galapagos Is.
G. of Guayaquil
Pta. Pariñas
Pta. Negra
Marañón
Ucayali
Juruá
Purus
Madeira
Aripuanã
Roosevelt
Tapajós
Teles Pires
Xingu
Tocantins
Araguaia
Parnaíba
Selvas
C. de São Roque
Plat. of Borborema
São Francisco
Huascarán 6768
Madre de Dios
Guaporé
Mamoré
Arinos
Plateau of Mato Grosso
Brazilian Highlands
Chincha Alta
L. Titicaca
Nevada Ancohuma 6550
Bolivian Plateau
L. de Poopó
Chile Peru Trench
Gran Chaco
Paraguay
Pilcomayo
Paraná
Abrolhos Bank
2890
Pico da Bandeira
Serra da Mantiqueira
C. Frio
Tropic of Capricorn
Tropic of Cancer
8050
Atacama Desert
Andes
Cerro Ojos del Salado 6863
San Félix
San Ambrosio
Iguaçu Falls
Uruguay
Serra do Mar
Salado
Entre Ríos
Salinas Grandes
L. Mar Chiquita
Sierra de Córdoba
Mt. Aconcagua 6960
L. dos Patos
Arch. de Juan Fernández
Pampas
Río de la Plata
Colorado
Bahía Blanca
Negro
G. San Matías
40
Valdés Peninsula
Chile Rise
Chiloé I.
Chubut
Patagonia
Chonos Archipelago
Mte. San Valentín 4058
Taitao Peninsula
Gulf of San Jorge
Argentine Basin
Gulf of Penas
6212
Wellington I.
Madre de Dios I.
Falkland Is.
West Falkland
East Falkland
Magellan's Str.
Santa Inés I.
Tierra del Fuego
Staten I.
Canal Cockburn
Canal Beagle
C. Horn
South Georgia
9200
West from Greenwich
Projection: Lambert's Azimuthal Equal Area
CARTOGRAPHY BY PHILIP'S.
km
miles
ft
m

NORTH ATLANTIC OCEAN
PACIFIC OCEAN
SOUTH ATLANTIC OCEAN
Caribbean Sea
BRAZIL
ARGENTINA
CHILE
PERU
BOLIVIA
COLOMBIA
VENEZUELA
ECUADOR
PARAGUAY
URUGUAY
GUYANA
SURINAM
FRENCH GUIANA
LIMA Capital Cities
Projection: Lambert's Azimuthal Equal Area
West from Greenwich
CARTOGRAPHY BY PHILIP'S.

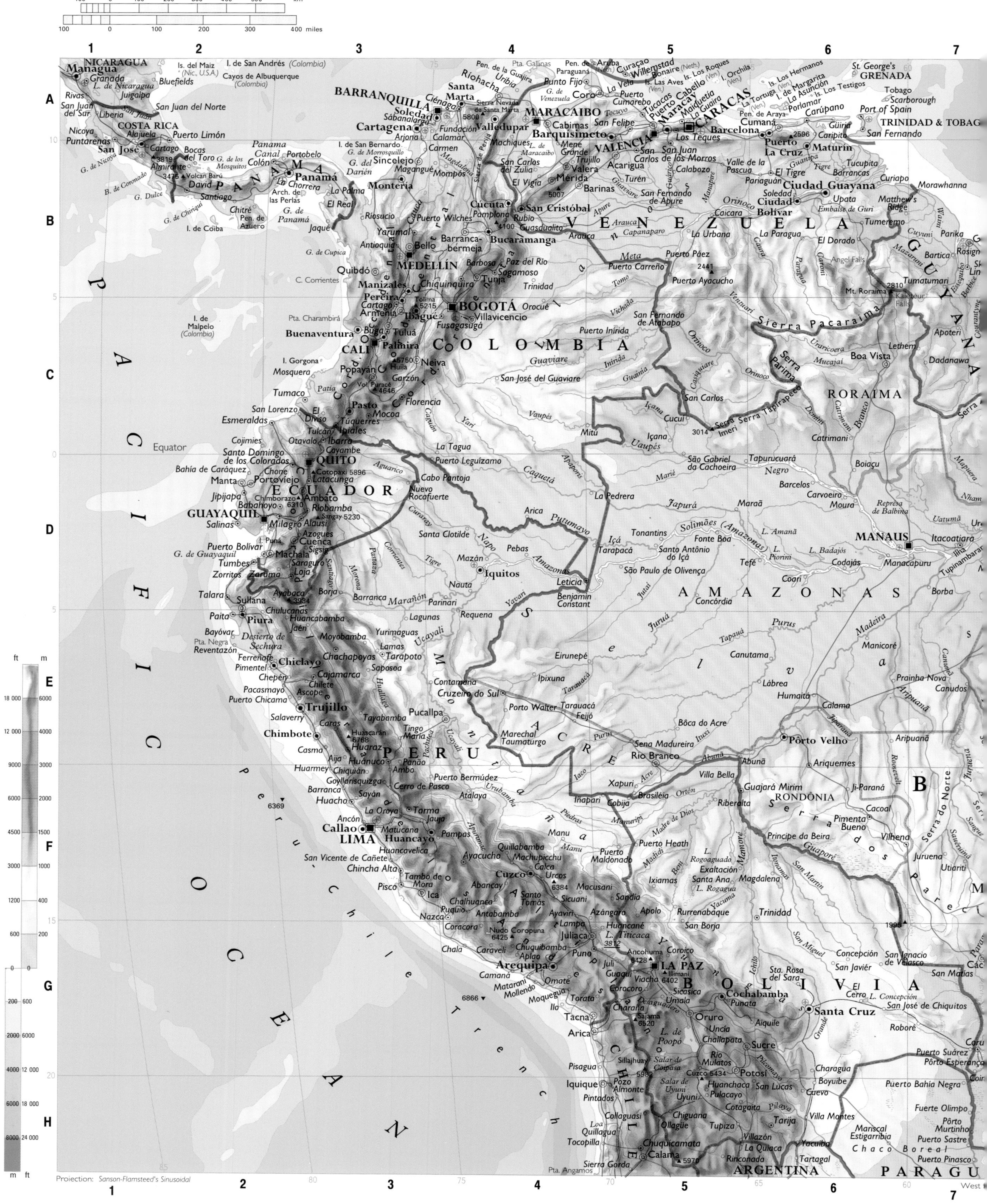

NICARAGUA
Managua
COSTA RICA
PANAMA
Panamá
BARRANQUILLA
Cartagena
MARACAIBO
CARACAS
Barcelona
Ciudad Guayana
TRINIDAD & TOBAGO
GRENADA
V E N E Z U E L A
MEDELLÍN
BOGOTÁ
C O L O M B I A
CALI
QUITO
E C U A D O R
GUAYAQUIL
Iquitos
MANAUS
A M A Z O N A S
Trujillo
Chiclayo
P E R U
Callao
LIMA
Arequipa
LA PAZ
B O L I V I A
Santa Cruz
Cochabamba
Sucre
Potosí
C H I L E
ARGENTINA
RONDÔNIA
RORAIMA
ACRE
P A C I F I C O C E A N
Peru-Chile Trench
Equator
Projection: Sanson-Flamsteed's Sinusoidal

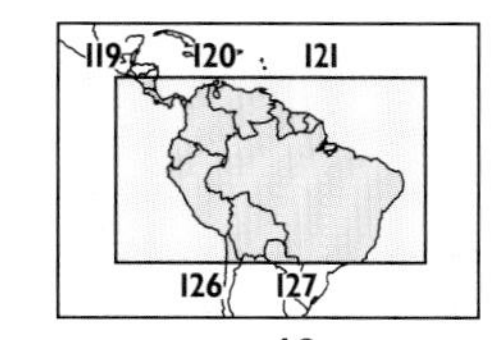

8 9 10 11 12 13

A B C D E F G H

ATLANTIC OCEAN

Equator

São Paulo (Braz.)
Rocas
Fernando de Noronha (Braz.)
Trindade (Braz.)
6059

Paramaribo
Nieuw Amsterdam
Moengo
St-Laurent
Iracoubo
Sinnamary
Kourou
Cayenne
Albina
C. Orange
St-Georges
Oiapoque
FRENCH GUIANA
Camopi
Serra Tumucumaque
Amapá
I. de Maracá
AMAPÁ
Merirumã
Serra do Navio
Macapá
I. Caviana
I. Mexiana
C. Maguarinho
Mazagão
Afuá
Chaves
Soure
Curuçá
Salinópolis
I. Grande de Gurupá
I. de Marajó
Vigia
Bragança
BELÉM
Castanhal
Viseu
Almeirim
Gurupá
Breves
Óbidos
Monte Alegre
Prainha
Pôrto de Móz
Curralinho
Abaetetuba
Turiaçu
Cururupu
Alenquer
Amazonas (Amazon)
Cametá
B. de São Marcos
São Luís
Barreirinhas
Tutóia
Santarém
Belterra
Altamira
Baião
Alcântara
Pinheiro
Rosário
Itapecuru-Mirim
Parnaíba
Luís Correia
Camocim
Granja
Itapipoca
Caucaia
FORTALEZA
Aveiro
Brasília Legal
PARÁ
Tucuruí
Santa Inês
Viana
Bacabal
Brejo
Coroatá
Codó
Piracuruca
Piripiri
Sobral
Maranguape
Cascavel
Itaituba
Represa de Tucuruí
Açailândia
Pedreiras
Caxias
Campo Maior
Oiticica
Ipu
Quixadá
Baturité
Russas
Aracati
Areia Branca
Mossoró
Macau
Ceará Mirim
C. de São Roque
Marabá
MARANHÃO
Imperatriz
Teresina
Crateús
Senador Pompeu
CEARÁ
RIO GRANDE DO NORTE
Natal
São João do Araguaia
Carajás
Barra do Corda
Grajaú
Pôrto Franco
Tocantinópolis
Estreito
Carolina
Colinas
Amarante
Floriano
Valença do Piauí
Oeiras
Picos
Iguatu
Caraúbas
Caicó
Currais Novos
Canguaretama
Mamanguape
Cajàzeiras
Cedro
Sousa
Patos
Alagoa Grande
Cabedelo
Araguaína
Loreto
Nova Iorque
PIAUÍ
Chapada do Araripe
Crato
Ouricuri
Juàzeiro do Norte
PARAÍBA
Campina Grande
João Pessoa
Olinda
Conceição do Araguaia
Riachão
Uruçuí
Salgueiro
Caruaru
RECIFE
Jaboatão
Paulistana
PERNAMBUCO
Pesqueira
Araguacema
Pedro Afonso
São João do Piauí
Santa Filomena
Caracol
Sa. Dois Irmãos
Petrolina
Garanhuns
Palmares
Vitória de Santo Antão
Novo Remanso
Juàzeiro
Nova Casa Nova
Represa de Sobradinho
Petrolândia
Palmeira dos Índios
Rio Largo
Maceió
Paulo Afonso
Arapiraca
ALAGOAS
Palmas
Parnaguá
Senhor-do-Bonfim
Propriá
SERGIPE
Penedo
BRAZIL
Pôrto Nacional
TOCANTINS
Barra
Xique-Xique
Jacobina
Aracaju
São Cristóvão
Santa Isabel do Morro
I. do Bananal
Gurupi
Peixe
Taguatinga
Barreiras
Ibotirama
Mundo Novo
Queimadas
Serrinha
Estância
Feira de Santana
Alagoinhas
BAHÍA
Itaberaba
Cachoeira
Santo Amaro
SALVADOR
Paranã
Campos Belos
São Domingos
Santa Maria da Vitória
Bom Jesus da Lapa
Serra do Sincorá
Castro Alves
Valença
Jequié
B. de Todos os Santos
Nazaré
MATO GROSSO
Planalto do Mato Grosso
Serra do Roncador
Serra Formosa
Serra Dourada
Caetité
Posse
Carinhanha
Brumado
Ubaitaba
Itabuna
Ilhéus
Niquelândia
1678
Uruaçu
Aruanã
Condeúba
Vitória da Conquista
Canavieiras
DIST. FED.
Formosa
BRASÍLIA
Januária
Monte Azul
São Francisco
Pedra Azul
Santo Antonio
Barra do Garças
Rondonópolis
Goiás
Taguatinga
Anápolis
Goiânia
Luziânia
Janaúba
Montes Claros
Salinas
Belmonte
Jequitinhonha
Pôrto Seguro
GOIÁS
Alto Araguaia
Vianópolis
Morrinhos
Paracatu
Pirapora
Araçuaí
Teófilo Otoni
Itamaraju
Prado
Caravelas
Nanuque
MATO GROSSO DO SUL
Coxim
Jataí
Rio Verde
Quirinópolis
Itumbiara
Ipameri
Catalão
Patos de Minas
Corinto
Diamantina
Governador Valadares
Nova Venécia
Mucuri
Conceição da Barra
São Mateus
MINAS GERAIS
Araguari
Uberlândia
Ituiutaba
Patrocínio
Curvelo
Ipatinga
Itabira
Colatina
Linhares
ESPÍRITO SANTO
Campo Grande
Paranaíba
Prata
Uberaba
Araxá
Ibiá
Sete Lagoas
BELO HORIZONTE
Sabará
Caratinga
Cariacica
Vitória
Vila Velha
Miranda
Santa Fé do Sul
Água Clara
São José do Barretos
Igarapava
Frutal
Divinópolis
Nova Lima
Ponte Nova
Aquidauana
Ribas do Rio Pardo
Três Lagoas
Rio Prêto
Andradina
Franca
Passos
Conselheiro Lafaiete
Ouro Prêto
Ubá
2890
Cachoeiro de Itapemirim
Ribeirão Prêto
Araçatuba
Panorama
Penápolis
Catanduva
Guaxupé
São João del Rei
Barbacena
Juiz de Fora
Itaperuna
Dourados
Presidente Epitácio
Presidente Prudente
Lins
SÃO PAULO
Araraquara
Poços de Caldas
Três Rios
Campos
Marília
São Carlos
São Lourenço
Ponta Porã
Assis
Bauru
Jaú
Moji-Mirim
2787
Nova Friburgo
Pedro Juan Caballero
Piracicaba
Limeira
Volta Redonda
Petrópolis
RIO DE JANEIRO
Botucatu
Campinas
Niterói
Cabo Frio
RIO DE JANEIRO

8 9 10 11 12 13

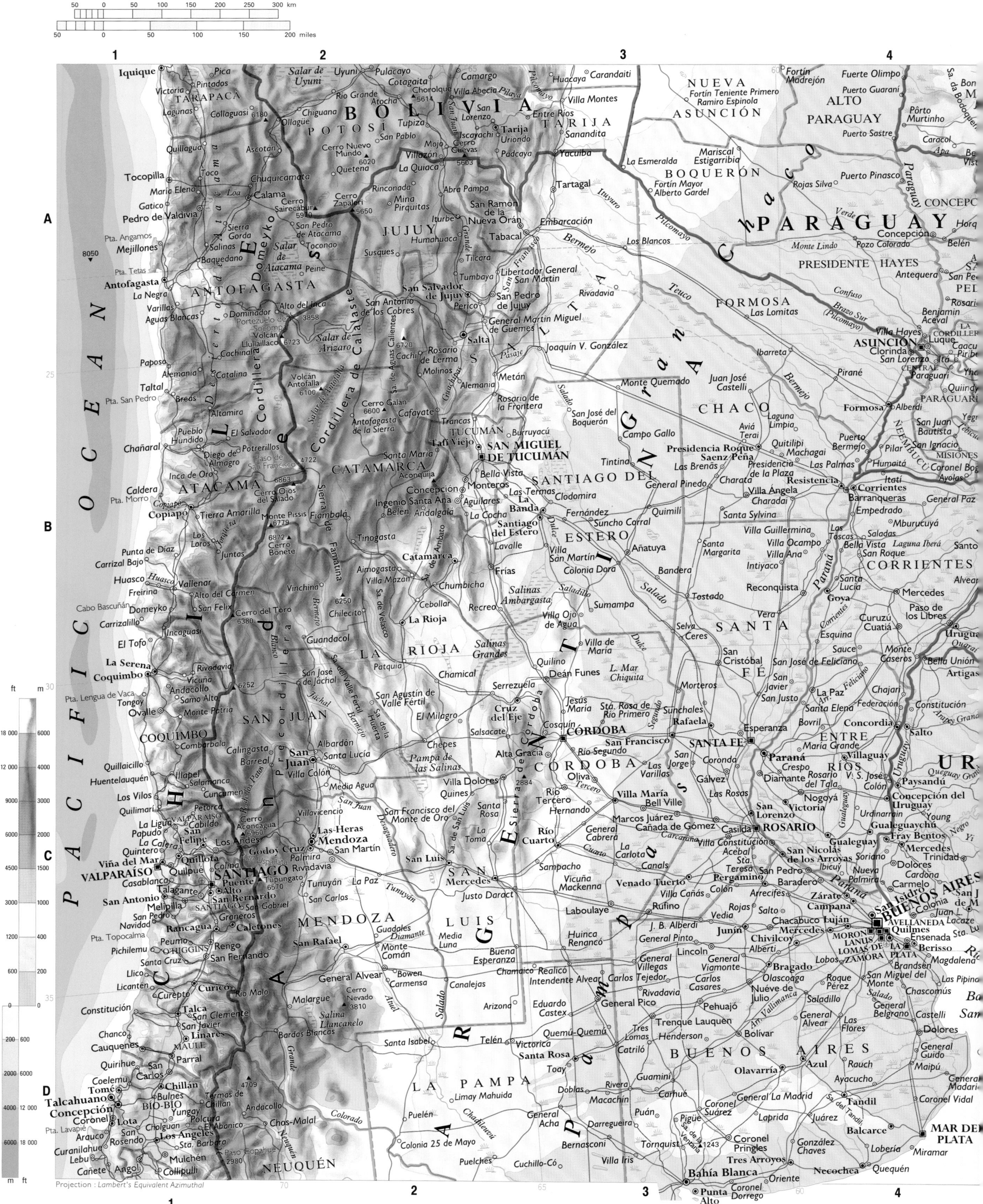

50 0 50 100 150 200 250 300 km
50 0 50 100 150 200 miles
PACIFIC OCEAN
BOLIVIA
PARAGUAY
ARGENTINA
CHILE
Gran Chaco
ANTOFAGASTA
ATACAMA
COQUIMBO
TARAPACÁ
POTOSÍ
TARIJA
JUJUY
SALTA
TUCUMÁN
CATAMARCA
SANTIAGO DEL ESTERO
LA RIOJA
SAN JUAN
CÓRDOBA
SANTA FÉ
CORRIENTES
ENTRE RÍOS
MENDOZA
SAN LUIS
LA PAMPA
BUENOS AIRES
NEUQUÉN
FORMOSA
CHACO
ALTO PARAGUAY
BOQUERÓN
PRESIDENTE HAYES
NUEVA ASUNCIÓN
Cordillera Domeyko
Cordillera de Calalaste
Salar de Uyuni
Salar de Atacama
ASUNCIÓN
SAN MIGUEL DE TUCUMÁN
CÓRDOBA
SANTA FE
ROSARIO
BUENOS AIRES
SANTIAGO
VALPARAÍSO
Mendoza
Antofagasta
Iquique
Copiapó
La Serena
Salta
Corrientes
Resistencia
Paraná
Concepción
Bahía Blanca
MAR DEL PLATA
Pto. Topocalma
Pta. Lavapié
Projection : Lambert's Equivalent Azimuthal

124
125
128
5
6
7
BELO HORIZONTE
Nova Lima
Itabirito
Vitória
Vila Velha
Guarapari
Três Lagoas
Andradina
Mirassol
São José do Rio Prêto
Olímpia
Barretos
Passos
Oliveira
Conselheiro Lafaiete
Ouro Prêto
Ponte Nova
Itaquari
Castelo
Cachoeiro de Itapemirim
Araçatuba
Birigui
Catanduva
Bebedouro
Ribeirão Prêto
São Sebastião do Paraíso
Campo Belo
São João del Rei
Ubá
Muriaé
Carangola
Alegre
Panorama
Presidente Epitácio
Adamantina
Penápolis
Lins
Jaboticabal
Guaxupé
Lavras
Barbacena
Cataguases
Itaperuna
Nova Alvorada do Sul
Maracaju
S Ã O P A U L O
Mococa
Alfenas
Varginha
Três Pontas
Santos Dumont
Juiz de Fora
Leopoldina
Campos
Dourados
Ponta Porã
Pedro Juan Caballero
Presidente Prudente
Tupã
Marília
Araraquara
São Carlos
São João da Boa Vista
Poços de Caldas
Pouso Alegre
Três Corações
Três Rios
Além Paraíba
RIO DE JANEIRO
Cabo de São Tomé
Amambaí
Naviraí
Rancharia
Bauru
Jaú
Rio Claro
Araras
Mogi-Mirim
Ouro Fino
Itajubá
Volta Redonda
Barra do Piraí
Nova Friburgo
Petrópolis
Macaé
Paranavaí
Londrina
Assis
Ourinhos
Piracicaba
Limeira
Americana
CAMPINAS
Cruzeiro
Guaratinguetá
Barra Mansa
NOVA IGUAÇU
DUQUE DE CAXIAS
SÃO GONÇALO
Cabo Frio
Maringá
Arapongas
Apucarana
Cornélio Procópio
Jacarèzinho
Avaré
Botucatu
Tatuí
Itu
Jundiaí
Bragança Paulista
Taubaté
São José dos C.
Angra dos Reis
NITERÓI
RIO DE JANEIRO
Umuarama
Cianorte
Itapetininga
Sorocaba
SÃO PAULO
SANTO ANDRÉ
Moji das Cruzes
Jacareí
Ilha Grande
Tropic of Capricorn
Cruzeiro do Oeste
Goio-Erê
Campo Mourão
São Bernardo do Campo
São Vicente
SANTOS
Guarujá
Ilha de São Sebastião
Pta. de Boi
Itanhaém
P A R A N Á
B R A Z I L
Toledo
Cascavel
Castro
Itararé
Registro
Iguape
Ilha Comprida
Ilha do Cardoso
Foz do Iguaçu
Ciudad del Este
Guarapuava
Ponta Grossa
CURITIBA
Antonina
Paranaguá
Matinhos
Guaratuba
Francisco Beltrão
União da Vitória
São Mateus do Sul
Rio Negro
Mafra
Joinville
São Francisco do Sul
Pato Branco
Palmas
Pôrto União
Caçador
MISIONES
Xanxerê
Chapecó
Joaçaba
SANTA CATARINA
Blumenau
Itajaí
Brusque
Posadas
Encarnación
Oberá
Erechim
Campos Novos
Curitibanos
Rio do Sul
São José
Ilha de Santa Catarina
Florianópolis
Santo Ângelo
Carazinho
Passo Fundo
Lajes
Lagoa Vermelha
Cruz Alta
Vacaria
Tubarão
Laguna
Cabo Santa Marta Grande
Criciúma
Araranguá
R I O G R A N D E
Santiago
Bento Gonçalves
Caxias do Sul
Torres
Santa Maria
Santa Cruz do Sul
Montenegro
Nôvo Hamburgo
Taquara
São Leopoldo
Canoas
Osorio
Alegrete
Cachoeira do Sul
Rio Pardo
PÔRTO ALEGRE
Viamão
D O S U L
São Gabriel
Santana do Livramento
Rivera
Dom Pedrito
Camaquã
Tapes
Bagé
Mostardas
Lagoa dos Patos
Pelotas
São José do Norte
Rio Grande
Jaguarão
Melo
Lagoa Mirim
Lagoa Mangueira
Santa Vitória do Palmar
Chuy
Treinta y Tres
Castillos
Rocha
Minas
San Carlos
Maldonado
MONTEVIDEO
A T L A N T I C
O C E A N
5304
West from Greenwich
A
B
C
D

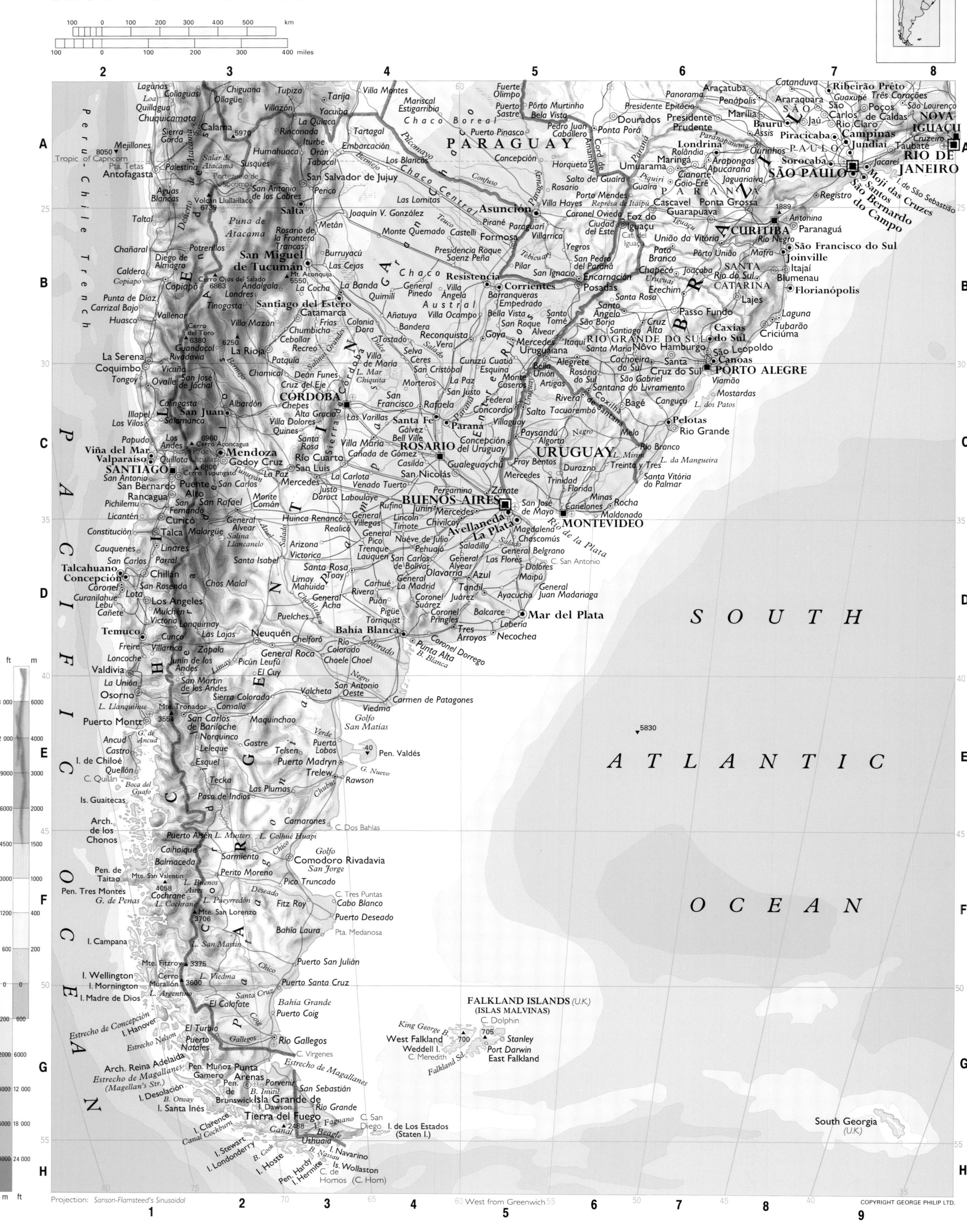

Projection: Sanson-Flamsteed's Sinusoidal

INDEX

The index contains the names of all the principal places and features shown on the World Maps. Each name is followed by an additional entry in italics giving the country or region within which it is located. The alphabetical order of names composed of two or more words is governed primarily by the first word and then by the second. This is an example of the rule:

Mīr Kūh, *Iran*	**71**	**E8**
Mīr Shahdād, *Iran*	**71**	**E8**
Mira, *Italy*	**29**	**C9**
Mira por vos Cay, *Bahamas*	**121**	**B5**
Miraj, *India*	**66**	**79**

Physical features composed of a proper name (Erie) and a description (Lake) are positioned alphabetically by the proper name. The description is positioned after the proper name and is usually abbreviated:

Erie, L., *N. Amer.* **110 D4**

Where a description forms part of a settlement or administrative name however, it is always written in full and put in its true alphabetic position:

Mount Morris, *U.S.A.* **110 D7**

Names beginning with M' and Mc are indexed as if they were spelled Mac. Names beginning St. are alphabetised under Saint, but Sankt, Sint, Sant', Santa and San are all spelt in full and are alphabetised accordingly. If the same place name occurs two or more times in the index and all are in the same country, each is followed by the name of the administrative subdivision in which it is located. The names are placed in the alphabetical order of the subdivisions. For example:

Jackson, *Ky., U.S.A.*	**108**	**G4**
Jackson, *Mich., U.S.A.*	**108**	**D3**
Jackson, *Minn., U.S.A.*	**112**	**D7**

The number in bold type which follows each name in the index refers to the number of the map page where that feature or place will be found. This is usually the largest scale at which the place or feature appears.

The letter and figure which are in bold type immediately after the page number give the grid square on the map page, within which the feature is situated. The letter represents the latitude and the figure the longitude.

In some cases the feature itself may fall within the specified square, while the name is outside. This is usually the case only with features which are larger than a grid square.

Rivers are indexed to their mouths or confluences, and carry the symbol → after their names. A solid square ■ follows the name of a country, while an open square □ refers to a first order administrative area.

ABBREVIATIONS USED IN THE INDEX

A.C.T. – Australian Capital Territory
A.R. – Autonomous Region
Afghan. – Afghanistan
Afr. – Africa
Ala. – Alabama
Alta. – Alberta
Amer. – America(n)
Arch. – Archipelago
Ariz. – Arizona
Ark. – Arkansas
Atl. Oc. – Atlantic Ocean
B. – Baie, Bahía, Bay, Bucht, Bugt
B.C. – British Columbia
Bangla. – Bangladesh
Barr. – Barrage
Bos.-H. – Bosnia-Herzegovina
C. – Cabo, Cap, Cape, Coast
C.A.R. – Central African Republic
C. Prov. – Cape Province
Calif. – California
Cat. – Catarata
Cent. – Central
Chan. – Channel
Colo. – Colorado
Conn. – Connecticut
Cord. – Cordillera
Cr. – Creek
Czech. – Czech Republic
D.C. – District of Columbia
Del. – Delaware
Dem. – Democratic
Dep. – Dependency
Des. – Desert
Dét. – Détroit
Dist. – District
Dj. – Djebel
Domin. – Dominica
Dom. Rep. – Dominican Republic
E. – East
E. Salv. – El Salvador
Eq. Guin. – Equatorial Guinea
Est. – Estrecho
Falk. Is. – Falkland Is.
Fd. – Fjord
Fla. – Florida
Fr. – French
G. – Golfe, Golfo, Gulf, Guba, Gebel
Ga. – Georgia
Gt. – Great, Greater
Guinea-Biss. – Guinea-Bissau
H.K. – Hong Kong
H.P. – Himachal Pradesh
Hants. – Hampshire
Harb. – Harbor, Harbour
Hd. – Head
Hts. – Heights
I.(s). – Île, Ilha, Insel, Isla, Island, Isle
Ill. – Illinois
Ind. – Indiana
Ind. Oc. – Indian Ocean
Ivory C. – Ivory Coast
J. – Jabal, Jebel
Jaz. – Jazīrah
Junc. – Junction
K. – Kap, Kapp
Kans. – Kansas
Kep. – Kepulauan
Ky. – Kentucky
L. – Lac, Lacul, Lago, Lagoa, Lake, Limni, Loch, Lough
La. – Louisiana
Ld. – Land
Liech. – Liechtenstein
Lux. – Luxembourg
Mad. P. – Madhya Pradesh
Madag. – Madagascar
Man. – Manitoba
Mass. – Massachusetts
Md. – Maryland
Me. – Maine
Medit. S. – Mediterranean Sea
Mich. – Michigan
Minn. – Minnesota
Miss. – Mississippi
Mo. – Missouri
Mont. – Montana
Mozam. – Mozambique
Mt.(s) – Mont, Montaña, Mountain
Mte. – Monte
Mti. – Monti
N. – Nord, Norte, North, Northern, Nouveau
N.B. – New Brunswick
N.C. – North Carolina
N. Cal. – New Caledonia
N. Dak. – North Dakota
N.H. – New Hampshire
N.I. – North Island
N.J. – New Jersey
N. Mex. – New Mexico
N.S. – Nova Scotia
N.S.W. – New South Wales
N.W.T. – North West Territory
N.Y. – New York
N.Z. – New Zealand
Nat. – National
Nebr. – Nebraska
Neths. – Netherlands
Nev. – Nevada
Nfld. – Newfoundland
Nic. – Nicaragua
O. – Oued, Ouadi
Occ. – Occidentale
Okla. – Oklahoma
Ont. – Ontario
Or. – Orientale
Oreg. – Oregon
Os. – Ostrov
Oz. – Ozero
P. – Pass, Passo, Pasul, Pulau
P.E.I. – Prince Edward Island
Pa. – Pennsylvania
Pac. Oc. – Pacific Ocean
Papua N.G. – Papua New Guinea
Pass. – Passage
Peg. – Pegunungan
Pen. – Peninsula, Péninsule
Phil. – Philippines
Pk. – Peak
Plat. – Plateau
Prov. – Province, Provincial
Pt. – Point
Pta. – Ponta, Punta
Pte. – Pointe
Qué. – Québec
Queens. – Queensland
R. – Rio, River
R.I. – Rhode Island
Ra. – Range
Raj. – Rajasthan
Recr. – Recreational, Récréatif
Reg. – Region
Rep. – Republic
Res. – Reserve, Reservoir
Rhld-Pfz. – Rheinland-Pfalz
S. – South, Southern, Sur
Si. Arabia – Saudi Arabia
S.C. – South Carolina
S. Dak. – South Dakota
S.I. – South Island
S. Leone – Sierra Leone
Sa. – Serra, Sierra
Sask. – Saskatchewan
Scot. – Scotland
Sd. – Sound
Sev. – Severnaya
Sib. – Siberia
Sprs. – Springs
St. – Saint
Sta. – Santa
Ste. – Sainte
Sto. – Santo
Str. – Strait, Stretto
Switz. – Switzerland
Tas. – Tasmania
Tenn. – Tennessee
Terr. – Territory, Territoire
Tex. – Texas
Tg. – Tanjung
Trin. & Tob. – Trinidad & Tobago
U.A.E. – United Arab Emirates
U.K. – United Kingdom
U.S.A. – United States of America
Ut. P. – Uttar Pradesh
Va. – Virginia
Vdkhr. – Vodokhranilishche
Vdskh. – Vodoskhovyshche
Vf. – Vîrful
Vic. – Victoria
Vol. – Volcano
Vt. – Vermont
W. – Wadi, West
W. Va. – West Virginia
Wall. & F. Is. – Wallis and Futuna Is.
Wash. – Washington
Wis. – Wisconsin
Wlkp. – Wielkopolski
Wyo. – Wyoming
Yorks. – Yorkshire
Yug. – Yugoslavia

A

A Baña, *Spain* 34 C2
A Cañiza, *Spain* 34 C2
A Coruña, *Spain* 34 B2
A Estrada, *Spain* 34 C2
A Fonsagrada, *Spain* 34 B3
A Guarda, *Spain* 34 D2
A Gudiña, *Spain* 34 C3
A Rúa, *Spain* 34 C3
Aachen, *Germany* 24 E2
Aalborg = Ålborg, *Denmark* 11 G3
Aalen, *Germany* 25 G6
A'âli an Nîl □, *Sudan* 81 F3
Aalst, *Belgium* 17 D4
Aalten, *Neths.* 17 C6
Aalter, *Belgium* 17 C3
Äänekoski, *Finland* 9 E21
Aarau, *Switz.* 25 H4
Aarberg, *Switz.* 25 H3
Aare →, *Switz.* 25 H4
Aargau □, *Switz.* 25 H4
Aarhus = Århus, *Denmark* 11 H4
Aarschot, *Belgium* 17 D4
Aba, *China* 58 A3
Aba, *Dem. Rep. of the Congo* 86 B3
Aba, *Nigeria* 83 D6
Âbâ, Jazîrat, *Sudan* 81 E3
Abadab, J., *Sudan* 80 D4
Ābādān, *Iran* 71 D6
Abade, *Ethiopia* 81 F4
Ābādeh, *Iran* 71 D7
Abadin, *Spain* 34 B3
Abadla, *Algeria* 78 B5
Abaetetuba, *Brazil* 125 D9
Abagnar Qi, *China* 56 C9
Abai, *Paraguay* 127 B4
Abak, *Nigeria* 83 E6
Abakaliki, *Nigeria* 83 D6
Abakan, *Russia* 51 D10
Abala, *Niger* 83 C5
Abalak, *Niger* 83 B6
Abalemma, *Niger* 83 B6
Abana, *Turkey* 72 B6
Abancay, *Peru* 124 F4
Abano Terme, *Italy* 29 C8
Abarán, *Spain* 33 G3
Abariringa, *Kiribati* 96 H10
Abarqū, *Iran* 71 D7
Abashiri, *Japan* 54 B12
Abashiri-Wan, *Japan* 54 C12
Abaújszántó, *Hungary* 42 B6
Abava →, *Latvia* 44 A8
Ābay = Nîl el Azraq →, *Sudan* 81 D3
Abay, *Kazakstan* 50 E8
Abaya, L., *Ethiopia* 81 F4
Abaza, *Russia* 50 D9
Abbadia San Salvatore, *Italy* 29 F8
'Abbāsābād, *Iran* 71 C8
Abbay = Nîl el Azraq →, *Sudan* 81 D3
Abbaye, Pt., *U.S.A.* 108 B1
Abbé, L., *Ethiopia* 81 E5
Abbeville, *France* 19 B8
Abbeville, *Ala., U.S.A.* 109 K3
Abbeville, *La., U.S.A.* 113 L8
Abbeville, *S.C., U.S.A.* 109 H4
Abbiategrasso, *Italy* 28 C5
Abbot Ice Shelf, *Antarctica* 5 D16
Abbottabad, *Pakistan* 68 B5
Abd al Kūrī, *Ind. Oc.* 74 E5
Ābdar, *Iran* 71 D7
'Abdolābād, *Iran* 71 C8
Abdulpur, *Bangla.* 69 G13
Abéché, *Chad* 79 F10
Abejar, *Spain* 32 D2
Abekr, *Sudan* 81 E2
Abengourou, *Ivory C.* 82 D4
Abenójar, *Spain* 35 G6
Åbenrå, *Denmark* 11 J3
Abensberg, *Germany* 25 G7
Abeokuta, *Nigeria* 83 D5
Aber, *Uganda* 86 B3
Aberaeron, *U.K.* 13 E3
Aberayron = Aberaeron, *U.K.* 13 E3
Aberchirder, *U.K.* 14 D6
Abercorn = Mbala, *Zambia* 87 D3
Abercorn, *Australia* 95 D5
Aberdare, *U.K.* 13 F4
Aberdare Ra., *Kenya* 86 C4
Aberdeen, *Australia* 95 E5
Aberdeen, *Canada* 105 C7
Aberdeen, *S. Africa* 88 E3
Aberdeen, *U.K.* 14 D6
Aberdeen, *Ala., U.S.A.* 109 J1
Aberdeen, *Idaho, U.S.A.* 114 E7
Aberdeen, *Md., U.S.A.* 108 F7
Aberdeen, *S. Dak., U.S.A.* 112 C5
Aberdeen, *Wash., U.S.A.* 116 D3
Aberdeen, City of □, *U.K.* 14 D6
Aberdeenshire □, *U.K.* 14 D6
Aberdovey = Aberdyfi, *U.K.* 13 E3
Aberdyfi, *U.K.* 13 E3
Aberfeldy, *U.K.* 14 E5
Abergavenny, *U.K.* 13 F4
Abergele, *U.K.* 12 D4
Abernathy, *U.S.A.* 113 J4
Abert, L., *U.S.A.* 114 E3
Aberystwyth, *U.K.* 13 E3
Abhā, *Si. Arabia* 74 D3
Abhar, *Iran* 71 B6
Abhayapuri, *India* 69 F14
Abia □, *Nigeria* 83 D6
Abide, *Turkey* 39 C11
Abidiya, *Sudan* 80 D3
Abidjan, *Ivory C.* 82 D4
Abilene, *Kans., U.S.A.* 112 F6
Abilene, *Tex., U.S.A.* 113 J5
Abingdon, *U.K.* 13 F6
Abingdon, *U.S.A.* 109 G5
Abington Reef, *Australia* 94 B4
Abitau →, *Canada* 105 B7
Abitibi →, *Canada* 102 B3
Abitibi, L., *Canada* 102 C4
Abiy Adi, *Ethiopia* 81 E4
Abkhaz Republic = Abkhazia □, *Georgia* 49 J5
Abkhazia □, *Georgia* 49 J5
Abminga, *Australia* 95 D1
Abnûb, *Egypt* 80 B3
Åbo = Turku, *Finland* 9 F20
Abocho, *Nigeria* 83 D6
Abohar, *India* 68 D6
Aboisso, *Ivory C.* 82 D4
Abomey, *Benin* 83 D5
Abong-Mbang, *Cameroon* 84 D2
Abonnema, *Nigeria* 83 E6
Abony, *Hungary* 42 C5
Aboso, *Ghana* 82 D4
Abou-Deïa, *Chad* 79 F9
Aboyne, *U.K.* 14 D6
Abra Pampa, *Argentina* 126 A2
Abraham L., *Canada* 104 C5
Abrantes, *Portugal* 35 F2
Abreojos, Pta., *Mexico* 118 B2
Abri, *Esh Shamâliya, Sudan* 80 C3
Abri, *Janub Kordofân, Sudan* 81 E3
Abrud, *Romania* 42 D8
Abruzzo □, *Italy* 29 F10
Absaroka Range, *U.S.A.* 114 D9
Abtenau, *Austria* 26 D6
Abu, *India* 68 G5
Abū al Abyad, *U.A.E.* 71 E7
Abū al Khaṣīb, *Iraq* 71 D6
Abū 'Alī, *Si. Arabia* 71 E6
Abū 'Alī →, *Lebanon* 75 A4
Abu Ballas, *Egypt* 80 C2
Abu Deleiq, *Sudan* 81 D3
Abu Dhabi = Abū Ẓāby, *U.A.E.* 71 E7
Abu Dis, *Sudan* 80 D3
Abu Dom, *Sudan* 81 D3
Abū Du'ān, *Syria* 70 B3
Abu el Gairi, W. →, *Egypt* 75 F2
Abu Fatma, Ras, *Sudan* 80 C4
Abu Gabra, *Sudan* 81 E2
Abu Ga'da, W. →, *Egypt* 75 F1
Abu Gelba, *Sudan* 81 E3
Abu Gubeiha, *Sudan* 81 E3
Abu Habl, Khawr →, *Sudan* 81 E3
Abū Ḥadrīyah, *Si. Arabia* 71 E6
Abu Hamed, *Sudan* 80 D3
Abu Haraz, *An Nîl el Azraq, Sudan* 80 D3
Abu Haraz, *El Gezira, Sudan* 81 E3
Abu Haraz, *Esh Shamâliya, Sudan* 80 D3
Abu Higar, *Sudan* 81 E3
Abū Kamāl, *Syria* 70 C4
Abu Kuleiwat, *Sudan* 81 E2
Abū Madd, Ra's, *Si. Arabia* 70 E3
Abu Matariq, *Sudan* 81 E2
Abu Mendi, *Ethiopia* 81 E4
Abū Mūsā, *U.A.E.* 71 E7
Abū Qaṣr, *Si. Arabia* 70 D3
Abu Qir, *Egypt* 80 H7
Abu Qireiya, *Egypt* 80 C4
Abu Qurqâs, *Egypt* 80 B3
Abu Şafāt, W. →, *Jordan* 75 E5
Abu Shagara, Ras, *Sudan* 80 C4
Abu Shanab, *Sudan* 81 E2
Abu Simbel, *Egypt* 80 C3
Abū Şukhayr, *Iraq* 70 D5
Abu Sultân, *Egypt* 80 H8
Abu Tabari, *Sudan* 80 D2
Abu Tig, *Egypt* 80 B3
Abu Tiga, *Sudan* 81 E3
Abu Tineitin, *Sudan* 81 E3
Abu Uruq, *Sudan* 81 D3
Abu Zabad, *Sudan* 81 E2
Abū Ẓāby, *U.A.E.* 71 E7
Abū Zeydābād, *Iran* 71 C6
Abuja, *Nigeria* 83 D6
Abukuma-Gawa →, *Japan* 54 E10
Abukuma-Sammyaku, *Japan* 54 F10
Abunã, *Brazil* 124 E5
Abunã →, *Brazil* 124 E5
Abune Yosef, *Ethiopia* 81 E4
Aburo, *Dem. Rep. of the Congo* 86 B3
Abut Hd., *N.Z.* 91 K3
Abuye Meda, *Ethiopia* 81 E4
Abwong, *Sudan* 81 F3
Åby, *Sweden* 11 F10
Aby, Lagune, *Ivory C.* 82 D4
Abyad, *Sudan* 81 E2
Åbybro, *Denmark* 11 G3
Acadia National Park, *U.S.A.* 109 C11
Açailândia, *Brazil* 125 D9
Acajutla, *El Salv.* 120 D2
Acámbaro, *Mexico* 118 D4
Acanthus, *Greece* 40 F7
Acaponeta, *Mexico* 118 C3
Acapulco, *Mexico* 119 D5
Acarai, Serra, *Brazil* 124 C7
Acarigua, *Venezuela* 124 B5
Acatlán, *Mexico* 119 D5
Acayucan, *Mexico* 119 D6
Accéglio, *Italy* 28 D4
Accomac, *U.S.A.* 108 G8
Accous, *France* 20 E3
Accra, *Ghana* 83 D4
Accrington, *U.K.* 12 D5
Acebal, *Argentina* 126 C3
Aceh □, *Indonesia* 62 D1
Acerra, *Italy* 31 B7
Aceuchal, *Spain* 35 G4
Achalpur, *India* 66 J10
Acheng, *China* 57 B14
Achenkirch, *Austria* 26 D4
Achensee, *Austria* 26 D4
Acher, *India* 68 H5
Achern, *Germany* 25 G4
Achill Hd., *Ireland* 15 C1
Achill I., *Ireland* 15 C1
Achim, *Germany* 24 B5
Achinsk, *Russia* 51 D10
Acıgöl, *Turkey* 39 D11
Acıpayam, *Turkey* 39 D11
Acireale, *Italy* 31 E8
Ackerman, *U.S.A.* 113 J10
Acklins I., *Bahamas* 121 B5
Acme, *Canada* 104 C6
Acme, *U.S.A.* 110 F5
Aconcagua, Cerro, *Argentina* 126 C2
Aconquija, Mt., *Argentina* 126 B2
Açores, Is. dos = Azores, *Atl. Oc.* 78 A1
Acornhoek, *S. Africa* 89 C5
Acquapendente, *Italy* 29 F8
Acquasanta Terme, *Italy* 29 F10
Acquasparta, *Italy* 29 F9
Acquaviva delle Fonti, *Italy* 31 B9
Ácqui Terme, *Italy* 28 D5
Acraman, L., *Australia* 95 E2
Acre = 'Akko, *Israel* 75 C4
Acre □, *Brazil* 124 E4
Acre →, *Brazil* 124 E5
Acri, *Italy* 31 C9
Acs, *Hungary* 42 C3
Actium, *Greece* 38 C2
Acton, *Canada* 110 C4
Acuña, *Mexico* 118 B4
Ad Dammām, *Si. Arabia* 71 E6
Ad Dāmūr, *Lebanon* 75 B4
Ad Dawādimī, *Si. Arabia* 70 E5
Ad Dawḥah, *Qatar* 71 E6
Ad Dawr, *Iraq* 70 C4
Ad Dir'īyah, *Si. Arabia* 70 E5
Ad Dīwānīyah, *Iraq* 70 D5
Ad Dujayl, *Iraq* 70 C5
Ad Duwayd, *Si. Arabia* 70 D4
Ada, *Ghana* 83 D5
Ada, *Serbia, Yug.* 42 E5
Ada, *Minn., U.S.A.* 112 B6
Ada, *Okla., U.S.A.* 113 H6
Adabiya, *Egypt* 75 F1
Adair, C., *Canada* 101 A12
Adaja →, *Spain* 34 D6
Adak I., *U.S.A.* 100 C2
Adamaoua, Massif de l', *Cameroon* 83 D7
Adamawa □, *Nigeria* 83 D7
Adamawa Highlands = Adamaoua, Massif de l', *Cameroon* 83 D7
Adamello, Mte., *Italy* 28 B7
Adami Tulu, *Ethiopia* 81 F4
Adaminaby, *Australia* 95 F4
Adams, *Mass., U.S.A.* 111 D11
Adams, *N.Y., U.S.A.* 111 C8
Adams, *Wis., U.S.A.* 112 D10
Adam's Bridge, *Sri Lanka* 66 Q11
Adams L., *Canada* 104 C5
Adams Mt., *U.S.A.* 116 D5
Adam's Peak, *Sri Lanka* 66 R12
Adamuz, *Spain* 35 G6
Adana, *Turkey* 70 B2
Adanero, *Spain* 34 E6
Adapazarı = Sakarya, *Turkey* 72 B4
Adar Gwagwa, J., *Sudan* 80 C4
Adarama, *Sudan* 81 D3
Adare, C., *Antarctica* 5 D11
Adarte, *Eritrea* 81 E5
Adaut, *Indonesia* 63 F8
Adavale, *Australia* 95 D3
Adda →, *Italy* 28 C6
Addis Ababa = Addis Abeba, *Ethiopia* 81 F4
Addis Abeba, *Ethiopia* 81 F4
Addis Alem, *Ethiopia* 81 F4
Addis Zemen, *Ethiopia* 81 E4
Addison, *U.S.A.* 110 D7
Addo, *S. Africa* 88 E4
Adebour, *Niger* 83 C7
Ādeh, *Iran* 70 B5
Adel, *U.S.A.* 109 K4
Adelaide, *Australia* 95 E2
Adelaide, *Bahamas* 120 A4
Adelaide, *S. Africa* 88 E4
Adelaide I., *Antarctica* 5 C17
Adelaide Pen., *Canada* 100 B10
Adelaide River, *Australia* 92 B5
Adelanto, *U.S.A.* 117 L9
Adele I., *Australia* 92 C3
Adélie, Terre, *Antarctica* 5 C10
Adélie Land = Adélie, Terre, *Antarctica* 5 C10
Ademuz, *Spain* 32 E3
Aden = Al 'Adan, *Yemen* 74 E4
Aden, G. of, *Asia* 74 E4
Adendorp, *S. Africa* 88 E3
Aderbissinat, *Niger* 83 B6
Adh Dhayd, *U.A.E.* 71 E7
Adhoi, *India* 68 H4
Adi, *Indonesia* 63 E8
Adi Arkai, *Ethiopia* 81 E4
Adi Daro, *Ethiopia* 81 E4
Adi Keyih, *Eritrea* 81 E4
Adi Kwala, *Eritrea* 81 E4
Adi Ugri, *Eritrea* 81 E4
Adieu, C., *Australia* 93 F5
Adieu Pt., *Australia* 92 C3
Adigala, *Ethiopia* 81 E5
Adige →, *Italy* 29 C9
Adigrat, *Ethiopia* 81 E4
Adıgüzel Barajı, *Turkey* 39 C11
Adilabad, *India* 66 K11
Adilcevaz, *Turkey* 73 C10
Adirondack Mts., *U.S.A.* 111 C10
Adıyaman, *Turkey* 73 D8
Adjohon, *Benin* 83 D5
Adjud, *Romania* 43 D12
Adjumani, *Uganda* 86 B3
Adlavik Is., *Canada* 103 A8
Adler, *Russia* 49 J4
Admer, *Algeria* 83 A6
Admiralty G., *Australia* 92 B4
Admiralty I., *U.S.A.* 104 B2
Admiralty Is., *Papua N. G.* 96 H6
Ado, *Nigeria* 83 D5
Ado-Ekiti, *Nigeria* 83 D6
Adok, *Sudan* 81 F3
Adola, *Ethiopia* 81 E5
Adonara, *Indonesia* 63 F6
Adoni, *India* 66 M10
Adony, *Hungary* 42 C3
Adour →, *France* 20 E2
Adra, *India* 69 H12
Adra, *Spain* 35 J7
Adrano, *Italy* 31 E7
Adrar, *Mauritania* 78 D3
Adrar des Iforas, *Algeria* 78 C5
Ádria, *Italy* 29 C9
Adrian, *Mich., U.S.A.* 108 E3
Adrian, *Tex., U.S.A.* 113 H3
Adriatic Sea, *Medit. S.* 6 G9
Adua, *Indonesia* 63 E7
Adwa, *Ethiopia* 81 E4
Adygea □, *Russia* 49 H5
Adzhar Republic = Ajaria □, *Georgia* 49 K6
Adzopé, *Ivory C.* 82 D4
Ægean Sea, *Medit. S.* 39 C7
Aerhtai Shan, *Mongolia* 60 B4
Ærø, *Denmark* 11 K4
Ærøskøbing, *Denmark* 11 K4
Aëtós, *Greece* 38 D3
'Afak, *Iraq* 70 C5
Afándou, *Greece* 36 C10
Afghanistan ■, *Asia* 66 C4
Afikpo, *Nigeria* 83 D6
Aflou, *Algeria* 78 B6
Afragóla, *Italy* 31 B7
Afram →, *Ghana* 83 D4
Afrera, *Ethiopia* 81 E5
Africa 76 E6
'Afrīn, *Syria* 70 B3
Afşin, *Turkey* 72 C7
Afton, *N.Y., U.S.A.* 111 D9
Afton, *Wyo., U.S.A.* 114 E8
Afuá, *Brazil* 125 D8
'Afula, *Israel* 75 C4
Afyon, *Turkey* 39 C12
Afyon □, *Turkey* 39 C12
Afyonkarahisar = Afyon, *Turkey* 39 C12
Aga, *Egypt* 80 H7
Agadès = Agadez, *Niger* 83 B6
Agadez, *Niger* 83 B6
Agadir, *Morocco* 78 B4
Agaete, *Canary Is.* 37 F4
Agaie, *Nigeria* 83 D6
Again, *Sudan* 81 F2
Ağapınar, *Turkey* 39 B12
Agar, *India* 68 H7
Agaro, *Ethiopia* 81 F4
Agartala, *India* 67 H17
Agăș, *Romania* 43 D11
Agassiz, *Canada* 104 D4
Agats, *Indonesia* 63 F9
Agawam, *U.S.A.* 111 D12
Agbélouvé, *Togo* 83 D5
Agboville, *Ivory C.* 82 D4
Ağcabädi, *Azerbaijan* 49 K8
Ağdam, *Azerbaijan* 49 L8
Ağdaş, *Azerbaijan* 49 K8
Agde, *France* 20 E7
Agde, C. d', *France* 20 E7
Agdzhabedi = Ağcabädi, *Azerbaijan* 49 K8
Agen, *France* 20 D4
Agerbæk, *Denmark* 11 J2
Agersø, *Denmark* 11 J5
Ageyevo, *Russia* 46 E9
Āgh Kand, *Iran* 71 B6
Aghireșu, *Romania* 43 D8
Aginskoye, *Russia* 51 D12
Ağlasun, *Turkey* 39 D12
Agly →, *France* 20 F7
Agnew, *Australia* 93 E3
Agnibilékrou, *Ivory C.* 82 D4
Agnita, *Romania* 43 E9
Agnone, *Italy* 29 G11
Agofie, *Ghana* 83 D5
Agogna →, *Italy* 28 C5
Agogo, *Sudan* 81 F2
Agön, *Sweden* 10 C11
Agon Coutainville, *France* 18 C5
Ágordo, *Italy* 29 B9
Agori, *India* 69 G10
Agouna, *Benin* 83 D5
Agout →, *France* 20 E5
Agra, *India* 68 F7
Agrakhanskiy Poluostrov, *Russia* 49 J8
Agramunt, *Spain* 32 D6
Agreda, *Spain* 32 D3
Ağri, *Turkey* 73 C10
Agri →, *Italy* 31 B9
Ağrı Dağı, *Turkey* 70 B5
Ağri Karakose = Ağri, *Turkey* 73 C10
Agriá, *Greece* 38 B5
Agrigento, *Italy* 30 E6
Agrínion, *Greece* 38 C3
Agrópoli, *Italy* 31 B7
Ağstafa, *Azerbaijan* 49 K7
Agua Caliente, *Baja Calif., Mexico* 117 N10
Agua Caliente, *Sinaloa, Mexico* 118 B3
Agua Caliente Springs, *U.S.A.* 117 N10
Água Clara, *Brazil* 125 H8
Agua Hechicero, *Mexico* 117 N10
Agua Prieta, *Mexico* 118 A3
Aguadilla, *Puerto Rico* 121 C6
Aguadulce, *Panama* 120 E3
Aguanga, *U.S.A.* 117 M10
Aguanish, *Canada* 103 B7
Aguanus →, *Canada* 103 B7
Aguapey →, *Argentina* 126 B4
Aguaray Guazú →, *Paraguay* 126 A4
Aguarico →, *Ecuador* 124 D3
Aguas →, *Spain* 32 D4
Aguas Blancas, *Chile* 126 A2
Aguas Calientes, Sierra de, *Argentina* 126 B2
Aguascalientes, *Mexico* 118 C4
Aguascalientes □, *Mexico* 118 C4
Agudo, *Spain* 35 G6
Águeda, *Portugal* 34 E2
Agueda →, *Spain* 34 D4
Aguelhok, *Mali* 83 B5
Aguié, *Niger* 83 C6
Aguilafuente, *Spain* 34 D6
Aguilar, *Spain* 35 H6
Aguilar de Campóo, *Spain* 34 C6
Aguilares, *Argentina* 126 B2
Aguilas, *Spain* 33 H3
Agüimes, *Canary Is.* 37 G4
Aguja, C. de la, *Colombia* 122 B3
Agulaa, *Ethiopia* 81 E4
Agulhas, C., *S. Africa* 88 E3
Agulo, *Canary Is.* 37 F2
Agung, *Indonesia* 62 F5
Agur, *Uganda* 86 B3
Agusan →, *Phil.* 61 G6
Ağva, *Turkey* 41 E13
Agvali, *Russia* 49 J8
Aha Mts., *Botswana* 88 B3
Ahaggar, *Algeria* 78 D7
Ahamansu, *Ghana* 83 D5
Ahar, *Iran* 70 B5
Ahat, *Turkey* 39 C11
Ahaus, *Germany* 24 C2
Ahipara B., *N.Z.* 91 F4
Ahir Dağı, *Turkey* 39 C12
Ahiri, *India* 66 K12
Ahlat, *Turkey* 73 C10
Ahlen, *Germany* 24 D3
Ahmad Wal, *Pakistan* 68 E1
Ahmadabad, *India* 68 H5
Aḥmadābād, *Khorāsān, Iran* 71 C9
Aḥmadābād, *Khorāsān, Iran* 71 C8
Aḥmadī, *Iran* 71 E8
Ahmadnagar, *India* 66 K9
Ahmadpur, *Pakistan* 68 E4
Ahmadpur Lamma, *Pakistan* 68 E4
Ahmar, *Ethiopia* 81 F5
Ahmedabad = Ahmadabad, *India* 68 H5
Ahmednagar = Ahmadnagar, *India* 66 K9
Ahmetbey, *Turkey* 41 E11
Ahmetler, *Turkey* 39 C11
Ahmetli, *Turkey* 39 C9
Ahoada, *Nigeria* 83 D6
Ahome, *Mexico* 118 B3
Ahoskie, *U.S.A.* 109 G7
Ahr →, *Germany* 24 E3
Ahram, *Iran* 71 D6
Ahrax Pt., *Malta* 36 D1
Ahrensbök, *Germany* 24 A6
Ahrensburg, *Germany* 24 B6
Āhū, *Iran* 71 C6
Ahuachapán, *El Salv.* 120 D2
Ahun, *France* 19 F9
Åhus, *Sweden* 11 J8
Ahvāz, *Iran* 71 D6
Ahvenanmaa = Åland, *Finland* 9 F19
Aḥwar, *Yemen* 74 E4
Ahzar →, *Mali* 83 B5
Ai →, *India* 69 F14
Ai-Ais, *Namibia* 88 D2
Aichach, *Germany* 25 G7
Aichi □, *Japan* 55 G8
Aigle, *Switz.* 25 J2
Aignay-le-Duc, *France* 19 E11
Aigoual, Mt., *France* 20 D7
Aigre, *France* 20 C4
Aigua, *Uruguay* 127 C5
Aigueperse, *France* 19 F10
Aigues →, *France* 21 D8
Aigues-Mortes, *France* 21 E8
Aigues-Mortes, G. d', *France* 21 E8
Aiguilles, *France* 21 D10
Aiguillon, *France* 20 D4
Aigurande, *France* 19 F8
Aihui, *China* 60 A7
Aija, *Peru* 124 E3
Aikawa, *Japan* 54 E9
Aiken, *U.S.A.* 109 J5
Ailao Shan, *China* 58 F3
Aileron, *Australia* 94 C1
Aillant-sur-Tholon, *France* 19 E10
Aillik, *Canada* 103 A8
Ailsa Craig, *U.K.* 14 F3
'Ailūn, *Jordan* 75 C4
Aim, *Russia* 51 D14

Aimere, *Indonesia* 63 F6
Aimogasta, *Argentina* 126 B2
Ain □, *France* 19 F12
Ain →, *France* 21 C9
Aïn Ben Tili, *Mauritania* 78 C4
Ain Dalla, *Egypt* 80 B2
Ain el Mafki, *Egypt* 80 B2
Ain Girba, *Egypt* 80 B2
Ain Murr, *Sudan* 80 C2
Ain Qeiqab, *Egypt* 80 B1
Aïn Sefra, *Algeria* 78 B5
Ain Sheikh Murzûk, *Egypt* 80 B2
Ain Sudr, *Egypt* 75 F2
Ain Sukhna, *Egypt* 80 J8
Ain Zeitûn, *Egypt* 80 B2
Ainaži, *Latvia* 9 H21
Aínos Óros, *Greece* 38 C2
Ainsworth, *U.S.A.* 112 D5
Aiquile, *Bolivia* 124 G5
Aïr, *Niger* 83 B6
Air Force I., *Canada* 101 B12
Air Hitam, *Malaysia* 65 M4
Airaines, *France* 19 C8
Airdrie, *Canada* 104 C6
Airdrie, *U.K.* 14 F5
Aire →, *France* 19 C11
Aire →, *U.K.* 12 D7
Aire, I. de l', *Spain* 37 B11
Aire-sur-la-Lys, *France* 19 B9
Aire-sur-l'Adour, *France* 20 E3
Airlie Beach, *Australia* 94 C4
Airvault, *France* 18 F6
Aisch →, *Germany* 25 F6
Aisne □, *France* 19 C10
Aisne →, *France* 19 C9
Ait, *India* 69 G8
Aitana, Sierra de, *Spain* 33 G4
Aitkin, *U.S.A.* 112 B8
Aitolía Kai Akarnanía □, *Greece* 38 C3
Aitolikón, *Greece* 38 C3
Aiud, *Romania* 43 D8
Aix-en-Provence, *France* 21 E9
Aix-la-Chapelle = Aachen, *Germany* 24 E2
Aix-les-Bains, *France* 21 C9
Aixe-sur-Vienne, *France* 20 C5
Aíyina, *Greece* 38 D5
Aiyínion, *Greece* 40 F6
Aíyion, *Greece* 38 C4
Aizawl, *India* 67 H18
Aizenay, *France* 18 F5
Aizkraukle, *Latvia* 9 H21
Aizpute, *Latvia* 9 H19
Aizuwakamatsu, *Japan* 54 F9
Ajaccio, *France* 21 G12
Ajaccio, G. d', *France* 21 G12
Ajaigarh, *India* 69 G9
Ajalpan, *Mexico* 119 D5
Ajanta Ra., *India* 66 J9
Ajari Rep. = Ajaria □, *Georgia* 49 K6
Ajaria □, *Georgia* 49 K6
Ajax, *Canada* 110 C5
Ajdābiyā, *Libya* 79 B10
Ajdovščina, *Slovenia* 29 C10
Ajibar, *Ethiopia* 81 E4
Ajka, *Hungary* 42 C2
'Ajmān, *U.A.E.* 71 E7
Ajmer, *India* 68 F6
Ajnala, *India* 68 D6
Ajo, *U.S.A.* 115 K7
Ajo, C. de, *Spain* 34 B7
Ajok, *Sudan* 81 F2
Ajuy, *Phil.* 61 F5
Ak Dağ, *Turkey* 39 E11
Ak Dağları, *Muğla, Turkey* 39 E11
Ak Dağları, *Sivas, Turkey* 72 C7
Akaba, *Togo* 83 D5
Akabira, *Japan* 54 C11
Akaki Beseka, *Ethiopia* 81 F4
Akala, *Sudan* 81 D4
Akamas □, *Cyprus* 36 D11
Akanthou, *Cyprus* 36 D12
Akarca, *Turkey* 39 C11
Akaroa, *N.Z.* 91 K4
Akasha, *Sudan* 80 C3
Akashi, *Japan* 55 G7
Akbarpur, *Bihar, India* 69 G10
Akbarpur, *Ut. P., India* 69 F10
Akçaabat, *Turkey* 73 B8
Akçadağ, *Turkey* 72 C7
Akçakale, *Turkey* 73 D8
Akçakoca, *Turkey* 72 B4
Akçaova, *Turkey* 41 E13
Akçay, *Turkey* 39 E11
Akçay →, *Turkey* 39 D10
Akdağ, *Turkey* 39 C8
Akdağmadeni, *Turkey* 72 C6
Akelamo, *Indonesia* 63 D7
Åkers styckebruk, *Sweden* 10 E11
Åkersberga, *Sweden* 10 E12
Aketi, *Dem. Rep. of the Congo* 84 D4
Akhaïa □, *Greece* 38 C3
Akhalkalaki, *Georgia* 49 K6
Akhaltsikhe, *Georgia* 49 K6
Akharnaí, *Greece* 38 C5
Akhelóös →, *Greece* 38 C3
Akhendriá, *Greece* 39 G7
Akhisar, *Turkey* 39 C9
Akhladhókambos, *Greece* 38 D4
Akhmîm, *Egypt* 80 B3
Akhnur, *India* 69 C6
Akhtopol, *Bulgaria* 41 D11
Akhtuba →, *Russia* 49 G8
Akhtubinsk, *Russia* 49 F8
Akhty, *Russia* 49 K8
Akhtyrka = Okhtyrka, *Ukraine* 47 G8
Aki, *Japan* 55 H6
Akimiski I., *Canada* 102 B3
Akimovka, *Ukraine* 47 J8
Åkirkeby, *Denmark* 11 J8
Akita, *Japan* 54 E10
Akita □, *Japan* 54 E10
Akjoujt, *Mauritania* 82 B2
Akka, *Mali* 82 B4
Akkaya Tepesi, *Turkey* 39 D11
Akkeshi, *Japan* 54 C12
'Akko, *Israel* 75 C4
Akköy, *Turkey* 39 D9
Aklampa, *Benin* 83 D5
Aklavik, *Canada* 100 B6
Aklera, *India* 68 G7
Akmenė, *Lithuania* 44 B9
Akmenrags, *Latvia* 44 B8
Akmolinsk = Astana, *Kazakstan* 50 D8
Akmonte = Almonte, *Spain* 35 H4
Akō, *Japan* 55 G7
Ako, *Nigeria* 83 C7
Akôbô, *Sudan* 81 F3
Akobo →, *Ethiopia* 81 F3
Akola, *India* 66 J10
Akonolinga, *Cameroon* 83 E7
Akor, *Mali* 82 C3
Akordat, *Eritrea* 81 D4
Akosombo Dam, *Ghana* 83 D5
Akot, *Sudan* 81 F3
Akoupé, *Ivory C.* 82 D4
Akpatok I., *Canada* 101 B13
Åkrahamn, *Norway* 9 G11
Akranes, *Iceland* 8 D2
Akreïjit, *Mauritania* 82 B3
Akrítas Venétiko, Ákra, *Greece* 38 E3
Akron, *Colo., U.S.A.* 112 E3
Akron, *Ohio, U.S.A.* 110 E3
Akrotiri, *Cyprus* 36 E11
Akrotíri, Ákra, *Greece* 41 F9
Akrotiri Bay, *Cyprus* 36 E12
Aksai Chin, *India* 69 B8
Aksaray, *Turkey* 70 B2
Aksay, *Kazakstan* 50 D6
Akşehir, *Turkey* 70 B1
Akşehir Gölü, *Turkey* 72 C4
Akstafa = Ağstafa, *Azerbaijan* 49 K7
Aksu, *China* 60 B3
Aksu →, *Turkey* 72 D4
Aksum, *Ethiopia* 81 E4
Aktash, *Russia* 48 C11
Aktogay, *Kazakstan* 50 E8
Aktsyabrski, *Belarus* 47 F5
Aktyubinsk = Aqtöbe, *Kazakstan* 50 D6
Aku, *Nigeria* 83 D6
Akure, *Nigeria* 83 D6
Akureyri, *Iceland* 8 D4
Akuseki-Shima, *Japan* 55 K4
Akusha, *Russia* 49 J8
Akwa-Ibom □, *Nigeria* 83 E6
Akyab = Sittwe, *Burma* 67 J18
Akyazı, *Turkey* 72 B4
Al 'Adan, *Yemen* 74 E4
Al Aḩsā = Hasa □, *Si. Arabia* 71 E6
Al Ajfar, *Si. Arabia* 70 E4
Al Amādīyah, *Iraq* 70 B4
Al 'Amārah, *Iraq* 70 D5
Al 'Aqabah, *Jordan* 75 F4
Al Arak, *Syria* 70 C3
Al 'Aramah, *Si. Arabia* 70 E5
Al Arṭāwīyah, *Si. Arabia* 70 E5
Al 'Āşimah = 'Ammān □, *Jordan* 75 D5
Al 'Assāfīyah, *Si. Arabia* 70 D3
Al 'Ayn, *Oman* 71 E7
Al 'Ayn, *Si. Arabia* 70 E3
Al 'Aẓamīyah, *Iraq* 70 C5
Al 'Azīzīyah, *Iraq* 70 C5
Al Bāb, *Syria* 70 B3
Al Bad', *Si. Arabia* 70 D2
Al Bādī, *Iraq* 70 C4
Al Baḩrah, *Kuwait* 70 D5
Al Baḩral Mayyit = Dead Sea, *Asia* 75 D4
Al Balqā' □, *Jordan* 75 C4
Al Bārūk, J., *Lebanon* 75 B4
Al Baṣrah, *Iraq* 70 D5
Al Baṭḩā, *Iraq* 70 D5
Al Batrūn, *Lebanon* 75 A4
Al Bayḑā, *Libya* 79 B10
Al Biqā, *Lebanon* 75 A5
Al Bi'r, *Si. Arabia* 70 D3
Al Burayj, *Syria* 75 A5
Al Faḑilī, *Si. Arabia* 71 E6
Al Fallūjah, *Iraq* 70 C4
Al Fāw, *Iraq* 71 D6
Al Fujayrah, *U.A.E.* 71 E8
Al Ghadaf, W. →, *Jordan* 75 D5
Al Ghammās, *Iraq* 70 D5
Al Ghazālah, *Si. Arabia* 70 E4
Al Ḩadīthah, *Iraq* 70 C4
Al Ḩadīthah, *Si. Arabia* 75 D6
Al Ḩaḑr, *Iraq* 70 C4
Al Ḩājānah, *Syria* 75 B5
Al Hajar al Gharbi, *Oman* 71 E8
Al Hāmad, *Si. Arabia* 70 D3
Al Hamdāniyah, *Syria* 70 C3
Al Ḩamīdīyah, *Syria* 75 A4
Al Ḩammār, *Iraq* 70 D5
Al Ḩamrā', *Si. Arabia* 70 E3
Al Ḩanākīyah, *Si. Arabia* 70 E4
Al Harīr, W. →, *Syria* 75 C4
Al Ḩasā, W. →, *Jordan* 75 D4
Al Ḩasakah, *Syria* 70 B4
Al Haydān, W. →, *Jordan* 75 D4
Al Ḩayy, *Iraq* 70 C5
Al Hijarah, *Asia* 70 D4
Al Ḩillah, *Iraq* 70 C5
Al Ḩillah, *Si. Arabia* 74 B4
Al Hindīyah, *Iraq* 70 C5
Al Hirmil, *Lebanon* 75 A5
Al Hoceïma, *Morocco* 78 A5
Al Ḩudaydah, *Yemen* 74 E3
Al Hufūf, *Si. Arabia* 71 E6
Al Ḩumayḑah, *Si. Arabia* 70 D2
Al Ḩunayy, *Si. Arabia* 71 E6
Al Īsāwīyah, *Si. Arabia* 70 D3
Al Jafr, *Jordan* 75 E5
Al Jāfūrah, *Si. Arabia* 71 E7
Al Jaghbūb, *Libya* 79 C10
Al Jahrah, *Kuwait* 70 D5
Al Jalāmīd, *Si. Arabia* 70 D3
Al Jamalīyah, *Qatar* 71 E6
Al Janūb □, *Lebanon* 75 B4
Al Jawf, *Libya* 79 D10
Al Jawf, *Si. Arabia* 70 D3
Al Jazirah, *Iraq* 70 C5
Al Jithāmīyah, *Si. Arabia* 70 E4
Al Jubayl, *Si. Arabia* 71 E6
Al Jubaylah, *Si. Arabia* 70 E5
Al Jubb, *Si. Arabia* 70 E4
Al Junaynah, *Sudan* 79 F10
Al Kabā'ish, *Iraq* 70 D5
Al Karak, *Jordan* 75 D4
Al Karak □, *Jordan* 75 E5
Al Kāẓim Tyah, *Iraq* 70 C5
Al Khābūra, *Oman* 71 F8
Al Khafji, *Si. Arabia* 71 E6
Al Khalīl, *West Bank* 75 D4
Al Khāliş, *Iraq* 70 C5
Al Kharsānīyah, *Si. Arabia* 71 E6
Al Khaşab, *Oman* 71 E8
Al Khawr, *Qatar* 71 E6
Al Khiḑr, *Iraq* 70 D5
Al Khiyām, *Lebanon* 75 B4
Al Kiswah, *Syria* 75 B5
Al Kūfah, *Iraq* 70 C5
Al Kufrah, *Libya* 79 D10
Al Kuhayfīyah, *Si. Arabia* 70 E4
Al Kūt, *Iraq* 70 C5
Al Kuwayt, *Kuwait* 70 D5
Al Labwah, *Lebanon* 75 A5
Al Lādhiqīyah, *Syria* 70 C2
Al Līth, *Si. Arabia* 74 C3
Al Liwā', *Oman* 71 E8
Al Luḩayyah, *Yemen* 74 D3
Al Madīnah, *Iraq* 70 D5
Al Madīnah, *Si. Arabia* 70 E3
Al Mafraq, *Jordan* 75 C5
Al Maḩmūdīyah, *Iraq* 70 C5
Al Majma'ah, *Si. Arabia* 70 E5
Al Makhruq, W. →, *Jordan* 75 D6
Al Makḩūl, *Si. Arabia* 70 E4
Al Manāmah, *Bahrain* 71 E6
Al Maqwa', *Kuwait* 70 D5
Al Marj, *Libya* 79 B10
Al Maṭlā, *Kuwait* 70 D5
Al Mawjib, W. →, *Jordan* 75 D4
Al Mawşil, *Iraq* 70 B4
Al Mayādin, *Syria* 70 C4
Al Mazār, *Jordan* 75 D4
Al Midhnab, *Si. Arabia* 70 E5
Al Minā', *Lebanon* 75 A4
Al Miqdādīyah, *Iraq* 70 C5
Al Mubarraz, *Si. Arabia* 71 E6
Al Mudawwarah, *Jordan* 75 F5
Al Mughayrā', *U.A.E.* 71 E7
Al Muḩarraq, *Bahrain* 71 E6
Al Mukallā, *Yemen* 74 E4
Al Mukhā, *Yemen* 74 E3
Al Musayjīd, *Si. Arabia* 70 E3
Al Musayyib, *Iraq* 70 C5
Al Muwayh, *Si. Arabia* 80 C5
Al Muwaylih, *Si. Arabia* 70 E2
Al Owuho = Otukpa, *Nigeria* 83 D6
Al Qā'im, *Iraq* 70 C4
Al Qalībah, *Si. Arabia* 70 D3
Al Qāmishlī, *Syria* 70 B4
Al Qaryatayn, *Syria* 75 A6
Al Qaşīm, *Si. Arabia* 70 E4
Al Qaṭ'ā, *Syria* 70 C4
Al Qaṭīf, *Si. Arabia* 71 E6
Al Qatrānah, *Jordan* 75 D5
Al Qaṭrūn, *Libya* 79 D9
Al Qayşūmah, *Si. Arabia* 70 D5
Al Quds = Jerusalem, *Israel* 75 D4
Al Qunayṭirah, *Syria* 75 C4
Al Qunfudhah, *Si. Arabia* 80 D5
Al Qurnah, *Iraq* 70 D5
Al Quşayr, *Iraq* 70 D5
Al Quşayr, *Syria* 75 A5
Al Qutayfah, *Syria* 75 B5
Al 'Ubaylah, *Si. Arabia* 74 C5
Al 'Uḑaylīyah, *Si. Arabia* 71 E6
Al 'Ulā, *Si. Arabia* 70 E3
Al 'Uqayr, *Si. Arabia* 71 E6
Al 'Uwaynid, *Si. Arabia* 70 E5
Al 'Uwayqīlah, *Si. Arabia* 70 D4
Al 'Uyūn, *Ḩijāz, Si. Arabia* 70 E3
Al 'Uyūn, *Najd, Si. Arabia* 70 E4
Al 'Uzayr, *Iraq* 70 D5
Al Wajh, *Si. Arabia* 70 E3
Al Wakrah, *Qatar* 71 E6
Al Waqbah, *Si. Arabia* 70 D5
Al Wari'āh, *Si. Arabia* 70 E5
Ala, *Italy* 28 C8
Ala Dağ, *Turkey* 70 B2
Ala Dağları, *Turkey* 73 C10
Alabama □, *U.S.A.* 109 J2
Alabama →, *U.S.A.* 109 K2
Alabaster, *U.S.A.* 109 J2
Alaca, *Turkey* 72 B6
Alacaatlı, *Turkey* 39 B10
Alaçam, *Turkey* 72 B6
Alaçam Dağları, *Turkey* 39 B10
Alaçatı, *Turkey* 39 C8
Alachua, *U.S.A.* 109 L4
Alaejos, *Spain* 34 D5
Alaérma, *Greece* 36 C9
Alagir, *Russia* 49 J7
Alagna Valsésia, *Italy* 28 C4
Alagoa Grande, *Brazil* 125 E11
Alagoas □, *Brazil* 125 E11
Alagoinhas, *Brazil* 125 F11
Alagón, *Spain* 32 D3
Alagón →, *Spain* 34 F4
Alaior, *Spain* 37 B11
Alajero, *Canary Is.* 37 F2
Alajuela, *Costa Rica* 120 D3
Alakamisy, *Madag.* 89 C8
Alaknanda →, *India* 69 D8
Alakol, Ozero, *Kazakstan* 60 B3
Alamarvdasht, *Iran* 71 E7
Alamata, *Ethiopia* 81 E4
Alameda, *Calif., U.S.A.* 116 H4
Alameda, *N. Mex., U.S.A.* 115 J10
Alaminos, *Phil.* 61 C3
Alamo, *U.S.A.* 117 J11
Alamo Crossing, *U.S.A.* 117 L13
Alamogordo, *U.S.A.* 115 K11
Alamos, *Mexico* 118 B3
Alamosa, *U.S.A.* 115 H11
Åland, *Finland* 9 F19
Alandroal, *Portugal* 35 G3
Ålands hav, *Sweden* 9 F18
Alange, Presa de, *Spain* 35 G4
Alania = North Ossetia □, *Russia* 49 J7
Alanís, *Spain* 35 G5
Alanya, *Turkey* 70 B1
Alaotra, Farihin', *Madag.* 89 B8
Alapayevsk, *Russia* 50 D7
Alappuzha = Alleppey, *India* 66 Q10
Alar del Rey, *Spain* 34 C6
Alaraz, *Spain* 34 E5
Alarcón, Embalse de, *Spain* 32 F2
Alarobia-Vohiposa, *Madag.* 89 C8
Alaşehir, *Turkey* 39 C10
Alaska □, *U.S.A.* 100 B5
Alaska, G. of, *Pac. Oc.* 100 C5
Alaska Peninsula, *U.S.A.* 100 C4
Alaska Range, *U.S.A.* 100 B4
Alássio, *Italy* 28 E5
Älät, *Azerbaijan* 49 L9
Alatri, *Italy* 29 G10
Alatyr, *Russia* 48 C8
Alatyr →, *Russia* 48 C8
Alausi, *Ecuador* 124 D3
Álava □, *Spain* 32 C2
Alava, C., *U.S.A.* 114 B1
Alaverdi, *Armenia* 49 K7
Alavus, *Finland* 9 E20
Alawoona, *Australia* 95 E3
'Alayh, *Lebanon* 75 B4
Alazani →, *Azerbaijan* 49 K8
Alba, *Italy* 28 D5
Alba □, *Romania* 43 D8
Alba Adriática, *Italy* 29 F10
Alba de Tormes, *Spain* 34 E5
Alba-Iulia, *Romania* 43 D8
Albac, *Romania* 42 D7
Albacete, *Spain* 33 F3
Albacete □, *Spain* 33 G3
Albacutya, L., *Australia* 95 F3
Ålbæk, *Denmark* 11 G4
Ålbæk Bugt, *Denmark* 11 G4
Albaida, *Spain* 33 G4
Albalate de las Nogueras, *Spain* 32 E2
Albalate del Arzobispo, *Spain* 32 D4
Alban, *France* 20 E6
Albanel, L., *Canada* 102 B5
Albania ■, *Europe* 40 E4
Albano Laziale, *Italy* 29 G9
Albany, *Australia* 93 G2
Albany, *Ga., U.S.A.* 109 K3
Albany, *N.Y., U.S.A.* 111 D11
Albany, *Oreg., U.S.A.* 114 D2
Albany, *Tex., U.S.A.* 113 J5
Albany →, *Canada* 102 B3
Albardón, *Argentina* 126 C2
Albarracín, *Spain* 32 E3
Albarracín, Sierra de, *Spain* 32 E3
Albatera, *Spain* 33 G4
Albatross B., *Australia* 94 A3
Albegna →, *Italy* 29 F8
Albemarle, *U.S.A.* 109 H5
Albemarle Sd., *U.S.A.* 109 H7
Albenga, *Italy* 28 D5
Alberche →, *Spain* 34 F6
Alberdi, *Paraguay* 126 B4
Alberes, Mts., *France* 20 F6
Ålberga, *Sweden* 11 F10
Albersdorf, *Germany* 24 A5
Albert, *France* 19 C9
Albert, L., *Africa* 86 B3
Albert, L., *Australia* 95 F2
Albert Edward Ra., *Australia* 92 C4
Albert Lea, *U.S.A.* 112 D8
Albert Nile →, *Uganda* 86 B3
Albert Town, *Bahamas* 121 B5
Alberta □, *Canada* 104 C6
Alberti, *Argentina* 126 D3
Albertinia, *S. Africa* 88 E3
Albertirsa, *Hungary* 42 C4
Alberton, *Canada* 103 C7
Albertville = Kalemie, *Dem. Rep. of the Congo* 86 D2
Albertville, *France* 21 C10
Albertville, *U.S.A.* 109 H2
Albi, *France* 20 E6
Albia, *U.S.A.* 112 E8
Albina, *Surinam* 125 B8
Albina, Ponta, *Angola* 88 B1
Albino, *Italy* 28 C6
Albion, *Mich., U.S.A.* 108 D3
Albion, *Nebr., U.S.A.* 112 E6
Albion, *Pa., U.S.A.* 110 E4
Albocácer, *Spain* 32 E5
Albolote, *Spain* 35 H7
Alborán, *Medit. S.* 35 K7
Alborea, *Spain* 33 F3
Ålborg, *Denmark* 11 G3
Ålborg Bugt, *Denmark* 11 H4
Alborz, Reshteh-ye Kūhhā-ye, *Iran* 71 C7
Albox, *Spain* 33 H2
Albufeira, *Portugal* 35 H2
Albula →, *Switz.* 25 J5
Albuñol, *Spain* 35 J7
Albuquerque, *U.S.A.* 115 J10
Albuquerque, Cayos de, *Caribbean* 120 D3
Alburg, *U.S.A.* 111 B11
Alburno, Mte., *Italy* 31 B8
Alburquerque, *Spain* 35 F4
Albury = Albury-Wodonga, *Australia* 95 F4
Albury-Wodonga, *Australia* 95 F4
Alcácer do Sal, *Portugal* 35 G2
Alcáçovas, *Portugal* 35 G2
Alcalá de Chivert, *Spain* 32 E5
Alcalá de Guadaira, *Spain* 35 H5
Alcalá de Henares, *Spain* 34 E7
Alcalá de los Gazules, *Spain* 35 J5
Alcalá del Júcar, *Spain* 33 F3
Alcalá del Río, *Spain* 35 H5
Alcalá del Valle, *Spain* 35 J5
Alcalá la Real, *Spain* 35 H7
Álcamo, *Italy* 30 E5
Alcanadre, *Spain* 32 C2
Alcanadre →, *Spain* 32 D4
Alcanar, *Spain* 32 E5
Alcanede, *Portugal* 35 F2
Alcanena, *Portugal* 35 F2
Alcañices, *Spain* 34 D4
Alcañiz, *Spain* 32 D4
Alcântara, *Brazil* 125 D10
Alcántara, *Spain* 34 F4
Alcántara, Embalse de, *Spain* 34 F4
Alcantarilla, *Spain* 33 H3
Alcaracejos, *Spain* 35 G6
Alcaraz, *Spain* 33 G2
Alcaraz, Sierra de, *Spain* 33 G2
Alcaudete, *Spain* 35 H6
Alcázar de San Juan, *Spain* 35 F7
Alchevsk, *Ukraine* 47 H10
Alcira = Alzira, *Spain* 33 F4
Alcobaça, *Portugal* 35 F2
Alcobendas, *Spain* 34 E7
Alcolea del Pinar, *Spain* 32 D2
Alcora, *Spain* 32 E4
Alcorcón, *Spain* 34 E7
Alcoutim, *Portugal* 35 H3
Alcova, *U.S.A.* 114 E10
Alcoy, *Spain* 33 G4
Alcubierre, Sierra de, *Spain* 32 D4
Alcublas, *Spain* 32 F4
Alcúdia, *Spain* 37 B10
Alcúdia, B. d', *Spain* 37 B10
Alcudia, Sierra de la, *Spain* 35 G6
Aldabra Is., *Seychelles* 77 G8
Aldama, *Mexico* 119 C5
Aldan, *Russia* 51 D13
Aldan →, *Russia* 51 C13
Aldea, Pta. de la, *Canary Is.* 37 G4
Aldeburgh, *U.K.* 13 E9
Alder Pk., *U.S.A.* 116 K5
Alderney, *U.K.* 13 H5
Aldershot, *U.K.* 13 F7
Åled, *Sweden* 11 H6
Aledo, *U.S.A.* 112 E9
Alefa, *Ethiopia* 81 E4
Aleg, *Mauritania* 82 B2
Alegranza, *Canary Is.* 37 E6
Alegranza, I., *Canary Is.* 37 E6
Alegre, *Brazil* 127 A7
Alegrete, *Brazil* 127 B4
Aleisk, *Russia* 50 D9
Aleksandriya = Oleksandriya, *Kirovohrad, Ukraine* 47 H7
Aleksandriya = Oleksandriya, *Rivne, Ukraine* 47 G4
Aleksandriyskaya, *Russia* 49 J8
Aleksandrov, *Russia* 46 D10
Aleksandrov Gay, *Russia* 48 E9
Aleksandrovac, *Serbia, Yug.* 40 C5
Aleksandrovac, *Serbia, Yug.* 40 B5
Aleksandrovka = Oleksandrovka, *Ukraine* 47 H7
Aleksandrovo, *Bulgaria* 41 C8
Aleksandrovsk-Sakhalinskiy, *Russia* 51 D15
Aleksandrów Kujawski, *Poland* 45 F5
Aleksandrów Łódźki, *Poland* 45 G6
Alekseyevka, *Samara, Russia* 48 D10
Alekseyevka, *Voronezh, Russia* 47 G10
Aleksin, *Russia* 46 E9
Aleksinac, *Serbia, Yug.* 40 C5
Além Paraíba, *Brazil* 127 A7
Alemania, *Argentina* 126 B2
Alemania, *Chile* 126 B2
Alençon, *France* 18 D7
Alenquer, *Brazil* 125 D8
Alenuihaha Channel, *U.S.A.* 106 H17
Alépé, *Ivory C.* 82 D4
Aleppo = Ḩalab, *Syria* 70 B3
Aléria, *France* 21 F13
Alès, *France* 21 D8
Aleşd, *Romania* 42 C7

Alessándria, *Italy* 28 D5
Ålestrup, *Denmark* 11 H3
Ålesund, *Norway* 9 E12
Alet-les-Bains, *France* 20 F6
Aletschhorn, *Switz.* 25 J4
Aleutian Is., *Pac. Oc.* 100 C2
Aleutian Trench, *Pac. Oc.* 96 C10
Alexander, *U.S.A.* 112 B3
Alexander, Mt., *Australia* 93 E3
Alexander Arch., *U.S.A.* 100 C6
Alexander Bay, *S. Africa* 88 D2
Alexander City, *U.S.A.* 109 J3
Alexander I., *Antarctica* 5 C17
Alexandra, *Australia* 95 F4
Alexandra, *N.Z.* 91 L2
Alexandra Falls, *Canada* 104 A5
Alexandria = El Iskandarîya, *Egypt* 80 H7
Alexandria, *B.C., Canada* 104 C4
Alexandria, *Ont., Canada* 102 C5
Alexandria, *Romania* 43 G10
Alexandria, *S. Africa* 88 E4
Alexandria, *U.K.* 14 F4
Alexandria, *La., U.S.A.* 113 K8
Alexandria, *Minn., U.S.A.* 112 C7
Alexandria, *S. Dak., U.S.A.* 112 D6
Alexandria, *Va., U.S.A.* 108 F7
Alexandria Bay, *U.S.A.* 111 B9
Alexandrina, L., *Australia* 95 F2
Alexandroúpolis, *Greece* 41 F9
Alexis →, *Canada* 103 B8
Alexis Creek, *Canada* 104 C4
Alfabia, *Spain* 37 B9
Alfambra, *Spain* 32 E3
Alfândega da Fé, *Portugal* 34 D4
Alfaro, *Spain* 32 C3
Alfatar, *Bulgaria* 41 C11
Alfaz del Pi, *Spain* 33 G4
Alfeld, *Germany* 24 D5
Alfenas, *Brazil* 127 A6
Alfiós →, *Greece* 38 D3
Alföld, *Hungary* 42 D5
Alfonsine, *Italy* 29 D9
Alford, *Aberds., U.K.* 14 D6
Alford, *Lincs., U.K.* 12 D8
Alfred, *Maine, U.S.A.* 111 C14
Alfred, *N.Y., U.S.A.* 110 D7
Alfreton, *U.K.* 12 D6
Alfta, *Sweden* 10 C10
Alga, *Kazakstan* 50 E6
Algaida, *Spain* 37 B9
Algar, *Spain* 35 J5
Ålgård, *Norway* 9 G11
Algarinejo, *Spain* 35 H6
Algarve, *Portugal* 35 J2
Algeciras, *Spain* 35 J5
Algemesí, *Spain* 33 F4
Alger, *Algeria* 78 A6
Algeria ■, *Africa* 78 C6
Alghero, *Italy* 30 B1
Älghult, *Sweden* 11 G9
Algiers = Alger, *Algeria* 78 A6
Algoa B., *S. Africa* 88 E4
Algodonales, *Spain* 35 J5
Algodor →, *Spain* 34 F7
Algoma, *U.S.A.* 108 C2
Algona, *U.S.A.* 112 D7
Algonac, *U.S.A.* 110 D2
Algonquin Prov. Park, *Canada* 102 C4
Algorta, *Uruguay* 128 C5
Alhama de Almería, *Spain* 35 J8
Alhama de Aragón, *Spain* 32 D3
Alhama de Granada, *Spain* 35 H7
Alhama de Murcia, *Spain* 33 H3
Alhambra, *U.S.A.* 117 L8
Alhaurín el Grande, *Spain* 35 J6
Alhucemas = Al Hoceïma, *Morocco* 78 A5
'Alī al Gharbī, *Iraq* 70 C5
'Alī ash Sharqī, *Iraq* 70 C5
Äli Bayramlı, *Azerbaijan* 49 L9
'Alī Khēl, *Afghan.* 68 C3
Ali Sahîh, *Djibouti* 81 E5
Alī Shāh, *Iran* 70 B5
Ália, *Italy* 30 E6
'Alīābād, *Khorāsān, Iran* 71 C8
'Alīābād, *Kordestān, Iran* 70 C5
'Alīābād, *Yazd, Iran* 71 D7
Aliaga, *Spain* 32 E4
Aliağa, *Turkey* 39 C8
Aliákmon →, *Greece* 40 F6
Alibo, *Ethiopia* 81 F4
Alibori →, *Benin* 83 C5
Alibunar, *Serbia, Yug.* 42 E5
Alicante, *Spain* 33 G4
Alicante □, *Spain* 33 G4
Alice, *S. Africa* 88 E4
Alice, *U.S.A.* 113 M5
Alice →, *Queens., Australia* 94 C3
Alice →, *Queens., Australia* 94 B3
Alice, Punta, *Italy* 31 C10
Alice Arm, *Canada* 104 B3
Alice Springs, *Australia* 94 C1
Alicedale, *S. Africa* 88 E4
Aliceville, *U.S.A.* 109 J1
Alicudi, *Italy* 31 D7
Aliganj, *India* 69 F8
Aligarh, *Raj., India* 68 G7
Aligarh, *Ut. P., India* 68 F8
Alīgūdarz, *Iran* 71 C6
Alijó, *Portugal* 34 D3
Alimnía, *Greece* 36 C9
Alingsås, *Sweden* 11 G6
Alipur, *Pakistan* 68 E4
Alipur Duar, *India* 67 F16
Aliquippa, *U.S.A.* 110 F4
Alishan, *Taiwan* 59 F13
Aliste →, *Spain* 34 D5
Alitus = Alytus, *Lithuania* 9 J21
Alivérion, *Greece* 38 C6
Aliwal North, *S. Africa* 88 E4
Alix, *Canada* 104 C6
Aljezur, *Portugal* 35 H2
Aljustrel, *Portugal* 35 H2
Alkamari, *Niger* 83 C7
Alkmaar, *Neths.* 17 B4
All American Canal, *U.S.A.* 115 K6
Allada, *Benin* 83 D5
Allagash →, *U.S.A.* 109 B11
Allah Dad, *Pakistan* 68 G2
Allahabad, *India* 69 G9
Allan, *Canada* 105 C7
Allanche, *France* 20 C6
Allanridge, *S. Africa* 88 D4
Allaqi, Wadi →, *Egypt* 80 C3
Allariz, *Spain* 34 C3
Allassac, *France* 20 C5
Ålleberg, *Sweden* 11 F7
Allegany, *U.S.A.* 110 D6
Allegheny →, *U.S.A.* 110 F5
Allegheny Mts., *U.S.A.* 108 G6
Allegheny Reservoir, *U.S.A.* 110 E6
Allègre, *France* 20 C7
Allen, Bog of, *Ireland* 15 C5
Allen, L., *Ireland* 15 B3
Allendale, *U.S.A.* 109 J5
Allende, *Mexico* 118 B4
Allentown, *U.S.A.* 111 F9
Allentsteig, *Austria* 26 C8
Alleppey, *India* 66 Q10
Allepuz, *Spain* 32 E4
Aller →, *Germany* 24 C5
Alliance, *Nebr., U.S.A.* 112 D3
Alliance, *Ohio, U.S.A.* 110 F3
Allier □, *France* 19 F9
Allier →, *France* 19 F10
Alliford Bay, *Canada* 104 C2
Allinge, *Denmark* 11 J8
Alliston, *Canada* 102 D4
Alloa, *U.K.* 14 E5
Allones, *France* 18 D8
Allora, *Australia* 95 D5
Allos, *France* 21 D10
Alluitsup Paa, *Greenland* 4 C5
Alma, *Canada* 103 C5
Alma, *Ga., U.S.A.* 109 K4
Alma, *Kans., U.S.A.* 112 F6
Alma, *Mich., U.S.A.* 108 D3
Alma, *Nebr., U.S.A.* 112 E5
Alma Ata = Almaty, *Kazakstan* 50 E8
Almacelles, *Spain* 32 D5
Almada, *Portugal* 35 G1
Almaden, *Australia* 94 B3
Almadén, *Spain* 35 G6
Almanor, L., *U.S.A.* 114 F3
Almansa, *Spain* 33 G3
Almanza, *Spain* 34 C5
Almanzor, Pico, *Spain* 34 E5
Almanzora →, *Spain* 33 H3
Almaş, Munţii, *Romania* 42 F7
Almassora, *Spain* 32 F4
Almaty, *Kazakstan* 50 E8
Almazán, *Spain* 32 D2
Almeirim, *Brazil* 125 D8
Almeirim, *Portugal* 35 F2
Almelo, *Neths.* 17 B6
Almenar de Soria, *Spain* 32 D2
Almenara, *Spain* 32 F4
Almenara, Sierra de la, *Spain* 33 H3
Almendra, Embalse de, *Spain* 34 D4
Almendralejo, *Spain* 35 G4
Almere-Stad, *Neths.* 17 B5
Almería, *Spain* 35 J8
Almería □, *Spain* 33 H2
Almería, G. de, *Spain* 33 J2
Almetyevsk, *Russia* 48 C11
Älmhult, *Sweden* 11 H8
Almirante, *Panama* 120 E3
Almiropótamos, *Greece* 38 C6
Almirós, *Greece* 38 B4
Almiroú, Kólpos, *Greece* 36 D6
Almodôvar, *Portugal* 35 H2
Almodóvar del Campo, *Spain* 35 G6
Almodóvar del Río, *Spain* 35 H5
Almond, *U.S.A.* 110 D7
Almont, *U.S.A.* 110 D1
Almonte, *Canada* 111 A8
Almonte, *Spain* 35 H4
Almora, *India* 69 E8
Almoradí, *Spain* 33 G4
Almorox, *Spain* 34 E6
Almoustarat, *Mali* 83 B5
Älmsta, *Sweden* 10 E12
Almudévar, *Spain* 32 C4
Almuñécar, *Spain* 35 J7
Almunge, *Sweden* 10 E12
Almuradiel, *Spain* 35 G7
Alness, *U.K.* 14 D4
Alnmouth, *U.K.* 12 B6
Alnwick, *U.K.* 12 B6
Aloi, *Uganda* 86 B3
Alon, *Burma* 67 H19
Alor, *Indonesia* 63 F6
Alor Setar, *Malaysia* 65 J3
Álora, *Spain* 35 J6
Alosno, *Spain* 35 H3
Alot, *India* 68 H6
Aloysius, Mt., *Australia* 93 E4
Alpaugh, *U.S.A.* 116 K7
Alpedrinha, *Portugal* 34 E3
Alpena, *U.S.A.* 108 C4
Alpes-de-Haute-Provence □, *France* 21 D10
Alpes-Maritimes □, *France* 21 E11
Alpha, *Australia* 94 C4
Alphen aan den Rijn, *Neths.* 17 B4
Alpiarça, *Portugal* 35 F2
Alpine, *Ariz., U.S.A.* 115 K9
Alpine, *Calif., U.S.A.* 117 N10
Alpine, *Tex., U.S.A.* 113 K3
Alps, *Europe* 6 F7
Alpu, *Turkey* 72 C4
Alqueta, Barragem do, *Portugal* 35 G3
Alrø, *Denmark* 11 J4
Als, *Denmark* 11 K3
Alsace, *France* 19 D14
Alsask, *Canada* 105 C7
Alsasua, *Spain* 32 C2
Alsek →, *U.S.A.* 104 B1
Alsfeld, *Germany* 24 E5
Alsten, *Norway* 8 D15
Alstermo, *Sweden* 11 H9
Alston, *U.K.* 12 C5
Alta, *Norway* 8 B20
Alta, Sierra, *Spain* 32 E3
Alta Gracia, *Argentina* 126 C3
Alta Sierra, *U.S.A.* 117 K8
Altaelva →, *Norway* 8 B20
Altafjorden, *Norway* 8 A20
Altai = Aerhtai Shan, *Mongolia* 60 B4
Altamaha →, *U.S.A.* 109 K5
Altamira, *Brazil* 125 D8
Altamira, *Chile* 126 B2
Altamira, *Mexico* 119 C5
Altamira, Cuevas de, *Spain* 34 B6
Altamont, *U.S.A.* 111 D10
Altamura, *Italy* 31 B9
Altanbulag, *Mongolia* 60 A5
Altar, *Mexico* 118 A2
Altar, Desierto de, *Mexico* 118 B2
Altata, *Mexico* 118 C3
Altavista, *U.S.A.* 108 G6
Altay, *China* 60 B3
Altdorf, *Switz.* 25 J4
Alte Mellum, *Germany* 24 B4
Altea, *Spain* 33 G4
Altenberg, *Germany* 24 E9
Altenbruch, *Germany* 24 B4
Altenburg, *Germany* 24 E8
Altenkirchen, *Mecklenburg-Vorpommern, Germany* 24 A9
Altenkirchen, *Rhld-Pfz., Germany* 24 E3
Altenmarkt, *Austria* 26 D7
Alter do Chão, *Portugal* 35 F3
Altınoluk, *Turkey* 39 B8
Altınova, *Turkey* 39 B8
Altıntaş, *Turkey* 39 B12
Altınyaka, *Turkey* 39 E12
Altınyayla, *Turkey* 39 D11
Altiplano = Bolivian Plateau, *S. Amer.* 122 E4
Altkirch, *France* 19 E14
Altmark, *Germany* 24 C7
Altmühl →, *Germany* 25 G7
Altmunster, *Austria* 26 D6
Alto Adige = Trentino-Alto Adige □, *Italy* 29 B8
Alto Araguaia, *Brazil* 125 G8
Alto Cuchumatanes = Cuchumatanes, Sierra de los, *Guatemala* 120 C1
Alto del Carmen, *Chile* 126 B1
Alto del Inca, *Chile* 126 A2
Alto Ligonha, *Mozam.* 87 F4
Alto Molocue, *Mozam.* 87 F4
Alto Paraguay □, *Paraguay* 126 A4
Alto Paraná □, *Paraguay* 127 B5
Alton, *Canada* 110 C4
Alton, *U.K.* 13 F7
Alton, *Ill., U.S.A.* 112 F9
Alton, *N.H., U.S.A.* 111 C13
Altoona, *U.S.A.* 110 F6
Altötting, *Germany* 25 G8
Altstätten, *Switz.* 25 H5
Altūn Kūprī, *Iraq* 70 C5
Altun Shan, *China* 60 C3
Alturas, *U.S.A.* 114 F3
Altus, *U.S.A.* 113 H5
Alubijid, *Phil.* 61 G6
Alucra, *Turkey* 73 B8
Aluk, *Sudan* 81 F2
Alūksne, *Latvia* 9 H22
Alunda, *Sweden* 10 D12
Alunite, *U.S.A.* 117 K12
Aluoro →, *Ethiopia* 81 F3
Alupka, *Ukraine* 47 K8
Alushta, *Ukraine* 47 K8
Alusi, *Indonesia* 63 F8
Alustante, *Spain* 32 E3
Alva, *U.S.A.* 113 G5
Alvaiázere, *Portugal* 34 F2
Älvängen, *Sweden* 11 G6
Alvarado, *Mexico* 119 D5
Alvarado, *U.S.A.* 113 J6
Alvaro Obregón, Presa, *Mexico* 118 B3
Älvdalen, *Sweden* 10 C8
Alvear, *Argentina* 126 B4
Alverca, *Portugal* 35 G1
Alvesta, *Sweden* 11 H8
Alvin, *U.S.A.* 113 L7
Alvinston, *Canada* 110 D3
Alvito, *Portugal* 35 G3
Älvkarleby, *Sweden* 10 D11
Alvord Desert, *U.S.A.* 114 E4
Älvros, *Sweden* 10 B8
Älvsbyn, *Sweden* 8 D19
Alwar, *India* 68 F7
Alxa Zuoqi, *China* 56 E3
Alyangula, *Australia* 94 A2
Alyata = Älät, *Azerbaijan* 49 L9
Alyth, *U.K.* 14 E5
Alytus, *Lithuania* 9 J21
Alzada, *U.S.A.* 112 C2
Alzey, *Germany* 25 F4
Alzira, *Spain* 33 F4
Am Timan, *Chad* 79 F10
Amadeus, L., *Australia* 93 D5
Amadi, *Dem. Rep. of the Congo* 86 B2
Amâdi, *Sudan* 81 F3
Amadjuak L., *Canada* 101 B12
Amadora, *Portugal* 35 G1
Amagansett, *U.S.A.* 111 F12
Amagasaki, *Japan* 55 G7
Amager, *Denmark* 11 J6
Amagunze, *Nigeria* 83 D6
Amahai, *Indonesia* 63 E7
Amakusa-Shotō, *Japan* 55 H5
Åmål, *Sweden* 10 E6
Amalfi, *Italy* 31 B7
Amaliás, *Greece* 38 D3
Amalner, *India* 66 J9
Amamapare, *Indonesia* 63 E9
Amambaí, *Brazil* 127 A4
Amambaí →, *Brazil* 127 A5
Amambay □, *Paraguay* 127 A4
Amambay, Cordillera de, *S. Amer.* 127 A4
Amami-Guntō, *Japan* 55 L4
Amami-Ō-Shima, *Japan* 55 L4
Amaná, L., *Brazil* 124 D6
Amanat →, *India* 69 G11
Amanda Park, *U.S.A.* 116 C3
Amangeldy, *Kazakstan* 50 D7
Amantea, *Italy* 31 C9
Amapá, *Brazil* 125 C8
Amapá □, *Brazil* 125 C8
Amara, *Sudan* 81 E3
Amarante, *Brazil* 125 E10
Amarante, *Portugal* 34 D2
Amaranth, *Canada* 105 C9
Amareleja, *Portugal* 35 G3
Amargosa →, *U.S.A.* 117 J10
Amargosa Range, *U.S.A.* 117 J10
Amári, *Greece* 36 D6
Amarillo, *U.S.A.* 113 H4
Amarkantak, *India* 69 H9
Amârna, Tell el', *Sudan* 80 B3
Amaro, Mte., *Italy* 29 F11
Amarpur, *India* 69 G12
Amarti, *Eritrea* 81 E5
Amarwara, *India* 69 H8
Amasra, *Turkey* 72 B5
Amassama, *Nigeria* 83 D6
Amasya, *Turkey* 72 B6
Amata, *Australia* 93 E5
Amatikulu, *S. Africa* 89 D5
Amatitlán, *Guatemala* 120 D1
Amatrice, *Italy* 29 F10
Amay, *Belgium* 17 D5
Amazon = Amazonas →, *S. Amer.* 122 D5
Amazonas □, *Brazil* 124 E6
Amazonas →, *S. Amer.* 122 D5
Amba Ferit, *Ethiopia* 81 E4
Ambah, *India* 68 F8
Ambahakily, *Madag.* 89 C7
Ambahita, *Madag.* 89 C8
Ambala, *India* 68 D7
Ambalavao, *Madag.* 89 C8
Ambanja, *Madag.* 89 A8
Ambararata, *Madag.* 89 B8
Ambarchik, *Russia* 51 C17
Ambarijeby, *Madag.* 89 A8
Ambaro, Helodranon', *Madag.* 89 A8
Ambato, *Ecuador* 124 D3
Ambato, *Madag.* 89 A8
Ambato, Sierra de, *Argentina* 126 B2
Ambato Boeny, *Madag.* 89 B8
Ambatofinandrahana, *Madag.* 89 C8
Ambatolampy, *Madag.* 89 B8
Ambatomainty, *Madag.* 89 B8
Ambatomanoina, *Madag.* 89 B8
Ambatondrazaka, *Madag.* 89 B8
Ambatosoratra, *Madag.* 89 B8
Ambelón, *Greece* 38 B4
Ambenja, *Madag.* 89 B8
Amberg, *Germany* 25 F7
Ambergris Cay, *Belize* 119 D7
Ambérieu-en-Bugey, *France* 21 C9
Amberley, *N.Z.* 91 K4
Ambert, *France* 20 C7
Ambidédi, *Mali* 82 C2
Ambikapur, *India* 69 H10
Ambikol, *Sudan* 80 C3
Ambilobé, *Madag.* 89 A8
Ambinanindrano, *Madag.* 89 C8
Ambinanitelo, *Madag.* 89 B8
Ambinda, *Madag.* 89 B8
Amble, *U.K.* 12 B6
Ambleside, *U.K.* 12 C5
Ambo, *Peru* 124 F3
Amboahangy, *Madag.* 89 C8
Ambodifototra, *Madag.* 89 B8
Ambodilazana, *Madag.* 89 B8
Ambodiriana, *Madag.* 89 B8
Ambohidratrimo, *Madag.* 89 B8
Ambohidray, *Madag.* 89 B8
Ambohimahamasina, *Madag.* 89 C8
Ambohimahasoa, *Madag.* 89 C8
Ambohimanga, *Madag.* 89 C8
Ambohimitombo, *Madag.* 89 C8
Ambohitra, *Madag.* 89 A8
Amboise, *France* 18 E8
Ambon, *Indonesia* 63 E7
Ambondro, *Madag.* 89 D8
Amboseli, L., *Kenya* 86 C4
Ambositra, *Madag.* 89 C8
Ambovombe, *Madag.* 89 D8
Amboy, *U.S.A.* 117 L11
Amboyna Cay, *S. China Sea* 62 C4
Ambridge, *U.S.A.* 110 F4
Ambriz, *Angola* 84 F2
Amchitka I., *U.S.A.* 100 C1
Amderma, *Russia* 50 C7
Amdhi, *India* 69 H9
Ameca, *Mexico* 118 C4
Ameca →, *Mexico* 118 C3
Amecameca, *Mexico* 119 D5
Ameland, *Neths.* 17 A5
Amélia, *Italy* 29 F9
Amendolara, *Italy* 31 C9
Amenia, *U.S.A.* 111 E11
American Falls, *U.S.A.* 114 E7
American Falls Reservoir, *U.S.A.* 114 E7
American Fork, *U.S.A.* 114 F8
American Highland, *Antarctica* 5 D6
American Samoa ■, *Pac. Oc.* 91 B13
Americana, *Brazil* 127 A6
Americus, *U.S.A.* 109 K3
Amersfoort, *Neths.* 17 B5
Amersfoort, *S. Africa* 89 D4
Amery Ice Shelf, *Antarctica* 5 C6
Ames, *Spain* 34 C2
Ames, *U.S.A.* 112 E8
Amesbury, *U.S.A.* 111 D14
Amet, *India* 68 G5
Amfíklia, *Greece* 38 C4
Amfilokhía, *Greece* 38 C3
Amfípolis, *Greece* 40 F7
Ámfissa, *Greece* 38 C4
Amga, *Russia* 51 C14
Amga →, *Russia* 51 C14
Amgu, *Russia* 51 E14
Amgun →, *Russia* 51 D14
Amherst, *Canada* 103 C7
Amherst, *Mass., U.S.A.* 111 D12
Amherst, *N.Y., U.S.A.* 110 D6
Amherst, *Ohio, U.S.A.* 110 E2
Amherst I., *Canada* 111 B8
Amherstburg, *Canada* 102 D3
Amiata, Mte., *Italy* 29 F8
Amidon, *U.S.A.* 112 B3
Amiens, *France* 19 C9
Amindaion, *Greece* 40 F5
Åminne, *Sweden* 11 G7
Amino, *Ethiopia* 81 G5
Aminuis, *Namibia* 88 C2
Amīrābād, *Iran* 70 C5
Amirante Is., *Seychelles* 52 K9
Amisk L., *Canada* 105 C8
Amistad, Presa de la, *Mexico* 118 B4
Amite, *U.S.A.* 113 K9
Amla, *India* 68 J8
Amlia I., *U.S.A.* 100 C2
Amlwch, *U.K.* 12 D3
Amm Adam, *Sudan* 81 D4
'Ammān, *Jordan* 75 D4
'Ammān □, *Jordan* 75 D5
Ammanford, *U.K.* 13 F4
Ammassalik = Tasiilaq, *Greenland* 4 C6
Ammerån →, *Sweden* 10 A10
Ammersee, *Germany* 25 G7
Ammon, *U.S.A.* 114 E8
Amnat Charoen, *Thailand* 64 E5
Amnura, *Bangla.* 69 G13
Amo Jiang →, *China* 58 F3
Āmol, *Iran* 71 B7
Amorgós, *Greece* 39 E7
Amory, *U.S.A.* 109 J1
Amos, *Canada* 102 C4
Åmot, *Norway* 9 G13
Åmotfors, *Sweden* 10 E6
Amoy = Xiamen, *China* 59 E12
Ampanavoana, *Madag.* 89 B9
Ampang, *Malaysia* 65 L3
Ampangalana, Lakandranon', *Madag.* 89 C8
Ampanihy, *Madag* 89 C7
Amparafaravola, *Madag.* 89 B8
Ampasinambo, *Madag.* 89 C8
Ampasindava, Helodranon', *Madag.* 89 A8
Ampasindava, Saikanosy, *Madag.* 89 A8
Ampenan, *Indonesia* 62 F5
Amper, *Nigeria* 83 D6
Amper →, *Germany* 25 G7
Ampezzo, *Italy* 29 B9
Ampitsikinana, *Réunion* 89 A8
Ampombiantambo, *Madag.* 89 A8
Amposta, *Spain* 32 E5
Ampotaka, *Madag.* 89 D7
Ampoza, *Madag.* 89 C7
Amqui, *Canada* 103 C6
Amravati, *India* 66 J10
Amreli, *India* 68 J4
Amritsar, *India* 68 D6
Amroha, *India* 69 E8
Amrum, *Germany* 24 A4
Amsterdam, *Neths.* 17 B4
Amsterdam, *U.S.A.* 111 D10
Amsterdam, I. = Nouvelle-Amsterdam, I., *Ind. Oc.* 3 F13
Amstetten, *Austria* 26 C7
Amudarya →, *Uzbekistan* 50 E6
Amundsen Gulf, *Canada* 100 A7
Amundsen Sea, *Antarctica* 5 D15
Amungen, *Sweden* 10 C9
Amuntai, *Indonesia* 62 E5
Amur →, *Russia* 51 D15
Amur, W. →, *Sudan* 80 D3

Amurang, *Indonesia* 63 D6
Amurrio, *Spain* 32 B1
Amursk, *Russia* 51 D14
Amusco, *Spain* 34 C6
Amvrakikós Kólpos, *Greece* 38 C2
Amvrosiyivka, *Ukraine* 47 J10
Amyderya = Amudarya →, *Uzbekistan* 50 E6
An Bien, *Vietnam* 65 H5
An Hoa, *Vietnam* 64 E7
An Nabatīyah at Tahta, *Lebanon* 75 B4
An Nabk, *Si. Arabia* 70 D3
An Nabk, *Syria* 75 A5
An Nafūd, *Si. Arabia* 70 D4
An Najaf, *Iraq* 70 C5
An Nāşirīyah, *Iraq* 70 D5
An Nhon, *Vietnam* 64 F7
An Nîl □, *Sudan* 80 D3
An Nîl el Abyad □, *Sudan* 81 E3
An Nîl el Azraq □, *Sudan* 81 E3
An Nu'ayrīyah, *Si. Arabia* 71 E6
An Nu'mānīyah, *Iraq* 73 F11
An Nuwayb'ī, W. →, *Si. Arabia* 75 F3
An Thoi, Dao, *Vietnam* 65 H4
An Uaimh, *Ireland* 15 C5
Anabar →, *Russia* 51 B12
'Anabtā, *West Bank* 75 C4
Anaconda, *U.S.A.* 114 C7
Anacortes, *U.S.A.* 116 B4
Anacuao, Mt., *Phil.* 61 C4
Anadarko, *U.S.A.* 113 H5
Anadia, *Portugal* 34 E2
Anadolu, *Turkey* 72 C5
Anadyr, *Russia* 51 C18
Anadyr →, *Russia* 51 C18
Anadyrskiy Zaliv, *Russia* 51 C19
Anáfi, *Greece* 39 E7
Anafópoulo, *Greece* 39 E7
Anaga, Pta. de, *Canary Is.* 37 F3
Anagni, *Italy* 29 G10
'Ānah, *Iraq* 70 C4
Anaheim, *U.S.A.* 117 M9
Anahim Lake, *Canada* 104 C3
Anáhuac, *Mexico* 118 B4
Anakapalle, *India* 67 L13
Anakie, *Australia* 94 C4
Anaklia, *Georgia* 49 J5
Analalava, *Madag.* 89 A8
Analavoka, *Madag.* 89 C8
Análipsis, *Greece* 36 A3
Anambar →, *Pakistan* 68 D3
Anambas, Kepulauan, *Indonesia* 65 L6
Anambas Is. = Anambas, Kepulauan, *Indonesia* 65 L6
Anambra □, *Nigeria* 83 D6
Anamosa, *U.S.A.* 112 D9
Anamur, *Turkey* 70 B2
Anamur Burnu, *Turkey* 72 D5
Anan, *Japan* 55 H7
Anand, *India* 68 H5
Anánes, *Greece* 38 E6
Anantnag, *India* 69 C6
Ananyiv, *Ukraine* 47 J5
Anapa, *Russia* 47 K9
Anapodháris →, *Greece* 36 E7
Anápolis, *Brazil* 125 G9
Anapu →, *Brazil* 125 D8
Anār, *Iran* 71 D7
Anārak, *Iran* 71 C7
Anarisfjällen, *Sweden* 10 A7
Anas →, *India* 68 H5
Anatolia = Anadolu, *Turkey* 72 C5
Anatsogno, *Madag.* 89 C7
Añatuya, *Argentina* 126 B3
Anaunethad L., *Canada* 105 A8
Anbyŏn, *N. Korea* 57 E14
Ancares, Sierra de, *Spain* 34 C4
Ancaster, *Canada* 110 C5
Ancenis, *France* 18 E5
Anchor Bay, *U.S.A.* 116 G3
Anchorage, *U.S.A.* 100 B5
Anci, *China* 56 E9
Ancohuma, Nevada, *Bolivia* 122 E4
Ancón, *Peru* 124 F3
Ancona, *Italy* 29 E10
Ancud, *Chile* 128 E2
Ancud, G. de, *Chile* 128 E2
Ancy-le-Franc, *France* 19 E11
Andacollo, *Argentina* 126 D1
Andacollo, *Chile* 126 C1
Andaingo, *Madag.* 89 B8
Andalgalá, *Argentina* 126 B2
Åndalsnes, *Norway* 9 E12
Andalucía □, *Spain* 35 H6
Andalusia = Andalucía □, *Spain* 35 H6
Andalusia, *U.S.A.* 109 K2
Andaman Is., *Ind. Oc.* 52 H13
Andaman Sea, *Ind. Oc.* 62 B1
Andamooka Opal Fields, *Australia* 95 E2
Andapa, *Madag.* 89 A8
Andara, *Namibia* 88 B3
Andelot-Blancheville, *France* 19 D12
Andenes, *Norway* 8 B17
Andenne, *Belgium* 17 D5
Andéranboukane, *Mali* 83 B5
Andermatt, *Switz.* 25 J4
Andernach, *Germany* 24 E3
Andernos-les-Bains, *France* 20 D2
Anderslöv, *Sweden* 11 J7
Anderson, *Alaska, U.S.A.* 100 B5
Anderson, *Calif., U.S.A.* 114 F2
Anderson, *Ind., U.S.A.* 108 E3
Anderson, *Mo., U.S.A.* 113 G7
Anderson, *S.C., U.S.A.* 109 H4
Anderson →, *Canada* 100 B7
Anderstorp, *Sweden* 11 G7
Andes, *U.S.A.* 111 D10
Andes, Cord. de los, *S. Amer.* 122 F4
Andfjorden, *Norway* 8 B17
Andhra Pradesh □, *India* 66 L11
Andijon, *Uzbekistan* 50 E8
Andikíthira, *Greece* 38 F5
Andilamena, *Madag.* 89 B8
Andīmeshk, *Iran* 71 C6
Andímilos, *Greece* 38 E6
Andíparos, *Greece* 39 D7
Andípaxoi, *Greece* 38 B2
Andípsara, *Greece* 39 C7
Andírrion, *Greece* 38 C3
Andizhan = Andijon, *Uzbekistan* 50 E8
Andoain, *Spain* 32 B2
Andoany, *Madag.* 89 A8
Andong, *S. Korea* 57 F15
Andongwei, *China* 57 G10
Andoom, *Australia* 94 A3
Andorra, *Spain* 32 E4
Andorra ■, *Europe* 20 F5
Andorra La Vella, *Andorra* 20 F5
Andover, *U.K.* 13 F6
Andover, *Maine, U.S.A.* 111 B14
Andover, *Mass., U.S.A.* 111 D13
Andover, *N.J., U.S.A.* 111 F10
Andover, *N.Y., U.S.A.* 110 D7
Andover, *Ohio, U.S.A.* 110 E4
Andøya, *Norway* 8 B16
Andradina, *Brazil* 125 H8
Andrahary, Mt., *Madag.* 89 A8
Andramasina, *Madag.* 89 B8
Andranopasy, *Madag.* 89 C7
Andranovory, *Madag.* 89 C7
Andratx, *Spain* 37 B9
Andreanof Is., *U.S.A.* 100 C2
Andreapol, *Russia* 46 D7
Andrews, *S.C., U.S.A.* 109 J6
Andrews, *Tex., U.S.A.* 113 J3
Andreyevka, *Russia* 48 D10
Ándria, *Italy* 31 A9
Andriamena, *Madag.* 89 B8
Andriandampy, *Madag.* 89 C8
Andriba, *Madag.* 89 B8
Andrijevica, *Montenegro, Yug.* 40 D3
Andrítsaina, *Greece* 38 D3
Androka, *Madag.* 89 C7
Andropov = Rybinsk, *Russia* 46 C10
Ándros, *Greece* 38 D6
Andros I., *Bahamas* 120 B4
Andros Town, *Bahamas* 120 B4
Androscoggin →, *U.S.A.* 111 C14
Andrychów, *Poland* 45 J6
Andselv, *Norway* 8 B18
Andújar, *Spain* 35 G6
Andulo, *Angola* 84 G3
Aneby, *Sweden* 11 G8
Anegada I., *U.S. Virgin Is.* 121 C7
Anegada Passage, *W. Indies* 121 C7
Anécho, *Togo* 83 D5
Anenni-Noi, *Moldova* 43 D14
Aneto, Pico de, *Spain* 32 C5
Anfu, *China* 59 D10
Ang Thong, *Thailand* 64 E3
Angamos, Punta, *Chile* 126 A1
Angara →, *Russia* 51 D10
Angara-Débou, *Benin* 83 C5
Angarab, *Ethiopia* 81 E4
Angarbaka, *Sudan* 81 F1
Angarsk, *Russia* 51 D11
Angas Hills, *Australia* 92 D4
Angaston, *Australia* 95 E2
Angaur I., *Pac. Oc.* 63 C8
Ånge, *Sweden* 10 B9
Ángel, Salto = Angel Falls, *Venezuela* 124 B6
Ángel de la Guarda, I., *Mexico* 118 B2
Angel Falls, *Venezuela* 124 B6
Angeles, *Phil.* 61 D4
Ängelholm, *Sweden* 11 H6
Angels Camp, *U.S.A.* 116 G6
Ängelsberg, *Sweden* 10 E10
Anger →, *Ethiopia* 81 F4
Angereb →, *Ethiopia* 81 E4
Ångermanälven →, *Sweden* 10 B11
Ångermanland, *Sweden* 8 E18
Angermünde, *Germany* 24 B9
Angers, *Canada* 111 A9
Angers, *France* 18 E6
Angerville, *France* 19 D9
Ängesån →, *Sweden* 8 C20
Angikuni L., *Canada* 105 A9
Angkor, *Cambodia* 64 F4
Anglès, *Spain* 32 D7
Anglesey, Isle of □, *U.K.* 12 D3
Anglet, *France* 20 E2
Anglin →, *France* 20 B4
Anglisidhes, *Cyprus* 36 E12
Anglure, *France* 19 D10
Angmagssalik = Tasiilaq, *Greenland* 4 C6
Ango, *Dem. Rep. of the Congo* 86 B2
Angoche, *Mozam.* 87 F4
Angoche, I., *Mozam.* 87 F4
Angol, *Chile* 126 D1
Angola, *Ind., U.S.A.* 108 E3
Angola, *N.Y., U.S.A.* 110 D5
Angola ■, *Africa* 85 G3
Angoulême, *France* 20 C4
Angoumois, *France* 20 C4
Angra dos Reis, *Brazil* 127 A7
Angren, *Uzbekistan* 50 E8
Angtassom, *Cambodia* 65 G5
Angu, *Dem. Rep. of the Congo* 86 B1
Anguang, *China* 57 B12
Anguilla ■, *W. Indies* 121 C7
Anguo, *China* 56 E8
Angurugu, *Australia* 94 A2
Angus □, *U.K.* 14 E6
Angwa →, *Zimbabwe* 89 B5
Anhanduí →, *Brazil* 127 A5
Anholt, *Denmark* 11 H5
Anhua, *China* 59 C8
Anhui □, *China* 59 B11
Anhwei = Anhui □, *China* 59 B11
Anichab, *Namibia* 88 C1
Ánidhros, *Greece* 39 E7
Anié, *Togo* 83 D5
Animas →, *U.S.A.* 115 H9
Anina, *Romania* 42 E6
Aninoasa, *Romania* 43 F9
Anivorano, *Madag.* 89 B8
Anjalankoski, *Finland* 9 F22
Anjar, *India* 68 H4
Anji, *China* 59 B12
Anjou, *France* 18 E6
Anjozorobe, *Madag.* 89 B8
Anju, *N. Korea* 57 E13
Anka, *Nigeria* 83 C6
Ankaboa, Tanjona, *Madag.* 89 C7
Ankang, *China* 56 H5
Ankara, *Turkey* 72 C5
Ankaramena, *Madag.* 89 C8
Ankaratra, *Madag.* 85 H9
Ankarsrum, *Sweden* 11 G10
Ankasakasa, *Madag.* 89 B7
Ankavandra, *Madag.* 89 B8
Ankazoabo, *Madag.* 89 C7
Ankazobe, *Madag.* 89 B8
Ankeny, *U.S.A.* 112 E8
Ankilimalinika, *Madag.* 89 C7
Ankilizato, *Madag.* 89 C8
Ankisabe, *Madag.* 89 B8
Anklam, *Germany* 24 B9
Ankober, *Ethiopia* 81 F4
Ankoro, *Dem. Rep. of the Congo* 86 D2
Ankororoka, *Madag.* 89 D8
Anlong, *China* 58 E5
Anlu, *China* 59 B9
Anmyŏn-do, *S. Korea* 57 F14
Ånn, *Sweden* 10 A6
Ann, C., *U.S.A.* 111 D14
Ann Arbor, *U.S.A.* 108 D4
Anna, *Russia* 48 E5
Anna, *U.S.A.* 113 G10
Annaba, *Algeria* 78 A7
Annaberg-Buchholz, *Germany* 24 E9
Annalee →, *Ireland* 15 B4
Annam, *Vietnam* 64 E7
Annamitique, Chaîne, *Asia* 64 D6
Annan, *U.K.* 14 G5
Annan →, *U.K.* 14 G5
Annapolis, *U.S.A.* 108 F7
Annapolis Royal, *Canada* 103 D6
Annapurna, *Nepal* 69 E10
Annean, L., *Australia* 93 E2
Anneberg, *Sweden* 11 G8
Annecy, *France* 21 C10
Annecy, Lac d', *France* 21 C10
Annemasse, *France* 19 F13
Annenskiy Most, *Russia* 46 B9
Anning, *China* 58 E4
Anniston, *U.S.A.* 109 J3
Annobón, *Atl. Oc.* 77 G4
Annonay, *France* 21 C8
Annot, *France* 21 E10
Annotto Bay, *Jamaica* 120 C4
Ånnsjön, *Sweden* 10 A6
Annville, *U.S.A.* 111 F8
Annweiler, *Germany* 25 F3
Áno Arkhánai, *Greece* 39 F7
Áno Porróia, *Greece* 40 E7
Áno Síros, *Greece* 38 D6
Áno Viánnos, *Greece* 36 D7
Anorotsangana, *Madag.* 89 A8
Anosibe, *Madag.* 89 B8
Anou Mellene, *Mali* 83 B5
Anoumaba, *Ivory C.* 82 D4
Anóyia, *Greece* 36 D6
Anping, *Hebei, China* 56 E8
Anping, *Liaoning, China* 57 D12
Anpu Gang, *China* 58 G7
Anqing, *China* 59 B11
Anqiu, *China* 57 F10
Anren, *China* 59 D9
Ansager, *Denmark* 11 J2
Ansai, *China* 56 F5
Ansbach, *Germany* 25 F6
Anseba →, *Eritrea* 81 D4
Ansfelden, *Austria* 26 C7
Anshan, *China* 57 D12
Anshun, *China* 58 D5
Ansião, *Portugal* 34 F2
Ansley, *U.S.A.* 112 E5
Ansó, *Spain* 32 C4
Ansoain, *Spain* 32 C3
Anson, *U.S.A.* 113 J5
Anson B., *Australia* 92 B5
Ansongo, *Mali* 83 B5
Ansonia, *U.S.A.* 111 E11
Anstruther, *U.K.* 14 E6
Ansudu, *Indonesia* 63 E9
Antabamba, *Peru* 124 F4
Antakya, *Turkey* 70 B3
Antalaha, *Madag.* 89 A9
Antalya, *Turkey* 72 D4
Antalya □, *Turkey* 39 E12
Antalya Körfezi, *Turkey* 72 D4
Antambohobe, *Madag.* 89 C8
Antanambao-Manampotsy, *Madag.* 89 B8
Antanambe, *Madag.* 89 B8
Antananarivo, *Madag.* 89 B8
Antananarivo □, *Madag.* 89 B8
Antanifotsy, *Madag.* 89 B8
Antanimbaribe, *Madag.* 89 C7
Antanimora, *Madag.* 89 C8
Antarctic Pen., *Antarctica* 5 C18
Antarctica 5 E3
Antelope, *Zimbabwe* 87 G2
Antequera, *Paraguay* 126 A4
Antequera, *Spain* 35 H6
Antero, Mt., *U.S.A.* 115 G10
Antevamena, *Madag.* 89 C7
Anthemoús, *Greece* 40 F7
Anthony, *Kans., U.S.A.* 113 G5
Anthony, *N. Mex., U.S.A.* 115 K10
Anti Atlas, *Morocco* 78 C4
Anti-Lebanon = Ash Sharqi, Al Jabal, *Lebanon* 75 B5
Antibes, *France* 21 E11
Antibes, C. d', *France* 21 E11
Anticosti, Î. d', *Canada* 103 C7
Antifer, C. d', *France* 18 C7
Antigo, *U.S.A.* 112 C10
Antigonish, *Canada* 103 C7
Antigua, *Canary Is.* 37 F5
Antigua, *W. Indies* 121 C7
Antigua & Barbuda ■, *W. Indies* 121 C7
Antigua Guatemala, *Guatemala* 120 D1
Antilla, *Cuba* 120 B4
Antilles = West Indies, *Cent. Amer.* 121 D7
Antioch, *U.S.A.* 116 G5
Antioche, Pertuis d', *France* 20 B2
Antioquia, *Colombia* 124 B3
Antipodes Is., *Pac. Oc.* 96 M9
Antlers, *U.S.A.* 113 H7
Antoetra, *Madag.* 89 C8
Antofagasta, *Chile* 126 A1
Antofagasta □, *Chile* 126 A2
Antofagasta de la Sierra, *Argentina* 126 B2
Antofalla, *Argentina* 126 B2
Antofalla, Salar de, *Argentina* 126 B2
Anton, *U.S.A.* 113 J3
Antongila, Helodrano, *Madag.* 89 B8
Antonibé, *Madag.* 89 B8
Antonibé, Presqu'île d', *Madag.* 89 A8
Antonina, *Brazil* 127 B6
Antrain, *France* 18 D5
Antrim, *U.K.* 15 B5
Antrim, *U.S.A.* 110 F3
Antrim □, *U.K.* 15 B5
Antrim, Mts. of, *U.K.* 15 A5
Antrim Plateau, *Australia* 92 C4
Antrodoco, *Italy* 29 F10
Antropovo, *Russia* 48 A6
Antsakabary, *Madag.* 89 B8
Antsalova, *Madag.* 89 B7
Antsenavolo, *Madag.* 89 C8
Antsiafabositra, *Madag.* 89 B8
Antsirabe, *Antananarivo, Madag.* 89 B8
Antsirabe, *Antsiranana, Madag.* 89 A8
Antsirabe, *Mahajanga, Madag.* 89 B8
Antsiranana, *Madag.* 89 A8
Antsiranana □, *Madag.* 89 A8
Antsohihy, *Madag.* 89 A8
Antsohimbondrona Seranana, *Madag.* 89 A8
Antu, *China* 57 C15
Antwerp = Antwerpen, *Belgium* 17 C4
Antwerp, *U.S.A.* 111 B9
Antwerpen, *Belgium* 17 C4
Antwerpen □, *Belgium* 17 C4
Anupgarh, *India* 68 E5
Anuppur, *India* 69 H9
Anuradhapura, *Sri Lanka* 66 Q12
Anveh, *Iran* 71 E7
Anvers = Antwerpen, *Belgium* 17 C4
Anvers I., *Antarctica* 5 C17
Anwen, *China* 59 C13
Anxi, *Fujian, China* 59 E12
Anxi, *Gansu, China* 60 B4
Anxian, *China* 58 B5
Anxiang, *China* 59 C9
Anxious B., *Australia* 95 E1
Anyama, *Ivory C.* 82 D4
Anyang, *China* 56 F8
Anyer-Kidul, *Indonesia* 63 G11
Anyi, *Jiangxi, China* 59 C10
Anyi, *Shanxi, China* 56 G6
Anyuan, *China* 59 E10
Anyue, *China* 58 B5
Anza, *U.S.A.* 117 M10
Anze, *China* 56 F7
Anzhero-Sudzhensk, *Russia* 50 D9
Ánzio, *Italy* 30 A5
Aoga-Shima, *Japan* 55 H9
Aoiz, *Spain* 32 C3
Aomen = Macau □, *China* 59 F9
Aomori, *Japan* 54 D10
Aomori □, *Japan* 54 D10
Aonla, *India* 69 E8
Aoraki Mount Cook, *N.Z.* 91 K3
Aosta, *Italy* 28 C4
Aoudéras, *Niger* 83 B6
Aoukâr, *Mauritania* 82 B3
Apa →, *S. Amer.* 126 A4
Apache, *U.S.A.* 113 H5
Apache Junction, *U.S.A.* 115 K8
Apalachee B., *U.S.A.* 109 L4
Apalachicola, *U.S.A.* 109 L3
Apalachicola →, *U.S.A.* 109 L3
Apam, *Ghana* 83 D4
Apapa, *Nigeria* 83 D5
Apaporis →, *Colombia* 124 D5
Aparri, *Phil.* 61 B4
Apateu, *Romania* 42 D6
Apatin, *Serbia, Yug.* 42 E4
Apatity, *Russia* 50 C4
Apatzingán, *Mexico* 118 D4
Apeldoorn, *Neths.* 17 B5
Apen, *Germany* 24 B3
Apennines = Appennini, *Italy* 28 E7
Aphrodisias, *Turkey* 39 D10
Apia, *Samoa* 91 A13
Apiacás, Serra dos, *Brazil* 124 E7
Apies →, *S. Africa* 89 D4
Apizaco, *Mexico* 119 D5
Aplao, *Peru* 124 G4
Apo, Mt., *Phil.* 63 C7
Apolakkiá, *Greece* 36 C9
Apolakkiá, Órmos, *Greece* 36 C9
Apolda, *Germany* 24 D7
Apollonia, *Greece* 38 E6
Apolo, *Bolivia* 124 F5
Aporé →, *Brazil* 125 G8
Apostle Is., *U.S.A.* 112 B9
Apóstoles, *Argentina* 127 B4
Apostolos Andreas, C., *Cyprus* 36 D13
Apostolovo, *Ukraine* 47 J7
Apoteri, *Guyana* 124 C7
Appalachian Mts., *U.S.A.* 108 G6
Äppelbo, *Sweden* 10 D8
Appennini, *Italy* 28 E7
Appennino Ligure, *Italy* 28 D6
Appenzell-Ausser Rhoden □, *Switz.* 25 H5
Appenzell-Inner Rhoden □, *Switz.* 25 H5
Appiano, *Italy* 29 B8
Apple Hill, *Canada* 111 A10
Apple Valley, *U.S.A.* 117 L9
Appleby-in-Westmorland, *U.K.* 12 C5
Appleton, *U.S.A.* 108 C1
Approuague →, *Fr. Guiana* 125 C8
Apricena, *Italy* 29 G12
Aprília, *Italy* 30 A5
Apsheronsk, *Russia* 49 H4
Apsley, *Canada* 110 B6
Apt, *France* 21 E9
Apuane, Alpi, *Italy* 28 D7
Apucarana, *Brazil* 127 A5
Apulia = Púglia □, *Italy* 31 A9
Apure →, *Venezuela* 124 B5
Apurimac →, *Peru* 124 F4
Apuseni, Munţii, *Romania* 42 D7
Āqā Jarī, *Iran* 71 D6
Aqaba = Al 'Aqabah, *Jordan* 75 F4
Aqaba, G. of, *Red Sea* 70 D2
'Aqabah, Khalīj al = Aqaba, G. of, *Red Sea* 70 D2
'Aqdā, *Iran* 71 C7
Aqîq, *Sudan* 80 D4
Aqîq, Khalîg, *Sudan* 80 D4
Aqmola = Astana, *Kazakstan* 50 D8
'Aqrah, *Iraq* 70 B4
Aqtaū, *Kazakstan* 50 E6
Aqtöbe, *Kazakstan* 50 D6
Aquidauana, *Brazil* 125 H7
Aquiles Serdán, *Mexico* 118 B3
Aquin, *Haiti* 121 C5
Aquitaine □, *France* 20 D3
Aqviligjuaq = Pelly Bay, *Canada* 101 B11
Ar Rachidiya = Er Rachidia, *Morocco* 78 B5
Ar Rafīd, *Syria* 75 C4
Ar Raḩḩālīyah, *Iraq* 70 C4
Ar Ramādī, *Iraq* 70 C4
Ar Ramthā, *Jordan* 75 C5
Ar Raqqah, *Syria* 70 C3
Ar Rass, *Si. Arabia* 70 E4
Ar Rawshān, *Si. Arabia* 80 C5
Ar Rifā'ī, *Iraq* 70 D5
Ar Riyāḑ, *Si. Arabia* 70 E5
Ar Ru'ays, *Qatar* 71 E6
Ar Rukhaymīyah, *Iraq* 70 D5
Ar Ruşāfah, *Syria* 70 C3
Ar Ruţbah, *Iraq* 70 C4
Ara, *India* 69 G11
Ara Goro, *Ethiopia* 81 F5
Ara Tera, *Ethiopia* 81 F5
Arab, *U.S.A.* 109 H2
'Arab, Bahr el →, *Sudan* 81 F2
Arab, Khalîg el, *Egypt* 80 A2
Arab, Shatt al →, *Asia* 71 D6
'Araba, W. →, *Egypt* 80 J8
'Arabābād, *Iran* 71 C8
Araban, *Turkey* 72 D7
Arabatskaya Strelka, *Ukraine* 47 K8
Arabba, *Italy* 29 B8
Arabia, *Asia* 52 G8
Arabian Desert = Es Sahrā' Esh Sharqîya, *Egypt* 80 B3
Arabian Gulf = Gulf, The, *Asia* 71 E6
Arabian Sea, *Ind. Oc.* 52 H10
Araç, *Turkey* 72 B5
Aracaju, *Brazil* 125 F11
Aracati, *Brazil* 125 D11
Araçatuba, *Brazil* 127 A5
Aracena, *Spain* 35 H4
Aracena, Sierra de, *Spain* 35 H4
Aračinovo, *Macedonia* 40 D5
Araçuaí, *Brazil* 125 G10
'Arad, *Israel* 75 D4
Arad, *Romania* 42 D6
Arad □, *Romania* 42 D6
Arādān, *Iran* 71 C7
Aradhippou, *Cyprus* 36 E12
Arafura Sea, *E. Indies* 52 K17
Aragats, *Armenia* 49 K7
Aragón □, *Spain* 32 D4
Aragón →, *Spain* 32 C3
Aragona, *Italy* 30 E6

Araguacema, *Brazil* 125 E9
Araguaia →, *Brazil* 122 D6
Araguaína, *Brazil* 125 E9
Araguari, *Brazil* 125 G9
Araguari →, *Brazil* 125 C9
Arain, *India* 68 F6
Arak, *Algeria* 78 C6
Arāk, *Iran* 71 C6
Araka, *Sudan* 81 G3
Arakan Coast, *Burma* 67 K19
Arakan Yoma, *Burma* 67 K19
Arákhova, *Greece* 38 C4
Arakli, *Turkey* 73 B8
Araks = Aras, Rūd-e →, *Asia* 49 K9
Aral, *Kazakstan* 50 E7
Aral Sea, *Asia* 50 E7
Aral Tengizi = Aral Sea, *Asia* 50 E7
Aralsk = Aral, *Kazakstan* 50 E7
Aralskoye More = Aral Sea, *Asia* 50 E7
Aralsor, Ozero, *Kazakstan* 49 F9
Aramac, *Australia* 94 C4
Aran I., *Ireland* 15 A3
Aran Is., *Ireland* 15 C2
Aranda de Duero, *Spain* 34 D7
Arandān, *Iran* 70 C5
Aranđelovac, *Serbia, Yug.* 40 B4
Aranjuez, *Spain* 34 E7
Aranos, *Namibia* 88 C2
Aransas Pass, *U.S.A.* 113 M6
Aranyaprathet, *Thailand* 64 F4
Araouane, *Mali* 82 B4
Arapahoe, *U.S.A.* 112 E5
Arapey Grande →, *Uruguay* 126 C4
Arapgir, *Turkey* 70 B3
Arapiraca, *Brazil* 125 E11
Arapongas, *Brazil* 127 A5
Ar'ar, *Si. Arabia* 70 D4
Araranguá, *Brazil* 127 B6
Araraquara, *Brazil* 125 H9
Ararás, Serra das, *Brazil* 127 B5
Ararat, *Armenia* 73 C11
Ararat, *Australia* 95 F3
Ararat, Mt. = Ağrı Dağı, *Turkey* 70 B5
Araria, *India* 69 F12
Araripe, Chapada do, *Brazil* 125 E11
Araruama, L. de, *Brazil* 127 A7
Aras, Rūd-e →, *Asia* 49 K9
Aratâne, *Mauritania* 82 B3
Arauca, *Colombia* 124 B4
Arauca →, *Venezuela* 124 B5
Arauco, *Chile* 126 D1
Arawa, *Ethiopia* 81 F5
Araxá, *Brazil* 125 G9
Araya, Pen. de, *Venezuela* 124 A6
Arba Gugu, *Ethiopia* 81 F5
Arba Minch, *Ethiopia* 81 F4
Arbat, *Iraq* 70 C5
Árbatax, *Italy* 30 C2
Arbi, *Ethiopia* 81 F4
Arbīl, *Iraq* 70 B5
Arboga, *Sweden* 10 E9
Arbois, *France* 19 F12
Arbore, *Ethiopia* 81 F4
Arboréa, *Italy* 30 C1
Arborfield, *Canada* 105 C8
Arborg, *Canada* 105 C9
Arbre du Ténéré, *Niger* 83 B7
Arbroath, *U.K.* 14 E6
Arbuckle, *U.S.A.* 116 F4
Arbus, *Italy* 30 C1
Arc →, *France* 21 C10
Arc-lès-Gray, *France* 19 E12
Arcachon, *France* 20 D2
Arcachon, Bassin d', *France* 20 D2
Arcade, *Calif., U.S.A.* 117 L8
Arcade, *N.Y., U.S.A.* 110 D6
Arcadia, *Fla., U.S.A.* 109 M5
Arcadia, *La., U.S.A.* 113 J8
Arcadia, *Pa., U.S.A.* 110 F6
Arcata, *U.S.A.* 114 F1
Arcévia, *Italy* 29 E9
Archangel = Arkhangelsk, *Russia* 50 C5
Archar, *Bulgaria* 40 C6
Archbald, *U.S.A.* 111 E9
Archena, *Spain* 33 G3
Archer →, *Australia* 94 A3
Archer B., *Australia* 94 A3
Archers Post, *Kenya* 86 B4
Arches National Park, *U.S.A.* 115 G9
Archidona, *Spain* 35 H6
Arci, Mte., *Italy* 30 C1
Arcidosso, *Italy* 29 F8
Arcis-sur-Aube, *France* 19 D11
Arckaringa Cr. →, *Australia* 95 D2
Arco, *Italy* 28 C7
Arco, *U.S.A.* 114 E7
Arcos = Arcos de Jalón, *Spain* 32 D2
Arcos de Jalón, *Spain* 32 D2
Arcos de la Frontera, *Spain* 35 J5
Arcos de Valdevez, *Portugal* 34 D2
Arcot, *India* 66 N11
Arcozelo, *Portugal* 34 E3
Arctic Bay, *Canada* 101 A11
Arctic Ocean, *Arctic* 4 B18
Arctic Red River = Tsiigehtchic, *Canada* 100 B6
Arda →, *Bulgaria* 41 E10
Arda →, *Italy* 28 C7
Ardabīl, *Iran* 71 B6
Ardahan, *Turkey* 73 B10
Ardakān = Sepīdān, *Iran* 71 D7
Ardakān, *Iran* 71 C7
Ardala, *Sweden* 11 F7
Ardales, *Spain* 35 J6
Ardèche □, *France* 21 D8
Ardèche →, *France* 21 D8
Ardee, *Ireland* 15 C5
Arden, *Canada* 110 B8
Arden, *Denmark* 11 H3
Arden, *Calif., U.S.A.* 116 G5
Arden, *Nev., U.S.A.* 117 J11
Ardenne, *Belgium* 6 F7
Ardennes = Ardenne, *Belgium* 6 F7
Ardennes □, *France* 19 C11
Ardentes, *France* 19 F8
Arderin, *Ireland* 15 C4
Ardeşen, *Turkey* 73 B9
Ardestān, *Iran* 71 C7
Árdhas →, *Greece* 41 E10
Ardhéa, *Greece* 40 F6
Ardila →, *Portugal* 35 G3
Ardino, *Bulgaria* 41 E9
Ardivachar Pt., *U.K.* 14 D1
Ardlethan, *Australia* 95 E4
Ardmore, *Okla., U.S.A.* 113 H6
Ardmore, *Pa., U.S.A.* 111 G9
Ardnamurchan, Pt. of, *U.K.* 14 E2
Ardnave Pt., *U.K.* 14 F2
Ardon, *Russia* 49 J7
Ardore, *Italy* 31 D9
Ardres, *France* 19 B8
Ardrossan, *Australia* 95 E2
Ardrossan, *U.K.* 14 F4
Ards Pen., *U.K.* 15 B6
Arduan, *Sudan* 80 D3
Ardud, *Romania* 42 C7
Åre, *Sweden* 10 A7
Arecibo, *Puerto Rico* 121 C6
Areia Branca, *Brazil* 125 E11
Arena, Pt., *U.S.A.* 116 G3
Arenal, *Honduras* 120 C2
Arenas = Las Arenas, *Spain* 34 B6
Arenas de San Pedro, *Spain* 34 E5
Arendal, *Norway* 9 G13
Arendsee, *Germany* 24 C7
Arenys de Mar, *Spain* 32 D7
Arenzano, *Italy* 28 D5
Areópolis, *Greece* 38 E4
Arequipa, *Peru* 124 G4
Arero, *Ethiopia* 81 G4
Arès, *France* 20 D2
Arévalo, *Spain* 34 D6
Arezzo, *Italy* 29 E8
Arga, *Turkey* 70 B3
Arga →, *Spain* 32 C3
Argalastí, *Greece* 38 B5
Argamasilla de Alba, *Spain* 35 F7
Argamasilla de Calatrava, *Spain* 35 G6
Arganda, *Spain* 34 E7
Arganil, *Portugal* 34 E2
Argedeb, *Ethiopia* 81 F5
Argelès-Gazost, *France* 20 E3
Argelès-sur-Mer, *France* 20 F7
Argens →, *France* 21 E10
Argent-sur-Sauldre, *France* 19 E9
Argenta, *Canada* 104 C5
Argenta, *Italy* 29 D8
Argentan, *France* 18 D6
Argentário, Mte., *Italy* 29 F8
Argentat, *France* 20 C5
Argentera, *Italy* 28 D4
Argenteuil, *France* 19 D9
Argentia, *Canada* 103 C9
Argentiera, C. dell', *Italy* 30 B1
Argentina ■, *S. Amer.* 128 D3
Argentina Is., *Antarctica* 5 C17
Argentino, L., *Argentina* 128 G2
Argenton-Château, *France* 18 F6
Argenton-sur-Creuse, *France* 19 F8
Argeş □, *Romania* 43 F9
Argeş →, *Romania* 43 F11
Arghandab →, *Afghan.* 68 D1
Argheile, *Ethiopia* 81 F5
Argo, *Sudan* 80 D3
Argolikós Kólpos, *Greece* 38 D4
Argolís □, *Greece* 38 D4
Argonne, *France* 19 C12
Árgos, *Greece* 38 D4
Árgos Orestikón, *Greece* 40 F5
Argostólion, *Greece* 38 C2
Arguedas, *Spain* 32 C3
Arguello, Pt., *U.S.A.* 117 L6
Arguineguín, *Canary Is.* 37 G4
Argun, *Russia* 49 J7
Argun →, *Russia* 51 D13
Argungu, *Nigeria* 83 C5
Argus Pk., *U.S.A.* 117 K9
Argyle, L., *Australia* 92 C4
Argyll & Bute □, *U.K.* 14 E3
Arhavi, *Turkey* 73 B9
Århus, *Denmark* 11 H4
Århus Amtskommune □, *Denmark* 11 H4
Ariadnoye, *Russia* 54 B7
Ariamsvlei, *Namibia* 88 D2
Ariano Irpino, *Italy* 31 A8
Aribinda, *Burkina Faso* 83 C4
Arica, *Chile* 124 G4
Arica, *Colombia* 124 D4
Arico, *Canary Is.* 37 F3
Arid, C., *Australia* 93 F3
Arida, *Japan* 55 G7
Ariège □, *France* 20 F5
Ariège →, *France* 20 E5
Arieş →, *Romania* 43 D8
Arihā, *Israel* 80 A4
Arilje, *Serbia, Yug.* 40 C4
Arílla, Ákra, *Greece* 36 A3
Arima, *Trin. & Tob.* 121 D7
Arinos →, *Brazil* 122 E5
Ario de Rosales, *Mexico* 118 D4
Ariogala, *Lithuania* 44 C10
Aripuanã, *Brazil* 124 E6
Aripuanã →, *Brazil* 122 D4
Ariquemes, *Brazil* 124 E6
Arisaig, *U.K.* 14 E3
Arîsh, W. el →, *Egypt* 80 A3
Arissa, *Ethiopia* 81 E5
Aristazabal I., *Canada* 104 C3
Arivonimamo, *Madag.* 89 B8
Ariza, *Spain* 32 D2
Arizaro, Salar de, *Argentina* 126 A2
Arizona, *Argentina* 126 D2
Arizona □, *U.S.A.* 115 J8
Arizpe, *Mexico* 118 A2
Årjäng, *Sweden* 10 E6
Arjeplog, *Sweden* 8 D18
Arjona, *Colombia* 124 A3
Arjona, *Spain* 35 H6
Arjuna, *Indonesia* 63 G15
Arka, *Russia* 51 C15
Arkadak, *Russia* 48 E6
Arkadelphia, *U.S.A.* 113 H8
Arkadhía □, *Greece* 38 D4
Arkaig, L., *U.K.* 14 E3
Arkalyk = Arqalyk, *Kazakstan* 50 D7
Arkansas □, *U.S.A.* 113 H8
Arkansas →, *U.S.A.* 113 J9
Arkansas City, *U.S.A.* 113 G6
Arkaroola, *Australia* 95 E2
Árkathos →, *Greece* 38 B3
Arkhángelos, *Greece* 36 C10
Arkhangelsk, *Russia* 50 C5
Arkhangelskoye, *Russia* 48 E5
Arki, *India* 68 D7
Arkiko, *Eritrea* 81 D4
Arklow, *Ireland* 15 D5
Árkoi, *Greece* 39 D8
Arkona, Kap, *Germany* 24 A9
Arkösund, *Sweden* 11 F10
Arkoúdhi, *Greece* 38 C2
Arkport, *U.S.A.* 110 D7
Arkticheskiy, Mys, *Russia* 51 A10
Arkul, *Russia* 48 B10
Arkville, *U.S.A.* 111 D10
Ärla, *Sweden* 10 E10
Arlanza →, *Spain* 34 C6
Arlanzón →, *Spain* 34 C6
Arlbergpass, *Austria* 26 D3
Arles, *France* 21 E8
Arlington, *S. Africa* 89 D4
Arlington, *N.Y., U.S.A.* 111 E11
Arlington, *Oreg., U.S.A.* 114 D3
Arlington, *S. Dak., U.S.A.* 112 C6
Arlington, *Tex., U.S.A.* 113 J6
Arlington, *Va., U.S.A.* 108 F7
Arlington, *Vt., U.S.A.* 111 C11
Arlington, *Wash., U.S.A.* 116 B4
Arlington Heights, *U.S.A.* 108 D2
Arlit, *Niger* 78 E7
Arlon, *Belgium* 17 E5
Arltunga, *Australia* 94 C1
Arly, *Burkina Faso* 83 C5
Armagh, *U.K.* 15 B5
Armagh □, *U.K.* 15 B5
Armagnac, *France* 20 E4
Armançon →, *France* 19 E10
Armavir, *Russia* 49 H5
Armenia, *Colombia* 124 C3
Armenia ■, *Asia* 49 K7
Armeniş, *Romania* 42 E7
Armenistís, Ákra, *Greece* 36 C9
Armentières, *France* 19 B9
Armidale, *Australia* 95 E5
Armilla, *Spain* 35 H7
Armour, *U.S.A.* 112 D5
Armstrong, *B.C., Canada* 104 C5
Armstrong, *Ont., Canada* 102 B2
Armutlu, *Bursa, Turkey* 41 F12
Armutlu, *İzmir, Turkey* 39 C9
Arnaía, *Greece* 40 F7
Arnarfjörður, *Iceland* 8 D2
Arnaud →, *Canada* 101 B12
Arnauti, C., *Cyprus* 36 D11
Arnay-le-Duc, *France* 19 E11
Arnedillo, *Spain* 32 C2
Arnedo, *Spain* 32 C2
Arnett, *U.S.A.* 113 G5
Arnhem, *Neths.* 17 C5
Arnhem, C., *Australia* 94 A2
Arnhem B., *Australia* 94 A2
Arnhem Land, *Australia* 94 A1
Árnissa, *Greece* 40 F5
Arno →, *Italy* 28 E7
Arno Bay, *Australia* 95 E2
Arnold, *U.K.* 12 D6
Arnold, *U.S.A.* 116 G6
Arnoldstein, *Austria* 26 E6
Arnon →, *France* 19 E9
Arnot, *Canada* 105 B9
Arnøy, *Norway* 8 A19
Arnprior, *Canada* 102 C4
Arnsberg, *Germany* 24 D4
Arnstadt, *Germany* 24 E6
Aroab, *Namibia* 88 D2
Aroánia Óri, *Greece* 38 D4
Aroche, *Spain* 35 H4
Arochuku, *Nigeria* 83 D6
Arolsen, *Germany* 24 D5
Aron, *India* 68 G6
Aron →, *France* 19 F10
Arona, *Italy* 28 C5
Aroroy, *Phil.* 61 E5
Arosa, Ría de, *Spain* 34 C2
Arpajon, *France* 19 D9
Arpajon-sur-Cère, *France* 20 D6
Arpaşu de Jos, *Romania* 43 E9
Arqalyk, *Kazakstan* 50 D7
Arrah = Ara, *India* 69 G11
Arrah, *Ivory C.* 82 D4
Arraiolos, *Portugal* 35 G3
Arran, *U.K.* 14 F3
Arras, *France* 19 B9
Arrasate, *Spain* 32 B2
Arrats →, *France* 20 D4
Arreau, *France* 20 F4
Arrecife, *Canary Is.* 37 F6
Arrecifes, *Argentina* 126 C3
Arrée, Mts. d', *France* 18 D3
Arresø, *Denmark* 11 J6
Arriaga, *Chiapas, Mexico* 119 D6
Arriaga, *San Luis Potosí, Mexico* 118 C4
Arrilalah, *Australia* 94 C3
Arrino, *Australia* 93 E2
Arriondas, *Spain* 34 B5
Arromanches-les-Bains, *France* 18 C6
Arronches, *Portugal* 35 F3
Arros →, *France* 20 E3
Arrow, L., *Ireland* 15 B3
Arrowhead, L., *U.S.A.* 117 L9
Arrowtown, *N.Z.* 91 L2
Arroyo de la Luz, *Spain* 35 F4
Arroyo Grande, *U.S.A.* 117 K6
Ars, *Denmark* 11 H3
Ars, *Iran* 70 B5
Ars-sur-Moselle, *France* 19 C13
Arsenault L., *Canada* 105 B7
Arsenev, *Russia* 54 B6
Arsi □, *Ethiopia* 81 F4
Arsiero, *Italy* 29 C8
Arsin, *Turkey* 73 B8
Arsk, *Russia* 48 B9
Arsunda, *Sweden* 10 D10
Árta, *Greece* 38 B3
Artà, *Spain* 37 B10
Árta □, *Greece* 38 B3
Arteaga, *Mexico* 118 D4
Arteche, *Phil.* 61 E6
Arteijo = Arteixo, *Spain* 34 B2
Arteixo, *Spain* 34 B2
Artem = Artyom, *Azerbaijan* 49 K10
Artem, *Russia* 54 C6
Artemovsk, *Russia* 51 D10
Artemovsk, *Ukraine* 47 H9
Artemovskiy, *Russia* 49 G5
Artenay, *France* 19 D8
Artern, *Germany* 24 D7
Artesa de Segre, *Spain* 32 D6
Artesia = Mosomane, *Botswana* 88 C4
Artesia, *U.S.A.* 113 J2
Arthington, *Liberia* 82 D2
Arthur, *Canada* 110 C4
Arthur →, *Australia* 94 G3
Arthur Cr. →, *Australia* 94 C2
Arthur Pt., *Australia* 94 C5
Arthur River, *Australia* 93 F2
Arthur's Pass, *N.Z.* 91 K3
Arthur's Town, *Bahamas* 121 B4
Artigas, *Uruguay* 126 C4
Artik, *Armenia* 49 K6
Artillery L., *Canada* 105 A7
Artois, *France* 19 B9
Artotína, *Greece* 38 C4
Artrutx, C. de, *Spain* 37 B10
Artsyz, *Ukraine* 47 J5
Artvin, *Turkey* 73 B9
Artyom, *Azerbaijan* 49 K10
Aru, Kepulauan, *Indonesia* 63 F8
Aru Is. = Aru, Kepulauan, *Indonesia* 63 F8
Arua, *Uganda* 86 B3
Aruanã, *Brazil* 125 F8
Aruba ■, *W. Indies* 121 D6
Arucas, *Canary Is.* 37 F4
Arudy, *France* 20 E3
Arun →, *Nepal* 69 F12
Arun →, *U.K.* 13 G7
Arunachal Pradesh □, *India* 67 F19
Arusha, *Tanzania* 86 C4
Arusha □, *Tanzania* 86 C4
Arusha Chini, *Tanzania* 86 C4
Aruwimi →, *Dem. Rep. of the Congo* 86 B1
Arvada, *Colo., U.S.A.* 112 F2
Arvada, *Wyo., U.S.A.* 114 D10
Arve →, *France* 19 F13
Árvi, *Greece* 36 E7
Arviat, *Canada* 105 A10
Arvidsjaur, *Sweden* 8 D18
Arvika, *Sweden* 10 E6
Arvin, *U.S.A.* 117 K8
Arwal, *India* 69 G11
Arxan, *China* 60 B6
Äryd, *Sweden* 11 H8
Aryirádhes, *Greece* 36 B3
Aryiroúpolis, *Greece* 36 D6
Arys, *Kazakstan* 50 E7
Arzachena, *Italy* 30 A2
Arzamas, *Russia* 48 C6
Arzgir, *Russia* 49 H7
Arzignano, *Italy* 29 C8
Arzúa, *Spain* 34 C2
Aš, *Czech Rep.* 26 A5
Ås, *Sweden* 10 A8
As Pontes de García Rodríguez, *Spain* 34 B3
Aş Şafā, *Syria* 75 B6
As Saffānīyah, *Si. Arabia* 71 E6
As Safīrah, *Syria* 70 B3
Aş Şahm, *Oman* 71 E8
As Sājir, *Si. Arabia* 70 E5
As Salamīyah, *Syria* 70 C3
As Salmān, *Iraq* 70 D5
As Salt, *Jordan* 75 C4
As Sal'w'a, *Qatar* 71 E6
As Samāwah, *Iraq* 70 D5
As Sanamayn, *Syria* 75 B5
As Sohar = Şuḩār, *Oman* 71 E8
As Sukhnah, *Syria* 70 C3
As Sulaymānīyah, *Iraq* 70 C5
As Sulaymī, *Si. Arabia* 70 E4
As Sulayyil, *Si. Arabia* 74 C4
As Summān, *Si. Arabia* 70 E5
As Suwaydā', *Syria* 75 C5
As Suwaydā' □, *Syria* 75 C5
As Suwayq, *Oman* 71 F8
As Şuwayrah, *Iraq* 70 C5
Åsa, *Sweden* 11 G6
Asab, *Namibia* 88 D2
Asaba, *Nigeria* 83 D6
Asad, Buḩayrat al, *Syria* 70 C3
Asadābād, *Iran* 73 E13
Asafo, *Ghana* 82 D4
Asahi-Gawa →, *Japan* 55 G6
Asahigawa, *Japan* 54 C11
Asale, L., *Ethiopia* 81 E5
Asamankese, *Ghana* 83 D4
Asan →, *India* 69 F8
Asansol, *India* 69 H12
Åsarna, *Sweden* 10 B8
Asayita, *Ethiopia* 81 E5
Asbe Teferi, *Ethiopia* 81 F5
Asbesberge, *S. Africa* 88 D3
Asbestos, *Canada* 103 C5
Asbury Park, *U.S.A.* 111 F10
Ascea, *Italy* 31 B8
Ascensión, *Mexico* 118 A3
Ascensión, B. de la, *Mexico* 119 D7
Ascension I., *Atl. Oc.* 77 G2
Aschach an der Donau, *Austria* 26 C7
Aschaffenburg, *Germany* 25 F5
Aschendorf, *Germany* 24 B3
Aschersleben, *Germany* 24 D7
Asciano, *Italy* 29 E8
Áscoli Piceno, *Italy* 29 F10
Áscoli Satriano, *Italy* 31 A8
Ascope, *Peru* 124 E3
Ascotán, *Chile* 126 A2
Aseb, *Eritrea* 81 E5
Åseda, *Sweden* 11 G9
Asela, *Ethiopia* 81 F4
Åsen, *Sweden* 10 C7
Asenovgrad, *Bulgaria* 41 D8
Aserradero, *Mexico* 118 C3
Asfeld, *France* 19 C11
Asfûn el Matâ'na, *Egypt* 80 B3
Asgata, *Cyprus* 36 E12
Ash Fork, *U.S.A.* 115 J7
Ash Grove, *U.S.A.* 113 G8
Ash Shabakah, *Iraq* 70 D4
Ash Shamāl □, *Lebanon* 75 A5
Ash Shāmīyah, *Iraq* 70 D5
Ash Shāriqah, *U.A.E.* 71 E7
Ash Sharmah, *Si. Arabia* 70 D2
Ash Sharqāt, *Iraq* 70 C4
Ash Sharqi, Al Jabal, *Lebanon* 75 B5
Ash Shaṭrah, *Iraq* 70 D5
Ash Shawbak, *Jordan* 70 D2
Ash Shawmari, J., *Jordan* 75 E5
Ash Shināfīyah, *Iraq* 70 D5
Ash Shu'bah, *Si. Arabia* 70 D5
Ash Shumlūl, *Si. Arabia* 70 E5
Ash Shūr'a, *Iraq* 70 C4
Ash Shurayf, *Si. Arabia* 70 E3
Ash Shuwayfāt, *Lebanon* 75 B4
Ashanti □, *Ghana* 83 D4
Ashau, *Vietnam* 64 D6
Ashbourne, *U.K.* 12 D6
Ashburn, *U.S.A.* 109 K4
Ashburton, *N.Z.* 91 K3
Ashburton →, *Australia* 92 D1
Ashcroft, *Canada* 104 C4
Ashdod, *Israel* 75 D3
Ashdown, *U.S.A.* 113 J7
Asheboro, *U.S.A.* 109 H6
Ashern, *Canada* 105 C9
Asherton, *U.S.A.* 113 L5
Asheville, *U.S.A.* 109 H4
Ashewat, *Pakistan* 68 D3
Asheweig →, *Canada* 102 B2
Ashford, *Australia* 95 D5
Ashford, *U.K.* 13 F8
Ashgabat, *Turkmenistan* 50 F6
Ashibetsu, *Japan* 54 C11
Ashikaga, *Japan* 55 F9
Ashington, *U.K.* 12 B6
Ashizuri-Zaki, *Japan* 55 H6
Ashkarkot, *Afghan.* 68 C2
Ashkhabad = Ashgabat, *Turkmenistan* 50 F6
Āshkhāneh, *Iran* 71 B8
Ashland, *Kans., U.S.A.* 113 G5
Ashland, *Ky., U.S.A.* 108 F4
Ashland, *Mont., U.S.A.* 114 D10
Ashland, *Ohio, U.S.A.* 110 F2
Ashland, *Oreg., U.S.A.* 114 E2
Ashland, *Pa., U.S.A.* 111 F8
Ashland, *Va., U.S.A.* 108 G7
Ashland, *Wis., U.S.A.* 112 B9
Ashley, *N. Dak., U.S.A.* 112 B5
Ashley, *Pa., U.S.A.* 111 E9
Ashmore Reef, *Australia* 92 B3
Ashmûn, *Egypt* 80 H7
Ashmyany, *Belarus* 9 J21
Ashokan Reservoir, *U.S.A.* 111 E10
Ashqelon, *Israel* 75 D3
Ashta, *India* 68 H7
Ashtabula, *U.S.A.* 110 E4
Ashton, *S. Africa* 88 E3
Ashton, *U.S.A.* 114 D8
Ashuanipi, L., *Canada* 103 B6
Ashville, *U.S.A.* 110 F6
'Āṣī →, *Asia* 72 D6

Asia 52 E11
Asia, Kepulauan, *Indonesia* 63 D8
Āsīā Bak, *Iran* 71 C6
Asiago, *Italy* 29 C8
Asifabad, *India* 66 K11
Asinara, *Italy* 30 A1
Asinara, G. dell', *Italy* 30 A1
Asino, *Russia* 50 D9
Asipovichy, *Belarus* 46 F5
'Asīr □, *Si. Arabia* 74 D3
Asir, Ras, *Somali Rep.* 74 E5
Aşkale, *Turkey* 73 C9
Askersund, *Sweden* 11 F8
Askham, *S. Africa* 88 D3
Askim, *Norway* 9 G14
Askja, *Iceland* 8 D5
Askøy, *Norway* 9 F11
Asl, *Egypt* 80 B3
Aslan Burnu, *Turkey* 39 C8
Aslanapa, *Turkey* 39 B11
Asmara = Asmera, *Eritrea* 81 D4
Asmera, *Eritrea* 81 D4
Asnæs, *Denmark* 11 J4
Åsnen, *Sweden* 11 H8
Asola, *Italy* 28 C7
Asosa, *Ethiopia* 81 E3
Asoteriba, Jebel, *Sudan* 80 C4
Aspe, *Spain* 33 G4
Aspen, *U.S.A.* 115 G10
Aspendos, *Turkey* 72 D4
Aspermont, *U.S.A.* 113 J4
Aspet, *France* 20 E4
Aspiring, Mt., *N.Z.* 91 L2
Aspres-sur-Buëch, *France* 21 D9
Asprókavos, Ákra, *Greece* 36 B4
Aspromonte, *Italy* 31 D9
Aspur, *India* 68 H6
Asquith, *Canada* 105 C7
Assâba, Massif de l', *Mauritania* 82 B2
Assaikio, *Nigeria* 83 D6
Assal, L., *Djibouti* 81 E5
Assam □, *India* 67 G18
Assamakka, *Niger* 83 B6
Asse, *Belgium* 17 D4
Assémini, *Italy* 30 C1
Assen, *Neths.* 17 A6
Assens, *Denmark* 11 J3
Assini, *Ivory C.* 82 D4
Assiniboia, *Canada* 105 D7
Assiniboine →, *Canada* 105 D9
Assiniboine, Mt., *Canada* 104 C5
Assis, *Brazil* 127 A5
Assisi, *Italy* 29 E9
Ássos, *Greece* 38 C2
Assynt, L., *U.K.* 14 C3
Astaffort, *France* 20 D4
Astakidha, *Greece* 39 F8
Astakós, *Greece* 38 C3
Astana, *Kazakstan* 50 D8
Āstāneh, *Iran* 71 B6
Astara, *Azerbaijan* 71 B6
Āstārā, *Iran* 73 C13
Asteroúsia, *Greece* 36 E7
Asti, *Italy* 28 D5
Astipálaia, *Greece* 39 E8
Astorga, *Spain* 34 C4
Astoria, *U.S.A.* 116 D3
Åstorp, *Sweden* 11 H6
Astrakhan, *Russia* 49 G9
Astudillo, *Spain* 34 C6
Asturias □, *Spain* 34 B5
Asunción, *Paraguay* 126 B4
Asunción Nochixtlán, *Mexico* 119 D5
Åsunden, *Sweden* 11 F9
Asutri, *Sudan* 81 D4
Aswa →, *Uganda* 86 B3
Aswad, Ra's al, *Si. Arabia* 80 C4
Aswân, *Egypt* 80 C3
Aswân High Dam = Sadd el Aali, *Egypt* 80 C3
Asyût, *Egypt* 80 B3
Asyûti, Wadi →, *Egypt* 80 B3
Aszód, *Hungary* 42 C4
At Ţafīlah, *Jordan* 75 E4
At Tā'if, *Si. Arabia* 74 C3
Aţ Ţirāq, *Si. Arabia* 70 E5
Aţ Tubayq, *Si. Arabia* 70 D3
Atabey, *Turkey* 39 D12
Atacama □, *Chile* 126 B2
Atacama, Desierto de, *Chile* 126 A2
Atacama, Salar de, *Chile* 126 A2
Atakpamé, *Togo* 83 D5
Atalándi, *Greece* 38 C4
Atalaya, *Peru* 124 F4
Atalaya de Femes, *Canary Is.* 37 F6
Atami, *Japan* 55 G9
Atapupu, *Indonesia* 63 F6
Atâr, *Mauritania* 78 D3
Atarfe, *Spain* 35 H7
Atari, *Pakistan* 68 D6
Atascadero, *U.S.A.* 116 K6
Atasu, *Kazakstan* 50 E8
Atatürk Barajı, *Turkey* 73 D8
Atauro, *Indonesia* 63 F7
'Atbara, *Sudan* 80 D3
'Atbara, Nahr →, *Sudan* 80 D3
Atbasar, *Kazakstan* 50 D7
Atça, *Turkey* 39 D10
Atchafalaya B., *U.S.A.* 113 L9
Atchison, *U.S.A.* 112 F7
Atebubu, *Ghana* 83 D4
Ateca, *Spain* 32 D3
Aterno →, *Italy* 29 F10
Āteshān, *Iran* 71 C7
Atesine, Alpi, *Italy* 29 B8
Atessa, *Italy* 29 F11
Atfîh, *Egypt* 80 J7
Ath, *Belgium* 17 D3
Athabasca, *Canada* 104 C6
Athabasca →, *Canada* 105 B6
Athabasca, L., *Canada* 105 B7
Athboy, *Ireland* 15 C5
Athenry, *Ireland* 15 C3
Athens = Athínai, *Greece* 38 D5
Athens, *Ala., U.S.A.* 109 H2
Athens, *Ga., U.S.A.* 109 J4
Athens, *N.Y., U.S.A.* 111 D11
Athens, *Ohio, U.S.A.* 108 F4
Athens, *Pa., U.S.A.* 111 E8
Athens, *Tenn., U.S.A.* 109 H3
Athens, *Tex., U.S.A.* 113 J7
Atherley, *Canada* 110 B5
Atherton, *Australia* 94 B4
Athiéme, *Benin* 83 D5
Athienou, *Cyprus* 36 D12
Athínai, *Greece* 38 D5
Athlone, *Ireland* 15 C4
Athna, *Cyprus* 36 D12
Athol, *U.S.A.* 111 D12
Atholl, Forest of, *U.K.* 14 E5
Atholville, *Canada* 103 C6
Áthos, *Greece* 41 F8
Athy, *Ireland* 15 C5
Ati, *Chad* 79 F9
Ati, *Sudan* 81 E2
Atiak, *Uganda* 86 B3
Atienza, *Spain* 32 D2
Atiit, *Sudan* 81 F3
Atik L., *Canada* 105 B9
Atikameg →, *Canada* 102 B3
Atikokan, *Canada* 102 C1
Atikonak L., *Canada* 103 B7
Atimonan, *Phil.* 61 E4
Atka, *Russia* 51 C16
Atka I., *U.S.A.* 100 C2
Atkarsk, *Russia* 48 E7
Atkinson, *U.S.A.* 112 D5
Atlanta, *Ga., U.S.A.* 109 J3
Atlanta, *Tex., U.S.A.* 113 J7
Atlantic, *U.S.A.* 112 E7
Atlantic City, *U.S.A.* 108 F8
Atlantic Ocean 2 E9
Atlas Mts. = Haut Atlas, *Morocco* 78 B4
Atlin, *Canada* 104 B2
Atlin, L., *Canada* 104 B2
Atlin Prov. Park, *Canada* 104 B2
Atmore, *U.S.A.* 109 K2
Atoka, *U.S.A.* 113 H6
Átokos, *Greece* 38 C2
Atolia, *U.S.A.* 117 K9
Atrai →, *Bangla.* 69 G13
Atrak = Atrek →, *Turkmenistan* 71 B8
Ätran, *Sweden* 11 G6
Ätran →, *Sweden* 11 H6
Atrauli, *India* 68 E8
Atrek →, *Turkmenistan* 71 B8
Atri, *Italy* 29 F10
Atsikí, *Greece* 39 B7
Atsoum, Mts., *Cameroon* 83 D7
Atsuta, *Japan* 54 C10
Attalla, *U.S.A.* 109 H2
Attapu, *Laos* 64 E6
Attáviros, *Greece* 36 C9
Attawapiskat, *Canada* 102 B3
Attawapiskat →, *Canada* 102 B3
Attawapiskat L., *Canada* 102 B2
Attersee, *Austria* 26 D6
Attica, *Ind., U.S.A.* 108 E2
Attica, *Ohio, U.S.A.* 110 E2
Attichy, *France* 19 C10
Attigny, *France* 19 C11
Attika = Attikí □, *Greece* 38 D5
Attikamagen L., *Canada* 103 B6
Attikí □, *Greece* 38 D5
Attleboro, *U.S.A.* 111 E13
Attock, *Pakistan* 68 C5
Attopeu = Attapu, *Laos* 64 E6
Attu I., *U.S.A.* 100 C1
Attur, *India* 66 P11
Atuel →, *Argentina* 126 D2
Åtvidaberg, *Sweden* 11 F10
Atwater, *U.S.A.* 116 H6
Atwood, *Canada* 110 C3
Atwood, *U.S.A.* 112 F4
Atyraū, *Kazakstan* 50 E6
Au Sable, *U.S.A.* 110 B1
Au Sable →, *U.S.A.* 108 C4
Au Sable Forks, *U.S.A.* 111 B11
Au Sable Pt., *U.S.A.* 110 B1
Aubagne, *France* 21 E9
Aubarca, C. d', *Spain* 37 B7
Aube □, *France* 19 D11
Aube →, *France* 19 D10
Aubenas, *France* 21 D8
Aubenton, *France* 19 C11
Auberry, *U.S.A.* 116 H7
Aubigny-sur-Nère, *France* 19 E9
Aubin, *France* 20 D6
Aubrac, Mts. d', *France* 20 D7
Auburn, *Ala., U.S.A.* 109 J3
Auburn, *Calif., U.S.A.* 116 G5
Auburn, *Ind., U.S.A.* 108 E3
Auburn, *Maine, U.S.A.* 109 C10
Auburn, *N.Y., U.S.A.* 111 D8
Auburn, *Nebr., U.S.A.* 112 E7
Auburn, *Pa., U.S.A.* 111 F8
Auburn, *Wash., U.S.A.* 116 C4
Auburn Ra., *Australia* 95 D5
Auburndale, *U.S.A.* 109 L5
Aubusson, *France* 20 C6
Auce, *Latvia* 44 B9
Auch, *France* 20 E4
Auchi, *Nigeria* 83 D6
Auckland, *N.Z.* 91 G5
Auckland Is., *Pac. Oc.* 96 N8
Aude □, *France* 20 E6
Aude →, *France* 20 E7
Auden, *Canada* 102 B2
Auderville, *France* 18 C5
Audierne, *France* 18 D2
Audincourt, *France* 19 E13
Audo, *Ethiopia* 81 F5
Audubon, *U.S.A.* 112 E7
Aue, *Germany* 24 E8
Auerbach, *Germany* 24 E8
Augathella, *Australia* 95 D4
Aughnacloy, *U.K.* 15 B5
Augrabies Falls, *S. Africa* 88 D3
Augsburg, *Germany* 25 G6
Augusta, *Australia* 93 F2
Augusta, *Italy* 31 E8
Augusta, *Ark., U.S.A.* 113 H9
Augusta, *Ga., U.S.A.* 109 J5
Augusta, *Kans., U.S.A.* 113 G6
Augusta, *Maine, U.S.A.* 101 D13
Augusta, *Mont., U.S.A.* 114 C7
Augustenborg, *Denmark* 11 K3
Augustów, *Poland* 44 E9
Augustus, Mt., *Australia* 93 D2
Augustus I., *Australia* 92 C3
Aukan, *Eritrea* 81 D5
Aukum, *U.S.A.* 116 G6
Auld, L., *Australia* 92 D3
Aulla, *Italy* 28 D6
Aulnay, *France* 20 B3
Aulne →, *France* 18 D2
Aulnoye-Aymeries, *France* 19 B10
Ault, *France* 18 B8
Ault, *U.S.A.* 112 E2
Aulus-les-Bains, *France* 20 F5
Aumale, *France* 19 C8
Aumont-Aubrac, *France* 20 D7
Auna, *Nigeria* 83 C5
Auning, *Denmark* 11 H4
Aunis, *France* 20 B3
Auponhia, *Indonesia* 63 E7
Aups, *France* 21 E10
Aur, Pulau, *Malaysia* 65 L5
Auraiya, *India* 69 F8
Aurangabad, *Bihar, India* 69 G11
Aurangabad, *Maharashtra, India* 66 K9
Auray, *France* 18 E4
Aurich, *Germany* 24 B3
Aurillac, *France* 20 D6
Auronzo di Cadore, *Italy* 29 B9
Aurora, *Canada* 110 C5
Aurora, *S. Africa* 88 E2
Aurora, *Colo., U.S.A.* 112 F2
Aurora, *Ill., U.S.A.* 108 E1
Aurora, *Mo., U.S.A.* 113 G8
Aurora, *N.Y., U.S.A.* 111 D8
Aurora, *Nebr., U.S.A.* 112 E6
Aurora, *Ohio, U.S.A.* 110 E3
Aurukun, *Australia* 94 A3
Aus, *Namibia* 88 D2
Ausable →, *Canada* 110 C3
Auschwitz = Oświęcim, *Poland* 45 H6
Austerlitz = Slavkov u Brna, *Czech Rep.* 27 B9
Austin, *Minn., U.S.A.* 112 D8
Austin, *Nev., U.S.A.* 114 G5
Austin, *Pa., U.S.A.* 110 E6
Austin, *Tex., U.S.A.* 113 K6
Austin, L., *Australia* 93 E2
Austin I., *Canada* 105 A10
Austra, *Norway* 8 D14
Austral Is. = Tubuai Is., *Pac. Oc.* 97 K13
Austral Seamount Chain, *Pac. Oc.* 97 K13
Australia ■, *Oceania* 96 K5
Australian Capital Territory □, *Australia* 95 F4
Australind, *Australia* 93 F2
Austria ■, *Europe* 26 E7
Austvågøy, *Norway* 8 B16
Auterive, *France* 20 E5
Authie →, *France* 19 B8
Authon-du-Perche, *France* 18 D7
Autlán, *Mexico* 118 D4
Autun, *France* 19 F11
Auvergne, *France* 20 C7
Auvergne, Mts. d', *France* 20 C6
Auvézère →, *France* 20 C4
Auxerre, *France* 19 E10
Auxi-le-Château, *France* 19 B9
Auxonne, *France* 19 E12
Auzances, *France* 19 F9
Ava, *U.S.A.* 113 G8
Avallon, *France* 19 E10
Avalon, *U.S.A.* 117 M8
Avalon Pen., *Canada* 103 C9
Avanos, *Turkey* 70 B2
Avaré, *Brazil* 127 A6
Ávas, *Greece* 41 F9
Avawatz Mts., *U.S.A.* 117 K10
Avdan Dağı, *Turkey* 41 F13
Aveiro, *Brazil* 125 D7
Aveiro, *Portugal* 34 E2
Aveiro □, *Portugal* 34 E2
Āvej, *Iran* 71 C6
Avellaneda, *Argentina* 126 C4
Avellino, *Italy* 31 B7
Avenal, *U.S.A.* 116 K6
Aversa, *Italy* 31 B7
Avery, *U.S.A.* 114 C6
Aves, Is. las, *Venezuela* 121 D6
Avesnes-sur-Helpe, *France* 19 B10
Avesta, *Sweden* 10 D10
Aveyron □, *France* 20 D6
Aveyron →, *France* 20 D5
Avezzano, *Italy* 29 F10
Avgó, *Greece* 39 F7
Aviá Terai, *Argentina* 126 B3
Aviano, *Italy* 29 B9
Aviemore, *U.K.* 14 D5
Avigliana, *Italy* 28 C4
Avigliano, *Italy* 31 B8
Avignon, *France* 21 E8
Ávila, *Spain* 34 E6
Ávila □, *Spain* 34 E6
Ávila, Sierra de, *Spain* 34 E5
Avila Beach, *U.S.A.* 117 K6
Avilés, *Spain* 34 B5
Avintes, *Portugal* 34 D2
Avionárion, *Greece* 38 C6
Avis, *Portugal* 35 F3
Avis, *U.S.A.* 110 E7
Avísio →, *Italy* 28 B8
Aviz = Avis, *Portugal* 35 F3
Avize, *France* 19 D11
Avlum, *Denmark* 11 H2
Avoca, *U.S.A.* 110 D7
Avoca →, *Australia* 95 F3
Avoca →, *Ireland* 15 D5
Avola, *Canada* 104 C5
Avola, *Italy* 31 F8
Avon, *U.S.A.* 110 D7
Avon →, *Australia* 93 F2
Avon →, *Bristol, U.K.* 13 F5
Avon →, *Dorset, U.K.* 13 G6
Avon →, *Warks., U.K.* 13 E5
Avon Park, *U.S.A.* 109 M5
Avondale, *Zimbabwe* 87 F3
Avonlea, *Canada* 105 D8
Avonmore, *Canada* 111 A10
Avramov, *Bulgaria* 41 D10
Avranches, *France* 18 D5
Avre →, *France* 18 D8
Avrig, *Romania* 43 E9
Avrillé, *France* 18 E6
Avtovac, *Bos.-H.* 40 C2
Awag el Baqar, *Sudan* 81 E3
A'waj →, *Syria* 75 B5
Awaji-Shima, *Japan* 55 G7
'Awālī, *Bahrain* 71 E6
Awantipur, *India* 69 C6
Awasa, *Ethiopia* 81 F4
Awasa, L., *Ethiopia* 81 F4
Awash, *Ethiopia* 81 F5
Awash →, *Ethiopia* 81 E5
Awaso, *Ghana* 82 D4
Awatere →, *N.Z.* 91 J5
Awbārī, *Libya* 79 C8
Awe, L., *U.K.* 14 E3
Aweil, *Sudan* 81 F2
Awgu, *Nigeria* 83 D6
Awjilah, *Libya* 79 C10
Awka, *Nigeria* 83 D6
Ax-les-Thermes, *France* 20 F5
Axat, *France* 20 F6
Axe →, *U.K.* 13 F5
Axel Heiberg I., *Canada* 4 B3
Axim, *Ghana* 82 E4
Axintele, *Romania* 43 F11
Axiós →, *Greece* 40 F6
Axminster, *U.K.* 13 G4
Axvall, *Sweden* 11 F7
Ay, *France* 19 C11
Ayabaca, *Peru* 124 D3
Ayabe, *Japan* 55 G7
Ayacucho, *Argentina* 126 D4
Ayacucho, *Peru* 124 F4
Ayaguz, *Kazakstan* 50 E9
Ayamé, *Ivory C.* 82 D4
Ayamonte, *Spain* 35 H3
Ayan, *Russia* 51 D14
Ayancık, *Turkey* 72 B6
Ayas, *Turkey* 72 B5
Ayaviri, *Peru* 124 F4
Aybastı, *Turkey* 72 B7
Aydın, *Turkey* 72 D2
Aydin □, *Turkey* 39 D9
Aydin Dağları, *Turkey* 39 D10
Ayelu, *Ethiopia* 81 E5
Ayenngré, *Togo* 83 D5
Ayer, *U.S.A.* 111 D13
Ayerbe, *Spain* 32 C4
Ayer's Cliff, *Canada* 111 A12
Ayers Rock, *Australia* 93 E5
Ayiá, *Greece* 38 B4
Ayia Aikateríni, Ákra, *Greece* 36 A3
Ayía Ánna, *Greece* 38 C5
Ayia Dhéka, *Greece* 36 D6
Ayia Gálini, *Greece* 36 D6
Ayía Marína, *Kásos, Greece* 39 F8
Ayía Marína, *Léros, Greece* 39 D8
Áyia Napa, *Cyprus* 36 E13
Ayía Paraskeví, *Greece* 39 B8
Áyia Phyla, *Cyprus* 36 E12
Ayía Rouméli, *Greece* 38 F5
Ayia Varvára, *Greece* 36 D7
Ayiássos, *Greece* 39 B8
Áyioi Theódhoroi, *Greece* 38 D5
Áyion Óros □, *Greece* 41 F8
Áyios Amvrósios, *Cyprus* 36 D12
Áyios Andréas, *Greece* 38 D4
Áyios Evstrátios, *Greece* 38 B6
Áyios Ioánnis, Ákra, *Greece* 36 D7
Áyios Isidhoros, *Greece* 36 C9
Áyios Kiríkos, *Greece* 39 D8
Áyios Matthaíos, *Greece* 36 B3
Áyios Mírono, *Greece* 39 F7
Áyios Nikólaos, *Greece* 36 D7
Áyios Pétros, *Greece* 38 C2
Áyios Seryios, *Cyprus* 36 D12
Áyios Theodhoros, *Cyprus* 36 D13
Áyios Yeóryios, *Greece* 38 D5
Aykathonisi, *Greece* 39 D8
Aykirikçi, *Turkey* 39 B12
Aylesbury, *U.K.* 13 F7
Aylmer, *Canada* 110 D4
Aylmer, L., *Canada* 100 B8
'Ayn, Wādī al, *Oman* 71 F7
Ayn Dār, *Si. Arabia* 71 E7
Ayn Zālah, *Iraq* 70 B4
Ayna, *Spain* 33 G2
Ayod, *Sudan* 81 F3
Ayolas, *Paraguay* 126 B4
Ayom, *Sudan* 81 F2
Ayon, Ostrov, *Russia* 51 C17
Ayora, *Spain* 33 F3
Ayorou, *Niger* 83 C5
'Ayoûn el 'Atroûs, *Mauritania* 82 B3
Ayr, *Australia* 94 B4
Ayr, *Canada* 110 C4
Ayr, *U.K.* 14 F4
Ayr →, *U.K.* 14 F4
Ayrancı, *Turkey* 72 D5
Ayrancılar, *Turkey* 39 C9
Ayre, Pt. of, *U.K.* 12 C3
Aysha, *Ethiopia* 81 E5
Ayton, *Australia* 94 B4
Aytos, *Bulgaria* 41 D11
Aytoska Planina, *Bulgaria* 41 D11
Ayu, Kepulauan, *Indonesia* 63 D8
Ayutla, *Guatemala* 120 D1
Ayutla, *Mexico* 119 D5
Ayvacık, *Turkey* 72 C2
Ayvalık, *Turkey* 39 B8
Az Zabadānī, *Syria* 75 B5
Aẓ Ẓāhirīyah, *West Bank* 75 D3
Aẓ Ẓahrān, *Si. Arabia* 71 E6
Az Zarqā, *Jordan* 75 C5
Az Zarqā', *U.A.E.* 71 E7
Az Zībār, *Iraq* 70 B5
Az Zilfī, *Si. Arabia* 70 E5
Az Zubayr, *Iraq* 70 D5
Az Zuqur, *Yemen* 81 E5
Azambuja, *Portugal* 35 F2
Azamgarh, *India* 69 F10
Azangaro, *Peru* 124 F4
Azaoua, *Niger* 83 B5
Azaouad, *Mali* 82 B4
Azaouak, Vallée de l', *Mali* 83 B5
Āzār Shahr, *Iran* 70 B5
Azara, *Nigeria* 83 D6
Azarān, *Iran* 70 B5
Azärbayjan = Azerbaijan ■, *Asia* 49 K9
Āzarbāyjān-e Gharbī □, *Iran* 70 B5
Āzarbāyjān-e Sharqī □, *Iran* 70 B5
Azare, *Nigeria* 83 C7
Azay-le-Rideau, *France* 18 E7
A'zāz, *Syria* 70 B3
Azbine = Aïr, *Niger* 83 B6
Azerbaijan ■, *Asia* 49 K9
Azerbaijchan = Azerbaijan ■, *Asia* 49 K9
Azezo, *Ethiopia* 81 E4
Azimganj, *India* 69 G13
Aznalcóllar, *Spain* 35 H4
Azogues, *Ecuador* 124 D3
Azores, *Atl. Oc.* 78 A1
Azov, *Russia* 49 G4
Azov, Sea of, *Europe* 47 J9
Azovskoye More = Azov, Sea of, *Europe* 47 J9
Azpeitia, *Spain* 32 B2
Azraq ash Shīshān, *Jordan* 75 D5
Aztec, *U.S.A.* 115 H10
Azúa de Compostela, *Dom. Rep.* 121 C5
Azuaga, *Spain* 35 G5
Azuara, *Spain* 32 D4
Azuer →, *Spain* 35 F7
Azuero, Pen. de, *Panama* 120 E3
Azuga, *Romania* 43 E10
Azul, *Argentina* 126 D4
Azusa, *U.S.A.* 117 L9
Azzano Décimo, *Italy* 29 C9

B

Ba Don, *Vietnam* 64 D6
Ba Dong, *Vietnam* 65 H6
Ba Ngoi = Cam Lam, *Vietnam* 65 G7
Ba Tri, *Vietnam* 65 G6
Ba Xian = Bazhou, *China* 56 E9
Baa, *Indonesia* 63 F6
Baamonde, *Spain* 34 B3
Baarle-Nassau, *Belgium* 17 C4
Bab el Mandeb, *Red Sea* 74 E3
Baba, *Bulgaria* 40 D7
Bābā, Koh-i-, *Afghan.* 66 B5
Baba Burnu, *Turkey* 39 B8
Baba dag, *Azerbaijan* 49 K9
Bābā Kalū, *Iran* 71 D6
Babadag, *Romania* 43 F13
Babadağ, *Turkey* 39 D10
Babadayhan, *Turkmenistan* 50 F7
Babaeski, *Turkey* 41 E11
Babahoyo, *Ecuador* 124 D3
Babai = Sarju →, *India* 69 F9
Babana, *Nigeria* 83 C5
Babanusa, *Sudan* 81 E2
Babar, *Indonesia* 63 F7
Babar, *Pakistan* 68 D3
Babarkach, *Pakistan* 68 E3
Babayevo, *Russia* 46 C8
Babb, *U.S.A.* 114 B7
Babelthuap, *Pac. Oc.* 63 C8
Babenhausen, *Germany* 25 F4
Băbeni, *Romania* 43 F9

Baberu, *India* 69 G9
Babi Besar, Pulau, *Malaysia* 65 L4
Babia Gora, *Europe* 45 J6
Babian Jiang →, *China* 58 F3
Babile, *Ethiopia* 81 F5
Babimost, *Poland* 45 F2
Babinda, *Australia* 94 B4
Babine, *Canada* 104 B3
Babine →, *Canada* 104 B3
Babine L., *Canada* 104 C3
Babo, *Indonesia* 63 E8
Babócsa, *Hungary* 42 D2
Bābol, *Iran* 71 B7
Bābol Sar, *Iran* 71 B7
Baborów, *Poland* 45 H5
Babruysk, *Belarus* 47 F5
Babuhri, *India* 68 F3
Babuna, *Macedonia* 40 E5
Babura, *Nigeria* 83 C6
Babusar Pass, *Pakistan* 69 B5
Babushkin, *Russia* 60 A5
Babušnica, *Serbia, Yug.* 40 C6
Babuyan Chan., *Phil.* 61 B4
Babylon, *Iraq* 70 C5
Bač, *Serbia, Yug.* 42 E4
Bâc →, *Moldova* 43 D14
Bac Can, *Vietnam* 58 F5
Bac Giang, *Vietnam* 58 G6
Bac Lieu, *Vietnam* 65 H5
Bac Ninh, *Vietnam* 58 G6
Bac Phan, *Vietnam* 64 B5
Bac Quang, *Vietnam* 58 F5
Bacabal, *Brazil* 125 D10
Bacalar, *Mexico* 119 D7
Bacan, Kepulauan, *Indonesia* 63 E7
Bacarra, *Phil.* 61 B4
Bacău, *Romania* 43 D11
Bacău □, *Romania* 43 D11
Baccarat, *France* 19 D13
Bacerac, *Mexico* 118 A3
Băceşti, *Romania* 43 D12
Bach Long Vi, Dao, *Vietnam* 64 B6
Bacharach, *Germany* 25 E3
Bachelina, *Russia* 50 D7
Bachhwara, *India* 69 G11
Bachuma, *Ethiopia* 81 F4
Bačina, *Serbia, Yug.* 40 C5
Back →, *Canada* 100 B9
Bačka Palanka, *Serbia, Yug.* 42 E4
Bačka Topola, *Serbia, Yug.* 42 E4
Bäckebo, *Sweden* 11 H10
Bäckefors, *Sweden* 11 F6
Bäckhammar, *Sweden* 10 E8
Bački Petrovac, *Serbia, Yug.* 42 E4
Backnang, *Germany* 25 G5
Baco, Mt., *Phil.* 61 E4
Bacolod, *Phil.* 61 F5
Bacqueville-en-Caux, *France* 18 C8
Bács-Kiskun □, *Hungary* 42 D4
Bácsalmás, *Hungary* 42 D4
Bacuag = Placer, *Phil.* 61 G6
Bacuk, *Malaysia* 65 J4
Bād, *Iran* 71 C7
Bad →, *U.S.A.* 112 C4
Bad Aussee, *Austria* 26 D6
Bad Axe, *U.S.A.* 110 C2
Bad Bergzabern, *Germany* 25 F3
Bad Berleburg, *Germany* 24 D4
Bad Bevensen, *Germany* 24 B6
Bad Bramstedt, *Germany* 24 B5
Bad Brückenau, *Germany* 25 E5
Bad Doberan, *Germany* 24 A7
Bad Driburg, *Germany* 24 D5
Bad Ems, *Germany* 25 E3
Bad Frankenhausen, *Germany* 24 D7
Bad Freienwalde, *Germany* 24 C10
Bad Goisern, *Austria* 26 D6
Bad Harzburg, *Germany* 24 D6
Bad Hersfeld, *Germany* 24 E5
Bad Hofgastein, *Austria* 26 D6
Bad Homburg, *Germany* 25 E4
Bad Honnef, *Germany* 24 E3
Bad Iburg, *Germany* 24 C4
Bad Ischl, *Austria* 26 D6
Bad Kissingen, *Germany* 25 E6
Bad Königshofen, *Germany* 25 E6
Bad Kreuznach, *Germany* 25 F3
Bad Krozingen, *Germany* 25 H3
Bad Laasphe, *Germany* 24 E4
Bad Lands, *U.S.A.* 112 D3
Bad Langensalza, *Germany* 24 D6
Bad Lauterberg, *Germany* 24 D6
Bad Leonfelden, *Austria* 26 C7
Bad Liebenwerda, *Germany* 24 D9
Bad Mergentheim, *Germany* 25 F5
Bad Münstereifel, *Germany* 24 E2
Bad Nauheim, *Germany* 25 E4
Bad Neuenahr-Ahrweiler, *Germany* 24 E3
Bad Neustadt, *Germany* 25 E6
Bad Oeynhausen, *Germany* 24 C4
Bad Oldesloe, *Germany* 24 B6
Bad Orb, *Germany* 25 E5
Bad Pyrmont, *Germany* 24 D5
Bad Reichenhall, *Germany* 25 H8
Bad Säckingen, *Germany* 25 H3
Bad Salzuflen, *Germany* 24 C4
Bad Salzungen, *Germany* 24 E6
Bad Schwartau, *Germany* 24 B6
Bad Segeberg, *Germany* 24 B6
Bad St. Leonhard, *Austria* 26 E7
Bad Tölz, *Germany* 25 H7
Bad Urach, *Germany* 25 G5
Bad Vöslau, *Austria* 27 D9
Bad Waldsee, *Germany* 25 H5
Bad Wildungen, *Germany* 24 D5
Bad Wimpfen, *Germany* 25 F5
Bad Windsheim, *Germany* 25 F6
Bad Zwischenahn, *Germany* 24 B4
Bada Barabil, *India* 69 H11
Badagara, *India* 66 P9
Badagri, *Nigeria* 83 D5
Badajós, L., *Brazil* 124 D6
Badajoz, *Spain* 35 G4
Badajoz □, *Spain* 35 G4
Badakhshān □, *Afghan.* 66 A7
Badalona, *Spain* 32 D7
Badalzai, *Afghan.* 68 E1
Badampahar, *India* 67 H15
Badanah, *Si. Arabia* 70 D4
Badarinath, *India* 69 D8
Badas, Kepulauan, *Indonesia* 62 D3
Baddo →, *Pakistan* 66 F4
Bade, *Indonesia* 63 F9
Badeggi, *Nigeria* 83 D6
Badéguichéri, *Niger* 83 C6
Baden, *Austria* 27 C9
Baden, *Switz.* 25 H4
Baden, *U.S.A.* 110 F4
Baden-Baden, *Germany* 25 G4
Baden-Württemberg □, *Germany* 25 G4
Badgastein, *Austria* 26 D6
Badger, *Canada* 103 C8
Badger, *U.S.A.* 116 J7
Bādghīs □, *Afghan.* 66 B3
Badgom, *India* 69 B6
Badia Polésine, *Italy* 29 C8
Badin, *Pakistan* 68 G3
Badlands National Park, *U.S.A.* 112 D3
Badogo, *Mali* 82 C3
Badoumbé, *Mali* 82 C2
Badrah, *Iraq* 70 C5
Badrinath, *India* 69 D8
Badulla, *Sri Lanka* 66 R12
Baena, *Spain* 35 H6
Baeza, *Spain* 35 H7
Bafang, *Cameroon* 83 D7
Bafatá, *Guinea-Biss.* 82 C2
Baffin B., *Canada* 101 A13
Baffin I., *Canada* 101 B12
Bafia, *Cameroon* 83 E7
Bafilo, *Togo* 83 D5
Bafing →, *Mali* 82 C2
Bafliyūn, *Syria* 70 B3
Bafoulabé, *Mali* 82 C2
Bafoussam, *Cameroon* 83 D7
Bāfq, *Iran* 71 D7
Bafra, *Turkey* 72 B6
Bafra Burnu, *Turkey* 72 B7
Bāft, *Iran* 71 D8
Bafut, *Cameroon* 83 D7
Bafwasende, *Dem. Rep. of the Congo* 86 B2
Bagam, *Niger* 83 B6
Bagamoyo, *Tanzania* 86 D4
Bagan Datoh, *Malaysia* 65 L3
Bagan Serai, *Malaysia* 65 K3
Baganga, *Phil.* 61 H7
Bagani, *Namibia* 88 B3
Bagansiapiapi, *Indonesia* 62 D2
Bagasra, *India* 68 J4
Bagaud, *India* 68 H6
Bagawi, *Sudan* 81 E3
Bagbag, *Sudan* 81 D3
Bagdad, *U.S.A.* 117 L11
Bagdarin, *Russia* 51 D12
Bagé, *Brazil* 127 C5
Bagenalstown = Muine Bheag, *Ireland* 15 D5
Baggs, *U.S.A.* 114 F10
Bagh, *Pakistan* 69 C5
Baghain →, *India* 69 G9
Baghdād, *Iraq* 70 C5
Bagheria, *Italy* 30 D6
Baghlān, *Afghan.* 66 A6
Baghlān □, *Afghan.* 66 B6
Bagley, *U.S.A.* 112 B7
Bagnara Cálabra, *Italy* 31 D8
Bagnasco, *Italy* 28 D5
Bagnères-de-Bigorre, *France* 20 E4
Bagnères-de-Luchon, *France* 20 F4
Bagni di Lucca, *Italy* 28 D7
Bagno di Romagna, *Italy* 29 E8
Bagnoles-de-l'Orne, *France* 18 D6
Bagnols-sur-Cèze, *France* 21 D8
Bagnorégio, *Italy* 29 F9
Bago = Pegu, *Burma* 67 L20
Bagodar, *India* 69 G11
Bagrationovsk, *Russia* 9 J19
Bagrdan, *Serbia, Yug.* 40 B5
Baguio, *Phil.* 61 C4
Bağyurdu, *Turkey* 39 C9
Bagzane, Monts, *Niger* 83 B6
Bah, *India* 69 F8
Bahabón de Esgueva, *Spain* 34 D7
Bahadurganj, *India* 69 F12
Bahadurgarh, *India* 68 E7
Bahama, Canal Viejo de, *W. Indies* 120 B4
Bahamas ■, *N. Amer.* 121 B5
Bahār, *Iran* 73 E13
Baharampur, *India* 69 G13
Baharîya, El Wâhât al, *Egypt* 80 B2
Bahawalnagar, *Pakistan* 68 E5
Bahawalpur, *Pakistan* 68 E4
Bahçe, *Turkey* 72 D7
Bahçecik, *Turkey* 41 F13
Baheri, *India* 69 E8
Bahgul →, *India* 69 F8
Bahi, *Tanzania* 86 D4
Bahi Swamp, *Tanzania* 86 D4
Bahía = Salvador, *Brazil* 125 F11
Bahía □, *Brazil* 125 F10
Bahía, Is. de la, *Honduras* 120 C2
Bahía Blanca, *Argentina* 126 D3
Bahía de Caráquez, *Ecuador* 124 D2
Bahía Honda, *Cuba* 120 B3
Bahía Laura, *Argentina* 128 F3
Bahía Negra, *Paraguay* 124 H7
Bahir Dar, *Ethiopia* 81 E4
Bahmanzād, *Iran* 71 D6
Bahr el Ahmar □, *Sudan* 80 D4
Bahr el Ghazâl □, *Sudan* 81 F2
Bahr el Jabal □, *Sudan* 81 G3
Bahr Yûsef →, *Egypt* 80 B3
Bahraich, *India* 69 F9
Bahrain ■, *Asia* 71 E6
Bahror, *India* 68 F7
Bāhū Kalāt, *Iran* 71 E9
Bai, *Mali* 82 C4
Bai Bung, Mui = Ca Mau, Mui, *Vietnam* 65 H5
Bai Duc, *Vietnam* 64 C5
Bai Thuong, *Vietnam* 64 C5
Baia de Aramă, *Romania* 42 E7
Baia Mare, *Romania* 43 C8
Baia-Sprie, *Romania* 43 C8
Baião, *Brazil* 125 D9
Baïbokoum, *Chad* 79 G9
Baicheng, *China* 57 B12
Băicoi, *Romania* 43 E10
Baidoa, *Somali Rep.* 74 G3
Baie Comeau, *Canada* 103 C6
Baie-St-Paul, *Canada* 103 C5
Baie Trinité, *Canada* 103 C6
Baie Verte, *Canada* 103 C8
Baignes-Ste-Radegonde, *France* 20 C3
Baigneux-les-Juifs, *France* 19 E11
Baihar, *India* 69 H9
Baihe, *China* 56 H6
Ba'ījī, *Iraq* 70 C4
Baijnath, *India* 69 E8
Baikal, L. = Baykal, Oz., *Russia* 51 D11
Baikunthpur, *India* 69 H10
Baile Atha Cliath = Dublin, *Ireland* 15 C5
Băile Govora, *Romania* 43 E9
Băile Herculane, *Romania* 42 F7
Băile Olăneşti, *Romania* 43 E9
Băile Tuşnad, *Romania* 43 D10
Bailén, *Spain* 35 G7
Băileşti, *Romania* 43 F8
Baima, *China* 58 A3
Bain-de-Bretagne, *France* 18 E5
Bainbridge, *Ga., U.S.A.* 109 K3
Bainbridge, *N.Y., U.S.A.* 111 D9
Baing, *Indonesia* 63 F6
Bainiu, *China* 56 H7
Baiona, *Spain* 34 C2
Bā'ir, *Jordan* 75 E5
Bairin Youqi, *China* 57 C10
Bairin Zuoqi, *China* 57 C10
Bairnsdale, *Australia* 95 F4
Bais, *Phil.* 61 G5
Baisha, *China* 56 G7
Baissa, *Nigeria* 83 D7
Baitadi, *Nepal* 69 E9
Baiyin, *China* 56 F3
Baiyü, *China* 58 B2
Baiyu Shan, *China* 56 F4
Baiyuda, *Sudan* 80 D3
Baj Baj, *India* 69 H13
Baja, *Hungary* 42 D3
Baja, Pta., *Mexico* 118 B1
Baja California, *Mexico* 118 A1
Baja California □, *Mexico* 118 B2
Baja California Sur □, *Mexico* 118 B2
Bajag, *India* 69 H9
Bajamar, *Canary Is.* 37 F3
Bajana, *India* 68 H4
Bājgīrān, *Iran* 71 B8
Bajimba, Mt., *Australia* 95 D5
Bajina Bašta, *Serbia, Yug.* 40 C3
Bajmok, *Serbia, Yug.* 42 E4
Bajo Nuevo, *Caribbean* 120 C4
Bajoga, *Nigeria* 83 C7
Bajool, *Australia* 94 C5
Bak, *Hungary* 42 D1
Bakar, *Croatia* 29 C11
Bakel, *Senegal* 82 C2
Baker, *Calif., U.S.A.* 117 K10
Baker, *Mont., U.S.A.* 112 B2
Baker, L., *Canada* 100 B10
Baker City, *U.S.A.* 114 D5
Baker I., *Pac. Oc.* 96 G10
Baker I., *U.S.A.* 104 B2
Baker L., *Australia* 93 E4
Baker Lake, *Canada* 100 B10
Baker Mt., *U.S.A.* 114 B3
Bakers Creek, *Australia* 94 C4
Baker's Dozen Is., *Canada* 102 A4
Bakersfield, *Calif., U.S.A.* 117 K8
Bakersfield, *Vt., U.S.A.* 111 B12
Bakhchysaray, *Ukraine* 47 K7
Bakhmach, *Ukraine* 47 G7
Bākhtarān, *Iran* 70 C5
Bākhtarān □, *Iran* 70 C5
Bakı, *Azerbaijan* 49 K9
Bakır →, *Turkey* 39 C9
Bakırdaği, *Turkey* 72 C6
Bakkafjörður, *Iceland* 8 C6
Baklan, *Turkey* 39 C11
Bako, *Ethiopia* 81 F4
Bako, *Ivory C.* 82 D3
Bakony, *Hungary* 42 C2
Bakony Forest = Bakony, *Hungary* 42 C2
Bakori, *Nigeria* 83 C6
Bakouma, *C.A.R.* 84 C4
Baksan, *Russia* 49 J6
Bakswaho, *India* 69 G8
Baku = Bakı, *Azerbaijan* 49 K9
Bakundi, *Nigeria* 83 D7
Bakutis Coast, *Antarctica* 5 D15
Baky = Bakı, *Azerbaijan* 49 K9
Bala, *Canada* 110 A5
Bala, *Senegal* 82 C2
Bâlâ, *Turkey* 72 C5
Bala, *U.K.* 12 E4
Bala, L., *U.K.* 12 E4
Balabac I., *Phil.* 62 C5
Balabac Str., *E. Indies* 62 C5
Balabagh, *Afghan.* 68 B4
Ba'labakk, *Lebanon* 75 B5
Balabalangan, Kepulauan, *Indonesia* 62 E5
Bălăciţa, *Romania* 43 F8
Balad, *Iraq* 70 C5
Balad Rūz, *Iraq* 70 C5
Bālādeh, *Fārs, Iran* 71 D6
Bālādeh, *Māzandaran, Iran* 71 B6
Balaghat, *India* 66 J12
Balaghat Ra., *India* 66 K10
Balaguer, *Spain* 32 D5
Balakhna, *Russia* 48 B6
Balaklava, *Ukraine* 47 K7
Balakliya, *Ukraine* 47 H9
Balakovo, *Russia* 48 D8
Balamau, *India* 69 F9
Bălan, *Romania* 43 D10
Balancán, *Mexico* 119 D6
Balashov, *Russia* 48 E6
Balasinor, *India* 68 H5
Balasore = Baleshwar, *India* 67 J15
Balassagyarmat, *Hungary* 42 B4
Balât, *Egypt* 80 B2
Balaton, *Hungary* 42 D2
Balatonboglár, *Hungary* 42 D2
Balatonfüred, *Hungary* 42 D2
Balatonszentgyörgy, *Hungary* 42 D2
Balayan, *Phil.* 61 E4
Balazote, *Spain* 33 G2
Balbieriškis, *Lithuania* 44 D10
Balbigny, *France* 21 C8
Balbina, Represa de, *Brazil* 124 D7
Balboa, *Panama* 120 E4
Balbriggan, *Ireland* 15 C5
Balcarce, *Argentina* 126 D4
Balcarres, *Canada* 105 C8
Bălceşti, *Romania* 43 F8
Balchik, *Bulgaria* 41 C12
Balclutha, *N.Z.* 91 M2
Balcones Escarpment, *U.S.A.* 113 L5
Balçova, *Turkey* 39 C9
Bald Hd., *Australia* 93 G2
Bald I., *Australia* 93 F2
Bald Knob, *U.S.A.* 113 H9
Baldock L., *Canada* 105 B9
Baldwin, *Mich., U.S.A.* 108 D3
Baldwin, *Pa., U.S.A.* 110 F5
Baldwinsville, *U.S.A.* 111 C8
Baldy Mt., *U.S.A.* 114 B9
Baldy Peak, *U.S.A.* 115 K9
Bale, *Croatia* 29 C10
Bale, *Ethiopia* 81 F5
Bale □, *Ethiopia* 81 F5
Baleares, Is., *Spain* 37 B10
Balearic Is. = Baleares, Is., *Spain* 37 B10
Baleine = Whale →, *Canada* 103 A6
Băleni, *Romania* 43 E12
Baler, *Phil.* 61 D4
Baler Bay, *Phil.* 61 D4
Baleshare, *U.K.* 14 D1
Baleshwar, *India* 67 J15
Balezino, *Russia* 48 B11
Balfate, *Honduras* 120 C2
Bali, *Cameroon* 83 D7
Balí, *Greece* 36 D6
Bali, *India* 68 G5
Bali, *Indonesia* 62 F4
Bali □, *Indonesia* 62 F5
Bali, Selat, *Indonesia* 63 H16
Balia, *S. Leone* 82 D2
Baliapal, *India* 69 J12
Baligród, *Poland* 45 J9
Balikeşir, *Turkey* 39 B9
Balikeşir □, *Turkey* 39 B9
Balıklıçeşme, *Turkey* 41 F11
Balikpapan, *Indonesia* 62 E5
Balimbing, *Phil.* 63 C5
Baling, *Malaysia* 65 K3
Balingen, *Germany* 25 G4
Balinţ, *Romania* 42 E6
Balintang Channel, *Phil.* 61 B4
Balipara, *India* 67 F18
Balkan Mts. = Stara Planina, *Bulgaria* 40 C7
Balkhash = Balqash, *Kazakstan* 50 E8
Balkhash, Ozero = Balqash Köl, *Kazakstan* 50 E8
Balla, *Bangla.* 67 G17
Ballachulish, *U.K.* 14 E3
Balladonia, *Australia* 93 F3
Ballaghaderreen, *Ireland* 15 C3
Ballarat, *Australia* 95 F3
Ballard, L., *Australia* 93 E3
Ballater, *U.K.* 14 D5
Ballé, *Mali* 82 B3
Ballenas, Canal de, *Mexico* 118 B2
Balleny Is., *Antarctica* 5 C11
Balleroy, *France* 18 C6
Ballerup, *Denmark* 11 J6
Ballı, *Turkey* 41 F11
Ballia, *India* 69 G11
Ballina, *Australia* 95 D5
Ballina, *Ireland* 15 B2
Ballinasloe, *Ireland* 15 C3
Ballinger, *U.S.A.* 113 K5
Ballinrobe, *Ireland* 15 C2
Ballinskelligs B., *Ireland* 15 E1
Ballon, *France* 18 D7
Ballsh, *Albania* 40 F3
Ballston Spa, *U.S.A.* 111 D11
Ballycastle, *U.K.* 15 A5
Ballyclare, *U.K.* 15 B5
Ballyhaunis, *Ireland* 15 C3
Ballymena, *U.K.* 15 B5
Ballymoney, *U.K.* 15 A5
Ballymote, *Ireland* 15 B3
Ballynahinch, *U.K.* 15 B6
Ballyquintin Pt., *U.K.* 15 B6
Ballyshannon, *Ireland* 15 B3
Balmaceda, *Chile* 128 F2
Balmaseda, *Spain* 32 B1
Balmazújváros, *Hungary* 42 C6
Balmertown, *Canada* 105 C10
Balmoral, *Australia* 95 F3
Balmorhea, *U.S.A.* 113 K3
Balonne →, *Australia* 95 D4
Balotra, *India* 68 G5
Balqash, *Kazakstan* 50 E8
Balqash Köl, *Kazakstan* 50 E8
Balrampur, *India* 69 F10
Balranald, *Australia* 95 E3
Balş, *Romania* 43 F9
Balsas, *Mexico* 119 D5
Balsas →, *Brazil* 125 E9
Balsas →, *Mexico* 118 D4
Bålsta, *Sweden* 10 E11
Balston Spa, *U.S.A.* 111 D11
Balta, *Romania* 42 F7
Balta, *Ukraine* 47 H5
Baltanás, *Spain* 34 D6
Bălţi, *Moldova* 43 C12
Baltic Sea, *Europe* 9 H18
Baltîm, *Egypt* 80 H7
Baltimore, *Ireland* 15 E2
Baltimore, *Md., U.S.A.* 108 F7
Baltimore, *Ohio, U.S.A.* 110 G2
Baltit, *Pakistan* 69 A6
Baltiysk, *Russia* 9 J18
Baltrum, *Germany* 24 B3
Baluchistan □, *Pakistan* 66 F4
Balurghat, *India* 69 G13
Balvi, *Latvia* 9 H22
Balya, *Turkey* 39 B9
Bam, *Iran* 71 D8
Bama, *China* 58 E6
Bama, *Nigeria* 83 C7
Bamaga, *Australia* 94 A3
Bamaji L., *Canada* 102 B1
Bamako, *Mali* 82 C3
Bamba, *Mali* 83 B4
Bambara Maoundé, *Mali* 82 B4
Bambari, *C.A.R.* 84 C4
Bambaroo, *Australia* 94 B4
Bambaya, *Guinea* 82 D2
Bamberg, *Germany* 25 F6
Bamberg, *U.S.A.* 109 J5
Bambesi, *Ethiopia* 81 F3
Bambey, *Senegal* 82 C1
Bambili, *Dem. Rep. of the Congo* 86 B2
Bamboi, *Ghana* 82 D4
Bamenda, *Cameroon* 83 D7
Bamfield, *Canada* 104 D3
Bāmīān □, *Afghan.* 66 B5
Bamiancheng, *China* 57 C13
Bamkin, *Cameroon* 83 D7
Bampūr, *Iran* 71 E9
Ban, *Burkina Faso* 82 C4
Ban Ban, *Laos* 64 C4
Ban Bang Hin, *Thailand* 65 H2
Ban Chiang Klang, *Thailand* 64 C3
Ban Chik, *Laos* 64 D4
Ban Choho, *Thailand* 64 E4
Ban Dan Lan Hoi, *Thailand* 64 D2
Ban Don = Surat Thani, *Thailand* 65 H2
Ban Don, *Vietnam* 64 F6
Ban Don, Ao →, *Thailand* 65 H2
Ban Dong, *Thailand* 64 C3
Ban Hong, *Thailand* 64 C2
Ban Kaeng, *Thailand* 64 D3
Ban Kantang, *Thailand* 65 J2
Ban Keun, *Laos* 64 C4
Ban Khai, *Thailand* 64 F3
Ban Kheun, *Laos* 64 B3
Ban Khlong Kua, *Thailand* 65 J3
Ban Khuan Mao, *Thailand* 65 J2
Ban Ko Yai Chim, *Thailand* 65 G2
Ban Kok, *Thailand* 64 D4
Ban Laem, *Thailand* 64 F2
Ban Lao Ngam, *Laos* 64 E6
Ban Le Kathe, *Thailand* 64 E2
Ban Mae Chedi, *Thailand* 64 C2
Ban Mae Laeng, *Thailand* 64 B2
Ban Mae Sariang, *Thailand* 64 C1
Ban Mê Thuôt = Buon Ma Thuot, *Vietnam* 64 F7
Ban Mi, *Thailand* 64 E3
Ban Muong Mo, *Laos* 64 C4
Ban Na Mo, *Laos* 64 D5
Ban Na San, *Thailand* 65 H2
Ban Na Tong, *Laos* 64 B3
Ban Nam Bac, *Laos* 64 B4
Ban Nam Ma, *Laos* 64 A3
Ban Ngang, *Laos* 64 E6
Ban Nong Bok, *Laos* 64 D5
Ban Nong Boua, *Laos* 64 E6
Ban Nong Pling, *Thailand* 64 E3
Ban Pak Chan, *Thailand* 65 G2
Ban Phai, *Thailand* 64 D4
Ban Pong, *Thailand* 64 F2
Ban Ron Phibun, *Thailand* 65 H2

Ban Sanam Chai, *Thailand* 65 J3
Ban Sangkha, *Thailand* 64 E4
Ban Tak, *Thailand* 64 D2
Ban Tako, *Thailand* 64 E4
Ban Tha Dua, *Thailand* 64 D2
Ban Tha Li, *Thailand* 64 D3
Ban Tha Nun, *Thailand* 65 H2
Ban Thahine, *Laos* 64 E5
Ban Xien Kok, *Laos* 64 B3
Ban Yen Nhan, *Vietnam* 64 B6
Banaba, *Kiribati* 96 H8
Banalia, *Dem. Rep. of the Congo* 86 B2
Banam, *Cambodia* 65 G5
Banamba, *Mali* 82 C3
Banana Is., *S. Leone* 82 D2
Bananal, I. do, *Brazil* 125 F8
Banaras = Varanasi, *India* ... 69 G10
Banas →, *Gujarat, India* 68 H4
Banas →, *Mad. P., India* 69 G9
Bânâs, Ras, *Egypt* 80 C4
Banaz, *Turkey* 39 C11
Banaz →, *Turkey* 39 C11
Banbridge, *U.K.* 15 B5
Banbury, *U.K.* 13 E6
Banchory, *U.K.* 14 D6
Banco, *Ethiopia* 81 F4
Bancroft, *Canada* 102 C4
Band, *Romania* 43 D9
Band Bonī, *Iran* 71 E8
Band Qīr, *Iran* 71 D6
Banda, *Mad. P., India* 69 G8
Banda, *Ut. P., India* 69 G9
Banda, Kepulauan, *Indonesia* .. 63 E7
Banda Aceh, *Indonesia* 62 C1
Banda Banda, Mt., *Australia* ... 95 E5
Banda Elat, *Indonesia* 63 F8
Banda Is. = Banda, Kepulauan, *Indonesia* 63 E7
Banda Sea, *Indonesia* 63 F7
Bandai-San, *Japan* 54 F10
Bandama →, *Ivory C.* 82 D3
Bandama Blanc →, *Ivory C.* .. 82 D3
Bandama Rouge →, *Ivory C.* .. 82 D4
Bandān, *Iran* 71 D9
Bandanaira, *Indonesia* 63 E7
Bandanwara, *India* 68 F6
Bandar = Machilipatnam, *India* 67 L12
Bandār 'Abbās, *Iran* 71 E8
Bandar-e Anzalī, *Iran* 71 B6
Bandar-e Bushehr = Būshehr, *Iran* 71 D6
Bandar-e Chārak, *Iran* 71 E7
Bandar-e Deylam, *Iran* 71 D6
Bandar-e Khomeynı, *Iran* 71 D6
Bandar-e Lengeh, *Iran* 71 E7
Bandar-e Maqām, *Iran* 71 E7
Bandar-e Ma'shur, *Iran* 71 D6
Bandar-e Rīg, *Iran* 71 D6
Bandar-e Torkeman, *Iran* 71 B7
Bandar Maharani = Muar, *Malaysia* 65 L4
Bandar Penggaram = Batu Pahat, *Malaysia* 65 M4
Bandar Seri Begawan, *Brunei* .. 62 C4
Bandar Sri Aman, *Malaysia* ... 62 D4
Bandawe, *Malawi* 87 E3
Bande, *Spain* 34 C3
Bandeira, Pico da, *Brazil* ... 127 A7
Bandera, *Argentina* 126 B3
Banderas, B. de, *Mexico* 118 C3
Bandhogarh, *India* 69 H9
Bandi →, *India* 68 F6
Bandiagara, *Mali* 82 C4
Bandikui, *India* 68 F7
Bandırma, *Turkey* 41 F11
Bandol, *France* 21 E9
Bandon, *Ireland* 15 E3
Bandon →, *Ireland* 15 E3
Bandula, *Mozam.* 87 F3
Bandundu, *Dem. Rep. of the Congo* 84 E3
Bandung, *Indonesia* 62 F3
Bané, *Burkina Faso* 83 C4
Băneasa, *Romania* 43 E12
Bāneh, *Iran* 70 C5
Bañeres, *Spain* 33 G4
Banes, *Cuba* 121 B4
Banff, *Canada* 104 C5
Banff, *U.K.* 14 D6
Banff Nat. Park, *Canada* .. 104 C5
Banfora, *Burkina Faso* 82 C4
Bang Fai →, *Laos* 64 D5
Bang Hieng →, *Laos* 64 D5
Bang Krathum, *Thailand* ... 64 D3
Bang Lamung, *Thailand* 64 F3
Bang Mun Nak, *Thailand* ... 64 D3
Bang Pa In, *Thailand* 64 E3
Bang Rakam, *Thailand* 64 D3
Bang Saphan, *Thailand* 65 G2
Bangaduni I., *India* 69 J13
Bangala Dam, *Zimbabwe* 87 G3
Bangalore, *India* 66 N10
Banganga →, *India* 68 F6
Bangangté, *Cameroon* 83 D7
Bangaon, *India* 69 H13
Bangassou, *C.A.R.* 84 D4
Banggai, *Indonesia* 63 E6
Banggai, Kepulauan, *Indonesia* 63 E6
Banggai Arch. = Banggai, Kepulauan, *Indonesia* 63 E6
Banggi, *Malaysia* 62 C5
Banghāzī, *Libya* 79 B10
Bangjang, *Sudan* 81 E3
Bangka, *Sulawesi, Indonesia* ... 63 D7
Bangka, *Sumatera, Indonesia* .. 62 E3
Bangka, Selat, *Indonesia* 62 E3
Bangkalan, *Indonesia* 63 G15
Bangkinang, *Indonesia* 62 D2
Bangko, *Indonesia* 62 E2
Bangkok, *Thailand* 64 F3
Bangladesh ■, *Asia* 67 H17
Bangolo, *Ivory C.* 82 D3
Bangong Co, *India* 69 B8
Bangor, *Down, U.K.* 15 B6
Bangor, *Gwynedd, U.K.* 12 D3
Bangor, *Maine, U.S.A.* 101 D13
Bangor, *Pa., U.S.A.* 111 F9
Bangued, *Phil.* 61 C4
Bangui, *C.A.R.* 84 D3
Bangui, *Phil.* 61 B4
Banguru, *Dem. Rep. of the Congo* 86 B2
Bangweulu, L., *Zambia* 87 E3
Bangweulu Swamp, *Zambia* ... 87 E3
Bani, *Dom. Rep.* 121 C5
Bani →, *Mali* 82 C4
Bani Bangou, *Niger* 83 B5
Banī Sa'd, *Iraq* 70 C5
Bania, *Ivory C.* 82 D4
Banihal Pass, *India* 69 C6
Banikoara, *Benin* 83 C5
Bāniyās, *Syria* 70 C3
Banja Luka, *Bos.-H.* 42 F2
Banjar, *India* 68 D7
Banjar →, *India* 69 H9
Banjarmasin, *Indonesia* 62 E4
Banjul, *Gambia* 82 C1
Banka, *India* 69 G12
Bankas, *Mali* 82 C4
Bankeryd, *Sweden* 11 G8
Banket, *Zimbabwe* 87 F3
Bankilaré, *Niger* 83 C5
Bankipore, *India* 67 G14
Banks I., *B.C., Canada* 104 C3
Banks I., *N.W.T., Canada* .. 100 A7
Banks Pen., *N.Z.* 91 K4
Banks Str., *Australia* 94 G4
Bankura, *India* 69 H12
Bankya, *Bulgaria* 40 D7
Banmankhi, *India* 69 G12
Bann →, *Arm., U.K.* 15 B5
Bann →, *L'derry., U.K.* .. 15 A5
Bannalec, *France* 18 E3
Bannang Sata, *Thailand* ... 65 J3
Banning, *U.S.A.* 117 M10
Banningville = Bandundu, *Dem. Rep. of the Congo* 84 E3
Banno, *Ethiopia* 81 G4
Bannockburn, *Canada* 110 B7
Bannockburn, *U.K.* 14 E5
Bannockburn, *Zimbabwe* 87 G2
Bannu, *Pakistan* 66 C7
Bano, *India* 69 H11
Bañolas = Banyoles, *Spain* .. 32 C7
Banon, *France* 21 D9
Baños de la Encina, *Spain* .. 35 G7
Baños de Molgas, *Spain* 34 C3
Bánovce nad Bebravou, *Slovak Rep.* 27 C11
Banovići, *Bos.-H.* 42 F3
Bansgaon, *India* 69 F10
Banská Bystrica, *Slovak Rep.* .. 27 C12
Banská Štiavnica, *Slovak Rep.* . 27 C11
Bansko, *Bulgaria* 40 E7
Banskobystrický □, *Slovak Rep.* 27 C12
Banswara, *India* 68 H6
Bantaeng, *Indonesia* 63 F5
Bantaji, *Nigeria* 83 D7
Bantayan, *Phil.* 61 F5
Bantry, *Ireland* 15 E2
Bantry B., *Ireland* 15 E2
Bantul, *Indonesia* 63 G14
Bantva, *India* 68 J4
Banya, *Bulgaria* 41 D8
Banyak, Kepulauan, *Indonesia* . 62 D1
Banyalbufar, *Spain* 37 B9
Banyo, *Cameroon* 83 D7
Banyoles, *Spain* 32 C7
Banyuls-sur-Mer, *France* .. 20 F7
Banyumas, *Indonesia* 63 G13
Banyuwangi, *Indonesia* ... 63 H16
Banzare Coast, *Antarctica* .. 5 C9
Banzyville = Mobayi, *Dem. Rep. of the Congo* 84 D4
Bao Ha, *Vietnam* 58 F5
Bao Lac, *Vietnam* 64 A5
Bao Loc, *Vietnam* 65 G6
Bao'an = Shenzhen, *China* .. 59 F10
Baocheng, *China* 56 H4
Baode, *China* 56 E6
Baodi, *China* 57 E9
Baoding, *China* 56 E8
Baoji, *China* 56 G4
Baojing, *China* 58 C7
Baokang, *China* 59 B8
Baoshan, *Shanghai, China* .. 59 B13
Baoshan, *Yunnan, China* ... 58 E2
Baotou, *China* 56 D6
Baoxing, *China* 58 B4
Baoying, *China* 57 H10
Bap, *India* 68 F5
Bapatla, *India* 67 M12
Bapaume, *France* 19 B9
Bāqerābād, *Iran* 71 C6
Ba'qūbah, *Iraq* 70 C5
Baquedano, *Chile* 126 A2
Bar, *Montenegro, Yug.* ... 40 D3
Bar, *Ukraine* 47 H4
Bar Bigha, *India* 69 G11
Bar Harbor, *U.S.A.* 109 C11
Bar-le-Duc, *France* 19 D12
Bar-sur-Aube, *France* .. 19 D11
Bar-sur-Seine, *France* . 19 D11
Bara, *India* 69 G9
Bâra, *Romania* 43 C12
Bara Banki, *India* 69 F9
Barabai, *Indonesia* ... 62 E5
Baraboo, *U.S.A.* 112 D10
Baracoa, *Cuba* 121 B5
Baradā →, *Syria* 75 B5
Baradero, *Argentina* .. 126 C4
Baraga, *U.S.A.* 112 B10
Bărăganul, *Romania* .. 43 F12
Barah →, *India* 68 F6
Barahona, *Dom. Rep.* .. 121 C5
Barahona, *Spain* 32 D2
Barail Range, *India* .. 67 G18
Baraka, *Sudan* 81 E2
Baraka →, *Sudan* 80 D4
Barakaldo, *Spain* ... 32 B2
Barakar →, *India* .. 69 G12
Barakhola, *India* ... 67 G18
Barakot, *India* 69 J11
Barakpur, *India* 69 H13
Baralaba, *Australia* .. 94 C4
Baralla, *Spain* 34 C3
Baralzon L., *Canada* .. 105 B9
Barameiya, *Sudan* 80 D4
Baramula, *India* 69 B6
Baran, *India* 68 G7
Baran →, *Pakistan* .. 68 G3
Barañain, *Spain* 32 C3
Baranavichy, *Belarus* .. 47 F4
Barani, *Burkina Faso* .. 82 C4
Baranof, *U.S.A.* 104 B2
Baranof I., *U.S.A.* ... 100 C6
Baranów Sandomierski, *Poland* 45 H8
Baranya □, *Hungary* .. 42 E3
Baraolt, *Romania* 43 D10
Barapasi, *Indonesia* .. 63 E9
Barasat, *India* 69 H13
Barat Daya, Kepulauan, *Indonesia* 63 F7
Barataria B., *U.S.A.* .. 113 L10
Barauda, *India* 68 H6
Baraut, *India* 68 E7
Barbacena, *Brazil* 127 A7
Barbados ■, *W. Indies* .. 121 D8
Barban, *Croatia* 29 C11
Barbària, C. de, *Spain* .. 37 C7
Barbaros, *Turkey* 41 F11
Barbastro, *Spain* 32 C5
Barbate = Barbate de Franco, *Spain* 35 J5
Barbate de Franco, *Spain* 35 J5
Barberino di Mugello, *Italy* 29 E8
Barberton, *S. Africa* 89 D5
Barberton, *U.S.A.* 110 E3
Barbezieux-St-Hilaire, *France* . 20 C3
Barbosa, *Colombia* 124 B4
Barbourville, *U.S.A.* 109 G4
Barbuda, *W. Indies* 121 C7
Bârca, *Romania* 43 G8
Barcaldine, *Australia* 94 C4
Barcarrota, *Spain* 35 G4
Barcellona Pozzo di Gotto, *Italy* 31 D8
Barcelona, *Spain* 32 D7
Barcelona, *Venezuela* 124 A6
Barcelona □, *Spain* 32 D7
Barcelonette, *France* 21 D10
Barcelos, *Brazil* 124 D6
Barcin, *Poland* 45 F4
Barclayville, *Liberia* 82 E3
Barcoo →, *Australia* 94 D3
Barcs, *Hungary* 42 E2
Barczewo, *Poland* 44 E7
Bärdä, *Azerbaijan* 49 K8
Bardaï, *Chad* 79 D9
Bardas Blancas, *Argentina* .. 126 D2
Barddhaman, *India* 69 H12
Bardejov, *Slovak Rep.* 27 B14
Bardera, *Somali Rep.* 74 G3
Bardi, *Italy* 28 D6
Bardīyah, *Libya* 79 B10
Bardolino, *Italy* 28 C7
Bardonécchia, *Italy* 28 C3
Bardsey I., *U.K.* 12 E3
Bardstown, *U.S.A.* 108 G3
Bareilly, *India* 69 E8
Barela, *India* 69 H9
Barentin, *France* 18 C7
Barenton, *France* 18 D6
Barents Sea, *Arctic* 4 B9
Barentu, *Eritrea* 81 D4
Barfleur, *France* 18 C5
Barfleur, Pte. de, *France* .. 18 C5
Barga, *Italy* 28 D7
Bargara, *Australia* 94 C5
Bargas, *Spain* 34 F6
Bârgăului Bistriţa, *Romania* .. 43 C9
Barge, *Italy* 28 D4
Bargnop, *Sudan* 81 F2
Bargteheide, *Germany* ... 24 B6
Barguzin, *Russia* 51 D11
Barh, *India* 69 G11
Barhaj, *India* 69 F10
Barharwa, *India* 69 G12
Barhi, *India* 69 G11
Bari, *India* 68 F7
Bari, *Italy* 31 A9
Bari Doab, *Pakistan* 68 D5
Bari Sadri, *India* 68 G6
Bari Sardo, *Italy* 30 C2
Barīdī, Ra's, *Si. Arabia* .. 70 E3
Barīm, *Yemen* 76 E8
Barinas, *Venezuela* 124 B4
Baring, C., *Canada* 100 B8
Baringo, *Kenya* 86 B4
Baringo, L., *Kenya* 86 B4
Bârîs, *Egypt* 80 C3
Barisal, *Bangla.* 67 H17
Barisal □, *Bangla.* 67 H17
Barisan, Bukit, *Indonesia* .. 62 E2
Barito →, *Indonesia* ... 62 E4
Barjac, *France* 21 D8
Barjols, *France* 21 E10
Bark L., *Canada* 110 A7
Barka = Baraka →, *Sudan* .. 80 D4
Barkakana, *India* 69 H11
Barkam, *China* 58 B4
Barker, *U.S.A.* 110 C6
Barkley, L., *U.S.A.* .. 109 G2
Barkley Sound, *Canada* .. 104 D3
Barkly East, *S. Africa* .. 88 E4
Barkly Roadhouse, *Australia* .. 94 B2
Barkly Tableland, *Australia* ... 94 B2
Barkly West, *S. Africa* 88 D3
Barkol, Wadi →, *Sudan* 80 D3
Barla Dağı, *Turkey* 39 C12
Bârlad, *Romania* 43 D12
Bârlad →, *Romania* 43 E12
Barlee, L., *Australia* 93 E2
Barlee, Mt., *Australia* 93 D4
Barletta, *Italy* 31 A9
Barlinek, *Poland* 45 F2
Barlovento, *Canary Is.* 37 F2
Barlow L., *Canada* 105 A8
Barmedman, *Australia* 95 E4
Barmer, *India* 68 G4
Barmera, *Australia* 95 E3
Barmouth, *U.K.* 12 E3
Barmstedt, *Germany* 24 B5
Barna →, *India* 69 G10
Barnagar, *India* 68 H6
Barnala, *India* 68 D6
Barnard Castle, *U.K.* 12 C6
Barnaul, *Russia* 50 D9
Barnesville, *U.S.A.* 109 J3
Barnet □, *U.K.* 13 F7
Barneveld, *Neths.* 17 B5
Barneveld, *U.S.A.* 111 C9
Barneville-Cartevert, *France* .. 18 C5
Barnhart, *U.S.A.* 113 K4
Barnsley, *U.K.* 12 D6
Barnstaple, *U.K.* 13 F3
Barnstaple Bay = Bideford Bay, *U.K.* 13 F3
Barnsville, *U.S.A.* 112 B6
Barnwell, *U.S.A.* 109 J5
Baro, *Nigeria* 83 D6
Baro →, *Ethiopia* 81 F3
Baroda = Vadodara, *India* .. 68 H5
Baroda, *India* 68 G7
Baroe, *S. Africa* 88 E3
Baron Ra., *Australia* 92 D4
Barong, *China* 58 B2
Barotseland, *Zambia* 85 H4
Barouéli, *Mali* 82 C3
Barpeta, *India* 67 F17
Barques, Pt. Aux, *U.S.A.* .. 110 B2
Barquísimeto, *Venezuela* .. 124 A5
Barr, Ras el, *Egypt* 80 H7
Barr Smith Range, *Australia* .. 93 E3
Barra, *Brazil* 125 F10
Barra, *U.K.* 14 E1
Barra, Sd. of, *U.K.* 14 D1
Barra de Navidad, *Mexico* .. 118 D4
Barra do Corda, *Brazil* ... 125 E9
Barra do Piraí, *Brazil* ... 127 A7
Barra Falsa, Pta. da, *Mozam.* .. 89 C6
Barra Hd., *U.K.* 14 E1
Barra Mansa, *Brazil* 127 A7
Barraba, *Australia* 95 E5
Barrackpur = Barakpur, *India* . 69 H13
Barradale Roadhouse, *Australia* 92 D1
Barrafranca, *Italy* 31 E7
Barraigh = Barra, *U.K.* ... 14 E1
Barranca, *Lima, Peru* 124 F3
Barranca, *Loreto, Peru* .. 124 D3
Barrancabermeja, *Colombia* .. 124 B4
Barrancas, *Venezuela* 124 B6
Barrancos, *Portugal* 35 G4
Barranqueras, *Argentina* .. 126 B4
Barranquilla, *Colombia* .. 124 A4
Barraute, *Canada* 102 C4
Barre, *Mass., U.S.A.* ... 111 D12
Barre, *Vt., U.S.A.* 111 B12
Barreal, *Argentina* 126 C2
Barreiras, *Brazil* 125 F10
Barreirinhas, *Brazil* ... 125 D10
Barreiro, *Portugal* 35 G1
Barrême, *France* 21 E10
Barren, Nosy, *Madag.* .. 89 B7
Barretos, *Brazil* 125 H9
Barrhead, *Canada* 104 C6
Barrie, *Canada* 102 D4
Barrier Ra., *Australia* .. 95 E3
Barrière, *Canada* 104 C4
Barrington, *U.S.A.* ... 111 E13
Barrington L., *Canada* .. 105 B8
Barrington Tops, *Australia* .. 95 E5
Barringun, *Australia* ... 95 D4
Barro do Garças, *Brazil* .. 125 G8
Barron, *U.S.A.* 112 C9
Barrow, *U.S.A.* 100 A4
Barrow →, *Ireland* 15 D5
Barrow, Pt., *U.S.A.* 98 B4
Barrow Creek, *Australia* .. 94 C1
Barrow I., *Australia* 92 D2
Barrow-in-Furness, *U.K.* .. 12 C4
Barrow Pt., *Australia* ... 94 A3
Barrow Ra., *Australia* .. 93 E4
Barrow Str., *Canada* 4 B3
Barruecopardo, *Spain* ... 34 D4
Barruelo de Santullán, *Spain* .. 34 C6
Barry, *U.K.* 13 F4
Barry's Bay, *Canada* ... 102 C4
Barsalogho, *Burkina Faso* .. 83 C4
Barsat, *Pakistan* 69 A5
Barsham, *Syria* 70 C4
Barsi, *India* 66 K9
Barsinghausen, *Germany* .. 24 C5
Barsoi, *India* 67 G15
Barstow, *U.S.A.* 117 L9
Barth, *Germany* 24 A8
Barthélemy, Col, *Vietnam* .. 64 C5
Bartica, *Guyana* 124 B7
Bartin, *Turkey* 72 B5
Bartlesville, *U.S.A.* .. 113 G7
Bartlett, *U.S.A.* 116 J8
Bartlett, L., *Canada* .. 104 A5
Bartolomeu Dias, *Mozam.* .. 87 G4
Barton, *U.S.A.* 111 B12
Barton upon Humber, *U.K.* .. 12 D7
Bartoszyce, *Poland* ... 44 D7
Bartow, *U.S.A.* 109 M5
Barú, Volcan, *Panama* .. 120 E3
Barumba, *Dem. Rep. of the Congo* 86 B1
Baruth, *Germany* 24 C9
Baruunsuu, *Mongolia* .. 56 C3
Barvinkove, *Ukraine* .. 47 H9
Barwani, *India* 68 H6
Barwice, *Poland* 44 E3
Barycz →, *Poland* .. 45 G3
Barysaw, *Belarus* .. 46 E5
Barysh, *Russia* 48 D8
Barzān, *Iraq* 70 B5
Bârzava, *Romania* .. 42 D6
Bas-Rhin □, *France* .. 19 D14
Bašaid, *Serbia, Yug.* .. 42 E5
Bāsa'idū, *Iran* 71 E7
Basal, *Pakistan* 68 C5
Basankusa, *Dem. Rep. of the Congo* 84 D3
Basarabeasca, *Moldova* .. 43 D13
Basarabi, *Romania* ... 43 F13
Basauri, *Spain* 32 B2
Basawa, *Afghan.* 68 B4
Bascuñán, C., *Chile* .. 126 B1
Basel, *Switz.* 25 H3
Basel-Landschaft □, *Switz.* .. 25 H3
Basento →, *Italy* .. 31 B9
Bashākerd, Kūhhā-ye, *Iran* .. 71 E8
Bashaw, *Canada* 104 C6
Bāshī, *Iran* 71 D6
Bashkir Republic = Bashkortostan □, *Russia* .. 50 D6
Bashkortostan □, *Russia* .. 50 D6
Basibasy, *Madag.* ... 89 C7
Basilan I., *Phil.* .. 61 H5
Basilan Str., *Phil.* .. 61 H5
Basildon, *U.K.* 13 F8
Basile, *Eq. Guin.* .. 83 E6
Basilicata □, *Italy* .. 31 B9
Basim = Washim, *India* .. 66 J10
Basin, *U.S.A.* 114 D9
Basingstoke, *U.K.* .. 13 F6
Baška, *Croatia* 29 D11
Başkale, *Turkey* ... 73 C10
Baskatong, Rés., *Canada* .. 102 C4
Basle = Basel, *Switz.* .. 25 H3
Başmakçı, *Turkey* .. 39 D12
Basoda, *India* 68 H7
Basoka, *Dem. Rep. of the Congo* 86 B1
Basque, Pays, *France* .. 20 E2
Basque Provinces = País Vasco □, *Spain* 32 C2
Basra = Al Başrah, *Iraq* .. 70 D5
Bass Str., *Australia* .. 94 F4
Bassano, *Canada* 104 C6
Bassano del Grappa, *Italy* .. 29 C8
Bassar, *Togo* 83 D5
Bassas da India, *Ind. Oc.* .. 85 J7
Basse-Normandie □, *France* .. 18 D6
Basse Santa-Su, *Gambia* .. 82 C2
Basse-Terre, *Guadeloupe* .. 121 C7
Bassein, *Burma* 67 L19
Basseterre, *St. Kitts & Nevis* .. 121 C7
Bassett, *U.S.A.* 112 D5
Bassi, *India* 68 D7
Bassigny, *France* 19 E12
Bassikounou, *Mauritania* .. 82 B3
Bassila, *Benin* 83 D5
Bassum, *Germany* 24 C4
Båstad, *Sweden* 11 H6
Bastak, *Iran* 71 E7
Baştām, *Iran* 71 B7
Bastar, *India* 67 K12
Bastelica, *France* 21 F13
Basti, *India* 69 F10
Bastia, *France* 21 F13
Bastogne, *Belgium* ... 17 D5
Bastrop, *La., U.S.A.* .. 113 J9
Bastrop, *Tex., U.S.A.* .. 113 K6
Bat Yam, *Israel* 75 C3
Bata, *Eq. Guin.* 84 D1
Bata, *Romania* 42 D7
Bataan □, *Phil.* 61 D4
Batabanó, *Cuba* 120 B3
Batabanó, G. de, *Cuba* .. 120 B3
Batac, *Phil.* 61 B4
Batagai, *Russia* 51 C14
Batajnica, *Serbia, Yug.* .. 40 B4
Batak, *Bulgaria* 41 E8
Batala, *India* 68 D6
Batalha, *Portugal* ... 34 F2
Batama, *Dem. Rep. of the Congo* 86 B2
Batamay, *Russia* 51 C13
Batang, *China* 58 B2
Batang, *Indonesia* .. 63 G13
Batangas, *Phil.* 61 E4
Batanta, *Indonesia* . 63 E8
Batatais, *Brazil* ... 127 A6
Batavia, *U.S.A.* ... 110 D6

Bataysk, *Russia* 47 J10
Batchelor, *Australia* 92 B5
Batdambang, *Cambodia* 64 F4
Batemans B., *Australia* 95 F5
Batemans Bay, *Australia* 95 F5
Bates Ra., *Australia* 93 E3
Batesburg-Leesville, *U.S.A.* 109 J5
Batesville, *Ark., U.S.A.* 113 H9
Batesville, *Miss., U.S.A.* 113 H10
Batesville, *Tex., U.S.A.* 113 L5
Bath, *Canada* 111 B8
Bath, *U.K.* 13 F5
Bath, *Maine, U.S.A.* 109 D11
Bath, *N.Y., U.S.A.* 110 D7
Bath & North East Somerset □, *U.K.* 13 F5
Batheay, *Cambodia* 65 G5
Bathurst = Banjul, *Gambia* 82 C1
Bathurst, *Australia* 95 E4
Bathurst, *Canada* 103 C6
Bathurst, *S. Africa* 88 E4
Bathurst, C., *Canada* 100 A7
Bathurst B., *Australia* 94 A3
Bathurst Harb., *Australia* 94 G4
Bathurst I., *Australia* 92 B5
Bathurst I., *Canada* 4 B2
Bathurst Inlet, *Canada* 100 B9
Bati, *Ethiopia* 81 E5
Batie, *Burkina Faso* 82 D4
Batlow, *Australia* 95 F4
Batman, *Turkey* 70 B4
Baṭn al Ghūl, *Jordan* 75 F4
Batna, *Algeria* 78 A7
Batobato = San Isidro, *Phil.* 61 H7
Batočina, *Serbia, Yug.* 40 B5
Batoka, *Zambia* 87 F2
Baton Rouge, *U.S.A.* 113 K9
Batong, Ko, *Thailand* 65 J2
Bátonyterenye, *Hungary* 42 C4
Batopilas, *Mexico* 118 B3
Batouri, *Cameroon* 84 D2
Båtsfjord, *Norway* 8 A23
Battambang = Batdambang, *Cambodia* 64 F4
Batticaloa, *Sri Lanka* 66 R12
Battipáglia, *Italy* 31 B7
Battle, *U.K.* 13 G8
Battle →, *Canada* 105 C7
Battle Creek, *U.S.A.* 108 D3
Battle Ground, *U.S.A.* 116 E4
Battle Harbour, *Canada* 103 B8
Battle Lake, *U.S.A.* 112 B7
Battle Mountain, *U.S.A.* 114 F5
Battlefields, *Zimbabwe* 87 F2
Battleford, *Canada* 105 C7
Battonya, *Hungary* 42 D6
Batu, *Ethiopia* 81 F4
Batu, Kepulauan, *Indonesia* 62 E1
Batu Caves, *Malaysia* 65 L3
Batu Gajah, *Malaysia* 65 K3
Batu Is. = Batu, Kepulauan, *Indonesia* 62 E1
Batu Pahat, *Malaysia* 65 M4
Batuata, *Indonesia* 63 F6
Batumi, *Georgia* 49 K5
Baturaja, *Indonesia* 62 E2
Baturité, *Brazil* 125 D11
Bau, *Malaysia* 62 D4
Baubau, *Indonesia* 63 F6
Bauchi, *Nigeria* 83 C6
Bauchi □, *Nigeria* 83 C7
Baud, *France* 18 E3
Baudette, *U.S.A.* 112 A7
Bauer, C., *Australia* 95 E1
Bauhinia, *Australia* 94 C4
Baukau, *E. Timor* 63 F7
Bauld, C., *Canada* 101 C14
Baume-les-Dames, *France* 19 E13
Baunatal, *Germany* 24 D5
Baunei, *Italy* 30 B2
Baure, *Nigeria* 83 C6
Bauru, *Brazil* 127 A6
Bausi, *India* 69 G12
Bauska, *Latvia* 9 H21
Bautino, *Kazakstan* 49 H10
Bautzen, *Germany* 24 D10
Bauya, *S. Leone* 82 D2
Bavānāt, *Iran* 71 D7
Bavanište, *Serbia, Yug.* 42 F5
Bavaria = Bayern □, *Germany* 25 G7
Båven, *Sweden* 10 E10
Bavispe →, *Mexico* 118 B3
Bawdwin, *Burma* 67 H20
Bawean, *Indonesia* 62 F4
Bawku, *Ghana* 83 C4
Bawlake, *Burma* 67 K20
Bawolung, *China* 58 C3
Baxley, *U.S.A.* 109 K4
Baxoi, *China* 58 B1
Baxter, *U.S.A.* 112 B7
Baxter Springs, *U.S.A.* 113 G7
Bay, L. de, *Phil.* 61 D4
Bay City, *Mich., U.S.A.* 108 D4
Bay City, *Tex., U.S.A.* 113 L7
Bay Minette, *U.S.A.* 109 K2
Bay Roberts, *Canada* 103 C9
Bay St. Louis, *U.S.A.* 113 K10
Bay Springs, *U.S.A.* 113 K10
Bay View, *N.Z.* 91 H6
Baya, *Dem. Rep. of the Congo* 87 E2
Bayamo, *Cuba* 120 B4
Bayamón, *Puerto Rico* 121 C6
Bayan Har Shan, *China* 60 C4
Bayan Hot = Alxa Zuoqi, *China* 56 E3
Bayan Obo, *China* 56 D5
Bayan-Ovoo = Erdenetsogt, *Mongolia* 56 C4
Bayana, *India* 68 F7
Bayanaüyl, *Kazakstan* 50 D8
Bayandalay, *Mongolia* 56 C2
Bayanhongor, *Mongolia* 60 B5
Bayard, *N. Mex., U.S.A.* 115 K9
Bayard, *Nebr., U.S.A.* 112 E3
Bayawan, *Phil.* 61 G5
Baybay, *Phil.* 61 F6
Bayburt, *Turkey* 73 B9
Bayelsa □, *Nigeria* 83 E6
Bayerische Alpen, *Germany* 25 H7
Bayerischer Wald, *Germany* 25 G8
Bayern □, *Germany* 25 G7
Bayeux, *France* 18 C6
Bayfield, *Canada* 110 C3
Bayfield, *U.S.A.* 112 B9
Bayındır, *Turkey* 39 C9
Baykal, Oz., *Russia* 51 D11
Baykan, *Turkey* 70 B4
Baykonur = Bayqongyr, *Kazakstan* 50 E7
Baynes Mts., *Namibia* 88 B1
Bayombong, *Phil.* 61 C4
Bayon, *France* 19 D13
Bayona = Baiona, *Spain* 34 C2
Bayonne, *France* 20 E2
Bayonne, *U.S.A.* 111 F10
Bayovar, *Peru* 124 E2
Bayqongyr, *Kazakstan* 50 E7
Bayram-Ali = Bayramaly, *Turkmenistan* 50 F7
Bayramaly, *Turkmenistan* 50 F7
Bayramiç, *Turkey* 39 B8
Bayreuth, *Germany* 25 F7
Bayrischzell, *Germany* 25 H8
Bayrūt, *Lebanon* 75 B4
Bays, L. of, *Canada* 110 A5
Baysville, *Canada* 110 A5
Bayt Lahm, *West Bank* 75 D4
Baytown, *U.S.A.* 113 L7
Bayzo, *Niger* 83 C5
Baza, *Spain* 35 H8
Bazar Dyuzi, *Russia* 49 K8
Bazardüzü = Bazar Dyuzi, *Russia* 49 K8
Bazarny Karabulak, *Russia* 48 D8
Bazarnyy Syzgan, *Russia* 48 D8
Bazaruto, I. do, *Mozam.* 89 C6
Bazas, *France* 20 D3
Bazhong, *China* 58 B6
Bazhou, *China* 56 E9
Bazmān, Kūh-e, *Iran* 71 D9
Beach, *U.S.A.* 112 B3
Beach City, *U.S.A.* 110 F3
Beachport, *Australia* 95 F3
Beachy Hd., *U.K.* 13 G8
Beacon, *Australia* 93 F2
Beacon, *U.S.A.* 111 E11
Beaconsfield, *Australia* 94 G4
Beagle, Canal, *S. Amer.* 122 J4
Beagle Bay, *Australia* 92 C3
Bealanana, *Madag.* 89 A8
Beals Cr. →, *U.S.A.* 113 J4
Beamsville, *Canada* 110 C5
Bear →, *Calif., U.S.A.* 116 G5
Bear →, *Utah, U.S.A.* 106 B4
Béar, C., *France* 20 F7
Bear I., *Ireland* 15 E2
Bear L., *Canada* 105 B9
Bear L., *U.S.A.* 114 F8
Beardmore, *Canada* 102 C2
Beardmore Glacier, *Antarctica* 5 E11
Beardstown, *U.S.A.* 112 F9
Bearma →, *India* 69 G8
Béarn, *France* 20 E3
Bearpaw Mts., *U.S.A.* 114 B9
Bearskin Lake, *Canada* 102 B1
Beas →, *India* 68 D6
Beas de Segura, *Spain* 35 G8
Beasain, *Spain* 32 B2
Beata, C., *Dom. Rep.* 121 C5
Beata, I., *Dom. Rep.* 121 C5
Beatrice, *U.S.A.* 112 E6
Beatrice, *Zimbabwe* 87 F3
Beatrice, C., *Australia* 94 A2
Beatton →, *Canada* 104 B4
Beatton River, *Canada* 104 B4
Beatty, *U.S.A.* 116 J10
Beaucaire, *France* 21 E8
Beauce, Plaine de la, *France* 19 D8
Beauceville, *Canada* 103 C5
Beaudesert, *Australia* 95 D5
Beaufort, *France* 21 C10
Beaufort, *Malaysia* 62 C5
Beaufort, *N.C., U.S.A.* 109 H7
Beaufort, *S.C., U.S.A.* 109 J5
Beaufort Sea, *Arctic* 4 B1
Beaufort West, *S. Africa* 88 E3
Beaugency, *France* 19 E8
Beauharnois, *Canada* 111 A11
Beaujeu, *France* 19 F11
Beaujolais, *France* 19 F11
Beaulieu →, *Canada* 104 A6
Beaulieu-sur-Dordogne, *France* 20 D5
Beaulieu-sur-Mer, *France* 21 E11
Beauly, *U.K.* 14 D4
Beauly →, *U.K.* 14 D4
Beaumaris, *U.K.* 12 D3
Beaumont, *Belgium* 17 D4
Beaumont, *France* 20 D4
Beaumont, *U.S.A.* 113 K7
Beaumont-de-Lomagne, *France* 20 E5
Beaumont-le-Roger, *France* 18 C7
Beaumont-sur-Sarthe, *France* 18 D7
Beaune, *France* 19 E11
Beaune-la-Rolande, *France* 19 D9
Beaupré, *Canada* 103 C5
Beaupréau, *France* 18 E6
Beauraing, *Belgium* 17 D4
Beaurepaire, *France* 21 C9
Beauséjour, *Canada* 105 C9
Beauvais, *France* 19 C9
Beauval, *Canada* 105 B7
Beauvoir-sur-Mer, *France* 18 F4
Beauvoir-sur-Niort, *France* 20 B3
Beaver, *Okla., U.S.A.* 113 G4
Beaver, *Pa., U.S.A.* 110 F4
Beaver, *Utah, U.S.A.* 115 G7
Beaver →, *B.C., Canada* 104 B4
Beaver →, *Ont., Canada* 102 A2
Beaver →, *Sask., Canada* 105 B7
Beaver →, *U.S.A.* 113 G5
Beaver City, *U.S.A.* 112 E5
Beaver Creek, *Canada* 100 B5
Beaver Dam, *U.S.A.* 112 D10
Beaver Falls, *U.S.A.* 110 F4
Beaver Hill L., *Canada* 105 C10
Beaver I., *U.S.A.* 108 C3
Beaverhill L., *Canada* 104 C6
Beaverlodge, *Canada* 104 B5
Beaverstone →, *Canada* 102 B2
Beaverton, *Canada* 110 B5
Beaverton, *U.S.A.* 116 E4
Beawar, *India* 68 F6
Bebedouro, *Brazil* 127 A6
Beboa, *Madag.* 89 B7
Bebra, *Germany* 24 E5
Beccles, *U.K.* 13 E9
Bečej, *Serbia, Yug.* 42 E5
Beceni, *Romania* 43 E11
Becerreá, *Spain* 34 C3
Béchar, *Algeria* 78 B5
Bechyně, *Czech Rep.* 26 B7
Beckley, *U.S.A.* 108 G5
Beckum, *Germany* 24 D4
Beclean, *Romania* 43 C9
Bečov nad Teplou, *Czech Rep.* 26 A5
Bečva →, *Czech Rep.* 27 B10
Bédar, *Spain* 33 H3
Bédarieux, *France* 20 E7
Beddouza, Ras, *Morocco* 78 B4
Bedele, *Ethiopia* 81 F4
Bederkesa, *Germany* 24 B4
Bedeso, *Ethiopia* 81 F5
Bedford, *Canada* 111 A12
Bedford, *S. Africa* 88 E4
Bedford, *U.K.* 13 E7
Bedford, *Ind., U.S.A.* 108 F2
Bedford, *Iowa, U.S.A.* 112 E7
Bedford, *Ohio, U.S.A.* 110 E3
Bedford, *Pa., U.S.A.* 110 F6
Bedford, *Va., U.S.A.* 108 G6
Bedford, C., *Australia* 94 B4
Bedfordshire □, *U.K.* 13 E7
Będków, *Poland* 45 G6
Bednja →, *Croatia* 29 B13
Bednodemyanovsk, *Russia* 48 D6
Bedónia, *Italy* 28 D6
Bedourie, *Australia* 94 C2
Bedum, *Neths.* 17 A6
Będzin, *Poland* 45 H6
Beebe Plain, *Canada* 111 A12
Beech Creek, *U.S.A.* 110 E7
Beelitz, *Germany* 24 C8
Beenleigh, *Australia* 95 D5
Be'er Menuḥa, *Israel* 70 D2
Be'er Sheva, *Israel* 75 D3
Beersheba = Be'er Sheva, *Israel* 75 D3
Beeskow, *Germany* 24 C10
Beestekraal, *S. Africa* 89 D4
Beeston, *U.K.* 12 E6
Beetzendorf, *Germany* 24 C7
Beeville, *U.S.A.* 113 L6
Befale, *Dem. Rep. of the Congo* 84 D4
Befandriana, *Mahajanga, Madag.* 89 B8
Befandriana, *Toliara, Madag.* 89 C7
Befasy, *Madag.* 89 C7
Befotaka, *Antsiranana, Madag.* 89 A8
Befotaka, *Fianarantsoa, Madag.* 89 C8
Bega, *Australia* 95 F4
Bega, Canalul, *Romania* 42 E5
Bégard, *France* 18 D3
Beğendik, *Turkey* 41 F10
Begoro, *Ghana* 83 D4
Begusarai, *India* 69 G12
Behābād, *Iran* 71 C8
Behala, *India* 69 H13
Behara, *Madag.* 89 C8
Behbehān, *Iran* 71 D6
Behm Canal, *U.S.A.* 104 B2
Behshahr, *Iran* 71 B7
Bei Jiang →, *China* 59 F9
Bei'an, *China* 60 B7
Beibei, *China* 58 C6
Beichuan, *China* 58 B5
Beihai, *China* 58 G7
Beijing, *China* 56 E9
Beijing □, *China* 56 E9
Beilen, *Neths.* 17 B6
Beiliu, *China* 59 F8
Beilngries, *Germany* 25 F7
Beilpajah, *Australia* 95 E3
Beilul, *Eritrea* 81 E5
Beinn na Faoghla = Benbecula, *U.K.* 14 D1
Beipan Jiang, *China* 58 E5
Beipiao, *China* 57 D11
Beira, *Mozam.* 87 F3
Beirut = Bayrūt, *Lebanon* 75 B4
Beiseker, *Canada* 104 C6
Beitaolaizhao, *China* 57 B13
Beitbridge, *Zimbabwe* 87 G3
Beiuş, *Romania* 42 D7
Beizhen = Binzhou, *China* 57 F10
Beizhen, *China* 57 D11
Beizhengzhen, *China* 57 B12
Beja, *Portugal* 35 G3
Béja, *Tunisia* 79 A7
Beja □, *Portugal* 35 H3
Bejaïa, *Algeria* 78 A7
Béjar, *Spain* 34 E5
Bejestān, *Iran* 71 C8
Bekçiler, *Turkey* 39 E11
Békés, *Hungary* 42 D6
Békés □, *Hungary* 42 D6
Békéscsaba, *Hungary* 42 D6
Bekilli, *Turkey* 39 C11
Bekily, *Madag.* 89 C8
Bekisopa, *Madag.* 89 C8
Bekitro, *Madag.* 89 C8
Bekodoka, *Madag.* 89 B8
Bekoji, *Ethiopia* 81 F4
Bekok, *Malaysia* 65 L4
Bekopaka, *Madag.* 89 B7
Bekwai, *Ghana* 83 D4
Bela, *India* 69 G10
Bela, *Pakistan* 68 F2
Bela Crkva, *Serbia, Yug.* 42 F6
Bela Palanka, *Serbia, Yug.* 40 C6
Bela Vista, *Brazil* 126 A4
Bela Vista, *Mozam.* 89 D5
Bélâbre, *France* 20 B5
Belalcázar, *Spain* 35 G5
Belan →, *India* 69 G9
Belanovica, *Serbia, Yug.* 40 B4
Belarus ■, *Europe* 46 F4
Belau = Palau ■, *Pac. Oc.* 52 J17
Belavenona, *Madag.* 89 C8
Belawan, *Indonesia* 62 D1
Belaya, *Ethiopia* 81 E4
Belaya Glina, *Russia* 49 G5
Belaya Kalitva, *Russia* 49 F5
Belaya Tserkov = Bila Tserkva, *Ukraine* 47 H6
Belceşti, *Romania* 43 C12
Bełchatów, *Poland* 45 G6
Belcher Is., *Canada* 102 A3
Belchite, *Spain* 32 D4
Belden, *U.S.A.* 116 E5
Belém, *Brazil* 125 D9
Belén, *Argentina* 126 B2
Belén, *Paraguay* 126 A4
Belen, *U.S.A.* 115 J10
Belene, *Bulgaria* 41 C9
Beleni, *Turkey* 72 D7
Bélesta, *France* 20 F5
Belet Uen, *Somali Rep.* 74 G4
Belev, *Russia* 46 F9
Belevi, *Turkey* 39 C9
Belfair, *U.S.A.* 116 C4
Belfast, *S. Africa* 89 D5
Belfast, *U.K.* 15 B6
Belfast, *Maine, U.S.A.* 109 C11
Belfast, *N.Y., U.S.A.* 110 D6
Belfast L., *U.K.* 15 B6
Belfield, *U.S.A.* 112 B3
Belfort, *France* 19 E13
Belfort, Territoire de □, *France* 19 E13
Belfry, *U.S.A.* 114 D9
Belgaum, *India* 66 M9
Belgioioso, *Italy* 28 C6
Belgium ■, *Europe* 17 D4
Belgodère, *France* 21 F13
Belgorod, *Russia* 47 G9
Belgorod-Dnestrovskiy = Bilhorod-Dnistrovskyy, *Ukraine* 47 J6
Belgrade = Beograd, *Serbia, Yug.* 40 B4
Belgrade, *U.S.A.* 114 D8
Belhaven, *U.S.A.* 109 H7
Beli Drim →, *Europe* 40 D4
Beli Manastir, *Croatia* 42 E3
Beli Timok →, *Serbia, Yug.* 40 C6
Bélice →, *Italy* 30 E5
Belinskiy, *Russia* 48 D6
Belinyu, *Indonesia* 62 E3
Beliton Is. = Belitung, *Indonesia* 62 E3
Belitung, *Indonesia* 62 E3
Beliu, *Romania* 42 D6
Belize ■, *Cent. Amer.* 119 D7
Belize City, *Belize* 119 D7
Beljakovci, *Macedonia* 40 D5
Beljanica, *Serbia, Yug.* 40 B5
Belkovskiy, Ostrov, *Russia* 51 B14
Bell →, *Canada* 102 C4
Bell I., *Canada* 103 B8
Bell-Irving →, *Canada* 104 B3
Bell Peninsula, *Canada* 101 B11
Bell Ville, *Argentina* 126 C3
Bella, *Italy* 31 B8
Bella Bella, *Canada* 104 C3
Bella Coola, *Canada* 104 C3
Bella Unión, *Uruguay* 126 C4
Bella Vista, *Corrientes, Argentina* 126 B4
Bella Vista, *Tucuman, Argentina* 126 B2
Bellac, *France* 20 B5
Bellágio, *Italy* 28 C6
Bellaire, *U.S.A.* 110 F4
Bellária, *Italy* 29 D9
Bellary, *India* 66 M10
Bellata, *Australia* 95 D4
Belle-Chasse, *U.S.A.* 113 L10
Belle Fourche, *U.S.A.* 112 C3
Belle Fourche →, *U.S.A.* 112 C3
Belle Glade, *U.S.A.* 109 M5
Belle-Île, *France* 18 E3
Belle Isle, *Canada* 103 B8
Belle Isle, Str. of, *Canada* 103 B8
Belle Plaine, *U.S.A.* 112 E8
Belle Yella, *Liberia* 82 D3
Belledonne, *France* 21 C10
Bellefontaine, *U.S.A.* 108 E4
Bellefonte, *U.S.A.* 110 F7
Bellegarde, *France* 19 E9
Bellegarde-en-Marche, *France* 20 C6
Bellegarde-sur-Valserine, *France* 19 F12
Bellême, *France* 18 D7
Belleoram, *Canada* 103 C8
Belleville, *Canada* 102 D4
Belleville, *France* 19 F11
Belleville, *Ill., U.S.A.* 112 F10
Belleville, *Kans., U.S.A.* 112 F6
Belleville, *N.Y., U.S.A.* 111 C8
Belleville-sur-Vie, *France* 18 F5
Bellevue, *Canada* 104 D6
Bellevue, *Idaho, U.S.A.* 114 E6
Bellevue, *Nebr., U.S.A.* 112 E7
Bellevue, *Ohio, U.S.A.* 110 E2
Bellevue, *Wash., U.S.A.* 116 C4
Belley, *France* 21 C9
Bellin = Kangirsuk, *Canada* 101 B13
Bellinge, *Denmark* 11 J4
Bellingen, *Australia* 95 E5
Bellingham, *U.S.A.* 100 D7
Bellingshausen Sea, *Antarctica* 5 C17
Bellinzona, *Switz.* 25 J5
Bello, *Colombia* 124 B3
Bellows Falls, *U.S.A.* 111 C12
Bellpat, *Pakistan* 68 E3
Bellpuig d'Urgell, *Spain* 32 D6
Belluno, *Italy* 29 B9
Bellwood, *U.S.A.* 110 F6
Bélmez, *Spain* 35 G5
Belmont, *Canada* 110 D3
Belmont, *S. Africa* 88 D3
Belmont, *U.S.A.* 110 D6
Belmonte, *Brazil* 125 G11
Belmonte, *Portugal* 34 E3
Belmonte, *Spain* 33 F2
Belmopan, *Belize* 119 D7
Belmullet, *Ireland* 15 B2
Belo Horizonte, *Brazil* 125 G10
Belo-sur-Mer, *Madag.* 89 C7
Belo-Tsiribihina, *Madag.* 89 B7
Belogorsk = Bilohirsk, *Ukraine* 47 K8
Belogorsk, *Russia* 51 D13
Belogradchik, *Bulgaria* 40 C6
Belogradets, *Bulgaria* 41 C11
Beloha, *Madag.* 89 D8
Beloit, *Kans., U.S.A.* 112 F5
Beloit, *Wis., U.S.A.* 112 D10
Belokorovichi, *Ukraine* 47 G5
Belomorsk, *Russia* 50 C4
Belonia, *India* 67 H17
Belopolye = Bilopillya, *Ukraine* 47 G8
Belorechensk, *Russia* 49 H4
Belorussia = Belarus ■, *Europe* 46 F4
Beloslav, *Bulgaria* 41 C11
Belovo, *Bulgaria* 41 D8
Belovo, *Russia* 50 D9
Belovodsk, *Ukraine* 47 H10
Beloye, Ozero, *Russia* 46 B9
Beloye More, *Russia* 50 C4
Belozem, *Bulgaria* 41 D9
Belozersk, *Russia* 46 B9
Belpasso, *Italy* 31 E7
Belpre, *U.S.A.* 108 F5
Belrain, *India* 69 E9
Belt, *U.S.A.* 114 C8
Beltana, *Australia* 95 E2
Belterra, *Brazil* 125 D8
Beltinci, *Slovenia* 29 B13
Belton, *U.S.A.* 113 K6
Belton L., *U.S.A.* 113 K6
Beltsy = Bălţi, *Moldova* 43 C12
Belturbet, *Ireland* 15 B4
Belukha, *Russia* 50 E9
Beluran, *Malaysia* 62 C5
Beluša, *Slovak Rep.* 27 B11
Belušić, *Serbia, Yug.* 40 C5
Belvedere Maríttimo, *Italy* 31 C8
Belvès, *France* 20 D5
Belvidere, *Ill., U.S.A.* 112 D10
Belvidere, *N.J., U.S.A.* 111 F9
Belvis de la Jara, *Spain* 34 F6
Belyando →, *Australia* 94 C4
Belyy, *Russia* 46 E7
Belyy, Ostrov, *Russia* 50 B8
Belyy Yar, *Russia* 50 D9
Bełżec, *Poland* 45 H10
Belzig, *Germany* 24 C8
Belzoni, *U.S.A.* 113 J9
Bełżyce, *Poland* 45 G9
Bemaraha, Lembalemban' i, *Madag.* 89 B7
Bemarivo, *Madag.* 89 C7
Bemarivo →, *Antsiranana, Madag.* 89 A9
Bemarivo →, *Mahajanga, Madag.* 89 B8
Bemavo, *Madag.* 89 C8
Bembéréke, *Benin* 83 C5
Bembesi, *Zimbabwe* 87 G2
Bembesi →, *Zimbabwe* 87 F2
Bembézar →, *Spain* 35 H5
Bembibre, *Spain* 34 C4
Bemetara, *India* 69 J9
Bemidji, *U.S.A.* 112 B7
Bemolanga, *Madag.* 89 B8
Ben, *Iran* 71 C6
Ben Cruachan, *U.K.* 14 E3
Ben Dearg, *U.K.* 14 D4
Ben Hope, *U.K.* 14 C4
Ben Lawers, *U.K.* 14 E4
Ben Lomond, *N.S.W., Australia* 95 E5

Ben Lomond, Tas., Australia 94 G4
Ben Lomond, U.K. 14 E4
Ben Luc, Vietnam 65 G6
Ben Macdhui, U.K. 14 D5
Ben Mhor, U.K. 14 D1
Ben More, Arg. & Bute, U.K. 14 E2
Ben More, Stirl., U.K. 14 E4
Ben More Assynt, U.K. 14 C4
Ben Nevis, U.K. 14 E3
Ben Quang, Vietnam 64 D6
Ben Vorlich, U.K. 14 E4
Ben Wyvis, U.K. 14 D4
Bena, Nigeria 83 C6
Benāb, Iran 73 D12
Benalla, Australia 95 F4
Benalmádena, Spain 35 J6
Benares = Varanasi, India 69 G10
Bénat, C., France 21 E10
Benavente, Portugal 35 G2
Benavente, Spain 34 C5
Benavides, U.S.A. 113 M5
Benavides de Órbigo, Spain 34 C5
Benbecula, U.K. 14 D1
Benbonyathe, Australia 95 E2
Bend, U.S.A. 114 D3
Bender Beila, Somali Rep. 74 F5
Bendery = Tighina, Moldova 43 D14
Bendigo, Australia 95 F3
Bendorf, Germany 24 E3
Benē Beraq, Israel 75 C3
Bénéna, Mali 82 C4
Benenitra, Madag. 89 C8
Benešov, Czech Rep. 26 B7
Benevento, Italy 31 A7
Benfeld, France 19 D14
Benga, Mozam. 87 F3
Bengal, Bay of, Ind. Oc. 67 M17
Bengbis, Cameroon 83 E7
Bengbu, China 57 H9
Benghazi = Banghāzī, Libya 79 B10
Bengkalis, Indonesia 62 D2
Bengkulu, Indonesia 62 E2
Bengkulu □, Indonesia 62 E2
Bengough, Canada 105 D7
Bengtsfors, Sweden 10 E6
Benguela, Angola 85 G2
Benguérua, I., Mozam. 89 C6
Benha, Egypt 80 H7
Beni, Dem. Rep. of the Congo 86 B2
Beni →, Bolivia 124 F5
Beni Mazâr, Egypt 80 B3
Beni Mellal, Morocco 78 B4
Beni Suef, Egypt 80 J7
Beniah L., Canada 104 A6
Benicarló, Spain 32 E5
Benicássim, Spain 32 E5
Benicia, U.S.A. 116 G4
Benidorm, Spain 33 G4
Benin ■, Africa 83 D5
Benin →, Nigeria 83 D6
Benin, Bight of, W. Afr. 83 E5
Benin City, Nigeria 83 D6
Benisa, Spain 33 G5
Benitses, Greece 36 A3
Benjamin Aceval, Paraguay 126 A4
Benjamin Constant, Brazil 124 D4
Benjamin Hill, Mexico 118 A2
Benkelman, U.S.A. 112 E4
Benkovac, Croatia 29 D12
Bennett, Canada 104 B2
Bennett, L., Australia 92 D5
Bennetta, Ostrov, Russia 51 B15
Bennettsville, U.S.A. 109 H6
Bennichchāb, Mauritania 82 B1
Bennington, N.H., U.S.A. 111 D11
Bennington, Vt., U.S.A. 111 D11
Bénodet, France 18 E2
Benoni, S. Africa 89 D4
Benque Viejo, Belize 119 D7
Bensheim, Germany 25 F4
Benson, Ariz., U.S.A. 115 L8
Benson, Minn., U.S.A. 112 C7
Bent, Iran 71 E8
Benteng, Indonesia 63 F6
Bentinck I., Australia 94 B2
Bentiu, Sudan 81 F2
Bento Gonçalves, Brazil 127 B5
Benton, Ark., U.S.A. 113 H8
Benton, Calif., U.S.A. 116 H8
Benton, Ill., U.S.A. 112 G10
Benton, Pa., U.S.A. 111 E8
Benton Harbor, U.S.A. 108 D2
Bentonville, U.S.A. 113 G7
Bentu Liben, Ethiopia 81 F4
Bentung, Malaysia 65 L3
Benue □, Nigeria 83 D6
Benue →, Nigeria 83 D6
Benxi, China 57 D12
Beo, Indonesia 63 D7
Beograd, Serbia, Yug. 40 B4
Beoumi, Ivory C. 82 D3
Bepan Jiang →, China 58 E6
Beppu, Japan 55 H5
Beqaa Valley = Al Biqā, Lebanon 75 A5
Ber Mota, India 68 H3
Berach →, India 68 G6
Beraketa, Madag. 89 C7
Berane, Montenegro, Yug. 40 D3
Berat, Albania 40 F3
Berau, Teluk, Indonesia 63 E8
Beravina, Madag. 89 B8
Berber, Sudan 80 D3
Berbera, Somali Rep. 74 E4
Berbérati, C.A.R. 84 D3
Berbice →, Guyana 124 B7
Berceto, Italy 28 D6
Berchidda, Italy 30 B2
Berchtesgaden, Germany 25 H8
Berck, France 19 B8
Berdichev = Berdychiv, Ukraine 47 H5
Berdsk, Russia 50 D9
Berdyansk, Ukraine 47 J9
Berdychiv, Ukraine 47 H5
Berea, U.S.A. 108 G3
Berebere, Indonesia 63 D7
Bereda, Somali Rep. 74 E5
Berehove, Ukraine 47 H2
Berekum, Ghana 82 D4
Berenice, Egypt 80 C4
Berens →, Canada 105 C9
Berens I., Canada 105 C9
Berens River, Canada 105 C9
Beresford, U.S.A. 112 D6
Berestechko, Ukraine 47 G3
Bereşti, Romania 43 D12
Beretău →, Romania 42 C6
Berettyó →, Hungary 42 D6
Berettyóújfalu, Hungary 42 C6
Berevo, Mahajanga, Madag. 89 B7
Berevo, Toliara, Madag. 89 B7
Bereza = Byaroza, Belarus 47 F3
Berezhany, Ukraine 47 H3
Berezina = Byarezina →, Belarus 47 F6
Berezivka, Ukraine 47 J6
Berezna, Ukraine 47 G6
Berezniki, Russia 50 C5
Berezniki, Russia 50 D6
Berezovo, Russia 50 C7
Berga, Spain 32 C6
Berga, Sweden 11 G10
Bergama, Turkey 39 B9
Bérgamo, Italy 28 C6
Bergara, Spain 32 B2
Bergby, Sweden 10 D11
Bergedorf, Germany 24 B6
Bergeforsen, Sweden 10 B11
Bergen, Mecklenburg-Vorpommern, Germany 24 A9
Bergen, Niedersachsen, Germany 24 C5
Bergen, Neths. 17 B4
Bergen, Norway 9 F11
Bergen, U.S.A. 110 C7
Bergen op Zoom, Neths. 17 C4
Bergerac, France 20 D4
Bergheim, Germany 24 E2
Bergholz, U.S.A. 110 F4
Bergisch Gladbach, Germany 17 D7
Bergkamen, Germany 24 D3
Bergkvara, Sweden 11 H10
Bergshamra, Sweden 10 E12
Bergsjö, Sweden 10 C11
Bergues, France 19 B9
Bergviken, Sweden 10 C10
Bergville, S. Africa 89 D4
Berhala, Selat, Indonesia 62 E2
Berhampore = Baharampur, India 69 G13
Berhampur = Brahmapur, India 67 K14
Berheci →, Romania 43 E12
Bering Sea, Pac. Oc. 100 C1
Bering Strait, Pac. Oc. 100 B3
Beringovskiy, Russia 51 C18
Berisso, Argentina 126 C4
Berja, Spain 35 J8
Berkeley, U.S.A. 116 H4
Berkner I., Antarctica 5 D18
Berkovitsa, Bulgaria 40 C7
Berkshire, U.S.A. 111 D8
Berkshire Downs, U.K. 13 F6
Berlanga, Spain 35 G5
Berlenga, I., Portugal 35 F1
Berlin, Germany 24 C9
Berlin, Md., U.S.A. 108 F8
Berlin, N.H., U.S.A. 111 B13
Berlin, N.Y., U.S.A. 111 D11
Berlin, Wis., U.S.A. 108 D1
Berlin □, Germany 24 C9
Berlin L., U.S.A. 110 E4
Bermeja, Sierra, Spain 35 J5
Bermejo →, Formosa, Argentina 126 B4
Bermejo →, San Juan, Argentina 126 C2
Bermen, L., Canada 103 B6
Bermeo, Spain 32 B2
Bermillo de Sayago, Spain 34 D4
Bermuda ■, Atl. Oc. 98 F13
Bern, Switz. 25 J3
Bern □, Switz. 25 J3
Bernalda, Italy 31 B9
Bernalillo, U.S.A. 115 J10
Bernardo de Irigoyen, Argentina 127 B5
Bernardo O'Higgins □, Chile 126 C1
Bernardsville, U.S.A. 111 F10
Bernasconi, Argentina 126 D3
Bernau, Bayern, Germany 25 H8
Bernau, Brandenburg, Germany 24 C9
Bernay, France 18 C7
Bernburg, Germany 24 D7
Berndorf, Austria 26 D9
Berne = Bern, Switz. 25 J3
Berne = Bern □, Switz. 25 J3
Berner Alpen, Switz. 25 J3
Berneray, U.K. 14 D1
Bernier I., Australia 93 D1
Bernina, Piz, Switz. 25 J5
Bernkastel-Kues, Germany 25 F3
Beroroha, Madag. 89 C8
Béroubouay, Benin 83 C5
Beroun, Czech Rep. 26 B7
Berounka →, Czech Rep. 26 B7
Berovo, Macedonia 40 E6
Berre, Étang de, France 21 E9
Berre-l'Étang, France 21 E9
Berri, Australia 95 E3
Berriane, Algeria 78 B6
Berry, Australia 95 E5
Berry, France 19 F8
Berry Is., Bahamas 120 A4
Berryessa L., U.S.A. 116 G4
Berryville, U.S.A. 113 G8
Berseba, Namibia 88 D2
Bersenbrück, Germany 24 C3
Bershad, Ukraine 47 H5
Berthold, U.S.A. 112 A4
Berthoud, U.S.A. 112 E2
Bertincourt, France 19 B9
Bertoua, Cameroon 84 D2
Bertraghboy B., Ireland 15 C2
Berwick, U.S.A. 111 E8
Berwick-upon-Tweed, U.K. 12 B6
Berwyn Mts., U.K. 12 E4
Beryslav, Ukraine 47 J7
Berzasca, Romania 42 F6
Berzence, Hungary 42 D2
Besal, Pakistan 69 B5
Besalampy, Madag. 89 B7
Besançon, France 19 E13
Besar, Indonesia 62 E5
Beshenkovichi, Belarus 46 E5
Beška, Serbia, Yug. 42 E5
Beslan, Russia 49 J7
Besna Kobila, Serbia, Yug. 40 D6
Besnard L., Canada 105 B7
Besni, Turkey 70 B3
Besor, N. →, Egypt 75 D3
Bessarabiya, Moldova 47 J5
Bessarabka = Basarabeasca, Moldova 43 D13
Bessèges, France 21 D8
Bessemer, Ala., U.S.A. 109 J2
Bessemer, Mich., U.S.A. 112 B9
Bessemer, Pa., U.S.A. 110 F4
Bessin, France 18 C6
Bessines-sur-Gartempe, France 20 B5
Beswick, Australia 92 B5
Bet She'an, Israel 75 C4
Bet Shemesh, Israel 75 D4
Betafo, Madag. 89 B8
Betancuria, Canary Is. 37 F5
Betanzos, Spain 34 B2
Bétaré Oya, Cameroon 84 C2
Betatao, Madag. 89 B8
Bétera, Spain 33 F4
Bétérou, Benin 83 D5
Bethal, S. Africa 89 D4
Bethanien, Namibia 88 D2
Bethany, Canada 110 B6
Bethany, U.S.A. 112 E7
Bethel, Alaska, U.S.A. 100 B3
Bethel, Conn., U.S.A. 111 E11
Bethel, Maine, U.S.A. 111 B14
Bethel, Vt., U.S.A. 111 C12
Bethel Park, U.S.A. 110 F4
Béthenville, France 19 C11
Bethlehem = Bayt Lahm, West Bank 75 D4
Bethlehem, S. Africa 89 D4
Bethlehem, U.S.A. 111 F9
Bethulie, S. Africa 88 E4
Béthune, France 19 B9
Béthune →, France 18 C8
Betioky, Madag. 89 C7
Betong, Thailand 65 K3
Betoota, Australia 94 D3
Betor, Ethiopia 81 E4
Betroka, Madag. 89 C8
Betsiamites, Canada 103 C6
Betsiamites →, Canada 103 C6
Betsiboka →, Madag. 89 B8
Bettendorf, U.S.A. 112 E9
Bettiah, India 69 F11
Bettna, Sweden 11 F10
Béttola, Italy 28 D6
Betul, India 66 J10
Betung, Malaysia 62 D4
Betws-y-Coed, U.K. 12 D4
Betxi, Spain 32 F4
Betzdorf, Germany 24 E3
Beuil, France 21 D10
Beulah, Mich., U.S.A. 108 C2
Beulah, N. Dak., U.S.A. 112 B4
Beuvron →, France 18 E8
Beveren, Belgium 17 C4
Beverley, Australia 93 F2
Beverley, U.K. 12 D7
Beverley Hills, U.S.A. 109 L4
Beverly, U.S.A. 111 D14
Beverly Hills, U.S.A. 117 L8
Beverungen, Germany 24 D5
Bevoalavo, Madag. 89 D7
Bewas →, India 69 H8
Bex, Switz. 25 J3
Bexhill, U.K. 13 G8
Bey Dağları, Turkey 39 E12
Beyānlū, Iran 70 C5
Beyazköy, Turkey 41 E11
Beyçayırı, Turkey 41 F10
Beydağ, Turkey 39 C10
Beyeğaç, Turkey 39 D10
Beyin, Ghana 82 D4
Beykoz, Turkey 41 E13
Beyla, Guinea 82 D3
Beynat, France 20 C5
Beyneu, Kazakstan 50 E6
Beyoba, Turkey 39 C9
Beyoğlu, Turkey 41 E12
Beypazarı, Turkey 72 B4
Beyşehir, Turkey 72 D4
Beyşehir Gölü, Turkey 70 B1
Beytüşşebap, Turkey 73 D10
Bezdan, Serbia, Yug. 42 E3
Bezhetsk, Russia 46 D9
Béziers, France 20 E7
Bezwada = Vijayawada, India 67 L12
Bhabua, India 69 G10
Bhachau, India 66 H7
Bhadar →, Gujarat, India 68 H5
Bhadar →, Gujarat, India 68 J3
Bhadarwah, India 69 C6
Bhadohi, India 69 G10
Bhadra, India 68 E6
Bhadrakh, India 67 J15
Bhadran, India 68 H5
Bhadravati, India 66 N9
Bhag, Pakistan 68 E2
Bhagalpur, India 69 G12
Bhagirathi →, Ut. P., India 69 D8
Bhagirathi →, W. Bengal, India 69 H13
Bhakkar, Pakistan 68 D4
Bhakra Dam, India 68 D7
Bhamo, Burma 67 G20
Bhandara, India 66 J11
Bhanpura, India 68 G6
Bhanrer Ra., India 69 H8
Bhaptiahi, India 69 F12
Bharat = India ■, Asia 66 K11
Bharatpur, Mad. P., India 69 H9
Bharatpur, Raj., India 68 F7
Bharno, India 69 H11
Bhatinda, India 68 D6
Bhatpara, India 69 H13
Bhattu, India 68 E6
Bhaun, Pakistan 68 C5
Bhaunagar = Bhavnagar, India 66 J8
Bhavnagar, India 66 J8
Bhawari, India 68 G5
Bhayavadar, India 68 J4
Bhera, Pakistan 68 C5
Bhikangaon, India 68 J6
Bhilsa = Vidisha, India 68 H7
Bhilwara, India 68 G6
Bhima →, India 66 L10
Bhimbar, Pakistan 69 C6
Bhind, India 69 F8
Bhinga, India 69 F9
Bhinmal, India 68 G5
Bhiwandi, India 66 K8
Bhiwani, India 68 E7
Bhogava →, India 68 H5
Bhola, Bangla. 67 H17
Bholari, Pakistan 68 G3
Bhopal, India 68 H7
Bhubaneshwar, India 67 J14
Bhuj, India 68 H3
Bhusaval, India 66 J9
Bhutan ■, Asia 67 F17
Biafra, B. of = Bonny, Bight of, Africa 83 E6
Biak, Indonesia 63 E9
Biała, Poland 45 H4
Biała →, Poland 45 H7
Biała Piska, Poland 44 E9
Biała Podlaska, Poland 45 F10
Biała Rawska, Poland 45 G7
Białobrzegi, Poland 45 G7
Białogard, Poland 44 D2
Białowieża, Poland 45 F10
Biały Bór, Poland 44 E3
Białystok, Poland 45 E10
Biancavilla, Italy 31 E7
Bianco, Italy 31 D9
Biankouma, Ivory C. 82 D3
Biaora, India 68 H7
Bīārjmand, Iran 71 B7
Biaro, Indonesia 63 D7
Biarritz, France 20 E2
Biasca, Switz. 25 J4
Biba, Egypt 80 J7
Bibai, Japan 54 C10
Bibbiena, Italy 29 E8
Bibby I., Canada 105 A10
Bibel →, Spain 34 C3
Biberach, Germany 25 G5
Bibiani, Ghana 82 D4
Bibungwa, Dem. Rep. of the Congo 86 C2
Bic, Canada 103 C6
Bicaj, Albania 40 E4
Bicaz, Romania 43 D11
Bicazu Ardelean, Romania 43 D10
Biccari, Italy 31 A8
Bicester, U.K. 13 F6
Bichena, Ethiopia 81 E4
Bicheno, Australia 94 G4
Bichia, India 69 H9
Bichvinta, Georgia 49 J5
Bickerton I., Australia 94 A2
Bicske, Hungary 42 C3
Bida, Nigeria 83 D6
Bidar, India 66 L10
Biddeford, U.S.A. 109 D10
Biddwara, Ethiopia 81 F4
Bideford, U.K. 13 F3
Bideford Bay, U.K. 13 F3
Bidhuna, India 69 F8
Bidor, Malaysia 65 K3
Bie, Sweden 10 E10
Bié, Planalto de, Angola 85 G3
Bieber, U.S.A. 114 F3
Biebrza →, Poland 45 E9
Biecz, Poland 45 J8
Biel, Switz. 25 H3
Bielawa, Poland 45 H3
Bielefeld, Germany 24 C4
Bielersee, Switz. 25 H3
Biella, Italy 28 C5
Bielsk Podlaski, Poland 45 F10
Bielsko-Biała, Poland 45 J6
Bien Hoa, Vietnam 65 G6
Bienne = Biel, Switz. 25 H3
Bienvenida, Spain 35 G4
Bienville, L., Canada 102 A5
Bierné, France 18 E6
Bierun, Poland 45 H6
Bierutów, Poland 45 G4
Biescas, Spain 32 C4
Biese →, Germany 24 C7
Biesiesfontein, S. Africa 88 E2
Bietigheim-Bissingen, Germany 25 G5
Bieżuń, Poland 45 F6
Biferno →, Italy 29 G12
Big →, Canada 103 B8
Big B., Canada 103 A7
Big Bear City, U.S.A. 117 L10
Big Bear Lake, U.S.A. 117 L10
Big Belt Mts., U.S.A. 114 C8
Big Bend, Swaziland 89 D5
Big Bend National Park, U.S.A. 113 L3
Big Black →, U.S.A. 113 K9
Big Blue →, U.S.A. 112 F6
Big Creek, U.S.A. 116 H7
Big Cypress National Preserve, U.S.A. 109 M5
Big Cypress Swamp, U.S.A. 109 M5
Big Falls, U.S.A. 112 A8
Big Fork →, U.S.A. 112 A8
Big Horn Mts. = Bighorn Mts., U.S.A. 114 D10
Big I., Canada 104 A5
Big Lake, U.S.A. 113 K4
Big Moose, U.S.A. 111 C10
Big Muddy Cr. →, U.S.A. 112 A2
Big Pine, U.S.A. 116 H8
Big Piney, U.S.A. 114 E8
Big Rapids, U.S.A. 108 D3
Big Rideau L., Canada 111 B8
Big River, Canada 105 C7
Big Run, U.S.A. 110 F6
Big Sable Pt., U.S.A. 108 C2
Big Salmon →, Canada 104 A2
Big Sand L., Canada 105 B9
Big Sandy, U.S.A. 114 B8
Big Sandy →, U.S.A. 108 F4
Big Sandy Cr. →, U.S.A. 112 F3
Big Sioux →, U.S.A. 112 D6
Big Spring, U.S.A. 113 J4
Big Stone City, U.S.A. 112 C6
Big Stone Gap, U.S.A. 109 G4
Big Stone L., U.S.A. 112 C6
Big Sur, U.S.A. 116 J5
Big Timber, U.S.A. 114 D9
Big Trout L., Canada 102 B2
Big Trout Lake, Canada 102 B2
Biğa, Turkey 41 F11
Biga →, Turkey 41 F11
Bigadiç, Turkey 39 B10
Biganos, France 20 D3
Biggar, Canada 105 C7
Biggar, U.K. 14 F5
Bigge I., Australia 92 B4
Biggenden, Australia 95 D5
Biggleswade, U.K. 13 E7
Biggs, U.S.A. 116 F5
Bighorn, U.S.A. 114 C10
Bighorn →, U.S.A. 114 C10
Bighorn L., U.S.A. 114 D9
Bighorn Mts., U.S.A. 114 D10
Bignona, Senegal 82 C1
Bigorre, France 20 E4
Bigstone L., Canada 105 C9
Biguglia, Étang de, France 21 F13
Bigwa, Tanzania 86 D4
Bihać, Bos.-H. 29 D12
Bihar, India 69 G11
Bihar □, India 69 G12
Biharamulo, Tanzania 86 C3
Bihariganj, India 69 G12
Biharkeresztes, Hungary 42 C6
Bihor □, Romania 42 D7
Bihor, Munţii, Romania 42 D7
Bijagós, Arquipélago dos, Guinea-Biss. 82 C1
Bijaipur, India 68 F7
Bijapur, Karnataka, India 66 L9
Bijapur, Mad. P., India 67 K12
Bījār, Iran 70 C5
Bijawar, India 69 G8
Bijeljina, Bos.-H. 42 F4
Bijelo Polje, Montenegro, Yug. 40 C3
Bijie, China 58 D5
Bijnor, India 68 E8
Bikaner, India 68 E5
Bikapur, India 69 F10
Bikeqi, China 56 D6
Bikfayyā, Lebanon 75 B4
Bikin, Russia 51 E14
Bikin →, Russia 54 A7
Bikini Atoll, Marshall Is. 96 F8
Bikita, Zimbabwe 89 C5
Bikoué, Cameroon 83 E7
Bila Tserkva, Ukraine 47 H6
Bilanga, Burkina Faso 83 C4
Bilara, India 68 F5
Bilaspur, Mad. P., India 69 H10
Bilaspur, Punjab, India 68 D7
Biläsuvar, Azerbaijan 73 C13
Bilauk Taungdan, Thailand 64 F2
Bilbao, Spain 32 B2
Bilbeis, Egypt 80 H7
Bilbo = Bilbao, Spain 32 B2
Bilbor, Romania 43 C10
Bilciureşti, Romania 43 F10

Bíldudalur, *Iceland* 8 D2
Bílé Karpaty, *Europe* 27 B11
Bileća, *Bos.-H.* 40 D2
Bilecik, *Turkey* 72 B4
Biłgoraj, *Poland* 45 H9
Bilgram, *India* 69 F9
Bilhaur, *India* 69 F9
Bilhorod-Dnistrovskyy, *Ukraine* 47 J6
Bilibino, *Russia* 51 C17
Bilibiza, *Mozam.* 87 E5
Bilisht, *Albania* 40 F5
Billabalong Roadhouse, *Australia* 93 E2
Billdal, *Sweden* 11 G5
Billiluna, *Australia* 92 C4
Billings, *U.S.A.* 114 D9
Billiton Is. = Belitung, *Indonesia* 62 E3
Billsta, *Sweden* 10 A12
Billund, *Denmark* 11 J3
Bilma, *Niger* 79 E8
Bilo Gora, *Croatia* 42 E2
Biloela, *Australia* 94 C5
Bilohirsk, *Ukraine* 47 K8
Bilopillya, *Ukraine* 47 G8
Biloxi, *U.S.A.* 113 K10
Bilpa Morea Claypan, *Australia* 94 D3
Biltine, *Chad* 79 F10
Bilyarsk, *Russia* 48 C10
Bima, *Indonesia* 63 F5
Bimban, *Egypt* 80 C3
Bimbila, *Ghana* 83 D5
Bimini Is., *Bahamas* 120 A4
Bin Xian, *Heilongjiang, China* 57 B14
Bin Xian, *Shaanxi, China* 56 G5
Bin Yauri, *Nigeria* 83 C5
Bina-Etawah, *India* 68 G8
Bīnāb, *Iran* 71 B6
Binalbagan, *Phil.* 61 F5
Binalong, *Australia* 95 E4
Bīnālūd, Kūh-e, *Iran* 71 B8
Binatang = Bintangor, *Malaysia* 62 D4
Binche, *Belgium* 17 D4
Binchuan, *China* 58 E3
Binder, *Chad* 83 D7
Bindki, *India* 69 F9
Bindslev, *Denmark* 11 G4
Bindura, *Zimbabwe* 87 F3
Binefar, *Spain* 32 D5
Bingara, *Australia* 95 D5
Bingen, *Germany* 25 F3
Bingerville, *Ivory C.* 82 D4
Bingham, *U.S.A.* 109 C11
Binghamton, *U.S.A.* 111 D9
Bingöl, *Turkey* 70 B4
Bingöl Dağları, *Turkey* 73 C9
Bingsjö, *Sweden* 10 C9
Binh Dinh = An Nhon, *Vietnam* 64 F7
Binh Khe, *Vietnam* 64 F7
Binh Son, *Vietnam* 64 E7
Binhai, *China* 57 G10
Binic, *France* 18 D4
Binisatua, *Spain* 37 B11
Binjai, *Indonesia* 62 D3
Binji, *Nigeria* 83 C5
Binnaway, *Australia* 95 E4
Binongko, *Indonesia* 63 F6
Binscarth, *Canada* 105 C8
Bint Goda, *Sudan* 81 E3
Bintan, *Indonesia* 62 D2
Bintangor, *Malaysia* 62 D4
Bintulu, *Malaysia* 62 D4
Bintuni, *Indonesia* 63 E8
Binyang, *China* 58 F7
Binz, *Germany* 24 A9
Binzert = Bizerte, *Tunisia* 79 A7
Binzhou, *China* 57 F10
Bío Bío □, *Chile* 126 D1
Biograd na Moru, *Croatia* 29 E12
Bioko, *Eq. Guin.* 83 E6
Biokovo, *Croatia* 29 E14
Bipindi, *Cameroon* 83 E7
Bir, *India* 66 K9
Bir, Ras, *Djibouti* 81 E5
Bîr Abu Hashim, *Egypt* 80 C3
Bîr Abu Minqar, *Egypt* 80 B2
Bîr Abu Muḩammad, *Egypt* 75 F3
Bi'r ad Dabbāghāt, *Jordan* 75 E4
Bîr Adal Deib, *Sudan* 80 C4
Bi'r al Butayyihāt, *Jordan* 75 F4
Bi'r al Mārī, *Jordan* 75 E4
Bi'r al Qattār, *Jordan* 75 F4
Bîr 'Asal, *Egypt* 80 B3
Bir Atrun, *Sudan* 80 D2
Bîr Beiḍa, *Egypt* 75 E3
Bîr Diqnash, *Egypt* 80 A2
Bîr el 'Abd, *Egypt* 75 D2
Bîr el Basur, *Egypt* 80 B2
Bîr el Biarât, *Egypt* 75 F3
Bîr el Duweidar, *Egypt* 75 E1
Bîr el Garârât, *Egypt* 75 D2
Bîr el Gellaz, *Egypt* 80 A2
Bîr el Heisi, *Egypt* 75 F3
Bîr el Jafir, *Egypt* 75 E1
Bîr el Mâlḩi, *Egypt* 75 E2
Bîr el Shaqqa, *Egypt* 80 A2
Bîr el Thamâda, *Egypt* 75 E2
Bîr Fuad, *Egypt* 80 A2
Bîr Gebeil Ḩişn, *Egypt* 75 E2
Bi'r Ghadīr, *Syria* 75 A6
Bîr Haimur, *Egypt* 80 C3
Bîr Ḩasana, *Egypt* 75 E2
Bîr Hööker, *Egypt* 80 H7
Bîr Kanayis, *Egypt* 80 C3
Bîr Kaseiba, *Egypt* 75 E2
Bîr Kerawein, *Egypt* 80 B2
Bîr Lahfân, *Egypt* 75 E2
Bîr Madkûr, *Egypt* 75 E1
Bîr Maql, *Egypt* 80 C3
Bîr Mîneiga, *Sudan* 80 C4
Bîr Misaha, *Egypt* 80 C2
Bîr Mogreïn, *Mauritania* 78 C3
Bîr Murr, *Egypt* 80 C3
Bi'r Muṭribah, *Kuwait* 70 D5
Bîr Nakheila, *Egypt* 80 C3
Bîr Qaṭia, *Egypt* 75 E1
Bîr Qatrani, *Egypt* 80 A2
Bîr Ranga, *Egypt* 80 C4
Bîr Sahara, *Egypt* 80 C2
Bîr Seiyâla, *Egypt* 80 B3
Bîr Shalatein, *Egypt* 80 C4
Bîr Shebb, *Egypt* 80 C2
Bîr Shût, *Egypt* 80 C4
Bîr Terfawi, *Egypt* 80 C2
Bîr Umm Qubûr, *Egypt* 80 C3
Bîr Ungât, *Egypt* 80 C3
Bîr Za'farâna, *Egypt* 80 J8
Bîr Zeidûn, *Egypt* 80 B3
Biramféro, *Guinea* 82 C3
Biratnagar, *Nepal* 69 F12
Birawa, *Dem. Rep. of the Congo* 86 C2
Birch →, *Canada* 104 B6
Birch Hills, *Canada* 105 C7
Birch I., *Canada* 105 C9
Birch L., *N.W.T., Canada* 104 A5
Birch L., *Ont., Canada* 102 B1
Birch Mts., *Canada* 104 B6
Birch River, *Canada* 105 C8
Birchip, *Australia* 95 F3
Birchiş, *Romania* 42 E7
Bird, *Canada* 105 B10
Bird I. = Las Aves, Is., *W. Indies* 121 C7
Birdsville, *Australia* 94 D2
Birdum Cr. →, *Australia* 92 C5
Birecik, *Turkey* 70 B3
Birein, *Israel* 75 E3
Bireuen, *Indonesia* 62 C1
Biri →, *Sudan* 81 F2
Birifo, *Gambia* 82 C2
Birigui, *Brazil* 127 A5
Birjand, *Iran* 71 C8
Birkenfeld, *Germany* 25 F3
Birkenhead, *U.K.* 12 D4
Birkerød, *Denmark* 11 J6
Birket Qârûn, *Egypt* 80 J7
Birkfeld, *Austria* 26 D8
Bîrlad = Bârlad, *Romania* 43 D12
Birmingham, *U.K.* 13 E6
Birmingham, *U.S.A.* 109 J2
Birmitrapur, *India* 67 H14
Birni Ngaouré, *Niger* 83 C5
Birni Nkonni, *Niger* 83 C6
Birnin Gwari, *Nigeria* 83 C6
Birnin Kebbi, *Nigeria* 83 C5
Birnin Kudu, *Nigeria* 83 C6
Birobidzhan, *Russia* 51 E14
Birr, *Ireland* 15 C4
Birrie →, *Australia* 95 D4
Birsilpur, *India* 68 E5
Birsk, *Russia* 50 D6
Birštonas, *Lithuania* 44 D11
Birtle, *Canada* 105 C8
Birur, *India* 66 N9
Biryuchiy, *Ukraine* 47 J8
Biržai, *Lithuania* 9 H21
Birzebbugga, *Malta* 36 D2
Bisa, *Indonesia* 63 E7
Bisáccia, *Italy* 31 A8
Bisacquino, *Italy* 30 E6
Bisalpur, *India* 69 E8
Bisbee, *U.S.A.* 115 L9
Biscarrosse, *France* 20 D2
Biscarrosse et de Parentis, Étang de, *France* 20 D2
Biscay, B. of, *Atl. Oc.* 6 F5
Biscayne B., *U.S.A.* 109 N5
Biscéglie, *Italy* 31 A9
Bischheim, *France* 19 D14
Bischofshofen, *Austria* 26 D6
Bischofswerda, *Germany* 24 D10
Bischwiller, *France* 19 D14
Biscoe Bay, *Antarctica* 5 D13
Biscoe Is., *Antarctica* 5 C17
Biscostasing, *Canada* 102 C3
Biševo, *Croatia* 29 F13
Bisha, *Eritrea* 81 D4
Bishah, W. →, *Si. Arabia* 80 C5
Bishan, *China* 58 C6
Bishkek, *Kyrgyzstan* 50 E8
Bishnupur, *India* 69 H12
Bisho, *S. Africa* 89 E4
Bishop, *Calif., U.S.A.* 116 H8
Bishop, *Tex., U.S.A.* 113 M6
Bishop Auckland, *U.K.* 12 C6
Bishop's Falls, *Canada* 103 C8
Bishop's Stortford, *U.K.* 13 F8
Bisignano, *Italy* 31 C9
Bisina, L., *Uganda* 86 B3
Biskra, *Algeria* 78 B7
Biskupiec, *Poland* 44 E7
Bismarck, *U.S.A.* 112 B4
Bismarck Arch., *Papua N. G.* 96 H7
Bismark, *Germany* 24 C7
Bismil, *Turkey* 73 D9
Biso, *Uganda* 86 B3
Bison, *U.S.A.* 112 C3
Bīsotūn, *Iran* 70 C5
Bispgården, *Sweden* 10 A10
Bissagos = Bijagós, Arquipélago dos, *Guinea-Biss.* 82 C1
Bissau, *Guinea-Biss.* 82 C1
Bissaula, *Nigeria* 83 D7
Bissikrima, *Guinea* 82 C2
Bissorã, *Guinea-Biss.* 82 C1
Bistcho L., *Canada* 104 B5
Bistreţ, *Romania* 43 G8
Bistrica = Ilirska-Bistrica, *Slovenia* 29 C11
Bistriţa, *Romania* 43 C9
Bistriţa →, *Romania* 43 D11
Bistriţa Năsăud □, *Romania* 43 C9
Bistriţei, Munţii, *Romania* 43 C10
Biswan, *India* 69 F9
Bisztynek, *Poland* 44 D7
Bitburg, *Germany* 25 F2
Bitche, *France* 19 C14
Bithynia, *Turkey* 72 B4
Bitlis, *Turkey* 70 B4
Bitola, *Macedonia* 40 E5
Bitolj = Bitola, *Macedonia* 40 E5
Bitonto, *Italy* 31 A9
Bitter Creek, *U.S.A.* 114 F9
Bitter L. = Buheirat-Murrat-el-Kubra, *Egypt* 80 H8
Bitterfeld, *Germany* 24 D8
Bitterfontein, *S. Africa* 88 E2
Bitterroot →, *U.S.A.* 114 C6
Bitterroot Range, *U.S.A.* 114 D6
Bitterwater, *U.S.A.* 116 J6
Bitti, *Italy* 30 B2
Bittou, *Burkina Faso* 83 C4
Biu, *Nigeria* 83 C7
Bivolari, *Romania* 43 C12
Bivolu, Vf., *Romania* 43 C10
Biwa-Ko, *Japan* 55 G8
Biwabik, *U.S.A.* 112 B8
Bixad, *Romania* 43 C8
Bixby, *U.S.A.* 113 H7
Biyang, *China* 56 H7
Biysk, *Russia* 50 D9
Bizana, *S. Africa* 89 E4
Bizen, *Japan* 55 G7
Bizerte, *Tunisia* 79 A7
Bjargtangar, *Iceland* 8 D1
Bjärnum, *Sweden* 11 H7
Bjästa, *Sweden* 10 A12
Bjelasica, *Montenegro, Yug.* 40 D3
Bjelašnica, *Bos.-H.* 42 G3
Bjelovar, *Croatia* 29 C13
Bjerringbro, *Denmark* 11 H3
Björbo, *Sweden* 10 D8
Björklinge, *Sweden* 10 D11
Björneborg, *Sweden* 10 E8
Bjørnevatn, *Norway* 8 B23
Bjørnøya, *Arctic* 4 B8
Bjursås, *Sweden* 10 D9
Bjuv, *Sweden* 11 H6
Bla, *Mali* 82 C3
Blace, *Serbia, Yug.* 40 C5
Blachownia, *Poland* 45 H5
Black = Da →, *Vietnam* 58 G5
Black →, *Canada* 110 B5
Black →, *Ariz., U.S.A.* 115 K8
Black →, *Ark., U.S.A.* 113 H9
Black →, *Mich., U.S.A.* 110 D2
Black →, *N.Y., U.S.A.* 111 C8
Black →, *Wis., U.S.A.* 112 D9
Black Bay Pen., *Canada* 102 C2
Black Birch L., *Canada* 105 B7
Black Diamond, *Canada* 104 C6
Black Duck →, *Canada* 102 A2
Black Forest = Schwarzwald, *Germany* 25 G4
Black Forest, *U.S.A.* 112 F2
Black Hd., *Ireland* 15 C2
Black Hills, *U.S.A.* 112 D3
Black I., *Canada* 105 C9
Black L., *Canada* 105 B7
Black L., *Mich., U.S.A.* 108 C3
Black L., *N.Y., U.S.A.* 111 B9
Black Lake, *Canada* 105 B7
Black Mesa, *U.S.A.* 113 G3
Black Mt. = Mynydd Du, *U.K.* 13 F4
Black Mts., *U.K.* 13 F4
Black Range, *U.S.A.* 115 K10
Black River, *Jamaica* 120 C4
Black River Falls, *U.S.A.* 112 C9
Black Sea, *Eurasia* 6 G12
Black Tickle, *Canada* 103 B8
Black Volta →, *Africa* 82 D4
Black Warrior →, *U.S.A.* 109 J2
Blackall, *Australia* 94 C4
Blackball, *N.Z.* 91 K3
Blackbull, *Australia* 94 B3
Blackburn, *U.K.* 12 D5
Blackburn with Darwen □, *U.K.* 12 D5
Blackfoot, *U.S.A.* 114 E7
Blackfoot →, *U.S.A.* 114 C7
Blackfoot River Reservoir, *U.S.A.* 114 E8
Blackpool, *U.K.* 12 D4
Blackpool □, *U.K.* 12 D4
Blackriver, *U.S.A.* 110 B1
Blacks Harbour, *Canada* 103 C6
Blacksburg, *U.S.A.* 108 G5
Blacksod B., *Ireland* 15 B1
Blackstone, *U.S.A.* 108 G7
Blackstone Ra., *Australia* 93 E4
Blackwater, *Australia* 94 C4
Blackwater →, *Meath, Ireland* 15 C4
Blackwater →, *Waterford, Ireland* 15 D4
Blackwater →, *U.K.* 15 B5
Blackwell, *U.S.A.* 113 G6
Blackwells Corner, *U.S.A.* 117 K7
Blaenau Ffestiniog, *U.K.* 12 E4
Blaenau Gwent □, *U.K.* 13 F4
Blagaj, *Bos.-H.* 40 C1
Blagnac, *France* 20 E5
Blagodarnoye = Blagodarnyy, *Russia* 49 H6
Blagodarnyy, *Russia* 49 H6
Blagoevgrad, *Bulgaria* 40 D7
Blagoveshchensk, *Russia* 51 D13
Blain, *France* 18 E5
Blain, *U.S.A.* 110 F7
Blaine, *Minn., U.S.A.* 112 C8
Blaine, *Wash., U.S.A.* 116 B4
Blaine Lake, *Canada* 105 C7
Blair, *U.S.A.* 112 E6
Blair Athol, *Australia* 94 C4
Blair Atholl, *U.K.* 14 E5
Blairgowrie, *U.K.* 14 E5
Blairsden, *U.S.A.* 116 F6
Blairsville, *U.S.A.* 110 F5
Blaj, *Romania* 43 D8
Blake Pt., *U.S.A.* 112 A10
Blakely, *Ga., U.S.A.* 109 K3
Blakely, *Pa., U.S.A.* 111 E9
Blâmont, *France* 19 D13
Blanc, C., *Spain* 37 B9
Blanc, Mont, *Alps* 21 C10
Blanc-Sablon, *Canada* 103 B8
Blanca, B., *Argentina* 122 G4
Blanca Peak, *U.S.A.* 115 H11
Blanche, C., *Australia* 95 E1
Blanche, L., *S. Austral., Australia* 95 D2
Blanche, L., *W. Austral., Australia* 92 D3
Blanco, *S. Africa* 88 E3
Blanco, *U.S.A.* 113 K5
Blanco →, *Argentina* 126 C2
Blanco, C., *Costa Rica* 120 E2
Blanco, C., *U.S.A.* 114 E1
Blanda →, *Iceland* 8 D3
Blandford Forum, *U.K.* 13 G5
Blanding, *U.S.A.* 115 H9
Blanes, *Spain* 32 D7
Blangy-sur-Bresle, *France* 19 C8
Blanice →, *Czech Rep.* 26 B7
Blankaholm, *Sweden* 11 G10
Blankenberge, *Belgium* 17 C3
Blankenburg, *Germany* 24 D6
Blanquefort, *France* 20 D3
Blanquilla, I., *Venezuela* 121 D7
Blanquillo, *Uruguay* 127 C4
Blansko, *Czech Rep.* 27 B9
Blantyre, *Malawi* 87 F4
Blarney, *Ireland* 15 E3
Blasdell, *U.S.A.* 110 D6
Błaszki, *Poland* 45 G5
Blatná, *Czech Rep.* 26 B6
Blato, *Croatia* 29 F13
Blaubeuren, *Germany* 25 G5
Blaustein, *Germany* 25 G5
Blåvands Huk, *Denmark* 11 J2
Blaydon, *U.K.* 12 C6
Blaye, *France* 20 C3
Blaye-les-Mines, *France* 20 D6
Blayney, *Australia* 95 E4
Blaze, Pt., *Australia* 92 B5
Błażowa, *Poland* 45 J9
Bleckede, *Germany* 24 B6
Bled, *Slovenia* 29 B11
Bleiburg, *Austria* 26 E7
Blejeşti, *Romania* 43 F10
Blekinge, *Sweden* 9 H16
Blekinge län □, *Sweden* 11 H9
Blenheim, *Canada* 110 D3
Blenheim, *N.Z.* 91 J4
Bléone →, *France* 21 D10
Blérancourt, *France* 19 C10
Bletchley, *U.K.* 13 F7
Blida, *Algeria* 78 A6
Blidö, *Sweden* 10 E12
Blidsberg, *Sweden* 11 G7
Blieskastel, *Germany* 25 F3
Bligh Sound, *N.Z.* 91 L1
Blind River, *Canada* 102 C3
Blinisht, *Albania* 40 E3
Bliss, *Idaho, U.S.A.* 114 E6
Bliss, *N.Y., U.S.A.* 110 D6
Blissfield, *U.S.A.* 110 F3
Blitar, *Indonesia* 63 H15
Blitta, *Togo* 83 D5
Block I., *U.S.A.* 111 E13
Block Island Sd., *U.S.A.* 111 E13
Blodgett Iceberg Tongue, *Antarctica* 5 C9
Bloemfontein, *S. Africa* 88 D4
Bloemhof, *S. Africa* 88 D4
Blois, *France* 18 E8
Blomskog, *Sweden* 10 E6
Blomstermåla, *Sweden* 11 H10
Blönduós, *Iceland* 8 D3
Błonie, *Poland* 45 F7
Bloodvein →, *Canada* 105 C9
Bloody Foreland, *Ireland* 15 A3
Bloomer, *U.S.A.* 112 C9
Bloomfield, *Canada* 110 C7
Bloomfield, *Iowa, U.S.A.* 112 E8
Bloomfield, *N. Mex., U.S.A.* 115 H10
Bloomfield, *Nebr., U.S.A.* 112 D6
Bloomington, *Ill., U.S.A.* 112 E10
Bloomington, *Ind., U.S.A.* 108 F2
Bloomington, *Minn., U.S.A.* 112 C8
Bloomsburg, *U.S.A.* 111 F8
Blora, *Indonesia* 63 G14
Blossburg, *U.S.A.* 110 E7
Blouberg, *S. Africa* 89 C4
Blountstown, *U.S.A.* 109 K3
Bludenz, *Austria* 26 D2
Blue Earth, *U.S.A.* 112 D8
Blue Mesa Reservoir, *U.S.A.* 115 G10
Blue Mountain Lake, *U.S.A.* 111 C10
Blue Mts., *Maine, U.S.A.* 111 B14
Blue Mts., *Oreg., U.S.A.* 114 D4
Blue Mts., *Pa., U.S.A.* 111 F8
Blue Mud B., *Australia* 94 A2
Blue Nile = Nîl el Azraq →, *Sudan* 81 D3
Blue Rapids, *U.S.A.* 112 F6
Blue Ridge Mts., *U.S.A.* 109 G5
Blue River, *Canada* 104 C5
Bluefield, *U.S.A.* 108 G5
Bluefields, *Nic.* 120 D3
Bluff, *Australia* 94 C4
Bluff, *N.Z.* 91 M2
Bluff, *U.S.A.* 115 H9
Bluff Knoll, *Australia* 93 F2
Bluff Pt., *Australia* 93 E1
Bluffton, *U.S.A.* 108 E3
Blumenau, *Brazil* 127 B6
Blunt, *U.S.A.* 112 C5
Bly, *U.S.A.* 114 E3
Blyth, *Canada* 110 C3
Blyth, *U.K.* 12 B6
Blythe, *U.S.A.* 117 M12
Blytheville, *U.S.A.* 113 H10
Bo, *S. Leone* 82 D2
Bo Duc, *Vietnam* 65 G6
Bo Hai, *China* 57 E10
Bo Xian = Bozhou, *China* 56 H8
Boa Vista, *Brazil* 124 C6
Boac, *Phil.* 61 E4
Boaco, *Nic.* 120 D2
Bo'ai, *China* 56 G7
Boal, *Spain* 34 B4
Boalsburg, *U.S.A.* 110 F7
Boane, *Mozam.* 89 D5
Boardman, *U.S.A.* 110 E4
Bobadah, *Australia* 95 E4
Bobai, *China* 58 F7
Bobbili, *India* 67 K13
Bòbbio, *Italy* 28 D6
Bobcaygeon, *Canada* 102 D4
Böblingen, *Germany* 25 G5
Bobo-Dioulasso, *Burkina Faso* 82 C4
Boboliçe, *Poland* 44 E3
Boboshevo, *Bulgaria* 40 D7
Bobov Dol, *Bulgaria* 40 D6
Bóbr →, *Poland* 45 F2
Bobraomby, Tanjon' i, *Madag.* 89 A8
Bobrinets, *Ukraine* 47 H7
Bobrov, *Russia* 48 E5
Bobrovitsa, *Ukraine* 47 G6
Bobruysk = Babruysk, *Belarus* 47 F5
Boby, Pic, *Madag.* 85 J9
Bôca do Acre, *Brazil* 124 E5
Boca Raton, *U.S.A.* 109 M5
Bocanda, *Ivory C.* 82 D4
Bocas del Toro, *Panama* 120 E3
Boceguillas, *Spain* 34 D7
Bochnia, *Poland* 45 J7
Bocholt, *Germany* 24 D2
Bochum, *Germany* 24 D3
Bockenem, *Germany* 24 C6
Boćki, *Poland* 45 F10
Bocognano, *France* 21 F13
Bocoyna, *Mexico* 118 B3
Bocşa, *Romania* 42 E6
Boda, *Dalarnas, Sweden* 10 C9
Böda, *Kalmar, Sweden* 11 G11
Boda, *Västernorrland, Sweden* 10 B10
Bodafors, *Sweden* 11 G8
Bodaybo, *Russia* 51 D12
Boddam, *U.K.* 14 B7
Boddington, *Australia* 93 F2
Bode Sadu, *Nigeria* 83 D5
Bodega Bay, *U.S.A.* 116 G3
Boden, *Sweden* 8 D19
Bodensee, *Europe* 25 H5
Bodenteich, *Germany* 24 C6
Bodhan, *India* 66 K10
Bodinga, *Nigeria* 83 C6
Bodmin, *U.K.* 13 G3
Bodmin Moor, *U.K.* 13 G3
Bodø, *Norway* 8 C16
Bodrog →, *Hungary* 42 B6
Bodrum, *Turkey* 39 D9
Bódva →, *Hungary* 42 B5
Boën, *France* 21 C8
Boende, *Dem. Rep. of the Congo* 84 E4
Boerne, *U.S.A.* 113 L5
Boesmans →, *S. Africa* 88 E4
Boffa, *Guinea* 82 C2
Bogalusa, *U.S.A.* 113 K10
Bogan →, *Australia* 95 D4
Bogan Gate, *Australia* 95 E4
Bogandé, *Burkina Faso* 83 C4
Bogantungan, *Australia* 94 C4
Bogata, *U.S.A.* 113 J7
Bogatić, *Serbia, Yug.* 40 B3
Boğazkale, *Turkey* 72 B6
Boğazlıyan, *Turkey* 72 C6
Bogen, *Sweden* 10 D6
Bogense, *Denmark* 11 J4
Bogetići, *Montenegro, Yug.* 40 D2
Boggabilla, *Australia* 95 D5
Boggabri, *Australia* 95 E5
Boggeragh Mts., *Ireland* 15 D3
Boglan = Solhan, *Turkey* 70 B4
Bognor Regis, *U.K.* 13 G7
Bogo, *Phil.* 61 F6
Bogodukhov = Bohodukhiv, *Ukraine* 47 G8
Bogol Manya, *Ethiopia* 81 G5
Bogong, Mt., *Australia* 95 F4
Bogor, *Indonesia* 62 F3
Bogoroditsk, *Russia* 46 F10
Bogorodsk, *Russia* 48 B6
Bogoso, *Ghana* 82 D4
Bogotá, *Colombia* 124 C4
Bogotol, *Russia* 50 D9
Bogou, *Togo* 83 C5

Bogra, Bangla. 67 G16
Boguchany, Russia 51 D10
Boguchar, Russia 48 F5
Bogué, Mauritania 82 B2
Boguslav, Ukraine 47 H6
Boguszów-Gorce, Poland 45 H3
Bohain-en-Vermandois, France 19 C10
Bohemian Forest =
Böhmerwald, Germany 25 F9
Bohinjska Bistrica, Slovenia 29 B11
Böhmerwald, Germany 25 F9
Bohmte, Germany 24 C4
Bohodukhiv, Ukraine 47 G8
Bohol □, Phil. 61 G6
Bohol Sea, Phil. 63 C6
Bohongou, Burkina Faso 83 C5
Böhönye, Hungary 42 D2
Bohuslän, Sweden 11 F5
Boi, Nigeria 83 D6
Boi, Pta. de, Brazil 127 A6
Boiaçu, Brazil 124 D6
Boileau, C., Australia 92 C3
Boing'o, Sudan 81 F3
Boiro, Spain 34 C2
Boise, U.S.A. 114 E5
Boise City, U.S.A. 113 G3
Boissevain, Canada 105 D8
Bóite →, Italy 29 B9
Boitzenburg, Germany 24 B9
Boizenburg, Germany 24 B6
Bojador C., W. Sahara 78 C3
Bojana →, Albania 40 E3
Bojano, Italy 31 A7
Bojanowo, Poland 45 G3
Bøjden, Denmark 11 J4
Bojnūrd, Iran 71 B8
Bojonegoro, Indonesia 63 G14
Boju, Nigeria 83 D6
Boka, Serbia, Yug. 42 E5
Boka Kotorska,
Montenegro, Yug. 40 D2
Bokala, Ivory C. 82 D4
Bokani, Nigeria 83 D6
Bokaro, India 69 H11
Boké, Guinea 82 C2
Bokhara →, Australia 95 D4
Bokkos, Nigeria 83 D6
Boknafjorden, Norway 9 G11
Bokoro, Chad 79 F9
Bokpyin, Burma 65 G2
Boksitogorsk, Russia 46 C7
Bol, Croatia 29 E13
Bolama, Guinea-Biss. 82 C1
Bolan →, Pakistan 68 E2
Bolan Pass, Pakistan 66 E5
Bolaños →, Mexico 118 C4
Bolaños de Calatrava, Spain 35 G7
Bolayır, Turkey 41 F10
Bolbec, France 18 C7
Boldājī, Iran 71 D6
Boldeşti-Scăeni, Romania 43 E11
Bole, China 60 B3
Bole, Ethiopia 81 F4
Bole, Ghana 82 D4
Bolekhiv, Ukraine 47 H2
Bolesławiec, Poland 45 G2
Bolgatanga, Ghana 83 C4
Bolgrad = Bolhrad, Ukraine 47 K5
Bolhrad, Ukraine 47 K5
Bolinao, Phil. 61 C3
Bolintin-Vale, Romania 43 F10
Bolívar, Argentina 126 D3
Bolivar, Mo., U.S.A. 113 G8
Bolivar, N.Y., U.S.A. 110 D6
Bolivar, Tenn., U.S.A. 113 H10
Bolivia ■, S. Amer. 124 G6
Bolivian Plateau, S. Amer. 122 E4
Boljevac, Serbia, Yug. 40 C5
Bolkhov, Russia 46 F9
Bolków, Poland 45 H3
Bollebygd, Sweden 11 G6
Bollène, France 21 D8
Bollnäs, Sweden 10 C10
Bollon, Australia 95 D4
Bollstabruk, Sweden 10 B11
Bolmen, Sweden 11 H7
Bolobo, Dem. Rep. of the Congo 84 E3
Bologna, Italy 29 D8
Bologoye, Russia 46 D8
Bolon, Ozero, Russia 60 B8
Bolonchenticul, Mexico 119 D7
Bolótana, Italy 30 B1
Boloven, Cao Nguyen, Laos 64 E6
Bolpur, India 69 H12
Bolsena, Italy 29 F8
Bolsena, L. di, Italy 29 F8
Bolshaya Chernigovka, Russia 48 D10
Bolshaya Glushitsa, Russia 48 D10
Bolshaya Martynovka, Russia 49 G5
Bolshaya Vradiyevka, Ukraine 47 J6
Bolshevik, Ostrov, Russia 51 B11
Bolshoi Kavkas = Caucasus
Mountains, Eurasia 49 J7
Bolshoy Anyuy →, Russia 51 C17
Bolshoy Begichev, Ostrov,
Russia 51 B12
Bolshoy Lyakhovskiy, Ostrov,
Russia 51 B15
Bolshoy Tokmak = Tokmak,
Ukraine 47 J8
Bolshoy Tyuters, Ostrov, Russia 9 G22
Bolsward, Neths. 17 A5
Bolt Head, U.K. 13 G4
Boltaña, Spain 32 C5
Boltigen, Switz. 25 J3
Bolton, Canada 110 C5
Bolton, U.K. 12 D5
Bolton Landing, U.S.A. 111 C11
Bolu, Turkey 72 B4
Bolungavík, Iceland 8 C2
Boluo, China 59 F10
Bolvadin, Turkey 70 B1
Bolzano, Italy 29 B8
Bom Jesus da Lapa, Brazil 125 F10
Boma, Dem. Rep. of the Congo 84 F2
Bombala, Australia 95 F4
Bombarral, Portugal 35 F1
Bombay = Mumbai, India 66 K8
Bomboma, Dem. Rep. of
the Congo 84 D3
Bombombwa, Dem. Rep. of
the Congo 86 B2
Bomi Hills, Liberia 82 D2
Bomili, Dem. Rep. of the Congo 86 B2
Bømlo, Norway 9 G11
Bomokandi →, Dem. Rep. of
the Congo 86 B2
Bomu →, C.A.R. 84 D4
Bon, C., Tunisia 76 C5
Bon Sar Pa, Vietnam 64 F6
Bonaigarh, India 69 J11
Bonaire, Neth. Ant. 121 D6
Bonang, Australia 95 F4
Bonanza, Nic. 120 D3
Bonaparte Arch., Australia 92 B3
Boñar, Spain 34 C5
Bonaventure, Canada 103 C6
Bonavista, Canada 103 C9
Bonavista, C., Canada 103 C9
Bonavista B., Canada 103 C9
Bondeno, Italy 29 D8
Bondo, Dem. Rep. of the Congo 86 B1
Bondoukou, Ivory C. 82 D4
Bondowoso, Indonesia 63 G15
Bone, Teluk, Indonesia 63 E6
Bonerate, Indonesia 63 F6
Bonerate, Kepulauan, Indonesia 63 F6
Bo'ness, U.K. 14 E5
Bonete, Cerro, Argentina 126 B2
Bong Son = Hoai Nhon, Vietnam 64 E7
Bonga, Ethiopia 81 F4
Bongabong, Phil. 61 E4
Bongor, Chad 79 F9
Bongouanou, Ivory C. 82 D4
Bonham, U.S.A. 113 J6
Boni, Mali 82 B4
Bonifacio, France 21 G13
Bonifacio, Bouches de, Medit. S. 30 A2
Bonin Is. = Ogasawara Gunto,
Pac. Oc. 52 G18
Bonke, Ethiopia 81 F4
Bonkoukou, Niger 83 C5
Bonn, Germany 24 E3
Bonnat, France 19 F8
Bonne Terre, U.S.A. 113 G9
Bonners Ferry, U.S.A. 114 B5
Bonnétable, France 18 D7
Bonneval, Eure-et-Loir, France 18 D8
Bonneval, Savoie, France 21 C11
Bonneville, France 19 F13
Bonney, L., Australia 95 F3
Bonnie Rock, Australia 93 F2
Bonny, Nigeria 83 E6
Bonny →, Nigeria 83 E6
Bonny, Bight of, Africa 83 E6
Bonny-sur-Loire, France 19 E9
Bonnyrigg, U.K. 14 F5
Bonnyville, Canada 105 C6
Bono, Italy 30 B2
Bonoi, Indonesia 63 E9
Bonorva, Italy 30 B1
Bonsall, U.S.A. 117 M9
Bontang, Indonesia 62 D5
Bonthe, S. Leone 82 D2
Bontoc, Phil. 61 C4
Bonyeri, Ghana 82 D4
Bonyhád, Hungary 42 D3
Bonython Ra., Australia 92 D4
Bookabie, Australia 93 F5
Booker, U.S.A. 113 G4
Boola, Guinea 82 D3
Boolaboolka L., Australia 95 E3
Booligal, Australia 95 E3
Boonah, Australia 95 D5
Boone, Iowa, U.S.A. 112 D8
Boone, N.C., U.S.A. 109 G5
Booneville, Ark., U.S.A. 113 H8
Booneville, Miss., U.S.A. 109 H1
Boonville, Calif., U.S.A. 116 F3
Boonville, Ind., U.S.A. 108 F2
Boonville, Mo., U.S.A. 112 F8
Boonville, N.Y., U.S.A. 111 C9
Boorindal, Australia 95 E4
Boorowa, Australia 95 E4
Boothia, Gulf of, Canada 101 A11
Boothia Pen., Canada 100 A10
Bootle, U.K. 12 D4
Booué, Gabon 84 E2
Boppard, Germany 25 E3
Boquete, Panama 120 E3
Boquilla, Presa de la, Mexico 118 B3
Boquillas del Carmen, Mexico 118 B4
Bor, Czech Rep. 26 B5
Bor, Russia 48 B7
Bor, Serbia, Yug. 40 B6
Bôr, Sudan 81 F3
Bor, Sweden 11 G8
Bor, Turkey 72 D6
Bor Mashash, Israel 75 D3
Borah Peak, U.S.A. 114 D7
Borang, Sudan 81 G3
Borås, Sweden 11 G6
Borāzjān, Iran 71 D6
Borba, Brazil 124 D7
Borba, Portugal 35 G3
Borborema, Planalto da, Brazil 122 D7
Borcea, Romania 43 F12
Borçka, Turkey 73 B9
Bord Khūn-e Now, Iran 71 D6
Borda, C., Australia 95 F2
Bordeaux, France 20 D3
Borden, Australia 93 F2
Borden, Canada 103 C7
Borden I., Canada 4 B2
Borden Pen., Canada 101 A11
Borders = Scottish Borders □,
U.K. 14 F6
Bordertown, Australia 95 F3
Borðeyri, Iceland 8 D3
Bordighera, Italy 28 E4
Bordj Fly Ste. Marie, Algeria 78 C5
Bordj-in-Eker, Algeria 78 D7
Bordj Omar Driss, Algeria 78 C7
Bore, Ethiopia 81 G4
Borehamwood, U.K. 13 F7
Borek Wielkopolski, Poland 45 G4
Borensberg, Sweden 11 F9
Borgå = Porvoo, Finland 9 F21
Borgarfjörður, Iceland 8 D7
Borgarnes, Iceland 8 D3
Børgefjellet, Norway 8 D15
Borger, Neths. 17 B6
Borger, U.S.A. 113 H4
Borgholm, Sweden 11 H10
Bórgia, Italy 31 D9
Borgo San Dalmazzo, Italy 28 D4
Borgo San Lorenzo, Italy 29 E8
Borgo Val di Taro, Italy 28 D6
Borgo Valsugana, Italy 29 B8
Borgomanero, Italy 28 C5
Borgorose, Italy 29 F10
Borgosésia, Italy 28 C5
Borhoyn Tal, Mongolia 56 C6
Bori, Nigeria 83 E6
Borikhane, Laos 64 C4
Borisoglebsk, Russia 48 E6
Borisov = Barysaw, Belarus 46 E5
Borisovka, Russia 47 G9
Borja, Peru 124 D3
Borja, Spain 32 D3
Borjas Blancas = Les Borges
Blanques, Spain 32 D5
Borjomi, Georgia 49 K6
Børkop, Denmark 11 J3
Borkou, Chad 79 E9
Borkum, Germany 24 B2
Borlänge, Sweden 10 D9
Borley, C., Antarctica 5 C5
Borlu, Turkey 39 C10
Bormida →, Italy 28 D5
Bórmio, Italy 28 B7
Borna, Germany 24 D8
Borne Sulinowo, Poland 44 E3
Borneo, E. Indies 62 D5
Bornholm, Denmark 11 J8
Bornholms Amtskommune □,
Denmark 11 J8
Bornholmsgattet, Europe 11 J8
Borno □, Nigeria 83 C7
Bornos, Spain 35 J5
Bornova, Turkey 39 C9
Bornu Yassa, Nigeria 83 C7
Boro →, Sudan 81 F2
Borodino, Russia 46 E8
Borogontsy, Russia 51 C14
Boromo, Burkina Faso 82 C4
Boron, U.S.A. 117 L9
Borongan, Phil. 61 F6
Borotangba Mts., C.A.R. 81 F2
Borotou, Ivory C. 82 D3
Borovan, Bulgaria 40 C7
Borovichi, Russia 46 C7
Borovsk, Russia 46 E9
Borrby, Sweden 11 J8
Borrego Springs, U.S.A. 117 M10
Borriol, Spain 32 E4
Borroloola, Australia 94 B2
Borşa, Cluj, Romania 43 D8
Borşa, Maramureş, Romania 43 C9
Borsad, India 68 H5
Borsec, Romania 43 D10
Borsod-Abaúj-Zemplén □,
Hungary 42 B6
Bort-les-Orgues, France 20 C6
Borth, U.K. 13 E3
Börtnan, Sweden 10 B7
Borūjerd, Iran 71 C6
Boryslav, Ukraine 47 H2
Boryspil, Ukraine 47 G6
Borzhomi = Borjomi, Georgia 49 K6
Borzna, Ukraine 47 G7
Borzya, Russia 51 D12
Bosa, Italy 30 B1
Bosanska Dubica, Bos.-H. 29 C13
Bosanska Gradiška, Bos.-H. 42 E2
Bosanska Kostajnica, Bos.-H. 29 C13
Bosanska Krupa, Bos.-H. 29 D13
Bosanski Brod, Bos.-H. 42 E2
Bosanski Novi, Bos.-H. 29 C13
Bosanski Petrovac, Bos.-H. 29 D13
Bosanski Šamac, Bos.-H. 42 E3
Bosansko Grahovo, Bos.-H. 29 D13
Bosaso, Somali Rep. 74 E4
Boscastle, U.K. 13 G3
Bose, China 58 F6
Boshan, China 57 F9
Boshof, S. Africa 88 D4
Boshrūyeh, Iran 71 C8
Bosilegrad, Serbia, Yug. 40 D6
Boskovice, Czech Rep. 27 B9
Bosna →, Bos.-H. 42 E3
Bosna i Hercegovina = Bosnia-
Herzegovina ■, Europe 42 G2
Bosnia-Herzegovina ■, Europe 42 G2
Bosnik, Indonesia 63 E9
Bosobolo, Dem. Rep. of
the Congo 84 D3
Bosporus = İstanbul Boğazı,
Turkey 41 E13
Bosque Farms, U.S.A. 115 J10
Bossangoa, C.A.R. 84 C3
Bossé Bangou, Niger 83 C5
Bossier City, U.S.A. 113 J8
Bosso, Niger 83 C7
Bosso, Dallol →, Niger 83 C5
Bostan, Pakistan 68 D2
Bostānābād, Iran 70 B5
Bosten Hu, China 60 B3
Boston, U.K. 12 E7
Boston, U.S.A. 111 D13
Boston Bar, Canada 104 D4
Boston Mts., U.S.A. 113 H8
Bosut →, Croatia 42 E3
Boswell, Canada 104 D5
Boswell, U.S.A. 110 F5
Botad, India 68 H4
Botan →, Turkey 73 D10
Botene, Laos 64 D3
Botev, Bulgaria 41 D8
Botevgrad, Bulgaria 40 D7
Bothaville, S. Africa 88 D4
Bothnia, G. of, Europe 8 E19
Bothwell, Australia 94 G4
Bothwell, Canada 110 D3
Boticas, Portugal 34 D3
Botletle →, Botswana 88 C3
Botlikh, Russia 49 J8
Botna →, Moldova 43 D14
Botoroaga, Romania 43 F10
Botoşani, Romania 43 C11
Botoşani □, Romania 43 C11
Botou, Burkina Faso 83 C5
Botricello, Italy 31 D9
Botro, Ivory C. 82 D3
Botswana ■, Africa 88 C3
Bottineau, U.S.A. 112 A4
Bottnaryd, Sweden 11 G7
Bottrop, Germany 17 C6
Botucatu, Brazil 127 A6
Botwood, Canada 103 C8
Bou Djébéha, Mali 82 B4
Bou Rjeïmât, Mauritania 82 B1
Bouaflé, Ivory C. 82 D3
Bouaké, Ivory C. 82 D3
Bouar, C.A.R. 84 C3
Bouârfa, Morocco 78 B5
Boucaut B., Australia 94 A1
Bouches-du-Rhône □, France 21 E9
Bougainville, C., Australia 92 B4
Bougainville I., Papua N. G. 96 H7
Bougainville Reef, Australia 94 B4
Bougie = Bejaïa, Algeria 78 A7
Bougouni, Mali 82 C3
Bouillon, Belgium 17 E5
Boukombé, Benin 83 C5
Boulal, Mali 82 B3
Boulazac, France 20 C4
Boulder, Colo., U.S.A. 112 E2
Boulder, Mont., U.S.A. 114 C7
Boulder City, U.S.A. 117 K12
Boulder Creek, U.S.A. 116 H4
Boulder Dam = Hoover Dam,
U.S.A. 117 K12
Bouli, Mauritania 82 B2
Boulia, Australia 94 C2
Bouligny, France 19 C12
Boulogne →, France 18 E5
Boulogne-sur-Gesse, France 20 E4
Boulogne-sur-Mer, France 19 B8
Bouloire, France 18 E7
Boulouli, Mali 82 B3
Boulsa, Burkina Faso 83 C4
Boultoum, Niger 83 C7
Boûmdeïd, Mauritania 82 B2
Boun Neua, Laos 64 B3
Boun Tai, Laos 64 B3
Bouna, Ivory C. 82 D4
Boundary Peak, U.S.A. 116 H8
Boundiali, Ivory C. 82 D3
Bountiful, U.S.A. 114 F8
Bounty Is., Pac. Oc. 96 M9
Boura, Mali 82 C4
Bourbon-Lancy, France 19 F10
Bourbon-l'Archambault, France 19 F10
Bourbonnais, France 19 F10
Bourbonne-les-Bains, France 19 E12
Bourbourg, France 19 B9
Bourdel L., Canada 102 A5
Bourem, Mali 83 B4
Bourg, France 20 C3
Bourg-Argental, France 21 C8
Bourg-de-Péage, France 21 C9
Bourg-en-Bresse, France 19 F12
Bourg-Lastic, France 20 C6
Bourg-Madame, France 20 F5
Bourg-St-Andéol, France 21 D8
Bourg-St-Maurice, France 21 C10
Bourganeuf, France 20 C5
Bourges, France 19 E9
Bourget, Canada 111 A9
Bourget, Lac du, France 21 C9
Bourgneuf, B. de, France 18 E4
Bourgneuf-en-Retz, France 18 E5
Bourgogne, France 19 F11
Bourgoin-Jallieu, France 21 C9
Bourgueil, France 18 E7
Bourke, Australia 95 E4
Bourne, U.K. 12 E7
Bournemouth, U.K. 13 G6
Bournemouth □, U.K. 13 G6
Bouroum, Burkina Faso 83 C4
Bouse, U.S.A. 117 M13
Boussac, France 19 F9
Boussé, Burkina Faso 83 C4
Boussouma, Burkina Faso 83 C4
Boutilimit, Mauritania 82 B2
Boutonne →, France 20 C3
Bouvet I. = Bouvetøya,
Antarctica 3 G10
Bouvetøya, Antarctica 3 G10
Bouxwiller, France 19 D14
Bouza, Niger 83 C6
Bouzonville, France 19 C13
Bova Marina, Italy 31 E8
Bovalino Marina, Italy 31 D9
Bovec, Slovenia 29 B10
Bovill, U.S.A. 114 C5
Bovino, Italy 31 A8
Bovril, Argentina 126 C4
Bow →, Canada 104 C6
Bow Island, Canada 104 D6
Bowbells, U.S.A. 112 A3
Bowdle, U.S.A. 112 C5
Bowelling, Australia 93 F2
Bowen, Argentina 126 D2
Bowen, Australia 94 C4
Bowen Mts., Australia 95 F4
Bowie, Ariz., U.S.A. 115 K9
Bowie, Tex., U.S.A. 113 J6
Bowkān, Iran 70 B5
Bowland, Forest of, U.K. 12 D5
Bowling Green, Ky., U.S.A. 108 G2
Bowling Green, Ohio, U.S.A. 108 E4
Bowling Green, C., Australia 94 B4
Bowman, U.S.A. 112 B3
Bowman I., Antarctica 5 C8
Bowmanville, Canada 110 C6
Bowmore, U.K. 14 F2
Bowral, Australia 95 E5
Bowraville, Australia 95 E5
Bowron →, Canada 104 C4
Bowron Lake Prov. Park,
Canada 104 C4
Bowser L., Canada 104 B3
Bowsman, Canada 105 C8
Bowwood, Zambia 87 F2
Box Cr. →, Australia 95 E3
Boxholm, Sweden 11 F9
Boxmeer, Neths. 17 C5
Boxtel, Neths. 17 C5
Boyabat, Turkey 72 B6
Boyalıca, Turkey 41 F13
Boyang, China 59 C11
Boyce, U.S.A. 113 K8
Boyd L., Canada 102 B4
Boyle, Canada 104 C6
Boyle, Ireland 15 C3
Boyne →, Ireland 15 C5
Boyne City, U.S.A. 108 C3
Boynitsa, Bulgaria 40 C6
Boynton Beach, U.S.A. 109 M5
Boyolali, Indonesia 63 G14
Boyoma, Chutes, Dem. Rep. of
the Congo 86 B2
Boysen Reservoir, U.S.A. 114 E9
Boyuibe, Bolivia 124 G6
Boyup Brook, Australia 93 F2
Boz Burun, Turkey 41 F12
Boz Dağ, Turkey 39 D11
Boz Dağları, Turkey 39 C10
Bozburun, Turkey 39 E10
Bozcaada, Turkey 72 C2
Bozdoğan, Turkey 39 D10
Bozeman, U.S.A. 114 D8
Bozen = Bolzano, Italy 29 B8
Boževac, Serbia, Yug. 40 B5
Bozhou, China 56 H8
Bozkır, Turkey 72 D5
Bozkurt, Turkey 39 D11
Bozouls, France 20 D6
Bozoum, C.A.R. 84 C3
Bozova, Antalya, Turkey 39 D12
Bozova, Sanliurfa, Turkey 73 D8
Bozovici, Romania 42 F7
Bozüyük, Turkey 39 B12
Bra, Italy 28 D4
Braås, Sweden 11 G9
Brabant □, Belgium 17 D4
Brabant L., Canada 105 B8
Brabrand, Denmark 11 H4
Brač, Croatia 29 E13
Bracadale, L., U.K. 14 D2
Bracciano, Italy 29 F9
Bracciano, L. di, Italy 29 F9
Bracebridge, Canada 102 C4
Brach, Libya 79 C8
Bracieux, France 18 E8
Bräcke, Sweden 10 B9
Brackettville, U.S.A. 113 L4
Bracki Kanal, Croatia 29 E13
Bracknell, U.K. 13 F7
Bracknell Forest □, U.K. 13 F7
Brad, Romania 42 D7
Brádano →, Italy 31 B9
Bradenton, U.S.A. 109 M4
Bradford, Canada 110 B5
Bradford, U.K. 12 D6
Bradford, Pa., U.S.A. 110 E6
Bradford, Vt., U.S.A. 111 C12
Bradley, Ark., U.S.A. 113 J8
Bradley, Calif., U.S.A. 116 K6
Bradley Institute, Zimbabwe 87 F3
Brady, U.S.A. 113 K5
Brædstrup, Denmark 11 J3
Braeside, Canada 111 A8

Braga, *Portugal* 34 D2
Braga □, *Portugal* 34 D2
Bragadiru, *Romania* 43 G10
Bragado, *Argentina* 126 D3
Bragança, *Brazil* 125 D9
Bragança, *Portugal* 34 D4
Bragança □, *Portugal* 34 D4
Bragança Paulista, *Brazil* 127 A6
Brahmanbaria, *Bangla.* 67 H17
Brahmani →, *India* 67 J15
Brahmapur, *India* 67 K14
Brahmaputra →, *India* 69 H13
Braich-y-pwll, *U.K.* 12 E3
Braidwood, *Australia* 95 F4
Brăila, *Romania* 43 E12
Brăila □, *Romania* 43 E12
Brainerd, *U.S.A.* 112 B7
Braintree, *U.K.* 13 F8
Braintree, *U.S.A.* 111 D14
Brak →, *S. Africa* 88 D3
Brake, *Germany* 24 B4
Brakel, *Germany* 24 D5
Bräkne-Hoby, *Sweden* 11 H9
Brakwater, *Namibia* 88 C2
Brålanda, *Sweden* 11 F6
Bramberg, *Germany* 25 E6
Bramdrupdam, *Denmark* 11 J3
Bramming, *Denmark* 11 J2
Brämön, *Sweden* 10 B11
Brampton, *Canada* 102 D4
Brampton, *U.K.* 12 C5
Bramsche, *Germany* 24 C3
Branco →, *Brazil* 122 D4
Brandberg, *Namibia* 88 B2
Brande, *Denmark* 11 J3
Brandenburg = Neubrandenburg, *Germany* 24 B9
Brandenburg, *Germany* 24 C8
Brandenburg □, *Germany* 24 C9
Brandfort, *S. Africa* 88 D4
Brando, *France* 21 F13
Brandon, *Canada* 105 D9
Brandon, *U.S.A.* 111 C11
Brandon B., *Ireland* 15 D1
Brandon Mt., *Ireland* 15 D1
Brandsen, *Argentina* 126 D4
Brandvlei, *S. Africa* 88 E3
Brandýs nad Labem, *Czech Rep.* 26 A7
Brănești, *Romania* 43 F11
Branford, *U.S.A.* 111 E12
Braniewo, *Poland* 44 D6
Bransfield Str., *Antarctica* 5 C18
Brańsk, *Poland* 45 F9
Branson, *U.S.A.* 113 G8
Brantford, *Canada* 102 D3
Brantôme, *France* 20 C4
Branzi, *Italy* 28 B6
Bras d'Or L., *Canada* 103 C7
Brasher Falls, *U.S.A.* 111 B10
Brasil, Planalto, *Brazil* 122 E6
Brasiléia, *Brazil* 124 F5
Brasília, *Brazil* 125 G9
Brasília Legal, *Brazil* 125 D7
Braslaw, *Belarus* 9 J22
Braslovče, *Slovenia* 29 B12
Brașov, *Romania* 43 E10
Brașov □, *Romania* 43 E10
Brass, *Nigeria* 83 E6
Brass →, *Nigeria* 83 E6
Brassac-les-Mines, *France* 20 C7
Brasschaat, *Belgium* 17 C4
Brassey, Banjaran, *Malaysia* 62 D5
Brassey Ra., *Australia* 93 E3
Brasstown Bald, *U.S.A.* 109 H4
Brastad, *Sweden* 11 F5
Brastavățu, *Romania* 43 G9
Bratan = Morozov, *Bulgaria* 41 D9
Brateș, *Romania* 43 E11
Bratislava, *Slovak Rep.* 27 C10
Bratislavský □, *Slovak Rep.* 27 C10
Bratsigovo, *Bulgaria* 41 D8
Bratsk, *Russia* 51 D11
Brattleboro, *U.S.A.* 111 D12
Bratunac, *Bos.-H.* 42 F4
Braunau, *Austria* 26 C6
Braunschweig, *Germany* 24 C6
Braunton, *U.K.* 13 F3
Bravicea, *Moldova* 43 C13
Bråviken, *Sweden* 11 F10
Bravo del Norte, Rio = Grande, Rio →, *U.S.A.* 113 N6
Brawley, *U.S.A.* 117 N11
Bray, *Ireland* 15 C5
Bray, Mt., *Australia* 94 A1
Bray-sur-Seine, *France* 19 D10
Brazeau →, *Canada* 104 C5
Brazil, *U.S.A.* 108 F2
Brazil ■, *S. Amer.* 125 F9
Brazilian Highlands = Brasil, Planalto, *Brazil* 122 E6
Brazo Sur →, *S. Amer.* 126 B4
Brazos →, *U.S.A.* 113 L7
Brazzaville, *Congo* 84 E3
Brčko, *Bos.-H.* 42 F3
Brda →, *Poland* 45 E5
Brdy, *Czech Rep.* 26 B6
Breaden, L., *Australia* 93 E4
Breaksea Sd., *N.Z.* 91 L1
Bream B., *N.Z.* 91 F5
Bream Hd., *N.Z.* 91 F5
Breas, *Chile* 126 B1
Breaza, *Romania* 43 E10
Brebes, *Indonesia* 63 G13
Brechin, *Canada* 110 B5
Brechin, *U.K.* 14 E6
Brecht, *Belgium* 17 C4
Breckenridge, *Colo., U.S.A.* 114 G10
Breckenridge, *Minn., U.S.A.* 112 B6
Breckenridge, *Tex., U.S.A.* 113 J5
Breckland, *U.K.* 13 E8
Břeclav, *Czech Rep.* 27 C9
Brecon, *U.K.* 13 F4
Brecon Beacons, *U.K.* 13 F4
Breda, *Neths.* 17 C4
Bredaryd, *Sweden* 11 G7
Bredasdorp, *S. Africa* 88 E3
Bredebro, *Denmark* 11 J2
Bredstedt, *Germany* 24 A4
Bree, *Belgium* 17 C5
Bregalnica →, *Macedonia* 40 E6
Bregenz, *Austria* 26 D2
Bregovo, *Bulgaria* 40 B6
Bréhal, *France* 18 D5
Bréhat, Î. de, *France* 18 D4
Breiðafjörður, *Iceland* 8 D2
Breil-sur-Roya, *France* 21 E11
Breisach, *Germany* 25 G3
Brejo, *Brazil* 125 D10
Bremen, *Germany* 24 B4
Bremen □, *Germany* 24 B4
Bremer Bay, *Australia* 93 F2
Bremer I., *Australia* 94 A2
Bremerhaven, *Germany* 24 B4
Bremerton, *U.S.A.* 116 C4
Bremervörde, *Germany* 24 B5
Brenes, *Spain* 35 H5
Brenham, *U.S.A.* 113 K6
Brenne, *France* 20 B5
Brennerpass, *Austria* 26 D4
Breno, *Italy* 28 C7
Brent, *U.S.A.* 109 J2
Brenta →, *Italy* 29 C9
Brentwood, *U.K.* 13 F8
Brentwood, *Calif., U.S.A.* 116 H5
Brentwood, *N.Y., U.S.A.* 111 F11
Bréscia, *Italy* 28 C7
Breskens, *Neths.* 17 C3
Breslau = Wrocław, *Poland* 45 G4
Bresle →, *France* 18 B8
Bressanone, *Italy* 29 B8
Bressay, *U.K.* 14 A7
Bresse, *France* 19 F12
Bressuire, *France* 18 F6
Brest, *Belarus* 47 F2
Brest, *France* 18 D2
Brest-Litovsk = Brest, *Belarus* 47 F2
Bretagne, *France* 18 D3
Bretçu, *Romania* 43 D11
Bretenoux, *France* 20 D5
Breteuil, *Eure, France* 18 D7
Breteuil, *Oise, France* 19 C9
Breton, *Canada* 104 C6
Breton, Pertuis, *France* 20 B2
Breton Sd., *U.S.A.* 113 L10
Brett, C., *N.Z.* 91 F5
Bretten, *Germany* 25 F4
Breuil-Cervínia, *Italy* 28 C4
Brevard, *U.S.A.* 109 H4
Breves, *Brazil* 125 D8
Brewarrina, *Australia* 95 E4
Brewer, *U.S.A.* 109 C11
Brewer, Mt., *U.S.A.* 116 J8
Brewerville, *Liberia* 82 D2
Brewster, *N.Y., U.S.A.* 111 E11
Brewster, *Ohio, U.S.A.* 110 F3
Brewster, *Wash., U.S.A.* 114 B4
Brewster, Kap = Kangikajik, *Greenland* 4 B6
Brewton, *U.S.A.* 109 K2
Breyten, *S. Africa* 89 D5
Breza, *Bos.-H.* 42 F3
Brezhnev = Naberezhnyye Chelny, *Russia* 48 C11
Brežice, *Slovenia* 29 C12
Březnice, *Czech Rep.* 26 B6
Breznik, *Bulgaria* 40 D6
Brezno, *Slovak Rep.* 27 C12
Brezoi, *Romania* 43 E9
Brezovica, *Kosovo, Yug.* 40 D5
Brezovo, *Bulgaria* 41 D9
Briançon, *France* 21 D10
Briare, *France* 19 E9
Briático, *Italy* 31 D9
Bribie I., *Australia* 95 D5
Bribri, *Costa Rica* 120 E3
Briceni, *Moldova* 43 B12
Bricquebec, *France* 18 C5
Bridgehampton, *U.S.A.* 111 F12
Bridgend, *U.K.* 13 F4
Bridgend □, *U.K.* 13 F4
Bridgeport, *Calif., U.S.A.* 116 G7
Bridgeport, *Conn., U.S.A.* 111 E11
Bridgeport, *Nebr., U.S.A.* 112 E3
Bridgeport, *Tex., U.S.A.* 113 J6
Bridger, *U.S.A.* 114 D9
Bridgeton, *U.S.A.* 108 F8
Bridgetown, *Australia* 93 F2
Bridgetown, *Barbados* 121 D8
Bridgetown, *Canada* 103 D6
Bridgewater, *Canada* 103 D7
Bridgewater, *Mass., U.S.A.* 111 E14
Bridgewater, *N.Y., U.S.A.* 111 D9
Bridgewater, C., *Australia* 95 F3
Bridgewater-Gagebrook, *Australia* 94 G4
Bridgnorth, *U.K.* 13 E5
Bridgton, *U.S.A.* 111 B14
Bridgwater, *U.K.* 13 F5
Bridgwater B., *U.K.* 13 F4
Bridlington, *U.K.* 12 C7
Bridlington B., *U.K.* 12 C7
Bridport, *Australia* 94 G4
Bridport, *U.K.* 13 G5
Briec, *France* 18 D2
Brienne-le-Château, *France* 19 D11
Brienon-sur-Armançon, *France* 19 E10
Brienz, *Switz.* 25 J4
Brienzersee, *Switz.* 25 J3
Brig, *Switz.* 25 J3
Brigg, *U.K.* 12 D7
Brigham City, *U.S.A.* 114 F7
Bright, *Australia* 95 F4
Brighton, *Australia* 95 F2
Brighton, *Canada* 110 B7
Brighton, *U.K.* 13 G7
Brighton, *Colo., U.S.A.* 112 F2
Brighton, *N.Y., U.S.A.* 110 C7
Brignogan-Plage, *France* 18 D2
Brignoles, *France* 21 E10
Brihuega, *Spain* 32 E2
Brikama, *Gambia* 82 C1
Brilliant, *U.S.A.* 110 F4
Brilon, *Germany* 24 D4
Bríndisi, *Italy* 31 B10
Brinje, *Croatia* 29 D12
Brinkley, *U.S.A.* 113 H9
Brinnon, *U.S.A.* 116 C4
Brion, I., *Canada* 103 C7
Brionne, *France* 18 C7
Brionski, *Croatia* 29 D10
Brioude, *France* 20 C7
Briouze, *France* 18 D6
Brisbane, *Australia* 95 D5
Brisbane →, *Australia* 95 D5
Brisighella, *Italy* 29 D8
Bristol, *U.K.* 13 F5
Bristol, *Conn., U.S.A.* 111 E12
Bristol, *Pa., U.S.A.* 111 F10
Bristol, *R.I., U.S.A.* 111 E13
Bristol, *Tenn., U.S.A.* 109 G4
Bristol, City of □, *U.K.* 13 F5
Bristol B., *U.S.A.* 100 C4
Bristol Channel, *U.K.* 13 F3
Bristol I., *Antarctica* 5 B1
Bristol L., *U.S.A.* 115 J5
Bristow, *U.S.A.* 113 H6
Britain = Great Britain, *Europe* 6 E5
British Columbia □, *Canada* 104 C3
British Indian Ocean Terr. = Chagos Arch., *Ind. Oc.* 52 K11
British Isles, *Europe* 6 E5
Brits, *S. Africa* 89 D4
Britstown, *S. Africa* 88 E3
Britt, *Canada* 102 C3
Brittany = Bretagne, *France* 18 D3
Britton, *U.S.A.* 112 C6
Brive-la-Gaillarde, *France* 20 C5
Briviesca, *Spain* 34 C7
Brixen = Bressanone, *Italy* 29 B8
Brixham, *U.K.* 13 G4
Brnaze, *Croatia* 29 E13
Brnenský □, *Czech Rep.* 27 B9
Brno, *Czech Rep.* 27 B9
Broad →, *U.S.A.* 109 J5
Broad Arrow, *Australia* 93 F3
Broad B., *U.K.* 14 C2
Broad Haven, *Ireland* 15 B2
Broad Law, *U.K.* 14 F5
Broad Sd., *Australia* 94 C4
Broadalbin, *U.S.A.* 111 C10
Broadback →, *Canada* 102 B4
Broadhurst Ra., *Australia* 92 D3
Broads, The, *U.K.* 12 E9
Broadus, *U.S.A.* 112 C2
Broager, *Denmark* 11 K3
Broby, *Sweden* 11 H8
Broceni, *Latvia* 44 B9
Brochet, *Canada* 105 B8
Brochet, L., *Canada* 105 B8
Brocken, *Germany* 24 D6
Brockport, *U.S.A.* 110 C7
Brockton, *U.S.A.* 111 D13
Brockville, *Canada* 102 D4
Brockway, *Mont., U.S.A.* 112 B2
Brockway, *Pa., U.S.A.* 110 E6
Brocton, *U.S.A.* 110 D5
Brod, *Macedonia* 40 E5
Brodarevo, *Serbia, Yug.* 40 C3
Brodeur Pen., *Canada* 101 A11
Brodhead, Mt., *U.S.A.* 110 E7
Brodick, *U.K.* 14 F3
Brodnica, *Poland* 45 E6
Brody, *Ukraine* 47 G3
Brogan, *U.S.A.* 114 D5
Broglie, *France* 18 C7
Brok, *Poland* 45 F8
Broken Arrow, *U.S.A.* 113 G7
Broken Bow, *Nebr., U.S.A.* 112 E5
Broken Bow, *Okla., U.S.A.* 113 H7
Broken Bow Lake, *U.S.A.* 113 H7
Broken Hill = Kabwe, *Zambia* 87 E2
Broken Hill, *Australia* 95 E3
Brokind, *Sweden* 11 F9
Bromley □, *U.K.* 13 F8
Bromölla, *Sweden* 11 H8
Bromsgrove, *U.K.* 13 E5
Brønderslev, *Denmark* 11 G3
Brong-Ahafo □, *Ghana* 82 D4
Broni, *Italy* 28 C6
Bronkhorstspruit, *S. Africa* 89 D4
Brønnøysund, *Norway* 8 D15
Bronte, *Italy* 31 E7
Brook Park, *U.S.A.* 110 E4
Brookhaven, *U.S.A.* 113 K9
Brookings, *Oreg., U.S.A.* 114 E1
Brookings, *S. Dak., U.S.A.* 112 C6
Brooklin, *Canada* 110 C6
Brooklyn Park, *U.S.A.* 112 C8
Brooks, *Canada* 104 C6
Brooks Range, *U.S.A.* 100 B5
Brooksville, *U.S.A.* 109 L4
Brookton, *Australia* 93 F2
Brookville, *U.S.A.* 110 E5
Broom, L., *U.K.* 14 D3
Broome, *Australia* 92 C3
Broons, *France* 18 D4
Brora, *U.K.* 14 C5
Brora →, *U.K.* 14 C5
Brørup, *Denmark* 11 J2
Brösarp, *Sweden* 11 J8
Brosna →, *Ireland* 15 C4
Broșteni, *Mehedinți, Romania* 42 F7
Broșteni, *Suceava, Romania* 43 C10
Brothers, *U.S.A.* 114 E3
Brou, *France* 18 D8
Brouage, *France* 20 C2
Brough, *U.K.* 12 C5
Brough Hd., *U.K.* 14 B5
Broughton Island = Qikiqtarjuaq, *Canada* 101 B13
Broumov, *Czech Rep.* 27 A9
Brovary, *Ukraine* 47 G6
Brovst, *Denmark* 11 G3
Brown, L., *Australia* 93 F2
Brown, Pt., *Australia* 95 E1
Brown City, *U.S.A.* 110 C2
Brown Willy, *U.K.* 13 G3
Brownfield, *U.S.A.* 113 J3
Browning, *U.S.A.* 114 B7
Brownsville, *Oreg., U.S.A.* 114 D2
Brownsville, *Pa., U.S.A.* 110 F5
Brownsville, *Tenn., U.S.A.* 113 H10
Brownsville, *Tex., U.S.A.* 113 N6
Brownville, *U.S.A.* 111 C9
Brownwood, *U.S.A.* 113 K5
Browse I., *Australia* 92 B3
Bruas, *Malaysia* 65 K3
Bruay-la-Buissière, *France* 19 B9
Bruce, Mt., *Australia* 92 D2
Bruce Pen., *Canada* 110 B3
Bruce Rock, *Australia* 93 F2
Bruche →, *France* 19 D14
Bruchsal, *Germany* 25 F4
Bruck an der Leitha, *Austria* 27 C9
Bruck an der Mur, *Austria* 26 D8
Brue →, *U.K.* 13 F5
Bruges = Brugge, *Belgium* 17 C3
Brugg, *Switz.* 25 H4
Brugge, *Belgium* 17 C3
Bruin, *U.S.A.* 110 E5
Brûlé, *Canada* 104 C5
Brûlon, *France* 18 E6
Brumado, *Brazil* 125 F10
Brumath, *France* 19 D14
Brumunddal, *Norway* 9 F14
Bruneau, *U.S.A.* 114 E6
Bruneau →, *U.S.A.* 114 E6
Bruneck = Brunico, *Italy* 29 B8
Brunei = Bandar Seri Begawan, *Brunei* 62 C4
Brunei ■, *Asia* 62 D4
Brunflo, *Sweden* 10 A8
Brunico, *Italy* 29 B8
Brunna, *Sweden* 10 E11
Brunnen, *Switz.* 25 J4
Brunner, L., *N.Z.* 91 K3
Brunsbüttel, *Germany* 24 B5
Brunssum, *Neths.* 17 D5
Brunswick = Braunschweig, *Germany* 24 C6
Brunswick, *Ga., U.S.A.* 109 K5
Brunswick, *Maine, U.S.A.* 109 D11
Brunswick, *Md., U.S.A.* 108 F7
Brunswick, *Mo., U.S.A.* 112 F8
Brunswick, *Ohio, U.S.A.* 110 E3
Brunswick, Pen. de, *Chile* 128 G2
Brunswick B., *Australia* 92 C3
Brunswick Junction, *Australia* 93 F2
Bruntál, *Czech Rep.* 27 B10
Bruny I., *Australia* 94 G4
Brus Laguna, *Honduras* 120 C3
Brusartsi, *Bulgaria* 40 C7
Brush, *U.S.A.* 112 E3
Brushton, *U.S.A.* 111 B10
Brusio, *Switz.* 25 J6
Brusque, *Brazil* 127 B6
Brussel, *Belgium* 17 D4
Brussels = Brussel, *Belgium* 17 D4
Brussels, *Canada* 110 C3
Brusy, *Poland* 44 E4
Bruthen, *Australia* 95 F4
Bruxelles = Brussel, *Belgium* 17 D4
Bruyères, *France* 19 D13
Bruz, *France* 18 D5
Brwinów, *Poland* 45 F7
Bryagovo, *Bulgaria* 41 E9
Bryan, *Ohio, U.S.A.* 108 E3
Bryan, *Tex., U.S.A.* 113 K6
Bryan, Mt., *Australia* 95 E2
Bryanka, *Ukraine* 47 H10
Bryansk, *Bryansk, Russia* 47 F8
Bryansk, *Dagestan, Russia* 49 H8
Bryanskoye = Bryansk, *Russia* 49 H8
Bryce Canyon National Park, *U.S.A.* 115 H7
Bryne, *Norway* 9 G11
Bryson City, *U.S.A.* 109 H4
Bryukhovetskaya, *Russia* 47 K10
Brza Palanka, *Serbia, Yug.* 40 B6
Brzeg, *Poland* 45 H4
Brzeg Dolny, *Poland* 45 G3
Brześć Kujawski, *Poland* 45 F5
Brzesko, *Poland* 45 J7
Brzeziny, *Poland* 45 G6
Brzozów, *Poland* 45 J9
Bsharri, *Lebanon* 75 A5
Bū Baqarah, *U.A.E.* 71 E8
Bu Craa, *W. Sahara* 78 C3
Bū Ḩasā, *U.A.E.* 71 F7
Bua, *Sweden* 11 G6
Bua Yai, *Thailand* 64 E4
Buapinang, *Indonesia* 63 E6
Buba, *Guinea-Biss.* 82 C2
Bubanza, *Burundi* 86 C2
Bubaque, *Guinea-Biss.* 82 C1
Bube, *Ethiopia* 81 F4
Būbiyān, *Kuwait* 71 D6
Buca, *Turkey* 39 C9
Bucak, *Turkey* 39 D12
Bucaramanga, *Colombia* 124 B4
Bucas Grande I., *Phil.* 61 G6
Bucasia, *Australia* 94 C4
Buccaneer Arch., *Australia* 92 C3
Buccino, *Italy* 31 B8
Bucecea, *Romania* 43 C11
Buchach, *Ukraine* 47 H3
Buchan, *U.K.* 14 D6
Buchan Ness, *U.K.* 14 D7
Buchanan, *Canada* 105 C8
Buchanan, *Liberia* 82 D2
Buchanan, L., *Queens., Australia* 94 C4
Buchanan, L., *W. Austral., Australia* 93 E3
Buchanan, L., *U.S.A.* 113 K5
Buchanan Cr. →, *Australia* 94 B2
Buchans, *Canada* 103 C8
Bucharest = București, *Romania* 43 F11
Buchen, *Germany* 25 F5
Buchholz, *Germany* 24 B5
Buchloe, *Germany* 25 G6
Buchon, Pt., *U.S.A.* 116 K6
Buciumi, *Romania* 42 C8
Buck Hill Falls, *U.S.A.* 111 E9
Bückeburg, *Germany* 24 C5
Buckeye, *U.S.A.* 115 K7
Buckeye Lake, *U.S.A.* 110 G2
Buckhannon, *U.S.A.* 108 F5
Buckhaven, *U.K.* 14 E5
Buckhorn L., *Canada* 110 B6
Buckie, *U.K.* 14 D6
Buckingham, *Canada* 102 C4
Buckingham, *U.K.* 13 F7
Buckingham B., *Australia* 94 A2
Buckinghamshire □, *U.K.* 13 F7
Buckle Hd., *Australia* 92 B4
Buckleboo, *Australia* 95 E2
Buckley, *U.K.* 12 D4
Buckley →, *Australia* 94 C2
Bucklin, *U.S.A.* 113 G5
Bucks L., *U.S.A.* 116 F5
Bucquoy, *France* 19 B9
Buctouche, *Canada* 103 C7
București, *Romania* 43 F11
Bucyrus, *U.S.A.* 108 E4
Budacu, Vf., *Romania* 43 C10
Budalin, *Burma* 67 H19
Budaörs, *Hungary* 42 C3
Budapest, *Hungary* 42 C4
Budapest □, *Hungary* 42 C4
Budaun, *India* 69 E8
Budd Coast, *Antarctica* 5 C8
Buddusò, *Italy* 30 B2
Bude, *U.K.* 13 G3
Budennovsk, *Russia* 49 H7
Budești, *Romania* 43 F11
Budge Budge = Baj Baj, *India* 69 H13
Budgewoi, *Australia* 95 E5
Budia, *Spain* 32 E2
Büdingen, *Germany* 25 E5
Budjala, *Dem. Rep. of the Congo* 84 D3
Budoni, *Italy* 30 B2
Búdrio, *Italy* 29 D8
Budva, *Montenegro, Yug.* 40 D2
Budzyń, *Poland* 45 F3
Buea, *Cameroon* 83 E6
Buellton, *U.S.A.* 117 L6
Buena Esperanza, *Argentina* 126 C2
Buena Park, *U.S.A.* 117 M9
Buena Vista, *Colo., U.S.A.* 115 G10
Buena Vista, *Va., U.S.A.* 108 G6
Buena Vista Lake Bed, *U.S.A.* 117 K7
Buenaventura, *Colombia* 124 C3
Buenaventura, *Mexico* 118 B3
Buendía, Embalse de, *Spain* 32 E2
Buenos Aires, *Argentina* 126 C4
Buenos Aires, *Costa Rica* 120 E3
Buenos Aires □, *Argentina* 126 D4
Buenos Aires, L., *Chile* 128 F2
Buffalo, *Mo., U.S.A.* 113 G8
Buffalo, *N.Y., U.S.A.* 110 D6
Buffalo, *Okla., U.S.A.* 113 G5
Buffalo, *S. Dak., U.S.A.* 112 C3
Buffalo, *Wyo., U.S.A.* 114 D10
Buffalo →, *Canada* 104 A5
Buffalo →, *S. Africa* 89 D5
Buffalo Head Hills, *Canada* 104 B5
Buffalo L., *Alta., Canada* 104 C6
Buffalo L., *N.W.T., Canada* 104 A5
Buffalo Narrows, *Canada* 105 B7
Buffels →, *S. Africa* 88 D2
Buford, *U.S.A.* 109 H4
Bug = Buh →, *Ukraine* 47 J6
Bug →, *Poland* 45 F8
Buga, *Colombia* 124 C3
Buganda, *Uganda* 86 C3
Buganga, *Uganda* 86 C3
Bugasong, *Phil.* 61 F5
Bugeat, *France* 20 C5
Bugel, Tanjung, *Indonesia* 63 G14
Bugibba, *Malta* 36 D1
Bugojno, *Bos.-H.* 42 F2
Bugsuk, *Phil.* 62 C5
Buguma, *Nigeria* 83 E6
Bugun Shara, *Mongolia* 60 B5
Buguruslan, *Russia* 50 D6

Buh →, *Ukraine* 47 J6
Buharkent, *Turkey* 39 D10
Buheirat-Murrat-el-Kubra, *Egypt* 80 H8
Buhera, *Zimbabwe* 89 B5
Bühl, *Germany* 25 G4
Buhl, *U.S.A.* 114 E6
Buhuşi, *Romania* 43 D11
Builth Wells, *U.K.* 13 E4
Buinsk, *Russia* 48 C9
Buir Nur, *Mongolia* 60 B6
Buis-les-Baronnies, *France* 21 D9
Buitrago = Buitrago del Lozoya, *Spain* 34 E7
Buitrago del Lozoya, *Spain* 34 E7
Bujalance, *Spain* 35 H6
Bujanovac, *Serbia, Yug.* 40 D5
Bujaraloz, *Spain* 32 D4
Buje, *Croatia* 29 C10
Bujumbura, *Burundi* 86 C2
Bük, *Hungary* 42 C1
Buk, *Poland* 45 F3
Bukachacha, *Russia* 51 D12
Bukama, *Dem. Rep. of the Congo* 87 D2
Bukavu, *Dem. Rep. of the Congo* 86 C2
Bukene, *Tanzania* 86 C3
Bukhara = Bukhoro, *Uzbekistan* 50 F7
Bukhoro, *Uzbekistan* 50 F7
Bukima, *Tanzania* 86 C3
Bukit Mertajam, *Malaysia* 65 K3
Bukittinggi, *Indonesia* 62 E2
Bükk, *Hungary* 42 B5
Bukoba, *Tanzania* 86 C3
Bukuru, *Nigeria* 83 D6
Bukuya, *Uganda* 86 B3
Būl, Kuh-e, *Iran* 71 D7
Bula, *Guinea-Biss.* 82 C1
Bula, *Indonesia* 63 E8
Bülach, *Switz.* 25 H4
Bulahdelah, *Australia* 95 E5
Bulan, *Phil.* 61 E5
Bulancak, *Turkey* 73 B8
Bulandshahr, *India* 68 E7
Bulanık, *Turkey* 73 C10
Bûlâq, *Egypt* 80 B3
Bulawayo, *Zimbabwe* 87 G2
Buldan, *Turkey* 39 C10
Bulgar, *Russia* 48 C9
Bulgaria ■, *Europe* 41 D9
Bulgheria, Monte, *Italy* 31 B8
Bulgurca, *Turkey* 39 C9
Buli, Teluk, *Indonesia* 63 D7
Buliluyan, C., *Phil.* 61 G2
Bulki, *Ethiopia* 81 F4
Bulkley →, *Canada* 104 B3
Bull Shoals L., *U.S.A.* 113 G8
Bullaque →, *Spain* 35 G6
Bullas, *Spain* 33 G3
Bulle, *Switz.* 25 J3
Bullhead City, *U.S.A.* 117 K12
Büllingen, *Belgium* 17 D6
Bullock Creek, *Australia* 94 B3
Bulloo →, *Australia* 95 D3
Bulloo L., *Australia* 95 D3
Bulls, *N.Z.* 91 J5
Bully-les-Mines, *France* 19 B9
Bulnes, *Chile* 126 D1
Bulqizë, *Albania* 40 E4
Bulsar = Valsad, *India* 66 J8
Bultfontein, *S. Africa* 88 D4
Bulukumba, *Indonesia* 63 F6
Bulun, *Russia* 51 B13
Bumba, *Dem. Rep. of the Congo* 84 D4
Bumbeşti-Jiu, *Romania* 43 E8
Bumbiri I., *Tanzania* 86 C3
Bumbuna, *S. Leone* 82 D2
Bumhpa Bum, *Burma* 67 F20
Bumi →, *Zimbabwe* 87 F2
Buna, *Kenya* 86 B4
Bunawan, *Phil.* 61 G6
Bunazi, *Tanzania* 86 C3
Bunbury, *Australia* 93 F2
Bunclody, *Ireland* 15 D5
Buncrana, *Ireland* 15 A4
Bundaberg, *Australia* 95 C5
Bünde, *Germany* 24 C4
Bundey →, *Australia* 94 C2
Bundi, *India* 68 G6
Bundoran, *Ireland* 15 B3
Bundukia, *Sudan* 81 F3
Bung Kan, *Thailand* 64 C4
Bunga →, *Nigeria* 83 C6
Bungay, *U.K.* 13 E9
Bungil Cr. →, *Australia* 95 D4
Bungo-Suidō, *Japan* 55 H6
Bungoma, *Kenya* 86 B3
Bungotakada, *Japan* 55 H5
Bungu, *Tanzania* 86 D4
Bunia, *Dem. Rep. of the Congo* 86 B3
Bunji, *Pakistan* 69 B6
Bunkie, *U.S.A.* 113 K8
Bunnell, *U.S.A.* 109 L5
Buñol, *Spain* 33 F4
Bunsuru, *Nigeria* 83 C5
Buntok, *Indonesia* 62 E4
Bununu Dass, *Nigeria* 83 C6
Bununu Kasa, *Nigeria* 83 D6
Bünyan, *Turkey* 72 C6
Bunyu, *Indonesia* 62 D5
Bunza, *Nigeria* 83 C5
Buol, *Indonesia* 63 D6
Buon Brieng, *Vietnam* 64 F7
Buon Ma Thuot, *Vietnam* 64 F7
Buong Long, *Cambodia* 64 F6
Buorkhaya, Mys, *Russia* 51 B14
Buqayq, *Si. Arabia* 71 E6
Buqbuq, *Egypt* 80 A2
Bur Acaba, *Somali Rep.* 74 G3
Bûr Fuad, *Egypt* 80 H8
Bûr Safâga, *Egypt* 70 E2
Bûr Sa'îd, *Egypt* 80 H8
Bûr Sûdân, *Sudan* 80 D4
Bûr Taufiq, *Egypt* 80 J8
Bura, *Kenya* 86 C4
Burakin, *Australia* 93 F2
Buram, *Sudan* 81 E2
Burao, *Somali Rep.* 74 F4
Burāq, *Syria* 75 B5
Buraydah, *Si. Arabia* 70 E4
Burbank, *U.S.A.* 117 L8
Burda, *India* 68 G6
Burdekin →, *Australia* 94 B4
Burdur, *Turkey* 39 D12
Burdur □, *Turkey* 39 D12
Burdur Gölü, *Turkey* 39 D12
Burdwan = Barddhaman, *India* 69 H12
Bure, *Gojam, Ethiopia* 81 E4
Bure, *Ilubabor, Ethiopia* 81 F4
Bure →, *U.K.* 12 E9
Büren, *Germany* 24 D4
Bureya →, *Russia* 51 E13
Burford, *Canada* 110 C4
Burg, *Germany* 24 C7
Burg auf Fehmarn, *Germany* 24 A7
Burg el Arab, *Egypt* 80 H6
Burg et Tuyur, *Sudan* 80 C2
Burg Stargard, *Germany* 24 B9
Burgas, *Bulgaria* 41 D11
Burgas □, *Bulgaria* 41 D10
Burgaski Zaliv, *Bulgaria* 41 D11
Burgdorf, *Germany* 24 C6
Burgdorf, *Switz.* 25 H3
Burgenland □, *Austria* 27 D9
Burgeo, *Canada* 103 C8
Burgersdorp, *S. Africa* 88 E4
Burges, Mt., *Australia* 93 F3
Burghausen, *Germany* 25 G8
Búrgio, *Italy* 30 E6
Burglengenfeld, *Germany* 25 F8
Burgohondo, *Spain* 34 E6
Burgos, *Spain* 34 C7
Burgos □, *Spain* 34 C7
Burgstädt, *Germany* 24 E8
Burgsvik, *Sweden* 11 G12
Burguillos del Cerro, *Spain* 35 G4
Burgundy = Bourgogne, *France* 19 F11
Burhaniye, *Turkey* 39 B8
Burhanpur, *India* 66 J10
Burhi Gandak →, *India* 69 G12
Burhner →, *India* 69 H9
Buri Pen., *Eritrea* 81 D4
Burias I., *Phil.* 61 E5
Burica, Pta., *Costa Rica* 120 E3
Burien, *U.S.A.* 116 C4
Burigi, L., *Tanzania* 86 C3
Burin, *Canada* 103 C8
Buriram, *Thailand* 64 E4
Burj Sāfitā, *Syria* 70 C3
Burji, *Ethiopia* 81 F4
Burkburnett, *U.S.A.* 113 H5
Burke →, *Australia* 94 C2
Burke Chan., *Canada* 104 C3
Burketown, *Australia* 94 B2
Burkina Faso ■, *Africa* 82 C4
Burk's Falls, *Canada* 102 C4
Burlada, *Spain* 32 C3
Burleigh Falls, *Canada* 110 B6
Burley, *U.S.A.* 114 E7
Burlingame, *U.S.A.* 116 H4
Burlington, *Canada* 102 D4
Burlington, *Colo., U.S.A.* 112 F3
Burlington, *Iowa, U.S.A.* 112 E9
Burlington, *Kans., U.S.A.* 112 F7
Burlington, *N.C., U.S.A.* 109 G6
Burlington, *N.J., U.S.A.* 111 F10
Burlington, *Vt., U.S.A.* 111 B11
Burlington, *Wash., U.S.A.* 116 B4
Burlington, *Wis., U.S.A.* 108 D1
Burlyu-Tyube, *Kazakstan* 50 E8
Burma ■, *Asia* 67 J20
Burnaby I., *Canada* 104 C2
Burnet, *U.S.A.* 113 K5
Burney, *U.S.A.* 114 F3
Burnham, *U.S.A.* 110 F7
Burnham-on-Sea, *U.K.* 13 F5
Burnie, *Australia* 94 G4
Burnley, *U.K.* 12 D5
Burns, *U.S.A.* 114 E4
Burns Lake, *Canada* 104 C3
Burnside →, *Canada* 100 B9
Burnside, L., *Australia* 93 E3
Burnsville, *U.S.A.* 112 C8
Burnt L., *Canada* 103 B7
Burnt River, *Canada* 110 B6
Burntwood →, *Canada* 105 B9
Burntwood L., *Canada* 105 B8
Burqān, *Kuwait* 70 D5
Burra, *Australia* 95 E2
Burra, *Nigeria* 83 C6
Burray, *U.K.* 14 C6
Burrel, *Albania* 40 E4
Burren Junction, *Australia* 95 E4
Burriana, *Spain* 32 F4
Burrinjuck Res., *Australia* 95 F4
Burro, Serranías del, *Mexico* 118 B4
Burrow Hd., *U.K.* 14 G4
Burruyacú, *Argentina* 126 B3
Burry Port, *U.K.* 13 F3
Bursa, *Turkey* 41 F13
Burseryd, *Sweden* 11 G7
Burstall, *Canada* 105 C7
Burton, *Ohio, U.S.A.* 110 E3
Burton, *S.C., U.S.A.* 109 J5
Burton, L., *Canada* 102 B4
Burton upon Trent, *U.K.* 12 E6
Buru, *Indonesia* 63 E7
Burullus, Bahra el, *Egypt* 80 H7
Burûn, Râs, *Egypt* 75 D2
Burundi ■, *Africa* 86 C3
Bururi, *Burundi* 86 C2
Burutu, *Nigeria* 83 D6
Burwell, *U.S.A.* 112 E5
Burwick, *U.K.* 14 C5
Bury, *U.K.* 12 D5
Bury St. Edmunds, *U.K.* 13 E8
Buryatia □, *Russia* 51 D11
Buryn, *Ukraine* 47 G7
Burzenin, *Poland* 45 G5
Busalla, *Italy* 28 D5
Busango Swamp, *Zambia* 87 E2
Buşayrah, *Syria* 70 C4
Busca, *Italy* 28 D4
Bushat, *Albania* 40 E3
Būshehr, *Iran* 71 D6
Būshehr □, *Iran* 71 D6
Bushell, *Canada* 105 B7
Bushenyi, *Uganda* 86 C3
Bushire = Būshehr, *Iran* 71 D6
Busie, *Ghana* 82 C4
Businga, *Dem. Rep. of the Congo* 84 D4
Busko-Zdrój, *Poland* 45 H7
Busovača, *Bos.-H.* 42 F2
Buşra ash Shām, *Syria* 75 C5
Busselton, *Australia* 93 F2
Busseri →, *Sudan* 81 F2
Busseto, *Italy* 28 D7
Bussière-Badil, *France* 20 C4
Bussolengo, *Italy* 28 C7
Bussum, *Neths.* 17 B5
Buşteni, *Romania* 43 E10
Busto, C., *Spain* 34 B4
Busto Arsízio, *Italy* 28 C5
Busu-Djanoa, *Dem. Rep. of the Congo* 84 D4
Busuanga I., *Phil.* 61 E3
Büsum, *Germany* 24 A4
Buta, *Dem. Rep. of the Congo* 86 B1
Butare, *Rwanda* 86 C2
Butaritari, *Kiribati* 96 G9
Bute, *U.K.* 14 F3
Bute Inlet, *Canada* 104 C4
Butemba, *Uganda* 86 B3
Butembo, *Dem. Rep. of the Congo* 86 B2
Buteni, *Romania* 42 D7
Butera, *Italy* 31 E7
Butha Qi, *China* 60 B7
Butiaba, *Uganda* 86 B3
Butler, *Mo., U.S.A.* 112 F7
Butler, *Pa., U.S.A.* 110 F5
Buton, *Indonesia* 63 E6
Butte, *Mont., U.S.A.* 114 C7
Butte, *Nebr., U.S.A.* 112 D5
Butte Creek →, *U.S.A.* 116 F5
Butterworth = Gcuwa, *S. Africa* 89 E4
Butterworth, *Malaysia* 65 K3
Buttevant, *Ireland* 15 D3
Buttfield, Mt., *Australia* 93 D4
Button B., *Canada* 105 B10
Buttonwillow, *U.S.A.* 117 K7
Butty Hd., *Australia* 93 F3
Butuan, *Phil.* 61 G6
Butuku-Luba, *Eq. Guin.* 83 E6
Butung = Buton, *Indonesia* 63 E6
Buturlinovka, *Russia* 48 E5
Butzbach, *Germany* 25 E4
Bützow, *Germany* 24 B7
Buxa Duar, *India* 69 F13
Buxar, *India* 69 G10
Buxtehude, *Germany* 24 B5
Buxton, *U.K.* 12 D6
Buxy, *France* 19 F11
Buy, *Russia* 48 A5
Buynaksk, *Russia* 49 J8
Buyo, *Ivory C.* 82 D3
Buyo, L. de, *Ivory C.* 82 D3
Büyük Menderes →, *Turkey* 39 D9
Büyükçekmece, *Turkey* 41 E12
Büyükkariştiran, *Turkey* 41 E11
Büyükkemikli Burnu, *Turkey* 41 F10
Büyükorhan, *Turkey* 39 B10
Büyükyoncalı, *Turkey* 41 E11
Buzançais, *France* 18 F8
Buzău, *Romania* 43 E11
Buzău □, *Romania* 43 E11
Buzău →, *Romania* 43 E12
Buzău, Pasul, *Romania* 43 E11
Buzen, *Japan* 55 H5
Buzet, *Croatia* 29 C10
Buzi →, *Mozam.* 87 F3
Buziaş, *Romania* 42 E6
Buzuluk, *Russia* 50 D6
Buzuluk →, *Russia* 48 E6
Buzzards B., *U.S.A.* 111 E14
Buzzards Bay, *U.S.A.* 111 E14
Bwana Mkubwe, *Dem. Rep. of the Congo* 87 E2
Byala, *Ruse, Bulgaria* 41 C9
Byala, *Varna, Bulgaria* 41 D11
Byala Slatina, *Bulgaria* 40 C7
Byarezina →, *Belarus* 47 F6
Byaroza, *Belarus* 47 F3
Bychawa, *Poland* 45 G9
Byczyna, *Poland* 45 G5
Bydgoszcz, *Poland* 45 E5
Byelarus = Belarus ■, *Europe* 46 F4
Byelorussia = Belarus ■, *Europe* 46 F4
Byers, *U.S.A.* 112 F2
Byesville, *U.S.A.* 110 G3
Byford, *Australia* 93 F2
Bykhaw, *Belarus* 46 F6
Bykhov = Bykhaw, *Belarus* 46 F6
Bykovo, *Russia* 48 F7
Bylas, *U.S.A.* 115 K8
Bylot, *Canada* 105 B10
Bylot I., *Canada* 101 A12
Byrd, C., *Antarctica* 5 C17
Byrock, *Australia* 95 E4
Byron Bay, *Australia* 95 D5
Byrranga, Gory, *Russia* 51 B11
Byrranga Mts. = Byrranga, Gory, *Russia* 51 B11
Byrum, *Denmark* 11 G5
Byske, *Sweden* 8 D19
Byske älv →, *Sweden* 8 D19
Bystrzyca →, *Dolnośląskie, Poland* 45 G3
Bystrzyca →, *Lubelskie, Poland* 45 G9
Bystrzyca Kłodzka, *Poland* 45 H3
Bytča, *Slovak Rep.* 27 B11
Bytom, *Poland* 45 H5
Bytom Odrzański, *Poland* 45 G2
Bytów, *Poland* 44 D4
Byumba, *Rwanda* 86 C3
Bzenec, *Czech Rep.* 27 C10
Bzura →, *Poland* 45 F7

C

Ca →, *Vietnam* 64 C5
Ca Mau, *Vietnam* 65 H5
Ca Mau, Mui, *Vietnam* 65 H5
Ca Na, *Vietnam* 65 G7
Caacupé, *Paraguay* 126 B4
Caála, *Angola* 85 G3
Caamano Sd., *Canada* 104 C3
Caazapá, *Paraguay* 126 B4
Caazapá □, *Paraguay* 127 B4
Cabadbaran, *Phil.* 61 G6
Cabalian = San Juan, *Phil.* 61 F6
Cabana, *Spain* 34 B2
Cabañaquinta, *Spain* 34 B5
Cabanatuan, *Phil.* 61 D4
Cabanes, *Spain* 32 E5
Cabano, *Canada* 103 C6
Čabar, *Croatia* 29 C11
Cabazon, *U.S.A.* 117 M10
Cabedelo, *Brazil* 125 E12
Cabeza del Buey, *Spain* 35 G5
Cabezón de la Sal, *Spain* 34 B6
Cabildo, *Chile* 126 C1
Cabimas, *Venezuela* 124 A4
Cabinda, *Angola* 84 F2
Cabinda □, *Angola* 84 F2
Cabinet Mts., *U.S.A.* 114 C6
Cabo Blanco, *Argentina* 128 F3
Cabo Frio, *Brazil* 127 A7
Cabo Pantoja, *Peru* 124 D3
Cabonga, Réservoir, *Canada* 102 C4
Cabool, *U.S.A.* 113 G8
Caboolture, *Australia* 95 D5
Cabora Bassa Dam = Cahora Bassa, Represa de, *Mozam.* 87 F3
Caborca, *Mexico* 118 A2
Cabot, Mt., *U.S.A.* 111 B13
Cabot Hd., *Canada* 110 A3
Cabot Str., *Canada* 103 C8
Cabra, *Spain* 35 H6
Cabra del Santo Cristo, *Spain* 35 H7
Cábras, *Italy* 30 C1
Cabrera, *Spain* 37 B9
Cabrera, Sierra, *Spain* 34 C4
Cabri, *Canada* 105 C7
Cabriel →, *Spain* 33 F3
Cabugao, *Phil.* 61 C4
Cacabelos, *Spain* 34 C4
Caçador, *Brazil* 127 B5
Čačak, *Serbia, Yug.* 40 C4
Caçapava do Sul, *Brazil* 127 C5
Cáccamo, *Italy* 30 E6
Cacém, *Portugal* 35 G1
Cáceres, *Brazil* 124 G7
Cáceres, *Spain* 35 F4
Cáceres □, *Spain* 34 F5
Cache Bay, *Canada* 102 C4
Cache Cr. →, *U.S.A.* 116 G5
Cache Creek, *Canada* 104 C4
Cacheu, *Guinea-Biss.* 82 C1
Cachi, *Argentina* 126 B2
Cachimbo, Serra do, *Brazil* 125 E7
Cachinal de la Sierra, *Chile* 126 A2
Cachoeira, *Brazil* 125 F11
Cachoeira do Sul, *Brazil* 127 C5
Cachoeiro de Itapemirim, *Brazil* 127 A7
Cachopo, *Portugal* 35 H3
Cacine, *Guinea-Biss.* 82 C1
Cacoal, *Brazil* 124 F6
Cacólo, *Angola* 84 G3
Caconda, *Angola* 85 G3
Čadca, *Slovak Rep.* 27 B11
Caddo, *U.S.A.* 113 H6
Cader Idris, *U.K.* 13 E4
Cadereyta, *Mexico* 118 B5
Cadí, Sierra del, *Spain* 32 C6
Cadibarrawirracanna, L., *Australia* 95 D2
Cadillac, *France* 20 D3
Cadillac, *U.S.A.* 108 C3
Cadiz, *Phil.* 61 F5
Cádiz, *Spain* 35 J4
Cadiz, *Calif., U.S.A.* 117 L11
Cadiz, *Ohio, U.S.A.* 110 F4
Cádiz □, *Spain* 35 J5
Cádiz, G. de, *Spain* 35 J3
Cadiz L., *U.S.A.* 115 J6
Cadney Park, *Australia* 95 D1
Cadomin, *Canada* 104 C5
Cadotte Lake, *Canada* 104 B5
Cadours, *France* 20 E5
Cadoux, *Australia* 93 F2
Caen, *France* 18 C6
Caernarfon, *U.K.* 12 D3
Caernarfon B., *U.K.* 12 D3
Caernarvon = Caernarfon, *U.K.* 12 D3
Caerphilly, *U.K.* 13 F4
Caerphilly □, *U.K.* 13 F4
Caesarea, *Israel* 75 C3
Caetité, *Brazil* 125 F10
Cafayate, *Argentina* 126 B2
Cafu, *Angola* 88 B2
Cagayan →, *Phil.* 61 B4
Cagayan de Oro, *Phil.* 61 G6
Cagayan Is., *Phil.* 61 G4
Cagayan Sulu I., *Phil.* 61 H3
Cagli, *Italy* 29 E9
Cágliari, *Italy* 30 C2
Cágliari, G. di, *Italy* 30 C2
Cagnano Varano, *Italy* 29 G12
Cagnes-sur-Mer, *France* 21 E11
Caguán →, *Colombia* 124 D4
Caguas, *Puerto Rico* 121 C6
Caha Mts., *Ireland* 15 E2
Cahama, *Angola* 88 B1
Caher, *Ireland* 15 D4
Caherciveen, *Ireland* 15 E1
Cahora Bassa, Represa de, *Mozam.* 87 F3
Cahore Pt., *Ireland* 15 D5
Cahors, *France* 20 D5
Cahul, *Moldova* 43 E13
Cai Bau, Dao, *Vietnam* 58 G6
Cai Nuoc, *Vietnam* 65 H5
Caia, *Mozam.* 87 F4
Caianda, *Angola* 87 E1
Caibarién, *Cuba* 120 B4
Caibiran, *Phil.* 61 F6
Caicara, *Venezuela* 124 B5
Caicó, *Brazil* 125 E11
Caicos Is., *Turks & Caicos* 121 B5
Caicos Passage, *W. Indies* 121 B5
Caidian, *China* 59 B10
Căinari, *Moldova* 43 D14
Caird Coast, *Antarctica* 5 D1
Cairn Gorm, *U.K.* 14 D5
Cairngorm Mts., *U.K.* 14 D5
Cairnryan, *U.K.* 14 G3
Cairns, *Australia* 94 B4
Cairns L., *Canada* 105 C10
Cairo = El Qâhira, *Egypt* 80 H7
Cairo, *Ga., U.S.A.* 109 K3
Cairo, *Ill., U.S.A.* 113 G10
Cairo, *N.Y., U.S.A.* 111 D11
Cairo Montenotte, *Italy* 28 D5
Caithness, Ord of, *U.K.* 14 C5
Cajamarca, *Peru* 124 E3
Cajarc, *France* 20 D5
Cajàzeiras, *Brazil* 125 E11
Čajetina, *Serbia, Yug.* 40 C3
Çakirgol, *Turkey* 73 B8
Çakırlar, *Turkey* 39 E12
Čakovec, *Croatia* 29 B13
Çal, *Turkey* 39 C11
Cala, *Spain* 35 H4
Cala →, *Spain* 35 H4
Cala Cadolar, Punta de = Rotja, Pta., *Spain* 33 G6
Cala d'Or, *Spain* 37 B10
Cala en Porter, *Spain* 37 B11
Cala Figuera, C. de, *Spain* 37 B9
Cala Forcat, *Spain* 37 B10
Cala Major, *Spain* 37 B9
Cala Mezquida = Sa Mesquida, *Spain* 37 B11
Cala Millor, *Spain* 37 B10
Cala Ratjada, *Spain* 37 B10
Cala Santa Galdana, *Spain* 37 B10
Calabanga, *Phil.* 61 E5
Calabar, *Nigeria* 83 E6
Calabogie, *Canada* 111 A8
Calabozo, *Venezuela* 124 B5
Calábria □, *Italy* 31 C9
Calaburras, Pta. de, *Spain* 35 J6
Calaceite, *Spain* 32 D5
Calacuccia, *France* 21 F13
Calafat, *Romania* 42 G7
Calafate, *Argentina* 128 G2
Calafell, *Spain* 32 D6
Calahorra, *Spain* 32 C3
Calais, *France* 19 B8
Calais, *U.S.A.* 109 C12
Calalaste, Cord. de, *Argentina* 126 B2
Calama, *Brazil* 124 E6
Calama, *Chile* 126 A2
Calamar, *Colombia* 124 A4
Calamian Group, *Phil.* 61 F3
Calamocha, *Spain* 32 E3
Calamonte, *Spain* 35 G4
Călan, *Romania* 42 E7
Calañas, *Spain* 35 H4
Calanda, *Spain* 32 E4
Calang, *Indonesia* 62 D1
Calangiánus, *Italy* 30 B2
Calapan, *Phil.* 61 E4
Călăraşi, *Moldova* 43 C13
Călăraşi, *Romania* 43 F12
Călăraşi □, *Romania* 43 F12
Calasparra, *Spain* 33 G3
Calatafimi, *Italy* 30 E5
Calatayud, *Spain* 32 D3
Călăţele, *Romania* 42 D8
Calato = Kálathos, *Greece* 39 E10
Calauag, *Phil.* 61 E5

Calavà, C., *Italy* 31 D7
Calavite, C., *Phil.* 61 E4
Calayan, *Phil.* 61 B4
Calbayog, *Phil.* 61 E6
Calca, *Peru* 124 F4
Calcasieu L., *U.S.A.* 113 L8
Calcutta = Kolkata, *India* 69 H13
Calcutta, *U.S.A.* 110 F4
Caldaro, *Italy* 29 B8
Caldas da Rainha, *Portugal* 35 F1
Caldas de Reis, *Spain* 34 C2
Calder →, *U.K.* 12 D6
Caldera, *Chile* 126 B1
Caldwell, *Idaho, U.S.A.* 114 E5
Caldwell, *Kans., U.S.A.* 113 G6
Caldwell, *Tex., U.S.A.* 113 K6
Caledon, *S. Africa* 88 E2
Caledon →, *S. Africa* 88 E4
Caledon B., *Australia* 94 A2
Caledonia, *Canada* 110 C5
Caledonia, *U.S.A.* 110 D7
Calella, *Spain* 32 D7
Calemba, *Angola* 88 B2
Calen, *Australia* 94 C4
Calenzana, *France* 21 F12
Caletones, *Chile* 126 C1
Calexico, *U.S.A.* 117 N11
Calf of Man, *U.K.* 12 C3
Calgary, *Canada* 104 C6
Calheta, *Madeira* 37 D2
Calhoun, *U.S.A.* 109 H3
Cali, *Colombia* 124 C3
Calicut, *India* 66 P9
Caliente, *U.S.A.* 115 H6
California, *Mo., U.S.A.* 112 F8
California, *Pa., U.S.A.* 110 F5
California □, *U.S.A.* 116 H7
California, Baja, *Mexico* 118 A1
California, Baja, T.N. = Baja California □, *Mexico* 118 B2
California, Baja, T.S. = Baja California Sur □, *Mexico* 118 B2
California, G. de, *Mexico* 118 B2
California City, *U.S.A.* 117 K9
California Hot Springs, *U.S.A.* 117 K8
Călimăneşti, *Romania* 43 E9
Călimani, Munţii, *Romania* 43 C10
Calingasta, *Argentina* 126 C2
Calipatria, *U.S.A.* 117 M11
Calistoga, *U.S.A.* 116 G4
Calitri, *Italy* 31 B8
Calitzdorp, *S. Africa* 88 E3
Callabonna, L., *Australia* 95 D3
Callac, *France* 18 D3
Callan, *Ireland* 15 D4
Callander, *U.K.* 14 E4
Callao, *Peru* 124 F3
Calles, *Mexico* 119 C5
Callicoon, *U.S.A.* 111 E9
Calling Lake, *Canada* 104 B6
Calliope, *Australia* 94 C5
Callosa de Ensarriá, *Spain* 33 G4
Callosa de Segura, *Spain* 33 G4
Calne, *U.K.* 13 F6
Calola, *Angola* 88 B2
Calolbon = San Andres, *Phil.* 61 E6
Calonge, *Spain* 32 D8
Caloocan, *Phil.* 61 D4
Calore →, *Italy* 31 A7
Caloundra, *Australia* 95 D5
Calpe, *Spain* 33 G5
Calpella, *U.S.A.* 116 F3
Calpine, *U.S.A.* 116 F6
Calstock, *Canada* 102 C3
Caltabellotta, *Italy* 30 E6
Caltagirone, *Italy* 31 E7
Caltanissetta, *Italy* 31 E7
Çaltılıbük, *Turkey* 41 G12
Caluire-et-Cuire, *France* 19 G11
Calulo, *Angola* 84 G2
Caluso, *Italy* 28 C4
Calvados □, *France* 18 C6
Calvert →, *Australia* 94 B2
Calvert I., *Canada* 104 C3
Calvert Ra., *Australia* 92 D3
Calvi, *France* 21 F12
Calviá, *Spain* 33 F7
Calvillo, *Mexico* 118 C4
Calvinia, *S. Africa* 88 E2
Calvo = Calvo, Mte., *Italy* 29 G12
Calvo, Mte., *Italy* 29 G12
Calwa, *U.S.A.* 116 J7
Calzada Almuradiel = Almuradiel, *Spain* 35 G7
Calzada de Calatrava, *Spain* 35 G7
Cam →, *U.K.* 13 E8
Cam Lam, *Vietnam* 65 G7
Cam Pha, *Vietnam* 58 G6
Cam Ranh, *Vietnam* 65 G7
Cam Xuyen, *Vietnam* 64 C6
Camabatela, *Angola* 84 F3
Camacha, *Madeira* 37 D3
Camacho, *Mexico* 118 C4
Camacupa, *Angola* 85 G3
Camagüey, *Cuba* 120 B4
Camaiore, *Italy* 28 E7
Camaná, *Peru* 124 G4
Camanche Reservoir, *U.S.A.* 116 G6
Camaquã, *Brazil* 127 C5
Camaquã →, *Brazil* 127 C5
Câmara de Lobos, *Madeira* 37 D3
Camarat, C., *France* 21 E10
Camarès, *France* 20 E6
Camaret-sur-Mer, *France* 18 D2
Camargo, *Mexico* 119 B5
Camargue, *France* 21 E8
Camarillo, *U.S.A.* 117 L7
Camariñas, *Spain* 34 B1
Camarón, C., *Honduras* 120 C2
Camarones, *Argentina* 128 E3
Camas, *Spain* 35 H4
Camas, *U.S.A.* 116 E4
Camas Valley, *U.S.A.* 114 E2
Camballin, *Australia* 92 C3
Cambará, *Brazil* 127 A5
Cambay = Khambhat, *India* 68 H5
Cambay, G. of = Khambhat, G. of, *India* 66 J8
Cambil, *Spain* 35 H7
Cambo-les-Bains, *France* 20 E2
Cambodia ■, *Asia* 64 F5
Camborne, *U.K.* 13 G2
Cambrai, *France* 19 B10
Cambre, *Spain* 34 B2
Cambria, *U.S.A.* 116 K5
Cambrian Mts., *U.K.* 13 E4
Cambridge, *Canada* 102 D3
Cambridge, *Jamaica* 120 C4
Cambridge, *N.Z.* 91 G5
Cambridge, *U.K.* 13 E8
Cambridge, *Mass., U.S.A.* 111 D13
Cambridge, *Minn., U.S.A.* 112 C8
Cambridge, *N.Y., U.S.A.* 111 C11
Cambridge, *Nebr., U.S.A.* 112 E4
Cambridge, *Ohio, U.S.A.* 110 F3
Cambridge Bay = Ikaluktutiak, *Canada* 100 B9
Cambridge G., *Australia* 92 B4
Cambridge Springs, *U.S.A.* 110 E4
Cambridgeshire □, *U.K.* 13 E7
Cambrils, *Spain* 32 D6
Cambuci, *Brazil* 127 A7
Cambundi-Catembo, *Angola* 84 G3
Camden, *Ala., U.S.A.* 109 K2
Camden, *Ark., U.S.A.* 113 J8
Camden, *Maine, U.S.A.* 109 C11
Camden, *N.J., U.S.A.* 111 G9
Camden, *N.Y., U.S.A.* 111 C9
Camden, *S.C., U.S.A.* 109 H5
Camden Sd., *Australia* 92 C3
Camdenton, *U.S.A.* 113 F8
Çameli, *Turkey* 39 D11
Camenca, *Moldova* 43 B13
Camerino, *Italy* 29 E10
Cameron, *Ariz., U.S.A.* 115 J8
Cameron, *La., U.S.A.* 113 L8
Cameron, *Mo., U.S.A.* 112 F7
Cameron, *Tex., U.S.A.* 113 K6
Cameron Highlands, *Malaysia* 65 K3
Cameron Hills, *Canada* 104 B5
Cameroon ■, *Africa* 84 C2
Camerota, *Italy* 31 B8
Cameroun →, *Cameroon* 83 E6
Cameroun, Mt., *Cameroon* 83 E6
Cametá, *Brazil* 125 D9
Çamiçi Gölü, *Turkey* 39 D9
Camiguin □, *Phil.* 61 G6
Camiguin I., *Phil.* 61 B4
Camiling, *Phil.* 61 D4
Camilla, *U.S.A.* 109 K3
Caminha, *Portugal* 34 D2
Camino, *U.S.A.* 116 G6
Camira Creek, *Australia* 95 D5
Cammal, *U.S.A.* 110 E7
Cammarata, *Italy* 30 E6
Camocim, *Brazil* 125 D10
Camooweal, *Australia* 94 B2
Camopi, *Fr. Guiana* 125 C8
Camotes Is., *Phil.* 61 F6
Camotes Sea, *Phil.* 61 F6
Camp Borden, *Canada* 110 B5
Camp Hill, *U.S.A.* 110 F8
Camp Nelson, *U.S.A.* 117 J8
Camp Pendleton, *U.S.A.* 117 M9
Camp Verde, *U.S.A.* 115 J8
Camp Wood, *U.S.A.* 113 L5
Campagna, *Italy* 31 B8
Campana, *Argentina* 126 C4
Campana, I., *Chile* 128 F1
Campanário, *Madeira* 37 D2
Campanario, *Spain* 35 G5
Campània □, *Italy* 31 B7
Campbell, *S. Africa* 88 D3
Campbell, *Calif., U.S.A.* 116 H5
Campbell, *Ohio, U.S.A.* 110 E4
Campbell I., *Pac. Oc.* 96 N8
Campbell L., *Canada* 105 A7
Campbell River, *Canada* 104 C3
Campbell Town, *Australia* 94 G4
Campbellford, *Canada* 110 B7
Campbellpur, *Pakistan* 68 C5
Campbellsville, *U.S.A.* 108 G3
Campbellton, *Canada* 103 C6
Campbelltown, *Australia* 95 E5
Campbeltown, *U.K.* 14 F3
Campeche, *Mexico* 119 D6
Campeche □, *Mexico* 119 D6
Campeche, Golfo de, *Mexico* 119 D6
Campello, *Spain* 33 G4
Câmpeni, *Romania* 42 D8
Camperdown, *Australia* 95 F3
Camperville, *Canada* 105 C8
Campi Salentina, *Italy* 31 B11
Câmpia Turzii, *Romania* 43 D8
Campidano, *Italy* 30 C1
Campíglia Maríttima, *Italy* 28 E7
Campillo de Altobuey, *Spain* 33 F3
Campillos, *Spain* 35 H6
Câmpina, *Romania* 43 E10
Campina Grande, *Brazil* 125 E11
Campinas, *Brazil* 127 A6
Campli, *Italy* 29 F10
Campo, *Spain* 32 C5
Campo de Criptana, *Spain* 35 F7
Campo de Gibraltar, *Spain* 35 J5
Campo Grande, *Brazil* 125 H8
Campo Maíor, *Brazil* 125 D10
Campo Maior, *Portugal* 35 F3
Campo Mourão, *Brazil* 127 A5
Campo Túres, *Italy* 29 B8
Campobasso, *Italy* 31 A7
Campobello di Licata, *Italy* 30 E6
Campobello di Mazara, *Italy* 30 E5
Campofelice di Roccella, *Italy* 30 E6
Campomarino, *Italy* 29 G12
Camporeale, *Italy* 30 E6
Camporrobles, *Spain* 32 F3
Campos, *Brazil* 127 A7
Campos Belos, *Brazil* 125 F9
Campos del Puerto, *Spain* 37 B10
Campos Novos, *Brazil* 127 B5
Camprodón, *Spain* 32 C7
Camptonville, *U.S.A.* 116 F5
Camptown, *U.S.A.* 111 E8
Câmpulung, *Argeş, Romania* 43 E10
Câmpulung, *Suceava, Romania* 43 C10
Câmpuri, *Romania* 43 D11
Camrose, *Canada* 104 C6
Camsell Portage, *Canada* 105 B7
Çamyuva, *Turkey* 39 E12
Çan, *Turkey* 41 F11
Can Clavo, *Spain* 37 C7
Can Creu, *Spain* 37 C7
Can Gio, *Vietnam* 65 G6
Can Tho, *Vietnam* 65 G5
Canaan, *U.S.A.* 111 D11
Canada ■, *N. Amer.* 100 C10
Cañada de Gómez, *Argentina* 126 C3
Canadian, *U.S.A.* 113 H4
Canadian →, *U.S.A.* 113 H7
Canajoharie, *U.S.A.* 111 D10
Çanakkale, *Turkey* 41 F10
Çanakkale □, *Turkey* 41 F10
Çanakkale Boğazı, *Turkey* 41 F10
Canal Flats, *Canada* 104 C5
Canalejas, *Argentina* 126 D2
Canals, *Argentina* 126 C3
Canals, *Spain* 33 G4
Canandaigua, *U.S.A.* 110 D7
Canandaigua L., *U.S.A.* 110 D7
Cananea, *Mexico* 118 A2
Canarias, Is., *Atl. Oc.* 37 F4
Canarreos, Arch. de los, *Cuba* 120 B3
Canary Is. = Canarias, Is., *Atl. Oc.* 37 F4
Canaseraga, *U.S.A.* 110 D7
Canatlán, *Mexico* 118 C4
Canaveral, C., *U.S.A.* 109 L5
Cañaveruelas, *Spain* 32 E2
Canavieiras, *Brazil* 125 G11
Canberra, *Australia* 95 F4
Canby, *Calif., U.S.A.* 114 F3
Canby, *Minn., U.S.A.* 112 C6
Canby, *Oreg., U.S.A.* 116 E4
Cancale, *France* 18 D5
Canche →, *France* 19 B8
Cancún, *Mexico* 119 C7
Candanchu, *Spain* 32 C4
Çandarlı, *Turkey* 39 C8
Çandarlı Körfezi, *Turkey* 39 C8
Candas, *Spain* 34 B5
Candé, *France* 18 E5
Candela, *Italy* 31 A8
Candelaria, *Argentina* 127 B4
Candelaria, *Canary Is.* 37 F3
Candeleda, *Spain* 34 E5
Candelo, *Australia* 95 F4
Candia = Iráklion, *Greece* 36 D7
Candia, Sea of = Crete, Sea of, *Greece* 39 E7
Candle L., *Canada* 105 C7
Candlemas I., *Antarctica* 5 B1
Cando, *U.S.A.* 112 A5
Candon, *Phil.* 61 C4
Canea = Khaniá, *Greece* 36 D6
Canelli, *Italy* 28 D5
Canelones, *Uruguay* 127 C4
Canet-Plage, *France* 20 F7
Cañete, *Chile* 126 D1
Cañete, *Peru* 124 F3
Cañete, *Spain* 32 E3
Cañete de las Torres, *Spain* 35 H6
Cangas, *Spain* 34 C2
Cangas de Narcea, *Spain* 34 B4
Cangas de Onís, *Spain* 34 B5
Cangnan, *China* 59 D13
Canguaretama, *Brazil* 125 E11
Canguçu, *Brazil* 127 C5
Canguçu, Serra do, *Brazil* 127 C5
Cangwu, *China* 59 F8
Cangxi, *China* 58 B5
Cangyuan, *China* 58 F2
Cangzhou, *China* 56 E9
Caniapiscau →, *Canada* 103 A6
Caniapiscau, Rés. de, *Canada* 103 B6
Canicattì, *Italy* 30 E6
Canicattini Bagni, *Italy* 31 E8
Caniles, *Spain* 35 H8
Canim Lake, *Canada* 104 C4
Canindeyu □, *Paraguay* 127 A5
Canino, *Italy* 29 F8
Canisteo, *U.S.A.* 110 D7
Canisteo →, *U.S.A.* 110 D7
Cañitas, *Mexico* 118 C4
Cañizal, *Spain* 34 D5
Canjáyar, *Spain* 35 H8
Çankırı, *Turkey* 72 B5
Cankuzo, *Burundi* 86 C3
Canmore, *Canada* 104 C5
Cann River, *Australia* 95 F4
Canna, *U.K.* 14 D2
Cannanore, *India* 66 P9
Cannes, *France* 21 E11
Canning Town = Port Canning, *India* 69 H13
Cannington, *Canada* 110 B5
Cannóbio, *Italy* 28 B5
Cannock, *U.K.* 13 E5
Cannon Ball →, *U.S.A.* 112 B4
Cannondale Mt., *Australia* 94 D4
Cannonsville Reservoir, *U.S.A.* 111 D9
Cannonvale, *Australia* 94 C4
Canoas, *Brazil* 127 B5
Canoe L., *Canada* 105 B7
Canon City, *U.S.A.* 112 F2
Canora, *Canada* 105 C8
Canosa di Púglia, *Italy* 31 A9
Canowindra, *Australia* 95 E4
Canso, *Canada* 103 C7
Cantabria □, *Spain* 34 B7
Cantabria, Sierra de, *Spain* 32 C2
Cantabrian Mts. = Cantábrica, Cordillera, *Spain* 34 C5
Cantábrica, Cordillera, *Spain* 34 C5
Cantal □, *France* 20 C6
Cantal, Plomb du, *France* 20 C6
Cantanhede, *Portugal* 34 E2
Cantavieja, *Spain* 32 E4
Čantavir, *Serbia, Yug.* 42 E4
Cantemir, *Moldova* 43 D13
Canterbury, *Australia* 94 D3
Canterbury, *U.K.* 13 F9
Canterbury Bight, *N.Z.* 91 L3
Canterbury Plains, *N.Z.* 91 K3
Cantil, *U.S.A.* 117 K9
Cantillana, *Spain* 35 H5
Canton = Guangzhou, *China* 59 F9
Canton, *Ga., U.S.A.* 109 H3
Canton, *Ill., U.S.A.* 112 E9
Canton, *Miss., U.S.A.* 113 J9
Canton, *Mo., U.S.A.* 112 E9
Canton, *N.Y., U.S.A.* 111 B9
Canton, *Ohio, U.S.A.* 110 F3
Canton, *Pa., U.S.A.* 110 E8
Canton, *S. Dak., U.S.A.* 112 D6
Canton L., *U.S.A.* 113 G5
Cantù, *Italy* 28 C6
Canudos, *Brazil* 124 E7
Canumã →, *Brazil* 124 D7
Canutama, *Brazil* 124 E6
Canutillo, *U.S.A.* 115 L10
Canvey, *U.K.* 13 F8
Canyon, *U.S.A.* 113 H4
Canyonlands National Park, *U.S.A.* 115 G9
Canyonville, *U.S.A.* 114 E2
Cao Bang, *Vietnam* 58 F6
Cao He →, *China* 57 D13
Cao Lanh, *Vietnam* 65 G5
Cao Xian, *China* 56 G8
Cáorle, *Italy* 29 C9
Cap-aux-Meules, *Canada* 103 C7
Cap-Chat, *Canada* 103 C6
Cap-de-la-Madeleine, *Canada* 102 C5
Cap-Haïtien, *Haiti* 121 C5
Capac, *U.S.A.* 110 C2
Capáccio, *Italy* 31 B8
Capaci, *Italy* 30 D6
Capanaparo →, *Venezuela* 124 B5
Capánnori, *Italy* 28 E7
Capbreton, *France* 20 E2
Capdenac, *France* 20 D6
Capdepera, *Spain* 32 F8
Cape →, *Australia* 94 C4
Cape Barren I., *Australia* 94 G4
Cape Breton Highlands Nat. Park, *Canada* 103 C7
Cape Breton I., *Canada* 103 C7
Cape Charles, *U.S.A.* 108 G8
Cape Coast, *Ghana* 83 D4
Cape Coral, *U.S.A.* 109 M5
Cape Dorset, *Canada* 101 B12
Cape Fear →, *U.S.A.* 109 H6
Cape Girardeau, *U.S.A.* 113 G10
Cape May, *U.S.A.* 108 F8
Cape May Point, *U.S.A.* 108 F8
Cape Province, *S. Africa* 85 L3
Cape Tormentine, *Canada* 103 C7
Cape Town, *S. Africa* 88 E2
Cape Verde Is. ■, *Atl. Oc.* 77 E1
Cape Vincent, *U.S.A.* 111 B8
Cape York Peninsula, *Australia* 94 A3
Capela, *Brazil* 125 F11
Capella, *Australia* 94 C4
Capendu, *France* 20 E6
Capestang, *France* 20 E7
Capim →, *Brazil* 125 D9
Capistrello, *Italy* 29 G10
Capitan, *U.S.A.* 115 K11
Capitol Reef National Park, *U.S.A.* 115 G8
Capitola, *U.S.A.* 116 J5
Capizzi, *Italy* 31 E7
Capoche →, *Mozam.* 87 F3
Capoterra, *Italy* 30 C1
Cappadocia, *Turkey* 72 C6
Capraia, *Italy* 28 E6
Caprara, Pta., *Italy* 30 A1
Caprarola, *Italy* 29 F9
Capreol, *Canada* 102 C3
Caprera, *Italy* 30 A2
Capri, *Italy* 31 B7
Capricorn Group, *Australia* 94 C5
Capricorn Ra., *Australia* 92 D2
Caprino Veronese, *Italy* 28 C7
Caprivi Strip, *Namibia* 88 B3
Captain's Flat, *Australia* 95 F4
Captieux, *France* 20 D3
Caquetá →, *Colombia* 122 D4
Caracal, *Romania* 43 F9
Caracas, *Venezuela* 124 A5
Caracol, *Mato Grosso do Sul, Brazil* 126 A4
Caracol, *Piauí, Brazil* 125 E10
Caráglio, *Italy* 28 D4
Carajas, *Brazil* 125 E8
Carajás, Serra dos, *Brazil* 125 E8
Carangola, *Brazil* 127 A7
Caransebeş, *Romania* 42 E7
Carantec, *France* 18 D3
Caraquet, *Canada* 103 C6
Caras, *Peru* 124 E3
Caraş Severin □, *Romania* 42 E7
Caraşova, *Romania* 42 E6
Caratasca, L., *Honduras* 120 C3
Caratinga, *Brazil* 125 G10
Caraúbas, *Brazil* 125 E11
Caravaca = Caravaca de la Cruz, *Spain* 33 G3
Caravaca de la Cruz, *Spain* 33 G3
Caravággio, *Italy* 28 C6
Caravela, *Guinea-Biss.* 82 C1
Caravelas, *Brazil* 125 G11
Caraveli, *Peru* 124 G4
Caràzinho, *Brazil* 127 B5
Carballino = O Carballiño, *Spain* 34 C2
Carballo, *Spain* 34 B2
Carberry, *Canada* 105 D9
Carbó, *Mexico* 118 B2
Carbonara, C., *Italy* 30 C2
Carbondale, *Colo., U.S.A.* 114 G10
Carbondale, *Ill., U.S.A.* 113 G10
Carbondale, *Pa., U.S.A.* 111 E9
Carbonear, *Canada* 103 C9
Carboneras, *Spain* 33 J3
Carboneras de Guadazaón, *Spain* 32 F3
Carbónia, *Italy* 30 C1
Carcabuey, *Spain* 35 H6
Carcagente = Carcaixent, *Spain* 33 F4
Carcaixent, *Spain* 33 F4
Carcajou, *Canada* 104 B5
Carcar, *Phil.* 61 F5
Carcarana →, *Argentina* 126 C3
Carcasse, C., *Haiti* 121 C5
Carcassonne, *France* 20 E6
Carcross, *Canada* 104 A2
Çardak, *Çanakkale, Turkey* 41 F10
Çardak, *Denizli, Turkey* 39 D11
Cardamon Hills, *India* 66 Q10
Cardeña, *Spain* 35 G6
Cárdenas, *Cuba* 120 B3
Cárdenas, *San Luis Potosí, Mexico* 119 C5
Cárdenas, *Tabasco, Mexico* 119 D6
Cardenete, *Spain* 32 F3
Cardiff, *U.K.* 13 F4
Cardiff □, *U.K.* 13 F4
Cardiff-by-the-Sea, *U.S.A.* 117 M9
Cardigan, *U.K.* 13 E3
Cardigan B., *U.K.* 13 E3
Cardinal, *Canada* 111 B9
Cardona, *Spain* 32 D6
Cardona, *Uruguay* 126 C4
Cardoner →, *Spain* 32 D6
Cardoso, Ilha do, *Brazil* 127 B5
Cardston, *Canada* 104 D6
Cardwell, *Australia* 94 B4
Careen L., *Canada* 105 B7
Carei, *Romania* 42 C7
Careme = Ciremai, *Indonesia* 63 G13
Carentan, *France* 18 C5
Carey, *U.S.A.* 114 E7
Carey, L., *Australia* 93 E3
Carey L., *Canada* 105 A8
Careysburg, *Liberia* 82 D2
Cargèse, *France* 21 F12
Carhaix-Plouguer, *France* 18 D3
Carhué, *Argentina* 126 D3
Caria, *Turkey* 39 D10
Cariacica, *Brazil* 125 H10
Cariati, *Italy* 31 C9
Caribbean Sea, *W. Indies* 121 D5
Cariboo Mts., *Canada* 104 C4
Caribou, *U.S.A.* 109 B12
Caribou →, *Man., Canada* 105 B10
Caribou →, *N.W.T., Canada* 104 A3
Caribou I., *Canada* 102 C2
Caribou Is., *Canada* 104 A6
Caribou L., *Man., Canada* 105 B9
Caribou L., *Ont., Canada* 102 B2
Caribou Mts., *Canada* 104 B5
Carichic, *Mexico* 118 B3
Carigara, *Phil.* 61 F6
Carignan, *France* 19 C12
Carignano, *Italy* 28 D4
Carillo, *Mexico* 118 B4
Carinda, *Australia* 95 E4
Cariñena, *Spain* 32 D3
Carinhanha, *Brazil* 125 F10
Carinhanha →, *Brazil* 125 F10
Carini, *Italy* 30 D6
Cariño, *Spain* 34 B3
Carínola, *Italy* 30 A6
Carinthia = Kärnten □, *Austria* 26 E6
Caripito, *Venezuela* 124 A6
Carlbrod = Dimitrovgrad, *Serbia, Yug.* 40 C6
Carlet, *Spain* 33 F4
Carleton, Mt., *Canada* 103 C6
Carleton Place, *Canada* 102 C4
Carletonville, *S. Africa* 88 D4
Cârlibaba, *Romania* 43 C10
Carlin, *U.S.A.* 114 F5
Carlingford L., *U.K.* 15 B5

Carlinville, U.S.A. 112 F10
Carlisle, U.K. 12 C5
Carlisle, U.S.A. 110 F7
Carlit, Pic, France 20 F5
Carloforte, Italy 30 C1
Carlos Casares, Argentina 126 D3
Carlos Tejedor, Argentina 126 D3
Carlow, Ireland 15 D5
Carlow □, Ireland 15 D5
Carlsbad, Calif., U.S.A. 117 M9
Carlsbad, N. Mex., U.S.A. 113 J2
Carlsbad Caverns National Park, U.S.A. 113 J2
Carluke, U.K. 14 F5
Carlyle, Canada 105 D8
Carmacks, Canada 100 B6
Carmagnola, Italy 28 D4
Carman, Canada 105 D9
Carmarthen, U.K. 13 F3
Carmarthen B., U.K. 13 F3
Carmarthenshire □, U.K. 13 F3
Carmaux, France 20 D6
Carmel, U.S.A. 111 E11
Carmel-by-the-Sea, U.S.A. 116 J5
Carmel Valley, U.S.A. 116 J5
Carmelo, Uruguay 126 C4
Carmen, Colombia 124 B3
Carmen, Paraguay 127 B4
Carmen →, Mexico 118 A3
Carmen, I., Mexico 118 B2
Carmen de Patagones, Argentina 128 E4
Cármenes, Spain 34 C5
Carmensa, Argentina 126 D2
Carmi, Canada 104 D5
Carmi, U.S.A. 108 F1
Carmichael, U.S.A. 116 G5
Carmila, Australia 94 C4
Carmona, Costa Rica 120 E2
Carmona, Spain 35 H5
Carn Ban, U.K. 14 D4
Carn Eige, U.K. 14 D3
Carnamah, Australia 93 E2
Carnarvon, Australia 93 D1
Carnarvon, S. Africa 88 E3
Carnarvon Ra., Queens., Australia 94 D4
Carnarvon Ra., W. Austral., Australia 93 E3
Carnation, U.S.A. 116 C5
Carndonagh, Ireland 15 A4
Carnduff, Canada 105 D8
Carnegie, U.S.A. 110 F4
Carnegie, L., Australia 93 E3
Carnic Alps = Karnische Alpen, Europe 26 E6
Carniche Alpi = Karnische Alpen, Europe 26 E6
Carnot, C.A.R. 84 D3
Carnot, C., Australia 95 E2
Carnot B., Australia 92 C3
Carnoustie, U.K. 14 E6
Carnsore Pt., Ireland 15 D5
Caro, U.S.A. 108 D4
Carol City, U.S.A. 109 N5
Carolina, Brazil 125 E9
Carolina, Puerto Rico 121 C6
Carolina, S. Africa 89 D5
Caroline I., Kiribati 97 H12
Caroline Is., Micronesia 52 J17
Caroni →, Venezuela 124 B6
Caroníe = Nébrodi, Monti, Italy 31 E7
Caroona, Australia 95 E5
Carpathians, Europe 6 F10
Carpaţii Meridionali, Romania 43 E9
Carpentaria, G. of, Australia 94 A2
Carpentras, France 21 D9
Carpi, Italy 28 D7
Cărpineni, Moldova 43 D13
Carpinteria, U.S.A. 117 L7
Carpio, Spain 34 D5
Carr Boyd Ra., Australia 92 C4
Carrabelle, U.S.A. 109 L3
Carral, Spain 34 B2
Carranza, Presa V., Mexico 118 B4
Carrara, Italy 28 D7
Carrascal, Phil. 61 G6
Carrascosa del Campo, Spain 32 E2
Carrauntoohill, Ireland 15 D2
Carrick-on-Shannon, Ireland 15 C3
Carrick-on-Suir, Ireland 15 D4
Carrickfergus, U.K. 15 B6
Carrickmacross, Ireland 15 C5
Carrieton, Australia 95 E2
Carrington, U.S.A. 112 B5
Carrión →, Spain 34 D6
Carrión de los Condes, Spain 34 C6
Carrizal Bajo, Chile 126 B1
Carrizalillo, Chile 126 B1
Carrizo Cr. →, U.S.A. 113 G3
Carrizo Springs, U.S.A. 113 L5
Carrizozo, U.S.A. 115 K11
Carroll, U.S.A. 112 D7
Carrollton, Ga., U.S.A. 109 J3
Carrollton, Ill., U.S.A. 112 F9
Carrollton, Ky., U.S.A. 108 F3
Carrollton, Mo., U.S.A. 112 F8
Carrollton, Ohio, U.S.A. 110 F3
Carron →, U.K. 14 D4
Carron, L., U.K. 14 D3
Carrot →, Canada 105 C8
Carrot River, Canada 105 C8
Carrouges, France 18 D6
Carrù, Italy 28 D4
Carruthers, Canada 105 C7
Carsa Dek, Ethiopia 81 F4
Çarşamba, Turkey 72 B7
Carsóli, Italy 29 F10
Carson, Calif., U.S.A. 117 M8
Carson, N. Dak., U.S.A. 112 B4
Carson →, U.S.A. 116 F8
Carson City, U.S.A. 116 F7
Carson Sink, U.S.A. 114 G4
Cartagena, Colombia 124 A3
Cartagena, Spain 33 H4
Cartago, Colombia 124 C3
Cartago, Costa Rica 120 E3
Cártama, Spain 35 J6
Cartaxo, Portugal 35 F2
Cartaya, Spain 35 H3
Cartersville, U.S.A. 109 H3
Carterton, N.Z. 91 J5
Carthage, Tunisia 30 F3
Carthage, Ill., U.S.A. 112 E9
Carthage, Mo., U.S.A. 113 G7
Carthage, N.Y., U.S.A. 108 D8
Carthage, Tex., U.S.A. 113 J7
Cartier I., Australia 92 B3
Cartwright, Canada 103 B8
Caruaru, Brazil 125 E11
Carúpano, Venezuela 124 A6
Caruthersville, U.S.A. 113 G10
Carvin, France 19 B9
Carvoeiro, Brazil 124 D6
Carvoeiro, C., Portugal 35 F1
Cary, U.S.A. 109 H6
Casa Branca, Portugal 35 G2
Casa Grande, U.S.A. 115 K8
Casablanca, Chile 126 C1
Casablanca, Morocco 78 B4
Casacalenda, Italy 29 G11
Casalbordino, Italy 29 F11
Casale Monferrato, Italy 28 C5
Casalmaggiore, Italy 28 D7
Casalpusterlengo, Italy 28 C6
Casamance →, Senegal 82 C1
Casarano, Italy 31 B11
Casares, Spain 35 J5
Casas Ibáñez, Spain 33 F3
Casasimarro, Spain 33 F2
Casatejada, Spain 34 F5
Casavieja, Spain 34 E6
Cascade, Idaho, U.S.A. 114 D5
Cascade, Mont., U.S.A. 114 C8
Cascade Locks, U.S.A. 116 E5
Cascade Ra., U.S.A. 116 D5
Cascade Reservoir, U.S.A. 114 D5
Cascais, Portugal 35 G1
Cascavel, Brazil 127 A5
Cáscina, Italy 28 E7
Casco B., U.S.A. 109 D10
Caselle Torinese, Italy 28 C4
Caserta, Italy 31 A7
Cashel, Ireland 15 D4
Casiguran, Phil. 61 C5
Casilda, Argentina 126 C3
Casimcea, Romania 43 F13
Casino, Australia 95 D5
Casiquiare →, Venezuela 124 C5
Čáslav, Czech Rep. 26 B8
Casma, Peru 124 E3
Casmalia, U.S.A. 117 L6
Cásola Valsénio, Italy 29 D8
Cásoli, Italy 29 F11
Caspe, Spain 32 D4
Casper, U.S.A. 114 E10
Caspian Depression, Eurasia 49 G9
Caspian Sea, Eurasia 50 E6
Cass Lake, U.S.A. 112 B7
Cassà de la Selva, Spain 32 D7
Cassadaga, U.S.A. 110 D5
Cassano allo Iónio, Italy 31 C9
Casse, Grande, France 21 C10
Cassel, France 19 B9
Casselman, Canada 111 A9
Casselton, U.S.A. 112 B6
Cassiar, Canada 104 B3
Cassiar Mts., Canada 104 B2
Cassino, Italy 30 A6
Cassis, France 21 E9
Cassville, U.S.A. 113 G8
Castagneto Carducci, Italy 28 E7
Castaic, U.S.A. 117 L8
Castalia, U.S.A. 110 E2
Castanhal, Brazil 125 D9
Castéggio, Italy 28 C6
Castejón de Monegros, Spain 32 D4
Castèl di Sangro, Italy 29 G11
Castèl San Giovanni, Italy 28 C6
Castèl San Pietro Terme, Italy 29 D8
Castelbuono, Italy 31 E7
Castelfidardo, Italy 29 E10
Castelfiorentino, Italy 28 E7
Castelfranco Emília, Italy 28 D8
Castelfranco Véneto, Italy 29 C8
Casteljaloux, France 20 D4
Castellabate, Italy 31 B7
Castellammare, G. di, Italy 30 D5
Castellammare del Golfo, Italy 30 D5
Castellammare di Stábia, Italy 31 B7
Castellamonte, Italy 28 C4
Castellane, France 21 E10
Castellaneta, Italy 31 B9
Castelli, Argentina 126 D4
Castelló de la Plana, Spain 32 F4
Castellón de la Plana □, Spain 32 E4
Castellote, Spain 32 E4
Castelmáuro, Italy 29 G11
Castelnau-de-Médoc, France 20 C3
Castelnau-Magnoac, France 20 E4
Castelnaudary, France 20 E5
Castelnovo ne' Monti, Italy 28 D7
Castelnuovo di Val di Cécina, Italy 28 E7
Castelo, Brazil 127 A7
Castelo Branco, Portugal 34 F3
Castelo Branco □, Portugal 34 F3
Castelo de Paiva, Portugal 34 D2
Castelo de Vide, Portugal 35 F3
Castelsardo, Italy 30 B1
Castelsarrasin, France 20 D5
Casteltérmini, Italy 30 E6
Castelvetrano, Italy 30 E5
Casterton, Australia 95 F3
Castets, France 20 E2
Castiglion Fiorentino, Italy 29 E8
Castiglione del Lago, Italy 29 E9
Castiglione della Pescáia, Italy 28 F7
Castiglione delle Stiviere, Italy 28 C7
Castilblanco, Spain 35 F5
Castile, U.S.A. 110 D6
Castilla, Playa de, Spain 35 J4
Castilla-La Mancha □, Spain 6 H5
Castilla y Leon □, Spain 34 D6
Castillo de Locubín, Spain 35 H7
Castillon-en-Couserans, France 20 F5
Castillonès, France 20 D4
Castillos, Uruguay 127 C5
Castle Dale, U.S.A. 114 G8
Castle Douglas, U.K. 14 G5
Castle Rock, Colo., U.S.A. 112 F2
Castle Rock, Wash., U.S.A. 116 D4
Castlebar, Ireland 15 C2
Castleblaney, Ireland 15 B5
Castlederg, U.K. 15 B4
Castleford, U.K. 12 D6
Castlegar, Canada 104 D5
Castlemaine, Australia 95 F3
Castlepollard, Ireland 15 C4
Castlerea, Ireland 15 C3
Castlereagh →, Australia 95 E4
Castlereagh B., Australia 94 A2
Castleton, U.S.A. 111 C11
Castletown, U.K. 12 C3
Castletown Bearhaven, Ireland 15 E2
Castor, Canada 104 C6
Castor →, Canada 102 B4
Castorland, U.S.A. 111 C9
Castres, France 20 E6
Castricum, Neths. 17 B4
Castries, St. Lucia 121 D7
Castril, Spain 35 H8
Castro, Brazil 127 A6
Castro, Chile 128 E2
Castro Alves, Brazil 125 F11
Castro del Río, Spain 35 H6
Castro-Urdiales, Spain 34 B7
Castro Verde, Portugal 35 H2
Castrojeriz, Spain 34 C6
Castropol, Spain 34 B4
Castroreale, Italy 31 D8
Castrovíllari, Italy 31 C9
Castroville, U.S.A. 116 J5
Castuera, Spain 35 G5
Çat, Turkey 73 C9
Cat Ba, Dao, Vietnam 64 B6
Cat I., Bahamas 121 B4
Cat L., Canada 102 B1
Cat Lake, Canada 102 B1
Čata, Slovak Rep. 27 D11
Catacamas, Honduras 120 D2
Cataguases, Brazil 127 A7
Çatak, Turkey 73 C10
Catalão, Brazil 125 G9
Çatalca, Turkey 41 E12
Catalina, Canada 103 C9
Catalina, Chile 126 B2
Catalina, U.S.A. 115 K8
Catalonia = Cataluña □, Spain 32 D6
Cataluña □, Spain 32 D6
Çatalzeytin, Turkey 72 B6
Catamarca, Argentina 126 B2
Catamarca □, Argentina 126 B2
Catanauan, Phil. 61 E5
Catanduanes □, Phil. 61 E6
Catanduva, Brazil 127 A6
Catánia, Italy 31 E8
Catánia, G. di, Italy 31 E8
Catanzaro, Italy 31 D9
Catarman, Phil. 61 E6
Catbalogan, Phil. 61 F6
Cateel, Phil. 61 H7
Catembe, Mozam. 89 D5
Caterham, U.K. 13 F7
Cathcart, S. Africa 88 E4
Cathlamet, U.S.A. 116 D3
Catio, Guinea-Biss. 82 C1
Catlettsburg, U.S.A. 108 F4
Çatma Dağı, Turkey 39 C11
Catoche, C., Mexico 119 C7
Cátria, Mte., Italy 29 E9
Catriló, Argentina 126 D3
Catrimani, Brazil 124 C6
Catrimani →, Brazil 124 C6
Catskill, U.S.A. 111 D11
Catskill Mts., U.S.A. 111 D10
Catt, Mt., Australia 94 A1
Cattaraugus, U.S.A. 110 D6
Cattólica, Italy 29 E9
Cattólica Eraclea, Italy 30 E6
Catuala, Angola 88 B2
Catuane, Mozam. 89 D5
Catur, Mozam. 87 E4
Catwick Is., Vietnam 65 G7
Cauca →, Colombia 124 B4
Caucaia, Brazil 125 D11
Caucasus Mountains, Eurasia 49 J7
Caudete, Spain 33 G3
Caudry, France 19 B10
Caulnes, France 18 D4
Caulónia, Italy 31 D9
Caungula, Angola 84 F3
Cauquenes, Chile 126 D1
Caura →, Venezuela 124 B6
Cauresi →, Mozam. 87 F3
Căuşani, Moldova 43 D14
Causapscal, Canada 103 C6
Caussade, France 20 D5
Causse-Méjean, France 20 D7
Cauterets, France 20 F3
Cauvery →, India 66 P11
Caux, Pays de, France 18 C7
Cava de' Tirreni, Italy 31 B7
Cávado →, Portugal 34 D2
Cavaillon, France 21 E9
Cavalaire-sur-Mer, France 21 E10
Cavalese, Italy 29 B8
Cavalier, U.S.A. 112 A6
Cavalla = Cavally →, Africa 82 E3
Cavalleria, C. de, Spain 37 A11
Cavallo, I. de, France 21 G13
Cavally →, Africa 82 E3
Cavan, Ireland 15 B4
Cavan □, Ireland 15 C4
Cavárzere, Italy 29 C9
Çavdarhisar, Turkey 39 B11
Çavdır, Turkey 39 D11
Cave Creek, U.S.A. 115 K7
Cavenagh Ra., Australia 93 E4
Cavendish, Australia 95 F3
Caviana, I., Brazil 125 C8
Cavite, Phil. 61 D4
Cavnic, Romania 43 C8
Cavour, Italy 28 D4
Cavtat, Croatia 40 D2
Cawndilla L., Australia 95 E3
Cawnpore = Kanpur, India 69 F9
Caxias, Brazil 125 D10
Caxias do Sul, Brazil 127 B5
Çay, Turkey 72 C4
Cay Sal Bank, Bahamas 120 B4
Cayambe, Ecuador 124 C3
Çaycuma, Turkey 72 B5
Çayeli, Turkey 73 B9
Cayenne, Fr. Guiana 125 B8
Caygören Barajı, Turkey 39 B10
Çayıralan, Turkey 72 C6
Caylus, France 20 D5
Cayman Brac, Cayman Is. 120 C4
Cayman Is. ■, W. Indies 120 C3
Cayo Romano, Cuba 120 B4
Cayres, France 20 D7
Cayuga, Canada 110 D5
Cayuga, U.S.A. 111 D8
Cayuga L., U.S.A. 111 D8
Cazalla de la Sierra, Spain 35 H5
Căzăneşti, Romania 43 F12
Cazaubon, France 20 E3
Cazaux et de Sanguinet, Étang de, France 20 D2
Cazenovia, U.S.A. 111 D9
Cazères, France 20 E5
Cazin, Bos.-H. 29 D12
Čazma, Croatia 29 C13
Cazombo, Angola 85 G4
Cazorla, Spain 35 H7
Cazorla, Sierra de, Spain 35 G8
Cea →, Spain 34 C5
Ceamurlia de Jos, Romania 43 F13
Ceanannus Mor, Ireland 15 C5
Ceará = Fortaleza, Brazil 125 D11
Ceará □, Brazil 125 E11
Ceará Mirim, Brazil 125 E11
Ceauru, L., Romania 43 F8
Cebaco, I. de, Panama 120 E3
Cebollar, Argentina 126 B2
Cebollera, Sierra de, Spain 32 D2
Cebreros, Spain 34 E6
Cebu, Phil. 61 F5
Čečava, Bos.-H. 42 F2
Ceccano, Italy 30 A6
Cece, Hungary 42 D3
Cechi, Ivory C. 82 D4
Cecil Plains, Australia 95 D5
Cécina, Italy 28 E7
Cécina →, Italy 28 E7
Ceclavín, Spain 34 F4
Cedar →, U.S.A. 112 E9
Cedar City, U.S.A. 115 H7
Cedar Creek Reservoir, U.S.A. 113 J6
Cedar Falls, Iowa, U.S.A. 112 D8
Cedar Falls, Wash., U.S.A. 116 C5
Cedar Key, U.S.A. 109 L4
Cedar L., Canada 105 C9
Cedar Rapids, U.S.A. 112 E9
Cedartown, U.S.A. 109 H3
Cedarvale, Canada 104 B3
Cedarville, S. Africa 89 E4
Cedeira, Spain 34 B2
Cedral, Mexico 118 C4
Cedrino →, Italy 30 B2
Cedro, Brazil 125 E11
Cedros, I. de, Mexico 118 B1
Ceduna, Australia 95 E1
Cedynia, Poland 45 F1
Cée, Spain 34 C1
Cefalù, Italy 31 D7
Cega →, Spain 34 D6
Cegléd, Hungary 42 C4
Céglie Messápico, Italy 31 B10
Cehegín, Spain 33 G3
Ceheng, China 58 E5
Cehu-Silvaniei, Romania 43 C8
Ceica, Romania 42 D7
Ceira →, Portugal 34 E2
Čelákovice, Czech Rep. 26 A7
Celano, Italy 29 F10
Celanova, Spain 34 C3
Celaya, Mexico 118 C4
Celebes Sea, Indonesia 63 D6
Čelić, Bos.-H. 42 F3
Celina, U.S.A. 108 E3
Celinac, Bos.-H. 42 F2
Celje, Slovenia 29 B12
Celldömölk, Hungary 42 C2
Celle, Germany 24 C6
Celorico da Beira, Portugal 34 E3
Çeltikçi, Turkey 39 D12
Çemişgezek, Turkey 73 C8
Cenderwasih, Teluk, Indonesia 63 E9
Cengong, China 58 D7
Ceno →, Italy 28 D7
Centallo, Italy 28 D4
Centelles, Spain 32 D7
Center, N. Dak., U.S.A. 112 B4
Center, Tex., U.S.A. 113 K7
Centerburg, U.S.A. 110 F2
Centerville, Calif., U.S.A. 116 J7
Centerville, Iowa, U.S.A. 112 E8
Centerville, Pa., U.S.A. 110 F5
Centerville, Tenn., U.S.A. 109 H2
Centerville, Tex., U.S.A. 113 K7
Cento, Italy 29 D8
Central □, Ghana 83 D4
Central □, Kenya 86 C4
Central □, Malawi 87 E3
Central □, Zambia 87 E2
Central, Cordillera, Colombia 122 C3
Central, Cordillera, Costa Rica 120 D3
Central, Cordillera, Dom. Rep. 121 C5
Central, Cordillera, Phil. 61 C4
Central African Rep. ■, Africa 84 C4
Central America, America 98 H11
Central Butte, Canada 105 C7
Central City, Colo., U.S.A. 114 G11
Central City, Ky., U.S.A. 108 G2
Central City, Nebr., U.S.A. 112 E6
Central I., Kenya 86 B4
Central Makran Range, Pakistan 66 F4
Central Patricia, Canada 102 B1
Central Point, U.S.A. 114 E2
Central Russian Uplands, Europe 6 E13
Central Siberian Plateau, Russia 52 C14
Central Square, U.S.A. 111 C8
Centralia, Ill., U.S.A. 112 F10
Centralia, Mo., U.S.A. 112 F8
Centralia, Wash., U.S.A. 116 D4
Cenxi, China 59 F8
Ceotina →, Bos.-H. 40 C2
Cephalonia = Kefallinía, Greece 38 C2
Čepin, Croatia 42 E3
Ceprano, Italy 30 A6
Ceptura, Romania 43 E11
Cepu, Indonesia 63 G14
Ceram = Seram, Indonesia 63 E7
Ceram Sea = Seram Sea, Indonesia 63 E7
Cerbère, France 20 F7
Cerbicales, Is., France 21 G13
Cercal, Portugal 35 H2
Cerdaña, Spain 32 C6
Cère →, France 20 D5
Cerea, Italy 29 C8
Ceredigion □, U.K. 13 E3
Ceres, Argentina 126 B3
Ceres, S. Africa 88 E2
Ceres, U.S.A. 116 H6
Céret, France 20 F6
Cergy, France 19 C9
Cerignola, Italy 31 A8
Cerigo = Kíthira, Greece 38 E5
Cérilly, France 19 F9
Cerisiers, France 19 D10
Cerizay, France 18 F6
Çerkeş, Turkey 72 B5
Çerkezköy, Turkey 41 E12
Cerknica, Slovenia 29 C11
Cerkovica, Bulgaria 41 C8
Cermerno, Serbia, Yug. 40 C4
Çermik, Turkey 73 C8
Cerna, Romania 43 E13
Cerna →, Romania 43 F8
Cernavodă, Romania 43 F13
Cernay, France 19 E14
Cernik, Croatia 42 E2
Cerralvo, I., Mexico 118 C3
Cërrik, Albania 40 E3
Cerritos, Mexico 118 C4
Cerro Chato, Uruguay 127 C4
Certaldo, Italy 28 E8
Cervaro →, Italy 31 A8
Cervati, Monte, Italy 31 B8
Cerventes, Australia 93 F2
Cervera, Spain 32 D6
Cervera de Pisuerga, Spain 34 C6
Cervera del Río Alhama, Spain 32 C3
Cervéteri, Italy 29 F9
Cérvia, Italy 29 D9
Cervignano del Friuli, Italy 29 C10
Cervinara, Italy 31 A7
Cervione, France 21 F13
Cervo, Spain 34 B3
Cesarò, Italy 31 E7
Cesena, Italy 29 D9
Cesenático, Italy 29 D9
Cēsis, Latvia 9 H21
Česká Lípa, Czech Rep. 26 A7
Česká Třebová, Czech Rep. 27 B9
České Budějovice, Czech Rep. 26 C7
České Velenice, Czech Rep. 26 C7
Českobudějovický □, Czech Rep. 26 B7
Českomoravská Vrchovina, Czech Rep. 26 B8
Český Brod, Czech Rep. 26 A7

Český Krumlov, *Czech Rep.* 26 C7
Český Těšín, *Czech Rep.* 27 B11
Česma →, *Croatia* 29 C13
Çeşme, *Turkey* 39 C8
Cessnock, *Australia* 95 E5
Cesson-Sévigné, *France* 18 D5
Cestas, *France* 20 D3
Cestos →, *Liberia* 82 D3
Cetate, *Romania* 42 F8
Cetin Grad, *Croatia* 29 C12
Cetina →, *Croatia* 29 E13
Cetinje, *Montenegro, Yug.* 40 D2
Cetraro, *Italy* 31 C8
Ceuta, *N. Afr.* 78 A4
Ceva, *Italy* 28 D5
Cévennes, *France* 20 D7
Ceyhan, *Turkey* 70 B2
Ceyhan →, *Turkey* 72 D6
Ceylânpınar, *Turkey* 73 D9
Ceylon = Sri Lanka ■, *Asia* 66 R12
Cèze →, *France* 21 D8
Cha-am, *Thailand* 64 F2
Cha Pa, *Vietnam* 64 A4
Chabanais, *France* 20 C4
Chabeuil, *France* 21 D9
Chablais, *France* 19 F13
Chablis, *France* 19 E10
Chacabuco, *Argentina* 126 C3
Chachapoyas, *Peru* 124 E3
Chachoengsao, *Thailand* 64 F3
Chachran, *Pakistan* 66 E7
Chachro, *Pakistan* 68 G4
Chaco □, *Argentina* 126 B3
Chaco □, *Paraguay* 126 B4
Chaco →, *U.S.A.* 115 H9
Chaco Austral, *S. Amer.* 128 B4
Chaco Boreal, *S. Amer.* 124 H6
Chaco Central, *S. Amer.* 128 A4
Chacon, C., *U.S.A.* 104 C2
Chad ■, *Africa* 79 F8
Chad, L. = Tchad, L., *Chad* 79 F8
Chadan, *Russia* 51 D10
Chadileuvú →, *Argentina* 126 D2
Chadiza, *Zambia* 87 E3
Chadron, *U.S.A.* 112 D3
Chadyr-Lunga = Ciadâr-Lunga, *Moldova* 43 D13
Chae Hom, *Thailand* 64 C2
Chaem →, *Thailand* 64 C2
Chaeryŏng, *N. Korea* 57 E13
Chagai Hills = Chāh Gay, *Afghan.* 66 E3
Chagda, *Russia* 51 D14
Chaghcharān, *Afghan.* 66 B4
Chagny, *France* 19 F11
Chagoda, *Russia* 46 C8
Chagos Arch., *Ind. Oc.* 52 K11
Chagrin Falls, *U.S.A.* 110 E3
Chāh Ākhvor, *Iran* 71 C8
Chāh Bahar, *Iran* 71 E9
Chāh-e Kavīr, *Iran* 71 C8
Chāh Gay, *Afghan.* 66 E3
Chahar Burjak, *Afghan.* 66 D3
Chahār Mahāll va Bakhtīarī □, *Iran* 71 C6
Chaibasa, *India* 67 H14
Chaillé-les-Marais, *France* 20 B2
Chainat, *Thailand* 64 E3
Chaiya, *Thailand* 65 H2
Chaj Doab, *Pakistan* 68 C5
Chajari, *Argentina* 126 C4
Chak Amru, *Pakistan* 68 C6
Chaka, *Sudan* 81 G3
Chakar →, *Pakistan* 68 E3
Chakari, *Zimbabwe* 89 B4
Chake Chake, *Tanzania* 86 D4
Chakhānsūr, *Afghan.* 66 D3
Chakonipau, L., *Canada* 103 A6
Chakradharpur, *India* 69 H11
Chakrata, *India* 68 D7
Chakwal, *Pakistan* 68 C5
Chala, *Peru* 124 G4
Chalais, *France* 20 C4
Chalchihuites, *Mexico* 118 C4
Chalcis = Khalkís, *Greece* 38 C5
Châlette-sur-Loing, *France* 19 D9
Chaleur B., *Canada* 103 C6
Chalfant, *U.S.A.* 116 H8
Chalhuanca, *Peru* 124 F4
Chalindrey, *France* 19 E12
Chaling, *China* 59 D9
Chalisgaon, *India* 66 J9
Chalk River, *Canada* 102 C4
Chalky Inlet, *N.Z.* 91 M1
Challans, *France* 18 F5
Challapata, *Bolivia* 124 G5
Challis, *U.S.A.* 114 D6
Chalmette, *U.S.A.* 113 L10
Chalon-sur-Saône, *France* 19 F11
Chalonnes-sur-Loire, *France* 18 E6
Châlons-en-Champagne, *France* 19 D11
Châlus, *France* 20 C4
Chalyaphum, *Thailand* 64 E4
Cham, *Germany* 25 F8
Cham, Cu Lao, *Vietnam* 64 E7
Chama, *U.S.A.* 115 H10
Chamaicó, *Argentina* 126 D3
Chaman, *Pakistan* 66 D5
Chamba, *India* 68 C7
Chamba, *Tanzania* 87 E4
Chambal →, *India* 69 F8
Chamberlain, *U.S.A.* 112 D5
Chamberlain →, *Australia* 92 C4
Chamberlain L., *U.S.A.* 109 B11
Chambers, *U.S.A.* 115 J9
Chambersburg, *U.S.A.* 108 F7
Chambéry, *France* 21 C9
Chambeshi →, *Zambia* 84 G6
Chambly, *Canada* 111 A11
Chambord, *Canada* 103 C5
Chamboulive, *France* 20 C5
Chamchamal, *Iraq* 70 C5
Chamela, *Mexico* 118 D3
Chamical, *Argentina* 126 C2
Chamkar Luong, *Cambodia* 65 G4
Chamoli, *India* 69 D8
Chamonix-Mont Blanc, *France* 21 C10
Chamouchouane →, *Canada* 102 C5
Champa, *India* 69 H10
Champagne, *Canada* 104 A1
Champagne, *France* 19 D11
Champagnole, *France* 19 F12
Champaign, *U.S.A.* 108 E1
Champassak, *Laos* 64 E5
Champaubert, *France* 19 D10
Champawat, *India* 69 E9
Champdeniers-St-Denis, *France* 20 B3
Champdoré, L., *Canada* 103 A6
Champeix, *France* 20 C7
Champion, *U.S.A.* 110 E4
Champlain, *U.S.A.* 111 B11
Champlain, L., *U.S.A.* 111 B11
Champlitte, *France* 19 E12
Champotón, *Mexico* 119 D6
Champua, *India* 69 H11
Chamusca, *Portugal* 35 F2
Chana, *Thailand* 65 J3
Chañaral, *Chile* 126 B1
Chanārān, *Iran* 71 B8
Chanasma, *India* 68 H5
Chanco, *Chile* 126 D1
Chand, *India* 69 J8
Chandan, *India* 69 G12
Chandan Chauki, *India* 69 E9
Chandannagar, *India* 69 H13
Chandausi, *India* 69 E8
Chandeleur Is., *U.S.A.* 113 L10
Chandeleur Sd., *U.S.A.* 113 L10
Chandigarh, *India* 68 D7
Chandil, *India* 69 H12
Chandler, *Australia* 95 D1
Chandler, *Canada* 103 C7
Chandler, *Ariz., U.S.A.* 115 K8
Chandler, *Okla., U.S.A.* 113 H6
Chandod, *India* 68 J5
Chandpur, *Bangla.* 67 H17
Chandrapur, *India* 66 K11
Chānf, *Iran* 71 E9
Chang, *Pakistan* 68 F3
Chang, Ko, *Thailand* 65 F4
Ch'ang Chiang = Chang Jiang →, *China* 59 B13
Chang Jiang →, *China* 59 B13
Changa, *India* 69 C7
Changanacheri, *India* 66 Q10
Changane →, *Mozam.* 89 C5
Changbai, *China* 57 D15
Changbai Shan, *China* 57 C15
Changchiak'ou = Zhangjiakou, *China* 56 D8
Ch'angchou = Changzhou, *China* 59 B12
Changchun, *China* 57 C13
Changchunling, *China* 57 B13
Changde, *China* 59 C8
Changdo-ri, *N. Korea* 57 E14
Changfeng, *China* 59 A11
Changhai = Shanghai, *China* 59 B13
Changhua, *China* 59 B12
Changhua, *Taiwan* 59 E13
Changhŭng, *S. Korea* 57 G14
Changhŭngni, *N. Korea* 57 D15
Changjiang, *China* 64 C7
Changjin, *N. Korea* 57 D14
Changjin-chŏsuji, *N. Korea* 57 D14
Changle, *China* 59 E12
Changli, *China* 57 E10
Changling, *China* 57 B12
Changlun, *Malaysia* 65 J3
Changning, *Hunan, China* 59 D9
Changning, *Sichuan, China* 58 C5
Changning, *Yunnan, China* 58 E2
Changping, *China* 56 D9
Changsha, *China* 59 C9
Changshan, *China* 59 C12
Changshu, *China* 59 B13
Changshun, *China* 58 D6
Changtai, *China* 59 E11
Changting, *China* 59 E11
Changwu, *China* 56 G4
Changxing, *China* 59 B12
Changyang, *China* 59 B8
Changyi, *China* 57 F10
Changyŏn, *N. Korea* 57 E13
Changyuan, *China* 56 G8
Changzhi, *China* 56 F7
Changzhou, *China* 59 B12
Chanhanga, *Angola* 88 B1
Chanlar = Xanlar, *Azerbaijan* 49 K8
Channapatna, *India* 66 N10
Channel Is., *U.K.* 13 H5
Channel Is., *U.S.A.* 117 M7
Channel Islands National Park, *U.S.A.* 117 M8
Channel-Port aux Basques, *Canada* 103 C8
Channel Tunnel, *Europe* 13 F9
Channing, *U.S.A.* 113 H3
Chantada, *Spain* 34 C3
Chanthaburi, *Thailand* 64 F4
Chantilly, *France* 19 C9
Chantonnay, *France* 18 F5
Chantrey Inlet, *Canada* 100 B10
Chanute, *U.S.A.* 113 G7
Chanza →, *Spain* 35 H3
Chao Hu, *China* 59 B11
Chao Phraya →, *Thailand* 64 F3
Chao Phraya Lowlands, *Thailand* 64 E3
Chaocheng, *China* 56 F8
Chaohu, *China* 59 B11
Chaoyang, *Guangdong, China* 59 F11
Chaoyang, *Liaoning, China* 57 D11
Chaozhou, *China* 59 F11
Chapais, *Canada* 102 C5
Chapala, *Mozam.* 87 F4
Chapala, L. de, *Mexico* 118 C4
Chapayev, *Kazakstan* 48 E10
Chapayevsk, *Russia* 48 D9
Chapecó, *Brazil* 127 B5
Chapel Hill, *U.S.A.* 109 H6
Chapleau, *Canada* 102 C3
Chaplin, *Canada* 105 C7
Chaplin L., *Canada* 105 C7
Chaplino, *Ukraine* 47 H9
Chaplygin, *Russia* 46 F11
Chappell, *U.S.A.* 112 E3
Chapra = Chhapra, *India* 69 G11
Chara, *Russia* 51 D12
Charadai, *Argentina* 126 B4
Charagua, *Bolivia* 124 G6
Charambirá, Punta, *Colombia* 124 C3
Charaña, *Bolivia* 124 G5
Charantsavan, *Armenia* 49 K7
Charanwala, *India* 68 F5
Charata, *Argentina* 126 B3
Charcas, *Mexico* 118 C4
Chard, *U.K.* 13 G5
Chardon, *U.S.A.* 110 E3
Chardzhou = Chärjew, *Turkmenistan* 50 F7
Charente □, *France* 20 C4
Charente →, *France* 20 C2
Charente-Maritime □, *France* 20 C3
Charenton-du-Cher, *France* 19 F9
Chari →, *Chad* 79 F8
Chārīkār, *Afghan.* 66 B6
Chariton →, *U.S.A.* 112 F8
Chärjew, *Turkmenistan* 50 F7
Charkhari, *India* 69 G8
Charkhi Dadri, *India* 68 E7
Charleroi, *Belgium* 17 D4
Charleroi, *U.S.A.* 110 F5
Charles, C., *U.S.A.* 108 G8
Charles City, *U.S.A.* 112 D8
Charles L., *Canada* 105 B6
Charles Town, *U.S.A.* 108 F7
Charleston, *Ill., U.S.A.* 108 F1
Charleston, *Miss., U.S.A.* 113 H9
Charleston, *Mo., U.S.A.* 113 G10
Charleston, *S.C., U.S.A.* 109 J6
Charleston, *W. Va., U.S.A.* 108 F5
Charleston L., *Canada* 111 B9
Charleston Peak, *U.S.A.* 117 J11
Charlestown, *Ireland* 15 C3
Charlestown, *S. Africa* 89 D4
Charlestown, *Ind., U.S.A.* 108 F3
Charlestown, *N.H., U.S.A.* 111 C12
Charleville = Rath Luirc, *Ireland* 15 D3
Charleville, *Australia* 95 D4
Charleville-Mézières, *France* 19 C11
Charlevoix, *U.S.A.* 108 C3
Charlieu, *France* 19 F11
Charlotte, *Mich., U.S.A.* 108 D3
Charlotte, *N.C., U.S.A.* 109 H5
Charlotte, *Vt., U.S.A.* 111 B11
Charlotte Amalie, *U.S. Virgin Is.* 121 C7
Charlotte Harbor, *U.S.A.* 109 M4
Charlotte L., *Canada* 104 C3
Charlottenberg, *Sweden* 10 E6
Charlottesville, *U.S.A.* 108 F6
Charlottetown, *Nfld., Canada* 103 B8
Charlottetown, *P.E.I., Canada* 103 C7
Charlton, *Australia* 95 F3
Charlton, *U.S.A.* 112 E8
Charlton I., *Canada* 102 B4
Charmes, *France* 19 D13
Charny, *Canada* 103 C5
Charolles, *France* 19 F11
Chârost, *France* 19 F9
Charre, *Mozam.* 87 F4
Charroux, *France* 20 B4
Charsadda, *Pakistan* 68 B4
Charters Towers, *Australia* 94 C4
Chartres, *France* 18 D8
Chascomús, *Argentina* 126 D4
Chasefu, *Zambia* 87 E3
Chashma Barrage, *Pakistan* 68 C4
Chasseneuil-sur-Bonnieure, *France* 20 C4
Chāt, *Iran* 71 B7
Chatal Balkan = Udvoy Balkan, *Bulgaria* 41 D10
Château-Arnoux, *France* 21 D10
Château-Chinon, *France* 19 E10
Château-d'Olonne, *France* 20 B2
Château-du-Loir, *France* 18 E7
Château-Gontier, *France* 18 E6
Château-la-Vallière, *France* 18 E7
Château-Landon, *France* 19 D9
Château-Renault, *France* 18 E7
Château-Salins, *France* 19 D13
Château-Thierry, *France* 19 C10
Châteaubourg, *France* 18 D5
Châteaubriant, *France* 18 E5
Châteaudun, *France* 18 D8
Chateaugay, *U.S.A.* 111 B10
Châteaugiron, *France* 18 D5
Châteauguay, L., *Canada* 103 A5
Châteaulin, *France* 18 D2
Châteaumeillant, *France* 19 F9
Châteauneuf-du-Faou, *France* 18 D3
Châteauneuf-sur-Charente, *France* 20 C3
Châteauneuf-sur-Cher, *France* 19 F9
Châteauneuf-sur-Loire, *France* 19 E9
Châteaurenard, *Bouches-du-Rhône, France* 21 E8
Châteaurenard, *Loiret, France* 19 E9
Châteauroux, *France* 19 F8
Châteauvillain, *France* 19 D11
Châtelaillon-Plage, *France* 20 B2
Châtelguyon, *France* 20 C7
Châtellerault, *France* 18 F7
Châtelus-Malvaleix, *France* 19 F9
Chatham = Miramichi, *Canada* 103 C6
Chatham, *Canada* 102 D3
Chatham, *U.K.* 13 F8
Chatham, *U.S.A.* 111 D11
Chatham Is., *Pac. Oc.* 96 M10
Châtillon, *Italy* 28 C4
Châtillon-Coligny, *France* 19 E9
Châtillon-en-Diois, *France* 21 D9
Châtillon-sur-Indre, *France* 18 F8
Châtillon-sur-Loire, *France* 19 E9
Châtillon-sur-Seine, *France* 19 E11
Chatmohar, *Bangla.* 69 G13
Chatra, *India* 69 G11
Chatrapur, *India* 67 K14
Chats, L. des, *Canada* 111 A8
Chatsu, *India* 68 F6
Chatsworth, *Canada* 110 B4
Chatsworth, *Zimbabwe* 87 F3
Chattahoochee, *U.S.A.* 109 K3
Chattahoochee →, *U.S.A.* 109 K3
Chattanooga, *U.S.A.* 109 H3
Chatteris, *U.K.* 13 E8
Chaturat, *Thailand* 64 E3
Chau Doc, *Vietnam* 65 G5
Chaudes-Aigues, *France* 20 D7
Chauffailles, *France* 19 F11
Chaukan Pass, *Burma* 67 F20
Chaumont, *France* 19 D12
Chaumont, *U.S.A.* 111 B8
Chaumont-en-Vexin, *France* 19 C8
Chaumont-sur-Loire, *France* 18 E8
Chaunay, *France* 20 B4
Chauny, *France* 19 C10
Chausey, Îs., *France* 18 D5
Chaussin, *France* 19 F12
Chautauqua L., *U.S.A.* 110 D5
Chauvigny, *France* 18 F7
Chauvin, *Canada* 105 C6
Chavanges, *France* 19 D11
Chaves, *Brazil* 125 D9
Chaves, *Portugal* 34 D3
Chawang, *Thailand* 65 H2
Chazelles-sur-Lyon, *France* 21 C8
Chazy, *U.S.A.* 111 B11
Cheb, *Czech Rep.* 26 A5
Cheboksarskoye Vdkhr., *Russia* 48 B8
Cheboksary, *Russia* 48 B8
Cheboygan, *U.S.A.* 108 C3
Chebsara, *Russia* 46 C10
Chech, Erg, *Africa* 78 D5
Chechen, Ostrov, *Russia* 49 H8
Chechenia □, *Russia* 49 J7
Checheno-Ingush Republic = Chechenia □, *Russia* 49 J7
Chechnya = Chechenia □, *Russia* 49 J7
Chech'ŏn, *S. Korea* 57 F15
Chęciny, *Poland* 45 H7
Checotah, *U.S.A.* 113 H7
Chedabucto B., *Canada* 103 C7
Cheduba I., *Burma* 67 K18
Cheepie, *Australia* 95 D4
Chef-Boutonne, *France* 20 B3
Chegdomyn, *Russia* 51 D14
Chegga, *Mauritania* 78 C4
Chegutu, *Zimbabwe* 87 F3
Chehalis, *U.S.A.* 116 D4
Chehalis →, *U.S.A.* 116 D3
Cheiron, Mt., *France* 21 E10
Cheju do, *S. Korea* 57 H14
Chekalin, *Russia* 46 E9
Chekiang = Zhejiang □, *China* 59 C13
Chel = Kuru, Bahr el →, *Sudan* 81 F2
Chela, Sa. da, *Angola* 88 B1
Chelan, *U.S.A.* 114 C4
Chelan, L., *U.S.A.* 114 B3
Cheleken, *Turkmenistan* 50 F6
Cheleken Yarymadasy, *Turkmenistan* 71 B7
Chelforó, *Argentina* 128 D3
Chelkar = Shalqar, *Kazakstan* 50 E6
Chelkar Tengiz, Solonchak, *Kazakstan* 50 E7
Chella, *Ethiopia* 81 F4
Chelles, *France* 19 D9
Chełm, *Poland* 45 G10
Chełmno, *Poland* 45 E5
Chelmsford, *U.K.* 13 F8
Chełmża, *Poland* 45 E5
Chelsea, *U.S.A.* 111 C12
Cheltenham, *U.K.* 13 F5
Chelva, *Spain* 32 F4
Chelyabinsk, *Russia* 50 D7
Chelyuskin, C., *Russia* 52 B14
Chemainus, *Canada* 116 B3
Chemba, *Mozam.* 85 H6
Chembar = Belinskiy, *Russia* 48 D6
Chemillé, *France* 18 E6
Chemnitz, *Germany* 24 E8
Chemult, *U.S.A.* 114 E3
Chen, Gora, *Russia* 51 C15
Chenab →, *Pakistan* 68 D4
Chenango Forks, *U.S.A.* 111 D9
Chencha, *Ethiopia* 81 F4
Chenchiang = Zhenjiang, *China* 59 A12
Cheney, *U.S.A.* 114 C5
Cheng Xian, *China* 56 H3
Chengbu, *China* 59 D8
Chengcheng, *China* 56 G5
Chengchou = Zhengzhou, *China* 56 G7
Chengde, *China* 57 D9
Chengdong Hu, *China* 59 A11
Chengdu, *China* 58 B5
Chenggong, *China* 58 E4
Chenggu, *China* 56 H4
Chenghai, *China* 59 F11
Chengjiang, *China* 58 E4
Chengkou, *China* 58 B7
Ch'engmai, *China* 64 C7
Ch'engtu = Chengdu, *China* 58 B5
Chengwu, *China* 56 G8
Chengxi Hu, *China* 59 A11
Chengyang, *China* 57 F11
Chenjiagang, *China* 57 G10
Chenkán, *Mexico* 119 D6
Chennai, *India* 66 N12
Chenôve, *France* 19 E12
Chenxi, *China* 59 C8
Chenzhou, *China* 59 E9
Cheo Reo, *Vietnam* 62 B3
Cheom Ksan, *Cambodia* 64 E5
Chepelare, *Bulgaria* 41 E8
Chepén, *Peru* 124 E3
Chepes, *Argentina* 126 C2
Chepo, *Panama* 120 E4
Chepstow, *U.K.* 13 F5
Cheptulil, Mt., *Kenya* 86 B4
Chequamegon B., *U.S.A.* 112 B9
Cher □, *France* 19 E9
Cher →, *France* 18 E7
Chéradi, *Italy* 31 B10
Cherasco, *Italy* 28 D4
Cheraw, *U.S.A.* 109 H6
Cherbourg, *France* 18 C5
Cherdakly, *Russia* 48 C9
Cherdyn, *Russia* 50 C6
Cheremkhovo, *Russia* 51 D11
Cherepanovo, *Russia* 50 D9
Cherepovets, *Russia* 46 C9
Chergui, Chott ech, *Algeria* 78 B6
Cherikov = Cherykaw, *Belarus* 46 F6
Cherkasy, *Ukraine* 47 H7
Cherkessk, *Russia* 49 H6
Cherlak, *Russia* 50 D8
Chernaya, *Russia* 51 B9
Cherni, *Bulgaria* 40 D7
Chernigov = Chernihiv, *Ukraine* 47 G6
Chernihiv, *Ukraine* 47 G6
Chernivtsi, *Ukraine* 47 H3
Chernobyl = Chornobyl, *Ukraine* 47 G6
Chernogorsk, *Russia* 51 D10
Chernomorskoye = Chornomorske, *Ukraine* 47 K7
Chernovtsy = Chernivtsi, *Ukraine* 47 H3
Chernyakhovsk, *Russia* 9 J19
Chernyanka, *Russia* 47 G9
Chernysheyskiy, *Russia* 51 C12
Chernyye Zemli, *Russia* 49 H8
Cherokee, *Iowa, U.S.A.* 112 D7
Cherokee, *Okla., U.S.A.* 113 G5
Cherokee Village, *U.S.A.* 113 G9
Cherokees, Grand Lake O' The, *U.S.A.* 113 G7
Cherrapunji, *India* 67 G17
Cherry Valley, *Calif., U.S.A.* 117 M10
Cherry Valley, *N.Y., U.S.A.* 111 D10
Cherskiy, *Russia* 51 C17
Cherskogo Khrebet, *Russia* 51 C15
Chertkovo, *Russia* 47 H11
Cherven, *Belarus* 46 F5
Cherven-Bryag, *Bulgaria* 41 C8
Chervonohrad, *Ukraine* 47 G3
Cherwell →, *U.K.* 13 F6
Cherykaw, *Belarus* 46 F6
Chesapeake, *U.S.A.* 108 G7
Chesapeake B., *U.S.A.* 108 G7
Cheshire □, *U.K.* 12 D5
Cheshskaya Guba, *Russia* 50 C5
Cheshunt, *U.K.* 13 F7
Chesil Beach, *U.K.* 13 G5
Chesley, *Canada* 110 B3
Cheste, *Spain* 33 F4
Chester, *U.K.* 12 D5
Chester, *Calif., U.S.A.* 114 F3
Chester, *Ill., U.S.A.* 113 G10
Chester, *Mont., U.S.A.* 114 B8
Chester, *Pa., U.S.A.* 108 F8
Chester, *S.C., U.S.A.* 109 H5
Chester, *Vt., U.S.A.* 111 C12
Chester, *W. Va., U.S.A.* 110 F4
Chester-le-Street, *U.K.* 12 C6
Chesterfield, *U.K.* 12 D6
Chesterfield, Is., *N. Cal.* 96 J7
Chesterfield Inlet, *Canada* 100 B10
Chesterton Ra., *Australia* 95 D4
Chestertown, *U.S.A.* 111 C11
Chesterville, *Canada* 111 A9
Chestnut Ridge, *U.S.A.* 110 F5
Chesuncook L., *U.S.A.* 109 C11
Chéticamp, *Canada* 103 C7
Chetrosu, *Moldova* 43 B12
Chetumal, *Mexico* 119 D7
Chetumal, B. de, *Mexico* 119 D7
Chetwynd, *Canada* 104 B4
Chevanceaux, *France* 20 C3
Cheviot, The, *U.K.* 12 B5
Cheviot Hills, *U.K.* 12 B5
Cheviot Ra., *Australia* 94 D3
Chew Bahir, *Ethiopia* 81 G4
Chewelah, *U.S.A.* 114 B5

Cheyenne, *Okla., U.S.A.* 113 H5
Cheyenne, *Wyo., U.S.A.* 112 E2
Cheyenne →, *U.S.A.* 112 C4
Cheyenne Wells, *U.S.A.* 112 F3
Cheyne B., *Australia* 93 F2
Chhabra, *India* 68 G7
Chhaktala, *India* 68 H6
Chhapra, *India* 69 G11
Chhata, *India* 68 F7
Chhatarpur, *Bihar, India* 69 G11
Chhatarpur, *Mad. P., India* 69 G8
Chhattisgarh □, *India* 69 J10
Chhep, *Cambodia* 64 F5
Chhindwara, *Mad. P., India* 69 H8
Chhindwara, *Mad. P., India* 69 H8
Chhlong, *Cambodia* 65 F5
Chhota Tawa →, *India* 68 H7
Chhoti Kali Sindh →, *India* 68 G6
Chhuikhadan, *India* 69 J9
Chhuk, *Cambodia* 65 G5
Chi →, *Thailand* 64 E5
Chiai, *Taiwan* 59 F13
Chiali, *Taiwan* 59 F13
Chiamboni, *Somali Rep.* 84 E8
Chiamussu = Jiamusi, *China* 60 B8
Chianciano Terme, *Italy* 29 E8
Chiang Dao, *Thailand* 64 C2
Chiang Kham, *Thailand* 64 C3
Chiang Khan, *Thailand* 64 D3
Chiang Khong, *Thailand* 58 G3
Chiang Mai, *Thailand* 64 C2
Chiang Rai, *Thailand* 58 H2
Chiang Saen, *Thailand* 58 G3
Chiapa →, *Mexico* 119 D6
Chiapa de Corzo, *Mexico* 119 D6
Chiapas □, *Mexico* 119 D6
Chiaramonte Gulfi, *Italy* 31 E7
Chiaravalle, *Italy* 29 E10
Chiaravalle Centrale, *Italy* 31 D9
Chiari, *Italy* 28 C6
Chiatura, *Georgia* 49 J6
Chiautla, *Mexico* 119 D5
Chiávari, *Italy* 28 D6
Chiavenna, *Italy* 28 B6
Chiba, *Japan* 55 G10
Chiba □, *Japan* 55 G10
Chibabava, *Mozam.* 89 C5
Chibemba, *Cunene, Angola* 85 H2
Chibemba, *Huila, Angola* 88 B2
Chibi, *Zimbabwe* 89 C5
Chibia, *Angola* 85 H2
Chibougamau, *Canada* 102 C5
Chibougamau, L., *Canada* 102 C5
Chibuk, *Nigeria* 83 C7
Chibuto, *Mozam.* 89 C5
Chic-Chocs, Mts., *Canada* 103 C6
Chicacole = Srikakulam, *India* 67 K13
Chicago, *U.S.A.* 108 E2
Chicago Heights, *U.S.A.* 108 E2
Chichagof I., *U.S.A.* 100 C6
Chichén-Itzá, *Mexico* 119 C7
Chicheng, *China* 56 D8
Chichester, *U.K.* 13 G7
Chichester Ra., *Australia* 92 D2
Chichibu, *Japan* 55 F9
Ch'ich'ihaerh = Qiqihar, *China* 51 E13
Chicholi, *India* 68 H8
Chickasha, *U.S.A.* 113 H6
Chiclana de la Frontera, *Spain* 35 J4
Chiclayo, *Peru* 124 E3
Chico, *U.S.A.* 116 F5
Chico →, *Chubut, Argentina* 128 E3
Chico →, *Santa Cruz, Argentina* 128 G3
Chicomo, *Mozam.* 89 C5
Chicontepec, *Mexico* 119 C5
Chicopee, *U.S.A.* 111 D12
Chicoutimi, *Canada* 103 C5
Chicualacuala, *Mozam.* 89 C5
Chidambaram, *India* 66 P11
Chidenguele, *Mozam.* 89 C5
Chidley, C., *Canada* 101 B13
Chiducuane, *Mozam.* 89 C5
Chiede, *Angola* 88 B2
Chiefs Pt., *Canada* 110 B3
Chiem Hoa, *Vietnam* 64 A5
Chiemsee, *Germany* 25 H8
Chiengi, *Zambia* 87 D2
Chiengmai = Chiang Mai, *Thailand* 64 C2
Chienti →, *Italy* 29 E10
Chieri, *Italy* 28 C4
Chiers →, *France* 19 C11
Chiesa in Valmalenco, *Italy* 28 B6
Chiese →, *Italy* 28 C7
Chieti, *Italy* 29 F11
Chifeng, *China* 57 C10
Chigirin, *Ukraine* 47 H7
Chignecto B., *Canada* 103 C7
Chiguana, *Bolivia* 126 A2
Chigwell, *U.K.* 13 F8
Chiha-ri, *N. Korea* 57 E14
Chihli, G. of = Bo Hai, *China* 57 E10
Chihuahua, *Mexico* 118 B3
Chihuahua □, *Mexico* 118 B3
Chiili = Shīeli, *Kazakstan* 50 E7
Chik Bollapur, *India* 66 N10
Chikmagalur, *India* 66 N9
Chikwawa, *Malawi* 87 F3
Chilac, *Mexico* 119 D5
Chilam Chavki, *Pakistan* 69 B6
Chilanga, *Zambia* 87 F2
Chilapa, *Mexico* 119 D5
Chilas, *Pakistan* 69 B6
Chilaw, *Sri Lanka* 66 R11
Chilcotin →, *Canada* 104 C4
Childers, *Australia* 95 D5
Childress, *U.S.A.* 113 H4
Chile ■, *S. Amer.* 128 D2
Chile Rise, *Pac. Oc.* 97 L18
Chilecito, *Argentina* 126 B2
Chilete, *Peru* 124 E3
Chilia, Bratul →, *Romania* 43 E14
Chililabombwe, *Zambia* 87 E2
Chilin = Jilin, *China* 57 C14
Chilka L., *India* 67 K14
Chilko →, *Canada* 104 C4
Chilko L., *Canada* 104 C4
Chillagoe, *Australia* 94 B3
Chillán, *Chile* 126 D1
Chillicothe, *Ill., U.S.A.* 112 E10
Chillicothe, *Mo., U.S.A.* 112 F8
Chillicothe, *Ohio, U.S.A.* 108 F4
Chilliwack, *Canada* 104 D4
Chilo, *India* 68 F5
Chiloane, I., *Mozam.* 89 C5
Chiloé, I. de, *Chile* 122 H3
Chilpancingo, *Mexico* 119 D5
Chiltern Hills, *U.K.* 13 F7
Chilton, *U.S.A.* 108 C1
Chilubi, *Zambia* 87 E2
Chilubula, *Zambia* 87 E3
Chilumba, *Malawi* 87 E3
Chilung, *Taiwan* 59 E13
Chilwa, L., *Malawi* 87 F4
Chimaltitán, *Mexico* 118 C4
Chimán, *Panama* 120 E4
Chimanimani, *Zimbabwe* 89 B5
Chimay, *Belgium* 17 D4
Chimayo, *U.S.A.* 115 H11
Chimbay, *Uzbekistan* 50 E6
Chimborazo, *Ecuador* 122 D3
Chimbote, *Peru* 124 E3
Chimkent = Shymkent, *Kazakstan* 50 E7
Chimoio, *Mozam.* 87 F3
Chimpembe, *Zambia* 87 D2
Chin □, *Burma* 67 J18
Chin Ling Shan = Qinling Shandi, *China* 56 H5
China, *Mexico* 119 B5
China ■, *Asia* 60 D6
China Lake, *U.S.A.* 117 K9
Chinan = Jinan, *China* 56 F9
Chinandega, *Nic.* 120 D2
Chinati Peak, *U.S.A.* 113 L2
Chincha Alta, *Peru* 122 E3
Chinchaga →, *Canada* 104 B5
Chinchilla, *Australia* 95 D5
Chinchilla de Monte Aragón, *Spain* 33 G3
Chinchorro, Banco, *Mexico* 119 D7
Chinchou = Jinzhou, *China* 57 D11
Chincoteague, *U.S.A.* 108 G8
Chinde, *Mozam.* 87 F4
Chindo, *S. Korea* 57 G14
Chindwin →, *Burma* 67 J19
Chineni, *India* 69 C6
Chinga, *Mozam.* 87 F4
Chingola, *Zambia* 87 E2
Chingole, *Malawi* 87 E3
Ch'ingtao = Qingdao, *China* 57 F11
Chinguetti, *Mauritania* 78 D3
Chingune, *Mozam.* 89 C5
Chinhae, *S. Korea* 57 G15
Chinhanguanine, *Mozam.* 89 D5
Chinhoyi, *Zimbabwe* 87 F3
Chini, *India* 68 D8
Chiniot, *Pakistan* 68 D5
Chínipas, *Mexico* 118 B3
Chinji, *Pakistan* 68 C5
Chinju, *S. Korea* 57 G15
Chinle, *U.S.A.* 115 H9
Chinmen, *Taiwan* 59 E13
Chinmen Tao, *Taiwan* 59 E12
Chinnampo = Namp'o, *N. Korea* 57 E13
Chino, *Japan* 55 G9
Chino, *U.S.A.* 117 L9
Chino Valley, *U.S.A.* 115 J7
Chinon, *France* 18 E7
Chinook, *U.S.A.* 114 B9
Chinsali, *Zambia* 87 E3
Chióggia, *Italy* 29 C9
Chíos = Khíos, *Greece* 39 C8
Chipata, *Zambia* 87 E3
Chiperceni, *Moldova* 43 C13
Chipinge, *Zimbabwe* 87 G3
Chipiona, *Spain* 35 J4
Chipley, *U.S.A.* 109 K3
Chipman, *Canada* 103 C6
Chipoka, *Malawi* 87 E3
Chippenham, *U.K.* 13 F5
Chippewa →, *U.S.A.* 112 C8
Chippewa Falls, *U.S.A.* 112 C9
Chipping Norton, *U.K.* 13 F6
Chiprovtsi, *Bulgaria* 40 C6
Chiputneticook Lakes, *U.S.A.* 109 C11
Chiquián, *Peru* 124 F3
Chiquimula, *Guatemala* 120 D2
Chiquinquira, *Colombia* 124 B4
Chir →, *Russia* 49 F6
Chirala, *India* 66 M12
Chiramba, *Mozam.* 87 F3
Chirawa, *India* 68 E6
Chirchiq, *Uzbekistan* 50 E7
Chiredzi, *Zimbabwe* 89 C5
Chiricahua Peak, *U.S.A.* 115 L9
Chiriquí, G. de, *Panama* 120 E3
Chiriquí, L. de, *Panama* 120 E3
Chirivira Falls, *Zimbabwe* 87 G3
Chirmiri, *India* 67 H13
Chirnogi, *Romania* 43 F11
Chirpan, *Bulgaria* 41 D9
Chirripó Grande, Cerro, *Costa Rica* 120 E3
Chirundu, *Zimbabwe* 89 B4
Chisamba, *Zambia* 87 E2
Chisapani Garhi, *Nepal* 67 F14
Chisasibi, *Canada* 102 B4
Ch'ishan, *Taiwan* 59 F13
Chisholm, *Canada* 104 C6
Chisholm, *U.S.A.* 112 B8
Chishtian Mandi, *Pakistan* 68 E5
Chishui, *China* 58 C5
Chishui He →, *China* 58 C5
Chisimaio, *Somali Rep.* 77 G8
Chisimba Falls, *Zambia* 87 E3
Chişinău, *Moldova* 43 C13
Chişineu Criş, *Romania* 42 D6
Chisone →, *Italy* 28 D4
Chisos Mts., *U.S.A.* 113 L3
Chistopol, *Russia* 48 C10
Chita, *Russia* 51 D12
Chitipa, *Malawi* 87 D3
Chitose, *Japan* 54 C10
Chitral, *Pakistan* 66 B7
Chitré, *Panama* 120 E3
Chittagong, *Bangla.* 67 H17
Chittagong □, *Bangla.* 67 G17
Chittaurgarh, *India* 68 G6
Chittoor, *India* 66 N11
Chitungwiza, *Zimbabwe* 87 F3
Chiusi, *Italy* 29 E8
Chiva, *Spain* 33 F4
Chivasso, *Italy* 28 C4
Chivhu, *Zimbabwe* 87 F3
Chivilcoy, *Argentina* 126 C4
Chiwanda, *Tanzania* 87 E3
Chixi, *China* 59 G9
Chizera, *Zambia* 87 E2
Chkalov = Orenburg, *Russia* 50 D6
Chkolovsk, *Russia* 48 B6
Chloride, *U.S.A.* 117 K12
Chlumec nad Cidlinou, *Czech Rep.* 26 A8
Chmielnik, *Poland* 45 H7
Cho Bo, *Vietnam* 58 G5
Cho-do, *N. Korea* 57 E13
Cho Phuoc Hai, *Vietnam* 65 G6
Choba, *Kenya* 86 B4
Chobe National Park, *Botswana* 88 B4
Choch'iwŏn, *S. Korea* 57 F14
Chocianów, *Poland* 45 G2
Chociwel, *Poland* 44 E2
Chocolate Mts., *U.S.A.* 117 M11
Choctawhatchee →, *U.S.A.* 109 K3
Chodecz, *Poland* 45 F6
Chodov, *Czech Rep.* 26 A5
Chodziez, *Poland* 45 F3
Choele Choel, *Argentina* 128 D3
Choix, *Mexico* 118 B3
Chojna, *Poland* 45 F1
Chojnice, *Poland* 44 E4
Chojnów, *Poland* 45 G2
Chŏkai-San, *Japan* 54 E10
Choke, *Ethiopia* 81 E4
Choke Canyon L., *U.S.A.* 113 L5
Chokurdakh, *Russia* 51 B15
Cholame, *U.S.A.* 116 K6
Cholet, *France* 18 E6
Cholguan, *Chile* 126 D1
Choluteca, *Honduras* 120 D2
Choluteca →, *Honduras* 120 D2
Chom Bung, *Thailand* 64 F2
Chom Thong, *Thailand* 64 C2
Choma, *Zambia* 87 F2
Chomen Swamp, *Ethiopia* 81 F4
Chomun, *India* 68 F6
Chomutov, *Czech Rep.* 26 A6
Chon Buri, *Thailand* 64 F3
Chon Thanh, *Vietnam* 65 G6
Ch'onan, *S. Korea* 57 F14
Chone, *Ecuador* 124 D3
Chong Kai, *Cambodia* 64 F4
Chong Mek, *Thailand* 64 E5
Chongde, *China* 59 B13
Chŏngdo, *S. Korea* 57 G15
Chŏngha, *S. Korea* 57 F15
Chŏngjin, *N. Korea* 57 D15
Chŏngjiu, *S. Korea* 57 F14
Chŏngju, *N. Korea* 57 E13
Chongli, *China* 56 D8
Chongming, *China* 59 B13
Chongming Dao, *China* 59 B13
Chongqing, *Chongqing, China* 58 C6
Chongqing, *Sichuan, China* 58 B4
Chongqing Shi □, *China* 58 C6
Chongren, *China* 59 D11
Chonguene, *Mozam.* 89 C5
Chŏngŭp, *S. Korea* 57 G14
Chongyi, *China* 59 E10
Chongzuo, *China* 58 F6
Chŏnju, *S. Korea* 57 G14
Chonos, Arch. de los, *Chile* 122 H3
Chop, *Ukraine* 47 H2
Chopim →, *Brazil* 127 B5
Chor, *Pakistan* 68 G3
Chorbat La, *India* 69 B7
Chorley, *U.K.* 12 D5
Chornobyl, *Ukraine* 47 G6
Chornomorske, *Ukraine* 47 K7
Chorolque, Cerro, *Bolivia* 126 A2
Choroszcz, *Poland* 45 E9
Chorregon, *Australia* 94 C3
Chortkiv, *Ukraine* 47 H3
Ch'ŏrwon, *S. Korea* 57 E14
Chorzele, *Poland* 45 E7
Chorzów, *Poland* 45 H5
Chos-Malal, *Argentina* 126 D1
Ch'osan, *N. Korea* 57 D13
Choszczno, *Poland* 45 E2
Choteau, *U.S.A.* 114 C7
Chotěboř, *Czech Rep.* 26 B8
Chotila, *India* 68 H4
Chotta Udepur, *India* 68 H6
Chowchilla, *U.S.A.* 116 H6
Choybalsan, *Mongolia* 60 B6
Christchurch, *N.Z.* 91 K4
Christchurch, *U.K.* 13 G6
Christian I., *Canada* 110 B4
Christiana, *S. Africa* 88 D4
Christiansfeld, *Denmark* 11 J3
Christiansted, *U.S. Virgin Is.* 121 C7
Christie B., *Canada* 105 A6
Christina →, *Canada* 105 B6
Christmas Cr. →, *Australia* 92 C4
Christmas I. = Kiritimati, *Kiribati* 97 G12
Christmas I., *Ind. Oc.* 96 J2
Christopher L., *Australia* 93 D4
Chrudim, *Czech Rep.* 26 B8
Chrzanów, *Poland* 45 H6
Chtimba, *Malawi* 87 E3
Chu = Shū, *Kazakstan* 50 E8
Chu →, *Vietnam* 64 C5
Chu Lai, *Vietnam* 64 E7
Ch'uanchou = Quanzhou, *China* 59 E12
Chuankou, *China* 56 G6
Chubbuck, *U.S.A.* 114 E7
Chūbu □, *Japan* 55 F8
Chubut →, *Argentina* 122 H4
Chuchi L., *Canada* 104 B4
Chuda, *India* 68 H4
Chudovo, *Russia* 46 C6
Chudskoye, Ozero, *Russia* 9 G22
Chūgoku □, *Japan* 55 G6
Chūgoku-Sanchi, *Japan* 55 G6
Chuguyev = Chuhuyiv, *Ukraine* 47 H9
Chugwater, *U.S.A.* 112 E2
Chuhuyiv, *Ukraine* 47 H9
Chukchi Sea, *Russia* 51 C19
Chukotskoye Nagorye, *Russia* 51 C18
Chula Vista, *U.S.A.* 117 N9
Chulucanas, *Peru* 124 E2
Chulym →, *Russia* 50 D9
Chum Phae, *Thailand* 64 D4
Chum Saeng, *Thailand* 64 E3
Chumar, *India* 69 C8
Chumbicha, *Argentina* 126 B2
Chumerna, *Bulgaria* 41 D9
Chumikan, *Russia* 51 D14
Chumphon, *Thailand* 65 G2
Chumuare, *Mozam.* 87 E3
Chumunjin, *S. Korea* 57 F15
Chuna →, *Russia* 51 D10
Chun'an, *China* 59 C12
Ch'unch'ŏn, *S. Korea* 57 F14
Chunchura, *India* 69 H13
Chunga, *Zambia* 87 F2
Chunggang-ŭp, *N. Korea* 57 D14
Chunghwa, *N. Korea* 57 E13
Ch'ungju, *S. Korea* 57 F14
Chungking = Chongqing, *China* 58 C6
Chungli, *Taiwan* 59 E13
Ch'ungmu, *S. Korea* 57 G15
Chungt'iaoshan = Zhongtiao Shan, *China* 56 G6
Chungyang Shanmo, *Taiwan* 59 F13
Chunian, *Pakistan* 68 D6
Chunya, *Tanzania* 87 D3
Chunyang, *China* 57 C15
Chuquibamba, *Peru* 124 G4
Chuquicamata, *Chile* 126 A2
Chur, *Switz.* 25 J5
Churachandpur, *India* 67 G18
Churchill, *Canada* 105 B10
Churchill →, *Man., Canada* 105 B10
Churchill →, *Nfld., Canada* 103 B7
Churchill, C., *Canada* 105 B10
Churchill Falls, *Canada* 103 B7
Churchill L., *Canada* 105 B7
Churchill Pk., *Canada* 104 B3
Churki, *India* 69 H10
Churu, *India* 68 E6
Churún Merú = Angel Falls, *Venezuela* 124 B6
Chushal, *India* 69 C8
Chuska Mts., *U.S.A.* 115 H9
Chusovoy, *Russia* 50 D6
Chute-aux-Outardes, *Canada* 103 C6
Chuuronjang, *N. Korea* 57 D15
Chuvash Republic = Chuvashia □, *Russia* 48 C8
Chuvashia □, *Russia* 48 C8
Chuwārtah, *Iraq* 70 C5
Chuxiong, *China* 58 E3
Chüy = Shū →, *Kazakstan* 52 E10
Chuy, *Uruguay* 127 C5
Chuzhou, *China* 59 A12
Ci Xian, *China* 56 F8
Ciacova, *Romania* 42 E6
Ciadâr-Lunga, *Moldova* 43 D13
Ciamis, *Indonesia* 63 G13
Cianjur, *Indonesia* 63 G12
Cianorte, *Brazil* 127 A5
Cibola, *U.S.A.* 117 M12
Cicero, *U.S.A.* 108 E2
Cidacos →, *Spain* 32 C3
Cide, *Turkey* 72 B5
Ciechanów, *Poland* 45 F7
Ciechanowiec, *Poland* 45 F9
Ciechocinek, *Poland* 45 F5
Ciego de Avila, *Cuba* 120 B4
Ciénaga, *Colombia* 124 A4
Cienfuegos, *Cuba* 120 B3
Cierp, *France* 20 F4
Cíes, Is., *Spain* 34 C2
Cieszanów, *Poland* 45 H10
Cieszyn, *Poland* 45 J5
Cieza, *Spain* 33 G3
Çifteler, *Turkey* 72 C4
Cifuentes, *Spain* 32 E2
Cihanbeyli, *Turkey* 72 C5
Cihuatlán, *Mexico* 118 D4
Cijara, Embalse de, *Spain* 35 F6
Cijulang, *Indonesia* 63 G13
Cilacap, *Indonesia* 63 G13
Çıldır, *Turkey* 73 B10
Çıldır Gölü, *Turkey* 73 B10
Cili, *China* 59 C8
Cilibia, *Romania* 43 E12
Cilicia, *Turkey* 72 D5
Cill Chainnigh = Kilkenny, *Ireland* 15 D4
Cilo Dağı, *Turkey* 73 D10
Cima, *U.S.A.* 117 K11
Cimarron, *Kans., U.S.A.* 113 G4
Cimarron, *N. Mex., U.S.A.* 113 G2
Cimarron →, *U.S.A.* 113 G6
Cimişlia, *Moldova* 43 D13
Cimone, Mte., *Italy* 28 D7
Çinar, *Turkey* 73 D9
Çınarcık, *Turkey* 41 F13
Cinca →, *Spain* 32 D5
Cincar, *Bos.-H.* 42 G2
Cincinnati, *U.S.A.* 108 F3
Cincinnatus, *U.S.A.* 111 D9
Çine, *Turkey* 39 D10
Ciney, *Belgium* 17 D5
Cíngoli, *Italy* 29 E10
Cinigiano, *Italy* 29 F8
Cinto, Mte., *France* 21 F12
Cintruénigo, *Spain* 32 C3
Ciocile, *Romania* 43 F12
Ciolănești din Deal, *Romania* 43 F10
Ciorani, *Romania* 43 F11
Čiovo, *Croatia* 29 E13
Circeo, Mte., *Italy* 30 A6
Çirçir, *Turkey* 72 C7
Circle, *Alaska, U.S.A.* 100 B5
Circle, *Mont., U.S.A.* 112 B2
Circleville, *U.S.A.* 108 F4
Cirebon, *Indonesia* 62 F3
Ciremai, *Indonesia* 63 G13
Cirencester, *U.K.* 13 F6
Cireșu, *Romania* 42 F7
Cirey-sur-Vezouze, *France* 19 D13
Ciriè, *Italy* 28 C4
Cirium, *Cyprus* 36 E11
Cirò, *Italy* 31 C10
Cirò Marina, *Italy* 31 C10
Ciron →, *France* 20 D3
Cisco, *U.S.A.* 113 J5
Cislău, *Romania* 43 E11
Cisna, *Poland* 45 J9
Cisnădie, *Romania* 43 E9
Cisterna di Latina, *Italy* 30 A5
Cisternino, *Italy* 31 B10
Cistierna, *Spain* 34 C5
Citeli-Ckaro = Tsiteli-Tsqaro, *Georgia* 49 K8
Citlaltépetl, *Mexico* 119 D5
Citrus Heights, *U.S.A.* 116 G5
Citrusdal, *S. Africa* 88 E2
Città della Pieve, *Italy* 29 F9
Città di Castello, *Italy* 29 E9
Città Sant' Angelo, *Italy* 29 F11
Cittadella, *Italy* 29 C8
Cittaducale, *Italy* 29 F9
Cittanova, *Italy* 31 D9
Ciuc, Munții, *Romania* 43 D11
Ciucaș, Vf., *Romania* 43 E10
Ciucea, *Romania* 42 D7
Ciuciulea, *Moldova* 43 C12
Ciuciuleni, *Moldova* 43 C13
Ciudad Altamirano, *Mexico* 118 D4
Ciudad Bolívar, *Venezuela* 124 B6
Ciudad Camargo, *Mexico* 118 B3
Ciudad de Valles, *Mexico* 119 C5
Ciudad del Carmen, *Mexico* 119 D6
Ciudad del Este, *Paraguay* 127 B5
Ciudad Delicias = Delicias, *Mexico* 118 B3
Ciudad Guayana, *Venezuela* 124 B6
Ciudad Guerrero, *Mexico* 118 B3
Ciudad Guzmán, *Mexico* 118 D4
Ciudad Juárez, *Mexico* 118 A3
Ciudad Madero, *Mexico* 119 C5
Ciudad Mante, *Mexico* 119 C5
Ciudad Obregón, *Mexico* 118 B3
Ciudad Real, *Spain* 35 G7
Ciudad Real □, *Spain* 35 G7
Ciudad Rodrigo, *Spain* 34 E4
Ciudad Trujillo = Santo Domingo, *Dom. Rep.* 121 C6
Ciudad Victoria, *Mexico* 119 C5
Ciudadela, *Spain* 37 B10
Ciulnița, *Romania* 43 F12
Ciumeghiu, *Romania* 42 D6
Ciuperceni, *Romania* 42 F8
Civa Burnu, *Turkey* 72 B7
Cividale del Friuli, *Italy* 29 B10
Civita Castellana, *Italy* 29 F9
Civitanova Marche, *Italy* 29 E10
Civitavécchia, *Italy* 29 F8
Civray, *France* 20 B4
Çivril, *Turkey* 39 C11
Cixerri →, *Italy* 30 C1
Cixi, *China* 59 B13
Cizre, *Turkey* 70 B4
Cizur Mayor, *Spain* 32 C3
Clackmannanshire □, *U.K.* 14 E5
Clacton-on-Sea, *U.K.* 13 F9
Clain →, *France* 18 F7
Claire, L., *Canada* 104 B6
Clairton, *U.S.A.* 110 F5

Clairvaux-les-Lacs, *France* 19 F12
Claise →, *France* 20 B5
Clallam Bay, *U.S.A.* 116 B2
Clamecy, *France* 19 E10
Clanton, *U.S.A.* 109 J2
Clanwilliam, *S. Africa* 88 E2
Clara, *Ireland* 15 C4
Claraville, *U.S.A.* 117 K8
Clare, *Australia* 95 E2
Clare, *U.S.A.* 108 D3
Clare □, *Ireland* 15 D3
Clare →, *Ireland* 15 C2
Clare I., *Ireland* 15 C1
Claremont, *Calif., U.S.A.* 117 L9
Claremont, *N.H., U.S.A.* 111 C12
Claremont Pt., *Australia* 94 A3
Claremore, *U.S.A.* 113 G7
Claremorris, *Ireland* 15 C3
Clarence →, *Australia* 95 D5
Clarence →, *N.Z.* 91 K4
Clarence, I., *Chile* 128 G2
Clarence I., *Antarctica* 5 C18
Clarence Str., *Australia* 92 B5
Clarence Town, *Bahamas* 121 B5
Clarendon, *Pa., U.S.A.* 110 E5
Clarendon, *Tex., U.S.A.* 113 H4
Clarenville, *Canada* 103 C9
Claresholm, *Canada* 104 D6
Clarie Coast, *Antarctica* 5 C9
Clarinda, *U.S.A.* 112 E7
Clarion, *Iowa, U.S.A.* 112 D8
Clarion, *Pa., U.S.A.* 110 E5
Clarion →, *U.S.A.* 110 E5
Clark, *U.S.A.* 112 C6
Clark, Pt., *Canada* 110 B3
Clark Fork, *U.S.A.* 114 B5
Clark Fork →, *U.S.A.* 114 B5
Clarkdale, *U.S.A.* 115 J7
Clarke City, *Canada* 103 B6
Clarke I., *Australia* 94 G4
Clarke Ra., *Australia* 94 C4
Clark's Fork →, *U.S.A.* 114 D9
Clark's Harbour, *Canada* 103 D6
Clarks Hill L., *U.S.A.* 109 J4
Clarks Summit, *U.S.A.* 111 E9
Clarksburg, *U.S.A.* 108 F5
Clarksdale, *U.S.A.* 113 H9
Clarksville, *Ark., U.S.A.* 113 H8
Clarksville, *Tenn., U.S.A.* 109 G2
Clarksville, *Tex., U.S.A.* 113 J7
Clatskanie, *U.S.A.* 116 D3
Claude, *U.S.A.* 113 H4
Claveria, *Phil.* 61 B4
Clay, *U.S.A.* 116 G5
Clay Center, *U.S.A.* 112 F6
Claypool, *U.S.A.* 115 K8
Claysburg, *U.S.A.* 110 F6
Claysville, *U.S.A.* 110 F4
Clayton, *N. Mex., U.S.A.* 113 G3
Clayton, *N.Y., U.S.A.* 111 B8
Clear, C., *Ireland* 15 E2
Clear, L., *Canada* 110 A7
Clear Hills, *Canada* 104 B5
Clear I., *Ireland* 15 E2
Clear L., *U.S.A.* 116 F4
Clear Lake, *Iowa, U.S.A.* 112 D8
Clear Lake, *S. Dak., U.S.A.* 112 C6
Clear Lake Reservoir, *U.S.A.* 114 F3
Clearfield, *Pa., U.S.A.* 110 E6
Clearfield, *Utah, U.S.A.* 114 F8
Clearlake, *U.S.A.* 114 G2
Clearlake Highlands, *U.S.A.* 116 G4
Clearwater, *Canada* 104 C4
Clearwater, *U.S.A.* 109 M4
Clearwater →, *Alta., Canada* 104 C6
Clearwater →, *Alta., Canada* 105 B6
Clearwater L., *Canada* 105 C9
Clearwater Mts., *U.S.A.* 114 C6
Clearwater Prov. Park, *Canada* 105 C8
Clearwater River Prov. Park, *Canada* 105 B7
Cleburne, *U.S.A.* 113 J6
Clee Hills, *U.K.* 13 E5
Cleethorpes, *U.K.* 12 D7
Cleeve Cloud, *U.K.* 13 F6
Clelles, *France* 21 D9
Clemson, *U.S.A.* 109 H4
Clerke Reef, *Australia* 92 C2
Clermont, *Australia* 94 C4
Clermont, *France* 19 C9
Clermont, *U.S.A.* 109 L5
Clermont-en-Argonne, *France* 19 C12
Clermont-Ferrand, *France* 20 C7
Clermont-l'Hérault, *France* 20 E7
Clerval, *France* 19 E13
Clervaux, *Lux.* 17 D6
Cles, *Italy* 28 B8
Clevedon, *U.K.* 13 F5
Cleveland, *Miss., U.S.A.* 113 J9
Cleveland, *Ohio, U.S.A.* 110 E3
Cleveland, *Okla., U.S.A.* 113 G6
Cleveland, *Tenn., U.S.A.* 109 H3
Cleveland, *Tex., U.S.A.* 113 K7
Cleveland, C., *Australia* 94 B4
Cleveland, Mt., *U.S.A.* 114 B7
Cleveland Heights, *U.S.A.* 110 E3
Clevelândia, *Brazil* 127 B5
Clew B., *Ireland* 15 C2
Clewiston, *U.S.A.* 109 M5
Clifden, *Ireland* 15 C1
Clifden, *N.Z.* 91 M1
Cliffdell, *U.S.A.* 116 D5
Cliffy Hd., *Australia* 93 G2
Clifton, *Australia* 95 D5
Clifton, *Ariz., U.S.A.* 115 K9
Clifton, *Colo., U.S.A.* 115 G9
Clifton, *Tex., U.S.A.* 113 K6
Clifton Beach, *Australia* 94 B4
Climax, *Canada* 105 D7
Clinch →, *U.S.A.* 109 H3
Clingmans Dome, *U.S.A.* 109 H4
Clint, *U.S.A.* 115 L10
Clinton, *B.C., Canada* 104 C4
Clinton, *Ont., Canada* 102 D3
Clinton, *N.Z.* 91 M2
Clinton, *Ark., U.S.A.* 113 H8
Clinton, *Conn., U.S.A.* 111 E12
Clinton, *Ill., U.S.A.* 112 E10
Clinton, *Ind., U.S.A.* 108 F2
Clinton, *Iowa, U.S.A.* 112 E9
Clinton, *Mass., U.S.A.* 111 D13
Clinton, *Miss., U.S.A.* 113 J9
Clinton, *Mo., U.S.A.* 112 F8
Clinton, *N.C., U.S.A.* 109 H6
Clinton, *Okla., U.S.A.* 113 H5
Clinton, *S.C., U.S.A.* 109 H5
Clinton, *Tenn., U.S.A.* 109 G3
Clinton, *Wash., U.S.A.* 116 C4
Clinton C., *Australia* 94 C5
Clinton Colden L., *Canada* 100 B9
Clintonville, *U.S.A.* 112 C10
Clipperton, I., *Pac. Oc.* 97 F17
Clisham, *U.K.* 14 D2
Clisson, *France* 18 E5
Clitheroe, *U.K.* 12 D5
Clo-oose, *Canada* 116 B2
Cloates, Pt., *Australia* 92 D1
Clocolan, *S. Africa* 89 D4
Clodomira, *Argentina* 126 B3
Clogher Hd., *Ireland* 15 C5
Clonakilty, *Ireland* 15 E3
Clonakilty B., *Ireland* 15 E3
Cloncurry, *Australia* 94 C3
Cloncurry →, *Australia* 94 B3
Clondalkin, *Ireland* 15 C5
Clones, *Ireland* 15 B4
Clonmel, *Ireland* 15 D4
Cloppenburg, *Germany* 24 C4
Cloquet, *U.S.A.* 112 B8
Clorinda, *Argentina* 126 B4
Cloud Bay, *Canada* 102 C2
Cloud Peak, *U.S.A.* 114 D10
Cloudcroft, *U.S.A.* 115 K11
Cloverdale, *U.S.A.* 116 G4
Clovis, *Calif., U.S.A.* 116 J7
Clovis, *N. Mex., U.S.A.* 113 H3
Cloyes-sur-le-Loir, *France* 18 E8
Cloyne, *Canada* 110 B7
Cluj □, *Romania* 43 D8
Cluj-Napoca, *Romania* 43 D8
Clunes, *Australia* 95 F3
Cluny, *France* 19 F11
Cluses, *France* 19 F13
Clusone, *Italy* 28 C6
Clutha →, *N.Z.* 91 M2
Clwyd →, *U.K.* 12 D4
Clyde, *Canada* 104 C6
Clyde, *N.Z.* 91 L2
Clyde, *U.S.A.* 110 C8
Clyde →, *U.K.* 14 F4
Clyde, Firth of, *U.K.* 14 F3
Clyde River, *Canada* 101 A13
Clydebank, *U.K.* 14 F4
Clymer, *N.Y., U.S.A.* 110 D5
Clymer, *Pa., U.S.A.* 110 D5
Ćmielów, *Poland* 45 H8
Côa →, *Portugal* 34 D3
Coachella, *U.S.A.* 117 M10
Coachella Canal, *U.S.A.* 117 N12
Coahoma, *U.S.A.* 113 J4
Coahuayana →, *Mexico* 118 D4
Coahuila □, *Mexico* 118 B4
Coal →, *Canada* 104 B3
Coalane, *Mozam.* 87 F4
Coalcomán, *Mexico* 118 D4
Coaldale, *Canada* 104 D6
Coalgate, *U.S.A.* 113 H6
Coalinga, *U.S.A.* 116 J6
Coalisland, *U.K.* 15 B5
Coalville, *U.K.* 12 E6
Coalville, *U.S.A.* 114 F8
Coari, *Brazil* 124 D6
Coast □, *Kenya* 86 C4
Coast Mts., *Canada* 104 C3
Coast Ranges, *U.S.A.* 116 G4
Coatbridge, *U.K.* 14 F4
Coatepec, *Mexico* 119 D5
Coatepeque, *Guatemala* 120 D1
Coatesville, *U.S.A.* 108 F8
Coaticook, *Canada* 103 C5
Coats I., *Canada* 101 B11
Coats Land, *Antarctica* 5 D1
Coatzacoalcos, *Mexico* 119 D6
Cobadin, *Romania* 43 F13
Cobalt, *Canada* 102 C4
Cobán, *Guatemala* 120 C1
Çobanlar, *Turkey* 39 C12
Cobar, *Australia* 95 E4
Cóbh, *Ireland* 15 E3
Cobija, *Bolivia* 124 F5
Cobleskill, *U.S.A.* 111 D10
Coboconk, *Canada* 110 B6
Cobourg, *Canada* 102 D4
Cobourg Pen., *Australia* 92 B5
Cobram, *Australia* 95 F4
Cóbué, *Mozam.* 87 E3
Coburg, *Germany* 25 E6
Coca, *Spain* 34 D6
Cocanada = Kakinada, *India* 67 L13
Cocentaina, *Spain* 33 G4
Cochabamba, *Bolivia* 124 G5
Cochem, *Germany* 25 E3
Cochemane, *Mozam.* 87 F3
Cochin, *India* 66 Q10
Cochin China = Nam-Phan, *Vietnam* 65 G6
Cochran, *U.S.A.* 109 J4
Cochrane, *Alta., Canada* 104 C6
Cochrane, *Ont., Canada* 102 C3
Cochrane, *Chile* 128 F2
Cochrane →, *Canada* 105 B8
Cochrane, L., *Chile* 128 F2
Cochranton, *U.S.A.* 110 E4
Cockburn, *Australia* 95 E3
Cockburn, Canal, *Chile* 122 J3
Cockburn I., *Canada* 102 C3
Cockburn Ra., *Australia* 92 C4
Cockermouth, *U.K.* 12 C4
Cocklebiddy, *Australia* 93 F4
Coco →, *Cent. Amer.* 120 D3
Coco, I. del, *Pac. Oc.* 97 G19
Cocoa, *U.S.A.* 109 L5
Cocobeach, *Gabon* 84 D1
Cocora, *Romania* 43 F12
Cocos Is., *Ind. Oc.* 96 J1
Cod, C., *U.S.A.* 108 D10
Codajás, *Brazil* 124 D6
Codigoro, *Italy* 29 D9
Codlea, *Romania* 43 E10
Codó, *Brazil* 125 D10
Codogno, *Italy* 28 C6
Codróipo, *Italy* 29 C10
Codru, Munţii, *Romania* 42 D7
Cody, *U.S.A.* 114 D9
Coe Hill, *Canada* 110 B7
Coelemu, *Chile* 126 D1
Coen, *Australia* 94 A3
Coesfeld, *Germany* 24 D3
Cœur d'Alene, *U.S.A.* 114 C5
Cœur d'Alene L., *U.S.A.* 114 C5
Coevorden, *Neths.* 17 B6
Cofete, *Canary Is.* 37 F5
Coffeyville, *U.S.A.* 113 G7
Coffin B., *Australia* 95 E2
Coffin Bay, *Australia* 95 E2
Coffin Bay Peninsula, *Australia* 95 E2
Coffs Harbour, *Australia* 95 E5
Cofrentes, *Spain* 33 F3
Cogalnic →, *Moldova* 43 E14
Cogealac, *Romania* 43 F13
Coghinas →, *Italy* 30 B1
Coghinas, L. del, *Italy* 30 B2
Cognac, *France* 20 C3
Cogne, *Italy* 28 C4
Cogolin, *France* 21 E10
Cogolludo, *Spain* 32 E1
Cohocton, *U.S.A.* 110 D7
Cohocton →, *U.S.A.* 110 D7
Cohoes, *U.S.A.* 111 D11
Cohuna, *Australia* 95 F3
Coiba, I., *Panama* 120 E3
Coig →, *Argentina* 128 G3
Coigeach, Rubha, *U.K.* 14 C3
Coihaique, *Chile* 128 F2
Coimbatore, *India* 66 P10
Coimbra, *Brazil* 124 G7
Coimbra, *Portugal* 34 E2
Coimbra □, *Portugal* 34 E2
Coín, *Spain* 35 J6
Coipasa, Salar de, *Bolivia* 124 G5
Cojimies, *Ecuador* 124 C3
Cojocna, *Romania* 43 D8
Cojutepequé, *El Salv.* 120 D2
Čoka, *Serbia, Yug.* 42 E5
Cokeville, *U.S.A.* 114 E8
Colac, *Australia* 95 F3
Colatina, *Brazil* 125 G10
Colbeck, C., *Antarctica* 5 D13
Colborne, *Canada* 110 C7
Colby, *U.S.A.* 112 F4
Colchester, *U.K.* 13 F8
Cold L., *Canada* 105 C7
Coldstream, *Canada* 104 C5
Coldstream, *U.K.* 14 F6
Coldwater, *Canada* 110 B5
Coldwater, *Kans., U.S.A.* 113 G5
Coldwater, *Mich., U.S.A.* 108 E3
Colebrook, *U.S.A.* 111 B13
Coleman, *U.S.A.* 113 K5
Coleman →, *Australia* 94 B3
Colenso, *S. Africa* 89 D4
Coleraine, *Australia* 95 F3
Coleraine, *U.K.* 15 A5
Coleridge, L., *N.Z.* 91 K3
Colesberg, *S. Africa* 88 E4
Coleville, *U.S.A.* 116 G7
Colfax, *Calif., U.S.A.* 116 F6
Colfax, *La., U.S.A.* 113 K8
Colfax, *Wash., U.S.A.* 114 C5
Colhué Huapi, L., *Argentina* 128 F3
Colibaşi, *Moldova* 43 E13
Colibaşi, *Romania* 43 F9
Cólico, *Italy* 28 B6
Coligny, *France* 19 F12
Coligny, *S. Africa* 89 D4
Colima, *Mexico* 118 D4
Colima □, *Mexico* 118 D4
Colima, Nevado de, *Mexico* 118 D4
Colina, *Chile* 126 C1
Colina do Norte, *Guinea-Biss.* 82 C2
Colinas, *Brazil* 125 E10
Colindres, *Spain* 34 B7
Coll, *U.K.* 14 E2
Collaguasi, *Chile* 126 A2
Collarada, Peña, *Spain* 32 C4
Collarenebri, *Australia* 95 D4
Colle di Val d'Elsa, *Italy* 28 E8
Collécchio, *Italy* 28 D7
Colleen Bawn, *Zimbabwe* 87 G2
College Park, *U.S.A.* 109 J3
College Station, *U.S.A.* 113 K6
Collesalvetti, *Italy* 28 E7
Collie, *Australia* 93 F2
Collier B., *Australia* 92 C3
Collier Ra., *Australia* 93 D2
Collina, Passo di, *Italy* 28 D7
Collingwood, *Canada* 102 D3
Collingwood, *N.Z.* 91 J4
Collins, *Canada* 102 B2
Collinsville, *Australia* 94 C4
Collipulli, *Chile* 126 D1
Collooney, *Ireland* 15 B3
Colmar, *France* 19 D14
Colmars, *France* 21 D10
Colmenar, *Spain* 35 J6
Colmenar de Oreja, *Spain* 34 E7
Colmenar Viejo, *Spain* 34 E7
Colo →, *Australia* 95 E5
Cologne = Köln, *Germany* 24 E2
Colom, I. d'en, *Spain* 37 B11
Coloma, *U.S.A.* 116 G6
Colomb-Béchar = Béchar, *Algeria* 78 B5
Colombey-les-Belles, *France* 19 D12
Colombey-les-Deux-Églises, *France* 19 D11
Colombia ■, *S. Amer.* 124 C4
Colombian Basin, *S. Amer.* 98 H12
Colombo, *Sri Lanka* 66 R11
Colomiers, *France* 20 E5
Colón, *Buenos Aires, Argentina* 126 C3
Colón, *Entre Ríos, Argentina* 126 C4
Colón, *Cuba* 120 B3
Colón, *Panama* 120 E4
Colonia de Sant Jordi, *Spain* 37 B9
Colonia del Sacramento, *Uruguay* 126 C4
Colonia Dora, *Argentina* 126 B3
Colonial Beach, *U.S.A.* 108 F7
Colonie, *U.S.A.* 111 D11
Colonna, C., *Italy* 31 C10
Colonsay, *Canada* 105 C7
Colonsay, *U.K.* 14 E2
Colorado □, *U.S.A.* 115 G10
Colorado →, *Argentina* 128 D4
Colorado →, *N. Amer.* 115 L6
Colorado →, *U.S.A.* 113 L7
Colorado City, *U.S.A.* 113 J4
Colorado Plateau, *U.S.A.* 115 H8
Colorado River Aqueduct, *U.S.A.* 117 L12
Colorado Springs, *U.S.A.* 112 F2
Colorno, *Italy* 28 D7
Colotlán, *Mexico* 118 C4
Colstrip, *U.S.A.* 114 D10
Colton, *U.S.A.* 111 B10
Columbia, *Ky., U.S.A.* 108 G3
Columbia, *La., U.S.A.* 113 J8
Columbia, *Miss., U.S.A.* 113 K10
Columbia, *Mo., U.S.A.* 112 F8
Columbia, *Pa., U.S.A.* 111 F8
Columbia, *S.C., U.S.A.* 109 J5
Columbia, *Tenn., U.S.A.* 109 H2
Columbia →, *N. Amer.* 116 D2
Columbia, C., *Canada* 4 A4
Columbia, District of □, *U.S.A.* 108 F7
Columbia, Mt., *Canada* 104 C5
Columbia Basin, *U.S.A.* 114 C4
Columbia Falls, *U.S.A.* 114 B6
Columbia Mts., *Canada* 104 C5
Columbia Plateau, *U.S.A.* 114 D5
Columbiana, *U.S.A.* 110 F4
Columbretes, Is., *Spain* 32 F5
Columbus, *Ga., U.S.A.* 109 J3
Columbus, *Ind., U.S.A.* 108 F3
Columbus, *Kans., U.S.A.* 113 G7
Columbus, *Miss., U.S.A.* 109 J1
Columbus, *Mont., U.S.A.* 114 D9
Columbus, *N. Mex., U.S.A.* 115 L10
Columbus, *Nebr., U.S.A.* 112 E6
Columbus, *Ohio, U.S.A.* 108 F4
Columbus, *Tex., U.S.A.* 113 L6
Colunga, *Spain* 34 B5
Colusa, *U.S.A.* 116 F4
Colville, *U.S.A.* 114 B5
Colville →, *U.S.A.* 100 A4
Colville, C., *N.Z.* 91 G5
Colwood, *Canada* 116 B3
Colwyn Bay, *U.K.* 12 D4
Coma, *Ethiopia* 81 F4
Comácchio, *Italy* 29 D9
Comalcalco, *Mexico* 119 D6
Comallo, *Argentina* 128 E2
Comana, *Romania* 43 F11
Comanche, *U.S.A.* 113 K5
Comăneşti, *Romania* 43 D11
Comarnic, *Romania* 43 E10
Comayagua, *Honduras* 120 D2
Combahee →, *U.S.A.* 109 J5
Combarbalá, *Chile* 126 C1
Combeaufontaine, *France* 19 E12
Comber, *Canada* 110 D2
Comber, *U.K.* 15 B6
Combermere, *Canada* 110 A7
Comblain-au-Pont, *Belgium* 17 D5
Combourg, *France* 18 D5
Combrailles, *France* 19 F9
Combronde, *France* 20 C7
Comeragh Mts., *Ireland* 15 D4
Comet, *Australia* 94 C4
Comilla, *Bangla.* 67 H17
Comino, *Malta* 36 C1
Comino, C., *Italy* 30 B2
Cómiso, *Italy* 31 F7
Comitán, *Mexico* 119 D6
Commentry, *France* 19 F9
Commerce, *Ga., U.S.A.* 109 H4
Commerce, *Tex., U.S.A.* 113 J7
Commercy, *France* 19 D12
Committee B., *Canada* 101 B11
Commonwealth B., *Antarctica* 5 C10
Commoron Cr. →, *Australia* 95 D5
Communism Pk. = Kommunizma, Pik, *Tajikistan* 50 F8
Como, *Italy* 28 C6
Como, Lago di, *Italy* 28 B6
Comodoro Rivadavia, *Argentina* 128 F3
Comorâşte, *Romania* 42 E6
Comorin, C., *India* 66 Q10
Comoro Is. = Comoros ■, *Ind. Oc.* 77 H8
Comoros ■, *Ind. Oc.* 77 H8
Comox, *Canada* 104 D4
Compiègne, *France* 19 C9
Comporta, *Portugal* 35 G2
Compostela, *Mexico* 118 C4
Comprida, I., *Brazil* 127 A6
Compton, *Canada* 111 A13
Compton, *U.S.A.* 117 M8
Comrat, *Moldova* 43 D13
Con Cuong, *Vietnam* 64 C5
Con Son, *Vietnam* 65 H6
Conakry, *Guinea* 82 D2
Conara, *Australia* 94 G4
Concarneau, *France* 18 E3
Conceição, *Mozam.* 87 F4
Conceição da Barra, *Brazil* 125 G11
Conceição do Araguaia, *Brazil* 125 E9
Concepción, *Argentina* 126 B2
Concepción, *Bolivia* 124 G6
Concepción, *Chile* 126 D1
Concepción, *Mexico* 119 D6
Concepción, *Paraguay* 126 A4
Concepción □, *Chile* 126 D1
Concepción →, *Mexico* 118 A2
Concepción, Est. de, *Chile* 128 G2
Concepción, L., *Bolivia* 124 G6
Concepción, Punta, *Mexico* 118 B2
Concepción del Oro, *Mexico* 118 C4
Concepción del Uruguay, *Argentina* 126 C4
Conception, Pt., *U.S.A.* 117 L6
Conception B., *Canada* 103 C9
Conception B., *Namibia* 88 C1
Conception I., *Bahamas* 121 B4
Concession, *Zimbabwe* 87 F3
Conchas Dam, *U.S.A.* 113 H2
Conches-en-Ouche, *France* 18 D7
Concho, *U.S.A.* 115 J9
Concho →, *U.S.A.* 113 K5
Conchos →, *Chihuahua, Mexico* 118 B4
Conchos →, *Tamaulipas, Mexico* 119 B5
Concord, *Calif., U.S.A.* 116 H4
Concord, *N.C., U.S.A.* 109 H5
Concord, *N.H., U.S.A.* 111 C13
Concordia, *Argentina* 126 C4
Concórdia, *Brazil* 124 D5
Concordia, *Mexico* 118 C3
Concordia, *U.S.A.* 112 F6
Concrete, *U.S.A.* 114 B3
Condamine, *Australia* 95 D5
Condat, *France* 20 C6
Conde, *U.S.A.* 112 C5
Condé-sur-Noireau, *France* 18 D6
Condeúba, *Brazil* 125 F10
Condobolin, *Australia* 95 E4
Condom, *France* 20 E4
Condon, *U.S.A.* 114 D3
Conegliano, *Italy* 29 C9
Conejera, I. = Conills, I. des, *Spain* 37 B9
Conejos, *Mexico* 118 B4
Confolens, *France* 20 B4
Confuso →, *Paraguay* 126 B4
Congaz, *Moldova* 43 D13
Conghua, *China* 59 F9
Congjiang, *China* 58 E7
Congleton, *U.K.* 12 D5
Congo (Kinshasa) = Congo, Dem. Rep. of the ■, *Africa* 84 E4
Congo ■, *Africa* 84 E3
Congo →, *Africa* 84 F2
Congo, Dem. Rep. of the ■, *Africa* 84 E4
Congo Basin, *Africa* 84 E4
Congonhas, *Brazil* 127 A7
Congress, *U.S.A.* 115 J7
Conil = Conil de la Frontera, *Spain* 35 J4
Conil de la Frontera, *Spain* 35 J4
Conills, I. des, *Spain* 37 B9
Coniston, *Canada* 102 C3
Conjeeveram = Kanchipuram, *India* 66 N11
Conklin, *Canada* 105 B6
Conklin, *U.S.A.* 111 D9
Conn, L., *Ireland* 15 B2
Connacht □, *Ireland* 15 C2
Conneaut, *U.S.A.* 110 E4
Connecticut □, *U.S.A.* 111 E12
Connecticut →, *U.S.A.* 111 E12
Connell, *U.S.A.* 114 C4
Connellsville, *U.S.A.* 110 F5
Connemara, *Ireland* 15 C2
Connemaugh →, *U.S.A.* 110 F5
Connerré, *France* 18 D7
Connersville, *U.S.A.* 108 F3
Connors Ra., *Australia* 94 C4
Conques, *France* 20 D6
Conquest, *Canada* 105 C7
Conrad, *U.S.A.* 114 B8
Conran, C., *Australia* 95 F4
Conroe, *U.S.A.* 113 K7
Consecon, *Canada* 110 C7

Conselheiro Lafaiete, *Brazil* 127 A7
Conselve, *Italy* 29 C8
Consett, *U.K.* 12 C6
Consort, *Canada* 105 C6
Constance = Konstanz, *Germany* 25 H5
Constance, L. = Bodensee, *Europe* 25 H5
Constanța, *Romania* 43 F13
Constanța □, *Romania* 43 F13
Constantia, *U.S.A.* 111 C8
Constantina, *Spain* 35 H5
Constantine, *Algeria* 78 A7
Constitución, *Chile* 126 D1
Constitución, *Uruguay* 126 C4
Consuegra, *Spain* 35 F7
Consul, *Canada* 105 D7
Contact, *U.S.A.* 114 F6
Contai, *India* 69 J12
Contamana, *Peru* 124 E4
Contarina, *Italy* 29 C9
Contas →, *Brazil* 125 F11
Contes, *France* 21 E11
Contoocook, *U.S.A.* 111 C13
Contra Costa, *Mozam.* 89 D5
Contres, *France* 18 E8
Contrexéville, *France* 19 D12
Contwoyto L., *Canada* 100 B8
Conversano, *Italy* 31 B10
Conway = Conwy, *U.K.* 12 D4
Conway = Conwy →, *U.K.* 12 D4
Conway, *Ark., U.S.A.* 113 H8
Conway, *N.H., U.S.A.* 111 C13
Conway, *S.C., U.S.A.* 109 J6
Conway, L., *Australia* 95 D2
Conwy, *U.K.* 12 D4
Conwy □, *U.K.* 12 D4
Conwy →, *U.K.* 12 D4
Coober Pedy, *Australia* 95 D1
Cooch Behar = Koch Bihar, *India* 67 F16
Cooinda, *Australia* 92 B5
Cook, *Australia* 93 F5
Cook, *U.S.A.* 112 B8
Cook, B., *Chile* 128 H3
Cook, C., *Canada* 104 C3
Cook, Mt. = Aoraki Mount Cook, *N.Z.* 91 K3
Cook Inlet, *U.S.A.* 100 C4
Cook Is., *Pac. Oc.* 97 J12
Cook Strait, *N.Z.* 91 J5
Cookeville, *U.S.A.* 109 G3
Cookhouse, *S. Africa* 88 E4
Cookshire, *Canada* 111 A13
Cookstown, *U.K.* 15 B5
Cooksville, *Canada* 110 C5
Cooktown, *Australia* 94 B4
Coolabah, *Australia* 95 E4
Cooladdi, *Australia* 95 D4
Coolah, *Australia* 95 E4
Coolamon, *Australia* 95 E4
Coolgardie, *Australia* 93 F3
Coolidge, *U.S.A.* 115 K8
Coolidge Dam, *U.S.A.* 115 K8
Cooma, *Australia* 95 F4
Coon Rapids, *U.S.A.* 112 C8
Coonabarabran, *Australia* 95 E4
Coonamble, *Australia* 95 E4
Coonana, *Australia* 93 F3
Coondapoor, *India* 66 N9
Cooninie, L., *Australia* 95 D2
Cooper, *U.S.A.* 113 J7
Cooper Cr. →, *Australia* 95 D2
Cooperstown, *N. Dak., U.S.A.* 112 B5
Cooperstown, *N.Y., U.S.A.* 111 D10
Coorabie, *Australia* 93 F5
Coorong, The, *Australia* 95 F2
Coorow, *Australia* 93 E2
Cooroy, *Australia* 95 D5
Coos Bay, *U.S.A.* 114 E1
Coosa →, *U.S.A.* 109 J2
Cootamundra, *Australia* 95 E4
Cootehill, *Ireland* 15 B4
Copahue Paso, *Argentina* 126 D1
Copainalá, *Mexico* 119 D6
Copake Falls, *U.S.A.* 111 D11
Copalnic Mănăștur, *Romania* 43 C8
Copán, *Honduras* 120 D2
Cope, *U.S.A.* 112 F3
Cope, C., *Spain* 33 H3
Copenhagen = København, *Denmark* 11 J6
Copenhagen, *U.S.A.* 111 C9
Copertino, *Italy* 31 B11
Copiapó, *Chile* 126 B1
Copiapó →, *Chile* 126 B1
Coplay, *U.S.A.* 111 F9
Copp L., *Canada* 104 A6
Copparo, *Italy* 29 D8
Coppename →, *Surinam* 125 B7
Copper Harbor, *U.S.A.* 108 B2
Copper Queen, *Zimbabwe* 87 F2
Copperas Cove, *U.S.A.* 113 K6
Copperbelt □, *Zambia* 87 E2
Coppermine = Kugluktuk, *Canada* 100 B8
Coppermine →, *Canada* 100 B8
Copperopolis, *U.S.A.* 116 H6
Copșa Mică, *Romania* 43 D9
Coquet →, *U.K.* 12 B6
Coquille, *U.S.A.* 114 E1
Coquimbo, *Chile* 126 C1
Coquimbo □, *Chile* 126 C1
Corabia, *Romania* 43 G9
Coracora, *Peru* 124 G4
Coraki, *Australia* 95 D5
Coral, *U.S.A.* 110 F5
Coral Gables, *U.S.A.* 109 N5
Coral Harbour = Salliq, *Canada* 101 B11
Coral Sea, *Pac. Oc.* 96 J7
Coral Springs, *U.S.A.* 109 M5
Coraopolis, *U.S.A.* 110 F4
Corato, *Italy* 31 A9
Corbeil-Essonnes, *France* 19 D9
Corbie, *France* 19 C9
Corbières, *France* 20 F6
Corbigny, *France* 19 E10
Corbin, *U.S.A.* 108 G3
Corbones →, *Spain* 35 H5
Corbu, *Romania* 43 F13
Corby, *U.K.* 13 E7
Corcaigh = Cork, *Ireland* 15 E3
Corcoran, *U.S.A.* 116 J7
Cordele, *U.S.A.* 109 K4
Cordell, *U.S.A.* 113 H5
Cordenòns, *Italy* 29 C9
Cordes, *France* 20 D5
Córdoba, *Argentina* 126 C3
Córdoba, *Mexico* 119 D5
Córdoba, *Spain* 35 H6
Córdoba □, *Argentina* 126 C3
Córdoba □, *Spain* 35 G6
Córdoba, Sierra de, *Argentina* 126 C3
Cordon, *Phil.* 61 C4
Cordova, *U.S.A.* 100 B5
Corella, *Spain* 32 C3
Corella →, *Australia* 94 B3
Corfield, *Australia* 94 C3
Corfu = Kérkira, *Greece* 36 A3
Corfu, Str. of, *Greece* 36 A4
Corgo = O Corgo, *Spain* 34 C3
Cori, *Italy* 30 A5
Coria, *Spain* 34 F4
Coria del Río, *Spain* 35 H4
Corigliano Cálabro, *Italy* 31 C9
Coringa Is., *Australia* 94 B4
Corinth = Kórinthos, *Greece* 38 D4
Corinth, *Miss., U.S.A.* 109 H1
Corinth, *N.Y., U.S.A.* 111 C11
Corinth, G. of = Korinthiakós Kólpos, *Greece* 38 C4
Corinth Canal, *Greece* 38 D4
Corinto, *Brazil* 125 G10
Corinto, *Nic.* 120 D2
Cork, *Ireland* 15 E3
Cork □, *Ireland* 15 E3
Cork Harbour, *Ireland* 15 E3
Corlay, *France* 18 D3
Corleone, *Italy* 30 E6
Corleto Perticara, *Italy* 31 B9
Çorlu, *Turkey* 41 E11
Cormack L., *Canada* 104 A4
Cormòns, *Italy* 29 C10
Cormorant, *Canada* 105 C8
Cormorant L., *Canada* 105 C8
Corn Is. = Maiz, Is. del, *Nic.* 120 D3
Cornélio Procópio, *Brazil* 127 A5
Corner Brook, *Canada* 103 C8
Cornești, *Moldova* 43 C13
Corníglio, *Italy* 28 D7
Corning, *Ark., U.S.A.* 113 G9
Corning, *Calif., U.S.A.* 114 G2
Corning, *Iowa, U.S.A.* 112 E7
Corning, *N.Y., U.S.A.* 110 D7
Corno Grande, *Italy* 29 F10
Cornwall, *Canada* 102 C5
Cornwall, *U.S.A.* 111 F8
Cornwall □, *U.K.* 13 G3
Corny Pt., *Australia* 95 E2
Coro, *Venezuela* 124 A5
Coroatá, *Brazil* 125 D10
Corocoro, *Bolivia* 124 G5
Coroico, *Bolivia* 124 G5
Coromandel, *N.Z.* 91 G5
Coromandel Coast, *India* 66 N12
Corona, *Calif., U.S.A.* 117 M9
Corona, *N. Mex., U.S.A.* 115 J11
Coronach, *Canada* 105 D7
Coronado, *U.S.A.* 117 N9
Coronado, B. de, *Costa Rica* 120 E3
Coronados, Is. los, *U.S.A.* 117 N9
Coronation, *Canada* 104 C6
Coronation Gulf, *Canada* 100 B8
Coronation I., *Antarctica* 5 C18
Coronation Is., *Australia* 92 B3
Coronda, *Argentina* 126 C3
Coronel, *Chile* 126 D1
Coronel Bogado, *Paraguay* 126 B4
Coronel Dorrego, *Argentina* 126 D3
Coronel Oviedo, *Paraguay* 126 B4
Coronel Pringles, *Argentina* 126 D3
Coronel Suárez, *Argentina* 126 D3
Coronel Vidal, *Argentina* 126 D4
Coropuna, Nevado, *Peru* 124 G4
Çorovodë, *Albania* 40 F4
Corowa, *Australia* 95 F4
Corozal, *Belize* 119 D7
Corps, *France* 21 D9
Corpus, *Argentina* 127 B4
Corpus Christi, *U.S.A.* 113 M6
Corpus Christi, L., *U.S.A.* 113 L6
Corral de Almaguer, *Spain* 34 F7
Corralejo, *Canary Is.* 37 F6
Corraun Pen., *Ireland* 15 C2
Corréggio, *Italy* 28 D7
Correntes, C. das, *Mozam.* 89 C6
Corrèze □, *France* 20 C5
Corrèze →, *France* 20 C5
Corrib, L., *Ireland* 15 C2
Corridónia, *Italy* 29 E10
Corrientes, *Argentina* 126 B4
Corrientes □, *Argentina* 126 B4
Corrientes →, *Argentina* 126 C4
Corrientes →, *Peru* 124 D4
Corrientes, C., *Colombia* 124 B3
Corrientes, C., *Cuba* 120 B3
Corrientes, C., *Mexico* 118 C3
Corrigan, *U.S.A.* 113 K7
Corrigin, *Australia* 93 F2
Corry, *U.S.A.* 110 E5
Corse, *France* 21 G13
Corse, C., *France* 21 E13
Corse-du-Sud □, *France* 21 G13
Corsica = Corse, *France* 21 G13
Corsicana, *U.S.A.* 113 J6
Corte, *France* 21 F13
Corte Pinto, *Portugal* 35 H3
Cortegana, *Spain* 35 H4
Cortez, *U.S.A.* 115 H9
Cortina d'Ampezzo, *Italy* 29 B9
Cortland, *N.Y., U.S.A.* 111 D8
Cortland, *Ohio, U.S.A.* 110 E4
Cortona, *Italy* 29 E8
Corubal →, *Guinea-Biss.* 82 C2
Coruche, *Portugal* 35 G2
Çoruh →, *Turkey* 49 K5
Çorum, *Turkey* 72 B6
Corumbá, *Brazil* 124 G7
Corund, *Romania* 43 D10
Corunna = A Coruña, *Spain* 34 B2
Corvallis, *U.S.A.* 114 D2
Corvette, L. de la, *Canada* 102 B5
Corydon, *U.S.A.* 112 E8
Cosalá, *Mexico* 118 C3
Cosamaloapan, *Mexico* 119 D5
Cosenza, *Italy* 31 C9
Coșereni, *Romania* 43 F11
Coshocton, *U.S.A.* 110 F3
Cosmo Newberry, *Australia* 93 E3
Cosne-Cours-sur-Loire, *France* 19 E9
Coso Junction, *U.S.A.* 117 J9
Coso Pk., *U.S.A.* 117 J9
Cospeito, *Spain* 34 B3
Cosquín, *Argentina* 126 C3
Cossato, *Italy* 28 C5
Cossé-le-Vivien, *France* 18 E6
Cosson →, *France* 18 E8
Costa Blanca, *Spain* 33 G4
Costa Brava, *Spain* 32 D8
Costa del Sol, *Spain* 35 J6
Costa Dorada, *Spain* 32 D6
Costa Mesa, *U.S.A.* 117 M9
Costa Rica ■, *Cent. Amer.* 120 E3
Costa Smeralda, *Italy* 30 A2
Costești, *Romania* 43 F9
Costigliole d'Asti, *Italy* 28 D5
Cosumnes →, *U.S.A.* 116 G5
Coswig, *Sachsen, Germany* 24 D9
Coswig, *Sachsen-Anhalt, Germany* 24 D8
Cotabato, *Phil.* 61 H6
Cotagaita, *Bolivia* 126 A2
Côte d'Azur, *France* 21 E11
Côte-d'Ivoire = Ivory Coast ■, *Africa* 82 D4
Côte d'Or, *France* 19 E11
Côte-d'Or □, *France* 19 E11
Coteau des Prairies, *U.S.A.* 112 C6
Coteau du Missouri, *U.S.A.* 112 B4
Coteau Landing, *Canada* 111 A10
Cotentin, *France* 18 C5
Côtes-d'Armor □, *France* 18 D4
Côtes de Meuse, *France* 19 C12
Côtes-du-Nord = Côtes-d'Armor □, *France* 18 D4
Cotiella, *Spain* 32 C5
Cotillo, *Canary Is.* 37 F5
Cotiujeni, *Moldova* 43 C13
Cotonou, *Benin* 83 D5
Cotopaxi, *Ecuador* 122 D3
Cotronei, *Italy* 31 C9
Cotswold Hills, *U.K.* 13 F5
Cottage Grove, *U.S.A.* 114 E2
Cottbus, *Germany* 24 D10
Cottonwood, *U.S.A.* 115 J7
Cotulla, *U.S.A.* 113 L5
Coubre, Pte. de la, *France* 20 C2
Couches, *France* 19 F11
Couço, *Portugal* 35 G2
Coudersport, *U.S.A.* 110 E6
Couedic, C. du, *Australia* 95 F2
Couëron, *France* 18 E5
Couesnon →, *France* 18 D5
Couhé, *France* 20 B4
Coulanges-sur-Yonne, *France* 19 E10
Coulee City, *U.S.A.* 114 C4
Coulman I., *Antarctica* 5 D11
Coulommiers, *France* 19 D10
Coulon →, *France* 21 E9
Coulonge →, *Canada* 102 C4
Coulonges-sur-l'Autize, *France* 20 B3
Coulounieix-Chamiers, *France* 20 C4
Coulterville, *U.S.A.* 116 H6
Council, *U.S.A.* 114 D5
Council Bluffs, *U.S.A.* 112 E7
Council Grove, *U.S.A.* 112 F6
Coupeville, *U.S.A.* 116 B4
Courantyne →, *S. Amer.* 122 C5
Courcelles, *Belgium* 17 D4
Courçon, *France* 20 B3
Courmayeur, *Italy* 28 C3
Couronne, C., *France* 21 E9
Cours-la-Ville, *France* 19 F11
Coursan, *France* 20 E7
Courseulles-sur-Mer, *France* 18 C6
Courtenay, *Canada* 104 D4
Courtenay, *France* 19 D10
Courtland, *U.S.A.* 116 G5
Courtrai = Kortrijk, *Belgium* 17 D3
Courtright, *Canada* 110 D2
Coushatta, *U.S.A.* 113 J8
Coutances, *France* 18 C5
Coutras, *France* 20 C3
Coutts Crossing, *Australia* 95 D5
Couvin, *Belgium* 17 D4
Covarrubias, *Spain* 34 C7
Covasna, *Romania* 43 E11
Covasna □, *Romania* 43 E10
Cove I., *Canada* 110 A3
Coventry, *U.K.* 13 E6
Covilhã, *Portugal* 34 E3
Covington, *Ga., U.S.A.* 109 J4
Covington, *Ky., U.S.A.* 108 F3
Covington, *Okla., U.S.A.* 113 G6
Covington, *Tenn., U.S.A.* 113 H10
Covington, *Va., U.S.A.* 108 G5
Cowal, L., *Australia* 95 E4
Cowan, L., *Australia* 93 F3
Cowan L., *Canada* 105 C7
Cowangie, *Australia* 95 F3
Cowansville, *Canada* 102 C5
Coward Springs, *Australia* 95 D2
Cowcowing Lakes, *Australia* 93 F2
Cowdenbeath, *U.K.* 14 E5
Cowell, *Australia* 95 E2
Cowes, *U.K.* 13 G6
Cowichan L., *Canada* 116 B2
Cowlitz →, *U.S.A.* 116 D4
Cowra, *Australia* 95 E4
Cox, *Spain* 33 G4
Coxilha Grande, *Brazil* 127 B5
Coxim, *Brazil* 125 G8
Cox's Bazar, *Bangla.* 67 J17
Coyote Wells, *U.S.A.* 117 N11
Coyuca de Benítez, *Mexico* 119 D4
Coyuca de Catalan, *Mexico* 118 D4
Cozad, *U.S.A.* 112 E5
Cozes, *France* 20 C3
Cozumel, *Mexico* 119 C7
Cozumel, Isla, *Mexico* 119 C7
Cracow = Kraków, *Poland* 45 H6
Cracow, *Australia* 95 D5
Cradock, *Australia* 95 E2
Cradock, *S. Africa* 88 E4
Craig, *U.S.A.* 114 F10
Craigavon, *U.K.* 15 B5
Craigmore, *Zimbabwe* 87 G3
Craik, *Canada* 105 C7
Crailsheim, *Germany* 25 F6
Craiova, *Romania* 43 F8
Cramsie, *Australia* 94 C3
Cranberry L., *U.S.A.* 111 B10
Cranberry Portage, *Canada* 105 C8
Cranbrook, *Australia* 93 F2
Cranbrook, *Canada* 104 D5
Crandon, *U.S.A.* 112 C10
Crane, *Oreg., U.S.A.* 114 E4
Crane, *Tex., U.S.A.* 113 K3
Cranston, *U.S.A.* 111 E13
Craon, *France* 18 E6
Craonne, *France* 19 C10
Craponne-sur-Arzon, *France* 20 C7
Crasna, *Romania* 43 D12
Crasna →, *Romania* 42 C7
Crasnei, Munții, *Romania* 43 C8
Crater L., *U.S.A.* 114 E2
Crater Lake National Park, *U.S.A.* 114 E2
Crateús, *Brazil* 125 E10
Crati →, *Italy* 31 C9
Crato, *Brazil* 125 E11
Crato, *Portugal* 35 F3
Craven, L., *Canada* 102 B4
Crawford, *U.S.A.* 112 D3
Crawfordsville, *U.S.A.* 108 E2
Crawley, *U.K.* 13 F7
Crazy Mts., *U.S.A.* 114 C8
Crean L., *Canada* 105 C7
Crécy-en-Ponthieu, *France* 19 B8
Crediton, *Canada* 110 C3
Cree →, *Canada* 105 B7
Cree →, *U.K.* 14 G4
Cree L., *Canada* 105 B7
Creede, *U.S.A.* 115 H10
Creekside, *U.S.A.* 110 F5
Creel, *Mexico* 118 B3
Creemore, *Canada* 110 B4
Creighton, *Canada* 105 C8
Creighton, *U.S.A.* 112 D6
Creil, *France* 19 C9
Crema, *Italy* 28 C6
Cremona, *Italy* 28 C7
Crepaja, *Serbia, Yug.* 42 E5
Crépy, *France* 19 C10
Crépy-en-Valois, *France* 19 C9
Cres, *Croatia* 29 D11
Crescent City, *U.S.A.* 114 F1
Crescentino, *Italy* 28 C5
Crespo, *Argentina* 126 C3
Cresson, *U.S.A.* 110 F6
Crest, *France* 21 D9
Cresta, Mt., *Phil.* 61 C5
Crestline, *Calif., U.S.A.* 117 L9
Crestline, *Ohio, U.S.A.* 110 F2
Creston, *Canada* 104 D5
Creston, *Calif., U.S.A.* 116 K6
Creston, *Iowa, U.S.A.* 112 E7
Crestview, *Calif., U.S.A.* 116 H8
Crestview, *Fla., U.S.A.* 109 K2
Crêt de la Neige, *France* 19 F12
Crete = Kríti, *Greece* 36 D7
Crete, *U.S.A.* 112 E6
Crete, Sea of, *Greece* 39 E7
Créteil, *France* 19 D9
Creus, C. de, *Spain* 32 C8
Creuse □, *France* 19 F9
Creuse →, *France* 20 B4
Creutzwald, *France* 19 C13
Creuzburg, *Germany* 24 D6
Crèvecœur-le-Grand, *France* 19 C9
Crevillente, *Spain* 33 G4
Crewe, *U.K.* 12 D5
Crewkerne, *U.K.* 13 G5
Criciúma, *Brazil* 127 B6
Cricova, *Moldova* 43 C13
Crieff, *U.K.* 14 E5
Crikvenica, *Croatia* 29 C11
Crimea □, *Ukraine* 47 K8
Crimean Pen. = Krymskyy Pivostriv, *Ukraine* 47 K8
Crimmitschau, *Germany* 24 E8
Cristuru Secuiesc, *Romania* 43 D10
Crișul Alb →, *Romania* 42 D6
Crișul Negru →, *Romania* 42 D6
Crișul Repede →, *Romania* 42 D5
Criuleni, *Moldova* 43 C14
Crivitz, *Germany* 24 B7
Crna →, *Macedonia* 40 E5
Crna Gora = Montenegro □, *Yugoslavia* 40 D3
Crna Gora, *Macedonia* 40 D5
Crna Reka = Crna →, *Macedonia* 40 E5
Crna Trava, *Serbia, Yug.* 40 D6
Crni Drim →, *Macedonia* 40 E4
Crni Timok →, *Serbia, Yug.* 40 C6
Crnoljeva Planina, *Kosovo, Yug.* 40 D5
Črnomelj, *Slovenia* 29 C12
Croagh Patrick, *Ireland* 15 C2
Croatia ■, *Europe* 29 C13
Crocker, Banjaran, *Malaysia* 62 C5
Crockett, *U.S.A.* 113 K7
Crocodile = Krokodil →, *Mozam.* 89 D5
Crocodile Is., *Australia* 94 A1
Crocq, *France* 20 C6
Crodo, *Italy* 28 B5
Crohy Hd., *Ireland* 15 B3
Croisette, C., *France* 21 E9
Croisic, Pte. du, *France* 18 E4
Croix, L. La, *Canada* 102 C1
Croker, C., *Australia* 92 B5
Croker, C., *Canada* 110 B4
Croker I., *Australia* 92 B5
Cromarty, *U.K.* 14 D4
Cromer, *U.K.* 12 E9
Cromwell, *N.Z.* 91 L2
Cromwell, *U.S.A.* 111 E12
Cronat, *France* 19 F10
Crook, *U.K.* 12 C6
Crooked →, *Canada* 104 C4
Crooked →, *U.S.A.* 114 D3
Crooked I., *Bahamas* 121 B5
Crooked Island Passage, *Bahamas* 121 B5
Crookston, *Minn., U.S.A.* 112 B6
Crookston, *Nebr., U.S.A.* 112 D4
Crookwell, *Australia* 95 E4
Crosby, *U.K.* 12 D4
Crosby, *N. Dak., U.S.A.* 112 A3
Crosby, *Pa., U.S.A.* 110 E6
Crosbyton, *U.S.A.* 113 J4
Crosía, *Italy* 31 C9
Cross →, *Nigeria* 83 E6
Cross City, *U.S.A.* 109 L4
Cross Fell, *U.K.* 12 C5
Cross L., *Canada* 105 C9
Cross Lake, *Canada* 105 C9
Cross River □, *Nigeria* 83 D6
Cross Sound, *U.S.A.* 100 C6
Crossett, *U.S.A.* 113 J9
Crosshaven, *Ireland* 15 E3
Crossville, *U.S.A.* 109 G3
Croswell, *U.S.A.* 110 C2
Croton-on-Hudson, *U.S.A.* 111 E11
Crotone, *Italy* 31 C10
Crow →, *Canada* 104 B4
Crow Agency, *U.S.A.* 114 D10
Crow Hd., *Ireland* 15 E1
Crowell, *U.S.A.* 113 J5
Crowley, *U.S.A.* 113 K8
Crowley, L., *U.S.A.* 116 H8
Crown Point, *Ind., U.S.A.* 108 E2
Crown Point, *N.Y., U.S.A.* 111 C11
Crownpoint, *U.S.A.* 115 J9
Crows Landing, *U.S.A.* 116 H5
Crows Nest, *Australia* 95 D5
Crowsnest Pass, *Canada* 104 D6
Croydon, *Australia* 94 B3
Croydon □, *U.K.* 13 F7
Crozet, Is., *Ind. Oc.* 3 G12
Crozon, *France* 18 D2
Cruz, C., *Cuba* 120 C4
Cruz Alta, *Brazil* 127 B5
Cruz de Incio, *Spain* 34 C3
Cruz del Eje, *Argentina* 126 C3
Cruzeiro, *Brazil* 127 A7
Cruzeiro do Oeste, *Brazil* 127 A5
Cruzeiro do Sul, *Brazil* 124 E4
Cry L., *Canada* 104 B3
Crystal Bay, *U.S.A.* 116 F7
Crystal Brook, *Australia* 95 E2
Crystal City, *U.S.A.* 113 L5
Crystal Falls, *U.S.A.* 108 B1
Crystal River, *U.S.A.* 109 L4
Crystal Springs, *U.S.A.* 113 K9
Csenger, *Hungary* 42 C7
Csongrád, *Hungary* 42 D5
Csongrád □, *Hungary* 42 D5
Csorna, *Hungary* 42 C2
Csurgo, *Hungary* 42 D2
Cu Lao Hon, *Vietnam* 65 G7
Cua Rao, *Vietnam* 64 C5
Cuácua →, *Mozam.* 87 F4
Cuamato, *Angola* 88 B2
Cuamba, *Mozam.* 87 E4

Cuando →, *Angola* 85 H4
Cuando Cubango □, *Angola* 88 B3
Cuangar, *Angola* 88 B2
Cuango = Kwango →, *Dem. Rep. of the Congo* 84 E3
Cuanza →, *Angola* 84 F2
Cuarto →, *Argentina* 126 C3
Cuatrociénegas, *Mexico* 118 B4
Cuauhtémoc, *Mexico* 118 B3
Cuba, *Portugal* 35 G3
Cuba, *N. Mex., U.S.A.* 115 J10
Cuba, *N.Y., U.S.A.* 110 D6
Cuba ■, *W. Indies* 120 B4
Cubango →, *Africa* 88 B3
Çubuk, *Turkey* 72 B5
Cuchumatanes, Sierra de los, *Guatemala* 120 C1
Cuckfield, *U.K.* 13 F7
Cucuí, *Brazil* 124 C5
Cucurpe, *Mexico* 118 A2
Cúcuta, *Colombia* 124 B4
Cudalbi, *Romania* 43 E12
Cuddalore, *India* 66 P11
Cuddapah, *India* 66 M11
Cuddapan, L., *Australia* 94 D3
Cudillero, *Spain* 34 B4
Cue, *Australia* 93 E2
Cuéllar, *Spain* 34 D6
Cuenca, *Ecuador* 124 D3
Cuenca, *Spain* 32 E2
Cuenca □, *Spain* 32 F3
Cuenca, Serranía de, *Spain* 32 F3
Cuerdo del Pozo, Embalse de la, *Spain* 32 D2
Cuernavaca, *Mexico* 119 D5
Cuero, *U.S.A.* 113 L6
Cuers, *France* 21 E10
Cuevas del Almanzora, *Spain* 33 H3
Cuevo, *Bolivia* 124 H6
Cugir, *Romania* 43 E8
Cugnaux, *France* 20 E5
Cuhai-Bakony →, *Hungary* 42 C2
Cuiabá, *Brazil* 125 G7
Cuiabá →, *Brazil* 125 G7
Cuijk, *Neths.* 17 C5
Cuilco, *Guatemala* 120 C1
Cuillin Hills, *U.K.* 14 D2
Cuillin Sd., *U.K.* 14 D2
Cuiseaux, *France* 19 F12
Cuito →, *Angola* 88 B3
Cuitzeo, L. de, *Mexico* 118 D4
Cujmir, *Romania* 42 F7
Cukai, *Malaysia* 65 K4
Culbertson, *U.S.A.* 112 A2
Culcairn, *Australia* 95 F4
Culebra, Sierra de la, *Spain* 34 D4
Culfa, *Azerbaijan* 73 C11
Culgoa →, *Australia* 95 D4
Culiacán, *Mexico* 118 C3
Culiacán →, *Mexico* 118 C3
Culion, *Phil.* 61 F4
Cúllar, *Spain* 35 H8
Cullarin Ra., *Australia* 95 E4
Cullen, *U.K.* 14 D6
Cullen Pt., *Australia* 94 A3
Cullera, *Spain* 33 F4
Cullman, *U.S.A.* 109 H2
Culoz, *France* 21 C9
Culpeper, *U.S.A.* 108 F7
Culuene →, *Brazil* 125 F8
Culver, Pt., *Australia* 93 F3
Culverden, *N.Z.* 91 K4
Cumaná, *Venezuela* 124 A6
Cumaovası, *Turkey* 39 C9
Cumberland, *B.C., Canada* 104 D4
Cumberland, *Ont., Canada* 111 A9
Cumberland, *U.S.A.* 108 F6
Cumberland →, *U.S.A.* 109 G2
Cumberland, L., *U.S.A.* 109 G3
Cumberland I., *U.S.A.* 109 K5
Cumberland Is., *Australia* 94 C4
Cumberland L., *Canada* 105 C8
Cumberland Pen., *Canada* 101 B13
Cumberland Plateau, *U.S.A.* 109 H3
Cumberland Sd., *Canada* 101 B13
Cumbernauld, *U.K.* 14 F5
Cumborah, *Australia* 95 D4
Cumbres Mayores, *Spain* 35 G4
Cumbria □, *U.K.* 12 C5
Cumbrian Mts., *U.K.* 12 C5
Cumbum, *India* 66 M11
Cuminá →, *Brazil* 125 D7
Cummings Mt., *U.S.A.* 117 K8
Cummins, *Australia* 95 E2
Cumnock, *Australia* 95 E4
Cumnock, *U.K.* 14 F4
Cumpas, *Mexico* 118 B3
Cumplida, Pta., *Canary Is.* 37 F2
Çumra, *Turkey* 72 D5
Cunco, *Chile* 128 D2
Cuncumén, *Chile* 126 C1
Cunderdin, *Australia* 93 F2
Cunene →, *Angola* 88 B1
Cúneo, *Italy* 28 D4
Çüngüş, *Turkey* 70 B3
Cunillera, I. = Sa Conillera, *Spain* 37 C7
Cunlhat, *France* 20 C7
Cunnamulla, *Australia* 95 D4
Cuorgnè, *Italy* 28 C4
Cupar, *Canada* 105 C8
Cupar, *U.K.* 14 E5
Cupcini, *Moldova* 43 B12
Cupica, G. de, *Colombia* 124 B3
Ćuprija, *Serbia, Yug.* 40 C5
Curaçao, *Neth. Ant.* 121 D6
Curanilahue, *Chile* 126 D1
Curaray →, *Peru* 124 D4
Cure →, *France* 19 E10
Curepto, *Chile* 126 D1
Curiapo, *Venezuela* 124 B6
Curicó, *Chile* 126 C1
Curinga, *Italy* 31 D9
Curitiba, *Brazil* 127 B6
Curitibanos, *Brazil* 127 B5
Currabubula, *Australia* 95 E5
Currais Novos, *Brazil* 125 E11
Curralinho, *Brazil* 125 D9
Currant, *U.S.A.* 114 G6
Current →, *U.S.A.* 113 G9
Currie, *Australia* 94 F3
Currie, *U.S.A.* 114 F6
Curtea de Argeş, *Romania* 43 E9
Curtici, *Romania* 42 D6
Curtis, *U.S.A.* 112 E4
Curtis Group, *Australia* 94 F4
Curtis I., *Australia* 94 C5
Curuápanema →, *Brazil* 125 D7
Curuçá, *Brazil* 125 D9
Curuguaty, *Paraguay* 127 A4
Curup, *Indonesia* 62 E2
Cururupu, *Brazil* 125 D10
Curuzú Cuatiá, *Argentina* 126 B4
Curvelo, *Brazil* 125 G10
Cushing, *U.S.A.* 113 H6
Cushing, Mt., *Canada* 104 B3
Cusihuiriáchic, *Mexico* 118 B3
Cusna, Mte., *Italy* 28 D7
Cusset, *France* 19 F10
Custer, *U.S.A.* 112 D3
Cut Bank, *U.S.A.* 114 B7
Cutchogue, *U.S.A.* 111 E12
Cuthbert, *U.S.A.* 109 K3
Cutler, *U.S.A.* 116 J7
Cutro, *Italy* 31 C9
Cuttaburra →, *Australia* 95 D3
Cuttack, *India* 67 J14
Cuvier, C., *Australia* 93 D1
Cuvier I., *N.Z.* 91 G5
Cuxhaven, *Germany* 24 B4
Cuyahoga Falls, *U.S.A.* 110 E3
Cuyapo, *Phil.* 61 D4
Cuyo, *Phil.* 61 F4
Cuyo East Pass, *Phil.* 61 F4
Cuyo West Pass, *Phil.* 61 F4
Cuyuni →, *Guyana* 124 B7
Cuzco, *Bolivia* 124 H5
Cuzco, *Peru* 124 F4
Čvrsnica, *Bos.-H.* 42 G2
Cwmbran, *U.K.* 13 F4
Cyangugu, *Rwanda* 86 C2
Cybinka, *Poland* 45 F1
Cyclades = Kikládhes, *Greece* 38 E6
Cygnet, *Australia* 94 G4
Cynthiana, *U.S.A.* 108 F3
Cypress Hills, *Canada* 105 D7
Cypress Hills Prov. Park, *Canada* 105 D7
Cyprus ■, *Asia* 36 E12
Cyrenaica, *Libya* 79 C10
Czaplinek, *Poland* 44 E3
Czar, *Canada* 105 C6
Czarna →, *Łódzkie, Poland* 45 G6
Czarna →, *Świętokrzyskie, Poland* 45 H8
Czarna Białostocka, *Poland* 45 E10
Czarna Woda, *Poland* 44 E5
Czarne, *Poland* 44 E3
Czarnków, *Poland* 45 F3
Czech Rep. ■, *Europe* 26 B8
Czechowice-Dziedzice, *Poland* 45 J5
Czempiń, *Poland* 45 F3
Czeremcha, *Poland* 45 F10
Czerniejewo, *Poland* 45 F4
Czersk, *Poland* 44 E4
Czerwieńsk, *Poland* 45 F2
Czerwionka-Leszczyny, *Poland* 45 H5
Częstochowa, *Poland* 45 H6
Człopa, *Poland* 45 E3
Człuchów, *Poland* 44 E4
Czyżew-Osada, *Poland* 45 F9

D

Da →, *Vietnam* 58 G5
Da Hinggan Ling, *China* 60 B7
Da Lat, *Vietnam* 65 G7
Da Nang, *Vietnam* 64 D7
Da Qaidam, *China* 60 C4
Da Yunhe →, *China* 57 G11
Da'an, *China* 57 B13
Dab'a, Ras el, *Egypt* 80 H6
Daba Shan, *China* 58 B7
Dabai, *Nigeria* 83 C6
Dabakala, *Ivory C.* 82 D4
Dabas, *Hungary* 42 C4
Dabat, *Ethiopia* 81 E4
Dabbagh, Jabal, *Si. Arabia* 70 E2
Dabhoi, *India* 68 H5
Dąbie, *Poland* 45 F5
Dabie Shan, *China* 59 B10
Dabilda, *Cameroon* 83 C7
Dabnou, *Niger* 83 C6
Dabo = Pasirkuning, *Indonesia* 62 E2
Dabola, *Guinea* 82 C2
Dabou, *Ivory C.* 82 D4
Daboya, *Ghana* 83 D4
Dąbrowa Białostocka, *Poland* 44 E10
Dąbrowa Górnicza, *Poland* 45 H6
Dąbrowa Tarnowska, *Poland* 45 H7
Dabu, *China* 59 E11
Dabung, *Malaysia* 65 K4
Dabus →, *Ethiopia* 81 E4
Dacato →, *Ethiopia* 81 F5
Dacca = Dhaka, *Bangla.* 69 H14
Dacca = Dhaka □, *Bangla.* 69 G14
Dachau, *Germany* 25 G7
Dachstein, Hoher, *Austria* 26 D6
Dačice, *Czech Rep.* 26 B8
Dadanawa, *Guyana* 124 C7
Daday, *Turkey* 72 B5
Dade City, *U.S.A.* 109 L4
Dadhar, *Pakistan* 68 E2
Dadiya, *Nigeria* 83 D7
Dadra & Nagar Haveli □, *India* 66 J8
Dadri = Charkhi Dadri, *India* 68 E7
Dadu, *Pakistan* 68 F2
Dadu He →, *China* 58 C4
Daet, *Phil.* 61 D5
Dafang, *China* 58 D5
Dağ, *Turkey* 39 D12
Dagana, *Senegal* 82 B1
Dagash, *Sudan* 80 D3
Dagestan □, *Russia* 49 J8
Dagestanskiye Ogni, *Russia* 49 J9
Daggett, *U.S.A.* 117 L10
Daghestan Republic = Dagestan □, *Russia* 49 J8
Daghfeli, *Sudan* 80 D3
Dağlıq Qarabağ = Nagorno-Karabakh, *Azerbaijan* 70 B5
Dagö = Hiiumaa, *Estonia* 9 G20
Dagu, *China* 57 E9
Daguan, *China* 58 D4
Dagupan, *Phil.* 61 C4
Daguragu, *Australia* 92 C5
Dahab, *Egypt* 80 B3
Dahlak Kebir, *Eritrea* 81 D5
Dahlenburg, *Germany* 24 B6
Dahlonega, *U.S.A.* 109 H4
Dahme, *Germany* 24 D9
Dahod, *India* 68 H6
Dahomey = Benin ■, *Africa* 83 D5
Dahong Shan, *China* 59 B9
Dahra, *Senegal* 82 B1
Dahshûr, *Egypt* 80 J7
Dahūk, *Iraq* 70 B3
Dai Hao, *Vietnam* 64 C6
Dai-Sen, *Japan* 55 G6
Dai Shan, *China* 59 B14
Dai Xian, *China* 56 E7
Daicheng, *China* 56 E9
Daimiel, *Spain* 35 F7
Daingean, *Ireland* 15 C4
Dainkog, *China* 58 A1
Daintree, *Australia* 94 B4
Daiō-Misaki, *Japan* 55 G8
Dair, J. ed, *Sudan* 81 E3
Dairût, *Egypt* 80 B3
Daisetsu-Zan, *Japan* 54 C11
Dajarra, *Australia* 94 C2
Dajin Chuan →, *China* 58 B3
Dak Dam, *Cambodia* 64 F6
Dak Nhe, *Vietnam* 64 E6
Dak Pek, *Vietnam* 64 E6
Dak Song, *Vietnam* 65 F6
Dak Sui, *Vietnam* 64 E6
Dakar, *Senegal* 82 C1
Dakhla, *W. Sahara* 78 D2
Dakhla, El Wâhât el-, *Egypt* 80 B2
Dakingari, *Nigeria* 83 C5
Dakor, *India* 68 H5
Dakoro, *Niger* 83 C6
Dakota City, *U.S.A.* 112 D6
Đakovica, *Kosovo, Yug.* 40 D4
Đakovo, *Croatia* 42 E3
Dalaba, *Guinea* 82 C2
Dalachi, *China* 56 F3
Dalai Nur, *China* 56 C9
Dālakī, *Iran* 71 D6
Dalälven →, *Sweden* 10 D10
Dalaman, *Turkey* 39 E10
Dalaman →, *Turkey* 39 E10
Dalandzadgad, *Mongolia* 56 C3
Dalap-Uliga-Darrit, *Marshall Is.* 96 G9
Dalarna, *Sweden* 10 D8
Dalarnas län □, *Sweden* 10 C8
Dālbandīn, *Pakistan* 66 E4
Dalbeattie, *U.K.* 14 G5
Dalbeg, *Australia* 94 C4
Dalbosjön, *Sweden* 11 F6
Dalby, *Australia* 95 D5
Dalby, *Sweden* 11 J7
Dale City, *U.S.A.* 108 F7
Dale Hollow L., *U.S.A.* 109 G3
Dalga, *Egypt* 80 B3
Dalgān, *Iran* 71 E8
Dalhart, *U.S.A.* 113 G3
Dalhousie, *Canada* 103 C6
Dalhousie, *India* 68 C6
Dali, *Shaanxi, China* 56 G5
Dali, *Yunnan, China* 58 E3
Dalian, *China* 57 E11
Daliang Shan, *China* 58 D4
Daling He →, *China* 57 D11
Dāliyat el Karmel, *Israel* 75 C4
Dalj, *Croatia* 42 E3
Dalkeith, *U.K.* 14 F5
Dallas, *Oreg., U.S.A.* 114 D2
Dallas, *Tex., U.S.A.* 113 J6
Dallol, *Ethiopia* 81 E5
Dalmā, *U.A.E.* 71 E7
Dalmacija, *Croatia* 29 E13
Dalmas, L., *Canada* 103 B5
Dalmatia = Dalmacija, *Croatia* 29 E13
Dalmau, *India* 69 F9
Dalmellington, *U.K.* 14 F4
Dalnegorsk, *Russia* 51 E14
Dalnerechensk, *Russia* 51 E14
Daloa, *Ivory C.* 82 D3
Dalou Shan, *China* 58 C6
Dalry, *U.K.* 14 F4
Dalrymple, L., *Australia* 94 C4
Dals Långed, *Sweden* 11 F6
Dalsjöfors, *Sweden* 11 G7
Dalsland, *Sweden* 11 F6
Daltenganj, *India* 69 H11
Dalton, *Ga., U.S.A.* 109 H3
Dalton, *Mass., U.S.A.* 111 D11
Dalton, *Nebr., U.S.A.* 112 E3
Dalton Iceberg Tongue, *Antarctica* 5 C9
Dalton-in-Furness, *U.K.* 12 C4
Dalupiri I., *Phil.* 61 B4
Dalvík, *Iceland* 8 D4
Dalwallinu, *Australia* 93 F2
Daly →, *Australia* 92 B5
Daly City, *U.S.A.* 116 H4
Daly L., *Canada* 105 B7
Daly River, *Australia* 92 B5
Daly Waters, *Australia* 94 B1
Dalyan, *Turkey* 39 E10
Dam Doi, *Vietnam* 65 H5
Dam Ha, *Vietnam* 64 B6
Daman, *India* 66 J8
Dāmaneh, *Iran* 71 C6
Damanhûr, *Egypt* 80 H7
Damant L., *Canada* 105 A7
Damanzhuang, *China* 56 E9
Damar, *Indonesia* 63 F7
Damaraland, *Namibia* 88 C2
Damascus = Dimashq, *Syria* 75 B5
Damaturu, *Nigeria* 83 C7
Damāvand, *Iran* 71 C7
Damāvand, Qolleh-ye, *Iran* 71 C7
Damba, *Angola* 84 F3
Dâmboviţa □, *Romania* 43 F10
Dâmboviţa →, *Romania* 43 F11
Dâmbovnic →, *Romania* 43 F10
Dame Marie, *Haiti* 121 C5
Dāmghān, *Iran* 71 B7
Dămienesti, *Romania* 43 D11
Damietta = Dumyât, *Egypt* 80 H7
Daming, *China* 56 F8
Damīr Qābū, *Syria* 70 B4
Dammam = Ad Dammām, *Si. Arabia* 71 E6
Dammarie-les-Lys, *France* 19 D9
Dammartin-en-Goële, *France* 19 C9
Damme, *Germany* 24 C4
Damodar →, *India* 69 H12
Damoh, *India* 69 H8
Dampier, *Australia* 92 D2
Dampier, Selat, *Indonesia* 63 E8
Dampier Arch., *Australia* 92 D2
Damrei, Chuor Phnum, *Cambodia* 65 G4
Damvillers, *France* 19 C12
Dan-Gulbi, *Nigeria* 83 C6
Dan Xian, *China* 64 C7
Dana, *Indonesia* 63 F6
Dana, L., *Canada* 102 B4
Dana, Mt., *U.S.A.* 116 H7
Danakil Desert, *Ethiopia* 81 E5
Danané, *Ivory C.* 82 D3
Danao, *Phil.* 61 F6
Danau Poso, *Indonesia* 63 E6
Danba, *China* 58 B3
Danbury, *U.S.A.* 111 E11
Danby L., *U.S.A.* 115 J6
Dand, *Afghan.* 68 D1
Dandeldhura, *Nepal* 69 E9
Dandeli, *India* 66 M9
Dandenong, *Australia* 95 F4
Dandîl, *Egypt* 80 J7
Dandong, *China* 57 D13
Danfeng, *China* 56 H6
Dangan Liedao, *China* 59 F10
Dangé-St-Romain, *France* 20 B4
Dângeni, *Romania* 43 C11
Danger Is. = Pukapuka, *Cook Is.* 97 J11
Danger Pt., *S. Africa* 88 E2
Dangla, *Ethiopia* 81 E4
Dangla Shan = Tanggula Shan, *China* 60 C4
Dangora, *Nigeria* 83 C6
Dangouadougou, *Burkina Faso* 82 D4
Dangrek, Phnom, *Thailand* 64 E5
Dangriga, *Belize* 119 D7
Dangshan, *China* 56 G9
Dangtu, *China* 59 B12
Dangyang, *China* 59 B8
Dani, *Burkina Faso* 83 C4
Daniel, *U.S.A.* 114 E8
Daniel's Harbour, *Canada* 103 B8
Danielskuil, *S. Africa* 88 D3
Danielson, *U.S.A.* 111 E13
Danilov, *Russia* 46 C11
Danilovgrad, *Montenegro, Yug.* 40 D3
Danilovka, *Russia* 48 E7
Daning, *China* 56 F6
Danissa, *Kenya* 86 B5
Danja, *Nigeria* 83 C6
Danjiangkou, *China* 59 A8
Danjiangkou Shuiku, *China* 59 A8
Dank, *Oman* 71 F8
Dankalwa, *Nigeria* 83 C7
Dankama, *Nigeria* 83 C6
Dankhar Gompa, *India* 66 C11
Dankov, *Russia* 46 F10
Danleng, *China* 58 B4
Danlí, *Honduras* 120 D2
Dannemora, *U.S.A.* 111 B11
Dannenberg, *Germany* 24 B7
Dannevirke, *N.Z.* 91 J6
Dannhauser, *S. Africa* 89 D5
Dansville, *U.S.A.* 110 D7
Danta, *India* 68 G5
Dantan, *India* 69 J12
Dante, *Somali Rep.* 74 E5
Danube = Dunărea →, *Europe* 43 E14
Danvers, *U.S.A.* 111 D14
Danville, *Ill., U.S.A.* 108 E2
Danville, *Ky., U.S.A.* 108 G3
Danville, *Pa., U.S.A.* 111 F8
Danville, *Va., U.S.A.* 109 G6
Danville, *Vt., U.S.A.* 111 B12
Danyang, *China* 59 B12
Danzhai, *China* 58 D6
Danzig = Gdańsk, *Poland* 44 D5
Dão →, *Portugal* 34 E2
Dao Xian, *China* 59 E8
Daocheng, *China* 58 C3
Daoukro, *Ivory C.* 82 D4
Dapaong, *Togo* 83 C5
Dapchi, *Nigeria* 83 C7
Dapitan, *Phil.* 61 G5
Daqing Shan, *China* 56 D6
Daqu Shan, *China* 59 B14
Dar Banda, *Africa* 76 F6
Dar el Beida = Casablanca, *Morocco* 78 B4
Dar es Salaam, *Tanzania* 86 D4
Dar Mazār, *Iran* 71 D8
Dar'ā, *Syria* 75 C5
Dar'ā □, *Syria* 75 C5
Dārāb, *Iran* 71 D7
Daraban, *Pakistan* 68 D4
Darabani, *Romania* 43 B11
Daraina, *Madag.* 89 A8
Daraj, *Libya* 79 B8
Dārān, *Iran* 71 C6
Daravica, *Kosovo, Yug.* 40 D4
Daraw, *Egypt* 80 C3
Dārayyā, *Syria* 75 B5
Darazo, *Nigeria* 83 C7
Darband, *Pakistan* 68 B5
Darband, Kūh-e, *Iran* 71 D8
Darbhanga, *India* 69 F11
D'Arcy, *Canada* 104 C4
Darda, *Croatia* 42 E3
Dardanelle, *Ark., U.S.A.* 113 H8
Dardanelle, *Calif., U.S.A.* 116 G7
Dardanelles = Çanakkale Boğazı, *Turkey* 41 F10
Dare →, *Ethiopia* 81 F5
Darende, *Turkey* 72 C7
Dārestān, *Iran* 71 D8
Darfo, *Italy* 28 C7
Dârfûr, *Sudan* 79 F10
Dargai, *Pakistan* 68 B4
Dargan Ata, *Turkmenistan* 50 E7
Dargaville, *N.Z.* 91 F4
Dargol, *Niger* 83 C5
Darhan Muminggan Lianheqi, *China* 56 D6
Dari, *Sudan* 81 F3
Darıca, *Turkey* 72 B3
Darién, G. del, *Colombia* 122 C3
Dariganga = Ovoot, *Mongolia* 56 B7
Darinskoye, *Kazakstan* 48 E10
Darjeeling = Darjiling, *India* 69 F13
Darjiling, *India* 69 F13
Darkan, *Australia* 93 F2
Darkhana, *Pakistan* 68 D5
Darkhazīneh, *Iran* 71 D6
Darkot Pass, *Pakistan* 69 A5
Darling Downs, *Australia* 95 D5
Darling Ra., *Australia* 93 F2
Darlington, *U.K.* 12 C6
Darlington, *U.S.A.* 109 H6
Darlington □, *U.K.* 12 C6
Darlington, L., *S. Africa* 88 E4
Darlot, L., *Australia* 93 E3
Darłowo, *Poland* 44 D3
Dărmăneşti, *Bacău, Romania* 43 D11
Dărmăneşti, *Suceava, Romania* 43 C11
Darmstadt, *Germany* 25 F4
Darnah, *Libya* 79 B10
Darnall, *S. Africa* 89 D5
Darney, *France* 19 D13
Darnley, C., *Antarctica* 5 C6
Darnley B., *Canada* 100 B7
Daroca, *Spain* 32 D3
Darou-Mousti, *Senegal* 82 B1
Darr →, *Australia* 94 C3
Darra Pezu, *Pakistan* 68 C4
Darrequeira, *Argentina* 126 D3
Darrington, *U.S.A.* 114 B3
Darsser Ort, *Germany* 24 A8
Dart →, *U.K.* 13 G4
Dart, C., *Antarctica* 5 D14
Dartford, *U.K.* 13 F8
Dartmoor, *U.K.* 13 G4
Dartmouth, *Canada* 103 D7
Dartmouth, *U.K.* 13 G4
Dartmouth, L., *Australia* 95 D4
Dartmouth Res., *Australia* 95 D4
Dartuch, C. = Artrutx, C. de, *Spain* 37 B10
Daruvar, *Croatia* 42 E2
Darvaza, *Turkmenistan* 50 E6
Darvel, Teluk = Lahad Datu, Teluk, *Malaysia* 63 D5
Darwen, *U.K.* 12 D5
Darwendale, *Zimbabwe* 89 B5
Darwha, *India* 66 J10
Darwin, *Australia* 92 B5
Darwin, *U.S.A.* 117 J9
Darya Khan, *Pakistan* 68 D4
Daryoi Amu = Amudarya →, *Uzbekistan* 50 E6
Dās, *U.A.E.* 71 E7

Dashen, Ras, *Ethiopia* 81 E4
Dashetai, *China* 56 D5
Dashhowuz, *Turkmenistan* 50 E6
Dashkesan = Daşkäsän, *Azerbaijan* 49 K7
Dashköpri, *Turkmenistan* 71 B9
Dasht, *Iran* 71 B8
Dasht →, *Pakistan* 66 G2
Daska, *Pakistan* 68 C6
Daşkäsän, *Azerbaijan* 49 K7
Dassa, *Benin* 83 D5
Dasuya, *India* 68 D6
Datça, *Turkey* 39 E9
Datia, *India* 69 G8
Datian, *China* 59 E11
Datong, *Anhui, China* 59 B11
Datong, *Shanxi, China* 56 D7
Dattakhel, *Pakistan* 68 C3
Datteln, *Germany* 24 D3
Datu, Tanjung, *Indonesia* 62 D3
Datu Piang, *Phil.* 61 H6
Datuk, Tanjong = Datu, Tanjung, *Indonesia* 62 D3
Daud Khel, *Pakistan* 68 C4
Daudnagar, *India* 69 G11
Daugava →, *Latvia* 9 H21
Daugavpils, *Latvia* 9 J22
Daulpur, *India* 68 F7
Daun, *Germany* 25 E2
Dauphin, *Canada* 105 C8
Dauphin, *U.S.A.* 110 F8
Dauphin L., *Canada* 105 C9
Dauphiné, *France* 21 C9
Daura, *Borno, Nigeria* 83 C7
Daura, *Katsina, Nigeria* 83 C6
Dausa, *India* 68 F7
Däväçi, *Azerbaijan* 49 K9
Davangere, *India* 66 M9
Davao, *Phil.* 61 H6
Davao G., *Phil.* 61 H6
Dāvar Panāh, *Iran* 71 E9
Davenport, *Calif., U.S.A.* 116 H4
Davenport, *Iowa, U.S.A.* 112 E9
Davenport, *Wash., U.S.A.* 114 C4
Davenport Ra., *Australia* 94 C1
Daventry, *U.K.* 13 E6
David, *Panama* 120 E3
David City, *U.S.A.* 112 E6
David Gorodok = Davyd Haradok, *Belarus* 47 F4
Davidson, *Canada* 105 C7
Davis, *U.S.A.* 116 G5
Davis Dam, *U.S.A.* 117 K12
Davis Inlet, *Canada* 103 A7
Davis Mts., *U.S.A.* 113 K2
Davis Sea, *Antarctica* 5 C7
Davis Str., *N. Amer.* 101 B14
Davo →, *Ivory C.* 82 D3
Davos, *Switz.* 25 J5
Davutlar, *Turkey* 39 D9
Davy L., *Canada* 105 B7
Davyd Haradok, *Belarus* 47 F4
Dawa →, *Ethiopia* 81 G5
Dawaki, *Bauchi, Nigeria* 83 D6
Dawaki, *Kano, Nigeria* 83 C6
Dawei, *Burma* 64 E2
Dawes Ra., *Australia* 94 C5
Dawlish, *U.K.* 13 G4
Dawna Ra., *Burma* 64 D2
Dawros Hd., *Ireland* 15 B3
Dawson, *Canada* 100 B6
Dawson, *U.S.A.* 109 K3
Dawson, I., *Chile* 128 G2
Dawson B., *Canada* 105 C8
Dawson Creek, *Canada* 104 B4
Dawson Inlet, *Canada* 105 A10
Dawson Ra., *Australia* 94 C4
Dawu, *Hubei, China* 59 B9
Dawu, *Sichuan, China* 58 B3
Dax, *France* 20 E2
Daxian, *China* 58 B6
Daxin, *China* 58 F6
Daxindian, *China* 57 F11
Daxinggou, *China* 57 C15
Daxue Shan, *Sichuan, China* 58 B3
Daxue Shan, *Yunnan, China* 58 F2
Dayao, *China* 58 E3
Daye, *China* 59 B10
Dayet en Naharat, *Mali* 82 B4
Dayi, *China* 58 B4
Daylesford, *Australia* 95 F3
Dayong, *China* 59 C8
Dayr az Zawr, *Syria* 70 C4
Daysland, *Canada* 104 C6
Dayton, *Nev., U.S.A.* 116 F7
Dayton, *Ohio, U.S.A.* 108 F3
Dayton, *Pa., U.S.A.* 110 F5
Dayton, *Tenn., U.S.A.* 109 H3
Dayton, *Wash., U.S.A.* 114 C4
Dayton, *Wyo., U.S.A.* 114 D10
Daytona Beach, *U.S.A.* 109 L5
Dayu, *China* 59 E10
Dayville, *U.S.A.* 114 D4
Dazhu, *China* 58 B6
Dazkırı, *Turkey* 39 D11
Dazu, *China* 58 C5
De Aar, *S. Africa* 88 E3
De Funiak Springs, *U.S.A.* 109 K2
De Grey →, *Australia* 92 D2
De Haan, *Belgium* 17 C3
De Kalb, *U.S.A.* 112 E10
De Land, *U.S.A.* 109 L5
De Leon, *U.S.A.* 113 J5
De Panne, *Belgium* 17 C2
De Pere, *U.S.A.* 108 C1
De Queen, *U.S.A.* 113 H7
De Quincy, *U.S.A.* 113 K8
De Ridder, *U.S.A.* 113 K8
De Smet, *U.S.A.* 112 C6
De Soto, *U.S.A.* 112 F9
De Tour Village, *U.S.A.* 108 C4
De Witt, *U.S.A.* 113 H9
Dead Sea, *Asia* 75 D4
Deadwood, *U.S.A.* 112 C3
Deadwood L., *Canada* 104 B3
Deal, *U.K.* 13 F9
Deal I., *Australia* 94 F4
Dealesville, *S. Africa* 88 D4
De'an, *China* 59 C10
Dean →, *Canada* 104 C3
Dean, Forest of, *U.K.* 13 F5
Dean Chan., *Canada* 104 C3
Deán Funes, *Argentina* 126 C3
Dease →, *Canada* 104 B3
Dease L., *Canada* 104 B2
Dease Lake, *Canada* 104 B2
Death Valley, *U.S.A.* 117 J10
Death Valley Junction, *U.S.A.* 117 J10
Death Valley National Park, *U.S.A.* 117 J10
Deauville, *France* 18 C7
Deba, *Spain* 32 B2
Deba Habe, *Nigeria* 83 C7
Debaltsevo, *Ukraine* 47 H10
Debao, *China* 58 F6
Debar, *Macedonia* 40 E4
Debden, *Canada* 105 C7
Dębica, *Poland* 45 H8
Dęblin, *Poland* 45 G8
Dębno, *Poland* 45 F1
Débo, L., *Mali* 82 B4
Debolt, *Canada* 104 B5
Deborah East, L., *Australia* 93 F2
Deborah West, L., *Australia* 93 F2
Debrc, *Serbia, Yug.* 40 B3
Debre Birhan, *Ethiopia* 81 F4
Debre Markos, *Ethiopia* 81 E4
Debre May, *Ethiopia* 81 E4
Debre Sina, *Ethiopia* 81 F4
Debre Tabor, *Ethiopia* 81 E4
Debre Zevit, *Ethiopia* 81 F4
Debre Zeyit, *Ethiopia* 81 E4
Debrecen, *Hungary* 42 C6
Debrzno, *Poland* 44 E4
Dečani, *Kosovo, Yug.* 40 D4
Decatur, *Ala., U.S.A.* 109 H2
Decatur, *Ga., U.S.A.* 109 J3
Decatur, *Ill., U.S.A.* 112 F10
Decatur, *Ind., U.S.A.* 108 E3
Decatur, *Tex., U.S.A.* 113 J6
Decazeville, *France* 20 D6
Deccan, *India* 66 L11
Deception Bay, *Australia* 95 D5
Deception L., *Canada* 105 B8
Dechang, *China* 58 D4
Dechhu, *India* 68 F5
Děčín, *Czech Rep.* 26 A7
Decize, *France* 19 F10
Deckerville, *U.S.A.* 110 C2
Decollatura, *Italy* 31 C9
Decorah, *U.S.A.* 112 D9
Deda, *Romania* 43 D9
Dedéagach = Alexandroúpolis, *Greece* 41 F9
Deder, *Ethiopia* 81 F5
Dedham, *U.S.A.* 111 D13
Dédougou, *Burkina Faso* 82 C4
Dedovichi, *Russia* 46 D5
Dedza, *Malawi* 87 E3
Dee →, *Aberds., U.K.* 14 D6
Dee →, *Dumf. & Gall., U.K.* 14 G4
Dee →, *Wales, U.K.* 12 D4
Deep B., *Canada* 104 A5
Deepwater, *Australia* 95 D5
Deer →, *Canada* 105 B10
Deer L., *Canada* 105 C10
Deer Lake, *Nfld., Canada* 103 C8
Deer Lake, *Ont., Canada* 105 C10
Deer Lodge, *U.S.A.* 114 C7
Deer Park, *U.S.A.* 114 C5
Deer River, *U.S.A.* 112 B8
Deeragun, *Australia* 94 B4
Deerdepoort, *S. Africa* 88 C4
Deferiet, *U.S.A.* 111 B9
Defiance, *U.S.A.* 108 E3
Degana, *India* 68 F6
Dêgê, *China* 58 B2
Degebe →, *Portugal* 35 G3
Degeberga, *Sweden* 11 J8
Dégelis, *Canada* 103 C6
Degema, *Nigeria* 83 E6
Degerfors, *Sweden* 10 E8
Degerhamn, *Sweden* 11 H10
Deggendorf, *Germany* 25 G8
Degh →, *Pakistan* 68 D5
Değirmendere, *Turkey* 41 F13
Deh Bīd, *Iran* 71 D7
Deh-e Shīr, *Iran* 71 D7
Dehaj, *Iran* 71 D7
Dehak, *Iran* 71 E9
Dehdez, *Iran* 71 D6
Dehej, *India* 68 J5
Dehestān, *Iran* 71 D7
Dehgolān, *Iran* 70 C5
Dehibat, *Tunisia* 79 B8
Dehlorān, *Iran* 70 C5
Dehnow-e Kūhestān, *Iran* 71 E8
Dehra Dun, *India* 68 D8
Dehri, *India* 69 G11
Dehua, *China* 59 E12
Dehui, *China* 57 B13
Deim Zubeir, *Sudan* 81 F2
Deinze, *Belgium* 17 D3
Dej, *Romania* 43 C8
Deje, *Sweden* 10 E7
Dejiang, *China* 58 C7
Deka →, *Zimbabwe* 88 B4
Dekemhare, *Eritrea* 81 D4
Dekese, *Dem. Rep. of the Congo* 84 E4
Del Mar, *U.S.A.* 117 N9
Del Norte, *U.S.A.* 115 H10
Del Rio, *U.S.A.* 113 L4
Delai, *Sudan* 80 D4
Delambre I., *Australia* 92 D2
Delami, *Sudan* 81 E3
Delano, *U.S.A.* 117 K7
Delano Peak, *U.S.A.* 115 G7
Delareyville, *S. Africa* 88 D4
Delaronde L., *Canada* 105 C7
Delavan, *U.S.A.* 112 D10
Delaware, *U.S.A.* 108 E4
Delaware □, *U.S.A.* 108 F8
Delaware →, *U.S.A.* 111 G9
Delaware B., *U.S.A.* 108 F8
Delay →, *Canada* 103 A5
Delbrück, *Germany* 24 D4
Delčevo, *Macedonia* 40 E6
Delegate, *Australia* 95 F4
Delémont, *Switz.* 25 H3
Delevan, *U.S.A.* 110 D6
Delft, *Neths.* 17 B4
Delfzijl, *Neths.* 17 A6
Delgado, C., *Mozam.* 87 E5
Delgerhet, *Mongolia* 56 B6
Delgo, *Sudan* 80 C3
Delhi, *Canada* 110 D4
Delhi, *India* 68 E7
Delhi, *La., U.S.A.* 113 J9
Delhi, *N.Y., U.S.A.* 111 D10
Deli Jovan, *Serbia, Yug.* 40 B6
Delia, *Canada* 104 C6
Delice, *Turkey* 72 C6
Delicias, *Mexico* 118 B3
Delījān, *Iran* 71 C6
Déline, *Canada* 100 B7
Delisle, *Canada* 105 C7
Delitzsch, *Germany* 24 D8
Dell City, *U.S.A.* 115 L11
Dell Rapids, *U.S.A.* 112 D6
Delle, *France* 19 E14
Delmar, *U.S.A.* 111 D11
Delmenhorst, *Germany* 24 B4
Delnice, *Croatia* 29 C11
Delonga, Ostrova, *Russia* 51 B15
Deloraine, *Australia* 94 G4
Deloraine, *Canada* 105 D8
Delphi, *Greece* 38 C4
Delphi, *U.S.A.* 108 E2
Delphos, *U.S.A.* 108 E3
Delportshoop, *S. Africa* 88 D3
Delray Beach, *U.S.A.* 109 M5
Delsbo, *Sweden* 10 C10
Delta, *Colo., U.S.A.* 115 G9
Delta, *Utah, U.S.A.* 114 G7
Delta □, *Nigeria* 83 D6
Delta Junction, *U.S.A.* 100 B5
Deltona, *U.S.A.* 109 L5
Delungra, *Australia* 95 D5
Delvada, *India* 68 J4
Delvinákion, *Greece* 38 B2
Delvinë, *Albania* 40 G4
Demak, *Indonesia* 63 G14
Demanda, Sierra de la, *Spain* 32 C2
Demavand = Damāvand, *Iran* 71 C7
Dembecha, *Ethiopia* 81 E4
Dembi, *Ethiopia* 81 F4
Dembia, *Dem. Rep. of the Congo* 86 B2
Dembidolo, *Ethiopia* 81 F3
Demchok, *India* 69 C8
Demer →, *Belgium* 17 D4
Demetrias, *Greece* 38 B5
Demidov, *Russia* 46 E6
Deming, *N. Mex., U.S.A.* 115 K10
Deming, *Wash., U.S.A.* 116 B4
Demini →, *Brazil* 124 D6
Demirci, *Turkey* 39 B10
Demirköprü Barajı, *Turkey* 39 C10
Demirköy, *Turkey* 41 E11
Demmin, *Germany* 24 B9
Demonte, *Italy* 28 D4
Demopolis, *U.S.A.* 109 J2
Dempo, *Indonesia* 62 E2
Demyansk, *Russia* 46 D7
Den Burg, *Neths.* 17 A4
Den Chai, *Thailand* 64 D3
Den Haag = 's-Gravenhage, *Neths.* 17 B4
Den Helder, *Neths.* 17 B4
Den Oever, *Neths.* 17 B5
Denain, *France* 19 B10
Denair, *U.S.A.* 116 H6
Denau, *Uzbekistan* 50 F7
Denbigh, *Canada* 110 A7
Denbigh, *U.K.* 12 D4
Denbighshire □, *U.K.* 12 D4
Dendang, *Indonesia* 62 E3
Dendermonde, *Belgium* 17 C4
Deneba, *Ethiopia* 81 F4
Dengchuan, *China* 58 E3
Denge, *Nigeria* 83 C6
Dengfeng, *China* 56 G7
Dengi, *Nigeria* 83 D6
Dengkou, *China* 56 D4
Dengzhou, *China* 59 A9
Denham, *Australia* 93 E1
Denham Ra., *Australia* 94 C4
Denham Sd., *Australia* 93 E1
Denholm, *Canada* 105 C7
Denia, *Spain* 33 G5
Denial B., *Australia* 95 E1
Deniliquin, *Australia* 95 F3
Denison, *Iowa, U.S.A.* 112 E7
Denison, *Tex., U.S.A.* 113 J6
Denison Plains, *Australia* 92 C4
Denizli, *Turkey* 39 D11
Denizli □, *Turkey* 39 D11
Denman Glacier, *Antarctica* 5 C7
Denmark, *Australia* 93 F2
Denmark ■, *Europe* 11 J3
Denmark Str., *Atl. Oc.* 4 C6
Dennison, *U.S.A.* 110 F3
Denny, *U.K.* 14 E5
Denpasar, *Indonesia* 62 F5
Denton, *Mont., U.S.A.* 114 C9
Denton, *Tex., U.S.A.* 113 J6
D'Entrecasteaux, Pt., *Australia* 93 F2
Denu, *Ghana* 83 D5
Denver, *Colo., U.S.A.* 112 F2
Denver, *Pa., U.S.A.* 111 F8
Denver City, *U.S.A.* 113 J3
Deoband, *India* 68 E7
Deogarh, *India* 68 G5
Deoghar, *India* 69 G12
Deolali, *India* 66 K8
Deoli = Devli, *India* 68 G6
Déols, *France* 19 F8
Deora, *India* 68 F4
Deori, *India* 69 H8
Deoria, *India* 69 F10
Deosai Mts., *Pakistan* 69 B6
Deosri, *India* 69 F14
Depalpur, *India* 68 H6
Deping, *China* 57 F9
Deposit, *U.S.A.* 111 D9
Depuch I., *Australia* 92 D2
Deputatskiy, *Russia* 51 C14
Dêqên, *China* 58 C2
Deqing, *China* 59 F8
Dera Ghazi Khan, *Pakistan* 68 D4
Dera Ismail Khan, *Pakistan* 68 D4
Derabugti, *Pakistan* 68 E3
Derawar Fort, *Pakistan* 68 E4
Derbent, *Russia* 49 J9
Derbent, *Turkey* 39 C10
Derby, *Australia* 92 C3
Derby, *U.K.* 12 E6
Derby, *Conn., U.S.A.* 111 E11
Derby, *Kans., U.S.A.* 113 G6
Derby, *N.Y., U.S.A.* 110 D6
Derby City □, *U.K.* 12 E6
Derby Line, *U.S.A.* 111 B12
Derbyshire □, *U.K.* 12 D6
Derecske, *Hungary* 42 C6
Dereköy, *Turkey* 41 E11
Dereli, *Turkey* 73 B8
Derg →, *U.K.* 15 B4
Derg, L., *Ireland* 15 D3
Dergachi = Derhaci, *Ukraine* 47 G9
Dergaon, *India* 67 F19
Derhaci, *Ukraine* 47 G9
Derik, *Turkey* 73 D9
Derinkuyu, *Turkey* 72 C6
Dermantsi, *Bulgaria* 41 C8
Dermott, *U.S.A.* 113 J9
Dêrong, *China* 58 C2
Derry = Londonderry, *U.K.* 15 B4
Derry = Londonderry □, *U.K.* 15 B4
Derry, *N.H., U.S.A.* 111 D13
Derry, *Pa., U.S.A.* 110 F5
Derryveagh Mts., *Ireland* 15 B3
Derudub, *Sudan* 80 D4
Derval, *France* 18 E5
Dervéni, *Greece* 38 C4
Derventa, *Bos.-H.* 42 F2
Derwent →, *Cumb., U.K.* 12 C4
Derwent →, *Derby, U.K.* 12 E6
Derwent →, *N. Yorks., U.K.* 12 D7
Derwent Water, *U.K.* 12 C4
Des Moines, *Iowa, U.S.A.* 112 E8
Des Moines, *N. Mex., U.S.A.* 113 G3
Des Moines →, *U.S.A.* 112 E9
Desa, *Romania* 42 G8
Desaguadero →, *Argentina* 126 C2
Desaguadero →, *Bolivia* 124 G5
Descanso, Pta., *Mexico* 117 N9
Descartes, *France* 20 B4
Deschaillons, *Canada* 103 C5
Deschambault L., *Canada* 105 C8
Deschutes →, *U.S.A.* 114 D3
Dese, *Ethiopia* 81 E4
Deseado →, *Argentina* 128 F3
Desenzano del Garda, *Italy* 28 C7
Desert Center, *U.S.A.* 117 M11
Desert Hot Springs, *U.S.A.* 117 M10
Deshnok, *India* 68 F5
Desna →, *Ukraine* 47 G6
Desnătui →, *Romania* 43 G8
Desolación, I., *Chile* 128 G2
Despeñaperros, Paso, *Spain* 35 G7
Despotovac, *Serbia, Yug.* 40 B5
Dessau, *Germany* 24 D8
Dessye = Dese, *Ethiopia* 81 E4
D'Estrees B., *Australia* 95 F2
Desuri, *India* 68 G5
Desvres, *France* 19 B8
Det Udom, *Thailand* 64 E5
Deta, *Romania* 42 E6
Dete, *Zimbabwe* 88 B4
Đetinja →, *Serbia, Yug.* 40 C4
Detmold, *Germany* 24 D4
Detour, Pt., *U.S.A.* 108 C2
Detroit, *U.S.A.* 110 D1
Detroit Lakes, *U.S.A.* 112 B7
Detva, *Slovak Rep.* 27 C12
Deurne, *Neths.* 17 C5
Deutsche Bucht, *Germany* 24 A4
Deutschlandsberg, *Austria* 26 E8
Deux-Sèvres □, *France* 18 F6
Deva, *Romania* 42 E7
Devakottai, *India* 66 Q11
Devaprayag, *India* 69 D8
Dévaványa, *Hungary* 42 C5
Deveci Dağları, *Turkey* 72 B7
Devecikonağı, *Turkey* 41 G12
Devecser, *Hungary* 42 C2
Develi, *Turkey* 72 C6
Deventer, *Neths.* 17 B6
Deveron →, *U.K.* 14 D6
Devesel, *Romania* 42 F7
Devgadh Bariya, *India* 68 H5
Devikot, *India* 68 F4
Devils Den, *U.S.A.* 116 K7
Devils Lake, *U.S.A.* 112 A5
Devils Paw, *Canada* 104 B2
Devils Tower Junction, *U.S.A.* 112 C2
Devin, *Bulgaria* 41 E8
Devine, *U.S.A.* 113 L5
Devizes, *U.K.* 13 F6
Devli, *India* 68 G6
Devnya, *Bulgaria* 41 C11
Devoll →, *Albania* 40 F4
Devon, *Canada* 104 C6
Devon □, *U.K.* 13 G4
Devon I., *Canada* 4 B3
Devonport, *Australia* 94 G4
Devonport, *N.Z.* 91 G5
Devrek, *Turkey* 72 B4
Devrekâni, *Turkey* 72 B5
Devrez →, *Turkey* 72 B6
Dewas, *India* 68 H7
Dewetsdorp, *S. Africa* 88 D4
Dexing, *China* 59 C11
Dexter, *Maine, U.S.A.* 109 C11
Dexter, *Mo., U.S.A.* 113 G10
Dexter, *N. Mex., U.S.A.* 113 J2
Dey-Dey, L., *Australia* 93 E5
Deyang, *China* 58 B5
Deyhūk, *Iran* 71 C8
Deyyer, *Iran* 71 E6
Dezadeash L., *Canada* 104 A1
Dezfūl, *Iran* 71 C6
Dezhneva, Mys, *Russia* 51 C19
Dezhou, *China* 56 F9
Dhadhar →, *India* 69 G11
Dháfni, *Kríti, Greece* 36 D7
Dháfni, *Pelóponnisos, Greece* 38 D4
Dhahabān, *Si. Arabia* 80 C4
Dhahiriya = Az Zāhirīyah, *West Bank* 75 D3
Dhahran = Az Zahrān, *Si. Arabia* 71 E6
Dhak, *Pakistan* 68 C5
Dhaka, *Bangla.* 69 H14
Dhaka □, *Bangla.* 69 G14
Dhali, *Cyprus* 36 D12
Dhamási, *Greece* 38 B4
Dhampur, *India* 69 E8
Dhamtari, *India* 67 J12
Dhanbad, *India* 69 H12
Dhangarhi, *Nepal* 67 E12
Dhankuta, *Nepal* 69 F12
Dhar, *India* 68 H6
Dharampur, *India* 68 H6
Dharamsala = Dharmsala, *India* 68 C7
Dhariwal, *India* 68 D6
Dharla →, *Bangla.* 69 G13
Dharmapuri, *India* 66 N11
Dharmjaygarh, *India* 69 H10
Dharmsala, *India* 68 C7
Dharni, *India* 68 J7
Dharwad, *India* 66 M9
Dhasan →, *India* 69 G8
Dhaulagiri, *Nepal* 69 E10
Dhebar, L., *India* 68 G6
Dheftera, *Cyprus* 36 D12
Dhenkanal, *India* 67 J14
Dhenoúsa, *Greece* 39 D7
Dherinia, *Cyprus* 36 D12
Dheskáti, *Greece* 40 G5
Dhespotikó, *Greece* 38 E6
Dhestina, *Greece* 38 C4
Dhiarrizos →, *Cyprus* 36 E11
Dhībān, *Jordan* 75 D4
Dhidhimótikhon, *Greece* 41 E10
Dhíkti Óros, *Greece* 36 D7
Dhilianáta, *Greece* 38 C2
Dhílos, *Greece* 39 D7
Dhilwan, *India* 68 D6
Dhimarkhera, *India* 69 H9
Dhimitsána, *Greece* 38 D4
Dhírfis Óros, *Greece* 38 C5
Dhodhekánisos, *Greece* 39 E8
Dhodhekánisos □, *Greece* 39 E8
Dhokós, *Greece* 38 D5
Dholiana, *Greece* 38 B2
Dholka, *India* 68 H5
Dhomokós, *Greece* 38 B4
Dhoraji, *India* 68 J4
Dhoxáton, *Greece* 41 E8
Dhragonísi, *Greece* 39 D7
Dhráhstis, Ákra, *Greece* 36 A3
Dhrangadhra, *India* 68 H4
Dhrápanon, Ákra, *Greece* 36 D6
Dhriopís, *Greece* 38 D6
Dhrol, *India* 68 H4
Dhuburi, *India* 67 F16
Dhule, *India* 66 J9
Di-ib, W. →, *Sudan* 80 C4
Di Linh, *Vietnam* 65 G7
Di Linh, Cao Nguyen, *Vietnam* 65 G7
Día, *Greece* 36 D7
Diabakania, *Guinea* 82 C2
Diablo, Mt., *U.S.A.* 116 H5
Diablo Range, *U.S.A.* 116 J5
Diafarabé, *Mali* 82 C4

Diala, *Mali* 82 C3
Dialakoro, *Mali* 82 C3
Dialakoto, *Senegal* 82 C2
Diallassagou, *Mali* 82 C4
Diamante, *Argentina* 126 C3
Diamante, *Italy* 31 C8
Diamante →, *Argentina* 126 C2
Diamantina, *Brazil* 125 G10
Diamantina →, *Australia* 95 D2
Diamantino, *Brazil* 125 F7
Diamond Bar, *U.S.A.* 117 L9
Diamond Harbour, *India* 69 H13
Diamond Is., *Australia* 94 B5
Diamond Mts., *U.S.A.* 114 G6
Diamond Springs, *U.S.A.* 116 G6
Dian Chi, *China* 58 E4
Dianalund, *Denmark* 11 J5
Dianbai, *China* 59 G8
Diancheng, *China* 59 G8
Dianjiang, *China* 58 B6
Diano Marina, *Italy* 28 E5
Dianra, *Ivory C.* 82 D3
Diapaga, *Burkina Faso* 83 C5
Diapangou, *Burkina Faso* 83 C5
Diariguila, *Guinea* 82 C2
Dībā, *Oman* 71 E8
Dibai, *India* 68 E8
Dibaya-Lubue, *Dem. Rep. of the Congo* 84 E3
Dibete, *Botswana* 88 C4
Dibrugarh, *India* 67 F19
Dickens, *U.S.A.* 113 J4
Dickinson, *U.S.A.* 112 B3
Dickson = Dikson, *Russia* 50 B9
Dickson, *U.S.A.* 109 G2
Dickson City, *U.S.A.* 111 E9
Dicle Nehri →, *Turkey* 73 D9
Dicomano, *Italy* 29 E8
Didesa, W. →, *Ethiopia* 81 E4
Didi, *Sudan* 81 F3
Didiéni, *Mali* 82 C3
Didsbury, *Canada* 104 C6
Didwana, *India* 68 F6
Die, *France* 21 D9
Diébougou, *Burkina Faso* 82 C4
Diecke, *Guinea* 82 D3
Diefenbaker, L., *Canada* 105 C7
Diego de Almagro, *Chile* 126 B1
Diego Garcia, *Ind. Oc.* 3 E13
Diekirch, *Lux.* 17 E6
Diéma, *Mali* 82 C3
Diembéring, *Senegal* 82 C1
Dien Ban, *Vietnam* 64 E7
Dien Bien, *Vietnam* 58 G4
Dien Khanh, *Vietnam* 65 F7
Diepholz, *Germany* 24 C4
Dieppe, *France* 18 C8
Dierks, *U.S.A.* 113 H8
Diest, *Belgium* 17 D5
Dietikon, *Switz.* 25 H4
Dieulefit, *France* 21 D9
Dieuze, *France* 19 D13
Dif, *Somali Rep.* 74 G3
Differdange, *Lux.* 17 E5
Dig, *India* 68 F7
Digba, *Dem. Rep. of the Congo* 86 B2
Digby, *Canada* 103 D6
Diggi, *India* 68 F6
Dighinala, *Bangla.* 67 H18
Dighton, *U.S.A.* 112 F4
Digna, *Mali* 82 C3
Digne-les-Bains, *France* 21 D10
Digoin, *France* 19 F11
Digor, *Turkey* 73 B10
Digos, *Phil.* 61 H6
Digranes, *Iceland* 8 C6
Digul →, *Indonesia* 63 F9
Dihang →, *India* 67 F19
Dijlah, Nahr →, *Asia* 70 D5
Dijon, *France* 19 E12
Dikhil, *Djibouti* 81 E5
Dikili, *Turkey* 39 B8
Dikirnis, *Egypt* 80 H7
Dikkil = Dikhil, *Djibouti* 81 E5
Dikodougou, *Ivory C.* 82 D3
Diksmuide, *Belgium* 17 C2
Dikson, *Russia* 50 B9
Dikwa, *Nigeria* 83 C7
Dila, *Ethiopia* 81 F4
Dili, *E. Timor* 63 F7
Dilijan, *Armenia* 49 K7
Dilizhan = Dilijan, *Armenia* 49 K7
Dilj, *Croatia* 42 E3
Dillenburg, *Germany* 24 E4
Dilley, *U.S.A.* 113 L5
Dilling, *Sudan* 81 E2
Dillingen, *Bayern, Germany* 25 G6
Dillingen, *Saarland, Germany* 25 F2
Dillingham, *U.S.A.* 100 C4
Dillon, *Canada* 105 B7
Dillon, *Mont., U.S.A.* 114 D7
Dillon, *S.C., U.S.A.* 109 H6
Dillon →, *Canada* 105 B7
Dillsburg, *U.S.A.* 110 F7
Dilly, *Mali* 82 C3
Dilolo, *Dem. Rep. of the Congo* 84 G4
Dimas, *Mexico* 118 C3
Dimashq, *Syria* 75 B5
Dimashq □, *Syria* 75 B5
Dimbaza, *S. Africa* 89 E4
Dimbokro, *Ivory C.* 82 D4
Dimboola, *Australia* 95 F3
Dîmbovița = Dâmbovița →, *Romania* 43 F11
Dimbulah, *Australia* 94 B4
Dimitrovgrad, *Bulgaria* 41 D9
Dimitrovgrad, *Russia* 48 C9
Dimitrovgrad, *Serbia, Yug.* 40 C6
Dimitrovo = Pernik, *Bulgaria* 40 D7
Dimmitt, *U.S.A.* 113 H3
Dimo, *Sudan* 81 F2
Dimona, *Israel* 75 D4
Dimovo, *Bulgaria* 40 C6
Dinagat, *Phil.* 61 F6
Dinajpur, *Bangla.* 67 G16
Dinan, *France* 18 D4
Dīnān Āb, *Iran* 71 C8
Dinant, *Belgium* 17 D4
Dinapur, *India* 69 G11
Dinar, *Turkey* 39 C12
Dīnār, Kūh-e, *Iran* 71 D6
Dinara Planina, *Croatia* 29 D13
Dinard, *France* 18 D4
Dinaric Alps = Dinara Planina, *Croatia* 29 D13
Dindanko, *Mali* 82 C3
Dinder, Nahr ed →, *Sudan* 81 E3
Dindigul, *India* 66 P11
Dindori, *India* 69 H9
Ding Xian = Dingzhou, *China* 56 E8
Dinga, *Pakistan* 68 G2
Dingalan, *Phil.* 61 D4
Dingbian, *China* 56 F4
Dingelstädt, *Germany* 24 D6
Dingle, *Ireland* 15 D1
Dingle, *Sweden* 11 F5
Dingle B., *Ireland* 15 D1
Dingmans Ferry, *U.S.A.* 111 E10
Dingnan, *China* 59 E10
Dingo, *Australia* 94 C4
Dingolfing, *Germany* 25 G8
Dingtao, *China* 56 G8
Dinguira, *Mali* 82 C2
Dinguiraye, *Guinea* 82 C2
Dingwall, *U.K.* 14 D4
Dingxi, *China* 56 G3
Dingxiang, *China* 56 E7
Dingyuan, *China* 59 A11
Dingzhou, *China* 56 E8
Dinh, Mui, *Vietnam* 65 G7
Dinh Lap, *Vietnam* 58 G6
Dinokwe, *Botswana* 88 C4
Dinorwic, *Canada* 105 D10
Dinosaur National Monument, *U.S.A.* 114 F9
Dinosaur Prov. Park, *Canada* 104 C6
Dinuba, *U.S.A.* 116 J7
Diö, *Sweden* 11 H8
Dioïla, *Mali* 82 C3
Dioka, *Mali* 82 C2
Diongoï, *Mali* 82 C3
Diósgyör, *Hungary* 42 B5
Diosig, *Romania* 42 C7
Diougani, *Mali* 82 C4
Diouloulou, *Senegal* 82 C1
Dioura, *Mali* 82 C3
Diourbel, *Senegal* 82 C1
Dipalpur, *Pakistan* 68 D5
Diplo, *Pakistan* 68 G3
Dipolog, *Phil.* 61 G5
Dir, *Pakistan* 66 B7
Diré, *Mali* 82 B4
Dire Dawa, *Ethiopia* 81 F5
Diriamba, *Nic.* 120 D2
Dirk Hartog I., *Australia* 93 E1
Dirranbandi, *Australia* 95 D4
Disa, *India* 68 G5
Disa, *Sudan* 81 E3
Disappointment, C., *U.S.A.* 114 C2
Disappointment, L., *Australia* 92 D3
Disaster B., *Australia* 95 F4
Discovery B., *Australia* 95 F3
Disentis Muster, *Switz.* 25 J4
Dishna, *Egypt* 80 B3
Disina, *Nigeria* 83 C6
Disko = Qeqertarsuaq, *Greenland* 101 B5
Disko Bugt, *Greenland* 4 C5
Disna = Dzisna →, *Belarus* 46 E5
Diss, *U.K.* 13 E9
Disteghil Sar, *Pakistan* 69 A6
Distrito Federal □, *Brazil* 125 G9
Distrito Federal □, *Mexico* 119 D5
Disūq, *Egypt* 80 H7
Diu, *India* 68 J4
Dīvāndarreh, *Iran* 70 C5
Dives →, *France* 18 C6
Dives-sur-Mer, *France* 18 C6
Divichi = Däväçi, *Azerbaijan* 49 K9
Divide, *U.S.A.* 114 D7
Dividing Ra., *Australia* 93 E2
Divinópolis, *Brazil* 125 H10
Divjake, *Albania* 40 F3
Divnoye, *Russia* 49 H6
Divo, *Ivory C.* 82 D3
Divriği, *Turkey* 73 C8
Dīwāl Kol, *Afghan.* 68 B2
Dixie Mt., *U.S.A.* 116 F6
Dixon, *Calif., U.S.A.* 116 G5
Dixon, *Ill., U.S.A.* 112 E10
Dixon Entrance, *U.S.A.* 100 C6
Dixville, *Canada* 111 A13
Diyadin, *Turkey* 73 C10
Diyālā →, *Iraq* 70 C5
Diyarbakır, *Turkey* 70 B4
Diyodar, *India* 68 G4
Djakarta = Jakarta, *Indonesia* 62 F3
Djamba, *Angola* 88 B1
Djambala, *Congo* 84 E2
Djanet, *Algeria* 78 D7
Djawa = Jawa, *Indonesia* 62 F3
Djelfa, *Algeria* 78 B6
Djema, *C.A.R.* 86 A2
Djenné, *Mali* 82 C4
Djerba, I. de, *Tunisia* 79 B8
Djerid, Chott, *Tunisia* 78 B7
Djibo, *Burkina Faso* 83 C4
Djibouti, *Djibouti* 81 E5
Djibouti ■, *Africa* 81 E5
Djolu, *Dem. Rep. of the Congo* 84 D4
Djougou, *Benin* 83 D5
Djoum, *Cameroon* 84 D2
Djourab, Erg du, *Chad* 79 E9
Djugu, *Dem. Rep. of the Congo* 86 B3
Djúpivogur, *Iceland* 8 D6
Djurås, *Sweden* 10 D9
Djursland, *Denmark* 11 H4
Dmitriya Lapteva, Proliv, *Russia* 51 B15
Dmitriyev Lgovskiy, *Russia* 47 F8
Dmitrov, *Russia* 46 D9
Dmitrovsk-Orlovskiy, *Russia* 47 F8
Dnepr → = Dnipro →, *Ukraine* 47 J7
Dneprodzerzhinsk = Dniprodzerzhynsk, *Ukraine* 47 H8
Dneprodzerzhinskoye Vdkhr. = Dniprodzerzhynske Vdskh., *Ukraine* 47 H8
Dnepropetrovsk = Dnipropetrovsk, *Ukraine* 47 H8
Dneprorudnoye = Dniprorudne, *Ukraine* 47 J8
Dnestr → = Dnister →, *Europe* 47 J6
Dnestrovski = Belgorod, *Russia* 47 G9
Dnieper = Dnipro →, *Ukraine* 47 J7
Dniester = Dnister →, *Europe* 47 J6
Dnipro →, *Ukraine* 47 J7
Dniprodzerzhynsk, *Ukraine* 47 H8
Dniprodzerzhynske Vdskh., *Ukraine* 47 H8
Dnipropetrovsk, *Ukraine* 47 H8
Dniprorudne, *Ukraine* 47 J8
Dnister →, *Europe* 47 J6
Dnistrovskyy Lyman, *Ukraine* 47 J6
Dno, *Russia* 46 D5
Dnyapro = Dnipro →, *Ukraine* 47 J7
Doaktown, *Canada* 103 C6
Doan Hung, *Vietnam* 58 G5
Doany, *Madag.* 89 A8
Doba, *Chad* 79 G9
Dobandi, *Pakistan* 68 D2
Dobbiaco, *Italy* 29 B9
Dobbyn, *Australia* 94 B3
Dobczyce, *Poland* 45 J7
Dobele, *Latvia* 9 H20
Dobele □, *Latvia* 44 B10
Döbeln, *Germany* 24 D9
Doberai, Jazirah, *Indonesia* 63 E8
Dobiegniew, *Poland* 45 F2
Doblas, *Argentina* 126 D3
Dobo, *Indonesia* 63 F8
Doboj, *Bos.-H.* 42 F3
Dobra, *Wielkopolskie, Poland* 45 G5
Dobra, *Zachodnio-Pomorskie, Poland* 44 E2
Dobra, *Dîmbovita, Romania* 43 F10
Dobra, *Hunedoara, Romania* 42 E7
Dobre Miasto, *Poland* 44 E7
Dobreşti, *Romania* 42 D7
Dobrich, *Bulgaria* 41 C11
Dobrinishta, *Bulgaria* 40 E7
Dobříš, *Czech Rep.* 26 B7
Dobrodzień, *Poland* 45 H5
Dobropole, *Ukraine* 47 H9
Dobruja, *Europe* 43 F13
Dobrush, *Belarus* 47 F6
Dobrzany, *Poland* 44 E2
Dobrzyń nad Wisłą, *Poland* 45 F6
Doc, Mui, *Vietnam* 64 D6
Docker River, *Australia* 93 D4
Dockste, *Sweden* 10 A12
Doctor Arroyo, *Mexico* 118 C4
Doda, *India* 69 C6
Doda, L., *Canada* 102 C4
Dodecanese = Dhodhekánisos, *Greece* 39 E8
Dodge City, *U.S.A.* 113 G5
Dodge L., *Canada* 105 B7
Dodgeville, *U.S.A.* 112 D9
Dodo, *Cameroon* 83 D7
Dodo, *Sudan* 81 F2
Dodola, *Ethiopia* 81 F4
Dodoma, *Tanzania* 86 D4
Dodoma □, *Tanzania* 86 D4
Dodona, *Greece* 38 B2
Dodsland, *Canada* 105 C7
Dodson, *U.S.A.* 114 B9
Dodurga, *Turkey* 39 B11
Doesburg, *Neths.* 17 B6
Doetinchem, *Neths.* 17 C6
Dog Creek, *Canada* 104 C4
Dog L., *Man., Canada* 105 C9
Dog L., *Ont., Canada* 102 C2
Doğanşehir, *Turkey* 72 C7
Dogliani, *Italy* 28 D4
Dogondoutchi, *Niger* 83 C5
Dogran, *Pakistan* 68 D5
Doğubayazıt, *Turkey* 70 B5
Doguéraoua, *Niger* 83 C6
Doha = Ad Dawḩah, *Qatar* 71 E6
Dohazari, *Bangla.* 67 H18
Dohrighat, *India* 69 F10
Doi, *Indonesia* 63 D7
Doi Luang, *Thailand* 64 C3
Doi Saket, *Thailand* 64 C2
Dois Irmãos, Sa., *Brazil* 125 E10
Dojransko Jezero, *Macedonia* 40 E6
Dokkum, *Neths.* 17 A5
Dokri, *Pakistan* 68 F3
Dokuchayevsk, *Ukraine* 47 J9
Dol-de-Bretagne, *France* 18 D5
Dolac, *Kosovo, Yug.* 40 D4
Dolak, Pulau, *Indonesia* 63 F9
Dolbeau, *Canada* 103 C5
Dole, *France* 19 E12
Doleib, Wadi →, *Sudan* 81 E3
Dolenji Logatec, *Slovenia* 29 C11
Dolgellau, *U.K.* 12 E4
Dolgelley = Dolgellau, *U.K.* 12 E4
Dolhasca, *Romania* 43 C11
Dolianova, *Italy* 30 C2
Dolinskaya = Dolynska, *Ukraine* 47 H7
Dolj □, *Romania* 43 F8
Dollard, *Neths.* 17 A7
Dolna Banya, *Bulgaria* 40 D7
Dolni Chiflik, *Bulgaria* 41 D11
Dolni Dŭbnik, *Bulgaria* 41 C8
Dolnośląskie □, *Poland* 45 G3
Dolný Kubín, *Slovak Rep.* 27 B12
Dolo, *Ethiopia* 81 G5
Dolo, *Italy* 29 C9
Dolomites = Dolomiti, *Italy* 29 B8
Dolomiti, *Italy* 29 B8
Dolores, *Argentina* 126 D4
Dolores, *Uruguay* 126 C4
Dolores, *U.S.A.* 115 H9
Dolores →, *U.S.A.* 115 G9
Dolovo, *Serbia, Yug.* 42 F5
Dolphin, C., *Falk. Is.* 128 G5
Dolphin and Union Str., *Canada* 100 B8
Dolsk, *Poland* 45 G4
Dolynska, *Ukraine* 47 H7
Dolzhanskaya, *Russia* 47 J9
Dom Pedrito, *Brazil* 127 C5
Doma, *Nigeria* 83 D6
Domaniç, *Turkey* 39 B11
Domariaganj →, *India* 69 F10
Domasi, *Malawi* 87 F4
Domažlice, *Czech Rep.* 26 B5
Dombarovskiy, *Russia* 50 D6
Dombås, *Norway* 9 E13
Dombasle-sur-Meurthe, *France* 19 D13
Dombes, *France* 21 C9
Dombóvár, *Hungary* 42 D3
Dombrád, *Hungary* 42 B6
Domel I. = Letsôk-aw Kyun, *Burma* 65 G2
Domérat, *France* 19 F9
Domeyko, *Chile* 126 B1
Domeyko, Cordillera, *Chile* 126 A2
Domfront, *France* 18 D6
Dominador, *Chile* 126 A2
Dominica ■, *W. Indies* 121 C7
Dominica Passage, *W. Indies* 121 C7
Dominican Rep. ■, *W. Indies* 121 C5
Dömitz, *Germany* 24 B7
Domme, *France* 20 D5
Domneşti, *Romania* 43 E9
Domodóssola, *Italy* 28 B5
Dompaire, *France* 19 D13
Dompierre-sur-Besbre, *France* 19 F10
Dompim, *Ghana* 82 D4
Domrémy-la-Pucelle, *France* 19 D12
Domville, Mt., *Australia* 95 D5
Domvraína, *Greece* 38 C4
Domžale, *Slovenia* 29 B11
Don →, *Russia* 47 J10
Don →, *Aberds., U.K.* 14 D6
Don →, *S. Yorks., U.K.* 12 D7
Don, C., *Australia* 92 B5
Don Benito, *Spain* 35 G5
Dona Ana = Nhamaabué, *Mozam.* 87 F4
Doña Mencía, *Spain* 35 H6
Donaghadee, *U.K.* 15 B6
Donald, *Australia* 95 F3
Donaldsonville, *U.S.A.* 113 K9
Donalsonville, *U.S.A.* 109 K3
Donau = Dunărea →, *Europe* 43 E14
Donau →, *Austria* 17 D3
Donaueschingen, *Germany* 25 H4
Donauwörth, *Germany* 25 G6
Doncaster, *U.K.* 12 D6
Dondo, *Mozam.* 87 F3
Dondo, Teluk, *Indonesia* 63 D6
Dondra Head, *Sri Lanka* 66 S12
Donduşeni, *Moldova* 43 B12
Donegal, *Ireland* 15 B3
Donegal □, *Ireland* 15 B4
Donegal B., *Ireland* 15 B3
Donets →, *Russia* 49 G5
Donetsk, *Ukraine* 47 J9
Dong Ba Thin, *Vietnam* 65 F7
Dong Dang, *Vietnam* 58 G6
Dong Giam, *Vietnam* 64 C5
Dong Ha, *Vietnam* 64 D6
Dong Hene, *Laos* 64 D5
Dong Hoi, *Vietnam* 64 D6
Dong Jiang →, *China* 59 F10
Dong Khe, *Vietnam* 64 A6
Dong Ujimqin Qi, *China* 56 B9
Dong Van, *Vietnam* 64 A5
Dong Xoai, *Vietnam* 65 G6
Donga, *Nigeria* 83 D7
Donga →, *Nigeria* 83 D7
Dong'an, *China* 59 D8
Dongara, *Australia* 93 E1
Dongbei, *China* 57 D13
Dongchuan, *China* 58 D4
Donges, *France* 18 E4
Dongfang, *China* 64 C7
Dongfeng, *China* 57 C13
Donggala, *Indonesia* 63 E5
Donggan, *China* 58 F5
Donggou, *China* 57 E13
Dongguan, *China* 59 F9
Dongguang, *China* 56 F9
Donghai Dao, *China* 59 G8
Dongjingcheng, *China* 57 B15
Dongkou, *China* 59 D8
Donglan, *China* 58 E6
Dongliu, *China* 59 B11
Dongmen, *China* 58 F6
Dongning, *China* 57 B16
Dongnyi, *China* 58 C3
Dongola, *Sudan* 80 D3
Dongping, *China* 56 G9
Dongshan, *China* 59 F11
Dongsheng, *China* 56 E6
Dongtai, *China* 57 H11
Dongting Hu, *China* 59 C9
Dongtou, *China* 59 D13
Dongxiang, *China* 59 C11
Dongxing, *China* 58 G7
Dongyang, *China* 59 C13
Dongzhi, *China* 59 B11
Donington, C., *Australia* 95 E2
Doniphan, *U.S.A.* 113 G9
Donja Stubica, *Croatia* 29 C12
Donji Dušnik, *Serbia, Yug.* 40 C6
Donji Miholjac, *Croatia* 42 E3
Donji Milanovac, *Serbia, Yug.* 40 B6
Donji Vakuf, *Bos.-H.* 42 F2
Dønna, *Norway* 8 C15
Donna, *U.S.A.* 113 M5
Donnaconna, *Canada* 103 C5
Donnelly's Crossing, *N.Z.* 91 F4
Donnybrook, *Australia* 93 F2
Donnybrook, *S. Africa* 89 D4
Donora, *U.S.A.* 110 F5
Donostia = Donostia-San Sebastián, *Spain* 32 B3
Donostia-San Sebastián, *Spain* 32 B3
Donskoy, *Russia* 46 F10
Donsol, *Phil.* 61 E5
Donzère, *France* 21 D8
Donzy, *France* 19 E10
Doon →, *U.K.* 14 F4
Dora, L., *Australia* 92 D3
Dora Báltea →, *Italy* 28 C5
Dora Ripária →, *Italy* 28 C4
Doran L., *Canada* 105 A7
Dorchester, *U.K.* 13 G5
Dorchester, C., *Canada* 101 B12
Dordabis, *Namibia* 88 C2
Dordogne □, *France* 20 C4
Dordogne →, *France* 20 C3
Dordrecht, *Neths.* 17 C4
Dordrecht, *S. Africa* 88 E4
Dore →, *France* 20 C7
Dore, Mts., *France* 20 C6
Doré L., *Canada* 105 C7
Doré Lake, *Canada* 105 C7
Dorfen, *Germany* 25 G8
Dorgali, *Italy* 30 B2
Dori, *Burkina Faso* 83 C4
Doring →, *S. Africa* 88 E2
Doringbos, *S. Africa* 88 E2
Dorion, *Canada* 111 A10
Dormaa-Ahenkro, *Ghana* 82 D4
Dormans, *France* 19 C10
Dormo, Ras, *Eritrea* 81 E5
Dornbirn, *Austria* 26 D2
Dornes, *France* 19 F10
Dorneşti, *Romania* 43 C11
Dornie, *U.K.* 14 D3
Dornoch, *U.K.* 14 D4
Dornoch Firth, *U.K.* 14 D4
Dornogovĭ □, *Mongolia* 56 C6
Doro, *Mali* 83 B4
Dorog, *Hungary* 42 C3
Dorogobuzh, *Russia* 46 E7
Dorohoi, *Romania* 43 C11
Döröö Nuur, *Mongolia* 60 B4
Dorr, *Iran* 71 C6
Dorre I., *Australia* 93 E1
Dorrigo, *Australia* 95 E5
Dorris, *U.S.A.* 114 F3
Dorset, *Canada* 110 A6
Dorset, *U.S.A.* 110 E4
Dorset □, *U.K.* 13 G5
Dorsten, *Germany* 24 D2
Dortmund, *Germany* 24 D3
Dortmund-Ems-Kanal →, *Germany* 24 D3
Dörtyol, *Turkey* 72 D7
Dorum, *Germany* 24 B4
Doruma, *Dem. Rep. of the Congo* 86 B2
Dorūneh, *Iran* 71 C8
Dos Bahías, C., *Argentina* 128 E3
Dos Hermanas, *Spain* 35 H5
Dos Palos, *U.S.A.* 116 J6
Döşemealtı, *Turkey* 39 D12
Dosso, *Niger* 83 C5
Dothan, *U.S.A.* 109 K3
Doty, *U.S.A.* 116 D3
Douai, *France* 19 B10
Douako, *Guinea* 82 D2
Douala, *Cameroon* 83 E6
Douarnenez, *France* 18 D2
Doubabougou, *Mali* 82 C3
Double Island Pt., *Australia* 95 D5
Double Mountain Fork →, *U.S.A.* 113 J4
Doubrava →, *Czech Rep.* 26 A8
Doubs □, *France* 19 E13
Doubs →, *France* 19 F12
Doubtful Sd., *N.Z.* 91 L1
Doubtless B., *N.Z.* 91 F4
Doudeville, *France* 18 C7
Doué-la-Fontaine, *France* 18 E6
Douentza, *Mali* 82 C4
Douglas, *S. Africa* 88 D3
Douglas, *U.K.* 12 C3
Douglas, *Ariz., U.S.A.* 115 L9

Douglas, *Ga., U.S.A.* 109 K4
Douglas, *Wyo., U.S.A.* 112 D2
Douglas Chan., *Canada* 104 C3
Douglas Pt., *Canada* 110 B3
Douglasville, *U.S.A.* 109 J3
Doukáton, Ákra, *Greece* 38 C2
Doulevant-le-Château, *France* 19 D11
Doullens, *France* 19 B9
Doumen, *China* 59 F9
Douna, *Mali* 82 C3
Douna, *Mali* 83 C4
Dounreay, *U.K.* 14 C5
Dourada, Serra, *Brazil* 125 F9
Dourados, *Brazil* 127 A5
Dourados →, *Brazil* 127 A5
Dourados, Serra dos, *Brazil* 127 A5
Dourdan, *France* 19 D9
Douro →, *Europe* 34 D2
Douvaine, *France* 19 F13
Douvres-la-Délivrande, *France* 18 C6
Douze →, *France* 20 E3
Dove →, *U.K.* 12 E6
Dove Creek, *U.S.A.* 115 H9
Dover, *Australia* 94 G4
Dover, *U.K.* 13 F9
Dover, *Del., U.S.A.* 108 F8
Dover, *N.H., U.S.A.* 111 C14
Dover, *N.J., U.S.A.* 111 F10
Dover, *Ohio, U.S.A.* 110 F3
Dover, Pt., *Australia* 93 F4
Dover, Str. of, *Europe* 13 G9
Dover-Foxcroft, *U.S.A.* 109 C11
Dover Plains, *U.S.A.* 111 E11
Dovey = Dyfi →, *U.K.* 13 E3
Dovrefjell, *Norway* 9 E13
Dow Rūd, *Iran* 71 C6
Dowa, *Malawi* 87 E3
Dowagiac, *U.S.A.* 108 E2
Dowerin, *Australia* 93 F2
Dowgha'i, *Iran* 71 B8
Dowlatābād, *Iran* 71 D8
Down □, *U.K.* 15 B5
Downey, *Calif., U.S.A.* 117 M8
Downey, *Idaho, U.S.A.* 114 E7
Downham Market, *U.K.* 13 E8
Downieville, *U.S.A.* 116 F6
Downpatrick, *U.K.* 15 B6
Downpatrick Hd., *Ireland* 15 B2
Downsville, *U.S.A.* 111 D10
Downton, Mt., *Canada* 104 C4
Dowsārī, *Iran* 71 D8
Doyle, *U.S.A.* 116 E6
Doylestown, *U.S.A.* 111 F9
Dozois, Rés., *Canada* 102 C4
Dra Khel, *Pakistan* 68 F2
Drac →, *France* 21 C9
Dračevo, *Macedonia* 40 E5
Drachten, *Neths.* 17 A6
Drăgănești, *Moldova* 43 C13
Drăgănești-Olt, *Romania* 43 F9
Drăgănești-Vlașca, *Romania* 43 F10
Dragaš, *Kosovo, Yug.* 40 D4
Drăgășani, *Romania* 43 F9
Dragichyn, *Belarus* 47 F3
Dragocvet, *Serbia, Yug.* 40 C5
Dragovishtitsa, *Bulgaria* 40 D6
Draguignan, *France* 21 E10
Drain, *U.S.A.* 114 E2
Drake, *U.S.A.* 112 B4
Drake Passage, *S. Ocean* 5 B17
Drakensberg, *S. Africa* 89 D4
Dráma, *Greece* 41 E8
Dráma □, *Greece* 41 E8
Drammen, *Norway* 9 G14
Drangajökull, *Iceland* 8 C2
Dranov, Ostrov, *Romania* 43 F14
Dras, *India* 69 B6
Drau = Drava →, *Croatia* 42 E3
Drava →, *Croatia* 42 E3
Dravograd, *Slovenia* 29 B12
Drawa →, *Poland* 45 F2
Drawno, *Poland* 45 E2
Drawsko Pomorskie, *Poland* 44 E2
Drayton Valley, *Canada* 104 C6
Dreieich, *Germany* 25 E4
Dren, *Kosovo, Yug.* 40 C4
Drenthe □, *Neths.* 17 B6
Drepanum, C., *Cyprus* 36 E11
Dresden, *Canada* 110 D2
Dresden, *Germany* 24 D9
Dreux, *France* 18 D8
Drezdenko, *Poland* 45 F2
Driffield, *U.K.* 12 C7
Driftwood, *U.S.A.* 110 E6
Driggs, *U.S.A.* 114 E8
Drin →, *Albania* 40 D3
Drin i Zi →, *Albania* 40 E4
Drina →, *Bos.-H.* 40 B3
Drincea →, *Romania* 42 F7
Drinjača →, *Bos.-H.* 42 F4
Drissa = Vyerkhnyadzvinsk, *Belarus* 46 E4
Drniš, *Croatia* 29 E13
Drøbak, *Norway* 9 G14
Drobeta-Turnu Severin, *Romania* 42 F7
Drobin, *Poland* 45 F6
Drochia, *Moldova* 43 B12
Drogheda, *Ireland* 15 C5
Drogichin = Dragichyn, *Belarus* 47 F3
Drogobych = Drohobych, *Ukraine* 47 H2
Drohiczyn, *Poland* 45 F9
Drohobych, *Ukraine* 47 H2
Droichead Atha = Drogheda, *Ireland* 15 C5
Droichead Nua, *Ireland* 15 C5
Droitwich, *U.K.* 13 E5
Drôme □, *France* 21 D9
Drôme →, *France* 21 D8
Dromedary, C., *Australia* 95 F5
Dromore, *U.K.* 15 B4
Dromore West, *Ireland* 15 B3
Dronero, *Italy* 28 D4
Dronfield, *U.K.* 12 D6
Dronne →, *France* 20 C3
Dronninglund, *Denmark* 11 G4
Dronten, *Neths.* 17 B5
Dropt →, *France* 20 D3
Drosendorf, *Austria* 26 C8
Droué, *France* 18 D8
Drumbo, *Canada* 110 C4
Drumheller, *Canada* 104 C6
Drummond, *U.S.A.* 114 C7
Drummond I., *U.S.A.* 108 C4
Drummond Pt., *Australia* 95 E2
Drummond Ra., *Australia* 94 C4
Drummondville, *Canada* 102 C5
Drumright, *U.S.A.* 113 H6
Druskininkai, *Lithuania* 9 J20
Drut →, *Belarus* 47 F6
Druya, *Belarus* 46 E4
Druzhba, *Bulgaria* 41 C12
Druzhina, *Russia* 51 C15
Drvar, *Bos.-H.* 29 D13
Drvenik, *Croatia* 29 E13
Drwęca →, *Poland* 45 E5
Dry Tortugas, *U.S.A.* 120 B3
Dryanovo, *Bulgaria* 41 D9
Dryden, *Canada* 105 D10
Dryden, *U.S.A.* 111 D8
Drygalski I., *Antarctica* 5 C7
Drysdale →, *Australia* 92 B4
Drysdale I., *Australia* 94 A2
Drzewica, *Poland* 45 G7
Drzewiczka →, *Poland* 45 G7
Dschang, *Cameroon* 83 D7
Du Bois, *U.S.A.* 110 E6
Du Gué →, *Canada* 102 A5
Du He, *China* 59 A8
Du Quoin, *U.S.A.* 112 G10
Du'an, *China* 58 F7
Duanesburg, *U.S.A.* 111 D10
Duaringa, *Australia* 94 C4
Ḍubā, *Si. Arabia* 70 E2
Dubai = Dubayy, *U.A.E.* 71 E7
Dubăsari, *Moldova* 43 C14
Dubăsari Vdkhr., *Moldova* 43 C13
Dubawnt →, *Canada* 105 A8
Dubawnt, L., *Canada* 105 A8
Dubayy, *U.A.E.* 71 E7
Dubbo, *Australia* 95 E4
Dubele, *Dem. Rep. of the Congo* 86 B2
Dübendorf, *Switz.* 25 H4
Dubica, *Croatia* 29 C13
Dublin, *Ireland* 15 C5
Dublin, *Ga., U.S.A.* 109 J4
Dublin, *Tex., U.S.A.* 113 J5
Dublin □, *Ireland* 15 C5
Dubna, *Russia* 46 D9
Dubnica nad Váhom, *Slovak Rep.* 27 C11
Dubno, *Ukraine* 47 G3
Dubois, *U.S.A.* 114 D7
Dubossary = Dubăsari, *Moldova* 43 C14
Dubossary Vdkhr. = Dubăsari Vdkhr., *Moldova* 43 C13
Dubovka, *Russia* 49 F7
Dubovskoye, *Russia* 49 G6
Dubrajpur, *India* 69 H12
Dubréka, *Guinea* 82 D2
Dubrovitsa = Dubrovytsya, *Ukraine* 47 G4
Dubrovnik, *Croatia* 40 D2
Dubrovytsya, *Ukraine* 47 G4
Dubuque, *U.S.A.* 112 D9
Dubysa →, *Lithuania* 44 C10
Duchang, *China* 59 C11
Duchesne, *U.S.A.* 114 F8
Duchess, *Australia* 94 C2
Ducie I., *Pac. Oc.* 97 K15
Duck →, *U.S.A.* 109 G2
Duck Cr. →, *Australia* 92 D2
Duck Lake, *Canada* 105 C7
Duck Mountain Prov. Park, *Canada* 105 C8
Duckwall, Mt., *U.S.A.* 116 H6
Duderstadt, *Germany* 24 D6
Dudhi, *India* 67 G13
Dudinka, *Russia* 51 C9
Dudley, *U.K.* 13 E5
Dudwa, *India* 69 E9
Duékoué, *Ivory C.* 82 D3
Dueñas, *Spain* 34 D6
Duero = Douro →, *Europe* 34 D2
Dufftown, *U.K.* 14 D5
Dufourspitz, *Switz.* 25 K3
Dūghī Kalā, *Afghan.* 66 C3
Dugi Otok, *Croatia* 29 D11
Dugo Selo, *Croatia* 29 C13
Duifken Pt., *Australia* 94 A3
Duisburg, *Germany* 24 D2
Duiwelskloof, *S. Africa* 89 C5
Dujiangyan, *China* 58 B4
Duk Fadiat, *Sudan* 81 F3
Duk Faiwil, *Sudan* 81 F3
Dukat, *Albania* 40 F3
Dūkdamīn, *Iran* 71 C8
Dukelský Průsmyk, *Slovak Rep.* 27 B14
Dukhān, *Qatar* 71 E6
Dukhovshchina, *Russia* 46 E7
Duki, *Pakistan* 66 D6
Dukla, *Poland* 45 J8
Duku, *Bauchi, Nigeria* 83 C7
Duku, *Sokoto, Nigeria* 83 C5
Dulag, *Phil.* 61 F6
Dulce, *U.S.A.* 115 H10
Dulce →, *Argentina* 126 C3
Dulce, G., *Costa Rica* 120 E3
Dulf, *Iraq* 70 C5
Dŭlgopol, *Bulgaria* 41 C11
Dulit, Banjaran, *Malaysia* 62 D4
Duliu, *China* 56 E9
Dullewala, *Pakistan* 68 D4
Dullstroom, *S. Africa* 89 D5
Dülmen, *Germany* 24 D3
Dulovo, *Bulgaria* 41 C11
Dulq Maghār, *Syria* 70 B3
Duluth, *U.S.A.* 112 B8
Dum Dum, *India* 69 H13
Dum Duma, *India* 67 F19
Dūmā, *Syria* 75 B5
Dumaguete, *Phil.* 61 G5
Dumai, *Indonesia* 62 D2
Dumaran, *Phil.* 61 F3
Dumas, *Ark., U.S.A.* 113 J9
Dumas, *Tex., U.S.A.* 113 H4
Ḍumayr, *Syria* 75 B5
Dumbarton, *U.K.* 14 F4
Ďumbier, *Slovak Rep.* 27 C12
Dumbleyung, *Australia* 93 F2
Dumboa, *Nigeria* 83 C7
Dumbrăveni, *Romania* 43 D9
Dumfries, *U.K.* 14 F5
Dumfries & Galloway □, *U.K.* 14 F5
Dumitrești, *Romania* 43 E11
Dumka, *India* 69 G12
Dumlupınar, *Turkey* 39 C12
Dümmer, *Germany* 24 C4
Dumoine →, *Canada* 102 C4
Dumoine, L., *Canada* 102 C4
Dumraon, *India* 69 G11
Dumyât, *Egypt* 80 H7
Dumyât, Masabb, *Egypt* 80 H7
Dún Dealgan = Dundalk, *Ireland* 15 B5
Dun Laoghaire, *Ireland* 15 C5
Dun-le-Palestel, *France* 19 F8
Dun-sur-Auron, *France* 19 F9
Dun-sur-Meuse, *France* 19 C12
Duna = Dunărea →, *Europe* 43 E14
Ḍunā, *Si. Arabia* 42 E3
Duna →, *Hungary* 42 E3
Duna-völgyi-főcsatorna, *Hungary* 42 D4
Dunaföldvár, *Hungary* 42 D3
Dunagiri, *India* 69 D8
Dunaj = Dunărea →, *Europe* 43 E14
Dunaj →, *Slovak Rep.* 27 D11
Dunajec →, *Poland* 45 H7
Dunajská Streda, *Slovak Rep.* 27 C10
Dunakeszi, *Hungary* 42 C4
Dunapataj, *Hungary* 42 D4
Dunărea →, *Europe* 43 E14
Dunaszekcső, *Hungary* 42 D3
Dunaújváros, *Hungary* 42 D3
Dunav = Dunărea →, *Europe* 43 E14
Dunavațu de Jos, *Romania* 43 F14
Dunavtsi, *Bulgaria* 40 C6
Dunay, *Russia* 54 C6
Dunback, *N.Z.* 91 L3
Dunbar, *U.K.* 14 E6
Dunblane, *U.K.* 14 E5
Duncan, *Canada* 104 D4
Duncan, *Ariz., U.S.A.* 115 K9
Duncan, *Okla., U.S.A.* 113 H6
Duncan, L., *Canada* 102 B4
Duncan L., *Canada* 104 A6
Duncan Town, *Bahamas* 120 B4
Duncannon, *U.S.A.* 110 F7
Duncansby Head, *U.K.* 14 C5
Duncansville, *U.S.A.* 110 F6
Dundaga, *Latvia* 44 A9
Dundalk, *Canada* 110 B4
Dundalk, *Ireland* 15 B5
Dundalk, *U.S.A.* 108 F7
Dundalk Bay, *Ireland* 15 C5
Dundas, *Canada* 110 C5
Dundas, L., *Australia* 93 F3
Dundas I., *Canada* 104 C2
Dundas Str., *Australia* 92 B5
Dundee, *S. Africa* 89 D5
Dundee, *U.K.* 14 E6
Dundee, *U.S.A.* 110 D8
Dundee City □, *U.K.* 14 E6
Dundgovĭ □, *Mongolia* 56 B4
Dundrum, *U.K.* 15 B6
Dundrum B., *U.K.* 15 B6
Dunedin, *N.Z.* 91 L3
Dunedin, *U.S.A.* 109 L4
Dunfermline, *U.K.* 14 E5
Dungannon, *Canada* 110 C3
Dungannon, *U.K.* 15 B5
Dungarpur, *India* 68 H5
Dungarvan, *Ireland* 15 D4
Dungarvan Harbour, *Ireland* 15 D4
Dungeness, *U.K.* 13 G8
Dungo, L. do, *Angola* 88 B2
Dungog, *Australia* 95 E5
Dungu, *Dem. Rep. of the Congo* 86 B2
Dungun, *Malaysia* 65 K4
Dunguñâb, *Sudan* 80 C4
Dunguñâb, Khalij, *Sudan* 80 C4
Dunhua, *China* 57 C15
Dunhuang, *China* 60 B4
Dunk I., *Australia* 94 B4
Dunkassa, *Benin* 83 C5
Dunkeld, *Australia* 95 E4
Dunkeld, *U.K.* 14 E5
Dunkerque, *France* 19 A9
Dunkery Beacon, *U.K.* 13 F4
Dunkirk = Dunkerque, *France* 19 A9
Dunkirk, *U.S.A.* 110 D5
Dunkuj, *Sudan* 81 E3
Dunkwa, *Central, Ghana* 82 D4
Dunkwa, *Central, Ghana* 83 D4
Dúnleary = Dun Laoghaire, *Ireland* 15 C5
Dunleer, *Ireland* 15 C5
Dunmanus B., *Ireland* 15 E2
Dunmanway, *Ireland* 15 E2
Dunmara, *Australia* 94 B1
Dunmore, *U.S.A.* 111 E9
Dunmore Hd., *Ireland* 15 D1
Dunmore Town, *Bahamas* 120 A4
Dunn, *U.S.A.* 109 H6
Dunnellon, *U.S.A.* 109 L4
Dunnet Hd., *U.K.* 14 C5
Dunning, *U.S.A.* 112 E4
Dunnville, *Canada* 110 D5
Dunolly, *Australia* 95 F3
Dunoon, *U.K.* 14 F4
Dunphy, *U.S.A.* 114 F5
Dunqul, *Egypt* 80 C3
Duns, *U.K.* 14 F6
Dunseith, *U.S.A.* 112 A4
Dunsmuir, *U.S.A.* 114 F2
Dunstable, *U.K.* 13 F7
Dunstan Mts., *N.Z.* 91 L2
Dunster, *Canada* 104 C5
Dunvegan L., *Canada* 105 A7
Duolun, *China* 56 C9
Duong Dong, *Vietnam* 65 G4
Dupree, *U.S.A.* 112 C4
Dupuyer, *U.S.A.* 114 B7
Duque de Caxias, *Brazil* 127 A7
Durack →, *Australia* 92 C4
Durack Ra., *Australia* 92 C4
Durağan, *Turkey* 72 B6
Durak, *Turkey* 39 B10
Đurakovac, *Kosovo, Yug.* 40 D4
Durance →, *France* 21 E8
Durand, *U.S.A.* 112 C9
Durango, *Mexico* 118 C4
Durango, *U.S.A.* 115 H10
Durango □, *Mexico* 118 C4
Durankulak, *Bulgaria* 41 C12
Durant, *Miss., U.S.A.* 113 J10
Durant, *Okla., U.S.A.* 113 J6
Duratón →, *Spain* 34 D6
Durazno, *Uruguay* 126 C4
Durazzo = Durrës, *Albania* 40 E3
Durban, *France* 20 F6
Durban, *S. Africa* 89 D5
Durbuy, *Belgium* 17 D5
Dúrcal, *Spain* 35 J7
Đurđevac, *Croatia* 42 D2
Düren, *Germany* 24 E2
Durg, *India* 67 J12
Durgapur, *India* 69 H12
Durham, *Canada* 102 D3
Durham, *U.K.* 12 C6
Durham, *Calif., U.S.A.* 116 F5
Durham, *N.C., U.S.A.* 109 H6
Durham, *N.H., U.S.A.* 111 C14
Durham □, *U.K.* 12 C6
Durlești, *Moldova* 43 C13
Ḍurmā, *Si. Arabia* 70 E5
Durmitor, *Montenegro, Yug.* 40 C2
Durness, *U.K.* 14 C4
Durrës, *Albania* 40 E3
Durrow, *Ireland* 15 D4
Dursey I., *Ireland* 15 E1
Dursunbey, *Turkey* 39 B10
Durtal, *France* 18 E6
Duru, *Dem. Rep. of the Congo* 86 B2
Duru Gölü, *Turkey* 41 E12
Durusu, *Turkey* 41 E12
Durūz, Jabal ad, *Jordan* 75 C5
D'Urville, Tanjung, *Indonesia* 63 E9
D'Urville I., *N.Z.* 91 J4
Duryea, *U.S.A.* 111 E9
Dûsh, *Egypt* 80 C3
Dushak, *Turkmenistan* 50 F7
Dushan, *China* 58 E6
Dushanbe, *Tajikistan* 50 F7
Dusheti, *Georgia* 49 J7
Dushore, *U.S.A.* 111 E8
Dusky Sd., *N.Z.* 91 L1
Dussejour, C., *Australia* 92 B4
Düsseldorf, *Germany* 24 D2
Duszniki-Zdrój, *Poland* 45 H3
Dutch Harbor, *U.S.A.* 100 C3
Dutlwe, *Botswana* 88 C3
Dutsan Wai, *Nigeria* 83 C6
Dutton, *Canada* 110 D3
Dutton →, *Australia* 94 C3
Duved, *Sweden* 10 A6
Düvertepe, *Turkey* 39 B10
Duwayhin, Khawr, *U.A.E.* 71 E6
Duyun, *China* 58 D6
Düzağac, *Turkey* 39 C12
Düzce, *Turkey* 72 B4
Duzdab = Zāhedān, *Iran* 71 D9
Dve Mogili, *Bulgaria* 41 C9
Dvina, Severnaya →, *Russia* 50 C5
Dvinsk = Daugavpils, *Latvia* 9 J22
Dvor, *Croatia* 29 C13
Dvůr Králové nad Labem, *Czech Rep.* 26 A8
Dwarka, *India* 68 H3
Dwellingup, *Australia* 93 F2
Dwight, *Canada* 110 A5
Dwight, *U.S.A.* 108 E1
Dyatkovo, *Russia* 46 F8
Dyatlovo = Dzyatlava, *Belarus* 46 F3
Dyce, *U.K.* 14 D6
Dyer, C., *Canada* 101 B13
Dyer Bay, *Canada* 110 A3
Dyer Plateau, *Antarctica* 5 D17
Dyersburg, *U.S.A.* 113 G10
Dyfi →, *U.K.* 13 E3
Dyje →, *Czech Rep.* 27 C9
Dymer, *Ukraine* 47 G6
Dynów, *Poland* 45 J9
Dysart, *Australia* 94 C4
Dzamin Üüd = Borhoyn Tal, *Mongolia* 56 C6
Dzerzhinsk, *Russia* 48 B6
Dzhalinda, *Russia* 51 D13
Dzhambul = Taraz, *Kazakstan* 50 E8
Dzhankoy, *Ukraine* 47 K8
Dzhanybek, *Kazakstan* 48 F8
Dzharylhach, Ostriv, *Ukraine* 47 J7
Dzhezkazgan = Zhezqazghan, *Kazakstan* 50 E7
Dzhizak = Jizzakh, *Uzbekistan* 50 E7
Dzhugdzur, Khrebet, *Russia* 51 D14
Dzhvari = Jvari, *Georgia* 49 J6
Działdowo, *Poland* 45 E7
Działoszyce, *Poland* 45 H7
Działoszyn, *Poland* 45 G5
Dzibilchaltun, *Mexico* 119 C7
Dzierzgoń, *Poland* 44 E6
Dzierżoniów, *Poland* 45 H3
Dzilam de Bravo, *Mexico* 119 C7
Dzisna, *Belarus* 46 E5
Dzisna →, *Belarus* 46 E5
Dziwnów, *Poland* 44 D1
Dzungaria = Junggar Pendi, *China* 60 B3
Dzuumod, *Mongolia* 60 B5
Dzyarzhynsk, *Belarus* 46 F4
Dzyatlava, *Belarus* 46 F3

E

Eabamet L., *Canada* 102 B2
Eads, *U.S.A.* 112 F3
Eagar, *U.S.A.* 115 J9
Eagle, *Alaska, U.S.A.* 100 B5
Eagle, *Colo., U.S.A.* 114 G10
Eagle →, *Canada* 103 B8
Eagle Butte, *U.S.A.* 112 C4
Eagle Grove, *U.S.A.* 112 D8
Eagle L., *Canada* 105 D10
Eagle L., *Calif., U.S.A.* 114 F3
Eagle L., *Maine, U.S.A.* 109 B11
Eagle Lake, *Canada* 110 A6
Eagle Lake, *Maine, U.S.A.* 109 B11
Eagle Lake, *Tex., U.S.A.* 113 L6
Eagle Mountain, *U.S.A.* 117 M11
Eagle Nest, *U.S.A.* 115 H11
Eagle Pass, *U.S.A.* 113 L4
Eagle Pk., *U.S.A.* 116 G7
Eagle Pt., *Australia* 92 C3
Eagle River, *Mich., U.S.A.* 108 B1
Eagle River, *Wis., U.S.A.* 112 C10
Eaglehawk, *Australia* 95 F3
Eagles Mere, *U.S.A.* 111 E8
Ealing □, *U.K.* 13 F7
Ear Falls, *Canada* 105 C10
Earle, *U.S.A.* 113 H9
Earlimart, *U.S.A.* 117 K7
Earn →, *U.K.* 14 E5
Earn, L., *U.K.* 14 E4
Earnslaw, Mt., *N.Z.* 91 L2
Earth, *U.S.A.* 113 H3
Easley, *U.S.A.* 109 H4
East Anglia, *U.K.* 12 E9
East Angus, *Canada* 103 C5
East Aurora, *U.S.A.* 110 D6
East Ayrshire □, *U.K.* 14 F4
East Bengal, *Bangla.* 67 H17
East Beskids = Vychodné Beskydy, *Europe* 27 B15
East Brady, *U.S.A.* 110 F5
East C., *N.Z.* 91 G7
East Chicago, *U.S.A.* 108 E2
East China Sea, *Asia* 60 C7
East Coulee, *Canada* 104 C6
East Dereham, *U.K.* 13 E8
East Dunbartonshire □, *U.K.* 14 F4
East Falkland, *Falk. Is.* 122 J5
East Grand Forks, *U.S.A.* 112 B6
East Greenwich, *U.S.A.* 111 E13
East Grinstead, *U.K.* 13 F8
East Hartford, *U.S.A.* 111 E12
East Helena, *U.S.A.* 114 C8
East Indies, *Asia* 52 K15
East Kilbride, *U.K.* 14 F4
East Lansing, *U.S.A.* 108 D3
East Liverpool, *U.S.A.* 110 F4
East London, *S. Africa* 89 E4
East Lothian □, *U.K.* 14 F6
East Main = Eastmain, *Canada* 102 B4
East Northport, *U.S.A.* 111 F11
East Orange, *U.S.A.* 111 F10
East Pacific Ridge, *Pac. Oc.* 97 J17
East Palestine, *U.S.A.* 110 F4
East Pine, *Canada* 104 B4
East Point, *U.S.A.* 109 J3
East Providence, *U.S.A.* 111 E13
East Pt., *Canada* 103 C7
East Renfrewshire □, *U.K.* 14 F4
East Retford = Retford, *U.K.* 12 D7
East Riding of Yorkshire □, *U.K.* 12 D7
East Rochester, *U.S.A.* 110 C7
East St. Louis, *U.S.A.* 112 F9
East Schelde = Oosterschelde →, *Neths.* 17 C4
East Sea = Japan, Sea of, *Asia* 54 E7
East Siberian Sea, *Russia* 51 B17

East Stroudsburg, *U.S.A.* 111 E9
East Sussex □, *U.K.* 13 G8
East Tawas, *U.S.A.* 108 C4
East Timor ■, *Asia* 63 F7
East Toorale, *Australia* 95 E4
East Walker →, *U.S.A.* 116 G7
East Windsor, *U.S.A.* 111 F10
Eastbourne, *N.Z.* 91 J5
Eastbourne, *U.K.* 13 G8
Eastend, *Canada* 105 D7
Easter I. = Pascua, I. de, *Pac. Oc.* 97 K17
Eastern □, *Ghana* 83 D4
Eastern □, *Kenya* 86 C4
Eastern Cape □, *S. Africa* 88 E4
Eastern Cr. →, *Australia* 94 C3
Eastern Ghats, *India* 66 N11
Eastern Group = Lau Group, *Fiji* 91 C9
Eastern Group, *Australia* 93 F3
Eastern Province □, *S. Leone* 82 D2
Eastern Transvaal = Mpumalanga □, *S. Africa* 89 B5
Easterville, *Canada* 105 C9
Easthampton, *U.S.A.* 111 D12
Eastlake, *U.S.A.* 110 E3
Eastland, *U.S.A.* 113 J5
Eastleigh, *U.K.* 13 G6
Eastmain, *Canada* 102 B4
Eastmain →, *Canada* 102 B4
Eastman, *Canada* 111 A12
Eastman, *U.S.A.* 109 J4
Easton, *Md., U.S.A.* 108 F7
Easton, *Pa., U.S.A.* 111 F9
Easton, *Wash., U.S.A.* 116 C5
Eastpointe, *U.S.A.* 110 D2
Eastport, *U.S.A.* 109 C12
Eastsound, *U.S.A.* 116 B4
Eaton, *U.S.A.* 112 E2
Eatonia, *Canada* 105 C7
Eatonton, *U.S.A.* 109 J4
Eatontown, *U.S.A.* 111 F10
Eatonville, *U.S.A.* 116 D4
Eau Claire, *U.S.A.* 112 C9
Eau Claire, L. à l', *Canada* 102 A5
Eauze, *France* 20 E4
Eban, *Nigeria* 83 D5
Ebbw Vale, *U.K.* 13 F4
Ebeltoft, *Denmark* 11 H4
Ebeltoft Vig, *Denmark* 11 H4
Ebensburg, *U.S.A.* 110 F6
Ebensee, *Austria* 26 D6
Eber Gölü, *Turkey* 72 C4
Eberbach, *Germany* 25 F4
Eberswalde-Finow, *Germany* 24 C9
Ebetsu, *Japan* 54 C10
Ebian, *China* 58 C4
Ebingen, *Germany* 25 G5
Éboli, *Italy* 31 B8
Ebolowa, *Cameroon* 83 E7
Ebonyi □, *Nigeria* 83 D6
Ebrach, *Germany* 25 F6
Ébrié, Lagune, *Ivory C.* 82 D4
Ebro →, *Spain* 32 E5
Ebro, Embalse del, *Spain* 34 C7
Ebstorf, *Germany* 24 B6
Eceabat, *Turkey* 41 F10
Ech Cheliff, *Algeria* 78 A6
Echigo-Sammyaku, *Japan* 55 F9
Échirolles, *France* 21 C9
Echizen-Misaki, *Japan* 55 G7
Echmiadzin = Yejmiadzin, *Armenia* 49 K7
Echo Bay, *N.W.T., Canada* 100 B8
Echo Bay, *Ont., Canada* 102 C3
Echoing →, *Canada* 102 B1
Echternach, *Lux.* 17 E6
Echuca, *Australia* 95 F3
Ecija, *Spain* 35 H5
Eckental, *Germany* 25 F7
Eckernförde, *Germany* 24 A5
Eclipse Is., *Australia* 92 B4
Eclipse Sd., *Canada* 101 A11
Écommoy, *France* 18 E7
Écouché, *France* 18 D6
Ecuador ■, *S. Amer.* 124 D3
Écueillé, *France* 18 E8
Ed, *Sweden* 11 F5
Ed Dabbura, *Sudan* 80 D3
Ed Da'ein, *Sudan* 81 E2
Ed Damazin, *Sudan* 79 F12
Ed Dâmer, *Sudan* 80 D3
Ed Debba, *Sudan* 80 D3
Ed-Déffa, *Egypt* 80 A2
Ed Deim, *Sudan* 81 E2
Ed Dueim, *Sudan* 81 E3
Edam, *Canada* 105 C7
Edam, *Neths.* 17 B5
Edane, *Sweden* 10 E6
Eday, *U.K.* 14 B6
Edd, *Eritrea* 81 E5
Eddrachillis B., *U.K.* 14 C3
Eddystone Pt., *Australia* 94 G4
Ede, *Neths.* 17 B5
Ede, *Nigeria* 83 D5
Edéa, *Cameroon* 83 E7
Edebäck, *Sweden* 10 D7
Edehon L., *Canada* 105 A9
Edelény, *Hungary* 42 B5
Eden, *Australia* 95 F4
Eden, *N.C., U.S.A.* 109 G6
Eden, *N.Y., U.S.A.* 110 D6
Eden, *Tex., U.S.A.* 113 K5
Eden →, *U.K.* 12 C4
Edenburg, *S. Africa* 88 D4
Edendale, *S. Africa* 89 D5
Edenderry, *Ireland* 15 C4
Edenton, *U.S.A.* 109 G7
Edenville, *S. Africa* 89 D4
Eder →, *Germany* 24 D5
Eder-Stausee, *Germany* 24 D4
Edewecht, *Germany* 24 B3
Edgar, *U.S.A.* 112 E6
Edgartown, *U.S.A.* 111 E14
Edge Hill, *U.K.* 13 E6
Edgefield, *U.S.A.* 109 J5
Edgeley, *U.S.A.* 112 B5
Edgemont, *U.S.A.* 112 D3
Edgeøya, *Svalbard* 4 B9
Édhessa, *Greece* 40 F6
Edievale, *N.Z.* 91 L2
Edina, *Liberia* 82 D2
Edina, *U.S.A.* 112 E8
Edinboro, *U.S.A.* 110 E4
Edinburg, *U.S.A.* 113 M5
Edinburgh, *U.K.* 14 F5
Edinburgh, City of □, *U.K.* 14 F5
Edineţ, *Moldova* 43 B12
Edirne, *Turkey* 41 E10
Edirne □, *Turkey* 41 E10
Edison, *U.S.A.* 116 B4
Edithburgh, *Australia* 95 F2
Edmeston, *U.S.A.* 111 D9
Edmond, *U.S.A.* 113 H6
Edmonds, *U.S.A.* 116 C4
Edmonton, *Australia* 94 B4
Edmonton, *Canada* 104 C6
Edmund L., *Canada* 102 B1
Edmundston, *Canada* 103 C6
Edna, *U.S.A.* 113 L6
Edo □, *Nigeria* 83 D6
Edolo, *Italy* 28 B7
Edremit, *Turkey* 39 B9
Edremit Körfezi, *Turkey* 39 B8
Edsbro, *Sweden* 10 E12
Edsbyn, *Sweden* 10 C9
Edson, *Canada* 104 C5
Eduardo Castex, *Argentina* 126 D3
Edward →, *Australia* 95 F3
Edward, L., *Africa* 86 C2
Edward River, *Australia* 94 A3
Edward VII Land, *Antarctica* 5 E13
Edwards, *Calif., U.S.A.* 117 L9
Edwards, *N.Y., U.S.A.* 111 B9
Edwards Air Force Base, *U.S.A.* 117 L9
Edwards Plateau, *U.S.A.* 113 K4
Edwardsville, *U.S.A.* 111 E9
Edzo, *Canada* 104 A5
Eeklo, *Belgium* 17 C3
Eferding, *Austria* 26 C7
Effingham, *U.S.A.* 108 F1
Eforie, *Romania* 43 F13
Ega →, *Spain* 32 C3
Égadi, Ísole, *Italy* 30 E5
Egan Range, *U.S.A.* 114 G6
Eganville, *Canada* 102 C4
Eger = Cheb, *Czech Rep.* 26 A5
Eger, *Hungary* 42 C5
Eger →, *Hungary* 42 C5
Egersund, *Norway* 9 G12
Egg L., *Canada* 105 B7
Eggenburg, *Austria* 26 C8
Eggenfelden, *Germany* 25 G8
Éghezée, *Belgium* 17 D4
Égletons, *France* 20 C6
Egmont, *Canada* 104 D4
Egmont, C., *N.Z.* 91 H4
Egmont, Mt. = Taranaki, Mt., *N.Z.* 91 H5
Egra, *India* 69 J12
Eğridir, *Turkey* 72 D4
Eğridir Gölü, *Turkey* 70 B1
Egtved, *Denmark* 11 J3
Egume, *Nigeria* 83 D6
Éguzon-Chantôme, *France* 19 F8
Egvekinot, *Russia* 51 C19
Egyek, *Hungary* 42 C5
Egypt ■, *Africa* 80 B3
Eha Amufu, *Nigeria* 83 D6
Ehime □, *Japan* 55 H6
Ehingen, *Germany* 25 G5
Ehrenberg, *U.S.A.* 117 M12
Ehrwald, *Austria* 26 D3
Eibar, *Spain* 32 B2
Eichstätt, *Germany* 25 G7
Eider →, *Germany* 24 A4
Eidsvold, *Australia* 95 D5
Eidsvoll, *Norway* 9 F14
Eifel, *Germany* 25 E2
Eiffel Flats, *Zimbabwe* 87 F3
Eiger, *Switz.* 28 B5
Eigg, *U.K.* 14 E2
Eighty Mile Beach, *Australia* 92 C3
Eil, *Somali Rep.* 74 F4
Eil, L., *U.K.* 14 E3
Eildon, L., *Australia* 95 F4
Eilenburg, *Germany* 24 D8
Ein el Luweiqa, *Sudan* 81 E3
Einasleigh, *Australia* 94 B3
Einasleigh →, *Australia* 94 B3
Einbeck, *Germany* 24 D5
Eindhoven, *Neths.* 17 C5
Einsiedeln, *Switz.* 25 H4
Eire = Ireland ■, *Europe* 15 C4
Eiríksjökull, *Iceland* 8 D3
Eirunepé, *Brazil* 124 E5
Eiseb →, *Namibia* 88 C2
Eisenach, *Germany* 24 E6
Eisenberg, *Germany* 24 E7
Eisenerz, *Austria* 26 D7
Eisenhüttenstadt, *Germany* 24 C10
Eisenkappel, *Austria* 26 E7
Eisenstadt, *Austria* 27 D9
Eisfeld, *Germany* 25 E6
Eisleben, *Germany* 24 D7
Eislingen, *Germany* 25 G5
Eivissa, *Spain* 37 C7
Eixe, Serra do, *Spain* 34 C4
Ejea de los Caballeros, *Spain* 32 C3
Ejeda, *Madag.* 89 C7
Ejura, *Ghana* 83 D4
Ejutla, *Mexico* 119 D5
Ekalaka, *U.S.A.* 112 C2
Ekenässjön, *Sweden* 11 G9
Ekerö, *Sweden* 10 E11
Eket, *Nigeria* 83 E6
Eketahuna, *N.Z.* 91 J5
Ekhínos, *Greece* 41 E9
Ekibastuz, *Kazakstan* 50 D8
Ekiti □, *Nigeria* 83 D6
Ekoli, *Dem. Rep. of the Congo* 86 C1
Ekoln, *Sweden* 10 E11
Ekshärad, *Sweden* 10 D7
Eksjö, *Sweden* 11 G8
Ekuma →, *Namibia* 88 B2
Ekwan →, *Canada* 102 B3
Ekwan Pt., *Canada* 102 B3
El Aaiún, *W. Sahara* 78 C3
El Abanico, *Chile* 126 D1
El Abbasiya, *Sudan* 81 E3
El 'Agrûd, *Egypt* 75 E3
El Ait, *Sudan* 81 E2
El 'Aiyat, *Egypt* 80 J7
El Alamein, *Egypt* 80 A2
El 'Aqaba, W. →, *Egypt* 75 E2
El 'Arag, *Egypt* 80 B2
El Arahal, *Spain* 35 H5
El Arīḥā, *West Bank* 75 D4
El 'Arîsh, *Egypt* 75 D2
El 'Arîsh, W. →, *Egypt* 75 D2
El Asnam = Ech Cheliff, *Algeria* 78 A6
El Astillero, *Spain* 34 B7
El Badâri, *Egypt* 80 B3
El Bahrein, *Egypt* 80 B2
El Ballâs, *Egypt* 80 B3
El Balyana, *Egypt* 80 B3
El Baqeir, *Sudan* 80 D3
El Barco de Ávila, *Spain* 34 E5
El Barco de Valdeorras = O Barco, *Spain* 34 C4
El Bauga, *Sudan* 80 D3
El Bawiti, *Egypt* 80 B2
El Bayadh, *Algeria* 78 B6
El Bierzo, *Spain* 34 C4
El Bluff, *Nic.* 120 D3
El Bonillo, *Spain* 33 G2
El Brûk, W. →, *Egypt* 75 E2
El Buheirat □, *Sudan* 81 F3
El Burgo de Osma, *Spain* 32 D1
El Cajon, *U.S.A.* 117 N10
El Campo, *U.S.A.* 113 L6
El Centro, *U.S.A.* 117 N11
El Cerro, *Bolivia* 124 G6
El Cerro de Andévalo, *Spain* 35 H4
El Compadre, *Mexico* 117 N10
El Coronil, *Spain* 35 H5
El Cuy, *Argentina* 128 D3
El Cuyo, *Mexico* 119 C7
El Dab'a, *Egypt* 80 H6
El Daheir, *Egypt* 75 D3
El Dátil, *Mexico* 118 B2
El Deir, *Egypt* 80 B3
El Dere, *Somali Rep.* 74 G4
El Descanso, *Mexico* 117 N10
El Desemboque, *Mexico* 118 A2
El Dilingat, *Egypt* 80 H7
El Diviso, *Colombia* 124 C3
El Djouf, *Mauritania* 78 D4
El Dorado, *Ark., U.S.A.* 113 J8
El Dorado, *Kans., U.S.A.* 113 G6
El Dorado, *Venezuela* 124 B6
El 'Ein, *Sudan* 81 D2
El Ejido, *Spain* 35 J8
El Escorial, *Spain* 34 E6
El Espinar, *Spain* 34 D6
El Faiyûm, *Egypt* 80 J7
El Fâsher, *Sudan* 81 E2
El Fashn, *Egypt* 80 J7
El Ferrol = Ferrol, *Spain* 34 B2
El Fifi, *Sudan* 81 E2
El Fuerte, *Mexico* 118 B3
El Ga'a, *Sudan* 81 E2
El Gal, *Somali Rep.* 74 E5
El Garef, *Sudan* 81 E3
El Gebir, *Sudan* 81 E2
El Gedida, *Egypt* 80 B2
El Geneina = Al Junaynah, *Sudan* 79 F10
El Geteina, *Sudan* 81 E3
El Gezira □, *Sudan* 81 E3
El Gir, *Sudan* 80 D2
El Gîza, *Egypt* 80 J7
El Goléa, *Algeria* 78 B6
El Grau, *Spain* 33 G4
El Hagiz, *Sudan* 81 D4
El Hâi, *Egypt* 80 J7
El Hammam, *Egypt* 80 A2
El Hawata, *Sudan* 81 E3
El Heiz, *Egypt* 80 B2
El Hideib, *Sudan* 81 E2
El Hilla, *Sudan* 81 E2
El 'Idisât, *Egypt* 80 B3
El Iskandarîya, *Egypt* 80 H7
El Istiwa'iya, *Sudan* 79 G11
El Jadida, *Morocco* 78 B4
El Jardal, *Honduras* 120 D2
El Jebelein, *Sudan* 81 E3
El Kab, *Sudan* 80 D3
El Kabrît, G., *Egypt* 75 F2
El Kafr el Sharqi, *Egypt* 80 H7
El Kamlin, *Sudan* 81 D3
El Karaba, *Sudan* 80 D3
El Kere, *Ethiopia* 81 F5
El Khandaq, *Sudan* 80 D3
El Khârga, *Egypt* 80 B3
El Khartûm, *Sudan* 81 D3
El Khartûm □, *Sudan* 81 D3
El Khartûm Bahrî, *Sudan* 81 D3
El Kuntilla, *Egypt* 75 E3
El Laqâwa, *Sudan* 81 E2
El Laqeita, *Egypt* 80 B3
El Leh, *Ethiopia* 81 G4
El Leiya, *Sudan* 81 D4
El Maestrazgo, *Spain* 32 E4
El Mafâza, *Sudan* 81 E3
El Maghra, *Egypt* 80 A2
El Mahalla el Kubra, *Egypt* 80 H7
El Mahârîq, *Egypt* 80 B3
El Maîmûn, *Egypt* 80 J7
El Maks el Bahari, *Egypt* 80 C3
El Manshâh, *Egypt* 80 B3
El Mansûra, *Egypt* 80 H7
El Manzala, *Egypt* 80 H7
El Marâgha, *Egypt* 80 B3
El Masid, *Sudan* 81 D3
El Masnou, *Spain* 32 D7
El Matariya, *Egypt* 80 H8
El Meda, *Ethiopia* 81 F5
El Medano, *Canary Is.* 37 F3
El Metemma, *Sudan* 81 D3
El Milagro, *Argentina* 126 C2
El Minyâ, *Egypt* 80 B3
El Monte, *U.S.A.* 117 L8
El Montseny, *Spain* 32 D7
El Mreyye, *Mauritania* 82 B3
El Niybo, *Ethiopia* 81 G4
El Obeid, *Sudan* 81 E3
El Odaiya, *Sudan* 81 E2
El Oro, *Mexico* 119 D4
El Oued, *Algeria* 78 B7
El Palmito, Presa, *Mexico* 118 B3
El Paso, *U.S.A.* 115 L10
El Paso Robles, *U.S.A.* 116 K6
El Pedernoso, *Spain* 33 F2
El Pedroso, *Spain* 35 H5
El Pobo de Dueñas, *Spain* 32 E3
El Portal, *U.S.A.* 116 H7
El Porvenir, *Mexico* 118 A3
El Prat de Llobregat, *Spain* 32 D7
El Progreso, *Honduras* 120 C2
El Pueblito, *Mexico* 118 B3
El Pueblo, *Canary Is.* 37 F2
El Puente del Arzobispo, *Spain* 34 F5
El Puerto de Santa María, *Spain* 35 J4
El Qâhira, *Egypt* 80 H7
El Qantara, *Egypt* 75 E1
El Qasr, *Egypt* 80 B2
El Qubâbât, *Egypt* 80 J7
El Quseima, *Egypt* 75 E3
El Qusîya, *Egypt* 80 B3
El Râshda, *Egypt* 80 B2
El Real, *Panama* 124 B3
El Reno, *U.S.A.* 113 H6
El Rîdisiya, *Egypt* 80 C3
El Rio, *U.S.A.* 117 L7
El Ronquillo, *Spain* 35 H4
El Roque, Pta., *Canary Is.* 37 F4
El Rosarito, *Mexico* 118 B2
El Rubio, *Spain* 35 H5
El Saff, *Egypt* 80 J7
El Saheira, W. →, *Egypt* 75 E2
El Salto, *Mexico* 118 C3
El Salvador ■, *Cent. Amer.* 120 D2
El Sauce, *Nic.* 120 D2
El Saucejo, *Spain* 35 H5
El Shallal, *Egypt* 80 C3
El Simbillawein, *Egypt* 80 H7
El Sueco, *Mexico* 118 B3
El Suweis, *Egypt* 80 J8
El Tabbîn, *Egypt* 80 J7
El Tamarâni, W. →, *Egypt* 75 E3
El Thamad, *Egypt* 75 F3
El Tigre, *Venezuela* 124 B6
El Tîh, Gebal, *Egypt* 75 F2
El Tîna, *Egypt* 80 H8
El Tîna, Khalîg, *Egypt* 75 D1
El Tofo, *Chile* 126 B1
El Tránsito, *Chile* 126 B1
El Tûr, *Egypt* 70 D2
El Turbio, *Argentina* 128 G2
El Uqsur, *Egypt* 80 B3
El Venado, *Mexico* 118 C4
El Vendrell, *Spain* 32 D6
El Vergel, *Mexico* 118 B3
El Vigía, *Venezuela* 124 B4
El Viso del Alcor, *Spain* 35 H5
El Wabeira, *Egypt* 75 F2
El Wak, *Kenya* 86 B5
El Waqf, *Egypt* 80 B3
El Weguet, *Ethiopia* 81 F5
El Wuz, *Sudan* 81 D3
Elafónisos, *Greece* 38 E4
Élancourt, *France* 19 D8
Élassa, *Greece* 39 F8
Elassón, *Greece* 38 B4
Elat, *Israel* 75 F3
Eláthia, *Greece* 38 C4
Elâzığ, *Turkey* 70 B3
Elba, *Italy* 28 F7
Elba, *U.S.A.* 109 K2
Elbasan, *Albania* 40 E4
Elbe, *U.S.A.* 116 D4
Elbe →, *Europe* 24 B4
Elbe-Seitenkanal, *Germany* 24 C6
Elbert, Mt., *U.S.A.* 115 G10
Elberton, *U.S.A.* 109 H4
Elbeuf, *France* 18 C8
Elbidtan, *Turkey* 70 B3
Elbing = Elbląg, *Poland* 44 D6
Elbistan, *Turkey* 72 C7
Elbląg, *Poland* 44 D6
Elbow, *Canada* 105 C7
Elbrus, *Asia* 49 J6
Elburz Mts. = Alborz, Reshteh-ye Kūhhā-ye, *Iran* 71 C7
Elche, *Spain* 33 G4
Elche de la Sierra, *Spain* 33 G2
Elcho I., *Australia* 94 A2
Elda, *Spain* 33 G4
Elde →, *Germany* 24 B7
Eldon, *Mo., U.S.A.* 112 F8
Eldon, *Wash., U.S.A.* 116 C3
Eldora, *U.S.A.* 112 D8
Eldorado, *Argentina* 127 B5
Eldorado, *Canada* 110 B7
Eldorado, *Mexico* 118 C3
Eldorado, *Ill., U.S.A.* 108 G1
Eldorado, *Tex., U.S.A.* 113 K4
Eldorado Springs, *U.S.A.* 113 G8
Eldoret, *Kenya* 86 B4
Eldred, *U.S.A.* 110 E6
Elea, C., *Cyprus* 36 D13
Eleanora, Pk., *Australia* 93 F3
Elefantes →, *Mozam.* 89 C5
Elektrogorsk, *Russia* 46 E10
Elektrostal, *Russia* 46 E10
Elele, *Nigeria* 83 D6
Elena, *Bulgaria* 41 D9
Elephant Butte Reservoir, *U.S.A.* 115 K10
Elephant I., *Antarctica* 5 C18
Eleshnitsa, *Bulgaria* 40 E7
Eleşkirt, *Turkey* 73 C10
Eleuthera, *Bahamas* 120 B4
Elevsís, *Greece* 38 C5
Elevtheroúpolis, *Greece* 41 F8
Elgin, *Canada* 111 B8
Elgin, *U.K.* 14 D5
Elgin, *Ill., U.S.A.* 108 D1
Elgin, *N. Dak., U.S.A.* 112 B4
Elgin, *Oreg., U.S.A.* 114 D5
Elgin, *Tex., U.S.A.* 113 K6
Elgoibar, *Spain* 32 B2
Elgon, Mt., *Africa* 86 B3
Eliase, *Indonesia* 63 F8
Elikón, *Greece* 38 C4
Elim, *Namibia* 88 B2
Elim, *S. Africa* 88 E2
Elin Pelin, *Bulgaria* 40 D7
Elista, *Russia* 49 G7
Elizabeth, *Australia* 95 E2
Elizabeth, *N.J., U.S.A.* 111 F10
Elizabeth, *N.J., U.S.A.* 111 F10
Elizabeth City, *U.S.A.* 109 G7
Elizabethton, *U.S.A.* 109 G4
Elizabethtown, *Ky., U.S.A.* 108 G3
Elizabethtown, *N.Y., U.S.A.* 111 B11
Elizabethtown, *Pa., U.S.A.* 111 F8
Elizondo, *Spain* 32 B3
Ełk, *Poland* 44 E9
Elk →, *Canada* 104 C5
Ełk →, *Poland* 44 E9
Elk →, *U.S.A.* 109 H2
Elk City, *U.S.A.* 113 H5
Elk Creek, *U.S.A.* 116 F4
Elk Grove, *U.S.A.* 116 G5
Elk Island Nat. Park, *Canada* 104 C6
Elk Lake, *Canada* 102 C3
Elk Point, *Canada* 105 C6
Elk River, *Idaho, U.S.A.* 114 C5
Elk River, *Minn., U.S.A.* 112 C8
Elkedra →, *Australia* 94 C2
Elkhart, *Ind., U.S.A.* 108 E3
Elkhart, *Kans., U.S.A.* 113 G4
Elkhorn, *Canada* 105 D8
Elkhorn →, *U.S.A.* 112 E6
Elkhovo, *Bulgaria* 41 D10
Elkin, *U.S.A.* 109 G5
Elkins, *U.S.A.* 108 F6
Elkland, *U.S.A.* 110 E7
Elko, *Canada* 104 D5
Elko, *U.S.A.* 114 F6
Elkton, *U.S.A.* 110 C1
Ell, L., *Australia* 93 E4
Ellef Ringnes I., *Canada* 4 B2
Ellen, Mt., *U.S.A.* 111 B12
Ellenburg, *U.S.A.* 111 B11
Ellendale, *U.S.A.* 112 B5
Ellensburg, *U.S.A.* 114 C3
Ellenville, *U.S.A.* 111 E10
Ellery, Mt., *Australia* 95 F4
Ellesmere, L., *N.Z.* 91 M4
Ellesmere I., *Canada* 4 B4
Ellesmere Port, *U.K.* 12 D5
Ellice Is. = Tuvalu ■, *Pac. Oc.* 96 H9
Ellicottville, *U.S.A.* 110 D6
Elliot, *Australia* 94 B1
Elliot, *S. Africa* 89 E4
Elliot Lake, *Canada* 102 C3
Elliotdale = Xhora, *S. Africa* 89 E4
Ellis, *U.S.A.* 112 F5
Elliston, *Australia* 95 E1
Ellisville, *U.S.A.* 113 K10
Ellon, *U.K.* 14 D6
Ellore = Eluru, *India* 67 L12
Ellsworth, *Kans., U.S.A.* 112 F5
Ellsworth, *Maine, U.S.A.* 109 C11
Ellsworth Land, *Antarctica* 5 D16
Ellsworth Mts., *Antarctica* 5 D16
Ellwangen, *Germany* 25 G6
Ellwood City, *U.S.A.* 110 F4
Elm, *Switz.* 25 J5
Elma, *Canada* 105 D9
Elma, *U.S.A.* 116 D3
Elmadağ, *Turkey* 72 C5

Elmalı, *Turkey* 39 E11
Elmhurst, *U.S.A.* 108 E2
Elmina, *Ghana* 83 D4
Elmira, *Canada* 110 C4
Elmira, *U.S.A.* 110 D8
Elmira Heights, *U.S.A.* 110 D8
Elmore, *Australia* 95 F3
Elmore, *U.S.A.* 117 M11
Elmshorn, *Germany* 24 B5
Elmvale, *Canada* 110 B5
Elne, *France* 20 F6
Elora, *Canada* 110 C4
Elos, *Greece* 38 E4
Eloúnda, *Greece* 36 D7
Eloy, *U.S.A.* 115 K8
Éloyes, *France* 19 D13
Elrose, *Canada* 105 C7
Elsdorf, *Germany* 24 E2
Elsie, *U.S.A.* 116 E3
Elsinore = Helsingør, *Denmark* 11 H6
Elster →, *Germany* 24 D7
Elsterwerda, *Germany* 24 D9
Eltham, *N.Z.* 91 H5
Elton, *Russia* 49 F8
Elton, Ozero, *Russia* 49 F8
Eltville, *Germany* 25 E4
Eluru, *India* 67 L12
Elvas, *Portugal* 35 G3
Elven, *France* 18 E4
Elverum, *Norway* 9 F14
Elvire →, *Australia* 92 C4
Elvire, Mt., *Australia* 93 E2
Elvo →, *Italy* 28 C5
Elwell, L., *U.S.A.* 114 B8
Elwood, *Ind., U.S.A.* 108 E3
Elwood, *Nebr., U.S.A.* 112 E5
Elx = Elche, *Spain* 33 G4
Ely, *U.K.* 13 E8
Ely, *Minn., U.S.A.* 112 B9
Ely, *Nev., U.S.A.* 114 G6
Elyria, *U.S.A.* 110 E2
Elyrus, *Greece* 38 F5
Elz →, *Germany* 25 G3
Emådalen, *Sweden* 10 C8
Emāmrūd, *Iran* 71 B7
Emån →, *Sweden* 11 G10
Emba, *Kazakstan* 50 E6
Emba →, *Kazakstan* 50 E6
Embarcación, *Argentina* 126 A3
Embarras Portage, *Canada* 105 B6
Embetsu, *Japan* 54 B10
Embi = Emba, *Kazakstan* 50 E6
Embi = Emba →, *Kazakstan* 50 E6
Embóna, *Greece* 36 C9
Embrun, *France* 21 D10
Embu, *Kenya* 86 C4
Emden, *Germany* 24 B3
Emecik, *Turkey* 39 E9
Emerald, *Australia* 94 C4
Emerson, *Canada* 105 D9
Emet, *Turkey* 39 B11
Emi Koussi, *Chad* 79 E9
Emília-Romagna □, *Italy* 28 D8
Emilius, Mte., *Italy* 28 C4
Eminabad, *Pakistan* 68 C6
Emine, Nos, *Bulgaria* 41 D11
Emirdağ, *Turkey* 72 C4
Emlenton, *U.S.A.* 110 E5
Emlichheim, *Germany* 24 C2
Emmaboda, *Sweden* 11 H9
Emmaus, *S. Africa* 88 D4
Emmaus, *U.S.A.* 111 F9
Emme →, *Switz.* 25 H3
Emmeloord, *Neths.* 17 B5
Emmen, *Neths.* 17 B6
Emmen, *Switz.* 25 H4
Emmendingen, *Germany* 25 G3
Emmental, *Switz.* 25 J3
Emmerich, *Germany* 24 D2
Emmet, *Australia* 94 C3
Emmetsburg, *U.S.A.* 112 D7
Emmett, *Idaho, U.S.A.* 114 E5
Emmett, *Mich., U.S.A.* 110 D2
Emmonak, *U.S.A.* 100 B3
Emo, *Canada* 105 D10
Emőd, *Hungary* 42 C5
Emona, *Bulgaria* 41 D11
Empalme, *Mexico* 118 B2
Empangeni, *S. Africa* 89 D5
Empedrado, *Argentina* 126 B4
Emperor Seamount Chain, *Pac. Oc.* 96 D9
Empoli, *Italy* 28 E7
Emporia, *Kans., U.S.A.* 112 F6
Emporia, *Va., U.S.A.* 109 G7
Emporium, *U.S.A.* 110 E6
Empress, *Canada* 105 C7
Empty Quarter = Rub' al Khālī, *Si. Arabia* 74 D4
Ems →, *Germany* 24 B3
Emsdale, *Canada* 110 A5
Emsdetten, *Germany* 24 C3
Emu, *China* 57 C15
Emu Park, *Australia* 94 C5
'En 'Avrona, *Israel* 75 F4
En Nahud, *Sudan* 81 E2
En Nofalab, *Sudan* 81 D3
Ena, *Japan* 55 G8
Enana, *Namibia* 88 B2
Enånger, *Sweden* 10 C11
Enard B., *U.K.* 14 C3
Enare = Inarijärvi, *Finland* 8 B22
Enarotali, *Indonesia* 63 E9
Encampment, *U.S.A.* 114 F10
Encantadas, Serra, *Brazil* 127 C5
Encarnación, *Paraguay* 127 B4
Encarnación de Diaz, *Mexico* 118 C4
Enchi, *Ghana* 82 D4
Encinitas, *U.S.A.* 117 M9
Encino, *U.S.A.* 115 J11
Encounter B., *Australia* 95 F2
Encs, *Hungary* 42 B6
Endako, *Canada* 104 C3
Ende, *Indonesia* 63 F6
Endeavour Str., *Australia* 94 A3
Endelave, *Denmark* 11 J4
Enderbury I., *Kiribati* 96 H10
Enderby, *Canada* 104 C5
Enderby I., *Australia* 92 D2
Enderby Land, *Antarctica* 5 C5
Enderlin, *U.S.A.* 112 B6
Endicott, *U.S.A.* 111 D8
Endwell, *U.S.A.* 111 D8
Endyalgout I., *Australia* 92 B5
Eneabba, *Australia* 93 E2
Enewetak Atoll, *Marshall Is.* 96 F8
Enez, *Turkey* 41 F10
Enfield, *Canada* 103 D7
Enfield, *Conn., U.S.A.* 111 E12
Enfield, *N.H., U.S.A.* 111 C12
Engadin, *Switz.* 25 J6
Engaño, C., *Dom. Rep.* 121 C6
Engaño, C., *Phil.* 63 A6
Engaru, *Japan* 54 B11
Engcobo, *S. Africa* 89 E4
Engelberg, *Switz.* 25 J4
Engels, *Russia* 48 E8
Engemann L., *Canada* 105 B7
Engershatu, *Eritrea* 81 D4
Enggano, *Indonesia* 62 F2
England, *U.S.A.* 113 H9
England □, *U.K.* 12 D7
Englee, *Canada* 103 B8
Englehart, *Canada* 102 C4
Englewood, *U.S.A.* 112 F2
English →, *Canada* 105 C10
English Bazar = Ingraj Bazar, *India* 69 G13
English Channel, *Europe* 13 G6
English River, *Canada* 102 C1
Engures ezers, *Latvia* 44 A10
Enguri →, *Georgia* 49 J5
Enid, *U.S.A.* 113 G6
Enipévs →, *Greece* 38 B4
Enkhuizen, *Neths.* 17 B5
Enköping, *Sweden* 10 E11
Enle, *China* 58 F3
Enna, *Italy* 31 E7
Ennadai, *Canada* 105 A8
Ennadai L., *Canada* 105 A8
Ennedi, *Chad* 79 E10
Enngonia, *Australia* 95 D4
Ennigerloh, *Germany* 24 D4
Ennis, *Ireland* 15 D3
Ennis, *Mont., U.S.A.* 114 D8
Ennis, *Tex., U.S.A.* 113 J6
Enniscorthy, *Ireland* 15 D5
Enniskillen, *U.K.* 15 B4
Ennistimon, *Ireland* 15 D2
Enns, *Austria* 26 C7
Enns →, *Austria* 26 C7
Enontekiö, *Finland* 8 B20
Enosburg Falls, *U.S.A.* 111 B12
Enping, *China* 59 F9
Enriquillo, L., *Dom. Rep.* 121 C5
Enschede, *Neths.* 17 B6
Ensenada, *Argentina* 126 C4
Ensenada, *Mexico* 118 A1
Ensenada de los Muertos, *Mexico* 118 C2
Enshi, *China* 58 B7
Ensiola, Pta. de n', *Spain* 37 B9
Ensisheim, *France* 19 E14
Entebbe, *Uganda* 86 B3
Enterprise, *Canada* 104 A5
Enterprise, *Ala., U.S.A.* 109 K3
Enterprise, *Oreg., U.S.A.* 114 D5
Entraygues-sur-Truyère, *France* 20 D6
Entre Ríos, *Bolivia* 126 A3
Entre Ríos □, *Argentina* 126 C4
Entrepeñas, Embalse de, *Spain* 32 E2
Entroncamento, *Portugal* 35 F2
Enugu, *Nigeria* 83 D6
Enugu □, *Nigeria* 83 D6
Enugu Ezike, *Nigeria* 83 D6
Enumclaw, *U.S.A.* 116 C5
Envermeu, *France* 18 C8
Enviken, *Sweden* 10 D9
Enying, *Hungary* 42 D3
Enza →, *Italy* 28 D7
Eólie, Ís., *Italy* 31 D7
Epanomí, *Greece* 40 F6
Epe, *Neths.* 17 B5
Epe, *Nigeria* 83 D5
Épernay, *France* 19 C10
Épernon, *France* 19 D8
Ephesus, *Turkey* 39 D9
Ephraim, *U.S.A.* 114 G8
Ephrata, *Pa., U.S.A.* 111 F8
Ephrata, *Wash., U.S.A.* 114 C4
Epidaurus Limera, *Greece* 38 E5
Épila, *Spain* 32 D3
Épinac, *France* 19 F11
Épinal, *France* 19 D13
Episkopi, *Cyprus* 36 E11
Episkopí, *Greece* 36 D6
Episkopi Bay, *Cyprus* 36 E11
Epitálion, *Greece* 38 D3
Eppan = Appiano, *Italy* 29 B8
Eppingen, *Germany* 25 F4
Epsom, *U.K.* 13 F7
Epukiro, *Namibia* 88 C2
Equatorial Guinea ■, *Africa* 84 D1
Er Hai, *China* 58 E3
Er Rachidia, *Morocco* 78 B5
Er Rahad, *Sudan* 81 E3
Er Rif, *Morocco* 78 A5
Er Rogel, *Sudan* 80 D4
Er Roseires, *Sudan* 81 E3
Er Rua'at, *Sudan* 81 E3
Eraclea, *Italy* 29 C9
Erāwadī Myit = Irrawaddy →, *Burma* 67 M19
Erāwadī Myitwanya = Irrawaddy, Mouths of the, *Burma* 67 M19
Erba, *Italy* 28 C6
Erba, *Sudan* 80 D4
Erba, J., *Sudan* 80 C4
Erbaa, *Turkey* 72 B7
Erbeskopf, *Germany* 25 F3
Erbil = Arbīl, *Iraq* 70 B5
Erbu, *Ethiopia* 81 E3
Erçek, *Turkey* 70 B4
Erçis, *Turkey* 73 C10
Erciyaş Dağı, *Turkey* 70 B2
Érd, *Hungary* 42 C3
Erdao Jiang →, *China* 57 C14
Erdek, *Turkey* 41 F11
Erdemli, *Turkey* 72 D6
Erdene = Ulaan-Uul, *Mongolia* 56 B6
Erdenetsogt, *Mongolia* 56 C4
Erding, *Germany* 25 G7
Erdre →, *France* 18 E5
Erebus, Mt., *Antarctica* 5 D11
Erechim, *Brazil* 127 B5
Ereğli, *Konya, Turkey* 70 B2
Ereğli, *Zonguldak, Turkey* 72 B4
Erei, Monti, *Italy* 31 E7
Erenhot, *China* 56 C7
Eresma →, *Spain* 34 D6
Eressós, *Greece* 39 B7
Erfenisdam, *S. Africa* 88 D4
Erfstadt, *Germany* 24 E2
Erft →, *Germany* 24 D2
Erfurt, *Germany* 24 E7
Erg Iguidi, *Africa* 78 C4
Ergani, *Turkey* 70 B3
Ergel, *Mongolia* 56 C5
Ergene →, *Turkey* 41 E10
Ergeni Vozvyshennost, *Russia* 49 G7
Ērgli, *Latvia* 9 H21
Erhlin, *Taiwan* 59 F13
Eria →, *Spain* 34 C5
Eriba, *Sudan* 81 D4
Eriboll, L., *U.K.* 14 C4
Érice, *Italy* 30 D5
Erie, *U.S.A.* 110 D4
Erie, L., *N. Amer.* 110 D4
Erie Canal, *U.S.A.* 110 C7
Erieau, *Canada* 110 D3
Erigavo, *Somali Rep.* 74 E4
Erikoúsa, *Greece* 36 A3
Eriksdale, *Canada* 105 C9
Erímanthos, *Greece* 38 D3
Erimo-misaki, *Japan* 54 D11
Erinpura, *India* 68 G5
Eriskay, *U.K.* 14 D1
Erithraí, *Greece* 38 C5
Eritrea ■, *Africa* 81 E4
Erjas →, *Portugal* 34 F3
Erkelenz, *Germany* 24 D2
Erkner, *Germany* 24 C9
Erlangen, *Germany* 25 F6
Erldunda, *Australia* 94 D1
Ermelo, *Neths.* 17 B5
Ermelo, *S. Africa* 89 D4
Ermenek, *Turkey* 70 B2
Ermil, *Sudan* 81 E2
Ermióni, *Greece* 38 D5
Ermones, *Greece* 36 A3
Ermoúpolis = Síros, *Greece* 38 D6
Ernakulam = Cochin, *India* 66 Q10
Erne →, *Ireland* 15 B3
Erne, Lower L., *U.K.* 15 B4
Erne, Upper L., *U.K.* 15 B4
Ernée, *France* 18 D6
Ernest Giles Ra., *Australia* 93 E3
Ernstberg, *Germany* 25 E2
Erode, *India* 66 P10
Eromanga, *Australia* 95 D3
Erongo, *Namibia* 88 C2
Erquy, *France* 18 D4
Erramala Hills, *India* 66 M11
Errer →, *Ethiopia* 81 F5
Errigal, *Ireland* 15 A3
Erris Hd., *Ireland* 15 B1
Ersekë, *Albania* 40 F4
Erskine, *U.S.A.* 112 B7
Erstein, *France* 19 D14
Ertholmene, *Denmark* 11 J9
Ertil, *Russia* 48 E5
Ertis = Irtysh →, *Russia* 50 C7
Eruh, *Turkey* 73 D10
Eruwa, *Nigeria* 83 D5
Ervy-le-Châtel, *France* 19 D10
Erwin, *U.S.A.* 109 G4
Eryuan, *China* 58 D2
Erzgebirge, *Germany* 24 E8
Erzin, *Russia* 51 D10
Erzincan, *Turkey* 70 B3
Erzurum, *Turkey* 70 B4
Es Caló, *Spain* 37 C8
Es Canar, *Spain* 37 B8
Es Mercadal, *Spain* 37 B11
Es Migjorn Gran, *Spain* 37 B11
Es Safiya, *Sudan* 81 D3
Es Sahrâ' Esh Sharqîya, *Egypt* 80 B3
Es Sînâ', *Egypt* 75 F3
Es Sûkî, *Sudan* 81 E3
Es Vedrà, *Spain* 37 C7
Esambo, *Dem. Rep. of the Congo* 86 C1
Esan-Misaki, *Japan* 54 D10
Esashi, *Hokkaidō, Japan* 54 B11
Esashi, *Hokkaidō, Japan* 54 D10
Esbjerg, *Denmark* 11 J2
Escalante, *U.S.A.* 115 H8
Escalante →, *U.S.A.* 115 H8
Escalón, *Mexico* 118 B4
Escambia →, *U.S.A.* 109 K2
Escanaba, *U.S.A.* 108 C2
Esch-sur-Alzette, *Lux.* 17 E6
Eschede, *Germany* 24 C6
Eschwege, *Germany* 24 D6
Eschweiler, *Germany* 24 E2
Escondido, *U.S.A.* 117 M9
Escravos →, *Nigeria* 83 D6
Escuinapa, *Mexico* 118 C3
Escuintla, *Guatemala* 120 D1
Eséka, *Cameroon* 83 E7
Eşen →, *Turkey* 39 E11
Esenguly, *Turkmenistan* 50 F6
Esens, *Germany* 24 B3
Esenyurt, *Turkey* 41 E12
Esera →, *Spain* 32 C5
Eşfahān, *Iran* 71 C6
Eşfahān □, *Iran* 71 C6
Esfarāyen, *Iran* 71 B8
Esfīdeh, *Iran* 71 C8
Esgueva →, *Spain* 34 D6
Esh Sham = Dimashq, *Syria* 75 B5
Esh Shamâlîya □, *Sudan* 80 D2
Esha Ness, *U.K.* 14 A7
Eshan, *China* 58 E4
Esher, *U.K.* 13 F7
Eshowe, *S. Africa* 89 D5
Esiama, *Ghana* 82 E4
Esigodini, *Zimbabwe* 89 C4
Esil = Ishim →, *Russia* 50 D8
Esino →, *Italy* 29 E10
Esira, *Madag.* 89 C8
Esk →, *Cumb., U.K.* 14 G5
Esk →, *N. Yorks., U.K.* 12 C7
Eskān, *Iran* 71 E9
Esker, *Canada* 103 B6
Eskifjörður, *Iceland* 8 D7
Eskilsäter, *Sweden* 11 F7
Eskilstuna, *Sweden* 10 E10
Eskimalatya, *Turkey* 73 C8
Eskimo Pt., *Canada* 100 B10
Eskişehir, *Turkey* 39 B12
Eskişehir □, *Turkey* 39 B12
Esla →, *Spain* 34 D4
Eslāmābād-e Gharb, *Iran* 70 C5
Eslāmshahr, *Iran* 71 C6
Eslöv, *Sweden* 11 J7
Eşme, *Turkey* 39 C10
Esmeraldas, *Ecuador* 124 C3
Esnagi L., *Canada* 102 C3
Espalion, *France* 20 D6
Espanola, *Canada* 102 C3
Espanola, *U.S.A.* 115 H10
Esparreguera, *Spain* 32 D6
Esparta, *Costa Rica* 120 E3
Espelkamp, *Germany* 24 C4
Esperance, *Australia* 93 F3
Esperance B., *Australia* 93 F3
Esperanza, *Argentina* 126 C3
Esperanza, *Phil.* 61 G6
Espéraza, *France* 20 F6
Espichel, C., *Portugal* 35 G1
Espiel, *Spain* 35 G5
Espigão, Serra do, *Brazil* 127 B5
Espinazo, Sierra del = Espinhaço, Serra do, *Brazil* 125 G10
Espinhaço, Serra do, *Brazil* 125 G10
Espinho, *Portugal* 34 D2
Espinilho, Serra do, *Brazil* 127 B5
Espinosa de los Monteros, *Spain* 34 B7
Espírito Santo □, *Brazil* 125 H10
Espíritu Santo, *Vanuatu* 96 J8
Espíritu Santo, B. del, *Mexico* 119 D7
Espíritu Santo, I., *Mexico* 118 C2
Espita, *Mexico* 119 C7
Espiye, *Turkey* 73 B8
Espluga de Francolí, *Spain* 32 D6
Espoo, *Finland* 9 F21
Espuña, Sierra de, *Spain* 33 H3
Espungabera, *Mozam.* 89 C5
Esquel, *Argentina* 128 E2
Esquimalt, *Canada* 104 D4
Esquina, *Argentina* 126 C4
Essaouira, *Morocco* 78 B4
Essebie, *Dem. Rep. of the Congo* 86 B3
Essen, *Belgium* 17 C4
Essen, *Germany* 24 D3
Essendon, Mt., *Australia* 93 E3
Essequibo →, *Guyana* 122 C5
Essex, *Canada* 110 D2
Essex, *Calif., U.S.A.* 117 L11
Essex, *N.Y., U.S.A.* 111 B11
Essex □, *U.K.* 13 F8
Essex Junction, *U.S.A.* 111 B11
Esslingen, *Germany* 25 G5
Essonne □, *France* 19 D9
Estaca de Bares, C. de, *Spain* 34 B3
Estadilla, *Spain* 32 C5
Estados, I. de Los, *Argentina* 122 J4
Estagel, *France* 20 F6
Eşţahbānāt, *Iran* 71 D7
Estância, *Brazil* 125 F11
Estancia, *U.S.A.* 115 J10
Estārm, *Iran* 71 D8
Estarreja, *Portugal* 34 E2
Estats, Pic d', *Spain* 32 C6
Estcourt, *S. Africa* 89 D4
Este, *Italy* 29 C8
Estelí, *Nic.* 120 D2
Estella, *Spain* 32 C2
Estellencs, *Spain* 37 B9
Estena →, *Spain* 35 F6
Estepa, *Spain* 35 H6
Estepona, *Spain* 35 J5
Esterhazy, *Canada* 105 C8
Esternay, *France* 19 D10
Esterri d'Aneu, *Spain* 32 C6
Estevan, *Canada* 105 D8
Estevan Group, *Canada* 104 C3
Estherville, *U.S.A.* 112 D7
Estissac, *France* 19 D10
Eston, *Canada* 105 C7
Estonia ■, *Europe* 9 G21
Estoril, *Portugal* 35 G1
Estouk, *Mali* 83 B5
Estreito, *Brazil* 125 E9
Estrela, Serra da, *Portugal* 34 E3
Estrella, *Spain* 35 G7
Estremoz, *Portugal* 35 G3
Estrondo, Serra do, *Brazil* 125 E9
Esztergom, *Hungary* 42 C3
Et Tîdra, *Mauritania* 82 B1
Etah, *India* 69 F8
Étain, *France* 19 C12
Étampes, *France* 19 D9
Etanga, *Namibia* 88 B1
Étaples, *France* 19 B8
Etawah, *India* 69 F8
Etawney L., *Canada* 105 B9
Ete, *Nigeria* 83 D6
Ethel, *U.S.A.* 116 D4
Ethelbert, *Canada* 105 C8
Ethiopia ■, *Africa* 74 F3
Ethiopian Highlands, *Ethiopia* 52 J7
Etili, *Turkey* 41 G10
Etive, L., *U.K.* 14 E3
Etna, *Italy* 31 E7
Etoile, *Dem. Rep. of the Congo* 87 E2
Etosha Nat. Park, *Namibia* 88 B2
Etosha Pan, *Namibia* 88 B2
Etowah, *U.S.A.* 109 H3
Étréchy, *France* 19 D9
Étrépagny, *France* 19 C8
Étretat, *France* 18 C7
Etropole, *Bulgaria* 41 D8
Ettelbruck, *Lux.* 17 E6
Ettlingen, *Germany* 25 G4
Ettrick Water →, *U.K.* 14 F6
Etuku, *Dem. Rep. of the Congo* 86 C2
Etulia, *Moldova* 43 E13
Etzatlán, *Mexico* 118 C4
Etzná, *Mexico* 119 D6
Eu, *France* 18 B8
Euboea = Évvoia, *Greece* 38 C6
Eucla, *Australia* 93 F4
Euclid, *U.S.A.* 110 E3
Eucumbene, L., *Australia* 95 F4
Eudora, *U.S.A.* 113 J9
Eufaula, *Ala., U.S.A.* 109 K3
Eufaula, *Okla., U.S.A.* 113 H7
Eufaula L., *U.S.A.* 113 H7
Eugene, *U.S.A.* 114 E2
Eugowra, *Australia* 95 E4
Eulo, *Australia* 95 D4
Eunice, *La., U.S.A.* 113 K8
Eunice, *N. Mex., U.S.A.* 113 J3
Eupen, *Belgium* 17 D6
Euphrates = Furāt, Nahr al →, *Asia* 70 D5
Eure □, *France* 18 C8
Eure →, *France* 18 C8
Eure-et-Loir □, *France* 18 D8
Eureka, *Canada* 4 B3
Eureka, *Calif., U.S.A.* 114 F1
Eureka, *Kans., U.S.A.* 113 G6
Eureka, *Mont., U.S.A.* 114 B6
Eureka, *Nev., U.S.A.* 114 G5
Eureka, *S. Dak., U.S.A.* 112 C5
Eureka, Mt., *Australia* 93 E3
Euroa, *Australia* 95 F4
Europa, Île, *Ind. Oc.* 85 J8
Europa, Picos de, *Spain* 34 B6
Europa, Pta. de, *Gib.* 35 J5
Europe 6 E10
Europoort, *Neths.* 17 C4
Euskirchen, *Germany* 24 E2
Eustis, *U.S.A.* 109 L5
Eutin, *Germany* 24 A6
Eutsuk L., *Canada* 104 C3
Evale, *Angola* 88 B2
Evans, *U.S.A.* 112 E2
Evans, L., *Canada* 102 B4
Evans City, *U.S.A.* 110 F4
Evans Head, *Australia* 95 D5
Evans Mills, *U.S.A.* 111 B9
Evansburg, *Canada* 104 C5
Evanston, *Ill., U.S.A.* 108 E2
Evanston, *Wyo., U.S.A.* 114 F8
Evansville, *U.S.A.* 108 G2
Évaux-les-Bains, *France* 19 F9
Evaz, *Iran* 71 E7
Evciler, *Afyon, Turkey* 39 C11
Evciler, *Çanakkale, Turkey* 39 B8
Eveleth, *U.S.A.* 112 B8
Evensk, *Russia* 51 C16
Everard, L., *Australia* 95 E2
Everard Ranges, *Australia* 93 E5
Everest, Mt., *Nepal* 69 E12
Everett, *Pa., U.S.A.* 110 F6
Everett, *Wash., U.S.A.* 116 C4
Everglades, The, *U.S.A.* 109 N5
Everglades City, *U.S.A.* 109 N5
Everglades National Park, *U.S.A.* 109 N5
Evergreen, *Ala., U.S.A.* 109 K2

Evergreen, *Mont., U.S.A.* **114 B6**
Everöd, *Sweden* **11 J8**
Evertsberg, *Sweden* **10 C7**
Evesham, *U.K.* **13 E6**
Évian-les-Bains, *France* **19 F13**
Évinos →, *Greece* **38 C3**
Évisa, *France* **21 F12**
Evje, *Norway* **9 G12**
Évora, *Portugal* **35 G3**
Évora □, *Portugal* **35 G3**
Evowghlī, *Iran* **70 B5**
Évreux, *France* **18 C8**
Evritanía □, *Greece* **38 B3**
Évron, *France* **18 D6**
Évros □, *Greece* **41 E10**
Évros →, *Greece* **72 B2**
Evrótas →, *Greece* **38 E4**
Évry, *France* **19 D9**
Évvoia, *Greece* **38 C6**
Évvoia □, *Greece* **38 C5**
Evxinoúpolis, *Greece* **38 B4**
Ewe, L., *U.K.* **14 D3**
Ewing, *U.S.A.* **112 D5**
Ewo, *Congo* **84 E2**
Exaltación, *Bolivia* **124 F5**
Excelsior Springs, *U.S.A.* **112 F7**
Excideuil, *France* **20 C5**
Exe →, *U.K.* **13 G4**
Exeter, *Canada* **110 C3**
Exeter, *U.K.* **13 G4**
Exeter, *Calif., U.S.A.* **116 J7**
Exeter, *N.H., U.S.A.* **111 D14**
Exmoor, *U.K.* **13 F4**
Exmouth, *Australia* **92 D1**
Exmouth, *U.K.* **13 G4**
Exmouth G., *Australia* **92 D1**
Expedition Ra., *Australia* **94 C4**
Extremadura □, *Spain* **35 F4**
Exuma Sound, *Bahamas* **120 B4**
Eyasi, L., *Tanzania* **86 C4**
Eye Pen., *U.K.* **14 C2**
Eyemouth, *U.K.* **14 F6**
Eygurande, *France* **19 G9**
Eyjafjörður, *Iceland* **8 C4**
Eymet, *France* **20 D4**
Eymoutiers, *France* **20 C5**
Eynesil, *Turkey* **73 B8**
Eyre (North), L., *Australia* **95 D2**
Eyre (South), L., *Australia* **95 D2**
Eyre Mts., *N.Z.* **91 L2**
Eyre Pen., *Australia* **95 E2**
Eysturoy, *Færoe Is.* **8 E9**
Eyvānkī, *Iran* **71 C6**
Ez Zeidab, *Sudan* **80 D3**
Ezcaray, *Spain* **32 C1**
Ežerėlis, *Lithuania* **44 D10**
Ezhou, *China* **59 B10**
Ezine, *Turkey* **39 B8**
Ezouza →, *Cyprus* **36 E11**

F

F.Y.R.O.M. = Macedonia ■, *Europe* **40 E5**
Fabala, *Guinea* **82 D3**
Fabens, *U.S.A.* **115 L10**
Fabero, *Spain* **34 C4**
Fåborg, *Denmark* **11 J4**
Fabriano, *Italy* **29 E9**
Făcăeni, *Romania* **43 F12**
Fachi, *Niger* **79 E8**
Fada, *Chad* **79 E10**
Fada-n-Gourma, *Burkina Faso* **83 C5**
Fadd, *Hungary* **42 D3**
Faddeyevskiy, Ostrov, *Russia* **51 B15**
Faddor, *Sudan* **81 F3**
Fadghāmī, *Syria* **70 C4**
Fadlab, *Sudan* **80 D3**
Faenza, *Italy* **29 D8**
Færoe Is. = Føroyar, *Atl. Oc.* **8 F9**
Fafa, *Mali* **83 B5**
Fafe, *Portugal* **34 D2**
Fagam, *Nigeria* **83 C7**
Făgăras, *Romania* **43 E9**
Făgăras, Munţii, *Romania* **43 E9**
Fågelmara, *Sweden* **11 H9**
Fagerhult, *Sweden* **11 G9**
Fagersta, *Sweden* **10 D9**
Făget, *Romania* **42 E7**
Făget, Munţii, *Romania* **43 C8**
Fagnano, L., *Argentina* **128 G3**
Fagnières, *France* **19 D11**
Faguibine, L., *Mali* **82 B4**
Fahlīān, *Iran* **71 D6**
Fahraj, *Kermān, Iran* **71 D8**
Fahraj, *Yazd, Iran* **71 D7**
Fai Tsi Long Archipelago, *Vietnam* **58 G6**
Faial, *Madeira* **37 D3**
Fair Haven, *U.S.A.* **108 D9**
Fair Hd., *U.K.* **15 A5**
Fair Oaks, *U.S.A.* **116 G5**
Fairbanks, *U.S.A.* **100 B5**
Fairbury, *U.S.A.* **112 E6**
Fairfax, *U.S.A.* **111 B11**
Fairfield, *Ala., U.S.A.* **109 J2**
Fairfield, *Calif., U.S.A.* **116 G4**
Fairfield, *Conn., U.S.A.* **111 E11**
Fairfield, *Idaho, U.S.A.* **114 E6**
Fairfield, *Ill., U.S.A.* **108 F1**
Fairfield, *Iowa, U.S.A.* **112 E9**
Fairfield, *Tex., U.S.A.* **113 K7**
Fairford, *Canada* **105 C9**
Fairhope, *U.S.A.* **109 K2**
Fairlie, *N.Z.* **91 L3**
Fairmead, *U.S.A.* **116 H6**
Fairmont, *Minn., U.S.A.* **112 D7**
Fairmont, *W. Va., U.S.A.* **108 F5**
Fairmount, *Calif., U.S.A.* **117 L8**
Fairmount, *N.Y., U.S.A.* **111 C8**
Fairplay, *U.S.A.* **115 G11**
Fairport, *U.S.A.* **110 C7**
Fairport Harbor, *U.S.A.* **110 E3**
Fairview, *Canada* **104 B5**
Fairview, *Mont., U.S.A.* **112 B2**
Fairview, *Okla., U.S.A.* **113 G5**
Fairweather, Mt., *U.S.A.* **104 B1**
Faisalabad, *Pakistan* **68 D5**
Faith, *U.S.A.* **112 C3**
Faizabad, *India* **69 F10**
Fajardo, *Puerto Rico* **121 C6**
Fajr, W. →, *Si. Arabia* **70 D3**
Fakenham, *U.K.* **12 E8**
Fåker, *Sweden* **10 A8**
Fakfak, *Indonesia* **63 E8**
Fakiya, *Bulgaria* **41 D11**
Fakobli, *Ivory C.* **82 D3**
Fakse, *Denmark* **11 J6**
Fakse Bugt, *Denmark* **11 J6**
Fakse Ladeplads, *Denmark* **11 J6**
Faku, *China* **57 C12**
Falaba, *S. Leone* **82 D2**
Falaise, *France* **18 D6**
Falaise, Mui, *Vietnam* **64 C5**
Falakrón Óros, *Greece* **40 E7**
Falam, *Burma* **67 H18**
Falces, *Spain* **32 C3**
Fălciu, *Romania* **43 D13**
Falcó, C. des, *Spain* **37 C7**
Falcón, Presa, *Mexico* **119 B5**
Falcon Lake, *Canada* **105 D9**
Falcon Reservoir, *U.S.A.* **113 M5**
Falconara Marittima, *Italy* **29 E10**
Falcone, C. del, *Italy* **30 B1**
Falconer, *U.S.A.* **110 D5**
Faléa, *Mali* **82 C2**
Falémé →, *Senegal* **82 C2**
Falerum, *Sweden* **11 F10**
Faleshty = Fălești, *Moldova* **43 C12**
Fălești, *Moldova* **43 C12**
Falfurrias, *U.S.A.* **113 M5**
Falher, *Canada* **104 B5**
Falirakí, *Greece* **36 C10**
Falkenberg, *Germany* **24 D9**
Falkenberg, *Sweden* **11 H6**
Falkensee, *Germany* **24 C9**
Falkirk, *U.K.* **14 F5**
Falkirk □, *U.K.* **14 F5**
Falkland, *U.K.* **14 E5**
Falkland Is. □, *Atl. Oc.* **128 G5**
Falkland Sd., *Falk. Is.* **128 G5**
Falkonéra, *Greece* **38 E5**
Falköping, *Sweden* **11 F7**
Fall River, *U.S.A.* **111 E13**
Fallbrook, *U.S.A.* **117 M9**
Fallon, *U.S.A.* **114 G4**
Falls City, *U.S.A.* **112 E7**
Falls Creek, *U.S.A.* **110 E6**
Falmouth, *Jamaica* **120 C4**
Falmouth, *U.K.* **13 G2**
Falmouth, *U.S.A.* **111 E14**
Falsa, Pta., *Mexico* **118 B1**
False B., *S. Africa* **88 E2**
Falso, C., *Honduras* **120 C3**
Falster, *Denmark* **11 K5**
Falsterbo, *Sweden* **9 J15**
Fălticeni, *Romania* **43 C11**
Falun, *Sweden* **10 D9**
Famagusta, *Cyprus* **36 D12**
Famagusta Bay, *Cyprus* **36 D13**
Famalé, *Niger* **78 F6**
Famatina, Sierra de, *Argentina* **126 B2**
Family L., *Canada* **105 C9**
Famoso, *U.S.A.* **117 K7**
Fan Xian, *China* **56 G8**
Fana, *Mali* **82 C3**
Fanad Hd., *Ireland* **15 A4**
Fanárion, *Greece* **38 B3**
Fandriana, *Madag.* **89 C8**
Fang, *Thailand* **58 H2**
Fang Xian, *China* **59 A8**
Fangaga, *Sudan* **80 D4**
Fangak, *Sudan* **81 F3**
Fangchang, *China* **59 B12**
Fangcheng, *China* **56 H7**
Fangchenggang, *China* **58 G7**
Fangliao, *Taiwan* **59 F13**
Fangshan, *China* **56 E6**
Fangzi, *China* **57 F10**
Fani i Madh →, *Albania* **40 E4**
Fanjakana, *Madag.* **89 C8**
Fanjiatun, *China* **57 C13**
Fannich, L., *U.K.* **14 D4**
Fannūj, *Iran* **71 E8**
Fanø, *Denmark* **11 J2**
Fano, *Italy* **29 E10**
Fanshi, *China* **56 E7**
Fao = Al Fāw, *Iraq* **71 D6**
Faqirwali, *Pakistan* **68 E5**
Fâqûs, *Egypt* **80 H7**
Fara in Sabina, *Italy* **29 F9**
Faradje, *Dem. Rep. of the Congo* **86 B2**
Farafangana, *Madag.* **89 C8**
Farâfra, El Wâhât el-, *Egypt* **80 B2**
Farāh, *Afghan.* **66 C3**
Farāh □, *Afghan.* **66 C3**
Farahalana, *Madag.* **89 A9**
Faraid, Gebel, *Egypt* **80 C4**
Farako, *Ivory C.* **82 D4**
Faramana, *Burkina Faso* **82 C4**
Faranah, *Guinea* **82 C2**
Farasān, Jazā'ir, *Si. Arabia* **74 D3**
Farasan Is. = Farasān, Jazā'ir, *Si. Arabia* **74 D3**
Faratsiho, *Madag.* **89 B8**
Fardes →, *Spain* **35 H7**
Fareham, *U.K.* **13 G6**
Farewell, C., *N.Z.* **91 J4**
Farewell C. = Nunap Isua, *Greenland* **101 C15**
Färgelanda, *Sweden* **11 F5**
Farghona, *Uzbekistan* **50 E8**
Fargo, *U.S.A.* **112 B6**
Fār'iah, W. al →, *West Bank* **75 C4**
Faribault, *U.S.A.* **112 C8**
Faridabad, *India* **68 E6**
Faridkot, *India* **68 D6**
Faridpur, *Bangla.* **69 H13**
Faridpur, *India* **69 E8**
Färila, *Sweden* **10 C9**
Farim, *Guinea-Biss.* **82 C1**
Farīmān, *Iran* **71 C8**
Farina, *Australia* **95 E2**
Fariones, Pta., *Canary Is.* **37 E6**
Fâriskûr, *Egypt* **80 H7**
Färjestaden, *Sweden* **11 H10**
Farkadhón, *Greece* **38 B4**
Farmakonisi, *Greece* **39 D9**
Farmerville, *U.S.A.* **113 J8**
Farmingdale, *U.S.A.* **111 F10**
Farmington, *Canada* **104 B4**
Farmington, *Calif., U.S.A.* **116 H6**
Farmington, *Maine, U.S.A.* **109 C10**
Farmington, *Mo., U.S.A.* **113 G9**
Farmington, *N.H., U.S.A.* **111 C13**
Farmington, *N. Mex., U.S.A.* **115 H9**
Farmington, *Utah, U.S.A.* **114 F8**
Farmington →, *U.S.A.* **111 E12**
Farmville, *U.S.A.* **108 G6**
Färnäs, *Sweden* **10 D8**
Farne Is., *U.K.* **12 B6**
Farnham, *Canada* **111 A12**
Farnham, Mt., *Canada* **104 C5**
Faro, *Brazil* **125 D7**
Faro, *Canada* **100 B6**
Faro, *Portugal* **35 H3**
Fårö, *Sweden* **9 H18**
Faro □, *Portugal* **35 H2**
Fårösund, *Sweden* **11 G13**
Farquhar, C., *Australia* **93 D1**
Farrars Cr. →, *Australia* **94 D3**
Farrāshband, *Iran* **71 D7**
Farrell, *U.S.A.* **110 E4**
Farrokhī, *Iran* **71 C8**
Farruch, C. = Ferrutx, C., *Spain* **37 B10**
Fārs □, *Iran* **71 D7**
Fársala, *Greece* **38 B4**
Farsø, *Denmark* **11 H3**
Farson, *U.S.A.* **114 E9**
Farsund, *Norway* **9 G12**
Fartak, Râs, *Si. Arabia* **70 D2**
Fartak, Ra's, *Yemen* **74 D5**
Fârţăneşti, *Romania* **43 E12**
Fartura, Serra da, *Brazil* **127 B5**
Faru, *Nigeria* **83 C6**
Fārūj, *Iran* **71 B8**
Fårup, *Denmark* **11 H3**
Farvel, Kap = Nunap Isua, *Greenland* **101 C15**
Farwell, *U.S.A.* **113 H3**
Fāryāb □, *Afghan.* **66 B4**
Fasā, *Iran* **71 D7**
Fasano, *Italy* **31 B10**
Fashoda, *Sudan* **81 F3**
Fassa, *Mali* **82 C3**
Fastiv, *Ukraine* **47 G5**
Fastov = Fastiv, *Ukraine* **47 G5**
Fatagar, Tanjung, *Indonesia* **63 E8**
Fatehabad, *Haryana, India* **68 E6**
Fatehabad, *Ut. P., India* **68 F8**
Fatehgarh, *India* **69 F8**
Fatehpur, *Bihar, India* **69 G11**
Fatehpur, *Raj., India* **68 F6**
Fatehpur, *Ut. P., India* **69 G9**
Fatehpur, *Ut. P., India* **69 F9**
Fatehpur Sikri, *India* **68 F6**
Fatesh, *Russia* **47 F8**
Fathai, *Sudan* **81 F3**
Fatick, *Senegal* **82 C1**
Fatima, *Canada* **103 C7**
Fátima, *Portugal* **35 F2**
Fatoya, *Guinea* **82 C3**
Fatsa, *Turkey* **72 B7**
Faucille, Col de la, *France* **19 F13**
Faulkton, *U.S.A.* **112 C5**
Faulquemont, *France* **19 C13**
Faure I., *Australia* **93 E1**
Făurei, *Romania* **43 E12**
Fauresmith, *S. Africa* **88 D4**
Fauske, *Norway* **8 C16**
Favara, *Italy* **30 E6**
Favàritx, C. de, *Spain* **37 B11**
Faverges, *France* **21 C10**
Favignana, *Italy* **30 E5**
Favignana, I., *Italy* **30 E5**
Fawcett, Pt., *Australia* **92 B5**
Fawn →, *Canada* **102 A2**
Fawnskin, *U.S.A.* **117 L10**
Faxaflói, *Iceland* **8 D2**
Faxälven →, *Sweden* **10 A10**
Faya-Largeau, *Chad* **79 E9**
Fayd, *Si. Arabia* **70 E4**
Fayence, *France* **21 E10**
Fayette, *Ala., U.S.A.* **109 J2**
Fayette, *Mo., U.S.A.* **112 F8**
Fayetteville, *Ark., U.S.A.* **113 G7**
Fayetteville, *N.C., U.S.A.* **109 H6**
Fayetteville, *Tenn., U.S.A.* **109 H2**
Fayied, *Egypt* **80 H8**
Fayón, *Spain* **32 D5**
Fazilka, *India* **68 D6**
Fazilpur, *Pakistan* **68 E4**
Fdérik, *Mauritania* **78 D3**
Feale →, *Ireland* **15 D2**
Fear, C., *U.S.A.* **109 J7**
Feather →, *U.S.A.* **114 G3**
Feather Falls, *U.S.A.* **116 F5**
Featherston, *N.Z.* **91 J5**
Featherstone, *Zimbabwe* **87 F3**
Fécamp, *France* **18 C7**
Fedala = Mohammedia, *Morocco* **78 B4**
Federación, *Argentina* **126 C4**
Féderal, *Argentina* **128 C5**
Federal Capital Terr. □, *Nigeria* **83 D6**
Federal Way, *U.S.A.* **116 C4**
Fedeshkūh, *Iran* **71 D7**
Fehérgyarmat, *Hungary* **42 C7**
Fehmarn, *Germany* **24 A7**
Fehmarn Bælt, *Europe* **11 K5**
Fehmarn Belt = Fehmarn Bælt, *Europe* **11 K5**
Fei Xian, *China* **57 G9**
Feijó, *Brazil* **124 E4**
Feilding, *N.Z.* **91 J5**
Feira de Santana, *Brazil* **125 F11**
Feixi, *China* **59 B11**
Feixiang, *China* **56 F8**
Fejér □, *Hungary* **42 C3**
Fejø, *Denmark* **11 K5**
Feke, *Turkey* **72 D6**
Fekete →, *Hungary* **42 E3**
Felanitx, *Spain* **37 B10**
Feldbach, *Austria* **26 E8**
Feldberg, *Baden-W., Germany* **25 H3**
Feldberg, *Mecklenburg-Vorpommern, Germany* **24 B9**
Feldkirch, *Austria* **26 D2**
Feldkirchen, *Austria* **26 E7**
Felipe Carrillo Puerto, *Mexico* **119 D7**
Felixburg, *Zimbabwe* **89 B5**
Felixstowe, *U.K.* **13 F9**
Felletin, *France* **20 C6**
Fellingsbro, *Sweden* **10 E9**
Felton, *U.S.A.* **116 H4**
Feltre, *Italy* **29 B8**
Femer Bælt = Fehmarn Bælt, *Europe* **11 K5**
Femø, *Denmark* **11 K5**
Femunden, *Norway* **9 E14**
Fen He →, *China* **56 G6**
Fene, *Spain* **34 B2**
Fenelon Falls, *Canada* **110 B6**
Fener Burnu, *Turkey* **39 E9**
Feneroa, *Ethiopia* **81 E4**
Feng Xian, *Jiangsu, China* **56 G9**
Feng Xian, *Shaanxi, China* **56 H4**
Fengári, *Greece* **41 F9**
Fengcheng, *Jiangxi, China* **59 C10**
Fengcheng, *Liaoning, China* **57 D13**
Fengfeng, *China* **56 F8**
Fenggang, *China* **58 D6**
Fenghua, *China* **59 C13**
Fenghuang, *China* **58 D7**
Fengkai, *China* **59 F8**
Fengkang, *Taiwan* **59 F13**
Fengle, *China* **59 B9**
Fenglin, *Taiwan* **59 F13**
Fengning, *China* **56 D9**
Fengqing, *China* **58 E2**
Fengqiu, *China* **56 G8**
Fengrun, *China* **57 E10**
Fengshan, *Guangxi Zhuangzu, China* **58 E7**
Fengshan, *Guangxi Zhuangzu, China* **58 E6**
Fengshan, *Taiwan* **59 F13**
Fengshun, *China* **59 F11**
Fengtai, *Anhui, China* **59 A11**
Fengtai, *Beijing, China* **56 E9**
Fengxian, *China* **59 B13**
Fengxiang, *China* **56 G4**
Fengxin, *China* **59 C10**
Fengyang, *China* **57 H9**
Fengyi, *China* **58 E3**
Fengyüan, *Taiwan* **59 E13**
Fengzhen, *China* **56 D7**
Feno, C. de, *France* **21 G12**
Fenoarivo, *Fianarantsoa, Madag.* **89 C8**
Fenoarivo, *Fianarantsoa, Madag.* **89 C8**
Fenoarivo Afovoany, *Madag.* **89 B8**
Fenoarivo Atsinanana, *Madag.* **89 B8**
Fens, The, *U.K.* **12 E7**
Fensmark, *Denmark* **11 J5**
Fenton, *U.S.A.* **108 D4**
Fenxi, *China* **56 F6**
Fenyang, *China* **56 F6**
Fenyi, *China* **59 D10**
Feodosiya, *Ukraine* **47 K8**
Ferdows, *Iran* **71 C8**
Fère-Champenoise, *France* **19 D10**
Fère-en-Tardenois, *France* **19 C10**
Ferentino, *Italy* **29 G10**
Ferfer, *Somali Rep.* **74 F4**
Fergana = Farghona, *Uzbekistan* **50 E8**
Fergus, *Canada* **110 C4**
Fergus Falls, *U.S.A.* **112 B6**
Feričanci, *Croatia* **42 E2**
Ferkéssédougou, *Ivory C.* **82 D3**
Ferlach, *Austria* **26 E7**
Ferland, *Canada* **102 B2**
Ferlo, Vallée du, *Senegal* **82 B2**
Fermanagh □, *U.K.* **15 B4**
Fermo, *Italy* **29 E10**
Fermont, *Canada* **103 B6**
Fermoselle, *Spain* **34 D4**
Fermoy, *Ireland* **15 D3**
Fernán Nuñéz, *Spain* **35 H6**
Fernández, *Argentina* **126 B3**
Fernandina Beach, *U.S.A.* **109 K5**
Fernando de Noronha, *Brazil* **125 D12**
Fernando Póo = Bioko, *Eq. Guin.* **83 E6**
Ferndale, *U.S.A.* **116 B4**
Fernie, *Canada* **104 D5**
Fernlees, *Australia* **94 C4**
Fernley, *U.S.A.* **114 G4**
Ferozepore = Firozpur, *India* **68 D6**
Férrai, *Greece* **41 F10**
Ferrandina, *Italy* **31 B9**
Ferrara, *Italy* **29 D8**
Ferrato, C., *Italy* **30 C2**
Ferreira do Alentejo, *Portugal* **35 G2**
Ferreñafe, *Peru* **124 E3**
Ferrerías, *Spain* **37 B11**
Ferret, C., *France* **20 D2**
Ferrette, *France* **19 E14**
Ferriday, *U.S.A.* **113 K9**
Ferriere, *Italy* **28 D6**
Ferrières, *France* **19 D9**
Ferro, Capo, *Italy* **30 A2**
Ferrol, *Spain* **34 B2**
Ferron, *U.S.A.* **115 G8**
Ferrutx, C., *Spain* **37 B10**
Ferryland, *Canada* **103 C9**
Fertile, *U.S.A.* **112 B6**
Fertőszentmiklós, *Hungary* **42 C1**
Fès, *Morocco* **78 B5**
Fessenden, *U.S.A.* **112 B5**
Festus, *U.S.A.* **112 F9**
Feté Bowé, *Senegal* **82 C2**
Feteşti, *Romania* **43 F12**
Fethiye, *Turkey* **39 E11**
Fethiye Körfezi, *Turkey* **39 E10**
Fetlar, *U.K.* **14 A8**
Feuilles →, *Canada* **101 C12**
Feurs, *France* **21 C8**
Fez = Fès, *Morocco* **78 B5**
Fezzan, *Libya* **79 C8**
Fiambalá, *Argentina* **126 B2**
Fianarantsoa, *Madag.* **89 C8**
Fianarantsoa □, *Madag.* **89 B8**
Fiche, *Ethiopia* **81 F4**
Fichtelgebirge, *Germany* **25 E7**
Ficksburg, *S. Africa* **89 D4**
Fidenza, *Italy* **28 D7**
Fiditi, *Nigeria* **83 D5**
Field →, *Australia* **94 C2**
Field I., *Australia* **92 B5**
Fieni, *Romania* **43 E10**
Fier, *Albania* **40 F3**
Fierzë, *Albania* **40 D4**
Fife □, *U.K.* **14 E5**
Fife Ness, *U.K.* **14 E6**
Fifth Cataract, *Sudan* **80 D3**
Figari, *France* **21 G13**
Figeac, *France* **20 D6**
Figeholm, *Sweden* **11 G10**
Figline Valdarno, *Italy* **29 E8**
Figtree, *Zimbabwe* **87 G2**
Figueira Castelo Rodrigo, *Portugal* **34 E4**
Figueira da Foz, *Portugal* **34 E2**
Figueiró dos Vinhos, *Portugal* **34 F2**
Figueres, *Spain* **32 C7**
Figuig, *Morocco* **78 B5**
Fihaonana, *Madag.* **89 B8**
Fiherenana, *Madag.* **89 B8**
Fiherenana →, *Madag.* **89 C7**
Fiji ■, *Pac. Oc.* **91 C8**
Fik, *Ethiopia* **81 F5**
Fika, *Nigeria* **83 C7**
Filabres, Sierra de los, *Spain* **35 H8**
Filabusi, *Zimbabwe* **89 C4**
Filadélfia, *Italy* **31 D9**
Fil'akovo, *Slovak Rep.* **27 C12**
Filey, *U.K.* **12 C7**
Filey B., *U.K.* **12 C7**
Filfla, *Malta* **36 D1**
Filiaşi, *Romania* **43 F8**
Filiátes, *Greece* **38 B2**
Filiatrá, *Greece* **38 D3**
Filicudi, *Italy* **31 D7**
Filingué, *Niger* **83 C5**
Filiourí →, *Greece* **41 E9**
Filipstad, *Sweden* **10 E8**
Filisur, *Switz.* **25 J5**
Fillmore, *Calif., U.S.A.* **117 L8**
Fillmore, *Utah, U.S.A.* **115 G7**
Filótion, *Greece* **39 D7**
Filottrano, *Italy* **29 E10**
Filtu, *Ethiopia* **81 F5**
Finale Emília, *Italy* **29 D8**
Finale Lígure, *Italy* **28 D5**
Fiñana, *Spain* **35 H8**
Finch, *Canada* **111 A9**
Findhorn →, *U.K.* **14 D5**
Findlay, *U.S.A.* **108 E4**
Finger L., *Canada* **102 B1**
Finger Lakes, *U.S.A.* **111 D8**
Fíngoè, *Mozam.* **87 E3**
Finike, *Turkey* **39 E12**
Finike Körfezi, *Turkey* **39 E12**
Finiq, *Albania* **40 G4**
Finistère □, *France* **18 D3**
Finisterre = Fisterra, *Spain* **34 C1**
Finisterre, C. = Fisterra, C., *Spain* **34 C1**
Finke, *Australia* **94 D1**
Finland ■, *Europe* **8 E22**
Finland, G. of, *Europe* **9 G21**
Finlay →, *Canada* **104 B3**

Finley, *Australia* 95 F4
Finley, *U.S.A.* 112 B6
Finn →, *Ireland* 15 B4
Finnerödja, *Sweden* 11 F8
Finnigan, Mt., *Australia* 94 B4
Finniss, C., *Australia* 95 E1
Finnmark, *Norway* 8 B20
Finnsnes, *Norway* 8 B18
Finspång, *Sweden* 11 F9
Finsteraarhorn, *Switz.* 25 J4
Finsterwalde, *Germany* 24 D9
Fiora →, *Italy* 29 F8
Fiorenzuola d'Arda, *Italy* 28 D6
Fiq, *Syria* 75 C4
Firat = Furāt, Nahr al →, *Asia* 70 D5
Firebag →, *Canada* 105 B6
Firebaugh, *U.S.A.* 116 J6
Firedrake L., *Canada* 105 A8
Firenze, *Italy* 29 E8
Firenzuola, *Italy* 29 D8
Firk →, *Iraq* 70 D5
Firmi, *France* 20 D6
Firminy, *France* 21 C8
Firozabad, *India* 69 F8
Firozpur, *India* 68 D6
Firozpur-Jhirka, *India* 68 F7
Fīrūzābād, *Iran* 71 D7
Fīrūzkūh, *Iran* 71 C7
Firvale, *Canada* 104 C3
Fish →, *Namibia* 88 D2
Fish →, *S. Africa* 88 E3
Fish River Canyon, *Namibia* 88 D2
Fisher, *Australia* 93 F5
Fisher B., *Canada* 105 C9
Fishers I., *U.S.A.* 111 E13
Fishguard, *U.K.* 13 E3
Fishing L., *Canada* 105 C9
Fishkill, *U.S.A.* 111 E11
Fismes, *France* 19 C10
Fisterra, *Spain* 34 C1
Fisterra, C., *Spain* 34 C1
Fitchburg, *U.S.A.* 111 D13
Fitz Roy, *Argentina* 128 F3
Fitzgerald, *Canada* 104 B6
Fitzgerald, *U.S.A.* 109 K4
Fitzmaurice →, *Australia* 92 B5
Fitzroy →, *Queens., Australia* 94 C5
Fitzroy →, *W. Austral., Australia* 92 C3
Fitzroy, Mte., *Argentina* 128 F2
Fitzroy Crossing, *Australia* 92 C4
Fitzwilliam I., *Canada* 110 A3
Fiuggi, *Italy* 29 G10
Fiume = Rijeka, *Croatia* 29 C11
Five Points, *U.S.A.* 116 J6
Fivizzano, *Italy* 28 D7
Fizi, *Dem. Rep. of the Congo* 86 C2
Fjällbacka, *Sweden* 11 F5
Fjärdhundra, *Sweden* 10 E10
Fjellerup, *Denmark* 11 H4
Fjerritslev, *Denmark* 11 G3
Fjugesta, *Sweden* 10 E8
Flagstaff, *U.S.A.* 115 J8
Flagstaff L., *U.S.A.* 109 C10
Flaherty I., *Canada* 102 A4
Flåm, *Norway* 9 F12
Flambeau →, *U.S.A.* 112 C9
Flamborough Hd., *U.K.* 12 C7
Fläming, *Germany* 24 C8
Flaming Gorge Reservoir, *U.S.A.* 114 F9
Flamingo, Teluk, *Indonesia* 63 F9
Flanders = Flandre, *Europe* 19 B9
Flandre, *Europe* 19 B9
Flandre Occidentale = West-Vlaanderen □, *Belgium* 17 D2
Flandre Orientale = Oost-Vlaanderen □, *Belgium* 17 C3
Flandreau, *U.S.A.* 112 C6
Flanigan, *U.S.A.* 116 E7
Flannan Is., *U.K.* 14 C1
Flåsjön, *Sweden* 8 D16
Flat →, *Canada* 104 A3
Flathead L., *U.S.A.* 114 C7
Flattery, C., *Australia* 94 A4
Flattery, C., *U.S.A.* 116 B2
Flatwoods, *U.S.A.* 108 F4
Fleetwood, *U.K.* 12 D4
Fleetwood, *U.S.A.* 111 F9
Flekkefjord, *Norway* 9 G12
Flemington, *U.S.A.* 110 E7
Flen, *Sweden* 10 E10
Flensburg, *Germany* 24 A5
Flers, *France* 18 D6
Flesherton, *Canada* 110 B4
Flesko, Tanjung, *Indonesia* 63 D6
Fleurance, *France* 20 E4
Fleurier, *Switz.* 25 J2
Fleurieu Pen., *Australia* 95 F2
Flevoland □, *Neths.* 17 B5
Flin Flon, *Canada* 105 C8
Flinders →, *Australia* 94 B3
Flinders B., *Australia* 93 F2
Flinders Group, *Australia* 94 A3
Flinders I., *S. Austral., Australia* 95 E1
Flinders I., *Tas., Australia* 94 G4
Flinders Ranges, *Australia* 95 E2
Flinders Reefs, *Australia* 94 B4
Flint, *U.K.* 12 D4
Flint, *U.S.A.* 108 D4
Flint →, *U.S.A.* 109 K3
Flint I., *Kiribati* 97 J12
Flintshire □, *U.K.* 12 D4
Fliseryd, *Sweden* 11 G10
Flix, *Spain* 32 D5
Flixecourt, *France* 19 B9
Floby, *Sweden* 11 F7
Floda, *Sweden* 11 G6
Flodden, *U.K.* 12 B5
Flogny-la-Chapelle, *France* 19 E10
Floodwood, *U.S.A.* 112 B8
Flora, *U.S.A.* 108 F1
Florac, *France* 20 D7
Florala, *U.S.A.* 109 K2
Florence = Firenze, *Italy* 29 E8
Florence, *Ala., U.S.A.* 109 H2
Florence, *Ariz., U.S.A.* 115 K8
Florence, *Colo., U.S.A.* 112 F2
Florence, *Oreg., U.S.A.* 114 E1
Florence, *S.C., U.S.A.* 109 H6
Florence, L., *Australia* 95 D2
Florencia, *Colombia* 124 C3
Florennes, *Belgium* 17 D4
Florensac, *France* 20 E7
Florenville, *Belgium* 17 E5
Flores, *Guatemala* 120 C2
Flores, *Indonesia* 63 F6
Flores I., *Canada* 104 D3
Flores Sea, *Indonesia* 63 F6
Floreşti, *Moldova* 43 C13
Floresville, *U.S.A.* 113 L5
Floriano, *Brazil* 125 E10
Florianópolis, *Brazil* 127 B6
Florida, *Cuba* 120 B4
Florida, *Uruguay* 127 C4
Florida □, *U.S.A.* 109 L5
Florida, Straits of, *U.S.A.* 120 B4
Florida B., *U.S.A.* 120 B3
Florida Keys, *U.S.A.* 109 N5
Florídia, *Italy* 31 E8
Flórina, *Greece* 40 F5
Flórina □, *Greece* 40 F5
Florø, *Norway* 9 F11
Flower Station, *Canada* 111 A8
Flowerpot I., *Canada* 110 A3
Floydada, *U.S.A.* 113 J4
Fluk, *Indonesia* 63 E7
Flúmen →, *Spain* 32 D4
Flumendosa →, *Italy* 30 C2
Fluminimaggiore, *Italy* 30 C1
Flushing = Vlissingen, *Neths.* 17 C3
Fluviá →, *Spain* 32 C8
Flying Fish, C., *Antarctica* 5 D15
Foam Lake, *Canada* 105 C8
Foča, *Bos.-H.* 40 C2
Foça, *Turkey* 39 C8
Focşani, *Romania* 43 E12
Fodécontéa, *Guinea* 82 C2
Fogang, *China* 59 F9
Fóggia, *Italy* 31 A8
Foggo, *Nigeria* 83 C6
Foglia →, *Italy* 29 E9
Fogo, *Canada* 103 C9
Fogo I., *Canada* 103 C9
Fohnsdorf, *Austria* 26 D7
Föhr, *Germany* 24 A4
Foia, *Portugal* 35 H2
Foix, *France* 20 E5
Fojnica, *Bos.-H.* 42 G2
Fokino, *Russia* 46 F8
Fokís □, *Greece* 38 C4
Fokku, *Nigeria* 83 C5
Folda, *Nord-Trøndelag, Norway* 8 D14
Folda, *Nordland, Norway* 8 C16
Főldeák, *Hungary* 42 D5
Folégandros, *Greece* 38 E6
Foley, *Botswana* 88 C4
Foley, *U.S.A.* 109 K2
Foleyet, *Canada* 102 C3
Folgefonni, *Norway* 9 F12
Foligno, *Italy* 29 F9
Folkestone, *U.K.* 13 F9
Folkston, *U.S.A.* 109 K5
Follansbee, *U.S.A.* 110 F4
Follónica, *Italy* 28 F7
Follónica, G. di, *Italy* 28 F7
Folsom L., *U.S.A.* 116 G5
Folteşti, *Romania* 43 E13
Fond-du-Lac, *Canada* 105 B7
Fond du Lac, *U.S.A.* 112 D10
Fond-du-Lac →, *Canada* 105 B7
Fonda, *U.S.A.* 111 D10
Fondi, *Italy* 30 A6
Fonfría, *Spain* 34 D4
Fongafale, *Tuvalu* 96 H9
Fonni, *Italy* 30 B2
Fonsagrada = A Fonsagrada, *Spain* 34 B3
Fonseca, G. de, *Cent. Amer.* 120 D2
Font-Romeu, *France* 20 F5
Fontaine-Française, *France* 19 E12
Fontainebleau, *France* 19 D9
Fontana, *U.S.A.* 117 L9
Fontas →, *Canada* 104 B4
Fonte Boa, *Brazil* 124 D5
Fontem, *Cameroon* 83 D6
Fontenay-le-Comte, *France* 20 B3
Fontenelle Reservoir, *U.S.A.* 114 E8
Fontur, *Iceland* 8 C6
Fonyód, *Hungary* 42 D2
Foochow = Fuzhou, *China* 59 D12
Foping, *China* 56 H5
Forbach, *France* 19 C13
Forbes, *Australia* 95 E4
Forbesganj, *India* 69 F12
Forcados, *Nigeria* 83 D6
Forcados →, *Nigeria* 83 D6
Forcalquier, *France* 21 E9
Forchheim, *Germany* 25 F7
Ford City, *Calif., U.S.A.* 117 K7
Ford City, *Pa., U.S.A.* 110 F5
Førde, *Norway* 9 F11
Ford's Bridge, *Australia* 95 D4
Fordyce, *U.S.A.* 113 J8
Forécariah, *Guinea* 82 D2
Forel, Mt., *Greenland* 4 C6
Foremost, *Canada* 104 D6
Forest, *Canada* 110 C3
Forest, *U.S.A.* 113 J10
Forest City, *Iowa, U.S.A.* 112 D8
Forest City, *N.C., U.S.A.* 109 H5
Forest City, *Pa., U.S.A.* 111 E9
Forest Grove, *U.S.A.* 116 E3
Forestburg, *Canada* 104 C6
Foresthill, *U.S.A.* 116 F6
Forestier Pen., *Australia* 94 G4
Forestville, *Canada* 103 C6
Forestville, *Calif., U.S.A.* 116 G4
Forestville, *N.Y., U.S.A.* 110 D5
Forez, Mts. du, *France* 20 C7
Forfar, *U.K.* 14 E6
Forks, *U.S.A.* 116 C2
Forksville, *U.S.A.* 111 E8
Forlì, *Italy* 29 D9
Forman, *U.S.A.* 112 B6
Formazza, *Italy* 28 B5
Formby Pt., *U.K.* 12 D4
Formentera, *Spain* 37 C7
Formentor, C. de, *Spain* 37 B10
Former Yugoslav Republic of Macedonia = Macedonia ■, *Europe* 40 E5
Fórmia, *Italy* 30 A6
Formígine, *Italy* 28 D7
Formosa = Taiwan ■, *Asia* 59 F13
Formosa, *Argentina* 126 B4
Formosa, *Brazil* 125 G9
Formosa □, *Argentina* 126 B4
Formosa, Serra, *Brazil* 125 F8
Formosa Bay, *Kenya* 86 C5
Formosa Strait = Taiwan Strait, *Asia* 59 E12
Fornells, *Spain* 37 A11
Fornos de Algodres, *Portugal* 34 E3
Fornovo di Taro, *Italy* 28 D7
Føroyar, *Atl. Oc.* 8 F9
Forres, *U.K.* 14 D5
Forrest, *Australia* 93 F4
Forrest, Mt., *Australia* 93 D4
Forrest City, *U.S.A.* 113 H9
Fors, *Sweden* 10 D10
Forsayth, *Australia* 94 B3
Forshaga, *Sweden* 10 E7
Förslöv, *Sweden* 11 H6
Forsmo, *Sweden* 10 A11
Forssa, *Finland* 9 F20
Forst, *Germany* 24 D10
Forsvik, *Sweden* 11 F8
Forsyth, *U.S.A.* 114 C10
Fort Abbas, *Pakistan* 68 E5
Fort Albany, *Canada* 102 B3
Fort Ann, *U.S.A.* 111 C11
Fort Assiniboine, *Canada* 104 C6
Fort Augustus, *U.K.* 14 D4
Fort Beaufort, *S. Africa* 88 E4
Fort Benton, *U.S.A.* 114 C8
Fort Bragg, *U.S.A.* 114 G2
Fort Bridger, *U.S.A.* 114 F8
Fort Chipewyan, *Canada* 105 B6
Fort Collins, *U.S.A.* 112 E2
Fort-Coulonge, *Canada* 102 C4
Fort Covington, *U.S.A.* 111 B10
Fort Davis, *U.S.A.* 113 K3
Fort-de-France, *Martinique* 121 D7
Fort Defiance, *U.S.A.* 115 J9
Fort Dodge, *U.S.A.* 112 D7
Fort Edward, *U.S.A.* 111 C11
Fort Erie, *Canada* 110 D6
Fort Fairfield, *U.S.A.* 109 B12
Fort Frances, *Canada* 105 D10
Fort Garland, *U.S.A.* 115 H11
Fort George = Chisasibi, *Canada* 102 B4
Fort Good-Hope, *Canada* 100 B7
Fort Hancock, *U.S.A.* 115 L11
Fort Hertz = Putao, *Burma* 67 F20
Fort Hope, *Canada* 102 B2
Fort Irwin, *U.S.A.* 117 K10
Fort Kent, *U.S.A.* 109 B11
Fort Klamath, *U.S.A.* 114 E3
Fort Laramie, *U.S.A.* 112 D2
Fort Lauderdale, *U.S.A.* 109 M5
Fort Liard, *Canada* 104 A4
Fort Liberté, *Haiti* 121 C5
Fort Lupton, *U.S.A.* 112 E2
Fort Mackay, *Canada* 104 B6
Fort Macleod, *Canada* 104 D6
Fort McMurray, *Canada* 104 B6
Fort McPherson, *Canada* 100 B6
Fort Madison, *U.S.A.* 112 E9
Fort Meade, *U.S.A.* 109 M5
Fort Morgan, *U.S.A.* 112 E3
Fort Myers, *U.S.A.* 109 M5
Fort Nelson, *Canada* 104 B4
Fort Nelson →, *Canada* 104 B4
Fort Norman = Tulita, *Canada* 100 B7
Fort Payne, *U.S.A.* 109 H3
Fort Peck, *U.S.A.* 114 B10
Fort Peck Dam, *U.S.A.* 114 C10
Fort Peck L., *U.S.A.* 114 C10
Fort Pierce, *U.S.A.* 109 M5
Fort Pierre, *U.S.A.* 112 C4
Fort Pierre Bordes = Ti-n-Zaouatene, *Algeria* 83 B5
Fort Plain, *U.S.A.* 111 D10
Fort Portal, *Uganda* 86 B3
Fort Providence, *Canada* 104 A5
Fort Qu'Appelle, *Canada* 105 C8
Fort Resolution, *Canada* 104 A6
Fort Rixon, *Zimbabwe* 87 G2
Fort Ross, *U.S.A.* 116 G3
Fort Rupert = Waskaganish, *Canada* 102 B4
Fort St. James, *Canada* 104 C4
Fort St. John, *Canada* 104 B4
Fort Saskatchewan, *Canada* 104 C6
Fort Scott, *U.S.A.* 113 G7
Fort Severn, *Canada* 102 A2
Fort Shevchenko, *Kazakstan* 49 H10
Fort Simpson, *Canada* 104 A4
Fort Smith, *Canada* 104 B6
Fort Smith, *U.S.A.* 113 H7
Fort Stockton, *U.S.A.* 113 K3
Fort Sumner, *U.S.A.* 113 H2
Fort Thompson, *U.S.A.* 112 C5
Fort Valley, *U.S.A.* 109 J4
Fort Vermilion, *Canada* 104 B5
Fort Walton Beach, *U.S.A.* 109 K2
Fort Wayne, *U.S.A.* 108 E3
Fort William, *U.K.* 14 E3
Fort Worth, *U.S.A.* 113 J6
Fort Yates, *U.S.A.* 112 B4
Fort Yukon, *U.S.A.* 100 B5
Fortaleza, *Brazil* 125 D11
Forteau, *Canada* 103 B8
Fortescue →, *Australia* 92 D2
Forth →, *U.K.* 14 E5
Forth, Firth of, *U.K.* 14 E6
Fortore →, *Italy* 29 G12
Fortrose, *U.K.* 14 D4
Fortuna, *Spain* 33 G3
Fortuna, *Calif., U.S.A.* 114 F1
Fortuna, *N. Dak., U.S.A.* 112 A3
Fortune, *Canada* 103 C8
Fortune B., *Canada* 103 C8
Forūr, *Iran* 71 E7
Fos-sur-Mer, *France* 21 E8
Foshan, *China* 59 F9
Fosna, *Norway* 8 E14
Fosnavåg, *Norway* 9 E11
Foso, *Ghana* 83 D4
Fossano, *Italy* 28 D4
Fossil, *U.S.A.* 114 D3
Fossombrone, *Italy* 29 E9
Foster, *Canada* 111 A12
Foster →, *Canada* 105 B7
Fosters Ra., *Australia* 94 C1
Fostoria, *U.S.A.* 108 E4
Fotadrevo, *Madag.* 89 C8
Fouesnant, *France* 18 E2
Fougères, *France* 18 D5
Foul Pt., *Sri Lanka* 66 Q12
Foula, *U.K.* 14 A6
Foulalaba, *Mali* 82 C3
Foulness I., *U.K.* 13 F8
Foulpointe, *Madag.* 89 B8
Foulweather, C., *U.S.A.* 106 B2
Foumban, *Cameroon* 83 D7
Foumbot, *Cameroon* 83 D7
Foundiougne, *Senegal* 82 C1
Fountain, *U.S.A.* 112 F2
Fountain Springs, *U.S.A.* 117 K8
Fourchambault, *France* 19 E10
Fouriesburg, *S. Africa* 88 D4
Fourmies, *France* 19 B11
Fournás, *Greece* 38 B3
Foúrnoi, *Greece* 39 D8
Fours, *France* 19 F10
Fourth Cataract, *Sudan* 80 D3
Fouta Djalon, *Guinea* 82 C2
Foux, Cap-à-, *Haiti* 121 C5
Foveaux Str., *N.Z.* 91 M2
Fowey, *U.K.* 13 G3
Fowler, *Calif., U.S.A.* 116 J7
Fowler, *Colo., U.S.A.* 112 F3
Fowlers B., *Australia* 93 F5
Fowman, *Iran* 71 B6
Fox →, *Canada* 105 B10
Fox Creek, *Canada* 104 C5
Fox Lake, *Canada* 104 B6
Fox Valley, *Canada* 105 C7
Foxboro, *U.S.A.* 111 D13
Foxe Basin, *Canada* 101 B12
Foxe Chan., *Canada* 101 B11
Foxe Pen., *Canada* 101 B12
Foxen, *Sweden* 10 E5
Foxton, *N.Z.* 91 J5
Foyle, Lough, *U.K.* 15 A4
Foynes, *Ireland* 15 D2
Foz, *Spain* 34 B3
Foz do Cunene, *Angola* 88 B1
Foz do Iguaçu, *Brazil* 127 B5
Frackville, *U.S.A.* 111 F8
Fraga, *Spain* 32 D5
Fraile Muerto, *Uruguay* 127 C5
Framingham, *U.S.A.* 111 D13
Frampol, *Poland* 45 H9
Franca, *Brazil* 125 H9
Francavilla al Mare, *Italy* 29 F11
Francavilla Fontana, *Italy* 31 B10
France ■, *Europe* 7 F6
Frances, *Australia* 95 F3
Frances →, *Canada* 104 A3
Frances L., *Canada* 104 A3
Franceville, *Gabon* 84 E2
Franche-Comté, *France* 19 F12
Francis Case, L., *U.S.A.* 112 D5
Francisco Beltrão, *Brazil* 127 B5
Francisco I. Madero, *Coahuila, Mexico* 118 B4
Francisco I. Madero, *Durango, Mexico* 118 C4
Francistown, *Botswana* 89 C4
Francofonte, *Italy* 31 E7
François, *Canada* 103 C8
François L., *Canada* 104 C3
Franeker, *Neths.* 17 A5
Frankado, *Djibouti* 81 E5
Frankenberg, *Germany* 24 D4
Frankenwald, *Germany* 25 E7
Frankford, *Canada* 110 B7
Frankfort, *S. Africa* 89 D4
Frankfort, *Ind., U.S.A.* 108 E2
Frankfort, *Kans., U.S.A.* 112 F6
Frankfort, *Ky., U.S.A.* 108 F3
Frankfort, *N.Y., U.S.A.* 111 C9
Frankfurt, *Brandenburg, Germany* 24 C10
Frankfurt, *Hessen, Germany* 25 E4
Fränkische Alb, *Germany* 25 F7
Fränkische Rezat →, *Germany* 25 F7
Fränkische Saale →, *Germany* 25 E5
Fränkische Schweiz, *Germany* 25 F7
Frankland →, *Australia* 93 G2
Franklin, *Ky., U.S.A.* 109 G2
Franklin, *La., U.S.A.* 113 L9
Franklin, *Mass., U.S.A.* 111 D13
Franklin, *N.H., U.S.A.* 111 C13
Franklin, *Nebr., U.S.A.* 112 E5
Franklin, *Pa., U.S.A.* 110 E5
Franklin, *Va., U.S.A.* 109 G7
Franklin, *W. Va., U.S.A.* 108 F6
Franklin B., *Canada* 100 B7
Franklin D. Roosevelt L., *U.S.A.* 114 B4
Franklin I., *Antarctica* 5 D11
Franklin L., *U.S.A.* 114 F6
Franklin Mts., *Canada* 100 B7
Franklin Str., *Canada* 100 A10
Franklinton, *U.S.A.* 113 K9
Franklinville, *U.S.A.* 110 D6
Franks Pk., *U.S.A.* 114 E9
Frankston, *Australia* 95 F4
Frånö, *Sweden* 10 B11
Fransfontein, *Namibia* 88 C2
Fränsta, *Sweden* 10 B10
Frantsa Iosifa, Zemlya, *Russia* 50 A6
Franz, *Canada* 102 C3
Franz Josef Land = Frantsa Iosifa, Zemlya, *Russia* 50 A6
Franzburg, *Germany* 24 A8
Frascati, *Italy* 29 G9
Fraser, *U.S.A.* 110 D2
Fraser →, *B.C., Canada* 104 D4
Fraser →, *Nfld., Canada* 103 A7
Fraser, Mt., *Australia* 93 E2
Fraser I., *Australia* 95 D5
Fraser Lake, *Canada* 104 C4
Fraserburg, *S. Africa* 88 E3
Fraserburgh, *U.K.* 14 D6
Fraserdale, *Canada* 102 C3
Frashër, *Albania* 40 F4
Frasne, *France* 19 F13
Frăteşti, *Romania* 43 G10
Frauenfeld, *Switz.* 25 H4
Fray Bentos, *Uruguay* 126 C4
Frechilla, *Spain* 34 C6
Fredericia, *Denmark* 11 J3
Frederick, *Md., U.S.A.* 108 F7
Frederick, *Okla., U.S.A.* 113 H5
Frederick, *S. Dak., U.S.A.* 112 C5
Fredericksburg, *Pa., U.S.A.* 111 F8
Fredericksburg, *Tex., U.S.A.* 113 K5
Fredericksburg, *Va., U.S.A.* 108 F7
Fredericktown, *Mo., U.S.A.* 113 G9
Fredericktown, *Ohio, U.S.A.* 110 F2
Frederico I. Madero, Presa, *Mexico* 118 B3
Frederico Westphalen, *Brazil* 127 B5
Fredericton, *Canada* 103 C6
Fredericton Junction, *Canada* 103 C6
Frederiksborg Amtskommune □, *Denmark* 11 J6
Frederikshåb = Paamiut, *Greenland* 4 C5
Frederikshavn, *Denmark* 11 G4
Frederikssund, *Denmark* 11 J6
Frederiksted, *U.S. Virgin Is.* 121 C7
Frederiksværk, *Denmark* 11 J6
Fredonia, *Ariz., U.S.A.* 115 H7
Fredonia, *Kans., U.S.A.* 113 G7
Fredonia, *N.Y., U.S.A.* 110 D5
Fredriksberg, *Sweden* 10 D8
Fredrikstad, *Norway* 9 G14
Free State □, *S. Africa* 88 D4
Freehold, *U.S.A.* 111 F10
Freel Peak, *U.S.A.* 116 G7
Freeland, *U.S.A.* 111 E9
Freels, C., *Canada* 103 C9
Freeman, *Calif., U.S.A.* 117 K9
Freeman, *S. Dak., U.S.A.* 112 D6
Freeport, *Bahamas* 120 A4
Freeport, *Ill., U.S.A.* 112 D10
Freeport, *N.Y., U.S.A.* 111 F11
Freeport, *Ohio, U.S.A.* 110 F3
Freeport, *Pa., U.S.A.* 110 F5
Freeport, *Tex., U.S.A.* 113 L7
Freetown, *S. Leone* 82 D2
Frégate, L., *Canada* 102 B5
Fregenal de la Sierra, *Spain* 35 G4
Fregene, *Italy* 29 G9
Fréhel, C., *France* 18 D4
Freiberg, *Germany* 24 E9
Freibourg = Fribourg, *Switz.* 25 J3
Freiburg, *Baden-W., Germany* 25 H3
Freiburg, *Niedersachsen, Germany* 24 B5
Freilassing, *Germany* 25 H8
Freire, *Chile* 128 D2
Freirina, *Chile* 126 B1
Freising, *Germany* 25 G7
Freistadt, *Austria* 26 C7
Freital, *Germany* 24 D9
Fréjus, *France* 21 E10
Fremantle, *Australia* 93 F2

Fremont, Calif., U.S.A. 116 H4
Fremont, Mich., U.S.A. 108 D3
Fremont, Nebr., U.S.A. 112 E6
Fremont, Ohio, U.S.A. 108 E4
Fremont →, U.S.A. 115 G8
French Camp, U.S.A. 116 H5
French Creek →, U.S.A. 110 E5
French Guiana ■, S. Amer. 125 C8
French Polynesia ■, Pac. Oc. 97 K13
Frenchman Cr. →, N. Amer. 114 B10
Frenchman Cr. →, U.S.A. 112 E4
Frenštát pod Radhoštěm, Czech Rep. 27 B11
Fresco, Ivory C. 82 D3
Fresco →, Brazil 125 E8
Freshfield, C., Antarctica 5 C10
Fresnay-sur-Sarthe, France 18 D7
Fresnillo, Mexico 118 C4
Fresno, U.S.A. 116 J7
Fresno Alhandiga, Spain 34 E5
Fresno Reservoir, U.S.A. 114 B9
Freudenstadt, Germany 25 G4
Frévent, France 19 B9
Frew →, Australia 94 C2
Frewsburg, U.S.A. 110 D5
Freycinet Pen., Australia 94 G4
Freyming-Merlebach, France 19 C13
Freyung, Germany 25 G9
Fria, Guinea 82 C2
Fria, C., Namibia 88 B1
Friant, U.S.A. 116 J7
Frías, Argentina 126 B2
Fribourg, Switz. 25 J3
Fribourg □, Switz. 25 J3
Fridafors, Sweden 11 H8
Friday Harbor, U.S.A. 116 B3
Friedberg, Bayern, Germany 25 G6
Friedberg, Hessen, Germany 25 E4
Friedens, U.S.A. 110 F6
Friedland, Germany 24 B9
Friedrichshafen, Germany 25 H5
Friedrichskoog, Germany 24 A4
Friedrichstadt, Germany 24 A5
Friendly Is. = Tonga ■, Pac. Oc. 91 D11
Friendship, U.S.A. 110 D6
Friesach, Austria 26 E7
Friesack, Germany 24 C8
Friesland □, Neths. 17 A5
Friesoythe, Germany 24 B3
Friggesund, Sweden 10 C10
Frillesås, Sweden 11 G6
Frinnaryd, Sweden 11 G8
Frio →, U.S.A. 113 L5
Frio, C., Brazil 122 F6
Friol, Spain 34 B3
Friona, U.S.A. 113 H3
Fristad, Sweden 11 G6
Fritch, U.S.A. 113 H4
Fritsla, Sweden 11 G6
Fritzlar, Germany 24 D5
Friuli-Venézia Giulia □, Italy 29 B9
Frobisher B., Canada 101 B13
Frobisher Bay = Iqaluit, Canada 101 B13
Frobisher L., Canada 105 B7
Frohavet, Norway 8 E13
Frohnleiten, Austria 26 D8
Frolovo, Russia 48 F6
Frombork, Poland 44 D6
Frome, U.K. 13 F5
Frome →, U.K. 13 G5
Frome, L., Australia 95 E2
Frómista, Spain 34 C6
Front Range, U.S.A. 106 C5
Front Royal, U.S.A. 108 F6
Fronteira, Portugal 35 F3
Frontera, Canary Is. 37 G2
Frontera, Mexico 119 D6
Fronteras, Mexico 118 A3
Frontignan, France 20 E7
Frosinone, Italy 30 A6
Frostburg, U.S.A. 108 F6
Frostisen, Norway 8 B17
Frouard, France 19 D13
Frövi, Sweden 10 E9
Frøya, Norway 8 E13
Frumoasa, Romania 43 D10
Frunze = Bishkek, Kyrgyzstan 50 E8
Fruška Gora, Serbia, Yug. 42 E4
Frutal, Brazil 125 H9
Frutigen, Switz. 25 J3
Frýdek-Místek, Czech Rep. 27 B11
Frýdlant, Czech Rep. 26 A8
Fryeburg, U.S.A. 111 B14
Fryvaldov = Jeseník, Czech Rep. 27 A10
Fthiótis □, Greece 38 C4
Fu Jiang →, China 58 C6
Fu Xian = Wafangdian, China 57 E11
Fu Xian, China 56 G5
Fu'an, China 59 D12
Fubian, China 58 B4
Fucécchio, Italy 28 E7
Fucheng, China 56 F9
Fuchou = Fuzhou, China 59 D12
Fuchū, Japan 55 G6
Fuchuan, China 59 E8
Fuchun Jiang →, China 59 B13
Fúcino, Piana del, Italy 29 F10
Fuding, China 59 D13
Fuencaliente, Canary Is. 37 F2
Fuencaliente, Spain 35 G6
Fuencaliente, Pta., Canary Is. 37 F2
Fuengirola, Spain 35 J6
Fuenlabrada, Spain 34 E7
Fuensalida, Spain 34 E6
Fuente-Alamo, Spain 33 G3
Fuente-Álamo de Murcia, Spain 33 H3
Fuente de Cantos, Spain 35 G4
Fuente del Maestre, Spain 35 G4
Fuente el Fresno, Spain 35 F7
Fuente Obejuna, Spain 35 G5
Fuente Palmera, Spain 35 H5
Fuentes de Andalucía, Spain 35 H5
Fuentes de Ebro, Spain 32 D4
Fuentes de León, Spain 35 G4
Fuentes de Oñoro, Spain 34 E4
Fuentesaúco, Spain 34 D5
Fuerte →, Mexico 118 B3
Fuerte Olimpo, Paraguay 126 A4
Fuerteventura, Canary Is. 37 F6
Fufeng, China 56 G5
Fuga I., Phil. 61 B4
Fugong, China 58 D2
Fugou, China 56 G8
Fugu, China 56 E6
Fuhai, China 60 B3
Fuḩaymī, Iraq 70 C4
Fuji, Japan 55 G9
Fuji-San, Japan 55 G9
Fuji-Yoshida, Japan 55 G9
Fujian □, China 59 E12
Fujinomiya, Japan 55 G9
Fujisawa, Japan 55 G9
Fujiyama, Mt. = Fuji-San, Japan 55 G9
Fukien = Fujian □, China 59 E12
Fukuchiyama, Japan 55 G7
Fukue-Shima, Japan 55 H4
Fukui, Japan 55 F8
Fukui □, Japan 55 G8
Fukuoka, Japan 55 H5
Fukuoka □, Japan 55 H5
Fukushima, Japan 54 F10
Fukushima □, Japan 54 F10
Fukuyama, Japan 55 G6
Fulacunda, Guinea-Biss. 82 C1
Fulda, Germany 24 E5
Fulda →, Germany 24 D5
Fulford Harbour, Canada 116 B3
Fuliang, China 59 C11
Fullerton, Calif., U.S.A. 117 M9
Fullerton, Nebr., U.S.A. 112 E6
Fulongquan, China 57 B13
Fülöpszállás, Hungary 42 D4
Fulton, Mo., U.S.A. 112 F9
Fulton, N.Y., U.S.A. 111 C8
Fuluälven →, Sweden 10 C7
Fulufjället, Sweden 10 C6
Fumay, France 19 C11
Fumel, France 20 D4
Fumin, China 58 E4
Funabashi, Japan 55 G10
Funafuti = Fongafale, Tuvalu 96 H9
Funäsdalen, Sweden 10 B6
Funchal, Madeira 37 D3
Fundación, Colombia 124 A4
Fundão, Portugal 34 E3
Fundu Moldovei, Romania 43 C10
Fundulea, Romania 43 F11
Fundy, B. of, Canada 103 D6
Funhalouro, Mozam. 89 C5
Funing, Hebei, China 57 E10
Funing, Jiangsu, China 57 H10
Funing, Yunnan, China 58 F5
Funiu Shan, China 56 H7
Funsi, Ghana 82 C4
Funtua, Nigeria 83 C6
Fuping, Hebei, China 56 E8
Fuping, Shaanxi, China 56 G5
Fuqing, China 59 E12
Fuquan, China 58 D6
Furano, Japan 54 C11
Furāt, Nahr al →, Asia 70 D5
Fūrg, Iran 71 D7
Furmanov, Russia 48 B5
Furmanovo, Kazakstan 48 F9
Furnás, Spain 37 B8
Furnas, Represa de, Brazil 127 A6
Furneaux Group, Australia 94 G4
Furqlus, Syria 75 A6
Fürstenau, Germany 24 C3
Fürstenberg, Germany 24 B9
Fürstenfeld, Austria 26 D9
Fürstenfeldbruck, Germany 25 G7
Fürstenwalde, Germany 24 C10
Fürth, Germany 25 F6
Furth im Wald, Germany 25 F8
Furtwangen, Germany 25 G4
Furudal, Sweden 10 C9
Furukawa, Japan 54 E10
Furulund, Sweden 11 J7
Fury and Hecla Str., Canada 101 B11
Fusagasuga, Colombia 124 C4
Fuscaldo, Italy 31 C9
Fushan, Shandong, China 57 F11
Fushan, Shanxi, China 56 G6
Fushë Arrëz, Albania 40 D4
Fushë-Krujë, Albania 40 E3
Fushun, Liaoning, China 57 D12
Fushun, Sichuan, China 58 C5
Fusong, China 57 C14
Füssen, Germany 25 H6
Fusui, China 58 F6
Futog, Yugoslavia 42 E4
Futuna, Wall. & F. Is. 91 B8
Fuwa, Egypt 80 H7
Fuxian Hu, China 58 E4
Fuxin, China 57 C11
Fuyang, Anhui, China 56 H8
Fuyang, Zhejiang, China 59 B12
Fuyang He →, China 56 E9
Fuying Dao, China 59 D13
Fuyu, China 57 B13
Fuyuan, China 58 E5
Füzesgyarmat, Hungary 42 C6
Fuzhou, China 59 D12
Fylde, U.K. 12 D5
Fyn, Denmark 11 J4
Fyne, L., U.K. 14 F3
Fyns Amtskommune □, Denmark 11 J4
Fynshav, Denmark 11 K3

G

Ga, Ghana 82 D4
Gaanda, Nigeria 83 C7
Gabarin, Nigeria 83 C7
Gabas →, France 20 E3
Gabela, Angola 84 G2
Gabès, Tunisia 79 B8
Gabès, G. de, Tunisia 79 B8
Gabgaba, W. →, Egypt 80 C3
Gąbin, Poland 45 F6
Gabon ■, Africa 84 E2
Gaborone, Botswana 88 C4
Gabriels, U.S.A. 111 B10
Gābrīk, Iran 71 E8
Gabrovo, Bulgaria 41 D9
Gacé, France 18 D7
Gāch Sār, Iran 71 B6
Gachsārān, Iran 71 D6
Gacko, Bos.-H. 40 C2
Gadag, India 66 M9
Gadamai, Sudan 81 D4
Gadap, Pakistan 68 G2
Gadarwara, India 69 H8
Gadebusch, Germany 24 B7
Gadein, Sudan 81 F2
Gadhada, India 68 J4
Gádor, Sierra de, Spain 35 J8
Gadra, Pakistan 68 G4
Gadsden, U.S.A. 109 H3
Gadwal, India 66 L10
Gadyach = Hadyach, Ukraine 47 G8
Găeşti, Romania 43 F10
Gaeta, Italy 30 A6
Gaeta, G. di, Italy 30 A6
Gaffney, U.S.A. 109 H5
Gafsa, Tunisia 78 B7
Gagarawa, Nigeria 83 C6
Gagaria, India 68 G4
Gagarin, Russia 46 E8
Gaggenau, Germany 25 G4
Gaghamni, Sudan 81 E2
Gagino, Russia 48 C7
Gagliano del Capo, Italy 31 C11
Gagnef, Sweden 10 D9
Gagnoa, Ivory C. 82 D3
Gagnon, Canada 103 B6
Gagnon, L., Canada 105 A6
Gagra, Georgia 49 J5
Gahini, Rwanda 86 C3
Gahmar, India 69 G10
Gai Xian = Gaizhou, China 57 D12
Gaïdhouronísi, Greece 36 E7
Gail, U.S.A. 113 J4
Gail →, Austria 26 E6
Gaillac, France 20 E5
Gaillimh = Galway, Ireland 15 C2
Gaillon, France 18 C8
Gaines, U.S.A. 110 E7
Gainesville, Fla., U.S.A. 109 L4
Gainesville, Ga., U.S.A. 109 H4
Gainesville, Mo., U.S.A. 113 G8
Gainesville, Tex., U.S.A. 113 J6
Gainsborough, U.K. 12 D7
Gairdner, L., Australia 95 E2
Gairloch, L., U.K. 14 D3
Gaizhou, China 57 D12
Gaj, Croatia 42 E2
Gaj →, Pakistan 68 F2
Gakuch, Pakistan 69 A5
Galala, Gebel el, Egypt 80 J8
Galán, Cerro, Argentina 126 B2
Galana →, Kenya 86 C5
Galanta, Slovak Rep. 27 C10
Galapagar, Spain 34 E7
Galápagos, Pac. Oc. 122 D1
Galashiels, U.K. 14 F6
Galatás, Greece 38 D5
Galaţi, Romania 43 E13
Galaţi □, Romania 43 E12
Galatia, Turkey 72 C5
Galatina, Italy 31 B11
Galátone, Italy 31 B11
Galax, U.S.A. 109 G5
Galaxídhion, Greece 38 C4
Galcaio, Somali Rep. 74 F4
Galdhøpiggen, Norway 9 F12
Galeana, Chihuahua, Mexico 118 A3
Galeana, Nuevo León, Mexico 118 A3
Galegu, Sudan 81 E4
Galela, Indonesia 63 D7
Galena, U.S.A. 100 B4
Galera, Spain 33 H2
Galera Pt., Trin. & Tob. 121 D7
Galesburg, U.S.A. 112 E9
Galeton, U.S.A. 110 E7
Galga, Ethiopia 81 F4
Gali, Georgia 49 J5
Galicea Mare, Romania 43 F8
Galich, Russia 48 A6
Galiche, Bulgaria 40 C7
Galicia □, Spain 34 C3
Galilee = Hagalil, Israel 75 C4
Galilee, L., Australia 94 C4
Galilee, Sea of = Yam Kinneret, Israel 75 C4
Galim, Cameroon 83 D7
Galinoporni, Cyprus 36 D13
Galion, U.S.A. 110 F2
Galiuro Mts., U.S.A. 115 K8
Galiwinku, Australia 94 A2
Gallabat, Sudan 81 E4
Gallan Hd., U.K. 14 C1
Gallarate, Italy 28 C5
Gallatin, U.S.A. 109 G2
Galle, Sri Lanka 66 R12
Gállego →, Spain 32 D4
Gallegos →, Argentina 128 G3
Galletti →, Ethiopia 81 F5
Galley Hd., Ireland 15 E3
Galliate, Italy 28 C5
Gallinas, Pta., Colombia 124 A4
Gallipoli = Gelibolu, Turkey 41 F10
Gallípoli, Italy 31 B10
Gallipolis, U.S.A. 108 F4
Gällivare, Sweden 8 C19
Gallneukirchen, Austria 26 C7
Gällö, Sweden 10 B9
Gallo, C., Italy 30 D6
Gallocanta, L. de, Spain 32 E3
Galloo I., U.S.A. 111 C8
Galloway, U.K. 14 F4
Galloway, Mull of, U.K. 14 G4
Gallup, U.S.A. 115 J9
Gallur, Spain 32 D3
Galoya, Sri Lanka 66 Q12
Galt, U.S.A. 116 G5
Galten, Denmark 11 H3
Galtür, Austria 26 E3
Galty Mts., Ireland 15 D3
Galtymore, Ireland 15 D3
Galva, U.S.A. 112 E9
Galve de Sorbe, Spain 32 D1
Galveston, U.S.A. 113 L7
Galveston B., U.S.A. 113 L7
Gálvez, Argentina 126 C3
Galway, Ireland 15 C2
Galway □, Ireland 15 C2
Galway B., Ireland 15 C2
Gam →, Vietnam 64 B5
Gamagōri, Japan 55 G8
Gamari, L., Ethiopia 81 E5
Gamawa, Nigeria 83 C7
Gamay, Phil. 61 E6
Gambaga, Ghana 83 C4
Gambat, Pakistan 68 F3
Gambela, Ethiopia 81 F3
Gambhir →, India 68 F6
Gambia ■, W. Afr. 82 C1
Gambia →, W. Afr. 82 C1
Gambier, U.S.A. 110 F2
Gambier, C., Australia 92 B5
Gambier Is., Australia 95 F2
Gambo, Canada 103 C9
Gamboli, Pakistan 68 E3
Gamboma, Congo 84 E3
Gamka →, S. Africa 88 E3
Gamkab →, Namibia 88 D2
Gamla Uppsala, Sweden 10 E11
Gamlakarleby = Kokkola, Finland 8 E20
Gamleby, Sweden 11 G10
Gammon →, Canada 105 C9
Gamo-Gofa □, Ethiopia 81 F4
Gamou, Niger 83 C6
Gamtoos →, S. Africa 88 E4
Gan, France 20 E3
Gan Goriama, Mts., Cameroon 83 D7
Gan Jiang →, China 59 C11
Ganado, U.S.A. 115 J9
Gananita, Sudan 80 D3
Gananoque, Canada 102 D4
Ganāveh, Iran 71 D6
Gäncä, Azerbaijan 49 K8
Gancheng, China 64 C7
Gand = Gent, Belgium 17 C3
Ganda, Angola 85 G2
Gandajika, Dem. Rep. of the Congo 84 F4
Gandak →, India 69 G11
Gandava, Pakistan 68 E2
Gander, Canada 103 C9
Gander L., Canada 103 C9
Ganderkesee, Germany 24 B4
Ganderowe Falls, Zimbabwe 87 F2
Gandesa, Spain 32 D5
Gandhi Sagar, India 68 G6
Gandhinagar, India 68 H5
Gandi, Nigeria 83 C6
Gandía, Spain 33 G4
Gandino, Italy 28 C6
Gando, Pta., Canary Is. 37 G4
Gandole, Nigeria 83 D7
Gâneb, Mauritania 82 B2
Ganedidalem = Gani, Indonesia 63 E7
Ganetti, Sudan 80 D3
Ganga →, India 69 H14
Ganga Sagar, India 69 J13
Gangafani, Mali 82 C4
Gangan →, India 69 E8
Ganganagar, India 68 E5
Gangapur, India 68 F7
Gangara, Niger 83 C6
Gangaw, Burma 67 H19
Gangdisê Shan, China 67 D12
Ganges = Ganga →, India 69 H14
Ganges, Canada 104 D4
Ganges, France 20 E7
Ganges, Mouths of the, India 69 J14
Gånghester, Sweden 11 G7
Gangi, Italy 31 E7
Gângiova, Romania 43 G8
Gangoh, India 68 E7
Gangroti, India 69 D8
Gangtok, India 67 F16
Gangu, China 56 G3
Gangyao, China 57 B14
Gani, Indonesia 63 E7
Ganj, India 69 F8
Ganluc, China 58 C4
Gannat, France 19 F10
Gannett Peak, U.S.A. 114 E9
Ganquan, China 56 F5
Gänserdorf, Austria 27 C9
Ganshui, China 58 C6
Gansu □, China 56 G3
Ganta, Liberia 82 D3
Gantheaume, C., Australia 95 F2
Gantheaume B., Australia 93 E1
Gantsevichi = Hantsavichy, Belarus 47 F4
Ganye, Nigeria 83 D7
Ganyem = Genyem, Indonesia 63 E10
Ganyu, China 57 G10
Ganyushkino, Kazakstan 49 G9
Ganzhou, China 59 E10
Gao, Mali 83 B4
Gao Xian, China 58 C5
Gao'an, China 59 C10
Gaochun, China 59 B12
Gaohe, China 59 F9
Gaohebu, China 59 B11
Gaokeng, China 59 D9
Gaolan Dao, China 59 G9
Gaoligong Shan, China 58 E2
Gaomi, China 57 F10
Gaoming, China 59 F9
Gaoping, China 56 G7
Gaotang, China 56 F9
Gaoua, Burkina Faso 82 C4
Gaoual, Guinea 82 C2
Gaoxiong = Kaohsiung, Taiwan 59 F13
Gaoyang, China 56 E8
Gaoyao, China 59 F9
Gaoyou, China 59 A12
Gaoyou Hu, China 57 H10
Gaoyuan, China 57 F9
Gaozhou, China 59 G8
Gap, France 21 D10
Gapan, Phil. 61 D4
Gapat →, India 69 G10
Gapuwiyak, Australia 94 A2
Gar, China 60 C2
Garabogazköl Aylagy, Turkmenistan 50 E6
Garachico, Canary Is. 37 F3
Garachiné, Panama 120 E4
Garafia, Canary Is. 37 F2
Garah, Australia 95 D4
Garajonay, Canary Is. 37 F2
Garango, Burkina Faso 83 C4
Garanhuns, Brazil 125 E11
Garautha, India 69 G8
Garawe, Liberia 82 E3
Garba Tula, Kenya 86 B4
Garberville, U.S.A. 114 F2
Garbiyang, India 69 D9
Garbsen, Germany 24 C5
Gard □, France 21 D8
Gard →, France 21 E8
Garda, L. di, Italy 28 C7
Gardanne, France 21 E9
Gårdby, Sweden 11 H10
Garde L., Canada 105 A7
Gardelegen, Germany 24 C7
Garden City, Ga., U.S.A. 109 J5
Garden City, Kans., U.S.A. 113 G4
Garden City, Tex., U.S.A. 113 K4
Garden Grove, U.S.A. 117 M9
Gardēz, Afghan. 68 C3
Gardhíki, Greece 38 C3
Gardiner, Maine, U.S.A. 109 C11
Gardiner, Mont., U.S.A. 114 D8
Gardiners I., U.S.A. 111 E12
Gardner, U.S.A. 111 D13
Gardner Canal, Canada 104 C3
Gardnerville, U.S.A. 116 G7
Gardno, Jezioro, Poland 44 D4
Gardo, Somali Rep. 74 F4
Gardone Val Trómpia, Italy 28 C7
Gárdony, Hungary 42 C3
Garešnica, Croatia 29 C13
Garéssio, Italy 28 D5
Garey, U.S.A. 117 L6
Garfield, U.S.A. 114 C5
Garforth, U.K. 12 D6
Gargaliánoi, Greece 38 D3
Gargan, Mt., France 20 C5
Gargouna, Mali 83 B5
Gargždai, Lithuania 44 C8
Garibaldi Prov. Park, Canada 104 D4
Gariep, L., S. Africa 88 E4
Garies, S. Africa 88 E2
Garigliano →, Italy 30 A6
Garissa, Kenya 86 C4
Garkida, Nigeria 83 C7
Garko, Nigeria 83 C6
Garland, Tex., U.S.A. 113 J6
Garland, Utah, U.S.A. 114 F7
Garlasco, Italy 28 C5
Garliava, Lithuania 44 D10
Garlin, France 20 E3
Garm, Tajikistan 50 F8
Garmāb, Iran 71 C8
Garmisch-Partenkirchen, Germany 25 H7
Garmo, Qullai = Kommunizma, Pik, Tajikistan 50 F8
Garmsār, Iran 71 C7
Garner, U.S.A. 112 D8
Garnett, U.S.A. 112 F7

Garo Hills, *India* 69 G14
Garoe, *Somali Rep.* 74 F4
Garonne →, *France* 20 C3
Garonne, Canal Latéral à la, *France* 20 D4
Garot, *India* 68 G6
Garoua, *Cameroon* 83 D7
Garpenberg, *Sweden* 10 D10
Garphyttan, *Sweden* 10 E8
Garrauli, *India* 69 G8
Garrel, *Germany* 24 C4
Garrigue = Garrigues, *France* 20 E7
Garrigues, *France* 20 E7
Garrison, *Mont., U.S.A.* 114 C7
Garrison, *N. Dak., U.S.A.* 112 B4
Garrison Res. = Sakakawea, L., *U.S.A.* 112 B4
Garron Pt., *U.K.* 15 A6
Garrovillas, *Spain* 35 F4
Garrucha, *Spain* 33 H3
Garry →, *U.K.* 14 E5
Garry, L., *Canada* 100 B9
Garsen, *Kenya* 86 C5
Gärsnäs, *Sweden* 11 J8
Garson L., *Canada* 105 B6
Gartempe →, *France* 20 B4
Gartz, *Germany* 24 B10
Garu, *Ghana* 83 C4
Garu, *India* 69 H11
Garub, *Namibia* 88 D2
Garut, *Indonesia* 63 G12
Garvão, *Portugal* 35 H2
Garvie Mts., *N.Z.* 91 L2
Garwa = Garoua, *Cameroon* 83 D7
Garwa, *India* 69 G10
Garwolin, *Poland* 45 G8
Gary, *U.S.A.* 108 E2
Garz, *Germany* 24 A9
Garzê, *China* 58 B3
Garzón, *Colombia* 124 C3
Gas-San, *Japan* 54 E10
Gasan Kuli = Esenguly, *Turkmenistan* 50 F6
Gascogne, *France* 20 E4
Gascogne, G. de, *Europe* 20 E2
Gascony = Gascogne, *France* 20 E4
Gascoyne →, *Australia* 93 D1
Gascoyne Junction, *Australia* 93 E2
Gascueña, *Spain* 32 E2
Gash, Wadi →, *Ethiopia* 81 D4
Gashagar, *Nigeria* 83 C7
Gashaka, *Nigeria* 83 D7
Gasherbrum, *Pakistan* 69 B7
Gashua, *Nigeria* 83 C7
Gaspé, *Canada* 103 C7
Gaspé, C. de, *Canada* 103 C7
Gaspé, Pén. de, *Canada* 103 C6
Gaspésie, Parc de Conservation de la, *Canada* 103 C6
Gassan, *Burkina Faso* 82 C4
Gassol, *Nigeria* 83 D7
Gasteiz = Vitoria-Gasteiz, *Spain* 32 C2
Gastonia, *U.S.A.* 109 H5
Gastoúni, *Greece* 38 D3
Gastoúri, *Greece* 38 B1
Gastre, *Argentina* 128 E3
Gästrikland, *Sweden* 10 D10
Gata, C., *Cyprus* 36 E12
Gata, C. de, *Spain* 33 J2
Gata, Sierra de, *Spain* 34 E4
Gataga →, *Canada* 104 B3
Gătaia, *Romania* 42 E6
Gatchina, *Russia* 46 C6
Gatehouse of Fleet, *U.K.* 14 G4
Gates, *U.S.A.* 110 C7
Gateshead, *U.K.* 12 C6
Gatesville, *U.S.A.* 113 K6
Gaths, *Zimbabwe* 87 G3
Gatico, *Chile* 126 A1
Gâtinais, *France* 19 D9
Gâtine, Hauteurs de, *France* 20 B3
Gatineau, *Canada* 111 A9
Gatineau →, *Canada* 102 C4
Gatineau, Parc Nat. de la, *Canada* 102 C4
Gattaran, *Phil.* 61 B4
Gattinara, *Italy* 28 C5
Gatton, *Australia* 95 D5
Gatun, L., *Panama* 120 E4
Gatyana, *S. Africa* 89 E4
Gau, *Fiji* 91 D8
Gaucín, *Spain* 35 J5
Gauer L., *Canada* 105 B9
Gauhati, *India* 67 F17
Gauja →, *Latvia* 9 H21
Gaula →, *Norway* 8 E14
Gauri Phanta, *India* 69 E9
Gausta, *Norway* 9 G13
Gauteng □, *S. Africa* 89 D4
Gāv Koshī, *Iran* 71 D8
Gāvakān, *Iran* 71 D7
Gavarnie, *France* 20 F3
Gavāter, *Iran* 71 E9
Gāvbandī, *Iran* 71 E7
Gavdhopoúla, *Greece* 36 E6
Gávdhos, *Greece* 36 E6
Gavi, *Italy* 28 D5
Gavião, *Portugal* 35 F3
Gaviota, *U.S.A.* 117 L6
Gāvkhūnī, Bāṭlāq-e, *Iran* 71 C7
Gävle, *Sweden* 10 D11
Gävleborgs län □, *Sweden* 10 C10
Gävlebukten, *Sweden* 10 D11
Gavorrano, *Italy* 28 F7
Gavray, *France* 18 D5
Gavrilov Yam, *Russia* 46 D10
Gávrion, *Greece* 38 D6
Gawachab, *Namibia* 88 D2
Gawilgarh Hills, *India* 66 J10
Gawler, *Australia* 95 E2
Gawu, *Nigeria* 83 D6
Gaxun Nur, *China* 60 B5
Gaya, *India* 69 G11
Gaya, *Niger* 83 C5
Gaya, *Nigeria* 83 C6
Gayéri, *Burkina Faso* 83 C5
Gaylord, *U.S.A.* 108 C3
Gayndah, *Australia* 95 D5
Gaysin = Haysyn, *Ukraine* 47 H5
Gayvoron = Hayvoron, *Ukraine* 47 H5
Gaza, *Gaza Strip* 75 D3
Gaza □, *Mozam.* 89 C5
Gaza Strip □, *Asia* 75 D3
Gazanjyk, *Turkmenistan* 71 B7
Gazaoua, *Niger* 83 C6
Gāzbor, *Iran* 71 D8
Gazi, *Dem. Rep. of the Congo* 86 B1
Gaziantep, *Turkey* 70 B3
Gazipaşa, *Turkey* 72 D5
Gbarnga, *Liberia* 82 D3
Gbekebo, *Nigeria* 83 D5
Gboko, *Nigeria* 83 D6
Gbongan, *Nigeria* 83 D5
Gcoverega, *Botswana* 88 B3
Gcuwa, *S. Africa* 89 E4
Gdańsk, *Poland* 44 D5
Gdańska, Zatoka, *Poland* 44 D6
Gdov, *Russia* 9 G22
Gdynia, *Poland* 44 D5
Geba →, *Guinea-Biss.* 82 C1
Gebe, *Indonesia* 63 D7
Gebeciler, *Turkey* 39 C12
Gebeit Mine, *Sudan* 80 C4
Gebel Abyad, *Sudan* 80 D2
Gebel Iweibid, *Egypt* 80 H8
Gebze, *Turkey* 41 F13
Gecha, *Ethiopia* 81 F4
Gedaref, *Sudan* 81 E4
Gedaref □, *Sudan* 81 E4
Gediz, *Turkey* 39 B11
Gediz →, *Turkey* 39 C8
Gedo, *Ethiopia* 81 F4
Gèdre, *France* 20 F4
Gedser, *Denmark* 11 K5
Geegully Cr. →, *Australia* 92 C3
Geel, *Belgium* 17 C4
Geelong, *Australia* 95 F3
Geelvink B. = Cenderwasih, Teluk, *Indonesia* 63 E9
Geelvink Chan., *Australia* 93 E1
Geesthacht, *Germany* 24 B6
Geidam, *Nigeria* 83 C7
Geikie →, *Canada* 105 B8
Geilenkirchen, *Germany* 24 E2
Geili, *Sudan* 81 D3
Geisingen, *Germany* 25 H4
Geislingen, *Germany* 25 G5
Geistown, *U.S.A.* 110 F6
Geita, *Tanzania* 86 C3
Gejiu, *China* 58 F4
Gel →, *Sudan* 81 F2
Gel, Meydān-e, *Iran* 71 D7
Gel River, *Sudan* 81 F2
Gela, *Italy* 31 E7
Gela, G. di, *Italy* 31 F7
Gelahun, *Liberia* 82 D2
Gelderland □, *Neths.* 17 B6
Geldern, *Germany* 24 D2
Geldrop, *Neths.* 17 C5
Geleen, *Neths.* 17 D5
Gelehun, *S. Leone* 82 D2
Gelembe, *Turkey* 39 B9
Gelemso, *Ethiopia* 81 F5
Gelendost, *Turkey* 72 C4
Gelendzhik, *Russia* 47 K10
Gelibolu, *Turkey* 41 F10
Gelibolu Yarımadası, *Turkey* 41 F10
Gelidonya Burnu, *Turkey* 72 D4
Gelnhausen, *Germany* 25 E5
Gelnica, *Slovak Rep.* 27 C13
Gelsenkirchen, *Germany* 24 D3
Gelting, *Germany* 24 A5
Gemas, *Malaysia* 65 L4
Gembloux, *Belgium* 17 D4
Gembu, *Nigeria* 83 D7
Gemena, *Dem. Rep. of the Congo* 84 D3
Gemerek, *Turkey* 70 B3
Gemla, *Sweden* 11 H8
Gemlik, *Turkey* 41 F13
Gemlik Körfezi, *Turkey* 41 F12
Gemona del Friuli, *Italy* 29 B10
Gemsa, *Egypt* 80 B3
Gemünden, *Germany* 25 E5
Genale →, *Ethiopia* 81 F4
Genç, *Turkey* 73 C9
Gençay, *France* 20 B4
Geneina, Gebel, *Egypt* 80 B3
General Acha, *Argentina* 126 D3
General Alvear, *Buenos Aires, Argentina* 126 D4
General Alvear, *Mendoza, Argentina* 126 D2
General Artigas, *Paraguay* 126 B4
General Belgrano, *Argentina* 126 D4
General Cabrera, *Argentina* 126 C3
General Cepeda, *Mexico* 118 B4
General Guido, *Argentina* 126 D4
General Juan Madariaga, *Argentina* 126 D4
General La Madrid, *Argentina* 126 D3
General MacArthur, *Phil.* 61 F6
General Martin Miguel de Güemes, *Argentina* 126 A3
General Paz, *Argentina* 126 B4
General Pico, *Argentina* 126 D3
General Pinedo, *Argentina* 126 B3
General Pinto, *Argentina* 126 C3
General Roca, *Argentina* 128 D3
General Santos, *Phil.* 61 H6
General Toshevo, *Bulgaria* 41 C12
General Trevino, *Mexico* 119 B5
General Trías, *Mexico* 118 B3
General Viamonte, *Argentina* 126 D3
General Villegas, *Argentina* 126 D3
Genesee, *Idaho, U.S.A.* 114 C5
Genesee, *Pa., U.S.A.* 110 E7
Genesee →, *U.S.A.* 110 C7
Geneseo, *Ill., U.S.A.* 112 E9
Geneseo, *N.Y., U.S.A.* 110 D7
Geneva = Genève, *Switz.* 25 J2
Geneva, *Ala., U.S.A.* 109 K3
Geneva, *N.Y., U.S.A.* 110 D8
Geneva, *Nebr., U.S.A.* 112 E6
Geneva, *Ohio, U.S.A.* 110 E4
Geneva, L. = Léman, L., *Europe* 19 F13
Geneva, L., *U.S.A.* 108 D1
Genève, *Switz.* 25 J2
Gengenbach, *Germany* 25 G4
Gengma, *China* 58 F2
Genichesk = Henichesk, *Ukraine* 47 J8
Genil →, *Spain* 35 H5
Genk, *Belgium* 17 D5
Genlis, *France* 19 E12
Gennargentu, Mti. del, *Italy* 30 B2
Gennes, *France* 18 E6
Genoa = Génova, *Italy* 28 D5
Genoa, *Australia* 95 F4
Genoa, *N.Y., U.S.A.* 111 D8
Genoa, *Nebr., U.S.A.* 112 E6
Genoa, *Nev., U.S.A.* 116 F7
Génova, *Italy* 28 D5
Génova, G. di, *Italy* 28 E6
Genriyetty, Ostrov, *Russia* 51 B16
Gent, *Belgium* 17 C3
Genteng, *Indonesia* 63 G12
Genthin, *Germany* 24 C8
Genyem, *Indonesia* 63 E10
Genzano di Lucánia, *Italy* 31 B9
Genzano di Roma, *Italy* 29 G9
Geoagiu, *Romania* 43 E8
Geographe B., *Australia* 93 F2
Geographe Chan., *Australia* 93 D1
Geokchay = Göyçay, *Azerbaijan* 49 K8
Geelvink, Zemlya, *Russia* 50 A5
George, *S. Africa* 88 E3
George →, *Canada* 103 A6
George, L., *N.S.W., Australia* 95 F4
George, L., *S. Austral., Australia* 95 F3
George, L., *W. Austral., Australia* 92 D3
George, L., *Uganda* 86 B3
George, L., *Fla., U.S.A.* 109 L5
George, L., *N.Y., U.S.A.* 111 C11
George Gill Ra., *Australia* 92 D5
George River = Kangiqsualujjuaq, *Canada* 101 C13
George Sound, *N.Z.* 91 L1
George Town, *Australia* 94 G4
George Town, *Bahamas* 120 B4
George Town, *Cayman Is.* 120 C3
George Town, *Malaysia* 65 K3
George V Land, *Antarctica* 5 C10
George VI Sound, *Antarctica* 5 D17
George West, *U.S.A.* 113 L5
Georgetown, *Australia* 94 B3
Georgetown, *Ont., Canada* 102 D4
Georgetown, *P.E.I., Canada* 103 C7
Georgetown, *Gambia* 82 C2
Georgetown, *Guyana* 124 B7
Georgetown, *Calif., U.S.A.* 116 G6
Georgetown, *Colo., U.S.A.* 114 G11
Georgetown, *Ky., U.S.A.* 108 F3
Georgetown, *N.Y., U.S.A.* 111 D9
Georgetown, *Ohio, U.S.A.* 108 F4
Georgetown, *S.C., U.S.A.* 109 J6
Georgetown, *Tex., U.S.A.* 113 K6
Georgia □, *U.S.A.* 109 K5
Georgia ■, *Asia* 49 J6
Georgia, Str. of, *Canada* 104 D4
Georgian B., *Canada* 102 C3
Georgina →, *Australia* 94 C2
Georgina I., *Canada* 110 B5
Georgiu-Dezh = Liski, *Russia* 47 G10
Georgiyevsk, *Russia* 49 H6
Georgsmarienhütte, *Germany* 24 C4
Gera, *Germany* 24 E8
Geraardsbergen, *Belgium* 17 D3
Geral, Serra, *Brazil* 127 B6
Geral de Goiás, Serra, *Brazil* 125 F9
Geraldine, *U.S.A.* 114 C8
Geraldton, *Australia* 93 E1
Geraldton, *Canada* 102 C2
Gérardmer, *France* 19 D13
Gercüş, *Turkey* 73 D9
Gerede, *Turkey* 72 B5
Gerês, Sierra do, *Portugal* 34 D3
Gereshk, *Afghan.* 66 D4
Geretsried, *Germany* 25 H7
Gérgal, *Spain* 33 H2
Gerik, *Malaysia* 65 K3
Gering, *U.S.A.* 112 E3
Gerlach, *U.S.A.* 114 F4
Gerlachovský štít, *Slovak Rep.* 27 B13
German Planina, *Macedonia* 40 D6
Germansen Landing, *Canada* 104 B4
Germantown, *U.S.A.* 113 M10
Germany ■, *Europe* 24 E6
Germencik, *Turkey* 39 D9
Germering, *Germany* 25 G7
Germersheim, *Germany* 25 F4
Germī, *Iran* 71 B6
Germiston, *S. Africa* 89 D4
Gernika-Lumo, *Spain* 32 B2
Gernsheim, *Germany* 25 F4
Gero, *Japan* 55 G8
Gerolzhofen, *Germany* 25 F6
Gerona = Girona, *Spain* 32 D7
Gerrard, *Canada* 104 C5
Gers □, *France* 20 E4
Gers →, *France* 20 D4
Gersfeld, *Germany* 24 E5
Gersthofen, *Germany* 25 G6
Gerzat, *France* 20 C7
Gerze, *Turkey* 72 B6
Geseke, *Germany* 24 D4
Geser, *Indonesia* 63 E8
Gesso →, *Italy* 28 D4
Gestro, Wabi →, *Ethiopia* 81 G5
Getafe, *Spain* 34 E7
Getinge, *Sweden* 11 H6
Gettysburg, *Pa., U.S.A.* 108 F7
Gettysburg, *S. Dak., U.S.A.* 112 C5
Getxo, *Spain* 32 B2
Getz Ice Shelf, *Antarctica* 5 D14
Gevaş, *Turkey* 73 C10
Gévaudan, *France* 20 D7
Gevgelija, *Macedonia* 40 E6
Gévora →, *Spain* 35 G4
Gewani, *Ethiopia* 81 E5
Gex, *France* 19 F13
Geyikli, *Turkey* 39 B8
Geyser, *U.S.A.* 114 C8
Geyserville, *U.S.A.* 116 G4
Geyve, *Turkey* 72 B4
Ghâbat el Arab = Wang Kai, *Sudan* 81 F2
Ghabeish, *Sudan* 81 E2
Ghaggar →, *India* 68 E6
Ghaghara →, *India* 69 G11
Ghaghat →, *Bangla.* 69 G13
Ghagra, *India* 69 H11
Ghagra →, *India* 69 F9
Ghalla, Wadi el →, *Sudan* 81 E2
Ghana ■, *W. Afr.* 83 D4
Ghansor, *India* 69 H9
Ghanzi, *Botswana* 88 C3
Gharb el Istiwa'iya □, *Sudan* 81 G3
Gharb Kordofân, *Sudan* 81 E2
Gharbîya, Es Sahrâ el, *Egypt* 80 B2
Ghardaïa, *Algeria* 78 B6
Ghârib, G., *Egypt* 80 B3
Gharig, *Sudan* 81 E2
Gharyān, *Libya* 79 B8
Ghat, *Libya* 79 D8
Ghatal, *India* 69 H12
Ghatampur, *India* 69 F9
Ghatsila, *India* 69 H12
Ghaṭṭī, *Si. Arabia* 70 D3
Ghawdex = Gozo, *Malta* 36 C1
Ghazal, Bahr el →, *Chad* 79 F9
Ghazâl, Bahr el →, *Sudan* 81 F3
Ghaziabad, *India* 68 E7
Ghazipur, *India* 69 G10
Ghaznī, *Afghan.* 68 C3
Ghaznī □, *Afghan.* 66 C6
Ghedi, *Italy* 28 C7
Ghelari, *Romania* 42 E7
Ghent = Gent, *Belgium* 17 C3
Gheorghe Gheorghiu-Dej = Onești, *Romania* 43 D11
Gheorgheni, *Romania* 43 D10
Gherla, *Romania* 43 C8
Ghidigeni, *Romania* 43 D12
Ghilarza, *Italy* 30 B1
Ghimeș-Făget, *Romania* 43 D11
Ghīnah, Wādī al →, *Si. Arabia* 70 D3
Ghisonaccia, *France* 21 F13
Ghisoni, *France* 21 F13
Ghizao, *Afghan.* 68 C1
Ghizar →, *Pakistan* 69 A5
Ghot Ogrein, *Egypt* 80 A2
Ghotaru, *India* 68 F4
Ghotki, *Pakistan* 68 E3
Ghowr □, *Afghan.* 66 C4
Ghudaf, W. al →, *Iraq* 70 C4
Ghudāmis, *Libya* 77 C4
Ghughri, *India* 69 H9
Ghugus, *India* 66 K11
Ghulam Mohammad Barrage, *Pakistan* 68 G3
Ghūriān, *Afghan.* 66 B2
Gia Dinh, *Vietnam* 65 G6
Gia Lai = Plei Ku, *Vietnam* 64 F7
Gia Nghia, *Vietnam* 65 G6
Gia Ngoc, *Vietnam* 64 E7
Gia Vuc, *Vietnam* 64 E7
Giannutri, *Italy* 28 F8
Giant Forest, *U.S.A.* 116 J8
Giant Mts. = Krkonoše, *Czech Rep.* 26 A8
Giants Causeway, *U.K.* 15 A5
Giarabub = Al Jaghbūb, *Libya* 79 C10
Giarre, *Italy* 31 E8
Giaveno, *Italy* 28 C4
Gibara, *Cuba* 120 B4
Gibb River, *Australia* 92 C4
Gibbon, *U.S.A.* 112 E5
Gibe →, *Ethiopia* 81 F4
Gibellina Nuova, *Italy* 30 E5
Gibeon, *Namibia* 88 D2
Gibraleón, *Spain* 35 H4
Gibraltar ■, *Europe* 35 J5
Gibraltar, Str. of, *Medit. S.* 35 K5
Gibson Desert, *Australia* 92 D4
Gibsons, *Canada* 104 D4
Gibsonville, *U.S.A.* 116 F6
Giddings, *U.S.A.* 113 K6
Gidole, *Ethiopia* 81 F4
Giebnegáisi = Kebnekaise, *Sweden* 8 C18
Gien, *France* 19 E9
Giengen, *Germany* 25 G6
Giessen, *Germany* 24 E4
Gīfān, *Iran* 71 B8
Gifatin, Geziret, *Egypt* 80 B3
Gifhorn, *Germany* 24 C6
Gift Lake, *Canada* 104 B5
Gifu, *Japan* 55 G8
Gifu □, *Japan* 55 G8
Gigant, *Russia* 49 G5
Giganta, Sa. de la, *Mexico* 118 B2
Gigen, *Bulgaria* 41 C8
Gigha, *U.K.* 14 F3
Gíglio, *Italy* 28 F7
Gignac, *France* 20 E7
Gigüela →, *Spain* 35 F7
Gijón, *Spain* 34 B5
Gil I., *Canada* 104 C3
Gila →, *U.S.A.* 115 K6
Gila Bend, *U.S.A.* 115 K7
Gila Bend Mts., *U.S.A.* 115 K7
Gīlān □, *Iran* 71 B6
Gilău, *Romania* 43 D8
Gilbert →, *Australia* 94 B3
Gilbert Is., *Kiribati* 96 G9
Gilbert River, *Australia* 94 B3
Gilead, *U.S.A.* 111 B14
Gilf el Kebîr, Hadabat el, *Egypt* 80 C2
Gilford I., *Canada* 104 C3
Gilgandra, *Australia* 95 E4
Gilgil, *Kenya* 86 C4
Gilgit, *India* 69 B6
Gilgit →, *Pakistan* 69 B6
Giljeva Planina, *Serbia, Yug.* 40 C3
Gillam, *Canada* 105 B10
Gilleleje, *Denmark* 11 H6
Gillen, L., *Australia* 93 E3
Gilles, L., *Australia* 95 E2
Gillette, *U.S.A.* 112 C2
Gilliat, *Australia* 94 C3
Gillingham, *U.K.* 13 F8
Gilmer, *U.S.A.* 113 J7
Gilmore, L., *Australia* 93 F3
Gilo →, *Ethiopia* 81 F3
Gilort →, *Romania* 43 F8
Gilroy, *U.S.A.* 116 H5
Gimbi, *Ethiopia* 81 F4
Gimli, *Canada* 105 C9
Gimo, *Sweden* 10 D12
Gimone →, *France* 20 E5
Gimont, *France* 20 E4
Gin Gin, *Australia* 95 D5
Ginâh, *Egypt* 80 B3
Gineifa, *Egypt* 80 H8
Gingin, *Australia* 93 F2
Gingindlovu, *S. Africa* 89 D5
Ginir, *Ethiopia* 81 F5
Ginosa, *Italy* 31 B9
Ginzo de Limia = Xinzo de Limia, *Spain* 34 C3
Gióia, G. di, *Italy* 31 D8
Gióia del Colle, *Italy* 31 B9
Gióia Táuro, *Italy* 31 D8
Gioiosa Iónica, *Italy* 31 D9
Gioiosa Marea, *Italy* 31 D7
Gióna, Óros, *Greece* 38 C4
Giovi, Passo dei, *Italy* 28 D5
Giovinazzo, *Italy* 31 A9
Gir Hills, *India* 68 J4
Girab, *India* 68 F4
Girâfi, W. →, *Egypt* 75 F3
Giraltovce, *Slovak Rep.* 27 B14
Girard, *Kans., U.S.A.* 113 G7
Girard, *Ohio, U.S.A.* 110 E4
Girard, *Pa., U.S.A.* 110 E4
Girdle Ness, *U.K.* 14 D6
Giresun, *Turkey* 73 B8
Girga, *Egypt* 80 B3
Giri →, *India* 68 D7
Giridih, *India* 69 G12
Girifalco, *Italy* 31 D9
Girne = Kyrenia, *Cyprus* 36 D12
Giro, *Nigeria* 83 C5
Giromagny, *France* 19 E13
Girona, *Spain* 32 D7
Girona □, *Spain* 32 C7
Gironde □, *France* 20 D3
Gironde →, *France* 20 C2
Gironella, *Spain* 32 C6
Giru, *Australia* 94 B4
Girvan, *U.K.* 14 F4
Gisborne, *N.Z.* 91 H7
Gisenyi, *Rwanda* 86 C2
Gislaved, *Sweden* 11 G7
Gisors, *France* 19 C8
Gitega, *Burundi* 86 C2
Giuba →, *Somali Rep.* 74 G3
Giugliano in Campania, *Italy* 31 B7
Giulianova, *Italy* 29 F10
Giurgeni, *Romania* 43 F12
Giurgiu, *Romania* 43 G10
Giurgiu □, *Romania* 43 F10
Giurgiulești, *Moldova* 43 E13
Give, *Denmark* 11 J3
Givet, *France* 19 B11
Givors, *France* 21 C8
Givry, *France* 19 F11
Giyon, *Ethiopia* 81 F4
Giza = El Gîza, *Egypt* 80 J7
Gizhiga, *Russia* 51 C17
Gizhiginskaya Guba, *Russia* 51 C16
Giżycko, *Poland* 44 D8
Gizzeria, *Italy* 31 D9
Gjalicë e Lumës, Mal., *Albania* 40 D4

Gjegjan, *Albania* 40 E4
Gjirokastër, *Albania* 40 F4
Gjoa Haven, *Canada* 100 B10
Gjøvik, *Norway* 9 F14
Gjuhës, Kep i, *Albania* 40 F3
Glace Bay, *Canada* 103 C8
Glacier Bay National Park and Preserve, *U.S.A.* 104 B1
Glacier National Park, *Canada* 104 C5
Glacier National Park, *U.S.A.* 114 B7
Glacier Peak, *U.S.A.* 114 B3
Gladewater, *U.S.A.* 113 J7
Gladstone, *Queens., Australia* 94 C5
Gladstone, *S. Austral., Australia* 95 E2
Gladstone, *Canada* 105 C9
Gladstone, *U.S.A.* 108 C2
Gladwin, *U.S.A.* 108 D3
Glafsfjorden, *Sweden* 10 E6
Głagów Małapolski, *Poland* 45 H8
Gläma = Glomma →, *Norway* 9 G14
Gláma, *Iceland* 8 D2
Glamis, *U.S.A.* 117 N11
Glamoč, *Bos.-H.* 29 D13
Glamsbjerg, *Denmark* 11 J4
Glarus, *Switz.* 25 H5
Glarus □, *Switz.* 25 J5
Glasco, *Kans., U.S.A.* 112 F6
Glasco, *N.Y., U.S.A.* 111 D11
Glasgow, *U.K.* 14 F4
Glasgow, *Ky., U.S.A.* 108 G3
Glasgow, *Mont., U.S.A.* 114 B10
Glasgow, City of □, *U.K.* 14 F4
Glaslyn, *Canada* 105 C7
Glastonbury, *U.K.* 13 F5
Glastonbury, *U.S.A.* 111 E12
Glauchau, *Germany* 24 E8
Glava, *Sweden* 10 E6
Glavice, *Croatia* 29 E13
Glazov, *Russia* 48 A11
Gleichen, *Canada* 104 C6
Gleisdorf, *Austria* 26 D8
Gleiwitz = Gliwice, *Poland* 45 H5
Glen, *U.S.A.* 111 B13
Glen Affric, *U.K.* 14 D3
Glen Canyon, *U.S.A.* 115 H8
Glen Canyon Dam, *U.S.A.* 115 H8
Glen Canyon National Recreation Area, *U.S.A.* 115 H8
Glen Coe, *U.K.* 14 E3
Glen Cove, *U.S.A.* 111 F11
Glen Garry, *U.K.* 14 D3
Glen Innes, *Australia* 95 D5
Glen Lyon, *U.S.A.* 111 E8
Glen Mor, *U.K.* 14 D4
Glen Moriston, *U.K.* 14 D4
Glen Robertson, *Canada* 111 A10
Glen Spean, *U.K.* 14 E4
Glen Ullin, *U.S.A.* 112 B4
Glénan, Îs. de, *France* 18 E3
Glencoe, *Canada* 110 D3
Glencoe, *S. Africa* 89 D5
Glencoe, *U.S.A.* 112 C7
Glendale, *Ariz., U.S.A.* 115 K7
Glendale, *Calif., U.S.A.* 117 L8
Glendale, *Zimbabwe* 87 F3
Glendive, *U.S.A.* 112 B2
Glendo, *U.S.A.* 112 D2
Glenelg →, *Australia* 95 F3
Glenfield, *U.S.A.* 111 C9
Glengarriff, *Ireland* 15 E2
Glenmont, *U.S.A.* 110 F2
Glenmorgan, *Australia* 95 D4
Glenn, *U.S.A.* 116 F4
Glennallen, *U.S.A.* 100 B5
Glennamaddy, *Ireland* 15 C3
Glenns Ferry, *U.S.A.* 114 E6
Glenore, *Australia* 94 B3
Glenreagh, *Australia* 95 E5
Glenrock, *U.S.A.* 114 E11
Glenrothes, *U.K.* 14 E5
Glens Falls, *U.S.A.* 111 C11
Glenside, *U.S.A.* 111 F9
Glenties, *Ireland* 15 B3
Glenville, *U.S.A.* 108 F5
Glenwood, *Canada* 103 C9
Glenwood, *Ark., U.S.A.* 113 H8
Glenwood, *Iowa, U.S.A.* 112 E7
Glenwood, *Minn., U.S.A.* 112 C7
Glenwood, *Wash., U.S.A.* 116 D5
Glenwood Springs, *U.S.A.* 114 G10
Glettinganes, *Iceland* 8 D7
Glifádha, *Greece* 38 D5
Glimåkra, *Sweden* 11 H8
Glina, *Croatia* 29 C13
Glinojeck, *Poland* 45 F7
Gliwice, *Poland* 45 H5
Globe, *U.S.A.* 115 K8
Glodeanu Siliştea, *Romania* 43 F11
Glodeni, *Moldova* 43 C12
Glödnitz, *Austria* 26 E7
Gloggnitz, *Austria* 26 D8
Głogów, *Poland* 45 G3
Głogówek, *Poland* 45 H4
Glomma →, *Norway* 9 G14
Glorieuses, Is., *Ind. Oc.* 89 A8
Glóssa, *Greece* 38 B5
Glossop, *U.K.* 12 D6
Gloucester, *Australia* 95 E5
Gloucester, *U.K.* 13 F5
Gloucester, *U.S.A.* 111 D14
Gloucester I., *Australia* 94 C4
Gloucester Point, *U.S.A.* 108 G7
Gloucestershire □, *U.K.* 13 F5
Gloversville, *U.S.A.* 111 C10
Glovertown, *Canada* 103 C9
Głowno, *Poland* 45 G6
Głubczyce, *Poland* 45 H4
Glubokiy, *Russia* 49 F5
Glubokoye = Hlybokaye, *Belarus* 46 E4
Głuchołazy, *Poland* 45 H4
Glücksburg, *Germany* 24 A5
Glückstadt, *Germany* 24 B5
Glukhov = Hlukhiv, *Ukraine* 47 G7
Glusk, *Belarus* 47 F5
Głuszyca, *Poland* 45 H3
Glyngøre, *Denmark* 11 H2
Gmünd, *Kärnten, Austria* 26 E6
Gmünd, *Niederösterreich, Austria* 26 C8
Gmunden, *Austria* 26 D6
Gnarp, *Sweden* 10 B11
Gnesta, *Sweden* 10 E11
Gniew, *Poland* 44 E5
Gniewkowo, *Poland* 45 F5
Gniezno, *Poland* 45 F4
Gnjilane, *Kosovo, Yug.* 40 D5
Gnoien, *Germany* 24 B8
Gnosjö, *Sweden* 11 G7
Gnowangerup, *Australia* 93 F2
Go Cong, *Vietnam* 65 G6
Gō-no-ura, *Japan* 55 H4
Goa, *India* 66 M8
Goa □, *India* 66 M8
Goalen Hd., *Australia* 95 F5
Goalpara, *India* 67 F17
Goaltor, *India* 69 H12
Goalundo Ghat, *Bangla.* 69 H13
Goaso, *Ghana* 82 D4
Goat Fell, *U.K.* 14 F3
Goba, *Ethiopia* 81 F4
Goba, *Mozam.* 89 D5
Gobabis, *Namibia* 88 C2
Göbel, *Turkey* 41 F12
Gobi, *Asia* 56 C6
Gobō, *Japan* 55 H7
Gobo, *Sudan* 81 F3
Göçbeyli, *Turkey* 39 B9
Goch, *Germany* 24 D2
Gochas, *Namibia* 88 C2
Godavari →, *India* 67 L13
Godavari Pt., *India* 67 L13
Godbout, *Canada* 103 C6
Godda, *India* 69 G12
Godech, *Bulgaria* 40 C7
Goderich, *Canada* 102 D3
Goderville, *France* 18 C7
Godfrey Ra., *Australia* 93 D2
Godhavn = Qeqertarsuaq, *Greenland* 4 C5
Godhra, *India* 68 H5
Gödöllő, *Hungary* 42 C4
Godoy Cruz, *Argentina* 126 C2
Gods →, *Canada* 102 A1
Gods L., *Canada* 102 B1
Gods River, *Canada* 105 C10
Godthåb = Nuuk, *Greenland* 101 B14
Godwin Austen = K2, *Pakistan* 69 B7
Goeie Hoop, Kaap die = Good Hope, C. of, *S. Africa* 88 E2
Goéland, L. au, *Canada* 102 C4
Goeree, *Neths.* 17 C3
Goes, *Neths.* 17 C3
Goffstown, *U.S.A.* 111 C13
Gogama, *Canada* 102 C3
Gogebic, L., *U.S.A.* 112 B10
Goggetti, *Ethiopia* 81 F4
Gogolin, *Poland* 45 H5
Gogonou, *Benin* 83 C5
Gogra = Ghaghara →, *India* 69 G11
Gogriâl, *Sudan* 81 F2
Gogti, *Ethiopia* 81 E5
Gohana, *India* 68 E7
Goharganj, *India* 68 H7
Goi →, *India* 68 H6
Goiânia, *Brazil* 125 G9
Goiás, *Brazil* 125 G8
Goiás □, *Brazil* 125 F9
Goio-Erê, *Brazil* 127 A5
Góis, *Portugal* 34 E2
Gojam □, *Ethiopia* 81 E4
Gojeb, Wabi →, *Ethiopia* 81 F4
Gojō, *Japan* 55 G7
Gojra, *Pakistan* 68 D5
Gökçeada, *Turkey* 41 F9
Gökçedağ, *Turkey* 39 B10
Gökçen, *Turkey* 39 C9
Gökçeören, *Turkey* 39 C10
Gökçeyazı, *Turkey* 39 B9
Gökırmak →, *Turkey* 72 B6
Gökova, *Turkey* 39 D10
Gökova Körfezi, *Turkey* 39 E9
Göksu →, *Turkey* 72 D6
Göksun, *Turkey* 72 C7
Gokteik, *Burma* 67 H20
Göktepe, *Turkey* 39 D10
Gokurt, *Pakistan* 68 E2
Gokwe, *Zimbabwe* 89 B4
Gola, *India* 69 E9
Golakganj, *India* 69 F13
Golan Heights = Hagolan, *Syria* 75 C4
Gołańcz, *Poland* 45 F4
Golāshkerd, *Iran* 71 E8
Golaya Pristen = Hola Pristan, *Ukraine* 47 J7
Gölbaşı, *Adiyaman, Turkey* 72 D7
Gölbaşı, *Ankara, Turkey* 72 C5
Golchikha, *Russia* 4 B12
Golconda, *U.S.A.* 114 F5
Gölcük, *Kocaeli, Turkey* 41 F13
Gölcük, *Niğde, Turkey* 72 C6
Gold, *U.S.A.* 110 E7
Gold Beach, *U.S.A.* 114 E1
Gold Coast, *W. Afr.* 83 E4
Gold Hill, *U.S.A.* 114 E2
Gold River, *Canada* 104 D3
Gołdap, *Poland* 44 D9
Goldberg, *Germany* 24 B8
Golden, *Canada* 104 C5
Golden B., *N.Z.* 91 J4
Golden Gate, *U.S.A.* 114 H2
Golden Hinde, *Canada* 104 D3
Golden Lake, *Canada* 110 A7
Golden Vale, *Ireland* 15 D3
Goldendale, *U.S.A.* 114 D3
Goldfield, *U.S.A.* 115 H5
Goldsand L., *Canada* 105 B8
Goldsboro, *U.S.A.* 109 H7
Goldsmith, *U.S.A.* 113 K3
Goldsworthy, *Australia* 92 D2
Goldthwaite, *U.S.A.* 113 K5
Golegã, *Portugal* 35 F2
Goleniów, *Poland* 44 E1
Golestānak, *Iran* 71 D7
Goleta, *U.S.A.* 117 L7
Golfito, *Costa Rica* 120 E3
Golfo Aranci, *Italy* 30 B2
Gölgeli Dağları, *Turkey* 39 D10
Gölhisar, *Turkey* 39 D11
Goliad, *U.S.A.* 113 L6
Golija, *Montenegro, Yug.* 40 C2
Golija, *Serbia, Yug.* 40 C4
Golina, *Poland* 45 F5
Gölköy, *Turkey* 72 B7
Göllersdorf, *Austria* 26 C9
Gölmarmara, *Turkey* 39 C9
Golo →, *France* 21 F13
Gölova, *Turkey* 39 E12
Golpāyegān, *Iran* 71 C6
Gölpazarı, *Turkey* 72 B4
Golra, *Pakistan* 68 C5
Golspie, *U.K.* 14 D5
Golub-Dobrzyń, *Poland* 45 E6
Golubac, *Serbia, Yug.* 40 B5
Golyam Perelik, *Bulgaria* 41 E8
Golyama Kamchiya →, *Bulgaria* 41 C11
Goma, *Dem. Rep. of the Congo* 86 C2
Gomal Pass, *Pakistan* 68 D3
Gomati →, *India* 69 G10
Gombari, *Dem. Rep. of the Congo* 86 B2
Gombe, *Nigeria* 83 C7
Gömbe, *Turkey* 39 E11
Gombe □, *Nigeria* 83 C7
Gombe →, *Tanzania* 86 C3
Gombi, *Nigeria* 83 C7
Gomel = Homyel, *Belarus* 47 F6
Gomera, *Canary Is.* 37 F2
Gómez Palacio, *Mexico* 118 B4
Gomīshān, *Iran* 71 B7
Gommern, *Germany* 24 C7
Gomogomo, *Indonesia* 63 F8
Gomoh, *India* 67 H15
Gomotartsi, *Bulgaria* 40 B6
Gompa = Ganta, *Liberia* 82 D3
Gomphi, *Greece* 38 B3
Gonābād, *Iran* 71 C8
Gonaïves, *Haiti* 121 C5
Gonâve, G. de la, *Haiti* 121 C5
Gonâve, I. de la, *Haiti* 121 C5
Gonbad-e Kāvūs, *Iran* 71 B7
Gönc, *Hungary* 42 B6
Gonda, *India* 69 F9
Gondal, *India* 68 J4
Gonder, *Ethiopia* 81 E4
Gonder □, *Ethiopia* 81 E4
Gondia, *India* 66 J12
Gondola, *Mozam.* 87 F3
Gondomar, *Portugal* 34 D2
Gondrecourt-le-Château, *France* 19 D12
Gönen, *Balıkesir, Turkey* 41 F11
Gönen, *Isparta, Turkey* 39 D12
Gönen →, *Turkey* 41 F11
Gong Xian, *China* 58 C5
Gong'an, *China* 59 B9
Gongcheng, *China* 59 E8
Gongga Shan, *China* 58 C3
Gongguan, *China* 58 G7
Gonghe, *China* 60 C5
Gongola →, *Nigeria* 83 D7
Gongolgon, *Australia* 95 E4
Gongshan, *China* 58 D2
Gongtan, *China* 58 C7
Gongzhuling, *China* 57 C13
Goniadz, *Poland* 44 E9
Goniri, *Nigeria* 83 C7
Gonjo, *China* 58 B2
Gonnesa, *Italy* 30 C1
Gónnos, *Greece* 38 B4
Gonnosfanádiga, *Italy* 30 C1
Gonzaga, *Phil.* 61 B5
Gonzales, *Calif., U.S.A.* 116 J5
Gonzales, *Tex., U.S.A.* 113 L6
González Chaves, *Argentina* 126 D3
Good Hope, C. of, *S. Africa* 88 E2
Gooderham, *Canada* 110 B6
Goodhouse, *S. Africa* 88 D2
Gooding, *U.S.A.* 114 E6
Goodland, *U.S.A.* 112 F4
Goodlow, *Canada* 104 B4
Goodooga, *Australia* 95 D4
Goodsprings, *U.S.A.* 117 K11
Goole, *U.K.* 12 D7
Goolgowi, *Australia* 95 E4
Goomalling, *Australia* 93 F2
Goomeri, *Australia* 95 D5
Goonda, *Mozam.* 87 F3
Goondiwindi, *Australia* 95 D5
Goongarrie, L., *Australia* 93 F3
Goonyella, *Australia* 94 C4
Goose →, *Canada* 103 B7
Goose Creek, *U.S.A.* 109 J5
Goose L., *U.S.A.* 114 F3
Gop, *India* 66 H6
Gopalganj, *India* 69 F11
Göppingen, *Germany* 25 G5
Gor, *Spain* 35 H8
Góra, *Dolnośląskie, Poland* 45 G3
Góra, *Mazowieckie, Poland* 45 F7
Góra Kalwaria, *Poland* 45 G8
Gorakhpur, *India* 69 F10
Goražde, *Bos.-H.* 42 G3
Gorbatov, *Russia* 48 B6
Gorbea, Peña, *Spain* 32 B2
Gorda, *U.S.A.* 116 K5
Gorda, Pta., *Canary Is.* 37 F2
Gorda, Pta., *Nic.* 120 D3
Gordan B., *Australia* 92 B5
Gördes, *Turkey* 39 C10
Gordon, *U.S.A.* 112 D3
Gordon →, *Australia* 94 G4
Gordon L., *Alta., Canada* 105 B6
Gordon L., *N.W.T., Canada* 104 A6
Gordonvale, *Australia* 94 B4
Gore, *Ethiopia* 81 F4
Gore, *N.Z.* 91 M2
Gore Bay, *Canada* 102 C3
Görele, *Turkey* 73 B8
Goreme, *Turkey* 72 C6
Gorey, *Ireland* 15 D5
Gorg, *Iran* 71 D8
Gorgān, *Iran* 71 B7
Gorgona, *Italy* 28 E6
Gorgona, I., *Colombia* 124 C3
Gorgora, *Ethiopia* 81 E4
Gorgoram, *Nigeria* 83 C7
Gorham, *U.S.A.* 111 B13
Gori, *Georgia* 49 J7
Goriganga →, *India* 69 E9
Gorinchem, *Neths.* 17 C4
Goris, *Armenia* 73 C12
Goritsy, *Russia* 46 D9
Gorízia, *Italy* 29 C10
Gorj □, *Romania* 43 E8
Gorki = Horki, *Belarus* 46 E6
Gorki = Nizhniy Novgorod, *Russia* 48 B7
Gorkiy = Nizhniy Novgorod, *Russia* 48 B7
Gorkovskoye Vdkhr., *Russia* 48 B6
Gorlice, *Poland* 45 J8
Görlitz, *Germany* 24 D10
Gorlovka = Horlivka, *Ukraine* 47 H10
Gorman, *U.S.A.* 117 L8
Gorna Dzhumayo = Blagoevgrad, *Bulgaria* 40 D7
Gorna Oryakhovitsa, *Bulgaria* 41 C9
Gornja Radgona, *Slovenia* 29 B13
Gornja Tuzla, *Bos.-H.* 42 F3
Gornji Grad, *Slovenia* 29 B11
Gornji Milanovac, *Serbia, Yug.* 40 B4
Gornji Vakuf, *Bos.-H.* 42 G2
Gorno Ablanovo, *Bulgaria* 41 C9
Gorno-Altay □, *Russia* 50 D9
Gorno-Altaysk, *Russia* 50 D9
Gornyatskiy, *Russia* 49 F5
Gornyy, *Saratov, Russia* 48 E9
Gornyy, *Sib., Russia* 54 B6
Gorodenka = Horodenka, *Ukraine* 47 H3
Gorodets, *Russia* 48 B6
Gorodishche = Horodyshche, *Ukraine* 47 H6
Gorodishche, *Russia* 48 D7
Gorodnya = Horodnya, *Ukraine* 47 G6
Gorodok = Haradok, *Belarus* 46 E6
Gorodok = Horodok, *Ukraine* 47 H2
Gorodovikovsk, *Russia* 49 G5
Gorokhov = Horokhiv, *Ukraine* 47 G3
Gorokhovets, *Russia* 48 B6
Gorom Gorom, *Burkina Faso* 83 C4
Goromonzi, *Zimbabwe* 87 F3
Gorong, Kepulauan, *Indonesia* 63 E8
Gorongose →, *Mozam.* 89 C5
Gorongoza, *Mozam.* 87 F3
Gorongoza, Sa. da, *Mozam.* 87 F3
Gorontalo, *Indonesia* 63 D6
Goronyo, *Nigeria* 83 C6
Górowo Iławeckie, *Poland* 44 D7
Gorron, *France* 18 D6
Gorshechnoye, *Russia* 47 G10
Gort, *Ireland* 15 C3
Gortis, *Greece* 36 D6
Góry Bystrzyckie, *Poland* 45 H3
Goryachiy Klyuch, *Russia* 49 H4
Gorzkowice, *Poland* 45 G6
Górzno, *Poland* 45 E6
Gorzów Śląski, *Poland* 45 G5
Gorzów Wielkopolski, *Poland* 45 F2
Gosford, *Australia* 95 E5
Goshen, *Calif., U.S.A.* 116 J7
Goshen, *Ind., U.S.A.* 108 E3
Goshen, *N.Y., U.S.A.* 111 E10
Goshogawara, *Japan* 54 D10
Goslar, *Germany* 24 D6
Gospič, *Croatia* 29 D12
Gosport, *U.K.* 13 G6
Gossas, *Senegal* 82 C1
Gosse →, *Australia* 94 B1
Gossi, *Mali* 83 B4
Gossinga, *Sudan* 81 F2
Gostivar, *Macedonia* 40 E4
Gostyń, *Poland* 45 G4
Gostynin, *Poland* 45 F6
Göta älv →, *Sweden* 11 G5
Göta kanal, *Sweden* 11 F9
Götaland, *Sweden* 11 G8
Göteborg, *Sweden* 11 G5
Götene, *Sweden* 11 F7
Goteşti, *Moldova* 43 D13
Gotha, *Germany* 24 E6
Gothenburg = Göteborg, *Sweden* 11 G5
Gothenburg, *U.S.A.* 112 E4
Gothèye, *Niger* 83 C5
Gotland, *Sweden* 11 G12
Gotlands län □, *Sweden* 11 G12
Gotō-Rettō, *Japan* 55 H4
Gotse Delchev, *Bulgaria* 40 E7
Gotska Sandön, *Sweden* 9 G18
Gōtsu, *Japan* 55 G6
Gott Pk., *Canada* 104 C4
Góttero, Monte, *Italy* 28 D6
Göttingen, *Germany* 24 D5
Gottwald = Zmiyev, *Ukraine* 47 H9
Gottwaldov = Zlín, *Czech Rep.* 27 B10
Goubangzi, *China* 57 D11
Gouda, *Neths.* 17 B4
Goúdhoura, Ákra, *Greece* 36 E8
Goudiry, *Senegal* 82 C2
Goudoumaria, *Niger* 83 C7
Gouéké, *Guinea* 82 D3
Gough I., *Atl. Oc.* 2 G9
Gouin, Rés., *Canada* 102 C5
Gouitafla, *Ivory C.* 82 D3
Goulburn, *Australia* 95 E4
Goulburn Is., *Australia* 94 A1
Goulia, *Ivory C.* 82 C3
Goulimine, *Morocco* 78 C3
Goumbou, *Mali* 82 B3
Gouménissa, *Greece* 40 F6
Goundam, *Mali* 82 B4
Goúra, *Greece* 38 D4
Gourbassi, *Mali* 82 C2
Gourdon, *France* 20 D5
Gouré, *Niger* 83 C7
Gourin, *France* 18 D3
Gourits →, *S. Africa* 88 E3
Gourma-Rharous, *Mali* 83 B4
Goúrnais, *Greece* 36 D7
Gournay-en-Bray, *France* 19 C8
Goursi, *Burkina Faso* 82 C4
Gouverneur, *U.S.A.* 111 B9
Gouviá, *Greece* 36 A3
Gouzon, *France* 19 F9
Governador Valadares, *Brazil* 125 G10
Governor's Harbour, *Bahamas* 120 A4
Govindgarh, *India* 69 G9
Gowan Ra., *Australia* 94 D4
Gowanda, *U.S.A.* 110 D6
Gower, *U.K.* 13 F3
Gowna, L., *Ireland* 15 C4
Goya, *Argentina* 126 B4
Göyçay, *Azerbaijan* 49 K8
Goyder Lagoon, *Australia* 95 D2
Goyllarisquisga, *Peru* 124 F3
Göynük, *Antalya, Turkey* 39 E12
Göynük, *Bolu, Turkey* 72 B4
Goz Beïda, *Chad* 79 F10
Goz Regeb, *Sudan* 81 D4
Gozdnica, *Poland* 45 G2
Gozo, *Malta* 36 C1
Graaff-Reinet, *S. Africa* 88 E3
Grabo, *Ivory C.* 82 D3
Grabow, *Germany* 24 B7
Grabów nad Prosną, *Poland* 45 G5
Gračac, *Croatia* 29 D12
Gračanica, *Bos.-H.* 42 F3
Graçay, *France* 19 E8
Gracias a Dios, C., *Honduras* 120 D3
Graciosa, I., *Canary Is.* 37 E6
Grad Sofiya □, *Bulgaria* 40 D7
Gradac, *Montenegro, Yug.* 40 C3
Gradačac, *Bos.-H.* 42 F3
Gradeška Planina, *Macedonia* 40 E6
Gradets, *Bulgaria* 41 D10
Gradišče, *Slovenia* 29 B12
Grădiştea de Munte, *Romania* 43 E8
Grado, *Italy* 29 C10
Grado, *Spain* 34 B4
Grady, *U.S.A.* 113 H3
Graeca, Lacul, *Romania* 43 F11
Grafenau, *Germany* 25 G9
Gräfenberg, *Germany* 25 F7
Grafham Water, *U.K.* 13 E7
Grafton, *Australia* 95 D5
Grafton, *N. Dak., U.S.A.* 112 A6
Grafton, *W. Va., U.S.A.* 108 F5
Graham, *Canada* 102 C1
Graham, *U.S.A.* 113 J5
Graham, Mt., *U.S.A.* 115 K9
Graham Bell, Ostrov = Greem-Bell, Ostrov, *Russia* 50 A7
Graham I., *Canada* 104 C2
Graham Land, *Antarctica* 5 C17
Grahamstown, *S. Africa* 88 E4
Grahamsville, *U.S.A.* 111 E10
Grahovo, *Montenegro, Yug.* 40 D2
Graie, Alpi, *Europe* 21 C11
Grain Coast, *W. Afr.* 82 E3
Grajaú, *Brazil* 125 E9
Grajaú →, *Brazil* 125 D10
Grajewo, *Poland* 44 E9
Gramada, *Bulgaria* 40 C6
Gramat, *France* 20 D5
Grammichele, *Italy* 31 E7
Grámmos, Óros, *Greece* 40 F4
Grampian, *U.S.A.* 110 F6
Grampian Highlands = Grampian Mts., *U.K.* 14 E5
Grampian Mts., *U.K.* 14 E5
Grampians, The, *Australia* 95 F3
Gramsh, *Albania* 40 F4
Gran Canaria, *Canary Is.* 37 G4
Gran Chaco, *S. Amer.* 126 B3

Gran Paradiso, *Italy* 28 C4
Gran Sasso d'Itália, *Italy* 29 F10
Granada, *Nic.* 120 D2
Granada, *Spain* 35 H7
Granada, *U.S.A.* 113 F3
Granada □, *Spain* 35 H7
Granadilla de Abona, *Canary Is.* 37 F3
Granard, *Ireland* 15 C4
Granbury, *U.S.A.* 113 J6
Granby, *Canada* 102 C5
Granby, *U.S.A.* 114 F11
Grand →, *Canada* 110 D5
Grand →, *Mo., U.S.A.* 112 F8
Grand →, *S. Dak., U.S.A.* 112 C4
Grand Bahama, *Bahamas* 120 A4
Grand Bank, *Canada* 103 C8
Grand Bassam, *Ivory C.* 82 D4
Grand Bérébу, *Ivory C.* 82 E3
Grand-Bourg, *Guadeloupe* 121 C7
Grand Canal = Yun He →, *China* 57 E9
Grand Canyon, *U.S.A.* 115 H7
Grand Canyon National Park, *U.S.A.* 115 H7
Grand Cayman, *Cayman Is.* 120 C3
Grand Centre, *Canada* 105 C6
Grand Cess, *Liberia* 82 E3
Grand Coulee, *U.S.A.* 114 C4
Grand Coulee Dam, *U.S.A.* 114 C4
Grand Erg Occidental, *Algeria* 78 B6
Grand Erg Oriental, *Algeria* 78 B7
Grand Falls, *Canada* 103 C6
Grand Falls-Windsor, *Canada* 103 C8
Grand Forks, *Canada* 104 D5
Grand Forks, *U.S.A.* 112 B6
Grand Gorge, *U.S.A.* 111 D10
Grand Haven, *U.S.A.* 108 D2
Grand I., *Mich., U.S.A.* 108 B2
Grand I., *N.Y., U.S.A.* 110 D6
Grand Island, *U.S.A.* 112 E5
Grand Isle, *La., U.S.A.* 113 L9
Grand Isle, *Vt., U.S.A.* 111 B11
Grand Junction, *U.S.A.* 115 G9
Grand L., *N.B., Canada* 103 C6
Grand L., *Nfld., Canada* 103 C8
Grand L., *Nfld., Canada* 103 B7
Grand L., *U.S.A.* 113 L8
Grand Lahou, *Ivory C.* 82 D3
Grand Lake, *U.S.A.* 114 F11
Grand-Lieu, L. de, *France* 18 E5
Grand Manan I., *Canada* 103 D6
Grand Marais, *Canada* 112 B9
Grand Marais, *U.S.A.* 108 B3
Grand-Mère, *Canada* 102 C5
Grand Popo, *Benin* 83 D5
Grand Portage, *U.S.A.* 112 B10
Grand Prairie, *U.S.A.* 113 J6
Grand Rapids, *Canada* 105 C9
Grand Rapids, *Mich., U.S.A.* 108 D2
Grand Rapids, *Minn., U.S.A.* 112 B8
Grand St-Bernard, Col du, *Europe* 25 K3
Grand Teton, *U.S.A.* 114 E8
Grand Teton National Park, *U.S.A.* 114 D8
Grand Union Canal, *U.K.* 13 E7
Grand View, *Canada* 105 C8
Grandas de Salime, *Spain* 34 B4
Grande →, *Jujuy, Argentina* 126 A2
Grande →, *Mendoza, Argentina* 126 D2
Grande →, *Bolivia* 124 G6
Grande →, *Bahia, Brazil* 125 F10
Grande →, *Minas Gerais, Brazil* 125 H8
Grande, B., *Argentina* 128 G3
Grande, Rio →, *U.S.A.* 113 N6
Grande Baleine, R. de la →, *Canada* 102 A4
Grande Cache, *Canada* 104 C5
Grande-Entrée, *Canada* 103 C7
Grande Prairie, *Canada* 104 B5
Grande-Rivière, *Canada* 103 C7
Grande-Vallée, *Canada* 103 C6
Grandfalls, *U.S.A.* 113 K3
Grândola, *Portugal* 35 G2
Grandpré, *France* 19 C11
Grandview, *U.S.A.* 114 C4
Grandvilliers, *France* 19 C8
Graneros, *Chile* 126 C1
Grangemouth, *U.K.* 14 E5
Granger, *U.S.A.* 114 F9
Grängesberg, *Sweden* 10 D9
Grangeville, *U.S.A.* 114 D5
Granisle, *Canada* 104 C3
Granite City, *U.S.A.* 112 F9
Granite Falls, *U.S.A.* 112 C7
Granite L., *Canada* 103 C8
Granite Mt., *U.S.A.* 117 M10
Granite Pk., *U.S.A.* 114 D9
Graniteville, *U.S.A.* 111 B12
Granitola, C., *Italy* 30 E5
Granity, *N.Z.* 91 J3
Granja, *Brazil* 125 D10
Granja de Moreruela, *Spain* 34 D5
Granja de Torrehermosa, *Spain* 35 G5
Gränna, *Sweden* 11 F8
Granollers, *Spain* 32 D7
Gransee, *Germany* 24 B9
Grant, *U.S.A.* 112 E4
Grant, Mt., *U.S.A.* 114 G4
Grant City, *U.S.A.* 112 E7
Grant I., *Australia* 92 B5
Grant Range, *U.S.A.* 115 G6
Grantham, *U.K.* 12 E7
Grantown-on-Spey, *U.K.* 14 D5
Grants, *U.S.A.* 115 J10
Grants Pass, *U.S.A.* 114 E2
Grantsville, *U.S.A.* 114 F7
Granville, *France* 18 D5
Granville, *N. Dak., U.S.A.* 112 A4
Granville, *N.Y., U.S.A.* 111 C11
Granville, *Ohio, U.S.A.* 110 F2
Granville L., *Canada* 105 B8
Graskop, *S. Africa* 89 C5
Gräsö, *Sweden* 10 D12
Grass →, *Canada* 105 B9
Grass Range, *U.S.A.* 114 C9
Grass River Prov. Park, *Canada* 105 C8
Grass Valley, *Calif., U.S.A.* 116 F6
Grass Valley, *Oreg., U.S.A.* 114 D3
Grassano, *Italy* 31 B9
Grasse, *France* 21 E10
Grassflat, *U.S.A.* 110 F6
Grasslands Nat. Park, *Canada* 105 D7
Grassy, *Australia* 94 G3
Gråsten, *Denmark* 11 K3
Grästorp, *Sweden* 11 F6
Gratkorn, *Austria* 26 D8
Graubünden □, *Switz.* 25 J5
Graulhet, *France* 20 E5
Graus, *Spain* 32 C5
Grave, Pte. de, *France* 20 C2
Gravelbourg, *Canada* 105 D7
Gravelines, *France* 19 A9
's-Gravenhage, *Neths.* 17 B4
Gravenhurst, *Canada* 102 D4
Gravesend, *Australia* 95 D5
Gravesend, *U.K.* 13 F8
Gravina in Púglia, *Italy* 31 B9
Gravois, Pointe-à-, *Haiti* 121 C5
Gravone →, *France* 21 G12
Gray, *France* 19 E12
Grayling, *U.S.A.* 108 C3
Grays Harbor, *U.S.A.* 114 C1
Grays L., *U.S.A.* 114 E8
Grays River, *U.S.A.* 116 D3
Grayvoron, *Russia* 47 G8
Graz, *Austria* 26 D8
Grdelica, *Serbia, Yug.* 40 D6
Greasy L., *Canada* 104 A4
Great Abaco I., *Bahamas* 120 A4
Great Artesian Basin, *Australia* 94 C3
Great Australian Bight, *Australia* 93 F5
Great Bahama Bank, *Bahamas* 120 B4
Great Barrier I., *N.Z.* 91 G5
Great Barrier Reef, *Australia* 94 B4
Great Barrington, *U.S.A.* 111 D11
Great Basin, *U.S.A.* 114 G5
Great Basin Nat. Park, *U.S.A.* 114 G6
Great Bear →, *Canada* 100 B7
Great Bear L., *Canada* 100 B7
Great Belt = Store Bælt, *Denmark* 11 J4
Great Bend, *Kans., U.S.A.* 112 F5
Great Bend, *Pa., U.S.A.* 111 E9
Great Blasket I., *Ireland* 15 D1
Great Britain, *Europe* 6 E5
Great Codroy, *Canada* 103 C8
Great Dividing Ra., *Australia* 94 C4
Great Driffield = Driffield, *U.K.* 12 C7
Great Exuma I., *Bahamas* 120 B4
Great Falls, *U.S.A.* 114 C8
Great Fish = Groot Vis →, *S. Africa* 88 E4
Great Guana Cay, *Bahamas* 120 B4
Great Inagua I., *Bahamas* 121 B5
Great Indian Desert = Thar Desert, *India* 68 F5
Great Karoo, *S. Africa* 88 E3
Great Lake, *Australia* 94 G4
Great Lakes, *N. Amer.* 98 E11
Great Malvern, *U.K.* 13 E5
Great Miami →, *U.S.A.* 108 F3
Great Ormes Head, *U.K.* 12 D4
Great Ouse →, *U.K.* 12 E8
Great Palm I., *Australia* 94 B4
Great Plains, *N. Amer.* 106 A6
Great Ruaha →, *Tanzania* 86 D4
Great Sacandaga Res., *U.S.A.* 111 C10
Great Saint Bernard Pass = Grand St-Bernard, Col du, *Europe* 25 K3
Great Salt L., *U.S.A.* 114 F7
Great Salt Lake Desert, *U.S.A.* 114 F7
Great Salt Plains L., *U.S.A.* 113 G5
Great Sandy Desert, *Australia* 92 D3
Great Sangi = Sangihe, Pulau, *Indonesia* 63 D7
Great Scarcies →, *S. Leone* 82 D2
Great Skellig, *Ireland* 15 E1
Great Slave L., *Canada* 104 A5
Great Smoky Mts. Nat. Park, *U.S.A.* 109 H4
Great Snow Mt., *Canada* 104 B4
Great Stour = Stour →, *U.K.* 13 F9
Great Victoria Desert, *Australia* 93 E4
Great Wall, *China* 56 E5
Great Whernside, *U.K.* 12 C6
Great Yarmouth, *U.K.* 13 E9
Greater Antilles, *W. Indies* 121 C5
Greater London □, *U.K.* 13 F7
Greater Manchester □, *U.K.* 12 D5
Greater Sunda Is., *Indonesia* 62 F4
Grebbestad, *Sweden* 11 F5
Grebenka = Hrebenka, *Ukraine* 47 G7
Greco, C., *Cyprus* 36 E13
Greco, Mte., *Italy* 29 G10
Gredos, Sierra de, *Spain* 34 E6
Greece, *U.S.A.* 110 C7
Greece ■, *Europe* 38 B3
Greeley, *Colo., U.S.A.* 112 E2
Greeley, *Nebr., U.S.A.* 112 E5
Greem-Bell, Ostrov, *Russia* 50 A7
Green, *U.S.A.* 114 E2
Green →, *Ky., U.S.A.* 108 G2
Green →, *Utah, U.S.A.* 115 G9
Green B., *U.S.A.* 108 C2
Green Bay, *U.S.A.* 108 C2
Green C., *Australia* 95 F5
Green Cove Springs, *U.S.A.* 109 L5
Green Lake, *Canada* 105 C7
Green Mts., *U.S.A.* 111 C12
Green River, *Utah, U.S.A.* 115 G8
Green River, *Wyo., U.S.A.* 114 F9
Green Valley, *U.S.A.* 115 L8
Greenbank, *U.S.A.* 116 B4
Greenbush, *Mich., U.S.A.* 110 B1
Greenbush, *Minn., U.S.A.* 112 A6
Greencastle, *U.S.A.* 108 F2
Greene, *U.S.A.* 111 D9
Greenfield, *Calif., U.S.A.* 116 J5
Greenfield, *Calif., U.S.A.* 117 K8
Greenfield, *Ind., U.S.A.* 108 F3
Greenfield, *Iowa, U.S.A.* 112 E7
Greenfield, *Mass., U.S.A.* 111 D12
Greenfield, *Mo., U.S.A.* 113 G8
Greenfield Park, *Canada* 111 A11
Greenland ■, *N. Amer.* 4 C5
Greenland Sea, *Arctic* 4 B7
Greenock, *U.K.* 14 F4
Greenore, *Ireland* 15 B5
Greenore Pt., *Ireland* 15 D5
Greenough, *Australia* 93 E1
Greenough →, *Australia* 93 E1
Greenough Pt., *Canada* 110 B3
Greenport, *U.S.A.* 111 E12
Greensboro, *Ga., U.S.A.* 109 J4
Greensboro, *N.C., U.S.A.* 109 G6
Greensboro, *Vt., U.S.A.* 111 B12
Greensburg, *Ind., U.S.A.* 108 F3
Greensburg, *Kans., U.S.A.* 113 G5
Greensburg, *Pa., U.S.A.* 110 F5
Greenstone Pt., *U.K.* 14 D3
Greenvale, *Australia* 94 B4
Greenville, *Liberia* 82 D3
Greenville, *Ala., U.S.A.* 109 K2
Greenville, *Calif., U.S.A.* 116 E6
Greenville, *Maine, U.S.A.* 109 C11
Greenville, *Mich., U.S.A.* 108 D3
Greenville, *Miss., U.S.A.* 113 J9
Greenville, *Mo., U.S.A.* 113 G9
Greenville, *N.C., U.S.A.* 109 H7
Greenville, *N.H., U.S.A.* 111 D13
Greenville, *N.Y., U.S.A.* 111 D10
Greenville, *Ohio, U.S.A.* 108 E3
Greenville, *Pa., U.S.A.* 110 E4
Greenville, *S.C., U.S.A.* 109 H4
Greenville, *Tenn., U.S.A.* 109 G4
Greenville, *Tex., U.S.A.* 113 J6
Greenwater Lake Prov. Park, *Canada* 105 C8
Greenwich, *Conn., U.S.A.* 111 E11
Greenwich, *N.Y., U.S.A.* 111 C11
Greenwich, *Ohio, U.S.A.* 110 E2
Greenwich □, *U.K.* 13 F8
Greenwood, *Canada* 104 D5
Greenwood, *Ark., U.S.A.* 113 H7
Greenwood, *Ind., U.S.A.* 108 F2
Greenwood, *Miss., U.S.A.* 113 J9
Greenwood, *S.C., U.S.A.* 109 H4
Greenwood, Mt., *Australia* 92 B5
Gregbe, *Ivory C.* 82 D3
Gregory, *U.S.A.* 112 D5
Gregory →, *Australia* 94 B2
Gregory, L., *S. Austral., Australia* 95 D2
Gregory, L., *W. Austral., Australia* 93 E2
Gregory Downs, *Australia* 94 B2
Gregory L., *Australia* 92 D4
Gregory Ra., *Queens., Australia* 94 B3
Gregory Ra., *W. Austral., Australia* 92 D3
Greiffenberg, *Germany* 24 B9
Greifswald, *Germany* 24 A9
Greifswalder Bodden, *Germany* 24 A9
Grein, *Austria* 26 C7
Greiz, *Germany* 24 E8
Gremikha, *Russia* 50 C4
Grenå, *Denmark* 11 H4
Grenada, *U.S.A.* 113 J10
Grenada ■, *W. Indies* 121 D7
Grenade, *France* 20 E5
Grenadier I., *U.S.A.* 111 B8
Grenadines, *St. Vincent* 121 D7
Grenchen, *Switz.* 25 H3
Grenen, *Denmark* 11 G4
Grenfell, *Australia* 95 E4
Grenfell, *Canada* 105 C8
Grenoble, *France* 21 C9
Grenville, C., *Australia* 94 A3
Grenville Chan., *Canada* 104 C3
Gréoux-les-Bains, *France* 21 E9
Gresham, *U.S.A.* 116 E4
Gresik, *Indonesia* 63 G15
Gretna, *U.K.* 14 F5
Greven, *Germany* 24 C3
Grevená, *Greece* 40 F5
Grevená □, *Greece* 40 F5
Grevenbroich, *Germany* 24 D2
Grevenmacher, *Lux.* 17 E6
Grevesmühlen, *Germany* 24 B7
Grevestrand, *Denmark* 11 J6
Grey →, *Canada* 103 C8
Grey →, *N.Z.* 91 K3
Grey, C., *Australia* 94 A2
Grey Ra., *Australia* 95 D3
Greybull, *U.S.A.* 114 D9
Greymouth, *N.Z.* 91 K3
Greystones, *Ireland* 15 C5
Greytown, *N.Z.* 91 J5
Greytown, *S. Africa* 89 D5
Gribanovskiy, *Russia* 48 E5
Gribbell I., *Canada* 104 C3
Gribës, Mal i, *Albania* 40 F3
Gridley, *U.S.A.* 116 F5
Griekwastad, *S. Africa* 88 D3
Griesheim, *Germany* 25 F4
Grieskirchen, *Austria* 26 C6
Griffin, *U.S.A.* 109 J3
Griffith, *Australia* 95 E4
Griffith, *Canada* 110 A7
Griffith I., *Canada* 110 B4
Grignols, *France* 20 D3
Grigoriopol, *Moldova* 43 C14
Grimaylov = Hrymayliv, *Ukraine* 47 H4
Grimes, *U.S.A.* 116 F5
Grimma, *Germany* 24 D8
Grimmen, *Germany* 24 A9
Grimsay, *U.K.* 14 D1
Grimsby, *Canada* 110 C5
Grimsby, *U.K.* 12 D7
Grímsey, *Iceland* 8 C5
Grimshaw, *Canada* 104 B5
Grimslöv, *Sweden* 11 H8
Grimstad, *Norway* 9 G13
Grindelwald, *Switz.* 25 J4
Grindsted, *Denmark* 11 J2
Grindstone I., *Canada* 111 B8
Grindu, *Romania* 43 F11
Grinnell, *U.S.A.* 112 E8
Grintavec, *Slovenia* 29 B11
Gris-Nez, C., *France* 19 B8
Grisolles, *France* 20 E5
Grisons = Graubünden □, *Switz.* 25 J5
Grisslehamn, *Sweden* 10 D12
Grmeč Planina, *Bos.-H.* 29 D13
Groais I., *Canada* 103 B8
Grobiņa, *Latvia* 44 B8
Groblersdal, *S. Africa* 89 D4
Grobming, *Austria* 26 D6
Grocka, *Serbia, Yug.* 40 B4
Gródek, *Poland* 45 E10
Grodków, *Poland* 45 H4
Grodno = Hrodna, *Belarus* 46 F2
Grodzisk Mazowiecki, *Poland* 45 F7
Grodzisk Wielkopolski, *Poland* 45 F3
Grodzyanka = Hrodzyanka, *Belarus* 46 F5
Groesbeck, *U.S.A.* 113 K6
Groix, *France* 18 E3
Groix, Î. de, *France* 18 E3
Grójec, *Poland* 45 G7
Gronau, *Niedersachsen, Germany* 24 C5
Gronau, *Nordrhein-Westfalen, Germany* 24 C3
Grong, *Norway* 8 D15
Grönhögen, *Sweden* 11 H10
Groningen, *Neths.* 17 A6
Groningen □, *Neths.* 17 A6
Groom, *U.S.A.* 113 H4
Groot →, *S. Africa* 88 E3
Groot Berg →, *S. Africa* 88 E2
Groot-Brakrivier, *S. Africa* 88 E3
Groot Karasberge, *Namibia* 88 D2
Groot-Kei →, *S. Africa* 89 E4
Groot Vis →, *S. Africa* 88 E4
Grootdrink, *S. Africa* 88 D3
Groote Eylandt, *Australia* 94 A2
Grootfontein, *Namibia* 88 B2
Grootlaagte →, *Africa* 88 C3
Grootvloer →, *S. Africa* 88 E3
Gros C., *Canada* 104 A6
Gros Morne Nat. Park, *Canada* 103 C8
Grósio, *Italy* 28 B7
Grosne →, *France* 19 F11
Grossa, Pta., *Spain* 37 B8
Grossenbrode, *Germany* 24 A7
Grossenhain, *Germany* 24 D9
Grosser Arber, *Germany* 25 F9
Grosser Plöner See, *Germany* 24 A6
Grosseto, *Italy* 29 F8
Grossgerungs, *Austria* 26 C7
Grossglockner, *Austria* 26 D5
Groswater B., *Canada* 103 B8
Groton, *Conn., U.S.A.* 111 E12
Groton, *N.Y., U.S.A.* 111 D8
Groton, *S. Dak., U.S.A.* 112 C5
Grottáglie, *Italy* 31 B10
Grottaminarda, *Italy* 31 A8
Grottammare, *Italy* 29 F10
Grouard Mission, *Canada* 104 B5
Grouin, Pte. du, *France* 18 D5
Groundhog →, *Canada* 102 C3
Grouw, *Neths.* 17 A5
Grove City, *U.S.A.* 110 E4
Grove Hill, *U.S.A.* 109 K2
Groveland, *U.S.A.* 116 H6
Grover City, *U.S.A.* 117 K6
Groves, *U.S.A.* 113 L8
Groveton, *U.S.A.* 111 B13
Grožnjan, *Croatia* 29 C10
Groznyy, *Russia* 49 J7
Grubišno Polje, *Croatia* 42 E2
Grudovo, *Bulgaria* 41 D11
Grudusk, *Poland* 45 E7
Grudziądz, *Poland* 44 E5
Gruinard B., *U.K.* 14 D3
Gruissan, *France* 20 E7
Grumo Áppula, *Italy* 31 A9
Grums, *Sweden* 10 E7
Grünberg, *Germany* 24 E4
Gründau, *Germany* 25 E5
Grundy Center, *U.S.A.* 112 D8
Grünstadt, *Germany* 25 F4
Gruvberget, *Sweden* 10 C10
Gruver, *U.S.A.* 113 G4
Gruyères, *Switz.* 25 J3
Gruža, *Serbia, Yug.* 40 C4
Gryazi, *Russia* 47 F10
Gryazovets, *Russia* 46 C11
Grybów, *Poland* 45 J7
Grycksbo, *Sweden* 10 D9
Gryfice, *Poland* 44 E2
Gryfino, *Poland* 45 E1
Gryfów Śląski, *Poland* 45 G2
Grythyttan, *Sweden* 10 E8
Gstaad, *Switz.* 25 J3
Gua, *India* 67 H14
Gua Musang, *Malaysia* 65 K3
Guacanayabo, G. de, *Cuba* 120 B4
Guachípas →, *Argentina* 126 B2
Guadajoz →, *Spain* 35 H6
Guadalajara, *Mexico* 118 C4
Guadalajara, *Spain* 32 E1
Guadalajara □, *Spain* 32 E2
Guadalcanal, *Solomon Is.* 96 H8
Guadalcanal, *Spain* 35 G5
Guadalén →, *Spain* 35 G7
Guadales, *Argentina* 126 C2
Guadalete →, *Spain* 35 J4
Guadalimar →, *Spain* 35 G7
Guadalmena →, *Spain* 35 G8
Guadalmez →, *Spain* 35 G5
Guadalope →, *Spain* 32 D4
Guadalquivir →, *Spain* 35 J4
Guadalupe = Guadeloupe ■, *W. Indies* 121 C7
Guadalupe, *Mexico* 117 N10
Guadalupe, *Spain* 35 F5
Guadalupe, *U.S.A.* 117 L6
Guadalupe →, *Mexico* 117 N10
Guadalupe →, *U.S.A.* 113 L6
Guadalupe, Sierra de, *Spain* 35 F5
Guadalupe Bravos, *Mexico* 118 A3
Guadalupe I., *Pac. Oc.* 98 G8
Guadalupe Mts. Nat. Park, *U.S.A.* 113 K2
Guadalupe Peak, *U.S.A.* 113 K2
Guadalupe y Calvo, *Mexico* 118 B3
Guadarrama, Sierra de, *Spain* 34 E7
Guadauta, *Georgia* 49 J5
Guadeloupe ■, *W. Indies* 121 C7
Guadeloupe Passage, *W. Indies* 121 C7
Guadiamar →, *Spain* 35 J4
Guadiana →, *Portugal* 35 H3
Guadiana Menor →, *Spain* 35 H7
Guadiaro →, *Spain* 35 J5
Guadiato →, *Spain* 35 H5
Guadiela →, *Spain* 32 E2
Guadix, *Spain* 35 H7
Guafo, Boca del, *Chile* 128 E2
Guainía →, *Colombia* 124 C5
Guaíra, *Brazil* 127 A5
Guaíra □, *Paraguay* 126 B4
Guaitecas, Is., *Chile* 128 E2
Guajará-Mirim, *Brazil* 124 F5
Guajira, Pen. de la, *Colombia* 124 A4
Gualán, *Guatemala* 120 C2
Gualdo Tadino, *Italy* 29 E9
Gualeguay, *Argentina* 126 C4
Gualeguaychú, *Argentina* 126 C4
Gualequay →, *Argentina* 126 C4
Guam ■, *Pac. Oc.* 96 F6
Guaminí, *Argentina* 126 D3
Guamúchil, *Mexico* 118 B3
Guanabacoa, *Cuba* 120 B3
Guanacaste, Cordillera del, *Costa Rica* 120 D2
Guanaceví, *Mexico* 118 B3
Guanahani = San Salvador I., *Bahamas* 121 B5
Guanajay, *Cuba* 120 B3
Guanajuato, *Mexico* 118 C4
Guanajuato □, *Mexico* 118 C4
Guandacol, *Argentina* 126 B2
Guane, *Cuba* 120 B3
Guang'an, *China* 58 B6
Guangchang, *China* 59 D11
Guangde, *China* 59 B12
Guangdong □, *China* 59 F9
Guangfeng, *China* 59 C12
Guanghan, *China* 58 B5
Guangling, *China* 56 E8
Guangnan, *China* 58 E5
Guangning, *China* 59 F9
Guangrao, *China* 57 F10
Guangshui, *China* 59 B9
Guangshun, *China* 58 D6
Guangwu, *China* 56 F3
Guangxi Zhuangzu Zizhiqu □, *China* 58 F7
Guangyuan, *China* 58 A5
Guangze, *China* 59 D11
Guangzhou, *China* 59 F9
Guanipa →, *Venezuela* 124 B6
Guanling, *China* 58 E5
Guannan, *China* 57 G10
Guantánamo, *Cuba* 121 B4
Guantao, *China* 56 F8
Guanyang, *China* 59 E8
Guanyun, *China* 57 G10
Guápiles, *Costa Rica* 120 D3
Guaporé, *Brazil* 127 B5
Guaporé →, *Brazil* 122 E4
Guaqui, *Bolivia* 124 G5
Guara, Sierra de, *Spain* 32 C4
Guarapari, *Brazil* 127 A7
Guarapuava, *Brazil* 127 B5
Guaratinguetá, *Brazil* 127 A6
Guaratuba, *Brazil* 127 B6
Guarda, *Portugal* 34 E3
Guarda □, *Portugal* 34 E3
Guardafui, C. = Asir, Ras,

Somali Rep. 74 E5
Guardamar del Segura, *Spain* 33 G4
Guardavalle, *Italy* 31 D9
Guárdia Sanframondi, *Italy* 31 A7
Guardiagrele, *Italy* 29 F11
Guardo, *Spain* 34 C6
Guareña, *Spain* 35 G4
Guareña →, *Spain* 34 D5
Guárico □, *Venezuela* 124 B5
Guarujá, *Brazil* 127 A6
Guarus, *Brazil* 127 A7
Guasave, *Mexico* 118 B3
Guasdualito, *Venezuela* 124 B4
Guastalla, *Italy* 28 D7
Guatemala, *Guatemala* 120 D1
Guatemala ■, *Cent. Amer.* 120 C1
Guaviare →, *Colombia* 122 C4
Guaxupé, *Brazil* 127 A6
Guayama, *Puerto Rico* 121 C6
Guayaquil, *Ecuador* 124 D3
Guayaquil, G. de, *Ecuador* 122 D2
Guaymas, *Mexico* 118 B2
Guba, *Dem. Rep. of the Congo* 87 E2
Guba, *Ethiopia* 81 E4
Gûbâl, Madîq, *Egypt* 80 B3
Gubat, *Phil.* 61 E6
Gúbbio, *Italy* 29 E9
Guben, *Germany* 24 D10
Gubin, *Poland* 45 G1
Gubio, *Nigeria* 83 C7
Gubkin, *Russia* 47 G9
Guča, *Serbia, Yug.* 40 C4
Gucheng, *China* 59 A8
Gudata = Guadauta, *Georgia* 49 J5
Gudbrandsdalen, *Norway* 9 F14
Guddu Barrage, *Pakistan* 66 E6
Gudenå →, *Denmark* 11 H4
Gudermes, *Russia* 49 J8
Gudhjem, *Denmark* 11 J8
Gudur, *India* 66 M11
Guebwiller, *France* 19 E14
Guecho = Getxo, *Spain* 32 B2
Guékédou, *Guinea* 82 D2
Guéle Mendouka, *Cameroon* 83 E7
Guelph, *Canada* 102 D3
Guéméné-Penfao, *France* 18 E5
Guéméné-sur-Scorff, *France* 18 D3
Guéné, *Benin* 83 C5
Guer, *France* 18 E4
Guérande, *France* 18 E4
Guéret, *France* 19 F8
Guérigny, *France* 19 E10
Guerneville, *U.S.A.* 116 G4
Guernica = Gernika-Lumo, *Spain* 32 B2
Guernsey, *U.K.* 13 H5
Guernsey, *U.S.A.* 112 D2
Guerrero □, *Mexico* 119 D5
Guessou-Sud, *Benin* 83 C5
Gueugnon, *France* 19 F11
Guéyo, *Ivory C.* 82 D3
Gughe, *Ethiopia* 81 F4
Gügher, *Iran* 71 D8
Guglionesi, *Italy* 29 G11
Guhakolak, Tanjung, *Indonesia* 63 G11
Gui Jiang →, *China* 59 F8
Guia, *Canary Is.* 37 F4
Guia de Isora, *Canary Is.* 37 F3
Guia Lopes da Laguna, *Brazil* 127 A4
Guiana, *S. Amer.* 122 C4
Guibéroua, *Ivory C.* 82 D3
Guichi, *China* 59 B11
Guider, *Cameroon* 83 D7
Guidiguir, *Niger* 83 C6
Guidimouni, *Niger* 83 C6
Guiding, *China* 58 D6
Guidong, *China* 59 D9
Guidónia-Montecélio, *Italy* 29 F9
Guiers, L. de, *Senegal* 82 B1
Guigang, *China* 58 F7
Guiglo, *Ivory C.* 82 D3
Guihulñgan, *Phil.* 61 F5
Guijá, *Mozam.* 89 C5
Guijuelo, *Spain* 34 E5
Guildford, *U.K.* 13 F7
Guilford, *U.S.A.* 111 E12
Guilin, *China* 59 E8
Guillaume-Delisle L., *Canada* 102 A4
Guillaumes, *France* 21 D10
Guillestre, *France* 21 D10
Guilvinec, *France* 18 E2
Güimar, *Canary Is.* 37 F3
Guimarães, *Portugal* 34 D2
Guimaras □, *Phil.* 61 F5
Guinda, *U.S.A.* 116 G4
Guinea, *Africa* 76 F4
Guinea ■, *W. Afr.* 82 C2
Guinea, Gulf of, *Atl. Oc.* 83 E5
Guinea-Bissau ■, *Africa* 82 C2
Güines, *Cuba* 120 B3
Guingamp, *France* 18 D3
Guinguinéo, *Senegal* 82 C1
Guipavas, *France* 18 D2
Guiping, *China* 59 F8
Guipúzcoa □, *Spain* 32 B2
Guir, *Mali* 82 B4
Guirel, *Mauritania* 82 B3
Güiria, *Venezuela* 124 A6
Guiscard, *France* 19 C10
Guise, *France* 19 C10
Guitiriz, *Spain* 34 B3
Guitri, *Ivory C.* 82 D3
Guiuan, *Phil.* 61 F6
Guixi, *China* 59 C11
Guiyang, *Guizhou, China* 58 D6
Guiyang, *Hunan, China* 59 E9
Guizhou □, *China* 58 D6
Gujan-Mestras, *France* 20 D2
Gujar Khan, *Pakistan* 68 C5
Gujarat □, *India* 68 H4
Gujiang, *China* 59 D10
Gujranwala, *Pakistan* 68 C6
Gujrat, *Pakistan* 68 C6
Gukovo, *Russia* 49 F5
Gulbarga, *India* 66 L10
Gulbene, *Latvia* 9 H22
Gulf, The, *Asia* 71 E6
Gulfport, *U.S.A.* 113 K10
Gulgong, *Australia* 95 E4
Gulin, *China* 58 C5
Gulistan, *Pakistan* 68 D2
Gull Lake, *Canada* 105 C7
Gullbrandstorp, *Sweden* 11 H6
Gullspång, *Sweden* 11 F8
Güllük, *Turkey* 39 D9
Güllük Korfezi, *Turkey* 39 D9
Gulma, *Nigeria* 83 C5
Gulmarg, *India* 69 B6
Gülnar, *Turkey* 72 D5
Gülpınar, *Turkey* 39 B8
Gülşehir, *Turkey* 72 C6
Gulshad, *Kazakstan* 50 E8
Gulu, *Uganda* 86 B3
Gŭlŭbovo, *Bulgaria* 41 D9
Gulud, J., *Sudan* 81 E2
Gulwe, *Tanzania* 86 D4
Gulyaypole = Hulyaypole, *Ukraine* 47 J9
Gumal →, *Pakistan* 68 D4
Gumbaz, *Pakistan* 68 D3
Gumel, *Nigeria* 83 C6
Gumiel de Hizán, *Spain* 34 D7
Gumla, *India* 69 H11
Gumlu, *Australia* 94 B4
Gumma □, *Japan* 55 F9
Gummersbach, *Germany* 24 D3
Gummi, *Nigeria* 83 C6
Gümüldür, *Turkey* 39 C9
Gümüşçay, *Turkey* 41 F11
Gümüşhaciköy, *Turkey* 72 B6
Gümüşhane, *Turkey* 73 B8
Gümüşsu, *Turkey* 39 C11
Gumzai, *Indonesia* 63 F8
Guna, *Ethiopia* 81 F4
Guna, *India* 68 G7
Gundelfingen, *Germany* 25 G6
Güney, *Burdur, Turkey* 39 D11
Güney, *Denizli, Turkey* 39 C11
Güneydoğu Toroslar, *Turkey* 73 C9
Gunisao →, *Canada* 105 C9
Gunisao L., *Canada* 105 C9
Gunjyal, *Pakistan* 68 C4
Günlüce, *Turkey* 39 E10
Gunnarskog, *Sweden* 10 E6
Gunnbjørn Fjeld, *Greenland* 4 C6
Gunnebo, *Sweden* 11 G10
Gunnedah, *Australia* 95 E5
Gunnewin, *Australia* 95 D4
Gunningbar Cr. →, *Australia* 95 E4
Gunnison, *Colo., U.S.A.* 115 G10
Gunnison, *Utah, U.S.A.* 114 G8
Gunnison →, *U.S.A.* 115 G9
Gunpowder, *Australia* 94 B2
Guntakal, *India* 66 M10
Guntersville, *U.S.A.* 109 H2
Guntong, *Malaysia* 65 K3
Guntur, *India* 67 L12
Gunungapi, *Indonesia* 63 F7
Gunungsitoli, *Indonesia* 62 D1
Günz →, *Germany* 25 G6
Gunza, *Angola* 84 G2
Günzburg, *Germany* 25 G6
Gunzenhausen, *Germany* 25 F6
Guo He →, *China* 57 H9
Guoyang, *China* 56 H9
Gupis, *Pakistan* 69 A5
Gura Humorului, *Romania* 43 C10
Gura-Teghii, *Romania* 43 E11
Gurag, *Ethiopia* 81 F4
Gurahonţ, *Romania* 42 D7
Gurdaspur, *India* 68 C6
Gurdon, *U.S.A.* 113 J8
Güre, *Balıkesir, Turkey* 39 B8
Güre, *Uşak, Turkey* 39 C11
Gurgaon, *India* 68 E7
Gürgentepe, *Turkey* 72 B7
Gurghiu, Munţii, *Romania* 43 D10
Gurgueia →, *Brazil* 125 E10
Gurha, *India* 68 G4
Guri, Embalse de, *Venezuela* 124 B6
Gurin, *Nigeria* 83 D7
Gurjaani, *Georgia* 49 K7
Gurk →, *Austria* 26 E7
Gurkha, *Nepal* 69 E11
Gurley, *Australia* 95 D4
Gurnet Point, *U.S.A.* 111 D14
Gürpınar, *Ist., Turkey* 41 F12
Gürpınar, *Van, Turkey* 73 C10
Gürsu, *Turkey* 41 F13
Guruè, *Mozam.* 87 F4
Gurun, *Malaysia* 65 K3
Gürün, *Turkey* 72 C7
Gurupá, *Brazil* 125 D8
Gurupá, I. Grande de, *Brazil* 125 D8
Gurupi, *Brazil* 125 F9
Gurupi →, *Brazil* 125 D9
Guruwe, *Zimbabwe* 89 B5
Guryev = Atyraū, *Kazakstan* 50 E6
Gus-Khrustalnyy, *Russia* 48 C5
Gusau, *Nigeria* 83 C6
Gusev, *Russia* 9 J20
Gushan, *China* 57 E12
Gushgy, *Turkmenistan* 50 F7
Gushi, *China* 59 A10
Gushiago, *Ghana* 83 D4
Gusinje, *Montenegro, Yug.* 40 D3
Gusinoozersk, *Russia* 51 D11
Gúspini, *Italy* 30 C1
Güssing, *Austria* 27 D9
Gustavsberg, *Sweden* 10 E12
Gustavus, *U.S.A.* 104 B1
Gustine, *U.S.A.* 116 H6
Güstrow, *Germany* 24 B8
Gusum, *Sweden* 11 F10
Guta = Kolárovo, *Slovak Rep.* 27 D10
Gütersloh, *Germany* 24 D4
Gutha, *Australia* 93 E2
Guthalungra, *Australia* 94 B4
Guthrie, *Okla., U.S.A.* 113 H6
Guthrie, *Tex., U.S.A.* 113 J4
Gutian, *China* 59 D12
Guttenberg, *U.S.A.* 112 D9
Gutu, *Zimbabwe* 89 B5
Guyana ■, *S. Amer.* 124 C7
Guyane française = French Guiana ■, *S. Amer.* 125 C8
Guyang, *China* 56 D6
Guyenne, *France* 20 D4
Guymon, *U.S.A.* 113 G4
Guyra, *Australia* 95 E5
Guyuan, *Hebei, China* 56 D8
Guyuan, *Ningxia Huizu, China* 56 G4
Güzelbahçe, *Turkey* 39 C8
Guzhang, *China* 58 C7
Guzhen, *China* 57 H9
Guzmán, L. de, *Mexico* 118 A3
Gvardeysk, *Russia* 9 J19
Gvardeyskoye, *Ukraine* 47 K8
Gwa, *Burma* 67 L19
Gwaai, *Zimbabwe* 87 F2
Gwabegar, *Australia* 95 E4
Gwadabawa, *Nigeria* 83 C6
Gwādar, *Pakistan* 66 G3
Gwagwada, *Nigeria* 83 C6
Gwalior, *India* 68 F8
Gwanara, *Nigeria* 83 D5
Gwanda, *Zimbabwe* 87 G2
Gwandu, *Nigeria* 83 C5
Gwane, *Dem. Rep. of the Congo* 86 B2
Gwaram, *Nigeria* 83 C7
Gwarzo, *Nigeria* 83 C6
Gwasero, *Nigeria* 83 D5
Gwda →, *Poland* 45 E3
Gweebarra B., *Ireland* 15 B3
Gweedore, *Ireland* 15 A3
Gweru, *Zimbabwe* 87 F2
Gwi, *Nigeria* 83 D6
Gwinn, *U.S.A.* 108 B2
Gwio Kura, *Nigeria* 83 C7
Gwoza, *Nigeria* 83 C7
Gwydir →, *Australia* 95 D4
Gwynedd □, *U.K.* 12 E3
Gyandzha = Gäncä, *Azerbaijan* 49 K8
Gyaring Hu, *China* 60 C4
Gydanskiy Poluostrov, *Russia* 50 C8
Gympie, *Australia* 95 D5
Gyomaendrőd, *Hungary* 42 D5
Gyöngyös, *Hungary* 42 C4
Győr, *Hungary* 42 C2
Győr-Moson-Sopron □, *Hungary* 42 C2
Gypsum Pt., *Canada* 104 A6
Gypsumville, *Canada* 105 C9
Gyueshevo, *Bulgaria* 40 D6
Gyula, *Hungary* 42 D6
Gyumri, *Armenia* 49 K6
Gyzylarbat, *Turkmenistan* 50 F6
Gyzyletrek, *Turkmenistan* 71 B7
Gzhatsk = Gagarin, *Russia* 46 E8

H

Ha 'Arava →, *Israel* 75 E4
Ha Coi, *Vietnam* 58 G6
Ha Dong, *Vietnam* 58 G5
Ha Giang, *Vietnam* 58 F5
Ha Tien, *Vietnam* 65 G5
Ha Tinh, *Vietnam* 64 C5
Ha Trung, *Vietnam* 64 C5
Haaksbergen, *Neths.* 17 B6
Haapsalu, *Estonia* 9 G20
Haarlem, *Neths.* 17 B4
Haast →, *N.Z.* 91 K2
Haast Bluff, *Australia* 92 D5
Hab →, *Pakistan* 68 G3
Hab Nadi Chauki, *Pakistan* 68 G2
Habaswein, *Kenya* 86 B4
Habay, *Canada* 104 B5
Ḩabbānīyah, *Iraq* 70 C4
Ḩabbānīyah, Hawr al, *Iraq* 73 F10
Habo, *Sweden* 11 G8
Haboro, *Japan* 54 B10
Ḩabshān, *U.A.E.* 71 F7
Hachenburg, *Germany* 24 E3
Hachijō-Jima, *Japan* 55 H9
Hachinohe, *Japan* 54 D10
Hachiōji, *Japan* 55 G9
Hachŏn, *N. Korea* 57 D15
Hacıbektaş, *Turkey* 72 C6
Hacılar, *Turkey* 72 C6
Hackås, *Sweden* 10 B8
Hackensack, *U.S.A.* 111 F10
Hackettstown, *U.S.A.* 111 F10
Hadali, *Pakistan* 68 C5
Hadarba, Ras, *Sudan* 80 C4
Hadarom □, *Israel* 75 E4
Hadd, Ra's al, *Oman* 74 C6
Hadejia, *Nigeria* 83 C7
Hadejia →, *Nigeria* 83 C7
Ḩadera, *Israel* 75 C3
Ḩadera, N. →, *Israel* 75 C3
Haderslev, *Denmark* 11 J3
Hadhramaut = Ḩaḑramawt, *Yemen* 74 D4
Hadibu, *Yemen* 74 E5
Hadım, *Turkey* 72 D5
Hadong, *S. Korea* 57 G14
Ḩaḑramawt, *Yemen* 74 D4
Ḩadrānīyah, *Iraq* 70 C4
Hadrian's Wall, *U.K.* 12 B5
Hadsten, *Denmark* 11 H4
Hadsund, *Denmark* 11 H4
Hadyach, *Ukraine* 47 G8
Haeju, *N. Korea* 57 E13
Haenam, *S. Korea* 57 G14
Haenertsburg, *S. Africa* 89 C4
Haerhpin = Harbin, *China* 57 B14
Hafar al Bāţin, *Si. Arabia* 70 D5
Hafik, *Turkey* 72 C7
Ḩafīrat al 'Aydā, *Si. Arabia* 70 E3
Ḩafit, *Oman* 71 F7
Hafizabad, *Pakistan* 68 C5
Haflong, *India* 67 G18
Hafnarfjörður, *Iceland* 8 D3
Haft Gel, *Iran* 71 D6
Hafun, Ras, *Somali Rep.* 74 E5
Hagalil, *Israel* 75 C4
Hagby, *Sweden* 11 H10
Hagen, *Germany* 24 D3
Hagenow, *Germany* 24 B7
Hagerman, *U.S.A.* 113 J2
Hagerstown, *U.S.A.* 108 F7
Hagersville, *Canada* 110 D4
Hagetmau, *France* 20 E3
Hagfors, *Sweden* 10 D7
Hagi, *Japan* 55 G5
Hagolan, *Syria* 75 C4
Hagondange, *France* 19 C13
Hags Hd., *Ireland* 15 D2
Hague, C. de la, *France* 18 C5
Hague, The = 's-Gravenhage, *Neths.* 17 B4
Haguenau, *France* 19 D14
Hai Duong, *Vietnam* 58 G6
Hai'an, *Guangdong, China* 59 G8
Hai'an, *Jiangsu, China* 59 A13
Haicheng, *Fujian, China* 59 E11
Haicheng, *Liaoning, China* 57 D12
Haidar Khel, *Afghan.* 68 C3
Haidargarh, *India* 69 F9
Haifa = Ḩefa, *Israel* 75 C4
Haifeng, *China* 59 F10
Haiger, *Germany* 24 E4
Haikou, *China* 60 D6
Ḩā'il, *Si. Arabia* 70 E4
Hailar, *China* 60 B6
Hailey, *U.S.A.* 114 E6
Haileybury, *Canada* 102 C4
Hailin, *China* 57 B15
Hailing Dao, *China* 59 G8
Hailong, *China* 57 C13
Hailuoto, *Finland* 8 D21
Haimen, *Guangdong, China* 59 F11
Haimen, *Jiangsu, China* 59 B13
Hainan □, *China* 60 E5
Hainaut □, *Belgium* 17 D4
Hainburg, *Austria* 27 C9
Haines, *Alaska, U.S.A.* 104 B1
Haines, *Oreg., U.S.A.* 114 D5
Haines City, *U.S.A.* 109 L5
Haines Junction, *Canada* 104 A1
Hainfeld, *Austria* 26 C8
Haining, *China* 59 B13
Haiphong, *Vietnam* 58 G6
Haitan Dao, *China* 59 E12
Haiti ■, *W. Indies* 121 C5
Haiya, *Sudan* 80 D4
Haiyan, *China* 59 B13
Haiyang, *China* 57 F11
Haiyuan, *Guangxi Zhuangzu, China* 58 F6
Haiyuan, *Ningxia Huizu, China* 56 F3
Haizhou, *China* 57 G10
Haizhou Wan, *China* 57 G10
Hajdú-Bihar □, *Hungary* 42 C6
Hajdúböszörmény, *Hungary* 42 C6
Hajdúdorog, *Hungary* 42 C6
Hajdúhadház, *Hungary* 42 C6
Hajdúnánás, *Hungary* 42 C6
Hajdúsámson, *Hungary* 42 C6
Hajdúszoboszló, *Hungary* 42 C6
Hajipur, *India* 69 G11
Hājjī Muḩsin, *Iraq* 70 C5
Ḩājjīābād, *Iran* 71 D7
Ḩājjīābād-e Zarrīn, *Iran* 71 C7
Hajnówka, *Poland* 45 F10
Hakansson, Mts., *Dem. Rep. of the Congo* 87 D2
Hakkâri, *Turkey* 70 B4
Hakkâri Dağları, *Turkey* 73 C10
Hakken-Zan, *Japan* 55 G7
Hakodate, *Japan* 54 D10
Hakos, *Namibia* 88 C2
Håksberg, *Sweden* 10 D9
Haku-San, *Japan* 55 F8
Hakui, *Japan* 55 F8
Hala, *Pakistan* 66 G6
Ḩalab, *Syria* 70 B3
Ḩalabjah, *Iraq* 70 C5
Halaib, *Sudan* 80 C4
Halasa, *Sudan* 81 E3
Hālat 'Ammār, *Si. Arabia* 70 D3
Halbā, *Lebanon* 75 A5
Halberstadt, *Germany* 24 D7
Halcombe, *N.Z.* 91 J5
Halcon, *Phil.* 63 B6
Halden, *Norway* 9 G14
Haldensleben, *Germany* 24 C7
Haldia, *India* 67 H16
Haldwani, *India* 69 E8
Hale →, *Australia* 94 C2
Halesowen, *U.K.* 13 E5
Haleyville, *U.S.A.* 109 H2
Half Assini, *Ghana* 82 D4
Halfmoon Bay, *N.Z.* 91 M2
Halfway →, *Canada* 104 B4
Halia, *India* 69 G10
Haliburton, *Canada* 102 C4
Halifax, *Australia* 94 B4
Halifax, *Canada* 103 D7
Halifax, *U.K.* 12 D6
Halifax, *U.S.A.* 110 F8
Halifax B., *Australia* 94 B4
Halifax I., *Namibia* 88 D2
Halīl →, *Iran* 71 E8
Halkirk, *U.K.* 14 C5
Hall Beach = Sanirajak, *Canada* 101 B11
Hall in Tirol, *Austria* 26 D4
Hall Pen., *Canada* 101 B13
Hall Pt., *Australia* 92 C3
Hallabro, *Sweden* 11 H9
Halland, *Sweden* 9 H15
Hallands län □, *Sweden* 11 H6
Hallands Väderö, *Sweden* 11 H6
Hallandsås, *Sweden* 11 H7
Hällbybrunn, *Sweden* 10 E10
Halle, *Belgium* 17 D4
Halle, *Nordrhein-Westfalen, Germany* 24 C4
Halle, *Sachsen-Anhalt, Germany* 24 D7
Hällefors, *Sweden* 10 E8
Hälleforsnäs, *Sweden* 10 E10
Hallein, *Austria* 26 D6
Hällekis, *Sweden* 11 F7
Hallen, *Sweden* 10 A8
Hallett, *Australia* 95 E2
Hallettsville, *U.S.A.* 113 L6
Hallim, *S. Korea* 57 H14
Hallingdalselvi →, *Norway* 9 F13
Hallock, *U.S.A.* 112 A6
Halls Creek, *Australia* 92 C4
Hallsberg, *Sweden* 10 E9
Hallstahammar, *Sweden* 10 E10
Hallstatt, *Austria* 26 D6
Hallstavik, *Sweden* 10 D12
Hallstead, *U.S.A.* 111 E9
Halmahera, *Indonesia* 63 D7
Halmeu, *Romania* 42 C8
Halmstad, *Sweden* 11 H6
Hals, *Denmark* 11 H4
Hälsingborg = Helsingborg, *Sweden* 11 H6
Hälsingland, *Sweden* 10 C10
Halstead, *U.K.* 13 F8
Haltern, *Germany* 24 D3
Halti, *Finland* 8 B19
Halton □, *U.K.* 12 D5
Haltwhistle, *U.K.* 12 C5
Ḩalul, *Qatar* 71 E7
Halvad, *India* 68 H4
Ḩalvān, *Iran* 71 C8
Ham, *France* 19 C10
Ham Tan, *Vietnam* 65 G6
Ham Yen, *Vietnam* 64 A5
Hamab, *Namibia* 88 D2
Hamad, *Sudan* 81 D3
Hamada, *Japan* 55 G6
Hamadān, *Iran* 71 C6
Hamadān □, *Iran* 71 C6
Hamāh, *Syria* 70 C3
Hamamatsu, *Japan* 55 G8
Hamar, *Norway* 9 F14
Hamâta, Gebel, *Egypt* 70 E2
Hambantota, *Sri Lanka* 66 R12
Hamber Prov. Park, *Canada* 104 C5
Hamburg, *Germany* 24 B5
Hamburg, *Ark., U.S.A.* 113 J9
Hamburg, *N.Y., U.S.A.* 110 D6
Hamburg, *Pa., U.S.A.* 111 F9
Hamburg □, *Germany* 24 B5
Ḩamḑ, W. al →, *Si. Arabia* 70 E3
Hamden, *U.S.A.* 111 E12
Hamdibey, *Turkey* 39 B9
Häme, *Finland* 9 F20
Hämeenlinna, *Finland* 9 F21
Hamélé, *Ghana* 82 C4
Hamelin Pool, *Australia* 93 E1
Hameln, *Germany* 24 C5
Hamerkaz □, *Israel* 75 C3
Hamersley Ra., *Australia* 92 D2
Hamhung, *N. Korea* 57 E14
Hami, *China* 60 B4
Hamilton, *Australia* 95 F3
Hamilton, *Canada* 102 D4
Hamilton, *N.Z.* 91 G5
Hamilton, *U.K.* 14 F4
Hamilton, *Ala., U.S.A.* 109 H1
Hamilton, *Mont., U.S.A.* 114 C6
Hamilton, *N.Y., U.S.A.* 111 D9
Hamilton, *Ohio, U.S.A.* 108 F3
Hamilton, *Tex., U.S.A.* 113 K5
Hamilton →, *Australia* 94 C2
Hamilton City, *U.S.A.* 116 F4
Hamilton Inlet, *Canada* 103 B8
Hamilton Mt., *U.S.A.* 111 C10
Hamina, *Finland* 9 F22
Hamirpur, *H.P., India* 68 D7
Hamirpur, *Ut. P., India* 69 G9
Hamitabat, *Turkey* 41 E11
Hamlet, *U.S.A.* 109 H6
Hamley Bridge, *Australia* 95 E2
Hamlin = Hameln, *Germany* 24 C5

Hamlin, N.Y., U.S.A. 110 C7
Hamlin, Tex., U.S.A. 113 J4
Hamm, Germany 24 D3
Ḩammār, Hawr al, Iraq 70 D5
Hammarstrand, Sweden 10 A10
Hammelburg, Germany 25 E5
Hammeren, Denmark 11 J8
Hammerfest, Norway 8 A20
Hammerum, Denmark 11 H3
Hamminkeln, Germany 24 D2
Hammond, Ind., U.S.A. 108 E2
Hammond, La., U.S.A. 113 K9
Hammond, N.Y., U.S.A. 111 B9
Hammondsport, U.S.A. 110 D7
Hammonton, U.S.A. 108 F8
Hamneda, Sweden 11 H7
Hamoyet, Jebel, Sudan 80 D4
Hampden, N.Z. 91 L3
Hampshire □, U.K. 13 F6
Hampshire Downs, U.K. 13 F6
Hampton, N.B., Canada 103 C6
Hampton, Ont., Canada 110 C6
Hampton, Ark., U.S.A. 113 J8
Hampton, Iowa, U.S.A. 112 D8
Hampton, N.H., U.S.A. 111 D14
Hampton, S.C., U.S.A. 109 J5
Hampton, Va., U.S.A. 108 G7
Hampton Bays, U.S.A. 111 F12
Hampton Tableland, Australia 93 F4
Hamra, Sweden 10 C8
Hamrat esh Sheykh, Sudan 81 E2
Hamur, Turkey 73 C10
Hamyang, S. Korea 57 G14
Han Jiang →, China 59 F11
Han Shui, China 58 A7
Han Shui →, China 59 B10
Hanak, Si. Arabia 70 E3
Hanamaki, Japan 54 E10
Hanang, Tanzania 86 C4
Hanau, Germany 25 E4
Hanbogd = Ihbulag, Mongolia 56 C4
Hançalar, Turkey 39 C11
Hânceşti, Moldova 43 D13
Hancheng, China 56 G6
Hanchuan, China 59 B9
Hancock, Mich., U.S.A. 112 B10
Hancock, N.Y., U.S.A. 111 E9
Handa, Japan 55 G8
Handan, China 56 F8
Handeni, Tanzania 86 D4
Handlová, Slovak Rep. 27 C11
Handub, Sudan 80 D4
Handwara, India 69 B6
Hanegev, Israel 75 E4
Hanford, U.S.A. 116 J7
Hang Chat, Thailand 64 C2
Hang Dong, Thailand 64 C2
Hangang →, S. Korea 57 F14
Hangayn Nuruu, Mongolia 60 B4
Hangchou = Hangzhou, China 59 B13
Hanggin Houqi, China 56 D4
Hanggin Qi, China 56 E5
Hangu, China 57 E9
Hangzhou, China 59 B13
Hangzhou Wan, China 59 B13
Hanhongor, Mongolia 56 C3
Ḩanīdh, Si. Arabia 71 E6
Ḩanīsh, Yemen 74 E3
Haniska, Slovak Rep. 27 C14
Hanjiang, China 59 E12
Hankinson, U.S.A. 112 B6
Hanko, Finland 9 G20
Hankou, China 59 B10
Hanksville, U.S.A. 115 G8
Hanle, India 69 C8
Hanmer Springs, N.Z. 91 K4
Hann →, Australia 92 C4
Hann, Mt., Australia 92 C4
Hanna, Canada 104 C6
Hanna, U.S.A. 114 F10
Hannah B., Canada 102 B4
Hannibal, Mo., U.S.A. 112 F9
Hannibal, N.Y., U.S.A. 111 C8
Hannik, Sudan 80 D3
Hannover, Germany 24 C5
Hanö, Sweden 11 H8
Hanöbukten, Sweden 11 J8
Hanoi, Vietnam 58 G5
Hanover = Hannover, Germany 24 C5
Hanover, Canada 102 D3
Hanover, S. Africa 88 E3
Hanover, N.H., U.S.A. 111 C12
Hanover, Ohio, U.S.A. 110 F2
Hanover, Pa., U.S.A. 108 F7
Hanover, I., Chile 128 G2
Hansdiha, India 69 G12
Hanshou, China 59 C8
Hansi, India 68 E6
Hanson, L., Australia 95 E2
Hanstholm, Denmark 11 G2
Hantsavichy, Belarus 47 F4
Hanumangarh, India 68 E6
Hanyin, China 58 A7
Hanyuan, China 58 C4
Hanzhong, China 56 H4
Hanzhuang, China 57 G9
Haora, India 69 H13
Haoxue, China 59 B9
Haparanda, Sweden 8 D21
Happy, U.S.A. 113 H4
Happy Camp, U.S.A. 114 F2
Happy Valley-Goose Bay, Canada 103 B7
Hapsu, N. Korea 57 D15
Hapur, India 68 E7
Ḩaql, Si. Arabia 75 F3
Har, Indonesia 63 F8
Har-Ayrag, Mongolia 56 B5
Har Hu, China 60 C4
Har Us Nuur, Mongolia 60 B4
Har Yehuda, Israel 75 D3
Ḩaraḑ, Si. Arabia 74 C4
Haradok, Belarus 46 E6
Häradsbäck, Sweden 11 H8
Haranomachi, Japan 54 F10
Harare, Zimbabwe 87 F3
Harat, Eritrea 81 D4
Harbin, China 57 B14
Harbiye, Turkey 72 D7
Harbo, Sweden 10 D11
Harboør, Denmark 11 H2
Harbor Beach, U.S.A. 110 C2
Harbour Breton, Canada 103 C8
Harbour Deep, Canada 103 B8
Harburg, Germany 24 B5
Hårby, Denmark 11 J4
Harda, India 68 H7
Hardangerfjorden, Norway 9 F12
Hardangervidda, Norway 9 F12
Hardap Dam, Namibia 88 C2
Hardenberg, Neths. 17 B6
Harderwijk, Neths. 17 B5
Hardey →, Australia 92 D2
Hardin, U.S.A. 114 D10
Harding, S. Africa 89 E4
Harding Ra., Australia 92 C3
Hardisty, Canada 104 C6
Hardoi, India 69 F9
Hardwar = Haridwar, India 68 E8
Hardwick, U.S.A. 111 B12
Hardy, Pen., Chile 128 H3
Hare B., Canada 103 B8
Hareid, Norway 9 E12
Haren, Germany 24 C3
Harer, Ethiopia 81 F5
Harerge □, Ethiopia 81 F5
Hareto, Ethiopia 81 F4
Harfleur, France 18 C7
Hargeisa, Somali Rep. 74 F3
Harghita □, Romania 43 D10
Harghita, Munţii, Romania 43 D10
Hargshamn, Sweden 10 D12
Hari →, Indonesia 62 E2
Haria, Canary Is. 37 E6
Haridwar, India 68 E8
Harim, Jabal al, Oman 71 E8
Haringhata →, Bangla. 67 J16
Harīrūd →, Asia 66 A2
Härjedalen, Sweden 10 B7
Harlan, Iowa, U.S.A. 112 E7
Harlan, Ky., U.S.A. 109 G4
Hârlău, Romania 43 C11
Harlech, U.K. 12 E3
Harlem, U.S.A. 114 B9
Hårlev, Denmark 11 J6
Harlingen, Neths. 17 A5
Harlingen, U.S.A. 113 M6
Harlow, U.K. 13 F8
Harlowton, U.S.A. 114 C9
Harmancık, Turkey 39 B11
Harmånger, Sweden 10 C11
Harmil, Eritrea 81 D5
Harnai, Pakistan 68 D2
Harney Basin, U.S.A. 114 E4
Harney L., U.S.A. 114 E4
Harney Peak, U.S.A. 112 D3
Härnön, Sweden 10 B12
Härnösand, Sweden 10 B11
Haro, Spain 32 C2
Haroldswick, U.K. 14 A8
Harp L., Canada 103 A7
Harper, Liberia 82 E3
Harplinge, Sweden 11 H6
Harr, Mauritania 82 B2
Harrai, India 69 H8
Harrand, Pakistan 68 E4
Ḩarrat Khaybar, Si. Arabia 80 B5
Ḩarrat Nawāşīf, Si. Arabia 80 C5
Harricana →, Canada 102 B4
Harriman, U.S.A. 109 H3
Harrington Harbour, Canada 103 B8
Harris, U.K. 14 D2
Harris, Sd. of, U.K. 14 D1
Harris L., Australia 95 E2
Harris Pt., Canada 110 C2
Harrisburg, Ill., U.S.A. 113 G10
Harrisburg, Nebr., U.S.A. 112 E3
Harrisburg, Pa., U.S.A. 110 F8
Harrismith, S. Africa 89 D4
Harrison, Ark., U.S.A. 113 G8
Harrison, Maine, U.S.A. 111 B14
Harrison, Nebr., U.S.A. 112 D3
Harrison, C., Canada 103 B8
Harrison L., Canada 104 D4
Harrisonburg, U.S.A. 108 F6
Harrisonville, U.S.A. 112 F7
Harriston, Canada 110 C4
Harrisville, Mich., U.S.A. 110 B1
Harrisville, N.Y., U.S.A. 111 B9
Harrisville, Pa., U.S.A. 110 E5
Harrodsburg, U.S.A. 108 G3
Harrogate, U.K. 12 C6
Harrow □, U.K. 13 F7
Harrowsmith, Canada 111 B8
Harry S. Truman Reservoir, U.S.A. 112 F7
Harsefeld, Germany 24 B5
Harsewinkel, Germany 24 D4
Harsīn, Iran 70 C5
Hârşova, Romania 43 F12
Harstad, Norway 8 B17
Harsud, India 68 H7
Hart, U.S.A. 108 D2
Hart, L., Australia 95 E2
Hartbees →, S. Africa 88 D3
Hartberg, Austria 26 D8
Hartford, Conn., U.S.A. 111 E12
Hartford, Ky., U.S.A. 108 G2
Hartford, S. Dak., U.S.A. 112 D6
Hartford, Wis., U.S.A. 112 D10
Hartford City, U.S.A. 108 E3
Hartland, Canada 103 C6
Hartland Pt., U.K. 13 F3
Hartlepool, U.K. 12 C6
Hartlepool □, U.K. 12 C6
Hartley Bay, Canada 104 C3
Hartmannberge, Namibia 88 B1
Hartney, Canada 105 D8
Hârtop, Moldova 43 D13
Harts →, S. Africa 88 D3
Hartselle, U.S.A. 109 H2
Hartshorne, U.S.A. 113 H7
Hartstown, U.S.A. 110 E4
Hartsville, U.S.A. 109 H5
Hartswater, S. Africa 88 D3
Hartwell, U.S.A. 109 H4
Harunabad, Pakistan 68 E5
Harvand, Iran 71 D7
Harvey, Australia 93 F2
Harvey, Ill., U.S.A. 108 E2
Harvey, N. Dak., U.S.A. 112 B5
Harwich, U.K. 13 F9
Haryana □, India 68 E7
Haryn →, Belarus 47 F4
Harz, Germany 24 D6
Harzgerode, Germany 24 D7
Hasa □, Si. Arabia 71 E6
Hasaheisa, Sudan 81 E3
Ḩasanābād, Iran 71 C7
Hasdo →, India 69 J10
Haselünne, Germany 24 C3
Hashimoto, Japan 55 G7
Hashtjerd, Iran 71 C6
Haskell, U.S.A. 113 J5
Hasköy, Turkey 41 E10
Haslach, Germany 25 G4
Hasle, Denmark 11 J8
Haslemere, U.K. 13 F7
Haslev, Denmark 11 J5
Hasparren, France 20 E2
Hassa, Turkey 72 D7
Hassela, Sweden 10 B10
Hasselt, Belgium 17 D5
Hassfurt, Germany 25 E6
Hassi Messaoud, Algeria 78 B7
Hässleholm, Sweden 11 H7
Hassloch, Germany 25 F4
Hästholmen, Sweden 11 F8
Hastings, N.Z. 91 H6
Hastings, U.K. 13 G8
Hastings, Mich., U.S.A. 108 D3
Hastings, Minn., U.S.A. 112 C8
Hastings, Nebr., U.S.A. 112 E5
Hastings Ra., Australia 95 E5
Hästveda, Sweden 11 H7
Hat Yai, Thailand 65 J3
Hatanbulag = Ergel, Mongolia 56 C5
Hatay = Antalya, Turkey 72 D4
Hatch, U.S.A. 115 K10
Hatchet L., Canada 105 B8
Haţeg, Romania 42 E7
Hateruma-Shima, Japan 55 M1
Hatfield P.O., Australia 95 E3
Hatgal, Mongolia 60 A5
Hathras, India 68 F8
Hatia, Bangla. 67 H17
Ḩāţibah, Ra's, Si. Arabia 80 C4
Hato Mayor, Dom. Rep. 121 C6
Hatta, India 69 G8
Hattah, Australia 95 E3
Hatteras, C., U.S.A. 109 H8
Hattiesburg, U.S.A. 113 K10
Hatvan, Hungary 42 C4
Hau Bon = Cheo Reo, Vietnam 62 B3
Hau Duc, Vietnam 64 E7
Haugesund, Norway 9 G11
Haukipudas, Finland 8 D21
Haultain →, Canada 105 B7
Hauraki G., N.Z. 91 G5
Hausruck, Austria 26 C6
Haut Atlas, Morocco 78 B4
Haut-Rhin □, France 19 E14
Haut-Zaïre = Orientale □, Dem. Rep. of the Congo 86 B2
Haute-Corse □, France 21 F13
Haute-Garonne □, France 20 E5
Haute-Loire □, France 20 C7
Haute-Marne □, France 19 D12
Haute-Normandie □, France 18 C7
Haute-Saône □, France 19 E13
Haute-Savoie □, France 21 C10
Haute-Vienne □, France 20 C5
Hautes-Alpes □, France 21 D10
Hautes Fagnes = Hohe Venn, Belgium 17 D6
Hautes-Pyrénées □, France 20 F4
Hauteville-Lompnès, France 21 C9
Hautmont, France 19 B10
Hauts-de-Seine □, France 19 D9
Hauts Plateaux, Algeria 76 C4
Hauzenberg, Germany 25 G9
Havana = La Habana, Cuba 120 B3
Havana, U.S.A. 112 E9
Havant, U.K. 13 G7
Havârna, Romania 43 B11
Havasu, L., U.S.A. 117 L12
Havdhem, Sweden 11 G12
Havel →, Germany 24 C8
Havelian, Pakistan 68 B5
Havelock, Canada 102 D4
Havelock, N.Z. 91 J4
Havelock, U.S.A. 109 H7
Haverfordwest, U.K. 13 F3
Haverhill, U.S.A. 111 D13
Haverstraw, U.S.A. 111 E11
Håverud, Sweden 11 F6
Havirga, Mongolia 56 B7
Havířov, Czech Rep. 27 B11
Havlíčkův Brod, Czech Rep. 26 B8
Havneby, Denmark 11 J2
Havran, Turkey 39 B9
Havre, U.S.A. 114 B9
Havre-Aubert, Canada 103 C7
Havre-St.-Pierre, Canada 103 B7
Havsa, Turkey 41 E10
Havza, Turkey 72 B6
Haw →, U.S.A. 109 H6
Hawaii □, U.S.A. 106 H16
Hawaii I., Pac. Oc. 106 J17
Hawaiian Is., Pac. Oc. 106 H17
Hawaiian Ridge, Pac. Oc. 97 E11
Hawarden, U.S.A. 112 D6
Hawea, L., N.Z. 91 L2
Hawera, N.Z. 91 H5
Hawick, U.K. 14 F6
Hawk Junction, Canada 102 C3
Hawke B., N.Z. 91 H6
Hawker, Australia 95 E2
Hawkesbury, Canada 102 C5
Hawkesbury I., Canada 104 C3
Hawkesbury Pt., Australia 94 A1
Hawkinsville, U.S.A. 109 J4
Hawley, Minn., U.S.A. 112 B6
Hawley, Pa., U.S.A. 111 E9
Ḩawrān, W. →, Iraq 70 C4
Hawsh Mūssá, Lebanon 75 B4
Hawthorne, U.S.A. 114 G4
Hay, Australia 95 E3
Hay →, Australia 94 C2
Hay →, Canada 104 A5
Hay, C., Australia 92 B4
Hay I., Canada 110 B4
Hay L., Canada 104 B5
Hay-on-Wye, U.K. 13 E4
Hay River, Canada 104 A5
Hay Springs, U.S.A. 112 D3
Haya = Tehoru, Indonesia 63 E7
Hayachine-San, Japan 54 E10
Hayange, France 19 C13
Haydarlı, Turkey 39 C12
Hayden, U.S.A. 114 F10
Haydon, Australia 94 B3
Hayes, U.S.A. 112 C4
Hayes →, Canada 102 A1
Hayes Creek, Australia 92 B5
Hayle, U.K. 13 G2
Hayling I., U.K. 13 G7
Haymana, Turkey 72 C5
Hayrabolu, Turkey 41 E11
Hays, Canada 104 C6
Hays, U.S.A. 112 F5
Haysyn, Ukraine 47 H5
Hayvoron, Ukraine 47 H5
Hayward, Calif., U.S.A. 116 H4
Hayward, Wis., U.S.A. 112 B9
Haywards Heath, U.K. 13 G7
Hazafon □, Israel 75 C4
Hazārān, Kūh-e, Iran 71 D8
Hazard, U.S.A. 108 G4
Hazaribag, India 69 H11
Hazaribag Road, India 69 G11
Hazebrouck, France 19 B9
Hazelton, Canada 104 B3
Hazelton, U.S.A. 112 B4
Hazen, U.S.A. 112 B4
Hazlehurst, Ga., U.S.A. 109 K4
Hazlehurst, Miss., U.S.A. 113 K9
Hazlet, U.S.A. 111 F10
Hazleton, U.S.A. 111 F9
Hazlett, L., Australia 92 D4
Hazro, Turkey 70 B4
He Xian, Anhui, China 59 B12
He Xian, Guangxi Zhuangzu, China 59 E8
Head of Bight, Australia 93 F5
Headlands, Zimbabwe 87 F3
Healdsburg, U.S.A. 116 G4
Healdton, U.S.A. 113 H6
Healesville, Australia 95 F4
Heany Junction, Zimbabwe 89 C4
Heard I., Ind. Oc. 3 G13
Hearne, U.S.A. 113 K6
Hearst, Canada 102 C3
Heart →, U.S.A. 112 B4
Heart's Content, Canada 103 C9
Heath Pt., Canada 103 C7
Heavener, U.S.A. 113 H7
Hebbronville, U.S.A. 113 M5
Hebei □, China 56 E9
Hebel, Australia 95 D4
Heber, U.S.A. 117 N11
Heber City, U.S.A. 114 F8
Heber Springs, U.S.A. 113 H9
Hebert, Canada 105 C7
Hebgen L., U.S.A. 114 D8
Hebi, China 56 G8
Hebrides, U.K. 6 D4
Hebrides, Sea of the, U.K. 14 D2
Hebron = Al Khalīl, West Bank 75 D4
Hebron, Canada 101 C13
Hebron, N. Dak., U.S.A. 112 B3
Hebron, Nebr., U.S.A. 112 E6
Heby, Sweden 10 E10
Hecate Str., Canada 104 C2
Hecate I., U.S.A. 104 B2
Hechi, China 58 E7
Hechingen, Germany 25 G4
Hechuan, China 58 B6
Hecla, U.S.A. 112 C5
Hecla I., Canada 105 C9
Hédé, France 18 D5
Hede, Sweden 10 B7
Hedemora, Sweden 10 D9
Hedensted, Denmark 11 J3
Hedesunda, Sweden 10 D10
Heerde, Neths. 17 B6
Heerenveen, Neths. 17 B5
Heerhugowaard, Neths. 17 B4
Heerlen, Neths. 17 D5
Ḩefa, Israel 75 C4
Ḩefa □, Israel 75 C4
Hefei, China 59 B11
Hefeng, China 59 C8
Hegalig, Sudan 81 E3
Hegang, China 60 B8
Heiban, Sudan 81 E3
Heichengzhen, China 56 F4
Heide, Germany 24 A5
Heidelberg, Germany 25 F4
Heidelberg, S. Africa 88 E3
Heidenau, Germany 24 E9
Heidenheim, Germany 25 G6
Heijing, China 58 E3
Heilbad Heiligenstadt, Germany 24 D6
Heilbron, S. Africa 89 D4
Heilbronn, Germany 25 F5
Heiligenblut, Austria 26 D5
Heiligenhafen, Germany 24 A6
Heilongjiang □, China 60 B7
Heilunkiang = Heilongjiang □, China 60 B7
Heimaey, Iceland 8 E3
Heinola, Finland 9 F22
Heinsberg, Germany 24 D2
Heinze Kyun, Burma 64 E1
Heishan, China 57 D12
Heishui, Liaoning, China 57 C10
Heishui, Sichuan, China 58 A4
Hejaz = Ḩijāz □, Si. Arabia 70 E3
Hejian, China 56 E9
Hejiang, China 58 C5
Hejin, China 56 G6
Hekımhan, Turkey 70 B3
Hekla, Iceland 8 E4
Hekou, Guangdong, China 59 F9
Hekou, Yunnan, China 58 F4
Hel, Poland 44 D5
Helagsfjället, Sweden 10 B6
Helan Shan, China 56 E3
Helechosa, Spain 35 F6
Helen Atoll, Pac. Oc. 63 D8
Helena, Ark., U.S.A. 113 H9
Helena, Mont., U.S.A. 114 C7
Helendale, U.S.A. 117 L9
Helensburgh, U.K. 14 E4
Helensville, N.Z. 91 G5
Helenvale, Australia 94 B4
Helgasjön, Sweden 11 H8
Helgeland, Norway 8 C15
Helgoland, Germany 24 A3
Heligoland = Helgoland, Germany 24 A3
Heligoland B. = Deutsche Bucht, Germany 24 A4
Heliopolis, Egypt 80 H7
Hella, Iceland 8 E3
Hellertown, U.S.A. 111 F9
Hellespont = Çanakkale Boğazı, Turkey 41 F10
Hellevoetsluis, Neths. 17 C4
Hellín, Spain 33 G3
Helmand □, Afghan. 66 D4
Helmand →, Afghan. 66 D2
Helme →, Germany 24 D7
Helmeringhausen, Namibia 88 D2
Helmond, Neths. 17 C5
Helmsdale, U.K. 14 C5
Helmsdale →, U.K. 14 C5
Helmstedt, Germany 24 C7
Helong, China 57 C15
Helper, U.S.A. 114 G8
Helsingborg, Sweden 11 H6
Helsinge, Denmark 11 H6
Helsingfors = Helsinki, Finland 9 F21
Helsingør, Denmark 11 H6
Helsinki, Finland 9 F21
Helska, Mierzeja, Poland 44 D5
Helston, U.K. 13 G2
Helvellyn, U.K. 12 C4
Helwân, Egypt 80 J7
Hemel Hempstead, U.K. 13 F7
Hemet, U.S.A. 117 M10
Hemingford, U.S.A. 112 D3
Hemmingford, Canada 111 A11
Hempstead, U.S.A. 113 K6
Hemse, Sweden 11 G12
Hemsön, Sweden 10 B12
Henån, Sweden 11 F5
Henan □, China 56 H8
Henares →, Spain 34 E7
Henashi-Misaki, Japan 54 D9
Hendaye, France 20 E2
Hendek, Turkey 72 B4
Henderson, Argentina 126 D3
Henderson, Ky., U.S.A. 108 G2
Henderson, N.C., U.S.A. 109 G6
Henderson, Nev., U.S.A. 117 J12
Henderson, Tenn., U.S.A. 109 H1
Henderson, Tex., U.S.A. 113 J7
Hendersonville, N.C., U.S.A. 109 H4
Hendersonville, Tenn., U.S.A. 109 G2
Hendījān, Iran 71 D6
Hendorābī, Iran 71 E7
Heng Jiang, China 58 C5
Heng Xian, China 58 F7

Hengcheng, China 56 E4
Hëngchun, Taiwan 59 F13
Hengdaohezi, China 57 B15
Hengelo, Neths. 17 B6
Hengfeng, China 59 C10
Hengshan, Hunan, China 59 D9
Hengshan, Shaanxi, China 56 F5
Hengshui, China 56 F8
Hengyang, China 59 D9
Henichesk, Ukraine 47 J8
Hénin-Beaumont, France 19 B9
Henlopen, C., U.S.A. 108 F8
Hennan, Sweden 10 B9
Hennebont, France 18 E3
Hennenman, S. Africa 88 D4
Hennessey, U.S.A. 113 G6
Hennigsdorf, Germany 24 C9
Henrietta, U.S.A. 113 J5
Henrietta, Ostrov = Genriyetty, Ostrov, Russia 51 B16
Henrietta Maria, C., Canada 102 A3
Henry, U.S.A. 112 E10
Henryetta, U.S.A. 113 H7
Henryville, Canada 111 A11
Hensall, Canada 110 C3
Henstedt-Ulzburg, Germany 24 B6
Hentiesbaai, Namibia 88 C1
Hentiyn Nuruu, Mongolia 60 B5
Henty, Australia 95 F4
Henzada, Burma 67 L19
Hephaestia, Greece 39 B7
Heping, China 59 E10
Heppner, U.S.A. 114 D4
Hepu, China 58 G7
Hepworth, Canada 110 B3
Heqing, China 58 D3
Hequ, China 56 E6
Héraðsflói, Iceland 8 D6
Héraðsvötn →, Iceland 8 D4
Herald Cays, Australia 94 B4
Herāt, Afghan. 66 B3
Herāt □, Afghan. 66 B3
Hérault □, France 20 E7
Hérault →, France 20 E7
Herbault, France 18 E8
Herbert →, Australia 94 B4
Herberton, Australia 94 B4
Herbertsdale, S. Africa 88 E3
Herbignac, France 18 E4
Herborn, Germany 24 E4
Herby, Poland 45 H5
Herceg-Novi, Montenegro, Yug. 40 D2
Herchmer, Canada 105 B10
Herðubreið, Iceland 8 D5
Hereford, U.K. 13 E5
Hereford, U.S.A. 113 H3
Herefordshire □, U.K. 13 E5
Hereke, Turkey 41 F13
Herencia, Spain 35 F7
Herentals, Belgium 17 C4
Herford, Germany 24 C4
Héricourt, France 19 E13
Herington, U.S.A. 112 F6
Herisau, Switz. 25 H5
Hérisson, France 19 F9
Herkimer, U.S.A. 111 D10
Herlong, U.S.A. 116 E6
Herm, U.K. 13 H5
Hermann, U.S.A. 112 F9
Hermannsburg, Australia 92 D5
Hermannsburg, Germany 24 C6
Hermanus, S. Africa 88 E2
Herment, France 20 C6
Hermidale, Australia 95 E4
Hermiston, U.S.A. 114 D4
Hermite, I., Chile 128 H3
Hermon, U.S.A. 111 B9
Hermon, Mt. = Shaykh, J. ash, Lebanon 75 B4
Hermosillo, Mexico 118 B2
Hernád →, Hungary 42 C6
Hernandarias, Paraguay 127 B5
Hernandez, U.S.A. 116 J6
Hernando, Argentina 126 C3
Hernando, U.S.A. 113 H10
Hernani, Spain 32 B3
Herndon, U.S.A. 110 F8
Herne, Germany 17 C7
Herne Bay, U.K. 13 F9
Herning, Denmark 11 H2
Heroica = Caborca, Mexico 118 A2
Heroica Nogales = Nogales, Mexico 118 A2
Heron Bay, Canada 102 C2
Herradura, Pta. de la, Canary Is. 37 F5
Herreid, U.S.A. 112 C4
Herrenberg, Germany 25 G4
Herrera, Spain 35 H6
Herrera de Alcántara, Spain 35 F3
Herrera de Pisuerga, Spain 34 C6
Herrera del Duque, Spain 35 F5
Herrestad, Sweden 11 F5
Herrin, U.S.A. 113 G10
Herriot, Canada 105 B8
Herrljunga, Sweden 11 F7
Hersbruck, Germany 25 F7
Hershey, U.S.A. 111 F8
Hersonissos, Greece 36 D7
Herstal, Belgium 17 D5
Hertford, U.K. 13 F7
Hertfordshire □, U.K. 13 F7
's-Hertogenbosch, Neths. 17 C5
Hertzogville, S. Africa 88 D4
Hervás, Spain 34 E5
Hervey B., Australia 94 C5
Herzberg, Brandenburg, Germany 24 D9
Herzberg, Niedersachsen, Germany 24 D6
Herzliyya, Israel 75 C3
Herzogenburg, Austria 26 C8
Ḩeşār, Fārs, Iran 71 D6
Ḩeşār, Markazī, Iran 71 C6
Hesdin, France 19 B9
Heshan, China 58 F7
Heshui, China 56 G5
Heshun, China 56 F7
Hesperia, U.S.A. 117 L9
Hesse = Hessen □, Germany 24 E4
Hessen □, Germany 24 E4
Hestra, Sweden 11 G7
Hetch Hetchy Aqueduct, U.S.A. 116 H5
Hettinger, U.S.A. 112 C3
Hettstedt, Germany 24 D7
Heuvelton, U.S.A. 111 B9
Heves, Hungary 42 C5
Heves □, Hungary 42 C5
Hewitt, U.S.A. 113 K6
Hexham, U.K. 12 C5
Hexi, Yunnan, China 58 E4
Hexi, Zhejiang, China 59 D12
Hexigten Qi, China 57 C9
Ḩeydarābād, Iran 71 D7
Heysham, U.K. 12 C5
Heyuan, China 59 F10
Heywood, Australia 95 F3
Heze, China 56 G8
Hezhang, China 58 D5
Hi Vista, U.S.A. 117 L9
Hialeah, U.S.A. 109 N5
Hiawatha, U.S.A. 112 F7
Hibbing, U.S.A. 112 B8
Hibbs B., Australia 94 G4
Hibernia Reef, Australia 92 B3
Hickman, U.S.A. 113 G10
Hickory, U.S.A. 109 H5
Hicks, Pt., Australia 95 F4
Hicks L., Canada 105 A9
Hicksville, U.S.A. 111 F11
Hida, Romania 43 C8
Hida-Gawa →, Japan 55 G8
Hida-Sammyaku, Japan 55 F8
Hidaka-Sammyaku, Japan 54 C11
Hidalgo, Mexico 119 C5
Hidalgo □, Mexico 119 C5
Hidalgo, Presa M., Mexico 118 B3
Hidalgo, Pta. del, Canary Is. 37 F3
Hidalgo del Parral, Mexico 118 B3
Hiddensee, Germany 24 A9
Hieflau, Austria 26 D7
Hiendelaencina, Spain 32 D2
Hierro, Canary Is. 37 G1
Higashiajima-San, Japan 54 F10
Higashiōsaka, Japan 55 G7
Higgins, U.S.A. 113 G4
Higgins Corner, U.S.A. 116 F5
High Atlas = Haut Atlas, Morocco 78 B4
High Bridge, U.S.A. 111 F10
High Level, Canada 104 B5
High Point, U.S.A. 109 H6
High Prairie, Canada 104 B5
High River, Canada 104 C6
High Tatra = Tatry, Slovak Rep. 27 B13
High Veld, Africa 76 J6
High Wycombe, U.K. 13 F7
Highland □, U.K. 14 D4
Highland Park, U.S.A. 108 D2
Highmore, U.S.A. 112 C5
Highrock L., Man., Canada 105 B8
Highrock L., Sask., Canada 105 B7
Higüey, Dom. Rep. 121 C6
Hihya, Egypt 80 H7
Hiiumaa, Estonia 9 G20
Híjar, Spain 32 D4
Ḩijāz □, Si. Arabia 70 E3
Hijo = Tagum, Phil. 61 H6
Hikari, Japan 55 H5
Hikmak, Ras el, Egypt 80 A2
Hiko, U.S.A. 116 H11
Hikone, Japan 55 G8
Hikurangi, N.Z. 91 F5
Hikurangi, Mt., N.Z. 91 H6
Hildburghausen, Germany 24 E6
Hildesheim, Germany 24 C5
Hill →, Australia 93 F2
Hill City, Idaho, U.S.A. 114 E6
Hill City, Kans., U.S.A. 112 F5
Hill City, S. Dak., U.S.A. 112 D3
Hill Island L., Canada 105 A7
Hillared, Sweden 11 G7
Hillcrest Center, U.S.A. 117 K8
Hillegom, Neths. 17 B4
Hillerød, Denmark 11 J6
Hillerstorp, Sweden 11 G7
Hillsboro, Kans., U.S.A. 112 F6
Hillsboro, N. Dak., U.S.A. 112 B6
Hillsboro, N.H., U.S.A. 111 C13
Hillsboro, Ohio, U.S.A. 108 F4
Hillsboro, Oreg., U.S.A. 116 E4
Hillsboro, Tex., U.S.A. 113 J6
Hillsborough, Grenada 121 D7
Hillsdale, Mich., U.S.A. 108 E3
Hillsdale, N.Y., U.S.A. 111 D11
Hillsport, Canada 102 C2
Hillston, Australia 95 E4
Hilo, U.S.A. 106 J17
Hilton, U.S.A. 110 C7
Hilton Head Island, U.S.A. 109 J5
Hilvan, Turkey 73 D8
Hilversum, Neths. 17 B5
Himachal Pradesh □, India 68 D7
Himalaya, Asia 69 E11
Himamaylan, Phil. 61 F5
Himarë, Albania 40 F3
Himatnagar, India 66 H8
Himeji, Japan 55 G7
Himi, Japan 55 F8
Himmerland, Denmark 11 H3
Ḩimş, Syria 75 A5
Ḩimş □, Syria 75 A6
Hinche, Haiti 121 C5
Hinchinbrook I., Australia 94 B4
Hinckley, U.K. 13 E6
Hinckley, U.S.A. 112 B8
Hindaun, India 68 F7
Hindmarsh, L., Australia 95 F3
Hindsholm, Denmark 11 J4
Hindu Bagh, Pakistan 68 D2
Hindu Kush, Asia 66 B7
Hindubagh, Pakistan 66 D5
Hindupur, India 66 N10
Hines Creek, Canada 104 B5
Hinesville, U.S.A. 109 K5
Hinganghat, India 66 J11
Hingham, U.S.A. 114 B8
Hingir, India 69 J10
Hingoli, India 66 K10
Hinigaran, Phil. 61 F5
Hinis, Turkey 73 C9
Hinna = Imi, Ethiopia 81 F5
Hinna, Nigeria 83 C7
Hinnerup, Denmark 11 H4
Hinnøya, Norway 8 B16
Hinojosa del Duque, Spain 35 G5
Hinsdale, U.S.A. 111 D12
Hinterrhein →, Switz. 25 J5
Hinton, Canada 104 C5
Hinton, U.S.A. 108 G5
Hınzır Burnu, Turkey 72 D6
Hirado, Japan 55 H4
Hirakud Dam, India 67 J13
Hiran →, India 69 H8
Hirapur, India 69 G8
Hiratsuka, Japan 55 G9
Hirfanlı Barajı, Turkey 72 C5
Hiroo, Japan 54 C11
Hirosaki, Japan 54 D10
Hiroshima, Japan 55 G6
Hiroshima □, Japan 55 G6
Hirson, France 19 C11
Hirtshals, Denmark 11 G3
Hisar, India 68 E6
Hisarcık, Turkey 39 B11
Hisaria, Bulgaria 41 D8
Hisb →, Iraq 70 D5
Ḩismá, Si. Arabia 70 D3
Hispaniola, W. Indies 121 C5
Hīt, Iraq 70 C4
Hita, Japan 55 H5
Hitachi, Japan 55 F10
Hitchin, U.K. 13 F7
Hitoyoshi, Japan 55 H5
Hitra, Norway 8 E13
Hitzacker, Germany 24 B7
Hixon, Canada 104 C4
Ḩiyyon, N. →, Israel 75 E4
Hjalmar L., Canada 105 A7
Hjälmaren, Sweden 10 E9
Hjältevad, Sweden 11 G9
Hjo, Sweden 11 F8
Hjørring, Denmark 11 G3
Hjortkvarn, Sweden 11 F9
Hkakabo Razi, Burma 67 E20
Hlinsko, Czech Rep. 26 B8
Hlobane, S. Africa 89 D5
Hlohovec, Slovak Rep. 27 C10
Hlučín, Czech Rep. 27 B11
Hluhluwe, S. Africa 89 D5
Hlukhiv, Ukraine 47 G7
Hlyboka, Ukraine 47 H3
Hlybokaye, Belarus 46 E4
Hnúšt'a, Slovak Rep. 27 C12
Ho, Ghana 83 D5
Ho Chi Minh City = Thanh Pho Ho Chi Minh, Vietnam 65 G6
Ho Thuong, Vietnam 64 C5
Hoa Binh, Vietnam 58 G5
Hoa Da, Vietnam 65 G7
Hoa Hiep, Vietnam 65 G5
Hoai Nhon, Vietnam 64 E7
Hoang Lien Son, Vietnam 58 F4
Hoanib →, Namibia 88 B2
Hoare B., Canada 101 B13
Hoarusib →, Namibia 88 B2
Hobart, Australia 94 G4
Hobart, U.S.A. 113 H5
Hobbs, U.S.A. 113 J3
Hobbs Coast, Antarctica 5 D14
Hobe Sound, U.S.A. 109 M5
Hoboken, U.S.A. 111 F10
Hobro, Denmark 11 H3
Hoburgen, Sweden 11 H12
Hocalar, Turkey 39 C11
Hochfeld, Namibia 88 C2
Hochschwab, Austria 26 D8
Höchstadt, Germany 25 F6
Hockenheim, Germany 25 F4
Hodaka-Dake, Japan 55 F8
Hodgeville, Canada 105 C7
Hodgson, Canada 105 C9
Hódmezővásárhely, Hungary 42 D5
Hodna, Chott el, Algeria 78 A6
Hodonín, Czech Rep. 27 C10
Hoeamdong, N. Korea 57 C16
Hœdic, Î. de, France 18 E4
Hoek van Holland, Neths. 17 C4
Hoengsŏng, S. Korea 57 F14
Hoeryong, N. Korea 57 C15
Hoeyang, N. Korea 57 E14
Hof, Germany 25 E7
Hofgeismar, Germany 24 D5
Hofheim, Germany 25 E4
Hofmeyr, S. Africa 88 E4
Höfn, Iceland 8 D6
Hofors, Sweden 10 D10
Hofsjökull, Iceland 8 D4
Hōfu, Japan 55 G5
Hogan Group, Australia 95 F4
Höganäs, Sweden 11 H6
Hogarth, Mt., Australia 94 C2
Hoggar = Ahaggar, Algeria 78 D7
Högsäter, Sweden 11 F6
Högsby, Sweden 11 G10
Högsjö, Sweden 10 E9
Hogsty Reef, Bahamas 121 B5
Hoh →, U.S.A. 116 C2
Hohe Acht, Germany 25 E3
Hohe Tauern, Austria 26 D5
Hohe Venn, Belgium 17 D6
Hohenau, Austria 27 C9
Hohenems, Austria 26 D2
Hohenloher Ebene, Germany 25 F5
Hohenwald, U.S.A. 109 H2
Hohenwestedt, Germany 24 A5
Hoher Rhön = Rhön, Germany 24 E5
Hohhot, China 56 D6
Hóhlakas, Greece 36 D9
Hohoe, Ghana 83 D5
Hoi An, Vietnam 64 E7
Hoi Xuan, Vietnam 58 G5
Hoisington, U.S.A. 112 F5
Højer, Denmark 11 K2
Hōjō, Japan 55 H6
Hok, Sweden 11 G8
Hökensås, Sweden 11 G8
Hökerum, Sweden 11 G7
Hokianga Harbour, N.Z. 91 F4
Hokitika, N.Z. 91 K3
Hokkaidō □, Japan 54 C11
Hol-Hol, Djibouti 81 E5
Hola Pristan, Ukraine 47 J7
Holbæk, Denmark 11 J5
Holbrook, Australia 95 F4
Holbrook, U.S.A. 115 J8
Holden, U.S.A. 114 G7
Holdenville, U.S.A. 113 H6
Holdrege, U.S.A. 112 E5
Holešov, Czech Rep. 27 B10
Holguín, Cuba 120 B4
Holíč, Slovak Rep. 27 C10
Holice, Czech Rep. 26 A8
Höljes, Sweden 10 D6
Hollabrunn, Austria 26 C9
Hollams Bird I., Namibia 88 C1
Holland, Mich., U.S.A. 108 D2
Holland, N.Y., U.S.A. 110 D6
Hollandale, U.S.A. 113 J9
Hollandia = Jayapura, Indonesia 63 E10
Holley, U.S.A. 110 C6
Hollfeld, Germany 25 F7
Hollidaysburg, U.S.A. 110 F6
Hollis, U.S.A. 113 H5
Hollister, Calif., U.S.A. 116 J5
Hollister, Idaho, U.S.A. 114 E6
Höllviken = Höllviksnäs, Sweden 11 J6
Höllviksnäs, Sweden 11 J6
Holly Hill, U.S.A. 109 L5
Holly Springs, U.S.A. 113 H10
Hollywood, U.S.A. 109 N5
Holman, Canada 100 A8
Hólmavík, Iceland 8 D3
Holmen, U.S.A. 112 D9
Holmes Reefs, Australia 94 B4
Holmsjö, Sweden 11 H9
Holmsjön, Västernorrland, Sweden 10 B10
Holmsjön, Västernorrland, Sweden 10 B9
Holmsland Klit, Denmark 11 J2
Holmsund, Sweden 8 E19
Holod, Romania 42 D7
Holroyd →, Australia 94 A3
Holstebro, Denmark 11 H2
Holsworthy, U.K. 13 G3
Holton, Canada 103 B8
Holton, U.S.A. 112 F7
Holtville, U.S.A. 117 N11
Holwerd, Neths. 17 A5
Holy I., Angl., U.K. 12 D3
Holy I., Northumb., U.K. 12 B6
Holyhead, U.K. 12 D3
Holyoke, Colo., U.S.A. 112 E3
Holyoke, Mass., U.S.A. 111 D12
Holyrood, Canada 103 C9
Holzkirchen, Germany 25 H7
Holzminden, Germany 24 D5
Homa Bay, Kenya 86 C3
Homalin, Burma 67 G19
Homand, Iran 71 C8
Homathko →, Canada 104 C4
Homberg, Germany 24 D5
Hombori, Mali 83 B4
Homburg, Germany 25 F3
Home B., Canada 101 B13
Home Hill, Australia 94 B4
Homedale, U.S.A. 114 E5
Homer, Alaska, U.S.A. 100 C4
Homer, La., U.S.A. 113 J8
Homer City, U.S.A. 110 F5
Homestead, Australia 94 C4
Homestead, U.S.A. 109 N5
Homewood, U.S.A. 116 F6
Homoine, Mozam. 89 C6
Homoljske Planina, Serbia, Yug. 40 B5
Homorod, Romania 43 D10
Homs = Ḩimş, Syria 75 A5
Homyel, Belarus 47 F6
Hon Chong, Vietnam 65 G5
Hon Me, Vietnam 64 C5
Honan = Henan □, China 56 H8
Honaz, Turkey 39 D11
Honbetsu, Japan 54 C11
Honcut, U.S.A. 116 F5
Honda Bay, Phil. 61 G3
Hondarribia, Spain 32 B3
Hondeklipbaai, S. Africa 88 E2
Hondo, Japan 55 H5
Hondo, U.S.A. 113 L5
Hondo →, Belize 119 D7
Honduras ■, Cent. Amer. 120 D2
Honduras, G. de, Caribbean 120 C2
Hønefoss, Norway 9 F14
Honesdale, U.S.A. 111 E9
Honey L., U.S.A. 116 E6
Honfleur, France 18 C7
Høng, Denmark 11 J5
Hong →, Vietnam 58 F5
Hong Gai, Vietnam 58 G6
Hong He →, China 56 H8
Hong Hu, China 59 C9
Hong Kong □, China 59 F10
Hong'an, China 59 B10
Hongch'ŏn, S. Korea 57 F14
Honghai Wan, China 59 F10
Honghe, China 58 F4
Honghu, China 59 C9
Hongjiang, China 58 D7
Hongliu He →, China 56 F5
Hongor, Mongolia 56 B7
Hongsa, Laos 64 C3
Hongshui He →, China 58 F7
Hongsŏng, S. Korea 57 F14
Hongtong, China 56 F6
Honguedo, Détroit d', Canada 103 C7
Hongwon, N. Korea 57 E14
Hongya, China 58 C4
Hongyuan, China 58 A4
Hongze Hu, China 57 H10
Honiara, Solomon Is. 96 H7
Honiton, U.K. 13 G4
Honjō, Japan 54 E10
Honkorâb, Ras, Egypt 80 C4
Honningsvåg, Norway 8 A21
Hönö, Sweden 11 G5
Honolulu, U.S.A. 106 H16
Hontoria del Pinar, Spain 32 D1
Hood, Mt., U.S.A. 114 D3
Hood, Pt., Australia 93 F2
Hood River, U.S.A. 114 D3
Hoodsport, U.S.A. 116 C3
Hooge, Germany 24 A4
Hoogeveen, Neths. 17 B6
Hoogezand-Sappemeer, Neths. 17 A6
Hooghly = Hugli →, India 69 J13
Hooghly-Chinsura = Chunchura, India 69 H13
Hook Hd., Ireland 15 D5
Hook I., Australia 94 C4
Hook of Holland = Hoek van Holland, Neths. 17 C4
Hooker, U.S.A. 113 G4
Hooker Creek, Australia 92 C5
Hoonah, U.S.A. 104 B1
Hooper Bay, U.S.A. 100 B3
Hoopeston, U.S.A. 108 E2
Hoopstad, S. Africa 88 D4
Höör, Sweden 11 J7
Hoorn, Neths. 17 B5
Hoover, U.S.A. 109 J2
Hoover Dam, U.S.A. 117 K12
Hooversville, U.S.A. 110 F6
Hop Bottom, U.S.A. 111 E9
Hopa, Turkey 73 B9
Hope, Canada 104 D4
Hope, Ariz., U.S.A. 117 M13
Hope, Ark., U.S.A. 113 J8
Hope, L., S. Austral., Australia 95 D2
Hope, L., W. Austral., Australia 93 F3
Hope I., Canada 110 B4
Hope Town, Bahamas 120 A4
Hopedale, Canada 103 A7
Hopedale, U.S.A. 111 D13
Hopefield, S. Africa 88 E2
Hopei = Hebei □, China 56 E9
Hopelchén, Mexico 119 D7
Hopetoun, Vic., Australia 95 F3
Hopetoun, W. Austral., Australia 93 F3
Hopetown, S. Africa 88 D3
Hopevale, Australia 94 B4
Hopewell, U.S.A. 108 G7
Hopfgarten, Austria 26 D5
Hopkins, L., Australia 92 D4
Hopkinsville, U.S.A. 109 G2
Hopland, U.S.A. 116 G3
Hoquiam, U.S.A. 116 D3
Horasan, Turkey 73 B10
Horažďovice, Czech Rep. 26 B6
Horb, Germany 25 G4
Hörby, Sweden 11 J7
Horcajo de Santiago, Spain 32 F1
Horden Hills, Australia 92 D5
Horezu, Romania 43 E8
Horgen, Switz. 25 H4
Horgoš, Serbia, Yug. 42 D4
Hořice, Czech Rep. 26 A8
Horinger, China 56 D6
Horki, Belarus 46 E6
Horlick Mts., Antarctica 5 E15
Horlivka, Ukraine 47 H10
Hormak, Iran 71 D9
Hormoz, Iran 71 E7
Hormoz, Jazy.-ye, Iran 71 E8
Hormozgān □, Iran 71 E8
Hormuz, Kūh-e, Iran 71 E7

Hormuz, Str. of, *The Gulf* 71 E8
Horn, *Austria* 26 C8
Horn, *Iceland* 8 C2
Horn, *Sweden* 11 G9
Horn →, *Canada* 104 A5
Horn, Cape = Hornos, C. de, *Chile* 122 J4
Horn Head, *Ireland* 15 A3
Horn I., *Australia* 94 A3
Horn Mts., *Canada* 104 A5
Hornachuelos, *Spain* 35 H5
Hornavan, *Sweden* 8 C17
Hornbeck, *U.S.A.* 113 K8
Hornbrook, *U.S.A.* 114 F2
Hornburg, *Germany* 24 C6
Horncastle, *U.K.* 12 D7
Horndal, *Sweden* 10 D10
Hornell, *U.S.A.* 110 D7
Hornell L., *Canada* 104 A5
Hornepayne, *Canada* 102 C3
Horní Planá, *Czech Rep.* 26 C7
Hornings Mills, *Canada* 110 B4
Hornitos, *U.S.A.* 116 H6
Hornos, C. de, *Chile* 122 J4
Hornoy-le-Bourg, *France* 19 C8
Hornsea, *U.K.* 12 D7
Hornslandet, *Sweden* 10 C11
Hörnum, *Germany* 24 A4
Horobetsu, *Japan* 54 C10
Horodenka, *Ukraine* 47 H3
Horodnya, *Ukraine* 47 G6
Horodok, *Khmelnytskyy, Ukraine* 47 H4
Horodok, *Lviv, Ukraine* 47 H2
Horodyshche, *Ukraine* 47 H6
Horokhiv, *Ukraine* 47 G3
Horovice, *Czech Rep.* 26 B6
Horqin Youyi Qianqi, *China* 57 A12
Horqueta, *Paraguay* 126 A4
Horred, *Sweden* 11 G6
Horse Creek, *U.S.A.* 112 E3
Horse Is., *Canada* 103 B8
Horsefly L., *Canada* 104 C4
Horseheads, *U.S.A.* 110 D8
Horsens, *Denmark* 11 J3
Horsham, *Australia* 95 F3
Horsham, *U.K.* 13 F7
Horšovský Týn, *Czech Rep.* 26 B5
Horten, *Norway* 9 G14
Hortobágy →, *Hungary* 42 C6
Horton, *U.S.A.* 112 F7
Horton →, *Canada* 100 B7
Horwood L., *Canada* 102 C3
Hosaina, *Ethiopia* 81 F4
Hose, Gunung-Gunung, *Malaysia* 62 D4
Ḥoseynābād, *Khuzestān, Iran* 71 C6
Ḥoseynābād, *Kordestān, Iran* 70 C5
Hoshangabad, *India* 68 H7
Hoshiarpur, *India* 68 D6
Hospet, *India* 66 M10
Hoste, I., *Chile* 128 H3
Hostens, *France* 20 D3
Hot, *Thailand* 64 C2
Hot Creek Range, *U.S.A.* 114 G6
Hot Springs, *Ark., U.S.A.* 113 H8
Hot Springs, *S. Dak., U.S.A.* 112 D3
Hotagen, *Sweden* 8 E16
Hotan, *China* 60 C2
Hotazel, *S. Africa* 88 D3
Hotchkiss, *U.S.A.* 115 G10
Hotham, C., *Australia* 92 B5
Hoting, *Sweden* 8 D17
Hotolisht, *Albania* 40 E4
Hotte, Massif de la, *Haiti* 121 C5
Hottentotsbaai, *Namibia* 88 D1
Houat, Î. de, *France* 18 E4
Houdan, *France* 19 D8
Houei Sai, *Laos* 58 G3
Houeillès, *France* 20 D4
Houffalize, *Belgium* 17 D5
Houghton, *Mich., U.S.A.* 112 B10
Houghton, *N.Y., U.S.A.* 110 D6
Houghton L., *U.S.A.* 108 C3
Houhora Heads, *N.Z.* 91 F4
Houlton, *U.S.A.* 109 B12
Houma, *U.S.A.* 113 L9
Houndé, *Burkina Faso* 82 C4
Hourtin, *France* 20 C2
Hourtin-Carcans, Étang d', *France* 20 C2
Housatonic →, *U.S.A.* 111 E11
Houston, *Canada* 104 C3
Houston, *Mo., U.S.A.* 113 G9
Houston, *Tex., U.S.A.* 113 L7
Hout →, *S. Africa* 89 C4
Houtkraal, *S. Africa* 88 E3
Houtman Abrolhos, *Australia* 93 E1
Hovd, *Mongolia* 60 B4
Hove, *U.K.* 13 G7
Hoveyzeh, *Iran* 71 D6
Hovmantorp, *Sweden* 11 H9
Hövsgöl, *Mongolia* 56 C5
Hövsgöl Nuur, *Mongolia* 60 A5
Hovsta, *Sweden* 10 E9
Howakil, *Eritrea* 81 D5
Howar, Wadi →, *Sudan* 81 D2
Howard, *Australia* 95 D5
Howard, *Pa., U.S.A.* 110 F7
Howard, *S. Dak., U.S.A.* 112 C6
Howe, *U.S.A.* 114 E7
Howe, C., *Australia* 95 F5
Howe I., *Canada* 111 B8
Howell, *U.S.A.* 108 D4
Howick, *Canada* 111 A11
Howick, *S. Africa* 89 D5
Howick Group, *Australia* 94 A4
Howitt, L., *Australia* 95 D2
Howland I., *Pac. Oc.* 96 G10
Howrah = Haora, *India* 69 H13
Howth Hd., *Ireland* 15 C5
Höxter, *Germany* 24 D5
Hoy, *U.K.* 14 C5
Hoya, *Germany* 24 C5
Høyanger, *Norway* 9 F12
Hoyerswerda, *Germany* 24 D10
Hoylake, *U.K.* 12 D4
Hoyos, *Spain* 34 E4
Hpa-an = Pa-an, *Burma* 67 L20
Hpungan Pass, *Burma* 67 F20
Hradec Králové, *Czech Rep.* 26 A8
Hrádek, *Czech Rep.* 27 C9
Hranice, *Czech Rep.* 27 B10
Hrazdan, *Armenia* 49 K7
Hrebenka, *Ukraine* 47 G7
Hrodna, *Belarus* 46 F2
Hrodzyanka, *Belarus* 46 F5
Hron →, *Slovak Rep.* 27 D11
Hrubieszów, *Poland* 45 H10
Hrubý Jeseník, *Czech Rep.* 27 A10
Hrvatska = Croatia ■, *Europe* 29 C13
Hrymayliv, *Ukraine* 47 H4
Hsenwi, *Burma* 67 H20
Hsiamen = Xiamen, *China* 59 E12
Hsian = Xi'an, *China* 56 G5
Hsinchu, *Taiwan* 59 E13
Hsinhailien = Lianyungang, *China* 57 G10
Hsinying, *Taiwan* 59 F13
Hsopket, *Burma* 58 F2
Hsüchou = Xuzhou, *China* 57 G9
Hu Xian, *China* 56 G5
Hua Hin, *Thailand* 64 F2
Hua Xian, *Henan, China* 56 G8
Hua Xian, *Shaanxi, China* 56 G5
Hua'an, *China* 59 E11
Huab →, *Namibia* 88 B2
Huacheng, *China* 59 E10
Huachinera, *Mexico* 118 A3
Huacho, *Peru* 124 F3
Huade, *China* 56 D7
Huadian, *China* 57 C14
Huadu, *China* 59 F9
Huai He →, *China* 59 A12
Huai Yot, *Thailand* 65 J2
Huai'an, *Hebei, China* 56 D8
Huai'an, *Jiangsu, China* 57 H10
Huaibei, *China* 56 G9
Huaibin, *China* 59 A10
Huaide = Gongzhuling, *China* 57 C13
Huaidezhen, *China* 57 C13
Huaihua, *China* 58 D7
Huaiji, *China* 59 F9
Huainan, *China* 59 A11
Huaining, *China* 59 B11
Huairen, *China* 56 E7
Huairou, *China* 56 D9
Huaiyang, *China* 56 H8
Huaiyin, *China* 57 H10
Huaiyuan, *Anhui, China* 57 H9
Huaiyuan, *Guangxi Zhuangzu, China* 58 E7
Huajianzi, *China* 57 D13
Huajuapan de Leon, *Mexico* 119 D5
Hualapai Peak, *U.S.A.* 115 J7
Hualien, *Taiwan* 59 E13
Huallaga →, *Peru* 124 E3
Huambo, *Angola* 85 G3
Huan Jiang →, *China* 56 G5
Huan Xian, *China* 56 F4
Huancabamba, *Peru* 124 E3
Huancane, *Peru* 124 G5
Huancavelica, *Peru* 124 F3
Huancayo, *Peru* 124 F3
Huanchaca, *Bolivia* 124 H5
Huang Hai = Yellow Sea, *China* 57 G12
Huang He →, *China* 57 F10
Huang Xian, *China* 57 F11
Huangchuan, *China* 59 A10
Huanggang, *China* 59 B10
Huangguoshu, *China* 58 E5
Huangling, *China* 56 G5
Huanglong, *China* 56 G5
Huanglongtan, *China* 59 A8
Huangmei, *China* 59 B10
Huangpi, *China* 59 B10
Huangping, *China* 58 D6
Huangshan, *China* 59 C12
Huangshi, *China* 59 B10
Huangsongdian, *China* 57 C14
Huangyan, *China* 59 C13
Huangyangsi, *China* 59 D8
Huaning, *China* 58 E4
Huanjiang, *China* 58 E7
Huantai, *China* 57 F9
Huánuco, *Peru* 124 E3
Huaping, *China* 58 D3
Huaraz, *Peru* 124 E3
Huarmey, *Peru* 124 F3
Huarong, *China* 59 C9
Huascarán, *Peru* 122 D3
Huasco, *Chile* 126 B1
Huasco →, *Chile* 126 B1
Huasna, *U.S.A.* 117 K6
Huatabampo, *Mexico* 118 B3
Huauchinango, *Mexico* 119 C5
Huautla de Jiménez, *Mexico* 119 D5
Huaxi, *China* 58 D6
Huay Namota, *Mexico* 118 C4
Huayin, *China* 56 G6
Huayuan, *China* 58 C7
Huayun, *China* 58 B6
Huazhou, *China* 59 G8
Hubbard, *Ohio, U.S.A.* 110 E4
Hubbard, *Tex., U.S.A.* 113 K6
Hubbart Pt., *Canada* 105 B10
Hubei □, *China* 59 B9
Huch'ang, *N. Korea* 57 D14
Hucknall, *U.K.* 12 D6
Huddersfield, *U.K.* 12 D6
Hude, *Germany* 24 B4
Hudi, *Sudan* 80 D3
Hudiksvall, *Sweden* 10 C11
Hudson, *Canada* 102 B1
Hudson, *Mass., U.S.A.* 111 D13
Hudson, *N.Y., U.S.A.* 111 D11
Hudson, *Wis., U.S.A.* 112 C8
Hudson, *Wyo., U.S.A.* 114 E9
Hudson →, *U.S.A.* 111 F10
Hudson Bay, *Nunavut, Canada* 101 C11
Hudson Bay, *Sask., Canada* 105 C8
Hudson Falls, *U.S.A.* 111 C11
Hudson Mts., *Antarctica* 5 D16
Hudson Str., *Canada* 101 B13
Hudson's Hope, *Canada* 104 B4
Hue, *Vietnam* 64 D6
Huebra →, *Spain* 34 D4
Huedin, *Romania* 42 D8
Huehuetenango, *Guatemala* 120 C1
Huejúcar, *Mexico* 118 C4
Huélamo, *Spain* 32 E3
Huelgoat, *France* 18 D3
Huelma, *Spain* 35 H7
Huelva, *Spain* 35 H4
Huelva □, *Spain* 35 H4
Huelva →, *Spain* 35 H5
Huentelauquén, *Chile* 126 C1
Huércal-Overa, *Spain* 33 H3
Huerta, Sa. de la, *Argentina* 126 C2
Huertas, C. de las, *Spain* 33 G4
Huerva →, *Spain* 32 D4
Huesca, *Spain* 32 C4
Huesca □, *Spain* 32 C5
Huéscar, *Spain* 33 H2
Huetamo, *Mexico* 118 D4
Huete, *Spain* 32 E2
Hugh →, *Australia* 94 D1
Hughenden, *Australia* 94 C3
Hughes, *Australia* 93 F4
Hughesville, *U.S.A.* 111 E8
Hugli →, *India* 69 J13
Hugo, *Colo., U.S.A.* 112 F3
Hugo, *Okla., U.S.A.* 113 H7
Hugoton, *U.S.A.* 113 G4
Hui Xian = Huixian, *China* 56 G7
Hui Xian, *China* 56 H4
Hui'an, *China* 59 E12
Hui'anbu, *China* 56 F4
Huichang, *China* 59 E10
Huichapán, *Mexico* 119 C5
Huidong, *Guangdong, China* 59 F10
Huidong, *Sichuan, China* 58 D4
Huifa He →, *China* 57 C14
Huila, Nevado del, *Colombia* 124 C3
Huilai, *China* 59 F11
Huili, *China* 58 D4
Huimin, *China* 57 F9
Huinan, *China* 57 C14
Huinca Renancó, *Argentina* 126 C3
Huining, *China* 56 G3
Huinong, *China* 56 E4
Huisache, *Mexico* 118 C4
Huishui, *China* 58 D6
Huisne →, *France* 18 E7
Huiting, *China* 56 G9
Huitong, *China* 58 D7
Huixian, *China* 56 G7
Huixtla, *Mexico* 119 D6
Huize, *China* 58 D4
Huizhou, *China* 59 F10
Hukawng Valley, *Burma* 67 F20
Hukou, *China* 59 C11
Hukuntsi, *Botswana* 88 C3
Ḥulayfā', *Si. Arabia* 70 E4
Huld = Ulaanjirem, *Mongolia* 56 B3
Hulin He →, *China* 57 B12
Hull = Kingston upon Hull, *U.K.* 12 D7
Hull, *Canada* 102 C4
Hull →, *U.K.* 12 D7
Hulst, *Neths.* 17 C4
Hultsfred, *Sweden* 11 G9
Hulun Nur, *China* 60 B6
Hulyaypole, *Ukraine* 47 J9
Humahuaca, *Argentina* 126 A2
Humaitá, *Brazil* 124 E6
Humaitá, *Paraguay* 126 B4
Humansdorp, *S. Africa* 88 E3
Humara, J., *Sudan* 81 D3
Humbe, *Angola* 88 B1
Humber →, *U.K.* 12 D7
Humboldt, *Canada* 105 C7
Humboldt, *Iowa, U.S.A.* 112 D7
Humboldt, *Tenn., U.S.A.* 113 H10
Humboldt →, *U.S.A.* 114 F4
Humboldt Gletscher, *Greenland* 4 B4
Hume, *U.S.A.* 116 J8
Hume, L., *Australia* 95 F4
Humenné, *Slovak Rep.* 27 C14
Hummelsta, *Sweden* 10 E10
Humphreys, Mt., *U.S.A.* 116 H8
Humphreys Peak, *U.S.A.* 115 J8
Humpolec, *Czech Rep.* 26 B8
Humptulips, *U.S.A.* 116 C3
Hūn, *Libya* 79 C9
Hun Jiang →, *China* 57 D13
Húnaflói, *Iceland* 8 D3
Hunan □, *China* 59 D9
Hunchun, *China* 57 C16
Hundested, *Denmark* 11 J5
Hundewali, *Pakistan* 68 D5
Hundred Mile House, *Canada* 104 C4
Hunedoara, *Romania* 42 E7
Hunedoara □, *Romania* 42 E7
Hünfeld, *Germany* 24 E5
Hung Yen, *Vietnam* 58 G6
Hungary ■, *Europe* 27 D12
Hungary, Plain of, *Europe* 6 F10
Hungerford, *Australia* 95 D3
Hŭngnam, *N. Korea* 57 E14
Hungt'ou Hsü, *Taiwan* 59 G13
Huni Valley, *Ghana* 82 D4
Hunneberg, *Sweden* 11 F6
Hunnebostrand, *Sweden* 11 F5
Hunsberge, *Namibia* 88 D2
Hunsrück, *Germany* 25 F3
Hunstanton, *U.K.* 12 E8
Hunte →, *Germany* 24 B4
Hunter, *U.S.A.* 111 D10
Hunter I., *Australia* 94 G3
Hunter I., *Canada* 104 C3
Hunter Ra., *Australia* 95 E5
Hunters Road, *Zimbabwe* 87 F2
Hunterville, *N.Z.* 91 H5
Huntingburg, *U.S.A.* 108 F2
Huntingdon, *Canada* 102 C5
Huntingdon, *U.K.* 13 E7
Huntingdon, *U.S.A.* 110 F6
Huntington, *Ind., U.S.A.* 108 E3
Huntington, *Oreg., U.S.A.* 114 D5
Huntington, *Utah, U.S.A.* 114 G8
Huntington, *W. Va., U.S.A.* 108 F4
Huntington Beach, *U.S.A.* 117 M9
Huntington Station, *U.S.A.* 111 F11
Huntly, *N.Z.* 91 G5
Huntly, *U.K.* 14 D6
Huntsville, *Canada* 102 C4
Huntsville, *Ala., U.S.A.* 109 H2
Huntsville, *Tex., U.S.A.* 113 K7
Hunyani →, *Zimbabwe* 87 F3
Hunyuan, *China* 56 E7
Hunza →, *India* 69 B6
Huo Xian = Huozhou, *China* 56 F6
Huong Hoa, *Vietnam* 64 D6
Huong Khe, *Vietnam* 64 C5
Huonville, *Australia* 94 G4
Huoqiu, *China* 59 A11
Huoshan, *Anhui, China* 59 A12
Huoshan, *Anhui, China* 59 B11
Huoshao Dao = Lü-Tao, *Taiwan* 59 F13
Huozhou, *China* 56 F6
Hupeh = Hubei □, *China* 59 B9
Ḥūr, *Iran* 71 D8
Hurbanovo, *Slovak Rep.* 27 D11
Hurd, C., *Canada* 110 A3
Hure Qi, *China* 57 C11
Hurezani, *Romania* 43 F8
Hurghada, *Egypt* 80 B3
Hurley, *N. Mex., U.S.A.* 115 K9
Hurley, *Wis., U.S.A.* 112 B9
Huron, *Calif., U.S.A.* 116 J6
Huron, *Ohio, U.S.A.* 110 E2
Huron, *S. Dak., U.S.A.* 112 C5
Huron, L., *U.S.A.* 110 B2
Hurricane, *U.S.A.* 115 H7
Hurso, *Ethiopia* 81 F5
Hurunui →, *N.Z.* 91 K4
Hurup, *Denmark* 11 H2
Húsavík, *Iceland* 8 C5
Huşi, *Romania* 43 D13
Huskvarna, *Sweden* 11 G8
Hustadvika, *Norway* 8 E12
Hustontown, *U.S.A.* 110 F6
Hustopeče, *Czech Rep.* 27 C9
Husum, *Germany* 24 A5
Husum, *Sweden* 10 A13
Hutchinson, *Kans., U.S.A.* 113 F6
Hutchinson, *Minn., U.S.A.* 112 C7
Hutte Sauvage, L. de la, *Canada* 103 A7
Hüttenberg, *Austria* 26 E7
Hutton, Mt., *Australia* 95 D4
Huwun, *Ethiopia* 81 G5
Huy, *Belgium* 17 D5
Huzhou, *China* 59 B13
Hvalpsund, *Denmark* 11 H3
Hvammstangi, *Iceland* 8 D3
Hvar, *Croatia* 29 E13
Hvarski Kanal, *Croatia* 29 E13
Hvítá →, *Iceland* 8 D3
Hwachŏn-chŏsuji, *S. Korea* 57 E14
Hwang Ho = Huang He →, *China* 57 F10
Hwange, *Zimbabwe* 87 F2
Hwange Nat. Park, *Zimbabwe* 88 B4
Hyannis, *Mass., U.S.A.* 108 E10
Hyannis, *Nebr., U.S.A.* 112 E4
Hyargas Nuur, *Mongolia* 60 B4
Hybo, *Sweden* 10 C10
Hydaburg, *U.S.A.* 104 B2
Hyde Park, *U.S.A.* 111 E11
Hyden, *Australia* 93 F2
Hyder, *U.S.A.* 104 B2
Hyderabad, *India* 66 L11
Hyderabad, *Pakistan* 68 G3
Hyères, *France* 21 E10
Hyères, Îs. d', *France* 21 F10
Hyesan, *N. Korea* 57 D15
Hyland →, *Canada* 104 B3
Hyltebruk, *Sweden* 11 H7
Hymia, *India* 69 C8
Hyndman Peak, *U.S.A.* 114 E6
Hyōgo □, *Japan* 55 G7
Hyrum, *U.S.A.* 114 F8
Hysham, *U.S.A.* 114 C10
Hythe, *U.K.* 13 F9
Hyūga, *Japan* 55 H5
Hyvinge = Hyvinkää, *Finland* 9 F21
Hyvinkää, *Finland* 9 F21

I

I-n-Gall, *Niger* 83 B6
I-n-Oudad, *Algeria* 83 A5
I-n-Ouzzal, *Algeria* 83 A5
I-n-Tadreft, *Niger* 83 B6
Iablaniţa, *Romania* 42 F7
Iaco →, *Brazil* 124 E5
Iacobeni, *Romania* 43 C10
Iakora, *Madag.* 89 C8
Ialomiţa □, *Romania* 43 F12
Ialomiţa →, *Romania* 43 F12
Ialoveni, *Moldova* 43 D13
Ialpug →, *Moldova* 43 E13
Ianca, *Romania* 43 E12
Iara, *Romania* 43 D8
Iarda, *Ethiopia* 81 E4
Iargara, *Moldova* 43 D13
Iaşi, *Romania* 43 C12
Iaşi □, *Romania* 43 C12
Iasmos, *Greece* 41 E9
Ib →, *India* 69 J10
Iba, *Phil.* 61 D3
Ibadan, *Nigeria* 83 D5
Ibagué, *Colombia* 124 C3
Iballë, *Albania* 40 D4
Ibăneşti, *Botoşani, Romania* 43 B11
Ibăneşti, *Mureş, Romania* 43 D9
Ibar →, *Serbia, Yug.* 40 C4
Ibaraki □, *Japan* 55 F10
Ibarra, *Ecuador* 124 C3
Ibba, *Sudan* 81 G2
Ibba, Bahr el →, *Sudan* 81 F2
Ibbenbüren, *Germany* 24 C3
Ibembo, *Dem. Rep. of the Congo* 86 B1
Ibera, L., *Argentina* 126 B4
Iberian Peninsula, *Europe* 6 H5
Iberville, *Canada* 102 C5
Iberville, Lac d', *Canada* 102 A5
Ibi, *Nigeria* 83 D6
Ibi, *Spain* 33 G4
Ibiá, *Brazil* 125 G9
Ibiapaba, Sa. da, *Brazil* 125 D10
Ibicuí →, *Brazil* 127 B4
Ibicuy, *Argentina* 126 C4
Ibiza = Eivissa, *Spain* 37 C7
Íblei, Monti, *Italy* 31 E7
Ibo, *Mozam.* 87 E5
Ibonma, *Indonesia* 63 E8
Ibotirama, *Brazil* 125 F10
Ibrāhīm →, *Lebanon* 75 A4
'Ibrī, *Oman* 71 F8
Ibriktepe, *Turkey* 41 E10
Ibshawâi, *Egypt* 80 J7
Ibu, *Indonesia* 63 D7
Ibusuki, *Japan* 55 J5
Ica, *Peru* 124 F3
Iça →, *Brazil* 124 D5
Içana, *Brazil* 124 C5
Içana →, *Brazil* 124 C5
Içel = Mersin, *Turkey* 70 B2
Iceland ■, *Europe* 8 D4
Ich'ang = Yichang, *China* 59 B8
Ichchapuram, *India* 67 K14
Ichhawar, *India* 68 H7
Ichihara, *Japan* 55 G10
Ichikawa, *Japan* 55 G9
Ichilo →, *Bolivia* 124 G6
Ichinohe, *Japan* 54 D10
Ichinomiya, *Japan* 55 G8
Ichinoseki, *Japan* 54 E10
Ichnya, *Ukraine* 47 G7
Icod, *Canary Is.* 37 F3
Ida Grove, *U.S.A.* 112 D7
Idabel, *U.S.A.* 113 J7
Idaga Hamus, *Ethiopia* 81 E4
Idah, *Nigeria* 83 D6
Idaho □, *U.S.A.* 114 D7
Idaho City, *U.S.A.* 114 E6
Idaho Falls, *U.S.A.* 114 E7
Idanha-a-Nova, *Portugal* 34 F3
Idar-Oberstein, *Germany* 25 F3
Idfû, *Egypt* 80 C3
Ídhi Óros, *Greece* 36 D6
Ídhra, *Greece* 38 D5
Idi, *Indonesia* 62 C1
Idiofa, *Dem. Rep. of the Congo* 84 E3
Idkerberget, *Sweden* 10 D9
Idku, Bahra el, *Egypt* 80 H7
Idlib, *Syria* 70 C3
Idre, *Sweden* 10 C6
Idria, *U.S.A.* 116 J6
Idrija, *Slovenia* 29 C11
Idritsa, *Russia* 46 D5
Idutywa, *S. Africa* 89 E4
Ieper, *Belgium* 17 D2
Ierápetra, *Greece* 36 E7
Ierissós, *Greece* 40 F7
Ierissóu Kólpos, *Greece* 40 F7
Iernut, *Romania* 43 D9
Iesi, *Italy* 29 E10
Iésolo, *Italy* 29 C9
Ifach, Peñón de, *Spain* 33 G5
Ifakara, *Tanzania* 84 F7
'Ifāl, W. al →, *Si. Arabia* 70 D2
Ifanadiana, *Madag.* 89 C8
Ife, *Nigeria* 83 D5
Iférouâne, *Niger* 83 B6
Iffley, *Australia* 94 B3
Ifon, *Nigeria* 83 D6
Iforas, Adrar des, *Africa* 83 B5
Ifould, L., *Australia* 93 F5
Iganga, *Uganda* 86 B3
Igarapava, *Brazil* 125 H9
Igarka, *Russia* 50 C9
Igatimi, *Paraguay* 127 A4

Igbetti, *Nigeria* 83 D5
Igbo-Ora, *Nigeria* 83 D5
Igboho, *Nigeria* 83 D5
Igbor, *Nigeria* 83 D6
Iğdır, *Turkey* 73 C11
Igelfors, *Sweden* 11 F9
Iggesund, *Sweden* 10 C11
Iglésias, *Italy* 30 C1
Igloolik, *Canada* 101 B11
Igluligaarjuk, *Canada* 101 B10
Iglulik = Igloolik, *Canada* 101 B11
'Igma, Gebel el, *Egypt* 80 B3
Ignace, *Canada* 102 C1
İğneada, *Turkey* 41 E11
İğneada Burnu, *Turkey* 41 E12
Igoumenítsa, *Greece* 38 B2
Igra, *Russia* 48 B11
Iguaçu →, *Brazil* 127 B5
Iguaçu, Cat. del, *Brazil* 127 B5
Iguaçu Falls = Iguaçu, Cat. del, *Brazil* 127 B5
Iguala, *Mexico* 119 D5
Igualada, *Spain* 32 D6
Iguassu = Iguaçu →, *Brazil* 127 B5
Iguatu, *Brazil* 125 E11
Iharana, *Madag.* 89 A9
Ihbulag, *Mongolia* 56 C4
Iheya-Shima, *Japan* 55 L3
Ihiala, *Nigeria* 83 D6
Ihosy, *Madag.* 89 C8
Ihotry, Farihy, *Madag.* 89 C7
Ihugh, *Nigeria* 83 D6
Ii, *Finland* 8 D21
Ii-Shima, *Japan* 55 L3
Iida, *Japan* 55 G8
Iijoki →, *Finland* 8 D21
Iisalmi, *Finland* 8 E22
Iiyama, *Japan* 55 F9
Iizuka, *Japan* 55 H5
Ijebu-Igbo, *Nigeria* 83 D5
Ijebu-Ode, *Nigeria* 83 D5
IJmuiden, *Neths.* 17 B4
IJssel →, *Neths.* 17 B5
IJsselmeer, *Neths.* 17 B5
Ijuí, *Brazil* 127 B5
Ijuí →, *Brazil* 127 B4
Ikalamavony, *Madag.* 89 C8
Ikale, *Nigeria* 83 D6
Ikaluktutiak, *Canada* 100 B9
Ikang, *Nigeria* 83 E6
Ikara, *Nigeria* 83 C6
Ikare, *Nigeria* 83 D6
Ikaría, *Greece* 39 D8
Ikast, *Denmark* 11 H3
Ikeda, *Japan* 55 G6
Ikeja, *Nigeria* 83 D5
Ikela, *Dem. Rep. of the Congo* 84 E4
Ikerre-Ekiti, *Nigeria* 83 D6
Ikhtiman, *Bulgaria* 40 D7
Iki, *Japan* 55 H4
Ikimba L., *Tanzania* 86 C3
Ikire, *Nigeria* 83 D5
İkizdere, *Turkey* 73 B9
Ikom, *Nigeria* 83 D6
Ikongo, *Madag.* 89 C8
Ikopa →, *Madag.* 89 B8
Ikot Ekpene, *Nigeria* 83 D6
Ikungu, *Tanzania* 86 C3
Ikurun, *Nigeria* 83 D5
Ila, *Nigeria* 83 D5
Ilagan, *Phil.* 61 C4
Ilaka, *Madag.* 89 B8
Īlām, *Iran* 70 C5
Ilam, *Nepal* 69 F12
Ilam □, *Iran* 70 C5
Ilan, *Taiwan* 59 E13
Ilanskiy, *Russia* 51 D10
Ilaro, *Nigeria* 83 D5
Ilatane, *Niger* 83 B5
Iława, *Poland* 44 E6
Ile →, *Kazakstan* 50 E8
Île-à-la-Crosse, *Canada* 105 B7
Île-à-la-Crosse, Lac, *Canada* 105 B7
Île-de-France □, *France* 19 D9
Ileanda, *Romania* 43 C8
Ilebo, *Dem. Rep. of the Congo* 84 E4
Ilek, *Russia* 50 D6
Ilero, *Nigeria* 83 D5
Ilesha, *Kwara, Nigeria* 83 D5
Ilesha, *Oyo, Nigeria* 83 D5
Ilford, *Canada* 105 B9
Ilfracombe, *Australia* 94 C3
Ilfracombe, *U.K.* 13 F3
Ilgaz, *Turkey* 72 B5
Ilgaz Dağları, *Turkey* 72 B5
Ilgın, *Turkey* 72 C4
Ílhavo, *Portugal* 34 E2
Ilhéus, *Brazil* 125 F11
Ili = Ile →, *Kazakstan* 50 E8
Ilia, *Romania* 42 E7
Ilia □, *Greece* 38 D3
Iliamna L., *U.S.A.* 100 C4
Iliç, *Turkey* 73 C8
Ilıca, *Turkey* 39 B9
Ilichevsk, *Azerbaijan* 73 C11
Iligan, *Phil.* 61 G6
Iligan Bay, *Phil.* 61 G6
Ilíkí, L., *Greece* 38 C5
Ilin I., *Phil.* 61 E4
Iliodhrómia, *Greece* 38 B5
Ilion, *U.S.A.* 111 D9
Ilirska-Bistrica, *Slovenia* 29 C11
Ilkeston, *U.K.* 12 E6
Ilkley, *U.K.* 12 D6
Illampu = Ancohuma, Nevada, *Bolivia* 122 E4
Illana B., *Phil.* 61 H5
Illapel, *Chile* 126 C1
Ille-et-Vilaine □, *France* 18 D5
Ille-sur-Têt, *France* 20 F6
Illéla, *Niger* 83 C6
Iller →, *Germany* 25 G5
Illertissen, *Germany* 25 G6
Illescas, *Spain* 34 E7
Illetas, *Spain* 37 B9
Illichivsk, *Ukraine* 47 J6
Illiers-Combray, *France* 18 D8
Illimani, Nevado, *Bolivia* 124 G5
Illinois □, *U.S.A.* 112 E10
Illinois →, *U.S.A.* 107 C8
Illium = Troy, *Turkey* 39 B8
Illizi, *Algeria* 78 C7
Illkirch-Graffenstaden, *France* 19 D14
Íllora, *Spain* 35 H7
Ilm →, *Germany* 24 D7
Ilmajoki, *Finland* 9 E20
Ilmen, Ozero, *Russia* 46 C6
Ilmenau, *Germany* 24 E6
Ilo, *Peru* 124 G4
Ilobu, *Nigeria* 83 D5
Iloilo, *Phil.* 61 F5
Ilora, *Nigeria* 83 D5
Ilorin, *Nigeria* 83 D5
Ilovatka, *Russia* 48 E7
Ilovlya, *Russia* 49 F7
Ilovlya →, *Russia* 49 F7
Iłowa, *Poland* 45 G2
Ilubabor □, *Ethiopia* 81 F4
Ilva Mică, *Romania* 43 C9
Ilwaco, *U.S.A.* 116 D2
Ilwaki, *Indonesia* 63 F7
Ilyichevsk = Illichivsk, *Ukraine* 47 J6
Iłża, *Poland* 45 G8
Iłżanka →, *Poland* 45 G8
Imabari, *Japan* 55 G6
Imaloto →, *Madag.* 89 C8
İmamoğlu, *Turkey* 72 D6
Imandra, Ozero, *Russia* 50 C4
Imanombo, *Madag.* 89 C8
Imari, *Japan* 55 H4
Imasa, *Sudan* 80 D4
Imathía □, *Greece* 40 F6
Imatra, *Finland* 46 B5
Imbil, *Australia* 95 D5
Iménas, *Mali* 83 B5
imeni 26 Bakinskikh Komissarov = Neftçala, *Azerbaijan* 71 B6
imeni 26 Bakinskikh Komissarov, *Turkmenistan* 71 B7
Imeri, Serra, *Brazil* 124 C5
Imerimandroso, *Madag.* 89 B8
Imi, *Ethiopia* 81 F5
Imishly = İmişli, *Azerbaijan* 49 L9
İmişli, *Azerbaijan* 49 L9
Imlay, *U.S.A.* 114 F4
Imlay City, *U.S.A.* 110 D1
Immaseri, *Sudan* 81 D2
Immenstadt, *Germany* 25 H6
Immingham, *U.K.* 12 D7
Immokalee, *U.S.A.* 109 M5
Imo □, *Nigeria* 83 D6
Imo →, *Nigeria* 83 E6
Ímola, *Italy* 29 D8
Imotski, *Croatia* 29 E14
Imperatriz, *Brazil* 125 E9
Impéria, *Italy* 28 E5
Imperial, *Canada* 105 C7
Imperial, *Calif., U.S.A.* 117 N11
Imperial, *Nebr., U.S.A.* 112 E4
Imperial Beach, *U.S.A.* 117 N9
Imperial Dam, *U.S.A.* 117 N12
Imperial Reservoir, *U.S.A.* 117 N12
Imperial Valley, *U.S.A.* 117 N11
Imperieuse Reef, *Australia* 92 C2
Impfondo, *Congo* 84 D3
Imphal, *India* 67 G18
Imphy, *France* 19 F10
Imranlı, *Turkey* 73 C8
İmroz = Gökçeada, *Turkey* 41 F9
İmroz, *Turkey* 41 F9
Imst, *Austria* 26 D3
Imuris, *Mexico* 118 A2
Imuruan B., *Phil.* 63 B5
In Akhmed, *Mali* 83 B4
In Aleï, *Mali* 82 B4
In Delimane, *Mali* 83 B5
In Guezzam, *Algeria* 83 B6
In Koufi, *Mali* 83 B5
In Salah, *Algeria* 78 C6
In Tallak, *Mali* 83 B5
In Tebezas, *Mali* 83 B5
Ina, *Japan* 55 G8
Inangahua, *N.Z.* 91 J3
Inanwatan, *Indonesia* 63 E8
Iñapari, *Peru* 124 F5
Inari, *Finland* 8 B22
Inarijärvi, *Finland* 8 B22
Inawashiro-Ko, *Japan* 54 F10
Inca, *Spain* 37 B9
Inca de Oro, *Chile* 126 B2
Incaguasi, *Chile* 126 B1
Ince Burun, *Turkey* 72 A6
İncekum Burnu, *Turkey* 72 D5
İncesu, *Turkey* 70 B2
Inch'ŏn, *S. Korea* 57 F14
Incio = Cruz de Incio, *Spain* 34 C3
İncirliova, *Turkey* 39 D9
Incline Village, *U.S.A.* 114 G4
Incomáti →, *Mozam.* 89 D5
Inda Silase, *Ethiopia* 81 E4
Indal, *Sweden* 10 B11
Indalsälven →, *Sweden* 10 B11
Indaw, *Burma* 67 G20
Indbir, *Ethiopia* 81 F4
Independence, *Calif., U.S.A.* 116 J8
Independence, *Iowa, U.S.A.* 112 D9
Independence, *Kans., U.S.A.* 113 G7
Independence, *Ky., U.S.A.* 108 F3
Independence, *Mo., U.S.A.* 112 F7
Independence Fjord, *Greenland* 4 A6
Independence Mts., *U.S.A.* 114 F5
Independenţa, *Romania* 43 E12
Index, *U.S.A.* 116 C5
India ■, *Asia* 66 K11
Indian →, *U.S.A.* 109 M5
Indian Cabins, *Canada* 104 B5
Indian Harbour, *Canada* 103 B8
Indian Head, *Canada* 105 C8
Indian Lake, *U.S.A.* 111 C10
Indian Ocean 52 K11
Indian Springs, *U.S.A.* 117 J11
Indiana, *U.S.A.* 110 F5
Indiana □, *U.S.A.* 108 F3
Indianapolis, *U.S.A.* 108 F2
Indianola, *Iowa, U.S.A.* 112 E8
Indianola, *Miss., U.S.A.* 113 J9
Indigirka →, *Russia* 51 B15
Inđija, *Serbia, Yug.* 42 E5
Indio, *U.S.A.* 117 M10
Indo-China, *Asia* 52 H14
Indonesia ■, *Asia* 62 F5
Indore, *India* 68 H6
Indramayu, *Indonesia* 63 G13
Indravati →, *India* 67 K12
Indre □, *France* 19 F8
Indre →, *France* 18 E7
Indre-et-Loire □, *France* 18 E7
Indulkana, *Australia* 95 D1
Indus →, *Pakistan* 68 G2
Indus, Mouth of the, *Pakistan* 68 H3
İnebolu, *Turkey* 72 B5
İnecik, *Turkey* 41 F11
İnegöl, *Turkey* 41 F13
Ineu, *Romania* 42 D6
Infantes = Villanueva de los Infantes, *Spain* 35 G7
Infiernillo, Presa del, *Mexico* 118 D4
Infiesto, *Spain* 34 B5
Ingelstad, *Sweden* 11 H8
Ingenio, *Canary Is.* 37 G4
Ingenio Santa Ana, *Argentina* 126 B2
Ingersoll, *Canada* 102 D3
Ingham, *Australia* 94 B4
Ingleborough, *U.K.* 12 C5
Inglewood, *Queens., Australia* 95 D5
Inglewood, *Vic., Australia* 95 F3
Inglewood, *N.Z.* 91 H5
Inglewood, *U.S.A.* 117 M8
Ingólfshöfði, *Iceland* 8 E5
Ingolstadt, *Germany* 25 G7
Ingomar, *U.S.A.* 114 C10
Ingonish, *Canada* 103 C7
Ingore, *Guinea-Biss.* 82 C1
Ingraj Bazar, *India* 69 G13
Ingrid Christensen Coast, *Antarctica* 5 C6
Ingul → = Inhul →, *Ukraine* 47 J7
Ingulec = Inhulec, *Ukraine* 47 J7
Ingulets → = Inhulets →, *Ukraine* 47 J7
Inguri → = Enguri →, *Georgia* 49 J5
Ingushetia □, *Russia* 49 J7
Ingwavuma, *S. Africa* 89 D5
Inhaca, *Mozam.* 89 D5
Inhafenga, *Mozam.* 89 C5
Inhambane, *Mozam.* 89 C6
Inhambane □, *Mozam.* 89 C5
Inhaminga, *Mozam.* 87 F4
Inharrime, *Mozam.* 89 C6
Inharrime →, *Mozam.* 89 C6
Inhisar, *Turkey* 39 A12
Inhul →, *Ukraine* 47 J7
Inhulec, *Ukraine* 47 J7
Inhulets →, *Ukraine* 47 J7
Iniesta, *Spain* 33 F3
Ining = Yining, *China* 50 E9
Inírida →, *Colombia* 124 C5
Inishbofin, *Ireland* 15 C1
Inisheer, *Ireland* 15 C2
Inishfree B., *Ireland* 15 A3
Inishkea North, *Ireland* 15 B1
Inishkea South, *Ireland* 15 B1
Inishmaan, *Ireland* 15 C2
Inishmore, *Ireland* 15 C2
Inishowen Pen., *Ireland* 15 A4
Inishshark, *Ireland* 15 C1
Inishturk, *Ireland* 15 C1
Inishvickillane, *Ireland* 15 D1
Injibara, *Ethiopia* 81 E4
Injune, *Australia* 95 D4
Inklin →, *Canada* 104 B2
Inland Sea = Setonaikai, *Japan* 55 G6
Inle L., *Burma* 67 J20
Inlet, *U.S.A.* 111 C10
Inn →, *Austria* 26 C6
Innamincka, *Australia* 95 D3
Inner Hebrides, *U.K.* 14 E2
Inner Mongolia = Nei Monggol Zizhiqu □, *China* 56 D7
Inner Sound, *U.K.* 14 D3
Innerkip, *Canada* 110 C4
Innetalling I., *Canada* 102 A4
Innisfail, *Australia* 94 B4
Innisfail, *Canada* 104 C6
In'noshima, *Japan* 55 G6
Innsbruck, *Austria* 26 D4
Innviertel, *Austria* 26 C6
Inny →, *Ireland* 15 C4
Inongo, *Dem. Rep. of the Congo* 84 E3
Inönü, *Turkey* 39 B12
Inoucdjouac = Inukjuak, *Canada* 101 C12
Inowrocław, *Poland* 45 F5
Inpundong, *N. Korea* 57 D14
Inscription, C., *Australia* 93 E1
Insein, *Burma* 67 L20
Insjön, *Sweden* 10 D9
Ińsko, *Poland* 44 E2
Însurăţei, *Romania* 43 F12
Inta, *Russia* 50 C6
Intendente Alvear, *Argentina* 126 D3
Intepe, *Turkey* 39 A8
Interlaken, *Switz.* 25 J3
Interlaken, *U.S.A.* 111 D8
International Falls, *U.S.A.* 112 A8
Intiyaco, *Argentina* 126 B3
Întorsura Buzăului, *Romania* 43 E11
Inukjuak, *Canada* 101 C12
Inútil, B., *Chile* 128 G2
Inuvik, *Canada* 100 B6
Inveraray, *U.K.* 14 E3
Inverbervie, *U.K.* 14 E6
Invercargill, *N.Z.* 91 M2
Inverclyde □, *U.K.* 14 F4
Inverell, *Australia* 95 D5
Invergordon, *U.K.* 14 D4
Inverloch, *Australia* 95 F4
Invermere, *Canada* 104 C5
Inverness, *Canada* 103 C7
Inverness, *U.K.* 14 D4
Inverness, *U.S.A.* 109 L4
Inverurie, *U.K.* 14 D6
Investigator Group, *Australia* 95 E1
Investigator Str., *Australia* 95 F2
Inya, *Russia* 50 D9
Inyanga, *Zimbabwe* 87 F3
Inyangani, *Zimbabwe* 87 F3
Inyantue, *Zimbabwe* 88 B4
Inyo Mts., *U.S.A.* 116 J9
Inyokern, *U.S.A.* 117 K9
Inza, *Russia* 48 D8
Inzhavino, *Russia* 48 D6
Iō-Jima, *Japan* 55 J5
Ioánnina, *Greece* 38 B2
Ioánnina □, *Greece* 38 B2
Iola, *U.S.A.* 113 G7
Ion Corvin, *Romania* 43 F12
Iona, *U.K.* 14 E2
Ione, *U.S.A.* 116 G6
Ionia, *U.S.A.* 108 D3
Ionian Is. = Iónioi Nísoi, *Greece* 38 C2
Ionian Sea, *Medit. S.* 6 H9
Iónioi Nísoi, *Greece* 38 C2
Iónioi Nísoi □, *Greece* 38 C2
Íos, *Greece* 39 E7
Iowa □, *U.S.A.* 112 D8
Iowa →, *U.S.A.* 112 E9
Iowa City, *U.S.A.* 112 E9
Iowa Falls, *U.S.A.* 112 D8
Iowa Park, *U.S.A.* 113 J5
Ipala, *Tanzania* 86 C3
Ipameri, *Brazil* 125 G9
Ipáti, *Greece* 38 C4
Ipatinga, *Brazil* 125 G10
Ipatovo, *Russia* 49 H6
Ipel' →, *Europe* 27 D11
Ipiales, *Colombia* 124 C3
Ipin = Yibin, *China* 58 C5
Ípiros □, *Greece* 38 B2
Ipixuna, *Brazil* 124 E4
Ipoh, *Malaysia* 65 K3
Ippy, *C.A.R.* 84 C4
İpsala, *Turkey* 41 F10
Ipsário, Óros, *Greece* 41 F8
Ipswich, *Australia* 95 D5
Ipswich, *U.K.* 13 E9
Ipswich, *Mass., U.S.A.* 111 D14
Ipswich, *S. Dak., U.S.A.* 112 C5
Ipu, *Brazil* 125 D10
Iqaluit, *Canada* 101 B13
Iquique, *Chile* 124 H4
Iquitos, *Peru* 124 D4
Irabu-Jima, *Japan* 55 M2
Iracoubo, *Fr. Guiana* 125 B8
Īrafshān, *Iran* 71 E9
Irahuan, *Phil.* 61 G3
Iráklia, *Kikládhes, Greece* 39 E7
Iráklia, *Sérrai, Greece* 40 E7
Iráklion, *Greece* 36 D7
Iráklion □, *Greece* 36 D7
Irala, *Paraguay* 127 B5
Iran ■, *Asia* 71 C7
Iran, Gunung-Gunung, *Malaysia* 62 D4
Iran, Plateau of, *Asia* 52 F9
Iran Ra. = Iran, Gunung-Gunung, *Malaysia* 62 D4
Īrānshahr, *Iran* 71 E9
Irapuato, *Mexico* 118 C4
Iraq ■, *Asia* 70 C5
Irati, *Brazil* 127 B5
Irbes saurums, *Latvia* 44 A9
Irbid, *Jordan* 75 C4
Irbid □, *Jordan* 75 C5
Iregua →, *Spain* 32 C7
Ireland ■, *Europe* 15 C4
Irele, *Nigeria* 83 D6
Irgiz, Bolshaya →, *Russia* 48 D9
Irhyangdong, *N. Korea* 57 D15
Iri, *S. Korea* 57 G14
Irian Jaya □, *Indonesia* 63 E9
Irié, *Guinea* 82 D3
Iriga, *Phil.* 61 E5
Iringa, *Tanzania* 86 D4
Iringa □, *Tanzania* 86 D4
Iriomote-Jima, *Japan* 55 M1
Iriona, *Honduras* 120 C2
Iriri →, *Brazil* 125 D8
Irish Republic ■, *Europe* 15 C3
Irish Sea, *U.K.* 12 D3
Irkutsk, *Russia* 51 D11
Irlıganlı, *Turkey* 39 D11
Irma, *Canada* 105 C6
Irō-Zaki, *Japan* 55 G9
Iroise, Mer d', *France* 18 D2
Iron Baron, *Australia* 95 E2
Iron Gate = Portile de Fier, *Europe* 42 F7
Iron Knob, *Australia* 95 E2
Iron Mountain, *U.S.A.* 108 C1
Iron River, *U.S.A.* 112 B10
Irondequoit, *U.S.A.* 110 C7
Ironton, *Mo., U.S.A.* 113 G9
Ironton, *Ohio, U.S.A.* 108 F4
Ironwood, *U.S.A.* 112 B9
Iroquois, *Canada* 111 B9
Iroquois Falls, *Canada* 102 C3
Irosin, *Phil.* 61 E6
Irpin, *Ukraine* 47 G6
Irrara Cr. →, *Australia* 95 D4
Irrawaddy □, *Burma* 67 L19
Irrawaddy →, *Burma* 67 M19
Irrawaddy, Mouths of the, *Burma* 67 M19
Irricana, *Canada* 104 C6
Irsina, *Italy* 31 B9
Irtysh →, *Russia* 50 C7
Irumu, *Dem. Rep. of the Congo* 86 B2
Irún, *Spain* 32 B3
Irunea = Pamplona, *Spain* 32 C3
Irurzun, *Spain* 32 C3
Irvine, *U.K.* 14 F4
Irvine, *Calif., U.S.A.* 117 M9
Irvine, *Ky., U.S.A.* 108 G4
Irvinestown, *U.K.* 15 B4
Irving, *U.S.A.* 113 J6
Irvona, *U.S.A.* 110 F6
Irwin →, *Australia* 93 E1
Irymple, *Australia* 95 E3
Is, Jebel, *Sudan* 80 C4
Is-sur-Tille, *France* 19 E12
Isa, *Nigeria* 83 C6
Isa Khel, *Pakistan* 68 C4
Isaac →, *Australia* 94 C4
Isabel, *U.S.A.* 112 C4
Isabela, *Phil.* 61 H5
Isabela, I., *Mexico* 118 C3
Isabelia, Cord., *Nic.* 120 D2
Isabella Ra., *Australia* 92 D3
Isaccea, *Romania* 43 E13
Ísafjarðardjúp, *Iceland* 8 C2
Ísafjörður, *Iceland* 8 C2
Isagarh, *India* 68 G7
Isahaya, *Japan* 55 H5
Isaka, *Tanzania* 86 C3
Isakly, *Russia* 48 C10
Işalniţa, *Romania* 43 F8
Isan →, *India* 69 F9
Isana = Içana →, *Brazil* 124 C5
Isanlu Makutu, *Nigeria* 83 D6
Isar →, *Germany* 25 G8
Isarco →, *Italy* 29 B8
Ísari, *Greece* 38 D3
Íscar, *Spain* 34 D6
İscehisar, *Turkey* 39 C12
Íschia, *Italy* 30 B6
Isdell →, *Australia* 92 C3
Ise, *Japan* 55 G8
Ise-Wan, *Japan* 55 G8
Isefjord, *Denmark* 11 J5
Isel →, *Austria* 26 E5
Iseo, *Italy* 28 C7
Iseo, L. d', *Italy* 28 C7
Iseramagazi, *Tanzania* 86 C3
Isère □, *France* 21 C9
Isère →, *France* 21 D8
Iserlohn, *Germany* 24 D3
Isérnia, *Italy* 31 A7
Iseyin, *Nigeria* 83 D5
Isfahan = Eşfahān, *Iran* 71 C6
Ishëm, *Albania* 40 E3
Ishigaki-Shima, *Japan* 55 M2
Ishikari-Gawa →, *Japan* 54 C10
Ishikari-Sammyaku, *Japan* 54 C11
Ishikari-Wan, *Japan* 54 C10
Ishikawa □, *Japan* 55 F8
Ishim, *Russia* 50 D7
Ishim →, *Russia* 50 D8
Ishinomaki, *Japan* 54 E10
Ishioka, *Japan* 55 F10
Ishkuman, *Pakistan* 69 A5
Ishpeming, *U.S.A.* 108 B2
Isigny-sur-Mer, *France* 18 C5
Isiklar Dağı, *Turkey* 41 F11
Işıklı, *Turkey* 39 C11
Isil Kul, *Russia* 50 D8
Ísili, *Italy* 30 C2
Isiolo, *Kenya* 86 B4
Isiro, *Dem. Rep. of the Congo* 86 B2
Isisford, *Australia* 94 C3
İskenderun, *Turkey* 70 B3
İskenderun Körfezi, *Turkey* 72 D6
İskilip, *Turkey* 72 B6
Iskŭr →, *Bulgaria* 41 C8
Iskŭr, Yazovir, *Bulgaria* 40 D7
Iskut →, *Canada* 104 B2
Isla →, *U.K.* 14 E5
Isla Cristina, *Spain* 35 H3
Isla Vista, *U.S.A.* 117 L7
İslâhiye, *Turkey* 72 D7
Islam Headworks, *Pakistan* 68 E5
Islamabad, *Pakistan* 68 C5
Islamgarh, *Pakistan* 68 F4
Islamkot, *Pakistan* 68 G4
Islampur, *India* 69 G11
Island L., *Canada* 105 C10

Island Lagoon, *Australia* 95 E2
Island Pond, *U.S.A.* 111 B13
Islands, B. of, *Canada* 103 C8
Islands, B. of, *N.Z.* 91 F5
Islay, *U.K.* 14 F2
Isle →, *France* 20 D3
Isle aux Morts, *Canada* 103 C8
Isle of Wight □, *U.K.* 13 G6
Isle Royale, *U.S.A.* 112 B10
Isle Royale National Park, *U.S.A.* 112 B10
Isleton, *U.S.A.* 116 G5
Ismail = Izmayil, *Ukraine* 47 K5
Ismâ'ilîya, *Egypt* 80 H8
Ismaning, *Germany* 25 G7
Isna, *Egypt* 80 B3
Isoanala, *Madag.* 89 C8
Isogstalo, *India* 69 B8
Ísola del Liri, *Italy* 29 G10
Ísola della Scala, *Italy* 28 C7
Ísola di Capo Rizzuto, *Italy* 31 D10
Isparta, *Turkey* 39 D12
Isperikh, *Bulgaria* 41 C10
Íspica, *Italy* 31 F7
Israel ■, *Asia* 75 D3
Isratu, *Eritrea* 81 D4
Issia, *Ivory C.* 82 D3
Issoire, *France* 20 C7
Issoudun, *France* 19 F8
Issyk-Kul, Ozero = Ysyk-Köl, *Kyrgyzstan* 50 E8
Ist, *Croatia* 29 D11
Istállós-kő, *Hungary* 42 B5
İstanbul, *Turkey* 41 E12
İstanbul □, *Turkey* 41 E12
İstanbul Boğazı, *Turkey* 41 E13
Istiaía, *Greece* 38 C5
Istok, *Kosovo, Yug.* 40 D4
Istokpoga, L., *U.S.A.* 109 M5
Istra, *Croatia* 29 C10
Istres, *France* 21 E8
Istria = Istra, *Croatia* 29 C10
Itá, *Paraguay* 126 B4
Itaberaba, *Brazil* 125 F10
Itabira, *Brazil* 125 G10
Itabirito, *Brazil* 127 A7
Itabuna, *Brazil* 125 F11
Itacaunas →, *Brazil* 125 E9
Itacoatiara, *Brazil* 124 D7
Itaipú, Représa de, *Brazil* 127 B5
Itaituba, *Brazil* 125 D7
Itajaí, *Brazil* 127 B6
Itajubá, *Brazil* 127 A6
Itaka, *Tanzania* 87 D3
Italy ■, *Europe* 7 G8
Itamaraju, *Brazil* 125 G11
Itampolo, *Madag.* 89 C7
Itandrano, *Madag.* 89 C8
Itapecuru-Mirim, *Brazil* 125 D10
Itaperuna, *Brazil* 127 A7
Itapetininga, *Brazil* 127 A6
Itapeva, *Brazil* 127 A6
Itapicuru →, *Bahia, Brazil* 125 F11
Itapicuru →, *Maranhão, Brazil* 125 D10
Itapipoca, *Brazil* 125 D11
Itapuá □, *Paraguay* 127 B4
Itaquari, *Brazil* 127 A7
Itaquí, *Brazil* 126 B4
Itararé, *Brazil* 127 A6
Itarsi, *India* 68 H7
Itatí, *Argentina* 126 B4
Itbayat, *Phil.* 61 A4
Itchen →, *U.K.* 13 G6
Itéa, *Greece* 38 C4
Itezhi Tezhi, L., *Zambia* 87 F2
Ithaca = Itháki, *Greece* 38 C2
Ithaca, *U.S.A.* 111 D8
Itháki, *Greece* 38 C2
Itiquira →, *Brazil* 125 G7
Itō, *Japan* 55 G9
Itoigawa, *Japan* 55 F8
Iton →, *France* 18 C8
Itonamas →, *Bolivia* 124 F6
Itri, *Italy* 30 A6
Itsa, *Egypt* 80 J7
Íttiri, *Italy* 30 B1
Ittoqqortoormiit, *Greenland* 4 B6
Itu, *Brazil* 127 A6
Itu, *Nigeria* 83 D6
Itu Aba I., *S. China Sea* 62 B4
Ituiutaba, *Brazil* 125 G9
Itumbiara, *Brazil* 125 G9
Ituna, *Canada* 105 C8
Itunge Port, *Tanzania* 87 D3
Iturbe, *Argentina* 126 A2
Ituri →, *Dem. Rep. of the Congo* 86 B2
Iturup, Ostrov, *Russia* 51 E15
Ituxi →, *Brazil* 124 E6
Ituyuro →, *Argentina* 126 A3
Itzehoe, *Germany* 24 B5
Ivahona, *Madag.* 89 C8
Ivaí →, *Brazil* 127 A5
Ivalo, *Finland* 8 B22
Ivalojoki →, *Finland* 8 B22
Ivanava, *Belarus* 47 F3
Ivančice, *Czech Rep.* 27 B9
Ivănești, *Romania* 43 D12
Ivangorod, *Russia* 46 C5
Ivanhoe, *Australia* 95 E3
Ivanhoe, *Calif., U.S.A.* 116 J7
Ivanhoe, *Minn., U.S.A.* 112 C6
Ivanić Grad, *Croatia* 29 C13
Ivanjica, *Serbia, Yug.* 40 C4
Ivanjska, *Bos.-H.* 42 F2
Ivankoyskoye Vdkhr., *Russia* 46 D9
Ivano-Frankivsk, *Ukraine* 47 H3
Ivano-Frankovsk = Ivano-Frankivsk, *Ukraine* 47 H3
Ivanovo = Ivanava, *Belarus* 47 F3
Ivanovo, *Russia* 46 D11
Ivanšćica, *Croatia* 29 B13
Ivato, *Madag.* 89 C8
Ivatsevichy, *Belarus* 47 F3
Ivaylovgrad, *Bulgaria* 41 E10
Ivinheima →, *Brazil* 127 A5
Ivinhema, *Brazil* 127 A5
Ivohibe, *Madag.* 89 C8
Ivory Coast, *W. Afr.* 82 E4
Ivory Coast ■, *Africa* 82 D4
Ivösjön, *Sweden* 11 H8
Ivrea, *Italy* 28 C4
Ivrindi, *Turkey* 39 B9
Ivujivik, *Canada* 101 B12
Ivybridge, *U.K.* 13 G4
Iwaizumi, *Japan* 54 E10
Iwaki, *Japan* 55 F10
Iwakuni, *Japan* 55 G6
Iwamizawa, *Japan* 54 C10
Iwanai, *Japan* 54 C10
Iwata, *Japan* 55 G8
Iwate □, *Japan* 54 E10
Iwate-San, *Japan* 54 E10
Iwo, *Nigeria* 83 D5
Iwonicz-Zdrój, *Poland* 45 J8
Ixiamas, *Bolivia* 124 F5
Ixopo, *S. Africa* 89 E5
Ixtepec, *Mexico* 119 D5
Ixtlán del Río, *Mexico* 118 C4
Iyal Bakhit, *Sudan* 81 E2
Iyo, *Japan* 55 H6
Izabal, L. de, *Guatemala* 120 C2
Izamal, *Mexico* 119 C7
Izberbash, *Russia* 49 J8
Izbica, *Poland* 45 H10
Izbica Kujawska, *Poland* 45 F5
Izbiceni, *Romania* 43 G9
Izena-Shima, *Japan* 55 L3
Izgrev, *Bulgaria* 41 C10
Izhevsk, *Russia* 50 D6
Izmayil, *Ukraine* 47 K5
İzmir, *Turkey* 39 C9
İzmir □, *Turkey* 39 C9
İzmir Körfezi, *Turkey* 39 C8
İzmit = Kocaeli, *Turkey* 41 F13
Iznájar, *Spain* 35 H6
Iznalloz, *Spain* 35 H7
İznik, *Turkey* 72 B3
İznik Gölü, *Turkey* 41 F13
Izobil'nyy, *Russia* 49 H5
Izola, *Slovenia* 29 C10
Izra, *Syria* 75 C5
Iztochni Rodopi, *Bulgaria* 41 E9
Izu-Shotō, *Japan* 55 G10
Izúcar de Matamoros, *Mexico* 119 D5
Izumi-Sano, *Japan* 55 G7
Izumo, *Japan* 55 G6
Izyaslav, *Ukraine* 47 G4
Izyum, *Ukraine* 47 H9

J

Jaba, *Ethiopia* 81 F4
Jabal at Tā'ir, *Red Sea* 81 D5
Jabalón →, *Spain* 35 G6
Jabalpur, *India* 69 H8
Jabbūl, *Syria* 70 B3
Jabiru, *Australia* 92 B5
Jablah, *Syria* 70 C3
Jablanac, *Croatia* 29 D11
Jablanica, *Bos.-H.* 42 G2
Jablonec nad Nisou, *Czech Rep.* 26 A8
Jablonica, *Slovak Rep.* 27 C10
Jabłonowo Pomorskie, *Poland* 44 E6
Jablunkov, *Czech Rep.* 27 B11
Jaboatão, *Brazil* 125 E11
Jaboticabal, *Brazil* 127 A6
Jabukovac, *Serbia, Yug.* 40 B6
Jaca, *Spain* 32 C4
Jacareí, *Brazil* 127 A6
Jacarèzinho, *Brazil* 127 A6
Jackman, *U.S.A.* 109 C10
Jacksboro, *U.S.A.* 113 J5
Jackson, *Ala., U.S.A.* 109 K2
Jackson, *Calif., U.S.A.* 116 G6
Jackson, *Ky., U.S.A.* 108 G4
Jackson, *Mich., U.S.A.* 108 D3
Jackson, *Minn., U.S.A.* 112 D7
Jackson, *Miss., U.S.A.* 113 J9
Jackson, *Mo., U.S.A.* 113 G10
Jackson, *N.H., U.S.A.* 111 B13
Jackson, *Ohio, U.S.A.* 108 F4
Jackson, *Tenn., U.S.A.* 109 H1
Jackson, *Wyo., U.S.A.* 114 E8
Jackson B., *N.Z.* 91 K2
Jackson L., *U.S.A.* 114 E8
Jacksons, *N.Z.* 91 K3
Jackson's Arm, *Canada* 103 C8
Jacksonville, *Ala., U.S.A.* 109 J3
Jacksonville, *Ark., U.S.A.* 113 H8
Jacksonville, *Calif., U.S.A.* 116 H6
Jacksonville, *Fla., U.S.A.* 109 K5
Jacksonville, *Ill., U.S.A.* 112 F9
Jacksonville, *N.C., U.S.A.* 109 H7
Jacksonville, *Tex., U.S.A.* 113 K7
Jacksonville Beach, *U.S.A.* 109 K5
Jacmel, *Haiti* 121 C5
Jacob Lake, *U.S.A.* 115 H7
Jacobabad, *Pakistan* 68 E3
Jacobina, *Brazil* 125 F10
Jacques Cartier, Dét. de, *Canada* 103 C7
Jacques Cartier, Mt., *Canada* 103 C6
Jacques Cartier, Parc Prov., *Canada* 103 C5
Jacqueville, *Ivory C.* 82 D4
Jacuí →, *Brazil* 127 C5
Jacumba, *U.S.A.* 117 N10
Jacundá →, *Brazil* 125 D8
Jade, *Germany* 24 B4
Jadebusen, *Germany* 24 B4
Jadotville = Likasi, *Dem. Rep. of the Congo* 87 E2
Jadovnik, *Serbia, Yug.* 40 C3
Jadraque, *Spain* 32 E2
Jaén, *Peru* 124 E3
Jaén, *Spain* 35 H7
Jaén □, *Spain* 35 H7
Jafarabad, *India* 68 J4
Jaffa = Tel Aviv-Yafo, *Israel* 75 C3
Jaffa, C., *Australia* 95 F2
Jaffna, *Sri Lanka* 66 Q12
Jaffrey, *U.S.A.* 111 D12
Jagadhri, *India* 68 D7
Jagadishpur, *India* 69 G11
Jagdalpur, *India* 67 K13
Jagersfontein, *S. Africa* 88 D4
Jaghīn →, *Iran* 71 E8
Jagodina, *Serbia, Yug.* 40 B5
Jagraon, *India* 66 D9
Jagst →, *Germany* 25 F5
Jagtial, *India* 66 K11
Jaguariaíva, *Brazil* 127 A6
Jaguaribe →, *Brazil* 125 D11
Jagüey Grande, *Cuba* 120 B3
Jahanabad, *India* 69 G11
Jahazpur, *India* 68 G6
Jahrom, *Iran* 71 D7
Jaijon, *India* 68 D7
Jailolo, *Indonesia* 63 D7
Jailolo, Selat, *Indonesia* 63 D7
Jaipur, *India* 68 F6
Jais, *India* 69 F9
Jaisalmer, *India* 68 F4
Jaisinghnagar, *India* 69 H8
Jaitaran, *India* 68 F5
Jaithari, *India* 69 H8
Jājarm, *Iran* 71 B8
Jajce, *Bos.-H.* 42 F2
Jakam →, *India* 68 H6
Jakarta, *Indonesia* 62 F3
Jakhal, *India* 68 E6
Jakhau, *India* 68 H3
Jakobstad = Pietarsaari, *Finland* 8 E20
Jakupica, *Macedonia* 40 E5
Jal, *U.S.A.* 113 J3
Jalālābād, *Afghan.* 68 B4
Jalalabad, *India* 69 F8
Jalalpur Jattan, *Pakistan* 68 C6
Jalama, *U.S.A.* 117 L6
Jalapa, *Guatemala* 120 D2
Jalapa Enríquez, *Mexico* 119 D5
Jalasjärvi, *Finland* 9 E20
Jalaun, *India* 69 F8
Jaldhaka →, *Bangla.* 69 F13
Jalesar, *India* 68 F8
Jaleswar, *Nepal* 69 F11
Jalgaon, *India* 66 J9
Jalībah, *Iraq* 70 D5
Jalingo, *Nigeria* 83 D7
Jalisco □, *Mexico* 118 D4
Jalkot, *Pakistan* 69 B5
Jallas →, *Spain* 34 C1
Jalna, *India* 66 K9
Jalón →, *Spain* 32 D3
Jalor, *India* 68 G5
Jalpa, *Mexico* 118 C4
Jalpaiguri, *India* 67 F16
Jaluit I., *Marshall Is.* 96 G8
Jalūlā, *Iraq* 70 C5
Jamaari, *Nigeria* 83 C6
Jamaica ■, *W. Indies* 120 C4
Jamalpur, *Bangla.* 67 G16
Jamalpur, *India* 69 G12
Jamalpurganj, *India* 69 H13
Jamanxim →, *Brazil* 125 D7
Jambi, *Indonesia* 62 E2
Jambi □, *Indonesia* 62 E2
Jambusar, *India* 68 H5
James →, *S. Dak., U.S.A.* 112 D6
James →, *Va., U.S.A.* 108 G7
James B., *Canada* 102 B3
James Ranges, *Australia* 92 D5
James Ross I., *Antarctica* 5 C18
Jamesabad, *Pakistan* 68 G3
Jamestown, *Australia* 95 E2
Jamestown, *S. Africa* 88 E4
Jamestown, *N. Dak., U.S.A.* 112 B5
Jamestown, *N.Y., U.S.A.* 110 D5
Jamestown, *Pa., U.S.A.* 110 E4
Jamīlābād, *Iran* 71 C6
Jamiltepec, *Mexico* 119 D5
Jamira →, *India* 69 J13
Jämjö, *Sweden* 11 H9
Jamkhandi, *India* 66 L9
Jammerbugt, *Denmark* 11 G3
Jammu, *India* 68 C6
Jammu & Kashmir □, *India* 69 B7
Jamnagar, *India* 68 H4
Jamni →, *India* 69 G8
Jampur, *Pakistan* 68 E4
Jamrud, *Pakistan* 68 C4
Jämsä, *Finland* 9 F21
Jamshedpur, *India* 69 H12
Jamtara, *India* 69 H12
Jämtland, *Sweden* 8 E15
Jämtlands län □, *Sweden* 10 B7
Jan L., *Canada* 105 C8
Jan Mayen, *Arctic* 4 B7
Janakkala, *Finland* 9 F21
Janaúba, *Brazil* 125 G10
Jand, *Pakistan* 68 C5
Jandaq, *Iran* 71 C7
Jandia, *Canary Is.* 37 F5
Jandia, Pta. de, *Canary Is.* 37 F5
Jandola, *Pakistan* 68 C4
Jandowae, *Australia* 95 D5
Jándula →, *Spain* 35 G6
Janesville, *U.S.A.* 112 D10
Janga, *Ghana* 83 C4
Jangamo, *Mozam.* 89 C6
Janghai, *India* 69 G10
Janikowo, *Poland* 45 F5
Janīn, *West Bank* 75 C4
Janinà = Ioánnina □, *Greece* 38 B2
Janja, *Bos.-H.* 42 F4
Janjevo, *Kosovo, Yug.* 40 D5
Janjgir, *India* 69 J10
Janjina, *Croatia* 29 F14
Janjina, *Madag.* 89 C8
Janos, *Mexico* 118 A3
Jánoshalma, *Hungary* 42 D4
Jánosháza, *Hungary* 42 C2
Jánossomorja, *Hungary* 42 C2
Janów, *Poland* 45 H6
Janów Lubelski, *Poland* 45 H9
Janów Podlaski, *Poland* 45 F10
Janowiec Wielkopolski, *Poland* 45 F4
Januária, *Brazil* 125 G10
Janub Dârfûr □, *Sudan* 81 E2
Janub Kordofân □, *Sudan* 81 E3
Janûb Sînî □, *Egypt* 75 F2
Janubio, *Canary Is.* 37 F6
Janville, *France* 19 D8
Janzé, *France* 18 E5
Jaora, *India* 68 H6
Japan ■, *Asia* 55 G8
Japan, Sea of, *Asia* 54 E7
Japan Trench, *Pac. Oc.* 52 F18
Japen = Yapen, *Indonesia* 63 E9
Japla, *India* 69 G11
Japurá →, *Brazil* 122 D4
Jaquarão, *Brazil* 127 C5
Jaqué, *Panama* 120 E4
Jarābulus, *Syria* 70 B3
Jaraicejo, *Spain* 35 F5
Jaraíz de la Vera, *Spain* 34 E5
Jarama →, *Spain* 34 E7
Jaramānah, *Syria* 72 F7
Jarandilla, *Spain* 34 E5
Jaranwala, *Pakistan* 68 D5
Jarash, *Jordan* 75 C4
Järbo, *Sweden* 10 D10
Jardim, *Brazil* 126 A4
Jardín →, *Spain* 33 G2
Jardines de la Reina, Arch. de los, *Cuba* 120 B4
Jargalang, *China* 57 C12
Jargalant = Hovd, *Mongolia* 60 B4
Jari →, *Brazil* 125 D8
Jarīr, W. al →, *Si. Arabia* 70 E4
Järlåsa, *Sweden* 10 E11
Jarmen, *Germany* 24 B9
Järna, *Dalarnas, Sweden* 10 D8
Järna, *Stockholm, Sweden* 10 E11
Jarnac, *France* 20 C3
Jarny, *France* 19 C12
Jarocin, *Poland* 45 G4
Jaroměř, *Czech Rep.* 26 A8
Jarosław, *Poland* 45 H9
Järpås, *Sweden* 11 F6
Järpen, *Sweden* 10 A7
Jarrahdale, *Australia* 93 F2
Jarrahi →, *Iran* 71 D6
Jarres, Plaine des, *Laos* 64 C4
Jarso, *Ethiopia* 81 F4
Jartai, *China* 56 E3
Jarud Qi, *China* 57 B11
Järvenpää, *Finland* 9 F21
Jarvis, *Canada* 110 D4
Jarvis I., *Pac. Oc.* 97 H12
Jarvorník, *Czech Rep.* 27 A10
Järvsö, *Sweden* 10 C10
Jarwa, *India* 69 F10
Jaša Tomić, *Serbia, Yug.* 42 E5
Jasdan, *India* 68 H4
Jashpurnagar, *India* 69 H11
Jasidih, *India* 69 G12
Jasień, *Poland* 45 G2
Jāsimīyah, *Iraq* 70 C5
Jasin, *Malaysia* 65 L4
Jāsk, *Iran* 71 E8
Jasło, *Poland* 45 J8
Jasmund, *Germany* 24 A9
Jaso, *India* 69 G9
Jasper, *Alta., Canada* 104 C5
Jasper, *Ont., Canada* 111 B9
Jasper, *Ala., U.S.A.* 109 J2
Jasper, *Fla., U.S.A.* 109 K4
Jasper, *Ind., U.S.A.* 108 F2
Jasper, *Tex., U.S.A.* 113 K8
Jasper Nat. Park, *Canada* 104 C5
Jasrasar, *India* 68 F5
Jastarnia, *Poland* 44 D5
Jastrebarsko, *Croatia* 29 C12
Jastrowie, *Poland* 44 E3
Jastrzębie Zdrój, *Poland* 45 J5
Jász-Nagykun-Szolnok □, *Hungary* 42 C5
Jászapáti, *Hungary* 42 C5
Jászárokszállás, *Hungary* 42 C4
Jászberény, *Hungary* 42 C4
Jászkisér, *Hungary* 42 C5
Jászladány, *Hungary* 42 C5
Jataí, *Brazil* 125 G8
Jati, *Pakistan* 68 G3
Jatibarang, *Indonesia* 63 G13
Jatinegara, *Indonesia* 63 G12
Játiva = Xátiva, *Spain* 33 G4
Jättendal, *Sweden* 10 C11
Jaú, *Brazil* 127 A6
Jauja, *Peru* 124 F3
Jaunpur, *India* 69 G10
Java = Jawa, *Indonesia* 62 F3
Java Barat □, *Indonesia* 63 G12
Java Sea, *Indonesia* 62 E3
Java Tengah □, *Indonesia* 63 G14
Java Timur □, *Indonesia* 63 G15
Java Trench, *Ind. Oc.* 62 F3
Javalambre, Sa. de, *Spain* 32 E4
Jávea, *Spain* 33 G5
Javhlant = Ulyasutay, *Mongolia* 60 B4
Jawa, *Indonesia* 62 F3
Jawad, *India* 68 G6
Jawor, *Poland* 45 G3
Jaworzno, *Poland* 45 H6
Jaworzyna Śląska, *Poland* 45 H3
Jay Peak, *U.S.A.* 111 B12
Jaya, Puncak, *Indonesia* 63 E9
Jayanti, *India* 67 F16
Jayapura, *Indonesia* 63 E10
Jayawijaya, Pegunungan, *Indonesia* 63 E9
Jaynagar, *India* 67 F15
Jayrūd, *Syria* 70 C3
Jayton, *U.S.A.* 113 J4
Jāz Mūrīān, Hāmūn-e, *Iran* 71 E8
Jazīreh-ye Shīf, *Iran* 71 D6
Jazminal, *Mexico* 118 C4
Jazzīn, *Lebanon* 75 B4
Jean, *U.S.A.* 117 K11
Jean Marie River, *Canada* 104 A4
Jean Rabel, *Haiti* 121 C5
Jeanerette, *U.S.A.* 113 L9
Jeanette, Ostrov = Zhannetty, Ostrov, *Russia* 51 B16
Jeannette, *U.S.A.* 110 F5
Jebāl Bārez, Kūh-e, *Iran* 71 D8
Jebba, *Nigeria* 83 D5
Jebel, Bahr el →, *Sudan* 81 F3
Jebel Dud, *Sudan* 81 E3
Jebel Qerri, *Sudan* 81 D3
Jedburgh, *U.K.* 14 F6
Jedda = Jiddah, *Si. Arabia* 74 C2
Jeddore L., *Canada* 103 C8
Jedlicze, *Poland* 45 J8
Jędrzejów, *Poland* 45 H7
Jedwabne, *Poland* 45 E9
Jeetzel →, *Germany* 24 B7
Jefferson, *Iowa, U.S.A.* 112 D7
Jefferson, *Ohio, U.S.A.* 110 E4
Jefferson, *Tex., U.S.A.* 113 J7
Jefferson, Mt., *Nev., U.S.A.* 114 G5
Jefferson, Mt., *Oreg., U.S.A.* 114 D3
Jefferson City, *Mo., U.S.A.* 112 F8
Jefferson City, *Tenn., U.S.A.* 109 G4
Jeffersontown, *U.S.A.* 108 F3
Jeffersonville, *U.S.A.* 108 F3
Jeffrey City, *U.S.A.* 114 E10
Jega, *Nigeria* 83 C5
Jēkabpils, *Latvia* 9 H21
Jekyll I., *U.S.A.* 109 K5
Jelcz-Laskowice, *Poland* 45 G4
Jelenia Góra, *Poland* 45 H2
Jelgava, *Latvia* 9 H20
Jelgava □, *Latvia* 44 B10
Jelica, *Serbia, Yug.* 40 C4
Jelli, *Sudan* 81 F3
Jelšava, *Slovak Rep.* 27 C13
Jemaja, *Indonesia* 65 L5
Jemaluang, *Malaysia* 65 L4
Jember, *Indonesia* 63 H15
Jembongan, *Malaysia* 62 C5
Jena, *Germany* 24 E7
Jena, *U.S.A.* 113 K8
Jenbach, *Austria* 26 D4
Jenkins, *U.S.A.* 108 G4
Jenner, *U.S.A.* 116 G3
Jennings, *U.S.A.* 113 K8
Jepara, *Indonesia* 63 G14
Jeparit, *Australia* 95 F3
Jequié, *Brazil* 125 F10
Jequitinhonha, *Brazil* 125 G10
Jequitinhonha →, *Brazil* 125 G11
Jerantut, *Malaysia* 65 L4
Jérémie, *Haiti* 121 C5
Jerez, Punta, *Mexico* 119 C5
Jerez de García Salinas, *Mexico* 118 C4
Jerez de la Frontera, *Spain* 35 J4
Jerez de los Caballeros, *Spain* 35 G4
Jericho = El Arīḥā, *West Bank* 75 D4
Jericho, *Australia* 94 C4
Jerichow, *Germany* 24 C8
Jerid, Chott = Djerid, Chott, *Tunisia* 78 B7
Jerilderie, *Australia* 95 F4
Jermyn, *U.S.A.* 111 E9
Jerome, *U.S.A.* 114 E6
Jerramungup, *Australia* 93 F2
Jersey, *U.K.* 13 H5
Jersey City, *U.S.A.* 111 F10
Jersey Shore, *U.S.A.* 110 E7
Jerseyville, *U.S.A.* 112 F9
Jerusalem, *Israel* 75 D4
Jervis B., *Australia* 95 F5
Jervis Inlet, *Canada* 104 C4
Jerzu, *Italy* 30 C2
Jesenice, *Slovenia* 29 B11
Jeseník, *Czech Rep.* 27 A10
Jesenké, *Slovak Rep.* 27 C13
Jesi = Iesi, *Italy* 29 E10
Jesselton = Kota Kinabalu, *Malaysia* 62 C5
Jessnitz, *Germany* 24 D8

Jessore, *Bangla.* 67 H16
Jesup, *U.S.A.* 109 K5
Jesús Carranza, *Mexico* 119 D5
Jesús María, *Argentina* 126 C3
Jetmore, *U.S.A.* 113 F5
Jetpur, *India* 68 J4
Jeumont, *France* 19 B11
Jevnaker, *Norway* 9 F14
Jewett, *U.S.A.* 110 F3
Jewett City, *U.S.A.* 111 E13
Jeyḩūnābād, *Iran* 71 C6
Jeypore, *India* 67 K13
Jeziorak, Jezioro, *Poland* 44 E6
Jeziorany, *Poland* 44 E7
Jeziorka →, *Poland* 45 F8
Jha Jha, *India* 69 G12
Jhaarkand = Jharkhand □, *India* 69 H11
Jhabua, *India* 68 H6
Jhajjar, *India* 68 E7
Jhal, *Pakistan* 68 E2
Jhal Jhao, *Pakistan* 66 F4
Jhalawar, *India* 68 G7
Jhalida, *India* 69 H11
Jhalrapatan, *India* 68 G7
Jhang Maghiana, *Pakistan* 68 D5
Jhansi, *India* 69 G8
Jhargram, *India* 69 H12
Jharia, *India* 69 H12
Jharkhand □, *India* 69 H11
Jharsuguda, *India* 67 J14
Jhelum, *Pakistan* 68 C5
Jhelum →, *Pakistan* 68 D5
Jhilmilli, *India* 69 H10
Jhudo, *Pakistan* 68 G3
Jhunjhunu, *India* 68 E6
Ji-Paraná, *Brazil* 124 F6
Ji Xian, *Hebei, China* 56 F8
Ji Xian, *Henan, China* 56 G8
Ji Xian, *Shanxi, China* 56 F6
Jia Xian, *Henan, China* 56 H7
Jia Xian, *Shaanxi, China* 56 E6
Jiading, *China* 59 B13
Jiahe, *China* 59 E9
Jialing Jiang →, *China* 58 C6
Jiamusi, *China* 60 B8
Ji'an, *Jiangxi, China* 59 D10
Ji'an, *Jilin, China* 57 D14
Jianchang, *China* 57 D11
Jianchangying, *China* 57 D10
Jianchuan, *China* 58 D2
Jiande, *China* 59 C12
Jiang'an, *China* 58 C5
Jiangbei, *China* 58 C6
Jiangcheng, *China* 58 F3
Jiangchuan, *China* 58 E4
Jiangdi, *China* 58 D4
Jiangdu, *China* 59 A12
Jiange, *China* 58 A5
Jianghua, *China* 59 E8
Jiangjin, *China* 58 C6
Jiangkou, *China* 58 D7
Jiangle, *China* 59 D11
Jiangling, *China* 59 B9
Jiangmen, *China* 59 F9
Jiangning, *China* 59 B12
Jiangshan, *China* 59 C12
Jiangsu □, *China* 57 H11
Jiangxi □, *China* 59 D11
Jiangyan, *China* 59 A13
Jiangyin, *China* 59 B13
Jiangyong, *China* 59 E8
Jiangyou, *China* 58 B5
Jianhe, *China* 58 D7
Jianli, *China* 59 C9
Jianning, *China* 59 D11
Jian'ou, *China* 59 D12
Jianshi, *China* 58 B7
Jianshui, *China* 58 F4
Jianyang, *Fujian, China* 59 D12
Jianyang, *Sichuan, China* 58 B5
Jiao Xian = Jiaozhou, *China* 57 F11
Jiaohe, *Hebei, China* 56 E9
Jiaohe, *Jilin, China* 57 C14
Jiaojiang, *China* 59 C13
Jiaoling, *China* 59 E11
Jiaozhou, *China* 57 F11
Jiaozhou Wan, *China* 57 F11
Jiaozuo, *China* 56 G7
Jiashan, *China* 59 B13
Jiawang, *China* 57 G9
Jiaxiang, *China* 56 G9
Jiaxing, *China* 59 B13
Jiayi = Chiai, *Taiwan* 59 F13
Jiayu, *China* 59 C9
Jibiya, *Nigeria* 83 C6
Jibou, *Romania* 43 C8
Jibuti = Djibouti ■, *Africa* 81 E5
Jicarón, I., *Panama* 120 E3
Jičín, *Czech Rep.* 26 A8
Jiddah, *Si. Arabia* 74 C2
Jido, *India* 67 E19
Jieshou, *China* 56 H8
Jiexiu, *China* 56 F6
Jieyang, *China* 59 F11
Jigawa □, *Nigeria* 83 C6
Jiggalong, *Australia* 92 D3
Jigni, *India* 69 G8
Jihlava, *Czech Rep.* 26 B8
Jihlava →, *Czech Rep.* 27 C9
Jihlavský □, *Czech Rep.* 26 B8
Jijiga, *Ethiopia* 74 F3
Jikamshi, *Nigeria* 83 C6
Jikau, *Sudan* 81 F3
Jilin, *China* 57 C14
Jilin □, *China* 57 C14
Jiloca →, *Spain* 32 D3
Jilong = Chilung, *Taiwan* 59 E13
Jim Thorpe, *U.S.A.* 111 F9
Jima, *Ethiopia* 81 F4
Jimbolia, *Romania* 42 E5
Jimena de la Frontera, *Spain* 35 J5
Jiménez, *Mexico* 118 B4
Jimo, *China* 57 F11
Jin Jiang →, *China* 59 C10
Jin Xian = Jinzhou, *China* 56 E8
Jin Xian, *China* 57 E11
Jinan, *China* 56 F9
Jincheng, *China* 56 G7
Jinchuan, *China* 58 B4
Jind, *India* 68 E7
Jindabyne, *Australia* 95 F4
Jindřichův Hradec, *Czech Rep.* 26 B8
Jing He →, *China* 56 G5
Jing Shan, *China* 59 B8
Jing Xian, *China* 59 B12
Jing'an, *China* 59 C10
Jingbian, *China* 56 F5
Jingchuan, *China* 56 G4
Jingde, *China* 59 B12
Jingdezhen, *China* 59 C11
Jingdong, *China* 58 E3
Jinggangshan, *China* 59 D10
Jinggu, *China* 58 F3
Jinghai, *China* 56 E9
Jinghong, *China* 58 G3
Jingjiang, *China* 59 A13
Jingle, *China* 56 E6
Jingmen, *China* 59 B9
Jingning, *China* 56 G3
Jingpo Hu, *China* 57 C15
Jingshan, *China* 59 B9
Jingtai, *China* 56 F3
Jingxi, *China* 58 F6
Jingxing, *China* 56 E8
Jingyang, *China* 56 G5
Jingyu, *China* 57 C14
Jingyuan, *China* 56 F3
Jingzhou, *China* 58 D7
Jingziguan, *China* 56 H6
Jinhua, *China* 59 C12
Jining, *Nei Monggol Zizhiqu, China* 56 D7
Jining, *Shandong, China* 56 G9
Jinja, *Uganda* 86 B3
Jinjang, *Malaysia* 65 L3
Jinji, *China* 56 F4
Jinjiang, *Fujian, China* 59 E12
Jinjiang, *Yunnan, China* 58 D3
Jinjini, *Ghana* 82 D4
Jinkou, *China* 59 B10
Jinkouhe, *China* 58 C4
Jinmen Dao, *China* 59 E12
Jinnah Barrage, *Pakistan* 66 C7
Jinning, *China* 58 E4
Jinotega, *Nic.* 120 D2
Jinotepe, *Nic.* 120 D2
Jinping, *Guizhou, China* 58 D7
Jinping, *Yunnan, China* 58 F4
Jinsha, *China* 58 D6
Jinsha Jiang →, *China* 58 C5
Jinshan, *China* 59 B13
Jinshi, *China* 59 C8
Jintan, *China* 59 B12
Jinxi, *Jiangxi, China* 59 D11
Jinxi, *Liaoning, China* 57 D11
Jinxian, *China* 59 C11
Jinxiang, *China* 56 G9
Jinyang, *China* 58 D4
Jinyun, *China* 59 C13
Jinzhai, *China* 59 B10
Jinzhou, *Hebei, China* 56 E8
Jinzhou, *Liaoning, China* 57 D11
Jiparaná →, *Brazil* 124 E6
Jipijapa, *Ecuador* 124 D2
Jiquilpan, *Mexico* 118 D4
Jishan, *China* 56 G6
Jishou, *China* 58 C7
Jishui, *China* 59 D10
Jisr ash Shughūr, *Syria* 70 C3
Jitarning, *Australia* 93 F2
Jitra, *Malaysia* 65 J3
Jiu →, *Romania* 43 G8
Jiudengkou, *China* 56 E4
Jiujiang, *Guangdong, China* 59 F9
Jiujiang, *Jiangxi, China* 59 C10
Jiuling Shan, *China* 59 C10
Jiulong, *China* 58 C3
Jiutai, *China* 57 B13
Jiuxincheng, *China* 56 E8
Jiuyuhang, *China* 59 B12
Jixi, *Anhui, China* 59 B12
Jixi, *Heilongjiang, China* 57 B16
Jiyang, *China* 57 F9
Jiyuan, *China* 56 G7
Jīzān, *Si. Arabia* 74 D3
Jize, *China* 56 F8
Jizera →, *Czech Rep.* 26 A7
Jizl, W. →, *Si. Arabia* 80 B4
Jizl, Wādī al, *Si. Arabia* 70 E3
Jizō-Zaki, *Japan* 55 G6
Jizzakh, *Uzbekistan* 50 E7
Joaçaba, *Brazil* 127 B5
Joal Fadiout, *Senegal* 82 C1
João Pessoa, *Brazil* 125 E12
Joaquín V. González, *Argentina* 126 B3
Jobat, *India* 68 H6
Jobourg, Nez de, *France* 18 C5
Jódar, *Spain* 35 H7
Jodhpur, *India* 68 F5
Jodiya, *India* 68 H4
Jōetsu, *Japan* 55 F9
Jœuf, *France* 19 C12
Jofane, *Mozam.* 89 C5
Jogbani, *India* 69 F12
Jõgeva, *Estonia* 9 G22
Jogjakarta = Yogyakarta, *Indonesia* 62 F4
Johannesburg, *S. Africa* 89 D4
Johannesburg, *U.S.A.* 117 K9
Johansfors, *Sweden* 11 H9
Johilla →, *India* 69 H9
John Day, *U.S.A.* 114 D4
John Day →, *U.S.A.* 114 D3
John D'Or Prairie, *Canada* 104 B5
John H. Kerr Reservoir, *U.S.A.* 109 G6
John o' Groats, *U.K.* 14 C5
Johnnie, *U.S.A.* 117 J10
John's Ra., *Australia* 94 C1
Johnson, *Kans., U.S.A.* 113 G4
Johnson, *Vt., U.S.A.* 111 B12
Johnson City, *N.Y., U.S.A.* 111 D9
Johnson City, *Tenn., U.S.A.* 109 G4
Johnson City, *Tex., U.S.A.* 113 K5
Johnsonburg, *U.S.A.* 110 E6
Johnsondale, *U.S.A.* 117 K8
Johnson's Crossing, *Canada* 104 A2
Johnston, L., *Australia* 93 F3
Johnston Falls = Mambilima Falls, *Zambia* 87 E2
Johnston I., *Pac. Oc.* 97 F11
Johnstone Str., *Canada* 104 C3
Johnstown, *N.Y., U.S.A.* 111 C10
Johnstown, *Ohio, U.S.A.* 110 F2
Johnstown, *Pa., U.S.A.* 110 F6
Johor Baharu, *Malaysia* 65 M4
Jõhvi, *Estonia* 9 G22
Joigny, *France* 19 E10
Joinville, *Brazil* 127 B6
Joinville, *France* 19 D12
Joinville I., *Antarctica* 5 C18
Jojutla, *Mexico* 119 D5
Jokkmokk, *Sweden* 8 C18
Jökulsá á Bru →, *Iceland* 8 D6
Jökulsá á Fjöllum →, *Iceland* 8 C5
Jolfā, *Āzarbājān-e Sharqī, Iran* 70 B5
Jolfā, *Eşfahan, Iran* 71 C6
Joliet, *U.S.A.* 108 E1
Joliette, *Canada* 102 C5
Jolo, *Phil.* 61 J4
Jolon, *U.S.A.* 116 K5
Jomalig I., *Phil.* 61 D5
Jombang, *Indonesia* 63 G15
Jomda, *China* 58 B2
Jonava, *Lithuania* 9 J21
Jones Sound, *Canada* 4 B3
Jonesboro, *Ark., U.S.A.* 113 H9
Jonesboro, *La., U.S.A.* 113 J8
Jong →, *S. Leone* 82 D2
Jonglei, *Sudan* 81 F3
Jonglei □, *Sudan* 81 F3
Joniškis, *Lithuania* 9 H20
Jönköping, *Sweden* 11 G8
Jönköpings län □, *Sweden* 11 G8
Jonquière, *Canada* 103 C5
Jonsered, *Sweden* 11 G6
Jonzac, *France* 20 C3
Joplin, *U.S.A.* 113 G7
Jora, *India* 68 F6
Jordan, *Mont., U.S.A.* 114 C10
Jordan, *N.Y., U.S.A.* 111 C8
Jordan ■, *Asia* 75 E5
Jordan →, *Asia* 75 D4
Jordan Valley, *U.S.A.* 114 E5
Jordanów, *Poland* 45 J6
Jorhat, *India* 67 F19
Jörn, *Sweden* 8 D19
Jorong, *Indonesia* 62 E4
Jørpeland, *Norway* 9 G11
Jorquera →, *Chile* 126 B2
Jos, *Nigeria* 83 D6
Jos Plateau, *Nigeria* 83 D6
Jošanička Banja, *Serbia, Yug.* 40 C4
José Batlle y Ordóñez, *Uruguay* 127 C4
Joseni, *Romania* 43 D10
Joseph, L., *Nfld., Canada* 103 B6
Joseph, L., *Ont., Canada* 110 A5
Joseph Bonaparte G., *Australia* 92 B4
Joshinath, *India* 69 D8
Joshua Tree, *U.S.A.* 117 L10
Joshua Tree National Park, *U.S.A.* 117 M10
Josselin, *France* 18 E4
Jostedalsbreen, *Norway* 9 F12
Jotunheimen, *Norway* 9 F13
Joubertberge, *Namibia* 88 B1
Joué-lès-Tours, *France* 18 E7
Jourdanton, *U.S.A.* 113 L5
Joutseno, *Finland* 46 B5
Jovellanos, *Cuba* 120 B3
Joyeuse, *France* 21 D8
Józefów, *Lubelskie, Poland* 45 H10
Józefów, *Mazowieckie, Poland* 45 F8
Ju Xian, *China* 57 F10
Juan Aldama, *Mexico* 118 C4
Juan Bautista Alberdi, *Argentina* 126 C3
Juan de Fuca Str., *Canada* 116 B3
Juan de Nova, *Ind. Oc.* 89 B7
Juan Fernández, Arch. de, *Pac. Oc.* 122 G2
Juan José Castelli, *Argentina* 126 B3
Juan L. Lacaze, *Uruguay* 126 C4
Juankoski, *Finland* 8 E23
Juárez, *Argentina* 126 D4
Juárez, *Mexico* 117 N11
Juárez, Sierra de, *Mexico* 118 A1
Juàzeiro, *Brazil* 125 E10
Juàzeiro do Norte, *Brazil* 125 E11
Juba, *Sudan* 81 G3
Jubayl, *Lebanon* 75 A4
Jubbah, *Si. Arabia* 70 D4
Jubbal, *India* 68 D7
Jubbulpore = Jabalpur, *India* 69 H8
Jübek, *Germany* 24 A5
Jubga, *Russia* 49 H4
Jubilee L., *Australia* 93 E4
Juby, C., *Morocco* 78 C3
Júcar = Xúquer →, *Spain* 33 F4
Júcaro, *Cuba* 120 B4
Juchitán, *Mexico* 119 D5
Judaea = Har Yehuda, *Israel* 75 D3
Judenburg, *Austria* 26 D7
Judith →, *U.S.A.* 114 C9
Judith, Pt., *U.S.A.* 111 E13
Judith Gap, *U.S.A.* 114 C9
Juelsminde, *Denmark* 11 J4
Jugoslavia = Yugoslavia ■, *Europe* 40 C4
Juigalpa, *Nic.* 120 D2
Juillac, *France* 20 C5
Juist, *Germany* 24 B2
Juiz de Fora, *Brazil* 127 A7
Jujuy □, *Argentina* 126 A2
Julesburg, *U.S.A.* 112 E3
Juli, *Peru* 124 G5
Julia Cr. →, *Australia* 94 C3
Julia Creek, *Australia* 94 C3
Juliaca, *Peru* 124 G4
Julian, *U.S.A.* 117 M10
Julian Alps = Julijske Alpe, *Slovenia* 29 B11
Julian L., *Canada* 102 B4
Julianatop, *Surinam* 125 C7
Julianehåb = Qaqortoq, *Greenland* 101 B6
Jülich, *Germany* 24 E2
Julijske Alpe, *Slovenia* 29 B11
Julimes, *Mexico* 118 B3
Jullundur, *India* 68 D6
Julu, *China* 56 F8
Jumbo, *Zimbabwe* 87 F3
Jumbo Pk., *U.S.A.* 117 J12
Jumentos Cays, *Bahamas* 120 B4
Jumilla, *Spain* 33 G3
Jumla, *Nepal* 69 E10
Jumna = Yamuna →, *India* 69 G9
Junagadh, *India* 68 J4
Junction, *Tex., U.S.A.* 113 K5
Junction, *Utah, U.S.A.* 115 G7
Junction B., *Australia* 94 A1
Junction City, *Kans., U.S.A.* 112 F6
Junction City, *Oreg., U.S.A.* 114 D2
Junction Pt., *Australia* 94 A1
Jundah, *Australia* 94 C3
Jundiaí, *Brazil* 127 A6
Juneau, *U.S.A.* 104 B2
Junee, *Australia* 95 E4
Jungfrau, *Switz.* 25 J3
Junggar Pendi, *China* 60 B3
Jungshahi, *Pakistan* 68 G2
Juniata →, *U.S.A.* 110 F7
Junín, *Argentina* 126 C3
Junín de los Andes, *Argentina* 128 D2
Jūniyah, *Lebanon* 75 B4
Junlian, *China* 58 C5
Juntas, *Chile* 126 B2
Juntura, *U.S.A.* 114 E4
Jur, Nahr el →, *Sudan* 81 F2
Jura = Jura, Mts. du, *Europe* 19 F13
Jura = Schwäbische Alb, *Germany* 25 G5
Jura, *U.K.* 14 F3
Jura □, *France* 19 F12
Jura □, *Switz.* 25 H3
Jūra →, *Lithuania* 44 C9
Jura, Mts. du, *Europe* 19 F13
Jura, Sd. of, *U.K.* 14 F3
Jurbarkas, *Lithuania* 9 J20
Jurien, *Australia* 93 F2
Jurilovca, *Romania* 43 F13
Jūrmala, *Latvia* 9 H20
Jurong, *China* 59 B12
Juruá →, *Brazil* 122 D4
Juruena, *Brazil* 124 F7
Juruena →, *Brazil* 124 E7
Juruti, *Brazil* 125 D7
Jussey, *France* 19 E12
Justo Daract, *Argentina* 126 C2
Jutaí →, *Brazil* 124 D5
Jüterbog, *Germany* 24 D9
Juticalpa, *Honduras* 120 D2
Jutland = Jylland, *Denmark* 11 H3
Juventud, I. de la, *Cuba* 120 B3
Juvigny-sous-Andaine, *France* 18 D6
Jūy Zar, *Iran* 70 C5
Juye, *China* 56 G9
Juzennecourt, *France* 19 D11
Jvari, *Georgia* 49 J6
Jwaneng, *Botswana* 85 J4
Jyderup, *Denmark* 11 J5
Jylland, *Denmark* 11 H3
Jyväskylä, *Finland* 9 E21

K

K2, *Pakistan* 69 B7
Ka →, *Nigeria* 83 C5
Kaap Plateau, *S. Africa* 88 D3
Kaapkruis, *Namibia* 88 C1
Kaapstad = Cape Town, *S. Africa* 88 E2
Kaba, *Guinea* 82 C2
Kabaena, *Indonesia* 63 F6
Kabala, *S. Leone* 82 D2
Kabale, *Uganda* 86 C3
Kabalo, *Dem. Rep. of the Congo* 86 D2
Kabambare, *Dem. Rep. of the Congo* 86 C2
Kabango, *Dem. Rep. of the Congo* 87 D2
Kabanjahe, *Indonesia* 62 D1
Kabankalan, *Phil.* 61 G5
Kabara, *Mali* 82 B4
Kabardinka, *Russia* 47 K10
Kabardino-Balkar Republic = Kabardino-Balkaria □, *Russia* 49 J6
Kabardino-Balkaria □, *Russia* 49 J6
Kabarega Falls = Murchison Falls, *Uganda* 86 B3
Kabasalan, *Phil.* 61 H5
Kabba, *Nigeria* 83 D6
Kabetogama, *U.S.A.* 112 A8
Kabi, *Niger* 83 C7
Kabin Buri, *Thailand* 64 F3
Kabinakagami L., *Canada* 102 C3
Kabinda, *Dem. Rep. of the Congo* 84 F4
Kabna, *Sudan* 80 D3
Kabompo, *Zambia* 87 E1
Kabompo →, *Zambia* 85 G4
Kabondo, *Dem. Rep. of the Congo* 87 D2
Kabongo, *Dem. Rep. of the Congo* 86 D2
Kabot, *Guinea* 82 C2
Kabou, *Togo* 83 D5
Kabr, *Sudan* 81 E2
Kabūd Gonbad, *Iran* 71 B8
Kabugao, *Phil.* 61 B4
Kābul, *Afghan.* 68 B3
Kābul □, *Afghan.* 66 B6
Kābul →, *Pakistan* 68 C5
Kabunga, *Dem. Rep. of the Congo* 86 C2
Kaburuang, *Indonesia* 63 D7
Kabushiya, *Sudan* 81 D3
Kabwe, *Zambia* 87 E2
Kačanik, *Kosovo, Yug.* 40 D5
Kačerginė, *Lithuania* 44 D10
Kachchh, Gulf of, *India* 68 H3
Kachchh, Rann of, *India* 68 H4
Kachchhidhana, *India* 69 J8
Kachebera, *Zambia* 87 E3
Kachia, *Nigeria* 83 D6
Kachikau, *Botswana* 88 B3
Kachin □, *Burma* 58 D1
Kachira, L., *Uganda* 86 C3
Kachiry, *Kazakstan* 50 D8
Kachisi, *Ethiopia* 81 F4
Kachnara, *India* 68 H6
Kachot, *Cambodia* 65 G4
Kaçkar, *Turkey* 73 B9
Kadan, *Czech Rep.* 26 A6
Kadan Kyun, *Burma* 64 F2
Kadanai →, *Afghan.* 68 D1
Kadarkút, *Hungary* 42 D2
Kade, *Ghana* 83 D4
Kadi, *India* 68 H5
Kadina, *Australia* 95 E2
Kadınhanı, *Turkey* 72 C5
Kadiolo, *Mali* 82 C3
Kadipur, *India* 69 F10
Kadirli, *Turkey* 70 B3
Kadiyevka = Stakhanov, *Ukraine* 47 H10
Kadodo, *Sudan* 81 E2
Kadoka, *U.S.A.* 112 D4
Kadom, *Russia* 48 C6
Kadoma, *Zimbabwe* 87 F2
Kâdugli, *Sudan* 81 E2
Kaduna, *Nigeria* 83 C6
Kaduna □, *Nigeria* 83 C6
Kaduy, *Russia* 46 C9
Kaédi, *Mauritania* 82 B2
Kaélé, *Cameroon* 83 C7
Kaeng Khoï, *Thailand* 64 E3
Kaesŏng, *N. Korea* 57 F14
Kāf, *Si. Arabia* 70 D3
Kafan = Kapan, *Armenia* 70 B5
Kafanchan, *Nigeria* 83 D6
Kafareti, *Nigeria* 83 C7
Kaffrine, *Senegal* 82 C1
Kafin, *Nigeria* 83 D6
Kafin Madaki, *Nigeria* 83 C6
Kafinda, *Zambia* 87 E3
Kafirévs, Ákra, *Greece* 38 C6
Kafr el Battikh, *Egypt* 80 H7
Kafr el Dauwâr, *Egypt* 80 H7
Kafr el Sheikh, *Egypt* 80 H7
Kafue, *Zambia* 87 F2
Kafue →, *Zambia* 85 H5
Kafue Flats, *Zambia* 87 F2
Kafue Nat. Park, *Zambia* 87 F2
Kafulwe, *Zambia* 87 D2
Kaga, *Afghan.* 68 B4
Kaga Bandoro, *C.A.R.* 84 C3
Kagan, *Uzbekistan* 50 F7
Kagarko, *Nigeria* 83 D6
Kagawa □, *Japan* 55 G7
Kagera = Ziwa Maghariba □, *Tanzania* 86 C3
Kagera →, *Uganda* 86 C3
Kağızman, *Turkey* 70 B4
Kagmar, *Sudan* 81 E3
Kagoshima, *Japan* 55 J5
Kagoshima □, *Japan* 55 J5
Kagul = Cahul, *Moldova* 43 E13
Kahak, *Iran* 71 B6
Kahama, *Tanzania* 86 C3
Kahan, *Pakistan* 68 E3
Kahang, *Malaysia* 65 L4
Kahayan →, *Indonesia* 62 E4
Kahe, *Tanzania* 86 C4
Kahnūj, *Iran* 71 E8

Kahoka, *U.S.A.* 112 E9
Kahoolawe, *U.S.A.* 106 H16
Kahramanmaraş, *Turkey* 70 B3
Kâhta, *Turkey* 73 D8
Kahuta, *Pakistan* 68 C5
Kai, Kepulauan, *Indonesia* 63 F8
Kai Besar, *Indonesia* 63 F8
Kai Is. = Kai, Kepulauan, *Indonesia* 63 F8
Kai Kecil, *Indonesia* 63 F8
Kai Xian, *China* 58 B7
Kaiama, *Nigeria* 83 D5
Kaiapoi, *N.Z.* 91 K4
Kaieteur Falls, *Guyana* 124 B7
Kaifeng, *China* 56 G8
Kaihua, *China* 59 C12
Kaijiang, *China* 58 B6
Kaikohe, *N.Z.* 91 F4
Kaikoura, *N.Z.* 91 K4
Kaikoura Ra., *N.Z.* 91 J4
Kailahun, *S. Leone* 82 D2
Kaili, *China* 58 D6
Kailu, *China* 57 C11
Kailua Kona, *U.S.A.* 106 J17
Kaimana, *Indonesia* 63 E8
Kaimanawa Mts., *N.Z.* 91 H5
Kaimganj, *India* 69 F8
Kaimur Hills, *India* 69 G10
Kainab →, *Namibia* 88 D2
Kainji Dam, *Nigeria* 83 D5
Kainji Res., *Nigeria* 83 C5
Kainuu, *Finland* 8 D23
Kaipara Harbour, *N.Z.* 91 G5
Kaiping, *China* 59 F9
Kaipokok B., *Canada* 103 B8
Kaira, *India* 68 H5
Kairana, *India* 68 E7
Kaironi, *Indonesia* 63 E8
Kairouan, *Tunisia* 79 A8
Kaiserslautern, *Germany* 25 F3
Kaiserstuhl, *Germany* 25 G3
Kaitaia, *N.Z.* 91 F4
Kaitangata, *N.Z.* 91 M2
Kaithal, *India* 68 E7
Kaitu →, *Pakistan* 68 C4
Kaiyang, *China* 58 D6
Kaiyuan, *Liaoning, China* 57 C13
Kaiyuan, *Yunnan, China* 58 F4
Kajaani, *Finland* 8 D22
Kajabbi, *Australia* 94 C3
Kajana = Kajaani, *Finland* 8 D22
Kajang, *Malaysia* 65 L3
Kajaran, *Armenia* 73 C12
Kajiado, *Kenya* 86 C4
Kajo Kaji, *Sudan* 81 G3
Kajuru, *Nigeria* 83 C6
Kaka, *Sudan* 81 E3
Kakabeka Falls, *Canada* 102 C2
Kakadu Nat. Park, *Australia* 92 B5
Kakamas, *S. Africa* 88 D3
Kakamega, *Kenya* 86 B3
Kakanj, *Bos.-H.* 42 F3
Kakanui Mts., *N.Z.* 91 L3
Kakata, *Liberia* 82 D2
Kakdwip, *India* 69 J13
Kake, *Japan* 55 G6
Kake, *U.S.A.* 104 B2
Kakegawa, *Japan* 55 G9
Kakeroma-Jima, *Japan* 55 K4
Kakhib, *Russia* 49 J8
Kakhovka, *Ukraine* 47 J7
Kakhovske Vdskh., *Ukraine* 47 J7
Kakinada, *India* 67 L13
Kakisa →, *Canada* 104 A5
Kakisa L., *Canada* 104 A5
Kakogawa, *Japan* 55 G7
Kakwa →, *Canada* 104 C5
Kāl Gūsheh, *Iran* 71 D8
Kal Safīd, *Iran* 70 C5
Kala, *Nigeria* 83 C7
Kalaallit Nunaat = Greenland ■, *N. Amer.* 4 C5
Kalabagh, *Pakistan* 68 C4
Kalabahi, *Indonesia* 63 F6
Kalabáka, *Greece* 38 B3
Kalabana, *Mali* 82 C3
Kalach, *Russia* 48 E5
Kalach na Donu, *Russia* 49 F6
Kaladan →, *Burma* 67 J18
Kaladar, *Canada* 102 D4
Kalahari, *Africa* 88 C3
Kalahari Gemsbok Nat. Park, *S. Africa* 88 D3
Kalajoki, *Finland* 8 D20
Kālak, *Iran* 71 E8
Kalakamati, *Botswana* 89 C4
Kalakan, *Russia* 51 D12
K'alak'unlun Shank'ou = Karakoram Pass, *Pakistan* 69 B7
Kalam, *Pakistan* 69 B5
Kalama, *Dem. Rep. of the Congo* 86 C2
Kalama, *U.S.A.* 116 E4
Kalámai, *Greece* 38 D4
Kalamariá, *Greece* 40 F6
Kalamata = Kalámai, *Greece* 38 D4
Kalamazoo, *U.S.A.* 108 D3
Kalamazoo →, *U.S.A.* 108 D2
Kalambo Falls, *Tanzania* 87 D3
Kálamos, *Attikí, Greece* 38 C5
Kálamos, *Iónioi Nísoi, Greece* 38 C2
Kalan, *Turkey* 70 B3
Kalankalan, *Guinea* 82 C3
Kalannie, *Australia* 93 F2
Kalāntarī, *Iran* 71 C7
Kalao, *Indonesia* 63 F6
Kalaotoa, *Indonesia* 63 F6
Kälarne, *Sweden* 10 E10
Kalasin, *Thailand* 64 D4
Kalat, *Pakistan* 66 E5
Kalāteh, *Iran* 71 B7
Kalāteh-ye Ganj, *Iran* 71 E8
Kálathos, *Greece* 39 E10
Kalaus →, *Russia* 49 H7
Kalávrita, *Greece* 38 C4
Kalbarri, *Australia* 93 E1
Kale, *Antalya, Turkey* 39 E12
Kale, *Denizli, Turkey* 39 D10
Kalecik, *Turkey* 72 B5
Kalegauk Kyun, *Burma* 67 M20
Kalehe, *Dem. Rep. of the Congo* 86 C2
Kalema, *Tanzania* 86 C3
Kalemie, *Dem. Rep. of the Congo* 86 D2
Kalety, *Poland* 45 H5
Kalewa, *Burma* 67 H19
Kaleybar, *Iran* 70 B5
Kalgan = Zhangjiakou, *China* 56 D8
Kalgoorlie-Boulder, *Australia* 93 F3
Kali →, *India* 69 F8
Kali Sindh →, *India* 68 G6
Kaliakra, Nos, *Bulgaria* 41 C12
Kalianda, *Indonesia* 62 F3
Kalibo, *Phil.* 61 F5
Kalima, *Dem. Rep. of the Congo* 86 C2
Kalimantan □, *Indonesia* 62 E4
Kalimantan Barat □, *Indonesia* 62 E4
Kalimantan Selatan □, *Indonesia* 62 E5
Kalimantan Tengah □, *Indonesia* 62 E4
Kalimantan Timur □, *Indonesia* 62 D5
Kálimnos, *Greece* 39 D8
Kalimpong, *India* 69 F13
Kalinin = Tver, *Russia* 46 D8
Kaliningrad, *Russia* 9 J19
Kalininsk, *Russia* 48 E7
Kalinkavichy, *Belarus* 47 F5
Kalinkovichi = Kalinkavichy, *Belarus* 47 F5
Kalinovik, *Bos.-H.* 40 C2
Kalipetrovo, *Bulgaria* 41 B11
Kaliro, *Uganda* 86 B3
Kalirrákhi, *Greece* 41 F8
Kalispell, *U.S.A.* 114 B6
Kalisz, *Poland* 45 G5
Kalisz Pomorski, *Poland* 45 E2
Kaliua, *Tanzania* 86 D3
Kalívia Thorikoú, *Greece* 38 D5
Kalix, *Sweden* 8 D20
Kalix →, *Sweden* 8 D20
Kalka, *India* 68 D7
Kalkan, *Turkey* 39 E11
Kalkarindji, *Australia* 92 C5
Kalkaska, *U.S.A.* 108 C3
Kalkfeld, *Namibia* 88 C2
Kalkfontein, *Botswana* 88 C3
Kalkım, *Turkey* 39 B9
Kalkrand, *Namibia* 88 C2
Kållandsö, *Sweden* 11 F7
Kallavesi, *Finland* 8 E22
Källby, *Sweden* 11 F7
Kållered, *Sweden* 11 G6
Kallimasiá, *Greece* 39 C8
Kallinge, *Sweden* 11 H9
Kallithéa, *Greece* 38 D5
Kallmet, *Albania* 40 E3
Kalloní, *Greece* 39 B8
Kallonís, Kólpos, *Greece* 39 B8
Kallsjön, *Sweden* 8 E15
Kalmalo, *Nigeria* 83 C6
Kalmar, *Sweden* 11 H10
Kalmar län □, *Sweden* 11 G10
Kalmar sund, *Sweden* 11 H10
Kalmyk Republic = Kalmykia □, *Russia* 49 G8
Kalmykia □, *Russia* 49 G8
Kalmykovo, *Kazakstan* 50 E6
Kalna, *India* 69 H13
Kalnai, *India* 69 H10
Kalocsa, *Hungary* 42 D4
Kalofer, *Bulgaria* 41 D8
Kalokhorio, *Cyprus* 36 E12
Kaloko, *Dem. Rep. of the Congo* 86 D2
Kalol, *Gujarat, India* 68 H5
Kalol, *Gujarat, India* 68 H5
Kalolímnos, *Greece* 39 D9
Kalomo, *Zambia* 87 F2
Kalonerón, *Greece* 38 D3
Kalpi, *India* 69 F8
Kaltern = Caldaro, *Italy* 29 B8
Kaltungo, *Nigeria* 83 D7
Kalu, *Pakistan* 68 G2
Kaluga, *Russia* 46 E9
Kalulushi, *Zambia* 87 E2
Kalundborg, *Denmark* 11 J5
Kalush, *Ukraine* 47 H3
Kałuszyn, *Poland* 45 F8
Kalutara, *Sri Lanka* 66 R12
Kalvarija, *Lithuania* 44 D10
Kalyazin, *Russia* 46 D9
Kam, *Albania* 40 D4
Kam →, *Nigeria* 83 D7
Kama, *Dem. Rep. of the Congo* 86 C2
Kama →, *Russia* 50 D6
Kamachumu, *Tanzania* 86 C3
Kamaishi, *Japan* 54 E10
Kamalia, *Pakistan* 68 D5
Kaman, *India* 68 F6
Kaman, *Turkey* 72 C5
Kamanjab, *Namibia* 88 B2
Kamapanda, *Zambia* 87 E1
Kamaran, *Yemen* 74 D3
Kamativi, *Zimbabwe* 88 B4
Kamba, *Nigeria* 83 C5
Kambalda, *Australia* 93 F3
Kambar, *Pakistan* 68 F3
Kambia, *S. Leone* 82 D2
Kambolé, *Togo* 83 D5
Kambolé, *Zambia* 87 D3
Kambos, *Cyprus* 36 D11
Kambove, *Dem. Rep. of the Congo* 87 E2
Kamchatka, Poluostrov, *Russia* 51 D16
Kamchatka Pen. = Kamchatka, Poluostrov, *Russia* 51 D16
Kamchiya →, *Bulgaria* 41 C11
Kamen, *Russia* 50 D9
Kamen-Rybolov, *Russia* 54 B6
Kamenica, *Serbia, Yug.* 40 C6
Kamenica, *Serbia, Yug.* 40 B3
Kamenice nad Lipou, *Czech Rep.* 26 B8
Kamenjak, Rt, *Croatia* 29 D10
Kamenka = Kaminka, *Ukraine* 47 H7
Kamenka, *Kazakstan* 48 E10
Kamenka, *Penza, Russia* 48 D6
Kamenka, *Voronezh, Russia* 47 G10
Kamenka Bugskaya = Kamyanka-Buzka, *Ukraine* 47 G3
Kamenka Dneprovskaya = Kamyanka-Dniprovska, *Ukraine* 47 J8
Kamennomostskiy, *Russia* 49 H5
Kameno, *Bulgaria* 41 D11
Kamenolomini, *Russia* 49 G5
Kamensk-Shakhtinskiy, *Russia* 49 F5
Kamensk Uralskiy, *Russia* 50 D7
Kamenskiy, *Russia* 48 E7
Kamenskoye, *Russia* 51 C17
Kamenyak, *Bulgaria* 41 C10
Kamenz, *Germany* 24 D10
Kameoka, *Japan* 55 G7
Kamiah, *U.S.A.* 114 C5
Kamień Krajeński, *Poland* 44 E4
Kamień Pomorski, *Poland* 44 E1
Kamienna →, *Poland* 45 G8
Kamienna Góra, *Poland* 45 H3
Kamieńsk, *Poland* 45 G6
Kamieskroon, *S. Africa* 88 E2
Kamilukuak, L., *Canada* 105 A8
Kamin-Kashyrskyy, *Ukraine* 47 G3
Kamina, *Dem. Rep. of the Congo* 87 D2
Kaminak L., *Canada* 105 A10
Kaministiquia, *Canada* 102 C1
Kaminka, *Ukraine* 47 H7
Kaminoyama, *Japan* 54 E10
Kamiros, *Greece* 36 C9
Kamituga, *Dem. Rep. of the Congo* 86 C2
Kamla →, *India* 69 G12
Kamloops, *Canada* 104 C4
Kamnik, *Slovenia* 29 B11
Kamo, *Armenia* 49 K7
Kamo, *Japan* 54 F9
Kamoke, *Pakistan* 68 C6
Kamp →, *Austria* 26 C8
Kampala, *Uganda* 86 B3
Kampang Chhnang, *Cambodia* 65 F5
Kampar, *Malaysia* 65 K3
Kampar →, *Indonesia* 62 D2
Kampen, *Neths.* 17 B5
Kampene, *Dem. Rep. of the Congo* 84 E5
Kamphaeng Phet, *Thailand* 64 D2
Kampolombo, L., *Zambia* 87 E2
Kampong Saom, *Cambodia* 65 G4
Kampong Saom, Chaak, *Cambodia* 65 G4
Kampong To, *Thailand* 65 J3
Kampot, *Cambodia* 65 G5
Kampti, *Burkina Faso* 82 C4
Kampuchea = Cambodia ■, *Asia* 64 F5
Kampung Air Putih, *Malaysia* 65 K4
Kampung Jerangau, *Malaysia* 65 K4
Kampung Raja, *Malaysia* 65 K4
Kampungbaru = Tolitoli, *Indonesia* 63 D6
Kamrau, Teluk, *Indonesia* 63 E8
Kamsack, *Canada* 105 C8
Kamsai, *Guinea* 82 C2
Kamskoye Ustye, *Russia* 48 C9
Kamuchawie L., *Canada* 105 B8
Kamui-Misaki, *Japan* 54 C10
Kamyanets-Podilskyy, *Ukraine* 47 H4
Kamyanka-Buzka, *Ukraine* 47 G3
Kamyanka-Dniprovska, *Ukraine* 47 J8
Kāmyārān, *Iran* 70 C5
Kamyshin, *Russia* 48 E7
Kamyzyak, *Russia* 49 G9
Kan, *Sudan* 81 F3
Kanaaupscow, *Canada* 102 B4
Kanaaupscow →, *Canada* 101 C12
Kanab, *U.S.A.* 115 H7
Kanab →, *U.S.A.* 115 H7
Kanagi, *Japan* 54 D10
Kanairiktok →, *Canada* 103 A7
Kanália, *Greece* 38 B4
Kananga, *Dem. Rep. of the Congo* 84 F4
Kanash, *Russia* 48 C8
Kanaskat, *U.S.A.* 116 C5
Kanastraíon, Ákra = Palioúrion, Ákra, *Greece* 40 G7
Kanawha →, *U.S.A.* 108 F4
Kanazawa, *Japan* 55 F8
Kanchanaburi, *Thailand* 64 E2
Kanchenjunga, *Nepal* 69 F13
Kanchipuram, *India* 66 N11
Kańczuga, *Poland* 45 J9
Kandaghat, *India* 68 D7
Kandahar = Qandahār, *Afghan.* 66 D4
Kandalaksha, *Russia* 50 C4
Kandangan, *Indonesia* 62 E5
Kandanghaur, *Indonesia* 63 G13
Kandanos, *Greece* 36 D5
Kandava, *Latvia* 44 A9
Kandavu, *Fiji* 91 D8
Kandhíla, *Greece* 38 D4
Kandhkot, *Pakistan* 68 E3
Kandhla, *India* 68 E7
Kandi, *Benin* 83 C5
Kandi, *India* 69 H13
Kandiaro, *Pakistan* 68 F3
Kandıra, *Turkey* 72 B4
Kandla, *India* 68 H4
Kandos, *Australia* 95 E4
Kandreho, *Madag.* 89 B8
Kandy, *Sri Lanka* 66 R12
Kane, *U.S.A.* 110 E6
Kane Basin, *Greenland* 4 B4
Kanel, *Senegal* 82 B2
Kaneohe, *U.S.A.* 106 H16
Kanevskaya, *Russia* 49 G4
Kanfanar, *Croatia* 29 C10
Kang, *Botswana* 88 C3
Kangaba, *Mali* 82 C3
Kangal, *Turkey* 72 C7
Kangān, *Fārs, Iran* 71 E7
Kangān, *Hormozgān, Iran* 71 E8
Kangar, *Malaysia* 65 J3
Kangaré, *Mali* 82 C3
Kangaroo I., *Australia* 95 F2
Kangaroo Mts., *Australia* 94 C3
Kangasala, *Finland* 9 F21
Kangāvar, *Iran* 71 C6
Kangding, *China* 58 B3
Kangdong, *N. Korea* 57 E14
Kangean, Kepulauan, *Indonesia* 62 F5
Kangean Is. = Kangean, Kepulauan, *Indonesia* 62 F5
Kangen →, *Sudan* 81 F3
Kanggye, *N. Korea* 57 D14
Kanggyŏng, *S. Korea* 57 F14
Kanghwa, *S. Korea* 57 F14
Kangikajik, *Greenland* 4 B6
Kangiqsliniq = Rankin Inlet, *Canada* 100 B10
Kangiqsualujjuaq, *Canada* 101 C13
Kangiqsujuaq, *Canada* 101 B12
Kangiqtugaapik = Clyde River, *Canada* 101 A13
Kangirsuk, *Canada* 101 B13
Kangnŭng, *S. Korea* 57 F15
Kangping, *China* 57 C12
Kangra, *India* 68 C7
Kangto, *India* 67 F18
Kanhar →, *India* 69 G10
Kani, *Ivory C.* 82 D3
Kaniama, *Dem. Rep. of the Congo* 86 D1
Kaniapiskau = Caniapiscau →, *Canada* 103 A6
Kaniapiskau, Res. = Caniapiscau, Rés. de, *Canada* 103 B6
Kanin, Poluostrov, *Russia* 50 C5
Kanin Nos, Mys, *Russia* 50 C5
Kanin Pen. = Kanin, Poluostrov, *Russia* 50 C5
Kaninë, *Albania* 40 F3
Kaniva, *Australia* 95 F3
Kanjiža, *Serbia, Yug.* 42 D5
Kanjut Sar, *Pakistan* 69 A6
Kankaanpää, *Finland* 9 F20
Kankakee, *U.S.A.* 108 E2
Kankakee →, *U.S.A.* 108 E1
Kankan, *Guinea* 82 C3
Kankendy = Xankändi, *Azerbaijan* 70 B5
Kanker, *India* 67 J12
Kankossa, *Mauritania* 82 B2
Kankroli, *India* 68 G5
Kannapolis, *U.S.A.* 109 H5
Kannauj, *India* 69 F8
Kannod, *India* 66 H10
Kano, *Nigeria* 83 C6
Kano □, *Nigeria* 83 C6
Kan onji, *Japan* 55 G6
Kanoroba, *Ivory C.* 82 D3
Kanowit, *Malaysia* 62 D4
Kanoya, *Japan* 55 J5
Kanpetlet, *Burma* 67 J18
Kanpur, *India* 69 F9
Kansas □, *U.S.A.* 112 F6
Kansas →, *U.S.A.* 112 F7
Kansas City, *Kans., U.S.A.* 112 F7
Kansas City, *Mo., U.S.A.* 112 F7
Kansenia, *Dem. Rep. of the Congo* 87 E2
Kansk, *Russia* 51 D10
Kansŏng, *S. Korea* 57 E15
Kansu = Gansu □, *China* 56 G3
Kantaphor, *India* 68 H7
Kantchari, *Burkina Faso* 83 C5
Kantché, *Niger* 83 C6
Kanté, *Togo* 83 D5
Kantemirovka, *Russia* 47 H10
Kantharalak, *Thailand* 64 E5
Kantli →, *India* 68 E6
Kantō □, *Japan* 55 F9
Kantō-Sanchi, *Japan* 55 G9
Kanturk, *Ireland* 15 D3
Kanuma, *Japan* 55 F9
Kanus, *Namibia* 88 D2
Kanye, *Botswana* 88 C4
Kanzenze, *Dem. Rep. of the Congo* 87 E2
Kanzi, Ras, *Tanzania* 86 D4
Kaohsiung, *Taiwan* 59 F13
Kaokoveld, *Namibia* 88 B1
Kaolack, *Senegal* 82 C1
Kaoshan, *China* 57 B13
Kapaa, *U.S.A.* 106 G15
Kapadvanj, *India* 68 H5
Kapaklı, *Turkey* 41 E11
Kapan, *Armenia* 70 B5
Kapanga, *Dem. Rep. of the Congo* 84 F4
Kapchagai = Qapshaghay, *Kazakstan* 50 E8
Kapela = Velika Kapela, *Croatia* 29 C12
Kapéllo, Ákra, *Greece* 38 E5
Kapema, *Dem. Rep. of the Congo* 87 E2
Kapfenberg, *Austria* 26 D8
Kapı Dağı, *Turkey* 41 F11
Kapiri Mposhi, *Zambia* 87 E2
Kāpīsā □, *Afghan.* 66 B6
Kapiskau →, *Canada* 102 B3
Kapit, *Malaysia* 62 D4
Kapiti I., *N.Z.* 91 J5
Kaplan, *U.S.A.* 113 K8
Kaplice, *Czech Rep.* 26 C7
Kapoe, *Thailand* 65 H2
Kapoeta, *Sudan* 81 G3
Kápolnásnyék, *Hungary* 42 C3
Kapos →, *Hungary* 42 D3
Kaposvár, *Hungary* 42 D2
Kapowsin, *U.S.A.* 116 D4
Kappeln, *Germany* 24 A5
Kappelshamn, *Sweden* 11 G12
Kapps, *Namibia* 88 C2
Kaprije, *Croatia* 29 E12
Kapsan, *N. Korea* 57 D15
Kapsukas = Marijampolė, *Lithuania* 9 J20
Kapuas →, *Indonesia* 62 E3
Kapuas Hulu, Pegunungan, *Malaysia* 62 D4
Kapuas Hulu Ra. = Kapuas Hulu, Pegunungan, *Malaysia* 62 D4
Kapulo, *Dem. Rep. of the Congo* 87 D2
Kapunda, *Australia* 95 E2
Kapuni, *N.Z.* 91 H5
Kapurthala, *India* 68 D6
Kapuskasing, *Canada* 102 C3
Kapuskasing →, *Canada* 102 C3
Kapustin Yar, *Russia* 49 F7
Kaputar, *Australia* 95 E5
Kaputir, *Kenya* 86 B4
Kapuvár, *Hungary* 42 C2
Kara, *Russia* 50 C7
Karā, W. →, *Si. Arabia* 80 C5
Kara Ada, *Turkey* 39 E9
Kara Bogaz Gol, Zaliv = Garabogazköl Aylagy, *Turkmenistan* 50 E6
Kara Burun, *Turkey* 39 E9
Kara Kalpak Republic = Qoraqalpoghistan □, *Uzbekistan* 50 E6
Kara Kum, *Turkmenistan* 50 F6
Kara Sea, *Russia* 50 B7
Karaadilli, *Turkey* 39 C12
Karabiğa, *Turkey* 41 F11
Karabük, *Turkey* 72 B5
Karaburun, *Albania* 40 F3
Karaburun, *Turkey* 39 C8
Karabutak = Qarabutaq, *Kazakstan* 50 E7
Karacabey, *Turkey* 41 F12
Karacakılavuz, *Turkey* 41 E11
Karacaköy, *Turkey* 41 E12
Karacasu, *Turkey* 39 D10
Karachala = Qaraçala, *Azerbaijan* 49 L9
Karachayevsk, *Russia* 49 J5
Karachev, *Russia* 47 F8
Karachey-Cherkessia □, *Russia* 49 J5
Karachi, *Pakistan* 68 G2
Karad, *India* 66 L9
Karadirek, *Turkey* 39 C12
Karaga, *Ghana* 83 D4
Karaganda = Qaraghandy, *Kazakstan* 50 E8
Karagayly, *Kazakstan* 50 E8
Karaginskiy, Ostrov, *Russia* 51 D17
Karagola Road, *India* 69 G12
Karagüney Dağları, *Turkey* 72 B6
Karahallı, *Turkey* 39 C11
Karaikal, *India* 66 P11
Karaikkudi, *India* 66 P11
Karaisali, *Turkey* 72 D6
Karaj, *Iran* 71 C6
Karak, *Malaysia* 65 L4
Karakalpakstan = Qoraqalpoghistan □, *Uzbekistan* 50 E6
Karakelong, *Indonesia* 63 D7
Karakitang, *Indonesia* 63 D7
Karaklis = Vanadzor, *Armenia* 49 K7
Karakoçan, *Turkey* 73 C9
Karakol, *Kyrgyzstan* 50 E8
Karakoram Pass, *Pakistan* 69 B7
Karakoram Ra., *Pakistan* 69 B7
Karakurt, *Turkey* 73 B10
Karakuwisa, *Namibia* 88 B2
Karalon, *Russia* 51 D12
Karama, *Jordan* 75 D4
Karaman, *Balıkesir, Turkey* 39 B9
Karaman, *Konya, Turkey* 70 B2
Karamanlı, *Turkey* 39 D11
Karamay, *China* 60 B3
Karambu, *Indonesia* 62 E5
Karamea Bight, *N.Z.* 91 J3
Karamnasa →, *India* 69 G10
Karamürsel, *Turkey* 41 F13

Karand, *Iran* 70 C5
Karangana, *Mali* 82 C3
Karanganyar, *Indonesia* 63 G13
Karanjia, *India* 69 J11
Karankasso, *Burkina Faso* 82 C4
Karaova, *Turkey* 39 D9
Karapınar, *Turkey* 72 D5
Karasburg, *Namibia* 88 D2
Karasino, *Russia* 50 C9
Karasjok, *Norway* 8 B21
Karasu, *Turkey* 72 B4
Karasu →, *Turkey* 39 E12
Karasuk, *Russia* 50 D8
Karasuyama, *Japan* 55 F10
Karataş, *Adana, Turkey* 72 D6
Karataş, *Manisa, Turkey* 39 C10
Karataş Burnu, *Turkey* 72 D6
Karatau, Khrebet = Qarataū, *Kazakstan* 50 E7
Karatoprak, *Turkey* 39 D9
Karatsu, *Japan* 55 H5
Karaul, *Russia* 50 B9
Karauli, *India* 68 F7
Karavastasë, L. e, *Albania* 40 F3
Karávi, *Greece* 38 E5
Karavostasi, *Cyprus* 36 D11
Karawang, *Indonesia* 63 G12
Karawanken, *Europe* 26 E7
Karayazı, *Turkey* 73 C10
Karazhal, *Kazakstan* 50 E8
Karbalā', *Iraq* 70 C5
Kårböle, *Sweden* 10 C9
Karcag, *Hungary* 42 C5
Karcha →, *Pakistan* 69 B7
Karchana, *India* 69 G9
Karczew, *Poland* 45 F8
Kardam, *Bulgaria* 41 C12
Kardeljovo = Ploče, *Croatia* 29 E14
Kardhámila, *Greece* 39 C8
Kardhamíli, *Greece* 38 E4
Kardhítsa, *Greece* 38 B3
Kardhítsa □, *Greece* 38 B3
Kärdla, *Estonia* 9 G20
Kareeberge, *S. Africa* 88 E3
Kareha →, *India* 69 G12
Kareima, *Sudan* 80 D3
Karelia □, *Russia* 50 C4
Karelian Republic = Karelia □, *Russia* 50 C4
Karera, *India* 68 G8
Kārevāndar, *Iran* 71 E9
Kargasok, *Russia* 50 D9
Kargat, *Russia* 50 D9
Kargı, *Turkey* 72 B6
Kargil, *India* 69 B7
Kargopol, *Russia* 46 B10
Kargowa, *Poland* 45 F2
Karguéri, *Niger* 83 C7
Karhal, *India* 69 F8
Kariá, *Greece* 38 C2
Kariaí, *Greece* 41 F8
Karīān, *Iran* 71 E8
Karianga, *Madag.* 89 C8
Kariba, *Zimbabwe* 87 F2
Kariba, L., *Zimbabwe* 87 F2
Kariba Dam, *Zimbabwe* 87 F2
Kariba Gorge, *Zambia* 87 F2
Karibib, *Namibia* 88 C2
Karimata, Kepulauan, *Indonesia* 62 E3
Karimata, Selat, *Indonesia* 62 E3
Karimata Is. = Karimata, Kepulauan, *Indonesia* 62 E3
Karimnagar, *India* 66 K11
Karimunjawa, Kepulauan, *Indonesia* 62 F4
Karin, *Somali Rep.* 74 E4
Káristos, *Greece* 38 C6
Karīt, *Iran* 71 C8
Kariya, *Japan* 55 G8
Kariyangwe, *Zimbabwe* 89 B4
Karjala, *Finland* 46 A5
Karkaralinsk = Qarqaraly, *Kazakstan* 50 E8
Karkheh →, *Iran* 70 D5
Karkinitska Zatoka, *Ukraine* 47 K7
Karkinitskiy Zaliv = Karkinitska Zatoka, *Ukraine* 47 K7
Karkur Tohl, *Egypt* 80 C2
Karl Liebknecht, *Russia* 47 G8
Karl-Marx-Stadt = Chemnitz, *Germany* 24 E8
Karlholmsbruk, *Sweden* 10 D11
Karlino, *Poland* 44 D2
Karlivka, *Ukraine* 47 H8
Karlobag, *Croatia* 29 D12
Karlovac, *Croatia* 29 C12
Karlovarský □, *Czech Rep.* 26 A5
Karlovka = Karlivka, *Ukraine* 47 H8
Karlovo, *Bulgaria* 41 D8
Karlovy Vary, *Czech Rep.* 26 A5
Karlsbad = Karlovy Vary, *Czech Rep.* 26 A5
Karlsborg, *Sweden* 11 F8
Karlshamn, *Sweden* 11 H8
Karlskoga, *Sweden* 10 E8
Karlskrona, *Sweden* 11 H9
Karlsruhe, *Germany* 25 F4
Karlstad, *Sweden* 10 E7
Karlstad, *U.S.A.* 112 A6
Karlstadt, *Germany* 25 F5
Karma, *Niger* 83 C5
Karmėlava, *Lithuania* 44 D11
Karmi'el, *Israel* 75 C4
Karnak, *Egypt* 79 C12
Karnal, *India* 68 E7
Karnali →, *Nepal* 69 E9
Karnaphuli Res., *Bangla.* 67 H18
Karnaprayag, *India* 69 D8
Karnataka □, *India* 66 N10
Karnes City, *U.S.A.* 113 L6
Karnische Alpen, *Europe* 26 E6
Karnobat, *Bulgaria* 41 D10
Kärnten □, *Austria* 26 E6
Karo, *Mali* 82 C4
Karoi, *Zimbabwe* 87 F2
Karonga, *Malawi* 87 D3
Karoonda, *Australia* 95 F2
Karor, *Pakistan* 68 D4
Karora, *Sudan* 80 D4
Káros, *Greece* 39 E7
Karounga, *Mali* 82 B3
Karousádhes, *Greece* 38 B1
Karpacz, *Poland* 45 H2
Karpasia □, *Cyprus* 36 D13
Kárpathos, *Greece* 39 F9
Kárpathos, Stenón, *Greece* 39 F9
Karpenísion, *Greece* 38 C3
Karpuz Burnu = Apostolos Andreas, C., *Cyprus* 36 D13
Karpuzlu, *Turkey* 39 D9
Karratha, *Australia* 92 D2
Kars, *Turkey* 73 B10
Karsakpay, *Kazakstan* 50 E7
Karsha, *Kazakstan* 48 F10
Karshi = Qarshi, *Uzbekistan* 50 F7
Karsiyang, *India* 69 F13
Karsog, *India* 68 D7
Karst = Kras, *Croatia* 29 C10
Kartal, *Turkey* 41 F13
Kartál Óros, *Greece* 41 E9
Kartaly, *Russia* 50 D7
Kartapur, *India* 68 D6
Karthaus, *U.S.A.* 110 E6
Kartuzy, *Poland* 44 D5
Karufa, *Indonesia* 63 E8
Karumba, *Australia* 94 B3
Karumo, *Tanzania* 86 C3
Karumwa, *Tanzania* 86 C3
Kārūn →, *Iran* 71 D6
Karungu, *Kenya* 86 C3
Karup, *Denmark* 11 H3
Karviná, *Czech Rep.* 27 B11
Karwan →, *India* 68 F8
Karwar, *India* 66 M9
Karwi, *India* 69 G9
Kaş, *Turkey* 39 E11
Kasaba, *Turkey* 39 E11
Kasache, *Malawi* 87 E3
Kasai →, *Dem. Rep. of the Congo* 84 E3
Kasaï-Oriental □, *Dem. Rep. of the Congo* 86 D1
Kasaji, *Dem. Rep. of the Congo* 87 E1
Kasama, *Zambia* 87 E3
Kasan-dong, *N. Korea* 57 D14
Kasane, *Namibia* 88 B3
Kasanga, *Tanzania* 87 D3
Kasar, Ras, *Sudan* 80 D4
Kasaragod, *India* 66 N9
Kasba L., *Canada* 105 A8
Kāseh Garān, *Iran* 70 C5
Kasempa, *Zambia* 87 E2
Kasenga, *Dem. Rep. of the Congo* 87 E2
Kasese, *Uganda* 86 B3
Kasewa, *Zambia* 87 E2
Kasganj, *India* 69 F8
Kashabowie, *Canada* 102 C1
Kashaf, *Iran* 71 C9
Kāshān, *Iran* 71 C6
Kashechewan, *Canada* 102 B3
Kashgar = Kashi, *China* 60 C2
Kashi, *China* 60 C2
Kashimbo, *Dem. Rep. of the Congo* 87 E2
Kashin, *Russia* 46 D9
Kashipur, *India* 69 E8
Kashira, *Russia* 46 E10
Kashiwazaki, *Japan* 55 F9
Kashk-e Kohneh, *Afghan.* 66 B3
Kashkū'īyeh, *Iran* 71 D7
Kāshmar, *Iran* 71 C8
Kashmir, *Asia* 69 C7
Kashmor, *Pakistan* 68 E3
Kashpirovka, *Russia* 48 D9
Kashun Noerh = Gaxun Nur, *China* 60 B5
Kasiari, *India* 69 H12
Kasimov, *Russia* 48 C5
Kasinge, *Dem. Rep. of the Congo* 86 D2
Kasiruta, *Indonesia* 63 E7
Kaskaskia →, *U.S.A.* 112 G10
Kaskattama →, *Canada* 105 B10
Kaskinen, *Finland* 9 E19
Kaslo, *Canada* 104 D5
Kasmere L., *Canada* 105 B8
Kasongo, *Dem. Rep. of the Congo* 86 C2
Kasongo Lunda, *Dem. Rep. of the Congo* 84 F3
Kásos, *Greece* 39 F8
Kásos, Stenón, *Greece* 39 F8
Kaspi, *Georgia* 49 K7
Kaspichan, *Bulgaria* 41 C11
Kaspiysk, *Russia* 49 J8
Kaspiyskiy, *Russia* 49 H8
Kassab ed Doleib, *Sudan* 81 E3
Kassaba, *Egypt* 80 C2
Kassalâ, *Sudan* 81 D4
Kassalâ □, *Sudan* 81 D4
Kassándra, *Greece* 40 F7
Kassándrinon, *Greece* 40 F7
Kassel, *Germany* 24 D5
Kassinger, *Sudan* 80 D3
Kassiópi, *Greece* 36 A3
Kasson, *U.S.A.* 112 C8
Kastamonu, *Turkey* 72 B5
Kastav, *Croatia* 29 C11
Kastélli, *Greece* 36 D5
Kastéllion, *Greece* 36 D7
Kastellórizon = Megiste, *Greece* 39 E11
Kástellos, *Greece* 39 E9
Kastellou, Ákra, *Greece* 39 F9
Kasterlee, *Belgium* 17 C4
Kastlösa, *Sweden* 11 H10
Kastóri, *Greece* 38 D4
Kastoría, *Greece* 40 F5
Kastoría □, *Greece* 40 F5
Kastorías, Límni, *Greece* 40 F5
Kastornoye, *Russia* 47 G10
Kastós, *Greece* 38 C2
Kastrosikiá, *Greece* 38 B2
Kastsyukovichy, *Belarus* 46 F7
Kasulu, *Tanzania* 86 C3
Kasumi, *Japan* 55 G7
Kasumkent, *Russia* 49 K9
Kasungu, *Malawi* 87 E3
Kasur, *Pakistan* 68 D6
Kataba, *Zambia* 87 F2
Katagum, *Nigeria* 83 C7
Katahdin, Mt., *U.S.A.* 109 C11
Katako Kombe, *Dem. Rep. of the Congo* 86 C1
Katákolon, *Greece* 38 D3
Katale, *Tanzania* 86 C3
Katanda, *Katanga, Dem. Rep. of the Congo* 86 D1
Katanda, *Nord-Kivu, Dem. Rep. of the Congo* 86 C2
Katanga □, *Dem. Rep. of the Congo* 86 D2
Katangi, *India* 66 J11
Katanning, *Australia* 93 F2
Katastári, *Greece* 38 D2
Katavi Swamp, *Tanzania* 86 D3
Kateríni, *Greece* 40 F6
Katghora, *India* 69 H10
Katha, *Burma* 67 G20
Katherîna, Gebel, *Egypt* 70 D2
Katherine, *Australia* 92 B5
Katherine Gorge, *Australia* 92 B5
Kathi, *India* 68 J6
Kathiawar, *India* 68 H4
Kathikas, *Cyprus* 36 E11
Kathua, *India* 68 C6
Kati, *Mali* 82 C3
Katihar, *India* 69 G12
Katima Mulilo, *Zambia* 88 B3
Katimbira, *Malawi* 87 E3
Katingan = Mendawai →, *Indonesia* 62 E4
Katiola, *Ivory C.* 82 D3
Katlanovo, *Macedonia* 40 E5
Katmandu, *Nepal* 69 F11
Katni, *India* 69 H9
Káto Akhaïa, *Greece* 38 C3
Káto Arkhánai, *Greece* 36 D7
Káto Khorió, *Greece* 36 D7
Káto Pyrgos, *Cyprus* 36 D11
Káto Stavros, *Greece* 40 F7
Katokhí, *Greece* 38 C3
Katompe, *Dem. Rep. of the Congo* 86 D2
Katonga →, *Uganda* 86 B3
Katoomba, *Australia* 95 E5
Katoúna, *Greece* 38 C3
Katowice, *Poland* 45 H6
Katrancı Dağı, *Turkey* 39 D12
Katrine, L., *U.K.* 14 E4
Katrineholm, *Sweden* 11 E10
Katsepe, *Madag.* 89 B8
Katsina, *Nigeria* 83 C6
Katsina □, *Nigeria* 83 C6
Katsina Ala, *Nigeria* 83 D6
Katsina Ala →, *Nigeria* 83 D6
Katsumoto, *Japan* 55 H4
Katsuura, *Japan* 55 G10
Katsuyama, *Japan* 55 F8
Kattaviá, *Greece* 36 D9
Kattegat, *Denmark* 11 H5
Katthammarsvik, *Sweden* 11 G12
Katul, J., *Sudan* 81 E2
Katumba, *Dem. Rep. of the Congo* 86 D2
Katungu, *Kenya* 86 C5
Katwa, *India* 69 H13
Katwijk, *Neths.* 17 B4
Kąty Wrocławskie, *Poland* 45 G3
Kauai, *U.S.A.* 106 H15
Kauai Channel, *U.S.A.* 106 H15
Kaub, *Germany* 25 E3
Kaufbeuren, *Germany* 25 H6
Kaufman, *U.S.A.* 113 J6
Kauhajoki, *Finland* 9 E20
Kaukauna, *U.S.A.* 108 C1
Kaukauveld, *Namibia* 88 C3
Kaunakakai, *U.S.A.* 106 H16
Kaunas, *Lithuania* 9 J20
Kaunia, *Bangla.* 69 G13
Kaunos, *Turkey* 39 E10
Kaura Namoda, *Nigeria* 83 C6
Kauru, *Nigeria* 83 C6
Kautokeino, *Norway* 8 B20
Kauwapur, *India* 69 F10
Kavacha, *Russia* 51 C17
Kavadarci, *Macedonia* 40 E6
Kavajë, *Albania* 40 E3
Kavak, *Turkey* 72 B7
Kavak Dağı, *Turkey* 39 D10
Kavaklı, *Turkey* 41 E11
Kavaklıdere, *Turkey* 39 D10
Kavalerovo, *Russia* 54 B7
Kavali, *India* 66 M12
Kavála, *Greece* 41 F8
Kavála □, *Greece* 41 E8
Kavála Kólpos, *Greece* 41 F8
Kavār, *Iran* 71 D7
Kavarna, *Bulgaria* 41 C12
Kavi, *India* 68 H5
Kavimba, *Botswana* 88 B3
Kavīr, Dasht-e, *Iran* 71 C7
Kavkaz, *Russia* 47 K9
Kävlinge, *Sweden* 11 J7
Kavos, *Greece* 36 B4
Kavoúsi, *Greece* 39 F7
Kaw, *Fr. Guiana* 125 C8
Kawa, *Sudan* 81 E3
Kawagama L., *Canada* 110 A6
Kawagoe, *Japan* 55 G9
Kawaguchi, *Japan* 55 G9
Kawambwa, *Zambia* 87 D2
Kawanoe, *Japan* 55 G6
Kawardha, *India* 69 J9
Kawasaki, *Japan* 55 G9
Kawasi, *Indonesia* 63 E7
Kawerau, *N.Z.* 91 H6
Kawhia Harbour, *N.Z.* 91 H5
Kawio, Kepulauan, *Indonesia* 63 D7
Kawnro, *Burma* 67 H21
Kawthaung, *Burma* 65 H2
Kawthoolei = Kayin □, *Burma* 67 L20
Kawthule = Kayin □, *Burma* 67 L20
Kaxholmen, *Sweden* 11 G8
Kaya, *Burkina Faso* 83 C4
Kayah □, *Burma* 67 K20
Kayalıköy Barajı, *Turkey* 41 E11
Kayan →, *Indonesia* 62 D5
Kaycee, *U.S.A.* 114 E10
Kayeli, *Indonesia* 63 E7
Kayenta, *U.S.A.* 115 H8
Kayes, *Mali* 82 C2
Kayı, *Turkey* 39 B12
Kayima, *S. Leone* 82 D2
Kayin □, *Burma* 67 L20
Kaymakçı, *Turkey* 39 C10
Kayoa, *Indonesia* 63 D7
Kayomba, *Zambia* 87 E1
Kaysatskoye, *Russia* 48 F8
Kayseri, *Turkey* 70 B2
Kaysville, *U.S.A.* 114 F8
Kaz Dağı, *Turkey* 39 B8
Kazachye, *Russia* 51 B14
Kazakstan ■, *Asia* 50 E7
Kazan, *Russia* 48 C9
Kazan →, *Canada* 105 A9
Kazan-Rettō, *Pac. Oc.* 96 E6
Kazanlŭk, *Bulgaria* 41 D9
Kazanskaya, *Russia* 48 F5
Kazatin = Kozyatyn, *Ukraine* 47 H5
Kazaure, *Nigeria* 83 C6
Kazbek, *Russia* 49 J7
Kāzerūn, *Iran* 71 D6
Kazi Magomed = Qazimämmäd, *Azerbaijan* 49 K9
Kazimierz Dolny, *Poland* 45 G8
Kazimierza Wielka, *Poland* 45 H7
Kazincbarcika, *Hungary* 42 B5
Kazlų Rūda, *Lithuania* 44 D10
Kaztalovka, *Kazakstan* 48 F9
Kazuno, *Japan* 54 D10
Kazym →, *Russia* 50 C7
Kcynia, *Poland* 45 F4
Ké-Macina, *Mali* 82 C3
Kéa, *Greece* 38 D6
Keady, *U.K.* 15 B5
Kearney, *U.S.A.* 112 E5
Kearny, *U.S.A.* 115 K8
Kearsarge, Mt., *U.S.A.* 111 C13
Keban, *Turkey* 73 C8
Keban Barajı, *Turkey* 70 B3
Kebbi □, *Nigeria* 83 C5
Kébi, *Ivory C.* 82 D3
Kebnekaise, *Sweden* 8 C18
Kebri Dehar, *Ethiopia* 74 F3
Kebumen, *Indonesia* 63 G13
Kecel, *Hungary* 42 D4
Kechika →, *Canada* 104 B3
Keçiborlu, *Turkey* 39 D12
Kecskemét, *Hungary* 42 D4
Kedada, *Ethiopia* 81 F4
Kėdainiai, *Lithuania* 9 J21
Kedarnath, *India* 69 D8
Kedgwick, *Canada* 103 C6
Kédhros Óros, *Greece* 36 D6
Kediri, *Indonesia* 62 F4
Kédjebi, *Ghana* 83 D5
Kédougou, *Senegal* 82 C2
Kędzierzyn-Koźle, *Poland* 45 H5
Keeler, *U.S.A.* 116 J9
Keeley L., *Canada* 105 C7
Keeling Is. = Cocos Is., *Ind. Oc.* 96 J1
Keelung = Chilung, *Taiwan* 59 E13
Keene, *Canada* 110 B6
Keene, *Calif., U.S.A.* 117 K8
Keene, *N.H., U.S.A.* 111 D12
Keene, *N.Y., U.S.A.* 111 B11
Keeper Hill, *Ireland* 15 D3
Keer-Weer, C., *Australia* 94 A3
Keeseville, *U.S.A.* 111 B11
Keetmanshoop, *Namibia* 88 D2
Keewatin, *Canada* 105 D10
Keewatin →, *Canada* 105 B8
Kefa □, *Ethiopia* 81 F4
Kefallinía, *Greece* 38 C2
Kefallinía □, *Greece* 38 C2
Kéfalos, *Greece* 39 E8
Kefamenanu, *Indonesia* 63 F6
Kefar Sava, *Israel* 75 C3
Keffi, *Nigeria* 83 D6
Keffin Hausa, *Nigeria* 83 C6
Keflavík, *Iceland* 8 D2
Keftya, *Ethiopia* 81 E4
Keg River, *Canada* 104 B5
Kegaska, *Canada* 103 B7
Keheili, *Sudan* 80 D3
Kehl, *Germany* 25 G3
Keighley, *U.K.* 12 D6
Keila, *Estonia* 9 G21
Keimoes, *S. Africa* 88 D3
Keita, *Niger* 83 C6
Keitele, *Finland* 8 E22
Keith, *Australia* 95 F3
Keith, *U.K.* 14 D6
Keizer, *U.S.A.* 114 D2
Kejimkujik Nat. Park, *Canada* 103 D6
Kejserr Franz Joseph Fd., *Greenland* 4 B6
Kekri, *India* 68 G6
Kelam, *Ethiopia* 81 G4
Kelamet, *Eritrea* 81 D4
Kelan, *China* 56 E6
Kelang, *Malaysia* 65 L3
Kelantan →, *Malaysia* 65 J4
Këlcyrë, *Albania* 40 F4
Kelekçi, *Turkey* 39 D11
Keles, *Turkey* 41 G13
Keleti-főcsatorna, *Hungary* 42 C6
Kelheim, *Germany* 25 G7
Kelkit, *Turkey* 73 B8
Kelkit →, *Turkey* 72 B7
Kellerberrin, *Australia* 93 F2
Kellett, C., *Canada* 4 B1
Kelleys I., *U.S.A.* 110 E2
Kellogg, *U.S.A.* 114 C5
Kells = Ceanannus Mor, *Ireland* 15 C5
Kelmė, *Lithuania* 44 C9
Kelokedhara, *Cyprus* 36 E11
Kelowna, *Canada* 104 D5
Kelseyville, *U.S.A.* 116 G4
Kelso, *N.Z.* 91 L2
Kelso, *U.K.* 14 F6
Kelso, *U.S.A.* 116 D4
Keluang, *Malaysia* 65 L4
Kelvington, *Canada* 105 C8
Kem, *Russia* 50 C4
Kema, *Indonesia* 63 D7
Kemah, *Turkey* 70 B3
Kemaliye, *Erzincan, Turkey* 73 C8
Kemaliye, *Manisa, Turkey* 39 C10
Kemalpaşa, *Turkey* 39 C9
Kemaman, *Malaysia* 62 D2
Kemano, *Canada* 104 C3
Kemasik, *Malaysia* 65 K4
Kembolcha, *Ethiopia* 81 E4
Kemer, *Antalya, Turkey* 39 E12
Kemer, *Burdur, Turkey* 39 D12
Kemer, *Muğla, Turkey* 39 E11
Kemer Barajı, *Turkey* 39 D10
Kemerovo, *Russia* 50 D9
Kemi, *Finland* 8 D21
Kemi älv = Kemijoki →, *Finland* 8 D21
Kemijärvi, *Finland* 8 C22
Kemijoki →, *Finland* 8 D21
Kemmerer, *U.S.A.* 114 F8
Kemmuna = Comino, *Malta* 36 C1
Kemp, L., *U.S.A.* 113 J5
Kemp Land, *Antarctica* 5 C5
Kempsey, *Australia* 95 E5
Kempt, L., *Canada* 102 C5
Kempten, *Germany* 25 H6
Kempton, *Australia* 94 G4
Kemptville, *Canada* 102 D4
Ken →, *India* 69 G9
Kenai, *U.S.A.* 100 B4
Kendai, *India* 69 H10
Kendal, *Indonesia* 63 G14
Kendal, *U.K.* 12 C5
Kendall, *Australia* 95 E5
Kendall, *U.S.A.* 109 N5
Kendall →, *Australia* 94 A3
Kendallville, *U.S.A.* 108 E3
Kendari, *Indonesia* 63 E6
Kendawangan, *Indonesia* 62 E4
Kende, *Nigeria* 83 C5
Kendrapara, *India* 67 J15
Këndrevicës, Maja e, *Albania* 40 F3
Kendrew, *S. Africa* 88 E3
Kene Thao, *Laos* 64 D3
Kenedy, *U.S.A.* 113 L6
Kenema, *S. Leone* 82 D2
Keng Kok, *Laos* 64 D5
Keng Tawng, *Burma* 67 J21
Keng Tung, *Burma* 58 G2
Kengeja, *Tanzania* 86 D4
Kenhardt, *S. Africa* 88 D3
Kéniéba, *Mali* 82 C2
Kenitra, *Morocco* 78 B4
Kenli, *China* 57 F10
Kenmare, *Ireland* 15 E2
Kenmare, *U.S.A.* 112 A3
Kenmare River, *Ireland* 15 E2
Kennebago Lake, *U.S.A.* 111 A14
Kennebec, *U.S.A.* 112 D5
Kennebec →, *U.S.A.* 109 D11
Kennebunk, *U.S.A.* 111 C14
Kennedy, *Zimbabwe* 88 B4
Kennedy Ra., *Australia* 93 D2
Kennedy Taungdeik, *Burma* 67 H18
Kenner, *U.S.A.* 113 L9
Kennet →, *U.K.* 13 F7
Kenneth Ra., *Australia* 93 D2
Kennett, *U.S.A.* 113 G9
Kennewick, *U.S.A.* 114 C4
Kenogami →, *Canada* 102 B3
Kenora, *Canada* 105 D10

Kenosha, *U.S.A.* 108 **D2**
Kensington, *Canada* 103 **C7**
Kent, *Ohio, U.S.A.* 110 **E3**
Kent, *Tex., U.S.A.* 113 **K2**
Kent, *Wash., U.S.A.* 116 **C4**
Kent □, *U.K.* 13 **F8**
Kent Group, *Australia* 94 **F4**
Kent Pen., *Canada* 100 **B9**
Kentaū, *Kazakstan* 50 **E7**
Kentland, *U.S.A.* 108 **E2**
Kenton, *U.S.A.* 108 **E4**
Kentucky □, *U.S.A.* 108 **G3**
Kentucky →, *U.S.A.* 108 **F3**
Kentucky L., *U.S.A.* 109 **G2**
Kentville, *Canada* 103 **C7**
Kentwood, *U.S.A.* 113 **K9**
Kenya ■, *Africa* 86 **B4**
Kenya, Mt., *Kenya* 86 **C4**
Keo Neua, Deo, *Vietnam* 64 **C5**
Keokuk, *U.S.A.* 112 **E9**
Keonjhargarh, *India* 69 **J11**
Kep, *Cambodia* 65 **G5**
Kep, *Vietnam* 64 **B6**
Kepez, *Turkey* 41 **F10**
Kepi, *Indonesia* 63 **F9**
Kępice, *Poland* 44 **D3**
Kępno, *Poland* 45 **G4**
Kepsut, *Turkey* 39 **B10**
Kerala □, *India* 66 **P10**
Kerama-Rettō, *Japan* 55 **L3**
Keran, *Pakistan* 69 **B5**
Kerang, *Australia* 95 **F3**
Keranyo, *Ethiopia* 81 **F4**
Kerao →, *Sudan* 81 **E3**
Keratéa, *Greece* 38 **D5**
Keraudren, C., *Australia* 92 **C2**
Kerava, *Finland* 9 **F21**
Kerch, *Ukraine* 47 **K9**
Kerchenskiy Proliv, *Black Sea* . 47 **K9**
Kerchoual, *Mali* 83 **B5**
Kerempe Burnu, *Turkey* 72 **A5**
Keren, *Eritrea* 81 **D4**
Kerewan, *Gambia* 82 **C1**
Kerguelen, *Ind. Oc.* 3 **G13**
Keri, *Greece* 38 **D2**
Keri Kera, *Sudan* 81 **E3**
Kericho, *Kenya* 86 **C4**
Kerinci, *Indonesia* 62 **E2**
Kerki, *Turkmenistan* 50 **F7**
Kerkinítis, Límni, *Greece* 40 **E7**
Kérkira, *Greece* 36 **A3**
Kérkira □, *Greece* 38 **B1**
Kerkrade, *Neths.* 17 **D6**
Kerma, *Sudan* 80 **D3**
Kermadec Is., *Pac. Oc.* 96 **L10**
Kermadec Trench, *Pac. Oc.* . . . 96 **L10**
Kermān, *Iran* 71 **D8**
Kerman, *U.S.A.* 116 **J6**
Kermān □, *Iran* 71 **D8**
Kermān, Bīābān-e, *Iran* 71 **D8**
Kermānshāh = Bākhtarān, *Iran* 70 **C5**
Kermen, *Bulgaria* 41 **D10**
Kermit, *U.S.A.* 113 **K3**
Kern →, *U.S.A.* 117 **K7**
Kernhof, *Austria* 26 **D8**
Kernow = Cornwall □, *U.K.* . . . 13 **G3**
Kernville, *U.S.A.* 117 **K8**
Keroh, *Malaysia* 65 **K3**
Kérou, *Benin* 83 **C5**
Kérouane, *Guinea* 82 **D3**
Kerpen, *Germany* 24 **E2**
Kerrera, *U.K.* 14 **E3**
Kerrobert, *Canada* 105 **C7**
Kerrville, *U.S.A.* 113 **K5**
Kerry □, *Ireland* 15 **D2**
Kerry Hd., *Ireland* 15 **D2**
Kersa, *Ethiopia* 81 **F5**
Kerulen →, *Asia* 60 **B6**
Kerzaz, *Algeria* 78 **C5**
Kesagami →, *Canada* 102 **B4**
Kesagami L., *Canada* 102 **B3**
Keşan, *Turkey* 41 **F10**
Kesennuma, *Japan* 54 **E10**
Keshit, *Iran* 71 **D8**
Keşiş Dağ, *Turkey* 73 **C8**
Keskin, *Turkey* 72 **C5**
Kestell, *S. Africa* 89 **D4**
Kestenga, *Russia* 50 **C4**
Keswick, *U.K.* 12 **C4**
Keszthely, *Hungary* 42 **D2**
Ket →, *Russia* 50 **D9**
Keta, *Ghana* 83 **D5**
Keta Lagoon, *Ghana* 83 **D5**
Ketapang, *Indonesia* 62 **E4**
Ketchikan, *U.S.A.* 104 **B2**
Ketchum, *U.S.A.* 114 **E6**
Kete Krachi, *Ghana* 83 **D4**
Ketef, Khalîg Umm el, *Egypt* . . 70 **F2**
Keti Bandar, *Pakistan* 68 **G2**
Kétou, *Benin* 83 **D5**
Ketri, *India* 68 **E6**
Kętrzyn, *Poland* 44 **D8**
Kettering, *U.K.* 13 **E7**
Kettering, *U.S.A.* 108 **F3**
Kettle →, *Canada* 105 **B11**
Kettle Falls, *U.S.A.* 114 **B4**
Kettle Pt., *Canada* 110 **C2**
Kettleman City, *U.S.A.* 116 **J7**
Kęty, *Poland* 45 **J6**
Keuka L., *U.S.A.* 110 **D7**
Keuruu, *Finland* 9 **E21**
Kevelaer, *Germany* 24 **D2**
Kewanee, *U.S.A.* 112 **E10**
Kewaunee, *U.S.A.* 108 **C2**
Keweenaw B., *U.S.A.* 108 **B1**
Keweenaw Pen., *U.S.A.* 108 **B2**
Keweenaw Pt., *U.S.A.* 108 **B2**
Key Largo, *U.S.A.* 109 **N5**
Key West, *U.S.A.* 107 **F10**
Keyala, *Sudan* 81 **G3**
Keynsham, *U.K.* 13 **F5**
Keyser, *U.S.A.* 108 **F6**
Kezhma, *Russia* 51 **D11**
Kezi, *Zimbabwe* 89 **C4**
Kežmarok, *Slovak Rep.* 27 **B13**
Khabarovsk, *Russia* 51 **E14**
Khabr, *Iran* 71 **D8**
Khābūr →, *Syria* 70 **C4**
Khachmas = Xaçmaz,
Azerbaijan 49 **K9**
Khachrod, *India* 68 **H6**
Khadari, W. el →, *Sudan* 81 **E2**
Khadro, *Pakistan* 68 **F3**
Khadyzhensk, *Russia* 49 **H4**
Khadzhilyangar, *India* 69 **B8**
Khaga, *India* 69 **G9**
Khagaria, *India* 69 **G12**
Khaipur, *Pakistan* 68 **E5**
Khair, *India* 68 **F7**
Khairabad, *India* 69 **F9**
Khairagarh, *India* 69 **J9**
Khairpur, *Pakistan* 68 **F3**
Khairpur Nathan Shah, *Pakistan* 68 **F2**
Khairwara, *India* 68 **H5**
Khaisor →, *Pakistan* 68 **D3**
Khajuri Kach, *Pakistan* 68 **C3**
Khakassia □, *Russia* 50 **D9**
Khakhea, *Botswana* 88 **C3**
Khalafābād, *Iran* 71 **D6**
Khalilabad, *India* 69 **F10**
Khalīlī, *Iran* 71 **E7**
Khalkhāl, *Iran* 71 **B6**
Khálki, *Dhodhekánisos, Greece* 39 **E9**
Khálki, *Thessalía, Greece* 38 **B4**
Khalkidhikí □, *Greece* 40 **F7**
Khalkís, *Greece* 38 **C5**
Khalmer-Sede = Tazovskiy,
Russia 50 **C8**
Khalmer Yu, *Russia* 50 **C7**
Khalūf, *Oman* 74 **C6**
Kham Keut, *Laos* 64 **C5**
Khamaria, *India* 69 **H9**
Khambhaliya, *India* 68 **H3**
Khambhat, *India* 68 **H5**
Khambhat, G. of, *India* 66 **J8**
Khamilonísion, *Greece* 39 **F8**
Khamīr, *Iran* 71 **E7**
Khamir, *Yemen* 74 **D3**
Khamsa, *Egypt* 75 **E1**
Khan →, *Namibia* 88 **C2**
Khān Abū Shāmat, *Syria* 75 **B5**
Khān Azād, *Iraq* 70 **C5**
Khān Mujiddah, *Iraq* 70 **C4**
Khān Shaykhūn, *Syria* 70 **C3**
Khān Yūnis, *Gaza Strip* 75 **D3**
Khanai, *Pakistan* 68 **D2**
Khānaqīn, *Iraq* 70 **C5**
Khānbāghī, *Iran* 71 **B7**
Khandrá, *Greece* 39 **F8**
Khandwa, *India* 66 **J10**
Khandyga, *Russia* 51 **C14**
Khāneh, *Iran* 70 **B5**
Khanewal, *Pakistan* 68 **D4**
Khangah Dogran, *Pakistan* 68 **D5**
Khanh Duong, *Vietnam* 64 **F7**
Khaniá, *Greece* 36 **D6**
Khaniá □, *Greece* 36 **D6**
Khaniadhana, *India* 68 **G8**
Khaníon, Kólpos, *Greece* 36 **D5**
Khanka, L., *Asia* 51 **E14**
Khankendy = Xankändi,
Azerbaijan 70 **B5**
Khanna, *India* 68 **D7**
Khanozai, *Pakistan* 68 **D2**
Khanpur, *Pakistan* 68 **E4**
Khanty-Mansiysk, *Russia* 50 **C7**
Khapalu, *Pakistan* 69 **B7**
Khapcheranga, *Russia* 51 **E12**
Kharabali, *Russia* 49 **G8**
Kharaghoda, *India* 68 **H4**
Kharagpur, *India* 69 **H12**
Khárakas, *Greece* 36 **D7**
Kharan Kalat, *Pakistan* 66 **E4**
Kharānaq, *Iran* 71 **C7**
Kharda, *India* 66 **K9**
Khardung La, *India* 69 **B7**
Khârga, El Wâhât-el, *Egypt* . . . 80 **B3**
Khargon, *India* 66 **J9**
Khari →, *India* 68 **G6**
Kharian, *Pakistan* 68 **C5**
Kharit, Wadi el →, *Egypt* 80 **C3**
Khārk, Jazīreh-ye, *Iran* 71 **D6**
Kharkiv, *Ukraine* 47 **H9**
Kharkov = Kharkiv, *Ukraine* . . 47 **H9**
Kharmanli, *Bulgaria* 41 **E9**
Kharovsk, *Russia* 46 **C11**
Kharsawangarh, *India* 69 **H11**
Kharta, *Turkey* 72 **B3**
Khartoum = El Khartûm, *Sudan* 81 **D3**
Khasan, *Russia* 54 **C5**
Khasavyurt, *Russia* 49 **J8**
Khāsh, *Iran* 66 **E2**
Khashm el Girba, *Sudan* 81 **E4**
Khashum, *Sudan* 81 **E2**
Khashuri, *Georgia* 49 **J6**
Khaskovo, *Bulgaria* 41 **E9**
Khaskovo □, *Bulgaria* 41 **E9**
Khatanga, *Russia* 51 **B11**
Khatanga →, *Russia* 51 **B11**
Khatauli, *India* 68 **E7**
Khatra, *India* 69 **H12**
Khātūnābād, *Iran* 71 **D7**
Khatyrka, *Russia* 51 **C18**
Khavda, *India* 68 **H3**
Khaybar, Ḩarrat, *Si. Arabia* . . . 70 **E4**
Khayelitsha, *S. Africa* 85 **L3**
Khāzimiyah, *Iraq* 70 **C4**
Khazzān Jabal al Awliyā, *Sudan* 81 **D3**
Khe Bo, *Vietnam* 64 **C5**
Khe Long, *Vietnam* 64 **B5**
Khed Brahma, *India* 66 **G8**
Khekra, *India* 68 **E7**
Khemarak Phouminville,
Cambodia 65 **G4**
Khemisset, *Morocco* 78 **B4**
Khemmarat, *Thailand* 64 **D5**
Khenāmān, *Iran* 71 **D8**
Khenchela, *Algeria* 78 **A7**
Khersān →, *Iran* 71 **D6**
Khérson, *Greece* 40 **E6**
Kherson, *Ukraine* 47 **J7**
Khersónisos Akrotíri, *Greece* . . 36 **D6**
Kheta →, *Russia* 51 **B11**
Khewari, *Pakistan* 68 **F3**
Khilchipur, *India* 68 **G7**
Khiliomódhion, *Greece* 38 **D4**
Khilok, *Russia* 51 **D12**
Khimki, *Russia* 46 **E9**
Khíos, *Greece* 39 **C8**
Khíos □, *Greece* 39 **C8**
Khirsadoh, *India* 69 **H8**
Khiuma = Hiiumaa, *Estonia* . . . 9 **G20**
Khiva, *Uzbekistan* 50 **E7**
Khīyāv, *Iran* 70 **B5**
Khlebarovo, *Bulgaria* 41 **C10**
Khlong Khlung, *Thailand* 64 **D2**
Khmelnik, *Ukraine* 47 **H4**
Khmelnitskiy = Khmelnytskyy,
Ukraine 47 **H4**
Khmelnytskyy, *Ukraine* 47 **H4**
Khmer Rep. = Cambodia ■,
Asia 64 **F5**
Khoai, Hon, *Vietnam* 65 **H5**
Khodoriv, *Ukraine* 47 **H3**
Khodzent = Khŭjand, *Tajikistan* 50 **E7**
Khojak Pass, *Afghan.* 68 **D2**
Khok Kloi, *Thailand* 65 **H2**
Khok Pho, *Thailand* 65 **J3**
Kholm, *Russia* 46 **D6**
Kholmsk, *Russia* 51 **E15**
Khomas Hochland, *Namibia* . . . 88 **C2**
Khombole, *Senegal* 82 **C1**
Khomeyn, *Iran* 71 **C6**
Khomeynī Shahr, *Iran* 71 **C6**
Khomodino, *Botswana* 88 **C3**
Khon Kaen, *Thailand* 64 **D4**
Khong →, *Cambodia* 64 **F5**
Khong Sedone, *Laos* 64 **E5**
Khonuu, *Russia* 51 **C15**
Khoper →, *Russia* 48 **F6**
Khor el 'Atash, *Sudan* 81 **E3**
Khóra, *Greece* 38 **D3**
Khóra Sfakíon, *Greece* 36 **D6**
Khorāsān □, *Iran* 71 **C8**
Khorat = Nakhon Ratchasima,
Thailand 64 **E4**
Khorat, Cao Nguyen, *Thailand* 64 **E4**
Khorixas, *Namibia* 88 **C1**
Khorol, *Ukraine* 47 **H7**
Khorramābād, *Khorāsān, Iran* . 71 **C8**
Khorramābād, *Lorestān, Iran* . . 71 **C6**
Khorrāmshahr, *Iran* 71 **D6**
Khorugh, *Tajikistan* 50 **F8**
Khosravī, *Iran* 71 **D6**
Khosrowābād, *Khuzestān, Iran* 71 **D6**
Khosrowābād, *Kordestān, Iran* . 70 **C5**
Khost, *Pakistan* 68 **D2**
Khosūyeh, *Iran* 71 **D7**
Khotyn, *Ukraine* 47 **H4**
Khouribga, *Morocco* 78 **B4**
Khowst, *Afghan.* 68 **C3**
Khowst □, *Afghan.* 66 **C6**
Khoyniki, *Belarus* 47 **G5**
Khrami →, *Georgia* 49 **K7**
Khrenovoye, *Russia* 48 **E5**
Khrisoúpolis, *Greece* 41 **F8**
Khristianá, *Greece* 39 **E7**
Khrysokhou B., *Cyprus* 36 **D11**
Khtapodhiá, *Greece* 39 **D7**
Khu Khan, *Thailand* 64 **E5**
Khudzhand = Khŭjand,
Tajikistan 50 **E7**
Khuff, *Si. Arabia* 70 **E5**
Khūgīānī, *Afghan.* 68 **D2**
Khuis, *Botswana* 88 **D3**
Khuiyala, *India* 68 **F4**
Khŭjand, *Tajikistan* 50 **E7**
Khujner, *India* 68 **H7**
Khulna, *Bangla.* 67 **H16**
Khulna □, *Bangla.* 67 **H16**
Khulo, *Georgia* 49 **K6**
Khumago, *Botswana* 88 **C3**
Khūnsorkh, *Iran* 71 **E8**
Khunti, *India* 69 **H11**
Khūr, *Iran* 71 **C8**
Khurai, *India* 68 **G8**
Khuraỳş, *Si. Arabia* 71 **E6**
Khureit, *Sudan* 81 **E2**
Khurīyā Murīyā, Jazā'ir, *Oman* 74 **D6**
Khurja, *India* 68 **E7**
Khūrmāl, *Iraq* 70 **C5**
Khurr, Wādī al, *Iraq* 70 **C4**
Khūsf, *Iran* 71 **C8**
Khush, *Afghan.* 66 **C3**
Khushab, *Pakistan* 68 **C5**
Khust, *Ukraine* 47 **H2**
Khuzdar, *Pakistan* 68 **F2**
Khūzestān □, *Iran* 71 **D6**
Khvāf, *Iran* 71 **C9**
Khvājeh, *Iran* 70 **B5**
Khvalynsk, *Russia* 48 **D9**
Khvānsār, *Iran* 71 **D7**
Khvatovka, *Russia* 48 **D8**
Khvor, *Iran* 71 **C7**
Khvorgū, *Iran* 71 **E8**
Khvormūj, *Iran* 71 **D6**
Khvoy, *Iran* 70 **B5**
Khvoynaya, *Russia* 46 **C8**
Khyber Pass, *Afghan.* 68 **B4**
Kiabukwa, *Dem. Rep. of*
the Congo 87 **D1**
Kiama, *Australia* 95 **E5**
Kiamba, *Phil.* 61 **H6**
Kiambi, *Dem. Rep. of the Congo* 86 **D2**
Kiambu, *Kenya* 86 **C4**
Kiangara, *Madag.* 89 **B8**
Kiangsi = Jiangxi □, *China* 59 **D11**
Kiangsu = Jiangsu □, *China* . . . 57 **H11**
Kiáton, *Greece* 38 **C4**
Kibæk, *Denmark* 11 **H2**
Kibanga Port, *Uganda* 86 **B3**
Kibara, *Tanzania* 86 **C3**
Kibare, Mts., *Dem. Rep. of*
the Congo 86 **D2**
Kibombo, *Dem. Rep. of*
the Congo 86 **C2**
Kibondo, *Tanzania* 86 **C3**
Kibre Mengist, *Ethiopia* 81 **F4**
Kibumbu, *Burundi* 86 **C2**
Kibungo, *Rwanda* 86 **C3**
Kibuye, *Burundi* 86 **C2**
Kibuye, *Rwanda* 86 **C2**
Kibwesa, *Tanzania* 86 **D2**
Kibwezi, *Kenya* 86 **C4**
Kicasalih, *Turkey* 41 **E10**
Kičevo, *Macedonia* 40 **E4**
Kichha, *India* 69 **E8**
Kichha →, *India* 69 **E8**
Kicking Horse Pass, *Canada* . . . 104 **C5**
Kidal, *Mali* 83 **B5**
Kidderminster, *U.K.* 13 **E5**
Kidete, *Tanzania* 86 **D4**
Kidira, *Senegal* 82 **C2**
Kidnappers, C., *N.Z.* 91 **H6**
Kidsgrove, *U.K.* 12 **D5**
Kidston, *Australia* 94 **B3**
Kidugallo, *Tanzania* 86 **D4**
Kiel, *Germany* 24 **A6**
Kiel Canal = Nord-Ostsee-
Kanal, *Germany* 24 **A5**
Kielce, *Poland* 45 **H7**
Kielder Water, *U.K.* 12 **B5**
Kieler Bucht, *Germany* 24 **A6**
Kiembara, *Burkina Faso* 82 **C4**
Kien Binh, *Vietnam* 65 **H5**
Kien Tan, *Vietnam* 65 **G5**
Kienge, *Dem. Rep. of the Congo* 87 **E2**
Kiessé, *Niger* 83 **C5**
Kiev = Kyyiv, *Ukraine* 47 **G6**
Kifaya, *Guinea* 82 **C2**
Kiffa, *Mauritania* 82 **B2**
Kifisiá, *Greece* 38 **C5**
Kifissós →, *Greece* 38 **C5**
Kifrī, *Iraq* 70 **C5**
Kigali, *Rwanda* 86 **C3**
Kigarama, *Tanzania* 86 **C3**
Kigelle, *Sudan* 81 **F3**
Kigoma □, *Tanzania* 86 **D3**
Kigoma-Ujiji, *Tanzania* 86 **C2**
Kigomasha, Ras, *Tanzania* 86 **C4**
Kığzı, *Turkey* 70 **B4**
Kihei, *U.S.A.* 106 **H16**
Kihnu, *Estonia* 9 **G21**
Kii-Sanchi, *Japan* 55 **G8**
Kii-Suidō, *Japan* 55 **H7**
Kikaiga-Shima, *Japan* 55 **K4**
Kikinda, *Serbia, Yug.* 42 **E5**
Kikládhes, *Greece* 38 **E6**
Kikládhes □, *Greece* 38 **D6**
Kikwit, *Dem. Rep. of the Congo* 84 **E3**
Kil, *Sweden* 10 **E7**
Kilafors, *Sweden* 10 **C10**
Kilar, *India* 68 **C7**
Kilauea Crater, *U.S.A.* 106 **J17**
Kilbrannan Sd., *U.K.* 14 **F3**
Kilchu, *N. Korea* 57 **D15**
Kilcoy, *Australia* 95 **D5**
Kildare, *Ireland* 15 **C5**
Kildare □, *Ireland* 15 **C5**
Kileikli, *Sudan* 81 **E2**
Kilfinnane, *Ireland* 15 **D3**
Kilgore, *U.S.A.* 113 **J7**
Kilibo, *Benin* 83 **D5**
Kilifi, *Kenya* 86 **C4**
Kilimanjaro, *Tanzania* 86 **C4**
Kilimanjaro □, *Tanzania* 86 **C4**
Kilimli, *Turkey* 72 **B4**
Kilindini, *Kenya* 86 **C4**
Kilis, *Turkey* 70 **B3**
Kiliya, *Ukraine* 47 **K5**
Kilkee, *Ireland* 15 **D2**
Kilkeel, *U.K.* 15 **B5**
Kilkenny, *Ireland* 15 **D4**
Kilkenny □, *Ireland* 15 **D4**
Kilkieran B., *Ireland* 15 **C2**
Kilkís, *Greece* 40 **F6**
Kilkís □, *Greece* 40 **E6**
Killala, *Ireland* 15 **B2**
Killala B., *Ireland* 15 **B2**
Killaloe, *Ireland* 15 **D3**
Killaloe Station, *Canada* 110 **A7**
Killarney, *Australia* 95 **D5**
Killarney, *Canada* 105 **D9**
Killarney, *Ireland* 15 **D2**
Killary Harbour, *Ireland* 15 **C2**
Killdeer, *U.S.A.* 112 **B3**
Killeberg, *Sweden* 11 **H8**
Killeen, *U.S.A.* 113 **K6**
Killin, *U.K.* 14 **E4**
Killíni, *Ilía, Greece* 38 **D3**
Killíni, *Korinthía, Greece* 38 **D4**
Killorglin, *Ireland* 15 **D2**
Killybegs, *Ireland* 15 **B3**
Kilmarnock, *U.K.* 14 **F4**
Kilmez, *Russia* 48 **B10**
Kilmez →, *Russia* 48 **B10**
Kilmore, *Australia* 95 **F3**
Kilondo, *Tanzania* 87 **D3**
Kilosa, *Tanzania* 86 **D4**
Kilrush, *Ireland* 15 **D2**
Kilwa Kisiwani, *Tanzania* 87 **D4**
Kilwa Kivinje, *Tanzania* 87 **D4**
Kilwa Masoko, *Tanzania* 87 **D4**
Kilwinning, *U.K.* 14 **F4**
Kim, *U.S.A.* 113 **G3**
Kim →, *Cameroon* 83 **D7**
Kimaam, *Indonesia* 63 **F9**
Kimamba, *Tanzania* 86 **D4**
Kimba, *Australia* 95 **E2**
Kimball, *Nebr., U.S.A.* 112 **E3**
Kimball, *S. Dak., U.S.A.* 112 **D5**
Kimberley, *Australia* 92 **C4**
Kimberley, *Canada* 104 **D5**
Kimberley, *S. Africa* 88 **D3**
Kimberly, *U.S.A.* 114 **E6**
Kimch'aek, *N. Korea* 57 **D15**
Kimch'ŏn, *S. Korea* 57 **F15**
Kími, *Greece* 38 **C6**
Kimje, *S. Korea* 57 **G14**
Kimmirut, *Canada* 101 **B13**
Kímolos, *Greece* 38 **E6**
Kimovsk, *Moskva, Russia* 46 **E9**
Kimovsk, *Tula, Russia* 46 **E10**
Kimparana, *Mali* 82 **C4**
Kimpese, *Dem. Rep. of*
the Congo 84 **F2**
Kimry, *Russia* 46 **D9**
Kimstad, *Sweden* 11 **F9**
Kinabalu, Gunong, *Malaysia* . . 62 **C5**
Kínaros, *Greece* 39 **E8**
Kinaskan L., *Canada* 104 **B2**
Kinbasket L., *Canada* 104 **C5**
Kincardine, *Canada* 102 **D3**
Kincolith, *Canada* 104 **B3**
Kinda, *Dem. Rep. of the Congo* 87 **D2**
Kindberg, *Austria* 26 **D8**
Kinde, *U.S.A.* 110 **C2**
Kinder Scout, *U.K.* 12 **D6**
Kindersley, *Canada* 105 **C7**
Kindia, *Guinea* 82 **D2**
Kindu, *Dem. Rep. of the Congo* 86 **C2**
Kinel, *Russia* 48 **D10**
Kineshma, *Russia* 48 **B6**
Kinesi, *Tanzania* 86 **C3**
King, L., *Australia* 93 **F2**
King, Mt., *Australia* 94 **D4**
King City, *U.S.A.* 116 **J5**
King Cr. →, *Australia* 94 **C2**
King Edward →, *Australia* 92 **B4**
King Frederick VI Land = Kong
Frederik VI Kyst, *Greenland* 4 **C5**
King George B., *Falk. Is.* 128 **G4**
King George I., *Antarctica* 5 **C18**
King George Is., *Canada* 101 **C11**
King I. = Kadan Kyun, *Burma* . 64 **F2**
King I., *Australia* 94 **F3**
King I., *Canada* 104 **C3**
King Leopold Ranges, *Australia* 92 **C4**
King of Prussia, *U.S.A.* 111 **F9**
King Sd., *Australia* 92 **C3**
King William I., *Canada* 100 **B10**
King William's Town, *S. Africa* 88 **E4**
Kingaok = Bathurst Inlet,
Canada 100 **B9**
Kingaroy, *Australia* 95 **D5**
Kingfisher, *U.S.A.* 113 **H6**
Kingirbān, *Iraq* 70 **C5**
Kingisepp = Kuressaare, *Estonia* 9 **G20**
Kingisepp, *Russia* 46 **C5**
Kingman, *Ariz., U.S.A.* 117 **K12**
Kingman, *Kans., U.S.A.* 113 **G5**
Kingoonya, *Australia* 95 **E2**
Kingri, *Pakistan* 68 **D3**
Kings →, *U.S.A.* 116 **J7**
Kings Canyon National Park,
U.S.A. 116 **J8**
King's Lynn, *U.K.* 12 **E8**
Kings Mountain, *U.S.A.* 109 **H5**
Kings Park, *U.S.A.* 111 **F11**
King's Peak, *U.S.A.* 114 **F8**
Kingsbridge, *U.K.* 13 **G4**
Kingsburg, *U.S.A.* 116 **J7**
Kingscote, *Australia* 95 **F2**
Kingscourt, *Ireland* 15 **C5**
Kingsford, *U.S.A.* 108 **C1**
Kingsland, *U.S.A.* 109 **K5**
Kingsley, *U.S.A.* 112 **D7**
Kingsport, *U.S.A.* 109 **G4**
Kingston, *Canada* 102 **D4**
Kingston, *Jamaica* 120 **C4**
Kingston, *N.Z.* 91 **L2**
Kingston, *N.H., U.S.A.* 111 **D13**
Kingston, *N.Y., U.S.A.* 111 **E11**
Kingston, *Pa., U.S.A.* 111 **E9**
Kingston, *R.I., U.S.A.* 111 **E13**
Kingston Pk., *U.S.A.* 117 **K11**
Kingston South East, *Australia* 95 **F2**
Kingston upon Hull, *U.K.* 12 **D7**
Kingston upon Hull □, *U.K.* . . . 12 **D7**
Kingston-upon-Thames □, *U.K.* 13 **F7**
Kingstown, *St. Vincent* 121 **D7**
Kingstree, *U.S.A.* 109 **J6**
Kingsville, *Canada* 102 **D3**
Kingsville, *U.S.A.* 113 **M6**
Kingussie, *U.K.* 14 **D4**

Kingwood, U.S.A. 113 K7
Kınık, Antalya, Turkey 39 E11
Kınık, İzmir, Turkey 39 B9
Kinistino, Canada 105 C7
Kinkala, Congo 84 E2
Kinki □, Japan 55 H8
Kinleith, N.Z. 91 H5
Kinmount, Canada 110 B6
Kinna, Sweden 11 G6
Kinnairds Hd., U.K. 14 D6
Kinnared, Sweden 11 G7
Kinnarodden, Norway 6 A11
Kinnarp, Sweden 11 F7
Kinneviken, Sweden 11 F7
Kinngait = Cape Dorset, Canada 101 B12
Kino, Mexico 118 B2
Kinoje →, Canada 102 B3
Kinomoto, Japan 55 G8
Kinoni, Uganda 86 C3
Kinoosao, Canada 105 B8
Kinross, U.K. 14 E5
Kinsale, Ireland 15 E3
Kinsale, Old Hd. of, Ireland 15 E3
Kinsha = Chang Jiang →, China 59 B13
Kinshasa, Dem. Rep. of the Congo 84 E3
Kinsley, U.S.A. 113 G5
Kinsman, U.S.A. 110 E4
Kinston, U.S.A. 109 H7
Kintampo, Ghana 83 D4
Kintore Ra., Australia 92 D4
Kintyre, U.K. 14 F3
Kintyre, Mull of, U.K. 14 F3
Kinushseo →, Canada 102 A3
Kinuso, Canada 104 B5
Kinyangiri, Tanzania 86 C3
Kinyeti, Sudan 81 G3
Kinzig →, Germany 25 G3
Kinzua, U.S.A. 110 E6
Kinzua Dam, U.S.A. 110 E6
Kióni, Greece 38 C2
Kiosk, Canada 102 C4
Kiowa, Kans., U.S.A. 113 G5
Kiowa, Okla., U.S.A. 113 H7
Kipahigan L., Canada 105 B8
Kipanga, Tanzania 86 D4
Kiparissía, Greece 38 D3
Kiparissiakós Kólpos, Greece 38 D3
Kipawa, L., Canada 102 C4
Kipembawe, Tanzania 86 D3
Kipengere Ra., Tanzania 87 D3
Kipili, Tanzania 86 D3
Kipini, Kenya 86 C5
Kipling, Canada 105 C8
Kippure, Ireland 15 C5
Kipushi, Dem. Rep. of the Congo 87 E2
Kirane, Mali 82 B2
Kiranomena, Madag. 89 B8
Kiraz, Turkey 39 C10
Kirazlı, Turkey 41 F10
Kirchhain, Germany 24 E4
Kirchheim, Germany 25 G5
Kirchheimbolanden, Germany 25 F3
Kirchschlag, Austria 27 D9
Kireç, Turkey 39 B10
Kirensk, Russia 51 D11
Kirghizia = Kyrgyzstan ■, Asia 50 E8
Kirghizstan = Kyrgyzstan ■, Asia 50 E8
Kiribati ■, Pac. Oc. 96 H10
Kırıkhan, Turkey 72 D7
Kırıkkale, Turkey 72 C5
Kirillov, Russia 46 C10
Kirin = Jilin, China 57 C14
Kirishi, Russia 46 C7
Kiritimati, Kiribati 97 G12
Kırka, Turkey 39 B12
Kırkağaç, Turkey 39 B9
Kirkby, U.K. 12 D5
Kirkby Lonsdale, U.K. 12 C5
Kirkcaldy, U.K. 14 E5
Kirkcudbright, U.K. 14 G4
Kirkee, India 66 K8
Kirkenes, Norway 8 B23
Kirkfield, Canada 110 B6
Kirkjubæjarklaustur, Iceland 8 E4
Kirkkonummi, Finland 9 F21
Kirkland Lake, Canada 102 C3
Kırklareli, Turkey 41 E11
Kırklareli □, Turkey 41 E11
Kirksville, U.S.A. 112 E8
Kirkūk, Iraq 70 C5
Kirkwall, U.K. 14 C6
Kirkwood, S. Africa 88 E4
Kirn, Germany 25 F3
Kirov, Kaluga, Russia 46 E8
Kirov, Kirov, Russia 50 D5
Kirovabad = Gäncä, Azerbaijan 49 K8
Kirovakan = Vanadzor, Armenia 49 K7
Kirovograd = Kirovohrad, Ukraine 47 H7
Kirovohrad, Ukraine 47 H7
Kirovsk = Babadayhan, Turkmenistan 50 F7
Kirovskiy, Astrakhan, Russia 49 H9
Kirovskiy, Kamchatka, Russia 51 D16
Kirovskiy, Primorsk, Russia 54 B6
Kirriemuir, U.K. 14 E5
Kirsanov, Russia 48 D6
Kırşehir, Turkey 70 B2
Kirtachi, Niger 83 C5
Kirthar Range, Pakistan 68 F2
Kirtland, U.S.A. 115 H9
Kiruna, Sweden 8 C19
Kirundu, Dem. Rep. of the Congo 86 C2
Kirya, Russia 48 C8
Kiryū, Japan 55 F9
Kisa, Sweden 11 G9
Kisaga, Tanzania 86 C3
Kisalaya, Nic. 120 D3
Kisalföld, Hungary 42 C2
Kisámou, Kólpos, Greece 36 D5
Kisanga, Dem. Rep. of the Congo 86 B2
Kisangani, Dem. Rep. of the Congo 86 B2
Kisar, Indonesia 63 F7
Kisarawe, Tanzania 86 D4
Kisarazu, Japan 55 G9
Kisbér, Hungary 42 C3
Kishanganga →, Pakistan 69 B5
Kishanganj, India 69 F13
Kishangarh, Raj., India 68 F6
Kishangarh, Raj., India 68 F4
Kishi, Nigeria 83 D5
Kishinev = Chişinău, Moldova 43 C13
Kishiwada, Japan 55 G7
Kishtwar, India 69 C6
Kisielice, Poland 44 E6
Kisii, Kenya 86 C3
Kisiju, Tanzania 86 D4
Kisir, Turkey 73 B10
Kisizi, Uganda 86 C2
Kiskomárom = Zalakomár, Hungary 42 D2
Kiskörei-víztároló, Hungary 42 C5
Kiskőrös, Hungary 42 D4
Kiskundorozsma, Hungary 42 D5
Kiskunfélegyháza, Hungary 42 D4
Kiskunhalas, Hungary 42 D4
Kiskunmajsa, Hungary 42 D4
Kislovodsk, Russia 49 J6
Kismayu = Chisimaio, Somali Rep. 77 G8
Kiso-Gawa →, Japan 55 G8
Kiso-Sammyaku, Japan 55 G8
Kisofukushima, Japan 55 G8
Kisoro, Uganda 86 C2
Kissidougou, Guinea 82 D2
Kissimmee, U.S.A. 109 L5
Kissimmee →, U.S.A. 109 M5
Kississing L., Canada 105 B8
Kissónerga, Cyprus 36 E11
Kissu, J., Sudan 80 C2
Kistanje, Croatia 29 E12
Kisújszállás, Hungary 42 C5
Kisumu, Kenya 86 C3
Kisvárda, Hungary 42 B7
Kiswani, Tanzania 86 C4
Kiswere, Tanzania 87 D4
Kit Carson, U.S.A. 112 F3
Kita, Mali 82 C3
Kitaibaraki, Japan 55 F10
Kitakami, Japan 54 E10
Kitakami-Gawa →, Japan 54 E10
Kitakami-Sammyaku, Japan 54 E10
Kitakata, Japan 54 F9
Kitakyūshū, Japan 55 H5
Kitale, Kenya 86 B4
Kitami, Japan 54 C11
Kitami-Sammyaku, Japan 54 B11
Kitangiri, L., Tanzania 86 C3
Kitaya, Tanzania 87 E5
Kitchener, Canada 102 D3
Kitee, Finland 46 A6
Kitega = Gitega, Burundi 86 C2
Kitengo, Dem. Rep. of the Congo 86 D1
Kitgum, Uganda 86 B3
Kíthira, Greece 38 E5
Kíthnos, Greece 38 D6
Kiti, Cyprus 36 E12
Kiti, C., Cyprus 36 E12
Kitimat, Canada 104 C3
Kitinen →, Finland 8 C22
Kitiyab, Sudan 81 D3
Kítros, Greece 40 F6
Kitsuki, Japan 55 H5
Kittakittaooloo, L., Australia 95 D2
Kittanning, U.S.A. 110 F5
Kittatinny Mts., U.S.A. 111 F10
Kittery, U.S.A. 109 D10
Kittilä, Finland 8 C21
Kitui, Kenya 86 C4
Kitwanga, Canada 104 B3
Kitwe, Zambia 87 E2
Kitzbühel, Austria 26 D5
Kitzbühler Alpen, Austria 26 D5
Kitzingen, Germany 25 F6
Kivarli, India 68 G5
Kivertsi, Ukraine 47 G3
Kividhes, Cyprus 36 E11
Kivik, Sweden 11 J8
Kivotós, Greece 40 F5
Kivu, L., Dem. Rep. of the Congo 86 C2
Kiyev = Kyyiv, Ukraine 47 G6
Kiyevskoye Vdkhr. = Kyyivske Vdskh., Ukraine 47 G6
Kıyıköy, Turkey 41 E12
Kiziguru, Rwanda 86 C3
Kızıl Adalar, Turkey 41 F13
Kızıl Irmak →, Turkey 72 B6
Kizil Jilga, India 69 B8
Kizil Yurt, Russia 49 J8
Kızılcabölük, Turkey 39 D11
Kızılcadağ, Turkey 39 D11
Kızılcahamam, Turkey 72 B5
Kızılhisar, Turkey 72 D3
Kızılırmak, Turkey 72 B5
Kızılkaya, Turkey 39 D12
Kızılören, Turkey 39 C12
Kızıltepe, Turkey 70 B4
Kizimkazi, Tanzania 86 D4
Kizlyar, Russia 49 J8
Kizyl-Arvat = Gyzylarbat, Turkmenistan 50 F6
Kjellerup, Denmark 11 H3
Kjölur, Iceland 8 D4
Kladanj, Bos.-H. 42 F3
Kladnica, Serbia, Yug. 40 C4
Kladno, Czech Rep. 26 A7
Kladovo, Serbia, Yug. 40 B6
Klaeng, Thailand 64 F3
Klagenfurt, Austria 26 E7
Klaipėda, Lithuania 9 J19
Klaipėda □, Lithuania 44 C8
Klaksvík, Færoe Is. 8 E9
Klamath →, U.S.A. 114 F1
Klamath Falls, U.S.A. 114 E3
Klamath Mts., U.S.A. 114 F2
Klamono, Indonesia 63 E8
Klanjec, Croatia 29 B12
Klappan →, Canada 104 B3
Klarälven →, Sweden 10 E7
Klässbol, Sweden 10 E6
Klatovy, Czech Rep. 26 B6
Klawer, S. Africa 88 E2
Klazienaveen, Neths. 17 B6
Klé, Mali 82 C3
Klecko, Poland 45 F4
Kleczew, Poland 45 F5
Kleena Kleene, Canada 104 C4
Klein-Karas, Namibia 88 D2
Klekovača, Bos.-H. 29 D13
Klenoec, Macedonia 40 E4
Klenovec, Slovak Rep. 27 C12
Klerksdorp, S. Africa 88 D4
Kleszczele, Poland 45 F10
Kletnya, Russia 46 F7
Kletsk = Klyetsk, Belarus 47 F4
Kletskiy, Russia 49 F6
Kleve, Germany 24 D2
Klickitat, U.S.A. 114 D3
Klickitat →, U.S.A. 116 E5
Klidhes, Cyprus 36 D13
Klimovichi, Belarus 46 F6
Klin, Russia 46 D9
Klina, Kosovo, Yug. 40 D4
Klinaklini →, Canada 104 C3
Klintehamn, Sweden 11 G12
Klintsy, Russia 47 F7
Klip →, S. Africa 89 D4
Klipdale, S. Africa 88 E2
Klippan, Sweden 11 H7
Klipplaat, S. Africa 88 E3
Klisura, Bulgaria 41 D8
Kljajićevo, Serbia, Yug. 42 E4
Ključ, Bos.-H. 29 D13
Kłobuck, Poland 45 H5
Klockestrand, Sweden 10 B11
Kłodawa, Poland 45 F5
Kłodzko, Poland 45 H3
Klos, Albania 40 E4
Klosterneuburg, Austria 27 C9
Klosters, Switz. 25 J5
Klötze, Germany 24 C7
Klouto, Togo 83 D5
Kluane L., Canada 100 B6
Kluane Nat. Park, Canada 104 A1
Kluczbork, Poland 45 H5
Klukwan, U.S.A. 104 B1
Klyetsk, Belarus 47 F4
Klyuchevskaya, Gora, Russia 51 D17
Knäred, Sweden 11 H7
Knaresborough, U.K. 12 C6
Knee L., Man., Canada 102 A1
Knee L., Sask., Canada 105 B7
Knezha, Bulgaria 41 C8
Knić, Serbia, Yug. 40 C4
Knight Inlet, Canada 104 C3
Knighton, U.K. 13 E4
Knights Ferry, U.S.A. 116 H6
Knights Landing, U.S.A. 116 G5
Knin, Croatia 29 D13
Knislinge, Sweden 11 H8
Knittelfeld, Austria 26 D7
Knivsta, Sweden 10 E11
Knjaževac, Serbia, Yug. 40 C6
Knob, C., Australia 93 F2
Knock, Ireland 15 C3
Knockmealdown Mts., Ireland 15 D4
Knokke-Heist, Belgium 17 C3
Knossós, Greece 36 D7
Knowlton, Canada 111 A12
Knox, U.S.A. 108 E2
Knox Coast, Antarctica 5 C8
Knoxville, Iowa, U.S.A. 112 E8
Knoxville, Pa., U.S.A. 110 E7
Knoxville, Tenn., U.S.A. 109 H4
Knysna, S. Africa 88 E3
Knyszyn, Poland 44 E9
Ko Kha, Thailand 64 C2
Koartac = Quaqtaq, Canada 101 B13
Koba, Indonesia 63 F8
Kobarid, Slovenia 29 B10
Kobayashi, Japan 55 J5
Kobdo = Hovd, Mongolia 60 B4
Kōbe, Japan 55 G7
Kobelyaky, Ukraine 47 H8
København, Denmark 11 J6
Københavns Amtskommune □, Denmark 11 J6
Kobenni, Mauritania 82 B3
Kōbi-Sho, Japan 55 M1
Koblenz, Germany 25 E3
Kobo, Ethiopia 81 E4
Kobryn, Belarus 47 F3
Kobuleti, Georgia 49 K5
Kobylin, Poland 45 G4
Kobyłka, Poland 45 F8
Kobylkino, Russia 48 C6
Koca →, Turkey 41 F11
Kocabaş, Turkey 39 D11
Kocaeli, Turkey 41 F13
Kocaeli □, Turkey 41 F13
Kočane, Serbia, Yug. 40 C5
Kočani, Macedonia 40 E6
Koçarlı, Turkey 39 D9
Koceljevo, Serbia, Yug. 40 B3
Kočevje, Slovenia 29 C11
Koch Bihar, India 67 F16
Kochang, S. Korea 57 G14
Kochas, India 69 G10
Kocher →, Germany 25 F5
Kochi = Cochin, India 66 Q10
Kōchi, Japan 55 H6
Kōchi □, Japan 55 H6
Kochiu = Gejiu, China 58 F4
Kock, Poland 45 G9
Kodarma, India 69 G11
Kode, Sweden 11 G5
Kodiak, U.S.A. 100 C4
Kodiak I., U.S.A. 100 C4
Kodinar, India 68 J4
Kodok, Sudan 81 F3
Kodori →, Georgia 49 J5
Koedoesberge, S. Africa 88 E3
Koes, Namibia 88 D2
Kofçaz, Turkey 41 E11
Koffiefontein, S. Africa 88 D4
Kofiau, Indonesia 63 E7
Köflach, Austria 26 D8
Koforidua, Ghana 83 D4
Kōfu, Japan 55 G9
Koga, Japan 55 F9
Kogaluk →, Canada 103 A7
Køge, Denmark 11 J6
Køge Bugt, Denmark 11 J6
Kogi □, Nigeria 83 D6
Kogin Baba, Nigeria 83 D7
Koh-i-Khurd, Afghan. 68 C1
Koh-i-Maran, Pakistan 68 E2
Kohat, Pakistan 68 C4
Kohima, India 67 G19
Kohkīlūyeh va Būyer Aḩmadi □, Iran 71 D6
Kohler Ra., Antarctica 5 D15
Kohlu, Pakistan 68 E3
Kohtla-Järve, Estonia 9 G22
Koillismaa, Finland 8 D23
Koin-dong, N. Korea 57 D14
Koinare, Bulgaria 41 C8
Koindu, S. Leone 82 D2
Kojetín, Czech Rep. 27 B10
Kojŏ, N. Korea 57 E14
Kojonup, Australia 93 F2
Kojūr, Iran 71 B6
Koka, Sudan 80 C3
Kokand = Qŭqon, Uzbekistan 50 E8
Kokas, Indonesia 63 E8
Kokava, Slovak Rep. 27 C12
Kokchetav = Kökshetaū, Kazakstan 50 D7
Kokemäenjoki →, Finland 9 F19
Kokhma, Russia 48 B5
Koki, Senegal 82 B1
Kokkola, Finland 8 E20
Koko, Nigeria 83 C5
Koko Kyunzu, Burma 67 M18
Kokolopozo, Ivory C. 82 D3
Kokomo, U.S.A. 108 E2
Kokoro, Niger 83 C5
Koksan, N. Korea 57 E14
Kökshetaū, Kazakstan 50 D7
Koksoak →, Canada 101 C13
Kokstad, S. Africa 89 E4
Kokubu, Japan 55 J5
Kola, Indonesia 63 F8
Kola Pen. = Kolskiy Poluostrov, Russia 50 C4
Kolachi →, Pakistan 68 F2
Kolahoi, India 69 B6
Kolahun, Liberia 82 D2
Kolaka, Indonesia 63 E6
Kolar, India 66 N11
Kolar Gold Fields, India 66 N11
Kolaras, India 68 G6
Kolari, Finland 8 C20
Kolárovo, Slovak Rep. 27 D10
Kolašin, Montenegro, Yug. 40 D3
Kolayat, India 66 F8
Kolbäck, Sweden 10 E10
Kolbäcksån →, Sweden 10 E10
Kolbermoor, Germany 25 H8
Kolbuszowa, Poland 45 H8
Kolchugino = Leninsk-Kuznetskiy, Russia 50 D9
Kolchugino, Russia 46 D10
Kolda, Senegal 82 C2
Koldegi, Sudan 81 E3
Kolding, Denmark 11 J3
Kolepom = Dolak, Pulau, Indonesia 63 F9
Kolguyev, Ostrov, Russia 50 C5
Kolhapur, India 66 L9
Kolia, Ivory C. 82 D3
Kolín, Czech Rep. 26 A8
Kolind, Denmark 11 H4
Kolkas rags, Latvia 9 H20
Kolkata, India 69 H13
Kollam = Quilon, India 66 Q10
Kölleda, Germany 24 D7
Kollum, Neths. 17 A6
Kolmanskop, Namibia 88 D2
Köln, Germany 24 E2
Kolno, Poland 44 E8
Koło, Poland 45 F5
Kołobrzeg, Poland 44 D2
Kolokani, Mali 82 C3
Koloko, Burkina Faso 82 C3
Kololo, Ethiopia 81 F5
Kolomna, Russia 46 E10
Kolomyya, Ukraine 47 H3
Kolondiéba, Mali 82 C3
Kolonodale, Indonesia 63 E6
Kolonowskie, Poland 45 H5
Kolosib, India 67 G18
Kolpashevo, Russia 50 D9
Kolpino, Russia 46 C6
Kolpny, Russia 47 F9
Kolskiy Poluostrov, Russia 50 C4
Kolsva, Sweden 10 E9
Kolubara →, Serbia, Yug. 40 B4
Koluszki, Poland 45 G6
Kolwezi, Dem. Rep. of the Congo 87 E2
Kolyma →, Russia 51 C17
Kolymskoye Nagorye, Russia 51 C16
Kôm Hamâda, Egypt 80 H7
Kôm Ombo, Egypt 80 C3
Komadugu Gana →, Nigeria 83 C7
Komandorskiye Is. = Komandorskiye Ostrova, Russia 51 D17
Komandorskiye Ostrova, Russia 51 D17
Komárno, Slovak Rep. 27 D11
Komárom, Hungary 42 C3
Komárom-Esztergom □, Hungary 42 C3
Komatipoort, S. Africa 89 D5
Komatou Yialou, Cyprus 36 D13
Komatsu, Japan 55 F8
Komatsushima, Japan 55 H7
Kombissiri, Burkina Faso 83 C4
Kombori, Burkina Faso 82 C4
Kombóti, Greece 38 B3
Komen, Slovenia 29 C10
Komenda, Ghana 83 D4
Komi □, Russia 50 C6
Komiža, Croatia 29 E13
Komló, Hungary 42 D3
Kommunarsk = Alchevsk, Ukraine 47 H10
Kommunizma, Pik, Tajikistan 50 F8
Komodo, Indonesia 63 F5
Komoé →, Ivory C. 82 D4
Komoran, Pulau, Indonesia 63 F9
Komoro, Japan 55 F9
Komotini, Greece 41 E9
Komovi, Montenegro, Yug. 40 D3
Kompasberg, S. Africa 88 E3
Kompong Bang, Cambodia 65 F5
Kompong Cham, Cambodia 65 F5
Kompong Chhnang = Kampong Chhnang, Cambodia 65 F5
Kompong Chikreng, Cambodia 64 F5
Kompong Kleang, Cambodia 64 F5
Kompong Luong, Cambodia 65 G5
Kompong Pranak, Cambodia 64 F5
Kompong Som = Kampong Saom, Cambodia 65 G4
Kompong Som, Chhung = Kampong Saom, Chaak, Cambodia 65 G4
Kompong Speu, Cambodia 65 G5
Kompong Sralao, Cambodia 64 E5
Kompong Thom, Cambodia 64 F5
Kompong Trabeck, Cambodia 64 F5
Kompong Trabeck, Cambodia 65 G5
Kompong Trach, Cambodia 65 G5
Kompong Tralach, Cambodia 65 G5
Komrat = Comrat, Moldova 43 D13
Komsberg, S. Africa 88 E3
Komsomolets, Ostrov, Russia 51 A10
Komsomolsk, Amur, Russia 51 D14
Komsomolsk, Ivanovo, Russia 46 D11
Komsomolskiy, Russia 48 C7
Kömür Burnu, Turkey 39 C8
Kon Tum, Vietnam 64 E7
Kon Tum, Plateau du, Vietnam 64 E7
Kona, Mali 82 C4
Konakovo, Russia 46 D9
Konarhā □, Afghan. 66 B7
Konārī, Iran 71 D6
Konch, India 69 G8
Konde, Tanzania 86 C4
Kondiá, Greece 39 B7
Kondinin, Australia 93 F2
Kondoa, Tanzania 86 C4
Kondókali, Greece 36 A3
Kondopaga, Russia 46 A8
Kondratyevo, Russia 51 D10
Kondrovo, Russia 46 E8
Köneürgench, Turkmenistan 50 E6
Konevo, Russia 46 A10
Kong = Khong →, Cambodia 64 F5
Kong, Ivory C. 82 D4
Kong, Koh, Cambodia 65 G4
Kong Christian IX Land, Greenland 4 C6
Kong Christian X Land, Greenland 4 B6
Kong Frederik IX Land, Greenland 4 C5
Kong Frederik VI Kyst, Greenland 4 C5
Kong Frederik VIII Land, Greenland 4 B6
Kong Oscar Fjord, Greenland 4 B6
Kongeå →, Denmark 11 J2
Kongerslev, Denmark 11 H4
Kongju, S. Korea 57 F14
Konglu, Burma 67 F20
Kongola, Namibia 88 B3

Kongolo, Kasai-Or., Dem. Rep. of the Congo 86 D1
Kongolo, Katanga, Dem. Rep. of the Congo 86 D2
Kongor, Sudan 81 F3
Kongoussi, Burkina Faso 83 C4
Kongsberg, Norway 9 G13
Kongsvinger, Norway 9 F15
Kongwa, Tanzania 86 D4
Koni, Dem. Rep. of the Congo 87 E2
Koni, Mts., Dem. Rep. of the Congo 87 E2
Koniakari, Mali 82 C2
Koniecpol, Poland 45 H6
Königs Wusterhausen, Germany 24 C9
Königsberg = Kaliningrad, Russia 9 J19
Königsbrunn, Germany 25 G6
Königslutter, Germany 24 C6
Konin, Poland 45 F5
Konispol, Albania 40 G4
Kónitsa, Greece 38 A2
Konjic, Bos.-H. 42 G2
Konkiep, Namibia 88 D2
Konkouré →, Guinea 82 D2
Könnern, Germany 24 D7
Kono, S. Leone 82 D2
Konongo, Ghana 83 D4
Konosha, Russia 46 B11
Kōnosu, Japan 55 F9
Konotop, Ukraine 47 G7
Konsankoro, Guinea 82 D3
Końskie, Poland 45 G7
Konstancin-Jeziorna, Poland 45 F8
Konstantinovka = Kostyantynivka, Ukraine 47 H9
Konstantinovsk, Russia 49 G5
Konstantynów Łódźki, Poland 45 G6
Konstanz, Germany 25 H5
Kont, Iran 71 E9
Kontagora, Nigeria 83 C6
Kontcha, Cameroon 83 D7
Konya, Turkey 70 B2
Konya Ovası, Turkey 72 C5
Konz, Germany 25 F2
Konza, Kenya 86 C4
Koocanusa, L., Canada 114 B6
Kookynie, Australia 93 E3
Koolyanobbing, Australia 93 F2
Koonibba, Australia 95 E1
Koorawatha, Australia 95 E4
Koorda, Australia 93 F2
Kooskia, U.S.A. 114 C6
Kootenay →, U.S.A. 104 D5
Kootenay L., Canada 104 D5
Kootenay Nat. Park, Canada 104 C5
Kootjieskolk, S. Africa 88 E3
Kopanovka, Russia 49 G8
Kopaonik, Yugoslavia 40 C4
Kópavogur, Iceland 8 D3
Koper, Slovenia 29 C10
Kopervik, Norway 9 G11
Kopet Dagh, Asia 71 B8
Kopi, Australia 95 E2
Köping, Sweden 10 E10
Köpingsvik, Sweden 11 H10
Kopište, Croatia 29 F13
Koplik, Albania 40 D3
Köpmanholmen, Sweden 10 A12
Kopparberg, Sweden 10 E9
Koppeh Dāgh = Kopet Dagh, Asia 71 B8
Koppies, S. Africa 89 D4
Koppom, Sweden 10 E6
Koprivlen, Bulgaria 40 E7
Koprivnica, Croatia 29 B13
Kopřivnice, Czech Rep. 27 B11
Koprivshtitsa, Bulgaria 41 D8
Köprübaşı, Turkey 39 C10
Kopychyntsi, Ukraine 47 H3
Korab, Macedonia 40 E4
Korakiána, Greece 36 A3
Koral, India 68 J5
Korarou, L., Mali 82 B4
Korba, India 69 H10
Korbach, Germany 24 D4
Korbu, G., Malaysia 65 K3
Korce = Korçë, Albania 40 F4
Korçë, Albania 40 F4
Korčula, Croatia 29 F13
Korčulanski Kanal, Croatia 29 E13
Kord Küy, Iran 71 B7
Kord Sheykh, Iran 71 D7
Kordestān □, Iran 70 C5
Kordofân, Sudan 79 F11
Koré Mayroua, Niger 83 C5
Korea, North ■, Asia 57 E14
Korea, South ■, Asia 57 G15
Korea Bay, Korea 57 E13
Korea Strait, Asia 57 H15
Korem, Ethiopia 81 E4
Korenevo, Russia 47 G8
Korenovsk, Russia 49 H4
Korets, Ukraine 47 G4
Korfantów, Poland 45 H4
Korgan, Turkey 72 B7
Korgus, Sudan 80 D3
Korhogo, Ivory C. 82 D3
Koribundu, S. Leone 82 D2
Korienzé, Mali 82 B4
Korinthía □, Greece 38 D4
Korinthiakós Kólpos, Greece 38 C4
Kórinthos, Greece 38 D4
Korioumé, Mali 82 B4
Koríssa, Límni, Greece 36 B3
Kōriyama, Japan 54 F10
Korkuteli, Turkey 39 D12
Kormakiti, C., Cyprus 36 D11
Körmend, Hungary 42 C1
Kornat, Croatia 29 E12
Korneshty = Corneşti, Moldova 43 C13
Korneuburg, Austria 27 C9
Kórnik, Poland 45 F4
Koro, Fiji 91 C8
Koro, Ivory C. 82 D3
Koro, Mali 82 C4
Koro Sea, Fiji 91 C9
Korocha, Russia 47 G9
Köroğlu Dağları, Turkey 72 B5
Korogwe, Tanzania 86 D4
Koronadal, Phil. 61 H6
Koróni, Greece 38 E3
Korónia, Límni, Greece 40 F7
Koronís, Greece 39 D7
Koronowo, Poland 45 E4
Koror, Palau 63 C8
Körös →, Hungary 42 D5
Köröstarcsa, Hungary 42 D6
Korosten, Ukraine 47 G5
Korostyshev, Ukraine 47 G5
Korotoyak, Russia 47 G10
Korraraika, Helodranon' i, Madag. 89 B7
Korsakov, Russia 51 E15
Korsberga, Sweden 11 G9
Korshunovo, Russia 51 D12
Korsør, Denmark 11 J5
Korsun Shevchenkovskiy, Ukraine 47 H6
Korsze, Poland 44 D8
Korti, Sudan 80 D3
Kortrijk, Belgium 17 D3
Korucu, Turkey 39 B9
Korwai, India 68 G8
Koryakskoye Nagorye, Russia 51 C18
Koryŏng, S. Korea 57 G15
Koryukovka, Ukraine 47 G7
Kos, Greece 39 E9
Kosa, Ethiopia 81 F4
Kosaya Gora, Russia 46 E9
Kościan, Poland 45 F3
Kościerzyna, Poland 44 D4
Kosciusko, U.S.A. 113 J10
Kosciuszko, Mt., Australia 95 F4
Kösély →, Hungary 42 C6
Kosha, Sudan 80 C3
Koshava, Bulgaria 40 B7
K'oshih = Kashi, China 60 C2
Koshiki-Rettō, Japan 55 J4
Kosi, India 68 F7
Kosi →, India 69 E8
Košice, Slovak Rep. 27 C14
Košický □, Slovak Rep. 27 C14
Kosjerić, Serbia, Yug. 40 B3
Köşk, Turkey 39 D10
Koskhinoú, Greece 36 C10
Koslan, Russia 50 C5
Kosŏng, N. Korea 57 E15
Kosovo □, Yugoslavia 40 D4
Kosovo Polje, Kosovo, Yug. 40 D5
Kosovska Kamenica, Kosovo, Yug. 40 D5
Kosovska Mitrovica, Kosovo, Yug. 40 D4
Kossou, L. de, Ivory C. 82 D3
Kosta, Sweden 11 H9
Kostajnica, Croatia 29 C13
Kostanjevica, Slovenia 29 C12
Kostenets, Bulgaria 40 D7
Koster, S. Africa 88 D4
Kôstî, Sudan 81 E3
Kostinbrod, Bulgaria 40 D7
Kostolac, Serbia, Yug. 40 B5
Kostopil, Ukraine 47 G4
Kostroma, Russia 46 D11
Kostromskoye Vdkhr., Russia 46 D11
Kostrzyn, Lubuskie, Poland 45 F1
Kostrzyn, Wielkopolskie, Poland 45 F4
Kostyantynivka, Ukraine 47 H9
Kostyukovichi = Kastsyukovichy, Belarus 46 F7
Koszalin, Poland 44 D3
Kőszeg, Hungary 42 C1
Kot Addu, Pakistan 68 D4
Kot Kapura, India 68 D6
Kot Moman, Pakistan 68 C5
Kot Sultan, Pakistan 68 D4
Kota, India 68 G6
Kota Baharu, Malaysia 65 J4
Kota Barrage, India 68 G6
Kota Belud, Malaysia 62 C5
Kota Kinabalu, Malaysia 62 C5
Kota Kubu Baharu, Malaysia 65 L3
Kota Tinggi, Malaysia 65 M4
Kotaagung, Indonesia 62 F2
Kotabaru, Indonesia 62 E5
Kotabumi, Indonesia 62 E2
Kotamobagu, Indonesia 63 D6
Kotcho L., Canada 104 B4
Kotdwara, India 69 E8
Kotel, Bulgaria 41 D10
Kotelnich, Russia 48 A9
Kotelnikovo, Russia 49 G6
Kotelnyy, Ostrov, Russia 51 B14
Kothari →, India 68 G6
Köthen, Germany 24 D7
Kothi, Mad. P., India 69 H10
Kothi, Mad. P., India 69 G9
Kotiro, Pakistan 68 F2
Kotka, Finland 9 F22
Kotlas, Russia 50 C5
Kotlenska Planina, Bulgaria 41 D10
Kotli, Pakistan 68 C5
Kotma, India 69 H9
Kotmul, Pakistan 69 B6
Koton-Karifi, Nigeria 83 D6
Kotonkoro, Nigeria 83 C6
Kotor, Montenegro, Yug. 40 D2
Kotor Varoš, Bos.-H. 42 F2
Kotoriba, Croatia 29 B13
Kotovo, Russia 48 E7
Kotovsk, Russia 48 D5
Kotovsk, Ukraine 47 J5
Kotputli, India 68 F7
Kotri, Pakistan 68 G3
Kótronas, Greece 38 E4
Kötschach-Mauthen, Austria 26 E6
Kotturu, India 66 M10
Kotuy →, Russia 51 B11
Kotzebue, U.S.A. 100 B3
Koudougou, Burkina Faso 82 C4
Koufonisi, Greece 36 E8
Koufonísia, Greece 39 E7
Kougaberge, S. Africa 88 E3
Kouibli, Ivory C. 82 D3
Kouilou →, Congo 84 E2
Koula Moutou, Gabon 84 E2
Koulen = Kulen, Cambodia 64 F5
Koulikoro, Mali 82 C3
Kouloúra, Greece 36 A3
Koúm-bournoú, Ákra, Greece 36 C10
Koumala, Australia 94 C4
Koumankou, Mali 82 C3
Koumbia, Burkina Faso 82 C4
Koumbia, Guinea 82 C2
Koumboum, Guinea 82 C2
Koumpenntoum, Senegal 82 C2
Koumra, Chad 79 G9
Koun-Fao, Ivory C. 82 D4
Koundara, Guinea 82 C2
Koundian, Guinea 82 C3
Koungheul, Senegal 82 C2
Kounradskiy, Kazakstan 50 E8
Kountze, U.S.A. 113 K7
Koupéla, Burkina Faso 83 C4
Kourémalé, Mali 82 C3
Kouris →, Cyprus 36 E11
Kourou, Fr. Guiana 125 B8
Kourouba, Mali 82 C2
Kouroukoto, Mali 82 C2
Kourouma, Burkina Faso 82 C4
Kourouninkoto, Mali 82 C3
Kouroussa, Guinea 82 C3
Koussanar, Senegal 82 C2
Koussané, Mali 82 C2
Koussane, Senegal 82 C2
Kousseri, Cameroon 79 F8
Koutiala, Mali 82 C3
Kouto, Ivory C. 82 D3
Kouvé, Togo 83 D5
Kouvola, Finland 9 F22
Kovačica, Serbia, Yug. 42 E5
Kovel, Ukraine 47 G3
Kovin, Serbia, Yug. 42 F5
Kovrov, Russia 48 B5
Kowal, Poland 45 F6
Kowalewo Pomorskie, Poland 45 E5
Kowanyama, Australia 94 B3
Kowloon, H.K. 59 F10
Kowŏn, N. Korea 57 E14
Köyceğiz, Turkey 39 E10
Köyceğiz Gölü, Turkey 39 E10
Koyulhisar, Turkey 72 B7
Koyunyeri, Turkey 41 F10
Koza, Japan 55 L3
Kozak, Turkey 39 B9
Kozan, Turkey 70 B2
Kozáni, Greece 40 F5
Kozáni □, Greece 40 F5
Kozara, Bos.-H. 29 D14
Kozarac, Bos.-H. 29 D13
Kozelets, Ukraine 47 G6
Kozelsk, Russia 46 E8
Kozhikode = Calicut, India 66 P9
Koziegłowy, Poland 45 H6
Kozienice, Poland 45 G8
Kozje, Slovenia 29 B12
Kozloduy, Bulgaria 40 C7
Kozlovets, Bulgaria 41 C9
Kozlovka, Russia 48 C9
Kozlu, Turkey 72 B4
Kozluk, Turkey 73 C9
Koźmin, Poland 45 G4
Kozmodemyansk, Russia 48 B8
Kożuchów, Poland 45 G2
Kozyatyn, Ukraine 47 H5
Kpabia, Ghana 83 D4
Kpalimé, Togo 83 D5
Kpandae, Ghana 83 D4
Kpessi, Togo 83 D5
Kra, Isthmus of = Kra, Kho Khot, Thailand 65 G2
Kra, Kho Khot, Thailand 65 G2
Kra Buri, Thailand 65 G2
Kraai →, S. Africa 88 E4
Krabi, Thailand 65 H2
Kracheh, Cambodia 64 F6
Kragan, Indonesia 63 G14
Kragerø, Norway 9 G13
Kragujevac, Serbia, Yug. 40 B4
Krajenka, Poland 45 E3
Krajina, Bos.-H. 29 D13
Krakatau = Rakata, Pulau, Indonesia 62 F3
Krakatoa = Rakata, Pulau, Indonesia 62 F3
Krakor, Cambodia 64 F5
Kraków, Poland 45 H6
Kralanh, Cambodia 64 F4
Králíky, Czech Rep. 27 A9
Kraljevo, Serbia, Yug. 40 C4
Královéhradecký □, Czech Rep. 26 A8
Královský Chlmec, Slovak Rep. 27 C14
Kralupy nad Vltavou, Czech Rep. 26 A7
Kramatorsk, Ukraine 47 H9
Kramfors, Sweden 10 B11
Kraniá, Greece 40 G5
Kranía Elassónas, Greece 38 B4
Kranídhion, Greece 38 D5
Kranj, Slovenia 29 B11
Kranjska Gora, Slovenia 29 B10
Krankskop, S. Africa 89 D5
Krapina, Croatia 29 B12
Krapina →, Croatia 29 C12
Krapkowice, Poland 45 H4
Kras, Croatia 29 C10
Kraskino, Russia 51 E14
Krāslava, Latvia 46 E4
Kraslice, Czech Rep. 26 A5
Krasnaya Gorbatka, Russia 48 C5
Krasnaya Polyana, Russia 49 J5
Kraśnik, Poland 45 H9
Krasnoarmeisk, Ukraine 47 H9
Krasnoarmeysk, Russia 48 E7
Krasnoarmeyskiy, Russia 49 G6
Krasnobrod, Poland 45 H10
Krasnodar, Russia 49 H4
Krasnodon, Ukraine 47 H10
Krasnogorskiy, Russia 48 B9
Krasnograd = Krasnohrad, Ukraine 47 H8
Krasnogvardeyskoye, Russia 49 H5
Krasnogvardyesk, Ukraine 47 K8
Krasnohrad, Ukraine 47 H8
Krasnokutsk, Ukraine 47 G8
Krasnolesnyy, Russia 47 G10
Krasnoperekopsk, Ukraine 47 J7
Krasnorechenskiy, Russia 54 B7
Krasnoselkup, Russia 50 C9
Krasnoslobodsk, Mordvinia, Russia 48 C6
Krasnoslobodsk, Volgograd, Russia 49 F7
Krasnoturinsk, Russia 50 D7
Krasnovodsk = Türkmenbashi, Turkmenistan 50 E6
Krasnoyarsk, Russia 51 D10
Krasnoye = Krasnyy, Russia 46 E6
Krasnozavodsk, Russia 46 D10
Krasny Sulin, Russia 47 J11
Krasnystaw, Poland 45 H10
Krasnyy, Russia 46 E6
Krasnyy Kholm, Russia 46 C9
Krasnyy Kut, Russia 48 E8
Krasnyy Liman, Ukraine 47 H9
Krasnyy Luch, Ukraine 47 H10
Krasnyy Profintern, Russia 46 D11
Krasnyy Yar, Astrakhan, Russia 49 G9
Krasnyy Yar, Samara, Russia 48 D10
Krasnyy Yar, Volgograd, Russia 48 E7
Krasnyye Baki, Russia 48 B7
Krasnyyoskolske Vdskh., Ukraine 47 H9
Kraszna →, Hungary 42 B7
Kratie = Kracheh, Cambodia 64 F6
Kratovo, Macedonia 40 D6
Krau, Indonesia 63 E10
Kravanh, Chuor Phnum, Cambodia 65 G4
Krefeld, Germany 24 D2
Kremasta, Límni, Greece 38 C3
Kremen, Croatia 29 D12
Kremenchug = Kremenchuk, Ukraine 47 H7
Kremenchuk, Ukraine 47 H7
Kremenchuksk Vdskh., Ukraine 47 H7
Kremenets, Ukraine 47 G3
Kremennaya, Ukraine 47 H10
Kremges = Svitlovodsk, Ukraine 47 H7
Kremmen, Germany 24 C9
Kremmling, U.S.A. 114 F10
Kremnica, Slovak Rep. 27 C11
Krems, Austria 26 C8
Kremsmünster, Austria 26 C7
Kretinga, Lithuania 9 J19
Krettsy, Russia 46 C7
Kreuzberg, Germany 25 E5
Kreuztal, Germany 24 E4
Kría Vrísi, Greece 40 F6
Kribi, Cameroon 83 E6
Krichem, Bulgaria 41 D8
Krichev = Krychaw, Belarus 46 F6
Krim, Slovenia 29 C11
Kriós, Ákra, Greece 36 D5
Krishna →, India 67 M12
Krishnanagar, India 69 H13
Kristdala, Sweden 11 G10
Kristiansand, Norway 9 G13
Kristianstad, Sweden 11 H8
Kristiansund, Norway 8 E12
Kristiinankaupunki, Finland 9 E19
Kristinehamn, Sweden 10 E8
Kristinestad = Kristiinankaupunki, Finland 9 E19
Kríti, Greece 36 D7
Kritsá, Greece 36 D7
Kriva →, Macedonia 40 D5
Kriva Palanka, Macedonia 40 D6
Krivaja →, Bos.-H. 42 F3
Krivelj, Serbia, Yug. 40 B6
Krivoy Rog = Kryvyy Rih, Ukraine 47 J7
Križevci, Croatia 29 B13
Krk, Croatia 29 C11
Krka →, Slovenia 29 C12
Krkonoše, Czech Rep. 26 A8
Krnov, Czech Rep. 27 A10
Krobia, Poland 45 G3
Krokeaí, Greece 38 E4
Krokek, Sweden 11 F10
Krokodil →, Mozam. 89 D5
Krokom, Sweden 10 A8
Krokowa, Poland 44 D5
Krolevets, Ukraine 47 G7
Kroměříž, Czech Rep. 27 B10
Krompachy, Slovak Rep. 27 C13
Kromy, Russia 47 F8
Kronach, Germany 25 E7
Krong Kaoh Kong, Cambodia 62 B2
Kronobergs län □, Sweden 11 H8
Kronprins Olav Kyst, Antarctica 5 C5
Kronshtadt, Russia 46 C5
Kroonstad, S. Africa 88 D4
Kröpelin, Germany 24 A7
Kropotkin, Russia 49 H5
Kropp, Germany 24 A5
Krosna, Lithuania 44 D10
Krośniewice, Poland 45 F6
Krosno, Poland 45 J8
Krosno Odrzańskie, Poland 45 F2
Krotoszyn, Poland 45 G4
Krotovka, Russia 48 D10
Kroussón, Greece 36 D6
Krrabë, Albania 40 E3
Krško, Slovenia 29 C12
Krstača, Serbia, Yug. 40 D4
Kruger Nat. Park, S. Africa 89 C5
Krugersdorp, S. Africa 89 D4
Kruisfontein, S. Africa 88 E3
Krujë, Albania 40 E3
Krulevshchina = Krulyewshchyna, Belarus 46 E4
Krulyewshchyna, Belarus 46 E4
Krumbach, Germany 25 G6
Krumë, Albania 40 D4
Krumovgrad, Bulgaria 41 E9
Krung Thep = Bangkok, Thailand 64 F3
Krupanj, Serbia, Yug. 40 B3
Krupina, Slovak Rep. 27 C12
Krupinica →, Slovak Rep. 27 C11
Krupki, Belarus 46 E5
Kruševac, Serbia, Yug. 40 C5
Kruševo, Macedonia 40 E5
Kruszwica, Poland 45 F5
Krychaw, Belarus 46 F6
Krymsk, Russia 47 K10
Krymskiy Poluostrov = Krymskyy Pivostriv, Ukraine 47 K8
Krymskyy Pivostriv, Ukraine 47 K8
Krynica, Poland 45 J7
Krynica Morska, Poland 44 D6
Krynki, Poland 45 E10
Kryvyy Rih, Ukraine 47 J7
Krzepice, Poland 45 H5
Krzeszów, Poland 45 H9
Krzna →, Poland 45 F10
Krzywiń, Poland 45 G3
Krzyż Wielkopolski, Poland 45 F2
Ksar el Kebir, Morocco 78 B4
Ksar es Souk = Er Rachidia, Morocco 78 B5
Książ Wielkopolski, Poland 45 F4
Kstovo, Russia 48 B7
Ku, W. el →, Sudan 81 E2
Kuala Belait, Malaysia 62 D4
Kuala Berang, Malaysia 65 K4
Kuala Dungun = Dungun, Malaysia 65 K4
Kuala Kangsar, Malaysia 65 K3
Kuala Kelawang, Malaysia 65 L4
Kuala Kerai, Malaysia 65 K4
Kuala Lipis, Malaysia 65 K4
Kuala Lumpur, Malaysia 65 L3
Kuala Nerang, Malaysia 65 J3
Kuala Pilah, Malaysia 65 L4
Kuala Rompin, Malaysia 65 L4
Kuala Selangor, Malaysia 65 L3
Kuala Sepetang, Malaysia 65 K3
Kuala Terengganu, Malaysia 65 K4
Kualajelai, Indonesia 62 E4
Kualakapuas, Indonesia 62 E4
Kualakurun, Indonesia 62 E4
Kualapembuang, Indonesia 62 E4
Kualasimpang, Indonesia 62 D1
Kuancheng, China 57 D10
Kuandang, Indonesia 63 D6
Kuandian, China 57 D13
Kuangchou = Guangzhou, China 59 F9
Kuanshan, Taiwan 59 F13
Kuantan, Malaysia 65 L4
Kuba = Quba, Azerbaijan 49 K9
Kuban →, Russia 47 K9
Kubenskoye, Ozero, Russia 46 C10
Kubokawa, Japan 55 H6
Kubrat, Bulgaria 41 C10
Kučevo, Serbia, Yug. 40 B5
Kucha Gompa, India 69 B7
Kuchaman, India 68 F6
Kuchenspitze, Austria 26 D3
Kuchinda, India 69 J11
Kuching, Malaysia 62 D4
Kuchino-eruba-Jima, Japan 55 J5
Kuchino-Shima, Japan 55 K4
Kuchinotsu, Japan 55 H5
Kuchl, Austria 26 D6
Kucing = Kuching, Malaysia 62 D4
Kuçovë, Albania 40 F3
Küçükbahçe, Turkey 39 C8
Küçükköy, Turkey 39 B8
Küçükkuyu, Turkey 39 B8
Küçükmenderes →, Turkey 39 D9
Kud →, Pakistan 68 F2
Kuda, India 66 H7

Kudat, *Malaysia* 62 C5
Kudirkos Naumiestis, *Lithuania* 44 D9
Kudowa-Zdrój, *Poland* 45 H3
Kudus, *Indonesia* 63 G14
Kudymkar, *Russia* 50 D6
Kueiyang = Guiyang, *China* 58 D6
Kufra Oasis = Al Kufrah, *Libya* 79 D10
Kufstein, *Austria* 26 D5
Kugluktuk, *Canada* 100 B8
Kugong I., *Canada* 102 A4
Kūhak, *Iran* 66 F3
Kuhan, *Pakistan* 68 E2
Kūhbonān, *Iran* 71 D8
Kūhestak, *Iran* 71 E8
Kuhin, *Iran* 71 B6
Kūhīrī, *Iran* 71 E9
Kuhnsdorf, *Austria* 26 E7
Kūhpāyeh, *Eşfahan, Iran* 71 C7
Kūhpāyeh, *Kermān, Iran* 71 D8
Kūhrān, Kūh-e, *Iran* 71 E8
Kui Buri, *Thailand* 65 F2
Kuiseb →, *Namibia* 88 B2
Kuito, *Angola* 85 G3
Kuiu I., *U.S.A.* 104 B2
Kujang, *N. Korea* 57 E14
Kujawsko-Pomorskie □, *Poland* 44 E5
Kuji, *Japan* 54 D10
Kujū-San, *Japan* 55 H5
Kukavica, *Serbia, Yug.* 40 D5
Kukawa, *Nigeria* 83 C7
Kukës, *Albania* 40 D4
Kukmor, *Russia* 48 B10
Kukup, *Malaysia* 65 M4
Kukvidze, *Russia* 48 E6
Kula, *Bulgaria* 40 C6
Kula, *Serbia, Yug.* 42 E4
Kula, *Turkey* 39 C10
Kulachi, *Pakistan* 68 D4
Kulai, *Malaysia* 65 M4
Kulal, Mt., *Kenya* 86 B4
Kulaly, Ostrov, *Kazakstan* 49 H10
Kulasekarappattinam, *India* 66 Q11
Kulautuva, *Lithuania* 44 D10
Kuldīga, *Latvia* 9 H19
Kuldīga □, *Latvia* 44 B8
Kuldja = Yining, *China* 50 E9
Kuldu, *Sudan* 81 E2
Kulebaki, *Russia* 48 C6
Kulen, *Cambodia* 64 F5
Kulen Vakuf, *Bos.-H.* 29 D13
Kulgam, *India* 69 C6
Kulgera, *Australia* 94 D1
Kulim, *Malaysia* 65 K3
Kulin, *Australia* 93 F2
Kullen, *Sweden* 11 H6
Kulmbach, *Germany* 25 E7
Kŭlob, *Tajikistan* 50 F7
Kulp, *Turkey* 73 C9
Kulpawn →, *Ghana* 83 D4
Kulsary, *Kazakstan* 50 E6
Kulti, *India* 69 H12
Kulu, *India* 68 D7
Kulu, *Turkey* 72 C5
Kulumbura, *Australia* 92 B4
Kulunda, *Russia* 50 D8
Kulungar, *Afghan.* 68 C3
Kūlvand, *Iran* 71 D7
Kulwin, *Australia* 95 F3
Kulyab = Kŭlob, *Tajikistan* 50 F7
Kuma →, *Russia* 49 H8
Kumafşarı, *Turkey* 39 D11
Kumaganum, *Nigeria* 83 C7
Kumagaya, *Japan* 55 F9
Kumai, *Indonesia* 62 E4
Kumalar Dağı, *Turkey* 39 C12
Kumamba, Kepulauan, *Indonesia* 63 E9
Kumamoto, *Japan* 55 H5
Kumamoto □, *Japan* 55 H5
Kumanovo, *Macedonia* 40 D5
Kumara, *N.Z.* 91 K3
Kumarina, *Australia* 93 D2
Kumasi, *Ghana* 82 D4
Kumayri = Gyumri, *Armenia* 49 K6
Kumba, *Cameroon* 83 E6
Kumbağ, *Turkey* 41 F11
Kumbakonam, *India* 66 P11
Kumbarilla, *Australia* 95 D5
Kumbhraj, *India* 68 G7
Kumbia, *Australia* 95 D5
Kumbo, *Cameroon* 83 D7
Kŭmch'ŏn, *N. Korea* 57 E14
Kumdok, *India* 69 C8
Kume-Shima, *Japan* 55 L3
Kumeny, *Russia* 48 A9
Kumharsain, *India* 68 D7
Kŭmhwa, *S. Korea* 57 E14
Kumi, *Uganda* 86 B3
Kumkale, *Turkey* 41 G10
Kumla, *Sweden* 10 E9
Kumluca, *Turkey* 39 E12
Kummerower See, *Germany* 24 B8
Kumo, *Nigeria* 83 C7
Kumon Bum, *Burma* 67 F20
Kumylzhenskaya, *Russia* 48 F6
Kunágota, *Hungary* 42 D6
Kunashir, Ostrov, *Russia* 51 E15
Kunda, *Estonia* 9 G22
Kunda, *India* 69 G9
Kundar →, *Pakistan* 68 D3
Kundian, *Pakistan* 68 C4
Kundla, *India* 68 J4
Kunga →, *Bangla.* 69 J13
Kungälv, *Sweden* 11 G5
Kunghit I., *Canada* 104 C2
Kungrad = Qŭnghirot, *Uzbekistan* 50 E6
Kungsängen, *Sweden* 10 E11
Kungsbacka, *Sweden* 11 G6
Kungsgården, *Sweden* 10 D10
Kungshamn, *Sweden* 11 F5
Kungsör, *Sweden* 10 E10
Kungur, *Russia* 50 D6
Kunhar →, *Pakistan* 69 B5
Kunhegyes, *Hungary* 42 C5
Kuningan, *Indonesia* 63 G13
Kunlong, *Burma* 58 F2
Kunlun Shan, *Asia* 60 C3
Kunmadaras, *Hungary* 42 C5
Kunming, *China* 58 E4
Kunów, *Poland* 45 H8
Kunsan, *S. Korea* 57 G14
Kunshan, *China* 59 B13
Kunszentmárton, *Hungary* 42 D5
Kunszentmiklós, *Hungary* 42 C4
Kuntaur, *Senegal* 82 C2
Kununurra, *Australia* 92 C4
Kunwari →, *India* 69 F8
Kunya-Urgench = Köneürgench, *Turkmenistan* 50 E6
Künzelsau, *Germany* 25 F5
Kuopio, *Finland* 8 E22
Kupa →, *Croatia* 29 C13
Kupang, *Indonesia* 63 F6
Kupreanof I., *U.S.A.* 104 B2
Kupres, *Bos.-H.* 42 G2
Kupyansk, *Ukraine* 47 H9
Kupyansk-Uzlovoi, *Ukraine* 47 H9
Kuqa, *China* 60 B3
Kür →, *Azerbaijan* 73 C13
Kür Dili, *Azerbaijan* 71 B6
Kura = Kür →, *Azerbaijan* 73 C13
Kuranda, *Australia* 94 B4
Kuranga, *India* 68 H3
Kurashiki, *Japan* 55 G6
Kurayoshi, *Japan* 55 G6
Kürdämir, *Azerbaijan* 49 K9
Kurdistan, *Asia* 73 D10
Kŭrdzhali, *Bulgaria* 41 E9
Kure, *Japan* 55 G6
Küre, *Turkey* 72 B5
Küre Dağları, *Turkey* 72 B6
Kuressaare, *Estonia* 9 G20
Kurgan, *Russia* 50 D7
Kurganinsk, *Russia* 49 H5
Kurgannaya = Kurganinsk, *Russia* 49 H5
Kuri, *India* 68 F4
Kuria Maria Is. = Khurīyā Murīyā, Jazā'ir, *Oman* 74 D6
Kuridala, *Australia* 94 C3
Kurigram, *Bangla.* 67 G16
Kurikka, *Finland* 9 E20
Kuril Is. = Kurilskiye Ostrova, *Russia* 51 E15
Kuril Trench, *Pac. Oc.* 52 E19
Kurilsk, *Russia* 51 E15
Kurilskiye Ostrova, *Russia* 51 E15
Kurino, *Japan* 55 J5
Kurinskaya Kosa = Kür Dili, *Azerbaijan* 71 B6
Kurkur, *Egypt* 80 C3
Kurlovskiy, *Russia* 48 C5
Kurmuk, *Sudan* 81 E3
Kurnool, *India* 66 M11
Kuro-Shima, *Kagoshima, Japan* 55 J4
Kuro-Shima, *Okinawa, Japan* 55 M2
Kuror, J., *Sudan* 80 C3
Kurow, *N.Z.* 91 L3
Kurów, *Poland* 45 G9
Kurram →, *Pakistan* 68 C4
Kurri Kurri, *Australia* 95 E5
Kurrimine, *Australia* 94 B4
Kursavka, *Russia* 49 H6
Kurshskiy Zaliv, *Russia* 9 J19
Kursk, *Russia* 47 G9
Kuršumlija, *Serbia, Yug.* 40 C5
Kuršumlijska Banja, *Serbia, Yug.* 40 C5
Kurşunlu, *Bursa, Turkey* 41 F13
Kurşunlu, *Çankırı, Turkey* 72 B5
Kurtalan, *Turkey* 73 D9
Kurtbey, *Turkey* 41 E10
Kuru, *Sudan* 81 F2
Kuru, Bahr el →, *Sudan* 81 F2
Kurucaşile, *Turkey* 72 B5
Kuruçay, *Turkey* 70 B3
Kuruktag, *China* 60 B3
Kuruman, *S. Africa* 88 D3
Kuruman →, *S. Africa* 88 D3
Kurume, *Japan* 55 H5
Kurun →, *Sudan* 81 F3
Kurunegala, *Sri Lanka* 66 R12
Kurya, *Russia* 50 C6
Kus Gölü, *Turkey* 41 F11
Kuşadası, *Turkey* 72 D2
Kuşadası Körfezi, *Turkey* 39 D8
Kusatsu, *Japan* 55 F9
Kusawa L., *Canada* 104 A1
Kusel, *Germany* 25 F3
Kushaka, *Nigeria* 83 C6
Kushalgarh, *India* 68 H6
Kushchevskaya, *Russia* 49 G4
Kusheriki, *Nigeria* 83 C6
Kushikino, *Japan* 55 J5
Kushima, *Japan* 55 J5
Kushimoto, *Japan* 55 H7
Kushiro, *Japan* 54 C12
Kushiro-Gawa →, *Japan* 54 C12
Kūshk, *Iran* 71 D8
Kushka = Gushgy, *Turkmenistan* 50 F7
Kūshkī, *Iran* 70 C5
Kushol, *India* 69 C7
Kushtia, *Bangla.* 67 H16
Kushum →, *Kazakstan* 48 F10
Kuskokwim B., *U.S.A.* 100 C3
Kusmi, *India* 69 H10
Kussharo-Ko, *Japan* 54 C12
Kustanay = Qostanay, *Kazakstan* 50 D7
Kut, Ko, *Thailand* 65 G4
Kütahya, *Turkey* 39 B12
Kütahya □, *Turkey* 39 B11
Kutaisi, *Georgia* 49 J6
Kutaraja = Banda Aceh, *Indonesia* 62 C1
Kutch, Gulf of = Kachchh, Gulf of, *India* 68 H3
Kutch, Rann of = Kachchh, Rann of, *India* 68 H4
Kutina, *Croatia* 29 C13
Kutiyana, *India* 68 J4
Kutjevo, *Croatia* 42 E2
Kutkashen, *Azerbaijan* 49 K8
Kutná Hora, *Czech Rep.* 26 B8
Kutno, *Poland* 45 F6
Kutse, *Botswana* 88 C3
Kutu, *Dem. Rep. of the Congo* 84 E3
Kutum, *Sudan* 81 E1
Kúty, *Slovak Rep.* 27 C10
Kuujjuaq, *Canada* 101 C13
Kuujjuarapik, *Canada* 102 A4
Kuŭp-tong, *N. Korea* 57 D14
Kuusamo, *Finland* 8 D23
Kuusankoski, *Finland* 9 F22
Kuvshinovo, *Russia* 46 D8
Kuwait = Al Kuwayt, *Kuwait* 70 D5
Kuwait ■, *Asia* 70 D5
Kuwana, *Japan* 55 G8
Kuwana →, *India* 69 F10
Kuybyshev = Samara, *Russia* 48 D10
Kuybyshev, *Russia* 50 D8
Kuybyshevo, *Ukraine* 47 J9
Kuybyshevskoye Vdkhr., *Russia* 48 C9
Kuye He →, *China* 56 E6
Kūyeh, *Iran* 70 B5
Kūysanjaq, *Iraq* 70 B5
Kuyucak, *Turkey* 39 D10
Kuyumba, *Russia* 51 C10
Kuzey Anadolu Dağları, *Turkey* 72 B7
Kuzmin, *Serbia, Yug.* 42 E4
Kuznetsk, *Russia* 48 D8
Kuzomen, *Russia* 50 C4
Kvænangen, *Norway* 8 A19
Kværndrup, *Denmark* 11 J4
Kvaløy, *Norway* 8 B18
Kvänum, *Sweden* 11 F7
Kvareli = Qvareli, *Georgia* 49 K7
Kvarner, *Croatia* 29 D11
Kvarnerič, *Croatia* 29 D11
Kvicksund, *Sweden* 10 E10
Kvillsfors, *Sweden* 11 G9
Kvismare kanal, *Sweden* 10 E9
Kvissleby, *Sweden* 10 B11
Kwa-Nobuhle, *S. Africa* 85 L5
Kwabhaca, *S. Africa* 89 E4
Kwakhanai, *Botswana* 88 C3
Kwakoegron, *Surinam* 125 B7
Kwale, *Kenya* 86 C4
Kwale, *Nigeria* 83 D6
KwaMashu, *S. Africa* 89 D5
Kwando →, *Africa* 88 B3
Kwangdaeri, *N. Korea* 57 D14
Kwangju, *S. Korea* 57 G14
Kwango →, *Dem. Rep. of the Congo* 84 E3
Kwangsi-Chuang = Guangxi Zhuangzu Zizhiqu □, *China* 58 F7
Kwangtung = Guangdong □, *China* 59 F9
Kwara □, *Nigeria* 83 D6
Kwataboahegan →, *Canada* 102 B3
Kwatisore, *Indonesia* 63 E8
KwaZulu Natal □, *S. Africa* 89 D5
Kweichow = Guizhou □, *China* 58 D6
Kwekwe, *Zimbabwe* 87 F2
Kwidzyn, *Poland* 44 E5
Kwiha, *Ethiopia* 81 E4
Kwinana New Town, *Australia* 93 F2
Kwisa →, *Poland* 45 G2
Kwoka, *Indonesia* 63 E8
Kwolla, *Nigeria* 83 D6
Kyabra Cr. →, *Australia* 95 D3
Kyabram, *Australia* 95 F4
Kyaikto, *Burma* 64 D1
Kyakhta, *Russia* 51 D11
Kyancutta, *Australia* 95 E2
Kyaukpadaung, *Burma* 67 J19
Kyaukpyu, *Burma* 67 K18
Kyaukse, *Burma* 67 J20
Kybartai, *Lithuania* 44 D9
Kyburz, *U.S.A.* 116 G6
Kyelang, *India* 68 C7
Kyenjojo, *Uganda* 86 B3
Kyjov, *Czech Rep.* 27 B10
Kyle, *Canada* 105 C7
Kyle Dam, *Zimbabwe* 87 G3
Kyle of Lochalsh, *U.K.* 14 D3
Kyll →, *Germany* 25 F2
Kyllburg, *Germany* 25 E2
Kymijoki →, *Finland* 9 F22
Kyneton, *Australia* 95 F3
Kynuna, *Australia* 94 C3
Kyō-ga-Saki, *Japan* 55 G7
Kyoga, L., *Uganda* 86 B3
Kyogle, *Australia* 95 D5
Kyom →, *Sudan* 81 F2
Kyongju, *S. Korea* 57 G15
Kyongpyaw, *Burma* 67 L19
Kyŏngsŏng, *N. Korea* 57 D15
Kyōto, *Japan* 55 G7
Kyōto □, *Japan* 55 G7
Kyparissovouno, *Cyprus* 36 D12
Kyperounda, *Cyprus* 36 E11
Kyrenia, *Cyprus* 36 D12
Kyrgyzstan ■, *Asia* 50 E8
Kyritz, *Germany* 24 C8
Kyrkhult, *Sweden* 11 H8
Kyrönjoki →, *Finland* 8 E19
Kystatyam, *Russia* 51 C13
Kysucké Nové Mesto, *Slovak Rep.* 27 B11
Kythréa, *Cyprus* 36 D12
Kyunhla, *Burma* 67 H19
Kyuquot Sound, *Canada* 104 D3
Kyurdamir = Kürdämir, *Azerbaijan* 49 K9
Kyūshū, *Japan* 55 H5
Kyūshū □, *Japan* 55 H5
Kyūshū-Sanchi, *Japan* 55 H5
Kyustendil, *Bulgaria* 40 D6
Kyusyur, *Russia* 51 B13
Kyyiv, *Ukraine* 47 G6
Kyyivske Vdskh., *Ukraine* 47 G6
Kyzyl, *Russia* 51 D10
Kyzyl Kum, *Uzbekistan* 50 E7
Kyzyl-Kyya, *Kyrgyzstan* 50 E8
Kzyl-Orda = Qyzylorda, *Kazakstan* 50 E7

L

La Albuera, *Spain* 35 G4
La Alcarria, *Spain* 32 E2
La Almarcha, *Spain* 32 F2
La Almunia de Doña Godina, *Spain* 32 D3
La Asunción, *Venezuela* 124 A6
La Baie, *Canada* 103 C5
La Banda, *Argentina* 126 B3
La Bañeza, *Spain* 34 C5
La Barca, *Mexico* 118 C4
La Barge, *U.S.A.* 114 E8
La Bastide-Puylaurent, *France* 20 D7
La Baule-Escoubiac, *France* 18 E4
La Belle, *U.S.A.* 109 M5
La Biche →, *Canada* 104 B4
La Biche, L., *Canada* 104 C6
La Bisbal d'Empordà, *Spain* 32 D8
La Bomba, *Mexico* 118 A1
La Brède, *France* 20 D3
La Bresse, *France* 19 D13
La Bureba, *Spain* 34 C7
La Calera, *Chile* 126 C1
La Campiña, *Spain* 35 H6
La Canal = Sa Canal, *Spain* 37 C7
La Cañiza = A Cañiza, *Spain* 34 C2
La Canourgue, *France* 20 D7
La Capelle, *France* 19 C10
La Carlota, *Argentina* 126 C3
La Carlota, *Phil.* 61 F5
La Carlota, *Spain* 35 H6
La Carolina, *Spain* 35 G7
La Cavalerie, *France* 20 D7
La Ceiba, *Honduras* 120 C2
La Chaise-Dieu, *France* 20 C7
La Chapelle d'Angillon, *France* 19 E9
La Chapelle-St-Luc, *France* 19 D11
La Chapelle-sur-Erdre, *France* 18 E5
La Charité-sur-Loire, *France* 19 E10
La Chartre-sur-le-Loir, *France* 18 E7
La Châtaigneraie, *France* 20 B3
La Châtre, *France* 19 F9
La Chaux-de-Fonds, *Switz.* 25 H2
La Chorrera, *Panama* 120 E4
La Ciotat, *France* 21 E9
La Clayette, *France* 19 F11
La Cocha, *Argentina* 126 B2
La Concepción = Ri-Aba, *Eq. Guin.* 83 E6
La Concepción, *Panama* 120 E3
La Concordia, *Mexico* 119 D6
La Coruña = A Coruña, *Spain* 34 B2
La Coruña □, *Spain* 34 B2
La Côte-St-André, *France* 21 C9
La Courtine-le-Trucq, *France* 20 C6
La Crau, *Bouches-du-Rhône, France* 21 E8
La Crau, *Var, France* 21 E10
La Crescent, *U.S.A.* 112 D9
La Crete, *Canada* 104 B5
La Crosse, *Kans., U.S.A.* 112 F5
La Crosse, *Wis., U.S.A.* 112 D9
La Cruz, *Costa Rica* 120 D2
La Cruz, *Mexico* 118 C3
La Désirade, *Guadeloupe* 121 C7
La Escondida, *Mexico* 118 C5
La Esmeralda, *Paraguay* 126 A3
La Esperanza, *Cuba* 120 B3
La Esperanza, *Honduras* 120 D2
La Estrada = A Estrada, *Spain* 34 C2
La Faouët, *France* 18 D3
La Fayette, *U.S.A.* 109 H3
La Fé, *Cuba* 120 B3
La Fère, *France* 19 C10
La Ferté-Bernard, *France* 18 D7
La Ferté-Gaucher, *France* 19 D10
La Ferté-Macé, *France* 18 D6
La Ferté-St-Aubin, *France* 19 E8
La Ferté-sous-Jouarre, *France* 19 D10
La Ferté-Vidame, *France* 18 D7
La Flèche, *France* 18 E6
La Follette, *U.S.A.* 109 G3
La Fregeneda, *Spain* 34 E4
La Fuente de San Esteban, *Spain* 34 E4
La Gacilly, *France* 18 E4
La Gineta, *Spain* 33 F2
La Grand-Combe, *France* 21 D8
La Grande, *U.S.A.* 114 D4
La Grande →, *Canada* 102 B5
La Grande Deux, Rés., *Canada* 102 B4
La Grande-Motte, *France* 21 E8
La Grande Quatre, Rés., *Canada* 102 B5
La Grande Trois, Rés., *Canada* 102 B4
La Grange, *Calif., U.S.A.* 116 H6
La Grange, *Ga., U.S.A.* 109 J3
La Grange, *Ky., U.S.A.* 108 F3
La Grange, *Tex., U.S.A.* 113 L6
La Grave, *France* 21 C10
La Guaira, *Venezuela* 124 A5
La Guardia = A Guarda, *Spain* 34 D2
La Gudiña = A Gudiña, *Spain* 34 C3
La Guerche-de-Bretagne, *France* 18 E5
La Guerche-sur-l'Aubois, *France* 19 F9
La Habana, *Cuba* 120 B3
La Haye-du-Puits, *France* 18 C5
La Horra, *Spain* 34 D7
La Independencia, *Mexico* 119 D6
La Isabela, *Dom. Rep.* 121 C5
La Jonquera, *Spain* 32 C7
La Junta, *U.S.A.* 113 F3
La Laguna, *Canary Is.* 37 F3
La Libertad, *Guatemala* 120 C1
La Libertad, *Mexico* 118 B2
La Ligua, *Chile* 126 C1
La Línea de la Concepción, *Spain* 35 J5
La Loche, *Canada* 105 B7
La Londe-les-Maures, *France* 21 E10
La Lora, *Spain* 34 C7
La Loupe, *France* 18 D8
La Louvière, *Belgium* 17 D4
La Machine, *France* 19 F10
La Maddalena, *Italy* 30 A2
La Malbaie, *Canada* 103 C5
La Mancha, *Spain* 33 F2
La Mariña, *Spain* 34 B3
La Martre, L., *Canada* 104 A5
La Mesa, *U.S.A.* 117 N9
La Misión, *Mexico* 118 A1
La Mothe-Achard, *France* 18 F5
La Motte, *France* 21 D10
La Motte-Chalançon, *France* 21 D9
La Motte-Servolex, *France* 21 C9
La Moure, *U.S.A.* 112 B5
La Muela, *Spain* 32 D3
La Mure, *France* 21 D9
La Negra, *Chile* 126 A1
La Oliva, *Canary Is.* 37 F6
La Orotava, *Canary Is.* 37 F3
La Oroya, *Peru* 124 F3
La Pacaudière, *France* 19 F10
La Palma, *Canary Is.* 37 F2
La Palma, *Panama* 120 E4
La Palma del Condado, *Spain* 35 H4
La Paloma, *Chile* 126 C1
La Pampa □, *Argentina* 126 D2
La Paragua, *Venezuela* 124 B6
La Paz, *Entre Ríos, Argentina* 126 C4
La Paz, *San Luis, Argentina* 126 C2
La Paz, *Bolivia* 124 G5
La Paz, *Honduras* 120 D2
La Paz, *Mexico* 118 C2
La Paz, *Phil.* 61 D4
La Paz Centro, *Nic.* 120 D2
La Pedrera, *Colombia* 124 D5
La Pérade, *Canada* 103 C5
La Perouse Str., *Asia* 54 B11
La Pesca, *Mexico* 119 C5
La Piedad, *Mexico* 118 C4
La Pine, *U.S.A.* 114 E3
La Plata, *Argentina* 126 D4
La Pobla de Lillet, *Spain* 32 C6
La Pocatière, *Canada* 103 C5
La Pola de Gordón, *Spain* 34 C5
La Porta, *France* 21 F13
La Porte, *Ind., U.S.A.* 108 E2
La Porte, *Tex., U.S.A.* 113 L7
La Presanella, *Italy* 28 B7
La Puebla = Sa Pobla, *Spain* 32 F8
La Puebla de Cazalla, *Spain* 35 H5
La Puebla de los Infantes, *Spain* 35 H5
La Puebla de Montalbán, *Spain* 34 F6
La Puebla del Río, *Spain* 35 H4
La Puerta de Segura, *Spain* 35 G8
La Purísima, *Mexico* 118 B2
La Push, *U.S.A.* 116 C2
La Quiaca, *Argentina* 126 A2
La Réole, *France* 20 D3
La Restinga, *Canary Is.* 37 G2
La Rioja, *Argentina* 126 B2
La Rioja □, *Argentina* 126 B2
La Rioja □, *Spain* 32 C2
La Robla, *Spain* 34 C5
La Roche-Bernard, *France* 18 E4
La Roche-Canillac, *France* 20 C5
La Roche-en-Ardenne, *Belgium* 17 D5
La Roche-sur-Foron, *France* 19 F13
La Roche-sur-Yon, *France* 18 F5
La Rochefoucauld, *France* 20 C4
La Rochelle, *France* 20 B2
La Roda, *Spain* 33 F2
La Roda de Andalucía, *Spain* 35 H6
La Romana, *Dom. Rep.* 121 C6
La Ronge, *Canada* 105 B7
La Rumorosa, *Mexico* 117 N10
La Sabina = Sa Savina, *Spain* 37 C7
La Sagra, *Spain* 33 H2
La Salle, *U.S.A.* 112 E10
La Sanabria, *Spain* 34 C4
La Santa, *Canary Is.* 37 E6
La Sarre, *Canada* 102 C4
La Scie, *Canada* 103 C8

La Selva, Spain 32 C7
La Selva Beach, U.S.A. 116 J5
La Selva del Camp, Spain 32 D6
La Serena, Chile 126 B1
La Serena, Spain 35 G5
La Seu d'Urgell, Spain 32 C6
La Seyne-sur-Mer, France 21 E9
La Sila, Italy 31 C9
La Solana, Spain 35 G7
La Soufrière, St. Vincent 121 D7
La Souterraine, France 19 F8
La Spézia, Italy 28 D6
La Suze-sur-Sarthe, France 18 E7
La Tagua, Colombia 124 C4
La Teste, France 20 D2
La Tortuga, Venezuela 121 D6
La Tour-du-Pin, France 21 C9
La Tranche-sur-Mer, France 18 F5
La Tremblade, France 20 C2
La Tuque, Canada 102 C5
La Unión, Chile 128 E2
La Unión, El Salv. 120 D2
La Unión, Mexico 118 D4
La Unión, Spain 33 H4
La Urbana, Venezuela 124 B5
La Vall d'Uixó, Spain 32 F4
La Vecilla de Curveño, Spain 34 C5
La Vega, Dom. Rep. 121 C5
La Vela de Coro, Venezuela 124 A5
La Veleta, Spain 35 H7
La Venta, Mexico 119 D6
La Ventura, Mexico 118 C4
La Voulte-sur-Rhône, France 21 D8
Laa an der Thaya, Austria 27 C9
Laaber, Grosse →, Germany 25 G8
Laage, Germany 24 B8
Laatzen, Germany 24 C5
Laba →, Russia 49 H4
Labasa, Fiji 91 C8
Labason, Phil. 61 G5
Labastide-Murat, France 20 D5
Labastide-Rouairoux, France 20 E6
Labbézenga, Mali 83 B5
Labe = Elbe →, Europe 24 B4
Labé, Guinea 82 C2
Laberge, L., Canada 104 A1
Labin, Croatia 29 C11
Labinsk, Russia 49 H5
Labis, Malaysia 65 L4
Łabiszyn, Poland 45 F4
Labo, Phil. 61 D5
Laboe, Germany 24 A6
Laborec →, Slovak Rep. 27 C14
Labouheyre, France 20 D3
Laboulaye, Argentina 126 C3
Labrador, Canada 103 B7
Labrador City, Canada 103 B6
Labrador Sea, Atl. Oc. 101 C14
Lábrea, Brazil 124 E6
Labruguière, France 20 E6
Labuan, Malaysia 62 C5
Labuan, Pulau, Malaysia 62 C5
Labuha, Indonesia 63 E7
Labuhan, Indonesia 63 G11
Labuhanbajo, Indonesia 63 F6
Labuk, Telok, Malaysia 62 C5
Labyrinth, L., Australia 95 E2
Labytnangi, Russia 50 C7
Laç, Albania 40 E3
Lac Bouchette, Canada 103 C5
Lac Édouard, Canada 102 C5
Lac La Biche, Canada 104 C6
Lac la Martre = Wha Ti, Canada 100 B8
Lac La Ronge Prov. Park, Canada 105 B7
Lac-Mégantic, Canada 103 C5
Lac Thien, Vietnam 64 F7
Lacanau, France 20 D2
Lacanau, Étang de, France 20 D2
Lacantúm →, Mexico 119 D6
Lacara →, Spain 35 G4
Lacaune, France 20 E6
Lacaune, Mts. de, France 20 E6
Laccadive Is. = Lakshadweep Is., India 52 H11
Lacepede B., Australia 95 F2
Lacepede Is., Australia 92 C3
Lacerdónia, Mozam. 87 F4
Lacey, U.S.A. 116 C4
Lachhmangarh, India 68 F6
Lachi, Pakistan 68 C4
Lachine, Canada 102 C5
Lachlan →, Australia 95 E3
Lachute, Canada 102 C5
Lackawanna, U.S.A. 110 D6
Lackawaxen, U.S.A. 111 E10
Lacolle, Canada 111 A11
Lacombe, Canada 104 C6
Lacona, U.S.A. 111 C8
Láconi, Italy 30 C2
Laconia, U.S.A. 111 C13
Lacq, France 20 E3
Ladakh Ra., India 69 C8
Lądek-Zdrój, Poland 45 H3
Ládhon →, Greece 38 D3
Ladik, Turkey 72 B6
Ladismith, S. Africa 88 E3
Ladíspoli, Italy 29 G9
Lādīz, Iran 71 D9
Ladnun, India 68 F6
Ladoga, L. = Ladozhskoye Ozero, Russia 46 B6
Ladozhskoye Ozero, Russia 46 B6
Lady Elliott I., Australia 94 C5
Lady Grey, S. Africa 88 E4
Ladybrand, S. Africa 88 D4
Ladysmith, Canada 104 D4
Ladysmith, S. Africa 89 D4
Ladysmith, U.S.A. 112 C9
Lae, Papua N. G. 96 H6
Laem Ngop, Thailand 65 F4
Laem Pho, Thailand 65 J3
Læsø, Denmark 11 G5
Læsø Rende, Denmark 11 G4
Lafayette, Colo., U.S.A. 112 F2
Lafayette, Ind., U.S.A. 108 E2
Lafayette, La., U.S.A. 113 K9
Lafayette, Tenn., U.S.A. 109 G2
Laferte →, Canada 104 A5
Lafia, Nigeria 83 D6
Lafiagi, Nigeria 83 D6
Lafleche, Canada 105 D7
Lafon, Sudan 81 F3
Lagan, Sweden 11 H7
Lagan →, Sweden 11 H6
Lagan →, U.K. 15 B6
Lagarfljót →, Iceland 8 D6
Lage, Germany 24 D4
Lågen →, Oppland, Norway 9 F14
Lågen →, Vestfold, Norway 9 G14
Lägerdorf, Germany 24 B5
Laghouat, Algeria 78 B6
Lagnieu, France 21 C9
Lagny-sur-Marne, France 19 D9
Lago, Italy 31 C9
Lagôa, Portugal 35 H2
Lagoa Vermelha, Brazil 127 B5
Lagoaça, Portugal 34 D4
Lagodekhi, Georgia 49 K8
Lagónegro, Italy 31 B8
Lagonoy G., Phil. 61 E5
Lagos, Nigeria 83 D5
Lagos, Portugal 35 H2
Lagos □, Nigeria 83 D5
Lagos de Moreno, Mexico 118 C4
Lagrange, Australia 92 C3
Lagrange B., Australia 92 C3
Laguardia, Spain 32 C2
Laguépie, France 20 D5
Laguna, Brazil 127 B6
Laguna, U.S.A. 115 J10
Laguna Beach, U.S.A. 117 M9
Laguna de Duera, Spain 34 D6
Laguna Limpia, Argentina 126 B4
Lagunas, Chile 126 A2
Lagunas, Peru 124 E3
Lahad Datu, Malaysia 63 C5
Lahad Datu, Teluk, Malaysia 63 D5
Lahan Sai, Thailand 64 E4
Lahanam, Laos 64 D5
Lahar, India 69 F8
Laharpur, India 69 F9
Lahat, Indonesia 62 E2
Lahewa, Indonesia 62 D1
Lāhījān, Iran 71 B6
Lahn →, Germany 25 E3
Lahnstein, Germany 25 E3
Laholm, Sweden 11 H7
Laholmsbukten, Sweden 11 H6
Lahore, Pakistan 68 D6
Lahr, Germany 25 G3
Lahri, Pakistan 68 E3
Lahti, Finland 9 F21
Lahtis = Lahti, Finland 9 F21
Laï, Chad 79 G9
Lai Chau, Vietnam 58 F4
Lai'an, China 59 A12
Laibin, China 58 F7
Laifeng, China 58 C7
L'Aigle, France 18 D7
Laignes, France 19 E11
L'Aiguillon-sur-Mer, France 20 B2
Laila = Laylá, Si. Arabia 74 C4
Laingsburg, S. Africa 88 E3
Lainio älv →, Sweden 8 C20
Lairg, U.K. 14 C4
Laishui, China 56 E8
Laissac, France 20 D6
Láives, Italy 29 B8
Laiwu, China 57 F9
Laixi, China 57 F11
Laiyang, China 57 F11
Laiyuan, China 56 E8
Laizhou, China 57 F10
Laizhou Wan, China 57 F10
Laja →, Mexico 118 C4
Lajere, Nigeria 83 C7
Lajes, Brazil 127 B5
Lajkovac, Serbia, Yug. 40 B4
Lajosmizse, Hungary 42 C4
Lak Sao, Laos 64 C5
Lakaband, Pakistan 68 D3
Lakamané, Mali 82 C3
Lake Alpine, U.S.A. 116 G7
Lake Andes, U.S.A. 112 D5
Lake Arthur, U.S.A. 113 K8
Lake Cargelligo, Australia 95 E4
Lake Charles, U.S.A. 113 K8
Lake City, Colo., U.S.A. 115 G10
Lake City, Fla., U.S.A. 109 K4
Lake City, Mich., U.S.A. 108 C3
Lake City, Minn., U.S.A. 112 C8
Lake City, Pa., U.S.A. 110 D4
Lake City, S.C., U.S.A. 109 J6
Lake Cowichan, Canada 104 D4
Lake District, U.K. 12 C4
Lake Elsinore, U.S.A. 117 M9
Lake George, U.S.A. 111 C11
Lake Grace, Australia 93 F2
Lake Harbour = Kimmirut, Canada 101 B13
Lake Havasu City, U.S.A. 117 L12
Lake Hughes, U.S.A. 117 L8
Lake Isabella, U.S.A. 117 K8
Lake Jackson, U.S.A. 113 L7
Lake Junction, U.S.A. 114 D8
Lake King, Australia 93 F2
Lake Lenore, Canada 105 C8
Lake Louise, Canada 104 C5
Lake Mead National Recreation Area, U.S.A. 117 K12
Lake Mills, U.S.A. 112 D8
Lake Placid, U.S.A. 111 B11
Lake Pleasant, U.S.A. 111 C10
Lake Providence, U.S.A. 113 J9
Lake St. Peter, Canada 110 A6
Lake Superior Prov. Park, Canada 102 C3
Lake Village, U.S.A. 113 J9
Lake Wales, U.S.A. 109 M5
Lake Worth, U.S.A. 109 M5
Lakeba, Fiji 91 D9
Lakefield, Canada 102 D4
Lakehurst, U.S.A. 111 F10
Lakeland, Australia 94 B3
Lakeland, U.S.A. 109 M5
Lakeport, Calif., U.S.A. 116 F4
Lakeport, Mich., U.S.A. 110 C2
Lakes Entrance, Australia 95 F4
Lakeside, Ariz., U.S.A. 115 J9
Lakeside, Calif., U.S.A. 117 N10
Lakeside, Nebr., U.S.A. 112 D3
Lakeside, Ohio, U.S.A. 110 E2
Lakeview, U.S.A. 114 E3
Lakeville, U.S.A. 112 C8
Lakewood, Colo., U.S.A. 112 F2
Lakewood, N.J., U.S.A. 111 F10
Lakewood, N.Y., U.S.A. 110 D5
Lakewood, Ohio, U.S.A. 110 E3
Lakewood, Wash., U.S.A. 116 C4
Lakha, India 68 F4
Lakhaniá, Greece 36 D9
Lakhimpur, India 69 F9
Lakhnadon, India 69 H8
Lakhonpheng, Laos 64 E5
Lakhpat, India 68 H3
Läki, Azerbaijan 49 K8
Lakin, U.S.A. 113 G4
Lakitusaki →, Canada 102 B3
Lakki, Pakistan 68 C4
Lákkoi, Greece 36 D5
Lakonía □, Greece 38 E4
Lakonikós Kólpos, Greece 38 E4
Lakor, Indonesia 63 F7
Lakota, Ivory C. 82 D3
Lakota, U.S.A. 112 A5
Laksar, India 68 E8
Laksefjorden, Norway 8 A22
Lakselv, Norway 8 A21
Lakshadweep Is., India 52 H11
Lakshmanpur, India 69 H10
Lakshmikantapur, India 69 H13
Lala Ghat, India 67 G18
Lala Musa, Pakistan 68 C5
Lalago, Tanzania 86 C3
Lalapanzi, Zimbabwe 87 F3
Lalapaşa, Turkey 41 E10
Lalbenque, France 20 D5
L'Albufera, Spain 33 F4
Lalganj, India 69 G11
Lalgola, India 69 G13
Lālī, Iran 71 C6
Lalibela, Ethiopia 81 E4
Lalin, China 57 B14
Lalín, Spain 34 C2
Lalin He →, China 57 B13
Lalinde, France 20 D4
Lalitpur, India 69 G8
Lalkua, India 69 E8
Lalsot, India 68 F7
Lam, Vietnam 64 B6
Lam Pao Res., Thailand 64 D4
Lama Kara, Togo 83 D5
Lamaing, Burma 67 M20
Lamar, Colo., U.S.A. 112 F3
Lamar, Mo., U.S.A. 113 G7
Lamas, Peru 124 E3
Lamastre, France 21 D8
Lambach, Austria 26 C6
Lamballe, France 18 D4
Lambaréné, Gabon 84 E2
Lambay I., Ireland 15 C5
Lambert Glacier, Antarctica 5 D6
Lambert's Bay, S. Africa 88 E2
Lambesc, France 21 E9
Lambeth, Canada 110 D3
Lámbia, Greece 38 D3
Lambomakondro, Madag. 89 C7
Lambro →, Italy 28 C6
Lame, Nigeria 83 C6
Lame Deer, U.S.A. 114 D10
Lamego, Portugal 34 D3
Lamèque, Canada 103 C7
Lameroo, Australia 95 F3
Lamesa, U.S.A. 113 J4
Lamía, Greece 38 C4
Lamitan, Phil. 61 H5
Lammermuir Hills, U.K. 14 F6
Lammhult, Sweden 11 G8
Lamoille →, U.S.A. 111 B11
Lamon B., Phil. 61 D5
Lamont, Canada 104 C6
Lamont, Calif., U.S.A. 117 K8
Lamont, Wyo., U.S.A. 114 E10
Lamotte-Beuvron, France 19 E9
Lampa, Peru 124 G4
Lampang, Thailand 64 C2
Lampasas, U.S.A. 113 K5
Lampazos de Naranjo, Mexico 118 B4
Lampertheim, Germany 25 F4
Lampeter, U.K. 13 E3
Lampman, Canada 105 D8
Lamprechtshausen, Austria 26 D5
Lampung □, Indonesia 62 F2
Lamta, India 69 H9
Lamu, Kenya 86 C5
Lamy, U.S.A. 115 J11
Lan Xian, China 56 E6
Lan Yu = Hung't'ou Hsü, Taiwan 59 G13
Lanak La, India 69 B8
Lanak'o Shank'ou = Lanak La, India 69 B8
Lanao, L., Phil. 61 H6
Lanark, Canada 111 A8
Lanark, U.K. 14 F5
Lanbi Kyun, Burma 65 G2
Lancang, China 58 F2
Lancang Jiang →, China 58 G3
Lancashire □, U.K. 12 D5
Lancaster, Canada 111 A10
Lancaster, U.K. 12 C5
Lancaster, Calif., U.S.A. 117 L8
Lancaster, Ky., U.S.A. 108 G3
Lancaster, N.H., U.S.A. 111 B13
Lancaster, N.Y., U.S.A. 110 D6
Lancaster, Ohio, U.S.A. 108 F4
Lancaster, Pa., U.S.A. 111 F8
Lancaster, S.C., U.S.A. 109 H5
Lancaster, Wis., U.S.A. 112 D9
Lancaster Sd., Canada 101 A11
Lancelin, Australia 93 F2
Lanchow = Lanzhou, China 56 F2
Lanciano, Italy 29 F11
Lancun, China 57 F11
Łańcut, Poland 45 H9
Landau, Bayern, Germany 25 G8
Landau, Rhld-Pfz., Germany 25 F4
Landeck, Austria 26 D3
Lander, U.S.A. 114 E9
Lander →, Australia 92 D5
Landerneau, France 18 D2
Landeryd, Sweden 11 G7
Landes, France 20 D2
Landes □, France 20 E3
Landete, Spain 32 F3
Landi Kotal, Pakistan 68 B4
Landisburg, U.S.A. 110 F7
Landivisiau, France 18 D2
Landquart, Switz. 25 J5
Landrecies, France 19 B10
Land's End, U.K. 13 G2
Landsberg, Germany 25 G6
Landsborough Cr. →, Australia 94 C3
Landsbro, Sweden 11 G8
Landshut, Germany 25 G8
Landskrona, Sweden 11 J6
Landstuhl, Germany 25 F3
Landvetter, Sweden 11 G6
Lanesboro, U.S.A. 111 E9
Lanester, France 18 E3
Lanett, U.S.A. 109 J3
Lang Qua, Vietnam 64 A5
Lang Shan, China 56 D4
Lang Son, Vietnam 58 G6
Lang Suan, Thailand 65 H2
Langå, Denmark 11 H3
La'nga Co, China 67 D12
Langadhás, Greece 40 F7
Langádhia, Greece 38 D4
Långan →, Sweden 10 A8
Langano, L., Ethiopia 81 F4
Langar, Iran 71 C9
Langara I., Canada 104 C2
Långås, Sweden 11 H6
Langcai, China 58 D5
Langdon, U.S.A. 112 A5
Långe Jan = Ölands södra udde, Sweden 11 H10
Langeac, France 20 C7
Langeais, France 18 E7
Langeb Baraka →, Sudan 80 D4
Langeberg, S. Africa 88 E3
Langeberge, S. Africa 88 D3
Langeland, Denmark 11 K4
Langelands Bælt, Denmark 11 K4
Langen, Hessen, Germany 25 F4
Langen, Niedersachsen, Germany 24 B4
Langenburg, Canada 105 C8
Langeneß, Germany 24 A4
Langenlois, Austria 26 C8
Langeoog, Germany 24 B3
Langeskov, Denmark 11 J4
Länghem, Sweden 11 G7
Langhirano, Italy 28 D7
Langholm, U.K. 14 F5
Langjökull, Iceland 8 D3
Langkawi, Pulau, Malaysia 65 J2
Langklip, S. Africa 88 D3
Langkon, Malaysia 62 C5
Langlade, St- P. & M. 103 C8
Langley, Canada 116 A4
Langnau, Switz. 25 J3
Langogne, France 20 D7
Langon, France 20 D3
Langøya, Norway 8 B16
Langreo, Spain 34 B5
Langres, France 19 E12
Langres, Plateau de, France 19 E12
Langsa, Indonesia 62 D1
Långsele, Sweden 10 A11
Långshyttan, Sweden 10 D10
Langtry, U.S.A. 113 L4
Langu, Thailand 65 J2
Languedoc, France 20 E7
Languedoc-Roussillon □, France 20 E6
Langxi, China 59 B12
Langxiangzhen, China 56 E9
Langzhong, China 58 B5
Lanigan, Canada 105 C7
Lankao, China 56 G8
Länkäran, Azerbaijan 71 B6
Lanmeur, France 18 D3
Lannemezan, France 20 E4
Lannilis, France 18 D2
Lannion, France 18 D3
L'Annonciation, Canada 102 C5
Lanouaille, France 20 C5
Lanping, China 58 D2
Lansdale, U.S.A. 111 F9
Lansdowne, Australia 95 E5
Lansdowne, Canada 111 B8
Lansdowne, India 69 E8
Lansdowne House, Canada 102 B2
L'Anse, U.S.A. 108 B1
L'Anse au Loup, Canada 103 B8
L'Anse aux Meadows, Canada 103 B8
Lansford, U.S.A. 111 F9
Lanshan, China 59 E9
Lansing, U.S.A. 108 D3
Lanslebourg-Mont-Cenis, France 21 C10
Lanta Yai, Ko, Thailand 65 J2
Lantewa, Nigeria 83 C7
Lantian, China 56 G5
Lanus, Argentina 126 C4
Lanusei, Italy 30 C2
Lanuza, Phil. 61 G7
Lanxi, China 59 C12
Lanzarote, Canary Is. 37 F6
Lanzhou, China 56 F2
Lanzo Torinese, Italy 28 C4
Lao →, Italy 31 C8
Lao Bao, Laos 64 D6
Lao Cai, Vietnam 58 F4
Laoag, Phil. 61 B4
Laoang, Phil. 61 E6
Laoha He →, China 57 C11
Laohekou, China 59 A8
Laois □, Ireland 15 D4
Laon, France 19 C10
Laona, U.S.A. 108 C1
Laos ■, Asia 64 D5
Lapa, Brazil 127 B6
Lapai, Nigeria 83 D6
Lapalisse, France 19 F10
Lapeer, U.S.A. 108 D4
Lapeyrade, France 20 D3
Lapithos, Cyprus 36 D12
Lapland = Lappland, Europe 8 B21
Laporte, U.S.A. 111 E8
Lapovo, Serbia, Yug. 40 B5
Lappeenranta, Finland 9 F23
Lappland, Europe 8 B21
Laprida, Argentina 126 D3
Lapseki, Turkey 41 F10
Laptev Sea, Russia 51 B13
Lapua, Finland 8 E20
Lăpuş →, Romania 43 C8
Lapuş, Munţii, Romania 43 C8
Lăpuşna, Moldova 43 D13
Łapy, Poland 45 F9
Laqiya Arba'in, Sudan 80 C2
Laqiya Umran, Sudan 80 D2
L'Aquila, Italy 29 F10
Lār, Āzarbājān-e Sharqī, Iran 70 B5
Lār, Fārs, Iran 71 E7
Larabanga, Ghana 82 D4
Laragne-Montéglin, France 21 D9
Laramie, U.S.A. 112 E2
Laramie →, U.S.A. 114 F11
Laramie Mts., U.S.A. 112 E2
Laranjeiras do Sul, Brazil 127 B5
Larantuka, Indonesia 63 F6
Larat, Indonesia 63 F8
L'Arbresle, France 21 C8
Lärbro, Sweden 11 G12
Larde, Mozam. 87 F4
Larder Lake, Canada 102 C4
Lardhos, Ákra = Líndhos, Ákra, Greece 36 C10
Lardhos, Órmos, Greece 36 C10
Laredo, Spain 34 B7
Laredo, U.S.A. 113 M5
Laredo Sd., Canada 104 C3
Largentière, France 21 D8
L'Argentière-la-Bessée, France 21 D10
Largo, U.S.A. 109 M4
Largs, U.K. 14 F4
Lari, Italy 28 E7
Lariang, Indonesia 63 E5
Larimore, U.S.A. 112 B6
Lārīn, Iran 71 C7
Larino, Italy 29 G11
Lárisa, Greece 38 B4
Lárisa □, Greece 38 B4
Larkana, Pakistan 68 F3
Larnaca, Cyprus 36 E12
Larnaca Bay, Cyprus 36 E12
Larne, U.K. 15 B6
Larned, U.S.A. 112 F5
Laroquebrou, France 20 D6
Larose, U.S.A. 113 L9
Larrimah, Australia 92 C5
Larsen Ice Shelf, Antarctica 5 C17
Laruns, France 20 F3
Larvik, Norway 9 G14
Larzac, Causse du, France 20 E7
Las Alpujarras, Spain 33 J1
Las Animas, U.S.A. 112 F3
Las Anod, Somali Rep. 74 F4
Las Arenas, Spain 34 B6
Las Aves, Is., W. Indies 121 C7
Las Brenãs, Argentina 126 B3
Las Cabezas de San Juan, Spain 35 J5
Las Cejas, Argentina 128 B4

Las Chimeneas, *Mexico* 117 N10
Las Cruces, *U.S.A.* 115 K10
Las Flores, *Argentina* 126 D4
Las Heras, *Argentina* 126 C2
Las Lajas, *Argentina* 128 D2
Las Lomitas, *Argentina* 126 A3
Las Marismas, *Spain* 35 H4
Las Minas, *Spain* 33 G3
Las Navas de la Concepción, *Spain* 35 H5
Las Navas del Marqués, *Spain* 34 E6
Las Palmas, *Argentina* 126 B4
Las Palmas, *Canary Is.* 37 F4
Las Palmas →, *Mexico* 117 N10
Las Pedroñas, *Spain* 33 F2
Las Piedras, *Uruguay* 127 C4
Las Pipinas, *Argentina* 126 D4
Las Plumas, *Argentina* 128 E3
Las Rosas, *Argentina* 126 C3
Las Rozas, *Spain* 34 E7
Las Tablas, *Panama* 120 E3
Las Termas, *Argentina* 126 B3
Las Toscas, *Argentina* 126 B4
Las Truchas, *Mexico* 118 D4
Las Varillas, *Argentina* 126 C3
Las Vegas, *N. Mex., U.S.A.* 115 J11
Las Vegas, *Nev., U.S.A.* 117 J11
Lasarte, *Spain* 32 B2
Lascano, *Uruguay* 127 C5
Lash-e Joveyn, *Afghan.* 66 D2
Lashburn, *Canada* 105 C7
Lashio, *Burma* 67 H20
Lashkar, *India* 68 F8
Łasin, *Poland* 44 E6
Lasíthi, *Greece* 36 D7
Lasíthi □, *Greece* 36 D7
Lāsjerd, *Iran* 71 C7
Lask, *Poland* 45 G6
Łaskarzew, *Poland* 45 G8
Laško, *Slovenia* 29 B12
Lassay-les-Châteaux, *France* 18 D6
Lassen Pk., *U.S.A.* 114 F3
Lassen Volcanic National Park, *U.S.A.* 114 F3
Last Mountain L., *Canada* 105 C7
Lastchance Cr. →, *U.S.A.* 116 E5
Lastoursville, *Gabon* 84 E2
Lastovo, *Croatia* 29 F13
Lastovski Kanal, *Croatia* 29 F14
Lat Yao, *Thailand* 64 E2
Latacunga, *Ecuador* 124 D3
Latakia = Al Lādhiqīyah, *Syria* 70 C2
Latchford, *Canada* 102 C4
Latehar, *India* 69 H11
Laterza, *Italy* 31 B9
Latham, *Australia* 93 E2
Lathen, *Germany* 24 C3
Lathi, *India* 68 F4
Lathrop Wells, *U.S.A.* 117 J10
Latiano, *Italy* 31 B10
Latina, *Italy* 30 A5
Latisana, *Italy* 29 C10
Latium = Lazio □, *Italy* 29 F9
Laton, *U.S.A.* 116 J7
Latorytsya →, *Slovak Rep.* 27 C14
Latouche Treville, C., *Australia* 92 C3
Latrobe, *Australia* 94 G4
Latrobe, *U.S.A.* 110 F5
Latrónico, *Italy* 31 B9
Latvia ■, *Europe* 9 H20
Lau, *Nigeria* 83 D7
Lau Group, *Fiji* 91 C9
Lauchhammer, *Germany* 24 D9
Lauda-Königshofen, *Germany* 25 F5
Lauenburg, *Germany* 24 B6
Lauf, *Germany* 25 F7
Laughlin, *U.S.A.* 115 J6
Laujar de Andarax, *Spain* 33 H2
Laukaa, *Finland* 9 E21
Launceston, *Australia* 94 G4
Launceston, *U.K.* 13 G3
Laune →, *Ireland* 15 D2
Launglon Bok, *Burma* 64 F1
Laupheim, *Germany* 25 G5
Laura, *Australia* 94 B3
Laureana di Borrello, *Italy* 31 D9
Laurel, *Miss., U.S.A.* 113 K10
Laurel, *Mont., U.S.A.* 114 D9
Laurencekirk, *U.K.* 14 E6
Laurens, *U.S.A.* 109 H4
Laurentian Plateau, *Canada* 103 B6
Lauria, *Italy* 31 B8
Laurie L., *Canada* 105 B8
Laurinburg, *U.S.A.* 109 H6
Laurium, *U.S.A.* 108 B1
Lausanne, *Switz.* 25 J2
Laut, *Indonesia* 65 K6
Laut, Pulau, *Indonesia* 62 E5
Laut Kecil, Kepulauan, *Indonesia* 62 E5
Lauterbach, *Germany* 24 E5
Lauterecken, *Germany* 25 F3
Lautoka, *Fiji* 91 C7
Lauzès, *France* 20 D5
Lavagh More, *Ireland* 15 B3
Lavagna, *Italy* 28 D6
Laval, *France* 18 D6
Lavalle, *Argentina* 126 B2
Lavant Station, *Canada* 111 A8
Lāvar Meydān, *Iran* 71 D7
Lávara, *Greece* 41 E10
Lavardac, *France* 20 D4
Lavaur, *France* 20 E5
Lavelanet, *France* 20 F5
Lavello, *Italy* 31 A8
Laverton, *Australia* 93 E3
Lavìs, *Italy* 28 B8
Lávkos, *Greece* 38 B5
Lavos, *Portugal* 34 E2
Lavradio, *Portugal* 35 G1
Lavras, *Brazil* 127 A7
Lavre, *Portugal* 35 G2
Lávrion, *Greece* 38 D6
Lávris, *Greece* 36 D6
Lavumisa, *Swaziland* 89 D5
Lawas, *Malaysia* 62 D5
Lawele, *Indonesia* 63 F6
Lawng Pit, *Burma* 67 G20
Lawqah, *Si. Arabia* 70 D4
Lawra, *Ghana* 82 C4
Lawrence, *N.Z.* 91 L2
Lawrence, *Kans., U.S.A.* 112 F7
Lawrence, *Mass., U.S.A.* 111 D13
Lawrenceburg, *Ind., U.S.A.* 108 F3
Lawrenceburg, *Tenn., U.S.A.* 109 H2
Lawrenceville, *Ga., U.S.A.* 109 J4
Lawrenceville, *Pa., U.S.A.* 110 E7
Laws, *U.S.A.* 116 H8
Lawton, *U.S.A.* 113 H5
Lawu, *Indonesia* 63 G14
Lawz, J. al, *Si. Arabia* 80 B4
Laxå, *Sweden* 11 F8
Laxford, L., *U.K.* 14 C3
Laxou, *France* 19 D13
Lay →, *France* 20 B2
Laylá, *Si. Arabia* 74 C4
Laylān, *Iraq* 70 C5
Layon →, *France* 18 E6
Layton, *U.S.A.* 114 F7
Laytonville, *U.S.A.* 114 G2
Lazarevac, *Serbia, Yug.* 40 B4
Lazarevskoye, *Russia* 49 J4
Lazarivo, *Madag.* 89 C8
Lazdijai, *Lithuania* 44 D10
Lazio □, *Italy* 29 F9
Lazo, *Moldova* 43 C13
Lazo, *Russia* 54 C6
Le Beausset, *France* 21 E9
Le Blanc, *France* 20 B5
Le Bleymard, *France* 20 D7
Le Bourgneuf-la-Fôret, *France* 18 D6
Le Bugue, *France* 20 D4
Le Canourgue = La Canourgue, *France* 20 D7
Le Cateau Cambrésis, *France* 19 B10
Le Caylar, *France* 20 E7
Le Chambon-Feugerolles, *France* 21 C8
Le Châtelet, *France* 19 F9
Le Chesne, *France* 19 C11
Le Cheylard, *France* 21 D8
Le Conquet, *France* 18 D2
Le Creusot, *France* 19 F11
Le Croisic, *France* 18 E4
Le Donjon, *France* 19 F10
Le Dorat, *France* 20 B5
Le François, *Martinique* 121 D7
Le Grand-Lucé, *France* 18 E7
Le Grand-Pressigny, *France* 18 F7
Le Grand-Quevilly, *France* 18 C8
Le Havre, *France* 18 C7
Le Lavandou, *France* 21 E10
Le Lion-d'Angers, *France* 18 E6
Le Louroux-Béconnais, *France* 18 E6
Le Luc, *France* 21 E10
Le Lude, *France* 18 E7
Le Mans, *France* 18 E7
Le Mars, *U.S.A.* 112 D6
Le Mayet-de-Montagne, *France* 19 F10
Le Mêle-sur-Sarthe, *France* 18 D7
Le Monastier-sur-Gazeille, *France* 20 D7
Le Monêtier-les-Bains, *France* 21 D10
Le Mont-Dore, *France* 20 C6
Le Mont-St-Michel, *France* 18 D5
Le Moule, *Guadeloupe* 121 C7
Le Muy, *France* 21 E10
Le Palais, *France* 18 E3
Le Perthus, *France* 20 F6
Le Puy-en-Velay, *France* 20 C7
Le Sueur, *U.S.A.* 112 C8
Le Teil, *France* 21 D8
Le Teilleul, *France* 18 D6
Le Theil, *France* 18 D7
Le Thillot, *France* 19 E13
Le Thuy, *Vietnam* 64 D6
Le Touquet-Paris-Plage, *France* 19 B8
Le Tréport, *France* 18 B8
Le Val-d'Ajol, *France* 19 E13
Le Verdon-sur-Mer, *France* 20 C2
Le Vigan, *France* 20 E7
Lea →, *U.K.* 13 F8
Leach, *Cambodia* 65 F4
Lead, *U.S.A.* 112 C3
Leader, *Canada* 105 C7
Leadville, *U.S.A.* 115 G10
Leaf →, *U.S.A.* 113 K10
Leaf Rapids, *Canada* 105 B9
Leamington, *Canada* 102 D3
Leamington, *U.S.A.* 114 G7
Leamington Spa = Royal Leamington Spa, *U.K.* 13 E6
Le'an, *China* 59 D10
Leandro Norte Alem, *Argentina* 127 B4
Leane, L., *Ireland* 15 D2
Learmonth, *Australia* 92 D1
Leask, *Canada* 105 C7
Leatherhead, *U.K.* 13 F7
Leavenworth, *Kans., U.S.A.* 112 F7
Leavenworth, *Wash., U.S.A.* 114 C3
Łeba, *Poland* 44 D4
Łeba →, *Poland* 44 D4
Lebach, *Germany* 25 F2
Lebak, *Phil.* 61 H6
Lebam, *U.S.A.* 116 D3
Lebane, *Serbia, Yug.* 40 D5
Lebanon, *Ind., U.S.A.* 108 E2
Lebanon, *Kans., U.S.A.* 112 F5
Lebanon, *Ky., U.S.A.* 108 G3
Lebanon, *Mo., U.S.A.* 113 G8
Lebanon, *N.H., U.S.A.* 111 C12
Lebanon, *Oreg., U.S.A.* 114 D2
Lebanon, *Pa., U.S.A.* 111 F8
Lebanon, *Tenn., U.S.A.* 109 G2
Lebanon ■, *Asia* 75 B5
Lebec, *U.S.A.* 117 L8
Lebedyan, *Russia* 47 F10
Lebedyn, *Ukraine* 47 G8
Lebel-sur-Quévillon, *Canada* 102 C4
Lebomboberge, *S. Africa* 89 C5
Lębork, *Poland* 44 D4
Lebrija, *Spain* 35 J4
Łebsko, Jezioro, *Poland* 44 D4
Lebu, *Chile* 126 D1
Leca da Palmeira, *Portugal* 34 D2
Lecce, *Italy* 31 B11
Lecco, *Italy* 28 C6
Lecco, L. di, *Italy* 28 C6
Lécera, *Spain* 32 D4
Lech, *Austria* 26 D3
Lech →, *Germany* 25 G6
Lechang, *China* 59 E9
Lechtaler Alpen, *Austria* 26 D3
Lecontes Mills, *U.S.A.* 110 E6
Lectoure, *France* 20 E4
Łęczna, *Poland* 45 G9
Łęczyca, *Poland* 45 F6
Ledesma, *Spain* 34 D5
Ledong, *China* 64 C7
Leduc, *Canada* 104 C6
Lee, *U.S.A.* 111 D11
Lee →, *Ireland* 15 E3
Lee Vining, *U.S.A.* 116 H7
Leech L., *U.S.A.* 112 B7
Leechburg, *U.S.A.* 110 F5
Leeds, *U.K.* 12 D6
Leeds, *U.S.A.* 109 J2
Leek, *Neths.* 17 A6
Leek, *U.K.* 12 D5
Leeman, *Australia* 93 E1
Leeper, *U.S.A.* 110 E5
Leer, *Germany* 24 B3
Leesburg, *U.S.A.* 109 L5
Leesville, *U.S.A.* 113 K8
Leeton, *Australia* 95 E4
Leetonia, *U.S.A.* 110 F4
Leeu Gamka, *S. Africa* 88 E3
Leeuwarden, *Neths.* 17 A5
Leeuwin, C., *Australia* 93 F2
Leeward Is., *Atl. Oc.* 121 C7
Lefka, *Cyprus* 36 D11
Lefkoniko, *Cyprus* 36 D12
Lefroy, *Canada* 110 B5
Lefroy, L., *Australia* 93 F3
Łeg →, *Poland* 45 H8
Leganés, *Spain* 34 E7
Legazpi, *Phil.* 61 E5
Lège-Cap-Ferret, *France* 20 D2
Lege Hida, *Ethiopia* 81 F5
Legendre I., *Australia* 92 D2
Leghorn = Livorno, *Italy* 28 E7
Legionowo, *Poland* 45 F7
Legnago, *Italy* 29 C8
Legnano, *Italy* 28 C5
Legnica, *Poland* 45 G3
Legrad, *Croatia* 29 B13
Leh, *India* 69 B7
Lehigh Acres, *U.S.A.* 109 M5
Lehighton, *U.S.A.* 111 F9
Lehliu, *Romania* 43 F11
Leho, *Sudan* 81 F3
Lehrte, *Germany* 24 C5
Lehututu, *Botswana* 88 C3
Lei Shui →, *China* 59 D9
Leiah, *Pakistan* 68 D4
Leibnitz, *Austria* 26 E8
Leibo, *China* 58 C4
Leicester, *U.K.* 13 E6
Leicester City □, *U.K.* 13 E6
Leicestershire □, *U.K.* 13 E6
Leichhardt →, *Australia* 94 B2
Leichhardt Ra., *Australia* 94 C4
Leiden, *Neths.* 17 B4
Leie →, *Belgium* 17 C3
Leifers = Láives, *Italy* 29 B8
Leimen, *Germany* 25 F4
Leine →, *Germany* 24 C5
Leinefelde, *Germany* 24 D6
Leinster, *Australia* 93 E3
Leinster □, *Ireland* 15 C4
Leinster, Mt., *Ireland* 15 D5
Leipalingis, *Lithuania* 44 D10
Leipzig, *Germany* 24 D8
Leiria, *Portugal* 34 F2
Leiria □, *Portugal* 34 F2
Leirvik, *Norway* 9 G11
Leishan, *China* 58 D7
Leisler, Mt., *Australia* 92 D4
Leith, *U.K.* 14 F5
Leith Hill, *U.K.* 13 F7
Leitha →, *Europe* 27 D10
Leitrim, *Ireland* 15 B3
Leitrim □, *Ireland* 15 B4
Leitza, *Spain* 32 B3
Leiyang, *China* 59 D9
Leizhou, *China* 59 G8
Leizhou Bandao, *China* 58 G7
Leizhou Wan, *China* 59 G8
Lek →, *Neths.* 17 C4
Leka, *Norway* 8 D14
Lekáni, *Greece* 41 E8
Lekbibaj, *Albania* 40 D3
Lekeitio, *Spain* 32 B2
Lekhainá, *Greece* 38 D3
Lekoui, *Burkina Faso* 82 C4
Leksand, *Sweden* 10 D9
Lékva Óros, *Greece* 36 D6
Leland, *Mich., U.S.A.* 108 C3
Leland, *Miss., U.S.A.* 113 J9
Lelång, *Sweden* 10 E6
Leleque, *Argentina* 128 E2
Lelystad, *Neths.* 17 B5
Lem, *Denmark* 11 H2
Lema, *Nigeria* 83 C5
Lema Shilindi, *Ethiopia* 81 G5
Léman, L., *Europe* 19 F13
Lemera, *Dem. Rep. of the Congo* 86 C2
Lemery, *Phil.* 61 E4
Lemhi Ra., *U.S.A.* 114 D7
Lemmer, *Neths.* 17 B5
Lemmon, *U.S.A.* 112 C3
Lemon Grove, *U.S.A.* 117 N9
Lemoore, *U.S.A.* 116 J7
Lempdes, *France* 20 C7
Lemvig, *Denmark* 11 H2
Lena →, *Russia* 51 B13
Lenart, *Slovenia* 29 B12
Lenartovce, *Slovak Rep.* 27 C13
Lencloître, *France* 18 F7
Léndas, *Greece* 36 E6
Lendava, *Slovenia* 29 B13
Lendeh, *Iran* 71 D6
Lendinara, *Italy* 29 C8
Lengerich, *Germany* 24 C3
Lenggong, *Malaysia* 65 K3
Lenggries, *Germany* 25 H7
Lengshuijiang, *China* 59 D8
Lengshuitan, *China* 59 D8
Lengua de Vaca, Pta., *Chile* 126 C1
Lengyeltóti, *Hungary* 42 D2
Lenhovda, *Sweden* 11 G9
Lenina, Kanal →, *Russia* 49 J7
Leninabad = Khŭjand, *Tajikistan* 50 E7
Leninakan = Gyumri, *Armenia* 49 K6
Leningrad = Sankt-Peterburg, *Russia* 46 C6
Lenino, *Ukraine* 47 K8
Leninogorsk, *Kazakstan* 50 D9
Leninsk, *Russia* 49 F7
Leninsk-Kuznetskiy, *Russia* 50 D9
Leninskoye, *Russia* 48 A8
Lenk, *Switz.* 25 J3
Lenkoran = Länkäran, *Azerbaijan* 71 B6
Lenmalu, *Indonesia* 63 E8
Lenne →, *Germany* 24 D3
Lennestadt, *Germany* 24 D4
Lennox, *U.S.A.* 112 D6
Lennoxville, *Canada* 111 A13
Leno, *Italy* 28 C7
Lenoir, *U.S.A.* 109 H5
Lenoir City, *U.S.A.* 109 H3
Lenore L., *Canada* 105 C8
Lenox, *U.S.A.* 111 D11
Lens, *France* 19 B9
Lensahn, *Germany* 24 A6
Lensk, *Russia* 51 C12
Lentekhi, *Georgia* 49 J6
Lenti, *Hungary* 42 D1
Lentini, *Italy* 31 E8
Lenwood, *U.S.A.* 117 L9
Lenya, *Burma* 62 B1
Lenzen, *Germany* 24 B7
Léo, *Burkina Faso* 82 C4
Leoben, *Austria* 26 D8
Leodhas = Lewis, *U.K.* 14 C2
Leola, *U.S.A.* 112 C5
Leominster, *U.K.* 13 E5
Leominster, *U.S.A.* 111 D13
Léon, *France* 20 E2
León, *Mexico* 118 C4
León, *Nic.* 120 D2
León, *Spain* 34 C5
Leon, *U.S.A.* 112 E8
León □, *Spain* 34 C5
Leon →, *U.S.A.* 113 K6
León, Montes de, *Spain* 34 C4
Leonardtown, *U.S.A.* 108 F7
Leonardville, *Namibia* 88 C2
Leonberg, *Germany* 25 G5
Leonding, *Austria* 26 C7
Leonessa, *Italy* 29 F9
Leonforte, *Italy* 31 E7
Leongatha, *Australia* 95 F4
Leonídhion, *Greece* 38 D4
Leonora, *Australia* 93 E3
Leopoldina, *Brazil* 127 A7
Leopoldsburg, *Belgium* 17 C5
Leoti, *U.S.A.* 112 F4
Leova, *Moldova* 43 D13
Leoville, *Canada* 105 C7
Lepe, *Spain* 35 H3
Lepel = Lyepyel, *Belarus* 46 E5
Lepenoú, *Greece* 38 C3
Leping, *China* 59 C11
Lépo, L. do, *Angola* 88 B2
Lepontine, Alpi, *Italy* 28 B5
Leppävirta, *Finland* 9 E22
Lepsény, *Hungary* 42 D3
Lequeitio = Lekeitio, *Spain* 32 B2
Lercara Friddi, *Italy* 30 E6
Lerdo, *Mexico* 118 B4
Léré, *Chad* 83 D7
Léré, *Mali* 82 B4
Lere, *Bauchi, Nigeria* 83 D6
Lere, *Kaduna, Nigeria* 83 C6
Leribe, *Lesotho* 89 D4
Lérici, *Italy* 28 D6
Lérida = Lleida, *Spain* 32 D5
Lérins, Îs. de, *France* 21 E11
Lerma, *Spain* 34 C7
Léros, *Greece* 39 D8
Lérouville, *France* 19 D12
Lerum, *Sweden* 11 G6
Lerwick, *U.K.* 14 A7
Leş, *Romania* 42 D6
Les Abrets, *France* 21 C9
Les Andelys, *France* 18 C8
Les Borges Blanques, *Spain* 32 D5
Les Cayes, *Haiti* 121 C5
Les Essarts, *France* 18 F5
Les Herbiers, *France* 18 F5
Les Minquiers, Plateau des, *Chan. Is.* 18 D4
Les Pieux, *France* 18 C5
Les Ponts-de-Cé, *France* 18 E6
Les Riceys, *France* 19 E11
Les Sables-d'Olonne, *France* 20 B2
Les Vans, *France* 21 D8
Lesbos = Lésvos, *Greece* 39 B8
L'Escala, *Spain* 32 C8
Leshan, *China* 58 C4
Lésina, *Italy* 29 G12
Lésina, L. di, *Italy* 29 G12
Lesjöfors, *Sweden* 10 E8
Lesko, *Poland* 45 J9
Leskov I., *Antarctica* 5 B1
Leskovac, *Serbia, Yug.* 40 C5
Leskovik, *Albania* 40 F4
Leśna, *Poland* 45 G2
Lesneven, *France* 18 D2
Leśnica, *Poland* 45 H5
Lešnica, *Serbia, Yug.* 40 B3
Lesnoye, *Russia* 46 C8
Lesopilnoye, *Russia* 54 A7
Lesotho ■, *Africa* 89 D4
Lesozavodsk, *Russia* 51 E14
Lesparre-Médoc, *France* 20 C3
Lessay, *France* 18 C5
Lesse →, *Belgium* 17 D4
Lessebo, *Sweden* 11 H9
Lesser Antilles, *W. Indies* 121 D7
Lesser Slave L., *Canada* 104 B5
Lesser Sunda Is., *Indonesia* 63 F6
Lessines, *Belgium* 17 D3
Lester, *U.S.A.* 116 C5
Lestock, *Canada* 105 C8
Lesuer I., *Australia* 92 B4
Lésvos, *Greece* 39 B8
Leszno, *Poland* 45 G3
Letaba, *S. Africa* 89 C5
Letälven, *Sweden* 10 E8
Létavértes, *Hungary* 42 C6
Letchworth, *U.K.* 13 F7
Letea, Ostrov, *Romania* 43 E14
Lethbridge, *Canada* 104 D6
Lethem, *Guyana* 124 C7
Leti, Kepulauan, *Indonesia* 63 F7
Leti Is. = Leti, Kepulauan, *Indonesia* 63 F7
Letiahau →, *Botswana* 88 C3
Leticia, *Colombia* 124 D5
Leting, *China* 57 E10
Letjiesbos, *S. Africa* 88 E3
Letlhakane, *Botswana* 88 C4
Letlhakeng, *Botswana* 88 C3
Letong, *Indonesia* 62 D3
Letpadan, *Burma* 67 L19
Letpan, *Burma* 67 K19
Letsôk-aw Kyun, *Burma* 65 G2
Letterkenny, *Ireland* 15 B4
Leu, *Romania* 43 F9
Leucadia, *U.S.A.* 117 M9
Leucate, *France* 20 F7
Leucate, Étang de, *France* 20 F7
Leuk, *Switz.* 25 J3
Leuşeni, *Moldova* 43 D13
Leuser, G., *Indonesia* 62 D1
Leutkirch, *Germany* 25 H6
Leuven, *Belgium* 17 D4
Leuze-en-Hainaut, *Belgium* 17 D3
Lev Tolstoy, *Russia* 46 F10
Levádhia, *Greece* 38 C4
Levan, *Albania* 40 F3
Levanger, *Norway* 8 E14
Levant, Î. du, *France* 21 E10
Lévanto, *Italy* 28 D6
Lévanzo, *Italy* 30 D5
Levelland, *U.S.A.* 113 J3
Leven, *U.K.* 14 E6
Leven, L., *U.K.* 14 E5
Leven, Toraka, *Madag.* 89 A8
Leveque C., *Australia* 92 C3
Leverano, *Italy* 31 B10
Leverkusen, *Germany* 24 D3
Levice, *Slovak Rep.* 27 C11
Lévico Terme, *Italy* 29 C8
Levie, *France* 21 G13
Levier, *France* 19 F13
Levin, *N.Z.* 91 J5
Lévis, *Canada* 103 C5
Levis, L., *Canada* 104 A5
Levítha, *Greece* 39 D8
Levittown, *N.Y., U.S.A.* 111 F11
Levittown, *Pa., U.S.A.* 111 F10
Levka, *Bulgaria* 41 E10
Levkás, *Greece* 38 C2
Levkás □, *Greece* 38 C2
Levkímmi, *Greece* 36 B4
Levkímmi, Ákra, *Greece* 36 B4
Levkôsia = Nicosia, *Cyprus* 36 D12
Levoča, *Slovak Rep.* 27 B13
Levroux, *France* 19 F8
Levski, *Bulgaria* 41 C9
Levskigrad = Karlovo, *Bulgaria* 41 D8

Levuka, *Fiji* 91 **C8**
Lewes, *U.K.* 13 **G8**
Lewes, *U.S.A.* 108 **F8**
Lewin Brzeski, *Poland* 45 **H4**
Lewis, *U.K.* 14 **C2**
Lewis →, *U.S.A.* 116 **E4**
Lewis, Butt of, *U.K.* 14 **C2**
Lewis Ra., *Australia* 92 **D4**
Lewis Range, *U.S.A.* 114 **C7**
Lewis Run, *U.S.A.* 110 **E6**
Lewisburg, *Pa., U.S.A.* 110 **F8**
Lewisburg, *Tenn., U.S.A.* 109 **H2**
Lewisburg, *W. Va., U.S.A.* 108 **G5**
Lewisporte, *Canada* 103 **C8**
Lewiston, *Idaho, U.S.A.* 114 **C5**
Lewiston, *Maine, U.S.A.* 109 **C11**
Lewiston, *N.Y., U.S.A.* 110 **C5**
Lewistown, *Mont., U.S.A.* 114 **C9**
Lewistown, *Pa., U.S.A.* 110 **F7**
Lexington, *Ill., U.S.A.* 112 **E10**
Lexington, *Ky., U.S.A.* 108 **F3**
Lexington, *Mich., U.S.A.* 110 **C2**
Lexington, *Mo., U.S.A.* 112 **F8**
Lexington, *N.C., U.S.A.* 109 **H5**
Lexington, *N.Y., U.S.A.* 111 **D10**
Lexington, *Nebr., U.S.A.* 112 **E5**
Lexington, *Ohio, U.S.A.* 110 **F2**
Lexington, *Tenn., U.S.A.* 109 **H1**
Lexington, *Va., U.S.A.* 108 **G6**
Lexington Park, *U.S.A.* 108 **F7**
Leyburn, *U.K.* 12 **C6**
Leye, *China* 58 **E6**
Leyland, *U.K.* 12 **D5**
Leyre →, *France* 20 **D2**
Leyte □, *Phil.* 61 **F6**
Leyte Gulf, *Phil.* 61 **F6**
Leżajsk, *Poland* 45 **H9**
Lezay, *France* 20 **B3**
Lezhë, *Albania* 40 **E3**
Lezhi, *China* 58 **B5**
Lézignan-Corbières, *France* 20 **E6**
Lezoux, *France* 20 **C7**
Lgov, *Russia* 47 **G8**
Lhasa, *China* 60 **D4**
Lhazê, *China* 60 **D3**
Lhokkruet, *Indonesia* 62 **D1**
Lhokseumawe, *Indonesia* 62 **C1**
L'Hospitalet de Llobregat, *Spain* 32 **D7**
Li, *Thailand* 64 **D2**
Li Shui →, *China* 59 **C9**
Li Xian, *Gansu, China* 56 **G3**
Li Xian, *Hebei, China* 56 **E8**
Li Xian, *Hunan, China* 59 **C8**
Liádhoi, *Greece* 39 **E8**
Liancheng, *China* 59 **E11**
Lianga, *Phil.* 61 **G7**
Liangcheng, *Nei Monggol Zizhiqu, China* 56 **D7**
Liangcheng, *Shandong, China* 57 **G10**
Liangdang, *China* 56 **H4**
Lianghe, *China* 58 **E2**
Lianghekou, *China* 58 **C7**
Liangping, *China* 58 **B6**
Liangpran, *Indonesia* 62 **D4**
Lianhua, *China* 59 **D9**
Lianjiang, *Fujian, China* 59 **D12**
Lianjiang, *Guangdong, China* 59 **G8**
Lianping, *China* 59 **E10**
Lianshan, *China* 59 **E9**
Lianshanguan, *China* 57 **D12**
Lianshui, *China* 57 **H10**
Lianyuan, *China* 59 **D8**
Lianyungang, *China* 57 **G10**
Lianzhou, *China* 59 **E9**
Liao He →, *China* 57 **D11**
Liaocheng, *China* 56 **F8**
Liaodong Bandao, *China* 57 **E12**
Liaodong Wan, *China* 57 **D11**
Liaoning □, *China* 57 **D12**
Liaoyang, *China* 57 **D12**
Liaoyuan, *China* 57 **C13**
Liaozhong, *China* 57 **D12**
Liapádhes, *Greece* 38 **B1**
Liard →, *Canada* 104 **A4**
Liard River, *Canada* 104 **B3**
Liari, *Pakistan* 68 **G2**
Libau = Liepāja, *Latvia* 9 **H19**
Libby, *U.S.A.* 114 **B6**
Libenge, *Dem. Rep. of the Congo* 84 **D3**
Liberal, *U.S.A.* 113 **G4**
Liberec, *Czech Rep.* 26 **A8**
Liberecký □, *Czech Rep.* 26 **A8**
Liberia, *Costa Rica* 120 **D2**
Liberia ■, *W. Afr.* 82 **D3**
Liberty, *Mo., U.S.A.* 112 **F7**
Liberty, *N.Y., U.S.A.* 111 **E10**
Liberty, *Pa., U.S.A.* 110 **E7**
Liberty, *Tex., U.S.A.* 113 **K7**
Libiąż, *Poland* 45 **H6**
Lîbîya, Sahrâ', *Africa* 79 **C10**
Libo, *China* 58 **E6**
Libobo, Tanjung, *Indonesia* 63 **E7**
Libode, *S. Africa* 89 **E4**
Libohovë, *Albania* 40 **F4**
Libourne, *France* 20 **D3**
Libramont, *Belgium* 17 **E5**
Librazhd, *Albania* 40 **E4**
Libreville, *Gabon* 84 **D1**
Libya ■, *N. Afr.* 79 **C9**
Libyan Desert = Lîbîya, Sahrâ', *Africa* 79 **C10**
Libyan Plateau = Ed-Déffa, *Egypt* 80 **A2**
Licantén, *Chile* 126 **D1**
Licata, *Italy* 30 **E6**
Lice, *Turkey* 73 **C9**
Licheng, *China* 56 **F7**
Lichfield, *U.K.* 13 **E6**
Lichinga, *Mozam.* 87 **E4**
Lichtenburg, *S. Africa* 88 **D4**
Lichtenfels, *Germany* 25 **E7**
Lichuan, *Hubei, China* 58 **B7**
Lichuan, *Jiangxi, China* 59 **D11**
Licking →, *U.S.A.* 108 **F3**
Licosa, Punta, *Italy* 31 **B7**
Lida, *Belarus* 9 **K21**
Liden, *Sweden* 10 **B10**
Lidhoríkion, *Greece* 38 **C4**
Lidhult, *Sweden* 11 **H7**
Lidköping, *Sweden* 11 **F7**
Lido, *Italy* 29 **C9**
Lido, *Niger* 83 **C5**
Lido di Roma = Óstia, Lido di, *Italy* 29 **G9**
Lidzbark, *Poland* 45 **E6**
Lidzbark Warmiński, *Poland* 44 **D7**
Liebenwalde, *Germany* 24 **C9**
Lieberose, *Germany* 24 **D10**
Liebig, Mt., *Australia* 92 **D5**
Liebling, *Romania* 42 **E6**
Liechtenstein ■, *Europe* 25 **H5**
Liège, *Belgium* 17 **D5**
Liège □, *Belgium* 17 **D5**
Liegnitz = Legnica, *Poland* 45 **G3**
Lienart, *Dem. Rep. of the Congo* 86 **B2**
Lienyünchiangshih = Lianyungang, *China* 57 **G10**
Lienz, *Austria* 26 **E5**
Liepāja, *Latvia* 9 **H19**
Liepāja □, *Latvia* 44 **B8**
Liepājas ezers, *Latvia* 44 **B8**
Lier, *Belgium* 17 **C4**
Liernais, *France* 19 **E11**
Lieşti, *Romania* 43 **E12**
Liévin, *France* 19 **B9**
Lièvre →, *Canada* 102 **C4**
Liezen, *Austria* 26 **D7**
Liffey →, *Ireland* 15 **C5**
Lifford, *Ireland* 15 **B4**
Liffré, *France* 18 **D5**
Lifudzin, *Russia* 54 **B7**
Ligao, *Phil.* 61 **E5**
Lightning Ridge, *Australia* 95 **D4**
Lignano Sabbiadoro, *Italy* 29 **C10**
Ligny-en-Barrois, *France* 19 **D12**
Ligonier, *U.S.A.* 110 **F5**
Ligoúrion, *Greece* 38 **D5**
Ligueil, *France* 18 **E7**
Liguria □, *Italy* 28 **D5**
Ligurian Sea, *Medit. S.* 6 **G7**
Lihou Reefs and Cays, *Australia* 94 **B5**
Lihue, *U.S.A.* 106 **H15**
Lijiang, *China* 58 **D3**
Likasi, *Dem. Rep. of the Congo* 87 **E2**
Likenäs, *Sweden* 10 **D8**
Likhoslavl, *Russia* 46 **D8**
Likhovskoy, *Russia* 47 **H11**
Likoma I., *Malawi* 87 **E3**
Likumburu, *Tanzania* 87 **D4**
L'Île-Bouchard, *France* 18 **E7**
L'Île-Rousse, *France* 21 **F12**
Liling, *China* 59 **D9**
Lilla Edet, *Sweden* 11 **F6**
Lille, *France* 19 **B10**
Lille Bælt, *Denmark* 11 **J3**
Lillebonne, *France* 18 **C7**
Lillehammer, *Norway* 9 **F14**
Lillesand, *Norway* 9 **G13**
Lillhärdal, *Sweden* 10 **C8**
Lillian Pt., *Australia* 93 **E4**
Lillo, *Spain* 34 **F7**
Lillooet, *Canada* 104 **C4**
Lillooet →, *Canada* 104 **D4**
Lilongwe, *Malawi* 87 **E3**
Liloy, *Phil.* 63 **C6**
Lim →, *Bos.-H.* 40 **C3**
Lima, *Indonesia* 63 **E7**
Lima, *Peru* 124 **F3**
Lima, *Mont., U.S.A.* 114 **D7**
Lima, *Ohio, U.S.A.* 108 **E3**
Lima →, *Portugal* 34 **D2**
Liman, *Indonesia* 63 **G14**
Liman, *Russia* 49 **H8**
Limanowa, *Poland* 45 **J7**
Limassol, *Cyprus* 36 **E12**
Limavady, *U.K.* 15 **A5**
Limay →, *Argentina* 128 **D3**
Limay Mahuida, *Argentina* 126 **D2**
Limbach-Oberfrohna, *Germany* 24 **E8**
Limbang, *Brunei* 62 **D5**
Limbara, Mte., *Italy* 30 **B2**
Limbaži, *Latvia* 9 **H21**
Limbdi, *India* 68 **H4**
Limbe, *Cameroon* 83 **E6**
Limburg, *Germany* 25 **E4**
Limburg □, *Belgium* 17 **C5**
Limburg □, *Neths.* 17 **C5**
Limedsforsen, *Sweden* 10 **D7**
Limeira, *Brazil* 127 **A6**
Limenária, *Greece* 41 **F8**
Limerick, *Ireland* 15 **D3**
Limerick, *U.S.A.* 111 **C14**
Limerick □, *Ireland* 15 **D3**
Limestone, *U.S.A.* 110 **D6**
Limestone →, *Canada* 105 **B10**
Limfjorden, *Denmark* 11 **H3**
Limia = Lima →, *Portugal* 34 **D2**
Limín Khersonísou, *Greece* 39 **F7**
Limingen, *Norway* 8 **D15**
Limmared, *Sweden* 11 **G7**
Limmen Bight, *Australia* 94 **A2**
Limmen Bight →, *Australia* 94 **B2**
Límni, *Greece* 38 **C5**
Límnos, *Greece* 39 **B7**
Limoges, *Canada* 111 **A9**
Limoges, *France* 20 **C5**
Limón, *Costa Rica* 120 **E3**
Limon, *U.S.A.* 112 **F3**
Limone Piemonte, *Italy* 28 **D4**
Limousin, *France* 20 **C5**
Limousin, Plateaux du, *France* 20 **C5**
Limoux, *France* 20 **E6**
Limpopo →, *Africa* 89 **D5**
Limuru, *Kenya* 86 **C4**
Lin Xian, *China* 56 **F6**
Lin'an, *China* 59 **B12**
Linapacan I., *Phil.* 61 **F3**
Linapacan Str., *Phil.* 61 **F3**
Linares, *Chile* 126 **D1**
Linares, *Mexico* 119 **C5**
Linares, *Spain* 35 **G7**
Linaro, Capo, *Italy* 29 **F8**
Línas Mte., *Italy* 30 **C1**
Lincang, *China* 58 **F3**
Lincheng, *China* 56 **F8**
Linchuan, *China* 59 **D11**
Lincoln, *Argentina* 126 **C3**
Lincoln, *N.Z.* 91 **K4**
Lincoln, *U.K.* 12 **D7**
Lincoln, *Calif., U.S.A.* 116 **G5**
Lincoln, *Ill., U.S.A.* 112 **E10**
Lincoln, *Kans., U.S.A.* 112 **F5**
Lincoln, *Maine, U.S.A.* 109 **C11**
Lincoln, *N.H., U.S.A.* 111 **B13**
Lincoln, *N. Mex., U.S.A.* 115 **K11**
Lincoln, *Nebr., U.S.A.* 112 **E6**
Lincoln City, *U.S.A.* 114 **D1**
Lincoln Hav = Lincoln Sea, *Arctic* 4 **A5**
Lincoln Sea, *Arctic* 4 **A5**
Lincolnshire □, *U.K.* 12 **D7**
Lincolnshire Wolds, *U.K.* 12 **D7**
Lincolnton, *U.S.A.* 109 **H5**
L'Incudine, *France* 21 **G13**
Lind, *U.S.A.* 114 **C4**
Linda, *U.S.A.* 116 **F5**
Lindau, *Germany* 25 **H5**
Linden, *Guyana* 124 **B7**
Linden, *Ala., U.S.A.* 109 **J2**
Linden, *Calif., U.S.A.* 116 **G5**
Linden, *Tex., U.S.A.* 113 **J7**
Lindenhurst, *U.S.A.* 111 **F11**
Lindesberg, *Sweden* 10 **E9**
Lindesnes, *Norway* 9 **H12**
Líndhos, *Greece* 36 **C10**
Líndhos, Ákra, *Greece* 36 **C10**
Lindi, *Tanzania* 87 **D4**
Lindi □, *Tanzania* 87 **D4**
Lindi →, *Dem. Rep. of the Congo* 86 **B2**
Lindö, *Sweden* 11 **F10**
Lindome, *Sweden* 11 **G6**
Lindoso, *Portugal* 34 **D2**
Lindow, *Germany* 24 **C8**
Lindsay, *Canada* 102 **D4**
Lindsay, *Calif., U.S.A.* 116 **J7**
Lindsay, *Okla., U.S.A.* 113 **H6**
Lindsborg, *U.S.A.* 112 **F6**
Lindsdal, *Sweden* 11 **H10**
Linesville, *U.S.A.* 110 **E4**
Linfen, *China* 56 **F6**
Ling Xian, *Hunan, China* 59 **D9**
Ling Xian, *Shandong, China* 56 **F9**
Lingao, *China* 64 **C7**
Lingayen, *Phil.* 63 **A6**
Lingayen G., *Phil.* 61 **C4**
Lingbi, *China* 57 **H9**
Lingbo, *Sweden* 10 **C10**
Lingchuan, *Guangxi Zhuangzu, China* 59 **E8**
Lingchuan, *Shanxi, China* 56 **G7**
Lingen, *Germany* 24 **C3**
Lingga, *Indonesia* 62 **E2**
Lingga, Kepulauan, *Indonesia* 62 **E2**
Lingga Arch. = Lingga, Kepulauan, *Indonesia* 62 **E2**
Linghem, *Sweden* 11 **F9**
Lingle, *U.S.A.* 112 **D2**
Lingqiu, *China* 56 **E8**
Lingshan, *China* 58 **F7**
Lingshi, *China* 56 **F6**
Lingshou, *China* 56 **E8**
Lingshui, *China* 64 **C8**
Lingtai, *China* 56 **G4**
Linguère, *Senegal* 82 **B1**
Lingui, *China* 59 **E8**
Lingwu, *China* 56 **E4**
Lingyuan, *China* 57 **D10**
Lingyun, *China* 58 **E6**
Linhai, *China* 59 **C13**
Linhares, *Brazil* 125 **G10**
Linhe, *China* 56 **D4**
Linjiang, *China* 57 **D14**
Linköping, *Sweden* 11 **F9**
Linkou, *China* 57 **B16**
Linli, *China* 59 **C8**
Linnhe, L., *U.K.* 14 **E3**
Linqi, *China* 56 **G7**
Linqing, *China* 56 **F8**
Linqu, *China* 57 **F10**
Linru, *China* 56 **G7**
Lins, *Brazil* 127 **A6**
Linshui, *China* 58 **B6**
Linta →, *Madag.* 89 **D7**
Linth →, *Switz.* 25 **H5**
Linthal, *Switz.* 25 **J5**
Linton, *Ind., U.S.A.* 108 **F2**
Linton, *N. Dak., U.S.A.* 112 **B4**
Lintong, *China* 56 **G5**
Linwood, *Canada* 110 **C4**
Linwu, *China* 59 **E9**
Linxi, *China* 57 **C10**
Linxia, *China* 60 **C5**
Linxiang, *China* 59 **C9**
Linyanti →, *Africa* 88 **B4**
Linyi, *China* 57 **G10**
Linz, *Austria* 26 **C7**
Linz, *Germany* 24 **E3**
Linzhenzhen, *China* 56 **F5**
Linzi, *China* 57 **F10**
Lion, G. du, *France* 20 **E7**
Lionárisso, *Cyprus* 36 **D13**
Lioni, *Italy* 31 **B8**
Lions, G. of = Lion, G. du, *France* 20 **E7**
Lion's Den, *Zimbabwe* 87 **F3**
Lion's Head, *Canada* 110 **B3**
Liozno = Lyozna, *Belarus* 46 **E6**
Lipa, *Phil.* 61 **E4**
Lipali, *Mozam.* 87 **F4**
Lipany, *Slovak Rep.* 27 **B13**
Lípari, *Italy* 31 **D7**
Lípari, I., *Italy* 31 **D7**
Lípari, Is. = Eólie, Ís., *Italy* 31 **D7**
Lipcani, *Moldova* 43 **B11**
Lipetsk, *Russia* 47 **F10**
Lipiany, *Poland* 45 **E1**
Liping, *China* 58 **D7**
Lipkany = Lipcani, *Moldova* 43 **B11**
Lipljan, *Kosovo, Yug.* 40 **D5**
Lipník nad Bečvou, *Czech Rep.* 27 **B10**
Lipno, *Poland* 45 **F6**
Lipova, *Romania* 42 **D6**
Lipovcy Manzovka, *Russia* 54 **B6**
Lipovets, *Ukraine* 47 **H5**
Lippe →, *Germany* 24 **D2**
Lippstadt, *Germany* 24 **D4**
Lipscomb, *U.S.A.* 113 **G4**
Lipsk, *Poland* 44 **E10**
Lipsko, *Poland* 45 **G8**
Lipsói, *Greece* 39 **D8**
Liptovský Hrádok, *Slovak Rep.* 27 **B12**
Liptovský Milkuláš, *Slovak Rep.* 27 **B12**
Liptrap C., *Australia* 95 **F4**
Lipu, *China* 59 **E8**
Lira, *Uganda* 86 **B3**
Liri →, *Italy* 30 **A6**
Liria = Lliria, *Spain* 33 **F4**
Lisala, *Dem. Rep. of the Congo* 84 **D4**
Lisboa, *Portugal* 35 **G1**
Lisboa □, *Portugal* 35 **F1**
Lisbon = Lisboa, *Portugal* 35 **G1**
Lisbon, *N. Dak., U.S.A.* 112 **B6**
Lisbon, *N.H., U.S.A.* 111 **B13**
Lisbon, *Ohio, U.S.A.* 110 **F4**
Lisbon Falls, *U.S.A.* 109 **D10**
Lisburn, *U.K.* 15 **B5**
Liscannor B., *Ireland* 15 **D2**
Liscia →, *Italy* 30 **A2**
Lishe Jiang →, *China* 58 **E3**
Lishi, *China* 56 **F6**
Lishu, *China* 57 **C13**
Lishui, *Jiangsu, China* 59 **B12**
Lishui, *Zhejiang, China* 59 **C12**
Lisianski I., *Pac. Oc.* 96 **E10**
Lisichansk = Lysychansk, *Ukraine* 47 **H10**
Lisieux, *France* 18 **C7**
Liski, *Russia* 47 **G10**
L'Isle-Jourdain, *Gers, France* 20 **E5**
L'Isle-Jourdain, *Vienne, France* 20 **B4**
L'Isle-sur-la-Sorgue, *France* 21 **E9**
Lisle-sur-Tarn, *France* 20 **E5**
Lismore, *Australia* 95 **D5**
Lismore, *Ireland* 15 **D4**
Lista, *Norway* 9 **G12**
Lister, Mt., *Antarctica* 5 **D11**
Liston, *Australia* 95 **D5**
Listowel, *Canada* 102 **D3**
Listowel, *Ireland* 15 **D2**
Lit, *Sweden* 10 **A8**
Lit-et-Mixe, *France* 20 **D2**
Litang, *Guangxi Zhuangzu, China* 58 **F7**
Litang, *Sichuan, China* 58 **B3**
Litang Qu →, *China* 58 **C3**
Litani →, *Lebanon* 75 **B4**
Litchfield, *Calif., U.S.A.* 116 **E6**
Litchfield, *Conn., U.S.A.* 111 **E11**
Litchfield, *Ill., U.S.A.* 112 **F10**
Litchfield, *Minn., U.S.A.* 112 **C7**
Liteni, *Romania* 43 **C11**
Lithgow, *Australia* 95 **E5**
Líthinon, Ákra, *Greece* 36 **E6**
Lithuania ■, *Europe* 9 **J20**
Litija, *Slovenia* 29 **B11**
Lititz, *U.S.A.* 111 **F8**
Litókhoron, *Greece* 40 **F6**
Litoměřice, *Czech Rep.* 26 **A7**
Litomyšl, *Czech Rep.* 27 **B9**
Litschau, *Austria* 26 **C8**
Little Abaco I., *Bahamas* 120 **A4**
Little Barrier I., *N.Z.* 91 **G5**
Little Belt Mts., *U.S.A.* 114 **C8**
Little Blue →, *U.S.A.* 112 **F6**
Little Buffalo →, *Canada* 104 **A6**
Little Cayman, *Cayman Is.* 120 **C3**
Little Churchill →, *Canada* 105 **B9**
Little Colorado →, *U.S.A.* 115 **H8**
Little Current, *Canada* 102 **C3**
Little Current →, *Canada* 102 **B3**
Little Falls, *Minn., U.S.A.* 112 **C7**
Little Falls, *N.Y., U.S.A.* 111 **C10**
Little Fork →, *U.S.A.* 112 **A8**
Little Grand Rapids, *Canada* 105 **C9**
Little Humboldt →, *U.S.A.* 114 **F5**
Little Inagua I., *Bahamas* 121 **B5**
Little Karoo, *S. Africa* 88 **E3**
Little Lake, *U.S.A.* 117 **K9**
Little Laut Is. = Laut Kecil, Kepulauan, *Indonesia* 62 **E5**
Little Mecatina = Petit-Mécatina →, *Canada* 103 **B8**
Little Minch, *U.K.* 14 **D2**
Little Missouri →, *U.S.A.* 112 **B3**
Little Ouse →, *U.K.* 13 **E9**
Little Rann, *India* 68 **H4**
Little Red →, *U.S.A.* 113 **H9**
Little River, *N.Z.* 91 **K4**
Little Rock, *U.S.A.* 113 **H8**
Little Ruaha →, *Tanzania* 86 **D4**
Little Sable Pt., *U.S.A.* 108 **D2**
Little Scarcies →, *S. Leone* 82 **D2**
Little Sioux →, *U.S.A.* 112 **E6**
Little Smoky →, *Canada* 104 **C5**
Little Snake →, *U.S.A.* 114 **F9**
Little Valley, *U.S.A.* 110 **D6**
Little Wabash →, *U.S.A.* 108 **G1**
Little White →, *U.S.A.* 112 **D4**
Littlefield, *U.S.A.* 113 **J3**
Littlehampton, *U.K.* 13 **G7**
Littleton, *U.S.A.* 111 **B13**
Litvinov, *Czech Rep.* 26 **A6**
Liu He →, *China* 57 **D11**
Liu Jiang →, *China* 58 **F7**
Liuba, *China* 56 **H4**
Liucheng, *China* 58 **E7**
Liugou, *China* 57 **D10**
Liuhe, *China* 57 **C13**
Liuheng Dao, *China* 59 **C14**
Liujiang, *China* 58 **E7**
Liukang Tenggaja = Sabalana, Kepulauan, *Indonesia* 63 **F5**
Liuli, *Tanzania* 87 **E3**
Liuwa Plain, *Zambia* 85 **G4**
Liuyang, *China* 59 **C9**
Liuzhou, *China* 58 **E7**
Liuzhuang, *China* 57 **H11**
Livada, *Romania* 42 **C8**
Livadherón, *Greece* 40 **F5**
Livadhia, *Cyprus* 36 **E12**
Liválhion, *Greece* 38 **A4**
Livarot, *France* 18 **D7**
Live Oak, *Calif., U.S.A.* 116 **F5**
Live Oak, *Fla., U.S.A.* 109 **K4**
Liveras, *Cyprus* 36 **D11**
Livermore, *U.S.A.* 116 **H5**
Livermore, Mt., *U.S.A.* 113 **K2**
Livermore Falls, *U.S.A.* 109 **C11**
Liverpool, *Canada* 103 **D7**
Liverpool, *U.K.* 12 **D4**
Liverpool, *U.S.A.* 111 **C8**
Liverpool Bay, *U.K.* 12 **D4**
Liverpool Plains, *Australia* 95 **E5**
Liverpool Ra., *Australia* 95 **E5**
Livigno, *Italy* 28 **B7**
Livingston, *Guatemala* 120 **C2**
Livingston, *U.K.* 14 **F5**
Livingston, *Ala., U.S.A.* 109 **J1**
Livingston, *Calif., U.S.A.* 116 **H6**
Livingston, *Mont., U.S.A.* 114 **D8**
Livingston, *S.C., U.S.A.* 109 **J5**
Livingston, *Tenn., U.S.A.* 109 **G3**
Livingston, *Tex., U.S.A.* 113 **K7**
Livingston, L., *U.S.A.* 113 **K7**
Livingston Manor, *U.S.A.* 111 **E10**
Livingstone, *Zambia* 87 **F2**
Livingstone Mts., *Tanzania* 87 **D3**
Livingstonia, *Malawi* 87 **E3**
Livno, *Bos.-H.* 42 **G2**
Livny, *Russia* 47 **F9**
Livonia, *Mich., U.S.A.* 108 **D4**
Livonia, *N.Y., U.S.A.* 110 **D7**
Livorno, *Italy* 28 **E7**
Livramento, *Brazil* 127 **C4**
Livron-sur-Drôme, *France* 21 **D8**
Liwale, *Tanzania* 87 **D4**
Liwiec →, *Poland* 45 **F8**
Lixi, *China* 58 **D3**
Lixian, *China* 58 **B4**
Lixoúrion, *Greece* 38 **C2**
Liyang, *China* 59 **B12**
Lizard I., *Australia* 94 **A4**
Lizard Pt., *U.K.* 13 **H2**
Lizzano, *Italy* 31 **B10**
Ljig, *Serbia, Yug.* 40 **B4**
Ljubija, *Bos.-H.* 29 **D13**
Ljubinje, *Bos.-H.* 40 **D2**
Ljubljana, *Slovenia* 29 **B11**
Ljubno, *Slovenia* 29 **B11**
Ljubovija, *Serbia, Yug.* 40 **B3**
Ljugarn, *Sweden* 11 **G12**
Ljung, *Sweden* 11 **G7**
Ljungan →, *Sweden* 10 **B11**
Ljungaverk, *Sweden* 10 **B10**
Ljungby, *Sweden* 9 **H15**
Ljungbyholm, *Sweden* 11 **H10**
Ljungdalen, *Sweden* 10 **B6**
Ljungsbro, *Sweden* 11 **F9**
Ljungskile, *Sweden* 11 **F5**
Ljusdal, *Sweden* 10 **C10**
Ljusfallshammar, *Sweden* 11 **F9**
Ljusnan →, *Sweden* 10 **C11**
Ljusne, *Sweden* 10 **C11**
Ljutomer, *Slovenia* 29 **B13**
Llagostera, *Spain* 32 **D7**
Llancanelo, Salina, *Argentina* 126 **D2**
Llandeilo, *U.K.* 13 **F4**
Llandovery, *U.K.* 13 **F4**
Llandrindod Wells, *U.K.* 13 **E4**
Llandudno, *U.K.* 12 **D4**
Llanelli, *U.K.* 13 **F3**
Llanes, *Spain* 34 **B6**
Llangollen, *U.K.* 12 **E4**

Llanidloes, U.K. 13 E4
Llano, U.S.A. 113 K5
Llano →, U.S.A. 113 K5
Llano Estacado, U.S.A. 113 J3
Llanos, S. Amer. 122 C3
Llanquihue, L., Chile 128 E1
Llanwrtyd Wells, U.K. 13 E4
Llebeig, C. des, Spain 37 B9
Lleida, Spain 32 D5
Lleida □, Spain 32 C6
Llentrisca, C., Spain 37 C7
Llera, Mexico 119 C5
Llerena, Spain 35 G5
Lleyn Peninsula, U.K. 12 E3
Llico, Chile 126 C1
Lliria, Spain 33 F4
Llobregat →, Spain 32 D7
Llodio, Spain 32 B2
Lloret de Mar, Spain 32 D7
Lloyd B., Australia 94 A3
Lloyd L., Canada 105 B7
Lloydminster, Canada 105 C7
Llucena del Cid, Spain 32 E4
Llucmajor, Spain 37 B9
Llullaillaco, Volcán, S. Amer. 126 A2
Lo →, Vietnam 64 B5
Loa, U.S.A. 115 G8
Loa →, Chile 126 A1
Loaita I., S. China Sea 62 B4
Loange →, Dem. Rep. of the Congo 84 E4
Loano, Italy 28 D5
Lobatse, Botswana 88 D4
Löbau, Germany 24 D10
Lobenstein, Germany 24 E7
Lobería, Argentina 126 D4
Löberöd, Sweden 11 J7
Łobez, Poland 44 E2
Lobito, Angola 85 G2
Lobo →, Ivory C. 82 D3
Lobos, Argentina 126 D4
Lobos, I., Mexico 118 B2
Lobos, I. de, Canary Is. 37 F6
Łobżenica, Poland 45 E4
Loc Binh, Vietnam 64 B6
Loc Ninh, Vietnam 65 G6
Locarno, Switz. 25 J4
Loch Baghasdail = Lochboisdale, U.K. 14 D1
Loch Garman = Wexford, Ireland 15 D5
Loch Nam Madadh = Lochmaddy, U.K. 14 D1
Lochaber, U.K. 14 E3
Locharbriggs, U.K. 14 F5
Lochboisdale, U.K. 14 D1
Loche, L. La, Canada 105 B7
Lochem, Neths. 17 B6
Loches, France 18 E7
Lochgilphead, U.K. 14 E3
Lochinver, U.K. 14 C3
Lochmaddy, U.K. 14 D1
Lochnagar, Australia 94 C4
Lochnagar, U.K. 14 E5
Łochów, Poland 45 F8
Lochy, L., U.K. 14 E4
Lock, Australia 95 E2
Lock Haven, U.S.A. 110 E7
Lockeford, U.S.A. 116 G5
Lockeport, Canada 103 D6
Lockerbie, U.K. 14 F5
Lockhart, U.S.A. 113 L6
Lockhart, L., Australia 93 F2
Lockhart River, Australia 94 A3
Lockney, U.S.A. 113 H4
Lockport, U.S.A. 110 C6
Locminé, France 18 E4
Locri, Italy 31 D9
Locronan, France 18 D2
Lod, Israel 75 D3
Lodeinoye Pole, Russia 46 B7
Lodève, France 20 E7
Lodge Bay, Canada 103 B8
Lodge Grass, U.S.A. 114 D10
Lodgepole Cr. →, U.S.A. 112 E2
Lodhran, Pakistan 68 E4
Lodi, Italy 28 C6
Lodi, Calif., U.S.A. 116 G5
Lodi, Ohio, U.S.A. 110 E3
Lodja, Dem. Rep. of the Congo 86 C1
Lodosa, Spain 32 C2
Lödöse, Sweden 11 F6
Lodwar, Kenya 86 B4
Łódź, Poland 45 G6
Łódzkie □, Poland 45 G6
Loei, Thailand 64 D3
Loengo, Dem. Rep. of the Congo 86 C2
Loeriesfontein, S. Africa 88 E2
Lofa →, Liberia 83 D2
Lofer, Austria 26 D5
Lofoten, Norway 8 B15
Lofsdalen, Sweden 10 B7
Lofsen →, Sweden 10 B7
Loftahammar, Sweden 11 G10
Loga, Niger 83 C5
Logan, Iowa, U.S.A. 112 E7
Logan, Ohio, U.S.A. 108 F4
Logan, Utah, U.S.A. 114 F8
Logan, W. Va., U.S.A. 108 G5
Logan, Mt., Canada 100 B5
Logandale, U.S.A. 117 J12
Logansport, Ind., U.S.A. 108 E2
Logansport, La., U.S.A. 113 K8
Logirim, Sudan 81 G3
Logo, Sudan 81 F3
Logone →, Chad 79 F9
Logroño, Spain 32 C2
Logrosán, Spain 35 F5
Løgstør, Denmark 11 H3
Løgumkloster, Denmark 11 J2
Lohals, Denmark 11 J4
Lohardaga, India 69 H11
Loharia, India 68 H6
Loharu, India 68 E6
Lohja, Finland 9 F21
Löhne, Germany 24 C4
Lohr, Germany 25 F5
Lohri Wah →, Pakistan 68 F2
Loi-kaw, Burma 67 K20
Loimaa, Finland 9 F20
Loir →, France 18 E6
Loir-et-Cher □, France 18 E8
Loire □, France 21 C8
Loire →, France 18 E4
Loire-Atlantique □, France 18 E5
Loiret □, France 19 E9
Loitz, Germany 24 B9
Loja, Ecuador 124 D3
Loja, Spain 35 H6
Loji = Kawasi, Indonesia 63 E7
Løjt Kirkeby, Denmark 11 J3
Lojung, China 58 E7
Loka, Sudan 81 G3
Lokandu, Dem. Rep. of the Congo 86 C2
Lokeren, Belgium 17 C3
Lokgwabe, Botswana 88 C3
Lokhvitsa, Ukraine 47 G7
Lokichokio, Kenya 86 B3
Lokitaung, Kenya 86 B4
Lokkan tekojärvi, Finland 8 C22
Løkken, Denmark 11 G3
Loknya, Russia 46 D6
Loko, Nigeria 83 D6
Lokoja, Nigeria 83 D6
Lokot, Russia 47 F8
Lol →, Sudan 81 F2
Lola, Guinea 82 D3
Lola, Mt., U.S.A. 116 F6
Lolibai, Gebel, Sudan 81 G3
Lolimi, Sudan 81 G3
Loliondo, Tanzania 86 C4
Lolland, Denmark 11 K5
Lollar, Germany 24 E4
Lolo, U.S.A. 114 C6
Lolodorf, Cameroon 83 E7
Lom, Bulgaria 40 C7
Lom →, Bulgaria 40 C7
Lom Kao, Thailand 64 D3
Lom Sak, Thailand 64 D3
Loma, U.S.A. 114 C8
Loma Linda, U.S.A. 117 L9
Lomami →, Dem. Rep. of the Congo 86 B1
Lomas de Zamóra, Argentina 126 C4
Lombadina, Australia 92 C3
Lombárdia □, Italy 28 C6
Lombardy = Lombárdia □, Italy 28 C6
Lombez, France 20 E4
Lomblen, Indonesia 63 F6
Lombok, Indonesia 62 F5
Lomé, Togo 83 D5
Lomela, Dem. Rep. of the Congo 84 E4
Lomela →, Dem. Rep. of the Congo 84 E4
Lomianki, Poland 45 F7
Lomma, Sweden 11 J7
Lommel, Belgium 17 C5
Lomond, Canada 104 C6
Lomond, L., U.K. 14 E4
Lomphat, Cambodia 64 F6
Lompobatang, Indonesia 63 F5
Lompoc, U.S.A. 117 L6
Łomża, Poland 45 E9
Loncoche, Chile 128 D2
Londa, India 66 M9
Londiani, Kenya 86 C4
Londinières, France 18 C8
London, Canada 102 D3
London, U.K. 13 F7
London, Ky., U.S.A. 108 G3
London, Ohio, U.S.A. 108 F4
London, Greater □, U.K. 13 F7
Londonderry, U.K. 15 B4
Londonderry □, U.K. 15 B4
Londonderry, C., Australia 92 B4
Londonderry, I., Chile 128 H2
Londres, Argentina 128 B3
Londrina, Brazil 127 A5
Lone Pine, U.S.A. 116 J8
Lonely Mine, Zimbabwe 89 B4
Long B., U.S.A. 109 J6
Long Beach, Calif., U.S.A. 117 M8
Long Beach, N.Y., U.S.A. 111 F11
Long Beach, Wash., U.S.A. 116 D2
Long Branch, U.S.A. 111 F11
Long Creek, U.S.A. 114 D4
Long Eaton, U.K. 12 E6
Long I., Australia 94 C4
Long I., Bahamas 121 B4
Long I., Canada 102 B4
Long I., Ireland 15 E2
Long I., U.S.A. 111 F11
Long Island Sd., U.S.A. 111 E12
Long L., Canada 102 C2
Long Lake, U.S.A. 111 C10
Long Point B., Canada 110 D4
Long Prairie →, U.S.A. 112 C7
Long Pt., Canada 110 D4
Long Range Mts., Canada 103 C8
Long Reef, Australia 92 B4
Long Spruce, Canada 105 B10
Long Str. = Longa, Proliv, Russia 4 C16
Long Thanh, Vietnam 65 G6
Long Xian, China 56 G4
Long Xuyen, Vietnam 65 G5
Longá, Greece 38 E3
Longa, Proliv, Russia 4 C16
Long'an, China 58 F6
Longarone, Italy 29 B9
Longbenton, U.K. 12 B6
Longboat Key, U.S.A. 109 M4
Longchang, China 58 C5
Longchi, China 58 C4
Longchuan, Guangdong, China 59 E10
Longchuan, Yunnan, China 58 E1
Longde, China 56 G4
Longeau, France 19 E12
Longford, Australia 94 G4
Longford, Ireland 15 C4
Longford □, Ireland 15 C4
Longhai, China 59 E11
Longhua, China 57 D9
Longhui, China 59 D8
Longido, Tanzania 86 C4
Longiram, Indonesia 62 E5
Longkou, Jiangxi, China 59 D10
Longkou, Shandong, China 57 F11
Longlac, Canada 102 C2
Longli, China 58 D6
Longlin, China 58 E5
Longling, China 58 E2
Longmeadow, U.S.A. 111 D12
Longmen, China 59 F10
Longming, China 58 F6
Longmont, U.S.A. 112 E2
Longnan, China 59 E10
Longnawan, Indonesia 62 D4
Longobucco, Italy 31 C9
Longquan, China 59 C12
Longreach, Australia 94 C3
Longshan, China 58 C7
Longsheng, China 59 E8
Longué-Jumelles, France 18 E6
Longueau, France 19 C9
Longueuil, Canada 111 A11
Longuyon, France 19 C12
Longvic, France 19 E12
Longview, Tex., U.S.A. 113 J7
Longview, Wash., U.S.A. 116 D4
Longwy, France 19 C12
Longxi, China 56 G3
Longyan, China 59 E11
Longyou, China 59 C12
Longzhou, China 58 F6
Lonigo, Italy 29 C8
Löningen, Germany 24 C3
Lonja →, Croatia 29 C13
Lonoke, U.S.A. 113 H9
Lonquimay, Chile 128 D2
Lons-le-Saunier, France 19 F12
Lönsboda, Sweden 11 H8
Looe, U.K. 13 G3
Lookout, C., Canada 102 A3
Lookout, C., U.S.A. 109 H7
Loolmalasin, Tanzania 86 C4
Loon →, Alta., Canada 104 B5
Loon →, Man., Canada 105 B8
Loon Lake, Canada 105 C7
Loongana, Australia 93 F4
Loop Hd., Ireland 15 D2
Lop Buri, Thailand 64 E3
Lop Nor = Lop Nur, China 60 B4
Lop Nur, China 60 B4
Lopare, Bos.-H. 42 F3
Lopatin, Russia 49 J8
Lopatina, Gora, Russia 51 D15
Lopaye, Sudan 81 F3
Lopez, Phil. 61 E5
Lopez, U.S.A. 111 E8
Lopez, C., Gabon 84 E1
Lopphavet, Norway 8 A19
Lora →, Afghan. 66 D4
Lora, Hāmūn-i-, Pakistan 66 E4
Lora Cr. →, Australia 95 D2
Lora del Río, Spain 35 H5
Lorain, U.S.A. 110 E2
Loralai, Pakistan 68 D3
Lorca, Spain 33 H3
Lord Howe I., Pac. Oc. 96 L7
Lord Howe Ridge, Pac. Oc. 96 L8
Lordsburg, U.S.A. 115 K9
Lorestan □, Iran 71 C6
Loreto, Brazil 125 E9
Loreto, Italy 29 E10
Loreto, Mexico 118 B2
Lorgues, France 21 E10
Lorhosso, Burkina Faso 82 C4
Lorient, France 18 E3
Lőrinci, Hungary 42 C4
Lormi, India 69 H9
Lorn, U.K. 14 E3
Lorn, Firth of, U.K. 14 E3
Lorne, Australia 95 F3
Loronyo, Sudan 81 G3
Lorovouno, Cyprus 36 D11
Lörrach, Germany 25 H3
Lorraine □, France 19 D13
Los, Sweden 10 C9
Los, Îles de, Guinea 82 D2
Los Alamos, Calif., U.S.A. 117 L6
Los Alamos, N. Mex., U.S.A. 115 J10
Los Altos, U.S.A. 116 H4
Los Andes, Chile 126 C1
Los Angeles, Chile 126 D1
Los Angeles, U.S.A. 117 M8
Los Angeles, Bahia de, Mexico 118 B2
Los Angeles Aqueduct, U.S.A. 117 K9
Los Banos, U.S.A. 116 H6
Los Barrios, Spain 35 J5
Los Blancos, Argentina 126 A3
Los Chiles, Costa Rica 120 D3
Los Corrales de Buelna, Spain 34 B6
Los Cristianos, Canary Is. 37 F3
Los Gallardos, Spain 33 H3
Los Gatos, U.S.A. 116 H5
Los Hermanos Is., Venezuela 121 D7
Los Islotes, Canary Is. 37 E6
Los Llanos de Aridane, Canary Is. 37 F2
Los Loros, Chile 126 B1
Los Lunas, U.S.A. 115 J10
Los Mochis, Mexico 118 B3
Los Monegros, Spain 32 D4
Los Nietos, Spain 33 H4
Los Olivos, U.S.A. 117 L6
Los Palacios, Cuba 120 B3
Los Palacios y Villafranca, Spain 35 H5
Los Reyes, Mexico 118 D4
Los Roques Is., Venezuela 121 D6
Los Santos de Maimona, Spain 35 G4
Los Teques, Venezuela 124 A5
Los Testigos, Is., Venezuela 124 A6
Los Vilos, Chile 126 C1
Los Yébenes, Spain 35 F7
Łosice, Poland 45 F9
Loskop Dam, S. Africa 89 D4
Løsning, Denmark 11 J3
Lossiemouth, U.K. 14 D5
Lostwithiel, U.K. 13 G3
Lot □, France 20 D5
Lot →, France 20 D4
Lot-et-Garonne □, France 20 D4
Lota, Chile 126 D1
Lotagipi Swamp, Sudan 81 G3
Lotfābād, Iran 71 B8
Lothair, S. Africa 89 D5
Lotorp, Sweden 11 F9
Lötschbergtunnel, Switz. 25 J3
Löttorp, Sweden 11 G11
Lotung, Taiwan 59 E13
Loubomo, Congo 84 E2
Loudéac, France 18 D4
Loudi, China 59 D8
Loudonville, U.S.A. 110 F2
Loudun, France 18 E7
Loue →, France 19 E12
Louga, Senegal 82 B1
Loughborough, U.K. 12 E6
Loughrea, Ireland 15 C3
Loughros More B., Ireland 15 B3
Louhans, France 19 F12
Louis Trichardt, S. Africa 89 C4
Louis XIV, Pte., Canada 102 B4
Louisa, U.S.A. 108 F4
Louisbourg, Canada 103 C8
Louise I., Canada 104 C2
Louiseville, Canada 102 C5
Louisiade Arch., Papua N. G. 96 J7
Louisiana, U.S.A. 112 F9
Louisiana □, U.S.A. 113 K9
Louisville, Ky., U.S.A. 108 F3
Louisville, Miss., U.S.A. 113 J10
Louisville, Ohio, U.S.A. 110 F3
Loulay, France 20 B3
Loulé, Portugal 35 H3
Louny, Czech Rep. 26 A6
Loup City, U.S.A. 112 E5
Loups Marins, Lacs des, Canada 102 A5
Lourdes, France 20 E3
Lourinhã, Portugal 35 F1
Lousã, Portugal 34 E2
Louta, Burkina Faso 82 C4
Louth, Australia 95 E4
Louth, Ireland 15 C5
Louth, U.K. 12 D7
Louth □, Ireland 15 C5
Loutrá Aidhipsoú, Greece 38 C5
Loutráki, Greece 38 D4
Louvain = Leuven, Belgium 17 D4
Louviers, France 18 C8
Louwsburg, S. Africa 89 D5
Lovat →, Russia 46 C6
Lovćen, Montenegro, Yug. 40 D2
Lovech, Bulgaria 41 C8
Lovech □, Bulgaria 41 C8
Loveland, U.S.A. 112 E2
Lovell, U.S.A. 114 D9
Lovelock, U.S.A. 114 F4
Lóvere, Italy 28 C7
Lövestad, Sweden 11 J7
Loviisa, Finland 9 F22
Loving, U.S.A. 113 J2
Lovington, U.S.A. 113 J3
Lovisa = Loviisa, Finland 9 F22
Lovosice, Czech Rep. 26 A7
Lovran, Croatia 29 C11
Lovrin, Romania 42 E5
Lövstabruk, Sweden 10 D11
Lövstabukten, Sweden 10 D11
Low, L., Canada 102 B4
Low Pt., Australia 93 F4
Low Tatra = Nízké Tatry, Slovak Rep. 27 C12
Lowa, Dem. Rep. of the Congo 86 C2
Lowa →, Dem. Rep. of the Congo 86 C2
Lowell, U.S.A. 111 D13
Lowellville, U.S.A. 110 E4
Löwen →, Namibia 88 D2
Lower Alkali L., U.S.A. 114 F3
Lower Arrow L., Canada 104 D5
Lower Austria = Niederösterreich □, Austria 26 C8
Lower California = Baja California, Mexico 118 A1
Lower Hutt, N.Z. 91 J5
Lower Lake, U.S.A. 116 G4
Lower Manitou L., Canada 105 D10
Lower Post, Canada 104 B3
Lower Red L., U.S.A. 112 B7
Lower Saxony = Niedersachsen □, Germany 24 C4
Lower Tunguska = Tunguska, Nizhnyaya →, Russia 51 C9
Lowestoft, U.K. 13 E9
Lowgar □, Afghan. 66 B6
Łowicz, Poland 45 F6
Lowville, U.S.A. 111 C9
Loxton, Australia 95 E3
Loxton, S. Africa 88 E3
Loyalton, U.S.A. 116 F6
Loyalty Is. = Loyauté, Is., N. Cal. 96 K8
Loyang = Luoyang, China 56 G7
Loyauté, Is., N. Cal. 96 K8
Loyev = Loyew, Belarus 47 G6
Loyew, Belarus 47 G6
Loyoro, Uganda 86 B3
Lož, Slovenia 29 C11
Lozère □, France 20 D7
Loznica, Serbia, Yug. 40 B3
Lozova, Ukraine 47 H9
Lü Shan, China 59 C11
Lü-Tao, Taiwan 59 F13
Luachimo, Angola 84 F4
Luajan →, India 69 G11
Lualaba →, Dem. Rep. of the Congo 86 B2
Luampa, Zambia 87 F1
Lu'an, China 59 B11
Luan Chau, Vietnam 58 G4
Luan He →, China 57 E10
Luan Xian, China 57 E10
Luancheng, Guangxi Zhuangzu, China 58 F7
Luancheng, Hebei, China 56 F8
Luanco, Spain 34 B5
Luanda, Angola 84 F2
Luang, Thale, Thailand 65 J3
Luang Prabang, Laos 58 H4
Luangwa, Zambia 87 F3
Luangwa →, Zambia 87 E3
Luangwa Valley, Zambia 87 E3
Luanne, China 57 D9
Luanping, China 57 D9
Luanshya, Zambia 87 E2
Luapula □, Zambia 87 E2
Luapula →, Africa 87 D2
Luarca, Spain 34 B4
Luashi, Dem. Rep. of the Congo 87 E1
Luau, Angola 84 G4
Lubaczów, Poland 45 H10
Lubań, Poland 45 G2
Lubana, Ozero = Lubānas Ezers, Latvia 9 H22
Lubānas Ezers, Latvia 9 H22
Lubang, Phil. 61 E4
Lubang Is., Phil. 63 B6
Lubartów, Poland 45 G9
Lubawa, Poland 44 E6
Lübbecke, Germany 24 C4
Lübben, Germany 24 D9
Lübbenau, Germany 24 D9
Lubbock, U.S.A. 113 J4
Lübeck, Germany 24 B6
Lübecker Bucht, Germany 24 A6
Lubefu, Dem. Rep. of the Congo 86 C1
Lubefu →, Dem. Rep. of the Congo 86 C1
Lubelskie □, Poland 45 G9
Lubero = Luofu, Dem. Rep. of the Congo 86 C2
Lubersac, France 20 C5
Lubicon L., Canada 104 B5
Lubień Kujawski, Poland 45 F6
Lubilash →, Dem. Rep. of the Congo 84 F4
Lubin, Poland 45 G3
Lublin, Poland 45 G9
Lubliniec, Poland 45 H5
Lubnān, Jabal, Lebanon 75 B4
Lubniewice, Poland 45 F2
Lubny, Ukraine 47 G7
Lubomierz, Poland 45 G2
Luboń, Poland 45 F3
Lubongola, Dem. Rep. of the Congo 86 C2
L'ubotín, Slovak Rep. 27 B13
Lubraniec, Poland 45 F5
Lubsko, Poland 45 G1
Lübtheen, Germany 24 B7
Lubuagan, Phil. 61 C4
Lubudi, Dem. Rep. of the Congo 84 F5
Lubudi →, Dem. Rep. of the Congo 87 D2
Lubuklinggau, Indonesia 62 E2
Lubuksikaping, Indonesia 62 D2
Lubumbashi, Dem. Rep. of the Congo 87 E2
Lubunda, Dem. Rep. of the Congo 86 D2
Lubungu, Zambia 87 E2
Lubuskie □, Poland 45 F2
Lubutu, Dem. Rep. of the Congo 86 C2
Luc An Chau, Vietnam 64 A5
Luc-en-Diois, France 21 D9
Lucan, Canada 110 C3
Lucania, Mt., Canada 100 B5
Lucas Channel, Canada 110 A3
Lucban, Phil. 61 D4
Lucca, Italy 28 E7
Lucé, France 18 D8
Luce Bay, U.K. 14 G4
Lucea, Jamaica 120 C4
Lucedale, U.S.A. 109 K1

Lucena, *Phil.* 61 E4
Lucena, *Spain* 35 H6
Lučenec, *Slovak Rep.* 27 C12
Lucera, *Italy* 31 A8
Lucerne = Luzern, *Switz.* 25 H4
Lucerne, *U.S.A.* 116 F4
Lucerne Valley, *U.S.A.* 117 L10
Lucero, *Mexico* 118 A3
Luchena →, *Spain* 33 H3
Lucheng, *China* 56 F7
Lucheringo →, *Mozam.* 87 E4
Lüchow, *Germany* 24 C7
Luchuan, *China* 59 F8
Lucia, *U.S.A.* 116 J5
Lucinda, *Australia* 94 B4
Luckau, *Germany* 24 D9
Luckenwalde, *Germany* 24 C9
Luckhoff, *S. Africa* 88 D3
Lucknow, *Canada* 110 C3
Lucknow, *India* 69 F9
Luçon, *France* 20 B2
Lüda = Dalian, *China* 57 E11
Luda Kamchiya →, *Bulgaria* 41 C11
Ludbreg, *Croatia* 29 B13
Lüdenscheid, *Germany* 24 D3
Lüderitz, *Namibia* 88 D2
Lüderitzbaai, *Namibia* 88 D2
Ludhiana, *India* 68 D6
Ludian, *China* 58 D4
Luding Qiao, *China* 58 C4
Lüdinghausen, *Germany* 24 D3
Ludington, *U.S.A.* 108 D2
Ludlow, *U.K.* 13 E5
Ludlow, *Calif., U.S.A.* 117 L10
Ludlow, *Pa., U.S.A.* 110 E6
Ludlow, *Vt., U.S.A.* 111 C12
Ludus, *Romania* 43 D9
Ludvika, *Sweden* 10 D9
Ludwigsburg, *Germany* 25 G5
Ludwigsfelde, *Germany* 24 C9
Ludwigshafen, *Germany* 25 F4
Ludwigslust, *Germany* 24 B7
Ludza, *Latvia* 46 D4
Lueki, *Dem. Rep. of the Congo* 86 C2
Luena, *Dem. Rep. of the Congo* 87 D2
Luena, *Zambia* 87 E3
Lüeyang, *China* 56 H4
Lufeng, *Guangdong, China* 59 F10
Lufeng, *Yunnan, China* 58 E4
Lufira →, *Dem. Rep. of the Congo* 87 D2
Lufkin, *U.S.A.* 113 K7
Lufupa, *Dem. Rep. of the Congo* 87 E1
Luga, *Russia* 46 C5
Luga →, *Russia* 46 C5
Lugano, *Switz.* 25 J4
Lugano, L. di, *Switz.* 28 C6
Lugansk = Luhansk, *Ukraine* 47 H10
Lugard's Falls, *Kenya* 86 C4
Lugela, *Mozam.* 87 F4
Lugenda →, *Mozam.* 87 E4
Lugh Ganana, *Somali Rep.* 74 G3
Lugnaquilla, *Ireland* 15 D5
Lugo, *Italy* 29 D8
Lugo, *Spain* 34 B3
Lugo □, *Spain* 34 C3
Lugoj, *Romania* 42 E6
Lugovoy = Qulan, *Kazakstan* 50 E8
Luhansk, *Ukraine* 47 H10
Luhe, *China* 59 A12
Luhe →, *Germany* 24 B6
Luhuo, *China* 58 B3
Luiana, *Angola* 88 B3
Luimneach = Limerick, *Ireland* 15 D3
Luing, *U.K.* 14 E3
Luino, *Italy* 28 C5
Luís Correia, *Brazil* 125 D10
Luitpold Coast, *Antarctica* 5 D1
Luiza, *Dem. Rep. of the Congo* 84 F4
Luizi, *Dem. Rep. of the Congo* 86 D2
Luján, *Argentina* 126 C4
Lujiang, *China* 59 B11
Lukang, *Taiwan* 59 E13
Lukanga Swamp, *Zambia* 87 E2
Lukavac, *Bos.-H.* 42 F3
Lukenie →, *Dem. Rep. of the Congo* 84 E3
Lukhisaral, *India* 69 G12
Lŭki, *Bulgaria* 41 E8
Lukolela, *Dem. Rep. of the Congo* 86 D1
Lukosi, *Zimbabwe* 87 F2
Lukovë, *Albania* 40 G3
Lukovit, *Bulgaria* 41 C8
Łuków, *Poland* 45 G9
Lukoyanov, *Russia* 48 C7
Lule älv →, *Sweden* 8 D19
Luleå, *Sweden* 8 D20
Lüleburgaz, *Turkey* 41 E11
Luliang, *China* 58 E4
Luling, *U.S.A.* 113 L6
Lulong, *China* 57 E10
Lulonga →, *Dem. Rep. of the Congo* 84 D3
Lulua →, *Dem. Rep. of the Congo* 84 E4
Lumajang, *Indonesia* 63 H15
Lumbala N'guimbo, *Angola* 85 G4
Lumberton, *U.S.A.* 109 H6
Lumbwa, *Kenya* 86 C4
Lumsden, *Canada* 105 C8
Lumsden, *N.Z.* 91 L2
Lumut, *Malaysia* 65 K3
Lumut, Tanjung, *Indonesia* 62 E3
Luna, *India* 68 H3
Lunan, *China* 58 E4
Lunavada, *India* 68 H5
Lunca, *Romania* 43 C10
Lunca Corbului, *Romania* 43 F9
Lund, *Sweden* 11 J7
Lundazi, *Zambia* 87 E3
Lunderskov, *Denmark* 11 J3
Lundi →, *Zimbabwe* 87 G3
Lundu, *Malaysia* 62 D3
Lundy, *U.K.* 13 F3
Lune →, *U.K.* 12 C5
Lüneburg, *Germany* 24 B6
Lüneburg Heath = Lüneburger Heide, *Germany* 24 B6
Lüneburger Heide, *Germany* 24 B6
Lunel, *France* 21 E8
Lünen, *Germany* 24 D3
Lunenburg, *Canada* 103 D7
Lunéville, *France* 19 D13
Lunga →, *Zambia* 87 E2
Lungi Airport, *S. Leone* 82 D2
Lunglei, *India* 67 H18
Luni, *India* 68 G5
Luni →, *India* 68 G4
Luninets = Luninyets, *Belarus* 47 F4
Luning, *U.S.A.* 114 G4
Lunino, *Russia* 48 D7
Luninyets, *Belarus* 47 F4
Lunkaransar, *India* 68 E5
Lunsemfwa →, *Zambia* 87 E3
Lunsemfwa Falls, *Zambia* 87 E2
Luo He →, *China* 56 G6
Luocheng, *China* 58 E7
Luochuan, *China* 56 G5
Luoci, *China* 58 E4
Luodian, *China* 58 E6
Luoding, *China* 59 F8
Luofu, *Dem. Rep. of the Congo* 86 C2
Luohe, *China* 56 H8
Luojiang, *China* 58 B5
Luonan, *China* 56 G6
Luoning, *China* 56 G6
Luoshan, *China* 59 A10
Luotian, *China* 59 B10
Luoxiao Shan, *China* 59 D10
Luoyang, *China* 56 G7
Luoyuan, *China* 59 D12
Luozigou, *China* 57 C16
Lupanshui, *China* 58 D5
Lupeni, *Romania* 43 E8
Lupilichi, *Mozam.* 87 E4
Łupków, *Poland* 45 J9
Lupoing, *China* 58 E5
Luquan, *China* 58 E4
Luque, *Paraguay* 126 B4
Lūras, *Italy* 30 B2
Luray, *U.S.A.* 108 F6
Lure, *France* 19 E13
Lurgan, *U.K.* 15 B5
Lusaka, *Zambia* 87 F2
Lusambo, *Dem. Rep. of the Congo* 86 C1
Lusangaye, *Dem. Rep. of the Congo* 86 C2
Luseland, *Canada* 105 C7
Lushan, *Henan, China* 56 H7
Lushan, *Sichuan, China* 58 B4
Lushi, *China* 56 G6
Lushnjë, *Albania* 40 F3
Lushoto, *Tanzania* 86 C4
Lushui, *China* 58 E2
Lüshun, *China* 57 E11
Lusignan, *France* 20 B4
Lusigny-sur-Barse, *France* 19 D11
Lusk, *U.S.A.* 112 D2
Lussac-les-Châteaux, *France* 20 B4
Lustenau, *Austria* 26 D2
Lūt, Dasht-e, *Iran* 71 D8
Luta = Dalian, *China* 57 E11
Lutherstadt Wittenberg, *Germany* 24 D8
Luton, *U.K.* 13 F7
Luton □, *U.K.* 13 F7
Lutselke, *Canada* 105 A6
Lutsk, *Ukraine* 47 G3
Lützow Holmbukta, *Antarctica* 5 C4
Lutzputs, *S. Africa* 88 D3
Luverne, *Ala., U.S.A.* 109 K2
Luverne, *Minn., U.S.A.* 112 D6
Luvua, *Dem. Rep. of the Congo* 87 D2
Luvua →, *Dem. Rep. of the Congo* 86 D2
Luvuvhu →, *S. Africa* 89 C5
Luwegu →, *Tanzania* 87 D4
Luwuk, *Indonesia* 63 E6
Luxembourg, *Lux.* 17 E6
Luxembourg □, *Belgium* 17 E5
Luxembourg ■, *Europe* 7 F7
Luxeuil-les-Bains, *France* 19 E13
Luxi, *Hunan, China* 59 C8
Luxi, *Yunnan, China* 58 E4
Luxi, *Yunnan, China* 58 E2
Luxor = El Uqsur, *Egypt* 80 B3
Luy-de-Béarn →, *France* 20 E3
Luy-de-France →, *France* 20 E3
Luyi, *China* 56 H8
Luz-St-Sauveur, *France* 20 F4
Luzern, *Switz.* 25 H4
Luzern □, *Switz.* 25 H3
Luzhai, *China* 58 E7
Luzhi, *China* 58 D5
Luzhou, *China* 58 C5
Luziânia, *Brazil* 125 G9
Lužnice →, *Czech Rep.* 26 B7
Luzon, *Phil.* 61 D4
Luzy, *France* 19 F10
Luzzi, *Italy* 31 C9
Lviv, *Ukraine* 47 H3
Lvov = Lviv, *Ukraine* 47 H3
Lwówek, *Poland* 45 F3
Lwówek Śląski, *Poland* 45 G2
Lyakhavichy, *Belarus* 47 F4
Lyakhovskiye, Ostrova, *Russia* 51 B15
Lyaki = Läki, *Azerbaijan* 49 K8
Lyal I., *Canada* 110 B3
Lyallpur = Faisalabad, *Pakistan* 68 D5
Lyaskovets, *Bulgaria* 41 C9
Lybster, *U.K.* 14 C5
Lycaonia, *Turkey* 72 D5
Lychen, *Germany* 24 B9
Lychkova, *Russia* 46 D7
Lycia, *Turkey* 39 E11
Lyckebyån →, *Sweden* 11 H9
Lycksele, *Sweden* 8 D18
Lycosura, *Greece* 38 D4
Lydda = Lod, *Israel* 75 D3
Lydenburg, *S. Africa* 89 D5
Lydia, *Turkey* 39 C10
Łydynia →, *Poland* 45 F7
Lyell, *N.Z.* 91 J4
Lyell I., *Canada* 104 C2
Lyepyel, *Belarus* 46 E5
Lygnern, *Sweden* 11 G6
Lykens, *U.S.A.* 111 F8
Lyman, *U.S.A.* 114 F8
Lyme B., *U.K.* 13 G4
Lyme Regis, *U.K.* 13 G5
Lymington, *U.K.* 13 G6
Łyna →, *Poland* 9 J19
Lynchburg, *U.S.A.* 108 G6
Lynd →, *Australia* 94 B3
Lynd Ra., *Australia* 95 D4
Lynden, *Canada* 110 C4
Lynden, *U.S.A.* 116 B4
Lyndhurst, *Australia* 95 E2
Lyndon →, *Australia* 93 D1
Lyndonville, *N.Y., U.S.A.* 110 C6
Lyndonville, *Vt., U.S.A.* 111 B12
Lyngen, *Norway* 8 B19
Lynher Reef, *Australia* 92 C3
Lynn, *U.S.A.* 111 D14
Lynn Lake, *Canada* 105 B8
Lynnwood, *U.S.A.* 116 C4
Lynton, *U.K.* 13 F4
Lyntupy, *Belarus* 9 J22
Lynx L., *Canada* 105 A7
Lyon, *France* 21 C8
Lyonnais, *France* 21 C8
Lyons = Lyon, *France* 21 C8
Lyons, *Ga., U.S.A.* 109 J4
Lyons, *Kans., U.S.A.* 112 F5
Lyons, *N.Y., U.S.A.* 110 C8
Lyons →, *Australia* 93 E2
Lyons Falls, *U.S.A.* 111 C9
Lyozna, *Belarus* 46 E6
Lys = Leie →, *Belgium* 17 C3
Lysá nad Labem, *Czech Rep.* 26 A7
Lysekil, *Sweden* 11 F5
Lyskovo, *Russia* 48 B7
Lystrup, *Denmark* 11 H4
Lysvik, *Sweden* 10 D7
Lysychansk, *Ukraine* 47 H10
Lytham St. Anne's, *U.K.* 12 D4
Lyttelton, *N.Z.* 91 K4
Lytton, *Canada* 104 C4
Lyuban, *Russia* 46 C6
Lyubertsy, *Russia* 46 E9
Lyubim, *Russia* 46 C11
Lyubimets, *Bulgaria* 41 E10
Lyuboml, *Ukraine* 47 G3
Lyubotyn, *Ukraine* 47 H8
Lyubytino, *Russia* 46 C7
Lyudinovo, *Russia* 46 F8

M

M.R. Gomez, Presa, *Mexico* 119 B5
Ma →, *Vietnam* 58 H5
Ma'adaba, *Jordan* 75 E4
Maamba, *Zambia* 88 B4
Ma'ān, *Jordan* 75 E4
Ma'ān □, *Jordan* 75 F5
Maanselkä, *Finland* 8 C23
Ma'anshan, *China* 59 B12
Maarianhamina, *Finland* 9 F18
Ma'arrat an Nu'mān, *Syria* 70 C3
Maas →, *Neths.* 17 C4
Maaseik, *Belgium* 17 C5
Maasin, *Phil.* 63 B6
Maastricht, *Neths.* 17 D5
Maave, *Mozam.* 89 C5
Mababe Depression, *Botswana* 88 B3
Mabalane, *Mozam.* 89 C5
Mabel L., *Canada* 104 C5
Mabenge, *Dem. Rep. of the Congo* 86 B1
Maberly, *Canada* 111 B8
Mabian, *China* 58 C4
Mabil, *Ethiopia* 81 E4
Mablethorpe, *U.K.* 12 D8
Mably, *France* 19 F11
Maboma, *Dem. Rep. of the Congo* 86 B2
Mabonto, *S. Leone* 82 D2
Mabrouk, *Mali* 83 B4
Mac Bac, *Vietnam* 65 H6
Macachín, *Argentina* 126 D3
Macaé, *Brazil* 127 A7
Macael, *Spain* 33 H2
McAlester, *U.S.A.* 113 H7
McAllen, *U.S.A.* 113 M5
MacAlpine L., *Canada* 100 B9
Macamic, *Canada* 102 C4
Macao = Macau □, *China* 59 F9
Macão, *Portugal* 35 F3
Macapá, *Brazil* 125 C8
McArthur →, *Australia* 94 B2
McArthur, Port, *Australia* 94 B2
Macau, *Brazil* 125 E11
Macau □, *China* 59 F9
McBride, *Canada* 104 C4
McCall, *U.S.A.* 114 D5
McCamey, *U.S.A.* 113 K3
McCammon, *U.S.A.* 114 E7
McCauley I., *Canada* 104 C2
McCleary, *U.S.A.* 116 C3
Macclenny, *U.S.A.* 109 K4
Macclesfield, *U.K.* 12 D5
M'Clintock Chan., *Canada* 100 A9
McClintock Ra., *Australia* 92 C4
McCloud, *U.S.A.* 114 F2
McCluer I., *Australia* 92 B5
McClure, *U.S.A.* 110 F7
McClure, L., *U.S.A.* 116 H6
M'Clure Str., *Canada* 4 B2
McClusky, *U.S.A.* 112 B4
McComb, *U.S.A.* 113 K9
McConaughy, L., *U.S.A.* 112 E4
McCook, *U.S.A.* 112 E4
McCreary, *Canada* 105 C9
McCullough Mt., *U.S.A.* 117 K11
McCusker →, *Canada* 105 B7
McDame, *Canada* 104 B3
McDermitt, *U.S.A.* 114 F5
McDonald, *U.S.A.* 110 F4
Macdonald, L., *Australia* 92 D4
McDonald Is., *Ind. Oc.* 3 G13
MacDonnell Ranges, *Australia* 92 D5
MacDowell L., *Canada* 102 B1
Macduff, *U.K.* 14 D6
Maceda, *Spain* 34 C3
Macedonia, *U.S.A.* 110 E3
Macedonia ■, *Europe* 40 E5
Maceió, *Brazil* 125 E11
Maceira, *Portugal* 34 F2
Macenta, *Guinea* 82 D3
Macerata, *Italy* 29 E10
McFarland, *U.S.A.* 117 K7
McFarlane →, *Canada* 105 B7
Macfarlane, L., *Australia* 95 E2
McGehee, *U.S.A.* 113 J9
McGill, *U.S.A.* 114 G6
Macgillycuddy's Reeks, *Ireland* 15 E2
McGraw, *U.S.A.* 111 D8
McGregor, *U.S.A.* 112 D9
McGregor Ra., *Australia* 95 D3
Mach, *Pakistan* 66 E5
Māch Kowr, *Iran* 71 E9
Machado = Jiparaná →, *Brazil* 124 E6
Machagai, *Argentina* 126 B3
Machakos, *Kenya* 86 C4
Machala, *Ecuador* 124 D3
Machanga, *Mozam.* 89 C6
Machattie, L., *Australia* 94 C2
Machault, *France* 19 C11
Machava, *Mozam.* 89 D5
Machece, *Mozam.* 87 F4
Machecoul, *France* 18 F5
Macheke, *Zimbabwe* 89 B5
Macheng, *China* 59 B10
Machero, *Spain* 35 F6
Machhu →, *India* 68 H4
Machias, *Maine, U.S.A.* 109 C12
Machias, *N.Y., U.S.A.* 110 D6
Machichi →, *Canada* 105 B10
Machico, *Madeira* 37 D3
Machilipatnam, *India* 67 L12
Machiques, *Venezuela* 124 A4
Machupicchu, *Peru* 124 F4
Machynlleth, *U.K.* 13 E4
Macia, *Mozam.* 89 D5
Maciejowice, *Poland* 45 G8
McIlwraith Ra., *Australia* 94 A3
Măcin, *Romania* 43 E13
Macina, *Mali* 82 C4
McInnes L., *Canada* 105 C10
McIntosh, *U.S.A.* 112 C4
McIntosh L., *Canada* 105 B8
Macintosh Ra., *Australia* 93 E4
Macintyre →, *Australia* 95 D5
Macizo Galaico, *Spain* 34 C3
Mackay, *Australia* 94 C4
Mackay, *U.S.A.* 114 E7
MacKay →, *Canada* 104 B6
Mackay, L., *Australia* 92 D4
McKay Ra., *Australia* 92 D3
McKeesport, *U.S.A.* 110 F5
McKellar, *Canada* 110 A5
McKenna, *U.S.A.* 116 D4
Mackenzie, *Canada* 104 B4
McKenzie, *U.S.A.* 109 G1
Mackenzie →, *Australia* 94 C4
Mackenzie →, *Canada* 100 B6
McKenzie →, *U.S.A.* 114 D2
Mackenzie Bay, *Canada* 4 B1
Mackenzie City = Linden, *Guyana* 124 B7
Mackenzie Mts., *Canada* 100 B6
Mackinaw City, *U.S.A.* 108 C3
McKinlay, *Australia* 94 C3
McKinlay →, *Australia* 94 C3
McKinley, Mt., *U.S.A.* 100 B4
McKinley Sea, *Arctic* 4 A7
McKinney, *U.S.A.* 113 J6
Mackinnon Road, *Kenya* 86 C4
McKittrick, *U.S.A.* 117 K7
Macklin, *Canada* 105 C7
Macksville, *Australia* 95 E5
McLaughlin, *U.S.A.* 112 C4
Maclean, *Australia* 95 D5
McLean, *U.S.A.* 113 H4
McLeansboro, *U.S.A.* 112 F10
Maclear, *S. Africa* 89 E4
Macleay →, *Australia* 95 E5
McLennan, *Canada* 104 B5
McLeod →, *Canada* 104 C5
MacLeod, B., *Canada* 105 A7
McLeod, L., *Australia* 93 D1
MacLeod Lake, *Canada* 104 C4
McLoughlin, Mt., *U.S.A.* 114 E2
McMechen, *U.S.A.* 110 G4
McMinnville, *Oreg., U.S.A.* 114 D2
McMinnville, *Tenn., U.S.A.* 109 H3
McMurdo Sd., *Antarctica* 5 D11
McMurray = Fort McMurray, *Canada* 104 B6
McMurray, *U.S.A.* 116 B4
Macodoene, *Mozam.* 89 C6
Macomb, *U.S.A.* 112 E9
Macomer, *Italy* 30 B1
Mâcon, *France* 19 F11
Macon, *Ga., U.S.A.* 109 J4
Macon, *Miss., U.S.A.* 109 J1
Macon, *Mo., U.S.A.* 112 F8
Macossa, *Mozam.* 87 F3
Macoun L., *Canada* 105 B8
Macovane, *Mozam.* 89 C6
McPherson, *U.S.A.* 112 F6
McPherson Pk., *U.S.A.* 117 L7
McPherson Ra., *Australia* 95 D5
Macquarie →, *Australia* 95 E4
Macquarie Harbour, *Australia* 94 G4
Macquarie Is., *Pac. Oc.* 96 N7
MacRobertson Land, *Antarctica* 5 D6
Macroom, *Ireland* 15 E3
MacTier, *Canada* 110 A5
Macubela, *Mozam.* 87 F4
Macugnaga, *Italy* 28 C4
Macuiza, *Mozam.* 87 F3
Macusani, *Peru* 124 F4
Macuse, *Mozam.* 87 F4
Macuspana, *Mexico* 119 D6
Macusse, *Angola* 88 B3
Mada →, *Nigeria* 83 D6
Madadeni, *S. Africa* 89 D5
Madagali, *Nigeria* 83 C7
Madagascar ■, *Africa* 89 C8
Madā'in Sālih, *Si. Arabia* 70 E3
Madama, *Niger* 79 D8
Madame I., *Canada* 103 C7
Madan, *Bulgaria* 41 E8
Madaoua, *Niger* 83 C6
Madara, *Nigeria* 83 C7
Madaripur, *Bangla.* 67 H17
Madauk, *Burma* 67 L20
Madawaska, *Canada* 110 A7
Madawaska →, *Canada* 102 C4
Madaya, *Burma* 67 H20
Madbar, *Sudan* 81 F3
Maddalena, *Italy* 30 A2
Maddaloni, *Italy* 31 A7
Madeira, *Atl. Oc.* 37 D3
Madeira →, *Brazil* 122 D5
Madeleine, Îs. de la, *Canada* 103 C7
Maden, *Turkey* 73 C8
Madera, *Mexico* 118 B3
Madera, *Calif., U.S.A.* 116 J6
Madera, *Pa., U.S.A.* 110 F6
Madha, *India* 66 L9
Madhavpur, *India* 68 J3
Madhepura, *India* 69 F12
Madhubani, *India* 69 F12
Madhupur, *India* 69 G12
Madhya Pradesh □, *India* 68 J8
Madidi →, *Bolivia* 124 F5
Madikeri, *India* 66 N9
Madill, *U.S.A.* 113 H6
Madimba, *Dem. Rep. of the Congo* 84 E3
Ma'din, *Syria* 70 C3
Madina, *Mali* 82 C3
Madinani, *Ivory C.* 82 D3
Madingou, *Congo* 84 E2
Madirovalo, *Madag.* 89 B8
Madison, *Calif., U.S.A.* 116 G5
Madison, *Fla., U.S.A.* 109 K4
Madison, *Ind., U.S.A.* 108 F3
Madison, *Nebr., U.S.A.* 112 E6
Madison, *Ohio, U.S.A.* 110 E3
Madison, *S. Dak., U.S.A.* 112 D6
Madison, *Wis., U.S.A.* 112 D10
Madison →, *U.S.A.* 114 D8
Madison Heights, *U.S.A.* 108 G6
Madisonville, *Ky., U.S.A.* 108 G2
Madisonville, *Tex., U.S.A.* 113 K7
Madista, *Botswana* 88 C4
Madiun, *Indonesia* 62 F4
Madoc, *Canada* 110 B7
Madol, *Sudan* 81 F2
Madon →, *France* 19 D13
Madona, *Latvia* 9 H22
Madonie, *Italy* 30 E6
Madonna di Campíglio, *Italy* 28 B7
Madra Dağı, *Turkey* 39 B9
Madrakah, Ra's al, *Oman* 74 D6
Madras = Chennai, *India* 66 N12
Madras = Tamil Nadu □, *India* 66 P10
Madras, *U.S.A.* 114 D3
Madre, Laguna, *U.S.A.* 113 M6
Madre, Sierra, *Phil.* 61 C5
Madre de Dios →, *Bolivia* 122 E4
Madre de Dios, I., *Chile* 122 J3
Madre del Sur, Sierra, *Mexico* 119 D5
Madre Occidental, Sierra, *Mexico* 118 B3
Madre Oriental, Sierra, *Mexico* 118 C5
Madri, *India* 68 G5
Madrid, *Spain* 34 E7

Madrid, *U.S.A.* 111 **B9**
Madrid □, *Spain* 34 **E7**
Madridejos, *Spain* 35 **F7**
Madrigal de las Altas Torres, *Spain* 34 **D6**
Madrona, Sierra, *Spain* 35 **G6**
Madroñera, *Spain* 35 **F5**
Madu, *Sudan* 81 **E2**
Madura, *Australia* 93 **F4**
Madura, *Indonesia* 63 **G15**
Madura, Selat, *Indonesia* 63 **G15**
Madurai, *India* 66 **Q11**
Madurantakam, *India* 66 **N11**
Madzhalis, *Russia* 49 **J8**
Mae Chan, *Thailand* 64 **B2**
Mae Hong Son, *Thailand* 64 **C2**
Mae Khlong →, *Thailand* 64 **F3**
Mae Phrik, *Thailand* 64 **D2**
Mae Ramat, *Thailand* 64 **D2**
Mae Rim, *Thailand* 64 **C2**
Mae Sot, *Thailand* 64 **D2**
Mae Suai, *Thailand* 58 **H2**
Mae Tha, *Thailand* 64 **C2**
Maebashi, *Japan* 55 **F9**
Maella, *Spain* 32 **D5**
Maesteg, *U.K.* 13 **F4**
Maestra, Sierra, *Cuba* 120 **B4**
Maevatanana, *Madag.* 89 **B8**
Mafeking = Mafikeng, *S. Africa* 88 **D4**
Mafeking, *Canada* 105 **C8**
Maféré, *Ivory C.* 82 **D4**
Mafeteng, *Lesotho* 88 **D4**
Maffra, *Australia* 95 **F4**
Mafia I., *Tanzania* 86 **D4**
Mafikeng, *S. Africa* 88 **D4**
Mafra, *Brazil* 127 **B6**
Mafra, *Portugal* 35 **G1**
Mafungabusi Plateau, *Zimbabwe* 87 **F2**
Magadan, *Russia* 51 **D16**
Magadi, *Kenya* 86 **C4**
Magadi, L., *Kenya* 86 **C4**
Magaliesburg, *S. Africa* 89 **D4**
Magallanes, Estrecho de, *Chile* 122 **J3**
Magaluf, *Spain* 33 **F7**
Magangué, *Colombia* 124 **B4**
Magaria, *Niger* 83 **C6**
Magburaka, *S. Leone* 82 **D2**
Magdalen Is. = Madeleine, Îs. de la, *Canada* 103 **C7**
Magdalena, *Argentina* 126 **D4**
Magdalena, *Bolivia* 124 **F6**
Magdalena, *Mexico* 118 **A2**
Magdalena, *U.S.A.* 115 **J10**
Magdalena →, *Colombia* 122 **B3**
Magdalena →, *Mexico* 118 **A2**
Magdalena, B., *Mexico* 118 **C2**
Magdalena, Llano de la, *Mexico* 118 **C2**
Magdeburg, *Germany* 24 **C7**
Magdelaine Cays, *Australia* 94 **B5**
Magdub, *Sudan* 81 **E2**
Magee, *U.S.A.* 113 **K10**
Magelang, *Indonesia* 62 **F4**
Magellan's Str. = Magallanes, Estrecho de, *Chile* 122 **J3**
Magenta, *Italy* 28 **C5**
Magenta, L., *Australia* 93 **F2**
Magerøya, *Norway* 8 **A21**
Maggia →, *Switz.* 25 **J4**
Maggiorasca, Mte., *Italy* 28 **D6**
Maggiore, Lago, *Italy* 28 **C5**
Maghâgha, *Egypt* 80 **B3**
Maghama, *Mauritania* 82 **B2**
Magherafelt, *U.K.* 15 **B5**
Maghreb, *N. Afr.* 78 **B5**
Magione, *Italy* 29 **E9**
Magistralnyy, *Russia* 51 **D11**
Maglaj, *Bos.-H.* 42 **F3**
Magliano in Toscana, *Italy* 29 **F8**
Máglie, *Italy* 31 **B11**
Magnac-Laval, *France* 20 **B5**
Magnetic Pole (North) = North Magnetic Pole, *Canada* 4 **B2**
Magnetic Pole (South) = South Magnetic Pole, *Antarctica* 5 **C9**
Magnisía □, *Greece* 38 **B5**
Magnitogorsk, *Russia* 50 **D6**
Magnolia, *Ark., U.S.A.* 113 **J8**
Magnolia, *Miss., U.S.A.* 113 **K9**
Magny-en-Vexin, *France* 19 **C8**
Magog, *Canada* 103 **C5**
Magoro, *Uganda* 86 **B3**
Magosa = Famagusta, *Cyprus* 36 **D12**
Magouládhes, *Greece* 36 **A3**
Magoye, *Zambia* 87 **F2**
Magozal, *Mexico* 119 **C5**
Magpie, L., *Canada* 103 **B7**
Magrath, *Canada* 104 **D6**
Magre →, *Spain* 33 **F4**
Magrur, *Sudan* 81 **E3**
Magrur, Wadi →, *Sudan* 81 **D2**
Magta Lahjar, *Mauritania* 82 **B2**
Maguan, *China* 58 **F5**
Maguarinho, C., *Brazil* 125 **D9**
Magude, *Mozam.* 89 **D5**
Mağusa = Famagusta, *Cyprus* 36 **D12**
Maguse L., *Canada* 105 **A9**
Maguse Pt., *Canada* 105 **A10**
Magvana, *India* 68 **H3**
Magwe, *Burma* 67 **J19**
Magwe, *Sudan* 81 **G3**
Maha Sarakham, *Thailand* 64 **D4**
Mahābād, *Iran* 70 **B5**
Mahabharat Lekh, *Nepal* 69 **E10**
Mahabo, *Madag.* 89 **C7**
Mahadeo Hills, *India* 69 **H8**
Mahaffey, *U.S.A.* 110 **F6**
Mahagi, *Dem. Rep. of the Congo* 86 **B3**
Mahajamba →, *Madag.* 89 **B8**
Mahajamba, Helodranon' i, *Madag.* 89 **B8**
Mahajan, *India* 68 **E5**
Mahajanga, *Madag.* 89 **B8**
Mahajanga □, *Madag.* 89 **B8**
Mahajilo →, *Madag.* 89 **B8**
Mahakam →, *Indonesia* 62 **E5**
Mahalapye, *Botswana* 88 **C4**
Maḥallāt, *Iran* 71 **C6**
Māhān, *Iran* 71 **D8**
Mahan →, *India* 69 **H10**
Mahanadi →, *India* 67 **J15**
Mahananda →, *India* 69 **G12**
Mahanoro, *Madag.* 89 **B8**
Mahanoy City, *U.S.A.* 111 **F8**
Maharashtra □, *India* 66 **J9**
Mahari Mts., *Tanzania* 86 **D3**
Mahasham, W. →, *Egypt* 75 **E3**
Mahasoa, *Madag.* 89 **C8**
Mahasolo, *Madag.* 89 **B8**
Mahattat ash Shīdīyah, *Jordan* 75 **F4**
Mahattat 'Unayzah, *Jordan* 75 **E4**
Mahavavy →, *Madag.* 89 **B8**
Mahaxay, *Laos* 64 **D5**
Mahbubnagar, *India* 66 **L10**
Maḥḍah, *Oman* 71 **E7**
Mahdia, *Tunisia* 79 **A8**
Mahe, *India* 69 **C8**
Mahendragarh, *India* 68 **E7**
Mahenge, *Tanzania* 87 **D4**
Maheno, *N.Z.* 91 **L3**
Mahesana, *India* 68 **H5**
Maheshwar, *India* 68 **H6**
Mahgawan, *India* 69 **F8**
Mahi →, *India* 68 **H5**
Mahia Pen., *N.Z.* 91 **H6**
Mahilyow, *Belarus* 46 **F6**
Mahmiya, *Sudan* 81 **D3**
Mahmud Kot, *Pakistan* 68 **D4**
Mahmudia, *Romania* 43 **E14**
Mahmudiye, *Turkey* 39 **B12**
Mahmutbey, *Turkey* 41 **E12**
Mahnomen, *U.S.A.* 112 **B7**
Mahoba, *India* 69 **G8**
Mahón = Maó, *Spain* 37 **B11**
Mahone Bay, *Canada* 103 **D7**
Mahopac, *U.S.A.* 111 **E11**
Mahuta, *Nigeria* 83 **C5**
Mahuva, *India* 68 **J4**
Mahya Dağı, *Turkey* 41 **E11**
Mai-Ndombe, L., *Dem. Rep. of the Congo* 84 **E3**
Mai-Sai, *Thailand* 58 **G2**
Maia, *Portugal* 34 **D2**
Maia, *Spain* 32 **B3**
Maials, *Spain* 32 **D5**
Maîche, *France* 19 **E13**
Maicurú →, *Brazil* 125 **D8**
Máida, *Italy* 31 **D9**
Maidan Khula, *Afghan.* 68 **C3**
Maidenhead, *U.K.* 13 **F7**
Maidstone, *Canada* 105 **C7**
Maidstone, *U.K.* 13 **F8**
Maiduguri, *Nigeria* 83 **C7**
Măieruş, *Romania* 43 **E10**
Maigatari, *Nigeria* 83 **C6**
Maignelay Montigny, *France* 19 **C9**
Maigo, *Phil.* 61 **G5**
Maigudo, *Ethiopia* 81 **F4**
Maihar, *India* 69 **G9**
Maijdi, *Bangla.* 67 **H17**
Maikala Ra., *India* 67 **J12**
Mailani, *India* 69 **E9**
Maillezais, *France* 20 **B3**
Mailsi, *Pakistan* 68 **E5**
Main →, *Germany* 25 **F4**
Main →, *U.K.* 15 **B5**
Mainburg, *Germany* 25 **G7**
Maine, *France* 18 **D6**
Maine □, *U.S.A.* 109 **C11**
Maine →, *Ireland* 15 **D2**
Maine-et-Loire □, *France* 18 **E6**
Maïne-Soroa, *Niger* 83 **C7**
Maingkwan, *Burma* 67 **F20**
Mainit, L., *Phil.* 61 **G6**
Mainland, *Orkney, U.K.* 14 **C5**
Mainland, *Shet., U.K.* 14 **A7**
Mainoru, *Australia* 94 **A1**
Mainpuri, *India* 69 **F8**
Maintal, *Germany* 25 **E4**
Maintenon, *France* 19 **D8**
Maintirano, *Madag.* 89 **B7**
Mainz, *Germany* 25 **E4**
Maipú, *Argentina* 126 **D4**
Maiquetía, *Venezuela* 124 **A5**
Máira →, *Italy* 28 **D4**
Mairabari, *India* 67 **F18**
Maisí, *Cuba* 121 **B5**
Maisí, Pta. de, *Cuba* 121 **B5**
Maitland, *N.S.W., Australia* 95 **E5**
Maitland, *S. Austral., Australia* 95 **E2**
Maitland →, *Canada* 110 **C3**
Maiyema, *Nigeria* 83 **C5**
Maiyuan, *China* 59 **E11**
Maiz, Is. del, *Nic.* 120 **D3**
Maizuru, *Japan* 55 **G7**
Majalengka, *Indonesia* 63 **G13**
Majene, *Indonesia* 63 **E5**
Majevica, *Bos.-H.* 42 **F3**
Maji, *Ethiopia* 81 **F4**
Majiang, *China* 58 **D6**
Majorca = Mallorca, *Spain* 37 **B10**
Maka, *Senegal* 82 **C2**
Makaha, *Zimbabwe* 89 **B5**
Makak, *Cameroon* 83 **E7**
Makalamabedi, *Botswana* 88 **C3**
Makale, *Indonesia* 63 **E5**
Makamba, *Burundi* 86 **C2**
Makari, *Cameroon* 83 **C7**
Makarikari = Makgadikgadi Salt Pans, *Botswana* 88 **C4**
Makarovo, *Russia* 51 **D11**
Makarska, *Croatia* 29 **E14**
Makaryev, *Russia* 48 **B6**
Makasar = Ujung Pandang, *Indonesia* 63 **F5**
Makasar, Selat, *Indonesia* 63 **E5**
Makasar, Str. of = Makasar, Selat, *Indonesia* 63 **E5**
Makat, *Kazakstan* 50 **E6**
Makedonija = Macedonia ■, *Europe* 40 **E5**
Makeni, *S. Leone* 82 **D2**
Makeyevka = Makiyivka, *Ukraine* 47 **H9**
Makgadikgadi Salt Pans, *Botswana* 88 **C4**
Makhachkala, *Russia* 49 **J8**
Makharadze = Ozurgeti, *Georgia* 49 **K5**
Makhmūr, *Iraq* 70 **C4**
Makian, *Indonesia* 63 **D7**
Makindu, *Kenya* 86 **C4**
Makinsk, *Kazakstan* 50 **D8**
Makiyivka, *Ukraine* 47 **H9**
Makkah, *Si. Arabia* 74 **C2**
Makkovik, *Canada* 103 **A8**
Makó, *Hungary* 42 **D5**
Mako, *Senegal* 82 **C2**
Makokou, *Gabon* 84 **D2**
Makongo, *Dem. Rep. of the Congo* 86 **B2**
Makoro, *Dem. Rep. of the Congo* 86 **B2**
Maków Mazowiecki, *Poland* 45 **F8**
Maków Podhalański, *Poland* 45 **J6**
Makrá, *Greece* 39 **E7**
Makrai, *India* 66 **H10**
Makran Coast Range, *Pakistan* 66 **G4**
Makrana, *India* 68 **F6**
Mákri, *Greece* 41 **F9**
Makriyialos, *Greece* 36 **D7**
Mākū, *Iran* 70 **B5**
Makunda, *Botswana* 88 **C3**
Makung, *Taiwan* 59 **F12**
Makurazaki, *Japan* 55 **J5**
Makurdi, *Nigeria* 83 **D6**
Makūyeh, *Iran* 71 **D7**
Makwassie, *S. Africa* 88 **D4**
Makwiro, *Zimbabwe* 89 **B5**
Mâl, *Mauritania* 82 **B2**
Mal B., *Ireland* 15 **D2**
Mala, Pta., *Panama* 120 **E3**
Mala Belozërka, *Ukraine* 47 **J8**
Mala Kapela, *Croatia* 29 **D12**
Mała Panew →, *Poland* 45 **H4**
Mala Vyska, *Ukraine* 47 **H6**
Malabang, *Phil.* 61 **H6**
Malabar Coast, *India* 66 **P9**
Malabo = Rey Malabo, *Eq. Guin.* 83 **E6**
Malabon, *Phil.* 61 **D4**
Malabu, *Nigeria* 83 **D7**
Malacca, Str. of, *Indonesia* 65 **L3**
Malacky, *Slovak Rep.* 27 **C10**
Malad City, *U.S.A.* 114 **E7**
Maladeta, *Spain* 32 **C5**
Maladzyechna, *Belarus* 46 **E4**
Málaga, *Spain* 35 **J6**
Málaga □, *Spain* 35 **J6**
Malagarasi, *Tanzania* 86 **D3**
Malagarasi →, *Tanzania* 86 **D2**
Malagasy Rep. = Madagascar ■, *Africa* 89 **C8**
Malagón, *Spain* 35 **F7**
Malagón →, *Spain* 35 **H3**
Malahide, *Ireland* 15 **C5**
Malaimbandy, *Madag.* 89 **C8**
Malakâl, *Sudan* 81 **F3**
Malakand, *Pakistan* 68 **B4**
Malakwal, *Pakistan* 68 **C5**
Malamala, *Indonesia* 63 **E6**
Malanda, *Australia* 94 **B4**
Malang, *Indonesia* 62 **F4**
Malangen, *Norway* 8 **B18**
Malanje, *Angola* 84 **F3**
Mälaren, *Sweden* 10 **E11**
Malargüe, *Argentina* 126 **D2**
Malartic, *Canada* 102 **C4**
Malaryta, *Belarus* 47 **G3**
Malatya, *Turkey* 70 **B3**
Malawi ■, *Africa* 87 **E3**
Malawi, L. = Nyasa, L., *Africa* 87 **E3**
Malay Pen., *Asia* 65 **J3**
Malaya Belozërka = Mala Belozërka, *Ukraine* 47 **J8**
Malaya Vishera, *Russia* 46 **C7**
Malaya Viska = Mala Vyska, *Ukraine* 47 **H6**
Malaybalay, *Phil.* 61 **G6**
Malāyer, *Iran* 71 **C6**
Malaysia ■, *Asia* 65 **K4**
Malazgirt, *Turkey* 70 **B4**
Malbaza, *Niger* 83 **C6**
Malbon, *Australia* 94 **C3**
Malbooma, *Australia* 95 **E1**
Malbork, *Poland* 44 **D6**
Malcésine, *Italy* 28 **C7**
Malchin, *Germany* 24 **B8**
Malchow, *Germany* 24 **B8**
Malcolm, *Australia* 93 **E3**
Malcolm, Pt., *Australia* 93 **F3**
Malczyce, *Poland* 45 **G3**
Maldah, *India* 69 **G13**
Maldegem, *Belgium* 17 **C3**
Malden, *Mass., U.S.A.* 111 **D13**
Malden, *Mo., U.S.A.* 113 **G10**
Malden I., *Kiribati* 97 **H12**
Maldives ■, *Ind. Oc.* 52 **J11**
Maldonado, *Uruguay* 127 **C5**
Maldonado, Punta, *Mexico* 119 **D5**
Malè, *Italy* 28 **B7**
Malé, *Maldives* 53 **J11**
Malé Karpaty, *Slovak Rep.* 27 **C10**
Maléa, Ákra, *Greece* 38 **E5**
Malegaon, *India* 66 **J9**
Malei, *Mozam.* 87 **F4**
Malek, *Sudan* 81 **F3**
Malek Kandī, *Iran* 70 **B5**
Malela, *Dem. Rep. of the Congo* 86 **C2**
Malema, *Mozam.* 87 **E4**
Máleme, *Greece* 36 **D5**
Maleny, *Australia* 95 **D5**
Målerås, *Sweden* 11 **H9**
Malerkotla, *India* 68 **D6**
Máles, *Greece* 36 **D7**
Malesherbes, *France* 19 **D9**
Maleshevska Planina, *Europe* 40 **E7**
Malesína, *Greece* 38 **C5**
Malestroit, *France* 18 **E4**
Malfa, *Italy* 31 **D7**
Malgobek, *Russia* 49 **J7**
Malgomaj, *Sweden* 8 **D17**
Malgrat = Malgrat de Mar, *Spain* 32 **D7**
Malgrat de Mar, *Spain* 32 **D7**
Malha, *Sudan* 81 **D2**
Malhargarh, *India* 68 **G6**
Malheur →, *U.S.A.* 114 **D5**
Malheur L., *U.S.A.* 114 **E4**
Mali, *Guinea* 82 **C2**
Mali ■, *Africa* 82 **B4**
Mali →, *Burma* 67 **G20**
Mali Kanal, *Serbia, Yug.* 42 **E4**
Mali Kyun, *Burma* 64 **F2**
Malibu, *U.S.A.* 117 **L8**
Maliku, *Indonesia* 63 **E6**
Malili, *Indonesia* 63 **E6**
Målilla, *Sweden* 11 **G9**
Malimba, Mts., *Dem. Rep. of the Congo* 86 **D2**
Malin Hd., *Ireland* 15 **A4**
Malin Pen., *Ireland* 15 **A4**
Malindi, *Kenya* 86 **C5**
Malines = Mechelen, *Belgium* 17 **C4**
Malino, *Indonesia* 63 **D6**
Malinyi, *Tanzania* 87 **D4**
Malipo, *China* 58 **F5**
Maliq, *Albania* 40 **F4**
Malita, *Phil.* 63 **C7**
Maliwun, *Burma* 62 **B1**
Maliya, *India* 68 **H4**
Maljenik, *Serbia, Yug.* 40 **C5**
Malkara, *Turkey* 41 **F10**
Małkinia Górna, *Poland* 45 **F9**
Malko Tŭrnovo, *Bulgaria* 41 **E11**
Mallacoota Inlet, *Australia* 95 **F4**
Mallaig, *U.K.* 14 **D3**
Mallaoua, *Niger* 83 **C6**
Mallawan, *India* 69 **F9**
Mallawi, *Egypt* 80 **B3**
Mallemort, *France* 21 **E9**
Málles Venosta, *Italy* 28 **B7**
Mállia, *Greece* 36 **D7**
Mallión, Kólpos, *Greece* 36 **D7**
Mallorca, *Spain* 37 **B10**
Mallorytown, *Canada* 111 **B9**
Mallow, *Ireland* 15 **D3**
Malmbäck, *Sweden* 11 **G8**
Malmberget, *Sweden* 8 **C19**
Malmédy, *Belgium* 17 **D6**
Malmesbury, *S. Africa* 88 **E2**
Malmköping, *Sweden* 10 **E10**
Malmö, *Sweden* 11 **J6**
Malmslätt, *Sweden* 11 **F9**
Malmyzh, *Russia* 48 **B10**
Malnaş, *Romania* 43 **D10**
Malo Konare, *Bulgaria* 41 **D8**
Maloarkhangelsk, *Russia* 47 **F9**
Malolos, *Phil.* 63 **B6**
Malombe L., *Malawi* 87 **E4**
Małomice, *Poland* 45 **G2**
Malomir, *Bulgaria* 41 **D10**
Malone, *U.S.A.* 111 **B10**
Malong, *China* 58 **E4**
Małopolskie □, *Poland* 45 **J7**
Malorad, *Bulgaria* 40 **C7**
Måløy, *Norway* 9 **F11**
Maloyaroslovets, *Russia* 46 **E9**
Malpartida, *Spain* 35 **F4**
Malpaso, *Canary Is.* 37 **G1**
Malpelo, I. de, *Colombia* 124 **C2**
Malpica de Bergantiños, *Spain* 34 **B2**
Malpur, *India* 68 **H5**
Malpura, *India* 68 **F6**
Mals = Málles Venosta, *Italy* 28 **B7**
Malta, *Idaho, U.S.A.* 114 **E7**
Malta, *Mont., U.S.A.* 114 **B10**
Malta ■, *Europe* 36 **D2**
Maltahöhe, *Namibia* 88 **C2**
Maltepe, *Turkey* 41 **F13**
Malton, *Canada* 110 **C5**
Malton, *U.K.* 12 **C7**
Maluku, *Indonesia* 63 **E7**
Maluku □, *Indonesia* 63 **E7**
Maluku Sea = Molucca Sea, *Indonesia* 63 **E6**
Malumfashi, *Nigeria* 83 **C6**
Malung, *Sweden* 10 **D7**
Malungsfors, *Sweden* 10 **D7**
Maluwe, *Ghana* 82 **D4**
Malvan, *India* 66 **L8**
Malvern, *U.S.A.* 113 **H8**
Malvern Hills, *U.K.* 13 **E5**
Malvinas, Is. = Falkland Is. □, *Atl. Oc.* 128 **G5**
Malý Dunaj →, *Slovak Rep.* 27 **D11**
Malya, *Tanzania* 86 **C3**
Malyn, *Ukraine* 47 **G5**
Malyy Lyakhovskiy, Ostrov, *Russia* 51 **B15**
Mama, *Russia* 51 **D12**
Mamadysh, *Russia* 48 **C10**
Mamanguape, *Brazil* 125 **E11**
Mamarr Mitlā, *Egypt* 75 **E1**
Mamasa, *Indonesia* 63 **E5**
Mambasa, *Dem. Rep. of the Congo* 86 **B2**
Mamberamo →, *Indonesia* 63 **E9**
Mambilima Falls, *Zambia* 87 **E2**
Mambirima, *Dem. Rep. of the Congo* 87 **E2**
Mambo, *Tanzania* 86 **C4**
Mambrui, *Kenya* 86 **C5**
Mamburao, *Phil.* 61 **E4**
Mameigwess L., *Canada* 102 **B2**
Mamers, *France* 18 **D7**
Mamfé, *Cameroon* 83 **D6**
Mammoth, *U.S.A.* 115 **K8**
Mammoth Cave National Park, *U.S.A.* 108 **G3**
Mamoré →, *Bolivia* 122 **E4**
Mamou, *Guinea* 82 **C2**
Mampatá, *Guinea-Biss.* 82 **C2**
Mampikony, *Madag.* 89 **B8**
Mampong, *Ghana* 83 **D4**
Mamry, Jezioro, *Poland* 44 **D8**
Mamuju, *Indonesia* 63 **E5**
Mamuno, *Botswana* 88 **C3**
Mamuras, *Albania* 40 **E3**
Man, *Ivory C.* 82 **D3**
Man, I. of, *U.K.* 12 **C3**
Man-Bazar, *India* 69 **H12**
Man Na, *Burma* 67 **H20**
Mana →, *Fr. Guiana* 125 **B8**
Manaar, G. of = Mannar, G. of, *Asia* 66 **Q11**
Manacapuru, *Brazil* 124 **D6**
Manacor, *Spain* 37 **B10**
Manado, *Indonesia* 63 **D6**
Managua, *Nic.* 120 **D2**
Managua, L. de, *Nic.* 120 **D2**
Manakara, *Madag.* 89 **C8**
Manali, *India* 68 **C7**
Manama = Al Manāmah, *Bahrain* 71 **E6**
Manambao →, *Madag.* 89 **B7**
Manambato, *Madag.* 89 **A8**
Manambolo →, *Madag.* 89 **B7**
Manambolosy, *Madag.* 89 **B8**
Mananara, *Madag.* 89 **B8**
Mananara →, *Madag.* 89 **C8**
Mananjary, *Madag.* 89 **C8**
Manankoro, *Mali* 82 **C3**
Manantenina, *Madag.* 89 **C8**
Manaos = Manaus, *Brazil* 124 **D7**
Manapire →, *Venezuela* 124 **B5**
Manapouri, *N.Z.* 91 **L1**
Manapouri, L., *N.Z.* 91 **L1**
Manaqil, *Sudan* 81 **E3**
Manār, Jabal, *Yemen* 74 **E3**
Manaravolo, *Madag.* 89 **C8**
Manas, *China* 60 **B3**
Manas →, *India* 67 **F17**
Manaslu, *Nepal* 69 **E11**
Manasquan, *U.S.A.* 111 **F10**
Manassa, *U.S.A.* 115 **H11**
Manaung, *Burma* 67 **K18**
Manaus, *Brazil* 124 **D7**
Manavgat, *Turkey* 72 **D4**
Manawan L., *Canada* 105 **B8**
Manay, *Phil.* 61 **H7**
Manbij, *Syria* 70 **B3**
Mancha Real, *Spain* 35 **H7**
Manche □, *France* 18 **C5**
Manchegorsk, *Russia* 50 **C4**
Manchester, *U.K.* 12 **D5**
Manchester, *Calif., U.S.A.* 116 **G3**
Manchester, *Conn., U.S.A.* 111 **E12**
Manchester, *Ga., U.S.A.* 109 **J3**
Manchester, *Iowa, U.S.A.* 112 **D9**
Manchester, *Ky., U.S.A.* 108 **G4**
Manchester, *N.H., U.S.A.* 111 **D13**
Manchester, *N.Y., U.S.A.* 110 **D7**
Manchester, *Pa., U.S.A.* 111 **F8**
Manchester, *Tenn., U.S.A.* 109 **H2**
Manchester, *Vt., U.S.A.* 111 **C11**
Manchester L., *Canada* 105 **A7**
Manchhar L., *Pakistan* 68 **F2**
Manchuria = Dongbei, *China* 57 **D13**
Manchurian Plain, *China* 52 **E16**
Manciano, *Italy* 29 **F8**
Mancifa, *Ethiopia* 81 **F5**
Mand →, *India* 69 **J10**
Mand →, *Iran* 71 **D7**
Manda, *Ludewe, Tanzania* 87 **E3**
Manda, *Mbeya, Tanzania* 86 **D3**
Manda, *Mbeya, Tanzania* 87 **D3**
Mandabé, *Madag.* 89 **C7**
Mandaguari, *Brazil* 127 **A5**
Mandah = Töhöm, *Mongolia* 56 **B5**
Mandal, *Norway* 9 **G12**
Mandala, Puncak, *Indonesia* 63 **E10**
Mandalay, *Burma* 67 **J20**
Mandale = Mandalay, *Burma* 67 **J20**
Mandalgarh, *India* 68 **G6**
Mandalgovi, *Mongolia* 56 **B4**
Mandalī, *Iraq* 70 **C5**
Mandan, *U.S.A.* 112 **B4**
Mandaon, *Phil.* 61 **E5**

Mandar, Teluk, *Indonesia* 63 E5
Mándas, *Italy* 30 C2
Mandaue, *Phil.* 61 F5
Mandelieu-la-Napoule, *France* 21 E10
Mandera, *Kenya* 86 B5
Mandi, *India* 68 D7
Mandi Dabwali, *India* 68 E6
Mandiana, *Guinea* 82 C3
Mandimba, *Mozam.* 87 E4
Mandioli, *Indonesia* 63 E7
Mandla, *India* 69 H9
Mandø, *Denmark* 11 J2
Mandorah, *Australia* 92 B5
Mandoto, *Madag.* 89 B8
Mandoúdhion, *Greece* 38 C5
Mándra, *Greece* 38 C5
Mandra, *Pakistan* 68 C5
Mandrákhi, *Greece* 39 E9
Mandrare →, *Madag.* 89 D8
Mandritsara, *Madag.* 89 B8
Mandronarivo, *Madag.* 89 C8
Mandsaur, *India* 68 G6
Mandurah, *Australia* 93 F2
Mandúria, *Italy* 31 B10
Mandvi, *India* 68 H3
Mandya, *India* 66 N10
Mandzai, *Pakistan* 68 D2
Mané, *Burkina Faso* 83 C4
Maneh, *Iran* 71 B8
Manengouba, Mts., *Cameroon* 83 E6
Manera, *Madag.* 89 C7
Manérbio, *Italy* 28 C7
Maneroo Cr. →, *Australia* 94 C3
Manfalût, *Egypt* 80 B3
Manfredónia, *Italy* 29 G12
Manfredónia, G. di, *Italy* 29 G13
Manga, *Burkina Faso* 83 C4
Manga, *Niger* 83 C7
Mangabeiras, Chapada das, *Brazil* 125 F9
Mangalia, *Romania* 43 G13
Mangalore, *India* 66 N9
Mangan, *India* 69 F13
Mangaung, *S. Africa* 85 K5
Mangawan, *India* 69 G9
Mangaweka, *N.Z.* 91 H5
Manggar, *Indonesia* 62 E3
Manggawitu, *Indonesia* 63 E8
Mangindrano, *Madag.* 89 A8
Mangkalihat, Tanjung, *Indonesia* 63 D5
Mangla, *Pakistan* 68 C5
Mangla Dam, *Pakistan* 69 C5
Manglaur, *India* 68 E7
Mangnai, *China* 60 C4
Mango, *Togo* 83 C5
Mangoche, *Malawi* 87 E4
Mangoky →, *Madag.* 89 C7
Mangole, *Indonesia* 63 E6
Mangombe, *Dem. Rep. of the Congo* 86 C2
Mangonui, *N.Z.* 91 F4
Mangoro →, *Madag.* 89 B8
Mangrol, *Mad. P., India* 68 J4
Mangrol, *Raj., India* 68 G6
Mangualde, *Portugal* 34 E3
Mangueira, L. da, *Brazil* 127 C5
Mangum, *U.S.A.* 113 H5
Mangyshlak Poluostrov, *Kazakstan* 50 E6
Manhattan, *U.S.A.* 112 F6
Manhiça, *Mozam.* 89 D5
Mania →, *Madag.* 89 B8
Maniago, *Italy* 29 B9
Manica, *Mozam.* 89 B5
Manica □, *Mozam.* 89 B5
Manicaland □, *Zimbabwe* 87 F3
Manicoré, *Brazil* 124 E6
Manicouagan →, *Canada* 103 C6
Manicouagan, Rés., *Canada* 103 B6
Maniema □, *Dem. Rep. of the Congo* 86 C2
Manīfah, *Si. Arabia* 71 E6
Manifold, C., *Australia* 94 C5
Maniganggo, *China* 58 B2
Manigotagan, *Canada* 105 C9
Manigotagan →, *Canada* 105 C9
Manihari, *India* 69 G12
Manihiki, *Cook Is.* 97 J11
Manika, Plateau de la, *Dem. Rep. of the Congo* 87 E2
Manikpur, *India* 69 G9
Manila, *Phil.* 61 D4
Manila, *U.S.A.* 114 F9
Manila B., *Phil.* 61 D4
Manilla, *Australia* 95 E5
Manimpé, *Mali* 82 C3
Maningrida, *Australia* 94 A1
Maninian, *Ivory C.* 82 C3
Manipur □, *India* 67 G19
Manipur →, *Burma* 67 H19
Manisa, *Turkey* 39 C9
Manisa □, *Turkey* 39 C9
Manistee, *U.S.A.* 108 C2
Manistee →, *U.S.A.* 108 C2
Manistique, *U.S.A.* 108 C2
Manito L., *Canada* 105 C7
Manitoba □, *Canada* 105 B9
Manitoba, L., *Canada* 105 C9
Manitou, *Canada* 105 D9
Manitou, L., *Canada* 103 B6
Manitou Is., *U.S.A.* 108 C3
Manitou Springs, *U.S.A.* 112 F2
Manitoulin I., *Canada* 102 C3
Manitouwadge, *Canada* 102 C2
Manitowoc, *U.S.A.* 108 C2
Manizales, *Colombia* 124 B3
Manja, *Madag.* 89 C7
Manjacaze, *Mozam.* 89 C5
Manjakandriana, *Madag.* 89 B8
Manjhand, *Pakistan* 68 G3
Manjil, *Iran* 71 B6
Manjimup, *Australia* 93 F2
Manjra →, *India* 66 K10
Mankato, *Kans., U.S.A.* 112 F5
Mankato, *Minn., U.S.A.* 112 C8
Mankayane, *Swaziland* 89 D5
Mankera, *Pakistan* 68 D4
Mankim, *Cameroon* 83 D7
Mankono, *Ivory C.* 82 D3
Mankota, *Canada* 105 D7
Manlay = Üydzin, *Mongolia* 56 B4
Manlleu, *Spain* 32 C7
Manmad, *India* 66 J9
Mann Ranges, *Australia* 93 E5
Manna, *Indonesia* 62 E2
Mannahill, *Australia* 95 E3
Mannar, *Sri Lanka* 66 Q11
Mannar, G. of, *Asia* 66 Q11
Mannar I., *Sri Lanka* 66 Q11
Mannheim, *Germany* 25 F4
Manning, *Canada* 104 B5
Manning, *Oreg., U.S.A.* 116 E3
Manning, *S.C., U.S.A.* 109 J5
Manning Prov. Park, *Canada* 104 D4
Mannu →, *Italy* 30 C2
Mannu, C., *Italy* 30 B1
Mannum, *Australia* 95 E2
Mano, *S. Leone* 82 D2
Mano →, *Liberia* 82 D2
Mano River, *Liberia* 82 D2
Manoharpur, *India* 69 H11
Manokwari, *Indonesia* 63 E8
Manolás, *Greece* 38 C3
Manombo, *Madag.* 89 C7
Manono, *Dem. Rep. of the Congo* 86 D2
Manoppello, *Italy* 29 F11
Manosque, *France* 21 E9
Manotick, *Canada* 111 A9
Manouane →, *Canada* 103 C5
Manouane, L., *Canada* 103 B5
Manp'o, *N. Korea* 57 D14
Manpojin = Manp'o, *N. Korea* 57 D14
Manpur, *Mad. P., India* 68 H6
Manpur, *Mad. P., India* 69 H10
Manresa, *Spain* 32 D6
Mansa, *Gujarat, India* 68 H5
Mansa, *Punjab, India* 68 E6
Mansa, *Zambia* 87 E2
Månsåsen, *Sweden* 10 A8
Mansehra, *Pakistan* 68 B5
Mansel I., *Canada* 101 B11
Mansfield, *Australia* 95 F4
Mansfield, *U.K.* 12 D6
Mansfield, *La., U.S.A.* 113 J8
Mansfield, *Mass., U.S.A.* 111 D13
Mansfield, *Ohio, U.S.A.* 110 F2
Mansfield, *Pa., U.S.A.* 110 E7
Mansfield, Mt., *U.S.A.* 111 B12
Mansilla de las Mulas, *Spain* 34 C5
Mansle, *France* 20 C4
Mansoa, *Guinea-Biss.* 82 C1
Manson Creek, *Canada* 104 B4
Manta, *Ecuador* 124 D2
Mantalingajan, Mt., *Phil.* 61 G2
Mantare, *Tanzania* 86 C3
Manteca, *U.S.A.* 116 H5
Manteo, *U.S.A.* 109 H8
Mantes-la-Jolie, *France* 19 D8
Manthani, *India* 66 K11
Manti, *U.S.A.* 114 G8
Mantiqueira, Serra da, *Brazil* 127 A7
Manton, *U.S.A.* 108 C3
Mantorp, *Sweden* 11 F9
Mántova, *Italy* 28 C7
Mänttä, *Finland* 9 E21
Mantua = Mántova, *Italy* 28 C7
Manturovo, *Russia* 48 A7
Manu, *Peru* 124 F4
Manu →, *Peru* 124 F4
Manua Is., *Amer. Samoa* 91 B14
Manuel Alves →, *Brazil* 125 F9
Manui, *Indonesia* 63 E6
Manukau, *N.Z.* 91 G5
Manuripi →, *Bolivia* 124 F5
Many, *U.S.A.* 113 K8
Manyara, L., *Tanzania* 86 C4
Manyas, *Turkey* 41 F11
Manych →, *Russia* 49 G5
Manych-Gudilo, Ozero, *Russia* 49 G6
Manyonga →, *Tanzania* 86 C3
Manyoni, *Tanzania* 86 D3
Manzai, *Pakistan* 68 C4
Manzala, Bahra el, *Egypt* 80 H7
Manzanares, *Spain* 35 F7
Manzaneda, *Spain* 34 C3
Manzanillo, *Cuba* 120 B4
Manzanillo, *Mexico* 118 D4
Manzanillo, Pta., *Panama* 120 E4
Manzano Mts., *U.S.A.* 115 J10
Manzarīyeh, *Iran* 71 C6
Manzhouli, *China* 60 B6
Manzini, *Swaziland* 89 D5
Mao, *Chad* 79 F9
Maó, *Spain* 37 B11
Maoke, Pegunungan, *Indonesia* 63 E9
Maolin, *China* 57 C12
Maoming, *China* 59 G8
Maopi T'ou, *China* 59 G13
Maouri, Dallol →, *Niger* 83 C5
Maoxian, *China* 58 B4
Maoxing, *China* 57 B13
Mapam Yumco, *China* 60 C3
Mapastepec, *Mexico* 119 D6
Mapia, Kepulauan, *Indonesia* 63 D8
Mapimí, *Mexico* 118 B4
Mapimí, Bolsón de, *Mexico* 118 B4
Maping, *China* 59 B9
Mapinga, *Tanzania* 86 D4
Mapinhane, *Mozam.* 89 C6
Maple Creek, *Canada* 105 D7
Maple Valley, *U.S.A.* 116 C4
Mapleton, *U.S.A.* 114 D2
Mapuera →, *Brazil* 124 D7
Mapulanguene, *Mozam.* 89 C5
Maputo, *Mozam.* 89 D5
Maputo □, *Mozam.* 89 D5
Maputo, B. de, *Mozam.* 89 D5
Maqiaohe, *China* 57 B16
Maqnā, *Si. Arabia* 70 D2
Maqueda, *Spain* 34 E6
Maquela do Zombo, *Angola* 84 F3
Maquinchao, *Argentina* 128 E3
Maquoketa, *U.S.A.* 112 D9
Mar, Serra do, *Brazil* 127 B6
Mar Chiquita, L., *Argentina* 126 C3
Mar del Plata, *Argentina* 126 D4
Mar Menor, *Spain* 33 H4
Mara, *Tanzania* 86 C3
Mara □, *Tanzania* 86 C3
Maraã, *Brazil* 124 D5
Marabá, *Brazil* 125 E9
Maracá, I. de, *Brazil* 125 C8
Maracaibo, *Venezuela* 124 A4
Maracaibo, L. de, *Venezuela* 122 C3
Maracaju, *Brazil* 127 A4
Maracay, *Venezuela* 124 A5
Maracena, *Spain* 35 H7
Maradi, *Niger* 83 C6
Marāgheh, *Iran* 70 B5
Marāh, *Si. Arabia* 70 E5
Marajó, I. de, *Brazil* 122 D6
Marākand, *Iran* 70 B5
Maralal, *Kenya* 86 B4
Maralinga, *Australia* 93 F5
Maramaraereğlisi, *Turkey* 41 F11
Marampa, *S. Leone* 82 D2
Maramureş □, *Romania* 43 C9
Maran, *Malaysia* 65 L4
Marana, *U.S.A.* 115 K8
Maranboy, *Australia* 92 B5
Maranchón, *Spain* 32 D2
Marand, *Iran* 70 B5
Marang, *Malaysia* 65 K4
Maranguape, *Brazil* 125 D11
Maranhão = São Luís, *Brazil* 125 D10
Maranhão □, *Brazil* 125 E9
Marano, L. di, *Italy* 29 C10
Maranoa →, *Australia* 95 D4
Marañón →, *Peru* 122 D3
Marão, *Mozam.* 89 C5
Maraş = Kahramanmaraş, *Turkey* 70 B3
Mărăşeşti, *Romania* 43 E12
Maratea, *Italy* 31 C8
Marateca, *Portugal* 35 G2
Marathasa □, *Cyprus* 36 E11
Marathókambos, *Greece* 39 D8
Marathon, *Australia* 94 C3
Marathon, *Canada* 102 C2
Marathón, *Greece* 38 C5
Marathon, *N.Y., U.S.A.* 111 D8
Marathon, *Tex., U.S.A.* 113 K3
Marathóvouno, *Cyprus* 36 D12
Maratua, *Indonesia* 63 D5
Maravatío, *Mexico* 118 D4
Marawi City, *Phil.* 61 G6
Marāwih, *U.A.E.* 71 E7
Marbella, *Spain* 35 J6
Marble Bar, *Australia* 92 D2
Marble Falls, *U.S.A.* 113 K5
Marblehead, *U.S.A.* 111 D14
Marburg, *Germany* 24 E4
Marcal →, *Hungary* 42 C2
Marcali, *Hungary* 42 D2
Marcaria, *Italy* 28 C7
Mărcăuţi, *Moldova* 43 B12
March, *U.K.* 13 E8
Marche, *France* 20 B5
Marche □, *Italy* 29 E10
Marche-en-Famenne, *Belgium* 17 D5
Marchena, *Spain* 35 H5
Marches = Marche □, *Italy* 29 E10
Marciana Marina, *Italy* 28 F7
Marcianise, *Italy* 31 A7
Marcigny, *France* 19 F11
Marcillat-en-Combraille, *France* 19 F9
Marck, *France* 19 B8
Marckolsheim, *France* 19 D14
Marco, *U.S.A.* 109 N5
Marcos Juárez, *Argentina* 126 C3
Mărculeşti, *Moldova* 43 C13
Marcus I. = Minami-Tori-Shima, *Pac. Oc.* 96 E7
Marcus Necker Ridge, *Pac. Oc.* 96 F9
Marcy, Mt., *U.S.A.* 111 B11
Mardan, *Pakistan* 68 B5
Mardin, *Turkey* 70 B4
Mårdsjön, *Sweden* 10 A9
Marécchia →, *Italy* 29 D9
Maree, L., *U.K.* 14 D3
Mareeba, *Australia* 94 B4
Mareetsane, *S. Africa* 88 D4
Maremma, *Italy* 29 F8
Maréna, *Mali* 82 C2
Maréna, *Mali* 82 C3
Marengo, *U.S.A.* 112 E8
Marennes, *France* 20 C2
Marenyi, *Kenya* 86 C4
Marerano, *Madag.* 89 C7
Maréttimo, *Italy* 30 E5
Mareuil, *France* 20 C4
Marfa, *U.S.A.* 113 K2
Marfa Pt., *Malta* 36 D1
Marganets = Marhanets, *Ukraine* 47 J8
Margaret →, *Australia* 92 C4
Margaret Bay, *Canada* 104 C3
Margaret L., *Canada* 104 B5
Margaret River, *Australia* 93 F2
Margarita, I. de, *Venezuela* 122 B4
Margarítion, *Greece* 38 B2
Margaritovo, *Russia* 54 C7
Margate, *S. Africa* 89 E5
Margate, *U.K.* 13 F9
Margeride, Mts. de la, *France* 20 D7
Margherita di Savóia, *Italy* 31 A9
Marghita, *Romania* 42 C7
Margonin, *Poland* 45 F4
Margosatubig, *Phil.* 61 H5
Mārgow, Dasht-e, *Afghan.* 66 D3
Marguerite, *Canada* 104 C4
Marhanets, *Ukraine* 47 J8
Mari El □, *Russia* 48 B8
Mari Indus, *Pakistan* 68 C4
Mari Republic = Mari El □, *Russia* 48 B8
María, Sa. de, *Spain* 33 H2
María Elena, *Chile* 126 A2
María Grande, *Argentina* 126 C4
Maria I., *N. Terr., Australia* 94 A2
Maria I., *Tas., Australia* 94 G4
Maria van Diemen, C., *N.Z.* 91 F4
Mariager, *Denmark* 11 H3
Mariager Fjord, *Denmark* 11 H4
Mariakani, *Kenya* 86 C4
Marian, *Australia* 94 C4
Marian L., *Canada* 104 A5
Mariana Trench, *Pac. Oc.* 52 H18
Marianao, *Cuba* 120 B3
Marianna, *Ark., U.S.A.* 113 H9
Marianna, *Fla., U.S.A.* 109 K3
Mariannelund, *Sweden* 11 G9
Mariánské Lázně, *Czech Rep.* 26 B5
Marias →, *U.S.A.* 114 C8
Mariato, Punta, *Panama* 120 E3
Mariazell, *Austria* 26 D8
Maribo, *Denmark* 11 K5
Maribor, *Slovenia* 29 B12
Marico →, *Africa* 88 C4
Maricopa, *Ariz., U.S.A.* 115 K7
Maricopa, *Calif., U.S.A.* 117 K7
Marîdî, *Sudan* 81 G2
Marîdî, Wadi →, *Sudan* 81 F2
Marié →, *Brazil* 124 D5
Marie Byrd Land, *Antarctica* 5 D14
Marie-Galante, *Guadeloupe* 121 C7
Mariecourt = Kangiqsujuaq, *Canada* 101 B12
Mariefred, *Sweden* 10 E11
Marieholm, *Sweden* 11 J7
Mariembourg, *Belgium* 17 D4
Marienbad = Mariánské Lázně, *Czech Rep.* 26 B5
Marienberg, *Germany* 24 E9
Mariental, *Namibia* 88 C2
Marienville, *U.S.A.* 110 E5
Mariestad, *Sweden* 11 F7
Marietta, *Ga., U.S.A.* 109 J3
Marietta, *Ohio, U.S.A.* 108 F5
Marieville, *Canada* 111 A11
Mariga →, *Nigeria* 83 C6
Marignane, *France* 21 E9
Marihatag, *Phil.* 61 G7
Mariinsk, *Russia* 50 D9
Mariinskiy Posad, *Russia* 48 B8
Marijampolė, *Lithuania* 9 J20
Marijampolės □, *Lithuania* 44 D10
Marília, *Brazil* 127 A6
Marín, *Spain* 34 C2
Marina, *U.S.A.* 116 J5
Marinduque, *Phil.* 63 B6
Marine City, *U.S.A.* 110 D2
Marineo, *Italy* 30 E6
Marinette, *U.S.A.* 108 C2
Maringá, *Brazil* 127 A5
Marinha Grande, *Portugal* 34 F2
Marino, *Italy* 29 G9
Marion, *Ala., U.S.A.* 109 J2
Marion, *Ill., U.S.A.* 113 G10
Marion, *Ind., U.S.A.* 108 E3
Marion, *Iowa, U.S.A.* 112 D9
Marion, *Kans., U.S.A.* 112 F6
Marion, *N.C., U.S.A.* 109 H5
Marion, *Ohio, U.S.A.* 108 E4
Marion, *S.C., U.S.A.* 109 H6
Marion, *Va., U.S.A.* 109 G5
Marion, L., *U.S.A.* 109 J5
Mariposa, *U.S.A.* 116 H7
Mariscal Estigarribia, *Paraguay* 126 A3
Maritime Alps = Maritimes, Alpes, *Europe* 21 D11
Maritimes, Alpes, *Europe* 21 D11
Maritsa = Évros →, *Greece* 72 B2
Maritsá, *Greece* 36 C10
Mariupol, *Ukraine* 47 J9
Marīvān, *Iran* 70 C5
Marj 'Uyūn, *Lebanon* 75 B4
Marka, *Si. Arabia* 80 D5
Markam, *China* 58 C2
Markaryd, *Sweden* 11 H7
Markazī □, *Iran* 71 C6
Markdale, *Canada* 110 B4
Marked Tree, *U.S.A.* 113 H9
Markesdorfer Huk, *Germany* 24 A7
Market Drayton, *U.K.* 12 E5
Market Harborough, *U.K.* 13 E7
Market Rasen, *U.K.* 12 D7
Markham, *Canada* 110 C5
Markham, Mt., *Antarctica* 5 E11
Marki, *Poland* 45 F8
Markkleeberg, *Germany* 24 D8
Markleeville, *U.S.A.* 116 G7
Markoupoulon, *Greece* 38 D5
Markovac, *Serbia, Yug.* 40 B5
Markovo, *Russia* 51 C17
Markoye, *Burkina Faso* 83 C5
Marks, *Russia* 48 E8
Marksville, *U.S.A.* 113 K8
Markt Schwaben, *Germany* 25 G7
Marktoberdorf, *Germany* 25 H6
Marktredwitz, *Germany* 25 E8
Marl, *Germany* 24 D3
Marla, *Australia* 95 D1
Marlbank, *Canada* 110 B7
Marlboro, *Mass., U.S.A.* 111 D13
Marlboro, *N.Y., U.S.A.* 111 E11
Marlborough, *Australia* 94 C4
Marlborough, *U.K.* 13 F6
Marlborough Downs, *U.K.* 13 F6
Marle, *France* 19 C10
Marlin, *U.S.A.* 113 K6
Marlow, *Germany* 24 A8
Marlow, *U.S.A.* 113 H6
Marmagao, *India* 66 M8
Marmande, *France* 20 D4
Marmara, *Turkey* 41 F11
Marmara, Sea of = Marmara Denizi, *Turkey* 41 F12
Marmara Denizi, *Turkey* 41 F12
Marmara Gölü, *Turkey* 39 C10
Marmaris, *Turkey* 39 E10
Marmaris Limanı, *Turkey* 39 E10
Marmion, Mt., *Australia* 93 E2
Marmion L., *Canada* 102 C1
Marmolada, Mte., *Italy* 29 B8
Marmolejo, *Spain* 35 G6
Marmora, *Canada* 102 D4
Mármora, La, *Italy* 30 C2
Marnay, *France* 19 E12
Marne, *Germany* 24 B5
Marne □, *France* 19 D11
Marne →, *France* 19 D9
Marneuli, *Georgia* 49 K7
Maroala, *Madag.* 89 B8
Maroantsetra, *Madag.* 89 B8
Maroelaboom, *Namibia* 88 B2
Marofandilia, *Madag.* 89 C7
Marolambo, *Madag.* 89 C8
Maromandia, *Madag.* 89 A8
Marondera, *Zimbabwe* 87 F3
Maroni →, *Fr. Guiana* 125 B8
Marónia, *Greece* 41 F9
Maronne →, *France* 20 C5
Maroochydore, *Australia* 95 D5
Maroona, *Australia* 95 F3
Maros →, *Hungary* 42 D5
Marosakoa, *Madag.* 89 B8
Maroseranana, *Madag.* 89 B8
Maróstica, *Italy* 29 C8
Marotandrano, *Madag.* 89 B8
Marotaolano, *Madag.* 89 A8
Maroua, *Cameroon* 83 C7
Marovato, *Madag.* 89 B8
Marovoay, *Madag.* 89 B8
Marquard, *S. Africa* 88 D4
Marquesas Is. = Marquises, Is., *Pac. Oc.* 97 H14
Marquette, *U.S.A.* 108 B2
Marquise, *France* 19 B8
Marquises, Is., *Pac. Oc.* 97 H14
Marra, Djebel, *Sudan* 79 F10
Marra, Gebel, *Sudan* 81 F2
Marracuene, *Mozam.* 89 D5
Marradi, *Italy* 29 D8
Marrakech, *Morocco* 78 B4
Marratxí, *Spain* 32 F7
Marrawah, *Australia* 94 G3
Marree, *Australia* 95 D2
Marrero, *U.S.A.* 113 L9
Marrimane, *Mozam.* 89 C5
Marromeu, *Mozam.* 89 B6
Marroquí, Punta, *Spain* 35 K5
Marrowie Cr. →, *Australia* 95 E4
Marrubane, *Mozam.* 87 F4
Marrúbiu, *Italy* 30 C1
Marrupa, *Mozam.* 87 E4
Mars Hill, *U.S.A.* 109 B12
Marsá 'Alam, *Egypt* 80 B3
Marsá Matrûh, *Egypt* 80 A2
Marsá Sha'b, *Sudan* 80 C4
Marsabit, *Kenya* 86 B4
Marsala, *Italy* 30 E5
Marsalforn, *Malta* 36 C1
Mărşani, *Romania* 43 F9
Marsberg, *Germany* 24 D4
Marsciano, *Italy* 29 F9
Marsden, *Australia* 95 E4
Marseillan, *France* 20 E7
Marseille, *France* 21 E9
Marseilles = Marseille, *France* 21 E9
Marsh I., *U.S.A.* 113 L9
Marshall, *Liberia* 82 D2
Marshall, *Ark., U.S.A.* 113 H8
Marshall, *Mich., U.S.A.* 108 D3
Marshall, *Minn., U.S.A.* 112 C7
Marshall, *Mo., U.S.A.* 112 F8
Marshall, *Tex., U.S.A.* 113 J7
Marshall →, *Australia* 94 C2
Marshall Is. ■, *Pac. Oc.* 96 G9
Marshalltown, *U.S.A.* 112 D8
Marshbrook, *Zimbabwe* 89 B5
Marshfield, *Mo., U.S.A.* 113 G8
Marshfield, *Vt., U.S.A.* 111 B12
Marshfield, *Wis., U.S.A.* 112 C9
Marshūn, *Iran* 71 B6

Mársico Nuovo, Italy 31 B8
Märsta, Sweden 10 E11
Marstal, Denmark 11 K4
Marstrand, Sweden 11 G5
Mart, U.S.A. 113 K6
Marta →, Italy 29 F8
Martaban, Burma 67 L20
Martaban, G. of, Burma 67 L20
Martano, Italy 31 B11
Martapura, Kalimantan, Indonesia 62 E4
Martapura, Sumatera, Indonesia 62 E2
Marte, Nigeria 83 C7
Martel, France 20 D5
Martelange, Belgium 17 E5
Martellago, Italy 29 C9
Martés, Sierra, Spain 33 F4
Martfű, Hungary 42 C5
Martha's Vineyard, U.S.A. 111 E14
Martigné-Ferchaud, France 18 E5
Martigny, Switz. 25 J3
Martigues, France 21 E9
Martin, Slovak Rep. 27 B11
Martin, S. Dak., U.S.A. 112 D4
Martin, Tenn., U.S.A. 113 G10
Martín →, Spain 32 D4
Martin, L., U.S.A. 109 J3
Martina Franca, Italy 31 B10
Martinborough, N.Z. 91 J5
Martinez, Calif., U.S.A. 116 G4
Martinez, Ga., U.S.A. 109 J4
Martinique ■, W. Indies 121 D7
Martinique Passage, W. Indies 121 C7
Martínon, Greece 38 C5
Martinópolis, Brazil 127 A5
Martins Ferry, U.S.A. 110 F4
Martinsberg, Austria 26 C8
Martinsburg, Pa., U.S.A. 110 F6
Martinsburg, W. Va., U.S.A. 108 F7
Martinsicuro, Italy 29 F10
Martinsville, Ind., U.S.A. 108 F2
Martinsville, Va., U.S.A. 109 G6
Marton, N.Z. 91 J5
Martorell, Spain 32 D6
Martos, Spain 35 H7
Martuni, Armenia 49 K7
Maru, Nigeria 83 C6
Marudi, Malaysia 62 D4
Maruf, Afghan. 66 D5
Marugame, Japan 55 G6
Marunga, Angola 88 B3
Marungu, Mts., Dem. Rep. of the Congo 86 D3
Marv Dasht, Iran 71 D7
Marvast, Iran 71 D7
Marvejols, France 20 D7
Marvel Loch, Australia 93 F2
Marwar, India 68 G5
Mary, Turkmenistan 50 F7
Maryborough = Port Laoise, Ireland 15 C4
Maryborough, Queens., Australia 95 D5
Maryborough, Vic., Australia 95 F3
Maryfield, Canada 105 D8
Maryland □, U.S.A. 108 F7
Maryland Junction, Zimbabwe 87 F3
Maryport, U.K. 12 C4
Mary's Harbour, Canada 103 B8
Marystown, Canada 103 C8
Marysville, Canada 104 D5
Marysville, Calif., U.S.A. 116 F5
Marysville, Kans., U.S.A. 112 F6
Marysville, Mich., U.S.A. 110 D2
Marysville, Ohio, U.S.A. 108 E4
Marysville, Wash., U.S.A. 116 B4
Maryville, Mo., U.S.A. 112 E7
Maryville, Tenn., U.S.A. 109 H4
Marzūq, Libya 79 C8
Masahunga, Tanzania 86 C3
Masai Steppe, Tanzania 86 C4
Masaka, Uganda 86 C3
Masalembo, Kepulauan, Indonesia 62 F4
Masalima, Kepulauan, Indonesia 62 F5
Masallı, Azerbaijan 73 C13
Masamba, Indonesia 63 E6
Masan, S. Korea 57 G15
Masandam, Ra's, Oman 71 E8
Masasi, Tanzania 87 E4
Masaya, Nic. 120 D2
Masba, Nigeria 83 C7
Masbate, Phil. 61 E5
Máscali, Italy 31 E8
Mascara, Algeria 78 A6
Mascota, Mexico 118 C4
Masela, Indonesia 63 F7
Maseru, Lesotho 88 D4
Mashaba, Zimbabwe 87 G3
Mashābih, Si. Arabia 70 E3
Mashan, China 58 F7
Mashar, Sudan 81 F2
Mashegu, Nigeria 83 D6
Masherbrum, Pakistan 69 B7
Mashhad, Iran 71 B8
Mashi, Nigeria 83 C6
Mashīz, Iran 71 D8
Māshkel, Hāmūn-i-, Pakistan 66 E3
Mashki Chāh, Pakistan 66 E3
Mashonaland, Zimbabwe 85 H6
Mashonaland Central □, Zimbabwe 89 B5
Mashonaland East □, Zimbabwe 89 B5
Mashonaland West □, Zimbabwe 89 B4
Mashrakh, India 69 F11
Mashtaga = Maştağa, Azerbaijan 49 K10
Masindi, Uganda 86 B3
Masindi Port, Uganda 86 B3
Maşīrah, Oman 74 C6
Maşīrah, Khalīj, Oman 74 C6
Masisi, Dem. Rep. of the Congo 86 C2
Masjed Soleyman, Iran 71 D6
Mask, L., Ireland 15 C2
Maskin, Oman 71 F8
Maslen Nos, Bulgaria 41 D11
Maslinica, Croatia 29 E13
Masnou = El Masnou, Spain 32 D7
Masoala, Tanjon' i, Madag. 89 B9
Masoarivo, Madag. 89 B7
Masohi = Amahai, Indonesia 63 E7
Masomeloka, Madag. 89 C8
Mason, Nev., U.S.A. 116 G7
Mason, Tex., U.S.A. 113 K5
Mason City, U.S.A. 112 D8
Maspalomas, Canary Is. 37 G4
Maspalomas, Pta., Canary Is. 37 G4
Masqat, Oman 74 C6
Massa, Italy 28 D7
Massa Maríttima, Italy 28 E7
Massachusetts □, U.S.A. 111 D13
Massachusetts B., U.S.A. 111 D14
Massafra, Italy 31 B10
Massakory, Chad 79 F9
Massanella, Spain 37 B9
Massangena, Mozam. 89 C5
Massango, Angola 84 F3
Massat, France 20 F5
Massawa = Mitsiwa, Eritrea 81 D4
Massena, U.S.A. 111 B10
Massénya, Chad 79 F9
Masset, Canada 104 C2
Masseube, France 20 E4
Massiac, France 20 C7
Massif Central, France 20 D7
Massigui, Mali 82 C3
Massillon, U.S.A. 110 F3
Massinga, Mozam. 89 C6
Massingir, Mozam. 89 C5
Mässlingen, Sweden 10 B6
Masson, Canada 111 A9
Masson I., Antarctica 5 C7
Maştağa, Azerbaijan 49 K10
Mastanli = Momchilgrad, Bulgaria 41 E9
Masterton, N.Z. 91 J5
Mastic, U.S.A. 111 F12
Mástikho, Ákra, Greece 39 C8
Mastuj, Pakistan 69 A5
Mastung, Pakistan 66 E5
Mastūrah, Si. Arabia 80 C4
Masty, Belarus 46 F3
Masuda, Japan 55 G5
Masvingo, Zimbabwe 87 G3
Masvingo □, Zimbabwe 87 G3
Maşyāf, Syria 70 C3
Maszewo, Poland 44 E2
Mat →, Albania 40 E3
Matabeleland, Zimbabwe 85 H5
Matabeleland North □, Zimbabwe 87 F2
Matabeleland South □, Zimbabwe 87 G2
Matachel →, Spain 35 G4
Matachewan, Canada 102 C3
Matadi, Dem. Rep. of the Congo 84 F2
Matagalpa, Nic. 120 D2
Matagami, Canada 102 C4
Matagami, L., Canada 102 C4
Matagorda B., U.S.A. 113 L6
Matagorda I., U.S.A. 113 L6
Matak, Indonesia 65 L6
Mátala, Greece 36 E6
Matam, Senegal 82 B2
Matameye, Niger 83 C6
Matamoros, Campeche, Mexico 119 D6
Matamoros, Coahuila, Mexico 118 B4
Matamoros, Tamaulipas, Mexico 119 B5
Ma'ţan as Sarra, Libya 79 D10
Matandu →, Tanzania 87 D3
Matane, Canada 103 C6
Matang, China 58 F5
Matankari, Niger 83 C5
Matanomadh, India 68 H3
Matanzas, Cuba 120 B3
Matapa, Botswana 88 C3
Matapan, C. = Taínaron, Ákra, Greece 38 E4
Matapédia, Canada 103 C6
Matara, Sri Lanka 66 S12
Mataram, Indonesia 62 F5
Matarani, Peru 124 G4
Mataranka, Australia 92 B5
Matarma, Râs, Egypt 75 E1
Mataró, Spain 32 D7
Matarraña →, Spain 32 D5
Mataruška Banja, Serbia, Yug. 40 C4
Matatiele, S. Africa 89 E4
Mataura, N.Z. 91 M2
Matehuala, Mexico 118 C4
Mateke Hills, Zimbabwe 87 G3
Matera, Italy 31 B9
Matese, Monti del, Italy 31 A7
Mátészalka, Hungary 42 C7
Matetsi, Zimbabwe 87 F2
Matfors, Sweden 10 B11
Matha, France 20 C3
Mathis, U.S.A. 113 L6
Mathráki, Greece 36 A3
Mathura, India 68 F7
Mati, Phil. 61 H7
Matiakoali, Burkina Faso 83 C5
Matiali, India 69 F13
Matías Romero, Mexico 119 D5
Matibane, Mozam. 87 E5
Matima, Botswana 88 C3
Matiri Ra., N.Z. 91 J4
Matjiesfontein, S. Africa 88 E3
Matla →, India 69 J13
Matlamanyane, Botswana 88 B4
Matli, Pakistan 68 G3
Matlock, U.K. 12 D6
Matna, Sudan 81 E4
Mato Grosso □, Brazil 125 F8
Mato Grosso, Planalto do, Brazil 122 E5
Mato Grosso do Sul □, Brazil 125 G8
Matochkin Shar, Russia 50 B6
Matopo Hills, Zimbabwe 87 G2
Matopos, Zimbabwe 87 G2
Matosinhos, Portugal 34 D2
Matour, France 19 F11
Matroosberg, S. Africa 88 E2
Maţruḩ, Oman 74 C6
Matsena, Nigeria 83 C7
Matsesta, Russia 49 J4
Matsu Tao, Taiwan 59 E13
Matsue, Japan 55 G6
Matsumae, Japan 54 D10
Matsumoto, Japan 55 F9
Matsusaka, Japan 55 G8
Matsuura, Japan 55 H4
Matsuyama, Japan 55 H6
Mattagami →, Canada 102 B3
Mattancheri, India 66 Q10
Mattawa, Canada 102 C4
Matterhorn, Switz. 25 K3
Mattersburg, Austria 27 D9
Matthew Town, Bahamas 121 B5
Matthew's Ridge, Guyana 124 B6
Mattice, Canada 102 C3
Mattituck, U.S.A. 111 F12
Mattō, Japan 55 F8
Mattoon, U.S.A. 108 F1
Matuba, Mozam. 89 C5
Matucana, Peru 124 F3
Matūn = Khowst, Afghan. 68 C3
Maturín, Venezuela 124 B6
Matveyev Kurgan, Russia 47 J10
Matxitxako, C., Spain 32 B2
Mau, Mad. P., India 69 F8
Mau, Ut. P., India 69 G10
Mau, Ut. P., India 69 G9
Mau Escarpment, Kenya 86 C4
Mau Ranipur, India 69 G8
Maubeuge, France 19 B10
Maubourguet, France 20 E4
Maud, Pt., Australia 92 D1
Maude, Australia 95 E3
Maudin Sun, Burma 67 M19
Maués, Brazil 124 D7
Mauganj, India 67 G12
Maughold Hd., U.K. 12 C3
Mauguio, France 20 E7
Maui, U.S.A. 106 H16
Maulamyaing = Moulmein, Burma 67 L20
Maule □, Chile 126 D1
Mauléon-Licharre, France 20 E3
Maumee, U.S.A. 108 E4
Maumee →, U.S.A. 108 E4
Maumere, Indonesia 63 F6
Maumusson, Pertuis de, France 20 C2
Maun, Botswana 88 C3
Mauna Kea, U.S.A. 106 J17
Mauna Loa, U.S.A. 106 J17
Maungmagan Kyunzu, Burma 64 E1
Maupin, U.S.A. 114 D3
Maure-de-Bretagne, France 18 E5
Maurepas, L., U.S.A. 113 K9
Maures, France 21 E10
Mauriac, France 20 C6
Maurice, L., Australia 93 E5
Mauricie, Parc Nat. de la, Canada 102 C5
Maurienne, France 21 C10
Mauritania ■, Africa 78 E3
Mauritius ■, Ind. Oc. 77 J9
Mauron, France 18 D4
Maurs, France 20 D6
Mauston, U.S.A. 112 D9
Mauterndorf, Austria 26 D6
Mauthen, Austria 26 E6
Mauvezin, France 20 E4
Mauzé-sur-le-Mignon, France 20 B3
Mavli, India 68 G5
Mavrovë, Albania 40 F3
Mavuradonha Mts., Zimbabwe 87 F3
Mawa, Dem. Rep. of the Congo 86 B2
Mawai, India 69 H9
Mawana, India 68 E7
Mawand, Pakistan 68 E3
Mawk Mai, Burma 67 J20
Mawlaik, Burma 67 H19
Mawlamyine = Moulmein, Burma 67 L20
Mawqaq, Si. Arabia 70 E4
Mawson Coast, Antarctica 5 C6
Max, U.S.A. 112 B4
Maxcanú, Mexico 119 C6
Maxesibeni, S. Africa 89 E4
Maxhamish L., Canada 104 B4
Maxixe, Mozam. 89 C6
Maxville, Canada 111 A10
Maxwell, U.S.A. 116 F4
Maxwelton, Australia 94 C3
May, C., U.S.A. 108 F8
May Pen, Jamaica 120 C4
Maya →, Russia 51 D14
Maya Mts., Belize 119 D7
Mayaguana, Bahamas 121 B5
Mayagüez, Puerto Rico 121 C6
Mayahi, Niger 83 C6
Mayals = Maials, Spain 32 D5
Mayāmey, Iran 71 B7
Mayang, China 58 D7
Mayanup, Australia 93 F2
Mayapan, Mexico 119 C7
Mayarí, Cuba 121 B4
Maybell, U.S.A. 114 F9
Maybole, U.K. 14 F4
Maychew, Ethiopia 81 E4
Maydān, Iraq 70 C5
Maydena, Australia 94 G4
Mayen, Germany 25 E3
Mayenne, France 18 D6
Mayenne □, France 18 D6
Mayenne →, France 18 E6
Mayer, U.S.A. 115 J7
Mayerthorpe, Canada 104 C5
Mayfield, Ky., U.S.A. 109 G1
Mayfield, N.Y., U.S.A. 111 C10
Mayhill, U.S.A. 115 K11
Maykop, Russia 49 H5
Maymyo, Burma 64 A1
Maynard, Mass., U.S.A. 111 D13
Maynard, Wash., U.S.A. 116 C4
Maynard Hills, Australia 93 E2
Mayne →, Australia 94 C3
Maynooth, Ireland 15 C5
Mayo, Canada 100 B6
Mayo □, Ireland 15 C2
Mayo Daga, Nigeria 83 D7
Mayo Faran, Nigeria 83 D7
Mayon Volcano, Phil. 61 E5
Mayor I., N.Z. 91 G6
Mayorga, Spain 34 C5
Mayotte, Ind. Oc. 85 G9
Mayraira Pt., Phil. 61 B4
Mayskiy, Russia 49 J7
Maysville, U.S.A. 108 F4
Mayu, Indonesia 63 D7
Mayville, N. Dak., U.S.A. 112 B6
Mayville, N.Y., U.S.A. 110 D5
Mayya, Russia 51 C14
Mazabuka, Zambia 87 F2
Mazagán = El Jadida, Morocco 78 B4
Mazagão, Brazil 125 D8
Mazamet, France 20 E6
Mazán, Peru 124 D4
Māzandarān □, Iran 71 B7
Mazapil, Mexico 118 C4
Mazara del Vallo, Italy 30 E5
Mazarrón, Spain 33 H3
Mazarrón, G. de, Spain 33 H3
Mazaruni →, Guyana 124 B7
Mazatán, Mexico 118 B2
Mazatenango, Guatemala 120 D1
Mazatlán, Mexico 118 C3
Mažeikiai, Lithuania 9 H20
Māzhān, Iran 71 C8
Mazīnān, Iran 71 B8
Mazoe, Mozam. 87 F3
Mazoe →, Mozam. 87 F3
Mazowe, Zimbabwe 87 F3
Mazowieckie □, Poland 45 F8
Mazrûb, Sudan 81 E2
Mazu Dao, China 59 D12
Mazurian Lakes = Mazurski, Pojezierze, Poland 44 E7
Mazurski, Pojezierze, Poland 44 E7
Mazyr, Belarus 47 F5
Mbaba, Senegal 82 C1
Mbabane, Swaziland 89 D5
Mbagne, Mauritania 82 B2
M'bahiakro, Ivory C. 82 D4
Mbaïki, C.A.R. 84 D3
Mbala, Zambia 87 D3
Mbalabala, Zimbabwe 89 C4
Mbale, Uganda 86 B3
Mbalmayo, Cameroon 83 E7
Mbam →, Cameroon 83 E7
Mbamba Bay, Tanzania 87 E3
Mbandaka, Dem. Rep. of the Congo 84 D3
Mbanga, Cameroon 83 E6
Mbanza Congo, Angola 84 F2
Mbanza Ngungu, Dem. Rep. of the Congo 84 F2
Mbarara, Uganda 86 C3
Mbashe →, S. Africa 89 E4
Mbatto, Ivory C. 82 D4
Mbenkuru →, Tanzania 87 D4
Mberengwa, Zimbabwe 87 G2
Mberengwa, Mt., Zimbabwe 87 G2
Mberubu, Nigeria 83 D6
Mbesuma, Zambia 87 E3
Mbeya, Tanzania 87 D3
Mbeya □, Tanzania 86 D3
M'bili, Sudan 81 F2
Mbinga, Tanzania 87 E4
Mbini □, Eq. Guin. 84 D2
Mboki, C.A.R. 81 F2
M'bonge, Cameroon 83 E6
Mboro, Senegal 82 B1
M'boukou Res., Cameroon 83 D7
Mboune, Senegal 82 C2
Mbour, Senegal 82 C1
Mbout, Mauritania 82 B2
Mbuji-Mayi, Dem. Rep. of the Congo 86 D1
Mbulu, Tanzania 86 C4
Mburucuyá, Argentina 126 B4
Mchinja, Tanzania 87 D4
Mchinji, Malawi 87 E3
Mdantsane, S. Africa 85 L5
Mead, L., U.S.A. 117 J12
Meade, U.S.A. 113 G4
Meadow Lake, Canada 105 C7
Meadow Lake Prov. Park, Canada 105 C7
Meadow Valley Wash →, U.S.A. 117 J12
Meadville, U.S.A. 110 E4
Meaford, Canada 102 D3
Mealhada, Portugal 34 E2
Mealy Mts., Canada 103 B8
Meander River, Canada 104 B5
Meares, C., U.S.A. 114 D2
Mearim →, Brazil 125 D10
Meath □, Ireland 15 C5
Meath Park, Canada 105 C7
Meaulne, France 19 F9
Meaux, France 19 D9
Mebechi-Gawa →, Japan 54 D10
Mecanhelas, Mozam. 87 F4
Mecca = Makkah, Si. Arabia 74 C2
Mecca, U.S.A. 117 M10
Mechanicsburg, U.S.A. 110 F8
Mechanicville, U.S.A. 111 D11
Mechara, Ethiopia 81 F5
Mechelen, Belgium 17 C4
Mecheria, Algeria 78 B5
Mechernich, Germany 24 E2
Mechetinskaya, Russia 49 G5
Mecidiye, Turkey 41 F10
Mecitözü, Turkey 72 B6
Mecklenburg-Vorpommern □, Germany 24 B8
Mecklenburger Bucht, Germany 24 A7
Meconta, Mozam. 87 E4
Mecsek, Hungary 42 D3
Meda, Portugal 34 E3
Medan, Indonesia 62 D1
Medanosa, Pta., Argentina 128 F3
Mede, Italy 28 C5
Médéa, Algeria 78 A6
Mededa, Bos.-H. 42 G4
Medellín, Colombia 124 B3
Medelpad, Sweden 10 B10
Medemblik, Neths. 17 B5
Mederdra, Mauritania 82 B1
Medford, Mass., U.S.A. 111 D13
Medford, Oreg., U.S.A. 114 E2
Medford, Wis., U.S.A. 112 C9
Medgidia, Romania 43 F13
Medi, Sudan 81 F3
Media Agua, Argentina 126 C2
Media Luna, Argentina 126 C2
Medianeira, Brazil 127 B5
Mediaş, Romania 43 D9
Medicina, Italy 29 D8
Medicine Bow, U.S.A. 114 F10
Medicine Bow Pk., U.S.A. 114 F10
Medicine Bow Ra., U.S.A. 114 F10
Medicine Hat, Canada 105 D6
Medicine Lake, U.S.A. 112 A2
Medicine Lodge, U.S.A. 113 G5
Medina = Al Madīnah, Si. Arabia 70 E3
Medina, N. Dak., U.S.A. 112 B5
Medina, N.Y., U.S.A. 110 C6
Medina, Ohio, U.S.A. 110 E3
Medina →, U.S.A. 113 L5
Medina de Pomar, Spain 34 C7
Medina de Ríoseco, Spain 34 D5
Medina del Campo, Spain 34 D6
Medina L., U.S.A. 113 L5
Medina Sidonia, Spain 35 J5
Medinaceli, Spain 32 D2
Medinipur, India 69 H12
Mediterranean Sea, Europe 6 H7
Médoc, France 20 C3
Medulin, Croatia 29 D10
Medveđa, Serbia, Yug. 40 D5
Medvedevo, Russia 48 B8
Medveditsa →, Tver, Russia 46 D9
Medveditsa →, Volgograd, Russia 48 F6
Medvedok, Russia 48 B10
Medvezhi, Ostrava, Russia 51 B17
Medvezhyegorsk, Russia 50 C4
Medway □, U.K. 13 F8
Medway →, U.K. 13 F8
Medzev, Slovak Rep. 27 C13
Medzilaborce, Slovak Rep. 27 B14
Medžitlija, Macedonia 40 F5
Meekatharra, Australia 93 E2
Meeker, U.S.A. 114 F10
Meelpaeg Res., Canada 103 C8
Meersburg, Germany 25 H5
Meerut, India 68 E7
Meeteetse, U.S.A. 114 D9
Mega, Ethiopia 81 G4
Megálo Khorío, Greece 39 E9
Megálo Petalí, Greece 38 D6
Megalópolis, Greece 38 D4
Meganísi, Greece 38 C2
Mégara, Greece 38 D5
Megasini, India 69 J12
Megdhova →, Greece 38 B3
Megève, France 21 C10
Meghalaya □, India 67 G17
Meghezez, Ethiopia 81 F4
Mégiscane, L., Canada 102 C4
Megiste, Greece 39 E11
Megra, Russia 46 B9
Mehadia, Romania 42 F7
Meharry, Mt., Australia 92 D2
Mehedeby, Sweden 10 D11
Mehedinţi □, Romania 42 F7
Meheisa, Sudan 80 D3
Mehlville, U.S.A. 112 F9
Mehndawal, India 69 F10
Mehr Jān, Iran 71 C7
Mehrābād, Iran 70 B5
Mehrān, Iran 70 C5

Mehrīz, *Iran* 71 D7
Mehun-sur-Yèvre, *France* 19 E9
Mei Jiang →, *China* 59 E11
Mei Xian, *China* 56 G4
Meicheng, *China* 59 C12
Meichengzhen, *China* 59 C8
Meichuan, *China* 59 B10
Meigu, *China* 58 C4
Meiktila, *Burma* 67 J19
Meinerzhagen, *Germany* 24 D3
Meiningen, *Germany* 24 E6
Meira, Serra de, *Spain* 34 B3
Meiringen, *Switz.* 25 J4
Meishan, *China* 58 B4
Meissen, *Germany* 24 D9
Meissner, *Germany* 24 D5
Meitan, *China* 58 D6
Meizhou, *China* 59 E11
Meja, *India* 69 G10
Mejillones, *Chile* 126 A1
Mekdela, *Ethiopia* 81 E4
Mekele, *Ethiopia* 81 E4
Mekhtar, *Pakistan* 66 D6
Meknès, *Morocco* 78 B4
Meko, *Nigeria* 83 D5
Mekong →, *Asia* 65 H6
Mekongga, *Indonesia* 63 E6
Mekrou →, *Benin* 83 C5
Mekvari = Kür →, *Azerbaijan* 73 C13
Mel, *Italy* 29 B9
Melagiri Hills, *India* 66 N10
Melaka, *Malaysia* 65 L4
Melalap, *Malaysia* 62 C5
Mélambes, *Greece* 36 D6
Melanesia, *Pac. Oc.* 96 H7
Melbourne, *Australia* 95 F4
Melbourne, *U.S.A.* 109 L5
Melchor Múzquiz, *Mexico* 118 B4
Melchor Ocampo, *Mexico* 118 C4
Méldola, *Italy* 29 D9
Meldorf, *Germany* 24 A5
Melegnano, *Italy* 28 C6
Melenci, *Serbia, Yug.* 42 E5
Melenki, *Russia* 48 C5
Mélèzes →, *Canada* 102 A5
Melfi, *Italy* 31 B8
Melfort, *Canada* 105 C8
Melfort, *Zimbabwe* 87 F3
Melgaço, *Portugal* 34 C2
Melgar de Fernamental, *Spain* 34 C6
Melhus, *Norway* 8 E14
Melide, *Spain* 34 C2
Meligalá, *Greece* 38 D3
Melilla, *N. Afr.* 78 A5
Melilli, *Italy* 31 E8
Melipilla, *Chile* 126 C1
Mélissa, Ákra, *Greece* 36 D6
Mélissa Óros, *Greece* 39 D8
Melita, *Canada* 105 D8
Mélito di Porto Salvo, *Italy* 31 E8
Melitopol, *Ukraine* 47 J8
Melk, *Austria* 26 C8
Mellan Fryken, *Sweden* 10 E7
Mellansel, *Sweden* 8 E18
Mellbystrand, *Sweden* 11 H6
Melle, *France* 20 B3
Melle, *Germany* 24 C4
Mellen, *U.S.A.* 112 B9
Mellerud, *Sweden* 11 F6
Mellette, *U.S.A.* 112 C5
Mellid = Melide, *Spain* 34 C2
Mellieha, *Malta* 36 D1
Mellit, *Sudan* 81 E2
Mellrichstadt, *Germany* 24 E6
Melnik, *Bulgaria* 40 E7
Mělník, *Czech Rep.* 26 A7
Melo, *Uruguay* 127 C5
Melolo, *Indonesia* 63 F6
Melouprey, *Cambodia* 64 F5
Melrose, *Australia* 95 E4
Melrose, *U.K.* 14 F6
Melrose, *Minn., U.S.A.* 112 C7
Melrose, *N. Mex., U.S.A.* 113 H3
Melstone, *U.S.A.* 114 C10
Melsungen, *Germany* 24 D5
Melton Mowbray, *U.K.* 12 E7
Melun, *France* 19 D9
Melut, *Sudan* 81 E3
Melville, *Canada* 105 C8
Melville, C., *Australia* 94 A3
Melville, L., *Canada* 103 B8
Melville B., *Australia* 94 A2
Melville I., *Australia* 92 B5
Melville I., *Canada* 4 B2
Melville Pen., *Canada* 101 B11
Mélykút, *Hungary* 42 D4
Memaliaj, *Albania* 40 F3
Memba, *Mozam.* 87 E5
Memboro, *Indonesia* 63 F5
Membrilla, *Spain* 35 G7
Memel = Klaipėda, *Lithuania* 9 J19
Memel, *S. Africa* 89 D4
Memmingen, *Germany* 25 H6
Mempawah, *Indonesia* 62 D3
Memphis, *Egypt* 80 J7
Memphis, *Mich., U.S.A.* 110 D2
Memphis, *Tenn., U.S.A.* 113 H10
Memphis, *Tex., U.S.A.* 113 H4
Memphremagog, L., *U.S.A.* 111 B12
Mena, *Ukraine* 47 G7
Mena, *U.S.A.* 113 H7
Mena →, *Ethiopia* 81 F5
Menai Strait, *U.K.* 12 D3
Ménaka, *Mali* 83 B5
Menan = Chao Phraya →, *Thailand* 64 F3
Menarandra →, *Madag.* 89 D7
Menard, *U.S.A.* 113 K5
Menawashei, *Sudan* 81 E1
Mendawai →, *Indonesia* 62 E4
Mende, *France* 20 D7
Mendebo, *Ethiopia* 81 F4
Menden, *Germany* 24 D3
Menderes, *Turkey* 39 C9
Mendez, *Mexico* 119 B5
Mendhar, *India* 69 C6
Mendi, *Ethiopia* 81 F4
Mendip Hills, *U.K.* 13 F5
Mendocino, *U.S.A.* 114 G2
Mendocino, C., *U.S.A.* 114 F1
Mendota, *Calif., U.S.A.* 116 J6
Mendota, *Ill., U.S.A.* 112 E10
Mendoza, *Argentina* 126 C2
Mendoza □, *Argentina* 126 C2
Mene Grande, *Venezuela* 124 B4
Menemen, *Turkey* 39 C9
Menen, *Belgium* 17 D3
Menfi, *Italy* 30 E5
Mengdingjie, *China* 58 F2
Mengeš, *Slovenia* 29 B11
Menggala, *Indonesia* 62 E3
Menghai, *China* 58 G3
Mengíbar, *Spain* 35 H7
Mengjin, *China* 56 G7
Mengla, *China* 58 G3
Menglian, *China* 58 F2
Mengshan, *China* 59 E8
Mengyin, *China* 57 G9
Mengzhe, *China* 58 F3
Mengzi, *China* 58 F4
Menihek, *Canada* 103 B6
Menihek L., *Canada* 103 B6
Menin = Menen, *Belgium* 17 D3
Menindee, *Australia* 95 E3
Menindee L., *Australia* 95 E3
Meningie, *Australia* 95 F2
Menlo Park, *U.S.A.* 116 H4
Menominee, *U.S.A.* 108 C2
Menominee →, *U.S.A.* 108 C2
Menomonie, *U.S.A.* 112 C9
Menongue, *Angola* 85 G3
Menorca, *Spain* 37 B11
Mentakab, *Malaysia* 65 L4
Mentawai, Kepulauan, *Indonesia* 62 E1
Menton, *France* 21 E11
Mentor, *U.S.A.* 110 E3
Menzies, *Australia* 93 E3
Meob B., *Namibia* 88 B2
Me'ona, *Israel* 75 B4
Meoqui, *Mexico* 118 B3
Mepaco, *Mozam.* 87 F3
Meppel, *Neths.* 17 B6
Meppen, *Germany* 24 C3
Mequinenza, *Spain* 32 D5
Mequinenza, Embalse de, *Spain* 32 D5
Mer, *France* 18 E8
Merabéllou, Kólpos, *Greece* 36 D7
Merak, *Indonesia* 63 F12
Meramangye, L., *Australia* 93 E5
Meran = Merano, *Italy* 29 B8
Merano, *Italy* 29 B8
Merate, *Italy* 28 C6
Merauke, *Indonesia* 63 F10
Merbein, *Australia* 95 E3
Merca, *Somali Rep.* 74 G3
Mercato Saraceno, *Italy* 29 E9
Merced, *U.S.A.* 116 H6
Merced →, *U.S.A.* 116 H6
Merced Pk., *U.S.A.* 116 H7
Mercedes, *Buenos Aires, Argentina* 126 C4
Mercedes, *Corrientes, Argentina* 126 B4
Mercedes, *San Luis, Argentina* 126 C2
Mercedes, *Uruguay* 126 C4
Mercedes, *U.S.A.* 113 M6
Merceditas, *Chile* 126 B1
Mercer, *N.Z.* 91 G5
Mercer, *U.S.A.* 110 E4
Mercer Island, *U.S.A.* 116 C4
Mercury, *U.S.A.* 117 J11
Mercy C., *Canada* 101 B13
Merdrignac, *France* 18 D4
Mere, *U.K.* 13 F5
Meredith, C., *Falk. Is.* 128 G4
Meredith, L., *U.S.A.* 113 H4
Merefa, *Ukraine* 47 H9
Merei, *Romania* 43 E11
Merga = Nukheila, *Sudan* 80 D2
Mergui, *Burma* 64 F2
Mergui Arch. = Myeik Kyunzu, *Burma* 65 G1
Meriç, *Turkey* 41 E10
Meriç →, *Turkey* 41 F10
Mérida, *Mexico* 119 C7
Mérida, *Spain* 35 G4
Mérida, *Venezuela* 124 B4
Mérida, Cord. de, *Venezuela* 122 C3
Meriden, *U.K.* 13 E6
Meriden, *U.S.A.* 111 E12
Meridian, *Calif., U.S.A.* 116 F5
Meridian, *Idaho, U.S.A.* 114 E5
Meridian, *Miss., U.S.A.* 109 J1
Mérignac, *France* 20 D3
Mérinaghène, *Senegal* 82 B1
Merinda, *Australia* 94 C4
Mering, *Germany* 25 G6
Meringa, *Nigeria* 83 C7
Merir, *Pac. Oc.* 63 D8
Merirumã, *Brazil* 125 C8
Merkel, *U.S.A.* 113 J5
Mermaid Reef, *Australia* 92 C2
Merowe, *Sudan* 80 D3
Merredin, *Australia* 93 F2
Merrick, *U.K.* 14 F4
Merrickville, *Canada* 111 B9
Merrill, *Oreg., U.S.A.* 114 E3
Merrill, *Wis., U.S.A.* 112 C10
Merrimack →, *U.S.A.* 111 D14
Merriman, *U.S.A.* 112 D4
Merritt, *Canada* 104 C4
Merritt Island, *U.S.A.* 109 L5
Merriwa, *Australia* 95 E5
Merry I., *Canada* 102 A4
Merryville, *U.S.A.* 113 K8
Mersa Fatma, *Eritrea* 81 E5
Mersch, *Lux.* 17 E6
Merse →, *Italy* 29 E8
Mersea I., *U.K.* 13 F8
Merseburg, *Germany* 24 D7
Mersey →, *U.K.* 12 D4
Merseyside □, *U.K.* 12 D4
Mersin, *Turkey* 70 B2
Mersing, *Malaysia* 65 L4
Merta, *India* 68 F6
Merta Road, *India* 68 F5
Merthyr Tydfil, *U.K.* 13 F4
Merthyr Tydfil □, *U.K.* 13 F4
Mértola, *Portugal* 35 H3
Mertzon, *U.S.A.* 113 K4
Méru, *France* 19 C9
Meru, *Kenya* 86 B4
Meru, *Tanzania* 86 C4
Merville, *France* 19 B9
Méry-sur-Seine, *France* 19 D10
Merzifon, *Turkey* 72 B6
Merzig, *Germany* 25 F2
Mesa, *U.S.A.* 115 K8
Mesa Verde National Park, *U.S.A.* 115 H9
Mesagne, *Italy* 31 B10
Mesanagrós, *Greece* 36 C9
Mesaoría □, *Cyprus* 36 D12
Mesarás, Kólpos, *Greece* 36 D6
Meschede, *Germany* 24 D4
Mescit, *Turkey* 73 B9
Mesfinto, *Ethiopia* 81 E4
Mesgouez, L., *Canada* 102 B5
Meshchovsk, *Russia* 46 E8
Meshed = Mashhad, *Iran* 71 B8
Meshoppen, *U.S.A.* 111 E8
Meshra er Req, *Sudan* 81 F2
Mesilinka →, *Canada* 104 B4
Mesilla, *U.S.A.* 115 K10
Meslay-du-Maine, *France* 18 E6
Mesocco, *Switz.* 25 J5
Mesolóngion, *Greece* 38 C3
Mesopotamia = Al Jazirah, *Iraq* 70 C5
Mesopotamia, *U.S.A.* 110 E4
Mesopótamon, *Greece* 38 B2
Mesoraca, *Italy* 31 C9
Mésou Volímais = Volímai, *Greece* 38 D2
Mesquite, *U.S.A.* 115 H6
Messaad, *Algeria* 78 B6
Messac, *France* 18 E5
Messalo →, *Mozam.* 87 E4
Méssaména, *Cameroon* 83 E7
Messeue, *Greece* 38 D3
Messina, *Italy* 31 D8
Messina, *S. Africa* 89 C5
Messina, Str. di, *Italy* 31 D8
Messíni, *Greece* 38 D4
Messínia □, *Greece* 38 D3
Messiniakós Kólpos, *Greece* 38 E4
Messkirch, *Germany* 25 H5
Messonghi, *Greece* 36 B3
Mesta →, *Bulgaria* 40 E7
Mestá, Ákra, *Greece* 39 C7
Mestanza, *Spain* 35 G6
Mestre, *Italy* 29 C9
Mesudiye, *Turkey* 72 B7
Meta →, *S. Amer.* 122 C4
Meta Incognita Peninsula, *Canada* 101 B13
Metabetchouan, *Canada* 103 C5
Metairie, *U.S.A.* 113 L9
Metalici, Munţii, *Romania* 42 D7
Metaline Falls, *U.S.A.* 114 B5
Metallifere, Colline, *Italy* 28 E8
Metán, *Argentina* 126 B3
Metangula, *Mozam.* 87 E3
Metauro →, *Italy* 29 E10
Metema, *Ethiopia* 81 E4
Metengobalame, *Mozam.* 87 E3
Méthana, *Greece* 38 D5
Methóni, *Greece* 38 E3
Methven, *N.Z.* 91 K3
Metil, *Mozam.* 87 F4
Metkovets, *Bulgaria* 40 C7
Metković, *Croatia* 29 E14
Metlakatla, *U.S.A.* 100 C6
Metlika, *Slovenia* 29 C12
Metropolis, *U.S.A.* 113 G10
Métsovon, *Greece* 38 B3
Metu, *Ethiopia* 81 F4
Metz, *France* 19 C13
Metzingen, *Germany* 25 G5
Meulaboh, *Indonesia* 62 D1
Meung-sur-Loire, *France* 19 E8
Meureudu, *Indonesia* 62 C1
Meurthe →, *France* 19 D13
Meurthe-et-Moselle □, *France* 19 D13
Meuse □, *France* 19 C12
Meuse →, *Europe* 17 D5
Meuselwitz, *Germany* 24 D8
Mexia, *U.S.A.* 113 K6
Mexiana, I., *Brazil* 125 D9
Mexicali, *Mexico* 117 N11
Mexican Plateau, *Mexico* 98 G9
Mexican Water, *U.S.A.* 115 H9
México, *Mexico* 119 D5
Mexico, *Maine, U.S.A.* 111 B14
Mexico, *Mo., U.S.A.* 112 F9
Mexico, *N.Y., U.S.A.* 111 C8
México □, *Mexico* 119 D5
Mexico ■, *Cent. Amer.* 118 C4
Mexico, G. of, *Cent. Amer.* 119 C7
Mexico B., *U.S.A.* 111 C8
Meydān-e Naftūn, *Iran* 71 D6
Meydani, Ra's-e, *Iran* 71 E8
Meyenburg, *Germany* 24 B8
Meymac, *France* 20 C6
Meymaneh, *Afghan.* 66 B4
Meyrueis, *France* 20 D7
Meyssac, *France* 20 C5
Meyzieu, *France* 21 C8
Mezdra, *Bulgaria* 40 C7
Mèze, *France* 20 E7
Mezen, *Russia* 50 C5
Mezen →, *Russia* 50 C5
Mézenc, Mt., *France* 21 D8
Mezeş, Munţii, *Romania* 42 C8
Mezha →, *Russia* 46 E6
Mezhdurechenskiy, *Russia* 50 D7
Mézidon-Canon, *France* 18 C6
Mézières-en-Brenne, *France* 20 B5
Mézilhac, *France* 21 D8
Mézin, *France* 20 D4
Mezöberény, *Hungary* 42 D6
Mezőfalva, *Hungary* 42 D3
Mezőhegyes, *Hungary* 42 D5
Mezőkovácsháza, *Hungary* 42 D5
Mezőkövesd, *Hungary* 42 C5
Mézos, *France* 20 D2
Mezőtúr, *Hungary* 42 C5
Mezquital, *Mexico* 118 C4
Mezzolombardo, *Italy* 28 B8
Mfolozi →, *S. Africa* 89 D5
Mgeta, *Tanzania* 87 D4
Mglin, *Russia* 47 F7
Mhlaba Hills, *Zimbabwe* 87 F3
Mhow, *India* 68 H6
Miahuatlán, *Mexico* 119 D5
Miajadas, *Spain* 35 F5
Miami, *Fla., U.S.A.* 109 N5
Miami, *Okla., U.S.A.* 113 G7
Miami, *Tex., U.S.A.* 113 H4
Miami Beach, *U.S.A.* 109 N5
Mian Xian, *China* 56 H4
Mianchi, *China* 56 G6
Mīāndarreh, *Iran* 71 C7
Mīāndowāb, *Iran* 70 B5
Miandrivazo, *Madag.* 89 B8
Mīāneh, *Iran* 70 B5
Mianning, *China* 58 C4
Mianwali, *Pakistan* 68 C4
Mianyang, *China* 58 B5
Mianzhu, *China* 58 B5
Miaoli, *Taiwan* 59 E13
Miarinarivo, *Antananarivo, Madag.* 89 B8
Miarinarivo, *Toamasina, Madag.* 89 B8
Miariravaratra, *Madag.* 89 C8
Miass, *Russia* 50 D7
Miasteczko Krajeńskie, *Poland* 45 E4
Miastko, *Poland* 44 E3
Mica, *S. Africa* 89 C5
Micăsasa, *Romania* 43 D9
Michalovce, *Slovak Rep.* 27 C14
Michigan □, *U.S.A.* 108 C3
Michigan, L., *U.S.A.* 108 D2
Michigan City, *U.S.A.* 108 E2
Michika, *Nigeria* 83 C7
Michipicoten I., *Canada* 102 C2
Michoacan □, *Mexico* 118 D4
Michurin, *Bulgaria* 41 D11
Michurinsk, *Russia* 48 D5
Mico, Pta., *Nic.* 120 D3
Micronesia, *Pac. Oc.* 96 G7
Micronesia, Federated States of ■, *Pac. Oc.* 96 G7
Midai, *Indonesia* 65 L6
Midale, *Canada* 105 D8
Middelburg, *Neths.* 17 C3
Middelburg, *Eastern Cape, S. Africa* 88 E4
Middelburg, *Mpumalanga, S. Africa* 89 D4
Middelfart, *Denmark* 11 J3
Middelpos, *S. Africa* 88 E3
Middelwit, *S. Africa* 88 C4
Middle Alkali L., *U.S.A.* 114 F3
Middle Bass I., *U.S.A.* 110 E2
Middle East, *Asia* 52 F7
Middle Fork Feather →, *U.S.A.* 116 F5
Middle I., *Australia* 93 F3
Middle Loup →, *U.S.A.* 112 E5
Middle Sackville, *Canada* 103 D7
Middleboro, *U.S.A.* 111 E14
Middleburg, *Fla., U.S.A.* 109 K5
Middleburg, *N.Y., U.S.A.* 111 D10
Middleburg, *Pa., U.S.A.* 110 F7
Middlebury, *U.S.A.* 111 B11
Middlemount, *Australia* 94 C4
Middleport, *N.Y., U.S.A.* 110 C6
Middleport, *Ohio, U.S.A.* 108 F4
Middlesboro, *U.S.A.* 109 G4
Middlesbrough, *U.K.* 12 C6
Middlesbrough □, *U.K.* 12 C6
Middlesex, *Belize* 120 C2
Middlesex, *N.J., U.S.A.* 111 F10
Middlesex, *N.Y., U.S.A.* 110 D7
Middleton, *Australia* 94 C3
Middleton, *Canada* 103 D6
Middleton Cr. →, *Australia* 94 C3
Middletown, *U.K.* 15 B5
Middletown, *Calif., U.S.A.* 116 G4
Middletown, *Conn., U.S.A.* 111 E12
Middletown, *N.Y., U.S.A.* 111 E10
Middletown, *Ohio, U.S.A.* 108 F3
Middletown, *Pa., U.S.A.* 111 F8
Midhurst, *U.K.* 13 G7
Mīdī, *Yemen* 81 D5
Midi, Canal du →, *France* 20 E5
Midi d'Ossau, Pic du, *France* 20 F3
Midi-Pyrénées □, *France* 20 E5
Midland, *Canada* 102 D4
Midland, *Calif., U.S.A.* 117 M12
Midland, *Mich., U.S.A.* 108 D3
Midland, *Pa., U.S.A.* 110 F4
Midland, *Tex., U.S.A.* 113 K3
Midlands □, *Zimbabwe* 87 F2
Midleton, *Ireland* 15 E3
Midlothian, *U.S.A.* 113 J6
Midlothian □, *U.K.* 14 F5
Midongy, Tangorombohitr' i, *Madag.* 89 C8
Midongy Atsimo, *Madag.* 89 C8
Midou →, *France* 20 E3
Midouze →, *France* 20 E3
Midsayap, *Phil.* 61 H6
Midu, *China* 58 E3
Midway Is., *Pac. Oc.* 96 E10
Midway Wells, *U.S.A.* 117 N11
Midwest, *U.S.A.* 114 E10
Midwest City, *U.S.A.* 113 H6
Midyat, *Turkey* 70 B4
Midžor, *Bulgaria* 40 C6
Mie □, *Japan* 55 G8
Miechów, *Poland* 45 H7
Miedwie, Jezioro, *Poland* 45 E1
Międzybórz, *Poland* 45 G4
Międzychód, *Poland* 45 F2
Międzylesie, *Poland* 45 H3
Międzyrzec Podlaski, *Poland* 45 G9
Międzyrzecz, *Poland* 45 F2
Międzyzdroje, *Poland* 44 E1
Miejska Górka, *Poland* 45 G3
Miélan, *France* 20 E4
Mielec, *Poland* 45 H8
Mienga, *Angola* 88 B2
Miercurea-Ciuc, *Romania* 43 D10
Miercurea Sibiului, *Romania* 43 E8
Mieres, *Spain* 34 B5
Mieroszów, *Poland* 45 H3
Mieso, *Ethiopia* 81 F5
Mieszkowice, *Poland* 45 F1
Mifflintown, *U.S.A.* 110 F7
Mifraz Hefa, *Israel* 75 C4
Migennes, *France* 19 E10
Migliarino, *Italy* 29 D8
Miguel Alemán, Presa, *Mexico* 119 D5
Miguelturra, *Spain* 35 G7
Mihăileni, *Romania* 43 C11
Mihăileşti, *Romania* 43 F10
Mihailovca, *Moldova* 43 D13
Mihalgazi, *Turkey* 39 A12
Mihaliççık, *Turkey* 72 C4
Mihara, *Japan* 55 G6
Miheşu de Cîmpie, *Romania* 43 D9
Mijas, *Spain* 35 J6
Mikese, *Tanzania* 86 D4
Mikha-Tskhakaya = Senaki, *Georgia* 49 J6
Mikhailovka = Mykhaylivka, *Ukraine* 47 J8
Mikhaylov, *Russia* 46 E10
Mikhaylovgrad = Montana, *Bulgaria* 40 C7
Mikhaylovka, *Russia* 48 E6
Mikhnevo, *Russia* 46 E9
Mikínai, *Greece* 38 D4
Mikkeli, *Finland* 9 F22
Mikkwa →, *Canada* 104 B6
Mikniya, *Sudan* 81 D3
Mikołajki, *Poland* 44 E8
Míkonos, *Greece* 39 D7
Mikrí Préspa, Límni, *Greece* 40 F5
Mikrón Dhérion, *Greece* 41 E10
Mikstat, *Poland* 45 G4
Mikulov, *Czech Rep.* 27 C9
Mikumi, *Tanzania* 86 D4
Milaca, *U.S.A.* 112 C8
Milagro, *Ecuador* 124 D3
Milagros, *Phil.* 61 E5
Milan = Milano, *Italy* 28 C6
Milan, *Mo., U.S.A.* 112 E8
Milan, *Tenn., U.S.A.* 109 H1
Milange, *Mozam.* 87 F4
Milano, *Italy* 28 C6
Milanoa, *Madag.* 89 A8
Milâs, *Turkey* 39 D9
Mílatos, *Greece* 36 D7
Milazzo, *Italy* 31 D8
Milbank, *U.S.A.* 112 C6
Milbanke Sd., *Canada* 104 C3
Milden, *Canada* 105 C7
Mildenhall, *U.K.* 13 E8
Mildmay, *Canada* 110 B3
Mildura, *Australia* 95 E3
Mile, *China* 58 E4
Miléai, *Greece* 38 B5
Miles, *Australia* 95 D5
Miles City, *U.S.A.* 112 B2
Mileşti, *Moldova* 43 C13
Milestone, *Canada* 105 D8
Mileto, *Italy* 31 D9
Miletto, Mte., *Italy* 31 A7
Miletus, *Turkey* 39 D9
Milevsko, *Czech Rep.* 26 B7
Milford, *Calif., U.S.A.* 116 E6
Milford, *Conn., U.S.A.* 111 E11
Milford, *Del., U.S.A.* 108 F8
Milford, *Mass., U.S.A.* 111 D13
Milford, *N.H., U.S.A.* 111 D13

Milford, *Pa., U.S.A.* 111 E10
Milford, *Utah, U.S.A.* 115 G7
Milford Haven, *U.K.* 13 F2
Milford Sd., *N.Z.* 91 L1
Milḩ, Baḩr al, *Iraq* 70 C4
Milicz, *Poland* 45 G4
Milikapiti, *Australia* 92 B5
Miling, *Australia* 93 F2
Militello in Val di Catánia, *Italy* 31 E7
Milk →, *U.S.A.* 114 B10
Milk, Wadi el →, *Sudan* 80 D3
Milk River, *Canada* 104 D6
Mill I., *Antarctica* 5 C8
Mill Valley, *U.S.A.* 116 H4
Millárs →, *Spain* 32 F4
Millau, *France* 20 D7
Millbridge, *Canada* 110 B7
Millbrook, *Canada* 110 B6
Millbrook, *U.S.A.* 111 E11
Mille Lacs, L. des, *Canada* 102 C1
Mille Lacs L., *U.S.A.* 112 B8
Milledgeville, *U.S.A.* 109 J4
Millen, *U.S.A.* 109 J5
Millennium I. = Caroline I., *Kiribati* 97 H12
Miller, *U.S.A.* 112 C5
Millerovo, *Russia* 49 F5
Millersburg, *Ohio, U.S.A.* 110 F3
Millersburg, *Pa., U.S.A.* 110 F8
Millerton, *U.S.A.* 111 E11
Millerton L., *U.S.A.* 116 J7
Millevaches, Plateau de, *France* 20 C6
Millheim, *U.S.A.* 110 F7
Millicent, *Australia* 95 F3
Millington, *U.S.A.* 113 H10
Millinocket, *U.S.A.* 109 C11
Millmerran, *Australia* 95 D5
Millom, *U.K.* 12 C4
Mills L., *Canada* 104 A5
Millsboro, *U.S.A.* 110 G5
Milltown Malbay, *Ireland* 15 D2
Millville, *N.J., U.S.A.* 108 F8
Millville, *Pa., U.S.A.* 111 E8
Millwood L., *U.S.A.* 113 J8
Milna, *Croatia* 29 E13
Milne →, *Australia* 94 C2
Milo, *U.S.A.* 109 C11
Mílos, *Greece* 38 E6
Miłosław, *Poland* 45 F4
Milot, *Albania* 40 E3
Milparinka, *Australia* 95 D3
Miltenberg, *Germany* 25 F5
Milton, *N.S., Canada* 103 D7
Milton, *Ont., Canada* 110 C5
Milton, *N.Z.* 91 M2
Milton, *Calif., U.S.A.* 116 G6
Milton, *Fla., U.S.A.* 109 K2
Milton, *Pa., U.S.A.* 110 F8
Milton, *Vt., U.S.A.* 111 B11
Milton-Freewater, *U.S.A.* 114 D4
Milton Keynes, *U.K.* 13 E7
Milton Keynes □, *U.K.* 13 E7
Miluo, *China* 59 C9
Milverton, *Canada* 110 C4
Milwaukee, *U.S.A.* 108 D2
Milwaukee Deep, *Atl. Oc.* 121 C6
Milwaukie, *U.S.A.* 116 E4
Mim, *Ghana* 82 D4
Mimizan, *France* 20 D2
Mimoň, *Czech Rep.* 26 A7
Min Jiang →, *Fujian, China* 59 E12
Min Jiang →, *Sichuan, China* 58 C5
Min Xian, *China* 56 G3
Mina Pirquitas, *Argentina* 126 A2
Mīnā Su'ud, *Si. Arabia* 71 D6
Mīnā'al Aḩmadī, *Kuwait* 71 D6
Minago →, *Canada* 105 C9
Minaki, *Canada* 105 D10
Minamata, *Japan* 55 H5
Minami-Tori-Shima, *Pac. Oc.* 96 E7
Minas, *Uruguay* 127 C4
Minas, Sierra de las, *Guatemala* 120 C2
Minas Basin, *Canada* 103 C7
Minas de Rio Tinto = Minas de Riotinto, *Spain* 35 H4
Minas de Riotinto, *Spain* 35 H4
Minas Gerais □, *Brazil* 125 G9
Minatitlán, *Mexico* 119 D6
Minbu, *Burma* 67 J19
Minchinabad, *Pakistan* 68 D5
Mincio →, *Italy* 28 C7
Minčol, *Slovak Rep.* 27 B13
Mindanao, *Phil.* 61 H6
Mindanao Sea = Bohol Sea, *Phil.* 63 C6
Mindanao Trench, *Pac. Oc.* 61 F7
Mindel →, *Germany* 25 G6
Mindelheim, *Germany* 25 G6
Minden, *Canada* 110 B6
Minden, *Germany* 24 C4
Minden, *La., U.S.A.* 113 J8
Minden, *Nev., U.S.A.* 116 G7
Mindiptana, *Indonesia* 63 F10
Mindoro, *Phil.* 61 E4
Mindoro Str., *Phil.* 61 E4
Mine, *Japan* 55 G5
Minehead, *U.K.* 13 F4
Mineola, *N.Y., U.S.A.* 111 F11
Mineola, *Tex., U.S.A.* 113 J7
Mineral King, *U.S.A.* 116 J8
Mineral Wells, *U.S.A.* 113 J5
Mineralnyye Vody, *Russia* 49 H6
Minersville, *U.S.A.* 111 F8
Minerva, *U.S.A.* 110 F3
Minervino Murge, *Italy* 31 A9
Minetto, *U.S.A.* 111 C8
Mingäçevir, *Azerbaijan* 49 K8
Mingäçevir Su Anbarı, *Azerbaijan* 49 K8
Mingan, *Canada* 103 B7
Mingechaur = Mingäçevir, *Azerbaijan* 49 K8
Mingechaurskoye Vdkhr. = Mingäçevir Su Anbarı, *Azerbaijan* 49 K8
Mingela, *Australia* 94 B4
Mingenew, *Australia* 93 E2
Mingera Cr. →, *Australia* 94 C2
Minggang, *China* 59 A10
Mingguang, *China* 59 A11
Mingin, *Burma* 67 H19
Mingir, *Moldova* 43 D13
Minglanilla, *Spain* 33 F3
Minglun, *China* 58 E7
Mingo Junction, *U.S.A.* 110 F4
Mingorria, *Spain* 34 E6
Mingshan, *China* 58 B4
Mingteke Daban = Mintaka Pass, *Pakistan* 69 A6
Mingxi, *China* 59 D11
Mingyuegue, *China* 57 C15
Minho = Miño →, *Spain* 34 D2
Minhou, *China* 59 E12
Minićevo, *Serbia, Yug.* 42 G7
Minidoka, *U.S.A.* 114 E7
Minigwal, L., *Australia* 93 E3
Minilya →, *Australia* 93 D1
Minilya Roadhouse, *Australia* 93 D1
Minipi L., *Canada* 103 B7
Mink L., *Canada* 104 A5
Minkammen, *Sudan* 81 F3
Minna, *Nigeria* 83 D6
Minneapolis, *Kans., U.S.A.* 112 F6
Minneapolis, *Minn., U.S.A.* 112 C8
Minnedosa, *Canada* 105 C9
Minnesota □, *U.S.A.* 112 B8
Minnesota →, *U.S.A.* 112 C8
Minnewaukan, *U.S.A.* 112 A5
Minnipa, *Australia* 95 E2
Minnitaki L., *Canada* 102 C1
Mino, *Japan* 55 G8
Miño, *Spain* 34 B2
Miño →, *Spain* 34 D2
Minoa, *Greece* 39 F7
Minorca = Menorca, *Spain* 37 B11
Minot, *U.S.A.* 112 A4
Minqin, *China* 56 E2
Minqing, *China* 59 D12
Minsen, *Germany* 24 B3
Minsk, *Belarus* 46 F4
Mińsk Mazowiecki, *Poland* 45 F8
Mintabie, *Australia* 95 D1
Mintaka Pass, *Pakistan* 69 A6
Minto, *Canada* 103 C6
Minto, L., *Canada* 102 A5
Minton, *Canada* 105 D8
Minturn, *U.S.A.* 114 G10
Minturno, *Italy* 30 A6
Minûf, *Egypt* 80 H7
Minusinsk, *Russia* 51 D10
Minutang, *India* 67 E20
Minya el Qamh, *Egypt* 80 H7
Mionica, *Bos.-H.* 42 F3
Mionica, *Serbia, Yug.* 40 B4
Miquelon, *Canada* 102 C4
Miquelon, *St- P. & M.* 103 C8
Mir, *Niger* 83 C7
Mīr Kūh, *Iran* 71 E8
Mīr Shahdād, *Iran* 71 E8
Mira, *Italy* 29 C9
Mira, *Portugal* 34 E2
Mira →, *Portugal* 35 H2
Mira por vos Cay, *Bahamas* 121 B5
Mirabella Eclano, *Italy* 31 A7
Miraj, *India* 66 L9
Miram Shah, *Pakistan* 68 C4
Miramar, *Argentina* 126 D4
Miramar, *Mozam.* 89 C6
Miramas, *France* 21 E8
Mirambeau, *France* 20 C3
Miramichi, *Canada* 103 C6
Miramichi B., *Canada* 103 C7
Miramont-de-Guyenne, *France* 20 D4
Miranda, *Brazil* 125 H7
Miranda →, *Brazil* 124 G7
Miranda de Ebro, *Spain* 32 C2
Miranda do Corvo, *Portugal* 34 E2
Miranda do Douro, *Portugal* 34 D4
Mirande, *France* 20 E4
Mirandela, *Portugal* 34 D3
Mirándola, *Italy* 28 D8
Mirandópolis, *Brazil* 127 A5
Mirango, *Malawi* 87 E3
Mirano, *Italy* 29 C9
Miras, *Albania* 40 F4
Mirassol, *Brazil* 127 A6
Mirbāţ, *Oman* 74 D5
Mirear, *Egypt* 80 C4
Mirebeau, *Côte-d'Or, France* 19 E12
Mirebeau, *Vienne, France* 18 F7
Mirecourt, *France* 19 D13
Mirgorod = Myrhorod, *Ukraine* 47 H7
Miri, *Malaysia* 62 D4
Miriam Vale, *Australia* 94 C5
Miribel, *France* 19 G11
Mirim, L., *S. Amer.* 127 C5
Mirnyy, *Russia* 51 C12
Miroč, *Serbia, Yug.* 40 B6
Mirokhan, *Pakistan* 68 F3
Mirond L., *Canada* 105 B8
Mirosławiec, *Poland* 44 E3
Mirpur, *Pakistan* 69 C5
Mirpur Batoro, *Pakistan* 68 G3
Mirpur Bibiwari, *Pakistan* 68 E2
Mirpur Khas, *Pakistan* 68 G3
Mirpur Sakro, *Pakistan* 68 G2
Mirria, *Niger* 83 C6
Mirsk, *Poland* 45 H2
Mirtağ, *Turkey* 70 B4
Miryang, *S. Korea* 57 G15
Mirzaani, *Georgia* 49 K8
Mirzapur, *India* 69 G10
Mirzapur-cum-Vindhyachal = Mirzapur, *India* 69 G10
Misantla, *Mexico* 119 D5
Misawa, *Japan* 54 D10
Miscou I., *Canada* 103 C7
Mish'āb, Ra's al, *Si. Arabia* 71 D6
Mishan, *China* 60 B8
Mishawaka, *U.S.A.* 108 E2
Mishbih, Gebel, *Egypt* 80 C3
Mishima, *Japan* 55 G9
Misión, *Mexico* 117 N10
Misiones □, *Argentina* 127 B5
Misiones □, *Paraguay* 126 B4
Miskah, *Si. Arabia* 70 E4
Miskitos, Cayos, *Nic.* 120 D3
Miskolc, *Hungary* 42 B5
Misoke, *Dem. Rep. of the Congo* 86 C2
Misool, *Indonesia* 63 E8
Mişrātah, *Libya* 79 B9
Missanabie, *Canada* 102 C3
Missinaibi →, *Canada* 102 B3
Missinaibi L., *Canada* 102 C3
Mission, *Canada* 104 D4
Mission, *S. Dak., U.S.A.* 112 D4
Mission, *Tex., U.S.A.* 113 M5
Mission Beach, *Australia* 94 B4
Mission Viejo, *U.S.A.* 117 M9
Missirah, *Senegal* 82 C1
Missisa L., *Canada* 102 B2
Missisicabi →, *Canada* 102 B4
Missisagi →, *Canada* 102 C3
Mississauga, *Canada* 110 C5
Mississippi □, *U.S.A.* 113 J10
Mississippi →, *U.S.A.* 113 L10
Mississippi L., *Canada* 111 A8
Mississippi River Delta, *U.S.A.* 113 L9
Mississippi Sd., *U.S.A.* 113 K10
Missoula, *U.S.A.* 114 C7
Missouri □, *U.S.A.* 112 F8
Missouri →, *U.S.A.* 112 F9
Missouri City, *U.S.A.* 113 L7
Missouri Valley, *U.S.A.* 112 E7
Mist, *U.S.A.* 116 E3
Mistassibi →, *Canada* 103 B5
Mistassini, *Canada* 103 C5
Mistassini →, *Canada* 103 C5
Mistassini, L., *Canada* 102 B5
Mistastin L., *Canada* 103 A7
Mistelbach, *Austria* 27 C9
Misterbianco, *Italy* 31 E8
Mistinibi, L., *Canada* 103 A7
Mistretta, *Italy* 31 E7
Misty L., *Canada* 105 B8
Misurata = Mişrātah, *Libya* 79 B9
Mît Ghamr, *Egypt* 80 H7
Mitatib, *Sudan* 81 D4
Mitchell, *Australia* 95 D4
Mitchell, *Canada* 110 C3
Mitchell, *Nebr., U.S.A.* 112 E3
Mitchell, *Oreg., U.S.A.* 114 D3
Mitchell, *S. Dak., U.S.A.* 112 D6
Mitchell →, *Australia* 94 B3
Mitchell, Mt., *U.S.A.* 109 H4
Mitchell Ranges, *Australia* 94 A2
Mitchelstown, *Ireland* 15 D3
Mitha Tiwana, *Pakistan* 68 C5
Mithi, *Pakistan* 68 G3
Míthimna, *Greece* 39 B8
Mithrao, *Pakistan* 68 F3
Mitilíni, *Greece* 39 B8
Mitilinoí, *Greece* 39 D8
Mito, *Japan* 55 F10
Mitrofanovka, *Russia* 47 H10
Mitrovica = Kosovska Mitrovica, *Kosovo, Yug.* 40 D4
Mitsinjo, *Madag.* 89 B8
Mitsiwa, *Eritrea* 81 D4
Mitsiwa Channel, *Eritrea* 81 D5
Mitsukaidō, *Japan* 55 F9
Mittagong, *Australia* 95 E5
Mittelberg, *Austria* 26 D3
Mittelfranken □, *Germany* 25 F6
Mittellandkanal →, *Germany* 24 C4
Mittenwalde, *Germany* 24 C9
Mittersill, *Austria* 26 D5
Mitterteich, *Germany* 25 F8
Mittimatalik = Pond Inlet, *Canada* 101 A12
Mittweida, *Germany* 24 E8
Mitú, *Colombia* 124 C4
Mitumba, *Tanzania* 86 D3
Mitumba, Mts., *Dem. Rep. of the Congo* 86 D2
Mitwaba, *Dem. Rep. of the Congo* 87 D2
Mityana, *Uganda* 86 B3
Mixteco →, *Mexico* 119 D5
Miyagi □, *Japan* 54 E10
Miyâh, W. el →, *Egypt* 80 C3
Miyāh, W. el →, *Syria* 70 C3
Miyake-Jima, *Japan* 55 G9
Miyako, *Japan* 54 E10
Miyako-Jima, *Japan* 55 M2
Miyako-Rettō, *Japan* 55 M2
Miyakonojō, *Japan* 55 J5
Miyani, *India* 68 J3
Miyanoura-Dake, *Japan* 55 J5
Miyazaki, *Japan* 55 J5
Miyazaki □, *Japan* 55 H5
Miyazu, *Japan* 55 G7
Miyet, Bahr el = Dead Sea, *Asia* 75 D4
Miyi, *China* 58 D4
Miyoshi, *Japan* 55 G6
Miyun, *China* 56 D9
Miyun Shuiku, *China* 57 D9
Mizan Teferi, *Ethiopia* 81 F4
Mizdah, *Libya* 79 B8
Mizen Hd., *Cork, Ireland* 15 E2
Mizen Hd., *Wick., Ireland* 15 D5
Mizhi, *China* 56 F6
Mizil, *Romania* 43 F11
Mizoram □, *India* 67 H18
Mizpe Ramon, *Israel* 75 E3
Mizusawa, *Japan* 54 E10
Mjällby, *Sweden* 11 H8
Mjöbäck, *Sweden* 11 G6
Mjölby, *Sweden* 11 F9
Mjörn, *Sweden* 11 G6
Mjøsa, *Norway* 9 F14
Mkata, *Tanzania* 86 D4
Mkokotoni, *Tanzania* 86 D4
Mkomazi, *Tanzania* 86 C4
Mkomazi →, *S. Africa* 89 E5
Mkulwe, *Tanzania* 87 D3
Mkumbi, Ras, *Tanzania* 86 D4
Mkushi, *Zambia* 87 E2
Mkushi River, *Zambia* 87 E2
Mkuze, *S. Africa* 89 D5
Mladá Boleslav, *Czech Rep.* 26 A7
Mladenovac, *Serbia, Yug.* 40 B4
Mlala Hills, *Tanzania* 86 D3
Mlange = Mulanje, *Malawi* 87 F4
Mlanje, Pic, *Malawi* 85 H7
Mlava →, *Serbia, Yug.* 40 B5
Mława, *Poland* 45 E7
Mlinište, *Bos.-H.* 29 D13
Mljet, *Croatia* 29 F14
Mljetski Kanal, *Croatia* 29 F14
Młynary, *Poland* 44 D6
Mmabatho, *S. Africa* 88 D4
Mme, *Cameroon* 83 D7
Mnichovo Hradiště, *Czech Rep.* 26 A7
Mo i Rana, *Norway* 8 C16
Moa, *Cuba* 121 B4
Moa, *Indonesia* 63 F7
Moa →, *S. Leone* 82 D2
Moab, *U.S.A.* 115 G9
Moala, *Fiji* 91 D8
Moama, *Australia* 95 F3
Moamba, *Mozam.* 89 D5
Moapa, *U.S.A.* 117 J12
Moate, *Ireland* 15 C4
Moba, *Dem. Rep. of the Congo* 86 D2
Mobārakābād, *Iran* 71 D7
Mobaye, *C.A.R.* 84 D4
Mobayi, *Dem. Rep. of the Congo* 84 D4
Moberley Lake, *Canada* 104 B4
Moberly, *U.S.A.* 112 F8
Mobile, *U.S.A.* 109 K1
Mobile B., *U.S.A.* 109 K2
Mobridge, *U.S.A.* 112 C4
Mobutu Sese Seko, L. = Albert, L., *Africa* 86 B3
Moc Chau, *Vietnam* 64 B5
Moc Hoa, *Vietnam* 65 G5
Mocabe Kasari, *Dem. Rep. of the Congo* 87 D2
Moçambique, *Mozam.* 87 F5
Moçâmedes = Namibe, *Angola* 85 H2
Mocanaqua, *U.S.A.* 111 E8
Mochudi, *Botswana* 88 C4
Mocimboa da Praia, *Mozam.* 87 E5
Mociu, *Romania* 43 D9
Möckeln, *Sweden* 11 H8
Mockfjärd, *Sweden* 10 D8
Moclips, *U.S.A.* 116 C2
Mocoa, *Colombia* 124 C3
Mococa, *Brazil* 127 A6
Mocorito, *Mexico* 118 B3
Moctezuma, *Mexico* 118 B3
Moctezuma →, *Mexico* 119 C5
Mocuba, *Mozam.* 87 F4
Mocúzari, Presa, *Mexico* 118 B3
Modane, *France* 21 C10
Modasa, *India* 68 H5
Modder →, *S. Africa* 88 D3
Modderrivier, *S. Africa* 88 D3
Módena, *Italy* 28 D7
Modena, *U.S.A.* 115 H7
Modesto, *U.S.A.* 116 H6
Módica, *Italy* 31 F7
Mödling, *Austria* 27 C9
Modo, *Sudan* 81 F3
Modra, *Slovak Rep.* 27 C10
Modriča, *Bos.-H.* 42 F3
Moe, *Australia* 95 F4
Moebase, *Mozam.* 87 F4
Moëlan-sur-Mer, *France* 18 E3
Moengo, *Surinam* 125 B8
Moffat, *U.K.* 14 F5
Moga, *India* 68 D6
Mogadishu = Muqdisho, *Somali Rep.* 74 G4
Mogador = Essaouira, *Morocco* 78 B4
Mogadouro, *Portugal* 34 D4
Mogalakwena →, *S. Africa* 89 C4
Mogami-Gawa →, *Japan* 54 E10
Mogán, *Canary Is.* 37 G4
Mogaung, *Burma* 67 G20
Mogente = Moixent, *Spain* 33 G4
Mogho, *Ethiopia* 81 G5
Mogi das Cruzes, *Brazil* 127 A6
Mogi-Guaçu →, *Brazil* 127 A6
Mogi-Mirim, *Brazil* 127 A6
Mogielnica, *Poland* 45 G7
Mogige, *Ethiopia* 81 F4
Mogilev = Mahilyow, *Belarus* 46 F6
Mogilev-Podolskiy = Mohyliv-Podilskyy, *Ukraine* 47 H4
Mogilno, *Poland* 45 F4
Mogincual, *Mozam.* 87 F5
Mogliano Véneto, *Italy* 29 C9
Mogocha, *Russia* 51 D12
Mogok, *Burma* 67 H20
Mogollon Rim, *U.S.A.* 115 J8
Mógoro, *Italy* 30 C1
Mograt, *Sudan* 80 D3
Moguer, *Spain* 35 H4
Mogumber, *Australia* 93 F2
Mohács, *Hungary* 42 E3
Mohales Hoek, *Lesotho* 88 E4
Mohall, *U.S.A.* 112 A4
Moḩammadābād, *Iran* 71 B8
Mohammedia, *Morocco* 78 B4
Mohana →, *India* 69 G11
Mohanlalganj, *India* 69 F9
Mohave, L., *U.S.A.* 117 K12
Mohawk →, *U.S.A.* 111 D11
Moheda, *Sweden* 11 G8
Mohenjodaro, *Pakistan* 68 F3
Mohicanville Reservoir, *U.S.A.* 110 F3
Möhne →, *Germany* 24 D3
Mohoro, *Tanzania* 86 D4
Mohyliv-Podilskyy, *Ukraine* 47 H4
Moia, *Sudan* 81 F2
Moidart, L., *U.K.* 14 E3
Moineşti, *Romania* 43 D11
Moira →, *Canada* 110 B7
Moirans, *France* 21 C9
Moirans-en-Montagne, *France* 19 F12
Moíres, *Greece* 36 D6
Moisaküla, *Estonia* 9 G21
Moisie, *Canada* 103 B6
Moisie →, *Canada* 103 B6
Moissac, *France* 20 D5
Moita, *Portugal* 35 G2
Moixent, *Spain* 33 G4
Möja, *Sweden* 10 E12
Mojácar, *Spain* 33 H3
Mojados, *Spain* 34 D6
Mojave, *U.S.A.* 117 K8
Mojave Desert, *U.S.A.* 117 L10
Mojiang, *China* 58 F3
Mojjo →, *Ethiopia* 81 F5
Mojkovac, *Montenegro, Yug.* 40 D3
Mojo, *Bolivia* 126 A2
Mojo, *Ethiopia* 81 F4
Mojokerto, *Indonesia* 63 G15
Mokai, *N.Z.* 91 H5
Mokambo, *Dem. Rep. of the Congo* 87 E2
Mokameh, *India* 69 G11
Mokau, *N.Z.* 91 H5
Mokelumne →, *U.S.A.* 116 G5
Mokelumne Hill, *U.S.A.* 116 G6
Mokhós, *Greece* 36 D7
Mokhotlong, *Lesotho* 89 D4
Möklinta, *Sweden* 10 D10
Mokokchung, *India* 67 F19
Mokolo, *Cameroon* 83 C7
Mokolo →, *S. Africa* 89 C4
Mokp'o, *S. Korea* 57 G14
Mokra Gora, *Yugoslavia* 40 D4
Mokronog, *Slovenia* 29 C12
Moksha →, *Russia* 48 C6
Mokshan, *Russia* 48 D7
Mokwa, *Nigeria* 83 D6
Mol, *Belgium* 17 C5
Mola di Bari, *Italy* 31 A10
Molale, *Ethiopia* 81 E4
Moláoi, *Greece* 38 E4
Molara, *Italy* 30 B2
Molat, *Croatia* 29 D11
Molchanovo, *Russia* 50 D9
Mold, *U.K.* 12 D4
Moldava nad Bodvou, *Slovak Rep.* 27 C14
Moldavia = Moldova ■, *Europe* 43 C13
Moldavia, *Romania* 43 D12
Molde, *Norway* 8 E12
Moldova ■, *Europe* 43 C13
Moldova Nouă, *Romania* 42 F6
Moldoveanu, Vf., *Romania* 43 E9
Moldoviţa, *Romania* 43 C10
Mole →, *U.K.* 13 F7
Mole Creek, *Australia* 94 G4
Molepolole, *Botswana* 88 C4
Molfetta, *Italy* 31 A9
Molina de Aragón, *Spain* 32 E3
Molina de Segura, *Spain* 33 G3
Moline, *U.S.A.* 112 E9
Molinella, *Italy* 29 D8
Molinos, *Argentina* 126 B2
Moliro, *Dem. Rep. of the Congo* 86 D3
Moliterno, *Italy* 31 B8
Molkom, *Sweden* 10 E7
Mölle, *Sweden* 11 H6
Molledo, *Spain* 34 B6
Mollendo, *Peru* 124 G4
Mollerin, L., *Australia* 93 F2
Mollerussa, *Spain* 32 D5
Mollina, *Spain* 35 H6
Mölln, *Germany* 24 B6
Mölltorp, *Sweden* 11 F8
Mölnlycke, *Sweden* 11 G6
Molochansk, *Ukraine* 47 J8
Molochnoye, Ozero, *Ukraine* 47 J8
Molodechno = Maladzyechna, *Belarus* 46 E4
Molokai, *U.S.A.* 106 H16
Molong, *Australia* 95 E4
Molopo →, *Africa* 88 D3
Mólos, *Greece* 38 C4

Molotov = Perm, *Russia* 50 D6
Molsheim, *France* 19 D14
Molson L., *Canada* 105 C9
Molteno, *S. Africa* 88 E4
Molu, *Indonesia* 63 F8
Molucca Sea, *Indonesia* 63 E6
Moluccas = Maluku, *Indonesia* 63 E7
Moma, *Dem. Rep. of the Congo* 86 C1
Moma, *Mozam.* 87 F4
Mombasa, *Kenya* 86 C4
Mombetsu, *Japan* 54 B11
Mombuey, *Spain* 34 C4
Momchilgrad, *Bulgaria* 41 E9
Momi, *Dem. Rep. of the Congo* 86 C2
Mompós, *Colombia* 124 B4
Møn, *Denmark* 11 K6
Mon □, *Burma* 67 L20
Mona, Canal de la, *W. Indies* 121 C6
Mona, Isla, *Puerto Rico* 121 C6
Mona, Pta., *Costa Rica* 120 E3
Monaca, *U.S.A.* 110 F4
Monaco ■, *Europe* 21 E11
Monadhliath Mts., *U.K.* 14 D4
Monadnock, Mt., *U.S.A.* 111 D12
Monaghan, *Ireland* 15 B5
Monaghan □, *Ireland* 15 B5
Monahans, *U.S.A.* 113 K3
Monapo, *Mozam.* 87 E5
Monar, L., *U.K.* 14 D3
Monarch Mt., *Canada* 104 C3
Monashee Mts., *Canada* 104 C5
Monasterevin, *Ireland* 15 C4
Monastir = Bitola, *Macedonia* 40 E5
Moncada, *Phil.* 61 D4
Moncalieri, *Italy* 28 D4
Moncalvo, *Italy* 28 C5
Moncão, *Portugal* 34 C2
Moncarapacho, *Portugal* 35 H3
Moncayo, Sierra del, *Spain* 32 D3
Mönchengladbach, *Germany* 24 D2
Monchique, *Portugal* 35 H2
Moncks Corner, *U.S.A.* 109 J5
Monclova, *Mexico* 118 B4
Moncontour, *France* 18 D4
Moncton, *Canada* 103 C7
Mondariz, *Spain* 34 C2
Mondego →, *Portugal* 34 E2
Mondego, C., *Portugal* 34 E2
Mondeodo, *Indonesia* 63 E6
Mondeville, *France* 18 C6
Mondolfo, *Italy* 29 E10
Mondoñedo, *Spain* 34 B3
Mondovì, *Italy* 28 D4
Mondragon, *Phil.* 61 E6
Mondragone, *Italy* 30 A6
Mondrain I., *Australia* 93 F3
Monemvasía, *Greece* 38 E5
Monessen, *U.S.A.* 110 F5
Monesterio, *Spain* 35 G4
Monestier-de-Clermont, *France* 21 D9
Monett, *U.S.A.* 113 G8
Moneymore, *U.K.* 15 B5
Monfalcone, *Italy* 29 C10
Monflanquin, *France* 20 D4
Monforte, *Portugal* 35 F3
Monforte de Lemos, *Spain* 34 C3
Mong Hsu, *Burma* 58 G2
Mong Kung, *Burma* 67 J20
Mong Nai, *Burma* 67 J20
Mong Pawk, *Burma* 67 H21
Mong Ping, *Burma* 58 G2
Mong Ton, *Burma* 67 J21
Mong Wa, *Burma* 67 J22
Mong Yai, *Burma* 67 H21
Mongalla, *Sudan* 81 F3
Mongers, L., *Australia* 93 E2
Monghyr = Munger, *India* 69 G12
Mongibello = Etna, *Italy* 31 E7
Mongo, *Chad* 79 F9
Mongo →, *S. Leone* 82 D2
Mongolia ■, *Asia* 51 E10
Mongonu, *Nigeria* 83 C7
Mongu, *Zambia* 85 H4
Mônguà, *Angola* 88 B2
Monifieth, *U.K.* 14 E6
Monistrol-sur-Loire, *France* 21 C8
Monkey Bay, *Malawi* 87 E4
Monkey Mia, *Australia* 93 E1
Monkey River, *Belize* 119 D7
Mońki, *Poland* 44 E9
Monkoto, *Dem. Rep. of the Congo* 84 E4
Monkton, *Canada* 110 C3
Monmouth, *U.K.* 13 F5
Monmouth, *Ill., U.S.A.* 112 E9
Monmouth, *Oreg., U.S.A.* 114 D2
Monmouthshire □, *U.K.* 13 F5
Mono L., *U.S.A.* 116 H7
Monolith, *U.S.A.* 117 K8
Monólithos, *Greece* 36 C9
Monongahela, *U.S.A.* 110 F5
Monópoli, *Italy* 31 B10
Monor, *Hungary* 42 C4
Monóvar, *Spain* 33 G4
Monreal del Campo, *Spain* 32 E3
Monreale, *Italy* 30 D6
Monroe, *Ga., U.S.A.* 109 J4
Monroe, *La., U.S.A.* 113 J8
Monroe, *Mich., U.S.A.* 108 E4
Monroe, *N.C., U.S.A.* 109 H5
Monroe, *N.Y., U.S.A.* 111 E10
Monroe, *Utah, U.S.A.* 115 G7
Monroe, *Wash., U.S.A.* 116 C5
Monroe, *Wis., U.S.A.* 112 D10
Monroe City, *U.S.A.* 112 F9
Monroeton, *U.S.A.* 111 E8
Monroeville, *Ala., U.S.A.* 109 K2
Monroeville, *Pa., U.S.A.* 110 F5
Monrovia, *Liberia* 82 D2
Mons, *Belgium* 17 D3
Møns Klint, *Denmark* 11 K6
Monsaraz, *Portugal* 35 G3
Monse, *Indonesia* 63 E6
Monségur, *France* 20 D4
Monsélice, *Italy* 29 C8
Mönsterås, *Sweden* 11 G10
Mont Cenis, Col du, *France* 21 C10
Mont-de-Marsan, *France* 20 E3
Mont-Joli, *Canada* 103 C6
Mont-Laurier, *Canada* 102 C4
Mont-Louis, *Canada* 103 C6
Mont-roig del Camp, *Spain* 32 D5
Mont-St-Michel, Le = Le Mont-St-Michel, *France* 18 D5
Mont Tremblant, Parc Recr. du, *Canada* 102 C5
Montabaur, *Germany* 24 E3
Montagnac, *France* 20 E7
Montagnana, *Italy* 29 C8
Montagu, *S. Africa* 88 E3
Montagu I., *Antarctica* 5 B1
Montague, *Canada* 103 C7
Montague, I., *Mexico* 118 A2
Montague Ra., *Australia* 93 E2
Montague Sd., *Australia* 92 B4
Montaigu, *France* 18 F5
Montalbán, *Spain* 32 E4
Montalbano Iónico, *Italy* 31 B9
Montalbo, *Spain* 32 F2
Montalcino, *Italy* 29 E8
Montalegre, *Portugal* 34 D3
Montalto, *Italy* 31 D8
Montalto di Castro, *Italy* 29 F8
Montalto Uffugo, *Italy* 31 C9
Montalvo, *U.S.A.* 117 L7
Montamarta, *Spain* 34 D5
Montana, *Bulgaria* 40 C7
Montaña, *Peru* 124 E4
Montana □, *Bulgaria* 40 C7
Montana □, *U.S.A.* 114 C9
Montaña Clara, I., *Canary Is.* 37 E6
Montánchez, *Spain* 35 F4
Montargil, *Portugal* 35 F2
Montargis, *France* 19 E9
Montauban, *France* 20 D5
Montauk, *U.S.A.* 111 E13
Montauk Pt., *U.S.A.* 111 E13
Montbard, *France* 19 E11
Montbarrey, *France* 19 E12
Montbéliard, *France* 19 E13
Montblanc, *Spain* 32 D6
Montbrison, *France* 21 C8
Montcalm, Pic de, *France* 20 F5
Montceau-les-Mines, *France* 19 F11
Montcenis, *France* 21 B8
Montclair, *U.S.A.* 111 F10
Montcornet, *France* 19 C11
Montcuq, *France* 20 D5
Montdidier, *France* 19 C9
Monte Albán, *Mexico* 119 D5
Monte Alegre, *Brazil* 125 D8
Monte Azul, *Brazil* 125 G10
Monte Bello Is., *Australia* 92 D2
Monte-Carlo, *Monaco* 21 E11
Monte Caseros, *Argentina* 126 C4
Monte Comán, *Argentina* 126 C2
Monte Cristi, *Dom. Rep.* 121 C5
Monte Lindo →, *Paraguay* 126 A4
Monte Patria, *Chile* 126 C1
Monte Quemado, *Argentina* 126 B3
Monte Redondo, *Portugal* 34 F2
Monte Rio, *U.S.A.* 116 G4
Monte San Giovanni Campano, *Italy* 30 A6
Monte San Savino, *Italy* 29 E8
Monte Sant' Ángelo, *Italy* 29 G12
Monte Santu, C. di, *Italy* 30 B2
Monte Vista, *U.S.A.* 115 H10
Monteagudo, *Argentina* 127 B5
Montealegre del Castillo, *Spain* 33 G3
Montebello, *Canada* 102 C5
Montebello Iónico, *Italy* 31 E8
Montebelluna, *Italy* 29 C9
Montebourg, *France* 18 C5
Montecastrilli, *Italy* 29 F9
Montecatini Terme, *Italy* 28 E7
Montecito, *U.S.A.* 117 L7
Montecristo, *Italy* 28 F7
Montefalco, *Italy* 29 F9
Montefiascone, *Italy* 29 F9
Montefrío, *Spain* 35 H7
Montegiórgio, *Italy* 29 E10
Montego Bay, *Jamaica* 120 C4
Montehermoso, *Spain* 34 E4
Montejicar, *Spain* 35 H7
Montélimar, *France* 21 D8
Montella, *Italy* 31 B8
Montellano, *Spain* 35 J5
Montello, *U.S.A.* 112 D10
Montemor-o-Novo, *Portugal* 35 G2
Montemor-o-Velho, *Portugal* 34 E2
Montemorelos, *Mexico* 119 B5
Montendre, *France* 20 C3
Montenegro, *Brazil* 127 B5
Montenegro □, *Yugoslavia* 40 D3
Montenero di Bisáccia, *Italy* 29 G11
Montepuez, *Mozam.* 87 E4
Montepuez →, *Mozam.* 87 E5
Montepulciano, *Italy* 29 E8
Montereale, *Italy* 29 F10
Montereau-Faut-Yonne, *France* 19 D9
Monterey, *U.S.A.* 116 J5
Monterey B., *U.S.A.* 116 J5
Montería, *Colombia* 124 B3
Monteros, *Argentina* 126 B2
Monterotondo, *Italy* 29 F9
Monterrey, *Mexico* 118 B4
Montes Claros, *Brazil* 125 G10
Montesano, *U.S.A.* 116 D3
Montesano sulla Marcellana, *Italy* 31 B8
Montesárchio, *Italy* 31 A7
Montescaglioso, *Italy* 31 B9
Montesilvano, *Italy* 29 F11
Montevarchi, *Italy* 29 E8
Montevideo, *Uruguay* 127 C4
Montevideo, *U.S.A.* 112 C7
Montezuma, *U.S.A.* 112 E8
Montfaucon, *France* 18 E5
Montfaucon-d'Argonne, *France* 19 C12
Montfaucon-en-Velay, *France* 21 C8
Montfort, *France* 18 D5
Montfort-le-Gesnois, *France* 18 D7
Montgenèvre, *France* 21 D10
Montgomery = Sahiwal, *Pakistan* 68 D5
Montgomery, *U.K.* 13 E4
Montgomery, *Ala., U.S.A.* 109 J2
Montgomery, *Pa., U.S.A.* 110 E8
Montgomery, *W. Va., U.S.A.* 108 F5
Montgomery City, *U.S.A.* 112 F9
Montguyon, *France* 20 C3
Monthermé, *France* 19 C11
Monthey, *Switz.* 25 J2
Monthois, *France* 19 C11
Monti, *Italy* 30 B2
Monticelli d'Ongina, *Italy* 28 C6
Monticello, *Ark., U.S.A.* 113 J9
Monticello, *Fla., U.S.A.* 109 K4
Monticello, *Ind., U.S.A.* 108 E2
Monticello, *Iowa, U.S.A.* 112 D9
Monticello, *Ky., U.S.A.* 109 G3
Monticello, *Minn., U.S.A.* 112 C8
Monticello, *Miss., U.S.A.* 113 K9
Monticello, *N.Y., U.S.A.* 111 E10
Monticello, *Utah, U.S.A.* 115 H9
Montichiari, *Italy* 28 C7
Montier-en-Der, *France* 19 D11
Montignac, *France* 20 C5
Montigny-les-Metz, *France* 19 C13
Montigny-sur-Aube, *France* 19 E11
Montijo, *Portugal* 35 G2
Montijo, *Spain* 35 G4
Montilla, *Spain* 35 H6
Montivilliers, *France* 18 C7
Montluçon, *France* 19 F9
Montmagny, *Canada* 103 C5
Montmarault, *France* 19 F9
Montmartre, *Canada* 105 C8
Montmédy, *France* 19 C12
Montmélian, *France* 21 C10
Montmirail, *France* 19 D10
Montmoreau-St-Cybard, *France* 20 C4
Montmorillon, *France* 20 B4
Montmort-Lucy, *France* 19 D10
Monto, *Australia* 94 C5
Montoire-sur-le-Loir, *France* 18 E7
Montório al Vomano, *Italy* 29 F10
Montoro, *Spain* 35 G6
Montour Falls, *U.S.A.* 110 D8
Montoursville, *U.S.A.* 110 E8
Montpelier, *Idaho, U.S.A.* 114 E8
Montpelier, *Vt., U.S.A.* 111 B12
Montpellier, *France* 20 E7
Montpezat-de-Quercy, *France* 20 D5
Montpon-Ménestérol, *France* 20 D4
Montréal, *Canada* 102 C5
Montréal, *Aude, France* 20 E6
Montréal, *Gers, France* 20 E4
Montreal →, *Canada* 102 C3
Montreal L., *Canada* 105 C7
Montreal Lake, *Canada* 105 C7
Montredon-Labessonnié, *France* 20 E6
Montrésor, *France* 18 E8
Montret, *France* 19 F12
Montreuil, *Pas-de-Calais, France* 19 B8
Montreuil, *Seine-St-Denis, France* 19 D9
Montreuil-Bellay, *France* 18 E6
Montreux, *Switz.* 25 J2
Montrevel-en-Bresse, *France* 19 F12
Montrichard, *France* 18 E8
Montrose, *U.K.* 14 E6
Montrose, *Colo., U.S.A.* 115 G10
Montrose, *Pa., U.S.A.* 111 E9
Monts, Pte. des, *Canada* 103 C6
Montsalvy, *France* 20 D6
Montsant, Serra de, *Spain* 32 D6
Montsauche-les-Settons, *France* 19 E11
Montsec, Serra del, *Spain* 32 C5
Montserrat, *Spain* 32 D6
Montserrat ■, *W. Indies* 121 C7
Montuenga, *Spain* 34 D6
Montuiri, *Spain* 37 B9
Monywa, *Burma* 67 H19
Monza, *Italy* 28 C6
Monze, *Zambia* 87 F2
Monze, C., *Pakistan* 68 G2
Monzón, *Spain* 32 D5
Mooers, *U.S.A.* 111 B11
Mooi →, *S. Africa* 89 D5
Mooi River, *S. Africa* 89 D4
Moonah →, *Australia* 94 C2
Moonda, L., *Australia* 94 D3
Moonie, *Australia* 95 D5
Moonie →, *Australia* 95 D4
Moonta, *Australia* 95 E2
Moora, *Australia* 93 F2
Moorcroft, *U.S.A.* 112 C2
Moore →, *Australia* 93 F2
Moore, L., *Australia* 93 E2
Moore Park, *Australia* 94 C5
Moore Reefs, *Australia* 94 B4
Moorefield, *U.S.A.* 108 F6
Moores Res., *U.S.A.* 111 B13
Moorfoot Hills, *U.K.* 14 F5
Moorhead, *U.S.A.* 112 B6
Moormerland, *Germany* 24 B3
Moorpark, *U.S.A.* 117 L8
Moorreesburg, *S. Africa* 88 E2
Moosburg, *Germany* 25 G7
Moose →, *Canada* 102 B3
Moose →, *U.S.A.* 111 C9
Moose Creek, *Canada* 111 A10
Moose Factory, *Canada* 102 B3
Moose Jaw, *Canada* 105 C7
Moose Jaw →, *Canada* 105 C7
Moose Lake, *Canada* 105 C8
Moose Lake, *U.S.A.* 112 B8
Moose Mountain Prov. Park, *Canada* 105 D8
Moosehead L., *U.S.A.* 109 C11
Mooselookmeguntic L., *U.S.A.* 109 C10
Moosilauke, Mt., *U.S.A.* 111 B13
Moosomin, *Canada* 105 C8
Moosonee, *Canada* 102 B3
Moosup, *U.S.A.* 111 E13
Mopane, *S. Africa* 89 C4
Mopeia Velha, *Mozam.* 87 F4
Mopipi, *Botswana* 88 C3
Mopoi, *C.A.R.* 86 A2
Mopti, *Mali* 82 C4
Moqatta, *Sudan* 81 E4
Moqor, *Afghan.* 68 C2
Moquegua, *Peru* 124 G4
Mór, *Hungary* 42 C3
Mora, *Cameroon* 83 C7
Móra, *Portugal* 35 G2
Mora, *Spain* 35 F7
Mora, *Sweden* 10 C8
Mora, *Minn., U.S.A.* 112 C8
Mora, *N. Mex., U.S.A.* 115 J11
Mora →, *U.S.A.* 113 H2
Mora de Ebro = Mòra d'Ebre, *Spain* 32 D5
Mora de Rubielos, *Spain* 32 E4
Mòra d'Ebre, *Spain* 32 D5
Mòra la Nova, *Spain* 32 D5
Morača →, *Montenegro, Yug.* 40 D3
Moradabad, *India* 69 E8
Morafenobe, *Madag.* 89 B7
Morąg, *Poland* 44 E6
Moral de Calatrava, *Spain* 35 G7
Moraleja, *Spain* 34 E4
Moramanga, *Madag.* 89 B8
Moran, *Kans., U.S.A.* 113 G7
Moran, *Wyo., U.S.A.* 114 E8
Moranbah, *Australia* 94 C4
Morano Cálabro, *Italy* 31 C9
Morant Cays, *Jamaica* 120 C4
Morant Pt., *Jamaica* 120 C4
Morar, *India* 68 F8
Morar, L., *U.K.* 14 E3
Moratalla, *Spain* 33 G3
Moratuwa, *Sri Lanka* 66 R11
Morava →, *Slovak Rep.* 27 C9
Moravia, *U.S.A.* 111 D8
Moravian Hts. = Českomoravská Vrchovina, *Czech Rep.* 26 B8
Moravica →, *Serbia, Yug.* 40 C4
Moravița, *Romania* 42 E6
Moravská Třebová, *Czech Rep.* 27 B9
Moravské Budějovice, *Czech Rep.* 26 B8
Morawa, *Australia* 93 E2
Morawhanna, *Guyana* 124 B7
Moray □, *U.K.* 14 D5
Moray Firth, *U.K.* 14 D5
Morbach, *Germany* 25 F3
Morbegno, *Italy* 28 B6
Morbi, *India* 68 H4
Morbihan □, *France* 18 E4
Mörbylånga, *Sweden* 11 H10
Morcenx, *France* 20 D3
Morcone, *Italy* 31 A7
Mordelles, *France* 18 D5
Morden, *Canada* 105 D9
Mordoğan, *Turkey* 39 C8
Mordovian Republic = Mordvinia □, *Russia* 48 C7
Mordovo, *Russia* 48 D5
Mordvinia □, *Russia* 48 C7
Mordy, *Poland* 45 F9
Morea, *Greece* 6 H10
Moreau →, *U.S.A.* 112 C4
Morecambe, *U.K.* 12 C5
Morecambe B., *U.K.* 12 C5
Moree, *Australia* 95 D4
Morehead, *U.S.A.* 108 F4
Morehead City, *U.S.A.* 109 H7
Morel →, *India* 68 F7
Morelia, *Mexico* 118 D4
Morella, *Australia* 94 C3
Morella, *Spain* 32 E4
Morelos, *Mexico* 118 B3
Morelos □, *Mexico* 119 D5
Morena, *India* 68 F8
Morena, Sierra, *Spain* 35 G7
Moreni, *Romania* 43 F10
Moreno Valley, *U.S.A.* 117 M10
Moresby I., *Canada* 104 C2
Morestel, *France* 21 C9
Moreton I., *Australia* 95 D5
Moreuil, *France* 19 C9
Morey, *Spain* 37 B10
Morez, *France* 19 F13
Morgan, *U.S.A.* 114 F8
Morgan City, *U.S.A.* 113 L9
Morgan Hill, *U.S.A.* 116 H5
Morganfield, *U.S.A.* 108 G2
Morganton, *U.S.A.* 109 H5
Morgantown, *U.S.A.* 108 F6
Morgenzon, *S. Africa* 89 D4
Morges, *Switz.* 25 J2
Morghak, *Iran* 71 D8
Morgongåva, *Sweden* 10 E10
Morhange, *France* 19 D13
Morhar →, *India* 69 G11
Mori, *Italy* 28 C7
Moriarty, *U.S.A.* 115 J10
Moribaya, *Guinea* 82 D3
Morice L., *Canada* 104 C3
Moriki, *Nigeria* 83 C6
Morinville, *Canada* 104 C6
Morioka, *Japan* 54 E10
Moris, *Mexico* 118 B3
Morlaàs, *France* 20 E3
Morlaix, *France* 18 D3
Mörlunda, *Sweden* 11 G9
Mormanno, *Italy* 31 C8
Mormant, *France* 19 D9
Mornington, *Australia* 95 F4
Mornington, I., *Chile* 128 F1
Mornington I., *Australia* 94 B2
Mórnos →, *Greece* 38 C3
Moro, *Pakistan* 68 F2
Moro, *Sudan* 81 E3
Moro →, *Pakistan* 68 E2
Moro G., *Phil.* 61 H5
Morocco ■, *N. Afr.* 78 B4
Morogoro, *Tanzania* 86 D4
Morogoro □, *Tanzania* 86 D4
Moroleón, *Mexico* 118 C4
Morombe, *Madag.* 89 C7
Moron, *Argentina* 126 C4
Morón, *Cuba* 120 B4
Morón de Almazán, *Spain* 32 D2
Morón de la Frontera, *Spain* 35 H5
Morona →, *Peru* 124 D3
Morondava, *Madag.* 89 C7
Morondo, *Ivory C.* 82 D3
Morongo Valley, *U.S.A.* 117 L10
Moroni, *Comoros Is.* 77 H8
Moroni, *U.S.A.* 114 G8
Moronou, *Ivory C.* 82 D4
Morotai, *Indonesia* 63 D7
Moroto, *Uganda* 86 B3
Moroto Summit, *Kenya* 86 B3
Morozov, *Bulgaria* 41 D9
Morozovsk, *Russia* 49 F5
Morpeth, *U.K.* 12 B6
Morphou, *Cyprus* 36 D11
Morphou Bay, *Cyprus* 36 D11
Morrilton, *U.S.A.* 113 H8
Morrinhos, *Brazil* 125 G9
Morrinsville, *N.Z.* 91 G5
Morris, *Canada* 105 D9
Morris, *Ill., U.S.A.* 112 E10
Morris, *Minn., U.S.A.* 112 C7
Morris, *N.Y., U.S.A.* 111 D9
Morris, *Pa., U.S.A.* 110 E7
Morris, Mt., *Australia* 93 E5
Morrisburg, *Canada* 111 B9
Morristown, *Ariz., U.S.A.* 115 K7
Morristown, *N.J., U.S.A.* 111 F10
Morristown, *N.Y., U.S.A.* 111 B9
Morristown, *Tenn., U.S.A.* 109 G4
Morrisville, *N.Y., U.S.A.* 111 D9
Morrisville, *Pa., U.S.A.* 111 F10
Morrisville, *Vt., U.S.A.* 111 B12
Morro, Pta., *Chile* 126 B1
Morro Bay, *U.S.A.* 116 K6
Morro del Jable, *Canary Is.* 37 F5
Morro Jable, Pta. de, *Canary Is.* 37 F5
Morrosquillo, G. de, *Colombia* 120 E4
Mörrum, *Sweden* 11 H8
Morrumbene, *Mozam.* 89 C6
Mörrumsån →, *Sweden* 11 H8
Mors, *Denmark* 11 H2
Morshansk, *Russia* 48 D5
Mörsil, *Sweden* 10 A7
Mortagne →, *France* 19 D13
Mortagne-au-Perche, *France* 18 D7
Mortagne-sur-Gironde, *France* 20 C3
Mortagne-sur-Sèvre, *France* 18 F6
Mortain, *France* 18 D6
Mortara, *Italy* 28 C5
Morteau, *France* 19 E13
Morteros, *Argentina* 126 C3
Mortlach, *Canada* 105 C7
Mortlake, *Australia* 95 F3
Morton, *Tex., U.S.A.* 113 J3
Morton, *Wash., U.S.A.* 116 D4
Morundah, *Australia* 95 E4
Moruya, *Australia* 95 F5
Morvan, *France* 19 E11
Morven, *Australia* 95 D4
Morvern, *U.K.* 14 E3
Morwell, *Australia* 95 F4
Moryń, *Poland* 45 F1
Morzine, *France* 19 F13
Mosalsk, *Russia* 46 E8
Mosbach, *Germany* 25 F5
Mošćenice, *Croatia* 29 C11
Mosciano Sant' Ángelo, *Italy* 29 F10
Moscos Is., *Burma* 64 E1
Moscow = Moskva, *Russia* 46 E9
Moscow, *Idaho, U.S.A.* 114 C5
Moscow, *Pa., U.S.A.* 111 E9
Mosel →, *Europe* 19 B14
Moselle = Mosel →, *Europe* 19 B14
Moselle □, *France* 19 D13
Moses Lake, *U.S.A.* 114 C4
Mosgiel, *N.Z.* 91 L3
Moshaweng →, *S. Africa* 88 D3
Moshi, *Tanzania* 86 C4

Moshupa, *Botswana* 88 C4
Mosina, *Poland* 45 F3
Mosjøen, *Norway* 8 D15
Moskenesøya, *Norway* 8 C15
Moskenstraumen, *Norway* 8 C15
Moskva, *Russia* 46 E9
Moskva →, *Russia* 46 E10
Moslavačka Gora, *Croatia* 29 C13
Mosomane, *Botswana* 88 C4
Mosonmagyaróvár, *Hungary* 42 C2
Mošorin, *Serbia, Yug.* 42 E5
Mospino, *Ukraine* 47 J9
Mosquera, *Colombia* 124 C3
Mosquero, *U.S.A.* 113 H3
Mosqueruela, *Spain* 32 E4
Mosquitia, *Honduras* 120 C3
Mosquito Coast = Mosquitia, *Honduras* 120 C3
Mosquito Creek L., *U.S.A.* 110 E4
Mosquito L., *Canada* 105 A8
Mosquitos, G. de los, *Panama* 120 E3
Moss, *Norway* 9 G14
Moss Vale, *Australia* 95 E5
Mossbank, *Canada* 105 D7
Mossburn, *N.Z.* 91 L2
Mosselbaai, *S. Africa* 88 E3
Mossendjo, *Congo* 84 E2
Mossgiel, *Australia* 95 E3
Mössingen, *Germany* 25 G5
Mossman, *Australia* 94 B4
Mossoró, *Brazil* 125 E11
Mossuril, *Mozam.* 87 E5
Most, *Czech Rep.* 26 A6
Mosta, *Malta* 36 D1
Mostaganem, *Algeria* 78 A6
Mostar, *Bos.-H.* 42 G2
Mostardas, *Brazil* 127 C5
Mostiska = Mostyska, *Ukraine* 47 H2
Móstoles, *Spain* 34 E7
Mosty = Masty, *Belarus* 46 F3
Mostyska, *Ukraine* 47 H2
Mosul = Al Mawşil, *Iraq* 70 B4
Mosŭlpo, *S. Korea* 57 H14
Mota, *Ethiopia* 81 E4
Mota del Cuervo, *Spain* 33 F2
Mota del Marqués, *Spain* 34 D5
Motagua →, *Guatemala* 120 C2
Motala, *Sweden* 11 F9
Motaze, *Mozam.* 89 C5
Moţca, *Romania* 43 C11
Moth, *India* 69 G8
Motherwell, *U.K.* 14 F5
Motihari, *India* 69 F11
Motilla del Palancar, *Spain* 33 F3
Motnik, *Slovenia* 29 B11
Motovun, *Croatia* 29 C10
Motozintla de Mendoza, *Mexico* 119 D6
Motril, *Spain* 35 J7
Motru, *Romania* 42 F7
Motru →, *Romania* 43 F8
Mott, *U.S.A.* 112 B3
Móttola, *Italy* 31 B10
Motueka, *N.Z.* 91 J4
Motueka →, *N.Z.* 91 J4
Motul, *Mexico* 119 C7
Mouchalagane →, *Canada* 103 B6
Moúdhros, *Greece* 39 B7
Mouding, *China* 58 E3
Moudjeria, *Mauritania* 82 B2
Moudon, *Switz.* 25 J2
Mouila, *Gabon* 84 E2
Moulamein, *Australia* 95 F3
Moulianá, *Greece* 36 D7
Moulins, *France* 19 F10
Moulmein, *Burma* 67 L20
Moulouya, O. →, *Morocco* 78 B5
Moultrie, *U.S.A.* 109 K4
Moultrie, L., *U.S.A.* 109 J5
Mound City, *Mo., U.S.A.* 112 E7
Mound City, *S. Dak., U.S.A.* 112 C4
Moúnda, Ákra, *Greece* 38 C2
Moundou, *Chad* 79 G9
Moundsville, *U.S.A.* 110 G4
Moung, *Cambodia* 64 F4
Mount Airy, *U.S.A.* 109 G5
Mount Albert, *Canada* 110 B5
Mount Barker, *S. Austral., Australia* 95 F2
Mount Barker, *W. Austral., Australia* 93 F2
Mount Brydges, *Canada* 110 D3
Mount Burr, *Australia* 95 F3
Mount Carmel, *Ill., U.S.A.* 108 F2
Mount Carmel, *Pa., U.S.A.* 111 F8
Mount Charleston, *U.S.A.* 117 J11
Mount Clemens, *U.S.A.* 110 D2
Mount Coolon, *Australia* 94 C4
Mount Darwin, *Zimbabwe* 87 F3
Mount Desert I., *U.S.A.* 109 C11
Mount Dora, *U.S.A.* 109 L5
Mount Edziza Prov. Park, *Canada* 104 B2
Mount Fletcher, *S. Africa* 89 E4
Mount Forest, *Canada* 102 D3
Mount Gambier, *Australia* 95 F3
Mount Garnet, *Australia* 94 B4
Mount Holly, *U.S.A.* 111 G10
Mount Holly Springs, *U.S.A.* 110 F7
Mount Hope, *N.S.W., Australia* 95 E4
Mount Hope, *S. Austral., Australia* 95 E2
Mount Isa, *Australia* 94 C2
Mount Jewett, *U.S.A.* 110 E6
Mount Kisco, *U.S.A.* 111 E11
Mount Laguna, *U.S.A.* 117 N10
Mount Larcom, *Australia* 94 C5
Mount Lofty Ra., *Australia* 95 E2
Mount Magnet, *Australia* 93 E2
Mount Maunganui, *N.Z.* 91 G6
Mount Molloy, *Australia* 94 B4
Mount Morgan, *Australia* 94 C5
Mount Morris, *U.S.A.* 110 D7
Mount Pearl, *Canada* 103 C9
Mount Penn, *U.S.A.* 111 F9
Mount Perry, *Australia* 95 D5
Mount Pleasant, *Iowa, U.S.A.* 112 E9
Mount Pleasant, *Mich., U.S.A.* 108 D3
Mount Pleasant, *Pa., U.S.A.* 110 F5
Mount Pleasant, *S.C., U.S.A.* 109 J6
Mount Pleasant, *Tenn., U.S.A.* 109 H2
Mount Pleasant, *Tex., U.S.A.* 113 J7
Mount Pleasant, *Utah, U.S.A.* 114 G8
Mount Pocono, *U.S.A.* 111 E9
Mount Rainier Nat. Park, *U.S.A.* 116 D5
Mount Revelstoke Nat. Park, *Canada* 104 C5
Mount Robson Prov. Park, *Canada* 104 C5
Mount Selinda, *Zimbabwe* 89 C5
Mount Shasta, *U.S.A.* 114 F2
Mount Signal, *U.S.A.* 117 N11
Mount Sterling, *Ill., U.S.A.* 112 F9
Mount Sterling, *Ky., U.S.A.* 108 F4
Mount Surprise, *Australia* 94 B3
Mount Union, *U.S.A.* 110 F7
Mount Upton, *U.S.A.* 111 D9
Mount Vernon, *Ill., U.S.A.* 108 F1
Mount Vernon, *Ind., U.S.A.* 112 F10
Mount Vernon, *N.Y., U.S.A.* 111 F11
Mount Vernon, *Ohio, U.S.A.* 110 F2
Mount Vernon, *Wash., U.S.A.* 116 B4
Mountain Ash, *U.K.* 13 F4
Mountain Center, *U.S.A.* 117 M10
Mountain City, *Nev., U.S.A.* 114 F6
Mountain City, *Tenn., U.S.A.* 109 G5
Mountain Dale, *U.S.A.* 111 E10
Mountain Grove, *U.S.A.* 113 G8
Mountain Home, *Ark., U.S.A.* 113 G8
Mountain Home, *Idaho, U.S.A.* 114 E6
Mountain Iron, *U.S.A.* 112 B8
Mountain Pass, *U.S.A.* 117 K11
Mountain View, *Ark., U.S.A.* 113 H8
Mountain View, *Calif., U.S.A.* 116 H4
Mountain View, *Hawaii, U.S.A.* 106 J17
Mountainair, *U.S.A.* 115 J10
Mountlake Terrace, *U.S.A.* 116 C4
Mountmellick, *Ireland* 15 C4
Mountrath, *Ireland* 15 D4
Moura, *Australia* 94 C4
Moura, *Brazil* 124 D6
Moura, *Portugal* 35 G3
Mourão, *Portugal* 35 G3
Mourdi, Dépression du, *Chad* 79 E10
Mourdiah, *Mali* 82 C3
Mourenx, *France* 20 E3
Mouri, *Ghana* 83 D4
Mourilyan, *Australia* 94 B4
Mourmelon-le-Grand, *France* 19 C11
Mourne →, *U.K.* 15 B4
Mourne Mts., *U.K.* 15 B5
Mourniaí, *Greece* 36 D6
Mournies = Mourniaí, *Greece* 36 D6
Mouscron, *Belgium* 17 D3
Moussoro, *Chad* 79 F9
Mouthe, *France* 19 F13
Moutier, *Switz.* 25 H3
Moûtiers, *France* 21 C10
Moutong, *Indonesia* 63 D6
Mouy, *France* 19 C9
Mouzáki, *Greece* 38 B3
Mouzon, *France* 19 C12
Movas, *Mexico* 118 B3
Moville, *Ireland* 15 A4
Mowandjum, *Australia* 92 C3
Moy →, *Ireland* 15 B2
Moyale, *Kenya* 81 G4
Moyamba, *S. Leone* 82 D2
Moyen Atlas, *Morocco* 78 B4
Moyne, L. le, *Canada* 103 A6
Moyo, *Indonesia* 62 F5
Moyobamba, *Peru* 124 E3
Moyyero →, *Russia* 51 C11
Moyynty, *Kazakstan* 50 E8
Mozambique = Moçambique, *Mozam.* 87 F5
Mozambique ■, *Africa* 87 F4
Mozambique Chan., *Africa* 89 B7
Mozdok, *Russia* 49 J7
Mozdūrān, *Iran* 71 B9
Mozhaysk, *Russia* 46 E9
Mozhga, *Russia* 48 B11
Mozhnābād, *Iran* 71 C9
Mozirje, *Slovenia* 29 B11
Mozyr = Mazyr, *Belarus* 47 F5
Mpanda, *Tanzania* 86 D3
Mpésoba, *Mali* 82 C3
Mphoengs, *Zimbabwe* 89 C4
Mpika, *Zambia* 87 E3
Mpulungu, *Zambia* 87 D3
Mpumalanga, *S. Africa* 89 D5
Mpumalanga □, *S. Africa* 89 B5
Mpwapwa, *Tanzania* 86 D4
Mqanduli, *S. Africa* 89 E4
Mqinvartsveri = Kazbek, *Russia* 49 J7
Mrągowo, *Poland* 44 E8
Mramor, *Serbia, Yug.* 40 C5
Mrkonjić Grad, *Bos.-H.* 42 F2
Mrkopalj, *Croatia* 29 C11
Mrocza, *Poland* 45 E4
Msambansovu, *Zimbabwe* 87 F3
M'sila →, *Algeria* 78 A6
Msoro, *Zambia* 87 E3
Msta →, *Russia* 46 C6
Mstislavl = Mstsislaw, *Belarus* 46 E6
Mstsislaw, *Belarus* 46 E6
Mszana Dolna, *Poland* 45 J7
Mszczonów, *Poland* 45 G7
Mtama, *Tanzania* 87 E4
Mtamvuna →, *S. Africa* 89 E5
Mtilikwe →, *Zimbabwe* 87 G3
Mtsensk, *Russia* 46 F9
Mtskheta, *Georgia* 49 K7
Mtubatuba, *S. Africa* 89 D5
Mtwalume, *S. Africa* 89 E5
Mtwara-Mikindani, *Tanzania* 87 E5
Mu Gia, Deo, *Vietnam* 64 D5
Mu Us Shamo, *China* 56 E5
Muang Chiang Rai = Chiang Rai, *Thailand* 58 H2
Muang Khong, *Laos* 64 E5
Muang Lamphun, *Thailand* 64 C2
Muang Pak Beng, *Laos* 58 H3
Muar, *Malaysia* 65 L4
Muarabungo, *Indonesia* 62 E2
Muaraenim, *Indonesia* 62 E2
Muarajuloi, *Indonesia* 62 E4
Muarakaman, *Indonesia* 62 E5
Muaratebo, *Indonesia* 62 E2
Muaratembesi, *Indonesia* 62 E2
Muaratewe, *Indonesia* 62 E4
Mubarakpur, *India* 69 F10
Mubarraz = Al Mubarraz, *Si. Arabia* 71 E6
Mubende, *Uganda* 86 B3
Mubi, *Nigeria* 83 C7
Mubur, Pulau, *Indonesia* 65 L6
Mucajaí →, *Brazil* 124 C6
Muchachos, Roque de los, *Canary Is.* 37 F2
Mücheln, *Germany* 24 D7
Muchinga Mts., *Zambia* 87 E3
Muchkapskiy, *Russia* 48 E6
Muchuan, *China* 58 C5
Muck, *U.K.* 14 E2
Muckadilla, *Australia* 95 D4
Mucur, *Turkey* 72 C6
Mucuri, *Brazil* 125 G11
Mucusso, *Angola* 88 B3
Muda, *Canary Is.* 37 F6
Mudanjiang, *China* 57 B15
Mudanya, *Turkey* 41 F12
Muddy Cr. →, *U.S.A.* 115 H8
Mudgee, *Australia* 95 E4
Mudjatik →, *Canada* 105 B7
Mudurnu, *Turkey* 72 B4
Muecate, *Mozam.* 87 E4
Mueda, *Mozam.* 87 E4
Mueller Ra., *Australia* 92 C4
Muende, *Mozam.* 87 E3
Muerto, Mar, *Mexico* 119 D6
Mufu Shan, *China* 59 C10
Mufulira, *Zambia* 87 E2
Mufumbiro Range, *Africa* 86 C2
Mugardos, *Spain* 34 B2
Muge →, *Portugal* 35 F2
Múggia, *Italy* 29 C10
Mughal Sarai, *India* 69 G10
Mughayrā', *Si. Arabia* 70 D3
Mugi, *Japan* 55 H7
Mugia = Muxía, *Spain* 34 B1
Mugila, Mts., *Dem. Rep. of the Congo* 86 D2
Muğla, *Turkey* 39 D10
Muğla □, *Turkey* 39 D10
Muglad, *Sudan* 81 E2
Müglizh, *Bulgaria* 41 D9
Mugu, *Nepal* 69 E10
Muhammad, Ras, *Egypt* 70 E2
Muhammad Qol, *Sudan* 80 C4
Muhammadabad, *India* 69 F10
Muhesi →, *Tanzania* 86 D4
Mühlacker, *Germany* 25 G4
Mühldorf, *Germany* 25 G8
Mühlhausen, *Germany* 24 D6
Mühlig Hofmann fjell, *Antarctica* 5 D3
Mühlviertel, *Austria* 26 C7
Muhos, *Finland* 8 D22
Muhu, *Estonia* 9 G20
Muhutwe, *Tanzania* 86 C3
Muine Bheag, *Ireland* 15 D5
Muir, L., *Australia* 93 F2
Mujnak = Muynak, *Uzbekistan* 50 E6
Mukacheve, *Ukraine* 47 H2
Mukachevo = Mukacheve, *Ukraine* 47 H2
Mukah, *Malaysia* 62 D4
Mukandwara, *India* 68 G6
Mukawwa, Geziret, *Egypt* 80 C4
Mukawwar, *Sudan* 80 C4
Mukdahan, *Thailand* 64 D5
Mukden = Shenyang, *China* 57 D12
Mukerian, *India* 68 D6
Mukhtolovo, *Russia* 48 C6
Mukhtuya = Lensk, *Russia* 51 C12
Mukinbudin, *Australia* 93 F2
Mukishi, *Dem. Rep. of the Congo* 87 D1
Mukomuko, *Indonesia* 62 E2
Mukomwenze, *Dem. Rep. of the Congo* 86 D2
Muktsar, *India* 68 D6
Mukur = Moqor, *Afghan.* 68 C2
Mukutawa →, *Canada* 105 C9
Mukwela, *Zambia* 87 F2
Mula, *Spain* 33 G3
Mula →, *Pakistan* 68 F2
Mulange, *Dem. Rep. of the Congo* 86 C2
Mulanje, *Malawi* 87 F4
Mulchén, *Chile* 126 D1
Mulde →, *Germany* 24 D8
Mule Creek Junction, *U.S.A.* 112 D2
Muleba, *Tanzania* 86 C3
Mulejé, *Mexico* 118 B2
Muleshoe, *U.S.A.* 113 H3
Muletta, Gara, *Ethiopia* 81 F5
Mulgrave, *Canada* 103 C7
Mulhacén, *Spain* 35 H7
Mülheim, *Germany* 24 D2
Mulhouse, *France* 19 E14
Muli, *China* 58 D3
Muling, *China* 57 B16
Mull, *U.K.* 14 E3
Mull, Sound of, *U.K.* 14 E3
Mullaittivu, *Sri Lanka* 66 Q12
Mullen, *U.S.A.* 112 D4
Mullens, *U.S.A.* 108 G5
Muller, Pegunungan, *Indonesia* 62 D4
Mullet Pen., *Ireland* 15 B1
Mullewa, *Australia* 93 E2
Müllheim, *Germany* 25 H3
Mulligan →, *Australia* 94 D2
Mullingar, *Ireland* 15 C4
Mullins, *U.S.A.* 109 H6
Mullsjö, *Sweden* 11 G7
Mullumbimby, *Australia* 95 D5
Mulobezi, *Zambia* 87 F2
Mulroy B., *Ireland* 15 A4
Multan, *Pakistan* 68 D4
Mulumbe, Mts., *Dem. Rep. of the Congo* 87 D2
Mulungushi Dam, *Zambia* 87 E2
Mulvane, *U.S.A.* 113 G6
Mulwad, *Sudan* 80 D3
Mumbai, *India* 66 K8
Mumbwa, *Zambia* 87 F2
Mumra, *Russia* 49 H8
Mun →, *Thailand* 64 E5
Muna, *Indonesia* 63 F6
Munabao, *India* 68 G4
Munamagi, *Estonia* 9 H22
Münchberg, *Germany* 25 E7
Müncheberg, *Germany* 24 C10
München, *Germany* 25 G7
Munchen-Gladbach = Mönchengladbach, *Germany* 24 D2
Muncho Lake, *Canada* 104 B3
Munch'ŏn, *N. Korea* 57 E14
Muncie, *U.S.A.* 108 E3
Muncoonie, L., *Australia* 94 D2
Mundabbera, *Australia* 95 D5
Munday, *U.S.A.* 113 J5
Münden, *Germany* 24 D5
Mundiwindi, *Australia* 92 D3
Mundo →, *Spain* 33 G2
Mundo Novo, *Brazil* 125 F10
Mundra, *India* 68 H3
Mundrabilla, *Australia* 93 F4
Munera, *Spain* 33 F2
Mungallala, *Australia* 95 D4
Mungallala Cr. →, *Australia* 95 D4
Mungana, *Australia* 94 B3
Mungaoli, *India* 68 G8
Mungari, *Mozam.* 87 F3
Mungbere, *Dem. Rep. of the Congo* 86 B2
Mungeli, *India* 69 H9
Munger, *India* 69 G12
Munich = München, *Germany* 25 G7
Munising, *U.S.A.* 108 B2
Munka-Ljungby, *Sweden* 11 H6
Munkebo, *Denmark* 11 J4
Munkedal, *Sweden* 11 F5
Munkfors, *Sweden* 10 E7
Munku-Sardyk, *Russia* 51 D11
Münnerstadt, *Germany* 25 E6
Muñoz Gamero, Pen., *Chile* 128 G2
Munroe L., *Canada* 105 B9
Munsan, *S. Korea* 57 F14
Munster, *France* 19 D14
Munster, *Niedersachsen, Germany* 24 C6
Münster, *Nordrhein-Westfalen, Germany* 24 D3
Munster □, *Ireland* 15 D3
Muntadgin, *Australia* 93 F2
Muntele Mare, Vf., *Romania* 43 D8
Muntok, *Indonesia* 62 E3
Munyama, *Zambia* 87 F2
Munzur Dağları, *Turkey* 73 C8
Muong Beng, *Laos* 58 G3
Muong Boum, *Vietnam* 58 F4
Muong Et, *Laos* 64 B5
Muong Hai, *Laos* 58 G3
Muong Hiem, *Laos* 64 B4
Muong Houn, *Laos* 58 G3
Muong Hung, *Vietnam* 58 G4
Muong Kau, *Laos* 64 E5
Muong Khao, *Laos* 64 C4
Muong Khoua, *Laos* 58 G4
Muong Liep, *Laos* 64 C3
Muong May, *Laos* 64 E6
Muong Ngeun, *Laos* 58 G3
Muong Ngoi, *Laos* 58 G4
Muong Nhie, *Vietnam* 58 F4
Muong Nong, *Laos* 64 D6
Muong Ou Tay, *Laos* 58 F3
Muong Oua, *Laos* 64 C3
Muong Peun, *Laos* 58 G4
Muong Phalane, *Laos* 64 D5
Muong Phieng, *Laos* 64 C3
Muong Phine, *Laos* 64 D6
Muong Sai, *Laos* 58 G3
Muong Saiapoun, *Laos* 64 C3
Muong Sen, *Vietnam* 64 C5
Muong Sing, *Laos* 58 G3
Muong Son, *Laos* 58 G4
Muong Soui, *Laos* 64 C4
Muong Va, *Laos* 58 G4
Muong Xia, *Vietnam* 64 B5
Muonio, *Finland* 8 C20
Muonionjoki →, *Finland* 8 C20
Muping, *China* 57 F11
Mupoi, *Sudan* 81 F2
Muqaddam, Wadi →, *Sudan* 80 D3
Muqdisho, *Somali Rep.* 74 G4
Mur →, *Austria* 27 E9
Mur-de-Bretagne, *France* 18 D4
Muradiye, *Manisa, Turkey* 39 C9
Muradiye, *Van, Turkey* 73 C10
Murakami, *Japan* 54 E9
Murallón, Cerro, *Chile* 128 F2
Muranda, *Rwanda* 86 C2
Murang'a, *Kenya* 86 C4
Murashi, *Russia* 50 D5
Murat, *France* 20 C6
Murat →, *Turkey* 73 C9
Murat Dağı, *Turkey* 39 C11
Muratlı, *Turkey* 41 E11
Murato, *France* 21 F13
Murau, *Austria* 26 D7
Muravera, *Italy* 30 C2
Murayama, *Japan* 54 E10
Murça, *Portugal* 34 D3
Murchison →, *Australia* 93 E1
Murchison, Mt., *Antarctica* 5 D11
Murchison Falls, *Uganda* 86 B3
Murchison Ra., *Australia* 94 C1
Murchison Rapids, *Malawi* 87 F3
Murcia, *Spain* 33 G3
Murcia □, *Spain* 33 H3
Murdo, *U.S.A.* 112 D4
Murdoch Pt., *Australia* 94 A3
Mürefte, *Turkey* 41 F11
Mureş □, *Romania* 43 D9
Mureş →, *Romania* 42 D5
Mureşul = Mureş →, *Romania* 42 D5
Muret, *France* 20 E5
Murewa, *Zimbabwe* 89 B5
Murfreesboro, *N.C., U.S.A.* 109 G7
Murfreesboro, *Tenn., U.S.A.* 109 H2
Murgab = Murghob, *Tajikistan* 50 F8
Murgab →, *Turkmenistan* 71 B9
Murgenella, *Australia* 92 B5
Murgeni, *Romania* 43 D13
Murgha Kibzai, *Pakistan* 68 D3
Murghob, *Tajikistan* 50 F8
Murgon, *Australia* 95 D5
Muri, *India* 69 H11
Muria, *Indonesia* 63 G14
Muriaé, *Brazil* 127 A7
Murias de Paredes, *Spain* 34 C4
Muriel Mine, *Zimbabwe* 87 F3
Müritz, *Germany* 24 B8
Murka, *Kenya* 86 C4
Murliganj, *India* 69 G12
Murmansk, *Russia* 50 C4
Murnau, *Germany* 25 H7
Muro, *France* 21 F12
Muro, *Spain* 37 B10
Muro, C. de, *France* 21 G12
Muro de Alcoy, *Spain* 33 G4
Muro Lucano, *Italy* 31 B8
Murom, *Russia* 48 C6
Muroran, *Japan* 54 C10
Muros, *Spain* 34 C1
Muros y de Noya, Ría de, *Spain* 34 C1
Muroto, *Japan* 55 H7
Muroto-Misaki, *Japan* 55 H7
Murowana Goślina, *Poland* 45 F3
Murphy, *U.S.A.* 114 E5
Murphys, *U.S.A.* 116 G6
Murrat, *Sudan* 80 D2
Murrat Wells, *Sudan* 80 C3
Murray, *Ky., U.S.A.* 109 G1
Murray, *Utah, U.S.A.* 114 F8
Murray →, *Australia* 95 F2
Murray, L., *U.S.A.* 109 H5
Murray Bridge, *Australia* 95 F2
Murray Harbour, *Canada* 103 C7
Murraysburg, *S. Africa* 88 E3
Murree, *Pakistan* 68 C5
Murrieta, *U.S.A.* 117 M9
Murro di Porco, Capo, *Italy* 31 F8
Murrumbidgee →, *Australia* 95 E3
Murrumburrah, *Australia* 95 E4
Murrurundi, *Australia* 95 E5
Murshid, *Sudan* 80 C3
Murshidabad, *India* 69 G13
Murska Sobota, *Slovenia* 29 B13
Murtle L., *Canada* 104 C5
Murtoa, *Australia* 95 F3
Murtosa, *Portugal* 34 E2
Murungu, *Tanzania* 86 C3
Mururoa, *Pac. Oc.* 97 K14
Murwara, *India* 69 H9
Murwillumbah, *Australia* 95 D5
Mürz →, *Austria* 26 D8
Mürzzuschlag, *Austria* 26 D8
Muş, *Turkey* 70 B4
Mûsa, Gebel, *Egypt* 70 D2
Musa Khel, *Pakistan* 68 D3
Mūsa Qal'eh, *Afghan.* 66 C4
Musafirkhana, *India* 69 F9
Musala, *Bulgaria* 40 D7
Musala, *Indonesia* 62 D1
Musan, *N. Korea* 57 C15
Musangu, *Dem. Rep. of the Congo* 87 E1
Musasa, *Tanzania* 86 C3
Musay'īd, *Qatar* 71 E6
Muscat = Masqat, *Oman* 74 C6
Muscat & Oman = Oman ■, *Asia* 74 C6

Muscatine, *U.S.A.* 112 E9
Musgrave Harbour, *Canada* 103 C9
Musgrave Ranges, *Australia* 93 E5
Mushie, *Dem. Rep. of the Congo* 84 E3
Mushin, *Nigeria* 83 D5
Musi →, *Indonesia* 62 E2
Muskeg →, *Canada* 104 A4
Muskegon, *U.S.A.* 108 D2
Muskegon →, *U.S.A.* 108 D2
Muskegon Heights, *U.S.A.* 108 D2
Muskogee, *U.S.A.* 113 H7
Muskoka, L., *Canada* 110 B5
Muskwa →, *Canada* 104 B4
Muslīmiyah, *Syria* 70 B3
Musmar, *Sudan* 80 D4
Musofu, *Zambia* 87 E2
Musoma, *Tanzania* 86 C3
Musquaro, L., *Canada* 103 B7
Musquodoboit Harbour, *Canada* 103 D7
Musselburgh, *U.K.* 14 F5
Musselshell →, *U.S.A.* 114 C10
Mussidan, *France* 20 C4
Mussomeli, *Italy* 30 E6
Mussoorie, *India* 68 D8
Mussuco, *Angola* 88 B2
Mustafakemalpaşa, *Turkey* 41 F12
Mustang, *Nepal* 69 E10
Musters, L., *Argentina* 128 F3
Musudan, *N. Korea* 57 D15
Muswellbrook, *Australia* 95 E5
Muszyna, *Poland* 45 J7
Mût, *Egypt* 80 B2
Mut, *Turkey* 70 B2
Mutanda, *Mozam.* 89 C5
Mutanda, *Zambia* 87 E2
Mutare, *Zimbabwe* 87 F3
Muting, *Indonesia* 63 F10
Mutoko, *Zimbabwe* 89 B5
Mutoray, *Russia* 51 C11
Mutshatsha, *Dem. Rep. of the Congo* 87 E1
Mutsu, *Japan* 54 D10
Mutsu-Wan, *Japan* 54 D10
Muttaburra, *Australia* 94 C3
Muttalip, *Turkey* 39 B12
Mutton I., *Ireland* 15 D2
Mutuáli, *Mozam.* 87 E4
Mutum Biyu, *Nigeria* 83 D7
Muweilih, *Egypt* 75 E3
Muxía, *Spain* 34 B1
Muy Muy, *Nic.* 120 D2
Muyinga, *Burundi* 86 C3
Muynak, *Uzbekistan* 50 E6
Muzaffarabad, *Pakistan* 69 B5
Muzaffargarh, *Pakistan* 68 D4
Muzaffarnagar, *India* 68 E7
Muzaffarpur, *India* 69 F11
Muzafirpur, *Pakistan* 68 D3
Muzhi, *Russia* 50 C7
Muzillac, *France* 18 E4
Muzūra, *Egypt* 80 J7
Mvôlô, *Sudan* 81 F2
Mvuma, *Zimbabwe* 87 F3
Mvurwi, *Zimbabwe* 87 F3
Mwadui, *Tanzania* 86 C3
Mwambo, *Tanzania* 87 E5
Mwandi, *Zambia* 87 F1
Mwanza, *Dem. Rep. of the Congo* 86 D2
Mwanza, *Tanzania* 86 C3
Mwanza, *Zambia* 87 F1
Mwanza □, *Tanzania* 86 C3
Mwaya, *Tanzania* 87 D3
Mweelrea, *Ireland* 15 C2
Mweka, *Dem. Rep. of the Congo* 84 E4
Mwenezi, *Zimbabwe* 87 G3
Mwenezi →, *Mozam.* 87 G3
Mwenga, *Dem. Rep. of the Congo* 86 C2
Mweru, L., *Zambia* 87 D2
Mweza Range, *Zimbabwe* 87 G3
Mwilambwe, *Dem. Rep. of the Congo* 86 D2
Mwimbi, *Tanzania* 87 D3
Mwinilunga, *Zambia* 87 E1
My Tho, *Vietnam* 65 G6
Myajlar, *India* 68 F4
Myanaung, *Burma* 67 K19
Myanmar = Burma ■, *Asia* 67 J20
Myaungmya, *Burma* 67 L19
Myeik Kyunzu, *Burma* 65 G1
Myers Chuck, *U.S.A.* 104 B2
Myerstown, *U.S.A.* 111 F8
Myingyan, *Burma* 67 J19
Myitkyina, *Burma* 67 G20
Myjava, *Slovak Rep.* 27 C10
Mykhaylivka, *Ukraine* 47 J8
Mykines, *Færoe Is.* 8 E9
Mykolayiv, *Ukraine* 47 J7
Mymensingh, *Bangla.* 67 G17
Mynydd Du, *U.K.* 13 F4
Mýrdalsjökull, *Iceland* 8 E4
Myrhorod, *Ukraine* 47 H7
Myrtle Beach, *U.S.A.* 109 J6
Myrtle Creek, *U.S.A.* 114 E2
Myrtle Point, *U.S.A.* 114 E1
Myrtou, *Cyprus* 36 D12
Mysia, *Turkey* 41 G11
Myślenice, *Poland* 45 J6
Myślibórz, *Poland* 45 F1
Mysłowice, *Poland* 45 H6
Mysore = Karnataka □, *India* 66 N10
Mysore, *India* 66 N10
Mystic, *U.S.A.* 111 E13
Myszków, *Poland* 45 H6
Myszyniec, *Poland* 44 E8
Mytishchi, *Russia* 46 E9
Mývatn, *Iceland* 8 D5
Mže →, *Czech Rep.* 26 B6
Mzimba, *Malawi* 87 E3
Mzimkulu →, *S. Africa* 89 E5
Mzimvubu →, *S. Africa* 89 E4
Mzuzu, *Malawi* 87 E3

N

Na Hearadh = Harris, *U.K.* 14 D2
Na Noi, *Thailand* 64 C3
Na Phao, *Laos* 64 D5
Na Sam, *Vietnam* 58 F6
Na San, *Vietnam* 64 B5
Naab →, *Germany* 25 F8
Na'am, *Sudan* 81 F2
Na'am →, *Sudan* 81 F2
Naantali, *Finland* 9 F19
Naas, *Ireland* 15 C5
Nababeep, *S. Africa* 88 D2
Nabadwip = Navadwip, *India* 69 H13
Nabari, *Japan* 55 G8
Nabawa, *Australia* 93 E1
Nabberu, L., *Australia* 93 E3
Nabburg, *Germany* 25 F8
Naberezhnyye Chelny, *Russia* 48 C11
Nabeul, *Tunisia* 79 A8
Nabha, *India* 68 D7
Nabīd, *Iran* 71 D8
Nabire, *Indonesia* 63 E9
Nabisar, *Pakistan* 68 G3
Nabisipi →, *Canada* 103 B7
Nabiswera, *Uganda* 86 B3
Nablus = Nābulus, *West Bank* 75 C4
Naboomspruit, *S. Africa* 89 C4
Nabou, *Burkina Faso* 82 C4
Nabua, *Phil.* 61 E5
Nābulus, *West Bank* 75 C4
Nacala, *Mozam.* 87 E5
Nacala-Velha, *Mozam.* 87 E5
Nacaome, *Honduras* 120 D2
Nacaroa, *Mozam.* 87 E4
Naches, *U.S.A.* 114 C3
Naches →, *U.S.A.* 116 D6
Nachicapau, L., *Canada* 103 A6
Nachingwea, *Tanzania* 87 E4
Nachna, *India* 68 F4
Náchod, *Czech Rep.* 26 A9
Nacimiento L., *U.S.A.* 116 K6
Naco, *Mexico* 118 A3
Nacogdoches, *U.S.A.* 113 K7
Nácori Chico, *Mexico* 118 B3
Nacozari, *Mexico* 118 A3
Nadi, *Sudan* 80 D3
Nadiad, *India* 68 H5
Nădlac, *Romania* 42 D5
Nador, *Morocco* 78 B5
Nadur, *Malta* 36 C1
Nadūshan, *Iran* 71 C7
Nadvirna, *Ukraine* 47 H3
Nadvornaya = Nadvirna, *Ukraine* 47 H3
Nadym, *Russia* 50 C8
Nadym →, *Russia* 50 C8
Nærbø, *Norway* 9 G11
Næstved, *Denmark* 11 J5
Nafada, *Nigeria* 83 C7
Naft-e Safīd, *Iran* 71 D6
Naftshahr, *Iran* 70 C5
Nafud Desert = An Nafūd, *Si. Arabia* 70 D4
Nag Hammâdi, *Egypt* 80 B3
Naga, *Phil.* 61 E5
Nagahama, *Japan* 55 G8
Nagai, *Japan* 54 E10
Nagaland □, *India* 67 G19
Nagano, *Japan* 55 F9
Nagano □, *Japan* 55 F9
Nagaoka, *Japan* 55 F9
Nagappattinam, *India* 66 P11
Nagar →, *Bangla.* 69 G13
Nagar Parkar, *Pakistan* 68 G4
Nagasaki, *Japan* 55 H4
Nagasaki □, *Japan* 55 H4
Nagato, *Japan* 55 G5
Nagaur, *India* 68 F5
Nagda, *India* 68 H6
Nagercoil, *India* 66 Q10
Nagina, *India* 69 E8
Nagīneh, *Iran* 71 C8
Nagir, *Pakistan* 69 A6
Naglarby, *Sweden* 10 D9
Nagod, *India* 69 G9
Nagold, *Germany* 25 G4
Nagold →, *Germany* 25 G4
Nagoorin, *Australia* 94 C5
Nagorno-Karabakh, *Azerbaijan* 70 B5
Nagornyy, *Russia* 51 D13
Nagoya, *Japan* 55 G8
Nagpur, *India* 66 J11
Nagua, *Dom. Rep.* 121 C6
Nagyatád, *Hungary* 42 D2
Nagyecsed, *Hungary* 42 C7
Nagykálló, *Hungary* 42 C6
Nagykanizsa, *Hungary* 42 D2
Nagykáta, *Hungary* 42 C4
Nagykőrös, *Hungary* 42 C4
Naha, *Japan* 55 L3
Nahan, *India* 68 D7
Nahanni Butte, *Canada* 104 A4
Nahanni Nat. Park, *Canada* 104 A4
Nahargarh, *Mad. P., India* 68 G6
Nahargarh, *Raj., India* 68 G7
Nahariyya, *Israel* 70 C2
Nahāvand, *Iran* 71 C6
Nahe →, *Germany* 25 F3
Nahīya, W. →, *Egypt* 80 B3
Naicá, *Mexico* 118 B3
Naicam, *Canada* 105 C8
Naikoon Prov. Park, *Canada* 104 C2
Naila, *Germany* 25 E7
Naimisharanya, *India* 69 F9
Nain, *Canada* 103 A7
Nā'īn, *Iran* 71 C7
Naini Tal, *India* 69 E8
Nainpur, *India* 66 H12
Naintré, *France* 18 F7
Nainwa, *India* 68 G6
Naipu, *Romania* 43 F10
Nairn, *U.K.* 14 D5
Nairobi, *Kenya* 86 C4
Naissaar, *Estonia* 9 G21
Naita, Mt., *Ethiopia* 81 F4
Naivasha, *Kenya* 86 C4
Naivasha, L., *Kenya* 86 C4
Najac, *France* 20 D5
Najafābād, *Iran* 71 C6
Najd, *Si. Arabia* 74 B3
Nájera, *Spain* 32 C2
Najerilla →, *Spain* 32 C2
Najibabad, *India* 68 E8
Najin, *N. Korea* 57 C16
Najmah, *Si. Arabia* 71 E6
Naju, *S. Korea* 57 G14
Nakadōri-Shima, *Japan* 55 H4
Nakalagba, *Dem. Rep. of the Congo* 86 B2
Nakaminato, *Japan* 55 F10
Nakamura, *Japan* 55 H6
Nakano, *Japan* 55 F9
Nakano-Shima, *Japan* 55 K4
Nakashibetsu, *Japan* 54 C12
Nakfa, *Eritrea* 81 D4
Nakhfar al Buşayyah, *Iraq* 70 D5
Nakhichevan = Naxçıvan, *Azerbaijan* 70 B5
Nakhichevan Republic = Naxçıvan □, *Azerbaijan* 50 F5
Nakhl, *Egypt* 75 F2
Nakhl-e Taqī, *Iran* 71 E7
Nakhodka, *Russia* 51 E14
Nakhon Nayok, *Thailand* 64 E3
Nakhon Pathom, *Thailand* 64 F3
Nakhon Phanom, *Thailand* 64 D5
Nakhon Ratchasima, *Thailand* 64 E4
Nakhon Sawan, *Thailand* 64 E3
Nakhon Si Thammarat, *Thailand* 65 H3
Nakhon Thai, *Thailand* 64 D3
Nakhtarana, *India* 68 H3
Nakina, *Canada* 102 B2
Nakło nad Notecią, *Poland* 45 E4
Nako, *Burkina Faso* 82 C4
Nakodar, *India* 68 D6
Nakskov, *Denmark* 11 K5
Naktong →, *S. Korea* 57 G15
Nakuru, *Kenya* 86 C4
Nakuru, L., *Kenya* 86 C4
Nakusp, *Canada* 104 C5
Nal, *Pakistan* 68 F2
Nal →, *Pakistan* 68 G1
Nalázi, *Mozam.* 89 C5
Nalchik, *Russia* 49 J6
Nałęczów, *Poland* 45 G9
Nalerigu, *Ghana* 83 C4
Nalgonda, *India* 66 L11
Nalhati, *India* 69 G12
Naliya, *India* 68 H3
Nallamalai Hills, *India* 66 M11
Nallıhan, *Turkey* 72 B4
Nalón →, *Spain* 34 B4
Nam Can, *Vietnam* 65 H5
Nam-ch'on, *N. Korea* 57 E14
Nam Co, *China* 60 C4
Nam Dinh, *Vietnam* 58 G6
Nam Du, Hon, *Vietnam* 65 H5
Nam Ngum Dam, *Laos* 64 C4
Nam-Phan, *Vietnam* 65 G6
Nam Phong, *Thailand* 64 D4
Nam Tha, *Laos* 58 G3
Nam Tok, *Thailand* 64 E2
Namacunde, *Angola* 88 B2
Namacurra, *Mozam.* 89 B6
Namak, Daryācheh-ye, *Iran* 71 C7
Namak, Kavir-e, *Iran* 71 C8
Namakzār, Daryācheh-ye, *Iran* 71 C9
Namaland, *Namibia* 88 C2
Namangan, *Uzbekistan* 50 E8
Namapa, *Mozam.* 87 E4
Namaqualand, *S. Africa* 88 E2
Namasagali, *Uganda* 86 B3
Namber, *Indonesia* 63 E8
Nambour, *Australia* 95 D5
Nambucca Heads, *Australia* 95 E5
Namche Bazar, *Nepal* 69 F12
Namchonjŏm = Nam-ch'on, *N. Korea* 57 E14
Namecunda, *Mozam.* 87 E4
Nameponda, *Mozam.* 87 F4
Náměšť nad Oslavou, *Czech Rep.* 27 B9
Námestovo, *Slovak Rep.* 27 B12
Nametil, *Mozam.* 87 F4
Namew L., *Canada* 105 C8
Namgia, *India* 69 D8
Namhkam, *Burma* 58 E1
Namib Desert, *Namibia* 88 C2
Namibe, *Angola* 85 H2
Namibe □, *Angola* 88 B1
Namibia ■, *Africa* 88 C2
Namibwoestyn = Namib Desert, *Namibia* 88 C2
Namīn, *Iran* 73 C13
Namlea, *Indonesia* 63 E7
Namoi →, *Australia* 95 E4
Nampa, *U.S.A.* 114 E5
Nampala, *Mali* 82 B3
Namp'o, *N. Korea* 57 E13
Nampō-Shotō, *Japan* 55 J10
Nampula, *Mozam.* 87 F4
Namrole, *Indonesia* 63 E7
Namse Shankou, *China* 67 E13
Namsen →, *Norway* 8 D14
Namsos, *Norway* 8 D14
Namtsy, *Russia* 51 C13
Namtu, *Burma* 67 H20
Namtumbo, *Tanzania* 87 E4
Namu, *Canada* 104 C3
Namur, *Belgium* 17 D4
Namur □, *Belgium* 17 D4
Namutoni, *Namibia* 88 B2
Namwala, *Zambia* 87 F2
Namwŏn, *S. Korea* 57 G14
Namysłów, *Poland* 45 G4
Nan, *Thailand* 64 C3
Nan →, *Thailand* 64 E3
Nan-ch'ang = Nanchang, *China* 59 C10
Nan Ling, *China* 59 E8
Nan Xian, *China* 59 C9
Nana, *Romania* 43 F11
Nana Kru, *Liberia* 82 E3
Nanaimo, *Canada* 104 D4
Nanam, *N. Korea* 57 D15
Nanan, *China* 59 E12
Nanango, *Australia* 95 D5
Nan'ao, *China* 59 F11
Nanao, *Japan* 55 F8
Nanbu, *China* 58 B6
Nanchang, *Jiangxi, China* 59 C10
Nanchang, *Kiangsi, China* 59 C10
Nancheng, *China* 59 D11
Nanching = Nanjing, *China* 59 A12
Nanchong, *China* 58 B6
Nanchuan, *China* 58 C6
Nancy, *France* 19 D13
Nanda Devi, *India* 69 D8
Nanda Kot, *India* 69 D9
Nandan, *China* 58 E6
Nandan, *Japan* 55 G7
Nanded, *India* 66 K10
Nandewar Ra., *Australia* 95 E5
Nandi, *Fiji* 91 C7
Nandigram, *India* 69 H12
Nandurbar, *India* 66 J9
Nandyal, *India* 66 M11
Nanfeng, *Guangdong, China* 59 F8
Nanfeng, *Jiangxi, China* 59 D11
Nanga-Eboko, *Cameroon* 83 E7
Nanga Parbat, *Pakistan* 69 B6
Nangade, *Mozam.* 87 E4
Nangapinoh, *Indonesia* 62 E4
Nangarhār □, *Afghan.* 66 B7
Nangatayap, *Indonesia* 62 E4
Nangeya Mts., *Uganda* 86 B3
Nangis, *France* 19 D10
Nangong, *China* 56 F8
Nanhua, *China* 58 E3
Nanhuang, *China* 57 F11
Nanhui, *China* 59 B13
Nanjeko, *Zambia* 87 F1
Nanji Shan, *China* 59 D13
Nanjian, *China* 58 E3
Nanjiang, *China* 58 A6
Nanjing, *Fujian, China* 59 E11
Nanjing, *Jiangsu, China* 59 A12
Nanjirinji, *Tanzania* 87 D4
Nankana Sahib, *Pakistan* 68 D5
Nankang, *China* 59 E10
Nanking = Nanjing, *China* 59 A12
Nankoku, *Japan* 55 H6
Nanling, *China* 59 B12
Nanning, *China* 58 F7
Nannup, *Australia* 93 F2
Nanpan Jiang →, *China* 58 E6
Nanpara, *India* 69 F9
Nanpi, *China* 56 E9
Nanping, *Fujian, China* 59 D12
Nanping, *Henan, China* 59 C9
Nanri Dao, *China* 59 E12
Nanripe, *Mozam.* 87 E4
Nansei-Shotō = Ryūkyū-rettō, *Japan* 55 M3
Nansen Sd., *Canada* 4 A3
Nanshan I., *S. China Sea* 62 B5
Nansio, *Tanzania* 86 C3
Nant, *France* 20 D7
Nanterre, *France* 19 D9
Nantes, *France* 18 E5
Nantiat, *France* 20 B5
Nanticoke, *U.S.A.* 111 E8
Nanton, *Canada* 104 C6
Nantong, *China* 59 A13
Nantou, *Taiwan* 59 F13
Nantua, *France* 19 F12
Nantucket I., *U.S.A.* 108 E10
Nantwich, *U.K.* 12 D5
Nanty Glo, *U.S.A.* 110 F6
Nanuque, *Brazil* 125 G10
Nanusa, Kepulauan, *Indonesia* 63 D7
Nanutarra Roadhouse, *Australia* 92 D2
Nanxi, *China* 58 C5
Nanxiong, *China* 59 E10
Nanyang, *China* 56 H7
Nanyi Hu, *China* 59 B12
Nanyuki, *Kenya* 86 B4
Nanzhang, *China* 59 B8
Nao, C. de la, *Spain* 33 G5
Naococane, L., *Canada* 103 B5
Náousa, *Imathía, Greece* 40 F6
Náousa, *Kikládhes, Greece* 39 D7
Naozhou Dao, *China* 59 G8
Napa, *U.S.A.* 116 G4
Napa →, *U.S.A.* 116 G4
Napanee, *Canada* 102 D4
Napanoch, *U.S.A.* 111 E10
Nape, *Laos* 64 C5
Nape Pass = Keo Neua, Deo, *Vietnam* 64 C5
Napier, *N.Z.* 91 H6
Napier Broome B., *Australia* 92 B4
Napier Pen., *Australia* 94 A2
Napierville, *Canada* 111 A11
Naples = Nápoli, *Italy* 31 B7
Naples, *U.S.A.* 109 M5
Napo, *China* 58 F5
Napo →, *Peru* 122 D3
Napoleon, *N. Dak., U.S.A.* 112 B5
Napoleon, *Ohio, U.S.A.* 108 E3
Nápoli, *Italy* 31 B7
Nápoli, G. di, *Italy* 31 B7
Napopo, *Dem. Rep. of the Congo* 86 B2
Naqâda, *Egypt* 80 B3
Naqadeh, *Iran* 73 D11
Naqb, Ra's an, *Jordan* 75 F4
Naqqāsh, *Iran* 71 C6
Nara, *Japan* 55 G7
Nara, *Mali* 82 B3
Nara □, *Japan* 55 G8
Nara Canal, *Pakistan* 68 G3
Nara Visa, *U.S.A.* 113 H3
Naracoorte, *Australia* 95 F3
Naradhan, *Australia* 95 E4
Naraini, *India* 69 G9
Narasapur, *India* 67 L12
Narathiwat, *Thailand* 65 J3
Narayanganj, *Bangla.* 67 H17
Narayanpet, *India* 66 L10
Narbonne, *France* 20 E7
Narcea →, *Spain* 34 B4
Nardīn, *Iran* 71 B7
Nardò, *Italy* 31 B11
Narembeen, *Australia* 93 F2
Narendranagar, *India* 68 D8
Nares Str., *Arctic* 98 A13
Naretha, *Australia* 93 F3
Narew →, *Poland* 45 F7
Nari →, *Pakistan* 68 F2
Narin, *Afghan.* 66 A6
Narindra, Helodranon' i, *Madag.* 89 A8
Narita, *Japan* 55 G10
Närke, *Sweden* 10 E8
Narmada →, *India* 68 J5
Narman, *Turkey* 73 B9
Narmland, *Sweden* 9 F15
Narnaul, *India* 68 E7
Narni, *Italy* 29 F9
Naro, *Ghana* 82 C4
Naro Fominsk, *Russia* 46 E9
Narodnaya, *Russia* 6 B17
Narok, *Kenya* 86 C4
Narón, *Spain* 34 B2
Narooma, *Australia* 95 F5
Narowal, *Pakistan* 68 C6
Narrabri, *Australia* 95 E4
Narran →, *Australia* 95 D4
Narrandera, *Australia* 95 E4
Narrogin, *Australia* 93 F2
Narromine, *Australia* 95 E4
Narrow Hills Prov. Park, *Canada* 105 C8
Narsimhapur, *India* 69 H8
Narsinghgarh, *India* 68 H7
Nartes, L. e, *Albania* 40 F3
Nartkala, *Russia* 49 J6
Naruto, *Japan* 55 G7
Narva, *Estonia* 46 C5
Narva →, *Russia* 9 G22
Narva Bay, *Estonia* 9 G19
Narvik, *Norway* 8 B17
Narvskoye Vdkhr., *Russia* 46 C5
Narwana, *India* 68 E7
Naryan-Mar, *Russia* 50 C6
Narym, *Russia* 50 D9
Naryn, *Kyrgyzstan* 50 E8
Nasa, *Norway* 8 C16
Nasarawa, *Nigeria* 83 D6
Năsăud, *Romania* 43 C9
Naseby, *N.Z.* 91 L3
Naselle, *U.S.A.* 116 D3
Naser, Buheirat en, *Egypt* 80 C3
Nashua, *Mont., U.S.A.* 114 B10
Nashua, *N.H., U.S.A.* 111 D13
Nashville, *Ark., U.S.A.* 113 J8
Nashville, *Ga., U.S.A.* 109 K4
Nashville, *Tenn., U.S.A.* 109 G2
Našice, *Croatia* 42 E3
Nasielsk, *Poland* 45 F7
Nasik, *India* 66 K8
Nasipit, *Phil.* 61 G6
Nasir, *Sudan* 81 F3
Nasirabad, *India* 68 F6
Nasirabad, *Pakistan* 68 E3
Naskaupi →, *Canada* 103 B7
Naso, *Italy* 31 D7
Naşrābād, *Iran* 71 C6
Naşriān-e Pā'īn, *Iran* 70 C5
Nass →, *Canada* 104 C3
Nassarawa □, *Nigeria* 83 D6
Nassau, *Bahamas* 120 A4
Nassau, *U.S.A.* 111 D11
Nassau, B., *Chile* 128 H3
Nasser, L. = Naser, Buheirat en, *Egypt* 80 C3
Nasser City = Kôm Ombo, *Egypt* 80 C3
Nassian, *Ivory C.* 82 D4
Nässjö, *Sweden* 11 G8
Nastapoka →, *Canada* 102 A4

Nastapoka, Is., Canada 102 A4
Nasugbu, Phil. 61 D4
Näsum, Sweden 11 H8
Näsviken, Sweden 10 C10
Nata, Botswana 88 C4
Nata →, Botswana 88 C4
Natal, Brazil 125 E11
Natal, Indonesia 62 D1
Natal, S. Africa 85 K6
Natalinci, Serbia, Yug. 42 F5
Naṭanz, Iran 71 C6
Natashquan, Canada 103 B7
Natashquan →, Canada 103 B7
Natchez, U.S.A. 113 K9
Natchitoches, U.S.A. 113 K8
Nathalia, Australia 95 F4
Nathdwara, India 68 G5
Nati, Pta., Spain 37 A10
Natimuk, Australia 95 F3
Nation →, Canada 104 B4
National City, U.S.A. 117 N9
Natitingou, Benin 83 C5
Natividad, I., Mexico 118 B1
Natkyizin, Burma 64 E1
Natron, L., Tanzania 86 C4
Natrona Heights, U.S.A. 110 F5
Natrûn, W. el →, Egypt 80 H7
Nättraby, Sweden 11 H9
Natukanaoka Pan, Namibia 88 B2
Natuna Besar, Kepulauan, Indonesia 65 L7
Natuna Is. = Natuna Besar, Kepulauan, Indonesia 65 L7
Natuna Selatan, Kepulauan, Indonesia 65 L7
Natural Bridge, U.S.A. 111 B9
Naturaliste, C., Australia 94 G4
Nau Qala, Afghan. 68 B3
Naucelle, France 20 D6
Nauders, Austria 26 E3
Nauen, Germany 24 C8
Naugatuck, U.S.A. 111 E11
Naujaat = Repulse Bay, Canada 101 B11
Naujoji Akmenė, Lithuania 44 B9
Naumburg, Germany 24 D7
Nā'ūr at Tunayb, Jordan 75 D4
Nauru ■, Pac. Oc. 96 H8
Naushahra = Nowshera, Pakistan 66 C8
Naushahro, Pakistan 68 F3
Naushon I., U.S.A. 111 E14
Nauta, Peru 124 D4
Nautanwa, India 67 F13
Nautla, Mexico 119 C5
Nava, Mexico 118 B4
Nava, Spain 34 B5
Nava del Rey, Spain 34 D5
Navadwip, India 69 H13
Navahermosa, Spain 35 F6
Navahrudak, Belarus 46 F3
Navajo Reservoir, U.S.A. 115 H10
Navalcarnero, Spain 34 E6
Navalmoral de la Mata, Spain 34 F5
Navalvillar de Pela, Spain 35 F5
Navan = An Uaimh, Ireland 15 C5
Navapolatsk, Belarus 46 E5
Navarino, I., Chile 128 H3
Navarra □, Spain 32 C3
Navarre, U.S.A. 110 F3
Navarro →, U.S.A. 116 F3
Navas de San Juan, Spain 35 G7
Navasota, U.S.A. 113 K6
Navassa I., W. Indies 121 C5
Nävekvarn, Sweden 11 F10
Naver →, U.K. 14 C4
Navia, Spain 34 B4
Navia →, Spain 34 B4
Navia de Suarna, Spain 34 C3
Navibandar, India 68 J3
Navidad, Chile 126 C1
Naviraí, Brazil 127 A5
Navlakhi, India 68 H4
Navlya, Russia 47 F8
Năvodari, Romania 43 F13
Navoi = Nawoiy, Uzbekistan 50 E7
Navojoa, Mexico 118 B3
Navolato, Mexico 118 C3
Návpaktos, Greece 38 C3
Návplion, Greece 38 D4
Navrongo, Ghana 83 C4
Navsari, India 66 J8
Nawa Kot, Pakistan 68 E4
Nawab Khan, Pakistan 68 D3
Nawabganj, Ut. P., India 69 F9
Nawabganj, Ut. P., India 69 E8
Nawabshah, Pakistan 68 F3
Nawada, India 69 G11
Nawakot, Nepal 69 F11
Nawalgarh, India 68 F6
Nawanshahr, India 69 C6
Nawar, Dasht-i-, Afghan. 68 C3
Nawi, Sudan 80 D3
Nawoiy, Uzbekistan 50 E7
Naxçıvan, Azerbaijan 70 B5
Naxçıvan □, Azerbaijan 50 F5
Náxos, Greece 39 D7
Nay, France 20 E3
Nay, Mui, Vietnam 62 B3
Nāy Band, Būshehr, Iran 71 E7
Nāy Band, Khorāsān, Iran 71 C8
Nayakhan, Russia 51 C16
Nayarit □, Mexico 118 C4
Nayé, Senegal 82 C2
Nayong, China 58 D5
Nayoro, Japan 54 B11
Nayyāl, W. →, Si. Arabia 70 D3
Nazaré, Brazil 125 F11
Nazaré, Portugal 35 F1
Nazareth = Nazerat, Israel 75 C4
Nazareth, U.S.A. 111 F9
Nazas, Mexico 118 B4
Nazas →, Mexico 118 B4
Nazca, Peru 124 F4
Naze, The, U.K. 13 F9
Nazerat, Israel 75 C4
Nāzīk, Iran 70 B5
Nazilli, Turkey 39 D10
Nazko, Canada 104 C4
Nazko →, Canada 104 C4
Nazret, Ethiopia 81 F4
Nazwá, Oman 74 C6
Nchanga, Zambia 87 E2
Ncheu, Malawi 87 E3
Ndala, Tanzania 86 C3
Ndalatando, Angola 84 F2
Ndali, Benin 83 D5
Ndareda, Tanzania 86 C4
Ndélé, C.A.R. 84 C4
Ndikinimeki, Cameroon 83 E7
N'Dioum, Senegal 82 B2
Ndjamena, Chad 79 F8
Ndola, Zambia 87 E2
Ndoto Mts., Kenya 86 B4
Nduguti, Tanzania 86 C3
Néa Alikarnassós, Greece 39 F7
Néa Ankhíalos, Greece 38 B4
Néa Epídhavros, Greece 38 D5
Néa Flippiás, Greece 38 B2
Néa Ionia, Greece 38 B4
Néa Kallikrátia, Greece 40 F7
Néa Mákri, Greece 38 C5
Néa Moudhaniá, Greece 40 F7
Néa Péramos, Attikí, Greece 38 C5
Néa Péramos, Kavála, Greece 41 F8
Néa Víssi, Greece 41 E10
Néa Zíkhna, Greece 40 E7
Neagh, Lough, U.K. 15 B5
Neah Bay, U.S.A. 116 B2
Neale, L., Australia 92 D5
Neamţ □, Romania 43 C11
Neápolis, Kozáni, Greece 40 F5
Neápolis, Kríti, Greece 36 D7
Neápolis, Lakonía, Greece 38 E5
Near Is., U.S.A. 100 C1
Neath, U.K. 13 F4
Neath Port Talbot □, U.K. 13 F4
Nebbou, Burkina Faso 83 C4
Nebelat el Hagana, Sudan 81 E2
Nebine Cr. →, Australia 95 D4
Nebitdag, Turkmenistan 50 F6
Nebo, Australia 94 C4
Nebolchy, Russia 46 C7
Nebraska □, U.S.A. 112 E5
Nebraska City, U.S.A. 112 E7
Nébrodi, Monti, Italy 31 E7
Necedah, U.S.A. 112 C9
Nechako →, Canada 104 C4
Neches →, U.S.A. 113 L8
Neckar →, Germany 25 F4
Necochea, Argentina 126 D4
Neda, Spain 34 B2
Nedelino, Bulgaria 41 E9
Nedelišće, Croatia 29 B13
Nédha →, Greece 38 D3
Needles, Canada 104 D5
Needles, U.S.A. 117 L12
Needles, The, U.K. 13 G6
Ñeembucú □, Paraguay 126 B4
Neemuch = Nimach, India 68 G6
Neenah, U.S.A. 108 C1
Neepawa, Canada 105 C9
Neftçala, Azerbaijan 71 B6
Neftegorsk, Russia 49 H4
Neftekumsk, Russia 49 H7
Nefyn, U.K. 12 E3
Négala, Mali 82 C3
Negapatam = Nagappattinam, India 66 P11
Negaunee, U.S.A. 108 B2
Negele, Ethiopia 81 F4
Negev Desert = Hanegev, Israel 75 E4
Negoiul, Vf., Romania 43 E9
Negombo, Sri Lanka 66 R11
Negotin, Serbia, Yug. 40 B6
Negotino, Macedonia 40 E6
Negra, Peña, Spain 34 C4
Negra, Pta., Peru 122 D2
Negrais, C. = Maudin Sun, Burma 67 M19
Negreşti, Romania 43 D12
Negreşti-Oaş, Romania 43 C8
Negril, Jamaica 120 C4
Negro →, Argentina 122 H4
Negro →, Brazil 122 D4
Negro →, Uruguay 127 C4
Negros, Phil. 61 G5
Negru Vodă, Romania 43 G13
Neguac, Canada 103 C6
Nehalem →, U.S.A. 116 E3
Nehāvand, Iran 71 C6
Nehbandān, Iran 71 D9
Nehoiu, Romania 43 E11
Nei Monggol Zizhiqu □, China 56 D7
Neijiang, China 58 C5
Neillsville, U.S.A. 112 C9
Neilton, U.S.A. 114 C2
Neiqiu, China 56 F8
Neiva, Colombia 124 C3
Neixiang, China 56 H6
Nejanilini L., Canada 105 B9
Nejd = Najd, Si. Arabia 74 B3
Nejo, Ethiopia 81 F4
Nekā, Iran 71 B7
Nekemte, Ethiopia 81 F4
Nêkheb, Egypt 80 B3
Neksø, Denmark 11 J9
Nelas, Portugal 34 E3
Nelia, Australia 94 C3
Nelidovo, Russia 46 D7
Neligh, U.S.A. 112 D5
Nelkan, Russia 51 D14
Nellore, India 66 M11
Nelson, Canada 104 D5
Nelson, N.Z. 91 J4
Nelson, U.K. 12 D5
Nelson, Ariz., U.S.A. 115 J7
Nelson, Nev., U.S.A. 117 K12
Nelson →, Canada 105 C9
Nelson, C., Australia 95 F3
Nelson, Estrecho, Chile 128 G2
Nelson Forks, Canada 104 B4
Nelson House, Canada 105 B9
Nelson L., Canada 105 B8
Nelspoort, S. Africa 88 E3
Nelspruit, S. Africa 89 D5
Néma, Mauritania 82 B3
Neman, Russia 9 J20
Neman →, Lithuania 9 J19
Neméa, Greece 38 D4
Nemeiben L., Canada 105 B7
Nemërçkë, Mal, Albania 40 F4
Nemira, Vf., Romania 43 D11
Némiscau, Canada 102 B4
Némiscau, L., Canada 102 B4
Nemours, France 19 D9
Nemšová, Slovak Rep. 27 C11
Nemunas = Neman →, Lithuania 9 J19
Nemuro, Japan 54 C12
Nemuro-Kaikyō, Japan 54 C12
Nen Jiang →, China 57 B13
Nenagh, Ireland 15 D3
Nenasi, Malaysia 65 L4
Nene →, U.K. 13 E8
Nénita, Greece 39 C8
Nenjiang, China 60 B7
Neno, Malawi 87 F3
Neodesha, U.S.A. 113 G7
Neokhórion, Aitolía kai Akarnanía, Greece 38 C3
Neokhórion, Árta, Greece 38 B2
Néon Karlovásion, Greece 39 D8
Néon Petrítsi, Greece 40 E7
Neosho, U.S.A. 113 G7
Neosho →, U.S.A. 113 H7
Nepal ■, Asia 69 F11
Nepalganj, Nepal 69 E9
Nepalganj Road, India 69 E9
Nephi, U.S.A. 114 G8
Nephin, Ireland 15 B2
Nepi, Italy 29 F9
Nepomuk, Czech Rep. 26 B6
Neptune, U.S.A. 111 F10
Nera →, Italy 29 F9
Nera →, Romania 42 F6
Nérac, France 20 D4
Nerang, Australia 95 D5
Neratovice, Czech Rep. 26 A7
Nerchinsk, Russia 51 D12
Nereju, Romania 43 E11
Nerekhta, Russia 46 D11
Néret, L., Canada 103 B5
Neretvanski Kanal, Croatia 29 E14
Neringa, Lithuania 9 J19
Nerja, Spain 35 J7
Nerl →, Russia 46 D11
Nerpio, Spain 33 G2
Nerva, Spain 35 H4
Nervi, Italy 28 D6
Neryungri, Russia 51 D13
Nescopeck, U.S.A. 111 E8
Nesebŭr, Bulgaria 41 D11
Ness, L., U.K. 14 D4
Ness City, U.S.A. 112 F5
Nesterov, Poland 47 G2
Nestórion, Greece 40 F5
Néstos →, Greece 41 E8
Nesvady, Slovak Rep. 27 D11
Nesvizh = Nyasvizh, Belarus 47 F4
Netanya, Israel 75 C3
Netarhat, India 69 H11
Nete →, Belgium 17 C4
Netherdale, Australia 94 C4
Netherlands ■, Europe 17 C5
Netherlands Antilles ■, W. Indies 124 A5
Neto →, Italy 31 C10
Netrang, India 68 J5
Nettancourt, France 19 D11
Nettetal, Germany 24 D2
Nettilling L., Canada 101 B12
Nettuno, Italy 30 A5
Netzahualcoyotl, Presa, Mexico 119 D6
Neu-Isenburg, Germany 25 E4
Neu-Ulm, Germany 25 G6
Neubrandenburg, Germany 24 B9
Neubukow, Germany 24 A7
Neuburg, Germany 25 G7
Neuchâtel, Switz. 25 J2
Neuchâtel □, Switz. 25 J2
Neuchâtel, Lac de, Switz. 25 J2
Neudau, Austria 26 D9
Neuenhagen, Germany 24 C9
Neuenhaus, Germany 24 C2
Neuf-Brisach, France 19 D14
Neufahrn, Bayern, Germany 25 G8
Neufahrn, Bayern, Germany 25 G7
Neufchâteau, Belgium 17 E5
Neufchâteau, France 19 D12
Neufchâtel-en-Bray, France 18 C8
Neufchâtel-sur-Aisne, France 19 C11
Neuhaus, Germany 24 B6
Neuillé-Pont-Pierre, France 18 E7
Neuilly-St-Front, France 19 C10
Neukalen, Germany 24 B8
Neumarkt, Germany 25 F7
Neumünster, Germany 24 A5
Neung-sur-Beuvron, France 19 E8
Neunkirchen, Austria 26 D9
Neunkirchen, Germany 25 F3
Neuquén, Argentina 128 D3
Neuquén □, Argentina 126 D2
Neuruppin, Germany 24 C8
Neusäss, Germany 25 G6
Neuse →, U.S.A. 109 H7
Neusiedl, Austria 27 D9
Neusiedler See, Austria 27 D9
Neuss, Germany 24 D2
Neussargues-Moissac, France 20 C7
Neustadt, Bayern, Germany 25 F8
Neustadt, Bayern, Germany 25 G7
Neustadt, Bayern, Germany 25 F6
Neustadt, Bayern, Germany 25 E7
Neustadt, Brandenburg, Germany 24 C8
Neustadt, Hessen, Germany 24 E5
Neustadt, Niedersachsen, Germany 24 C5
Neustadt, Rhld-Pfz., Germany 25 F4
Neustadt, Sachsen, Germany 24 D10
Neustadt, Schleswig-Holstein, Germany 24 A6
Neustadt, Thüringen, Germany 24 E7
Neustrelitz, Germany 24 B9
Neuvic, France 20 C6
Neuville-sur-Saône, France 21 C8
Neuvy-le-Roi, France 18 E7
Neuvy-St-Sépulchre, France 19 F8
Neuvy-sur-Barangeon, France 19 E9
Neuwerk, Germany 24 B4
Neuwied, Germany 24 E3
Neva →, Russia 46 C6
Nevada, Iowa, U.S.A. 112 D8
Nevada, Mo., U.S.A. 113 G7
Nevada □, U.S.A. 114 G5
Nevada City, U.S.A. 116 F6
Nevado, Cerro, Argentina 126 D2
Nevel, Russia 46 D5
Nevers, France 19 F10
Nevertire, Australia 95 E4
Nevesinje, Bos.-H. 40 C2
Neville, Canada 105 D7
Nevinnomyssk, Russia 49 H6
Nevis, St. Kitts & Nevis 121 C7
Nevrokop = Gotse Delchev, Bulgaria 40 E7
Nevşehir, Turkey 70 B2
New →, U.S.A. 108 F5
New Aiyansh, Canada 104 B3
New Albany, Ind., U.S.A. 108 F3
New Albany, Miss., U.S.A. 113 H10
New Albany, Pa., U.S.A. 111 E8
New Amsterdam, Guyana 124 B7
New Angledool, Australia 95 D4
New Baltimore, U.S.A. 110 D2
New Bedford, U.S.A. 111 E14
New Berlin, N.Y., U.S.A. 111 D9
New Berlin, Pa., U.S.A. 110 F8
New Bern, U.S.A. 109 H7
New Bethlehem, U.S.A. 110 F5
New Bloomfield, U.S.A. 110 F7
New Boston, U.S.A. 113 J7
New Braunfels, U.S.A. 113 L5
New Brighton, N.Z. 91 K4
New Brighton, U.S.A. 110 F4
New Britain, Papua N. G. 96 H7
New Britain, U.S.A. 111 E12
New Brunswick, U.S.A. 111 F10
New Brunswick □, Canada 103 C6
New Bussa, Nigeria 83 D5
New Caledonia ■, Pac. Oc. 96 K8
New Castile = Castilla-La Mancha □, Spain 6 H5
New Castle, Ind., U.S.A. 108 F3
New Castle, Pa., U.S.A. 110 F4
New City, U.S.A. 111 E11
New Concord, U.S.A. 110 G3
New Cumberland, U.S.A. 110 F4
New Cuyama, U.S.A. 117 L7
New Delhi, India 68 E7
New Denver, Canada 104 D5
New Don Pedro Reservoir, U.S.A. 116 H6
New England, U.S.A. 112 B3
New England Ra., Australia 95 E5
New Forest, U.K. 13 G6
New Galloway, U.K. 14 F4
New Glasgow, Canada 103 C7
New Guinea, Oceania 52 K17
New Hamburg, Canada 110 C4
New Hampshire □, U.S.A. 111 C13
New Hampton, U.S.A. 112 D8
New Hanover, S. Africa 89 D5
New Hartford, U.S.A. 111 C9
New Haven, Conn., U.S.A. 111 E12
New Haven, Mich., U.S.A. 110 D2
New Hazelton, Canada 104 B3
New Hebrides = Vanuatu ■, Pac. Oc. 96 J8
New Holland, U.S.A. 111 F8
New Iberia, U.S.A. 113 K9
New Ireland, Papua N. G. 96 H7
New Jersey □, U.S.A. 108 E8
New Kensington, U.S.A. 110 F5
New Lexington, U.S.A. 108 F4
New Liskeard, Canada 102 C4
New London, Conn., U.S.A. 111 E12
New London, Ohio, U.S.A. 110 E2
New London, Wis., U.S.A. 112 C10
New Madrid, U.S.A. 113 G10
New Martinsville, U.S.A. 108 F5
New Meadows, U.S.A. 114 D5
New Melones L., U.S.A. 116 H6
New Mexico □, U.S.A. 115 J10
New Milford, Conn., U.S.A. 111 E11
New Milford, Pa., U.S.A. 111 E9
New Norcia, Australia 93 F2
New Norfolk, Australia 94 G4
New Orleans, U.S.A. 113 L9
New Philadelphia, U.S.A. 110 F3
New Plymouth, N.Z. 91 H5
New Plymouth, U.S.A. 114 E5
New Port Richey, U.S.A. 109 L4
New Providence, Bahamas 120 A4
New Quay, U.K. 13 E3
New Radnor, U.K. 13 E4
New Richmond, Canada 103 C6
New Richmond, U.S.A. 112 C8
New Roads, U.S.A. 113 K9
New Rochelle, U.S.A. 111 F11
New Rockford, U.S.A. 112 B5
New Romney, U.K. 13 G8
New Ross, Ireland 15 D5
New Salem, U.S.A. 112 B4
New Scone, U.K. 14 E5
New Siberian I. = Novaya Sibir, Ostrov, Russia 51 B16
New Siberian Is. = Novosibirskiye Ostrova, Russia 51 B15
New Smyrna Beach, U.S.A. 109 L5
New South Wales □, Australia 95 E4
New Town, U.S.A. 112 B3
New Tredegar, U.K. 13 F4
New Ulm, U.S.A. 112 C7
New Waterford, Canada 103 C7
New Westminster, Canada 116 A4
New York, U.S.A. 111 F11
New York □, U.S.A. 111 D9
New York Mts., U.S.A. 115 J6
New Zealand ■, Oceania 91 J6
Newaj →, India 68 G7
Newala, Tanzania 87 E4
Newark, Del., U.S.A. 108 F8
Newark, N.J., U.S.A. 111 F10
Newark, N.Y., U.S.A. 110 C7
Newark, Ohio, U.S.A. 110 F2
Newark-on-Trent, U.K. 12 D7
Newark Valley, U.S.A. 111 D8
Newberg, U.S.A. 114 D2
Newberry, Mich., U.S.A. 108 B3
Newberry, S.C., U.S.A. 109 H5
Newberry Springs, U.S.A. 117 L10
Newboro L., Canada 111 B8
Newbridge = Droichead Nua, Ireland 15 C5
Newburgh, Canada 110 B8
Newburgh, U.S.A. 111 E10
Newbury, U.K. 13 F6
Newbury, N.H., U.S.A. 111 B12
Newbury, Vt., U.S.A. 111 B12
Newburyport, U.S.A. 109 D10
Newcastle, Australia 95 E5
Newcastle, N.B., Canada 103 C6
Newcastle, Ont., Canada 102 D4
Newcastle, S. Africa 89 D4
Newcastle, U.K. 15 B6
Newcastle, Calif., U.S.A. 116 G5
Newcastle, Wyo., U.S.A. 112 D2
Newcastle Emlyn, U.K. 13 E3
Newcastle Ra., Australia 92 C5
Newcastle-under-Lyme, U.K. 12 D5
Newcastle-upon-Tyne, U.K. 12 C6
Newcastle Waters, Australia 94 B1
Newcastle West, Ireland 15 D2
Newcomb, U.S.A. 111 C10
Newcomerstown, U.S.A. 110 F3
Newdegate, Australia 93 F2
Newell, Australia 94 B4
Newell, U.S.A. 112 C3
Newfane, U.S.A. 110 C6
Newfield, U.S.A. 111 D8
Newfound L., U.S.A. 111 C13
Newfoundland, Canada 98 E14
Newfoundland, U.S.A. 111 E9
Newfoundland □, Canada 103 B8
Newhall, U.S.A. 117 L8
Newhaven, U.K. 13 G8
Newkirk, U.S.A. 113 G6
Newlyn, U.K. 13 G2
Newman, Australia 92 D2
Newman, U.S.A. 116 H5
Newmarket, Canada 110 B5
Newmarket, Ireland 15 D2
Newmarket, U.K. 13 E8
Newmarket, U.S.A. 111 C14
Newnan, U.S.A. 109 J3
Newport, Ireland 15 C2
Newport, I. of W., U.K. 13 G6
Newport, Newp., U.K. 13 F5
Newport, Ark., U.S.A. 113 H9
Newport, Ky., U.S.A. 108 F3
Newport, N.H., U.S.A. 111 C12
Newport, N.Y., U.S.A. 111 C9
Newport, Oreg., U.S.A. 114 D1
Newport, Pa., U.S.A. 110 F7
Newport, R.I., U.S.A. 111 E13
Newport, Tenn., U.S.A. 109 H4
Newport, Vt., U.S.A. 111 B12
Newport, Wash., U.S.A. 114 B5
Newport □, U.K. 13 F4
Newport Beach, U.S.A. 117 M9
Newport News, U.S.A. 108 G7
Newport Pagnell, U.K. 13 E7
Newquay, U.K. 13 G2

Newry, *U.K.* 15 B5
Newton, *Ill., U.S.A.* 112 F10
Newton, *Iowa, U.S.A.* 112 E8
Newton, *Kans., U.S.A.* 113 F6
Newton, *Mass., U.S.A.* 111 D13
Newton, *Miss., U.S.A.* 113 J10
Newton, *N.C., U.S.A.* 109 H5
Newton, *N.J., U.S.A.* 111 E10
Newton, *Tex., U.S.A.* 113 K8
Newton Abbot, *U.K.* 13 G4
Newton Aycliffe, *U.K.* 12 C6
Newton Falls, *U.S.A.* 110 E4
Newton Stewart, *U.K.* 14 G4
Newtonmore, *U.K.* 14 D4
Newtown, *U.K.* 13 E4
Newtownabbey, *U.K.* 15 B6
Newtownards, *U.K.* 15 B6
Newtownbarry = Bunclody, *Ireland* 15 D5
Newtownstewart, *U.K.* 15 B4
Newville, *U.S.A.* 110 F7
Nexon, *France* 20 C5
Neya, *Russia* 48 A6
Neyrīz, *Iran* 71 D7
Neyshābūr, *Iran* 71 B8
Nezhin = Nizhyn, *Ukraine* 47 G6
Nezperce, *U.S.A.* 114 C5
Ngabang, *Indonesia* 62 D3
Ngabordamlu, Tanjung, *Indonesia* 63 F8
N'Gage, *Angola* 84 F3
Ngala, *Nigeria* 83 C7
Ngambé, *Cameroon* 83 D7
Ngambé, *Cameroon* 83 E7
Ngami Depression, *Botswana* 88 C3
Ngamo, *Zimbabwe* 87 F2
Ngangala, *Sudan* 81 G3
Nganglong Kangri, *China* 67 C12
Ngao, *Thailand* 64 C2
Ngaoundéré, *Cameroon* 84 C2
Ngapara, *N.Z.* 91 L3
Ngara, *Tanzania* 86 C3
Ngawi, *Indonesia* 63 G14
Nghia Lo, *Vietnam* 58 G5
Ngoboli, *Sudan* 81 G3
Ngoma, *Malawi* 87 E3
Ngomahura, *Zimbabwe* 87 G3
Ngomba, *Tanzania* 87 D3
Ngop, *Sudan* 81 F3
Ngoring Hu, *China* 60 C4
Ngorkou, *Mali* 82 B4
Ngorongoro, *Tanzania* 86 C4
Ngozi, *Burundi* 86 C2
Ngudu, *Tanzania* 86 C3
Nguigmi, *Niger* 79 F8
Nguila, *Cameroon* 83 E7
Nguiu, *Australia* 92 B5
Ngukurr, *Australia* 94 A1
Ngulu Atoll, *Pac. Oc.* 63 C9
Ngunga, *Tanzania* 86 C3
Nguru, *Nigeria* 83 C7
Nguru Mts., *Tanzania* 86 D4
Nguyen Binh, *Vietnam* 58 F5
Nha Trang, *Vietnam* 65 F7
Nhacoongo, *Mozam.* 89 C6
Nhamaabué, *Mozam.* 87 F4
Nhamundá →, *Brazil* 125 D7
Nhangulaze, L., *Mozam.* 89 C5
Nhill, *Australia* 95 F3
Nho Quan, *Vietnam* 58 G5
Nhulunbuy, *Australia* 94 A2
Nia-nia, *Dem. Rep. of the Congo* 86 B2
Niafounké, *Mali* 82 B4
Niagara Falls, *Canada* 102 D4
Niagara Falls, *U.S.A.* 110 C6
Niagara-on-the-Lake, *Canada* 110 C5
Niah, *Malaysia* 62 D4
Niamey, *Niger* 83 C5
Niandan-Koro, *Guinea* 82 C3
Nianforando, *Guinea* 82 D2
Niangara, *Dem. Rep. of the Congo* 86 B2
Niangbo, *Ivory C.* 82 D3
Niangoloko, *Burkina Faso* 82 C4
Niantic, *U.S.A.* 111 E12
Niaro, *Sudan* 81 E3
Nias, *Indonesia* 62 D1
Niassa □, *Mozam.* 87 E4
Nibāk, *Si. Arabia* 71 E7
Nibe, *Denmark* 11 H3
Nicaragua ■, *Cent. Amer.* 120 D2
Nicaragua, L. de, *Nic.* 120 D2
Nicastro, *Italy* 31 D9
Nice, *France* 21 E11
Niceville, *U.S.A.* 109 K2
Nichicun, L., *Canada* 103 B5
Nichinan, *Japan* 55 J5
Nicholás, Canal, *W. Indies* 120 B3
Nicholasville, *U.S.A.* 108 G3
Nichols, *U.S.A.* 111 D8
Nicholson, *Australia* 92 C4
Nicholson, *U.S.A.* 111 E9
Nicholson →, *Australia* 94 B2
Nicholson L., *Canada* 105 A8
Nicholson Ra., *Australia* 93 E2
Nicholville, *U.S.A.* 111 B10
Nicobar Is., *Ind. Oc.* 52 J13
Nicola, *Canada* 104 C4
Nicolls Town, *Bahamas* 120 A4
Nicopolis, *Greece* 38 B2
Nicosia, *Cyprus* 36 D12
Nicosia, *Italy* 31 E7
Nicótera, *Italy* 31 D8
Nicoya, *Costa Rica* 120 D2
Nicoya, G. de, *Costa Rica* 120 E3
Nicoya, Pen. de, *Costa Rica* 120 E2
Nidd →, *U.K.* 12 D6
Nidda, *Germany* 25 E5
Nidda →, *Germany* 25 E4
Nidwalden □, *Switz.* 25 J4
Nidzica, *Poland* 45 E7
Niebüll, *Germany* 24 A4
Nied →, *Germany* 19 C13
Niederaula, *Germany* 24 E5
Niederbayern □, *Germany* 25 G8
Niederbronn-les-Bains, *France* 19 D14
Niedere Tauern, *Austria* 26 D7
Niederlausitz, *Germany* 24 D9
Niederösterreich □, *Austria* 26 C8
Niedersachsen □, *Germany* 24 C4
Niekerkshoop, *S. Africa* 88 D3
Niellé, *Ivory C.* 82 C3
Niemba, *Dem. Rep. of the Congo* 86 D2
Niemen = Neman →, *Lithuania* 9 J19
Niemodlin, *Poland* 45 H4
Nienburg, *Germany* 24 C5
Niepołomice, *Poland* 45 H7
Niers →, *Germany* 24 D1
Niesky, *Germany* 24 D10
Nieszawa, *Poland* 45 F5
Nieu Bethesda, *S. Africa* 88 E3
Nieuw Amsterdam, *Surinam* 125 B7
Nieuw Nickerie, *Surinam* 125 B7
Nieuwoudtville, *S. Africa* 88 E2
Nieuwpoort, *Belgium* 17 C2
Nieves, Pico de las, *Canary Is.* 37 G4
Nièvre □, *France* 19 E10
Niga, *Mali* 82 C3
Niğde, *Turkey* 70 B2
Nigel, *S. Africa* 89 D4
Niger □, *Nigeria* 83 D6
Niger ■, *W. Afr.* 83 B7
Niger →, *W. Afr.* 83 D6
Niger Delta, *Africa* 83 E6
Nigeria ■, *W. Afr.* 83 D6
Nighasin, *India* 69 E9
Nightcaps, *N.Z.* 91 L2
Nigríta, *Greece* 40 F7
Nii-Jima, *Japan* 55 G9
Niigata, *Japan* 54 F9
Niigata □, *Japan* 55 F9
Niihama, *Japan* 55 H6
Niihau, *U.S.A.* 106 H14
Niimi, *Japan* 55 G6
Niitsu, *Japan* 54 F9
Nījar, *Spain* 33 J2
Nijil, *Jordan* 75 E4
Nijkerk, *Neths.* 17 B5
Nijmegen, *Neths.* 17 C5
Nijverdal, *Neths.* 17 B6
Nīk Pey, *Iran* 71 B6
Nike, *Nigeria* 83 D6
Nikiniki, *Indonesia* 63 F6
Nikísiani, *Greece* 41 F8
Nikítas, *Greece* 40 F7
Nikki, *Benin* 83 D5
Nikkō, *Japan* 55 F9
Nikolayev = Mykolayiv, *Ukraine* 47 J7
Nikolayevsk, *Russia* 48 E7
Nikolayevsk-na-Amur, *Russia* 51 D15
Nikolsk, *Russia* 48 D8
Nikolskoye, *Russia* 51 D17
Nikopol, *Bulgaria* 41 C8
Nikopol, *Ukraine* 47 J8
Niksar, *Turkey* 72 B7
Nīkshahr, *Iran* 71 E9
Nikšić, *Montenegro, Yug.* 40 D2
Nîl, Nahr en →, *Africa* 80 H7
Nîl el Abyad →, *Sudan* 81 D3
Nîl el Azraq →, *Sudan* 81 D3
Nila, *Indonesia* 63 F7
Niland, *U.S.A.* 117 M11
Nile = Nîl, Nahr en →, *Africa* 80 H7
Niles, *Mich., U.S.A.* 108 E2
Niles, *Ohio, U.S.A.* 110 E4
Nilüfer →, *Turkey* 41 F12
Nim Ka Thana, *India* 68 F6
Nimach, *India* 68 G6
Nimbahera, *India* 68 G6
Nîmes, *France* 21 E8
Nimfaíon, Ákra = Pínnes, Ákra, *Greece* 41 F8
Nimmitabel, *Australia* 95 F4
Nimule, *Sudan* 81 G3
Nin, *Croatia* 29 D12
Nīnawá, *Iraq* 70 B4
Nindigully, *Australia* 95 D4
Nineveh = Nīnawá, *Iraq* 70 B4
Ning Xian, *China* 56 G4
Ning'an, *China* 57 B15
Ningbo, *China* 59 C13
Ningcheng, *China* 57 D10
Ningde, *China* 59 D12
Ningdu, *China* 59 D10
Ninggang, *China* 59 D9
Ningguo, *China* 59 B12
Ninghai, *China* 59 C13
Ninghua, *China* 59 D11
Ningi, *Nigeria* 83 C6
Ningjin, *China* 56 F8
Ningjing Shan, *China* 58 C2
Ninglang, *China* 58 D3
Ningling, *China* 56 G8
Ningming, *China* 58 F6
Ningnan, *China* 58 D4
Ningpo = Ningbo, *China* 59 C13
Ningqiang, *China* 56 H4
Ningshan, *China* 56 H5
Ningsia Hui A.R. = Ningxia Huizu Zizhiqu □, *China* 56 F4
Ningwu, *China* 56 E7
Ningxia Huizu Zizhiqu □, *China* 56 F4
Ningxiang, *China* 59 C9
Ningyang, *China* 56 G9
Ningyuan, *China* 59 E8
Ninh Binh, *Vietnam* 58 G5
Ninh Giang, *Vietnam* 64 B6
Ninh Hoa, *Vietnam* 64 F7
Ninh Ma, *Vietnam* 64 F7
Ninove, *Belgium* 17 D4
Nioaque, *Brazil* 127 A4
Niobrara, *U.S.A.* 112 D6
Niobrara →, *U.S.A.* 112 D6
Niono, *Mali* 82 C3
Nionsamoridougou, *Guinea* 82 D3
Nioro du Rip, *Senegal* 82 C1
Nioro du Sahel, *Mali* 82 B3
Niort, *France* 20 B3
Nipawin, *Canada* 105 C8
Nipfjället, *Sweden* 10 C6
Nipigon, *Canada* 102 C2
Nipigon, L., *Canada* 102 C2
Nipishish L., *Canada* 103 B7
Nipissing, L., *Canada* 102 C4
Nipomo, *U.S.A.* 117 K6
Nipton, *U.S.A.* 117 K11
Niquelândia, *Brazil* 125 F9
Nīr, *Iran* 70 B5
Nirasaki, *Japan* 55 G9
Nirmal, *India* 66 K11
Nirmali, *India* 69 F12
Niš, *Serbia, Yug.* 40 C5
Nisa, *Portugal* 35 F3
Niṣāb, *Si. Arabia* 70 D5
Niṣāb, *Yemen* 74 E4
Nišava →, *Serbia, Yug.* 40 C5
Niscemi, *Italy* 31 E7
Nishinomiya, *Japan* 55 G7
Nishino'omote, *Japan* 55 J5
Nishiwaki, *Japan* 55 G7
Nísíros, *Greece* 39 E9
Niška Banja, *Serbia, Yug.* 40 C6
Niskibi →, *Canada* 102 A2
Nisko, *Poland* 45 H9
Nisporeni, *Moldova* 43 C13
Nisqually →, *U.S.A.* 116 C4
Nissáki, *Greece* 36 A3
Nissan →, *Sweden* 11 H6
Nissum Bredning, *Denmark* 11 H2
Nissum Fjord, *Denmark* 11 H2
Nistru = Dnister →, *Europe* 47 J6
Nisutlin →, *Canada* 104 A2
Nitchequon, *Canada* 103 B5
Niterói, *Brazil* 127 A7
Nith →, *Canada* 110 C4
Nith →, *U.K.* 14 F5
Nitra, *Slovak Rep.* 27 C11
Nitra →, *Slovak Rep.* 27 D11
Nitriansky □, *Slovak Rep.* 27 C11
Nittenau, *Germany* 25 F8
Niuafo'ou, *Tonga* 91 B11
Niue, *Cook Is.* 97 J11
Niulan Jiang →, *China* 58 D4
Niut, *Indonesia* 62 D4
Niutou Shan, *China* 59 C13
Niuzhuang, *China* 57 D12
Nivala, *Finland* 8 E21
Nivelles, *Belgium* 17 D4
Nivernais, *France* 19 E10
Niwas, *India* 69 H9
Nixon, *U.S.A.* 113 L6
Nizamabad, *India* 66 K11
Nizamghat, *India* 67 E19
Nizhne Kolymsk, *Russia* 51 C17
Nizhnegorskiy = Nyzhnohirskyy, *Ukraine* 47 K8
Nizhnekamsk, *Russia* 48 C10
Nizhneudinsk, *Russia* 51 D10
Nizhnevartovsk, *Russia* 50 C8
Nizhniy Chir, *Russia* 49 F6
Nizhniy Lomov, *Russia* 48 D6
Nizhniy Novgorod, *Russia* 48 B7
Nizhniy Tagil, *Russia* 50 D6
Nizhyn, *Ukraine* 47 G6
Nizina Mazowiecka, *Poland* 45 F8
Nizip, *Turkey* 70 B3
Nízké Tatry, *Slovak Rep.* 27 C12
Nízký Jeseník, *Czech Rep.* 27 B10
Nizza Monferrato, *Italy* 28 D5
Njakwa, *Malawi* 87 E3
Njanji, *Zambia* 87 E3
Njegoš, *Montenegro, Yug.* 40 D2
Njinjo, *Tanzania* 87 D4
Njombe, *Tanzania* 87 D3
Njombe →, *Tanzania* 86 D4
Njurundabommen, *Sweden* 10 B11
Nkambe, *Cameroon* 83 D7
Nkana, *Zambia* 87 E2
Nkandla, *S. Africa* 89 D5
Nkawkaw, *Ghana* 83 D4
Nkayi, *Zimbabwe* 87 F2
Nkhotakota, *Malawi* 87 E3
Nkongsamba, *Cameroon* 83 E6
Nkurenkuru, *Namibia* 88 B2
Nkwanta, *Ghana* 82 D4
Nmai →, *Burma* 58 F2
Noakhali = Maijdi, *Bangla.* 67 H17
Nobel, *Canada* 110 A4
Nobeoka, *Japan* 55 H5
Noblejas, *Spain* 34 F7
Noblesville, *U.S.A.* 108 E3
Noce →, *Italy* 28 B8
Nocera Inferiore, *Italy* 31 B7
Nocera Umbra, *Italy* 29 E9
Noci, *Italy* 31 B10
Nocona, *U.S.A.* 113 J6
Nocrich, *Romania* 43 E9
Noda, *Japan* 55 G9
Nogales, *Mexico* 118 A2
Nogales, *U.S.A.* 115 L8
Nogaro, *France* 20 E3
Nogat →, *Poland* 44 D6
Nōgata, *Japan* 55 H5
Nogent, *France* 19 D12
Nogent-le-Rotrou, *France* 18 D7
Nogent-sur-Seine, *France* 19 D10
Noggerup, *Australia* 93 F2
Noginsk, *Moskva, Russia* 46 E10
Noginsk, *Tunguska, Russia* 51 C10
Nogoa →, *Australia* 94 C4
Nogoyá, *Argentina* 126 C4
Nógrád □, *Hungary* 42 C4
Noguera Pallaresa →, *Spain* 32 D5
Noguera Ribagorzana →, *Spain* 32 D5
Nohar, *India* 68 E6
Nohfelden, *Germany* 25 F3
Nohta, *India* 69 H8
Noia, *Spain* 34 C2
Noire, Montagne, *France* 20 E6
Noires, Mts., *France* 18 D3
Noirétable, *France* 20 C7
Noirmoutier, Î. de, *France* 18 F4
Noirmoutier-en-l'Île, *France* 18 F4
Nojane, *Botswana* 88 C3
Nojima-Zaki, *Japan* 55 G9
Nok Kundi, *Pakistan* 66 E3
Nokaneng, *Botswana* 88 B3
Nokia, *Finland* 9 F20
Nokomis, *Canada* 105 C8
Nokomis L., *Canada* 105 B8
Nol, *Sweden* 11 G6
Nola, *C.A.R.* 84 D3
Nola, *Italy* 31 B7
Nolay, *France* 19 F11
Noli, C. di, *Italy* 28 D5
Nolinsk, *Russia* 48 B9
Noma Omuramba →, *Namibia* 88 B3
Nombre de Dios, *Panama* 120 E4
Nome, *U.S.A.* 100 B3
Nomo-Zaki, *Japan* 55 H4
Nonacho L., *Canada* 105 A7
Nonancourt, *France* 18 D8
Nonda, *Australia* 94 C3
None, *Italy* 28 D4
Nong Chang, *Thailand* 64 E2
Nong Het, *Laos* 64 C4
Nong Khai, *Thailand* 64 D4
Nong'an, *China* 57 B13
Nongoma, *S. Africa* 89 D5
Nonoava, *Mexico* 118 B3
Nonoava →, *Mexico* 118 B3
Nonthaburi, *Thailand* 64 F3
Nontron, *France* 20 C4
Nonza, *France* 21 F13
Noonamah, *Australia* 92 B5
Noord Brabant □, *Neths.* 17 C5
Noord Holland □, *Neths.* 17 B4
Noordbeveland, *Neths.* 17 C3
Noordoostpolder, *Neths.* 17 B5
Noordwijk, *Neths.* 17 B4
Nootka I., *Canada* 104 D3
Nopiming Prov. Park, *Canada* 105 C9
Nora, *Eritrea* 81 D5
Nora, *Sweden* 10 E9
Noralee, *Canada* 104 C3
Noranda = Rouyn-Noranda, *Canada* 102 C4
Norberg, *Sweden* 10 D9
Nórcia, *Italy* 29 F10
Norco, *U.S.A.* 117 M9
Nord □, *France* 19 B10
Nord-Kivu □, *Dem. Rep. of the Congo* 86 C2
Nord-Ostsee-Kanal, *Germany* 24 A5
Nord-Pas-de-Calais □, *France* 19 B9
Nordaustlandet, *Svalbard* 4 B9
Nordborg, *Denmark* 11 J3
Nordby, *Denmark* 11 J2
Norddeich, *Germany* 24 B3
Nordegg, *Canada* 104 C5
Norden, *Germany* 24 B3
Nordenham, *Germany* 24 B4
Norderney, *Germany* 24 B3
Norderstedt, *Germany* 24 B6
Nordfjord, *Norway* 9 F11
Nordfriesische Inseln, *Germany* 24 A4
Nordhausen, *Germany* 24 D6
Nordhorn, *Germany* 24 C3
Norðoyar, *Færoe Is.* 8 E9
Nordingrå, *Sweden* 10 B12
Nordjyllands Amtskommune □, *Denmark* 11 G4
Nordkapp, *Norway* 8 A21
Nordkapp, *Svalbard* 4 A9
Nordkinn = Kinnarodden, *Norway* 6 A11
Nordkinn-halvøya, *Norway* 8 A22
Nördlingen, *Germany* 25 G6
Nordrhein-Westfalen □, *Germany* 24 D3
Nordstrand, *Germany* 24 A4
Nordvik, *Russia* 51 B12
Nore →, *Ireland* 15 D4
Norfolk, *Nebr., U.S.A.* 112 D6
Norfolk, *Va., U.S.A.* 108 G7
Norfolk □, *U.K.* 13 E8
Norfolk I., *Pac. Oc.* 96 K8
Norfork L., *U.S.A.* 113 G8
Norilsk, *Russia* 51 C9
Norma, Mt., *Australia* 94 C3
Normal, *U.S.A.* 112 E10
Norman, *U.S.A.* 113 H6
Norman →, *Australia* 94 B3
Norman Wells, *Canada* 100 B7
Normanby →, *Australia* 94 A3
Normandin, *Canada* 102 C5
Normanhurst, Mt., *Australia* 93 E3
Normanton, *Australia* 94 B3
Normétal, *Canada* 102 C4
Norquay, *Canada* 105 C8
Norquinco, *Argentina* 128 E2
Norra Dellen, *Sweden* 10 C10
Norra Ulvön, *Sweden* 10 A12
Norrahammar, *Sweden* 11 G8
Norrbotten □, *Sweden* 8 C19
Nørre Åby, *Denmark* 11 J3
Nørre Alslev, *Denmark* 11 K5
Nørresundby, *Denmark* 11 G3
Norrhult, *Sweden* 11 G9
Norris Point, *Canada* 103 C8
Norristown, *U.S.A.* 111 F9
Norrköping, *Sweden* 11 F10
Norrland, *Sweden* 9 E16
Norrsundet, *Sweden* 10 D11
Norrtälje, *Sweden* 10 E12
Norseman, *Australia* 93 F3
Norsk, *Russia* 51 D14
Norte, Pta. del, *Canary Is.* 37 G2
Norte, Serra do, *Brazil* 124 F7
North, C., *Canada* 103 C7
North Adams, *U.S.A.* 111 D11
North Arm, *Canada* 104 A5
North Augusta, *U.S.A.* 109 J5
North Ayrshire □, *U.K.* 14 F4
North Bass I., *U.S.A.* 110 E2
North Battleford, *Canada* 105 C7
North Bay, *Canada* 102 C4
North Belcher Is., *Canada* 102 A4
North Bend, *Oreg., U.S.A.* 114 E1
North Bend, *Pa., U.S.A.* 110 E7
North Bend, *Wash., U.S.A.* 116 C5
North Bennington, *U.S.A.* 111 D11
North Berwick, *U.K.* 14 E6
North Berwick, *U.S.A.* 111 C14
North C., *Canada* 103 C7
North C., *N.Z.* 91 F4
North Canadian →, *U.S.A.* 113 H7
North Canton, *U.S.A.* 110 F3
North Cape = Nordkapp, *Norway* 8 A21
North Cape = Nordkapp, *Svalbard* 4 A9
North Caribou L., *Canada* 102 B1
North Carolina □, *U.S.A.* 109 H6
North Cascades National Park, *U.S.A.* 114 B3
North Channel, *Canada* 102 C3
North Channel, *U.K.* 14 F3
North Charleston, *U.S.A.* 109 J6
North Chicago, *U.S.A.* 108 D2
North Creek, *U.S.A.* 111 C11
North Dakota □, *U.S.A.* 112 B5
North Downs, *U.K.* 13 F8
North East, *U.S.A.* 110 D5
North East Frontier Agency = Arunachal Pradesh □, *India* 67 F19
North East Lincolnshire □, *U.K.* 12 D7
North Eastern □, *Kenya* 86 B5
North Esk →, *U.K.* 14 E6
North European Plain, *Europe* 6 E10
North Foreland, *U.K.* 13 F9
North Fork, *U.S.A.* 116 H7
North Fork American →, *U.S.A.* 116 G5
North Fork Feather →, *U.S.A.* 116 F5
North Fork Grand →, *U.S.A.* 112 C3
North Fork Red →, *U.S.A.* 113 H5
North Frisian Is. = Nordfriesische Inseln, *Germany* 24 A4
North Gower, *Canada* 111 A9
North Hd., *Australia* 93 F1
North Henik L., *Canada* 105 A9
North Highlands, *U.S.A.* 116 G5
North Horr, *Kenya* 86 B4
North I., *Kenya* 86 B4
North I., *N.Z.* 91 H5
North Kingsville, *U.S.A.* 110 E4
North Knife →, *Canada* 105 B10
North Koel →, *India* 69 G10
North Korea ■, *Asia* 57 E14
North Lakhimpur, *India* 67 F19
North Lanarkshire □, *U.K.* 14 F5
North Las Vegas, *U.S.A.* 117 J11
North Lincolnshire □, *U.K.* 12 D7
North Little Rock, *U.S.A.* 113 H8
North Loup →, *U.S.A.* 112 E5
North Magnetic Pole, *Canada* 4 B2
North Minch, *U.K.* 14 C3
North Moose L., *Canada* 105 C8
North Myrtle Beach, *U.S.A.* 109 J6
North Nahanni →, *Canada* 104 A4
North Olmsted, *U.S.A.* 110 E3
North Ossetia □, *Russia* 49 J7
North Pagai, I. = Pagai Utara, Pulau, *Indonesia* 62 E2
North Palisade, *U.S.A.* 116 H8
North Platte, *U.S.A.* 112 E4
North Platte →, *U.S.A.* 112 E4
North Pole, *Arctic* 4 A
North Portal, *Canada* 105 D8
North Powder, *U.S.A.* 114 D5
North Pt., *U.S.A.* 110 A1
North Rhine Westphalia = Nordrhein-Westfalen □, *Germany* 24 D3
North River, *Canada* 103 B8
North Ronaldsay, *U.K.* 14 B6
North Saskatchewan →, *Canada* 105 C7
North Sea, *Europe* 6 D6
North Seal →, *Canada* 105 B9
North Somerset □, *U.K.* 13 F5
North Sporades = Vóriai Sporádhes, *Greece* 38 B5
North Sydney, *Canada* 103 C7
North Syracuse, *U.S.A.* 111 C8

North Taranaki Bight, *N.Z.* ... **91 H5**
North Thompson →, *Canada* .. **104 C4**
North Tonawanda, *U.S.A.* **110 C6**
North Troy, *U.S.A.* **111 B12**
North Truchas Pk., *U.S.A.* **115 J11**
North Twin I., *Canada* **102 B4**
North Tyne →, *U.K.* **12 B5**
North Uist, *U.K.* **14 D1**
North Vancouver, *Canada* **104 D4**
North Vernon, *U.S.A.* **108 F3**
North Wabasca L., *Canada* **104 B6**
North Walsham, *U.K.* **12 E9**
North-West □, *S. Africa* **88 D4**
North West C., *Australia* **92 D1**
North West Christmas I. Ridge, *Pac. Oc.* **97 G11**
North West Frontier □, *Pakistan* **68 C4**
North West Highlands, *U.K.* ... **14 D4**
North West River, *Canada* **103 B7**
North Western □, *Zambia* **87 E2**
North Wildwood, *U.S.A.* **108 F8**
North York Moors, *U.K.* **12 C7**
North Yorkshire □, *U.K.* **12 C6**
Northallerton, *U.K.* **12 C6**
Northam, *Australia* **93 F2**
Northam, *S. Africa* **88 C4**
Northampton, *Australia* **93 E1**
Northampton, *U.K.* **13 E7**
Northampton, *Mass., U.S.A.* ... **111 D12**
Northampton, *Pa., U.S.A.* **111 F9**
Northamptonshire □, *U.K.* **13 E7**
Northbridge, *U.S.A.* **111 D13**
Northcliffe, *Australia* **93 F2**
Northeast Providence Chan., *W. Indies* **120 A4**
Northeim, *Germany* **24 D6**
Northern □, *Ghana* **83 D4**
Northern □, *Malawi* **87 E3**
Northern □, *Zambia* **87 E3**
Northern Areas □, *Pakistan* ... **69 A5**
Northern Cape □, *S. Africa* ... **88 D3**
Northern Circars, *India* **67 L13**
Northern Indian L., *Canada* ... **105 B9**
Northern Ireland □, *U.K.* **15 B5**
Northern Light L., *Canada* **102 C1**
Northern Marianas ■, *Pac. Oc.* **96 F6**
Northern Province □, *S. Leone* **82 D2**
Northern Province □, *S. Africa* **89 C4**
Northern Territory □, *Australia* **92 D5**
Northfield, *Minn., U.S.A.* **112 C8**
Northfield, *Vt., U.S.A.* **111 B12**
Northland □, *N.Z.* **91 F4**
Northome, *U.S.A.* **112 B7**
Northport, *Ala., U.S.A.* **109 J2**
Northport, *Wash., U.S.A.* **114 B5**
Northumberland □, *U.K.* **12 B6**
Northumberland, C., *Australia* . **95 F3**
Northumberland Is., *Australia* . **94 C4**
Northumberland Str., *Canada* . **103 C7**
Northville, *U.S.A.* **111 C10**
Northwest Providence Channel, *W. Indies* **120 A4**
Northwest Territories □, *Canada* **100 B9**
Northwood, *Iowa, U.S.A.* **112 D8**
Northwood, *N. Dak., U.S.A.* ... **112 B6**
Norton, *U.S.A.* **112 F5**
Norton, *Zimbabwe* **87 F3**
Norton Sd., *U.S.A.* **100 B3**
Nortorf, *Germany* **24 A5**
Norwalk, *Calif., U.S.A.* **117 M8**
Norwalk, *Conn., U.S.A.* **111 E11**
Norwalk, *Iowa, U.S.A.* **112 E8**
Norwalk, *Ohio, U.S.A.* **110 E2**
Norway, *Maine, U.S.A.* **109 C10**
Norway, *Mich., U.S.A.* **108 C2**
Norway ■, *Europe* **8 E14**
Norway House, *Canada* **105 C9**
Norwegian Sea, *Atl. Oc.* **4 C8**
Norwich, *Canada* **110 D4**
Norwich, *U.K.* **13 E9**
Norwich, *Conn., U.S.A.* **111 E12**
Norwich, *N.Y., U.S.A.* **111 D9**
Norwood, *Canada* **110 B7**
Norwood, *U.S.A.* **111 B10**
Noshiro, *Japan* **54 D10**
Nosivka, *Ukraine* **47 G6**
Nosovka = Nosivka, *Ukraine* .. **47 G6**
Noşratābād, *Iran* **71 D8**
Noss Hd., *U.K.* **14 C5**
Nossebro, *Sweden* **11 F6**
Nossob →, *S. Africa* **88 D3**
Nossombougou, *Mali* **82 C3**
Nosy Barren, *Madag.* **85 H8**
Nosy Be, *Madag.* **85 G9**
Nosy Boraha, *Madag.* **89 B8**
Nosy Lava, *Madag.* **89 A8**
Nosy Varika, *Madag.* **89 C8**
Noteć →, *Poland* **45 F2**
Notikewin →, *Canada* **104 B5**
Notio Aigaio = Notios Aiyaíon □ **39 E7**
Notios Aiyaíon □ **39 E7**
Notios Evvoïkos Kólpos, *Greece* **38 C5**
Noto, *Italy* **31 F8**
Noto, G. di, *Italy* **31 F8**
Notodden, *Norway* **9 G13**
Notre Dame B., *Canada* **103 C8**
Notre Dame de Koartac = Quaqtaq, *Canada* **101 B13**
Notre-Dame-des-Bois, *Canada* **111 A13**
Notre Dame d'Ivugivic = Ivujivik, *Canada* **101 B12**
Notre-Dame-du-Nord, *Canada* **102 C4**
Notsé, *Togo* **83 D5**
Nottawasaga B., *Canada* **110 B4**
Nottaway →, *Canada* **102 B4**
Nottingham, *U.K.* **12 E6**
Nottingham, City of □, *U.K.* ... **12 E6**
Nottingham I., *Canada* **101 B12**
Nottinghamshire □, *U.K.* **12 D6**
Nottoway →, *U.S.A.* **108 G7**
Notwane →, *Botswana* **88 C4**
Nouâdhibou, *Mauritania* **78 D2**
Nouâdhibou, Ras, *Mauritania* . **78 D2**
Nouakchott, *Mauritania* **82 B1**
Nouâmghâr, *Mauritania* **82 B1**
Nouméa, *N. Cal.* **96 K8**
Nouna, *Burkina Faso* **82 C4**
Noupoort, *S. Africa* **88 E3**
Nouveau Comptoir = Wemindji, *Canada* **102 B4**
Nouvelle-Amsterdam, I., *Ind. Oc.* **3 F13**
Nouvelle-Calédonie = New Caledonia ■, *Pac. Oc.* **96 K8**
Nouzonville, *France* **19 C11**
Nová Baňa, *Slovak Rep.* **27 C11**
Nová Bystřice, *Czech Rep.* **26 B8**
Nova Casa Nova, *Brazil* **125 E10**
Nova Esperança, *Brazil* **127 A5**
Nova Friburgo, *Brazil* **127 A7**
Nova Gaia = Cambundi-Catembo, *Angola* **84 G3**
Nova Gorica, *Slovenia* **29 C10**
Nova Gradiška, *Croatia* **42 E2**
Nova Iguaçu, *Brazil* **127 A7**
Nova Iorque, *Brazil* **125 E10**
Nova Kakhovka, *Ukraine* **47 J7**
Nova Lamego, *Guinea-Biss.* ... **82 C2**
Nova Lima, *Brazil* **127 A7**
Nova Lisboa = Huambo, *Angola* **85 G3**
Nova Lusitânia, *Mozam.* **87 F3**
Nova Mambone, *Mozam.* **89 C6**
Nova Odesa, *Ukraine* **47 J6**
Nová Paka, *Czech Rep.* **26 A8**
Nova Pavova, *Serbia, Yug.* **42 F5**
Nova Scotia □, *Canada* **103 C7**
Nova Siri, *Italy* **31 B9**
Nova Sofala, *Mozam.* **89 C5**
Nova Varoš, *Serbia, Yug.* **40 C3**
Nova Venécia, *Brazil* **125 G10**
Nova Zagora, *Bulgaria* **41 D10**
Novaci, *Macedonia* **40 E5**
Novaci, *Romania* **43 E8**
Novafeltria, *Italy* **29 E9**
Novaleksandrovskaya = Novoaleksandrovsk, *Russia* . **49 H5**
Novannenskiy = Novoannenskiy, *Russia* **48 E6**
Novar, *Canada* **110 A5**
Novara, *Italy* **28 C5**
Novato, *U.S.A.* **116 G4**
Novaya Kakhovka = Nova Kakhovka, *Ukraine* **47 J7**
Novaya Kazanka, *Kazakstan* .. **49 F9**
Novaya Ladoga, *Russia* **46 B7**
Novaya Lyalya, *Russia* **50 D7**
Novaya Sibir, Ostrov, *Russia* .. **51 B16**
Novaya Zemlya, *Russia* **50 B6**
Nové Město, *Slovak Rep.* **27 C10**
Nové Město na Moravě, *Czech Rep.* **26 B9**
Nové Město nad Metují, *Czech Rep.* **27 A9**
Nové Zámky, *Slovak Rep.* **27 C11**
Novelda, *Spain* **33 G4**
Novellara, *Italy* **28 D7**
Noventa Vicentina, *Italy* **29 C8**
Novgorod, *Russia* **46 C6**
Novgorod-Severskiy = Novhorod-Siverskyy, *Ukraine* **47 G7**
Novhorod-Siverskyy, *Ukraine* . **47 G7**
Novi Bečej, *Serbia, Yug.* **42 E5**
Novi Iskar, *Bulgaria* **40 D7**
Novi Kneževac, *Serbia, Yug.* ... **42 D5**
Novi Lígure, *Italy* **28 D5**
Novi Pazar, *Bulgaria* **41 C11**
Novi Pazar, *Serbia, Yug.* **40 C4**
Novi Sad, *Serbia, Yug.* **42 E4**
Novi Slankamen, *Serbia, Yug.* . **42 E5**
Novi Travnik, *Bos.-H.* **42 F2**
Novi Vinodolski, *Croatia* **29 C11**
Novigrad, *Istra, Croatia* **29 C10**
Novigrad, *Zadar, Croatia* **29 D12**
Novigradsko More, *Croatia* ... **29 D12**
Nôvo Hamburgo, *Brazil* **127 B5**
Novo Mesto, *Slovenia* **29 C12**
Novo Miloševo, *Serbia, Yug.* ... **42 E5**
Novo Remanso, *Brazil* **125 E10**
Novoaleksandrovsk, *Russia* ... **49 H5**
Novoannenskiy, *Russia* **48 E6**
Novoataysk, *Russia* **50 D9**
Novoazovsk, *Ukraine* **47 J10**
Novocheboksarsk, *Russia* **48 B8**
Novocherkassk, *Russia* **49 G5**
Novodevichye, *Russia* **48 D9**
Novogrudok = Navahrudak, *Belarus* **46 F3**
Novohrad-Volynskyy, *Ukraine* . **47 G4**
Novokachalinsk, *Russia* **54 B6**
Novokazalinsk = Zhangaqazaly, *Kazakstan* **50 E7**
Novokhopersk, *Russia* **48 E5**
Novokuybyshevsk, *Russia* **48 D9**
Novokuznetsk, *Russia* **50 D9**
Novomirgorod, *Ukraine* **47 H6**
Novomoskovsk, *Russia* **46 E10**
Novomoskovsk, *Ukraine* **47 H8**
Novopolotsk = Navapolatsk, *Belarus* **46 E5**
Novorossiysk, *Russia* **47 K9**
Novorybnoye, *Russia* **51 B11**
Novorzhev, *Russia* **46 D5**
Novosej, *Albania* **40 E4**
Novoselytsya, *Ukraine* **47 H4**
Novoshakhtinsk, *Russia* **47 J10**
Novosibirsk, *Russia* **50 D9**
Novosibirskiye Ostrova, *Russia* **51 B15**
Novosil, *Russia* **47 F9**
Novosokolniki, *Russia* **46 D6**
Novotitarovskaya, *Russia* **49 H4**
Novotroitsk, *Russia* **50 D6**
Novoukrayinka, *Ukraine* **47 H6**
Novouljanovsk, *Russia* **48 C9**
Novouzensk, *Russia* **48 E9**
Novovolynsk, *Ukraine* **47 G3**
Novovoronezhskiy, *Russia* **47 G10**
Novozybkov, *Russia* **47 F6**
Novska, *Croatia* **29 C14**
Novvy Urengoy, *Russia* **50 C8**
Nový Bor, *Czech Rep.* **26 A7**
Novy Bug = Novyy Buh, *Ukraine* **47 J7**
Nový Bydžov, *Czech Rep.* **26 A8**
Novy Dwór Mazowiecki, *Poland* **45 F7**
Nový Jičín, *Czech Rep.* **27 B11**
Novyy Afon, *Georgia* **49 J5**
Novyy Buh, *Ukraine* **47 J7**
Novyy Oskol, *Russia* **47 G9**
Novyy Port, *Russia* **50 C8**
Now Shahr, *Iran* **71 B6**
Nowa Deba, *Poland* **45 H8**
Nowa Ruda, *Poland* **45 H3**
Nowa Sarzyna, *Poland* **45 H9**
Nowa Sól, *Poland* **45 G2**
Nowata, *U.S.A.* **113 G7**
Nowbarān, *Iran* **71 C6**
Nowe, *Poland* **44 E5**
Nowe Miasteczko, *Poland* **45 G2**
Nowe Miasto, *Poland* **45 G7**
Nowe Miasto Lubawskie, *Poland* **44 E6**
Nowe Skalmierzyce, *Poland* ... **45 G4**
Nowe Warpno, *Poland* **44 E1**
Nowghāb, *Iran* **71 C8**
Nowgong, *Assam, India* **67 F18**
Nowgong, *Mad. P., India* **69 G8**
Nowogard, *Poland* **44 E2**
Nowogród, *Poland* **45 E8**
Nowogród Bobrzanski, *Poland* **45 G2**
Nowogrodziec, *Poland* **45 G2**
Nowra, *Australia* **95 E5**
Nowshera, *Pakistan* **66 C8**
Nowy Dwór Gdański, *Poland* .. **44 D6**
Nowy Sącz, *Poland* **45 J7**
Nowy Staw, *Poland* **44 D6**
Nowy Targ, *Poland* **45 J7**
Nowy Tomyśl, *Poland* **45 F3**
Nowy Wiśnicz, *Poland* **45 J7**
Noxen, *U.S.A.* **111 E8**
Noxon, *U.S.A.* **114 C6**
Noyabr'sk, *Russia* **50 C8**
Noyant, *France* **18 E7**
Noyers, *France* **19 E10**
Noyon, *France* **19 C9**
Noyon, *Mongolia* **56 C2**
Nozay, *France* **18 E5**
Nqutu, *S. Africa* **89 D5**
Nsanje, *Malawi* **87 F4**
Nsawam, *Ghana* **83 D4**
Nsomba, *Zambia* **87 E2**
Nsukka, *Nigeria* **83 D6**
Ntui, *Cameroon* **83 E7**
Nu Jiang →, *China* **58 E2**
Nu Shan, *China* **58 E2**
Nuba Mts. = Nubah, Jibalan, *Sudan* **81 E3**
Nubah, Jibalan, *Sudan* **81 E3**
Nubia, *Africa* **76 D7**
Nubian Desert = Nûbîya, Es Sahrâ en, *Sudan* **80 C3**
Nûbîya, Es Sahrâ en, *Sudan* .. **80 C3**
Nubledo, *Spain* **34 B5**
Nuboai, *Indonesia* **63 E9**
Nubra →, *India* **69 B7**
Nucet, *Romania* **42 D7**
Nueces →, *U.S.A.* **113 M6**
Nueltin L., *Canada* **105 A9**
Nueva Asunción □, *Paraguay* . **126 A3**
Nueva Carteya, *Spain* **35 H6**
Nueva Gerona, *Cuba* **120 B3**
Nueva Palmira, *Uruguay* **126 C4**
Nueva Rosita, *Mexico* **118 B4**
Nueva San Salvador, *El Salv.* .. **120 D2**
Nueva Tabarca, *Spain* **33 G4**
Nuéve de Julio, *Argentina* **126 D3**
Nuevitas, *Cuba* **120 B4**
Nuevo, G., *Argentina* **128 E4**
Nuevo Casas Grandes, *Mexico* . **118 A3**
Nuevo Guerrero, *Mexico* **119 B5**
Nuevo Laredo, *Mexico* **119 B5**
Nuevo León □, *Mexico* **118 C5**
Nuevo Rocafuerte, *Ecuador* ... **124 D3**
Nugget Pt., *N.Z.* **91 M2**
Nugrus, Gebel, *Egypt* **80 C3**
Nuhaka, *N.Z.* **91 H6**
Nuits-St-Georges, *France* **19 E11**
Nukey Bluff, *Australia* **95 E2**
Nukheila, *Sudan* **80 D2**
Nukhuyb, *Iraq* **70 C4**
Nuku'alofa, *Tonga* **91 E12**
Nukus, *Uzbekistan* **50 E6**
Nules, *Spain* **32 F4**
Nullagine, *Australia* **92 D3**
Nullagine →, *Australia* **92 D3**
Nullarbor, *Australia* **93 F5**
Nullarbor Plain, *Australia* **93 F4**
Numalla, L., *Australia* **95 D3**
Numan, *Nigeria* **83 D7**
Numata, *Japan* **55 F9**
Numatinna →, *Sudan* **81 F2**
Numazu, *Japan* **55 G9**
Numbulwar, *Australia* **94 A2**
Numfoor, *Indonesia* **63 E8**
Numurkah, *Australia* **95 F4**
Nunaksaluk I., *Canada* **103 A7**
Nunap Isua, *Greenland* **101 C15**
Nunavut □, *Canada* **101 B11**
Nunda, *U.S.A.* **110 D7**
Nungarin, *Australia* **93 F2**
Nungo, *Mozam.* **87 E4**
Nungwe, *Tanzania* **86 C3**
Nunivak I., *U.S.A.* **100 B3**
Nunkun, *India* **69 C7**
Núoro, *Italy* **30 B2**
Nūrābād, *Iran* **71 E8**
Nure →, *Italy* **28 C6**
Nuremberg = Nürnberg, *Germany* **25 F7**
Nuri, *Mexico* **118 B3**
Nuriootpa, *Australia* **95 E2**
Nuristān □, *Afghan.* **66 B7**
Nurlat, *Russia* **48 C10**
Nurmes, *Finland* **8 E23**
Nürnberg, *Germany* **25 F7**
Nurpur, *Pakistan* **68 D4**
Nurra, La, *Italy* **30 B1**
Nurran, L. = Terewah, L., *Australia* **95 D4**
Nurrari Lakes, *Australia* **93 E5**
Nurri, *Italy* **30 C2**
Nürtingen, *Germany* **25 G5**
Nurzec →, *Poland* **45 F9**
Nus, *Italy* **28 C4**
Nusa Barung, *Indonesia* **63 H15**
Nusa Kambangan, *Indonesia* .. **63 G13**
Nusa Tenggara Barat □, *Indonesia* **62 F5**
Nusa Tenggara Timur □, *Indonesia* **63 F6**
Nusaybin, *Turkey* **73 D9**
Nushki, *Pakistan* **68 E2**
Nuuk, *Greenland* **101 B14**
Nuwakot, *Nepal* **69 E10**
Nuweiba', *Egypt* **70 D2**
Nuwerus, *S. Africa* **88 E2**
Nuweveldberge, *S. Africa* **88 E3**
Nuyts, C., *Australia* **93 F5**
Nuyts, Pt., *Australia* **93 G2**
Nuyts Arch., *Australia* **95 E1**
Nxau-Nxau, *Botswana* **88 B3**
Nyaake, *Liberia* **82 E3**
Nyabing, *Australia* **93 F2**
Nyack, *U.S.A.* **111 E11**
Nyagan, *Russia* **50 C7**
Nyahanga, *Tanzania* **86 C3**
Nyahua, *Tanzania* **86 D3**
Nyahururu, *Kenya* **86 B4**
Nyainqentanglha Shan, *China* . **60 C4**
Nyakanazi, *Tanzania* **86 C3**
Nyakrom, *Ghana* **83 D4**
Nyâlâ, *Sudan* **81 E1**
Nyamandhlovu, *Zimbabwe* **87 F2**
Nyambiti, *Tanzania* **86 C3**
Nyamlell, *Sudan* **81 F2**
Nyamwaga, *Tanzania* **86 C3**
Nyandekwa, *Tanzania* **86 C3**
Nyanding →, *Sudan* **81 F3**
Nyandoma, *Russia* **46 B11**
Nyangana, *Namibia* **88 B3**
Nyanguge, *Tanzania* **86 C3**
Nyankpala, *Ghana* **83 D4**
Nyanza, *Rwanda* **86 C2**
Nyanza □, *Kenya* **86 C3**
Nyanza-Lac, *Burundi* **86 C2**
Nyaponges, *Sudan* **81 F3**
Nyasa, L., *Africa* **87 E3**
Nyasvizh, *Belarus* **47 F4**
Nyazura, *Zimbabwe* **87 F3**
Nyazwidzi →, *Zimbabwe* **87 G3**
Nyborg, *Denmark* **11 J4**
Nybro, *Sweden* **11 H9**
Nyda, *Russia* **50 C8**
Nyeri, *Kenya* **86 C4**
Nyerol, *Sudan* **81 F3**
Nyhammar, *Sweden* **10 D8**
Nyinahin, *Ghana* **82 D4**
Nyíradony, *Hungary* **42 C6**
Nyírbátor, *Hungary* **42 C7**
Nyíregyháza, *Hungary* **42 C6**
Nykøbing, *Storstrøm, Denmark* **11 K5**
Nykøbing, *Vestsjælland, Denmark* **11 J5**
Nykøbing, *Viborg, Denmark* ... **11 H2**
Nyköping, *Sweden* **11 F11**
Nykroppa, *Sweden* **10 E8**
Nykvarn, *Sweden* **10 E11**
Nyland, *Sweden* **10 A11**
Nylstroom, *S. Africa* **89 C4**
Nymagee, *Australia* **95 E4**
Nymburk, *Czech Rep.* **26 A8**
Nynäshamn, *Sweden* **11 F11**
Nyngan, *Australia* **95 E4**
Nyoma Rap, *India* **69 C8**
Nyoman = Neman →, *Lithuania* **9 J19**
Nyon, *Switz.* **25 J2**
Nyong →, *Cameroon* **83 E6**
Nyons, *France* **21 D9**
Nyou, *Burkina Faso* **83 C4**
Nýrsko, *Czech Rep.* **26 B6**
Nysa, *Poland* **45 H4**
Nysa →, *Europe* **24 C10**
Nysa Kłodzka →, *Poland* **45 H4**
Nysäter, *Sweden* **10 E6**
Nyssa, *U.S.A.* **114 E5**
Nysted, *Denmark* **11 K5**
Nyunzu, *Dem. Rep. of the Congo* **86 D2**
Nyurba, *Russia* **51 C12**
Nyzhnohirskyy, *Ukraine* **47 K8**
Nzébéla, *Guinea* **82 D3**
Nzega, *Tanzania* **86 C3**
Nzérékoré, *Guinea* **82 D3**
Nzeto, *Angola* **84 F2**
Nzilo, Chutes de, *Dem. Rep. of the Congo* **87 E2**
Nzo →, *Ivory C.* **82 D3**
Nzubuka, *Tanzania* **86 C3**

O

O Barco, *Spain* **34 C4**
O Carballiño, *Spain* **34 C2**
O Corgo, *Spain* **34 C3**
O Pino, *Spain* **34 C2**
O Porriño, *Spain* **34 C2**
Ō-Shima, *Japan* **55 G9**
Oa, Mull of, *U.K.* **14 F2**
Oacoma, *U.S.A.* **112 D5**
Oahe, L., *U.S.A.* **112 C4**
Oahe Dam, *U.S.A.* **112 C4**
Oahu, *U.S.A.* **106 H16**
Oak Harbor, *U.S.A.* **116 B4**
Oak Hill, *U.S.A.* **108 G5**
Oak Ridge, *U.S.A.* **109 G3**
Oak View, *U.S.A.* **117 L7**
Oakan-Dake, *Japan* **54 C12**
Oakdale, *Calif., U.S.A.* **116 H6**
Oakdale, *La., U.S.A.* **113 K8**
Oakes, *U.S.A.* **112 B5**
Oakesdale, *U.S.A.* **114 C5**
Oakey, *Australia* **95 D5**
Oakfield, *U.S.A.* **110 C6**
Oakham, *U.K.* **13 E7**
Oakhurst, *U.S.A.* **116 H7**
Oakland, *U.S.A.* **116 H4**
Oakley, *Idaho, U.S.A.* **114 E7**
Oakley, *Kans., U.S.A.* **112 F4**
Oakover →, *Australia* **92 D3**
Oakridge, *U.S.A.* **114 E2**
Oakville, *Canada* **110 C5**
Oakville, *U.S.A.* **116 D3**
Oamaru, *N.Z.* **91 L3**
Oancea, *Romania* **43 E12**
Oasis, *Calif., U.S.A.* **117 M10**
Oasis, *Nev., U.S.A.* **116 H9**
Oates Land, *Antarctica* **5 C11**
Oatlands, *Australia* **94 G4**
Oatman, *U.S.A.* **117 K12**
Oaxaca, *Mexico* **119 D5**
Oaxaca □, *Mexico* **119 D5**
Ob →, *Russia* **50 C7**
Oba, *Canada* **102 C3**
Obala, *Cameroon* **83 E7**
Obama, *Japan* **55 G7**
Oban, *Nigeria* **83 D6**
Oban, *U.K.* **14 E3**
Obbia, *Somali Rep.* **74 F4**
Obera, *Argentina* **127 B4**
Oberammergau, *Germany* **25 H7**
Oberasbach, *Germany* **25 F6**
Oberbayern □, *Germany* **25 G7**
Oberdrauburg, *Austria* **26 E5**
Oberfranken □, *Germany* **25 E7**
Oberhausen, *Germany* **24 D2**
Oberkirch, *Germany* **25 G4**
Oberlausitz, *Germany* **24 D10**
Oberlin, *Kans., U.S.A.* **112 F4**
Oberlin, *La., U.S.A.* **113 K8**
Oberlin, *Ohio, U.S.A.* **110 E2**
Obernai, *France* **19 D14**
Oberndorf, *Germany* **25 G4**
Oberon, *Australia* **95 E4**
Oberösterreich □, *Austria* **26 C7**
Oberpfalz □, *Germany* **25 F8**
Oberpfälzer Wald, *Germany* ... **25 F8**
Oberstdorf, *Germany* **25 H6**
Oberursel, *Germany* **25 E4**
Oberwart, *Austria* **27 D9**
Obi, Kepulauan, *Indonesia* **63 E7**
Obi Is. = Obi, Kepulauan, *Indonesia* **63 E7**
Obiaruku, *Nigeria* **83 D6**
Óbidos, *Brazil* **125 D7**
Óbidos, *Portugal* **35 F1**
Obihiro, *Japan* **54 C11**
Obilatu, *Indonesia* **63 E7**
Obilnoye, *Russia* **49 G7**
Obing, *Germany* **25 G8**
Objat, *France* **20 C5**
Obluchye, *Russia* **51 E14**
Obninsk, *Russia* **46 E9**
Obo, *C.A.R.* **86 A2**
Oboa, Mt., *Uganda* **86 B3**
Obock, *Djibouti* **81 E5**
Oborniki, *Poland* **45 F3**
Oborniki Śląskie, *Poland* **45 G3**
Oboyan, *Russia* **47 G9**
Obozerskaya = Obozerskiy, *Russia* **50 C5**
Obozerskiy, *Russia* **50 C5**
Obrenovac, *Serbia, Yug.* **40 B4**
Obrovac, *Croatia* **29 D12**
Obruk, *Turkey* **72 C5**
Obrzycko, *Poland* **45 F3**
Observatory Inlet, *Canada* ... **104 B3**
Obshchi Syrt, *Russia* **6 E16**
Obskaya Guba, *Russia* **50 C8**
Obuasi, *Ghana* **83 D4**
Obubra, *Nigeria* **83 D6**
Obudu, *Nigeria* **83 D6**
Obwalden □, *Switz.* **25 J4**
Obzor, *Bulgaria* **41 D11**
Ocala, *U.S.A.* **109 L4**
Ocampo, *Chihuahua, Mexico* .. **118 B3**

Ocampo, *Tamaulipas, Mexico* 119 C5
Ocaña, *Spain* 34 F7
Ocanomowoc, *U.S.A.* 112 D10
Occidental, Cordillera, *Colombia* 122 C3
Ocean City, *Md., U.S.A.* 108 F8
Ocean City, *N.J., U.S.A.* 108 F8
Ocean City, *Wash., U.S.A.* 116 C2
Ocean Falls, *Canada* 104 C3
Ocean I. = Banaba, *Kiribati* 96 H8
Ocean Park, *U.S.A.* 116 D2
Oceano, *U.S.A.* 117 K6
Oceanport, *U.S.A.* 111 F10
Oceanside, *U.S.A.* 117 M9
Ochagavía, *Spain* 32 C3
Ochakiv, *Ukraine* 47 J6
Ochamchira, *Georgia* 49 J5
Ochil Hills, *U.K.* 14 E5
Ochsenfurt, *Germany* 25 F6
Ochsenhausen, *Germany* 25 G5
Ocilla, *U.S.A.* 109 K4
Ockelbo, *Sweden* 10 D10
Ocmulgee →, *U.S.A.* 109 K4
Ocna Mureş, *Romania* 43 D8
Ocna Sibiului, *Romania* 43 E9
Ocnele Mari, *Romania* 43 E9
Ocniţa, *Moldova* 43 B12
Oconee →, *U.S.A.* 109 K4
Oconto, *U.S.A.* 108 C2
Oconto Falls, *U.S.A.* 108 C1
Ocosingo, *Mexico* 119 D6
Ocotal, *Nic.* 120 D2
Ocotlán, *Mexico* 118 C4
Ocotlán de Morelos, *Mexico* 119 D5
Ocreza →, *Portugal* 35 F3
Ócsa, *Hungary* 42 C4
Octeville, *France* 18 C5
Oda, *Ghana* 83 D4
Ōda, *Japan* 55 G6
Oda, J., *Sudan* 80 C4
Ódáðahraun, *Iceland* 8 D5
Ödåkra, *Sweden* 11 H6
Odate, *Japan* 54 D10
Odawara, *Japan* 55 G9
Odda, *Norway* 9 F12
Odder, *Denmark* 11 J4
Odei →, *Canada* 105 B9
Odemira, *Portugal* 35 H2
Ödemiş, *Turkey* 39 C9
Odendaalsrus, *S. Africa* 88 D4
Odensbacken, *Sweden* 10 E9
Odense, *Denmark* 11 J4
Odenwald, *Germany* 25 F5
Oder →, *Europe* 24 B10
Oder-Havel Kanal, *Germany* 24 C10
Oderzo, *Italy* 29 C9
Odesa, *Ukraine* 47 J6
Ödeshög, *Sweden* 11 F8
Odessa = Odesa, *Ukraine* 47 J6
Odessa, *Canada* 111 B8
Odessa, *Tex., U.S.A.* 113 K3
Odessa, *Wash., U.S.A.* 114 C4
Odiakwe, *Botswana* 88 C4
Odiel →, *Spain* 35 H4
Odienné, *Ivory C.* 82 D3
Odintsovo, *Russia* 46 E9
Odiongan, *Phil.* 61 E4
Odobeşti, *Romania* 43 E12
Odolanów, *Poland* 45 G4
O'Donnell, *U.S.A.* 113 J4
Odorheiu Secuiesc, *Romania* 43 D10
Odoyevo, *Russia* 46 F9
Odra = Oder →, *Europe* 24 B10
Odra →, *Spain* 34 C6
Odžaci, *Serbia, Yug.* 42 E4
Odžak, *Bos.-H.* 42 E3
Odzi, *Zimbabwe* 89 B5
Odzi →, *Zimbabwe* 89 B5
Oebisfelde, *Germany* 24 C6
Oeiras, *Brazil* 125 E10
Oeiras, *Portugal* 35 G1
Oelrichs, *U.S.A.* 112 D3
Oelsnitz, *Germany* 25 E8
Oelwein, *U.S.A.* 112 D9
Oenpelli, *Australia* 92 B5
Oetz, *Austria* 26 D3
Of, *Turkey* 73 B9
Ofanto →, *Italy* 31 A9
Offa, *Nigeria* 83 D5
Offaly □, *Ireland* 15 C4
Offenbach, *Germany* 25 E4
Offenburg, *Germany* 25 G3
Offida, *Italy* 29 F10
Ofidhousa, *Greece* 39 E8
Ofotfjorden, *Norway* 8 B17
Ōfunato, *Japan* 54 E10
Oga, *Japan* 54 E9
Oga-Hantō, *Japan* 54 E9
Ogaden, *Ethiopia* 74 F3
Ōgaki, *Japan* 55 G8
Ogallala, *U.S.A.* 112 E4
Ogasawara Gunto, *Pac. Oc.* 52 G18
Ogbomosho, *Nigeria* 83 D5
Ogden, *U.S.A.* 114 F7
Ogdensburg, *U.S.A.* 111 B9
Ogeechee →, *U.S.A.* 109 K5
Ogilby, *U.S.A.* 117 N12
Oglio →, *Italy* 28 C7
Ogmore, *Australia* 94 C4
Ognon →, *France* 19 E12
Ogoja, *Nigeria* 83 D6
Ogoki, *Canada* 102 B2
Ogoki →, *Canada* 102 B2
Ogoki L., *Canada* 102 B2
Ogoki Res., *Canada* 102 B2
Ogooué →, *Gabon* 84 E1
Ogosta →, *Bulgaria* 40 C7
Ogowe = Ogooué →, *Gabon* 84 E1
Ogr = Sharafa, *Sudan* 81 E2
Ograźden, *Macedonia* 40 E6
Ogre, *Latvia* 9 H21
Ogrein, *Sudan* 80 D3
Ogulin, *Croatia* 29 C12
Ogun □, *Nigeria* 83 D5
Ogurchinskiy, Ostrov, *Turkmenistan* 71 B7
Oguta, *Nigeria* 83 D6
Ogwashi-Uku, *Nigeria* 83 D6
Ogwe, *Nigeria* 83 E6
Ohai, *N.Z.* 91 L2
Ohakune, *N.Z.* 91 H5
Ohata, *Japan* 54 D10
Ohau, L., *N.Z.* 91 L2
Ohio □, *U.S.A.* 110 F2
Ohio →, *U.S.A.* 108 G1
Ohře →, *Czech Rep.* 26 A7
Ohre →, *Germany* 24 C7
Ohrid, *Macedonia* 40 E4
Ohridsko Jezero, *Macedonia* 40 E4
Ohrigstad, *S. Africa* 89 C5
Öhringen, *Germany* 25 F5
Oi Qu, *China* 58 C2
Oiapoque, *Brazil* 125
Oikou, *China* 57 E9
Oil City, *U.S.A.* 110 E5
Oil Springs, *Canada* 110 D2
Oildale, *U.S.A.* 117 K7
Oinousa, *Greece* 39 C8
Oise □, *France* 19 C9
Oise →, *France* 19 C9
Ōita, *Japan* 55 H5
Ōita □, *Japan* 55 H5
Oiticica, *Brazil* 125 E10
Ojacaliente, *Mexico* 118 C4
Ojai, *U.S.A.* 117 L7
Ojinaga, *Mexico* 118 B4
Ojiya, *Japan* 55 F9
Ojos del Salado, Cerro, *Argentina* 126 B2
Oka →, *Russia* 48 B7
Okaba, *Indonesia* 63 F9
Okahandja, *Namibia* 88 C2
Okanagan L., *Canada* 104 D5
Okanogan, *U.S.A.* 114 B4
Okanogan →, *U.S.A.* 114 B4
Okány, *Hungary* 42 D6
Okaputa, *Namibia* 88 C2
Okara, *Pakistan* 68 D5
Okaukuejo, *Namibia* 88 B2
Okavango Swamps, *Botswana* 88 B3
Okaya, *Japan* 55 F9
Okayama, *Japan* 55 G6
Okayama □, *Japan* 55 G6
Okazaki, *Japan* 55 G8
Oke-Iho, *Nigeria* 83 D5
Okeechobee, *U.S.A.* 109 M5
Okeechobee, L., *U.S.A.* 109 M5
Okefenokee Swamp, *U.S.A.* 109 K4
Okehampton, *U.K.* 13 G4
Okene, *Nigeria* 83 D6
Oker →, *Germany* 24 C6
Okha, *India* 68 H3
Okha, *Russia* 51 D15
Ókhi Óros, *Greece* 38 C6
Okhotsk, *Russia* 51 D15
Okhotsk, Sea of, *Asia* 51 D15
Okhotskiy Perevoz, *Russia* 51 C14
Okhtyrka, *Ukraine* 47 G8
Oki-Shotō, *Japan* 55 F6
Okiep, *S. Africa* 88 D2
Okigwi, *Nigeria* 83 D6
Okija, *Nigeria* 83 D6
Okinawa □, *Japan* 55 L4
Okinawa-Guntō, *Japan* 55 L4
Okinawa-Jima, *Japan* 55 L4
Okino-erabu-Shima, *Japan* 55 L4
Okitipupa, *Nigeria* 83 D5
Oklahoma □, *U.S.A.* 113 H6
Oklahoma City, *U.S.A.* 113 H6
Okmulgee, *U.S.A.* 113 H7
Oknitsa = Ocniţa, *Moldova* 43 B12
Oko, W. →, *Sudan* 80 C4
Okolo, *Uganda* 86 B3
Okolona, *U.S.A.* 113 J10
Okombahe, *Namibia* 88 C2
Okonek, *Poland* 44 E3
Okotoks, *Canada* 104 C6
Okrika, *Nigeria* 83 E6
Oksibil, *Indonesia* 63 E10
Oktabrsk = Oktyabrsk, *Kazakstan* 50 E6
Oktyabrsk, *Kazakstan* 50 E6
Oktyabrsk, *Russia* 48 D9
Oktyabrskiy = Aktsyabrski, *Belarus* 47 F5
Oktyabrskiy, *Russia* 49 G5
Oktyabrskoy Revolyutsii, Ostrov, *Russia* 51 B10
Oktyabrskoye = Zhovtneve, *Ukraine* 47 J7
Okulovka, *Russia* 46 C7
Okuru, *N.Z.* 91 K2
Okushiri-Tō, *Japan* 54 C9
Okuta, *Nigeria* 83 D5
Okwa →, *Botswana* 88 C3
Ola, *U.S.A.* 113 H8
Ólafsfjörður, *Iceland* 8 C4
Ólafsvík, *Iceland* 8 D2
Olaine, *Latvia* 44 B10
Olancha, *U.S.A.* 117 J8
Olancha Pk., *U.S.A.* 117 J8
Olanchito, *Honduras* 120 C2
Öland, *Sweden* 11 H10
Ölands norra udde, *Sweden* 11 G11
Ölands södra udde, *Sweden* 11 H10
Olargues, *France* 20 E6
Olary, *Australia* 95 E3
Olascoaga, *Argentina* 126 D3
Olathe, *U.S.A.* 112 F7
Olavarría, *Argentina* 126 D3
Oława, *Poland* 45 H4
Olbernhau, *Germany* 24 E9
Ólbia, *Italy* 30 B2
Ólbia, G. di, *Italy* 30 B2
Olching, *Germany* 25 G7
Olcott, *U.S.A.* 110 C6
Old Bahama Chan. = Bahama, Canal Viejo de, *W. Indies* 120 B4
Old Baldy Pk. = San Antonio, Mt., *U.S.A.* 117 L9
Old Castile = Castilla y Leon □, *Spain* 34 D6
Old Crow, *Canada* 100 B6
Old Dale, *U.S.A.* 117 L11
Old Dongola, *Sudan* 80 D3
Old Forge, *N.Y., U.S.A.* 111 C10
Old Forge, *Pa., U.S.A.* 111 E9
Old Perlican, *Canada* 103 C9
Old Shinyanga, *Tanzania* 86 C3
Old Speck Mt., *U.S.A.* 111 B14
Old Town, *U.S.A.* 109 C11
Old Washington, *U.S.A.* 110 F3
Old Wives L., *Canada* 105 C7
Oldbury, *U.K.* 13 F5
Oldcastle, *Ireland* 15 C4
Oldeani, *Tanzania* 86 C4
Oldenburg, *Niedersachsen, Germany* 24 B4
Oldenburg, *Schleswig-Holstein, Germany* 24 A6
Oldenzaal, *Neths.* 17 B6
Oldham, *U.K.* 12 D5
Oldman →, *Canada* 104 D6
Oldmeldrum, *U.K.* 14 D6
Olds, *Canada* 104 C6
Oldziyt, *Mongolia* 56 B5
Olean, *U.S.A.* 110 D6
Olecko, *Poland* 44 D9
Oléggio, *Italy* 28 C5
Oleiros, *Portugal* 34 F3
Oleiros, *Spain* 34 B2
Olekma →, *Russia* 51 C13
Olekminsk, *Russia* 51 C13
Oleksandriya, *Kirovohrad, Ukraine* 47 H7
Oleksandriya, *Rivne, Ukraine* 47 G4
Oleksandrovka, *Ukraine* 47 H7
Olema, *U.S.A.* 116 G4
Olenek, *Russia* 51 C12
Olenek →, *Russia* 51 B13
Olenino, *Russia* 46 D7
Oléron, Î. d', *France* 20 C2
Oleśnica, *Poland* 45 G4
Olesno, *Poland* 45 H5
Olevsk, *Ukraine* 47 G4
Olga, *Russia* 51 E14
Olga, L., *Canada* 102 C4
Olga, Mt., *Australia* 93 E5
Ølgod, *Denmark* 11 J2
Olhão, *Portugal* 35 H3
Olib, *Croatia* 29 D11
Oliena, *Italy* 30 B2
Oliete, *Spain* 32 D4
Olifants →, *Africa* 89 C5
Olifants →, *Namibia* 88 C2
Olifantshoek, *S. Africa* 88 D3
Ólimbos, *Greece* 39 F9
Ólimbos, Óros, *Greece* 40 F6
Olímpia, *Brazil* 127 A6
Olinda, *Brazil* 125 E12
Olite, *Spain* 32 C3
Oliva, *Argentina* 126 C3
Oliva, *Spain* 33 G4
Oliva, Punta del, *Spain* 34 B5
Oliva de la Frontera, *Spain* 35 G4
Olivares, *Spain* 32 F2
Olivehurst, *U.S.A.* 116 F5
Oliveira de Azeméis, *Portugal* 34 E2
Oliveira do Douro, *Portugal* 34 D2
Olivenza, *Spain* 35 G3
Oliver, *Canada* 104 D5
Oliver L., *Canada* 105 B8
Olivet, *France* 19 E8
Olkhovka, *Russia* 48 F7
Olkusz, *Poland* 45 H6
Ollagüe, *Chile* 126 A2
Olmedo, *Spain* 34 D6
Olmeto, *France* 21 G12
Olney, *Ill., U.S.A.* 108 F1
Olney, *Tex., U.S.A.* 113 J5
Olofström, *Sweden* 11 H8
Oloma, *Cameroon* 83 E7
Olomane →, *Canada* 103 B7
Olomouc, *Czech Rep.* 27 B10
Olomoucký □, *Czech Rep.* 27 B10
Olonets, *Russia* 46 B7
Olongapo, *Phil.* 61 D4
Olonne-sur-Mer, *France* 20 B2
Oloron, Gave d' →, *France* 20 E2
Oloron-Ste-Marie, *France* 20 E3
Olot, *Spain* 32 C7
Olovo, *Bos.-H.* 42 F3
Olovyannaya, *Russia* 51 D12
Oloy →, *Russia* 51 C16
Olsberg, *Germany* 24 D4
Olshammar, *Sweden* 11 F8
Olshanka, *Ukraine* 47 H6
Olshany, *Ukraine* 47 G8
Olsztyn, *Poland* 44 E7
Olsztynek, *Poland* 44 E7
Olt □, *Romania* 43 F9
Olt →, *Romania* 43 G9
Olten, *Switz.* 25 H3
Olteniţa, *Romania* 43 F11
Olton, *U.S.A.* 113 H3
Oltu, *Turkey* 73 B9
Oluanpi, *Taiwan* 59 G13
Olula del Rio, *Spain* 33 H2
Olur, *Turkey* 73 B10
Olutanga, *Phil.* 61 H5
Olvega, *Spain* 32 D2
Olvera, *Spain* 35 J5
Olymbos, *Cyprus* 36 D12
Olympia, *Greece* 38 D3
Olympia, *U.S.A.* 116 D4
Olympic Dam, *Australia* 95 E2
Olympic Mts., *U.S.A.* 116 C3
Olympic Nat. Park, *U.S.A.* 116 C3
Olympus, *Cyprus* 36 E11
Olympus, Mt. = Ólimbos, Óros, *Greece* 40 F6
Olympus, Mt. = Uludağ, *Turkey* 41 F13
Olympus, Mt., *U.S.A.* 116 C3
Olyphant, *U.S.A.* 111 E9
Om →, *Russia* 50 D8
Om Hajer, *Eritrea* 81 E4
Om Koi, *Thailand* 64 D2
Ōma, *Japan* 54 D10
Ōmachi, *Japan* 55 F8
Omae-Zaki, *Japan* 55 G9
Ōmagari, *Japan* 54 E10
Omagh, *U.K.* 15 B4
Omagh □, *U.K.* 15 B4
Omaha, *U.S.A.* 112 E7
Omak, *U.S.A.* 114 B4
Omalos, *Greece* 36 D5
Oman ■, *Asia* 74 C6
Oman, G. of, *Asia* 71 E8
Omaruru, *Namibia* 88 C2
Omaruru →, *Namibia* 88 C1
Omate, *Peru* 124 G4
Ombai, Selat, *Indonesia* 63 F6
Omboué, *Gabon* 84 E1
Ombrone →, *Italy* 28 F8
Omdurmân, *Sudan* 81 D3
Omegna, *Italy* 28 C5
Omemee, *Canada* 110 B6
Omeonga, *Dem. Rep. of the Congo* 86 C1
Ometepe, I. de, *Nic.* 120 D2
Ometepec, *Mexico* 119 D5
Ominato, *Japan* 54 D10
Omineca →, *Canada* 104 B4
Omiš, *Croatia* 29 E13
Omišalj, *Croatia* 29 C11
Omitara, *Namibia* 88 C2
Ōmiya, *Japan* 55 G9
Omme Å →, *Denmark* 11 J2
Ommen, *Neths.* 17 B6
Ömnögovĭ □, *Mongolia* 56 C3
Omo →, *Ethiopia* 81 F4
Omodeo, L., *Italy* 30 B1
Omodhos, *Cyprus* 36 E11
Omoko, *Nigeria* 83 D6
Omolon →, *Russia* 51 C16
Omono-Gawa →, *Japan* 54 E10
Omsk, *Russia* 50 D8
Omsukchan, *Russia* 51 C16
Ōmu, *Japan* 54 B11
Omul, Vf., *Romania* 43 E10
Omulew →, *Poland* 45 E8
Ōmura, *Japan* 55 H4
Omuramba Omatako →, *Namibia* 88 B2
Omuramba Ovambo →, *Namibia* 88 B2
Omurtag, *Bulgaria* 41 C10
Ōmuta, *Japan* 55 H5
Oña, *Spain* 34 C7
Onaga, *U.S.A.* 112 F6
Onalaska, *U.S.A.* 112 D9
Onancock, *U.S.A.* 108 G8
Onang, *Indonesia* 63 E5
Onaping L., *Canada* 102 C3
Oñati, *Spain* 32 B2
Onavas, *Mexico* 118 B3
Onawa, *U.S.A.* 112 D6
Oncócua, *Angola* 88 B1
Onda, *Spain* 32 F4
Ondaejin, *N. Korea* 57 D15
Ondangwa, *Namibia* 88 B2
Ondarroa, *Spain* 32 B2
Ondava →, *Slovak Rep.* 27 C14
Ondjiva, *Angola* 88 B2
Ondo, *Nigeria* 83 D5
Ondo □, *Nigeria* 83 D6
Öndörshil, *Mongolia* 56 B5
Öndverðarnes, *Iceland* 8 D1
One Tree, *Australia* 95 E3
Onega, *Russia* 50 C4
Onega →, *Russia* 6 C13
Onega, L. = Onezhskoye Ozero, *Russia* 46 B8
Oneida, *U.S.A.* 111 C9
Oneida L., *U.S.A.* 111 C9
O'Neill, *U.S.A.* 112 D5
Onekotan, Ostrov, *Russia* 51 E16
Onema, *Dem. Rep. of the Congo* 86 C1
Oneonta, *U.S.A.* 111 D9
Oneşti, *Romania* 43 D11
Onezhskoye Ozero, *Russia* 46 B8
Ongarue, *N.Z.* 91 H5
Ongers →, *S. Africa* 88 E3
Ongerup, *Australia* 93 F2
Ongjin, *N. Korea* 57 F13
Ongkharak, *Thailand* 64 E3
Ongniud Qi, *China* 57 C10
Ongoka, *Dem. Rep. of the Congo* 86 C2
Ongole, *India* 66 M12
Ongon = Havirga, *Mongolia* 56 B7
Oni, *Georgia* 49 J6
Onida, *U.S.A.* 112 C4
Onilahy →, *Madag.* 89 C7
Onitsha, *Nigeria* 83 D6
Onoda, *Japan* 55 G5
Onpyŏng-ni, *S. Korea* 57 H14
Ons, I. de, *Spain* 34 C2
Onslow, *Australia* 92 D2
Onslow B., *U.S.A.* 109 H7
Ontake-San, *Japan* 55 G8
Ontario, *Calif., U.S.A.* 117 L9
Ontario, *Oreg., U.S.A.* 114 D5
Ontario □, *Canada* 102 B2
Ontario, L., *N. Amer.* 110 C7
Ontinyent, *Spain* 33 G4
Ontonagon, *U.S.A.* 112 B10
Ontur, *Spain* 33 G3
Onyx, *U.S.A.* 117 K8
Oodnadatta, *Australia* 95 D2
Ooldea, *Australia* 93 F5
Oombulgurri, *Australia* 92 C4
Oorindi, *Australia* 94 C3
Oost-Vlaanderen □, *Belgium* 17 C3
Oostende, *Belgium* 17 C2
Oosterhout, *Neths.* 17 C4
Oosterschelde →, *Neths.* 17 C4
Oosterwolde, *Neths.* 17 B6
Ootacamund = Udagamandalam, *India* 66 P10
Ootsa L., *Canada* 104 C3
Opaka, *Bulgaria* 41 C10
Opala, *Dem. Rep. of the Congo* 86 C1
Opalenica, *Poland* 45 F3
Opan, *Bulgaria* 41 D9
Opanake, *Sri Lanka* 66 R12
Opasatika, *Canada* 102 C3
Opasquia Prov. Park, *Canada* 102 B1
Opatija, *Croatia* 29 C11
Opatów, *Poland* 45 H8
Opava, *Czech Rep.* 27 B10
Opelika, *U.S.A.* 109 J3
Opelousas, *U.S.A.* 113 K8
Opémisca, L., *Canada* 102 C5
Opheim, *U.S.A.* 114 B10
Ophthalmia Ra., *Australia* 92 D2
Opi, *Nigeria* 83 D6
Opinaca →, *Canada* 102 B4
Opinaca, Rés., *Canada* 102 B4
Opinnagau →, *Canada* 102 B3
Opiscoteo, L., *Canada* 103 B6
Opobo, *Nigeria* 83 E6
Opochka, *Russia* 46 D5
Opoczno, *Poland* 45 G7
Opol, *Phil.* 61 G6
Opole, *Poland* 45 H4
Opole Lubelskie, *Poland* 45 G8
Opolskie □, *Poland* 45 H5
Oponono L., *Namibia* 88 B2
Oporto = Porto, *Portugal* 34 D2
Opotiki, *N.Z.* 91 H6
Opp, *U.S.A.* 109 K2
Oppdal, *Norway* 9 E13
Óppido Mamertina, *Italy* 31 D8
Opportunity, *U.S.A.* 114 C5
Oprişor, *Romania* 42 F8
Oprtalj, *Croatia* 29 C10
Opua, *N.Z.* 91 F5
Opunake, *N.Z.* 91 H4
Opuwo, *Namibia* 88 B1
Opuzen, *Croatia* 29 E14
Ora, *Cyprus* 36 E12
Oracle, *U.S.A.* 115 K8
Oradea, *Romania* 42 C6
Öræfajökull, *Iceland* 8 D5
Orahovac, *Kosovo, Yug.* 40 D4
Orahovica, *Croatia* 42 E2
Orai, *India* 69 G8
Oraison, *France* 21 E9
Oral = Zhayyq →, *Kazakstan* 50 E6
Oral, *Kazakstan* 48 E10
Oran, *Algeria* 78 A5
Orange, *Australia* 95 E4
Orange, *France* 21 D8
Orange, *Calif., U.S.A.* 117 M9
Orange, *Mass., U.S.A.* 111 D12
Orange, *Tex., U.S.A.* 113 K8
Orange, *Va., U.S.A.* 108 F6
Orange →, *S. Africa* 88 D2
Orange, C., *Brazil* 122 C5
Orange Cove, *U.S.A.* 116 J7
Orange Free State = Free State □, *S. Africa* 88 D4
Orange Grove, *U.S.A.* 113 M6
Orange Walk, *Belize* 119 D7
Orangeburg, *U.S.A.* 109 J5
Orangeville, *Canada* 102 D3
Orango, *Guinea-Biss.* 82 C1
Orani, *Phil.* 61 D4
Oranienburg, *Germany* 24 C9
Oranje = Orange →, *S. Africa* 88 D2
Oranje Vrystaat = Free State □, *S. Africa* 88 D4
Oranjemund, *Namibia* 88 D2
Oranjerivier, *S. Africa* 88 D3
Orapa, *Botswana* 85 J5
Orarak, *Sudan* 81 F3
Oras, *Phil.* 61 E6
Orašje, *Bos.-H.* 42 E3
Orăştie, *Romania* 43 E8
Oraşul Stalin = Braşov, *Romania* 43 E10
Orava →, *Slovak Rep.* 27 B12

Orava, Vodna nádriž, *Slovak Rep.* 27 B12
Oraviţa, *Romania* 42 E6
Orb →, *France* 20 E7
Orba →, *Italy* 28 D5
Ørbæk, *Denmark* 11 J4
Orbe, *Switz.* 25 J2
Orbec, *France* 18 C7
Orbetello, *Italy* 29 F8
Órbigo →, *Spain* 34 C5
Orbisonia, *U.S.A.* 110 F7
Orbost, *Australia* 95 F4
Örbyhus, *Sweden* 10 D11
Orcas I., *U.S.A.* 116 B4
Orce, *Spain* 33 H2
Orce →, *Spain* 33 H2
Orchard City, *U.S.A.* 115 G10
Orchies, *France* 19 B10
Orchila, I., *Venezuela* 121 D6
Òrcia →, *Italy* 29 F8
Orco →, *Italy* 28 C4
Orcutt, *U.S.A.* 117 L6
Ord, *U.S.A.* 112 E5
Ord →, *Australia* 92 C4
Ord, Mt., *Australia* 92 C4
Ordenes = Ordes, *Spain* 34 B2
Orderville, *U.S.A.* 115 H7
Ordes, *Spain* 34 B2
Ording = St-Peter-Ording, *Germany* 24 A4
Ordos = Mu Us Shamo, *China* 56 E5
Ordu, *Turkey* 72 B7
Ordubad, *Azerbaijan* 73 C12
Orduña, *Álava, Spain* 32 C2
Orduña, *Granada, Spain* 35 H7
Ordway, *U.S.A.* 112 F3
Ordzhonikidze = Vladikavkaz, *Russia* 49 J7
Ordzhonikidze, *Ukraine* 47 J8
Ore, *Dem. Rep. of the Congo* 86 B2
Ore Mts. = Erzgebirge, *Germany* 24 E8
Orebić, *Croatia* 29 F14
Örebro, *Sweden* 10 E9
Örebro län □, *Sweden* 10 E8
Oregon, *U.S.A.* 112 D10
Oregon □, *U.S.A.* 114 E3
Oregon City, *U.S.A.* 116 E4
Öregrund, *Sweden* 10 D12
Öregrundsgrepen, *Sweden* 10 D12
Orekhov = Orikhiv, *Ukraine* 47 J8
Orekhovo-Zuyevo, *Russia* 46 E10
Orel, *Russia* 47 F9
Orel →, *Ukraine* 47 H8
Orellana, *Spain* 35 F5
Orellana, Canal de, *Spain* 35 F5
Orellana, Embalse de, *Spain* 35 F5
Orem, *U.S.A.* 114 F8
Ören, *Turkey* 39 D9
Orenburg, *Russia* 50 D6
Örencik, *Turkey* 39 B11
Orense = Ourense, *Spain* 34 C3
Orense □, *Spain* 34 C3
Orepuki, *N.Z.* 91 M1
Orestiás, *Greece* 41 E10
Orestos Pereyra, *Mexico* 118 B3
Øresund, *Europe* 11 J6
Orford Ness, *U.K.* 13 E9
Orgañà = Organyà, *Spain* 32 C6
Organos, Pta. de los, *Canary Is.* 37 F2
Organyà, *Spain* 32 C6
Orgaz, *Spain* 35 F7
Orgeyev = Orhei, *Moldova* 43 C13
Orhaneli, *Turkey* 41 G12
Orhaneli →, *Turkey* 41 G12
Orhangazi, *Turkey* 41 F13
Orhei, *Moldova* 43 C13
Orhon Gol →, *Mongolia* 60 A5
Òria, *Italy* 31 B10
Oriental, Cordillera, *Colombia* 122 C3
Orientale □, *Dem. Rep. of the Congo* 86 B2
Oriente, *Argentina* 126 D3
Orihuela, *Spain* 33 G4
Orihuela del Tremedal, *Spain* 32 E3
Orikhiv, *Ukraine* 47 J8
Orikum, *Albania* 40 F3
Orillia, *Canada* 102 D4
Orinoco →, *Venezuela* 122 C4
Orion, *Canada* 105 D6
Oriskany, *U.S.A.* 111 C9
Orissa □, *India* 67 K14
Orissaare, *Estonia* 9 G20
Oristano, *Italy* 30 C1
Oristano, G. di, *Italy* 30 C1
Orizaba, *Mexico* 119 D5
Orizare, *Bulgaria* 41 D11
Orjen, *Bos.-H.* 40 D2
Orjiva, *Spain* 35 J7
Orkanger, *Norway* 8 E13
Örkelljunga, *Sweden* 11 H7
Örken, *Sweden* 11 G9
Örkény, *Hungary* 42 C4
Orkla →, *Norway* 8 E13
Orkney, *S. Africa* 88 D4
Orkney □, *U.K.* 14 B5
Orkney Is., *U.K.* 14 B6
Orland, *U.S.A.* 116 F4
Orlando, *U.S.A.* 109 L5
Orlando, C. d', *Italy* 31 D7
Orléanais, *France* 19 E9
Orléans, *France* 19 E8
Orleans, *U.S.A.* 111 B12
Orléans, I. d', *Canada* 103 C5
Orlice →, *Czech Rep.* 26 A8
Orlov, *Slovak Rep.* 27 B13
Orlov Gay, *Russia* 48 E9
Orlová, *Czech Rep.* 27 B11
Orlovat, *Serbia, Yug.* 42 E5
Ormara, *Pakistan* 66 G4
Ormea, *Italy* 28 D4
Ormília, *Greece* 40 F7
Ormoc, *Phil.* 61 F6
Ormond, *N.Z.* 91 H6
Ormond Beach, *U.S.A.* 109 L5
Ormož, *Slovenia* 29 B13
Ormskirk, *U.K.* 12 D5
Ormstown, *Canada* 111 A11
Ornans, *France* 19 E13
Orne □, *France* 18 D7
Orne →, *France* 18 C6
Orneta, *Poland* 44 D7
Ornö, *Sweden* 10 E12
Örnsköldsvik, *Sweden* 10 A12
Oro, *N. Korea* 57 D14
Oro →, *Mexico* 118 B3
Oro Grande, *U.S.A.* 117 L9
Oro Valley, *U.S.A.* 115 K8
Orobie, Alpi, *Italy* 28 B6
Orocué, *Colombia* 124 C4
Orodara, *Burkina Faso* 82 C4
Orodo, *Nigeria* 83 D6
Orofino, *U.S.A.* 114 C5
Orol Dengizi = Aral Sea, *Asia* 50 E7
Oromocto, *Canada* 103 C6
Oron, *Nigeria* 83 E6
Orono, *Canada* 110 C6
Orono, *U.S.A.* 109 C11
Oronsay, *U.K.* 14 E2
Oropesa, *Spain* 34 F5
Oroquieta, *Phil.* 61 G5
Orosei, *Italy* 30 B2
Orosei, G. di, *Italy* 30 B2
Orosháza, *Hungary* 42 D5
Oroszlány, *Hungary* 42 C3
Orotukan, *Russia* 51 C16
Oroville, *Calif., U.S.A.* 116 F5
Oroville, *Wash., U.S.A.* 114 B4
Oroville, L., *U.S.A.* 116 F5
Orrefors, *Sweden* 11 H9
Orroroo, *Australia* 95 E2
Orrviken, *Sweden* 10 A8
Orrville, *U.S.A.* 110 F3
Orsa, *Sweden* 10 C8
Orsara di Púglia, *Italy* 31 A8
Orsasjön, *Sweden* 10 C8
Orsha, *Belarus* 46 E6
Orsjö, *Sweden* 11 H9
Orsk, *Russia* 50 D6
Orşova, *Romania* 42 F7
Ørsted, *Denmark* 11 H4
Örsundsbro, *Sweden* 10 E11
Orta, L. d', *Italy* 28 C5
Orta Nova, *Italy* 31 A8
Ortaca, *Turkey* 39 E10
Ortakent, *Turkey* 39 D9
Ortaklar, *Turkey* 39 D9
Ortaköy, *Çorum, Turkey* 72 B6
Ortaköy, *Niğde, Turkey* 72 C6
Orte, *Italy* 29 F9
Ortegal, C., *Spain* 34 B3
Orthez, *France* 20 E3
Ortigueira, *Spain* 34 B3
Orting, *U.S.A.* 116 C4
Ortisei, *Italy* 29 B8
Ortles, *Italy* 28 B7
Ortón →, *Bolivia* 124 F5
Ortona, *Italy* 29 F11
Ortonville, *U.S.A.* 112 C6
Orūmīyeh, *Iran* 70 B5
Orūmīyeh, Daryācheh-ye, *Iran* 70 B5
Orune, *Italy* 30 B2
Oruro, *Bolivia* 124 G5
Orust, *Sweden* 11 F5
Oruzgān □, *Afghan.* 66 C5
Orvault, *France* 18 E5
Orvieto, *Italy* 29 F9
Orwell, *N.Y., U.S.A.* 111 C9
Orwell, *Ohio, U.S.A.* 110 E4
Orwell →, *U.K.* 13 F9
Orwigsburg, *U.S.A.* 111 F8
Oryakhovo, *Bulgaria* 40 C7
Orzinuovi, *Italy* 28 C6
Orzyc →, *Poland* 45 F8
Orzysz, *Poland* 44 E8
Osa →, *Poland* 44 E5
Osa, Pen. de, *Costa Rica* 120 E3
Osage, *U.S.A.* 112 D8
Osage →, *U.S.A.* 112 F9
Osage City, *U.S.A.* 112 F7
Ōsaka, *Japan* 55 G7
Osan, *S. Korea* 57 F14
Osawatomie, *U.S.A.* 112 F7
Osborne, *U.S.A.* 112 F5
Osby, *Sweden* 11 H7
Osceola, *Ark., U.S.A.* 113 H10
Osceola, *Iowa, U.S.A.* 112 E8
Oschatz, *Germany* 24 D9
Oschersleben, *Germany* 24 C7
Óschiri, *Italy* 30 B2
Oscoda, *U.S.A.* 110 B1
Osečina, *Serbia, Yug.* 40 B3
Ösel = Saaremaa, *Estonia* 9 G20
Osery, *Russia* 46 E10
Osgoode, *Canada* 111 A9
Osh, *Kyrgyzstan* 50 E8
Oshakati, *Namibia* 85 H3
Oshawa, *Canada* 102 D4
Oshigambo, *Namibia* 88 B2
Oshkosh, *Nebr., U.S.A.* 112 E3
Oshkosh, *Wis., U.S.A.* 112 C10
Oshmyany = Ashmyany, *Belarus* 9 J21
Oshnovīyeh, *Iran* 70 B5
Oshogbo, *Nigeria* 83 D5
Oshtorīnān, *Iran* 71 C6
Oshwe, *Dem. Rep. of the Congo* 84 E3
Osi, *Nigeria* 83 D6
Osieczna, *Poland* 45 G3
Osijek, *Croatia* 42 E3
Ósilo, *Italy* 30 B1
Ósimo, *Italy* 29 E10
Osintorf, *Belarus* 46 E6
Osipenko = Berdyansk, *Ukraine* 47 J9
Osipovichi = Asipovichy, *Belarus* 46 F5
Osiyan, *India* 68 F5
Osizweni, *S. Africa* 89 D5
Oskaloosa, *U.S.A.* 112 E8
Oskarshamn, *Sweden* 11 G10
Oskarström, *Sweden* 11 H6
Oskélanéo, *Canada* 102 C4
Öskemen, *Kazakstan* 50 E9
Oskol →, *Ukraine* 47 H9
Oslo, *Norway* 9 G14
Oslob, *Phil.* 61 G5
Oslofjorden, *Norway* 9 G14
Osmanabad, *India* 66 K10
Osmancık, *Turkey* 72 B6
Osmaniye, *Turkey* 70 B3
Osmanlı, *Turkey* 41 E10
Ösmo, *Sweden* 10 F11
Osnabrück, *Germany* 24 C4
Ośno Lubuskie, *Poland* 45 F1
Osoblaha, *Czech Rep.* 27 A10
Osogovska Planina, *Macedonia* 40 D6
Osor, *Italy* 29 D11
Osorio, *Brazil* 127 B5
Osorno, *Chile* 128 E2
Osorno, *Spain* 34 C6
Osoyoos, *Canada* 104 D5
Osøyro, *Norway* 9 F11
Ospika →, *Canada* 104 B4
Osprey Reef, *Australia* 94 A4
Oss, *Neths.* 17 C5
Ossa, Mt., *Australia* 94 G4
Óssa, Óros, *Greece* 38 B4
Ossa de Montiel, *Spain* 33 G2
Ossabaw I., *U.S.A.* 109 K5
Osse →, *France* 20 D4
Osse →, *Nigeria* 83 D6
Ossi, *Italy* 30 B1
Ossining, *U.S.A.* 111 E11
Ossipee, *U.S.A.* 111 C13
Ossokmanuan L., *Canada* 103 B7
Ossora, *Russia* 51 D17
Ostashkov, *Russia* 46 D7
Östavall, *Sweden* 10 B9
Oste →, *Germany* 24 B5
Ostend = Oostende, *Belgium* 17 C2
Oster, *Ukraine* 47 G6
Osterburg, *Germany* 24 C7
Osterburg, *U.S.A.* 110 F6
Osterburken, *Germany* 25 F5
Österbybruk, *Sweden* 10 D11
Österbymo, *Sweden* 11 G9
Österdalälven, *Sweden* 10 C7
Østerdalen, *Norway* 9 F14
Österfärnebo, *Sweden* 10 D10
Österforse, *Sweden* 10 A11
Östergötlands län □, *Sweden* 11 F9
Osterholz-Scharmbeck, *Germany* 24 B4
Østerild, *Denmark* 11 G2
Osterode, *Germany* 24 D6
Östersund, *Sweden* 10 A8
Östervåla, *Sweden* 10 D11
Ostfriesische Inseln, *Germany* 24 B3
Ostfriesland, *Germany* 24 B3
Östhammar, *Sweden* 10 D12
Ostia, Lido di, *Italy* 29 G9
Ostíglia, *Italy* 29 C8
Östmark, *Sweden* 10 D6
Östra Husby, *Sweden* 11 F10
Ostrava, *Czech Rep.* 27 B11
Ostravský □, *Czech Rep.* 27 B10
Ostróda, *Poland* 44 E6
Ostrogozhsk, *Russia* 47 G10
Ostroh, *Ukraine* 47 G4
Ostrołęka, *Poland* 45 E8
Ostrov, *Bulgaria* 41 C8
Ostrov, *Czech Rep.* 26 A5
Ostrov, *Romania* 43 F12
Ostrov, *Russia* 46 D5
Ostrów Lubelski, *Poland* 45 G9
Ostrów Mazowiecka, *Poland* 45 F8
Ostrów Wielkopolski, *Poland* 45 G4
Ostrowiec-Świętokrzyski, *Poland* 45 H8
Ostrožac, *Bos.-H.* 42 G2
Ostrzeszów, *Poland* 45 G4
Ostseebad Kühlungsborn, *Germany* 24 A7
Osttirol □, *Austria* 26 E5
Ostuni, *Italy* 31 B10
Osum →, *Albania* 40 F4
Osŭm →, *Bulgaria* 41 C8
Ōsumi-Kaikyō, *Japan* 55 J5
Ōsumi-Shotō, *Japan* 55 J5
Osun □, *Nigeria* 83 D5
Osuna, *Spain* 35 H5
Oswegatchie →, *U.S.A.* 111 B9
Oswego, *U.S.A.* 111 C8
Oswego →, *U.S.A.* 111 C8
Oswestry, *U.K.* 12 E4
Oświęcim, *Poland* 45 H6
Otaci, *Moldova* 43 B12
Otago □, *N.Z.* 91 L2
Otago Harbour, *N.Z.* 91 L3
Ōtake, *Japan* 55 G6
Otaki, *N.Z.* 91 J5
Otaru, *Japan* 54 C10
Otaru-Wan = Ishikari-Wan, *Japan* 54 C10
Otava →, *Czech Rep.* 26 B7
Otavalo, *Ecuador* 124 C3
Otavi, *Namibia* 88 B2
Otchinjau, *Angola* 88 B1
Otelec, *Romania* 42 E5
Otelnuk L., *Canada* 103 A6
Oţelu Roşu, *Romania* 42 E7
Otero de Rey = Outeiro de Rei, *Spain* 34 B3
Othello, *U.S.A.* 114 C4
Othonoí, *Greece* 38 B1
Óthris, Óros, *Greece* 38 B4
Otjiwarongo, *Namibia* 88 C2
Otmuchów, *Poland* 45 H4
Otočac, *Croatia* 29 D12
Otoineppu, *Japan* 54 B11
Otok, *Croatia* 29 E13
Otorohanga, *N.Z.* 91 H5
Otoskwin →, *Canada* 102 B2
Otra →, *Norway* 9 G13
Otradnyy, *Russia* 48 D10
Otranto, *Italy* 31 B11
Otranto, C. d', *Italy* 31 B11
Otranto, Str. of, *Italy* 31 B11
Otrokovice, *Czech Rep.* 27 B10
Otse, *S. Africa* 88 D4
Ōtsu, *Japan* 55 G7
Ōtsuki, *Japan* 55 G9
Ottawa = Outaouais →, *Canada* 102 C5
Ottawa, *Canada* 102 C4
Ottawa, *Ill., U.S.A.* 112 E10
Ottawa, *Kans., U.S.A.* 112 F7
Ottawa Is., *Canada* 101 C11
Ottélé, *Cameroon* 83 E7
Ottensheim, *Austria* 26 C7
Otter Cr. →, *U.S.A.* 111 B11
Otter L., *Canada* 105 B8
Otterndorf, *Germany* 24 B4
Otterup, *Denmark* 11 J4
Otterville, *Canada* 110 D4
Ottery St. Mary, *U.K.* 13 G4
Otto Beit Bridge, *Zimbabwe* 87 F2
Ottosdal, *S. Africa* 88 D4
Ottumwa, *U.S.A.* 112 E8
Otu, *Nigeria* 83 D5
Otukpa, *Nigeria* 83 D6
Oturkpo, *Nigeria* 83 D6
Otway, B., *Chile* 128 G2
Otway, C., *Australia* 95 F3
Otwock, *Poland* 45 F8
Ötztaler Ache →, *Austria* 26 D3
Ötztaler Alpen, *Austria* 26 E3
Ou →, *Laos* 64 B4
Ou Neua, *Laos* 58 F3
Ou-Sammyaku, *Japan* 54 E10
Ouachita →, *U.S.A.* 113 K9
Ouachita, L., *U.S.A.* 113 H8
Ouachita Mts., *U.S.A.* 113 H7
Ouagadougou, *Burkina Faso* 83 C4
Ouahigouya, *Burkina Faso* 82 C4
Ouahran = Oran, *Algeria* 78 A5
Oualâta, *Mauritania* 82 B3
Ouallam, *Niger* 83 C5
Ouallene, *Algeria* 78 D6
Ouargaye, *Burkina Faso* 83 C5
Ouargla, *Algeria* 78 B7
Ouarkoye, *Burkina Faso* 82 C4
Ouarzazate, *Morocco* 78 B4
Ouassouas, *Mali* 83 B5
Ouatagouna, *Mali* 83 B5
Oubangi →, *Dem. Rep. of the Congo* 84 E3
Ouche →, *France* 19 E12
Ouddorp, *Neths.* 17 C3
Oude Rijn →, *Neths.* 17 B4
Oudeïka, *Mali* 83 B4
Oudenaarde, *Belgium* 17 D3
Oudon →, *France* 18 E6
Oudtshoorn, *S. Africa* 88 E3
Ouellé, *Ivory C.* 82 D4
Ouémé →, *Benin* 83 D5
Ouessa, *Burkina Faso* 82 C4
Ouessant, Î. d', *France* 18 D1
Ouesso, *Congo* 84 D3
Ouest, Pte. de l', *Canada* 103 C7
Ouezzane, *Morocco* 78 B4
Ougarou, *Burkina Faso* 83 C5
Oughterard, *Ireland* 15 C2
Ouidah, *Benin* 83 D5
Ouidi, *Niger* 83 C7
Ouistreham, *France* 18 C6
Oujda, *Morocco* 78 B5
Oujeft, *Mauritania* 82 A2
Oulainen, *Finland* 8 D21
Ould Yenjé, *Mauritania* 82 B2
Oullins, *France* 21 C8
Oulu, *Finland* 8 D21
Oulujärvi, *Finland* 8 D22
Oulujoki →, *Finland* 8 D21
Oulx, *Italy* 28 C3
Oum Chalouba, *Chad* 79 E10
Oum Hadjer, *Chad* 79 F9
Oumé, *Ivory C.* 82 D3
Ounasjoki →, *Finland* 8 C21
Ounguati, *Namibia* 88 C2
Ounianga Sérir, *Chad* 79 E10
Our →, *Lux.* 17 E6
Ouranópolis, *Greece* 40 F7
Ourârene, *Niger* 83 B6
Ouray, *U.S.A.* 115 G10
Ourcq →, *France* 19 C10
Ourense, *Spain* 34 C3
Ouricuri, *Brazil* 125 E10
Ourinhos, *Brazil* 127 A6
Ourique, *Portugal* 35 H2
Ouro Fino, *Brazil* 127 A6
Ouro-Ndia, *Mali* 82 B4
Ouro Prêto, *Brazil* 127 A7
Ouro Sogui, *Senegal* 82 B2
Oursi, *Burkina Faso* 83 C4
Ourthe →, *Belgium* 17 D5
Ouse →, *E. Susx., U.K.* 13 G8
Ouse →, *N. Yorks., U.K.* 12 D7
Oust, *France* 20 F5
Oust →, *France* 18 E4
Outaouais →, *Canada* 102 C5
Outardes →, *Canada* 103 C6
Outeiro de Rei, *Spain* 34 B3
Outer Hebrides, *U.K.* 14 D1
Outes = Serra de Outes, *Spain* 34 C2
Outjo, *Namibia* 88 C2
Outlook, *Canada* 105 C7
Outokumpu, *Finland* 8 E23
Outreau, *France* 19 B8
Ouvèze →, *France* 21 E8
Ouyen, *Australia* 95 F3
Ouzouer-le-Marché, *France* 19 E8
Ovada, *Italy* 28 D5
Ovalau, *Fiji* 91 C8
Ovalle, *Chile* 126 C1
Ovamboland, *Namibia* 88 B2
Ovar, *Portugal* 34 E2
Overath, *Germany* 24 E3
Overflakkee, *Neths.* 17 C4
Overijssel □, *Neths.* 17 B6
Overland Park, *U.S.A.* 112 F7
Overton, *U.S.A.* 117 J12
Övertorneå, *Sweden* 8 C20
Överum, *Sweden* 11 F10
Ovid, *U.S.A.* 111 D8
Ovidiopol, *Ukraine* 47 J6
Ovidiu, *Romania* 43 F13
Oviedo, *Spain* 34 B5
Oviksfjällen, *Sweden* 10 A7
Oviši, *Latvia* 9 H19
Ovoot, *Mongolia* 56 B7
Övör Hangay □, *Mongolia* 56 B2
Ovoro, *Nigeria* 83 D6
Øvre Årdal, *Norway* 9 F12
Övre Fryken, *Sweden* 10 E7
Ovruch, *Ukraine* 47 G5
Owaka, *N.Z.* 91 M2
Owambo = Ovamboland, *Namibia* 88 B2
Owasco L., *U.S.A.* 111 D8
Owase, *Japan* 55 G8
Owatonna, *U.S.A.* 112 C8
Owbeh, *Afghan.* 66 B3
Owego, *U.S.A.* 111 D8
Owen Falls Dam, *Uganda* 86 B3
Owen Sound, *Canada* 102 D3
Owens →, *U.S.A.* 116 J9
Owens L., *U.S.A.* 117 J9
Owensboro, *U.S.A.* 108 G2
Owerri, *Nigeria* 83 D6
Owl →, *Canada* 105 B10
Owo, *Nigeria* 83 D6
Owosso, *U.S.A.* 108 D3
Owyhee, *U.S.A.* 114 F5
Owyhee →, *U.S.A.* 114 E5
Owyhee, L., *U.S.A.* 114 E5
Ox Mts. = Slieve Gamph, *Ireland* 15 B3
Öxarfjörður, *Iceland* 8 C5
Oxbow, *Canada* 105 D8
Oxelösund, *Sweden* 11 F11
Oxford, *N.Z.* 91 K4
Oxford, *U.K.* 13 F6
Oxford, *Mass., U.S.A.* 111 D13
Oxford, *Miss., U.S.A.* 113 H10
Oxford, *N.C., U.S.A.* 109 G6
Oxford, *N.Y., U.S.A.* 111 D9
Oxford, *Ohio, U.S.A.* 108 F3
Oxford L., *Canada* 105 C9
Oxfordshire □, *U.K.* 13 F6
Oxía, *Greece* 38 C3
Oxie, *Sweden* 11 J7
Oxílithos, *Greece* 38 C6
Oxnard, *U.S.A.* 117 L7
Oxsjövålen, *Sweden* 10 B7
Oxus = Amudarya →, *Uzbekistan* 50 E6
Oya, *Malaysia* 62 D4
Oyama, *Japan* 55 F9
Oyem, *Gabon* 84 D2
Oyen, *Canada* 105 C6
Oykel →, *U.K.* 14 D4
Oymyakon, *Russia* 51 C15
Oyo, *Nigeria* 83 D5
Oyo □, *Nigeria* 83 D5
Oyonnax, *France* 19 F12
Oyster Bay, *U.S.A.* 111 F11
Ōyūbari, *Japan* 54 C11
Özalp, *Turkey* 73 C10
Ozamiz, *Phil.* 61 G5
Ozark, *Ala., U.S.A.* 109 K3
Ozark, *Ark., U.S.A.* 113 H8
Ozark, *Mo., U.S.A.* 113 G8
Ozark Plateau, *U.S.A.* 113 G9
Ozarks, L. of the, *U.S.A.* 112 F8
Ożarów, *Poland* 45 H8
Ózd, *Hungary* 42 B5
Ozernoye, *Russia* 48 E10
Ozette L., *U.S.A.* 116 B2
Ozieri, *Italy* 30 B2
Ozimek, *Poland* 45 H5
Ozinki, *Russia* 48 E9
Ozona, *U.S.A.* 113 K4
Ozorków, *Poland* 45 G6
Ozren, *Bos.-H.* 42 G3
Ozuluama, *Mexico* 119 C5
Ozun, *Romania* 43 E10
Ozurgeti, *Georgia* 49 K5

P

Pa, *Burkina Faso* 82 C4
Pa-an, *Burma* 67 L20
Pa Mong Dam, *Thailand* 64 D4
Pa Sak →, *Thailand* 62 B2
Paamiut, *Greenland* 4 C5
Paar →, *Germany* 25 G7
Paarl, *S. Africa* 88 E2
Pab Hills, *Pakistan* 68 F2
Pabbay, *U.K.* 14 D1
Pabianice, *Poland* 45 G6
Pabna, *Bangla.* 67 G16
Pabo, *Uganda* 86 B3
Pacaja →, *Brazil* 125 D8
Pacaraima, Sa., *S. Amer.* 122 C4
Pacasmayo, *Peru* 124 E3
Paceco, *Italy* 30 E5
Pachhar, *India* 68 G7
Pachino, *Italy* 31 F8
Pachitea →, *Peru* 124 E4
Pachmarhi, *India* 69 H8
Pachpadra, *India* 66 G8
Pachuca, *Mexico* 119 C5
Pacific, *Canada* 104 C3
Pacific-Antarctic Ridge, *Pac Oc.* 97 M16
Pacific Grove, *U.S.A.* 116 J5
Pacific Ocean, *Pac. Oc.* 97 G14
Pacific Rim Nat. Park, *Canada* 116 B2
Pacifica, *U.S.A.* 116 H4
Pacitan, *Indonesia* 63 H14
Packwood, *U.S.A.* 116 D5
Pacov, *Czech Rep.* 26 B8
Pacy-sur-Eure, *France* 18 C8
Padaido, Kepulauan, *Indonesia* 63 E9
Padang, *Indonesia* 62 E2
Padang Endau, *Malaysia* 65 L4
Padangpanjang, *Indonesia* 62 E2
Padangsidempuan, *Indonesia* 62 D1
Padborg, *Denmark* 11 K3
Paddle Prairie, *Canada* 104 B5
Paddockwood, *Canada* 105 C7
Paderborn, *Germany* 24 D4
Padeş, Vf., *Romania* 42 E7
Padina, *Romania* 43 F12
Padma, *India* 69 G11
Pádova, *Italy* 29 C8
Padra, *India* 68 H5
Padrauna, *India* 69 F10
Padre I., *U.S.A.* 113 M6
Padrón, *Spain* 34 C2
Padstow, *U.K.* 13 G3
Padua = Pádova, *Italy* 29 C8
Paducah, *Ky., U.S.A.* 108 G1
Paducah, *Tex., U.S.A.* 113 H4
Padul, *Spain* 35 H7
Paengnyŏng-do, *S. Korea* 57 F13
Paeroa, *N.Z.* 91 G5
Paesana, *Italy* 28 D4
Pafúri, *Mozam.* 89 C5
Pag, *Croatia* 29 D12
Paga, *Ghana* 83 C4
Pagadian, *Phil.* 61 H5
Pagai Selatan, Pulau, *Indonesia* 62 E2
Pagai Utara, Pulau, *Indonesia* 62 E2
Pagalu = Annobón, *Atl. Oc.* 77 G4
Pagara, *India* 69 G9
Pagastikós Kólpos, *Greece* 38 B5
Pagatan, *Indonesia* 62 E5
Page, *U.S.A.* 115 H8
Pagėgiai, *Lithuania* 44 C8
Pago Pago, *Amer. Samoa* 91 B13
Pagosa Springs, *U.S.A.* 115 H10
Pagwa River, *Canada* 102 B2
Pahala, *U.S.A.* 106 J17
Pahang →, *Malaysia* 65 L4
Pahiatua, *N.Z.* 91 J5
Pahokee, *U.S.A.* 109 M5
Pahrump, *U.S.A.* 117 J11
Pahute Mesa, *U.S.A.* 116 H10
Pai, *Thailand* 64 C2
Paicines, *U.S.A.* 116 J5
Paide, *Estonia* 9 G21
Paignton, *U.K.* 13 G4
Paiho, *Taiwan* 59 F13
Päijänne, *Finland* 9 F21
Pailani, *India* 69 G9
Pailin, *Cambodia* 64 F4
Paimpol, *France* 18 D3
Painan, *Indonesia* 62 E2
Painesville, *U.S.A.* 110 E3
Paint Hills = Wemindji, *Canada* 102 B4
Paint L., *Canada* 105 B9
Painted Desert, *U.S.A.* 115 J8
Paintsville, *U.S.A.* 108 G4
País Vasco □, *Spain* 32 C2
Paisley, *Canada* 110 B3
Paisley, *U.K.* 14 F4
Paisley, *U.S.A.* 114 E3
Paita, *Peru* 124 E2
Paiva →, *Portugal* 34 D2
Paizhou, *China* 59 B9
Pajares, *Spain* 34 B5
Pajares, Puerto de, *Spain* 34 C5
Pajęczno, *Poland* 45 G5
Pak Lay, *Laos* 64 C3
Pak Phanang, *Thailand* 65 H3
Pak Sane, *Laos* 64 C4
Pak Song, *Laos* 64 E6
Pak Suong, *Laos* 58 H4
Pakaur, *India* 69 G12
Pakenham, *Canada* 111 A8
Pákhnes, *Greece* 36 D6
Pakhuis, *S. Africa* 88 E2
Pakistan ■, *Asia* 68 E4
Pakkading, *Laos* 64 C4
Pakokku, *Burma* 67 J19
Pakość, *Poland* 45 F5
Pakowki L., *Canada* 105 D6
Pakpattan, *Pakistan* 68 D5
Pakrac, *Croatia* 42 E2
Pakruojis, *Lithuania* 44 C10
Paks, *Hungary* 42 D3
Paktīā □, *Afghan.* 66 C6
Paktīkā □, *Afghan.* 66 C6
Pakwach, *Uganda* 86 B3
Pakxe, *Laos* 64 E5
Pal Lahara, *India* 69 J11
Pala, *Chad* 79 G9
Pala, *Dem. Rep. of the Congo* 86 D2
Pala, *U.S.A.* 117 M9
Palabek, *Uganda* 86 B3
Palacios, *U.S.A.* 113 L6
Palafrugell, *Spain* 32 D8
Palagiano, *Italy* 31 B10
Palagonía, *Italy* 31 E7
Palagruža, *Croatia* 29 F13
Palaiókastron, *Greece* 36 D8
Palaiokhóra, *Greece* 36 D5
Pálairos, *Greece* 38 C2
Palaiseau, *France* 19 D9
Palam, *India* 66 K10
Palamás, *Greece* 38 B4
Palamós, *Spain* 32 D8
Palampur, *India* 68 C7
Palamut, *Turkey* 39 C9
Palana, *Australia* 94 F4
Palana, *Russia* 51 D16
Palanan, *Phil.* 61 C5
Palanan Pt., *Phil.* 61 C5
Palandri, *Pakistan* 69 C5
Palanga, *Lithuania* 9 J19
Palangkaraya, *Indonesia* 62 E4
Palani Hills, *India* 66 P10
Palanpur, *India* 68 G5
Palapye, *Botswana* 88 C4
Palas, *Pakistan* 69 B5
Palas de Rei, *Spain* 34 C3
Palashi, *India* 69 H13
Palasponga, *India* 69 J11
Palatka, *Russia* 51 C16
Palatka, *U.S.A.* 109 L5
Palau, *Italy* 30 A2
Palau ■, *Pac. Oc.* 52 J17
Palauk, *Burma* 64 F2
Palawan, *Phil.* 61 G3
Palayankottai, *India* 66 Q10
Palazzo, Pte., *France* 21 F12
Palazzo San Gervásio, *Italy* 31 B8
Palazzolo Acréide, *Italy* 31 E7
Paldiski, *Estonia* 9 G21
Pale, *Bos.-H.* 42 G3
Paleleh, *Indonesia* 63 D6
Palembang, *Indonesia* 62 E2
Palencia, *Spain* 34 C6
Palencia □, *Spain* 34 C6
Palenque, *Mexico* 119 D6
Paleokastrítsa, *Greece* 36 A3
Paleometokho, *Cyprus* 36 D12
Palermo, *Italy* 30 D6
Palermo, *U.S.A.* 114 G3
Palestina, *Chile* 128 A3
Palestine, *Asia* 75 D4
Palestine, *U.S.A.* 113 K7
Palestrina, *Italy* 29 G9
Paletwa, *Burma* 67 J18
Palghat, *India* 66 P10
Palgrave, Mt., *Australia* 92 D2
Pali, *India* 68 G5
Palikir, *Micronesia* 96 G7
Palinuro, *Italy* 31 B8
Palinuro, C., *Italy* 31 B8
Palioúrion, Ákra, *Greece* 40 G7
Palisades Reservoir, *U.S.A.* 114 E8
Paliseul, *Belgium* 17 E5
Palitana, *India* 68 J4
Palizada, *Mexico* 119 D6
Palk Bay, *Asia* 66 Q11
Palk Strait, *Asia* 66 Q11
Palkānah, *Iraq* 70 C5
Palkot, *India* 69 H11
Palla Road = Dinokwe, *Botswana* 88 C4
Pallanza = Verbánia, *Italy* 28 C5
Pallarenda, *Australia* 94 B4
Pallasovka, *Russia* 48 E8
Pallës, Bishti i, *Albania* 40 E3
Pallinup →, *Australia* 93 F2
Pallisa, *Uganda* 86 B3
Pallu, *India* 68 E6
Palm Bay, *U.S.A.* 109 L5
Palm Beach, *U.S.A.* 109 M6
Palm Coast, *U.S.A.* 109 L5
Palm Desert, *U.S.A.* 117 M10
Palm Is., *Australia* 94 B4
Palm Springs, *U.S.A.* 117 M10
Palma, *Mozam.* 87 E5
Palma, B. de, *Spain* 37 B9
Palma de Mallorca, *Spain* 37 B9
Palma del Río, *Spain* 35 H5
Palma di Montechiaro, *Italy* 30 E6
Palma Soriano, *Cuba* 120 B4
Palmares, *Brazil* 125 E11
Palmarola, *Italy* 30 B5
Palmas, *Brazil* 127 B5
Palmas, C., *Liberia* 82 E3
Pálmas, G. di, *Italy* 30 D1
Palmdale, *U.S.A.* 117 L8
Palmeira das Missões, *Brazil* 127 B5
Palmeira dos Índios, *Brazil* 125 E11
Palmela, *Portugal* 35 G2
Palmer, *U.S.A.* 100 B5
Palmer →, *Australia* 94 B3
Palmer Arch., *Antarctica* 5 C17
Palmer Lake, *U.S.A.* 112 F2
Palmer Land, *Antarctica* 5 D18
Palmerston, *Canada* 110 C4
Palmerston, *N.Z.* 91 L3
Palmerston North, *N.Z.* 91 J5
Palmerton, *U.S.A.* 111 F9
Palmetto, *U.S.A.* 109 M4
Palmi, *Italy* 31 D8
Palmira, *Argentina* 126 C2
Palmira, *Colombia* 124 C3
Palmyra = Tudmur, *Syria* 70 C3
Palmyra, *Mo., U.S.A.* 112 F9
Palmyra, *N.J., U.S.A.* 111 F9
Palmyra, *N.Y., U.S.A.* 110 C7
Palmyra, *Pa., U.S.A.* 111 F8
Palmyra Is., *Pac. Oc.* 97 G11
Palo Alto, *U.S.A.* 116 H4
Palo Verde, *U.S.A.* 117 M12
Paloich, *Sudan* 81 E3
Palompon, *Phil.* 61 F6
Palopo, *Indonesia* 63 E6
Palos, C. de, *Spain* 33 H4
Palos de la Frontera, *Spain* 35 H4
Palos Verdes, *U.S.A.* 117 M8
Palos Verdes, Pt., *U.S.A.* 117 M8
Pålsboda, *Sweden* 10 E9
Palu, *Indonesia* 63 E5
Palu, *Turkey* 70 B3
Paluke, *Liberia* 82 D3
Paluzza, *Italy* 29 B10
Palwal, *India* 68 E7
Pama, *Burkina Faso* 83 C5
Pamanukan, *Indonesia* 63 G12
Pamiers, *France* 20 E5
Pamir, *Tajikistan* 50 F8
Pamlico →, *U.S.A.* 109 H7
Pamlico Sd., *U.S.A.* 109 H8
Pampa, *U.S.A.* 113 H4
Pampa de las Salinas, *Argentina* 126 C2
Pampanua, *Indonesia* 63 E6
Pampas, *Argentina* 126 D3
Pampas, *Peru* 124 F4
Pamphylia, *Turkey* 72 D4
Pamplona, *Colombia* 124 B4
Pamplona, *Spain* 32 C3
Pampoenpoort, *S. Africa* 88 E3
Pamukçu, *Turkey* 39 B9
Pamukkale, *Turkey* 39 D11
Pan Xian, *China* 58 E5
Pana, *U.S.A.* 112 F10
Panabo, *Phil.* 61 H6
Panaca, *U.S.A.* 115 H6
Panagyurishte, *Bulgaria* 41 D8
Panaitan, *Indonesia* 63 G11
Panaji, *India* 66 M8
Panamá, *Panama* 120 E4
Panama ■, *Cent. Amer.* 120 E4
Panamá, G. de, *Panama* 120 E4
Panama Canal, *Panama* 120 E4
Panama City, *U.S.A.* 109 K3
Panamint Range, *U.S.A.* 117 J9
Panamint Springs, *U.S.A.* 117 J9
Panão, *Peru* 124 E3
Panaon I., *Phil.* 61 F6
Panare, *Thailand* 65 J3
Panarea, *Italy* 31 D8
Panaro →, *Italy* 29 D8
Panay, *Phil.* 61 F5
Panay, G., *Phil.* 63 B6
Pančevo, *Serbia, Yug.* 42 F5
Panch'iao, *Taiwan* 59 E13
Panciu, *Romania* 43 E12
Pancorbo, Desfiladero, *Spain* 34 C7
Pâncota, *Romania* 42 D6
Panda, *Mozam.* 89 C5
Pandan, *Antique, Phil.* 61 F5
Pandan, *Catanduanes, Phil.* 61 D6
Pandegelang, *Indonesia* 63 G12
Pandhana, *India* 68 J7
Pandharpur, *India* 66 L9
Pando, *Uruguay* 127 C4
Pando, L. = Hope, L., *Australia* 95 D2
Pandokrátor, *Greece* 36 A3
Pandora, *Costa Rica* 120 E3
Pandrup, *Denmark* 11 G3
Panevėžys, *Lithuania* 9 J21
Panfilov, *Kazakstan* 50 E8
Panfilovo, *Russia* 48 E6
Pang-Long, *Burma* 67 H21
Pang-Yang, *Burma* 67 H21
Panga, *Dem. Rep. of the Congo* 86 B2
Pangaíon Óros, *Greece* 41 F8
Pangalanes, Canal des = Ampangalana, Lakandranon', *Madag.* 89 C8
Pangani, *Tanzania* 86 D4
Pangani →, *Tanzania* 86 D4
Pangfou = Bengbu, *China* 57 H9
Pangil, *Dem. Rep. of the Congo* 86 C2
Pangkah, Tanjung, *Indonesia* 63 G15
Pangkajene, *Indonesia* 63 E5
Pangkalanbrandan, *Indonesia* 62 D1
Pangkalanbuun, *Indonesia* 62 E4
Pangkalpinang, *Indonesia* 62 E3
Pangnirtung, *Canada* 101 B13
Pangong Tso, *India* 68 B8
Panguitch, *U.S.A.* 115 H7
Pangutaran Group, *Phil.* 61 H4
Panhandle, *U.S.A.* 113 H4
Pani Mines, *India* 68 H5
Pania-Mutombo, *Dem. Rep. of the Congo* 86 D1
Panikota I., *India* 68 J4
Panipat, *India* 68 E7
Panjal Range, *India* 68 C7
Panjang, Hon, *Vietnam* 65 H4
Panjgur, *Pakistan* 66 F4
Panjim = Panaji, *India* 66 M8
Panjin, *China* 57 D12
Panjinad Barrage, *Pakistan* 66 E7
Panjnad →, *Pakistan* 68 E4
Panjwai, *Afghan.* 68 D1
Pankshin, *Nigeria* 83 D6
Panmunjŏm, *N. Korea* 57 F14
Panna, *India* 69 G9
Panna Hills, *India* 69 G9
Pannawonica, *Australia* 92 D2
Pannirtuuq = Pangnirtung, *Canada* 101 B13
Pano Akil, *Pakistan* 68 F3
Pano Lefkara, *Cyprus* 36 E12
Pano Panayia, *Cyprus* 36 E11
Panorama, *Brazil* 127 A5
Pánormon, *Greece* 36 D6
Pansemal, *India* 68 J6
Panshan = Panjin, *China* 57 D12
Panshi, *China* 57 C14
Pantanal, *Brazil* 124 H7
Pantar, *Indonesia* 63 F6
Pante Macassar, *E. Timor* 63 F6
Pante Makasar = Pante Macassar, *E. Timor* 63 F6
Pantelleria, *Italy* 30 F4
Pantón, *Spain* 34 C3
Pánuco, *Mexico* 119 C5
Panyam, *Nigeria* 83 D6
Panyu, *China* 59 F9
Panzhihua, *China* 58 D3
Páola, *Italy* 31 C9
Paola, *Malta* 36 D2
Paola, *U.S.A.* 112 F7
Paonia, *U.S.A.* 115 G10
Paoting = Baoding, *China* 56 E8
Paot'ou = Baotou, *China* 56 D6
Paoua, *C.A.R.* 84 C3
Pápa, *Hungary* 42 C2
Papa Stour, *U.K.* 14 A7
Papa Westray, *U.K.* 14 B6
Papagayo →, *Mexico* 119 D5
Papagayo, G. de, *Costa Rica* 120 D2
Papakura, *N.Z.* 91 G5
Papantla, *Mexico* 119 C5
Papar, *Malaysia* 62 C5
Pápas, Ákra, *Greece* 38 C3
Papeete, *Tahiti* 97 J13
Papenburg, *Germany* 24 B3
Paphlagonia, *Turkey* 72 B5
Paphos, *Cyprus* 36 E11
Papien Chiang = Da →, *Vietnam* 58 G5
Papigochic →, *Mexico* 118 B3
Paposo, *Chile* 126 B1
Papoutsa, *Cyprus* 36 E12
Papua New Guinea ■, *Oceania* 96 H6
Papudo, *Chile* 126 C1
Papuk, *Croatia* 42 E2
Papun, *Burma* 67 K20
Papunya, *Australia* 92 D5
Pará = Belém, *Brazil* 125 D9
Pará □, *Brazil* 125 D8
Paraburdoo, *Australia* 92 D2
Paracale, *Phil.* 61 D5
Paracatu, *Brazil* 125 G9
Paracel Is., *S. China Sea* 62 A4
Parachilna, *Australia* 95 E2
Parachinar, *Pakistan* 68 C4
Paraćin, *Serbia, Yug.* 40 C5
Paradas, *Spain* 35 H5
Paradela, *Spain* 34 C3
Paradhísi, *Greece* 36 C10
Paradip, *India* 67 J15
Paradise, *Calif., U.S.A.* 116 F5
Paradise, *Nev., U.S.A.* 117 J11
Paradise →, *Canada* 103 B8
Paradise Hill, *Canada* 105 C7
Paradise River, *Canada* 103 B8
Paradise Valley, *U.S.A.* 114 F5
Parado, *Indonesia* 63 F5
Paragould, *U.S.A.* 113 G9
Paragua →, *Venezuela* 124 B6
Paraguaçu →, *Brazil* 125 F11
Paraguaçu Paulista, *Brazil* 127 A5
Paraguaná, Pen. de, *Venezuela* 124 A5
Paraguarí, *Paraguay* 126 B4
Paraguarí □, *Paraguay* 126 B4
Paraguay ■, *S. Amer.* 126 A4
Paraguay →, *Paraguay* 126 B4
Paraíba = João Pessoa, *Brazil* 125 E12
Paraíba □, *Brazil* 125 E11
Paraíba do Sul →, *Brazil* 127 A7
Parainen, *Finland* 9 F20
Paraíso, *Mexico* 119 D6
Parak, *Iran* 71 E7
Parakhino Paddubye, *Russia* 46 C7
Parakou, *Benin* 83 D5
Paralimni, *Cyprus* 36 D12
Parálion-Astrous, *Greece* 38 D4
Paramaribo, *Surinam* 125 B7
Paramithiá, *Greece* 38 B2
Paramushir, Ostrov, *Russia* 51 D16
Paran →, *Israel* 75 E4
Paraná, *Argentina* 126 C3
Paraná, *Brazil* 125 F9
Paraná □, *Brazil* 127 A5
Paraná →, *Argentina* 126 C4
Paranaguá, *Brazil* 127 B6
Paranaíba, *Brazil* 125 G8
Paranaíba →, *Brazil* 125 H8
Paranapanema →, *Brazil* 127 A5
Paranapiacaba, Serra do, *Brazil* 127 A6
Paranas, *Phil.* 61 F6
Paranavaí, *Brazil* 127 A5
Parang, *Maguindanao, Phil.* 63 C6
Parang, *Sulu, Phil.* 61 J4
Parângul Mare, Vf., *Romania* 43 E8
Paraparaumu, *N.Z.* 91 J5
Parapóla, *Greece* 38 E5
Paraspóri, Ákra, *Greece* 39 F9
Paray-le-Monial, *France* 19 F11
Parbati →, *Mad. P., India* 68 G7
Parbati →, *Raj., India* 68 F7
Parbhani, *India* 66 K10
Parchim, *Germany* 24 B7
Parczew, *Poland* 45 G9
Pardes Hanna-Karkur, *Israel* 75 C3
Pardilla, *Spain* 34 D7
Pardo →, *Bahia, Brazil* 125 G11
Pardo →, *Mato Grosso, Brazil* 127 A5
Pardubice, *Czech Rep.* 26 A8
Pardubický □, *Czech Rep.* 26 B8
Pare, *Indonesia* 63 G15
Pare Mts., *Tanzania* 86 C4
Parecis, Serra dos, *Brazil* 124 F7
Paredes de Nava, *Spain* 34 C6
Paren, *Russia* 51 C17
Parent, *Canada* 102 C5
Parent, L., *Canada* 102 C4
Parentis-en-Born, *France* 20 D2
Parepare, *Indonesia* 63 E5
Parfino, *Russia* 46 D6
Párga, *Greece* 38 B2
Pargo, Pta. do, *Madeira* 37 D2
Pariaguán, *Venezuela* 124 B6
Paricutín, Cerro, *Mexico* 118 D4
Parigi, *Indonesia* 63 E6
Parika, *Guyana* 124 B7
Parikkala, *Finland* 46 B5
Parima, Serra, *Brazil* 124 C6
Parinari, *Peru* 124 D4
Pariñas, Pta., *S. Amer.* 122 D2
Parincea, *Romania* 43 D12
Parintins, *Brazil* 125 D7
Pariparit Kyun, *Burma* 67 M18
Paris, *Canada* 110 C4
Paris, *France* 19 D9
Paris, *Idaho, U.S.A.* 114 E8
Paris, *Ky., U.S.A.* 108 F3
Paris, *Tenn., U.S.A.* 109 G1
Paris, *Tex., U.S.A.* 113 J7
Paris, Ville de □, *France* 19 D9
Parish, *U.S.A.* 111 C8
Parishville, *U.S.A.* 111 B10
Park, *U.S.A.* 116 B4
Park City, *U.S.A.* 113 G6
Park Falls, *U.S.A.* 112 C9
Park Head, *Canada* 110 B3
Park Hills, *U.S.A.* 113 G9
Park Range, *U.S.A.* 114 G10
Park Rapids, *U.S.A.* 112 B7
Park River, *U.S.A.* 112 A6
Park Rynie, *S. Africa* 89 E5
Parkā Bandar, *Iran* 71 E8
Parkano, *Finland* 9 E20
Parker, *Ariz., U.S.A.* 117 L12
Parker, *Pa., U.S.A.* 110 E5
Parker Dam, *U.S.A.* 117 L12
Parkersburg, *U.S.A.* 108 F5
Parkes, *Australia* 95 E4
Parkfield, *U.S.A.* 116 K6
Parkhill, *Canada* 110 C3
Parkland, *U.S.A.* 116 C4
Parkston, *U.S.A.* 112 D6
Parksville, *Canada* 104 D4
Parla, *Spain* 34 E7
Pârliţa, *Moldova* 43 C12
Parma, *Italy* 28 D7
Parma, *Idaho, U.S.A.* 114 E5
Parma, *Ohio, U.S.A.* 110 E3
Parma →, *Italy* 28 D7
Parnaguá, *Brazil* 125 F10
Parnaíba, *Brazil* 125 D10
Parnaíba →, *Brazil* 122 D6
Parnassós, *Greece* 38 C4
Párnis, *Greece* 38 C5
Párnon Óros, *Greece* 38 D4
Pärnu, *Estonia* 9 G21
Paroo →, *Australia* 95 E3
Páros, *Greece* 39 D7
Parowan, *U.S.A.* 115 H7
Parpaillon, *France* 21 D10
Parral, *Chile* 126 D1
Parras, *Mexico* 118 B4
Parrett →, *U.K.* 13 F4
Parris I., *U.S.A.* 109 J5
Parrsboro, *Canada* 103 C7
Parry I., *Canada* 110 A4
Parry Is., *Canada* 4 B2
Parry Sound, *Canada* 102 C4
Parsberg, *Germany* 25 F7
Parsęta →, *Poland* 44 D2
Parsnip →, *Canada* 104 B4
Parsons, *U.S.A.* 113 G7
Parsons Ra., *Australia* 94 A2
Partanna, *Italy* 30 E5
Parthenay, *France* 18 F6
Partinico, *Italy* 30 D6
Partizánske, *Slovak Rep.* 27 C11
Partridge I., *Canada* 102 A2
Paru →, *Brazil* 125 D8
Parvān □, *Afghan.* 66 B6
Parvatipuram, *India* 67 K13
Parvatsar, *India* 68 F6
Påryd, *Sweden* 11 H9
Parys, *S. Africa* 88 D4
Pas, Pta. des, *Spain* 37 C7
Pas-de-Calais □, *France* 19 B9
Pasada, *Spain* 34 B5
Pasadena, *Canada* 103 C8
Pasadena, *Calif., U.S.A.* 117 L8
Pasadena, *Tex., U.S.A.* 113 L7
Pasaje →, *Argentina* 126 B3

Paşalimanı, *Turkey* 41 F11
Pasay, *Phil.* 61 D4
Pascagoula, *U.S.A.* 113 K10
Pascagoula →, *U.S.A.* 113 K10
Paşcani, *Romania* 43 C11
Pasco, *U.S.A.* 114 C4
Pasco, Cerro de, *Peru* 124 F3
Pasco I., *Australia* 92 D2
Pascoag, *U.S.A.* 111 E13
Pascua, I. de, *Pac. Oc.* 97 K17
Pasewalk, *Germany* 24 B9
Pasfield L., *Canada* 105 B7
Pasha →, *Russia* 46 B7
Pashmakli = Smolyan, *Bulgaria* 41 E8
Pasinler, *Turkey* 73 C9
Pasir Mas, *Malaysia* 65 J4
Pasir Putih, *Malaysia* 65 K4
Pasirian, *Indonesia* 63 H15
Pasirkuning, *Indonesia* 62 E2
Påskallavik, *Sweden* 11 G10
Pasküh, *Iran* 71 E9
Pasłęk, *Poland* 44 D6
Pasłęka →, *Poland* 44 D6
Pasley, C., *Australia* 93 F3
Pašman, *Croatia* 29 E12
Pasni, *Pakistan* 66 G3
Paso Cantinela, *Mexico* 117 N11
Paso de Indios, *Argentina* 128 E3
Paso de los Libres, *Argentina* 126 B4
Paso de los Toros, *Uruguay* 126 C4
Paso Robles, *U.S.A.* 115 J3
Paspébiac, *Canada* 103 C6
Pasrur, *Pakistan* 68 C6
Passage West, *Ireland* 15 E3
Passaic, *U.S.A.* 111 F10
Passau, *Germany* 25 G9
Passero, C., *Italy* 31 F8
Passo Fundo, *Brazil* 127 B5
Passos, *Brazil* 125 H9
Passow, *Germany* 24 B10
Passy, *France* 21 C10
Pastavy, *Belarus* 9 J22
Pastaza →, *Peru* 124 D3
Pasto, *Colombia* 124 C3
Pastrana, *Spain* 32 E2
Pasuruan, *Indonesia* 63 G15
Pasym, *Poland* 44 E7
Pásztó, *Hungary* 42 C4
Patagonia, *Argentina* 122 H4
Patagonia, *U.S.A.* 115 L8
Patambar, *Iran* 71 D9
Patan, *Gujarat, India* 66 H8
Patan, *Maharashtra, India* 68 H5
Patani, *Indonesia* 63 D7
Pătârlagele, *Romania* 43 E11
Pataudi, *India* 68 E7
Patchewollock, *Australia* 95 F3
Patchogue, *U.S.A.* 111 F11
Patea, *N.Z.* 91 H5
Pategi, *Nigeria* 83 D6
Patensie, *S. Africa* 88 E3
Paterna, *Spain* 33 F4
Paternion, *Austria* 26 E6
Paternò, *Italy* 31 E7
Pateros, *U.S.A.* 114 B4
Paterson, *U.S.A.* 111 F10
Paterson Ra., *Australia* 92 D3
Pathankot, *India* 68 C6
Pathfinder Reservoir, *U.S.A.* 114 E10
Pathiu, *Thailand* 65 G2
Pathum Thani, *Thailand* 64 E3
Pati, *Indonesia* 63 G14
Patía →, *Colombia* 124 C3
Patiala, *Punjab, India* 68 D7
Patiala, *Ut. P., India* 69 F8
Patine Kouka, *Senegal* 82 C2
Patitíríon, *Greece* 38 B5
Patkai Bum, *India* 67 F19
Pátmos, *Greece* 39 D8
Patna, *India* 69 G11
Patnos, *Turkey* 73 C10
Pato Branco, *Brazil* 127 B5
Patonga, *Uganda* 86 B3
Patos, *Albania* 40 F3
Patos, *Brazil* 125 E11
Patos, L. dos, *Brazil* 127 C5
Patos, Río de los →, *Argentina* 126 C2
Patos de Minas, *Brazil* 125 G9
Patquía, *Argentina* 126 C2
Pátrai, *Greece* 38 C3
Pátraikós Kólpos, *Greece* 38 C3
Patras = Pátrai, *Greece* 38 C3
Patrocínio, *Brazil* 125 G9
Patta, *Kenya* 86 C5
Pattada, *Italy* 30 B2
Pattani, *Thailand* 65 J3
Pattaya, *Thailand* 62 B2
Patten, *U.S.A.* 109 C11
Patterson, *Calif., U.S.A.* 116 H5
Patterson, *La., U.S.A.* 113 L9
Patterson, Mt., *U.S.A.* 116 G7
Patti, *Punjab, India* 68 D6
Patti, *Ut. P., India* 69 G10
Patti, *Italy* 31 D7
Pattoki, *Pakistan* 68 D5
Patton, *U.S.A.* 110 F6
Patuakhali, *Bangla.* 67 H17
Patuanak, *Canada* 105 B7
Patuca →, *Honduras* 120 C3
Patuca, Punta, *Honduras* 120 C3
Pătulele, *Romania* 42 F7
Pátzcuaro, *Mexico* 118 D4
Pau, *France* 20 E3
Pau, Gave de →, *France* 20 E2
Pauillac, *France* 20 C3
Pauk, *Burma* 67 J19
Paul I., *Canada* 103 A7
Paul Smiths, *U.S.A.* 111 B10
Paulatuk, *Canada* 100 B7
Paulhan, *France* 20 E7
Paulis = Isiro, *Dem. Rep. of the Congo* 86 B2
Paulistana, *Brazil* 125 E10
Paulo Afonso, *Brazil* 125 E11
Paulpietersburg, *S. Africa* 89 D5
Pauls Valley, *U.S.A.* 113 H6
Pauma Valley, *U.S.A.* 117 M10
Pauri, *India* 69 D8
Pāveh, *Iran* 70 C5
Pavelets, *Russia* 46 F10
Pavia, *Italy* 28 C6
Pavilion, *U.S.A.* 110 D6
Pavilly, *France* 18 C7
Pāvilosta, *Latvia* 9 H19
Pavlikeni, *Bulgaria* 41 C9
Pavlodar, *Kazakstan* 50 D8
Pavlograd = Pavlohrad, *Ukraine* 47 H8
Pavlohrad, *Ukraine* 47 H8
Pavlovo, *Russia* 48 C6
Pavlovsk, *Russia* 48 E5
Pavlovskaya, *Russia* 49 G4
Pavlovskiy-Posad, *Russia* 46 E10
Pavullo nel Frignano, *Italy* 28 D7
Pawayan, *India* 69 E9
Pawhuska, *U.S.A.* 113 G6
Pawling, *U.S.A.* 111 E11
Pawnee, *U.S.A.* 113 G6
Pawnee City, *U.S.A.* 112 E6
Pawtucket, *U.S.A.* 111 E13
Paximádhia, *Greece* 36 E6
Paxoí, *Greece* 38 B2
Paxton, *Ill., U.S.A.* 108 E1
Paxton, *Nebr., U.S.A.* 112 E4
Payakumbuh, *Indonesia* 62 E2
Payerne, *Switz.* 25 J2
Payette, *U.S.A.* 114 D5
Paymogo, *Spain* 35 H3
Payne Bay = Kangirsuk, *Canada* 101 B13
Payne L., *Canada* 101 C12
Paynes Find, *Australia* 93 E2
Paynesville, *Liberia* 82 D2
Paynesville, *U.S.A.* 112 C7
Pays de la Loire □, *France* 18 E6
Paysandú, *Uruguay* 126 C4
Payson, *U.S.A.* 115 J8
Paz →, *Guatemala* 120 D1
Paz, B. de la, *Mexico* 118 C2
Pāzanān, *Iran* 71 D6
Pazar, *Turkey* 73 B9
Pazarcık, *Turkey* 72 D7
Pazardzhik, *Bulgaria* 41 D8
Pazarköy, *Turkey* 39 B9
Pazarlar, *Turkey* 39 C11
Pazaryeri, *Turkey* 39 B11
Pazaryolu, *Turkey* 73 B9
Pazin, *Croatia* 29 C10
Pčinja →, *Macedonia* 40 E5
Pe Ell, *U.S.A.* 116 D3
Peabody, *U.S.A.* 111 D14
Peace →, *Canada* 104 B6
Peace Point, *Canada* 104 B6
Peace River, *Canada* 104 B5
Peach Springs, *U.S.A.* 115 J7
Peachland, *Canada* 104 D5
Peachtree City, *U.S.A.* 109 J3
Peak, The = Kinder Scout, *U.K.* 12 D6
Peak District, *U.K.* 12 D6
Peak Hill, *N.S.W., Australia* 95 E4
Peak Hill, *W. Austral., Australia* 93 E2
Peak Ra., *Australia* 94 C4
Peake Cr. →, *Australia* 95 D2
Peal de Becerro, *Spain* 35 H7
Peale, Mt., *U.S.A.* 115 G9
Pearblossom, *U.S.A.* 117 L9
Pearl →, *U.S.A.* 113 K10
Pearl City, *U.S.A.* 106 H16
Pearl Harbor, *U.S.A.* 106 H16
Pearl River, *U.S.A.* 111 E10
Pearsall, *U.S.A.* 113 L5
Peary Land, *Greenland* 4 A6
Pease →, *U.S.A.* 113 H5
Peawanuck, *Canada* 101 C11
Pebane, *Mozam.* 87 F4
Pebas, *Peru* 124 D4
Pebble Beach, *U.S.A.* 116 J5
Peć, *Kosovo, Yug.* 40 D4
Péccioli, *Italy* 28 E7
Pechea, *Romania* 43 E12
Pechenga, *Russia* 50 C4
Pechenizhyn, *Ukraine* 47 H3
Pechiguera, Pta., *Canary Is.* 37 F6
Pechnezhskoye Vdkhr., *Ukraine* 47 G9
Pechora, *Russia* 50 C6
Pechora →, *Russia* 50 C6
Pechorskaya Guba, *Russia* 50 C6
Pecica, *Romania* 42 D6
Pecka, *Serbia, Yug.* 40 B3
Pécora, C., *Italy* 30 C1
Pečory, *Russia* 9 H22
Pecos, *U.S.A.* 113 K3
Pecos →, *U.S.A.* 113 L3
Pécs, *Hungary* 42 D3
Pedder, L., *Australia* 94 G4
Peddie, *S. Africa* 89 E4
Pedernales, *Dom. Rep.* 121 C5
Pedieos →, *Cyprus* 36 D12
Pedirka, *Australia* 95 D2
Pedra Azul, *Brazil* 125 G10
Pedreguer, *Spain* 33 G5
Pedreiras, *Brazil* 125 D10
Pedro Afonso, *Brazil* 125 E9
Pedro Cays, *Jamaica* 120 C4
Pedro de Valdivia, *Chile* 126 A2
Pedro Juan Caballero, *Paraguay* 127 A4
Pedro Muñoz, *Spain* 35 F8
Pedrógão Grande, *Portugal* 34 F2
Pee Dee →, *U.S.A.* 109 J6
Peebinga, *Australia* 95 E3
Peebles, *U.K.* 14 F5
Peekskill, *U.S.A.* 111 E11
Peel, *U.K.* 12 C3
Peel →, *Australia* 95 E5
Peel →, *Canada* 100 B6
Peel Sound, *Canada* 100 A10
Peene →, *Germany* 24 A9
Peera Peera Poolanna L., *Australia* 95 D2
Peerless Lake, *Canada* 104 B6
Peers, *Canada* 104 C5
Pegasus Bay, *N.Z.* 91 K4
Peggau, *Austria* 26 D8
Pegnitz, *Germany* 25 F7
Pegnitz →, *Germany* 25 F6
Pego, *Spain* 33 G4
Pegu, *Burma* 67 L20
Pegu Yoma, *Burma* 67 K20
Pehčevo, *Macedonia* 40 E6
Pehlivanköy, *Turkey* 41 E10
Pehuajó, *Argentina* 126 D3
Pei Xian = Pizhou, *China* 56 G9
Peine, *Chile* 126 A2
Peine, *Germany* 24 C6
Peip'ing = Beijing, *China* 56 E9
Peipus, L. = Chudskoye, Ozero, *Russia* 9 G22
Peissenberg, *Germany* 25 H7
Peitz, *Germany* 24 D10
Peixe, *Brazil* 125 F9
Peixe →, *Brazil* 125 H8
Pek →, *Serbia, Yug.* 40 B5
Pekalongan, *Indonesia* 62 F3
Pekan, *Malaysia* 65 L4
Pekanbaru, *Indonesia* 62 D2
Pekang, *Taiwan* 59 F13
Pekin, *U.S.A.* 112 E10
Peking = Beijing, *China* 56 E9
Péla, *Guinea* 82 D3
Pelabuhan Kelang, *Malaysia* 65 L3
Pelabuhan Ratu, Teluk, *Indonesia* 63 G12
Pelabuhanratu, *Indonesia* 63 G12
Pélagos, *Greece* 38 B6
Pelaihari, *Indonesia* 62 E4
Pelat, Mt., *France* 21 D10
Pełczyce, *Poland* 45 E2
Peleaga, Vf., *Romania* 42 E7
Pelée, Mt., *Martinique* 121 D7
Pelee, Pt., *Canada* 102 D3
Pelee I., *Canada* 102 D3
Pelekech, *Kenya* 86 B4
Peleng, *Indonesia* 63 E6
Pélézi, *Ivory C.* 82 D3
Pelhřimov, *Czech Rep.* 26 B8
Pelican, *U.S.A.* 104 B1
Pelican L., *Canada* 105 C8
Pelican Narrows, *Canada* 105 B8
Pelješac, *Croatia* 29 F14
Pelkosenniemi, *Finland* 8 C22
Pella, *Greece* 40 F6
Pella, *S. Africa* 88 D2
Pella, *U.S.A.* 112 E8
Pélla □, *Greece* 40 F6
Pello, *Finland* 8 C21
Pellworm, *Germany* 24 A4
Pelly →, *Canada* 100 B6
Pelly Bay, *Canada* 101 B11
Peloponnese = Pelopónnisos □, *Greece* 38 D4
Pelopónnisos □, *Greece* 38 D4
Peloritani, Monti, *Italy* 31 D8
Pelorus Sd., *N.Z.* 91 J4
Pelotas, *Brazil* 127 C5
Pelotas →, *Brazil* 127 B5
Pelovo, *Bulgaria* 41 C8
Pelplin, *Poland* 44 E5
Pelvoux, Massif du, *France* 21 D10
Pemalang, *Indonesia* 63 G13
Pemanggil, Pulau, *Malaysia* 65 L5
Pematangsiantar, *Indonesia* 62 D1
Pemba, *Mozam.* 87 E5
Pemba, *Zambia* 87 F2
Pemba Channel, *Tanzania* 86 D4
Pemba I., *Tanzania* 86 D4
Pemberton, *Australia* 93 F2
Pemberton, *Canada* 104 C4
Pembina, *U.S.A.* 112 A6
Pembroke, *Canada* 102 C4
Pembroke, *U.K.* 13 F3
Pembrokeshire □, *U.K.* 13 F3
Pen-y-Ghent, *U.K.* 12 C5
Peña, Sierra de la, *Spain* 32 C4
Peña de Francia, Sierra de la, *Spain* 34 E4
Penafiel, *Portugal* 34 D2
Peñafiel, *Spain* 34 D6
Peñaflor, *Spain* 35 H5
Peñalara, *Spain* 34 E7
Penamacôr, *Portugal* 34 E3
Penang = Pinang, *Malaysia* 65 K3
Penápolis, *Brazil* 127 A6
Peñaranda de Bracamonte, *Spain* 34 E5
Peñarroya, *Spain* 32 E4
Peñarroya-Pueblonuevo, *Spain* 35 G5
Penarth, *U.K.* 13 F4
Peñas, C. de, *Spain* 34 B5
Penas, G. de, *Chile* 122 H3
Peñas de San Pedro, *Spain* 33 G3
Peñas del Chache, *Canary Is.* 37 E6
Peñausende, *Spain* 34 D5
Pench'i = Benxi, *China* 57 D12
Pend Oreille →, *U.S.A.* 114 B5
Pend Oreille, L., *U.S.A.* 114 C5
Pendálofon, *Greece* 40 F5
Pendembu, *Eastern, S. Leone* 82 D2
Pendembu, *Northern, S. Leone* 82 D2
Pender B., *Australia* 92 C3
Pendik, *Turkey* 41 F13
Pendjari →, *Benin* 83 C5
Pendleton, *U.S.A.* 114 D4
Pendra, *India* 69 H9
Penedo, *Brazil* 125 F11
Penetanguishene, *Canada* 102 D4
Penfield, *U.S.A.* 110 E6
Pengalengan, *Indonesia* 63 G12
Penge, *Kasai-Or., Dem. Rep. of the Congo* 86 D1
Penge, *Sud-Kivu, Dem. Rep. of the Congo* 86 C2
Penghu, *Taiwan* 59 F12
Penglai, *China* 57 F11
Pengshan, *China* 58 B4
Pengshui, *China* 58 C7
Penguin, *Australia* 94 G4
Pengxi, *China* 58 B5
Pengze, *China* 59 C11
Penhalonga, *Zimbabwe* 87 F3
Peniche, *Portugal* 35 F1
Penicuik, *U.K.* 14 F5
Penida, *Indonesia* 62 F5
Peninnes, Alpes = Pennine, Alpi, *Alps* 25 J3
Peninsular Malaysia □, *Malaysia* 65 L4
Peñíscola, *Spain* 32 E5
Penitente, Serra do, *Brazil* 125 E9
Penkridge, *U.K.* 12 E5
Penmarch, *France* 18 E2
Penmarch, Pte. de, *France* 18 E2
Penn Hills, *U.S.A.* 110 F5
Penn Yan, *U.S.A.* 110 D7
Penna, Punta della, *Italy* 29 F11
Pennant, *Canada* 105 C7
Penne, *Italy* 29 F10
Penner →, *India* 66 M12
Pennine, Alpi, *Alps* 25 J3
Pennines, *U.K.* 12 C5
Pennington, *U.S.A.* 116 F5
Pennington →, *Nigeria* 83 E6
Pennino, Mte., *Italy* 29 E9
Pennsburg, *U.S.A.* 111 F9
Pennsylvania □, *U.S.A.* 108 E7
Penny, *Canada* 104 C4
Peno, *Russia* 46 D7
Penobscot →, *U.S.A.* 109 C11
Penobscot B., *U.S.A.* 109 C11
Penola, *Australia* 95 F3
Penong, *Australia* 93 F5
Penonomé, *Panama* 120 E3
Penrith, *Australia* 95 E5
Penrith, *U.K.* 12 C5
Penryn, *U.K.* 13 G2
Pensacola, *U.S.A.* 109 K2
Pensacola Mts., *Antarctica* 5 E1
Pense, *Canada* 105 C8
Penshurst, *Australia* 95 F3
Penticton, *Canada* 104 D5
Pentland, *Australia* 94 C4
Pentland Firth, *U.K.* 14 C5
Pentland Hills, *U.K.* 14 F5
Penza, *Russia* 48 D7
Penzance, *U.K.* 13 G2
Penzberg, *Germany* 25 H7
Penzhino, *Russia* 51 C17
Penzhinskaya Guba, *Russia* 51 C17
Penzhou, *China* 58 B4
Penzlin, *Germany* 24 B9
Peoria, *Ariz., U.S.A.* 115 K7
Peoria, *Ill., U.S.A.* 112 E10
Pepacton Reservoir, *U.S.A.* 111 D10
Pepani →, *S. Africa* 88 D3
Pepel, *S. Leone* 82 D2
Peqin, *Albania* 40 E3
Pera Hd., *Australia* 94 A3
Perabumulih, *Indonesia* 62 E2
Perak →, *Malaysia* 65 K3
Perakhóra, *Greece* 38 C4
Perales de Alfambra, *Spain* 32 E4
Perales del Puerto, *Spain* 34 E4
Pérama, *Kérkira, Greece* 36 A3
Pérama, *Kríti, Greece* 36 D6
Peräpohjola, *Finland* 8 C22
Perast, *Montenegro, Yug.* 40 D2
Percé, *Canada* 103 C7
Perche, *France* 18 D8
Perchtoldsdorf, *Austria* 27 C9
Percival Lakes, *Australia* 92 D4
Percy, *France* 18 D5
Percy Is., *Australia* 94 C5
Perdido, Mte., *Spain* 32 C5
Perdu, Mt. = Perdido, Mte., *Spain* 32 C5
Pereira, *Colombia* 124 C3
Perelazovskiy, *Russia* 49 F6
Perenjori, *Australia* 93 E2
Peresecina, *Moldova* 43 C13
Pereslavl-Zalesskiy, *Russia* 46 D10
Peretu, *Romania* 43 F10
Pereyaslav-Khmelnytskyy, *Ukraine* 47 G6
Pérez, I., *Mexico* 119 C7
Perg, *Austria* 26 C7
Pergamino, *Argentina* 126 C3
Pergau →, *Malaysia* 65 K3
Pérgine Valsugana, *Italy* 29 B8
Pérgola, *Italy* 29 E9
Perham, *U.S.A.* 112 B7
Perhentian, Kepulauan, *Malaysia* 62 C2
Periam, *Romania* 42 D5
Péribonca →, *Canada* 103 C5
Péribonca, L., *Canada* 103 B5
Perico, *Argentina* 126 A2
Pericos, *Mexico* 118 B3
Périers, *France* 18 C5
Périgord, *France* 20 D4
Périgueux, *France* 20 C4
Perijá, Sierra de, *Colombia* 124 B4
Peristéra, *Greece* 38 B5
Peristerona →, *Cyprus* 36 D12
Perito Moreno, *Argentina* 128 F2
Perivol = Dragovishtitsa, *Bulgaria* 40 D6
Perkasie, *U.S.A.* 111 F9
Perković, *Croatia* 29 E13
Perlas, Arch. de las, *Panama* 120 E4
Perlas, Punta de, *Nic.* 120 D3
Perleberg, *Germany* 24 B7
Perlez, *Serbia, Yug.* 42 E5
Perm, *Russia* 50 D6
Përmet, *Albania* 40 F4
Pernambuco = Recife, *Brazil* 125 E12
Pernambuco □, *Brazil* 125 E11
Pernatty Lagoon, *Australia* 95 E2
Pernik, *Bulgaria* 40 D7
Peron Is., *Australia* 92 B5
Peron Pen., *Australia* 93 E1
Péronne, *France* 19 C9
Perosa Argentina, *Italy* 28 D4
Perow, *Canada* 104 C3
Perpendicular Pt., *Australia* 95 E5
Perpignan, *France* 20 F6
Perris, *U.S.A.* 117 M9
Perros-Guirec, *France* 18 D3
Perry, *Fla., U.S.A.* 109 K4
Perry, *Ga., U.S.A.* 109 J4
Perry, *Iowa, U.S.A.* 112 E7
Perry, *Okla., U.S.A.* 113 G6
Perryton, *U.S.A.* 113 G4
Perryville, *U.S.A.* 113 G10
Persan, *France* 19 C9
Persberg, *Sweden* 10 E8
Perşembe, *Turkey* 72 B7
Persepolis, *Iran* 71 D7
Pershotravensk, *Ukraine* 47 G4
Persia = Iran ■, *Asia* 71 C7
Persian Gulf = Gulf, The, *Asia* 71 E6
Perstorp, *Sweden* 11 H7
Pertek, *Turkey* 73 C8
Perth, *Australia* 93 F2
Perth, *Canada* 102 D4
Perth, *U.K.* 14 E5
Perth & Kinross □, *U.K.* 14 E5
Perth Amboy, *U.S.A.* 111 F10
Perth-Andover, *Canada* 103 C6
Pertuis, *France* 21 E9
Pertusato, C., *France* 21 G13
Peru, *Ind., U.S.A.* 108 E2
Peru, *N.Y., U.S.A.* 111 B11
Peru ■, *S. Amer.* 124 D4
Peru Basin, *Pac. Oc.* 97 J18
Peru-Chile Trench, *Pac. Oc.* 124 G3
Perúgia, *Italy* 29 E9
Perušić, *Croatia* 29 D12
Pervomaysk, *Russia* 48 C6
Pervomaysk, *Ukraine* 47 H6
Pervouralsk, *Russia* 50 D6
Pésaro, *Italy* 29 E9
Pescadores = Penghu, *Taiwan* 59 F12
Pescara, *Italy* 29 F11
Pescara →, *Italy* 29 F11
Peschanokopskoye, *Russia* 49 G5
Péscia, *Italy* 28 E7
Pescina, *Italy* 29 F10
Peshawar, *Pakistan* 68 B4
Peshkopi, *Albania* 40 E4
Peshtera, *Bulgaria* 41 D8
Peshtigo, *U.S.A.* 108 C2
Peski, *Russia* 48 E6
Pêso da Régua, *Portugal* 34 D3
Pesqueira, *Brazil* 125 E11
Pessac, *France* 20 D3
Pest □, *Hungary* 42 C4
Pestovo, *Russia* 46 C8
Pestravka, *Russia* 48 D9
Péta, *Greece* 38 B3
Petah Tiqwa, *Israel* 75 C3
Petalídhion, *Greece* 38 E3
Petaling Jaya, *Malaysia* 65 L3
Petaloudhes, *Greece* 36 C10
Petaluma, *U.S.A.* 116 G4
Pétange, *Lux.* 17 E5
Petaro, *Pakistan* 68 G3
Petatlán, *Mexico* 118 D4
Petauke, *Zambia* 87 E3
Petawawa, *Canada* 102 C4
Petén Itzá, L., *Guatemala* 120 C2
Peter I.s Øy, *Antarctica* 5 C16
Peter Pond L., *Canada* 105 B7
Peterbell, *Canada* 102 C3
Peterborough, *Australia* 95 E2
Peterborough, *Canada* 102 D4
Peterborough, *U.K.* 13 E7
Peterborough, *U.S.A.* 111 D13
Peterborough □, *U.K.* 13 E7
Peterculter, *U.K.* 14 D6
Peterhead, *U.K.* 14 D7
Peterlee, *U.K.* 12 C6
Petermann Bjerg, *Greenland* 98 B17
Petermann Ranges, *Australia* 92 E5
Petersburg, *Alaska, U.S.A.* 100 C6
Petersburg, *Pa., U.S.A.* 110 F6
Petersburg, *Va., U.S.A.* 108 G7
Petersburg, *W. Va., U.S.A.* 108 F6
Petersfield, *U.K.* 13 F7
Petershagen, *Germany* 24 C4

Petília Policastro, *Italy* 31 C9
Petit Goâve, *Haiti* 121 C5
Petit Jardin, *Canada* 103 C8
Petit Lac Manicouagan, *Canada* 103 B6
Petit-Mécatina →, *Canada* 103 B8
Petit-Mécatina, I. du, *Canada* 103 B8
Petit Saint Bernard, Col du, *Italy* 21 C10
Petitcodiac, *Canada* 103 C6
Petite Baleine →, *Canada* 102 A4
Petite Saguenay, *Canada* 103 C5
Petitot →, *Canada* 104 A4
Petitsikapau L., *Canada* 103 B6
Petlad, *India* 68 H5
Peto, *Mexico* 119 C7
Petone, *N.Z.* 91 J5
Petorca, *Chile* 126 C1
Petoskey, *U.S.A.* 108 C3
Petra, *Jordan* 75 E4
Petra, *Spain* 37 B10
Petra, Ostrova, *Russia* 4 B13
Petra Velikogo, Zaliv, *Russia* 54 C6
Petrel = Petrer, *Spain* 33 G4
Petrella, Monte, *Italy* 30 A6
Petrer, *Spain* 33 G4
Petreto-Bicchisano, *France* 21 G12
Petrich, *Bulgaria* 40 E7
Petrified Forest National Park, *U.S.A.* 115 J9
Petrijanec, *Croatia* 29 B13
Petrikov = Pyetrikaw, *Belarus* 47 F5
Petrila, *Romania* 43 E8
Petrinja, *Croatia* 29 C13
Petrodvorets, *Russia* 46 C5
Petrograd = Sankt-Peterburg, *Russia* 46 C6
Petrolândia, *Brazil* 125 E11
Petrolia, *Canada* 102 D3
Petrolina, *Brazil* 125 E10
Petropavl, *Kazakstan* 50 D7
Petropavlovsk = Petropavl, *Kazakstan* 50 D7
Petropavlovsk-Kamchatskiy, *Russia* 51 D16
Petropavlovskiy = Akhtubinsk, *Russia* 49 F8
Petrópolis, *Brazil* 127 A7
Petroşani, *Romania* 43 E8
Petrova Gora, *Croatia* 29 C12
Petrovac, *Montenegro, Yug.* 40 D2
Petrovac, *Serbia, Yug.* 40 B5
Petrovaradin, *Serbia, Yug.* 42 E4
Petrovsk, *Russia* 48 D7
Petrovsk-Zabaykalskiy, *Russia* 51 D11
Petrovskaya, *Russia* 47 K9
Petrovskoye = Svetlograd, *Russia* 49 H6
Petrozavodsk, *Russia* 46 B8
Petrus Steyn, *S. Africa* 89 D4
Petrusburg, *S. Africa* 88 D4
Petzeck, *Austria* 26 E5
Peumo, *Chile* 126 C1
Peureulak, *Indonesia* 62 D1
Pevek, *Russia* 51 C18
Peveragno, *Italy* 28 D4
Peyrehorade, *France* 20 E2
Peyruis, *France* 21 D9
Pézenas, *France* 20 E7
Pezinok, *Slovak Rep.* 27 C10
Pfaffenhofen, *Germany* 25 G7
Pfarrkirchen, *Germany* 25 G8
Pfeffenhausen, *Germany* 25 G7
Pforzheim, *Germany* 25 G4
Pfullendorf, *Germany* 25 H5
Pfungstadt, *Germany* 25 F4
Phagwara, *India* 66 D9
Phaistós, *Greece* 36 D6
Phala, *Botswana* 88 C4
Phalera = Phulera, *India* 68 F6
Phalodi, *India* 68 F5
Phalsbourg, *France* 19 D14
Phan, *Thailand* 64 C2
Phan Rang, *Vietnam* 65 G7
Phan Ri = Hoa Da, *Vietnam* 65 G7
Phan Thiet, *Vietnam* 65 G7
Phanae, *Greece* 39 C7
Phanat Nikhom, *Thailand* 64 F3
Phangan, Ko, *Thailand* 65 H3
Phangnga, *Thailand* 65 H2
Phanom Sarakham, *Thailand* 64 F3
Phaphund, *India* 69 F8
Pharenda, *India* 69 F10
Pharr, *U.S.A.* 113 M5
Phatthalung, *Thailand* 65 J3
Phayao, *Thailand* 64 C2
Phelps, *U.S.A.* 110 D7
Phelps L., *Canada* 105 B8
Phenix City, *U.S.A.* 109 J3
Phet Buri, *Thailand* 64 F2
Phetchabun, *Thailand* 64 D3
Phetchabun, Thiu Khao, *Thailand* 64 E3
Phetchaburi = Phet Buri, *Thailand* 64 F2
Phi Phi, Ko, *Thailand* 65 J2
Phiafay, *Laos* 64 E6
Phibun Mangsahan, *Thailand* 64 E5
Phichai, *Thailand* 64 D3
Phichit, *Thailand* 64 D3
Philadelphia, *Miss., U.S.A.* 113 J10
Philadelphia, *N.Y., U.S.A.* 111 B9
Philadelphia, *Pa., U.S.A.* 111 G9
Philip, *U.S.A.* 112 C4
Philippeville, *Belgium* 17 D4
Philippi, *Greece* 41 E8
Philippi, *U.S.A.* 108 F5
Philippi L., *Australia* 94 C2
Philippines ■, *Asia* 61 F5
Philippolis, *S. Africa* 88 E4
Philippopolis = Plovdiv, *Bulgaria* 41 D8
Philipsburg, *Canada* 111 A11
Philipsburg, *Mont., U.S.A.* 114 C7
Philipsburg, *Pa., U.S.A.* 110 F6
Philipstown = Daingean, *Ireland* 15 C4
Philipstown, *S. Africa* 88 E3
Phillip I., *Australia* 95 F4
Phillips, *U.S.A.* 112 C9
Phillipsburg, *Kans., U.S.A.* 112 F5
Phillipsburg, *N.J., U.S.A.* 111 F9
Philmont, *U.S.A.* 111 D11
Philomath, *U.S.A.* 114 D2
Phimai, *Thailand* 64 E4
Phitsanulok, *Thailand* 64 D3
Phnom Dangrek, *Thailand* 62 B2
Phnom Penh, *Cambodia* 65 G5
Phnum Penh = Phnom Penh, *Cambodia* 65 G5
Phoenicia, *U.S.A.* 111 D10
Phoenix, *Ariz., U.S.A.* 115 K7
Phoenix, *N.Y., U.S.A.* 111 C8
Phoenix Is., *Kiribati* 96 H10
Phoenixville, *U.S.A.* 111 F9
Phon, *Thailand* 64 E4
Phon Tiou, *Laos* 64 D5
Phong →, *Thailand* 64 D4
Phong Saly, *Laos* 58 G4
Phong Tho, *Vietnam* 64 A4
Phonhong, *Laos* 64 C4
Phonum, *Thailand* 65 H2
Phosphate Hill, *Australia* 94 C2
Photharam, *Thailand* 64 F2
Phra Nakhon Si Ayutthaya, *Thailand* 64 E3
Phra Thong, Ko, *Thailand* 65 H2
Phrae, *Thailand* 64 C3
Phrom Phiram, *Thailand* 64 D3
Phrygia, *Turkey* 72 C4
Phu Dien, *Vietnam* 64 C5
Phu Loi, *Laos* 64 B4
Phu Ly, *Vietnam* 58 G5
Phu Quoc, Dao, *Vietnam* 65 G4
Phu Tho, *Vietnam* 58 G5
Phuc Yen, *Vietnam* 58 G5
Phuket, *Thailand* 65 J2
Phuket, Ko, *Thailand* 65 J2
Phul, *India* 68 D6
Phulad, *India* 68 G5
Phulchari, *Bangla.* 69 G13
Phulera, *India* 68 F6
Phulpur, *India* 69 G10
Phun Phin, *Thailand* 65 H2
Piacenza, *Italy* 28 C6
Pian Cr. →, *Australia* 95 E4
Piana, *France* 21 F12
Pianella, *Italy* 29 F11
Pianosa, *Puglia, Italy* 29 F12
Pianosa, *Toscana, Italy* 28 F7
Piapot, *Canada* 105 D7
Pias, *Portugal* 35 G3
Piaseczno, *Poland* 45 F8
Piaski, *Poland* 45 G9
Piastów, *Poland* 45 F7
Piatra, *Romania* 43 G10
Piatra Neamţ, *Romania* 43 D11
Piatra Olt, *Romania* 43 F9
Piauí □, *Brazil* 125 E10
Piauí →, *Brazil* 125 E10
Piave →, *Italy* 29 C9
Piazza Ármerina, *Italy* 31 E7
Pibor →, *Sudan* 81 F3
Pibor Post, *Sudan* 81 F3
Picardie, *France* 19 C10
Picardie, Plaine de, *France* 19 C9
Picardy = Picardie, *France* 19 C10
Picayune, *U.S.A.* 113 K10
Picerno, *Italy* 31 B8
Pichhor, *India* 69 G8
Pichilemu, *Chile* 126 C1
Pichor, *India* 68 G8
Pickerel L., *Canada* 102 C1
Pickering, *U.K.* 12 C7
Pickering, Vale of, *U.K.* 12 C7
Pickle Lake, *Canada* 102 B1
Pickwick L., *U.S.A.* 109 H1
Pico Truncado, *Argentina* 128 F3
Picos, *Brazil* 125 E10
Picton, *Australia* 95 E5
Picton, *Canada* 102 D4
Picton, *N.Z.* 91 J5
Pictou, *Canada* 103 C7
Picture Butte, *Canada* 104 D6
Picún Leufú, *Argentina* 128 D3
Pidurutalagala, *Sri Lanka* 66 R12
Piechowice, *Poland* 45 H2
Piedmont = Piemonte □, *Italy* 28 D5
Piedmont, *Ala., U.S.A.* 109 J3
Piedmont, *S.C., U.S.A.* 107 D10
Piedmonte Matese, *Italy* 31 A7
Piedra →, *Spain* 32 D3
Piedrabuena, *Spain* 35 G6
Piedrahita, *Spain* 34 E5
Piedralaves, *Spain* 34 E6
Piedras Blancas, *Spain* 34 B5
Piedras Negras, *Mexico* 118 B4
Piekary Śląskie, *Poland* 45 H5
Pieksämäki, *Finland* 9 E22
Piemonte □, *Italy* 28 D5
Pienaarsrivier, *S. Africa* 89 D4
Pieniężno, *Poland* 44 D7
Pieńsk, *Poland* 45 G2
Piercefield, *U.S.A.* 111 B10
Pierceland, *Canada* 105 C7
Piería □, *Greece* 40 F6
Pierpont, *U.S.A.* 110 E4
Pierre, *U.S.A.* 112 C4
Pierre-Buffière, *France* 20 C5
Pierre-de-Bresse, *France* 19 F12
Pierre E. Trudeau, Mt. = Logan, Mt., *Canada* 100 B5
Pierrefontaine-les-Varans, *France* 19 E13
Pierrefort, *France* 20 D6
Pierrelatte, *France* 21 D8
Piešťany, *Slovak Rep.* 27 C10
Piesting →, *Austria* 27 C9
Pieszyce, *Poland* 45 H3
Piet Retief, *S. Africa* 89 D5
Pietarsaari, *Finland* 8 E20
Pietermaritzburg, *S. Africa* 89 D5
Pietersburg, *S. Africa* 89 C4
Pietragalla, *Italy* 31 B8
Pietrasanta, *Italy* 28 E7
Pietroşiţa, *Romania* 43 E10
Pietrosul, Vf., *Maramureş, Romania* 43 C9
Pietrosul, Vf., *Suceava, Romania* 43 C10
Pieve di Cadore, *Italy* 29 B9
Pieve di Teco, *Italy* 28 D4
Pievepélago, *Italy* 28 D7
Pigadhítsa, *Greece* 40 G5
Pigeon L., *Canada* 110 B6
Piggott, *U.S.A.* 113 G9
Pigna, *Italy* 28 E4
Pigüe, *Argentina* 126 D3
Pihani, *India* 69 F9
Pihlajavesi, *Finland* 9 F23
Pijijiapan, *Mexico* 119 D6
Pikalevo, *Russia* 46 C8
Pikangikum Berens, *Canada* 105 C10
Pikes Peak, *U.S.A.* 112 F2
Piketberg, *S. Africa* 88 E2
Pikeville, *U.S.A.* 108 G4
Pikou, *China* 57 E12
Pikwitonei, *Canada* 105 B9
Piła, *Poland* 45 E3
Pila, *Spain* 33 G3
Pilaía, *Greece* 40 F6
Pilani, *India* 68 E6
Pilar, *Paraguay* 126 B4
Pilar de la Horadada, *Spain* 33 H4
Pilawa, *Poland* 45 G8
Pilaya →, *Bolivia* 124 H6
Pilbara, *Australia* 92 D2
Pilcomayo →, *Paraguay* 126 B4
Pilgrim's Rest, *S. Africa* 89 C5
Pilgrimstad, *Sweden* 10 B9
Píli, *Greece* 39 E9
Pilibhit, *India* 69 E8
Pilica →, *Poland* 45 G8
Pilion, *Greece* 38 B5
Pilis, *Hungary* 42 C4
Pilisvörösvár, *Hungary* 42 C3
Pilkhawa, *India* 68 E7
Pilliga, *Australia* 95 E4
Pílos, *Greece* 38 E3
Pilot Mound, *Canada* 105 D9
Pilot Point, *U.S.A.* 113 J6
Pilot Rock, *U.S.A.* 114 D4
Pilsen = Plzeň, *Czech Rep.* 26 B6
Pilštanj, *Slovenia* 29 B12
Piltene, *Latvia* 44 A8
Pilzno, *Poland* 45 J8
Pima, *U.S.A.* 115 K9
Pimba, *Australia* 95 E2
Pimenta Bueno, *Brazil* 124 F6
Pimentel, *Peru* 124 E3
Pina de Ebro, *Spain* 32 D4
Pinamalayan, *Phil.* 61 E4
Pinang, *Malaysia* 65 K3
Pinar, C. des, *Spain* 37 B10
Pinar del Río, *Cuba* 120 B3
Pınarbaşı, *Çanakkale, Turkey* 39 B8
Pınarbaşı, *Kayseri, Turkey* 72 C7
Pınarhisar, *Turkey* 41 E11
Pinatubo, Mt., *Phil.* 61 D3
Pincehely, *Hungary* 42 D3
Pinchang, *China* 58 B6
Pincher Creek, *Canada* 104 D6
Pinchi L., *Canada* 104 C4
Pinckneyville, *U.S.A.* 112 F10
Pińczów, *Poland* 45 H7
Pindar, *Australia* 93 E2
Pindi Gheb, *Pakistan* 68 C5
Pindiga, *Nigeria* 83 D7
Pindos Óros, *Greece* 38 B3
Pindus Mts. = Pindos Óros, *Greece* 38 B3
Pine →, *B.C., Canada* 104 B4
Pine →, *Sask., Canada* 105 B7
Pine, C., *Canada* 103 C9
Pine Bluff, *U.S.A.* 113 H9
Pine Bluffs, *U.S.A.* 112 E2
Pine City, *U.S.A.* 112 C8
Pine Cr. →, *U.S.A.* 110 E7
Pine Creek, *Australia* 92 B5
Pine Falls, *Canada* 105 C9
Pine Flat Res., *U.S.A.* 116 J7
Pine Grove, *U.S.A.* 111 F8
Pine Pass, *Canada* 104 B4
Pine Point, *Canada* 104 A6
Pine Ridge, *U.S.A.* 112 D3
Pine River, *Canada* 105 C8
Pine River, *U.S.A.* 112 B7
Pine Valley, *U.S.A.* 117 N10
Pinecrest, *U.S.A.* 116 G6
Pineda de Mar, *Spain* 32 D7
Pinedale, *Calif., U.S.A.* 116 J7
Pinedale, *Wyo., U.S.A.* 114 E9
Pinega →, *Russia* 50 C5
Pinehill, *Australia* 94 C4
Pinehouse L., *Canada* 105 B7
Pineimuta →, *Canada* 102 B1
Pinerolo, *Italy* 28 D4
Pineto, *Italy* 29 F11
Pinetop, *U.S.A.* 115 J9
Pinetown, *S. Africa* 89 D5
Pineville, *U.S.A.* 113 K8
Piney, *France* 19 D11
Ping →, *Thailand* 64 E3
Pingaring, *Australia* 93 F2
Pingba, *China* 58 D6
Pingbian, *China* 58 F4
Pingchuan, *China* 58 D3
Pingding, *China* 56 F7
Pingdingshan, *China* 56 H7
Pingdong, *Taiwan* 59 F13
Pingdu, *China* 57 F10
Pingelly, *Australia* 93 F2
Pingguo, *China* 58 F6
Pinghe, *China* 59 E11
Pinghu, *China* 59 B13
Pingjiang, *China* 59 C9
Pingle, *China* 59 E8
Pingli, *China* 58 A7
Pingliang, *China* 56 G4
Pinglu, *China* 56 E7
Pingluo, *China* 56 E4
Pingnan, *Fujian, China* 59 D12
Pingnan, *Guangxi Zhuangzu, China* 59 F8
Pingquan, *China* 57 D10
Pingrup, *Australia* 93 F2
Pingshan, *China* 58 C5
Pingtan, *China* 59 E12
Pingtang, *China* 58 E6
P'ingtung, *Taiwan* 59 F13
Pingwu, *China* 56 H3
Pingxiang, *Guangxi Zhuangzu, China* 58 F6
Pingxiang, *Jiangxi, China* 59 D9
Pingyao, *China* 56 F7
Pingyi, *China* 57 G9
Pingyin, *China* 56 F9
Pingyuan, *Guangdong, China* 59 E10
Pingyuan, *Shandong, China* 56 F9
Pingyuanjie, *China* 58 F4
Pinhal, *Brazil* 127 A6
Pinhal Novo, *Portugal* 35 G2
Pinheiro, *Brazil* 125 D9
Pinheiro Machado, *Brazil* 127 C5
Pinhel, *Portugal* 34 E3
Pini, *Indonesia* 62 D1
Piniós →, *Ilía, Greece* 38 D3
Piniós →, *Trikkala, Greece* 38 B4
Pinjarra, *Australia* 93 F2
Pink Mountain, *Canada* 104 B4
Pinkafeld, *Austria* 27 D9
Pinnacles, *U.S.A.* 116 J5
Pinnaroo, *Australia* 95 F3
Pinneberg, *Germany* 24 B5
Pínnes, Ákra, *Greece* 41 F8
Pinon Hills, *U.S.A.* 117 L9
Pinos, *Mexico* 118 C4
Pinos, Mt., *U.S.A.* 117 L7
Pinos Pt., *U.S.A.* 115 H3
Pinos Puente, *Spain* 35 H7
Pinotepa Nacional, *Mexico* 119 D5
Pinrang, *Indonesia* 63 E5
Pins, Pte. aux, *Canada* 110 D3
Pinsk, *Belarus* 47 F4
Pintados, *Chile* 124 H5
Pinyang, *China* 59 D13
Pinyug, *Russia* 50 C5
Pioche, *U.S.A.* 115 H6
Piombino, *Italy* 28 F7
Piombino, Canale di, *Italy* 28 F7
Pioner, Ostrov, *Russia* 51 B10
Pionki, *Poland* 45 G8
Piorini, L., *Brazil* 124 D6
Piotrków Trybunalski, *Poland* 45 G6
Piove di Sacco, *Italy* 29 C9
Pīp, *Iran* 71 E9
Pipar, *India* 68 F5
Pipar Road, *India* 68 F5
Piparia, *Mad. P., India* 68 H8
Piparia, *Mad. P., India* 68 J7
Pipéri, *Greece* 38 B6
Pipestone, *U.S.A.* 112 D6
Pipestone →, *Canada* 102 B2
Pipestone Cr. →, *Canada* 105 D8
Piplan, *Pakistan* 68 C4
Piploda, *India* 68 H6
Pipmuacan, Rés., *Canada* 103 C5
Pippingarra, *Australia* 92 D2
Pipriac, *France* 18 E5
Piqua, *U.S.A.* 108 E3
Piquiri →, *Brazil* 127 A5
Pīr Sohrāb, *Iran* 71 E9
Pira, *Benin* 83 D5
Piracicaba, *Brazil* 127 A6
Piracuruca, *Brazil* 125 D10
Piræus = Piraiévs, *Greece* 38 D5
Piraiévs, *Greece* 38 D5
Piraju, *Brazil* 127 A6
Piram I., *India* 68 J5
Piran, *Slovenia* 29 C10
Pirané, *Argentina* 126 B4
Pirano = Piran, *Slovenia* 29 C10
Pirapora, *Brazil* 125 G10
Pirawa, *India* 68 G7
Pircop, *Bulgaria* 41 D8
Pírgos, *Ilía, Greece* 38 D3
Pírgos, *Kríti, Greece* 39 F7
Pirgovo, *Bulgaria* 41 C9
Piribebuy, *Paraguay* 126 B4
Pirimapun, *Indonesia* 63 F9
Pirin Planina, *Bulgaria* 40 E7
Pirineos = Pyrénées, *Europe* 20 F4
Piripiri, *Brazil* 125 D10
Pirmasens, *Germany* 25 F3
Pirna, *Germany* 24 E9
Pirot, *Serbia, Yug.* 40 C6
Piru, *Indonesia* 63 E7
Piru, *U.S.A.* 117 L8
Piryatin = Pyryatyn, *Ukraine* 47 G7
Piryí, *Greece* 39 C7
Pisa, *Italy* 28 E7
Pisa →, *Poland* 45 E8
Pisagne, *Italy* 28 C7
Pisagua, *Chile* 124 G4
Pisarovina, *Croatia* 29 C12
Pisco, *Peru* 124 F3
Piscu, *Romania* 43 E12
Písek, *Czech Rep.* 26 B7
Pishan, *China* 60 C2
Pīshīn, *Iran* 71 E9
Pishin, *Pakistan* 68 D2
Pishin Lora →, *Pakistan* 68 E1
Pisidia, *Turkey* 72 D4
Pising, *Indonesia* 63 F6
Pismo Beach, *U.S.A.* 117 K6
Piso, L., *Liberia* 82 D2
Pissila, *Burkina Faso* 83 C4
Pissis, Cerro, *Argentina* 126 B2
Pissos, *France* 20 D3
Pissouri, *Cyprus* 36 E11
Pisticci, *Italy* 31 B9
Pistóia, *Italy* 28 E7
Pistol B., *Canada* 105 A10
Pisuerga →, *Spain* 34 D6
Pisz, *Poland* 44 E8
Pit →, *U.S.A.* 114 F2
Pita, *Guinea* 82 C2
Pitarpunga, L., *Australia* 95 E3
Pitcairn I., *Pac. Oc.* 97 K14
Pite älv →, *Sweden* 8 D19
Piteå, *Sweden* 8 D19
Piterka, *Russia* 48 E8
Piteşti, *Romania* 43 F9
Pithapuram, *India* 67 L13
Pithara, *Australia* 93 F2
Píthion, *Greece* 41 E10
Pithiviers, *France* 19 D9
Pithoragarh, *India* 69 E9
Pithoro, *Pakistan* 68 G3
Pitigliano, *Italy* 29 F8
Pitkyaranta, *Russia* 46 B6
Pitlochry, *U.K.* 14 E5
Pitsilia □, *Cyprus* 36 E12
Pitt I., *Canada* 104 C3
Pittsburg, *Calif., U.S.A.* 116 G5
Pittsburg, *Kans., U.S.A.* 113 G7
Pittsburg, *Tex., U.S.A.* 113 J7
Pittsburgh, *U.S.A.* 110 F5
Pittsfield, *Ill., U.S.A.* 112 F9
Pittsfield, *Maine, U.S.A.* 109 C11
Pittsfield, *Mass., U.S.A.* 111 D11
Pittsfield, *N.H., U.S.A.* 111 C13
Pittston, *U.S.A.* 111 E9
Pittsworth, *Australia* 95 D5
Pituri →, *Australia* 94 C2
Piura, *Peru* 124 E2
Piva →, *Montenegro, Yug.* 40 C2
Piwniczna, *Poland* 45 J7
Pixley, *U.S.A.* 116 K7
Piyai, *Greece* 38 B3
Pizarra, *Spain* 35 J6
Pizhou, *China* 56 G9
Pizzo, *Italy* 31 D9
Placentia, *Canada* 103 C9
Placentia B., *Canada* 103 C9
Placer, *Masbate, Phil.* 61 F5
Placer, *Surigao N., Phil.* 61 G6
Placerville, *U.S.A.* 116 G6
Placetas, *Cuba* 120 B4
Plačkovica, *Macedonia* 40 E6
Plainfield, *N.J., U.S.A.* 111 F10
Plainfield, *Ohio, U.S.A.* 110 F3
Plainfield, *Vt., U.S.A.* 111 B12
Plains, *Mont., U.S.A.* 114 C6
Plains, *Tex., U.S.A.* 113 J3
Plainview, *Nebr., U.S.A.* 112 D6
Plainview, *Tex., U.S.A.* 113 H4
Plainwell, *U.S.A.* 108 D3
Plaisance, *France* 20 E4
Plaistow, *U.S.A.* 111 D13
Pláka, *Greece* 39 B7
Pláka, Ákra, *Greece* 36 D8
Plakenska Planina, *Macedonia* 40 E5
Planá, *Czech Rep.* 26 B5
Plana Cays, *Bahamas* 121 B5
Planada, *U.S.A.* 116 H6
Plancoët, *France* 18 D4
Plandište, *Serbia, Yug.* 42 E6
Plano, *U.S.A.* 113 J6
Plant City, *U.S.A.* 109 M4
Plaquemine, *U.S.A.* 113 K9
Plasencia, *Spain* 34 E4
Plaški, *Croatia* 29 C12
Plaster City, *U.S.A.* 117 N11
Plaster Rock, *Canada* 103 C6
Plastun, *Russia* 54 B8
Plasy, *Czech Rep.* 26 B6
Plata, Río de la, *S. Amer.* 126 C4
Plátani →, *Italy* 30 E6
Plátanos, *Greece* 36 D5
Plateau □, *Nigeria* 83 D6
Platí, Ákra, *Greece* 41 F8
Platte, *U.S.A.* 112 D5
Platte →, *Mo., U.S.A.* 112 F7
Platte →, *Nebr., U.S.A.* 112 E7
Platteville, *U.S.A.* 112 D9
Plattling, *Germany* 25 G8
Plattsburgh, *U.S.A.* 111 B11
Plattsmouth, *U.S.A.* 112 E7
Plau, *Germany* 24 B8

Plauen, *Germany* 24 E8
Plauer See, *Germany* 24 B8
Plav, *Montenegro, Yug.* 40 D3
Plavinas, *Latvia* 9 H21
Plavnica, *Montenegro, Yug.* 40 D3
Plavno, *Croatia* 29 D13
Plavsk, *Russia* 46 F9
Playa Blanca, *Canary Is.* 37 F6
Playa Blanca Sur, *Canary Is.* 37 F6
Playa de las Americas, *Canary Is.* 37 F3
Playa de Mogán, *Canary Is.* 37 G4
Playa del Inglés, *Canary Is.* 37 G4
Playa Esmerelda, *Canary Is.* 37 F5
Playgreen L., *Canada* 105 C9
Pleasant Bay, *Canada* 103 C7
Pleasant Hill, *U.S.A.* 116 H4
Pleasant Mount, *U.S.A.* 111 E9
Pleasanton, *Calif., U.S.A.* 116 H5
Pleasanton, *Tex., U.S.A.* 113 L5
Pleasantville, *N.J., U.S.A.* 108 F8
Pleasantville, *Pa., U.S.A.* 110 E5
Pléaux, *France* 20 C6
Plei Ku, *Vietnam* 64 F7
Plélan-le-Grand, *France* 18 D4
Pléneuf-Val-André, *France* 18 D4
Plenița, *Romania* 43 F8
Plenty →, *Australia* 94 C2
Plenty, B. of, *N.Z.* 91 G6
Plentywood, *U.S.A.* 112 A2
Plérin, *France* 18 D4
Plessisville, *Canada* 103 C5
Plestin-les-Grèves, *France* 18 D3
Pleszew, *Poland* 45 G4
Pleternica, *Croatia* 42 E2
Plétipi, L., *Canada* 103 B5
Pleven, *Bulgaria* 41 C8
Plevlja, *Montenegro, Yug.* 40 C3
Plevna, *Canada* 110 B8
Plješevica, *Croatia* 29 D12
Ploaghe, *Italy* 30 B1
Ploče, *Croatia* 29 E14
Płock, *Poland* 45 F6
Plöckenpass, *Italy* 29 B9
Plöckenstein, *Germany* 25 G9
Ploemeur, *France* 18 E3
Ploërmel, *France* 18 E4
Ploiești, *Romania* 43 F11
Plomárion, *Greece* 39 C8
Plombières-les-Bains, *France* 19 E13
Plomin, *Croatia* 29 C11
Plön, *Germany* 24 A6
Plonge, Lac la, *Canada* 105 B7
Płońsk, *Poland* 45 F7
Plopeni, *Romania* 43 E10
Plopișului, Munții, *Romania* 42 C7
Płoty, *Poland* 44 E2
Plouaret, *France* 18 D3
Plouay, *France* 18 E3
Ploučnice →, *Czech Rep.* 26 A7
Ploudalmézeau, *France* 18 D2
Plouescat, *France* 18 D2
Plougasnou, *France* 18 D3
Plougastel-Daoulas, *France* 18 D2
Plouguerneau, *France* 18 D2
Plouha, *France* 18 D4
Plouhinec, *France* 18 E2
Plovdiv, *Bulgaria* 41 D8
Plovdiv □, *Bulgaria* 41 D8
Plum, *U.S.A.* 110 F5
Plum I., *U.S.A.* 111 E12
Plumas, *U.S.A.* 116 F7
Plummer, *U.S.A.* 114 C5
Plumtree, *Zimbabwe* 87 G2
Plungė, *Lithuania* 9 J19
Pluvigner, *France* 18 E3
Plymouth, *U.K.* 13 G3
Plymouth, *Calif., U.S.A.* 116 G6
Plymouth, *Ind., U.S.A.* 108 E2
Plymouth, *Mass., U.S.A.* 111 E14
Plymouth, *N.C., U.S.A.* 109 H7
Plymouth, *N.H., U.S.A.* 111 C13
Plymouth, *Pa., U.S.A.* 111 E9
Plymouth, *Wis., U.S.A.* 108 D2
Plynlimon = Pumlumon Fawr, *U.K.* 13 E4
Plyusa, *Russia* 46 C5
Plyusa →, *Russia* 46 C5
Plyussa = Plyusa, *Russia* 46 C5
Plyussa → = Plyusa →, *Russia* 46 C5
Plzeň, *Czech Rep.* 26 B6
Plzeňský □, *Czech Rep.* 26 B6
Pniewy, *Poland* 45 F3
Pô, *Burkina Faso* 83 C4
Po →, *Italy* 29 D9
Po, Foci del, *Italy* 29 D9
Po Hai = Bo Hai, *China* 57 E10
Pobé, *Benin* 83 D5
Pobé, *Burkina Faso* 83 C4
Pobeda, *Russia* 51 C15
Pobedy, Pik, *Kyrgyzstan* 50 E8
Pobiedziska, *Poland* 45 F4
Pobla de Segur, *Spain* 32 C5
Pobladura del Valle, *Spain* 34 C5
Pobra de Trives, *Spain* 34 C3
Pocahontas, *Ark., U.S.A.* 113 G9
Pocahontas, *Iowa, U.S.A.* 112 D7
Pocatello, *U.S.A.* 114 E7
Počátky, *Czech Rep.* 26 B8
Pochep, *Russia* 47 F7
Pochinki, *Russia* 48 C7
Pochinok, *Russia* 46 E7
Pöchlarn, *Austria* 26 C8
Pochutla, *Mexico* 119 D5
Pocito Casas, *Mexico* 118 B2
Pocking, *Germany* 25 G9
Pocomoke City, *U.S.A.* 108 F8
Poços de Caldas, *Brazil* 127 A6
Podbořany, *Czech Rep.* 26 A6
Poddębice, *Poland* 45 G5
Poděbrady, *Czech Rep.* 26 A8
Podensac, *France* 20 D3
Podenzano, *Italy* 28 D6
Podgorač, *Croatia* 42 E3
Podgorica, *Montenegro, Yug.* 40 D3
Podgorie, *Albania* 40 F4
Podilska Vysochyna, *Ukraine* 47 H4
Podkarpackie □, *Poland* 45 H9
Podkova, *Bulgaria* 41 E9
Podlapača, *Croatia* 29 D12
Podlaskie □, *Poland* 45 E10
Podoleni, *Romania* 43 D11
Podolínec, *Slovak Rep.* 27 B13
Podolsk, *Russia* 46 E9
Podor, *Senegal* 82 B1
Podporozhye, *Russia* 46 B8
Podu Iloaiei, *Romania* 43 C12
Podu Turcului, *Romania* 43 D12
Podujevo, *Kosovo, Yug.* 40 D5
Poel, *Germany* 24 B6
Pofadder, *S. Africa* 88 D2
Poggiardo, *Italy* 31 B11
Poggibonsi, *Italy* 28 E8
Póggio Mirteto, *Italy* 29 F9
Pogoanele, *Romania* 43 F12
Pogorzela, *Poland* 45 G4
Pogradec, *Albania* 40 F4
Pogranitšnyi, *Russia* 54 B5
Poh, *Indonesia* 63 E6
P'ohang, *S. Korea* 57 F15
Pohjanmaa, *Finland* 8 E20
Pohnpei, *Micronesia* 96 G7
Pohorelá, *Slovak Rep.* 27 C13
Pohořelice, *Czech Rep.* 27 C9
Pohorje, *Slovenia* 29 B12
Pohri, *India* 68 G6
Poiana Mare, *Romania* 42 G8
Poiana Ruscăi, Munții, *Romania* 42 E7
Poiana Stampei, *Romania* 43 C10
Poinsett, C., *Antarctica* 5 C8
Point Arena, *U.S.A.* 116 G3
Point Baker, *U.S.A.* 104 B2
Point Edward, *Canada* 102 D3
Point Hope, *U.S.A.* 100 B3
Point L., *Canada* 100 B8
Point Pedro, *Sri Lanka* 66 Q12
Point Pleasant, *N.J., U.S.A.* 111 F10
Point Pleasant, *W. Va., U.S.A.* 108 F4
Pointe-à-Pitre, *Guadeloupe* 121 C7
Pointe-Claire, *Canada* 111 A11
Pointe-Gatineau, *Canada* 111 A9
Pointe-Noire, *Congo* 84 E2
Poio, *Spain* 34 C2
Poirino, *Italy* 28 D4
Poisonbush Ra., *Australia* 92 D3
Poissonnier Pt., *Australia* 92 C2
Poitiers, *France* 18 F7
Poitou, *France* 20 B3
Poitou-Charentes □, *France* 20 B4
Poix-de-Picardie, *France* 19 C8
Poix-Terron, *France* 19 C11
Pojoaque, *U.S.A.* 115 J11
Pokaran, *India* 66 F7
Pokataroo, *Australia* 95 D4
Pokhara, *Nepal* 69 E10
Pokhvistnevo, *Russia* 48 D11
Poko, *Dem. Rep. of the Congo* 86 B2
Poko, *Sudan* 81 F3
Pokrov, *Russia* 46 E10
Pokrovsk = Engels, *Russia* 48 E8
Pokrovsk, *Russia* 51 C13
Pokrovskoye, *Russia* 47 J10
Pola = Pula, *Croatia* 29 D10
Pola, *Russia* 46 D7
Pola de Allande, *Spain* 34 B4
Pola de Lena, *Spain* 34 B5
Pola de Siero, *Spain* 34 B5
Pola de Somiedo, *Spain* 34 B4
Polacca, *U.S.A.* 115 J8
Polan, *Iran* 71 E9
Pol'ana, *Slovak Rep.* 27 C12
Poland ■, *Europe* 45 G3
Polanica-Zdrój, *Poland* 45 H3
Połaniec, *Poland* 45 H8
Polanów, *Poland* 44 D3
Polar Bear Prov. Park, *Canada* 102 A2
Polatlı, *Turkey* 72 C5
Polatsk, *Belarus* 46 E5
Polcura, *Chile* 126 D1
Połczyn-Zdrój, *Poland* 44 E3
Polessk, *Russia* 9 J19
Polesye = Pripet Marshes, *Europe* 47 F5
Polgar, *Hungary* 42 C6
Pŏlgyo-ri, *S. Korea* 57 G14
Poli, *Cameroon* 83 C7
Políaigos, *Greece* 38 E6
Policastro, G. di, *Italy* 31 C8
Police, *Poland* 44 E1
Polička, *Czech Rep.* 27 B9
Policoro, *Italy* 31 B9
Polignano a Mare, *Italy* 31 A9
Poligny, *France* 19 F12
Políkhnitas, *Greece* 39 B8
Polillo Is., *Phil.* 61 D4
Polillo Strait, *Phil.* 61 D4
Polis, *Cyprus* 36 D11
Polístena, *Italy* 31 D9
Políyiros, *Greece* 40 F7
Polk, *U.S.A.* 110 E5
Polkowice, *Poland* 45 G3
Polla, *Italy* 31 B8
Pollachi, *India* 66 P10
Pollença, *Spain* 37 B10
Pollença, B. de, *Spain* 37 B10
Póllica, *Italy* 31 B8
Pollino, Mte., *Italy* 31 C9
Polna, *Russia* 46 C5
Polnovat, *Russia* 50 C7
Pology, *Ukraine* 47 J9
Polonne, *Ukraine* 47 G4
Polonnoye = Polonne, *Ukraine* 47 G4
Polski Trŭmbesh, *Bulgaria* 41 C9
Polsko Kosovo, *Bulgaria* 41 C9
Polson, *U.S.A.* 114 C6
Poltár, *Slovak Rep.* 27 C12
Poltava, *Ukraine* 47 H8
Põltsamaa, *Estonia* 9 G21
Polunochnoye, *Russia* 50 C7
Põlva, *Estonia* 9 G22
Polynesia, *Pac. Oc.* 97 J11
Polynésie française = French Polynesia ■, *Pac. Oc.* 97 K13
Pomarance, *Italy* 28 E7
Pomaro, *Mexico* 118 D4
Pombal, *Portugal* 34 F2
Pómbia, *Greece* 36 E6
Pomene, *Mozam.* 89 C6
Pomeroy, *Ohio, U.S.A.* 108 F4
Pomeroy, *Wash., U.S.A.* 114 C5
Pomézia, *Italy* 30 A5
Pomichna, *Ukraine* 47 H6
Pomona, *Australia* 95 D5
Pomona, *U.S.A.* 117 L9
Pomorie, *Bulgaria* 41 D11
Pomorskie □, *Poland* 44 D5
Pomorskie, Pojezierze, *Poland* 44 E3
Pomos, *Cyprus* 36 D11
Pomos, C., *Cyprus* 36 D11
Pompano Beach, *U.S.A.* 109 M5
Pompei, *Italy* 31 B7
Pompey, *France* 19 D13
Pompeys Pillar, *U.S.A.* 114 D10
Pompton Lakes, *U.S.A.* 111 F10
Ponape = Pohnpei, *Micronesia* 96 G7
Ponask L., *Canada* 102 B1
Ponca, *U.S.A.* 112 D6
Ponca City, *U.S.A.* 113 G6
Ponce, *Puerto Rico* 121 C6
Ponchatoula, *U.S.A.* 113 K9
Poncheville, L., *Canada* 102 B4
Pond, *U.S.A.* 117 K7
Pond Inlet, *Canada* 101 A12
Pondicherry, *India* 66 P11
Ponds, I. of, *Canada* 103 B8
Ponferrada, *Spain* 34 C4
Pongo, Wadi →, *Sudan* 81 F2
Poniatowa, *Poland* 45 G9
Poniec, *Poland* 45 G3
Ponikva, *Slovenia* 29 B12
Ponnani, *India* 66 P9
Ponoka, *Canada* 104 C6
Ponorogo, *Indonesia* 63 G14
Pons = Ponts, *Spain* 32 D6
Pons, *France* 20 C3
Ponsul →, *Portugal* 34 F3
Pont-à-Mousson, *France* 19 D13
Pont-Audemer, *France* 18 C7
Pont-Aven, *France* 18 E3
Pont Canavese, *Italy* 28 C4
Pont-d'Ain, *France* 19 F12
Pont-de-Roide, *France* 19 E13
Pont-de-Salars, *France* 20 D6
Pont-de-Vaux, *France* 19 F11
Pont-de-Veyle, *France* 19 F11
Pont-du-Château, *France* 19 G10
Pont-l'Abbé, *France* 18 E2
Pont-l'Évêque, *France* 18 C7
Pont-St-Esprit, *France* 21 D8
Pont-St-Martin, *Italy* 28 C4
Pont-Ste-Maxence, *France* 19 C9
Pont-sur-Yonne, *France* 19 D10
Ponta do Sol, *Madeira* 37 D2
Ponta Grossa, *Brazil* 127 B5
Ponta Pora, *Brazil* 127 A4
Pontacq, *France* 20 E3
Pontailler-sur-Saône, *France* 19 E12
Pontarlier, *France* 19 F13
Pontassieve, *Italy* 29 E8
Pontaumur, *France* 20 C6
Pontcharra, *France* 21 C10
Pontchartrain L., *U.S.A.* 113 K10
Pontchâteau, *France* 18 E4
Ponte da Barca, *Portugal* 34 D2
Ponte de Sor, *Portugal* 35 F2
Ponte dell'Ólio, *Italy* 28 D6
Ponte di Legno, *Italy* 28 B7
Ponte do Lima, *Portugal* 34 D2
Ponte do Pungué, *Mozam.* 87 F3
Ponte-Leccia, *France* 21 F13
Ponte nelle Alpi, *Italy* 29 B9
Ponte Nova, *Brazil* 127 A7
Ponteareas, *Spain* 34 C2
Pontebba, *Italy* 29 B10
Ponteceso, *Spain* 34 B2
Pontecorvo, *Italy* 30 A6
Pontedeume, *Spain* 34 B2
Ponteix, *Canada* 105 D7
Pontevedra, *Spain* 34 C2
Pontevedra □, *Spain* 34 C2
Pontevedra, R. de →, *Spain* 34 C2
Pontevico, *Italy* 28 C7
Pontiac, *Ill., U.S.A.* 112 E10
Pontiac, *Mich., U.S.A.* 108 D4
Pontian Kecil, *Malaysia* 65 M4
Pontianak, *Indonesia* 62 E3
Pontine Is. = Ponziane, Ísole, *Italy* 30 B5
Pontine Mts. = Kuzey Anadolu Dağları, *Turkey* 72 B7
Pontínia, *Italy* 30 A6
Pontivy, *France* 18 D4
Pontoise, *France* 19 C9
Ponton →, *Canada* 104 B5
Pontorson, *France* 18 D5
Pontrémoli, *Italy* 28 D6
Pontrieux, *France* 18 D3
Ponts, *Spain* 32 D6
Pontypool, *Canada* 110 B6
Pontypool, *U.K.* 13 F4
Ponza, *Italy* 30 B5
Ponziane, Ísole, *Italy* 30 B5
Poochera, *Australia* 95 E1
Poole, *U.K.* 13 G6
Poole □, *U.K.* 13 G6
Poona = Pune, *India* 66 K8
Pooncarie, *Australia* 95 E3
Poopelloe L., *Australia* 95 E3
Poopó, L. de, *Bolivia* 122 E4
Popayán, *Colombia* 124 C3
Poperinge, *Belgium* 17 D2
Popilta L., *Australia* 95 E3
Popina, *Bulgaria* 41 B10
Popio L., *Australia* 95 E3
Poplar, *U.S.A.* 112 A2
Poplar →, *Canada* 105 C9
Poplar Bluff, *U.S.A.* 113 G9
Poplarville, *U.S.A.* 113 K10
Popocatépetl, Volcán, *Mexico* 119 D5
Popokabaka, *Dem. Rep. of the Congo* 84 F3
Pópoli, *Italy* 29 F10
Popovača, *Croatia* 29 C13
Popovo, *Bulgaria* 41 C10
Poppberg, *Germany* 25 F7
Poppi, *Italy* 29 E8
Poprad, *Slovak Rep.* 27 B13
Poprad →, *Slovak Rep.* 27 B13
Porali →, *Pakistan* 68 G2
Porbandar, *India* 66 J6
Porcher I., *Canada* 104 C2
Porcuna, *Spain* 35 H6
Porcupine →, *Canada* 105 B8
Porcupine →, *U.S.A.* 100 B5
Pordenone, *Italy* 29 C9
Pordim, *Bulgaria* 41 C8
Poreč, *Croatia* 29 C10
Poretskoye, *Russia* 48 C8
Pori, *Finland* 9 F19
Porí, *Greece* 38 F5
Porkhov, *Russia* 46 D5
Porlamar, *Venezuela* 124 A6
Porlezza, *Italy* 28 B6
Porma →, *Spain* 34 C5
Pornic, *France* 18 E4
Poronaysk, *Russia* 51 E15
Póros, *Greece* 38 D5
Poroshiri-Dake, *Japan* 54 C11
Poroszló, *Hungary* 42 C5
Poroto Mts., *Tanzania* 87 D3
Porpoise B., *Antarctica* 5 C9
Porquerolles, Î. de, *France* 21 F10
Porrentruy, *Switz.* 25 H3
Porreres, *Spain* 37 B10
Porsangen, *Norway* 8 A21
Porsgrunn, *Norway* 9 G13
Port Alberni, *Canada* 104 D4
Port Alfred, *S. Africa* 88 E4
Port Alice, *Canada* 104 C3
Port Allegany, *U.S.A.* 110 E6
Port Allen, *U.S.A.* 113 K9
Port Alma, *Australia* 94 C5
Port Angeles, *U.S.A.* 116 B3
Port Antonio, *Jamaica* 120 C4
Port Aransas, *U.S.A.* 113 M6
Port Arthur = Lüshun, *China* 57 E11
Port Arthur, *Australia* 94 G4
Port Arthur, *U.S.A.* 113 L8
Port au Choix, *Canada* 103 B8
Port au Port B., *Canada* 103 C8
Port-au-Prince, *Haiti* 121 C5
Port Augusta, *Australia* 95 E2
Port Austin, *U.S.A.* 110 B2
Port Bell, *Uganda* 86 B3
Port Bergé Vaovao, *Madag.* 89 B8
Port Blandford, *Canada* 103 C9
Port-Bouët, *Ivory C.* 82 D4
Port Bradshaw, *Australia* 94 A2
Port Broughton, *Australia* 95 E2
Port Burwell, *Canada* 110 D4
Port Canning, *India* 69 H13
Port-Cartier, *Canada* 103 B6
Port Chalmers, *N.Z.* 91 L3
Port Charlotte, *U.S.A.* 109 M4
Port Chester, *U.S.A.* 111 F11
Port Clements, *Canada* 104 C2
Port Clinton, *U.S.A.* 108 E4
Port Colborne, *Canada* 102 D4
Port Coquitlam, *Canada* 104 D4
Port Credit, *Canada* 110 C5
Port Curtis, *Australia* 94 C5
Port d'Alcúdia, *Spain* 37 B10
Port Dalhousie, *Canada* 110 C5
Port Darwin, *Australia* 92 B5
Port Darwin, *Falk. Is.* 128 G5
Port Davey, *Australia* 94 G4
Port-de-Bouc, *France* 21 E8
Port-de-Paix, *Haiti* 121 C5
Port de Pollença, *Spain* 37 B10
Port de Sóller, *Spain* 37 B9
Port Dickson, *Malaysia* 65 L3
Port Douglas, *Australia* 94 B4
Port Dover, *Canada* 110 D4
Port Edward, *Canada* 104 C2
Port Elgin, *Canada* 102 D3
Port Elizabeth, *S. Africa* 88 E4
Port Ellen, *U.K.* 14 F2
Port-en-Bessin, *France* 18 C6
Port Erin, *U.K.* 12 C3
Port Essington, *Australia* 92 B5
Port Etienne = Nouâdhibou, *Mauritania* 78 D2
Port Ewen, *U.S.A.* 111 E11
Port Fairy, *Australia* 95 F3
Port Fouâd = Bûr Fuad, *Egypt* 80 H8
Port Gamble, *U.S.A.* 116 C4
Port-Gentil, *Gabon* 84 E1
Port Germein, *Australia* 95 E2
Port Gibson, *U.S.A.* 113 K9
Port Glasgow, *U.K.* 14 F4
Port Harcourt, *Nigeria* 83 E6
Port Hardy, *Canada* 104 C3
Port Harrison = Inukjuak, *Canada* 101 C12
Port Hawkesbury, *Canada* 103 C7
Port Hedland, *Australia* 92 D2
Port Henry, *U.S.A.* 111 B11
Port Hood, *Canada* 103 C7
Port Hope, *Canada* 102 D4
Port Hope, *U.S.A.* 110 C2
Port Hope Simpson, *Canada* 103 B8
Port Hueneme, *U.S.A.* 117 L7
Port Huron, *U.S.A.* 110 D2
Port Iliç, *Azerbaijan* 73 C13
Port Jefferson, *U.S.A.* 111 F11
Port Jervis, *U.S.A.* 111 E10
Port-Joinville, *France* 18 F4
Port Katon, *Russia* 47 J10
Port Kelang = Pelabuhan Kelang, *Malaysia* 65 L3
Port Kenny, *Australia* 95 E1
Port-la-Nouvelle, *France* 20 E7
Port Lairge = Waterford, *Ireland* 15 D4
Port Laoise, *Ireland* 15 C4
Port Lavaca, *U.S.A.* 113 L6
Port Leyden, *U.S.A.* 111 C9
Port Lincoln, *Australia* 95 E2
Port Loko, *S. Leone* 82 D2
Port Louis, *France* 18 E3
Port Louis, *Mauritius* 77 H9
Port Lyautey = Kenitra, *Morocco* 78 B4
Port MacDonnell, *Australia* 95 F3
Port McNeill, *Canada* 104 C3
Port Macquarie, *Australia* 95 E5
Port Maria, *Jamaica* 120 C4
Port Matilda, *U.S.A.* 110 F6
Port Mellon, *Canada* 104 D4
Port-Menier, *Canada* 103 C7
Port Moody, *Canada* 116 A4
Port Morant, *Jamaica* 120 C4
Port Moresby, *Papua N. G.* 96 H6
Port Musgrave, *Australia* 94 A3
Port-Navalo, *France* 18 E4
Port Neches, *U.S.A.* 113 L8
Port Nolloth, *S. Africa* 88 D2
Port Nouveau-Québec = Kangiqsualujjuaq, *Canada* 101 C13
Port of Spain, *Trin. & Tob.* 121 D7
Port Orange, *U.S.A.* 109 L5
Port Orchard, *U.S.A.* 116 C4
Port Orford, *U.S.A.* 114 E1
Port Pegasus, *N.Z.* 91 M1
Port Perry, *Canada* 102 D4
Port Phillip B., *Australia* 95 F3
Port Pirie, *Australia* 95 E2
Port Radium = Echo Bay, *Canada* 100 B8
Port Renfrew, *Canada* 104 D4
Port Roper, *Australia* 94 A2
Port Rowan, *Canada* 110 D4
Port Safaga = Bûr Safâga, *Egypt* 70 E2
Port Said = Bûr Sa'îd, *Egypt* 80 H8
Port St. Joe, *U.S.A.* 109 L3
Port St. Johns = Umzimvubu, *S. Africa* 89 E4
Port-St-Louis-du-Rhône, *France* 21 E8
Port St. Lucie, *U.S.A.* 109 M5
Port-Ste-Marie, *France* 20 D4
Port Sanilac, *U.S.A.* 110 C2
Port Severn, *Canada* 110 B5
Port Shepstone, *S. Africa* 89 E5
Port Simpson, *Canada* 104 C2
Port Stanley = Stanley, *Falk. Is.* 128 G5
Port Stanley, *Canada* 102 D3
Port Sudan = Bûr Sûdân, *Sudan* 80 D4
Port Sulphur, *U.S.A.* 113 L10
Port-sur-Saône, *France* 19 E13
Port Talbot, *U.K.* 13 F4
Port Taufiq = Bûr Taufiq, *Egypt* 80 J8
Port Townsend, *U.S.A.* 116 B4
Port-Vendres, *France* 20 F7
Port Vila, *Vanuatu* 96 J8
Port Wakefield, *Australia* 95 E2
Port Washington, *U.S.A.* 108 D2
Port Weld = Kuala Sepetang, *Malaysia* 65 K3
Portadown, *U.K.* 15 B5
Portaferry, *U.K.* 15 B6
Portage, *Pa., U.S.A.* 110 F6
Portage, *Wis., U.S.A.* 112 D10
Portage La Prairie, *Canada* 105 D9
Portageville, *U.S.A.* 113 G10
Portalegre, *Portugal* 35 F3
Portalegre □, *Portugal* 35 F3
Portales, *U.S.A.* 113 H3
Portarlington, *Ireland* 15 C4
Portbou, *Spain* 32 C8
Portel, *Portugal* 35 G3
Porter L., *N.W.T., Canada* 105 A7
Porter L., *Sask., Canada* 105 B7
Porterville, *S. Africa* 88 E2
Porterville, *U.S.A.* 116 J8
Portes-lès-Valence, *France* 21 D8
Porthcawl, *U.K.* 13 F4

Porthill, *U.S.A.* 114 B5
Porthmadog, *U.K.* 12 E3
Portile de Fier, *Europe* 42 F7
Portimão, *Portugal* 35 H2
Portishead, *U.K.* 13 F5
Portiţei, Gura, *Romania* 43 F14
Portknockie, *U.K.* 14 D6
Portland, *N.S.W., Australia* 95 E5
Portland, *Vic., Australia* 95 F3
Portland, *Canada* 111 B8
Portland, *Conn., U.S.A.* 111 E12
Portland, *Maine, U.S.A.* 101 D12
Portland, *Mich., U.S.A.* 108 D3
Portland, *Oreg., U.S.A.* 116 E4
Portland, *Pa., U.S.A.* 111 F9
Portland, *Tex., U.S.A.* 113 M6
Portland, I. of, *U.K.* 13 G5
Portland B., *Australia* 95 F3
Portland Bill, *U.K.* 13 G5
Portland Canal, *U.S.A.* 104 B2
Portmadoc = Porthmadog, *U.K.* 12 E3
Porto, *France* 21 F12
Porto, *Portugal* 34 D2
Porto □, *Portugal* 34 D2
Porto, G. de, *France* 21 F12
Pôrto Alegre, *Brazil* 127 C5
Porto Amboim = Gunza, *Angola* 84 G2
Porto Azzurro, *Italy* 28 F7
Porto Cristo, *Spain* 37 B10
Pôrto de Móz, *Brazil* 125 D8
Porto Empédocle, *Italy* 30 E6
Pôrto Esperança, *Brazil* 124 G7
Pôrto Franco, *Brazil* 125 E9
Pórto Lágos, *Greece* 41 E9
Porto Mendes, *Brazil* 127 A5
Porto Moniz, *Madeira* 37 D2
Pôrto Murtinho, *Brazil* 124 H7
Pôrto Nacional, *Brazil* 125 F9
Porto-Novo, *Benin* 83 D5
Porto Petro, *Spain* 37 B10
Porto San Giórgio, *Italy* 29 E10
Porto Sant' Elpídio, *Italy* 29 E10
Porto Santo, I. de, *Madeira* 78 B2
Porto Santo Stéfano, *Italy* 28 F8
Pôrto São José, *Brazil* 127 A5
Pôrto Seguro, *Brazil* 125 G11
Porto Tolle, *Italy* 29 D9
Porto Tórres, *Italy* 30 B1
Pôrto União, *Brazil* 127 B5
Pôrto Válter, *Brazil* 124 E4
Porto-Vecchio, *France* 21 G13
Pôrto Velho, *Brazil* 124 E6
Portobelo, *Panama* 120 E4
Portoferráio, *Italy* 28 F7
Portogruaro, *Italy* 29 C9
Portola, *U.S.A.* 116 F6
Portomaggiore, *Italy* 29 D8
Portoscuso, *Italy* 30 C1
Portovénere, *Italy* 28 D6
Portoviejo, *Ecuador* 124 D2
Portpatrick, *U.K.* 14 G3
Portree, *U.K.* 14 D2
Portrush, *U.K.* 15 A5
Portsmouth, *Domin.* 121 C7
Portsmouth, *U.K.* 13 G6
Portsmouth, *N.H., U.S.A.* 109 D10
Portsmouth, *Ohio, U.S.A.* 108 F4
Portsmouth, *R.I., U.S.A.* 111 E13
Portsmouth, *Va., U.S.A.* 108 G7
Portsmouth □, *U.K.* 13 G6
Portsoy, *U.K.* 14 D6
Portstewart, *U.K.* 15 A5
Porttipahtan tekojärvi, *Finland* 8 B22
Portugal ■, *Europe* 34 F3
Portugalete, *Spain* 32 B1
Portumna, *Ireland* 15 C3
Portville, *U.S.A.* 110 D6
Porvenir, *Chile* 128 G2
Porvoo, *Finland* 9 F21
Porzuna, *Spain* 35 F6
Posada, *Italy* 30 B2
Posada →, *Italy* 30 B2
Posadas, *Argentina* 127 B4
Posadas, *Spain* 35 H5
Poschiavo, *Switz.* 25 J6
Posets, *Spain* 32 C5
Poshan = Boshan, *China* 57 F9
Posht-e-Badam, *Iran* 71 C7
Posídhion, Ákra, *Greece* 40 G7
Posidium, *Greece* 39 F9
Poso, *Indonesia* 63 E6
Posong, *S. Korea* 57 G14
Posse, *Brazil* 125 F9
Possession I., *Antarctica* 5 D11
Pössneck, *Germany* 24 E7
Possum Kingdom L., *U.S.A.* 113 J5
Post, *U.S.A.* 113 J4
Post Falls, *U.S.A.* 114 C5
Postavy = Pastavy, *Belarus* 9 J22
Poste-de-la-Baleine = Kuujjuarapik, *Canada* 102 A4
Postmasburg, *S. Africa* 88 D3
Postojna, *Slovenia* 29 C11
Poston, *U.S.A.* 117 M12
Postville, *Canada* 103 B8
Potamós, *Andikíthira, Greece* 38 F5
Potamós, *Kíthira, Greece* 38 E4
Potchefstroom, *S. Africa* 88 D4
Potcoava, *Romania* 43 F9
Poteau, *U.S.A.* 113 H7
Poteet, *U.S.A.* 113 L5
Potenza, *Italy* 31 B8
Potenza →, *Italy* 29 E10
Potenza Picena, *Italy* 29 E10
Poteriteri, L., *N.Z.* 91 M1
Potgietersrus, *S. Africa* 89 C4
Poti, *Georgia* 49 J5
Potiskum, *Nigeria* 83 C7
Potlogi, *Romania* 43 F10
Potomac →, *U.S.A.* 108 G7
Potosí, *Bolivia* 124 G5
Potosi Mt., *U.S.A.* 117 K11
Pototan, *Phil.* 61 F5
Potrerillos, *Chile* 126 B2
Potsdam, *Germany* 24 C9
Potsdam, *U.S.A.* 111 B10
Pottenstein, *Germany* 25 F7
Pottersville, *U.S.A.* 111 C11
Pottery Hill = Abu Ballas, *Egypt* 80 C2
Pottstown, *U.S.A.* 111 F9
Pottsville, *U.S.A.* 111 F8
Pottuvil, *Sri Lanka* 66 R12
P'otzu, *Taiwan* 59 F13
Pouancé, *France* 18 E5
Pouce Coupé, *Canada* 104 B4
Poughkeepsie, *U.S.A.* 111 E11
Pouilly-sur-Loire, *France* 19 E9
Poulaphouca Res., *Ireland* 15 C5
Poulsbo, *U.S.A.* 116 C4
Poultney, *U.S.A.* 111 C11
Poulton-le-Fylde, *U.K.* 12 D5
Pouso Alegre, *Brazil* 127 A6
Pout, *Senegal* 82 C1
Pouthisat, *Cambodia* 64 F4
Pouzauges, *France* 18 F6
Pova de Sta. Iria, *Portugal* 35 G1
Považská Bystrica, *Slovak Rep.* 27 B11
Poverty B., *N.Z.* 91 H7
Povlen, *Serbia, Yug.* 40 B3
Póvoa de Lanhosa, *Portugal* 34 D2
Póvoa de Varzim, *Portugal* 34 D2
Povorino, *Russia* 48 E6
Povungnituk = Puvirnituq, *Canada* 101 B12
Powassan, *Canada* 102 C4
Poway, *U.S.A.* 117 N9
Powder →, *U.S.A.* 112 B2
Powder River, *U.S.A.* 114 E10
Powell, *U.S.A.* 114 D9
Powell, L., *U.S.A.* 115 H8
Powell River, *Canada* 104 D4
Powers, *U.S.A.* 108 C2
Powys □, *U.K.* 13 E4
Poyang Hu, *China* 59 C11
Poyarkovo, *Russia* 51 E13
Poysdorf, *Austria* 27 C9
Poza de la Sal, *Spain* 34 C7
Poza Rica, *Mexico* 119 C5
Pozanti, *Turkey* 72 D6
Požarevac, *Serbia, Yug.* 40 B5
Pozazal, Puerto, *Spain* 34 C6
Požega, *Croatia* 42 E2
Požega, *Serbia, Yug.* 40 C4
Poznań, *Poland* 45 F3
Pozo, *U.S.A.* 117 K6
Pozo Alcón, *Spain* 35 H8
Pozo Almonte, *Chile* 124 H5
Pozo Colorado, *Paraguay* 126 A4
Pozoblanco, *Spain* 35 G6
Pozzallo, *Italy* 31 F7
Pozzomaggiore, *Italy* 30 B1
Pozzuoli, *Italy* 31 B7
Pra →, *Ghana* 83 D4
Prabuty, *Poland* 44 E6
Prača, *Bos.-H.* 42 G3
Prachatice, *Czech Rep.* 26 B6
Prachin Buri, *Thailand* 64 E3
Prachuap Khiri Khan, *Thailand* 65 G2
Pradelles, *France* 20 D7
Prades, *France* 20 F6
Prado, *Brazil* 125 G11
Prado del Rey, *Spain* 35 J5
Præstø, *Denmark* 11 J6
Pragersko, *Slovenia* 29 B12
Prague = Praha, *Czech Rep.* 26 A7
Praha, *Czech Rep.* 26 A7
Prahecq, *France* 20 B3
Prahova □, *Romania* 43 E10
Prahova →, *Romania* 43 F10
Prahovo, *Serbia, Yug.* 40 B6
Praia, *C. Verde Is.* 77 E1
Práia a Mare, *Italy* 31 C8
Praid, *Romania* 43 D10
Prainha, *Amazonas, Brazil* 124 E6
Prainha, *Pará, Brazil* 125 D8
Prairie, *Australia* 94 C3
Prairie City, *U.S.A.* 114 D4
Prairie Dog Town Fork →, *U.S.A.* 113 H5
Prairie du Chien, *U.S.A.* 112 D9
Prairies, L. of the, *Canada* 105 C8
Pramánda, *Greece* 38 B3
Prampram, *Ghana* 83 D5
Pran Buri, *Thailand* 64 F2
Prang, *Ghana* 83 D4
Prapat, *Indonesia* 62 D1
Prasonísi, Ákra, *Greece* 36 D9
Prästmon, *Sweden* 10 A11
Praszka, *Poland* 45 G5
Prata, *Brazil* 125 G9
Pratabpur, *India* 69 H10
Pratapgarh, *Raj., India* 68 G6
Pratapgarh, *Ut. P., India* 69 G9
Prato, *Italy* 28 E8
Prátola Peligna, *Italy* 29 F10
Prats-de-Mollo-la-Preste, *France* 20 F6
Pratt, *U.S.A.* 113 G5
Prattville, *U.S.A.* 109 J2
Pravdinsk, *Russia* 48 B6
Pravets, *Bulgaria* 40 D7
Pravia, *Spain* 34 B4
Praya, *Indonesia* 62 F5
Pré-en-Pail, *France* 18 D6
Precordillera, *Argentina* 126 C2
Predáppio, *Italy* 29 D8
Predazzo, *Italy* 29 B8
Predeal, *Romania* 43 E10
Predejane, *Serbia, Yug.* 40 D6
Preeceville, *Canada* 105 C8
Preetz, *Germany* 24 A6
Pregrada, *Croatia* 29 B12
Preiļi, *Latvia* 9 H22
Preko, *Croatia* 29 D12
Prelog, *Croatia* 29 B13
Prémery, *France* 19 E10
Premià de Mar, *Spain* 32 D7
Premont, *U.S.A.* 113 M5
Premuda, *Croatia* 29 D11
Prentice, *U.S.A.* 112 C9
Prenzlau, *Germany* 24 B9
Preobrazheniye, *Russia* 54 C6
Preparis North Channel, *Ind. Oc.* 67 M18
Preparis South Channel, *Ind. Oc.* 67 M18
Přerov, *Czech Rep.* 27 B10
Prescott, *Canada* 102 D4
Prescott, *Ariz., U.S.A.* 115 J7
Prescott, *Ark., U.S.A.* 113 J8
Prescott Valley, *U.S.A.* 115 J7
Preservation Inlet, *N.Z.* 91 M1
Preševo, *Serbia, Yug.* 40 D5
Presho, *U.S.A.* 112 D4
Presicce, *Italy* 31 C11
Presidencia de la Plaza, *Argentina* 126 B4
Presidencia Roque Saenz Peña, *Argentina* 126 B3
Presidente Epitácio, *Brazil* 125 H8
Presidente Hayes □, *Paraguay* 126 A4
Presidente Prudente, *Brazil* 127 A5
Presidio, *Mexico* 118 B4
Presidio, *U.S.A.* 113 L2
Preslav, *Bulgaria* 41 C10
Preslavska Planina, *Bulgaria* 41 C10
Prešov, *Slovak Rep.* 27 B14
Prešovský □, *Slovak Rep.* 27 B13
Prespa, *Bulgaria* 41 E8
Prespa, L. = Prespansko Jezero, *Macedonia* 40 F5
Prespansko Jezero, *Macedonia* 40 F5
Presque I., *U.S.A.* 110 D4
Presque Isle, *U.S.A.* 109 B12
Prestatyn, *U.K.* 12 D4
Prestea, *Ghana* 82 D4
Presteigne, *U.K.* 13 E5
Přeštice, *Czech Rep.* 26 B6
Preston, *Canada* 110 C4
Preston, *U.K.* 12 D5
Preston, *Idaho, U.S.A.* 114 E8
Preston, *Minn., U.S.A.* 112 D8
Preston, C., *Australia* 92 D2
Prestonburg, *U.S.A.* 108 G4
Prestwick, *U.K.* 14 F4
Pretoria, *S. Africa* 89 D4
Preuilly-sur-Claise, *France* 18 F7
Préveza, *Greece* 38 C2
Préveza □, *Greece* 38 B2
Prey Veng, *Cambodia* 65 G5
Priazovskoye, *Ukraine* 47 J8
Pribilof Is., *U.S.A.* 100 C2
Priboj, *Serbia, Yug.* 40 C3
Příbram, *Czech Rep.* 26 B7
Price, *U.S.A.* 114 G8
Price I., *Canada* 104 C3
Prichard, *U.S.A.* 109 K1
Priego, *Spain* 32 E2
Priego de Córdoba, *Spain* 35 H6
Priekule, *Latvia* 9 H19
Prien, *Germany* 25 H8
Prienai, *Lithuania* 9 J20
Prieska, *S. Africa* 88 D3
Priest L., *U.S.A.* 114 B5
Priest River, *U.S.A.* 114 B5
Priest Valley, *U.S.A.* 116 J6
Prievidza, *Slovak Rep.* 27 C11
Prignitz, *Germany* 24 B7
Prijedor, *Bos.-H.* 29 D13
Prijepolje, *Serbia, Yug.* 40 C3
Prikaspiyskaya Nizmennost = Caspian Depression, *Eurasia* 49 G9
Prikro, *Ivory C.* 82 D4
Prikubanskaya Nizmennost, *Russia* 49 H4
Prilep, *Macedonia* 40 E5
Priluki = Pryluky, *Ukraine* 47 G7
Prime Seal I., *Australia* 94 G4
Primorsk, *Russia* 46 B5
Primorsko, *Bulgaria* 41 D11
Primorsko-Akhtarsk, *Russia* 47 J10
Primorskoye, *Ukraine* 47 J9
Primrose L., *Canada* 105 C7
Prince Albert, *Canada* 105 C7
Prince Albert, *S. Africa* 88 E3
Prince Albert Mts., *Antarctica* 5 D11
Prince Albert Nat. Park, *Canada* 105 C7
Prince Albert Pen., *Canada* 100 A8
Prince Albert Sd., *Canada* 100 A8
Prince Alfred, C., *Canada* 4 B1
Prince Charles I., *Canada* 101 B12
Prince Charles Mts., *Antarctica* 5 D6
Prince Edward I. □, *Canada* 103 C7
Prince Edward Is., *Ind. Oc.* 3 G11
Prince Edward Pt., *Canada* 110 C8
Prince George, *Canada* 104 C4
Prince of Wales, C., *U.S.A.* 98 C3
Prince of Wales I., *Australia* 94 A3
Prince of Wales I., *Canada* 100 A10
Prince of Wales I., *U.S.A.* 100 C6
Prince Patrick I., *Canada* 4 B2
Prince Regent Inlet, *Canada* 4 B3
Prince Rupert, *Canada* 104 C2
Princess Charlotte B., *Australia* 94 A3
Princess May Ranges, *Australia* 92 C4
Princess Royal I., *Canada* 104 C3
Princeton, *Canada* 104 D4
Princeton, *Calif., U.S.A.* 116 F4
Princeton, *Ill., U.S.A.* 112 E10
Princeton, *Ind., U.S.A.* 108 F2
Princeton, *Ky., U.S.A.* 108 G2
Princeton, *Mo., U.S.A.* 112 E8
Princeton, *N.J., U.S.A.* 111 F10
Princeton, *W. Va., U.S.A.* 108 G5
Principe, I. de, *Atl. Oc.* 76 F4
Principe da Beira, *Brazil* 124 F6
Prineville, *U.S.A.* 114 D3
Prins Harald Kyst, *Antarctica* 5 D4
Prinsesse Astrid Kyst, *Antarctica* 5 D3
Prinsesse Ragnhild Kyst, *Antarctica* 5 D4
Prinzapolca, *Nic.* 120 D3
Prior, C., *Spain* 34 B2
Priozersk, *Russia* 46 B6
Pripet = Prypyat →, *Europe* 47 G6
Pripet Marshes, *Europe* 47 F5
Pripyat Marshes = Pripet Marshes, *Europe* 47 F5
Pripyats = Prypyat →, *Europe* 47 G6
Prislop, Pasul, *Romania* 43 C9
Pristen, *Russia* 47 G9
Priština, *Kosovo, Yug.* 40 D5
Pritzwalk, *Germany* 24 B8
Privas, *France* 21 D8
Priverno, *Italy* 30 A6
Privolzhsk, *Russia* 48 B5
Privolzhskaya Vozvyshennost, *Russia* 48 E7
Privolzhskiy, *Russia* 48 E8
Privolzhye, *Russia* 48 D9
Priyutnoye, *Russia* 49 G6
Prizren, *Kosovo, Yug.* 40 D4
Prizzi, *Italy* 30 E6
Prnjavor, *Bos.-H.* 42 F2
Probolinggo, *Indonesia* 63 G15
Prochowice, *Poland* 45 G3
Proctor, *U.S.A.* 111 C11
Proddatur, *India* 66 M11
Prodhromos, *Cyprus* 36 E11
Proença-a-Nova, *Portugal* 34 F3
Profítis Ilías, *Greece* 36 C9
Profondeville, *Belgium* 17 D4
Progreso, *Coahuila, Mexico* 118 B4
Progreso, *Yucatán, Mexico* 119 C7
Prokhladnyy, *Russia* 49 J7
Prokletije, *Albania* 40 D3
Prokopyevsk, *Russia* 50 D9
Prokuplje, *Serbia, Yug.* 40 C5
Proletarsk, *Russia* 49 G5
Proletarskaya = Proletarsk, *Russia* 49 G5
Prome = Pyè, *Burma* 67 K19
Prophet →, *Canada* 104 B4
Prophet River, *Canada* 104 B4
Propriá, *Brazil* 125 F11
Propriano, *France* 21 G12
Proserpine, *Australia* 94 C4
Prosna →, *Poland* 45 F4
Prospect, *U.S.A.* 111 C9
Prosser, *U.S.A.* 114 C4
Prostějov, *Czech Rep.* 27 B10
Prostki, *Poland* 44 E9
Proston, *Australia* 95 D5
Proszowice, *Poland* 45 H7
Proti, *Greece* 38 D3
Provadiya, *Bulgaria* 41 C11
Provence, *France* 21 E9
Provence-Alpes-Côte d'Azur □, *France* 21 D10
Providence, *Ky., U.S.A.* 108 G2
Providence, *R.I., U.S.A.* 111 E13
Providence Bay, *Canada* 102 C3
Providence Mts., *U.S.A.* 117 K11
Providencia, I. de, *Colombia* 120 D3
Provideniya, *Russia* 51 C19
Provins, *France* 19 D10
Provo, *U.S.A.* 114 F8
Provost, *Canada* 105 C6
Prozor, *Bos.-H.* 42 G2
Prrenjas, *Albania* 40 E4
Prudhoe Bay, *U.S.A.* 100 A5
Prudhoe I., *Australia* 94 C4
Prud'homme, *Canada* 105 C7
Prudnik, *Poland* 45 H4
Prüm, *Germany* 25 E2
Prundu, *Romania* 43 F11
Pruszcz Gdański, *Poland* 44 D5
Pruszków, *Poland* 45 F7
Prut →, *Romania* 43 E13
Pruzhany, *Belarus* 47 F3
Prvič, *Croatia* 29 D11
Prydz B., *Antarctica* 5 C6
Pryluky, *Ukraine* 47 G7
Pryor, *U.S.A.* 113 G7
Prypyat →, *Europe* 47 G6
Przasnysz, *Poland* 45 E7
Przedbórz, *Poland* 45 G6
Przedecz, *Poland* 45 F5
Przemków, *Poland* 45 G2
Przemyśl, *Poland* 45 J9
Przeworsk, *Poland* 45 H9
Przewóz, *Poland* 45 G1
Przhevalsk = Karakol, *Kyrgyzstan* 50 E8
Przysucha, *Poland* 45 G7
Psakhná, *Greece* 38 C5
Psará, *Greece* 39 C7
Psathoúra, *Greece* 38 B6
Psel →, *Ukraine* 47 H7
Pserimos, *Greece* 39 E9
Psíra, *Greece* 36 D7
Pskov, *Russia* 46 D5
Pskovskoye, Ozero, *Russia* 46 D5
Psunj, *Croatia* 42 E2
Pteleón, *Greece* 38 B4
Ptich = Ptsich →, *Belarus* 47 F5
Ptolemaís, *Greece* 40 F5
Ptsich →, *Belarus* 47 F5
Ptuj, *Slovenia* 29 B12
Ptujska Gora, *Slovenia* 29 B12
Pu Xian, *China* 56 F6
Pua, *Thailand* 64 C3
Puán, *Argentina* 126 D3
Pu'an, *China* 58 E5
Puan, *S. Korea* 57 G14
Pubei, *China* 58 F7
Pucallpa, *Peru* 124 E4
Pucheng, *China* 59 D12
Pucheni, *Romania* 43 E10
Puchheim, *Germany* 25 G7
Púchov, *Slovak Rep.* 27 B11
Pucioasa, *Romania* 43 E10
Pučišća, *Croatia* 29 E13
Puck, *Poland* 44 D5
Pucka, Zatoka, *Poland* 44 D5
Puçol, *Spain* 33 F4
Pudasjärvi, *Finland* 8 D22
Puding, *China* 58 D5
Pudozh, *Russia* 46 B9
Pudukkottai, *India* 66 P11
Puebla, *Mexico* 119 D5
Puebla □, *Mexico* 119 D5
Puebla de Alcocer, *Spain* 35 G5
Puebla de Don Fadrique, *Spain* 33 H2
Puebla de Don Rodrigo, *Spain* 35 F6
Puebla de Guzmán, *Spain* 35 H3
Puebla de la Calzada, *Spain* 35 G4
Puebla de Sanabria, *Spain* 34 C4
Puebla de Trives = Pobra de Trives, *Spain* 34 C3
Pueblo, *U.S.A.* 112 F2
Pueblo Hundido, *Chile* 126 B1
Puelches, *Argentina* 126 D2
Puelén, *Argentina* 126 D2
Puente Alto, *Chile* 126 C1
Puente-Genil, *Spain* 35 H6
Puente la Reina, *Spain* 32 C3
Puenteareas = Ponteareas, *Spain* 34 C2
Puentedeume = Pontedeume, *Spain* 34 B2
Puentes de Garcia Rodriguez = As Pontes de García Rodríguez, *Spain* 34 B3
Pu'er, *China* 58 F3
Puerco →, *U.S.A.* 115 J10
Puerto, *Canary Is.* 37 F2
Puerto Aisén, *Chile* 128 F2
Puerto Ángel, *Mexico* 119 D5
Puerto Arista, *Mexico* 119 D6
Puerto Armuelles, *Panama* 120 E3
Puerto Ayacucho, *Venezuela* 124 B5
Puerto Barrios, *Guatemala* 120 C2
Puerto Bermejo, *Argentina* 126 B4
Puerto Bermúdez, *Peru* 124 F4
Puerto Bolívar, *Ecuador* 124 D3
Puerto Cabello, *Venezuela* 124 A5
Puerto Cabezas, *Nic.* 120 D3
Puerto Cabo Gracias á Dios, *Nic.* 120 D3
Puerto Carreño, *Colombia* 124 B5
Puerto Castilla, *Honduras* 120 C2
Puerto Chicama, *Peru* 124 E3
Puerto Coig, *Argentina* 128 G3
Puerto Cortés, *Costa Rica* 120 E3
Puerto Cortés, *Honduras* 120 C2
Puerto Cumarebo, *Venezuela* 124 A5
Puerto de Alcudia = Port d'Alcúdia, *Spain* 37 B10
Puerto de Andraitx, *Spain* 37 B9
Puerto de Cabrera, *Spain* 37 B9
Puerto de Gran Tarajal, *Canary Is.* 37 F5
Puerto de la Cruz, *Canary Is.* 37 F3
Puerto de Mazarrón, *Spain* 33 H3
Puerto de Pozo Negro, *Canary Is.* 37 F6
Puerto de Sóller = Port de Sóller, *Spain* 37 B9
Puerto de Somosierra, *Spain* 34 D7
Puerto del Carmen, *Canary Is.* 37 F6
Puerto del Rosario, *Canary Is.* 37 F6
Puerto Deseado, *Argentina* 128 F3
Puerto Escondido, *Mexico* 119 D5
Puerto Heath, *Bolivia* 124 F5
Puerto Inírida, *Colombia* 124 C5
Puerto Juárez, *Mexico* 119 C7
Puerto La Cruz, *Venezuela* 124 A6
Puerto Leguízamo, *Colombia* 124 D4
Puerto Limón, *Colombia* 124 C4
Puerto Lobos, *Argentina* 128 E3
Puerto Lumbreras, *Spain* 33 H3
Puerto Madryn, *Argentina* 128 E3
Puerto Maldonado, *Peru* 124 F5
Puerto Manotí, *Cuba* 120 B4
Puerto Mazarrón = Puerto de Mazarrón, *Spain* 33 H3
Puerto Montt, *Chile* 128 E2
Puerto Morazán, *Nic.* 120 D2
Puerto Morelos, *Mexico* 119 C7
Puerto Natales, *Chile* 128 G2
Puerto Padre, *Cuba* 120 B4
Puerto Páez, *Venezuela* 124 B5
Puerto Peñasco, *Mexico* 118 A2
Puerto Pinasco, *Paraguay* 126 A4
Puerto Plata, *Dom. Rep.* 121 C5
Puerto Pollensa = Port de Pollença, *Spain* 37 B10

Puerto Princesa, *Phil.* 61 G3
Puerto Quepos, *Costa Rica* 120 E3
Puerto Real, *Spain* 35 J4
Puerto Rico, *Canary Is.* 37 G4
Puerto Rico ■, *W. Indies* 121 C6
Puerto Rico Trench, *Atl. Oc.* 121 C6
Puerto San Julián, *Argentina* 128 F3
Puerto Sastre, *Paraguay* 126 A4
Puerto Serrano, *Spain* 35 J5
Puerto Suárez, *Bolivia* 124 G7
Puerto Vallarta, *Mexico* 118 C3
Puerto Wilches, *Colombia* 124 B4
Puertollano, *Spain* 35 G6
Pueyrredón, L., *Argentina* 128 F2
Puffin I., *Ireland* 15 E1
Pugachev, *Russia* 48 D9
Pugal, *India* 68 E5
Puge, *China* 58 D4
Puge, *Tanzania* 86 C3
Puget Sound, *U.S.A.* 114 C2
Puget-Théniers, *France* 21 E10
Púglia □, *Italy* 31 A9
Pugŏdong, *N. Korea* 57 C16
Pugu, *Tanzania* 86 D4
Pūgūnzī, *Iran* 71 E8
Pui, *Romania* 42 E8
Puieşti, *Romania* 43 D12
Puig Major, *Spain* 37 B9
Puigcerdà, *Spain* 32 C6
Puigmal, *Spain* 32 C7
Puigpunyent, *Spain* 37 B9
Puijiang, *China* 58 B4
Puisaye, Collines de la, *France* 19 E10
Puiseaux, *France* 19 D9
Pujehun, *S. Leone* 82 D2
Pujiang, *China* 59 C12
Pujols, *France* 20 D3
Pujon-chŏsuji, *N. Korea* 57 D14
Pukaki L., *N.Z.* 91 L3
Pukapuka, *Cook Is.* 97 J11
Pukaskwa Nat. Park, *Canada* 102 C2
Pukatawagan, *Canada* 105 B8
Pukchin, *N. Korea* 57 D13
Pukch'ŏng, *N. Korea* 57 D15
Pukë, *Albania* 40 D3
Pukekohe, *N.Z.* 91 G5
Pukhrayan, *India* 69 F8
Pukou, *China* 59 A12
Pula, *Croatia* 29 D10
Pula, *Italy* 30 C1
Pulacayo, *Bolivia* 124 H5
Pulandian, *China* 57 E11
Pularumpi, *Australia* 92 B5
Pulaski, *N.Y., U.S.A.* 111 C8
Pulaski, *Tenn., U.S.A.* 109 H2
Pulaski, *Va., U.S.A.* 108 G5
Pulau →, *Indonesia* 63 F9
Puławy, *Poland* 45 G8
Pulga, *U.S.A.* 116 F5
Pulicat L., *India* 66 N12
Pullman, *U.S.A.* 114 C5
Pulo-Anna, *Pac. Oc.* 63 D8
Pulog, Mt., *Phil.* 61 C4
Pułtusk, *Poland* 45 F8
Pülümür, *Turkey* 73 C8
Pumlumon Fawr, *U.K.* 13 E4
Puná, I., *Ecuador* 124 D2
Punakha, *Bhutan* 67 F16
Punasar, *India* 68 F5
Punata, *Bolivia* 124 G5
Punch, *India* 69 C6
Punch →, *Pakistan* 68 C5
Punda Maria, *S. Africa* 89 C5
Pune, *India* 66 K8
P'ungsan, *N. Korea* 57 D15
Pungue, Ponte de, *Mozam.* 87 F3
Puning, *China* 59 F11
Punjab □, *India* 68 D7
Punjab □, *Pakistan* 68 E6
Puno, *Peru* 124 G4
Punpun →, *India* 69 G11
Punta Alta, *Argentina* 128 D4
Punta Arenas, *Chile* 128 G2
Punta de Díaz, *Chile* 126 B1
Punta Gorda, *Belize* 119 D7
Punta Gorda, *U.S.A.* 109 M5
Punta Prieta, *Mexico* 118 B2
Punta Prima, *Spain* 37 B11
Punta Umbría, *Spain* 35 H4
Puntarenas, *Costa Rica* 120 E3
Punto Fijo, *Venezuela* 124 A4
Punxsatawney, *U.S.A.* 110 F6
Puqi, *China* 59 C9
Puquio, *Peru* 124 F4
Pur →, *Russia* 50 C8
Purace, Vol., *Colombia* 124 C3
Puračić, *Bos.-H.* 42 F3
Puralia = Puruliya, *India* 69 H12
Puranpur, *India* 69 E9
Purbeck, Isle of, *U.K.* 13 G6
Purcell, *U.S.A.* 113 H6
Purcell Mts., *Canada* 104 D5
Puri, *India* 67 K14
Purmerend, *Neths.* 17 B4
Purnia, *India* 69 G12
Pursat = Pouthisat, *Cambodia* 64 F4
Purukcahu, *Indonesia* 62 E4
Puruliya, *India* 69 H12
Purus →, *Brazil* 122 D4
Puruvesi, *Finland* 46 B5
Purvis, *U.S.A.* 113 K10
Pŭrvomay, *Bulgaria* 41 D9
Purwa, *India* 69 F9
Purwakarta, *Indonesia* 63 G12
Purwodadi, *Indonesia* 63 G14
Purwokerto, *Indonesia* 63 G13
Puryŏng, *N. Korea* 57 C15
Pusa, *India* 69 G11
Pusan, *S. Korea* 57 G15
Pushkin, *Russia* 46 C6
Pushkino, *Moskva, Russia* 46 D9
Pushkino, *Saratov, Russia* 48 E8
Püspökladány, *Hungary* 42 C6
Pustoshka, *Russia* 46 D5
Puszczykowo, *Poland* 45 F3
Putahow L., *Canada* 105 B8
Putao, *Burma* 67 F20
Putaruru, *N.Z.* 91 H5
Putbus, *Germany* 24 A9
Putian, *China* 59 E12
Putignano, *Italy* 31 B10
Puting, Tanjung, *Indonesia* 62 E4
Putlitz, *Germany* 24 B8
Putna, *Romania* 43 C10
Putna →, *Romania* 43 E12
Putnam, *U.S.A.* 111 E13
Putnok, *Hungary* 42 B5
Putorana, Gory, *Russia* 51 C10
Puttalam, *Sri Lanka* 66 Q11
Puttgarden, *Germany* 24 A7
Püttlingen, *Germany* 25 F2
Putumayo →, *S. Amer.* 122 D4
Putuo, *China* 59 C14
Putussibau, *Indonesia* 62 D4
Puvirnituq, *Canada* 101 B12
Puy-de-Dôme, *France* 20 C6
Puy-de-Dôme □, *France* 20 C7
Puy-l'Évêque, *France* 20 D5
Puyallup, *U.S.A.* 116 C4
Puyang, *China* 56 G8
Puylaurens, *France* 20 E6
Pūzeh Rīg, *Iran* 71 E8
Pwani □, *Tanzania* 86 D4
Pweto, *Dem. Rep. of the Congo* 87 D2
Pwllheli, *U.K.* 12 E3
Pyana →, *Russia* 48 C8
Pyapon, *Burma* 67 L19
Pyasina →, *Russia* 51 B9
Pyatigorsk, *Russia* 49 H6
Pyatykhatky, *Ukraine* 47 H7
Pydna, *Greece* 40 F6
Pyè, *Burma* 67 K19
Pyetrikaw, *Belarus* 47 F5
Pyhäjoki, *Finland* 8 D21
Pyinmana, *Burma* 67 K20
Pyla, C., *Cyprus* 36 E12
Pymatuning Reservoir, *U.S.A.* 110 E4
Pyŏktong, *N. Korea* 57 D13
Pyŏnggang, *N. Korea* 57 E14
P'yŏngt'aek, *S. Korea* 57 F14
P'yŏngyang, *N. Korea* 57 E13
Pyote, *U.S.A.* 113 K3
Pyramid L., *U.S.A.* 114 G4
Pyramid Pk., *U.S.A.* 117 J10
Pyramids, *Egypt* 80 J7
Pyrénées, *Europe* 20 F4
Pyrénées-Atlantiques □, *France* 20 E3
Pyrénées-Orientales □, *France* 20 F6
Pyryatyn, *Ukraine* 47 G7
Pyrzyce, *Poland* 45 E1
Pyskowice, *Poland* 45 H5
Pytalovo, *Russia* 46 D4
Pyu, *Burma* 67 K20
Pyzdry, *Poland* 45 F4

Q

Qaanaaq, *Greenland* 4 B4
Qabirri →, *Azerbaijan* 49 K8
Qachasnek, *S. Africa* 89 E4
Qa'el Jafr, *Jordan* 75 E5
Qa'emābād, *Iran* 71 D9
Qā'emshahr, *Iran* 71 B7
Qagan Nur, *China* 56 C8
Qahar Youyi Zhongqi, *China* 56 D7
Qahremānshahr = Bākhtarān, *Iran* 70 C5
Qaidam Pendi, *China* 60 C4
Qajarīyeh, *Iran* 71 D6
Qala, Ras il, *Malta* 36 C1
Qala-i-Jadid = Spīn Búldak, *Afghan.* 68 D2
Qala Viala, *Pakistan* 68 D2
Qala Yangi, *Afghan.* 68 B2
Qal'at al Akhḑar, *Si. Arabia* 70 E3
Qal'at Dīzah, *Iraq* 70 B5
Qal'at Şāliḩ, *Iraq* 70 D5
Qal'at Sukkar, *Iraq* 70 D5
Qalyûb, *Egypt* 80 H7
Qamani'tuaq = Baker Lake, *Canada* 100 B10
Qamdo, *China* 58 B1
Qamruddin Karez, *Pakistan* 68 D3
Qandahār, *Afghan.* 66 D4
Qandahār □, *Afghan.* 66 D4
Qapān, *Iran* 71 B7
Qapshaghay, *Kazakstan* 50 E8
Qaqortoq, *Greenland* 101 B6
Qâra, *Egypt* 80 B2
Qara Qash →, *India* 69 B8
Qarabutaq, *Kazakstan* 50 E7
Qaraçala, *Azerbaijan* 49 L9
Qaraghandy, *Kazakstan* 50 E8
Qārah, *Si. Arabia* 70 D4
Qarataū, *Kazakstan* 50 E8
Qarataū, *Kazakstan* 50 E7
Qardud, *Sudan* 81 E2
Qareh →, *Iran* 70 B5
Qareh Tekān, *Iran* 71 B6
Qarqan He →, *China* 60 C3
Qarqaraly, *Kazakstan* 50 E8
Qarrasa, *Sudan* 81 E3
Qarshi, *Uzbekistan* 50 F7
Qartabā, *Lebanon* 75 A4
Qaryat al Gharab, *Iraq* 70 D5
Qaryat al 'Ulyā, *Si. Arabia* 70 E5
Qasr 'Amra, *Jordan* 70 D3
Qaşr-e Qand, *Iran* 71 E9
Qasr Farâfra, *Egypt* 80 B2
Qatanā, *Syria* 75 B5
Qatar ■, *Asia* 71 E6
Qatlīsh, *Iran* 71 B8
Qattâra, *Egypt* 80 A2
Qattâra, Munkhafed el, *Egypt* 80 B2
Qattâra Depression = Qattâra, Munkhafed el, *Egypt* 80 B2
Qawām al Ḩamzah, *Iraq* 70 D5
Qāyen, *Iran* 71 C8
Qazaqstan = Kazakstan ■, *Asia* 50 E7
Qazimämmäd, *Azerbaijan* 49 K9
Qazvin, *Iran* 71 B6
Qeissan, *Sudan* 81 E3
Qena, *Egypt* 80 B3
Qena, W. →, *Egypt* 80 B3
Qeqertarsuaq, *Greenland* 101 B5
Qeqertarsuaq, *Greenland* 4 C5
Qeshlāq, *Iran* 70 C5
Qeshm, *Iran* 71 E8
Qeys, *Iran* 71 E7
Qezel Owzen →, *Iran* 71 B6
Qezi'ot, *Israel* 75 E3
Qi Xian, *China* 56 G8
Qian Gorlos, *China* 57 B13
Qian Xian, *China* 56 G5
Qiancheng, *China* 58 D7
Qianjiang, *Guangxi Zhuangzu, China* 58 F7
Qianjiang, *Hubei, China* 59 B9
Qianjiang, *Sichuan, China* 58 C7
Qianshan, *China* 59 B11
Qianwei, *China* 58 C4
Qianxi, *China* 58 D6
Qianyang, *Hunan, China* 59 D8
Qianyang, *Shaanxi, China* 56 G4
Qianyang, *Zhejiang, China* 59 B12
Qiaojia, *China* 58 D4
Qichun, *China* 59 B10
Qidong, *Hunan, China* 59 D9
Qidong, *Jiangsu, China* 59 B13
Qijiang, *China* 58 C6
Qikiqtarjuaq, *Canada* 101 B13
Qila Safed, *Pakistan* 66 E2
Qila Saifullāh, *Pakistan* 68 D3
Qilian Shan, *China* 60 C4
Qimen, *China* 59 C11
Qin He →, *China* 56 G7
Qin Jiang →, *Guangxi Zhuangzu, China* 58 F7
Qin Jiang →, *Jiangxi, China* 59 D10
Qin Ling = Qinling Shandi, *China* 56 H5
Qin'an, *China* 56 G3
Qing Xian, *China* 56 E9
Qingcheng, *China* 57 F9
Qingdao, *China* 57 F11
Qingfeng, *China* 56 G8
Qinghai □, *China* 60 C4
Qinghai Hu, *China* 60 C5
Qinghecheng, *China* 57 D13
Qinghemen, *China* 57 D11
Qingjian, *China* 56 F6
Qingjiang = Huaiyin, *China* 57 H10
Qingliu, *China* 59 D11
Qinglong, *China* 58 E5
Qingping, *China* 58 D6
Qingpu, *China* 59 B13
Qingshui, *China* 56 G4
Qingshuihe, *China* 56 E6
Qingtian, *China* 59 C13
Qingtongxia Shuiku, *China* 56 F3
Qingxi, *China* 58 D7
Qingxu, *China* 56 F7
Qingyang, *Anhui, China* 59 B11
Qingyang, *Gansu, China* 56 F4
Qingyi Jiang →, *China* 58 C4
Qingyuan, *Guangdong, China* 59 F9
Qingyuan, *Liaoning, China* 57 C13
Qingyuan, *Zhejiang, China* 59 D12
Qingyun, *China* 57 F9
Qingzhen, *China* 58 D6
Qinhuangdao, *China* 57 E10
Qinling Shandi, *China* 56 H5
Qinshui, *China* 56 G7
Qinyang = Jiyuan, *China* 56 G7
Qinyuan, *China* 56 F7
Qinzhou, *China* 58 G7
Qionghai, *China* 64 C8
Qionglai, *China* 58 B4
Qionglai Shan, *China* 58 B4
Qiongzhou Haixia, *China* 64 B8
Qiqihar, *China* 51 E13
Qirâiya, W. →, *Egypt* 75 E3
Qiryat Ata, *Israel* 75 C4
Qiryat Gat, *Israel* 75 D3
Qiryat Mal'akhi, *Israel* 75 D3
Qiryat Shemona, *Israel* 75 B4
Qiryat Yam, *Israel* 75 C4
Qishan, *China* 56 G4
Qitai, *China* 60 B3
Qiubei, *China* 58 E5
Qixia, *China* 57 F11
Qiyang, *China* 59 D8
Qızılağac Körfäzi, *Azerbaijan* 71 B6
Qojūr, *Iran* 70 B5
Qom, *Iran* 71 C6
Qomolangma Feng = Everest, Mt., *Nepal* 69 E12
Qomsheh, *Iran* 71 D6
Qoraqalpoghistan □, *Uzbekistan* 50 E6
Qorveh, *Iran* 73 E12
Qostanay, *Kazakstan* 50 D7
Qoţūr, *Iran* 73 C11
Qu Jiang →, *China* 58 B6
Qu Xian, *China* 58 B6
Quabbin Reservoir, *U.S.A.* 111 D12
Quairading, *Australia* 93 F2
Quakenbrück, *Germany* 24 C3
Quakertown, *U.S.A.* 111 F9
Qualicum Beach, *Canada* 104 D4
Quambatook, *Australia* 95 F3
Quambone, *Australia* 95 E4
Quamby, *Australia* 94 C3
Quan Long = Ca Mau, *Vietnam* 65 H5
Quanah, *U.S.A.* 113 H5
Quang Ngai, *Vietnam* 64 E7
Quang Tri, *Vietnam* 64 D6
Quang Yen, *Vietnam* 58 G6
Quannan, *China* 59 E10
Quantock Hills, *U.K.* 13 F4
Quanzhou, *Fujian, China* 59 E12
Quanzhou, *Guangxi Zhuangzu, China* 59 E8
Qu'Appelle, *Canada* 105 C8
Quaqtaq, *Canada* 101 B13
Quaraí, *Brazil* 126 C4
Quarré-les-Tombes, *France* 19 E11
Quarteira, *Portugal* 35 H2
Quartu Sant'Élena, *Italy* 30 C2
Quartzsite, *U.S.A.* 117 M12
Quatsino Sd., *Canada* 104 C3
Quba, *Azerbaijan* 49 K9
Qūchān, *Iran* 71 B8
Queanbeyan, *Australia* 95 F4
Québec, *Canada* 103 C5
Québec □, *Canada* 103 C6
Quedlinburg, *Germany* 24 D7
Queen Alexandra Ra., *Antarctica* 5 E11
Queen Charlotte City, *Canada* 104 C2
Queen Charlotte Is., *Canada* 104 C2
Queen Charlotte Sd., *Canada* 104 C3
Queen Charlotte Strait, *Canada* 104 C3
Queen Elizabeth Is., *Canada* 98 B10
Queen Elizabeth Nat. Park, *Uganda* 86 C3
Queen Mary Land, *Antarctica* 5 D7
Queen Maud G., *Canada* 100 B9
Queen Maud Land, *Antarctica* 5 D3
Queen Maud Mts., *Antarctica* 5 E13
Queens Chan., *Australia* 92 C4
Queenscliff, *Australia* 95 F3
Queensland □, *Australia* 94 C3
Queenstown, *Australia* 94 G4
Queenstown, *N.Z.* 91 L2
Queenstown, *S. Africa* 88 E4
Queets, *U.S.A.* 116 C2
Queguay Grande →, *Uruguay* 126 C4
Queimadas, *Brazil* 125 F11
Quelimane, *Mozam.* 87 F4
Quellón, *Chile* 128 E2
Quelpart = Cheju do, *S. Korea* 57 H14
Queluz, *Portugal* 35 G1
Quemado, *N. Mex., U.S.A.* 115 J9
Quemado, *Tex., U.S.A.* 113 L4
Quemoy = Chinmen, *Taiwan* 59 E13
Quemú-Quemú, *Argentina* 126 D3
Quequén, *Argentina* 126 D4
Querétaro, *Mexico* 118 C4
Querétaro □, *Mexico* 118 C5
Querfurt, *Germany* 24 D7
Quérigut, *France* 20 F6
Querqueville, *France* 18 C5
Quesada, *Spain* 35 H7
Queshan, *China* 56 H8
Quesnel, *Canada* 104 C4
Quesnel →, *Canada* 104 C4
Quesnel L., *Canada* 104 C4
Questa, *U.S.A.* 115 H11
Questembert, *France* 18 E4
Quetico Prov. Park, *Canada* 102 C1
Quetta, *Pakistan* 68 D2
Quezaltenango, *Guatemala* 120 D1
Quezon City, *Phil.* 61 D4
Qufār, *Si. Arabia* 70 E4
Qui Nhon, *Vietnam* 64 F7
Quibaxe, *Angola* 84 F2
Quibdo, *Colombia* 124 B3
Quiberon, *France* 18 E3
Quiberon, Presqu'île de, *France* 18 E3
Quickborn, *Germany* 24 B5
Quiet L., *Canada* 104 A2
Quiindy, *Paraguay* 126 B4
Quila, *Mexico* 118 C3
Quilán, C., *Chile* 128 E2
Quilcene, *U.S.A.* 116 C4
Quilimarí, *Chile* 126 C1
Quilino, *Argentina* 126 C3
Quill Lakes, *Canada* 105 C8
Quillabamba, *Peru* 124 F4
Quillagua, *Chile* 126 A2
Quillaicillo, *Chile* 126 C1
Quillan, *France* 20 F6
Quillota, *Chile* 126 C1
Quilmes, *Argentina* 126 C4
Quilon, *India* 66 Q10
Quilpie, *Australia* 95 D3
Quilpué, *Chile* 126 C1
Quilua, *Mozam.* 87 F4
Quimilí, *Argentina* 126 B3
Quimper, *France* 18 E2
Quimperlé, *France* 18 E3
Quinault →, *U.S.A.* 116 C2
Quincy, *Calif., U.S.A.* 116 F6
Quincy, *Fla., U.S.A.* 109 K3
Quincy, *Ill., U.S.A.* 112 F9
Quincy, *Mass., U.S.A.* 111 D14
Quincy, *Wash., U.S.A.* 114 C4
Quines, *Argentina* 126 C2
Quinga, *Mozam.* 87 F5
Quingey, *France* 19 E12
Quinns Rocks, *Australia* 93 F2
Quintana de la Serena, *Spain* 35 G5
Quintana Roo □, *Mexico* 119 D7
Quintanar de la Orden, *Spain* 35 F7
Quintanar de la Sierra, *Spain* 32 D2
Quintanar del Rey, *Spain* 33 F3
Quintero, *Chile* 126 C1
Quintin, *France* 18 D4
Quinto, *Spain* 32 D4
Quípar →, *Spain* 33 G3
Quirihue, *Chile* 126 D1
Quirindi, *Australia* 95 E5
Quirinópolis, *Brazil* 125 G8
Quiroga, *Spain* 34 C3
Quissac, *France* 21 E8
Quissanga, *Mozam.* 87 E5
Quissico, *Mozam.* 89 C5
Quitilipi, *Argentina* 126 B3
Quitman, *U.S.A.* 109 K4
Quito, *Ecuador* 124 D3
Quixadá, *Brazil* 125 D11
Quixaxe, *Mozam.* 87 F5
Qujing, *China* 58 E4
Qulan, *Kazakstan* 50 E8
Qul'ân, Jazâ'ir, *Egypt* 70 E2
Qumbu, *S. Africa* 89 E4
Quneitra, *Syria* 75 B4
Qŭnghirot, *Uzbekistan* 50 E6
Qu'nyido, *China* 58 B2
Quoin I., *Australia* 92 B4
Quoin Pt., *S. Africa* 88 E2
Quorn, *Australia* 95 E2
Qŭqon, *Uzbekistan* 50 E8
Qurein, *Sudan* 81 E3
Qurnat as Sawdā', *Lebanon* 75 A5
Qûs, *Egypt* 80 B3
Qusar, *Azerbaijan* 49 K9
Quşaybā', *Si. Arabia* 70 E4
Qusaybah, *Iraq* 70 C4
Quseir, *Egypt* 70 E2
Qūshchī, *Iran* 70 B5
Quthing, *Lesotho* 89 E4
Qūţīābād, *Iran* 71 C6
Quwo, *China* 56 G6
Quyang, *China* 56 E8
Quynh Nhai, *Vietnam* 64 B4
Quyon, *Canada* 111 A8
Quzhou, *China* 59 C12
Quzi, *China* 56 F4
Qvareli, *Georgia* 49 K7
Qytet Stalin = Kuçovë, *Albania* 40 F3
Qyzylorda, *Kazakstan* 50 E7

R

Ra, Ko, *Thailand* 65 H2
Raab, *Austria* 26 C6
Raahe, *Finland* 8 D21
Raalte, *Neths.* 17 B6
Raasay, *U.K.* 14 D2
Raasay, Sd. of, *U.K.* 14 D2
Rab, *Croatia* 29 D11
Raba, *Indonesia* 63 F5
Rába →, *Hungary* 42 C2
Raba →, *Poland* 45 H7
Rabaçal →, *Portugal* 34 D3
Rabah, *Nigeria* 83 C6
Rabai, *Kenya* 86 C4
Rabak, *Sudan* 81 E3
Rabastens, *France* 20 E5
Rabastens-de-Bigorre, *France* 20 E4
Rabat, *Malta* 36 D1
Rabat, *Morocco* 78 B4
Rabaul, *Papua N. G.* 96 H7
Rābigh, *Si. Arabia* 74 C2
Rabka, *Poland* 45 J6
Râbniţa, *Moldova* 43 C14
Rābor, *Iran* 71 D8
Rača, *Serbia, Yug.* 40 B4
Răcăciuni, *Romania* 43 D11
Răcăşdia, *Romania* 42 F6
Racconigi, *Italy* 28 D4
Race, C., *Canada* 103 C9
Rach Gia, *Vietnam* 65 G5
Rachid, *Mauritania* 82 B2
Raciąż, *Poland* 45 F7
Racibórz, *Poland* 45 H5
Racine, *U.S.A.* 108 D2
Rackerby, *U.S.A.* 116 F5
Radama, Nosy, *Madag.* 89 A8
Radama, Saikanosy, *Madag.* 89 A8
Radan, *Serbia, Yug.* 40 D5
Rădăuţi, *Romania* 43 C10
Rădăuţi-Prut, *Romania* 43 B11
Radbuza →, *Czech Rep.* 26 B6
Radcliff, *U.S.A.* 108 G3
Radeberg, *Germany* 24 D9
Radebeul, *Germany* 24 D9
Radeče, *Slovenia* 29 B12
Radekhiv, *Ukraine* 47 G3
Radekhov = Radekhiv, *Ukraine* 47 G3
Radenthein, *Austria* 26 E6
Radew →, *Poland* 44 D2
Radford, *U.S.A.* 108 G5
Radhanpur, *India* 68 H4
Radhwa, Jabal, *Si. Arabia* 70 E3
Radika →, *Macedonia* 40 E4
Radisson, *Qué., Canada* 102 B4
Radisson, *Sask., Canada* 105 C7
Radium Hot Springs, *Canada* 104 C5
Radlje ob Dravi, *Slovenia* 29 B12

Radnevo, *Bulgaria* 41 D9
Radnice, *Czech Rep.* 26 B6
Radnor Forest, *U.K.* 13 E4
Radolfzell, *Germany* 25 H4
Radom, *Poland* 45 G8
Radomir, *Bulgaria* 40 D6
Radomka →, *Poland* 45 G8
Radomsko, *Poland* 45 G6
Radomyshl, *Ukraine* 47 G5
Radomyśl Wielki, *Poland* 45 H8
Radoszyce, *Poland* 45 G7
Radoviš, *Macedonia* 40 E6
Radovljica, *Slovenia* 29 B11
Radstadt, *Austria* 26 D6
Radstock, C., *Australia* 95 E1
Răducăneni, *Romania* 43 D12
Raduša, *Macedonia* 40 D5
Radviliškis, *Lithuania* 9 J20
Radville, *Canada* 105 D8
Raḑwá, J., *Si. Arabia* 80 C4
Radymno, *Poland* 45 J9
Radzanów, *Poland* 45 F7
Radziejów, *Poland* 45 F5
Radzyń Chełmiński, *Poland* 44 E5
Radzyń Podlaski, *Poland* 45 G9
Rae, *Canada* 104 A5
Rae Bareli, *India* 69 F9
Rae Isthmus, *Canada* 101 B11
Raeren, *Belgium* 17 D6
Raeside, L., *Australia* 93 E3
Raetihi, *N.Z.* 91 H5
Rafaela, *Argentina* 126 C3
Rafah, *Gaza Strip* 75 D3
Rafai, *C.A.R.* 86 B1
Raffadali, *Italy* 30 E6
Raffili, *Sudan* 81 F2
Rafḩā, *Si. Arabia* 70 D4
Rafsanjān, *Iran* 71 D8
Raft Pt., *Australia* 92 C3
Râgâ, *Sudan* 81 F2
Raga →, *Sudan* 81 F2
Ragachow, *Belarus* 47 F6
Ragag, *Sudan* 81 E1
Ragama, *Sri Lanka* 66 R11
Ragged, Mt., *Australia* 93 F3
Raghunathpalli, *India* 69 H11
Raghunathpur, *India* 69 H12
Raglan, *N.Z.* 91 G5
Ragusa, *Italy* 31 F7
Raha, *Indonesia* 63 E6
Rahad, Nahr ed →, *Sudan* 81 E3
Rahaeng = Tak, *Thailand* 64 D2
Rahatgarh, *India* 69 H8
Rahden, *Germany* 24 C4
Raheita, *Eritrea* 81 E5
Rahimyar Khan, *Pakistan* 68 E4
Rāhjerd, *Iran* 71 C6
Rahon, *India* 68 D7
Raichur, *India* 66 L10
Raiganj, *India* 69 G13
Raigarh, *India* 67 J13
Raijua, *Indonesia* 63 F6
Raikot, *India* 68 D6
Railton, *Australia* 94 G4
Rainbow Lake, *Canada* 104 B5
Rainier, *U.S.A.* 116 D4
Rainier, Mt., *U.S.A.* 116 D5
Rainy L., *Canada* 105 D10
Rainy River, *Canada* 105 D10
Raippaluoto, *Finland* 8 E19
Raipur, *India* 67 J12
Ra'is, *Si. Arabia* 80 C4
Raisen, *India* 68 H8
Raisio, *Finland* 9 F20
Raj Nandgaon, *India* 67 J12
Raj Nilgiri, *India* 69 J12
Raja, Ujung, *Indonesia* 62 D1
Raja Ampat, Kepulauan, *Indonesia* 63 E7
Rajahmundry, *India* 67 L12
Rajang →, *Malaysia* 62 D4
Rajanpur, *Pakistan* 68 E4
Rajapalaiyam, *India* 66 Q10
Rajasthan □, *India* 68 F5
Rajasthan Canal, *India* 68 F5
Rajauri, *India* 69 C6
Rajgarh, *Mad. P., India* 68 G7
Rajgarh, *Raj., India* 68 F7
Rajgarh, *Raj., India* 68 E6
Rajgir, *India* 69 G11
Rajgród, *Poland* 44 E9
Rajkot, *India* 68 H4
Rajmahal Hills, *India* 69 G12
Rajpipla, *India* 66 J8
Rajpur, *India* 68 H6
Rajpura, *India* 68 D7
Rajshahi, *Bangla.* 67 G16
Rajshahi □, *Bangla.* 69 G13
Rajula, *India* 68 J4
Rakaia, *N.Z.* 91 K4
Rakaia →, *N.Z.* 91 K4
Rakan, Ra's, *Qatar* 71 E6
Rakaposhi, *Pakistan* 69 A6
Rakata, Pulau, *Indonesia* 62 F3
Rakhiv, *Ukraine* 47 H3
Rakhni, *Pakistan* 68 D3
Rakhni →, *Pakistan* 68 E3
Rakitnoye, *Russia* 54 B7
Rakitovo, *Bulgaria* 41 E8
Rakoniewice, *Poland* 45 F3
Rakops, *Botswana* 88 C3
Rakovica, *Croatia* 29 D12
Rakovník, *Czech Rep.* 26 A6
Rakovski, *Bulgaria* 41 D8
Rakvere, *Estonia* 9 G22
Raleigh, *U.S.A.* 109 H6
Ralja, *Serbia, Yug.* 40 B4
Ralls, *U.S.A.* 113 J4
Ralston, *U.S.A.* 110 E8
Ram →, *Canada* 104 A4
Rām Allāh, *West Bank* 75 D4
Rama, *Nic.* 120 D3
Ramacca, *Italy* 31 E7
Ramakona, *India* 69 J8
Ramales de la Victoria, *Spain* 34 B7
Raman, *Thailand* 65 J3
Ramanathapuram, *India* 66 Q11
Ramanetaka, B. de, *Madag.* 89 A8
Ramanujganj, *India* 69 H10
Ramat Gan, *Israel* 75 C3
Ramatlhabama, *S. Africa* 88 D4
Ramban, *India* 69 C6
Rambervillers, *France* 19 D13
Rambipuji, *Indonesia* 63 H15
Rambouillet, *France* 19 D8
Rame Hd., *Australia* 95 F4
Ramechhap, *Nepal* 69 F12
Ramenskoye, *Russia* 46 E10
Ramganga →, *India* 69 F8
Ramgarh, *Bihar, India* 69 H11
Ramgarh, *Raj., India* 68 F6
Ramgarh, *Raj., India* 68 F4
Rāmhormoz, *Iran* 71 D6
Ramīān, *Iran* 71 B7
Ramingining, *Australia* 94 A2
Ramla, *Israel* 75 D3
Ramlu, *Eritrea* 81 E5
Râmna →, *Romania* 43 E12
Ramnad = Ramanathapuram, *India* 66 Q11
Ramnagar, *Jammu & Kashmir, India* 69 C6
Ramnagar, *Ut. P., India* 69 E8
Ramnäs, *Sweden* 10 E10
Râmnicu Sărat, *Romania* 43 E12
Râmnicu Vâlcea, *Romania* 43 E9
Ramon, *Russia* 47 G10
Ramona, *U.S.A.* 117 M10
Ramonville-St-Agne, *France* 20 E5
Ramore, *Canada* 102 C3
Ramos →, *Nigeria* 83 D6
Ramotswa, *Botswana* 88 C4
Rampur, *H.P., India* 68 D7
Rampur, *Mad. P., India* 68 H5
Rampur, *Ut. P., India* 69 E8
Rampur Hat, *India* 69 G12
Rampura, *India* 68 G6
Ramrama Tola, *India* 69 J8
Ramree I., *Burma* 67 K19
Rāmsar, *Iran* 71 B6
Ramsey, *U.K.* 12 C3
Ramsey, *U.S.A.* 111 E10
Ramsey L., *Canada* 102 C3
Ramsgate, *U.K.* 13 F9
Ramsjö, *Sweden* 10 B9
Ramstein, *Germany* 25 F3
Ramtek, *India* 66 J11
Ramvik, *Sweden* 10 B11
Rana Pratap Sagar Dam, *India* 68 G6
Ranaghat, *India* 69 H13
Ranahu, *Pakistan* 68 G3
Ranau, *Malaysia* 62 C5
Rancagua, *Chile* 126 C1
Rance →, *France* 18 D5
Rancheria →, *Canada* 104 A3
Ranchester, *U.S.A.* 114 D10
Ranchi, *India* 69 H11
Rancho Cucamonga, *U.S.A.* 117 L9
Randalstown, *U.K.* 15 B5
Randan, *France* 19 F10
Randazzo, *Italy* 31 E7
Randers, *Denmark* 11 H4
Randers Fjord, *Denmark* 11 H4
Randfontein, *S. Africa* 89 D4
Randle, *U.S.A.* 116 D5
Randolph, *Mass., U.S.A.* 111 D13
Randolph, *N.Y., U.S.A.* 110 D6
Randolph, *Utah, U.S.A.* 114 F8
Randolph, *Vt., U.S.A.* 111 C12
Randsburg, *U.S.A.* 117 K9
Råne älv →, *Sweden* 8 D20
Rangae, *Thailand* 65 J3
Rangaunu B., *N.Z.* 91 F4
Rangeley, *U.S.A.* 111 B14
Rangeley L., *U.S.A.* 111 B14
Rangely, *U.S.A.* 114 F9
Ranger, *U.S.A.* 113 J5
Rangia, *India* 67 F17
Rangiora, *N.Z.* 91 K4
Rangitaiki →, *N.Z.* 91 G6
Rangitata →, *N.Z.* 91 K3
Rangkasbitung, *Indonesia* 63 G12
Rangon →, *Burma* 67 L20
Rangoon, *Burma* 67 L20
Rangpur, *Bangla.* 67 G16
Rangsit, *Thailand* 64 F3
Ranibennur, *India* 66 M9
Raniganj, *Ut. P., India* 69 F9
Raniganj, *W. Bengal, India* 67 H15
Ranikhet, *India* 69 E8
Raniwara, *India* 66 G8
Rāniyah, *Iraq* 70 B5
Ranka, *India* 69 H10
Ranken →, *Australia* 94 C2
Rankin, *U.S.A.* 113 K4
Rankin Inlet, *Canada* 100 B10
Rankins Springs, *Australia* 95 E4
Rankweil, *Austria* 26 D2
Rannoch, L., *U.K.* 14 E4
Rannoch Moor, *U.K.* 14 E4
Ranobe, Helodranon' i, *Madag.* 89 C7
Ranohira, *Madag.* 89 C8
Ranomafana, *Toamasina, Madag.* 89 B8
Ranomafana, *Toliara, Madag.* 89 C8
Ranomena, *Madag.* 89 C8
Ranong, *Thailand* 65 H2
Ranotsara Nord, *Madag.* 89 C8
Rānsa, *Iran* 71 C6
Ransiki, *Indonesia* 63 E8
Rantabe, *Madag.* 89 B8
Rantauprapat, *Indonesia* 62 D1
Rantemario, *Indonesia* 63 E5
Rantoul, *U.S.A.* 108 E1
Ranum, *Denmark* 11 H3
Ranyah, W. →, *Si. Arabia* 80 C5
Raon l'Étape, *France* 19 D13
Raoping, *China* 59 F11
Raoyang, *China* 56 E8
Rapa, *Pac. Oc.* 97 K13
Rapallo, *Italy* 28 D6
Rapar, *India* 68 H4
Rāpch, *Iran* 71 E8
Raper, C., *Canada* 101 B13
Rapid City, *U.S.A.* 112 D3
Rapid River, *U.S.A.* 108 C2
Rapla, *Estonia* 9 G21
Rapti →, *India* 69 F10
Rapu Rapu I., *Phil.* 61 E6
Raqaba ez Zarqa →, *Sudan* 81 F2
Raquette →, *U.S.A.* 111 B10
Raquette Lake, *U.S.A.* 111 C10
Rarotonga, *Cook Is.* 97 K12
Ra's al 'Ayn, *Syria* 70 B4
Ra's al Khaymah, *U.A.E.* 71 E7
Râs el Mâ, *Mali* 82 B4
Ras Ghârib, *Egypt* 80 B3
Ras Mallap, *Egypt* 80 B3
Rasca, Pta. de la, *Canary Is.* 37 G3
Răşcani, *Moldova* 43 C12
Raseiniai, *Lithuania* 9 J20
Rashad, *Sudan* 81 E3
Rashîd, *Egypt* 80 H7
Rashîd, Masabb, *Egypt* 80 H7
Rashmi, *India* 68 G6
Rasht, *Iran* 71 B6
Rasi Salai, *Thailand* 64 E5
Raška, *Serbia, Yug.* 40 C4
Râsnov, *Romania* 43 E10
Rason L., *Australia* 93 E3
Raşova, *Romania* 43 F12
Rasovo, *Bulgaria* 40 C7
Rasra, *India* 69 G10
Rasskazovo, *Russia* 48 D5
Rast, *Romania* 43 G8
Rastatt, *Germany* 25 G4
Rastede, *Germany* 24 B4
Răstoliţa, *Romania* 43 D9
Rasul, *Pakistan* 68 C5
Raszków, *Poland* 45 G4
Rat Buri, *Thailand* 64 F2
Rat Islands, *U.S.A.* 100 C1
Rat L., *Canada* 105 B9
Ratangarh, *India* 68 E6
Rätansbyn, *Sweden* 10 B8
Raţāwī, *Iraq* 70 D5
Rath, *India* 69 G8
Rath Luirc, *Ireland* 15 D3
Rathdrum, *Ireland* 15 D5
Rathenow, *Germany* 24 C8
Rathkeale, *Ireland* 15 D3
Rathlin I., *U.K.* 15 A5
Rathmelton, *Ireland* 15 A4
Ratibor = Racibórz, *Poland* 45 H5
Rätikon, *Austria* 26 D2
Ratingen, *Germany* 24 D2
Ratlam, *India* 68 H6
Ratnagiri, *India* 66 L8
Ratodero, *Pakistan* 68 F3
Raton, *U.S.A.* 113 G2
Rattaphum, *Thailand* 65 J3
Ratten, *Austria* 26 D8
Rattray Hd., *U.K.* 14 D7
Rättvik, *Sweden* 10 D9
Ratz, Mt., *Canada* 104 B2
Ratzeburg, *Germany* 24 B6
Raub, *Malaysia* 65 L3
Rauch, *Argentina* 126 D4
Raudales de Malpaso, *Mexico* 119 D6
Raufarhöfn, *Iceland* 8 C6
Raufoss, *Norway* 9 F14
Raukumara Ra., *N.Z.* 91 H6
Rauma, *Finland* 9 F19
Raurkela, *India* 69 H11
Rausu-Dake, *Japan* 54 B12
Răut →, *Moldova* 43 C14
Rava-Ruska, *Poland* 47 G2
Rava Russkaya = Rava-Ruska, *Poland* 47 G2
Ravalli, *U.S.A.* 114 C6
Ravānsar, *Iran* 70 C5
Ravanusa, *Italy* 30 E6
Rāvar, *Iran* 71 D8
Ravena, *U.S.A.* 111 D11
Ravenna, *Italy* 29 D9
Ravenna, *Nebr., U.S.A.* 112 E5
Ravenna, *Ohio, U.S.A.* 110 E3
Ravensburg, *Germany* 25 H5
Ravenshoe, *Australia* 94 B4
Ravensthorpe, *Australia* 93 F3
Ravenswood, *Australia* 94 C4
Ravenswood, *U.S.A.* 108 F5
Ravi →, *Pakistan* 68 D4
Ravna Gora, *Croatia* 29 C11
Ravna Reka, *Serbia, Yug.* 40 B5
Ravne na Koroškem, *Slovenia* 29 B11
Rawa Mazowiecka, *Poland* 45 G7
Rawalpindi, *Pakistan* 68 C5
Rawāndūz, *Iraq* 70 B5
Rawang, *Malaysia* 65 L3
Rawene, *N.Z.* 91 F4
Rawicz, *Poland* 45 G3
Rawka →, *Poland* 45 F7
Rawlinna, *Australia* 93 F4
Rawlins, *U.S.A.* 114 F10
Rawlinson Ra., *Australia* 93 D4
Rawson, *Argentina* 128 E3
Raxaul, *India* 69 F11
Ray, *U.S.A.* 112 A3
Ray, C., *Canada* 103 C8
Rayadurg, *India* 66 M10
Rayagada, *India* 67 K13
Raychikhinsk, *Russia* 51 E13
Rāyen, *Iran* 71 D8
Rayleigh, *U.K.* 13 F8
Raymond, *Canada* 104 D6
Raymond, *Calif., U.S.A.* 116 H7
Raymond, *N.H., U.S.A.* 111 C13
Raymond, *Wash., U.S.A.* 116 D3
Raymondville, *U.S.A.* 113 M6
Raymore, *Canada* 105 C8
Rayón, *Mexico* 118 B2
Rayong, *Thailand* 64 F3
Rayville, *U.S.A.* 113 J9
Raz, Pte. du, *France* 18 D2
Razan, *Iran* 71 C6
Ražana, *Serbia, Yug.* 40 B3
Ražanj, *Serbia, Yug.* 40 C5
Razdelna, *Bulgaria* 41 C11
Razdel'naya = Rozdilna, *Ukraine* 47 J6
Razdolnoye, *Russia* 54 C5
Razdolnoye, *Ukraine* 47 K7
Razeh, *Iran* 71 C6
Razgrad, *Bulgaria* 41 C10
Razim, Lacul, *Romania* 43 F14
Razlog, *Bulgaria* 40 E7
Razmak, *Pakistan* 68 C3
Ré, Î. de, *France* 20 B2
Reading, *U.K.* 13 F7
Reading, *U.S.A.* 111 F9
Reading □, *U.K.* 13 F7
Realicó, *Argentina* 126 D3
Réalmont, *France* 20 E6
Ream, *Cambodia* 65 G4
Reata, *Mexico* 118 B4
Reay Forest, *U.K.* 14 C4
Rebais, *France* 19 D10
Rebi, *Indonesia* 63 F8
Rebiana, *Libya* 79 D10
Rebun-Tō, *Japan* 54 B10
Recanati, *Italy* 29 E10
Recaş, *Romania* 42 E6
Recco, *Italy* 28 D6
Recherche, Arch. of the, *Australia* 93 F3
Rechna Doab, *Pakistan* 68 D5
Rechytsa, *Belarus* 47 F6
Recife, *Brazil* 125 E12
Recklinghausen, *Germany* 17 C7
Reconquista, *Argentina* 126 B4
Recreo, *Argentina* 126 B2
Recz, *Poland* 45 E2
Red →, *La., U.S.A.* 113 K9
Red →, *N. Dak., U.S.A.* 100 C10
Red Bank, *U.S.A.* 111 F10
Red Bay, *Canada* 103 B8
Red Bluff, *U.S.A.* 114 F2
Red Bluff L., *U.S.A.* 113 K3
Red Cliffs, *Australia* 95 E3
Red Cloud, *U.S.A.* 112 E5
Red Creek, *U.S.A.* 111 C8
Red Deer, *Canada* 104 C6
Red Deer →, *Alta., Canada* 105 C7
Red Deer →, *Man., Canada* 105 C8
Red Deer L., *Canada* 105 C8
Red Hook, *U.S.A.* 111 E11
Red Indian L., *Canada* 103 C8
Red L., *Canada* 105 C10
Red Lake, *Canada* 105 C10
Red Lake Falls, *U.S.A.* 112 B6
Red Lake Road, *Canada* 105 C10
Red Lodge, *U.S.A.* 114 D9
Red Mountain, *U.S.A.* 117 K9
Red Oak, *U.S.A.* 112 E7
Red Rock, *Canada* 102 C2
Red Rock, L., *U.S.A.* 112 E8
Red Rocks Pt., *Australia* 93 F4
Red Sea, *Asia* 74 C2
Red Slate Mt., *U.S.A.* 116 H8
Red Sucker L., *Canada* 102 B1
Red Tower Pass = Turnu Roşu, P., *Romania* 43 E9
Red Wing, *U.S.A.* 112 C8
Reda, *Poland* 44 D5
Redang, *Malaysia* 62 C2
Redange, *Lux.* 17 E5
Redcar, *U.K.* 12 C6
Redcar & Cleveland □, *U.K.* 12 C7
Redcliff, *Canada* 105 C6
Redcliffe, *Australia* 95 D5
Redcliffe, Mt., *Australia* 93 E3
Reddersburg, *S. Africa* 88 D4
Redding, *U.S.A.* 114 F2
Redditch, *U.K.* 13 E6
Redfield, *U.S.A.* 112 C5
Redford, *U.S.A.* 111 B11
Redkino, *Russia* 46 D9
Redlands, *U.S.A.* 117 M9
Redmond, *Oreg., U.S.A.* 114 D3
Redmond, *Wash., U.S.A.* 116 C4
Redon, *France* 18 E4
Redonda, *Antigua* 121 C7
Redondela, *Spain* 34 C2
Redondo, *Portugal* 35 G3
Redondo Beach, *U.S.A.* 117 M8
Redruth, *U.K.* 13 G2
Redvers, *Canada* 105 D8
Redwater, *Canada* 104 C6
Redwood, *U.S.A.* 111 B9
Redwood City, *U.S.A.* 116 H4
Redwood Falls, *U.S.A.* 112 C7
Redwood National Park, *U.S.A.* 114 F1
Ree, L., *Ireland* 15 C3
Reed, L., *Canada* 105 C8
Reed City, *U.S.A.* 108 D3
Reedley, *U.S.A.* 116 J7
Reedsburg, *U.S.A.* 112 D9
Reedsport, *U.S.A.* 114 E1
Reedsville, *U.S.A.* 110 F7
Reefton, *N.Z.* 91 K3
Rees, *Germany* 24 D2
Reese →, *U.S.A.* 114 F5
Refahiye, *Turkey* 73 C8
Reftele, *Sweden* 11 G7
Refugio, *U.S.A.* 113 L6
Rega →, *Poland* 44 D2
Regalbuto, *Italy* 31 E7
Regen, *Germany* 25 G9
Regen →, *Germany* 25 F8
Regensburg, *Germany* 25 F8
Regenstauf, *Germany* 25 F8
Reggâne = Zaouiet Reggâne, *Algeria* 78 C6
Reggello, *Italy* 29 E8
Réggio di Calábria, *Italy* 31 D8
Réggio nell'Emília, *Italy* 28 D7
Reghin, *Romania* 43 D9
Regina, *Canada* 105 C8
Regina Beach, *Canada* 105 C8
Registro, *Brazil* 127 A6
Reguengos de Monsaraz, *Portugal* 35 G3
Rehar →, *India* 69 H10
Rehli, *India* 69 H8
Rehoboth, *Namibia* 88 C2
Rehovot, *Israel* 75 D3
Reichenbach, *Germany* 24 E8
Reid, *Australia* 93 F4
Reidsville, *U.S.A.* 109 G6
Reigate, *U.K.* 13 F7
Reillo, *Spain* 32 F3
Reims, *France* 19 C11
Reina Adelaida, Arch., *Chile* 128 G2
Reinbek, *Germany* 24 B6
Reindeer →, *Canada* 105 B8
Reindeer I., *Canada* 105 C9
Reindeer L., *Canada* 105 B8
Reinga, C., *N.Z.* 91 F4
Reinosa, *Spain* 34 B6
Reitz, *S. Africa* 89 D4
Reivilo, *S. Africa* 88 D3
Rejaf, *Sudan* 81 G3
Rejmyre, *Sweden* 11 F9
Rejowiec Fabryczny, *Poland* 45 G10
Reka →, *Slovenia* 29 C11
Rekovac, *Serbia, Yug.* 40 C5
Reliance, *Canada* 105 A7
Rémalard, *France* 18 D7
Remarkable, Mt., *Australia* 95 E2
Rembang, *Indonesia* 63 G14
Remedios, *Panama* 120 E3
Remeshk, *Iran* 71 E8
Remetea, *Romania* 43 D10
Remich, *Lux.* 17 E6
Remiremont, *France* 19 D13
Remo, *Ethiopia* 81 F5
Remontnoye, *Russia* 49 G6
Remoulins, *France* 21 E8
Remscheid, *Germany* 17 C7
Ren Xian, *China* 56 F8
Rende, *Italy* 31 C9
Rendína, *Greece* 38 B3
Rendsburg, *Germany* 24 A5
Renfrew, *Canada* 102 C4
Renfrewshire □, *U.K.* 14 F4
Rengat, *Indonesia* 62 E2
Rengo, *Chile* 126 C1
Renhua, *China* 59 E9
Renhuai, *China* 58 D6
Reni, *Ukraine* 47 K5
Renk, *Sudan* 81 E3
Renmark, *Australia* 95 E3
Rennell Sd., *Canada* 104 C2
Renner Springs, *Australia* 94 B1
Rennes, *France* 18 D5
Rennie L., *Canada* 105 A7
Reno, *U.S.A.* 116 F7
Reno →, *Italy* 29 D9
Renovo, *U.S.A.* 110 E7
Renqiu, *China* 56 E9
Rens, *Denmark* 11 K3
Renshou, *China* 58 C5
Rensselaer, *Ind., U.S.A.* 108 E2
Rensselaer, *N.Y., U.S.A.* 111 D11
Rentería, *Spain* 32 B3
Renton, *U.S.A.* 116 C4
Réo, *Burkina Faso* 82 C4
Reocín, *Spain* 34 B6
Reotipur, *India* 69 G10
Répcelak, *Hungary* 42 C2
Republic, *Mo., U.S.A.* 113 G8
Republic, *Wash., U.S.A.* 114 B4
Republican →, *U.S.A.* 112 F6
Repulse Bay, *Canada* 101 B11
Requena, *Peru* 124 E4
Requena, *Spain* 33 F3
Réquista, *France* 20 D6
Reşadiye = Datça, *Turkey* 39 E9
Reşadiye, *Turkey* 72 B7
Reşadiye Yarımadası, *Turkey* 39 E9
Resavica, *Serbia, Yug.* 40 B5
Resen, *Macedonia* 40 E5
Reserve, *U.S.A.* 115 K9
Resht = Rasht, *Iran* 71 B6

Resistencia, *Argentina* 126 B4
Reşiţa, *Romania* 42 E6
Resko, *Poland* 44 E2
Resolution I., *Canada* 101 B13
Resolution I., *N.Z.* 91 L1
Ressano Garcia, *Mozam.* 89 D5
Reston, *Canada* 105 D8
Reszel, *Poland* 44 D8
Retalhuleu, *Guatemala* 120 D1
Retenue, L. de, *Dem. Rep. of the Congo* 87 E2
Retezat, Munţii, *Romania* 42 E8
Retford, *U.K.* 12 D7
Rethel, *France* 19 C11
Rethem, *Germany* 24 C5
Réthímnon, *Greece* 36 D6
Réthímnon □, *Greece* 36 D6
Reti, *Pakistan* 68 E3
Retiche, Alpi, *Switz.* 25 J6
Retiers, *France* 18 E5
Retortillo, *Spain* 34 E4
Retournac, *France* 21 C8
Rétság, *Hungary* 42 C4
Réunion ■, *Ind. Oc.* 77 J9
Reus, *Spain* 32 D6
Reuterstadt Stavenhagen, *Germany* 24 B8
Reutlingen, *Germany* 25 G5
Reutte, *Austria* 26 D3
Reval = Tallinn, *Estonia* 9 G21
Revel, *France* 20 E6
Revelganj, *India* 69 G11
Revelstoke, *Canada* 104 C5
Reventazón, *Peru* 124 E2
Revigny-sur-Ornain, *France* 19 D11
Revillagigedo, Is. de, *Pac. Oc.* 118 D2
Revin, *France* 19 C11
Revúca, *Slovak Rep.* 27 C13
Revuè →, *Mozam.* 87 F3
Rewa, *India* 69 G9
Rewari, *India* 68 E7
Rexburg, *U.S.A.* 114 E8
Rey, *Iran* 71 C6
Rey, I. del, *Panama* 120 E4
Rey Malabo, *Eq. Guin.* 83 E6
Reyðarfjörður, *Iceland* 8 D6
Reyes, Pt., *U.S.A.* 116 H3
Reyhanlı, *Turkey* 72 D7
Reykjahlið, *Iceland* 8 D5
Reykjanes, *Iceland* 8 E2
Reykjavík, *Iceland* 8 D3
Reynolds Ra., *Australia* 92 D5
Reynoldsville, *U.S.A.* 110 E6
Reynosa, *Mexico* 119 B5
Rēzekne, *Latvia* 9 H22
Rezina, *Moldova* 43 C13
Rezovo, *Bulgaria* 41 D12
Rezvān, *Iran* 71 E8
Rgotina, *Serbia, Yug.* 40 B6
Rhamnus, *Greece* 38 C6
Rhayader, *U.K.* 13 E4
Rheda-Wiedenbrück, *Germany* 24 D4
Rhede, *Germany* 24 D2
Rhein →, *Europe* 17 C6
Rhein-Main-Donau-Kanal, *Germany* 25 F7
Rheinbach, *Germany* 24 E2
Rheine, *Germany* 24 C3
Rheinfelden, *Germany* 25 H3
Rheinhessen-Pfalz □, *Germany* 25 F3
Rheinland-Pfalz □, *Germany* 25 E2
Rheinsberg, *Germany* 24 B8
Rhin = Rhein →, *Europe* 17 C6
Rhine = Rhein →, *Europe* 17 C6
Rhinebeck, *U.S.A.* 111 E11
Rhineland-Palatinate = Rheinland-Pfalz □, *Germany* 25 E2
Rhinelander, *U.S.A.* 112 C10
Rhinns Pt., *U.K.* 14 F2
Rhino Camp, *Uganda* 86 B3
Rhir, Cap, *Morocco* 78 B4
Rho, *Italy* 28 C6
Rhode Island □, *U.S.A.* 111 E13
Rhodes = Ródhos, *Greece* 36 C10
Rhodesia = Zimbabwe ■, *Africa* 87 F3
Rhodope Mts. = Rhodopi Planina, *Bulgaria* 41 E8
Rhodopi Planina, *Bulgaria* 41 E8
Rhön, *Germany* 24 E5
Rhondda, *U.K.* 13 F4
Rhondda Cynon Taff □, *U.K.* 13 F4
Rhône □, *France* 21 C8
Rhône →, *France* 21 E8
Rhône-Alpes □, *France* 21 C9
Rhum, *U.K.* 14 E2
Rhyl, *U.K.* 12 D4
Ri-Aba, *Eq. Guin.* 83 E6
Riachão, *Brazil* 125 E9
Riangnom, *Sudan* 81 F3
Riaño, *Spain* 34 C6
Rians, *France* 21 E9
Riansáres →, *Spain* 35 F7
Riasi, *India* 69 C6
Riau □, *Indonesia* 62 D2
Riau, Kepulauan, *Indonesia* 62 D2
Riau Arch. = Riau, Kepulauan, *Indonesia* 62 D2
Riaza, *Spain* 34 D7
Riaza →, *Spain* 34 D7
Riba de Saelices, *Spain* 32 E2
Riba-Roja de Turia, *Spain* 33 F4
Ribadavia, *Spain* 34 C2
Ribadeo, *Spain* 34 B3
Ribadesella, *Spain* 34 B5
Ribado, *Nigeria* 83 D7
Ribao, *Cameroon* 83 D7
Ribas = Ribes de Freser, *Spain* 32 C7
Ribas do Rio Pardo, *Brazil* 125 H8
Ribble →, *U.K.* 12 D5
Ribe, *Denmark* 11 J2
Ribe Amtskommune □, *Denmark* 11 J2
Ribeauvillé, *France* 19 D14
Ribécourt-Dreslincourt, *France* 19 C9
Ribeira = Santa Uxía, *Spain* 34 C2
Ribeira Brava, *Madeira* 37 D2
Ribeirão Prêto, *Brazil* 127 A6
Ribemont, *France* 19 C10
Ribera, *Italy* 30 E6
Ribérac, *France* 20 C4
Riberalta, *Bolivia* 124 F5
Ribes de Freser, *Spain* 32 C7
Ribnica, *Slovenia* 29 C11
Ribnitz-Damgarten, *Germany* 24 A8
Ričany, *Czech Rep.* 26 B7
Riccarton, *N.Z.* 91 K4
Ríccia, *Italy* 31 A7
Riccione, *Italy* 29 E9
Rice, *U.S.A.* 117 L12
Rice L., *Canada* 110 B6
Rice Lake, *U.S.A.* 112 C9
Rich, C., *Canada* 110 B4
Richard Toll, *Senegal* 82 B1
Richards Bay, *S. Africa* 89 D5
Richardson →, *Canada* 105 B6
Richardson Lakes, *U.S.A.* 108 C10
Richardson Springs, *U.S.A.* 116 F5
Riche, C., *Australia* 93 F2
Richelieu, *France* 18 E7
Richey, *U.S.A.* 112 B2
Richfield, *U.S.A.* 115 G8
Richfield Springs, *U.S.A.* 111 D10
Richford, *U.S.A.* 111 B12
Richibucto, *Canada* 103 C7
Richland, *Ga., U.S.A.* 109 J3
Richland, *Wash., U.S.A.* 114 C4
Richland Center, *U.S.A.* 112 D9
Richlands, *U.S.A.* 108 G5
Richmond, *Australia* 94 C3
Richmond, *N.Z.* 91 J4
Richmond, *U.K.* 12 C6
Richmond, *Calif., U.S.A.* 116 H4
Richmond, *Ind., U.S.A.* 108 F3
Richmond, *Ky., U.S.A.* 108 G3
Richmond, *Mich., U.S.A.* 110 D2
Richmond, *Mo., U.S.A.* 112 F8
Richmond, *Tex., U.S.A.* 113 L7
Richmond, *Utah, U.S.A.* 114 F8
Richmond, *Va., U.S.A.* 108 G7
Richmond, *Vt., U.S.A.* 111 B12
Richmond Hill, *Canada* 110 C5
Richmond Ra., *Australia* 95 D5
Richwood, *U.S.A.* 108 F5
Ricla, *Spain* 32 D3
Ridder = Leninogorsk, *Kazakstan* 50 D9
Riddlesburg, *U.S.A.* 110 F6
Ridgecrest, *U.S.A.* 117 K9
Ridgefield, *Conn., U.S.A.* 111 E11
Ridgefield, *Wash., U.S.A.* 116 E4
Ridgeland, *U.S.A.* 109 J5
Ridgetown, *Canada* 102 D3
Ridgewood, *U.S.A.* 111 F10
Ridgway, *U.S.A.* 110 E6
Riding Mountain Nat. Park, *Canada* 105 C9
Ridley, Mt., *Australia* 93 F3
Riebeek-Oos, *S. Africa* 88 E4
Ried, *Austria* 26 C6
Riedlingen, *Germany* 25 G5
Riedstadt, *Germany* 25 F4
Rienza →, *Italy* 29 B8
Riesa, *Germany* 24 D9
Riesi, *Italy* 31 E7
Riet →, *S. Africa* 88 D3
Rietavas, *Lithuania* 44 C8
Rietbron, *S. Africa* 88 E3
Rietfontein, *Namibia* 88 C3
Rieti, *Italy* 29 F9
Rieupeyroux, *France* 20 D6
Riez, *France* 21 E10
Riffe L., *U.S.A.* 116 D4
Rifle, *U.S.A.* 114 G10
Rift Valley □, *Kenya* 86 B4
Rīga, *Latvia* 9 H21
Riga, G. of, *Latvia* 9 H20
Rigacikun, *Nigeria* 83 C6
Rīgān, *Iran* 71 D8
Rīgas Jūras Līcis = Riga, G. of, *Latvia* 9 H20
Rigaud, *Canada* 111 A10
Rigby, *U.S.A.* 114 E8
Rīgestān, *Afghan.* 66 D4
Riggins, *U.S.A.* 114 D5
Rignac, *France* 20 D6
Rigolet, *Canada* 103 B8
Rihand Dam, *India* 69 G10
Riihimäki, *Finland* 9 F21
Riiser-Larsen-halvøya, *Antarctica* 5 C4
Rijau, *Nigeria* 83 C6
Rijeka, *Croatia* 29 C11
Rijeka Crnojevića, *Montenegro, Yug.* 40 D3
Rijssen, *Neths.* 17 B6
Rike, *Ethiopia* 81 E4
Rikuzentakada, *Japan* 54 E10
Rila, *Bulgaria* 40 D7
Rila Planina, *Bulgaria* 40 D7
Riley, *U.S.A.* 114 E4
Rima →, *Nigeria* 83 C6
Rimah, Wadi ar →, *Si. Arabia* 70 E4
Rimavská Sobota, *Slovak Rep.* 27 C13
Rimbey, *Canada* 104 C6
Rimbo, *Sweden* 10 E12
Rimersburg, *U.S.A.* 110 E5
Rimforsa, *Sweden* 11 F9
Rimi, *Nigeria* 83 C6
Rímini, *Italy* 29 D9
Rimouski, *Canada* 103 C6
Rimrock, *U.S.A.* 116 D5
Rinca, *Indonesia* 63 F5
Rincón de la Victoria, *Spain* 35 J6
Rincón de Romos, *Mexico* 118 C4
Rinconada, *Argentina* 126 A2
Rind →, *India* 69 G9
Ringarum, *Sweden* 11 F10
Ringas, *India* 68 F6
Ringe, *Denmark* 11 J4
Ringim, *Nigeria* 83 C6
Ringkøbing, *Denmark* 11 H2
Ringkøbing Amtskommune □, *Denmark* 11 H2
Ringkøbing Fjord, *Denmark* 11 H2
Ringsjön, *Sweden* 11 J7
Ringsted, *Denmark* 11 J5
Ringvassøy, *Norway* 8 B18
Ringwood, *U.S.A.* 111 E10
Rinía, *Greece* 39 D7
Rinjani, *Indonesia* 62 F5
Rinteln, *Germany* 24 C5
Río, Punta del, *Spain* 33 J2
Rio Branco, *Brazil* 124 E5
Río Branco, *Uruguay* 127 C5
Río Bravo del Norte →, *Mexico* 119 B5
Rio Brilhante, *Brazil* 127 A5
Rio Claro, *Brazil* 127 A6
Rio Claro, *Trin. & Tob.* 121 D7
Río Colorado, *Argentina* 128 D4
Río Cuarto, *Argentina* 126 C3
Rio das Pedras, *Mozam.* 89 C6
Rio de Janeiro, *Brazil* 127 A7
Rio de Janeiro □, *Brazil* 127 A7
Rio do Sul, *Brazil* 127 B6
Río Gallegos, *Argentina* 128 G3
Rio Grande = Grande, Rio →, *U.S.A.* 113 N6
Río Grande, *Argentina* 128 G3
Rio Grande, *Brazil* 127 C5
Río Grande, *Mexico* 118 C4
Río Grande, *Nic.* 120 D3
Rio Grande City, *U.S.A.* 113 M5
Río Grande de Santiago →, *Mexico* 118 C3
Rio Grande do Norte □, *Brazil* 125 E11
Rio Grande do Sul □, *Brazil* 127 C5
Río Hato, *Panama* 120 E3
Río Lagartos, *Mexico* 119 C7
Rio Largo, *Brazil* 125 E11
Rio Maior, *Portugal* 35 F2
Rio Marina, *Italy* 28 F7
Rio Mulatos, *Bolivia* 124 G5
Río Muni = Mbini □, *Eq. Guin.* 84 D2
Rio Negro, *Brazil* 127 B6
Rio Pardo, *Brazil* 127 C5
Rio Rancho, *U.S.A.* 115 J10
Río Segundo, *Argentina* 126 C3
Río Tercero, *Argentina* 126 C3
Rio Tinto, *Portugal* 34 D2
Rio Verde, *Brazil* 125 G8
Río Verde, *Mexico* 119 C5
Rio Vista, *U.S.A.* 116 G5
Ríobamba, *Ecuador* 124 D3
Ríohacha, *Colombia* 124 A4
Riom, *France* 20 C7
Riom-ès-Montagnes, *France* 20 C6
Rion-des-Landes, *France* 20 E3
Rionero in Vúlture, *Italy* 31 B8
Rioni →, *Georgia* 49 J5
Riós, *Spain* 34 D3
Ríosucio, *Colombia* 124 B3
Riou L., *Canada* 105 B7
Rioz, *France* 19 E13
Ripatransone, *Italy* 29 F10
Ripley, *Canada* 110 B3
Ripley, *Calif., U.S.A.* 117 M12
Ripley, *N.Y., U.S.A.* 110 D5
Ripley, *Tenn., U.S.A.* 113 H10
Ripley, *W. Va., U.S.A.* 108 F5
Ripoll, *Spain* 32 C7
Ripon, *U.K.* 12 C6
Ripon, *Calif., U.S.A.* 116 H5
Ripon, *Wis., U.S.A.* 108 D1
Riposto, *Italy* 31 E8
Risan, *Montenegro, Yug.* 40 D2
Riscle, *France* 20 E3
Rishā', W. ar →, *Si. Arabia* 70 E5
Rishiri-Tō, *Japan* 54 B10
Rishon le Ẓiyyon, *Israel* 75 D3
Risle →, *France* 18 C7
Rison, *U.S.A.* 113 J8
Risør, *Norway* 9 G13
Rita Blanca Cr. →, *U.S.A.* 113 H3
Riti, *Nigeria* 83 D6
Ritter, Mt., *U.S.A.* 116 H7
Rittman, *U.S.A.* 110 F3
Ritzville, *U.S.A.* 114 C4
Riva del Garda, *Italy* 28 C7
Riva Lígure, *Italy* 28 E4
Rivadavia, *Buenos Aires, Argentina* 126 D3
Rivadavia, *Mendoza, Argentina* 126 C2
Rivadavia, *Salta, Argentina* 126 A3
Rivadavia, *Chile* 126 B1
Rivarolo Canavese, *Italy* 28 C4
Rivas, *Nic.* 120 D2
Rive-de-Gier, *France* 21 C8
River Cess, *Liberia* 82 D3
River Jordan, *Canada* 116 B2
Rivera, *Argentina* 126 D3
Rivera, *Uruguay* 127 C4
Riverbank, *U.S.A.* 116 H6
Riverdale, *U.S.A.* 116 J7
Riverhead, *U.S.A.* 111 F12
Riverhurst, *Canada* 105 C7
Rivers, *Canada* 105 C8
Rivers □, *Nigeria* 83 E6
Rivers Inlet, *Canada* 104 C3
Riversdale, *S. Africa* 88 E3
Riverside, *U.S.A.* 117 M9
Riverton, *Australia* 95 E2
Riverton, *Canada* 105 C9
Riverton, *N.Z.* 91 M2
Riverton, *U.S.A.* 114 E9
Riverton Heights, *U.S.A.* 116 C4
Rives, *France* 21 C9
Rivesaltes, *France* 20 F6
Riviera, *U.S.A.* 117 K12
Riviera di Levante, *Italy* 28 D6
Riviera di Ponente, *Italy* 28 D5
Rivière-au-Renard, *Canada* 103 C7
Rivière-du-Loup, *Canada* 103 C6
Rivière-Pentecôte, *Canada* 103 C6
Rivière-Pilote, *Martinique* 121 D7
Rivière St. Paul, *Canada* 103 B8
Rivne, *Ukraine* 47 G4
Rívoli, *Italy* 28 C4
Rivoli B., *Australia* 95 F3
Rixheim, *France* 19 E14
Riyadh = Ar Riyāḍ, *Si. Arabia* 70 E5
Rize, *Turkey* 73 B9
Rizhao, *China* 57 G10
Rizokarpaso, *Cyprus* 36 D13
Rizzuto, C., *Italy* 31 D10
Rjukan, *Norway* 9 G13
Ro, *Greece* 39 E11
Roa, *Spain* 34 D7
Road Town, *Br. Virgin Is.* 121 C7
Roan Plateau, *U.S.A.* 114 G9
Roanne, *France* 19 F11
Roanoke, *Ala., U.S.A.* 109 J3
Roanoke, *Va., U.S.A.* 108 G6
Roanoke →, *U.S.A.* 109 H7
Roanoke I., *U.S.A.* 109 H8
Roanoke Rapids, *U.S.A.* 109 G7
Roatán, *Honduras* 120 C2
Robāt Sang, *Iran* 71 C8
Robbins I., *Australia* 94 G4
Róbbio, *Italy* 28 C5
Robe →, *Australia* 92 D2
Röbel, *Germany* 24 B8
Robert Lee, *U.S.A.* 113 K4
Robertsdale, *U.S.A.* 110 F6
Robertsganj, *India* 69 G10
Robertson, *S. Africa* 88 E2
Robertson I., *Antarctica* 5 C18
Robertson Ra., *Australia* 92 D3
Robertsport, *Liberia* 82 D2
Robertstown, *Australia* 95 E2
Roberval, *Canada* 103 C5
Robeson Chan., *Greenland* 4 A4
Robesonia, *U.S.A.* 111 F8
Robi, *Ethiopia* 81 F4
Robinson, *U.S.A.* 108 F2
Robinson →, *Australia* 94 B2
Robinson Ra., *Australia* 93 E2
Robinvale, *Australia* 95 E3
Robledo, *Spain* 33 G2
Roblin, *Canada* 105 C8
Roboré, *Bolivia* 124 G7
Robson, *Canada* 104 D5
Robson, Mt., *Canada* 104 C5
Robstown, *U.S.A.* 113 M6
Roca, C. da, *Portugal* 35 G1
Roca Partida, I., *Mexico* 118 D2
Rocamadour, *France* 20 D5
Rocas, I., *Brazil* 125 D12
Rocca San Casciano, *Italy* 29 D8
Roccadáspide, *Italy* 31 B8
Roccastrada, *Italy* 29 F8
Roccella Iónica, *Italy* 31 D9
Rocha, *Uruguay* 127 C5
Rochdale, *U.K.* 12 D5
Rochechouart, *France* 20 C4
Rochefort, *Belgium* 17 D5
Rochefort, *France* 20 C3
Rochefort-en-Terre, *France* 18 E4
Rochelle, *U.S.A.* 112 E10
Rocher River, *Canada* 104 A6
Rocheservière, *France* 18 F5
Rochester, *U.K.* 13 F8
Rochester, *Ind., U.S.A.* 108 E2
Rochester, *Minn., U.S.A.* 112 C8
Rochester, *N.H., U.S.A.* 111 C14
Rochester, *N.Y., U.S.A.* 110 C7
Rociu, *Romania* 43 F10
Rock →, *Canada* 104 A3
Rock Creek, *U.S.A.* 110 E4
Rock Falls, *U.S.A.* 112 E10
Rock Hill, *U.S.A.* 109 H5
Rock Island, *U.S.A.* 112 E9
Rock Rapids, *U.S.A.* 112 D6
Rock Sound, *Bahamas* 120 B4
Rock Springs, *Mont., U.S.A.* 114 C10
Rock Springs, *Wyo., U.S.A.* 114 F9
Rock Valley, *U.S.A.* 112 D6
Rockall, *Atl. Oc.* 6 D3
Rockdale, *Tex., U.S.A.* 113 K6
Rockdale, *Wash., U.S.A.* 116 C5
Rockefeller Plateau, *Antarctica* 5 E14
Rockford, *U.S.A.* 112 D10
Rockglen, *Canada* 105 D7
Rockhampton, *Australia* 94 C5
Rockingham, *Australia* 93 F2
Rockingham, *U.S.A.* 109 H6
Rockingham B., *Australia* 94 B4
Rocklake, *U.S.A.* 112 A5
Rockland, *Canada* 111 A9
Rockland, *Idaho, U.S.A.* 114 E7
Rockland, *Maine, U.S.A.* 109 C11
Rockland, *Mich., U.S.A.* 112 B10
Rocklin, *U.S.A.* 116 G5
Rockmart, *U.S.A.* 109 H3
Rockport, *Mass., U.S.A.* 111 D14
Rockport, *Mo., U.S.A.* 112 E7
Rockport, *Tex., U.S.A.* 113 L6
Rocksprings, *U.S.A.* 113 K4
Rockville, *Conn., U.S.A.* 111 E12
Rockville, *Md., U.S.A.* 108 F7
Rockwall, *U.S.A.* 113 J6
Rockwell City, *U.S.A.* 112 D7
Rockwood, *Canada* 110 C4
Rockwood, *Maine, U.S.A.* 109 C11
Rockwood, *Tenn., U.S.A.* 109 H3
Rocky Ford, *U.S.A.* 112 F3
Rocky Gully, *Australia* 93 F2
Rocky Harbour, *Canada* 103 C8
Rocky Island L., *Canada* 102 C3
Rocky Lane, *Canada* 104 B5
Rocky Mount, *U.S.A.* 109 H7
Rocky Mountain House, *Canada* 104 C6
Rocky Mountain National Park, *U.S.A.* 114 F11
Rocky Mts., *N. Amer.* 114 G10
Rocky Point, *Namibia* 88 B2
Rocroi, *France* 19 C11
Rod, *Pakistan* 66 E3
Rødby, *Denmark* 11 K5
Rødbyhavn, *Denmark* 11 K5
Roddickton, *Canada* 103 B8
Rødding, *Denmark* 11 J3
Rödeby, *Sweden* 11 H9
Rødekro, *Denmark* 11 J3
Rodenkirchen, *Germany* 24 B4
Rodez, *France* 20 D6
Rodholívas, *Greece* 40 F7
Rodhópi □, *Greece* 41 E9
Rodhopoú, *Greece* 36 D5
Ródhos, *Greece* 36 C10
Rodi Gargánico, *Italy* 29 G12
Rodna, *Romania* 43 C9
Rodnei, Munţii, *Romania* 43 C9
Rodney, *Canada* 110 D3
Rodney, C., *N.Z.* 91 G5
Rodniki, *Russia* 48 B5
Rodonit, Kepi i, *Albania* 40 E3
Rodriguez, *Ind. Oc.* 3 E13
Roe →, *U.K.* 15 A5
Roebling, *U.S.A.* 111 F10
Roebourne, *Australia* 92 D2
Roebuck B., *Australia* 92 C3
Roermond, *Neths.* 17 C6
Roes Welcome Sd., *Canada* 101 B11
Roeselare, *Belgium* 17 D3
Rogachev = Ragachow, *Belarus* 47 F6
Rogačica, *Serbia, Yug.* 40 B3
Rogagua, L., *Bolivia* 124 F5
Rogaška Slatina, *Slovenia* 29 B12
Rogatec, *Slovenia* 29 B12
Rogatica, *Bos.-H.* 42 G4
Rogatyn, *Ukraine* 47 H3
Rogdhia, *Greece* 36 D7
Rogers, *U.S.A.* 113 G7
Rogers City, *U.S.A.* 108 C4
Rogersville, *Canada* 103 C6
Roggan →, *Canada* 102 B4
Roggan L., *Canada* 102 B4
Roggeveldberge, *S. Africa* 88 E3
Roggiano Gravina, *Italy* 31 C9
Rogliano, *France* 21 F13
Rogliano, *Italy* 31 C9
Rogoaguado, L., *Bolivia* 124 F5
Rogoźno, *Poland* 45 F3
Rogue →, *U.S.A.* 114 E1
Rohan, *France* 18 D4
Róhda, *Greece* 36 A3
Rohnert Park, *U.S.A.* 116 G4
Rohri, *Pakistan* 68 F3
Rohri Canal, *Pakistan* 68 F3
Rohtak, *India* 68 E7
Roi Et, *Thailand* 64 D4
Roja, *Latvia* 9 H20
Rojas, *Argentina* 126 C3
Rojiște, *Romania* 43 F8
Rojo, C., *Mexico* 119 C5
Rokan →, *Indonesia* 62 D2
Rokel →, *S. Leone* 82 D2
Rokiškis, *Lithuania* 9 J21
Rokitno, *Russia* 47 G8
Rokycany, *Czech Rep.* 26 B6
Rolândia, *Brazil* 127 A5
Rolla, *U.S.A.* 113 G9
Rolleston, *Australia* 94 C4
Rollingstone, *Australia* 94 B4
Rom, *Sudan* 81 F3
Roma, *Australia* 95 D4
Roma, *Italy* 29 G9
Roma, *Sweden* 11 G12
Roma, *U.S.A.* 113 M5
Romain C., *U.S.A.* 109 J6
Romaine, *Canada* 103 B7
Romaine →, *Canada* 103 B7
Roman, *Bulgaria* 40 C7
Roman, *Romania* 43 D11
Roman-Kosh, Gora, *Ukraine* 47 K8
Romanche →, *France* 21 C9
Romang, *Indonesia* 63 F7
Români, *Egypt* 75 E1
Romania ■, *Europe* 43 D10
Romanija, *Bos.-H.* 42 G3
Romano, Cayo, *Cuba* 120 B4
Romanovka = Basarabeasca, *Moldova* 43 D13
Romans-sur-Isère, *France* 21 C9
Romanshorn, *Switz.* 25 H5

Rombari, *Sudan* 81 G3
Romblon, *Phil.* 61 E5
Rome = Roma, *Italy* 29 G9
Rome, *Ga., U.S.A.* 109 H3
Rome, *N.Y., U.S.A.* 111 C9
Rome, *Pa., U.S.A.* 111 E8
Rometta, *Italy* 31 D8
Romilly-sur-Seine, *France* 19 D10
Romney, *U.S.A.* 108 F6
Romney Marsh, *U.K.* 13 F8
Romny, *Ukraine* 47 G7
Rømø, *Denmark* 11 J2
Romodan, *Ukraine* 47 G7
Romodanovo, *Russia* 48 C7
Romont, *Switz.* 25 J2
Romorantin-Lanthenay, *France* 19 E8
Romsdalen, *Norway* 9 E12
Romsey, *U.K.* 13 G6
Ron, *Vietnam* 64 D6
Rona, *U.K.* 14 D3
Ronan, *U.S.A.* 114 C6
Roncador, Cayos, *Caribbean* 120 D3
Roncador, Serra do, *Brazil* 125 F8
Ronciglione, *Italy* 29 F9
Ronco →, *Italy* 29 D9
Ronda, *Spain* 35 J5
Ronda, Serranía de, *Spain* 35 J5
Rondane, *Norway* 9 F13
Rondônia □, *Brazil* 124 F6
Rondonópolis, *Brazil* 125 G8
Rong, Koh, *Cambodia* 65 G4
Rong Jiang →, *China* 58 E7
Rong Xian, *Guangxi Zhuangzu, China* 59 F8
Rong Xian, *Sichuan, China* 58 C5
Rong'an, *China* 58 E7
Rongchang, *China* 58 C5
Ronge, L. la, *Canada* 105 B7
Rongjiang, *China* 58 E7
Rongshui, *China* 58 E7
Rønne, *Denmark* 11 J8
Ronne Ice Shelf, *Antarctica* 5 D18
Ronneby, *Sweden* 11 H9
Ronnebyån →, *Sweden* 11 H9
Rönneshytta, *Sweden* 11 F9
Ronsard, C., *Australia* 93 D1
Ronse, *Belgium* 17 D3
Roodepoort, *S. Africa* 89 D4
Roof Butte, *U.S.A.* 115 H9
Rooiboklaagte →, *Namibia* 88 C3
Roorkee, *India* 68 E7
Roosendaal, *Neths.* 17 C4
Roosevelt, *U.S.A.* 114 F8
Roosevelt →, *Brazil* 122 D4
Roosevelt, Mt., *Canada* 104 B3
Roosevelt I., *Antarctica* 5 D12
Ropczyce, *Poland* 45 H8
Roper →, *Australia* 94 A2
Roper Bar, *Australia* 94 A1
Roque Pérez, *Argentina* 126 D4
Roquefort, *France* 20 D3
Roquemaure, *France* 21 D8
Roquetas de Mar, *Spain* 33 J2
Roquetes, *Spain* 32 E5
Roquevaire, *France* 21 E9
Roraima □, *Brazil* 124 C6
Roraima, Mt., *Venezuela* 122 C4
Røros, *Norway* 9 E14
Rorschach, *Switz.* 25 H5
Rosa, *Zambia* 87 D3
Rosa, L., *Bahamas* 121 B5
Rosa, Monte, *Italy* 28 C4
Rosal de la Frontera, *Spain* 35 H3
Rosalia, *U.S.A.* 114 C5
Rosamond, *U.S.A.* 117 L8
Rosans, *France* 21 D9
Rosario, *Argentina* 126 C3
Rosário, *Brazil* 125 D10
Rosario, *Baja Calif., Mexico* 118 B1
Rosario, *Sinaloa, Mexico* 118 C3
Rosario, *Paraguay* 126 A4
Rosario de la Frontera, *Argentina* 126 B3
Rosario de Lerma, *Argentina* 126 A2
Rosario del Tala, *Argentina* 126 C4
Rosário do Sul, *Brazil* 127 C5
Rosarito, *Mexico* 117 N9
Rosarno, *Italy* 31 D8
Rosas = Roses, *Spain* 32 C8
Roscoe, *U.S.A.* 111 E10
Roscoff, *France* 18 D3
Roscommon, *Ireland* 15 C3
Roscommon □, *Ireland* 15 C3
Roscrea, *Ireland* 15 D4
Rose →, *Australia* 94 A2
Rose Blanche, *Canada* 103 C8
Rose Pt., *Canada* 104 C2
Rose Valley, *Canada* 105 C8
Roseau, *Domin.* 121 C7
Roseau, *U.S.A.* 112 A7
Rosebery, *Australia* 94 G4
Rosebud, *S. Dak., U.S.A.* 112 D4
Rosebud, *Tex., U.S.A.* 113 K6
Roseburg, *U.S.A.* 114 E2
Rosedale, *U.S.A.* 113 J9
Roseland, *U.S.A.* 116 G4
Rosemary, *Canada* 104 C6
Rosenberg, *U.S.A.* 113 L7
Rosendaël, *France* 19 A9
Rosenheim, *Germany* 25 H8
Roses, *Spain* 32 C8
Roses, G. de, *Spain* 32 C8
Roseto degli Abruzzi, *Italy* 29 F11
Rosetown, *Canada* 105 C7
Rosetta = Rashîd, *Egypt* 80 H7
Roseville, *Calif., U.S.A.* 116 G5
Roseville, *Mich., U.S.A.* 110 D2
Rosewood, *Australia* 95 D5
Roshkhvār, *Iran* 71 C8
Rosières-en-Santerre, *France* 19 C9
Rosignano Maríttimo, *Italy* 28 E7
Rosignol, *Guyana* 124 B7
Roşiori de Vede, *Romania* 43 F10
Rositsa, *Bulgaria* 41 C11
Rositsa →, *Bulgaria* 41 C9
Roskilde, *Denmark* 11 J6
Roskilde Amtskommune □, *Denmark* 11 J6
Roskovec, *Albania* 40 F3
Roslavl, *Russia* 46 F7
Rosmaninhal, *Portugal* 34 F3
Rosmead, *S. Africa* 88 E4
Røsnæs, *Denmark* 11 J4
Rosolini, *Italy* 31 F7
Rosporden, *France* 18 E3
Ross, *Australia* 94 G4
Ross, *N.Z.* 91 K3
Ross Béthio, *Mauritania* 82 B1
Ross I., *Antarctica* 5 D11
Ross Ice Shelf, *Antarctica* 5 E12
Ross L., *U.S.A.* 114 B3
Ross-on-Wye, *U.K.* 13 F5
Ross River, *Australia* 94 C1
Ross River, *Canada* 104 A2
Ross Sea, *Antarctica* 5 D11
Rossall Pt., *U.K.* 12 D4
Rossan Pt., *Ireland* 15 B3
Rossano, *Italy* 31 C9
Rossburn, *Canada* 105 C8
Rosseau, *Canada* 110 A5
Rosseau L., *Canada* 110 A5
Rosses, The, *Ireland* 15 A3
Rossignol, L., *Canada* 102 B5
Rossignol Res., *Canada* 103 D6
Rossland, *Canada* 104 D5
Rosslare, *Ireland* 15 D5
Rosslau, *Germany* 24 D8
Rosso, *Mauritania* 82 B1
Rosso, C., *France* 21 F12
Rossosh, *Russia* 47 G10
Røssvatnet, *Norway* 8 D16
Røst, *Norway* 8 C15
Rosthern, *Canada* 105 C7
Rostock, *Germany* 24 A8
Rostov, *Don, Russia* 47 J10
Rostov, *Yaroslavl, Russia* 46 D10
Rostrenen, *France* 18 D3
Roswell, *Ga., U.S.A.* 109 H3
Roswell, *N. Mex., U.S.A.* 113 J2
Rota, *Spain* 35 J4
Rotan, *U.S.A.* 113 J4
Rotenburg, *Hessen, Germany* 24 E5
Rotenburg, *Niedersachsen, Germany* 24 B5
Roth, *Germany* 25 F7
Rothaargebirge, *Germany* 24 D4
Rothenburg ob der Tauber, *Germany* 25 F6
Rother →, *U.K.* 13 G8
Rotherham, *U.K.* 12 D6
Rothes, *U.K.* 14 D5
Rothesay, *Canada* 103 C6
Rothesay, *U.K.* 14 F3
Roti, *Indonesia* 63 F6
Rotja, Pta., *Spain* 33 G6
Roto, *Australia* 95 E4
Rotondo, Mte., *France* 21 F13
Rotoroa, L., *N.Z.* 91 J4
Rotorua, *N.Z.* 91 H6
Rotorua, L., *N.Z.* 91 H6
Rott →, *Germany* 25 G9
Rottenburg, *Germany* 25 G4
Rottenmann, *Austria* 26 D7
Rotterdam, *Neths.* 17 C4
Rotterdam, *U.S.A.* 111 D10
Rottne, *Sweden* 11 G8
Rottnest I., *Australia* 93 F2
Rottumeroog, *Neths.* 17 A6
Rottweil, *Germany* 25 G4
Rotuma, *Fiji* 96 J9
Roubaix, *France* 19 B10
Roudnice nad Labem, *Czech Rep.* 26 A7
Rouen, *France* 18 C8
Rouergue, *France* 20 D5
Rouillac, *France* 20 C3
Rouleau, *Canada* 105 C8
Round Mountain, *U.S.A.* 114 G5
Round Mt., *Australia* 95 E5
Round Rock, *U.S.A.* 113 K6
Roundup, *U.S.A.* 114 C9
Rousay, *U.K.* 14 B5
Rouses Point, *U.S.A.* 111 B11
Rouseville, *U.S.A.* 110 E5
Roussillon, *Isère, France* 21 C8
Roussillon, *Pyrénées-Or., France* 20 F6
Rouxville, *S. Africa* 88 E4
Rouyn-Noranda, *Canada* 102 C4
Rovaniemi, *Finland* 8 C21
Rovato, *Italy* 28 C7
Rovenki, *Ukraine* 47 H10
Rovereto, *Italy* 28 C8
Rovigo, *Italy* 29 C8
Rovinj, *Croatia* 29 C10
Rovno = Rivne, *Ukraine* 47 G4
Rovnoye, *Russia* 48 E8
Rovuma = Ruvuma →, *Tanzania* 87 E5
Row'ān, *Iran* 71 C6
Rowena, *Australia* 95 D4
Rowley Shoals, *Australia* 92 C2
Roxa, *Guinea-Biss.* 82 C1
Roxas, *Capiz, Phil.* 61 F5
Roxas, *Isabela, Phil.* 61 C4
Roxas, *Mind. Or., Phil.* 61 E4
Roxboro, *U.S.A.* 109 G6
Roxburgh, *N.Z.* 91 L2
Roxbury, *U.S.A.* 110 F7
Roxen, *Sweden* 11 F9
Roy, *Mont., U.S.A.* 114 C9
Roy, *N. Mex., U.S.A.* 113 H2
Roy, *Utah, U.S.A.* 114 F7
Royal Canal, *Ireland* 15 C4
Royal Leamington Spa, *U.K.* 13 E6
Royal Tunbridge Wells, *U.K.* 13 F8
Royan, *France* 20 C2
Roye, *France* 19 C9
Royston, *U.K.* 13 E7
Rožaj, *Montenegro, Yug.* 40 D4
Różan, *Poland* 45 F8
Rozay-en-Brie, *France* 19 D9
Rozdilna, *Ukraine* 47 J6
Rozhyshche, *Ukraine* 47 G3
Rožmitál pod Třemšínem, *Czech Rep.* 26 B6
Rožňava, *Slovak Rep.* 27 C13
Rozogi, *Poland* 44 E8
Rozoy-sur-Serre, *France* 19 C11
Rozzano, *Italy* 28 C6
Rrëshen, *Albania* 40 E3
Rrogozhine, *Albania* 40 E3
Rtanj, *Serbia, Yug.* 40 C5
Rtishchevo, *Russia* 48 D5
Rúa = A Rúa, *Spain* 34 C3
Ruacaná, *Namibia* 88 B1
Ruahine Ra., *N.Z.* 91 H6
Ruapehu, *N.Z.* 91 H5
Ruapuke I., *N.Z.* 91 M2
Ruâq, W. →, *Egypt* 75 F2
Rub' al Khālī, *Si. Arabia* 74 D4
Rubeho Mts., *Tanzania* 86 D4
Rubezhnoye = Rubizhne, *Ukraine* 47 H10
Rubh a' Mhail, *U.K.* 14 F2
Rubha Hunish, *U.K.* 14 D2
Rubha Robhanais = Lewis, Butt of, *U.K.* 14 C2
Rubí, *Spain* 32 D7
Rubicon →, *U.S.A.* 116 G5
Rubicone →, *Italy* 29 D9
Rubik, *Albania* 40 E3
Rubino, *Ivory C.* 82 D4
Rubio, *Venezuela* 124 B4
Rubizhne, *Ukraine* 47 H10
Rubtsovsk, *Russia* 50 D9
Ruby L., *U.S.A.* 114 F6
Ruby Mts., *U.S.A.* 114 F6
Rubyvale, *Australia* 94 C4
Rucheng, *China* 59 E9
Ruciane-Nida, *Poland* 44 E8
Rūd Sar, *Iran* 71 B6
Ruda, *Sweden* 11 G10
Ruda Śląska, *Poland* 45 H5
Rudall, *Australia* 95 E2
Rudall →, *Australia* 92 D3
Rüdersdorf, *Germany* 24 C9
Rudewa, *Tanzania* 87 E3
Rudkøbing, *Denmark* 11 K4
Rudna, *Poland* 45 G3
Rudnik, *Bulgaria* 41 D11
Rudnik, *Poland* 45 H9
Rudnik, *Serbia, Yug.* 40 B4
Rudnya, *Russia* 46 E6
Rudnyy, *Kazakstan* 50 D7
Rudo, *Bos.-H.* 42 G4
Rudolfa, Ostrov, *Russia* 50 A6
Rudolstadt, *Germany* 24 E7
Rudong, *China* 59 A13
Rudozem, *Bulgaria* 41 E8
Rudyard, *U.S.A.* 108 B3
Rue, *France* 19 B8
Rufa'a, *Sudan* 81 E3
Rufiji →, *Tanzania* 86 D4
Rufino, *Argentina* 126 C3
Rufisque, *Senegal* 82 C1
Rufunsa, *Zambia* 87 F2
Rugao, *China* 59 A13
Rugby, *U.K.* 13 E6
Rugby, *U.S.A.* 112 A5
Rügen, *Germany* 24 A9
Rugles, *France* 18 D7
Ruhengeri, *Rwanda* 86 C2
Ruhla, *Germany* 24 E6
Ruhland, *Germany* 24 D9
Ruhnu, *Estonia* 9 H20
Ruhr →, *Germany* 24 D2
Ruhuhu →, *Tanzania* 87 E3
Rui'an, *China* 59 D13
Ruichang, *China* 59 C10
Ruidoso, *U.S.A.* 115 K11
Ruijin, *China* 59 E10
Ruili, *China* 58 E1
Ruivo, Pico, *Madeira* 37 D3
Ruj, *Bulgaria* 40 D6
Rujen, *Macedonia* 40 D6
Rujm Tal'at al Jamā'ah, *Jordan* 75 E4
Ruk, *Pakistan* 68 F3
Rukhla, *Pakistan* 68 C4
Ruki →, *Dem. Rep. of the Congo* 84 E3
Rukwa □, *Tanzania* 86 D3
Rukwa, L., *Tanzania* 86 D3
Rulhieres, C., *Australia* 92 B4
Rum = Rhum, *U.K.* 14 E2
Rum Cay, *Bahamas* 121 B5
Rum Jungle, *Australia* 92 B5
Ruma, *Serbia, Yug.* 42 E4
Rumāḥ, *Si. Arabia* 70 E5
Rumania = Romania ■, *Europe* 43 D10
Rumaylah, *Iraq* 70 D5
Rumbêk, *Sudan* 81 F2
Rumburk, *Czech Rep.* 26 A7
Rumford, *U.S.A.* 109 C10
Rumia, *Poland* 44 D5
Rumilly, *France* 21 C9
Rumoi, *Japan* 54 C10
Rumonge, *Burundi* 86 C2
Rumson, *U.S.A.* 111 F11
Rumuruti, *Kenya* 86 B4
Runan, *China* 56 H8
Runanga, *N.Z.* 91 K3
Runaway, C., *N.Z.* 91 G6
Runcorn, *U.K.* 12 D5
Rundu, *Namibia* 88 B2
Rungwa, *Tanzania* 86 D3
Rungwa →, *Tanzania* 86 D3
Rungwe, *Tanzania* 87 D3
Rungwe, Mt., *Tanzania* 84 F6
Runka, *Nigeria* 83 C6
Runn, *Sweden* 10 D9
Running Ra., *Australia* 92 D3
Ruokolahti, *Finland* 46 B5
Ruoqiang, *China* 60 C3
Rupa, *India* 67 F18
Rupar, *India* 68 D7
Rupat, *Indonesia* 62 D2
Rupea, *Romania* 43 D10
Rupen →, *India* 68 H4
Rupert, *U.S.A.* 114 E7
Rupert →, *Canada* 102 B4
Rupert B., *Canada* 102 B4
Rupert House = Waskaganish, *Canada* 102 B4
Rupsa, *India* 69 J12
Rur →, *Germany* 24 D1
Rurrenabaque, *Bolivia* 124 F5
Rus →, *Spain* 33 F2
Rusambo, *Zimbabwe* 87 F3
Rusape, *Zimbabwe* 87 F3
Ruschuk = Ruse, *Bulgaria* 41 C9
Ruse, *Bulgaria* 41 C9
Ruse □, *Bulgaria* 41 C10
Ruşeţu, *Romania* 43 F12
Rush, *Ireland* 15 C5
Rushan, *China* 57 F11
Rushden, *U.K.* 13 E7
Rushmore, Mt., *U.S.A.* 112 D3
Rushville, *Ill., U.S.A.* 112 E9
Rushville, *Ind., U.S.A.* 108 F3
Rushville, *Nebr., U.S.A.* 112 D3
Russas, *Brazil* 125 D11
Russell, *Canada* 105 C8
Russell, *Kans., U.S.A.* 112 F5
Russell, *N.Y., U.S.A.* 111 B9
Russell, *Pa., U.S.A.* 110 E5
Russell L., *Man., Canada* 105 B8
Russell L., *N.W.T., Canada* 104 A5
Russellkonda, *India* 67 K14
Russellville, *Ala., U.S.A.* 109 H2
Russellville, *Ark., U.S.A.* 113 H8
Russellville, *Ky., U.S.A.* 109 G2
Rüsselsheim, *Germany* 25 F4
Russi, *Italy* 29 D9
Russia ■, *Eurasia* 51 C11
Russian →, *U.S.A.* 116 G3
Russkoye Ustie, *Russia* 4 B15
Rust, *Austria* 27 D9
Rustam, *Pakistan* 68 B5
Rustam Shahr, *Pakistan* 68 F2
Rustavi, *Georgia* 49 K7
Rustenburg, *S. Africa* 88 D4
Ruston, *U.S.A.* 113 J8
Rutana, *Burundi* 86 C3
Rute, *Spain* 35 H6
Ruteng, *Indonesia* 63 F6
Ruth, *U.S.A.* 110 C2
Rutherford, *U.S.A.* 116 G4
Rutland, *U.S.A.* 111 C12
Rutland □, *U.K.* 13 E7
Rutland Water, *U.K.* 13 E7
Rutledge →, *Canada* 105 A6
Rutledge L., *Canada* 105 A6
Rutqa, W. →, *Syria* 73 E9
Rutshuru, *Dem. Rep. of the Congo* 86 C2
Ruvo di Púglia, *Italy* 31 A9
Ruvu, *Tanzania* 86 D4
Ruvu →, *Tanzania* 86 D4
Ruvuma □, *Tanzania* 87 E4
Ruvuma →, *Tanzania* 87 E5
Ruwais, *U.A.E.* 71 E7
Ruwenzori, *Africa* 86 B2
Ruya →, *Zimbabwe* 89 B5
Ruyigi, *Burundi* 86 C3
Ruyuan, *China* 59 E9
Ruzayevka, *Russia* 48 C7
Ružhevo Konare, *Bulgaria* 41 D8
Ružomberok, *Slovak Rep.* 27 B12
Rwanda ■, *Africa* 86 C3
Ryakhovo, *Bulgaria* 41 C10
Ryan, L., *U.K.* 14 G3
Ryazan, *Russia* 46 E10
Ryazhsk, *Russia* 46 F11
Rybache = Rybachye, *Kazakstan* 50 E9
Rybachye, *Kazakstan* 50 E9
Rybinsk, *Russia* 46 C10
Rybinskoye Vdkhr., *Russia* 46 C10
Rybnik, *Poland* 45 H5
Rybnitsa = Râbniţa, *Moldova* 43 C14
Rybnoye, *Russia* 46 E10
Rychnov nad Kněžnou, *Czech Rep.* 27 A9
Rychwał, *Poland* 45 F5
Rycroft, *Canada* 104 B5
Ryd, *Sweden* 11 H8
Rydaholm, *Sweden* 11 H8
Ryde, *U.K.* 13 G6
Ryderwood, *U.S.A.* 116 D3
Rydzyna, *Poland* 45 G3
Rye, *U.K.* 13 G8
Rye →, *U.K.* 12 C7
Rye Bay, *U.K.* 13 G8
Rye Patch Reservoir, *U.S.A.* 114 F4
Ryegate, *U.S.A.* 114 C9
Ryki, *Poland* 45 G8
Ryley, *Canada* 104 C6
Rylsk, *Russia* 47 G8
Rylstone, *Australia* 95 E4
Rymanów, *Poland* 45 J8
Ryn, *Poland* 44 E8
Ryn Peski, *Kazakstan* 49 G9
Ryōtsu, *Japan* 54 E9
Rypin, *Poland* 45 E6
Ryssby, *Sweden* 11 H8
Ryūgasaki, *Japan* 55 G10
Ryūkyū Is. = Ryūkyū-rettō, *Japan* 55 M3
Ryūkyū-rettō, *Japan* 55 M3
Rzepin, *Poland* 45 F1
Rzeszów, *Poland* 45 H8
Rzhev, *Russia* 46 D8

S

Sa, *Thailand* 64 C3
Sa Canal, *Spain* 37 C7
Sa Conillera, *Spain* 37 C7
Sa Dec, *Vietnam* 65 G5
Sa Dragonera, *Spain* 37 B9
Sa Mesquida, *Spain* 37 B11
Sa Pobla, *Spain* 32 F8
Sa Savina, *Spain* 37 C7
Sa'ādatābād, *Fārs, Iran* 71 D7
Sa'ādatābād, *Hormozgān, Iran* 71 D7
Sa'ādatābād, *Kermān, Iran* 71 D7
Saale →, *Germany* 24 D7
Saaler Bodden, *Germany* 24 A8
Saalfeld, *Germany* 24 E7
Saalfelden, *Austria* 26 D5
Saane →, *Switz.* 25 H3
Saar →, *Europe* 17 E6
Saarbrücken, *Germany* 25 F2
Saarburg, *Germany* 25 F2
Saaremaa, *Estonia* 9 G20
Saarijärvi, *Finland* 9 E21
Saariselkä, *Finland* 8 B23
Saarland □, *Germany* 25 F2
Saarlouis, *Germany* 25 F2
Sab 'Ābar, *Syria* 70 C3
Saba, *W. Indies* 121 C7
Šabac, *Serbia, Yug.* 40 B3
Sabadell, *Spain* 32 D7
Sabah □, *Malaysia* 62 C5
Sabak Bernam, *Malaysia* 65 L3
Sabalān, Kūhhā-ye, *Iran* 70 B5
Sabalana, Kepulauan, *Indonesia* 63 F5
Sábana de la Mar, *Dom. Rep.* 121 C6
Sábanalarga, *Colombia* 124 A4
Sabang, *Indonesia* 62 C1
Săbăoani, *Romania* 43 C11
Sabará, *Brazil* 125 G10
Sabarmati →, *India* 68 H5
Sabattis, *U.S.A.* 111 B10
Sabáudia, *Italy* 30 A6
Saberania, *Indonesia* 63 E9
Sabhah, *Libya* 79 C8
Sabi →, *India* 68 E7
Sabidana, J., *Sudan* 80 D4
Sabie, *S. Africa* 89 D5
Sabinal, *Mexico* 118 A3
Sabinal, *U.S.A.* 113 L5
Sabiñánigo, *Spain* 32 C4
Sabinar, Punta del, *Spain* 33 J2
Sabinas, *Mexico* 118 B4
Sabinas →, *Mexico* 118 B4
Sabinas Hidalgo, *Mexico* 118 B4
Sabine →, *U.S.A.* 113 L8
Sabine L., *U.S.A.* 113 L8
Sabine Pass, *U.S.A.* 113 L8
Sabinov, *Slovak Rep.* 27 B14
Sabinsville, *U.S.A.* 110 E7
Sabirabad, *Azerbaijan* 49 K9
Sabkhet el Bardawîl, *Egypt* 75 D2
Sablayan, *Phil.* 61 E4
Sable, *Canada* 103 A6
Sable, C., *Canada* 103 D6
Sable, C., *U.S.A.* 107 E10
Sable I., *Canada* 103 D8
Sablé-sur-Sarthe, *France* 18 E6
Sabonkafi, *Niger* 83 C6
Sabor →, *Portugal* 34 D3
Sabou, *Burkina Faso* 82 C4
Sabres, *France* 20 D3
Sabrina Coast, *Antarctica* 5 C9
Sabugal, *Portugal* 34 E3
Sabulubbek, *Indonesia* 62 E1
Sabuncu, *Turkey* 39 B12
Sabzevār, *Iran* 71 B8
Sabzvārān, *Iran* 71 D8
Sac City, *U.S.A.* 112 D7
Sacedón, *Spain* 32 E2
Săcele, *Romania* 43 E10
Sachigo →, *Canada* 102 A2
Sachigo, L., *Canada* 102 B1
Sachkhere, *Georgia* 49 J6
Sachsen □, *Germany* 24 E9
Sachsen-Anhalt □, *Germany* 24 D7
Sacile, *Italy* 29 C9
Sackets Harbor, *U.S.A.* 111 C8
Sackville, *Canada* 103 C7
Saco, *Maine, U.S.A.* 109 D10
Saco, *Mont., U.S.A.* 114 B10
Sacramento, *U.S.A.* 116 G5

Sacramento →, U.S.A. 116 G5
Sacramento Mts., U.S.A. 115 K11
Sacramento Valley, U.S.A. 116 G5
Sacratif, C., Spain 35 J7
Săcueni, Romania 42 C7
Sada, Spain 34 B2
Sada-Misaki, Japan 55 H6
Sádaba, Spain 32 C3
Sadabad, India 68 F8
Sadani, Tanzania 86 D4
Sadao, Thailand 65 J3
Sadd el Aali, Egypt 80 C3
Saddle Mt., U.S.A. 116 E3
Sade, Nigeria 83 C7
Sadimi, Dem. Rep. of the Congo 87 D1
Sadiola, Mali 82 C2
Sa'dīyah, Hawr as, Iraq 73 F12
Sado, Japan 54 F9
Sado →, Portugal 35 G2
Sadon, Burma 67 G20
Sadon, Russia 49 J6
Sadra, India 68 H5
Sadri, India 68 G5
Sæby, Denmark 11 G4
Saegertown, U.S.A. 110 E4
Saelices, Spain 32 F2
Safaalan, Turkey 41 E12
Safaga, Egypt 80 B3
Şafājah, Si. Arabia 70 E3
Šafárikovo = Tornal'a, Slovak Rep. 27 C13
Säffle, Sweden 10 E6
Safford, U.S.A. 115 K9
Saffron Walden, U.K. 13 E8
Safi, Morocco 78 B4
Şafīābād, Iran 71 B8
Safīd Dasht, Iran 71 C6
Safīd Kūh, Afghan. 66 B3
Safīd Rūd →, Iran 71 B6
Safipur, India 69 F9
Safonovo, Russia 46 E7
Safranbolu, Turkey 72 B5
Saft Rashîn, Egypt 80 J7
Safwān, Iraq 70 D5
Sag Harbor, U.S.A. 111 F12
Saga, Japan 55 H5
Saga □, Japan 55 H5
Sagae, Japan 54 E10
Sagala, Mali 82 C3
Sagamore, U.S.A. 110 F5
Sagar, Karnataka, India 66 M9
Sagar, Mad. P., India 69 H8
Sagara, L., Tanzania 86 D3
Sagay, Phil. 61 F5
Saginaw, U.S.A. 108 D4
Saginaw →, U.S.A. 108 D4
Saginaw B., U.S.A. 108 D4
Sagleipie, Liberia 82 D3
Saglouc = Salluit, Canada 101 B12
Sagŏ-ri, S. Korea 57 G14
Sagone, France 21 F12
Sagone, G. de, France 21 F12
Sagres, Portugal 35 J2
Sagua la Grande, Cuba 120 B3
Saguache, U.S.A. 115 G10
Saguaro Nat. Park, U.S.A. 115 K8
Saguenay →, Canada 103 C5
Sagunt, Spain 32 F4
Sagunto = Sagunt, Spain 32 F4
Sagwara, India 68 H6
Sahaba, Sudan 80 D3
Sahagún, Spain 34 C5
Saḥam al Jawlān, Syria 75 C4
Sahamandrevo, Madag. 89 C8
Sahand, Kūh-e, Iran 70 B5
Sahara, Africa 78 D6
Saharan Atlas = Saharien, Atlas, Algeria 78 B6
Saharanpur, India 68 E7
Saharien, Atlas, Algeria 78 B6
Saharsa, India 69 G12
Sahasinaka, Madag. 89 C8
Sahaswan, India 69 E8
Sahel, Africa 78 E5
Sahel, Canal du, Mali 82 C3
Sahibganj, India 69 G12
Sāḥilīyah, Iraq 70 C4
Sahiwal, Pakistan 68 D5
Şaḥneh, Iran 70 C5
Sahuaripa, Mexico 118 B3
Sahuarita, U.S.A. 115 L8
Sahuayo, Mexico 118 C4
Šahy, Slovak Rep. 27 C11
Sai →, India 69 G10
Sai Buri, Thailand 65 J3
Sa'id Bundas, Sudan 79 G10
Sa'īdābād, Kermān, Iran 71 D7
Sa'īdābād, Semnān, Iran 71 B7
Sa'īdīyeh, Iran 71 B6
Saidpur, Bangla. 67 G16
Saidpur, India 69 G10
Saidu, Pakistan 69 B5
Saignes, France 20 C6
Saigon = Thanh Pho Ho Chi Minh, Vietnam 65 G6
Saijō, Japan 55 H6
Saikanosy Masoala, Madag. 89 B9
Saikhoa Ghat, India 67 F19
Saiki, Japan 55 H5
Sailana, India 68 H6
Saillans, France 21 D9
Sailolof, Indonesia 63 E8
Saimaa, Finland 9 F23
Saimbeyli, Turkey 72 D7
Şa'in Dezh, Iran 70 B5
St. Abb's Head, U.K. 14 F6
St-Affrique, France 20 E6
St-Agrève, France 21 C8
St-Aignan, France 18 E8
St. Alban's, Canada 103 C8
St. Albans, U.K. 13 F7
St. Albans, Vt., U.S.A. 111 B11
St. Albans, W. Va., U.S.A. 108 F5
St. Alban's Head, U.K. 13 G5
St. Albert, Canada 104 C6
St-Amand-en-Puisaye, France 19 E10
St-Amand-les-Eaux, France 19 B10
St-Amand-Montrond, France 19 F9
St-Amarin, France 19 E14
St-Amour, France 19 F12
St-André-de-Cubzac, France 20 D3
St-André-les-Alpes, France 21 E10
St. Andrew's, Canada 103 C8
St. Andrews, U.K. 14 E6
St-Anicet, Canada 111 A10
St. Ann B., Canada 103 C7
St. Ann's Bay, Jamaica 120 C4
St. Anthony, Canada 103 B8
St. Anthony, U.S.A. 114 E8
St. Antoine, Canada 103 C7
St-Antonin-Noble-Val, France 20 D5
St. Arnaud, Australia 95 F3
St-Astier, France 20 C4
St-Aubin-du-Cormier, France 18 D5
St-Augustin →, Canada 103 B8
St-Augustin-Saguenay, Canada 103 B8
St. Augustine, U.S.A. 109 L5
St-Aulaye, France 20 C4
St. Austell, U.K. 13 G3
St-Avold, France 19 C13
St. Barbe, Canada 103 B8
St-Barthélemy, W. Indies 121 C7
St-Béat, France 20 F4
St. Bees Hd., U.K. 12 C4
St-Benoît-du-Sault, France 20 B5
St-Bonnet, France 21 D10
St-Brévin-les-Pins, France 18 E4
St-Brice-en-Coglès, France 18 D5
St. Bride's, Canada 103 C9
St. Brides B., U.K. 13 F2
St-Brieuc, France 18 D4
St-Calais, France 18 E7
St-Cast-le-Guildo, France 18 D4
St. Catharines, Canada 102 D4
St. Catherines I., U.S.A. 109 K5
St. Catherine's Pt., U.K. 13 G6
St-Céré, France 20 D5
St-Cergue, Switz. 25 J2
St-Cernin, France 20 C6
St-Chamond, France 21 C8
St. Charles, Ill., U.S.A. 108 E1
St. Charles, Mo., U.S.A. 112 F9
St. Charles, Va., U.S.A. 108 F7
St-Chély-d'Apcher, France 20 D7
St-Chinian, France 20 E6
St. Christopher-Nevis = St. Kitts & Nevis ■, W. Indies 121 C7
St-Ciers-sur-Gironde, France 20 C3
St. Clair, Mich., U.S.A. 110 D2
St. Clair, Pa., U.S.A. 111 F8
St. Clair →, U.S.A. 110 D2
St. Clair, L., Canada 102 D3
St. Clair, L., U.S.A. 110 D2
St. Clairsville, U.S.A. 110 F4
St-Claud, France 20 C4
St. Claude, Canada 105 D9
St-Claude, France 19 F12
St-Clet, Canada 111 A10
St. Cloud, Fla., U.S.A. 109 L5
St. Cloud, Minn., U.S.A. 112 C7
St. Cricq, C., Australia 93 E1
St. Croix, U.S. Virgin Is. 121 C7
St. Croix →, U.S.A. 112 C8
St. Croix Falls, U.S.A. 112 C8
St-Cyprien, France 20 F7
St-Cyr-sur-Mer, France 21 E9
St. David's, Canada 103 C8
St. David's, U.K. 13 F2
St. David's Head, U.K. 13 F2
St-Denis, France 19 D9
St-Dié, France 19 D13
St-Dizier, France 19 D11
St-Égrève, France 21 C9
St. Elias, Mt., U.S.A. 100 B5
St. Elias Mts., Canada 104 A1
St. Elias Mts., U.S.A. 100 C6
St-Eloy-les-Mines, France 19 F9
St-Émilion, France 20 D3
St-Étienne, France 21 C8
St-Étienne-de-Tinée, France 21 D10
St-Étienne-du-Rouvray, France 18 C8
St. Eugène, Canada 111 A10
St. Eustatius, W. Indies 121 C7
St-Fargeau, France 19 E10
St-Félicien, Canada 102 C5
St-Florent, France 21 F13
St-Florent, G. de, France 21 F13
St-Florent-sur-Cher, France 19 F9
St-Florentin, France 19 E10
St-Flour, France 20 C7
St. Francis, U.S.A. 112 F4
St. Francis →, U.S.A. 113 H9
St. Francis, C., S. Africa 88 E3
St. Francisville, U.S.A. 113 K9
St-François, L., Canada 111 A10
St-Fulgent, France 18 F5
St-Gabriel, Canada 102 C5
St. Gallen = Sankt Gallen, Switz. 25 H5
St-Galmier, France 19 G11
St-Gaudens, France 20 E4
St-Gaultier, France 18 F8
St-Gengoux-le-National, France 19 F11
St-Geniez-d'Olt, France 20 D6
St. George, Australia 95 D4
St. George, Canada 103 C6
St. George, S.C., U.S.A. 109 J5
St. George, Utah, U.S.A. 115 H7
St. George, C., Canada 103 C8
St. George, C., U.S.A. 109 L3
St. George Ra., Australia 92 C4
St. George's, Canada 103 C8
St-Georges, Canada 103 C5
St. George's, Grenada 121 D7
St. George's B., Canada 103 C8
St. Georges Basin, N.S.W., Australia 95 F5
St. Georges Basin, W. Austral., Australia 92 C4
St. George's Channel, Europe 15 E6
St. Georges Hd., Australia 95 F5
St-Georges-lès-Baillargeaux, France 20 B4
St-Germain-de-Calberte, France 20 D7
St-Germain-en-Laye, France 19 D9
St-Germain-Lembron, France 20 C7
St-Gervais-d'Auvergne, France 19 F9
St-Gervais-les-Bains, France 21 C10
St-Gildas, Pte. de, France 18 E4
St-Gilles, France 21 E8
St-Girons, Ariège, France 20 F5
St-Girons, Landes, France 20 E2
St. Gotthard P. = San Gottardo, P. del, Switz. 25 J4
St. Helena, U.S.A. 114 G2
St. Helena ■, Atl. Oc. 76 H3
St. Helena, Mt., U.S.A. 116 G4
St. Helena B., S. Africa 88 E2
St. Helens, Australia 94 G4
St. Helens, U.K. 12 D5
St. Helens, U.S.A. 116 E4
St. Helens, Mt., U.S.A. 116 D4
St. Helier, U.K. 13 H5
St-Herblain, France 18 E5
St-Hilaire-du-Harcouët, France 18 D5
St-Hippolyte, France 19 E13
St-Hippolyte-du-Fort, France 20 E7
St-Honoré-les-Bains, France 19 F10
St-Hubert, Belgium 17 D5
St-Hyacinthe, Canada 102 C5
St. Ignace, U.S.A. 108 C3
St. Ignace I., Canada 102 C2
St. Ignatius, U.S.A. 114 C6
St-Imier, Switz. 25 H2
St. Ives, U.K. 13 G2
St-James, France 18 D5
St. James, U.S.A. 112 D7
St-Jean →, Canada 103 B7
St-Jean, L., Canada 103 C5
St-Jean-d'Angély, France 20 C3
St-Jean-de-Braye, France 19 E8
St-Jean-de-Luz, France 20 E2
St-Jean-de-Maurienne, France 21 C10
St-Jean-de-Monts, France 18 F4
St-Jean-du-Gard, France 20 D7
St-Jean-en-Royans, France 21 C9
St-Jean-Pied-de-Port, France 20 E2
St-Jean-Port-Joli, Canada 103 C5
St-Jean-sur-Richelieu, Canada 102 C5
St-Jérôme, Canada 102 C5
St. John, Canada 103 C6
St. John, U.S.A. 113 G5
St. John →, Liberia 82 D2
St. John →, U.S.A. 109 C12
St. John, C., Canada 103 C8
St. John's, Antigua 121 C7
St. John's, Canada 103 C9
St. Johns, Ariz., U.S.A. 115 J9
St. Johns, Mich., U.S.A. 108 D3
St. Johns →, U.S.A. 109 K5
St. John's Pt., Ireland 15 B3
St. Johnsbury, U.S.A. 111 B12
St. Johnsville, U.S.A. 111 D10
St. Joseph, La., U.S.A. 113 K9
St. Joseph, Mo., U.S.A. 112 F7
St. Joseph →, U.S.A. 108 D2
St. Joseph, I., Canada 102 C3
St. Joseph, L., Canada 102 B1
St-Jovite, Canada 102 C5
St-Juéry, France 20 E6
St-Julien-Chapteuil, France 21 C8
St-Julien-de-Vouvantes, France 18 E5
St-Julien-en-Genevois, France 19 F13
St-Junien, France 20 C4
St-Just-en-Chaussée, France 19 C9
St-Just-en-Chevalet, France 20 C7
St. Kitts & Nevis ■, W. Indies 121 C7
St. Laurent, Canada 105 C9
St-Laurent-de-la-Salanque, France 20 F6
St-Laurent-du-Pont, France 21 C9
St-Laurent-en-Grandvaux, France 19 F12
St-Laurent-Médoc, France 20 C3
St. Lawrence, Australia 94 C4
St. Lawrence, Canada 103 C8
St. Lawrence →, Canada 103 C6
St. Lawrence, Gulf of, Canada 103 C7
St. Lawrence I., U.S.A. 100 B3
St. Leonard, Canada 103 C6
St-Léonard-de-Noblat, France 20 C5
St. Lewis →, Canada 103 B8
St-Lô, France 18 C5
St-Louis, France 19 E14
St. Louis, Senegal 82 B1
St. Louis, U.S.A. 112 F9
St. Louis →, U.S.A. 112 B8
St-Loup-sur-Semouse, France 19 E13
St. Lucia ■, W. Indies 121 D7
St. Lucia, L., S. Africa 89 D5
St. Lucia Channel, W. Indies 121 D7
St. Maarten, W. Indies 121 C7
St. Magnus B., U.K. 14 A7
St-Maixent-l'École, France 20 B3
St-Malo, France 18 D4
St-Malo, G. de, France 18 D4
St-Mandrier-sur-Mer, France 21 E9
St-Marc, Haiti 121 C5
St-Marcellin, France 21 C9
St-Marcouf, Îs., France 18 C5
St. Maries, U.S.A. 114 C5
St-Martin, W. Indies 121 C7
St. Martin, L., Canada 105 C9
St-Martin-de-Crau, France 21 E8
St-Martin-de-Ré, France 20 B2
St-Martin-d'Hères, France 21 C9
St-Martin-Vésubie, France 21 D11
St-Martory, France 20 E4
St. Mary Pk., Australia 95 E2
St. Marys, Australia 94 G4
St. Marys, Canada 110 C3
St. Mary's, Corn., U.K. 13 H1
St. Mary's, Orkney, U.K. 14 C6
St. Marys, Ga., U.S.A. 109 K5
St. Marys, Pa., U.S.A. 110 E6
St. Mary's, C., Canada 103 C9
St. Mary's B., Canada 103 C9
St. Marys Bay, Canada 103 D6
St-Mathieu, Pte., France 18 D2
St. Matthew I., U.S.A. 100 B2
St. Matthews, I. = Zadetkyi Kyun, Burma 65 G1
St-Maurice →, Canada 102 C5
St-Maximin-la-Ste-Baume, France 21 E9
St-Médard-en-Jalles, France 20 D3
St-Méen-le-Grand, France 18 D4
St-Mihiel, France 19 D12
St. Moritz, Switz. 25 J5
St-Nazaire, France 18 E4
St. Neots, U.K. 13 E7
St-Nicolas-de-Port, France 19 D13
St-Niklaas, Belgium 17 C4
St-Omer, France 19 B9
St-Palais-sur-Mer, France 20 C2
St-Pamphile, Canada 103 C6
St-Pardoux-la-Rivière, France 20 C4
St. Pascal, Canada 103 C6
St. Paul, Canada 104 C6
St-Paul, France 21 D10
St. Paul, Minn., U.S.A. 112 C8
St. Paul, Nebr., U.S.A. 112 E5
St-Paul →, Canada 103 B8
St. Paul →, Liberia 82 D2
St. Paul, I., Ind. Oc. 3 F13
St-Paul-de-Fenouillet, France 20 F6
St. Paul I., Canada 103 C7
St-Paul-lès-Dax, France 20 E2
St-Péray, France 21 D8
St. Peter, U.S.A. 112 C8
St-Peter-Ording, Germany 24 A4
St. Peter Port, U.K. 13 H5
St. Peters, N.S., Canada 103 C7
St. Peters, P.E.I., Canada 103 C7
St. Petersburg = Sankt-Peterburg, Russia 46 C6
St. Petersburg, U.S.A. 109 M4
St-Philbert-de-Grand-Lieu, France 18 E5
St-Pie, Canada 111 A12
St-Pierre, St- P. & M. 103 C8
St-Pierre, L., Canada 102 C5
St-Pierre-d'Oléron, France 20 C2
St-Pierre-en-Port, France 18 C7
St-Pierre et Miquelon □, St- P. & M. 103 C8
St-Pierre-le-Moûtier, France 19 F10
St-Pierre-sur-Dives, France 18 C6
St-Pol-de-Léon, France 18 D3
St-Pol-sur-Mer, France 19 A9
St-Pol-sur-Ternoise, France 19 B9
St-Pons, France 20 E6
St-Pourçain-sur-Sioule, France 19 F10
St-Priest, France 21 C8
St-Quay-Portrieux, France 18 D4
St. Quentin, Canada 103 C6
St-Quentin, France 19 C10
St-Rambert-d'Albon, France 21 C8
St-Raphaël, France 21 E10
St. Regis, U.S.A. 114 C6
St-Renan, France 18 D2
St-Saëns, France 18 C8
St-Savin, France 20 B4
St-Savinien, France 20 C3
St. Sebastien, Tanjon' i, Madag. 89 A8
St-Seine-l'Abbaye, France 19 E11
St-Sernin-sur-Rance, France 20 E6
St-Sever, France 20 E3
St-Siméon, Canada 103 C6
St. Simons I., U.S.A. 109 K5
St. Simons Island, U.S.A. 109 K5
St. Stephen, Canada 103 C6
St-Sulpice, France 20 E5
St-Sulpice-Laurière, France 20 B5
St-Sulpice-les-Feuilles, France 20 B5
St-Syprien = St-Cyprien, France 20 F7
St-Thégonnec, France 18 D3
St. Thomas, Canada 102 D3
St. Thomas I., U.S. Virgin Is. 121 C7
St-Tite, Canada 102 C5
St-Tropez, France 21 E10
St. Troud = St. Truiden, Belgium 17 D5
St. Truiden, Belgium 17 D5
St-Vaast-la-Hougue, France 18 C5
St-Valery-en-Caux, France 18 C7
St-Valéry-sur-Somme, France 19 B8
St-Vallier, France 19 F11
St-Vallier-de-Thiey, France 21 E10
St-Varent, France 18 F6
St-Vaury, France 20 B5
St. Vincent, Italy 28 C4
St. Vincent, G., Australia 95 F2
St. Vincent & the Grenadines ■, W. Indies 121 D7
St-Vincent-de-Tyrosse, France 20 E2
St. Vincent Passage, W. Indies 121 D7
St-Vith, Belgium 17 D6
St-Vivien-de-Médoc, France 20 C2
St. Walburg, Canada 105 C7
St-Yrieix-la-Perche, France 20 C5
Ste-Adresse, France 18 C7
Ste-Agathe-des-Monts, Canada 102 C5
Ste-Anne, L., Canada 103 B6
Ste-Anne-des-Monts, Canada 103 C6
Ste-Croix, Switz. 25 J2
Ste-Enimie, France 20 D7
Ste-Foy-la-Grande, France 20 D4
Ste. Genevieve, U.S.A. 112 G9
Ste-Hermine, France 20 B2
Ste-Livrade-sur-Lot, France 20 D4
Ste-Marguerite →, Canada 103 B6
Ste-Marie, Martinique 121 D7
Ste-Marie-aux-Mines, France 19 D14
Ste-Marie de la Madeleine, Canada 103 C5
Ste-Maure-de-Touraine, France 18 E7
Ste-Maxime, France 21 E10
Ste-Menehould, France 19 C11
Ste-Mère-Église, France 18 C5
Ste-Rose, Guadeloupe 121 C7
Ste. Rose du Lac, Canada 105 C9
Ste-Savine, France 19 D11
Ste-Sigolène, France 21 C8
Saintes, France 20 C3
Saintes, I. des, Guadeloupe 121 C7
Stes-Maries-de-la-Mer, France 21 E8
Saintfield, U.K. 15 B6
Saintonge, France 20 C3
Saipan, Pac. Oc. 96 F6
Sairang, India 67 H18
Sairecábur, Cerro, Bolivia 126 A2
Saitama □, Japan 55 F9
Saiteli = Kadınhanı, Turkey 72 C5
Saiţi, Moldova 43 D14
Saiyid, Pakistan 68 C5
Sajama, Bolivia 124 G5
Sajan, Serbia, Yug. 42 E5
Sajó →, Hungary 42 C6
Sajószentpéter, Hungary 42 B5
Sajum, India 69 C8
Sak →, S. Africa 88 E3
Sakaba, Nigeria 83 C6
Sakai, Japan 55 G7
Sakaide, Japan 55 G6
Sakaiminato, Japan 55 G6
Sakākah, Si. Arabia 70 D4
Sakakawea, L., U.S.A. 112 B4
Sakami →, Canada 102 B4
Sakami, L., Canada 102 B4
Sâkâne, 'Erg i-n, Mali 83 A4
Sakania, Dem. Rep. of the Congo 87 E2
Sakaraha, Madag. 89 C7
Sakarya, Turkey 72 B4
Sakarya →, Turkey 72 B4
Sakashima-Guntō, Japan 55 M2
Sakassou, Ivory C. 82 D3
Sakata, Japan 54 E9
Sakchu, N. Korea 57 D13
Sakeny →, Madag. 89 C8
Sakété, Benin 83 D5
Sakha □, Russia 51 C13
Sakhalin, Russia 51 D15
Sakhalinskiy Zaliv, Russia 51 D15
Şaki, Azerbaijan 49 K8
Šakiai, Lithuania 9 J20
Sakon Nakhon, Thailand 64 D5
Sakrand, Pakistan 68 F3
Sakri, India 69 F12
Sakrivier, S. Africa 88 E3
Sakskøbing, Denmark 11 K5
Sakti, India 69 H10
Sakuma, Japan 55 G8
Sakurai, Japan 55 G7
Saky, Ukraine 47 K7
Sal →, Russia 49 G5
Sala, Eritrea 81 D4
Šal'a, Slovak Rep. 27 C10
Sala, Sweden 10 E10
Sala →, Eritrea 81 D4
Sala Consilina, Italy 31 B8
Sala-y-Gómez, Pac. Oc. 97 K17
Salaberry-de-Valleyfield, Canada 102 C5
Saladas, Argentina 126 B4
Saladillo, Argentina 126 D4
Salado →, Buenos Aires, Argentina 126 D4
Salado →, La Pampa, Argentina 128 D3
Salado →, Santa Fe, Argentina 126 C3
Salado →, Mexico 113 M5
Salaga, Ghana 83 D4
Salāh, Syria 75 C5
Sălaj □, Romania 42 C8
Sálakhos, Greece 36 C9
Salala, Liberia 82 D2
Salala, Sudan 80 C4
Salālah, Oman 74 D5
Salamanca, Chile 126 C1
Salamanca, Spain 34 E5
Salamanca, U.S.A. 110 D6
Salamanca □, Spain 34 E5
Salāmatābād, Iran 70 C5
Salamis, Cyprus 36 D12
Salamís, Greece 38 D5
Salar de Atacama, Chile 126 A2
Salar de Uyuni, Bolivia 124 H5

Sălard, *Romania* 42 C7
Salas, *Spain* 34 B4
Salas de los Infantes, *Spain* 34 C7
Salatiga, *Indonesia* 63 G14
Salaverry, *Peru* 124 E3
Salawati, *Indonesia* 63 E8
Salaya, *India* 68 H3
Salayar, *Indonesia* 63 F6
Salazar ✈, *Spain* 32 C3
Salbris, *France* 19 E9
Salcia, *Romania* 43 G9
Sălciua, *Romania* 43 D8
Salcombe, *U.K.* 13 G4
Saldaña, *Spain* 34 C6
Saldanha, *S. Africa* 88 E2
Saldanha B., *S. Africa* 88 E2
Saldus, *Latvia* 9 H20
Saldus □, *Latvia* 44 B9
Sale, *Australia* 95 F4
Sale, *Italy* 28 D5
Salé, *Morocco* 78 B4
Sale, *U.K.* 12 D5
Salekhard, *Russia* 50 C7
Salem, *India* 66 P11
Salem, *Ill., U.S.A.* 108 F1
Salem, *Ind., U.S.A.* 108 F2
Salem, *Mass., U.S.A.* 111 D14
Salem, *Mo., U.S.A.* 113 G9
Salem, *N.H., U.S.A.* 111 D13
Salem, *N.J., U.S.A.* 108 F8
Salem, *N.Y., U.S.A.* 111 C11
Salem, *Ohio, U.S.A.* 110 F4
Salem, *Oreg., U.S.A.* 114 D2
Salem, *S. Dak., U.S.A.* 112 D6
Salem, *Va., U.S.A.* 108 G5
Salemi, *Italy* 30 E5
Sälen, *Sweden* 10 C7
Salernes, *France* 21 E10
Salerno, *Italy* 31 B7
Salerno, G. di, *Italy* 31 B7
Salford, *U.K.* 12 D5
Salgir ✈, *Ukraine* 47 K8
Salgótarján, *Hungary* 42 B4
Salgueiro, *Brazil* 125 E11
Salibabu, *Indonesia* 63 D7
Salida, *U.S.A.* 106 C5
Salies-de-Béarn, *France* 20 E3
Salihli, *Turkey* 72 C3
Salihorsk, *Belarus* 47 F4
Salima, *Malawi* 85 G6
Salina, *Italy* 31 D7
Salina, *Kans., U.S.A.* 112 F6
Salina, *Utah, U.S.A.* 115 G8
Salina Cruz, *Mexico* 119 D5
Salinas, *Brazil* 125 G10
Salinas, *Chile* 126 A2
Salinas, *Ecuador* 124 D2
Salinas, *U.S.A.* 116 J5
Salinas ✈, *Guatemala* 119 D6
Salinas ✈, *U.S.A.* 116 J5
Salinas, B. de, *Nic.* 120 D2
Salinas, Pampa de las, *Argentina* 126 C2
Salinas Ambargasta, *Argentina* 126 B3
Salinas de Hidalgo, *Mexico* 118 C4
Salinas Grandes, *Argentina* 126 C3
Saline ✈, *Ark., U.S.A.* 113 J8
Saline ✈, *Kans., U.S.A.* 112 F6
Salines, *Spain* 37 B10
Salines, C. de ses, *Spain* 37 B10
Salinópolis, *Brazil* 125 D9
Salins-les-Bains, *France* 19 F12
Salir, *Portugal* 35 H2
Salisbury = Harare, *Zimbabwe* 87 F3
Salisbury, *U.K.* 13 F6
Salisbury, *Md., U.S.A.* 108 F8
Salisbury, *N.C., U.S.A.* 109 H5
Salisbury I., *Canada* 101 B12
Salisbury Plain, *U.K.* 13 F6
Săliște, *Romania* 43 E8
Salka, *Nigeria* 83 C5
Şalkhad, *Syria* 75 C5
Salla, *Finland* 8 C23
Sallanches, *France* 21 C10
Sallent, *Spain* 32 D6
Salles, *France* 20 D3
Salles-Curan, *France* 20 D6
Salling, *Denmark* 11 H2
Salliq, *Canada* 101 B11
Sallisaw, *U.S.A.* 113 H7
Sallom Junction, *Sudan* 80 D4
Salluit, *Canada* 101 B12
Salmās, *Iran* 70 B5
Salmerón, *Spain* 32 E2
Salmo, *Canada* 104 D5
Salmon, *U.S.A.* 114 D7
Salmon ✈, *Canada* 104 C4
Salmon ✈, *U.S.A.* 114 D5
Salmon Arm, *Canada* 104 C5
Salmon Gums, *Australia* 93 F3
Salmon River Mts., *U.S.A.* 114 D6
Salo, *Finland* 9 F20
Salò, *Italy* 28 C7
Salobreña, *Spain* 35 J7
Salome, *U.S.A.* 117 M13
Salon, *India* 69 F9
Salon-de-Provence, *France* 21 E9
Salonica = Thessaloníki, *Greece* 40 F6
Salonta, *Romania* 42 D6
Salor ✈, *Spain* 35 F3
Salou, *Spain* 32 D6
Salou, C. de, *Spain* 32 D6
Saloum ✈, *Senegal* 82 C1
Salpausselkä, *Finland* 9 F22
Salsacate, *Argentina* 126 C2
Salses, *France* 20 F6
Salsk, *Russia* 49 G5
Salso ✈, *Italy* 30 E6
Salsomaggiore Terme, *Italy* 28 D6
Salt, *Spain* 32 D7
Salt ✈, *Canada* 104 B6
Salt ✈, *U.S.A.* 115 K7
Salt Lake City, *U.S.A.* 114 F8
Salt Range, *Pakistan* 68 C5
Salta, *Argentina* 126 A2
Salta □, *Argentina* 126 A2
Saltara, *Italy* 29 E9
Saltash, *U.K.* 13 G3
Saltburn by the Sea, *U.K.* 12 C7
Saltcoats, *U.K.* 14 F4
Saltee Is., *Ireland* 15 D5
Saltfjellet, *Norway* 8 C16
Saltfjorden, *Norway* 8 C16
Saltholm, *Denmark* 11 J6
Saltillo, *Mexico* 118 B4
Salto, *Argentina* 126 C3
Salto, *Uruguay* 126 C4
Salto del Guaíra, *Paraguay* 127 A5
Salton City, *U.S.A.* 117 M11
Salton Sea, *U.S.A.* 117 M11
Saltpond, *Ghana* 83 D4
Saltsburg, *U.S.A.* 110 F5
Saltsjöbaden, *Sweden* 10 E12
Saluda ✈, *U.S.A.* 109 J5
Salûm, *Egypt* 80 A2
Salûm, Khâlig el, *Egypt* 80 A2
Salur, *India* 67 K13
Saluzzo, *Italy* 28 D4
Salvador, *Brazil* 125 F11
Salvador, *Canada* 105 C7
Salvador, L., *U.S.A.* 113 L9
Salvaterra de Magos, *Portugal* 35 F2
Sálvora, I. de, *Spain* 34 C2
Salween ✈, *Burma* 67 L20
Salyan, *Azerbaijan* 50 F5
Salza ✈, *Austria* 26 D7
Salzach ✈, *Austria* 26 C5
Salzburg, *Austria* 26 D6
Salzburg □, *Austria* 26 D6
Salzgitter, *Germany* 24 C6
Salzkotten, *Germany* 24 D4
Salzwedel, *Germany* 24 C7
Sam, *India* 68 F4
Sam Neua, *Laos* 58 G5
Sam Ngao, *Thailand* 64 D2
Sam Rayburn Reservoir, *U.S.A.* 113 K7
Sam Son, *Vietnam* 64 C5
Sam Teu, *Laos* 64 C5
Sama de Langreo = Langreo, *Spain* 34 B5
Samagaltay, *Russia* 51 D10
Samales Group, *Phil.* 61 J4
Samâlût, *Egypt* 80 B3
Samana, *India* 68 D7
Samana Cay, *Bahamas* 121 B5
Samandağı, *Turkey* 72 D6
Samandıra, *Turkey* 41 F13
Samanga, *Tanzania* 87 D4
Samangān □, *Afghan.* 66 B5
Samangwa, *Dem. Rep. of the Congo* 86 C1
Samani, *Japan* 54 C11
Samanli Dağları, *Turkey* 41 F13
Samar, *Phil.* 61 F6
Samara, *Russia* 48 D10
Samara ✈, *Russia* 48 D10
Samara ✈, *Ukraine* 47 H8
Samaria = Shōmrōn, *West Bank* 75 C4
Samariá, *Greece* 36 D5
Samarinda, *Indonesia* 62 E5
Samarkand = Samarqand, *Uzbekistan* 50 F7
Samarqand, *Uzbekistan* 50 F7
Sāmarrā, *Iraq* 70 C4
Samastipur, *India* 69 G11
Şamaxi, *Azerbaijan* 49 K9
Samba, *Dem. Rep. of the Congo* 86 C2
Samba, *India* 69 C6
Sambalpur, *India* 67 J14
Sambar, Tanjung, *Indonesia* 62 E4
Sambas, *Indonesia* 62 D3
Sambava, *Madag.* 89 A9
Sambawizi, *Zimbabwe* 87 F2
Sambhal, *India* 69 E8
Sambhar, *India* 68 F6
Sambhar L., *India* 68 F6
Sambiase, *Italy* 31 D9
Sambir, *Ukraine* 47 H2
Sambor, *Cambodia* 64 F6
Samborombón, B., *Argentina* 126 D4
Sambuca di Sicília, *Italy* 30 E6
Samch'ŏk, *S. Korea* 57 F15
Samch'onp'o, *S. Korea* 57 G15
Same, *Tanzania* 86 C4
Samer, *France* 19 B8
Samfya, *Zambia* 87 E2
Sámi, *Greece* 38 C2
Şämkir, *Azerbaijan* 49 K8
Şamlı, *Turkey* 39 B9
Samnah, *Si. Arabia* 70 E3
Samo Alto, *Chile* 126 C1
Samoa ■, *Pac. Oc.* 91 B13
Samobor, *Croatia* 29 C12
Samoëns, *France* 19 F13
Samokov, *Bulgaria* 40 D7
Šamorín, *Slovak Rep.* 27 C10
Samorogouan, *Burkina Faso* 82 C4
Sámos, *Greece* 39 D8
Samoš, *Serbia, Yug.* 42 E5
Samos, *Spain* 34 C3
Sámos □, *Greece* 39 D8
Samothráki = Mathráki, *Greece* 36 A3
Samothráki, *Évros, Greece* 41 F9
Samothráki, *Évros, Greece* 41 F9
Samoylovka, *Russia* 48 E6
Sampa, *Ghana* 82 D4
Sampacho, *Argentina* 126 C3
Sampang, *Indonesia* 63 G15
Samper de Calanda, *Spain* 32 D4
Sampéyre, *Italy* 28 D4
Sampit, *Indonesia* 62 E4
Sampit, Teluk, *Indonesia* 62 E4
Samrong, *Cambodia* 64 E4
Samrong, *Thailand* 64 E3
Samsø, *Denmark* 11 J4
Samsø Bælt, *Denmark* 11 J4
Samsun, *Turkey* 72 B7
Samtredia, *Georgia* 49 J6
Samui, Ko, *Thailand* 65 H3
Samur ✈, *Russia* 49 K9
Samurskiy Khrebet, *Russia* 49 K8
Samusole, *Dem. Rep. of the Congo* 87 E1
Samut Prakan, *Thailand* 64 F3
Samut Songkhram ✈, *Thailand* 62 B1
Samwari, *Pakistan* 68 E2
San, *Mali* 82 C4
San ✈, *Cambodia* 64 F5
San ✈, *Poland* 45 H8
San Adrián, *Spain* 32 C3
San Adrián, C. de, *Spain* 34 B2
San Agustin, C., *Phil.* 61 H7
San Agustín de Valle Fértil, *Argentina* 126 C2
San Ambrosio, *Pac. Oc.* 122 F3
San Andreas, *U.S.A.* 116 G6
San Andres, *Phil.* 61 E6
San Andrés, I. de, *Caribbean* 120 D3
San Andrès del Rabanedo, *Spain* 34 C5
San Andres Mts., *U.S.A.* 115 K10
San Andrés Tuxtla, *Mexico* 119 D5
San Angelo, *U.S.A.* 113 K4
San Anselmo, *U.S.A.* 116 H4
San Antonio, *Belize* 119 D7
San Antonio, *Chile* 126 C1
San Antonio, *Phil.* 61 D4
San Antonio, *N. Mex., U.S.A.* 115 K10
San Antonio, *Tex., U.S.A.* 113 L5
San Antonio ✈, *U.S.A.* 113 L6
San Antonio, C., *Argentina* 126 D4
San Antonio, C., *Cuba* 120 B3
San Antonio, C. de, *Spain* 33 G5
San Antonio, Mt., *U.S.A.* 117 L9
San Antonio de los Baños, *Cuba* 120 B3
San Antonio de los Cobres, *Argentina* 126 A2
San Antonio Oeste, *Argentina* 128 E4
San Arcángelo, *Italy* 31 B9
San Ardo, *U.S.A.* 116 J6
San Augustin, *Canary Is.* 37 G4
San Augustine, *U.S.A.* 113 K7
San Bartolomé, *Canary Is.* 37 F6
San Bartolomé de Tirajana, *Canary Is.* 37 G4
San Bartolomeo in Galdo, *Italy* 31 A8
San Benedetto del Tronto, *Italy* 29 F10
San Benedetto Po, *Italy* 28 C7
San Benedicto, I., *Mexico* 118 D2
San Benito, *U.S.A.* 113 M5
San Benito ✈, *U.S.A.* 116 J5
San Benito Mt., *U.S.A.* 116 J6
San Bernardino, *U.S.A.* 117 L9
San Bernardino Mts., *U.S.A.* 117 L10
San Bernardino Str., *Phil.* 61 E6
San Bernardo, *Chile* 126 C1
San Bernardo, I. de, *Colombia* 124 B3
San Blas, *Mexico* 118 B3
San Blas, Arch. de, *Panama* 120 E4
San Blas, C., *U.S.A.* 109 L3
San Bonifacio, *Italy* 29 C8
San Borja, *Bolivia* 124 F5
San Buenaventura, *Mexico* 118 B4
San Carlos = Butuku-Luba, *Eq. Guin.* 83 E6
San Carlos = Sant Carles, *Spain* 37 B8
San Carlos, *Argentina* 126 C2
San Carlos, *Chile* 126 D1
San Carlos, *Baja Calif. S., Mexico* 118 C2
San Carlos, *Coahuila, Mexico* 118 B4
San Carlos, *Nic.* 120 D3
San Carlos, *Neg. Occ., Phil.* 61 F5
San Carlos, *Pangasinan, Phil.* 61 D4
San Carlos, *Uruguay* 127 C5
San Carlos, *U.S.A.* 115 K8
San Carlos, *Venezuela* 124 B5
San Carlos de Bariloche, *Argentina* 128 E2
San Carlos de Bolívar, *Argentina* 128 D4
San Carlos de la Ràpita = Sant Carles de la Ràpita, *Spain* 32 E5
San Carlos del Zulia, *Venezuela* 124 B4
San Carlos L., *U.S.A.* 115 K8
San Cataldo, *Italy* 30 E6
San Celoni = Sant Celoni, *Spain* 32 D7
San Clemente, *Chile* 126 D1
San Clemente, *Spain* 33 F2
San Clemente, *U.S.A.* 117 M9
San Clemente I., *U.S.A.* 117 N8
San Cristóbal = Es Migjorn Gran, *Spain* 37 B11
San Cristóbal, *Argentina* 126 C3
San Cristóbal, *Dom. Rep.* 121 C5
San Cristóbal, *Venezuela* 124 B4
San Cristóbal de la Casas, *Mexico* 119 D6
San Damiano d'Asti, *Italy* 28 D5
San Daniele del Friuli, *Italy* 29 B10
San Diego, *Calif., U.S.A.* 117 N9
San Diego, *Tex., U.S.A.* 113 M5
San Diego, C., *Argentina* 128 G3
San Diego de la Unión, *Mexico* 118 C4
San Dimitri, Ras, *Malta* 36 C1
San Donà di Piave, *Italy* 29 C9
San Estanislao, *Paraguay* 126 A4
San Esteban de Gormaz, *Spain* 32 D1
San Felice Circeo, *Italy* 30 A6
San Felice sul Panaro, *Italy* 29 D8
San Felipe, *Chile* 126 C1
San Felipe, *Mexico* 118 A2
San Felipe, *Venezuela* 124 A5
San Felipe ✈, *U.S.A.* 117 M11
San Felix, *Chile* 126 B1
San Félix, *Pac. Oc.* 122 F2
San Fernando = Sant Ferran, *Spain* 37 C7
San Fernando, *Chile* 126 C1
San Fernando, *Baja Calif., Mexico* 118 B1
San Fernando, *Tamaulipas, Mexico* 119 C5
San Fernando, *La Union, Phil.* 61 C4
San Fernando, *Pampanga, Phil.* 61 D4
San Fernando, *Spain* 35 J4
San Fernando, *Trin. & Tob.* 121 D7
San Fernando, *U.S.A.* 117 L8
San Fernando de Apure, *Venezuela* 124 B5
San Fernando de Atabapo, *Venezuela* 124 C5
San Fernando di Púglia, *Italy* 31 A9
San Francisco, *Argentina* 126 C3
San Francisco, *U.S.A.* 116 H4
San Francisco ✈, *U.S.A.* 115 K9
San Francisco, Paso de, *S. Amer.* 126 B2
San Francisco de Macorís, *Dom. Rep.* 121 C5
San Francisco del Monte de Oro, *Argentina* 126 C2
San Francisco del Oro, *Mexico* 118 B3
San Francisco Javier = Sant Francesc de Formentera, *Spain* 37 C7
San Francisco Solano, Pta., *Colombia* 122 C3
San Fratello, *Italy* 31 D7
San Gabriel, *Chile* 126 C1
San Gabriel Mts., *U.S.A.* 117 L9
San Gavino Monreale, *Italy* 30 C1
San Gimignano, *Italy* 28 E8
San Giórgio di Nogaro, *Italy* 29 C10
San Giórgio Iónico, *Italy* 31 B10
San Giovanni Bianco, *Italy* 28 C6
San Giovanni in Fiore, *Italy* 31 C9
San Giovanni in Persiceto, *Italy* 29 D8
San Giovanni Rotondo, *Italy* 29 G12
San Giovanni Valdarno, *Italy* 29 E8
San Giuliano Terme, *Italy* 28 E7
San Gorgonio Mt., *U.S.A.* 117 L10
San Gottardo, P. del, *Switz.* 25 J4
San Gregorio, *Uruguay* 127 C4
San Gregorio, *U.S.A.* 116 H4
San Guiseppe Jato, *Italy* 30 E6
San Ignacio, *Belize* 119 D7
San Ignacio, *Bolivia* 124 G6
San Ignacio, *Mexico* 118 B2
San Ignacio, *Paraguay* 120 C2
San Ignacio, L., *Mexico* 118 B2
San Ildefonso, C., *Phil.* 61 C5
San Isidro, *Argentina* 126 C4
San Isidro, *Phil.* 61 H7
San Jacinto, *U.S.A.* 117 M10
San Jaime = Sant Jaume, *Spain* 37 B11
San Javier, *Misiones, Argentina* 127 B4
San Javier, *Santa Fe, Argentina* 126 C4
San Javier, *Bolivia* 124 G6
San Javier, *Chile* 126 D1
San Javier, *Spain* 33 H4
San Jeronimo Taviche, *Mexico* 119 D5
San Joaquin, *U.S.A.* 116 J6
San Joaquin ✈, *U.S.A.* 116 G5
San Joaquin Valley, *U.S.A.* 116 J6
San Jon, *U.S.A.* 113 H3
San Jordi = Sant Jordi, *Spain* 37 B9
San Jorge, *Argentina* 126 C3
San Jorge, *Spain* 37 C7
San Jorge, B. de, *Mexico* 118 A2
San Jorge, G., *Argentina* 128 F3
San Jorge, G. of, *Argentina* 122 H4
San José = San Josep, *Spain* 37 C7
San José, *Costa Rica* 120 E3
San José, *Guatemala* 120 D1
San José, *Mexico* 118 C2
San Jose, *Mind. Occ., Phil.* 61 E4
San Jose, *Nueva Ecija, Phil.* 61 D4
San Jose, *U.S.A.* 116 H5
San Jose ✈, *U.S.A.* 115 J10
San Jose de Buenavista, *Phil.* 63 B6
San José de Chiquitos, *Bolivia* 124 G6
San José de Feliciano, *Argentina* 126 C4
San José de Jáchal, *Argentina* 126 C2
San José de Mayo, *Uruguay* 126 C4
San José del Cabo, *Mexico* 118 C3
San José del Guaviare, *Colombia* 124 C4
San Josep, *Spain* 37 C7
San Juan, *Argentina* 126 C2
San Juan, *Mexico* 118 C4
San Juan, *Phil.* 61 F6
San Juan, *Puerto Rico* 121 C6
San Juan □, *Argentina* 126 C2
San Juan ✈, *Argentina* 126 C2
San Juan ✈, *Nic.* 120 D3
San Juan ✈, *U.S.A.* 115 H8
San Juan Bautista = Sant Joan Baptista, *Spain* 37 B8
San Juan Bautista, *Paraguay* 126 B4
San Juan Bautista, *U.S.A.* 116 J5
San Juan Bautista Valle Nacional, *Mexico* 119 D5
San Juan Capistrano, *U.S.A.* 117 M9
San Juan Cr. ✈, *U.S.A.* 116 J5
San Juan de Alicante, *Spain* 33 G4
San Juan de Guadalupe, *Mexico* 118 C4
San Juan de la Costa, *Mexico* 118 C2
San Juan de los Morros, *Venezuela* 124 B5
San Juan del Norte, *Nic.* 120 D3
San Juan del Norte, B. de, *Nic.* 120 D3
San Juan del Río, *Mexico* 119 C5
San Juan del Sur, *Nic.* 120 D2
San Juan I., *U.S.A.* 116 B3
San Juan Mts., *U.S.A.* 115 H10
San Just, Sierra de, *Spain* 32 E4
San Justo, *Argentina* 126 C3
San Kamphaeng, *Thailand* 64 C2
San Lázaro, C., *Mexico* 118 C2
San Lázaro, Sa., *Mexico* 118 C3
San Leandro, *U.S.A.* 116 H4
San Leonardo de Yagüe, *Spain* 32 D1
San Lorenzo = Sant Llorenç des Cardassar, *Spain* 37 B10
San Lorenzo, *Argentina* 126 C3
San Lorenzo, *Ecuador* 124 C3
San Lorenzo, *Paraguay* 126 B4
San Lorenzo ✈, *Mexico* 118 C3
San Lorenzo, I., *Mexico* 118 B2
San Lorenzo, Mte., *Argentina* 128 F2
San Lorenzo de la Parrilla, *Spain* 32 F2
San Lorenzo de Morunys = Sant Llorenç de Morunys, *Spain* 32 C6
San Lucas, *Bolivia* 124 H5
San Lucas, *Baja Calif. S., Mexico* 118 C3
San Lucas, *Baja Calif. S., Mexico* 118 B2
San Lucas, *U.S.A.* 116 J5
San Lucas, C., *Mexico* 118 C3
San Lúcido, *Italy* 31 C9
San Luis, *Argentina* 126 C2
San Luis, *Cuba* 120 B3
San Luis, *Guatemala* 120 C2
San Luis, *Ariz., U.S.A.* 115 K6
San Luis, *Colo., U.S.A.* 115 H11
San Luis □, *Argentina* 126 C2
San Luis, I., *Mexico* 118 B2
San Luis, Sierra de, *Argentina* 126 C2
San Luis de la Paz, *Mexico* 118 C4
San Luis Obispo, *U.S.A.* 117 K6
San Luis Potosí, *Mexico* 118 C4
San Luis Potosí □, *Mexico* 118 C4
San Luis Reservoir, *U.S.A.* 116 H5
San Luis Río Colorado, *Mexico* 118 A2
San Manuel, *U.S.A.* 115 K8
San Marco, C., *Italy* 30 C1
San Marco Argentano, *Italy* 31 C9
San Marco in Lámis, *Italy* 29 G12
San Marcos, *Guatemala* 120 D1
San Marcos, *Mexico* 118 B2
San Marcos, *Calif., U.S.A.* 117 M9
San Marcos, *Tex., U.S.A.* 113 L6
San Marino, *San Marino* 29 E9
San Marino ■, *Europe* 29 E9
San Martín, *Argentina* 126 C2
San Martin ✈, *Bolivia* 124 F6
San Martín, L., *Argentina* 128 F2
San Martín de la Vega, *Spain* 34 E7
San Martin de los Andes, *Argentina* 128 E2
San Martín de Valdeiglesias, *Spain* 34 E6
San Mateo = Sant Mateu, *Baleares, Spain* 37 B7
San Mateo = Sant Mateu, *Valencia, Spain* 32 E5
San Mateo, *Phil.* 61 C4
San Mateo, *U.S.A.* 116 H4
San Matías, *Bolivia* 124 G7
San Matías, G., *Argentina* 122 H4
San Miguel = Sant Miquel, *Spain* 37 B7
San Miguel, *El Salv.* 120 D2
San Miguel, *Panama* 120 E4
San Miguel, *U.S.A.* 116 K6
San Miguel ✈, *Bolivia* 124 F6
San Miguel de Tucumán, *Argentina* 126 B2
San Miguel del Monte, *Argentina* 126 D4
San Miguel I., *U.S.A.* 117 L6
San Miniato, *Italy* 28 E7
San Nicolás, *Canary Is.* 37 G4
San Nicolas, *Phil.* 61 B4
San Nicolás de los Arroyas, *Argentina* 126 C3
San Nicolas I., *U.S.A.* 117 M7
San Onofre, *U.S.A.* 117 M9
San Pablo, *Bolivia* 126 A2
San Pablo, *Phil.* 61 D4
San Pablo, *U.S.A.* 116 H4
San Páolo di Civitate, *Italy* 29 G12
San Pedro, *Buenos Aires, Argentina* 126 C4
San Pedro, *Misiones, Argentina* 127 B5
San Pedro, *Chile* 126 C1
San Pédro, *Ivory C.* 82 E3
San Pedro, *Mexico* 118 C2
San Pedro □, *Paraguay* 126 A4
San Pedro ✈, *Chihuahua, Mexico* 118 B3
San Pedro ✈, *Nayarit, Mexico* 118 C3
San Pedro ✈, *U.S.A.* 115 K8
San Pedro, Pta., *Chile* 126 B1
San Pedro, Sierra de, *Spain* 35 F4
San Pedro Channel, *U.S.A.* 117 M8
San Pedro de Atacama, *Chile* 126 A2
San Pedro de Jujuy, *Argentina* 126 A3

San Pedro de las Colonias, *Mexico* 118 B4
San Pedro de Macorís, *Dom. Rep.* 121 C6
San Pedro del Norte, *Nic.* 120 D3
San Pedro del Paraná, *Paraguay* 126 B4
San Pedro del Pinatar, *Spain* 33 H4
San Pedro Mártir, Sierra, *Mexico* 118 A1
San Pedro Mixtepec, *Mexico* 119 D5
San Pedro Ocampo = Melchor Ocampo, *Mexico* 118 C4
San Pedro Sula, *Honduras* 120 C2
San Pietro, *Italy* 30 C1
San Pietro Vernótico, *Italy* 31 B11
San Quintín, *Mexico* 118 A1
San Rafael, *Argentina* 126 C2
San Rafael, *Calif., U.S.A.* 116 H4
San Rafael, *N. Mex., U.S.A.* 115 J10
San Rafael Mt., *U.S.A.* 117 L7
San Rafael Mts., *U.S.A.* 117 L7
San Ramón de la Nueva Orán, *Argentina* 126 A3
San Remo, *Italy* 28 E4
San Roque, *Argentina* 126 B4
San Roque, *Spain* 35 J5
San Rosendo, *Chile* 126 D1
San Saba, *U.S.A.* 113 K5
San Salvador, *El Salv.* 120 D2
San Salvador, *Spain* 37 B10
San Salvador de Jujuy, *Argentina* 126 A3
San Salvador I., *Bahamas* 121 B5
San Salvo, *Italy* 29 F11
San Sebastián = Donostia-San Sebastián, *Spain* 32 B3
San Sebastián, *Argentina* 128 G3
San Sebastian de la Gomera, *Canary Is.* 37 F2
San Serra = Son Serra, *Spain* 37 B10
San Serverino Marche, *Italy* 29 E10
San Severo, *Italy* 29 G12
San Simeon, *U.S.A.* 116 K5
San Simon, *U.S.A.* 115 K9
San Stéfano di Cadore, *Italy* 29 B9
San Stino di Livenza, *Italy* 29 C9
San Telmo = Sant Telm, *Spain* 37 B9
San Telmo, *Mexico* 118 A1
San Tiburcio, *Mexico* 118 C4
San Valentin, Mte., *Chile* 122 H3
San Vicente de Alcántara, *Spain* 35 F3
San Vicente de la Barquera, *Spain* 34 B6
San Vincente del Raspeig, *Spain* 33 G4
San Vincenzo, *Italy* 28 E7
San Vito, *Costa Rica* 120 E3
San Vito, *Italy* 30 C2
San Vito, C., *Italy* 30 D5
San Vito al Tagliamento, *Italy* 29 C9
San Vito Chietino, *Italy* 29 F11
San Vito dei Normanni, *Italy* 31 B10
Sana', *Yemen* 74 D3
Sana →, *Bos.-H.* 29 C13
Sanaba, *Burkina Faso* 82 C4
Şanāfīr, *Si. Arabia* 80 B3
Sanaga →, *Cameroon* 83 E6
Sanaloa, Presa, *Mexico* 118 C3
Sanana, *Indonesia* 63 E7
Sanand, *India* 68 H5
Sanandaj, *Iran* 70 C5
Sanandita, *Bolivia* 126 A3
Sanary-sur-Mer, *France* 21 E9
Sanawad, *India* 68 H7
Sancellas = Sencelles, *Spain* 37 B9
Sancergues, *France* 19 E9
Sancerre, *France* 19 E9
Sancerrois, Collines du, *France* 19 E9
Sancha He →, *China* 58 D6
Sanchahe, *China* 57 B14
Sánchez, *Dom. Rep.* 121 C6
Sanchor, *India* 68 G4
Sancoins, *France* 19 F9
Sancti Spíritus, *Cuba* 120 B4
Sancy, Puy de, *France* 20 C6
Sand →, *S. Africa* 89 C5
Sand Hills, *U.S.A.* 112 D4
Sand Springs, *U.S.A.* 113 G6
Sanda, *Japan* 55 G7
Sandakan, *Malaysia* 62 C5
Sandan = Sambor, *Cambodia* 64 F6
Sandanski, *Bulgaria* 40 E7
Sandaré, *Mali* 82 C2
Sandared, *Sweden* 11 G6
Sandarne, *Sweden* 10 C11
Sanday, *U.K.* 14 B6
Sandefjord, *Norway* 9 G14
Sanders, *U.S.A.* 115 J9
Sanderson, *U.S.A.* 113 K3
Sandersville, *U.S.A.* 109 J4
Sandfire Roadhouse, *Australia* 92 C3
Sandfly L., *Canada* 105 B7
Sandfontein, *Namibia* 88 C2
Sandhammaren, C., *Sweden* 11 J8
Sandía, *Peru* 124 F5
Sandıklı, *Turkey* 39 C12
Sandila, *India* 69 F9
Sandnes, *Norway* 9 G11
Sandnessjøen, *Norway* 8 C15
Sandoa, *Dem. Rep. of the Congo* 84 F4
Sandomierz, *Poland* 45 H8
Sândominic, *Romania* 43 D10
Sandover →, *Australia* 94 C2
Sandoway, *Burma* 67 K19
Sandoy, *Færoe Is.* 8 F9
Sandpoint, *U.S.A.* 114 B5
Sandray, *U.K.* 14 E1
Sandringham, *U.K.* 12 E8
Sandstone, *Australia* 93 E2
Sandu, *China* 58 E6
Sandusky, *Mich., U.S.A.* 110 C2
Sandusky, *Ohio, U.S.A.* 110 E2
Sandvig, *Sweden* 11 J8
Sandviken, *Sweden* 10 D10
Sandwich, C., *Australia* 94 B4
Sandwich B., *Canada* 103 B8
Sandwich B., *Namibia* 88 C1
Sandy, *Oreg., U.S.A.* 116 E4
Sandy, *Pa., U.S.A.* 110 E6
Sandy, *Utah, U.S.A.* 114 F8
Sandy Bay, *Canada* 105 B8
Sandy Bight, *Australia* 93 F3
Sandy C., *Queens., Australia* 94 C5
Sandy C., *Tas., Australia* 94 G3
Sandy Cay, *Bahamas* 121 B4
Sandy Cr. →, *U.S.A.* 114 F9
Sandy L., *Canada* 102 B1
Sandy Lake, *Canada* 102 B1
Sandy Valley, *U.S.A.* 117 K11
Sanford, *Fla., U.S.A.* 109 L5
Sanford, *Maine, U.S.A.* 109 D10
Sanford, *N.C., U.S.A.* 109 H6
Sanford →, *Australia* 93 E2
Sanford, Mt., *U.S.A.* 100 B5
Sang-i-Masha, *Afghan.* 68 C2
Sanga, *Mozam.* 87 E4
Sanga →, *Congo* 84 E3
Sangamner, *India* 66 K9
Sangar, *Afghan.* 68 C1
Sangar, *Russia* 51 C13
Sangar Sarai, *Afghan.* 68 B4
Sangaredi, *Guinea* 82 C2
Sangarh →, *Pakistan* 68 D4
Sangasso, *Mali* 82 C3
Sangatte, *France* 19 B8
Sangay, *Ecuador* 124 D3
Sange, *Dem. Rep. of the Congo* 86 D2
Sangeang, *Indonesia* 63 F5
Sângeorz-Băi, *Romania* 43 C9
Sanger, *U.S.A.* 116 J7
Sângera, *Moldova* 43 D13
Sangerhausen, *Germany* 24 D7
Sanggan He →, *China* 56 E9
Sanggau, *Indonesia* 62 D4
Sanghar, *Pakistan* 68 F3
Sangihe, Kepulauan, *Indonesia* 63 D7
Sangihe, Pulau, *Indonesia* 63 D7
Sangju, *S. Korea* 57 F15
Sangkapura, *Indonesia* 62 F4
Sangkhla, *Thailand* 64 E2
Sangkulirang, *Indonesia* 62 D5
Sangla, *Pakistan* 68 D5
Sangli, *India* 66 L9
Sangmélima, *Cameroon* 83 E7
Sangod, *India* 68 G7
Sangre de Cristo Mts., *U.S.A.* 113 G2
Sangro →, *Italy* 29 F11
Sangrur, *India* 68 D6
Sangudo, *Canada* 104 C6
Sangue →, *Brazil* 124 F7
Sangüesa, *Spain* 32 C3
Sanguinaires, Îs., *France* 21 G12
Sangzhi, *China* 59 C8
Sanhala, *Ivory C.* 82 C3
Sanibel, *U.S.A.* 109 M4
Sanirajak, *Canada* 101 B11
Sanjawi, *Pakistan* 68 D3
Sanje, *Uganda* 86 C3
Sanjiang, *China* 58 E7
Sanjo, *Japan* 54 F9
Sankh →, *India* 69 H11
Sankt Andrä, *Austria* 26 E7
Sankt Augustin, *Germany* 24 E3
Sankt Blasien, *Germany* 25 H4
Sankt Gallen, *Switz.* 25 H5
Sankt Gallen □, *Switz.* 25 H5
Sankt Goar, *Germany* 25 E3
Sankt Ingbert, *Germany* 25 F3
Sankt Johann im Pongau, *Austria* 26 D6
Sankt Johann in Tirol, *Austria* 26 D5
Sankt-Peterburg, *Russia* 46 C6
Sankt Pölten, *Austria* 26 C8
Sankt Ulrich = Ortisei, *Italy* 29 B8
Sankt Valentin, *Austria* 26 C7
Sankt Veit an der Glan, *Austria* 26 E7
Sankt Wendel, *Germany* 25 F3
Sankt Wolfgang, *Austria* 26 D6
Sankuru →, *Dem. Rep. of the Congo* 84 E4
Sanliurfa, *Turkey* 70 B3
Sanlúcar de Barrameda, *Spain* 35 J4
Sanluri, *Italy* 30 C1
Sânmartin, *Romania* 43 D10
Sanmen, *China* 59 C13
Sanmenxia, *China* 56 G6
Sanming, *China* 59 D11
Sannaspos, *S. Africa* 88 D4
Sannicandro Gargánico, *Italy* 29 G12
Sânnicolau Mare, *Romania* 42 D5
Sannieshof, *S. Africa* 88 D4
Sannīn, J., *Lebanon* 75 B4
Sanniquellie, *Liberia* 82 D3
Sannûr, W. →, *Egypt* 80 B3
Sanok, *Poland* 45 J9
Sanquhar, *U.K.* 14 F5
Sansanding, *Mali* 82 C3
Sansepolcro, *Italy* 29 E9
Sansha, *China* 59 D13
Sanshui, *China* 59 F9
Sanski Most, *Bos.-H.* 29 D13
Sansui, *China* 58 D7
Sant Antoni Abat, *Spain* 37 C7
Sant Boi de Llobregat, *Spain* 32 D7
Sant Carles, *Spain* 37 B8
Sant Carles de la Ràpita, *Spain* 32 E5
Sant Celoni, *Spain* 32 D7
Sant Feliu de Guíxols, *Spain* 32 D8
Sant Feliu de Llobregat, *Spain* 32 D7
Sant Ferran, *Spain* 37 C7
Sant Francesc de Formentera, *Spain* 37 C7
Sant Jaume, *Spain* 37 B11
Sant Joan Baptista, *Spain* 37 B8
Sant Jordi, *Spain* 37 B9
Sant Jordi, G. de, *Spain* 32 E6
Sant Llorenç de Morunys, *Spain* 32 C6
Sant Llorenç des Cardassar, *Spain* 37 B10
Sant Mateu, *Baleares, Spain* 37 B7
Sant Mateu, *Valencia, Spain* 32 E5
Sant Miquel, *Spain* 37 B7
Sant Telm, *Spain* 37 B9
Sant' Ágata Militello, *Italy* 31 D7
Santa Agnés, *Spain* 37 B7
Santa Ana, *Bolivia* 124 F5
Santa Ana, *El Salv.* 120 D2
Santa Ana, *Mexico* 118 A2
Santa Ana, *U.S.A.* 117 M9
Sant' Ángelo Lodigiano, *Italy* 28 C6
Sant' Antíoco, *Italy* 30 C1
Santa Barbara, *Chile* 126 D1
Santa Barbara, *Honduras* 120 D2
Santa Bárbara, *Mexico* 118 B3
Santa Bárbara, *Spain* 32 E5
Santa Barbara, *U.S.A.* 117 L7
Santa Bárbara, Mt., *Spain* 33 H2
Santa Barbara Channel, *U.S.A.* 117 L7
Santa Barbara I., *U.S.A.* 117 M7
Santa Catalina, Gulf of, *U.S.A.* 117 N9
Santa Catalina, I., *Mexico* 118 B2
Santa Catalina I., *U.S.A.* 117 M8
Santa Catarina □, *Brazil* 127 B6
Santa Catarina, I. de, *Brazil* 127 B6
Santa Caterina di Pittinuri, *Italy* 30 B1
Santa Caterina Villarmosa, *Italy* 31 E7
Santa Cecília, *Brazil* 127 B5
Santa Clara, *Cuba* 120 B4
Santa Clara, *Calif., U.S.A.* 116 H5
Santa Clara, *Utah, U.S.A.* 115 H7
Santa Clara, El Golfo de, *Mexico* 118 A2
Santa Clara de Olimar, *Uruguay* 127 C5
Santa Clarita, *U.S.A.* 117 L8
Santa Clotilde, *Peru* 124 D4
Santa Coloma de Farners, *Spain* 32 D7
Santa Coloma de Gramenet, *Spain* 32 D7
Santa Comba, *Spain* 34 B2
Santa Croce Camerina, *Italy* 31 F7
Santa Croce di Magliano, *Italy* 29 G11
Santa Cruz, *Argentina* 128 G3
Santa Cruz, *Bolivia* 124 G6
Santa Cruz, *Chile* 126 C1
Santa Cruz, *Costa Rica* 120 D2
Santa Cruz, *Madeira* 37 D3
Santa Cruz, *Phil.* 61 D4
Santa Cruz, *U.S.A.* 116 J4
Santa Cruz →, *Argentina* 128 G3
Santa Cruz de la Palma, *Canary Is.* 37 F2
Santa Cruz de Mudela, *Spain* 35 G7
Santa Cruz de Tenerife, *Canary Is.* 37 F3
Santa Cruz del Norte, *Cuba* 120 B3
Santa Cruz del Retamar, *Spain* 34 E6
Santa Cruz del Sur, *Cuba* 120 B4
Santa Cruz do Rio Pardo, *Brazil* 127 A6
Santa Cruz do Sul, *Brazil* 127 B5
Santa Cruz I., *U.S.A.* 117 M7
Santa Cruz Is., *Solomon Is.* 96 J8
Santa Domingo, Cay, *Bahamas* 120 B4
Sant' Egídio alla Vibrata, *Italy* 29 F10
Santa Elena, *Argentina* 126 C4
Santa Elena, C., *Costa Rica* 120 D2
Sant' Eufémia, G. di, *Italy* 31 D9
Santa Eulàlia des Riu, *Spain* 37 C8
Santa Fe, *Argentina* 126 C3
Santa Fe, *Spain* 35 H7
Santa Fe, *U.S.A.* 115 J11
Santa Fé □, *Argentina* 126 C3
Santa Fé do Sul, *Brazil* 125 H8
Santa Filomena, *Brazil* 125 E9
Santa Fiora, *Italy* 29 F8
Santa Gertrudis, *Spain* 37 C7
Santa Giustina, *Italy* 29 B9
Santa Inês, *Brazil* 125 F11
Santa Inés, *Spain* 35 G5
Santa Inés, I., *Chile* 122 J3
Santa Isabel = Rey Malabo, *Eq. Guin.* 83 E6
Santa Isabel, *Argentina* 126 D2
Santa Isabel, Pico, *Eq. Guin.* 83 E6
Santa Isabel do Morro, *Brazil* 125 F8
Santa Lucía, *Corrientes, Argentina* 126 B4
Santa Lucía, *San Juan, Argentina* 126 C2
Santa Lucía, *Spain* 33 H4
Santa Lucia, *Uruguay* 126 C4
Santa Lucia Range, *U.S.A.* 116 K5
Santa Magdalena, I., *Mexico* 118 C2
Santa Margarita, *Argentina* 126 D3
Santa Margarita, *Spain* 37 B10
Santa Margarita, *U.S.A.* 116 K6
Santa Margarita →, *U.S.A.* 117 M9
Santa Margarita, I., *Mexico* 118 C2
Santa Margherita, *Italy* 30 D1
Santa Margherita Ligure, *Italy* 28 D6
Santa María, *Argentina* 126 B2
Santa Maria, *Brazil* 127 B5
Santa Maria, *Phil.* 61 C4
Santa Maria, *U.S.A.* 117 L6
Santa María →, *Mexico* 118 A3
Santa María, B. de, *Mexico* 118 B3
Santa Maria, C. de, *Portugal* 35 J3
Santa Maria Cápua Vétere, *Italy* 31 A7
Santa Maria da Feira, *Portugal* 34 E2
Santa Maria da Vitória, *Brazil* 125 F10
Santa Maria del Camí, *Spain* 37 B9
Santa Maria di Léuca, C., *Italy* 31 C11
Santa María la Real de Nieva, *Spain* 34 D6
Santa Marinella, *Italy* 29 F8
Santa Marta, *Colombia* 124 A4
Santa Marta, Sierra Nevada de, *Colombia* 122 B3
Santa Marta de Tormes, *Spain* 34 E5
Santa Marta Grande, C., *Brazil* 127 B6
Santa Marta Ortigueira, Ría de, *Spain* 34 B3
Santa Maura = Levkás, *Greece* 38 C2
Santa Monica, *U.S.A.* 117 M8
Santa Olalla, *Huelva, Spain* 35 H4
Santa Olalla, *Toledo, Spain* 34 E6
Santa Paula, *U.S.A.* 117 L7
Santa Pola, *Spain* 33 G4
Santa Ponsa, *Spain* 37 B9
Santa Rita, *U.S.A.* 115 K10
Santa Rosa, *La Pampa, Argentina* 126 D3
Santa Rosa, *San Luis, Argentina* 126 C2
Santa Rosa, *Brazil* 127 B5
Santa Rosa, *Calif., U.S.A.* 116 G4
Santa Rosa, *N. Mex., U.S.A.* 113 H2
Santa Rosa de Copán, *Honduras* 120 D2
Santa Rosa de Río Primero, *Argentina* 126 C3
Santa Rosa del Sara, *Bolivia* 124 G6
Santa Rosa I., *Calif., U.S.A.* 117 M6
Santa Rosa I., *Fla., U.S.A.* 109 K2
Santa Rosa Range, *U.S.A.* 114 F5
Santa Rosalía, *Mexico* 118 B2
Santa Sylvina, *Argentina* 126 B3
Santa Tecla = Nueva San Salvador, *El Salv.* 120 D2
Santa Teresa, *Argentina* 126 C3
Santa Teresa, *Australia* 94 C1
Santa Teresa, *Mexico* 119 B5
Santa Teresa di Riva, *Italy* 31 E8
Santa Teresa Gallura, *Italy* 30 A2
Santa Uxía, *Spain* 34 C2
Santa Vitória do Palmar, *Brazil* 127 C5
Santa Ynez →, *U.S.A.* 117 L6
Santa Ynez Mts., *U.S.A.* 117 L6
Santa Ysabel, *U.S.A.* 117 M10
Santadi, *Italy* 30 C1
Santaella, *Spain* 35 H6
Santai, *China* 58 B5
Santana, *Madeira* 37 D3
Sântana, *Romania* 42 D6
Santana, Coxilha de, *Brazil* 127 C4
Santana do Livramento, *Brazil* 127 C4
Santander, *Spain* 34 B7
Santander Jiménez, *Mexico* 119 C5
Santanyí, *Spain* 37 B10
Santaquin, *U.S.A.* 114 G8
Santarcángelo di Romagna, *Italy* 29 D9
Santarém, *Brazil* 125 D8
Santarém, *Portugal* 35 F2
Santarém □, *Portugal* 35 F2
Santaren Channel, *W. Indies* 120 B4
Santee, *U.S.A.* 117 N10
Santee →, *U.S.A.* 109 J6
Santéramo in Colle, *Italy* 31 B9
Santerno →, *Italy* 29 D8
Santhià, *Italy* 28 C5
Santiago, *Brazil* 127 B5
Santiago, *Chile* 126 C1
Santiago, *Panama* 120 E3
Santiago, *Phil.* 61 C4
Santiago □, *Chile* 126 C1
Santiago →, *Mexico* 98 G9
Santiago →, *Peru* 124 D3
Santiago, Punta de, *Eq. Guin.* 83 E6
Santiago de Compostela, *Spain* 34 C2
Santiago de Cuba, *Cuba* 120 C4
Santiago de los Cabelleros, *Dom. Rep.* 121 C5
Santiago del Estero, *Argentina* 126 B3
Santiago del Estero □, *Argentina* 126 B3
Santiago del Teide, *Canary Is.* 37 F3
Santiago do Cacém, *Portugal* 35 G2
Santiago Ixcuintla, *Mexico* 118 C3
Santiago Papasquiaro, *Mexico* 118 C3
Santiaguillo, L. de, *Mexico* 118 C4
Santiguila, *Mali* 82 C3
Santillana, *Spain* 34 B6
Santisteban del Puerto, *Spain* 35 G7
Santo Amaro, *Brazil* 125 F11
Santo Anastácio, *Brazil* 127 A5
Santo André, *Brazil* 127 A6
Santo Ângelo, *Brazil* 127 B5
Santo Antônio do Içá, *Brazil* 124 D5
Santo Antônio do Leverger, *Brazil* 125 G7
Santo Domingo, *Dom. Rep.* 121 C6
Santo Domingo, *Baja Calif., Mexico* 118 A1
Santo Domingo, *Baja Calif. S., Mexico* 118 B2
Santo Domingo, *Nic.* 120 D3
Santo Domingo de la Calzada, *Spain* 32 C2
Santo Domingo de los Colorados, *Ecuador* 124 D3
Santo Domingo Pueblo, *U.S.A.* 115 J10
Santo Stéfano di Camastro, *Italy* 31 D7
Santo Tirso, *Portugal* 34 D2
Santo Tomás, *Mexico* 118 A1
Santo Tomás, *Peru* 124 F4
Santo Tomé, *Argentina* 127 B4
Santo Tomé de Guayana = Ciudad Guayana, *Venezuela* 124 B6
Santomera, *Spain* 33 G3
Santoña, *Spain* 34 B7
Santoríni = Thíra, *Greece* 39 E7
Santos, *Brazil* 127 A6
Santos, Sierra de los, *Spain* 35 G5
Santos Dumont, *Brazil* 127 A7
Sanwer, *India* 68 H6
Sanxenxo, *Spain* 34 C2
Sanyuan, *China* 56 G5
São Bartolomeu de Messines, *Portugal* 35 H2
São Bernardo do Campo, *Brazil* 127 A6
São Borja, *Brazil* 127 B4
São Brás de Alportel, *Portugal* 35 H3
São Carlos, *Brazil* 127 A6
São Cristóvão, *Brazil* 125 F11
São Domingos, *Brazil* 125 F9
São Domingos, *Guinea-Biss.* 82 C1
São Francisco, *Brazil* 125 G10
São Francisco →, *Brazil* 122 E7
São Francisco do Sul, *Brazil* 127 B6
São Gabriel, *Brazil* 127 C5
São Gonçalo, *Brazil* 127 A7
Sao Hill, *Tanzania* 87 D4
São João, *Guinea-Biss.* 82 C1
São João da Boa Vista, *Brazil* 127 A6
São João da Madeira, *Portugal* 34 E2
São João da Pesqueira, *Portugal* 34 D3
São João del Rei, *Brazil* 127 A7
São João do Araguaia, *Brazil* 125 E9
São João do Piauí, *Brazil* 125 E10
São Joaquim, *Brazil* 127 B6
São Jorge, Pta. de, *Madeira* 37 D3
São José, *Brazil* 127 B5
São José do Norte, *Brazil* 127 C5
São José do Rio Prêto, *Brazil* 127 A6
São José dos Campos, *Brazil* 127 A6
São Leopoldo, *Brazil* 127 B5
São Lourenço, *Brazil* 127 A6
São Lourenço →, *Brazil* 125 G7
São Lourenço, Pta. de, *Madeira* 37 D3
São Lourenço do Sul, *Brazil* 127 C5
São Luís, *Brazil* 125 D10
São Luís Gonzaga, *Brazil* 127 B5
São Marcos →, *Brazil* 125 G9
São Marcos, B. de, *Brazil* 125 D10
São Martinho da Cortiça, *Portugal* 34 E2
São Mateus, *Brazil* 125 G11
São Mateus do Sul, *Brazil* 127 B5
São Miguel do Oeste, *Brazil* 127 B5
São Paulo, *Brazil* 127 A6
São Paulo □, *Brazil* 127 A6
São Paulo, I., *Atl. Oc.* 2 D8
São Paulo de Olivença, *Brazil* 124 D5
São Pedro do Sul, *Portugal* 34 E2
São Roque, *Madeira* 37 D3
São Roque, C. de, *Brazil* 122 D7
São Sebastião, I. de, *Brazil* 127 A6
São Sebastião do Paraíso, *Brazil* 127 A6
São Teotónio, *Portugal* 35 H2
São Tomé, *Atl. Oc.* 76 F4
São Tomé, C. de, *Brazil* 127 A7
São Tomé & Principe ■, *Africa* 77 F4
São Vicente, *Brazil* 127 A6
São Vicente, *Madeira* 37 D2
São Vicente, C. de, *Portugal* 35 H1
Saona, I., *Dom. Rep.* 121 C6
Saône →, *France* 19 G11
Saône-et-Loire □, *France* 19 F11
Saonek, *Indonesia* 63 E8
Sápai, *Greece* 41 E9
Sapanca, *Turkey* 72 B4
Saparua, *Indonesia* 63 E7
Sapele, *Nigeria* 83 D6
Sapelo I., *U.S.A.* 109 K5
Şaphane, *Turkey* 39 B11
Sapiéntza, *Greece* 38 E3
Sapone, *Burkina Faso* 83 C4
Saposoa, *Peru* 124 E3
Sapouy, *Burkina Faso* 83 C4
Sapozhok, *Russia* 48 D5
Sapphire, *Australia* 94 C4
Sappho, *U.S.A.* 116 B2
Sapporo, *Japan* 54 C10
Sapri, *Italy* 31 B8
Sapulpa, *U.S.A.* 113 H6
Saqqez, *Iran* 70 B5
Sar Dasht, *Iran* 71 C6
Sar-e Pol □, *Afghan.* 66 B4
Sar Gachīneh = Yāsūj, *Iran* 71 D6
Sar Planina, *Macedonia* 40 E4
Sara, *Burkina Faso* 82 C4
Sara, *Phil.* 61 F5
Sara Buri = Saraburi, *Thailand* 64 E3
Sarāb, *Iran* 70 B5
Sarabadi, *Iraq* 70 C5
Saraburi, *Thailand* 64 E3
Saradiya, *India* 68 J4
Saraféré, *Mali* 82 B4
Saragossa = Zaragoza, *Spain* 32 D4
Saraguro, *Ecuador* 124 D3
Sarai Naurang, *Pakistan* 68 C4
Saraikela, *India* 69 H11
Saraiu, *Romania* 43 F13
Sarajevo, *Bos.-H.* 42 G3
Sarakhs, *Turkmenistan* 71 B9
Saran, Gunung, *Indonesia* 62 E4
Saranac L., *U.S.A.* 111 B10
Saranac Lake, *U.S.A.* 111 B10
Saranda, *Tanzania* 86 D3
Sarandë, *Albania* 40 G3
Sarandí del Yi, *Uruguay* 127 C4
Sarandí Grande, *Uruguay* 126 C4
Sarangani B., *Phil.* 61 J6

Sarangani Is., *Phil.* 61 J6
Sarangarh, *India* 67 J13
Saransk, *Russia* 48 C7
Sarapul, *Russia* 50 D6
Sarasota, *U.S.A.* 109 M4
Saratoga, *Calif., U.S.A.* 116 H4
Saratoga, *Wyo., U.S.A.* 114 F10
Saratoga Springs, *U.S.A* 111 C11
Saratok, *Malaysia* 62 D4
Saratov, *Russia* 48 E7
Saravane, *Laos* 64 E6
Sarawak □, *Malaysia* 62 D4
Saray, *Tekirdağ, Turkey* 41 E11
Saray, *Van, Turkey* 73 C11
Saraya, *Guinea* 82 C2
Saraya, *Senegal* 82 C2
Saraycık, *Turkey* 39 B11
Sarayköy, *Turkey* 39 D10
Saraylar, *Turkey* 41 F11
Sarayönü, *Turkey* 72 C5
Sarbāz, *Iran* 71 E9
Sarbīsheh, *Iran* 71 C8
Sárbogárd, *Hungary* 42 D3
Sarca →, *Italy* 28 C7
Sarcelles, *France* 19 D9
Sarda →, *India* 67 F12
Sardarshahr, *India* 68 E6
Sardegna □, *Italy* 30 B1
Sardhana, *India* 68 E7
Sardina, Pta., *Canary Is.* 37 F4
Sardinia = Sardegna □, *Italy* 30 B1
Sardis, *Turkey* 39 C10
Sārdūīyeh = Dar Mazār, *Iran* 71 D8
S'Arenal, *Spain* 37 B9
Sarentino, *Italy* 29 B8
Saréyamou, *Mali* 82 B4
Sargasso Sea, *Atl. Oc.* 97 D20
Sargodha, *Pakistan* 68 C5
Sarh, *Chad* 79 G9
Sarhala, *Ivory C.* 82 D3
Sārī, *Iran* 71 B7
Sari d'Orcino, *France* 21 F12
Sária, *Greece* 39 F9
Saria, *India* 69 J10
Sariab, *Pakistan* 68 D2
Sarıbeyler, *Turkey* 39 B9
Sarıgöl, *Turkey* 72 C3
Sarıkamiş, *Turkey* 73 B10
Sarıkaya, *Turkey* 72 C6
Sarikei, *Malaysia* 62 D4
Sarıköy, *Turkey* 41 F11
Sarila, *India* 69 G8
Sarina, *Australia* 94 C4
Sariñena, *Spain* 32 D4
Sarita, *U.S.A.* 113 M6
Sariwŏn, *N. Korea* 57 E13
Sariyar Barajı, *Turkey* 72 B4
Sariyer, *Turkey* 41 E13
Sarju →, *India* 69 F9
Sark, *U.K.* 13 H5
Sarkad, *Hungary* 42 D6
Sarkari Tala, *India* 68 F4
Şarkışla, *Turkey* 72 C7
Şarköy, *Turkey* 41 F11
Sarlat-la-Canéda, *France* 20 D5
Sărmăşag, *Romania* 42 C7
Sărmaşu, *Romania* 43 D9
Sarmi, *Indonesia* 63 E9
Sarmiento, *Argentina* 128 F3
Sarmizegetusa, *Romania* 42 E7
Särna, *Sweden* 10 C7
Sarnano, *Italy* 29 E10
Sarnen, *Switz.* 25 J4
Sarnia, *Canada* 102 D3
Sarno, *Italy* 31 B7
Sarnthein = Sarentino, *Italy* 29 B8
Särö, *Sweden* 11 G5
Sarolangun, *Indonesia* 62 E2
Saronikós Kólpos, *Greece* 38 D5
Saronno, *Italy* 28 C6
Saros Körfezi, *Turkey* 41 F10
Sárospatak, *Hungary* 42 B6
Sarpsborg, *Norway* 9 G14
Sarracín, *Spain* 34 C7
Sarralbe, *France* 19 D14
Sarre = Saar →, *Europe* 17 E6
Sarre, *Italy* 28 C4
Sarre-Union, *France* 19 D14
Sarrebourg, *France* 19 D14
Sarreguemines, *France* 19 C14
Sarria, *Spain* 34 C3
Sarrión, *Spain* 32 E4
Sarro, *Mali* 82 C3
Sarstedt, *Germany* 24 C5
Sartène, *France* 21 G12
Sarthe □, *France* 18 D7
Sarthe →, *France* 18 E6
Sartilly, *France* 18 D5
Saruhanlı, *Turkey* 39 C9
Săruleşti, *Romania* 43 F11
Saruna →, *Pakistan* 68 F2
Sárvár, *Hungary* 42 C1
Sarvar, *India* 68 F6
Sarvestān, *Iran* 71 D7
Sărvfjället, *Sweden* 10 B7
Sárvíz →, *Hungary* 42 D3
Sary-Tash, *Kyrgyzstan* 50 F8
Sarych, Mys, *Ukraine* 47 K7
Saryshagan, *Kazakstan* 50 E8
Sarzana, *Italy* 28 D6
Sarzeau, *France* 18 E4
Sasan Gir, *India* 68 J4
Sasaram, *India* 69 G11
Sasebo, *Japan* 55 H4
Saser, *India* 69 B7
Saskatchewan □, *Canada* 105 C7
Saskatchewan →, *Canada* 105 C8
Saskatoon, *Canada* 105 C7
Saskylakh, *Russia* 51 B12
Sasolburg, *S. Africa* 89 D4
Sasovo, *Russia* 48 C5
Sassandra, *Ivory C.* 82 E3
Sassandra →, *Ivory C.* 82 E3
Sássari, *Italy* 30 B1
Sassnitz, *Germany* 24 A9
Sasso Marconi, *Italy* 29 D8
Sassocorvaro, *Italy* 29 E9
Sassoferrato, *Italy* 29 E9
Sasstown, *Liberia* 82 E3
Sassuolo, *Italy* 28 D7
Sástago, *Spain* 32 D4
Sasumua Dam, *Kenya* 86 C4
Sasyk, Ozero, *Ukraine* 47 K5
Sata-Misaki, *Japan* 55 J5
Satadougou, *Mali* 82 C2
Satakunta, *Finland* 9 F20
Satama-Soukoura, *Ivory C.* 82 D4
Satara, *India* 66 L8
Satara, *S. Africa* 89 C5
Satbarwa, *India* 69 H11
Såtenäs, *Sweden* 11 F6
Säter, *Sweden* 10 D9
Satevó, *Mexico* 118 B3
Satilla →, *U.S.A.* 109 K5
Satmala Hills, *India* 66 J9
Satna, *India* 69 G9
Šator, *Bos.-H.* 29 D13
Sátoraljaújhely, *Hungary* 42 B6
Satpura Ra., *India* 66 J10
Satrup, *Germany* 24 A5
Satsuna-Shotō, *Japan* 55 K5
Sattahip, *Thailand* 64 F3
Satu Mare, *Romania* 42 C7
Satu Mare □, *Romania* 42 C8
Satui, *Indonesia* 62 E5
Satun, *Thailand* 65 J3
Saturnina →, *Brazil* 124 F7
Sauce, *Argentina* 126 C4
Sauceda, *Mexico* 118 B4
Saucillo, *Mexico* 118 B3
Sauda, *Norway* 9 G12
Sauðarkrókur, *Iceland* 8 D4
Saudi Arabia ■, *Asia* 70 B3
Saugeen →, *Canada* 110 B3
Saugerties, *U.S.A.* 111 D11
Saugues, *France* 20 D7
Saugus, *U.S.A.* 117 L8
Saujon, *France* 20 C3
Sauk Centre, *U.S.A.* 112 C7
Sauk Rapids, *U.S.A.* 112 C7
Saulgau, *Germany* 25 G5
Saulieu, *France* 19 E11
Sault, *France* 21 D9
Sault Ste. Marie, *Canada* 102 C3
Sault Ste. Marie, *U.S.A.* 101 D11
Saumlaki, *Indonesia* 63 F8
Saumur, *France* 18 E6
Saunders C., *N.Z.* 91 L3
Saunders I., *Antarctica* 5 B1
Saunders Point, *Australia* 93 E4
Sauri, *Nigeria* 83 C6
Saurimo, *Angola* 84 F4
Sausalito, *U.S.A.* 116 H4
Sauveterre-de-Béarn, *France* 20 E3
Sauzé-Vaussais, *France* 20 B4
Savá, *Honduras* 120 C2
Sava, *Italy* 31 B10
Sava →, *Serbia, Yug.* 42 F5
Savage, *U.S.A.* 112 B2
Savage I. = Niue, *Cook Is.* 97 J11
Savage River, *Australia* 94 G4
Savai'i, *Samoa* 91 A12
Savalou, *Benin* 83 D5
Savane, *Mozam.* 87 F4
Savanna, *U.S.A.* 112 D9
Savanna-la-Mar, *Jamaica* 120 C4
Savannah, *Ga., U.S.A.* 109 J5
Savannah, *Mo., U.S.A.* 112 F7
Savannah, *Tenn., U.S.A.* 109 H1
Savannah →, *U.S.A.* 109 J5
Savannakhet, *Laos* 64 D5
Savant L., *Canada* 102 B1
Savant Lake, *Canada* 102 B1
Săvârşin, *Romania* 42 D7
Savaştepe, *Turkey* 39 B9
Savé, *Benin* 83 D5
Save →, *France* 20 E5
Save →, *Mozam.* 89 C5
Sāveh, *Iran* 71 C6
Savelugu, *Ghana* 83 D4
Savenay, *France* 18 E5
Săveni, *Romania* 43 C11
Saverdun, *France* 20 E5
Saverne, *France* 19 D14
Savigliano, *Italy* 28 D4
Savigny-sur-Braye, *France* 18 E7
Sávio →, *Italy* 29 D9
Šavnik, *Montenegro, Yug.* 40 D3
Savo, *Finland* 8 E22
Savoie □, *France* 21 C10
Savona, *Italy* 28 D5
Savona, *U.S.A.* 110 D7
Savonlinna, *Finland* 46 B5
Savoy = Savoie □, *France* 21 C10
Şavşat, *Turkey* 73 B10
Sävsjö, *Sweden* 11 G8
Savur, *Turkey* 70 B4
Sawahlunto, *Indonesia* 62 E2
Sawai, *Indonesia* 63 E7
Sawai Madhopur, *India* 68 G7
Sawang Daen Din, *Thailand* 64 D4
Sawankhalok, *Thailand* 64 D2
Sawara, *Japan* 55 G10
Sawatch Range, *U.S.A.* 115 G10
Sawel Mt., *U.K.* 15 B4
Sawi, *Thailand* 65 G2
Sawla, *Ghana* 82 D4
Sawmills, *Zimbabwe* 87 F2
Sawtooth Range, *U.S.A.* 114 E6
Sawu, *Indonesia* 63 F6
Sawu Sea, *Indonesia* 63 F6
Saxby →, *Australia* 94 B3
Saxmundham, *U.K.* 13 E9
Saxony = Sachsen □, *Germany* 24 E9
Saxony, Lower = Niedersachsen □, *Germany* 24 C4
Saxton, *U.S.A.* 110 F6
Say, *Mali* 82 C4
Say, *Niger* 83 C5
Saya, *Nigeria* 83 D5
Sayabec, *Canada* 103 C6
Sayaboury, *Laos* 64 C3
Sayán, *Peru* 124 F3
Sayan, Vostochnyy, *Russia* 51 D10
Sayan, Zapadnyy, *Russia* 51 D10
Saydā, *Lebanon* 75 B4
Sayhandulaan = Oldziyt, *Mongolia* 56 B5
Sayhūt, *Yemen* 74 D5
Saykhin, *Kazakstan* 49 F8
Saynshand, *Mongolia* 60 B6
Sayre, *Okla., U.S.A.* 113 H5
Sayre, *Pa., U.S.A.* 111 E8
Sayreville, *U.S.A.* 111 F10
Sayula, *Mexico* 118 D4
Sayward, *Canada* 104 C3
Sazanit, *Albania* 40 F3
Sázava →, *Czech Rep.* 26 B7
Sazin, *Pakistan* 69 B5
Sazlika →, *Bulgaria* 41 E9
Scaër, *France* 18 D3
Scafell Pike, *U.K.* 12 C4
Scalea, *Italy* 31 C8
Scalloway, *U.K.* 14 A7
Scalpay, *U.K.* 14 D3
Scandia, *Canada* 104 C6
Scandiano, *Italy* 28 D7
Scandicci, *Italy* 29 E8
Scandinavia, *Europe* 8 E16
Scansano, *Italy* 29 F8
Scapa Flow, *U.K.* 14 C5
Scappoose, *U.S.A.* 116 E4
Scarámia, Capo, *Italy* 31 F7
Scarba, *U.K.* 14 E3
Scarborough, *Trin. & Tob.* 121 D7
Scarborough, *U.K.* 12 C7
Scariff I., *Ireland* 15 E1
Scarp, *U.K.* 14 C1
Scebeli, Wabi →, *Somali Rep.* 74 G3
Šćedro, *Croatia* 29 E13
Schaal See, *Germany* 24 B6
Schaffhausen, *Switz.* 25 H4
Schagen, *Neths.* 17 B4
Schaghticoke, *U.S.A.* 111 D11
Schärding, *Austria* 26 C6
Scharhörn, *Germany* 24 B4
Scheessel, *Germany* 24 B5
Schefferville, *Canada* 103 B6
Scheibbs, *Austria* 26 C8
Schelde →, *Belgium* 17 C4
Schell Creek Ra., *U.S.A.* 114 G6
Schellsburg, *U.S.A.* 110 F6
Schenectady, *U.S.A.* 111 D11
Schenevus, *U.S.A.* 111 D10
Scherfede, *Germany* 24 D5
Schesslitz, *Germany* 25 F7
Schiedam, *Neths.* 17 C4
Schiermonnikoog, *Neths.* 17 A6
Schiltigheim, *France* 19 D14
Schio, *Italy* 29 C8
Schladming, *Austria* 26 D6
Schlanders = Silandro, *Italy* 28 B7
Schlei →, *Germany* 24 A5
Schleiden, *Germany* 24 E2
Schleiz, *Germany* 24 E7
Schleswig, *Germany* 24 A5
Schleswig-Holstein □, *Germany* 24 A5
Schlüchtern, *Germany* 25 E5
Schmalkalden, *Germany* 24 E6
Schmölln, *Germany* 24 E8
Schneeberg, *Austria* 26 D8
Schneeberg, *Germany* 24 E8
Schneverdingen, *Germany* 24 B5
Schoharie, *U.S.A.* 111 D10
Schoharie →, *U.S.A.* 111 D10
Scholls, *U.S.A.* 116 E4
Schönberg, *Mecklenburg-Vorpommern, Germany* 24 B6
Schönberg, *Schleswig-Holstein, Germany* 24 A6
Schönebeck, *Germany* 24 C7
Schongau, *Germany* 25 H6
Schöningen, *Germany* 24 C6
Schopfheim, *Germany* 25 H3
Schorndorf, *Germany* 25 G5
Schortens, *Germany* 24 B3
Schouten I., *Australia* 94 G4
Schouten Is. = Supiori, *Indonesia* 63 E9
Schouwen, *Neths.* 17 C3
Schramberg, *Germany* 25 G4
Schrankogel, *Austria* 26 D4
Schreiber, *Canada* 102 C2
Schrems, *Austria* 26 C8
Schrobenhausen, *Germany* 25 G7
Schroffenstein, *Namibia* 88 D2
Schroon Lake, *U.S.A.* 111 C11
Schruns, *Austria* 26 D2
Schuler, *Canada* 105 C6
Schumacher, *Canada* 102 C3
Schurz, *U.S.A.* 114 G4
Schuyler, *U.S.A.* 112 E6
Schuylerville, *U.S.A.* 111 C11
Schuylkill →, *U.S.A.* 111 G9
Schuylkill Haven, *U.S.A.* 111 F8
Schwabach, *Germany* 25 F7
Schwaben □, *Germany* 25 G6
Schwäbisch Gmünd, *Germany* 25 G5
Schwäbisch Hall, *Germany* 25 F5
Schwäbische Alb, *Germany* 25 G5
Schwabmünchen, *Germany* 25 G6
Schwalmstadt, *Germany* 24 E5
Schwandorf, *Germany* 25 F8
Schwaner, Pegunungan, *Indonesia* 62 E4
Schwanewede, *Germany* 24 B4
Schwarmstedt, *Germany* 24 C5
Schwarze Elster →, *Germany* 24 D8
Schwarzenberg, *Germany* 24 E8
Schwarzrand, *Namibia* 88 D2
Schwarzwald, *Germany* 25 G4
Schwaz, *Austria* 26 D4
Schwechat, *Austria* 27 C9
Schwedt, *Germany* 24 B10
Schweinfurt, *Germany* 25 E6
Schweizer-Reneke, *S. Africa* 88 D4
Schwenningen = Villingen-Schwenningen, *Germany* 25 G4
Schwerin, *Germany* 24 B7
Schweriner See, *Germany* 24 B7
Schwetzingen, *Germany* 25 F4
Schwyz, *Switz.* 25 H4
Schwyz □, *Switz.* 25 H4
Sciacca, *Italy* 30 E6
Scicli, *Italy* 31 F7
Scilla, *Italy* 31 D8
Scilly, Isles of, *U.K.* 13 H1
Ścinawa, *Poland* 45 G3
Scione, *Greece* 40 G7
Scioto →, *U.S.A.* 108 F4
Scituate, *U.S.A.* 111 D14
Scobey, *U.S.A.* 112 A2
Scone, *Australia* 95 E5
Scordia, *Italy* 31 E7
Scoresbysund = Ittoqqortoormiit, *Greenland* 4 B6
Scorniceşti, *Romania* 43 F9
Scotia, *Calif., U.S.A.* 114 F1
Scotia, *N.Y., U.S.A.* 111 D11
Scotia Sea, *Antarctica* 5 B18
Scotland, *Canada* 110 C4
Scotland □, *U.K.* 14 E5
Scott, C., *Australia* 92 B4
Scott City, *U.S.A.* 112 F4
Scott Glacier, *Antarctica* 5 C8
Scott I., *Antarctica* 5 C11
Scott Is., *Canada* 104 C3
Scott L., *Canada* 105 B7
Scott Reef, *Australia* 92 B3
Scottburgh, *S. Africa* 89 E5
Scottdale, *U.S.A.* 110 F5
Scottish Borders □, *U.K.* 14 F6
Scottsbluff, *U.S.A.* 112 E3
Scottsboro, *U.S.A.* 109 H3
Scottsburg, *U.S.A.* 108 F3
Scottsdale, *Australia* 94 G4
Scottsdale, *U.S.A.* 115 K7
Scottsville, *Ky., U.S.A.* 109 G2
Scottsville, *N.Y., U.S.A.* 110 C7
Scottville, *U.S.A.* 108 D2
Scranton, *U.S.A.* 111 E9
Scugog, L., *Canada* 110 B6
Sculeni, *Moldova* 43 C12
Scunthorpe, *U.K.* 12 D7
Scuol Schuls, *Switz.* 25 J6
Scutari = Üsküdar, *Turkey* 41 F13
Seabrook, L., *Australia* 93 F2
Seaford, *U.K.* 13 G8
Seaford, *U.S.A.* 108 F8
Seaforth, *Australia* 94 C4
Seaforth, *Canada* 110 C3
Seaforth, L., *U.K.* 14 D2
Seagraves, *U.S.A.* 113 J3
Seaham, *U.K.* 12 C6
Seal →, *Canada* 105 B10
Seal L., *Canada* 103 B7
Sealy, *U.S.A.* 113 L6
Searchlight, *U.S.A.* 117 K12
Searcy, *U.S.A.* 113 H9
Searles L., *U.S.A.* 117 K9
Seascale, *U.K.* 12 C4
Seaside, *Calif., U.S.A.* 116 J5
Seaside, *Oreg., U.S.A.* 116 E3
Seaspray, *Australia* 95 F4
Seattle, *U.S.A.* 116 C4
Seaview Ra., *Australia* 94 B4
Sebago L., *U.S.A.* 111 C14
Sebago Lake, *U.S.A.* 111 C14
Sebastián Vizcaíno, B., *Mexico* 118 B2
Sebastopol = Sevastopol, *Ukraine* 47 K7
Sebastopol, *U.S.A.* 116 G4
Sebba, *Burkina Faso* 83 C5
Sebderat, *Eritrea* 81 D4
Sébékoro, *Mali* 82 C3
Seben, *Turkey* 72 B4
Sebeş, *Romania* 43 E8
Sebeşului, Munţii, *Romania* 43 E8
Sebewaing, *U.S.A.* 108 D4
Sebezh, *Russia* 46 D5
Sebha = Sabhah, *Libya* 79 C8
Sébi, *Mali* 82 B4
Şebinkarahisar, *Turkey* 73 B8
Sebiş, *Romania* 42 D7
Sebnitz, *Germany* 24 E10
Sebring, *Fla., U.S.A.* 109 M5
Sebring, *Ohio, U.S.A.* 110 F3
Sebringville, *Canada* 110 C3
Sebta = Ceuta, *N. Afr.* 78 A4
Sebuku, *Indonesia* 62 E5
Sebuku, Teluk, *Malaysia* 62 D5
Sečanj, *Serbia, Yug.* 42 E5
Secchia →, *Italy* 28 C8
Sechelt, *Canada* 104 D4
Sechura, Desierto de, *Peru* 124 E2
Seclin, *France* 19 B10
Secondigny, *France* 18 F6
Sečovce, *Slovak Rep.* 27 C14
Secretary I., *N.Z.* 91 L1
Secunderabad, *India* 66 L11
Security-Widefield, *U.S.A.* 112 F2
Sedalia, *U.S.A.* 112 F8
Sedan, *France* 19 C11
Sedan, *U.S.A.* 113 G6
Sedano, *Spain* 34 C7
Seddon, *N.Z.* 91 J5
Seddonville, *N.Z.* 91 J4
Sedé Boqér, *Israel* 75 E3
Sedeh, *Fārs, Iran* 71 D7
Sedeh, *Khorāsān, Iran* 71 C8
Séderon, *France* 21 D9
Sederot, *Israel* 75 D3
Sédhiou, *Senegal* 82 C1
Sedico, *Italy* 29 B9
Sedlčany, *Czech Rep.* 26 B7
Sedley, *Canada* 105 C8
Sedona, *U.S.A.* 115 J8
Sedova, Pik, *Russia* 50 B6
Sedro Woolley, *U.S.A.* 116 B4
Šeduva, *Lithuania* 44 C10
Sędziszów, *Poland* 45 H7
Sędziszów Małapolski, *Poland* 45 H8
Seebad Ahlbeck, *Germany* 24 B10
Seefeld in Tirol, *Austria* 26 D4
Seehausen, *Germany* 24 C7
Seeheim, *Namibia* 88 D2
Seeheim-Jugenheim, *Germany* 25 F4
Seeis, *Namibia* 88 C2
Seekoei →, *S. Africa* 88 E4
Seeley's Bay, *Canada* 111 B8
Seelow, *Germany* 24 C10
Sées, *France* 18 D7
Seesen, *Germany* 24 D6
Seevetal, *Germany* 24 B6
Sefadu, *S. Leone* 82 D2
Seferihisar, *Turkey* 39 C8
Séfeto, *Mali* 82 C3
Sefwi Bekwai, *Ghana* 82 D4
Segamat, *Malaysia* 65 L4
Şegarcea, *Romania* 43 F8
Ségbana, *Benin* 83 C5
Segbwema, *S. Leone* 82 D2
Seget, *Indonesia* 63 E8
Segonzac, *France* 20 C3
Segorbe, *Spain* 32 F4
Ségou, *Mali* 82 C3
Segovia = Coco →, *Cent. Amer.* 120 D3
Segovia, *Spain* 34 E6
Segovia □, *Spain* 34 E6
Segré, *France* 18 E6
Segre →, *Spain* 32 D5
Séguéla, *Ivory C.* 82 D3
Séguénéga, *Burkina Faso* 83 C4
Seguin, *U.S.A.* 113 L6
Segundo →, *Argentina* 126 C3
Segura →, *Spain* 33 G4
Segura, Sierra de, *Spain* 33 G2
Seh Konj, Kūh-e, *Iran* 71 D8
Seh Qal'eh, *Iran* 71 C8
Sehitwa, *Botswana* 88 C3
Sehore, *India* 68 H7
Sehwan, *Pakistan* 68 F2
Şeica Mare, *Romania* 43 D9
Seil, *U.K.* 14 E3
Seiland, *Norway* 8 A20
Seilhac, *France* 20 C5
Seiling, *U.S.A.* 113 G5
Seille →, *Moselle, France* 19 C13
Seille →, *Saône-et-Loire, France* 19 F11
Sein, Î. de, *France* 18 D2
Seinäjoki, *Finland* 9 E20
Seine →, *France* 18 C7
Seine, B. de la, *France* 18 C6
Seine-et-Marne □, *France* 19 D10
Seine-Maritime □, *France* 18 C7
Seine-St-Denis □, *France* 19 D9
Seini, *Romania* 43 C8
Seirijai, *Lithuania* 44 D10
Seistan = Sīstān, *Asia* 71 D9
Seistan, Daryācheh-ye = Sīstān, Daryācheh-ye, *Iran* 71 D9
Sejerø, *Denmark* 11 J5
Sejerø Bugt, *Denmark* 11 J5
Sejny, *Poland* 44 D10
Seka, *Ethiopia* 81 F4
Sekayu, *Indonesia* 62 E2
Seke, *Tanzania* 86 C3
Sekenke, *Tanzania* 86 C3
Seki, *Turkey* 39 E11
Sekondi-Takoradi, *Ghana* 82 E4
Sekota, *Ethiopia* 81 E4
Seksna, *Russia* 46 C10
Sekuma, *Botswana* 88 C3
Selah, *U.S.A.* 114 C3
Selama, *Malaysia* 65 K3
Selárgius, *Italy* 30 C2
Selaru, *Indonesia* 63 F8
Selb, *Germany* 25 E8
Selby, *U.K.* 12 D6
Selby, *U.S.A.* 112 C4
Selca, *Croatia* 29 E13
Selçuk, *Turkey* 39 D9
Selden, *U.S.A.* 112 F4
Sele →, *Italy* 31 B7
Selebi-Pikwe, *Botswana* 89 C4

Selemdzha →, *Russia* 51 D13
Selendi, *Manisa, Turkey* 39 C10
Selendi, *Manisa, Turkey* 39 C9
Selenga = Selenge Mörön →, *Asia* 60 A5
Selenge Mörön →, *Asia* 60 A5
Selenicë, *Albania* 40 F3
Selenter See, *Germany* 24 A6
Sélestat, *France* 19 D14
Seletan, Tanjung, *Indonesia* 62 E4
Selevac, *Serbia, Yug.* 40 B4
Sélibabi, *Mauritania* 82 B2
Seliger, Ozero, *Russia* 46 D7
Seligman, *U.S.A.* 115 J7
Şelim, *Turkey* 73 B10
Selîma, El Wâhât el, *Sudan* 80 C2
Selimiye, *Turkey* 39 D9
Selinda Spillway →, *Botswana* 88 B3
Selinoús, *Greece* 38 D3
Selinsgrove, *U.S.A.* 110 F8
Selizharovo, *Russia* 46 D7
Selkirk, *Canada* 105 C9
Selkirk, *U.K.* 14 F6
Selkirk I., *Canada* 105 C9
Selkirk Mts., *Canada* 100 C8
Sellama, *Sudan* 81 E2
Selliá, *Greece* 36 D6
Sellières, *France* 19 F12
Sells, *U.S.A.* 115 L8
Sellye, *Hungary* 42 E2
Selma, *Ala., U.S.A.* 109 J2
Selma, *Calif., U.S.A.* 116 J7
Selma, *N.C., U.S.A.* 109 H6
Selmer, *U.S.A.* 109 H1
Selongey, *France* 19 E12
Selowandoma Falls, *Zimbabwe* 87 G3
Selpele, *Indonesia* 63 E8
Selsey Bill, *U.K.* 13 G7
Seltso, *Russia* 46 F8
Seltz, *France* 19 D15
Selu, *Indonesia* 63 F8
Sélune →, *France* 18 D5
Selva = La Selva del Camp, *Spain* 32 D6
Selva, *Argentina* 126 B3
Selvas, *Brazil* 122 D4
Selwyn L., *Canada* 105 B8
Selwyn Mts., *Canada* 100 B6
Selwyn Ra., *Australia* 94 C3
Seman →, *Albania* 40 F3
Semarang, *Indonesia* 62 F4
Sembabule, *Uganda* 86 C3
Şemdinli, *Turkey* 73 D11
Sémé, *Senegal* 82 B2
Semeih, *Sudan* 81 E3
Semenov, *Russia* 48 B7
Semenovka, *Chernihiv, Ukraine* 47 F7
Semenovka, *Kremenchuk, Ukraine* 47 H7
Semeru, *Indonesia* 63 H15
Semey, *Kazakstan* 50 D9
Semikarakorskiy, *Russia* 49 G5
Semiluki, *Russia* 47 G10
Seminoe Reservoir, *U.S.A.* 114 F10
Seminole, *Okla., U.S.A.* 113 H6
Seminole, *Tex., U.S.A.* 113 J3
Seminole Draw →, *U.S.A.* 113 J3
Semipalatinsk = Semey, *Kazakstan* 50 D9
Semirara Is., *Phil.* 61 F4
Semitau, *Indonesia* 62 D4
Semiyarka, *Kazakstan* 50 D8
Semiyarskoye = Semiyarka, *Kazakstan* 50 D8
Semmering P., *Austria* 26 D8
Semnān, *Iran* 71 C7
Semnān □, *Iran* 71 C7
Semporna, *Malaysia* 63 D5
Semuda, *Indonesia* 62 E4
Semur-en-Auxois, *France* 19 E11
Sen →, *Cambodia* 62 B3
Senā, *Iran* 71 D6
Sena, *Mozam.* 87 F4
Sena Madureira, *Brazil* 124 E5
Senador Pompeu, *Brazil* 125 E11
Senaki, *Georgia* 49 J6
Senanga, *Zambia* 85 H4
Senatobia, *U.S.A.* 113 H10
Sencelles, *Spain* 37 B9
Sendafa, *Ethiopia* 81 F4
Sendai, *Kagoshima, Japan* 55 J5
Sendai, *Miyagi, Japan* 54 E10
Sendai-Wan, *Japan* 54 E10
Senden, *Bayern, Germany* 25 G6
Senden, *Nordrhein-Westfalen, Germany* 24 D3
Sendhwa, *India* 68 J6
Sene →, *Ghana* 83 D4
Senec, *Slovak Rep.* 27 C10
Seneca, *U.S.A.* 109 H4
Seneca Falls, *U.S.A.* 111 D8
Seneca L., *U.S.A.* 110 D8
Senecaville L., *U.S.A.* 110 G3
Senegal ■, *W. Afr.* 82 C2
Sénégal →, *W. Afr.* 82 B1
Senegambia, *Africa* 76 E2
Senekal, *S. Africa* 89 D4
Senftenberg, *Germany* 24 D10
Senga Hill, *Zambia* 87 D3
Senge Khambab = Indus →, *Pakistan* 68 G2
Sengiley, *Russia* 48 D9
Sengua →, *Zimbabwe* 87 F2
Senhor-do-Bonfim, *Brazil* 125 F10
Senica, *Slovak Rep.* 27 C10
Senigállia, *Italy* 29 E10
Senio →, *Italy* 29 D9
Senirkent, *Turkey* 39 C12
Senise, *Italy* 31 B9
Senj, *Croatia* 29 D11
Senja, *Norway* 8 B17
Senkaku-Shotō, *Japan* 55 L1
Senlis, *France* 19 C9
Senmonorom, *Cambodia* 64 F6
Sennâr, *Sudan* 81 E3
Sennar □, *Sudan* 81 E3
Senneterre, *Canada* 102 C4
Senno, *Belarus* 46 E5
Sénnori, *Italy* 30 B1
Seno, *Laos* 64 D5
Senonches, *France* 18 D8
Senorbì, *Italy* 30 C2
Senožeče, *Slovenia* 29 C11
Sens, *France* 19 D10
Senta, *Serbia, Yug.* 42 E5
Sentani, *Indonesia* 63 E10
Sentery, *Dem. Rep. of the Congo* 86 D2
Sentinel, *U.S.A.* 115 K7
Šentjur, *Slovenia* 29 B12
Senya Beraku, *Ghana* 83 D4
Seo de Urgel = La Seu d'Urgell, *Spain* 32 C6
Seohara, *India* 69 E8
Seonath →, *India* 69 J10
Seondha, *India* 69 F8
Seoni, *India* 69 H8
Seoni Malwa, *India* 68 H8
Seoul = Sŏul, *S. Korea* 57 F14
Sepīdān, *Iran* 71 D7
Sepo-ri, *N. Korea* 57 E14
Sępólno Krajeńskie, *Poland* 44 E4
Sepone, *Laos* 64 D6
Sępopol, *Poland* 44 D8
Sept-Îles, *Canada* 103 B6
Septemvri, *Bulgaria* 41 D8
Sepúlveda, *Spain* 34 D7
Sequeros, *Spain* 34 E4
Sequim, *U.S.A.* 116 B3
Sequoia National Park, *U.S.A.* 116 J8
Serafimovich, *Russia* 48 F6
Seraing, *Belgium* 17 D5
Seraja, *Indonesia* 65 L7
Serakhis →, *Cyprus* 36 D11
Seram, *Indonesia* 63 E7
Seram Sea, *Indonesia* 63 E7
Seranantsara, *Madag.* 89 B8
Serang, *Indonesia* 63 G12
Serasan, *Indonesia* 65 L7
Seravezza, *Italy* 28 E7
Şerbettar, *Turkey* 41 E10
Serbia □, *Yugoslavia* 40 C5
Şercaia, *Romania* 43 E10
Serdo, *Ethiopia* 81 E5
Serdobsk, *Russia* 48 D7
Sered', *Slovak Rep.* 27 C10
Seredka, *Russia* 46 C5
Şereflikoçhisar, *Turkey* 72 C5
Seregno, *Italy* 28 C6
Seremban, *Malaysia* 65 L3
Serengeti Plain, *Tanzania* 86 C4
Serenje, *Zambia* 87 E3
Sereth = Siret →, *Romania* 43 E12
Sergach, *Russia* 48 C7
Sergen, *Turkey* 41 E11
Sergino, *Russia* 50 C7
Sergipe □, *Brazil* 125 F11
Sergiyev Posad, *Russia* 46 D10
Seria, *Brunei* 62 D4
Serian, *Malaysia* 62 D4
Seriate, *Italy* 28 C6
Seribu, Kepulauan, *Indonesia* 62 F3
Sérifontaine, *France* 19 C8
Sérifos, *Greece* 38 D6
Sérignan, *France* 20 E7
Sérigny →, *Canada* 103 A6
Serik, *Turkey* 72 D4
Seringapatam Reef, *Australia* 92 B3
Serinhisar, *Turkey* 39 D11
Sermaize-les-Bains, *France* 19 D11
Sermata, *Indonesia* 63 F7
Sérmide, *Italy* 29 D8
Sernovodsk, *Russia* 48 D10
Sernur, *Russia* 48 B9
Serock, *Poland* 45 F8
Serón, *Spain* 33 H2
Serós, *Spain* 32 D5
Serov, *Russia* 50 D7
Serowe, *Botswana* 88 C4
Serpa, *Portugal* 35 H3
Serpeddí, Punta, *Italy* 30 C2
Serpentara, *Italy* 30 C2
Serpentine Lakes, *Australia* 93 E4
Serpis →, *Spain* 33 G4
Serpukhov, *Russia* 46 E9
Serra de Outes, *Spain* 34 C2
Serra do Navio, *Brazil* 125 C8
Serra San Bruno, *Italy* 31 D9
Serradilla, *Spain* 34 F4
Sérrai, *Greece* 40 E7
Sérrai □, *Greece* 40 E7
Serramanna, *Italy* 30 C1
Serravalle Scrívia, *Italy* 28 D5
Serre-Ponçon, L. de, *France* 21 D10
Serres, *France* 21 D9
Serrezuela, *Argentina* 126 C2
Serrinha, *Brazil* 125 F11
Sersale, *Italy* 31 C9
Sertã, *Portugal* 34 F2
Sertanópolis, *Brazil* 127 A5
Sêrtar, *China* 58 A3
Serua, *Indonesia* 63 F8
Serui, *Indonesia* 63 E9
Serule, *Botswana* 88 C4
Sérvia, *Greece* 40 F6
Serzedelo, *Portugal* 34 D2
Sese Is., *Uganda* 86 C3
Sesepe, *Indonesia* 63 E7
Sesfontein, *Namibia* 88 B1
Sesheke, *Zambia* 88 B3
Sésia →, *Italy* 28 C5
Sesimbra, *Portugal* 35 G1
S'Espalmador, *Spain* 37 C7
S'Espardell, *Spain* 37 C7
Sessa Aurunca, *Italy* 30 A6
S'Estanyol, *Spain* 37 B9
Sestao, *Spain* 32 B2
Sesto Calende, *Italy* 28 C5
Sesto San Giovanni, *Italy* 28 C6
Sestri Levante, *Italy* 28 D6
Sestriere, *Italy* 28 D3
Sestroretsk, *Russia* 46 B6
Sestrunj, *Croatia* 29 D11
Sestu, *Italy* 30 C2
Setana, *Japan* 54 C9
Sète, *France* 20 E7
Sete Lagôas, *Brazil* 125 G10
Sétif, *Algeria* 78 A7
Seto, *Japan* 55 G8
Setonaikai, *Japan* 55 G6
Settat, *Morocco* 78 B4
Séttimo Torinese, *Italy* 28 C4
Setting L., *Canada* 105 C9
Settle, *U.K.* 12 C5
Settlement Pt., *Bahamas* 109 M6
Settlers, *S. Africa* 89 C4
Setúbal, *Portugal* 35 G2
Setúbal □, *Portugal* 35 G2
Setúbal, B. de, *Portugal* 35 G2
Seugne →, *France* 20 C3
Seul, Lac, *Canada* 102 B1
Seurre, *France* 19 F12
Sevan, *Armenia* 49 K7
Sevan, Ozero = Sevana Lich, *Armenia* 49 K7
Sevana Lich, *Armenia* 49 K7
Sevastopol, *Ukraine* 47 K7
Seven Sisters, *Canada* 104 C3
Sever →, *Spain* 35 F3
Sévérac-le-Château, *France* 20 D7
Severn →, *Canada* 102 A2
Severn →, *U.K.* 13 F5
Severn L., *Canada* 102 B1
Severnaya Zemlya, *Russia* 51 B10
Severo-Kurilsk, *Russia* 51 D16
Severo-Yeniseyskiy, *Russia* 51 C10
Severodonetsk = Syeverodonetsk, *Ukraine* 47 H10
Severodvinsk, *Russia* 50 C4
Sevier, *U.S.A.* 115 G7
Sevier →, *U.S.A.* 115 G7
Sevier Desert, *U.S.A.* 114 G7
Sevier L., *U.S.A.* 114 G7
Sevilla, *Spain* 35 H5
Sevilla □, *Spain* 35 H5
Seville = Sevilla, *Spain* 35 H5
Sevlievo, *Bulgaria* 41 C9
Sevnica, *Slovenia* 29 B12
Sèvre-Nantaise →, *France* 18 E5
Sèvre-Niortaise →, *France* 20 B3
Sevsk, *Russia* 47 F8
Sewa →, *S. Leone* 82 D2
Sewani, *India* 68 E6
Seward, *Alaska, U.S.A.* 100 B5
Seward, *Nebr., U.S.A.* 112 E6
Seward, *Pa., U.S.A.* 110 F5
Seward Peninsula, *U.S.A.* 100 B3
Sewell, *Chile* 126 C1
Sewer, *Indonesia* 63 F8
Sewickley, *U.S.A.* 110 F4
Sexsmith, *Canada* 104 B5
Seychelles ■, *Ind. Oc.* 52 K9
Seyðisfjörður, *Iceland* 8 D6
Seydişehir, *Turkey* 72 D4
Seydvān, *Iran* 70 B5
Seyhan →, *Turkey* 70 B2
Seyhan Barajı, *Turkey* 72 D6
Seyitgazi, *Turkey* 39 B12
Seyitömer, *Turkey* 39 B11
Seym →, *Ukraine* 47 G7
Seymen, *Turkey* 41 E11
Seymour, *Australia* 95 F4
Seymour, *S. Africa* 89 E4
Seymour, *Conn., U.S.A.* 111 E11
Seymour, *Ind., U.S.A.* 108 F3
Seymour, *Tex., U.S.A.* 113 J5
Seyne, *France* 21 D10
Seyssel, *France* 21 C9
Sežana, *Slovenia* 29 C10
Sézanne, *France* 19 D10
Sezze, *Italy* 30 A6
Sfântu Gheorghe, *Covasna, Romania* 43 E10
Sfântu Gheorghe, *Tulcea, Romania* 43 F14
Sfântu Gheorghe, Braţul →, *Romania* 43 F14
Sfax, *Tunisia* 79 B8
Sha Xi →, *China* 59 D12
Sha Xian, *China* 59 D11
Shaanxi □, *China* 56 G5
Shaba = Katanga □, *Dem. Rep. of the Congo* 86 D2
Shabla, *Bulgaria* 41 C12
Shabogamo L., *Canada* 103 B6
Shabunda, *Dem. Rep. of the Congo* 86 C2
Shache, *China* 60 C2
Shackleton Ice Shelf, *Antarctica* 5 C8
Shackleton Inlet, *Antarctica* 5 E11
Shādegān, *Iran* 71 D6
Shadi, *China* 59 D10
Shadi, *India* 69 C7
Shadrinsk, *Russia* 50 D7
Shadyside, *U.S.A.* 110 G4
Shaffa, *Nigeria* 83 C7
Shafter, *U.S.A.* 117 K7
Shaftesbury, *U.K.* 13 F5
Shagamu, *Nigeria* 83 D5
Shagram, *Pakistan* 69 A5
Shah Alizai, *Pakistan* 68 E2
Shah Bunder, *Pakistan* 68 G2
Shahabad, *Punjab, India* 68 D7
Shahabad, *Raj., India* 68 G7
Shahabad, *Ut. P., India* 69 F8
Shahadpur, *Pakistan* 68 G3
Shahba, *Syria* 75 C5
Shahdād, *Iran* 71 D8
Shahdād, Namakzār-e, *Iran* 71 D8
Shahdadkot, *Pakistan* 68 F2
Shahdol, *India* 69 H9
Shahe, *China* 56 F8
Shahganj, *India* 69 F10
Shahgarh, *India* 66 F6
Shahjahanpur, *India* 69 F8
Shahpur, *India* 68 H7
Shahpur, *Baluchistan, Pakistan* 68 E3
Shahpur, *Punjab, Pakistan* 68 C5
Shahpur Chakar, *Pakistan* 68 F3
Shahpura, *Mad. P., India* 69 H9
Shahpura, *Raj., India* 68 G6
Shahr-e Bābak, *Iran* 71 D7
Shahr-e Kord, *Iran* 71 C6
Shāhrakht, *Iran* 71 C9
Shahrig, *Pakistan* 68 D2
Shahukou, *China* 56 D7
Shaikhabad, *Afghan.* 68 B3
Shajapur, *India* 68 H7
Shakargarh, *Pakistan* 68 C6
Shakawe, *Botswana* 88 B3
Shaker Heights, *U.S.A.* 110 E3
Shakhty, *Russia* 49 G5
Shakhunya, *Russia* 48 B8
Shaki, *Nigeria* 83 D5
Shākir, *Egypt* 80 B3
Shala, L., *Ethiopia* 81 F4
Shali, *Russia* 49 J7
Shallow Lake, *Canada* 110 B3
Shalqar, *Kazakstan* 50 E6
Shalskiy, *Russia* 46 B8
Shaluli Shan, *China* 58 B2
Shām, *Iran* 71 E8
Shām, Bādiyat ash, *Asia* 70 C3
Shamâl Bahr el Ghazal □, *Sudan* 81 F2
Shamâl Dârfûr □, *Sudan* 81 E2
Shamâl Kordofân □, *Sudan* 81 E3
Shamâl Sînî □, *Egypt* 75 E2
Shamattawa, *Canada* 102 A1
Shamattawa →, *Canada* 102 A2
Shambe, *Sudan* 81 F3
Shambu, *Ethiopia* 81 F4
Shamīl, *Iran* 71 E8
Shamkhor = Şämkir, *Azerbaijan* 49 K8
Shāmkūh, *Iran* 71 C8
Shamli, *India* 68 E7
Shammar, Jabal, *Si. Arabia* 70 E4
Shamo = Gobi, *Asia* 56 C6
Shamo, L., *Ethiopia* 81 F4
Shamokin, *U.S.A.* 111 F8
Shamrock, *U.S.A.* 113 H4
Shamva, *Zimbabwe* 87 F3
Shan □, *Burma* 67 J21
Shan Xian, *China* 56 G9
Shanan →, *Ethiopia* 81 F5
Shanchengzhen, *China* 57 C13
Shāndak, *Iran* 71 D9
Shandon, *U.S.A.* 116 K6
Shandong □, *China* 57 G10
Shandong Bandao, *China* 57 F11
Shang Xian = Shangzhou, *China* 56 H5
Shanga, *Nigeria* 78 F6
Shangalowe, *Dem. Rep. of the Congo* 87 E2
Shangani, *Zimbabwe* 89 B4
Shangani →, *Zimbabwe* 87 F2
Shangbancheng, *China* 57 D10
Shangcheng, *China* 59 B10
Shangchuan Dao, *China* 59 G9
Shangdu, *China* 56 D7
Shanggao, *China* 59 C10
Shanghai, *China* 59 B13
Shanghai Shi □, *China* 59 B13
Shanghang, *China* 59 E11
Shanghe, *China* 57 F9
Shanglin, *China* 58 F7
Shangnan, *China* 56 H6
Shangqiu, *China* 56 G8
Shangrao, *China* 59 C11
Shangshui, *China* 60 C6
Shangsi, *China* 58 F6
Shangyou, *China* 59 E10
Shangyu, *China* 59 B13
Shangzhi, *China* 57 B14
Shangzhou, *China* 56 H5
Shanhetun, *China* 57 B14
Shani, *Nigeria* 83 C7
Shannon, *N.Z.* 91 J5
Shannon →, *Ireland* 15 D2
Shannon, Mouth of the, *Ireland* 15 D2
Shannon Airport, *Ireland* 15 D3
Shansi = Shanxi □, *China* 56 F7
Shantar, Ostrov Bolshoy, *Russia* 51 D14
Shantipur, *India* 69 H13
Shantou, *China* 59 F11
Shantung = Shandong □, *China* 57 G10
Shanwei, *China* 59 F10
Shanxi □, *China* 56 F7
Shanyang, *China* 56 H5
Shanyin, *China* 56 E7
Shaodong, *China* 59 D8
Shaoguan, *China* 59 E9
Shaoshan, *China* 59 D9
Shaowu, *China* 59 D11
Shaoxing, *China* 59 C13
Shaoyang, *Hunan, China* 59 D8
Shaoyang, *Hunan, China* 59 D8
Shap, *U.K.* 12 C5
Shapinsay, *U.K.* 14 B6
Shaqq el Gi'eifer →, *Sudan* 81 D2
Shaqra', *Si. Arabia* 70 E5
Shaqrā', *Yemen* 74 E4
Sharafa, *Sudan* 81 E2
Sharafkhāneh, *Iran* 70 B5
Sharbot Lake, *Canada* 111 B8
Shari, *Japan* 54 C12
Sharjah = Ash Shāriqah, *U.A.E.* 71 E7
Shark B., *Australia* 93 E1
Sharm el Sheikh, *Egypt* 80 B3
Sharon, *Mass., U.S.A.* 111 D13
Sharon, *Pa., U.S.A.* 110 E4
Sharon Springs, *Kans., U.S.A.* 112 F4
Sharon Springs, *N.Y., U.S.A.* 111 D10
Sharp Pt., *Australia* 94 A3
Sharpe L., *Canada* 102 B1
Sharpsville, *U.S.A.* 110 E4
Sharq el Istiwa'iya □, *Sudan* 81 G3
Sharya, *Russia* 48 A7
Shasha, *Ethiopia* 81 F4
Shashemene, *Ethiopia* 81 F4
Shashi, *Botswana* 89 C4
Shashi, *China* 59 B9
Shashi →, *Africa* 87 G2
Shasta, Mt., *U.S.A.* 114 F2
Shasta L., *U.S.A.* 114 F2
Shatawi, *Sudan* 81 E3
Shatsk, *Russia* 48 C5
Shatt al Arab = Arab, Shatt al →, *Asia* 71 D6
Shatura, *Russia* 46 E10
Shaumyani = Shulaveri, *Georgia* 49 K7
Shaunavon, *Canada* 105 D7
Shaver L., *U.S.A.* 116 H7
Shaw →, *Australia* 92 D2
Shaw I., *Australia* 94 C4
Shawanaga, *Canada* 110 A4
Shawangunk Mts., *U.S.A.* 111 E10
Shawano, *U.S.A.* 108 C1
Shawinigan, *Canada* 102 C5
Shawnee, *U.S.A.* 113 H6
Shay Gap, *Australia* 92 D3
Shayang, *China* 59 B9
Shaybārā, *Si. Arabia* 70 E3
Shayib el Banat, Gebel, *Egypt* 80 B3
Shaykh, J. ash, *Lebanon* 75 B4
Shaykh Miskīn, *Syria* 75 C5
Shaykh Sa'īd, *Iraq* 70 C5
Shchekino, *Russia* 46 E9
Shcherbakov = Rybinsk, *Russia* 46 C10
Shchigry, *Russia* 47 G9
Shchors, *Ukraine* 47 G6
Shchuchinsk, *Kazakstan* 50 D8
She Xian, *Anhui, China* 59 C12
She Xian, *Hebei, China* 56 F7
Shebekino, *Russia* 47 G9
Shebele = Scebeli, Wabi →, *Somali Rep.* 74 G3
Sheboygan, *U.S.A.* 108 D2
Shebshi Mts., *Nigeria* 83 D7
Shediac, *Canada* 103 C7
Sheelin, L., *Ireland* 15 C4
Sheep Haven, *Ireland* 15 A4
Sheerness, *U.K.* 13 F8
Sheet Harbour, *Canada* 103 D7
Sheffield, *U.K.* 12 D6
Sheffield, *Ala., U.S.A.* 109 H2
Sheffield, *Mass., U.S.A.* 111 D11
Sheffield, *Pa., U.S.A.* 110 E5
Shehojele, *Ethiopia* 81 E4
Shehong, *China* 58 B5
Sheikh Idris, *Sudan* 81 E3
Sheikhpura, *India* 69 G11
Shek Hasan, *Ethiopia* 81 E4
Shekhupura, *Pakistan* 68 D5
Sheki = Şaki, *Azerbaijan* 49 K8
Shelburne, *N.S., Canada* 103 D6
Shelburne, *Ont., Canada* 102 D3
Shelburne, *U.S.A.* 111 B11
Shelburne B., *Australia* 94 A3
Shelburne Falls, *U.S.A.* 111 D12
Shelby, *Mich., U.S.A.* 108 D2
Shelby, *Miss., U.S.A.* 113 J9
Shelby, *Mont., U.S.A.* 114 B8
Shelby, *N.C., U.S.A.* 109 H5
Shelby, *Ohio, U.S.A.* 110 F2
Shelbyville, *Ill., U.S.A.* 112 F10
Shelbyville, *Ind., U.S.A.* 108 F3
Shelbyville, *Ky., U.S.A.* 108 F3
Shelbyville, *Tenn., U.S.A.* 109 H2
Sheldon, *U.S.A.* 112 D7
Sheldrake, *Canada* 103 B7
Shelengo, Khawr →, *Sudan* 81 E2
Shelikhova, Zaliv, *Russia* 51 D16
Shell Lakes, *Australia* 93 E4
Shellbrook, *Canada* 105 C7
Shellharbour, *Australia* 95 E5
Shelon →, *Russia* 46 C6
Shelter I, *U.S.A.* 111 E12
Shelton, *Conn., U.S.A.* 111 E11
Shelton, *Wash., U.S.A.* 116 C3
Shemakha = Şamaxi, *Azerbaijan* 49 K9
Shëmri, *Albania* 40 D4
Shemsi, *Sudan* 80 D2
Shen Xian, *China* 56 F8
Shenandoah, *Iowa, U.S.A.* 112 E7
Shenandoah, *Pa., U.S.A.* 111 F8
Shenandoah, *Va., U.S.A.* 108 F6

Shenandoah →, *U.S.A.* 108 F7
Shenandoah National Park, *U.S.A.* 108 F6
Shenchi, *China* 56 E7
Shendam, *Nigeria* 83 D6
Shendī, *Sudan* 81 D3
Shenge, *S. Leone* 82 D2
Shengfang, *China* 56 E9
Shëngjergj, *Albania* 40 E4
Shëngjin, *Albania* 40 E3
Shengzhou, *China* 59 C13
Shenjingzi, *China* 57 B13
Shenmu, *China* 56 E6
Shennongjia, *China* 59 B8
Shenqiu, *China* 56 H8
Shensi = Shaanxi □, *China* 56 G5
Shenyang, *China* 57 D12
Shenzhen, *China* 59 F10
Sheo, *India* 68 F4
Sheopur Kalan, *India* 66 G10
Shepetivka, *Ukraine* 47 G4
Shepetovka = Shepetivka, *Ukraine* 47 G4
Shepparton, *Australia* 95 F4
Sheppey, I. of, *U.K.* 13 F8
Shepton Mallet, *U.K.* 13 F5
Sheqi, *China* 56 H7
Sher Qila, *Pakistan* 69 A6
Sherab, *Sudan* 81 E1
Sherborne, *U.K.* 13 G5
Sherbro →, *S. Leone* 82 D2
Sherbro I., *S. Leone* 82 D2
Sherbrooke, *N.S., Canada* 103 C7
Sherbrooke, *Qué., Canada* 103 C5
Sherburne, *U.S.A.* 111 D9
Shereik, *Sudan* 80 D3
Shergarh, *India* 68 F5
Sherghati, *India* 69 G11
Sheridan, *Ark., U.S.A.* 113 H8
Sheridan, *Wyo., U.S.A.* 114 D10
Sheringham, *U.K.* 12 E9
Sherkin I., *Ireland* 15 E2
Sherkot, *India* 69 E8
Sherman, *U.S.A.* 113 J6
Sherpur, *India* 69 G10
Sherridon, *Canada* 105 B8
Sherwood Forest, *U.K.* 12 D6
Sherwood Park, *Canada* 104 C6
Sheslay →, *Canada* 104 B2
Shethanei L., *Canada* 105 B9
Shetland □, *U.K.* 14 A7
Shetland Is., *U.K.* 14 A7
Shetrunji →, *India* 68 J5
Shewa □, *Ethiopia* 81 F4
Shewa Gimira, *Ethiopia* 81 F4
Sheyenne →, *U.S.A.* 112 B6
Shibām, *Yemen* 74 D4
Shibata, *Japan* 54 F9
Shibecha, *Japan* 54 C12
Shibetsu, *Japan* 54 B11
Shibîn el Kôm, *Egypt* 80 H7
Shibîn el Qanâtir, *Egypt* 80 H7
Shibing, *China* 58 D7
Shibogama L., *Canada* 102 B2
Shibushi, *Japan* 55 J5
Shicheng, *China* 59 D11
Shickshinny, *U.S.A.* 111 E8
Shickshock Mts. = Chic-Chocs, Mts., *Canada* 103 C6
Shidao, *China* 57 F12
Shidian, *China* 58 E2
Shido, *Japan* 55 G7
Shiel, L., *U.K.* 14 E3
Shield, C., *Australia* 94 A2
Shīeli, *Kazakstan* 50 E7
Shifang, *China* 58 B5
Shiga □, *Japan* 55 G8
Shigu, *China* 58 D2
Shiguaigou, *China* 56 D6
Shihchiachuangi = Shijiazhuang, *China* 56 E8
Shijak, *Albania* 40 E3
Shijiazhuang, *China* 56 E8
Shijiu Hu, *China* 59 B12
Shikarpur, *India* 68 E8
Shikarpur, *Pakistan* 68 F3
Shikohabad, *India* 69 F8
Shikoku □, *Japan* 55 H6
Shikoku-Sanchi, *Japan* 55 H6
Shiliguri, *India* 67 F16
Shilka, *Russia* 51 D12
Shilka →, *Russia* 51 D13
Shillelagh, *Ireland* 15 D5
Shillington, *U.S.A.* 111 F9
Shillong, *India* 67 G17
Shilo, *West Bank* 75 C4
Shilong, *China* 59 F9
Shilou, *China* 56 F6
Shilovo, *Russia* 48 C5
Shimabara, *Japan* 55 H5
Shimada, *Japan* 55 G9
Shimane □, *Japan* 55 G6
Shimanovsk, *Russia* 51 D13
Shimen, *China* 59 C8
Shimenjie, *China* 59 C11
Shimian, *China* 58 C4
Shimizu, *Japan* 55 G9
Shimodate, *Japan* 55 F9
Shimoga, *India* 66 N9
Shimoni, *Kenya* 86 C4
Shimonoseki, *Japan* 55 H5
Shimpuru Rapids, *Angola* 88 B2
Shimsk, *Russia* 46 C6
Shin, L., *U.K.* 14 C4
Shinan, *China* 58 F7
Shinano-Gawa →, *Japan* 55 F9
Shināş, *Oman* 71 E8
Shīndand, *Afghan.* 66 C3
Shinglehouse, *U.S.A.* 110 E6
Shingū, *Japan* 55 H7
Shingwidzi, *S. Africa* 89 C5
Shinjō, *Japan* 54 E10
Shinkafe, *Nigeria* 83 C6
Shinshār, *Syria* 75 A5
Shinyanga, *Tanzania* 86 C3
Shinyanga □, *Tanzania* 86 C3
Shio-no-Misaki, *Japan* 55 H7
Shiogama, *Japan* 54 E10
Shiojiri, *Japan* 55 F8
Shipchenski Prokhod, *Bulgaria* 41 D9
Shiping, *China* 58 F4
Shippegan, *Canada* 103 C7
Shippensburg, *U.S.A.* 110 F7
Shippenville, *U.S.A.* 110 E5
Shiprock, *U.S.A.* 115 H9
Shiqian, *China* 58 D7
Shiqma, N. →, *Israel* 75 D3
Shiquan, *China* 56 H5
Shiquan He = Indus →, *Pakistan* 68 G2
Shīr Kūh, *Iran* 71 D7
Shiragami-Misaki, *Japan* 54 D10
Shirakawa, *Fukushima, Japan* 55 F10
Shirakawa, *Gifu, Japan* 55 F8
Shirane-San, *Gumma, Japan* 55 F9
Shirane-San, *Yamanashi, Japan* 55 G9
Shiraoi, *Japan* 54 C10
Shīrāz, *Iran* 71 D7
Shirbīn, *Egypt* 80 H7
Shire →, *Africa* 87 F4
Shiretoko-Misaki, *Japan* 54 B12
Shirinab →, *Pakistan* 68 D2
Shiriya-Zaki, *Japan* 54 D10
Shiroishi, *Japan* 54 F10
Shīrvān, *Iran* 71 B8
Shirwa, L. = Chilwa, L., *Malawi* 87 F4
Shishi, *China* 59 E12
Shishou, *China* 59 C9
Shitai, *China* 59 B11
Shivpuri, *India* 68 G7
Shixian, *China* 57 C15
Shixing, *China* 59 E10
Shiyan, *China* 59 A8
Shiyata, *Egypt* 80 B2
Shizhu, *China* 58 C7
Shizong, *China* 58 E5
Shizuishan, *China* 56 E4
Shizuoka, *Japan* 55 G9
Shizuoka □, *Japan* 55 G9
Shklov = Shklow, *Belarus* 46 E6
Shklow, *Belarus* 46 E6
Shkoder = Shkodër, *Albania* 40 D3
Shkodër, *Albania* 40 D3
Shkumbini →, *Albania* 40 E3
Shmidta, Ostrov, *Russia* 51 A10
Shō-Gawa →, *Japan* 55 F8
Shoal L., *Canada* 105 D9
Shoal Lake, *Canada* 105 C8
Shōdo-Shima, *Japan* 55 G7
Sholapur = Solapur, *India* 66 L9
Shologontsy, *Russia* 51 C12
Shōmrōn, *West Bank* 75 C4
Shoreham by Sea, *U.K.* 13 G7
Shori →, *Pakistan* 68 E3
Shorkot Road, *Pakistan* 68 D5
Shoshone, *Calif., U.S.A.* 117 K10
Shoshone, *Idaho, U.S.A.* 114 E6
Shoshone L., *U.S.A.* 114 D8
Shoshone Mts., *U.S.A.* 114 G5
Shoshong, *Botswana* 88 C4
Shoshoni, *U.S.A.* 114 E9
Shostka, *Ukraine* 47 G7
Shou Xian, *China* 59 A11
Shouchang, *China* 59 C12
Shouguang, *China* 57 F10
Shouning, *China* 59 D12
Shouyang, *China* 56 F7
Show Low, *U.S.A.* 115 J9
Shpola, *Ukraine* 47 H6
Shreveport, *U.S.A.* 113 J8
Shrewsbury, *U.K.* 13 E5
Shri Mohangarh, *India* 68 F4
Shrirampur, *India* 69 H13
Shropshire □, *U.K.* 13 E5
Shū, *Kazakstan* 50 E8
Shū →, *Kazakstan* 52 E10
Shuangbai, *China* 58 E3
Shuangcheng, *China* 57 B14
Shuangfeng, *China* 59 D9
Shuanggou, *China* 57 G9
Shuangjiang, *China* 58 F2
Shuangliao, *China* 57 C12
Shuangshanzi, *China* 57 D10
Shuangyang, *China* 57 C13
Shuangyashan, *China* 60 B8
Shubra Khit, *Egypt* 80 H7
Shucheng, *China* 59 B11
Shugozero, *Russia* 46 C8
Shuguri Falls, *Tanzania* 87 D4
Shuiji, *China* 59 D12
Shuiye, *China* 56 F8
Shujalpur, *India* 68 H7
Shukpa Kunzang, *India* 69 B8
Shulan, *China* 57 B14
Shulaveri, *Georgia* 49 K7
Shule, *China* 60 C2
Shumagin Is., *U.S.A.* 100 C4
Shumen, *Bulgaria* 41 C10
Shumerlya, *Russia* 48 C8
Shumikha, *Russia* 50 D7
Shunchang, *China* 59 D11
Shunde, *China* 59 F9
Shungay, *Kazakstan* 49 F8
Shuo Xian = Shuozhou, *China* 56 E7
Shuozhou, *China* 56 E7
Shūr →, *Fārs, Iran* 71 D7
Shūr →, *Kermān, Iran* 71 D8
Shūr →, *Yazd, Iran* 71 D7
Shūr Āb, *Iran* 71 C6
Shūr Gaz, *Iran* 71 D8
Shūrāb, *Iran* 71 C8
Shūrjestān, *Iran* 71 D7
Shurugwi, *Zimbabwe* 87 F3
Shūsf, *Iran* 71 D9
Shūsh, *Iran* 73 F13
Shūshtar, *Iran* 71 D6
Shuswap L., *Canada* 104 C5
Shuya, *Russia* 48 B5
Shuyang, *China* 57 G10
Shūzū, *Iran* 71 D7
Shwebo, *Burma* 67 H19
Shwegu, *Burma* 67 G20
Shweli →, *Burma* 67 H20
Shymkent, *Kazakstan* 50 E7
Shyok, *India* 69 B8
Shyok →, *Pakistan* 69 B6
Si Chon, *Thailand* 65 H2
Si Kiang = Xi Jiang →, *China* 59 F9
Si-ngan = Xi'an, *China* 56 G5
Si Prachan, *Thailand* 64 E3
Si Racha, *Thailand* 64 F3
Si Xian, *China* 57 H9
Siahaf →, *Pakistan* 68 E3
Siahan Range, *Pakistan* 66 F4
Siaksriindrapura, *Indonesia* 62 D2
Sialkot, *Pakistan* 68 C6
Siam = Thailand ■, *Asia* 64 E4
Sian = Xi'an, *China* 56 G5
Sianów, *Poland* 44 D3
Siantan, *Indonesia* 62 D3
Siāreh, *Iran* 71 D9
Siargao I., *Phil.* 61 G7
Siari, *Pakistan* 69 B7
Siasi, *Phil.* 63 C6
Siasi I., *Phil.* 61 J4
Siátista, *Greece* 40 F5
Siau, *Indonesia* 63 D7
Šiauliai, *Lithuania* 9 J20
Šiauliai □, *Lithuania* 44 C10
Siazan = Siyäzän, *Azerbaijan* 49 K9
Sibâi, Gebel el, *Egypt* 70 E2
Sibayi, L., *S. Africa* 89 D5
Sibdu, *Sudan* 81 E2
Šibenik, *Croatia* 29 E12
Siberia, *Russia* 4 D13
Siberut, *Indonesia* 62 E1
Sibi, *Pakistan* 68 E2
Sibil = Oksibil, *Indonesia* 63 E10
Sibiti, *Congo* 84 E2
Sibiu, *Romania* 43 E9
Sibiu □, *Romania* 43 E9
Sibley, *U.S.A.* 112 D7
Sibolga, *Indonesia* 62 D1
Sibsagar, *India* 67 F19
Sibu, *Malaysia* 62 D4
Sibuco, *Phil.* 61 H5
Sibuguey B., *Phil.* 61 H5
Sibut, *C.A.R.* 84 C3
Sibutu, *Phil.* 63 D5
Sibutu Group, *Phil.* 61 J3
Sibutu Passage, *E. Indies* 63 D5
Sibuyan I., *Phil.* 61 E5
Sibuyan Sea, *Phil.* 61 E5
Sic, *Romania* 43 D8
Sicamous, *Canada* 104 C5
Siccus →, *Australia* 95 E2
Sichuan □, *China* 58 B5
Sichuan Pendi, *China* 58 B5
Sicilia, *Italy* 31 E7
Sicilia □, *Italy* 31 E7
Sicily = Sicilia, *Italy* 31 E7
Sicuani, *Peru* 124 F4
Šid, *Serbia, Yug.* 42 E4
Sidamo □, *Ethiopia* 81 G4
Sidaouet, *Niger* 83 B6
Sidári, *Greece* 36 A3
Siddhapur, *India* 68 H5
Siddipet, *India* 66 K11
Sidensjö, *Sweden* 10 A12
Sidéradougou, *Burkina Faso* 82 C4
Siderno, *Italy* 31 D9
Sidhauli, *India* 69 F9
Sídheros, Ákra, *Greece* 36 D8
Sidhi, *India* 69 G9
Sidhirókastron, *Greece* 40 E7
Sîdi Abd el Rahmân, *Egypt* 80 A2
Sîdi Barrâni, *Egypt* 80 A2
Sidi-bel-Abbès, *Algeria* 78 A5
Sidi Haneish, *Egypt* 80 A2
Sidi Ifni, *Morocco* 78 C3
Sidi Omar, *Egypt* 80 A1
Sidlaw Hills, *U.K.* 14 E5
Sidley, Mt., *Antarctica* 5 D14
Sidmouth, *U.K.* 13 G4
Sidmouth, C., *Australia* 94 A3
Sidney, *Canada* 104 D4
Sidney, *Mont., U.S.A.* 112 B2
Sidney, *N.Y., U.S.A.* 111 D9
Sidney, *Nebr., U.S.A.* 112 E3
Sidney, *Ohio, U.S.A.* 108 E3
Sidney Lanier, L., *U.S.A.* 109 H4
Sido, *Mali* 82 C3
Sidoarjo, *Indonesia* 63 G15
Sidon = Saydā, *Lebanon* 75 B4
Sidra, G. of = Surt, Khalīj, *Libya* 79 B9
Siedlce, *Poland* 45 F9
Sieg →, *Germany* 24 E3
Siegburg, *Germany* 24 E3
Siegen, *Germany* 24 E4
Siem Pang, *Cambodia* 64 E6
Siem Reap = Siemreab, *Cambodia* 64 F4
Siemiatycze, *Poland* 45 F9
Siemreab, *Cambodia* 64 F4
Siena, *Italy* 29 E8
Sieniawa, *Poland* 45 H9
Sieradz, *Poland* 45 G5
Sieraków, *Poland* 45 F3
Sierck-les-Bains, *France* 19 C13
Sierning, *Austria* 26 C7
Sierpc, *Poland* 45 F6
Sierra Blanca, *U.S.A.* 115 L11
Sierra Blanca Peak, *U.S.A.* 115 K11
Sierra City, *U.S.A.* 116 F6
Sierra Colorada, *Argentina* 128 E3
Sierra de Yeguas, *Spain* 35 H6
Sierra Gorda, *Chile* 126 A2
Sierra Leone ■, *W. Afr.* 82 D2
Sierra Madre, *Mexico* 119 D6
Sierra Mojada, *Mexico* 118 B4
Sierra Nevada, *Spain* 35 H7
Sierra Nevada, *U.S.A.* 116 H8
Sierra Vista, *U.S.A.* 115 L8
Sierraville, *U.S.A.* 116 F6
Sierre, *Switz.* 25 J3
Sifani, *Ethiopia* 81 E5
Sifié, *Ivory C.* 82 D3
Sífnos, *Greece* 38 E6
Sifton, *Canada* 105 C8
Sifton Pass, *Canada* 104 B3
Sigean, *France* 20 E6
Sighetu-Marmaţiei, *Romania* 43 C8
Sighişoara, *Romania* 43 D9
Sigli, *Indonesia* 62 C1
Siglufjörður, *Iceland* 8 C4
Sigmaringen, *Germany* 25 G5
Signa, *Italy* 28 E8
Signakhi = Tsnori, *Georgia* 49 K7
Signal, *U.S.A.* 117 L13
Signal Pk., *U.S.A.* 117 M12
Signy-l'Abbaye, *France* 19 C11
Sigsig, *Ecuador* 124 D3
Sigüenza, *Spain* 32 D2
Siguiri, *Guinea* 82 C3
Sigulda, *Latvia* 9 H21
Sihanoukville = Kampong Saom, *Cambodia* 65 G4
Sihora, *India* 69 H9
Sihui, *China* 59 F9
Siikajoki →, *Finland* 8 D21
Siilinjärvi, *Finland* 8 E22
Siirt, *Turkey* 73 D9
Sijarira Ra., *Zimbabwe* 87 F2
Sika, *India* 68 H3
Sikao, *Thailand* 65 J2
Sikar, *India* 68 F6
Sikasso, *Mali* 82 C3
Sikeston, *U.S.A.* 113 G10
Sikhote Alin, Khrebet, *Russia* 51 E14
Sikhote Alin Ra. = Sikhote Alin, Khrebet, *Russia* 51 E14
Sikiá., *Greece* 40 F7
Síkinos, *Greece* 39 E7
Sikkani Chief →, *Canada* 104 B4
Sikkim □, *India* 67 F16
Siklós, *Hungary* 42 E3
Sikotu-Ko, *Japan* 54 C10
Sil →, *Spain* 34 C3
Silacayoapan, *Mexico* 119 D5
Šilalė, *Lithuania* 44 C9
Silandro, *Italy* 28 B7
Silawad, *India* 68 J6
Silay, *Phil.* 61 F5
Silba, *Croatia* 29 D11
Silchar, *India* 67 G18
Şile, *Turkey* 41 E13
Siler City, *U.S.A.* 109 H6
Silgarhi Doti, *Nepal* 69 E9
Silghat, *India* 67 F18
Sili, *Burkina Faso* 82 C4
Silifke, *Turkey* 70 B2
Siliguri = Shiliguri, *India* 67 F16
Siling Co, *China* 60 C3
Silistea Nouă, *Romania* 43 F10
Silistra, *Bulgaria* 41 B11
Silivri, *Turkey* 41 E12
Siljan, *Sweden* 10 D8
Siljansnäs, *Sweden* 10 D8
Silkeborg, *Denmark* 11 H3
Silkwood, *Australia* 94 B4
Silla, *Spain* 33 F4
Sillajhuay, Cordillera, *Chile* 124 G5
Sillamäe, *Estonia* 9 G22
Sillé-le-Guillaume, *France* 18 D6
Silleda, *Spain* 34 C2
Silloth, *U.K.* 12 C4
Sílo, *Greece* 41 E9
Siloam Springs, *U.S.A.* 113 G7
Silopi, *Turkey* 73 D10
Silsbee, *U.S.A.* 113 K7
Siluko, *Nigeria* 83 D6
Šilutė, *Lithuania* 9 J19
Silva Porto = Kuito, *Angola* 85 G3
Silvan, *Turkey* 73 C9
Silvani, *India* 69 H8
Silver City, *U.S.A.* 115 K9
Silver Cr. →, *U.S.A.* 114 E4
Silver Creek, *U.S.A.* 110 D5
Silver L., *U.S.A.* 116 G6
Silver Lake, *Calif., U.S.A.* 117 K10
Silver Lake, *Oreg., U.S.A.* 114 E3
Silverdalen, *Sweden* 11 G9
Silverton, *Colo., U.S.A.* 115 H10
Silverton, *Tex., U.S.A.* 113 H4
Silves, *Portugal* 35 H2
Silvi Marina, *Italy* 29 F11
Silvies →, *U.S.A.* 114 E4
Silvrettahorn, *Switz.* 28 B7
Silwa Bahari, *Egypt* 80 C3
Silz, *Austria* 26 D3
Simaltala, *India* 69 G12
Simanggang = Bandar Sri Aman, *Malaysia* 62 D4
Simao, *China* 58 F3
Simard, L., *Canada* 102 C4
Şīmareh →, *Iran* 73 F12
Simav, *Turkey* 39 B10
Simav →, *Turkey* 41 F12
Simav Dağları, *Turkey* 39 B10
Simba, *Tanzania* 86 C4
Simbach, *Germany* 25 G9
Simbirsk, *Russia* 48 C9
Simbo, *Tanzania* 86 C2
Simcoe, *Canada* 102 D3
Simcoe, L., *Canada* 102 D4
Simdega, *India* 69 H11
Simeonovgrad, *Bulgaria* 41 D9
Simeria, *Romania* 42 E8
Simeto →, *Italy* 31 E8
Simeulue, *Indonesia* 62 D1
Simferopol, *Ukraine* 47 K8
Sími, *Greece* 39 E9
Simi Valley, *U.S.A.* 117 L8
Simikot, *Nepal* 69 E9
Simitli, *Bulgaria* 40 E7
Simla, *India* 68 D7
Simlångsdalen, *Sweden* 11 H7
Şimleu-Silvaniei, *Romania* 42 C7
Simmern, *Germany* 25 F3
Simmie, *Canada* 105 D7
Simmler, *U.S.A.* 117 K7
Simnas, *Lithuania* 44 D10
Simojoki →, *Finland* 8 D21
Simojovel, *Mexico* 119 D6
Simonette →, *Canada* 104 B5
Simonstown, *S. Africa* 88 E2
Simontornya, *Hungary* 42 D3
Simplonpass, *Switz.* 25 J4
Simplontunnel, *Switz.* 25 J4
Simpson Desert, *Australia* 94 D2
Simpson Pen., *Canada* 101 B11
Simpungdong, *N. Korea* 57 D15
Simrishamn, *Sweden* 11 J8
Simsbury, *U.S.A.* 111 E12
Simushir, Ostrov, *Russia* 51 E16
Sin Cowe I., *S. China Sea* 62 C4
Sinabang, *Indonesia* 62 D1
Sinadogo, *Somali Rep.* 74 F4
Sinai = Es Sînâ', *Egypt* 75 F3
Sinai, Mt. = Mûsa, Gebel, *Egypt* 70 D2
Sinai Peninsula, *Egypt* 75 F3
Sinaia, *Romania* 43 E10
Sinaloa □, *Mexico* 118 C3
Sinaloa de Leyva, *Mexico* 118 B3
Sinalunga, *Italy* 29 E8
Sinan, *China* 58 D7
Sînandrei, *Romania* 42 E6
Sinarádhes, *Greece* 36 A3
Sincan, *Turkey* 72 B5
Sincanlı, *Turkey* 39 C12
Sincelejo, *Colombia* 124 B3
Sinch'ang, *N. Korea* 57 D15
Sinchang-ni, *N. Korea* 57 E14
Sinclair, *U.S.A.* 114 F10
Sinclair Mills, *Canada* 104 C4
Sinclair's B., *U.K.* 14 C5
Sinclairville, *U.S.A.* 110 D5
Sincorá, Serra do, *Brazil* 125 F10
Sind, *Pakistan* 68 G3
Sind □, *Pakistan* 68 G3
Sind →, *Jammu & Kashmir, India* 69 B6
Sind →, *Mad. P., India* 69 F8
Sind Sagar Doab, *Pakistan* 68 D4
Sindal, *Denmark* 11 G4
Sindangan, *Phil.* 61 G5
Sindangbarang, *Indonesia* 63 G12
Sinde, *Zambia* 87 F2
Sindelfingen, *Germany* 25 G4
Sındırgı, *Turkey* 39 B10
Sindou, *Burkina Faso* 82 C3
Sindri, *India* 69 H12
Sine →, *Senegal* 82 C1
Sinegorskiy, *Russia* 49 G5
Sinekli, *Turkey* 41 E12
Sinelnikovo = Synelnykove, *Ukraine* 47 H8
Sinendé, *Benin* 83 C5
Sines, *Portugal* 35 H2
Sines, C. de, *Portugal* 35 H2
Sineu, *Spain* 37 B10
Sinfra, *Ivory C.* 82 D3
Sing Buri, *Thailand* 64 E3
Singa, *Sudan* 81 E3
Singapore ■, *Asia* 65 M4
Singapore, Straits of, *Asia* 65 M5
Singaraja, *Indonesia* 62 F5
Singen, *Germany* 25 H4
Singida, *Tanzania* 86 C3
Singida □, *Tanzania* 86 D3
Singitikós Kólpos, *Greece* 40 F7
Singkaling Hkamti, *Burma* 67 G19
Singkang, *Indonesia* 63 E6
Singkawang, *Indonesia* 62 D3
Singkep, *Indonesia* 62 E2
Singleton, *Australia* 95 E5
Singleton, Mt., *N. Terr., Australia* 92 D5
Singleton, Mt., *W. Austral., Australia* 93 E2
Singö, *Sweden* 10 D12
Singoli, *India* 68 G6
Singora = Songkhla, *Thailand* 65 J3
Singosan, *N. Korea* 57 E14
Sinhung, *N. Korea* 57 D14
Siniátsikon, Óros, *Greece* 40 F5

Siniscóla, *Italy* 30 B2
Sinj, *Croatia* 29 E13
Sinjai, *Indonesia* 63 F6
Sinjajevina, *Montenegro, Yug.* 40 D3
Sinjār, *Iraq* 70 B4
Sinkat, *Sudan* 80 D4
Sinkiang Uighur = Xinjiang Uygur Zizhiqu □, *China* 60 B3
Sinmak, *N. Korea* 57 E14
Sinnai, *Italy* 30 C2
Sinnamary, *Fr. Guiana* 125 B8
Sinni →, *Italy* 31 B9
Sinnuris, *Egypt* 80 J7
Sinoie, Lacul, *Romania* 43 F13
Sinop, *Turkey* 72 A6
Sinor, *India* 68 J5
Sinp'o, *N. Korea* 57 E15
Sinsheim, *Germany* 25 F4
Sinsk, *Russia* 51 C13
Sintang, *Indonesia* 62 D4
Sinton, *U.S.A.* 113 L6
Sintra, *Portugal* 35 G1
Sinŭiju, *N. Korea* 57 D13
Sinyukha →, *Ukraine* 47 H6
Sinzig, *Germany* 24 E3
Sio →, *Hungary* 42 D3
Siocon, *Phil.* 61 H5
Siófok, *Hungary* 42 D3
Sion, *Switz.* 25 J3
Sion Mills, *U.K.* 15 B4
Sioux City, *U.S.A.* 112 D6
Sioux Falls, *U.S.A.* 112 D6
Sioux Lookout, *Canada* 102 B1
Sioux Narrows, *Canada* 105 D10
Sipalay, *Phil.* 61 G5
Šipan, *Croatia* 40 D1
Siping, *China* 57 C13
Sipiwesk L., *Canada* 105 B9
Šipovo, *Bos.-H.* 42 F2
Sipra →, *India* 68 H6
Sipura, *Indonesia* 62 E1
Siquia →, *Nic.* 120 D3
Siquijor, *Phil.* 61 G5
Siquirres, *Costa Rica* 120 D3
Şīr Banī Yās, *U.A.E.* 71 E7
Sir Edward Pellew Group, *Australia* 94 B2
Sir Graham Moore Is., *Australia* 92 B4
Sir James MacBrien, Mt., *Canada* 100 B7
Sira →, *Norway* 9 G12
Siracusa, *Italy* 31 E8
Sirajganj, *Bangla.* 69 G13
Sirakoro, *Mali* 82 C3
Şiran, *Turkey* 73 B8
Sirasso, *Ivory C.* 82 D3
Sirathu, *India* 69 G9
Sīrdān, *Iran* 71 B6
Sirdaryo = Syrdarya →, *Kazakstan* 50 E7
Sire, *Ethiopia* 81 F4
Siren, *U.S.A.* 112 C8
Sirer, *Spain* 37 C7
Siret, *Romania* 43 C11
Siret →, *Romania* 43 E12
Sirghāyā, *Syria* 75 B5
Şiria, *Romania* 42 D6
Sirino, Mte., *Italy* 31 B8
Sirmaur, *India* 69 G9
Sírna, *Greece* 39 E8
Şirnak, *Turkey* 73 D10
Sirohi, *India* 68 G5
Sironj, *India* 68 G7
Síros, *Greece* 38 D6
Sirretta Pk., *U.S.A.* 117 K8
Sīrrī, *Iran* 71 E7
Sirsa, *India* 68 E6
Sirsa →, *India* 69 F8
Siruela, *Spain* 35 G5
Sisak, *Croatia* 29 C13
Sisaket, *Thailand* 64 E5
Sisante, *Spain* 33 F2
Sisargas, Is., *Spain* 34 B2
Sishen, *S. Africa* 88 D3
Sishui, *Henan, China* 56 G7
Sishui, *Shandong, China* 57 G9
Sisipuk L., *Canada* 105 B8
Sisophon, *Cambodia* 64 F4
Sisseton, *U.S.A.* 112 C6
Sissonne, *France* 19 C10
Sīstān, *Asia* 71 D9
Sīstān, Daryācheh-ye, *Iran* 71 D9
Sīstān va Balūchestān □, *Iran* 71 E9
Sisteron, *France* 21 D9
Sisters, *U.S.A.* 114 D3
Siswa Bazar, *India* 69 F10
Sitakili, *Mali* 82 C2
Sitamarhi, *India* 69 F11
Sitampiky, *Madag.* 89 B8
Sitapur, *India* 69 F9
Siteki, *Swaziland* 89 D5
Sitges, *Spain* 32 D6
Sithoniá, *Greece* 40 F7
Sitía, *Greece* 36 D8
Sitka, *U.S.A.* 104 B1
Sitoti, *Botswana* 88 C3
Sitra, *Egypt* 80 B2
Sittang Myit →, *Burma* 67 L20
Sittard, *Neths.* 17 C5
Sittensen, *Germany* 24 B5
Sittingbourne, *U.K.* 13 F8
Sittona, *Eritrea* 81 E4
Sittoung = Sittang Myit →, *Burma* 67 L20
Sittwe, *Burma* 67 J18
Situbondo, *Indonesia* 63 G16
Siuna, *Nic.* 120 D3
Siuri, *India* 69 H12
Siutghiol, Lacul, *Romania* 43 F13
Sīvand, *Iran* 71 D7
Sivas, *Turkey* 70 B3
Sivaslı, *Turkey* 39 C11
Siverek, *Turkey* 70 B3
Sivrihisar, *Turkey* 72 C4
Sīwa, *Egypt* 80 B2
Sīwa, El Wâhât es, *Egypt* 80 B2
Siwa Oasis = Sīwa, El Wâhât es, *Egypt* 80 B2
Siwalik Range, *Nepal* 69 F10
Siwan, *India* 69 F11
Siwana, *India* 68 G5
Sixmilebridge, *Ireland* 15 D3
Sixth Cataract, *Sudan* 81 D3
Siyâl, Jazâ'ir, *Egypt* 80 C4
Siyäzän, *Azerbaijan* 49 K9
Siziwang Qi, *China* 56 D6
Sjælland, *Denmark* 11 J5
Sjællands Odde, *Denmark* 11 J5
Sjenica, *Serbia, Yug.* 40 C3
Sjöbo, *Sweden* 11 J7
Sjötofta, *Sweden* 11 G7
Sjötorp, *Sweden* 11 F8
Sjumen = Shumen, *Bulgaria* 41 C10
Sjuntorp, *Sweden* 11 F6
Skadarsko Jezero, *Montenegro, Yug.* 40 D3
Skadovsk, *Ukraine* 47 J7
Skælskør, *Denmark* 11 J5
Skærbæk, *Denmark* 11 J2
Skaftafell, *Iceland* 8 D5
Skagafjörður, *Iceland* 8 D4
Skagastølstindane, *Norway* 9 F12
Skagaströnd, *Iceland* 8 D3
Skagen, *Denmark* 11 G4
Skagern, *Sweden* 10 F8
Skagerrak, *Denmark* 11 G2
Skagit →, *U.S.A.* 116 B4
Skagway, *U.S.A.* 100 C6
Skala-Podilska, *Ukraine* 47 H4
Skala Podolskaya = Skala-Podilska, *Ukraine* 47 H4
Skalat, *Ukraine* 47 H3
Skalbmierz, *Poland* 45 H7
Skälderviken, *Sweden* 11 H6
Skalica, *Slovak Rep.* 27 C10
Skallingen, *Denmark* 11 J2
Skalni Dol = Kamenyak, *Bulgaria* 41 C10
Skanderborg, *Denmark* 11 H3
Skåne, *Sweden* 11 J7
Skåne län □, *Sweden* 11 H7
Skaneateles, *U.S.A.* 111 D8
Skaneateles L., *U.S.A.* 111 D8
Skänninge, *Sweden* 11 F9
Skanör med Falsterbo, *Sweden* 11 J6
Skantzoúra, *Greece* 38 B6
Skara, *Sweden* 11 F7
Skärblacka, *Sweden* 11 F9
Skardu, *Pakistan* 69 B6
Skåre, *Sweden* 10 E7
Skärhamn, *Sweden* 11 G5
Skarszewy, *Poland* 44 D5
Skaryszew, *Poland* 45 G8
Skarżysko-Kamienna, *Poland* 45 G7
Skattkärr, *Sweden* 10 E7
Skattungbyn, *Sweden* 10 C8
Skawina, *Poland* 45 J6
Skebobruk, *Sweden* 10 E12
Skeena →, *Canada* 104 C2
Skeena Mts., *Canada* 104 B3
Skegness, *U.K.* 12 D8
Skeldon, *Guyana* 124 B7
Skeleton Coast Park, *Namibia* 88 C1
Skellefte älv →, *Sweden* 8 D19
Skellefteå, *Sweden* 8 D19
Skelleftehamn, *Sweden* 8 D19
Skender Vakuf, *Bos.-H.* 42 F2
Skerries, The, *U.K.* 12 D3
Skhíza, *Greece* 38 E3
Skhoinoúsa, *Greece* 39 E7
Ski, *Norway* 9 G14
Skíathos, *Greece* 38 B5
Skibbereen, *Ireland* 15 E2
Skiddaw, *U.K.* 12 C4
Skidegate, *Canada* 104 C2
Skídhra, *Greece* 40 F6
Skien, *Norway* 9 G13
Skierniewice, *Poland* 45 G7
Skikda, *Algeria* 78 A7
Skillingaryd, *Sweden* 11 G8
Skillinge, *Sweden* 11 J8
Skilloura, *Cyprus* 36 D12
Skinári, Ákra, *Greece* 38 D2
Skinnskatteberg, *Sweden* 10 E9
Skipton, *U.K.* 12 D5
Skirmish Pt., *Australia* 94 A1
Skiropoúla, *Greece* 38 C6
Skíros, *Greece* 38 C6
Skivarp, *Sweden* 11 J7
Skive, *Denmark* 11 H3
Skjálfandafljót →, *Iceland* 8 D5
Skjálfandi, *Iceland* 8 C5
Skjern, *Denmark* 11 J2
Skoczów, *Poland* 45 J5
Škofja Loka, *Slovenia* 29 B11
Skoghall, *Sweden* 10 E7
Skogstorp, *Sweden* 10 E10
Skoki, *Poland* 45 F4
Skole, *Ukraine* 47 H2
Skópelos, *Greece* 38 B5
Skopí, *Greece* 36 D8
Skopin, *Russia* 46 F10
Skopje, *Macedonia* 40 D5
Skórcz, *Poland* 44 E5
Skørping, *Denmark* 11 H3
Skövde, *Sweden* 11 F7
Skovorodino, *Russia* 51 D13
Skowhegan, *U.S.A.* 109 C11
Skradin, *Croatia* 29 E12
Skrea, *Sweden* 11 H6
Skrunda, *Latvia* 44 B9
Skrwa →, *Poland* 45 F6
Skull, *Ireland* 15 E2
Skultorp, *Sweden* 11 F7
Skultuna, *Sweden* 10 E10
Skunk →, *U.S.A.* 112 E9
Skuodas, *Lithuania* 9 H19
Skurup, *Sweden* 11 J7
Skutskär, *Sweden* 10 D11
Skvyra, *Ukraine* 47 H5
Skwierzyna, *Poland* 45 F2
Skye, *U.K.* 14 D2
Skykomish, *U.S.A.* 114 C3
Skyros = Skíros, *Greece* 38 C6
Skyttorp, *Sweden* 10 D11
Slættaratindur, *Færoe Is.* 8 E9
Slagelse, *Denmark* 11 J5
Slamet, *Indonesia* 63 G13
Slaney →, *Ireland* 15 D5
Slangberge, *S. Africa* 88 E3
Slănic, *Romania* 43 E10
Slano, *Croatia* 40 D1
Slantsy, *Russia* 46 C5
Slaný, *Czech Rep.* 26 A7
Śląskie □, *Poland* 45 H6
Slätbaken, *Sweden* 11 F10
Slate Is., *Canada* 102 C2
Slatina, *Croatia* 42 E2
Slatina, *Romania* 43 F9
Slatina Timiş, *Romania* 42 E7
Slatington, *U.S.A.* 111 F9
Slaton, *U.S.A.* 113 J4
Slave →, *Canada* 104 A6
Slave Coast, *W. Afr.* 83 D5
Slave Lake, *Canada* 104 B6
Slave Pt., *Canada* 104 A5
Slavgorod, *Russia* 50 D8
Slavinja, *Serbia, Yug.* 40 C6
Slavkov u Brna, *Czech Rep.* 27 B9
Slavonija, *Europe* 42 E2
Slavonski Brod, *Croatia* 42 E3
Slavuta, *Ukraine* 47 G4
Slavyanka, *Russia* 54 C5
Slavyanovo, *Bulgaria* 41 C8
Slavyansk = Slovyansk, *Ukraine* 47 H9
Slavyansk-na-Kubani, *Russia* 47 K10
Sława, *Poland* 45 G3
Slawharad, *Belarus* 46 F6
Sławno, *Poland* 44 D3
Sławoborze, *Poland* 44 E2
Sleaford, *U.K.* 12 D7
Sleaford B., *Australia* 95 E2
Sleat, Sd. of, *U.K.* 14 D3
Sleeper Is., *Canada* 101 C11
Sleepy Eye, *U.S.A.* 112 C7
Slemon L., *Canada* 104 A5
Ślesin, *Poland* 45 F5
Slide Mt., *U.S.A.* 111 E10
Slidell, *U.S.A.* 113 K10
Sliema, *Malta* 36 D2
Slieve Aughty, *Ireland* 15 C3
Slieve Bloom, *Ireland* 15 C4
Slieve Donard, *U.K.* 15 B6
Slieve Gamph, *Ireland* 15 B3
Slieve Gullion, *U.K.* 15 B5
Slieve Mish, *Ireland* 15 D2
Slievenamon, *Ireland* 15 D4
Sligeach = Sligo, *Ireland* 15 B3
Sligo, *Ireland* 15 B3
Sligo, *U.S.A.* 110 E5
Sligo □, *Ireland* 15 B3
Sligo B., *Ireland* 15 B3
Slippery Rock, *U.S.A.* 110 E4
Slite, *Sweden* 11 G12
Sliven, *Bulgaria* 41 D10
Slivnitsa, *Bulgaria* 40 D7
Sljeme, *Croatia* 29 C12
Sloan, *U.S.A.* 117 K11
Sloansville, *U.S.A.* 111 D10
Slobozia, *Moldova* 43 D14
Slobozia, *Argeş, Romania* 43 F10
Slobozia, *Ialomiţa, Romania* 43 F12
Slocan, *Canada* 104 D5
Słomniki, *Poland* 45 H7
Slonim, *Belarus* 47 F3
Slough, *U.K.* 13 F7
Slough □, *U.K.* 13 F7
Sloughhouse, *U.S.A.* 116 G5
Slovak Rep. ■, *Europe* 27 C13
Slovakia = Slovak Rep. ■, *Europe* 27 C13
Slovakian Ore Mts. = Slovenské Rudohorie, *Slovak Rep.* 27 C12
Slovenia ■, *Europe* 29 C11
Slovenija = Slovenia ■, *Europe* 29 C11
Slovenj Gradec, *Slovenia* 29 B12
Slovenska Bistrica, *Slovenia* 29 B12
Slovenske Konjice, *Slovenia* 29 B12
Slovenské Rudohorie, *Slovak Rep.* 27 C12
Slovyansk, *Ukraine* 47 H9
Słubice, *Poland* 45 F1
Sluch →, *Ukraine* 47 G4
Sluis, *Neths.* 17 C3
Slŭnchev Bryag, *Bulgaria* 41 D11
Slunj, *Croatia* 29 C12
Słupca, *Poland* 45 F4
Słupia →, *Poland* 44 D3
Słupsk, *Poland* 44 D4
Slurry, *S. Africa* 88 D4
Slutsk, *Belarus* 47 F4
Slyne Hd., *Ireland* 15 C1
Slyudyanka, *Russia* 51 D11
Småland, *Sweden* 11 G9
Smålandsfarvandet, *Denmark* 11 J5
Smålandsstenar, *Sweden* 11 G7
Smalltree L., *Canada* 105 A8
Smallwood Res., *Canada* 103 B7
Smarhon, *Belarus* 46 E4
Smarje, *Slovenia* 29 B12
Smartt Syndicate Dam, *S. Africa* 88 E3
Smartville, *U.S.A.* 116 F5
Smeaton, *Canada* 105 C8
Smedby, *Sweden* 11 H10
Smederevo, *Serbia, Yug.* 40 B4
Smederevska Palanka, *Serbia, Yug.* 40 B4
Smedjebacken, *Sweden* 10 D9
Smela = Smila, *Ukraine* 47 H6
Smerwick Harbour, *Ireland* 15 D1
Smethport, *U.S.A.* 110 E6
Smidovich, *Russia* 51 E14
Śmigiel, *Poland* 45 F3
Smila, *Ukraine* 47 H6
Smilyan, *Bulgaria* 41 E8
Smith, *Canada* 104 B6
Smith Center, *U.S.A.* 112 F5
Smith Sund, *Greenland* 4 B4
Smithburne →, *Australia* 94 B3
Smithers, *Canada* 104 C3
Smithfield, *S. Africa* 89 E4
Smithfield, *N.C., U.S.A.* 109 H6
Smithfield, *Utah, U.S.A.* 114 F8
Smiths Falls, *Canada* 102 D4
Smithton, *Australia* 94 G4
Smithville, *Canada* 110 C5
Smithville, *U.S.A.* 113 K6
Smoky →, *Canada* 104 B5
Smoky Bay, *Australia* 95 E1
Smoky Hill →, *U.S.A.* 112 F6
Smoky Hills, *U.S.A.* 112 F5
Smoky Lake, *Canada* 104 C6
Smøla, *Norway* 8 E13
Smolensk, *Russia* 46 E7
Smolikas, Óros, *Greece* 40 F4
Smolník, *Slovak Rep.* 27 C13
Smolyan, *Bulgaria* 41 E8
Smooth Rock Falls, *Canada* 102 C3
Smoothstone L., *Canada* 105 C7
Smorgon = Smarhon, *Belarus* 46 E4
Smulţi, *Romania* 43 E12
Smyadovo, *Bulgaria* 41 C11
Smygehamn, *Sweden* 11 J7
Smyrna = İzmir, *Turkey* 39 C9
Smyrna, *U.S.A.* 108 F8
Snæfell, *Iceland* 8 D6
Snaefell, *U.K.* 12 C3
Snæfellsjökull, *Iceland* 8 D2
Snake →, *U.S.A.* 114 C4
Snake I., *Australia* 95 F4
Snake Range, *U.S.A.* 114 G6
Snake River Plain, *U.S.A.* 114 E7
Snasahögarna, *Sweden* 10 A6
Snåsavatnet, *Norway* 8 D14
Snedsted, *Denmark* 11 H2
Sneek, *Neths.* 17 A5
Sneeuberge, *S. Africa* 88 E3
Snejbjerg, *Denmark* 11 H2
Snelling, *U.S.A.* 116 H6
Snezhnoye, *Ukraine* 47 J10
Snežnik, *Slovenia* 29 C11
Śniadowo, *Poland* 45 E8
Sniardwy, Jezioro, *Poland* 44 E8
Śnieżka, *Europe* 26 A8
Snigirevka = Snihurivka, *Ukraine* 47 J7
Snihurivka, *Ukraine* 47 J7
Snina, *Slovak Rep.* 27 C15
Snizort, L., *U.K.* 14 D2
Snøhetta, *Norway* 9 E13
Snohomish, *U.S.A.* 116 C4
Snoul, *Cambodia* 65 F6
Snow Hill, *U.S.A.* 108 F8
Snow Lake, *Canada* 105 C8
Snow Mt., *Calif., U.S.A.* 116 F4
Snow Mt., *Maine, U.S.A.* 111 A14
Snow Shoe, *U.S.A.* 110 E7
Snowbird L., *Canada* 105 A8
Snowdon, *U.K.* 12 D3
Snowdrift →, *Canada* 105 A6
Snowflake, *U.S.A.* 115 J8
Snowshoe Pk., *U.S.A.* 114 B6
Snowtown, *Australia* 95 E2
Snowville, *U.S.A.* 114 F7
Snowy →, *Australia* 95 F4
Snowy Mt., *U.S.A.* 111 C10
Snowy Mts., *Australia* 95 F4
Snug Corner, *Bahamas* 121 B5
Snyatyn, *Ukraine* 47 H3
Snyder, *Okla., U.S.A.* 113 H5
Snyder, *Tex., U.S.A.* 113 J4
Soahanina, *Madag.* 89 B7
Soalala, *Madag.* 89 B8
Soaloka, *Madag.* 89 B8
Soamanonga, *Madag.* 89 C7
Soan →, *Pakistan* 68 C4
Soanierana-Ivongo, *Madag.* 89 B8
Soanindraniny, *Madag.* 89 B8
Şoarş, *Romania* 43 E9
Soavina, *Madag.* 89 C8
Soavinandriana, *Madag.* 89 B8
Soba, *Nigeria* 83 C6
Sobat, Nahr →, *Sudan* 81 F3
Soběslav, *Czech Rep.* 26 B7
Sobhapur, *India* 68 H8
Sobinka, *Russia* 46 E11
Sobótka, *Poland* 45 H3
Sobra, *Croatia* 29 F14
Sobradinho, Reprêsa de, *Brazil* 125 E10
Sobral, *Brazil* 125 D10
Sobrance, *Slovak Rep.* 27 C15
Sobreira Formosa, *Portugal* 34 F3
Soc Giang, *Vietnam* 58 F6
Soc Trang, *Vietnam* 65 H5
Soča →, *Europe* 26 E6
Socastee, *U.S.A.* 109 J6
Sochaczew, *Poland* 45 F7
Soch'e = Shache, *China* 60 C2
Sochi, *Russia* 49 J4
Société, Is. de la, *Pac. Oc.* 97 J12
Society Is. = Société, Is. de la, *Pac. Oc.* 97 J12
Socompa, Portezuelo de, *Chile* 126 A2
Socorro, *N. Mex., U.S.A.* 115 J10
Socorro, *Tex., U.S.A.* 115 L10
Socorro, I., *Mexico* 118 D2
Socotra, *Yemen* 74 E5
Socovos, *Spain* 33 G3
Socuéllamos, *Spain* 33 F2
Soda L., *U.S.A.* 115 J5
Soda Plains, *India* 69 B8
Soda Springs, *U.S.A.* 114 E8
Sodankylä, *Finland* 8 C22
Soddy-Daisy, *U.S.A.* 109 H3
Söderala, *Sweden* 10 C10
Söderbärke, *Sweden* 10 D9
Söderfors, *Sweden* 10 D11
Söderhamn, *Sweden* 10 C11
Söderköping, *Sweden* 11 F10
Södermanland, *Sweden* 9 G17
Södermanlands län □, *Sweden* 10 E10
Södertälje, *Sweden* 10 E11
Sodiri, *Sudan* 81 E2
Sodo, *Ethiopia* 81 F4
Södra Dellen, *Sweden* 10 C10
Södra Finnskoga, *Sweden* 10 D6
Södra Sandby, *Sweden* 11 J7
Södra Ulvön, *Sweden* 10 B12
Södra Vi, *Sweden* 11 G9
Sodražica, *Slovenia* 29 C11
Sodus, *U.S.A.* 110 C7
Soekmekaar, *S. Africa* 89 C4
Soest, *Germany* 24 D4
Soest, *Neths.* 17 B5
Sofádhes, *Greece* 38 B4
Sofala □, *Mozam.* 89 B5
Sofara, *Mali* 82 C4
Sofia = Sofiya, *Bulgaria* 40 D7
Sofia →, *Madag.* 89 B8
Sofievka, *Ukraine* 47 H7
Sofikón, *Greece* 38 D5
Sofiya, *Bulgaria* 40 D7
Sofiya □, *Bulgaria* 40 D7
Sōfu-Gan, *Japan* 55 K10
Sogakofe, *Ghana* 83 D5
Sogamoso, *Colombia* 124 B4
Sogār, *Iran* 71 E8
Sögel, *Germany* 24 C3
Sogndalsfjøra, *Norway* 9 F12
Søgne, *Norway* 9 G12
Sognefjorden, *Norway* 9 F11
Söğüt, *Bilecik, Turkey* 39 A12
Söğüt, *Burdur, Turkey* 39 D11
Söğüt Dağı, *Turkey* 39 D11
Söğütköy, *Turkey* 39 E10
Sŏgwipo, *S. Korea* 57 H14
Soh, *Iran* 71 C6
Sohâg, *Egypt* 80 B3
Sohagpur, *India* 68 H8
Sŏhori, *N. Korea* 57 D15
Soignies, *Belgium* 17 D4
Soin, *Burkina Faso* 82 C4
Soira, *Eritrea* 81 E4
Soissons, *France* 19 C10
Sōja, *Japan* 55 G6
Sojat, *India* 68 G5
Sok →, *Russia* 48 D10
Sokal, *Ukraine* 47 G3
Söke, *Turkey* 39 D9
Sokelo, *Dem. Rep. of the Congo* 87 D1
Sokhós, *Greece* 40 F7
Sokhumi, *Georgia* 49 J5
Soko Banja, *Serbia, Yug.* 40 C5
Sokodé, *Togo* 83 D5
Sokol, *Russia* 46 C11
Sokolac, *Bos.-H.* 42 G3
Sokółka, *Poland* 44 E10
Sokolo, *Mali* 82 C3
Sokolo, *Mali* 82 C3
Sokolov, *Czech Rep.* 26 A5
Sokołów Małpolski, *Poland* 45 H9
Sokołów Podlaski, *Poland* 45 F9
Sokoły, *Poland* 45 F9
Sokoto, *Nigeria* 83 C6
Sokoto □, *Nigeria* 83 C6
Sokoto →, *Nigeria* 83 C5
Sol Iletsk, *Russia* 50 D6
Sola →, *Poland* 45 H6
Solai, *Kenya* 86 B4
Solan, *India* 68 D7
Solano, *Phil.* 61 C4
Solapur, *India* 66 L9
Solca, *Romania* 43 C10
Solda Gölü, *Turkey* 39 D11
Soldăneşti, *Moldova* 43 C13
Soldotna, *U.S.A.* 100 B4
Soléa □, *Cyprus* 36 D12
Solec Kujawski, *Poland* 45 E5
Soledad, *Colombia* 124 A4
Soledad, *U.S.A.* 116 J5
Soledad, *Venezuela* 124 B6
Solent, The, *U.K.* 13 G6
Solenzara, *France* 21 G13
Solesmes, *France* 19 B10
Solfonn, *Norway* 9 F12

Solhan, *Turkey* 70 B4
Soligorsk = Salihorsk, *Belarus* 47 F4
Solihull, *U.K.* 13 E6
Solikamsk, *Russia* 50 D6
Solila, *Madag.* 89 C8
Solimões = Amazonas →, *S. Amer.* 122 D5
Solin, *Croatia* 29 E13
Solingen, *Germany* 24 D3
Sollebrunn, *Sweden* 11 F6
Sollefteå, *Sweden* 10 A11
Sollentuna, *Sweden* 10 E11
Sóller, *Spain* 37 B9
Sollerön, *Sweden* 10 D8
Solling, *Germany* 24 D5
Solnechnogorsk, *Russia* 46 D9
Solo →, *Indonesia* 63 G15
Solofra, *Italy* 31 B7
Sologne, *France* 19 E8
Solok, *Indonesia* 62 E2
Sololá, *Guatemala* 120 D1
Solomon, N. Fork →, *U.S.A.* 112 F5
Solomon, S. Fork →, *U.S.A.* 112 F5
Solomon Is. ■, *Pac. Oc.* 96 H7
Solon, *China* 60 B7
Solon Springs, *U.S.A.* 112 B9
Solor, *Indonesia* 63 F6
Solotcha, *Russia* 46 E10
Solothurn, *Switz.* 25 H3
Solothurn □, *Switz.* 25 H3
Solsona, *Spain* 32 C6
Solt, *Hungary* 42 D4
Šolta, *Croatia* 29 E13
Solṭānābād, *Khorāsān, Iran* 71 C8
Solṭānābād, *Khorāsān, Iran* 71 B8
Soltau, *Germany* 24 C5
Soltsy, *Russia* 46 C6
Solunska Glava, *Macedonia* 40 E5
Solvang, *U.S.A.* 117 L6
Solvay, *U.S.A.* 111 C8
Sölvesborg, *Sweden* 11 H8
Solway Firth, *U.K.* 12 C4
Solwezi, *Zambia* 87 E2
Sōma, *Japan* 54 F10
Soma, *Turkey* 39 B9
Somabhula, *Zimbabwe* 89 B4
Somali Pen., *Africa* 76 F8
Somali Rep. ■, *Africa* 74 F4
Somalia = Somali Rep. ■, *Africa* 74 F4
Sombernon, *France* 19 E11
Sombor, *Serbia, Yug.* 42 E4
Sombra, *Canada* 110 D2
Sombrerete, *Mexico* 118 C4
Sombrero, *Anguilla* 121 C7
Şomcuta Mare, *Romania* 43 C8
Somdari, *India* 68 G5
Somers, *U.S.A.* 114 B6
Somerset, *Ky., U.S.A.* 108 G3
Somerset, *Mass., U.S.A.* 111 E13
Somerset, *Pa., U.S.A.* 110 F5
Somerset □, *U.K.* 13 F5
Somerset East, *S. Africa* 88 E4
Somerset I., *Canada* 100 A10
Somerset West, *S. Africa* 88 E2
Somersworth, *U.S.A.* 111 C14
Somerton, *U.S.A.* 115 K6
Somerville, *U.S.A.* 111 F10
Someş →, *Romania* 42 C7
Someşul Mare →, *Romania* 43 C8
Somme □, *France* 19 C9
Somme →, *France* 19 B8
Somme, B. de la, *France* 18 B8
Sommen, *Jönköping, Sweden* 11 F8
Sommen, *Östergötland, Sweden* 11 F9
Sommepy-Tahure, *France* 19 C11
Sömmerda, *Germany* 24 D7
Sommesous, *France* 19 D11
Sommières, *France* 21 E8
Somnath, *India* 68 J4
Somogy □, *Hungary* 42 D2
Somogyszob, *Hungary* 42 D2
Somoto, *Nic.* 120 D2
Sompolno, *Poland* 45 F5
Somport, Puerto de, *Spain* 32 C4
Son →, *India* 69 G11
Son Ha, *Vietnam* 64 E7
Son Hoa, *Vietnam* 64 F7
Son La, *Vietnam* 58 G4
Son Serra, *Spain* 37 B10
Son Servera, *Spain* 32 F8
Son Tay, *Vietnam* 58 G5
Soná, *Panama* 120 E3
Sonamarg, *India* 69 B6
Sonamukhi, *India* 69 H12
Sonar →, *India* 69 G8
Sŏnch'ŏn, *N. Korea* 57 E13
Sondags →, *S. Africa* 88 E4
Sondalo, *Italy* 28 B7
Sondar, *India* 69 C6
Sønder Felding, *Denmark* 11 J2
Sønder Omme, *Denmark* 11 J2
Sønderborg, *Denmark* 11 K3
Sønderjyllands Amtskommune □, *Denmark* 11 J3
Sondershausen, *Germany* 24 D6
Sóndrio, *Italy* 28 B6
Sone, *Mozam.* 87 F3
Sonepur, *India* 67 J13
Song, *Nigeria* 83 D7
Song, *Thailand* 64 C3
Song Cau, *Vietnam* 64 F7
Song Xian, *China* 56 G7
Songch'ŏn, *N. Korea* 57 E14
Songea, *Tanzania* 87 E4
Songeons, *France* 19 C8
Songhua Hu, *China* 57 C14
Songhua Jiang →, *China* 60 B8
Songjiang, *China* 59 B13
Songjin, *N. Korea* 57 D15
Songjŏng-ni, *S. Korea* 57 G14
Songkan, *China* 58 C6
Songkhla, *Thailand* 65 J3
Songming, *China* 58 E4
Songnim, *N. Korea* 57 E13
Songo, *Mozam.* 85 H6
Songo, *Sudan* 79 G10
Songpan, *China* 58 A4
Songtao, *China* 58 C7
Songwe, *Dem. Rep. of the Congo* 86 C2
Songwe →, *Africa* 87 D3
Songxi, *China* 59 D12
Songzi, *China* 59 B8
Sonhat, *India* 69 H10
Sonid Youqi, *China* 56 C7
Sonipat, *India* 68 E7
Sonkach, *India* 68 H7
Sonkovo, *Russia* 46 D9
Sonmiani, *Pakistan* 68 G2
Sonmiani B., *Pakistan* 68 G2
Sonnino, *Italy* 30 A6
Sono →, *Brazil* 125 E9
Sonoma, *U.S.A.* 116 G4
Sonora, *Calif., U.S.A.* 116 H6
Sonora, *Tex., U.S.A.* 113 K4
Sonora □, *Mexico* 118 B2
Sonora →, *Mexico* 118 B2
Sonoran Desert, *U.S.A.* 117 L12
Sonoyta, *Mexico* 118 A2
Sonqor, *Iran* 73 E12
Sŏnsan, *S. Korea* 57 F15
Sonseca, *Spain* 35 F7
Sonsonate, *El Salv.* 120 D2
Sonsorol Is., *Pac. Oc.* 63 C8
Sonstorp, *Sweden* 11 F9
Sonthofen, *Germany* 25 H6
Soochow = Suzhou, *China* 59 B13
Sooke, *Canada* 116 B3
Sop Hao, *Laos* 58 G5
Sop Prap, *Thailand* 64 D2
Sopelana, *Spain* 32 B2
Sopi, *Indonesia* 63 D7
Sopo, Nahr →, *Sudan* 81 F2
Sopot, *Bulgaria* 41 D8
Sopot, *Poland* 44 D5
Sopot, *Serbia, Yug.* 40 B4
Sopotnica, *Macedonia* 40 E5
Sopron, *Hungary* 42 C1
Sopur, *India* 69 B6
Sør-Rondane, *Antarctica* 5 D4
Sora, *Italy* 29 G10
Sorah, *Pakistan* 68 F3
Söråker, *Sweden* 10 B11
Sorano, *Italy* 29 F8
Soraon, *India* 69 G9
Sorbas, *Spain* 33 H2
Sörbygden, *Sweden* 10 B10
Sore, *France* 20 D3
Sorel, *Canada* 102 C5
Soresina, *Italy* 28 C6
Sörforsa, *Sweden* 10 C10
Sórgono, *Italy* 30 B2
Sorgues, *France* 21 D8
Sorgun, *Turkey* 72 C6
Soria, *Spain* 32 D2
Soria □, *Spain* 32 D2
Soriano, *Uruguay* 126 C4
Soriano nel Cimino, *Italy* 29 F9
Sorkh, Kuh-e, *Iran* 71 C8
Sorø, *Denmark* 11 J5
Soro, *Guinea* 82 C3
Soroca, *Moldova* 43 B13
Sorocaba, *Brazil* 127 A6
Soroki = Soroca, *Moldova* 43 B13
Sorol Atoll, *Pac. Oc.* 63 C10
Sorong, *Indonesia* 63 E8
Soroní, *Greece* 36 C10
Soroti, *Uganda* 86 B3
Sørøya, *Norway* 8 A20
Sørøysundet, *Norway* 8 A20
Sorraia →, *Portugal* 35 G2
Sorrell, *Australia* 94 G4
Sorrento, *Italy* 31 B7
Sorsele, *Sweden* 8 D17
Sörsjön, *Sweden* 10 C7
Sorso, *Italy* 30 B1
Sorsogon, *Phil.* 61 E6
Sortavala, *Russia* 46 B6
Sortino, *Italy* 31 E8
Sortland, *Norway* 8 B16
Sorvizhi, *Russia* 48 B9
Sos = Sos del Rey Católico, *Spain* 32 C3
Sos del Rey Católico, *Spain* 32 C3
Sŏsan, *S. Korea* 57 F14
Soscumica, L., *Canada* 102 B4
Sösdala, *Sweden* 11 H7
Sosna →, *Russia* 47 F10
Sosnovka, *Kirov, Russia* 48 B10
Sosnovka, *Tambov, Russia* 48 D5
Sosnovyy Bor, *Russia* 46 C5
Sosnowiec, *Poland* 45 H6
Sospel, *France* 21 E11
Sossus Vlei, *Namibia* 88 C2
Šoštanj, *Slovenia* 29 B12
Sŏsura, *N. Korea* 57 C16
Sot →, *India* 69 F8
Sotkamo, *Finland* 8 D23
Soto del Barco, *Spain* 34 B4
Soto la Marina →, *Mexico* 119 C5
Soto y Amío, *Spain* 34 C5
Sotrondio, *Spain* 34 B5
Sotuta, *Mexico* 119 C7
Souanké, *Congo* 84 D2
Soubré, *Ivory C.* 82 D3
Souderton, *U.S.A.* 111 F9
Soúdha, *Greece* 36 D6
Soúdhas, Kólpos, *Greece* 36 D6
Souflíon, *Greece* 41 E10
Soufrière, *St. Lucia* 121 D7
Souillac, *France* 20 D5
Souilly, *France* 19 C12
Soukhouma, *Laos* 64 E5
Sŏul, *S. Korea* 57 F14
Soulac-sur-Mer, *France* 20 C2
Soulougou, *Burkina Faso* 83 C5
Soultz-sous-Forêts, *France* 19 D14
Sound, The = Øresund, *Europe* 11 J6
Sound, The, *U.K.* 13 G3
Soúnion, Ákra, *Greece* 38 D6
Sources, Mt. aux, *Lesotho* 89 D4
Soure, *Brazil* 125 D9
Soure, *Portugal* 34 E2
Souris, *Man., Canada* 105 D8
Souris, *P.E.I., Canada* 103 C7
Souris →, *Canada* 112 A5
Sourou →, *Africa* 82 C4
Soúrpi, *Greece* 38 B4
Sousa, *Brazil* 125 E11
Sousel, *Portugal* 35 G3
Sousse, *Tunisia* 79 A8
Soustons, *France* 20 E2
Sout →, *S. Africa* 88 E2
South Africa ■, *Africa* 88 E3
South America 122 E5
South Atlantic Ocean 122 H7
South Aulatsivik I., *Canada* 103 A7
South Australia □, *Australia* 95 E2
South Ayrshire □, *U.K.* 14 F4
South Baldy, *U.S.A.* 115 J10
South Bass I., *U.S.A.* 110 E2
South Bend, *Ind., U.S.A.* 108 E2
South Bend, *Wash., U.S.A.* 116 D3
South Boston, *U.S.A.* 109 G6
South Branch, *Canada* 103 C8
South Brook, *Canada* 103 C8
South Carolina □, *U.S.A.* 109 J5
South Charleston, *U.S.A.* 108 F5
South China Sea, *Asia* 62 C4
South Dakota □, *U.S.A.* 112 C5
South Deerfield, *U.S.A.* 111 D12
South Downs, *U.K.* 13 G7
South East C., *Australia* 94 G4
South East Is., *Australia* 93 F3
South Esk →, *U.K.* 14 E6
South Foreland, *U.K.* 13 F9
South Fork American →, *U.S.A.* 116 G5
South Fork Feather →, *U.S.A.* 116 F5
South Fork Grand →, *U.S.A.* 112 C3
South Fork Republican →, *U.S.A.* 112 E4
South Georgia, *Antarctica* 122 J7
South Gloucestershire □, *U.K.* 13 F5
South Hadley, *U.S.A.* 111 D12
South Haven, *U.S.A.* 108 D2
South Henik, L., *Canada* 105 A9
South Honshu Ridge, *Pac. Oc.* 96 E6
South Horr, *Kenya* 86 B4
South I., *Kenya* 86 B4
South I., *N.Z.* 91 L3
South Indian Lake, *Canada* 105 B9
South Invercargill, *N.Z.* 91 M2
South Knife →, *Canada* 105 B10
South Koel →, *India* 69 H11
South Korea ■, *Asia* 57 G15
South Lake Tahoe, *U.S.A.* 116 G6
South Lanarkshire □, *U.K.* 14 F5
South Loup →, *U.S.A.* 112 E5
South Magnetic Pole, *Antarctica* 5 C9
South Milwaukee, *U.S.A.* 108 D2
South Molton, *U.K.* 13 F4
South Moose L., *Canada* 105 C8
South Nahanni →, *Canada* 104 A4
South Nation →, *Canada* 111 A9
South Natuna Is. = Natuna Selatan, Kepulauan, *Indonesia* 65 L7
South Negril Pt., *Jamaica* 120 C4
South Orkney Is., *Antarctica* 5 C18
South Ossetia □, *Georgia* 49 J7
South Pagai, I. = Pagai Selatan, Pulau, *Indonesia* 62 E2
South Paris, *U.S.A.* 111 B14
South Pittsburg, *U.S.A.* 109 H3
South Platte →, *U.S.A.* 112 E4
South Pole, *Antarctica* 5 E
South Porcupine, *Canada* 102 C3
South Portland, *U.S.A.* 109 D10
South Pt., *U.S.A.* 110 B1
South River, *Canada* 102 C4
South River, *U.S.A.* 111 F10
South Ronaldsay, *U.K.* 14 C6
South Sandwich Is., *Antarctica* 5 B1
South Saskatchewan →, *Canada* 105 C7
South Seal →, *Canada* 105 B9
South Shetland Is., *Antarctica* 5 C18
South Shields, *U.K.* 12 C6
South Sioux City, *U.S.A.* 112 D6
South Taranaki Bight, *N.Z.* 91 H5
South Thompson →, *Canada* 104 C4
South Twin I., *Canada* 102 B4
South Tyne →, *U.K.* 12 C5
South Uist, *U.K.* 14 D1
South West Africa = Namibia ■, *Africa* 88 C2
South West C., *Australia* 94 G4
South Williamsport, *U.S.A.* 110 E8
South Yorkshire □, *U.K.* 12 D6
Southampton, *Canada* 102 D3
Southampton, *U.K.* 13 G6
Southampton, *U.S.A.* 111 F12
Southampton □, *U.K.* 13 G6
Southampton I., *Canada* 101 B11
Southaven, *U.S.A.* 113 H9
Southbank, *Canada* 104 C3
Southbridge, *N.Z.* 91 K4
Southbridge, *U.S.A.* 111 D12
Southend, *Canada* 105 B8
Southend-on-Sea, *U.K.* 13 F8
Southend-on-Sea □, *U.K.* 13 F8
Southern □, *Malawi* 87 F4
Southern □, *S. Leone* 82 D2
Southern □, *Zambia* 87 F2
Southern Alps, *N.Z.* 91 K3
Southern Cross, *Australia* 93 F2
Southern Indian L., *Canada* 105 B9
Southern Ocean, *Antarctica* 5 C6
Southern Pines, *U.S.A.* 109 H6
Southern Uplands, *U.K.* 14 F5
Southington, *U.S.A.* 111 E12
Southland □, *N.Z.* 91 L1
Southold, *U.S.A.* 111 E12
Southport, *Australia* 95 D5
Southport, *U.K.* 12 D4
Southport, *Fla., U.S.A.* 109 K3
Southport, *N.Y., U.S.A.* 110 D8
Southwest C., *N.Z.* 91 M1
Southwold, *U.K.* 13 E9
Soutpansberg, *S. Africa* 89 C4
Souvigny, *France* 19 F10
Sovata, *Romania* 43 D10
Soverato, *Italy* 31 D9
Sovetsk, *Kaliningd., Russia* 9 J19
Sovetsk, *Kirov, Russia* 48 B9
Sovetskaya Gavan = Vanino, *Russia* 51 E15
Sovicille, *Italy* 29 E8
Soweto, *S. Africa* 89 D4
Sōya-Kaikyō = La Perouse Str., *Asia* 54 B11
Sōya-Misaki, *Japan* 54 B10
Soyaux, *France* 20 C4
Sozh →, *Belarus* 47 F6
Sozopol, *Bulgaria* 41 D11
Spa, *Belgium* 17 D5
Spain ■, *Europe* 7 H5
Spalding, *Australia* 95 E2
Spalding, *U.K.* 12 E7
Spangler, *U.S.A.* 110 F6
Spanish, *Canada* 102 C3
Spanish Fork, *U.S.A.* 114 F8
Spanish Town, *Jamaica* 120 C4
Sparks, *U.S.A.* 116 F7
Sparreholm, *Sweden* 10 E10
Sparta = Spárti, *Greece* 38 D4
Sparta, *Mich., U.S.A.* 108 D3
Sparta, *N.J., U.S.A.* 111 E10
Sparta, *Wis., U.S.A.* 112 D9
Spartanburg, *U.S.A.* 109 H5
Spartansburg, *U.S.A.* 110 E5
Spárti, *Greece* 38 D4
Spartivento, C., *Calabria, Italy* 31 E9
Spartivento, C., *Sard., Italy* 30 D1
Spas-Demensk, *Russia* 46 E7
Spas-Klepiki, *Russia* 46 E11
Spassk Dalniy, *Russia* 51 E14
Spassk-Ryazanskiy, *Russia* 46 E11
Spátha, Ákra, *Greece* 36 D5
Spatsizi →, *Canada* 104 B3
Spatsizi Plateau Wilderness Park, *Canada* 104 B3
Spean →, *U.K.* 14 E4
Spearfish, *U.S.A.* 112 C3
Spearman, *U.S.A.* 113 G4
Speculator, *U.S.A.* 111 C10
Speia, *Moldova* 43 D14
Speightstown, *Barbados* 121 D8
Speke Gulf, *Tanzania* 86 C3
Spello, *Italy* 29 F9
Spencer, *Idaho, U.S.A.* 114 D7
Spencer, *Iowa, U.S.A.* 112 D7
Spencer, *N.Y., U.S.A.* 111 D8
Spencer, *Nebr., U.S.A.* 112 D5
Spencer, C., *Australia* 95 F2
Spencer B., *Namibia* 88 D1
Spencer G., *Australia* 95 E2
Spencerville, *Canada* 111 B9
Spences Bridge, *Canada* 104 C4
Spennymoor, *U.K.* 12 C6
Spenser Mts., *N.Z.* 91 K4
Spentrup, *Denmark* 11 H4
Sperkhiós →, *Greece* 38 C4
Sperrin Mts., *U.K.* 15 B5
Spessart, *Germany* 25 F5
Spétsai, *Greece* 38 D5
Spey →, *U.K.* 14 D5
Speyer, *Germany* 25 F4
Spezand, *Pakistan* 68 E2
Spezzano Albanese, *Italy* 31 C9
Spiekeroog, *Germany* 24 B3
Spiez, *Switz.* 25 J3
Spíli, *Greece* 36 D6
Spilimbergo, *Italy* 29 B9
Spīn Būldak, *Afghan.* 68 D2
Spinalónga, *Greece* 36 D7
Spinazzola, *Italy* 31 B9
Spineni, *Romania* 43 F9
Spirit Lake, *U.S.A.* 116 D4
Spirit River, *Canada* 104 B5
Spiritwood, *Canada* 105 C7
Spišská Nová Ves, *Slovak Rep.* 27 C13
Spišské Podhradie, *Slovak Rep.* 27 B13
Spital, *Austria* 26 D7
Spithead, *U.K.* 13 G6
Spittal an der Drau, *Austria* 26 E6
Spitzbergen = Svalbard, *Arctic* 4 B8
Spjelkavik, *Norway* 9 E12
Split, *Croatia* 29 E13
Split L., *Canada* 105 B9
Split Lake, *Canada* 105 B9
Splitski Kanal, *Croatia* 29 E13
Splügenpass, *Switz.* 25 J5
Spofford, *U.S.A.* 113 L4
Spokane, *U.S.A.* 114 C5
Spoleto, *Italy* 29 F9
Spooner, *U.S.A.* 112 C9
Sporyy Navolok, Mys, *Russia* 50 B7
Sprague, *U.S.A.* 114 C5
Spratly I., *S. China Sea* 62 C4
Spratly Is., *S. China Sea* 62 C4
Spray, *U.S.A.* 114 D4
Spreča →, *Bos.-H.* 42 F3
Spree →, *Germany* 24 C9
Spreewald, *Germany* 24 D9
Spremberg, *Germany* 24 D10
Sprengisandur, *Iceland* 8 D5
Spring City, *U.S.A.* 111 F9
Spring Creek, *U.S.A.* 114 F6
Spring Garden, *U.S.A.* 116 F6
Spring Hill, *U.S.A.* 109 L4
Spring Mts., *U.S.A.* 115 H6
Spring Valley, *U.S.A.* 117 N10
Springbok, *S. Africa* 88 D2
Springboro, *U.S.A.* 110 E4
Springdale, *Canada* 103 C8
Springdale, *U.S.A.* 113 G7
Springe, *Germany* 24 C5
Springer, *U.S.A.* 113 G2
Springerville, *U.S.A.* 115 J9
Springfield, *Canada* 110 D4
Springfield, *N.Z.* 91 K3
Springfield, *Colo., U.S.A.* 113 G3
Springfield, *Ill., U.S.A.* 112 F10
Springfield, *Mass., U.S.A.* 111 D12
Springfield, *Mo., U.S.A.* 113 G8
Springfield, *Ohio, U.S.A.* 108 F4
Springfield, *Oreg., U.S.A.* 114 D2
Springfield, *Tenn., U.S.A.* 109 G2
Springfield, *Vt., U.S.A.* 111 C12
Springfontein, *S. Africa* 88 E4
Springhill, *Canada* 103 C7
Springhill, *U.S.A.* 113 J8
Springhouse, *Canada* 104 C4
Springs, *S. Africa* 89 D4
Springsure, *Australia* 94 C4
Springvale, *U.S.A.* 111 C14
Springville, *Calif., U.S.A.* 116 J8
Springville, *N.Y., U.S.A.* 110 D6
Springville, *Utah, U.S.A.* 114 F8
Springwater, *U.S.A.* 110 D7
Spruce-Creek, *U.S.A.* 110 F6
Spruce Mt., *U.S.A.* 111 B12
Spur, *U.S.A.* 113 J4
Spurn Hd., *U.K.* 12 D8
Spuž, *Montenegro, Yug.* 40 D3
Spuzzum, *Canada* 104 D4
Squam L., *U.S.A.* 111 C13
Squamish, *Canada* 104 D4
Square Islands, *Canada* 103 B8
Squillace, G. di, *Italy* 31 D9
Squinzano, *Italy* 31 B11
Squires, Mt., *Australia* 93 E4
Srbac, *Bos.-H.* 42 E2
Srbica, *Kosovo, Yug.* 40 D4
Srbija = Serbia □, *Yugoslavia* 40 C5
Srbobran, *Serbia, Yug.* 42 E4
Sre Ambel, *Cambodia* 65 G4
Sre Khtum, *Cambodia* 65 F6
Sre Umbell = Sre Ambel, *Cambodia* 65 G4
Srebrenica, *Bos.-H.* 42 F4
Sredinny Ra. = Sredinnyy Khrebet, *Russia* 51 D16
Sredinnyy Khrebet, *Russia* 51 D16
Središče, *Slovenia* 29 B13
Sredna Gora, *Bulgaria* 41 D8
Srednekolymsk, *Russia* 51 C16
Sredni Rodopi, *Bulgaria* 41 E8
Srednogorie, *Bulgaria* 41 D8
Śrem, *Poland* 45 F4
Sremska Mitrovica, *Serbia, Yug.* 42 F4
Sremski Karlovci, *Serbia, Yug.* 42 E4
Srepok →, *Cambodia* 64 F6
Sretensk, *Russia* 51 D12
Sri Lanka ■, *Asia* 66 R12
Srikakulam, *India* 67 K13
Srinagar, *India* 69 B6
Środa Śląska, *Poland* 45 G3
Środa Wielkopolski, *Poland* 45 F4
Srpska Crnja, *Serbia, Yug.* 42 E5
Srpski Itebej, *Serbia, Yug.* 42 E5
Staaten →, *Australia* 94 B3
Staberhuk, *Germany* 24 A7
Stade, *Germany* 24 B5
Stadskanaal, *Neths.* 17 A6
Stadtallendorf, *Germany* 24 E5
Stadthagen, *Germany* 24 C5
Stadtlohn, *Germany* 24 D2
Stadtroda, *Germany* 24 E7
Staffa, *U.K.* 14 E2
Staffanstorp, *Sweden* 11 J7
Stafford, *U.K.* 12 E5
Stafford, *U.S.A.* 113 G5
Stafford Springs, *U.S.A.* 111 E12
Staffordshire □, *U.K.* 12 E5
Stagnone, *Italy* 30 E5
Staines, *U.K.* 13 F7
Stainz, *Austria* 26 E8
Stakhanov, *Ukraine* 47 H10
Stalać, *Serbia, Yug.* 40 C5
Stalingrad = Volgograd, *Russia* 49 F7
Staliniri = Tskhinvali, *Georgia* 49 J7
Stalino = Donetsk, *Ukraine* 47 J9
Stalinogorsk = Novomoskovsk, *Russia* 46 E10
Stalis, *Greece* 36 D7

Stallarholmen, Sweden 10 E11
Ställdalen, Sweden 10 E8
Stalowa Wola, Poland 45 H9
Stalybridge, U.K. 12 D5
Stamford, Australia 94 C3
Stamford, U.K. 13 E7
Stamford, Conn., U.S.A. 111 E11
Stamford, N.Y., U.S.A. 111 D10
Stamford, Tex., U.S.A. 113 J5
Stampriet, Namibia 88 C2
Stamps, U.S.A. 113 J8
Stančevo = Kalipetrovo, Bulgaria 41 B11
Standerton, S. Africa 89 D4
Standish, U.S.A. 108 D4
Stanford, S. Africa 88 E2
Stanford, U.S.A. 114 C8
Stånga, Sweden 11 G12
Stanger, S. Africa 89 D5
Stanišić, Serbia, Yug. 42 E4
Stanislaus →, U.S.A. 116 H5
Stanislav = Ivano-Frankivsk, Ukraine 47 H3
Stanisławów, Poland 45 F8
Stanley, Australia 94 G4
Stanley, Canada 105 B8
Stanley, Falk. Is. 128 G5
Stanley, U.K. 12 C6
Stanley, Idaho, U.S.A. 114 D6
Stanley, N. Dak., U.S.A. 112 A3
Stanley, N.Y., U.S.A. 110 D7
Stanovoy Khrebet, Russia 51 D13
Stanovoy Ra. = Stanovoy Khrebet, Russia 51 D13
Stansmore Ra., Australia 92 D4
Stanthorpe, Australia 95 D5
Stanton, U.S.A. 113 J4
Stanwood, U.S.A. 116 B4
Staples, U.S.A. 112 B7
Stąporków, Poland 45 G7
Star City, Canada 105 C8
Star Lake, U.S.A. 111 B9
Stará L'ubovňa, Slovak Rep. 27 B13
Stara Moravica, Serbia, Yug. 42 E4
Stara Pazova, Serbia, Yug. 42 F5
Stara Planina, Bulgaria 40 C7
Stará Turá, Slovak Rep. 27 C10
Stara Zagora, Bulgaria 41 D9
Starachowice, Poland 45 G8
Staraya Russa, Russia 46 D6
Starbuck I., Kiribati 97 H12
Starchiojd, Romania 43 E11
Stargard Szczeciński, Poland 44 E2
Stari Bar, Montenegro, Yug. 40 D3
Stari Trg, Slovenia 29 C12
Staritsa, Russia 46 D8
Starke, U.S.A. 109 L4
Starnberg, Germany 25 H7
Starnberger See, Germany 25 H7
Starobilsk, Ukraine 47 H10
Starodub, Russia 47 F7
Starogard Gdański, Poland 44 E5
Starokonstantinov = Starokonstyantyniv, Ukraine 47 H4
Starokonstyantyniv, Ukraine 47 H4
Starominskaya, Russia 47 J10
Staroshcherbinovskaya, Russia 47 J10
Start Pt., U.K. 13 G4
Stary Sącz, Poland 45 J7
Staryy Biryuzyak, Russia 49 H8
Staryy Chartoriysk, Ukraine 47 G3
Staryy Krym, Ukraine 47 K8
Staryy Oskol, Russia 47 G9
Stassfurt, Germany 24 D7
Staszów, Poland 45 H8
State College, U.S.A. 110 F7
Stateline, U.S.A. 116 G7
Staten, I. = Estados, I. de Los, Argentina 122 J4
Staten I., U.S.A. 111 F10
Statesboro, U.S.A. 109 J5
Statesville, U.S.A. 109 H5
Stauffer, U.S.A. 117 L7
Staunton, Ill., U.S.A. 112 F10
Staunton, Va., U.S.A. 108 F6
Stavanger, Norway 9 G11
Staveley, N.Z. 91 K3
Stavelot, Belgium 17 D5
Stavern, Norway 9 G14
Stavoren, Neths. 17 B5
Stavropol, Russia 49 H6
Stavros, Cyprus 36 D11
Stavrós, Greece 36 D6
Stavrós, Ákra, Greece 36 D6
Stavroúpolis, Greece 41 E8
Stawell, Australia 95 F3
Stawell →, Australia 94 C3
Stawiski, Poland 44 E9
Stawiszyn, Poland 45 G5
Stayner, Canada 110 B4
Stayton, U.S.A. 114 D2
Steamboat Springs, U.S.A. 114 F10
Steblevë, Albania 40 E4
Steele, U.S.A. 112 B5
Steelton, U.S.A. 110 F8
Steen River, Canada 104 B5
Steenkool = Bintuni, Indonesia 63 E8
Steens Mt., U.S.A. 114 E4
Steenwijk, Neths. 17 B6
Steep Pt., Australia 93 E1
Steep Rock, Canada 105 C9
Ştefan Vodă, Moldova 43 D14
Ştefăneşti, Romania 43 C12
Stefanie L. = Chew Bahir, Ethiopia 81 G4
Stefansson Bay, Antarctica 5 C5
Stege, Denmark 11 K6
Ştei, Romania 42 D7
Steiermark □, Austria 26 D8
Steigerwald, Germany 25 F6
Steilacoom, U.S.A. 116 C4
Steilrandberge, Namibia 88 B1
Steinbach, Canada 105 D9
Steinfurt, Germany 24 C3
Steinhausen, Namibia 88 C2
Steinheim, Germany 24 D5
Steinhuder Meer, Germany 24 C5
Steinkjer, Norway 8 D14
Steinkopf, S. Africa 88 D2
Stellarton, Canada 103 C7
Stellenbosch, S. Africa 88 E2
Stelvio, Paso dello, Italy 28 B7
Stenay, France 19 C12
Stendal, Germany 24 C7
Stende, Latvia 44 A9
Stenhamra, Sweden 10 E11
Stenstorp, Sweden 11 F7
Stenungsund, Sweden 11 F5
Steornabhaigh = Stornoway, U.K. 14 C2
Stepanakert = Xankändi, Azerbaijan 70 B5
Stepanavan, Armenia 49 K7
Stephens Creek, Australia 95 E3
Stephens I., Canada 104 C2
Stephens L., Canada 105 B9
Stephenville, Canada 103 C8
Stephenville, U.S.A. 113 J5
Stepnica, Poland 44 E1
Stepnoi = Elista, Russia 49 G7
Steppe, Asia 52 D9
Stereá Ellas □, Greece 38 C4
Sterkstroom, S. Africa 88 E4
Sterling, Colo., U.S.A. 112 E3
Sterling, Ill., U.S.A. 112 E10
Sterling, Kans., U.S.A. 112 F5
Sterling City, U.S.A. 113 K4
Sterling Heights, U.S.A. 108 D4
Sterling Run, U.S.A. 110 E6
Sterlitamak, Russia 50 D6
Sternberg, Germany 24 B7
Šternberk, Czech Rep. 27 B10
Stérnes, Greece 36 D6
Sterzing = Vipiteno, Italy 29 B8
Stettin = Szczecin, Poland 44 E1
Stettiner Haff, Germany 24 B10
Stettler, Canada 104 C6
Steubenville, U.S.A. 110 F4
Stevenage, U.K. 13 F7
Stevens Point, U.S.A. 112 C10
Stevenson, U.S.A. 116 E5
Stevenson L., Canada 105 C9
Stevensville, U.S.A. 114 C6
Stevns Klint, Denmark 11 J6
Stewart, Canada 104 B3
Stewart, U.S.A. 116 F7
Stewart →, Canada 100 B6
Stewart, C., Australia 94 A1
Stewart, I., Chile 128 G2
Stewart I., N.Z. 91 M1
Stewarts Point, U.S.A. 116 G3
Stewartville, U.S.A. 112 D8
Stewiacke, Canada 103 C7
Steynsburg, S. Africa 88 E4
Steyr, Austria 26 C7
Steyr →, Austria 26 C7
Steytlerville, S. Africa 88 E3
Stia, Italy 29 E8
Stigler, U.S.A. 113 H7
Stigliano, Italy 31 B9
Stigtomta, Sweden 11 F10
Stikine →, Canada 104 B2
Stilfontein, S. Africa 88 D4
Stílis, Greece 38 C4
Stillwater, N.Z. 91 K3
Stillwater, Minn., U.S.A. 112 C8
Stillwater, N.Y., U.S.A. 111 D11
Stillwater, Okla., U.S.A. 113 G6
Stillwater Range, U.S.A. 114 G4
Stillwater Reservoir, U.S.A. 111 C9
Stilo, Pta., Italy 31 D9
Stilwell, U.S.A. 113 H7
Štip, Macedonia 40 E6
Stíra, Greece 38 C6
Stirling, Canada 110 B7
Stirling, U.K. 14 E5
Stirling □, U.K. 14 E4
Stirling Ra., Australia 93 F2
Stittsville, Canada 111 A9
Stjernøya, Norway 8 A20
Stjørdalshalsen, Norway 8 E14
Stockach, Germany 25 H5
Stockaryd, Sweden 11 G8
Stockerau, Austria 27 C9
Stockholm, Sweden 10 E12
Stockholms län □, Sweden 10 E12
Stockport, U.K. 12 D5
Stocksbridge, U.K. 12 D6
Stockton, Calif., U.S.A. 116 H5
Stockton, Kans., U.S.A. 112 F5
Stockton, Mo., U.S.A. 113 G8
Stockton-on-Tees, U.K. 12 C6
Stockton-on-Tees □, U.K. 12 C6
Stockton Plateau, U.S.A. 113 K3
Stoczek Łukowski, Poland 45 G8
Stöde, Sweden 10 B10
Stoeng Treng, Cambodia 64 F5
Stoer, Pt. of, U.K. 14 C3
Stogovo, Macedonia 40 E4
Stoholm, Denmark 11 H3
Stoke-on-Trent, U.K. 12 D5
Stoke-on-Trent □, U.K. 12 D5
Stokes Pt., Australia 94 G3
Stokes Ra., Australia 92 C5
Stokksnes, Iceland 8 D6
Stokmarknes, Norway 8 B16
Stolac, Bos.-H. 40 C1
Stolberg, Germany 24 E2
Stolbovoy, Ostrov, Russia 51 B14
Stolbtsy = Stowbtsy, Belarus 46 F4
Stolin, Belarus 47 G4
Stöllet, Sweden 10 D7
Stolnici, Romania 43 F9
Stomíon, Greece 36 D5
Ston, Croatia 29 F14
Stone, U.K. 12 E5
Stoneboro, U.S.A. 110 E4
Stonehaven, U.K. 14 E6
Stonehenge, Australia 94 C3
Stonehenge, U.K. 13 F6
Stonewall, Canada 105 C9
Stony L., Man., Canada 105 B9
Stony L., Ont., Canada 110 B6
Stony Point, U.S.A. 111 E11
Stony Pt., U.S.A. 111 C8
Stony Rapids, Canada 105 B7
Stony Tunguska = Tunguska, Podkamennaya →, Russia 51 C10
Stonyford, U.S.A. 116 F4
Stopnica, Poland 45 H7
Storå, Sweden 10 E9
Storå →, Denmark 11 H2
Stora Gla, Sweden 10 E6
Stora Le, Sweden 10 E5
Stora Lulevatten, Sweden 8 C18
Storavan, Sweden 8 D18
Stord, Norway 9 G11
Store Bælt, Denmark 11 J4
Store Heddinge, Denmark 11 J6
Storebro, Sweden 11 G9
Storfors, Sweden 10 E8
Storlien, Sweden 10 A6
Storm B., Australia 94 G4
Storm Lake, U.S.A. 112 D7
Stormberge, S. Africa 88 E4
Stormsrivier, S. Africa 88 E3
Stornoway, U.K. 14 C2
Storo, Italy 28 C7
Storozhinets = Storozhynets, Ukraine 47 H3
Storozhynets, Ukraine 47 H3
Storrs, U.S.A. 111 E12
Storsjön, Gävleborg, Sweden 10 D10
Storsjön, Jämtland, Sweden 10 B7
Storsjön, Jämtland, Sweden 10 A8
Storstrøms Amtskommune □, Denmark 11 J5
Storuman, Sweden 8 D17
Storuman, sjö, Sweden 8 D17
Storvätteshågna, Sweden 10 B6
Storvik, Sweden 10 D10
Storvreta, Sweden 10 E11
Stouffville, Canada 110 C5
Stoughton, Canada 105 D8
Stour →, Dorset, U.K. 13 G6
Stour →, Kent, U.K. 13 F9
Stour →, Suffolk, U.K. 13 F9
Stourbridge, U.K. 13 E5
Stout L., Canada 105 C10
Stove Pipe Wells Village, U.S.A. 117 J9
Støvring, Denmark 11 H3
Stow, U.S.A. 110 E3
Stowbtsy, Belarus 46 F4
Stowmarket, U.K. 13 E9
Strabane, U.K. 15 B4
Stracin, Macedonia 40 D6
Stradella, Italy 28 C6
Strahan, Australia 94 G4
Strajitsa, Bulgaria 41 C9
Strakonice, Czech Rep. 26 B6
Straldzha, Bulgaria 41 D10
Stralsund, Germany 24 A9
Strand, S. Africa 88 E2
Stranda, Møre og Romsdal, Norway 9 E12
Stranda, Nord-Trøndelag, Norway 8 E14
Strandby, Denmark 11 G4
Strangford L., U.K. 15 B6
Strängnäs, Sweden 10 E11
Stranraer, U.K. 14 G3
Strasbourg, Canada 105 C8
Strasbourg, France 19 D14
Strasburg, Germany 24 B9
Strășeni, Moldova 43 C13
Stråssa, Sweden 10 E9
Stratford, Canada 102 D3
Stratford, N.Z. 91 H5
Stratford, Calif., U.S.A. 116 J7
Stratford, Conn., U.S.A. 111 E11
Stratford, Tex., U.S.A. 113 G3
Stratford-upon-Avon, U.K. 13 E6
Strath Spey, U.K. 14 D5
Strathalbyn, Australia 95 F2
Strathaven, U.K. 14 F4
Strathcona Prov. Park, Canada 104 D3
Strathmore, Canada 104 C6
Strathmore, U.K. 14 E5
Strathmore, U.S.A. 116 J7
Strathnaver, Canada 104 C4
Strathpeffer, U.K. 14 D4
Strathroy, Canada 102 D3
Strathy Pt., U.K. 14 C4
Strattanville, U.S.A. 110 E5
Stratton, U.S.A. 111 A14
Stratton Mt., U.S.A. 111 C12
Straubing, Germany 25 G8
Straumnes, Iceland 8 C2
Strausberg, Germany 24 C9
Strawberry →, U.S.A. 114 F8
Strážnice, Czech Rep. 27 C10
Streaky B., Australia 95 E1
Streaky Bay, Australia 95 E1
Streator, U.S.A. 112 E10
Streetsboro, U.S.A. 110 E3
Streetsville, Canada 110 C5
Strehaia, Romania 43 F8
Strelcha, Bulgaria 41 D8
Strelka, Russia 51 D10
Streng →, Cambodia 64 F4
Stresa, Italy 28 C5
Streymoy, Færoe Is. 8 E9
Strezhevoy, Russia 50 C8
Stříbro, Czech Rep. 26 A6
Strimón →, Greece 40 F7
Strimonikós Kólpos, Greece 40 F7
Strofádhes, Greece 38 D3
Stroma, U.K. 14 C5
Strómboli, Italy 31 D8
Stromeferry, U.K. 14 D3
Stromness, U.K. 14 C5
Strömsbruk, Sweden 10 C11
Stromsburg, U.S.A. 112 E6
Strömsnäsbruk, Sweden 11 H7
Strömstad, Sweden 11 F5
Strömsund, Sweden 8 E16
Strongilí, Greece 39 E11
Stróngoli, Italy 31 C10
Strongsville, U.S.A. 110 E3
Stronie Śląskie, Poland 45 H3
Stronsay, U.K. 14 B6
Stropkov, Slovak Rep. 27 B14
Stroud, U.K. 13 F5
Stroud Road, Australia 95 E5
Stroudsburg, U.S.A. 111 F9
Stroumbi, Cyprus 36 E11
Struer, Denmark 11 H2
Struga, Macedonia 40 E4
Strugi Krasnyye, Russia 46 C5
Strumica, Macedonia 40 E6
Strumica →, Europe 40 E7
Struthers, Canada 102 C2
Struthers, U.S.A. 110 E4
Stryama, Bulgaria 41 D8
Stryker, U.S.A. 114 B6
Stryków, Poland 45 G6
Stryy, Ukraine 47 H2
Strzegom, Poland 45 H3
Strzelce Krajeńskie, Poland 45 F2
Strzelce Opolskie, Poland 45 H5
Strzelecki Cr. →, Australia 95 D2
Strzelin, Poland 45 H4
Strzelno, Poland 45 F5
Strzybnica, Poland 45 H5
Strzyżów, Poland 45 J8
Stuart, Fla., U.S.A. 109 M5
Stuart, Nebr., U.S.A. 112 D5
Stuart →, Canada 104 C4
Stuart Bluff Ra., Australia 92 D5
Stuart L., Canada 104 C4
Stuart Ra., Australia 95 D1
Stubbekøbing, Denmark 11 K6
Stuben, Austria 26 D3
Studen Kladenets, Yazovir, Bulgaria 41 E9
Studenka, Czech Rep. 27 B11
Stugun, Sweden 10 A9
Stuhr, Germany 24 B4
Stull L., Canada 102 B1
Stung Treng = Stoeng Treng, Cambodia 64 F5
Stupart →, Canada 102 A1
Stupava, Slovak Rep. 27 C10
Stupino, Russia 46 E10
Sturgeon B., Canada 105 C9
Sturgeon Bay, U.S.A. 108 C2
Sturgeon Falls, Canada 102 C4
Sturgeon L., Alta., Canada 104 B5
Sturgeon L., Ont., Canada 102 C1
Sturgeon L., Ont., Canada 110 B6
Sturgis, Canada 105 C8
Sturgis, Mich., U.S.A. 108 E3
Sturgis, S. Dak., U.S.A. 112 C3
Sturkö, Sweden 11 H9
Štúrovo, Slovak Rep. 27 D11
Sturt Cr. →, Australia 92 C4
Stutterheim, S. Africa 88 E4
Stuttgart, Germany 25 G5
Stuttgart, U.S.A. 113 H9
Stuyvesant, U.S.A. 111 D11
Stykkishólmur, Iceland 8 D2
Styria = Steiermark □, Austria 26 D8
Styrsö, Sweden 11 G5
Su Xian = Suzhou, China 56 H9
Suakin, Sudan 80 D4
Suan, N. Korea 57 E14
Suaqui, Mexico 118 B3
Suar, India 69 E8
Subang, Indonesia 63 G12
Subansiri →, India 67 F18
Subarnarekha →, India 69 H12
Subayhah, Si. Arabia 70 D3
Subcetate, Romania 42 E8
Subi, Indonesia 65 L7
Subiaco, Italy 29 G10
Subotica, Serbia, Yug. 42 D4
Suca, Ethiopia 81 F4
Suceava, Romania 43 C11
Suceava □, Romania 43 C10
Suceava →, Romania 43 C11
Sucha-Beskidzka, Poland 45 J6
Suchań, Poland 45 E2
Suchan, Russia 54 C6
Suchedniów, Poland 45 G7
Suchitoto, El Salv. 120 D2
Suchou = Suzhou, China 59 B13
Süchow = Xuzhou, China 57 G9
Suchowola, Poland 44 E10
Suck →, Ireland 15 C3
Sucre, Bolivia 124 G5
Sućuraj, Croatia 29 E14
Sucuriú →, Brazil 125 H8
Sud, Pte. du, Canada 103 C7
Sud-Kivu □, Dem. Rep. of the Congo 86 C2
Sud-Ouest, Pte. du, Canada 103 C7
Suda →, Russia 46 C9
Sudak, Ukraine 47 K8
Sudan, U.S.A. 113 H3
Sudan ■, Africa 81 E3
Sudbury, Canada 102 C3
Sudbury, U.K. 13 E8
Sûdd, Sudan 81 F3
Süderbrarup, Germany 24 A5
Süderlügum, Germany 24 A4
Süderoogsand, Germany 24 A4
Sudeten Mts. = Sudety, Europe 27 A9
Sudety, Europe 27 A9
Suðuroy, Færoe Is. 8 F9
Sudi, Tanzania 87 E4
Sudirman, Pegunungan, Indonesia 63 E9
Sudiţi, Romania 43 F12
Sudogda, Russia 48 C5
Sudr, Egypt 80 B3
Sudzha, Russia 47 G8
Sue →, Sudan 81 F2
Sueca, Spain 33 F4
Suedinenie, Bulgaria 41 D8
Suemez I., U.S.A. 104 B2
Suez = El Suweis, Egypt 80 J8
Suez, G. of = Suweis, Khalîg el, Egypt 80 J8
Suez Canal = Suweis, Qanâ es, Egypt 80 H8
Suffield, Canada 104 C6
Suffolk, U.S.A. 108 G7
Suffolk □, U.K. 13 E9
Şugag, Romania 43 E8
Sugargrove, U.S.A. 110 E5
Sugarive →, India 69 F12
Suğla Gölü, Turkey 72 D5
Sugluk = Salluit, Canada 101 B12
Suhaia, Lacul, Romania 43 G10
Şuḩār, Oman 71 E8
Sühbaatar □, Mongolia 56 B8
Suhl, Germany 24 E6
Şuhut, Turkey 39 C12
Sui, Pakistan 68 E3
Sui Xian, China 56 G8
Šuica, Bos.-H. 42 G2
Suichang, China 59 C12
Suichuan, China 59 D10
Suide, China 56 F6
Suifenhe, China 57 B16
Suihua, China 60 B7
Suijiang, China 58 C4
Suining, Hunan, China 59 D8
Suining, Jiangsu, China 57 H9
Suining, Sichuan, China 58 B5
Suiping, China 56 H7
Suippes, France 19 C11
Suir →, Ireland 15 D4
Suisun City, U.S.A. 116 G4
Suixi, China 59 G8
Suiyang, Guizhou, China 58 D6
Suiyang, Heilongjiang, China 57 B16
Suizhong, China 57 D11
Suizhou, China 59 B9
Sujangarh, India 68 F6
Sukabumi, Indonesia 63 G12
Sukadana, Indonesia 62 E3
Sukagawa, Japan 55 F10
Sukaraja, Indonesia 62 E4
Sukarnapura = Jayapura, Indonesia 63 E10
Sukch'ŏn, N. Korea 57 E13
Sukhindol, Bulgaria 41 C9
Sukhinichi, Russia 46 E8
Sukhona →, Russia 50 D4
Sukhothai, Thailand 64 D2
Sukhumi = Sokhumi, Georgia 49 J5
Sukkur, Pakistan 68 F3
Sukkur Barrage, Pakistan 68 F3
Sukovo, Serbia, Yug. 40 C6
Sukri →, India 68 G4
Sukumo, Japan 55 H6
Sukunka →, Canada 104 B4
Sula →, Ukraine 47 H7
Sula, Kepulauan, Indonesia 63 E7
Sulaco →, Honduras 120 C2
Sulaiman Range, Pakistan 68 D3
Sulak →, Russia 49 J8
Sūlār, Iran 71 D6
Sulawesi Sea = Celebes Sea, Indonesia 63 D6
Sulawesi Selatan □, Indonesia 63 E6
Sulawesi Utara □, Indonesia 63 D6
Sulechów, Poland 45 F2
Sulęcin, Poland 45 F2
Sulejów, Poland 45 G6
Sulejówek, Poland 45 F8
Süleymanlı, Turkey 39 C9
Sulima, S. Leone 82 D2
Sulina, Romania 43 E14
Sulina, Braţul →, Romania 43 E14
Sulingen, Germany 24 C4
Suliţa, Romania 43 C11
Sulitjelma, Norway 8 C17
Sułkowice, Poland 45 J6
Sullana, Peru 124 D2
Süller, Turkey 39 C11
Sullivan, Ill., U.S.A. 112 F10
Sullivan, Ind., U.S.A. 108 F2
Sullivan, Mo., U.S.A. 112 F9

Sullivan Bay, *Canada* 104 C3
Sullivan I. = Lanbi Kyun, *Burma* 65 G2
Sully-sur-Loire, *France* 19 E9
Sulmierzyce, *Poland* 45 G4
Sulmona, *Italy* 29 F10
Süloğlu, *Turkey* 41 E10
Sulphur, *La., U.S.A.* 113 K8
Sulphur, *Okla., U.S.A.* 113 H6
Sulphur Pt., *Canada* 104 A6
Sulphur Springs, *U.S.A.* 113 J7
Sultan, *Canada* 102 C3
Sultan, *U.S.A.* 116 C5
Sultan Dağları, *Turkey* 72 C4
Sultanhisar, *Turkey* 39 D10
Sultaniça, *Turkey* 41 F10
Sultaniye, *Turkey* 41 F12
Sultanpur, *Mad. P., India* 68 H8
Sultanpur, *Punjab, India* 68 D6
Sultanpur, *Ut. P., India* 69 F10
Sulu Arch., *Phil.* 61 J4
Sulu Sea, *E. Indies* 61 G4
Sülüklü, *Turkey* 72 C5
Sululta, *Ethiopia* 81 F4
Suluova, *Turkey* 72 B6
Suluq, *Libya* 79 B10
Sulzbach, *Germany* 25 F3
Sulzbach-Rosenberg, *Germany* 25 F7
Sulzberger Ice Shelf, *Antarctica* 5 D10
Sumalata, *Indonesia* 63 D6
Sumampa, *Argentina* 126 B3
Sumatera □, *Indonesia* 62 D2
Sumatera Barat □, *Indonesia* 62 E2
Sumatera Utara □, *Indonesia* 62 D1
Sumatra = Sumatera □, *Indonesia* 62 D2
Sumba, *Indonesia* 63 F5
Sumba, Selat, *Indonesia* 63 F5
Sumbawa, *Indonesia* 62 F5
Sumbawa Besar, *Indonesia* 62 F5
Sumbawanga □, *Tanzania* 84 F6
Sumbe, *Angola* 84 G2
Sumburgh Hd., *U.K.* 14 B7
Sumdeo, *India* 69 D8
Sumdo, *India* 69 B8
Sumedang, *Indonesia* 63 G12
Sümeg, *Hungary* 42 D2
Sumeih, *Sudan* 81 F2
Šumen = Shumen, *Bulgaria* 41 C10
Sumenep, *Indonesia* 63 G15
Sumgait = Sumqayıt, *Azerbaijan* 49 K9
Summer L., *U.S.A.* 114 E3
Summerland, *Canada* 104 D5
Summerside, *Canada* 103 C7
Summersville, *U.S.A.* 108 F5
Summerville, *Ga., U.S.A.* 109 H3
Summerville, *S.C., U.S.A.* 109 J5
Summit Lake, *Canada* 104 C4
Summit Peak, *U.S.A.* 115 H10
Sumner, *Iowa, U.S.A.* 112 D8
Sumner, *Wash., U.S.A.* 116 C4
Sumoto, *Japan* 55 G7
Šumperk, *Czech Rep.* 27 B9
Sumqayıt, *Azerbaijan* 49 K9
Sumter, *U.S.A.* 109 J5
Sumy, *Ukraine* 47 G8
Sun City, *Ariz., U.S.A.* 115 K7
Sun City, *Calif., U.S.A.* 117 M9
Sun City Center, *U.S.A.* 109 M4
Sun Lakes, *U.S.A.* 115 K8
Sun Valley, *U.S.A.* 114 E6
Sunagawa, *Japan* 54 C10
Sunan, *N. Korea* 57 E13
Sunart, L., *U.K.* 14 E3
Sunburst, *U.S.A.* 114 B8
Sunbury, *Australia* 95 F3
Sunbury, *U.S.A.* 111 F8
Sunchales, *Argentina* 126 C3
Suncho Corral, *Argentina* 126 B3
Sunch'ŏn, *S. Korea* 57 G14
Suncook, *U.S.A.* 111 C13
Sunda, Selat, *Indonesia* 62 F3
Sunda Is., *Indonesia* 52 K14
Sunda Str. = Sunda, Selat, *Indonesia* 62 F3
Sundance, *Canada* 105 B10
Sundance, *U.S.A.* 112 C2
Sundar Nagar, *India* 68 D7
Sundarbans, The, *Asia* 67 J16
Sundargarh, *India* 67 H14
Sundays = Sondags →, *S. Africa* 88 E4
Sunderland, *Canada* 110 B5
Sunderland, *U.K.* 12 C6
Sundre, *Canada* 104 C6
Sunds, *Denmark* 11 H3
Sundsvall, *Sweden* 10 B11
Sundsvallsbukten, *Sweden* 10 B11
Sung Hei, *Vietnam* 65 G6
Sungai Kolok, *Thailand* 65 J3
Sungai Lembing, *Malaysia* 65 L4
Sungai Petani, *Malaysia* 65 K3
Sungaigerong, *Indonesia* 62 E2
Sungailiat, *Indonesia* 62 E3
Sungaipenuh, *Indonesia* 62 E2
Sungari = Songhua Jiang →, *China* 60 B8
Sunghua Chiang = Songhua Jiang →, *China* 60 B8
Sungikai, *Sudan* 81 E2
Sungurlu, *Turkey* 72 B6
Sunja, *Croatia* 29 C13
Sunland Park, *U.S.A.* 115 L10
Sunnansjö, *Sweden* 10 D8
Sunndalsøra, *Norway* 9 E13
Sunne, *Sweden* 10 E7
Sunnemo, *Sweden* 10 E7
Sunnyside, *U.S.A.* 114 C3
Sunnyvale, *U.S.A.* 116 H4
Suntar, *Russia* 51 C12
Sunyani, *Ghana* 82 D4
Suomenselkä, *Finland* 8 E21
Suomussalmi, *Finland* 8 D23
Suoyarvi, *Russia* 46 A7
Supai, *U.S.A.* 115 H7
Supaul, *India* 69 F12
Superior, *Ariz., U.S.A.* 115 K8
Superior, *Mont., U.S.A.* 114 C6
Superior, *Nebr., U.S.A.* 112 E5
Superior, *Wis., U.S.A.* 112 B8
Superior, L., *N. Amer.* 102 C2
Supetar, *Croatia* 29 E13
Suphan Buri, *Thailand* 64 E3
Suphan Dağı, *Turkey* 70 B4
Supiori, *Indonesia* 63 E9
Supraśl, *Poland* 45 E10
Supraśl →, *Poland* 45 E9
Supung Shuiku, *China* 57 D13
Sūq Suwayq, *Si. Arabia* 70 E3
Suqian, *China* 57 H10
Sūr, *Lebanon* 75 B4
Şūr, *Oman* 74 C6
Sur, Pt., *U.S.A.* 116 J5
Sura →, *Russia* 48 C8
Surab, *Pakistan* 68 E2
Surabaja = Surabaya, *Indonesia* 62 F4
Surabaya, *Indonesia* 62 F4
Surahammar, *Sweden* 10 E10
Suraia, *Romania* 43 E12
Surakarta, *Indonesia* 62 F4
Surakhany, *Azerbaijan* 49 K10
Šurany, *Slovak Rep.* 27 C11
Surat, *Australia* 95 D4
Surat, *India* 66 J8
Surat Thani, *Thailand* 65 H2
Suratgarh, *India* 68 E5
Suraž, *Poland* 45 F9
Surazh, *Belarus* 46 E6
Surazh, *Russia* 47 F7
Surduc, *Romania* 43 C8
Surduc Pasul, *Romania* 43 E8
Surdulica, *Serbia, Yug.* 40 D6
Surendranagar, *India* 68 H4
Surf, *U.S.A.* 117 L6
Surgères, *France* 20 B3
Surgut, *Russia* 50 C8
Sùria, *Spain* 32 D6
Suriapet, *India* 66 L11
Surigao, *Phil.* 61 G6
Surigao Strait, *Phil.* 61 F6
Surin, *Thailand* 64 E4
Surin Nua, Ko, *Thailand* 65 H1
Surinam ■, *S. Amer.* 125 C7
Suriname = Surinam ■, *S. Amer.* 125 C7
Suriname →, *Surinam* 125 B7
Sürmaq, *Iran* 71 D7
Sürmene, *Turkey* 73 B9
Surovikino, *Russia* 49 F6
Surrey □, *U.K.* 13 F7
Sursand, *India* 69 F11
Sursar →, *India* 69 F12
Sursee, *Switz.* 25 H4
Sursk, *Russia* 48 D7
Surskoye, *Russia* 48 C8
Surt, *Libya* 79 B9
Surt, Khalīj, *Libya* 79 B9
Surtanahu, *Pakistan* 68 F4
Surte, *Sweden* 11 G6
Surtsey, *Iceland* 8 E3
Sürüç, *Turkey* 73 D8
Suruga-Wan, *Japan* 55 G9
Susa, *Italy* 28 C4
Susâ →, *Denmark* 11 J5
Sušac, *Croatia* 29 F13
Susak, *Croatia* 29 D11
Susaki, *Japan* 55 H6
Sūsangerd, *Iran* 71 D6
Susanville, *U.S.A.* 114 F3
Susch, *Switz.* 25 J6
Suşehri, *Turkey* 73 B8
Sušice, *Czech Rep.* 26 B6
Susleni, *Moldova* 43 C13
Susner, *India* 68 H7
Susong, *China* 59 B11
Susquehanna, *U.S.A.* 111 E9
Susquehanna →, *U.S.A.* 111 G8
Susques, *Argentina* 126 A2
Sussex, *Canada* 103 C6
Sussex, *U.S.A.* 111 E10
Sussex, E. □, *U.K.* 13 G8
Sussex, W. □, *U.K.* 13 G7
Sustut →, *Canada* 104 B3
Susuman, *Russia* 51 C15
Susunu, *Indonesia* 63 E8
Susurluk, *Turkey* 39 B10
Susuz, *Turkey* 73 B10
Susz, *Poland* 44 E6
Sütçüler, *Turkey* 72 D4
Şuţeşti, *Romania* 43 E12
Sutherland, *S. Africa* 88 E3
Sutherland, *U.S.A.* 112 E4
Sutherland Falls, *N.Z.* 91 L1
Sutherlin, *U.S.A.* 114 E2
Suthri, *India* 68 H3
Sutlej →, *Pakistan* 68 E4
Sutter, *U.S.A.* 116 F5
Sutter Creek, *U.S.A.* 116 G6
Sutton, *Canada* 111 A12
Sutton, *Nebr., U.S.A.* 112 E6
Sutton, *W. Va., U.S.A.* 108 F5
Sutton →, *Canada* 102 A3
Sutton Coldfield, *U.K.* 13 E6
Sutton in Ashfield, *U.K.* 12 D6
Sutton L., *Canada* 102 B3
Suttor →, *Australia* 94 C4
Suttsu, *Japan* 54 C10
Suva, *Fiji* 91 D8
Suva Gora, *Macedonia* 40 E5
Suva Planina, *Serbia, Yug.* 40 C6
Suva Reka, *Kosovo, Yug.* 40 D4
Suvorov, *Russia* 46 E9
Suvorov Is. = Suwarrow Is., *Cook Is.* 97 J11
Suvorovo, *Bulgaria* 41 C11
Suwałki, *Poland* 44 D9
Suwannaphum, *Thailand* 64 E4
Suwannee →, *U.S.A.* 109 L4
Suwanose-Jima, *Japan* 55 K4
Suwarrow Is., *Cook Is.* 97 J11
Suwayq aş Şuqban, *Iraq* 70 D5
Suweis, Khalîg el, *Egypt* 80 J8
Suweis, Qanâ es, *Egypt* 80 H8
Suwŏn, *S. Korea* 57 F14
Suzdal, *Russia* 46 D11
Suzhou, *Anhui, China* 56 H9
Suzhou, *Jiangsu, China* 59 B13
Suzu, *Japan* 55 F8
Suzu-Misaki, *Japan* 55 F8
Suzuka, *Japan* 55 G8
Suzzara, *Italy* 28 D7
Svalbard, *Arctic* 4 B8
Svalöv, *Sweden* 11 J7
Svaneke, *Denmark* 11 J9
Svängsta, *Sweden* 11 H8
Svanskog, *Sweden* 10 E6
Svappavaara, *Sweden* 8 C19
Svärdsjö, *Sweden* 10 D9
Svartå, *Sweden* 10 E8
Svartisen, *Norway* 8 C15
Svartvik, *Sweden* 10 B11
Svatove, *Ukraine* 47 H10
Svatovo = Svatove, *Ukraine* 47 H10
Svay Chek, *Cambodia* 64 F4
Svay Rieng, *Cambodia* 65 G5
Svealand □, *Sweden* 10 D9
Svedala, *Sweden* 11 J7
Sveg, *Sweden* 10 B8
Svendborg, *Denmark* 11 J4
Svenljunga, *Sweden* 11 G7
Svenstavik, *Sweden* 10 B8
Svenstrup, *Denmark* 11 H3
Sverdlovsk = Yekaterinburg, *Russia* 50 D7
Sverdlovsk, *Ukraine* 47 H10
Sverdrup Is., *Canada* 4 B3
Svetac, *Croatia* 29 E12
Sveti Nikola, Prokhad, *Europe* 40 C6
Sveti Nikole, *Macedonia* 40 E5
Sveti Rok, *Croatia* 29 D12
Svetlaya, *Russia* 54 A9
Svetlogorsk = Svyetlahorsk, *Belarus* 47 F5
Svetlograd, *Russia* 49 H6
Svetlovodsk = Svitlovodsk, *Ukraine* 47 H7
Svidník, *Slovak Rep.* 27 B14
Svilaja Planina, *Croatia* 29 E13
Svilajnac, *Serbia, Yug.* 40 B5
Svilengrad, *Bulgaria* 41 E10
Svir →, *Russia* 46 B7
Sviritsa, *Russia* 46 B7
Svishtov, *Bulgaria* 41 C9
Svislach, *Belarus* 47 F3
Svitava →, *Czech Rep.* 27 B9
Svitavy, *Czech Rep.* 27 B9
Svitlovodsk, *Ukraine* 47 H7
Svobodnyy, *Russia* 51 D13
Svoge, *Bulgaria* 40 D7
Svolvær, *Norway* 8 B16
Svratka →, *Czech Rep.* 27 B9
Svrljig, *Serbia, Yug.* 40 C6
Svyetlahorsk, *Belarus* 47 F5
Swabian Alps = Schwäbische Alb, *Germany* 25 G5
Swainsboro, *U.S.A.* 109 J4
Swakop →, *Namibia* 88 C2
Swakopmund, *Namibia* 88 C1
Swale →, *U.K.* 12 C6
Swan →, *Australia* 93 F2
Swan →, *Canada* 105 C8
Swan Hill, *Australia* 95 F3
Swan Hills, *Canada* 104 C5
Swan Is., *W. Indies* 120 C3
Swan L., *Canada* 105 C8
Swan Peak, *U.S.A.* 114 C7
Swan Ra., *U.S.A.* 114 C7
Swan River, *Canada* 105 C8
Swanage, *U.K.* 13 G6
Swansea, *Australia* 94 G4
Swansea, *Canada* 110 C5
Swansea, *U.K.* 13 F4
Swansea □, *U.K.* 13 F3
Swar →, *Pakistan* 69 B5
Swartberge, *S. Africa* 88 E3
Swartmodder, *S. Africa* 88 D3
Swartnossob →, *Namibia* 88 C2
Swartruggens, *S. Africa* 88 D4
Swarzędz, *Poland* 45 F4
Swastika, *Canada* 102 C3
Swatow = Shantou, *China* 59 F11
Swaziland ■, *Africa* 89 D5
Sweden ■, *Europe* 9 G16
Swedru, *Ghana* 83 D4
Sweet Home, *U.S.A.* 114 D2
Sweetgrass, *U.S.A.* 114 B8
Sweetwater, *Nev., U.S.A.* 116 G7
Sweetwater, *Tenn., U.S.A.* 109 H3
Sweetwater, *Tex., U.S.A.* 113 J4
Sweetwater →, *U.S.A.* 114 E10
Swellendam, *S. Africa* 88 E3
Swider →, *Poland* 45 F8
Świdnica, *Poland* 45 H3
Świdnik, *Poland* 45 G9
Świdwin, *Poland* 44 E2
Świebodzice, *Poland* 45 H3
Świebodzin, *Poland* 45 F2
Świecie, *Poland* 44 E5
Świerzawa, *Poland* 45 G2
Świętokrzyskie □, *Poland* 45 H7
Świętokrzyskie, Góry, *Poland* 45 H7
Swift Current, *Canada* 105 C7
Swiftcurrent →, *Canada* 105 C7
Swilly, L., *Ireland* 15 A4
Swindon, *U.K.* 13 F6
Swindon □, *U.K.* 13 F6
Swinemünde = Świnoujście, *Poland* 44 E1
Swinford, *Ireland* 15 C3
Świnoujście, *Poland* 44 E1
Switzerland ■, *Europe* 25 J4
Swords, *Ireland* 15 C5
Swoyerville, *U.S.A.* 111 E9
Syasstroy, *Russia* 46 B7
Sychevka, *Russia* 46 E8
Syców, *Poland* 45 G4
Sydenham →, *Canada* 110 D2
Sydney, *Australia* 95 E5
Sydney, *Canada* 103 C7
Sydney L., *Canada* 105 C10
Sydney Mines, *Canada* 103 C7
Sydprøven = Alluitsup Paa, *Greenland* 4 C5
Sydra, G. of = Surt, Khalīj, *Libya* 79 B9
Syeverodonetsk, *Ukraine* 47 H10
Syke, *Germany* 24 C4
Sykesville, *U.S.A.* 110 E6
Syktyvkar, *Russia* 50 C6
Sylacauga, *U.S.A.* 109 J2
Sylarna, *Sweden* 8 E15
Sylhet, *Bangla.* 67 G17
Sylhet □, *Bangla.* 67 G17
Sylt, *Germany* 24 A4
Sylvan Beach, *U.S.A.* 111 C9
Sylvan Lake, *Canada* 104 C6
Sylvania, *U.S.A.* 109 J5
Sylvester, *U.S.A.* 109 K4
Sym, *Russia* 50 C9
Symón, *Mexico* 118 C4
Synelnykove, *Ukraine* 47 H8
Synnott Ra., *Australia* 92 C4
Syracuse, *Kans., U.S.A.* 113 G4
Syracuse, *N.Y., U.S.A.* 111 C8
Syracuse, *Nebr., U.S.A.* 112 E6
Syrdarya →, *Kazakstan* 50 E7
Syria ■, *Asia* 70 C3
Syrian Desert = Shām, Bādiyat ash, *Asia* 70 C3
Sysslebäck, *Sweden* 10 D6
Syzran, *Russia* 48 D9
Szabolcs-Szatmár-Bereg □, *Hungary* 42 B6
Szadek, *Poland* 45 G5
Szamocin, *Poland* 45 E4
Szamos →, *Hungary* 42 B7
Szamotuły, *Poland* 45 F3
Száraz →, *Hungary* 42 D6
Szarvas, *Hungary* 42 D5
Százhalombatta, *Hungary* 42 C3
Szczawnica, *Poland* 45 J7
Szczebrzeszyn, *Poland* 45 H9
Szczecin, *Poland* 44 E1
Szczecinek, *Poland* 44 E3
Szczeciński, Zalew = Stettiner Haff, *Germany* 24 B10
Szczekociny, *Poland* 45 H6
Szczucin, *Poland* 45 H8
Szczuczyn, *Poland* 44 E9
Szczyrk, *Poland* 45 J6
Szczytna, *Poland* 45 H3
Szczytno, *Poland* 44 E7
Szechwan = Sichuan □, *China* 58 B5
Szécsény, *Hungary* 42 B4
Szeged, *Hungary* 42 D5
Szeghalom, *Hungary* 42 C6
Székesfehérvár, *Hungary* 42 C3
Szekszárd, *Hungary* 42 D3
Szendrő, *Hungary* 42 B5
Szentendre, *Hungary* 42 C4
Szentes, *Hungary* 42 D5
Szentgotthárd, *Hungary* 42 D1
Szentlőrinc, *Hungary* 42 D3
Szerencs, *Hungary* 42 B6
Szigetszentmiklós, *Hungary* 42 C4
Szigetvár, *Hungary* 42 D2
Szikszó, *Hungary* 42 B5
Szklarska Poreba, *Poland* 45 H2
Szkwa →, *Poland* 45 E8
Szlichtyngowa, *Poland* 45 G3
Szob, *Hungary* 42 C3
Szolnok, *Hungary* 42 C5
Szombathely, *Hungary* 42 C1
Szprotawa, *Poland* 45 G2
Sztum, *Poland* 44 E6
Sztutowo, *Poland* 44 D6
Szubin, *Poland* 45 E4
Szydłowiec, *Poland* 45 G7
Szypliszki, *Poland* 44 D10

T

Ta Khli Khok, *Thailand* 64 E3
Ta Lai, *Vietnam* 65 G6
Tab, *Hungary* 42 D3
Tabacal, *Argentina* 126 A3
Tabaco, *Phil.* 61 E5
Tabagné, *Ivory C.* 82 D4
Ţābah, *Si. Arabia* 70 E4
Tabankort, *Niger* 83 B5
Ţabas, *Khorāsān, Iran* 71 C9
Ţabas, *Khorāsān, Iran* 71 C8
Tabasará, Serranía de, *Panama* 120 E3
Tabasco □, *Mexico* 119 D6
Tabāsīn, *Iran* 71 D8
Tabatinga, Serra da, *Brazil* 125 F10
Taber, *Canada* 104 D6
Taberg, *Sweden* 11 G8
Taberg, *U.S.A.* 111 C9
Tabla, *Niger* 83 C5
Tablas I., *Phil.* 61 E5
Tablas Strait, *Phil.* 61 E4
Table B. = Tafelbaai, *S. Africa* 88 E2
Table B., *Canada* 103 B8
Table Mt., *S. Africa* 88 E2
Table Rock L., *U.S.A.* 113 G8
Tabletop, Mt., *Australia* 94 C4
Tábor, *Czech Rep.* 26 B7
Tabora, *Tanzania* 86 D3
Tabora □, *Tanzania* 86 D3
Tabou, *Ivory C.* 82 E3
Tabrīz, *Iran* 70 B5
Tabuaeran, *Kiribati* 97 G12
Tabuenca, *Spain* 32 D3
Tabūk, *Si. Arabia* 70 D3
Täby, *Sweden* 10 E12
Tacámbaro de Codallos, *Mexico* 118 D4
Tacheng, *China* 60 B3
Tach'i, *Taiwan* 59 E13
Tachia, *Taiwan* 59 E13
Tach'ing Shan = Daqing Shan, *China* 56 D6
Tachov, *Czech Rep.* 26 B5
Tácina →, *Italy* 31 D9
Tacloban, *Phil.* 61 F6
Tacna, *Peru* 124 G4
Tacoma, *U.S.A.* 116 C4
Tacuarembó, *Uruguay* 127 C4
Tademaït, Plateau du, *Algeria* 78 C6
Tadio, L., *Ivory C.* 82 D3
Tadjoura, *Djibouti* 81 E5
Tadjoura, Golfe de, *Djibouti* 81 E5
Tadmor, *N.Z.* 91 J4
Tadoule, L., *Canada* 105 B9
Tadoussac, *Canada* 103 C6
Tadzhikistan = Tajikistan ■, *Asia* 50 F8
Taechŏn-ni, *S. Korea* 57 F14
Taegu, *S. Korea* 57 G15
Taegwan, *N. Korea* 57 D13
Taejŏn, *S. Korea* 57 F14
Tafalla, *Spain* 32 C3
Tafar, *Sudan* 81 F2
Tafelbaai, *S. Africa* 88 E2
Tafermaar, *Indonesia* 63 F8
Tafí Viejo, *Argentina* 126 B2
Tafīhān, *Iran* 71 D7
Tafiré, *Ivory C.* 82 D3
Tafo, *Ghana* 83 D4
Tafresh, *Iran* 71 C6
Taft, *Iran* 71 D7
Taft, *Phil.* 61 F6
Taft, *U.S.A.* 117 K7
Taftān, Kūh-e, *Iran* 71 D9
Taga Dzong, *Bhutan* 67 F16
Taganrog, *Russia* 47 J10
Taganrogskiy Zaliv, *Russia* 47 J10
Tagânt, *Mauritania* 82 B2
Tagatay, *Phil.* 61 D4
Tagbilaran, *Phil.* 61 G5
Tággia, *Italy* 28 E4
Tagish, *Canada* 104 A2
Tagish L., *Canada* 104 A2
Tagliacozzo, *Italy* 29 F10
Tagliamento →, *Italy* 29 C10
Táglio di Po, *Italy* 29 D9
Tago, *Phil.* 61 G7
Tagomago, *Spain* 37 B8
Tagourâret, *Mauritania* 82 B3
Taguatinga, *Brazil* 125 F10
Tagudin, *Phil.* 61 C4
Tagum, *Phil.* 61 H6
Tagus = Tejo →, *Europe* 35 F2
Tahakopa, *N.Z.* 91 M2
Tahan, Gunong, *Malaysia* 65 K4
Tahat, *Algeria* 78 D7
Tāherī, *Iran* 71 E7
Tahiti, *Pac. Oc.* 97 J13
Tahlequah, *U.S.A.* 113 H7
Tahoe, L., *U.S.A.* 116 G6
Tahoe City, *U.S.A.* 116 F6
Tahoka, *U.S.A.* 113 J4
Taholah, *U.S.A.* 116 C2
Tahoua, *Niger* 83 C6
Tahrūd, *Iran* 71 D8
Tahsis, *Canada* 104 D3
Tahta, *Egypt* 80 B3
Tahtaköprü, *Turkey* 41 G13
Tahtalı Dağları, *Turkey* 72 C7
Tahulandang, *Indonesia* 63 D7
Tahuna, *Indonesia* 63 D7
Taï, *Ivory C.* 82 D3
Tai Hu, *China* 59 B12
Tai Shan, *China* 57 F9
Tai'an, *China* 57 F9
Taibei = T'aipei, *Taiwan* 59 E13
Taibique, *Canary Is.* 37 G2
Taibus Qi, *China* 56 D8
Taicang, *China* 59 B13
T'aichung, *Taiwan* 59 E13
Taieri →, *N.Z.* 91 M3
Taigu, *China* 56 F7
Taihang Shan, *China* 56 G7
Taihape, *N.Z.* 91 H5
Taihe, *Anhui, China* 56 H8
Taihe, *Jiangxi, China* 59 D10

Taihu, *China* 59 **B11**
Taijiang, *China* 58 **D7**
Taikang, *China* 56 **G8**
Tailem Bend, *Australia* 95 **F2**
Tailfingen, *Germany* 25 **G5**
Tailuko, *Taiwan* 59 **E13**
Taimyr Peninsula = Taymyr, Poluostrov, *Russia* 51 **B11**
Tain, *U.K.* 14 **D4**
T'ainan, *Taiwan* 59 **F13**
Taínaron, Ákra, *Greece* 38 **E4**
Taining, *China* 59 **D11**
T'aipei, *Taiwan* 59 **E13**
Taiping, *China* 59 **B12**
Taiping, *Malaysia* 65 **K3**
Taipingzhen, *China* 56 **H6**
Tairbeart = Tarbert, *U.K.* 14 **D2**
Taishan, *China* 59 **F9**
Taishun, *China* 59 **D12**
Taita Hills, *Kenya* 86 **C4**
Taitao, Pen. de, *Chile* 122 **H3**
T'aitung, *Taiwan* 59 **F13**
Taivalkoski, *Finland* 8 **D23**
Taiwan ■, *Asia* 59 **F13**
Taiwan Strait, *Asia* 59 **E12**
Taixing, *China* 59 **A13**
Taiyara, *Sudan* 81 **E3**
Taïyetos Óros, *Greece* 38 **D4**
Taiyiba, *Israel* 75 **C4**
Taiyuan, *China* 56 **F7**
Taizhong = T'aichung, *Taiwan* 59 **E13**
Taizhou, *China* 59 **A12**
Taizhou Liedao, *China* 59 **C13**
Ta'izz, *Yemen* 74 **E3**
Tājābād, *Iran* 71 **D7**
Tajikistan ■, *Asia* 50 **F8**
Tajima, *Japan* 55 **F9**
Tajo = Tejo →, *Europe* 35 **F2**
Tajrīsh, *Iran* 71 **C6**
Tak, *Thailand* 64 **D2**
Takāb, *Iran* 70 **B5**
Takachiho, *Japan* 55 **H5**
Takachu, *Botswana* 88 **C3**
Takada, *Japan* 55 **F9**
Takahagi, *Japan* 55 **F10**
Takaka, *N.Z.* 91 **J4**
Takamatsu, *Japan* 55 **G7**
Takaoka, *Japan* 55 **F8**
Takapuna, *N.Z.* 91 **G5**
Takasaki, *Japan* 55 **F9**
Takatsuki, *Japan* 55 **G7**
Takaungu, *Kenya* 86 **C4**
Takayama, *Japan* 55 **F8**
Take-Shima, *Japan* 55 **J5**
Takefu, *Japan* 55 **G8**
Takengon, *Indonesia* 62 **D1**
Takeo, *Japan* 55 **H5**
Tåkern, *Sweden* 11 **F8**
Tākestān, *Iran* 71 **C6**
Taketa, *Japan* 55 **H5**
Takev, *Cambodia* 65 **G5**
Takh, *India* 69 **C7**
Takht-Sulaiman, *Pakistan* 68 **D3**
Takikawa, *Japan* 54 **C10**
Takla L., *Canada* 104 **B3**
Takla Landing, *Canada* 104 **B3**
Takla Makan = Taklamakan Shamo, *China* 60 **C3**
Taklamakan Shamo, *China* 60 **C3**
Taku →, *Canada* 104 **B2**
Takum, *Nigeria* 83 **D6**
Tal Halāl, *Iran* 71 **D7**
Tala, *Uruguay* 127 **C4**
Talachyn, *Belarus* 46 **E5**
Talacogan, *Phil.* 61 **G6**
Talagang, *Pakistan* 68 **C5**
Talagante, *Chile* 126 **C1**
Talak, *Niger* 83 **B6**
Talamanca, Cordillera de, *Cent. Amer.* 120 **E3**
Talant, *France* 19 **E11**
Talara, *Peru* 124 **D2**
Talas, *Kyrgyzstan* 50 **E8**
Talas, *Turkey* 72 **C6**
Talâta, *Egypt* 75 **E1**
Talata Mafara, *Nigeria* 83 **C6**
Talaud, Kepulauan, *Indonesia* 63 **D7**
Talaud Is. = Talaud, Kepulauan, *Indonesia* 63 **D7**
Talavera de la Reina, *Spain* 34 **F6**
Talavera la Real, *Spain* 35 **G4**
Talayan, *Phil.* 61 **H6**
Talayuela, *Spain* 34 **F5**
Talbandh, *India* 69 **H12**
Talbert, Sillon de, *France* 18 **D3**
Talbot, C., *Australia* 92 **B4**
Talbragar →, *Australia* 95 **E4**
Talca, *Chile* 126 **D1**
Talcahuano, *Chile* 126 **D1**
Talcher, *India* 67 **J14**
Talcho, *Niger* 83 **C5**
Taldy Kurgan = Taldyqorghan, *Kazakstan* 50 **E8**
Taldyqorghan, *Kazakstan* 50 **E8**
Tālesh, *Iran* 71 **B6**
Tālesh, Kūhhā-ye, *Iran* 71 **B6**
Talguharai, *Sudan* 80 **D4**
Tali Post, *Sudan* 81 **F3**
Taliabu, *Indonesia* 63 **E6**
Talibon, *Phil.* 63 **B6**
Talibong, Ko, *Thailand* 65 **J2**
Talihina, *U.S.A.* 113 **H7**
Talisayan, *Phil.* 61 **G6**
Taliwang, *Indonesia* 62 **F5**
Tall 'Afar, *Iraq* 70 **B4**
Tall Kalakh, *Syria* 75 **A5**
Talla, *Egypt* 80 **B3**
Talladega, *U.S.A.* 109 **J2**
Tallahassee, *U.S.A.* 109 **K3**
Tallangatta, *Australia* 95 **F4**
Tallard, *France* 21 **D10**
Tällberg, *Sweden* 10 **D9**
Tallering Pk., *Australia* 93 **E2**
Talli, *Pakistan* 68 **E3**
Tallinn, *Estonia* 9 **G21**
Tallmadge, *U.S.A.* 110 **E3**
Tallulah, *U.S.A.* 113 **J9**
Tălmaciu, *Romania* 43 **E9**
Talmont-St-Hilaire, *France* 20 **B2**
Talne, *Ukraine* 47 **H6**
Talnoye = Talne, *Ukraine* 47 **H6**
Talodi, *Sudan* 81 **E3**
Talovaya, *Russia* 48 **E5**
Taloyoak, *Canada* 100 **B10**
Talpa de Allende, *Mexico* 118 **C4**
Talsi, *Latvia* 9 **H20**
Talsi □, *Latvia* 44 **A9**
Taltal, *Chile* 126 **B1**
Taltson →, *Canada* 104 **A6**
Talurqjuak = Taloyoak, *Canada* 100 **B10**
Talwood, *Australia* 95 **D4**
Talyawalka Cr. →, *Australia* 95 **E3**
Tam Chau, *Vietnam* 65 **G5**
Tam Ky, *Vietnam* 64 **E7**
Tam Quan, *Vietnam* 64 **E7**
Tama, *U.S.A.* 112 **E8**
Tamale, *Ghana* 83 **D4**
Taman, *Russia* 47 **K9**
Tamani, *Mali* 82 **C3**
Tamano, *Japan* 55 **G6**
Tamanrasset, *Algeria* 78 **D7**
Tamaqua, *U.S.A.* 111 **F9**
Tamar →, *U.K.* 13 **G3**
Tamarinda, *Spain* 37 **B10**
Tamarite de Litera, *Spain* 32 **D5**
Tamashima, *Japan* 55 **G6**
Tamási, *Hungary* 42 **D3**
Tamaské, *Niger* 83 **C6**
Tamaulipas □, *Mexico* 119 **C5**
Tamaulipas, Sierra de, *Mexico* 119 **C5**
Tamazula, *Mexico* 118 **C3**
Tamazunchale, *Mexico* 119 **C5**
Tamba-Dabatou, *Guinea* 82 **C2**
Tambacounda, *Senegal* 82 **C2**
Tambelan, Kepulauan, *Indonesia* 62 **D3**
Tambellup, *Australia* 93 **F2**
Tambo, *Australia* 94 **C4**
Tambo de Mora, *Peru* 124 **F3**
Tambohorano, *Madag.* 89 **B7**
Tambora, *Indonesia* 62 **F5**
Tambov, *Russia* 48 **D5**
Tambre →, *Spain* 34 **C2**
Tambuku, *Indonesia* 63 **G15**
Tamburâ, *Sudan* 81 **F2**
Tâmchekket, *Mauritania* 82 **B2**
Tâmega →, *Portugal* 34 **D2**
Tamenglong, *India* 67 **G18**
Tamgué, Massif du, *Guinea* 82 **C2**
Tamiahua, L. de, *Mexico* 119 **C5**
Tamil Nadu □, *India* 66 **P10**
Tamis →, *Serbia, Yug.* 42 **F5**
Tamluk, *India* 69 **H12**
Tammerfors = Tampere, *Finland* 9 **F20**
Tammisaari, *Finland* 9 **F20**
Tämnaren, *Sweden* 10 **D11**
Tamo Abu, Pegunungan, *Malaysia* 62 **D5**
Tampa, *U.S.A.* 109 **M4**
Tampa B., *U.S.A.* 109 **M4**
Tampere, *Finland* 9 **F20**
Tampico, *Mexico* 119 **C5**
Tampin, *Malaysia* 65 **L4**
Tamsweg, *Austria* 26 **D6**
Tamu, *Burma* 67 **G19**
Tamuja →, *Spain* 35 **F4**
Tamworth, *Australia* 95 **E5**
Tamworth, *Canada* 110 **B8**
Tamworth, *U.K.* 13 **E6**
Tamyang, *S. Korea* 57 **G14**
Tan An, *Vietnam* 65 **G6**
Tan-Tan, *Morocco* 78 **C3**
Tana →, *Kenya* 86 **C5**
Tana →, *Norway* 8 **A23**
Tana, L., *Ethiopia* 81 **E4**
Tana River, *Kenya* 86 **C4**
Tanabe, *Japan* 55 **H7**
Tanafjorden, *Norway* 8 **A23**
Tanaga, Pta., *Canary Is.* 37 **G1**
Tanahbala, *Indonesia* 62 **E1**
Tanahgrogot, *Indonesia* 62 **E5**
Tanahjampea, *Indonesia* 63 **F6**
Tanahmasa, *Indonesia* 62 **E1**
Tanahmerah, *Indonesia* 63 **F10**
Tanakpur, *India* 69 **E9**
Tanakura, *Japan* 55 **F10**
Tanami, *Australia* 92 **C4**
Tanami Desert, *Australia* 92 **C5**
Tanana →, *U.S.A.* 100 **B4**
Tananarive = Antananarivo, *Madag.* 89 **B8**
Tánaro →, *Italy* 28 **D5**
Tancheng, *China* 57 **G10**
Tanch'ŏn, *N. Korea* 57 **D15**
Tanda, *Ut. P., India* 69 **F10**
Tanda, *Ut. P., India* 69 **E8**
Tanda, *Ivory C.* 82 **D4**
Tandag, *Phil.* 61 **G7**
Tandaia, *Tanzania* 87 **D3**
Tăndărei, *Romania* 43 **F12**
Tandaué, *Angola* 88 **B2**
Tandil, *Argentina* 126 **D4**
Tandil, Sa. del, *Argentina* 126 **D4**
Tandlianwala, *Pakistan* 68 **D5**
Tando Adam, *Pakistan* 68 **G3**
Tando Allahyar, *Pakistan* 68 **G3**
Tando Bago, *Pakistan* 68 **G3**
Tando Mohommed Khan, *Pakistan* 68 **G3**
Tandou L., *Australia* 95 **E3**
Tandragee, *U.K.* 15 **B5**
Tandsjöborg, *Sweden* 10 **C8**
Tane-ga-Shima, *Japan* 55 **J5**
Taneatua, *N.Z.* 91 **H6**
Tanen Tong Dan = Dawna Ra., *Burma* 64 **D2**
Tanew →, *Poland* 45 **H9**
Tanezrouft, *Algeria* 78 **D6**
Tang, Koh, *Cambodia* 65 **G4**
Tang, Ra's-e, *Iran* 71 **E8**
Tang Krasang, *Cambodia* 64 **F5**
Tanga, *Tanzania* 86 **D4**
Tanga □, *Tanzania* 86 **D4**
Tanganyika, L., *Africa* 86 **D3**
Tangaza, *Nigeria* 83 **C5**
Tanger, *Morocco* 78 **A4**
Tangerang, *Indonesia* 63 **G12**
Tangerhütte, *Germany* 24 **C7**
Tangermünde, *Germany* 24 **C7**
Tanggu, *China* 57 **E9**
Tanggula Shan, *China* 60 **C4**
Tanghe, *China* 56 **H7**
Tangier = Tanger, *Morocco* 78 **A4**
Tangorin, *Australia* 94 **C3**
Tangorombohitr'i Makay, *Madag.* 89 **C8**
Tangshan, *China* 57 **E10**
Tangtou, *China* 57 **G10**
Tanguiéta, *Benin* 83 **C5**
Tangxi, *China* 59 **C12**
Tangyan He →, *China* 58 **C7**
Tanimbar, Kepulauan, *Indonesia* 63 **F8**
Tanimbar Is. = Tanimbar, Kepulauan, *Indonesia* 63 **F8**
Taninthari = Tenasserim □, *Burma* 64 **F2**
Tanjay, *Phil.* 61 **G5**
Tanjong Malim, *Malaysia* 65 **L3**
Tanjore = Thanjavur, *India* 66 **P11**
Tanjung, *Indonesia* 62 **E5**
Tanjungbalai, *Indonesia* 62 **D1**
Tanjungbatu, *Indonesia* 62 **D5**
Tanjungkarang Telukbetung, *Indonesia* 62 **F3**
Tanjungpandan, *Indonesia* 62 **E3**
Tanjungpinang, *Indonesia* 62 **D2**
Tanjungredeb, *Indonesia* 62 **D5**
Tanjungselor, *Indonesia* 62 **D5**
Tank, *Pakistan* 68 **C4**
Tankhala, *India* 68 **J5**
Tännäs, *Sweden* 10 **B6**
Tannersville, *U.S.A.* 111 **E9**
Tannis Bugt, *Denmark* 11 **G4**
Tannu-Ola, *Russia* 51 **D10**
Tannum Sands, *Australia* 94 **C5**
Tano →, *Ghana* 82 **D4**
Tanon Str., *Phil.* 61 **F5**
Tanout, *Niger* 83 **C6**
Tanshui, *Taiwan* 59 **E13**
Tansilla, *Burkina Faso* 82 **C4**
Tanta, *Egypt* 80 **H7**
Tantoyuca, *Mexico* 119 **C5**
Tantung = Dandong, *China* 57 **D13**
Tanumshede, *Sweden* 11 **F5**
Tanunda, *Australia* 95 **E2**
Tanus, *France* 20 **D6**
Tanzania ■, *Africa* 86 **D3**
Tanzilla →, *Canada* 104 **B2**
Tao, Ko, *Thailand* 65 **G2**
Tao'an = Taonan, *China* 57 **B12**
Tao'er He →, *China* 57 **B13**
Taohua Dao, *China* 59 **C14**
Taolanaro, *Madag.* 89 **D8**
Taole, *China* 56 **E4**
Taonan, *China* 57 **B12**
Taormina, *Italy* 31 **E8**
Taos, *U.S.A.* 115 **H11**
Taoudenni, *Mali* 78 **D5**
Taoyuan, *China* 59 **C8**
T'aoyüan, *Taiwan* 59 **E13**
Tapa, *Estonia* 9 **G21**
Tapa Shan = Daba Shan, *China* 58 **B7**
Tapachula, *Mexico* 119 **E6**
Tapah, *Malaysia* 65 **K3**
Tapajós →, *Brazil* 122 **D5**
Tapaktuan, *Indonesia* 62 **D1**
Tapanahoni →, *Surinam* 125 **C8**
Tapanui, *N.Z.* 91 **L2**
Tapauá →, *Brazil* 124 **E6**
Tapes, *Brazil* 127 **C5**
Tapeta, *Liberia* 82 **D3**
Taphan Hin, *Thailand* 64 **D3**
Tapi →, *India* 66 **J8**
Tapia de Casariego, *Spain* 34 **B4**
Tapirapecó, Serra, *Venezuela* 124 **C6**
Tapolca, *Hungary* 42 **D2**
Tapuaenuku, Mt., *N.Z.* 91 **K4**
Tapul Group, *Phil.* 61 **J4**
Tapurucuará, *Brazil* 124 **D5**
Ţaqţaq, *Iraq* 70 **C5**
Taquara, *Brazil* 127 **B5**
Taquari →, *Brazil* 124 **G7**
Tara, *Australia* 95 **D5**
Tara, *Canada* 110 **B3**
Tara, *Russia* 50 **D8**
Tara, *Zambia* 87 **F2**
Tara →, *Montenegro, Yug.* 40 **C2**
Taraba □, *Nigeria* 83 **D7**
Taraba →, *Nigeria* 83 **D7**
Tarabagatay, Khrebet, *Kazakstan* 50 **E9**
Tarābulus, *Lebanon* 75 **A4**
Tarābulus, *Libya* 79 **B8**
Taraclia, *Moldova* 43 **D14**
Taraclia, *Moldova* 43 **E13**
Taradehi, *India* 69 **H8**
Tarajalejo, *Canary Is.* 37 **F5**
Tarakan, *Indonesia* 62 **D5**
Tarakit, Mt., *Kenya* 86 **B4**
Tarama-Jima, *Japan* 55 **M2**
Taran, Mys, *Russia* 9 **J18**
Taranagar, *India* 68 **E6**
Taranaki □, *N.Z.* 91 **H5**
Taranaki, Mt., *N.Z.* 91 **H5**
Tarancón, *Spain* 32 **E1**
Taransay, *U.K.* 14 **D1**
Táranto, *Italy* 31 **B10**
Táranto, G. di, *Italy* 31 **B10**
Tarapacá, *Colombia* 124 **D5**
Tarapacá □, *Chile* 126 **A2**
Tarapoto, *Peru* 124 **E3**
Tarare, *France* 21 **C8**
Tararua Ra., *N.Z.* 91 **J5**
Tarascon, *France* 21 **E8**
Tarascon-sur-Ariège, *France* 20 **F5**
Tarashcha, *Ukraine* 47 **H6**
Tarauacá, *Brazil* 124 **E4**
Tarauacá →, *Brazil* 124 **E5**
Taravo →, *France* 21 **G12**
Tarawa, *Kiribati* 96 **G9**
Tarawera, *N.Z.* 91 **H6**
Tarawera L., *N.Z.* 91 **H6**
Taraz, *Kazakstan* 50 **E8**
Tarazona, *Spain* 32 **D3**
Tarazona de la Mancha, *Spain* 33 **F3**
Tarbat Ness, *U.K.* 14 **D5**
Tarbela Dam, *Pakistan* 68 **B5**
Tarbert, *Arg. & Bute, U.K.* 14 **F3**
Tarbert, *W. Isles, U.K.* 14 **D2**
Tarbes, *France* 20 **E4**
Tarboro, *U.S.A.* 109 **H7**
Tărcău, Munţii, *Romania* 43 **D11**
Tarcento, *Italy* 29 **B10**
Tarcoola, *Australia* 95 **E1**
Tarcoon, *Australia* 95 **E4**
Tardets-Sorholus, *France* 20 **E3**
Tardoire →, *France* 20 **C4**
Taree, *Australia* 95 **E5**
Tarfa, W. el →, *Egypt* 80 **B3**
Tarfaya, *Morocco* 78 **C3**
Târgovişte, *Romania* 43 **F10**
Târgu Bujor, *Romania* 43 **E12**
Târgu Cărbuneşti, *Romania* 43 **F8**
Târgu Frumos, *Romania* 43 **C12**
Târgu-Jiu, *Romania* 43 **E8**
Târgu Lăpuş, *Romania* 43 **C8**
Târgu Mureş, *Romania* 43 **D9**
Târgu Neamţ, *Romania* 43 **C11**
Târgu Ocna, *Romania* 43 **D11**
Târgu Secuiesc, *Romania* 43 **E11**
Târguşor, *Romania* 43 **F13**
Tărhăus, Vf., *Romania* 43 **D11**
Ţarif, *U.A.E.* 71 **E7**
Tarifa, *Spain* 35 **J5**
Tarija, *Bolivia* 126 **A3**
Tarija □, *Bolivia* 126 **A3**
Tariku →, *Indonesia* 63 **E9**
Tarim Basin = Tarim Pendi, *China* 60 **C3**
Tarim He →, *China* 60 **C3**
Tarim Pendi, *China* 60 **C3**
Taritatu →, *Indonesia* 63 **E9**
Tarka →, *S. Africa* 88 **E4**
Tarkastad, *S. Africa* 88 **E4**
Tarkhankut, Mys, *Ukraine* 47 **K7**
Tarko Sale, *Russia* 50 **C8**
Tarkwa, *Ghana* 82 **D4**
Tarlac, *Phil.* 61 **D4**
Tarm, *Denmark* 11 **J2**
Tarma, *Peru* 124 **F3**
Tarn □, *France* 20 **E6**
Tarn →, *France* 20 **D5**
Tarn-et-Garonne □, *France* 20 **D5**
Tarna →, *Hungary* 42 **C4**
Târnava Mare →, *Romania* 43 **D8**
Târnava Mică →, *Romania* 43 **D8**
Târnăveni, *Romania* 43 **D9**
Tarnica, *Poland* 45 **J9**
Tarnobrzeg, *Poland* 45 **H8**
Tarnogród, *Poland* 45 **H9**
Tarnos, *France* 20 **E2**
Târnova, *Moldova* 43 **B12**
Târnova, *Romania* 42 **E6**
Tarnów, *Poland* 45 **H8**
Tarnowskie Góry, *Poland* 45 **H5**
Tärnsjö, *Sweden* 10 **D10**
Táro →, *Italy* 28 **C7**
Ţarom, *Iran* 71 **D7**
Taroom, *Australia* 95 **D4**
Taroudannt, *Morocco* 78 **B4**
Tarp, *Germany* 24 **A5**
Tarpon Springs, *U.S.A.* 109 **L4**
Tarquínia, *Italy* 29 **F8**
Tarragona, *Spain* 32 **D6**
Tarragona □, *Spain* 32 **D6**
Tarraleah, *Australia* 94 **G4**
Tarrasa = Terrassa, *Spain* 32 **D7**
Tàrrega, *Spain* 32 **D6**
Tarrytown, *U.S.A.* 111 **E11**
Tårs, *Denmark* 11 **G4**
Tarshiha = Me'ona, *Israel* 75 **B4**
Tarso Emissi, *Chad* 79 **D9**
Tarsus, *Turkey* 70 **B2**
Tartagal, *Argentina* 126 **A3**
Tärtär, *Azerbaijan* 49 **K8**
Tärtär →, *Azerbaijan* 49 **K8**
Tartas, *France* 20 **E3**
Tartu, *Estonia* 9 **G22**
Ţarţūs, *Syria* 70 **C2**
Tarumizu, *Japan* 55 **J5**
Tarussa, *Russia* 46 **E9**
Tarutao, Ko, *Thailand* 65 **J2**
Tarutung, *Indonesia* 62 **D1**
Tarvísio, *Italy* 29 **B10**
Taseko →, *Canada* 104 **C4**
Tash-Kömür, *Kyrgyzstan* 50 **E8**
Tash-Kumyr = Tash-Kömür, *Kyrgyzstan* 50 **E8**
Tashauz = Dashhowuz, *Turkmenistan* 50 **E6**
Tashi Chho Dzong = Thimphu, *Bhutan* 67 **F16**
Ţashk, Daryācheh-ye, *Iran* 71 **D7**
Tashkent = Toshkent, *Uzbekistan* 50 **E7**
Tashtagol, *Russia* 50 **D9**
Tasiilaq, *Greenland* 4 **C6**
Tasikmalaya, *Indonesia* 63 **G13**
Tåsinge, *Denmark* 11 **J4**
Tåsjön, *Sweden* 8 **D16**
Taskan, *Russia* 51 **C16**
Tasker, *Niger* 83 **C7**
Taşköprü, *Turkey* 72 **B6**
Taşlâc, *Moldova* 43 **C14**
Tasman B., *N.Z.* 91 **J4**
Tasman Mts., *N.Z.* 91 **J4**
Tasman Pen., *Australia* 94 **G4**
Tasman Sea, *Pac. Oc.* 96 **L8**
Tasmania □, *Australia* 94 **G4**
Tăşnad, *Romania* 42 **C7**
Tassili n'Ajjer, *Algeria* 78 **C7**
Tassili Tin-Rerhoh, *Algeria* 83 **A5**
Tata, *Hungary* 42 **C3**
Tatabánya, *Hungary* 42 **C3**
Tatahouine, *Tunisia* 79 **B8**
Tatar Republic = Tatarstan □, *Russia* 48 **C10**
Tatarbunary, *Ukraine* 47 **K5**
Tatarsk, *Russia* 50 **D8**
Tatarstan □, *Russia* 48 **C10**
Tateyama, *Japan* 55 **G9**
Tathlina L., *Canada* 104 **A5**
Tathra, *Australia* 95 **F4**
Tatinnai L., *Canada* 105 **A9**
Tatla L., *Canada* 104 **C4**
Tatlısu, *Turkey* 41 **F11**
Tatnam, C., *Canada* 105 **B10**
Tatra = Tatry, *Slovak Rep.* 27 **B13**
Tatry, *Slovak Rep.* 27 **B13**
Tatshenshini →, *Canada* 104 **B1**
Tatsuno, *Japan* 55 **G7**
Tatta, *Pakistan* 68 **G2**
Tatuí, *Brazil* 127 **A6**
Tatum, *U.S.A.* 113 **J3**
Tat'ung = Datong, *China* 56 **D7**
Tatvan, *Turkey* 70 **B4**
Taubaté, *Brazil* 127 **A6**
Tauberbischofsheim, *Germany* 25 **F5**
Taucha, *Germany* 24 **D8**
Tauern-tunnel, *Austria* 26 **D6**
Taufikia, *Sudan* 81 **F3**
Taulé, *France* 18 **D3**
Taumarunui, *N.Z.* 91 **H5**
Taumaturgo, *Brazil* 124 **E4**
Taung, *S. Africa* 88 **D3**
Taungdwingyi, *Burma* 67 **J19**
Taunggyi, *Burma* 67 **J20**
Taungup, *Burma* 67 **K19**
Taungup Taunggya, *Burma* 67 **K18**
Taunsa, *Pakistan* 68 **D4**
Taunsa Barrage, *Pakistan* 68 **D4**
Taunton, *U.K.* 13 **F4**
Taunton, *U.S.A.* 111 **E13**
Taunus, *Germany* 25 **E4**
Taupo, *N.Z.* 91 **H6**
Taupo, L., *N.Z.* 91 **H5**
Tauragė, *Lithuania* 9 **J20**
Tauragė □, *Lithuania* 44 **C9**
Tauranga, *N.Z.* 91 **G6**
Tauranga Harb., *N.Z.* 91 **G6**
Taureau, Rés., *Canada* 102 **C5**
Taurianova, *Italy* 31 **D9**
Taurus Mts. = Toros Dağları, *Turkey* 70 **B2**
Tauste, *Spain* 32 **D3**
Tauz = Tovuz, *Azerbaijan* 49 **K7**
Tavas, *Turkey* 39 **D11**
Tavda, *Russia* 50 **D7**
Tavda →, *Russia* 50 **D7**
Tavernes de la Valldigna, *Spain* 33 **F4**
Taveta, *Tanzania* 86 **C4**
Taveuni, *Fiji* 91 **C9**
Taviano, *Italy* 31 **C11**
Tavignano →, *France* 21 **F13**
Tavira, *Portugal* 35 **H3**
Tavistock, *Canada* 110 **C4**
Tavistock, *U.K.* 13 **G3**
Tavolara, *Italy* 30 **B2**
Távora →, *Portugal* 34 **D3**
Tavoy = Dawei, *Burma* 64 **E2**
Tavşanlı, *Turkey* 39 **B11**
Taw →, *U.K.* 13 **F3**
Tawa →, *India* 68 **H8**
Tawas City, *U.S.A.* 108 **C4**
Tawau, *Malaysia* 62 **D5**
Taweisha, *Sudan* 81 **E2**
Tawitawi, *Phil.* 63 **B6**
Tawu, *Taiwan* 59 **F13**
Taxco de Alarcón, *Mexico* 119 **D5**
Taxila, *Pakistan* 68 **C5**
Tay →, *U.K.* 14 **E5**
Tay, Firth of, *U.K.* 14 **E5**
Tay, L., *Australia* 93 **F3**
Tay, L., *U.K.* 14 **E4**
Tay Ninh, *Vietnam* 65 **G6**

Tayabamba, *Peru* 124 E3
Tayabas Bay, *Phil.* 61 E4
Taylakova, *Russia* 50 D8
Taylakovy = Taylakova, *Russia* 50 D8
Taylor, *Canada* 104 B4
Taylor, *Nebr., U.S.A.* 112 E5
Taylor, *Pa., U.S.A.* 111 E9
Taylor, *Tex., U.S.A.* 113 K6
Taylor, Mt., *U.S.A.* 115 J10
Taylorville, *U.S.A.* 112 F10
Taymā, *Si. Arabia* 70 E3
Taymyr, Oz., *Russia* 51 B11
Taymyr, Poluostrov, *Russia* 51 B11
Tayport, *U.K.* 14 E6
Tayshet, *Russia* 51 D10
Taytay, *Phil.* 61 F3
Taz →, *Russia* 50 C8
Taza, *Morocco* 78 B5
Tāzah Khurmātū, *Iraq* 70 C5
Tazawa-Ko, *Japan* 54 E10
Tazin, *Canada* 105 B7
Tazin L., *Canada* 105 B7
Tazovskiy, *Russia* 50 C8
Tbilisi, *Georgia* 49 K7
Tchad = Chad ■, *Africa* 79 F8
Tchad, L., *Chad* 79 F8
Tchaourou, *Benin* 83 D5
Tch'eng-tou = Chengdu, *China* 58 B5
Tchentlo L., *Canada* 104 B4
Tchetti, *Benin* 83 D5
Tchibanga, *Gabon* 84 E2
Tchien, *Liberia* 82 D3
Tchin Tabaraden, *Niger* 83 B6
Tch'ong-k'ing = Chongqing, *China* 58 C6
Tczew, *Poland* 44 D5
Te Anau, *N.Z.* 91 L1
Te Anau, L., *N.Z.* 91 L1
Te Aroha, *N.Z.* 91 G5
Te Awamutu, *N.Z.* 91 H5
Te Kuiti, *N.Z.* 91 H5
Te-n-Dghâmcha, Sebkhet, *Mauritania* 82 B1
Te Puke, *N.Z.* 91 G6
Te Waewae B., *N.Z.* 91 M1
Teaca, *Romania* 43 D9
Teague, *U.S.A.* 113 K6
Teano, *Italy* 31 A7
Teapa, *Mexico* 119 D6
Teba, *Spain* 35 J6
Tebakang, *Malaysia* 62 D4
Teberda, *Russia* 49 J5
Tébessa, *Algeria* 78 A7
Tebicuary →, *Paraguay* 126 B4
Tebingtinggi, *Indonesia* 62 D1
Tebintingii, *Indonesia* 62 E2
Tebulos, *Georgia* 49 J7
Tecate, *Mexico* 117 N10
Tecer Dağları, *Turkey* 72 C7
Tech →, *France* 20 F7
Techiman, *Ghana* 82 D4
Techirghiol, *Romania* 43 F13
Tecka, *Argentina* 128 E2
Tecomán, *Mexico* 118 D4
Tecopa, *U.S.A.* 117 K10
Tecoripa, *Mexico* 118 B3
Tecuala, *Mexico* 118 C3
Tecuci, *Romania* 43 E12
Tecumseh, *Canada* 110 D2
Tecumseh, *Mich., U.S.A.* 108 D4
Tecumseh, *Okla., U.S.A.* 113 H6
Tedzhen = Tejen, *Turkmenistan* 50 F7
Tees →, *U.K.* 12 C6
Tees B., *U.K.* 12 C6
Teeswater, *Canada* 110 C3
Tefé, *Brazil* 124 D6
Tefenni, *Turkey* 39 D11
Tegal, *Indonesia* 62 F3
Tegernsee, *Germany* 25 H7
Teggiano, *Italy* 31 B8
Tegid, L. = Bala, L., *U.K.* 12 E4
Tegina, *Nigeria* 83 C6
Tegucigalpa, *Honduras* 120 D2
Teguidda i-n-Tessoum, *Niger* 83 B6
Tehachapi, *U.S.A.* 117 K8
Tehachapi Mts., *U.S.A.* 117 L8
Tehamiyam, *Sudan* 80 D4
Tehilla, *Sudan* 80 D4
Téhini, *Ivory C.* 82 D4
Tehoru, *Indonesia* 63 E7
Tehrān, *Iran* 71 C6
Tehri, *India* 69 D8
Tehuacán, *Mexico* 119 D5
Tehuantepec, *Mexico* 119 D5
Tehuantepec, G. de, *Mexico* 119 D5
Tehuantepec, Istmo de, *Mexico* 119 D6
Teide, *Canary Is.* 37 F3
Teifi →, *U.K.* 13 E3
Teign →, *U.K.* 13 G4
Teignmouth, *U.K.* 13 G4
Teiuş, *Romania* 43 D8
Teixeira Pinto, *Guinea-Biss.* 82 C1
Tejam, *India* 69 E9
Tejen, *Turkmenistan* 50 F7
Tejen →, *Turkmenistan* 71 B9
Tejo →, *Europe* 35 F2
Tejon Pass, *U.S.A.* 117 L8
Tekamah, *U.S.A.* 112 E6
Tekapo, L., *N.Z.* 91 K3
Tekax, *Mexico* 119 C7
Teke, *Turkey* 41 E13
Tekeli, *Kazakstan* 50 E8
Tekeze →, *Ethiopia* 81 E4
Tekija, *Serbia, Yug.* 40 B6
Tekirdağ, *Turkey* 41 F11
Tekirdağ □, *Turkey* 41 E11
Tekirova, *Turkey* 39 E12
Tekkali, *India* 67 K14
Tekke, *Turkey* 72 B7
Tekman, *Turkey* 73 C9
Tekoa, *U.S.A.* 114 C5
Tel Aviv-Yafo, *Israel* 75 C3
Tel Lakhish, *Israel* 75 D3
Tel Megiddo, *Israel* 75 C4
Tela, *Honduras* 120 C2
Telanaipura = Jambi, *Indonesia* 62 E2
Telavi, *Georgia* 49 J7
Telč, *Czech Rep.* 26 B8
Telciu, *Romania* 43 C9
Telde, *Canary Is.* 37 G4
Telegraph Creek, *Canada* 104 B2
Telekhany = Tsyelyakhany, *Belarus* 47 F3
Telemark, *Norway* 9 G12
Telén, *Argentina* 126 D2
Teleneşti, *Moldova* 43 C13
Teleng, *Iran* 71 E9
Teleño, *Spain* 34 C4
Teleorman □, *Romania* 43 G10
Teleorman →, *Romania* 43 G10
Teles Pires →, *Brazil* 122 D5
Telescope Pk., *U.S.A.* 117 J9
Teletaye, *Mali* 83 B5
Telfer Mine, *Australia* 92 C3
Telford, *U.K.* 13 E5
Telford and Wrekin □, *U.K.* 12 E5
Telfs, *Austria* 26 D4
Télimélé, *Guinea* 82 C2
Teljo, J., *Sudan* 81 E2
Telkwa, *Canada* 104 C3
Tell City, *U.S.A.* 108 G2
Tellicherry, *India* 66 P9
Telluride, *U.S.A.* 115 H10
Teloloapán, *Mexico* 119 D5
Telpos Iz, *Russia* 6 C17
Telsen, *Argentina* 128 E3
Telšiai, *Lithuania* 9 H20
Telšiai □, *Lithuania* 44 C9
Teltow, *Germany* 24 C9
Teluk Anson = Teluk Intan, *Malaysia* 65 K3
Teluk Betung = Tanjungkarang Telukbetung, *Indonesia* 62 F3
Teluk Intan, *Malaysia* 65 K3
Telukbutun, *Indonesia* 65 K7
Telukdalem, *Indonesia* 62 D1
Tema, *Ghana* 83 D5
Temax, *Mexico* 119 C7
Temba, *S. Africa* 89 D4
Tembagapura, *Indonesia* 63 E9
Tembe, *Dem. Rep. of the Congo* 86 C2
Tembleque, *Spain* 34 F7
Temblor Range, *U.S.A.* 117 K7
Teme →, *U.K.* 13 E5
Temecula, *U.S.A.* 117 M9
Temerloh, *Malaysia* 62 D2
Teminabuan, *Indonesia* 63 E8
Temir, *Kazakstan* 50 E6
Temirtau, *Kazakstan* 50 D8
Temirtau, *Russia* 50 D9
Temiscamie →, *Canada* 103 B5
Témiscaming, *Canada* 102 C4
Témiscamingue, L., *Canada* 102 C4
Temnikov, *Russia* 48 C6
Temo →, *Italy* 30 B1
Temosachic, *Mexico* 118 B3
Tempe, *U.S.A.* 115 K8
Témpio Pausánia, *Italy* 30 B2
Tempiute, *U.S.A.* 116 H11
Temple, *U.S.A.* 113 K6
Temple B., *Australia* 94 A3
Templemore, *Ireland* 15 D4
Templeton, *U.S.A.* 116 K6
Templeton →, *Australia* 94 C2
Templin, *Germany* 24 B9
Tempoal, *Mexico* 119 C5
Temryuk, *Russia* 47 K9
Temska →, *Serbia, Yug.* 40 C6
Temuco, *Chile* 128 D2
Temuka, *N.Z.* 91 L3
Tenabo, *Mexico* 119 C6
Tenaha, *U.S.A.* 113 K7
Tenakee Springs, *U.S.A.* 104 B1
Tenali, *India* 67 L12
Tenancingo, *Mexico* 119 D5
Tenango, *Mexico* 119 D5
Tenasserim, *Burma* 65 F2
Tenasserim □, *Burma* 64 F2
Tenby, *U.K.* 13 F3
Tenda, Colle di, *France* 21 D11
Tendaho, *Ethiopia* 81 E5
Tende, *France* 21 D11
Tendelti, *Sudan* 81 E3
Tendrovskaya Kosa, *Ukraine* 47 J6
Tendukhera, *India* 69 H8
Teneida, *Egypt* 80 B2
Tenenkou, *Mali* 82 C4
Ténéré, *Niger* 83 B7
Tenerife, *Canary Is.* 37 F3
Tenerife, Pico, *Canary Is.* 37 G1
Teng Xian, *Guangxi Zhuangzu, China* 59 F8
Teng Xian, *Shandong, China* 57 G9
Tengah □, *Indonesia* 63 E6
Tengah, Kepulauan, *Indonesia* 62 F5
Tengchong, *China* 58 E2
Tengchowfu = Penglai, *China* 57 F11
Tenggara □, *Indonesia* 63 E6
Tenggarong, *Indonesia* 62 E5
Tenggol, Pulau, *Malaysia* 65 K4
Tengiz, Ozero, *Kazakstan* 50 D7
Tenhult, *Sweden* 11 G8
Tenino, *U.S.A.* 116 D4
Tenkasi, *India* 66 Q10
Tenke, *Katanga, Dem. Rep. of the Congo* 87 E2
Tenke, *Katanga, Dem. Rep. of the Congo* 87 E2
Tenkodogo, *Burkina Faso* 83 C4
Tenna →, *Italy* 29 E10
Tennant Creek, *Australia* 94 B1
Tennessee □, *U.S.A.* 109 H2
Tennessee →, *U.S.A.* 108 G1
Teno, Pta. de, *Canary Is.* 37 F3
Tenom, *Malaysia* 62 C5
Tenosique, *Mexico* 119 D6
Tenryū-Gawa →, *Japan* 55 G8
Tenterden, *U.K.* 13 F8
Tenterfield, *Australia* 95 D5
Teo, *Spain* 34 C2
Teófilo Otoni, *Brazil* 125 G10
Tepa, *Indonesia* 63 F7
Tepalcatepec →, *Mexico* 118 D4
Tepecik, *Bursa, Turkey* 41 F12
Tepecik, *Kütahya, Turkey* 39 B11
Tepehuanes, *Mexico* 118 B3
Tepelenë, *Albania* 40 F4
Tepetongo, *Mexico* 118 C4
Tepic, *Mexico* 118 C4
Teplá, *Czech Rep.* 26 B5
Teplice, *Czech Rep.* 26 A6
Tepoca, C., *Mexico* 118 A2
Tequila, *Mexico* 118 C4
Ter →, *Spain* 32 C8
Ter Apel, *Neths.* 17 B7
Téra, *Niger* 83 C5
Tera →, *Spain* 34 D5
Teraina, *Kiribati* 97 G11
Terakeka, *Sudan* 81 F3
Téramo, *Italy* 29 F10
Terang, *Australia* 95 F3
Terazit, Massif de, *Niger* 83 A6
Tercan, *Turkey* 73 C9
Tercero →, *Argentina* 126 C3
Terebovlya, *Ukraine* 47 H3
Teregova, *Romania* 42 E7
Tereida, *Sudan* 81 E3
Terek →, *Russia* 49 J8
Tereshka →, *Russia* 48 E8
Teresina, *Brazil* 125 E10
Terespol, *Poland* 45 F10
Terewah, L., *Australia* 95 D4
Terges →, *Portugal* 35 H3
Tergnier, *France* 19 C10
Teridgerie Cr. →, *Australia* 95 E4
Terlizzi, *Italy* 31 A9
Terme, *Turkey* 72 B7
Termez = Termiz, *Uzbekistan* 50 F7
Términi Imerese, *Italy* 30 E6
Términos, L. de, *Mexico* 119 D6
Termiz, *Uzbekistan* 50 F7
Térmoli, *Italy* 29 F12
Ternate, *Indonesia* 63 D7
Terneuzen, *Neths.* 17 C3
Terney, *Russia* 51 E14
Terni, *Italy* 29 F9
Ternitz, *Austria* 26 D9
Ternopil, *Ukraine* 47 H3
Ternopol = Ternopil, *Ukraine* 47 H3
Terowie, *Australia* 95 E2
Terpní, *Greece* 40 F7
Terra Bella, *U.S.A.* 117 K7
Terra Nova Nat. Park, *Canada* 103 C9
Terrace, *Canada* 104 C3
Terrace Bay, *Canada* 102 C2
Terracina, *Italy* 30 A6
Terralba, *Italy* 30 C1
Terranova = Ólbia, *Italy* 30 B2
Terrasini, *Italy* 30 D6
Terrassa, *Spain* 32 D7
Terrasson-la-Villedieu, *France* 20 C5
Terre Haute, *U.S.A.* 108 F2
Terrebonne B., *U.S.A.* 113 L9
Terrell, *U.S.A.* 113 J6
Terrenceville, *Canada* 103 C9
Terry, *U.S.A.* 112 B2
Terryville, *U.S.A.* 111 E11
Terschelling, *Neths.* 17 A5
Tersko-Kumskiy Kanal →, *Russia* 49 H7
Tertenía, *Italy* 30 C2
Terter → = Tärtär →, *Azerbaijan* 49 K8
Teruel, *Spain* 32 E3
Teruel □, *Spain* 32 E4
Tervel, *Bulgaria* 41 C11
Tervola, *Finland* 8 C21
Teryaweyna L., *Australia* 95 E3
Tešanj, *Bos.-H.* 42 F3
Teseney, *Eritrea* 81 D4
Tesha →, *Russia* 48 C6
Teshio, *Japan* 54 B10
Teshio-Gawa →, *Japan* 54 B10
Tešica, *Serbia, Yug.* 40 C5
Tesiyn Gol →, *Mongolia* 60 A4
Teslić, *Bos.-H.* 42 F2
Teslin, *Canada* 104 A2
Teslin →, *Canada* 104 A2
Teslin L., *Canada* 104 A2
Tessalit, *Mali* 83 A5
Tessaoua, *Niger* 83 C6
Tessin, *Germany* 24 A8
Tessit, *Mali* 83 B5
Test →, *U.K.* 13 G6
Testa del Gargano, *Italy* 29 G13
Testigos, Is. Las, *Venezuela* 121 D7
Tét, *Hungary* 42 C2
Têt →, *France* 20 F7
Tetachuck L., *Canada* 104 C3
Tetas, Pta., *Chile* 126 A1
Tete, *Mozam.* 87 F3
Tete □, *Mozam.* 87 F3
Teterev →, *Ukraine* 47 G6
Teterow, *Germany* 24 B8
Teteven, *Bulgaria* 41 D8
Tethul →, *Canada* 104 A6
Tetiyev, *Ukraine* 47 H5
Teton →, *U.S.A.* 114 C8
Tétouan, *Morocco* 78 A4
Tetovo, *Macedonia* 40 D4
Tetyushi, *Russia* 48 C9
Teuco →, *Argentina* 126 B3
Teulada, *Italy* 30 D1
Teulon, *Canada* 105 C9
Teun, *Indonesia* 63 F7
Teutoburger Wald, *Germany* 24 C4
Tevere →, *Italy* 29 G9
Teverya, *Israel* 75 C4
Teviot →, *U.K.* 14 F6
Tewantin, *Australia* 95 D5
Tewkesbury, *U.K.* 13 F5
Texada I., *Canada* 104 D4
Texarkana, *Ark., U.S.A.* 113 J8
Texarkana, *Tex., U.S.A.* 113 J7
Texas, *Australia* 95 D5
Texas □, *U.S.A.* 113 K5
Texas City, *U.S.A.* 113 L7
Texel, *Neths.* 17 A4
Texline, *U.S.A.* 113 G3
Texoma, L., *U.S.A.* 113 J6
Teykovo, *Russia* 46 D11
Teza →, *Russia* 48 B5
Tezin, *Afghan.* 68 B3
Teziutlán, *Mexico* 119 D5
Tezpur, *India* 67 F18
Tezzeron L., *Canada* 104 C4
Tha-anne →, *Canada* 105 A10
Tha Deua, *Laos* 64 D4
Tha Deua, *Laos* 64 C3
Tha Pla, *Thailand* 64 D3
Tha Rua, *Thailand* 64 E3
Tha Sala, *Thailand* 65 H2
Tha Song Yang, *Thailand* 64 D1
Thaba Putsoa, *Lesotho* 89 D4
Thabana Ntlenyana, *Lesotho* 89 D4
Thabazimbi, *S. Africa* 89 C4
Thādiq, *Si. Arabia* 70 E5
Thai Binh, *Vietnam* 58 G6
Thai Muang, *Thailand* 65 H2
Thai Nguyen, *Vietnam* 58 G5
Thailand ■, *Asia* 64 E4
Thailand, G. of, *Asia* 65 G3
Thakhek, *Laos* 64 D5
Thal, *Pakistan* 68 C4
Thal Desert, *Pakistan* 68 D4
Thala La = Hkakabo Razi, *Burma* 67 E20
Thalabarivat, *Cambodia* 64 F5
Thallon, *Australia* 95 D4
Thalwil, *Switz.* 25 H4
Thames, *N.Z.* 91 G5
Thames →, *Canada* 102 D3
Thames →, *U.K.* 13 F8
Thames →, *U.S.A.* 111 E12
Thames Estuary, *U.K.* 13 F8
Thamesford, *Canada* 110 C4
Thamesville, *Canada* 110 D3
Than, *India* 68 H4
Than Uyen, *Vietnam* 64 B4
Thana Gazi, *India* 68 F7
Thandla, *India* 68 H6
Thane, *India* 66 K8
Thanesar, *India* 68 D7
Thanet, I. of, *U.K.* 13 F9
Thangool, *Australia* 94 C5
Thanh Hoa, *Vietnam* 64 C5
Thanh Hung, *Vietnam* 65 H5
Thanh Pho Ho Chi Minh, *Vietnam* 65 G6
Thanh Thuy, *Vietnam* 64 A5
Thanjavur, *India* 66 P11
Thann, *France* 19 E14
Thano Bula Khan, *Pakistan* 68 G2
Thaolinta L., *Canada* 105 A9
Thaon-les-Vosges, *France* 19 D13
Thap Sakae, *Thailand* 65 G2
Thap Than, *Thailand* 64 E2
Thar Desert, *India* 68 F5
Tharad, *India* 68 G4
Thargomindah, *Australia* 95 D3
Tharrawaddy, *Burma* 67 L19
Tharthār, Mileh, *Iraq* 70 C4
Tharthār, W. ath →, *Iraq* 70 C4
Thasopoúla, *Greece* 41 F8
Thásos, *Greece* 41 F8
That Khe, *Vietnam* 58 F6
Thatcher, *Ariz., U.S.A.* 115 K9
Thatcher, *Colo., U.S.A.* 113 G2
Thaton, *Burma* 67 L20
Thau, Bassin de, *France* 20 E7
Thaungdut, *Burma* 67 G19
Thayer, *U.S.A.* 113 G9
Thayetmyo, *Burma* 67 K19
Thazi, *Burma* 67 J20
The Alberga →, *Australia* 95 D2
The Bight, *Bahamas* 121 B4
The Dalles, *U.S.A.* 114 D3
The English Company's Is., *Australia* 94 A2
The Frome →, *Australia* 95 D2
The Great Divide = Great Dividing Ra., *Australia* 94 C4
The Hague = 's-Gravenhage, *Neths.* 17 B4
The Hamilton →, *Australia* 95 D2
The Macumba →, *Australia* 95 D2
The Neales →, *Australia* 95 D2
The Officer →, *Australia* 93 E5
The Pas, *Canada* 105 C8
The Range, *Zimbabwe* 87 F3
The Rock, *Australia* 95 F4
The Salt L., *Australia* 95 E3
The Sandheads, *India* 69 J13
The Stevenson →, *Australia* 95 D2
The Warburton →, *Australia* 95 D2
The Woodlands, *U.S.A.* 113 K7
Thebes = Thívai, *Greece* 38 C5
Thebes, *Egypt* 80 B3
Thedford, *Canada* 110 C3
Thedford, *U.S.A.* 112 E4
Theebine, *Australia* 95 D5
Thekulthili L., *Canada* 105 A7
Thelon →, *Canada* 105 A8
Thénezay, *France* 18 F6
Thenon, *France* 20 C5
Theodore, *Australia* 94 C5
Theodore, *Canada* 105 C8
Theodore, *U.S.A.* 109 K1
Theodore Roosevelt National Memorial Park, *U.S.A.* 112 B3
Theodore Roosevelt Res., *U.S.A.* 115 K8
Thepha, *Thailand* 65 J3
Thérain →, *France* 19 C9
Theresa, *U.S.A.* 111 B9
Thermaïkós Kólpos, *Greece* 40 F6
Thermí, *Greece* 39 B8
Thermopolis, *U.S.A.* 114 E9
Thermopylae P., *Greece* 38 C4
Thesprotía □, *Greece* 38 B2
Thessalía □, *Greece* 38 B4
Thessalon, *Canada* 102 C3
Thessaloníki, *Greece* 40 F6
Thessaloníki □, *Greece* 40 F7
Thessaloniki, Gulf of = Thermaïkós Kólpos, *Greece* 40 F6
Thessaly = Thessalía □, *Greece* 38 B4
Thetford, *U.K.* 13 E8
Thetford Mines, *Canada* 103 C5
Theun →, *Laos* 64 C5
Theunissen, *S. Africa* 88 D4
Thevenard, *Australia* 95 E1
Thiámis →, *Greece* 38 B2
Thiberville, *France* 18 C7
Thibodaux, *U.S.A.* 113 L9
Thicket Portage, *Canada* 105 B9
Thief River Falls, *U.S.A.* 112 A6
Thiel Mts., *Antarctica* 5 E16
Thiene, *Italy* 29 C8
Thiérache, *France* 19 C10
Thiers, *France* 20 C7
Thiès, *Senegal* 82 C1
Thiesi, *Italy* 30 B1
Thiet, *Sudan* 81 F2
Thika, *Kenya* 86 C4
Thikombia, *Fiji* 91 B9
Thille-Boubacar, *Senegal* 82 B1
Thimphu, *Bhutan* 67 F16
Þingvallavatn, *Iceland* 8 D3
Thionville, *France* 19 C13
Thíra, *Greece* 39 E7
Thirasía, *Greece* 39 E7
Third Cataract, *Sudan* 80 D3
Thirsk, *U.K.* 12 C6
Thiruvananthapuram = Trivandrum, *India* 66 Q10
Thisted, *Denmark* 11 H2
Thistle I., *Australia* 95 F2
Thívai, *Greece* 38 C5
Thiviers, *France* 20 C4
Thizy, *France* 19 F11
Þjórsá →, *Iceland* 8 E3
Thlewiaza →, *Man., Canada* 105 B8
Thlewiaza →, *N.W.T., Canada* 105 A10
Thmar Puok, *Cambodia* 64 F4
Tho Vinh, *Vietnam* 64 C5
Thoa →, *Canada* 105 A7
Thoen, *Thailand* 64 D2
Thoeng, *Thailand* 64 C3
Thohoyandou, *S. Africa* 85 J6
Tholdi, *Pakistan* 69 B7
Thomas, *U.S.A.* 113 H5
Thomas, L., *Australia* 95 D2
Thomaston, *U.S.A.* 109 J3
Thomasville, *Ala., U.S.A.* 109 K2
Thomasville, *Ga., U.S.A.* 109 K4
Thomasville, *N.C., U.S.A.* 109 H5
Thompson, *Canada* 105 B9
Thompson, *U.S.A.* 111 E9
Thompson →, *Canada* 104 C4
Thompson →, *U.S.A.* 112 F8
Thompson Falls, *U.S.A.* 114 C6
Thompson Pk., *U.S.A.* 114 F2
Thompson Springs, *U.S.A.* 115 G9
Thompsontown, *U.S.A.* 110 F7
Thomson, *U.S.A.* 109 J4
Thomson →, *Australia* 94 C3
Thomson's Falls = Nyahururu, *Kenya* 86 B4
Thônes, *France* 21 C10
Thonon-les-Bains, *France* 19 F13
Thorez, *Ukraine* 47 H10
Þórisvatn, *Iceland* 8 D4
Thornaby on Tees, *U.K.* 12 C6
Thornbury, *Canada* 110 B4
Thorne, *U.K.* 12 D7
Thornhill, *Canada* 110 C5
Thorold, *Canada* 110 C5
Þórshöfn, *Iceland* 8 C6
Thouarcé, *France* 18 E6
Thouars, *France* 18 F6
Thouet →, *France* 18 E6
Thouin, C., *Australia* 92 D2
Thousand Oaks, *U.S.A.* 117 L8
Thrace, *Turkey* 41 F10

Thrakikón Pélagos, *Greece* **41 F8**
Three Forks, *U.S.A.* **114 D8**
Three Gorges Dam, *China* **59 B8**
Three Hills, *Canada* **104 C6**
Three Hummock I., *Australia* **94 G3**
Three Points, C., *Ghana* **82 E4**
Three Rivers, *Calif., U.S.A.* **116 J8**
Three Rivers, *Tex., U.S.A.* **113 L5**
Three Sisters, *U.S.A.* **114 D3**
Three Springs, *Australia* **93 E2**
Throssell, L., *Australia* **93 E3**
Throssell Ra., *Australia* **92 D3**
Thuan Hoa, *Vietnam* **65 H5**
Thubun Lakes, *Canada* **105 A6**
Thueyts, *France* **21 D8**
Thuin, *Belgium* **17 D4**
Thuir, *France* **20 F6**
Thule = Qaanaaq, *Greenland* **4 B4**
Thun, *Switz.* **25 J3**
Thunder B., *U.S.A.* **110 B1**
Thunder Bay, *Canada* **102 C2**
Thunersee, *Switz.* **25 J3**
Thung Song, *Thailand* **65 H2**
Thunkar, *Bhutan* **67 F17**
Thuong Tra, *Vietnam* **64 D6**
Thur →, *Switz.* **25 H5**
Thurgau □, *Switz.* **25 H5**
Thüringen □, *Germany* **24 D6**
Thüringer Wald, *Germany* **24 E6**
Thurles, *Ireland* **15 D4**
Thurn P., *Austria* **26 D5**
Thurrock □, *U.K.* **13 F8**
Thursday I., *Australia* **94 A3**
Thurso, *Canada* **102 C4**
Thurso, *U.K.* **14 C5**
Thurso →, *U.K.* **14 C5**
Thurston I., *Antarctica* **5 D16**
Thury-Harcourt, *France* **18 D6**
Thutade L., *Canada* **104 B3**
Thy, *Denmark* **11 H2**
Thyborøn, *Denmark* **11 H2**
Thyolo, *Malawi* **87 F4**
Thysville = Mbanza Ngungu, *Dem. Rep. of the Congo* **84 F2**
Ti-n-Amzi →, *Niger* **83 B5**
Ti-n-Barraouene, O. →, *Africa* **83 B5**
Ti-n-Zaouatene, *Algeria* **83 B5**
Ti Tree, *Australia* **94 C1**
Tiadiaye, *Senegal* **82 C1**
Tian Shan, *Asia* **60 B3**
Tianchang, *China* **59 A12**
Tiandeng, *China* **58 F6**
Tiandong, *China* **58 F6**
Tian'e, *China* **58 E6**
Tianhe, *China* **58 E7**
Tianjin, *China* **57 E9**
Tiankoura, *Burkina Faso* **82 C4**
Tianlin, *China* **58 E6**
Tianmen, *China* **59 B9**
Tianquan, *China* **58 B4**
Tianshui, *China* **56 G3**
Tiantai, *China* **59 C13**
Tianyang, *China* **58 F6**
Tianzhen, *China* **56 D8**
Tianzhu, *China* **58 D7**
Tianzhuangtai, *China* **57 D12**
Tiaret, *Algeria* **78 A6**
Tiassalé, *Ivory C.* **82 D4**
Tibagi, *Brazil* **127 A5**
Tibagi →, *Brazil* **127 A5**
Tibati, *Cameroon* **83 D7**
Tibe, *Ethiopia* **81 F4**
Tiber = Tevere →, *Italy* **29 G9**
Tiberias = Teverya, *Israel* **75 C4**
Tiberias, L. = Yam Kinneret, *Israel* **75 C4**
Tibesti, *Chad* **79 D9**
Tibet = Xizang Zizhiqu □, *China* **60 C3**
Tibet, Plateau of, *Asia* **52 F12**
Tibiao, *Phil.* **61 F5**
Tibiri, *Niger* **83 C6**
Ţibleş, Vf., *Romania* **43 C9**
Ţibleşului, Munţii, *Romania* **43 C9**
Tibnī, *Syria* **70 C3**
Tibooburra, *Australia* **95 D3**
Tibro, *Sweden* **11 F8**
Tiburón, I., *Mexico* **118 B2**
Ticao I., *Phil.* **61 E5**
Tîchît, *Mauritania* **82 B3**
Ticho, *Ethiopia* **81 F4**
Ticino □, *Switz.* **25 J4**
Ticino →, *Italy* **25 K5**
Ticleni, *Romania* **43 F8**
Ticonderoga, *U.S.A.* **111 C11**
Ticul, *Mexico* **119 C7**
Tidaholm, *Sweden* **11 F7**
Tidan, *Sweden* **11 F8**
Tiddim, *Burma* **67 H18**
Tidioute, *U.S.A.* **110 E5**
Tidjikja, *Mauritania* **82 B2**
Tidore, *Indonesia* **63 D7**
Tiébissou, *Ivory C.* **82 D3**
Tiel, *Neths.* **17 C5**
Tiel, *Senegal* **82 C1**
Tieling, *China* **57 C12**
Tielt, *Belgium* **17 C3**
Tien Shan = Tian Shan, *Asia* **60 B3**
Tien-tsin = Tianjin, *China* **57 E9**
Tien Yen, *Vietnam* **64 B6**
T'ienching = Tianjin, *China* **57 E9**
Tienen, *Belgium* **17 D4**
Tiénigbé, *Ivory C.* **82 D3**
Tientsin = Tianjin, *China* **57 E9**
Tieri, *Australia* **94 C4**
Tierp, *Sweden* **10 D11**
Tierra Amarilla, *Chile* **126 B1**
Tierra Amarilla, *U.S.A.* **115 H10**
Tierra Colorada, *Mexico* **119 D5**
Tierra de Barros, *Spain* **35 G4**
Tierra de Campos, *Spain* **34 C6**
Tierra del Fuego, I. Gr. de, *Argentina* **122 J4**
Tiétar →, *Spain* **34 F4**
Tieté →, *Brazil* **127 A5**
Tiffin, *U.S.A.* **108 E4**
Tiflis = Tbilisi, *Georgia* **49 K7**
Tifton, *U.S.A.* **109 K4**
Tifu, *Indonesia* **63 E7**
Tighina, *Moldova* **43 D14**
Tigil, *Russia* **51 D16**
Tignish, *Canada* **103 C7**
Tigray □, *Ethiopia* **81 E4**
Tigre →, *Peru* **124 D4**
Tigre →, *Venezuela* **124 B6**
Tigris = Dijlah, Nahr →, *Asia* **70 D5**
Tigveni, *Romania* **43 E9**
Tigyaing, *Burma* **67 H20**
Tîh, Gebel el, *Egypt* **80 B3**
Tijara, *India* **68 F7**
Tijuana, *Mexico* **117 N9**
Tikal, *Guatemala* **120 C2**
Tikamgarh, *India* **69 G8**
Tikaré, *Burkina Faso* **83 C4**
Tikhoretsk, *Russia* **49 H5**
Tikhvin, *Russia* **46 C7**
Tiko, *Cameroon* **83 E6**
Tikrīt, *Iraq* **70 C4**
Tiksi, *Russia* **51 B13**
Tilamuta, *Indonesia* **63 D6**
Tilburg, *Neths.* **17 C5**
Tilbury, *Canada* **102 D3**
Tilbury, *U.K.* **13 F8**
Tilcara, *Argentina* **126 A2**
Tilden, *U.S.A.* **112 D6**
Tilemses, *Niger* **83 B5**
Tilemsi, Vallée du, *Mali* **83 B5**
Tilhar, *India* **69 F8**
Tilichiki, *Russia* **51 C17**
Tílissos, *Greece* **36 D7**
Till →, *U.K.* **12 B5**
Tillabéri, *Niger* **83 C5**
Tillamook, *U.S.A.* **114 D2**
Tillberga, *Sweden* **10 E10**
Tillia, *Niger* **83 B5**
Tillsonburg, *Canada* **102 D3**
Tillyeria □, *Cyprus* **36 D11**
Tilogne, *Senegal* **82 B2**
Tílos, *Greece* **39 E9**
Tilpa, *Australia* **95 E3**
Tilsit = Sovetsk, *Russia* **9 J19**
Tilt →, *U.K.* **14 E5**
Tilton, *U.S.A.* **111 C13**
Tiltonsville, *U.S.A.* **110 F4**
Tim, *Denmark* **11 H2**
Timagami, L., *Canada* **102 C3**
Timaru, *N.Z.* **91 L3**
Timashevo, *Russia* **48 D10**
Timashevsk, *Russia* **49 H4**
Timau, *Kenya* **86 B4**
Timbákion, *Greece* **36 D6**
Timbedgha, *Mauritania* **82 B3**
Timber Creek, *Australia* **92 C5**
Timber Lake, *U.S.A.* **112 C4**
Timber Mt., *U.S.A.* **116 H10**
Timbo, *Guinea* **82 C2**
Timbo, *Liberia* **82 D3**
Timbuktu = Tombouctou, *Mali* **82 B4**
Timeiaouine, *Algeria* **83 A5**
Timétrine, Mts., *Mali* **83 B4**
Timfi Óros, *Greece* **38 B2**
Timfristós, Óros, *Greece* **38 C3**
Timi, *Cyprus* **36 E11**
Timia, *Niger* **83 B6**
Timimoun, *Algeria* **78 C6**
Timirist, Râs, *Mauritania* **82 B1**
Timiş = Tamis →, *Serbia, Yug.* **42 F5**
Timiş □, *Romania* **42 E6**
Timişoara, *Romania* **42 E6**
Timmersdala, *Sweden* **11 F7**
Timmins, *Canada* **102 C3**
Timok →, *Serbia, Yug.* **40 B6**
Timor, *Indonesia* **63 F7**
Timor Sea, *Ind. Oc.* **92 B4**
Timor Timur = East Timor ■, *Asia* **63 F7**
Timrå, *Sweden* **10 B11**
Tin Can Bay, *Australia* **95 D5**
Tin Ethisane, *Mali* **83 B4**
Tin Gornai, *Mali* **83 B4**
Tin Mt., *U.S.A.* **116 J9**
Tina →, *S. Africa* **89 E4**
Tîna, Khalîg el, *Egypt* **80 A3**
Tinaca Pt., *Phil.* **61 J6**
Tinajo, *Canary Is.* **37 E6**
Tinca, *Romania* **42 D6**
Tindal, *Australia* **92 B5**
Tindouf, *Algeria* **78 C4**
Tinée →, *France* **21 E11**
Tineo, *Spain* **34 B4**
Ting Jiang →, *China* **59 E11**
Tinggi, Pulau, *Malaysia* **65 L5**
Tinglev, *Denmark* **11 K3**
Tingo Maria, *Peru* **124 E3**
Tingrela, *Ivory C.* **82 C3**
Tingsryd, *Sweden* **11 H9**
Tingstäde, *Sweden* **11 G12**
Tinh Bien, *Vietnam* **65 G5**
Tinnevelly = Tirunelveli, *India* **66 Q10**
Tinogasta, *Argentina* **126 B2**
Tínos, *Greece* **39 D7**
Tiñoso, C., *Spain* **33 H3**
Tinpahar, *India* **69 G12**
Tintina, *Argentina* **126 B3**
Tintinara, *Australia* **95 F3**
Tintioulé, *Guinea* **82 C3**
Tinto →, *Spain* **35 H4**
Tioga, *N. Dak., U.S.A.* **112 A3**
Tioga, *Pa., U.S.A.* **110 E7**
Tioman, Pulau, *Malaysia* **65 L5**
Tione di Trento, *Italy* **28 B7**
Tionesta, *U.S.A.* **110 E5**
Tior, *Sudan* **81 F3**
Tipongpani, *India* **67 F19**
Tipperary, *Ireland* **15 D3**
Tipperary □, *Ireland* **15 D4**
Tipton, *Calif., U.S.A.* **116 J7**
Tipton, *Iowa, U.S.A.* **112 E9**
Tipton Mt., *U.S.A.* **117 K12**
Tiptonville, *U.S.A.* **113 G10**
Tīrān, *Iran* **71 C6**
Tīrān, *Si. Arabia* **80 B3**
Tiranë, *Albania* **40 E3**
Tirano, *Italy* **28 B7**
Tiraspol, *Moldova* **43 D14**
Tirdout, *Mali* **83 B4**
Tire, *Turkey* **39 C9**
Tirebolu, *Turkey* **73 B8**
Tiree, *U.K.* **14 E2**
Tiree, Passage of, *U.K.* **14 E2**
Tîrgovişte = Târgovişte, *Romania* **43 F10**
Tîrgu-Jiu = Târgu-Jiu, *Romania* **43 E8**
Tîrgu Mureş = Târgu Mureş, *Romania* **43 D9**
Tirich Mir, *Pakistan* **66 A7**
Tiriolo, *Italy* **31 D9**
Tiriro, *Guinea* **82 C3**
Tírnavos, *Greece* **38 B4**
Tirodi, *India* **66 J11**
Tirol □, *Austria* **26 D3**
Tirschenreuth, *Germany* **25 F8**
Tirso →, *Italy* **30 C1**
Tirstrup, *Denmark* **11 H4**
Tiruchchirappalli, *India* **66 P11**
Tirunelveli, *India* **66 Q10**
Tirupati, *India* **66 N11**
Tiruppur, *India* **66 P10**
Tiruvannamalai, *India* **66 N11**
Tisa, *India* **68 C7**
Tisa →, *Serbia, Yug.* **42 E5**
Tisdale, *Canada* **105 C8**
Tishomingo, *U.S.A.* **113 H6**
Tisjön, *Sweden* **10 D7**
Tisnaren, *Sweden* **11 F9**
Tišnov, *Czech Rep.* **27 B9**
Tisovec, *Slovak Rep.* **27 C12**
Tisza = Tisa →, *Serbia, Yug.* **42 E5**
Tiszaföldvár, *Hungary* **42 D5**
Tiszafüred, *Hungary* **42 C5**
Tiszalök, *Hungary* **42 B6**
Tiszavasvári, *Hungary* **42 C6**
Tit-Ary, *Russia* **51 B13**
Titaguas, *Spain* **32 F3**
Titao, *Burkina Faso* **83 C4**
Titel, *Serbia, Yug.* **42 E5**
Tithwal, *Pakistan* **69 B5**
Titicaca, L., *S. Amer.* **122 E4**
Titisee, *Germany* **25 H4**
Titiwa, *Nigeria* **83 C7**
Tito, *Italy* **31 B8**
Titograd = Podgorica, *Montenegro, Yug.* **40 D3**
Titova Korenica, *Croatia* **29 D12**
Titu, *Romania* **43 F10**
Titule, *Dem. Rep. of the Congo* **86 B2**
Titusville, *Fla., U.S.A.* **109 L5**
Titusville, *Pa., U.S.A.* **110 E5**
Tivaouane, *Senegal* **82 C1**
Tivat, *Montenegro, Yug.* **40 D2**
Tiverton, *U.K.* **13 G4**
Tívoli, *Italy* **29 G9**
Tiyo, *Eritrea* **81 E5**
Tizi-Ouzou, *Algeria* **78 A6**
Tizimín, *Mexico* **119 C7**
Tjæreborg, *Denmark* **11 J2**
Tjällmo, *Sweden* **11 F9**
Tjeggelvas, *Sweden* **8 C17**
Tjirebon = Cirebon, *Indonesia* **62 F3**
Tjörn, *Sweden* **11 F5**
Tkibuli = Tqibuli, *Georgia* **49 J6**
Tkvarcheli = Tqvarcheli, *Georgia* **49 J5**
Tlacotalpan, *Mexico* **119 D5**
Tlahualilo, *Mexico* **118 B4**
Tlaquepaque, *Mexico* **118 C4**
Tlaxcala, *Mexico* **119 D5**
Tlaxcala □, *Mexico* **119 D5**
Tlaxiaco, *Mexico* **119 D5**
Tlemcen, *Algeria* **78 B5**
Tłuszcz, *Poland* **45 F8**
Tlyarata, *Russia* **49 J8**
To Bong, *Vietnam* **64 F7**
Toad →, *Canada* **104 B4**
Toad River, *Canada* **104 B3**
Toamasina, *Madag.* **89 B8**
Toamasina □, *Madag.* **89 B8**
Toay, *Argentina* **126 D3**
Toba, *China* **58 B1**
Toba, *Japan* **55 G8**
Toba, Danau, *Indonesia* **62 D1**
Toba Kakar, *Pakistan* **68 D3**
Toba Tek Singh, *Pakistan* **68 D5**
Tobago, *Trin. & Tob.* **121 D7**
Tobarra, *Spain* **33 G3**
Tobelo, *Indonesia* **63 D7**
Tobermory, *Canada* **102 C3**
Tobermory, *U.K.* **14 E2**
Tobi, *Pac. Oc.* **63 D8**
Tobin, *U.S.A.* **116 F5**
Tobin, L., *Australia* **92 D4**
Tobin L., *Canada* **105 C8**
Toblach = Dobbiaco, *Italy* **29 B9**
Toboali, *Indonesia* **62 E3**
Tobol →, *Russia* **50 D7**
Toboli, *Indonesia* **63 E6**
Tobolsk, *Russia* **50 D7**
Tobor, *Senegal* **82 C1**
Tobruk = Tubruq, *Libya* **79 B10**
Tobyhanna, *U.S.A.* **111 E9**
Tobyl = Tobol →, *Russia* **50 D7**
Tocantinópolis, *Brazil* **125 E9**
Tocantins □, *Brazil* **125 F9**
Tocantins →, *Brazil* **122 D6**
Toccoa, *U.S.A.* **109 H4**
Toce →, *Italy* **28 C5**
Tochi →, *Pakistan* **68 C4**
Tochigi, *Japan* **55 F9**
Tochigi □, *Japan* **55 F9**
Tocina, *Spain* **35 H5**
Töcksfors, *Sweden* **10 E5**
Toconao, *Chile* **126 A2**
Tocopilla, *Chile* **126 A1**
Tocumwal, *Australia* **95 F4**
Tocuyo →, *Venezuela* **124 A5**
Todd →, *Australia* **94 C2**
Todeli, *Indonesia* **63 E6**
Todenyang, *Kenya* **86 B4**
Todgarh, *India* **68 G5**
Todi, *Italy* **29 F9**
Todos os Santos, B. de, *Brazil* **125 F11**
Todos Santos, *Mexico* **118 C2**
Todtnau, *Germany* **25 H3**
Toe Hd., *U.K.* **14 D1**
Toecé, *Burkina Faso* **83 C4**
Tofield, *Canada* **104 C6**
Tofino, *Canada* **104 D3**
Tofua, *Tonga* **91 D11**
Tōgane, *Japan* **55 G10**
Togba, *Mauritania* **82 B2**
Togian, Kepulauan, *Indonesia* **63 E6**
Togliatti, *Russia* **48 D9**
Togo ■, *W. Afr.* **83 D5**
Togtoh, *China* **56 D6**
Tohma →, *Turkey* **72 C7**
Tōhoku □, *Japan* **54 E10**
Töhöm, *Mongolia* **56 B5**
Toinya, *Sudan* **81 F2**
Toiyabe Range, *U.S.A.* **114 G5**
Tojikiston = Tajikistan ■, *Asia* **50 F8**
Tojo, *Indonesia* **63 E6**
Tōjō, *Japan* **55 G6**
Tok, *U.S.A.* **100 B5**
Tok-do, *Japan* **55 F5**
Tokachi-Dake, *Japan* **54 C11**
Tokachi-Gawa →, *Japan* **54 C11**
Tokaj, *Hungary* **42 B6**
Tokala, *Indonesia* **63 E6**
Tōkamachi, *Japan* **55 F9**
Tokanui, *N.Z.* **91 M2**
Tokar, *Sudan* **80 D4**
Tokara-Rettō, *Japan* **55 K4**
Tokarahi, *N.Z.* **91 L3**
Tokashiki-Shima, *Japan* **55 L3**
Tokat, *Turkey* **72 B7**
Tŏkch'ŏn, *N. Korea* **57 E14**
Tokeland, *U.S.A.* **116 D3**
Tokelau Is., *Pac. Oc.* **96 H10**
Tokmak, *Kyrgyzstan* **50 E8**
Tokmak, *Ukraine* **47 J8**
Toko Ra., *Australia* **94 C2**
Tokoro-Gawa →, *Japan* **54 B12**
Tokuno-Shima, *Japan* **55 L4**
Tokushima, *Japan* **55 G7**
Tokushima □, *Japan* **55 H7**
Tokuyama, *Japan* **55 G5**
Tōkyō, *Japan* **55 G9**
Tolaga Bay, *N.Z.* **91 H7**
Tolbukhin = Dobrich, *Bulgaria* **41 C11**
Toledo, *Brazil* **127 A5**
Toledo, *Spain* **34 F6**
Toledo, *Ohio, U.S.A.* **108 E4**
Toledo, *Oreg., U.S.A.* **114 D2**
Toledo, *Wash., U.S.A.* **114 C2**
Toledo, Montes de, *Spain* **35 F6**
Toledo Bend Reservoir, *U.S.A.* **113 K8**
Tolentino, *Italy* **29 E10**
Tolfa, *Italy* **29 F8**
Tolga, *Australia* **94 B4**
Toliara, *Madag.* **89 C7**
Toliara □, *Madag.* **89 C8**
Tolima, *Colombia* **124 C3**
Tolitoli, *Indonesia* **63 D6**
Tolkmicko, *Poland* **44 D6**
Tollarp, *Sweden* **11 J7**
Tollensesee, *Germany* **24 B9**
Tollhouse, *U.S.A.* **116 H7**
Tolmachevo, *Russia* **46 C5**
Tolmezzo, *Italy* **29 B10**
Tolmin, *Slovenia* **29 B10**
Tolna, *Hungary* **42 D3**
Tolna □, *Hungary* **42 D3**
Tolo, Teluk, *Indonesia* **63 E6**
Tolochin = Talachyn, *Belarus* **46 E5**
Tolosa, *Spain* **32 B2**
Tolox, *Spain* **35 J6**
Toluca, *Mexico* **119 D5**
Tom Burke, *S. Africa* **89 C4**
Tom Price, *Australia* **92 D2**
Toma, *Burkina Faso* **82 C4**
Tomah, *U.S.A.* **112 D9**
Tomahawk, *U.S.A.* **112 C10**
Tomai, *Moldova* **43 D13**
Tomakomai, *Japan* **54 C10**
Tomales, *U.S.A.* **116 G4**
Tomales B., *U.S.A.* **116 G3**
Tomar, *Portugal* **35 F2**
Tómaros, Óros, *Greece* **38 B2**
Tomarza, *Turkey* **72 C6**
Tomaszów Lubelski, *Poland* **45 H10**
Tomaszów Mazowiecki, *Poland* **45 G7**
Tomatlán, *Mexico* **118 D3**
Tombadonkéa, *Guinea* **82 C2**
Tombador, Serra do, *Brazil* **124 F7**
Tombe, *Sudan* **81 F3**
Tombigbee →, *U.S.A.* **109 K2**
Tombouctou, *Mali* **82 B4**
Tombstone, *U.S.A.* **115 L8**
Tombua, *Angola* **88 B1**
Tomé, *Chile* **126 D1**
Tomelilla, *Sweden* **11 J7**
Tomelloso, *Spain* **35 F7**
Tomini, *Indonesia* **63 D6**
Tomini, Teluk, *Indonesia* **63 E6**
Tominian, *Mali* **82 C4**
Tomiño, *Spain* **34 D2**
Tomintoul, *U.K.* **14 D5**
Tomislavgrad, *Bos.-H.* **42 G2**
Tomkinson Ranges, *Australia* **93 E4**
Tommot, *Russia* **51 D13**
Tomnop Ta Suos, *Cambodia* **65 G5**
Tomo →, *Colombia* **124 B5**
Toms Place, *U.S.A.* **116 H8**
Toms River, *U.S.A.* **111 G10**
Tomsk, *Russia* **50 D9**
Tomtabacken, *Sweden* **11 G8**
Tona, *Spain* **32 D7**
Tonalá, *Mexico* **119 D6**
Tonale, Passo del, *Italy* **28 B7**
Tonantins, *Brazil* **124 D5**
Tonasket, *U.S.A.* **114 B4**
Tonawanda, *U.S.A.* **110 D6**
Tonbridge, *U.K.* **13 F8**
Tondano, *Indonesia* **63 D6**
Tondela, *Portugal* **34 E2**
Tønder, *Denmark* **11 K2**
Tondi Kiwindi, *Niger* **83 C5**
Tondibi, *Mali* **83 B4**
Tondoro, *Namibia* **88 B2**
Tone →, *Australia* **93 F2**
Tone-Gawa →, *Japan* **55 F9**
Tonekābon, *Iran* **71 B6**
Tong Xian, *China* **56 E9**
Tōngā, *Sudan* **81 F3**
Tonga ■, *Pac. Oc.* **91 D11**
Tonga Trench, *Pac. Oc.* **96 J10**
Tongaat, *S. Africa* **89 D5**
Tong'an, *China* **59 E12**
Tongareva, *Cook Is.* **97 H12**
Tongatapu Group, *Tonga* **91 E12**
Tongbai, *China* **59 A9**
Tongcheng, *Anhui, China* **59 B11**
Tongcheng, *Hubei, China* **59 C9**
Tongchŏn-ni, *N. Korea* **57 E14**
Tongchuan, *China* **56 G5**
Tongdao, *China* **58 D7**
Tongeren, *Belgium* **17 D5**
Tonggu, *China* **59 C10**
Tongguan, *China* **56 G6**
Tonghai, *China* **58 E4**
Tonghua, *China* **57 D13**
Tongjiang, *China* **58 B6**
Tongjosŏn Man, *N. Korea* **57 E15**
Tongking, G. of = Tonkin, G. of, *Asia* **60 E5**
Tongliang, *China* **58 C6**
Tongliao, *China* **57 C12**
Tongling, *China* **59 B11**
Tonglu, *China* **59 C12**
Tongnae, *S. Korea* **57 G15**
Tongnan = Anyue, *China* **58 B5**
Tongobory, *Madag.* **89 C7**
Tongoy, *Chile* **126 C1**
Tongren, *China* **58 D7**
Tongres = Tongeren, *Belgium* **17 D5**
Tongsa Dzong, *Bhutan* **67 F17**
Tongue, *U.K.* **14 C4**
Tongue →, *U.S.A.* **112 B2**
Tongwei, *China* **56 G3**
Tongxiang, *China* **59 B13**
Tongxin, *China* **56 F3**
Tongyang, *N. Korea* **57 E14**
Tongyu, *China* **57 B12**
Tongzi, *China* **58 C6**
Tonj, *Sudan* **81 F2**
Tonj →, *Sudan* **81 F2**
Tonk, *India* **68 F6**
Tonkawa, *U.S.A.* **113 G6**
Tonkin = Bac Phan, *Vietnam* **64 B5**
Tonkin, G. of, *Asia* **60 E5**
Tonle Sap, *Cambodia* **64 F4**
Tonnay-Charente, *France* **20 C3**
Tonneins, *France* **20 D4**
Tonnerre, *France* **19 E10**
Tönning, *Germany* **24 A4**
Tono, *Japan* **54 E10**
Tonopah, *U.S.A.* **115 G5**
Tonosí, *Panama* **120 E3**
Tons →, *Haryana, India* **68 D7**
Tons →, *Ut. P., India* **69 F10**
Tønsberg, *Norway* **9 G14**
Tonya, *Turkey* **73 B8**
Toobanna, *Australia* **94 B4**
Toodyay, *Australia* **93 F2**
Tooele, *U.S.A.* **114 F7**
Toompine, *Australia* **95 D3**
Toora, *Australia* **95 F4**
Toora-Khem, *Russia* **51 D10**
Toowoomba, *Australia* **95 D5**
Top Springs, *Australia* **92 C5**
Topalu, *Romania* **43 F13**
Topaz, *U.S.A.* **116 G7**
Topeka, *U.S.A.* **112 F7**
Topl'a →, *Slovak Rep.* **27 C14**
Topley, *Canada* **104 C3**
Toplica →, *Serbia, Yug.* **40 C5**

Toplița, *Romania* 43 D10
Topocalma, Pta., *Chile* 126 C1
Topock, *U.S.A.* 117 L12
Topola, *Serbia, Yug.* 40 B4
Topolčani, *Macedonia* 40 E5
Topol'čany, *Slovak Rep.* 27 C11
Topolnitsa →, *Bulgaria* 41 D8
Topolobampo, *Mexico* 118 B3
Topoloveni, *Romania* 43 F10
Topolovgrad, *Bulgaria* 41 D10
Topolvățu Mare, *Romania* 42 E6
Toppenish, *U.S.A.* 114 C3
Topraisar, *Romania* 43 F13
Topusko, *Croatia* 29 C12
Torà, *Spain* 32 D6
Tora Kit, *Sudan* 81 E3
Toraka Vestale, *Madag.* 89 B7
Torata, *Peru* 124 G4
Torbalı, *Turkey* 39 C9
Torbat-e Heydārīyeh, *Iran* 71 C8
Torbat-e Jām, *Iran* 71 C9
Torbay, *Canada* 103 C9
Torbay □, *U.K.* 13 G4
Torbjörntorp, *Sweden* 11 F7
Tordesillas, *Spain* 34 D6
Töreboda, *Sweden* 11 F8
Torekov, *Sweden* 11 H6
Torellò, *Spain* 32 C7
Toreno, *Spain* 34 C4
Torfaen □, *U.K.* 13 F4
Torgau, *Germany* 24 D8
Torgelow, *Germany* 24 B10
Torhamn, *Sweden* 11 H9
Torhout, *Belgium* 17 C3
Tori, *Ethiopia* 81 F3
Tori-Shima, *Japan* 55 J10
Torigni-sur-Vire, *France* 18 C6
Torija, *Spain* 32 E1
Torin, *Mexico* 118 B2
Torino, *Italy* 28 C4
Torit, *Sudan* 81 G3
Torkamān, *Iran* 70 B5
Torkovichi, *Russia* 46 C6
Tormac, *Romania* 42 E6
Tormes →, *Spain* 34 D4
Tornado Mt., *Canada* 104 D6
Tornal'a, *Slovak Rep.* 27 C13
Torne älv →, *Sweden* 8 D21
Torneå = Tornio, *Finland* 8 D21
Torneträsk, *Sweden* 8 B18
Tornio, *Finland* 8 D21
Tornionjoki →, *Finland* 8 D21
Tornquist, *Argentina* 126 D3
Toro, *Baleares, Spain* 37 B11
Toro, *Zamora, Spain* 34 D5
Torö, *Sweden* 11 F11
Toro, Cerro del, *Chile* 126 B2
Toro Pk., *U.S.A.* 117 M10
Törökszentmiklós, *Hungary* 42 C5
Toroníos Kólpos, *Greece* 40 F7
Toronto, *Canada* 102 D4
Toronto, *U.S.A.* 110 F4
Toropets, *Russia* 46 D6
Tororo, *Uganda* 86 B3
Toros Dağları, *Turkey* 70 B2
Torpa, *India* 69 H11
Torquay, *U.K.* 13 G4
Torquemada, *Spain* 34 C6
Torrance, *U.S.A.* 117 M8
Torrão, *Portugal* 35 G2
Torre Annunziata, *Italy* 31 B7
Torre de Moncorvo, *Portugal* 34 D3
Torre del Campo, *Spain* 35 H7
Torre del Greco, *Italy* 31 B7
Torre del Mar, *Spain* 35 J6
Torre-Pacheco, *Spain* 33 H4
Torre Pellice, *Italy* 28 D4
Torreblanca, *Spain* 32 E5
Torrecampo, *Spain* 35 G6
Torrecilla en Cameros, *Spain* 32 C2
Torredembarra, *Spain* 32 D6
Torredonjimeno, *Spain* 35 H7
Torrejón de Ardoz, *Spain* 34 E7
Torrejoncillo, *Spain* 34 F4
Torrelaguna, *Spain* 34 E7
Torrelavega, *Spain* 34 B6
Torremaggiore, *Italy* 29 G12
Torremolinos, *Spain* 35 J6
Torrens, L., *Australia* 95 E2
Torrens Cr. →, *Australia* 94 C4
Torrens Creek, *Australia* 94 C4
Torrent, *Spain* 33 F4
Torrenueva, *Spain* 35 G7
Torreón, *Mexico* 118 B4
Torreperogil, *Spain* 35 G7
Torres, *Brazil* 127 B5
Torres, *Mexico* 118 B2
Torres Novas, *Portugal* 35 F2
Torres Strait, *Australia* 96 H6
Torres Vedras, *Portugal* 35 F1
Torrevieja, *Spain* 33 H4
Torrey, *U.S.A.* 115 G8
Torridge →, *U.K.* 13 G3
Torridon, L., *U.K.* 14 D3
Torrijos, *Spain* 34 F6
Tørring, *Denmark* 11 J3
Torrington, *Conn., U.S.A.* 111 E11
Torrington, *Wyo., U.S.A.* 112 D2
Torroella de Montgrì, *Spain* 32 C8
Torrox, *Spain* 35 J7
Torsås, *Sweden* 11 H9
Torsby, *Sweden* 10 D6
Torshälla, *Sweden* 10 E10
Tórshavn, *Færoe Is.* 8 E9
Torslanda, *Sweden* 11 G5
Torsö, *Sweden* 11 F7
Tortola, *Br. Virgin Is.* 121 C7
Tórtoles de Esgueva, *Spain* 34 D6
Tortolì, *Italy* 30 C2
Tortona, *Italy* 28 D5
Tortorici, *Italy* 31 D7
Tortosa, *Spain* 32 E5
Tortosa, C., *Spain* 32 E5
Tortosendo, *Portugal* 34 E3
Tortue, I. de la, *Haiti* 121 B5
Tortum, *Turkey* 73 B9
Torūd, *Iran* 71 C7
Torul, *Turkey* 73 B8
Toruń, *Poland* 45 E5
Tory I., *Ireland* 15 A3
Torysa →, *Slovak Rep.* 27 C14
Torzhok, *Russia* 46 D8
Torzym, *Poland* 45 F2
Tosa, *Japan* 55 H6
Tosa-Shimizu, *Japan* 55 H6
Tosa-Wan, *Japan* 55 H6
Toscana □, *Italy* 28 E8
Toscano, Arcipelago, *Italy* 28 F7
Toshkent, *Uzbekistan* 50 E7
Tosno, *Russia* 46 C6
Tossa de Mar, *Spain* 32 D7
Tösse, *Sweden* 11 F6
Tostado, *Argentina* 126 B3
Tostedt, *Germany* 24 B5
Tostón, Pta. de, *Canary Is.* 37 F5
Tosu, *Japan* 55 H5
Tosya, *Turkey* 72 B6
Toszek, *Poland* 45 H5
Totana, *Spain* 33 H3
Totebo, *Sweden* 11 G10
Toteng, *Botswana* 88 C3
Tôtes, *France* 18 C8
Tótkomlós, *Hungary* 42 D5
Totma, *Russia* 50 C5
Totnes, *U.K.* 13 G4
Totness, *Surinam* 125 B7
Toto, *Nigeria* 83 D6
Totonicapán, *Guatemala* 120 D1
Totten Glacier, *Antarctica* 5 C8
Tottenham, *Australia* 95 E4
Tottenham, *Canada* 110 B5
Tottori, *Japan* 55 G7
Tottori □, *Japan* 55 G7
Touaret, *Niger* 83 A6
Touba, *Ivory C.* 82 D3
Touba, *Senegal* 82 C1
Toubkal, Djebel, *Morocco* 78 B4
Toucy, *France* 19 E10
Tougan, *Burkina Faso* 82 C4
Touggourt, *Algeria* 78 B7
Tougouri, *Burkina Faso* 83 C4
Tougué, *Guinea* 82 C2
Toukoto, *Mali* 82 C3
Toul, *France* 19 D12
Toulepleu, *Ivory C.* 82 D3
Toulon, *France* 21 E9
Toulouse, *France* 20 E5
Toummo, *Niger* 79 D8
Toumodi, *Ivory C.* 82 D3
Tounan, *Taiwan* 59 F13
Toungo, *Nigeria* 83 D7
Toungoo, *Burma* 67 K20
Touques →, *France* 18 C7
Touraine, *France* 18 E7
Tourane = Da Nang, *Vietnam* 64 D7
Tourcoing, *France* 19 B10
Touriñán, C., *Spain* 34 B1
Tournai, *Belgium* 17 D3
Tournan-en-Brie, *France* 19 D9
Tournay, *France* 20 E4
Tournon-St-Martin, *France* 18 F7
Tournon-sur-Rhône, *France* 21 C8
Tournus, *France* 19 F11
Tours, *France* 18 E7
Toussora, Mt., *C.A.R.* 84 C4
Touws →, *S. Africa* 88 E3
Touwsrivier, *S. Africa* 88 E3
Tovarkovskiy, *Russia* 46 F10
Tovuz, *Azerbaijan* 49 K7
Towada, *Japan* 54 D10
Towada-Ko, *Japan* 54 D10
Towanda, *U.S.A.* 111 E8
Towang, *India* 67 F17
Tower, *U.S.A.* 112 B8
Towerhill Cr. →, *Australia* 94 C3
Towner, *U.S.A.* 112 A4
Townsend, *U.S.A.* 114 C8
Townshend I., *Australia* 94 C5
Townsville, *Australia* 94 B4
Towraghondi, *Afghan.* 66 B3
Towson, *U.S.A.* 108 F7
Towuti, Danau, *Indonesia* 63 E6
Toya-Ko, *Japan* 54 C10
Toyama, *Japan* 55 F8
Toyama □, *Japan* 55 F8
Toyama-Wan, *Japan* 55 F8
Toyohashi, *Japan* 55 G8
Toyokawa, *Japan* 55 G8
Toyonaka, *Japan* 55 G7
Toyooka, *Japan* 55 G7
Toyota, *Japan* 55 G8
Tozeur, *Tunisia* 78 B7
Tqibuli, *Georgia* 49 J6
Tqvarcheli, *Georgia* 49 J5
Trá Li = Tralee, *Ireland* 15 D2
Tra On, *Vietnam* 65 H5
Trabancos →, *Spain* 34 D5
Traben-Trarbach, *Germany* 25 F3
Trabzon, *Turkey* 73 B8
Tracadie, *Canada* 103 C7
Tracy, *Calif., U.S.A.* 116 H5
Tracy, *Minn., U.S.A.* 112 C7
Tradate, *Italy* 28 C5
Trade Town, *Liberia* 82 D3
Trafalgar, C., *Spain* 35 J4
Traian, *Brăila, Romania* 43 E12
Traian, *Tulcea, Romania* 43 E13
Trail, *Canada* 104 D5
Trainor L., *Canada* 104 A4
Trákhonas, *Cyprus* 36 D12
Tralee, *Ireland* 15 D2
Tralee B., *Ireland* 15 D2
Tramore, *Ireland* 15 D4
Tramore B., *Ireland* 15 D4
Tran Ninh, Cao Nguyen, *Laos* 64 C4
Tranås, *Sweden* 11 F8
Tranbjerg, *Denmark* 11 H4
Trancas, *Argentina* 126 B2
Trancoso, *Portugal* 34 E3
Tranebjerg, *Denmark* 11 J4
Tranemo, *Sweden* 11 G7
Trang, *Thailand* 65 J2
Trangahy, *Madag.* 89 B7
Trangan, *Indonesia* 63 F8
Trangie, *Australia* 95 E4
Trångsviken, *Sweden* 10 A7
Trani, *Italy* 31 A9
Tranoroa, *Madag.* 89 C8
Tranqueras, *Uruguay* 127 C4
Transantarctic Mts., *Antarctica* 5 E12
Transilvania, *Romania* 43 D9
Transilvanian Alps = Carpații Meridionali, *Romania* 43 E9
Transtrand, *Sweden* 10 C7
Transtrandsfjällen, *Sweden* 10 C6
Transvaal, *S. Africa* 85 K5
Transylvania = Transilvania, *Romania* 43 D9
Trápani, *Italy* 30 D5
Trapper Pk., *U.S.A.* 114 D6
Traralgon, *Australia* 95 F4
Trarza, *Mauritania* 82 B2
Trasacco, *Italy* 29 G10
Trăscău, Munții, *Romania* 43 D8
Trasimeno, L., *Italy* 29 E9
Träslövsläge, *Sweden* 11 G6
Trasvase Tajo-Segura, Canal de, *Spain* 32 E2
Trat, *Thailand* 65 F4
Tratani →, *Pakistan* 68 E3
Traun, *Austria* 26 C7
Traunreut, *Germany* 25 H8
Traunsee, *Austria* 26 D6
Traunstein, *Germany* 25 H8
Traveller's L., *Australia* 95 E3
Travemünde, *Germany* 24 B6
Travers, Mt., *N.Z.* 91 K4
Traverse City, *U.S.A.* 108 C3
Travis, L., *U.S.A.* 113 K5
Travnik, *Bos.-H.* 42 F2
Trbovlje, *Slovenia* 29 B12
Trébbia →, *Italy* 28 C6
Trebel →, *Germany* 24 B9
Trébeurden, *France* 18 D3
Třebíč, *Czech Rep.* 26 B8
Trebinje, *Bos.-H.* 40 D2
Trebisacce, *Italy* 31 C9
Trebišnjica →, *Bos.-H.* 40 D2
Trebišov, *Slovak Rep.* 27 C14
Trebižat →, *Bos.-H.* 29 E14
Trebnje, *Slovenia* 29 C12
Třeboň, *Czech Rep.* 26 B7
Trebonne, *Australia* 94 B4
Trebujena, *Spain* 35 J4
Trecate, *Italy* 28 C5
Tregaron, *U.K.* 13 E4
Tregnago, *Italy* 29 C8
Tregrosse Is., *Australia* 94 B5
Tréguier, *France* 18 D3
Trégunc, *France* 18 E3
Treherne, *Canada* 105 D9
Tréia, *Italy* 29 E10
Treignac, *France* 20 C5
Treinta y Tres, *Uruguay* 127 C5
Treis-karden, *Germany* 25 E3
Treklyano, *Bulgaria* 40 D6
Trelawney, *Zimbabwe* 89 B5
Trélazé, *France* 18 E6
Trelew, *Argentina* 128 E3
Trélissac, *France* 20 C4
Trelleborg, *Sweden* 11 J7
Tremadog Bay, *U.K.* 12 E3
Trémiti, *Italy* 29 F12
Tremonton, *U.S.A.* 114 F7
Tremp, *Spain* 32 C5
Trenche →, *Canada* 102 C5
Trenčiansky □, *Slovak Rep.* 27 C11
Trenčín, *Slovak Rep.* 27 C11
Trenggalek, *Indonesia* 63 H14
Trenque Lauquen, *Argentina* 126 D3
Trent →, *Canada* 110 B7
Trent →, *U.K.* 12 D7
Trentino-Alto Adige □, *Italy* 29 B8
Trento, *Italy* 28 B8
Trenton, *Canada* 102 D4
Trenton, *Mo., U.S.A.* 112 E8
Trenton, *N.J., U.S.A.* 111 F10
Trenton, *Nebr., U.S.A.* 112 E4
Trepassey, *Canada* 103 C9
Trepuzzi, *Italy* 31 B11
Tres Arroyos, *Argentina* 126 D3
Três Corações, *Brazil* 127 A6
Três Lagoas, *Brazil* 125 H8
Tres Lomas, *Argentina* 126 D3
Tres Marías, Islas, *Mexico* 118 C3
Tres Montes, C., *Chile* 128 F1
Tres Pinos, *U.S.A.* 116 J5
Três Pontas, *Brazil* 127 A6
Tres Puentes, *Chile* 126 B1
Tres Puntas, C., *Argentina* 128 F3
Três Rios, *Brazil* 127 A7
Tres Valles, *Mexico* 119 D5
Tresco, *U.K.* 13 H1
Treska →, *Macedonia* 40 E5
Treskavica, *Bos.-H.* 42 G3
Trespaderne, *Spain* 34 C7
Trets, *France* 21 E9
Treuchtlingen, *Germany* 25 G6
Treuenbrietzen, *Germany* 24 C8
Trevi, *Italy* 29 F9
Trevíglio, *Italy* 28 C6
Trevínca, Peña, *Spain* 34 C4
Treviso, *Italy* 29 C9
Trévoux, *France* 21 C8
Trgovište, *Serbia, Yug.* 40 D6
Triabunna, *Australia* 94 G4
Triánda, *Greece* 36 C10
Triangle, *Zimbabwe* 89 C5
Triaucourt-en-Argonne, *France* 19 D12
Tribal Areas □, *Pakistan* 68 C4
Tribsees, *Germany* 24 A8
Tribulation, C., *Australia* 94 B4
Tribune, *U.S.A.* 112 F4
Tricárico, *Italy* 31 B9
Tricase, *Italy* 31 C11
Trichinopoly = Tiruchchirappalli, *India* 66 P11
Trichur, *India* 66 P10
Trida, *Australia* 95 E4
Trier, *Germany* 25 F2
Trieste, *Italy* 29 C10
Trieste, G. di, *Italy* 29 C10
Trieux →, *France* 18 D3
Triggiano, *Italy* 31 A9
Triglav, *Slovenia* 29 B10
Trigno →, *Italy* 29 F11
Trigueros, *Spain* 35 H4
Tríkeri, *Greece* 38 B5
Trikhonis, Límni, *Greece* 38 C3
Tríkkala, *Greece* 38 B3
Tríkkala □, *Greece* 38 B3
Trikomo, *Cyprus* 36 D12
Trikora, Puncak, *Indonesia* 63 E9
Trilj, *Croatia* 29 E13
Trillo, *Spain* 32 E2
Trim, *Ireland* 15 C5
Trincomalee, *Sri Lanka* 66 Q12
Trindade, *Brazil* 125 G9
Trindade, I., *Atl. Oc.* 2 F8
Třinec, *Czech Rep.* 27 B11
Trinidad, *Bolivia* 124 F6
Trinidad, *Cuba* 120 B4
Trinidad, *Trin. & Tob.* 121 D7
Trinidad, *Uruguay* 126 C4
Trinidad, *U.S.A.* 113 G2
Trinidad →, *Mexico* 119 D5
Trinidad & Tobago ■, *W. Indies* 121 D7
Trinitápoli, *Italy* 31 A9
Trinity, *Canada* 103 C9
Trinity, *U.S.A.* 113 K7
Trinity →, *Calif., U.S.A.* 114 F2
Trinity →, *Tex., U.S.A.* 113 L7
Trinity B., *Canada* 103 C9
Trinity Is., *U.S.A.* 100 C4
Trinity Range, *U.S.A.* 114 F4
Trinkitat, *Sudan* 80 D4
Trino, *Italy* 28 C5
Trinway, *U.S.A.* 110 F2
Trionto, C., *Italy* 31 C9
Triora, *Italy* 28 D4
Tripoli = Tarābulus, *Lebanon* 75 A4
Tripoli = Tarābulus, *Libya* 79 B8
Trípolis, *Greece* 38 D4
Tripolitania, *N. Afr.* 79 B8
Tripura □, *India* 67 H18
Tripylos, *Cyprus* 36 E11
Trischen, *Germany* 24 A4
Tristan da Cunha, *Atl. Oc.* 77 K2
Trisul, *India* 69 D8
Trivandrum, *India* 66 Q10
Trivento, *Italy* 29 G11
Trnava, *Slovak Rep.* 27 C10
Trnavský □, *Slovak Rep.* 27 C10
Troarn, *France* 18 C6
Trochu, *Canada* 104 C6
Trodely I., *Canada* 102 B4
Troezen, *Greece* 38 D5
Trogir, *Croatia* 29 E13
Troglav, *Croatia* 29 E13
Tróia, *Italy* 31 A8
Troilus, L., *Canada* 102 B5
Troina, *Italy* 31 E7
Trois-Pistoles, *Canada* 103 C6
Trois-Rivières, *Canada* 102 C5
Troisdorf, *Germany* 24 E3
Troitsk, *Russia* 50 D7
Troitsko Pechorsk, *Russia* 50 C6
Trölladyngja, *Iceland* 8 D5
Trollhättan, *Sweden* 11 F6
Trollheimen, *Norway* 8 E13
Trombetas →, *Brazil* 125 D7
Tromsø, *Norway* 8 B18
Trona, *U.S.A.* 117 K9
Tronador, Mte., *Argentina* 128 E2
Trøndelag, *Norway* 8 D14
Trondheim, *Norway* 8 E14
Trondheimsfjorden, *Norway* 8 E14
Trönninge, *Sweden* 11 H6
Tronto →, *Italy* 29 F10
Troodos, *Cyprus* 36 E11
Troon, *U.K.* 14 F4
Tropea, *Italy* 31 D8
Tropic, *U.S.A.* 115 H7
Tropojë, *Albania* 40 D4
Trosa, *Sweden* 11 F11
Trostan, *U.K.* 15 A5
Trostberg, *Germany* 25 G8
Trostyanets, *Ukraine* 47 G8
Trout →, *Canada* 104 A5
Trout L., *N.W.T., Canada* 104 A4
Trout L., *Ont., Canada* 105 C10
Trout Lake, *Canada* 104 B6
Trout Lake, *U.S.A.* 116 E5
Trout River, *Canada* 103 C8
Trout Run, *U.S.A.* 110 E7
Trouville-sur-Mer, *France* 18 C7
Trowbridge, *U.K.* 13 F5
Troy, *Turkey* 39 B8
Troy, *Ala., U.S.A.* 109 K3
Troy, *Kans., U.S.A.* 112 F7
Troy, *Mo., U.S.A.* 112 F9
Troy, *Mont., U.S.A.* 114 B6
Troy, *N.Y., U.S.A.* 111 D11
Troy, *Ohio, U.S.A.* 108 E3
Troy, *Pa., U.S.A.* 111 E8
Troyan, *Bulgaria* 41 D8
Troyes, *France* 19 D11
Trpanj, *Croatia* 29 E14
Trstenik, *Serbia, Yug.* 40 C5
Trubchevsk, *Russia* 47 F7
Truchas Peak, *U.S.A.* 113 H2
Trucial States = United Arab Emirates ■, *Asia* 71 F7
Truckee, *U.S.A.* 116 F6
Trudfront, *Russia* 49 H8
Trudovoye, *Russia* 54 C6
Trujillo, *Honduras* 120 C2
Trujillo, *Peru* 124 E3
Trujillo, *Spain* 35 F5
Trujillo, *U.S.A.* 113 H2
Trujillo, *Venezuela* 124 B4
Truk, *Micronesia* 96 G7
Trumann, *U.S.A.* 113 H9
Trumansburg, *U.S.A.* 111 D8
Trumbull, Mt., *U.S.A.* 115 H7
Trŭn, *Bulgaria* 40 D6
Trun, *France* 18 D7
Trundle, *Australia* 95 E4
Trung-Phan = Annam, *Vietnam* 64 E7
Truro, *Canada* 103 C7
Truro, *U.K.* 13 G2
Truskavets, *Ukraine* 47 H2
Trŭstenik, *Bulgaria* 41 C8
Trustrup, *Denmark* 11 H4
Trutch, *Canada* 104 B4
Truth or Consequences, *U.S.A.* 115 K10
Trutnov, *Czech Rep.* 26 A8
Truxton, *U.S.A.* 111 D8
Truyère →, *France* 20 D6
Tryavna, *Bulgaria* 41 D9
Tryonville, *U.S.A.* 110 E5
Trzcianka, *Poland* 45 E3
Trzciel, *Poland* 45 F2
Trzcińsko Zdrój, *Poland* 45 F1
Trzebiatów, *Poland* 44 D2
Trzebiez, *Poland* 44 E1
Trzebnica, *Poland* 45 G4
Trzemeszno, *Poland* 45 F4
Tržič, *Slovenia* 29 B11
Tsagan Aman, *Russia* 49 G8
Tsamandás, *Greece* 38 B2
Tsandi, *Namibia* 88 B1
Tsaratanana, *Madag.* 89 B8
Tsaratanana, Mt. de, *Madag.* 89 A8
Tsarevo = Michurin, *Bulgaria* 41 D11
Tsarevo, *Bulgaria* 41 D9
Tsaritsáni, *Greece* 38 B4
Tsau, *Botswana* 88 C3
Tsebrykove, *Ukraine* 47 J6
Tselinograd = Astana, *Kazakstan* 50 D8
Tses, *Namibia* 88 D2
Tsetserleg, *Mongolia* 60 B5
Tsévié, *Togo* 83 D5
Tshabong, *Botswana* 88 D3
Tshane, *Botswana* 88 C3
Tshela, *Dem. Rep. of the Congo* 84 E2
Tshesebe, *Botswana* 89 C4
Tshibeke, *Dem. Rep. of the Congo* 86 C2
Tshibinda, *Dem. Rep. of the Congo* 86 C2
Tshikapa, *Dem. Rep. of the Congo* 84 F4
Tshilenge, *Dem. Rep. of the Congo* 86 D1
Tshinsenda, *Dem. Rep. of the Congo* 87 E2
Tshofa, *Dem. Rep. of the Congo* 86 D2
Tshwane, *Botswana* 88 C3
Tsigara, *Botswana* 88 C4
Tsihombe, *Madag.* 89 D8
Tsiigehtchic, *Canada* 100 B6
Tsimlyansk, *Russia* 49 G6
Tsimlyansk Res. = Tsimlyanskoye Vdkhr., *Russia* 49 F6
Tsimlyanskoye Vdkhr., *Russia* 49 F6
Tsinan = Jinan, *China* 56 F9
Tsineng, *S. Africa* 88 D3
Tsínga, *Greece* 41 E8
Tsinghai = Qinghai □, *China* 60 C4
Tsingtao = Qingdao, *China* 57 F11
Tsinjoarivo, *Madag.* 89 B8
Tsinjomitondraka, *Madag.* 89 B8
Tsiroanomandidy, *Madag.* 89 B8
Tsiteli-Tsqaro, *Georgia* 49 K8
Tsitondroina, *Madag.* 89 C8
Tsivilsk, *Russia* 48 C8
Tsivory, *Madag.* 89 C8
Tskhinvali, *Georgia* 49 J7
Tsna →, *Russia* 48 C6
Tsnori, *Georgia* 49 K7
Tso Moriri, L., *India* 69 C8
Tsobis, *Namibia* 88 B2
Tsodilo Hill, *Botswana* 88 B3

Tsogttsetsiy = Baruunsuu, *Mongolia* 56 C3
Tsolo, *S. Africa* 89 E4
Tsomo, *S. Africa* 89 E4
Tsu, *Japan* 55 G8
Tsu L., *Canada* 104 A6
Tsuchiura, *Japan* 55 F10
Tsuen Wan, *H.K.* 59 F10
Tsugaru-Kaikyō, *Japan* 54 D10
Tsumeb, *Namibia* 88 B2
Tsumis, *Namibia* 88 C2
Tsuruga, *Japan* 55 G8
Tsurugi-San, *Japan* 55 H7
Tsuruoka, *Japan* 54 E9
Tsushima, *Gifu, Japan* 55 G8
Tsushima, *Nagasaki, Japan* 55 G4
Tsuyama, *Japan* 55 G7
Tsvetkovo, *Ukraine* 47 H6
Tsyelyakhany, *Belarus* 47 F3
Tua →, *Portugal* 34 D3
Tual, *Indonesia* 63 F8
Tuam, *Ireland* 15 C3
Tuamotu Arch. = Tuamotu Is., *Pac. Oc.* 97 J13
Tuamotu Is., *Pac. Oc.* 97 J13
Tuamotu Ridge, *Pac. Oc.* 97 K14
Tuanfeng, *China* 59 B10
Tuanxi, *China* 58 D6
Tuao, *Phil.* 61 C4
Tuapse, *Russia* 49 H4
Tuatapere, *N.Z.* 91 M1
Tuba City, *U.S.A.* 115 H8
Tuban, *Indonesia* 63 G15
Tubani, *Botswana* 88 C3
Tubarão, *Brazil* 127 B6
Tūbās, *West Bank* 75 C4
Tubas →, *Namibia* 88 C2
Tübingen, *Germany* 25 G5
Tubruq, *Libya* 79 B10
Tubuai Is., *Pac. Oc.* 97 K13
Tuc Trung, *Vietnam* 65 G6
Tucacas, *Venezuela* 124 A5
T'uch'ang, *Taiwan* 59 E13
Tuchodi →, *Canada* 104 B4
Tuchola, *Poland* 44 E4
Tuchów, *Poland* 45 J8
Tuckanarra, *Australia* 93 E2
Tucson, *U.S.A.* 115 K8
Tucumán □, *Argentina* 126 B2
Tucumcari, *U.S.A.* 113 H3
Tucupita, *Venezuela* 124 B6
Tucuruí, *Brazil* 125 D9
Tucuruí, Reprêsa de, *Brazil* 125 D9
Tuczno, *Poland* 45 E3
Tudela, *Spain* 32 C3
Tudmur, *Syria* 70 C3
Tudor, L., *Canada* 103 A6
Tudora, *Romania* 43 C11
Tuella →, *Portugal* 34 D3
Tugela →, *S. Africa* 89 D5
Tuguegarao, *Phil.* 61 C4
Tugur, *Russia* 51 D14
Tui, *Spain* 34 C2
Tuineje, *Canary Is.* 37 F5
Tukangbesi, Kepulauan, *Indonesia* 63 F6
Tukarak I., *Canada* 102 A4
Tukayyid, *Iraq* 70 D5
Tûkh, *Egypt* 80 H7
Tukobo, *Ghana* 82 D4
Tuktoyaktuk, *Canada* 100 B6
Tukums, *Latvia* 9 H20
Tukums □, *Latvia* 44 B10
Tukuyu, *Tanzania* 87 D3
Tula, *Hidalgo, Mexico* 119 C5
Tula, *Tamaulipas, Mexico* 119 C5
Tula, *Nigeria* 83 D7
Tula, *Russia* 46 E9
Tulancingo, *Mexico* 119 C5
Tulare, *Serbia, Yug.* 40 D5
Tulare, *U.S.A.* 116 J7
Tulare Lake Bed, *U.S.A.* 116 K7
Tularosa, *U.S.A.* 115 K10
Tulbagh, *S. Africa* 88 E2
Tulcán, *Ecuador* 124 C3
Tulcea, *Romania* 43 E13
Tulcea □, *Romania* 43 E13
Tulchyn, *Ukraine* 47 H5
Tūleh, *Iran* 71 C7
Tulemalu L., *Canada* 105 A9
Tulgheş, *Romania* 43 D10
Tuli, *Zimbabwe* 87 G2
Tulia, *U.S.A.* 113 H4
Tuliszków, *Poland* 45 F5
Tulita, *Canada* 100 B7
Ţūlkarm, *West Bank* 75 C4
Tulla, *Ireland* 15 D3
Tullahoma, *U.S.A.* 109 H2
Tullamore, *Australia* 95 E4
Tullamore, *Ireland* 15 C4
Tulle, *France* 20 C5
Tulln, *Austria* 26 C9
Tullow, *Ireland* 15 D5
Tullus, *Sudan* 81 E1
Tully, *Australia* 94 B4
Tully, *U.S.A.* 111 D8
Tulnici, *Romania* 43 E11
Tulovo, *Bulgaria* 41 D9
Tulsa, *U.S.A.* 113 G7
Tulsequah, *Canada* 104 B2
Tulu Milki, *Ethiopia* 81 F4
Tulu Welel, *Ethiopia* 81 F3
Tulua, *Colombia* 124 C3
Tuluceşti, *Romania* 43 E13
Tulun, *Russia* 51 D11
Tulungagung, *Indonesia* 63 H14
Tuma, *Russia* 46 E11
Tuma →, *Nic.* 120 D3
Tumaco, *Colombia* 124 C3
Tumatumari, *Guyana* 124 B7
Tumba, *Sweden* 10 E11
Tumba, L., *Dem. Rep. of the Congo* 84 E3
Tumbarumba, *Australia* 95 F4
Tumbaya, *Argentina* 126 A2
Tumbes, *Peru* 124 D2
Tumbur, *Sudan* 81 G3
Tumbwe, *Dem. Rep. of the Congo* 87 E2
Tumby Bay, *Australia* 95 E2
Tumd Youqi, *China* 56 D6
Tumen, *China* 57 C15
Tumen Jiang →, *China* 57 C16
Tumeremo, *Venezuela* 124 B6
Tumkur, *India* 66 N10
Tump, *Pakistan* 66 F3
Tumpat, *Malaysia* 65 J4
Tumu, *Ghana* 82 C4
Tumucumaque, Serra, *Brazil* 122 C5
Tumut, *Australia* 95 F4
Tumwater, *U.S.A.* 116 C4
Tuna, *India* 68 H4
Tunadal, *Sweden* 10 B11
Tunas de Zaza, *Cuba* 120 B4
Tunbridge Wells = Royal Tunbridge Wells, *U.K.* 13 F8
Tunçbilek, *Turkey* 39 B11
Tunceli, *Turkey* 73 C8
Tuncurry, *Australia* 95 E5
Tundla, *India* 68 F8
Tundubai, *Sudan* 80 D2
Tunduru, *Tanzania* 87 E4
Tundzha →, *Bulgaria* 41 E10
Tungabhadra →, *India* 66 M11
Tungaru, *Sudan* 81 E3
Tungla, *Nic.* 120 D3
Tungsha Tao, *Taiwan* 59 G11
Tungshih, *Taiwan* 59 E13
Tungsten, *Canada* 104 A3
Tunguska, Nizhnyaya →, *Russia* 51 C9
Tunguska, Podkamennaya →, *Russia* 51 C10
Tunica, *U.S.A.* 113 H9
Tunis, *Tunisia* 78 A7
Tunisia ■, *Africa* 78 B6
Tunja, *Colombia* 124 B4
Tunkhannock, *U.S.A.* 111 E9
Tunliu, *China* 56 F7
Tunnsjøen, *Norway* 8 D15
Tunø, *Denmark* 11 J4
Tunungayualok I., *Canada* 103 A7
Tununirusiq = Arctic Bay, *Canada* 101 A11
Tunuyán, *Argentina* 126 C2
Tunuyán →, *Argentina* 126 C2
Tuo Jiang →, *China* 58 C5
Tuolumne, *U.S.A.* 116 H6
Tuolumne →, *U.S.A.* 116 H5
Tūp Āghāj, *Iran* 70 B5
Tupã, *Brazil* 127 A5
Tupelo, *U.S.A.* 109 H1
Tupik, *Russia* 46 E7
Tupinambaranas, *Brazil* 124 D7
Tupiza, *Bolivia* 126 A2
Tupižnica, *Serbia, Yug.* 40 C6
Tupman, *U.S.A.* 117 K7
Tupper, *Canada* 104 B4
Tupper Lake, *U.S.A.* 111 B10
Tupungato, Cerro, *S. Amer.* 126 C2
Tuquan, *China* 57 B11
Túquerres, *Colombia* 124 C3
Tura, *Russia* 51 C11
Turabah, *Si. Arabia* 70 D4
Turabah, *Si. Arabia* 80 C5
Tūrān, *Iran* 71 C8
Turan, *Russia* 51 D10
Ţurayf, *Si. Arabia* 70 D3
Turbacz, *Poland* 45 J7
Turbe, *Bos.-H.* 42 F2
Turčianske Teplice, *Slovak Rep.* 27 C11
Turcoaia, *Romania* 43 E13
Turda, *Romania* 43 D8
Turek, *Poland* 45 F5
Turen, *Venezuela* 124 B5
Turfan = Turpan, *China* 60 B3
Turfan Depression = Turpan Hami, *China* 52 E12
Turgeon →, *Canada* 102 C4
Tŭrgovishte, *Bulgaria* 41 C10
Turgut, *Turkey* 39 D10
Turgutlu, *Turkey* 39 C9
Turgwe →, *Zimbabwe* 89 C5
Turhal, *Turkey* 72 B7
Turia →, *Spain* 33 F4
Turiaçu, *Brazil* 125 D9
Turiaçu →, *Brazil* 125 D9
Turiec →, *Slovak Rep.* 27 B11
Turin = Torino, *Italy* 28 C4
Turkana, L., *Africa* 86 B4
Türkeli, *Turkey* 41 F11
Turkestan = Türkistan, *Kazakstan* 50 E7
Túrkeve, *Hungary* 42 C5
Turkey ■, *Eurasia* 72 C7
Turkey Creek, *Australia* 92 C4
Turki, *Russia* 48 D6
Türkistan, *Kazakstan* 50 E7
Türkmenbashi, *Turkmenistan* 50 E6
Turkmenistan ■, *Asia* 50 F6
Türkmenli, *Turkey* 39 B8
Türkoğlu, *Turkey* 72 D7
Turks & Caicos Is. ■, *W. Indies* 121 B5
Turks Island Passage, *W. Indies* 121 B5
Turku, *Finland* 9 F20
Turkwel →, *Kenya* 86 B4
Turlock, *U.S.A.* 116 H6
Turnagain →, *Canada* 104 B3
Turnagain, C., *N.Z.* 91 J6
Turneffe Is., *Belize* 119 D7
Turner, *U.S.A.* 114 B9
Turner Pt., *Australia* 94 A1
Turner Valley, *Canada* 104 C6
Turners Falls, *U.S.A.* 111 D12
Turnhout, *Belgium* 17 C4
Türnitz, *Austria* 26 D8
Turnor L., *Canada* 105 B7
Turnov, *Czech Rep.* 26 A8
Tŭrnovo = Veliko Tŭrnovo, *Bulgaria* 41 C9
Turnu Măgurele, *Romania* 43 G9
Turnu Roşu, P., *Romania* 43 E9
Turobin, *Poland* 45 H9
Turpan, *China* 60 B3
Turpan Hami, *China* 52 E12
Turrës, Kala e, *Albania* 40 E3
Turriff, *U.K.* 14 D6
Tursāq, *Iraq* 70 C5
Tursi, *Italy* 31 B9
Turtle Head I., *Australia* 94 A3
Turtle Is., *S. Leone* 82 D2
Turtle L., *Canada* 105 C7
Turtle Lake, *U.S.A.* 112 B4
Turtleford, *Canada* 105 C7
Turukhansk, *Russia* 51 C9
Turzovka, *Slovak Rep.* 27 B11
Tuscaloosa, *U.S.A.* 109 J2
Tuscánia, *Italy* 29 F8
Tuscany = Toscana □, *Italy* 28 E8
Tuscarawas →, *U.S.A.* 110 F3
Tuscarora Mt., *U.S.A.* 110 F7
Tuscola, *Ill., U.S.A.* 108 F1
Tuscola, *Tex., U.S.A.* 113 J5
Tuscumbia, *U.S.A.* 109 H2
Tuskegee, *U.S.A.* 109 J3
Tustin, *U.S.A.* 117 M9
Tuszyn, *Poland* 45 G6
Tutak, *Turkey* 73 C10
Tutayev, *Russia* 46 D10
Tuticorin, *India* 66 Q11
Tutin, *Serbia, Yug.* 40 D4
Tutóia, *Brazil* 125 D10
Tutong, *Brunei* 62 D4
Tutova →, *Romania* 43 D12
Tutrakan, *Bulgaria* 41 B10
Tuttle Creek L., *U.S.A.* 112 F6
Tuttlingen, *Germany* 25 H4
Tutuala, *Indonesia* 63 F7
Tutuila, *Amer. Samoa* 91 B13
Tutume, *Botswana* 85 J5
Tutun, *Egypt* 80 J7
Tututepec, *Mexico* 119 D5
Tuva □, *Russia* 51 D10
Tuvalu ■, *Pac. Oc.* 96 H9
Tuxer Alpen, *Austria* 26 D4
Tuxpan, *Mexico* 119 C5
Tuxtla Gutiérrez, *Mexico* 119 D6
Tuy = Tui, *Spain* 34 C2
Tuy An, *Vietnam* 64 F7
Tuy Duc, *Vietnam* 65 F6
Tuy Hoa, *Vietnam* 64 F7
Tuy Phong, *Vietnam* 65 G7
Tuya L., *Canada* 104 B2
Tuyen Hoa, *Vietnam* 64 D6
Tuyen Quang, *Vietnam* 58 G5
Tūysarkān, *Iran* 71 C6
Tuz Gölü, *Turkey* 72 C5
Ţūz Khurmātū, *Iraq* 70 C5
Tuzi, *Montenegro, Yug.* 40 D3
Tuzla, *Bos.-H.* 42 F3
Tuzlov →, *Russia* 47 J10
Tuzluca, *Turkey* 73 B10
Tvååker, *Sweden* 11 G6
Tvardiţa, *Moldova* 43 D13
Tver, *Russia* 46 D8
Tvrdošin, *Slovak Rep.* 27 B12
Tvrdošovce, *Slovak Rep.* 27 C11
Tvŭrditsa, *Bulgaria* 41 D9
Twain, *U.S.A.* 116 E5
Twain Harte, *U.S.A.* 116 G6
Twardogóra, *Poland* 45 G4
Tweed, *Canada* 110 B7
Tweed →, *U.K.* 14 F6
Tweed Heads, *Australia* 95 D5
Tweedsmuir Prov. Park, *Canada* 104 C3
Twentynine Palms, *U.S.A.* 117 L10
Twillingate, *Canada* 103 C9
Twin Bridges, *U.S.A.* 114 D7
Twin Falls, *Canada* 103 B7
Twin Falls, *U.S.A.* 114 E6
Twin Valley, *U.S.A.* 112 B6
Twinsburg, *U.S.A.* 110 E3
Twistringen, *Germany* 24 C4
Twitchell Reservoir, *U.S.A.* 117 L6
Two Harbors, *U.S.A.* 112 B9
Two Hills, *Canada* 104 C6
Two Rivers, *U.S.A.* 108 C2
Two Rocks, *Australia* 93 F2
Twofold B., *Australia* 95 F4
Tyachiv, *Ukraine* 47 H2
Tychy, *Poland* 45 H5
Tyczyn, *Poland* 45 J9
Tykocin, *Poland* 45 E9
Tyler, *Minn., U.S.A.* 112 C6
Tyler, *Tex., U.S.A.* 113 J7
Tyligul →, *Ukraine* 47 J6
Týn nad Vltavou, *Czech Rep.* 26 B7
Tynda, *Russia* 51 D13
Tyndall, *U.S.A.* 112 D6
Tyne →, *U.K.* 12 C6
Tyne & Wear □, *U.K.* 12 B6
Týnec nad Sázavou, *Czech Rep.* 26 B7
Tynemouth, *U.K.* 12 B6
Tyre = Sūr, *Lebanon* 75 B4
Tyrifjorden, *Norway* 9 F14
Tyringe, *Sweden* 11 H7
Tyrnyauz, *Russia* 49 J6
Tyrol = Tirol □, *Austria* 26 D3
Tyrone, *U.S.A.* 110 F6
Tyrone □, *U.K.* 15 B4
Tyrrell →, *Australia* 95 F3
Tyrrell, L., *Australia* 95 F3
Tyrrell L., *Canada* 105 A7
Tyrrhenian Sea, *Medit. S.* 6 G8
Tysfjorden, *Norway* 8 B17
Tystberga, *Sweden* 11 F11
Tytuvėnai, *Lithuania* 44 C10
Tyub Karagan, Mys, *Kazakstan* 49 H10
Tyuleni, Ostrova, *Kazakstan* 49 H10
Tyuleniy, *Russia* 49 H8
Tyuleniy, Mys, *Azerbaijan* 49 K10
Tyumen, *Russia* 50 D7
Tywi →, *U.K.* 13 F3
Tywyn, *U.K.* 13 E3
Tzaneen, *S. Africa* 89 C5
Tzermiádhes, *Greece* 36 D7
Tzoumérka, Óros, *Greece* 38 B3
Tzukong = Zigong, *China* 58 C5

U

U Taphao, *Thailand* 64 F3
U.S.A. = United States of America ■, *N. Amer.* 106 C7
Uatumã →, *Brazil* 124 D7
Uaupés, *Brazil* 124 D5
Uaupés →, *Brazil* 124 C5
Uaxactún, *Guatemala* 120 C2
Ub, *Serbia, Yug.* 40 B4
Ubá, *Brazil* 127 A7
Uba, *Nigeria* 83 C7
Ubaitaba, *Brazil* 125 F11
Ubangi = Oubangi →, *Dem. Rep. of the Congo* 84 E3
Ubauro, *Pakistan* 68 E3
Ubaye →, *France* 21 D10
Ubayyiḍ, W. al →, *Iraq* 70 C4
Ube, *Japan* 55 H5
Úbeda, *Spain* 35 G7
Uberaba, *Brazil* 125 G9
Uberlândia, *Brazil* 125 G9
Überlingen, *Germany* 25 H5
Ubiaja, *Nigeria* 83 D6
Ubolratna Res., *Thailand* 64 D4
Ubombo, *S. Africa* 89 D5
Ubon Ratchathani, *Thailand* 64 E5
Ubondo, *Dem. Rep. of the Congo* 86 C2
Ubort →, *Belarus* 47 F5
Ubrique, *Spain* 35 J5
Ubundu, *Dem. Rep. of the Congo* 86 C2
Ucayali →, *Peru* 122 D3
Uchab, *Namibia* 88 B2
Uchiura-Wan, *Japan* 54 C10
Uchquduq, *Uzbekistan* 50 E7
Uchte, *Germany* 24 C4
Uchur →, *Russia* 51 D14
Uckermark, *Germany* 24 B9
Ucluelet, *Canada* 104 D3
Uda →, *Russia* 51 D14
Udagamandalam, *India* 66 P10
Udainagar, *India* 68 H7
Udaipur, *India* 68 G5
Udaipur Garhi, *Nepal* 69 F12
Udala, *India* 69 J12
Udbina, *Croatia* 29 D12
Uddeholm, *Sweden* 10 D7
Uddevalla, *Sweden* 11 F5
Uddjaur, *Sweden* 8 D17
Uden, *Neths.* 17 C5
Udgir, *India* 66 K10
Udhampur, *India* 69 C6
Udi, *Nigeria* 83 D6
Údine, *Italy* 29 B10
Udmurtia □, *Russia* 50 D6
Udon Thani, *Thailand* 64 D4
Udupi, *India* 66 N9
Udvoy Balkan, *Bulgaria* 41 D10
Udzungwa Range, *Tanzania* 87 D4
Ueckermünde, *Germany* 24 B10
Ueda, *Japan* 55 F9
Uedineniya, Os., *Russia* 4 B12
Uele →, *Dem. Rep. of the Congo* 84 D4
Uelen, *Russia* 51 C19
Uelzen, *Germany* 24 C6
Uetersen, *Germany* 24 B5
Uetze, *Germany* 24 C6
Ufa, *Russia* 50 D6
Uffenheim, *Germany* 25 F6
Ugab →, *Namibia* 88 C1
Ugalla →, *Tanzania* 86 D3
Uganda ■, *Africa* 86 B3
Ugento, *Italy* 31 C11
Ugep, *Nigeria* 83 D6
Ughelli, *Nigeria* 83 D6
Ugie, *S. Africa* 89 E4
Ugíjar, *Spain* 35 J7
Ugine, *France* 21 C10
Uglegorsk, *Russia* 51 E15
Uglich, *Russia* 46 D10
Ugljan, *Croatia* 29 D12
Ugljane, *Croatia* 29 E13
Ugra →, *Russia* 46 E9
Ugŭrchin, *Bulgaria* 41 C8
Uh →, *Slovak Rep.* 27 C15
Uherské Hradiště, *Czech Rep.* 27 B10
Uherský Brod, *Czech Rep.* 27 B10
Úhlava →, *Czech Rep.* 26 B6
Uhlenhorst, *Namibia* 88 C2
Uhrichsville, *U.S.A.* 110 F3
Uibhist a Deas = South Uist, *U.K.* 14 D1
Uibhist a Tuath = North Uist, *U.K.* 14 D1
Uig, *U.K.* 14 D2
Uíge, *Angola* 84 F2
Uijŏngbu, *S. Korea* 57 F14
Ŭiju, *N. Korea* 57 D13
Uinta Mts., *U.S.A.* 114 F8
Uis, *Namibia* 88 B2
Uitenhage, *S. Africa* 88 E4
Uithuizen, *Neths.* 17 A6
Ujazd, *Poland* 45 H5
Újfehértó, *Hungary* 42 C6
Ujh →, *India* 68 C6
Ujhani, *India* 69 F8
Uji-guntō, *Japan* 55 J4
Ujjain, *India* 68 H6
Ujście, *Poland* 45 E3
Újszász, *Hungary* 42 C5
Ujung Pandang, *Indonesia* 63 F5
Uka, *Russia* 51 D17
Ukara I., *Tanzania* 86 C3
Uke-Shima, *Japan* 55 K4
Ukerewe I., *Tanzania* 86 C3
Ukholovo, *Russia* 48 D5
Ukhrul, *India* 67 G19
Ukhta, *Russia* 50 C6
Ukiah, *U.S.A.* 116 F3
Ukki Fort, *India* 69 C7
Ukmergė, *Lithuania* 9 J21
Ukraine ■, *Europe* 47 H7
Ukwi, *Botswana* 88 C3
Ulaan-Uul, *Mongolia* 56 B6
Ulaanbaatar, *Mongolia* 51 E11
Ulaangom, *Mongolia* 60 A4
Ulaanjirem, *Mongolia* 56 B3
Ulamba, *Dem. Rep. of the Congo* 87 D1
Ulan Bator = Ulaanbaatar, *Mongolia* 51 E11
Ulan Erge, *Russia* 49 G7
Ulan Khol, *Russia* 49 H8
Ulan Ude, *Russia* 51 D11
Ulanów, *Poland* 45 H9
Ulaş, *Sivas, Turkey* 72 C7
Ulaş, *Tekirdağ, Turkey* 41 E11
Ulaya, *Morogoro, Tanzania* 86 D4
Ulaya, *Tabora, Tanzania* 86 C3
Ulcinj, *Montenegro, Yug.* 40 E3
Ulco, *S. Africa* 88 D3
Ulefoss, *Norway* 9 G13
Ulëz, *Albania* 40 E3
Ulfborg, *Denmark* 11 H2
Ulhasnagar, *India* 66 K8
Uliastay = Ulyasutay, *Mongolia* 60 B4
Ulithi Atoll, *Pac. Oc.* 63 B9
Uljma, *Serbia, Yug.* 42 E6
Ulla →, *Spain* 34 C2
Ulladulla, *Australia* 95 F5
Ullapool, *U.K.* 14 D3
Ullared, *Sweden* 11 G6
Ulldecona, *Spain* 32 E5
Ullswater, *U.K.* 12 C5
Ullŭng-do, *S. Korea* 55 F5
Ulm, *Germany* 25 G5
Ulmarra, *Australia* 95 D5
Ulmeni, *Buzău, Romania* 43 E11
Ulmeni, *Maramureş, Romania* 43 C8
Ulonguè, *Mozam.* 87 E3
Ulricehamn, *Sweden* 11 G7
Ulrika, *Sweden* 11 F9
Ulsan, *S. Korea* 57 G15
Ulsta, *U.K.* 14 A7
Ulster □, *U.K.* 15 B5
Ulstrem, *Bulgaria* 41 D10
Ulubat Gölü, *Turkey* 41 F12
Ulubey, *Turkey* 39 C11
Uluborlu, *Turkey* 39 C12
Uluçinar, *Turkey* 72 D6
Uludağ, *Turkey* 41 F13
Uludere, *Turkey* 73 D10
Uluguru Mts., *Tanzania* 86 D4
Ulukışla, *Turkey* 72 D6
Ulungur He →, *China* 60 B3
Uluru = Ayers Rock, *Australia* 93 E5
Uluru Nat. Park, *Australia* 93 E5
Ulutau, *Kazakstan* 50 E7
Ulva, *U.K.* 14 E2
Ulverston, *U.K.* 12 C4
Ulverstone, *Australia* 94 G4
Ulya, *Russia* 51 D15
Ulyanovsk = Simbirsk, *Russia* 48 C9
Ulyasutay, *Mongolia* 60 B4
Ulysses, *U.S.A.* 113 G4
Umag, *Croatia* 29 C10
Umala, *Bolivia* 124 G5
Uman, *Ukraine* 47 H6
Umaria, *India* 67 H12
Umarkot, *Pakistan* 66 G6
Umarpada, *India* 68 J5
Umatilla, *U.S.A.* 114 D4
Umbagog L., *U.S.A.* 111 B13
Umbakumba, *Australia* 94 A2
Umbértide, *Italy* 29 E9
Umbrella Mts., *N.Z.* 91 L2
Umbria □, *Italy* 29 F9
Ume älv →, *Sweden* 8 E19
Umeå, *Sweden* 8 E19
Umera, *Indonesia* 63 E7
Umfuli →, *Zimbabwe* 87 F2
Umgusa, *Zimbabwe* 87 F2
Umim Urūmah, *Si. Arabia* 80 B4

Umka, *Serbia, Yug.* 40 B4
Umkomaas, *S. Africa* 89 E5
Umlazi, *S. Africa* 85 L6
Umm ad Daraj, J., *Jordan* 75 C4
Umm al Qaywayn, *U.A.E.* 71 E7
Umm al Qittayn, *Jordan* 75 C5
Umm Arda, *Sudan* 81 D3
Umm Bāb, *Qatar* 71 E6
Umm Badr, *Sudan* 81 E2
Umm Baiyud, *Sudan* 81 E3
Umm Bel, *Sudan* 81 E2
Umm Birkah, *Si. Arabia* 80 B4
Umm Boim, *Sudan* 81 E2
Umm Dam, *Sudan* 81 E3
Umm Debi, *Sudan* 81 E3
Umm Dubban, *Sudan* 81 D3
Umm el Fahm, *Israel* 75 C4
Umm Gafala, *Sudan* 81 E2
Umm Gimala, *Sudan* 81 E2
Umm Inderaba, *Sudan* 80 D3
Umm Keddada, *Sudan* 81 E2
Umm Koweika, *Sudan* 81 E3
Umm Lajj, *Si. Arabia* 70 E3
Umm Merwa, *Sudan* 80 D3
Umm Qantur, *Sudan* 81 E3
Umm Qurein, *Sudan* 81 F2
Umm Ruwaba, *Sudan* 81 E3
Umm Saiyala, *Sudan* 81 E3
Umm Shanqa, *Sudan* 81 E2
Umm Shutur, *Sudan* 81 F3
Umm Sidr, *Sudan* 81 E2
Umm Zehetir, *Egypt* 80 J8
Umnak I., *U.S.A.* 100 C3
Umniati →, *Zimbabwe* 87 F2
Umpqua →, *U.S.A.* 114 E1
Umreth, *India* 68 H5
Umtata, *S. Africa* 89 E4
Umuahia, *Nigeria* 83 D6
Umuarama, *Brazil* 127 A5
Umurbey, *Turkey* 41 F10
Umvukwe Ra., *Zimbabwe* 87 F3
Umzimvubu, *S. Africa* 89 E4
Umzingwane →, *Zimbabwe* 87 G2
Umzinto, *S. Africa* 89 E5
Una, *India* 68 J4
Una →, *Bos.-H.* 29 D13
Unac →, *Bos.-H.* 29 D13
Unadilla, *U.S.A.* 111 D9
Unalakleet, *U.S.A.* 100 B3
Unalaska, *U.S.A.* 100 C3
Unalaska I., *U.S.A.* 100 C3
'Unayzah, *Si. Arabia* 70 E4
'Unāzah, J., *Asia* 70 C3
Uncastillo, *Spain* 32 C3
Uncía, *Bolivia* 124 G5
Uncompahgre Peak, *U.S.A.* 115 G10
Uncompahgre Plateau, *U.S.A.* 115 G9
Unden, *Sweden* 11 F8
Underbool, *Australia* 95 F3
Undersaker, *Sweden* 10 A7
Unecha, *Russia* 47 F7
Ungarie, *Australia* 95 E4
Ungarra, *Australia* 95 E2
Ungava, Pén. d', *Canada* 101 C12
Ungava B., *Canada* 101 C13
Ungeny = Ungheni, *Moldova* 43 C12
Unggi, *N. Korea* 57 C16
Ungheni, *Moldova* 43 C12
Unguala →, *Ethiopia* 81 F5
Ungwatiri, *Sudan* 81 D4
Uni, *Russia* 48 B10
União da Vitória, *Brazil* 127 B5
Uničov, *Czech Rep.* 27 B10
Uniejów, *Poland* 45 G5
Unije, *Croatia* 29 D11
Unimak I., *U.S.A.* 100 C3
Union, *Miss., U.S.A.* 113 J10
Union, *Mo., U.S.A.* 112 F9
Union, *S.C., U.S.A.* 109 H5
Union City, *Calif., U.S.A.* 116 H4
Union City, *N.J., U.S.A.* 111 F10
Union City, *Pa., U.S.A.* 110 E5
Union City, *Tenn., U.S.A.* 113 G10
Union Gap, *U.S.A.* 114 C3
Union Springs, *U.S.A.* 109 J3
Uniondale, *S. Africa* 88 E3
Uniontown, *U.S.A.* 108 F6
Unionville, *U.S.A.* 112 E8
Unirea, *Romania* 43 F12
United Arab Emirates ■, *Asia* 71 F7
United Kingdom ■, *Europe* 7 E5
United States of America ■, *N. Amer.* 106 C7
Unity, *Canada* 105 C7
Universales, Mtes., *Spain* 32 E3
University Park, *U.S.A.* 115 K10
Unjha, *India* 68 H5
Unna, *Germany* 24 D3
Unnao, *India* 69 F9
Uno, Ilha, *Guinea-Biss.* 82 C1
Unst, *U.K.* 14 A8
Unstrut →, *Germany* 24 D7
Unterfranken □, *Germany* 25 F5
Unterschleissheim, *Germany* 25 G7
Unuk →, *Canada* 104 B2
Ünye, *Turkey* 72 B7
Unzha, *Russia* 48 A7
Unzha →, *Russia* 48 B6
Uozu, *Japan* 55 F8
Upata, *Venezuela* 124 B6
Upemba, L., *Dem. Rep. of the Congo* 87 D2
Upernavik, *Greenland* 4 B5
Upington, *S. Africa* 88 D3
Upleta, *India* 68 J4
Upolu, *Samoa* 91 A13
Upper □, *Ghana* 83 C4
Upper Alkali L., *U.S.A.* 114 F3
Upper Arrow L., *Canada* 104 C5
Upper Austria = Oberösterreich □, *Austria* 26 C7
Upper Foster L., *Canada* 105 B7
Upper Hutt, *N.Z.* 91 J5
Upper Klamath L., *U.S.A.* 114 E3
Upper Lake, *U.S.A.* 116 F4
Upper Musquodoboit, *Canada* 103 C7
Upper Red L., *U.S.A.* 112 A7
Upper Sandusky, *U.S.A.* 108 E4
Upper Volta = Burkina Faso ■, *Africa* 82 C4
Upphärad, *Sweden* 11 F6
Uppland, *Sweden* 10 E11
Upplands-Väsby, *Sweden* 10 E11
Uppsala, *Sweden* 10 E11
Uppsala län □, *Sweden* 10 D11
Upshi, *India* 69 C7
Upstart, C., *Australia* 94 B4
Upton, *U.S.A.* 112 C2
Ur, *Iraq* 70 D5
Urad Qianqi, *China* 56 D5
Urakawa, *Japan* 54 C11
Ural = Zhayyq →, *Kazakstan* 50 E6
Ural, *Australia* 95 E4
Ural Mts. = Uralskie Gory, *Eurasia* 50 D6
Uralla, *Australia* 95 E5
Uralsk = Oral, *Kazakstan* 48 E10
Uralskie Gory, *Eurasia* 50 D6
Urambo, *Tanzania* 86 D3
Urandangi, *Australia* 94 C2
Uranium City, *Canada* 105 B7
Uraricoera →, *Brazil* 124 C6
Urawa, *Japan* 55 G9
Uray, *Russia* 50 C7
'Uray'irah, *Si. Arabia* 71 E6
Urbana, *Ill., U.S.A.* 108 E1
Urbana, *Ohio, U.S.A.* 108 E4
Urbánia, *Italy* 29 E9
Urbel →, *Spain* 34 C7
Urbino, *Italy* 29 E9
Urbión, Picos de, *Spain* 32 C2
Urcos, *Peru* 124 F4
Urdinarrain, *Argentina* 126 C4
Urdos, *France* 20 F3
Urdzhar, *Kazakstan* 50 E9
Ure →, *U.K.* 12 C6
Uren, *Russia* 48 B7
Ures, *Mexico* 118 B2
Urfa = Sanliurfa, *Turkey* 70 B3
Urganch, *Uzbekistan* 50 E7
Urgench = Urganch, *Uzbekistan* 50 E7
Ürgüp, *Turkey* 70 B2
Uri, *India* 69 B6
Uri □, *Switz.* 25 J4
Uribia, *Colombia* 124 A4
Uricani, *Romania* 42 E8
Uriondo, *Bolivia* 126 A3
Urique, *Mexico* 118 B3
Urique →, *Mexico* 118 B3
Urk, *Neths.* 17 B5
Urla, *Turkey* 39 C8
Urlați, *Romania* 43 F11
Urmia = Orūmīyeh, *Iran* 70 B5
Urmia, L. = Orūmīyeh, Daryācheh-ye, *Iran* 70 B5
Uroševac, *Kosovo, Yug.* 40 D5
Urshult, *Sweden* 11 H8
Uruaçu, *Brazil* 125 F9
Uruapan, *Mexico* 118 D4
Urubamba →, *Peru* 124 F4
Uruçara, *Brazil* 124 D7
Uruçuí, *Brazil* 125 E10
Uruguai →, *Brazil* 127 B5
Uruguaiana, *Brazil* 126 B4
Uruguay ■, *S. Amer.* 126 C4
Uruguay →, *S. Amer.* 126 C4
Urumchi = Ürümqi, *China* 50 E9
Ürümqi, *China* 50 E9
Urup →, *Russia* 49 H5
Urup, Ostrov, *Russia* 51 E16
Uryupinsk, *Russia* 48 E5
Urzhum, *Russia* 48 B9
Urziceni, *Romania* 43 F11
Usa →, *Russia* 50 C6
Uşak, *Turkey* 39 C11
Uşak □, *Turkey* 39 C11
Usakos, *Namibia* 88 C2
Ušće, *Serbia, Yug.* 40 C4
Usedom, *Germany* 24 B10
Useless Loop, *Australia* 93 E1
'Usfān, *Si. Arabia* 80 C4
Ush-Tobe, *Kazakstan* 50 E8
Ushakova, Ostrov, *Russia* 4 A12
Ushant = Ouessant, Î. d', *France* 18 D1
Ushashi, *Tanzania* 86 C3
Ushat, *Sudan* 81 F2
'Ushayrah, *Si. Arabia* 80 C5
Ushibuka, *Japan* 55 H5
Ushuaia, *Argentina* 128 G3
Ushumun, *Russia* 51 D13
Usk, *Canada* 104 C3
Usk →, *U.K.* 13 F5
Uska, *India* 69 F10
Üsküdar, *Turkey* 41 F13
Uslar, *Germany* 24 D5
Usman, *Russia* 47 F10
Usoke, *Tanzania* 86 D3
Usolye Sibirskoye, *Russia* 51 D11
Usoro, *Nigeria* 83 D6
Uspallata, P. de, *Argentina* 126 C2
Uspenskiy, *Kazakstan* 50 E8
Ussel, *France* 20 C6
Usson-du-Poitou, *France* 20 B4
Ussuri →, *Asia* 54 A7
Ussuriysk, *Russia* 51 E14
Ussurka, *Russia* 54 B6
Ust-Aldan = Batamay, *Russia* 51 C13
Ust-Amginskoye = Khandyga, *Russia* 51 C14
Ust-Bolsheretsk, *Russia* 51 D16
Ust-Buzulukskaya, *Russia* 48 E6
Ust-Chaun, *Russia* 51 C18
Ust-Donetskiy, *Russia* 49 G5
Ust-Ilimpeya = Yukta, *Russia* 51 C11
Ust-Ilimsk, *Russia* 51 D11
Ust-Ishim, *Russia* 50 D8
Ust-Kamchatsk, *Russia* 51 D17
Ust-Kamenogorsk = Öskemen, *Kazakstan* 50 E9
Ust-Khayryuzovo, *Russia* 51 D16
Ust-Kut, *Russia* 51 D11
Ust-Kuyga, *Russia* 51 B14
Ust-Labinsk, *Russia* 49 H4
Ust-Luga, *Russia* 46 C5
Ust-Maya, *Russia* 51 C14
Ust-Mil, *Russia* 51 D14
Ust-Nera, *Russia* 51 C15
Ust-Nyukzha, *Russia* 51 D13
Ust-Olenek, *Russia* 51 B12
Ust-Omchug, *Russia* 51 C15
Ust-Port, *Russia* 50 C9
Ust-Tsilma, *Russia* 50 C6
Ust Urt = Ustyurt Plateau, *Asia* 50 E6
Ustaritz, *France* 20 E2
Ustecký □, *Czech Rep.* 26 A7
Uster, *Switz.* 25 H4
Ústí nad Labem, *Czech Rep.* 26 A7
Ústí nad Orlicí, *Czech Rep.* 27 B9
Ústica, *Italy* 30 D6
Ustinov = Izhevsk, *Russia* 50 D6
Ustka, *Poland* 44 D3
Ustroń, *Poland* 45 J5
Ustrzyki Dolne, *Poland* 45 J9
Ustyurt Plateau, *Asia* 50 E6
Ustyuzhna, *Russia* 46 C9
Usu, *China* 60 B3
Usuki, *Japan* 55 H5
Usulután, *El Salv.* 120 D2
Usumacinta →, *Mexico* 119 D6
Usumbura = Bujumbura, *Burundi* 86 C2
Usure, *Tanzania* 86 C3
Usutuo →, *Mozam.* 89 D5
Uta, *Indonesia* 63 E9
Utah □, *U.S.A.* 114 G8
Utah L., *U.S.A.* 114 F8
Utansjö, *Sweden* 10 B11
Utarni, *India* 68 F4
Utatlan, *Guatemala* 120 C1
Ute Creek →, *U.S.A.* 113 H3
Utebo, *Spain* 32 D3
Utena, *Lithuania* 9 J21
Utete, *Tanzania* 86 D4
Uthai Thani, *Thailand* 64 E3
Uthal, *Pakistan* 68 G2
Utiariti, *Brazil* 124 F7
Utica, *N.Y., U.S.A.* 111 C9
Utica, *Ohio, U.S.A.* 110 F2
Utiel, *Spain* 33 F3
Utikuma L., *Canada* 104 B5
Utö, *Sweden* 10 F12
Utopia, *Australia* 94 C1
Utraula, *India* 69 F10
Utrecht, *Neths.* 17 B5
Utrecht, *S. Africa* 89 D5
Utrecht □, *Neths.* 17 B5
Utrera, *Spain* 35 H5
Utsjoki, *Finland* 8 B22
Utsunomiya, *Japan* 55 F9
Uttar Pradesh □, *India* 69 F9
Uttaradit, *Thailand* 64 D3
Uttaranchal □, *India* 69 D8
Uttoxeter, *U.K.* 12 E6
Uummannarsuaq = Nunap Isua, *Greenland* 101 C15
Uusikaarlepyy, *Finland* 8 E20
Uusikaupunki, *Finland* 9 F19
Uva, *Russia* 48 B11
Uvac →, *Serbia, Yug.* 40 C3
Uvalde, *U.S.A.* 113 L5
Uvarovo, *Russia* 48 E6
Uvat, *Russia* 50 D7
Uvinza, *Tanzania* 86 D3
Uvira, *Dem. Rep. of the Congo* 86 C2
Uvs Nuur, *Mongolia* 60 A4
'Uwairidh, Ḩarrat al, *Si. Arabia* 70 E3
Uwajima, *Japan* 55 H6
Uweinat, Jebel, *Sudan* 80 C1
Uxbridge, *Canada* 110 B5
Uxin Qi, *China* 56 E5
Uxmal, *Mexico* 119 C7
Üydzin, *Mongolia* 56 B4
Uyo, *Nigeria* 83 D6
Üyüklü Tepe, *Turkey* 39 D9
Uyûn Mûsa, *Egypt* 75 F1
Uyuni, *Bolivia* 124 H5
Uzbekistan ■, *Asia* 50 E7
Uzen, Bolshoi →, *Kazakstan* 49 F9
Uzen, Mal →, *Kazakstan* 49 F9
Uzerche, *France* 20 C5
Uzès, *France* 21 D8
Uzh →, *Ukraine* 47 G6
Uzhgorod = Uzhhorod, *Ukraine* 47 H2
Uzhhorod, *Ukraine* 47 H2
Užice, *Serbia, Yug.* 40 C3
Uzlovaya, *Russia* 46 F10
Üzümlü, *Turkey* 39 E11
Uzunköprü, *Turkey* 41 E10
Uzunkuyu, *Turkey* 39 C8

V

Vaal →, *S. Africa* 88 D3
Vaal Dam, *S. Africa* 89 D4
Vaalwater, *S. Africa* 89 C4
Vaasa, *Finland* 8 E19
Vabre, *France* 20 E6
Vác, *Hungary* 42 C4
Vacaria, *Brazil* 127 B5
Vacaville, *U.S.A.* 116 G5
Vaccarès, Étang de, *France* 21 E8
Vach = Vakh →, *Russia* 50 C8
Vache, Î. à, *Haiti* 121 C5
Väckelsång, *Sweden* 11 H8
Väddö, *Sweden* 10 D12
Väderstad, *Sweden* 11 F8
Vadnagar, *India* 68 H5
Vado Lígure, *Italy* 28 D5
Vadodara, *India* 68 H5
Vadsø, *Norway* 8 A23
Vadstena, *Sweden* 11 F8
Vaduz, *Liech.* 25 H5
Værøy, *Norway* 8 C15
Vágar, *Færoe Is.* 8 E9
Vaggeryd, *Sweden* 11 G8
Vagney, *France* 19 D13
Vagnhärad, *Sweden* 11 F11
Vagos, *Portugal* 34 E2
Vågsfjorden, *Norway* 8 B17
Váh →, *Slovak Rep.* 27 D11
Vahsel B., *Antarctica* 5 D1
Váï, *Greece* 36 D8
Vaigach, *Russia* 50 B6
Vaiges, *France* 18 D6
Vaihingen, *Germany* 25 G4
Vail, *U.S.A.* 106 C5
Vailly-sur-Aisne, *France* 19 C10
Vaisali →, *India* 69 F8
Vaison-la-Romaine, *France* 21 D9
Vakarel, *Bulgaria* 40 D7
Vakfikebir, *Turkey* 73 B8
Vakh →, *Russia* 50 C8
Vakhtan, *Russia* 48 B8
Vál, *Hungary* 42 C3
Val-de-Marne □, *France* 19 D9
Val-d'Isère, *France* 21 C10
Val-d'Oise □, *France* 19 C9
Val-d'Or, *Canada* 102 C4
Val Marie, *Canada* 105 D7
Valaam, *Russia* 46 B6
Valadares, *Portugal* 34 D2
Valahia, *Romania* 43 F9
Valais □, *Switz.* 25 J3
Valais, Alpes du, *Switz.* 25 J3
Valandovo, *Macedonia* 40 E6
Valašské Meziříčí, *Czech Rep.* 27 B10
Valáxa, *Greece* 38 C6
Vålberg, *Sweden* 10 E7
Valbo, *Sweden* 10 D10
Valbondione, *Italy* 28 B7
Vâlcani, *Romania* 42 D5
Vâlcea □, *Romania* 43 F9
Valcheta, *Argentina* 128 E3
Valdagno, *Italy* 29 C8
Valdahon, *France* 19 E13
Valday, *Russia* 46 D7
Valdayskaya Vozvyshennost, *Russia* 46 D7
Valdeazogues →, *Spain* 35 G6
Valdecañas, Embalse de, *Spain* 34 F5
Valdemarsvik, *Sweden* 11 F10
Valdemoro, *Spain* 34 E7
Valdepeñas, *Spain* 35 G7
Valderaduey →, *Spain* 34 D5
Valdérice, *Italy* 30 D5
Valderrobres, *Spain* 32 E5
Valdés, Pen., *Argentina* 122 H4
Valdez, *U.S.A.* 100 B5
Valdivia, *Chile* 128 D2
Valdobbiádene, *Italy* 29 C8
Valdosta, *U.S.A.* 109 K4
Valdoviño, *Spain* 34 B2
Valdres, *Norway* 9 F13
Vale, *Georgia* 49 K6
Vale, *U.S.A.* 114 E5
Vale of Glamorgan □, *U.K.* 13 F4
Valea lui Mihai, *Romania* 42 C7
Valea Mărului, *Romania* 43 E12
Valemount, *Canada* 104 C5
Valença, *Brazil* 125 F11
Valença, *Portugal* 34 C2
Valença do Piauí, *Brazil* 125 E10
Valençay, *France* 19 E8
Valence = Valence d'Agen, *France* 20 D4
Valence, *France* 21 D8
Valence d'Agen, *France* 20 D4
Valencia, *Spain* 33 F4
Valencia, *U.S.A.* 115 J10
Valencia, *Venezuela* 124 A5
Valencia □, *Spain* 33 F4
Valencia, G. de, *Spain* 33 F5
Valencia de Alcántara, *Spain* 35 F3
Valencia de Don Juan, *Spain* 34 C5
Valencia I., *Ireland* 15 E1
Valenciennes, *France* 19 B10
Văleni, *Romania* 43 F9
Vălenii de Munte, *Romania* 43 E11
Valensole, *France* 21 E9
Valentigney, *France* 19 E13
Valentim, Sa. do, *Brazil* 125 E10
Valentin, *Russia* 54 C7
Valentine, *U.S.A.* 113 K2
Valenza, *Italy* 28 C5
Valera, *Venezuela* 124 B4
Valga, *Estonia* 9 H22
Valguarnera Caropepe, *Italy* 31 E7
Valier, *U.S.A.* 114 B7
Valinco, G. de, *France* 21 G12
Valjevo, *Serbia, Yug.* 40 B3
Valka, *Latvia* 9 H21
Valkeakoski, *Finland* 9 F20
Valkenswaard, *Neths.* 17 C5
Vall de Uxó = La Vall d'Uixó, *Spain* 32 F4
Valla, *Sweden* 10 E10
Valladolid, *Mexico* 119 C7
Valladolid, *Spain* 34 D6
Valladolid □, *Spain* 34 D6
Vallata, *Italy* 31 A8
Valldemossa, *Spain* 37 B9
Valle d'Aosta □, *Italy* 28 C4
Valle de Arán, *Spain* 32 C5
Valle de la Pascua, *Venezuela* 124 B5
Valle de las Palmas, *Mexico* 117 N10
Valle de Santiago, *Mexico* 118 C4
Valle de Suchil, *Mexico* 118 C4
Valle de Zaragoza, *Mexico* 118 B3
Valle Fértil, Sierra del, *Argentina* 126 C2
Valle Hermoso, *Mexico* 119 B5
Valledupar, *Colombia* 124 A4
Vallehermoso, *Canary Is.* 37 F2
Vallejo, *U.S.A.* 116 G4
Vallenar, *Chile* 126 B1
Vallentuna, *Sweden* 10 E12
Valleraugue, *France* 20 D7
Vallet, *France* 18 E5
Valletta, *Malta* 36 D2
Valley Center, *U.S.A.* 117 M9
Valley City, *U.S.A.* 112 B6
Valley Falls, *Oreg., U.S.A.* 114 E3
Valley Falls, *R.I., U.S.A.* 111 E13
Valley Springs, *U.S.A.* 116 G6
Valley View, *U.S.A.* 111 F8
Valley Wells, *U.S.A.* 117 K11
Valleyview, *Canada* 104 B5
Valli di Comácchio, *Italy* 29 D9
Vallimanca, Arroyo, *Argentina* 126 D4
Vallo della Lucánia, *Italy* 31 B8
Vallon-Pont-d'Arc, *France* 21 D8
Vallorbe, *Switz.* 25 J2
Valls, *Spain* 32 D6
Valmaseda = Balmaseda, *Spain* 32 B1
Valmiera, *Latvia* 9 H21
Valnera, *Spain* 34 B7
Valognes, *France* 18 C5
Valona = Vlorë, *Albania* 40 F3
Valongo, *Portugal* 34 D2
Valozhyn, *Belarus* 46 E4
Valpaços, *Portugal* 34 D3
Valparaíso, *Chile* 126 C1
Valparaíso, *Mexico* 118 C4
Valparaiso, *U.S.A.* 108 E2
Valparaíso □, *Chile* 126 C1
Valpovo, *Croatia* 42 E3
Valréas, *France* 21 D9
Vals, *Switz.* 25 J5
Vals →, *S. Africa* 88 D4
Vals, Tanjung, *Indonesia* 63 F9
Vals-les-Bains, *France* 21 D8
Valsad, *India* 66 J8
Valtellina, *Italy* 28 B6
Valuyki, *Russia* 47 G10
Valverde, *Canary Is.* 37 G2
Valverde del Camino, *Spain* 35 H4
Valverde del Fresno, *Spain* 34 E4
Vama, *Romania* 43 C10
Vamdrup, *Denmark* 11 J3
Våmhus, *Sweden* 10 C8
Vammala, *Finland* 9 F20
Vámos, *Greece* 36 D6
Van, *Turkey* 70 B4
Van, L. = Van Gölü, *Turkey* 70 B4
Van Alstyne, *U.S.A.* 113 J6
Van Blommestein Meer, *Surinam* 125 C7
Van Buren, *Canada* 103 C6
Van Buren, *Ark., U.S.A.* 113 H7
Van Buren, *Maine, U.S.A.* 109 B11
Van Buren, *Mo., U.S.A.* 113 G9
Van Canh, *Vietnam* 64 F7
Van Diemen, C., *N. Terr., Australia* 92 B5
Van Diemen, C., *Queens., Australia* 94 B2
Van Diemen G., *Australia* 92 B5
Van Gölü, *Turkey* 70 B4
Van Horn, *U.S.A.* 113 K2
Van Ninh, *Vietnam* 64 F7
Van Rees, Pegunungan, *Indonesia* 63 E9
Van Wert, *U.S.A.* 108 E3
Van Yen, *Vietnam* 58 G5
Vanadzor, *Armenia* 49 K7
Vanavara, *Russia* 51 C11
Vancouver, *Canada* 104 D4
Vancouver, *U.S.A.* 116 E4
Vancouver, C., *Australia* 93 G2
Vancouver I., *Canada* 104 D3
Vandalia, *Ill., U.S.A.* 112 F10
Vandalia, *Mo., U.S.A.* 112 F9
Vandenburg, *U.S.A.* 117 L6
Vanderbijlpark, *S. Africa* 89 D4
Vandergrift, *U.S.A.* 110 F5
Vanderhoof, *Canada* 104 C4
Vanderkloof Dam, *S. Africa* 88 E3
Vanderlin I., *Australia* 94 B2
Vänern, *Sweden* 11 F7
Vänersborg, *Sweden* 11 F6
Vang Vieng, *Laos* 64 C4
Vanga, *Kenya* 86 C4
Vangaindrano, *Madag.* 89 C8

Vanguard, *Canada* 105 D7
Vanino, *Russia* 51 E15
Vânju Mare, *Romania* 42 F7
Vanna, *Norway* 8 A18
Vännäs, *Sweden* 8 E18
Vannes, *France* 18 E4
Vanoise, *France* 21 C10
Vanrhynsdorp, *S. Africa* 88 E2
Vansbro, *Sweden* 10 D8
Vansittart B., *Australia* 92 B4
Vantaa, *Finland* 9 F21
Vanua Balavu, *Fiji* 91 C9
Vanua Levu, *Fiji* 91 C8
Vanuatu ■, *Pac. Oc.* 96 J8
Vanwyksvlei, *S. Africa* 88 E3
Vanzylsrus, *S. Africa* 88 D3
Vapnyarka, *Ukraine* 47 H5
Var □, *France* 21 E10
Var →, *France* 21 E11
Vara, *Sweden* 11 F6
Varades, *France* 18 E5
Varáita →, *Italy* 28 D4
Varallo, *Italy* 28 C5
Varanasi, *India* 69 G10
Varangerfjorden, *Norway* 8 A23
Varangerhalvøya, *Norway* 8 A23
Varano, Lago di, *Italy* 29 G12
Varaždin, *Croatia* 29 B13
Varazze, *Italy* 28 D5
Varberg, *Sweden* 11 G6
Vardak □, *Afghan.* 66 B6
Vardar = Axiós →, *Greece* 40 F6
Varde, *Denmark* 11 J2
Varde Å →, *Denmark* 11 J2
Vardø, *Norway* 8 A24
Varel, *Germany* 24 B4
Varella, Mui, *Vietnam* 64 F7
Varėna, *Lithuania* 9 J21
Varennes-sur-Allier, *France* 19 F10
Varennes-Vauzelles, *France* 19 E10
Vareš, *Bos.-H.* 42 F3
Varese, *Italy* 28 C5
Vârfurile, *Romania* 42 D7
Vårgårda, *Sweden* 11 F6
Varginha, *Brazil* 127 A6
Vargön, *Sweden* 11 F6
Varillas, *Chile* 126 A1
Varkaus, *Finland* 9 E22
Värmdölandet, *Sweden* 10 E12
Värmeln, *Sweden* 10 E6
Värmlands Bro, *Sweden* 10 E7
Värmlands län □, *Sweden* 10 E6
Varna, *Bulgaria* 41 C11
Varna □, *Bulgaria* 41 C11
Värnamo, *Sweden* 11 G8
Varnsdorf, *Czech Rep.* 26 A7
Várpalota, *Hungary* 42 C3
Vars, *Canada* 111 A9
Vars, *France* 21 D10
Varto, *Turkey* 73 C9
Varvarin, *Serbia, Yug.* 40 C5
Varysburg, *U.S.A.* 110 D6
Varzaneh, *Iran* 71 C7
Varzi, *Italy* 28 D6
Varzo, *Italy* 28 B5
Varzy, *France* 19 E10
Vas □, *Hungary* 42 C1
Vasa Barris →, *Brazil* 125 F11
Vásárosnamény, *Hungary* 42 B7
Vascão →, *Portugal* 35 H3
Vaşcău, *Romania* 42 D7
Vascongadas = País Vasco □, *Spain* 32 C2
Vasht = Khāsh, *Iran* 66 E2
Vasilevichi, *Belarus* 47 F5
Vasilikón, *Greece* 38 C5
Vasilkov = Vasylkiv, *Ukraine* 47 G6
Vaslui, *Romania* 43 D12
Vaslui □, *Romania* 43 D12
Väsman, *Sweden* 10 D9
Vassar, *Canada* 105 D9
Vassar, *U.S.A.* 108 D4
Västerås, *Sweden* 10 E10
Västerbotten, *Sweden* 8 D18
Västerdalälven →, *Sweden* 10 D8
Västergötland, *Sweden* 11 F7
Västerhaninge, *Sweden* 10 E12
Västervik, *Sweden* 11 G10
Västmanland, *Sweden* 9 G16
Västmanlands län □, *Sweden* 10 E10
Vasto, *Italy* 29 F11
Västra Götalands Län □, *Sweden* 11 F6
Vasvár, *Hungary* 42 C1
Vasylkiv, *Ukraine* 47 G6
Vatan, *France* 19 E8
Vatersay, *U.K.* 14 E1
Váthia, *Greece* 38 E4
Vatican City ■, *Europe* 29 G9
Vaticano, C., *Italy* 31 D8
Vatili, *Cyprus* 36 D12
Vatin, *Serbia, Yug.* 42 E6
Vatnajökull, *Iceland* 8 D5
Vatoa, *Fiji* 91 D9
Vatólakkos, *Greece* 36 D5
Vatoloha, *Madag.* 89 B8
Vatomandry, *Madag.* 89 B8
Vatra-Dornei, *Romania* 43 C10
Vatrak →, *India* 68 H5
Vättern, *Sweden* 11 F8
Vaucluse □, *France* 21 E9
Vaucouleurs, *France* 19 D12
Vaud □, *Switz.* 25 J2
Vaughn, *Mont., U.S.A.* 114 C8
Vaughn, *N. Mex., U.S.A.* 115 J11
Vaujours L., *Canada* 102 A5
Vaupés = Uaupés →, *Brazil* 124 C5
Vaupes □, *Colombia* 124 C4
Vauvert, *France* 21 E8
Vauxhall, *Canada* 104 C6
Vav, *India* 68 G4
Vavatenina, *Madag.* 89 B8
Vava'u, *Tonga* 91 D12
Vavoua, *Ivory C.* 82 D3
Vawkavysk, *Belarus* 47 F3
Vaxholm, *Sweden* 10 E12
Växjö, *Sweden* 11 H8
Våxtorp, *Sweden* 11 H7
Vaygach, Ostrov, *Russia* 50 C6
Váyia, *Greece* 38 C5
Váyia, Ákra, *Greece* 36 C10
Vechelde, *Germany* 24 C6
Vechta, *Germany* 24 C4
Vechte →, *Neths.* 17 B6
Vecsés, *Hungary* 42 C4
Veddige, *Sweden* 11 G6
Vedea →, *Romania* 43 G10
Vedia, *Argentina* 126 C3
Vedum, *Sweden* 11 F7
Veendam, *Neths.* 17 A6
Veenendaal, *Neths.* 17 B5
Vefsna →, *Norway* 8 D15
Vega, *Norway* 8 D14
Vega, *U.S.A.* 113 H3
Vegadeo, *Spain* 34 B3
Vegorrítis, Límni, *Greece* 40 F5
Vegreville, *Canada* 104 C6
Veinge, *Sweden* 11 H7
Veisiejai, *Lithuania* 44 D10
Vejbystrand, *Sweden* 11 H6
Vejen, *Denmark* 11 J3
Vejer de la Frontera, *Spain* 35 J5
Vejle, *Denmark* 11 J3
Vejle Amtskommune □, *Denmark* 11 J3
Vejle Fjord, *Denmark* 11 J3
Vela Luka, *Croatia* 29 F13
Velas, C., *Costa Rica* 120 D2
Velasco, Sierra de, *Argentina* 126 B2
Velay, Mts. du, *France* 20 D7
Velbert, *Germany* 24 D3
Velddrif, *S. Africa* 88 E2
Velebit Planina, *Croatia* 29 D12
Velebitski Kanal, *Croatia* 29 D11
Veleka →, *Bulgaria* 41 D11
Velencei-tó, *Hungary* 42 C3
Velenje, *Slovenia* 29 B12
Veles, *Macedonia* 40 E5
Velestínon, *Greece* 38 B4
Vélez-Málaga, *Spain* 35 J6
Vélez Rubio, *Spain* 33 H2
Velhas →, *Brazil* 125 G10
Velika, *Croatia* 42 E2
Velika Gorica, *Croatia* 29 C13
Velika Kapela, *Croatia* 29 C12
Velika Kladuša, *Bos.-H.* 29 C12
Velika Kruša, *Kosovo, Yug.* 40 D4
Velika Morava →, *Serbia, Yug.* 40 B5
Velika Plana, *Serbia, Yug.* 40 B5
Velikaya →, *Russia* 46 D5
Velikaya Kema, *Russia* 54 B8
Velikaya Lepetikha, *Ukraine* 47 J7
Veliké Kapušany, *Slovak Rep.* 27 C15
Velike Lašče, *Slovenia* 29 C11
Veliki Jastrebac, *Serbia, Yug.* 40 C5
Veliki Kanal, *Serbia, Yug.* 42 E4
Veliki Popović, *Serbia, Yug.* 40 B5
Velikiye Luki, *Russia* 46 D6
Veliko Gradište, *Serbia, Yug.* 40 B5
Veliko Tŭrnovo, *Bulgaria* 41 C9
Velikonda Range, *India* 66 M11
Vélingara, *Senegal* 82 C2
Vélingara, *Senegal* 82 B2
Velingrad, *Bulgaria* 40 D7
Velino, Mte., *Italy* 29 F10
Velizh, *Russia* 46 E6
Velké Karlovice, *Czech Rep.* 27 B11
Velké Meziřící, *Czech Rep.* 26 B9
Vel'ký Javorník, *Slovak Rep.* 27 B11
Vel'ký Krtíš, *Slovak Rep.* 27 C12
Vel'ký Meder, *Slovak Rep.* 27 D10
Vel'ký Tribeč, *Slovak Rep.* 27 C11
Velletri, *Italy* 30 A5
Vellinge, *Sweden* 11 J6
Vellmar, *Germany* 24 D5
Vellore, *India* 66 N11
Velsk, *Russia* 46 B11
Velten, *Germany* 24 C9
Velva, *U.S.A.* 112 A4
Velvendós, *Greece* 40 F6
Vemb, *Denmark* 11 H2
Vemdalen, *Sweden* 10 B7
Ven, *Sweden* 11 J6
Venaco, *France* 21 F13
Venado Tuerto, *Argentina* 126 C3
Venafro, *Italy* 31 A7
Venarey-les-Laumes, *France* 19 E11
Venaría, *Italy* 28 C4
Venčane, *Serbia, Yug.* 40 B4
Vence, *France* 21 E11
Vendas Novas, *Portugal* 35 G2
Vendée □, *France* 18 F5
Vendée →, *France* 18 F5
Vendéen, Bocage, *France* 20 B2
Vendeuvre-sur-Barse, *France* 19 D11
Vendôme, *France* 18 E8
Vendrell = El Vendrell, *Spain* 32 D6
Vendsyssel, *Denmark* 11 G4
Venelles, *France* 21 E9
Véneta, L., *Italy* 29 C9
Véneto □, *Italy* 29 C9
Venev, *Russia* 46 E10
Venézia, *Italy* 29 C9
Venézia, G. di, *Italy* 29 C10
Venezuela ■, *S. Amer.* 124 B5
Venezuela, G. de, *Venezuela* 122 B3
Vengurla, *India* 66 M8
Venice = Venézia, *Italy* 29 C9
Venice, *U.S.A.* 109 M4
Vénissieux, *France* 21 C8
Venjansjön, *Sweden* 10 D8
Venkatapuram, *India* 67 K12
Venlo, *Neths.* 17 C6
Vennesla, *Norway* 9 G12
Venosa, *Italy* 31 B8
Venray, *Neths.* 17 C6
Venta, *Lithuania* 44 B9
Venta →, *Latvia* 44 A8
Venta de Baños, *Spain* 34 D6
Venta de Cardeña = Cardeña, *Spain* 35 G6
Ventana, Punta de la, *Mexico* 118 C3
Ventana, Sa. de la, *Argentina* 126 D3
Ventersburg, *S. Africa* 88 D4
Venterstad, *S. Africa* 88 E4
Ventimíglia, *Italy* 28 E4
Ventnor, *U.K.* 13 G6
Ventoténe, *Italy* 30 B6
Ventoux, Mt., *France* 21 D9
Ventspils, *Latvia* 9 H19
Ventspils □, *Latvia* 44 A8
Ventuarí →, *Venezuela* 124 C5
Ventucopa, *U.S.A.* 117 L7
Ventura, *U.S.A.* 117 L7
Venus B., *Australia* 95 F4
Vera, *Argentina* 126 B3
Vera, *Spain* 33 H3
Veracruz, *Mexico* 119 D5
Veracruz □, *Mexico* 119 D5
Veraval, *India* 68 J4
Verbánia, *Italy* 28 C5
Verbicaro, *Italy* 31 C8
Verbier, *Switz.* 25 J3
Vercelli, *Italy* 28 C5
Verchovchevo, *Ukraine* 47 H8
Verdalsøra, *Norway* 8 E14
Verde →, *Argentina* 128 E3
Verde →, *Goiás, Brazil* 125 G8
Verde →, *Mato Grosso do Sul, Brazil* 125 H8
Verde →, *Chihuahua, Mexico* 118 B3
Verde →, *Oaxaca, Mexico* 119 D5
Verde →, *Veracruz, Mexico* 118 C4
Verde →, *Paraguay* 126 A4
Verde →, *U.S.A.* 106 D4
Verde, Cay, *Bahamas* 120 B4
Verde Island Pass, *Phil.* 61 E4
Verden, *Germany* 24 C5
Verdhikoúsa, *Greece* 38 B3
Verdi, *U.S.A.* 116 F7
Verdon →, *France* 21 E9
Verdun, *France* 19 C12
Verdun-sur-le-Doubs, *France* 19 F12
Vereeniging, *S. Africa* 89 D4
Verga, C., *Guinea* 82 C2
Vergara, *Uruguay* 127 C5
Vergato, *Italy* 28 D8
Vergemont Cr. →, *Australia* 94 C3
Vergennes, *U.S.A.* 111 B11
Vergt, *France* 20 C4
Verín, *Spain* 34 D3
Verkhnedvinsk = Vyerkhnyadzvinsk, *Belarus* 46 E4
Verkhnevilyuysk, *Russia* 51 C13
Verkhniy Baskunchak, *Russia* 49 F8
Verkhovye, *Russia* 47 F9
Verkhoyansk, *Russia* 51 C14
Verkhoyansk Ra. = Verkhoyanskiy Khrebet, *Russia* 51 C13
Verkhoyanskiy Khrebet, *Russia* 51 C13
Vermenton, *France* 19 E10
Vermilion, *Canada* 105 C6
Vermilion, *U.S.A.* 110 E2
Vermilion →, *Alta., Canada* 105 C6
Vermilion →, *Qué., Canada* 102 C5
Vermilion, B., *U.S.A.* 113 L9
Vermilion Bay, *Canada* 105 D10
Vermilion L., *U.S.A.* 112 B8
Vermillion, *U.S.A.* 112 D6
Vermont □, *U.S.A.* 111 C12
Vermosh, *Albania* 40 D3
Vernal, *U.S.A.* 114 F9
Vernalis, *U.S.A.* 116 H5
Vernazza, *Italy* 28 D6
Verner, *Canada* 102 C3
Verneuil-sur-Avre, *France* 18 D7
Verneukpan, *S. Africa* 88 E3
Vernier, *Switz.* 25 J2
Vérnio, *Italy* 28 D8
Vernon, *Canada* 104 C5
Vernon, *France* 18 C8
Vernon, *U.S.A.* 113 H5
Vernonia, *U.S.A.* 116 E3
Vernouillet, *France* 18 D8
Vero Beach, *U.S.A.* 109 M5
Véroia, *Greece* 40 F6
Véroli, *Italy* 29 G10
Verona, *Canada* 111 B8
Verona, *Italy* 28 C7
Verona, *U.S.A.* 112 D10
Verrès, *Italy* 28 C4
Versailles, *France* 19 D9
Versmold, *Germany* 24 C4
Vert, C., *Senegal* 82 C1
Vertou, *France* 18 E5
Vertus, *France* 19 D11
Verulam, *S. Africa* 89 D5
Verviers, *Belgium* 17 D5
Vervins, *France* 19 C10
Veržej, *Slovenia* 29 B13
Verzy, *France* 19 C11
Vescovato, *France* 21 F13
Veselí nad Lužnicí, *Czech Rep.* 26 B7
Veselie, *Bulgaria* 41 D11
Veselovskoye Vdkhr., *Russia* 49 G5
Veshenskaya, *Russia* 48 F5
Vesle →, *France* 19 C10
Vesoul, *France* 19 E13
Vessigebro, *Sweden* 11 H6
Vesterålen, *Norway* 8 B16
Vestfjorden, *Norway* 8 C15
Vestmannaeyjar, *Iceland* 8 E3
Vestsjællands Amtskommune □, *Denmark* 11 J5
Vestspitsbergen, *Svalbard* 4 B8
Vestvågøy, *Norway* 8 B15
Vesuvio, *Italy* 31 B7
Vesuvius, Mt. = Vesuvio, *Italy* 31 B7
Vesyegonsk, *Russia* 46 C9
Veszprém, *Hungary* 42 C2
Veszprém □, *Hungary* 42 C2
Vésztő, *Hungary* 42 D6
Vetlanda, *Sweden* 11 G9
Vetluga, *Russia* 48 B7
Vetluga →, *Russia* 48 B8
Vetluzhskiy, *Kostroma, Russia* 48 A7
Vetluzhskiy, *Nizhniy Novgorod, Russia* 48 B7
Vetovo, *Bulgaria* 41 C10
Vetralla, *Italy* 29 F9
Vetren, *Bulgaria* 41 D8
Vettore, Mte., *Italy* 29 F10
Veurne, *Belgium* 17 C2
Veveno →, *Sudan* 81 F3
Vevey, *Switz.* 25 J2
Vévi, *Greece* 40 F5
Veynes, *France* 21 D9
Veys, *Iran* 71 D6
Vézelay, *France* 19 E10
Vézelise, *France* 19 D13
Vézère →, *France* 20 D4
Vezhen, *Bulgaria* 41 D8
Vezirköprü, *Turkey* 72 B6
Vezzani, *France* 21 F13
Vi Thanh, *Vietnam* 65 H5
Viacha, *Bolivia* 124 G5
Viadana, *Italy* 28 D7
Viamão, *Brazil* 127 C5
Viana, *Brazil* 125 D10
Viana, *Spain* 32 C2
Viana do Alentejo, *Portugal* 35 G3
Viana do Bolo, *Spain* 34 C3
Viana do Castelo, *Portugal* 34 D2
Viana do Castelo □, *Portugal* 34 D2
Vianden, *Lux.* 17 E6
Viangchan = Vientiane, *Laos* 64 D4
Vianópolis, *Brazil* 125 G9
Viar →, *Spain* 35 H5
Viaréggio, *Italy* 28 E7
Viaur →, *France* 20 D5
Vibble, *Sweden* 11 G12
Vibo Valéntia, *Italy* 31 D9
Viborg, *Denmark* 11 H3
Viborg Amtskommune □, *Denmark* 11 H3
Vibraye, *France* 18 D7
Vic, *Spain* 32 D7
Vic, Étang de, *France* 20 E7
Vic-en-Bigorre, *France* 20 E4
Vic-Fézensac, *France* 20 E4
Vic-le-Comte, *France* 19 G10
Vic-sur-Cère, *France* 20 D6
Vícar, *Spain* 33 J2
Vicenza, *Italy* 29 C8
Vich = Vic, *Spain* 32 D7
Vichada →, *Colombia* 124 C5
Vichuga, *Russia* 48 B5
Vichy, *France* 19 F10
Vicksburg, *Ariz., U.S.A.* 117 M13
Vicksburg, *Miss., U.S.A.* 113 J9
Vico, *France* 21 F12
Vico, L. di, *Italy* 29 F9
Vico del Gargano, *Italy* 29 G12
Vicovu de Sus, *Romania* 43 C10
Victor, *India* 68 J4
Victor, *U.S.A.* 110 D7
Victor Harbor, *Australia* 95 F2
Victoria = Labuan, *Malaysia* 62 C5
Victoria, *Argentina* 126 C3
Victoria, *Canada* 104 D4
Victoria, *Chile* 128 D2
Victoria, *Guinea* 82 C2
Victoria, *Malta* 36 C1
Victoria, *Phil.* 61 D4
Victoria, *Romania* 43 E9
Victoria, *Kans., U.S.A.* 112 F5
Victoria, *Tex., U.S.A.* 113 L6
Victoria □, *Australia* 95 F3
Victoria →, *Australia* 92 C4
Victoria, Grand L., *Canada* 102 C4
Victoria, L., *Africa* 86 C3
Victoria, L., *Australia* 95 E3
Victoria, Mt., *Burma* 67 J18
Victoria Beach, *Canada* 105 C9
Victoria de Durango = Durango, *Mexico* 118 C4
Victoria de las Tunas, *Cuba* 120 B4
Victoria Falls, *Zimbabwe* 87 F2
Victoria Harbour, *Canada* 110 B5
Victoria I., *Canada* 100 A8
Victoria L., *Canada* 103 C8
Victoria Ld., *Antarctica* 5 D11
Victoria Nile →, *Uganda* 86 B3
Victoria River, *Australia* 92 C5
Victoria Str., *Canada* 100 B9
Victoria West, *S. Africa* 88 E3
Victorias, *Phil.* 61 F5
Victoriaville, *Canada* 103 C5
Victorica, *Argentina* 126 D2
Victorville, *U.S.A.* 117 L9
Vicuña, *Chile* 126 C1
Vicuña Mackenna, *Argentina* 126 C3
Vidal, *U.S.A.* 117 L12
Vidal Junction, *U.S.A.* 117 L12
Vidalia, *U.S.A.* 109 J4
Vidauban, *France* 21 E10
Videbæk, *Denmark* 11 H2
Videle, *Romania* 43 F10
Vídho, *Greece* 36 A3
Vidigueira, *Portugal* 35 G3
Vidin, *Bulgaria* 40 C6
Vidio, C., *Spain* 34 B4
Vidisha, *India* 68 H7
Vidra, *Romania* 43 E11
Viduša, *Bos.-H.* 40 D2
Vidzy, *Belarus* 9 J22
Viechtach, *Germany* 25 F8
Viedma, *Argentina* 128 E4
Viedma, L., *Argentina* 128 F2
Vieira do Minho, *Portugal* 34 D2
Vielha, *Spain* 32 C5
Viella = Vielha, *Spain* 32 C5
Vielsalm, *Belgium* 17 D5
Vienenburg, *Germany* 24 D6
Vieng Pou Kha, *Laos* 58 G3
Vienna = Wien, *Austria* 27 C9
Vienna, *Ill., U.S.A.* 113 G10
Vienna, *Mo., U.S.A.* 112 F9
Vienne, *France* 21 C8
Vienne □, *France* 20 B4
Vienne →, *France* 18 E7
Vientiane, *Laos* 64 D4
Vientos, Paso de los, *Caribbean* 121 C5
Viernheim, *Germany* 25 F4
Viersen, *Germany* 24 D2
Vierwaldstättersee, *Switz.* 25 J4
Vierzon, *France* 19 E9
Vieste, *Italy* 29 G13
Vietnam ■, *Asia* 64 C6
Vieux-Boucau-les-Bains, *France* 20 E2
Vif, *France* 21 C9
Vigan, *Phil.* 61 C4
Vigévano, *Italy* 28 C5
Vigia, *Brazil* 125 D9
Vigía Chico, *Mexico* 119 D7
Víglas, Ákra, *Greece* 36 D9
Vignemalle, *France* 20 F3
Vigneulles-lès-Hattonchâtel, *France* 19 D12
Vignola, *Italy* 28 D8
Vigo, *Spain* 34 C2
Vigo, Ría de, *Spain* 34 C2
Vigsø Bugt, *Denmark* 11 G2
Vihiers, *France* 18 E6
Vihowa, *Pakistan* 68 D4
Vihowa →, *Pakistan* 68 D4
Vijayawada, *India* 67 L12
Vijosë →, *Albania* 40 F3
Vík, *Iceland* 8 E4
Vika, *Sweden* 10 D8
Vikarbyn, *Sweden* 10 D9
Vikeke, *E. Timor* 63 F7
Viken, *Skåne, Sweden* 11 H6
Viken, *Västra Götaland, Sweden* 11 F8
Viking, *Canada* 104 C6
Vikmanshyttan, *Sweden* 10 D9
Vikna, *Norway* 8 D14
Vila da Maganja, *Mozam.* 87 F4
Vila de João Belo = Xai-Xai, *Mozam.* 89 D5
Vila de Rei, *Portugal* 34 F2
Vila do Bispo, *Portugal* 35 H2
Vila do Conde, *Portugal* 34 D2
Vila Franca de Xira, *Portugal* 35 G2
Vila Gamito, *Mozam.* 87 E3
Vila Gomes da Costa, *Mozam.* 89 C5
Vila Machado, *Mozam.* 87 F3
Vila Mouzinho, *Mozam.* 87 E3
Vila Nova de Famalicão, *Portugal* 34 D2
Vila Nova de Fos Côa, *Portugal* 34 D3
Vila Nova de Foscôa = Vila Nova de Fos Côa, *Portugal* 34 D3
Vila Nova de Gaia, *Portugal* 34 D2
Vila Nova de Ourém, *Portugal* 34 F2
Vila Pouca de Aguiar, *Portugal* 34 D3
Vila Real, *Portugal* 34 D3
Vila Real □, *Portugal* 34 D3
Vila-real de los Infantes, *Spain* 32 F4
Vila Real de Santo António, *Portugal* 35 H3
Vila Vasco da Gama, *Mozam.* 87 E3
Vila Velha, *Brazil* 127 A7
Vila Viçosa, *Portugal* 35 G3
Vilafranca del Maestrat, *Spain* 32 E4
Vilafranca del Penedès, *Spain* 32 D6
Vilagarcía de Arousa, *Spain* 34 C2
Vilaine →, *France* 18 E4
Vilanandro, Tanjona, *Madag.* 89 B7
Vilanculos, *Mozam.* 89 C6
Vilanova de Castelló, *Spain* 33 F4
Vilanova i la Geltrú, *Spain* 32 D6
Vilar Formosa, *Portugal* 34 E4
Vilaseca, *Spain* 32 D6
Vilaseca-Salou = Vilaseca, *Spain* 32 D6
Vilbjerg, *Denmark* 11 H2
Vilches, *Spain* 35 G7
Vileyka, *Belarus* 46 E4
Vilhelmina, *Sweden* 8 D17
Vilhena, *Brazil* 124 F6
Viliga, *Russia* 51 C16
Viliya →, *Lithuania* 9 J21
Viljandi, *Estonia* 9 G21
Vilkaviškis, *Lithuania* 44 D10

Vilkija, *Lithuania* 44 C10
Vilkitskogo, Proliv, *Russia* 51 B11
Vilkovo = Vylkove, *Ukraine* 47 K5
Villa Abecia, *Bolivia* 126 A2
Villa Ahumada, *Mexico* 118 A3
Villa Ana, *Argentina* 126 B4
Villa Ángela, *Argentina* 126 B3
Villa Bella, *Bolivia* 124 F5
Villa Bens = Tarfaya, *Morocco* 78 C3
Villa Cañás, *Argentina* 126 C3
Villa Cisneros = Dakhla, *W. Sahara* 78 D2
Villa Colón, *Argentina* 126 C2
Villa Constitución, *Argentina* 126 C3
Villa de María, *Argentina* 126 B3
Villa del Rio, *Spain* 35 H6
Villa Dolores, *Argentina* 126 C2
Villa Frontera, *Mexico* 118 B4
Villa Guillermina, *Argentina* 126 B4
Villa Hayes, *Paraguay* 126 B4
Villa Iris, *Argentina* 126 D3
Villa Juárez, *Mexico* 118 B4
Villa María, *Argentina* 126 C3
Villa Mazán, *Argentina* 126 B2
Villa Minozzo, *Italy* 28 D7
Villa Montes, *Bolivia* 126 A3
Villa Ocampo, *Argentina* 126 B4
Villa Ocampo, *Mexico* 118 B3
Villa Ojo de Agua, *Argentina* 126 B3
Villa San Giovanni, *Italy* 31 D8
Villa San José, *Argentina* 126 C4
Villa San Martín, *Argentina* 126 B3
Villa Santina, *Italy* 29 B9
Villa Unión, *Mexico* 118 C3
Villablino, *Spain* 34 C4
Villacarlos, *Spain* 37 B11
Villacarriedo, *Spain* 34 B7
Villacarrillo, *Spain* 35 G7
Villacastín, *Spain* 34 E6
Villach, *Austria* 26 E6
Villacidro, *Italy* 30 C1
Villada, *Spain* 34 C6
Villadiego, *Spain* 34 C6
Villadóssola, *Italy* 28 B5
Villafeliche, *Spain* 32 D3
Villafranca, *Spain* 32 C3
Villafranca de los Barros, *Spain* 35 G4
Villafranca de los Caballeros, *Baleares, Spain* 37 B10
Villafranca de los Caballeros, *Toledo, Spain* 35 F7
Villafranca del Cid = Vilafranca del Maestrat, *Spain* 32 E4
Villafranca del Panadés = Vilafranca del Penedès, *Spain* 32 D6
Villafranca di Verona, *Italy* 28 C7
Villafranca Tirrena, *Italy* 31 D8
Villagrán, *Mexico* 119 C5
Villaguay, *Argentina* 126 C4
Villaharta, *Spain* 35 G6
Villahermosa, *Mexico* 119 D6
Villahermosa, *Spain* 33 G2
Villaines-la-Juhel, *France* 18 D6
Villajoyosa, *Spain* 33 G4
Villalba, *Spain* 34 B3
Villalba de Guardo, *Spain* 34 C6
Villalón de Campos, *Spain* 34 C5
Villalpando, *Spain* 34 D5
Villaluenga, *Spain* 34 E7
Villamanán, *Spain* 34 C5
Villamartín, *Spain* 35 J5
Villamayor de Santiago, *Spain* 32 F2
Villamblard, *France* 20 C4
Villanova Monteleone, *Italy* 30 B1
Villanueva, *U.S.A.* 113 H2
Villanueva de Castellón = Vilanova de Castelló, *Spain* 33 F4
Villanueva de Córdoba, *Spain* 35 G6
Villanueva de la Fuente, *Spain* 33 G2
Villanueva de la Serena, *Spain* 35 G5
Villanueva de la Sierra, *Spain* 34 E4
Villanueva de los Castillejos, *Spain* 35 H3
Villanueva de los Infantes, *Spain* 35 G7
Villanueva del Arzobispo, *Spain* 33 G2
Villanueva del Fresno, *Spain* 35 G3
Villanueva y Geltrú = Vilanova i la Geltrú, *Spain* 32 D6
Villaputzu, *Italy* 30 C2
Villaquilambre, *Spain* 34 C5
Villar del Arzobispo, *Spain* 32 F4
Villar del Rey, *Spain* 35 F4
Villard-de-Lans, *France* 21 C9
Villarramiel, *Spain* 34 C6
Villarreal = Vila-real de los Infantes, *Spain* 33 F4
Villarrica, *Chile* 128 D2
Villarrica, *Paraguay* 126 B4
Villarrobledo, *Spain* 33 F2
Villarroya de la Sierra, *Spain* 32 D3
Villarrubia de los Ojos, *Spain* 35 F7
Villars-les-Dombes, *France* 19 F12
Villasayas, *Spain* 32 D2
Villaseca de los Gamitos = Villaseco de los Gamitos, *Spain* 34 D4
Villaseco de los Gamitos, *Spain* 34 D4
Villasimíus, *Italy* 30 C2
Villastar, *Spain* 32 E3
Villatobas, *Spain* 34 F7
Villavicencio, *Argentina* 126 C2
Villavicencio, *Colombia* 124 C4
Villaviciosa, *Spain* 34 B5
Villazón, *Bolivia* 126 A2
Ville-Marie, *Canada* 102 C4
Ville Platte, *U.S.A.* 113 K8
Villedieu-les-Poêles, *France* 18 D5
Villefort, *France* 20 D7
Villefranche-de-Lauragais, *France* 20 E5
Villefranche-de-Rouergue, *France* 20 D6
Villefranche-du-Périgord, *France* 20 D5
Villefranche-sur-Saône, *France* 21 C8
Villel, *Spain* 32 E3
Villemur-sur-Tarn, *France* 20 E5
Villena, *Spain* 33 G4
Villenauxe-la-Grande, *France* 19 D10
Villenave-d'Ornon, *France* 20 D3
Villeneuve-d'Ascq, *France* 19 B10
Villeneuve-l'Archevêque, *France* 19 D10
Villeneuve-lès-Avignon, *France* 21 E8
Villeneuve-sur-Allier, *France* 19 F10
Villeneuve-sur-Lot, *France* 20 D4
Villeneuve-sur-Yonne, *France* 19 D10
Villeréal, *France* 20 D4
Villers-Bocage, *France* 18 C6
Villers-Cotterêts, *France* 19 C10
Villers-sur-Mer, *France* 18 C6
Villersexel, *France* 19 E13
Villerupt, *France* 19 C12
Villeurbanne, *France* 21 C8
Villiers, *S. Africa* 89 D4
Villingen-Schwenningen, *Germany* 25 G4
Vilna, *Canada* 104 C6
Vilnius, *Lithuania* 9 J21
Vils, *Austria* 26 D3
Vils →, *Bayern, Germany* 25 G9
Vils →, *Bayern, Germany* 25 F7
Vilsbiburg, *Germany* 25 G8
Vilshofen, *Germany* 25 G9
Vilusi, *Montenegro, Yug.* 40 D2
Vilvoorde, *Belgium* 17 D4
Vilyuy →, *Russia* 51 C13
Vilyuysk, *Russia* 51 C13
Vimianzo, *Spain* 34 B1
Vimioso, *Portugal* 34 D4
Vimmerby, *Sweden* 11 G9
Vimoutiers, *France* 18 D7
Vimperk, *Czech Rep.* 26 B6
Viña del Mar, *Chile* 126 C1
Vinarós, *Spain* 32 E5
Vincennes, *U.S.A.* 108 F2
Vincent, *U.S.A.* 117 L8
Vinchina, *Argentina* 126 B2
Vindelälven →, *Sweden* 8 E18
Vindeln, *Sweden* 8 D18
Vinderup, *Denmark* 11 H2
Vindhya Ra., *India* 68 H7
Vineland, *U.S.A.* 108 F8
Vineuil, *France* 18
Vinga, *Romania* 42 D6
Vingåker, *Sweden* 10 E9
Vinh, *Vietnam* 64 C5
Vinh Linh, *Vietnam* 64 D6
Vinh Long, *Vietnam* 65 G5
Vinh Yen, *Vietnam* 58 G5
Vinhais, *Portugal* 34 D3
Vinica, *Croatia* 29 B13
Vinica, *Macedonia* 40 E6
Vinica, *Slovenia* 29 C12
Vinita, *U.S.A.* 113 G7
Vinkovci, *Croatia* 42 E3
Vinnitsa = Vinnytsya, *Ukraine* 47 H5
Vinnytsya, *Ukraine* 47 H5
Vinslöv, *Sweden* 11 H7
Vintjärn, *Sweden* 10 D10
Vinton, *Calif., U.S.A.* 116 F6
Vinton, *Iowa, U.S.A.* 112 D8
Vinton, *La., U.S.A.* 113 K8
Vinţu de Jos, *Romania* 43 D8
Viöl, *Germany* 24 A5
Vipava, *Slovenia* 29 C10
Vipiteno, *Italy* 29 B8
Vir, *Croatia* 29 D12
Virac, *Phil.* 61 E6
Virachei, *Cambodia* 64 F6
Virago Sd., *Canada* 104 C2
Viramgam, *India* 68 H5
Viranşehir, *Turkey* 70 B3
Virawah, *Pakistan* 68 G4
Virbalis, *Lithuania* 44 D9
Virden, *Canada* 105 D8
Vire, *France* 18 D6
Vire →, *France* 18 C5
Vírgenes, C., *Argentina* 128 G3
Virgin →, *U.S.A.* 115 H6
Virgin Gorda, *Br. Virgin Is.* 121 C7
Virgin Is. (British) ■, *W. Indies* 121 C7
Virgin Is. (U.S.) ■, *W. Indies* 121 C7
Virginia, *S. Africa* 88 D4
Virginia, *U.S.A.* 112 B8
Virginia □, *U.S.A.* 108 G7
Virginia Beach, *U.S.A.* 108 G8
Virginia City, *Mont., U.S.A.* 114 D8
Virginia City, *Nev., U.S.A.* 116 F7
Virginia Falls, *Canada* 104 A3
Virginiatown, *Canada* 102 C4
Virje, *Croatia* 29 B13
Viroqua, *U.S.A.* 112 D9
Virovitica, *Croatia* 42 E2
Virpazar, *Montenegro, Yug.* 40 D3
Virpur, *India* 68 J4
Virserum, *Sweden* 11 G9
Virton, *Belgium* 17 E5
Virudunagar, *India* 66 Q10
Vis, *Croatia* 29 E13
Visalia, *U.S.A.* 116 J7
Visayan Sea, *Phil.* 61 F5
Visby, *Sweden* 11 G12
Viscount Melville Sd., *Canada* 4 B2
Visé, *Belgium* 17 D5
Višegrad, *Bos.-H.* 42 G4
Viseu, *Brazil* 125 D9
Viseu, *Portugal* 34 E3
Viseu □, *Portugal* 34 E3
Vişeu de Sus, *Romania* 43 C9
Vishakhapatnam, *India* 67 L13
Vişina, *Romania* 43 G9
Vişineşti, *Moldova* 43 D13
Visingsö, *Sweden* 11 F8
Viskafors, *Sweden* 11 G6
Viskan →, *Sweden* 11 G6
Viški Kanal, *Croatia* 29 E13
Vislanda, *Sweden* 11 H8
Visnagar, *India* 68 H5
Višnja Gora, *Slovenia* 29 C11
Viso, Mte., *Italy* 28 D4
Viso del Marqués, *Spain* 35 G7
Visoko, *Bos.-H.* 42 G3
Visokoi I., *Antarctica* 5 B1
Visp, *Switz.* 25 J3
Vissefjärda, *Sweden* 11 H9
Visselhövede, *Germany* 24 C5
Vissenbjerg, *Denmark* 11 J4
Vista, *U.S.A.* 117 M9
Vistonikos, Ormos = Vistonís, Límni, *Greece* 41 E9
Vistonís, Límni, *Greece* 41 E9
Vistula = Wisła →, *Poland* 44 D5
Vit →, *Bulgaria* 41 C8
Vitanje, *Slovenia* 29 B12
Vitebsk = Vitsyebsk, *Belarus* 46 E6
Viterbo, *Italy* 29 F9
Vitez, *Bos.-H.* 42 F2
Viti Levu, *Fiji* 91 C7
Vitigudino, *Spain* 34 D4
Vitim, *Russia* 51 D12
Vitim →, *Russia* 51 D12
Vitina, *Bos.-H.* 29 E14
Vitína, *Greece* 38 D4
Vítkov, *Czech Rep.* 27 B10
Vitória, *Brazil* 125 H10
Vitória da Conquista, *Brazil* 125 F10
Vitória de São Antão, *Brazil* 125 E11
Vitoria-Gasteiz, *Spain* 32 C2
Vitré, *France* 18 D5
Vitry-le-François, *France* 19 D11
Vitry-sur-Seine, *France* 19 D9
Vitsand, *Sweden* 10 D7
Vitsi, Óros, *Greece* 40 F5
Vitsyebsk, *Belarus* 46 E6
Vittaryd, *Sweden* 11 H7
Vitteaux, *France* 19 E11
Vittel, *France* 19 D12
Vittória, *Italy* 31 F7
Vittório Véneto, *Italy* 29 C9
Vittsjö, *Sweden* 11 H7
Viveiro, *Spain* 34 B3
Vivian, *U.S.A.* 113 J8
Viviers, *France* 21 D8
Vivonne, *France* 20 B4
Vizcaíno, Desierto de, *Mexico* 118 B2
Vizcaíno, Sierra, *Mexico* 118 B2
Vizcaya □, *Spain* 32 B2
Vize, *Turkey* 41 E11
Vizianagaram, *India* 67 K13
Vizille, *France* 21 C9
Viziňada, *Croatia* 29 C10
Viziru, *Romania* 43 E12
Vizzini, *Italy* 31 E7
Vlaardingen, *Neths.* 17 C4
Vlădeasa, Vf., *Romania* 42 D7
Vladičin Han, *Serbia, Yug.* 40 D6
Vladikavkaz, *Russia* 49 J7
Vladimir, *Russia* 46 D11
Vladimir Volynskiy = Volodymyr-Volynskyy, *Ukraine* 47 G3
Vladimirci, *Serbia, Yug.* 40 B3
Vladimirovac, *Serbia, Yug.* 42 E5
Vladimirovka, *Russia* 49 F8
Vladimirovo, *Bulgaria* 40 C7
Vladimirovka, *Kazakstan* 48 E10
Vladislavovka, *Ukraine* 47 K8
Vladivostok, *Russia* 51 E14
Vlăhiţa, *Romania* 43 D10
Vlakhiótis, *Greece* 38 E4
Vlasenica, *Bos.-H.* 42 F3
Vlašić, *Bos.-H.* 42 F2
Vlašim, *Czech Rep.* 26 B7
Vlasinsko Jezero, *Serbia, Yug.* 40 D6
Vlasotince, *Serbia, Yug.* 40 D6
Vlieland, *Neths.* 17 A4
Vlissingen, *Neths.* 17 C3
Vlorë, *Albania* 40 F3
Vlorës, Gjiri i, *Albania* 40 F3
Vltava →, *Czech Rep.* 26 A7
Vo Dat, *Vietnam* 65 G6
Vobarno, *Italy* 28 C7
Voćin, *Croatia* 42 E2
Vöcklabruck, *Austria* 26 C6
Vodice, *Croatia* 29 E12
Vodňany, *Czech Rep.* 26 B7
Vodnjan, *Croatia* 29 D10
Voe, *U.K.* 14 A7
Vogel Pk., *Nigeria* 83 D7
Vogelkop = Doberai, Jazirah, *Indonesia* 63 E8
Vogelsberg, *Germany* 24 E5
Voghera, *Italy* 28 D6
Vohibinany, *Madag.* 89 B8
Vohilava, *Madag.* 89 C8
Vohimarina = Iharana, *Madag.* 89 A9
Vohimena, Tanjon' i, *Madag.* 89 D8
Vohipeno, *Madag.* 89 C8
Voi, *Kenya* 86 C4
Void-Vacon, *France* 19 D12
Voineşti, *Iaşi, Romania* 43 C12
Voineşti, *Prahova, Romania* 43 E10
Voíotía □, *Greece* 38 C5
Voiron, *France* 21 C9
Voisey B., *Canada* 103 A7
Voitsberg, *Austria* 26 D8
Vojens, *Denmark* 11 J3
Vojmsjön, *Sweden* 8 D17
Vojnić, *Croatia* 29 C12
Vojnik, *Italy* 29 B12
Vojvodina □, *Serbia, Yug.* 42 E5
Vokhtoga, *Russia* 46 C11
Volary, *Czech Rep.* 26 C6
Volborg, *U.S.A.* 112 C2
Volcano Is. = Kazan-Rettō, *Pac. Oc.* 96 E6
Volchansk = Vovchansk, *Ukraine* 47 G9
Volchya →, *Ukraine* 47 H8
Volda, *Norway* 9 E12
Volga, *Russia* 46 C10
Volga →, *Russia* 49 G9
Volga Hts. = Privolzhskaya Vozvyshennost, *Russia* 48 E7
Volgo-Baltiyskiy Kanal, *Russia* 46 B9
Volgo-Donskoy Kanal, *Russia* 49 F7
Volgodonsk, *Russia* 49 G6
Volgograd, *Russia* 49 F7
Volgogradskoye Vdkhr., *Russia* 48 E8
Volgorechensk, *Russia* 48 B5
Volímai, *Greece* 38 D2
Volintiri, *Moldova* 43 D14
Volissós, *Greece* 39 C7
Volkach, *Germany* 25 F6
Völkermarkt, *Austria* 26 E7
Volkhov, *Russia* 46 C7
Volkhov →, *Russia* 46 B7
Völklingen, *Germany* 25 F2
Volkovysk = Vawkavysk, *Belarus* 47 F3
Volksrust, *S. Africa* 89 D4
Volnansk, *Ukraine* 47 H8
Volnovakha, *Ukraine* 47 J9
Volochanka, *Russia* 51 B10
Volodarsk, *Russia* 48 B6
Volodymyr-Volynskyy, *Ukraine* 47 G3
Vologda, *Russia* 46 C10
Volokolamsk, *Russia* 46 D8
Volokonovka, *Russia* 47 G9
Vólos, *Greece* 38 B4
Volosovo, *Russia* 46 C5
Volovets, *Ukraine* 47 H2
Volovo, *Russia* 46 F10
Volozhin = Valozhyn, *Belarus* 46 E4
Volsk, *Russia* 48 D8
Volta □, *Ghana* 83 D5
Volta →, *Ghana* 83 D5
Volta, L., *Ghana* 83 D5
Volta Blanche = White Volta →, *Ghana* 83 D4
Volta Redonda, *Brazil* 127 A7
Voltaire, C., *Australia* 92 B4
Volterra, *Italy* 28 E7
Voltri, *Italy* 28 D5
Volturno →, *Italy* 30 A6
Vólvi, L., *Greece* 40 F7
Volyně, *Czech Rep.* 26 B6
Volzhsk, *Russia* 48 C9
Volzhskiy, *Russia* 49 F7
Vondrozo, *Madag.* 89 C8
Vónitsa, *Greece* 38 C2
Vopnafjörður, *Iceland* 8 D6
Vorarlberg □, *Austria* 26 D2
Vóras Óros, *Greece* 40 F5
Vorbasse, *Denmark* 11 J3
Vorchdorf, *Austria* 26 C6
Vorderrhein →, *Switz.* 25 J5
Vordingborg, *Denmark* 11 J5
Vorë, *Albania* 40 E3
Voreio Aigaio = Vórios Aiyaíon □, *Greece* 39 C7
Voreppe, *France* 21 C9
Vóriai Sporádhes, *Greece* 38 B5
Vórios Aiyaíon □, *Greece* 39 C7
Vórios Evvoïkos Kólpos, *Greece* 38 C5
Vorkuta, *Russia* 50 C7
Vormsi, *Estonia* 9 G20
Vorona →, *Russia* 48 E6
Voronezh, *Russia* 47 G10
Voronezh, *Ukraine* 47 G7
Voronezh →, *Russia* 47 G10
Vorontsovo-Aleksandrovskoye = Zelenokumsk, *Russia* 49 H6
Voroshilovgrad = Luhansk, *Ukraine* 47 H10
Voroshilovsk = Alchevsk, *Ukraine* 47 H10
Vórroi, *Greece* 38 F6
Vorskla →, *Ukraine* 47 H8
Võrts Järv, *Estonia* 9 G22
Võru, *Estonia* 9 H22
Vosges, *France* 19 D14
Vosges □, *France* 19 D13
Voskopojë, *Albania* 40 F4
Voskresensk, *Russia* 46 E10
Voskresenskoye, *Russia* 48 B7
Voss, *Norway* 9 F12
Vostok I., *Kiribati* 97 J12
Votice, *Czech Rep.* 26 B7
Votsuri-Shima, *Japan* 55 M1
Vouga →, *Portugal* 34 E2
Vouillé, *France* 18 F7
Voúxa, Ákra, *Greece* 36 D5
Vouzela, *Portugal* 34 E2
Vouziers, *France* 19 C11
Vovchansk, *Ukraine* 47 G9
Vozhe, Ozero, *Russia* 46 B10
Vozhega, *Russia* 46 B11
Voznesensk, *Ukraine* 47 J6
Voznesenye, *Russia* 46 B8
Vrå, *Denmark* 11 G3
Vráble, *Slovak Rep.* 27 C11
Vraćevšnica, *Serbia, Yug.* 40 B4
Vrakhnéïka, *Greece* 38 C3
Vrancea □, *Romania* 43 E11
Vrancei, Munţii, *Romania* 43 E11
Vrangelya, Ostrov, *Russia* 51 B19
Vranica, *Bos.-H.* 42 G2
Vranje, *Serbia, Yug.* 40 D5
Vranjska Banja, *Serbia, Yug.* 40 D6
Vranov nad Topľou, *Slovak Rep.* 27 C14
Vransko, *Slovenia* 29 B11
Vransko Jezero, *Croatia* 29 E12
Vrapčište, *Macedonia* 40 E4
Vratsa, *Bulgaria* 40 C7
Vrbas, *Serbia, Yug.* 42 E4
Vrbas →, *Bos.-H.* 42 E2
Vrbnik, *Croatia* 29 C11
Vrbovec, *Croatia* 29 C13
Vrbovsko, *Croatia* 29 C12
Vrchlabí, *Czech Rep.* 26 A8
Vrede, *S. Africa* 89 D4
Vredefort, *S. Africa* 88 D4
Vreden, *Germany* 24 C2
Vredenburg, *S. Africa* 88 E2
Vredendal, *S. Africa* 88 E2
Vretstorp, *Sweden* 10 E8
Vrgorac, *Croatia* 29 E14
Vrhnika, *Slovenia* 29 C11
Vrïdi, *Ivory C.* 82 D4
Vrigstad, *Sweden* 11 G8
Vrindavan, *India* 68 F7
Vríses, *Greece* 36 D6
Vrnograč, *Bos.-H.* 29 C12
Vrondádhes, *Greece* 39 C8
Vrpolje, *Croatia* 42 E3
Vršac, *Serbia, Yug.* 42 E6
Vrsacki Kanal, *Serbia, Yug.* 42 E5
Vrútky, *Slovak Rep.* 27 B11
Vryburg, *S. Africa* 88 D3
Vryheid, *S. Africa* 89 D5
Vsetín, *Czech Rep.* 27 B11
Vu Liet, *Vietnam* 64 C5
Vŭcha →, *Bulgaria* 41 D8
Vučitrn, *Kosovo, Yug.* 40 D4
Vukovar, *Croatia* 42 E3
Vulcan, *Canada* 104 C6
Vulcan, *Romania* 43 E8
Vulcaneşti, *Moldova* 43 E13
Vulcano, *Italy* 31 D7
Vŭlchedruma, *Bulgaria* 40 C7
Vulkaneshty = Vulcaneşti, *Moldova* 43 E13
Vunduzi →, *Mozam.* 87 F3
Vung Tau, *Vietnam* 65 G6
Vŭrbitsa, *Bulgaria* 41 D10
Vurshets, *Bulgaria* 40 C7
Vutcani, *Romania* 43 D12
Vuya, *Sudan* 81 F2
Vyartsilya, *Russia* 46 A6
Vyatka = Kirov, *Russia* 50 D5
Vyatka →, *Russia* 48 C10
Vyatskiye Polyany, *Russia* 48 B10
Vyazemskiy, *Russia* 51 E14
Vyazma, *Russia* 46 E8
Vyazniki, *Russia* 48 B6
Vyborg, *Russia* 46 B5
Vychegda →, *Russia* 50 C5
Vychodné Beskydy, *Europe* 27 B15
Vyerkhnyadzvinsk, *Belarus* 46 E4
Vyksa, *Russia* 48 C6
Vylkove, *Ukraine* 47 K5
Vynohradiv, *Ukraine* 47 H2
Vyrnwy, L., *U.K.* 12 E4
Vyshniy Volochek, *Russia* 46 D8
Vyshzha = imeni 26 Bakinskikh Komissarov, *Turkmenistan* 71 B7
Vyškov, *Czech Rep.* 27 B9
Vysoké Mýto, *Czech Rep.* 27 B9
Vysokovsk, *Russia* 46 D9
Vyšší Brod, *Czech Rep.* 26 C7
Vytegra, *Russia* 46 B9

W

W.A.C. Bennett Dam, *Canada* 104 B4
Wa, *Ghana* 82 C4
Waal →, *Neths.* 17 C5
Waalwijk, *Neths.* 17 C5
Waat, *Sudan* 81 F3
Wabana, *Canada* 103 C9
Wabasca →, *Canada* 104 B5
Wabasca-Desmarais, *Canada* 104 B6
Wabash, *U.S.A.* 108 E3
Wabash →, *U.S.A.* 108 G1
Wabi →, *Ethiopia* 81 F5
Wabigoon L., *Canada* 105 D10
Wabowden, *Canada* 105 C9
Wąbrzeźno, *Poland* 45 E5
Wabu Hu, *China* 59 A11
Wabuk Pt., *Canada* 102 A2
Wabush, *Canada* 103 B6
Wąchock, *Poland* 45 G8
Wächtersbach, *Germany* 25 E5
Waco, *U.S.A.* 113 K6
Waconichi, L., *Canada* 102 B5
Wad Ban Naqa, *Sudan* 81 D3
Wad Banda, *Sudan* 81 E2
Wad el Haddad, *Sudan* 81 E3
Wad en Nau, *Sudan* 81 E3
Wad Hamid, *Sudan* 81 D3

Wad Medanî, *Sudan* 81 E3
Wad Thana, *Pakistan* 68 F2
Wadai, *Africa* 76 E5
Wadayama, *Japan* 55 G7
Waddeneilanden, *Neths.* 17 A5
Waddenzee, *Neths.* 17 A5
Waddington, *U.S.A.* 111 B9
Waddington, Mt., *Canada* 104 C3
Waddy Pt., *Australia* 95 C5
Wadebridge, *U.K.* 13 G3
Wadena, *Canada* 105 C8
Wadena, *U.S.A.* 112 B7
Wädenswil, *Switz.* 25 H4
Wadern, *Germany* 25 F2
Wadeye, *Australia* 92 B4
Wadhams, *Canada* 104 C3
Wādī as Sīr, *Jordan* 75 D4
Wadi Gemâl, *Egypt* 80 C4
Wadi Halfa, *Sudan* 80 C3
Wadian, *China* 59 A9
Wadlew, *Poland* 45 G6
Wadowice, *Poland* 45 J6
Wadsworth, *Nev., U.S.A.* 114 G4
Wadsworth, *Ohio, U.S.A.* 110 E3
Waegwan, *S. Korea* 57 G15
Wafangdian, *China* 57 E11
Wafrah, *Si. Arabia* 70 D5
Wageningen, *Neths.* 17 C5
Wager B., *Canada* 101 B11
Wagga Wagga, *Australia* 95 F4
Waghete, *Indonesia* 63 E9
Wagin, *Australia* 93 F2
Wagner, *U.S.A.* 112 D5
Wagon Mound, *U.S.A.* 113 G2
Wagoner, *U.S.A.* 113 H7
Wagrowiec, *Poland* 45 F4
Wah, *Pakistan* 68 C5
Wahai, *Indonesia* 63 E7
Wahiawa, *U.S.A.* 106 H15
Wâḥid, *Egypt* 75 E1
Wahnai, *Afghan.* 68 C1
Wahni, *Ethiopia* 81 E4
Wahoo, *U.S.A.* 112 E6
Wahpeton, *U.S.A.* 112 B6
Waiau →, *N.Z.* 91 K4
Waibeem, *Indonesia* 63 E8
Waiblingen, *Germany* 25 G5
Waidhofen an der Thaya, *Austria* 26 C8
Waidhofen an der Ybbs, *Austria* 26 D7
Waigeo, *Indonesia* 63 E8
Waihi, *N.Z.* 91 G5
Waihou →, *N.Z.* 91 G5
Waika, *Dem. Rep. of the Congo* 86 C2
Waikabubak, *Indonesia* 63 F5
Waikari, *N.Z.* 91 K4
Waikato →, *N.Z.* 91 G5
Waikerie, *Australia* 95 E3
Waikokopu, *N.Z.* 91 H6
Waikouaiti, *N.Z.* 91 L3
Wailuku, *U.S.A.* 106 H16
Waimakariri →, *N.Z.* 91 K4
Waimate, *N.Z.* 91 L3
Wainganga →, *India* 66 K11
Waingapu, *Indonesia* 63 F6
Waini →, *Guyana* 124 B7
Wainwright, *Canada* 105 C6
Waiouru, *N.Z.* 91 H5
Waipara, *N.Z.* 91 K4
Waipawa, *N.Z.* 91 H6
Waipiro, *N.Z.* 91 H7
Waipu, *N.Z.* 91 F5
Waipukurau, *N.Z.* 91 J6
Wairakei, *N.Z.* 91 H6
Wairarapa, L., *N.Z.* 91 J5
Wairoa, *N.Z.* 91 H6
Waitaki →, *N.Z.* 91 L3
Waitara, *N.Z.* 91 H5
Waitsburg, *U.S.A.* 114 C5
Waiuku, *N.Z.* 91 G5
Wajima, *Japan* 55 F8
Wajir, *Kenya* 86 B5
Waka, *Ethiopia* 81 F4
Wakasa, *Japan* 55 G7
Wakasa-Wan, *Japan* 55 G7
Wakatipu, L., *N.Z.* 91 L2
Wakaw, *Canada* 105 C7
Wakayama, *Japan* 55 G7
Wakayama □, *Japan* 55 H7
Wake Forest, *U.S.A.* 109 H6
Wake I., *Pac. Oc.* 96 F8
WaKeeney, *U.S.A.* 112 F5
Wakefield, *N.Z.* 91 J4
Wakefield, *U.K.* 12 D6
Wakefield, *Mass., U.S.A.* 111 D13
Wakefield, *Mich., U.S.A.* 112 B10
Wakkanai, *Japan* 54 B10
Wakkerstroom, *S. Africa* 89 D5
Wakool, *Australia* 95 F3
Wakool →, *Australia* 95 F3
Wakre, *Indonesia* 63 E8
Wakuach, L., *Canada* 103 A6
Walamba, *Zambia* 87 E2
Wałbrzych, *Poland* 45 H3
Walbury Hill, *U.K.* 13 F6
Walcha, *Australia* 95 E5
Walcheren, *Neths.* 17 C3
Walcott, *U.S.A.* 114 F10
Wałcz, *Poland* 45 E3
Waldbröl, *Germany* 24 E3
Waldburg Ra., *Australia* 93 D2
Waldeck, *Germany* 24 D5
Walden, *Colo., U.S.A.* 114 F10
Walden, *N.Y., U.S.A.* 111 E10
Waldkirch, *Germany* 25 G3
Waldkirchen, *Germany* 25 G9
Waldkraiburg, *Germany* 25 G8
Waldport, *U.S.A.* 114 D1
Waldron, *U.S.A.* 113 H7
Waldviertel, *Austria* 26 C8
Walebing, *Australia* 93 F2
Walembele, *Ghana* 82 C4
Walensee, *Switz.* 25 H5
Wales □, *U.K.* 13 E3
Walewale, *Ghana* 83 C4
Walgett, *Australia* 95 E4
Walgreen Coast, *Antarctica* 5 D15
Walker, *U.S.A.* 112 B7
Walker, L., *Canada* 103 B6
Walker L., *Canada* 105 C9
Walker L., *U.S.A.* 114 G4
Walkerston, *Australia* 94 C4
Walkerton, *Canada* 102 D3
Wall, *U.S.A.* 112 D3
Walla Walla, *U.S.A.* 114 C4
Wallace, *Idaho, U.S.A.* 114 C6
Wallace, *N.C., U.S.A.* 109 H7
Wallaceburg, *Canada* 102 D3
Wallachia = Valahia, *Romania* 43 F9
Wallal, *Australia* 95 D4
Wallam Cr. →, *Australia* 95 D4
Wallambin, L., *Australia* 93 F2
Wallangarra, *Australia* 95 D5
Wallaroo, *Australia* 95 E2
Walldürn, *Germany* 25 F5
Wallenhorst, *Germany* 24 C4
Wallenpaupack, L., *U.S.A.* 111 E9
Wallingford, *U.S.A.* 111 E12
Wallis & Futuna, Is., *Pac. Oc.* 96 J10
Wallowa, *U.S.A.* 114 D5
Wallowa Mts., *U.S.A.* 114 D5
Walls, *U.K.* 14 A7
Wallula, *U.S.A.* 114 C4
Wallumbilla, *Australia* 95 D4
Walmsley, L., *Canada* 105 A7
Walney, I. of, *U.K.* 12 C4
Walnut Creek, *U.S.A.* 116 H4
Walnut Ridge, *U.S.A.* 113 G9
Walpole, *Australia* 93 F2
Walpole, *U.S.A.* 111 D13
Wals, *Austria* 26 D5
Walsall, *U.K.* 13 E6
Walsenburg, *U.S.A.* 113 G2
Walsh, *U.S.A.* 113 G3
Walsh →, *Australia* 94 B3
Walsrode, *Germany* 24 C5
Walterboro, *U.S.A.* 109 J5
Walters, *U.S.A.* 113 H5
Waltershausen, *Germany* 24 E6
Waltham, *U.S.A.* 111 D13
Waltman, *U.S.A.* 114 E10
Walton, *U.S.A.* 111 D9
Walton-on-the-Naze, *U.K.* 13 F9
Walvis Bay, *Namibia* 88 C1
Walvisbaai = Walvis Bay, *Namibia* 88 C1
Wamba, *Dem. Rep. of the Congo* 86 B2
Wamba, *Kenya* 86 B4
Wamba, *Nigeria* 83 D6
Wamego, *U.S.A.* 112 F6
Wamena, *Indonesia* 63 E9
Wamsutter, *U.S.A.* 114 F9
Wamulan, *Indonesia* 63 E7
Wan Xian, *China* 56 E8
Wana, *Pakistan* 68 C3
Wanaaring, *Australia* 95 D3
Wanaka, *N.Z.* 91 L2
Wanaka L., *N.Z.* 91 L2
Wan'an, *China* 59 D10
Wanapitei L., *Canada* 102 C3
Wandel Sea = McKinley Sea, *Arctic* 4 A7
Wandérama, *Ivory C.* 82 D4
Wanderer, *Zimbabwe* 87 F3
Wandhari, *Pakistan* 68 F2
Wanding, *China* 58 E2
Wandoan, *Australia* 95 D4
Wanfu, *China* 57 D12
Wang →, *Thailand* 64 D2
Wang Kai, *Sudan* 81 F2
Wang Noi, *Thailand* 64 E3
Wang Saphung, *Thailand* 64 D3
Wang Thong, *Thailand* 64 D3
Wanga, *Dem. Rep. of the Congo* 86 B2
Wangal, *Indonesia* 63 F8
Wanganella, *Australia* 95 F3
Wanganui, *N.Z.* 91 H5
Wangaratta, *Australia* 95 F4
Wangary, *Australia* 95 E2
Wangcang, *China* 58 A6
Wangcheng, *China* 59 C9
Wangdu, *China* 56 E8
Wangen, *Germany* 25 H5
Wangerooge, *Germany* 24 B3
Wangi, *Kenya* 86 C5
Wangiwangi, *Indonesia* 63 F6
Wangjiang, *China* 59 B11
Wangmo, *China* 58 E6
Wangolodougou, *Ivory C.* 82 D3
Wangqing, *China* 57 C15
Wankaner, *India* 68 H4
Wanless, *Canada* 105 C8
Wannian, *China* 59 C11
Wanning, *China* 64 C8
Wanon Niwat, *Thailand* 64 D4
Wanquan, *China* 56 D8
Wanrong, *China* 56 G6
Wanshan, *China* 58 D7
Wanshengchang, *China* 58 C6
Wantage, *U.K.* 13 F6
Wanyuan, *China* 58 A7
Wanzai, *China* 59 C10
Wapakoneta, *U.S.A.* 108 E3
Wapato, *U.S.A.* 114 C3
Wapawekka L., *Canada* 105 C8
Wapikopa L., *Canada* 102 B2
Wapiti →, *Canada* 104 B5
Wappingers Falls, *U.S.A.* 111 E11
Wapsipinicon →, *U.S.A.* 112 E9
Warab □, *Sudan* 81 F2
Warangal, *India* 66 L11
Waraseoni, *India* 69 J9
Waratah, *Australia* 94 G4
Waratah B., *Australia* 95 F4
Warburg, *Germany* 24 D5
Warburton, *Vic., Australia* 95 F4
Warburton, *W. Austral., Australia* 93 E4
Warburton Ra., *Australia* 93 E4
Ward, *N.Z.* 91 J5
Ward →, *Australia* 95 D4
Ward Mt., *U.S.A.* 116 H8
Warden, *S. Africa* 89 D4
Wardha, *India* 66 J11
Wardha →, *India* 66 K11
Ware, *Canada* 104 B3
Ware, *U.S.A.* 111 D12
Waregem, *Belgium* 17 D3
Wareham, *U.S.A.* 111 E14
Waremme, *Belgium* 17 D5
Waren, *Germany* 24 B8
Warendorf, *Germany* 24 D4
Warialda, *Australia* 95 D5
Wariap, *Indonesia* 63 E8
Warin Chamrap, *Thailand* 64 E5
Warka, *Poland* 45 G8
Warkopi, *Indonesia* 63 E8
Warm Springs, *U.S.A.* 115 G5
Warman, *Canada* 105 C7
Warmbad, *Namibia* 88 D2
Warmbad, *S. Africa* 89 C4
Warmińsko-Mazurskie □, *Poland* 44 D8
Warminster, *U.K.* 13 F5
Warminster, *U.S.A.* 111 F9
Warnemünde, *Germany* 24 A8
Warner Mts., *U.S.A.* 114 F3
Warner Robins, *U.S.A.* 109 J4
Warnow →, *Germany* 24 A8
Waroona, *Australia* 93 F2
Warracknabeal, *Australia* 95 F3
Warragul, *Australia* 95 F4
Warrego →, *Australia* 95 E4
Warrego Ra., *Australia* 94 C4
Warren, *Australia* 95 E4
Warren, *Ark., U.S.A.* 113 J8
Warren, *Mich., U.S.A.* 108 D4
Warren, *Minn., U.S.A.* 112 A6
Warren, *Ohio, U.S.A.* 110 E4
Warren, *Pa., U.S.A.* 110 E5
Warrenpoint, *U.K.* 15 B5
Warrensburg, *Mo., U.S.A.* 112 F8
Warrensburg, *N.Y., U.S.A.* 111 C11
Warrenton, *S. Africa* 88 D3
Warrenton, *U.S.A.* 116 D3
Warri, *Nigeria* 83 D6
Warrina, *Australia* 95 D2
Warrington, *U.K.* 12 D5
Warrington, *U.S.A.* 109 K2
Warrington □, *U.K.* 12 D5
Warrnambool, *Australia* 95 F3
Warroad, *U.S.A.* 112 A7
Warruwi, *Australia* 94 A1
Warsa, *Indonesia* 63 E9
Warsak Dam, *Pakistan* 68 B4
Warsaw = Warszawa, *Poland* 45 F8
Warsaw, *Ind., U.S.A.* 108 E3
Warsaw, *N.Y., U.S.A.* 110 D6
Warsaw, *Ohio, U.S.A.* 110 F3
Warstein, *Germany* 24 D4
Warszawa, *Poland* 45 F8
Warta, *Poland* 45 G5
Warta →, *Poland* 45 F1
Warthe = Warta →, *Poland* 45 F1
Waru, *Indonesia* 63 E8
Warwick, *Australia* 95 D5
Warwick, *U.K.* 13 E6
Warwick, *N.Y., U.S.A.* 111 E10
Warwick, *R.I., U.S.A.* 111 E13
Warwickshire □, *U.K.* 13 E6
Wasaga Beach, *Canada* 110 B4
Wasagaming, *Canada* 105 C9
Wasatch Ra., *U.S.A.* 114 F8
Wasbank, *S. Africa* 89 D5
Wasco, *Calif., U.S.A.* 117 K7
Wasco, *Oreg., U.S.A.* 114 D3
Wase, *Nigeria* 83 D6
Waseca, *U.S.A.* 112 C8
Wasekamio L., *Canada* 105 B7
Wash, The, *U.K.* 12 E8
Washago, *Canada* 110 B5
Washburn, *N. Dak., U.S.A.* 112 B4
Washburn, *Wis., U.S.A.* 112 B9
Washim, *India* 66 J10
Washington, *U.K.* 12 C6
Washington, *D.C., U.S.A.* 108 F7
Washington, *Ga., U.S.A.* 109 J4
Washington, *Ind., U.S.A.* 108 F2
Washington, *Iowa, U.S.A.* 112 E9
Washington, *Mo., U.S.A.* 112 F9
Washington, *N.C., U.S.A.* 109 H7
Washington, *N.J., U.S.A.* 111 F10
Washington, *Pa., U.S.A.* 110 F4
Washington, *Utah, U.S.A.* 115 H7
Washington □, *U.S.A.* 114 C3
Washington, Mt., *U.S.A.* 111 B13
Washington Court House, *U.S.A.* 108 F4
Washington I., *U.S.A.* 108 C2
Washougal, *U.S.A.* 116 E4
Wasian, *Indonesia* 63 E8
Wasilków, *Poland* 45 E10
Wasilla, *U.S.A.* 100 B5
Wasior, *Indonesia* 63 E8
Waskaganish, *Canada* 102 B4
Waskaiowaka, L., *Canada* 105 B9
Waskesiu Lake, *Canada* 105 C7
Wasserburg, *Germany* 25 G8
Wasserkuppe, *Germany* 24 E5
Wassy, *France* 19 D11
Waswanipi, *Canada* 102 C4
Waswanipi, L., *Canada* 102 C4
Watampone, *Indonesia* 63 E6
Water Park Pt., *Australia* 94 C5
Water Valley, *U.S.A.* 113 H10
Waterberge, *S. Africa* 89 C4
Waterbury, *Conn., U.S.A.* 111 E11
Waterbury, *Vt., U.S.A.* 111 B12
Waterbury L., *Canada* 105 B8
Waterdown, *Canada* 110 C5
Waterford, *Canada* 110 D4
Waterford, *Ireland* 15 D4
Waterford, *Calif., U.S.A.* 116 H6
Waterford, *Pa., U.S.A.* 110 E5
Waterford □, *Ireland* 15 D4
Waterford Harbour, *Ireland* 15 D5
Waterhen L., *Canada* 105 C9
Waterloo, *Belgium* 17 D4
Waterloo, *Ont., Canada* 102 D3
Waterloo, *Qué., Canada* 111 A12
Waterloo, *S. Leone* 82 D2
Waterloo, *Ill., U.S.A.* 112 F9
Waterloo, *Iowa, U.S.A.* 112 D8
Waterloo, *N.Y., U.S.A.* 110 D8
Watersmeet, *U.S.A.* 112 B10
Waterton Lakes Nat. Park, *U.S.A.* 114 B7
Watertown, *Conn., U.S.A.* 111 E11
Watertown, *N.Y., U.S.A.* 111 C9
Watertown, *S. Dak., U.S.A.* 112 C6
Watertown, *Wis., U.S.A.* 112 D10
Waterval-Boven, *S. Africa* 89 D5
Waterville, *Canada* 111 A13
Waterville, *Maine, U.S.A.* 109 C11
Waterville, *N.Y., U.S.A.* 111 D9
Waterville, *Pa., U.S.A.* 110 E7
Waterville, *Wash., U.S.A.* 114 C3
Watervliet, *U.S.A.* 111 D11
Wates, *Indonesia* 63 G14
Watford, *Canada* 110 D3
Watford, *U.K.* 13 F7
Watford City, *U.S.A.* 112 B3
Wathaman →, *Canada* 105 B8
Wathaman L., *Canada* 105 B8
Watheroo, *Australia* 93 F2
Wating, *China* 56 G4
Watkins Glen, *U.S.A.* 110 D8
Watling I. = San Salvador I., *Bahamas* 121 B5
Watonga, *U.S.A.* 113 H5
Watrous, *Canada* 105 C7
Watrous, *U.S.A.* 113 H2
Watsa, *Dem. Rep. of the Congo* 86 B2
Watseka, *U.S.A.* 108 E2
Watson, *Australia* 93 F5
Watson, *Canada* 105 C8
Watson Lake, *Canada* 104 A3
Watsontown, *U.S.A.* 110 E8
Watsonville, *U.S.A.* 116 J5
Wattiwarriganna Cr. →, *Australia* 95 D2
Wattwil, *Switz.* 25 H5
Watuata = Batuata, *Indonesia* 63 F6
Watubela, Kepulauan, *Indonesia* 63 E8
Watubela Is. = Watubela, Kepulauan, *Indonesia* 63 E8
Wau = Wâw, *Sudan* 81 F2
Waubamik, *Canada* 110 A4
Waubay, *U.S.A.* 112 C6
Wauchope, *N.S.W., Australia* 95 E5
Wauchope, *N. Terr., Australia* 94 C1
Wauchula, *U.S.A.* 109 M5
Waukarlycarly, L., *Australia* 92 D3
Waukegan, *U.S.A.* 108 D2
Waukesha, *U.S.A.* 108 D1
Waukon, *U.S.A.* 112 D9
Waupaca, *U.S.A.* 112 C10
Waupun, *U.S.A.* 112 D10
Waurika, *U.S.A.* 113 H6
Wausau, *U.S.A.* 112 C10
Wautoma, *U.S.A.* 112 C10
Wauwatosa, *U.S.A.* 108 D2
Waveney →, *U.K.* 13 E9
Waverley, *N.Z.* 91 H5
Waverly, *Iowa, U.S.A.* 112 D8
Waverly, *N.Y., U.S.A.* 111 E8
Wavre, *Belgium* 17 D4
Wâw, *Sudan* 81 F2
Wāw al Kabīr, *Libya* 79 C9
Wawa, *Canada* 102 C3
Wawa, *Nigeria* 83 D5
Wawa, *Sudan* 80 C3
Wawanesa, *Canada* 105 D9
Wawona, *U.S.A.* 116 H7
Waxahachie, *U.S.A.* 113 J6
Way, L., *Australia* 93 E3
Waycross, *U.S.A.* 109 K4
Wayi, *Sudan* 81 F3
Wayland, *U.S.A.* 110 D7
Wayne, *Nebr., U.S.A.* 112 D6
Wayne, *W. Va., U.S.A.* 108 F4
Waynesboro, *Ga., U.S.A.* 109 J4
Waynesboro, *Miss., U.S.A.* 109 K1
Waynesboro, *Pa., U.S.A.* 108 F7
Waynesboro, *Va., U.S.A.* 108 F6
Waynesburg, *U.S.A.* 108 F5
Waynesville, *U.S.A.* 109 H4
Waynoka, *U.S.A.* 113 G5
Wazirabad, *Pakistan* 68 C6
Wda →, *Poland* 44 E5
We, *Indonesia* 62 C1
Weald, The, *U.K.* 13 F8
Wear →, *U.K.* 12 C6
Weatherford, *Okla., U.S.A.* 113 H5
Weatherford, *Tex., U.S.A.* 113 J6
Weaverville, *U.S.A.* 114 F2
Webb City, *U.S.A.* 113 G7
Webequie, *Canada* 102 B2
Webo = Nyaake, *Liberia* 82 E3
Webster, *Mass., U.S.A.* 111 D13
Webster, *N.Y., U.S.A.* 110 C7
Webster, *S. Dak., U.S.A.* 112 C6
Webster City, *U.S.A.* 112 D8
Webster Springs, *U.S.A.* 108 F5
Weda, *Indonesia* 63 D7
Weda, Teluk, *Indonesia* 63 D7
Weddell I., *Falk. Is.* 128 G4
Weddell Sea, *Antarctica* 5 D1
Wedderburn, *Australia* 95 F3
Wedel, *Germany* 24 B5
Wedemark, *Germany* 24 C5
Wedgeport, *Canada* 103 D6
Wedza, *Zimbabwe* 87 F3
Wee Waa, *Australia* 95 E4
Weed, *U.S.A.* 114 F2
Weed Heights, *U.S.A.* 116 G7
Weedsport, *U.S.A.* 111 C8
Weedville, *U.S.A.* 110 E6
Weenen, *S. Africa* 89 D5
Weener, *Germany* 24 B3
Weert, *Neths.* 17 C5
Węgierska-Górka, *Poland* 45 J6
Węgliniec, *Poland* 45 G2
Węgorzewo, *Poland* 44 D8
Węgorzyno, *Poland* 44 E2
Węgrów, *Poland* 45 F9
Wehda □, *Sudan* 81 F3
Wei He →, *Hebei, China* 56 F8
Wei He →, *Shaanxi, China* 56 G6
Weichang, *China* 57 D9
Weichuan, *China* 56 G7
Weida, *Germany* 24 E8
Weiden, *Germany* 25 F8
Weifang, *China* 57 F10
Weihai, *China* 57 F12
Weil, *Germany* 25 H3
Weilburg, *Germany* 24 E4
Weilheim, *Germany* 25 H7
Weimar, *Germany* 24 E7
Weinan, *China* 56 G5
Weingarten, *Germany* 25 F4
Weinheim, *Germany* 25 F4
Weining, *China* 58 D5
Weipa, *Australia* 94 A3
Weir →, *Australia* 95 D4
Weir →, *Canada* 105 B10
Weir River, *Canada* 105 B10
Weirton, *U.S.A.* 110 F4
Weiser, *U.S.A.* 114 D5
Weishan, *Shandong, China* 57 G9
Weishan, *Yunnan, China* 58 E3
Weissenburg, *Germany* 25 F6
Weissenfels, *Germany* 24 D7
Weisswasser, *Germany* 24 D10
Weitra, *Austria* 26 C7
Weixi, *China* 58 D2
Weixin, *China* 58 D5
Weiyuan, *China* 56 G3
Weiz, *Austria* 26 D8
Weizhou Dao, *China* 58 G7
Wejherowo, *Poland* 44 D5
Wekusko L., *Canada* 105 C9
Welch, *U.S.A.* 108 G5
Weldya, *Ethiopia* 81 E4
Welega □, *Ethiopia* 81 F3
Welkite, *Ethiopia* 81 F4
Welkom, *S. Africa* 88 D4
Welland, *Canada* 102 D4
Welland →, *U.K.* 13 E7
Wellesley Is., *Australia* 94 B2
Wellingborough, *U.K.* 13 E7
Wellington, *Australia* 95 E4
Wellington, *Canada* 110 C7
Wellington, *N.Z.* 91 J5
Wellington, *S. Africa* 88 E2
Wellington, *Somst., U.K.* 13 G4
Wellington, *Telford & Wrekin, U.K.* 13 E5
Wellington, *Colo., U.S.A.* 112 E2
Wellington, *Kans., U.S.A.* 113 G6
Wellington, *Nev., U.S.A.* 116 G7
Wellington, *Ohio, U.S.A.* 110 E2
Wellington, *Tex., U.S.A.* 113 H4
Wellington, I., *Chile* 122 H3
Wellington, L., *Australia* 95 F4
Wells, *U.K.* 13 F5
Wells, *Maine, U.S.A.* 111 C14
Wells, *N.Y., U.S.A.* 111 C10
Wells, *Nev., U.S.A.* 114 F6
Wells, L., *Australia* 93 E3
Wells, Mt., *Australia* 92 C4
Wells Gray Prov. Park, *Canada* 104 C4
Wells-next-the-Sea, *U.K.* 12 E8
Wells River, *U.S.A.* 111 B12
Wellsboro, *U.S.A.* 110 E7
Wellsburg, *U.S.A.* 110 F4
Wellsville, *N.Y., U.S.A.* 110 D7
Wellsville, *Ohio, U.S.A.* 110 F4
Wellsville, *Utah, U.S.A.* 114 F8
Wellton, *U.S.A.* 115 K6
Welmel, Wabi →, *Ethiopia* 81 F5
Welo □, *Ethiopia* 81 E4
Wels, *Austria* 26 C7
Welshpool, *U.K.* 13 E4
Welwyn Garden City, *U.K.* 13 F7

Wem, *U.K.* 12 E5
Wembere →, *Tanzania* 86 C3
Wemindji, *Canada* 102 B4
Wen Xian, *China* 56 G7
Wenatchee, *U.S.A.* 114 C3
Wenchang, *China* 64 C8
Wencheng, *China* 59 D13
Wenchi, *Ghana* 82 D4
Wenchow = Wenzhou, *China* 59 D13
Wenchuan, *China* 58 B4
Wenden, *U.S.A.* 117 M13
Wendeng, *China* 57 F12
Wendesi, *Indonesia* 63 E8
Wendo, *Ethiopia* 81 F4
Wendover, *U.S.A.* 114 F6
Weng'an, *China* 58 D6
Wengcheng, *China* 59 E9
Wengyuan, *China* 59 E10
Wenjiang, *China* 58 B4
Wenling, *China* 59 C13
Wenlock →, *Australia* 94 A3
Wenshan, *China* 58 F5
Wenshang, *China* 56 G9
Wenshui, *China* 56 F7
Wensleydale, *U.K.* 12 C6
Wensu, *China* 60 B3
Wensum →, *U.K.* 12 E8
Wentworth, *Australia* 95 E3
Wentzel L., *Canada* 104 B6
Wenut, *Indonesia* 63 E8
Wenxi, *China* 56 G6
Wenxian, *China* 56 H3
Wenzhou, *China* 59 D13
Weott, *U.S.A.* 114 F2
Wepener, *S. Africa* 88 D4
Werda, *Botswana* 88 D3
Werdau, *Germany* 24 E8
Werder, *Germany* 24 C8
Werdohl, *Germany* 24 D3
Wereilu, *Ethiopia* 81 E4
Weri, *Indonesia* 63 E8
Werneck, *Germany* 25 F6
Wernigerode, *Germany* 24 D6
Werra →, *Germany* 24 D5
Werrimull, *Australia* 95 E3
Werris Creek, *Australia* 95 E5
Wertach →, *Germany* 25 G6
Wertheim, *Germany* 25 F5
Wertingen, *Germany* 25 G6
Wesel, *Germany* 24 D2
Weser →, *Germany* 24 B4
Weser-Ems □, *Germany* 24 C3
Weserbergland, *Germany* 24 C5
Wesiri, *Indonesia* 63 F7
Weslemkoon L., *Canada* 110 A7
Wesleyville, *Canada* 103 C9
Wesleyville, *U.S.A.* 110 D4
Wessel, C., *Australia* 94 A2
Wessel Is., *Australia* 94 A2
Wesselburen, *Germany* 24 A4
Wessington Springs, *U.S.A.* 112 C5
West, *U.S.A.* 113 K6
West →, *U.S.A.* 111 D12
West Baines →, *Australia* 92 C4
West Bank □, *Asia* 75 C4
West Bend, *U.S.A.* 108 D1
West Bengal □, *India* 69 H13
West Berkshire □, *U.K.* 13 F6
West Beskids = Západné Beskydy, *Europe* 27 B12
West Branch, *U.S.A.* 108 C3
West Branch Susquehanna →, *U.S.A.* 111 F8
West Bromwich, *U.K.* 13 E6
West Burra, *U.K.* 14 A7
West Canada Cr. →, *U.S.A.* 111 C10
West Cape Howe, *Australia* 93 G2
West Chazy, *U.S.A.* 111 B11
West Chester, *U.S.A.* 111 G9
West Columbia, *U.S.A.* 113 L7
West Covina, *U.S.A.* 117 L9
West Des Moines, *U.S.A.* 112 E8
West Dunbartonshire □, *U.K.* 14 F4
West End, *Bahamas* 120 A4
West Falkland, *Falk. Is.* 122 J4
West Fargo, *U.S.A.* 112 B6
West Farmington, *U.S.A.* 110 E4
West Fjord = Vestfjorden, *Norway* 8 C15
West Fork Trinity →, *U.S.A.* 113 J6
West Frankfort, *U.S.A.* 112 G10
West Hartford, *U.S.A.* 111 E12
West Haven, *U.S.A.* 111 E12
West Hazleton, *U.S.A.* 111 F9
West Helena, *U.S.A.* 113 H9
West Hurley, *U.S.A.* 111 E10
West Ice Shelf, *Antarctica* 5 C7
West Indies, *Cent. Amer.* 121 D7
West Jordan, *U.S.A.* 114 F8
West Lorne, *Canada* 110 D3
West Lothian □, *U.K.* 14 F5
West Lunga →, *Zambia* 87 E1
West Memphis, *U.S.A.* 113 H9
West Midlands □, *U.K.* 13 E6
West Mifflin, *U.S.A.* 110 F5
West Milton, *U.S.A.* 110 E8
West Monroe, *U.S.A.* 113 J8
West Newton, *U.S.A.* 110 F5
West Nicholson, *Zimbabwe* 87 G2
West Palm Beach, *U.S.A.* 109 M5
West Plains, *U.S.A.* 113 G9
West Point, *N.Y., U.S.A.* 111 E11
West Point, *Nebr., U.S.A.* 112 E6
West Point, *Va., U.S.A.* 108 G7
West Pt. = Ouest, Pte. de l', *Canada* 103 C7
West Pt., *Australia* 95 F2
West Road →, *Canada* 104 C4
West Rutland, *U.S.A.* 111 C11
West Schelde = Westerschelde →, *Neths.* 17 C3
West Seneca, *U.S.A.* 110 D6
West Siberian Plain, *Russia* 52 C11
West Sussex □, *U.K.* 13 G7
West-Terschelling, *Neths.* 17 A5
West Valley City, *U.S.A.* 114 F8
West Virginia □, *U.S.A.* 108 F5
West-Vlaanderen □, *Belgium* 17 D2
West Walker →, *U.S.A.* 116 G7
West Wyalong, *Australia* 95 E4
West Yellowstone, *U.S.A.* 114 D8
West Yorkshire □, *U.K.* 12 D6
Westall Pt., *Australia* 95 E1
Westbrook, *U.S.A.* 109 D10
Westbury, *Australia* 94 G4
Westby, *U.S.A.* 112 A2
Westend, *U.S.A.* 117 K9
Westerland, *Germany* 9 J13
Westerly, *U.S.A.* 111 E13
Western □, *Ghana* 82 D4
Western □, *Kenya* 86 B3
Western □, *S. Leone* 82 D2
Western □, *Zambia* 87 F1
Western Australia □, *Australia* 93 E2
Western Cape □, *S. Africa* 88 E3
Western Dvina = Daugava →, *Latvia* 9 H21
Western Ghats, *India* 66 N9
Western Isles □, *U.K.* 14 D1
Western Sahara ■, *Africa* 78 D3
Western Samoa = Samoa ■, *Pac. Oc.* 91 B13
Westernport, *U.S.A.* 108 F6
Westerschelde →, *Neths.* 17 C3
Westerstede, *Germany* 24 B3
Westerwald, *Germany* 24 E3
Westfield, *Mass., U.S.A.* 111 D12
Westfield, *N.Y., U.S.A.* 110 D5
Westfield, *Pa., U.S.A.* 110 E7
Westhill, *U.K.* 14 D6
Westhope, *U.S.A.* 112 A4
Westland Bight, *N.Z.* 91 K3
Westlock, *Canada* 104 C6
Westmar, *Australia* 95 D4
Westmeath □, *Ireland* 15 C4
Westminster, *U.S.A.* 108 F7
Westmont, *U.S.A.* 110 F6
Westmorland, *U.S.A.* 117 M11
Weston, *Oreg., U.S.A.* 114 D4
Weston, *W. Va., U.S.A.* 108 F5
Weston I., *Canada* 102 B4
Weston-super-Mare, *U.K.* 13 F5
Westover, *U.S.A.* 110 F6
Westport, *Canada* 111 B8
Westport, *Ireland* 15 C2
Westport, *N.Z.* 91 J3
Westport, *N.Y., U.S.A.* 111 B11
Westport, *Oreg., U.S.A.* 116 D3
Westport, *Wash., U.S.A.* 116 D2
Westray, *Canada* 105 C8
Westray, *U.K.* 14 B5
Westree, *Canada* 102 C3
Westville, *U.S.A.* 116 F6
Westwood, *U.S.A.* 114 F3
Wetar, *Indonesia* 63 F7
Wetaskiwin, *Canada* 104 C6
Wete, *Tanzania* 84 F7
Wetherby, *U.K.* 12 D6
Wethersfield, *U.S.A.* 111 E12
Wetteren, *Belgium* 17 D3
Wetzlar, *Germany* 24 E4
Wewoka, *U.S.A.* 113 H6
Wexford, *Ireland* 15 D5
Wexford □, *Ireland* 15 D5
Wexford Harbour, *Ireland* 15 D5
Weyburn, *Canada* 105 D8
Weyer Markt, *Austria* 26 D7
Weyhe, *Germany* 24 C4
Weyib →, *Ethiopia* 81 F5
Weymouth, *Canada* 103 D6
Weymouth, *U.K.* 13 G5
Weymouth, *U.S.A.* 111 D14
Weymouth, C., *Australia* 94 A3
Wha Ti, *Canada* 100 B8
Whakatane, *N.Z.* 91 G6
Whale →, *Canada* 103 A6
Whale Cove, *Canada* 105 A10
Whales, B. of, *Antarctica* 5 D12
Whalsay, *U.K.* 14 A8
Whangamomona, *N.Z.* 91 H5
Whangarei, *N.Z.* 91 F5
Whangarei Harb., *N.Z.* 91 F5
Wharfe →, *U.K.* 12 D6
Wharfedale, *U.K.* 12 C5
Wharton, *N.J., U.S.A.* 111 F10
Wharton, *Pa., U.S.A.* 110 E6
Wharton, *Tex., U.S.A.* 113 L6
Wheatland, *Calif., U.S.A.* 116 F5
Wheatland, *Wyo., U.S.A.* 112 D2
Wheatley, *Canada* 110 D2
Wheaton, *Md., U.S.A.* 108 F7
Wheaton, *Minn., U.S.A.* 112 C6
Wheelbarrow Pk., *U.S.A.* 116 H10
Wheeler, *Oreg., U.S.A.* 114 D2
Wheeler, *Tex., U.S.A.* 113 H4
Wheeler →, *Canada* 103 A6
Wheeler L., *U.S.A.* 109 H2
Wheeler Pk., *N. Mex., U.S.A.* 115 H11
Wheeler Pk., *Nev., U.S.A.* 115 G6
Wheeler Ridge, *U.S.A.* 117 L8
Wheeling, *U.S.A.* 110 F4
Whernside, *U.K.* 12 C5
Whiskey Jack L., *Canada* 105 B8
Whistleduck Cr. →, *Australia* 94 C2
Whistler, *Canada* 104 C4
Whitby, *Canada* 110 C6
Whitby, *U.K.* 12 C7
White →, *Ark., U.S.A.* 113 J9
White →, *Ind., U.S.A.* 108 F2
White →, *S. Dak., U.S.A.* 112 D5
White →, *Tex., U.S.A.* 113 J4
White →, *Utah, U.S.A.* 114 F9
White →, *Vt., U.S.A.* 111 C12
White →, *Wash., U.S.A.* 116 C4
White, L., *Australia* 92 D4
White B., *Canada* 103 C8
White Bird, *U.S.A.* 114 D5
White Butte, *U.S.A.* 112 B3
White City, *U.S.A.* 114 E2
White Cliffs, *Australia* 95 E3
White Hall, *U.S.A.* 112 F9
White Haven, *U.S.A.* 111 E9
White Horse, Vale of, *U.K.* 13 F6
White I., *N.Z.* 91 G6
White L., *Canada* 111 A8
White L., *U.S.A.* 113 L8
White Mountain Peak, *U.S.A.* 115 G4
White Mts., *Calif., U.S.A.* 116 H8
White Mts., *N.H., U.S.A.* 111 B13
White Nile = Nîl el Abyad →, *Sudan* 81 D3
White Nile Dam = Khazzān Jabal al Awliyā, *Sudan* 81 D3
White Otter L., *Canada* 102 C1
White Pass, *U.S.A.* 116 D5
White Plains, *U.S.A.* 111 E11
White River, *Canada* 102 C2
White River, *S. Africa* 89 D5
White River, *U.S.A.* 112 D4
White Rock, *Canada* 116 A4
White Russia = Belarus ■, *Europe* 46 F4
White Sea = Beloye More, *Russia* 50 C4
White Sulphur Springs, *Mont., U.S.A.* 114 C8
White Sulphur Springs, *W. Va., U.S.A.* 108 G5
White Swan, *U.S.A.* 116 D6
White Volta →, *Ghana* 83 D4
Whitecliffs, *N.Z.* 91 K3
Whitecourt, *Canada* 104 C5
Whiteface Mt., *U.S.A.* 111 B11
Whitefield, *U.S.A.* 111 B13
Whitefish, *U.S.A.* 114 B6
Whitefish L., *Canada* 105 A7
Whitefish Point, *U.S.A.* 108 B3
Whitegull, L., *Canada* 103 A7
Whitehall, *Mich., U.S.A.* 108 D2
Whitehall, *Mont., U.S.A.* 114 D7
Whitehall, *N.Y., U.S.A.* 111 C11
Whitehall, *Wis., U.S.A.* 112 C9
Whitehaven, *U.K.* 12 C4
Whitehorse, *Canada* 104 A1
Whitemark, *Australia* 94 G4
Whiteplains, *Liberia* 82 D2
Whiteriver, *U.S.A.* 115 K9
Whitesand →, *Canada* 104 A5
Whitesands, *S. Africa* 88 E3
Whitesboro, *N.Y., U.S.A.* 111 C9
Whitesboro, *Tex., U.S.A.* 113 J6
Whiteshell Prov. Park, *Canada* 105 D9
Whitesville, *U.S.A.* 110 D7
Whiteville, *U.S.A.* 109 H6
Whitewater, *U.S.A.* 108 D1
Whitewater Baldy, *U.S.A.* 115 K9
Whitewater L., *Canada* 102 B2
Whitewood, *Australia* 94 C3
Whitewood, *Canada* 105 C8
Whithorn, *U.K.* 14 G4
Whitianga, *N.Z.* 91 G5
Whitman, *U.S.A.* 111 D14
Whitney, *Canada* 102 C4
Whitney, Mt., *U.S.A.* 116 J8
Whitney Point, *U.S.A.* 111 D9
Whitstable, *U.K.* 13 F9
Whitsunday I., *Australia* 94 C4
Whittier, *U.S.A.* 117 M8
Whittlesea, *Australia* 95 F4
Wholdaia L., *Canada* 105 A8
Whyalla, *Australia* 95 E2
Wiarton, *Canada* 102 D3
Wiawso, *Ghana* 82 D4
Wiay, *U.K.* 14 D1
Wiązów, *Poland* 45 H4
Wibaux, *U.S.A.* 112 B2
Wichian Buri, *Thailand* 64 E3
Wichita, *U.S.A.* 113 G6
Wichita Falls, *U.S.A.* 113 J5
Wick, *U.K.* 14 C5
Wicked Pt., *Canada* 110 C7
Wickenburg, *U.S.A.* 115 K7
Wickepin, *Australia* 93 F2
Wickham, *Australia* 92 D2
Wickham, C., *Australia* 94 F3
Wickliffe, *U.S.A.* 110 E3
Wicklow, *Ireland* 15 D5
Wicklow □, *Ireland* 15 D5
Wicklow Hd., *Ireland* 15 D6
Wicklow Mts., *Ireland* 15 C5
Widawa, *Poland* 45 G5
Widawka →, *Poland* 45 G5
Widgeegoara Cr. →, *Australia* 95 D4
Widgiemooltha, *Australia* 93 F3
Widnes, *U.K.* 12 D5
Więcbork, *Poland* 45 E4
Wiehl, *Germany* 24 E3
Wiek, *Germany* 24 A9
Wielbark, *Poland* 44 E7
Wieleń, *Poland* 45 F3
Wielichowo, *Poland* 45 F3
Wieliczka, *Poland* 45 J7
Wielkopolskie □, *Poland* 45 F4
Wieluń, *Poland* 45 G5
Wien, *Austria* 27 C9
Wiener Neustadt, *Austria* 27 D9
Wieprz →, *Poland* 45 G8
Wieprza →, *Poland* 44 D3
Wieruszów, *Poland* 45 G5
Wiesbaden, *Germany* 25 E4
Wiesental, *Germany* 25 F4
Wiesloch, *Germany* 25 F4
Wiesmoor, *Germany* 24 B3
Wieżyca, *Poland* 44 D5
Wigan, *U.K.* 12 D5
Wiggins, *Colo., U.S.A.* 112 E2
Wiggins, *Miss., U.S.A.* 113 K10
Wight, I. of □, *U.K.* 13 G6
Wigry, Jezioro, *Poland* 44 D10
Wigston, *U.K.* 13 E6
Wigton, *U.K.* 12 C4
Wigtown, *U.K.* 14 G4
Wigtown B., *U.K.* 14 G4
Wil, *Switz.* 25 H5
Wilamowice, *Poland* 45 J6
Wilber, *U.S.A.* 112 E6
Wilberforce, *Canada* 110 A6
Wilberforce, C., *Australia* 94 A2
Wilburton, *U.S.A.* 113 H7
Wilcannia, *Australia* 95 E3
Wilcox, *U.S.A.* 110 E6
Wildbad, *Germany* 25 G4
Wildeshausen, *Germany* 24 C4
Wildon, *Austria* 26 E8
Wildrose, *U.S.A.* 117 J9
Wildspitze, *Austria* 26 E3
Wilga →, *Poland* 45 G8
Wilge →, *S. Africa* 89 D4
Wilhelm II Coast, *Antarctica* 5 C7
Wilhelmsburg, *Austria* 26 C8
Wilhelmshaven, *Germany* 24 B4
Wilhelmstal, *Namibia* 88 C2
Wilkes-Barre, *U.S.A.* 111 E9
Wilkie, *Canada* 105 C7
Wilkinsburg, *U.S.A.* 110 F5
Wilkinson Lakes, *Australia* 93 E5
Willandra Creek →, *Australia* 95 E4
Willapa B., *U.S.A.* 114 C2
Willapa Hills, *U.S.A.* 116 D3
Willard, *N.Y., U.S.A.* 110 D8
Willard, *Ohio, U.S.A.* 110 E2
Willcox, *U.S.A.* 115 K9
Willemstad, *Neth. Ant.* 121 D6
Willet, *U.S.A.* 111 D9
William →, *Canada* 105 B7
William 'Bill' Dannely Res., *U.S.A.* 109 J2
William Creek, *Australia* 95 D2
Williams, *Australia* 93 F2
Williams, *Ariz., U.S.A.* 115 J7
Williams, *Calif., U.S.A.* 116 F4
Williams Harbour, *Canada* 103 B8
Williams Lake, *Canada* 104 C4
Williamsburg, *Ky., U.S.A.* 109 G3
Williamsburg, *Pa., U.S.A.* 110 F6
Williamsburg, *Va., U.S.A.* 108 G7
Williamson, *N.Y., U.S.A.* 110 C7
Williamson, *W. Va., U.S.A.* 108 G4
Williamsport, *U.S.A.* 110 E7
Williamston, *U.S.A.* 109 H7
Williamstown, *Australia* 95 F3
Williamstown, *Ky., U.S.A.* 108 F3
Williamstown, *Mass., U.S.A.* 111 D11
Williamstown, *N.Y., U.S.A.* 111 C9
Willimantic, *U.S.A.* 111 E12
Willingboro, *U.S.A.* 108 E8
Willis Group, *Australia* 94 B5
Williston, *S. Africa* 88 E3
Williston, *Fla., U.S.A.* 109 L4
Williston, *N. Dak., U.S.A.* 112 A3
Williston L., *Canada* 104 B4
Willits, *U.S.A.* 114 G2
Willmar, *U.S.A.* 112 C7
Willoughby, *U.S.A.* 110 E3
Willow Bunch, *Canada* 105 D7
Willow L., *Canada* 104 A5
Willow Wall, The, *China* 57 C12
Willowick, *U.S.A.* 110 E3
Willowlake →, *Canada* 104 A4
Willowmore, *S. Africa* 88 E3
Willows, *U.S.A.* 116 F4
Willowvale = Gatyana, *S. Africa* 89 E4
Wills, L., *Australia* 92 D4
Wills Cr. →, *Australia* 94 C3
Willsboro, *U.S.A.* 111 B11
Willunga, *Australia* 95 F2
Wilmette, *U.S.A.* 108 D2
Wilmington, *Australia* 95 E2
Wilmington, *Del., U.S.A.* 108 F8
Wilmington, *N.C., U.S.A.* 109 H7
Wilmington, *Ohio, U.S.A.* 108 F4
Wilmington, *Vt., U.S.A.* 111 D12
Wilmslow, *U.K.* 12 D5
Wilpena Cr. →, *Australia* 95 E2
Wilsall, *U.S.A.* 114 D8
Wilson, *N.C., U.S.A.* 109 H7
Wilson, *N.Y., U.S.A.* 110 C6
Wilson, *Pa., U.S.A.* 111 F9
Wilson →, *Australia* 92 C4
Wilson Bluff, *Australia* 93 F4
Wilson Inlet, *Australia* 93 G2
Wilsons Promontory, *Australia* 95 F4
Wilster, *Germany* 24 B5
Wilton, *U.S.A.* 112 B4
Wilton →, *Australia* 94 A1
Wiltshire □, *U.K.* 13 F6
Wiltz, *Lux.* 17 E5
Wiluna, *Australia* 93 E3
Wimborne Minster, *U.K.* 13 G6
Wimereux, *France* 19 B8
Wimmera →, *Australia* 95 F3
Winam G., *Kenya* 86 C3
Winburg, *S. Africa* 88 D4
Winchendon, *U.S.A.* 111 D12
Winchester, *U.K.* 13 F6
Winchester, *Conn., U.S.A.* 111 E11
Winchester, *Idaho, U.S.A.* 114 C5
Winchester, *Ind., U.S.A.* 108 E3
Winchester, *Ky., U.S.A.* 108 G3
Winchester, *N.H., U.S.A.* 111 D12
Winchester, *Nev., U.S.A.* 117 J11
Winchester, *Tenn., U.S.A.* 109 H2
Winchester, *Va., U.S.A.* 108 F6
Wind →, *U.S.A.* 114 E9
Wind River Range, *U.S.A.* 114 E9
Windau = Ventspils, *Latvia* 9 H19
Windber, *U.S.A.* 110 F6
Winder, *U.S.A.* 109 J4
Windermere, *U.K.* 12 C5
Windhoek, *Namibia* 88 C2
Windischgarsten, *Austria* 26 D7
Windom, *U.S.A.* 112 D7
Windorah, *Australia* 94 D3
Window Rock, *U.S.A.* 115 J9
Windrush →, *U.K.* 13 F6
Windsor, *Australia* 95 E5
Windsor, *N.S., Canada* 103 D7
Windsor, *Ont., Canada* 102 D3
Windsor, *U.K.* 13 F7
Windsor, *Colo., U.S.A.* 112 E2
Windsor, *Conn., U.S.A.* 111 E12
Windsor, *Mo., U.S.A.* 112 F8
Windsor, *N.Y., U.S.A.* 111 D9
Windsor, *Vt., U.S.A.* 111 C12
Windsor & Maidenhead □, *U.K.* 13 F7
Windsorton, *S. Africa* 88 D3
Windward Is., *W. Indies* 121 D7
Windward Passage = Vientos, Paso de los, *Caribbean* 121 C5
Winefred L., *Canada* 105 B6
Winejok, *Sudan* 81 F2
Winfield, *U.S.A.* 113 G6
Wingate Mts., *Australia* 92 B5
Wingham, *Australia* 95 E5
Wingham, *Canada* 102 D3
Winisk, *Canada* 102 A2
Winisk →, *Canada* 102 A2
Winisk L., *Canada* 102 B2
Wink, *U.S.A.* 113 K3
Winkler, *Canada* 105 D9
Winklern, *Austria* 26 E5
Winlock, *U.S.A.* 116 D4
Winneba, *Ghana* 83 D4
Winnebago, L., *U.S.A.* 108 D1
Winnecke Cr. →, *Australia* 92 C5
Winnemucca, *U.S.A.* 114 F5
Winnemucca L., *U.S.A.* 114 F4
Winnett, *U.S.A.* 114 C9
Winnfield, *U.S.A.* 113 K8
Winnibigoshish, L., *U.S.A.* 112 B7
Winnipeg, *Canada* 105 D9
Winnipeg →, *Canada* 105 C9
Winnipeg, L., *Canada* 105 C9
Winnipeg Beach, *Canada* 105 C9
Winnipegosis, *Canada* 105 C9
Winnipegosis L., *Canada* 105 C9
Winnipesaukee, L., *U.S.A.* 111 C13
Winnisquam L., *U.S.A.* 111 C13
Winnsboro, *La., U.S.A.* 113 J9
Winnsboro, *S.C., U.S.A.* 109 H5
Winnsboro, *Tex., U.S.A.* 113 J7
Winokapau, L., *Canada* 103 B7
Winona, *Minn., U.S.A.* 112 C9
Winona, *Miss., U.S.A.* 113 J10
Winooski, *U.S.A.* 111 B11
Winooski →, *U.S.A.* 111 B11
Winschoten, *Neths.* 17 A7
Winsen, *Germany* 24 B6
Winsford, *U.K.* 12 D5
Winslow, *Ariz., U.S.A.* 115 J8
Winslow, *Wash., U.S.A.* 116 C4
Winsted, *U.S.A.* 111 E11
Winston-Salem, *U.S.A.* 109 G5
Winter Garden, *U.S.A.* 109 L5
Winter Haven, *U.S.A.* 109 M5
Winter Park, *U.S.A.* 109 L5
Winterberg, *Germany* 24 D4
Winterhaven, *U.S.A.* 117 N12
Winters, *U.S.A.* 116 G5
Wintersville, *U.S.A.* 110 F4
Winterswijk, *Neths.* 17 C6
Winterthur, *Switz.* 25 H4
Winthrop, *U.S.A.* 114 B3
Winton, *Australia* 94 C3
Winton, *N.Z.* 91 M2
Wipper →, *Germany* 24 D7
Wirrulla, *Australia* 95 E1
Wisbech, *U.K.* 13 E8
Wisconsin □, *U.S.A.* 112 C10
Wisconsin →, *U.S.A.* 112 D9
Wisconsin Rapids, *U.S.A.* 112 C10
Wisdom, *U.S.A.* 114 D7
Wishaw, *U.K.* 14 F5
Wishek, *U.S.A.* 112 B5
Wisła, *Poland* 45 J5
Wisła →, *Poland* 44 D5
Wisłok →, *Poland* 45 H9
Wisłoka →, *Poland* 45 H8
Wismar, *Germany* 24 B7
Wisner, *U.S.A.* 112 E6
Wissant, *France* 19 B8
Wissembourg, *France* 19 C14
Wisznice, *Poland* 45 G10
Witbank, *S. Africa* 89 D4
Witdraai, *S. Africa* 88 D3

Witham, *U.K.* 13 F8
Witham →, *U.K.* 12 E7
Withernsea, *U.K.* 12 D8
Witkowo, *Poland* 45 F4
Witney, *U.K.* 13 F6
Witnica, *Poland* 45 F1
Witnossob →, *Namibia* 88 D3
Wittdün, *Germany* 24 A4
Witten, *Germany* 24 D3
Wittenberge, *Germany* 24 B7
Wittenburg, *Germany* 24 B7
Wittenheim, *France* 19 E14
Wittenoom, *Australia* 92 D2
Wittingen, *Germany* 24 C6
Wittlich, *Germany* 25 F2
Wittmund, *Germany* 24 B3
Wittow, *Germany* 24 A9
Wittstock, *Germany* 24 B8
Witvlei, *Namibia* 88 C2
Witzenhausen, *Germany* 24 D5
Wkra →, *Poland* 45 F7
Władysławowo, *Poland* 44 D5
Wleń, *Poland* 45 G2
Wlingi, *Indonesia* 63 H15
Włocławek, *Poland* 45 F6
Włodawa, *Poland* 45 G10
Włoszczowa, *Poland* 45 H6
Woburn, *U.S.A.* 111 D13
Wodian, *China* 56 H7
Wodonga = Albury-Wodonga, *Australia* 95 F4
Wodzisław Śląski, *Poland* 45 H5
Wœrth, *France* 19 D14
Woinbogoin, *China* 58 A2
Woippy, *France* 19 C13
Wojcieszow, *Poland* 45 H2
Wokam, *Indonesia* 63 F8
Woking, *U.K.* 13 F7
Wokingham □, *U.K.* 13 F7
Wolbrom, *Poland* 45 H6
Wołczyn, *Poland* 45 G5
Woldegk, *Germany* 24 B9
Wolf →, *Canada* 104 A2
Wolf Creek, *U.S.A.* 114 C7
Wolf L., *Canada* 104 A2
Wolf Point, *U.S.A.* 112 A2
Wolfe I., *Canada* 102 D4
Wolfeboro, *U.S.A.* 111 C13
Wolfen, *Germany* 24 D8
Wolfenbüttel, *Germany* 24 C6
Wolfratshausen, *Germany* 25 H7
Wolfsberg, *Austria* 26 E7
Wolfsburg, *Germany* 24 C6
Wolgast, *Germany* 24 A9
Wolhusen, *Switz.* 25 H4
Wolin, *Poland* 44 E1
Wollaston, Is., *Chile* 128 H3
Wollaston L., *Canada* 105 B8
Wollaston Lake, *Canada* 105 B8
Wollaston Pen., *Canada* 100 B8
Wollongong, *Australia* 95 E5
Wolmaransstad, *S. Africa* 88 D4
Wolmirstedt, *Germany* 24 C7
Wołomin, *Poland* 45 F8
Wołów, *Poland* 45 G3
Wolseley, *S. Africa* 88 E2
Wolsey, *U.S.A.* 112 C5
Wolstenholme, C., *Canada* 98 C12
Wolsztyn, *Poland* 45 F3
Wolvega, *Neths.* 17 B6
Wolverhampton, *U.K.* 13 E5
Wondai, *Australia* 95 D5
Wongalarroo L., *Australia* 95 E3
Wongan Hills, *Australia* 93 F2
Wŏnju, *S. Korea* 57 F14
Wonosari, *Indonesia* 63 G14
Wonosobo, *Indonesia* 63 G13
Wonowon, *Canada* 104 B4
Wŏnsan, *N. Korea* 57 E14
Wonthaggi, *Australia* 95 F4
Wood Buffalo Nat. Park, *Canada* 104 B6
Wood Is., *Australia* 92 C3
Wood L., *Canada* 105 B8
Woodah I., *Australia* 94 A2
Woodbourne, *U.S.A.* 111 E10
Woodbridge, *Canada* 110 C5
Woodbridge, *U.K.* 13 E9
Woodburn, *U.S.A.* 114 D2
Woodenbong, *Australia* 95 D5
Woodend, *Australia* 95 F3
Woodford, *Australia* 95 D5
Woodfords, *U.S.A.* 116 G7
Woodlake, *U.S.A.* 116 J7
Woodland, *Calif., U.S.A.* 116 G5
Woodland, *Maine, U.S.A.* 109 C12
Woodland, *Pa., U.S.A.* 110 F6
Woodland, *Wash., U.S.A.* 116 E4
Woodland Caribou Prov. Park, *Canada* 105 C10
Woodridge, *Canada* 105 D9
Woodroffe, Mt., *Australia* 93 E5
Woods, L., *Australia* 94 B1
Woods, L. of the, *Canada* 105 D10
Woodstock, *Australia* 94 B4
Woodstock, *N.B., Canada* 103 C6
Woodstock, *Ont., Canada* 102 D3
Woodstock, *U.K.* 13 F6
Woodstock, *Ill., U.S.A.* 112 D10
Woodstock, *Vt., U.S.A.* 111 C12
Woodsville, *U.S.A.* 111 B13
Woodville, *N.Z.* 91 J5
Woodville, *Miss., U.S.A.* 113 K9
Woodville, *Tex., U.S.A.* 113 K7
Woodward, *U.S.A.* 113 G5
Woody, *U.S.A.* 117 K8
Woody →, *Canada* 105 C8
Woolamai, C., *Australia* 95 F4
Wooler, *U.K.* 12 B5
Woolgoolga, *Australia* 95 E5
Woomera, *Australia* 95 E2
Woonsocket, *R.I., U.S.A.* 111 E13
Woonsocket, *S. Dak., U.S.A.* 112 C5
Wooramel →, *Australia* 93 E1
Wooramel Roadhouse, *Australia* 93 E1
Wooster, *U.S.A.* 110 F3
Worcester, *S. Africa* 88 E2
Worcester, *U.K.* 13 E5
Worcester, *Mass., U.S.A.* 111 D13
Worcester, *N.Y., U.S.A.* 111 D10
Worcestershire □, *U.K.* 13 E5
Wörgl, *Austria* 26 D5
Workington, *U.K.* 12 C4
Worksop, *U.K.* 12 D6
Workum, *Neths.* 17 B5
Worland, *U.S.A.* 114 D10
Wormhout, *France* 19 B9
Worms, *Germany* 25 F4
Worsley, *Canada* 104 B5
Wörth, *Germany* 25 F8
Wortham, *U.S.A.* 113 K6
Wörther See, *Austria* 26 E7
Worthing, *U.K.* 13 G7
Worthington, *Minn., U.S.A.* 112 D7
Worthington, *Pa., U.S.A.* 110 F5
Wosi, *Indonesia* 63 E7
Wou-han = Wuhan, *China* 59 B10
Wousi = Wuxi, *China* 59 B13
Wowoni, *Indonesia* 63 E6
Wrangel I. = Vrangelya, Ostrov, *Russia* 51 B19
Wrangell, *U.S.A.* 104 B2
Wrangell Mts., *U.S.A.* 100 B5
Wrath, C., *U.K.* 14 C3
Wray, *U.S.A.* 112 E3
Wrekin, The, *U.K.* 13 E5
Wrens, *U.S.A.* 109 J4
Wrexham, *U.K.* 12 D4
Wrexham □, *U.K.* 12 D5
Wriezen, *Germany* 24 C10
Wright = Paranas, *Phil.* 61 F6
Wright, *U.S.A.* 112 D2
Wright Pt., *Canada* 110 C3
Wrightson Mt., *U.S.A.* 115 L8
Wrightwood, *U.S.A.* 117 L9
Wrigley, *Canada* 100 B7
Wrocław, *Poland* 45 G4
Wronki, *Poland* 45 F3
Września, *Poland* 45 F4
Wschowa, *Poland* 45 G3
Wu Jiang →, *China* 58 C6
Wu'an, *China* 56 F8
Wubin, *Australia* 93 F2
Wubu, *China* 56 F6
Wuchang, *China* 57 B14
Wucheng, *China* 56 F9
Wuchuan, *Guangdong, China* 59 G8
Wuchuan, *Guizhou, China* 58 C7
Wuchuan, *Nei Monggol Zizhiqu, China* 56 D6
Wudi, *China* 57 F9
Wuding, *China* 58 E4
Wuding He →, *China* 56 F6
Wudinna, *Australia* 95 E2
Wudu, *China* 56 H3
Wufeng, *China* 59 B8
Wugang, *China* 59 D8
Wugong Shan, *China* 59 D9
Wuhan, *China* 59 B10
Wuhe, *China* 57 H9
Wuhsi = Wuxi, *China* 59 B13
Wuhu, *China* 59 B12
Wujiang, *China* 59 B13
Wukari, *Nigeria* 83 D6
Wulajie, *China* 57 B14
Wulanbulang, *China* 56 D6
Wular L., *India* 69 B6
Wulehe, *Ghana* 83 D5
Wulian, *China* 57 G10
Wuliang Shan, *China* 58 E3
Wuliaru, *Indonesia* 63 F8
Wuling Shan, *China* 58 C7
Wulong, *China* 58 C6
Wulumuchi = Ürümqi, *China* 50 E9
Wum, *Cameroon* 83 D7
Wuming, *China* 58 F7
Wun Rog, *Sudan* 81 F2
Wundowie, *Australia* 93 F2
Wuning, *China* 59 C10
Wunnummin L., *Canada* 102 B2
Wunsiedel, *Germany* 25 E8
Wunstorf, *Germany* 24 C5
Wuntho, *Burma* 67 H19
Wuping, *China* 59 E11
Wuppertal, *Germany* 24 D3
Wuppertal, *S. Africa* 88 E2
Wuqing, *China* 57 E9
Wurtsboro, *U.S.A.* 111 E10
Würzburg, *Germany* 25 F5
Wurzen, *Germany* 24 D8
Wushan, *China* 56 G3
Wushishi, *Nigeria* 83 D6
Wusuli Jiang = Ussuri →, *Asia* 54 A7
Wutach →, *Germany* 25 H4
Wutai, *China* 56 E7
Wuting = Huimin, *China* 57 F9
Wutong, *China* 59 E8
Wutonghaolai, *China* 57 C11
Wutongqiao, *China* 58 C4
Wuwei, *Anhui, China* 59 B11
Wuwei, *Gansu, China* 60 C5
Wuxi, *Jiangsu, China* 59 B13
Wuxi, *Sichuan, China* 58 B7
Wuxiang, *China* 56 F7
Wuxuan, *China* 58 F7
Wuxue, *China* 59 C10
Wuyang, *China* 56 H7
Wuyi, *Hebei, China* 56 F8
Wuyi, *Zhejiang, China* 59 C12
Wuyi Shan, *China* 59 D11
Wuyishan, *China* 59 D12
Wuyo, *Nigeria* 83 C7
Wuyuan, *Jiangxi, China* 59 C11
Wuyuan, *Nei Monggol Zizhiqu, China* 56 D5
Wuzhai, *China* 56 E6
Wuzhi Shan, *China* 64 C7
Wuzhong, *China* 56 E4
Wuzhou, *China* 59 F8
Wyaaba Cr. →, *Australia* 94 B3
Wyalkatchem, *Australia* 93 F2
Wyalusing, *U.S.A.* 111 E8
Wyandotte, *U.S.A.* 108 D4
Wyandra, *Australia* 95 D4
Wyangala, L., *Australia* 95 E4
Wyara, L., *Australia* 95 D3
Wycheproof, *Australia* 95 F3
Wye →, *U.K.* 13 F5
Wyemandoo, *Australia* 93 E2
Wyk, *Germany* 24 A4
Wymondham, *U.K.* 13 E9
Wymore, *U.S.A.* 112 E6
Wyndham, *Australia* 92 C4
Wyndham, *N.Z.* 91 M2
Wynne, *U.S.A.* 113 H9
Wynyard, *Australia* 94 G4
Wynyard, *Canada* 105 C8
Wyola L., *Australia* 93 E5
Wyoming, *Canada* 110 D2
Wyoming □, *U.S.A.* 114 E10
Wyomissing, *U.S.A.* 111 F9
Wyong, *Australia* 95 E5
Wyrzysk, *Poland* 45 E4
Wyśmierzyce, *Poland* 45 G7
Wysoka, *Poland* 45 E4
Wysokie, *Poland* 45 H9
Wysokie Mazowieckie, *Poland* 45 F9
Wyszków, *Poland* 45 F8
Wyszogród, *Poland* 45 F7
Wytheville, *U.S.A.* 108 G5
Wyżyna Małopolska, *Poland* 45 H7

X

Xaçmaz, *Azerbaijan* 49 K9
Xai-Xai, *Mozam.* 89 D5
Xainza, *China* 60 C3
Xangongo, *Angola* 88 B2
Xankändi, *Azerbaijan* 70 B5
Xanlar, *Azerbaijan* 49 K8
Xanten, *Germany* 24 D2
Xánthi, *Greece* 41 E8
Xánthi □, *Greece* 41 E8
Xanthos, *Turkey* 39 E11
Xanxerê, *Brazil* 127 B5
Xapuri, *Brazil* 124 F5
Xar Moron He →, *China* 57 C11
Xarrë, *Albania* 40 G4
Xátiva, *Spain* 33 G4
Xau, L., *Botswana* 88 C3
Xavantina, *Brazil* 127 A5
Xenia, *U.S.A.* 108 F4
Xeropotamos →, *Cyprus* 36 E11
Xertigny, *France* 19 D13
Xhora, *S. Africa* 89 E4
Xhumo, *Botswana* 88 C3
Xi Jiang →, *China* 59 F9
Xi Xian, *Henan, China* 59 A10
Xi Xian, *Shanxi, China* 56 F6
Xia Xian, *China* 56 G6
Xiachengzi, *China* 57 B16
Xiachuan Dao, *China* 59 G9
Xiaguan, *China* 60 D5
Xiajiang, *China* 59 D10
Xiajin, *China* 56 F9
Xiamen, *China* 59 E12
Xi'an, *China* 56 G5
Xian Xian, *China* 56 E9
Xianfeng, *China* 58 C7
Xiang Jiang →, *China* 59 C9
Xiangcheng, *Henan, China* 56 H8
Xiangcheng, *Henan, China* 56 H7
Xiangcheng, *Sichuan, China* 58 C2
Xiangdu, *China* 58 F6
Xiangfan, *China* 59 A9
Xianggang = Hong Kong □, *China* 59 F10
Xianghuang Qi, *China* 56 C7
Xiangning, *China* 56 G6
Xiangquan, *China* 56 F7
Xiangquan He = Sutlej →, *Pakistan* 68 E4
Xiangshan, *China* 59 C13
Xiangshui, *China* 57 G10
Xiangtan, *China* 59 D9
Xiangxiang, *China* 59 D9
Xiangyin, *China* 59 C9
Xiangyun, *China* 58 E3
Xiangzhou, *China* 58 F7
Xianju, *China* 59 C13
Xianning, *China* 59 C10
Xianshui He →, *China* 58 B3
Xiantao, *China* 59 B9
Xianyang, *China* 56 G5
Xianyou, *China* 59 E12
Xiao Hinggan Ling, *China* 60 B7
Xiao Xian, *China* 56 G9
Xiaofeng, *China* 59 B12
Xiaogan, *China* 59 B9
Xiaojin, *China* 58 B4
Xiaolan, *China* 59 F9
Xiaoshan, *China* 59 B13
Xiaoyi, *China* 56 F6
Xiapu, *China* 59 D12
Xiawa, *China* 57 C11
Xiayi, *China* 56 G9
Xichang, *China* 58 D4
Xichong, *China* 58 B5
Xichou, *China* 58 E5
Xichuan, *China* 56 H6
Xide, *China* 58 C4
Xiemahe, *China* 59 B8
Xieng Khouang, *Laos* 64 C4
Xifei He →, *China* 56 H9
Xifeng, *Gansu, China* 56 G4
Xifeng, *Guizhou, China* 58 D6
Xifeng, *Liaoning, China* 57 C13
Xifengzhen = Xifeng, *China* 56 G4
Xigazê, *China* 60 D3
Xihe, *China* 56 G3
Xihua, *China* 56 H8
Xilaganí, *Greece* 41 F9
Xiliao He →, *China* 57 C12
Xilin, *China* 58 E5
Xilókastron, *Greece* 38 C4
Xime, *Guinea-Biss.* 82 C2
Ximeng, *China* 58 F2
Xin Jiang →, *China* 59 C11
Xin Xian = Xinzhou, *China* 56 E7
Xinavane, *Mozam.* 89 D5
Xinbin, *China* 57 D13
Xincai, *China* 59 A10
Xinchang, *China* 59 C13
Xincheng, *Guangxi Zhuangzu, China* 58 E7
Xincheng, *Jiangxi, China* 59 D10
Xindu, *China* 58 B5
Xinfeng, *Guangdong, China* 59 E10
Xinfeng, *Jiangxi, China* 59 D11
Xinfeng, *Jiangxi, China* 59 E10
Xinfengjiang Skuiku, *China* 59 F10
Xing Xian, *China* 56 E6
Xing'an, *Guangxi Zhuangzu, China* 59 E8
Xingan, *Jiangxi, China* 59 D10
Xingcheng, *China* 57 D11
Xingguo, *China* 59 D10
Xinghe, *China* 56 D7
Xinghua, *China* 57 H10
Xinghua Wan, *China* 59 E12
Xinglong, *China* 57 D9
Xingning, *China* 59 E10
Xingping, *China* 56 G5
Xingren, *China* 58 E5
Xingshan, *China* 59 B8
Xingtai, *China* 56 F8
Xingu →, *Brazil* 122 D5
Xingwen, *China* 58 C5
Xingyang, *China* 56 G7
Xinhe, *China* 56 F8
Xinhua, *China* 59 D8
Xinhuang, *China* 58 D7
Xinhui, *China* 59 F9
Xining, *China* 60 C5
Xinjian, *China* 59 C10
Xinjiang, *China* 56 G6
Xinjiang Uygur Zizhiqu □, *China* 60 B3
Xinjie, *China* 58 D3
Xinjin = Pulandian, *China* 57 E11
Xinjin, *China* 58 B4
Xinkai He →, *China* 57 C12
Xinle, *China* 56 E8
Xinlitun, *China* 57 D12
Xinlong, *China* 58 B3
Xinmin, *China* 57 D12
Xinning, *China* 59 D8
Xinping, *China* 58 E3
Xinshao, *China* 59 D8
Xintai, *China* 57 G9
Xintian, *China* 59 E9
Xinxian, *China* 59 B10
Xinxiang, *China* 56 G7
Xinxing, *China* 59 F9
Xinyang, *China* 59 A10
Xinye, *China* 59 A9
Xinyi, *China* 59 F8
Xinyu, *China* 59 D10
Xinzhan, *China* 57 C14
Xinzheng, *China* 56 G7
Xinzhou, *Hubei, China* 59 B10
Xinzhou, *Shanxi, China* 56 E7
Xinzo de Limia, *Spain* 34 C3
Xiongyuecheng, *China* 57 D12
Xiping, *Henan, China* 56 H8
Xiping, *Henan, China* 56 H6
Xiping, *Zhejiang, China* 59 C12
Xique-Xique, *Brazil* 125 F10
Xisha Qundao = Paracel Is., *S. China Sea* 62 A4
Xishui, *Guizhou, China* 58 C6
Xishui, *Hubei, China* 59 B10
Xitole, *Guinea-Biss.* 82 C2
Xiu Shui →, *China* 59 C10
Xiuning, *China* 59 C12
Xiuren, *China* 59 E8
Xiushan, *China* 58 C7
Xiushui, *China* 59 C10
Xiuwen, *China* 58 D6
Xiuyan, *China* 57 D12
Xixabangma Feng, *China* 67 E14
Xixia, *China* 56 H6
Xixiang, *China* 56 H4
Xiyang, *China* 56 F7
Xizang Zizhiqu □, *China* 60 C3
Xlendi, *Malta* 36 C1
Xu Jiang →, *China* 59 D11
Xuan Loc, *Vietnam* 65 G6
Xuan'en, *China* 58 C7
Xuanhan, *China* 58 B6
Xuanhua, *China* 56 D8
Xuanwei, *China* 58 C5
Xuanzhou, *China* 59 B12
Xuchang, *China* 56 G7
Xudat, *Azerbaijan* 49 K9
Xuefeng Shan, *China* 59 D8
Xuejiaping, *China* 59 B8
Xun Jiang →, *China* 59 F8
Xun Xian, *China* 56 G8
Xundian, *China* 58 E4
Xunwu, *China* 59 E10
Xunyang, *China* 56 H5
Xunyi, *China* 56 G5
Xupu, *China* 59 D8
Xúquer →, *Spain* 33 F4
Xushui, *China* 56 E8
Xuwen, *China* 59 G8
Xuyen Moc, *Vietnam* 65 G6
Xuyong, *China* 58 C5
Xuzhou, *China* 57 G9
Xylophagou, *Cyprus* 36 E12

Y

Ya Xian, *China* 64 C7
Yaamba, *Australia* 94 C5
Ya'an, *China* 58 C4
Yaapeet, *Australia* 95 F3
Yabassi, *Cameroon* 83 E6
Yabelo, *Ethiopia* 81 G4
Yablanitsa, *Bulgaria* 41 C8
Yablonovy Ra. = Yablonovyy Khrebet, *Russia* 51 D12
Yablonovyy Khrebet, *Russia* 51 D12
Yabrai Shan, *China* 56 E2
Yabrūd, *Syria* 75 B5
Yacheng, *China* 64 C7
Yacuiba, *Bolivia* 126 A3
Yacuma →, *Bolivia* 124 F5
Yadgir, *India* 66 L10
Yadkin →, *U.S.A.* 109 H5
Yadrin, *Russia* 48 C8
Yaeyama-Rettō, *Japan* 55 M1
Yagaba, *Ghana* 83 C4
Yağcılar, *Turkey* 39 B10
Yagodnoye, *Russia* 51 C15
Yahila, *Dem. Rep. of the Congo* 86 B1
Yahk, *Canada* 104 D5
Yahotyn, *Ukraine* 47 G6
Yahuma, *Dem. Rep. of the Congo* 84 D4
Yahyalı, *Turkey* 72 C6
Yaita, *Japan* 55 F9
Yaiza, *Canary Is.* 37 F6
Yajiang, *China* 58 B3
Yajua, *Nigeria* 83 C7
Yakima, *U.S.A.* 114 C3
Yakima →, *U.S.A.* 114 C3
Yako, *Burkina Faso* 82 C4
Yakobi I., *U.S.A.* 104 B1
Yakoruda, *Bulgaria* 40 D7
Yakovlevka, *Russia* 54 B6
Yaku-Shima, *Japan* 55 J5
Yakumo, *Japan* 54 C10
Yakutat, *U.S.A.* 100 C6
Yakutia = Sakha □, *Russia* 51 C13
Yakutsk, *Russia* 51 C13
Yala, *Thailand* 65 J3
Yale, *U.S.A.* 110 C2
Yalgoo, *Australia* 93 E2
Yalinga, *C.A.R.* 84 C4
Yalkubul, Punta, *Mexico* 119 C7
Yalleroi, *Australia* 94 C4
Yalobusha →, *U.S.A.* 113 J9
Yalong Jiang →, *China* 58 D3
Yalova, *Turkey* 41 F13
Yalta, *Ukraine* 47 K8
Yalu Jiang →, *China* 57 E13
Yalvaç, *Turkey* 72 C4
Yam Ha Melaḥ = Dead Sea, *Asia* 75 D4
Yam Kinneret, *Israel* 75 C4
Yamada, *Japan* 55 H5
Yamagata, *Japan* 54 E10
Yamagata □, *Japan* 54 E10
Yamaguchi, *Japan* 55 G5
Yamaguchi □, *Japan* 55 G5
Yamal, Poluostrov, *Russia* 50 B8
Yamal Pen. = Yamal, Poluostrov, *Russia* 50 B8
Yamanashi □, *Japan* 55 G9
Yamba, *Australia* 95 D5
Yambarran Ra., *Australia* 92 C5
Yambéring, *Guinea* 82 C2
Yâmbiô, *Sudan* 81 G2
Yambol, *Bulgaria* 41 D10
Yamdena, *Indonesia* 63 F8
Yame, *Japan* 55 H5
Yamethin, *Burma* 67 J20
Yamma-Yamma, L., *Australia* 95 D3
Yamoussoukro, *Ivory C.* 82 D3
Yampa →, *U.S.A.* 114 F9
Yampi Sd., *Australia* 92 C3
Yampil, *Moldova* 47 H5
Yampol = Yampil, *Moldova* 47 H5
Yamrat, *Nigeria* 83 C6
Yamrukchal = Botev, *Bulgaria* 41 D8
Yamuna →, *India* 69 G9
Yamunanagar, *India* 68 D7
Yamzho Yumco, *China* 60 D4
Yan, *Nigeria* 83 C7

Yana →, *Russia* 51 B14
Yanagawa, *Japan* 55 H5
Yanai, *Japan* 55 H6
Yan'an, *China* 56 F5
Yanbian, *China* 58 D3
Yanbu 'al Baḥr, *Si. Arabia* 70 F3
Yanchang, *China* 56 F6
Yancheng, *Henan, China* 56 H8
Yancheng, *Jiangsu, China* 57 H11
Yanchep Beach, *Australia* 93 F2
Yanchi, *China* 56 F4
Yanchuan, *China* 56 F6
Yanco Cr. →, *Australia* 95 F4
Yandoon, *Burma* 67 L19
Yanfeng, *China* 58 E3
Yanfolila, *Mali* 82 C3
Yang Xian, *China* 56 H4
Yang-Yang, *Senegal* 82 B1
Yangambi, *Dem. Rep. of the Congo* 86 B1
Yangbi, *China* 58 E2
Yangcheng, *China* 56 G7
Yangch'ü = Taiyuan, *China* 56 F7
Yangchun, *China* 59 F8
Yanggao, *China* 56 D7
Yanggu, *China* 56 F8
Yangjiang, *China* 59 G8
Yangliuqing, *China* 57 E9
Yangon = Rangoon, *Burma* 67 L20
Yangping, *China* 59 B8
Yangpingguan, *China* 56 H4
Yangquan, *China* 56 F7
Yangshan, *China* 59 E9
Yangshuo, *China* 59 E8
Yangtse = Chang Jiang →, *China* 59 B13
Yangtze Kiang = Chang Jiang →, *China* 59 B13
Yangxin, *China* 59 C10
Yangyang, *S. Korea* 57 E15
Yangyuan, *China* 56 D8
Yangzhong, *China* 59 A12
Yangzhou, *China* 59 A12
Yanhe, *China* 58 C7
Yanji, *China* 57 C15
Yanjin, *China* 58 C5
Yanjing, *China* 58 C2
Yankton, *U.S.A.* 112 D6
Yanonge, *Dem. Rep. of the Congo* 86 B1
Yanqi, *China* 60 B3
Yanqing, *China* 56 D8
Yanshan, *Hebei, China* 57 E9
Yanshan, *Jiangxi, China* 59 C11
Yanshan, *Yunnan, China* 58 F5
Yanshou, *China* 57 B15
Yantabulla, *Australia* 95 D4
Yantai, *China* 57 F11
Yanting, *China* 58 B5
Yantra →, *Bulgaria* 41 C9
Yanwa, *China* 58 D2
Yanyuan, *China* 58 D3
Yanzhou, *China* 56 G9
Yao Xian, *China* 56 G5
Yao Yai, Ko, *Thailand* 65 J2
Yao'an, *China* 58 E3
Yaodu, *China* 58 A5
Yaoundé, *Cameroon* 83 E7
Yaowan, *China* 57 G10
Yap I., *Pac. Oc.* 96 G5
Yapen, *Indonesia* 63 E9
Yapen, Selat, *Indonesia* 63 E9
Yapero, *Indonesia* 63 E9
Yappar →, *Australia* 94 B3
Yaqui →, *Mexico* 118 B2
Yar-Sale, *Russia* 50 C8
Yaraka, *Australia* 94 C3
Yaransk, *Russia* 48 B8
Yarbasan, *Turkey* 39 C10
Yardımcı Burnu, *Turkey* 39 E12
Yare →, *U.K.* 13 E9
Yaremcha, *Ukraine* 47 H3
Yarensk, *Russia* 50 C5
Yarfa, *Si. Arabia* 80 C4
Yarí →, *Colombia* 124 D4
Yarkand = Shache, *China* 60 C2
Yarker, *Canada* 111 B8
Yarkhun →, *Pakistan* 69 A5
Yarmouth, *Canada* 103 D6
Yarmūk →, *Syria* 75 C4
Yaroslavl, *Russia* 46 D10
Yarqa, W. →, *Egypt* 75 F2
Yarra Yarra Lakes, *Australia* 93 E2
Yarram, *Australia* 95 F4
Yarraman, *Australia* 95 D5
Yarras, *Australia* 95 E5
Yartsevo, *Sib., Russia* 51 C10
Yartsevo, *Smolensk, Russia* 46 E7
Yarumal, *Colombia* 124 B3
Yasawa Group, *Fiji* 91 C7
Yaselda, *Belarus* 47 F4
Yashi, *Nigeria* 83 C6
Yashikera, *Nigeria* 83 D5
Yashkul, *Russia* 49 G7
Yasin, *Pakistan* 69 A5
Yasinovataya, *Ukraine* 47 H9
Yasinski, L., *Canada* 102 B4
Yasinya, *Ukraine* 47 H3
Yasothon, *Thailand* 64 E5
Yass, *Australia* 95 E4
Yāsūj, *Iran* 71 D6
Yatağan, *Turkey* 39 D10
Yatakala, *Niger* 83 C5
Yates Center, *U.S.A.* 113 G7
Yathkyed L., *Canada* 105 A9
Yatsushiro, *Japan* 55 H5
Yatta Plateau, *Kenya* 86 C4
Yavari →, *Peru* 124 D4
Yávaros, *Mexico* 118 B3
Yavatmal, *India* 66 J11
Yavne, *Israel* 75 D3
Yavoriv, *Ukraine* 47 H2
Yavorov = Yavoriv, *Ukraine* 47 H2
Yavuzeli, *Turkey* 72 D7
Yawatahama, *Japan* 55 H6
Yawri B., *S. Leone* 82 D2
Yaxi, *China* 58 D6
Yazd, *Iran* 71 D7
Yazd □, *Iran* 71 D7
Yazd-e Khvāst, *Iran* 71 D7
Yazıköy, *Turkey* 39 E9
Yazman, *Pakistan* 68 E4
Yazoo →, *U.S.A.* 113 J9
Yazoo City, *U.S.A.* 113 J9
Ybbs, *Austria* 26 C8
Yding Skovhøj, *Denmark* 11 J3
Ye Xian = Laizhou, *China* 57 F10
Ye Xian, *China* 56 H7
Yebyu, *Burma* 64 E2
Yechŏn, *S. Korea* 57 F15
Yecla, *Spain* 33 G3
Yécora, *Mexico* 118 B3
Yedintsy = Edineţ, *Moldova* 43 B12
Yedseram →, *Nigeria* 83 C7
Yefremov, *Russia* 46 F10
Yeghegnadzor, *Armenia* 73 C11
Yegorlyk →, *Russia* 49 G5
Yegorlykskaya, *Russia* 49 G5
Yegoryevsk, *Russia* 46 E10
Yegros, *Paraguay* 126 B4
Yehuda, Midbar, *Israel* 75 D4
Yei, *Sudan* 81 G3
Yei, Nahr →, *Sudan* 81 F3
Yejmiadzin, *Armenia* 49 K7
Yekaterinburg, *Russia* 50 D7
Yekaterinodar = Krasnodar, *Russia* 49 H4
Yelabuga, *Russia* 48 C11
Yelan, *Russia* 48 E6
Yelarbon, *Australia* 95 D5
Yelatma, *Russia* 48 C5
Yelets, *Russia* 47 F10
Yélimané, *Mali* 82 B2
Yelizavetgrad = Kirovohrad, *Ukraine* 47 H7
Yell, *U.K.* 14 A7
Yell Sd., *U.K.* 14 A7
Yellow Sea, *China* 57 G12
Yellowhead Pass, *Canada* 104 C5
Yellowknife, *Canada* 104 A6
Yellowknife →, *Canada* 104 A6
Yellowstone →, *U.S.A.* 112 B3
Yellowstone L., *U.S.A.* 114 D8
Yellowstone National Park, *U.S.A.* 114 D9
Yelnya, *Russia* 46 E7
Yelsk, *Belarus* 47 G5
Yelwa, *Nigeria* 83 C5
Yemen ■, *Asia* 74 E3
Yen Bai, *Vietnam* 58 G5
Yenagoa, *Nigeria* 83 E6
Yenakiyeve, *Ukraine* 47 H10
Yenakiyevo = Yenakiyeve, *Ukraine* 47 H10
Yenangyaung, *Burma* 67 J19
Yenbo = Yanbu 'al Baḥr, *Si. Arabia* 70 F3
Yenda, *Australia* 95 E4
Yende Millimou, *Guinea* 82 D2
Yendéré, *Burkina Faso* 82 C4
Yendi, *Ghana* 83 D4
Yéni, *Niger* 83 C5
Yenice, *Ankara, Turkey* 72 C5
Yenice, *Aydın, Turkey* 39 D10
Yenice, *Çanakkale, Turkey* 39 B9
Yenice, *Edirne, Turkey* 41 F10
Yenice →, *Turkey* 72 D6
Yenifoça, *Turkey* 39 C8
Yenihisar, *Turkey* 39 D9
Yeniköy, *Bursa, Turkey* 41 F13
Yeniköy, *Çanakkale, Turkey* 39 B8
Yeniköy, *Kütahya, Turkey* 39 C11
Yenipazar, *Turkey* 39 D10
Yenisaía, *Greece* 41 E8
Yenişehir, *Turkey* 41 F13
Yenisey →, *Russia* 50 B9
Yeniseysk, *Russia* 51 D10
Yeniseyskiy Zaliv, *Russia* 50 B9
Yennádhi, *Greece* 36 C9
Yenne, *France* 21 C9
Yenotayevka, *Russia* 49 G8
Yenyuka, *Russia* 51 D13
Yeo →, *U.K.* 13 G5
Yeo, L., *Australia* 93 E3
Yeo I., *Canada* 110 A3
Yeola, *India* 66 J9
Yeoryioúpolis, *Greece* 36 D6
Yeovil, *U.K.* 13 G5
Yepes, *Spain* 34 F7
Yeppoon, *Australia* 94 C5
Yeráki, *Greece* 38 D4
Yerbent, *Turkmenistan* 50 F6
Yerbogachen, *Russia* 51 C11
Yerevan, *Armenia* 49 K7
Yerington, *U.S.A.* 114 G4
Yerkesik, *Turkey* 39 D10
Yerköy, *Turkey* 72 C6
Yermak, *Kazakstan* 50 D8
Yermo, *U.S.A.* 117 L10
Yerólakkos, *Cyprus* 36 D12
Yeropol, *Russia* 51 C17
Yeropótamos →, *Greece* 36 D6
Yeroskipos, *Cyprus* 36 E11
Yershov, *Russia* 48 E9
Yerushalayim = Jerusalem, *Israel* 75 D4
Yerville, *France* 18 C7
Yes Tor, *U.K.* 13 G4
Yesan, *S. Korea* 57 F14
Yeşilhisar, *Turkey* 72 C6
Yeşilırmak →, *Turkey* 72 B7
Yeşilkent, *Turkey* 72 D7
Yeşilköy, *Turkey* 41 F12
Yeşilova, *Turkey* 39 D11
Yeşilyurt, *Manisa, Turkey* 39 C10
Yeşilyurt, *Muğla, Turkey* 39 D10
Yesnogorsk, *Russia* 46 E9
Yeso, *U.S.A.* 113 H2
Yessentuki, *Russia* 49 H6
Yessey, *Russia* 51 C11
Yeste, *Spain* 33 G2
Yetman, *Australia* 95 D5
Yeu, Î. d', *France* 18 F4
Yevlakh = Yevlax, *Azerbaijan* 49 K8
Yevlax, *Azerbaijan* 49 K8
Yevpatoriya, *Ukraine* 47 K7
Yeya →, *Russia* 47 J10
Yeysk, *Russia* 47 J10
Yezd = Yazd, *Iran* 71 D7
Yezerishche, *Belarus* 46 E5
Yhati, *Paraguay* 126 B4
Yhú, *Paraguay* 127 B4
Yi →, *Uruguay* 126 C4
Yi 'Allaq, G., *Egypt* 75 E2
Yi He →, *China* 57 G10
Yi Xian, *Anhui, China* 59 C11
Yi Xian, *Hebei, China* 56 E8
Yi Xian, *Liaoning, China* 57 D11
Yialí, *Greece* 39 E9
Yialiás →, *Cyprus* 36 D12
Yi'allaq, G., *Egypt* 80 A3
Yialousa, *Cyprus* 36 D13
Yiáltra, *Greece* 38 C4
Yianisádhes, *Greece* 36 D8
Yiannitsa, *Greece* 40 F6
Yibin, *China* 58 C5
Yichang, *China* 59 B8
Yicheng, *Henan, China* 59 B9
Yicheng, *Shanxi, China* 56 G6
Yichuan, *China* 56 F6
Yichun, *Heilongjiang, China* 60 B7
Yichun, *Jiangxi, China* 59 D10
Yidu, *China* 57 F10
Yidun, *China* 58 B2
Yifag, *Ethiopia* 81 E4
Yifeng, *China* 59 C10
Yihuang, *China* 59 D11
Yijun, *China* 56 G5
Yıldız Dağları, *Turkey* 41 E11
Yıldızeli, *Turkey* 72 C7
Yiliang, *Yunnan, China* 58 D5
Yiliang, *Yunnan, China* 58 E4
Yilong, *China* 58 B6
Yimen, *China* 58 E4
Yimianpo, *China* 57 B15
Yinchuan, *China* 56 E4
Yindarlgooda, L., *Australia* 93 F3
Ying He →, *China* 56 H9
Ying Xian, *China* 56 E7
Yingcheng, *China* 59 B9
Yingde, *China* 59 E9
Yingjiang, *China* 58 E1
Yingjing, *China* 58 C4
Yingkou, *China* 57 D12
Yingshan, *Henan, China* 59 B9
Yingshan, *Hubei, China* 59 B10
Yingshan, *Sichuan, China* 58 B6
Yingshang, *China* 59 A11
Yingtan, *China* 59 C11
Yining, *China* 50 E9
Yinjiang, *China* 58 C7
Yinmabin, *Burma* 67 H19
Yiofiros →, *Greece* 36 D7
Yioúra, *Nótios Aiyaíon, Greece* 38 D6
Yioúra, *Thessalía, Greece* 38 B6
Yipinglang, *China* 58 E3
Yirba Muda, *Ethiopia* 81 F4
Yirga Alem, *Ethiopia* 81 F4
Yirol, *Sudan* 81 F3
Yirrkala, *Australia* 94 A2
Yishan, *China* 58 E7
Yishui, *China* 57 G10
Yíthion, *Greece* 38 E4
Yitong, *China* 57 C13
Yiwu, *China* 59 C13
Yixing, *China* 59 B12
Yiyang, *Henan, China* 56 G7
Yiyang, *Hunan, China* 59 C9
Yiyang, *Jiangxi, China* 59 C11
Yizhang, *China* 59 E9
Yizheng, *China* 59 A12
Yli-Kitka, *Finland* 8 C23
Ylitornio, *Finland* 8 C20
Ylivieska, *Finland* 8 D21
Yngaren, *Sweden* 11 F10
Yoakum, *U.S.A.* 113 L6
Yobe □, *Nigeria* 83 C7
Yog Pt., *Phil.* 63 B6
Yogan, *Togo* 83 D5
Yoğuntaş, *Turkey* 41 E11
Yogyakarta, *Indonesia* 62 F4
Yoho Nat. Park, *Canada* 104 C5
Yojoa, L. de, *Honduras* 120 D2
Yŏju, *S. Korea* 57 F14
Yokadouma, *Cameroon* 84 D2
Yokkaichi, *Japan* 55 G8
Yoko, *Cameroon* 83 D7
Yokohama, *Japan* 55 G9
Yokosuka, *Japan* 55 G9
Yokote, *Japan* 54 E10
Yola, *Nigeria* 83 D7
Yolaina, Cordillera de, *Nic.* 120 D3
Yoloten, *Turkmenistan* 71 B9
Yom →, *Thailand* 62 A2
Yonago, *Japan* 55 G6
Yonaguni-Jima, *Japan* 55 M1
Yŏnan, *N. Korea* 57 F14
Yonezawa, *Japan* 54 F10
Yong Peng, *Malaysia* 65 L4
Yong Sata, *Thailand* 65 J2
Yongamp'o, *N. Korea* 57 E13
Yong'an, *China* 59 E11
Yongcheng, *China* 56 H9
Yŏngch'ŏn, *S. Korea* 57 G15
Yongchuan, *China* 58 C5
Yongchun, *China* 59 E12
Yongde, *China* 58 E2
Yongdeng, *China* 56 F2
Yongding, *China* 59 E11
Yŏngdŏk, *S. Korea* 57 F15
Yŏngdŭngpo, *S. Korea* 57 F14
Yongfeng, *China* 59 D10
Yongfu, *China* 58 E7
Yonghe, *China* 56 F6
Yŏnghŭng, *N. Korea* 57 E14
Yongji, *China* 56 G6
Yongjia, *China* 59 C13
Yŏngju, *S. Korea* 57 F15
Yongkang, *Yunnan, China* 58 E2
Yongkang, *Zhejiang, China* 59 C13
Yongnian, *China* 56 F8
Yongning, *Guangxi Zhuangzu, China* 58 F7
Yongning, *Ningxia Huizu, China* 56 E4
Yongping, *China* 58 E2
Yongqing, *China* 56 E9
Yongren, *China* 58 D3
Yongshan, *China* 58 C4
Yongsheng, *China* 58 D3
Yongshun, *China* 58 C7
Yongtai, *China* 59 E12
Yŏngwŏl, *S. Korea* 57 F15
Yongxin = Jinggangshan, *China* 59 D10
Yongxing, *China* 59 D9
Yongxiu, *China* 59 C10
Yongzhou, *China* 59 D8
Yonibana, *S. Leone* 82 D2
Yonkers, *U.S.A.* 111 F11
Yonne □, *France* 19 E10
Yonne →, *France* 19 D9
York, *Australia* 93 F2
York, *U.K.* 12 D6
York, *Ala., U.S.A.* 113 J10
York, *Nebr., U.S.A.* 112 E6
York, *Pa., U.S.A.* 108 F7
York, C., *Australia* 94 A3
York, City of □, *U.K.* 12 D6
York, Kap, *Greenland* 4 B4
York, Vale of, *U.K.* 12 C6
York Haven, *U.S.A.* 110 F8
York Sd., *Australia* 92 C4
Yorke Pen., *Australia* 95 E2
Yorkshire Wolds, *U.K.* 12 C7
Yorkton, *Canada* 105 C8
Yorkville, *U.S.A.* 116 G3
Yoro, *Honduras* 120 C2
Yoron-Jima, *Japan* 55 L4
Yorosso, *Mali* 82 C4
Yos Sudarso, Pulau = Dolak, Pulau, *Indonesia* 63 F9
Yosemite National Park, *U.S.A.* 116 H7
Yosemite Village, *U.S.A.* 116 H7
Yoshkar Ola, *Russia* 48 B8
Yŏsu, *S. Korea* 57 G14
Yotvata, *Israel* 75 F4
You Jiang →, *China* 58 F6
You Xian, *China* 59 D9
Youbou, *Canada* 116 B2
Youghal, *Ireland* 15 E4
Youghal B., *Ireland* 15 E4
Youkounkoun, *Guinea* 82 C2
Young, *Australia* 95 E4
Young, *Canada* 105 C7
Young, *Uruguay* 126 C4
Younghusband, L., *Australia* 95 E2
Younghusband Pen., *Australia* 95 F2
Youngstown, *Canada* 105 C6
Youngstown, *N.Y., U.S.A.* 110 C5
Youngstown, *Ohio, U.S.A.* 110 E4
Youngsville, *U.S.A.* 110 E5
Youngwood, *U.S.A.* 110 F5
Youxi, *China* 59 D12
Youyang, *China* 58 C7
Youyu, *China* 56 D7
Yozgat, *Turkey* 72 C6
Ypané →, *Paraguay* 126 A4
Yport, *France* 18 C7
Ypres = Ieper, *Belgium* 17 D2
Yreka, *U.S.A.* 114 F2
Yssingeaux, *France* 21 C8
Ystad, *Sweden* 11 J7
Ysyk-Köl, *Kyrgyzstan* 50 E8
Ythan →, *U.K.* 14 D7
Ytterhogdal, *Sweden* 10 B8
Ytyk-Kyuyel, *Russia* 51 C14
Yu Jiang →, *China* 58 F7
Yu Xian = Yuzhou, *China* 56 G7
Yu Xian, *Hebei, China* 56 E8
Yu Xian, *Shanxi, China* 56 E7
Yuan Jiang →, *Hunan, China* 59 C8
Yuan Jiang →, *Yunnan, China* 58 F4
Yuan'an, *China* 59 B8
Yuanjiang, *Hunan, China* 59 C9
Yuanjiang, *Yunnan, China* 58 F4
Yüanli, *Taiwan* 59 E13
Yüanlin, *Taiwan* 59 F13
Yuanling, *China* 59 C8
Yuanmou, *China* 58 E3
Yuanqu, *China* 56 G6
Yuanyang, *Henan, China* 56 G7
Yuanyang, *Yunnan, China* 58 F4
Yuba →, *U.S.A.* 116 F5
Yuba City, *U.S.A.* 116 F5
Yūbari, *Japan* 54 C10
Yubdo, *Ethiopia* 81 F4
Yūbetsu, *Japan* 54 B11
Yubo, *Sudan* 81 F2
Yucatán □, *Mexico* 119 C7
Yucatán, Canal de, *Caribbean* 120 B2
Yucatán, Península de, *Mexico* 98 H11
Yucatán Basin, *Cent. Amer.* 98 H11
Yucatan Str. = Yucatán, Canal de, *Caribbean* 120 B2
Yucca, *U.S.A.* 117 L12
Yucca Valley, *U.S.A.* 117 L10
Yucheng, *China* 56 F9
Yuci, *China* 56 F7
Yudu, *China* 59 E10
Yuechi, *China* 58 B6
Yuendumu, *Australia* 92 D5
Yueqing, *China* 59 C13
Yueqing Wan, *China* 59 D13
Yuexi, *Anhui, China* 59 B11
Yuexi, *Sichuan, China* 58 C4
Yueyang, *China* 59 C9
Yugan, *China* 59 C11
Yugoslavia ■, *Europe* 40 C4
Yuhuan, *China* 59 C13
Yuhuan Dao, *China* 59 C13
Yujiang, *China* 59 C11
Yukhnov, *Russia* 46 E8
Yukon →, *U.S.A.* 100 B3
Yukon Territory □, *Canada* 100 B6
Yüksekova, *Turkey* 73 D11
Yukta, *Russia* 51 C11
Yukuhashi, *Japan* 55 H5
Yulara, *Australia* 93 E5
Yule →, *Australia* 92 D2
Yuleba, *Australia* 95 D4
Yuli, *Nigeria* 83 D7
Yuli, *Taiwan* 59 F13
Yulin, *Guangxi Zhuangzu, China* 59 F8
Yülin, *Hainan, China* 65 C7
Yulin, *Shaanxi, China* 56 E5
Yuma, *Ariz., U.S.A.* 117 N12
Yuma, *Colo., U.S.A.* 112 E3
Yuma, B. de, *Dom. Rep.* 121 C6
Yumbe, *Uganda* 86 B3
Yumbi, *Dem. Rep. of the Congo* 86 C2
Yumen, *China* 60 C4
Yumurtalık, *Turkey* 72 D6
Yun Gui Gaoyuan, *China* 58 E3
Yun Ho →, *China* 57 E9
Yun Ling, *China* 58 D2
Yun Xian, *Hubei, China* 59 A8
Yun Xian, *Yunnan, China* 58 E3
Yuna, *Australia* 93 E2
Yunak, *Turkey* 72 C4
Yunan, *China* 59 F8
Yuncheng, *Henan, China* 56 G8
Yuncheng, *Shanxi, China* 56 G6
Yunfu, *China* 59 F9
Yungas, *Bolivia* 124 G5
Yungay, *Chile* 126 D1
Yunhe, *China* 59 C12
Yunkai Dashan, *China* 59 F8
Yunlin, *Taiwan* 59 F13
Yunlong, *China* 58 E2
Yunmeng, *China* 59 B9
Yunnan □, *China* 58 E4
Yunquera de Henares, *Spain* 32 E1
Yunt Dağı, *Turkey* 39 C9
Yunta, *Australia* 95 E2
Yunxi, *China* 56 H6
Yunxiao, *China* 59 F11
Yuping, *China* 58 D7
Yupyongdong, *N. Korea* 57 D15
Yuqing, *China* 58 D6
Yurga, *Russia* 50 D9
Yurimaguas, *Peru* 124 E3
Yuryev-Polskiy, *Russia* 46 D10
Yuryevets, *Russia* 48 B6
Yuscarán, *Honduras* 120 D2
Yushan, *China* 59 C12
Yushanzhen, *China* 58 C7
Yushe, *China* 56 F7
Yushu, *Jilin, China* 57 B14
Yushu, *Qinghai, China* 60 C4
Yusufeli, *Turkey* 73 B9
Yutai, *China* 56 G9
Yutian, *China* 57 E9
Yuxarı Qarabağ = Nagorno-Karabakh, *Azerbaijan* 70 B5
Yuxi, *China* 58 E4
Yuyao, *China* 59 B13
Yuzawa, *Japan* 54 E10
Yuzha, *Russia* 48 B6
Yuzhno-Sakhalinsk, *Russia* 51 E15
Yuzhou, *China* 56 G7
Yvelines □, *France* 19 D8
Yverdon-les-Bains, *Switz.* 25 J2
Yvetot, *France* 18 C7
Yzeure, *France* 19 F10

Z

Zaanstad, *Neths.* 17 B4
Zāb al Kabīr →, *Iraq* 70 C4
Zāb aş Şagīr →, *Iraq* 70 C4
Žabalj, *Serbia, Yug.* 42 E5
Žabari, *Serbia, Yug.* 40 B5
Zabarjad, *Egypt* 80 C4

Zabaykalsk, *Russia* 51 E12
Zabki, *Poland* 45 F8
Ząbkowice Śląskie, *Poland* 45 H3
Žabljak, *Montenegro, Yug.* 40 C3
Zabłudów, *Poland* 45 F9
Žabno, *Poland* 45 H7
Zābol, *Iran* 71 D9
Zābol □, *Afghan.* 66 D5
Zābolī, *Iran* 71 E9
Zabré, *Burkina Faso* 83 C4
Zábřeh, *Czech Rep.* 27 B9
Zabrze, *Poland* 45 H5
Zabzuga, *Ghana* 83 D5
Zacapa, *Guatemala* 120 D2
Zacapu, *Mexico* 118 D4
Zacatecas, *Mexico* 118 C4
Zacatecas □, *Mexico* 118 C4
Zacatecoluca, *El Salv.* 120 D2
Zachary, *U.S.A.* 113 K9
Zachodnio-Pomorskie □, *Poland* 44 E2
Zacoalco, *Mexico* 118 C4
Zacualtipán, *Mexico* 119 C5
Zadar, *Croatia* 29 D12
Zadawa, *Nigeria* 83 C7
Zadetkyi Kyun, *Burma* 65 G1
Zadonsk, *Russia* 47 F10
Zafarqand, *Iran* 71 C7
Zafora, *Greece* 39 E8
Zafra, *Spain* 35 G4
Żagań, *Poland* 45 G2
Zagaoua, *Chad* 79 E10
Žagarė, *Lithuania* 44 B10
Zagazig, *Egypt* 80 H7
Zāgheh, *Iran* 71 C6
Zaglivérion, *Greece* 40 F7
Zagnanado, *Benin* 83 D5
Zagorá, *Greece* 38 B5
Zagorje, *Slovenia* 29 B11
Zagórów, *Poland* 45 F4
Zagorsk = Sergiyev Posad, *Russia* 46 D10
Zagórz, *Poland* 45 J9
Zagreb, *Croatia* 29 C12
Zāgros, Kūhhā-ye, *Iran* 71 C6
Zagros Mts. = Zāgros, Kūhhā-ye, *Iran* 71 C6
Žagubica, *Serbia, Yug.* 40 B5
Zaguinaso, *Ivory C.* 82 C3
Zagyva →, *Hungary* 42 C5
Zāhedān, *Fārs, Iran* 71 D7
Zāhedān, *Sīstān va Balūchestān, Iran* 71 D9
Zahlah, *Lebanon* 75 B4
Zahna, *Germany* 24 D8
Záhony, *Hungary* 42 B7
Zainsk, *Russia* 48 C11
Zaïre = Congo →, *Africa* 84 F2
Zaječar, *Serbia, Yug.* 40 C6
Zaka, *Zimbabwe* 89 C5
Zakamensk, *Russia* 51 D11
Zakataly = Zaqatala, *Azerbaijan* 49 K8
Zakháro, *Greece* 38 D3
Zakhodnaya Dzvina = Daugava →, *Latvia* 9 H21
Zākhū, *Iraq* 70 B4
Zákinthos, *Greece* 38 D2
Zákinthos □, *Greece* 38 D2
Zakopane, *Poland* 45 J6
Zakroczym, *Poland* 45 F7
Zákros, *Greece* 36 D8
Zala, *Ethiopia* 81 F4
Zala □, *Hungary* 42 D1
Zala →, *Hungary* 42 D2
Zalaegerszeg, *Hungary* 42 D1
Zalakomár, *Hungary* 42 D2
Zalalövő, *Hungary* 42 D1
Zalamea de la Serena, *Spain* 35 G5
Zalamea la Real, *Spain* 35 H4
Zalău, *Romania* 42 C8
Žalec, *Slovenia* 29 B12
Zaleshchiki = Zalishchyky, *Ukraine* 47 H3
Zalew Wiślany, *Poland* 44 D6
Zalewo, *Poland* 44 E6
Zalingei, *Sudan* 79 F10
Zalishchyky, *Ukraine* 47 H3
Zama L., *Canada* 104 B5
Zambeke, *Dem. Rep. of the Congo* 86 B2
Zambeze →, *Africa* 87 F4
Zambezi = Zambeze →, *Africa* 87 F4
Zambezi, *Zambia* 85 G4
Zambezia □, *Mozam.* 87 F4
Zambia ■, *Africa* 87 F2
Zamboanga, *Phil.* 61 H5
Zambrów, *Poland* 45 F9
Zametchino, *Russia* 48 D6
Zamfara □, *Nigeria* 83 C6
Zamfara →, *Nigeria* 83 C5
Zamora, *Mexico* 118 D4
Zamora, *Spain* 34 D5
Zamora □, *Spain* 34 D5
Zamość, *Poland* 45 H10
Zamtang, *China* 58 A3
Zan, *Ghana* 83 D4
Záncara →, *Spain* 33 F1
Zandvoort, *Neths.* 17 B4
Zanesville, *U.S.A.* 110 G2
Zangābād, *Iran* 70 B5
Zangue →, *Mozam.* 87 F4
Zanjān, *Iran* 71 B6
Zanjān □, *Iran* 71 B6
Zanjān →, *Iran* 71 B6
Zannone, *Italy* 30 B6
Zante = Zákinthos, *Greece* 38 D2
Zanthus, *Australia* 93 F3
Zanzibar, *Tanzania* 86 D4
Zaouiet El-Kala = Bordj Omar Driss, *Algeria* 78 C7
Zaouiet Reggâne, *Algeria* 78 C6
Zaoyang, *China* 59 A9
Zaozhuang, *China* 57 G9
Zap Suyu = Zāb al Kabīr →, *Iraq* 70 C4
Zapadna Morava →, *Serbia, Yug.* 40 C5
Zapadnaya Dvina = Daugava →, *Latvia* 9 H21
Zapadnaya Dvina, *Russia* 46 D7
Západné Beskydy, *Europe* 27 B12
Zapadni Rodopi, *Bulgaria* 40 E7
Zapala, *Argentina* 128 D2
Zapaleri, Cerro, *Bolivia* 126 A2
Zapata, *U.S.A.* 113 M5
Zapatón →, *Spain* 35 F4
Zaporizhzhya, *Ukraine* 47 J8
Zaporozhye = Zaporizhzhya, *Ukraine* 47 J8
Zaqatala, *Azerbaijan* 49 K8
Zara, *Turkey* 70 B3
Zaragoza, *Coahuila, Mexico* 118 B4
Zaragoza, *Nuevo León, Mexico* 119 C5
Zaragoza, *Spain* 32 D4
Zaragoza □, *Spain* 32 D4
Zarand, *Kermān, Iran* 71 D8
Zarand, *Markazī, Iran* 71 C6
Zărandului, Munții, *Romania* 42 D7
Zaranj, *Afghan.* 66 D2
Zarasai, *Lithuania* 9 J22
Zarate, *Argentina* 126 C4
Zarautz, *Spain* 32 B2
Zaraysk, *Russia* 46 E10
Zard, Kūh-e, *Iran* 71 C6
Zāreh, *Iran* 71 C6
Zari, *Nigeria* 83 C7
Zaria, *Nigeria* 83 C6
Żarki, *Poland* 45 H6
Zárkon, *Greece* 38 B4
Zarneh, *Iran* 70 C5
Zărnești, *Romania* 43 E10
Zarós, *Greece* 36 D6
Żarów, *Poland* 45 H3
Zarqā', Nahr az →, *Jordan* 75 C4
Zarrīn, *Iran* 71 C7
Zaruma, *Ecuador* 124 D3
Żary, *Poland* 45 G2
Zarza de Granadilla, *Spain* 34 E4
Zarzis, *Tunisia* 79 B8
Zas, *Spain* 34 B2
Zaskar →, *India* 69 B7
Zaskar Mts., *India* 69 C7
Zastron, *S. Africa* 88 E4
Žatec, *Czech Rep.* 26 A6
Zaterechnyy, *Russia* 49 H7
Zator, *Poland* 45 J6
Zavala, *Bos.-H.* 40 D1
Zavāreh, *Iran* 71 C7
Zave, *Zimbabwe* 89 B5
Zavetnoye, *Russia* 49 G6
Zavidovići, *Bos.-H.* 42 F3
Zavitinsk, *Russia* 51 D13
Zavodovski, I., *Antarctica* 5 B1
Zavolzhsk, *Russia* 48 B6
Zavolzhye, *Russia* 48 B6
Zawadzkie, *Poland* 45 H5
Zawichost, *Poland* 45 H8
Zawidów, *Poland* 45 G2
Zawiercie, *Poland* 45 H6
Zāwiyat al Bayḍā = Al Bayḍā, *Libya* 79 B10
Zâwyet Shammas, *Egypt* 80 A2
Zâwyet Um el Rakham, *Egypt* 80 A2
Zâwyet Ungeîla, *Egypt* 80 A2
Zāyā, *Iraq* 70 C5
Zāyandeh →, *Iran* 71 C7
Zaysan, *Kazakstan* 50 E9
Zaysan, Oz., *Kazakstan* 50 E9
Zayü, *China* 58 C1
Zazafotsy, *Madag.* 89 C8
Zázrivá, *Slovak Rep.* 27 B12
Zbarazh, *Ukraine* 47 H3
Zbąszyń, *Poland* 45 F2
Zbąszynek, *Poland* 45 F2
Zblewo, *Poland* 44 E5
Žďár nad Sázavou, *Czech Rep.* 26 B8
Zdolbuniv, *Ukraine* 47 G4
Ždrelo, *Serbia, Yug.* 40 B5
Zduńska Wola, *Poland* 45 G5
Zduny, *Poland* 45 G4
Zeballos, *Canada* 104 D3
Zebediela, *S. Africa* 89 C4
Zebila, *Ghana* 83 C4
Zeebrugge, *Belgium* 17 C3
Zeehan, *Australia* 94 G4
Zeeland □, *Neths.* 17 C3
Zeerust, *S. Africa* 88 D4
Zefat, *Israel* 75 C4
Zege, *Ethiopia* 81 E4
Zeggerene, Iracher, *Mali* 83 B5
Zégoua, *Mali* 82 C3
Zehdenick, *Germany* 24 C9
Zeil, Mt., *Australia* 92 D5
Zeila, *Somali Rep.* 74 E3
Zeist, *Neths.* 17 B5
Zeitz, *Germany* 24 D8
Zelechów, *Poland* 45 G8
Zelengora, *Bos.-H.* 40 C2
Zelenodolsk, *Russia* 48 C9
Zelenogorsk, *Russia* 46 B5
Zelenograd, *Russia* 46 D9
Zelenogradsk, *Russia* 9 J19
Zelenokumsk, *Russia* 49 H6
Železná Ruda, *Czech Rep.* 26 B6
Železnik, *Serbia, Yug.* 40 B4
Zelienople, *U.S.A.* 110 F4
Želiezovce, *Slovak Rep.* 27 C11
Zelina, *Croatia* 29 C13
Zell, *Baden-W., Germany* 25 H3
Zell, *Rhld-Pfz., Germany* 25 E3
Zell am See, *Austria* 26 D5
Zella-Mehlis, *Germany* 24 E6
Zelów, *Poland* 45 G6
Zeltweg, *Austria* 26 D7
Zémio, *C.A.R.* 86 A2
Zempléni-hegység, *Hungary* 42 B6
Zemplínska šírava, *Slovak Rep.* 27 C15
Zemun, *Serbia, Yug.* 40 B4
Zengbé, *Cameroon* 83 D7
Zengcheng, *China* 59 F9
Zenica, *Bos.-H.* 42 F2
Žepče, *Bos.-H.* 42 F3
Zeraf, Bahr ez →, *Sudan* 81 F3
Zerbst, *Germany* 24 D8
Żerków, *Poland* 45 F4
Zermatt, *Switz.* 25 J3
Zernez, *Switz.* 25 J6
Zernograd, *Russia* 49 G5
Zerqan, *Albania* 40 E4
Zestaponi, *Georgia* 49 J6
Zetel, *Germany* 24 B3
Zeulenroda, *Germany* 24 E7
Zeven, *Germany* 24 B5
Zevenaar, *Neths.* 17 C6
Zévio, *Italy* 28 C8
Zeya, *Russia* 51 D13
Zeya →, *Russia* 51 D13
Zeytinbaği, *Turkey* 41 F12
Zeytindağ, *Turkey* 39 C9
Zghartā, *Lebanon* 75 A4
Zgierz, *Poland* 45 G6
Zgorzelec, *Poland* 45 G2
Zgurița, *Moldova* 43 B13
Zhabinka, *Belarus* 47 F3
Zhailma, *Kazakstan* 50 D7
Zhambyl = Taraz, *Kazakstan* 50 E8
Zhangaly, *Kazakstan* 49 G10
Zhangaqazaly, *Kazakstan* 50 E7
Zhangbei, *China* 56 D8
Zhangguangcai Ling, *China* 57 B15
Zhangjiakou, *China* 56 D8
Zhangping, *China* 59 E11
Zhangpu, *China* 59 E11
Zhangshu, *China* 59 C10
Zhangwu, *China* 57 C12
Zhangye, *China* 60 C5
Zhangzhou, *China* 59 E11
Zhanhua, *China* 57 F10
Zhanjiang, *China* 59 G8
Zhannetty, Ostrov, *Russia* 51 B16
Zhanyi, *China* 58 E4
Zhanyu, *China* 57 B12
Zhao Xian, *China* 56 F8
Zhao'an, *China* 59 F11
Zhaocheng, *China* 56 F6
Zhaojue, *China* 58 C4
Zhaoping, *China* 59 E8
Zhaoqing, *China* 59 F9
Zhaotong, *China* 58 D4
Zhaoyuan, *Heilongjiang, China* 57 B13
Zhaoyuan, *Shandong, China* 57 F11
Zharkovskiy, *Russia* 46 E7
Zhashkiv, *Ukraine* 47 H6
Zhashui, *China* 56 H5
Zhayyq →, *Kazakstan* 50 E6
Zhdanov = Mariupol, *Ukraine* 47 J9
Zhecheng, *China* 56 G8
Zhegao, *China* 59 B11
Zhejiang □, *China* 59 C13
Zheleznogorsk, *Russia* 47 F8
Zheleznogorsk-Ilimskiy, *Russia* 51 D11
Zheltyye Vody = Zhovti Vody, *Ukraine* 47 H7
Zhen'an, *China* 56 H5
Zhenba, *China* 58 A6
Zhenfeng, *China* 58 E5
Zheng'an, *China* 58 C6
Zhengding, *China* 56 E8
Zhenghe, *China* 59 D12
Zhengyang, *China* 59 A10
Zhengyangguan, *China* 59 A11
Zhengzhou, *China* 56 G7
Zhenhai, *China* 59 C13
Zhenjiang, *China* 59 A12
Zhenkang, *China* 58 F2
Zhenlai, *China* 57 B12
Zhenning, *China* 58 D5
Zhenping, *Henan, China* 56 H7
Zhenping, *Shaanxi, China* 58 B7
Zhenxiong, *China* 58 D5
Zhenyuan, *Gansu, China* 56 G4
Zhenyuan, *Guizhou, China* 58 D7
Zherdevka, *Russia* 48 E5
Zherong, *China* 59 D12
Zhetiqara, *Kazakstan* 50 D7
Zhezqazghan, *Kazakstan* 50 E7
Zhicheng, *China* 59 B8
Zhidan, *China* 56 F5
Zhigansk, *Russia* 51 C13
Zhigulevsk, *Russia* 48 D9
Zhijiang, *Hubei, China* 59 B8
Zhijiang, *Hunan, China* 58 D7
Zhijin, *China* 58 D5
Zhilinda, *Russia* 51 C12
Zhirnovsk, *Russia* 48 E7
Zhitomir = Zhytomyr, *Ukraine* 47 G5
Zhizdra, *Russia* 46 F8
Zhlobin, *Belarus* 47 F6
Zhmerinka = Zhmerynka, *Ukraine* 47 H5
Zhmerynka, *Ukraine* 47 H5
Zhob, *Pakistan* 68 D3
Zhob →, *Pakistan* 68 C3
Zhodino = Zhodzina, *Belarus* 46 E5
Zhodzina, *Belarus* 46 E5
Zhokhova, Ostrov, *Russia* 51 B16
Zhongdian, *China* 58 D2
Zhongdong, *China* 58 F6
Zhongdu, *China* 58 E7
Zhongning, *China* 56 F3
Zhongshan, *Guangdong, China* 59 F9
Zhongshan, *Guangxi Zhuangzu, China* 59 E8
Zhongtiao Shan, *China* 56 G6
Zhongwei, *China* 56 F3
Zhongxiang, *China* 59 B9
Zhongyang, *China* 56 F6
Zhoucun, *China* 57 F9
Zhouning, *China* 59 D12
Zhoushan, *China* 59 B14
Zhoushan Dao, *China* 59 C14
Zhouzhi, *China* 56 G5
Zhovti Vody, *Ukraine* 47 H7
Zhovtneve, *Ukraine* 47 J7
Zhovtnevoye = Zhovtneve, *Ukraine* 47 J7
Zhu Jiang →, *China* 59 F9
Zhuanghe, *China* 57 E12
Zhucheng, *China* 57 G10
Zhugqu, *China* 56 H3
Zhuhai, *China* 59 F9
Zhuji, *China* 59 C13
Zhukovka, *Russia* 46 F7
Zhumadian, *China* 56 H8
Zhuo Xian = Zhuozhou, *China* 56 E8
Zhuolu, *China* 56 D8
Zhuozhou, *China* 56 E8
Zhuozi, *China* 56 D7
Zhushan, *China* 59 A8
Zhuxi, *China* 58 A7
Zhuzhou, *China* 59 D9
Zhytomyr, *Ukraine* 47 G5
Zi Shui →, *China* 59 C9
Žiar nad Hronom, *Slovak Rep.* 27 C11
Zīārān, *Iran* 71 B6
Ziarat, *Pakistan* 68 D2
Zibo, *China* 57 F10
Zichang, *China* 56 F5
Zidarovo, *Bulgaria* 41 D11
Ziębice, *Poland* 45 H4
Zielona Góra, *Poland* 45 G2
Zierikzee, *Neths.* 17 C3
Ziesar, *Germany* 24 C8
Zifta, *Egypt* 80 H7
Zigey, *Chad* 79 F9
Zigong, *China* 58 C5
Ziguinchor, *Senegal* 82 C1
Zihuatanejo, *Mexico* 118 D4
Zijin, *China* 59 F10
Zile, *Turkey* 72 B6
Žilina, *Slovak Rep.* 27 B11
Žilinský □, *Slovak Rep.* 27 B12
Zillah, *Libya* 79 C9
Zillertaler Alpen, *Austria* 26 D4
Zima, *Russia* 51 D11
Zimapán, *Mexico* 119 C5
Zimba, *Zambia* 87 F2
Zimbabwe, *Zimbabwe* 87 G3
Zimbabwe ■, *Africa* 87 F3
Zimi, *S. Leone* 82 D2
Zimnicea, *Romania* 43 G10
Zimovniki, *Russia* 49 G6
Zinder, *Niger* 83 C6
Zinga, *Tanzania* 87 D4
Zingst, *Germany* 24 A8
Ziniaré, *Burkina Faso* 83 C4
Zinnowitz, *Germany* 24 A9
Zion National Park, *U.S.A.* 115 H7
Zirbitzkogel, *Austria* 26 D7
Zirc, *Hungary* 42 C2
Žiri, *Slovenia* 29 B11
Žirje, *Croatia* 29 E12
Zirl, *Austria* 26 D4
Zirndorf, *Germany* 25 F6
Ziros, *Greece* 36 D8
Zirreh, Gowd-e, *Afghan.* 66 E3
Zisterdorf, *Austria* 27 C9
Zitácuaro, *Mexico* 118 D4
Žitava →, *Slovak Rep.* 27 C11
Žitište, *Serbia, Yug.* 42 E5
Zitong, *China* 58 B5
Zítsa, *Greece* 38 B2
Zittau, *Germany* 24 E10
Zitundo, *Mozam.* 89 D5
Živinice, *Bos.-H.* 42 F3
Ziwa Magharibi □, *Tanzania* 86 C3
Ziway, L., *Ethiopia* 81 F4
Zixi, *China* 59 D11
Zixing, *China* 59 E9
Ziyang, *Shaanxi, China* 56 H5
Ziyang, *Sichuan, China* 58 B5
Ziyuan, *China* 59 D8
Ziyun, *China* 58 E6
Zizhong, *China* 58 C5
Zlarin, *Croatia* 29 E12
Zlatar, *Croatia* 29 B13
Zlatar, *Serbia, Yug.* 40 C3
Zlataritsa, *Bulgaria* 41 C9
Zlaté Moravce, *Slovak Rep.* 27 C11
Zlatibor, *Serbia, Yug.* 40 C3
Zlatitsa, *Bulgaria* 41 D8
Zlatna, *Romania* 43 D8
Zlatna Panega, *Bulgaria* 41 C8
Zlatni Pyasŭtsi, *Bulgaria* 41 C12
Zlatograd, *Bulgaria* 41 E9
Zlatoust, *Russia* 50 D6
Zletovo, *Macedonia* 40 E6
Zlín, *Czech Rep.* 27 B10
Zlínský □, *Czech Rep.* 27 B10
Złocieniec, *Poland* 44 E3
Złoczew, *Poland* 45 G5
Zlot, *Serbia, Yug.* 40 B5
Złotoryja, *Poland* 45 G2
Złotów, *Poland* 44 E4
Zmeinogorsk, *Kazakstan* 50 D9
Żmigród, *Poland* 45 G3
Zmiyev, *Ukraine* 47 H9
Znamenka = Znamyanka, *Ukraine* 47 H7
Znamyanka, *Ukraine* 47 H7
Żnin, *Poland* 45 F4
Znojmo, *Czech Rep.* 26 C9
Zobeyrī, *Iran* 70 C5
Zobia, *Dem. Rep. of the Congo* 86 B2
Zoetermeer, *Neths.* 17 B4
Zogang, *China* 58 C1
Zogno, *Italy* 28 C6
Zogqên, *China* 58 A2
Zolochev = Zolochiv, *Ukraine* 47 H3
Zolochiv, *Ukraine* 47 H3
Zolotonosha, *Ukraine* 47 H7
Zomba, *Malawi* 87 F4
Zongo, *Dem. Rep. of the Congo* 84 D3
Zonguldak, *Turkey* 72 B4
Zongyang, *China* 59 B11
Zonqor Pt., *Malta* 36 D2
Zonza, *France* 21 G13
Zorgo, *Burkina Faso* 83 C4
Zorita, *Spain* 35 F5
Zorleni, *Romania* 43 D12
Zornitsa, *Bulgaria* 41 D10
Zorritos, *Peru* 124 D2
Żory, *Poland* 45 H5
Zorzor, *Liberia* 82 D3
Zossen, *Germany* 24 C9
Zou Xiang, *China* 56 G9
Zouan-Hounien, *Ivory C.* 82 D3
Zouar, *Chad* 79 D9
Zouérate = Zouîrât, *Mauritania* 78 D3
Zouîrât, *Mauritania* 78 D3
Zourika, *Niger* 83 B6
Zourma, *Burkina Faso* 83 C4
Zoushan Dao, *China* 59 B14
Zoutkamp, *Neths.* 17 A6
Zrenjanin, *Serbia, Yug.* 42 E5
Zuarungu, *Ghana* 83 C4
Zuba, *Nigeria* 83 D6
Zubayr, *Yemen* 81 D5
Zubtsov, *Russia* 46 D8
Zuénoula, *Ivory C.* 82 D3
Zuera, *Spain* 32 D4
Zufār, *Oman* 74 D5
Zug □, *Switz.* 25 H4
Zugdidi, *Georgia* 49 J5
Zugersee, *Switz.* 25 H4
Zugspitze, *Germany* 25 H6
Zuid-Holland □, *Neths.* 17 C4
Zuidbeveland, *Neths.* 17 C3
Zuidhorn, *Neths.* 17 A6
Zújar, *Spain* 35 H8
Zújar →, *Spain* 35 G5
Żukowo, *Poland* 44 D5
Zula, *Eritrea* 81 D4
Zülpich, *Germany* 24 E2
Zumaia, *Spain* 32 B2
Zumárraga, *Spain* 32 B2
Zumbo, *Mozam.* 87 F3
Zummo, *Nigeria* 83 D7
Zumpango, *Mexico* 119 D5
Zungeru, *Nigeria* 83 D6
Zunhua, *China* 57 D9
Zuni, *U.S.A.* 115 J9
Zunyi, *China* 58 D6
Zuo Jiang →, *China* 58 F6
Zuozhou, *China* 58 F6
Županja, *Croatia* 42 E3
Žur, *Kosovo, Yug.* 40 D4
Zurbātīyah, *Iraq* 70 C5
Zürich, *Switz.* 25 H4
Zürich □, *Switz.* 25 H4
Zürichsee, *Switz.* 25 H4
Żuromin, *Poland* 45 E6
Žut, *Croatia* 29 E12
Zutphen, *Neths.* 17 B6
Zuwārah, *Libya* 79 B8
Zūzan, *Iran* 71 C8
Žužemberk, *Slovenia* 29 C11
Zvenigorodka = Zvenyhorodka, *Ukraine* 47 H6
Zvenyhorodka, *Ukraine* 47 H6
Zverinogolovskoye, *Russia* 50 D7
Zvezdets, *Bulgaria* 41 D11
Zvishavane, *Zimbabwe* 87 G3
Zvolen, *Slovak Rep.* 27 C12
Zvonce, *Serbia, Yug.* 40 D6
Zvornik, *Bos.-H.* 42 F4
Zwedru = Tchien, *Liberia* 82 D3
Zweibrücken, *Germany* 25 F3
Zwenkau, *Germany* 24 D8
Zwettl, *Austria* 26 C8
Zwickau, *Germany* 24 E8
Zwierzyniec, *Poland* 45 H9
Zwiesel, *Germany* 25 F9
Zwoleń, *Poland* 45 G8
Zwolle, *Neths.* 17 B6
Zwolle, *U.S.A.* 113 K8
Żychlin, *Poland* 45 F6
Żyrardów, *Poland* 45 F7
Zyryan, *Kazakstan* 50 E9
Zyryanka, *Russia* 51 C16
Zyryanovsk = Zyryan, *Kazakstan* 50 E9
Żywiec, *Poland* 45 J6
Zyyi, *Cyprus* 36 E12

Key to World Map Pages

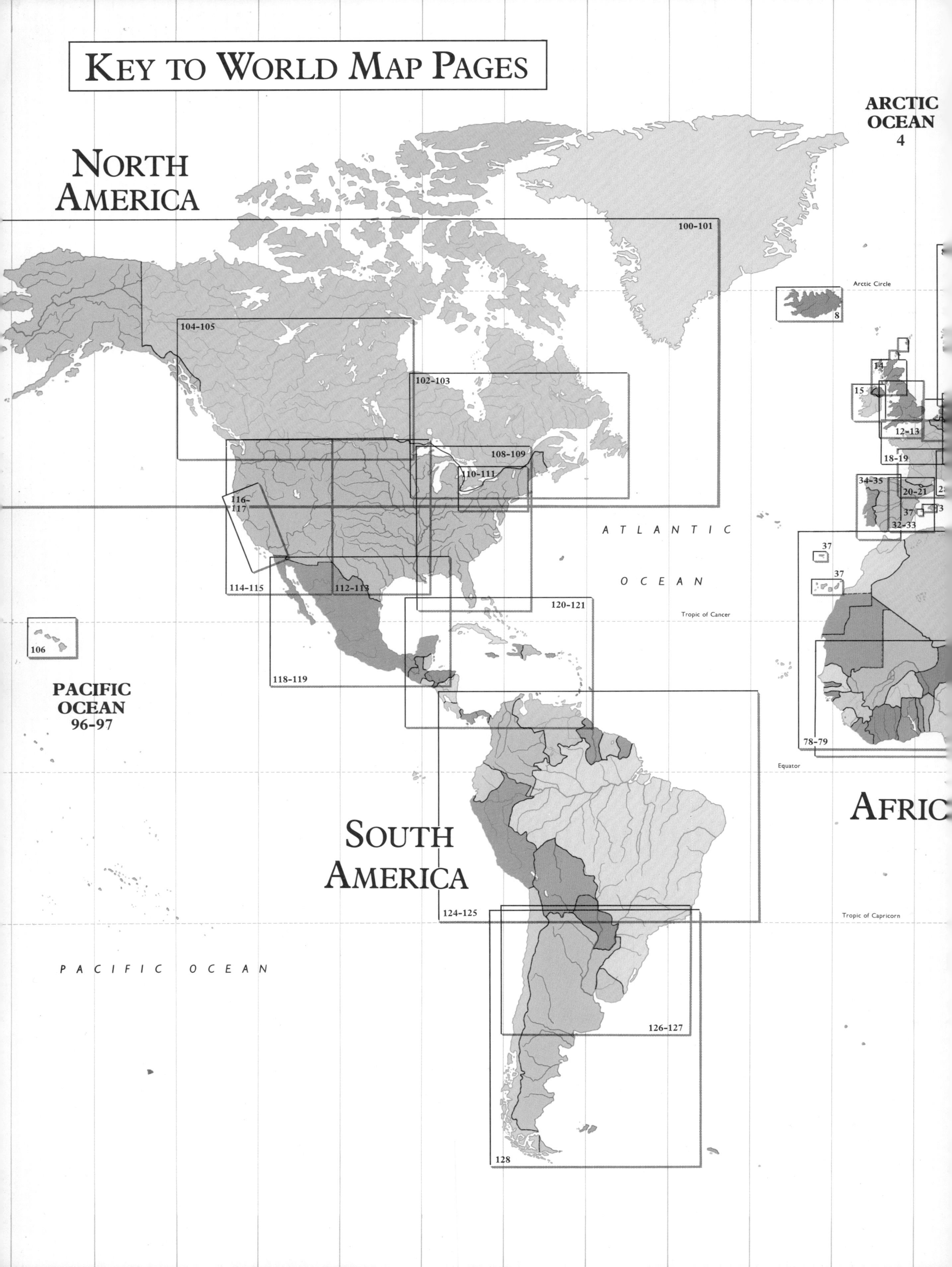

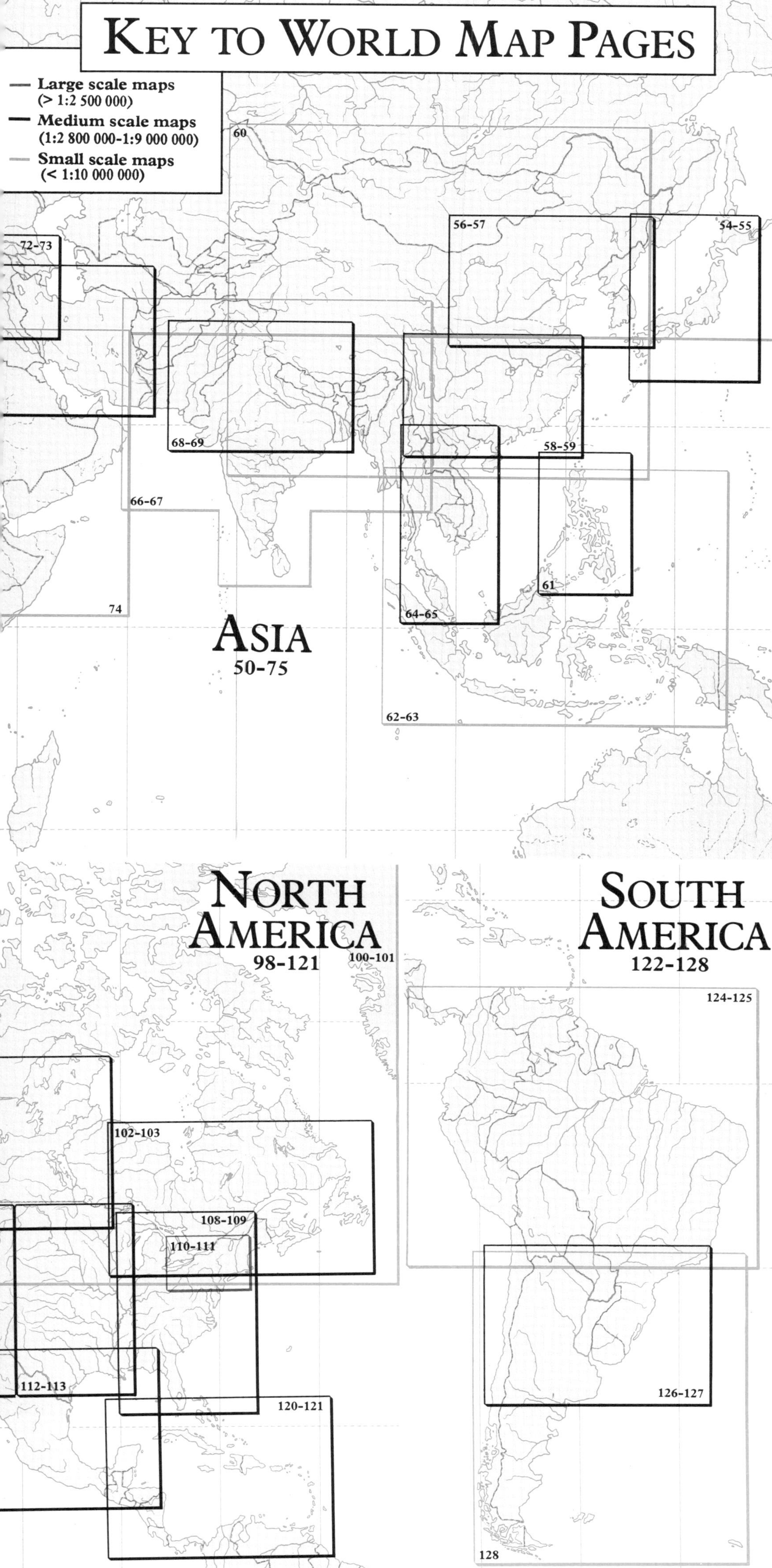

COUNTRY INDEX

Afghanistan 66
Albania 40
Algeria 78
Angola 84–85
Argentina 126, 128
Armenia 73
Australia 92-95
Austria 26-27
Azerbaijan 73

Bahamas 120–121
Bahrain 71
Bangladesh 67
Barbados 121
Belarus 46–47
Belgium 17
Belize 120
Benin 83
Bhutan 67
Bolivia 124
Bosnia-Herzegovina 29, 40
Botswana 88-89
Brazil 124–127
Brunei 78
Bulgaria 40–41
Burkina Faso 82–83
Burma 67
Burundi 86

Cambodia 64–65
Cameroon 84
Canada 100–101
Central African Republic 84
Chad 79
Chile 124, 128
China 56–60
Colombia 124
Congo 84
Congo, Dem. Rep. of the 84–85
Costa Rica 120
Croatia 29, 42
Cuba 120–121
Cyprus 36
Czech Republic 26–27

Denmark 11
Djibouti 74
Dominican Republic 121

Ecuador 124
Egypt 80
El Salvador 120
England 12–13
Equatorial Guinea 84
Eritrea 80–81
Estonia 46
Ethiopia 74, 81

Fiji 91
Finland 8–9
France 18–21
French Guiana 125

Gabon 84
Gambia 82
Georgia 73
Germany 24–25
Ghana 82-83
Greece 38–41
Greenland 4
Guatemala 120
Guinea 82
Guinea-Bissau 82
Guyana 124

Haiti 121
Honduras 120
Hungary 42

Iceland 8
India 66–69
Indonesia 62–63
Iran 70–71
Iraq 70–71
Irish Republic 15
Israel 75
Italy 28–31
Ivory Coast 82

Jamaica 120
Japan 54–55
Jordan 75

Kazakstan 50
Kenya 86
Korea, North 57
Korea, South 57
Kuwait 70–71
Kyrgyzstan 50

Laos 64
Latvia 46
Lebanon 75
Lesotho 88–89
Liberia 82
Libya 79
Lithuania 46
Luxembourg 17

Macedonia 40
Madagascar 89
Malawi 87
Malaysia 62–63
Mali 78, 82–83
Malta 36
Mauritania 78, 82
Mauritius 77
Mexico 118–119
Moldova 43
Mongolia 60
Morocco 78
Mozambique 85, 87

Namibia 88
Nepal 69
Netherlands 17
New Zealand 91
Nicaragua 120
Niger 83
Nigeria 83
Northern Ireland 15
Norway 8–9

Oman 74

Pakistan 68
Panama 120
Papua New Guinea 90
Paraguay 126–127
Peru 124
Philippines 61
Poland 44–45
Portugal 34–35
Puerto Rico 121

Qatar 71

Romania 42–43
Russia 50–51
Rwanda 86

Saudi Arabia 74
Scotland 14
Senegal 82
Sierra Leone 82
Singapore 65
Slovak Republic 27
Slovenia 29
Somali Republic 74
South Africa 88–89
Spain 32–35, 37
Sri Lanka 66
Sudan 79, 81
Surinam 124–125
Swaziland 89
Sweden 8–9
Switzerland 25
Syria 72–73

Taiwan 59
Tajikistan 50
Tanzania 86–87
Thailand 64–65
Togo 83
Trinidad and Tobago 121
Tunisia 78–79
Turkey 72–73
Turkmenistan 50

Uganda 86
Ukraine 47
United Arab Emirates 71
United Kingdom 12–15
USA 106–117
Uruguay 126–127
Uzbekistan 50

Venezuela 124
Vietnam 64–65

Wales 12–13

Yemen 74
Yugoslavia 40, 42

Zambia 84–85, 87
Zimbabwe 87

PHILIP'S

CONCISE WORLD ATLAS